Literature of the Western World

Volume I

The Ancient World Through the Renaissance

Fifth Edition

Brian Wilkie
University of Arkansas

James Hurt
University of Illinois

Upper Saddle River, New Jersey 07458

Library of Congress Cataloging-in-Publication Data

Literature of the Western World/[compiled by] Brian Wilkie, James Hurt.—5th ed.
p. cm.
Includes bibliographical references and index.
Contents: v. 1. The ancient world through the Renaissance—v. 2. Neoclassicism through the modern period.
ISBN 0-13-018666-X (v. 1)—ISBN 0-13-018667-8 (v. 2)
1. Literature—Collections. I. Wilkie, Brian. II. Hurt, James.

PN6014.L615 2000
808.8—dc21 00-042759

Editor in chief: Leah Jewell
Senior acquisitions editor: Carrie Brandon
Editorial assistant: Sandy Hrasdzira
AVP/Director of production and manufacturing: Barbara Kittle
Managing editor: Mary Rottino
Production editor: Kari Callaghan Mazzola
Project liaison: Randy Pettit
Marketing manager: Rachel Falk
Prepress and manufacturing manager: Nick Sklitsis
Prepress and manufacturing buyer: Mary Ann Gloriande
Electronic page makeup: Kari Callaghan Mazzola and John P. Mazzola
Cover director: Jayne Conte
Cover design: Bruce Kenselaar
Cover art: The Granger Collection

This book was set in 10/11 New Baskerville by Big Sky Composition and was printed and bound by Courier Companies, Inc.
The cover was printed by Phoenix Color Corp.

Grateful acknowledgment is made to the copyright holders on pages 2317–2320, which are hereby a continuation of this copyright page.

Printed in the United States of America
10 9 8 7 6 5 4 3

ISBN 0-13-018666-X

PRENTICE-HALL INTERNATIONAL (UK) LIMITED, *London*
PRENTICE-HALL OF AUSTRALIA PTY. LIMITED, *Sydney*
PRENTICE-HALL CANADA INC., *Toronto*
PRENTICE-HALL HISPANOAMERICANA, S.A., *Mexico*
PRENTICE-HALL OF INDIA PRIVATE LIMITED, *New Delhi*
PRENTICE-HALL OF JAPAN, INC., *Tokyo*
PEARSON EDUCATION ASIA PTE. LTD., *Singapore*
EDITORA PRENTICE-HALL DO BRASIL, LTDA., *Rio de Janeiro*

Contents

AESOP 595
(Sixth Century B.C.)

AESCHYLUS 612
(c. 525–456 B.C.)

The New Testament 1130

(First and Second Centuries A.D.)

Greek and Latin Lyric Poetry 1138

(Seventh Century B.C. to Second Century A.D.)

Sappho 1141

(Early Sixth Century B.C.)

Pindar 1148

(518–438 B.C.)

Theocritus 1153

(Third Century B.C.)

Catullus 1158

(c. 84–c. 54 B.C.)

Lope de Vega 2240
(1562–1635)

Michael Drayton 2245
(1563–1631)

William Shakespeare 2246
(1564–1616)

Thomas Campion 2249
(1567–1620)

John Donne 2250
(1572–1631)

Preface

This fifth edition of *Literature of the Western World* is intended, as its predecessors were, to provide the best possible materials for courses in the literatures of Europe and America from the earliest times to the present. It is a textbook in the broad sense of "a book of texts," rather than in the narrow one of a book arranged along the lines of a single course. It is a small library of Western literature upon which a wide range of courses might be based and which students might preserve after a particular class is over as a useful part of their personal libraries. Through the successive incarnations of the book, the editors have clung to a quite personal conception of their roles as participants in a conversation with instructors and students who use the book, and they have made choices of texts and presentation accordingly.

In such a conversation, the first question is, inevitably, "What shall we read?" This text is limited to the literatures of Europe and America and thus is designed either for courses in Western literature or for the Western portions of courses in global literature. The editors are acutely aware that the West is not the world and that a course in Western literature, even a two-semester one, should be part of a curriculum that includes non-Western literature as well, preferably with books that treat the literatures of East Asia, South Asia, the Middle East, Africa, and South America as thoroughly as this one does Western literature.

Even within Western literature, two volumes, thick as they are, can include only a tiny fraction of the most highly regarded and most influential works. The editors have adopted principles of both balance and range in making their hard choices. The text goes from about 2000 B.C. to 2000 A.D., and the editors have tried to represent the earlier periods as fully and fairly as the later ones. The temporal range and balance are matched by a range and balance of literary modes. If the works included were divided into the modes of lyric, narrative, and drama, the result would be three substantial anthologies of poems, stories, and plays. The national literatures within the boundaries of the subject have been represented in a balanced way as well, as far as possible. Balance, too, has been the goal in the representation of "high" and "low" literature (both *Oedipus Rex* and Aesop's *Fables*) and literature by women and men (Marguerite de Navarre as well as Boccaccio, Anna Akhmatova as well as Rainer Maria Rilke).

The way the texts are presented has been as important to the editors as their selection. The editors are aware that most students who use *Literature of the Western World* are encountering the works in it for the first time. Therefore, they try to make the initial encounter as rich and meaningful as possible. This means that translations of works in languages other than

English must be carefully chosen, not only for accuracy but also for readability and, above all, for capturing the literary quality of the original as vividly as possible. Robert Fitzgerald's translations of the *Iliad* and the *Odyssey*, the longest selection from a single author in the anthology, achieve these goals, as do Robert Fagles's and Phillip Vellacott's translations of Greek tragedy, H. R. Huse's translation of the *Divine Comedy*, Louise and Aylmer Maude's translations of Tolstoy, and Stephen Mitchell's translations of Rilke. In a number of cases, we have been able to include translations by distinguished writers in their own right. Thus the Irish poets Thomas Kinsella and Derek Mahon translate the Irish *Tain* and the poems of Gerard de Nerval; the American poets Henry Wadsworth Longfellow, William Cullen Bryant, W. S. Merwin, and Denise Levertov translate some of the Renaissance lyrics; Marianne Moore and Richard Wilbur translate La Fontaine and Moliére respectively; and Randall Jarrell translates *Faust.* The great English novelist Tobias Smollett translates Voltaire, his contemporary; and D. M. Thomas translates both Alexander Pushkin and Anna Akhmatova. Such pairings of congenial temperaments often result in happy blendings that read like original works.

Introductions and annotations are also intended to help the student feel at home in the often remote and unfamiliar worlds of the writers. Extensive period introductions survey historical events and provide syntheses of the thematic and aesthetic preoccupations of each period. Detailed introductions to individual authors and works place each work in the context of its author's life and times and suggest what to look out for in a first reading without giving away the content or imposing a single interpretation. Annotations are economical and factual rather than interpretive but ample enough to minimize trips to the dictionary or encyclopedia.

The fifth edition retains much from the previous editions, especially texts that instructors told us were especially important in a course in Western literature, but it also includes a great deal of new material. The most striking innovation is perhaps the sections of "Cultural Texts" for each period. These are made up of selections that, though they may have considerable literary value themselves, are likely to be read principally for their ideas rather than their literary merits. A few of these are works of literary theory, such as Aristotle's *Poetics*, Boileau's *Art of Poetry*, and the selection from Raymond Williams's *The Long Revolution.* Most, though, are works of philosophy, history, political science, and other non-literary fields that express directly some of the ideas that poets, storytellers, and playwrights express indirectly. A total of forty-three of these cultural texts appear in the two volumes as illuminating companion pieces to the works of literature proper.

A second structural change is not strictly new but represents an expansion of features of the earlier editions: a number of sections of lyric poetry in both volumes, a series of mini-anthologies within the anthology. The fourth edition included such a section of French Symbolist and Modernist Poetry. This edition adds similar sections of Greek and Latin Lyric Poetry, Renaissance Lyric Poetry, and Romantic Lyric Poetry. Some of the poets included in these sections appeared separately in previous editions; placing them in the contexts of their contemporaries considerably enriches our reading of them.

A third new feature of the book is greater attention to popular literature. There is a temptation in compressing all of Western literature into two volumes to focus on the most heroic works, often aristocratic in origin. But the "high" literature of the West has always been accompanied by the "low," and we have tried to acknowledge its presence by including such popular forms as folktales, beast fables, and tales of wonder throughout the two volumes. Thus in Volume I Aesop's fables follow the *Odyssey*, the medieval beast-epic *Renard the Fox* follows the *Lais* of Marie de France, and the *Thousand and One Nights* follows the *Divine Comedy*. Folk tales in sophisticated retellings appear near the beginning and near the end of Volume II, in La Fontaine's suave, ironic *Fables* and Calvino's *Italian Folktales*, in which folk tradition meets postmodernism.

A number of other changes are local rather than structural. Euripides's extraordinary *Helen* is a metaplay that forms a good companion piece not only to the horrific *Medea* but also to Homer's account of Helen in the *Iliad* and the *Odyssey*. *Beowulf* has given way to a selection from the Irish national epic *The Cattle Raid of Cooley* and an Icelandic saga. Strong recent postcolonialist readings of Shakespeare's *The Tempest* led us to substitute it for *Henry IV, Part 1* (though postcolonial themes are not absent from that play, either).

Changes in Volume II are just as extensive. Diderot's *Rameau's Nephew* is a hilarious, unsettling counter-voice to the Enlightenment texts grouped with it. Pushkin's *The Bronze Horseman* is a better sample of Pushkin than *The Queen of Spades*, since it is for his poetry that the Russians chiefly treasure him. Balzac's *Colonel Chabert* strengthens our representation of nineteenth-century French fiction. Tolstoy's *The Kreutzer Sonata* has replaced *The Death of Ivan Ilyich* as a better example of the interesting complexities and conflicts of Tolstoy's thought and art. The twentieth century has been bolstered by the addition of the poems of Rilke and Akhmatova and of Eliot's *The Waste Land*, by Sartre's *No Exit*, and by Richard Wright's *The Man Who Lived Underground*. As a conclusion (for the moment) to four thousand years of literary history the editors have chosen Chinua Achebe's *Things Fall Apart*, a wonderful novel which, set in Nigeria but drawing on the full resources of the European novel, connects the literature of "the Western world" to the rest of the world, a significant note on which to begin a new century and a new millennium.

Among the participants in the ongoing conversation that resulted in this book are friends who took an active part in planning and advising on this edition. They include the following: Randy Malamud, Georgia State University; David L. Middleton, Trinity University; Christopher Trogan, Julliard University; Nancy J. Wright, Blinn College; Kamala Edwards, Montgomery College; Fidel Fajardo-Acosta, Creighton University; William F. Naufftus, Winthrop University; Reiner Smolinski, Georgia State University; Edward E. Baldwin, University of Nevada at Las Vegas; and Linda Camarasana, Baruch College.

For advice on particular authors and periods we warmly thank Charles Hansford Adams, Lynn Altenbernd, John Bateman, Susan Bazargan, Barbara Bowen, Vincent Bowen, Edward Brandabur, David Bright, Jackson Campbell, Joseph Candido, Robert Cochran, Howard Cole, John Dussinger, Karen Ford, Chester Fontenot, Eva Frayne, John Frayne, John Friedman, Stanley Gray,

Achsah Guibbory, Jan Hinely, Bernard Hirsch, Frank Hodgins, Allan Holaday, Anthony Kaufman, David Kay, Keneth Kinnamon, Joan Klein, Dale Kramer, John Locke, James Marchand, Donald Masterson, Linda Mazer, Michael Mullin, Cary Nelson, John K. Newman, Michael Palencia-Roth, William Quinn, Arnold Stein, Dorothy Stephens, Jack Stillinger, Zohreh Sullivan, Benjamin Uroff, Leon Waldoff, Emily Watts, and Richard Wheeler.

We also owe debts to Carrie Brandon, our editor at Prentice Hall, and to Kari Callaghan Mazzola, our production editor. Finally, we thank Ann Hall, who undertook a number of tasks of manuscript preparation expertly and cheerfully.

Brian Wilkie

James Hurt

The Ancient World

The "ancient world," as it is represented in this book, consists mainly of three civilizations that flourished in the millennium before Christ in a comparatively small area around the Mediterranean Sea: those of the ancient Hebrews, the Greeks, and the Romans. One of our selections, the *Gilgamesh* epic, opens a window on the even older Mesopotamian world out of which the Hebrew culture emerged and which was to condition that culture in many ways. To the farsighted anthropologist taking a long view of time, such a sampling of the ancient world would be too limited both chronologically and geographically. By the second millennium B.C., humankind was already old upon the earth and had created many other civilizations, some of them highly developed. Some of them, too, flourished in areas far from the Mediterranean—in the Orient, in Africa, and in the Americas. Nevertheless, it is to the Hebrews, the Greeks, and the Romans that we look for the main literary traditions of Western culture that concern this anthology. These traditions are the riverhead of Western literature, although we can discern other contributions near the source and continuing tributary streams from Africa and the East.

The core of Hebrew culture has always been religion, and it is through religion that it has most strongly influenced the Western world. It would be neither possible nor very useful to review here the course of the development of the Hebrews' culture and conception of God. But much of their view of the world is summed up in the prophet Micah's deceptively simple words: "He has showed you, O man, what is good; and what does the Lord require of you but to do justice, and to love kindness, and to walk humbly with your God?" No Greek or Roman could have written, or even have understood, these words. They imply a cluster of ideas wholly alien to the Greek and Roman worldviews but at the very heart of Hebraism: the existence of a single God, from whom the idea of "the good" derives, and a moral role for human beings in which they, along with everything else, are subordinated to God. (Micah's terms for ethical behavior in this world—"justice" and "kindness"—would not have puzzled either a Greek or a Roman, but both would have defined these words differently.) The Hebrew "Yahveh" came to be the God of all mankind and, at the same time, the God of each individual. The result of this personal relationship was a stress upon individual experience, an emphasis upon conscience (including a social conscience), and a concentration upon introspection and the spiritual life. The Hebrews were continually involved in negotiations, individual and collective, with a father-God.

The course of Greek thought was significantly different. When the people we now know as Greeks began to filter into the Greek peninsula about

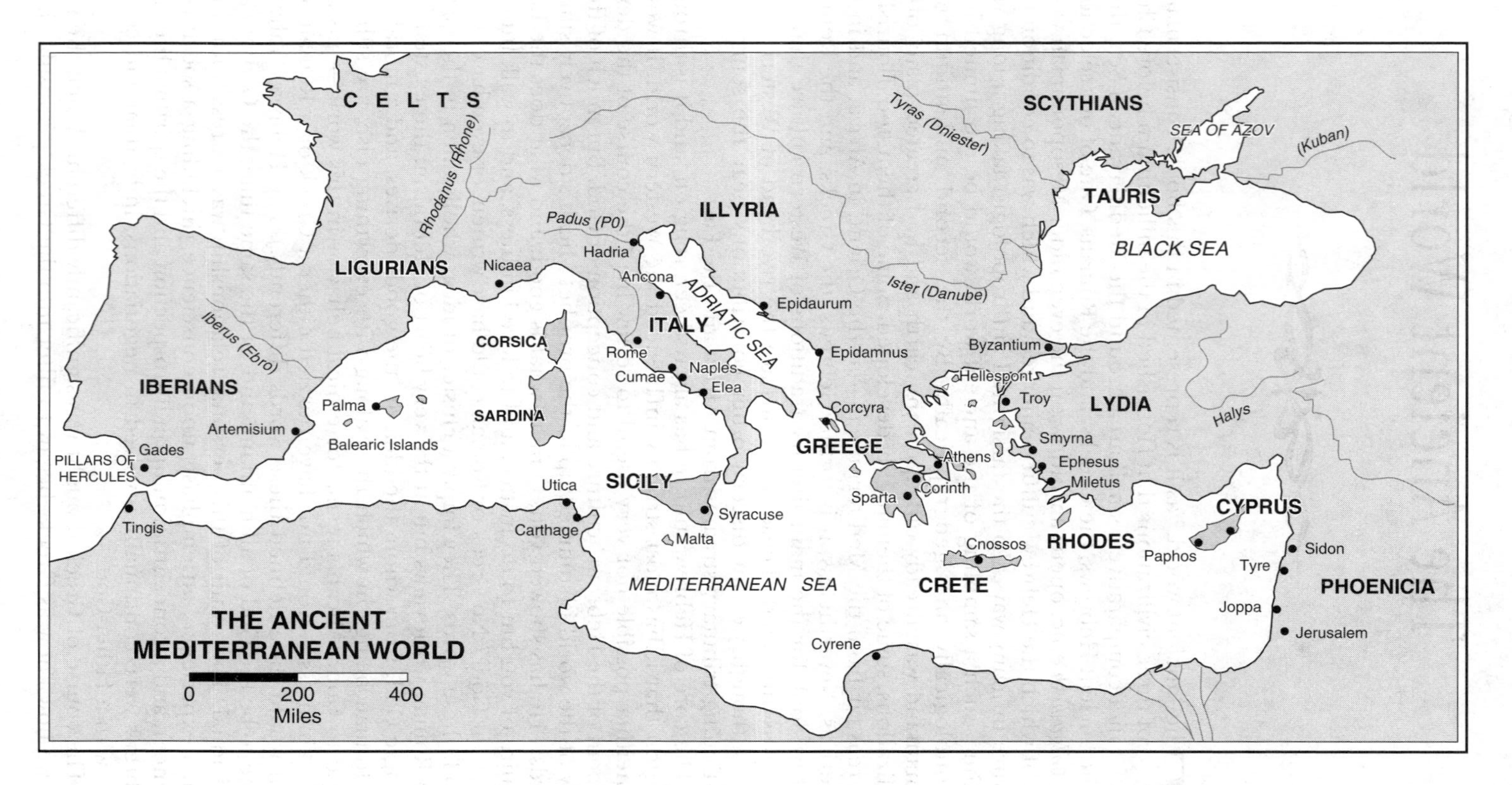
C E L T S
SCYTHIANS
Tyras (Dniester)
SEA OF AZOV
(Kuban)
Rhodanus (Rhone)
TAURIS
ILLYRIA
Padus (P0)
BLACK SEA
Hadria
LIGURIANS
Nicaea
Ancona
ADRIATIC SEA
Ister (Danube)
Epidaurum
Iberus (Ebro)
ITALY
CORSICA
Rome
Epidamnus
Byzantium
Naples
Cumae
Hellespont
IBERIANS
Elea
Troy
LYDIA
Palma
SARDINA
Corcyra
Halys
Artemisium
Smyrna
Balearic Islands
GREECE
Gades
Athens
Ephesus
PILLARS OF HERCULES
SICILY
Corinth
Miletus
Utica
Sparta
CYPRUS
Syracuse
Tingis
Carthage
Malta
Cnossos
RHODES
Sidon
Paphos
Tyre
MEDITERRANEAN SEA
CRETE
PHOENICIA
Joppa
THE ANCIENT MEDITERRANEAN WORLD
Jerusalem
Cyrene
0
200
400
Miles

2000 B.C., they brought with them a primitive polytheism based on personifications of natural forces, which they humanized and attempted to propitiate by means of prayers, libations, and sacrifices. Greek religion changed and developed, of course, over its long history, but even in its most fully developed form it carried few if any implications for morality or conscience in the Hebrew sense. The Greek gods were superior to humans, in power, beauty, and immortality, but they were not ethically superior, and, unlike Yahveh, they did not demand that people follow an exacting code of morality. The Greeks looked not to their gods for an ethical code, but to their own reason and innate sense of the good. The result was a culture that seems, even to a modern "post-Christian" reader, remarkably serene and guiltfree. The Greeks, it has been said, had a strong sense of crime, but none at all of sin.

The Greeks found the main significance of life not in the relation of human beings with God, but in human beings' relations with themselves and with their fellows. If, for the sake of focus, we simplify the Greek view of the world as we did the Hebrew, we may find it stated best in the mottoes the Greeks inscribed over the gates of the temple to Apollo at Delphi: "Know thyself" and "Nothing too much." An ancient Hebrew would have misunderstood these phrases as badly as an ancient Greek would have misunderstood Micah's words. "Knowing" oneself implied to a Greek none of the spiritual struggles or the wrestling with angels with which the Hebrew was preoccupied. People came to know themselves in Greece through experience, through involvement in the world. The crucial tableau in Hebrew history is one person alone on a mountaintop, learning directly from God "what is good." The Greeks had their mountaintops, too, but the messages they received there from the gods were characteristically riddling and enigmatic; the responsibility for knowledge was thrown squarely back upon the questioner. The Greek tableau corresponding to the person on the mountaintop is a group of people in lively, earnest conversation, exercising the privilege Socrates said was characteristic of free citizens: "They can have their talk out in peace, wandering at will from one subject to another, their only aim to attain the truth."

Or the emblematic tableau might be a group of people at the great Olympic Games, competing in athletics or in horseracing, drama, music, or poetry; or it could be the audience at a production of an Aeschylean tragedy at the City Dionysia in the theater of Dionysus in Athens. For to the Greeks there were no sharp divisions between the intellectual, physical, and spiritual sides of human nature. To "know oneself" was to know one's mind, body, and spirit as a harmonious balanced system. The Greek view of human nature as a seamless unity was so deep and so thoroughgoing that it provides a stumbling block to our understanding of their institutions and their literature. We attend class, or watch the Rose Bowl on television, or go to a play or to church, and all of these are separate activities, each carried on by specialists and directed at different aspects of our personalities. It is hard for us to understand the very different Greek attitude toward, for example, the Great Games, in which the same contestants might compete in the five athletic events of the *pentathlon* and in music and poetry. The Games were a religious festival as well, dedicated to the worship of Zeus or Apollo or Poseidon. And were the great dramatic festivals artistic events or religious ceremonies? The Greeks would not have understood such a question, any more than they would have understood our attempts to distinguish between "sin" and "error" in

ANCIENT GREECE
0 25 50
Miles
ILLYRIA
Mt. Olympus
Vale of Tempe
Mt. Ossa
Mt. Pelion
Mt. Athos
LEMNOS
TENEDOS
Troy
MYSIA
Scamander
Mt. Ida
CORCYRA
(CORFU)
Dodona
EPIRUS
Achelous
THESSALY
Pherae
Pergamum
Mytilene
LESBOS
Cape Artemisium
Thermopylae
ACARNANIA
LEUCAS
DORIS
AETOLIA
PHOCIS
SCYROS
BOEOTIA
EUBOEA
Mt. Parnassus
LOCRIS
ITHACA
Delphi
Mt. Helicon
Chalcis
AEGEAN
SEA
Smyrna
CHIOS
LYDIA
Thebes
Delium
Plataea
Mt. Hymettus
ATTICA
Marathon
CEPHALLENIA
ACHAEA
Megara
Eleusis
Athens
Piraeus
IONIA
Ephesus
ELIS
ARCADIA
Corinth
SALAMIS
ANDROS
SAMOS
Mycenae
AEGINA
Olympia
Alpheus
Argos
Epidaurus
Mt. Laurium
Cape Sunium
TENOS
ICARIA
ZACYNTHOS
Tiryns
PELOPONNESUS
ARGOLIS
Miletus
Didyma
IONIAN
SEA
MESSENIA
Taygetus Mts.
Eurotas
DELOS
PATMOS
PAROS
Pylos
Halicarnassus
Sparta
LACONIA
NAXOS
COS
Cnidus
Cape Malea
MELOS
THERA
Cape Taenarum
CYTHERA

Ancient Greece. NOTE: Some of the names below are spelled in various ways by translators. Asterisks (*) indicate the places described in the list.

ARCADIA. Setting of much ancient pastoral poetry.

ARGOS. In Aeschylus, the city of Agamemnon, Clytemnestra, Orestes, and Electra.

CORCYRA (Corfu). Conjectural home island of the Phaeacians in Homer's *Odyssey*.

CORINTH. Center of wealth, commerce, and shipbuilding; setting of Euripides' *Medea*.

CYTHERA. Island where Aphrodite came to land after being born of the sea foam.

DELOS. Birthplace of Apollo and Artemis.

DELPHI. Site of the great oracle of Apollo; the center of Greek prophetic utterance. The Omphalos (Navelstone), believed to be the center of the earth, was located there.

DODONA. Site of the great oracle of Zeus.

HELICON. Mountain sacred to the Muses; location of the Hippocrene, the fountain of poetic inspiration.

ITHACA. Home island of Odysseus.

LESBOS. Home island of Sappho.

MARATHON. Plain (26 miles from Athens) where the Greeks defeated the Persians in 490 B.C.

MYCENAE. Center of a great ancient culture; in Homer, the city of Agamemnon.

OLYMPIA. With Delphi, one of the two greatest religious centers of Greece; site of the ancient Olympic Games.

OLYMPUS. Mountain home of the gods.

OSSA, PELION. Mountains piled atop one another in an attempt by the Titans to take the gods by storm.

PARNASSUS. Mountain associated with Apollo and the Muses and hence with learning and the arts.

PELION. See Ossa.

PLATAEA. Site of victory by the Greeks, under Pausanias, over the Persians in 479 B.C.

PYLOS. Home of Nestor; visited by Telemachus in Homer's *Odyssey*.

SALAMIS. Site of defeat of Xerxes and the Persian navy by the Greeks in 480 B.C.

SPARTA. Principal enemy of Athens in the Peloponnesian War (431–404 B.C.); home of Menelaus and Helen of Troy in Homer's *Odyssey*.

THEBES. City of Oedipus and Antigone.

THERMOPYLAE. A mountain pass heroically defended in 480 B.C. by the Spartans, under Leonidas, against the Persian invaders.

TROY. Site of the Trojan War, fought by the Greeks to reclaim Helen.

such dramatic characters as King Oedipus. In institutions, as in human personalities, the Greeks did not differentiate the spirit, the mind, and the flesh.

The other Delphic inscription, "Nothing too much," is also a deceptively simple statement. The concept does not suggest a timid moderation, "playing it safe," but something almost the opposite. It insists that people confront reality unflinchingly, refusing the temptation to retreat into defensive and self-deluding inflations and exaggerations. This principle is consistent with "knowing oneself," since self-knowledge ends in accepting what it is to be human and avoiding the temptation to be either less or more than human. Morally, exaggeration and excess manifest themselves in *hubris,* which is not just pride but also a self-deluding rejection of human limitations. To the fifth-century Greeks, the luxurious and despotic Persian emperor Xerxes represented the sort of overweening man who closed his eyes to human boundaries and whom the gods delighted in cutting down. Greek tragedy is full of parallel examples of people who fall through their attempts to be something other than human. Artistically, the principle of "nothing too much" was also expressed in a deep dislike of any elaboration or ornamentation that shielded the viewer from a direct view of "the thing itself." Greek art, whether it be the epics of Homer, the architecture of the Parthenon, or a sculpted Apollo, is characterized by a direct, unblinking view of reality and a combination of passion and restraint that is the essence of classicism. This is not to say that Greek art was "realistic" in the modern sense. Idealization—the attempt to capture the essence of a thing—was also fundamental to Greek art. But the ideal originated in the recognizable.

The leisure which made possible the Greeks' passionate but clear-eyed exploration of themselves and the world around them had a price: slavery and the subjugation of women. The Greek male was freed from demanding physical labor by the existence of a sizable slave class, made up mostly of "barbarians" (non-Greeks) captured in war. The institution of slavery was rarely questioned by the Greeks; one of the ironies of history is that its most freedom-loving culture accepted slavery, for the most part, as a matter of course. Nor did women share in the free exploration of the world men enjoyed. Greek women had few rights and were confined to the home. They managed domestic matters, and they bore and raised the children (at least in Athens; customs differed among the city-states). Greek children were almost exclusively in the company of women until the age of seven and then were rigidly segregated by sex; the result, predictably, was a perpetuation of traditional attitudes on the part of Greek women and a deep-seated distrust and even fear of women on the part of Greek men. This fear expressed itself in widespread homosexuality ("Greek love"), a rigid compartmentalization of sexual qualities, a glorification of "male" at the expense of "female" qualities, and a mythology full of female fright-figures, from the shrewish Hera to the Medusa, whose gaze turned men to stone, to the fearsome Furies, goddesses of blood vengeance, to the fierce Medea, who killed her children to avenge herself upon her faithless husband. (There were, of course, idealized women in myth, too: Athena, the patroness of Athens, was the goddess of wisdom.) The tragedian Euripides, in many ways an ironic commentator upon the ways of his contemporaries, questioned his culture's attitudes toward both slaves and women, but his was a rare voice in an intensely male-oriented society.

Greek culture reached its peak in the fifth century B.C. and was centered in Athens, which dominated the city-states of the peninsula and its islands for most of the century. But the power of Athens and Greece alike was severely eroded during a series of bitter internecine wars which ended in 338 B.C. when the kingdom of Macedonia conquered Greece. Greek art and learning had a brief Indian summer, the third-century "Hellenistic" (as opposed to the earlier "Hellenic") period, in the city of Alexandria in northern Egypt. Greek culture maintained some of its integrity through the days of the Roman Empire, and it passed on part of its legacy to Christianity. But the deathblow to even nominal Greek political independence came in 146 B.C., when the armies of the rising Republic of Rome marched into Greece and turned it into a mere province for the growing Roman Empire.

If the Hebrews looked to God for the meaning of life and the Greeks looked for it in the world around them, the Romans looked to earthly, human authority. It was a Roman, Horace, who wrote that it is "sweet and seemly to die for one's country," a phrase which encapsulates a number of Roman attitudes, including the subordination of the individual to the state, an obsession with death, and the cultivation of a stoic denial of personal feeling. Many Greeks suffered or risked death for their country, but it is hard to imagine their idealizing their sacrifice in this way. The Roman tableau to match the Hebrew on a mountaintop and the Greek talking with friends might be the uniformed centurion marching in a column behind his commander to triumph or death. The Roman Empire took shape over centuries of constant war; in our first glimpse of Rome at the end of the sixth century B.C., it is at war, attacking neighbor after neighbor until by 133 B.C. the nation was the undisputed ruler of the whole Mediterranean. The Roman virtues were those of the soldier: discipline, control, and obedience to authority.

Authority hedged the Roman around from earliest childhood. The Roman family was a miniature of the state, headed by a stern father whose power was almost absolute. He owned all the property and could, by writing a letter, divorce his wife or even condemn her to death. The Greek family, male-oriented as it was, was never patriarchal in the Roman sense; the Greek grew up thinking of himself as an individual, but the Roman was above all else a member of a family and, later, of a clan and a nation. Roman religion reinforced these feelings of subordination to authority. The earliest Roman religion, which continued to be the domestic religion throughout the years of the empire, rested on a belief in spirits that inhabited particular localities; each household had its own *lares, penates,* and *manes,* which, respectively, watched over its lands and buildings, guarded the family's other possessions, and embodied the spirits of its male ancestors. Romans must have grown up feeling that they were constantly observed by such spirits. When the more generalized gods of the Romans—Jupiter, Juno, Venus, and Mars—were merged, under Greek influence, with the Greek pantheon of Zeus, Hera, Aphrodite, and Ares, the result was a state religion the outward observances of which were enforced with a rigidity totally alien to the Greek mentality. In the late Empire, Stoic philosophy deeply influenced thoughtful Romans; it has been called the true Roman religion. Although Stoicism originated with a Greek—Zeno of Citium—its emphasis on endurance and the repression of feeling made a strong appeal to the Romans' instinct for authority. The version of Stoicism developed in Rome taught the individual to subordinate his own will to the family, to the state, and to God. He was to do his duty without question, cultivating self-denial and impassive reserve. Altogether, the Stoic view of the world was ideally suited to the Roman temperament.

The great Roman contribution to civilization was the instrument of social organization—law. The Romans were able to extend their sway over so much of the world and maintain it so long because wherever they went they brought with them the concept of authority. In their system, no one was wholly exempt from the rule of an impersonal force. Forbidding as such impersonality may seem, it also left a cherished legacy to posterity. We owe to the Romans the principles that a person must be assumed innocent until proven guilty, that the law must be applied judiciously, with due regard to the particular situation, and that all individuals are equal before the law.

Roman art was largely derivative from the Greeks. After 272 B.C., when the Romans captured the Greek city of Tarentum, Greek artists and scholars poured into Rome, and as Horace expressed it, "Conquered Greece took captive her fierce conqueror." Roman architecture, sculpture, drama, poetry, and painting were all copied from Greek models, often with a considerable distortion through inflation, as in the gigantic Roman temples copied from small Greek originals, or through refinement, as in Seneca's polished imitations of Greek tragedy.

In a survey of ancient literature (even that of the cultures represented in this book), variety is more apparent than unity. But we can follow a few threads related to the development of the major literary genres: narrative, drama, poetry, and expository literary prose.

The characteristic narrative forms of the ancient world are the folktale, the epic, and the history. We may pass over the folktale fairly quickly, since our knowledge of it in the ancient world is indirect and inferential. We know that a large body of folk narrative must have been in oral circulation since earliest times among the Hebrews, the Greeks, and the Romans. But these tales have reached us only as they were incorporated into written narratives. We can detect signs of them in, for example, *Gilgamesh,* the Hebrew Bible, Homer, and Virgil. Even the fables of "Aesop," though they seem to stand in a closer relationship to an oral tradition of "people's" literature, have been mediated by the written tradition.

In narrative, the greatest achievement of the ancient world was the epic. Long heroic poems seem to be a natural form in most early literatures. There are the Exodus epic in the Bible and the *Iliad* and the *Odyssey* at the dawn of Greek literature. But we can also point to, among others, the Babylonian *Gilgamesh* (c. 2000 B.C.), the Indian *Mahabharata* (A.D. 350–500), the Old English *Beowulf* (eighth century A.D.), and the German *Nibelungenlied* (c. A.D. 1200). These are all "folk epics"—that is, although they may have been put into final form by single authors, they were developed by folk poets, over extended periods of time, from traditional materials that dealt with the legendary histories of their peoples.

The folk epics have a wide variety of forms, but they are linked by certain recurring characteristics. Though not all are regarded as, like the Bible, "sacred books," all hold special places in their cultures as major statements of national or cultural identity. They purport to tell the stories of the formation or the early history of an entire people; thus they are never regarded as mere fictional entertainment but are held in some degree of reverence.

All of them, too, center on heroes, drawn from history or legend, who are regarded not merely as individuals but as embodiments of the special values of their cultures. The settings are vast, ranging across nations or the entire world. Even when the action is confined to a limited place, as in Homer's *Iliad,* that place is the scene of great events determining the fate of nations. The action is similarly grand, involving deeds that exemplify extraordinary qualities treasured by the culture, especially military prowess, physical strength, and spiritual force. Often the action takes the hero on a journey which consists of a series of trials testing his heroism. The gods of the culture often involve themselves in the action, as the Lord does in the Exodus story, or as, in a very different way, the Olympian gods enter the plots of the Homeric epics. The style is at once exalted and simple, grand but not highly embellished. And the point of view is objective; the action is seen from an impersonal angle, without authorial intrusion and with the emphasis on external action rather than inner motivations.

The epic form captured the imaginations of a great many poets who attempted to incorporate its qualities in original works, or art epics. In addition to employing the features of folk epics, these poets developed a number of epic conventions, which refine and develop the features inherent in the folk epic, especially the epics of Homer. The art epic opens with a statement of a grand governing theme and an invocation to an appropriate muse to inspire and instruct the poet. The poet plunges *in medias res,* or "into the middle of things," with earlier action recounted at a later point in the epic. There are, characteristically, catalogs of warriors, ships, armies; extended formal speeches by the main characters; and epic similes, extended set-pieces which develop comparisons at length. The greatest ancient art epic is Virgil's *Aeneid;* Ovid's *Metamorphoses* is another, in some ways, though he introduces the epic conventions in a playful and deliberately trivializing way.

The other major narrative form of the ancient world is the history. The dividing line between epic and history is not always precise; the epic finds its roots in legendary history, and history is often seen through epic lenses. About half of the Old Testament is presented as a history of the Hebrews, though a good part of it—the Exodus saga—blends history with folk epic. But we cannot reconstruct from the Old Testament a factual account of early Israel such as a modern historian would write. Hebrew history is history seen through faith; and the purpose of the Hebrew Bible is not to record precise dates and circumstances but, rather, to trace out the underlying design of history as a revelation of religious truth.

History in the modern sense begins in the fifth century B.C. with Herodotus and his Greek history of the Persian Wars. Here, too, fact and fancy are often mingled; Herodotus begins with a lively travelogue of the Persian Empire, reporting everything he has seen and heard, though he is careful to say he does not necessarily believe all of it. The modern critical and scientific treatment of history begins with Herodotus' younger contemporary Thucydides, whose history of the Peloponnesian War makes a quite modern attempt not only at factual accuracy but also at historical interpretation. The Romans carried on the tradition of historical writing. The romantic and patriotic Livy's *History of Rome* is the historical counterpart to Virgil's epic *Aeneid,* while Tacitus' *Histories* and *Annals* chronicle Rome's later degeneracy, in a savage parallel to the contemporary verse satires of Juvenal. The beginning of modern notions of how to organize and develop a sustained narrative lies as much in the work of these historians as in that of the more frankly "literary" writers.

Of the major literary kinds, drama has had the most sporadic history. Perhaps because a fairly complex set of social and intellectual circumstances are necessary to make theatrical production possible, drama has flourished in only three fairly brief periods in Western history, and the first of these is in the Greece of the fifth century B.C. (the other two ages are the late Renaissance and early neoclassical period, between about 1580 and 1700, and the modern period, since about 1860).

There is some evidence that a dramatic tradition existed in Egypt as early as 3000 B.C., but practically nothing is known of it. The Hebrews had no theater, although the Book of Job shows some evidence of the influence of Greek tragedy, and the Song of Solomon may have some relation to a quasi-dramatic wedding performance. It is to Greece that we look for the beginnings of Western drama.

Greek drama originated in the sixth century B.C., in the worship of Dionysus. Four annual festivals were consecrated to him: the Rural Dionysia (in December), the Lenaia (in January), the Anthesteria (in February), and the City or Great Dionysia (in March). The god was worshipped at these festivals through the performances of dithyrambs, which were hymns of ecstasy narrating an incident in the life of the god and performed by choruses of singers and dancers. The step from narration to drama presumably was taken when a chorus leader moved from telling about the god to impersonating him and acting out his story. The Greeks believed that this revolutionary innovator was a man named Thespis, who is therefore traditionally regarded as the first actor in history. It was Thespis, too, who won the prize for tragedy in 534 B.C., when the City Dionysia was reorganized and a contest for tragedy was established. Dithyrambic performances took place on the circular stone platforms which were used as threshing floors in the center of Greek villages; these platforms seem to have provided the model for the *orchestra,* or circular dancing place, which served as the central acting area of the fully developed Greek theater.

It is in the fifth century that we emerge from theatrical legend into theatrical history. By the time Aeschylus, the oldest of the Greek dramatists whose works survive, began competing in the tragedy contests in 499 B.C., the contests had been held for about thirty-five years and the methods of production had assumed essentially the form they kept throughout the great age of the Greek theater. The festivals were civic and religious rituals, occasions for exploring the fundamental ideas and values that made Athens a unified community. The annual dramatic festivals were organized, and the plays produced, by a cooperative effort of the civic leaders of the city, eminent private sponsors, and the artists themselves, in accordance with rules that by the fifth century had become standard. The audience consisted, in effect, of the whole citizenry, brought together not in a spirit of playgoing whim but of communal solidarity. (Women attended the tragedies but not the comedies.) During the fifth century, the Great Dionysia, the most important of the annual festivals, included four days devoted to plays. On the first day, five comedies, by different authors, were presented. On each of the next three days, plays by a single author were acted: three

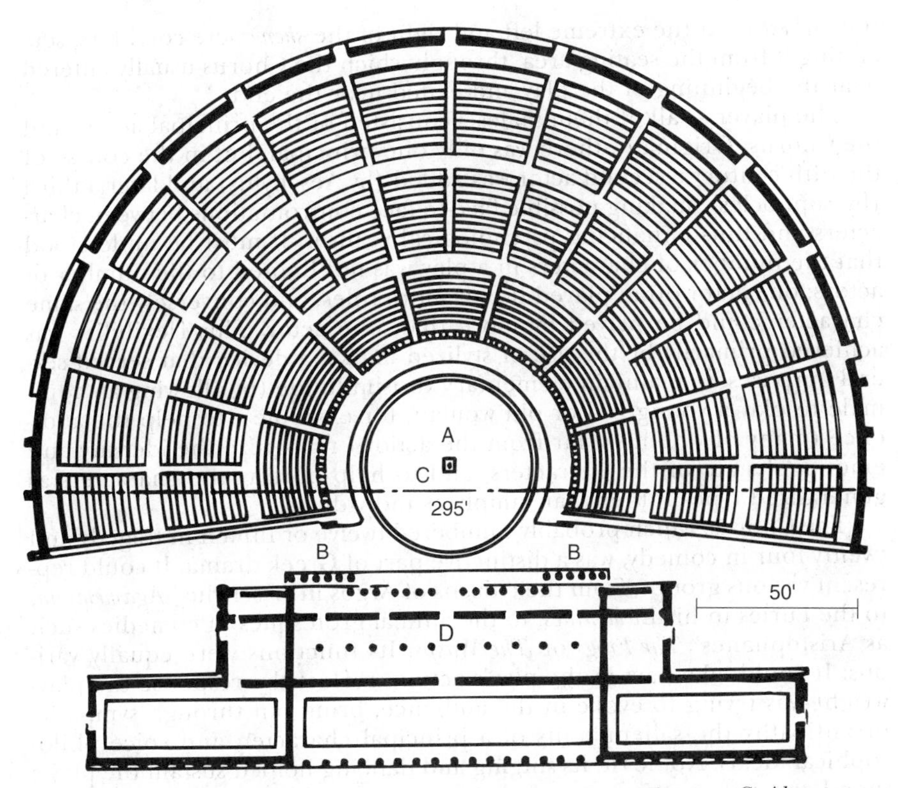

Plan of the theater of Dionysus at Athens. A. Orchestra B. Chorus Entrance C. Altar to Dionysus D. Skene.

tragedies, followed by a broadly comic "satyr play" designed to relieve the intensity of the tragedies. Prizes were awarded to the best actor and to the best combination of playwright and producer.

At Athens, plays were acted in the Theater of Dionysus, a vast outdoor arena located on sloping ground near the Acropolis. Between the sixth and fourth centuries, the most important era of Greek drama, the theater evolved considerably. At first it was little more than a circular acting space, or *orchestra,* at the foot of a concave hillside where the audience sat on the ground. By the fifth century, permanent seats for the audience had been built and a long building called the *skene* had been constructed behind the *orchestra.* The *skene,* which became increasingly elaborate architecturally as time passed, provided dressing rooms, a backdrop for the action (scenery was apparently minimal), and a place through which the principal actors could make their entrances and exits. The *skene* often represented an edifice, integral to the story, where indoor actions could be imagined to happen, offstage—in Agamemnon's palace, for example. (The direct presentation of indoor scenes is unusual in Greek plays, as are killings and other violent episodes.) It is possible, though not certain, that a raised platform directly in front of the *skene* formed a stage slightly elevated above the *orchestra.* At the extreme left and right of the *skene* were corridors, separating it from the seating area, through which the Chorus usually entered near the beginning of the play and exited near the end.

The players—all of them males—consisted of the principal actors and the Chorus. Originally, there was only one principal, but in the course of the fifth century a second actor was added (by Aeschylus) and later a third (by Sophocles), making possible face-to-face confrontations between characters and thus enhancing psychological realism. It must be understood that the number of characters in a play was not limited to the number of actors; one actor often played two or more roles, and conversely the same character could be played by more than one actor. This flexibility was achieved primarily by the use of stylized masks, a device that served several purposes: to maintain elementary verisimilitude (by allowing an adult male to play a young girl or old woman, for example); to help the audience (many of whom sat far from the action) recognize the identity and emotional state of the characters; and to help portray the characters as generalized types rather than simply as individuals.

The Chorus, which probably numbered twelve or fifteen in tragedy and twenty-four in comedy, was a distinctive part of Greek drama. It could represent various groups, from the citizens of Argos in Aeschylus' *Agamemnon,* to the Furies in his *Eumenides,* to the animal grotesques in comedies such as Aristophanes' *The Frogs* or *The Wasps.* Its functions were equally various: It could take part in the play's action, reflect the response the playwright was trying to evoke in the audience, bring out through sympathy or antipathy the salient traits of a principal character, and voice philosophical ideals. Not least, its singing and dancing helped sustain the play's mood and enhance it as spectacle.

Music and dance were important in both tragedy and comedy, helping to create elevated, festive, or ceremonial effects. The choral poems were sung, in a variety of lyric verse forms, to the accompaniment of dance and of musical instruments including the flute. Ordinary dialogue was probably delivered as a quasi-musical chant or in some other way that distinguished it from the tone of ordinary speech. A number of people have pointed out that, in its stylized manner, its spectacle, and its integration of different art media, Greek drama has its closest modern analogue in grand opera. (And indeed, opera originated in a seventeenth-century attempt to reconstruct the staging of Greek drama.)

Only forty-five Greek plays have survived: seven tragedies by Aeschylus, seven tragedies by Sophocles, seventeen tragedies and one satyr play by Euripides, eleven comedies by Aristophanes, and two comedies by Menander (only one of which is intact). Even this small sampling, hardly likely to encompass the full range of Greek drama, is highly varied. Tragedy ranges from the titanic culture-histories of Aeschylus, through the marvelously crafted humanistic dramas of Sophocles, to Euripides' ironic dramas of inner division and self-deception (some of which are more like comedies of manners than like tragedies). Aristophanes' Old Comedy is the Greek dramatic form most remote from modern drama. He strings upon a sketchy, fantastic, often perfunctory plot, scenes of farce, parody, and topical satire, punctuated with choruses of beautiful lyric poetry. It was not Old Comedy but New Comedy—surviving only in the works of the fourth-century Menander—that was to establish the pattern of later comedy. New Comedy turned from fantasy and satire to deal with contemporary middle-class private life. The choruses were subordinated to intrigue-plots, which usually dealt with a young man's attempt to marry against his father's opposition.

The Roman theater, like many aspects of Roman culture, was modeled on that of the Greeks. In Rome, where Greek-inspired plays began to be performed in the third century B.C., plays were performed at festivals honoring the gods or for special occasions, such as a state funeral or a military victory. The theaters were constructed along Greek lines, although by the first century A.D. they had come to be much larger and more elaborate than the Greek theaters, reflecting the Roman love of excess. Thirty-seven Roman plays survive: twenty-one comedies by Plautus (c. 254–184 B.C.); six comedies by Terence (195–159 B.C.); nine tragedies by Seneca (4 B.C.–65 A.D.), the Stoic philosopher and adviser to the Emperor Nero; and one tragedy formerly attributed to Seneca but now agreed to be the work of a later, anonymous author. Roman comedy, like Greek New Comedy, dealt with intrigues arising from middle-class life, while Seneca's stiff, melodramatic dramas, not meant for production, are reworkings of Greek tragedies. (Five of his nine extant plays are adapted from Euripides.)

Greek tragedy expressed the Greek spirit both in its unflinching treatment of basic issues in human life ("Know thyself") and in its strict economy of means ("Nothing too much"). Greek comedy embodied the Greeks' freedom of thought and expression, as well as their involvement in public life. Roman drama carried on the Greek achievement and was to be the version of classical drama that initially influenced the theater when it was reborn during the Renaissance.

Of all the genres, lyric poetry travels least well. Narrative and drama lose a great deal with the passage of time and loss of cultural associations. Subtleties disappear with translation into other languages. But the broad outlines of a story and the power of the stage are rugged—thus epic and drama can survive the passing of time and changes in language better than lyric poetry, which depends so much on nuance and the precise word.

"Lyric" originally meant "sung to the lyre," and perhaps the central fact about lyric poetry in the ancient world is its close connection with music. The lyric poet was literally a "lyricist" in Hebrew and Greek cultures, as we are reminded by stories about David as a harpist and of Sappho's skill upon the lyre.

The Hebrew Bible is full of song, and the lyric portions of it should be read with imaginary, if not real, music in the background. The role of music and poetry in Hebrew worship is suggested by many passages in the Old Testament, among them the description of David's bringing of the ark to Jerusalem (I Chron. 16:7–36) and the descriptions of worship in the Psalms. In Psalm 42, the speaker tells of leading the throng to the House of God "with glad shouts and songs of thanksgiving," while in Psalm 68 another procession is described, "the singers in front, the minstrels last, between them maidens playing timbrels."

Hebrew poetry, like most ancient Near Eastern poetry, did not depend on rhyme or a fixed line length but, rather, on a loose rhythm and parallelism. A unit of Hebrew verse characteristically consists of two lines, each with three or four heavily stressed syllables, the second line parallel to the first in that it either paraphrases, develops, or completes it:

> What is man, that thou art mindful of him?
> and the son of man, that thou visitest him? [PSALMS 8:4]

The simple, exalted power of this form is perceptible even in English translation.

The early Greeks described poetry as either "lyric" or "choric." Lyric poetry was the expression of a single singer accompanied by the lyre, while choric poetry was a group expression, sung by a chorus, usually also with instrumental accompaniment. The greatest school of lyric poets in Greece was centered among the Aeolians, on the eastern coast of the Aegean Sea and on the island of Lesbos, in the sixth century B.C. The great Aeolian lyricists, Sappho and Alcaeus, also inspired an Ionian school of lyricists on the mainland of Greece. The major successor to Sappho and Alcaeus was Anacreon, who was born in Teos in Asia Minor but spent much of his life in Athens. The leader of the Dorian school of the fifth century was the "choric" poet Pindar. Late Greek poetry of the Hellenistic period is best represented by Theocritus, whose *Idylls* established the pattern for centuries to come of pastoral poetry, in which the subject matter, whatever it may be, is cast in terms of rural scenes and characters.

In lyric poetry, as in much else, the Greeks set out on paths we still follow. The very conception of a "lyric" voice, intensely individual and personal, uncovering the subtle movements of thought and emotion and linking them to musicality, was Greek. Perhaps the most direct heir to Greek lyricism among the Romans was the first-century B.C. Catullus, whose most famous poems, those about his mistress "Lesbia," seem to explore all the convolutions of a self in the grip of an ambivalent passion. The other great Latin lyricists seem tame by comparison—they are polished and even elegant but they lack the naked self-revelation of the Greeks and of Catullus. Virgil is almost as well known for his *Eclogues* as for the *Aeneid;* in these poems he follows Theocritus in urbanely surveying many subjects under the cloak of the pastoral idiom. The other great Augustan lyricist was Horace, whose polished style, charm, and tone of detached common sense made him the most imitated classical poet of the European Enlightenment. Ovid was primarily a storyteller rather than a lyricist, but in his *Art of Love, Amores,* and *Metamorphoses,* we see again the Greek lyric inspiration, translated into Roman smartness and a cynical, amusing detachment.

Finally, a narrow definition of literary genres should not rule out such masterpieces of discursive prose as we find in much of the Old Testament and in Plato and Aristotle. Such works have had an incalculable impact upon later literature. The voices of the Hebrew prophets, of Plato's genial and humane Socrates, and of Aristotle, the indefatigable analyst of the nature and meaning of almost everything, must be included among the voices of the ancient world.

FURTHER READING: *The Oxford History of the Classical World,* ed. by John Boardman, Jasper Griffin, and Oswyn Murray, 1986, is a very fine comprehensive treatment of the ancient Greek and Roman world, lavishly illustrated, combining history and sociology with good essays on ancient literature, art, and philosophy. An excellent overview of ancient history is provided by Chester G. Starr, *A History of the Ancient World,* 1965. The transition from ancient agriculture-myth cultures to urban ones is well treated in William Irwin Thompson, *The Time Falling Bodies Take to Light: Mythology, Sexuality, and the Origins of Culture,* 1981. A standard brief introduction to Hebrew history is John Bright, *A History of Israel,* 2nd ed., 1972. Even briefer and very useful are B. K. Rattey, *A Short History of the Hebrews,* 2nd ed., 1964, and Harry Orlinsky, *Ancient Israel,* 2nd ed., 1960. J. B. Bury's *History of Greece,* revised by R. Meiggs, 1951, and Michael Grant's *History of Rome,* 1978, are recommended for what their titles promise. Classical Greece is well treated in S. Hornblower, *The Greek World, 479–323,* 1983, and J. K. Davies, *Democracy and Classical Greece,* 1978. T. Cornell and J. Matthews, *Atlas of the Roman World,* 1982, includes, besides good maps and illustrations, a general history of Rome. Also useful are studies of the history of ideas in the ancient world. For the Hebrews, see James Muilenburg, *The Way of Israel,* 1961, and Norman Snaith, *Distinctive Ideas of the Old Testament,* 1947. Important special topics are treated in Frank M. Cross, *Canaanite Myth and Hebrew Epic,* 1973; Dennis J. McCarthy, *Old Testament Covenant: A Survey of Current Opinions,* 1972; and John H. Otwell, *And Sarah Laughed,* 1977, which examines the role of women in the Old Testament. Of many feminist perspectives on the ancient world, especially noteworthy are Jane E. Burns, *Bodytalk,* 1994 (which addresses the medieval world also); Gerda Lerner, *The Creation of Patriarchy,* 1986; and Eva Cantarella, *Pandora's Daughters,* trans. Maureen B. Fant, 1987. Of special importance in understanding the literary practice of the Hebrews, as well as individual books of the Bible, is Northrop Frye's *The Great Code: The Bible and Literature,* 1982. H. D. F. Kitto's *The Greeks,* 1951, C. M. Bowra's *The Greek Experience,* 1957, A. Andrewes' *The Greeks,* 1967, and K. J. Dover's lavishly illustrated *The Greeks,* 1981, are all clear, accurate introductions to Greek ideas and culture. An important literary history of Greece is Albin Lesky, *A History of Greek Literature,* 1963, trans. James Willis and Cornelis de Heer, 1966. Briefer, but still valuable, overviews are provided by C. M. Bowra, *Ancient Greek Literature,* 1933, and K. J. Dover, ed., *Ancient Greek Literature,* 1980. On Greek drama and the Greek theater, T. B. L. Webster's *Greek Theatre Production,* 1962, Peter Arnott's *Greek Scenic Conventions,* 1962, and Margarete Bieber's *The History of the Greek and Roman Theater,* 2nd ed., 1961, are authoritative. Albin Lesky's *Greek Tragic Poetry,* 1983, is a comprehensive account. H. D. F. Kitto's *Greek Tragedy,* 3rd ed., 1961, is a standard critical survey; Jan Kott's *The Eating of the Gods,* 1973, surveys the plays from a more recent perspective. Hugh Lloyd-Jones, *The Justice of Zeus,* 2nd ed., 1984, puts Greek tragic drama in a broad perspective. M. I. Finley, ed., *The Legacy of Greece,* 1981, collects major essays reappraising the Greek heritage. R. H. Barrow's *The Romans,* 1949, is a useful brief introduction to Roman thought and culture. J. Wight Duff's two-volume history of Roman literature has not been superseded: *A Literary History of Rome from the Origins to the Close of the Golden Age,* 3rd ed., 1953; and *A Literary History of Rome in the Silver Age,* 3rd ed., 1964. Michael Grant's *Roman Literature,* 1954, is also accurate and readable, as is Moses Hadas's *History of Latin Literature,* 1952. Hadas's *Ancilla to Classical Reading,* 1954, is a thoughtful and lively handbook for the student of both Greek and Roman literature. R. M. Ogilvie's *Roman Literature and Society,* 1980, is a good author-by-author introduction and survey. On the forging of the ancient epic tradition and its modern heritage, see John Kevin Newman, *The Classical Epic Tradition,* 1986.

Gilgamesh

(c. 2000 B.C.)

Consider this: If we traveled backward in time, twenty centuries would take us to the era of Christ. We would then be only halfway back to the era when the epic *Gilgamesh* was coming into existence, and much less than halfway back in time to the civilization and culture out of which the poem arose. It would seem that we had approached the very border of primitive history.

But consider this, too: The poet Herbert Mason published in 1970 an English rendering of *Gilgamesh,* testifying in an autobiographical postscript to a feeling of deep affinity with the poem. His absorption with it, he reveals, dates to his discovery of *Gilgamesh* in a course on oral epic at Harvard in the 1950s. The course, taught by the distinguished scholar Albert Lord, discriminated between primitive and sophisticated epics. *Gilgamesh* was classified among the sophisticated ones.

When we put these two observations together, the inference to be drawn is obvious: It is a mistake to assume that what is historically early must be, as literature, rough-hewn. Of *Gilgamesh* the opposite is emphatically true, as Lord maintained. For well over a thousand years the poem was familiar, loved, and admired over a wide geographic area, not only in its place of origin but also through much of the Near Eastern world. At the other end of the vast time line we are drawing, the poem has had a special fascination for twentieth-century readers. *Gilgamesh* is a heroic poem, affirming the intensity that human life derives from its very brevity. At the same time, it is almost an antiheroic poem, obsessed with the bitterly agonizing puzzle of inescapable human mortality. Many centuries after *Gilgamesh,* Homer was to examine these same existential themes—when, in the *Odyssey,* Odysseus chooses temporal life in lieu of the goddess Kalypso's offer of immortality; when the dead Akhilleus tells Odysseus in the Underworld that the lowliest station among the living is better than supremacy among the dead; and when, at the end of the *Iliad,* Akhilleus broods over his own mortality in the presence of Priam, who has come to retrieve the corpse of his son from the man who has slain him. It seems safe to say, then, that the enduring appeal of *Gilgamesh,* though its world and atmosphere are in many ways unique and utterly strange, arises largely from the universal interest inherent in its themes and worldview.

In light of what has just been said, it is all the more astonishing that *Gilgamesh* sank into oblivion for two and a half thousand years. The way in which it was rediscovered, in the mid-nineteenth century, constitutes one of the most exciting chapters in the annals of archaeology. The poem originated in the region, corresponding roughly to modern Iraq, called Mesopotamia, a word that means "between the rivers," the rivers being the Tigris and Euphrates. During the three or four millennia before Christ, Mesopotamia was ruled in succession by a number of ancient peoples and dynasties. The written languages of the region, among the earliest in human history, used cuneiform ("wedge-shaped") characters, the meaning of which was lost to the world for more than two thousand years. In 1839, Austen Henry Layard, a young Englishman, happened on the ruins of the ancient Mesopotamian city of Nineveh. Among the things he discovered in excavating the site were thousands of pieces of broken clay tablets, covered with cuneiform characters, which he delivered to the British Museum. In 1853, Layard's colleague Hormuzd Rassam unearthed at Nineveh part of the extensive ancient library amassed by the last great Assyrian king, Assurbanipal, who reigned in the seventh century B.C. This library contained, on its clay tablets, a fragmentary but substantially complete version of the work later recognized as *Gilgamesh*, written in cuneiform in Akkadian, which over a long period had been the main international language of the Near Eastern world. The setting of the poem is the ancient Mesopotamian city of Uruk, much of which was to be excavated in the 1920s and 1930s by German archaeologists. Uruk, which the epic declares was built and ruled by Gilgamesh, is called Erech in the Hebrew Bible and, as part of modern Iraq, is called Warka. Gilgamesh himself may well have been a historical person who lived in the twenty-seventh century B.C. American experts, from the University of Pennsylvania especially, also played a key role, through their Mesopotamian researches late in the nineteenth century, in discovering far more ancient versions, in Sumerian, of the main episodes in *Gilgamesh.*

Discoveries had been made, but they would have meant little if the meaning of cuneiform had remained a mystery. The main breakthrough on this front was made by the English soldier and diplomat Henry Rawlinson, who broke the cuneiform code by analyzing the "Record of Darius," a multilingual Persian inscription in stone. (A similar method had been used earlier in the nineteenth century to decipher ancient Egyptian hieroglyphics with the aid of the Rosetta Stone, discovered by one of Napoleon's soldiers, which was inscribed in both hieroglyphics and Greek.) The major significance of the unearthed cuneiform tablets was first recognized by George Smith, who, in 1872, noted that they recorded a prebiblical account of the Flood.

The textual study of *Gilgamesh* is enormously complicated. Since the first find at Nineveh (and even there, more than one copy was found), many further pertinent fragments have been unearthed. Some passages of the "standard" version from Assurbanipal's excavated library appear in that version only, but many episodes of the poem are found also in the much older Sumerian texts, which go back past 2000 B.C. Still other fragments of the poem, in large numbers, have been found over a wide area of the Near East, written in several different ancient languages. (Some of these fragments represent schoolboy exercises, done with the varying degrees of accuracy one can expect from schoolboys.) The version from Assurbanipal's library is sometimes attributed to a poet named Sin-leque-unninni, who lived during the Kassite period (about 1650–1150 B.C.), but, as with Homer later, it is unclear just what role he may have played in putting the poem together.

If we could be sure there was an "ideal" text of *Gilgamesh*, the various fragments discovered here and there by archaeologists could be expected to firm up, progressively, an authentic version of the poem. In fact, though, newly discovered pieces of it often do the opposite, introducing new variants and textual bypaths. It seems very possible that there has never been a single authoritative version, the poem having evolved and branched rather than being composed in the ordinary sense of the word. *Gilgamesh* has been transmitted in writing but also orally, after the fashion of other works of folk literature the appeal of which often lies, precisely, in the variety of their retellings.

Because all the versions of *Gilgamesh* are, in one sense or another, fragmentary, one might expect that reading it would be a disjointed experience. That is not the case, however; translations of *Gilgamesh* can differ significantly from one another, but they all relate essentially the same powerfully unified story. The "standard" version is fairly consistent in its style, the verse having a highly fluid and flexible meter. The poem is also framed effectively—for example, by nearly identical passages at beginning and end inviting the reader to take in the glories of the city of Uruk.

The main unifying element, though, is thematic. The heroic motif of comradeship in performing awesome feats blends organically with the motif of coping with death, of achieving—figuratively or more literally—immortality. Much of the existential appeal of *Gilgamesh* lies in its uncompromising, unglamorized presentation of the brute fact of death. Heroic achievement is heroic because it faces unflinchingly the obscenity of death, and the stakes are literally infinite; no gardens of the blessed or Elysian Fields or Valhallas await the slain hero. One can leave great achievements behind—a great city, for example, if one is Gilgamesh—but they *are* left behind. The intimate, recognizably human psychology of *Gilgamesh* is striking: Enkidu comes to see some of his noblest achievements, in bitter retrospect, as follies or disasters. The quest for eternal life undertaken by Gilgamesh in the latter part of the poem is not idle fantasy; at the deepest level it reflects the unthinkableness that almost everyone feels at the prospect of simply ceasing to exist, of leaving behind—in Thomas Gray's words—"the warm precincts of the cheerful day."

Gilgamesh is about what it means to be human. Among other things, that involves being civilized, becoming part of a city, a human community. We catch only brief glimpses of nature in the poem, and then mainly as a mocking mirage such as Gilgamesh finds when he reaches the oceanside paradise over which the female vintner Siduri presides, or as the forbidding territory of the monster Humbaba. The most telling episode in this respect is Enkidu's encounter with the temple harlot sent out to cope with him. The sexual initiation she affords Enkidu is not an indulgence of "nature" but quite the opposite: Thereafter he is alienated from the communion with animals he had hitherto experienced. Sexual union brings him into a human world, a world that, as for Gilgamesh too, makes the career of heroism possible and meaningful but also, by the same token, makes it tragic, in a mode available only to members of a generically human collectivity.

NOTE ON THE TEXT AND TRANSLATION

Because *Gilgamesh* has to be recaptured from fragmentary tablets, scrupulously faithful scholarly translations (for example, Stephanie Dalley's in *Myths from Mesopotamia*, 1989) must use an elaborate system of brackets, blank spaces, and the like. Danny P. Jackson's translation, like a number of other modern ones, attempts to draw the fragments together into a coherent, readable text by making occasional conjectures, incorporating supplementary readings from versions other than the "standard" one, condensing or omitting obscure passages, and taking other such necessary liberties. Jackson's inclusion of Tablet XII is especially problematical. Scholars generally agree that Tablet XII, in which a "resurrected" Enkidu speaks to Gilgamesh from the land of the dead, is an appendage added to the other Gilgamesh stories at a later date. Jackson acknowledges its inconsistency with the rest of the epic but includes it because it offers "our first recorded vision of an afterlife" and thus further complicates the poem's treatment of mortality.

FURTHER READING: An authoritative and succinct discussion of *Gilgamesh* is included in Stephanie Dalley, *Myths from Mesopotamia*, 1989. As the title indicates, this book also includes several other myths deriving from related languages and cultures. A less recent but fuller and very clearly written account of the poem, including the story of its discovery and the historic deciphering of cuneiform, is the long Introduction to N. K. Sandars's translation, *The Epic of Gilgamesh*, 1960. An even fuller account of the archaeological adventures appears, along with much else, in Lewis Spence, *Myths and Legends: Babylonia and Assyria*, n.d. Provocative critical insights into the poem are among the good points of the Introduction to *Gilgamesh*, trans. John Gardner, John Maier, and Richard A. Henshaw. Valuable treatments of Mesopotamian culture and civilization include A. Leo Oppenheim, *Ancient Mesopotamia*, 1977; Thorkild Jacobsen, *The Treasure of Darkness: A History of Mesopotamian Religion*, 1976; William Irwin Thompson, *The Time Falling Bodies Take to Light: Mythology, Sexuality, and the Origins of Culture*, 1981; and Samuel Noah Kramer, *Sumerian Mythology*, 1944. On *Gilgamesh* and the Bible, see Alexander Heidel, *The Gilgamesh Epic and Old Testament Parallels*, 1963. In *Somewhere I Have Travelled*, 1992, Thomas Van Nortwick discusses *Gilgamesh* (and Virgil) in terms of personal growth and self-realization. Since the standard text is imperfect and translators therefore often have to resort to creative intuition, it is useful and enjoyable to compare different translations; their number continues to grow.

GILGAMESH

Translated by Danny P. Jackson

MAIN CHARACTERS OF THE EPIC

GILGAMESH (gil' gah mesh): *the hero and king of Uruk.*
ENKIDU (en' kee doo): *his new friend.*
NINSUN (neen' soon): *wise goddess and mother of Gilgamesh.*
SHAMBAT (shahm' baht): *sacred girl who brought the two friends together.*
ANU (ah' noo): *father of the gods and patron of Uruk.*
HUMBABA (hoom bah' bah): *monster god who must be killed.*
ISHTAR (eesh' tar): *the king's spurned and vengeful suitor-goddess.*
ENLIL (en' lil): *god who unleashes the great flood.*
SIDURI (see door' ee): *the barmaid with worldly advice.*
URSHANABI (oor shah nah' bee): *the boatman who gives passage to paradise.*
UTNAPISHTIM (oot nah peesh' teem): *who holds the secret of eternal life.*

TABLET I

Gilgamesh, the King
The Creation of Enkidu
The Civilization of Enkidu
Gilgamesh Dreams of Enkidu

COLUMN I

Fame haunts the man who visits Hell,
who lives to tell my entire tale identically.
So like a sage, a trickster or saint,
GILGAMESH
was a hero who knew secrets and saw forbidden places,
who could even speak of the time before the
Flood because he lived long, learned much,
and spoke his life to those who first
cut into clay his bird-like words.

He commanded walls for Uruk and for Eanna, 10
our holy ground,
walls that you can see still; walls where weep
the weary widows of dead soldiers.
Go to them and touch their immovable presence
with gentle finger to find yourself.
No one else ever built such walls
Climb Uruk's Tower and walk about on a
windy night. Look. Touch. Taste. Sense.
What force creates such mass?
Open up the special box that's hidden in the wall 20
and read aloud the story of Gilgamesh's life.
Learn what sorrow taught him; learn of those
he overcame by wit or force or fear as he,
a town's best child, acted nobly in the way
one should to lead and acted wisely too
as one who sought no fame.
Child of Lugalbanda's wife and some great force,
Gilgamesh is a fate alive, the
finest babe of Ninsun, she who never
let a man touch her, indeed
so pure and heavenly, so without sin. 30
He knew the secret paths that reached the eagle's
nest above the mountain and he knew too how
just to drop a well into the chilly earth.
He sailed the sea to where Shamash comes,
explored the world, sought life, and came at last
to Utnapishtim far away who did bring
back to life the flooded earth.

Is there anywhere a greater king
who can say, as Gilgamesh may, 40
"I am supreme"?

COLUMN II

The bigger part of him was made in heaven
and the smaller part somewhere on earth.
She-who-must-be-obeyed fashioned his body's self.
She endowed him.

Gilgamesh watches the flocks of Uruk himself
as if he were a loose bull, nose up in open field.
No one else could come close to fighting like that.
His clan is roused by powdery dreams
And with them all he goes howling through sanctuaries. 50
But would he ever let his child come
To see him ravish others?
"Is this the shepherd of Uruk's flocks,
our strength, our light, our reason,
who hoards the girls of other men
for his own purpose?"
A prayer of opposition rose from Uruk's other men to heaven;
and the attentive gods asked:
"Who created this awesome beast
with an unmatched strength and a 60
chant that fosters armies?
This warrior keeps boys from fathers
in the night and in the day.
Is this Gilgamesh,
is this the shepherd of Uruk's flocks,
our strength, our light, our reason,
who hoards the girls of other men
for his own purpose?"

When Anu in the sky heard this,
he said to Aruru, great goddess of creation that she is: 70
"You created humans; create again in the
image of Gilgamesh and let this imitation be
as quick in heart and as strong in arm
so that these counterforces might first engage,
then disengage, and finally let Uruk's children
live in peace."
Hearing that, Aruru thought of Anu. Then she
wet her creative fingers, fashioned a rock, and tossed it
as far as she could into the woods.
Thus she fathered Enkidu, a forester, and gave birth 80
in terror and in fright without a single cry of pain,
bringing forth another likeness of Ninurta, god of war.

Hair covered his body and his curls resembled
those of any good girl, growing swiftly like the
fair hair of Nisaba-giver-of-grain.
This Enkidu had neither clan nor race. He went
clothed as one who shepherds well, eating the food
of grass, drinking from the watery holes of herds
and racing swift as wind or silent water.
Then Enkidu met a hunter at the watery hole 90
on three consecutive days.
And each time the face of the hunter signaled
recognition of Enkidu.
For the herds were uninvited at
the hunter's oasis and the hunter was
disturbed by this intrusion. His quiet heart
rushed up in trouble. His eyes darkened.
Fear leaped forth onto a face that looks
as if it expects to doubt for a long, long time.

COLUMN III

Then with trembling lips the hunter told his father this complaint: 100
"Sir, one has come to my watery hole from afar and he
is the biggest and best throughout the land. He feels power.
His is a strength like that of Anu's swift star, and
tirelessly does he roam across the land.
He eats the food of beasts and, like the beasts,
he comes at will to drink from my watery hole.
In fear do I see him come to undo
what I have done by wrecking traps, by
bursting mounds, by letting animals slip through my
grasp, beasts that I would bind." 110

Then with hateful lips, the father told the hunter his reply:
"Boy, your answer lies in Uruk where
there stalks a man of endless strength named Gilgamesh.
He is the biggest and best throughout the land. He feels power.
His is a strength like that of Anu's swift star.
Start out toward Uruk's ancient palace
and tell your tale to Gilgamesh.
In turn he'll say to set a trap, take back with
you a fine lover, some sacred temple girl,
who might let him see what force and charm a girl can have. 120
Then as Enkidu comes again to the watery hole,
let her strip in nearby isolation to show him all her grace.
If he is drawn toward her, and leaves the herd to mate,
his beasts on high will leave him then behind."
The hunter heard his father well and went that very night
to Uruk where he said this to Gilgamesh:
"There is someone from afar whose
force is great throughout our land.
His is a strength throughout the land. He feels power. 130

His is a strength like that of Anu's swift star, and
tirelessly does he roam across the land.
He eats the food of beasts and, like the beasts,
he comes at will to drink from my watery hole.
In fear do I see him come to undo
what I have done by wrecking traps, by
bursting mounds, by letting animals slip through my
grasp, beasts that I would bind."

So Gilgamesh replied:
"Go set a trap; take back with
you a fine lover, Shamhat, the sacred temple girl. 140
who might let him see what charm and force a girl can have.
Then as Enkidu comes again to the watery hole,
let her strip in nearby isolation to show him all her grace.
If he is drawn toward her, and leaves the herd to mate,
his beasts on high will leave him then behind."

The hunter returned, bringing with him the sacred temple girl,
and swift was their journey.
Three days later, at the watery hole, they set their
trap for Enkidu and spoke no word for two
whole days waiting and waiting and waiting. 150
Then the herd came slowly in to drink.

COLUMN IV

Beasts arose and sleepy limbs began to flutter then.
Enkidu, the boy who walked on mountains,
who eats the food of beasts and, like the beasts,
comes down at will to drink from the watery hole,
with the beasts arose and stretched
his tired limbs to start the day.
She beheld him then, as he was in his beginning,
the one who gave and took life from the far woods.
"Here is he, fine lover; be set to wet him with 160
your tongue and chest and loins.
Spread forth your happiness. Display your hidden charm.
Jump him fast and kneel upon his shoulders.
Without his wind then, he'll enter near your entrance.
Take off your robe to let him in.
Let him see what force a girl can have.
The friends he has from on wild will exile him
if he presses his person, as he will, into your scented bush."
Shamhat let her garments loose and spread forth
her happiness which Enkidu entered as gusts of wind 170
enter tunnels bound for Hell.
Hot and swollen first, she jumped him fast
knocking out his rapid breath with
thrust after loving thrust.
She let him see what force a girl can have,

and he stayed within her scented bush for
seven nights, leaping, seeping, weeping, and sleeping there.

After that week of pleasure,
Enkidu returned to the herds
but the beasts fled from him in haste. 180
They stampeded away from his new self.
He could no longer race as he had once,
legs soft now and ankles stiff. The beasts
left him behind and he grew sad
that he could no longer speed with them.
But he enjoyed the memory that no virgin has
and, returning to his fine lover, he once
more knelt between her legs
as she spoke these words to him:
"Now you are as if a god, my boy, 190
with no more need of dumb beasts, however fair.
We can now ascend the road to Uruk's palace,
the immaculate domicile, where Anu and Ishtar dwell,
and there we will see Gilgamesh, the powerful,
who rides over the herd like any great king."
These words he heard and he stared at her.
For the first time he wished for just one friend.
Then Enkidu asked the love who was so fine:
"Please come with me and be my love
at the immaculate domicile, where Anu and Ishtar dwell, 200
and there we will see Gilgamesh, the powerful,
who rides over the herd like any great king.
I wish to call on him; to proclaim all things
aloud and find a friend in him."

COLUMN V

Enkidu continued:
"Uruk will hear me say, 'I am the strongest.
I alone can do all I wish.'
Forester that I am, a mountainous power is mine.
We should march together, face-by-face,
so I can promote your fame." 210
Then fine lover said these words in invitation:
"Enter Uruk of the herds, Enkidu,
where costumes bright are worn,
where it is always time to party,
where merry music never fades,
where graceful girls do ever play
with toys and boys and men;
for in the night these revelers do
their best to rule the town.
There, with a smile, Enkidu 220
will see his other self, great Gilgamesh.

Watch him all, please. Note his
face, his fists, his fairest sword,
and all the strength that dwells in him.
Could he be greater than you,
this one who's up and down all day and night?
Fear your own anger, boy; for great Gilgamesh
adores fair Shamash and is adored in turn.
Anu of the blue sky, Enlil from the clouds
and clever Ea have empowered him. 230
And before he even sees you,
this great Gilgamesh will have first envisioned you
in Uruk as a rival in a dream."

Gilgamesh awakens to ask his mother, Ninsun,
to leave off the dream.
"Mother," says he, "I saw a star
within my head in sleep just now
that fell at me like Anu's dart
and I could not escape.
Uruk was on high of it, 240
our people did applaud,
and gathered up to praise his force.
Men clenched fists; women danced.
And I too embraced this rising star,
as a man does the woman he loves best,
then took the new one here to you
so that you could see us both at once."

Gilgamesh's mother, who is wise in all and worries not, replied:
"This bright, new star is your true friend
who fell at you like Anu's dart, 250
whom you could not escape."

COLUMN VI

Then she who is wise in all and worries not continued:
"So say this friend is one who is almighty,
with strength renowned around the world,
like Anu's dart his force is real
so that he draws you in, as does a wife,
though he is sure to race away, like
that most distant star, with the secrets of your origin.
This dissolves your sleep."

Then again, Gilgamesh said to her in reply: 260
"Mother, I slept when some with axes then
attacked the herds of Uruk."
So Ninsun reassured the frightened king:
"Enkidu will help.
He will guard his loves
or rescue them from danger;

he is your most faithful friend.
Expect him to shepherd you
and to be sure that all goes well."

Gilgamesh said to his fond source:
"I pray for fortune and for fate 270
to send me such a one
that I may have a friend who's as kind
and patient as a brother."

Then in sleep full of repose
the temple girl enchanted Enkidu
where they lay smiling.

TABLET II

The Meeting of Gilgamesh and Enkidu

COLUMN I

Then Gilgamesh explained his dream to Ninsun:
"Last night a vision filled my head
with sights of stars and one sent down from heaven.
At first I tried and failed to carry forth
these signs with me. Then all citizens
of Uruk here assisted in my efforts.
So I was able then to bring these omens near to you."

And she said in reply:
"Wisely done, fair son, and rightly so
for one well reared as you were. 10
All others too will soon acclaim
this god-sent gift to you."

Then Gilgamesh concluded:
"In another dream I saw an ax
and bent toward it with manly interest;
so fair was its appearance
that it seemed wholesome, young and
ready as a woman."

COLUMN II

Soon the day came when the fine lover of Enkidu said:
"Now come with me to enter into Uruk 20
where we shall meet the mighty king,
enormous Gilgamesh.
Now you are as if a god, my boy,
with no more need of dumb beasts, however fair.

We can ascend the road to Uruk's palace,
the immaculate domicile, where Anu and Ishtar dwell
and there we will see Gilgamesh, the powerful,
who rides over the herd like any great king.
You will see in him a power rare
and fairly learn to love him like yourself." 30

They journeyed from the forest far and wide
to venture on toward Uruk.
The girl led forth the naked boy
as gently as a mother would,
tearing her garment right in two
to hide their native beauty
and clothed his splendid body then
with her own cloak as they approached.

COLUMN III

Along the way he learned new human ways 40
tracking down the gentle sheep
and using weapons for the first time
to fight away the savage beasts
that do attack the herds and
farms of men.

COLUMN IV

Along the way he also learned to eat and drink
as men and women do. The girl did
teach all these things too for Enkidu's first lessons.

And with a man upon the road they spoke
to learn of customs new to one from 50
far off woods. So Enkidu came then
to know of Gilgamesh who harshly
ruled and was not loved by those men whose girls
he often played with all night long.

And before they entered through the
gates of Uruk's mighty walls, Enkidu
was hailed as one who might
be sent to rival any king who
might treat gentle folk unfairly.

COLUMN V

In the alleys of Uruk
during a display of force 60
the approach of Enkidu stopped everything.
Uruk rose before him.
The mountain beyond stretched skyward.

All creatures worshiped him.
Youths rallied round.
People adored him as they adore a newborn babe.
For so it is when one comes from nowhere
to do what no one thought could be done.
For Ishara then a wedding bed is set this night
because a guest has come who is as strong as any king. 70
And Enkidu stood before the gate where new lovers go
and stopped Gilgamesh from coming with nighttime girls.
It is there where they first fight
throughout the night and round about Uruk's walls
which they chipped and wrecked in places.

COLUMN VI

So the mighty brothers fought at first
pushing and shoving each other
for hours and hours enraged.
Then a calm force gently soothed
their well-matched spirits
to bring a peace and rest their strife. 80

It was Enkidu who sued for rest saying:
"Gilgamesh, enough! I am here to
match some fate with you, not
to destroy or rival any king."

TABLET III

A Sacred Friendship Forged
The Plot to Conquer Humbaba

COLUMN I

Then Enkidu and Gilgamesh joined in
sacred friendship and sealed their solemn
bond with noble kiss.

COLUMN II

Enkidu and Gilgamesh often sat then together,
visited Ninsun's shrine, conversed
of many plans and fashioned a future together.
Once, informed by fears of
future sorrow, Enkidu began

to weep and warn his friend of
coming horror. He said: 10
"If we go there beyond here to where
Humbaba-the-awful lives,
there will be a gruesome war
in a place no one calls home,
where no one wants to stay for long
or go to rest or rest to gain
the strength to reach the forests."

The Great One rose within
and robed herself appropriately
covering herself, 20
ringing her curls beneath her crown
to ascend the altar, where she stood
lighting the first signals of charcoal for the incense
and preparing sacred cups that hold the
precious liquids which will be spilled.
Then Ninsun asked Shamash:
"Why?
Why have you called my only son away
and shaped his mind in so disturbed a way?
For now, he says, you invite him to begin a 30
pilgrimage that ends where Humbaba
directs a never ending battle,
along a foreign, lonely road
far within the forests dark and damp
where a man like him might just kill
a god like Humbaba or be killed
to dissolve the pain that you, Shamash, oppose."

COLUMN III

Humbaba stirs within the darkened wood
and in the hearts of men there rises fear.
When Enkidu spoke at last to Gilgamesh 40
he said these words of warning:
"I knew this monster's reputation long ago.
Fire and death mix in his breath,
and I for one do not wish now
to challenge such a demon."
But Gilgamesh retorted: "All glory
will be ours if now we conquer
this unprecedented foe and risk the
woe that frightens others."
And Enkidu said then in swift reply: 50
"How shall we go towards woods
so fiercely guarded?"

COLUMN IV

Enlil it was who sent Humbaba there
to scare away intruders with fierce
and frightening howls. Great Gilgamesh
remembered that when he spoke words like these
to Enkidu: "Only gods live forever
with Shamash, my friend; for even our
longest days are numbered. Why worry over
being like dust in the wind? Leap up for 60
this great threat. Fear not. Even if I were
to fail and fall in combat,
all future clans would say I did the job."
Special weapons then were ordered to be made
for their assault upon Humbaba.
Axes, swords, and combat saddles were prepared
and all of Uruk's population flocked round
their great departure.

COLUMN V

The awful monster's reputation
made Uruk's gentle people fear 70
for their great king. And after
all the plans were made to start
out to fight Humbaba, a group
came forward to see the king.
The elders spoke to Gilgamesh:
"Fear the force that you control, hot-headed boy;
Be sure you watch where you direct
your every, heavy swing in battle.
Vanguards protect.
Friends save friends. 80
Let Enkidu lead on the way
through forests that he knows.
He knows how to fight in woodlands;
he knows where to pick his fight.
Enkidu will shield his bosom too
as well as that of his companion
so as to protect them both.
He'll traverse any ditch of any width.
Enkidu will guard our king.
Be sure to bring him safely back." 90
Gilgamesh said to Enkidu:
"Arise, my other self, and speed your way to Egalmah
to where my mother sits, kind Ninsun,.
She understands all I need to know.
She'll tell us where we should go and what to do."
Again the men embraced as teammates do.
Gilgamesh and Enkidu set out to Egalmah.

COLUMN VI

Upset by all his thoughts of coming battles
and concerned by his consultations with the gods,
Gilgamesh then sadly set his palace rooms in order. 100
His weapons were prepared, his helmet shined
and garments freshly cleaned.
Citizens of Uruk came to say good-bye and
wish their daring king farewell.
"Go careful through this risky, bold adventure,
mighty lord. Be sure of your own safety first of all."
So spoke the elders of his town and then continued:
"Let Enkidu take risks for you and have him
lead the way through woods he knows so well.
Pray that Shamash show him, as your guide, 110
the nearest path and choicest route to
where you dare to go.
May great Lugalbanda favor you in combat with Humbaba."
Then Enkidu himself spoke finally to his king:
"The time is right for us to now depart.
Follow me, sir, along the savage way
to where a worthy opponent,
the awful beast Humbaba,
waits for your challenge in the
dark woodlands that he guards. 120
Do not fear this. Rely on me
in every matter and let me act
as careful guide for your most daring venture."

TABLET IV

A Mother's Prayer
Journey to the Cedar Forest
An Ominous Wound

COLUMNS I, II

Ten miles into the march, they stopped to eat.
After thirty miles, they rested,
then finished another twenty miles that day.
Within three days they covered
what would take others a month and a half to travel.
They dug for water where
there appeared to be none
in the dry desert on their way
to challenge Humbaba.

COLUMNS III, IV

Onward ventured Gilgamesh and Enkidu
And they both knew where danger lurked 10
at their first destination.
As up they climbed upon the final hill,
they saw a guard put out by Humbaba
as fierce as any watchdog.
Gilgamesh pursued first.

COLUMN V

Gilgamesh heard shouts from
Enkidu who said to his companion:
"Remember promises we made
in the city where we live. Recall
the courage and the force 20
we vowed to bring upon this mission."
These words dispelled the fear felt
in his heart and Gilgamesh in
return then shouted back:
"Quick. Grab the guard
and don't let go.
Race fearlessly and don't let go.
Our enemy, Humbaba, has set out seven uniforms
but has only dressed in one
so far. So six layers of strength 30
are yet unused by him."
As one mad brute he is enraged,
bellowing loudly while the foresters warn each other
what he's like.

COLUMN VI

Wounded in combat with the guard they killed,
Enkidu uses words to say:
"I lost my strength in this crushed hand when the gate slammed shut.
What shall I do?"
Then Gilgamesh spoke: "Brother,
as a man in tears would, 40
you transcend all the rest who've gathered,
for you can cry and kill
with equal force.
Hold my hand in yours,
and we will not fear what hands like ours can do.
Scream in unison, we will ascend
to death or love, to say in song what we shall do.
Our cry will shoot afar so
this new weakness, awful doubt,
will pass through you. 50
Stay, brother, let us ascend as one."

TABLET V

A Dream of Battle
Humbaba Slain

COLUMN I

Gilgamesh and Enkidu froze and stared into the woods'
great depth and height. When they spied
Humbaba's path, they found the opening toward
straight passage. Then they were able to find and see
the home of the gods, the paradise of Ishtar's other self,
called Imini-most-attractive.
All beauty true is ever there
where gods do dwell, where there is
cool shade and harmony and
sweet-odored food to match their mood. 10

COLUMN III

Then Gilgamesh envisioned yet again
another dream
high up in the hills
where boulders crashed.
Again Enkidu said to his brother,
as he unraveled his dreary story for his king:
"Brother, your song is a fine omen.
This dream will make you well.
Brother, that vision you saw is rich
for on that mountain top 20
we can capture Humbaba and
hurl his earthly form from
towering cliffs through sky to
earth, making his shape
as flat and wide as it is round and high."

"Mountain, mountain in the sky,
Break the god and make him die."

COLUMN IV

Mountain-on-high then sent the myth into Enkidu's sleep,
and a chill from the high winds forced him to rest,
since he was blown around as grain is on open field. 30
Curled up in a ball, Gilgamesh rested
in blessed sleep, the best of friends at the worst of time.
But by the moon's half-way course, he rose
and then began to speak:
"Brother, if you made no noise, what sound woke me?
If you didn't jostle me, what shook my body?
There was no god nearby, so why am I so stunned?

Brother, I've had a third vision in sleep
and I am deeply frightened to recall it all.
Sky screamed. And Mother Earth moaned.
Sun went out of light and blackest night 40
enveloped the heavens.
Then came flashes of lightning, source of fire.
Storm clouds raced nearby and swept all life away
from out of the sky above our heads.
Brightness dissolved, light evaporated;
cinders turned to ash.
When we leave the mountain, this is what we will remember."

When Enkidu learned this myth as told,
he replied to Gilgamesh:
"Shamash, your god, creates a great attraction 50
for both of us. Shamash now approves
of this attack upon Humbaba. Take the sign
as some divine dream to urge us on."
Shamash himself said such words to Gilgamesh
as if in prayer:
"Do not balk now, favored one.
Brace yourself for battle and proceed."

Heavenly winds blasted down from out of the sky
about and all around Humbaba. From east and 60
west, with sand and grain, they blew him
back and forth. His giant self became
fatigued. His awesome strength dwindled.
Not even his great right foot could step away in flight.
So in this way, by Shamash's intervention,
Humbaba-the-awful beast was brought so low.

COLUMN VI

The dying beast called out for mercy once
and part of what he said could still be heard over the howling winds:
"Please, Gilgamesh! Have mercy on me, wounded.
I shall freely give you all the lumber of my mighty realm 70
and work for you both day and night."
It was Enkidu then who shouted louder
than the beast and with his words he
urged a swift conclusion:
"Kill the beast now, Gilgamesh. Show
no weak or silly mercy toward so sly a foe."
Taking his companion's mean advice, Gilgamesh
swiftly cut the beast, splattering blood upon
his cloak and sandals then. Soiled by this
violent conflict, the friends began their 80
journey back to Uruk's towering walls
expecting now to be received as heroes who
had fought and won a legendary battle.

TABLET VI

Ishtar's Proposal
A Scathing Rejection
Ishtar's Revenge: The Bull of Heaven
The Slaughter of the Bull
Enkidu's Ominous Dream

Gilgamesh bathed himself and cleaned his hair,
as beautiful as it was long.
He cast off bloodied robes and put on his favorite gown,
secured the cincture and stood royal.
Then Gilgamesh put on his crown.

Ishtar looked up at Gilgamesh's handsome pride.
"Come to me," she whispered. "Come to me and be my groom.
Let me taste all parts of you,
treat you as husband, be treated as your wife.
And as a gift I'd give to you 10
one regal coach of gold and blue
with wheels of yellow and all so new
that I would flatter all your might
with the sight of demons driven off
by my own god, by my own man.
Come to my home, most sweetly scented of all places,
where holy faces wash your feet with tears as
do the priests and priestesses of gods like Anu.
All mighty hands of kings and queens
will open doors for you. 20
So too will all the countryside donate
in duplicate to your fold.
And the slow will race ahead for you,
so that by association, all that you touch
will turn to gold."
Gilgamesh replied to mighty Ishtar thus:
"But how could I repay you as a wife
and still avoid the bitterness and strife that follow you?
Is it perfume for a dress you want, or me?
My self or something wrapped around a tree? 30
Do I offer you food, sweet nuts or grapes?
Are those for gods or for the savage apes?
And who will pour a treat to us in bed,
you dressed for life and me as if I'm dead?
Here's a song I made for you
(a little crude, a little rude):

Ishtar's the hearth gone cold,
a broken door, without the gold;
a fort that shuts its soldiers out,
a water well that's filled with doubt; 40

tar that can't be washed away,
a broken cup, stained and gray;
rock that shatters to dust and sand,
a useless weapon in the hand;
and worse than that or even this,
a god's own sandal filled with piss.
You've had your share of boys, that's true,
but which of them came twice for you?
Let me now list the ones that you just blew away.
First was Tammuz, the virgin boy you took 50
after a three-year-long seductive look.
Then you lusted for a fancy, colored bird
and cut its wing so it could not herd.
Thus in the lovely woods at night
bird sings, 'I'm blind. I have no sight.'
You trapped a lion, too, back then.
Its cock went in your form-as-hen.
And then you dug him seven holes
in which to fall on sharpened poles.
You let a horse in your back door 60
by laying on a stable floor;
but then you built the world's first chain
to choke his throat and end his reign.
You let him run with all his might,
as boys will sometimes do at night,
before you harnessed his brute force
with labor fierce, a mean divorce.
So did his mother weep and wail
to see her child's foot set with a nail.
You fondled once a shepherd boy 70
who baked buns for your tongue's joy
and daily killed his lambs so coy.
So in return for gifts like those
you chose to lupinize his toy.
And when his brothers saw his penis
they knew you'd done something heinous.
Ishullanu trimmed your father's trees
and brought you carrots, dates and peas.
So mighty you sat down to feasts,
then turned your thoughts to raping beasts. 80
You saw him naked once and said:
'Come, Ishullanu, into my bed
and force your force into my head.
place your fingers where men dread
to touch a girl who's dead.'
And he in turn said this to you:
'What is it that you'd have me do?
I know, kind mother, I won't eat
if I can't match your female heat.
But would you have me sing and sin 90

as my whistle goes both out and in?'
So since he balked to play that role,
you switched his jewel into a mole;
stuck in the muck of a marshy town
his pleasure can't go up or down.
And that is how you'd deal with me
if we got friendly, warm, and free."

When Ishtar heard his words so cruel,
she lost her cool and played the fool
by blasting off for daddy's distant star, 100
where she said: "Daddy, daddy, daddy, please,
Gilgamesh called me a tease."

"Gilgamesh said I sinned and lived
without faith in myself or others," she pouted.

Her father, Anu, said these exact words to Ishtar:
"Now, daughter, did you first insult him,
this Gilgamesh who then began to taunt you
with jibes about your inclinations?"
Ishtar shouted back at him-who-is-her-father:
"You! Now! Make him stop! Loose the 110
bull who could trample him at once.
Let the bull spill his blood.
And you'd better do this now or I'll
wreak havoc of my own right down to Hell.
I'll loose the goddamn devil. I'll rain corpses.
I'll make zombies eat infants and there will be
more dead souls than living ones!"

Her father, Anu, said these exact words to Ishtar:
"But if I do what you seem now to want,
there would be long years of drought 120
and sorrow. Have you stored enough
reserve to feed the people who
deserve your close protection?"

And she said:
"Yes, I have reserved a plan
for those I love. Now do as I demand
and punish all who insult me."

Then her father, Anu, heard Ishtar's cry
and Ishtar forced her will.

Anu set loose a bull from out of the sky and, 130
at the bull's proclamation, there cracks the
earth to swallow up nine dozen citizens of Uruk!
An earthquake fixed a grave for nine dozen citizens of Uruk.

Two or three or four hundred victims,
maybe more than that, fell into Hell.
And when the quake returned for a third time,
it was near to Enkidu,
he who fell upon the Abyss so wide and grim.
Enkidu collapsed near the earth-shaking bull.
Then he leaped to grab the bull by his long horns 140
even with spit upon his face from out the savage mouth,
even with the stench of bowels near his nose.

Then Enkidu said to Gilgamesh:
"Brother, you and I are now hailed as one.
How could we defeat a god?
Brother, I see great challenge here, but can we dare defy such force?
Let's kill it if we can right now.

Be unrelenting and hope that god
gives us the strength.
We must be cold and strong 150
to cut our enemy's weak neck."
Enkidu surrounds the bull, pursuing Heaven's beast
and finally catches him.

So Gilgamesh, like a bull dancer,
svelte and mighty then,
plunged his sword into the throat held fast by Enkidu.
They butchered and bled the bull and then cut out its heart
to offer as sacrifice before Shamash.
Then Gilgamesh and Enkidu retreated
from the altar itself and stood afar 160
in deep respect as they did pray.
At last the two sat down, bound by war, bound by worship.

Ishtar appeared upon Uruk's walls
looking like a wailing widow.
She shrieked this curse aloud:
"Damn Gilgamesh, who injured me,
by slaughtering a divine bull."
Enkidu reacted to these words of Ishtar quick
by hurling at her head a hunk of meat from the bull's thigh.
And from afar he shouted up to her: 170
"This bloody mess of a plain bull would
be about what I could make of you
if you came near. I'd tie
your hands with these rope-like intestines."
Ishtar signaled then for her attendants:
coiffured bishops, cantors, and girls
whose charms keep worshippers coming.

Then atop the great wall above the city high
standing by the severed part of its right thigh,

she had them shriek laments for the bull who'd died. 180
So to complete this ritual and adorn his throne
Gilgamesh summoned artisans of all kinds.
Some measured the diameter of the bull's horns,
each containing thirty pounds of lapis lazuli.
Together those horns could hollow hold
half a dozen quarts of oil.
And that is what Gilgamesh brought as potion
to the altar of Lugalbanda, his special protector.
He carried the horns and enshrined them in a palace
of honor where his clan held rites. 190
Then Enkidu and Gilgamesh absolved their
bloody hands in the forgiving river,
the deep, eternal Euphrates that does not change.

At last relieved of such a stain, the friends renew
their vows with a brief embrace
before riding through Uruk's crowded streets
amid acclaim. There Gilgamesh stops to
give this speech to gathered girls:
"What man is most impressive now?
Who is finest, firmest, and most fair? 200
Isn't Gilgamesh that man above men
and isn't Enkidu the strongest of all?"
Then they party loudly throughout the day
so that, come night, they drop down dead in sleep.
But Enkidu is resurrected quickly
to relieve his soul of fright
and sadly he asks Gilgamesh in tears:
"Oh, brother, why would I dream that gods sat round to set my fate?"

TABLET VII

The Death of Enkidu

COLUMN I

Enkidu confessed this dream to Gilgamesh:
"The gods all gathered round last night
and Anu told Enlil that one of us should die
because of what we've done against their names.
Though Shamash intervened for us,
saying we had slain Humbaba and the bull
with his consent, the others sought revenge."

Then Enkidu fell ill and soon lost his full strength.
Saying words like these as his friend lay dying,
Gilgamesh intoned: 10
"Why should you be so condemned and why should
I go right on living?

Will my own sad eyes soon never look on you again?
Shall I descend to depths beneath
this earth to visit worlds reserved
for those who've died?"

Enkidu glanced up, addressing the entryway
on which his hand was morbidly crushed:
"Door of all forests, that confuses wind and rain,
deaf, dumb, and blind portal; 20
I admired your firm texture
before I first saw the mighty trees
aloft that gave force to you.
There is nothing on earth that could replace
your splendor or your worth.
At two hundred feet in height, at forty feet around are
your mighty posts, your priceless hinge
cut and crafted in Nippur's holy ground.
If I had guessed that you'd become this,
I would have shattered you to pieces 30
with my ax and have been more careful not
to wound my hand so badly on your frame."

COLUMN III

Then cursing the hunter whom he first met
and the girl whom he first loved, Enkidu raged:
"Slash him. Cut half his face.
Raise up floods beneath his feet
so that no animal is safe."
And at his sacred, former lover Enkidu did swear:
"Get up, witch, and hear your fortune
guaranteed now and forever. 40
I damn you off and damn you down.
I'd break your teeth with stones and let
your mouth hang open
until you'd say thanks to your killer
who would favor you by letting you
lie homeless on an open road
in some foul ditch.
May all and any who can hurt you now
often cross the paths you take.
I hope you live in fright, unsure of hope 50
and starved always for the touch of love."

Shamash responded from on high:
"The fine lover, my Enkidu, is cursed by you
who gave you bread and meat and stew,
the same who offered you some wine,
food and drink almost divine
so that you were taken for a god.
The fine lover, my thoughtless boy, invested you

with robes of gold, robes of blue
and, more important, gave your dear friend 60
the thought that he should do whatever need
be done and still more too.
Did your brother, Gilgamesh, give you as fine a bed
as any on earth or any there in heaven?
Did he promote the likes of you to fame
unrivaled, so that rulers kneel to kiss
the ground you walk upon?
He will also show the Uruk people how to mourn for you.
And entire people will cry upon your death
and he will go in tears 70
ignoring the dirt and dust and mud
that stain his hands and hair.
So in despair will his mind be
as off he roams in lonely woods wearing rags."

When Enkidu heard these sad words
he was speechless and in his heart
he knew that Shamash spoke the truth.
His anger fled and Enkidu resolved
to die in peace.

COLUMN IV

With these last words the dying Enkidu did pray 80
and say to his beloved companion:
"In dreams last night
the heavens and the earth poured out
great groans while I alone
stood facing devastation. Some fierce
and threatening creature flew down at me
and pushed me with its talons toward
the horror-filled house of death
wherein Irkalla, queen of shades,
stands in command. 90
There is darkness which lets no person
again see light of day.
There is a road leading away from
bright and lively life.
There dwell those who eat dry dust
and have no cooling water to quench their awful thirst.

As I stood there I saw all those who've died
and even kings among those darkened souls
have none of their remote and former glory.
All earthly greatness was forfeit 100
and I entered then into the house of death.
Others who have been there long
did rise to welcome me."

Hearing this, great Gilgamesh said to his handsome mother:
"My friend, dear Enkidu, has seen his passing now
and he lies dying here upon a sad and lonely cot.
Each day he weakens more and wonders how much more
life may yet belong to his hands and eyes and tongue."

Then Enkidu resumed his last remarks and said:
"Oh Gilgamesh, some destiny has robbed me 110
of the honor fixed for those who die in battle.
I lie now in slow disgrace, withering day by day,
deprived as I am of the peace that comes to one
who dies suddenly in a swift clash of arms."

TABLET VIII

Gilgamesh's Lament
The Specter of Mortality
Farewell to Enkidu

COLUMN I

Then once again at break of day
did Gilgamesh conclude the silent night
by being first to raise his hands and voice
and he said:
"Oh Enkidu, whose own mother's grace
was every bit as sweet as any deer's
and whose father
raced just as swift and stood as strong
as any horse that ever ran,
accept all natural customs 10
within the limitless confines of the wild
where you were raised by those with
tails, by those with hooves, by
those with fur and whiskers.
All the roads in and out of your great forest
now lie silent, but for the sobbing done by your wild friends.
The aged men and women of Uruk mourn today
and raise their withered palms in prayer
as we carry you by, toward Mount Kur.
Grottos weep for you and valleys too 20
and so do those great trees
upon the shore where you loved to run.
And also crying now are
large bears, little dogs, baby cubs
of lions and of tigers, and even
the hyena now has ceased its laugh.
Wild bull and the rapidest of deer
All, all, all sigh,

All, all, all cry for you.
Ulay's lovely riverbanks are swollen on this day 30
where you did walk as boys alone can do
upon the banks of rivers that mother
their young thoughts about life and death.
Yes, that great brown god, the river Ulay,
today mourns for you as does the
true Euphrates eternal and silent.
Uruk's rugged men mourn for you
who killed that sacrificial bull.
They all weep tears today
and those in Eridu, who loved your fame, 40
and say your name aloud,
they too weep tears today
and all in days to come, even those who knew
you not, all may weep tears someday
for your sad lot.
Your favorite aunt, your blessed servant,
your first girlfriend,
your inspiration, your companion, your darling
dear and she you feared to be alone with,
all women who ever sat and ate with you, 50
all men you ever helped with food or drink,
every one and all,
lovers fast and strangers slow.
Those you touched or who touched you
and those who never knew just how you felt.
All and every burst into tears
today because they heard that
you were suddenly dead."

COLUMN II

"I'll cry now, citizens of Uruk, and you
will finally hear what no one else 60
has ever had the nerve to say in sorrow.
I was family and friend to Enkidu and I shall
fill the woodlands where we stalked with loud, sad sobs today.
I cry now, Enkidu, like some crazed woman. I howl.
I screech for you because you were the ax upon my belt
and the bow in my weak hand; the sword within my sheath,
the shield that covered me in battle; my happiest robe,
the finest clothes I ever wore,
the ones that made me look best in the eyes of the world.
That is what you were; that is what you'll always be. 70
What devil came to take you off from me?

Brother, you chased down the strongest mule,
the swiftest horse on mountains high,
the quickest panthers in the flatlands.
And they in turn will weep for you.

Birds in the air cry aloud.
Fish in the lake gather together near the shore.
What else heeds this sorrow?
The leaves of the trees and the paths you loved
in the forest grow dark. 80
Night itself murmurs and so too does the day.
All the eyes of the city that once saw your kind face begin to weep.
Why? Because you were my brother and you died.
When we met and fought and loved,
we went up on mountains high to where we dared to capture
god's own strength in one great beast and then to cut its throat,
thus humbling Humbaba, green god of woodlands steep.
Now there is a sleep-like spell on you, and you
are dark as well as deaf."

Enkidu can move no more. 90
Enkidu can lift his head no more.

"Now there is a sound throughout the land
that can mean only one thing.
I hear the voice of grief and I know that you have been taken
somewhere by death.
Weep. Let the roads we walked together flood themselves with tears.
Let the beasts we hunted cry out for this:
the lion and the leopard, the tiger and the panther.
Let their strength be put into their tears.
Let the cloud-like mountain where you killed 100
the guardian of woodland treasures
place grief upon its sky-blue top.
Let the river which soothed our feet overflow its banks
as tears do that swell and rush across my dusty cheeks.
Let the clouds and stars race swiftly with you into death.
Let the rain that makes us dream
tell the story of your life tonight.
Who mourns for you now, Brother?
Everyone who knew you does.
The harvesters and the farmers who used to bring you grain 110
are standing alone in their fields.
The servants who worked in your house
today whispered your name in empty rooms.
The lover who kissed every part of you
touches her chilled lips with scented fingers.
The women of the palace sit
and stare at the queen of the city.
She sobs and sobs and sobs.
The men with whom you played so bold
speak fondly of your name. 120
Thus they deal with this misfortune.
But what do I do? I only know that a cruel fate robbed me
of my dearest friend too soon.

What state of being holds you now? Are you lost forever?
Do you hear my song?"

"I placed my hand upon your quiet heart."
One brother covered the set face of another
with a bride-white veil.

"I flew above you then as if I were an eagle."

Then, like some great cat whose darling young have sadly died, 130
Gilgamesh slides back and forth fixed mindlessly on grief.
He commands many men to erect statues of honor, saying:
"Make his chest a noble blue and on his honored body place a jewel
as will allow all viewers then to see how great he was,
how great he'll always be."

Next day, Gilgamesh rose from a restless sleep.

COLUMN III

Then Gilgamesh continued with his bird-like words:
"On a pedestal I will honor your corpse
by setting you
above all earthly princes who will celebrate you 140
when people from all distant lands
both rich and poor in spirit
acclaim your memory.
And when you are gone,
never again to wear good clothes or care for food,
I'll still remember how you dressed and how you ate."
When day did break again next morn,
Gilgamesh stripped off the lion's cloak and
rose to say this prayer:
"Your funeral is a precious 150
gesture I made to hide my own guilt."

Goodbye, dear brother
Ave atque vale, frater[1]
Sat sri akai meri pra[2]
Dehna hune wood wordema[3]
Slan agat, seanchara[4]
Shalom.[5]

COLUMN V

Still grieving reverently
after he arose next day, Gilgamesh imagined the Annunaki

[1]Latin: Hail and farewell, Brother
[2]Bengali (India): Goodbye, Brother
[3]Amharic (Ethiopia): Farewell, sweet Brother
[4]Gaelic: Go fairly, old Friend
[5]Hebrew: Peace

who decide the fate of
those who go to the underworld. 160
After learning how to pause his heart,
Gilgamesh created just the same image
in the face of a river.
At break of day,
on the sacred table made of special wood,
the grieving king placed a consecrated bowl of blue
filled with butter and with honey too
and this he offered up in solemn prayer
to Shamash, lord god. 170

TABLET IX

The Quest for Immortality
The Scorpion

COLUMN I

Then Gilgamesh wept some more
for his dead friend. He wandered
over barren hills, mumbling to his own spirit:
"Will you too die as Enkidu did?
Will grief become your food? Will we both
fear the lonely hills, so vacant?
I now race from place to place,
dissatisfied with wherever I am and
turn my step toward Utnapishtim,
godchild of Ubaratutu, 10
who lives a pious life in fair Dilmun
where the morning sun arises as it
does in paradises lost and won.
As if in sleep I come upon the mountain door at midnight
where I face wild-eyed lions and I am afraid.
Then to Sin, the god of mighty light,
I raise my solemn chant to beg:
'Save me, please, my god.' "

Despite respite
he could not sleep or dream that night. 20
Instead he wandered through the woods
so like a savage beast just then
did he bring death again and again
upon the lions' heads
with an ax he drew
from off his belt.

COLUMN II

When he finally reached the base of
Mt. Mashu, Gilgamesh began to

climb the double cliff
that guides the rising and setting of Shamash. 30
Now these identical towers touch
the distant, distant sky,
and far below, their breasts descend toward Hell.
Those who guard the gate are
poison scorpions
who terrorize all, whose spells bring death.
And then resplendent power
thrives all across the town
where I was born
and rises farther still to 40
mountain tops.
At dawn and dark they shield Shamash.
And when he sensed them there,
Gilgamesh could not dare to look
upon their threat;
but held his glance away,
suspended fear,
and then approached in dread.
One among the guardians there
said this to his wife: 50
"The one who comes toward us
is partly divine, my dear."
And then the same one said
to the god-like part of Gilgamesh:
"Eternal heart, why make
this long, long trip
trying to come to us
through travail? Speak now."

COLUMN III

Gilgamesh said: "I come by here
to visit my elder, my Utnapishtim, 60
the epitome of both life everlasting and
death that is eternal."

The poison scorpion guardian said:
"No mortal man has ever
come to know what you seek
here. Not one of all your kind
has come so far, the distance
you would fall if you fell
all day and all night into the pit
and through great darkness 70
where there is no light
without Shamash who raises
and lowers the sun;
to where I let no one go,
to where I forbid anyone to enter."

COLUMN IV

Heartachest pain abounds
with ice or fire all around.
The scorpion one,
I do not know whether a man or a woman,
said then:
"Gilgamesh, I command you 80
to proceed
to highest peaks
over hills toward heaven.
Godspeed!
With all permissions given here, I approve your venture."
So Gilgamesh set out then over
that sacred, sacred path within the mountains of Mashu,
near that incarnate ray of sunshine
precious to Shamash.
Oh dark, dark, dark, dark. 90
Oh the night, unholy and blind,
that wrapped him as soon as he stepped
forth upon that path.

COLUMN V

DARKNESS
Beneath a moonless, starless sky,
Gilgamesh was frozen and unseeing
by time before midnight;
by midnight's hollow eye
he was unseen and frozen. 100
At 1 A.M. he tripped and fell
blinded and frozen.
At 2 A.M. he staggered on
blinded and frozen.
At 3 A.M. he faltered not
blinded and frozen.
By 4 A.M. his second wind warmed him who still was
blinded and frozen.
And at your final dawn,
son of man, you will see only 110
a heap of broken images in an ascending
light that gives you sight you may not want,
for you will then behold all precious goods
and gardens sweet as home to you, as exile,
boughs of blue, oh unforgotten gem,
as true as any other memory from any other previous life.

COLUMN VI

Then along the path
Gilgamesh traveled fast
and came at length to

shorelines fresh with dew. 120
And there he met a maiden,
one who knows the secrets of the sea.

TABLET X

Siduri Whose Drinks Refresh the Soul
The Boatman, Urshanabi
Gilgamesh Implores Utnapishtim

COLUMN I

This gentle girl is called Siduri
and she sits by the sea
where she sways from side to side.
She made the water pale; she crafted the first gold bowl
while peeking at the sun
through a slit across her face veil.

King Gilgamesh approached the girl's small cottage by the sea
dressed as a mountain man,
a meat-eater,
with an aching heart 10
and the stare of one setting out upon some
arduous, horrid trek.
The girl who gives her men lifesaving drinks
said to herself, "Beware of the one
coming now. He walks as if he'd kill."
And so Siduri locked the door,
put stones in place, lay on the floor.
When Gilgamesh heard sounds inside
he yelled at her. "Why do you hide?
Shall I have to break through this door?" 20

The girl whose drinks refresh the soul
then said these words to Gilgamesh:
"Is there a simple reason, sir, why you're so sad
or why your face is drawn and thin?
Has chance worn out your youth or did some
wicked sorrow consume you like food?
You look like one setting out on some arduous, horrid trek,
like one exposed to extremes of hot and cold,
like one who searches everywhere for grace.
He responded then to her who gives her men 30
lifesaving drinks:
"Girl, there is no simple reason why I'm so sad
or why my face is drawn and thin.
Chance alone did not wear out my youth. Some
wicked sorrow consumes me like food.
But I do look like one setting out on some
arduous, horrid trek, like one exposed

to extreme hot or cold,
like one who searches everywhere
for the breath of life 40
because my brother, my only true friend, met death;
he who raced wild horses there,
who caught orange tigers here.
This was Enkidu, my soul's good half,
who raced wild horses there,
who caught orange tigers here;
who did all things while he conquered mountains
and divine bulls that race
across the sky like clouds;
who gave Humbaba, the woodland god, 50
reason to weep when he stole through
the wooded path to slaughter lions."

COLUMN II

Gilgamesh continued:
"I greatly loved my friend who was always there for me.
I loved Enkidu who was always there for me.
What awaits us all caught him first
and I did thirst for one whole week to
see him once again in splendor until his body decomposed.
Then I wept for my future death
and I fled home for mountaintops to breathe 60
when my friend's death choked off my wind.
On mountaintops I roamed content to breathe
again when my friend's death choked off my wind.
Walking. Walking. Walking over hills.
Could I sit down to rest?
Could I stop crying then
when my best friend had died
as I will someday do?"

Then Gilgamesh said to the fair girl
whose saving drinks gave life to men: 70
"Tell me, girl, how to get to Utnapishtim.
Where do I look for signs? Show me directions. Help.
Please let me have safe passage over seas.
Give me advice to guide me on my way."
She said to him in swift reply:
"No man has ever gone that way
and lived to say he crossed the sea.
Shamash only ventures there,
only Shamash would dare
to stare into the sun. 80
Pain joins the voyager soon,
and soon the traveler grows weary
where death surrounds the path
on every side with danger."

COLUMN III

The girl whose drinks refresh the soul
then said these words to Gilgamesh:
"Remember always, mighty king,
that gods decreed the fates of all
many years ago. They alone are let
to be eternal, while we frail humans die 90
as you yourself must someday do.
What is best for us to do
is now to sing and dance.
Relish warm food and cool drinks.
Cherish children to whom your love gives life.
Bathe easily in sweet, refreshing waters.
Play joyfully with your chosen wife."

"It is the will of the gods for you to smile
on simple pleasure in the leisure time of your short days."

"And what, after all, my fellow man, 100
would you do when you got to that
far side where Urshanabi dwells
among the hills of Utnapishtim?
He knows only the dead weight of what is dead
and he is one who plays with deadly snakes.
Would you put your lips near his?
If he befriends you then, go on.
But if he walks away, return to me."
With that in mind
Gilgamesh took up his chore, 110
unsheathed his sword, slipped toward the shore
and there joined one who rows the seas of death.
Gilgamesh sliced through the underbrush as an arrow goes through air
while cracking the stones of the sacred columns.
And Urshanabi barely saw the arrow's glint
and too late heard the ax's thud.
And so surprised was he that
there was never any chance to
hide or to deny the daring man
at least a chance at 120
some safe passage.

Gilgamesh traveled on to where he next
found the ferryman of Utnapishtim. This man,
Urshanabi, said to Gilgamesh:
"Your face seems tense; your eyes do not glance well
and Hell itself is part of how you look.
Grief hangs from your shoulders.
You look like one who's been without a home, without a bed
or roof for a long time, wandering the wilds on some random search.
Gilgamesh replied to the ferryman: 130
"Yes, sir, it's true my face is tense

and that my eyes seem harsh.
My looks are now so hellish,
for I wear my grief as ill as any other.
I'm not this way as some refugee
without a bed or roof for a long time,
and I don't wander the wilds randomly.
I grieve for Enkidu, my fair companion and true friend,
who chased the strongest mule, the swiftest horse
on mountain high, the quickest panther of the flatland. 140
Together we did all things, climbing sky-high peaks,
stealing divine cattle, humbling the gods, killing Humbaba
and the precious lions, guardians of the sky.
All this I did with my best friend who now is dead.
Mortality reached him first and I am left this week
to weep and wail for his shriveling corpse which scares me.
I roam aloft and alone now, by death enthralled,
and think of nothing but my dear friend.
I roam the lonely path with death upon my mind
and think of nothing but my dear friend. 150
Over many seas and across many mountains I roam.
I can't stop pacing. I can't stop crying.
My friend has died and half my heart is torn from me.
Won't I soon be like him, stone-cold and dead, for all the days to come?"

Urshanabi replied as he had done before:
"Your face seems tense; your eyes do not glance well
and Hell itself is part of how you look.
Grief hangs from your shoulders.
You look like one who's been without a home, without a bed
or roof for a long time, wandering the wilds on some random search." 160

And Gilgamesh said to him then in swift reply:
"Of course my face seems tense and my eyes seem harsh.
Of course I'm worn out weeping. Why should I not cry?
I've come to ask directions to Utnapishtim, who lives so
free beyond death's deep, deep lake. Where can he be?
Tell me how to venture there where I may learn his secrets."

Finally, Urshanabi uttered these last words to Gilgamesh:
"You yourself have hurt this effort most, sir,
by blasphemy and sacrilege,
by breaking idols and by holding the untouchably sacred stones. 170
You broke stone images!
So now, Mr. Gilgamesh, raise high your ax.

Thus chastised, Gilgamesh
raised high his ax, unsheathed his sword,
did penance too as he chopped down many trees;
prepared them then, and then brought them
to Urshanabi.
After this, they cast off together,
with push and pull they launched the skiff

upon the waving sea. 180
They leaped quick, in three short days
covering a span that any other would
traverse only after months of passage
and soon they sailed on to Death's own sea.

COLUMN IV

Still directing the king's new efforts, Urshanabi called:
"Give me another pull, Gilgamesh, upon the mighty oar
and then another. Give ten times twenty
and then give twenty times ten pulls upon the
mighty oars; then ten more twice; then twice
more ten and then confuse the number of 190
the pulls you put upon the oar
by losing count aloud and starting over."
Halfway through all that pulling,
Gilgamesh had worn the oars to bits
and torn his shirt from off his back
to raise a helping sail upon the mast.
Then Utnapishtim glared down from stars and clouds
and mused aloud, as if to coach the world:
"How could any human dare to break the idols
or steer the craft that gods and goddesses use? 200
This stranger is not fit to tie the shoes of servants.
I do see, but I am blind.
I do know, but cannot understand
how he behaves like
the beasts of here and there."

COLUMN V

Gilgamesh spoke many words to Utnapishtim
and told of strife-in-life and
battles rare. He hailed his friend Enkidu,
acclaimed their pride and grieved the
death that saddened his great heart. 210
Gilgamesh raised his prayer to the remote Utnapishtim:
"Oh myth-filled god,
I have traveled many roads,
crossed many rivers and mountains.
I never rested. I never slept. Grief consumed me.
My clothing was ragged by the time I met
the girl who would help me.
I killed all manner of animal in order
to eat and clothe myself.
When I was rejected, I stooped to squalor. 220
Cursed I went,
being unholy."
Utnapishtim replied:
"Why cry over your fate and nature?

Chance fathered you. Your conception was
an accidental combination
of the divine and mortal.
I do not presume to know how to help
the likes of you."

COLUMN VI

Utnapishtim continued: 230
"No man has ever seen Death.
No one ever heard Death's voice
but Death is real and Death is loud.
How many times must a home be restored
or a contract revised and approved?
How many times must two brothers agree
not to dispute what is theirs?
How many wars and how many floods must there be
with plague and exile in their wake?
Shamash is the one who can say. 240
But there is no one else who can
see what Shamash only can see within the sun.

Behold the cold, cold corpse from a distance,
and then regard the body of one who sleeps.
There seems no difference. How can we say
which is good and which is bad?
And it is also like that with other things as well.

Somewhere above us, where the goddess Mammetum decides all things,
Mother Chance sits with the Anunnaki
and there she settles all decrees of fable and of fortune. 250
There they issue lengths of lives;
then they issue times of death.
But the last, last matter
is always veiled from human beings.
The length of lives can only be guessed."
Thus spoke Utnapishtim.

TABLET XI

The Flood
Trial of Sleeplessness
Plant of Eternal Life
Foiled by the Serpent
Triumphant Return

COLUMN I

To the most distant and removed of semi-gods, to Utnapishtim,
Gilgamesh said:

"When I regard you now, my god-like man,
it's like seeing my own face on calm water
where I dare to study myself.
Like me, you are first of all a fighter
who prefers to war-no-more.
How could one like you, so human, all-too-human,
ascend to be at one with other gods?"

Utnapishtim said to him in swift reply: 10
"Only one as bold as you would dare expect
such knowledge. But I shall tell you what
no person has ever been told.
High up the constant Euphrates
there rests a place you call Shuruppak
where gods and goddesses recline.
Then came the flood, sent by gods' intent.
Mama, Anu, and Enlil were at Shuruppak.
So too was their coachman, Ninurta,
and Ennugi, the beastiarius, 20
and one who watches over precious infants, the ever vigilant Ea.
And Ea refrained their chant to the high-grown reeds
upon the shore, giving this advice to me:
'Arise! Arise! Oh wall-like reeds.
Arise and hear my words:
Citizen of Shuruppak, child of Ubaratutu,
abandon your home and build a boat.
Reject the corpse-like stench of wealth.
Choose to live and choose to love;
choose to rise above and give back 30
what you yourself were given.
Be moderate as you flee for survival
in a boat that has no place for riches.
Take the seed of all you need aboard
with you and carefully weigh anchor
after securing a roof that will let in no water.'

"Then I said back in reverent prayer:
'I understand, great Ea.
I shall do just as you say to honor god,
but for myself 40
I'll have to find a reason to give the people.'
"Then Ea voiced a fair reply:
'Tell those who'll need to know
that Enlil hates you.
Say: "I must flee the city now
and go by sea to where Enlil waits to take my life.
I will descend to the brink of Hell
to be with Ea, god,
who will send riches to you like the rain:
all manner of birds; 50
birds . . . bords . . . burds . . .

and the rarest of rare fish.
The land will fill with crops full grown at break of day.
Ea will begin to shower
gifts of life upon you all".'"

COLUMN II

Then Utnapishtim continued, saying words like these:
"By week's end I engineered designs
for an acre's worth of floor upon the ark we built
so that its walls rose straight toward heaven;
with decks all round did I design its space; 120 cubits measured its deck. 60
With division of six and of seven
I patterned its squares and stairs;
left space for portals too,
secured its beams and stockpiled
all that ever could be used.
Pitch for the hull I poured into the kiln
and ordered three full volumes of oil
to start with and two times three more yet.
For what is security?
Each day I sacrificed the holy bulls 70
and chosen sheep for the people
and pushed the laborers to great fatigue
and thirst, allayed alone by wine
which they drank as if it were water running
from barrels set up for holding cheer
in preparation for a New Year's party they expected.
I set up an ointment box
and cleaned my fingers with its cream.

"After one week, the ark was done,
though launching was more work than fun 80
since hull boards caught and snapped
until the water burst most of its great ton.
I supplied the craft with all I owned
of silver, gold, and seed.
My clan brought on the food they'd eat
and all the things we thought we'd need.
At last, it was my turn just then
to shepherd beasts and birds and
babies wet and loud.
It was Shamash who ordained the time, saying: 90
'Prepare the way for your whole boat
and set to sail when the storm
begins to threaten you.'

"The Anunnaki too then cried for them.
The gods themselves, finally suffering, sat up
and let their first tears flow down
cheeks and over lips pressed closed.

COLUMN III

"For the whole next week
the sky screamed and storms wrecked the earth
and finally broke the war 100
which groaned as one in labor's throes.
Even Ishtar then bemoaned the
fates of her sad people.
Ocean silent.
Winds dead.
Flood ended.
Then I see a dawn so still;
all humans beaten to dirt
and earth itself like some vast roof.
I peeked through the portal into a morning sun 110
then turned, knelt and cried.
Tears flooded down my face.

"Then I searched high and low for the shoreline,
finally spotting an island near and dear.
Our boat stuck fast beside Mt. Nimush.
Mt. Nimush held the hull that could not sway for one whole week.

"I released the watch-bird, to soar in search of land.
The bird came back within a day
exhausted, unrelieved from lack of rest.
I then released a swallow, to soar in search of land. 120
The bird came back within a day
exhausted, unrelieved from lack of rest.
I then released a raven, to soar in search of land.
The bird took flight above more shallow seas,
found food and found release and found no
need to fly on back to me.

"These birds I then released to earth's four corners
and offered sacrifice,
a small libation to the heights of many mountains,
from numbered chalices that I arranged. 130
Under these I spread the scents that gods favored
and when the gods smelled the sweet perfume of sacrifice,
they gathered in flight all above, like apparitions.

COLUMN IV

"From distant heights with heavenly sights,
the female of all female gods descended then;
Aruru who aroused the wry thought
that Anu made for intercourse.
'Great gods from far and wide
keep always in my mind

this thought for intercourse, 140
tokened by the sacred blue medallion on my neck.
Let me recall with smiles
these days in days to come.
Gods of my shoreline, gods of my sky,
come round this food that I prepared for you;
but do not let Enlil enjoy this too,
since he's the one who drowned my relatives
without telling the gods what he set out to do.'
When Enlil saw the boat, he released
his calm reason and let in the Igigi, monsters of blood. 150
'What force dares defy my anger!?
How dare a man be still alive!?'
Then with these words Ninurta said to Enlil:
'Can any of us besides Ea, maker of words,
create such things as speech?'
Then with these words Ea himself said to Enlil:
'Sly god,
sky darkener,
and tough fighter,
how dare you drown so many little people 160
without consulting me?
Why not just kill the one who offended you,
drown only the sinner?
Keep hold of his lifecord; harness his destiny.
Rather than killing rains, set cats at people's throats.
Rather than killing rains, set starvation on dry, parched throats.
Rather than killing rains, set sickness on the minds and hearts of people.
I was not the one who revealed our god-awful secrets.
Blame Utnapishtim, Mr. Know-it-all,
who sees everything, 170
who knows everything.' "

"Reflect on these stories, my Gilgamesh."

"Then Enlil swooped down around my boat;
he gently raised me from the slime,
placed my wife beside my kneeling form
and blessed us both at once with hands upon our bowed heads.
So was it ordained.
So we were ordained."

Earlier than that time, Utnapishtim was not divine.
Then with his wife he was deified 180
and sent to rule the place where rivers start.
"Gods sent me everywhere to rule the place where rivers start."

"As for you, Gilgamesh, which gods will be called on
to direct your path and future life?
Arise! Be alert! Stay up with stars for

seven long and sleepless nights!"
But even as he tried to stay awake,
fog-like sleep rolled over his eyes.
Then Utnapishtim said these words:
"Dear wife, behold the one who tries to pray 190
while fog-like sleep rolls over his eyes."
She said to him who rarely talks:
"Arouse him now and let him
leave unharmed. Permit that one
to go back home at last."

COLUMN V

Then Utnapishtim said these words:
"An upset soul can upset many gods.
Be kind with food and generous to him.
But keep a count of how he
sleeps and what he eats." 200
She was kind with food and gentle with the man
and she kept count of how he slept.
"*One, two, three, alarie,*
he slept with death-the-fairy.
Four, five, six, alarie,
he looked so cold and wary."
Then he returned from death to breath!

So Gilgamesh said to the One-who-rarely-spoke:
"Just as I slipped toward sleep,
you sent my dream." 210
And to him in reply, Utnapishtim said these words:
"*One, two, three, alarie,*
you slept with death-the-fairy.
Four, five, six, alarie,
you looked so cold and wary.
Then you arose from death to breath."
So Gilgamesh said to the One-who-rarely-speaks:
"Help me, Utnapishtim. Where is
home for one like me whose self
was robbed of life? My own 220
bed is where death sleeps and
I crack her spine on every line
where my foot falls."
Utnapishtim calls out to the sailor-god:
"Urshanabi, dear, you will never land
again easily or easily sail the seas
to shores where you no more will find safe harbor.
Sandy and disheveled hair does not become
the one you nearly drowned.
Shingles now spoil his hidden beauty. 230
Better find a place to clean him up.

Better race to pools of saltless water soon
so that by noon he'll shine again for all of us to see.
Tie up his curly hair with ribbon fair.
Place on his shoulders broad the happy robe
so that he may return to his native city easily in triumph.
Allow him to wear the sacred elder's cloak
and see that it is always kept as clean
as it can be."

The sailor-god brought Gilgamesh
to where they cleaned his wounds.
By noon he shone again for all to see. 240
He tied his curly hair with ribbon fair,
and placed upon his shoulder broad the happy robe
so he would return to Uruk easily in triumph
with a cloak unstained and unstainable.
Urshanabi and Gilgamesh launched the boat
over the breakers on the beach and
started to depart across the seas.

COLUMN VI

To her distant husband, Utnapishtim's wife said:
"This Gilgamesh has labored much to come here. 250
Can you reward him for traveling back?"
At that very moment, Gilgamesh used paddles
to return his craft along the shore.
Then Utnapishtim called out to him:
"Gilgamesh! You labored much to come here.
How can I reward you for traveling back?
May I share a special secret, one
that the gods alone do know?
There is a plant that hides somewhere among the rocks
that thirsts and thrusts itself deep
in the earth, with thistles that sting. 260
That plant contains eternal life for you."
Immediately, Gilgamesh set out in search.
Weighed down carefully, he dove beneath
the cold, cold waters and saw the plant.
Although it stung him when he grabbed its leaf,
he held it fast as he then slipped off his weights
and soared back to the surface.

Then Gilgamesh said this to Urshanabi, the sailor-god:
"Here is the leaf that begins
all life worth having. 270
I am bound now for Uruk,
town-so-full-of-shepherds,
and there I'll dare to give
this plant to aged men as food

and they will call it life-giving.
I too intend to eat it
and to be made forever young."
After 10 miles they ate.
After 15 miles they set up camp 280
where Gilgamesh slipped into a pool;
but in the pool, a cruel snake slithered by
and stole the plant from Gilgamesh
who saw the snake grow young again,
as off it raced with the special, special plant.
Right there and then Gilgamesh began to weep
and, between sobs, said to the sailor-god who held his hand:
"Why do I bother working for nothing?
Who even notices what I do?
I don't value what I did 290
and now only the snake has
won eternal life. In minutes,
swift currents will lose forever
that special sign that god had left for me."

Then they set out again,
This time upon the land.
After 10 miles they stopped to eat.
After 30 miles they set up camp.
Next day they came to Uruk, full of shepherds.
Then Gilgamesh said this to the boatman: 300
"Rise up now, Urshanabi, and examine
Uruk's wall. Study the base, the brick,
the old design. Is it permanent as can be?
Does it look like wisdom designed it?
The house of Ishtar in
Uruk is divided into three parts:
the town itself, the palm grove, and the prairie."

TABLET XII

Descent to the Underworld
The Afterlife

"If only I'd have protected our instruments in the
safe home of the drum-maker;
If only I'd have given so precious a harp to the
craftsman's wife, she who shepherds such jewel-like children.
God, has your heart forgotten me?
Who shall descend to Hell and redeem the
drum from where it rests unused?

Who shall risk his life to retrieve
the precious gifts of Ishtar from death?"
And for this quest his friend alone did pledge. 10
So Gilgamesh said this to Enkidu:
"Descend, descend to Hell where life does end
but listen now to words you need to know.
Go slow to where death rules, my brother dear,
and then arise again above and over fear."
And, once more, Gilgamesh said this to Enkidu:
"Let all who would be saved today, take heed,
and listen to god's words in time of need.
When walking with the strong or with the dead,
do not wear clothes of purple or of red. 20
Shun make-up that presents a holy face
for they attack the phony and the base.
Leave here with me your knife and rock and club;
such weapons only add to their own strife.
Put down your bow, as you would leave a wife.
The souls of death will soil your hands and feet.
Go naked, filthy, tearful, when you meet.
Be quiet, mild, remote, and distant too
as those who will surround and follow you.
Greet no girl with kiss so kind upon her lips; 30
push none away from you with fingertips.
Hold no child's hand as you descend to Hell
and strike no boy who chooses there to dwell.
Around you, Enkidu, the lament of the dead
will whirl and scream,
for she alone, in that good place, is at home who,
having given birth to beauty,
has watched that beauty die.
No graceful robe any longer graces her naked self
and her kind breasts, once warm with milk, 40
have turned into bowls of cold stone."

But Enkidu refused to heed his friend
as he set out that day to then descend
to where the dead who-do-not-live do stay.
He wore bright clothes of celebrative red,
the sight of which offended all the dead.
His colored face made him seem fair and good
but spirits hate the flesh that would dare
remind us of the beauty they have lost.
He brought with him his club and rock and knife 50
and did cause strife with those whom he did mock.

There, too, is where he showed off;
where he went clothed among the naked,
where he wasted food beside the starving,
where he danced beside the grief-stricken.

He kissed a happy girl.
He struck a good woman.
He enjoyed his fatherhood.
He fought with his son.

Around him, the lament for the dead arose; 60
for she alone, in that sad place, is at home who,
having given birth to beauty,
has watched that beauty die.
No graceful robe any longer graces her naked self
and her kind breasts, once warm with milk,
have turned into bowls of cold stone.
She never even dreamed once of letting him return
to life. Namtar, the decision-maker,
would not help Enkidu. Nor would illness
help. Hell became his home. 70
Nergal, chief-enforcer, would not help.
Dirges and laments rose all around.
Not even the soldier's death-in-battle,
with all its false and phony honor,
helped Enkidu. Death just swallowed him, unrecognized.
So the great son of Ninsun, proud Gilgamesh,
cried for his beloved friend
and went to the temple of Enlil,
the savage god of soldiers,
to say: "My god, when death 80
called for me, my best friend went
in my place and he is now no longer living."
But the savage god of soldiers, Enlil, was mute.
So Gilgamesh turned next to one who flies alone,
and to the moon he said: "My god, when death
called for me, my best friend went
in my place and he is now no longer living."
But the moon, who flies alone, was also mute;
so he went next to Ea, whose waters fill
the desert oasis even when no rain falls. 90
"My god," he cried, "when death
called for me, my best friend went
in my place and he is now no longer living."

And Ea, whose waters keep us alive as we journey over desert sands
said this to Nergal, great soldier in arms.
"Go now, mighty follower; free Enkidu to speak once to kin
and show this Gilgamesh how to descend halfway
to Hell through the bowels of earth."
And Nergal, accustomed to absurd orders,
obeyed as soldiers do. 100
He freed Enkidu to speak once to kin
and showed Gilgamesh how to descend halfway
to Hell through the bowels of earth.

Enkidu's shadow rose slowly toward the living
and the brothers, tearful and weak,
tried to hug, tried to speak,
tried and failed to do anything but sob.

"Speak to me please, dear brother,"
whispered Gilgamesh.
"Tell me of death and where you are." 110
"Not willingly do I speak of death,"
said Enkidu in slow reply.
"But if you wish to sit for a brief
time, I will describe where I do stay."
"Yes," his brother said in early grief.
"All my skin and all my bones are dead now.
All my skin and all my bones are now dead."
"Oh no," cried Gilgamesh without relief.
"Oh no," sobbed one enclosed by grief.
"Did you see there a man who never fathered any child?" 120
"I saw there a no-man who died."
"Did you see there a man whose one son died?"
"I saw him sobbing all alone in open fields."
"Did you see there a man with two grown sons?"
"I did indeed and he smiles all day long."
"Did you see there a man with three of his own boys?"
"I did, I did; and his heart's full of joys."
"Did you there see a king with four full kids?"
"I did see one whose pleasure is supreme."
"Did you see there anyone with five children?" 130
"Oh yes, they go about with laughs and shouts."
"And could you find a man with six or seven boys?"
"You could and they are treated as the gods."
"Have you seen one who died too soon?"
"Oh yes; that one sips water fair and rests
each night upon a couch."
"Have you seen one who died in War?"
"Oh yes; his aged father weeps and his young widow visits graves."
"Have you seen one buried poor, with other homeless nomads?"
"Oh yes; that one knows rest that is not sure, 140
far from the proper place."
"Have you seen a brother crying among relatives
who chose to ignore his prayers?"
"Oh yes; he brings bread to the hungry from
the dumps of those who feed their dogs
with food they keep from people
and he eats trash that no other man would want."

The Old Testament (Hebrew Bible)

(Tenth Century B.C. to Second Century B.C.)

The Old Testament develops a single central theme: the history of the ancient Hebrews' evolving perceptions of God. (The term Old Testament is used in this anthology as being the most familiar term for the pre-Christian part of the Bible. Some people, however, including many Jews and biblical scholars, prefer the more theologically neutral term Hebrew Bible.) The setting is the tiny land of Palestine, the characters are the members of a small group of nomadic, Semitic tribes, and the time is a span of about fourteen centuries, from about 1800 B.C. to about 400 B.C. The story is above all a history, for the Hebrews—the ancient people whose culture has been transmitted by the Jews—were unusual, though not unique, among early peoples in conceiving of their religion not as the product of a single magnificent revelation, but as the result of a long series of experiences with their God. To the Hebrews, history was the story of a series of transactions with a stern but loving deity.

Although the Book of Genesis deals with the earliest events in the history of humankind, it was, in its final form, one of the last written books of the Old Testament. A group of Priestly revisers constructed the book, in about the middle of the fourth century B.C. Their sources were a much earlier version (the "J document") and an undetermined number of intermediate accounts.

The book as we have it divides into two parts. The first section is an account of prehistorical racial beginnings, and the second is a history of the origin of the Hebrews, descendants of the three patriarchs Abraham, Isaac, and Jacob. The account of the Creation that opens the book is a poetic treatment that in concrete narrative embodies certain basic Hebrew beliefs. Some of the matters "explained" in this account are fairly trivial: why snakes crawl on the ground, for example, and why women are afraid of them. But most of the questions raised are of the grandest magnitude: Who rules the world? What is humanity's relationship to God? How can we account for the presence of suffering in the world? Why do people wage war against each other? Genesis provides no final answers to these questions; the rest of the Old Testament, and the New Testament as well, is devoted to exploring the questions more fully, and people today are still engaged in debating some of the issues raised by the Creation story: Should women be subordinate to men, and must there be mistrust between men and women? Is work to be conceived of as a punishment? Are human beings by nature sinful, and is their natural relation to God that of suppliants seeking to atone for their sins?

Such questions do not obscure the major assumptions about the world that the first part of Genesis establishes. The Hebrews maintained that there is a Supreme Being, that He makes certain ethical demands upon human beings, and that their chief duty is to serve God and to carry out His will.

With the eleventh chapter of Genesis, the focus abruptly narrows from the prehistory of humankind as a whole to the Hebrew people in particular and to their origins in the family of Abraham. The following stories of Abraham, Isaac, Jacob, Esau, and Joseph bear, like the earlier part of Genesis, the marks of primitive, folktale origins and later, more sophisticated revision. The key episodes, as in the earlier portion, are those in which God reveals Himself to humanity and establishes a series of "covenants," or agreements. These covenants represent a series of unfolding or developing perceptions of God, from the first (broken) covenant in the Garden, through the covenant of the rainbow, to the great covenant made with Abraham, and subsequently repeatedly renewed, that He would "make of thee a great nation."

It is generally agreed that the Book of Job is the literary masterpiece of the Old Testament and one of the great works of all literature. It contains some of the most magnificent poetry in the Bible, and its seemingly simple structure, on rereading, reveals itself as endlessly resonant in its implications. And yet it is somewhat surprising that this book should be in the Bible at all, so sharp is its questioning of traditional Hebrew thought. Its subject is an eternal one—why do the good suffer?—and although of course it arrives at no answer to the unanswerable question, its reasoning is so keen and its emotional power so deep that the careful reader of Job can never again accept easy and shallow answers to the question.

Nothing is known of the author of Job, and its precise date is uncertain, but scholars now generally date it in the fifth century B.C. Such dating would make it roughly contemporary with Aeschylus' *Prometheus Bound* and Sophocles' *Oedipus Rex,* both of which also deal profoundly with the question of human suffering. This common theme and the book's dramatic form have tempted critics to speculate that the author was directly influenced by Greek tragedy, though there is no external evidence of such influence.

Job's debate with his conventional friends Eliphaz, Bildad, and Zophar sharply challenges the traditional Deuteronomic view of human suffering. Job and his "Comforters" agree that his suffering comes from God, but they differ radically on its meaning. The Comforters reconcile God's absolute power and absolute goodness by insisting that Job's suffering is a just punishment for sin. Job insists with equal vehemence that he has not deserved his fate and that no simple equation can be made between sin and suffering. But his lament is directed as much to God Himself as to the Comforters, as he calls into question not only their facile explanations but also the fundamental idea of any sort of justice or "covenant" between limited man and limitless God. "How should man be just with God?" he cries, "If he will contend with Him, he cannot answer Him one of a thousand."

The resolution of the book comes when God speaks "out of the whirlwind" in a theophany that recalls God's other appearances to human beings throughout the Old Testament. God's reply is simultaneously a rebuke to Job and a vindication of his position that God's power is too great to be reckoned in human terms. Ultimately, God approves the tormented questioner more than the complacent moralizers: "My wrath is kindled against thee, and against thy two friends," He tells Eliphaz, "for ye have not spoken of me the thing that is right, as my servant Job hath." The wager won, God restores to Job all that he has lost, and the book ends. The central question is still unanswered, but the issue has been dramatized more vividly than ever before or since.

The Psalms (a word that literally means "Songs") are thoroughly and obviously an expression of Hebrew ideas, expressed in some of the most beautiful lyric poetry in world literature. Martin Luther called these 150 songs "a Bible in miniature," and indeed they do encapsulate much of Hebrew history, psychology, and theology. Written over almost the entire time span of the Old Testament, they were used in ancient times for liturgical purposes (the exact nature of which is a subject of controversy) and continue to be so used in modern Jewish and Christian worship. They include hymns, meditations, exhortations, songs of praise, and commentaries on the significance of historical events for the Hebrew people. In tone they range widely, from quietude to rage, from exultation to deep grief. They are deeply Hebraic in their celebration of nature, not for its own sake but as God's handiwork, in their portrayal of God as transcendently great and powerful but in intimate touch with His people, and in their expression of communal ideals through an intensely personal tone.

NOTE ON THE TEXT

These selections from the Old Testament are from the King James Version of 1611. There are a number of more accurate, modern translations, but none has had comparable influence upon English speech and literature. Genesis has been condensed for the sake of narrative continuity. Omissions of large sections are marked in footnotes.

FURTHER READING: The 1975 revision, by Allen C. Myers et al., of *The Eerdmans Bible Dictionary,* repr. 1987, is an excellent one-volume comprehensive reference work on the Bible, arranged alphabetically. Good introductions to the Bible include Stephen L. Harris, *Understanding the Bible,* 1992; and Bernhard Anderson, *Understanding the Old Testament,* 1986. George A. Buttrick, ed., *The Interpreter's Bible,* 12 vols., 1952, gives, in addition to background material on the Old Testament (vol. 7), introductions, exegesis, and exposition on individual books. John E. Steinmueller and Kathryn Sullivan, eds., *Catholic Biblical Encyclopedia: Old Testament,* 1956, have compiled a valuable work of reference. Dealing with the books as literary types is Georg Fohrer's *Introduction to the Old Testament,* 1965, trans. David E. Green, 1968. The relationship between literary art and biblical strategy and meaning is explored incisively in Meir Sternberg's *The Poetics of Biblical Narrative: Ideological Literature and the Drama of Reading,* 1985, and in two books by Robert Alter: *The Art of Biblical Narrative,* 1981, and *The Art of Biblical Poetry,* 1985. Alter has also edited, with Frank Kermode, *The Literary Guide to the Bible,* 1987, a collection of authoritative essays. John B. Gabel and Charles B. Wheeler, *The Bible as Literature: An Introduction,* 1986, is especially useful for basic background. Kenneth R. R. Gros Louis, ed., *Literary Interpretations of Biblical Narratives,* 1982, is accurately described by its title. General studies, including information on background, canon, literary merits and individual books, are offered by Otto Eissfeldt, *The Old Testament,* 1934, trans. Peter R. Ackroyd, 1965, repr. 1974; and by Aage Bentzen, *Introduction to the Old Testament,* 1948, 7th ed., 1967. Gabriel Josipovici, *The Book of God,* 1988, is a literary-critical study of biblical narrative, including the relationships between books. Jon Douglas Levinson, *The Death and Resurrection of the Beloved Son,* 1994, examines the roles of sons and heirs in the Bible. Harold Bloom, *The Book of J,* 1990, is a startlingly provocative reading of the "J" author's contributions to the Pentateuch, suggesting the possibility that a woman wrote them; the volume includes also a boldly original translation of the passages, by David Rosenberg. Charlotte Mandel, *The Marriage of Jacob,* 1992, is a novella-poem rendering the Jacob story in a way that vividly portrays the culture of the era.

THE OLD TESTAMENT

King James Version (1611)

from GENESIS

THE CREATION OF THE WORLD

(Genesis I:1–2:3)
In the beginning God created the heaven and the earth. And the earth was without form, and void; and darkness was upon the face of the deep. And the Spirit of God moved upon the face of the waters. And God said, "Let there be light": and there was light. And God saw the light, that it was good: and God divided the light from the darkness. And God called the light Day, and the darkness he called Night. And the evening and the morning were the first day.

And God said, "Let there be a firmament in the midst of the waters, and let it divide the waters from the waters." And God made the firmament, and divided the waters which were under the firmament from the waters which were above the firmament: and it was so.[1] And God called the firmament Heaven. And the evening and the morning were the second day.

And God said, "Let the waters under the heaven be gathered together unto one place, and let the dry land appear": and it was so. And God called the dry land Earth; and the gathering together of the waters called he Seas: and God saw that it was good. And God said, "Let the earth bring forth grass, the herb yielding seed, and the fruit tree yielding fruit after his kind, whose seed is in itself, upon the earth": and it was so. And the earth brought forth grass, and herb yielding seed after his kind, and the tree yielding fruit, whose seed was in itself, after his kind: and God saw that it was good. And the evening and the morning were the third day.

And God said: "Let there be lights in the firmament of the heaven to divide the day from the night; and let them be for signs, and for seasons, and for days, and years; and let them be for lights in the firmament of the heaven to give light upon the earth." And it was so. And God made two great lights; the greater light to rule the day, and the lesser light to rule the night: he made the stars also. And God set them in the firmament of the heaven to give light upon the earth. And to rule over the day and over the night, and to divide the light from the darkness: and God saw that it was good. And the evening and the morning were the fourth day.

And God said, "Let the waters bring forth abundantly the moving creature that hath life, and fowl that may fly above the earth in the open firmament of heaven." And God created great whales, and every living creature that moveth, which the waters brought forth abundantly, after their kind, and every winged fowl after his kind: and God saw that it was good. And God blessed them, saying, "Be fruitful, and multiply, and fill the waters in

[1]These lines rest upon a belief that the world was created out of a watery chaos. The "firmament" was thought of as a solid dome that divided the "waters above" from the "waters below."

the seas, and let fowl multiply in the earth." And the evening and the morning were the fifth day.

And God said, "Let the earth bring forth the living creature after his kind, cattle,[2] and creeping thing, and beast of the earth after his kind": and it was so. And God made the beast of the earth after his kind, and cattle after their kind, and every thing that creepeth upon the earth after his kind: and God saw that it was good.

And God said, "Let us make man in our image, after our likeness: and let them have dominion over the fish of the sea, and over the fowl of the air, and over the cattle, and over all the earth, and over every creeping thing that creepeth upon the earth." So God created man in his own image, in the image of God created he him; male and female created he them. And God blessed them, and God said unto them, "Be fruitful, and multiply, and replenish the earth, and subdue it: and have dominion over the fish of the sea, and over the fowl of the air, and over every living thing that moveth upon the earth." And God said, "Behold, I have given you every herb bearing seed, which is upon the face of all the earth, and every tree, in the which is the fruit of a tree yielding seed; to you it shall be for meat. And to every beast of the earth, and to every fowl of the air, and to every thing that creepeth upon the earth, wherein there is life, I have given every green herb for meat." And it was so. And God saw every thing that he had made, and, behold, it was very good. And the evening and the morning were the sixth day.

Thus the heavens and the earth were finished, and all the host of them. And on the seventh day God ended his work which he had made; and he rested on the seventh day from all his work which he had made. And God blessed the seventh day, and sanctified it: because that in it he had rested from all his work which God created and made. . . .

THE FALL

(Genesis 2:4–3:24)

In the day that the Lord God made the earth and the heavens, and every plant of the field before it was in the earth, and every herb of the field before it grew (for the Lord God had not caused it to rain upon the earth, and there was not a man to till the ground) there went up a mist from the earth, and watered the whole face of the ground. And the Lord God formed man of the dust of the ground, and breathed into his nostrils the breath of life; and man became a living soul. And the Lord God planted a garden eastward in Eden; and there he put the man whom he had formed. And out of the ground made the Lord God to grow every tree that is pleasant to the sight, and good for food; the tree of life also in the midst of the garden, and the tree of knowledge of good and evil. And a river went out of Eden to water the garden; and from thence it was parted, and became into four heads. The name of the first is Pison: that is it which compasseth the whole land of Havilah, where there is gold; and the gold of that land is good: there is bdellium[3] and the onyx stone. And the name of the second river

[2] All domestic animals.

[3] The meaning of this word is obscure. It may be either a fragrant gum resin or a precious stone such as carbuncle, crystal, or pearl.

is Gihon: the same is it that compasseth the whole land of Ethiopia. And the name of the third river is Hiddekel: that is it which goeth toward the east of Assyria. And the fourth river is Euphrates.

And the Lord God took the man, and put him into the garden of Eden to dress[4] it and to keep it. And the Lord God commanded the man, saying, "Of every tree of the garden thou mayest freely eat: but of the tree of the knowledge of good and evil, thou shalt not eat of it: for in the day that thou eatest thereof thou shalt surely die."

And the Lord God said, "It is not good that the man should be alone; I will make him a help meet for him." And out of the ground the Lord God formed every beast of the field, and every fowl of the air; and brought them unto Adam[5] to see what he would call them: and whatsoever Adam called every living creature, that was the name thereof. And Adam gave names to all cattle, and to the fowl of the air, and to every beast of the field; but for Adam there was not found a help meet for him. And the Lord God caused a deep sleep to fall upon Adam, and he slept: and he took one of his ribs, and closed up the flesh instead thereof; and the rib, which the Lord God had taken from man, made he a woman, and brought her unto the man.

And Adam said,

> "This is now bone of my bones,
>   and flesh of my flesh:
> She shall be called Woman,
>   because she was taken out of Man."

Therefore shall a man leave his father and his mother, and shall cleave unto his wife: and they shall be one flesh. And they were both naked, the man and his wife, and were not ashamed.

Now the serpent was more subtil than any beast of the field which the Lord God had made. And he said unto the woman, "Yea, hath God said, 'Ye shall not eat of every tree of the garden'?" And the woman said unto the serpent, "We may eat of the fruit of the trees of the garden: but of the fruit of the tree which is in the midst of the garden, God hath said, 'Ye shall not eat of it, neither shall ye touch it, lest ye die.'" And the serpent said unto the woman, "Ye shall not surely die: for God doth know that in the day ye eat thereof, then your eyes shall be opened, and ye shall be as gods, knowing good and evil."[6]

And when the woman saw that the tree was good for food, and that it was pleasant to the eyes, and a tree to be desired to make one wise, she took of the fruit thereof, and did eat, and gave also unto her husband with her; and he did eat. And the eyes of them both were opened, and they knew that they were naked; and they sewed fig leaves together, and made themselves aprons.

And they heard the voice of the Lord God walking in the garden in the cool of the day: and Adam and his wife hid themselves from the presence of the Lord God amongst the trees of the garden. And the Lord God called

[4] Tend or cultivate. [5] "Adam" means "man."

[6] Only the tree of "the knowledge of good and evil" is mentioned in the temptation story. The previously mentioned "tree of life" does not appear.

unto Adam, and said unto him, "Where art thou?" And he said, "I heard thy voice in the garden, and I was afraid, because I was naked; and I hid myself." And he said, "Who told thee that thou wast naked? Hast thou eaten of the tree, whereof I commanded thee that thou shouldest not eat?" And the man said, "The woman whom thou gavest to be with me, she gave me of the tree, and I did eat." And the Lord God said unto the woman, "What is this that thou hast done?" And the woman said, "The serpent beguiled me, and I did eat." And the Lord God said unto the serpent,

"Because thou hast done this,
thou are cursed above all cattle,
and above every beast of the field.
Upon thy belly shalt thou go,
and dust shalt thou eat
all the days of thy life:
And I will put enmity between thee and the woman,
and between thy seed[7] and her seed;
It shall bruise thy head,
and thou shalt bruise his heel."

Unto the woman he said,

"I will greatly multiply thy sorrow and thy conception;
In sorrow thou shalt bring forth children;
And thy desire shall be to thy husband,
And he shall rule over thee."

And unto Adam he said, "Because thou hast hearkened unto the voice of thy wife, and hast eaten of the tree, of which I commanded thee, saying, 'Thou shalt not eat of it':

"Cursed is the ground for thy sake;
in sorrow shalt thou eat of it all the days of thy life.
Thorns also and thistles shall it bring forth to thee;
and thou shalt eat the herb of the field;
In the sweat of thy face
shalt thou eat bread,
Till thou return unto the ground;
for out of it wast thou taken:
For dust thou art,
and unto dust shalt thou return."

And Adam called his wife's name Eve; because she was the mother of all living.[8] Unto Adam also and to his wife did the Lord God make coats of skins, and clothed them.

And the Lord God said, "Behold, the man is become as one of us, to know good and evil: and now, lest he put forth his hand, and take also of

[7]Descendants.
[8]"Eve" in Hebrew resembles the word for "living."

the tree of life, and eat, and live for ever—" therefore the Lord God sent him forth from the garden of Eden, to till the ground from whence he was taken. So he drove out the man; and he placed at the east of the garden of Eden Cherubims,[9] and a flaming sword which turned every way, to keep the way of the tree of life.

CAIN AND ABEL

(Genesis 4:1–5:5)
And Adam knew[10] Eve his wife; and she conceived, and bore Cain, and said, "I have gotten a man from the Lord." And she again bore his brother Abel. And Abel was a keeper of sheep, but Cain was a tiller of the ground. And in process of time it came to pass that Cain brought of the fruit of the ground an offering unto the Lord. And Abel, he also brought of the firstlings of his flock and of the fat thereof. And the Lord had respect unto Abel and to his offering: but unto Cain and to his offering he had not respect.[11] And Cain was very wroth, and his countenance fell. And the Lord said unto Cain, "Why are thou wroth? and why is thy countenance fallen? If thou doest well, shalt thou not be accepted? and if thou doest not well, sin lieth at the door. And unto thee shall be his desire, and thou shalt rule over him."

And Cain talked with Abel his brother: and it came to pass, when they were in the field, that Cain rose up against Abel his brother, and slew him. And the Lord said unto Cain, "Where is Abel thy brother?" And he said, "I know not: am I my brother's keeper?" And he said, "What hast thou done? the voice of thy brother's blood crieth unto me from the ground. And now art thou cursed from the earth, which hath opened her mouth to receive thy brother's blood from thy hand. When thou tillest the ground, it shall not henceforth yield unto thee her strength; a fugitive and a vagabond shalt thou be in the earth." And Cain said unto the Lord, "My punishment is greater than I can bear. Behold, thou hast driven me out this day from the face of the earth; and from thy face shall I be hid; and I shall be a fugitive and a vagabond in the earth; and it shall come to pass that every one that findeth me shall slay me." And the Lord said unto him, "Therefore whosoever slayeth Cain, vengeance shall be taken on him sevenfold." And the Lord set a mark upon Cain, lest any finding him should kill him. And Cain went out from the presence of the Lord, and dwelt in the land of Nod, on the east of Eden. . . .

And Adam knew his wife again; and she bore a son, and called his name Seth: "For God," said she, "hath appointed me another seed instead of Abel, whom Cain slew." And to Seth, to him also there was born a son; and he called his name Enos; then began men to call upon the name of the Lord. . . .

[9]Guardians of sacred areas, depicted as winged creatures, half human and half lion.

[10]Had sexual intercourse with.

[11]The Cain and Abel story reflects the tensions between nomadic shepherds and farmers. (Compare the tension between hunter and shepherd in the story of Jacob and Esau.) No reason is given for God's refusal of Cain's offering.

And the days of Adam after he had begotten Seth were eight hundred years: and he begot sons and daughters. And all the days that Adam lived were nine hundred and thirty years: and he died. . . .[12]

THE FLOOD

(Genesis 6:1–9:29)

And it came to pass, when men began to multiply on the face of the earth, and daughters were born unto them, that the sons of God saw the daughters of men that they were fair; and they took them wives of all which they chose.[13] And the Lord said, "My spirit shall not always strive with man, for that he also is flesh: yet his days shall be a hundred and twenty years." There were giants in the earth in those days; and also after that, when the sons of God came in unto the daughters of men, and they bore children to them, the same became mighty men which were of old, men of renown. And God saw that the wickedness of man was great in the earth, and that every imagination of the thoughts of his heart was only evil continually. And it repented the Lord that he had made man on the earth, and it grieved him at his heart. And the Lord said, "I will destroy man whom I have created from the face of the earth; both man, and beast, and the creeping thing, and the fowls of the air; for it repenteth me that I have made them." But Noah found grace in the eyes of the Lord. . . .

Noah was a just man and perfect in his generations, and Noah walked with God. And Noah begot three sons, Shem, Ham, and Japheth. . . .

And God said unto Noah, "The end of all flesh is come before me; for the earth is filled with violence through them; and, behold, I will destroy them with the earth.[14] Make thee an ark of gopher wood;[15] rooms shalt thou make in the ark, and shalt pitch it within and without with pitch. And this is the fashion which thou shalt make it of: the length of the ark shall be three hundred cubits,[16] the breadth of it fifty cubits, and the height of it thirty cubits. A window shalt thou make to the ark, and in a cubit shalt thou finish it above; and the door of the ark shalt thou set in the side thereof; with lower, second, and third stories shalt thou make it. And, behold, I, even I, do bring a flood of waters upon the earth, to destroy all flesh, wherein is

[12] Various explanations have been offered to account for the extraordinary life spans attributed to figures of the Old Testament. The simplest is that they are exaggerations—such as appear in other national legends—intended to glorify the beginnings of the race.

[13] This account of the mating of "the sons of God" and "the daughters of men" is a good example of the primitive conceptions of divinity that still survive in the Old Testament. The story was perhaps originally intended to account for the existence of the Nephilim, a tribe of men of gigantic size and strength; this narrative may be compared to the stories of the matings of gods and mortal women in Greek mythology.

[14] The biblical account of the Flood has much in common with other accounts of great floods, especially in the Babylonian *Gilgamesh* epic. In this other work, the hero also builds an ark, it comes to rest on a mountain, birds are sent out to see if the flood is subsiding, and the hero makes burnt offerings for his deliverance. The Genesis version differs, however, in that the Flood is not sent capriciously but as a punishment for human wickedness.

[15] An ark is a large ship. The kind of wood used is unidentified; "gopher" simply means "tree" in Hebrew.

[16] A cubit is an ancient unit of measurement based on the length of the forearm, usually about 20 inches.

the breath of life, from under heaven; and everything that is in the earth shall die. But with thee will I establish my covenant;[17] and thou shalt come into the ark, thou, and thy sons, and thy wife, and thy sons' wives with thee. And of every living thing of all flesh, two of every sort shalt thou bring into the ark, to keep them alive with thee; they shall be male and female. Of fowls after their kind, and of cattle after their kind, of every creeping thing of the earth after his kind, two of every sort shall come unto thee, to keep them alive. And take thou unto thee of all food that is eaten, and thou shalt gather it to thee; and it shall be for food for thee, and for them." Thus did Noah; according to all that God commanded him, so did he. And the Lord said unto Noah, "Come thou and all thy house into the ark; for thee have I seen righteous before me in this generation. Of every clean beast thou shalt take to thee by sevens, the male and his female; and of beasts that are not clean by two, the male and his female.[18] Of fowls also of the air by sevens, the male and the female; to keep seed alive upon the face of all the earth. For yet seven days, and I will cause it to rain upon the earth forty days and forty nights; and every living substance that I have made will I destroy from off the face of the earth."

And Noah did according unto all that the Lord commanded him. And Noah went in, and his sons, and his wife, and his sons' wives with him, into the ark, because of the waters of the flood. Of clean beasts, and of beasts that are not clean, and of fowls, and of every thing that creepeth upon the earth, there went in two and two unto Noah into the ark, the male and the female, as God had commanded Noah. And it came to pass after seven days that the waters of the flood were upon the earth. In the six hundredth year of Noah's life in the second month, the seventeenth day of the month, the same day were all the fountains of the great deep broken up, and the windows of heaven were opened.[19] And the waters prevailed, and were increased greatly upon the earth; and the ark went upon the face of the waters. And the waters prevailed exceedingly upon the earth; and all the high hills, that were under the whole heaven, were covered. Fifteen cubits upward did the waters prevail; and the mountains were covered. And all flesh died that moved upon the earth, both of fowl, and of cattle, and of beast, and of every creeping thing that creepeth upon the earth, and every man. All in whose nostrils was the breath of life, of all that was in the dry land, died. And every living substance was destroyed which was upon the face of the ground, both man, and cattle, and the creeping things, and the fowl of the heaven; and they were destroyed from the earth: and Noah only remained alive, and they

[17] This "covenant," or agreement, between God and Noah, which is expanded after the Flood and marked with the sign of the rainbow, is the first of several such covenants in the Old Testament. The agreements culminate in the repeated covenant with Abraham and his descendants, which has become the central idea in Judaism. The conditions under which God allowed Adam and Eve to live in the Garden are an implicit covenant that anticipates these later covenants.

[18] "Clean beasts" include those that have cloven hooves and chew a cud. See Leviticus, Chapter 11. The distinction between clean and unclean here is apparently a later addition, not harmonized with the rest of the text, since Noah takes in two of each animal, regardless of status.

[19] As a result of the blending of different accounts, two explanations are given for the Flood. The first is that it rained for forty days and forty nights, while here it is said that "all the fountains of the great deep [were] broken up, and the windows of heaven were opened." In other words, chaos returned through the opening up of subterranean seas and the opening of the domelike firmament that restrained "the waters above." See the beginning of Genesis.

that were with him in the ark. And the waters prevailed upon the earth a hundred and fifty days.

And God remembered Noah, and every living thing, and all the cattle that was with him in the ark: and God made a wind to pass over the earth, and the waters assuaged. The fountains also of the deep and the windows of heaven were stopped, and the rain from heaven was restrained; and the waters returned from off the earth continually: and after the end of the hundred and fifty days the waters were abated. And the ark rested in the seventh month, on the seventeenth day of the month, upon the mountains of Ararat. And the waters decreased continually until the tenth month: in the tenth month, on the first day of the month, were the tops of the mountains seen.

And it came to pass at the end of forty days that Noah opened the window of the ark which he had made: and he sent forth a raven, which went forth to and fro, until the waters were dried up from off the earth. Also he sent forth a dove from him, to see if the waters were abated from off the face of the ground; but the dove found no rest for the sole of her foot, and she returned unto him into the ark, for the waters were on the face of the whole earth: then he put forth his hand, and took her, and pulled her in unto him into the ark. And he stayed yet other seven days; and again he sent forth the dove out of the ark; and the dove came in to him in the evening; and, lo, in her mouth was an olive leaf plucked off: so Noah knew that the waters were abated from off the earth. And he stayed yet other seven days; and sent forth the dove; which returned not again unto him any more.

And it came to pass in the six hundredth and first year, in the first month, the first day of the month, the waters were dried up from off the earth: and Noah removed the covering of the ark, and looked, and, behold the face of the ground was dry. And in the second month, on the seven and twentieth day of the month, was the earth dried. And God spoke unto Noah, saying, "Go forth of the ark, thou, and thy wife, and thy sons, and thy sons' wives with thee. Bring forth with thee every living thing that is with thee, of all flesh, both of fowl, and of cattle, and of every creeping thing that creepeth upon the earth; that they may breed abundantly in the earth, and be fruitful, and multiply upon the earth." And Noah went forth, and his sons, and his wife, and his sons' wives with him. Every beast, every creeping thing, and every fowl, and whatsoever creepeth upon the earth, after their kinds, went forth out of the ark.

And Noah builded an altar unto the Lord; and took of every clean beast, and of every clean fowl, and offered burnt offerings on the altar. And the Lord smelled a sweet savor; and the Lord said in his heart, "I will not again curse the ground any more for man's sake; for the imagination of man's heart is evil from his youth; neither will I again smite any more every thing living, as I have done. While the earth remaineth, seedtime and harvest, and cold and heat, and summer and winter, and day and night shall not cease."

And God blessed Noah and his sons, and said unto them, "Be fruitful, and multiply, and replenish the earth. And the fear of you and the dread of you shall be upon every beast of the earth, and upon every fowl of the air, upon all that moveth upon the earth, and upon all the fishes of the sea; into your hand are they delivered. Every moving thing that liveth shall be meat for you; even as the green herb have I given you all things. But flesh with the life thereof, which is the blood thereof, shall ye not eat. And surely your blood of your lives will I require; at the hand of every beast will I require it, and at the hand of man; at the hand of every man's brother will I require the life of man. Whoso sheddeth man's blood, by man shall his blood be shed: for in the image of God made he man." . . . And God spoke unto Noah, and to his sons with him, saying, "And I, behold, I establish my covenant with you, and with your seed after you; and with every living creature that is with you, of the fowl, of the cattle, and of every beast of the earth with you; from all that go out of the ark, to every beast of the earth. And I will establish my covenant with you; neither shall all flesh be cut off any more by the waters of a flood; neither shall there any more be a flood to destroy the earth."

And God said, "This is the token of the covenant which I make between me and you and every living creature that is with you, for perpetual generations: I do set my bow in the cloud, and it shall be for a token of a covenant between me and the earth. And it shall come to pass, when I bring a cloud over the earth, that the bow shall be seen in the cloud: and I will remember my covenant, which is between me and you and every living creature of all flesh; and the waters shall no more become a flood to destroy all flesh. And the bow shall be in the cloud; and I will look upon it, that I may remember the everlasting covenant between God and every living creature of all flesh that is upon the earth."[20] And God said unto Noah, "This is the token of the covenant, which I have established between me and all flesh that is upon the earth." . . .

And Noah began to be a husbandman, and he planted a vineyard: and he drank of the wine, and was drunken; and he was uncovered within his tent. And Ham, the father of Canaan, saw the nakedness of his father, and told his two brethren without. And Shem and Japheth took a garment, and laid it upon both their shoulders, and went backward, and covered the nakedness of their father; and their faces were backward, and they saw not their father's nakedness.[21] And Noah awoke from his wine, and knew what his younger son had done unto him. And he said, "Cursed be Canaan; a servant of servants shall he be unto his brethren." And he said, "Blessed be the Lord God of Shem; and Canaan shall be his servant. God shall enlarge Japheth, and he shall dwell in the tents of Shem; and Canaan shall be his servant."

And Noah lived after the flood three hundred and fifty years. And all the days of Noah were nine hundred and fifty years: and he died. . . .

THE TOWER OF BABEL

(Genesis II:I–II:9)

And the whole earth was of one language, and of one speech. And it came to pass, as they journeyed from the east, that they found a plain in the land

[20] The rainbow was often regarded by primitive peoples as God's bow from which he shot arrows of lightning. Here it becomes rather a sign in the heavens that God's anger has abated.

[21] There is some confusion here in names. God places the curse on Canaan rather than on Ham, who is said to have committed the offense. The incident implies that Israel's later subjugation of Canaan was the consequence of the Canaanites' sexual perversions.

of Shinar; and they dwelt there. And they said one to another, "Go to, let us make brick, and burn them thoroughly." And they had brick for stone, and slime had they for mortar. And they said, "Go to, let us build us a city and a tower, whose top may reach unto heaven; and let us make us a name, lest we be scattered abroad upon the face of the whole earth."[22] And the Lord came down to see the city and the tower, which the children of men builded. And the Lord said, "Behold, the people is one, and they have all one language; and this they begin to do: and now nothing will be restrained from them, which they have imagined to do. Go to, let us go down, and there confound their language, that they may not understand one another's speech." So the Lord scattered them abroad from thence upon the face of all the earth: and they left off to build the city. Therefore is the name of it called Babel; because the Lord did there confound the language of all the earth: and from thence did the Lord scatter them abroad upon the face of all the earth. . . .

THE STORY OF ABRAHAM AND ISAAC

(Genesis II:27–25:28)

Now these are the generations of Terah: Terah begot Abram, Nahor and Haran; and Haran begot Lot. And Haran died before his father Terah in the land of his nativity, in Ur of the Chaldees. And Abram and Nahor took them wives: the name of Abram's wife was Sarai; and the name of Nahor's wife, Milcah, the daughter of Haran, the father of Milcah, and the father of Iscah. But Sarai was barren; she had no child.

And Terah took Abram his son, and Lot the son of Haran his son's son, and Sarai his daughter-in-law, his son Abram's wife; and they went forth with them from Ur of the Chaldees, to go into the land of Canaan; and they came unto Haran, and dwelt there. And the days of Terah were two hundred and five years: and Terah died in Haran.

Now the Lord had said unto Abram, "Get thee out of thy country, and from thy kindred, and from thy father's house, unto a land that I will show thee: and I will make of thee a great nation, and I will bless thee, and make thy name great; and thou shalt be a blessing. And I will bless them that bless thee, and curse him that curseth thee: and in thee shall all families of the earth be blessed."[23]

So Abram departed, as the Lord had spoken unto him; and Lot went with him: and Abram was seventy and five years old when he departed out of Haran. And Abram took Sarai his wife, and Lot his brother's son, and all their substance that they had gathered, and the souls that they had gotten in Haran; and they went forth to go into the land of Canaan; and into

[22] Mesopotamian cities were marked by ziggurats, pyramidlike towers regarded as the gateways to heaven. The story of the Tower of Babel not only alludes to such structures but also is an etiological story accounting for the origin of languages and the cultural magnificence of Babylon. The episode also emphasizes humanity's continuing pride and sinfulness even after the Flood.

[23] This is the first statement of the often-repeated "covenant" with Israel around which much of Old Testament history revolves.

the land of Canaan they came. And Abram passed through the land unto the place of Sichem, unto the plain of Moreh. And the Canaanite was then in the land. And the Lord appeared unto Abram, and said, "Unto thy seed will I give this land." And there builded he an altar unto the Lord, who appeared unto him. And he removed from thence unto a mountain on the east of Beth-el, and pitched his tent, having Beth-el on the west, and Hai on the east: and there he builded an altar unto the Lord, and called upon the name of the Lord. And Abram journeyed, going on still toward the south. . . .[24]

And it came to pass after these things that God did tempt Abraham, and said unto him, "Abraham": and he said, "Behold, here I am." And he said, "Take now thy son, thine only son Isaac, whom thou lovest, and get thee into the land of Moriah; and offer him there for a burnt offering upon one of the mountains which I will tell thee of." And Abraham rose up early in the morning, and saddled his ass, and took two of his young men with him, and Isaac his son, and cleft the wood for the burnt offering, and rose up, and went unto the place of which God had told him. Then on the third day Abraham lifted up his eyes, and saw the place afar off. And Abraham said unto his young men, "Abide ye here with the ass; and I and the lad will go yonder and worship, and come again to you." And Abraham took the wood of the burnt offering, and laid it upon Isaac his son; and he took the fire in his hand, and a knife; and they went both of them together.

And Isaac spoke unto Abraham his father, and said, "My father": and he said, "Here am I, my son." And he said, "Behold the fire and the wood: but where is the lamb for a burnt offering?" And Abraham said, "My son, God will provide himself a lamb for a burnt offering": so they went both of them together. And they came to the place which God had told him of; and Abraham built an altar there, and laid the wood in order, and bound Isaac his son, and laid him on the altar upon the wood. And Abraham stretched forth his hand, and took the knife to slay his son. And the angel of the Lord called unto him out of heaven, and said, "Abraham, Abraham": and he said, "Here am I." And he said, "Lay not thine hand upon the lad, neither do thou any thing unto him: for now I know that thou fearest God, seeing thou hast not withheld thy son, thine only son from me." And Abraham lifted up his eyes, and looked, and beheld behind him a ram caught in a thicket by his horns: and Abraham went and took the ram, and offered him up for a burnt offering in the stead of his son. And Abraham called the name of that place Jehovah-jireh: as it is said to this day, "In the mount of the Lord it shall be seen. . . .[25]

[24] Abram and his family migrate to Egypt and then return to Canaan. His nephew Lot settles in the cities of the fertile plain of Jordan. To mark His covenant with the Hebrews, God changes Abram's name to Abraham and Sarai's to Sarah, requires that all males of Abraham's line be circumcised, and miraculously causes Sarah to bear a son, Isaac, in her very old age. Angered by the practice of sodomy, God sends down fire and brimstone to destroy the cities of the plain, Sodom and Gomorrah, sparing only Lot and some of his kin.

[25] The story of the near-sacrifice of Isaac has many analogues in other religions and literatures, including the story of Agamemnon's sacrifice of his daughter Iphigenia, referred to in the *Iliad* and in Aeschylus' *Agamemnon.* The form the story takes here seems to celebrate perfect faith and to condemn human sacrifice.

So Abraham returned unto his young men, and they rose up and went together to Beer-sheba; and Abraham dwelt at Beer-sheba. . . .[26]

And Isaac was forty years old when he took Rebekah to wife, the daughter of Bethuel the Syrian of Padan-aram, the sister to Laban the Syrian. And Isaac intreated the Lord for his wife, because she was barren: and the Lord was intreated of him, and Rebekah his wife conceived. And the children struggled together within her; and she said, "If it be so, why am I thus?" And she went to enquire of the Lord. And the Lord said unto her,

"Two nations are in thy womb,
  and two manner of people shall be separated from thy bowels;
And the one people shall be stronger than the other people;
  and the elder shall serve the younger."

And when her days to be delivered were fulfilled, behold, there were twins in her womb. And the first came out red, all over like a hairy garment; and they called his name Esau. And after that came his brother out, and his hand took hold on Esau's heel; and his name was called Jacob:[27] and Isaac was threescore years old when she bore them. And the boys grew: and Esau was a cunning hunter, a man of the field; and Jacob was a plain man, dwelling in tents. And Isaac loved Esau, because he did eat of his venison: but Rebekah loved Jacob.

THE STORY OF JACOB

(Genesis 25:29–35:29)

And Jacob sod pottage:[28] and Esau came from the field, and he was faint: and Esau said to Jacob, "Feed me, I pray thee, with that same red pottage; for I am faint" (therefore was his name called Edom). And Jacob said, "Sell me this day thy birthright." And Esau said, "Behold, I am at the point to die: and what profit shall this birthright do to me?" And Jacob said, "Swear to me this day!" And he swore unto him: and he sold his birthright unto Jacob. Then Jacob gave Esau bread and pottage of lentils; and he did eat and drink, and rose up, and went his way: thus Esau despised his birthright. . . .

And Esau was forty years old when he took to wife Judith the daughter of Beeri the Hittite, and Bashemath the daughter of Elon the Hittite: which were a grief of mind unto Isaac and to Rebekah.

And it came to pass that when Isaac was old, and his eyes were dim, so that he could not see, he called Esau his eldest son, and said unto him, "My

[26]After Sarah dies, Abraham seeks a bride for Isaac. Resolved that his son shall marry a woman of his own Mesopotamian people rather than any of the local Canaanite women, Abraham sends his steward to his former homeland. While stopping by a well, the steward providentially encounters Rebekah, Isaac's first cousin. She travels to her new homeland in Canaan and is married to Isaac. Abraham dies and is buried beside Sarah.

[27]The name Jacob can mean either "he takes by the heel" or "he supplants." The second meaning is particularly relevant in the light of Jacob's later history. The character of Jacob is a version of the "trickster hero," and his often rather crudely comic exploits in the sections that follow still betray their origins in folktales.

[28]Cooked food.

son": and he said unto him, "Behold, here am I." And he said, "Behold now, I am old, I know not the day of my death. Now therefore take, I pray thee, thy weapons, thy quiver and thy bow, and go out to the field, and take me some venison; and make me savory meat, such as I love, and bring it to me, that I may eat; that my soul may bless thee before I die."

And Rebekah heard when Isaac spoke to Esau his son. And Esau went to the field to hunt for venison, and to bring it. And Rebekah spoke unto Jacob her son, saying, "Behold, I heard thy father speak unto Esau thy brother, saying, 'Bring me venison, and make me savory meat, that I may eat, and bless thee before the Lord before my death.' Now therefore, my son, obey my voice according to that which I command thee. Go now to the flock, and fetch me from thence two good kids of the goats; and I will make them savory meat for thy father, such as he loveth: and thou shalt bring it to thy father, that he may eat, and that he may bless thee before his death." And Jacob said to Rebekah his mother, "Behold, Esau my brother is a hairy man, and I am a smooth man. My father peradventure will feel me, and I shall seem to him as a deceiver; and I shall bring a curse upon me, and not a blessing." And his mother said unto him, "Upon me be thy curse, my son; only obey my voice, and go fetch me them." And he went, and fetched, and brought them to his mother; and his mother made savory meat, such as his father loved. And Rebekah took goodly raiment of her eldest son Esau, which were with her in the house, and put them upon Jacob her younger son; and she put the skins of the kids of the goats upon his hands, and upon the smooth of his neck; and she gave the savory meat and the bread, which she had prepared, into the hand of her son Jacob.

And he came unto his father, and said, "My father": and he said, "Here am I; who art thou, my son?" And Jacob said unto his father, "I am Esau thy firstborn; I have done according as thou badest me: arise, I pray thee, sit and eat of my venison, that thy soul may bless me." And Isaac said unto his son, "How is it that thou hast found it so quickly, my son?" And he said, "Because the Lord thy God brought it to me." And Isaac said unto Jacob, "Come near, I pray thee, that I may feel thee, my son, whether thou be my very son Esau or not." And Jacob went near unto Isaac his father; and he felt him, and said, "The voice is Jacob's voice, but the hands are the hands of Esau." And he discerned him not, because his hands were hairy, as his brother Esau's hands; so he blessed him. And he said, "Art thou my very son Esau?" And he said, "I am." And he said, "Bring it near to me, and I will eat of my son's venison, that my soul may bless thee." And he brought it near to him, and he did eat: and he brought the wine, and he drank. And his father Isaac said unto him, "Come near now, and kiss me, my son." And he came near, and kissed him: and he smelled the smell of his raiment, and blessed him, and said,

"See, the smell of my son
    is as the smell of a field which the Lord hath blessed:
Therefore God give thee of the dew of heaven,
    and the fatness of the earth,
    and plenty of corn and wine:
Let people serve thee,
    and nations bow down to thee:

Be lord over thy brethren,
 and let thy mother's sons bow down to thee:
Cursed be every one that curseth thee,
 and blessed be he that blesseth thee."

And it came to pass, as soon as Isaac had made an end of blessing Jacob, and Jacob was yet scarce gone out from the presence of Isaac his father, that Esau his brother came in from his hunting. And he also had made savory meat, and brought it unto his father, and said unto his father, "Let my father arise, and eat of his son's venison, that thy soul may bless me." And Isaac his father said unto him, "Who art thou?" And he said, "I am thy son, thy firstborn Esau." And Isaac trembled very exceedingly, and said, "Who? where is he that hath taken venison, and brought it me, and I have eaten of all before thou camest, and have blessed him? yea, and he shall be blessed." And when Esau heard the words of his father, he cried with a great and exceeding bitter cry, and said unto his father, "Bless me, even me also, O my father." And he said, "Thy brother came with subtilty, and hath taken away thy blessing." And he said, "Is not he rightly named Jacob? for he hath supplanted me these two times: he took away my birthright; and, behold, now he hath taken away my blessing." And he said, "Hast thou not reserved a blessing for me?" And Isaac answered and said unto Esau, "Behold, I have made him thy lord, and all his brethren have I given to him for servants; and with corn and wine have I sustained him: and what shall I do now unto thee, my son?" And Esau said unto his father, "Hast thou but one blessing, my father? bless me, even me also, O my father." And Esau lifted up his voice, and wept. And Isaac his father answered and said unto him,

"Behold, thy dwelling shall be the fatness of the earth,
 and of the dew of heaven from above;
And by thy sword shalt thou live,
 and shalt serve thy brother;
And it shall come to pass when thou shalt have the dominion,
 that thou shalt break his yoke from off thy neck."

And Esau hated Jacob because of the blessing wherewith his father blessed him: and Esau said in his heart, "The days of mourning for my father are at hand; then will I slay my brother Jacob."[29] And these words of Esau her elder son were told to Rebekah: and she sent and called Jacob her younger son, and said unto him, "Behold, thy brother Esau, as touching thee, doth comfort himself, purposing to kill thee. Now therefore, my son, obey my voice; and arise, flee thou to Laban my brother to Haran. And tarry with him a few days, until thy brother's fury turn away; until thy brother's anger turn away from thee, and he forget that which thou hast done to him. Then I will send, and fetch thee from thence: why should I be deprived also of you both in one day?"

[29]Jacob's hoodwinking of Isaac reflects the ancient belief in the magical nature of formal blessings and curses; once a blessing had been pronounced, even in error, it could not be withdrawn.

And Rebekah said to Isaac, "I am weary of my life because of the daughters of Heth: if Jacob take a wife of the daughters of Heth, such as these which are of the daughters of the land, what good shall my life do me?" And Isaac called Jacob, and blessed him, and charged him, and said unto him, "Thou shalt not take a wife of the daughters of Canaan. Arise, go to Padan-aram, to the house of Bethuel thy mother's father; and take thee a wife from thence of the daughters of Laban thy mother's brother. And God Almighty bless thee, and make thee fruitful, and multiply thee, that thou mayest be a multitude of people; and give thee the blessing of Abraham, to thee, and to thy seed with thee; that thou mayest inherit the land wherein thou art a stranger, which God gave unto Abraham." . . .

And Jacob went out from Beer-sheba, and went toward Haran. And he lighted upon a certain place, and tarried there all night, because the sun was set; and he took of the stones of that place, and put them for his pillows, and lay down in that place to sleep. And he dreamed, and, behold, a ladder set up on the earth, and the top of it reached to heaven: and, behold, the angels of God ascending and descending on it. And, behold, the Lord stood above it, and said, "I am the Lord God of Abraham thy father, and the God of Isaac: the land whereon thou liest, to thee will I give it, and to thy seed; and thy seed shall be as the dust of the earth, and thou shalt spread abroad to the west, and to the east, and to the north, and to the south: and in thee and in thy seed shall all the families of the earth be blessed. And, behold, I am with thee, and will keep thee in all places whither thou goest, and will bring thee again into this land; for I will not leave thee until I have done that which I have spoken to thee of." And Jacob awaked out of his sleep, and he said, "Surely the Lord is in this place; and I knew it not." And he was afraid, and said, "How dreadful is this place! this is none other but the house of God, and this is the gate of heaven."

And Jacob rose up early in the morning, and took the stone that he had put for his pillows, and set it up for a pillar, and poured oil upon the top of it. And he called the name of that place Beth-el:[30] but the name of that city was called Luz at the first. And Jacob vowed a vow, saying, "If God will be with me, and will keep me in this way that I go, and will give me bread to eat, and raiment to put on, so that I come again to my father's house in peace; then shall the Lord be my God: and this stone, which I have set for a pillar, shall be God's house: and of all that thou shalt give me I will surely give the tenth unto thee."

Then Jacob went on his journey, and came into the land of the people of the east. And he looked, and beheld a well in the field, and, lo, there were three flocks of sheep lying by it; for out of that well they watered the flocks: and a great stone was upon the well's mouth. And thither were all the flocks gathered: and they rolled the stone from the well's mouth, and watered the sheep, and put the stone again upon the well's mouth in his place. And Jacob said unto them, "My brethren, whence be ye?" And they said, "Of Haran are we." And he said unto them, "Know ye Laban the son of Nahor?" And they said, "We know him." And he said unto them, "Is he well?" And they said, "He is well: and, behold, Rachel his daughter cometh with the sheep." And he said, "Lo, it is yet high day, neither is it time that

[30] "The House of God."

the cattle should be gathered together: water ye the sheep, and go and feed them." And they said, "We cannot, until all the flocks be gathered together, and till they roll the stone from the well's mouth; then we water the sheep." And while he yet spoke with them, Rachel came with her father's sheep: for she kept them. And it came to pass, when Jacob saw Rachel the daughter of Laban his mother's brother, and the sheep of Laban his mother's brother, that Jacob went near, and rolled the stone from the well's mouth; and watered the flock of Laban his mother's brother. And Jacob kissed Rachel, and lifted up his voice, and wept. And Jacob told Rachel that he was her father's brother, and that he was Rebekah's son: and she ran and told her father.

And it came to pass, when Laban heard the tidings of Jacob his sister's son, that he ran to meet him, and embraced him, and kissed him, and brought him to his house. And he told Laban all these things. And Laban said to him, "Surely thou art my bone and my flesh." And he abode with him the space of a month. And Laban said unto Jacob, "Because thou art my brother, shouldest thou therefore serve me for nought? tell me, what shall thy wages be?" And Laban had two daughters: the name of the elder was Leah, and the name of the younger was Rachel. Leah was tender-eyed;[31] but Rachel was beautiful and well favored. And Jacob loved Rachel; and said, "I will serve thee seven years for Rachel thy younger daughter." And Laban said, "It is better that I give her to thee than that I should give her to another man. Abide with me."

And Jacob served seven years for Rachel; and they seemed unto him but a few days, for the love he had to her. And Jacob said unto Laban, "Give me my wife, for my days are fulfilled, that I may go in unto her." And Laban gathered together all the men of the place, and made a feast. And it came to pass in the evening that he took Leah his daughter, and brought her to him; and he went in unto her. And Laban gave unto his daughter Leah Zilpah his maid for a handmaid. And it came to pass that in the morning, behold, it was Leah: and he said to Laban, "What is this thou hast done unto me? did not I serve with thee for Rachel? wherefore then hast thou beguiled me?" And Laban said, "It must not be so done in our country, to give the younger before the firstborn. Fulfil her week, and we will give thee this also for the service which thou shalt serve with me yet seven other years."[32] And Jacob did so, and fulfilled her week: and he gave him Rachel his daughter to wife also. And Laban gave to Rachel his daughter Bilhah his handmaid to be her maid. And he went in also unto Rachel, and he loved also Rachel more than Leah, and served with him yet seven other years.

And when the Lord saw that Leah was hated, he opened her womb: but Rachel was barren. And Leah conceived, and bore a son, and she called his name Reuben: for she said, "Surely the Lord hath looked upon my affliction; now therefore my husband will love me."[33] And she conceived again, and bore a son; and said, "Because the Lord hath heard that I was hated, he hath therefore given me this son also": and she called his name Simeon. And she conceived again, and bore a son; and said, "Now this time will my

[31] The word here translated "tender-eyed" apparently means, more precisely, "dull-eyed."

[32] Laban's cheating of Jacob, an example of "the trickster out-tricked," succeeds because of the custom of leading the bride to the bridal tent in darkness.

[33] "Reuben" means "See, a son!"

husband be joined unto me, because I have borne him three sons": therefore was his name called Levi. And she conceived again, and bore a son: and she said, "Now will I praise the Lord": therefore she called his name Judah; and left bearing.

And when Rachel saw that she bore Jacob no children, Rachel envied her sister; and said unto Jacob, "Give me children, or else I die." And Jacob's anger was kindled against Rachel: and he said "Am I in God's stead, who hath withheld from thee the fruit of the womb?" And she said, "Behold my maid Bilhah, go in unto her; and she shall bear upon my knees, that I may also have children by her." And she gave him Bilhah her handmaid to wife: and Jacob went in unto her. And Bilhah conceived, and bore Jacob a son. And Rachel said, "God hath judged me, and hath also heard my voice, and hath given me a son": therefore called she his name Dan.[34] And Bilhah Rachel's maid conceived again, and bore Jacob a second son. And Rachel said, "With great wrestlings have I wrestled with my sister, and I have prevailed": and she called his name Naphtali.

When Leah saw that she had left bearing, she took Zilpah her maid, and gave her Jacob to wife. And Zilpah Leah's maid bore Jacob a son. And Leah said, "A troop cometh": and she called his name Gad.[35] And Zilpah Leah's maid bore Jacob a second son. And Leah said, "Happy am I, for the daughters will call me blessed": and she called his name Asher.[36]

And Reuben went in the days of wheat harvest, and found mandrakes in the field, and brought them unto his mother Leah. Then Rachel said to Leah, "Give me, I pray thee, of thy son's mandrakes."[37] And she said unto her, "Is it a small matter that thou hast taken my husband? and wouldest thou take away my son's mandrakes also?" And Rachel said, "Therefore he shall lie with thee to-night for thy son's mandrakes." And Jacob came out of the field in the evening, and Leah went out to meet him, and said, "Thou must come in unto me; for surely I have hired thee with my son's mandrakes." And he lay with her that night. And God hearkened unto Leah, and she conceived, and bore Jacob the fifth son. And Leah said, "God hath given me my hire, because I have given my maiden to my husband": and she called his name Issachar. And Leah conceived again, and bore Jacob the sixth son. And Leah said, "God hath endued me with a good dowry; now will my husband dwell with me, because I have borne him six sons": and she called his name Zebulun. And afterwards she bore a daughter, and called her name Dinah. And God remembered Rachel, and God hearkened to her, and opened her womb. And she conceived, and bore a son; and said, "God hath taken away my reproach": and she called his name Joseph; and said, "The Lord shall add to me another son."[38]

And it came to pass, when Rachel had borne Joseph, that Jacob said unto Laban, "Send me away, that I may go unto mine own place, and to my country. Give me my wives and my children, for whom I have served thee, and let me go: for thou knowest my service which I have done thee." And Laban

[34] "Dan" means "He judged." [35] "Gad" means "Fortune."

[36] "Asher" means "Happy."

[37] Mandrakes are the roots of a potatolike plant that were thought to have aphrodisiac qualities and to stimulate conception.

[38] "Joseph" means "He adds."

said unto him, "I pray thee, if I have found favor in thine eyes, tarry: for I have learned by experience that the Lord hath blessed me for thy sake." And he said, "Appoint me thy wages, and I will give it." And he said unto him, "Thou knowest how I have served thee, and how thy cattle was with me. For it was little which thou hadst before I came, and it is now increased unto a multitude; and the Lord hath blessed thee since my coming: and now when shall I provide for mine own house also?" And he said, "What shall I give thee?" And Jacob said, "Thou shalt not give me any thing: if thou wilt do this thing for me, I will again feed and keep thy flock. I will pass through all thy flock to-day, removing from thence all the speckled and spotted cattle, and all the brown cattle among the sheep, and the spotted and speckled among the goats: and of such shall be my hire. So shall my righteousness answer for me in time to come, when it shall come for my hire before thy face: everyone that is not speckled and spotted among the goats, and brown among the sheep, that shall be counted stolen with me." And Laban said, "Behold, I would it might be according to thy word." And he removed that day the he-goats that were ringstreaked and spotted, and all the she-goats that were speckled and spotted, and every one that had some white in it, and all the brown among the sheep, and gave them into the hand of his sons. And he set three days' journey betwixt himself and Jacob: and Jacob fed the rest of Laban's flocks.

And Jacob took him rods of green poplar, and of the hazel and chestnut tree; and peeled white strakes in them, and made the white appear which was in the rods. And he set the rods which he had peeled before the flocks in the gutters in the watering troughs when the flocks came to drink, that they should conceive when they came to drink. And the flocks conceived before the rods, and brought forth cattle ringstreaked, speckled, and spotted.[39] And Jacob did separate the lambs, and set the faces of the flocks toward the ringstreaked, and all the brown in the flock of Laban; and he put his own flocks by themselves, and put them not unto Laban's cattle. And it came to pass, whensoever the stronger cattle did conceive, that Jacob laid the rods before the eyes of the cattle in the gutters, that they might conceive among the rods. But when the cattle were feeble, he put them not in: so the feebler were Laban's, and the stronger Jacob's. And the man increased exceedingly, and had much cattle, and maidservants, and menservants, and camels, and asses.

And he heard the words of Laban's sons, saying, "Jacob hath taken away all that was our father's; and of that which was our father's hath he gotten all this glory." And Jacob beheld the countenance of Laban and, behold, it was not toward him as before. And the Lord said unto Jacob, "Return unto the land of thy fathers, and to thy kindred; and I will be with thee." And Jacob sent and called Rachel and Leah to the field unto his flock and said unto them, "I see your father's countenance, that it is not toward me as before; but the God of my father hath been with me. And ye know that with all my power I have served your father. And your father hath deceived me, and changed my wages ten times; but God suffered him not to hurt me. If he

[39]Jacob's trick depends upon the notion of prenatal influence, the belief that a pregnant animal's experiences influence her offspring. The cows and ewes see spotted rods and give birth to spotted offspring.

said thus, 'The speckled shall be thy wages'; then all the cattle bore speckled: and if he said thus, 'The ringstreaked shall be thy hire'; then bore all the cattle ringstreaked. Thus God hath taken away the cattle of your father, and given them to me. And it came to pass at the time that the cattle conceived, that I lifted up mine eyes, and saw in a dream, and, behold, the rams which leaped upon the cattle were ringstreaked, speckled, and grisled. And the angel of God spoke unto me in a dream, saying, 'Jacob.' And I said, 'Here am I.' And he said, 'Lift up now thine eyes, and see, all the rams which leap upon the cattle are ringstreaked, speckled, and grisled: for I have seen all that Laban doeth unto thee. I am the God of Beth-el, where thou anointedst the pillar, and where thou vowedst a vow unto me: now arise, get thee out from this land, and return unto the land of thy kindred.'" And Rachel and Leah answered and said unto him, "Is there yet any portion or inheritance for us in our father's house? Are we not counted of him strangers? for he hath sold us, and hath quite devoured also our money. For all the riches which God hath taken from our father, that is ours, and our children's: now then, whatsoever God hath said unto thee, do."

Then Jacob rose up, and set his sons and his wives upon camels; and he carried away all his cattle, and all his goods which he had gotten, the cattle of his getting, which he had gotten in Padan-aram, for to go to Isaac his father in the land of Canaan. And Laban went to shear his sheep: and Rachel had stolen the images that were her father's.[40] And Jacob stole away unawares to Laban the Syrian, in that he told him not that he fled. So he fled with all that he had; and he rose up, and passed over the river, and set his face toward the mount Gilead.

And it was told Laban on the third day that Jacob was fled. And he took his brethren with him, and pursued after him seven days' journey; and they overtook him in the mount Gilead. And God came to Laban the Syrian in a dream by night, and said unto him, "Take heed that thou speak not to Jacob either good or bad."

Then Laban overtook Jacob. Now Jacob had pitched his tent in the mount: and Laban with his brethren pitched in the Mount of Gilead. And Laban said to Jacob, "What hast thou done, that thou hast stolen away unawares to me, and carried away my daughters, as captives taken with the sword? Wherefore didst thou flee away secretly, and steal away from me; and didst not tell me, that I might have sent thee away with mirth, and with songs, with tabret, and with harp? And hast not suffered me to kiss my sons and my daughters? thou has now done foolishly in so doing. It is in the power of my hand to do you hurt: but the God of your father spoke unto me yesternight, saying, 'Take thou heed that thou speak not to Jacob either good or bad.' And now, though thou wouldest needs be gone, because thou sore longedst after thy father's house, yet wherefore hast thou stolen my gods?" And Jacob answered and said to Laban, "Because I was afraid: for I said, 'Peradventure thou wouldest take by force thy daughters from me.' With whomsoever thou findest thy gods, let him not live: before our brethren discern thou what is thine with me, and take it to thee." For Jacob knew not that Rachel had stolen them.

[40] These "images," later called "gods," are either small statues of household deities (like the Roman Lares and Penates) or images of ancestors.

And Laban went into Jacob's tent, and into Leah's tent, and into the two maidservants' tents; but he found them not. Then went he out of Leah's tent, and entered into Rachel's tent. Now Rachel had taken the images, and put them in the camel's furniture, and sat upon them. And Laban searched all the tent, but found them not. And she said to her father, "Let it not displease my lord that I cannot rise up before thee; for the custom of women is upon me."[41] And he searched, but found not the images.

And Jacob was wroth, and chid with Laban: and Jacob answered and said to Laban, "What is my trespass? what is my sin, that thou hast so hotly pursued after me? Whereas thou hast searched all my stuff, what hast thou found of all thy household stuff? set it here before my brethren and thy brethren, that they may judge betwixt us both. This twenty years have I been with thee; thy ewes and thy she-goats have not cast their young, and the rams of thy flock have I not eaten. That which was torn of beasts I brought not unto thee;[42] I bore the loss of it; of my hand didst thou require it, whether stolen by day, or stolen by night. Thus I was; in the day the drought consumed me, and the frost by night; and my sleep departed from mine eyes. Thus have I been twenty years in thy house; I served thee fourteen years for thy two daughters, and six years for thy cattle: and thou hast changed my wages ten times. Except the God of my father, the God of Abraham, and the fear of Isaac, had been with me, surely thou hadst sent me away now empty. God hath seen mine affliction and the labor of my hands, and rebuked thee yesternight."

And Laban answered and said unto Jacob, "These daughters are my daughters, and these children are my children, and these cattle are my cattle, and all that thou seest is mine: and what can I do this day unto these my daughters, or unto their children which they have borne? Now therefore come thou, let us make a covenant, I and thou; and let it be for a witness between me and thee." And Jacob took a stone, and set it up for a pillar. And Jacob said unto his brethren, "Gather stones"; and they took stones, and made a heap: and they did eat there upon the heap. And Laban called it Jegar-sahadutha: but Jacob called it Galeed.[43] And Laban said, "This heap is a witness between me and thee this day." Therefore was the name of it called Galeed and Mizpah,[44] for he said, "The Lord watch between me and thee, when we are absent one from another. If thou shalt afflict my daughters, or if thou shalt take other wives beside my daughters, no man is with us; see, God is witness betwixt me and thee."

And Laban said to Jacob, "Behold this heap, and behold this pillar, which I have cast betwixt me and thee! This heap be witness, and this pillar be witness, that I will not pass over this heap to thee, and that thou shalt not pass over this heap and this pillar unto me, for harm. The God of Abraham, and the God of Nahor, the God of their father, judge betwixt us." Then Jacob offered sacrifice upon the mount, and called his brethren to eat bread: and

[41] That is, she is menstruating.

[42] According to the Code of Hammurabi, then the law in Mesopotamia, a shepherd was not responsible to his employer for animals "torn by beasts." Despite his trickery and sharp dealing, Jacob represents himself as one who goes even beyond the law in his honesty and hard work.

[43] Both these names mean "the heap of witness," in Laban's Aramaic and Jacob's Hebrew.

[44] "Mizpah" means "Watchpost."

they did eat bread, and tarried all night in the mount. And early in the morning Laban rose up, and kissed his sons and his daughters, and blessed them: and Laban departed, and returned unto his place.

And Jacob went on his way, and the angels of God met him. And when Jacob saw them, he said, "This is God's host": and he called the name of that place Mahanaim.[45] And Jacob sent messengers before him to Esau his brother unto the land of Seir, the country of Edom. And he commanded them, saying, "Thus shall ye speak unto my lord Esau: 'Thy servant Jacob saith thus, "I have sojourned with Laban, and stayed there until now; and I have oxen, and asses, flocks, and menservants, and womenservants; and I have sent to tell my lord, that I may find grace in thy sight."'"

And the messengers returned to Jacob, saying, "We came to thy brother Esau, and also he cometh to meet thee, and four hundred men with him." Then Jacob was greatly afraid and distressed; and he divided the people that was with him, and the flocks, and herds, and the camels, into two bands; and said, "If Esau come to the one company, and smite it, then the other company which is left shall escape."

And Jacob said, "O God of my father Abraham, and God of my father Isaac, the Lord which saidst unto me, 'Return unto thy country, and to thy kindred, and I will deal well with thee!' I am not worthy of the least of all the mercies, and of all the truth, which thou hast showed unto thy servant; for with my staff I passed over this Jordan; and now I am become two bands. Deliver me, I pray thee, from the hand of my brother, from the hand of Esau: for I fear him, lest he will come and smite me, and the mother with the children. And thou saidst, 'I will surely do thee good, and make thy seed as the sand of the sea, which cannot be numbered for multitude.'"

And he lodged there that same night; and took of that which came to his hand a present for Esau his brother: two hundred she-goats, and twenty he-goats, two hundred ewes, and twenty rams, thirty milch camels with their colts, forty kine, and ten bulls, twenty she-asses, and ten foals. And he delivered them into the hand of his servants, every drove by themselves; and said unto his servants, "Pass over before me, and put a space betwixt drove and drove." And he commanded the foremost, saying, "When Esau my brother meeteth thee, and asketh thee, saying, 'Whose art thou? and whither goest thou? and whose are these before thee?' then thou shalt say, 'They be thy servant Jacob's; it is a present sent unto my lord Esau: and, behold, also he is behind us.'" And so commanded he the second, and the third, and all that followed the droves, saying, "On this manner shall ye speak unto Esau, when ye find him. And say ye moreover, 'Behold, thy servant Jacob is behind us.'" For he said, "I will appease him with the present that goeth before me, and afterward I will see his face; peradventure he will accept of me." So went the present over before him: and himself lodged that night in the company.

And he rose up that night, and took his two wives, and his two womenservants, and his eleven sons, and passed over the ford Jabbok. And he took them, and sent them over the brook, and sent over that he had. And Jacob was left alone; and there wrestled a man with him until the breaking of the day. And when he saw that he prevailed not against him, he touched the hollow of his thigh; and the hollow of Jacob's thigh was out of joint, as

[45] "Two armies."

he wrestled with him. And he said, "Let me go, for the day breaketh." And he said, "I will not let thee go, except thou bless me." And he said unto him, "What is thy name?" And he said "Jacob." And he said, "Thy name shall be called no more Jacob, but Israel: for as a prince hast thou power with God and with men, and hast prevailed." And Jacob asked him, and said, "Tell me, I pray thee, thy name." And he said, "Wherefore is it that thou dost ask after my name?" And he blessed him there. And Jacob called the name of the place Peniel: "For I have seen God face to face, and my life is preserved." And as he passed over Peniel the sun rose upon him, and he halted upon his thigh. Therefore the children of Israel eat not of the sinew which shrank, which is upon the hollow of the thigh, unto this day: because he touched the hollow of Jacob's thigh in the sinew that shrank.[46]

And Jacob lifted up his eyes, and looked, and, behold, Esau came, and with him four hundred men. And he divided the children unto Leah, and unto Rachel, and unto the two handmaids. And he put the handmaids and their children foremost, and Leah and her children after, and Rachel and Joseph hindermost. And he passed over before them, and bowed himself to the ground seven times, until he came near to his brother.

And Esau ran to meet him, and embraced him, and fell on his neck, and kissed him: and they wept. And he lifted up his eyes, and saw the women and the children; and said, "Who are those with thee?" And he said, "The children which God hath graciously given thy servant." Then the handmaidens came near, they and their children and they bowed themselves. And Leah also with her children came near, and bowed themselves: and after came Joseph near and Rachel, and they bowed themselves. And he said, "What meanest thou by all this drove which I met?" And he said, "These are to find grace in the sight of my lord."

And Esau said, "I have enough, my brother; keep that thou hast unto thyself." And Jacob said, "Nay, I pray thee, if now I have found grace in thy sight, then receive my present at my hand: for therefore I have seen thy face, as though I had seen the face of God, and thou wast pleased with me. Take, I pray thee, my blessing that is brought to thee; because God hath dealt graciously with me, and because I have enough."

And he said, "Let us take our journey, and let us go, and I will go before thee." And he said unto him, "My lord knoweth that the children are tender, and the flocks and herds with young are with me: and if men should overdrive them one day, all the flock will die. Let my lord, I pray thee, pass over before his servant: and I will lead on softly, according as the cattle that goeth before me and the children be able to endure, until I come unto my lord unto Seir."

And Esau said, "Let me now leave with thee some of the folk that are with me." And he said, "What needeth it? let me find grace in the sight of my lord." So Esau returned that day on his way unto Seir. And Jacob journeyed

[46] The meaning of this strange wrestling episode is rather obscure. Jacob's wrestling with God may be intended to represent symbolically his own inner struggle to throw off his rather defective past character and become a worthier man. The reference to the "sinew which shrank" in "the hollow of the thigh" seems to be an attempt to account for the Jewish ritual of removing the sciatic nerves, with the arteries and tendons of the thigh, in meat intended to be eaten.

to Succoth, and built him a house, and made booths for his cattle: therefore the name of the place is called Succoth.[47] And Jacob came to Shalem, a city of Shechem, which is in the land of Canaan, when he came from Padan-aram; and pitched his tent before the city. And he bought a parcel of a field, where he had spread his tent, at the hand of the children of Hamor, Shechem's father, for a hundred pieces of money. And he erected there an altar, and called it El-elohe-Israel. . . .[48]

And God said unto Jacob, "Arise, go up to Beth-el, and dwell there: and make there an altar unto God, that appeared unto thee when thou fleddest from the face of Esau thy brother." Then Jacob said unto his household, and to all that were with him, "Put away the strange gods that are among you, and be clean, and change your garments: and let us arise, and go up to Beth-el; and I will make there an altar unto God, who answered me in the day of my distress, and was with me in the way which I went." And they gave unto Jacob all the strange gods which were in their hand, and all their earrings which were in their ears; and Jacob hid them under the oak which was by Shechem.[49] And they journeyed: and the terror of God[50] was upon the cities that were round about them, and they did not pursue after the sons of Jacob.

So Jacob came to Luz, which is in the land of Canaan, that is, Beth-el, he and all the people that were with him. And he built there an altar, and called the place El-beth-el: because there God appeared unto him, when he fled from the face of his brother. But Deborah Rebekah's nurse died, and she was buried beneath Beth-el under an oak: and the name of it was called Allon-bachuth.

And God appeared unto Jacob again, when he came out of Padan-aram, and blessed him. And God said unto him, "Thy name is Jacob: thy name shall not be called any more Jacob, but Israel shall be thy name": and he called his name Israel. And God said unto him, "I am God Almighty: be fruitful and multiply; a nation and a company of nations shall be of thee, and kings shall come out of thy loins; and the land which I gave Abraham and Isaac, to thee I will give it, and to thy seed after thee will I give the land." And God went up from him in the place where he talked with him. And Jacob set up a pillar in the place where he talked with him, even a pillar of stone: and he poured a drink offering thereon, and he poured oil thereon. And Jacob called the name of the place where God spoke with him, Beth-el.

And they journeyed from Beth-el; and there was but a little way to come to Ephrath: and Rachel travailed, and she had hard labor. And it came to pass, when she was in hard labor, that the midwife said unto her, "Fear not; thou shalt have this son also." And it came to pass, as her soul was in departing (for she died), that she called his name Ben-oni: but his father called

[47] "Booths."

[48] "God, the God of Israel."

[49] The worshipers had to undergo ceremonial purification (washing and changing clothes), and they were required to renounce strange (or foreign) gods. The earrings that they surrendered were magical amulets used in pagan worship.

[50] The "Terror of God" was a mysterious panic said to seize and paralyze the enemy in early accounts of holy wars.

him Benjamin.[51] And Rachel died, and was buried in the way to Ephrath, which is Beth-lehem. And Jacob set a pillar upon her grave: that is the pillar of Rachel's grave unto this day. And Israel journeyed, and spread his tent beyond the tower of Edar.

And it came to pass, when Israel dwelt in that land, that Reuben went and lay with Bilhah his father's concubine: and Israel heard it. . . .[52]

And Jacob came unto Isaac his father unto Mamre, unto the city of Arbah, which is Hebron, where Abraham and Isaac sojourned. And the days of Isaac were a hundred and fourscore years. And Isaac gave up the ghost, and died, and was gathered unto his people, being old and full of days: and his sons Esau and Jacob buried him. . . .[53]

from JOB

CHAPTER 1

There was a man in the land of Uz, whose name was Job; and that man was perfect and upright, and one that feared God, and eschewed evil. And there were born unto him seven sons and three daughters. His substance also was seven thousand sheep, and three thousand camels, and five hundred yoke of oxen, and five hundred she asses, and a very great household; so that this man was the greatest of all the men of the east.

And his sons went and feasted in their houses, every one his day; and sent and called for their three sisters to eat and to drink with them. And it was so, when the days of their feasting were gone about, that Job sent and sanctified them, and rose up early in the morning, and offered burnt offerings according to the number of them all: for Job said, "It may be that my sons have sinned, and cursed God in their hearts." Thus did Job continually.

Now there was a day when the sons of God came to present themselves before the Lord, and Satan[1] came also among them. And the Lord said unto Satan, "Whence comest thou?" Then Satan answered the Lord, and said, "From going to and fro in the earth, and from walking up and down in it." And the Lord said unto Satan, "Hast thou considered my servant Job, that there is none like him in the earth, a perfect and an upright man, one that feareth God, and escheweth evil?" Then Satan answered the Lord, and said, "Doth Job fear God for nought? Hast not thou made an hedge about him, and about his house, and about all that he hath on every side? thou hast blessed the

[51] "Ben-oni" means "son of my sorrow," but "Benjamin" means "son of my right hand" or "son of the South."

[52] This mysterious episode apparently accounts for Reuben's loss of prestige as the first-born son.

[53] The last fourteen chapters of Genesis, here omitted, tell the story of Jacob's son Joseph and his rise to power in the land of Egypt.

[1] As the ruler of a band of evil spirits opposed to God, Satan appears by name only three times in the King James Version of the Old Testament, though he appears frequently in the New Testament. In Job, he appears in the Prologue but is never mentioned in the debate with the Comforters.

work of his hands, and his substance is increased in the land. But put forth thine hand now, and touch all that he hath, and he will curse thee to thy face." And the Lord said unto Satan, "Behold, all that he hath is in thy power; only upon himself put not forth thine hand." So Satan went forth from the presence of the Lord.

And there was a day when his sons and his daughters were eating and drinking wine in their eldest brother's house: and there came a messenger unto Job, and said, "The oxen were plowing, and the asses feeding beside them: and the Sabeans fell upon them, and took them away; yea, they have slain the servants with the edge of the sword; and I only am escaped alone to tell thee." While he was yet speaking, there came also another, and said, "The fire of God is fallen from heaven, and hath burned up the sheep, and the servants, and consumed them; and I only am escaped alone to tell thee." While he was yet speaking, there came also another, and said, "The Chaldeans made out three bands, and fell upon the camels, and have carried them away, yea, and slain the servants with the edge of the sword; and I only am escaped alone to tell thee." While he was yet speaking, there came also another, and said, "Thy sons and thy daughters were eating and drinking wine in their eldest brother's house: and, behold, there came a great wind from the wilderness, and smote the four corners of the house, and it fell upon the young men, and they are dead; and I only am escaped alone to tell thee."

Then Job arose, and rent his mantle, and shaved his head, and fell down upon the ground, and worshipped, and said,

> "Naked came I out of my mother's womb,
> And naked shall I return thither:
> The Lord gave, and the Lord hath taken away;
> Blessed be the name of the Lord."

In all this Job sinned not, nor charged God foolishly.

CHAPTER 2

Again there was a day when the sons of God came to present themselves before the Lord, and Satan came also among them to present himself before the Lord. And the Lord said unto Satan, "From whence comest thou?" And Satan answered the Lord, and said, "From going to and fro in the earth, and from walking up and down in it." And the Lord said unto Satan, "Hast thou considered my servant Job, that there is none like him in the earth, a perfect and an upright man, one that feareth God, and escheweth evil? and still he holdeth fast his integrity, although thou movedst me against him, to destroy him without cause." And Satan answered the Lord, and said, "Skin for skin,[2] yea, all that a man hath will he give for his life. But put forth thine hand now, and touch his bone and his flesh, and he will curse thee to thy face." And the Lord said unto Satan, "Behold, he is in thine hand; but save his life."

So went Satan forth from the presence of the Lord, and smote Job with sore boils from the sole of his foot unto his crown. And he took him a

[2] "A hide for a hide"—a proverbial expression used by tradesmen.

potsherd[3] to scrape himself withal; and he sat down among the ashes. Then said his wife unto him, "Dost thou still retain thine integrity? curse God, and die." But he said unto her, "Thou speakest as one of the foolish women speaketh. What? shall we receive good at the hand of God, and shall we not receive evil?" In all this did not Job sin with his lips.

Now when Job's three friends heard of all this evil that was come upon him, they came every one from his own place; Eliphaz the Temanite, and Bildad the Shuhite, and Zophar the Naamathite: for they had made an appointment together to come to mourn with him and to comfort him. And when they lifted up their eyes afar off, and knew him not, they lifted up their voice, and wept; and they rent every one his mantle, and sprinkled dust upon their heads toward heaven. So they sat down with him upon the ground seven days and seven nights, and none spake a word unto him: for they saw that his grief was very great.

CHAPTER 3

After this opened Job his mouth, and cursed his day. And Job spake, and said,

"Let the day perish wherein I was born,
    and the night in which it was said, There is a man child conceived.
Let that day be darkness;
    Let not God regard it from above,
    neither let the light shine upon it.
Let darkness and the shadow of death stain it;
    let a cloud dwell upon it;
    let the blackness of the day terrify it.
As for that night, let darkness seize upon it;
    let it not be joined unto the days of the year,
    let it not come into the number of the months.
Lo, let that night be solitary,
    let no joyful voice come therein.
Let them curse it that curse the day,
    who are ready to raise up their mourning.
Let the stars of the twilight thereof be dark;
    let it look for light, but have none;
    neither let it see the dawning of the day:
Because it shut not up the doors of my mother's womb,
    nor hid sorrow from mine eyes.

"Why died I not from the womb?
    why did I not give up the ghost when I came out of the belly?
Why did the knees prevent me?
    or why the breasts that I should suck?
For now should I have lain still and been quiet,
    I should have slept: then had I been at rest,

[3]A piece of broken pottery.

With kings and counsellors of the earth,
which built desolate places for themselves;
Or with princes that had gold,
who filled their houses with silver:
Or as an hidden untimely birth I had not been;
as infants which never saw light.
There the wicked cease from troubling;
and there the weary be at rest.
There the prisoners rest together;
they hear not the voice of the oppressor.
The small and great are there;
And the servant is free from his master.

"Wherefore is light given to him that is in misery,
and life unto the bitter in soul;
Which long for death, but it cometh not;
and dig for it more than for hid treasures;
Which rejoice exceedingly,
and are glad, when they can find the grave?
Why is light given to a man whose way is hid,
and whom God hath hedged in?
For my sighing cometh before I eat,
and my roarings are poured out like the waters.
For the thing which I greatly feared is come upon me,
and that which I was afraid of is come unto me.
I was not in safety, neither had I rest,
neither was I quiet; yet trouble came."

CHAPTER 4

Then Eliphaz the Temanite answered and said,

"If we assay to commune with thee, wilt thou be grieved?
but who can withhold himself from speaking?
Behold, thou hast instructed many,
and thou hast strengthened the weak hands.
Thy words have upholden him that was falling,
and thou hast strengthened the feeble knees.
But now it is come upon thee, and thou faintest;
it toucheth thee, and thou art troubled.
Is not this thy fear, thy confidence, thy hope,
and the uprightness of thy ways?
Remember, I pray thee, who ever perished, being innocent?
or where were the righteous cut off?[4]
Even as I have seen, they that plow iniquity,
and sow wickedness, reap the same.

[4]Here, as throughout, Eliphaz upholds the doctrine that the good prosper and the wicked are punished in this world. Suffering is thus a proof of sin.

By the blast of God they perish,
and by the breath of his nostrils are they consumed.
The roaring of the lion, and the voice of the fierce lion,
and the teeth of the young lions, are broken.
The old lion perisheth for lack of prey,
and the stout lion's whelps are scattered abroad.

"Now a thing was secretly brought to me,
and mine ear received a little thereof.
In thoughts from the visions of the night,
when deep sleep falleth on men,
Fear came upon me, and trembling,
which made all my bones to shake.
Then a spirit passed before my face;
the hair of my flesh stood up:
It stood still,
but I could not discern the form thereof:
An image was before mine eyes,
there was silence, and I heard a voice, saying,
Shall mortal man be more just than God?
shall a man be more pure than his maker?
Behold, he put no trust in his servants;
and his angels he charged with folly:
How much less in them that dwell in houses of clay,
whose foundation is in the dust,
which are crushed before the moth?
They are destroyed from morning to evening:
they perish for ever without any regarding it.
Doth not their excellency which is in them go away?
they die, even without wisdom."

CHAPTER 5

"Call now, if there be any that will answer thee;
and to which of the saints wilt thou turn?
For wrath killeth the foolish man,
and envy slayeth the silly one.
I have seen the foolish taking root:
but suddenly I cursed his habitation.
His children are far from safety,
and they are crushed in the gate,
neither is there any to deliver them.
Whose harvest the hungry eateth up,
and taketh it even out of the thorns,
and the robber swalloweth up their substance.
Although affliction cometh not forth of the dust,
neither doth trouble spring out of the ground;
Yet man is born unto trouble,
as the sparks fly upward.

"I would seek unto God,
and unto God would I commit my cause:
Which doeth great things and unsearchable;
marvellous things without number:
Who giveth rain upon the earth,
and sendeth waters upon the fields:
To set up on high those that be low;
that those which mourn may be exalted to safety.
He disappointeth the devices of the crafty,
so that their hands cannot perform their enterprise.
He taketh the wise in their own craftiness:
and the counsel of the froward is carried headlong.
They meet with darkness in the daytime,
and grope in the noonday as in the night.
But he saveth the poor from the sword,
from their mouth, and from the hand of the mighty.
So the poor hath hope,
And iniquity stoppeth her mouth.

"Behold, happy is the man whom God correcteth:
therefore despise not thou the chastening of the Almighty:[5]
For he maketh sore, and bindeth up:
he woundeth, and his hands make whole.
He shall deliver thee in six troubles:
yea, in seven there shall no evil touch thee.
In famine he shall redeem thee from death:
and in war from the power of the sword.
Thou shalt be hid from the scourge of the tongue:
neither shalt thou be afraid of destruction when it cometh.
At destruction and famine thou shalt laugh:
neither shalt thou be afraid of the beasts of the earth.
For thou shalt be in league with the stones of the field:
and the beasts of the field shall be at peace with thee.
And thou shalt know that thy tabernacle shall be in peace;
and thou shalt visit thy habitation, and shalt not sin.
Thou shalt know also that thy seed shall be great,
and thine offspring as the grass of the earth.
Thou shalt come to thy grave in a full age,
like as a shock of corn cometh in in his season.
Lo this, we have searched it, so it is;
hear it, and know thou it for thy good."

CHAPTER 6

But Job answered and said,

"Oh that my grief were thoroughly weighed,
and my calamity laid in the balances together!

[5] This is the orthodox Jewish doctrine of *musar;* God imposes suffering to chasten or correct.

For now it would be heavier than the sand of the sea:
therefore my words are swallowed up.[6]
For the arrows of the Almighty are within me,
the poison whereof drinketh up my spirit:
the terrors of God do set themselves in array against me.
Doth the wild ass bray when he hath grass?
or loweth the ox over his fodder?
Can that which is unsavory be eaten without salt?
or is there any taste in the white of an egg?
The things that my soul refused to touch
are as my sorrowful meat.
Oh that I might have my request;
and that God would grant me the thing that I long for!
Even that it would please God to destroy me;
that he would let loose his hand, and cut me off!
Then should I yet have comfort;
yea, I would harden myself in sorrow: let him not spare;
for I have not concealed the words of the Holy One.
What is my strength, that I should hope?
and what is mine end, that I should prolong my life?
Is my strength the strength of stones?
or is my flesh of brass?
Is not my help in me?
and is wisdom driven quite from me?

"To him that is afflicted pity should be showed from his friend;
but he forsaketh the fear of the Almighty.
My brethren have dealt deceitfully as a brook,
and as the stream of brooks they pass away;
Which are blackish by reason of the ice,
and wherein the snow is hid:
What time they wax warm, they vanish:
when it is hot, they are consumed out of their place.
The paths of their way are turned aside;
they go to nothing, and perish.
The troops of Tema looked,
the companies of Sheba waited for them.
They were confounded because they had hoped;
they came thither, and were ashamed.
For now ye are nothing;
ye see my casting down, and are afraid.
Did I say, 'Bring unto me'?
or, 'Give a reward for me of your substance'?
Or, 'Deliver me from the enemy's hand'?
or, 'Redeem me from the hand of the mighty'?

[6] Job replies to Eliphaz by saying that the orthodox explanation cannot be valid in his case, since his suffering exceeds any possible cause.

"Teach me, and I will hold my tongue:
and cause me to understand wherein I have erred.
How forcible are right words!
but what doth your arguing reprove?
Do ye imagine to reprove words,
and the speeches of one that is desperate, which are as wind?
Yea, ye overwhelm the fatherless,
and ye dig a pit for your friend.

"Now therefore be content, look upon me;
for it is evident unto you if I lie.
Return, I pray you, let it not be iniquity;
yea, return again, my righteousness is in it.[7]
Is there iniquity in my tongue?
cannot my taste discern perverse things?"

CHAPTER 7

"Is there not an appointed time to man upon earth?
are not his days also like the days of an hireling?
As a servant earnestly desireth the shadow,
and as an hireling looketh for the reward of his work:
So am I made to possess months of vanity,
and wearisome nights are appointed to me.
When I lie down, I say, 'When shall I arise, and the night be gone?'
and I am full of tossings to and fro unto the dawning of the day.
My flesh is clothed with worms and clods of dust;
my skin is broken, and become loathsome.
My days are swifter than a weaver's shuttle,
and are spent without hope.

"O remember that my life is wind:
mine eye shall no more see good.
The eye of him that hath seen me shall see me no more:
thine eyes are upon me, and I am not.
As the cloud is consumed and vanisheth away:
so he that goeth down to the grave shall come up no more.
He shall return no more to his house,
neither shall his place know him any more.

"Therefore I will not refrain my mouth;
I will speak in the anguish of my spirit;
I will complain in the bitterness of my soul.
Am I a sea, or a whale,
that thou settest a watch over me?

[7] This line would be clearer if translated "Let no injustice be done; my cause is righteous."

When I say, 'My bed shall comfort me,
my couch shall ease my complaint';
Then thou scarest me with dreams,
and terrifiest me through visions:
So that my soul chooseth strangling,
and death rather than my life.
I loathe it; I would not live alway:
let me alone; for my days are vanity.
What is man, that thou shouldest magnify him?
and that thou shouldest set thine heart upon him?
And that thou shouldest visit him every morning,
and try him every moment?
How long wilt thou not depart from me,
nor let me alone till I swallow down my spittle?
I have sinned; what shall I do unto thee, O thou preserver of men?
why hast thou set me as a mark against thee,
so that I am a burden to myself?
And why dost thou not pardon my transgression,
and take away mine iniquity?
For now shall I sleep in the dust;
and thou shalt seek me in the morning, but I shall not be."

CHAPTER 8

Then answered Bildad the Shuhite, and said,

"How long wilt thou speak these things?
and how long shall the words of thy mouth be like a strong wind?
Doth God pervert judgment?
or doth the Almighty pervert justice?
If thy children have sinned against him,
and he have cast them away for their transgression;
If thou wouldest seek unto God betimes,
and make thy supplication to the Almighty;
If thou wert pure and upright;
surely now he would awake for thee,
and make the habitation of thy righteousness prosperous.
Though thy beginning was small,
yet thy latter end should greatly increase.

"For enquire, I pray thee, of the former age,
and prepare thyself to the search of their fathers:[8]
(For we are but of yesterday, and know nothing,
because our days upon earth are a shadow:)
Shall not they teach thee, and tell thee,
and utter words out of their heart?

[8]In his eagerness to uphold orthodoxy, Bildad suggests that the cause of Job's suffering may be not in his own sins but in those of his family.

Can the rush grow up without mire?
    can the flag grow without water?
Whilst it is yet in his greenness, and not cut down,
    It withereth before any other herb.
So are the paths of all that forget God;
    and the hypocrite's hope shall perish:
Whose hope shall be cut off,
    and whose trust shall be a spider's web.
He shall lean upon his house, but it shall not stand:
    he shall hold it fast, but it shall not endure.
He is green before the sun,
    and his branch shooteth forth in his garden.
His roots are wrapped about the heap,
    and seeth the place of stones.
If he destroy him from his place,
    then it shall deny him, saying, 'I have not seen thee.'
Behold, this is the joy of his way,
    and out of the earth shall others grow.

"Behold, God will not cast away a perfect man,
    neither will he help the evil doers:
Till he fill thy mouth with laughing,
    and thy lips with rejoicing.
They that hate thee shall be clothed with shame;
    and the dwelling place of the wicked shall come to nought."

CHAPTER 9

Then Job answered and said,

"I know it is so of a truth:
    but how should man be just with God?
If he will contend with him,
    he cannot answer him one of a thousand.
He is wise in heart, and mighty in strength:
    who hath hardened himself against him, and hath prospered?
Which removeth the mountains, and they know not:
    which overturneth them in his anger.
Which shaketh the earth out of her place,
    and the pillars thereof tremble.
Which commandeth the sun, and it riseth not;
    and sealeth up the stars.
Which alone spreadeth out the heavens,
    and treadeth upon the waves of the sea.
Which maketh Arcturus, Orion, and Pleiades,
    and the chambers of the south.
Which doeth great things past finding out;
    yea, and wonders without number.

Lo, he goeth by me, and I see him not:
he passeth on also, but I perceive him not.
Behold, he taketh away, who can hinder him?
Who will say unto him, 'What doest thou?'

"If God will not withdraw his anger,
the proud helpers do stoop under him.
How much less shall I answer him,
and choose out my words to reason with him?
Whom, though I were righteous, yet would I not answer,
but I would make supplication to my judge.
If I had called, and he had answered me;
yet would I not believe that he had hearkened unto my voice.
For he breaketh me with a tempest,
and multiplieth my wounds without cause.
He will not suffer me to take my breath,
but filleth me with bitterness.
If I speak of strength, lo, he is strong:
and if of judgment, who shall set me a time to plead?
If I justify myself, mine own mouth shall condemn me:
if I say, I am perfect, it shall also prove me perverse.
Though I were perfect, yet would I not know my soul:
I would despise my life.
This is one thing, therefore I said it,
he destroyeth the perfect and the wicked.
If the scourge slay suddenly,
he will laugh at the trial of the innocent.
The earth is given into the hand of the wicked:
he covereth the faces of the judges thereof;
if not, where, and who is he?

"Now my days are swifter than a post:[9]
they flee away, they see no good.
They are passed away as the swift ships:
as the eagle that hasteth to the prey.
If I say, 'I will forget my complaint,
I will leave off my heaviness, and comfort myself':
I am afraid of all my sorrows,
I know that thou wilt not hold me innocent.
If I be wicked, why then labor I in vain?
If I wash myself with snow water,
and make my hands never so clean;
Yet shalt thou plunge me in the ditch,
and mine own clothes shall abhor me.
For he is not a man, as I am, that I should answer him,
and we should come together in judgment.
Neither is there any daysman[10] betwixt us,
that might lay his hand upon us both.

[9]Runner. [10]Umpire.

Let him take his rod away from me,
and let not his fear terrify me:
Then would I speak, and not fear him;
but it is not so with me.

CHAPTER 10

"My soul is weary of my life; I will leave my complaint upon myself;
I will speak in the bitterness of my soul.
I will say unto God, 'Do not condemn me;
show me wherefore thou contendest with me.
Is it good unto thee that thou shouldest oppress,
that thou shouldest despise the work of thine hands,
and shine upon the counsel of the wicked?
Hast thou eyes of flesh?
or seest thou as man seeth?
Are thy days as the days of man?
are thy years as man's days,
That thou enquirest after mine iniquity,
and searchest after my sin?
Thou knowest that I am not wicked;
and there is none that can deliver out of thine hand.
Thine hands have made me and fashioned me together round about;
yet thou dost destroy me.
Remember, I beseech thee, that thou hast made me as the clay;
And wilt thou bring me into dust again?
Hast thou not poured me out as milk,
and curdled me like cheese?
Thou hast clothed me with skin and flesh,
and hast fenced me with bones and sinews:
Thou hast granted me life and favor,
and thy visitation hath preserved my spirit.
And these things hast thou hid in thine heart:
I know that this is with thee.
If I sin, then thou markest me,
and thou wilt not acquit me from mine iniquity.
If I be wicked, woe unto me;
and if I be righteous, yet will I not lift up my head.
I am full of confusion;
therefore see thou mine affliction;
For it increaseth. Thou huntest me as a fierce lion:
and again thou showest thyself marvellous upon me.
Thou renewest thy witnesses against me,
and increasest thine indignation upon me;
changes and war are against me.

"Wherefore then hast thou brought me forth out of the womb?
Oh that I had given up the ghost, and no eye had seen me!
I should have been as though I had not been;
I should have been carried from the womb to the grave.

Are not my days few? cease then,
and let me alone, that I may take comfort a little,
Before I go whence I shall not return,
even to the land of darkness[11] and the shadow of death;
A land of darkness, as darkness itself;
and of the shadow of death, without any order,
and where the light is as darkness."

CHAPTER 11

Then answered Zophar the Naamathite, and said,

"Should not the multitude of words be answered?
and should a man full of talk be justified?
Should thy lies make men hold their peace?
and when thou mockest, shall no man make thee ashamed?
For thou hast said, 'My doctrine is pure,
and I am clean in thine eyes.'
But oh that God would speak,
and open his lips against thee;
And that he would show thee the secrets of wisdom,
that they are double to that which is!
Know therefore that God exacteth of thee less than thine iniquity
deserveth.[12]

"Canst thou by searching find out God?
canst thou find out the Almighty unto perfection?
It is as high as heaven; what canst thou do?
deeper than hell; what canst thou know?
The measure thereof is longer than the earth,
and broader than the sea.
If he cut off, and shut up,
or gather together, then who can hinder him?
For he knoweth vain men:
he seeth wickedness also; will he not then consider it?
For vain man would be wise,
though man be born like a wild ass's colt.

"If thou prepare thine heart,
and stretch out thine hands toward him;
If iniquity be in thine hand, put it far away,
and let not wickedness dwell in thy tabernacles.
For then shalt thou lift up thy face without spot;
yea, thou shalt be steadfast, and shalt not fear:

[11] The concept of hell, like the figure of Satan, is late in developing in the Old Testament period. The "land of darkness" mentioned here is the Hebrew *sheol,* a shadowy place where the dead go, similar to the Greek Hades. It does not imply reward or punishment for one's life on earth.

[12] Zophar, too, insists that Job has deserved his suffering and that God dispenses justice on earth.

Because thou shalt forget thy misery,
and remember it as waters that pass away:
And thine age shall be clearer than the noonday;
thou shalt shine forth, thou shalt be as the morning.
And thou shalt be secure, because there is hope;
yea thou shalt dig about thee, and thou shalt take thy rest in safety.
Also thou shalt lie down, and none shall make thee afraid;
yea, many shall make suit unto thee.
But the eyes of the wicked shall fail, and they shall not escape,
and their hope shall be as the giving up of the ghost."

CHAPTER 12

And Job answered and said,

"No doubt but ye are the people,
and wisdom shall die with you.
But I have understanding as well as you;
I am not inferior to you:
yea, who knoweth not such things as these?
I am as one mocked of his neighbor,
who calleth upon God, and he answereth him:
the just upright man is laughed to scorn.
He that is ready to slip with his feet
is as a lamp despised in the thought of him that is at ease.
The tabernacles of robbers prosper,
and they that provoke God are secure;
into whose hand God bringeth abundantly.

"But ask now the beasts, and they shall teach thee;
and the fowls of the air, and they shall tell thee:
Or speak to the earth, and it shall teach thee:
and the fishes of the sea shall declare unto thee.
Who knoweth not in all these
that the hand of the Lord hath wrought this?
In whose hand is the soul of every living thing,
and the breath of all mankind.
Doth not the ear try words?
and the mouth taste his meat?
With the ancient is wisdom;
and in length of days understanding.

"With him is wisdom and strength,
he hath counsel and understanding.
Behold, he breaketh down, and it cannot be built again:
he shutteth up a man, and there can be no opening.
Behold, he withholdeth the waters, and they dry up:
also he sendeth them out, and they overturn the earth.
With him is strength and wisdom:
the deceived and the deceiver are his.

He leadeth counsellors away spoiled,
and maketh the judges fools.
He looseth the bond of kings,
and girdeth their loins with a girdle.
He leadeth princes away spoiled,
and overthroweth the mighty.
He removeth away the speech of the trusty,
and taketh away the understanding of the aged.
He poureth contempt upon princes,
and weakeneth the strength of the mighty.
He discovereth deep things out of darkness,
and bringeth out to light the shadow of death.
He increaseth the nations, and destroyeth them:
he enlargeth the nations, and straiteneth them again.
He taketh away the heart of the chief of the people of the earth,
and causeth them to wander in a wilderness where there is no way.
They grope in the dark without light,
and he maketh them to stagger like a drunken man."

CHAPTER 13

"Lo, mine eye hath seen all this,
mine ear hath heard and understood it.
What ye know, the same do I know also:
I am not inferior unto you.

Surely I would speak to the Almighty,
and I desire to reason with God.
But ye are forgers of lies,
ye are all physicians of no value.

O that ye would altogether hold your peace!
and it should be your wisdom.
Hear now my reasoning,
and hearken to the pleadings of my lips.
Will ye speak wickedly for God?
and talk deceitfully for him?
Will ye accept his person?
will ye contend for God?
Is it good that he should search you out?
or as one man mocketh another, do ye so mock him?
He will surely reprove you,
if ye do secretly accept persons.
Shall not his excellency make you afraid?
and his dread fall upon you?
Your remembrances are like unto ashes,
your bodies to bodies of clay.
Hold your peace, let me alone, that I may speak,
and let come on me what will.
Wherefore do I take my flesh in my teeth,
and put my life in mine hand?

Though he slay me, yet will I trust in him:[13]
but I will maintain mine own ways before him.
He also shall be my salvation:
for an hypocrite shall not come before him.[14]
Hear diligently my speech,
and my declaration with your ears.
Behold now, I have ordered my cause;
I know that I shall be justified.
Who is he that will plead with me?
for now, if I hold my tongue, I shall give up the ghost.
Only do not two things unto me:
then will I not hide myself from thee.
Withdraw thine hand far from me:
and let not thy dread make me afraid.
Then call thou, and I will answer:
or let me speak, and answer thou me.
How many are mine iniquities and sins?
make me to know my transgression and my sin.
Wherefore hidest thou thy face,
and holdest me for thine enemy?
Wilt thou break a leaf driven to and fro?
and wilt thou pursue the dry stubble?
For thou writest bitter things against me,
and makest me to possess the iniquities of my youth.
Thou puttest my feet also in the stocks,
and lookest narrowly unto all my paths;
thou settest a print upon the heels of my feet.
And he, as a rotten thing, consumeth,
as a garment that is moth eaten."

CHAPTER 14

"Man that is born of a woman
is of few days, and full of trouble.
He cometh forth like a flower, and is cut down:
he fleeth also as a shadow, and continueth not.
And dost thou open thine eyes upon such an one,
and bringest me into judgment with thee?
Who can bring a clean thing out of an unclean?
not one.
Seeing his days are determined,
the number of his months are with thee,
thou hast appointed his bounds that he cannot pass;

[13] The latter part of this line should read "I have no hope," a more defiant and despairing statement.

[14] Job argues that his eagerness to confront God is a proof of his blamelessness, for a guilty man would not dare to come before Him.

Turn from him, that he may rest,
till he shall accomplish, as an hireling, his day.

"For there is hope of a tree, if it be cut down, that it will sprout again,
and that the tender branch thereof will not cease.
Though the root thereof wax old in the earth,
and the stock thereof die in the ground;
Yet through the scent of water it will bud,
and bring forth boughs like a plant.
But man dieth, and wasteth away:
yea, man giveth up the ghost, and where is he?
As the waters fail from the sea,
and the flood decayeth and drieth up:
So man lieth down, and riseth not:
till the heavens be no more, they shall not awake,
nor be raised out of their sleep.
O that thou wouldest hide me in the grave,
that thou wouldest keep me secret, until thy wrath be past,
that thou wouldest appoint me a set time, and remember me!
If a man die, shall he live again?
all the days of my appointed time will I wait,
till my change come.
Thou shalt call, and I will answer thee:
thou wilt have a desire to the work of thine hands.
For now thou numberest my steps:
dost thou not watch over my sin?
My transgression is sealed up in a bag,
and thou sewest up mine iniquity.

"And surely the mountain falling cometh to nought,
and the rock is removed out of his place.
The waters wear the stones:
thou washest away the things which grow out of the dust of the earth;
and thou destroyest the hope of man.
Thou prevailest for ever against him, and he passeth:
thou changest his countenance, and sendest him away.
His sons come to honor, and he knoweth it not;
and they are brought low, but he perceiveth it not of them.
But his flesh upon him shall have pain,
and his soul within him shall mourn."

CHAPTER 19

Then Job answered [the Comforters] and said,

"How long will ye vex my soul,
and break me in pieces with words?
These ten times have ye reproached me:
ye are not ashamed that ye make yourselves strange to me.

And be it indeed that I have erred,
 mine error remaineth with myself.
If indeed ye will magnify yourselves against me,
 and plead against me my reproach:
Know now that God hath overthrown me,
 and hath compassed me with his net.
Behold, I cry out of wrong, but I am not heard:
 I cry aloud, but there is no judgment.
He hath fenced up my way that I cannot pass,
 and he hath set darkness in my paths.
He hath stripped me of my glory,
 and taken the crown from my head.
He hath destroyed me on every side, and I am gone:
 and mine hope hath he removed like a tree.
He hath also kindled his wrath against me,
 and he counteth me unto him as one of his enemies.
His troops come together,
 and raise up their way against me,
 and encamp round about my tabernacle.

"He hath put my brethren far from me,
 and mine acquaintance are verily estranged from me.
My kinsfolk have failed,
 and my familiar friends have forgotten me.
They that dwell in mine house, and my maids, count me for a stranger:
 I am an alien in their sight.
I called my servant, and he gave me no answer;
 I intreated him with my mouth.
My breath is strange to my wife,
 though I intreated for the children's sake of mine own body.
Yea, young children despised me;
 I arose, and they spake against me.
All my inward friends abhorred me:
 and they whom I loved are turned against me.
My bone cleaveth to my skin and to my flesh,
 and I am escaped with the skin of my teeth.
Have pity upon me, have pity upon me, O ye my friends;
 for the hand of God hath touched me.
Why do ye persecute me as God,
 and are not satisfied with my flesh?

"Oh that my words were now written!
 Oh that they were printed in a book!
That they were graven with an iron pen
 and lead in the rock for ever!
For I know that my redeemer liveth,
 and that he shall stand at the latter day upon the earth:
And though after my skin worms destroy this body,
 yet in my flesh shall I see God:

Whom I shall see for myself,
and mine eyes shall behold, and not another;[15]
though my reins be consumed within me.
But ye should say, 'Why persecute we him,
seeing the root of the matter is found in me?'
Be ye afraid of the sword:
for wrath bringeth the punishments of the sword,
that ye may know there is a judgment."

CHAPTER 29

Moreover Job continued his parable, and said,

"Oh that I were as in months past,
as in the days when God preserved me;
When his candle shined upon my head,
and when by his light I walked through darkness;
As I was in the days of my youth,
when the secret of God was upon my tabernacle;
When the Almighty was yet with me,
when my children were about me;
When I washed my steps with butter,
and the rock poured me out rivers of oil;
When I went out to the gate through the city,
when I prepared my seat in the street!
The young men saw me, and hid themselves:
and the aged arose, and stood up.
The princes refrained talking,
and laid their hand on their mouth.
The nobles held their peace,
and their tongue cleaved to the roof of their mouth.
When the ear heard me, then it blessed me;
and when the eye saw me, it gave witness to me:
Because I delivered the poor that cried,
and the fatherless, and him that had none to help him.
The blessing of him that was ready to perish came upon me:
and I caused the widow's heart to sing for joy.
I put on righteousness, and it clothed me:
my judgment was as a robe and a diadem.
I was eyes to the blind,
and feet was I to the lame.
I was a father to the poor:
and the cause which I knew not I searched out.
And I brake the jaws of the wicked,
and plucked the spoil out of his teeth.

[15]The Hebrew text is unclear at this point. The word translated "Redeemer" here was a legal term meaning "avenger" or "vindicator." Job probably is saying that after his death he will see God, in the role of "avenger," vindicate him posthumously in the eyes of the world.

Then I said, 'I shall die in my nest,
and I shall multiply my days as the sand.'
My root was spread out by the waters,
and the dew lay all night upon my branch.
My glory was fresh in me,
and my bow was renewed in my hand.

"Unto me men gave ear,
and waited, and kept silence at my counsel.
After my words they spake not again;
and my speech dropped upon them.
And they waited for me as for the rain;
and they opened their mouth wide as for the latter rain.
If I laughed on them, they believed it not;
and the light of my countenance they cast not down.
I chose out their way, and sat chief,
and dwelt as a king in the army,
as one that comforteth the mourners."

CHAPTER 30

"But now they that are younger than I
have me in derision,
Whose fathers I would have disdained
to have set with the dogs of my flock.
Yea, whereto might the strength of their hands profit me,
in whom old age was perished?
For want and famine they were solitary;
fleeing into the wilderness in former time desolate and waste.
Who cut up mallows by the bushes,
and juniper roots for their meat.
They were driven forth from among men,
(they cried after them as after a thief;)
To dwell in the cliffs of the valleys,
in caves of the earth, and in the rocks.
Among the bushes they brayed;
under the nettles they were gathered together.
They were children of fools, yea, children of base men:
they were viler than the earth.

"And now am I their song,
yea, I am their byword.
They abhor me, they flee far from me,
and spare not to spit in my face.
Because he hath loosed my cord, and afflicted me,
they have also let loose the bridle before me.
Upon my right hand rise the youth;
they push away my feet,
And they raise up against me
the ways of their destruction.

They mar my path,
they set forward my calamity, they have no helper.
They came upon me as a wide breaking in of waters:
in the desolation they rolled themselves upon me.
Terrors are turned upon me:
they pursue my soul as the wind:
and my welfare passeth away as a cloud.

"And now my soul is poured out upon me;
the days of affliction have taken hold upon me.
My bones are pierced in me in the night season:
and my sinews take no rest.
By the great force of my disease is my garment changed:
it bindeth me about as the collar of my coat.
He hath cast me into the mire,
and I am become like dust and ashes.
I cry unto thee, and thou dost not hear me:
I stand up, and thou regards me not.
Thou art become cruel to me:
with thy strong hand thou opposest thyself against me.
Thou liftest me up to the wind;
thou causest me to ride upon it,
and dissolvest my substance.
For I know that thou wilt bring me to death,
and to the house appointed for all living.

"Howbeit he will not stretch out his hand to the grave,
though they cry in his destruction.
Did not I weep for him that was in trouble?
was not my soul grieved for the poor?
When I looked for good, then evil came unto me:
and when I waited for light, there came darkness.
My bowels boiled, and rested not:
the days of affliction prevented me.
I went mourning without the sun:
I stood up, and I cried in the congregation.
I am a brother to dragons,
and a companion to owls.
My skin is black upon me,
and my bones are burned with heat.
My harp also is turned to mourning,
and my organ into the voice of them that weep."

CHAPTER 31

"I made a covenant with mine eyes;
why then should I think upon a maid?
For what portion of God is there from above?
and what inheritance of the Almighty from on high?

Is not destruction to the wicked?
and a strange punishment to the workers of iniquity?
Doth not he see my ways,
and count all my steps?

If I have walked with vanity,
or if my foot hath hasted to deceit;
Let me be weighed in an even balance,
that God may know mine integrity.
If my step hath turned out of the way,
and mine heart walked after mine eyes,
and if any blot hath cleaved to mine hands;
Then let me sow, and let another eat;
yea, let my offspring be rooted out.

"If mine heart have been deceived by a woman,
or if I have laid wait at my neighbor's door;
Then let my wife grind unto another,[16]
and let others bow down upon her.
For this is an heinous crime;
yea, it is an iniquity to be punished by the judges.
For it is a fire that consumeth to destruction,
and would root out all mine increase.

"If I did despise the cause of my manservant or of my maidservant,
when they contended with me;
What then shall I do when God riseth up?
and when he visiteth, what shall I answer him?
Did not he that made me in the womb make him?
and did not one fashion us in the womb?

"If I have withheld the poor from their desire,
or have caused the eyes of the widow to fail;
Or have eaten my morsel myself alone,
and the fatherless hath not eaten thereof;
(For from my youth he was brought up with me, as with a father,
and I have guided her from my mother's womb;)
If I have seen any perish for want of clothing,
or any poor without covering;
If his loins have not blessed me,
and if he were not warmed with the fleece of my sheep;
If I have lifted up my hand against the fatherless,
when I saw my help in the gate:
Then let mine arm fall from my shoulder blade,
and mine arm be broken from the bone.
For destruction from God was a terror to me,
and by reason of his highness I could not endure.

[16]That is, grind grain as a servant for someone else.

"If I have made gold my hope,
or have said to the fine gold, 'Thou art my confidence';
If I rejoiced because my wealth was great,
and because my hand had gotten much:
If I beheld the sun when it shined,
or the moon walking in brightness;
And my heart hath been secretly enticed,
or my mouth hath kissed my hand:
This also were an iniquity to be punished by the judge:
for I should have denied the God that is above.

"If I rejoiced at the destruction of him that hated me,
or lifted up myself when evil found him:
Neither have I suffered my mouth to sin
by wishing a curse to his soul.
If the men of my tabernacle said not,
'Oh that we had of his flesh! we cannot be satisfied.'
The stranger did not lodge in the street:
but I opened my doors to the traveller.
If I covered my transgressions as Adam,
by hiding mine iniquity in my bosom:
Did I fear a great multitude,
or did the contempt of families terrify me,
that I kept silence, and went not out of the door?
Oh that one would hear me!
behold, my desire is, that the Almighty would answer me,
and that mine adversary had written a book.
Surely I would take it upon my shoulder,
and bind it as a crown to me.
I would declare unto him the number of my steps;
as a prince would I go near unto him.

"If my land cry against me,
or that the furrows likewise thereof complain;
If I have eaten the fruits thereof without money,
or have caused the owners thereof to lose their life:
Let thistles grow instead of wheat,
and cockle instead of barley."

The words of Job are ended.

CHAPTER 38

Then the Lord answered Job out of the whirlwind,[17] and said,

"Who is this that darkeneth counsel
by words without knowledge?

[17]God appears in a whirlwind elsewhere in the Old Testament as well, notably in Nahum 1:3 and Psalms 18:7–15.

Gird up now thy loins like a man;
  for I will demand of thee, and answer thou me.

"Where wast thou when I laid the foundations of the earth?
  declare, if thou hast understanding.
Who hath laid the measures thereof, if thou knowest?
  or who hath stretched the line upon it?
Whereupon are the foundations thereof fastened?
  or who laid the corner stone thereof;
When the morning stars sang together,
  and all the sons of God shouted for joy?

"Or who shut up the sea with doors,
  when it brake forth, as if it had issued out of the womb?
When I made the cloud the garment thereof,
  and thick darkness a swaddlingband for it,
And brake up for it my decreed place,
  and set bars and doors,
And said, 'Hitherto shalt thou come, but no further:
  and here shall thy proud waves be stayed'?
Hast thou commanded the morning since thy days;
  and caused the dayspring[18] to know his place;
That it might take hold of the ends of the earth,
  that the wicked might be shaken out of it?
It is turned as clay to the seal;
  and they stand as a garment.
And from the wicked their light is withholden,
  and the high arm shall be broken.

"Hast thou entered into the springs of the sea?
  or hast thou walked in the search of the depth?
Have the gates of death been opened unto thee?
  or hast thou seen the doors of the shadow of death?
Hast thou perceived the breadth of the earth?
  declare if thou knowest it all.

"Where is the way where light dwelleth?
  and as for darkness, where is the place thereof,
That thou shouldest take it to the bound thereof,
  and that thou shouldest know the paths to the house thereof?
Knowest thou it, because thou wast then born?
  or because the number of thy days is great?

"Hast thou entered into the treasures of the snow?
  or hast thou seen the treasures of the hail,
Which I have reserved against the time of trouble,
  against the day of battle and war?

[18] Dawn.

By what way is the light parted,
which scattereth the east wind upon the earth?
Who hath divided a watercourse for the overflowing of waters,
or a way for the lightning of thunder;
To cause it to rain on the earth, where no man is;
on the wilderness, wherein there is no man;
To satisfy the desolate and waste ground;
and to cause the bud of the tender herb to spring forth?

"Hath the rain a father?
or who hath begotten the drops of dew?
Out of whose womb came the ice?
and the hoary frost of heaven, who hath gendered it?
The waters are hid as with a stone,
and the face of the deep is frozen.

"Canst thou bind the sweet influences of Pleiades,
or loose the bands of Orion?
Canst thou bring forth Mazzaroth in his season?
or canst thou guide Arcturus with his sons?[19]
Knowest thou the ordinances of heaven?
canst thou set the dominion thereof in the earth?

"Canst thou lift up thy voice to the clouds,
that abundance of waters may cover thee?
Canst thou send lightnings, that they may go,
and say unto thee, 'Here we are'?
Who hath put wisdom in the inward parts?
or who hath given understanding to the heart?
Who can number the clouds in wisdom?
or who can stay the bottles of heaven,
When the dust groweth into hardness,
and the clods cleave fast together?

"Wilt thou hunt the prey for the lion?
or fill the appetite of the young lions,
When they couch in their dens,
and abide in the covert to lie in wait?
Who provideth for the raven his food?
when his young ones cry unto God,
they wander for lack of meat."

CHAPTER 39

"Knowest thou the time when the wild goats of the rock bring forth?
or canst thou mark when the hinds do calve?
Canst thou number the months that they fulfil?
or knowest thou the time when they bring forth?

[19] These are all stars or constellations.

They bow themselves, they bring forth their young ones,
they cast out their sorrows.
Their young ones are in good liking, they grow up with corn;
they go forth, and return not unto them.

"Who hath sent out the wild ass free?
or who hath loosed the bands of the wild ass?
Whose house I have made the wilderness,
and the barren land his dwellings.
He scorneth the multitude of the city,
neither regardeth he the crying of the driver.
The range of the mountains is his pasture,
and he searcheth after every green thing.

"Will the unicorn[20] be willing to serve thee,
or abide by thy crib?
Canst thou bind the unicorn with his band in the furrow?
or will he harrow the valleys after thee?
Wilt thou trust him, because his strength is great?
or wilt thou leave thy labor to him?
Wilt thou believe him, that he will bring home thy seed,
and gather it into thy barn?

"Gavest thou the goodly wings unto the peacocks?
or wings and feathers unto the ostrich?
Which leaveth her eggs in the earth,
and warmeth them in dust,
And forgetteth that the foot may crush them,
or that the wild beast may break them.
She is hardened against her young ones, as though they were not hers:
her labor is in vain without fear;
Because God hath deprived her of wisdom,
neither hath he imparted to her understanding.
What time she lifteth up herself on high,
she scorneth the horse and his rider.

"Hast thou given the horse strength?
hast thou clothed his neck with thunder?
Canst thou make him afraid as a grasshopper?
the glory of his nostrils is terrible.
He paweth in the valley, and rejoiceth in his strength:
he goeth on to meet the armed men.
He mocketh at fear, and is not affrighted;
neither turneth he back from the sword.
The quiver rattleth against him,
the glittering spear and the shield.

[20]Or wild ox.

He swalloweth the ground with fierceness and rage:
    neither believeth he that it is the sound of the trumpet.
He saith among the trumpets, 'Ha, ha';
    and he smelleth the battle afar off,
    the thunder of the captains, and the shouting.

"Doth the hawk fly by thy wisdom,
    and stretch her wings toward the south?
Doth the eagle mount up at thy command,
    and make her nest on high?
She dwelleth and abideth on the rock,
    upon the crag of the rock, and the strong place.
From thence she seeketh the prey,
    and her eyes behold afar off.
Her young ones also suck up blood:
    and where the slain are, there is she."

CHAPTER 40

Moreover the Lord answered Job, and said,

"Shall he that contendeth with the Almighty instruct him?
He that reproveth God, let him answer it."

Then Job answered the Lord, and said,

"Behold, I am vile; what shall I answer thee?
    I will lay mine hand upon my mouth.
Once have I spoken; but I will not answer:
    yea, twice; but I will proceed no further."

Then answered the Lord unto Job out of the whirlwind, and said,

"Gird up thy loins now like a man:
    I will demand of thee, and declare thou unto me.
Wilt thou also disannul my judgment?
    wilt thou condemn me, that thou mayest be righteous?
Hast thou an arm like God?
    or canst thou thunder with a voice like him?

"Deck thyself now with majesty and excellency;
    and array thyself with glory and beauty.
Cast abroad the rage of thy wrath:
    and behold every one that is proud, and abase him.
Look on every one that is proud, and bring him low;
    and tread down the wicked in their place.
Hide them in the dust together;
    and bind their faces in secret.

Then will I also confess unto thee
that thine own right hand can save thee.

"Behold now behemoth,[21] which I made with thee;
he eateth grass as an ox.
Lo now, his strength is in his loins,
and his force is in the navel of his belly.
He moveth his tail like a cedar:
the sinews of his stones are wrapped together.
His bones are as strong pieces of brass;
his bones are like bars of iron.

"He is the chief of the ways of God:
he that made him can make his sword to approach unto him.
Surely the mountains bring him forth food,
where all the beasts of the field play.
He lieth under the shady trees,
in the covert of the reed, and fens.
The shady trees cover him with their shadow;
the willows of the brook compass him about.
Behold, he drinketh up a river, and hasteth not:
he trusteth that he can draw up Jordan into his mouth.
He taketh it with his eyes:
his nose pierceth through snares."

CHAPTER 41

"Canst thou draw out leviathan[22] with an hook?
or his tongue with a cord which thou lettest down?
Canst thou put an hook into his nose?
or bore his jaw through with a thorn?
Will he make many supplications unto thee?
will he speak soft words unto thee?
Will he make a covenant with thee?
wilt thou take him for a servant for ever?
Wilt thou play with him as with a bird?
or wilt thou bind him for thy maidens?
Shall the companions make a banquet of him?
shall they part him among the merchants?
Canst thou fill his skin with barbed irons?
or his head with fish spears?
Lay thine hand upon him,
remember the battle, do no more.

[21] Probably the hippopotamus, here presented as a primeval monster.
[22] A mythological version of the crocodile, here presented as a sea monster emblematic of primeval chaos.

Behold, the hope of him is in vain:
    shall not one be cast down even at the sight of him?
None is so fierce that dare stir him up:
    who then is able to stand before me?
Who hath prevented me, that I should repay him?
    whatsoever is under the whole heaven is mine.
"I will not conceal his parts,
    nor his power, nor his comely proportion.
Who can discover the face of his garment?
    or who can come to him with his double bridle?
Who can open the doors of his face?
    his teeth are terrible round about.
His scales are his pride,
    shut up together as with a close seal.
One is so near to another,
    that no air can come between them.
They are joined one to another,
    they stick together, that they cannot be sundered.
By his neesings[23] a light doth shine,
    and his eyes are like the eyelids of the morning.
Out of his mouth go burning lamps,
    and sparks of fire leap out.
Out of his nostrils goeth smoke,
    as out of a seething pot or caldron.
His breath kindleth coals,
    and a flame goeth out of his mouth.
In his neck remaineth strength,
    and sorrow is turned into joy before him.
The flakes of his flesh are joined together:
    they are firm in themselves; they cannot be moved.
His heart is as firm as a stone;
    yea, as hard as a piece of the nether millstone.
When he raiseth up himself, the mighty are afraid:
    by reason of breakings they purify themselves.
The sword of him that layeth at him cannot hold:
    the spear, the dart, nor the habergeon.
He esteemeth iron as straw,
    and brass as rotten wood.
The arrow cannot make him flee:
    slingstones are turned with him into stubble.
Darts are counted as stubble:
    he laugheth at the shaking of a spear.
Sharp stones are under him:
    he spreadeth sharp pointed things upon the mire.
He maketh the deep to boil like a pot:
    he maketh the sea like a pot of ointment.

[23] Sneezes (which send out drops of water reflecting the sun).

He maketh a path to shine after him;
    one would think the deep to be hoary.
Upon earth there is not his like,
    who is made without fear.
He beholdeth all high things:
    he is a king over all the children of pride."

CHAPTER 42

Then Job answered the Lord, and said,

"I know that thou canst do every thing,
    and that no thought can be withholden from thee.
'Who is he that hideth counsel without knowledge?'
Therefore have I uttered that I understood not;
    things too wonderful for me, which I knew not.
'Hear, I beseech thee, and I will speak:
    I will demand of thee, and declare thou unto me.'
I have heard of thee by the hearing of the ear:
    but now mine eye seeth thee.
Wherefore I abhor myself, and repent
    in dust and ashes."

And it was so, that after the Lord had spoken these words unto Job, the Lord said to Eliphaz the Temanite, "My wrath is kindled against thee, and against thy two friends: for ye have not spoken of me the thing that is right, as my servant Job hath. Therefore take unto you now seven bullocks and seven rams, and go to my servant Job, and offer up for yourselves a burnt offering; and my servant Job shall pray for you: for him will I accept: lest I deal with you after your folly, in that ye have not spoken of me the thing which is right, like my servant Job." So Eliphaz the Temanite and Bildad the Shuhite and Zophar the Naamathite went, and did according as the Lord commanded them: the Lord also accepted Job. And the Lord turned the captivity of Job, when he prayed for his friends: also the Lord gave Job twice as much as he had before. Then came there unto him all his brethren, and all his sisters, and all they that had been of his acquaintance before, and did eat bread with him in his house: and they bemoaned him, and comforted him over all the evil that the Lord had brought upon him: every man also gave him a piece of money, and every one an earring of gold. So the Lord blessed the latter end of Job more than his beginning: for he had fourteen thousand sheep, and six thousand camels, and a thousand yoke of oxen, and a thousand she asses. He had also seven sons and three daughters. And he called the name of the first, Jemima; and the name of the second, Kezia; and the name of the third, Keren-happuch. And in all the land were no women found so fair as the daughters of Job: and their father gave them inheritance among their brethren. After this lived Job an hundred and forty years, and saw his sons, and his sons' sons, even four generations. So Job died, being old and full of days.

from PSALMS

PSALM 8

1 O Lord our Lord,[1]
how excellent is thy name in all the earth!
who has set thy glory above the heavens.
2 Out of the mouth of babes and sucklings[2] hast thou ordained strength
because of thine enemies,
that thou mightest still the enemy and the avenger.

3 When I consider thy heavens, the work of thy fingers,
the moon and the stars, which thou hast ordained;

4 What is man, that thou art mindful of him?
and the son of man,[3] that thou visitest him?

5 For thou hast made him a little lower than the angels,
and hast crowned him with glory and honor.
6 Thou madest him to have dominion over the works of thy hands;
thou hast put all things under his feet:
7 All sheep and oxen,
yea, and the beasts of the field;
8 The fowl of the air, and the fish of the sea,
and whatsoever passeth through the paths of the sea.

9 O Lord our Lord,
how excellent is thy name in all the earth!

PSALM 23

1 The Lord is my shepherd;
I shall not want.
2 He maketh me to lie down in green pastures:
he leadeth me beside the still waters.
3 He restoreth my soul:
he leadeth me in the paths of righteousness for his name's sake.

4 Yea, though I walk through the valley of the shadow of death,
I will fear no evil: for thou art with me;
thy rod and thy staff[4] they comfort me.

[1] Numbers in left margin are biblical verse numbers.
[2] Infants at the breast.
[3] "Son of man" means any individual person.
[4] The rod keeps off enemies; the staff is an emblem of protection.

5 Thou preparest a table before me in the presence of mine enemies:
thou anointest my head with oil;
my cup runneth over.[5]

6 Surely goodness and mercy shall follow me all the days of my life:
and I will dwell in the house of the Lord for ever.[6]

PSALM 91

1 He that dwelleth in the secret place of the Most High[7]
shall abide under the shadow of the Almighty.

2 I will say of the Lord, He is my refuge and my fortress:
my God; in him will I trust.

3 Surely he shall deliver thee from the snare of the fowler,[8]
and from the noisome[9] pestilence.

4 He shall cover thee with his feathers,
and under his wings shalt thou trust:
his truth shall be thy shield and buckler.[10]

5 Thou shalt not be afraid for the terror by night;
nor for the arrow that flieth by day;

6 Nor for the pestilence that walketh in darkness;
nor for the destruction that wasteth at noonday.

7 A thousand shall fall[11] at thy side,
and ten thousand at thy right hand;
but it shall not come nigh thee.

8 Only with thine eyes shalt thou behold
and see the reward of the wicked.

9 Because thou hast made the Lord, which is my refuge,
even the Most High, thy habitation;

10 There shall no evil befall thee,
neither shall any plague come nigh thy dwelling.

11 For he shall give his angels charge over thee,
to keep thee in all thy ways.

12 They shall bear thee up in their hands,
lest thou dash thy foot against a stone.

13 Thou shalt tread upon the lion and adder:
the young lion and the dragon shalt thou trample under feet.

14 Because he hath set his love upon me,[12]
therefore will I deliver him:
I will set him on high, because he hath known my name.

[5] In verse 5, the metaphor shifts; God is a host lavishing attentions on a dinner guest.
[6] One possible meaning is "I will spend my life worshipping in God's temple."
[7] Dwells in God's presence, or perhaps, more specifically, in the Temple.
[8] Hunter of game birds. [9] Harmful. [10] Shield; defense.
[11] Shall be stricken by the plague.
[12] Verses 14–16 are thought of as spoken by God.

15 He shall call upon me, and I will answer him:
I will be with him in trouble;
I will deliver him, and honor him.
16 With long life will I satisfy him,
and show him my salvation.

PSALM 103

1 Bless the Lord, O my soul:
and all that is within me, bless his holy name.
2 Bless the Lord, O my soul,
and forget not all his benefits:
3 Who forgiveth all thine iniquities;
Who healeth all thy diseases;
4 Who redeemeth thy life from destruction;
who crowneth thee with loving-kindness and tender mercies;
5 Who satisfieth thy mouth with good things;
so that thy youth is renewed like the eagle's.

6 The Lord executeth righteousness
and judgment for all that are oppressed.
7 He made known his ways unto Moses,
his acts unto the children of Israel.
8 The Lord is merciful and gracious,
slow to anger, and plenteous in mercy.
9 He will not always chide:
neither will he keep his anger for ever.
10 He hath not dealt with us after [13] our sins;
nor rewarded us according to our iniquities.

11 For as the heaven is high above the earth,
so great is his mercy toward them that fear him.
12 As far as the east is from the west,
so far hath he removed our transgressions from us.
13 Like as a father pitieth his children,
so the Lord pitieth them that fear him.
14 For he knoweth our frame;
he remembereth that we are dust.

15 As for man, his days are as grass:
as a flower of the field, so he flourisheth.
16 For the wind passeth over it, and it is gone;
and the place thereof shall know it no more.
17 But the mercy of the Lord is from everlasting to everlasting
upon them that fear him,
and his righteousness unto children's children;
18 To such as keep his covenant,
and to those that remember his commandments to do them.

[13] In proportion to.

19 The Lord hath prepared his throne[14] in the heavens;
and his kingdom ruleth over all.
20 Bless the Lord, ye his angels, that excel in strength,
that do his commandments, hearkening unto the voice of his word.
21 Bless ye the Lord, all ye his hosts;
ye ministers of his, that do his pleasure.
22 Bless the Lord, all his works in all places of his dominion:
bless the Lord, O my soul.

PSALM 114

1 When Israel went out of Egypt,
the house of Jacob from a people of strange language;
2 Judah was his sanctuary,
and Israel[15] his dominion.

3 The sea saw it,[16] and fled:
Jordan was driven back.
4 The mountains skipped like rams,
and the little hills like lambs.

5 What ailed thee, O thou sea, that thou fleddest?
thou Jordan, that thou wast driven back?
6 Ye mountains, that ye skipped like rams;
and ye little hills, like lambs?

7 Tremble, thou earth, at the presence of the Lord,
at the presence of the God of Jacob;
8 Which turned the rock into a standing water,[17]
the flint into a fountain of waters.

PSALM 130

1 Out of the depths have I cried unto thee, O Lord.
2 Lord, hear my voice:
let thine ears be attentive to the voice of my supplications.

3 If thou, Lord, shouldest mark iniquities,
O Lord, who shall stand?

[14] Established His (God's own) throne.

[15] Judah was the southern kingdom of Palestine, settled by the tribes of Judah and Benjamin; Israel was the northern kingdom, settled by the tribes descended from Jacob's ten other sons.

[16] Saw God's presence. The reference is to the miraculous dividing of the waters when the Hebrews escaped from Egypt (Exodus 14); Jordan, in the following line, is the river crossed by the Hebrews forty years later, when they entered the Promised Land (Joshua 3). The Jordan too was miraculously dried up to allow a crossing.

[17] A pool. During the Hebrews' forty years of wandering, God empowered Moses to draw water from a rock by striking it with his staff (Exodus 17).

4 But there is forgiveness with thee,
that thou mayest be feared.

5 I wait for the Lord,
my soul doth wait, and in his word do I hope.
6 My soul waiteth for the Lord more than they that watch for the morning:
I say, more than they that watch for the morning.

7 Let Israel hope in the Lord:
for with the Lord there is mercy,
and with him is plenteous redemption.
8 And he shall redeem Israel from all his iniquities.

PSALM 137

1 By the rivers of Babylon,[18] there we sat down,
yea, we wept, when we remembered Zion.
2 We hanged our harps upon the willows in the midst thereof.
3 For there they that carried us away captive required of us a song;
and they that wasted[19] us required of us mirth, saying,
Sing us one of the songs of Zion.
4 How shall we sing the Lord's song in a strange land?

5 If I forget thee, O Jerusalem,
let my right hand forget her cunning.
6 If I do not remember thee,
let my tongue cleave to the roof of my mouth;
if I prefer not Jerusalem above my chief joy.

7 Remember, O Lord, the children of Edom[20]
in the day of Jerusalem;
who said, Rase[21] it, rase it,
even to the foundation thereof.
8 O daughter of Babylon, who are to be destroyed;
happy shall he be, that rewardeth thee as thou hast served us.
9 Happy shall he be, that taketh and dasheth
thy little ones against the stones.

[18] The irrigation canals of the Tigris and Euphrates rivers, in Babylonia. The Babylonians conquered the Hebrews' homeland (Zion) in 597 B.C., inaugurating sixty years of exile and captivity.
[19] Laid waste.
[20] A land south of the Dead Sea; an ally of the Babylonians in the sack of Jerusalem.
[21] Raze; demolish.

PSALM 139

1 O Lord, thou hast searched me, and known me.
2 Thou knowest my downsitting and mine uprising;
thou understandest my thought afar off.
3 Thou compassest my path and my lying down,
and art acquainted with all my ways.
4 For there is not a word in my tongue,
but, lo, O Lord, thou knowest it altogether.
5 Thou hast beset me behind and before,
and laid thine hand upon me.
6 Such knowledge is too wonderful for me;
it is high, I cannot attain unto it.
7 Whither shall I go from thy Spirit?
or whither shall I flee from thy presence?
8 If I ascend up into heaven, thou art there:
if I make my bed in hell,[22] behold, thou art there.
9 If I take the wings of the morning,[23]
and dwell in the uttermost parts of the sea;
10 Even there shall thy hand lead me,
and thy right hand shall hold me.
11 If I say, Surely the darkness shall cover me;
even the night shall be light about me.
12 Yea, the darkness hideth not from thee;
but the night shineth as the day:
the darkness and the light are both alike to thee.

13 For thou hast possessed my reins:[24]
thou has covered me in my mother's womb.
14 I will praise thee; for I am fearfully and wonderfully made:
marvelous are thy works; and that my soul knoweth right well.
15 My substance was not hid from thee
when I was made in secret,
and curiously wrought in the lowest parts of the earth.[25]
16 Thine eyes did see my substance, yet being unperfect;
and in thy book all my members were written,
which in continuance were fashioned,
when as yet there was none of them.
17 How precious also are thy thoughts unto me, O God!
How great is the sum of them!
18 If I should count them, they are more in number than the sand:
when I awake, I am still with thee.

19 Surely thou wilt slay the wicked, O God:
depart from me therefore, ye bloody men.

[22] Sheol, the place of the dead (roughly equivalent to the Greek Hades).
[23] Travel as fast as the dawn spreads.
[24] "Didst form my inward parts" (Revised Standard Version).
[25] A metaphor for the womb.

20 For they speak against thee wickedly,
and thine enemies take thy name in vain.
21 Do not I hate them, O Lord, that hate thee?
And am not I grieved with those that rise up against thee?
22 I hate them with perfect hatred:
I count them mine enemies.
23 Search me, O God, and know my heart:
try me, and know my thoughts:
24 And see if there be any wicked way in me,
and lead me in the way everlasting.

Homer

(Eighth Century B.C.)

Like the Bible, Homer's *Iliad* and *Odyssey* are fundamental sources of the culture and literature of the Western world. These epics have been revered not only as masterpieces of language and narrative but also as expressions of central truths about human beings and their place in the scheme of things. They grow out of a story the elements of which are as follows: While a guest at the palace of Meneláos (*Menelaus* in the more familiar English spelling), who was king of Sparta in southern Greece, the Trojan prince Paris fell in love with Helen, his host's supremely beautiful wife, and carried her off to Troy, apparently with her consent. Under the command of Meneláos' brother Agamémnon, the Greeks organized an army and sailed to Troy in order to recapture Helen, to avenge the dishonor of her husband, and to punish Paris for his violation of the sacred code of hospitality. But, despite outnumbering the Trojans, the Greeks were long frustrated in their attempt to take the city, which was to fall only after ten years of siege. The *Iliad* focuses on one important episode in the war, a quarrel between Agamémnon and Akhilleus (Achilles) over ownership of a prisoner slavegirl. The epic then records the tragic consequences of the quarrel: It describes the death of Akhilleus' beloved companion Patróklos (Patroclus) while Akhilleus was sulking on the sidelines and the subsequent revenge taken by Akhilleus on the Trojan hero Hektor (Hector), who had killed his friend. The action of the *Odyssey* takes place after the war is over. The poem concentrates on one of the foremost Greek warriors against Troy, the resourceful Odysseus, who must overcome many obstacles and tribulations in order to return to his wife and homeland. The actual fall of Troy is not described in either of the two Homeric poems. (One ancient account of the city's fall was written many centuries later by the Roman poet Virgil in his *Aeneid,* Book II.)

Again like the Bible, the two Homeric epics have for centuries caused controversy. Debates continue today as strongly as ever. To say that the *Iliad* and *Odyssey* were written by Homer is in fact almost a nonstatement, since the meaning of its very terms is ambiguous. What exactly *are* the two poems?

Are some parts more authentic than others? Were they composed as wholes or did they evolve? Was Homer a real person or is his name merely a convenient label for a legendary figure or group? Are both poems the work of the same author? If he was an individual, when and where did he live? At what stage of their history were the poems (originally meant to be sung or recited) put into the written form we know? To what extent does the written version preserve the oral version? Were Troy and the Trojan War as described in the *Iliad* historical? Many of these questions, some of which date to early antiquity, still cannot be answered with complete certainty.

Some probabilities have emerged, however. In the later nineteenth century, the great amateur archaeologist Heinrich Schliemann proved by his excavations that Troy did indeed once exist. A war similar to the one Homer describes probably did occur, around the early twelfth century B.C. Most authorities now believe also that Homer was a single person, who lived around the eighth century B.C. and was a professional bard or minstrel like Demódokos and Phêmios in the *Odyssey*. His homeland was probably Ionia, a region south of Troy in Asia Minor (modern Turkey) that faces Greece across the Aegean Sea. Tradition says that he was blind.

His role in composing the *Iliad* and *Odyssey* is harder to define. Undoubtedly he inherited a large store of traditional material that included many prominent incidents and characters of the tale of Troy. He regarded this material as history, and many poems on the subject would have been familiar to him and to his audience. But he probably deserves the main credit at least for shaping and refining this material into the monumental works we know, giving to them the unity, power, and artistry that Aristotle later praised so highly in his *Poetics*. These qualities have caused Homer to be honored as one of the supreme poets of the world. Whether the *Iliad* and *Odyssey* were actually put in written form by him (he lived in an age and place barely emerging from several centuries of illiteracy), were recorded by a scribe to whom he dictated, or were written down only after a considerable period of oral transmission is still much debated.

That the *Iliad* and *Odyssey* were originally intended to be heard rather than read is the first thing new readers need to know about the poems. The fact explains, for example, the frequent repetitions—of single phrases, of whole lines, and sometimes of long passages. Such repetition is characteristic of all forms of oral communication, since—as lecturers, auctioneers, playwrights, and orators know—repetition enhances clarity and helps achieve the desired emphasis. The repetition may even be, as some scholars now believe, a key to the poems' origins, in the oral-formulaic method, a process by which singers improvised by combining traditional phrases with original ones to flesh out a memorized narrative outline. If we ignore the poems' oral manner we put an unnecessary distance between ourselves and their original audience. Moreover, we can misinterpret many of their strategies, especially the "Homeric epithets," the recurrent brief phrases used to describe things or persons. The reader may wonder why Hera, the queen of the gods, is called "white-armed" in some passages and "Goddess of the Golden Chair" in others, where either label (or neither) would seem appropriate, or why Akhilleus is "the great runner" even when he is not running, or why the striking phrase "tamer of horses" should be applied to two different men. The answer is that Homer inserted such phrases in places where they fit the poetic rhythm, even where they are not especially relevant to the narrative context. (The Greek meter, dactyllic hexameter, combines long [—] and short [˘] syllables in the pattern —˘ ˘ —˘ ˘—˘ ˘ — ˘ ˘—˘ ˘ — —, with certain substitutions permitted.) It is a mistake, then, to read too much into such phrases or to use them to interpret particular passages, even when the phrases do sound appropriate.

An even more serious error is to look down on Homer as a simple, primitive poet, one whose accomplishments, like those of a precocious child, are impressive mainly because of his early age. In fact, there have been few if any greater artists than Homer. The stories he tells are vivid and powerful in their sweep, but they are also subtle and skillfully shaded. For example, all the principal men in the *Iliad,* Greeks and Trojans, are brave in battle, but their styles of bravery are distinctive: Agamémnon is savage, Akhilleus is proud and supremely confident, Hektor is patriotic, Odysseus is pragmatic (as in the *Odyssey* as well). Seemingly fleeting details can be quite significant. When, in Book IV of the *Odyssey,* Telémakhos approaches the palace of Meneláos, one of the king's men hesitates to admit the young man as the code of hospitality would dictate. Meneláos is furious, but we can guess why his man is nervous: Years before, another guest named Paris had been welcomed by Meneláos but had gone on to abduct his beautiful wife, Helen, and thus had set off the entire Trojan War. We must be alert to such subtleties, since Homer's objective manner usually leaves connections unstated. Characterizations are fully individualized. Penélopê in the *Odyssey* is not merely the object of the suitors' lust and greed but also a fully imagined, resourceful wife and woman, a fit mate for the crafty Odysseus. The green young man Telémakhos and the inexperienced but enterprising Phaiákian princess Nausikaa (Nausicaä) are richly realized characters in themselves and also effective foils for Odysseus, the seasoned veteran of life and experience. One of the major achievements of the Homeric poems is that they combine richness of detail and nuance with a masterful control of the poems' general movement and pattern.

Homer's control results partly, as Aristotle later pointed out, from his careful limiting of his material; the *Iliad* treats a single episode in the ten-year Trojan War and the *Odyssey* centers on the troubled homecoming of a single warrior. But the poems have also a far more ambitious aim: to describe as fully as possible the heroic world. Heroism is the theme of both poems. Since the *Iliad* is a tragedy and a war poem, it celebrates the heroism that faces and suffers death. The *Odyssey* is a kind of comedy, and the heroism it celebrates is that of survival, the triumph over death. The *Iliad* derives much of its intensity from its almost claustrophobic atmosphere, its setting confined to a few square miles in and around the besieged city of Troy where thousands of men are cramped together. The closeness of atmosphere is relieved only occasionally by scenes involving the Olympian gods and through similes reminding the audience of the world of nature and peacetime. The *Odyssey* is wholly different. Its geographic vistas are almost endless, taking in the far, romantic reaches of the known and fabled Mediterranean world and even the realm of the dead. In intriguing contrast is the second half of the poem, where the setting narrows to that of a domestic drama on Odysseus' home island. Here the arena of heroism is neither the defeat of an army nor the perils of distant travel but a struggle to reassert private rights to home and property. The suspense of Odysseus' plot against the suitors emerges from a context not of the cosmic but of familiar human detail—a world of good and bad servants, favorite beds, kitchen logistics. In different ways, then, the *Odyssey* is both more panoramic and more intimate than the *Iliad.*

The Homeric divinities, similarly, seem both remote and familiar. Their role and relationship to human beings are very difficult to define. In some ways they seem like projections (often in a comic vein) of human activities and the human environment: Poseidon of the sea, Hephaistos of fire and metalworking, Apollo of medicine and archery, Athêna of resourcefulness, Aphrodítê of love and sex, and so forth. They are thoroughly humanized, and in their rivalries, loyalties, plots, and bickerings they sometimes seem to parody the human beings, on a scale actually smaller than life. On the other hand, they are utterly superior to human beings, in power and above all in their exemption from death. (Paradoxically, the strictest limitation of their power is their inability to share their immortality with their human protégés.) They continually intervene, especially at key moments, to shape the course of events on earth. In doing so they would seem to limit human freedom. Yet the poems also make it clear that humans are responsible for their deeds and that they do have choices. The immortals' actions frequently seem to be confirmations rather than causes of what happens; we can say that Odysseus is resourceful because the goddess Athena aids him or that she aids him because, like her, he is resourceful. In any event, the presence of the divinities in the world of the poems emphasizes both the brevity and the urgency of human life and thus enhances our sense of the mystery in the world.

The *Iliad* and *Odyssey* are the definitive epics in the Western tradition. Seven centuries after Homer, Virgil creatively imitated and synthesized the two Homeric epics in the *Aeneid,* a story of the Trojan survivors who, under Ainéias, or Aeneas, journeyed like Odysseus through hardships to lay in Italy the foundations of Roman greatness after a battle resembling that in the *Iliad.* Virgil sophisticated the epic, making it a more strictly literary form and using it for doctrinal purposes, as a vehicle for fostering Roman political and religious values. Seventeen hundred years after Virgil, Milton wrote the definitive English epic, *Paradise Lost,* in an attempt to "justify the ways of God to men" and to preach an essentially Christian heroism. Both Milton and Virgil depict a universe governed by an ultimately just providential force, and each either implies or states that his form of heroism has superseded earlier epic values. Each found a model in Homer, despite the vast differences between their metaphysics and Homer's apparent unconcern with it. That indebtedness testifies that Homer was not only a great poet but also one whose vision has universal application.

FURTHER READING: Oliver Taplin provides an introductory essay on Homer, with a useful bibliography, in *The Oxford History of the Classical World,* ed. John Boardman, Jasper Griffin, and Oswyn Murray, 1986. A description of the life and culture of pre-Homeric civilization is given by John Chadwick, *The Decipherment of Linear B,* 1960. Howard Clarke's *Homer's Readers,* 1981, surveys clearly what is known of the circumstances under which the Homeric epics were composed. Two introductory works on Homer are W. A. Camps, *An Introduction to Homer,* 1980; and Jasper Griffin, *Homer* (in the Past Masters series), 1980. On the Homeric problem, G. S. Kirk, *Homer and the Oral Tradition,* 1976, is useful. A stimulating sampling of essays by artists such as Tolstoy, Pound, and Cavafy has been edited by George Steiner and Robert Fagles,

Homer: A Collection of Critical Essays, 1962; while learned studies by classical scholars such as Bowra, Lord, and Blegen have been assembled by Alan J. B. Wace and Frank H. Stubbings, *A Companion to Homer,* 1962. An informative and readable critical commentary on the *Iliad,* based specifically on the Robert Fitzgerald translation and including a foreword by him, is James C. Hogan's *A Guide to the Iliad,* 1979. Martin Mueller, *The Iliad,* 1984, is a fine introduction. Mark W. Edwards, *Homer: Poet of the Iliad,* 1987, is also recommended for its valuable insights. Katherine Callan King discusses the Achilles myth in *Achilles,* 1987. On the *Iliad* as tragedy, see C. W. Macleod's introduction to his edition of and commentary on the *Iliad,* Book XXIV, 1982. For a treatment of human mortality in the poem, along with discussion of the Homeric deities, see J. Griffin's *Homer on Life and Death,* 1980. Analysis of individual scenes in the *Odyssey* as they contribute to the poem's effect appears in B. Fenik, *Studies in the Odyssey,* 1974. The poem's effect is also well captured in N. Austin, *Archery at the Dark of the Moon,* 1975. M. I. Finley, *The World of Odysseus,* 1964, discusses the sociology of the *Odyssey.* Charles Taylor, ed., *Essays on the Odyssey: Selected Modern Criticism,* 1963, provides twentieth-century interpretations of the work. Jasper Griffin, *Homer: The Odyssey,* 1987, is a good introduction to the poem. George E. Dimock, *The Unity of the Odyssey,* 1989, is especially good on the coherence of the poem. On the motif of hospitality in the *Odyssey,* see Steve Reece, *The Stranger's Welcome,* 1993. The multiple roles of Penelope are the subject of Nancy Felson-Rubin, *Regarding Penelope,* 1994. The latter half of the poem is well treated in Sheila Murnagham, *Disguise and Recognition in the Odyssey,* 1987.

THE ILIAD

Translated by Robert Fitzgerald

For the events leading up to the Trojan War, see the first paragraph of the Introduction to Homer. As the *Iliad* opens, Troy is undergoing its tenth year of siege by the Greek coalition (called at different times Akhaians, Danáäns, and Argives). Although they outnumber the Trojans, the Greeks have not been able to take Troy and win back Helen—this despite the presence on the Greek side of the great warrior Akhilleus (Achilles) and the Myrmidons, his tough and disciplined army.

The gods take a strong interest in the war and are divided in their allegiances, some supporting the Greeks and some the Trojans. The division is explained in part by a mythological episode that occurred before Paris and Helen eloped. Paris had judged a dispute among Hêra (queen of the gods), the warlike goddess Athêna, and Aphrodítê (goddess of love and beauty) over which of the three was most beautiful. He decided for Aphrodítê, who had promised him as a reward the most beautiful woman in the world and then kept her promise by giving him Helen. As a result, Aphrodítê sides with Paris and his people while Hêra and Athêna oppose them bitterly.

Many persons and places in the *Iliad* are best known to readers by their Latinized names, such as *Achilles* and *Ajax.* The present translator has used forms (*Akhilleus, Aías*) closer to the Greek spelling and pronunciation. An acute accent (´) indicates stress; thus *Aías* is accented on the first syllable, *Agamémnon* on the third one. A circumflex accent (ˆ) indicates that the vowel sound is long; thus *Lêto* is pronounced Laytoe. A dieresis (¨) indicates pronunciation as a separate syllable; thus *Danáäns* has three syllables rather than two. [*Editors' headnote.*]

BOOK ONE: QUARREL, OATH, AND PROMISE

Anger be now your song, immortal one,[1]
Akhilleus' anger, doomed and ruinous,
that caused the Akhaians[2] loss on bitter loss
and crowded brave souls into the undergloom,[3]
leaving so many dead men—carrion
for dogs and birds; and the will of Zeus was done.[4]
Begin it when the two men first contending
broke with one another—
the Lord Marshal
Agamémnon, Atreus' son, and Prince Akhilleus.
Among the gods, who brought this quarrel on? 10
The son of Zeus by Lêto.[5] Agamémnon
angered him, so he made a burning wind
of plague rise in the army: rank and file
sickened and died for the ill their chief had done
in despising a man of prayer.
This priest, Khrysês, had come down to the ships[6]
with gifts, no end of ransom for his daughter;
on a golden staff he carried the god's white bands[7]
and sued for grace from the men of all Akhaia,
the two Atreidai[8] most of all:
"O Captains 20
Meneláos and Agamémnon, and you other
Akhaians under arms!
The gods who hold Olympos,[9] may they grant you
plunder of Priam's[10] town and a fair wind home,
but let me have my daughter back for ransom
as you revere Apollo, son of Zeus!"

Then all the soldiers murmured their assent:

"Behave well to the priest. And take the ransom!"

[1]The first lines are the model for the "opening formula" used by epic poets after Homer: the invocation of the Muse, or spirit of inspiration; the request that she "sing" the poem; the statement of the main theme, along with a hint at its consequences; the abrupt leap into the story itself. Compare the opening lines of Homer's *Odyssey,* Virgil's *Aeneid,* and Milton's *Paradise Lost.*

[2]The Greek forces. [3]Aïdês (Hades), the shadowy realm of the dead.

[4]Zeus was the king of the gods. Homer considers all events in the poem and life in general as manifestations of Zeus's will, although human beings do have a limited but significant freedom to choose and are responsible for their actions; the interrelationship of human and divine will is complex and ambiguous. Even Zeus is to some extent limited by fate; in later Greek literature fate is regarded as an even more mysterious and impersonal force.

[5]*son . . . Lêto.* Apollo, god of archery, prophecy, and healing (as well as its opposite, disease).

[6]The Greek fleet is drawn up on the beach bordering the plain of Troy.

[7]The staff and ribbons are symbolic of Apollo, who as god of prophecy is patron of the prophet-priest Khrysês.

[8]Sons of Atreus. For the history of the house of Atreus, see Aeschylus' *Oresteia.*

[9]The mountain where the gods live. [10]The king of Troy.

But Agamémnon would not. It went against his desire,
and brutally he ordered the man away: 30

"Let me not find you here by the long ships
loitering this time or returning later,
old man; if I do,
the staff and ribbons of the god will fail you.
Give up the girl? I swear she will grow old
at home in Argos,[11] far from her own country,
working my loom and visiting my bed.
Leave me in peace and go, while you can, in safety."

So harsh he was, the old man feared and obeyed him,
in silence trailing away 40
by the shore of the tumbling clamorous whispering sea,
and he prayed and prayed again, as he withdrew,
to the god whom silken-braided Lêto bore:

"O hear me, master of the silver bow,
protector of Ténedos and the holy towns,
Apollo, Sminthian,[12] if to your liking
ever in any grove I roofed a shrine
or burnt thighbones in fat upon your altar—
bullock or goat flesh—let my wish come true:
your arrows on the Danáäns[13] for my tears!" 50

Now when he heard this prayer, Phoibos Apollo
walked with storm in his heart from Olympos' crest,
quiver and bow at his back, and the bundled arrows
clanged on the sky behind as he rocked in his anger,
descending like night itself. Apart from the ships
he halted and let fly, and the bowstring slammed
as the silver bow sprang, rolling in thunder away.
Pack animals were his target first, and dogs,
but soldiers, too, soon felt transfixing pain
from his hard shots, and pyres[14] burned night and day. 60
Nine days the arrows of the god came down
broadside upon the army. On the tenth,
Akhilleus called all ranks to assembly. Hêra,[15]
whose arms are white as ivory, moved him to it,
as she took pity on Danáäns dying.

[11]A region of southern Greece, ruled by Agamémnon.

[12]*Ténedos.* An island nearby. *Sminthian.* A name of Apollo meaning "mouse god," perhaps a reference to the god's ability to bring on plague, rodents being carriers.

[13]Another name for the Greek forces.

[14]Bonfires for cremating the dead.

[15]Queen of the gods who strongly supports the Greeks. See headnote to the *Iliad.* The phrase "whose arms are white as ivory" is one of many repeated verbal formulas; some of them can have a particular, appropriate effect, but most of them are used more automatically, in accordance with the needs of poetic meter in oral poetry.

All being mustered, all in place and quiet,
Akhilleus, fast in battle as a lion,
rose and said:

"Agamémnon, now, I take it,
the siege is broken, we are going to sail,
and even so may not leave death behind: 70
if war spares anyone, disease will take him . . .
We might, though, ask some priest or some diviner,
even some fellow good at dreams—for dreams
come down from Zeus as well—
why all this anger of the god Apollo?

Has he some quarrel with us for a failure
in vows or hekatombs?[16] Would mutton burned
or smoking goat flesh make him lift the plague?"

Putting the question, down he sat. And Kalkhas,
Kalkhas Thestórides,[17] came forward, wisest 80
by far of all who scanned the flight of birds.[18]
He knew what was, what had been, what would be,
Kalkhas, who brought Akhaia's ships to Ilion[19]
by the diviner's gift Apollo gave him.
Now for their benefit he said:

"Akhilleus,
dear to Zeus, it is on me you call
to tell you why the Archer God is angry.
Well, I can tell you. Are you listening? Swear
by heaven that you will back me and defend me,
because I fear my answer will enrage 90
a man with power in Argos, one whose word
Ákhaian troops obey.

A great man in his rage is formidable
for underlings: though he may keep it down,
he cherishes the burning in his belly
until a reckoning day. Think well
if you will save me."

Said Akhilleus:

"Courage.
Tell what you know, what you have light to know.
I swear by Apollo, the lord god to whom
you pray when you uncover truth, 100
never while I draw breath, while I have eyes to see,

[16]Lavish sacrifices to the gods.
[17]The suffix *-ides* means "son of."
[18]Prophets, or diviners, discovered the gods' will by observing omens such as the direction of birds in flight.
[19]Troy.

shall any man upon this beachhead dare
lay hands on you—not one of all the army,
not Agamémnon, if it is he you mean,
though he is first in rank of all Akhaians."

The diviner then took heart and said:

"No failure
in hekatombs or vows is held against us.
It is the man of prayer whom Agamémnon
treated with contempt: he kept his daughter,
spurned his gifts: for that man's sake the Archer 110
visited grief upon us and will again.
Relieve the Danáäns of this plague he will not
until the girl who turns the eyes of men
shall be restored to her own father—freely,
with no demand for ransom—and until
we offer up a hekatomb at Khrysê.[20]
Then only can we calm him and persuade him."

He finished and sat down. The son of Atreus,
ruler of the great plain, Agamémnon,
rose, furious. Round his heart resentment 120
welled, and his eyes shone out like licking fire.
Then, with a long and boding look at Kalkhas,
he growled at him:

"You visionary of hell,
never have I had fair play in your forecasts.
Calamity is all you care about, or see,
no happy portents; and you bring to pass
nothing agreeable. Here you stand again
before the army, giving it out as oracle
the Archer made them suffer because of me,
because I would not take the gifts 130
and let the girl Khrysêis go; I'd have her
mine, at home. Yes, if you like, I rate her
higher than Klytaimnestra, my own wife!
She loses nothing by comparison
in beauty or womanhood, in mind or skill.

For all of that, I am willing now to yield her
if it is best; I want the army saved
and not destroyed. You must prepare, however,
a prize of honor for me, and at once,
that I may not be left without my portion— 140
I, of all Argives. It is not fitting so.

[20]Khrysês' town; the names of priest, town, and daughter (Khrysêis) are virtually the same word.

While every man of you looks on, my girl
goes elsewhere."

Prince Akhilleus answered him:

"Lord Marshall, most insatiate of men,
how can the army make you a new gift?
Where is our store of booty? Can you see it?
Everything plundered from the towns has been
distributed; should troops turn all that in?[21]
Just let the girl go, in the god's name, now; 150
we'll make it up to you, twice over, three
times over, on that day Zeus gives us leave
to plunder Troy behind her rings of stone."

Agamémnon answered:

"Not that way
will I be gulled, brave as you are, Akhilleus.
Take me in, would you? Try to get around me?
What do you really ask? That you may keep
your own winnings, I am to give up mine
and sit here wanting her? Oh, no:
the army will award a prize to me 160
and make sure that it measures up, or if
they do not, I will take a girl myself,
your own, or Aías', or Odysseus' prize![22]
Take her, yes, to keep. The man I visit
may choke with rage; well, let him.
But this, I say, we can decide on later.

Look to it now, we launch on the great sea
a well-found ship, and get her manned with oarsmen,
load her with sacrificial beasts and put aboard
Khrysêis in her loveliness. My deputy, 170
Aías, Idómeneus,[23] or Prince Odysseus,
or you, Akhilleus, fearsome as you are,
will make the hekatomb and quiet the Archer."

Akhilleus frowned and looked at him, then said:

"You thick-skinned, shameless, greedy fool!
Can any Akhaian care for you, or obey you,
after this on marches or in battle?
As for myself, when I came here to fight,
I had no quarrel with Troy or Trojan spearmen:

[21] The Greeks have made several side raids on towns near Troy.

[22] *Aías, Odysseus.* Two of the principal Greek warriors and leaders. There are two Aíases; the one referred to here is the "greater" Aías, son of Télamôn. Odysseus, noted for his resourcefulness, is the hero of Homer's other epic, the *Odyssey.*

[23] Ruler of Krete (Crete); another prominent leader among the Greeks.

they never stole my cattle or my horses, 180
never in the black farmland of Phthía[24]
ravaged my crops. How many miles there are
of shadowy hills between, and foaming seas!
No, no, we joined for you, you insolent boor,
to please you, fighting for your brother's sake
and yours, to get revenge upon the Trojans.
You overlook this, dogface, or don't care,
and now in the end you threaten to take my girl,
a prize I sweated for, and soldiers gave me!

Never have I had plunder like your own 190
from any Trojan stronghold battered down
by the Akhaians. I have seen more action
hand to hand in those assaults than you have,
but when the time for sharing comes, the greater
share is always yours. Worn out with battle
I carry off some trifle to my ships.
Well, this time I make sail for home.
Better to take now to my ships. Why linger,
cheated of winnings, to make wealth for you?"

To this the high commander made reply: 200

"Desért, if that's the way the wind blows. Will I
beg you to stay on my account? I will not.
Others will honor me, and Zeus who views
the wide world most of all.

No officer
is hateful to my sight as you are, none
given like you to faction,[25] as to battle—
rugged you are, I grant, by some god's favor.
Sail, then, in your ships, and lord it over
your own battalion of Myrmidons.[26] I do not
give a curse for you, or for your anger. 210
But here is warning for you:

Khrysêis
being required of me by Phoibos Apollo,
she will be sent back in a ship of mine,
manned by my people. That done, I myself
will call for Brisêis at your hut, and take her,
flower of young girls that she is, your prize,
to show you here and now who is the stronger
and make the next man sick at heart—if any
think of claiming equal place with me."

[24]Akhilleus' homeland, in northern Greece.
[25]Insubordination; subversive dissent.
[26]Akhilleus' troops.

A pain like grief weighed on the son of Pêleus,[27] 220
and in his shaggy chest this way and that
the passion of his heart ran: should he draw
longsword from hip, stand off the rest, and kill
in single combat the great son of Atreus,
or hold his rage in check and give it time?
And as this tumult swayed him, as he slid
the big blade slowly from the sheath, Athêna
came to him from the sky.[28] The white-armed goddess,
Hêra, sent her, being fond of both,
concerned for both men. And Athêna, stepping 230
up behind him, visible to no one
except Akhilleus, gripped his red-gold hair.

Startled, he made a half turn, and he knew her
upon the instant for Athêna: terribly
her grey eyes blazed at him. And speaking softly
but rapidly aside to her he said:

"What now, O daughter of the god of heaven
who bears the stormcloud, why are you here? To see
the wolfishness of Agamémnon?
Well, I give you my word: this time, and soon, 240
he pays for his behavior with his blood."

The grey-eyed goddess Athêna said to him:

"It was to check this killing rage I came
from heaven, if you will listen. Hêra sent me,
being fond of both of you, concerned for both.
Enough: break off this combat, stay your hand
upon the sword hilt. Let him have a lashing
with words, instead: tell him how things will be.
Here is my promise, and it will be kept:
winnings three times as rich, in due season, 250
you shall have in requital for his arrogance.
But hold your hand. Obey."

The great runner,
Akhilleus, answered:

"Nothing for it, goddess,
but when you two immortals speak, a man
complies, though his heart burst. Just as well.
Honor the gods' will, they may honor ours."

[27]Akhilleus' father.

[28]Associated with crafts, resourcefulness, and skill in general, Athêna is a powerful agent of divine assistance to the Greeks in the *Iliad* and the faithful patron of Odysseus in the *Odyssey*. For her opposition to Troy and allegiance to the Greeks, see the headnote to the *Iliad*.

On this he stayed his massive hand
upon the silver pommel, and the blade
of his great weapon slid back in the scabbard.
The man had done her bidding. Off to Olympos, 260
gaining the air, she went to join the rest,
the powers of heaven in the home of Zeus.

But now the son of Pêleus turned on Agamémnon
and lashed out at him, letting his anger ride
in execration:

"Sack of wine,
you with your cur's eyes and your antelope heart!
You've never had the kidney to buckle on
armor among the troops, or make a sortie
with picked men—oh, no; that way death might lie.
Safer, by god, in the middle of the army— 270
is it not?—to commandeer the prize
of any man who stands up to you! Leech!
Commander of trash! If not, I swear,
you never could abuse one soldier more!

But here is what I say: my oath upon it
by this great staff: look: leaf or shoot
it cannot sprout again, once lopped away
from the log it left behind in the timbered hills;
it cannot flower, peeled of bark and leaves;
instead, Akhaian officers in council 280
take it in hand by turns, when they observe
by the will of Zeus due order in debate:[29]
let this be what I swear by then: I swear
a day will come when every Akhaian soldier
will groan to have Akhilleus back. That day
you shall no more prevail on me than this
dry wood shall flourish—driven though you are,
and though a thousand men perish before
the killer, Hektor.[30] You will eat your heart out,
raging with remorse for this dishonor 290
done by you to the bravest of Akhaians."

He hurled the staff, studded with golden nails,
before him on the ground. Then down he sat,
and fury filled Agamémnon, looking across at him.
But for the sake of both men Nestor arose,
the Pylians' orator, eloquent and clear;
argument sweeter than honey rolled from his tongue.
By now he had outlived two generations

[29] To hold the staff signifies that one has the floor in the discussion.
[30] Son of Priam and chief warrior on the Trojan side; a central character in the *Iliad*.

of mortal men, his own and the one after,
in Pylos land, and still ruled in the third. 300
In kind reproof he said:

"A black day, this.
Bitter distress comes this way to Akhaia.
How happy Priam and Priam's sons would be,
and all the Trojans—wild with joy—if they
got wind of all these fighting words between you,
foremost in council as you are, foremost
in battle. Give me your attention. Both
are younger men than I, and in my time
men who were even greater have I known
and none of them disdained me. Men like those 310
I have not seen again, nor shall: Peiríthoös,
the Lord Marshal Dryas, Kaineus, Exádios,
Polyphêmos, Theseus—Aigeus' son,
a man like the immortal gods. I speak
of champions among men of earth, who fought
with champions, with wild things of the mountains,
great centaurs[31] whom they broke and overpowered.
Among these men I say I had my place
when I sailed out of Pylos, my far country,
because they called for me. I fought 320
for my own hand among them. Not one man
alive now upon earth could stand against them.
And I repeat: they listened to my reasoning,
took my advice. Well, then, you take it too.
It is far better so.

Lord Agamémnon,
do not deprive him of the girl, renounce her.
The army had allotted her to him.
Akhilleus, for your part, do not defy
your King and Captain. No one vies in honor
with him who holds authority from Zeus. 330
You have more prowess, for a goddess bore you;[32]
his power over men surpasses yours.

But, Agamémnon, let your anger cool.
I beg you to relent, knowing Akhilleus
a sea wall for Akhaians in the black waves of war."

Lord Agamémnon answered:

"All you say
is fairly said, sir, but this man's ambition,
remember, is to lead, to lord it over
everyone, hold power over everyone,

[31]Mythological beings, shaped like horses but having human torsos and heads.
[32]Thetis, a sea nymph, had been the mate of Akhilleus' father, Pêleus.

give orders to the rest of us! Well, one 340
will never take his orders! If the gods
who live forever made a spearman of him,
have they put insults on his lips as well?"

Akhilleus interrupted:

"What a poltroon,[33]
how lily-livered I should be called, if I
knuckled under to all you do or say!
Give your commands to someone else, not me!
And one more thing I have to tell you: think it
over: this time, for the girl, I will not
wrangle in arms with you or anyone, 350
though I am robbed of what was given me;
but as for any other thing I have
alongside my black ship, you shall not take it
against my will. Try it. Hear this, everyone:
that instant your hot blood blackens my spear!"

They quarreled in this way, face to face, and then
broke off the assembly by the ships. Akhilleus
made his way to his squadron and his quarters,
Patróklos[34] by his side, with his companions.

Agamémnon proceeded to launch a ship, 360
assigned her twenty oarsmen, loaded beasts
for sacrifice to the god, then set aboard
Khrysêis in her loveliness. The versatile
Odysseus took the deck, and, all oars manned,
they pulled out on the drenching ways of sea.
The troops meanwhile were ordered to police camp
and did so, throwing refuse in the water;
then to Apollo by the barren surf
they carried out full-tally hekatombs,
and the savor curled in crooked smoke toward heaven. 370

That was the day's work in the army.

Agamémnon
had kept his threat in mind, and now he acted,
called Eurýbatês and Talthýbios,
his aides and criers:[35]

"Go along," he said,
"both of you, to the quarters of Akhilleus
and take his charming Brisêis by the hand

[33]Coward.
[34]Akhilleus' chariot driver and dearest friend; a central character in the *Iliad*.
[35]Heralds.

to bring to me. And if he balks at giving her
I shall be there myself with men-at-arms
in force to take her—all the more gall for him."

So, ominously, he sent them on their way, 380
and they who had no stomach for it went
along the waste sea shingle toward the ships
and shelters of the Myrmidons. Not far
from his black ship and hut they found the prince
in the open, seated. And seeing these two come
was cheerless to Akhilleus. Shamefast, pale
with fear of him, they stood without a word;
but he knew what they felt and called out:

"Peace to you,
criers and couriers of Zeus and men!
Come forward. Not one thing have I against you: 390
Agamémnon is the man who sent you
for Brisêis. Here then, my lord Patróklos,
bring out the girl and give her to these men.
And let them both bear witness before the gods
who live in bliss, as before men who die,
including this harsh king, if ever hereafter
a need for me arises to keep the rest
from black defeat and ruin.

Lost in folly,
the man cannot think back or think ahead
how to come through a battle by the ships." 400

Patróklos did the bidding of his friend,
led from the hut Brisêis in her beauty
and gave her to them. Back along the ships
they took their way, and the girl went, loath to go.

Leaving his friends in haste, Akhilleus wept,
and sat apart by the grey wave, scanning the endless sea.
Often he spread his hands in prayer to his mother:

"As my life came from you, though it is brief,
honor at least from Zeus who storms in heaven
I call my due. He gives me precious little. 410
See how the lord of the great plains, Agamémnon,
humiliated me! He has my prize,
by his own whim, for himself."

Eyes wet with tears,
he spoke, and her ladyship his mother heard him
in green deeps where she lolled near her old father.[36]

[36]Nêreus, father of the Nereids (sea nymphs).

Gliding she rose and broke like mist from the inshore
grey sea face, to sit down softly before him,
her son in tears; and fondling him she said:

"Child, why do you weep? What grief is this?
Out with it, tell me, both of us should know." 420
Akhilleus, fast in battle as a lion,
groaned and said:

"Why tell you what you know?
We sailed out raiding, and we took by storm
that ancient town of Eëtíôn called Thêbê,
plundered the place, brought slaves and spoils away.[37]
At the division, later,
they chose a young girl, Khrysêis, for the king.
Then Khrysês, priest of the Archer God, Apollo,
came to the beachhead we Akhaians hold,
bringing no end of ransom for his daughter; 430
he had the god's white bands on a golden staff
and sued for grace from the army of Akhaia,
mostly the two Atreidai, corps commanders.
All of our soldiers murmured in assent:
'Behave well to the priest. And take the ransom!'
But Agamémnon would not. It went against his desire,
and brutally he ordered the man away.
So the old man withdrew in grief and anger.
Apollo cared for him: he heard his prayer
and let black bolts of plague fly on the Argives. 440

One by one our men came down with it
and died hard as the god's shots raked the army
broadside. But our priest divined the cause
and told us what the god meant by the plague.

I said, 'Appease the god!' but Agamémnon
could not contain his rage; he threatened me,
and what he threatened is now done—
one girl the Akhaians are embarking now
for Khrysê beach with gifts for Lord Apollo;
the other, just now, from my hut—the criers 450
came and took her, Briseus' girl, my prize,
given by the army.

If you can, stand by me:
go to Olympos, pray to Zeus, if ever
by word or deed you served him—
and so you did, I often heard you tell it
in Father's house: that time when you alone
of all the gods shielded the son of Krónos[38]

[37] Elaborate, sometimes verbatim, repetitions of earlier material are frequent in Homer. Eëtíôn is the father of Andrómakhê, wife of the Trojan hero Hektor.

[38] Krónos was father of Zeus and ruler of the gods in the divine generation overthrown by Zeus and the Olympians.

from peril and disgrace—when other gods,
Pallas Athêna, Hêra, and Poseidon,[39]
wished him in irons, wished to keep him bound, 460
you had the will to free him of that bondage,
and called up to Olympos in all haste
Aigaion, whom the gods call Briareus,
the giant with a hundred arms, more powerful
than the sea-god, his father. Down he sat
by the son of Krónos, glorying in that place.
For fear of him the blissful gods forbore
to manacle Zeus.
Remind him of these things,
cling to his knees and tell him your good pleasure
if he will take the Trojan side 470
and roll the Akhaians back to the water's edge,
back on the ships with slaughter! All the troops
may savor what their king has won for them,
and he may know his madness, what he lost
when he dishonored me, peerless among Akhaians."

Her eyes filled, and a tear fell as she answered:

"Alas, my child, why did I rear you, doomed
the day I bore you?[40] Ah, could you only be
serene upon this beachhead through the siege,
your life runs out so soon. 480
Oh early death! Oh broken heart! No destiny
so cruel! And I bore you to this evil!
But what you wish I will propose
To Zeus, lord of the lightning, going up
myself into the snow-glare of Olympos
with hope for his consent.
Be quiet now
beside the long ships, keep your anger bright
against the army, quit the war.
Last night
Zeus made a journey to the shore of Ocean
to feast among the Sunburned,[41] and the gods 490
accompanied him. In twelve days he will come
back to Olympos. Then I shall be there
to cross his bronze doorsill and take his knees.
I trust I'll move him."

[39] God of the ocean, brother of Zeus, and a supporter of the Greeks in the war.

[40] Akhilleus is fated to die young and will in fact be killed in the Trojan War, though his death is not described in the *Iliad*. See also Akhilleus' somewhat different account in Book IX of his "two possible destinies."

[41] The Ethiopians, a people believed to live at the edge of the world, which was envisaged as flat and surrounded by a body of water called Ocean.

Thetis left her son
still burning for the softly belted girl
whom they had wrested from him.

Meanwhile Odysseus
with his shipload of offerings came to Khrysê.
Entering the deep harbor there
they furled the sails and stowed them, and unbent
forestays to ease the mast down quickly aft 500
into its rest; then rowed her to a mooring.
Bow-stones were dropped, and they tied up astern,
and all stepped out into the wash and ebb,
then disembarked their cattle for the Archer,
and Khrysêis, from the deepsea ship. Odysseus,
the great tactician, led her to the altar,
putting her in her father's hands, and said:

"Khrysês, as Agamémnon's emissary
I bring your child to you, and for Apollo
a hekatomb in the Danáäns' name. 510
We trust in this way to appease your lord,
who sent down pain and sorrow on the Argives."

So he delivered her, and the priest received her,
the child so dear to him, in joy. Then hastening
to give the god his hekatomb, they led
bullocks to crowd around the compact altar,
rinsed their hands and delved in barley baskets,
as open-armed to heaven Khrysês prayed:

"Oh hear me, master of the silver bow,
protector of Ténedos and the holy towns, 520
if while I prayed you listened once before
and honored me, and punished the Akhaians,
now let my wish come true again. But turn
your plague away this time from the Danáäns."

And this petition, too, Apollo heard.
When prayers were said and grains of barley strewn,
they held the bullocks for the knife, and flayed them,
cutting out joints and wrapping these in fat,
two layers, folded, with raw strips of flesh,
for the old man to burn on cloven faggots, 530
wetting it all with wine.

Around him stood
young men with five-tined forks in hand, and when
the vitals had been tasted, joints consumed,
they sliced the chines and quarters for the spits,
roasted them evenly and drew them off.
Their meal being now prepared and all work done,

they feasted to their hearts' content and made
desire for meat and drink recede again,
then young men filled their winebowls to the brim,
ladling drops for the god in every cup. 540
Propitiatory songs rose clear and strong
until day's end, to praise the god, Apollo,
as One Who Keeps the Plague Afar; and listening
the god took joy.
After the sun went down
and darkness came, at last Odysseus' men
lay down to rest under the stern hawsers.

When Dawn spread out her finger tips of rose
they put to sea for the main camp of Akhaians,
and the Archer God sent them a following wind.
Stepping the mast they shook their canvas out, 550
and wind caught, bellying the sail. A foaming
dark blue wave sang backward from the bow
as the running ship made way against the sea,
until they came offshore of the encampment.
Here they put in and hauled the black ship high,
far up the sand, braced her with shoring timbers,
and then disbanded, each to his own hut.

Meanwhile unstirring and with smoldering heart,
the godlike athlete, son of Pêleus, Prince
Akhilleus waited by his racing ships. 560
He would not enter the assembly
of emulous men, nor ever go to war,
but felt his valor staling in his breast
with idleness, and missed the cries of battle.
Now when in fact twelve days had passed, the gods
who live forever turned back to Olympos,
with Zeus in power supreme among them.
Thetis
had kept in mind her mission for her son,
and rising like a dawn mist from the sea
into a cloud she soared aloft in heaven 570
to high Olympos. Zeus with massive brows
she found apart, on the chief crest enthroned,
and slipping down before him, her left hand
placed on his knees and her right hand held up
to cup his chin, she made her plea to him:[42]

"O Father Zeus, if ever amid immortals
by word or deed I served you, grant my wish

[42] This posture—one hand on the knees, the other on the chin—was conventional for seekers of help from the powerful.

and see to my son's honor! Doom for him
of all men comes on quickest.
Now Lord Marshal
Agamémnon has been highhanded with him, 580
has commandeered and holds his prize of war.
But you can make him pay for this, profound
mind of Olympos!
Lend the Trojans power,
until the Akhaians recompense my son
and heap new honor upon him!"

When she finished,
the gatherer of cloud said never a word
but sat unmoving for a long time, silent.
Thetis clung to his knees then spoke again:

"Give your infallible word, and bow your head,
or else reject me. Can you be afraid 590
to let me see how low in your esteem
I am of all the gods?"

Greatly perturbed,
Lord Zeus who masses cloud said:

"Here is trouble,
You drive me into open war with Hêra
sooner or later:
she will be at me, scolding all day long.
Even as matters stand she never rests
from badgering me before the gods: I take
the Trojan side in battle, so she says.

Go home before you are seen. But you can trust me 600
to put my mind on this; I shall arrange it.
Here let me bow my head, then be content
to see me bound by that most solemn act
before the gods. My word is not revocable
nor ineffectual, once I nod upon it."

He bent his ponderous black brows down, and locks
ambrosial[43] of his immortal head
swung over them, as all Olympos trembled.
After this pact they parted: misty Thetis
from glittering Olympos leapt away 610
into the deep sea; Zeus to his hall retired.
There all the gods rose from their seats in deference
before their father; not one dared

[43]Celestial; literally, ambrosia is the food of the gods. Their drink is nectar, which is later served to them.

face him unmoved, but all stood up before him,
and thus he took his throne.
But Hêra knew
he had new interests; she had seen
the goddess Thetis, silvery-footed daughter
of the Old One of the sea, conferring with him,
and, nagging, she inquired of Zeus Kroníon:

"Who is it this time, schemer? Who has your ear? 620
How fond you are of secret plans, of taking
decisions privately! You could not bring yourself,
could you, to favor me with any word
of your new plot?"

The father of gods and men
said in reply:

"Hêra, all my provisions
you must not itch to know.
You'll find them rigorous, consort though you are.
In all appropriate matters no one else,
no god or man, shall be advised before you.
But when I choose to think alone, 630
don't harry me about it with your questions."

The Lady Hêra answered with wide eyes:

"Majesty, what a thing to say. I have not
'harried' you before with questions, surely;
you are quite free to tell what you will tell.
This time I dreadfully fear—I have a feeling—
Thetis, the silvery-footed daughter
of the Old One of the sea, led you astray.
Just now at daybreak, anyway, she came
to sit with you and take your knees; my guess is 640
you bowed your head for her in solemn pact
that you will see to the honor of Akhilleus—
that is, to Akhaian carnage near the ships."

Now Zeus the gatherer of cloud said:

"Marvelous,
you and your guesses; you are near it, too.
But there is not one thing that you can do about it,
only estrange yourself still more from me—
all the more gall for you. If what you say
is true, you may be sure it pleases me.
And now you just sit down, be still, obey me, 650
or else not all the gods upon Olympos
can help in the least when I approach your chair
to lay my inexorable hands upon you."

At this the wide-eyed Lady Hêra feared him,
and sat quite still, and bent her will to his.
Up through the hall of Zeus now all the lords
of heaven were sullen and looked askance. Hêphaistos,[44]
master artificer, broke the silence,
doing a kindness to the snowy-armed
lady, his mother Hêra.

He began: 660

"Ah, what a miserable day, if you two
raise your voices over mortal creatures!
More than enough already! Must you bring
your noisy bickering among the gods?
What pleasure can we take in a fine dinner
when baser matters gain the upper hand?
To Mother my advice is—what she knows—
better make up to Father, or he'll start
his thundering and shake our feast to bits.
You know how he can shock us if he cares to— 670
out of our seats with lightning bolts!
Supreme power is his. Oh, soothe him, please,
take a soft tone, get back in his good graces.
Then he'll be benign to us again."
He lurched up as he spoke, and held a winecup
out to her, a double-handed one,
and said:

"Dear Mother, patience, hold your tongue,
no matter how upset you are. I would not
see you battered, dearest.
It would hurt me,
and yet I could not help you, not a bit. 680
The Olympian is difficult to oppose.
One other time I took your part he caught me
around one foot and flung me
into the sky from our tremendous terrace.
I soared all day! Just as the sun dropped down
I dropped down, too, on Lemnos—nearly dead.
The island people nursed a fallen god."

He made her smile—and the goddess, white-armed Hêra,
smiling took the winecup from his hand.
Then, dipping from the winebowl, round he went 690
from left to right, serving the other gods
nectar of sweet delight.

[44] The lame god of fire and of metal crafts. He had once before been thrown from Olympos for taking Hêra's side against Zeus, landing on the Aegean island of Lemnos.

And quenchless laughter
broke out among the blissful gods
to see Hêphaistos wheezing down the hall.
So all day long until the sun went down
they spent in feasting, and the measured feast
matched well their hearts' desire.
So did the flawless harp held by Apollo
and heavenly songs in choiring antiphon
that all the Muses sang.
And when the shining 700
sun of day sank in the west, they turned
homeward each one to rest, each to that home
the bandy-legged wondrous artisan
Hêphaistos fashioned for them with his craft.
The lord of storm and lightning, Zeus, retired
and shut his eyes where sweet sleep ever came to him,
and at his side lay Hêra, Goddess of the Golden Chair.

BOOK II. *Persuaded by Thetis to side with Akhilleus, Zeus sends a deceiving dream to Agamémnon which leads him to believe that the fall of Troy is at hand. As a test of his army's determination, Agamémnon calls the troops together and tells them that they must abandon the siege of Troy and admit defeat despite their superior numbers. The soldiers, all too happy to go home, rush toward the ships; but Odysseus, under the influence of Hêra and Athêna, rallies them. Thersítês, a repulsive common soldier, reviles Agamémnon for his greed, lust, and ill-treatment of Akhilleus. Nestor proposes that, to foster loyalty and discipline, the army should be mustered by nation and clan. A long catalog follows, listing the Greek commanders, giving information about their geographic and family backgrounds, and specifying the number of ships each leader commands. (The total number of ships is over 1,200.) A briefer catalog of the Trojans and of their allies from other regions concludes the Book.*

BOOK III. *As the armies approach each other, Paris offers single combat; he is soon recognized by Meneláos, the husband whom Paris has cuckolded. At first Paris is cowed, but after Hektor expresses contempt for his softness he agrees to face Meneláos. (We learn in this Book that Paris is hated or despised by both armies and even by Helen.) A treaty is proposed by which the victor in the duel is to have Helen and the armies are to end the war, without further fighting. Next we see Helen herself in Troy; the aged counselors of Priam, the Trojan king, are awed by Helen's beauty but desire that she should go back to her husband so that the war can end. Priam himself, however, is fond of Helen. From atop the city walls she points out to him, at his request, the chief leaders of the Greeks. Priam goes out onto the plain to ratify the treaty but returns before the duel, which he considers too painful to watch. The single combat begins; Meneláos is about to triumph when Aphrodítê, goddess of love and protector of Paris, rescues Paris and returns him to the safety of his bedchamber in Troy. The goddess then sends to him the reluctant Helen, who goes to bed with Paris but only after taunting him. Since the mysteriously vanished Paris cannot be found, the Greeks claim victory and demand that Helen and other agreed-upon compensation be delivered up to them.*

BOOK IV. *The gods are feasting on Mount Olympos. Zeus deliberately provokes his wife, Hêra, by suggesting that, since Meneláos has won the duel, he should be awarded Helen and the war should end now, with Troy spared. Predictably, the fiercely vindictive goddess is angered; she wins from Zeus permission for Athêna to incite some Trojan to break the pledged truce agreement and thus rekindle the hostilities. Athêna, in disguise, tempts the archer Pándaros, who is fighting for the Trojans, to launch an arrow at Meneláos; he is slightly wounded by the shot. The truce broken, Agamémnon rouses the Greeks to battle through a combination of flattery and taunts. Fierce fighting breaks out between the two armies.*

BOOK V. *The war continues to rage—man against man, man against god, god against god. Athêna and Hêra aid the Greeks; Apollo, Aphrodítê, and Arês aid the Trojans. The central human figure is the great Greek warrior Diomêdês; he kills the truce-breaker Pándaros after being wounded by an arrow from him and puts the Trojan hero Aineías in grave danger before Aineías is assisted by Apollo and his mother Aphrodítê. Aphrodítê and Arês are both wounded by Diomêdês and retire to Olympos; the beautiful goddess is told by Zeus, affectionately, that she is too soft for battle, but Zeus expresses loathing for the universally hated war god. The battle itself is indecisive.*

from BOOK SIX: INTERLUDES IN FIELD AND CITY

The immortals having retired from the field, battle continues; the Trojans begin to retreat. Agamémnon vows to kill the whole Trojan people, including children. Hektor's brother Hélenos, a prophet, urges him to return to Troy and have the women offer propitiatory offerings to Athêna so that the goddess may restrain her protégé Diomêdês. Diomêdês is about to fight a stranger (Glaukos) when they discover that their grandfathers were sworn friends; the two agree not to fight each other. Hektor arrives at Troy. Book VI continues:

Now, when Hektor reached the Skaian Gates[1]
daughters and wives of Trojans rushed to greet him
with questions about friends, sons, husbands, brothers.
"Pray to the gods!" he said to each in turn,
as grief awaited many. He walked on
and into Priam's palace, fair and still,
made all of ashlar,[2] with bright colonnades.
Inside were fifty rooms of polished stone
one by another, where the sons of Priam
slept beside their wives;[3] apart from these 290
across an inner court were twelve rooms more
all in one line, of polished stone, where slept
the sons-in-law of Priam and their wives.
Approaching these, he met his gentle mother
going in with Laódikê, most beautiful
of all her daughters. Both hands clasping his,
she looked at him and said:

"Why have you come
from battle, child? Those fiends, the Akhaians, fighting

[1] The main portal of the city.
[2] Rectangular building blocks.
[3] Priam had fifty sons, by his queen, Hékabê, and by other women.

around the town, have worn you out; you come
to climb our Rock[4] and lift your palms to Zeus! 300
Wait, and I'll serve you honeyed wine.
First you may offer up a drop to Zeus,
to the immortal gods, then slake your thirst.
Wine will restore a man when he is weary
as you are, fighting to defend your own."

Hektor answered her, his helmet flashing:

"No, my dear mother, ladle me no wine;
You'd make my nerve go slack: I'd lose my edge.
May I tip wine to Zeus with hands unwashed?
I fear to—a bespattered man, and bloody, 310
may not address the lord of gloomy cloud.
No, it is you I wish would bring together
our older women, with offerings, and go visit
the temple of Athêna, Hope of Soldiers.
Pick out a robe, most lovely and luxurious,
most to your liking in the women's hall;
place it upon Athêna's knees;[5] assure her
a sacrifice of heifers, twelve young ones
ungoaded ever in their lives, if in her mercy
relenting toward our town, our wives and children, 320
she keeps Diomêdês out of holy Troy.
He is a wild beast now in combat and pursuit.
Make your way to her shrine, visit Athêna,
Hope of Soldiers.
As for me, I go
for Paris, to arouse him, if he listens.
If only earth would swallow him here and now!
What an affliction the Olympian
brought up for us in him—a curse for Priam
and Priam's children![6] Could I see that man
dwindle into Death's night, I'd feel my soul 330
relieved of its distress!"

So Hektor spoke, and she walked slowly on
into the mégaron.[7] She called her maids,
who then assembled women from the city.
But Hékabê went down to the low chamber
fragrant with cedar, where her robes were kept,
embroidered work by women of Sidonia

[4]The hill on which the city stands.
[5]The knees of her statue.
[6]It is worth remembering that Paris as well as Hektor is a son of Hékabê, the addressee here.
[7]The great hall of the house.

Aléxandros[8] had brought, that time he sailed
and ravished Helen, princess, pearl of kings.
Hékabê lifted out her loveliest robe, 340
most ample, most luxurious in brocade,
and glittering like starlight under all.
This offering she carried to Athêna
with a long line of women in her train.
On the Akrópolis,[9] Athêna's shrine
was opened for them by Theanô, stately
daughter of Kisseus, wife to Antênor,[10]
and chosen priestess of Athêna. Now
all crying loud stretched out their arms in prayer,
while Theanô with grace took up the robe 350
to place it on fair-haired Athêna's knees.
She made petition then to Zeus's daughter:

"Lady,
excellent goddess, towering friend of Troy,
smash Diomêdês' lance-haft! Throw him hard
below the Skaian Gates, before our eyes!
Upon this altar we'll make offering
of twelve young heifers never scarred!
Only show mercy to our town,
mercy to Trojan men, their wives and children."

These were Theanô's prayers, her vain prayers. 360
Pallas Athêna turned away her head.

During the supplication at the shrine,
Hektor approached the beautiful house Aléxandros
himself had made, with men who in that time
were master-builders in the land of Troy.
Bedchamber, hall, and court, in the upper town,
they built for him near Priam's hall and Hektor's.
Now Hektor dear to Zeus went in, his hand
gripping a spear eleven forearms long,
whose bronze head shone before him in the air 370
as shone, around the neck, a golden ring.
He found his brother in the bedchamber
handling a magnificent cuirass[11] and shield
and pulling at his bent-horn bow, while Helen
among her household women sat nearby,
directing needlecraft and splendid weaving.
At sight of him, to shame him, Hektor said:

[8]Another name for Paris. He and Helen had stopped in Sidonia (Phoenicia) on their way to Troy.
[9]The most elevated part of the city.
[10]A Trojan lord and counselor.
[11]A piece of armor designed to cover the chest and back.

"Unquiet soul, why be aggrieved in private?
Our troops are dying out there where they fight
around our city, under our high walls. 380
The hue and cry of war, because of you,
comes in like surf upon this town.
You'd be at odds with any other man
you might see quitting your accursèd war.
Up; into action, before torches thrown
make the town flare!"

And shining like a god
Aléxandros replied:

"Ah, Hektor,
this call to order is no more than just.
So let me tell you something: hear me out.
No pettishness, resentment toward the Trojans, 390
kept me in this bedchamber so long,
but rather my desire, on being routed,
to taste grief to the full.
In her sweet way
my lady rouses me to fight again—
and I myself consider it better so.
Victory falls to one man, then another.
Wait, while I put on the wargod's gear,
or else go back; I'll follow, sure to find you."

For answer, Hektor in his shining helm
said not a word, but in low tones 400
enticing Helen murmured:

"Brother dear—
dear to a whore, a nightmare of a woman!
That day my mother gave me to the world
I wish a hurricane blast had torn me away
to wild mountains, or into tumbling sea
to be washed under by a breaking wave,
before these evil days could come!—or, granted
terrible years were in the gods' design,
I wish I had had a good man for a lover
who knew the sharp tongues and just rage of men. 410
This one—his heart's unsound, and always will be,
and he will win what he deserves. Come here
and rest upon this couch with me, dear brother.
You are the one afflicted most
by harlotry in me and by his madness,
our portion, all of misery, given by Zeus
that we may live in song for men to come."

Great Hektor shook his head, his helmet flashing,
and said:

"No, Helen, offer me no rest;
I know you are fond of me. I cannot rest. 420
Time presses, and I grow impatient now
to lend a hand to Trojans in the field
who feel a gap when I am gone. Your part
can be to urge him—let him feel the urgency
to join me in the city. He has time:
I must go home to visit my own people,
my own dear wife and my small son. Who knows
if I shall be reprieved again to see them,
or beaten down under Akhaian blows
as the immortals will."

He turned away 430
and quickly entered his own hall, but found
Princess Andrómakhê was not at home.
With one nursemaid and her small child, she stood
upon the tower of Ilion, in tears,
bemoaning what she saw.
Now Hektor halted
upon his threshold, calling to his maids:

"Tell me at once, and clearly, please,
my lady Andrómakhê, where has she gone?
To see my sisters, or my brothers' wives?
Or to Athêna's temple? Ladies of Troy 440
are there to make petition to the goddess."

The busy mistress of the larder answered:

"Hektor, to put it clearly as you ask,
she did not go to see your sisters, nor
your brothers' wives, nor to Athêna's shrine
where others are petitioning the goddess.
Up to the great square tower of Ilion
she took her way, because she heard our men
were spent in battle by Akhaian power.
In haste, like a madwoman, to the wall 450
she went, and Nurse went too, carrying the child."
At this word Hektor whirled and left his hall,
taking the same path he had come by,
along byways, walled lanes, all through the town
until he reached the Skaian Gates, whereby
before long he would issue on the field.
There his warmhearted lady
came to meet him, running: Andrómakhê,
whose father, Eëtíôn, once had ruled
the land under Mount Plakos, dark with forest, 460
at Thêbê under Plakos—lord and king
of the Kilikians. Hektor was her lord now,

head to foot in bronze; and now she joined him.
Behind her came the maid, who held the child
against her breast, a rosy baby still,
Hektoridês, the world's delight, as fresh
as a pure shining star. Skamándrios[12]
his father named him; other men would say
Astýanax, "Lord of the Lower Town,"
as Hektor singlehandedly guarded Troy. 470
How brilliantly the warrior smiled, in silence,
his eyes upon the child! Andrómakhê
rested against him, shook away a tear,
and pressed his hand in both her own, to say:

"Oh, my wild one, your bravery will be
your own undoing! No pity for our child,
poor little one, or me in my sad lot—
soon to be deprived of you! soon, soon
Akhaians as one man will set upon you
and cut you down! Better for me, without you, 480
to take cold earth for mantle. No more comfort,
no other warmth, after you meet your doom,
but heartbreak only. Father is dead, and Mother.[13]
My father great Akhilleus killed when he
besieged and plundered Thêbê, our high town,
citadel of Kilikians. He killed him,
but, reverent at least in this, did not
despoil him. Body, gear, and weapons forged
so handsomely, he burned, and heaped a barrow
over the ashes. Elms were planted round 490
by mountain-nymphs of him who bears the stormcloud.[14]
Then seven brothers that I had at home
in one day entered Death's dark place. Akhilleus,
prince and powerful runner, killed all seven
amid their shambling cattle and silvery sheep.
Mother, who had been queen of wooded Plakos,
he brought with other winnings home, and freed her,
taking no end of ransom. Artemis
the Huntress shot her in her father's house.[15]
Father and mother—I have none but you, 500
nor brother, Hektor; lover none but you!
Be merciful! Stay here upon the tower!
Do not bereave your child and widow me!
Draw up your troops by the wild figtree; that way
the city lies most open, men most easily

[12] Hektor's son is named for Skamánder, a river on the Trojan plain.

[13] Khryseîs, the woman awarded to Agamémnon, was also taken during the raid on Thêbê that Andrómakhê describes in the following lines; the same expedition included a raid on another city where Akhilleus captured Briseîs, whom he has given up to Agamémnon.

[14] Nymphs associated with Zeus.

[15] The arrows of Artemis, goddess of the hunt, were a symbol of death for women.

could swarm the wall where it is low:
three times, at least, their best men tried it there
in company of the two called Aías, with
Idómeneus, the Atreidai, Diomêdes—
whether someone who had it from oracles 510
had told them, or their own hearts urged them on."

Great Hektor in his shimmering helmet answered:

"Lady, these many things beset my mind
no less than yours. But I should die of shame
before our Trojan men and noblewomen
if like a coward I avoided battle,
nor am I moved to. Long ago I learned
how to be brave, how to go forward always
and to contend for honor, Father's and mine.
Honor—for in my heart and soul I know 520
a day will come when ancient Ilion falls,
when Priam and the folk of Priam perish.
Not by the Trojans' anguish on that day
am I so overborne in mind—the pain
of Hékabê herself, or Priam king,
or of my brothers, many and valorous,
who will have fallen in dust before our enemies—
as by your own grief, when some armed Akhaian
takes you in tears, your free life stripped away.
Before another woman's loom in Argos 530
it may be you will pass, or at Messêis
or Hypereiê fountain, carrying water,
against your will—iron constraint upon you.
And seeing you in tears, a man may say:
'There is the wife of Hektor, who fought best
of Trojan horsemen when they fought at Troy.'
So he may say—and you will ache again
for one man who could keep you out of bondage.
Let me be hidden dark down in my grave
before I hear you cry or know you captive!" 540

As he said this, Hektor held out his arms
to take his baby. But the child squirmed round
on the nurse's bosom and began to wail,
terrified by his father's great war helm—
the flashing bronze, the crest with horsehair plume
tossed like a living thing at every nod.
His father began laughing, and his mother
laughed as well. Then from his handsome head
Hektor lifted off his helm and bent
to place it, bright with sunlight, on the ground. 550
When he had kissed his child and swung him high
to dandle him, he said this prayer:

"O Zeus
and all immortals, may this child, my son,
become like me a prince among the Trojans.[16]
Let him be strong and brave and rule in power
at Ilion; then someday men will say
'This fellow is far better than his father!'
seeing him home from war, and his arms
the bloodstained gear of some tall warrior slain—
making his mother proud."
After this prayer, 560
into his dear wife's arms he gave his baby,
whom on her fragrant breast
she held and cherished, laughing through her tears.
Hektor pitied her now. Caressing her,
he said:

"Unquiet soul, do not be too distressed
by thoughts of me. You know no man dispatches me
into the undergloom against my fate;
no mortal, either, can escape his fate,
coward or brave man, once he comes to be.
Go home, attend to your own handiwork 570
at loom and spindle, and command the maids
to busy themselves, too. As for the war,
that is for men, all who were born at Ilion,
to put their minds on—most of all for me."

He stooped now to recover his plumed helm
as she, his dear wife, drew away, her head
turned and her eyes upon him, brimming tears.
She made her way in haste then to the ordered
house of Hektor and rejoined her maids,
moving them all to weep at sight of her. 580
In Hektor's home they mourned him, living still
but not, they feared, again to leave the war
or be delivered from Akhaian fury.

Paris in the meantime had not lingered:
after he buckled his bright war-gear on
he ran through Troy, sure-footed with long strides.
Think how a stallion fed on clover and barley,
mettlesome, thundering in a stall, may snap
his picket rope and canter down a field
to bathe as he would daily in the river— 590
glorying in freedom! Head held high
with mane over his shoulders flying,
his dazzling work of finely jointed knees

[16]Hektor's prayer for his son would seem to contradict what he has just said about the inevitable destruction of the Trojans. His mood changes during this episode.

takes him around the pasture haunts of horses.[17]
That was the way the son of Priam, Paris,
ran from the height of Pergamos,[18] his gear
ablaze like the great sun,
and laughed aloud. He sprinted on, and quickly
met his brother, who was slow to leave
the place where he had discoursed with his lady. 600
Aléxandros was first to speak:

"Dear fellow,"
he said, "have I delayed you, kept you waiting?
Have I not come at the right time, as you asked?"

And Hektor in his shimmering helm replied:

"My strange brother! No man with justice in him
would underrate your handiwork in battle;
you have a powerful arm. But you give way
too easily, and lose interest, lose your will.
My heart aches in me when I hear our men,
who have such toil of battle on your account, 610
talk of you with contempt. Well, come along.
Someday we'll make amends for that, if ever
we drive the Akhaians from the land of Troy—
if ever Zeus permit us, in our hall,
to set before the gods of heaven, undying
and ever young, our winebowl of deliverance."[19]

BOOK VII. *Athêna and Apollo collaborate to arrange a temporary halt in the fighting, by instigating another single combat, this time between Hektor and a Greek opponent. Hektor utters the challenge, stipulating that the corpse of the man defeated is to be given proper rites. After the Greeks hesitate, Meneláos comes forward, but he is then dissuaded and the foremost Greek warriors volunteer. The greater Aías is chosen by lot to face Hektor. Their duel ends indecisively, and the two men exchange gifts. A truce is arranged during which both armies are to recover their dead and give them proper funerals. The Greeks intend also to build a wall around their encampment near the ships. During a council of the Trojans it is proposed that Helen be surrendered; Paris insists that he will keep her, though he is willing to give up the treasure he had brought to Troy with her. When that offer is made to the Greeks, they refuse it and indicate that even the restoration of Helen will not satisfy them. The dead are cremated and the Greeks build their ramparts.*

BOOK VIII. *Asserting his supreme power over the other deities, Zeus commands them not to intervene in the fighting. Led by the exultant Hektor, the Trojans drive the Greeks back to their seaside encampment behind the walls. When Hêra and Athêna prepare to enter the battle on the Greek side, Zeus again asserts his will, forcing them to return reluctantly to Olympos.*

[17] This extended comparison is an example of the "Homeric simile," which typically illustrates an action or state of mind but is also, to some extent, a small, self-contained picture or story. Most of Homer's similes are drawn from nature (storms, the sea, etc.) or from the familiar activities of shepherd, farmer, or hunter.

[18] The citadel of Troy.

[19] Hektor hopes that some day they may celebrate a ritual thanksgiving to the gods for the city's survival.

Zeus decrees that Hektor shall give the Greeks no respite until the time when Akhilleus, roused by the death of his good friend Patróklos, shall return to action. At nightfall the Trojans do not return to the city as usual but encamp on the field, preparing what they hope will be a decisive attack the next day.

BOOK NINE: A VISIT OF EMISSARIES

So Trojans kept their watch that night.
To seaward
Panic that attends blood-chilling Rout
now ruled the Akhaians. All their finest men
were shaken by this fear, in bitter throes,
as when a shifting gale
blows up over the cold fish-breeding sea,
north wind and west wind wailing out of Thrace
in squall on squall, and dark waves crest, and shoreward
masses of weed are cast up by the surf:
so were Akhaian hearts torn in their breasts. 10

By that great gloom hard hit, the son of Atreus[1]
made his way amid his criers and told them
to bid each man in person to assembly
but not raise a general cry. He led them,
making the rounds himself, and soon the soldiers
grimly took their places. Then he rose,
with slow tears trickling, as from a hidden spring
dark water runs down, staining a rock wall;
and groaning heavily he addressed the Argives:

"Friends, leaders of Argives, all my captains, 20
Zeus Kronidês entangled me in folly
to my undoing. Wayward god, he promised
solemnly that I should not sail away
before I stormed the inner town of Troy.
Crookedness and duplicity, I see now!
He calls me to return to Argos beaten
after these many losses. That must be
his will and his good pleasure, who knows why?
Many a great town's height has he destroyed
and will destroy, being supreme in power. 30
Enough. Now let us act on what I say:
Board ship for our own fatherland! Retreat!
We cannot hope any longer to take Troy!"

At this a stillness overcame them all,
the Akhaian soldiers. Long they sat in silence,

[1]Agamémnon (the higher-ranking son), not Meneláos.

hearing their own hearts beat. Then Diomêdês
rose at last to speak. He said:

"My lord,
I must contend with you for letting go,
for losing balance. I may do so here
in assembly lawfully. Spare me your anger. 40
Before this you have held me up to scorn
for lack of fighting spirit;[2] old and young,
everyone knows the truth of that. In your case,
the son of crooked-minded Krónos gave you
one gift and not both: a staff of kingship
honored by all men, but no staying power—
the greatest gift of all.
What has come over you, to make you think
the Akhaians weak and craven as you say?
If you are in a passion to sail home, 50
sail on: the way is clear, the many ships
that made the voyage from Mykênê[3] with you
stand near the sea's edge. Others here will stay
until we plunder Troy! Or if they, too,
would like to, let them sail for their own country!
Sthênelos[4] and I will fight alone
until we see the destined end of Ilion.
We came here under god."

When Diomêdês
finished, a cry went up from all Akhaians
in wonder at his words. Then Nestor stood 60
and spoke among them:

"Son of Tydeus, formidable
above the rest in war, in council, too,
you have more weight than others of your age.
No one will cry down what you say, no true
Akhaian will, or contradict you. Still,
you did not push on to the end.
I know you are young; in years you might well be
my last-born son, and yet for all of that
you kept your head and said what needed saying
before the Argive captains. My own part, 70
as I am older, is to drive it home.
No one will show contempt for what I say,
surely not Agamémnon, our commander.
Alien to clan and custom and hearth fire

[2]Agamémnon made this charge in Book IV; in fact, Diomêdês is one of the bravest warriors among the Greeks.
[3]Agamémnon's chief city (also spelled *Mycenae*).
[4]Diomêdês' comrade and charioteer.

is he who longs for war—heartbreaking war—
with his own people.
Let us yield to darkness
and make our evening meal. But let the sentries
take their rest on watch outside the rampart
near the moat;[5] those are my orders for them.
Afterward, you direct us, Agamémnon, 80
by right of royal power. Provide a feast
for older men, your counselors. That is duty
and no difficulty: your huts are full of wine
brought over daily in our ships from Thrace
across the wide sea, and all provender
for guests is yours, as you are high commander.
Your counselors being met, pay heed to him
who counsels best. The army of Akhaia
bitterly needs a well-found plan of action.
The enemy is upon us, near the ships, 90
burning his thousand fires. What Akhaian
could be highhearted in that glare? This night
will see the army saved or brought to ruin."

They heeded him and did his will. Well-armed,
the sentries left to take their posts, one company
formed around Thrasymêdês, Nestor's son,
another mustered by Askálaphos
and Iálmenos, others commanded by
Meríonês, Aphareus, Dêípyros,
and Kreion's son, the princely Lykomêdês. 100
Seven lieutenants, each with a hundred men,
carrying long spears, issued from the camp
for outposts chosen between ditch and rampart.
Campfires were kindled, and they took their meal.
The son of Atreus led the elder men
together to his hut, where he served dinner,
and each man's hand went out upon the meal.
When they had driven hunger and thirst away,
Old Nestor opened their deliberations—
Nestor, whose counsel had seemed best before, 110
point by point weaving his argument:

"Lord Marshal of the army, Agamémnon,
as I shall end with you, so I begin,
since you hold power over a great army
and are responsible for it: the Lord Zeus
put in your keeping staff and precedent
that you might gather counsel for your men.
You should be first in discourse, but attentive
to what another may propose, to act on it

[5] The defensive ditch outside the walls.

if he speak out for the good of all. Whatever 120
he may initiate, action is yours.
On this rule, let me speak as I think best.
A better view than mine no man can have,
the same view that I've held these many days
since that occasion when, my lord, for all
Akhilleus' rage, you took the girl Brisêis
out of his lodge—but not with our consent.
Far from it; I for one had begged you not to.
Just the same, you gave way to your pride,
and you dishonored a great prince, 130
a hero to whom the gods themselves do honor.
Taking his prize, you kept her and still do.
But even so, and even now, we may
contrive some way of making peace with him
by friendly gifts, and by affectionate words."

Then Agamémnon, the Lord Marshal, answered:

"Sir, there is nothing false in your account
of my blind errors. I committed them;
I will not now deny it. Troops of soldiers
are worth no more than one man cherished by Zeus 140
as he has cherished this man and avenged him,
overpowering the army of Akhaians.
I lost my head, I yielded to black anger,
but now I would retract it and appease him
with all munificence. Here before everyone
I may enumerate the gifts I'll give.
Seven new tripods and ten bars of gold,
then twenty shining caldrons, and twelve horses,
thoroughbreds, who by their wind and legs
have won me prizes: any man who owned 150
what these have brought me could not lack resources,
could not be pinched for precious gold—so many
prizes have these horses carried home.
Then I shall give him seven women, deft
in household handicraft—women of Lesbos
I chose when he himself took Lesbos town,
as they outshone all womankind in beauty.
These I shall give him, and one more, whom I
took away from him then: Briseus' daughter.
Concerning her, I add my solemn oath 160
I never went to bed or coupled with her,
as custom is with men and women.
These will be his at once. If the immortals
grant us the plundering of Priam's town,
let him come forward when the spoils are shared
and load his ship with bars of gold and bronze.
Then he may choose among the Trojan women

twenty that are most lovely, after Helen.
If we return to Argos of Akhaia,
flowing with good things of the earth, he'll be 170
my own adopted son, dear as Orestês,
born long ago and reared in bounteous peace.[6]
I have three daughters now at home, Khrysóthemis,
Laódikê, and Iphiánassa.
He may take whom he will to be his bride
and pay no bridal gift, leading her home
to Pêleus' hall. But I shall add a dowry
such as no man has given to his daughter.
Seven flourishing strongholds I'll give him:
Kardamylê and Enopê and Hirê 180
in the wild grassland; holy Phêrai too,
and the deep meadowland of Ántheia,
Aipeia and the vineyard slope of Pêdasos,
all lying near the sea in the far west
of sandy Pylos. In these lands are men
who own great flocks and herds; now as his liegemen,
they will pay tithes[7] and sumptuous honor to him,
prospering as they carry out his plans.
These are the gifts I shall arrange if he
desists from anger. Let him be subdued! 190
Lord Death indeed is deaf to appeal, implacable;
of all gods therefore he is most abhorrent
to mortal men. So let Akhilleus bow to me,
considering that I hold higher rank
and claim the precedence of age."

To this
Lord Nestor of Gerênia replied:

"Lord Marshal of the army, Agamémnon,
this time the gifts you offer Lord Akhilleus
are not to be despised. Come, we'll dispatch
our chosen emissaries to his quarters 200
as quickly as possible. Those men whom I
may designate, let them perform the mission.
Phoinix,[8] dear to Zeus, may lead the way.
Let Aías follow him, and Prince Odysseus.
The criers, Hódios and Eurýbatês,
may go as escorts. Bowls for their hands here!

[6] The murder of Agamémnon by his wife, and his son Orestês' later murder of her in revenge, are mentioned in Homer's *Odyssey* and are the central incidents of Aeschylus' *Oresteia*. The following lines fail to mention Agamémnon's best-known daughters, Iphigeneia and Electra. The sacrifice of Iphigeneia by Agamémnon in order to gain favorable winds for the voyage to Troy and Electra's support of her brother in the murder of their mother are important in Aeschylus' plays.

[7] Shares of crops, animals, and so on.

[8] Akhilleus' tutor.

Tell them to keep silence, while we pray
that Zeus the son of Krónos will be merciful."

Nestor's proposal fell on willing ears,
and criers came at once to tip out water 210
over their hands, while young men filled the winebowls
and dipped a measure into every cup.
They spilt their offerings[9] and drank their fill,
then briskly left the hut of Agamémnon.
Nestor accompanied them with final words
and sage looks, especially for Odysseus,
as to the effort they should make to bring
the son of Pêleus round.

Following Phoinix,
Aías and Odysseus walked together
beside the tumbling clamorous whispering sea, 220
praying hard to the girdler of the islands[10]
that they might easily sway their great friend's heart.
Amid the ships and huts of the Myrmidons
they found him, taking joy in a sweet harp
of rich and delicate make—the crossbar set
to hold the strings being silver. He had won it
when he destroyed the city of Eëtíôn,
and plucking it he took his joy: he sang
old tales of heroes, while across the room
alone and silent sat Patróklos, waiting 230
until Akhilleus should be done with song.
Phoinix had come in unremarked,[11] but when
the two new visitors, Odysseus leading,
entered and stood before him, then Akhilleus
rose in wonderment, and left his chair,
his harp still in his hand. So did Patróklos
rise at sight of the two men. Akhilleus
made both welcome with a gesture, saying:

"Peace! My two great friends, I greet your coming.
How I have needed it! Even in my anger, 240
of all Akhaians, you are closest to me."

And Prince Akhilleus led them in. He seated them
on easy chairs with purple coverlets,
and to Patróklos who stood near he said:

[9]That is, as tribute to the gods.
[10]Poseidon, god of the ocean.
[11]*Phoinix . . . unremarked.* Like "Following Phoinix" a few lines earlier, these words are inserted by the translator as a way of coping with a major problem in the Greek text, which does not mention Phoinix as walking from Agamémnon's hut to that of Akhilleus.

"Put out an ampler winebowl, use more wine
for stronger drink,[12] and place a cup for each.
Here are my dearest friends beneath my roof."

Patróklos did as his companion bade him.
Meanwhile the host set down a carving block
within the fire's rays; a chine of mutton 250
and a fat chine of goat he placed upon it,
as well as savory pork chine. Automédôn[13]
steadied the meat for him, Akhilleus carved,
then sliced it well and forked it on the spits.
Meanwhile Patróklos, like a god in firelight,
made the hearth blaze up. When the leaping flame
had ebbed and died away, he raked the coals
and in the glow extended spits of meat,
lifting these at times from the firestones
to season with pure salt. When all was done 260
and the roast meat apportioned into platters,
loaves of bread were passed round by Patróklos
in fine baskets. Akhilleus served the meat.
He took his place then opposite Odysseus,
back to the other wall, and told
Patróklos to make offering to the gods.
This he did with meat tossed in the fire,
then each man's hand went out upon the meal.
When they had put their hunger and thirst away,
Aías nodded silently to Phoinix, 270
but Prince Odysseus caught the nod. He filled
a cup of wine and lifted it to Akhilleus,
saying:

"Health, Akhilleus. We've no lack
of generous feasts this evening—in the lodge
of Agamémnon first, and now with you,
good fare and plentiful each time.
It is not feasting that concerns us now,
however, but a ruinous defeat.
Before our very eyes we see it coming
and are afraid. By a blade's turn, our good ships 280
are saved or lost, unless you arm your valor.
Trojans and allies are encamped tonight
in pride before our ramparts, at our sterns,
and through their army burn a thousand fires.
These men are sure they cannot now be stopped
but will get through to our good ships. Lord Zeus
flashes and thunders for them on the right,[14]
and Hektor in his ecstasy of power

[12]Wine was usually served mixed, often with water.
[13]Third-ranking man among the Myrmidons, after Akhilleus and Patróklos.
[14]Favorable omens appeared on the observer's right.

is mad for battle, confident in Zeus,
deferring to neither men nor gods. Pure frenzy 290
fills him, and he prays for the bright dawn
when he will shear our stern-post beaks away
and fire all our ships, while in the shipways
amid that holocaust he carries death
among our men, driven out by smoke. All this
I gravely fear; I fear the gods will make
good his threatenings, and our fate will be
to die here, far from the pastureland of Argos.
Rouse yourself, if even at this hour
you'll pitch in for the Akhaians and deliver them 300
from Trojan havoc. In the years to come
this day will be remembered pain for you
if you do not. No remedy, no remedy
will come to hand, once the great ill is done.
While there is time, think how to keep this evil
day from the Danáäns!
My dear lad,
how rightly in your case your father, Pêleus,
put it in his farewell, sending you out
from Phthía to take ship with Agamémnon!
'Now as to fighting power, child,' he said, 310
'if Hêra and Athêna wish, they'll give it.
Control your passion, though, and your proud heart,
for gentle courtesy is a better thing.
Break off insidious quarrels, and young and old,
the Argives will respect you for it more.'
That was your old father's admonition:
you have forgotten. Still, even now, abandon
heart-wounding anger. If you will relent,
Agamémnon will match this change of heart
with gifts. Now listen and let me list for you 320
what just now in his quarters he proposed:
seven new tripods, and ten bars of gold,
then twenty shining caldrons, and twelve horses,
thoroughbreds, that by their wind and legs
have won him prizes: any man who owned
what these have brought him would not lack resources,
could not be pinched for precious gold—so many
prizes have these horses carried home.
Then he will give you seven women, deft
in household handicraft: women of Lesbos 330
chosen when you yourself took Lesbos town,
as they outshone all womankind in beauty.
These he will give you, and one more, whom he
took away from you then: Briseus' daughter,
concerning whom he adds a solemn oath
never to have gone to bed or coupled with her,
as custom is, my lord, with men and women.

These are all yours at once. If the immortals
grant us the pillaging of Priam's town,
you may come forward when the spoils are shared 340
and load your ship with bars of gold and bronze.
Then you may choose among the Trojan women
twenty that are most lovely, after Helen.
And then, if we reach Argos of Akhaia,
flowing with good things of the earth, you'll be
his own adopted son, dear as Orestês,
born long ago and reared in bounteous peace.
He has three daughters now at home, Khrysóthemis,
Laódikê, and Iphiánassa.
You may take whom you will to be your bride 350
and pay no gift when you conduct her home
to your ancestral hall. He'll add a dowry
such as no man has given to his daughter.
Seven flourishing strongholds he'll give to you:
Kardamylê and Enopê and Hirê
in the wild grassland; holy Phêrai too,
and the deep meadowland of Ántheia,
Aipeia and the vineyard slope of Pêdasos,
all lying near the sea in the far west
of sandy Pylos. In these lands are men 360
who own great flocks and herds; now as your liegemen,
they will pay tithes and sumptuous honor to you,
prospering as they carry out your plans.
These are the gifts he will arrange if you
desist from anger.
Even if you abhor
the son of Atreus all the more bitterly,
with all his gifts, take pity on the rest,
all the old army, worn to rags in battle.
These will honor you as gods are honored!
And ah, for these, what glory you may win! 370
Think: Hektor is your man this time: being crazed
with ruinous pride, believing there's no fighter
equal to him among those that our ships
brought here by sea, he'll put himself in range!"

Akhilleus the great runner answered him:

"Son of Laërtês and the gods of old,
Odysseus, master soldier and mariner,
I owe you a straight answer, as to how
I see this thing, and how it is to end.
No need to sit with me like mourning doves 380
making your gentle noise by turns. I hate
as I hate Hell's own gate that man who hides
one thought within him while he speaks another.
What I shall say is what I see and think.

Give in to Agamémnon? I think not,
neither to him nor to the rest. I had
small thanks for fighting, fighting without truce
against hard enemies here. The portion's equal
whether a man hangs back or fights his best;
the same respect, or lack of it, is given 390
brave man and coward. One who's active dies
like the do-nothing. What least thing have I
to show for it, for harsh days undergone
and my life gambled, all these years of war?
A bird will give her fledglings every scrap
she comes by, and go hungry, foraging.
That is the case with me.
Many a sleepless night I've spent afield
and many a day in bloodshed, hand to hand
in battle for the wives of other men. 400
In sea raids I plundered a dozen towns,
eleven in expeditions overland
through Trojan country, and the treasure taken
out of them all, great heaps of handsome things,
I carried back each time to Agamémnon.
He sat tight on the beachhead, and shared out
a little treasure; most of it he kept.
He gave prizes of war to his officers;
the rest have theirs, not I; from me alone
of all Akhaians, he pre-empted her. 410
He holds my bride,[15] dear to my heart. Aye, let him
sleep with her and enjoy her!
Why must Argives
fight the Trojans? Why did he raise an army
and lead it here? For Helen, was it not?
Are the Atreidai of all mortal men
the only ones who love their wives? I think not.
Every sane decent fellow loves his own
and cares for her, as in my heart I loved
Brisêis, though I won her by the spear.
Now, as he took my prize out of my hands, 420
tricked and defrauded me, he need not tempt me;
I know him, and he cannot change my mind.
Let him take thought, Odysseus, with you
and others how the ships may be defended
against incendiary attack. By god,
he has achieved imposing work without me,
a rampart piled up overnight, a ditch
running beyond it, broad and deep,
with stakes implanted in it! All no use!
He cannot hold against the killer's charge. 430

[15] Brisêis; she is not literally his wife, however.

As long as I was in the battle, Hektor
never cared for a fight far from the walls;
his limit was the oak tree by the gate.
When I was alone one day he waited there,
but barely got away when I went after him.
Now it is I who do not care to fight.
Tomorrow at dawn when I have made offering
to Zeus and all the gods, and hauled my ships
for loading in the shallows, if you like
and if it interests you, look out and see 440
my ships on Hellê's waters in the offing,[16]
oarsmen in line making the sea-foam scud!
And if the great Earthshaker[17] gives a breeze,
the third day out I'll make it home to Phthía.
Rich possessions are there I left behind
when I was mad enough to come here; now
I take home gold and ruddy bronze, and women
belted luxuriously, and hoary iron,
all that came to me here. As for my prize,
he who gave her took her outrageously back. 450
Well, you can tell him all this to his face,
and let the other Akhaians burn
if he in his thick hide of shamelessness
picks out another man to cheat. He would not
look me in the eye, dog that he is!
I will not share one word of counsel with him,
nor will I act with him; he robbed me blind,
broke faith with me: he gets no second chance
to play me for a fool. Once is enough.
To hell with him, Zeus took his brains away! 460
His gifts I abominate, and I would give
not one dry shuck for him. I would not change,
not if he multiplied his gifts by ten,
by twenty times what he has now, and more,
no matter where they came from: if he gave
what enters through Orkhómenos' town gate
or Thebes of Egypt, where the treasures lie—
that city where through each of a hundred gates
two hundred men drive out in chariots.[18]
Not if his gifts outnumbered the sea sands 470
or all the dust grains in the world could Agamémnon
ever appease me—not till he pays me back
full measure, pain for pain, dishonor for dishonor.
The daughter of Agamémnon, son of Atreus,
I will not take in marriage. Let her be
as beautiful as pale-gold Aphrodítê,
skilled as Athêna of the sea-grey eyes,

[16] *Hellê's waters:* the Hellespont (the modern Dardanelles). *offing:* horizon.
[17] Poseidon.
[18] *Orkhómenos:* an important city northwest of Athens. *Thebes:* an ancient, royal city of Egypt.

I will not have her, at any price. No, let him
find someone else, an eligible Akhaian,
kinglier than I.
Now if the gods 480
preserve me and I make it home, my father
Pêleus will select a bride for me.
In Hellas[19] and in Phthîa there are many
daughters of strong men who defend the towns.
I'll take the one I wish to be my wife.
There in my manhood I have longed, indeed,
to marry someone of congenial mind
and take my ease, enjoying the great estate
my father had acquired.
Now I think
no riches can compare with being alive, 490
not even those they say this well-built Ilion
stored up in peace before the Akhaians came.
Neither could all the Archer's shrine contains
at rocky Pytho,[20] in the crypt of stone.
A man may come by cattle and sheep in raids;
tripods he buys, and tawny-headed horses;
but his life's breath cannot be hunted back
or be recaptured once it pass his lips.
My mother, Thetis of the silvery feet,
tells me of two possible destinies 500
carrying me toward death: two ways:
if on the one hand I remain to fight
around Troy town, I lose all hope of home
but gain unfading glory; on the other,
if I sail back to my own land my glory
fails—but a long life lies ahead for me.
To all the rest of you I say: 'Sail home:
you will not now see Ilion's last hour,'
for Zeus who views the wide world held his sheltering
hand over that city, and her troops 510
have taken heart.
Return, then, emissaries,
deliver my answer to the Akhaian peers—
it is the senior officer's privilege—
and let them plan some other way, and better,
to save their ships and save the Akhaian army.
This one cannot be put into effect—
their scheme this evening—while my anger holds.
Phoinix may stay and lodge the night with us,
then take ship and sail homeward at my side
tomorrow, if he wills. I'll not constrain him." 520

[19] This word later came to mean all of Greece; here it refers to a region in northern Greece.
[20] Temple of Apollo at Delphi in Greece; visitors seeking the god's oracular guidance made rich offerings.

After Akhilleus finished, all were silent,
awed, for he spoke with power.
Then the old master-charioteer, Lord Phoinix,
answered at last, and let his tears come shining,
fearing for the Akhaian ships:

"Akhilleus,
if it is true you set your heart on home
and will not stir a finger to save the ships
from being engulfed by fire—all for this rage
that has swept over you—how, child, could I
be sundered from you, left behind alone? 530
For your sake the old master-charioteer,
Pêleus, made provision that I should come,
that day he gave you godspeed out of Phthía
to go with Agamémnon. Still a boy,
you knew nothing of war that levels men
to the same testing, nothing of assembly
where men become illustrious. That is why
he sent me, to instruct you in these matters,
to be a man of eloquence and action.
After all that, dear child, I should not wish 540
to be left here apart from you—not even
if god himself should undertake to smooth
my wrinkled age and make me fresh and young,
as when for the first time I left the land
of lovely women, Hellas. I went north
to avoid a feud with Father, Amyntor
Orménidês. His anger against me rose
over a fair-haired slave girl whom he fancied,
without respect for his own wife, my mother.
Mother embraced my knees and begged that I 550
make love to this girl, so that afterward
she might be cold to the aging man. I did it.
My father guessed the truth at once, and cursed me,
praying the ghostly Furies[21] that no son
of mine should ever rest upon his knees:
a curse fulfilled by the immortals—Lord
Zeus of undergloom and cold Perséphonê.[22]
I planned to put a sword in him, and would have,
had not some god unstrung my rage, reminding me
of country gossip and the frowns of men; 560
I shrank from being called a parricide
among the Akhaians. But from that time on
I felt no tie with home, no love for lingering
under the rooftree of a raging father.
Our household and our neighbors, it is true,
urged me to stay. They made a handsome feast

[21]Spirits who avenge sins, especially against blood kindred.
[22]*Zeus of undergloom:* Aïdês (Hades), ruler of the dead. *Perséphonê:* his queen.

of shambling cattle butchered, and fat sheep;
young porkers by the litter, crisp with fat,
were singed and spitted in Hêphaistos' fire,
rivers of wine drunk from the old man's store. 570
Nine times they spent the night and slept beside me,
taking the watch by turns, leaving a fire
to flicker under the entrance colonnade,
and one more in the court outside my room.
But when the tenth night came, starless and black,
I cracked the tight bolt on my chamber door,
pushed out, and scaled the courtyard wall, unseen
by household men on watch or women slaves.
Then I escaped from that place, made my way
through Hellas where the dancing floors are wide, 580
until I came to Phthía's fertile plain,
mother of flocks, and Pêleus the king.
He gave me welcome, treated me with love,
as a father would an only son, his heir
to rich possessions. And he made me rich,
appointing me great numbers of retainers
on the frontier of Phthía, where I lived
as lord of Dolopês. Now, it was I
who formed your manhood, handsome as a god's,
Akhilleus: I who loved you from the heart; 590
for never in another's company
would you attend a feast or dine in hall—
never, unless I took you on my knees
and cut your meat, and held your cup of wine.
Many a time you wet my shirt, hiccuping
wine-bubbles in distress, when you were small.
Patient and laborious as a nurse
I had to be for you, bearing in mind
that never would the gods bring into being
any son of mine. Godlike Akhilleus, 600
you were the manchild that I made my own
to save me someday, so I thought, from misery.
Quell your anger, Akhilleus! You must not
be pitiless! The gods themselves relent,
and are they not still greater in bravery,
in honor and in strength? Burnt offerings,
courteous prayer, libation, smoke of sacrifice,
with all of these, men can placate the gods
when someone oversteps and errs. The truth is,
prayers[23] are daughters of almighty Zeus— 610
one may imagine them lame, wrinkled things

[23]*prayers:* pleas for forgiveness, uttered by a man who, after harming another while possessed by a kind of madness (Folly), repents of his misdeed. If the injured man accepts the plea or prayer he is rewarded, but if he rejects it he may himself be visited by a fit of Folly that drives him to a ruinous act. The allegory is prophetic of what will happen to Akhilleus.

with eyes cast down, that toil to follow after
passionate Folly. Folly is strong and swift,
outrunning all the prayers, and everywhere
arriving first to injure mortal men;
still they come healing after. If a man
reveres the daughters of Zeus when they come near,
he is rewarded, and his prayers are heard;
but if he spurns them and dismisses them,
they make their way to Zeus again and ask 620
that Folly dog that man till suffering
has taken arrogance out of him.
Relent,
be courteous to the daughters of Zeus, you too,
as courtesy sways others, and the best.
If Agamémnon had no gifts for you,
named none to follow, but inveighed against you
still in fury, then I could never say,
'Discard your anger and defend the Argives—'
never, no matter how they craved your help.
But this is not so: he will give many things 630
at once; he promised others; he has sent
his noblest men to intercede with you,
the flower of the army, and your friends,
dearest among the Argives. Will you turn
their words, their coming, into humiliation?
Until this moment, no one took it ill
that you should suffer anger; we learned this
from the old stories of how towering wrath
could overcome great men; but they were still
amenable to gifts and to persuasion. 640
Here is an instance I myself remember
not from our own time but in ancient days:
I'll tell it to you all, for all are friends.
The Kourêtês were fighting a warlike race,[24]
Aitolians, around the walls of Kálydôn,
with slaughter on both sides: Aitolians
defending their beloved Kálydôn
while the Kourêtês longed to sack the town.
The truth is, Artemis of the Golden Chair
had brought the scourge of war on the Aitolians; 650

[24]The story Phoinix proceeds to tell is a parable, drawn from mythology and adapted here to make it fit Akhilleus' situation. Reordered chronologically, the story is as follows: Artemis, goddess of the hunt and of wild life ("Mistress of Long Arrows"), was offended by the failure of Oineus, king of the Aitolians, to honor her. In revenge, she sent a great boar to ravage his land. The king's son, Meléagros, organized a band of men to kill the boar. After it was killed, the Aitolians quarreled with the Kourêtês, a neighboring people, over the animal's head and hide; in the ensuing war the Kourêtês threatened Kálydôn, Oineus' city. In the fighting Meléagros killed his mother Althaiê's brother, who was fighting on the Kourêtês' side. She cursed her son, who therefore retired from battle, putting his city in peril. His people and family implored him to defend it and offered him gifts, but he resisted their pleas until his wife Kleopátrê persuaded him. He then saved the city, but only after it was too late for him to receive the gifts.

she had been angered because Oineus made
no harvest offering from his vineyard slope.
While other gods enjoyed his hekatombs
he made her none, either forgetful of it
or careless—a great error, either way.
In her anger, the Mistress of Long Arrows
roused against him a boar with gleaming tusks
out of his wild grass bed, a monstrous thing
that ravaged the man's vineyard many times
and felled entire orchards, roots, 660
blooms, apples and all. Now this great boar
Meléagros, the son of Oineus, killed
by gathering men and hounds from far and near.
So huge the boar was, no small band could master him,
and he brought many to the dolorous pyre.[25]
Around the dead beast Artemis set on
a clash with battlecries between Kourêtês
and proud Aitolians over the boar's head
and shaggy hide. As long, then, as Meléagros,
backed by the wargod, fought, the Kourêtês 670
had the worst of it for all their numbers
and could not hold a line outside the walls.
But then a day came when Meléagros
was stung by venomous anger that infects
the coolest thinker's heart: swollen with rage
at his own mother, Althaiê, he languished
in idleness at home beside his lady,
Kleopátrê.

This lovely girl was born
to Marpessê of ravishing pale ankles,[26]
Euênos' child, and Idês, who had been 680
most powerful of men on earth. He drew
the bow against the Lord Phoibos Apollo
over his love, Marpessê, whom her father
and gentle mother called Alkýonê,
since for her sake her mother gave that seabird's
forlorn cry when Apollo ravished her.
With Kleopátrê lay Meléagros,
nursing the bitterness his mother stirred,
when in her anguish over a brother slain
she cursed her son. She called upon the gods, 690
beating the grassy earth with both her hands
as she pitched forward on her knees, with cries
to the Lord of Undergloom and cold Perséphonê,
while tears wetted her veils—in her entreaty

[25] The fire in which the dead were cremated.

[26] The poem digresses for a few lines to describe the parents of Meléagros' wife, Kleopátrê. Her father Idês and the god Apollo had been rivals for the love of her mother Marpessê (who chose her human lover), also called Alkýonê, a name denoting a seabird with a mournful cry.

that death come to her son. Inexorable
in Érebos[27] a vampire Fury listened.
Soon, then, about the gates of the Aitolians
tumult and din of war grew loud; their towers
rang with blows. And now the elder men
implored Meléagros to leave his room, 700
and sent the high priests of the gods, imploring him
to help defend the town. They promised him
a large reward: in the green countryside
of Kálydôn, wherever it was richest,
there he might choose a beautiful garden plot
of fifty acres, half in vineyard, half
in virgin prairie for the plow to cut.
Oineus, master of horsemen, came with prayers
upon the doorsill of the chamber, often
rattling the locked doors, pleading with his son. 710
His sisters, too, and then his gentle mother
pleaded with him. Only the more fiercely
he turned away. His oldest friends, his dearest,
not even they could move him—not until
his room was shaken by a hail of stones
as Kourêtês began to scale the walls
and fire the city.
Then at last his lady
in her soft-belted gown besought him weeping,
speaking of all the ills that come to men
whose town is taken: soldiers put to the sword; 720
the city razed by fire; alien hands
carrying off the children and the women.
Hearing these fearful things, his heart was stirred
to action: he put on his shining gear
and fought off ruin from the Aitolians.
Mercy prevailed in him. His folk no longer
cared to award him gifts and luxuries,
yet even so he saved that terrible day.
Oh, do not let your mind go so astray!
Let no malignant spirit 730
turn you that way, dear son! It will be worse
to fight for ships already set afire!
Value the gifts; rejoin the war; Akhaians
afterward will give you a god's honor.
If you reject the gifts and then, later,
enter the deadly fight, you will not be
accorded the same honor, even though
you turn the tide of war!"

But the great runner
Akhilleus answered:

[27]Part of the realm of the dead.

"Old uncle Phoinix, bless you,
that is an honor I can live without. 740
Honored I think I am by Zeus's justice,
justice that will sustain me by the ships
as long as breath is in me and I can stand.
Here is another point: ponder it well:
best not confuse my heart with lamentation
for Agamémnon, whom you must not honor;
you would be hateful to me, dear as you are.
Loyalty should array you at my side
in giving pain to him who gives me pain.
Rule with me equally, share half my honor,[28] 750
but do not ask my help for Agamémnon.
My answer will be reported by these two.
Lodge here in a soft bed, and at first light
we can decide whether to sail or stay."

He knit his brows and nodded to Patróklos
to pile up rugs for Phoinix' bed—a sign
for the others to be quick about departing.
Aías, however, noble son of Télamôn
made the last appeal. He said:

"Odysseus,
master soldier and mariner, let us go. 760
I do not see the end of this affair
achieved by this night's visit. Nothing for it
but to report our talk for what it's worth
to the Danáäns, who sit waiting there.
Akhilleus hardened his great heart against us,
wayward and savage as he is, unmoved
by the affections of his friends who made him
honored above all others on the beachhead.
There is no pity in him. A normal man
will take the penalty for a brother slain 770
or a dead son. By paying much, the one
who did the deed may stay unharmed at home.
Fury and pride in the bereaved are curbed
when he accepts the penalty. Not you.
Cruel and unappeasable rage the gods
put in you for one girl alone. We offer
seven beauties, and much more besides!
Be gentler, and respect your own rooftree
whereunder we are guests who speak for all
Danáäns as a body. Our desire 780
is to be closest to you of them all."

[28] This is not meant literally; Akhilleus is saying, in effect, "Ask any favor except that I help Agamémnon."

Akhilleus the great runner answered him:

"Scion[29] of Télamôn and gods of old,
Aías, lord of fighting men, you seemed
to echo my own mind in what you said!
And yet my heart grows large and hot with fury
remembering that affair: as though I were
some riffraff or camp follower, he taunted me
before them all!
Go back, report the news:
I will not think of carnage or of war 790
until Prince Hektor, son of Priam, reaches
Myrmidon huts and ships in his attack,
slashing through Argives, burning down their ships.
Around my hut, my black ship, I foresee
for all his fury, Hektor will break off combat."[30]

That was his answer. Each of the emissaries
took up a double-handed cup and poured
libation by the shipways. Then Odysseus
led the way on their return. Patróklos
commanded his retainers and the maids 800
to make at once a deep-piled bed for Phoinix.
Obediently they did so, spreading out
fleeces and coverlet and a linen sheet,
and down the old man lay, awaiting Dawn.
Akhilleus slept in the well-built hut's recess,
and with him lay a woman he had brought
from Lesbos, Phorbas' daughter, Diomêdê.
Patróklos went to bed at the other end,
and with him, too, a woman lay—soft-belted
Iphis, who had been given to him by Akhilleus 810
when he took Skyros, ringed by cliff, the mountain
fastness of Enyéus.
Now the emissaries
arrived at Agamémnon's lodge. With cups
of gold held up, and rising to their feet
on every side, the Akhaians greeted them,
curious for the news. Lord Agamémnon
put the question first:

"Come, tell me, sir,
Odysseus, glory of Akhaia—will Akhilleus
fight off ravenous fire from the ships
or does he still refuse, does anger still 820
hold sway in his great heart?"

[29] Offspring.
[30] Akhilleus is apparently modifying his earlier resolve to sail away the next morning.

That patient man,
the Prince Odysseus, made reply:

"Excellency,
Lord Marshal of the army, son of Atreus,
the man has no desire to quench his rage.
On the contrary, he is more than ever
full of anger, spurns you and your gifts,
calls on you to work out your own defense
to save the ships and the Akhaian army.
As for himself, he threatens at daybreak
to drag his well-found ships into the surf, 830
and says he would advise the rest as well
to sail for home. 'You shall not see,' he says,
'the last hour that awaits tall Ilion,
for Zeus who views the wide world held his sheltering
hand over the city, and her troops
have taken heart.' That was Akhilleus' answer.
Those who were with me can confirm all this,
Aías can, and the two clearheaded criers.
As to old Phoinix, he is sleeping there
by invitation, so that he may sail 840
to his own country, homeward with Akhilleus,
tomorrow, if he wills, without constraint."

When he had finished everyone was still,
sitting in silence and in perturbation
for a long time. At last brave Diomêdês,
lord of the warcry, said:

"Excellency,
Lord Marshal of the army, Agamémnon,
you never should have pled with him, or given
so many gifts to him. At the best of times
he is a proud man; now you have pushed him far 850
deeper into his vanity and pride.
By god, let us have done with him—
whether he goes or stays! He'll fight again
when the time comes, whenever his blood is up
or the god rouses him. As for ourselves,
let everyone now do as I advise
and go to rest. Your hearts have been refreshed
with bread and wine, the pith and nerve of men.
When the fair Dawn with finger tips of rose
makes heaven bright, deploy your men and horses 860
before the ships at once, and cheer them on,
and take your place, yourself, in the front line
to join the battle."

All gave their assent
in admiration of Diomêdês,

breaker of horses. When they had spilt their wine
they all dispersed, each man to his own hut,
and lying down they took the gift of sleep.

BOOK X. *The troubled Agamémnon and his brother Meneláos, unable to sleep, assemble the Greek chieftains in the night. After they inspect the sentries, Nestor proposes that a reconnaissance patrol try to discover the Trojan plans. Diomêdês volunteers for the dangerous mission, choosing the wily Odysseus as his partner. Meanwhile the Trojans too decide to send out a scout, a man named Dolôn. Diomêdês and Odysseus capture him, lead him to believe he will be taken prisoner alive, get information from him, and then kill him. The two Greeks, acting on what they have learned, raid the camp of King Rhésos of Thrace, a newcomer to the war, kill him and several of his men, steal his wondrous horses, and then return triumphantly to the ships.*

BOOK XI. *The next day brings fierce general fighting, gods and goddesses remaining out of action. At first Agamémnon inflicts severe damage on the Trojans, who retreat before him. Zeus sends his messenger goddess, Iris, to tell Hektor that he should not engage the enemy himself until Agamémnon shall be wounded. Soon thereafter the Greek commander is in fact wounded and forced to return to the camp. Hektor leads a counterattack. Diomêdês is wounded, by an arrow from Paris, and then Odysseus is wounded too. Meneláos and the greater Aías come to Odysseus' aid. Nestor takes the wounded Greek physician Makháôn back to the camp as Aías slowly retreats before a swarm of Trojans. At this point almost all the important Greek leaders have been put out of action. Akhilleus, aboard his ship, exults over the Greeks' plight but sends his friend Patróklos to Nestor for information about the wounded man he is attending. Nestor reminds Patróklos that the latter's proper mission is to counsel Akhilleus and goes on to suggest that Akhilleus authorize Patróklos to lead the Myrmidons, Akhilleus' rested troops, against the Trojans. Patróklos feels sympathy for the desperate Greeks.*

from BOOK TWELVE: THE RAMPART BREACHED

The immortals still inactive, Hektor leads an assault on the palisaded fort that protects the Greek camp and ships. (The main defenders are now the two Aíases and the archer Teukros.) Poulýdamas, a Trojan, suggests to Hektor that the Trojan forces should breach the moat on foot rather than with chariots; Hektor accepts the advice. But a later suggestion by Poulýdamas, that the army should retreat in accordance with an apparent ill omen, is scornfully rejected by Hektor. Sarpêdôn—king of Lykia, son of Zeus, and ally of the Trojans—prepares to attack the wall.

But even so, and even now, the Trojans
led by great Hektor could not yet have breached
the wall and gate with massive bar, had not
Lord Zeus impelled Sarpêdôn, his own son, 330
against the Argives like a lion on cattle.
Circular was the shield he held before him,
hammered out of pure bronze: aye, the smith
had hammered it, and riveted the plates
to thick bull's hide on golden rods rigged out
to the full circumference. Now gripping this,
hefting a pair of spears, he joined the battle,
formidable as some hill-bred lion, ravenous

for meat after long abstinence. His valor
summons him to attempt homesteads and flocks— 340
and though he find herdsmen on hand with dogs
and spears to guard the sheep, he will not turn
without a fling at the stockade. One thing
or the other: a mighty leap and a fresh kill,
or he will fall at the spearmen's feet, brought down
by a javelin thrown hard.
So valor drove
Sarpêdôn to the wall to make a breakthrough.
Turning to Glaukos, Hippólokhos' son, he said:

"What is the point of being honored so
with precedence at table, choice of meat, 350
and brimming cups, at home in Lykia,
like gods at ease in everyone's regard?
And why have lands been granted you and me
on Xánthos bank: to each his own demesne,
with vines and fields of grain?
So that we two
at times like this in the Lykian front line
may face the blaze of battle and fight well,
that Lykian men-at-arms may say:
'They are no common men, our lords who rule
in Lykia. They eat fat lamb at feasts 360
and drink rare vintages, but the main thing is
their fighting power, when they lead in combat!'
Ah, cousin, could we but survive this war
to live forever deathless, without age,
I would not ever go again to battle,
nor would I send you there for honor's sake!
But now a thousand shapes of death surround us,
and no man can escape them, or be safe.
Let us attack—whether to give some fellow
glory or to win it from him." 370

BOOK XII. (continued). *After this speech to Glaukos, Sarpêdôn assaults the wall and is partially successful. It is Hektor, however, who finally breaks down one of the gates. His troops swarm into the fort after him, the Greeks fleeing toward the ships.*

BOOK XIII. *Confident that his earlier prohibition will keep the other gods from interfering in the war, Zeus relaxes his vigilance. The sea god, Poseidon, however, takes advantage of the opportunity and comes covertly to the Greeks' aid, inciting them to stiff resistance. Fierce battle continues, reflected in many scattered engagements. Zeus' plan, we learn, is to give the Trojans a limited victory in answer to Thetis' plea in Book I that Akhilleus be vindicated, but the god will not let the Greeks be utterly defeated. Idómeneus the king of Krete (Crete) performs valiant deeds on the Greek side. The Trojans falter, but Hektor rallies them. The Book ends as the Greeks prepare to resist still another Trojan offensive.*

BOOK XIV. *With Agamémnon, Diomêdês, and Odysseus all wounded, the Greeks are on the point of being routed. Agamémnon proposes to launch the ships, but Odysseus scorns the idea as cowardice and bad strategy. Diomêdês urges that the three return to the fight, at least to encourage their comrades. Poseidon continues to help the Greeks; to support him, Hêra decides to hoodwink Zeus by seducing him and then making him fall asleep—a project in which she wins the help of Aphrodítê by deception and of the god Sleep by bribes. With Zeus asleep, Poseidon is able to help the Greeks even more than before, and the tide of battle is turned. The greater Aías wounds Hektor with a large stone so that he has to be carried out of battle. The Trojans withdraw in panic.*

BOOK XV. *Zeus awakens, sees the Trojans being routed by the Greeks and Poseidon, and is enraged at the trick Hêra has played on him. He predicts the future course of the war: the Greeks will be driven back to the ships again, Akhilleus will send Patróklos into the fight, Hektor will kill Patróklos and then be killed by Akhilleus, the Greeks will take Troy. But for the time being Zeus will continue to humiliate the Greeks as part of his plan to vindicate Akhilleus. He sends Hêra back to Olympos with instructions to summon Iris and Apollo. When they come to him, he sends Iris to order Poseidon out of the action and Apollo to reinvigorate the wounded Hektor. Poseidon angrily and reluctantly obeys, and Apollo leads Hektor and the Trojans back to the ships, leveling the protective walls and making a causeway across the moat. The dismayed Patróklos, who since the end of Book XI has been attending one of the wounded in the Greeks' camp, hurries away to persuade Akhilleus to come to the rescue. Zeus' will is that the Trojans shall set fire to part of the Grecian fleet.*

BOOK SIXTEEN: A SHIP FIRED, A TIDE TURNED

That was the way the fighting went
for one seagoing ship. Meanwhile Patróklos
approached Akhilleus his commander, streaming
warm tears—like a shaded mountain spring
that makes a rockledge run with dusky water.
Akhilleus watched him come, and felt a pang for him.
Then the great prince and runner said:

"Patróklos,
why all the weeping? Like a small girlchild
who runs beside her mother and cries and cries
to be taken up, and catches at her gown, 10
and will not let her go, looking up in tears
until she has her wish: that's how you seem,
Patróklos, winking out your glimmering tears.
Have you something to tell the Myrmidons
or me? Some message you alone have heard
from Phthía? But they say that Aktor's son,
Menoitios, is living still, and Pêleus,
the son of Aíakos, lives on
amid his Myrmidons.[1] If one of these
were dead, we should be grieved.
Or is this weeping 20
over the Argives, seeing how they perish

[1] *Menoitios, Pêleus.* The fathers of, respectively, Patróklos and Akhilleus.

at the long ships by their own bloody fault!
Speak out now, don't conceal it, let us share it."

And groaning, Patróklos, you replied:

"Akhilleus, prince and greatest of Akhaians,
be forbearing. They are badly hurt.
All who were the best fighters are now lying
among the ships with spear or arrow wounds.
Diomêdês, Tydeus' rugged son, was shot;
Odysseus and Agamémnon, the great spearman, 30
have spear wounds; Eurýpylos[2]
took an arrow shot deep in his thigh.
Surgeons with medicines are attending them
to ease their wounds.
But you are a hard case,
Akhilleus! God forbid this rage you nurse
should master me. You and your fearsome pride!
What good will come of it to anyone, later,
unless you keep disaster from the Argives?
Have you no pity?
Pêleus, master of horse, was not your father, 40
Thetis was not your mother! Cold grey sea
and sea-cliffs bore you, making a mind so harsh.
If in your heart you fear some oracle,
some word of Zeus, told by your gentle mother,
then send me out at least, and send me quickly,[3]
give me a company of Myrmidons,
and I may be a beacon to Danáäns!
Lend me your gear to strap over my shoulders;
Trojans then may take me for yourself
and break off battle, giving our worn-out men 50
a chance to breathe. Respites are brief in war.
We fresh troops with one battlecry might easily
push their tired men back on the town,
away from ships and huts."

So he petitioned,
witless as a child that what he begged for
was his own death, hard death and doom.
Akhilleus
out of his deep anger made reply:

"Hard words, dear prince. There is no oracle
I know of that I must respect, no word

[2]A wounded Greek warrior whom Patróklos has been tending since the action of Book XI.
[3]This suggestion, like certain other points in Patróklos' speech, was made first by Nestor in Book XI.

from Zeus reported by my gentle mother.[4] 60
Only this bitterness eats at my heart
when one man would deprive and shame his equal,
taking back his prize by abuse of power.
The girl whom the Akhaians chose for me
I won by my own spear. A town with walls
I stormed and sacked for her. Then Agamémnon
stole her back, out of my hands, as though
I were some vagabond held cheap.
All that
we can let pass as being over and done with;
I could not rage forever. And yet, by heaven, I swore 70
I would not rest from anger till the cries
and clangor of battle reached my very ships!
But you, now, you can strap my famous gear
on your own shoulders, and then take command
of Myrmidons on edge and ripe for combat,
now that like a dark stormcloud the Trojans
have poured round the first ships, and Argive troops
have almost no room for maneuver left,
with nothing to their rear but sea. The whole
townful of Trojans joins in, sure of winning, 80
because they cannot see my helmet's brow
aflash in range of them. They'd fill the gullies
with dead men soon, in flight up through the plain,
if Agamémnon were on good terms with me.
As things are, they've outflanked the camp. A mercy
for them that in the hands of Diomêdês
no great spear goes berserk, warding death
from the Danáäns! Not yet have I heard
the voice of Agamémnon, either, shouting
out of his hateful skull. The shout of Hektor, 90
the killer, calling Trojans, makes a roar
like breaking surf, and with long answering cries
they hold the whole plain where they drove the Akhaians.
Even so, defend the ships, Patróklos.
Attack the enemy in force, or they
will set the ships ablaze with whirling fire
and rob Akhaians of their dear return.
Now carry out the purpose I confide,
so that you'll win great honor for me, and glory
among Danáäns; then they'll send me back 100
my lovely girl, with bright new gifts as well.
Once you expel the enemy from the ships,
rejoin me here. If Hêra's lord,
the lord of thunder, grants you the day's honor,

[4]These words seem to contradict what Akhilleus has said in Book IX about his "two possible destinies"; possibly the excited Akhilleus means something like "That is not the point right now."

covet no further combat far from me
with Trojan soldiers. That way you'd deny me
recompense of honor. You must not,
for joy of battle, joy of killing Trojans,
carry the fight to Ilion![5] Some power
out of Olympos, one of the immortal gods, 110
might intervene for them. The Lord Apollo
loves the Trojans. Turn back, then, as soon
as you restore the safety of the ships,
and let the rest contend, out on the plain.
Ah, Father Zeus, Athêna, and Apollo!
If not one Trojan of them all
should get away from death, and not one Argive
save ourselves were spared, we two alone
could pull down Troy's old coronet of towers!"

These were the speeches they exchanged. Now Aías 120
could no longer hold:[6] he was dislodged
by spear-throws, beaten by the mind of Zeus
and Trojan shots. His shining helm rang out
around his temples dangerously with hits
as his helmplates were struck and struck again;
he felt his shoulder galled on the left side
hugging the glittering shield—and yet they could not
shake it, putting all their weight in throws.
In painful gasps his breath came, sweat ran down
in rivers off his body everywhere; 130
no rest for him, but trouble upon trouble.

Now tell me, Muses, dwellers on Olympos,
how fire first fell on the Akhaian ships!
Hektor moved in to slash with his long blade
at Aías' ashwood shaft, and near the spearhead
lopped it off. Then Telamônian Aías
wielded a pointless shaft, while far away
the flying bronze head rang upon the ground,
and Aías shivered knowing in his heart
the work of gods: how Zeus, the lord of thunder, 140
cut off his war-craft in that fight, and willed
victory to the Trojans. He gave way
before their missiles as they rushed in throwing
untiring fire into the ship. It caught
at once, a-gush with flame, and fire lapped
about the stern.
Akhilleus smote his thighs
and said to Patróklos:

[5] To the city of Troy itself.
[6] Aías is aboard one of the beached ships, using a long spear to ward off attackers.

"Now go into action,
prince and horseman! I see roaring fire
burst at the ships. Action, or they'll destroy them,
leaving no means of getting home. Be quick, 150
strap on my gear, while I alert the troops!"

Patróklos now put on the flashing bronze.
Greaves were the first thing, beautifully fitted
to calf and shin with silver ankle chains,
and next he buckled round his ribs the cuirass,
blazoned with stars, of swift Aiákidês;[7]
then slung the silver-studded blade of bronze
about his shoulders, and the vast solid shield;
then on his noble head he placed the helm,
its plume of terror nodding high above, 160
and took two burly spears with his own handgrip.
He did not take the great spear of Akhilleus,
weighty, long, and tough. No other Akhaian
had the strength to wield it, only Akhilleus.
It was a Pêlian ash, cut on the crest
of Pêlion, given to Akhilleus' father
by Kheirôn[8] to deal death to soldiery.
He then ordered his war-team put in harness
by Automédôn,[9] whom he most admired
after Prince Akhilleus, breaker of men, 170
for waiting steadfast at his call in battle.
Automédôn yoked the fast horses for him—
Xánthos and Balíos, racers in wind.
The stormgust Podargê, who once had grazed
green meadowland by the Ocean stream, conceived
and bore them to the west wind, Zephyros.
In the side-traces Pêdasos, a thoroughbred,
was added to the team; Akhilleus took him
when he destroyed the city of Eëtíôn.
Mortal, he ran beside immortal horses. 180
Akhilleus put the Myrmidons in arms,
the whole detachment near the huts. Like wolves,
carnivorous and fierce and tireless,
who rend a great stag on a mountainside
and feed on him, their jaws reddened with blood,
loping in a pack to drink springwater,
lapping the dark rim up with slender tongues,
their chops a-drip with fresh blood, their hearts
unshaken ever, and their bellies glutted:
such were the Myrmidons and their officers, 190

[7]Akhilleus' father, Pêleus (son of Aíakos).
[8]A centaur who had tutored Akhilleus; also spelled *Chiron*.
[9]When Patróklos assumes command, his normal post as charioteer is assumed by Automédôn, the third-ranking among Akhilleus' Myrmidons.

running to form up round Akhilleus' brave
companion-in-arms.
And like the god of war
among them was Akhilleus: he stood tall
and sped the chariots and shieldmen onward.

Fifty ships there were that Lord Akhilleus,
favored of heaven, led to Troy. In each
were fifty soldiers, shipmates at the rowlocks.
Five he entrusted with command and made
lieutenants, while he ruled them all as king.
One company was headed by Menésthios 200
in his glittering breastplate, son of Spérkheios,
a river fed by heaven. Pêleus' daughter,
beautiful Polydôrê, had conceived him
lying with Spérkheios, untiring stream,
a woman with a god; but the world thought
she bore her child to Periêrês' son,
Bôros, who married her in the eyes of men
and offered countless bridal gifts. A second
company was commanded by Eudôros,
whose mother was unmarried: Polymêlê, 210
Phylas' daughter, a beautiful dancer
with whom the strong god Hermês fell in love,
seeing her among singing girls who moved
in measure for the lady of belling hounds,
Artemis of the golden shaft. And Hermês,
pure Deliverer, ascending soon
to an upper room, lay secretly with her
who was to bear his brilliant son, Eudôros,
a first-rate man at running and in war.
When Eileithyía,[10] sending pangs of labor, 220
brought him forth to see the sun-rays, then
strong-minded Ekheklêos, Aktor's son,
led the girl home with countless bridal gifts;
but Phylas in his age brought up the boy
with all kind care, as though he were a son.
Company three was led by Peísandros
Maimálidês, the best man with a spear,
of all Myrmidons after Patróklos.
Company four the old man, master of horse,
Phoinix, commanded. Alkimédôn, son 230
of Laërkês, commanded company five.
When all were mustered under their officers,
Akhilleus had strict orders to impart:

"Myrmidons, let not one man forget
how menacing you were against the Trojans

[10]Goddess of childbirth.

during my anger and seclusion: how
each one reproached me, saying, 'Ironhearted
son of Pêleus, now we see: your mother
brought you up on rage, merciless man,
the way you keep your men confined to camp 240
against their will! We might as well sail home
in our seagoing ships, now this infernal
anger has come over you!' That way
you often talked, in groups around our fires.
Now the great task of battle is at hand
that you were longing for! Now every soldier
keep a fighting heart and face the Trojans!"

He stirred and braced their spirit; every rank
fell in more sharply when it heard its king.
As when a builder fitting stone on stone 250
lays well a high house wall to buffet back
the might of winds, just so
they fitted helms and studded shields together:
shield-rim on shield-rim, helmet on helmet, men
all pressed on one another, horsehair plumes
brushed on the bright crests as the soldiers nodded,
densely packed as they were.
Before them all
two captains stood in gear of war: Patróklos
and Automédôn, of one mind, resolved
to open combat in the lead.
Akhilleus 260
went to his hut. He lifted up the lid
of a seachest, all intricately wrought,
that Thetis of the silver feet had stowed
aboard his ship for him to take to Ilion,
filled to the brim with shirts, wind-breaking cloaks,
and fleecy rugs. His hammered cup was there,
from which no other man drank the bright wine,
and he made offering to no god but Zeus.
Lifting it from the chest, he purified it
first with brimstone,[11] washed it with clear water, 270
and washed his hands, then dipped it full of wine.
Now standing in the forecourt, looking up
toward heaven, he prayed and poured his offering out,
and Zeus who plays in thunder heard his prayer:

"Zeus of Dôdôna,[12] god of Pelasgians,
O god whose home lies far! Ruler of wintry
harsh Dôdôna! Your interpreters,

[11]Sulfur.

[12]A shrine of Zeus near Akhilleus' homeland, supervised by the Selloi, primitive people who interpreted the god's oracles.

the Selloi, live with feet like roots, unwashed,
and sleep on the hard ground. My lord, you heard me
praying before this, and honored me 280
by punishing the Akhaian army. Now,
again, accomplish what I most desire.
I shall stay on the beach, behind the ships,
but send my dear friend with a mass of soldiers,
Myrmidons, into combat. Let your glory,
Zeus who views the wide world, go beside him.
Sir, exalt his heart,
so Hektor too may see whether my friend
can only fight when I am in the field,
or whether singlehanded he can scatter them 290
before his fury! When he has thrown back
their shouting onslaught from the ships, then let him
return unhurt to the shipways and to me,
his gear intact, with all his fighting men."

That was his prayer, and Zeus who views the wide world
heard him. Part he granted, part denied:
he let Patróklos push the heavy fighting
back from the ships, but would not let him come
unscathed from battle.
Now, after Akhilleus
had made his prayer and offering to Zeus, 300
he entered his hut again, restored the cup
to his seachest, and took his place outside—
desiring still to watch the savage combat
of Trojans and Akhaians. Brave Patróklos'
men moved forward with high hearts until
they charged the Trojans—Myrmidons in waves,
like hornets that small boys, as boys will do,
the idiots, poke up with constant teasing
in their daub chambers on the road,
to give everyone trouble. If some traveler 310
who passes unaware should then excite them,
all the swarm comes raging out
to defend their young. So hot, so angrily
the Myrmidons came pouring from the ships
in a quenchless din of shouting. And Patróklos
cried above them all:

"O Myrmidons,
brothers-in-arms of Pêleus' son, Akhilleus,
fight like men, dear friends, remember courage,
let us win honor for the son of Pêleus!
He is the greatest captain on the beach, 320
his officers and soldiers are the bravest!
Let King Agamémnon learn his folly
in holding cheap the best of the Akhaians!"

Shouting so, he stirred their hearts. They fell
as one man on the Trojans, and the ships
around them echoed the onrush and the cries.
On seeing Menoitios' powerful son, and with him
Automédôn, aflash with brazen gear,
the Trojan ranks broke, and they caught their breath,
imagining that Akhilleus the swift fighter 330
had put aside his wrath for friendship's sake.
Now each man kept an eye out for retreat
from sudden death. Patróklos drove ahead
against their center with his shining spear,
into the huddling mass, around the stern
of Prôtesílaos' burning ship. He hit
Pyraikhmês, who had led the Paiônês
from Amydôn, from Áxios' wide river—
hit him in the right shoulder. Backward in dust
he tumbled groaning, and his men at-arms, 340
the Paiônês, fell back around him. Dealing
death to a chief and champion, Patróklos
drove them in confusion from the ship,
and doused the tigerish fire. The hull half-burnt
lay smoking on the shipway. Now the Trojans
wlth a great outcry streamed away; Danáäns
poured along the curved ships, and the din
of war kept on. As when the lightning master,
Zeus, removes a dense cloud from the peak
of some great mountain, and the lookout points 350
and spurs and clearings are distinctly seen
as though pure space had broken through from heaven:
so when the dangerous fire had been repelled
Danáäns took breath for a space. The battle
had not ended, though; not yet were Trojans
put to rout by the Akhaian charge
or out of range of the black ships. They withdrew
but by regrouping tried to make a stand.

In broken
ranks the captains sought and killed each other,
Menoitios' son making the first kill. 360
As Arêilykos wheeled around to fight,
he caught him with his spearhead in the hip,
and drove the bronze through, shattering the bone.
He sprawled face downward on the ground.

Now veteran
Meneláos thrusting past the shield
of Thoas to the bare chest brought him down.[13]
Rushed by Ámphiklos, the alert Mégês
got his thrust in first, hitting his thigh

[13] The victors in lines 365–409 are all Greeks.

where a man's muscles bunch. Around the spearhead
tendons were split, and darkness veiled his eyes. 370
Nestor's sons were in action: Antílokhos
with his good spear brought down Atýmnios,
laying open his flank; he fell headfirst.
Now Maris moved in, raging for his brother,
lunging over the dead man with his spear,
but Thrasymêdês had already lunged
and did not miss, but smashed his shoulder squarely,
tearing his upper arm out of the socket,
severing muscles, breaking through the bone.
He thudded down and darkness veiled his eyes. 380
So these two, overcome by the two brothers,[14]
dropped to the underworld of Érebos.
They were Sarpêdôn's true brothers-in-arms
and sons of Amisôdaros, who reared
the fierce Khimaira,[15] nightmare to many men.
Aías,[16] Oïleus' son, drove at Kleóboulos
and took him alive, encumbered in the press,
but killed him on the spot with a sword stroke
across the nape—the whole blade running hot
with blood, as welling death and his harsh destiny 390
possessed him. Now Pênéleos
and Lykôn clashed; as both had cast and missed
and lunged and missed with spears,
they fought again with swords. The stroke of Lykôn
came down on the other's helmet ridge
but his blade broke at the hilt. Pênéleos
thrust at his neck below the ear and drove
the blade clear in and through; his head toppled,
held only by skin, and his knees gave way.
Meríonês on the run overtook Akámas 400
mounting behind his horses and hit his shoulder,
knocking him from the car. Mist swathed his eyes.
Idómeneus thrust hard at Erýmas' mouth
with his hard bronze. The spearhead passed on through
beneath his brain and split the white brain-pan.
His teeth were dashed out, blood filled both his eyes,
and from his mouth and nostrils as he gaped
he spurted blood. Death's cloud enveloped him.
There each Danäan captain killed his man.
As ravenous wolves come down on lambs and kids 410
astray from some flock that in hilly country
splits in two by a shepherd's negligence,
and quickly wolves bear off the defenseless things,

[14]Antílokhos and Thrasymêdes, the sons of Nestor.
[15]In fable, the Khimaira (or Chimera) was a monster having a lion's head, a goat's body, and a dragon's tail.
[16]This is the "lesser" Aías.

so when Danáäns fell on Trojans, shrieking
flight was all they thought of, not of combat.
Aías the Tall[17] kept after bronze-helmed Hektor,
casting his lance, but Hektor, skilled in war,
would fit his shoulders under the bull's-hide shield,
and watch for whizzing arrows, thudding spears.
Aye, though he knew the tide of battle turned, 420
he kept his discipline and saved his friends.
As when Lord Zeus would hang the sky with storm,
a cloud may enter heaven from Olympos
out of crystalline space, so terror and cries
increased about the shipways. In disorder
men withdrew. Then Hektor's chariot team
cantering bore him off with all his gear,
leaving the Trojans whom the moat confined;
and many chariot horses in that ditch,
breaking their poles off at the tip, abandoned 430
war-cars and masters. Hard on their heels
Patróklos kept on calling all Danáäns
onward with slaughter in his heart. The Trojans,
yelling and clattering, filled all the ways,
their companies cut in pieces. High in air
a blast of wind swept on, under the clouds,
as chariot horses raced back toward the town
away from the encampment. And Patróklos
rode shouting where he saw the enemy mass
in uproar: men fell from their chariots 440
under the wheels and cars jounced over them,
and running horses leapt over the ditch—
immortal horses, whom the gods gave Pêleus,
galloping as their mettle called them onward
after Hektor, target of Patróklos.
But Hektor's battle-team bore him away.

As under a great storm black earth is drenched
on an autumn day, when Zeus pours down the rain
in scudding gusts to punish men, annoyed
because they will enforce their crooked judgments 450
and banish justice from the market place,
thoughtless of the gods' vengeance; all their streams
run high and full, and torrents cut their way
down dry declivities into the swollen sea
with a hoarse clamor, headlong out of hills,
while cultivated fields erode away—
such was the gasping flight of the Trojan horses.

[17] The "greater" Aías.

When he had cut their first wave off, Patróklos
forced it back again upon the ships
as the men fought toward the city. In between 460
the ships and river and the parapet[18]
he swept among them killing, taking toll
for many dead Akhaians. First,
thrusting past Prónoös' shield, he hit him
on the bare chest, and made him crumple: down
he tumbled with a crash. Then he rushed Thestôr,
Enop's son, who sat all doubled up
in a polished war-car, shocked out of his wits,
the reins flown from his hands—and the Akhaian
got home his thrust on the right jawbone, driving 470
through his teeth. He hooked him by the spearhead
over the chariot rail, as a fisherman
on a point of rock will hook a splendid fish
with line and dazzling bronze out of the ocean:
so from his chariot on the shining spear
he hooked him gaping and face downward threw him,
life going out of him as he fell.
Patróklos
now met Erýlaos' rush and hit him square
mid-skull with a big stone. Within his helm
the skull was cleft asunder, and down he went 480
headfirst to earth; heartbreaking death engulfed him.
Next Erýmas, Amphóteros, Epaltês,
Tlêpolemos Damastoridês, Ekhíos,
Pyris, Ipheus, Euíppos, Polymêlos,
all in quick succession he brought down
to the once peaceful pastureland.
Sarpêdôn,
seeing his brothers-in-arms in their unbelted
battle jackets downed at Patróklos' hands,
called in bitterness to the Lykians:[19]

"Shame, O Lykians, where are you running? 490
Now you show your speed!
I'll take on this one,
and learn what man he is that has the power
to do such havoc as he has done among us,
cutting down so many, and such good men."

He vaulted from his car with all his gear,
and on his side Patróklos, when he saw him,
leapt from his car. Like two great birds of prey
with hooked talons and angled beaks, who screech
and clash on a high ridge of rock, these two

[18] The wall of Troy. The river Skamánder, also called Xánthos, flows by the plain.
[19] Lykia, of which Sarpêdôn is king, is a region about two hundred miles southeast of Troy.

rushed one another with hoarse cries. But Zeus, 500
the son of crooked-minded Krónos, watched,
and pitied them. He said to Hêra:

"Ai!
Sorrow for me, that in the scheme of things
the dearest of men to me must lie in dust
before the son of Menoitios, Patróklos.
My heart goes two ways as I ponder this:
shall I catch up Sarpêdôn
out of the mortal fight with all its woe
and put him down alive in Lykia,
in that rich land? Or shall I make him fall 510
beneath Patróklos' hard-thrown spear?"

Then Hêra
of the wide eyes answered him:

"O fearsome power,
my Lord Zeus, what a curious thing to say.
A man who is born to die, long destined for it,
would you set free from that unspeakable end?
Do so; but not all of us will praise you.
And this, too, I may tell you: ponder this:
should you dispatch Sarpêdôn home alive,
anticipate some other god's desire
to pluck a man he loves out of the battle. 520
Many who fight around the town of Priam
sprang from immortals; you'll infuriate these.
No, dear to you though he is, and though you mourn him,
let him fall, even so, in the rough battle,
killed by the son of Menoitios, Patróklos.
Afterward, when his soul is gone, his lifetime
ended, Death and sweetest Sleep can bear him
homeward to the broad domain of Lykia.
There friends and kin may give him funeral
with tomb and stone, the trophies of the dead." 530

To this the father of gods and men agreed,
but showered bloody drops upon the earth
for the dear son Patróklos would destroy
in fertile Ilion, far from his home.
When the two men had come in range, Patróklos
turned like lightning against Thrasydêmos,
a tough man ever at Sarpêdôn's side,
and gave him a death-wound in the underbelly.
Sarpêdôn's counterthrust went wide, but hit
the trace horse, Pêdasos, in the right shoulder.[20] 540
Screaming harshly, panting his life away,

[20] Pêdasos is the third, auxiliary horse harnessed with Akhilleus' two immortal horses.

he crashed and whinnied in the dust; the spirit
left him with a wingbeat. The team shied
and strained apart with a great creak of the yoke
as reins were tangled over the dead weight
of their outrider fallen. Automédôn,
the good soldier, found a way to end it:
pulling his long blade from his hip
he jumped in fast and cut the trace horse free.
The team then ranged themselves beside the pole, 550
drawing the reins taut, and once more,
devoured by fighting madness, the two men clashed.
Sarpêdôn missed again. He drove his spearhead
over the left shoulder of Patróklos,
not even grazing him. Patróklos then
made his last throw, and the weapon left his hand
with flawless aim. He hit his enemy
just where the muscles of the diaphragm
encased his throbbing heart. Sarpêdôn fell
the way an oak or poplar or tall pine 560
goes down, when shipwrights in the wooded hills
with whetted axes chop it down for timber.
So, full length, before his war-car lay
Sarpêdôn raging, clutching the bloody dust.
Imagine a greathearted sultry bull
a lion kills amid a shambling herd:
with choking groans he dies under the claws.
So, mortally wounded by Patróklos
the chief of Lykian shieldsmen lay in agony
and called his friend by name:

"Glaukos, old man, 570
old war-dog, now's the time to be a spearman!
Put your heart in combat! Let grim war
be all your longing! Quickly, if you can,
arouse the Lykian captains, round them up
to fight over Sarpêdôn. You, too, fight
to keep my body, else in later days
this day will be your shame.[21] You'll hang your head
all your life long, if these Akhaians take
my armor here, where I have gone down fighting
before the ships. Hold hard; cheer on the troops!" 580

The end of life came on him as he spoke,
closing his eyes and nostrils. And Patróklos
with one foot on his chest drew from his belly
spearhead and spear; the diaphragm came out,
so he extracted life and blade together.

[21] Proper funeral rites were essential for the honor of the dead man and for his well-being after death—an important theme in the poem.

Myrmidons clung to the panting Lykian horses,
rearing to turn the car left by their lords.

But bitter anguish at Sarpêdôn's voice
had come to Glaukos, and his heart despaired
because he had not helped his friend. He gripped 590
his own right arm and squeezed it, being numb
where Teukros with a bowshot from the rampart
had hit him while he fought for his own men,[22]
and he spoke out in prayer to Lord Apollo:

"Hear me, O lord, somewhere in Lykian farmland
or else in Troy: for you have power to listen
the whole world round to a man hard pressed as I!
I have my sore wound, all my length of arm
a-throb with lancing pain; the flow of blood
cannot be stanched; my shoulder's heavy with it. 600
I cannot hold my spear right or do battle,
cannot attack them. Here's a great man destroyed,
Sarpêdôn, son of Zeus. Zeus let his own son
die undefended. O my lord, heal this wound,
lull me my pains, put vigor in me! Let me
shout to my Lykians, move them into combat!
Let me give battle for the dead man here!"

This way he prayed, and Phoibos Apollo heard him,
cutting his pain and making the dark blood dry
on his deep wound, then filled his heart with valor. 610
Glaukos felt the change, and knew with joy
how swiftly the great god had heard his prayer.
First he appealed to the Lykian captains, going
right and left, to defend Sarpêdôn's body,
then on the run he followed other Trojans,
Poulýdamas, Pánthoös' son, Agênor,
and caught up with Aineías and with Hektor,
shoulder to shoulder, urgently appealing:

"Hektor, you've put your allies out of mind,
those men who give their lives here for your sake 620
so distant from their friends and lands: you will not
come to their aid! Sarpêdôn lies there dead,
commander of the Lykians, who kept
his country safe by his firm hand, in justice!
Arês in bronze has brought him down: the spear
belonged to Patróklos. Come, stand with me, friends,
and count it shame if they strip off his gear
or bring dishonor on his body—these

[22] Teukros had wounded Glaukos in Book XII.

fresh Myrmidons enraged for the Danáäns
cut down at the shipways by our spears!" 630

At this, grief and remorse possessed the Trojans,
grief not to be borne, because Sarpêdôn
had been a bastion of the town of Troy,
foreigner though he was. A host came with him,
but he had fought most gallantly of all.
They made straight for the Danáäns, and Hektor
led them, hot with anger for Sarpêdôn.
Patróklos in his savagery cheered on
the Akhaians, first the two named Aías, both
already aflame for war:

"Aías and Aías, 640
let it be sweet to you to stand and fight!
You always do; be lionhearted, now.
The man who crossed the rampart of Akhaians
first of all lies dead: Sarpêdôn.[23] May we
take him, dishonor him, and strip his arms,
and hurl any friend who would defend him
into the dust with our hard bronze!"

At this they burned to throw the Trojans back.
And both sides reinforced their battle lines,
Trojans and Lykians, Myrmidons and Akhaians, 650
moving up to fight around the dead
with fierce cries and clanging of men's armor.
Zeus unfurled a deathly gloom of night
over the combat, making battle toil
about his dear son's body a fearsome thing.
At first, the Trojans drove back the Akhaians,
fiery-eyed as they were; one Myrmidon,
and not the least, was killed: noble Epeigeus,
a son of Agaklês. In Boudeion,
a flourishing town, he ruled before the war. 660
but slew a kinsman. So he came as suppliant
to Pêleus and to Thetis, who enlisted him
along with Lord Akhilleus, breaker of men,
to make war in the wild-horse country of Ilion
against the Trojans. Even as he touched the dead man,
Hektor hit him square upon the crest
with a great stone: his skull split in the helmet,
and he fell prone upon the corpse. Death's cloud
poured round him, heart-corroding. Grief and pain
for this friend dying came to Lord Patróklos, 670
who pounced through spear-play like a diving hawk

[23]The reference is to Book XII; it was actually Hektor who first broke through the defensive wall around the ships, though Sarpêdôn had threatened and damaged it.

that puts jackdaws and starlings wildly to flight:
straight through Lykians, through Trojans, too,
you drove, Patróklos, master of horse,
in fury for your friend. Sthenélaos
the son of Ithaiménês was the victim:
Patróklos with a great stone broke his nape-cord.

Backward the line bent, Hektor too gave way,
as far as a hunting spear may hurtle, thrown
by a man in practice or in competition 680
or matched with deadly foes in war. So far
the Trojans ebbed, as the Akhaians drove them.
Glaukos, commander of Lykians, turned first,
to bring down valorous Báthyklês, the son
of Khalkôn, one who had his home in Hellas,
fortunate and rich among the Myrmidons.
Whirling as this man caught him, Glaukos hit him
full in the breastbone with his spear, and down
he thudded on his face. The Akhaians grieved
to see their champion fallen, but great joy 690
came to the Trojans, and they thronged about him.
Not that Akhaians now forgot their courage,
no, for their momentum carried them on.
Meríonês brought down a Trojan soldier,
Laógonos, Onêtor's rugged son,
a priest of Zeus on Ida, honored there
as gods are. Gashed now under jaw and ear
his life ran out, and hateful darkness took him.
Then at Meríonês Aineías cast
his bronze-shod spear, thinking to reach his body 700
under the shield as he came on. But he
looked out for it and swerved, slipping the spear-throw,
bowing forward, so the long shaft stuck
in earth behind him and the butt quivered;
the god Arês deprived it of its power.
Aineías raged and sneered:

"Meríonês,
fast dodger that you are, if I had hit you
my spearhead would have stopped your dance for good!"

Meríonês, good spearman, answered him:

"For all your power, Aineías, you could hardly 710
quench the fighting spirit of every man
defending himself against you. You are made
of mortal stuff like me. I, too, can say,
if I could hit you square, then tough and sure
as you may be, you would concede the game
and give your soul to the lord of nightmare, Death."

Patróklos said to him sharply:

"Meríonês,
you have your skill, why make a speech about it?
No, old friend, rough words will make no Trojans
back away from the body. Many a one 720
will be embraced by earth before they do.
War is the use of arms, words are for council.
More talk's pointless now; we need more fighting!"

He pushed on, and godlike Meríonês
fought at his side. Think of the sound of strokes
woodcutters make in mountain glens, the echoes
ringing for listeners far away: just so
the battering din of these in combat rose
from earth where the living go their ways—the clang
of bronze, hard blows on leather, on bull's hide, 730
as longsword blades and spearheads met their marks.
And an observer could not by now have seen
the Prince Sarpêdôn, since from head to foot
he lay enwrapped in weapons, dust, and blood.
Men kept crowding around the corpse. Like flies
that swarm and drone in farmyards round the milkpails
on spring days, when the pails are splashed with milk:
just so they thronged around the corpse. And Zeus
would never turn his shining eyes away
from this mêlée, but watched them all and pondered 740
long over the slaughter of Patróklos—
whether in that place, on Sarpêdôn's body,
Hektor should kill the man and take his gear,
or whether he, Zeus, should augment the moil[24]
of battle for still other men. He weighed it
and thought this best: that for a while Akhilleus'
shining brother-in-arms should drive his foes
and Hektor in the bronze helm toward the city,
taking the lives of many. First of all
he weakened Hektor, made him mount his car 750
and turn away, retreating, crying out
to others to retreat: for he perceived
the dipping scales of Zeus.[25] At this the Lykians
themselves could not stand fast, but all turned back,
once they had seen their king struck to the heart,
lying amid swales of dead—for many
fell to earth beside him when Lord Zeus
had drawn the savage battle line. So now

[24] Turmoil.
[25] Zeus uses a balance scale to weigh alternative results of a conflict. The loser's side of the scale tips down, the winner's up.

Akhaians lifted from Sarpêdôn's shoulders
gleaming arms of bronze, and these Patróklos 760
gave to his soldiers to be carried back
to the decked ships. At this point, to Apollo
Zeus who gathers cloud said:

"Come, dear Phoibos,
wipe away the blood mantling Sarpêdôn;
take him up, out of the play of spears,
a long way off, and wash him in the river,
anoint him with ambrosia, put ambrosial
clothing on him. Then have him conveyed
by those escorting spirits quick as wind,
sweet Sleep and Death, who are twin brothers. These 770
will set him down in the rich broad land of Lykia,
and there his kin and friends may bury him
with tomb and stone, the trophies of the dead."

Attentive to his father, Lord Apollo
went down the foothills of Ida[26] to the field
and lifted Prince Sarpêdôn clear of it.
He bore him far and bathed him in the river,
scented him with ambrosia, put ambrosial
clothing on him, then had him conveyed
by those escorting spirits quick as wind, 780
sweet Sleep and Death, who are twin brothers. These
returned him to the rich broad land of Lykia.

Patróklos, calling to his team, commanding
Automédôn, rode on after the Trojans
and Lykians—all this to his undoing,
the blunderer. By keeping Akhilleus' mandate,
he might have fled black fate and cruel death.
But overpowering is the mind of Zeus
forever, matched with man's. He turns in fright
the powerful man and robs him of his victory 790
easily, though he drove him on himself.
So now he stirred Patróklos' heart to fury.

Whom first, whom later did you kill in battle,
Patróklos, when the gods were calling deathward?
First it was Adrêstos, Autônoös,
and Ekheklos; then Périmos Megadês,
Eristôr, Melánippos; afterward,
Elasos, Moulios, Pylartês. These
he cut down, while the rest looked to their flight.
Troy of the towering gates was on the verge 800
of being taken by the Akhaians, under

[26]A mountain near Troy from whieh Zeus often observes the war.

Patróklos' drive: he raced with blooded spear
ahead and around it. On the massive tower
Phoibos Apollo stood as Troy's defender,
deadly toward him. Now three times Patróklos
assaulted the high wall at the tower joint,
and three times Lord Apollo threw him back
with counterblows of his immortal hands
against the resplendent shield. The Akhaian then
a fourth time flung himself against the wall, 810
more than human in fury. But Apollo
thundered:

"Back, Patróklos, lordly man!
Destiny will not let this fortress town
of Trojans fall to you! Not to Akhilleus,
either, greater far though he is in war!"[27]

Patróklos now retired, a long way off
and out of range of Lord Apollo's anger.
Hektor had held his team at the Skaian Gates,
being of two minds: should he re-engage,
or call his troops to shelter behind the wall? 820
While he debated this, Phoibos Apollo
stood at his shoulder in a strong man's guise:
Ásïos, his maternal uncle, brother
of Hékabê and son of Dymas, dweller
in Phrygia on Sangaríos river.
Taking his semblance now, Apollo said:

"Why break off battle, Hektor? You need not.
Were I superior to you in the measure
that I am now inferior, you'd suffer
from turning back so wretchedly from battle. 830
Action! Lash your team against Patróklos,
and see if you can take him. May Apollo
grant you the glory!"

And at this, once more
he joined the mêlée, entering it as a god.
Hektor in splendor called Kebríonês
to whip the horses toward the fight. Apollo,
disappearing into the ranks, aroused
confusion in the Argives, but on Hektor
and on the Trojans he conferred his glory.
Letting the rest go, Hektor drove his team 840
straight at Patróklos; and Patróklos faced him
vaulting from his war-car, with his spear
gripped in his left hand; in his right

[27]Akhilleus will be slain before the city is finally taken.

he held enfolded a sparkling jagged stone.
Not for long in awe of the other man,
he aimed and braced himself and threw the stone
and scored a direct hit on Hektor's driver,
Kebríonês, a bastard son of Priam,
smashing his forehead with the jagged stone.
Both brows were hit at once, the frontal bone 850
gave way, and both his eyes burst from their sockets
dropping into the dust before his feet,
as like a diver from the handsome car
he plummeted, and life ebbed from his bones.
You jeered at him then, master of horse, Patróklos:

"God, what a nimble fellow, somersaulting!
If he were out at sea in the fishing grounds
this man could feed a crew, diving for oysters,
going overboard even in rough water,
the way he took that earth-dive from his car. 860
The Trojans have their acrobats, I see."

With this, he went for the dead man with a spring
like a lion, one that has taken a chest wound
while ravaging a cattle pen—his valor
his undoing. So you sprang, Patróklos,
on Kebríonês. Then Hektor, too, leapt down
out of his chariot, and the two men fought
over the body like two mountain lions
over the carcass of a buck, both famished,
both in pride of combat. So these two 870
fought now for Kebríonês, two champions,
Patróklos son of Menoitios, and Hektor,
hurling their bronze to tear each other's flesh.
Hektor caught hold of the dead man's head and held,
while his antagonist clung to a single foot,
as Trojans and Danáäns pressed the fight.
As south wind and the southeast wind, contending
in mountain groves, make all the forest thrash,
beech trees and ash trees and the slender cornel
swaying their pointed boughs toward one another 880
in roaring wind, and snapping branches crack:
so Trojans and Akhaians made a din
as lunging they destroyed each other. Neither
considered ruinous flight. Many sharp spears
and arrows trued by feathers from the strings
were fixed in flesh around Kebríonês,
and boulders crashed on shields, as they fought on
around him. And a dustcloud wrought
by a whirlwind hid the greatness of him slain,
minding no more the mastery of horses. 890
Until the sun stood at high noon in heaven

spears bit on both sides, and the soldiers fell;
but when the sun passed toward unyoking time,
the Akhaians outfought destiny to prevail.
Now they dragged off gallant Kebríonês
out of range, away from the shouting Trojans,
to strip his shoulders of his gear. And fierce
Patróklos hurled himself upon the Trojans
in onslaughts fast as Arês, three times, wild
yells in his throat. Each time he killed nine men. 900
But on the fourth demonic foray, then
the end of life loomed up for you, Patróklos.
Into the combat dangerous Phoibos came
against him, but Patróklos could not see
the god, enwrapped in cloud as he came near.
He stood behind and struck with open hand
the man's back and broad shoulders, and the eyes
of the fighting man were dizzied by the blow.
Then Phoibos sent the captain's helmet rolling
under the horses' hooves, making the ridge 910
ring out, and dirtying all the horsehair plume
with blood and dust. Never in time before
had this plumed helmet been befouled with dust,
the helmet that had kept a hero's brow
unmarred, shielding Akhilleus' head. Now Zeus
bestowed it upon Hektor, let him wear it,
though his destruction waited. For Patróklos
felt his great spearshaft shattered in his hands,
long, tough, well-shod, and seasoned though it was;
his shield and strap fell to the ground; the Lord 920
Apollo, son of Zeus, broke off his cuirass.
Shock ran through him, and his good legs failed,
so that he stood agape. Then from behind
at close quarters, between the shoulder blades,
a Dardan fighter speared him: Pánthoös' son,
Euphórbos, the best Trojan of his age
at handling spears, in horsemanship and running:
he had brought twenty chariot fighters down
since entering combat in his chariot,
already skilled in the craft of war. This man 930
was first to wound you with a spear, Patróklos,
but did not bring you down. Instead, he ran back
into the mêlée, pulling from the flesh
his ashen spear, and would not face his enemy,
even disarmed, in battle. Then Patróklos,
disabled by the god's blow and the spear wound,
moved back to save himself amid his men.
But Hektor, seeing that his brave adversary
tried to retire, hurt by the spear wound, charged
straight at him through the ranks and lunged for him 940
low in the flank, driving the spearhead through.

He crashed, and all Akhaian troops turned pale.
Think how a lion in his pride brings down
a tireless boar; magnificently they fight
on a mountain crest for a small gushing spring—
both in desire to drink—and by sheer power
the lion conquers the great panting boar:
that was the way the son of Priam, Hektor,
closed with Patróklos, son of Menoitios,
killer of many, and took his life away. 950
Then glorying above him he addressed him:

"Easy to guess, Patróklos, how you swore
to ravage Troy, to take the sweet daylight
of liberty from our women, and to drag them
off in ships to your own land—you fool!
Between you and those women there is Hektor's
war-team, thundering out to fight! My spear
has pride of place among the Trojan warriors,
keeping their evil hour at bay.
The kites[28] will feed on you, here on this field. 960
Poor devil, what has that great prince, Akhilleus,
done for you? He must have told you often
as you were leaving and he stayed behind,
'Never come back to me, to the deepsea ships,
Patróklos, till you cut to rags
the bloody tunic on the chest of Hektor!'
That must have been the way he talked, and won
your mind to mindlessness."

In a low faint voice,
Patróklos, master of horse, you answered him:

"This is your hour to glory over me, 970
Hektor. The Lord Zeus and Apollo gave you
the upper hand and put me down with ease.
They stripped me of my arms. No one else did.
Say twenty men like you had come against me,
all would have died before my spear.
No, Lêto's son and fatal destiny
have killed me; if we speak of men, Euphórbos.
You were in third place, only in at the death.
I'll tell you one thing more; take it to heart.
No long life is ahead for you. This day 980
your death stands near, and your immutable end,
at Prince Akhilleus' hands."

His own death
came on him as he spoke, and soul from body,
bemoaning severance from youth and manhood,

[28] Birds of prey.

slipped to be wafted to the underworld.
Even in death Prince Hektor still addressed him:

"Why prophesy my sudden death, Patróklos?
Who knows, Akhilleus, son of bright-haired Thetis,
might be hit first; he might be killed by me."

At this he pulled his spearhead from the wound, 990
setting his heel upon him; then he pushed him
over on his back, clear of the spear,
and lifting it at once sought Automédôn,
companion of the great runner, Akhilleus,
longing to strike him. But the immortal horses,
gift of the gods to Pêleus, bore him away.

from BOOK SEVENTEEN: CONTENDING FOR A SOLDIER FALLEN

Hektor has seized the armor of Akhilleus that the dead Patróklos had worn. A long and bitter struggle ensues for possession of his body. The Greeks want to return it to Akhilleus, the Trojans to desecrate it; moreover, Glaukos, mistakenly believing that the Greeks now have the corpse of his dead comrade Sarpêdôn, hopes they may trade it for the corpse of Patróklos. Meneláos defends Patróklos' body with the help of the greater Aías and other warriors. Glaukos charges Hektor with cowardice; Hektor, aroused, puts on the armor of Akhilleus/Patróklos (as Zeus predicts Hektor's death) and leads his followers into the fight for the body. Aineías joins in. This part of the battlefield has been shrouded in near-darkness by Zeus, though in other places the sky is clear. Akhilleus is still unaware of his friend's death.

At the end of Book XVI Automédôn, charioteer for Patróklos, withdrew from the battle along with Akhilleus' immortal horses. We see them again:

Out of range,
the horses of Akhilleus, from the time
they sensed their charioteer[1] downed in the dust 480
at the hands of deadly Hektor, had been weeping.
Automédôn, the son of Diorês,
laid often on their backs his flickering whip,
pled often in a low tone—or he swore at them—
but neither toward the shipways and the beach
by Hellê's waters would they budge, nor follow
Akhaians into battle. No: stock-still
as a gravestone, fixed above the tomb
of a dead man or woman, they stood fast,
holding the beautiful war-car still: their heads 490
curved over to the ground, and warm tears flowed

[1]Patróklos, who normally serves as charioteer (that is, when Akhilleus is in action).

from under eyelids earthward as they mourned
their longed-for driver. Manes along the yoke
were soiled as they hung forward under yokepads.
Seeing their tears flow, pitying them, Lord Zeus
bent his head and murmured in his heart:

"Poor things, why did I give you to King Pêleus,
a mortal, you who never age nor die,
to let you ache with men in their hard lot?
For of all creatures that breathe and move on earth 500
none is more to be pitied than a man.
Never at least shall Hektor, son of Priam,
ride behind you in your painted car.
That I will not allow. Is it not enough
that he both has the gear and brags about it?
I shall put fire in your knees and hearts
to rescue Automédôn, bear him away
from battle to the decked ships. Glory of killing,
even so, I reserve to his enemies
until they reach the ships, until sundown, 510
until the dusk comes, full of stars."

BOOK XVII (continued). *Hektor and Aineías try to capture Akhilleus' horses but are driven back by the two Aíases. Zeus allows Athêna to encourage Meneláos; Apollo encourages Hektor once more. Zeus now gives victory to the Trojans. The greater Aías and Meneláos send a runner to Akhilleus with the news of Patróklos' death. With immense difficulty, and sustained by the two Aíases, the Greeks carry Patróklos' body to the rear as the triumphant Trojans advance again, led by Hektor and Aineías.*

BOOK EIGHTEEN: THE IMMORTAL SHIELD

While they were still in combat, fighting seaward
raggedly as fire, Antílokhos[1]
ran far ahead with tidings for Akhilleus.
In shelter of the curled, high prows he found him
envisioning what had come to pass,
in gloom and anger saying to himself:

"Ai! why are they turning tail once more,
unmanned, outfought, and driven from the field
back on the beach and ships? I pray the gods
this may not be the last twist of the knife! 10
My mother warned me once that, while I lived,
the most admirable of Myrmidons
would quit the sunlight under Trojan blows.
It could indeed be so. He has gone down,
my dear and wayward friend!

[1]Son of Nestor, sent in Book XVII to inform Akhilleus of Patróklos' death.

Push their deadly fire away, I told him,
then return! You must not fight with Hektor!"

And while he called it all to mind,
the son of gallant Nestor came up weeping
to give his cruel news:

"Here's desolation, 20
son of Pêleus, the worst news for you—
would god it had not happened!—Lord Patróklos
fell, and they are fighting over his body,
stripped of armor. Hektor has your gear."

A black stormcloud of pain shrouded Akhilleus.
On his bowed head he scattered dust and ash
in handfuls and befouled his beautiful face,
letting black ash sift on his fragrant khiton.[2]
Then in the dust he stretched his giant length
and tore his hair with both hands.

From the hut 30
the women who had been spoils of war to him
and to Patróklos flocked in haste around him,
crying loud in grief. All beat their breasts,
and trembling came upon their knees.

Antílokhos
wept where he stood, bending to hold the hero's
hands when groaning shook his heart: he feared
the man might use sharp iron to slash his throat.
And now Akhilleus gave a dreadful cry.

Her ladyship
his mother heard him, in the depths offshore
lolling near her ancient father.[3] Nymphs 40
were gathered round her: all Nêrêïdês
who haunted the green chambers of the sea.
Glaukê, Thaleia, and Kymodokê,
Nesaiê, Speiô, Thoê, Haliê
with her wide eyes; Kymothoê, Aktaiê,
Limnôreia, Melitê, and Iaira,
Amphitoê, Agauê, Dôtô, Prôtô,
Pherousa, Dynaménê, Dexaménê,
Amphinomê, Kallianeira, Dôris,
Panopê, and storied Galateia, 50
Nêmertês and Apseudês, Kallianassa,
Klyméne, Ianeira, Ianassa,
Maira, Oreithyia, Amathyia,
and other Nêrêïdês of the deep sea,

[2] A loose, knee-length garment.
[3] Nêreus, a sea-god.

filling her glimmering silvery cave. All these
now beat their breasts as Thetis cried in sorrow:

"Sisters, daughters of Nêreus, hear and know
how sore my heart is! Now my life is pain
for my great son's dark destiny! I bore
a child flawless and strong beyond all men. 60
He flourished like a green shoot, and I brought him
to manhood like a blossoming orchard tree,
only to send him in the ships to Ilion
to war with Trojans. Now I shall never see him
entering Pêleus' hall, his home, again.
But even while he lives, beholding sunlight,
suffering is his lot. I have no power
to help him, though I go to him. Even so,
I'll visit my dear child and learn what sorrow
came to him while he held aloof from war." 70

On this she left the cave, and all in tears
her company swam aloft with her. Around them
a billow broke and foamed on the open sea.
As they made land at the fertile plain of Troy,
they went up one by one in line to where,
in close order, Myrmidon ships were beached
to right and left of Akhilleus. Bending near
her groaning son, the gentle goddess wailed
and took his head between her hands in pity,
saying softly:

"Child, why are you weeping? 80
What great sorrow came to you? Speak out,
do not conceal it. Zeus
did all you asked: Akhaian troops,
for want of you, were all forced back again
upon the ship sterns, taking heavy losses
none of them could wish."

The great runner
groaned and answered:

"Mother, yes, the master
of high Olympos brought it all about,
but how have I benefited? My greatest friend
is gone: Patróklos, comrade in arms, whom I 90
held dear above all others—dear as myself—
now gone, lost; Hektor cut him down, despoiled him
of my own arms, massive and fine, a wonder
in all men's eyes. The gods gave them to Pêleus
that day they put you in a mortal's bed—
how I wish the immortals of the sea
had been your only consorts! How I wish
Pêleus had taken a mortal queen! Sorrow

immeasurable is in store for you as well,
when your own child is lost: never again 100
on his homecoming day will you embrace him!
I must reject this life, my heart tells me,
reject the world of men,
if Hektor does not feel my battering spear
tear the life out of him, making him pay
in his own blood for the slaughter of Patróklos!"

Letting a tear fall, Thetis said:

"You'll be
swift to meet your end, child, as you say:
your doom comes close on the heels of Hektor's own."

Akhilleus the great runner ground his teeth 110
and said:

"May it come quickly. As things were,
I could not help my friend in his extremity.
Far from his home he died; he needed me
to shield him or to parry the death stroke.
For me there's no return to my own country.
Not the slightest gleam of hope did I
afford Patróklos or the other men
whom Hektor overpowered. Here I sat,
my weight a useless burden to the earth,
and I am one who has no peer in war 120
among Akhaian captains—

though in council
there are wiser. Ai! let strife and rancor
perish from the lives of gods and men,
with anger that envenoms even the wise
and is far sweeter than slow-dripping honey,
clouding the hearts of men like smoke: just so
the marshal of the army, Agamémnon,
moved me to anger. But we'll let that go,
though I'm still sore at heart; it is all past,
and I have quelled my passion as I must. 130

Now I must go to look for the destroyer
of my great friend. I shall confront the dark
drear spirit of death at any hour Zeus
and the other gods may wish to make an end.
Not even Hêraklês[4] escaped that terror
though cherished by the Lord Zeus. Destiny
and Hêra's bitter anger mastered him.
Likewise with me, if destiny like his
awaits me, I shall rest when I have fallen!

[4]In myth, Hêraklês (Hercules) was a great Greek hero, a kind of superman. In some versions he was deified at the end of his life.

Now, though, may I win my perfect glory 140
and make some wife of Troy break down,
or some deep-breasted Dardan[5] woman sob
and wipe tears from her soft cheeks. They'll know then
how long they had been spared the deaths of men,
while I abstained from war!
Do not attempt to keep me from the fight,
though you love me; you cannot make me listen."

Thetis, goddess of the silvery feet,
answered:

"Yes, of course, child: very true.
You do no wrong to fight for tired soldiers 150
and keep them from defeat. But still, your gear,
all shining bronze, remains in Trojan hands.
Hektor himself is armed with it in pride!—
Not that he'll glory in it long, I know,
for violent death is near him.

Patience, then.
Better not plunge into the moil of Arês
until you see me here once more. At dawn,
at sunrise, I shall come
with splendid arms for you from Lord Hêphaistos."

She rose at this and, turning from her son, 160
told her sister Nêrêïdês:

"Go down
into the cool broad body of the sea
to the sea's Ancient; visit Father's hall,
and make all known to him. Meanwhile, I'll visit
Olympos' great height and the lord of crafts,
Hêphaistos, hoping he will give me
new and shining armor for my son."

At this they vanished in the offshore swell,
and to Olympos Thetis the silvery-footed
went once more, to fetch for her dear son 170
new-forged and finer arms.

Meanwhile, Akhaians,
wildly crying, pressed by deadly Hektor,
reached the ships, beached above Hellê's water.
None had been able to pull Patróklos clear
of spear- and swordplay: troops and chariots
and Hektor, son of Priam, strong as fire,
once more gained upon the body. Hektor
three times had the feet within his grasp

[5] From the vicinity of Troy.

and strove to wrest Patróklos backward, shouting
to all the Trojans—but three times the pair 180
named Aías in their valor shook him off.
Still he pushed on, sure of his own power,
sometimes lunging through the battle-din,
or holding fast with a great shout: not one step
would he give way. As from a fresh carcass
herdsmen in the wilds cannot dislodge
a tawny lion, famished: so those two
with fearsome crests could not affright the son
of Priam or repel him from the body.
He might have won it, might have won unending 190
glory, but Iris running on the wind
came from Olympos to the son of Pêleus,
bidding him gird for battle. All unknown
to Zeus and the other gods she came, for Hêra
sent her down. And at his side she said:

"Up with you, Pêleidês, who strike cold fear
into men's blood! Protect your friend Patróklos,
for whom, beyond the ships, desperate combat
rages now. They are killing one another
on both sides: the Akhaians to defend him, 200
Trojans fighting for that prize
to drag to windy Ilion. And Hektor
burns to take it more than anyone—
to sever and impale Patróklos' head
on Trojan battlements. Lie here no longer.
It would be shameful if wild dogs of Troy
made him their plaything! If that body suffers
mutilation, you will be infamous!"

Prince Akhilleus answered:

"Iris of heaven,
what immortal sent you to tell me this?" 210

And she who runs upon the wind replied:

"Hêra, illustrious wife of Zeus,
but he on his high throne knows nothing of it.
Neither does any one of the gods undying
who haunt Olympos of eternal snows."

Akhilleus asked:

"And now how shall I go
into the fighting? Those men have my gear.
My dear mother allows me no rearming
until I see her again here.
She promises fine arms from Lord Hêphaistos. 220
I don't know whose armor I can wear,

unless I take Aías' big shield.
But I feel sure he's in the thick of it,
contending with his spear over Patróklos."

Then she who runs upon the wind replied:

"We know they have your arms, and know it well.
Just as you are, then, stand at the moat; let Trojans
take that in; they will be so dismayed
they may break off the battle, and Akhaians
in their fatigue may win a breathing spell, 230
however brief, a respite from the war."

At this,
Iris left him, running downwind. Akhilleus,
whom Zeus loved, now rose. Around his shoulders
Athêna hung her shield,[6] like a thunderhead
with trailing fringe. Goddess of goddesses,
she bound his head with golden cloud, and made
his very body blaze with fiery light.
Imagine how the pyre of a burning town
will tower to heaven and be seen for miles
from the island under attack, while all day long 240
outside their town, in brutal combat, pikemen
suffer the wargod's winnowing; at sundown
flare on flare is lit, the signal fires
shoot up for other islanders to see,
that some relieving force in ships may come:
just so the baleful radiance from Akhilleus
lit the sky. Moving from parapet
to moat, without a nod for the Akhaians,
keeping clear, in deference to his mother,
he halted and gave tongue. Not far from him 250
Athêna shrieked. The great sound shocked the Trojans
into tumult, as a trumpet blown
by a savage foe shocks an encircled town,
so harsh and clarion was Akhilleus' cry.
The hearts of men quailed, hearing that brazen voice.
Teams, foreknowing danger, turned their cars
and charioteers blanched, seeing unearthly fire,
kindled by the grey-eyed goddess Athêna,
brilliant over Akhilleus. Three great cries
he gave above the moat. Three times they shuddered, 260
whirling backward, Trojans and allies,
and twelve good men took mortal hurt
from cars and weapons in the rank behind.
Now the Akhaians leapt at the chance

[6] The aegis, a terror-inspiring shield given by Hêphaistos to Zeus and often used by Athêna.

to bear Patróklos' body out of range.
They placed it on his bed,
and old companions there with brimming eyes
surrounded him. Into their midst Akhilleus
came then, and he wept hot tears to see
his faithful friend, torn by the sharp spearhead, 270
lying cold upon his cot. Alas,
the man he sent to war with team and chariot
he could not welcome back alive.

Her majesty,
wide-eyed Hêra, made the reluctant sun,
unwearied still, sink in the streams of Ocean.
Down he dropped, and the Akhaian soldiers
broke off combat, resting from the war.[7]
The Trojans, too, retired. Unharnessing
teams from war-cars, before making supper,
they came together on the assembly ground, 280
every man on his feet; not one could sit,
each being still in a tremor—for Akhilleus,
absent so long, had once again appeared.
Clearheaded Poulýdamas, son of Pánthoös,
spoke up first, as he alone could see
what lay ahead and all that lay behind.
He and Hektor were companions-in-arms,
born, as it happened, on the same night; but one
excelled in handling weapons, one with words.
Now for the good of all he spoke among them: 290

"Think well of our alternatives, my friends.
What I say is, retire upon the town,
instead of camping on the field till dawn
here by the ships. We are a long way
from our stone wall. As long as that man raged
at royal Agamémnon, we could fight
the Akhaians with advantage. I was happy
to spend last night so near the beach and think
of capturing ships today. Now, though, I fear
the son of Pêleus to my very marrow! 300
There are no bounds to the passion of that man.
He will not be contained by the flat ground
where Trojans and Akhaians share between them
raging war: he will strive on to fight
to win our town, our women. Back to Troy!
Believe me, this is what we face!
Now, starry night has made Akhilleus pause,
but when day comes, when he sorties in arms
to find us lingering here, there will be men
who learn too well what he is made of. Aye, 310

[7] This day's fighting had begun in Book XI.

I daresay those who get away will reach
walled Ilion thankfully, but dogs and kites
of Troy will feed on many. May that story
never reach my ears! If we can follow
my battle plan, though galled by it, tonight
we'll husband strength, at rest in the market place.
Towers, high gates, great doors of fitted planking,
bolted tight, will keep the town secure.
Early tomorrow we shall arm ourselves
and man the walls. Worse luck then for Akhilleus, 320
if he comes looking for a head-on fight
on the field around the wall! He can do nothing
but trot back, after all, to the encampment,
his proud team in a lather from their run,
from scouring every quarter below the town.
Rage as he will, he cannot force an entrance,
cannot take all Troy by storm. Wild dogs
will eat him first!"

Under his shimmering helmet
Hektor glared at the speaker. Then he said:

"Poulýdamas, what you propose no longer 330
serves my turn. To go on the defensive
inside the town again? Is anyone
not sick of being huddled in those towers?
In past days men told tales of Priam's city,
rich in gold and rich in bronze, but now
those beautiful treasures of our home are lost.[8]
Many have gone for sale to Phrygia
and fair Mêïonie, since Lord Zeus
grew hostile toward us.

Now when the son of Krónos
Crooked Wit has given me a chance 340
of winning glory, pinning the Akhaians
back on the sea—now is no time to publish
notions like these to troops, you fool! No Trojan
goes along with you, I will not have it!
Come, let each man act as I propose.
Take your evening meal by companies;
remember sentries; keep good watch; and any
Trojan tired of his wealth, who wants
to lose everything, let him turn it over
to the army stores to be consumed in common! 350
Better our men enjoy it than Akhaians.
At first light we shall buckle armor on
and bring the ships under attack. Suppose
the man who stood astern there was indeed

[8] *treasures . . . are lost.* That is, sold to pay the expenses of the war.

Akhilleus, then worse luck for him,
if he will have it so. Shall I retreat
from him, from clash of combat? No, I will not.
Here I'll stand, though he should win; I might
just win, myself: the battle-god's impartial,
dealing death to the death-dealing man." 360

This was Hektor's speech. The Trojans roared
approval of it—fools, for Pallas Athêna
took away their wits. They all applauded
Hektor's poor tactics, but Poulýdamas
with his good judgment got not one assent.
They took their evening meal now, through the army,
while all night long Akhaians mourned Patróklos.

Akhilleus led them in their lamentation,
laying those hands deadly to enemies
upon the breast of his old friend, with groans 370
at every breath, bereft as a lioness
whose whelps a hunter seized out of a thicket;
late in returning, she will grieve, and roam
through many meandering valleys on his track
in hope of finding him; heart-stinging anger
carries her away. Now with a groan
he cried out to the Myrmidons:

"Ah, god,
what empty prophecy I made that day
to cheer Menoitios in his mégaron!
I promised him his honored son, brought back 380
to Opoeis,[9] as pillager of Ilion
bearing his share of spoils,
But Zeus will not fulfill what men design,
not all of it. Both he and I were destined
to stain the same earth dark red here at Troy.
No going home for me; no welcome there
from Pêleus, master of horse, or from my mother,
Thetis. Here the earth will hold me under.
Therefore, as I must follow you into the grave,
I will not give you burial, Patróklos, 390
until I carry back the gear and head
of him who killed you, noble friend.
Before your funeral pyre I'll cut the throats
of twelve resplendent children of the Trojans—
that is my murdering fury at your death.
But while you lie here by the swanlike ships,
night and day, close by, deep-breasted women
of Troy, and Dardan women, must lament

[9] The home of Menoitios, Patróklos' father.

and weep hot tears, all those whom we acquired
by labor in assault, by the long spear, 400
pillaging the fat market towns of men."

With this Akhilleus called the company
to place over the campfire a big tripod
and bathe Patróklos of his clotted blood.
Setting tripod and caldron on the blaze
they poured it full, and fed the fire beneath,
and flames licked round the belly of the vessel
until the water warmed and bubbled up
in the bright bronze. They bathed him then, and took
sweet oil for his anointing, laying nard[10] 410
in the open wounds; and on his bed they placed him,
covering him with fine linen, head to foot,
and a white shroud over it.

So all that night
beside Akhilleus the great runner,
the Myrmidons held mourning for Patróklos.
Now Zeus observed to Hêra, wife and sister:

"You had your way; my lady, after all,
my wide-eyed one! You brought him to his feet,
the great runner! One would say the Akhaian
gentlemen were progeny of yours." 420

And Hêra with wide eyes replied:

"Dread majesty,
Lord Zeus, why do you take this tone? May not
an ordinary mortal have his way,
though death awaits him, and his mind is dim?
Would anyone suppose that I, who rank
in two respects highest of goddesses—
by birth[11] and by my station, queen to thee,
lord of all gods—that I should not devise
ill fortune for the Trojans whom I loathe?"

So ran their brief exchange. Meanwhile 430
the silvery-footed Thetis reached Hêphaistos'
lodging, indestructible and starry,
framed in bronze by the bandy-legged god.
She found him sweating, as from side to side
he plied his bellows; on his forge were twenty
tripods to be finished, then to stand
around his mégaron. And he wrought wheels
of gold for the base of each, that each might roll
as of itself into the gods' assembly,

[10] Balm made from the aromatic spikenard plant.
[11] Hêra and Zeus are both children of the former supreme deity, Krónos.

then roll home, a marvel to the eyes. 440
The caldrons were all shaped but had no handles.
These he applied now, hammering rivets in;
and as he toiled surehandedly at this,
Thetis arrived.
Grace in her shining veil
just going out encountered her—that Grace
the bowlegged god had taken to wife.[12] She greeted
Thetis with a warm handclasp and said:

"My lady Thetis, gracious goddess, what
has brought you here? You almost never honor us!
Please come in, and let me give you welcome." 450

Loveliest of goddesses, she led the way,
to seat her guest on a silver-studded chair,
elaborately fashioned, with a footrest.
Then she called to Hêphaistos:

"Come and see!
Thetis is here, in need of something from you!"

To this the Great Gamelegs replied:

"Ah, then we have a visitor I honor.
She was my savior, after the long fall
and fractures that I had to bear, when Mother,[13]
bitch that she is, wanted to hide her cripple. 460
That would have been a dangerous time, had not
Thetis and Eurýnomê[14] taken me in—
Eurýnomê, daughter of the tidal Ocean.
Nine years I stayed, and fashioned works of art,
brooches and spiral bracelets, necklaces,
in their smooth cave, round which the stream of Ocean
flows with a foaming roar: and no one else
knew of it, gods or mortals. Only Thetis
knew, and Eurýnomê, the two who saved me.
Now she has come to us. Well, what I owe 470
for life to her ladyship in her soft braids
I must repay. Serve her our choicest fare
while I put up my bellows and my tools."

At this he left the anvil block, and hobbled
with monstrous bulk on skinny legs to take
his bellows from the fire. Then all the tools
he had been toiling with he stowed
in a silver chest.

[12] Hêphaistos' wife is generally identified as Aphrodítê. Here she is identified as Grace, perhaps to indicate that metalworking entails not just strength but also elegant beauty.
[13] Hêra. [14] Thetis' aunt.

That done, he sponged himself,
his face, both arms, bull-neck and hairy chest,
put on a tunic, took a weighty staff, 480
and limped out of his workshop. Round their lord
came fluttering maids of gold, like living girls:
intelligences, voices, power of motion
these maids have, and skills learnt from immortals.
Now they came rustling to support their lord,
and he moved on toward Thetis, where she sat
upon the silvery chair. He took her hand
and warmly said:

"My Lady Thetis, gracious
goddess, why have you come? You almost never honor us.
Tell me the favor that you have in mind, 490
for I desire to do it if I can,
and if it is a thing that one may do."

Thetis answered, tear on cheek:

"Hêphaístos,
who among all Olympian goddesses
endured anxiety and pain like mine?
Zeus chose me, from all of them, for this!
Of sea-nymphs I alone was given in thrall
to a mortal warrior, Pêleus Aiákidês,
and I endured a mortal warrior's bed
many a time, without desire. Now Pêleus 500
lies far gone in age in his great hall,
and I have other pain. Our son, bestowed
on me and nursed by me, became a hero
unsurpassed. He grew like a green shoot;
I cherished him like a flowering orchard tree,
only to send him in the ships to Ilion
to war with Trojans. Now I shall never see him
entering Pêleus' hall, his home, again.
But even while he lives, beholding sunlight,
suffering is his lot. I have no power 510
to help him, though I go to him. A girl,
his prize from the Akhaians, Agamémnon
took out of his hands to make his own,
and ah, he pined with burning heart! The Trojans
rolled the Akhaians back on the ship sterns,
and left them no escape. Then Argive officers
begged my son's help, offering every gift,
but he would not defend them from disaster.
Arming Patróklos in his own war-gear,
he sent him with his people into battle. 520
All day long, around the Skaian Gates,
they fought, and would have won the city, too,
had not Apollo, seeing the brave son

of Menoitios wreaking havoc on the Trojans,
killed him in action, and then given Hektor
the honor of that deed.
On this account
I am here to beg you: if you will, provide
for my doomed son a shield and crested helm,
good legging-greaves, fitted with ankle clasps,
a cuirass, too. His own armor was lost 530
when his great friend went down before the Trojans.
Now my son lies prone on the hard ground in grief."

The illustrious lame god replied:
"Take heart.
No trouble about the arms. I only wish
that I could hide him from the power of death
in his black hour—wish I were sure of that
as of the splendid gear he'll get, a wonder
to any one of the many men there are!"

He left her there, returning to his bellows,
training them on the fire, crying, "To work!" 540
In crucibles the twenty bellows breathed
every degree of fiery air: to serve him
a great blast when he labored might and main,
or a faint puff, according to his wish
and what the work demanded.
Durable
fine bronze and tin he threw into the blaze
with silver and with honorable gold,
then mounted a big anvil in his block
and in his right hand took a powerful hammer,
managing with his tongs in his left hand. 550

His first job was a shield, a broad one, thick,
well-fashioned everywhere.[15] A shining rim
he gave it, triple-ply, and hung from this
a silver shoulder strap. Five welded layers
composed the body of the shield. The maker
used all his art adorning this expanse.
He pictured on it earth, heaven, and sea,
unwearied sun, moon waxing, all the stars
that heaven bears for garland: Plêïadês,
Hyadês, Oriôn in his might, 560
the Great Bear, too, that some have called the Wain,

[15] The pictures on the shield are an attempt to describe comprehensively life in Homer's time and the cosmos as then conceived. Though in its physical structure the shield is modeled on man-made shields as described elsewhere in the *Iliad,* both the craftsmanship and the content clearly go beyond what a human artisan could achieve.

pivoting there, attentive to Oriôn,
and unbathed ever in the Ocean stream.[16]

He pictured, then, two cities, noble scenes:
weddings in one, and wedding feasts, and brides
led out through town by torchlight from their chambers
amid chorales, amid the young men turning
round and round in dances: flutes and harps
among them, keeping up a tune, and women
coming outdoors to stare as they went by. 570
A crowd, then, in a market place, and there
two men at odds over satisfaction owed
for a murder done:[17] one claimed that all was paid,
and publicly declared it; his opponent
turned the reparation down, and both
demanded a verdict from an arbiter,
as people clamored in support of each,
and criers restrained the crowd. The town elders
sat in a ring, on chairs of polished stone,
the staves of clarion criers in their hands, 580
with which they sprang up, each to speak in turn,
and in the middle were two golden measures
to be awarded him whose argument
would be the most straightforward.
Wartime then;
around the other city were emplaced
two columns of besiegers, bright in arms,
as yet divided on which plan they liked:
whether to sack the town, or treat for half
of all the treasure stored in the citadel.
The townsmen would not bow to either: secretly 590
they armed to break the siege-line. Women and children
stationed on the walls kept watch, with men
whom age disabled. All the rest filed out,
as Arês led the way, and Pallas Athêna,
figured in gold, with golden trappings, both
magnificent in arms, as the gods are,
in high relief, while men were small beside them.
When these had come to a likely place for ambush,
a river with a watering place for flocks,
they there disposed themselves, compact in bronze. 600
Two lookouts at a distance from the troops
took their posts, awaiting sight of sheep

[16]The Great Bear (Ursa Major), also called the Wain and the Big Dipper, is close to the North Star, or Polaris, and therefore seems to rotate around it; for people in the northern latitudes, then, the constellation is always above the northern horizon, regardless of season or time of day.

[17]The penalty for a killing could be paid by a gift of money to the dead man's kin. Here the elders and arbiter argue and judge the case, two measures of gold being awarded for the best argument or solution.

and shambling cattle. Both now came in view,
trailed by two herdsmen playing pipes, no hidden
danger in their minds. The ambush party
took them by surprise in a sudden rush;
swiftly they cut off herds and beautiful flocks
of silvery grey sheep, then killed the herdsmen.
When the besiegers from their parleying ground
heard sounds of cattle in stampede, they mounted 610
behind mettlesome teams, following the sound,
and came up quickly. Battle lines were drawn,
and on the riverbanks the fight began
as each side rifled javelins at the other.
Here then Strife and Uproar joined the fray,
and ghastly Fate, that kept a man with wounds
alive, and one unwounded, and another
dragged by the heels through battle-din in death.
This figure wore a mantle dyed with blood,
and all the figures clashed and fought 620
like living men, and pulled their dead away.

Upon the shield, soft terrain, freshly plowed,
he pictured: a broad field, and many plowmen
here and there upon it. Some were turning
ox teams at the plowland's edge, and there
as one arrived and turned, a man came forward
putting a cup of sweet wine in his hands.
They made their turns-around, then up the furrows
drove again, eager to reach the deep field's
limit; and the earth looked black behind them, 630
as though turned up by plows. But it was gold,
all gold—a wonder of the artist's craft.

He put there, too, a king's field. Harvest hands
were swinging whetted scythes to mow the grain,
and stalks were falling along the swath
while binders girded others up in sheaves
with bands of straw—three binders, and behind them
children came as gleaners, proffering
their eager armfuls. And amid them all
the king stood quietly with staff in hand, 640
happy at heart, upon a new-mown swath.
To one side, under an oak tree his attendants
worked at a harvest banquet. They had killed
a great ox, and were dressing it; their wives
made supper for the hands, with barley strewn.

A vineyard then he pictured, weighted down
with grapes: this all in gold; and yet the clusters
hung dark purple, while the spreading vines
were propped on silver vine-poles. Blue enamel

he made the enclosing ditch, and tin the fence, 650
and one path only led into the vineyard
on which the loaded vintagers took their way
at vintage time. Lighthearted boys and girls
were harvesting the grapes in woven baskets,
while on a resonant harp a boy among them
played a tune of longing, singing low
with delicate voice a summer dirge. The others,
breaking out in song for the joy of it,
kept time together as they skipped along.

The artisan made next a herd of longhorns, 660
fashioned in gold and tin: away they shambled,
lowing, from byre[18] to pasture by a stream
that sang and rippled in a reedy bed.
Four cowherds all of gold were plodding after
with nine lithe dogs beside them.
On the assault,
in two tremendous bounds, a pair of lions
caught in the van a bellowing bull, and off
they dragged him, followed by the dogs and men.
Rending the belly of the bull, the two
gulped down his blood and guts, even as the herdsmen 670
tried to set on their hunting dogs, but failed:
no trading bites with lions for those dogs,
who halted close up, barking, then ran back.

And on the shield the great bowlegged god
designed a pasture in a lovely valley,
wide, with silvery sheep, and huts and sheds
and sheepfolds there.
A dancing floor as well
he fashioned, like that one in royal Knossos[19]
Daidalos made for the Princess Ariadnê.
Here young men and the most desired young girls 680
were dancing, linked, touching each other's wrists,
the girls in linen, in soft gowns, the men
in well-knit khitons given a gloss with oil;
the girls wore garlands, and the men had daggers
golden-hilted, hung on silver lanyards.
Trained and adept, they circled there with ease
the way a potter sitting at his wheel
will give it a practice twirl between his palms
to see it run; or else, again, in lines
as though in ranks, they moved on one another: 690

[18]Barn.

[19]A city in Krete, ruled by the legendary king Minos and renowned for, among other things, dancing. Daidalos (Daedalus) was a master craftsman best known for constructing a labyrinth to contain the Minotaur, a monster half man and half bull.

magical dancing! All around, a crowd
stood spellbound as two tumblers led the beat
with spins and handsprings through the company.

Then, running round the shield-rim, triple-ply,
he pictured all the might of the Ocean stream.

Besides the densely plated shield, he made
a cuirass, brighter far than fire light,
a massive helmet, measured for his temples,
handsomely figured, with a crest of gold;
then greaves[20] of pliant tin.

Now when the crippled god 700
had done his work, he picked up all the arms
and laid them down before Akhilleus' mother,
and swift as a hawk from snowy Olympos' height
she bore the brilliant gear made by Hêphaistos.

BOOK NINETEEN: THE AVENGER FASTS AND ARMS

Dawn in her yellow robe rose in the east
out of the flowing Ocean, bearing light
for deathless gods and mortal men. And Thetis
brought to the beach her gifts from the god of fire.
She found her dear son lying beside Patróklos,
wailing, while his men stood by
in tears around him. Now amid that throng
the lovely goddess bent to touch his shoulder
and said to him:

"Ah, child, let him lie dead,
for all our grief and pain, we must allow it; 10
he fell by the gods' will.
But you, now—take the war-gear from Hêphaistos.
No man ever bore upon his shoulders
gear so magnificent."

And she laid the armor
down before Akhilleus, clanging loud
in all its various glory. Myrmidons
began to tremble at the sound, and dared not
look straight at the armor; their knees shook.
But anger entered Akhilleus as he gazed,
his eyes grown wide and bright as blazing fire, 20
with fierce joy as he handled the god's gifts.

[20]Armor for the lower legs.

After appraising them in his delight
he spoke out to his mother swiftly:

"Mother,
these the god gave are miraculous arms,
handiwork of immortals, plainly—far
beyond the craft of men. By heaven, I'll wear them!
Only, I feel the dread that while I fight
black carrion flies may settle on Patróklos'
wounds, where the spearheads marked him, and I fear
they may breed maggots to defile the corpse, 30
now life is torn from it. His flesh may rot."

But silvery-footed Thetis answered:

"Child,
you must not let that prey on you. I'll find
a way to shield him from the black fly hordes
that eat the bodies of men killed in battle.
Though he should lie unburied a long year,
his flesh will be intact and firm. Now, though,
for your part, call the Akhaians to assembly.
Tell them your anger against Agamémnon
is over and done with! 40
After that, at once
put on your gear, prepare your heart, for war!"

Her promise gave her son wholehearted valor.
Then, turning to Patróklos, she instilled
red nectar and ambrosia[1] in his nostrils
to keep his body whole.

And Prince Akhilleus
passed along the surf-line with a shout
that split the air and roused men of Akhaia,
even those who, up to now, had stayed
amid the massed ships—navigators, helmsmen, 50
men in charge of rations and ship stores.
Aye, even these now headed for assembly,
since he who for so long had shunned the battle,
Akhilleus, now appeared upon the field.
Resolute Diomêdês and Odysseus,
familiars[2] of the wargod, limped along,
leaning on spears, for both had painful wounds.
They made their way to the forefront and sat down,
and last behind them entered the Lord Marshal
Agamémnon, favoring his wound: he too 60
had taken a slash, from Antênor's son, Koôn.

[1]Literally, the drink and food of the gods.
[2]Attendants.

When everyone had crowded in, Akhilleus,
the great battlefield runner, rose and said:

"Agamémnon, was it better for us
in any way, when we were sore at heart,
to waste ourselves in strife over a girl?
If only Artemis had shot her down[3]
among the ships on the day I made her mine,
after I took Lyrnessos!
Fewer Akhaians would have died hard 70
at enemy hands, while I abstained in anger—
Hektor's gain, the Trojans' gain. Akhaians
years hence will remember our high words,
mine and yours. But now we can forget them,
and, as we must, forego our passion. Aye,
by heaven, I drop my anger now!
No need to smolder in my heart forever! Come,
send your long-haired Akhaians into combat,
and let me see how Trojans will hold out,
if camping near the beachhead's their desire! 80
I rather think some will be glad to rest,
provided they get home, away from danger,
out of my spear's range!"

These were his words,
and all the Akhaians gave a roar of joy
to hear the prince abjure his rage.
Lord Marshal Agamémnon then addressed them,
standing up, not in the midst of them,
but where he had been sitting:

"Friends, fighters,
Danáäns, companions of Arês: it is fair
to listen to a man when he has risen 90
and not to interrupt him. That's vexation
to any speaker, able though he may be.
In a great hubbub how can any man
attend or speak? A fine voice will be muffled.
While I open my mind to the son of Pêleus,
Argives, attention! Each man weigh my words!
The Akhaians often brought this up against me,
and chided me. But I am not to blame.[4]
Zeus and Fate and a nightmare Fury are,
for putting savage Folly in my mind 100
in the assembly that day, when I wrested

[3] Had brought death to her.
[4] *I am not to blame.* Despite these words and his accusation of Folly, Agamémnon does to some extent admit his fault. His account is roughly analogous to modern expressions like "What possessed me to do that?"

Akhilleus' prize of war from him. In truth,
what could I do? Divine will shapes these things.
Ruinous Folly, eldest daughter of Zeus,
beguiles us all. Her feet are soft, from walking
not on earth but over the heads of men
to do them hurt. She traps one man or another.
Once indeed she deluded Zeus, most noble
of gods and men, they say. But feminine
Hêra with her underhanded ways 110
tricked him, the day Alkmênê, in high Thebes,
was to have given birth to Hêraklês.[5]
Then glorying Zeus remarked to all the gods:
"Hear me, all gods and goddesses, I'll tell you
of something my heart dwells upon. This day
the childbirth goddess, Eileithyía, brings
into the light a man who will command
all those around him, being of the race of men
who come of my own blood!' But in her guile
the Lady Hêra said: 'You may be wrong, 120
unable to seal your word with truth hereafter.
Come, Olympian, swear me a great oath
he will indeed be lord of all his neighbors,
the child of your own stock in the race of men
who drops between a woman's legs today!'

Zeus failed to see her crookedness: he swore
a mighty oath, and mightily went astray,
for flashing downward from Olympos crest
Hêra visited Argos of Akhaia,
aware that the strong wife of Perseus' son, 130
Sthénelos, was big with child,
just entering her seventh month. But Hêra
brought this child into the world's daylight
beforehand by two months, and checked Alkmênê's
labor, to delay the birth of hers.
To Zeus the son of Krónos then she said:
'Zeus of the bright bolt, father, let me add
a new event to your deliberations.
Even now a superior man is born
to be a lord of Argives: Eurýstheus, 140
a son of Sthénelos, the son of Perseus,
of your own stock. And it is not unfitting
for him to rule the Argives.' This report
sharply wounded the deep heart of Zeus.
He picked up Folly by her shining braids

[5]Alkmênê was a mortal woman who, after being seduced by Zeus in the guise of her husband, gave birth to the hero Hêraklês, whom Hêra hated out of jealousy of his mother. During one period of his life he was required to serve Eurýstheus (grandson of Perseus, another son of Zeus) by performing twelve superhumanly difficult labors.

in sudden anger—swearing a great oath
that never to starred heaven or Olympos
Folly, who tricks us all, should come again.
With this he whirled her with one hand and flung her
out of the sky. So to men's earth she came, 150
but ever thereafter made Zeus groan to see
his dear son toil at labors for Eurýstheus.

So, too, with me: when in his shimmering helm
great Hektor slaughtered Argives near the ships,
could I ignore my folly, my delusion?
Zeus had stolen my wits, my act was blind.
But now I wish to make amends, to give
all possible satisfaction. Rouse for war,
send in your troops! I here repeat my offer
of all that Odysseus promised yesterday![6] 160
Stay if you will, though the wargod presses you.
Men in my service will unload the gifts
from my own ship, that you may see how richly
I reward you!"

Akhilleus answered:

"Excellency,
Lord Marshal Agamémnon, make the gifts
if you are keen to—gifts are due; or keep them.
It is for you to say. Let us recover
joy of battle soon, that's all!
No need to dither here and lose our time,
our great work still undone. When each man sees 170
Akhilleus in a charge, crumpling the ranks
of Trojans with his bronze-shod spear, let each
remember that is the way to fight his man!"

Replied Odysseus, the shrewd field commander:

"Brave as you are, and like a god in looks,
Akhilleus, do not send Akhaian soldiers
into the fight unfed! Today's mêlée
will not be brief, when rank meets rank, and heaven
breathes fighting spirit into both contenders.
No, tell all troops who are near the ships to take 180
roast meat and wine, for heart and staying power.
No soldier can fight hand to hand, in hunger,
all day long until the sun goes down!
Though in his heart he yearns for war, his legs
go slack before he knows it: thirst and famine
search him out, and his knees fail as he moves.
But that man stayed with victualing and wine

[6]Agamémnon refers to the offer he made in Book IX.

can fight his enemies all day: his heart
is bold and happy in his chest, his legs
hold out until both sides break off the battle! 190
Come, then, dismiss the ranks to make their breakfast.
Let the Lord Marshal Agamémnon
bring his gifts to the assembly ground
where all may see them; may your heart be warmed.
Then let him swear to you, before the Argives,
never to have made love to her, my lord,
as men and women by their nature do.
So may your heart be peaceable toward him!
And let him sate your hunger with rich fare
in his own shelter, that you may lack nothing 200
due you in justice. Afterward, Agamémnon,
you'll be more just to others, too. There is
no fault in a king's wish to conciliate
a man with whom he has been quick to anger!"

And the Lord Marshal Agamémnon answered:

"Glad I am to hear you, son of Laërtês,
finding the right word at the right time
for all these matters. And the oath you speak of
I'll take willingly, with all my heart,
and will not, before heaven, be forsworn. 210
Now let Akhilleus wait here, though the wargod
tug his arm; and all the rest of you
wait here assembled till the gifts have come
down from our quarters, and our peace is made.
For you, Odysseus, here is my command:
choose the finest young peers of all Akhaia
to fetch out of my ship those gifts we pledged
Akhilleus yesterday; and bring the women.
Let Talthýbios[7] prepare for sacrifice,
in the army's name, a boar to Zeus and Hêlios."[8] 220

Replied Akhilleus:

"Excellency, Lord Marshal,
another time were better for these ceremonies,
some interval in the war, and when I feel
less passion in me. Look, those men lie dead
whom Hektor killed when Zeus allowed him glory,
and yet you two propose a meal! By god,
I'd send our soldiers into action now
unfed and hungry. Have a feast, I'd say,
at sundown, when our shame has been avenged!

[7]Agamémnon's crier, or herald.
[8]The sun or sun god.

Before that, for my part, I will not swallow 230
food or drink—my dear friend being dead,
lying before my eyes, bled white by spear-cuts,
feet turned to his hut's door, his friends in mourning
around him. Your concerns are none of mine.
Slaughter and blood are what I crave, and groans
of anguished men!"

But the shrewd field commander
Odysseus answered:

"Akhilleus, flower and pride
of the Akhaians, you are more powerful
than I am—and a better spearman, too—
only in sizing matters up I'd say 240
I'm just as far beyond you, being older,
knowing more of the world. So bear with me.
Men quickly reach satiety with battle
in which the reaping bronze will bring to earth
big harvests, but a scanty yield, when Zeus,
war's overseer for mankind, tips the scales.
How can a fasting belly mourn our dead?
So many die, so often, every day,
when would soldiers come to an end of fasting?
No, we must dispose of him who dies 250
and keep hard hearts, and weep that day alone.
And those whom the foul war has left unhurt
will do well to remember food and drink,
so that we may again close with our enemies,
our dangerous enemies, and be tough soldiers,
hardened in mail of bronze. Let no one, now,
be held back waiting for another summons:
here is your summons! Woe to the man who lingers
beside the Argive ships! No, all together,
let us take up the fight against the Trojans!" 260

He took as escort sons of illustrious Nestor:
Phyleus' son Mégês, Thoas, and Meríonês,
and the son of Kreion, Lykomêdês, and
Melánippos, to Agamémnon's quarters.
No sooner was the work assigned than done:
they brought the seven tripods Agamémnon
promised Akhilleus, and the twenty caldrons
shining, and the horses, a full dozen;
then they conducted seven women, skilled
in housecraft, with Brisêis in her beauty. 270
Odysseus weighed ten bars of purest gold
and turned back, followed by his young Akhaians,
bearing the gifts to place in mid-assembly.

Now Agamémnon rose. Talthýbios
the crier, with his wondrous voice, stood near him,
holding the boar. The son of Atreus drew
the sheath knife that he carried, hung
beside the big sheath of his sword, and cut
first bristles from the boar. Arms wide to heaven
he prayed to Zeus, as all the troops kept still, 280
all sitting in due order in their places,
hearing their king. In prayer he raised his eyes
to the broad sky and said:

"May Zeus, all-highest
and first of gods, be witness first, then Earth
and Hêlios and the Furies underground
who punish men for having broken oaths,
I never laid a hand on your Brisêis,
proposing bed or any other pleasure;
in my quarters the girl has been untouched.
If one word that I swear is false, 290
may the gods plague me for a perjured liar!"

He slit the boar's throat with his blade of bronze.
Then Talthýbios, wheeling, flung the victim
into the offshore water, bait for fish.
Akhilleus rose amid the Argive warriors,
saying:

"Father Zeus, you send mankind
prodigious follies. Never otherwise
had Agamémnon stung me through and through;
never would he have been so empty-headed
as to defy my will and take the girl! 300
No, for some reason Zeus had death at heart
for the Akhaians, and for many.

Well:
go to your meat, then we'll resume the fighting."

Thus he dismissed the assembly. All the men
were quick to scatter, each to his own ship.
As for the gifts, the Myrmidons took over
and bore them all to Akhilleus' ship, to stow
within his shelter. There they left the women
and drove the horses to the herd.

The girl
Brisêis, in her grace like Aphrodítê, 310
on entering saw Patróklos lying dead
of spear wounds, and she sank down to embrace him
with a sharp sobbing cry, lifting her hands
to tear her breast, soft throat, and lovely face,
this girl, shaped like the goddesses of heaven.

Weeping, she said:

"Patróklos, very dear,
most dear to me, cursed as I am, you were
alive still when I left you, left this place!
Now I come back to find you dead, my captain!
Evil follows evil so, for me. 320
The husband to whom father and mother gave me
I saw brought down by spears before our town,
with my three brothers, whom my mother bore.
Dear brothers, all three met their day of wrath.
But when Akhilleus killed my lord, and sacked
the city of royal Mynês, not a tear
would you permit me: no, you undertook
to see me married to the Prince Akhilleus,[9]
conveyed by ship to Phthía, given a wedding
among the Myrmidons. Now must I mourn 330
your death forever, who were ever gentle."

She wailed again, and women sobbed about her,
first for Patróklos, then for each one's grief.
Meanwhile Akhaian counselors were gathered
begging Akhilleus to take food. He spurned it,
groaning:

"No, I pray you, my dear friends,
if anyone will listen!—do not nag me
to glut and dull my heart with food and drink!
A burning pain is in me. I'll hold out
till sundown without food. I say I'll bear it." 340

With this he sent the peers away, except
the two Atreidai[10] and the great Odysseus,
Nestor, Idómeneus, and old Lord Phoinix.
These would have comforted him, but none
could quiet or comfort him until he entered
the bloody jaws of war. Now pierced by memory,
he sighed and sighed again, and said:

"Ah, once
you, too, poor fated friend, and best of friends,
would set a savory meal deftly before us
in our field shelter, when the Akhaians wished 350
no time lost between onsets against Trojans.
Now there you lie, broken in battle. Ah,
lacking you, my heart will fast this day

[9] Patróklos was presumably trying to console Brisêis; for Akhilleus to marry a woman taken captive would be unlikely.

[10] Sons of Atreus—that is, Agamémnon and Meneláos.

from meat and drink as well. No greater ill
could come to me, not news of Father's death—
my father, weeping soft tears now in Phthía
for want of that son in a distant land
who wars on Troy for Helen's sake—that woman
who makes the blood run cold. No greater ill,
even should my son die, who is being reared 360
on Skyros, Neoptólemos, if indeed
he's living still.[11] My heart's desire had been
that I alone should perish far from Argos
here at Troy; that you should sail to Phthía,
taking my son aboard your swift black ship
at Skyros, to introduce him to his heritage,
my wide lands, my servants, my great hall.
In this late year Pêleus may well be dead
and buried, or have few days yet to live,
beset by racking age, always awaiting 370
dire news of me, of my own death."

As he said this he wept. The counselors groaned,
remembering each what he had left at home;
and seeing them sorrow, Zeus took pity on them,
saying quickly to Athêna:

"Daughter,
you seem to have left your fighting man alone.
Should one suppose you care no more for Akhilleus?
There he sits, before the curving prows,
and grieves for his dear friend. The other soldiers
flock to meat; he thirsts and hungers. Come, 380
infuse in him sweet nectar and ambrosia,
that an empty belly may not weaken him."

He urged Athêna to her own desire,
and like a gliding sea hawk, shrilling high,
she soared from heaven through the upper air,
while the Akhaians armed throughout the ranks.
Nectar and ambrosia she instilled
within Akhilleus, that his knees be not
assailed by hollow famine; then she withdrew
to her mighty father's house. Meanwhile the troops 390
were pouring from the shipways to the field.
As when cold snowflakes fly from Zeus in heaven,
thick and fast under the blowing north wind,
just so, that multitude of gleaming helms

[11]Skyros was an island east of Greece, in the Aegean Sea. According to some versions of the legend, the mother of Neoptólemos was a princess of Skyros whom Akhilleus had loved while hiding out there to avoid the Trojan War. Neoptólemos (also called Pyrrhus) joined the Greek forces after his father's death and killed Priam when Troy was finally taken (compare the account in Virgil's *Aeneid,* Book II).

and bossed shields issued from the ships, with plated
cuirasses and ashwood spears. Reflected
glintings flashed to heaven, as the plain
in all directions shone with glare of bronze
and shook with trampling feet of men. Among them
Prince Akhilleus armed. One heard his teeth 400
grind hard together, and his eyes blazed out
like licking fire, for unbearable pain
had fixed upon his heart. Raging at Trojans,
he buckled on the arms Hêphaistos forged.
The beautiful greaves, fitted with silver anklets
first he put upon his legs, and next
the cuirass on his ribs; then over his shoulder
he slung the sword of bronze with silver scabbard;
finally he took up the massive shield
whence came a radiance like the round full moon. 410
As when at sea to men on shipboard comes
the shining of a campfire on a mountain
in a lone sheepfold, while the gusts of nightwind
take them, loath to go, far from their friends
over the teeming sea: just so
Akhilleus' finely modeled shield sent light
into the heavens: Lifting his great helm
he placed it on his brows, and like a star
the helm shone with its horsetail blowing free,
all golden, that Hêphaistos had set in 420
upon the crest. Akhilleus tried his armor,
shrugging and flexing, making sure it fitted,
sure that his gleaming legs had play. Indeed
the gear sat on him light as wings: it buoyed him!
Now from a spear-case he withdrew a spear—
his father's—weighty, long, and tough. No other
Akhaian had the strength to handle it,
this great Pêlian shaft
of ashwood, given his father by the centaur
Kheirôn from the crest of Pêlion 430
to be the death of heroes.

Automédôn
and Álkimos with swift hands yoked his team,
making firm the collars on the horses,
placing the bits between their teeth, and pulling
reins to the war-car. Automédôn then
took in hand the shining whip and mounted
the chariot, and at his back Akhilleus
mounted in full armor, shining bright
as the blinding Lord of Noon.[12] In a clarion voice
he shouted to the horses of his father: 440

[12] The sun.

"Xánthos and Balíos! Known to the world
as foals of great Podargê! In this charge
care for your driver in another way!
Pull him back, I mean, to the Danáäns,
back to the main body of the army,
once we are through with battle; this time,
no leaving him there dead, like Lord Patróklos!"

To this, from under the yoke, the nimble Xánthos
answered, and hung his head, so that his mane
dropped forward from the yokepad to the ground— 450
Hêra whose arms are white as ivory
gave him a voice to say:

"Yes, we shall save you,
this time, too, Akhilleus in your strength!
And yet the day of your destruction comes,
and it is nearer. We are not the cause,
but rather a great god is, and mighty Fate.
Nor was it by our sloth or sluggishness
the Trojans stripped Patróklos of his armor.
No, the magnificent god[13] that Lêto bore
killed him in action and gave Hektor glory. 460
We might run swiftly as the west wind blows,
most rapid of all winds, they say; but still
it is your destiny to be brought low
by force, a god's force and a man's!"[14]

On this,
the Furies put a stop to Xánthos' voice.[15]
In anger and gloom Akhilleus said to him:

"Xánthos, why prophesy my death? No need.
What is in store for me I know, know well:
to die here, far away from my dear father,
my mother, too. No matter. All that matters 470
is that I shall not call a halt today
till I have made the Trojans sick of war!"

And with a shout he drove his team
of trim-hooved horses into the front line.

BOOK XX. *Zeus assembles the gods and tells them that they now have a free hand to intervene in the war. A brief catalog of the gods follows: on the Greek side Hêra, Athêna, Poseidon, Hermês, and Hêphaistos; on the Trojan side Arês, Apollo, Artemis (Apollo's sister and goddess of the hunt), Lêto (mother of Apollo and Artemis), the river god Xánthos, and Aphrodítê.*

[13]Apollo.
[14]Akhilleus will one day be slain by the bow of Paris with the help of Apollo, god of archers.
[15]That a horse should speak violates natural law, of which the Furies are guardians. (Xánthos is also the name of a river god who appears in Books XX and XXI.)

(For the time being, however, most of the gods stay out of action.) Aineías, incited by Apollo, engages Akhilleus; Poseidon (though he favors the Greeks) saves the Trojan hero by spiriting him away, since Aineías is fated to live and rule over the Trojan survivors of the war. Akhilleus and Hektor exhort their respective armies to fight. At Apollo's suggestion, Hektor stays out of Akhilleus' range, but when one of Hektor's brothers is slain he attacks Akhilleus. Hektor is saved when Apollo hides him in a cloud. Cheated of his prey a second time, Akhilleus rages, killing many Trojans.

BOOK XXI. *Akhilleus divides the Trojan forces, driving half of them toward the city, half into the river Xánthos (also called Skamánder), which flows by the plain. In the river he kills many men and takes twelve alive who are to pay later for the death of Patróklos. Xánthos, the god and personification of the river, angered by the pollution of his waters and by Akhilleus' slaughter of Trojans, attacks him and puts him in sore danger of drowning. Poseidon, Athêna, and Hêra come to Akhilleus' aid, and the fire god Hêphaistos uses his flames to overcome the raging river, which bubbles with the heat. Now the gods begin a general battle with one another: Athêna against Arês, Athêna against Aphrodítê, Hêra against Artemis. Challenged halfheartedly by Poseidon, Apollo declines to fight, remarking that it is foolish for gods to fight one another for the sake of mere mortals. The deities who favor the Greeks having emerged as victors, all the gods return to Olympos except Apollo, who helps the fleeing Trojans to withdraw safely within the city walls, by impersonating a Trojan and leading Akhilleus on a wild-goose chase. But Hektor remains outside the walls, stranded.*

BOOK TWENTY-TWO: DESOLATION BEFORE TROY

Once in the town, those who had fled like deer
wiped off their sweat and drank their thirst away,
leaning against the cool stone of the ramparts.
Meanwhile Akhaians with bright shields aslant
came up the plain and nearer. As for Hektor,
fatal destiny pinned him where he stood
before the Skaian Gates, outside the city.

Now Akhilleus heard Apollo calling
back to him:

"Why run so hard, Akhilleus,
mortal as you are, after a god? 10
Can you not comprehend it? I am immortal.
You are so hot to catch me, you no longer
think of finishing off the men you routed.
They are all in the town by now, packed in
while you were being diverted here. And yet
you cannot kill me; I am no man's quarry."

Akhilleus bit his lip and said:

"Archer of heaven, deadliest
of immortal gods, you put me off the track,
turning me from the wall this way. A hundred 20
might have sunk their teeth into the dust
before one man took cover in Ilion!

You saved my enemies with ease and stole
my glory, having no punishment to fear.
I'd take it out of you, if I had the power."
Then toward the town with might and main he ran,
magnificent, like a racing chariot horse
that holds its form at full stretch on the plain.
So light-footed Akhilleus held the pace.
And aging Priam was the first to see him 30
sparkling on the plain, bright as that star
in autumn rising, whose unclouded rays
shine out amid a throng of stars at dusk—
the one they call Oríôn's dog, most brilliant,
yes, but baleful as a sign: it brings
great fever to frail men.[1] So pure and bright
the bronze gear blazed upon him as he ran.
The old man gave a cry. With both his hands
thrown up on high he struck his head, then shouted,
groaning, appealing to his dear son. Unmoved, 40
Lord Hektor stood in the gateway, resolute
to fight Akhilleus.
Stretching out his hands,
old Priam said, imploring him:
"No, Hector!
Cut off as you are, alone, dear son,
don't try to hold your ground against this man,
or soon you'll meet the shock of doom, borne down
by the son of Pêleus. He is more powerful
by far than you, and pitiless. Ah, were he
but dear to the gods as he is dear to me!
Wild dogs and kites would eat him where he lay 50
within the hour, and ease me of my torment.
Many tall sons he killed, bereaving me,
or sold them to far islands. Even now
I cannot see two sons of mine, Lykáôn
and Polydôros,[2] among the Trojans massed
inside the town. A queen, Laóthoé,
conceived and bore them. If they are alive
amid the Akhaian host, I'll ransom them
with bronze and gold: both I have, piled at home,
rich treasures that old Altês, the renowned, 60
gave for his daughter's dowry. If they died,
if they went under to the homes of Death,
sorrow has come to me and to their mother.
But to our townsmen all this pain is brief,

[1] Sirius, the brightest of the stars, reappears in the eastern skies in the "dog days" of August, a time associated with disease.

[2] They were slain by Akhilleus in, respectively, Books XXI and XX. Laóthoê, daughter of Altês, is one of Priam's concubines. (Hektor's mother, Hékabê, is Priam's principal wife and queen of Troy.)

unless you too go down before Akhilleus.
Come inside the wall, child; here you may
fight on to save our Trojan men and women.
Do not resign the glory to Akhilleus,
losing your own dear life! Take pity, too,
on me and my hard fate, while I live still. 70
Upon the threshold of my age, in misery,
the son[3] of Krónos will destroy my life
after the evil days I shall have seen—
my sons brought down, my daughters dragged away,
bedchambers ravaged, and small children hurled
to earth in the atrocity of war,
as my sons' wives are taken by Akhaians'
ruinous hands. And at the end, I too—
when someone with a sword-cut or a spear
has had my life—I shall be torn apart 80
on my own doorstep by the hounds
I trained as watchdogs, fed from my own table.
These will lap my blood with ravenous hearts
and lie in the entranceway.
Everything done
to a young man killed in war becomes his glory,
once he is riven by the whetted bronze:
dead though he be, it is all fair, whatever
happens then. But when an old man falls,
and dogs disfigure his grey head and cheek
and genitals, that is most harrowing 90
of all that men in their hard lives endure."

The old man wrenched at his grey hair and pulled out
hanks of it in both hands, but moved
Lord Hektor not at all. The young man's mother
wailed from the tower across, above the portal,
streaming tears, and loosening her robe
with one hand, held her breast out in the other,
saying:

"Hektor, my child, be moved by this,
and pity me, if ever I unbound
a quieting breast for you. Think of these things, 100
dear child; defend yourself against the killer
this side of the wall, not hand to hand.
He has no pity. If he brings you down,
I shall no longer be allowed to mourn you
laid out on your bed, dear branch in flower,
born of me! And neither will your lady,
so endowed with gifts. Far from us both,
dogs will devour you by the Argive ships."

[3] Zeus.

With tears and cries the two implored their son,
and made their prayers again, but could not shake him. 110
Hektor stood firm, as huge Akhilleus neared.
The way a serpent, fed on poisonous herbs,
coiled at his lair upon a mountainside,
with all his length of hate awaits a man
and eyes him evilly: so Hektor, grim
and narrow-eyed, refused to yield. He leaned
his brilliant shield against a spur of wall
and in his brave heart bitterly reflected:
"Here I am badly caught. If I take cover,
slipping inside the gate and wall, the first 120
to accuse me for it will be Poulýdamas,
he who told me I should lead the Trojans
back to the city on that cursed night
Akhilleus joined the battle. No, I would not,
would not, wiser though it would have been.
Now troops have perished for my foolish pride,
I am ashamed to face townsmen and women.
Someone inferior to me may say:
'He kept his pride and lost his men, this Hektor!'
So it will go. Better, when that time comes, 130
that I appear as he who killed Akhilleus
man to man, or else that I went down
fighting him to the end before the city.
Suppose, though, that I lay my shield and helm
aside, and prop my spear against the wall,
and go meet the noble Prince Akhilleus,
promising Helen, promising with her
all treasures that Aléxandros[4] brought home
by ship to Troy—the first cause of our quarrel—
that he may give these things to the Atreidai? 140
Then I might add, apart from these, a portion
of all the secret wealth the city owns.
Yes, later I might take our counselors' oath
to hide no stores, but share and share alike
to halve all wealth our lovely city holds,
all that is here within the walls. Ah, no,
why even put the question to myself?
I must not go before him and receive
no quarter, no respect! Aye, then and there
he'll kill me, unprotected as I am, 150
my gear laid by, defenseless as a woman.
No chance, now, for charms[5] from oak or stone
in parley with him—charms a girl and boy
might use when they enchant each other talking!

[4]Paris.
[5]Pleasing words. The meaning of the phrase "from oak or stone" is uncertain.

Better we duel, now at once, and see
to whom the Olympian awards the glory."

These were his shifts of mood. Now close at hand
Akhilleus like the implacable god of war
came on with blowing crest, hefting the dreaded
beam of Pêlian ash on his right shoulder. 160
Bronze light played around him, like the glare
of a great fire or the great sun rising,
and Hektor, as he watched, began to tremble.
Then he could hold his ground no more. He ran,
leaving the gate behind him, with Akhilleus
hard on his heels, sure of his own speed.
When that most lightning-like of birds, a hawk
bred on a mountain, swoops upon a dove,
the quarry dips in terror, but the hunter,
screaming, dips behind and gains upon it, 170
passionate for prey. Just so, Akhilleus
murderously cleft the air, as Hektor
ran with flashing knees along the wall.
They passed the lookout point, the wild figtree
with wind in all its leaves, then veered away
along the curving wagon road, and came
to where the double fountains well, the source
of eddying Skamánder. One hot spring
flows out, and from the water fumes arise
as though from fire burning; but the other 180
even in summer gushes chill as hail
or snow or crystal ice frozen on water.
Near these fountains are wide washing pools
of smooth-laid stone, where Trojan wives and daughters
laundered their smooth linen in the days
of peace before the Akhaians came. Past these
the two men ran, pursuer and pursued,
and he who fled was noble, he behind
a greater man by far. They ran full speed,
and not for bull's hide or a ritual beast 190
or any prize that men compete for: no,
but for the life of Hektor, tamer of horses.
Just as when chariot-teams around a course
go wheeling swiftly, for the prize is great,
a tripod or a woman,[6] in the games
held for a dead man, so three times these two
at full speed made their course round Priam's town,
as all the gods looked on. And now the father
of gods and men turned to the rest and said:

[6]In Book XXIII these prizes are offered to the winner of the chariot race in the ceremonial funeral games honoring Patróklos.

"How sad that this beloved man is hunted 200
around the wall before my eyes! My heart
is touched for Hektor; he has burned thigh flesh
of oxen for me often, high on Ida,
at other times on the high point of Troy.
Now Prince Akhilleus with devouring stride
is pressing him around the town of Priam.
Come, gods, put your minds on it, consider
whether we may deliver him from death
or see him, noble as he is, brought down
by Pêleus' son, Akhilleus."

Grey-eyed Athêna 210
said to him:

"Father of the blinding bolt,
the dark stormcloud, what words are these? The man
is mortal, and his doom fixed, long ago.
Would you release him from his painful death?
Then do so, but not all of us will praise you."

Zeus who gathers cloud replied:

"Take heart,
my dear and honored child. I am not bent
on my suggestion, and I would indulge you.
Act as your thought inclines, refrain no longer."

So he encouraged her in her desire, 220
and down she swept from ridges of Olympos.
Great Akhilleus, hard on Hektor's heels,
kept after him, the way a hound will harry
a deer's fawn he has startled from its bed
to chase through gorge and open glade, and when
the quarry goes to earth under a bush
he holds the scent and quarters till he finds it;
so with Hektor: he could not shake off
the great runner, Akhilleus. Every time
he tried to spring hard for the Dardan gates 230
under the towers, hoping men could help him,
sending missiles down, Akhilleus loomed
to cut him off and turn him toward the plain,
as he himself ran always near the city.
As in a dream a man chasing another
cannot catch him, nor can he in flight
escape from his pursuer, so Akhilleus
could not by his swiftness overtake him,
nor could Hektor pull away. How could he
run so long from death, had not Apollo 240
for the last time, the very last, come near
to give him stamina and speed?

Akhilleus
shook his head at the rest of the Akhaians,
allowing none to shoot or cast at Hektor—
none to forestall him, and to win the honor.
But when, for the fourth time, they reached the springs,
the Father poised his golden scales.

He placed
two shapes of death, death prone and cold, upon them,
one of Akhilleus, one of the horseman, Hektor,
and held the midpoint, pulling upward. Down 250
sank Hektor's fatal day, the pan went down
toward undergloom, and Phoibos Apollo left him.
Then came Athêna, grey-eyed, to the son
of Pêleus, falling in with him, and near him,
saying swiftly:

"Now at last I think
the two of us, Akhilleus loved by Zeus,
shall bring Akhaians triumph at the ships
by killing Hektor—unappeased
though he was ever in his thirst for war.
There is no way he may escape us now, 260
not though Apollo, lord of distances,
should suffer all indignity for him
before his father Zeus who bears the stormcloud,
rolling back and forth and begging for him.
Now you can halt and take your breath, while I
persuade him into combat face to face."

These were Athêna's orders. He complied,
relieved, and leaning hard upon the spearshaft
armed with its head of bronze. She left him there
and overtook Lord Hektor—but she seemed 270
Dêíphobos in form and resonant voice,
appearing at his shoulder, saying swiftly:

"Ai! Dear brother, how he runs, Akhilleus,
harrying you around the town of Priam!
Come, we'll stand and take him on."

To this,
great Hektor in his shimmering helm replied:

"Dêíphobos, you were the closest to me
in the old days, of all my brothers, sons
of Hékabê and Priam. Now I can say
I honor you still more 280
because you dared this foray for my sake,
seeing me run. The rest stay under cover."

Again the grey-eyed goddess spoke:

"Dear brother, how your father and gentle mother
begged and begged me to remain! So did
the soldiers round me, all undone by fear.
But in my heart I ached for you.
Now let us fight him, and fight hard.
No holding back. We'll see if this Akhilleus
conquers both, to take our armor seaward, 290
or if he can be brought down by your spear."

This way, by guile, Athêna led him on.
And when at last the two men faced each other,
Hektor was the first to speak. He said:

"I will no longer fear you as before,
son of Pêleus, though I ran from you
round Priam's town three times and could not face you.
Now my soul would have me stand and fight,
whether I kill you or am killed. So come,
we'll summon gods here as our witnesses, 300
none higher, arbiters of a pact: I swear
that, terrible as you are,
I'll not insult your corpse should Zeus allow me
victory in the end, your life as prize.
Once I have your gear, I'll give your body
back to Akhaians. Grant me, too, this grace."

But swift Akhilleus frowned at him and said:

"Hektor, I'll have no talk of pacts with you,
forever unforgiven as you are.
As between men and lions there are none, 310
no concord between wolves and sheep, but all
hold one another hateful through and through,
so there can be no courtesy between us,
no sworn truce, till one of us is down
and glutting with his blood the wargod Arês.
Summon up what skills you have. By god,
you'd better be a spearman and a fighter!
Now there is no way out. Pallas Athêna
will have the upper hand of you. The weapon
belongs to me. You'll pay the reckoning 320
in full for all the pain my men have borne,
who met death by your spear."

He twirled and cast
his shaft with its long shadow. Splendid Hektor,
keeping his eye upon the point, eluded it
by ducking at the instant of the cast,
so shaft and bronze shank passed him overhead
and punched into the earth. But unperceived
by Hektor, Pallas Athêna plucked it out

and gave it back to Akhilleus. Hektor said:

"A clean miss. Godlike as you are, 330
you have not yet known doom for me from Zeus.
You thought you had, by heaven. Then you turned
into a word-thrower, hoping to make me lose
my fighting heart and head in fear of you.
You cannot plant your spear between my shoulders
while I am running. If you have the gift,
just put it through my chest as I come forward.
Now it's for you to dodge my own. Would god
you'd give the whole shaft lodging in your body!
War for the Trojans would be eased 340
if you were blotted out, bane that you are."

With this he twirled his long spearshaft and cast it,
hitting his enemy mid-shield, but off
and away the spear rebounded. Furious
that he had lost it, made his throw for nothing,
Hektor stood bemused. He had no other.
Then he gave a great shout to Dêíphobos
to ask for a long spear. But there was no one
near him, not a soul. Now in his heart
the Trojan realized the truth and said: 350

"This is the end. The gods are calling deathward.
I had thought
a good soldier, Dêíphobos, was with me.
He is inside the walls. Athêna tricked me.
Death is near, and black, not at a distance,
not to be evaded. Long ago
this hour must have been to Zeus's liking
and to the liking of his archer son.
They have been well disposed before, but now
the appointed time's upon me. Still, I would not 360
die without delivering a stroke,
or die ingloriously, but in some action
memorable to men in days to come."

With this he drew the whetted blade that hung
upon his left flank, ponderous and long,
collecting all his might the way an eagle
narrows himself to dive through shady cloud
and strike a lamb or cowering hare: so Hektor
lanced ahead and swung his whetted blade.
Akhilleus with wild fury in his heart 370
pulled in upon his chest his beautiful shield—
his helmet with four burnished metal ridges
nodding above it, and the golden crest
Hêphaistos locked there tossing in the wind.
Conspicuous as the evening star that comes,

amid the first in heaven, at fall of night,
and stands most lovely in the west, so shone
in sunlight the fine-pointed spear
Akhilleus poised in his right hand, with deadly
aim at Hektor, at the skin where most 380
it lay exposed. But nearly all was covered
by the bronze gear he took from slain Patróklos,
showing only, where his collarbones
divided neck and shoulders, the bare throat
where the destruction of a life is quickest.
Here, then, as the Trojan charged, Akhilleus
drove his point straight through the tender neck,
but did not cut the windpipe, leaving Hektor
able to speak and to respond. He fell
aside into the dust. And Prince Akhilleus 390
now exulted:

"Hektor, had you thought
that you could kill Patróklos and be safe?
Nothing to dread from me; I was not there.
All childishness. Though distant then, Patróklos'
comrade in arms was greater far than he—
and it is I who had been left behind
that day beside the deepsea ships who now
have made your knees give way. The dogs and kites
will rip your body. His will lie in honor
when the Akhaians give him funeral." 400

Hektor, barely whispering, replied:

"I beg you by your soul and by your parents,
do not let the dogs feed on me
in your encampment by the ships. Accept
the bronze and gold my father will provide
as gifts, my father and her ladyship
my mother. Let them have my body back,
so that our men and women may accord me
decency of fire when I am dead."

Akhilleus the great runner scowled and said: 410

"Beg me no beggary by soul or parents,
whining dog! Would god my passion drove me
to slaughter you and eat you raw, you've caused
such agony to me! No man exists
who could defend you from the carrion pack—
not if they spread for me ten times your ransom,
twenty times, and promise more as well;
aye, not if Priam, son of Dárdanos,
tells them to buy you for your weight in gold!
You'll have no bed of death, nor will you be 420

laid out and mourned by her who gave you birth.
Dogs and birds will have you, every scrap."

Then at the point of death Lord Hektor said:

"I see you now for what you are. No chance
to win you over. Iron in your breast
your heart is. Think a bit, though: this may be
a thing the gods in anger hold against you
on that day when Paris and Apollo
destroy you at the Gates,[7] great as you are."

Even as he spoke, the end came, and death hid him; 430
spirit from body fluttered to undergloom,
bewailing fate that made him leave his youth
and manhood in the world. And as he died
Akhilleus spoke again. He said:

"Die, make an end. I shall accept my own
whenever Zeus and the other gods desire."

At this he pulled his spearhead from the body,
laying it aside, and stripped
the bloodstained shield and cuirass from his shoulders.
Other Akhaians hastened round to see 440
Hektor's fine body and his comely face,
and no one came who did not stab the body.
Glancing at one another they would say:

"Now Hektor has turned vulnerable, softer
than when he put the torches to the ships!"

And he who said this would inflict a wound.
When the great master of pursuit, Akhilleus,
had the body stripped, he stood among them,
saying swiftly:

"Friends, my lords and captains
of Argives, now that the gods at last have let me 450
bring to earth this man who wrought
havoc among us—more than all the rest—
come, we'll offer battle around the city,
to learn the intentions of the Trojans now.
Will they give up their strongpoint at this loss?
Can they fight on, though Hektor's dead?

But wait:
why do I ponder, why take up these questions?
Down by the ships Patróklos' body lies

[7] The gates of Troy.

unwept, unburied. I shall not forget him
while I can keep my feet among the living. 460
If in the dead world they forget the dead,
I say there, too, I shall remember him,
my friend. Men of Akhaia, lift a song!
Down to the ships we go, and take this body,
our glory. We have beaten Hektor down,
to whom as to a god the Trojans prayed."

Indeed, he had in mind for Hektor's body
outrage and shame. Behind both feet he pierced
the tendons, heel to ankle. Rawhide cords
he drew through both and lashed them to his chariot, 470
letting the man's head trail. Stepping aboard,
bearing the great trophy of the arms,
he shook the reins, and whipped the team ahead
into a willing run. A dustcloud rose
above the furrowing body; the dark tresses
flowed behind, and the head so princely once
lay back in dust. Zeus gave him to his enemies
to be defiled in his own fatherland.
So his whole head was blackened. Looking down,
his mother tore her braids, threw off her veil, 480
and wailed, heartbroken to behold her son.
Piteously his father groaned, and round him
lamentation spread throughout the town,
most like the clamor to be heard if Ilion's
towers, top to bottom, seethed in flames.
They barely stayed the old man, mad with grief,
from passing through the gates. Then in the mire
he rolled, and begged them all, each man by name:

"Relent, friends. It is hard; but let me go
out of the city to the Akhaian ships. 490
I'll make my plea to that demonic heart.
He may feel shame before his peers, or pity
my old age. His father, too, is old,
Pêleus, who brought him up to be a scourge
to Trojans, cruel to all, but most to me,
so many of my sons in flower of youth
he cut away. And, though I grieve, I cannot
mourn them all as much as I do one,
for whom my grief will take me to the grave—
and that is Hektor. Why could he not have died 500
where I might hold him? In our weeping, then,
his mother, now so destitute, and I
might have had surfeit and relief of tears."

These were the words of Priam as he wept,
and all his people groaned. Then in her turn
Hékabê led the women in lamentation:

"Child, I am lost now. Can I bear my life
after the death of suffering your death?
You were my pride in all my nights and days,
pride of the city, pillar to the Trojans 510
and Trojan women. Everyone looked to you
as though you were a god, and rightly so.
You were their greatest glory while you lived.
Now your doom and death have come upon you."

These were her mournful words. But Hektor's lady
still knew nothing; no one came to tell her
of Hektor's stand outside the gates. She wove
upon her loom, deep in the lofty house,
a double purple web with rose design.
Calling her maids in waiting, 520
she ordered a big caldron on a tripod
set on the hearthfire, to provide a bath
for Hektor when he came home from the fight.
Poor wife, how far removed from baths he was
she could not know, as at Akhilleus' hands
Athêna brought him down.

Then from the tower
she heard a wailing and a distant moan.
Her knees shook, and she let her shuttle fall,
and called out to her maids again:

"Come here.
Two must follow me, to see this action. 530
I heard my husband's queenly mother cry.
I feel my heart rise, throbbing in my throat.
My knees are like stone under me. Some blow
is coming home to Priam's sons and daughters.
Ah, could it never reach my ears! I die
of dread that Akhilleus may have cut off Hektor,
blocked my bold husband from the city wall,
to drive him down the plain alone! By now
he may have ended Hektor's deathly pride.
He never kept his place amid the chariots 540
but drove ahead. He would not be outdone
by anyone in courage."

Saying this, she ran
like a madwoman through the mégaron,
her heart convulsed. Her maids kept at her side.
On reaching the great tower and the soldiers,
Andrómakhê stood gazing from the wall
and saw him being dragged before the city.
Chariot horses at a brutal gallop
pulled the torn body toward the decked ships.
Blackness of night covered her eyes; she fell 550
backward swooning, sighing out her life,

and let her shining headdress fall, her hood
and diadem, her plaited band and veil
that Aphrodítê once had given her,
on that day when, from Eëtíôn's house,
for a thousand bridal gifts, Lord Hektor led her.
Now, at her side, kinswomen of her lord
supported her among them, dazed and faint
to the point of death. But when she breathed again
and her stunned heart recovered, in a burst 560
of sobbing she called out among the women:

"Hektor! Here is my desolation. Both
had this in store from birth—from yours in Troy
in Priam's palace, mine by wooded Plakos
at Thêbê in the home of Eëtíôn,
my father, who took care of me in childhood,
a man cursed by fate, a fated daughter.
How I could wish I never had been born!
Now under earth's roof to the house of Death
you go your way and leave me here, bereft, 570
lonely, in anguish without end. The child
we wretches had is still in infancy;
you cannot be a pillar to him, Hektor,
now you are dead, nor he to you. And should
this boy escape the misery of the war,
there will be toil and sorrow for him later,
as when strangers move his boundary stones.[8]
The day that orphans him will leave him lonely,
downcast in everything, cheeks wet with tears,
in hunger going to his father's friends 580
to tug at one man's cloak, another's khiton.
Some will be kindly: one may lift a cup
to wet his lips at least, though not his throat;
but from the board some child with living parents
gives him a push, a slap, with biting words:
'Outside, you there! Your father is not with us
here at our feast!' And the boy Astýanax
will run to his forlorn mother. Once he fed
on marrow only and the fat of lamb,
high on his father's knees. And when sleep came 590
to end his play, he slept in a nurse's arms,
brimful of happiness, in a soft bed.
But now he'll know sad days and many of them,
missing his father. 'Lord of the lower town'[9]
the Trojans call him. They know, you alone,
Lord Hektor, kept their gates and their long walls.

[8] Encroach on his land.
[9] The meaning of the child's nickname, Astýanax.

Beside the beaked ships now, far from your kin,
the blowflies' maggots in a swarm will eat you
naked, after the dogs have had their fill.
Ah, there are folded garments in your chambers, 600
delicate and fine, of women's weaving.
These, by heaven, I'll burn to the last thread
in blazing fire! They are no good to you,
they cannot cover you in death. So let them
go, let them be burnt as an offering
from Trojans and their women in your honor."

Thus she mourned, and the women wailed in answer.

BOOK XXIII. *Led by Akhilleus and his Myrmidons, the Greeks mourn Patróklos. Akhilleus continues to dishonor Hektor's corpse. Patróklos' ghost appears to Akhilleus, asks for speedy burial so that he may be accepted among the dead, and reminds Akhilleus of his own approaching death in the Trojan War. The Greeks conduct Patróklos' funeral rites, which include the slaying by Akhilleus of the twelve Trojans he earlier captured for that purpose. (Hektor's body, meanwhile, is being preserved by Aphrodítê and Apollo from defacement and corruption.) Akhilleus presides over ceremonial athletic contests (the gods still intervening on occasion): chariot racing, boxing, wrestling, foot racing, armed combat, weight throwing, archery, javelin throwing. But the last of these contests is not actually held; Akhilleus awards the victory to Agamémnon in advance.*

BOOK TWENTY-FOUR: A GRACE GIVEN IN SORROW

The funeral games were over. Men dispersed
and turned their thoughts to supper in their quarters,
then to the boon of slumber. But Akhilleus
thought of his friend, and sleep that quiets all things
would not take hold of him. He tossed and turned
remembering with pain Patróklos' courage,
his buoyant heart; how in his company
he fought out many a rough day full of danger,
cutting through ranks in war and the bitter sea.
With memory his eyes grew wet. He lay 10
on his right side, then on his back, and then
face downward—but at last he rose, to wander
distractedly along the line of surf.
This for eleven nights. The first dawn, brightening
sea and shore, became familiar to him,
as at that hour he yoked his team, with Hektor
tied behind, to drag him out, three times
around Patróklos' tomb. By day he rested
in his own hut, abandoning Hektor's body
to lie full-length in dust—though Lord Apollo, 20
pitying the man, even in death,
kept his flesh free of disfigurement.

He wrapped him in his great shield's[1] flap of gold
to save him from laceration. But Akhilleus
in rage visited indignity on Hektor
day after day, and, looking on,
the blessed gods were moved. Day after day
they urged the Wayfinder[2] to steal the body—
a thought agreeable to all but Hêra,
Poseidon, and the grey-eyed one, Athêna. 30
These opposed it, and held out, since Ilion
and Priam and his people had incurred
their hatred first, the day Aléxandros
made his mad choice and piqued two goddesses,
visitors in his sheepfold: he praised
a third, who offered ruinous lust.[3]
Now when Dawn grew bright for the twelfth day,
Phoibos Apollo spoke among the gods:

"How heartless and how malevolent you are!
Did Hektor never make burnt offering 40
of bulls' thighbones to you, and unflawed goats?
Even in death you would not stir to save him
for his dear wife to see, and for his mother,
his child, his father, Priam, and his men:
they'd burn the corpse at once and give him burial.
Murderous Akhilleus has your willing help—
a man who shows no decency, implacable,
barbarous in his ways as a wild lion
whose power and intrepid heart
sway him to raid the flocks of men for meat. 50
The man has lost all mercy;
he has no shame—that gift that hinders mortals
but helps them, too. A sane one may endure
an even dearer loss: a blood brother,
a son; and yet, by heaven, having grieved
and passed through mourning, he will let it go.
The Fates have given patient hearts to men.
Not this one: first he took Prince Hektor's life
and now he drags the body, lashed to his car,
around the barrow[4] of his friend, performing 60
something neither nobler in report
nor better in itself. Let him take care,
or, brave as he is, we gods will turn against him,
seeing him outrage the insensate earth!"

[1] The aegis, or shield of Zeus, sometimes lent by him to other immortals.
[2] Hermês, messenger of the gods and also the patron of tricksters and thieves.
[3] For the decision by Paris (Aléxandros) that had offended Hêra and Athêna, see the headnote to the *Iliad*. Paris had been a shepherd at the time of the incident. Poseidon's hatred of the Trojans originated when he was forced to serve as a laborer under Priam's father, Laomédôn, who added insult to injury by withholding the god's wages.
[4] A large mound covering a grave.

Hêra whose arms are white as ivory
grew angry at Apollo. She retorted:

"Lord of the silver bow, your words would be
acceptable if one had a mind to honor
Hektor and Akhilleus equally.
But Hektor suckled at a woman's breast, 70
Akhilleus is the first-born of a goddess—
one I nursed myself. I reared her, gave her
to Pêleus, a strong man whom the gods loved.
All of you were present at their wedding—
you too—friend of the base, forever slippery!—
came with your harp and dined there!

Zeus the stormking

answered her:

"Hêra, don't lose your temper
altogether. Clearly the same high honor
cannot be due both men. And yet Lord Hektor
of all the mortal men in Ilion, 80
was dearest to the gods, or was to me.
He never failed in the right gift; my altar
never lacked a feast
of wine poured out and smoke of sacrifice—
the share assigned as ours. We shall renounce
the theft of Hektor's body; there is no way;
there would be no eluding Akhilleus' eye,
as night and day his mother comes to him.
Will one of you now call her to my presence?
I have a solemn message to impart: 90
Akhilleus is to take fine gifts from Priam,
and in return give back Prince Hektor's body."

At this, Iris who runs on the rainy wind
with word from Zeus departed. Midway between
Samos and rocky Imbros,[5] down she plunged
into the dark grey sea, and the brimming tide
roared over her as she sank into the depth—
as rapidly as a leaden sinker, fixed
on a lure of wild bull's horn, that glimmers down
with a fatal hook among the ravening fish. 100
Soon Iris came on Thetis in a cave,
surrounded by a company of Nereids
lolling there, while she bewailed the fate
of her magnificent son, now soon to perish
on Troy's rich earth, far from his fatherland.
Halting before her, Iris said:

[5]Islands in the Aegean Sea, northwest of Troy.

"Come, Thetis,
Zeus of eternal forethought summons you."

Silvery-footed Thetis answered:

"Why?
Why does the great one call me to him now,
when I am shy of mingling with immortals, 110
being so heavyhearted? But I'll go.
Whatever he may say will have its weight."

That loveliest of goddesses now put on
a veil so black no garment could be blacker,
and swam where windswift Iris led. Before them
on either hand the ground swell fell away.
They rose to a beach, then soared into the sky
and found the viewer of the wide world, Zeus,
with all the blissful gods who live forever
around him seated. Athêna yielded place, 120
and Thetis sat down by her father, Zeus,
while Hêra handed her a cup of gold
and spoke a comforting word. When she had drunk,
Thetis held out the cup again to Hêra.
The father of gods and men began:

"You've come
to Olympos, Thetis, though your mind is troubled
and insatiable pain preys on your heart.
I know, I too. But let me, even so,
explain why I have called you here. Nine days
of quarreling we've had among the gods 130
concerning Hektor's body and Akhilleus.
They wish the Wayfinder to make off with it.
I, however, accord Akhilleus honor
as I now tell you—in respect for you
whose love I hope to keep hereafter. Go, now,
down to the army, tell this to your son:
the gods are sullen toward him, and I, too,
more than the rest, am angered at his madness,
holding the body by the beaked ships
and not releasing it. In fear of me 140
let him relent and give back Hektor's body!
At the same time I'll send Iris to Priam,
directing him to go down to the beachhead
and ransom his dear son. He must bring gifts
to melt Akhilleus' rage."

Thetis obeyed,
leaving Olympos' ridge and flashing down
to her son's hut. She found him groaning there,

inconsolable, while men-at-arms
went to and fro, making their breakfast ready—
having just put to the knife a fleecy sheep. 150
His gentle mother sat down at his side,
caressed him, and said tenderly:

"My child,
will you forever feed on your own heart
in grief and pain, and take no thought of sleep
or sustenance? It would be comforting
to make love with a woman. No long time
will you live on for me: Death even now
stands near you, appointed and all-powerful.
But be alert and listen: I am a messenger
from Zeus, who tells me the gods are sullen toward you 160
and he himself most angered at your madness,
holding the body by the beaked ships
and not releasing it. Give Hektor back.
Take ransom for the body."

Said Akhilleus:

"Let it be so. Let someone bring the ransom
and take the dead away, if the Olympian
commands this in his wisdom."

So, that morning,
in camp, amid the ships, mother and son
conversed together, and their talk was long.
Lord Zeus meanwhile sent Iris to Ilion. 170

"Off with you, lightfoot, leave Olympos, take
my message to the majesty of Priam
at Ilion. He is to journey down
and ransom his dear son upon the beachhead.
He shall take gifts to melt Akhilleus' rage,
and let him go alone, no soldier with him,
only some crier, some old man, to drive
his wagon team and guide the nimble wagon,
and afterward to carry home the body
of him that Prince Akhilleus overcame. 180
Let him not think of death, or suffer dread,
as I'll provide him with a wondrous guide,
the Wayfinder, to bring him across the lines
into the very presence of Akhilleus.
And he, when he sees Priam within his hut,
will neither take his life nor let another
enemy come near. He is no madman,
no blind brute, nor one to flout the gods,
but dutiful toward men who beg his mercy."

Then Iris at his bidding ran 190
on the rainy winds to bear the word of Zeus,
until she came to Priam's house and heard
voices in lamentation. In the court
she found the princes huddled around their father,
faces and clothing wet with tears. The old man,
fiercely wrapped and hooded in his mantle,
sat like a figure graven—caked in filth
his own hands had swept over head and neck
when he lay rolling on the ground. Indoors
his daughters and his sons' wives were weeping, 200
remembering how many and how brave
the young men were who had gone down to death
before the Argive spearmen.
Zeus's courier,
appearing now to Priam's eyes alone,
alighted whispering, so the old man trembled:

"Priam, heir of Dárdanos,[6] take heart,
and have no fear of me; I bode no evil,
but bring you friendly word from Zeus,
who is distressed for you and pities you
though distant far upon Olympos. He 210
commands that you shall ransom the Prince Hektor,
taking fine gifts to melt Akhilleus' rage.
And go alone: no soldier may go with you,
only some crier, some old man, to drive
your wagon team and guide the nimble wagon,
and afterward to carry home the body
of him that Prince Akhilleus overcame.
Put away thoughts of death, shake off your dread,
for you shall have a wondrous guide,
the Wayfinder, to bring you across the lines 220
into the very presence of Akhilleus.
He, for his part, seeing you in his quarters,
will neither take your life nor let another
enemy come near. He is no madman,
no blind brute, nor one to flout the gods,
but dutiful toward men who beg his mercy."

Iris left him, swift as a veering wind.
Then Priam spoke, telling the men to rig
a four-wheeled wagon with a wicker box,
while he withdrew to his chamber roofed in cedar, 230
high and fragrant, rich in precious things.
He called to Hékabê, his lady:

[6]A son of Zeus and ancestor of Priam (five generations earlier).

"Princess,
word from Olympian Zeus has come to me
to go down to the ships of the Akhaians
and ransom our dead son. I am to take
gifts that will melt Akhilleus' anger. Tell me
how this appears to you, tell me your mind,
for I am torn with longing, now, to pass
inside the great encampment by the ships."

The woman's voice broke as she answered:

"Sorrow, 240
sorrow. Where is the wisdom now that made you
famous in the old days, near and far?
How can you ever face the Akhaian ships
or wish to go alone before those eyes,
the eyes of one who stripped your sons in battle,
how many, and how brave? Iron[7] must be
the heart within you. If he sees you, takes you,
savage and wayward as the man is,
he'll have no mercy and no shame. Better
that we should mourn together in our hall. 250
Almighty fate spun this thing for our son
the day I bore him: destined him to feed
the wild dogs after death, being far from us
when he went down before the stronger man.
I could devour the vitals of that man,
leeching into his living flesh! He'd know
pain then—pain like mine for my dead son.
It was no coward the Akhaian killed;
he stood and fought for the sweet wives of Troy,
with no more thought of flight or taking cover." 260

In majesty old Priam said:

"My heart
is fixed on going. Do not hold me back,
and do not make yourself a raven[8] crying
calamity at home. You will not move me.
If any man on earth had urged this on me—
reader of altar smoke,[9] prophet or priest—
we'd say it was a lie, and hold aloof.
But no: with my own ears I heard the voice,
I saw the god before me. Go I shall,
and no more words. If I must die alongside 270
the ships of the Akhaians in their bronze,

[7]Courageous.
[8]Traditionally, the bird forebodes evil.
[9]Interpreter of omens.

I die gladly. May I but hold my son
and spend my grief; then let Akhilleus kill me."

Throwing open the lids of treasure boxes
he picked out twelve great robes of state, and twelve
light cloaks for men, and rugs, an equal number,
and just as many capes of snowy linen,
adding a dozen khitons to the lot;
then set in order ten pure bars of gold,
a pair of shining tripods, four great caldrons, 280
and finally one splendid cup, a gift
Thracians had made him on an embassy.
He would not keep this, either—as he cared
for nothing now but ransoming his son.

And now, from the colonnade,
he made his Trojan people keep their distance,
berating and abusing them:

"Away,
you craven fools and rubbish! In your own homes
have you no one to mourn, that you crowd here,
to make more trouble for me? Is this a show, 290
that Zeus has crushed me, that he took the life
of my most noble son? You'll soon know what it means,
as you become child's play for the Akhaians
to kill in battle, now that Hektor's gone.
As for myself, before I see my city
taken and ravaged, let me go down blind
to Death's cold kingdom!"

Staff in hand,
he herded them, until they turned away
and left the furious old man. He lashed out
now at his sons, at Hélenos and Paris, 300
Agathôn, Pammôn, Antíphonos,
Polítês, Dêíphobos, Hippóthoös,
and Dios—to these nine the old man cried:

"Bestir yourselves, you misbegotten whelps,
shame of my house! Would god you had been killed
instead of Hektor at the line of ships.
How curst I am in everything! I fathered
first-rate men, in our great Troy; but now
I swear not one is left: Mêstôr, Trôïlos,
laughing amid the war-cars; and then Hektor— 310
a god to soldiers, and a god among them,
seeming not a man's child, but a god's.
Arês[10] killed them. These poltroons are left,

[10] Here, as often, the word is not so much the name of a god as a synonym for war itself.

hollow men, dancers, heroes of the dance,
light-fingered pillagers of lambs and kids
from the town pens!
Now will you get a wagon
ready for me, and quickly? Load these gifts
aboard it, so that we can take the road."

Dreading the rough edge of their father's tongue,
they lifted out a cart, a cargo wagon, 320
neat and maneuverable, and newly made,
and fixed upon it a wicker box; then took
a mule yoke from a peg, a yoke of boxwood
knobbed in front, with rings to hold the reins.
They brought out, too, the band nine forearms long
called the yoke-fastener, and placed the yoke
forward at the shank of the polished pole,
shoving the yoke-pin firmly in. They looped
three turns of the yoke-fastener round the knob
and wound it over and over down the pole, 330
tucking the tab end under. Next, the ransom:
bearing the weight of gifts for Hektor's person
out of the inner room, they piled them up
on the polished wagon. It was time to yoke
the mule-team, strong in harness, with hard hooves,
a team the Mysians had given Priam.
Then for the king's own chariot they harnessed
a team of horses of the line of Tros,[11]
reared by the old king in his royal stable.
So the impatient king and his sage crier 340
had their animals yoked in the palace yard
when Hékabê in her agitation joined them,
carrying in her right hand a golden cup
of honeyed wine, with which, before they left,
they might make offering. At the horses' heads
she stood to tell them:

"Here, tip wine to Zeus,
the father of gods. Pray for a safe return
from the enemy army, seeing your heart is set
on venturing to the camp against my will.
Pray in the second place to Zeus the stormking, 350
gloomy over Ida, who looks down
on all Troy country. Beg for an omen-bird,
the courier dearest of all birds to Zeus
and sovereign in power of flight,[12]
that he appear upon our right in heaven.

[11] Great-grandfather of Priam. The horses of Trôs, which he received from Zeus, were the best in the world.
[12] The eagle. Good omens appeared on the right side.

When you have seen him with your own eyes, then,
under that sign, you may approach the ships.
If Zeus who views the wide world will not give you
vision of his bird, then I at least
cannot bid godspeed to your journey, 360
bent on it though you are."

In majesty,
Priam replied:

"My lady, in this matter
I am disposed to trust you and agree.
It is an excellent thing and salutary
to lift our hands to Zeus, invoking mercy."

The old king motioned to his housekeeper,
who stood nearby with a basin and a jug,
to pour clear water on his hands. He washed them,
took the cup his lady held, and prayed
while standing there, midway in the walled court. 370
Then he tipped out the wine, looking toward heaven,
saying:

"Zeus, our Father, reigning from Ida,
god of glory and power, grant I come
to Akhilleus' door as one to be received
with kindliness and mercy. And dispatch
your courier bird, the nearest to your heart
of all birds, and the first in power of flight.
Let him appear upon our right in heaven
that I may see him with my own eyes
and under that sign journey to the ships." 380

Zeus all-foreseeing listened to this prayer
and put an eagle, king
of winged creatures, instantly in flight:
a swamp eagle, a hunter, one they call
the duskwing. Wide as a doorway in a chamber
spacious and high, built for a man of wealth,
a door with long bars fitted well, so wide
spread out each pinion. The great bird appeared
winging through the town on their right hand,
and all their hearts lifted with joy to see him. 390
In haste the old king boarded his bright car
and clattered out of the echoing colonnade.
Ahead, the mule-team drew the four-wheeled wagon,
driven by Idaíos,[13] and behind
the chariot rolled, with horses that the old man
whipped into a fast trot through the town.

[13] Priam's crier, or herald.

Family and friends all followed weeping
as though for Priam's last and deathward ride.
Into the lower town they passed, and reached
the plain of Troy. Here those who followed after 400
turned back, sons and sons-in-law. And Zeus
who views the wide world saw the car and wagon
brave the plain. He felt a pang for Priam
and quickly said to Hermês, his own son:

"Hermês, as you go most happily
of all the gods with mortals,[14] and give heed
to whom you will, be on your way this time
as guide for Priam to the deepsea ships.
Guide him so that not one of the Danáäns
may know or see him till he reach Akhilleus." 410

Argeiphontês[15] the Wayfinder obeyed.
He bent to tie his beautiful sandals on,
ambrosial, golden, that carry him over water
and over endless land on a puff of wind,
and took the wand with which he charms asleep—
or, when he wills, awake—the eyes of men.
So, wand in hand, the strong god glittering
paced into the air. Quick as a thought
he came to Hellê's waters and to Troy,
appearing as a boy whose lip was downy 420
in the first bloom of manhood, a young prince,
all graciousness.

After the travelers
drove past the mound of Ilos,[16] at the ford
they let the mules and horses pause to drink
the running stream. Now darkness had come on
when, looking round, the crier
saw Hermês near at hand. He said to Priam:

"You must think hard and fast, your grace;
there is new danger; we need care and prudence.
I see a man-at-arms there—ready, I think, 430
to prey on us. Come, shall we whip the team
and make a run for it? Or take his knees
and beg for mercy?"

Now the old man's mind
gave way to confusion and to terror.
On his gnarled arms and legs the hair stood up,

[14]Hermês often acts as a guide, and one of his functions is to conduct the spirits of the dead to the Underworld.

[15]A name for Hermês; see Homer's *Odyssey,* I.53 and note.

[16]Ilos' burial mound. He was grandfather of Priam and founder of Troy (which is therefore sometimes called Ilion).

and he stared, breathless. But the affable god
came over and took his hand and asked:

"Old father,
where do you journey, with your cart and car,
while others rest, below the evening star?
Do you not fear the Akhaians where they lie 440
encamped, hard, hostile outlanders, nearby?
Should someone see you, bearing stores like these
by night, how would you deal with enemies?
You are not young, your escort's ancient, too.
Could you beat off an attacker, either of you?
I'll do no hurt to you but defend you here.
You remind me of my father, whom I hold dear."

Old Priam answered him:

"Indeed, dear boy,
the case is as you say. And yet some god
stretched out his hand above me, he who sent 450
before me here—and just at the right time—
a traveler like yourself, well-made, well-spoken,
clearheaded, too. You come of some good family."

The Wayfinder rejoined:

"You speak with courtesy,
dear sir. But on this point enlighten me:
are you removing treasure here amassed
for safety abroad, until the war is past?
Or can you be abandoning Ilion
in fear, after he perished, that great one
who never shirked a battle, your own princely son?" 460

Old Priam replied:

"My brave young friend, who are you?
Born of whom? How nobly you acknowledge
the dreadful end of my unfortunate son."

To this the Wayfinder replied:

"Dear sir,
you question me about him? Never surmise
I have not seen him with my very eyes,
and often, on the field. I saw him chase
Argives with carnage to their own shipways,
while we stood wondering, forbidden war
by the great anger that Akhilleus bore 470
Lord Agamémnon. I am of that company
Akhilleus led. His own ship carried me

as one of the Myrmidons. My father is old,
as you are, and his name's Polyktôr;[17] gold
and other wealth he owns;
and I am seventh and last of all his sons.
When I cast lots among them, my lot fell
to join the siege against Troy citadel.
Tonight I've left the camp to scout this way
where, circling Troy, we'll fight at break of day; 480
our men are tired of waiting and will not stand
for any postponement by the high command."

Responded royal Priam:

"If you belong
to the company of Akhilleus, son of Pêleus,
tell me this, and tell me the whole truth:
is my son even now beside the ships?
Or has Akhilleus by this time dismembered him
and thrown him to the wild dogs?"

The Wayfinder
made reply again:

"Dear sir,
no dogs or birds have yet devoured your son. 490
Beside Akhilleus' ship, out of the sun,
he lies in a place of shelter. Now twelve days
the man has lain there, yet no part decays,
nor have the blowfly's maggots, that devour
dead men in war, fed on him to this hour.
True that around his dear friend's barrow tomb
Akhilleus drags him when dawn-shadows come,
driving pitilessly; but he mars him not.
You might yourself be witness, on the spot,
how fresh with dew he lies, washed of his gore, 500
unstained, for the deep gashes that he bore
have all closed up—and many thrust their bronze
into his body. The blest immortal ones
favor your prince, and care for every limb
even in death, as they so cherished him."

The old king's heart exulted, and he said:

"Child, it was well to honor the immortals.
He never forgot, at home in Ilion—
ah, did my son exist? was he a dream?—
the gods who own Olympos. They in turn 510
were mindful of him when he met his end.

[17]The name means "having wealth."

Here is a goblet as a gift from me.
Protect me, give me escort, if the gods
attend us, till I reach Akhilleus' hut."

And in response Hermês the Wayfinder
said:

"You are putting a young man to the test,
dear sir, but I may not, as you request,
accept a gift behind Akhilleus' back.
Fearing, honoring him, I could not lack
discretion to that point. The consequence, too, 520
could be unwelcome. As for escorting you,
even to Argos' famous land I'd ride
a deck with you, or journey at your side.
No cutthroat ever will disdain your guide."

With this, Hermês who lights the way for mortals
leapt into the driver's place. He caught up
reins and whip, and breathed a second wind
into the mule-team and the team of horses.
Onward they ran toward parapet and ships,
and pulled up to the moat.

Now night had fallen, 530
bringing the sentries to their supper fire,
but the glimmering god Hermês, the Wayfinder,
showered a mist of slumber on them all.
As quick as thought, he had the gates unbarred
and open to let the wagon enter, bearing
the old king and the ransom.

Going seaward
they came to the lofty quarters of Akhilleus,
a lodge the Myrmidons built for their lord
of pine trees cut and trimmed, and shaggy thatch
from mowings in deep meadows. Posts were driven 540
round the wide courtyard in a palisade,
whose gate one crossbar held, one beam of pine.
It took three men to slam this home, and three
to draw the bolt again—but great Akhilleus
worked his entryway alone with ease.
And now Hermês, who lights the way for mortals,
opened for Priam, took him safely in
with all his rich gifts for the son of Pêleus.
Then the god dropped the reins, and stepping down
he said:

"I am no mortal wagoner, 550
but Hermês, sir. My father sent me here
to be your guide amid the Akhaian men.
Now that is done, I'm off to heaven again

and will not visit Akhilleus. That would be
to compromise an immortal's dignity—
to be received with guests of mortal station.
Go take his knees, and make your supplication:
invoke his father, his mother, and his child;
pray that his heart be touched, that he be reconciled."

Now Hermês turned, departing for Olympos, 560
and Priam vaulted down. He left Idaíos
to hold the teams in check, while he went forward
into the lodge. He found Akhilleus, dear
to Zeus, there in his chair, with officers
at ease across the room. Only Automédôn
and Álkimos were busy near Akhilleus,
for he had just now made an end of dinner,
eating and drinking, and the laden boards
lay near him still upon the trestles.
Priam,
the great king of Troy, passed by the others, 570
knelt down, took in his arms Akhilleus' knees,
and kissed the hands of wrath that killed his sons.

When, taken with mad Folly in his own land,
a man does murder and in exile finds
refuge in some rich house, then all who see him
stand in awe.
So these men stood.
Akhilleus
gazed in wonder at the splendid king,
and his companions marveled too, all silent,
with glances to and fro. Now Priam prayed 580
to the man before him:

"Remember your own father,
Akhilleus, in your godlike youth: his years
like mine are many, and he stands upon
the fearful doorstep of old age.[18] He, too,
is hard pressed, it may be, by those around him,
there being no one able to defend him
from bane of war and ruin. Ah, but he
may nonetheless hear news of you alive,
and so with glad heart hope through all his days
for sight of his dear son, come back from Troy, 590
while I have deathly fortune.
Noble sons
I fathered here, but scarce one man is left me.
Fifty I had when the Akhaians came,

[18]Upon the threshold of death.

nineteen out of a single belly, others
born of attendant women. Most are gone.
Raging Arês cut their knees from under them.
And he who stood alone among them all,
their champion, and Troy's, ten days ago
you killed him, fighting for his land, my prince,
Hektor.
It is for him that I have come 600
among these ships, to beg him back from you,
and I bring ransom without stint.
Akhilleus,
be reverent toward the great gods! And take
pity on me, remember your own father.
Think me more pitiful by far, since I
have brought myself to do what no man else
has done before—to lift to my lips the hand
of one who killed my son."

Now in Akhilleus
the evocation of his father stirred
new longing, and an ache of grief. He lifted 610
the old man's hand and gently put him by.
Then both were overborne as they remembered:
the old king huddled at Akhilleus' feet
wept, and wept for Hektor, killer of men,
while great Akhilleus wept for his own father
as for Patróklos once again; and sobbing
filled the room.
But when Akhilleus' heart
had known the luxury of tears, and pain
within his breast and bones had passed away,
he stood then, raised the old king up, in pity 620
for his grey head and greybeard cheek, and spoke
in a warm rush of words:

"Ah, sad and old!
Trouble and pain you've borne, and bear, aplenty.
Only a great will could have brought you here
among the Akhaian ships, and here alone
before the eyes of one who stripped your sons,
your many sons, in battle. Iron must be
the heart within you. Come, then, and sit down.
We'll probe our wounds no more but let them rest,
though grief lies heavy on us. Tears heal nothing, 630
drying so stiff and cold. This is the way
the gods ordained the destiny of men,
to bear such burdens in our lives, while they
feel no affliction. At the door of Zeus
are those two urns of good and evil gifts

that he may choose for us; and one for whom
the lightning's joyous king dips in both urns
will have by turns bad luck and good. But one
to whom he sends all evil[19]—that man goes
contemptible by the will of Zeus; ravenous 640
hunger drives him over the wondrous earth,
unresting, without honor from gods or men.
Mixed fortune came to Pêleus. Shining gifts
at the gods' hands he had from birth: felicity,
wealth overflowing, rule of the Myrmidons,
a bride immortal at his mortal side.
But then Zeus gave afflictions too—no family
of powerful sons grew up for him at home,
but one child, of all seasons and of none.
Can I stand by him in his age? Far from my country 650
I sit at Troy to grieve you and your children.
You, too, sir, in time past were fortunate,
we hear men say. From Makar's isle of Lesbos
northward, and south of Phrygia and the Straits,
no one had wealth like yours, or sons like yours.[20]
Then gods out of the sky sent you this bitterness:
the years of siege, the battles and the losses.
Endure it, then. And do not mourn forever
for your dead son. There is no remedy.
You will not make him stand again. Rather 660
await some new misfortune to be suffered."

The old king in his majesty replied:

"Never give me a chair, my lord, while Hektor
lies in your camp uncared for. Yield him to me
now. Allow me sight of him. Accept
the many gifts I bring. May they reward you,
and may you see your home again.
You spared my life at once and let me live."

Akhilleus, the great runner, frowned and eyed him
under his brows:

"Do not vex me, sir," he said. 670
"I have intended, in my own good time,
to yield up Hektor to you. She who bore me,
the daughter of the Ancient of the sea,
has come with word to me from Zeus. I know
in your case, too—though you say nothing, Priam—
that some god guided you to the shipways here.

[19]Misfortune.

[20]Lesbos (of which Makar was a legendary king) is an island off the coastline, south of Troy; Phrygia lies inland, to the east; the Straits (the Hellespont, or modern Dardanelles) lie to the north.

No strong man in his best days could make entry
into this camp. How could he pass the guard,
or force our gateway?

Therefore, *let me be.*

Sting my sore heart again, and even here, 680
under my own roof, suppliant though you are,
I may not spare you, sir, but trample on
the express command of Zeus!"

When he heard this,

the old man feared him and obeyed with silence.
Now like a lion at one bound Akhilleus
left the room. Close at his back the officers
Automédôn and Álkimos went out—
comrades in arms whom he esteemed the most
after the dead Patróklos. They unharnessed
mules and horses, led the old king's crier 690
to a low bench and sat him down.
Then from the polished wagon
they took the piled-up price of Hektor's body.
One khiton and two capes they left aside
as dress and shrouding for the homeward journey.
Then, calling to the women slaves, Akhilleus
ordered the body bathed and rubbed with oil—
but lifted, too, and placed apart, where Priam
could not see his son—for seeing Hektor
he might in his great pain give way to rage, 700
and fury then might rise up in Akhilleus
to slay the old king, flouting Zeus's word.
So after bathing and anointing Hektor
they drew the shirt and beautiful shrouding over him.
Then with his own hands lifting him, Akhilleus
laid him upon a couch, and with his two
companions aiding, placed him in the wagon.
Now a bitter groan burst from Akhilleus,
who stood and prayed to his own dead friend:

"Patróklos,

do not be angry with me, if somehow 710
even in the world of Death you learn of this—
that I released Prince Hektor to his father.[21]
The gifts he gave were not unworthy. Aye,
and you shall have your share, this time as well."[22]

[21] When Patróklos' funeral was held, in Book XXIII, Akhilleus had promised his dead friend that he would not return Hektor's body to Priam or allow it to be burned or buried.

[22] The gifts are more than a bribe given to Akhilleus; they are valued not only in themselves but also—as in many primitive heroic cultures—as an outward symbol of the recipient's honor. Moreover, Akhilleus promises to give Patróklos his share—by burning it as he had burned other treasures at the funeral.

The Prince Akhilleus turned back to his quarters.
He took again the splendid chair that stood
against the farther wall, then looked at Priam
and made his declaration:

"As you wished, sir,
the body of your son is now set free.
He lies in state. At the first sight of Dawn 720
you shall take charge of him yourself and see him.
Now let us think of supper. We are told
that even Niobê in her extremity
took thought for bread—though all her brood had perished,
her six young girls and six tall sons.[23] Apollo,
making his silver longbow whip and sing,
shot the lads down, and Artemis with raining
arrows killed the daughters—all this after
Niobê had compared herself with Lêto,
the smooth-cheeked goddess.

She has borne two children, 730
Niobê said, How many have I borne!
But soon those two destroyed the twelve.

Besides,
nine days the dead lay stark, no one could bury them,
for Zeus had turned all folk of theirs to stone.
The gods made graves for them on the tenth day,
and then at last, being weak and spent with weeping,
Niobê thought of food. Among the rocks
of Sipylos' lonely mountainside, where nymphs
who race Akhelôïos river go to rest,
she, too, long turned to stone, somewhere broods on 740
the gall immortal gods gave her to drink.

Like her we'll think of supper, noble sir.
Weep for your son again when you have borne him
back to Troy; there he'll be mourned indeed."

In one swift movement now Akhilleus caught
and slaughtered a white lamb. His officers
flayed it, skillful in their butchering
to dress the flesh; they cut bits for the skewers,
roasted, and drew them off, done to a turn.
Automédôn dealt loaves into the baskets 750
on the great board; Akhilleus served the meat.
Then all their hands went out upon the supper.
When thirst and appetite were turned away,

[23]Niobê's presumptuous boast of superiority to Lêto (mother of Artemis and Apollo) and the transformation of the grieving mother to stone are traditional elements of the myth, but much of the story as given here was invented by Homer in order to create a parallel with Priam and Hektor. The poet does something similar with the Meléagros story in Book IX.

Priam, the heir of Dárdanos, gazed long
in wonder at Akhilleus' form and scale—
so like the gods in aspect. And Akhilleus
in his turn gazed in wonder upon Priam,
royal in visage as in speech. Both men
in contemplation found rest for their eyes,
till the old hero, Priam, broke the silence: 760

"Make a bed ready for me, son of Thetis,
and let us know the luxury of sleep.
From that hour when my son died at your hands
till now, my eyelids have not closed in slumber
over my eyes, but groaning where I sat
I tasted pain and grief a thousandfold,
or lay down rolling in my courtyard mire.
Here for the first time I have swallowed bread
and made myself drink wine.
Before, I could not."

Akhilleus ordered men and serving women 770
to make a bed outside, in the covered forecourt,
with purple rugs piled up and sheets outspread
and coverings of fleeces laid on top.
The girls went out with torches in their hands
and soon deftly made up a double bed.
Then Akhilleus, defiant of Agamémnon,
told his guest:

"Dear venerable sir,
you'll sleep outside tonight, in case an Akhaian
officer turns up, one of those men
who are forever taking counsel with me— 780
as well they may. If one should see you here
as the dark night runs on, he would report it
to the Lord Marshal Agamémnon. Then
return of the body would only be delayed.
Now tell me this, and give me a straight answer:
How many days do you require
for the funeral of Prince Hektor?—I should know
how long to wait, and hold the Akhaian army."

Old Priam in his majesty replied:

"If you would have me carry out the burial, 790
Akhilleus, here is the way to do me grace.
As we are penned in the town, but must bring wood
from the distant hills, the Trojans are afraid.
We should have mourning for nine days in hall,
then on the tenth conduct his funeral
and feast the troops and commons;
on the eleventh we should make his tomb,

and on the twelfth give battle, if we must."

Akhilleus said:

"As you command, old Priam,
the thing is done. I shall suspend the war 800
for those eleven days that you require."

He took the old man's right hand by the wrist
and held it, to allay his fear.

Now crier
and king with hearts brimful retired to rest
in the sheltered forecourt, while Akhilleus slept
deep in his palisaded lodge. Beside him,
lovely in her youth, Brisêis lay.
And other gods and soldiers all night long,
by slumber quieted, slept on. But slumber
would not come to Hermês the Good Companion, 810
as he considered how to ease the way
for Priam from the camp, to send him through
unseen by the formidable gatekeepers.
Then Hermês came to Priam's pillow, saying:

"Sir, no thought of danger shakes your rest,
as you sleep on, being great Akhilleus' guest,
amid men fierce as hunters in a ring.
You triumphed in a costly ransoming,
but three times costlier your own would be
to your surviving sons—a monarch's fee— 820
if this should come to Agamémnon's ear
and all the Akhaian host should learn that you are here."

The old king started up in fright, and woke
his herald. Hermês yoked the mules and horses,
took the reins, then inland like the wind
he drove through all the encampment, seen by no one.
When they reached Xánthos, eddying and running
god-begotten river, at the ford,
Hermês departed for Olympos. Dawn
spread out her yellow robe on all the earth, 830
as they drove on toward Troy, with groans and sighs,
and the mule-team pulled the wagon and the body.
And no one saw them, not a man or woman,
before Kassandra.[24] Tall as the pale-gold
goddess Aphrodítê, she had climbed

[24]A daughter of Priam and Hékabê. She is prominent in later Greek literature as a prophetess doomed to have her prophecies disbelieved. See, for example, Aeschylus' *Agamémnon,* which shows her as a captive taken from Troy by Agamémnon.

the citadel of Pergamos at dawn.
Now looking down she saw her father come
in his war-car, and saw the crier there,
and saw Lord Hektor on his bed of death
upon the mulecart. The girl wailed and cried 840
to all the city:

"Oh, look down, look down,
go to your windows, men of Troy, and women,
see Lord Hektor now! Remember joy
at seeing him return alive from battle,
exalting all our city and our land!"

Now, at the sight of Hektor, all gave way
to loss and longing, and all crowded down
to meet the escort and body near the gates,
till no one in the town was left at home.
There Hektor's lady and his gentle mother 850
tore their hair for him, flinging themselves
upon the wagon to embrace his person
while the crowd groaned. All that long day
until the sun went down they might have mourned
in tears before the gateway. But old Priam
spoke to them from his chariot:

"Make way,
let the mules pass. You'll have your fill of weeping
later, when I've brought the body home."

They parted then, and made way for the wagon,
allowing Priam to reach the famous hall. 860
They laid the body of Hektor in his bed,
and brought in minstrels, men to lead the dirge.
While these wailed out, the women answered, moaning.
Andrómakhê of the ivory-white arms
held in her lap between her hands
the head of Hektor who had killed so many.
Now she lamented:

"You've been torn from life,
my husband, in young manhood, and you leave me
empty in our hall. The boy's a child
whom you and I, poor souls, conceived; I doubt 870
he'll come to manhood. Long before, great Troy
will go down plundered, citadel and all,
now that you are lost, who guarded it
and kept it, and preserved its wives and children.
They will be shipped off in the murmuring hulls
one day, and I along with all the rest.
You, my little one, either you come with me
to do some grinding labor, some base toil

for a harsh master, or an Akhaian soldier
will grip you by the arm and hurl you down 880
from a tower here to a miserable death—
out of his anger for a brother, a father,
or even a son that Hektor killed. Akhaians
in hundreds mouthed black dust under his blows.
He was no moderate man in war, your father,
and that is why they mourn him through the city.
Hektor, you gave your parents grief and pain
but left me loneliest, and heartbroken.
You could not open your strong arms to me
from your deathbed, or say a thoughtful word, 890
for me to cherish all my life long
as I weep for you night and day."
Her voice broke,
and a wail came from the women. Hékabê
lifted her lamenting voice among them:

"Hektor, dearest of sons to me, in life
you had the favor of the immortal gods,
and they have cared for you in death as well.
Akhilleus captured other sons of mine
in other years, and sold them overseas
to Samos, Imbros, and the smoky island, 900
Lemnos. That was not his way with you.
After he took your life, cutting you down
with his sharp-bladed spear, he trussed and dragged you
many times round the barrow of his friend,
Patróklos, whom you killed—though not by this
could that friend live again. But now I find you
fresh as pale dew, seeming newly dead,
like one to whom Apollo of the silver bow
had given easy death with his mild arrows."[25]

Hékabê sobbed again, and the wails redoubled. 910
Then it was Helen's turn to make lament:

"Dear Hektor, dearest brother to me by far!
My husband is Aléxandros,
who brought me here to Troy—God, that I might
have died sooner! This is the twentieth year
since I left home, and left my fatherland.[26]
But never did I have an evil word
or gesture from you. No—and when some other
brother-in-law or sister would revile me,
or if my mother-in-law spoke to me bitterly— 920

[25] The arrows of Apollo bring death to men as those of his sister, Artemis, do to women.

[26] This statement is puzzling, since the war lasted only ten years. Perhaps we are to understand that the Greeks spent ten years in preparation or that the expedition was delayed ten years en route.

but Priam never did, being as mild
as my own father—you would bring her round
with your kind heart and gentle speech. Therefore
I weep for you and for myself as well,
given this fate, this grief. In all wide Troy
no one is left who will befriend me, none;
they all shudder at me."

Helen wept,
and a moan came from the people, hearing her.
Then Priam, the old king, commanded them:

"Trojans, bring firewood to the edge of town. 930
No need to fear an ambush of the Argives.
When he dismissed me from the camp, Akhilleus
told me clearly they will not harass us,
not until dawn comes for the twelfth day."

Then yoking mules and oxen to their wagons
the people thronged before the city gates.
Nine days they labored, bringing countless loads
of firewood to the town. When Dawn that lights
the world of mortals came for the tenth day,
they carried greathearted Hektor out at last, 940
and all in tears placed his dead body high
upon its pyre, then cast a torch below.
When the young Dawn with finger tips of rose
made heaven bright, the Trojan people massed
about Prince Hektor's ritual fire.
All being gathered and assembled, first
they quenched the smoking pyre with tawny wine
wherever flames had licked their way, then friends
and brothers picked his white bones from the char
in sorrow, while the tears rolled down their cheeks. 950
In a golden urn they put the bones,
shrouding the urn with veiling of soft purple.
Then in a grave dug deep they placed it
and heaped it with great stones. The men were quick
to raise the death-mound, while in every quarter
lookouts were posted to ensure against
an Akhaian surprise attack. When they had finished
raising the barrow, they returned to Ilion,
where all sat down to banquet in his honor
in the hall of Priam king. So they performed 960
the funeral rites of Hektor, tamer of horses.

THE ODYSSEY

Translated by Robert Fitzgerald

The ten-year war waged by the Greeks against Troy, culminating in the overthrow of the city, is now itself ten years in the past. Helen, whose flight to Troy with the Trojan prince Paris had prompted the Greek expedition to seek revenge and reclaim her, is now home in Sparta, living harmoniously once more with her husband Meneláos (Menelaus). His brother Agamémnon, commander in chief of the Greek forces, was murdered on his return from the war by his wife and her paramour. Of the Greek chieftains who have survived both the war and the perilous homeward voyage, all have returned except Odysseus, the crafty and astute ruler of Ithaka (Ithaca), an island in the Ionian Sea off western Greece. Since he is presumed dead, suitors from Ithaka and other regions have overrun his house, paying court to his attractive wife Penélopê, endangering the position of his son, Telémakhos (Telemachus), corrupting many of the servants, and literally eating up Odysseus' estate. Penélopê has stalled for time but is finding it increasingly difficult to deny the suitors' demands that she marry one of them; Telémakhos, who is just approaching young manhood, is becoming actively resentful of the indignities suffered by his household.

Many persons and places in the *Odyssey* are best known to readers by their Latinized names, such as *Telemachus.* The present translator has used forms (*Telémakhos*) closer to the Greek spelling and pronunciation. A slanted accent mark (´) indicates stress; thus *Agamémnon* is accented on the third syllable. A circumflex accent (ˆ) indicates that the vowel sound is long; thus *Kêrês* is pronounced "Care-ace." A dieresis (¨) indicates pronunciation as a separate syllable; thus, *Thoösa* has three syllables rather than two. [*Editors' headnote.*]

BOOK ONE: A GODDESS INTERVENES

Sing in me, Muse, and through me tell the story
of that man skilled in all ways of contending,
the wanderer, harried for years on end,
after he plundered the stronghold
on the proud height of Troy.[1]
He saw the townlands
and learned the minds of many distant men,
and weathered many bitter nights and days
in his deep heart at sea, while he fought only
to save his life, to bring his shipmates home.
But not by will nor valor could he save them, 10
for their own recklessness destroyed them all—

[1] These lines contain the traditional epic "opening formula" that includes the invocation of the inspiring Muse, the statement of the theme, the identification of the hero (in this case Odysseus), and a glance at the significance of the story.

children and fools, they killed and feasted on
the cattle of Lord Hêlios,[2] the Sun,
and he who moves all day through heaven
took from their eyes the dawn of their return.

Of these adventures, Muse, daughter of Zeus,
tell us in our time, lift the great song again.
Begin when all the rest who left behind them
headlong death in battle or at sea
had long ago returned, while he alone still hungered 20
for home and wife. Her ladyship Kalypso
clung to him in her sea-hollowed caves—
a nymph, immortal and most beautiful,
who craved him for her own.
And when long years and seasons
wheeling brought around that point of time
ordained for him to make his passage homeward,
trials and dangers, even so, attended him
even in Ithaka,[3] near those he loved.
Yet all the gods had pitied Lord Odysseus,
all but Poseidon,[4] raging cold and rough 30
against the brave king till he came ashore
at last on his own land.
But now that god
had gone far off among the sunburnt races,
most remote of men, at earth's two verges,
in sunset lands and lands of the rising sun,
to be regaled by smoke of thighbones burning,
haunches of rams and bulls, a hundred fold.
He lingered delighted at the banquet side.

In the bright hall of Zeus upon Olympos
the other gods were all at home, and Zeus, 40
the father of gods and men, made conversation.
For he had meditated on Aigísthos,[5] dead
by the hand of Agamémnon's son, Orestês,
and spoke his thought aloud before them all:

"My word, how mortals take the gods to task!
All their afflictions come from us, we hear.

[2] The offense against Hêlios is described in Book XII.

[3] Odysseus' island homeland, in the Ionian Sea off western Greece (sometimes the spelling is *Ithaca*).

[4] God of the ocean and brother of the chief of the gods who dwelled on Mount Olympos (Olympus), Zeus.

[5] While the Greek commander Agamémnon was away fighting against Troy, Aigísthos (Aegisthus) entered into an adulterous union with Klytaimnéstra (Clytaemnestra), Agamémnon's wife; they murdered Agamémnon upon his return. The murder was later avenged by Orestês, son of Agamémnon and Klytaimnéstra, as is related in Aeschylus' trilogy of plays known as the *Oresteia*.

And what of their own failings? Greed and folly
double the suffering in the lot of man.
See how Aigísthos, for his double portion,
stole Agamémnon's wife and killed the soldier 50
on his homecoming day. And yet Aigísthos
knew that his own doom lay in this. We gods
had warned him, sent down Hermês Argeiphontês,[6]
our most observant courier, to say:
'Don't kill the man, don't touch his wife,
or face a reckoning with Orestês
the day he comes of age and wants his patrimony.'
Friendly advice—but would Aigísthos take it?
Now he has paid the reckoning in full."

The grey-eyed goddess Athena replied to Zeus: 60

"O Majesty, O Father of us all,
that man is in the dust indeed, and justly.
So perish all who do what he had done.
But my own heart is broken for Odysseus,
the master mind of war, so long a castaway
upon an island in the running sea;
a wooded island, in the sea's middle,
and there's a goddess in the place, the daughter
of one whose baleful mind knows all the deeps
of the blue sea—Atlas,[7] who holds the columns 70
that bear from land the great thrust of the sky.
His daughter will not let Odysseus go,
poor mournful man; she keeps on coaxing him
with her beguiling talk, to turn his mind
from Ithaka. But such desire is in him
merely to see the hearthsmoke leaping upward
from his own island, that he longs to die.
Are you not moved by this, Lord of Olympos?
Had you no pleasure from Odysseus' offerings
beside the Argive[8] ships, on Troy's wide seaboard? 80
O Zeus, what do you hold against him now?"

To this the summoner of cloud replied:

"My child, what strange remarks you let escape you.
Could I forget that kingly man, Odysseus?
There is no mortal half so wise; no mortal
gave so much to the lords of open sky.
Only the god who laps the land in water,

[6] God of messengers and messenger of the gods; he was also associated sometimes with the wind. "Argeiphontês" connotes brightness or the ability to clear the sky of clouds.

[7] In myth, Atlas is the titanic being who supports the sky. Here he is described as father of the nymph Kalypso, who is holding Odysseus prisoner on her island, Ogýgia.

[8] The collective name for the Greek forces who fought under Agamémnon against Troy.

Poseidon, bears the fighter an old grudge
since he poked out the eye of Polyphêmos,
brawniest of the Kyklopês.[9] Who bore 90
that giant lout? Thoösa, daughter of Phorkys,
an offshore sea lord: for this nymph had lain
with Lord Poseidon in her hollow caves.
Naturally, the god, after the blinding—
mind you, he does not kill the man;
he only buffets him away from home.
But come now, we are all at leisure here,
let us take up this matter of his return,
that he may sail. Poseidon must relent
for being quarrelsome will get him nowhere, 100
one god, flouting the will of all the gods."

The grey-eyed goddess Athena answered him:

"O Majesty, O Father of us all,
if it now please the blissful gods
that wise Odysseus reach his home again,
let the Wayfinder, Hermês, cross the sea
to the island of Ogýgia; let him tell
our fixed intent to the nymph with pretty braids,
and let the steadfast man depart for home.
For my part, I shall visit Ithaka 110
to put more courage in the son, and rouse him
to call an assembly of the islanders,
Akhaian[10] gentlemen with flowing hair.
He must warn off that wolf pack of the suitors
who prey upon his flocks and dusky cattle.
I'll send him to the mainland then, to Sparta
by the sand beach of Pylos;[11] let him find
news of his dear father where he may
and win his own renown about the world."

She bent to tie her beautiful sandals on, 120
ambrosial, golden, that carry her over water
or over endless land on the wings of the wind,
and took the great haft of her spear in hand—
that bronzeshod spear this child of Power can use
to break in wrath long battle lines of fighters.

Flashing down from Olympos' height she went
to stand in Ithaka, before the Manor,

[9] The encounter with these one-eyed giants (also spelled *Polyphemus* and *Cyclops*) is described in Book IX.
[10] In a general sense, "Greek"; more especially, descriptive of men living in a region not far from Ithaka.
[11] A city and region of southern Greece ruled by Nestor, an aged king and counselor.

just at the doorsill of the court. She seemed
a family friend, the Taphian captain, Mentês,
waiting, with a light hand on her spear. 130
Before her eyes she found the lusty suitors
casting dice inside the gate, at ease
on hides of oxen—oxen they had killed.
Their own retainers made a busy sight
with houseboys, mixing bowls of water and wine,
or sopping water up in sponges, wiping
tables to be placed about in hall,
or butchering whole carcasses for roasting.

Long before anyone else, the prince Telémakhos
now caught sight of Athena—for he, too, 140
was sitting there, unhappy among the suitors,
a boy, daydreaming. What if his great father
came from the unknown world and drove these men
like dead leaves through the place, recovering
honor and lordship in his own domains?
Then he who dreamed in the crowd gazed out at Athena.
Straight to the door he came, irked with himself
to think a visitor had been kept there waiting,
and took her right hand, grasping with his left
her tall bronze-bladed spear. Then he said warmly: 150

"Greetings, stranger! Welcome to our feast.
There will be time to tell your errand later."

He led the way, and Pallas Athena followed
into the lofty hall. The boy reached up
and thrust her spear high in a polished rack
against a pillar, where tough spear on spear
of the old soldier, his father, stood in order.
Then, shaking out a splendid coverlet,
he seated her on a throne with footrest—all
finely carved—and drew his painted armchair 160
near her, at a distance from the rest.
To be amid the din, the suitors' riot,
would ruin his guest's appetite, he thought,
and he wished privacy to ask for news
about his father, gone for years.
A maid
brought them a silver finger bowl and filled it
out of a beautiful spouting golden jug,
then drew a polished table to their side.
The larder mistress with her tray came by
and served them generously. A carver lifted 170
cuts of each roast meat to put on trenchers[12]
before the two. He gave them cups of gold,

[12] Plates.

and these the steward as he went his rounds
filled and filled again.
Now came the suitors,
young bloods trooping in to their own seats
on thrones or easy chairs. Attendants poured
water over their fingers, while the maids
piled baskets full of brown loaves near at hand,
and houseboys brimmed the bowls with wine.
Now they laid hands upon the ready feast 180
and thought of nothing more. Not till desire
for food and drink had left them were they mindful
of dance and song, that are the grace of feasting.
A herald gave a shapely cithern harp
to Phêmios,[13] whom they compelled to sing—
and what a storm he plucked upon the strings
for prelude! High and clear the song arose.

Telémakhos now spoke to grey-eyed Athena,
his head bent close, so no one else might hear:

"Dear guest, will this offend you, if I speak? 190
It is easy for these men to like these things,
harping and song; they have an easy life,
scot free, eating the livestock of another—
a man whose bones are rotting somewhere now,
white in the rain on dark earth where they lie,
or tumbling in the groundswell of the sea.
If he returned, if these men ever saw him,
faster legs they'd pray for, to a man,
and not more wealth in handsome robes or gold.
But he is lost; he came to grief and perished, 200
and there's no help for us in someone's hoping
he still may come; that sun has long gone down.
But tell me now, and put it for me clearly—
who are you? Where do you come from? Where's your home
and family? What kind of ship is yours,
and what course brought you here? Who are your sailors?
I don't suppose you walked here on the sea.
Another thing—this too I ought to know—
is Ithaka new to you, or were you ever
a guest here in the old days? Far and near 210
friends knew this house; for he whose home it was
had much acquaintance in the world."

To this
the grey-eyed goddess answered:

[13] The house bard, or minstrel.

"As you ask,
I can account most clearly for myself.
Mentês I'm called, son of the veteran
Ankhíalos; I rule seafaring Taphos.
I came by ship, with a ship's company,
sailing the winedark[14] sea for ports of call
on alien shores—to Témesê, for copper,
bringing bright bars of iron in exchange. 220
My ship is moored on a wild strip of coast
in Reithron Bight, under the wooded mountain.
Years back, my family and yours were friends,
as Lord Laërtês[15] knows; ask when you see him.
I hear the old man comes to town no longer,
stays up country, ailing, with only one
old woman to prepare his meat and drink
when pain and stiffness take him in the legs
from working on his terraced plot, his vineyard.
As for my sailing here— 230
the tale was that your father had come home,
therefore I came. I see the gods delay him.
But never in this world is Odysseus dead—
only detained somewhere on the wide sea,
upon some island, with wild islanders;
savages, they must be, to hold him captive.
Well, I will forecast for you, as the gods
put the strong feeling in me—I see it all,
and I'm no prophet, no adept in bird-signs.
He will not, now, be long away from Ithaka, 240
his father's dear land; though he be in chains
he'll scheme a way to come; he can do anything.

But tell me this now, make it clear to me:
You must be, by your looks, Odysseus' boy?
The way your head is shaped, the fine eyes—yes,
how like him! We took meals like this together
many a time, before he sailed for Troy
with all the lords of Argos in the ships.
I have not seen him since, nor has he seen me."

And thoughtfully Telémakhos replied: 250

"Friend, let me put it in the plainest way.
My mother says I am his son; I know not
surely. Who has known his own engendering?
I wish at least I had some happy man
as father, growing old in his own house—

[14] This adjective is repeatedly used by Homer to describe the sea. Such "Homeric epithets" are taken as one sign that the *Iliad* and *Odyssey* were designed for oral delivery.
[15] Father of Odysseus. At this point Laërtês is living in retirement on a farm.

but unknown death and silence are the fate
of him that, since you ask, they call my father."

Then grey-eyed Athena said:

"The gods decreed
no lack of honor in this generation:
such is the son Penélopê bore in you. 260
But tell me now, and make this clear to me:
what gathering, what feast is this? Why here?
A wedding? Revel? At the expense of all?
Not that, I think. How arrogant they seem,
these gluttons, making free here in your house!
A sensible man would blush to be among them."

To this Telémakhos answered:

"Friend, now that you ask about these matters,
our house was always princely, a great house,
as long as he of whom we speak remained here. 270
But evil days the gods have brought upon it,
making him vanish, as they have, so strangely.
Were his death known, I could not feel such pain—
if he had died of wounds in Trojan country
or in the arms of friends, after the war.
They would have made a tomb for him, the Akhaians,
and I should have all honor as his son.
Instead, the whirlwinds got him, and no glory.
He's gone, no sign, no word of him; and I inherit
trouble and tears—and not for him alone, 280
the gods have laid such other burdens on me.
For now the lords of the islands,
Doulíkhion and Samê, wooded Zakynthos,
and rocky Ithaka's young lords as well,
are here courting my mother; and they use
our house as if it were a house to plunder.
Spurn them she dare not, though she hates that marriage,
nor can she bring herself to choose among them.
Meanwhile they eat their way through all we have,
and when they will, they can demolish me." 290

Pallas Athena was disturbed, and said:

"Ah, bitterly you need Odysseus, then!
High time he came back to engage these upstarts.
I wish we saw him standing helmeted
there in the doorway, holding shield and spear,
looking the way he did when I first knew him.
That was at our house, where he drank and feasted
after he left Ephyra, homeward bound
from a visit to the son of Mérmeris, Ilos.

He took his fast ship down the gulf that time 300
for a fatal drug to dip his arrows in
and poison the bronze points; but young Ilos
turned him away, fearing the gods' wrath.
My father gave it, for he loved him well.
I wish these men could meet the man of those days!
They'd know their fortune quickly: a cold bed.
Aye! but it lies upon the gods' great knees
whether he can return and force a reckoning
in his own house, or not.
If I were you,
I should take steps to make these men disperse. 310
Listen, now, and attend to what I say:
at daybreak call the islanders to assembly,
and speak your will, and call the gods to witness:
the suitors must go scattering to their homes.
Then here's a course for you, if you agree:
get a sound craft afloat with twenty oars
and go abroad for news of your lost father—
perhaps a traveller's tale, or rumored fame
issued from Zeus abroad in the world of men.
Talk to that noble sage at Pylos, Nestor, 320
then go to Meneláos,[16] the red-haired king
at Sparta, last man home of all the Akhaians.
If you should learn your father is alive
and coming home, you could hold out a year.
Or if you learn that he is dead and gone,
then you can come back to your own dear country
and raise a mound for him, and burn his gear,
with all the funeral honors due the man,
and give your mother to another husband.

When you have done all this, or seen it done 330
it will be time to ponder
concerning these contenders[17] in your house—
how you should kill them, outright or by guile.
You need not bear this insolence of theirs,
you are a child no longer. Have you heard
what glory young Orestês won
when he cut down that two-faced man, Aigísthos,
for killing his illustrious father?
Dear friend, you are tall and well set up, I see;
be brave—you, too—and men in times to come 340
will speak of you respectfully.

[16] Brother of Agamémnon and husband of Helen of Troy. Also spelled *Menelaus.* Helen's elopement with their Trojan guest, Paris, precipitated the Trojan War.

[17] Suitors for the hand in marriage of the presumably widowed Penélopê, wife of Odysseus.

Now I must join my ship;
my crew will grumble if I keep them waiting.
Look to yourself; remember what I told you."

Telémakhos replied:

"Friend, you have done me
kindness, like a father to his son,
and I shall not forget your counsel ever.
You must get back to sea, I know, but come
take a hot bath, and rest; accept a gift
to make your heart lift up when you embark—
some precious thing, and beautiful, from me, 350
a keepsake, such as dear friends give their friends."

But the grey-eyed goddess Athena answered him:

"Do not delay me, for I love the sea ways.
As for the gift your heart is set on giving,
let me accept it on my passage home,
and you shall have a choice gift in exchange."

With this Athena left him
as a bird rustles upward, off and gone.
But as she went she put new spirit in him,
a new dream of his father, clearer now, 360
so that he marvelled to himself
divining that a god had been his guest.
Then godlike in his turn he joined the suitors.

The famous minstrel still sang on before them,
and they sat still and listened, while he sang
that bitter song, the Homecoming of Akhaians—
how by Athena's will they fared from Troy;
and in her high room careful Penélopê,
Ikários' daughter, heeded the holy song.
She came, then, down the long stairs of her house, 370
this beautiful lady, with two maids in train
attending her as she approached the suitors;
and near a pillar of the roof she paused,
her shining veil drawn over across her cheeks,
the two girls close to her and still,
and through her tears spoke to the noble minstrel:

"Phêmios, other spells you know, high deeds
of gods and heroes, as the poets tell them;
let these men hear some other; let them sit
silent and drink their wine. But sing no more 380
this bitter tale that wears my heart away.
It opens in me again the wound of longing

for one incomparable, ever in my mind—
his fame all Hellas[18] knows, and midland Argos."

But Telémakhos intervened and said to her:

"Mother, why do you grudge our own dear minstrel
joy of song, wherever his thought may lead?
Poets are not to blame, but Zeus who gives
what fate he pleases to adventurous men.
Here is no reason for reproof: to sing 390
the news of the Danaans![19] Men like best
a song that rings like morning on the ear.
But you must nerve yourself and try to listen.
Odysseus was not the only one at Troy
never to know the day of his homecoming.
Others, how many others, lost their lives!"

The lady gazed in wonder and withdrew,
her son's clear wisdom echoing in her mind.
But when she had mounted to her rooms again
with her two handmaids, then she fell to weeping 400
for Odysseus, her husband. Grey-eyed Athena
presently cast a sweet sleep on her eyes.

Meanwhile the din grew loud in the shadowy hall
as every suitor swore to lie beside her,
but Telémakhos turned now and spoke to them:

"You suitors of my mother! Insolent men,
now we have dined, let us have entertainment
and no more shouting. There can be no pleasure
so fair as giving heed to a great minstrel
like ours, whose voice itself is pure delight. 410
At daybreak we shall sit down in assembly
and I shall tell you—take it as you will—
you are to leave this hall. Go feasting elsewhere,
consume your own stores. Turn and turn about,
use one another's houses. If you choose
to slaughter one man's livestock and pay nothing,
this is rapine; and by the eternal gods
I beg Zeus you shall get what you deserve:
a slaughter here, and nothing paid for it!"

By now their teeth seemed fixed in their under-lips, 420
Telémakhos' bold speaking stunned them so.
Antínoös, Eupeithês' son, made answer:

[18] Greece.
[19] The Greeks who fought against the Trojans.

"Telémakhos, no doubt the gods themselves
are teaching you this high and mighty manner.
Zeus forbid you should be king in Ithaka,[20]
though you are eligible as your father's son."

Telémakhos kept his head and answered him:

"Antínoös, you may not like my answer,
but I would happily be king, if Zeus
conferred the prize. Or do you think it wretched? 430
I shouldn't call it bad at all. A king
will be respected, and his house will flourish.
But there are eligible men enough,
heaven knows, on the island, young and old,
and one of them perhaps may come to power
after the death of King Odysseus.
All I insist on is that I rule our house
and rule the slaves my father won for me."

Eurýmakhos, Pólybos' son, replied:

"Telémakhos, it is on the gods' great knees 440
who will be king in sea-girt Ithaka.
But keep your property, and rule your house,
and let no man, against your will, make havoc
of your possessions, while there's life on Ithaka.
But now, my brave young friend,
a question or two about the stranger.
Where did your guest come from? Of what country?
Where does he say his home is, and his family?
Has he some message of your father's coming,
or business of his own, asking a favor? 450
He left so quickly that one hadn't time
to meet him, but he seemed a gentleman."

Telémakhos made answer, cool enough:

"Eurýmakhos, there's no hope for my father.
I would not trust a message, if one came,
nor any forecaster my mother invites
to tell by divination of time to come.
My guest, however, was a family friend,
Mentês, son of Ankhíalos.
He rules the Taphian people of the sea." 460

So said Telémakhos, though in his heart
he knew his visitor had been immortal.

[20]At the time of the poem's action, the rulership of most Greek city-states was not automatically passed from father to son.

But now the suitors turned to play again
with dance and haunting song. They stayed till nightfall,
indeed black night came on them at their pleasure,
and half asleep they left, each for his home.

Telémakhos' bedroom was above the court,
a kind of tower, with a view all round;
here he retired to ponder in the silence,
while carrying brands of pine alight beside him 470
Eurýkleia went padding, sage and old.
Her father had been Ops, Peisênor's son,
and she had been a purchase of Laërtês
when she was still a blossoming girl. He gave
the price of twenty oxen[21] for her, kept her
as kindly in his house as his own wife,
though, for the sake of peace, he never touched her.
No servant loved Telémakhos as she did,
she who had nursed him in his infancy.
So now she held the light, as he swung open 480
the door of his neat freshly painted chamber.
There he sat down, pulling his tunic off,
and tossed it into the wise old woman's hands.
She folded it and smoothed it, and then hung it
beside the inlaid bed upon a bar;
then, drawing the door shut by its silver handle
she slid the catch in place and went away.
And all night long, wrapped in the finest fleece,
he took in thought the course Athena gave him.

BOOK TWO: A HERO'S SON AWAKENS

When primal Dawn spread on the eastern sky
her fingers of pink light, Odysseus' true son
stood up, drew on his tunic and his mantle,
slung on a sword-belt and a new-edged sword,
tied his smooth feet into good rawhide sandals,
and left his room, a god's brilliance upon him.
He found the criers with clarion voices and told them
to muster the unshorn[1] Akhaians in full assembly.
The call sang out, and the men came streaming in;
and when they filled the assembly ground, he entered, 10
spear in hand, with two quick hounds at heel;
Athena lavished on him a sunlit grace

[21] In the Greek civilization of Homeric times, the ox was a common standard of value. Articles of clothing, weapons, women taken as war prizes, and servants were evaluated in terms of how many oxen they were worth.

[1] Having long or flowing hair.

that held the eye of the multitude. Old men
made way for him as he took his father's chair.

Now Lord Aigýptios, bent down and sage with years,
opened the assembly. This man's son
had served under the great Odysseus, gone
in the decked ships with him to the wild horse country
of Troy—a spearman, Ántiphos by name.
The ravenous Kyklops in the cave destroyed him[2] 20
last in his feast of men. Three other sons
the old man had, and one, Eurýnomos,
went with the suitors; two farmed for their father;
but even so the old man pined, remembering
the absent one, and a tear welled up as he spoke:

"Hear me, Ithakans! Hear what I have to say.
No meeting has been held here since our king,
Odysseus, left port in the decked ships.
Who finds occasion for assembly, now?
one of the young men? one of the older lot? 30
Has he had word our fighters are returning[3]—
news to report if he got wind of it—
or is it something else, touching the realm?
The man has vigor, I should say; more power to him.
Whatever he desires, may Zeus fulfill it."

The old man's words delighted the son of Odysseus,
who kept his chair no longer but stood up,
eager to speak, in the midst of all the men.
The crier, Peisênor, master of debate,
brought him the staff[4] and placed it in his hand; 40
then the boy touched the old man's shoulder, and said:

"No need to wonder any more, Sir,
who called this session. The distress is mine.
As to our troops returning, I have no news—
news to report if I got wind of it—
nor have I public business to propose;
only my need, and the trouble of my house—
the troubles.

My distinguished father is lost,
who ruled among you once, mild as a father,
and there is now this greater evil still: 50
my home and all I have are being ruined.

[2] This incident is described in Book IX.

[3] Except for Odysseus and his Ithakans, all the Greek warriors against Troy had by this time returned home or were known to be dead.

[4] The emblem that, placed by the herald in the speaker's hand, gave him the right to speak as a public official.

Mother wanted no suitors, but like a pack
they came—sons of the best men here among them—
lads with no stomach for an introduction
to Ikários, her father across the sea;
he would require a wedding gift, and give her
to someone who found favor in her eyes.
No; these men spend their days around our house
killing our beeves and sheep and fatted goats,
carousing, soaking up our good dark wine, 60
not caring what they do. They squander everything.
We have no strong Odysseus to defend us,
and as to putting up a fight ourselves—
we'd only show our incompetence in arms.
Expel them, yes, if I only had the power;
the whole thing's out of hand, insufferable.
My house is being plundered: is this courtesy?
Where is your indignation? Where is your shame?
Think of the talk in the islands all around us,
and fear the wrath of the gods, 70
or they may turn, and send you some devilry.
Friends, by Olympian Zeus and holy Justice
that holds men in assembly and sets them free,
make an end of this! Let me lament in peace
my private loss. Or did my father, Odysseus,
ever do injury to the armed Akhaians?
Is this your way of taking it out on me,
giving free rein to these young men?
I might as well—might better—see my treasure
and livestock taken over by you all; 80
then, if you fed on them, I'd have some remedy,
and when we met, in public, in the town,
I'd press my claim; you might make restitution.
This way you hurt me when my hands are tied."

And in hot anger now he threw the staff to the ground,
his eyes grown bright with tears. A wave of sympathy
ran through the crowd, all hushed; and no one there
had the audacity to answer harshly
except Antínoös, who said:

"What high and mighty
talk, Telémakhos! No holding you! 90
You want to shame us, and humiliate us,
but you should know the suitors are not to blame—
it is your own dear, incomparably cunning mother.
For three years now—and it will soon be four—
she has been breaking the hearts of the Akhaians,
holding out hope to all, and sending promises
to each man privately—but thinking otherwise.

Here is an instance of her trickery:
she had her great loom standing in the hall
and the fine warp of some vast fabric on it; 100
we were attending her, and she said to us:
'Young men, my suitors, now my lord is dead,
let me finish my weaving before I marry,
or else my thread will have been spun in vain.
It is a shroud I weave for Lord Laërtês,
when cold death comes to lay him on his bier.
The country wives would hold me in dishonor
if he, with all his fortune, lay unshrouded.'
We have men's hearts; she touched them; we agreed.
So every day she wove on the great loom— 110
but every night by torchlight she unwove it;
and so for three years she deceived the Akhaians.
But when the seasons brought the fourth around,
one of her maids, who knew the secret, told us;
we found her unraveling the splendid shroud.
She had to finish then, although she hated it.

Now here is the suitors' answer—
you and all the Akhaians, mark it well:
dismiss your mother from the house, or make her marry
the man her father names and she prefers. 120
Does she intend to keep us dangling forever?
She may rely too long on Athena's gifts—
talent in handicraft and a clever mind;
so cunning—history cannot show the like
among the ringleted ladies of Akhaia,
Mykênê with her coronet, Alkmênê, Tyro.
Wits like Penélopê's never were before,
but this time—well, she made poor use of them.
For here are suitors eating up your property
as long as she holds out—a plan some god 130
put in her mind. She makes a name for herself,
but you can feel the loss it means for you.
Our own affairs can wait; we'll never go anywhere else,
until she takes an Akhaian to her liking."

But clear-headed Telémakhos replied:

"Antínoös, can I banish against her will
the mother who bore me and took care of me?
My father is either dead or far away,
but dearly I should pay for this
at Ikários' hands, if ever I sent her back. 140
The powers of darkness would requite it, too,
my mother's parting curse would call hell's furies[5]

[5] In mythology, the primitive female agents of retribution for evil, especially for evil committed against blood kindred.

to punish me, along with the scorn of men.
No: I can never give the word for this.
But if your hearts are capable of shame,
leave my great hall, and take your dinner elsewhere,
consume your own stores. Turn and turn about,
use one another's houses. If you choose
to slaughter one man's livestock and pay nothing,
this is rapine; and by the eternal gods 150
I beg Zeus you shall get what you deserve:
a slaughter here, and nothing paid for it!"

Now Zeus who views the wide world sent a sign to him,
launching a pair of eagles from a mountain crest
in gliding flight down the soft blowing wind,
wing-tip to wing-tip quivering taut, companions,
till high above the assembly of many voices
they wheeled, their dense wings beating, and in havoc
dropped on the heads of the crowd—a deathly omen—
wielding their talons, tearing cheeks and throats; 160
then veered away on the right hand through the city.
Astonished, gaping after the birds, the men
felt their hearts flood, foreboding things to come.
And now they heard the old lord Halithersês,
son of Mastor, keenest among the old
at reading birdflight into accurate speech;
in his anxiety for them, he rose and said:

"Hear me, Ithakans! Hear what I have to say,
and may I hope to open the suitors' eyes
to the black wave towering over them. Odysseus 170
will not be absent from his family long:
he is already near, carrying in him
a bloody doom for all these men, and sorrow
for many more on our high seamark, Ithaka.
Let us think how to stop it; let the suitors
drop their suit; they had better, without delay.
I am old enough to know a sign when I see one,
and I say all has come to pass for Odysseus
as I foretold when the Argives massed on Troy,
and he, the great tactician, joined the rest. 180
My forecast was that after nineteen years,[6]
many blows weathered, all his shipmates lost,
himself unrecognized by anyone,
he would come home. I see this all fulfilled."

[6] These include the ten years of war against Troy.

But Pólybos' son, Eurýmakhos, retorted:

"Old man, go tell the omens for your children
at home, and try to keep them out of trouble.
I am more fit to interpret this than you are.
Bird life aplenty is found in the sunny air,
not all of it significant. As for Odysseus, 190
he perished far from home. You should have perished with him—
then we'd be spared this nonsense in assembly,
as good as telling Telémakhos to rage on;
do you think you can gamble on a gift from him?
Here is what I foretell, and it's quite certain:
if you, with what you know of ancient lore,
encourage bitterness in this young man,
it means, for him, only the more frustration—
he can do nothing whatever with two eagles—
and as for you, old man, we'll fix a penalty 200
that you will groan to pay.
Before the whole assembly I advise Telémakhos
to send his mother to her father's house;
let them arrange her wedding there, and fix
a portion suitable for a valued daughter.
Until he does this, courtship is our business,
vexing though it may be; we fear no one,
certainly not Telémakhos, with his talk;
and we care nothing for your divining, uncle,
useless talk; you win more hatred by it. 210
We'll share his meat, no thanks or fee to him,
as long as she delays and maddens us.
It is a long, long time we have been waiting
in rivalry for this beauty. We could have gone
elsewhere and found ourselves very decent wives."

Clear-headed Telémakhos replied to this:

"Eurýmakhos, and noble suitors all,
I am finished with appeals and argument.
The gods know, and the Akhaians know, these things.
But give me a fast ship and a crew of twenty 220
who will see me through a voyage, out and back.
I'll go to sandy Pylos, then to Sparta,
for news of Father since he sailed from Troy—
some traveller's tale, perhaps, or rumored fame
issued from Zeus himself into the world.
If he's alive, and beating his way home,
I might hold out for another weary year;
but if they tell me that he's dead and gone,
then I can come back to my own dear country
and raise a mound for him, and burn his gear, 230
with all the funeral honors that befit him,
and give my mother to another husband."

The boy sat down in silence. Next to stand
was Mentor, comrade in arms of the prince Odysseus,
an old man now. Odysseus left him authority
over his house and slaves, to guard them well.
In his concern, he spoke to the assembly:

"Hear me, Ithakans! Hear what I have to say.
Let no man holding scepter as a king
be thoughtful, mild, kindly, or virtuous; 240
let him be cruel, and practice evil ways;
it is so clear that no one here remembers
how like a gentle father Odysseus ruled you.
I find it less revolting that the suitors
carry their malice into violent acts;
at least they stake their lives
when they go pillaging the house of Odysseus—
their lives upon it, he will not come again.
What sickens me is to see the whole community
sitting still, and never a voice or a hand raised 250
against them—a mere handful compared with you."

Leókritos, Euênor's son, replied to him:

"Mentor, what mischief are you raking up?
Will this crowd risk the sword's edge over a dinner?
Suppose Odysseus himself indeed
came in and found the suitors at his table:
he might be hot to drive them out. What then?
Never would he enjoy his wife again—
the wife who loves him well; he'd only bring down
abject death on himself against those odds. 260
Madness, to talk of fighting in either case.
Now let all present go about their business!
Halithersês and Mentor will speed the traveller;
they can help him: they were his father's friends.
I rather think he will be sitting here
a long time yet, waiting for news on Ithaka;
that seafaring he spoke of is beyond him."

On this note they were quick to end their parley.
The assembly broke up; everyone went home—
the suitors home to Odysseus' house again. 270
But Telémakhos walked down along the shore
and washed his hands in the foam of the grey sea,
then said this prayer:

"O god of yesterday,
guest in our house, who told me to take ship
on the hazy sea for news of my lost father,
listen to me, be near me:
The Akhaians only wait, or hope to hinder me,
the damned insolent suitors most of all."

Athena was nearby and came to him,
putting on Mentor's figure and his tone, 280
the warm voice in a lucid flight of words:

"You'll never be fainthearted or a fool,
Telémakhos, if you have your father's spirit;
he finished what he cared to say,
and what he took in hand he brought to pass.
The sea routes will yield their distances
to his true son, Penélopê's true son,—
I doubt another's luck would hold so far.
The son is rare who measures with his father,
and one in a thousand is a better man, 290
but you will have the sap and wit
and prudence—for you get that from Odysseus—
to give you a fair chance of winning through.
So never mind the suitors and their ways,
there is no judgment in them, neither do they
know anything of death and the black terror
close upon them—doom's day on them all.
You need not linger over going to sea.
I sailed beside your father in the old days,
I'll find a ship for you, and help you sail her. 300
So go on home, as if to join the suitors,
but get provisions ready in containers—
wine in two-handled jugs and barley meal,
the staying power of oarsmen,
in skin bags, watertight. I'll go the rounds
and call a crew of volunteers together.
Hundreds of ships are beached on sea-girt Ithaka;
let me but choose the soundest, old or new,
we'll rig her and take her out on the broad sea."

This was the divine speech Telémakhos heard 310
from Athena, Zeus's daughter. He stayed no longer,
but took his heartache home,
and found the robust suitors there at work,
skinning goats and roasting pigs in the courtyard.
Antínoös came straight over, laughing at him,
and took him by the hand with a bold greeting:

"High-handed Telémakhos, control your temper!
Come on, get over it, no more grim thoughts,
but feast and drink with me, the way you used to.
The Akhaians will attend to all you ask for— 320
ship, crew, and crossing to the holy land
of Pylos, for the news about your father."

Telémakhos replied with no confusion:

"Antínoös, I cannot see myself again
taking a quiet dinner in this company.

Isn't it enough that you could strip my house
under my very nose when I was young?
Now that I know, being grown, what others say,
I understand it all, and my heart is full.
I'll bring black doom upon you if I can— 330
either in Pylos, if I go, or in this country.
And I will go, go all the way, if only
as someone's passenger. I have no ship,
no oarsmen: and it suits you that I have none."

Calmly he drew his hand from Antínoös' hand.
At this the suitors, while they dressed their meat,
began to exchange loud mocking talk about him.
One young toplofty gallant set the tone:

"Well, think of that!
Telémakhos has a mind to murder us.
He's going to lead avengers out of Pylos, 340
or Sparta, maybe; oh, he's wild to do it.
Or else he'll try the fat land of Ephyra—
he can get poison there, and bring it home,
doctor the wine jar and dispatch us all."

Another took the cue:

"Well now, who knows?
He might be lost at sea, just like Odysseus,
knocking around in a ship, far from his friends.
And what a lot of trouble that would give us,
making the right division of his things!
We'd keep his house as dowry for his mother— 350
his mother and the man who marries her."

That was the drift of it. Telémakhos
went on through to the storeroom of his father,
a great vault where gold and bronze lay piled
along with chests of clothes, and fragrant oil.
And there were jars of earthenware in rows
holding an old wine,
mellow, unmixed, and rare; cool stood the jars
against the wall, kept for whatever day
Odysseus, worn by hardships, might come home. 360
The double folding doors were tightly locked
and guarded, night and day, by the serving woman,
Eurýkleia, grand-daughter of Peisênor,
in all her duty vigilant and shrewd.
Telémakhos called her to the storeroom, saying:

"Nurse, get a few two-handled travelling jugs
filled up with wine—the second best, not that
you keep for your unlucky lord and king,

hoping he may have slipped away from death
and may yet come again—royal Odysseus. 370
Twelve amphorai[7] will do; seal them up tight.
And pour out barley into leather bags—
twenty bushels of barley meal ground fine.
Now keep this to yourself! Collect these things,
and after dark, when mother has retired
and gone upstairs to bed, I'll come for them.
I sail to sandy Pylos, then to Sparta,
to see what news there is of Father's voyage."

His loving nurse Eurýkleia gave a cry,
and tears sprang to her eyes as she wailed softly: 380

"Dear child, whatever put this in your head?
Why do you want to go so far in the world—
and you our only darling? Lord Odysseus
died in some strange place, far from his homeland.
Think how, when you have turned your back, these men
will plot to kill you and share all your things!
Stay with your own, dear, do. Why should you suffer
hardship and homelessness on the wild sea?"

But seeing all clear, Telémakhos replied:

"Take heart, Nurse, there's a god behind this plan. 390
And you must swear to keep it from my mother,
until the eleventh day, or twelfth, or till
she misses me, or hears that I am gone.
She must not tear her lovely skin lamenting."

So the old woman vowed by all the gods,
and vowed again, to carry out his wishes;
then she filled up the amphorai with wine
and sifted barley meal into leather bags.
Telémakhos rejoined the suitors.
Meanwhile
the goddess with grey eyes had other business: 400
disguised as Telémakhos, she roamed the town
taking each likely man aside and telling him:
"Meet us at nightfall at the ship!" Indeed,
she asked Noêmon, Phronios' wealthy son,
to lend her a fast ship, and he complied.
Now when at sundown shadows crossed the lanes
she dragged the cutter to the sea and launched it,
fitted out with tough seagoing gear,
and tied it up, away at the harbor's edge.

[7] Plural form of "amphora," a jar with two handles and a thin neck.

The crewmen gathered, sent there by the goddess. 410
Then it occurred to the grey-eyed goddess Athena
to pass inside the house of the hero Odysseus,
showering a sweet drowsiness on the suitors,
whom she had presently wandering in their wine;
and soon, as they could hold their cups no longer,
they straggled off to find their beds in town,
eyes heavy-lidded, laden down with sleep.
Then to Telémakhos the grey-eyed goddess
appeared again with Mentor's form and voice,
calling him out of the lofty emptied hall: 420

"Telémakhos, your crew of fighting men
is ready at the oars, and waiting for you;
come on, no point in holding up the sailing."

And Pallas Athena turned like the wind, running
ahead of him. He followed in her footsteps
down to the seaside, where they found the ship,
and oarsmen with flowing hair at the water's edge.
Telémakhos, now strong in the magic, cried:

"Come with me, friends, and get our rations down!
They are all packed at home, and my own mother 430
knows nothing!—only one maid was told."

He turned and led the way, and they came after,
carried and stowed all in the well-trimmed ship
as the dear son of Odysseus commanded.
Telémakhos then stepped aboard; Athena
took her position aft, and he sat by her.
The two stroke oars cast off the stern hawsers
and vaulted over the gunnels to their benches.
Grey-eyed Athena stirred them a following wind,
soughing from the north-west on the winedark sea, 440
and as he felt the wind, Telémakhos
called to all hands to break out mast and sail.
They pushed the fir mast high and stepped it firm
amidships in the box, made fast the forestays,
then hoisted up the white sail on its halyards
until the wind caught, booming in the sail;
and a flushing wave sang backward from the bow
on either side, as the ship got way upon her,
holding her steady course.
Now they made all secure in the fast black ship, 450
and, setting out the winebowls all a-brim,
they made libation to the gods,
the undying, the ever-new,
most of all to the grey-eyed daughter of Zeus.
And the prow sheared through the night into the dawn.

BOOK THREE: THE LORD OF THE WESTERN APPROACHES

The sun rose on the flawless brimming sea
into a sky all brazen—all one brightening
for gods immortal and for mortal men
on plowlands kind with grain.
And facing sunrise
the voyagers now lay off Pylos town,
compact stronghold of Neleus.[1] On the shore
black bulls were being offered by the people
to the blue-maned god who makes the islands tremble:
nine congregations, each five hundred strong,
led out nine bulls apiece to sacrifice, 10
taking the tripes to eat, while on their altars
thighbones in fat lay burning for the god.
Here they put in, furled sail, and beached the ship;
but Telémakhos hung back in disembarking,
so that Athena turned and said:

"Not the least shyness, now, Telémakhos.
You came across the open sea for this—
to find out where the great earth hides your father
and what the doom was that he came upon.
Go to old Nestor, master charioteer, 20
so we may broach the storehouse of his mind.
Ask him with courtesy, and in his wisdom
he will tell you history and no lies."

But clear-headed Telémakhos replied:

"Mentor, how can I do it, how approach him?
I have no practice in elaborate speeches, and
for a young man to interrogate an old man
seems disrespectful—"

But the grey-eyed goddess said:

"Reason and heart will give you words, Telémakhos;
and a spirit will counsel others. I should say 30
the gods were never indifferent to your life."

She went on quickly, and he followed her
to where the men of Pylos had their altars.
Nestor appeared enthroned among his sons,

[1] Son of the sea god Poseidon (the "blue-maned god"), he was the founder of Pylos and the father of Nestor.

while friends around them skewered the red beef
or held it scorching. When they saw the strangers
a hail went up, and all that crowd came forward
calling out invitations to the feast.
Peisístratos in the lead, the young prince,
caught up their hands in his and gave them places 40
on curly lambskins flat on the sea sand
near Thrasymêdês, his brother, and his father;
he passed them bits of the food of sacrifice,
and, pouring wine in a golden cup,
he said to Pallas Athena, daughter of Zeus:

"Friend, I must ask you to invoke Poseidon:
you find us at this feast, kept in his honor.
Make the appointed offering then, and pray,
and give the honeyed winecup to your friend
so he may do the same. He, too, 50
must pray to the gods on whom all men depend,
but he is just my age, you are the senior,
so here, I give the goblet first to you."

And he put the cup of sweet wine in her hand.
Athena liked his manners, and the equity
that gave her precedence with the cup of gold,
so she besought Poseidon at some length:

"Earthshaker, listen and be well disposed.
Grant your petitioners everything they ask:
above all, honor to Nestor and his sons; 60
second, to every man of Pylos town
a fair gift in exchange for this hekatomb;[2]
third, may Telémakhos and I perform
the errand on which last night we put to sea."

This was the prayer of Athena—
granted in every particular by herself.
She passed the beautiful wine cup to Telémakhos,
who tipped the wine and prayed as she had done.
Meanwhile the spits were taken off the fire,
portions of crisp meat for all. They feasted, 70
and when they had eaten and drunk their fill, at last
they heard from Nestor, prince of charioteers:

"Now is the time,"[3] he said, "for a few questions,
now that our young guests have enjoyed their dinner.
Who are you, strangers? Where are you sailing from,
and where to, down the highways of sea water?

[2] A grand public sacrifice and offering to the gods.
[3] Hospitality required that no such questions be asked of guests until they had been welcomed and fed.

Have you some business here? or are you, now,
reckless wanderers of the sea, like those corsairs
who risk their lives to prey on other men?"

Clear-headed Telémakhos responded cheerfully, 80
for Athena gave him heart. By her design
his quest for news about his father's wandering
would bring him fame in the world's eyes. So he said:

"Nestor, pride of Akhaians, Neleus' son,
you ask where we are from, and I can tell you:
our home port is under Mount Neion, Ithaka.
We are not here on Ithakan business, though,
but on my own. I want news of my father,
Odysseus, known for his great heart, and I
will comb the wide world for it. People say 90
he fought along with you when Troy was taken.
As to the other men who fought that war,
we know where each one died, and how he died;
but Zeus allotted my father death and mystery.
No one can say for sure where he was killed,
whether some hostile landsmen or the sea,
the stormwaves on the deep sea, got the best of him.
And this is why I come to you for help.
Tell me of his death, sir, if perhaps
you witnessed it, or have heard some wanderer 100
tell the tale. The man was born for trouble.
Spare me no part of it for kindness' sake,
but put the scene before me as you saw it.
If ever Odysseus my noble father
served you by promise kept or work accomplished
in the land of Troy, where you Akhaians suffered,
recall those things for me the way they were."

Then Nestor, prince of charioteers, made answer:

"Dear friend, you take me back to all the trouble
we went through in that country, we Akhaians: 110
rough days aboard ship on the cloudy sea
cruising away for pillage after Akhilleus;[4]
rough days of battle around Priam's[5] town.
Our losses, then—so many good men gone:
Arês' great Aias[6] lies there, Akhilleus lies there,
Patróklos,[7] too, the wondrous counselor,
and my own strong and princely son, Antílokhos—

[4] The foremost Greek warrior, central figure of the *Iliad.*

[5] King of Troy.

[6] Another great Greek warrior (also spelled *Ajax*), associated here with Arês, the god of war.

[7] The closest friend of Akhilleus; it was to avenge his death at the hand of the Trojan leader Hektor that Akhilleus—as is narrated in the *Iliad*—re-entered the battle and killed Hektor.

fastest man of them all, and a born fighter.
Other miseries, and many, we endured there.
Could any mortal man tell the whole story? 120
Not if you stayed five years or six to hear
how hard it was for the flower of the Akhaians;
you'd go home weary, and the tale untold.
Think: we were there nine years, and we tried everything,
all stratagems against them,
up to the bitter end that Zeus begrudged us.
And as to stratagems, no man would claim
Odysseus' gift for those. He had no rivals,
your father, at the tricks of war.
Your father?
Well, I must say I marvel at the sight of you: 130
your manner of speech couldn't be more like his;
one would say No; no boy could speak so well.
And all that time at Ilion,[8] he and I
were never at odds in council or assembly—
saw things the same way, had one mind between us
in all the good advice we gave the Argives.
But when we plundered Priam's town and tower
and took to the ships, God scattered the Akhaians.
He had a mind to make homecoming hard for them,
seeing they would not think straight nor behave, 140
or some would not. So evil days came on them,
and she who had been angered,
Zeus's dangerous grey-eyed daughter, did it,
starting a fight between the sons of Atreus.[9]
First they were fools enough to call assembly
at sundown, unheard of hour;
the Akhaian soldiers turned out, soaked with wine,
to hear talk, talk about it from their commanders:
Meneláos harangued them to get organized—
time to ride home on the sea's broad back, he said; 150
but Agamémnon wouldn't hear of it. He wanted
to hold the troops, make sacrifice, a hekatomb,
something to pacify Athena's rage.
Folly again, to think that he could move her.
Will you change the will of the everlasting gods
in a night or a day's time?
The two men stood there hammering at each other
until the army got to its feet with a roar,
and no decision, wanting it both ways.

[8] Troy.

[9] Atreus was father of Agamémnon and Meneláos, the brothers who commanded the Greek forces. Athena's hostility to the Greeks (whom she generally favored and aided) was occasioned by outrages committed against the Trojan princess and prophetess Kassandra, who during the sack of Troy had tried to take refuge at Athena's shrine.

That night no one slept well, everyone cursing 160
someone else. Here was the bane[10] from Zeus.
At dawn we dragged our ships to the lordly water,
stowed aboard all our plunder
and the slave women in their low hip girdles.
But half the army elected to stay behind
with Agamémnon as their corps commander;
the other half embarked and pulled away.
We made good time, the huge sea smoothed before us,
and held our rites when we reached Ténedos,[11]
being wild for home. But Zeus, not willing yet, 170
now cruelly set us at odds a second time,
and one lot turned, put back in the rolling ships,
under command of the subtle captain, Odysseus;
their notion was to please Lord Agamémnon.
Not I. I fled, with every ship I had;
I knew fate had some devilment brewing there.
Diomêdês roused his company and fled, too,
and later Meneláos, the red-haired captain,
caught up with us at Lesbos,
while we mulled over the long sea route, unsure 180
whether to lay our course northward of Khios,
keeping the Isle of Psyria off to port,
or inside Khios, coasting by windy Mimas.
We asked for a sign from heaven, and the sign came
to cut across the open sea to Euboia,
and lose no time putting our ills behind us.
The wind freshened astern, and the ships ran
before the wind on paths of the deep sea fish,
making Geraistos before dawn. We thanked Poseidon
with many a charred thighbone for that crossing. 190
On the fourth day, Diomêdês' company
under full sail put in at Argos port,
and I held on for Pylos. The fair wind,
once heaven set it blowing, never failed.

So this, dear child, was how I came from Troy,
and saw no more of the others, lost or saved.
But you are welcome to all I've heard since then
at home; I have no reason to keep it from you.
The Myrmidon spearfighters returned, they say,
under the son of lionhearted Akhilleus; 200
and so did Poias' great son, Philoktêtês.

[10] Ruin; poison

[11] The problem described by Nestor in the following lines is whether the part of the Greek fleet that decided to sail immediately should follow a circuitous course homeward among the islands of the Aegean Sea or head straight across it, by a course that was shorter but farther removed from ports.

Idómeneus brought his company back to Krete;[12]
the sea took not a man from him, of all
who lived through the long war.
And even as far away as Ithaka
you've heard of Agamémnon—how he came
home, how Aigísthos waited to destroy him
but paid a bitter price for it in the end.
That is a good thing, now, for a man to leave
a son behind him, like the son who punished 210
Aigísthos for the murder of his great father.
You, too, are tall and well set-up, I see;
be brave, you too, so men in times to come
will speak well of you."

Then Telémakhos said:

"Nestor, pride of Akhaians, Neleus' son,
that was revenge, and far and wide the Akhaians
will tell the tale in song for generations.
I wish the gods would buckle his arms on me!
I'd be revenged for outrage
on my insidious and brazen enemies. 220
But no such happy lot was given to me
or to my father. Still, I must hold fast."

To this Lord Nestor of Gerênia said:

"My dear young friend, now that you speak of it,
I hear a crowd of suitors for your mother
lives with you, uninvited, making trouble.
Now tell me how you take this. Do the people
side against you, hearkening to some oracle?
Who knows, your father might come home someday
alone or backed by troops, and have it out with them. 230
If grey-eyed Athena loved you
the way she did Odysseus in the old days,
in Troy country, where we all went through so much—
never have I seen the gods help any man
as openly as Athena did your father—
well, as I say, if she cared for you that way,
there would be those to quit this marriage game."

But prudently Telémakhos replied:

"I can't think what you say will ever happen, sir.
It is a dazzling hope. But not for me. 240

[12] The Myrmidons were Akhilleus' troops; his son was Pyrrhus, also called Neoptólemus. Philoktêtês was a Greek warrior who, after having been abandoned on the way to Troy because of a malodorous wound, later rejoined the Greek forces and was crucial to their success in the war. Idómeneus, an ally of the Greeks against the Trojans, was king of Krete (Crete).

It could not be—even if the gods willed it."

At this grey-eyed Athena broke in, saying:

"What strange talk you permit yourself, Telémakhos.
A god could save the man by simply wishing it—
from the farthest shore in the world.
If I were he, I should prefer to suffer
years at sea, and then be safe at home;
better that than a knife at my hearthside
where Agamémnon found it—killed by adulterers.
Though as for death, of course all men must suffer it: 250
the gods may love a man, but they can't help him
when cold death comes to lay him on his bier."[13]

Telémakhos replied:

"Mentor, grievously though we miss my father, why
go on as if that homecoming could happen?
You know the gods had settled it already,
years ago, when dark death came for him.
But there is something else I imagine Nestor
can tell us, knowing as he does the ways of men.
They say his rule goes back over three generations, 260
so long, so old, it seems death cannot touch him.
Nestor, Neleus' son, true sage, say how
did the Lord of the Great Plains, Agamémnon, die?
What was the trick Aigísthos used
to kill the better man? And Meneláos,
where was he? Not at Argos[14] in Akhaia,
but blown off course, held up in some far country,
is that what gave the killer nerve to strike?"

Lord Nestor of Gerênia made answer:

"Well, now, my son, I'll tell you the whole story. 270
You know, yourself, what would have come to pass
if red-haired Meneláos, back from Troy,
had caught Aigísthos in that house alive.
There would have been no burial mound for him,
but dogs and carrion birds to huddle on him

[13] This final sentence is a definitive expression of the ancient Greek understanding of the difference between human beings and deities. Though gods may be champions and even comrades of mortals, the latter are doomed to die and the gods are not. The distinction has little to do with morality or metaphysics. The gods belong to a different order of beings, though not necessarily to a superior order.

[14] The region ruled by Agamémnon, brother to Meneláos, whose wife Helen had run off with the Trojan prince Paris. Homer's account of the slaying of Agamémnon at his homecoming is at this point a fairly simple justification of Agamémnon and his avenging son Orestês; Aeschylus' account in the *Oresteia* is more psychologically complex. For other accounts of the story, by the Ancient of the Salt Sea and by Agamémnon himself, see Books IV and XI of the *Odyssey.*

in the fields beyond the wall, and not a soul
bewailing him, for the great wrong he committed.
While we were hard-pressed in the war at Troy
he stayed safe inland in the grazing country,
making light talk to win Agamémnon's queen. 280
But the Lady Klytaimnéstra, in the first days,
rebuffed him, being faithful still;
then, too, she had at hand as her companion
a minstrel Agamémnon left attending her,
charged with her care, when he took ship for Troy.
Then came the fated hour when she gave in.[15]
Her lover tricked the poet and marooned him
on a bare island for the seabirds' picking,
and took her home, as he and she desired.
Many thighbones he burned on the gods' altars 290
and many a woven and golden ornament
hung to bedeck them, in his satisfaction;
he had not thought life held such glory for him.

Now Meneláos and I sailed home together
on friendly terms, from Troy,
but when we came off Sunion Point[16] in Attika,
the ships still running free, Onêtor's son
Phrontis, the steersman of Meneláos' ship,
fell over with a death grip on the tiller:
some unseen arrow from Apollo hit him. 300
No man handled a ship better than he did
in a high wind and sea, so Meneláos
put down his longing to get on, and landed
to give this man full honor in funeral.
His own luck turned then. Out on the winedark sea
in the murmuring hulls again, he made Cape Malea,[17]
but Zeus who views the wide world sent a gloom
over the ocean, and a howling gale
came on with seas increasing, mountainous,
parting the ships and driving half toward Krete 310
where the Kydonians live by Iardanos river,
Off Gortyn's coastline in the misty sea there
a reef, a razorback, cuts through the water,
and every westerly piles up a pounding
surf along the left side, going toward Phaistos—
big seas buffeted back by the narrow stone.

[15] This passage presents both Klytaimnéstra and her paramour Aigísthos as frivolous and irresponsible dalliers; in other versions of the story, notably in Aeschylus' *Oresteia,* both these adulterers are given an understandable, if not necessarily justifiable, motive for revenge against Agamémnon.

[16] The tip of a promontory, near Athens, in southeastern Greece. The fleet is trying to sail westward around the southern coast.

[17] Located at the extreme southern point of the Greek mainland, directly north of the western end of the island of Krete.

They were blown here, and fought in vain for sea room;
the ships kept going in to their destruction,
slammed on the reef. The crews were saved. But now
those five that weathered it got off to southward, 320
taken by wind and current on to Egypt;
and there Meneláos stayed. He made a fortune
in sea traffic among those distant races,
but while he did so, the foul crime was planned
and carried out in Argos by Aigísthos,
who ruled over golden Mykênai[18] seven years.
Seven long years, with Agamémnon dead,
he held the people down, before the vengeance.
But in the eighth year, back from exile in Attika,
Orestês killed the snake who killed his father. 330
He gave his hateful mother and her soft man
a tomb together, and proclaimed the funeral day
a festal day for all the Argive people.
That day Lord Meneláos of the great war cry
made port with all the gold his ships could carry.
And this should give you pause, my son:
don't stay too long away from home, leaving
your treasure there, and brazen suitors near;
they'll squander all you have or take it from you,
and then how will your journey serve? 340
I urge you, though, to call on Meneláos,
he being but lately home from distant parts
in the wide world. A man could well despair
of getting home at all, if the winds blew him
over the Great South Sea—that weary waste,
even the wintering birds delay
one winter more before the northward crossing.
Well, take your ship and crew and go by water,
or if you'd rather go by land, here are
horses, a car, and my own sons for company 350
as far as the ancient land of Lakedaimon[19]
and Meneláos, the red-haired captain there.
Ask him with courtesy, and in his wisdom
he will tell you history and no lies."

While Nestor talked, the sun went down the sky
and gloom came on the land,
and now the grey-eyed goddess Athena said:

"Sir, this is all most welcome and to the point,
but why not slice the bulls' tongues now, and mix
libations for Poseidon and the gods? 360

[18] The capital city of the plain of Argos, ruled over by Agamémnon. Also spelled *Mycenae*.
[19] Sparta; in the far south of Greece. Also spelled *Lacedaemon*.

Then we can all retire; high time we did;
the light is going under the dark world's rim,
better not linger at the sacred feast."

When Zeus's daughter spoke, they turned to listen
and soon the squires brought water for their hands,
while stewards filled the winebowls and poured out
a fresh cup full for every man. The company
stood up to fling the tongues and a shower of wine
over the flames, then drank their thirst away.
Now finally Telémakhos and Athena 370
bestirred themselves, turning away to the ship,
but Nestor put a hand on each, and said:

"Now Zeus forbid, and the other gods as well,
that you should spend the night on board, and leave me
as though I were some pauper without a stitch,
no blankets in his house, no piles of rugs,
no sleeping soft for host or guest! Far from it!
I have all these, blankets and deep-piled rugs,
and while I live the only son of Odysseus
will never make his bed on a ship's deck— 380
no, not while sons of mine are left at home
to welcome any guest who comes to us."

The grey-eyed goddess Athena answered him:

"You are very kind, sir, and Telémakhos
should do as you ask. That is the best thing.
He will go with you, and will spend the night
under your roof. But I must join our ship
and talk to the crew, to keep their spirits up,
since I'm the only senior in the company.
The rest are boys who shipped for friendship's sake, 390
no older than Telémakhos, any of them.
Let me sleep out, then, by the black hull's side,
this night at least. At daybreak I'll be off
to see the Kaukonians[20] about a debt they owe me,
an old one and no trifle. As for your guest,
send him off in a car, with one of your sons,
and give him thoroughbreds, a racing team."

Even as she spoke, Athena left them—seeming
a seahawk, in a clap of wings,—and all
the Akhaians of Pylos town looked up astounded. 400
Awed then by what his eyes had seen, the old man
took Telémakhos' hand and said warmly:

[20] A people who lived near Pylos.

"My dear child, I can have no fears for you,
no doubt about your conduct or your heart,
if, at your age, the gods are your companions.
Here we had someone from Olympos—clearly
the glorious daughter of Zeus, his third child,
who held your father dear among the Argives.
O, Lady, hear me! Grant an illustrious name
to me and to my children and my dear wife! 410
A noble heifer shall be yours in sacrifice,
one that no man has ever yoked or driven;
my gift to you—her horns all sheathed in gold."

So he ended, praying; and Athena heard him.
Then Nestor of Gerênia led them all,
his sons and sons-in-law, to his great house;
and in they went to the famous hall of Nestor,
taking their seats on thrones and easy chairs,
while the old man mixed water in a wine bowl
with sweet red wine, mellowed eleven years 420
before his housekeeper uncapped the jar.
He mixed and poured his offering, repeating
prayers to Athena, daughter of royal Zeus.
The others made libation, and drank deep,
then all the company went to their quarters,
and Nestor of Gerênia showed Telémakhos
under the echoing eastern entrance hall
to a fine bed near the bed of Peisístratos,
captain of spearmen, his unmarried son.
Then he lay down in his own inner chamber 430
where his dear faithful wife had smoothed his bed.

When Dawn spread out her finger tips of rose,
Lord Nestor of Gerênia, charioteer,
left his room for a throne of polished stone,
white and gleaming as though with oil, that stood
before the main gate of the palace; Neleus here
had sat before him—masterful in kingship,
Neleus, long ago a prey to death, gone down
to the night of the underworld.
So Nestor held his throne and scepter now, 440
lord of the western approaches to Akhaia.
And presently his sons came out to join him,
leaving the palace: Ekhéphron and Stratíos,
Perseus and Arêtós and Thrasymêdês,
and after them the prince Peisístratos,
bringing Telémakhos along with him.
Seeing all present, the old lord Nestor said:

"Dear sons, here is my wish, and do it briskly
to please the gods, Athena first of all,

my guest in daylight at our holy feast. 450
One of you must go for a young heifer
and have the cowherd lead her from the pasture.
Another call on Lord Telémakhos' ship
to invite his crewmen, leaving two behind;
and someone else again send for the goldsmith,
Laerkês, to gild the horns.
The rest stay here together. Tell the servants
a ritual feast will be prepared in hall.
Tell them to bring seats, firewood and fresh water."

Before he finished, they were about these errands. 460
The heifer came from pasture,
the crewmen of Telémakhos from the ship,
the smith arrived, bearing the tools of his trade—
hammer and anvil, and the precision tongs
he handled fiery gold with,—and Athena
came as a god comes, numinous, to the rites.

The smith now gloved each horn in a pure foil
beaten out of the gold that Nestor gave him—
a glory and delight for the goddess' eyes—
while Ekhéphron and Stratíos held the horns. 470
Arêtós brought clear lustral water
in a bowl quivering with fresh-cut flowers,
a basket of barley in his other hand.
Thrasymêdês, who could stand his ground in war,
stood ready, with a sharp two-bladed axe,
for the stroke of sacrifice, and Perseus
held a bowl for the blood. And now Nestor,
strewing the barley grains, and water drops,
pronounced his invocation to Athena
and burned a pinch of bristles from the victim. 480
When prayers were said and all the grain was scattered
great-hearted Thrasymêdês in a flash
swung the axe, at one blow cutting through
the neck tendons. The heifer's spirit failed.
Then all the women gave a wail of joy—
daughters, daughters-in-law, and the Lady Eurydíkê,
Klyménos' eldest daughter. But the men
still held the heifer, shored her up
from the wide earth where the living go their ways,
until Peisístratos cut her throat across, 490
the black blood ran, and life ebbed from her marrow.
The carcass now sank down, and they disjointed
shoulder and thigh bone, wrapping them in fat,
two layers, folded, with raw strips of flesh.
These offerings Nestor burned on the split-wood fire
and moistened with red wine. His sons took up
five-tined forks in their hands, while the altar flame

ate through the bones, and bits of tripe went round.
Then came the carving of the quarters, and they spitted
morsels of lean meat on the long sharp tines 500
and broiled them at arm's length upon the fire.

Polykástê, a fair girl, Nestor's youngest,
had meanwhile given a bath to Telémakhos—
bathing him first, then rubbing him with oil.
She held fine clothes and a cloak to put around him
when he came godlike from the bathing place;
then out he went to take his place with Nestor.
When the best cuts were broiled and off the spits,
they all sat down to banquet. Gentle squires
kept every golden wine cup brimming full. 510
And so they feasted to their heart's content,
until the prince of charioteers commanded:

"Sons, harness the blood mares for Telémakhos;
hitch up the car, and let him take the road."

They swung out smartly to do the work, and hooked
the handsome horses to a chariot shaft.
The mistress of the stores brought up provisions
of bread and wine, with victuals fit for kings,
and Telémakhos stepped up on the painted car.
Just at his elbow stood Peisístratos, 520
captain of spearmen, reins in hand. He gave
a flick to the horses, and with streaming manes
they ran for the open country. The tall town
of Pylos sank behind them in the distance,
as all day long they kept the harness shaking.

The sun was low and shadows crossed the lanes
when they arrived at Phêrai.[21] There Dióklês,
son of Ortílokhos whom Alpheios fathered,
welcomed the young men, and they slept the night.
But up when the young Dawn's finger tips of rose 530
opened in the east, they hitched the team
once more to the painted car,
and steered out eastward through the echoing gate,
whipping their fresh horses into a run.
That day they made the grainlands of Lakedaimon,
where, as the horses held to a fast clip,
they kept on to their journey's end. Behind them
the sun went down and all the roads grew dark.

[21]A stopping place on the eastward route from Pylos to Lakedaimon.

BOOK FOUR: THE RED-HAIRED KING AND HIS LADY

By vales and sharp ravines in Lakedaimon
the travellers drove to Meneláos' mansion,
and found him at a double wedding feast
for son and daughter.
Long ago at Troy
he pledged her to the heir of great Akhilleus,
breaker of men—a match the gods had ripened;
so he must send her with a chariot train
to the town and glory of the Myrmidons.
And that day, too, he brought Alektor's daughter
to marry his tall scion,[1] Megapénthês, 10
born of a slave girl during the long war—
for the gods had never after granted Helen
a child to bring into the sunlit world
after the first, rose-lipped Hermionê,
a girl like the pale-gold goddess Aphroditê.[2]

Down the great hall in happiness they feasted,
neighbors of Meneláos, and his kin,
for whom a holy minstrel harped and sang;
and two lithe tumblers moved out on the song
with spins and handsprings through the company. 20
Now when Telémakhos and Nestor's son
pulled up their horses at the main gate,
one of the king's companions in arms, Eteóneus,
going outside, caught sight of them. He turned
and passed through court and hall to tell the master,
stepping up close to get his ear. Said he:

"Two men are here—two strangers,[3] Meneláos,
but nobly born Akhaians, they appear.
What do you say, shall we unhitch their team,
or send them on to someone free to receive them?" 30

The red-haired captain answered him in anger:

"You were no idiot before, Eteóneus,
but here you are talking like a child of ten.
Could we have made it home again—and Zeus
give us no more hard roving!—if other men
had never fed us, given us lodging?
Bring
these men to be our guests: unhitch their team!"

[1] Descendant; son.
[2] Goddess of love and beauty.
[3] The near-breach of hospitality by Eteóneus, which angers Meneláos, is probably explained by wariness; another guest, Paris, had once abducted Helen and thus set off the war.

Eteóneus left the long room like an arrow,
calling equerries[4] after him, on the run.
Outside, they freed the sweating team from harness, 40
stabled the horses, tied them up, and showered
bushels of wheat and barley in the feed box;
then leaned the chariot pole
against the gleaming entry wall of stone
and took the guests in. What a brilliant place
that mansion of the great prince seemed to them!
A-glitter everywhere, as though with fiery
points of sunlight, lusters of the moon.
The young men gazed in joy before they entered
into a room of polished tubs to bathe. 50
Maidservants gave them baths, anointed them,
held out fresh tunics, cloaked them warm; and soon
they took tall thrones beside the son of Atreus.
Here a maid tipped out water for their hands
from a golden pitcher into a silver bowl,
and set a polished table near at hand;
the larder mistress with her tray of loaves
and savories came, dispensing all her best,
and then a carver heaped their platters high
with various meats, and put down cups of gold. 60
Now said the red-haired captain, Meneláos,
gesturing:

"Welcome; and fall to; in time,
when you have supped, we hope to hear your names,
forbears and families—in your case, it seems,
no anonymities, but lordly men.
Lads like yourselves are not base born."

At this,
he lifted in his own hands the king's portion,
a chine of beef, and set it down before them.
Seeing all ready then, they took their dinner;
but when they had feasted well, 70
Telémakhos could not keep still, but whispered,
his head bent close, so the others might not hear:

"My dear friend, can you believe your eyes?—
the murmuring hall, how luminous it is
with bronze, gold, amber, silver, and ivory!
This is the way the court of Zeus must be,
inside, upon Olympos. What a wonder!"

[4] Men who tended to the horses.

But splendid Meneláos had overheard him
and spoke out on the instant to them both:

"Young friends, no mortal man can vie with Zeus. 80
His home and all his treasures are for ever.
But as for men, it may well be that few
have more than I. How painfully I wandered
before I brought it home! Seven years at sea,
Kypros, Phoinikia, Egypt, and still farther
among the sun-burnt races.
I saw the men of Sidon[5] and Arabia
and Libya, too, where lambs are horned at birth.
In every year they have three lambing seasons,
so no man, chief or shepherd, ever goes 90
hungry for want of mutton, cheese, or milk—
all year at milking time there are fresh ewes.
But while I made my fortune on those travels
a stranger killed my brother, in cold blood,—
tricked blind, caught in the web of his deadly queen.
What pleasure can I take, then, being lord
over these costly things?
You must have heard your fathers tell my story,
whoever your fathers are; you must know of my life,
the anguish I once had, and the great house 100
full of my treasure, left in desolation.
How gladly I should live one third as rich
to have my friends back safe at home!—my friends
who died on Troy's wide seaboard, far
from the grazing lands of Argos.
But as things are, nothing but grief is left me
for those companions. While I sit at home
sometimes hot tears come, and I revel in them,
or stop before the surfeit makes me shiver.
And there is one I miss more than the other 110
dead I mourn for; sleep and food alike
grow hateful when I think of him. No soldier
took on so much, went through so much, as Odysseus.
That seems to have been his destiny, and this mine—
to feel each day the emptiness of his absence,
ignorant, even, whether he lived or died.
How his old father and his quiet wife,
Penélopê, must miss him still!
And Telémakhos, whom he left as a new-born child."

Now hearing these things said, the boy's heart rose 120
in a long pang for his father, and he wept,

[5] An important city in Phoinikia (Phoenicia), an area along the Syrian coast noted for commerce and craftsmanship.

holding his purple mantle with both hands
before his eyes. Meneláos knew him now,
and so fell silent with uncertainty
whether to let him speak and name his father
in his own time, or to inquire, and prompt him.
And while he pondered, Helen came
out of her scented chamber, a moving grace
like Artemis,[6] straight as a shaft of gold.
Beside her came Adrastê, to place her armchair, 130
Alkippê, with a rug of downy wool,
and Phylo, bringing a silver basket, once
given by Alkandrê, the wife of Pólybos,
in the treasure city, Thebes of distant Egypt.
He gave two silver bathtubs to Meneláos
and a pair of tripods, with ten pure gold bars,
and she, then, made these beautiful gifts to Helen:
a golden distaff,[7] and the silver basket
rimmed in hammered gold, with wheels to run on.
So Phylo rolled it in to stand beside her, 140
heaped with fine spun stuff, and cradled on it
the distaff swathed in dusky violet wool.
Reclining in her light chair with its footrest,
Helen gazed at her husband and demanded:

"Meneláos, my lord, have we yet heard
our new guests introduce themselves? Shall I
dissemble what I feel? No, I must say it.
Never, anywhere, have I seen so great a likeness
in man or woman—but it is truly strange!
This boy must be the son of Odysseus, 150
Telémakhos, the child he left at home
that year the Akhaian host made war on Troy—
daring all for the wanton that I was."

And the red-haired captain, Meneláos, answered:

"My dear, I see the likeness as well as you do.
Odysseus' hands and feet were like this boy's;
his head, and hair, and the glinting of his eyes.
Not only that, but when I spoke, just now,
of Odysseus' years of toil on my behalf
and all he had to endure—the boy broke down 160
and wept into his cloak."

Now Nestor's son,
Peisístratos, spoke up in answer to him:

"My lord marshal, Meneláos, son of Atreus,
this is that hero's son as you surmise,

[6] Goddess of the hunt.
[7] A staff used in spinning thread.

but he is gentle, and would be ashamed
to clamor for attention before your grace
whose words have been so moving to us both.
Nestor, Lord of Gerênia, sent me with him
as guide and escort; he had wished to see you,
to be advised by you or assisted somehow. 170
A father far from home means difficulty
for an only son, with no one else to help him;
so with Telémakhos:
his father left the house without defenders."

The king with flaming hair now spoke again:

"His son, in my house! How I loved the man,
And how he fought through hardship for my sake!
I swore I'd cherish him above all others
if Zeus, who views the wide world, gave us passage
homeward across the sea in the fast ships. 180
I would have settled him in Argos, brought him
over with herds and household out of Ithaka,
his child and all his people. I could have cleaned out
one of my towns to be his new domain.
And so we might have been together often
in feasts and entertainments, never parted
till the dark mist of death lapped over one of us.
But God himself must have been envious,
to batter the bruised man so that he alone
should fail in his return." 190

A twinging ache of grief rose up in everyone,
and Helen of Argos wept, the daughter of Zeus,[8]
Telémakhos and Meneláos wept,
and tears came to the eyes of Nestor's son—
remembering, for his part, Antílokhos,
whom the son of shining Dawn[9] had killed in battle.
But thinking of that brother, he broke out:

"O son of Atreus, when we spoke of you
at home, and asked about you, my old father
would say you have the clearest mind of all. 200
If it is not too much to ask, then, let us not
weep away these hours after supper;
I feel we should not: Dawn will soon be here!
You understand, I would not grudge a man
right mourning when he comes to death and doom:
what else can one bestow on the poor dead?—

[8] Helen was daughter of Zeus by the mortal woman Lêda. (Lêda was ravished by the god, who took the form of a swan.)

[9] Memnon, an Ethiopian king, was the son of Eos, the goddess of the dawn.

a lock of hair sheared,[10] and a tear let fall.
For that matter, I, too,
lost someone in the war at Troy—my brother,
and no mean soldier, whom you must have known, 210
although I never did,—Antílokhos.
He ranked high as a runner and fighting man."

The red-haired captain Meneláos answered:

"My lad, what you have said is only sensible,
and you did well to speak. Yes, that was worthy
a wise man and an older man than you are:
you speak for all the world like Nestor's son.
How easily one can tell the man whose father
had true felicity, marrying and begetting!
And that was true of Nestor, all his days, 220
down to his sleek old age in peace at home,
with clever sons, good spearmen into the bargain.
Come, we'll shake off this mourning mood of ours
and think of supper. Let the men at arms
rinse our hands again! There will be time
for a long talk with Telémakhos in the morning."

The hero Meneláos' companion in arms,
Asphalion, poured water for their hands,
and once again they touched the food before them.
But now it entered Helen's mind 230
to drop into the wine that they were drinking
an anodyne, mild magic of forgetfulness.
Whoever drank this mixture in the wine bowl
would be incapable of tears that day—
though he should lose mother and father both,
or see, with his own eyes, a son or brother
mauled by weapons of bronze at his own gate.
The opiate of Zeus's daughter bore
this canny power. It had been supplied her
by Polydamna, mistress of Lord Thôn, 240
in Egypt, where the rich plantations grow
herbs of all kinds, maleficent and healthful;
and no one else knows medicine as they do,
Egyptian heirs of Paian,[11] the healing god.
She drugged the wine, then, had it served, and said—
taking again her part in the conversation—

"O Meneláos, Atreus' royal son,
and you that are great heroes' sons, you know
how Zeus gives all of us in turn
good luck and bad luck, being all powerful. 250

[10] To strew a lock of one's hair on the dead was a customary part of funeral ritual.
[11] An epithet for Apollo in his role as god of physicians.

So take refreshment, take your ease in hall,
and cheer the time with stories. I'll begin.
Not that I think of naming, far less telling,
every feat of that rugged man, Odysseus,
but here is something that he dared to do
at Troy, where you Akhaians endured the war.
He had, first, given himself an outrageous beating
and thrown some rags on—like a household slave—
then slipped into that city of wide lanes
among his enemies. So changed, he looked 260
as never before upon the Akhaian beachhead,
but like a beggar, merged in the townspeople;
and no one there remarked him. But I knew him—
even as he was, I knew him,
and questioned him. How shrewdly he put me off!
But in the end I bathed him and anointed him,
put a fresh cloak around him, and swore an oath
not to give him away as Odysseus to the Trojans,
till he got back to camp where the long ships lay.
He spoke up then, and told me 270
all about the Akhaians, and their plans—
then sworded many Trojans through the body
on his way out with what he learned of theirs.
The Trojan women raised a cry—but my heart
sang—for I had come round, long before,
to dreams of sailing home, and I repented
the mad day Aphroditê
drew me away from my dear fatherland,
forsaking all—child, bridal bed, and husband—
a man without defect in form or mind." 280

Replied the red-haired captain, Meneláos:

"An excellent tale, my dear, and most becoming.
In my life I have met, in many countries,
foresight and wit in many first rate men,
but never have I seen one like Odysseus
for steadiness and a stout heart. Here, for instance,
is what he did—had the cold nerve to do—
inside the hollow horse,[12] where we were waiting,
picked men all of us, for the Trojan slaughter,
when all of a sudden, you came by—I dare say 290
drawn by some superhuman
power that planned an exploit for the Trojans;
and Deïphobos,[13] that handsome man, came with you.
Three times you walked around it, patting it everywhere,

[12] The Greeks had hidden some of their best warriors inside a huge wooden horse, which the Trojans hauled into their city, thus precipitating its overthrow. For a detailed version of the incident, see Virgil's *Aeneid*, Book II.

[13] By the time of the fall of Troy, Helen had been married to this Trojan prince.

and called by name the flower of our fighters,
making your voice sound like their wives, calling.
Diomêdês and I crouched in the center
along with Odysseus; we could hear you plainly;
and listening, we two were swept
by waves of longing—to reply, or go. 300
Odysseus fought us down, despite our craving,
and all the Akhaians kept their lips shut tight,
all but Antiklos. Desire moved his throat
to hail you, but Odysseus' great hands clamped
over his jaws, and held. So he saved us all,
till Pallas Athena led you away at last."

Then clear-headed Telémakhos addressed him:

"My lord marshal, Meneláos, son of Atreus,
all the more pity, since these valors
could not defend him from annihilation— 310
not if his heart were iron in his breast.
But will you not dismiss us for the night now?
Sweet sleep will be a pleasure, drifting over us."

He said no more, but Helen called the maids
and sent them to make beds, with purple rugs
piled up, and sheets outspread, and fleecy
coverlets, in the porch inside the gate.
The girls went out with torches in their hands,
and presently a squire led the guests—
Telémakhos and Nestor's radiant son— 320
under the entrance colonnade, to bed.
Then deep in the great mansion, in his chamber,
Meneláos went to rest, and Helen,
queenly in her long gown, lay beside him.

When the young Dawn with finger tips of rose
made heaven bright, the deep-lunged man of battle
stood up, pulled on his tunic and his mantle,
slung on a swordbelt and a new edged sword,
tied his smooth feet into fine rawhide sandals
and left his room, a god's brilliance upon him. 330
He sat down by Telémakhos, asking gently:

"Telémakhos, why did you come, sir, riding
the sea's broad back to reach old Lakedaimon?
A public errand or private? Why, precisely?"

Telémakhos replied:

"My lord marshal Meneláos, son of Atreus,
I came to hear what news you had of Father.
My house, my good estates are being ruined.

Each day my mother's bullying suitors come
to slaughter flocks of mine and my black cattle; 340
enemies crowd our home. And this is why
I come to you for news of him who owned it.
Tell me of his death, sir, if perhaps
you witnessed it, or have heard some wanderer
tell the tale. The man was born for trouble.
Spare me no part for kindness' sake; be harsh;
but put the scene before me as you saw it.
If ever Odysseus my noble father
served you by promise kept or work accomplished
in the land of Troy, where you Akhaians suffered, 350
recall those things for me the way they were."

Stirred now to anger, Meneláos said:

"Intolerable—that soft men, as those are,
should think to lie in that great captain's bed.
Fawns in a lion's lair! As if a doe
put down her litter of sucklings there, while she
quested a glen or cropped some grassy hollow.
Ha! Then the lord returns to his own bed
and deals out wretched doom on both alike.
So will Odysseus deal out doom on these. 360
O Father Zeus, Athena, and Apollo!
I pray he comes as once he was, in Lesbos,
when he stood up to wrestle Philomeleidês—
champion and Island King—
and smashed him down. How the Akhaians cheered!
If only that Odysseus met the suitors,
they'd have their consummation, a cold bed!
Now for your questions, let me come to the point.
I would not misreport it for you; let me
tell you what the Ancient of the Sea,[14] 370
who is infallible, said to me—every word.

During my first try at a passage homeward
the gods detained me, tied me down to Egypt—
for I had been too scant in hekatombs,
and gods will have the rules each time remembered.
There is an island washed by the open sea
lying off Nile mouth—seamen call it Pharos—
distant a day's sail in a clean hull
with a brisk land breeze behind. It has a harbor,
a sheltered bay, where shipmasters 380
take on dark water for the outward voyage.
Here the gods held me twenty days becalmed.

[14] Proteus, who is described in the following passage.

No winds came up, seaward escorting winds
for ships that ride the sea's broad back, and so
my stores and men were used up; we were failing
had not one goddess intervened in pity—
Eidothea, daughter of Proteus,
the Ancient of the Sea. How I distressed her!
I had been walking out alone that day—
my sailors, thin-bellied from the long fast, 390
were off with fish hooks, angling on the shore—
then she appeared to me, and her voice sang:

'What fool is here, what drooping dunce of dreams?
Or can it be, friend, that you love to suffer?
How can you linger on this island, aimless
and shiftless, while your people waste away?'

To this I quickly answered:

'Let me tell you,
goddess, whatever goddess you may be,
these doldrums are no will of mine. I take it
the gods who own broad heaven are offended. 400
Why don't you tell me—since the gods know everything—
who has me pinned down here?
How am I going to make my voyage home?'

Now she replied in her immortal beauty:

'I'll put it for you clearly as may be, friend.
The Ancient of the Salt Sea haunts this place,
immortal Proteus of Egypt; all the deeps
are known to him; he serves under Poseidon,
and is, they say, my father.
If you could take him by surprise and hold him, 410
he'd give you course and distance for your sailing
homeward across the cold fish-breeding sea.
And should you wish it, noble friend, he'd tell you
all that occurred at home, both good and evil,
while you were gone so long and hard a journey.'

To this I said:

'But you, now—you must tell me
how I can trap this venerable sea-god.
He will elude me if he takes alarm;
no man—god knows—can quell a god with ease.'

That fairest of unearthly nymphs replied: 420

'I'll tell you this, too, clearly as may be.
When the sun hangs at high noon in heaven,
the Ancient glides ashore under the Westwind,

hidden by shivering glooms on the clear water,
and rests in caverns hollowed by the sea.
There flippered seals, brine children, shining come
from silvery foam in crowds to lie around him,
exhaling rankness from the deep sea floor.
Tomorrow dawn I'll take you to those caves
and bed you down there. Choose three officers 430
for company—brave men they had better be—
the old one has strange powers, I must tell you.
He goes amid the seals to check their number,
and when he sees them all, and counts them all,
he lies down like a shepherd with his flock.
Here is your opportunity: at this point
gather yourselves, with all your heart and strength,
and tackle him before he bursts away.
He'll make you fight—for he can take the forms
of all the beasts, and water, and blinding fire; 440
but you must hold on, even so, and crush him
until he breaks the silence. When he does,
he will be in that shape you saw asleep.
Relax your grip, then, set the Ancient free,
and put your questions, hero:
Who is the god so hostile to you,
and how will you go home on the fish-cold sea.'

At this she dove under a swell and left me.
Back to the ships in the sandy cove I went,
my heart within me like a high surf running; 450
but there I joined my men once more
at supper, as the sacred Night came on,
and slept at last beside the lapping water.
When Dawn spread out her finger tips of rose
I started, by the sea's wide level ways,
praying the gods for help, and took along
three lads I counted on in any fight.
Meanwhile the nereid[15] swam from the lap of Ocean
laden with four sealskins, new flayed
for the hoax she thought of playing on her father. 460
In the sand she scooped out hollows for our bodies
and sat down, waiting. We came close to touch her,
and, bedding us, she threw the sealskins over us—
a strong disguise; oh, yes, terribly strong
as I recall the stench of those damned seals.
Would any man lie snug with a sea monster?
But here the nymph, again, came to our rescue,
dabbing ambrosia under each man's nose—
a perfume drowning out the bestial odor.

[15]A sea nymph.

So there we lay with beating hearts all morning 470
while seals came shoreward out of ripples, jostling
to take their places, flopping on the sand.
At noon the Ancient issued from the sea
and held inspection, counting off the sea-beasts.
We were the first he numbered; he went by,
detecting nothing. When at last he slept
we gave a battlecry and plunged for him,
locking our hands behind him. But the old one's
tricks were not knocked out of him; far from it.
First he took on a whiskered lion's shape, 480
a serpent then; a leopard; a great boar;
then sousing water; then a tall green tree.
Still we hung on, by hook or crook, through everything,
until the Ancient saw defeat, and grimly
opened his lips to ask me:

'Son of Atreus,
who counselled you to this? A god: what god?
Set a trap for me, overpower me—why?'

He bit it off, then, and I answered:

'Old one,
you know the reason—why feign not to know?
High and dry so long upon this island 490
I'm at my wits' end, and my heart is sore.
You gods know everything; now you can tell me:
which of the immortals chained me here?
And how will I get home on the fish-cold sea?'

He made reply at once:

'You should have paid
honor to Zeus and the other gods, performing
a proper sacrifice before embarking:
that was your short way home on the winedark sea.
You may not see your friends, your own fine house,
or enter your own land again, 500
unless you first remount the Nile in flood
and pay your hekatomb to the gods of heaven.
Then, and then only,
the gods will grant the passage you desire.'

Ah, how my heart sank, hearing this—
hearing him send me back on the cloudy sea
in my own track, the long hard way of Egypt.
Nevertheless, I answered him and said:

'Ancient, I shall do all as you command.
But tell me, now, the others— 510
had they a safe return, all those Akhaians

who stayed behind when Nestor and I left Troy?
Or were there any lost at sea—what bitterness!—
any who died in camp, after the war?'

To this he said:

'For you to know these things
goes beyond all necessity, Meneláos.
Why must you ask?—you should not know my mind,
and you will grieve to learn it, I can tell you.
Many there were who died, many remain,
but two high officers alone were lost— 520
on the passage home, I mean; you saw the war.
One is alive, a castaway at sea;
the other, Aîas, perished with all hands—
though first Poseidon landed him on Gyrai[16]
promontory, and saved him from the ocean.
Despite Athena's hate, he had lived on,
but the great sinner in his insolence
yelled that the gods' will and the sea were beaten,
and this loud brag came to Poseidon's ears.
He swung the trident[17] in his massive hands 530
and in one shock from top to bottom split
that promontory, toppling into the sea
the fragment where the great fool sat.
So the vast ocean had its will with Aîas,
drunk in the end on salt spume as he drowned.
Meanwhile your brother left that doom astern
in his decked ships—the Lady Hera[18] saved him;
but as he came round Malea
a fresh squall caught him, bearing him away
over the cold sea, groaning in disgust, 540
to the Land's End of Argos, where Thyestês[19]
lived in the days of old, and then his son,
Aigísthos. Now, again, return seemed easy:
the high gods wound the wind into the east,
and back he sailed, this time to his own coast.
He went ashore and kissed the earth in joy,
hot tears blinding his eyes at sight of home.

[16]An island in the Aegean. Aîas, who in the following lines is described as punished for his insolent and sacrilegious boasting, is the "lesser," "Locrian" Aîas (Ajax), the son of Oileus; he is not the "greater" Aîas, who was the son of Télamon.

[17]The three-pronged spear wielded by the sea god Poseidon.

[18]Consort of Zeus; queen of the gods. She consistently sided with the Greeks against the Trojans.

[19]Brother of Atreus (the father of Agamémnon and Meneláos). See the headnote to Aeschylus' *Oresteia.* Homer's account here of the murder of Agamémnon differs considerably from the version in Aeschylus; in the *Oresteia,* Agamémnon's wife Klytaimnéstra plays a more significant role than does Aigísthos in the murder.

But there were eyes that watched him from a height—
a lookout, paid two bars of gold to keep
vigil the year round for Aigísthos' sake, 550
that he should be forewarned, and Agamémnon's
furious valor sleep unroused.
Now this man with his news ran to the tyrant,
who made his crooked arrangements in a flash,
stationed picked men at arms, a score of men
in hiding; set a feast in the next room;
then he went out with chariots and horses
to hail the king and welcome him to evil.
He led him in to banquet, all serene,
and killed him, like an ox felled at the trough; 560
and not a man of either company
survived that ambush in Aigísthos' house.'

Before the end my heart was broken down.
I slumped on the trampled sand and cried aloud,
caring no more for life or the light of day,
and rolled there weeping, till my tears were spent.
Then the unerring Ancient said at last:

'No more, no more; how long must you persist?
Nothing is gained by grieving so. How soon
can you return to Argos? You may take him 570
alive there still—or else meanwhile Orestês
will have despatched him. You'll attend the feast.'

At this my heart revived, and I recovered
the self command to question him once more:

'Of two companions now I know. The third?
Tell me his name, the one marooned at sea;
living, you say, or dead? Even in pain
I wish to hear.'

And this is all he answered:

'Laërtês' son, whose home is Ithaka.
I saw him weeping, weeping on an island. 580
The nymph Kalypso has him, in her hall.
No means of faring home are left him now;
no ship with oars, and no ship's company
to pull him on the broad back of the sea.
As to your own destiny, prince Meneláos,
you shall not die in the bluegrass land of Argos;
rather the gods intend you for Elysion[20]

[20]As presented here in Homer, this realm (also called *Elysium*) is not part of the underground Hades which Odysseus visits later in the *Odyssey.* It is, rather, a happy land on the extreme western surface of the earth.

with golden Rhadamanthos[21] at the world's end,
where all existence is a dream of ease.
Snowfall is never known there, neither long 590
frost of winter, nor torrential rain,
but only mild and lulling airs from Ocean
bearing refreshment for the souls of men—
the West Wind always blowing.
For the gods
hold you, as Helen's lord, a son of Zeus.'

At this he dove under a swell and left me,
and I went back to the ship with my companions,
feeling my heart's blood in me running high;
but in the long hull's shadow, near the sea,
we supped again as sacred Night came on 600
and slept at last beside the lapping water.

When Dawn spread out her finger tips of rose,
in first light we launched on the courtly breakers,
setting up masts and yards in the well-found ships;
went all on board, and braced on planks athwart
oarsmen in line dipped oars in the grey sea.
Soon I drew in to the great stream[22] fed by heaven
and, laying by, slew bulls in the proper number,
until the immortal gods were thus appeased;
then heaped a death mound on that shore against 610
all-quenching time for Agamémnon's honor,
and put to sea once more. The gods sent down
a sternwind for a racing passage homeward.

So ends the story. Now you must stay with me
and be my guest eleven or twelve days more.
I'll send you on your way with gifts, and fine ones:
three chariot horses, and a polished car;
a hammered cup, too, so that all your days,
tipping the red wine for the deathless gods,
you will remember me."

Telémakhos answered: 620

"Lord, son of Atreus, no, you must not keep me.
Not that a year with you would be too long:
I never could be homesick here—I find
your tales and all you say so marvellous.
But time hangs heavy on my shipmates' hands
at holy Pylos, if you make me stay.

[21]Ruler of Elysion (sometimes portrayed in ancient literature as a judge of the dead in Hades).
[22]The Nile, believed to have a divine source in the sky.

As for your gift, now, let it be some keepsake.
Horses I cannot take to Ithaka;
let me bestow them back on you, to serve
your glory here. My lord, you rule wide country, 630
rolling and rich with clover, galingale
and all the grains: red wheat and hoary barley.
home we have no level runs or meadows,
but highland, goat land—prettier than plains, though.
Grasses, and pasture land, are hard to come by
upon the islands tilted in the sea,
and Ithaka is the island of them all."

At this the deep-lunged man of battle smiled.
Then he said kindly, patting the boy's hand:

"You come of good stock, lad. That was well spoken. 640
I'll change the gift, then—as indeed I can.
Let me see what is costliest and most beautiful
of all the precious things my house contains:
a wine bowl, mixing bowl, all wrought of silver,
but rimmed with hammered gold. Let this be yours.
It is Hephaistos'[23] work, given me by Phaidimos,
captain and king of Sidon. He received me
during my travels. Let it be yours, I say."

This was their discourse on that morning. Meanwhile
guests were arriving at the great lord's house, 650
bringing their sheep, and wine, the ease of men,
with loaves their comely kerchiefed women sent,
to make a feast in hall.
At that same hour,
before the distant manor of Odysseus,
the suitors were competing at the discus throw
and javelin, on a measured field they used,
arrogant lords at play. The two best men,
Antínoös and Eurýmakhos, presided.
Now Phronios' son, Noêmon, came to see them
with a question for Antínoös. He said: 660

"Do any of us know, or not, Antínoös,
what day Telémakhos will be home from Pylos?
He took my ship, but now I need it back
to make a cruise to Elis, where the plains are.
I have a dozen mares at pasture there
with mule colts yet unweaned. My notion is
to bring one home and break him in for labor."

[23] The god of fire and of metalworking. Also spelled *Hephaestus.*

His first words made them stare—for they knew well
Telémakhos could not have gone to Pylos,
but inland with his flocks, or to the swineherd. 670
Eupeithês' son, Antínoös, quickly answered:

"Tell the story straight. He sailed? Who joined him—
a crew he picked up here in Ithaka,
or his own slaves? He might have done it that way.
And will you make it clear
whether he took the ship against your will?
Did he ask for it, did you lend it to him?"

Now said the son of Phronios in reply:

"Lent it to him, and freely. Who would not,
when a prince of that house asked for it, in trouble? 680
Hard to refuse the favor, it seems to me.
As for his crew, the best men on the island,
after ourselves, went with him. Mentor I noted
going aboard—or a god who looked like Mentor.
The strange thing is, I saw Lord Mentor here
in the first light yesterday—although he sailed
five days ago for Pylos."

Turning away,
Noêmon took the path to his father's house,
leaving the two men there, baffled and hostile.
They called the rest in from the playing field 690
and made them all sit down, so that Antínoös
could speak out from the stormcloud of his heart,
swollen with anger; and his eyes blazed:

"A bad business. Telémakhos had the gall
to make that crossing, though we said he could not.
So the young cub rounds up a first rate crew
in spite of all our crowd, and puts to sea.
What devilment will he be up to next time?—
Zeus blast the life out of him before he's grown!
Just give me a fast ship and twenty men; 700
I'll intercept him, board him in the strait
between the crags of Samê[24] and this island.
He'll fnd his sea adventure after his father
swamping work in the end!"

They all cried "Aye!"
and "After him!" and trailed back to the manor.

[24]An island, modern Cephalonia, south and west of Ithaka; also called Kephallênia in this poem.

Now not much time went by before Penélopê
learned what was afoot among the suitors.
Medôn the crier told her. He had been
outside the wall, and heard them in the court
conspiring. Into the house and up the stairs 710
he ran to her with his news upon his tongue—
but at the door Penélopê met him, crying:

"Why have they sent you up here now? To tell
the maids of King Odysseus—'Leave your spinning:
Time to go down and slave to feed those men?'
I wish this were the last time they came feasting,
courting me or consorting here! The last!
Each day you crowd this house like wolves
to eat away my brave son's patrimony.
When you were boys, did your own fathers tell you 720
nothing of what Odysseus was for them?
In word and act impeccable, disinterested
toward all the realm—though it is king's justice
to hold one man abhorred and love another;
no man alive could say Odysseus wronged him.
But your own hearts—how different!—and your deeds!
How soon are benefactions all forgotten!"

Now Medôn, the alert and cool man, answered:

"I wish that were the worst of it, my Lady,
but they intend something more terrible— 730
may Zeus forfend and spare us!
They plan to drive the keen bronze through Telémakhos
when he comes home. He sailed away, you know,
to hallowed Pylos and old Lakedaimon
for news about his father."

Her knees failed,
and her heart failed as she listened to the words,
and all her power of speech went out of her.
Tears came; but the rich voice could not come.
Only after a long while she made answer:

"Why has my child left me? He had no need 740
of those long ships on which men shake out sail
to tug like horses, breasting miles of sea.
Why did he go? Must he, too, be forgotten?"

Then Medôn, the perceptive man, replied:

"A god moved him—who knows?—or his own heart
sent him to learn, at Pylos, if his father
roams the wide world still, or what befell him."

He left her then, and went down through the house.
And now the pain around her heart benumbed her;
chairs were a step away, but far beyond her; 750
she sank down on the door sill of the chamber,
wailing, and all her women young and old
made a low murmur of lament around her,
until at last she broke out through her tears:

"Dearest companions, what has Zeus given me?
Pain—more pain than any living woman.
My lord, my lion heart, gone, long ago—
the bravest man, and best, of the Danaans,
famous through Hellas and the Argive midlands—
and now the squalls have blown my son, my dear one, 760
an unknown boy, southward. No one told me.
O brute creatures, not one soul would dare
to wake me from my sleep; you knew
the hour he took the black ship out to sea!
If I had seen that sailing in his eyes
he should have stayed with me, for all his longing,
stayed—or left me dead in the great hall.
Go, someone, now, and call old Dólios,
the slave my father gave me before I came,
my orchard keeper—tell him to make haste 770
and put these things before Laërtês; he
may plan some kind of action; let him come
to cry shame on these ruffians who would murder
Odysseus' son and heir, and end his line!"

The dear old nurse, Eurýkleia, answered her:

"Sweet mistress, have my throat cut without mercy
or what you will; it's true, I won't conceal it,
I knew the whole thing; gave him his provisions;
grain and sweet wine I gave, and a great oath
to tell you nothing till twelve days went by, 780
or till you heard of it yourself, or missed him;
he hoped you would not tear your skin lamenting.
Come, bathe and dress your loveliness afresh,
and go to the upper rooms with all your maids
to ask help from Athena, Zeus's daughter.
She it will be who saves this boy from death.
Spare the old man this further suffering;
the blissful gods cannot so hate his line,
heirs of Arkêsios; one will yet again
be lord of the tall house and the far fields." 790

She hushed her weeping in this way, and soothed her.
The Lady Penélopê arose and bathed,
dressing her body in her freshest linen,

filled a basket with barley, and led her maids
to the upper rooms, where she besought Athena:

"Tireless child of Zeus, graciously hear me!
If ever Odysseus burned at our altar fire
thighbones of beef or mutton in sacrifice,
remember it for my sake! Save my son!
Shield him, and make the killers go astray!" 800

She ended with a cry, and the goddess heard her.
Now voices rose from the shadowy hall below
where the suitors were assuring one another:

"Our so-long-courted Queen is even now
of a mind to marry one of us, and knows
nothing of what is destined for her son."

Of what was destined they in fact knew nothing,
But Antínoös addressed them in a whisper:

"No boasting—are you mad?—and no loud talk:
someone might hear it and alarm the house. 810
Come along now, be quiet, this way; come,
we'll carry out the plan our hearts are set on."

Picking out twenty of the strongest seamen,
he led them to a ship at the sea's edge,
and down they dragged her into deeper water,
stepping a mast in her, with furled sails,
and oars a-trail from thongs looped over thole pins,
ready all; then tried the white sail, hoisting,
while men at arms carried their gear aboard.
They moored the ship some way off shore, and left her 820
to take their evening meal there, waiting for night to come.

Penélopê at that hour in her high chamber
lay silent, tasting neither food nor drink,
and thought of nothing but her princely son—
could he escape, or would they find and kill him?—
her mind turning at bay, like a cornered lion
in whom fear comes as hunters close the ring.
But in her sick thought sweet sleep overtook her,
and she dozed off, her body slack and still.

Now it occurred to the grey-eyed goddess Athena 830
to make a figure of dream in a woman's form—
Iphthimê, great Ikários' other daughter,
whom Eumêlos of Phêrai took as bride.
The goddess sent this dream to Odysseus' house
to quiet Penélopê and end her grieving.

So, passing by the strap-slit[25] through the door,
the image came a-gliding down the room
to stand at her bedside and murmur to her:

"Sleepest thou, sorrowing Penélopê?
The gods whose life is ease no longer suffer thee 840
to pine and weep, then; he returns unharmed,
thy little one; no way hath he offended."

Then pensive Penélopê made this reply,
slumbering sweetly in the gates of dream:

"Sister, hast thou come hither? Why? Aforetime
never wouldst come, so far away thy dwelling.
And am I bid be done with all my grieving?
But see what anguish hath my heart and soul!
My lord, my lion heart, gone, long ago—
the bravest man, and best, of the Danaans, 850
famous through Hellas and the Argive midlands—
and now my son, my dear one, gone seafaring,
a child, untrained in hardship or in council.
Aye, 'tis for him I weep, more than his father!
Aye, how I tremble for him, lest some blow
befall him at men's hands or on the sea!
Cruel are they and many who plot against him,
to take his life before he can return."

Now the dim phantom spoke to her once more:

"Lift up thy heart, and fear not overmuch. 860
For by his side one goes whom all men else
invoke as their defender, one so powerful—
Pallas Athena; in thy tears she pitied thee
and now hath sent me that I so assure thee."

Then said Penélopê the wise:

"If thou art
numinous[26] and hast ears for divine speech,
O tell me, what of Odysseus, man of woe?
Is he alive still somewhere, seeth he day light still?
Or gone in death to the sunless underworld?"

The dim phantom said only this in answer: 870

"Of him I may not tell thee in this discourse,
alive or dead. And empty words are evil."

[25]A hole in a door through which a strap was passed. It allowed a person outside to bolt the door on the inside.

[26]Gifted with uncanny spiritual powers.

The wavering form withdrew along the doorbolt
into a draft of wind, and out of sleep
Penélopê awoke, in better heart
for that clear dream in the twilight of the night.

Meanwhile the suitors had got under way,
planning the death plunge for Telémakhos.
Between the Isles of Ithaka and Samê
the sea is broken by an islet, Asteris, 880
with access to both channels from a cove.
In ambush here that night the Akhaians lay.

BOOK FIVE: SWEET NYMPH AND OPEN SEA

Dawn came up from the couch of her reclining,
leaving her lord Tithonos'[1] brilliant side
with fresh light in her arms for gods and men.
And the master of heaven and high thunder, Zeus,
went to his place among the gods assembled
hearing Athena tell Odysseus' woe.
For she, being vexed that he was still sojourning
in the sea chambers of Kalypso,[2] said:

"O Father Zeus and gods in bliss forever,
let no man holding scepter as a king 10
think to be mild, or kind, or virtuous;
let him be cruel, and practice evil ways,
for those Odysseus ruled cannot remember
the fatherhood and mercy of his reign.
Meanwhile he lives and grieves upon that island
in thralldom to the nymph; he cannot stir,
cannot fare homeward, for no ship is left him,
fitted with oars—no crewmen or companions
to pull him on the broad back of the sea.
And now murder is hatched on the high sea 20
against his son, who sought news of his father
in the holy lands of Pylos and Lakedaimon."

To this the summoner of cloud replied:

"My child, what odd complaints you let escape you.
Have you not, you yourself, arranged this matter—
as we all know—so that Odysseus
will bring these men to book, on his return?

[1] The lover of Eos, goddess of the dawn. No mention is made here of the most famous version of his myth, in which Eos wins for him the gift of immortality but forgets, fatefully, to ensure that Tithonos will never grow older. See Tennyson's poem "Tithonus."

[2] The nymph's island, Ogýgia, is located in a western region of the Mediterranean. The geography of Odysseus' wanderings west of Greece is uncertain.

And are you not the one to give Telémakhos
a safe route for sailing? Let his enemies
encounter no one and row home again." 30

He turned then to his favorite son and said:

"Hermês, you have much practice on our missions,
go make it known to the softly-braided nymph
that we, whose will is not subject to error,
order Odysseus home; let him depart.
But let him have no company, gods or men,
only a raft that he must lash together,
and after twenty days, worn out at sea,
he shall make land upon the garden isle,
Skhería,[3] of our kinsmen, the Phaiákians. 40
Let these men take him to their hearts in honor
and berth him in a ship, and send him home,
with gifts of garments, gold, and bronze—
so much he had not counted on from Troy
could he have carried home his share of plunder.
His destiny is to see his friends again
under his own roof, in his father's country."

No words were lost on Hermês the Wayfinder,
who bent to tie his beautiful sandals on,
ambrosial, golden, that carry him over water 50
or over endless land in a swish of the wind,
and took the wand with which he charms asleep—
or when he wills, awake—the eyes of men.
So wand in hand he paced into the air,
shot from Pieria[4] down, down to sea level,
and veered to skim the swell. A gull patrolling
between the wave crests of the desolate sea
will dip to catch a fish, and douse his wings;
no higher above the whitecaps Hermês flew
until the distant island lay ahead, 60
then rising shoreward from the violet ocean
he stepped up to the cave. Divine Kalypso,
the mistress of the isle, was now at home.
Upon her hearthstone a great fire blazing
scented the farthest shores with cedar smoke
and smoke of thyme, and singing high and low
in her sweet voice, before her loom a-weaving,
she passed her golden shuttle to and fro.
A deep wood grew outside, with summer leaves
of alder and black poplar, pungent cypress. 70

[3]The land (also spelled *Scheria*) of the Phaiákians (Phaeacians), possibly located on the southern shore of the Mediterranean, opposite Ithaka, more probably Corfu, an island north-west of Ithaka off the west coast of Greece.

[4]An area on the slopes of Mount Olympos.

Ornate birds here rested their stretched wings—
horned owls, falcons, cormorants—long-tongued
beachcombing birds, and followers of the sea.
Around the smoothwalled cave a crooking vine
held purple clusters under ply of green;
and four springs, bubbling up near one another
shallow and clear, took channels here and there
through beds of violets and tender parsley.
Even a god who found this place
would gaze, and feel his heart beat with delight: 80
so Hermês did; but when he had gazed his fill
he entered the wide cave. Now face to face
the magical Kalypso recognized him,
as all immortal gods know one another
on sight—though seeming strangers, far from home.
but he saw nothing of the great Odysseus,
who sat apart, as a thousand times before,
and racked his own heart groaning, with eyes wet
scanning the bare horizon of the sea.
Kalypso, lovely nymph, seated her guest 90
in a bright chair all shimmering, and asked:

"O Hermês, ever with your golden wand,
what brings you to my island?
Your awesome visits in the past were few.
Now tell me what request you have in mind;
for I desire to do it, if I can,
and if it is a proper thing to do.
But wait a while, and let me serve my friend."

She drew a table of ambrosia near him
and stirred a cup of ruby-colored nectar[5]— 100
food and drink for the luminous Wayfinder,
who took both at his leisure, and replied:

"Goddess to god, you greet me, questioning me?
Well, here is truth for you in courtesy.
Zeus made me come, and not my inclination;
who cares to cross that tract of desolation,
the bitter sea, all mortal towns behind
where gods have beef and honors from mankind?
But it is not to be thought of—and no use—
for any god to elude the will of Zeus. 110

He notes your friend, most ill-starred by renown
of all the peers who fought for Priam's town—
nine years of war they had, before great Troy was down.
Homing, they wronged the goddess[6] with grey eyes,

[5] Ambrosia and nectar were the food and drink of the gods.
[6] Compare the passage in Book IV alluding to the insolence of the lesser Aîas, or Ajax.

who made a black wind blow and the seas rise,
in which his troops were lost, and all his gear,
while easterlies and current washed him here.
Now the command is: send him back in haste.
His life may not in exile go to waste.
His destiny, his homecoming, is at hand, 120
when he shall see his dearest, and walk on his own land."

That goddess most divinely made
shuddered before him, and her warm voice rose:

"Oh you vile gods, in jealousy supernal!
You hate it when we choose to lie with men—
immortal flesh by some dear mortal side.
So radiant Dawn once took to bed Orion[7]
until you easeful gods grew peevish at it,
and holy Artemis, Artemis throned in gold,
hunted him down in Delos with her arrows. 130
Then Dêmêtêr of the tasseled tresses yielded
to Iasion,[8] mingling and making love
in a furrow three times plowed; but Zeus found out
and killed him with a white-hot thunderbolt.
So now you grudge me, too, my mortal friend.
But it was I who saved him—saw him straddle
his own keel board, the one man left afloat
when Zeus rent wide his ship with chain lightning
and overturned him in the winedark sea.
Then all his troops were lost, his good companions, 140
but wind and current washed him here to me.
I fed him, loved him, sang that he should not die
nor grow old, ever, in all the days to come.
But now there's no eluding Zeus's will.
If this thing be ordained by him, I say
so be it, let the man strike out alone
on the vast water. Surely I cannot 'send' him.
I have no long-oared ships, no company
to pull him on the broad back of the sea.
My counsel he shall have, and nothing hidden, 150
to help him homeward without harm."

To this the Wayfinder made answer briefly:

"Thus you shall send him, then. And show more grace
in your obedience, or be chastised by Zeus."

[7]A gigantic hunter, loved by Eos.

[8]Probably symbolic of harvest wealth, since the offspring of his union with Dêmêtêr, goddess of the fields, was Plutus, who symbolized wealth.

The strong god glittering left her as he spoke,
and now her ladyship, having given heed
to Zeus's mandate, went to find Odysseus
in his stone seat to seaward—tear on tear
brimming his eyes. The sweet days of his life time
were running out in anguish over his exile, 160
for long ago the nymph had ceased to please.
Though he fought shy of her and her desire,
he lay with her each night, for she compelled him.
But when day came he sat on the rocky shore
and broke his own heart groaning, with eyes wet
scanning the bare horizon of the sea.
Now she stood near him in her beauty, saying:

"O forlorn man, be still.
Here you need grieve no more; you need not feel
your life consumed here; I have pondered it, 170
and I shall help you go.
Come and cut down high timber for a raft
or flatboat; make her broad-beamed, and decked over,
so you can ride her on the misty sea.
Stores I shall put aboard for you—bread, water,
and ruby-colored wine, to stay your hunger—
give you a seacloak and a following wind
to help you homeward without harm—provided
the gods who rule wide heaven wish it so.
Stronger than I they are, in mind and power." 180

For all he had endured, Odysseus shuddered.
But when he spoke, his words went to the mark:

"After these years, a helping hand? O goddess,
what guile is hidden here?
A raft, you say, to cross the Western Ocean,[9]
rough water, and unknown? Seaworthy ships
that glory in god's wind will never cross it.
I take no raft you grudge me out to sea.
Or yield me first a great oath, if I do,
to work no more enchantment to my harm." 190

At this the beautiful nymph Kalypso smiled
and answered sweetly, laying her hand upon him:

"What a dog you are! And not for nothing learned,
having the wit to ask this thing of me!
My witness then be earth and sky
and dripping Styx[10] that I swear by—

[9] The western Mediterranean.
[10] A river in Hades, the realm of the dead. To swear by Styx was the most solemn oath a deity could utter.

the gay gods cannot swear more seriously—
I have no further spells to work against you.
But what I shall devise, and what I tell you,
will be the same as if your need were mine. 200
Fairness is all I think of. There are hearts
made of cold iron—but my heart is kind."

Swiftly she turned and led him to her cave,
and they went in, the mortal and immortal.
He took the chair left empty now by Hermês,
where the divine Kalypso placed before him
victuals and drink of men; then she sat down
facing Odysseus, while her serving maids
brought nectar and ambrosia to her side.
Then each one's hands went out on each one's feast 210
until they had had their pleasure; and she said:

"Son of Laërtês, versatile Odysseus,
after these years with me, you still desire
your old home? Even so, I wish you well.
If you could see it all, before you go—
all the adversity you face at sea—
you would stay here, and guard this house, and be
immortal—though you wanted her forever,
that bride for whom you pine each day.
Can I be less desirable than she is? 220
Less interesting? Less beautiful? Can mortals
compare with goddesses in grace and form?"

To this the strategist Odysseus answered:

"My lady goddess, here is no cause for anger.
My quiet Penélopê—how well I know—

would seem a shade before your majesty,
death and old age being unknown to you,
while she must die. Yet, it is true, each day
I long for home, long for the sight of home.
If any god has marked me out again 230
for shipwreck, my tough heart can undergo it.
What hardship have I not long since endured
at sea, in battle! Let the trial come."

Now as he spoke the sun set, dusk drew on,
and they retired, this pair, to the inner cave
to revel and rest softly, side by side.

When Dawn spread out her finger tips of rose
Odysseus pulled his tunic and his cloak on,
while the sea nymph dressed in a silvery gown
of subtle tissue, drew about her waist 240
a golden belt, and veiled her head, and then

took thought for the great-hearted hero's voyage.
A brazen axehead first she had to give him,
two-bladed, and agreeable to the palm
with a smooth-fitting haft of olive wood;
next a well-polished adze; and then she led him
to the island's tip where bigger timber grew—
besides the alder and poplar, tall pine trees,
long dead and seasoned, that would float him high.
Showing him in that place her stand of timber 250
the loveliest of nymphs took her way home.
Now the man fell to chopping; when he paused
twenty tall trees were down. He lopped the branches,
split the trunks, and trimmed his puncheons true.
Meanwhile Kalypso brought him an auger tool
with which he drilled through all his planks, then drove.
stout pins to bolt them, fitted side by side.
A master shipwright, building a cargo vessel,
lays down a broad and shallow hull; just so
Odysseus shaped the bottom of his craft. 260
He made his decking fast to close-set ribs
before he closed the side with longer planking,
then cut a mast pole, and proper yard,
and shaped a steering oar to hold her steady.
He drove long strands of willow in all the seams
to keep out waves, and ballasted with logs.
As for a sail, the lovely nymph Kalypso
brought him a cloth so he could make that, too.
Then he ran up his rigging—halyards, braces—
and hauled the boat on rollers to the water. 270

This was the fourth day, when he had all ready;
on the fifth day, she sent him out to sea.
But first she bathed him, gave him a scented cloak,
and put on board a skin of dusky wine
with water in a bigger skin, and stores—
boiled meats and other victuals—in a bag.
Then she conjured a warm landbreeze to blowing—
joy for Odysseus when he shook out sail!
Now the great seaman, leaning on his oar,
steered all the night unsleeping, and his eyes 280
picked out the Pleiadês, the laggard Ploughman,
and the Great Bear, that some have called the Wain,
pivoting in the sky before Orion;
of all the night's pure figures, she alone
would never bathe or dip in the Ocean stream.[11]

[11]In northern latitudes, the Big Dipper (the Great Bear, or Wain) never sets but rather circles around Polaris, the North Star. For Odysseus to keep the constellation on his left would require him to sail eastward.

These stars the beautiful Kalypso bade him
hold on his left hand as he crossed the main.
Seventeen nights and days in the open water
he sailed, before a dark shoreline appeared;
Skhería then came slowly into view 290
like a rough shield of bull's hide on the sea.

But now the god of earthquake, storming home
over the mountains of Asia from the Sunburned land,
sighted him far away. The god grew sullen
and tossed his great head, muttering to himself:

"Here is a pretty cruise! While I was gone
the gods have changed their minds about Odysseus.
Look at him now, just offshore of that island
that frees him from the bondage of his exile!
Still I can give him a rough ride in, and will." 300

Brewing high thunderheads, he churned the deep
with both hands on his trident—called up wind
from every quarter, and sent a wall of rain
to blot out land and sea in torrential night.
Hurricane winds now struck from the South and East
shifting North West in a great spume of seas,
on which Odysseus' knees grew slack, his heart
sickened, and he said within himself:

"Rag of man that I am, is this the end of me?
I fear the goddess told it all too well— 310
predicting great adversity at sea
and far from home. Now all things bear her out:
the whole rondure[12] of heaven hooded so
by Zeus in woeful cloud, and the sea raging
under such winds. I am going down, that's sure.
How lucky those Danaans were who perished
on Troy's wide seaboard, serving the Atreidai![13]
Would God I, too, had died there—met my end
that time the Trojans made so many casts at me
when I stood by Akhilleus after death. 320
I should have had a soldier's burial
and praise from the Akhaians—not this choking
waiting for me at sea, unmarked and lonely."

A great wave drove at him with toppling crest
spinning him round, in one tremendous blow,
and he went plunging overboard, the oar-haft
wrenched from his grip. A gust that came on howling
at the same instant broke his mast in two,

[12] Circle or sphere.
[13] Sons of Atreus—Agamémnon and Meneláos.

hurling his yard and sail far out to leeward.
Now the big wave a long time kept him under, 330
helpless to surface, held by tons of water,
tangled, too, by the seacloak of Kalypso.
Long, long, until he came up spouting brine,
with streamlets gushing from his head and beard;
but still bethought him, half-drowned as he was,
to flounder for the boat and get a handhold
into the bilge—to crouch there, foiling death.
Across the foaming water, to and fro,
the boat careered like a ball of tumbleweed
blown on the autumn plains, but intact still. 340
So the winds drove this wreck over the deep,
East Wind and North Wind, then South Wind and West,
coursing each in turn to the brutal harry.

But Ino[14] saw him—Ino, Kadmos' daughter,
slim-legged, lovely, once an earthling girl,
now in the seas a nereid, Leukothea.
Touched by Odysseus' painful buffeting
she broke the surface, like a diving bird,
to rest upon the tossing raft and say:

"O forlorn man, I wonder 350
why the Earthshaker, Lord Poseidon, holds
this fearful grudge—father of all your woes.
He will not drown you, though, despite his rage.
You seem clear-headed still; do what I tell you.
Shed that cloak, let the gale take your craft,
and swim for it—swim hard to get ashore
upon Skhería, yonder,
where it is fated that you find a shelter.
Here: make my veil your sash; it is not mortal;
you cannot, now, be drowned or suffer harm. 360
Only, the instant you lay hold of earth,
discard it, cast it far, far out from shore
in the winedark sea again, and turn away."

After she had bestowed her veil, the nereid
dove like a gull to windward
where a dark waveside closed over her whiteness.
But in perplexity Odysseus
said to himself, his great heart laboring:

"O damned confusion! Can this be a ruse
to trick me from the boat for some god's pleasure? 370
No I'll not swim; with my own eyes I saw
how far the land lies that she called my shelter.

[14]Maddened by Hera, who was jealous of her for helping to rear the young god Dionysos, Ino leaped into the sea and was transformed into a nereid, or sea nymph.

Better to do the wise thing, as I see it.
While this poor planking holds, I stay aboard;
I may ride out the pounding of the storm,
or if she cracks up, take to the water then;
I cannot think it through a better way."

But even while he pondered and decided,
the god of earthquake heaved a wave against him
high as a rooftree and of awful gloom. 380
A gust of wind, hitting a pile of chaff,
will scatter all the parched stuff far and wide;
just so, when this gigantic billow struck
the boat's big timbers flew apart. Odysseus
clung to a single beam, like a jockey riding,
meanwhile stripping Kalypso's cloak away;
then he slung round his chest the veil of Ino
and plunged headfirst into the sea. His hands
went out to stroke, and he gave a swimmer's kick.
But the strong Earthshaker had him under his eye, 390
and nodded as he said:

"Go on, go on;
wander the high seas this way, take your blows,
before you join that race the gods have nurtured.[15]
Nor will you grumble, even then, I think,
for want of trouble."

Whipping his glossy team
he rode off to his glorious home at Aigai.[16]
But Zeus's daughter Athena countered him:
she checked the course of all the winds but one,
commanding them, "Be quiet and go to sleep."
Then sent a long swell running under a norther 400
to bear the prince Odysseus, back from danger,
to join the Phaiákians, people of the sea.

Two nights, two days, in the solid deep-sea swell
he drifted, many times awaiting death,
until with shining ringlets in the East
the dawn confirmed a third day, breaking clear
over a high and windless sea; and mounting
a rolling wave he caught a glimpse of land.
What a dear welcome thing life seems to children
whose father, in the extremity, recovers 410
after some weakening and malignant illness:
his pangs are gone, the gods have delivered him.
So dear and welcome to Odysseus
the sight of land, of woodland, on that morning.

[15] The Phaiákians, or Phaeacians. [16] An Akhaian city.

It made him swim again, to get a foothold
on solid ground. But when he came in earshot
he heard the trampling roar of sea on rock,
where combers, rising shoreward, thudded down
on the sucking ebb—all sheeted with salt foam.
Here were no coves or harborage or shelter, 420
only steep headlands, rockfallen reefs and crags.
Odysseus' knees grew slack, his heart faint,
a heaviness came over him, and he said:

"A cruel turn, this. Never had I thought
to see this land, but Zeus has let me see it—
and let me, too, traverse the Western Ocean—
only to find no exit from these breakers.
Here are sharp rocks off shore, and the sea a smother
rushing around them; rock face rising sheer
from deep water; nowhere could I stand up 430
on my two feet and fight free of the welter.
No matter how I try it, the surf may throw me
against the cliffside; no good fighting there.
If I swim down the coast, outside the breakers,
I may find shelving shore and quiet water—
but what if another gale comes on to blow?
Then I go cursing out to sea once more.
Or then again, some shark of Amphitritê's[17]
may hunt me, sent by the genius of the deep.
I know how he who makes earth tremble hates me." 440

During this meditation a heavy surge
was taking him, in fact, straight on the rocks.
He had been flayed there, and his bones broken,
had not grey-eyed Athena instructed him:
he gripped a rock-ledge with both hands in passing
and held on, groaning, as the surge went by,
to keep clear of its breaking. Then the backwash
hit him, ripping him under and far out.
An octopus, when you drag one from his chamber,
comes up with suckers full of tiny stones: 450
Odysseus left the skin of his great hands
torn on that rock-ledge as the wave submerged him.
And now at last Odysseus would have perished,
battered inhumanly, but he had the gift
of self-possession from grey-eyed Athena.
So, when the backwash spewed him up again,
he swam out and along, and scanned the coast
for some landspit that made a breakwater.

[17]A sea nymph, consort of Poseidon and thus queen of the ocean.

Lo and behold, the mouth of a calm river
at length came into view, with level shores 460
unbroken, free from rock, shielded from wind—
by far the best place he had found.
But as he felt the current flowing seaward
he prayed in his heart:

"O hear me, lord of the stream:
how sorely I depend upon your mercy!
derelict as I am by the sea's anger.
Is he not sacred, even to the gods,
the wandering man who comes, as I have come,
in weariness before your knees, your waters?
Here is your servant; lord, have mercy on me." 470

Now even as he prayed the tide at ebb
had turned, and the river god made quiet water,
drawing him in to safety in the shallows.
His knees buckled, his arms gave way beneath him,
all vital force now conquered by the sea.
Swollen from head to foot he was, and seawater
gushed from his mouth and nostrils. There he lay,
scarce drawing breath, unstirring, deathly spent.
In time, as air came back into his lungs
and warmth around his heart, he loosed the veil, 480
letting it drift away on the estuary
downstream to where a white wave took it under
and Ino's hands received it. Then the man
crawled to the river bank among the reeds
where, face down, he could kiss the soil of earth,
in his exhaustion murmuring to himself:

"What more can this hulk suffer? What comes now?
In vigil through the night here by the river
how can I not succumb, being weak and sick,
to the night's damp and hoarfrost of the morning? 490
The air comes cold from rivers before dawn.
But if I climb the slope and fall asleep
in the dark forest's undergrowth—supposing
cold and fatigue will go, and sweet sleep come—
I fear I make the wild beasts easy prey."

But this seemed best to him, as he thought it over.
He made his way to a grove above the water
on open ground, and crept under twin bushes
grown from the same spot—olive and wild olive—
a thicket proof against the stinging wind 500
or Sun's blaze, fine soever the needling sunlight;
nor could a downpour wet it through, so dense
those plants were interwoven. Here Odysseus
tunnelled, and raked together with his hands

a wide bed—for a fall of leaves was there,
enough to save two men or maybe three
on a winter night, a night of bitter cold.
Odysseus' heart laughed when he saw his leaf-bed,
and down he lay, heaping more leaves above him.

A man in a distant field, no hearthfires near, 510
will hide a fresh brand in his bed of embers
to keep a spark alive for the next day;
so in the leaves Odysseus hid himself,
while over him Athena showered sleep
that his distress should end, and soon, soon.
In quiet sleep she sealed his cherished eyes.

BOOK SIX: THE PRINCESS AT THE RIVER

Far gone in weariness, in oblivion,
the noble and enduring man slept on;
but Athena in the night went down the land
of the Phaiákians, entering their city.
In days gone by, these men held Hypereia,
a country of wide dancing grounds, but near them
were overbearing Kyklopês,[1] whose power
could not be turned from pillage. So the Phaiákians
migrated thence under Nausíthoös
to settle a New World across the sea, 10
Skhería Island. That first captain walled
their promontory, built their homes and shrines,
and parcelled out the black land for the plow.
But he had gone down long ago to Death.
Alkínoös ruled, and Heaven gave him wisdom,
so on this night the goddess, grey-eyed Athena,
entered the palace of Alkínoös
to make sure of Odysseus' voyage home.
She took her way to a painted bedchamber
where a young girl lay fast asleep—so fine 20
in mould and feature that she seemed a goddess—
the daughter of Alkínoös, Nausikaa.
On either side, as Graces[2] might have slept,
her maids were sleeping. The bright doors were shut,
but like a sudden stir of wind, Athena
moved to the bedside of the girl, and grew

[1] These monstrous giants of Sicily are described in Book IX. *Hypereia* means "highlands"; their location is uncertain.
[2] Three goddesses who personify grace and beauty.

visible as the shipman Dymas' daughter,
a girl the princess' age, and her dear friend.
In this form grey-eyed Athena said to her:

"How so remiss, and yet thy mother's daughter? 30
leaving thy clothes uncared for, Nausikaa,
when soon thou must have store of marriage linen,
and put thy minstrelsy in wedding dress!
Beauty, in these, will make folk admire,
and bring thy father and gentle mother joy.
Let us go washing in the shine of morning!
Beside thee will I drub, so wedding chests
will brim by evening. Maidenhood must end!
Have not the noblest born Phaiákians
paid court to thee, whose birth none can excel? 40
Go beg thy sovereign father, even at dawn,
to have the mule cart and the mules brought round
to take thy body-linen, gowns and mantles.
Thou shouldst ride, for it becomes thee more,
the washing pools are found so far from home."

On this word she departed, grey-eyed Athena,
to where the gods have their eternal dwelling—
as men say—in the fastness of Olympos.
Never a tremor of wind, or a splash of rain,
no errant snowflake comes to stain that heaven, 50
so calm, so vaporless, the world of light.
Here, where the gay gods live their days of pleasure,
the grey-eyed one withdrew, leaving the princess.

And now Dawn took her own fair throne, awaking
the girl in the sweet gown, still charmed by dream.
Down through the rooms she went to tell her parents,
whom she found still at home: her mother seated
near the great hearth among her maids—and twirling
out of her distaff yarn dyed like the sea—;
her father at the door, bound for a council 60
of princes on petition of the gentry.
She went up close to him and softly said:

"My dear Papà, could you not send the mule cart
around for me—the gig with pretty wheels?
I must take all our things and get them washed
at the river pools; our linen is all soiled.
And you should wear fresh clothing, going to council
with counselors and first men of the realm.
Remember your five sons at home: though two
are married, we have still three bachelor sprigs; 70
they will have none but laundered clothes each time
they go to the dancing. See what I must think of!"

She had no word to say of her own wedding,
though her keen father saw her blush. Said he:

"No mules would I deny you, child, nor anything.
Go along, now; the grooms will bring your gig
with pretty wheels and the cargo box upon it."

He spoke to the stableman, who soon brought round
the cart, low-wheeled and nimble;
harnessed the mules, and backed them in their traces. 80
Meanwhile the girl fetched all her soiled apparel
to bundle in the polished wagon box.
Her mother, for their luncheon, packed a hamper
with picnic fare, and filled a skin of wine,
and, when the princess had been handed up,
gave her a golden bottle of olive oil
for softening girls' bodies, after bathing.
Nausikaa took the reins and raised her whip,
lashing the mules. What jingling! What a clatter!
But off they went in a ground-covering trot, 90
with princess, maids, and laundry drawn behind.
By the lower river where the wagon came
were washing pools, with water all year flowing
in limpid spillways that no grime withstood.
The girls unhitched the mules, and sent them down
along the eddying stream to crop sweet grass.
Then sliding out the cart's tail board, they took
armloads of clothing to the dusky water,
and trod them in the pits, making a race of it.
All being drubbed, all blemish rinsed away, 100
they spread them, piece by piece, along the beach
whose pebbles had been laundered by the sea;
then took a dip themselves, and, all anointed
with golden oil, ate lunch beside the river
while the bright burning sun dried out their linen.
Princess and maids delighted in that feast;
then, putting off their veils,
they ran and passed a ball to a rhythmic beat,
Nausikaa flashing first with her white arms.

So Artemis goes flying after her arrows flown 110
down some tremendous valley-side—
Taÿgetos, Erymanthos—
chasing the mountain goats or ghosting deer,
with nymphs of the wild places flanking her;
and Lêto's[3] heart delights to see them running,
for, taller by a head than nymphs can be,

[3] Mother of Artemis, goddess of the hunt. Taÿgetos and Erymanthos are mountainous places in Greece.

the goddess shows more stately, all being beautiful.
So one could tell the princess from the maids.

Soon it was time, she knew, for riding homeward—
mules to be harnessed, linen folded smooth—
but the grey-eyed goddess Athena made her tarry, 120
so that Odysseus might behold her beauty
and win her guidance to the town.
It happened
when the king's daughter threw her ball off line
and missed, and put it in the whirling stream,—
at which they all gave such a shout, Odysseus
awoke and sat up, saying to himself:

"Now, by my life, mankind again! But who?
Savages, are they, strangers to courtesy?
Or gentle folk, who know and fear the gods?
That was a lust cry of tall young girls— 130
most like the cry of nymphs, who haunt the peaks,
and springs of brooks, and inland grassy places.
Or am I amid people of human speech?
Up again, man; and let me see for myself."

He pushed aside the bushes, breaking off
with his great hand a single branch of olive,
whose leaves might shield him in his nakedness;
so came out rustling, like a mountain lion,
rain-drenched, wind-buffeted, but in his might at ease,
with burning eyes—who prowls among the herds 140
or flocks, or after game, his hungry belly
taking him near stout homesteads for his prey.
Odysseus had this look, in his rough skin
advancing on the girls with pretty braids;
and he was driven on by hunger, too.
Streaked with brine, and swollen, he terrified them,
so that they fled, this way and that. Only
Alkínoös' daughter stood her ground, being given
a bold heart by Athena, and steady knees.

She faced him, waiting. And Odysseus came, 150
debating inwardly what he should do:
embrace this beauty's knees in supplication?
or stand apart, and, using honeyed speech,
inquire the way to town, and beg some clothing?
In his swift reckoning, he thought it best
to trust in words to please her—and keep away;
he might anger the girl, touching her knees.
So he began, and let the soft words fall:

"Mistress: please: are you divine, or mortal?
If one of those who dwell in the wide heaven, 160

you are most near to Artemis, I should say—
great Zeus's daughter—in your grace and presence.
If you are one of earth's inhabitants,
how blest your father, and your gentle mother,
blest all your kin. I know what happiness
must send the warm tears to their eyes, each time
they see their wondrous child go to the dancing!
But one man's destiny is more than blest—
he who prevails, and takes you as his bride.
Never have I laid eyes on equal beauty 170
in man or woman. I am hushed indeed.
So fair, one time, I thought a young palm tree
at Delos[4] near the altar of Apollo—
I had troops under me when I was there
on the sea route that later brought me grief—
but that slim palm tree filled my heart with wonder:
never came shoot from earth so beautiful.
So now, my lady, I stand in awe so great
I cannot take your knees. And yet my case is desperate:
twenty days, yesterday, in the winedark sea, 180
on the ever-lunging swell, under gale winds,
getting away from the Island of Ogýgia.
And now the terror of Storm has left me stranded
upon this shore—with more blows yet to suffer,
I must believe, before the gods relent.
Mistress, do me a kindness!
After much weary toil, I come to you,
and you are the first soul I have seen—I know
no others here. Direct me to the town,
give me a rag that I can throw around me, 190
some cloth or wrapping that you brought along.
And may the gods accomplish your desire:
a home, a husband, and harmonious
converse with him—the best thing in the world
being a strong house held in serenity
where man and wife agree. Woe to their enemies,
joy to their friends! But all this they know best."

Then she of the white arms, Nausikaa, replied:

"Stranger, there is no quirk or evil in you
that I can see. You know Zeus metes out fortune 200
to good and bad men as it pleases him.
Hardship he sent to you, and you must bear it.
But now that you have taken refuge here
you shall not lack for clothing, or any other
comfort due to a poor man in distress.

[4]An island in the Aegean Sea, birthplace of Apollo and sacred to him.

The town lies this way, and the men are called
Phaiákians, who own the land and city.
I am daughter to the Prince Alkínoös,
by whom the power of our people stands."
Turning, she called out to her maids-in-waiting: 210

"Stay with me! Does the sight of a man scare you?
Or do you take this one for an enemy?
Why, there's no fool so brash, and never will be,
as to bring war or pillage to this coast,
for we are dear to the immortal gods,
living here, in the sea that rolls forever,
distant from other lands and other men.
No: this man is a castaway, poor fellow;
we must take care of him. Strangers and beggars
come from Zeus: a small gift, then, is friendly. 220
Give our new guest some food and drink, and take him
into the river, out of the wind, to bathe."

They stood up now, and called to one another
to go on back. Quite soon they led Odysseus
under the river bank, as they were bidden;
and there laid out a tunic, and a cloak,
and gave him olive oil in the golden flask.
"Here," they said, "go bathe in the flowing water."
But heard now from that kingly man, Odysseus:

"Maids," he said, "keep away a little; let me 230
wash the brine from my own back, and rub on
plenty of oil. It is long since my anointing.
I take no bath, however, where you can see me—
naked before young girls with pretty braids."

They left him, then, and went to tell the princess.
And now Odysseus, dousing in the river,
scrubbed the coat of brine from back and shoulders
and rinsed the clot of sea-spume from his hair;
got himself all rubbed down, from head to foot,
then he put on the clothes the princess gave him. 240
Athena lent a hand, making him seem
taller, and massive too, with crisping hair
in curls like petals of wild hyacinth,
but all red-golden. Think of gold infused
on silver by a craftsman, whose fine art
Hephaistos taught him, or Athena: one
whose work moves to delight: just so she lavished
beauty over Odysseus' head and shoulders.
Then he went down to sit on the sea beach
in his new splendor. There the girl regarded him, 250
and after a time she said to the maids beside her:

"My gentlewomen, I have a thing to tell you.
The Olympian gods cannot be all averse
to this man's coming here among our islanders.
Uncouth he seemed, I thought so, too, before;
but now he looks like one of heaven's people.
I wish my husband could be fine as he
and glad to stay forever on Skhería!
But have you given refreshment to our guest?"

At this the maids, all gravely listening, hastened 260
to set out bread and wine before Odysseus,
and ah! how ravenously that patient man
took food and drink, his long fast at an end.

The princess Nausikaa now turned aside
to fold her linens; in the pretty cart
she stowed them, put the mule team under harness,
mounted the driver's seat, and then looked down
to say with cheerful prompting to Odysseus:

"Up with you now, friend; back to town we go;
and I shall send you in before my father 270
who is wondrous wise; there in our house with him
you'll meet the noblest of the Phaiákians.
You have good sense, I think; here's how to do it:
while we go through the countryside and farmland
stay with my maids, behind the wagon, walking
briskly enough to follow where I lead.
But near the town—well, there's a wall with towers
around the Isle, and beautiful ship basins
right and left of the causeway of approach;
seagoing craft are beached beside the road 280
each on its launching ways. The agora,[5]
with fieldstone benches bedded in the earth,
lies either side Poseidon's shrine—for there
men are at work on pitch-black hulls and rigging,
cables and sails, and tapering of oars.
The archer's craft is not for the Phaiákians,
but ship designing, modes of oaring cutters
in which they love to cross the foaming sea.
From these fellows I will have no salty talk,
no gossip later. Plenty are insolent. 290
And some seadog might say, after we passed:
'Who is this handsome stranger trailing Nausikaa?
Where did she find him? Will he be her husband?
Or is she being hospitable to some rover
come off his ship from lands across the sea—
there being no lands nearer. A god, maybe?

[5] Public meeting place.

a god from heaven, the answer to her prayer,
descending now—to make her his forever?
Better, if she's roamed and found a husband
somewhere else: none of our own will suit her, 300
though many come to court her, and those the best.'
This is the way they might make light of me.
And I myself should hold it shame
for any girl to flout her own dear parents,
taking up with a man, before her marriage.

Note well, now, what I say, friend, and your chances
are excellent for safe conduct from my father.
You'll find black poplars in a roadside park
around a meadow and fountain—all Athena's—
but Father has a garden in the place— 310
this within earshot of the city wall.
Go in there and sit down, giving us time
to pass through town and reach my father's house.
And when you can imagine we're at home,
then take the road into the city, asking
directions to the palace of Alkínoös.
You'll find it easily: any small boy
can take you there; no family has a mansion
half so grand as he does, being king.
As soon as you are safe inside, cross over 320
and go straight through into the mégaron[6]
to find my mother. She'll be there in firelight
before a column, with her maids in shadow,
spinning a wool dyed richly as the sea.
My father's great chair faces the fire, too;
there like a god he sits and takes his wine.
Go past him; cast yourself before my mother,
embrace her knees—and you may wake up soon
at home rejoicing, though your home be far.
On Mother's feeling much depends; if she 330
looks on you kindly, you shall see your friends
under your own roof in your father's country."

At this she raised her glistening whip, lashing
the team into a run; they left the river
cantering beautifully, then trotted smartly.
But then she reined them in, and spared the whip,
so that her maids could follow with Odysseus.
The sun was going down when they went by
Athena's grove. Here, then, Odysseus rested,
and lifted up his prayer to Zeus's daughter: 340

[6] The great hall of the house.

"Hear me, unwearied child of royal Zeus!
O listen to me now—thou so aloof
while the Earthshaker wrecked and battered me.
May I find love and mercy among these people."

He prayed for that, and Pallas Athena heard him—
although in deference to her father's brother[7]
she would not show her true form to Odysseus,
at whom Poseidon smoldered on
until the kingly man came home to his own shore.

BOOK SEVEN: GARDENS AND FIRELIGHT

As Lord Odysseus prayed there in the grove
the girl rode on, behind her strapping team,
and came late to the mansion of her father,
where she reined in at the courtyard gate. Her brothers
awaited her like tall gods in the court,
circling to lead the mules away and carry
the laundered things inside. But she withdrew
to her own bedroom, where a fire soon shone,
kindled by her old nurse, Eurymedousa.
Years ago, from a raid on the continent, 10
the rolling ships had brought this woman over
to be Alkínoös' share—fit spoil for him
whose realm hung on his word as on a god's.
And she had schooled the princess, Nausikaa,
whose fire she tended now, making her supper.

Odysseus, when the time had passed, arose
and turned into the city. But Athena
poured a sea fog around him as he went—
her love's expedient, that no jeering sailor
should halt the man or challenge him for luck. 20
Instead, as he set foot in the pleasant city,
the grey-eyed goddess came to him, in figure
a small girl child, hugging a water jug.

Confronted by her, Lord Odysseus asked:

"Little one, could you take me to the house
of that Alkínoös, king among these people?
You see, I am a poor old stranger here;
my home is far away; here there is no one
known to me, in countryside or city."

[7] Poseidon, brother of Athena's father, Zeus.

The grey-eyed goddess Athena replied to him: 30

"Oh, yes, good grandfer, sir, I know, I'll show you
the house you mean; it is quite near my father's.
But come now, hush, like this, and follow me.
You must not stare at people, or be inquisitive.
They do not care for strangers in this neighborhood;
a foreign man will get no welcome here.
The only things they trust are the racing ships
Poseidon gave, to sail the deep blue sea
like white wings in the sky, or a flashing thought."

Pallas Athena turned like the wind, running 40
ahead of him, and he followed in her footsteps.
And no seafaring men of Phaiákia
perceived Odysseus passing through their town:
the awesome one in pigtails barred their sight
with folds of sacred mist. And yet Odysseus
gazed out marvelling at the ships and harbors,
public squares, and ramparts towering up
with pointed palisades along the top.
When they were near the mansion of the king,
grey-eyed Athena in the child cried out: 50

"Here it is, grandfer, sir—that mansion house
you asked to see. You'll find our king and queen
at supper, but you must not be dismayed;
go in to them. A cheerful man does best
in every enterprise—even a stranger.
You'll see our lady just inside the hall—
her name is Arêtê; her grandfather
was our good king Alkínoös's father—
Nausithoös by name, son of Poseidon
and Periboia. That was a great beauty, 60
the daughter of Eurymedon, commander
of the Gigantês[1] in the olden days,
who led those wild things to their doom and his.
Poseidon then made love to Periboia,
and she bore Nausíthoös, Phaiákia's lord,
whose sons in turn were Rhêxênor and Alkínoös.
Rhêxênor had no sons; even as a bridegroom
he fell before the silver bow of Apollo,
his only child a daughter, Arêtê.
When she grew up, Alkínoös married her 70
and holds her dear. No lady in the world,
no other mistress of a man's household,
is honored as our mistress is, and loved,
by her own children, by Alkínoös,

[1] The Giants, enormous semihuman beings, offspring of Ge, an ancient earth goddess.

and by the people. When she walks the town
they murmur and gaze, as though she were a goddess.
No grace or wisdom fails in her; indeed
just men in quarrels come to her for equity.
Supposing, then, she looks upon you kindly,
the chances are that you shall see your friends 80
under your own roof, in your father's country."

At this the grey-eyed goddess Athena left him
and left that comely land, going over sea
to Marathon, to the wide roadways of Athens
and her retreat in the stronghold of Erekhtheus.[2]
Odysseus, now alone before the palace,
meditated a long time before crossing
the brazen threshold of the great courtyard.
High rooms he saw ahead, airy and luminous
as though with lusters of the sun and moon, 90
bronze-paneled walls, at several distances,
making a vista, with an azure molding
of lapis lazuli.[3] The doors were golden
guardians of the great room. Shining bronze
plated the wide door sill; the posts and lintel
were silver upon silver; golden handles
curved on the doors, and golden, too, and silver
were sculptured hounds, flanking the entrance way,
cast by the skill and ardor of Hephaistos
to guard the prince Alkínoös's house— 100
undying dogs that never could grow old.
Through all the rooms, as far as he could see,
tall chairs were placed around the walls, and strewn
with fine embroidered stuff made by the women.
Here were enthroned the leaders of Phaiákia
drinking and dining, with abundant fare.
Here, too, were boys of gold on pedestals
holding aloft bright torches of pitch pine
to light the great rooms, and the night-time feasting.
And fifty maids-in-waiting of the household 110
sat by the round mill, grinding yellow corn,
or wove upon their looms, or twirled their distaffs,
flickering like the leaves of a poplar tree;
while drops of oil glistened on linen weft.
Skillful as were the men of Phaiákia
in ship handling at sea, so were these women
skilled at the loom, having this lovely craft
and artistry as talents from Athena.

[2] Legendary ruler of Athens, Athena's city. Marathon (several centuries after Homer's time the site of a great Greek victory over the Persians) was a plain near Athens, cherished by Athena.
[3] Fine blue stone.

To left and right, outside, he saw an orchard
closed by a pale—four spacious acres planted 120
with trees in bloom or weighted down for picking:
pear trees, pomegranates, brilliant apples,
luscious figs, and olives ripe and dark.
Fruit never failed upon these trees: winter
and summer time they bore, for through the year
the breathing Westwind ripened all in turn—
so one pear came to prime, and then another,
and so with apples, figs, and the vine's fruit
empurpled in the royal vineyard there.
Currants were dried at one end, on a platform 130
bare to the sun, beyond the vintage arbors
and vats the vintners trod; while near at hand
were new grapes barely formed as the green bloom fell,
or half-ripe clusters, faintly coloring.
After the vines came rows of vegetables
of all the kinds that flourish in every season,
and through the garden plots and orchard ran
channels from one clear fountain, while another
gushed through a pipe under the courtyard entrance
to serve the house and all who came for water. 140
These were the gifts of heaven to Alkínoös.

Odysseus, who had borne the barren sea,
stood in the gateway and surveyed this bounty.
He gazed his fill, then swiftly he went in.
The lords and nobles of Phaiákia
were tipping wine to the wakeful god, to Hermês—
a last libation before going to bed—
but down the hall Odysseus went unseen,
still in the cloud Athena cloaked him in,
until he reached Arêtê, and the king. 150
He threw his great hands round Arêtê's knees,
whereon the sacred mist curled back;
they saw him; and the diners hushed amazed
to see an unknown man inside the palace.
Under their eyes Odysseus made his plea:

"Arêtê, admirable Rhêxênor's daughter,
here is a man bruised by adversity, thrown
upon your mercy and the king your husband's,
begging indulgence of this company—
may the gods' blessing rest on them! May life 160
be kind to all! Let each one leave his children
every good thing this realm confers upon him!
But grant me passage to my father land.
My home and friends lie far. My life is pain."

He moved, then, toward the fire, and sat him down
amid the ashes. No one stirred or spoke
until Ekhenêos broke the spell—an old man,
eldest of the Phaiákians, an oracle,
versed in the laws and manners of old time.
He rose among them now and spoke out kindly: 170

"Alkínoös, this will not pass for courtesy:
a guest abased in ashes at our hearth?
Everyone here awaits your word; so come, then,
lift the man up; give him a seat of honor,
a silver-studded chair. Then tell the stewards
we'll have another wine bowl for libation
to Zeus, lord of the lightning—advocate
of honorable petitioners. And supper
may be supplied our friend by the larder mistress."

Alkínoös, calm in power, heard him out, 180
then took the great adventurer by the hand
and led him from the fire. Nearest his throne
the son whom he loved best, Laódamas,
had long held place; now the king bade him rise
and gave his shining chair to Lord Odysseus.
A serving maid poured water for his hands
from a gold pitcher into a silver bowl,
and spead a polished table at his side;
the mistress of provisions came with bread
and other victuals, generous with her store. 190
So Lord Odysseus drank, and tasted supper.
Seeing this done, the king in majesty
said to his squire:

"A fresh bowl, Pontónoös;
we make libation to the lord of lightning,
who seconds honorable petitioners."

Mixing the honey-hearted wine, Pontónoös
went on his rounds and poured fresh cups for all,
whereof when all had spilt they drank their fill.
Alkínoös then spoke to the company:

"My lords and leaders of Phaiákia: 200
hear now, all that my heart would have me say.
Our banquet's ended, so you may retire;
but let our seniors gather in the morning
to give this guest a festal day, and make
fair offerings to the gods. In due course we
shall put our minds upon the means at hand
to take him safely, comfortably, well
and happily, with speed, to his own country,

distant though it may lie. And may no trouble
come to him here or on the way; his fate 210
he shall pay out at home, even as the Spinners[4]
spun for him on the day his mother bore him.
If, as may be, he is some god, come down
from heaven's height, the gods are working strangely:
until now, they have shown themselves in glory
only after great hekatombs—those figures
banqueting at our side, throned like ourselves.
Or if some traveller met them when alone
they bore no least disguise; we are their kin; Gigantês,
Kyklopês, rank no nearer gods than we." 220

Odysseus' wits were ready, and he replied:

"Alkínoös, you may set your mind at rest.
Body and birth, a most unlikely god
am I, being all of earth and mortal nature.
I should say, rather, I am like those men
who suffer the worst trials that you know,
and miseries greater yet, as I might tell you—
hundreds; indeed the gods could send no more.
You will indulge me if I finish dinner—?
grieved though I am to say it. There's no part 230
of man more like a dog than brazen Belly,
crying to be remembered—and it must be—
when we are mortal weary and sick at heart;
and that is my condition. Yet my hunger
drives me to take this food, and think no more
of my afflictions. Belly must be filled.
Be equally impelled, my lords, tomorrow
to berth me in a ship and send me home!
Rough years I've had; now may I see once more
my hall, my lands, my people before I die!" 240

Now all who heard cried out assent to this:
the guest had spoken well; he must have passage.
Then tipping wine they drank their thirst away,
and one by one went homeward for the night.
So Lord Odysseus kept his place alone
with Arêtê and the king Alkínoös
beside him, while the maids went to and fro
clearing away the wine cups and the tables.
Presently the ivory-skinned lady
turned to him—for she knew his cloak and tunic 250
to be her own fine work, done with her maids—
and arrowy came her words upon the air:

[4]The Fates, mythological women who determined the span of a human life by spinning, measuring, and cutting the thread symbolic of it.

"Friend, I, for one, have certain questions for you.
Who are you, and who has given you this clothing?
Did you not say you wandered here by sea?"

The great tactician carefully replied:

"Ah, majesty, what labor it would be
to go through the whole story! All my years
of misadventures, given by those on high!
But this you ask about is quickly told: 260
in mid-ocean lies Ogýgia, the island
haunt of Kalypso, Atlas' guileful daughter,
a lovely goddess and a dangerous one.
No one, no god or man, consorts with her;
but supernatural power brought me there
to be her solitary guest: for Zeus
let fly with his bright bolt and split my ship,
rolling me over in the winedark sea.
There all my shipmates, friends were drowned, while I
hung on the keelboard of the wreck and drifted 270
nine full days. Then in the dead of night
the gods brought me ashore upon Ogýgia
into her hands. The enchantress in her beauty
fed and caressed me, promised me I should be
immortal, youthful, all the days to come;
but in my heart I never gave consent
though seven years detained. Immortal clothing
I had from her, and kept it wet with tears.
Then came the eighth year on the wheel of heaven
and word to her from Zeus, or a change of heart, 280
so that she now commanded me to sail,
sending me out to sea on a craft I made
with timber and tools of hers. She gave me stores,
victuals and wine, a cloak divinely woven,
and made a warm land breeze come up astern.
Seventeen days I sailed in the open water
before I saw your country's shore, a shadow
upon the sea rim. Then my heart rejoiced—
pitiable as I am! For blows aplenty
awaited me from the god who shakes the earth. 290
Cross gales he blew, making me lose my bearings,
and heaved up seas beyond imagination—
huge and foundering seas. All I could do
was hold hard, groaning under every shock,
until my craft broke up in the hurricane.
I kept afloat and swam your sea, or drifted,
taken by wind and current to this coast
where I went in on big swells running landward.
But cliffs and rock shoals made that place forbidding,

so I turned back, swimming off shore, and came 300
in the end to a river, to auspicious water,
with smooth beach and a rise that broke the wind.
I lay there where I fell till strength returned.
Then sacred night came on, and I went inland
to high ground and a leaf bed in a thicket.
Heaven sent slumber in an endless tide
submerging my sad heart among the leaves.
That night and next day's dawn and noon I slept;
the sun went west; and then sweet sleep unbound me,
when I became aware of maids—your daughter's— 310
playing along the beach; the princess, too,
most beautiful. I prayed her to assist me,
and her good sense was perfect; one could hope
for no behavior like it from the young,
thoughtless as they most often are. But she
gave me good provender and good red wine,
a river bath, and finally this clothing.
There is the bitter tale. These are the facts."

But in reply Alkínoös observed:

"Friend, my child's good judgment failed in this— 320
not to have brought you in her company home.
Once you approached her, you became her charge."

To this Odysseus tactfully replied:

"Sir, as to that, you should not blame the princess.
She did tell me to follow with her maids,
but I would not. I felt abashed, and feared
the sight would somehow ruffle or offend you.
All of us on this earth are plagued by jealousy."

Alkínoös' answer was a declaration:

"Friend, I am not a man for trivial anger: 330
better a sense of measure in everything.
No anger here. I say that if it should please
our father Zeus, Athena, and Apollo—
seeing the man you are, seeing your thoughts
are my own thoughts—my daughter should be yours
and you my son-in-law, if you remained.
A home, lands, riches you should have from me
if you could be contented here. If not,
by Father Zeus, let none of our men hold you!
On the contrary, I can assure you now 340
of passage late tomorrow: while you sleep
my men will row you through the tranquil night
to your own land and home or where you please.

It may be, even, far beyond Euboia—
called most remote by seamen of our isle
who landed there, conveying Rhadamanthos
when he sought Títyos, the son of Gaia.[5]
They put about, with neither pause nor rest,
and entered their home port the selfsame day.
But this you, too, will see: what ships I have, 350
how my young oarsmen send the foam a-scudding!"

Now joy welled up in the patient Lord Odysseus
who said devoutly in the warmest tones:

"O Father Zeus, let all this be fulfilled
as spoken by Alkínoös! Earth of harvests
remember him! Return me to my homeland!"

In this manner they conversed with one another;
but the great lady called her maids, and sent them
to make a kingly bed, with purple rugs
piled up, and sheets outspread, and fleecy 360
coverlets, in an eastern colonnade.
The girls went out with torches in their hands,
swift at their work of bedmaking; returning
they whispered at the lord Odysseus' shoulder:

"Sir, you may come; your bed has been prepared."

How welcome the word "bed" came to his ears!
Now, then, Odysseus laid him down and slept
in luxury under the Porch of Morning,
while in his inner chamber Alkínoös
retired to rest where his dear consort lay. 370

BOOK EIGHT: THE SONGS OF THE HARPER

Under the opening fingers of the dawn
Alkínoös, the sacred prince, arose,
and then arose Odysseus, raider of cities.
As the king willed, they went down by the shipways
to the assembly ground of the Phaiákians.
Side by side the two men took their ease there
on smooth stone benches. Meanwhile Pallas Athena
roamed through the byways of the town, contriving
Odysseus' voyage home—in voice and feature

[5]The lines "It may be . . . Gaia" are somewhat obscure, since Rhadamanthos is pictured in Book IV as dwelling in Elysion, and Títyos, in Book XI, is punished in Hades. The main point is clear, though: Alkínoös is boasting of the nautical range and speed of his seafaring people. Euboia is an island east of Greece. Gaia is another name for Ge, the earth deity.

the crier of the king Alkínoös 10
who stopped and passed the word to every man:

"Phaiákian lords and counselors, this way!
Come to assembly: learn about the stranger,
the new guest at the palace of Alkínoös—
a man the sea drove, but a comely man;
the gods' own light is on him."

She aroused them,
and soon the assembly ground and seats were filled
with curious men, a throng who peered and saw
the master mind of war, Laërtês' son.
Athena now poured out her grace upon him, 20
head and shoulders, height and mass—a splendor
awesome to the eyes of the Phaiákians;
she put him in a fettle to win the day,
mastering every trial they set to test him.
When all the crowd sat marshalled, quieted,
Alkínoös addressed the full assembly:

"Hear me, lords and captains of the Phaiákians!
Hear what my heart would have me say!
Our guest and new friend—nameless to me still—
comes to my house after long wandering 30
in Dawn lands, or among the Sunset races.
Now he appeals to me for conveyance home.
As in the past, therefore, let us provide
passage, and quickly, for no guest of mine
languishes here for lack of it. Look to it:
get a black ship afloat on the noble sea,
and pick our fastest sailer; draft a crew
of two and fifty from our younger townsmen—
men who have made their names at sea. Loop oars
well to your tholepins,[1] lads, then leave the ship, 40
come to our house, fall to, and take your supper:
we'll furnish out a feast for every crewman.
These are your orders. As for my older peers
and princes of the realm, let them foregather
in festival for our friend in my great hall;
and let no man refuse. Call in our minstrel,
Demódokos, whom God made lord of song,
heart-easing, sing upon what theme he will."

He turned, led the procession, and those princes
followed, while his herald sought the minstrel. 50
Young oarsmen from the assembly chose a crew
of two and fifty, as the king commanded,

[1] Pegs on the side of a boat, used as oarlocks.

and these filed off along the waterside
to where the ship lay, poised above open water.
They hauled the black hull down to ride the sea,
rigging a mast and spar in the black ship,
with oars at trail from corded rawhide, all
seamanly; then tried the white sail, hoisting,
and moored her off the beach. Then going ashore
the crew went up to the great house of Alkínoös. 60

Here the enclosures, entrance ways, and rooms
were filled with men, young men and old, for whom
Alkínoös had put twelve sheep to sacrifice,
eight tuskers[2] and a pair of shambling oxen.
These, now, they flayed and dressed to make their banquet.

The crier soon came, leading that man of song
whom the Muse cherished; by her gift he knew
the good of life, and evil—
for she who lent him sweetness made him blind.[3]
Pontónoös fixed a studded chair for him 70
hard by a pillar amid the banqueters,
hanging the taut harp from a peg above him,
and guided up his hands upon the strings;
placed a bread basket at his side, and poured
wine in a cup, that he might drink his fill.
Now each man's hand went out upon the banquet.

In time, when hunger and thirst were turned away,
the Muse brought to the minstrel's mind a song
of heroes whose great fame rang under heaven:
the clash between Odysseus and Akhilleus, 80
how one time they contended[4] at the godfeast
raging, and the marshal, Agamémnon,
felt inward joy over his captains' quarrel;
for such had been foretold him by Apollo
at Pytho[5]—hallowed height—when the Akhaian
crossed that portal of rock to ask a sign—
in the old days when grim war lay ahead
for Trojans and Danaans, by God's will.
So ran the tale the minstrel sang. Odysseus
with massive hand drew his rich mantle down 90
over his brow, cloaking his face with it,
to make the Phaiákians miss the secret tears
that started to his eyes. How skillfully
he dried them when the song came to a pause!

[2]Animals with tusks, such as boars.
[3]According to tradition, Homer himself was blind.
[4]This incident probably took place before the action of the *Iliad*.
[5]The shrine of Apollo at Delphi, on Mount Parnassos (Parnassus); the god uttered oracular pronouncements there.

threw back his mantle, spilt his gout of wine!
But soon the minstrel plucked his note once more
to please the Phaiákian lords, who loved the song;
then in his cloak Odysseus wept again.
His tears flowed in the mantle unperceived:
only Alkínoös, at his elbow, saw them, 100
and caught the low groan in the man's breathing.
At once he spoke to all the seafolk round him:

"Hear me, lords and captains of the Phaiákians.
Our meat is shared, our hearts are full of pleasure
from the clear harp tone that accords with feasting;
now for the field and track; we shall have trials
in the pentathlon.[6] Let our guest go home
and tell his friends what champions we are
at boxing, wrestling, broadjump and foot racing."

On this he led the way and all went after. 110
The crier unslung and pegged the shining harp
and, taking Demódokos's hand,
led him along with all the rest—Phaiákian
peers, gay amateurs of the great games.
They gained the common, where a crowd was forming,
and many a young athlete now came forward
with seaside names like Tipmast, Tiderace, Sparwood,
Hullman, Sternman, Beacher and Pullerman,
Bluewater, Shearwater, Runningwake, Boardalee,
Seabelt, son of Grandfleet Shipwrightson; 120
Seareach stepped up, son of the Launching Master,
rugged as Arês,[7] bane of men; his build
excelled all but the Prince Laódamas;
and Laódamas made entry with his brothers,
Halios and Klytóneus, sons of the king.
The runners, first, must have their quarter mile.
All lined up tense; then Go! and down the track
they raised the dust in a flying bunch, strung out
longer and longer behind Prince Klytóneus.
By just so far as a mule team, breaking ground, 130
will distance oxen, he left all behind
and came up to the crowd, an easy winner.
Then they made room for wrestling—grinding bouts
that Seareach won, pinning the strongest men;
then the broadjump; first place went to Seabelt;
Sparwood gave the discus the mightiest fling,
and Prince Laódamas outboxed them all.

Now it was he, the son of Alkínoös,
who said when they had run through these diversions:

[6]An athletic contest consisting of five events.
[7]God of war.

"Look here, friends, we ought to ask the stranger 140
if he competes in something. He's no cripple;
look at his leg muscles and his forearms.
Neck like a bollard;[8] strong as a bull, he seems;
and not old, though he may have gone stale under
the rough times he had. Nothing like the sea
for wearing out the toughest man alive."

Then Seareach took him up at once, and said:

"Laódamas, you're right, by all the powers.
Go up to him, yourself, and put the question."

At this, Alkínoös' tall son advanced 150
to the center ground, and there addressed Odysseus:

"Friend, Excellency, come join our competition,
if you are practiced, as you seem to be.
While a man lives he wins no greater honor
than footwork and the skill of hands can bring him.
Enter our games, then; ease your heart of trouble.
Your journey home is not far off, remember;
the ship is launched, the crew all primed for sea."

Odysseus, canniest of men, replied:

"Laódamas, why do you young chaps challenge me? 160
I have more on my mind than track and field—
hard days, and many, have I seen, and suffered.
I sit here at your field meet, yes; but only
as one who begs your king to send him home."

Now Seareach put his word in, and contentiously:

"The reason being, as I see it, friend,
you never learned a sport, and have no skill
in any of the contests of fighting men.
You must have been the skipper of some tramp
that crawled from one port to the next, jam full 170
of chaffering hands: a tallier of cargoes,
itching for gold—not, by your looks, an athlete."

Odysseus frowned, and eyed him coldly, saying:

"That was uncalled for, friend, you talk like a fool.
The gods deal out no gift, this one or any—
birth, brains, or speech—to every man alike.
In looks a man may be a shade, a specter,
and yet be master of speech so crowned with beauty
that people gaze at him with pleasure. Courteous,

[8]A sturdy post to which a ship's ropes were tied.

sure of himself, he can command assemblies, 180
and when he comes to town, the crowds gather.
A handsome man, contrariwise, may lack
grace and good sense in everything he says.
You now, for instance, with your fine physique—
a god's, indeed—you have an empty noddle.[9]
I find my heart inside my ribs aroused
by your impertinence. I am no stranger
to contests, as you fancy. I rated well
when I could count on youth and my two hands.
Now pain has cramped me, and my years of combat 190
hacking through ranks in war, and the bitter sea.
Aye. Even so I'll give your games a trial.
You spoke heart-wounding words. You shall be answered."

He leapt out, cloaked as he was, and picked a discus,
a rounded stone, more ponderous than those
already used by the Phaiákian throwers,
and, whirling, let it fly from his great hand
with a low hum. The crowd went flat on the ground—
all those oar-pulling, seafaring Phaiákians—
under the rushing noise. The spinning disk 200
soared out, light as a bird, beyond all others.
Disguised now as a Phaiákian, Athena
staked it and called out:

"Even a blind man,
friend, could judge this, finding with his fingers
one discus, quite alone, beyond the cluster.
Congratulations; this event is yours;
not a man here can beat you or come near you."

That was a cheering hail, Odysseus thought,
seeing one friend there on the emulous field,
so, in relief, he turned among the Phaiákians 210
and said:

"Now come alongside that one, lads.
The next I'll send as far, I think, or farther.
Anyone else on edge for competition
try me now. By heaven, you angered me.
Racing, wrestling, boxing—I bar nothing
with any man except Laódamas,
for he's my host. Who quarrels with his host?
Only a madman—or no man at all—
would challenge his protector among strangers,
cutting the ground away under his feet. 220
Here are no others I will not engage,
none but I hope to know what he is made of.

[9] Head.

Inept at combat, am I? Not entirely.
Give me a smooth bow; I can handle it,
and I might well be first to hit my man
amid a swarm of enemies, though archers
in company around me drew together.
Philoktêtês[10] alone, at Troy, when we
Akhaians took the bow, used to outshoot me.
Of men who now eat bread upon the earth 230
I hold myself the best hand with a bow—
conceding mastery to the men of old,
Heraklês, or Eurýtos[11] of Oikhalía,
heroes who vied with gods in bowmanship.
Eurýtos came to grief, it's true; old age
never crept over him in his long hall;
Apollo took his challenge ill, and killed him.
What then, the spear? I'll plant it like an arrow.
Only in sprinting, I'm afraid, I may
be passed by someone. Roll of the sea waves 240
wearied me, and the victuals in my ship
ran low; my legs are flabby."

When he finished,
the rest were silent, but Alkínoös answered:

"Friend, we take your challenge in good part,
for this man angered and affronted you
here at our peaceful games. You'd have us note
the prowess that is in you, and so clearly,
no man of sense would ever cry it down!
Come, turn your mind, now, on a thing to tell
among your peers when you are home again, 250
dining in hall, beside your wife and children:
I mean our prowess, as you may remember it,
for we, too, have our skills, given by Zeus,
and practiced from our father's time to this—
not in the boxing ring nor the palestra[12]
conspicuous, but in racing, land or sea;
and all our days we set great store by feasting,
harpers, and the grace of dancing choirs,
changes of dress, warm baths, and downy beds.
O master dancers of the Phaiákians! 260
Perform now: let our guest on his return
tell his companions we excel the world
in dance and song, as in our ships and running.

[10]Philoktêtês had inherited the magical bow of the fabled hero Heraklês (Hercules); a version of his story is dramatized in Sophocles' *Philoctetes*.

[11]Grandson of Apollo, and Heraklês' instructor in bowmanship. He was killed in a competition with Apollo, god of archery. Eurýtos' bow descended to Odysseus.

[12]A public athletics ground.

Someone go find the gittern harp in hall
and bring it quickly to Demódokos!"

At the serene king's word, a squire ran
to bring the polished harp out of the palace,
and place was given to nine referees—
peers of the realm, masters of ceremony—
who cleared a space and smoothed a dancing floor. 270
The squire brought down, and gave Demódokos,
the clear-toned harp; and centering on the minstrel
magical young dancers formed a circle
with a light beat, and stamp of feet. Beholding,
Odysseus marvelled at the flashing ring.

Now to his harp the blinded minstrel sang
of Arês' dalliance with Aphroditê:
how hidden in Hephaistos'[13] house they played
at love together, and the gifts of Arês,
dishonoring Hephaistos' bed—and how 280
the word that wounds the heart came to the master
from Hêlios,[14] who had seen the two embrace;
and when he learned it, Lord Hephaistos went
with baleful calculation to his forge.
There mightily he armed his anvil block
and hammered out a chain, whose tempered links
could not be sprung or bent; he meant that they should hold.
Those shackles fashioned, hot in wrath Hephaistos
climbed to the bower and the bed of love,
pooled all his net of chain around the bed posts 290
and swung it from the rafters overhead—
light as a cobweb even gods in bliss
could not perceive, so wonderful his cunning.
Seeing his bed now made a snare, he feigned
a journey to the trim stronghold of Lemnos,[15]
the dearest of earth's towns to him. And Arês?
Ah, golden Arês' watch had its reward
when he beheld the great smith leaving home.
How promptly to the famous door he came,
intent on pleasure with sweet Kythereia![16] 300
She, who had left her father's side but now,
sat in her chamber when her lover entered;
and tenderly he pressed her hand and said:

[13]The lame god of fire and metalworking, husband of Aphroditê.
[14]The sun god.
[15]An island in the Aegean, center of the worship of Hephaistos; it was there that he fell after Zeus, during a fit of anger, threw him out of heaven.
[16]Aphroditê. Also spelled *Cytherea.*

"Come and lie down, my darling, and be happy!
Hephaistos is no longer here, but gone
to see his grunting Sintian[17] friends on Lemnos."

As she, too, thought repose would be most welcome,
the pair went in to bed—into a shower
of clever chains, the netting of Hephaistos.
So trussed, they could not move apart, nor rise, 310
at last they knew there could be no escape,
they were to see the glorious cripple now—
for Hêlios had spied for him, and told him;
so he turned back, this side of Lemnos Isle,
sick at heart, making his way homeward.
Now in the doorway of the room he stood
while deadly rage took hold of him; his voice,
hoarse and terrible, reached all the gods:

"O Father Zeus, O gods in bliss forever,
here is indecorous entertainment for you, 320
Aphroditê, Zeus's daughter,
caught in the act, cheating me, her cripple,
with Arês—devastating Arês.
Cleanlimbed beauty is her joy, not these
bandylegs I came into the world with:
no one to blame but the two gods[18] who bred me!
Come see this pair entwining here
in my own bed! How hot it makes me burn!
I think they may not care to lie much longer,
pressing on one another, passionate lovers; 330
they'll have enough of bed together soon.
And yet the chain that bagged them holds them down
till Father sends me back my wedding gifts—
all that I poured out for his damned pigeon,
so lovely, and so wanton."

All the others
were crowding in, now, to the brazen house—
Poseidon who embraces earth, and Hermês
the runner, and Apollo, lord of Distance.
The goddesses stayed home for shame; but these
munificences ranged there in the doorway, 340
and irrepressible among them all
arose the laughter of the happy gods.
Gazing hard at Hephaistos' handiwork
the gods in turn remarked among themselves:

"No dash in adultery now."

[17] The Sintians, of Lemnos, had a reputation for crudity.
[18] Zeus and Hera.

"The tortoise tags the hare—
Hephaistos catches Arês—and Arês outran the wind."

"The lame god's craft has pinned him. Now shall he
pay what is due from gods taken in cuckoldry."

They made these improving remarks to one another,
but Apollo leaned aside to say to Hermês: 350

"Son of Zeus, beneficent Wayfinder,
would you accept a coverlet of chain, if only
you lay by Aphroditê's golden side?"

To this the Wayfinder replied, shining:

"Would I not, though, Apollo of distances!
Wrap me in chains three times the weight of these,
come goddesses and gods to see the fun;
only let me lie beside the pale-golden one!"

The gods gave way again to peals of laughter,
all but Poseidon, and he never smiled, 360
but urged Hephaistos to unpinion Arês,
saying emphatically, in a loud voice:

"Free him:
you will be paid, I swear; ask what you will;
he pays up every jot the gods decree."

To this the Great Gamelegs replied:

"Poseidon,
lord of the earth-surrounding sea, I should not
swear to a scoundrel's honor. What have I
as surety from you, if Arês leaves me
empty-handed, with my empty chain?"

The Earth-shaker for answer urged again: 370

"Hephaistos, let us grant he goes, and leaves
the fine unpaid; I swear, then, I shall pay it."

Then said the Great Gamelegs at last:

"No more:
you offer terms I cannot well refuse."

And down the strong god bent to set them free,
till disencumbered of their bond, the chain,
the lovers leapt away—he into Thrace,
while Aphroditê, laughter's darling, fled

to Kypros Isle and Paphos,[19] to her meadow
and altar dim with incense. There the Graces 380
bathed and anointed her with golden oil—
a bloom that clings upon immortal flesh alone—
and let her folds of mantle fall in glory.

So ran the song the minstrel sang.

Odysseus
listening, found sweet pleasure in the tale,
among the Phaiákian mariners and oarsmen.
And next Alkínoös called upon his sons,
Halios and Laódamas, to show
the dance no one could do as well as they—
handling a purple ball carven by Pólybos. 390
One made it shoot up under the shadowing clouds
as he leaned backward; bounding high in air
the other cut its flight far off the ground—
and neither missed a step as the ball soared.

The next turn was to keep it low, and shuttling
hard between them, while the ring of boys
gave them a steady stamping beat.
Odysseus now addressed Alkínoös:

"O majesty, model of all your folk,
your promise was to show me peerless dancers; 400
here is the promise kept. I am all wonder."

At this Alkínoös in his might rejoicing
said to the seafarers of Phaiákia:

"Attend me now, Phaiákian lords and captains:
our guest appears a clear-eyed man and wise.
Come, let him feel our bounty as he should.
Here are twelve princes of the kingdom—lords
paramount, and I who make thirteen;
let each one bring a laundered cloak and tunic,
and add one bar of honorable gold. 410
Heap all our gifts together; load his arms;
let him go joyous to our evening feast!
As for Seareach—why, man to man
he'll make amends, and handsomely; he blundered."

Now all as one acclaimed the king's good pleasure,
and each one sent a squire to bring his gifts.
Meanwhile Seareach found speech again, saying:

[19] A city in ancient Cyprus (Kypros), an island south of Turkey where Aphroditê had a cult.

"My lord and model of us all, Alkínoös,
as you require of me, in satisfaction,
this broadsword of clear bronze goes to our guest. 420
Its hilt is silver, and the ringed sheath
of new-sawn ivory—a costly weapon."

He turned to give the broadsword to Odysseus,
facing him, saying blithely:

"Sir, my best
wishes, my respects; if I offended,
I hope the seawinds blow it out of mind.
God send you see your lady and your homeland
soon again, after the pain of exile."

Odysseus, the great tactician, answered:

"My hand, friend; may the gods award you fortune. 430
I hope no pressing need comes on you ever
for this fine blade you give me in amends."

He slung it, glinting silver, from his shoulder,
as the light shone from sundown. Messengers
were bearing gifts and treasure to the palace,
where the king's sons received them all, and made
a glittering pile at their grave mother's side;
then, as Alkínoös took his throne of power,
each went to his own high-backed chair in turn,
and said Alkínoös to Arêtê: 440

"Lady, bring here a chest, the finest one;
a clean cloak and tunic; stow these things;
and warm a cauldron for him. Let him bathe,
when he has seen the gifts of the Phaiákians,
and so dine happily to a running song.
My own wine-cup of gold intaglio[20]
I'll give him, too; through all the days to come,
tipping his wine to Zeus or other gods
in his great hall, he shall remember me."

Then said Arêtê to her maids:

"The tripod: 450
stand the great tripod legs about the fire."

They swung the cauldron on the fire's heart,
poured water in, and fed the blaze beneath
until the basin simmered, cupped in flame.

[20]A design cut into the surface.

The queen set out a rich chest from her chamber
and folded in the gifts—clothing and gold
given Odysseus by the Phaiákians;
then she put in the royal cloak and tunic,
briskly saying to her guest:

"Now here, sir,
look to the lid yourself, and tie it down 460
against light fingers, if there be any,
on the black ship tonight while you are sleeping."

Noble Odysseus, expert in adversity,
battened the lid down with a lightning knot
learned, once, long ago, from the Lady Kirkê.[21]
And soon a call came from the Bathing Mistress
who led him to a hip-bath, warm and clear—
a happy sight, and rare in his immersions
after he left Kalypso's home—where, surely,
the luxuries of a god were ever his. 470
When the bath maids had washed him, rubbed him down,
put a fresh tunic and a cloak around him,
he left the bathing place to join the men
at wine in hall.

The princess Nausikaa,
exquisite figure, as of heaven's shaping,
waited beside a pillar as he passed
and said swiftly, with wonder in her look:

"Fare well, stranger; in your land remember me
who met and saved you. It is worth your thought."

The man of all occasions now met this: 480

"Daughter of great Alkínoös, Nausikaa,
may Zeus the lord of thunder, Hera's consort,
grant me daybreak again in my own country!
But there and all my days until I die
may I invoke you as I would a goddess,
princess, to whom I owe my life."

He left her
and went to take his place beside the king.

Now when the roasts were cut, the winebowls full,
a herald led the minstrel down the room
amid the deference of the crowd, and paused 490
to seat him near a pillar in the center—
whereupon that resourceful man, Odysseus,

[21]A sorceress; Odysseus' encounter with her is described in Book X. Also spelled *Circe.*

carved out a quarter from his chine of pork,
crisp with fat, and called the blind man's guide:

"Herald! here, take this to Demódokos:
let him feast and be merry, with my compliments.
All men owe honor to the poets—honor
and awe, for they are dearest to the Muse
who puts upon their lips the ways of life."

Gentle Demódokos took the proffered gift 500
and inwardly rejoiced. When all were served,
every man's hand went out upon the banquet,
repelling hunger and thirst, until at length
Odysseus spoke again to the blind minstrel:

"Demódokos, accept my utmost praise.
The Muse, daughter of Zeus in radiance,
or else Apollo[22] gave you skill to shape
with such great style your songs of the Akhaians—
their hard lot, how they fought and suffered war.
You shared it, one would say, or heard it all. 510
Now shift your theme, and sing that wooden horse
Epeios built, inspired by Athena—
the ambuscade Odysseus filled with fighters
and sent to take the inner town of Troy.
Sing only this for me, sing me this well,
and I shall say at once before the world
the grace of heaven has given us a song."

The minstrel stirred, murmuring to the god, and soon
clear words and notes came one by one, a vision
of the Akhaians in their graceful ships 520
drawing away from shore: the torches flung
and shelters flaring: Argive soldiers crouched
in the close dark around Odysseus: and
the horse, tall on the assembly ground of Troy.
For when the Trojans pulled it in, themselves,
up to the citadel, they sat nearby
with long-drawn-out and hapless argument—
favoring, in the end, one course of three:
either to stave the vault with brazen axes,
or haul it to a cliff and pitch it down, 530
or else to save it for the gods, a votive glory—
the plan that could not but prevail.
For Troy must perish, as ordained, that day
she harbored the great horse of timber; hidden
the flower of Akhaia lay, and bore
slaughter and death upon the men of Troy.

[22]God of music and prophecy. He would naturally have an affinity with bards.

He sang, then, of the town sacked by Akhaians
pouring down from the horse's hollow cave,
this way and that way raping the steep city,
and how Odysseus came like Arês to 540
the door of Deïphobos,[23] with Meneláos,
and braved the desperate fight there—
conquering once more by Athena's power.

The splendid minstrel sang it.
And Odysseus
let the bright molten tears run down his cheeks,
weeping the way a wife mourns for her lord
on the lost field where he has gone down fighting
the day of wrath that came upon his children.
At sight of the man panting and dying there,
she slips down to enfold him, crying out; 550
then feels the spears, prodding her back and shoulders,
and goes bound into slavery and grief.
Piteous weeping wears away her cheeks:
but no more piteous than Odysseus' tears,
cloaked as they were, now, from the company.
Only Alkínoös, at his elbow, knew—
hearing the low sob in the man's breathing—
and when he knew, he spoke:

"Hear me, lords and captains of Phaiákia!
And let Demódokos touch his harp no more. 560
His theme has not been pleasing to all here.
During the feast, since our fine poet sang,
our guest has never left off weeping. Grief
seems fixed upon his heart. Break off the song!
Let everyone be easy, host and guest;
there's more decorum in a smiling banquet!
We had prepared here, on our friend's behalf,
safe conduct in a ship, and gifts to cheer him,
holding that any man with a grain of wit
will treat a decent suppliant like a brother. 570
Now by the same rule, friend, you must not be
secretive any longer! Come, in fairness,
tell me the name you bore in that far country;
how were you known to family, and neighbors?
No man is nameless—no man, good or bad,
but gets a name in his first infancy,
none being born, unless a mother bears him!
Tell me your native land, your coast and city—
sailing directions for the ships, you know—
for those Phaiákian ships of ours 580
that have no steersman, and no steering oar,

[23]Meneláos' wife, Helen, had in Troy been given in marriage to Deïphobos.

divining the crew's wishes, as they do,
and knowing, as they do, the ports of call
about the world. Hidden in mist or cloud
they scud the open sea, with never a thought
of being in distress or going down.
There is, however, something I once heard
Nausíthoös, my father, say: Poseidon
holds it against us that our deep sea ships
are sure conveyance for all passengers. 590
My father said, some day one of our cutters
homeward bound over the cloudy sea
would be wrecked by the god, and a range of hills
thrown round our city. So, in his age, he said,
and let it be, or not, as the god please.
But come, now, put it for me clearly, tell me
the sea ways that you wandered, and the shores
you touched; the cities, and the men therein,
uncivilized, if such there were, and hostile,
and those godfearing who had kindly manners. 600
Tell me why you should grieve so terribly
over the Argives and the fall of Troy.
That was all gods' work, weaving ruin there
so it should make a song for men to come!
Some kin of yours, then, died at Ilion,
some first rate man, by marriage near to you,
next your own blood most dear?
Or some companion of congenial mind
and valor? True it is, a wise friend
can take a brother's place in our affection." 610

BOOK NINE: NEW COASTS AND POSEIDON'S SON

Now this was the reply Odysseus made:

"Alkínoös, king and admiration of men,
how beautiful this is, to hear a minstrel
gifted as yours: a god he might be, singing!
There is no boon in life more sweet, I say,
than when a summer joy holds all the realm,
and banqueters sit listening to a harper
in a great hall, by rows of tables heaped
with bread and roast meat, while a steward goes
to dip up wine and brim your cups again. 10
Here is the flower of life, it seems to me!
But now you wish to know my cause for sorrow—
and thereby give me cause for more.
What shall I
say first? What shall I keep until the end?

The gods have tried me in a thousand ways.
But first my name: let that be known to you,
and if I pull away from pitiless death,
friendship will bind us, though my land lies far.

I am Laërtês' son, Odysseus.
Men hold me
formidable for guile in peace and war: 20
this fame has gone abroad to the sky's rim.
My home is on the peaked sea-mark of Ithaka
under Mount Neion's wind-blown robe of leaves,
in sight of other islands—Doulíkhion,
Samê, wooded Zakynthos—Ithaka
being most lofty in that coastal sea,
and northwest, while the rest lie east and south.
A rocky isle, but good for a boy's training;
I shall not see on earth a place more dear,
though I have been detained long by Kalypso, 30
loveliest among goddesses, who held me
in her smooth caves, to be her heart's delight,
as Kirkê of Aiaia, the enchantress,
desired me, and detained me in her hall.
But in my heart I never gave consent.
Where shall a man find sweetness to surpass
his own home and his parents? In far lands
he shall not, though he find a house of gold.

What of my sailing, then, from Troy?
What of those years
of rough adventure, weathered under Zeus? 40
The wind that carried west from Ilion
brought me to Ísmaros,[1] on the far shore,
a strongpoint on the coast of the Kikonês.
I stormed that place and killed the men who fought.
Plunder we took, and we enslaved the women,
to make division, equal shares to all—
but on the spot I told them: 'Back, and quickly!
Out to sea again!' My men were mutinous,
fools, on stores of wine. Sheep after sheep
they butchered by the surf, and shambling cattle, 50
feasting,—while fugitives went inland, running
to call to arms the main force of Kikonês.
This was an army, trained to fight on horseback
or, where the ground required, on foot. They came
with dawn over that terrain like the leaves
and blades of spring. So doom appeared to us,
dark word of Zeus for us, our evil days.

[1]The land of the Kikonês, in Thrace (on the northern coast of the Aegean Sea).

My men stood up and made a fight of it—
backed on the ships, with lances kept in play,
from bright morning through the blaze of noon 60
holding our beach, although so far outnumbered;
but when the sun passed toward unyoking time,
then the Akhaians, one by one, gave way.
Six benches were left empty in every ship
that evening when we pulled away from death.
And this new grief we bore with us to sea:
our precious lives we had, but not our friends.
No ship made sail next day until some shipmate
had raised a cry, three times, for each poor ghost
unfleshed by the Kikonês on that field. 70

Now Zeus the lord of cloud roused in the north
a storm against the ships, and driving veils
of squall moved down like night on land and sea.
The bows went plunging at the gust; sails
cracked and lashed out strips in the big wind.
We saw death in that fury, dropped the yards,
unshipped the oars, and pulled for the nearest lee:
then two long days and nights we lay offshore
worn out and sick at heart, tasting our grief,
until a third Dawn came with ringlets shining. 80
Then we put up our masts, hauled sail, and rested,
letting the steersmen and the breeze take over.

I might have made it safely home, that time,
but as I came round Malea[2] the current
took me out to sea, and from the north
a fresh gale drove me on, past Kythera.
Nine days I drifted on the teeming sea
before dangerous high winds. Upon the tenth
we came to the coastline of the Lotos Eaters,
who live upon that flower. We landed there 90
to take on water. All ships' companies
mustered alongside for the mid-day meal.
Then I sent out two picked men and a runner
to learn what race of men that land sustained.
They fell in, soon enough, with Lotos Eaters,
who showed no will to do us harm, only
offering the sweet Lotos to our friends—
but those who ate this honeyed plant, the Lotos,
never cared to report, nor to return:
they longed to stay forever, browsing on 100
the native bloom, forgetful of their homeland.
I drove them, all three wailing, to the ships,

[2]The cape at the southernmost end of Greece; Kythera, mentioned two lines below, is a sizable island just southwest of Malea.

tied them down under their rowing benches,
and called the rest: 'All hands aboard;
come, clear the beach and no one taste
the Lotos, or you lose your hope of home.'
Filing in to their places by the rowlocks
my oarsmen dipped their long oars in the surf,
and we moved out again on our sea faring.

In the next land we found were Kyklopês,[3] 110
giants, louts, without a law to bless them.
In ignorance leaving the fruitage of the earth in mystery
to the immortal gods, they neither plow
nor sow by hand, nor till the ground, though grain—
wild wheat and barley—grows untended, and
wine-grapes, in clusters, ripen in heaven's rain.
Kyklopês have no muster and no meeting,
no consultation or old tribal ways,
but each one dwells in his own mountain cave
dealing out rough justice to wife and child, 120
indifferent to what the others do.
Well, then:
across the wide bay from the mainland
there lies a desert island, not far out,
but still not close inshore. Wild goats in hundreds
breed there; and no human being comes
upon the isle to startle them—no hunter
of all who ever tracked with hounds through forests
or had rough going over mountain trails.
The isle, unplanted and untilled, a wilderness,
pastures goats alone. And this is why: 130
good ships like ours with cheekpaint at the bows
are far beyond the Kyklopês. No shipwright
toils among them, shaping and building up
symmetrical trim hulls to cross the sea
and visit all the seaboard towns, as men do
who go and come in commerce over water.
This isle—seagoing folk would have annexed it
and built their homesteads on it: all good land,
fertile for every crop in season: lush
well-watered meads along the shore, vines in profusion, 140
prairie, clear for the plow, where grain would grow
chin high by harvest time, and rich sub-soil.
The island cove is landlocked, so you need
no hawsers out astern, bow-stones or mooring:
run in and ride there till the day your crews
chafe to be under sail, and a fair wind blows.
You'll find good water flowing from a cavern
through dusky poplars into the upper bay.

[3] One-eyed giants, inhabitants of Sicily. Also spelled *Cyclops*.

Here we made harbor. Some god guided us
that night, for we could barely see our bows 150
in the dense fog around us, and no moonlight
filtered through the overcast. No look-out,
nobody saw the island dead ahead,
nor even the great landward rolling billow
that took us in: we found ourselves in shallows,
keels grazing shore: so furled our sails
and disembarked where the low ripples broke.
There on the beach we lay, and slept till morning.

When Dawn spread out her finger tips of rose
we turned out marvelling, to tour the isle, 160
while Zeus's shy nymph daughters flushed wild goats
down from the heights—a breakfast for my men.
We ran to fetch our hunting bows and long-shanked
lances from the ships, and in three companies
we took our shots. Heaven gave us game a-plenty:
for every one of twelve ships in my squadron
nine goats fell to be shared; my lot was ten.
So there all day, until the sun went down,
we made our feast on meat galore, and wine—
wine from the ship, for our supply held out, 170
so many jars were filled at Ísmaros
from stores of the Kikonês that we plundered.
We gazed, too, at Kyklopês Land, so near,
we saw their smoke, heard bleating from their flocks.
But after sundown, in the gathering dusk,
we slept again above the wash of ripples.

When the young Dawn with finger tips of rose
came in the east, I called my men together
and made a speech to them:

'Old shipmates, friends,
the rest of you stand by; I'll make the crossing 180
in my own ship, with my own company,
and find out what the mainland natives are—
for they may be wild savages, and lawless,
or hospitable and god fearing men.'

At this I went aboard, and gave the word
to cast off by the stern. My oarsmen followed,
filing in to their benches by the rowlocks,
and all in line dipped oars in the grey sea.

As we rowed on, and nearer to the mainland,
at one end of the bay, we saw a cavern 190
yawning above the water, screened with laurel,
and many rams and goats about the place

inside a sheepfold—made from slabs of stone
earthfast between tall trunks of pine and rugged
towering oak trees.
A prodigious man
slept in this cave alone, and took his flocks
to graze afield—remote from all companions,
knowing none but savage ways, a brute
so huge, he seemed no man at all of those
who eat good wheaten bread; but he seemed rather 200
a shaggy mountain reared in solitude.
We beached there, and I told the crew
to stand by and keep watch over the ship;
as for myself I took my twelve best fighters
and went ahead. I had a goatskin full
of that sweet liquor that Euanthês' son,
Maron, had given me. He kept Apollo's
holy grove at Ísmaros; for kindness
we showed him there, and showed his wife and child,
he gave me seven shining golden talents 210
perfectly formed, a solid silver winebowl,
and then this liquor—twelve two-handled jars
of brandy, pure and fiery. Not a slave
in Maron's household knew this drink; only
he, his wife and the storeroom mistress knew;
and they would put one cupful—ruby-colored,
honey-smooth—in twenty more of water,
but still the sweet scent hovered like a fume
over the winebowl. No man turned away
when cups of this came round.
A wineskin full 220
I brought along, and victuals in a bag,
for in my bones I knew some towering brute
would be upon us soon—all outward power,
a wild man, ignorant of civility.

We climbed, then, briskly to the cave. But Kyklops
had gone afield, to pasture his fat sheep,
so we looked round at everything inside:
a drying rack that sagged with cheeses, pens
crowded with lambs and kids, each in its class:
firstlings apart from middlings, and the 'dewdrops,' 230
or newborn lambkins, penned apart from both.
And vessels full of whey were brimming there—
bowls of earthenware and pails for milking.
My men came pressing round me, pleading:

'Why not
take these cheeses, get them stowed, come back,
throw open all the pens, and make a run for it?
We'll drive the kids and lambs aboard. We say
put out again on good salt water!'

Ah,
how sound that was! Yet I refused. I wished
to see the caveman, what he had to offer— 240
no pretty sight, it turned out, for my friends.
We lit a fire, burnt an offering,
and took some cheese to eat; then sat in silence
around the embers, waiting. When he came
he had a load of dry boughs on his shoulder
to stoke his fire at suppertime. He dumped it
with a great crash into that hollow cave,
and we all scattered fast to the far wall.
Then over the broad cavern floor he ushered
the ewes he meant to milk. He left his rams 250
and he-goats in the yard outside, and swung
high overhead a slab of solid rock
to close the cave. Two dozen four-wheeled wagons,
with heaving wagon teams, could not have stirred
the tonnage of that rock from where he wedged it
over the doorsill. Next he took his seat
and milked his bleating ewes. A practiced job
he made of it, giving each ewe her suckling;
thickened his milk, then, into curds and whey,[4]
sieved out the curds to drip in withy baskets, 260
and poured the whey to stand in bowls
cooling until he drank it for his supper.
When all these chores were done, he poked the fire,
heaping on brushwood. In the glare he saw us.

'Strangers,' he said, 'who are you? And where from?
What brings you here by sea ways—a fair traffic?
Or are you wandering rogues, who cast your lives
like dice, and ravage other folk by sea?'

We felt a pressure on our hearts, in dread
of that deep rumble and that mighty man. 270
But all the same I spoke up in reply:

'We are from Troy, Akhaians, blown off course
by shifting gales on the Great South Sea;
homeward bound, but taking routes and ways
uncommon; so the will of Zeus would have it.
We served under Agamémnon, son of Atreus—
the whole world knows what city
he laid waste, what armies he destroyed.
It was our luck to come here; here we stand,
beholden for your help, or any gifts 280
you give—as custom is to honor strangers.
We would entreat you, great Sir, have a care

[4]The liquid part of separated milk, as distinguished from the lumpy curds.

for the gods' courtesy; Zeus will avenge
the unoffending guest.'[5]

He answered this
from his brute chest, unmoved:

'You are a ninny,
or else you come from the other end of nowhere,
telling me, mind the gods! We Kyklopês
care not a whistle for your thundering Zeus
or all the gods in bliss; we have more force by far.
I would not let you go for fear of Zeus— 290
you or your friends—unless I had a whim to.
Tell me, where was it, now, you left your ship—
around the point, or down the shore, I wonder?'

He thought he'd find out, but I saw through this,
and answered with a ready lie:

'My ship?
Poseidon Lord, who sets the earth a-tremble,
broke it up on the rocks at your land's end.
A wind from seaward served him, drove us there.
We are survivors, these good men and I.'

Neither reply nor pity came from him, 300
but in one stride he clutched at my companions
and caught two in his hands like squirming puppies
to beat their brains out, spattering the floor.
Then he dismembered them and made his meal,
gaping and crunching like a mountain lion—
everything: innards, flesh, and marrow bones.
We cried aloud, lifting our hands to Zeus,
powerless, looking on at this, appalled;
but Kyklops[6] went on filling up his belly
with manflesh and great gulps of whey, 310
then lay down like a mast among his sheep.
My heart beat high now at the chance of action,
and drawing the sharp sword from my hip I went
along his flank to stab him where the midriff
holds the liver. I had touched the spot
when sudden fear stayed me: if I killed him
we perished there as well, for we could never
move his ponderous doorway slab aside.
So we were left to groan and wait for morning.

[5] Zeus was the protector and guarantor of the laws of hospitality.
[6] Here used as a singular; his name, we learn later, is Polyphêmos.

When the young Dawn with finger tips of rose 320
lit up the world, the Kyklops built a fire
and milked his handsome ewes, all in due order,
putting the sucklings to the mothers. Then,
his chores being all dispatched, he caught
another brace of men to make his breakfast,
and whisked away his great door slab
to let his sheep go through—but he, behind,
reset the stone as one would cap a quiver.
There was a din of whistling as the Kyklops
rounded his flock to higher ground, then stillness. 330
And now I pondered how to hurt him worst,
if but Athena granted what I prayed for.
Here are the means I thought would serve my turn:

a club, or staff, lay there along the fold—
an olive tree, felled green and left to season
for Kyklops' hand. And it was like a mast
a lugger of twenty oars, broad in the beam—
a deep-sea-going craft—might carry:
so long, so big around, it seemed. Now I
chopped out a six foot section of this pole 340
and set it down before my men, who scraped it;
and when they had it smooth, I hewed again
to make a stake with pointed end. I held this
in the fire's heart and turned it, toughening it,
then hid it, well back in the cavern, under
one of the dung piles in profusion there.
Now came the time to toss for it: who ventured
along with me? whose hand could bear to thrust
and grind that spike in Kyklops' eye, when mild
sleep had mastered him? As luck would have it, 350
the men I would have chosen won the toss—
four strong men, and I made five as captain.

At evening came the shepherd with his flock,
his woolly flock. The rams as well, this time,
entered the cave: by some sheep-herding whim—
or a god's bidding—none were left outside.
He hefted his great boulder into place
and sat him down to milk the bleating ewes
in proper order, put the lambs to suck,
and swiftly ran through all his evening chores. 360
Then he caught two more men and feasted on them.
My moment was at hand, and I went forward
holding an ivy bowl of my dark drink,
looking up, saying:

'Kyklops, try some wine.
Here's liquor to wash down your scraps of men.
Taste it, and see the kind of drink we carried

under our planks. I meant it for an offering
if you would help us home. But you are mad,
unbearable, a bloody monster! After this,
will any other traveller come to see you?' 370

He seized and drained the bowl, and it went down
so fiery and smooth he called for more:

'Give me another, thank you kindly. Tell me,
how are you called? I'll make a gift will please you.
Even Kyklopês know the wine-grapes grow
out of grassland and loam in heaven's rain,
but here's a bit of nectar and ambrosia!'

Three bowls I brought him, and he poured them down.
I saw the fuddle and flush come over him,
then I sang out in cordial tones:

'Kyklops, 380
you ask my honorable name? Remember
the gift you promised me, and I shall tell you.
My name is Nohbdy: mother, father, and friends,
everyone calls me Nohbdy.'

And he said:

'Nohbdy's my meat, then, after I eat his friends.
Others come first. There's a noble gift, now.'

Even as he spoke, he reeled and tumbled backward,
his great head lolling to one side; and sleep
took him like any creature. Drunk, hiccuping,
he dribbled streams of liquor and bits of men. 390

Now, by the gods, I drove my big hand spike
deep in the embers, charring it again,
and cheered my men along with battle talk
to keep their courage up: no quitting now.
The pike of olive, green though it had been,
reddened and glowed as if about to catch.
I drew it from the coals and my four fellows
gave me a hand, lugging it near the Kyklops
as more than natural force nerved them; straight
forward they sprinted, lifted it, and rammed it 400
deep in his crater eye, and I leaned on it
turning it as a shipwright turns a drill
in planking, having men below to swing
the two-handled strap that spins it in the groove.
So with our brand we bored that great eye socket
while blood ran out around the red hot bar.
Eyelid and lash were seared; the pierced ball
hissed broiling, and the roots popped.

In a smithy
one sees a white-hot axehead or an adze
plunged and wrung in a cold tub, screeching steam— 410
the way they make soft iron hale and hard—:
just so that eyeball hissed around the spike.
The Kyklops bellowed and the rock roared round him,
and we fell back in fear. Clawing his face
he tugged the bloody spike out of his eye,
threw it away, and his wild hands went groping;
then he set up a howl for Kyklopês
who lived in caves on windy peaks nearby.
Some heard him; and they came by divers ways
to clump around outside and call:

'What ails you, 420
Polyphêmos? Why do you cry so sore
in the starry night? You will not let us sleep.
Sure no man's driving off your flock? No man
has tricked you, ruined you?'

Out of the cave
the mammoth Polyphêmos roared in answer:

'Nohbdy, Nohbdy's tricked me, Nohbdy's ruined me!'

To this rough shout they made a sage reply:

'Ah well, if nobody has played you foul
there in your lonely bed, we are no use in pain
given by great Zeus. Let it be your father, 430
Poseidon Lord, to whom you pray.'

So saying
they trailed away. And I was filled with laughter
to see how like a charm the name deceived them.
Now Kyklops, wheezing as the pain came on him,
fumbled to wrench away the great doorstone
and squatted in the breach with arms thrown wide
for any silly beast or man who bolted—
hoping somehow I might be such a fool.
But I kept thinking how to win the game:
death sat there huge; how could we slip away? 440
I drew on all my wits, and ran through tactics,
reasoning as a man will for dear life,
until a trick came—and it pleased me well.
The Kyklops' rams were handsome, fat, with heavy
fleeces, a dark violet.

Three abreast
I tied them silently together, twining
cords of willow from the ogre's bed;
then slung a man under each middle one

to ride there safely, shielded left and right.
So three sheep could convey each man. I took 450
the woolliest ram, the choicest of the flock,
and hung myself under his kinky belly,
pulled up tight, with fingers twisted deep
in sheepskin ringlets for an iron grip.
So, breathing hard, we waited until morning.

When Dawn spread out her finger tips of rose
the rams began to stir, moving for pasture,
and peals of bleating echoed round the pens
where dams with udders full called for a milking.
Blinded, and sick with pain from his head wound, 460
the master stroked each ram, then let it pass,
but my men riding on the pectoral fleece
the giant's blind hands blundering never found.
Last of them all my ram, the leader, came,
weighted by wool and me with my meditations.
The Kyklops patted him, and then he said:

'Sweet cousin ram, why lag behind the rest
in the night cave? You never linger so,
but graze before them all, and go afar
to crop sweet grass, and take your stately way 470
leading along the streams, until at evening
you run to be the first one in the fold.
Why, now, so far behind? Can you be grieving
over your Master's eye? That carrion rogue
and his accurst companions burnt it out
when he had conquered all my wits with wine.
Nohbdy will not get out alive, I swear.
Oh, had you brain and voice to tell
where he may be now, dodging all my fury!
Bashed by this hand and bashed on this rock wall 480
his brains would strew the floor, and I should have
rest from the outrage Nohbdy worked upon me.'

He sent us into the open, then. Close by,
I dropped and rolled clear of the ram's belly,
going this way and that to untie the men.
With many glances back, we rounded up
his fat, stiff-legged sheep to take aboard,
and drove them down to where the good ship lay.
We saw, as we came near, our fellows' faces
shining; then we saw them turn to grief 490
tallying those who had not fled from death.
I hushed them, jerking head and eyebrows up,
and in a low voice told them: 'Load this herd;
move fast, and put the ship's head toward the breakers.'
They all pitched in at loading, then embarked

and struck their oars into the sea. Far out,
as far off shore as shouted words would carry,
I sent a few back to the adversary:

'O Kyklops! Would you feast on my companions?
Puny, am I, in a Caveman's hands? 500
How do you like the beating that we gave you,
you damned cannibal? Eater of guests
under your roof! Zeus and the gods have paid you!'

The blind thing in his doubled fury broke
a hilltop in his hands and heaved it after us.
Ahead of our black prow it struck and sank
whelmed in a spuming geyser, a giant wave
that washed the ship stern foremost back to shore.
I got the longest boathook out and stood
fending us off, with furious nods to all 510
to put their backs into a racing stroke—
row, row, or perish. So the long oars bent
kicking the foam sternward, making head
until we drew away, and twice as far.
Now when I cupped my hands I heard the crew
in low voices protesting:

'Godsake, Captain!
Why bait the beast again? Let him alone!'

'That tidal wave he made on the first throw
all but beached us.'

'All but stove us in!'

'Give him our bearing with your trumpeting, 520
he'll get the range and lob a boulder.'

'Aye
He'll smash our timbers and our heads together!'

I would not heed them in my glorying spirit,
but let my anger flare and yelled:

'Kyklops,
if ever mortal man inquire
how you were put to shame and blinded, tell him
Odysseus, raider of cities, took your eye:
Laërtês' son, whose home's on Ithaka!'

At this he gave a mighty sob and rumbled:

'Now comes the weird[7] upon me, spoken of old. 530
A wizard, grand and wondrous, lived here—Télemos,

[7] Inescapable destiny.

a son of Eurymos; great length of days
he had in wizardry among the Kyklopês,
and these things he foretold for time to come:
my great eye lost, and at Odysseus' hands.
Always I had in mind some giant, armed
in giant force, would come against me here.
But this, but you—small, pitiful and twiggy—
you put me down with wine, you blinded me.
Come back, Odysseus, and I'll treat you well, 540
praying the god of earthquake to befriend you—
his son I am, for he by his avowal
fathered me, and, if he will, he may
heal me of this black wound—he and no other
of all the happy gods or mortal men.'

Few words I shouted in reply to him:

'If I could take your life I would and take
your time away, and hurl you down to hell!
The god of earthquake could not heal you there!'

At this he stretched his hands out in his darkness 550
toward the sky of stars, and prayed Poseidon:

'O hear me, lord, blue girdler of the islands,
if I am thine indeed, and thou art father:
grant that Odysseus, raider of cities, never
see his home: Laërtês' son, I mean,
who kept his hall on Ithaka. Should destiny
intend that he shall see his roof again
among his family in his father land,
far be that day, and dark the years between.
Let him lose all companions, and return 560
under strange sail to bitter days at home.'

In these words he prayed, and the god heard him.
Now he laid hands upon a bigger stone
and wheeled around, titanic for the cast,
to let it fly in the black-prowed vessel's track.
But it fell short, just aft the steering oar,
and whelming seas rose giant above the stone
to bear us onward toward the island.
There
as we ran in we saw the squadron waiting,
the trim ships drawn up side by side, and all 570
our troubled friends who waited, looking seaward.
We beached her, grinding keel in the soft sand,
and waded in, ourselves, on the sandy beach.
Then we unloaded all the Kyklops' flock
to make division, share and share alike,
only my fighters voted that my ram,

the prize of all, should go to me. I slew him
by the sea side and burnt his long thighbones
to Zeus beyond the stormcloud, Kronos'[8] son,
who rules the world. But Zeus disdained my offering; 580
destruction for my ships he had in store
and death for those who sailed them, my companions.
Now all day long until the sun went down
we made our feast on mutton and sweet wine,
till after sunset in the gathering dark
we went to sleep above the wash of ripples.

When the young Dawn with finger tips of rose
touched the world, I roused the men, gave orders
to man the ships, cast off the mooring lines;
and filing in to sit beside the rowlocks 590
oarsmen in line dipped oars in the grey sea.
So we moved out, sad in the vast offing,
having our precious lives, but not our friends.

BOOK TEN: THE GRACE OF THE WITCH

We made our landfall on Aiolia Island,
domain of Aiolos[1] Hippotadês,
the wind king, dear to the gods who never die—
an isle adrift upon the sea, ringed round
with brazen ramparts on a sheer cliffside.
Twelve children had old Aiolos at home—
six daughters and six lusty sons—and he
gave girls to boys to be their gentle brides;
now those lords, in their parents' company,
sup every day in hall—a royal feast 10
with fumes of sacrifice and winds that pipe
'round hollow courts; and all the night they sleep
on beds of filigree beside their ladies.
Here we put in, lodged in the town and palace,
while Aiolos played host to me. He kept me
one full month to hear the tale of Troy,
the ships and the return of the Akhaians,
all which I told him point by point in order.
When in return I asked his leave to sail
and asked provisioning, he stinted nothing, 20
adding a bull's hide sewn from neck to tail
into a mighty bag, bottling storm winds;

[8] Equivalent of the Roman Saturn. Chief of the gods in the divine generation preceding Zeus and the Olympian dynasty; dethroned by his son Zeus.

[1] God of the winds, son of Hippotês. Commonly spelled *Aeolus*. A tradition locates his island off the north coast of Sicily.

for Zeus had long ago made Aiolos
warden of winds, to rouse or calm at will.
He wedged this bag under my afterdeck,
lashing the neck with shining silver wire
so not a breath go through; only the west wind
he lofted for me in a quartering breeze
to take my squadron spanking home.
No luck:
the fair wind failed us when our prudence failed. 30

Nine days and nights we sailed without event,
till on the tenth we raised our land. We neared it,
and saw men building fires along the shore;
but now, being weary to the bone, I fell
into deep slumber; I had worked the sheet
nine days alone, and given it to no one,
wishing to spill no wind on the homeward run.
But while I slept, the crew began to parley:
silver and gold, they guessed, were in that bag
bestowed on me by Aiolos' great heart; 40
and one would glance at his benchmate and say:
'It never fails. He's welcome everywhere:
hail to the captain when he goes ashore!
He brought along so many presents, plunder
out of Troy, that's it. How about ourselves—
his shipmates all the way? Nigh home we are
with empty hands. And who has gifts from Aiolos?
He has. I say we ought to crack that bag,
there's gold and silver, plenty, in that bag!'

Temptation had its way with my companions, 50
and they untied the bag.
Then every wind
roared into hurricane; the ships went pitching
west with many cries; our land was lost.
Roused up, despairing in that gloom, I thought:
'Should I go overside for a quick finish
or clench my teeth and stay among the living?'
Down in the bilge I lay, pulling my sea cloak
over my head, while the rough gale blew the ships
and rueful crews clear back to Aiolia.

We put ashore for water; then all hands 60
gathered alongside for a mid-day meal.
When we had taken bread and drink, I picked
one soldier, and one herald, to go with me
and called again on Aiolos. I found him
at meat with his young princes and his lady,
but there beside the pillars, in his portico,

we sat down silent at the open door.
The sight amazed them, and they all exclaimed:

'Why back again, Odysseus?'

'What sea fiend
rose in your path?'

'Did we not launch you well 70
for home, or for whatever land you chose?'

Out of my melancholy I replied:

'Mischief aboard and nodding at the tiller—
a damned drowse—did for me. Make good my loss,
dear friends! You have the power!'

Gently I pleaded,
but they turned cold and still. Said Father Aiolos:

'Take yourself out of this island, creeping thing—
no law, no wisdom, lays it on me now
to help a man the blessed gods detest—
out! Your voyage here was cursed by heaven!' 80

He drove me from the place, groan as I would,
and comfortless we went again to sea,
days of it, till the men flagged at the oars—
no breeze, no help in sight, by our own folly—
six indistinguishable nights and days
before we raised the Laistrygonian height
and far stronghold of Lamos.[2] In that land
the daybreak follows dusk, and so the shepherd
homing calls to the cowherd setting out;
and he who never slept could earn two wages, 90
tending oxen, pasturing silvery flocks,
where the low night path of the sun is near
the sun's path by day. Here, then, we found
a curious bay with mountain walls of stone
to left and right, and reaching far inland,—
a narrow entrance opening from the sea
where cliffs converged as though to touch and close.
All of my squadron sheltered here, inside
the cavern of this bay.

Black prow by prow
those hulls were made fast in a limpid calm 100
without a ripple, stillness all around them.

[2] Son of Poseidon and king of the Laistrygonians. Traditions place their land in southwest Italy or in Sicily. The following lines describe the almost continuous daylight of summer in the far north, but it would have been impossible for Odysseus and his men to reach such latitudes. Traditionally, the shepherd grazes his flock during the night.

My own black ship I chose to moor alone
on the sea side, using a rock for bollard;
and climbed a rocky point to get my bearings.
No farms, no cultivated land appeared,
but puffs of smoke rose in the wilderness;
so I sent out two picked men and a herald
to learn what race of men this land sustained.

My party found a track—a wagon road
for bringing wood down from the heights to town; 110
and near the settlement they met a daughter
of Antiphatês the Laistrygon—a stalwart
young girl taking her pail to Artakía,
the fountain where these people go for water.
My fellows hailed her, put their questions to her:
who might the king be? ruling over whom?
She waved her hand, showing her father's lodge,
so they approached it. In its gloom they saw
a woman like a mountain crag, the queen—
and loathed the sight of her. But she, for greeting, 120
called from the meeting ground her lord and master,
Antiphatês, who came to drink their blood.
He seized one man and tore him on the spot,
making a meal of him; the other two
leaped out of doors and ran to join the ships.
Behind, he raised the whole tribe howling, countless
Laistrygonês—and more than men they seemed,
gigantic when they gathered on the sky line
to shoot great boulders down from slings; and hell's own
crashing rose, and crying from the ships, 130
as planks and men were smashed to bits—poor gobbets[3]
the wildmen speared like fish and bore away.
But long before it ended in the anchorage—
havoc and slaughter—I had drawn my sword
and cut my own ship's cable. 'Men,' I shouted,
'man the oars and pull till your hearts break
if you would put this butchery behind!'
The oarsmen rent the sea in mortal fear
and my ship spurted out of range, far out
from that deep canyon where the rest were lost. 140
So we fared onward, and death fell behind,
and we took breath to grieve for our companions.

Our next landfall was on Aiaia,[4] island
of Kirkê, dire beauty and divine,

[3] Lumps of raw meat.

[4] Later legend placed this island, home of Kirkê (Circe), near the west coast of Italy, near Rome. Aiêtês was the king of Colchis who lost the magical Golden Fleece to Iêson (Jason) and the Argonauts; see the headnote to Euripides' *Medea.* Medea, Aiêtês' daughter, was also a sorceress; witchcraft ran in the family.

sister of baleful Aiêtês, like him
fathered by Hêlios the light of mortals
on Persê, child of the Ocean stream.
We came
washed in our silent ship upon her shore,
and found a cove, a haven for the ship—
some god, invisible, conned us in. We landed, 150
to lie down in that place two days and nights,
worn out and sick at heart, tasting our grief.
But when Dawn set another day a-shining
I took my spear and broadsword, and I climbed
a rocky point above the ship, for sight
or sound of human labor. Gazing out
from that high place over a land of thicket,
oaks and wide watercourses, I could see
a smoke wisp from the woodland hall of Kirkê.
So I took counsel with myself: should I 160
go inland scouting out that reddish smoke?
No: better not, I thought, but first return
to waterside and ship, and give the men
breakfast before I sent them to explore.
Now as I went down quite alone, and came
a bowshot from the ship, some god's compassion
set a big buck in motion to cross my path—
a stag with noble antlers, pacing down
from pasture in the woods to the riverside,
as long thirst and the power of sun constrained him. 170
He started from the bush and wheeled: I hit him
square in the spine midway along his back
and the bronze point broke through it. In the dust
he fell and whinnied as life bled away.
I set one foot against him, pulling hard
to wrench my weapon from the wound, then left it,
butt-end on the ground. I plucked some withies
and twined a double strand into a rope—
enough to tie the hocks of my huge trophy;
then pickaback I lugged him to the ship, 180
leaning on my long spearshaft; I could not
haul that mighty carcass on one shoulder.
Beside the ship I let him drop, and spoke
gently and low to each man standing near:

'Come, friends, though hard beset, we'll not go down
into the House of Death before our time.
As long as food and drink remain aboard
let us rely on it, not die of hunger.'

At this those faces, cloaked in desolation
upon the waste sea beach, were bared; 190
their eyes turned toward me and the mighty trophy,

lighting, foreseeing pleasure, one by one.
So hands were washed to take what heaven sent us.
And all that day until the sun went down
we had our fill of venison and wine,
till after sunset in the gathering dusk
we slept at last above the line of breakers.
When the young Dawn with finger tips of rose
made heaven bright, I called them round and said:

'Shipmates, companions in disastrous time, 200
O my dear friends, where Dawn lies, and the West,
and where the great Sun, light of men, may go
under the earth by night, and where he rises—
of these things we know nothing. Do we know
any least thing to serve us now? I wonder.
All that I saw when I went up the rock
was one more island in the boundless main,
a low landscape, covered with woods and scrub,
and puffs of smoke ascending in mid-forest.'

They were all silent, but their hearts contracted, 210
remembering Antiphatês the Laistrygon
and that prodigious cannibal, the Kyklops.
They cried out, and the salt tears wet their eyes.
But seeing our time for action lost in weeping,
I mustered those Akhaians under arms,
counting them off in two platoons, myself
and my godlike Eurýlokhos commanding.
We shook lots in a soldier's dogskin cap
and his came bounding out—valiant Eurýlokhos!—
So off he went, with twenty-two companions 220
weeping, as mine wept, too, who stayed behind.

In the wild wood they found an open glade,
around a smooth stone house—the hall of Kirkê—
and wolves and mountain lions lay there, mild
in her soft spell, fed on her drug of evil.
None would attack—oh, it was strange, I tell you—
but switching their long tails they faced our men
like hounds, who look up when their master comes
with tidbits for them—as he will—from table.
Humbly those wolves and lions with mighty paws 230
fawned on our men—who met their yellow eyes
and feared them.

In the entrance way they stayed
to listen there: inside her quiet house
they heard the goddess Kirkê.

Low she sang
in her beguiling voice, while on her loom
she wove ambrosial fabric sheer and bright,

by that craft known to the goddesses of heaven.
No one would speak, until Polítês—most
faithful and likable of my officers, said:

'Dear friends, no need for stealth: here's a young weaver 240
singing a pretty song to set the air
a-tingle on these lawns and paven courts.
Goddess she is, or lady. Shall we greet her?'

So reassured, they all cried out together,
and she came swiftly to the shining doors
to call them in. All but Eurýlokhos—
who feared a snare—the innocents went after her.
On thrones she seated them, and lounging chairs,
while she prepared a meal of cheese and barley
and amber honey mixed with Pramnian wine, 250
adding her own vile pinch, to make them lose
desire or thought of our dear father land.
Scarce had they drunk when she flew after them
with her long stick and shut them in a pigsty—
bodies, voices, heads, and bristles, all
swinish now, though minds were still unchanged.
So, squealing, in they went. And Kirkê tossed them
acorns, mast, and cornel berries—fodder
for hogs who rut and slumber on the earth.

Down to the ship Eurýlokhos came running. 260
to cry alarm, foul magic doomed his men!
But working with dry lips to speak a word
he could not, being so shaken; blinding tears
welled in his eyes; foreboding filled his heart.
When we were frantic questioning him, at last
we heard the tale: our friends were gone. Said he:

"We went up through the oak scrub where you sent us,
Odysseus, glory of commanders,
until we found a palace in a glade,
a marble house on open ground, and someone 270
singing before her loom a chill, sweet song—
goddess or girl, we could not tell. They hailed her,
and then she stepped through shining doors and said,
"Come, come in!" Like sheep they followed her,
but I saw cruel deceit, and stayed behind.
Then all our fellows vanished. Not a sound,
and nothing stirred, although I watched for hours.'

When I heard this I slung my silver-hilted
broadsword on, and shouldered my long bow,
and said, "Come, take me back the way you came.' 280
But he put both his hands around my knees
in desperate woe, and said in supplication:

"Not back there, O my lord! Oh, leave me here!
You, even you, cannot return, I know it,
I know you cannot bring away our shipmates;
better make sail with these men, quickly too,
and save ourselves from horror while we may.'

But I replied:

'By heaven, Eurýlokhos,
rest here then; take food and wine;
stay in the black hull's shelter. Let me go, 290
as I see nothing for it but to go.'

I turned and left him, left the shore and ship,
and went up through the woodland hushed and shady
to find the subtle witch in her long hall.
But Hermês met me, with his golden wand,
barring the way—a boy whose lip was downy
in the first bloom of manhood, so he seemed.
He took my hand and spoke as though he knew me:

'Why take the inland path alone,
poor seafarer, by hill and dale 300
upon this island all unknown?
Your friends are locked in Kirkê's pale;[5]
all are become like swine to see;
and if you go to set them free
you go to stay, and never more make sail
for your old home upon Thaki.[6]

But I can tell you what to do
to come unchanged from Kirkê's power
and disenthrall your fighting crew:
take with you to her bower 310
as amulet, this plant I know—
it will defeat her horrid show,
so pure and potent is the flower;
no mortal herb was ever so.

Your cup with numbing drops of night
and evil, stilled of all remorse,
she will infuse to charm your sight;
but this great herb with holy force
will keep your mind and senses clear:
when she turns cruel, coming near 320
with her long stick to whip you out of doors,
then let your cutting blade appear,

[5] An enclosed area. [6] Ithaka.

Let instant death upon it shine,
and she will cower and yield her bed—
a pleasure you must not decline,
so may her lust and fear bestead
you and your friends, and break her spell;
but make her swear by heaven and hell
no witches' tricks, or else, your harness shed,
you'll be unmanned by her as well.' 330

He bent down glittering for the magic plant
and pulled it up, black root and milky flower—
a *molü*[7] in the language of the gods—
fatigue and pain for mortals to uproot;
but gods do this, and everything, with ease.

Then toward Olympos through the island trees
Hermês departed, and I sought out Kirkê,
my heart high with excitement, beating hard.
Before her mansion in the porch I stood
to call her, all being still. Quick as a cat 340
she opened her bright doors and sighed a welcome;
then I strode after her with heavy heart
down the long hall, and took the chair she gave me,
silver-studded, intricately carved,
made with a low footrest. The lady Kirkê
mixed me a golden cup of honeyed wine,
adding in mischief her unholy drug.
I drank, and the drink failed. But she came forward
aiming a stroke with her long stick, and whispered:

'Down in the sty and snore among the rest!' 350

Without a word, I drew my sharpened sword
and in one bound held it against her throat.
She cried out, then slid under to take my knees,
catching her breath to say, in her distress:

'What champion, of what country, can you be?
Where are your kinsmen and your city?
Are you not sluggish with my wine? Ah, wonder!
Never a mortal man that drank this cup
but when it passed his lips he had succumbed.
Hale must your heart be and your tempered will. 360
Odysseus then you are, O great contender,
of whom the glittering god with golden wand
spoke to me ever, and foretold
the black swift ship would carry you from Troy.
Put up your weapon in the sheath. We two

[7] Usually spelled *moly.*

shall mingle and make love upon our bed.
So mutual trust may come of play and love.'

To this I said:

'Kirkê, am I a boy,
that you should make me soft and doting now?
Here in this house you turned my men to swine; 370
now it is I myself you hold, enticing
into your chamber, to your dangerous bed,
to take my manhood when you have me stripped.
I mount no bed of love with you upon it.
Or swear me first a great oath, if I do,
you'll work no more enchantment to my harm.'

She swore at once, outright, as I demanded,
and after she had sworn, and bound herself,
I entered Kirkê's flawless bed of love.

Presently in the hall her maids were busy, 380
the nymphs who waited upon Kirkê: four,
whose cradles were in fountains, under boughs,
or in the glassy seaward-gliding streams.
One came with richly colored rugs to throw
on seat and chairback, over linen covers;
a second pulled the tables out, all silver,
and loaded them with baskets all of gold;
a third mixed wine as tawny-mild as honey
in a bright bowl, and set out golden cups.
The fourth came bearing water, and lit a blaze 390
under a cauldron. By and by it bubbled,
and when the dazzling brazen vessel seethed
she filled a bathtub to my waist, and bathed me,
pouring a soothing blend on head and shoulders,
warming the soreness of my joints away.
When she had done, and smoothed me with sweet oil,
she put a tunic and a cloak around me
and took me to a silver-studded chair
with footrest, all elaborately carven.
Now came a maid to tip a golden jug 400
of water into a silver finger bowl,
and draw a polished table to my side.
The larder mistress brought her tray of loaves
with many savory slices, and she gave
the best, to tempt me. But no pleasure came;
I huddled with my mind elsewhere, oppressed.

Kirkê regarded me, as there I sat
disconsolate, and never touched a crust.
Then she stood over me and chided me:

'Why sit at table mute, Odysseus? 410
Are you mistrustful of my bread and drink?
Can it be treachery that you fear again,
after the gods' great oath I swore for you?'

I turned to her at once, and said:

'Kirkê,
where is the captain who could bear to touch
this banquet, in my place? A decent man
would see his company before him first.
Put heart in me to eat and drink—you may,
by freeing my companions. I must see them.'

But Kirkê had already turned away. 420
Her long staff in her hand, she left the hall
and opened up the sty. I saw her enter,
driving those men turned swine to stand before me.
She stroked them, each in turn, with some new chrism;[8]
and then, behold! their bristles fell away,
the course pelt grown upon them by her drug
melted away, and they were men again,
younger, more handsome, taller than before.
Their eyes upon me, each one took my hands,
and wild regret and longing pierced them through, 430
so the room rang with sobs, and even Kirkê
pitied that transformation. Exquisite
the goddess looked as she stood near me, saying:

'Son of Laërtês and the gods of old,
Odysseus, master mariner and soldier,
go to the sea beach and sea-breasting ship;
drag it ashore, full length upon the land;
stow gear and stores in rock-holes under cover;
return; be quick; bring all your dear companions.'

Now, being a man, I could not help consenting. 440
So I went down to the sea beach and the ship,
where I found all my other men on board,
weeping, in despair along the benches.
Sometimes in farmyards when the cows return
well fed from pasture to the barn, one sees
the pens give way before the calves in tumult,
breaking through to cluster about their mothers,
bumping together, bawling. Just that way
my crew poured round me when they saw me come—
their faces wet with tears as if they saw 450
their homeland, and the crags of Ithaka,

[8] An oil, usually having sacred or supernatural properties.

even the very town where they were born.
And weeping still they all cried out in greeting:

'Prince, what joy this is, your safe return!
Now Ithaka seems here, and we in Ithaka!
But tell us now, what death befell our friends?'

And, speaking gently, I replied:

'First we must get the ship high on the shingle,
and stow our gear and stores in clefts of rock
for cover. Then come follow me, to see 460
your shipmates in the magic house of Kirkê
eating and drinking, endlessly regaled.'

They turned back, as commanded, to this work;
only one lagged, and tried to hold the others:
Eurýlokhos it was, who blurted out:

'Where now, poor remnants? is it devil's work
you long for? Will you go to Kirkê's hall?
Swine, wolves, and lions she will make us all,
beasts of her courtyard, bound by her enchantment.
Remember those the Kyklops held, remember 470
shipmates who made that visit with Odysseus!
The daring man! They died for his foolishness!'

When I heard this I had a mind to draw
the blade that swung against my side and chop him,
bowling his head upon the ground—kinsman
or no kinsman, close to me though he was.
But others came between, saying, to stop me,

'Prince, we can leave him, if you say the word;
let him stay here on guard. As for ourselves,
show us the way to Kirkê's magic hall.' 480

So all turned inland, leaving shore and ship,
and Eurýlokhos—he, too, came on behind,
fearing the rough edge of my tongue. Meanwhile
at Kirkê's hands the rest were gently bathed,
anointed with sweet oil, and dressed afresh
in tunics and new cloaks with fleecy linings.
We found them all at supper when we came.
But greeting their old friends once more, the crew
could not hold back their tears; and now again
the rooms rang with sobs. Then Kirkê, loveliest 490
of all immortals, came to counsel me:

'Son of Laërtês and the gods of old,
Odysseus, master mariner and soldier,

enough of weeping fits. I know—I, too—
what you endured upon the inhuman sea,
what odds you met on land from hostile men.
Remain with me, and share my meat and wine;
restore behind your ribs those gallant hearts
that served you in the old days, when you sailed
from stony Ithaka. Now parched and spent, 500
your cruel wandering is all you think of,
never of joy, after so many blows.'

As we were men we could not help consenting.
So day by day we lingered, feasting long
on roasts and wine, until a year grew fat.
But when the passing months and wheeling seasons
brought the long summery days, the pause of summer,
my shipmates one day summoned me and said:

'Captain, shake off this trance, and think of home—
if home indeed awaits us,
if we shall ever see 510
your own well-timbered hall on Ithaka.'

They made me feel a pang, and I agreed.
That day, and all day long, from dawn to sundown,
we feasted on roast meat and ruddy wine,
and after sunset when the dusk came on
my men slept in the shadowy hall, but I
went through the dark to Kirkê's flawless bed
and took the goddess' knees in supplication,
urging, as she bent to hear:
'O Kirkê,
now you must keep your promise; it is time. 520
Help me make sail for home. Day after day
my longing quickens, and my company
give me no peace, but wear my heart away
pleading when you are not at hand to hear.'

The loveliest of goddesses replied:

'Son of Laërtês and the gods of old,
Odysseus, master mariner and soldier,
you shall not stay here longer against your will;
but home you may not go
unless you take a strange way round and come 530
to the cold homes of Death and pale Perséphonê.[9]
You shall hear prophecy from the rapt shade

[9] *Death* refers to Hades, ruler of the land of the dead. *Perséphonê* was his consort.

of blind Teirêsias[10] of Thebes, forever
charged with reason even among the dead;
to him alone, of all the flitting ghosts,
Perséphonê has given a mind undarkened.'

At this I felt a weight like stone within me,
and, moaning, pressed my length against the bed,
with no desire to see the daylight more.
But when I had wept and tossed and had my fill 540
of this despair, at last I answered her:

'Kirkê, who pilots me upon this journey?
No man has ever sailed to the land of Death.'

That loveliest of goddesses replied:

'Son of Laërtês and the gods of old,
Odysseus, master of land ways and sea ways,
feel no dismay because you lack a pilot;
only set up your mast and haul your canvas
to the fresh blowing North; sit down and steer,
and hold that wind, even to the bourne of Ocean, 550
Perséphonê's deserted strand and grove,
dusky with poplars and the drooping willow.
Run through the tide-rip, bring your ship to shore,
land there, and find the crumbling homes of Death.
Here, toward the Sorrowing Water, run the streams
of Wailing, out of Styx, and quenchless Burning—
torrents[11] that join in thunder at the Rock.
Here then, great soldier, setting foot obey me:
dig a well shaft a forearm square; pour out
libations round it to the unnumbered dead: 560
sweet milk and honey, then sweet wine, and last
clear water, scattering handfulls of white barley.
Pray now, with all your heart, to the faint dead;
swear you will sacrifice your finest heifer,
at home in Ithaka, and burn for them
her tenderest parts in sacrifice; and vow
to the lord Teirêsias, apart from all,
a black lamb, handsomest of all your flock—
thus to appease the nations of the dead.
Then slash a black ewe's throat, and a black ram, 570
facing the gloom of Erebos;[12] but turn
your head away toward Ocean. You shall see, now

[10] A famous soothsayer who figures in many Greek myths and legends; see, for example, Sophocles' *Oedipus the King*.

[11] The rivers of Hades. The Sorrowing Water is Acheron; the river of Wailing is Cocytus; the Burning river is Phlegethon.

[12] Part of the realm of Hades; the equivalent of primitive darkness. Also spelled *Erebus*.

souls of the buried dead in shadowy hosts,
and now you must call out to your companions
to flay those sheep the bronze knife has cut down,
for offerings, burnt flesh to those below,
to sovereign Death and pale Perséphonê.
Meanwhile draw sword from hip, crouch down, ward off
the surging phantoms from the bloody pit
until you know the presence of Teirêsias. 580
He will come soon, great captain; be it he
who gives you course and distance for your sailing
homeward across the cold fish-breeding sea.'

As the goddess ended, Dawn came stitched in gold.
Now Kirkê dressed me in my shirt and cloak,
put on a gown of subtle tissue, silvery,
then wound a golden belt about her waist
and veiled her head in linen,
while I went through the hall to rouse my crew.
I bent above each one, and gently said: 590

'Wake from your sleep: no more sweet slumber. Come,
we sail: the Lady Kirkê so ordains it.'

They were soon up, and ready at that word;
but I was not to take my men unharmed
from this place, even from this. Among them all
the youngest was Elpênor—
no mainstay in a fight nor very clever—
and this one, having climbed on Kirkê's roof
to taste the cool night, fell asleep with wine.
Waked by our morning voices, and the tramp 600
of men below, he started up, but missed
his footing on the long steep backward ladder
and fell that height headlong. The blow smashed
the nape cord, and his ghost fled to the dark.
But I was outside, walking with the rest,
saying:

'Homeward you think we must be sailing
to our own land; no, elsewhere is the voyage
Kirkê has laid upon me. We must go
to the cold homes of Death and pale Perséphonê
to hear Teirêsias tell of time to come.' 610

They felt so stricken, upon hearing this,
they sat down wailing loud, and tore their hair.
But nothing came of giving way to grief.
Down to the shore and ship at last we went,
bowed with anguish, cheeks all wet with tears,
to find that Kirkê had been there before us

and tied nearby a black ewe and a ram:
she had gone by like air.
For who could see the passage of a goddess
unless she wished his mortal eyes aware? 620

BOOK ELEVEN: A GATHERING OF SHADES

We bore down on the ship at the sea's edge
and launched her on the salt immortal sea,
stepping our mast and spar in the black ship;
embarked the ram and ewe and went aboard
in tears, with bitter and sore dread upon us.
But now a breeze came up for us astern—
a canvas-bellying landbreeze, hale shipmate
sent by the singing nymph with sun-bright hair;
so we made fast the braces, took our thwarts,
and let the wind and steersman work the ship 10
with full sail spread all day above our coursing,
till the sun dipped, and all the ways grew dark
upon the fathomless unresting sea.

By night
our ship ran onward toward the Ocean's[1] bourne,
the realm and region of the Men of Winter,
hidden in mist and cloud. Never the flaming
eye of Hêlios lights on those men
at morning, when he climbs the sky of stars,
nor in descending earthward out of heaven;
ruinous night being rove[2] over those wretches. 20
We made the land, put ram and ewe ashore,
and took our way along the Ocean stream
to find the place foretold for us by Kirkê.
There Perimêdês and Eurýlokhos
pinioned the sacred beasts. With my drawn blade
I spaded up the votive pit, and poured
libations round it to the unnumbered dead:
sweet milk and honey, then sweet wine, and last
clear water; and I scattered barley down.
Then I addressed the blurred and breathless dead, 30
vowing to slaughter my best heifer for them
before she calved, at home in Ithaka,
and burn the choice bits on the altar fire;
as for Teirêsias, I swore to sacrifice
a black lamb, handsomest of all our flock.

[1] The great river believed to encompass the entire (flat) world. In the present passage, Homer locates Hades in the north and not, as is more usual, beneath the surface of the earth.
[2] Fastened; a nautical term. Hêlios is the sun god.

Thus to assuage the nations of the dead
I pledged these rites, then slashed the lamb and ewe,
letting their black blood stream into the wellpit.
Now the souls gathered, stirring out of Erebos,
brides and young men, and men grown old in pain, 40
and tender girls whose hearts were new to grief;
many were there, too, torn by brazen lanceheads,
battle-slain, bearing still their bloody gear.
From every side they came and sought the pit
with rustling cries; and I grew sick with fear.
But presently I gave command to my officers
to flay those sheep the bronze cut down, and make
burnt offerings of flesh to the gods below—
to sovereign Death, to pale Perséphonê.
Meanwhile I crouched with my drawn sword to keep 50
the surging phantoms from the bloody pit
till I should know the presence of Teirêsias.

One shade came first—Elpênor, of our company,
who lay unburied still on the wide earth
as we had left him—dead in Kirkê's hall,
untouched, unmourned, when other cares compelled us.
Now when I saw him there I wept for pity
and called out to him:

'How is this, Elpênor,
how could you journey to the western gloom
swifter afoot than I in the black lugger?' 60

He sighed, and answered:

'Son of great Laërtês,
Odysseus, master mariner and soldier,
bad luck shadowed me, and no kindly power;
ignoble death I drank with so much wine.
I slept on Kirkê's roof, then could not see
the long steep backward ladder, coming down,
and fell that height. My neck bone, buckled under,
snapped, and my spirit found this well of dark.
Now hear the grace I pray for, in the name
of those back in the world, not here—your wife 70
and father, he who gave you bread in childhood,
and your own child, your only son, Telémakhos,
long ago left at home.

When you make sail
and put these lodgings of dim Death behind,
you will moor ship, I know, upon Aiaia Island;
there, O my lord, remember me, I pray,
do not abandon me unwept, unburied,

to tempt the gods' wrath,[3] while you sail for home;
but fire my corpse, and all the gear I had,
and build a cairn for me above the breakers— 80
an unknown sailor's mark for men to come.
Heap up the mound there, and implant upon it
the oar I pulled in life with my companions.'

He ceased, and I replied:

'Unhappy spirit,
I promise you the barrow and the burial.'

So we conversed, and grimly, at a distance,
with my long sword between, guarding the blood,
while the faint image of the lad spoke on.

Now came the soul of Antikleía, dead,
my mother, daughter of Autólykos, 90
dead now, though living still when I took ship
for holy Troy. Seeing this ghost I grieved,
but held her off, through pang on pang of tears,
till I should know the presence of Teirêsias.
Soon from the dark that prince of Thebes came forward
bearing a golden staff; and he addressed me:

'Son of Laërtês and the gods of old,
Odysseus, master of land ways and sea ways,
why leave the blazing sun, O man of woe,
to see the cold dead and the joyless region? 100
Stand clear, put up your sword;
let me but taste of blood, I shall speak true.'

At this I stepped aside, and in the scabbard
let my long sword ring home to the pommel silver,
as he bent down to the sombre blood. Then spoke
the prince of those with gift of speech:

'Great captain,
a fair wind and the honey lights of home
are all you seek. But anguish lies ahead;
the god who thunders on the land prepares it,
not to be shaken from your track, implacable, 110
in rancor for the son whose eye you blinded.
One narrow strait may take you through his blows:
denial of yourself, restraint of shipmates.
When you make landfall on Thrinákia[4] first
and quit the violet sea, dark on the land

[3] The wrath of the gods would be provoked if a body on earth was left unburied and visible.

[4] Sicily. For the outcome of this prophetic warning about molesting the sun god's cattle, see Book XII.

you'll find the grazing herds of Hêlios
by whom all things are seen, all speech is known.
Avoid those kine, hold fast to your intent,
and hard seafaring brings you all to Ithaka.
But if you raid the beeves, I see destruction 120
for ship and crew. Though you survive alone,
bereft of all companions, lost for years,
under strange sail shall you come home, to find
your own house filled with trouble: insolent men
eating your livestock as they court your lady.
Aye, you shall make those men atone in blood!
But after you have dealt out death—in open
combat or by stealth—to all the suitors,
go overland on foot, and take an oar,
until one day you come where men have lived 130
with meat unsalted, never known the sea,
nor seen seagoing ships, with crimson bows
and oars that fledge light hulls for dipping flight.
The spot will soon be plain to you, and I
can tell you how: some passerby will say,
"What winnowing fan[5] is that upon your shoulder?"
Halt, and implant your smooth oar in the turf
and make fair sacrifice to Lord Poseidon:
a ram, a bull, a great buck boar; turn back,
and carry out pure hekatombs at home 140
to all wide heaven's lords, the undying gods,
to each in order. Then a seaborne death
soft as this hand of mist will come upon you
when you are wearied out with rich old age,
your country folk in blessed peace around you.
And all this shall be just as I foretell.'

When he had done, I said at once,

'Teirêsias,
my life runs on then as the gods have spun it.
But come, now, tell me this; make this thing clear:
I see my mother's ghost among the dead 150
sitting in silence near the blood. Not once
has she glanced this way toward her son, nor spoken.
Tell me, my lord,
may she in some way come to know my presence?'

To this he answered:

'I shall make it clear
in a few words and simply. Any dead man
whom you allow to enter where the blood is

[5]A tool used to separate grain from chaff.

will speak to you, and speak the truth; but those
deprived will grow remote again and fade.'

When he had prophesied, Teirêsias' shade 160
retired lordly to the halls of Death;
but I stood fast until my mother stirred,
moving to sip the black blood; then she knew me
and called out sorrowfully to me:

'Child,
how could you cross alive into this gloom
at the world's end?—No sight for living eyes;
great currents run between, desolate waters,
the Ocean first, where no man goes a journey
without ship's timber under him.

Say, now,
is it from Troy, still wandering, after years, 170
that you come here with ship and company?
Have you not gone at all to Ithaka?
Have you not seen your lady in your hall?'

She put these questions, and I answered her:

'Mother, I came here, driven to the land of death
in want of prophecy from Teirêsias' shade;
nor have I yet coasted Akhaia's hills
nor touched my own land, but have had hard roving
since first I joined Lord Agamémnon's host
by sea for Ilion, the wild horse country, 180
to fight the men of Troy.
But come now, tell me this, and tell me clearly,
what was the bane that pinned you down in Death?
Some ravaging long illness, or mild arrows
a-flying down one day from Artemis?[6]
Tell me of Father, tell me of the son
I left behind me; have they still my place,
my honors, or have other men assumed them?
Do they not say that I shall come no more?
And tell me of my wife: how runs her thought, 190
still with her child, still keeping our domains,
or bride again to the best of the Akhaians?'

To this my noble mother quickly answered:

'Still with her child indeed she is, poor heart,
still in your palace hall. Forlorn her nights
and days go by, her life used up in weeping.
But no man takes your honored place. Telémakhos
has care of all your garden plots and fields,

[6] As archer goddess, Artemis provided the gift of painless death. Among other things, she was protectress of the weak.

and holds the public honor of a magistrate,
feasting and being feasted. But your father 200
is country bound and comes to town no more.
He owns no bedding, rugs, or fleecy mantles,
but lies down, winter nights, among the slaves,
rolled in old cloaks for cover, near the embers.
Or when the heat comes at the end of summer,
the fallen leaves, all round his vineyard plot,
heaped into windrows,[7] make his lowly bed.
He lies now even so, with aching heart,
and longs for your return, while age comes on him.
So I, too, pined away, so doom befell me, 210
not that the keen-eyed huntress with her shafts
had marked me down and shot to kill me; not
that illness overtook me—no true illness
wasting the body to undo the spirit;
only my loneliness for you, Odysseus,
for your kind heart and counsel, gentle Odysseus,
took my own life away.'

I bit my lip,
rising perplexed, with longing to embrace her,
and tried three times, putting my arms around her,
but she went sifting through my hands, impalpable 220
as shadows are, and wavering like a dream.
Now this embittered all the pain I bore,
and I cried in the darkness:

'O my mother,
will you not stay, be still, here in my arms,
may we not, in this place of Death, as well,
hold one another, touch with love, and taste
salt tears' relief, the twinge of welling tears?
Or is this all hallucination, sent
against me by the iron queen, Perséphonê,
to make me groan again?'

My noble mother 230
answered quickly:

'O my child—alas,
most sorely tried of men—great Zeus's daughter,
Perséphonê, knits no illusion for you.
All mortals meet this judgment when they die.
No flesh and bone are here, none bound by sinew,
since the bright-hearted pyre consumed them down—
the white bones long exanimate[8]—to ash;
dreamlike the soul flies, insubstantial.
You must crave sunlight soon.

[7] Drifted heaps, as of leaves or snow.
[8] Separated from the vital spirit, or "soul."

Note all things strange
seen here, to tell your lady in after days.' 240

So went our talk; then other shadows came,
ladies in company, sent by Perséphonê—
consorts or daughters of illustrious men—
crowding about the black blood.
I took thought
how best to separate and question them,
and saw no help for it, but drew once more
the long bright edge of broadsword from my hip,
that none should sip the blood in company
but one by one, in order; so it fell
that each declared her lineage and name. 250

Here was great loveliness of ghosts! I saw
before them all, that princess of great ladies,
Tyro,[9] Salmoneus' daughter, as she told me,
and queen to Krêtheus, a son of Aiolos.
She had gone daft for the river Enipeus,
most graceful of all running streams, and ranged
all day by Enipeus' limpid side,
whose form the foaming girdler of the islands,
the god who makes earth tremble, took and so
lay down with her where he went flooding seaward, 260
their bower a purple billow, arching round
to hide them in a sea-vale, god and lady.
Now when his pleasure was complete, the god
spoke to her softly, holding fast her hand:

'Dear mortal, go in joy! At the turn of seasons,
winter to summer, you shall bear me sons;
no lovemaking of gods can be in vain.
Nurse our sweet children tenderly, and rear them.
Home with you now, and hold your tongue, and tell
no one your lover's name—though I am yours, 270
Poseidon, lord of surf that makes earth tremble.'

He plunged away into the deep sea swell,
and she grew big with Pelias and Neleus,
powerful vassals, in their time, of Zeus.
Pelias lived on broad Iolkos seaboard
rich in flocks, and Neleus at Pylos.
As for the sons borne by that queen of women
to Krêtheus, their names were Aison, Pherês,
and Amytháon, expert charioteer.

[9]A queen of Thessaly, enamored of the river god Enipeus, in whose guise Poseidon made love to her. She bore him two sons: Pelias, the usurper-king of Iolkos (see headnote to Euripides' *Medea*), and Neleus (the father of Nestor, who appears earlier in the *Odyssey*).

Next after her I saw Antiopê, 280
daughter of Ásopos. She too could boast
a god for lover, having lain with Zeus
and borne two sons to him: Amphion and
Zêthos, who founded Thebes, the upper city,
and built the ancient citadel. They sheltered
no life upon that plain, for all their power,
without a fortress wall.

And next I saw
Amphitrion's true wife, Alkmênê,[10] mother,
as all men know, of lionish Heraklês,
conceived when she lay close in Zeus's arms; 290
and Megarê, high-hearted Kreon's daughter,
wife of Amphitrion's unwearying son.

I saw the mother of Oidipous, Epikastê,[11]
whose great unwitting deed it was
to marry her own son. He took that prize
from a slain father; presently the gods
brought all to light that made the famous story.
But by their fearsome wills he kept his throne
in dearest Thebes, all through his evil days,
while she descended to the place of Death, 300
god of the locked and iron door. Steep down
from a high rafter, throttled in her noose,
she swung, carried away by pain, and left him
endless agony from a mother's Furies.

And I saw Khloris, that most lovely lady,
whom for her beauty in the olden time
Neleus wooed with countless gifts, and married.
She was the youngest daughter of Amphion,
son of Iasos. In those days he held
power at Orkhómenos, over the Minyai. 310
At Pylos then as queen she bore her children—
Nestor, Khromios, Periklýmenos,
and Pêro, too, who turned the heads of men
with her magnificence. A host of princes
from nearby lands came courting her; but Neleus
would hear of no one, not unless the suitor
could drive the steers of giant Íphiklos
from Phylakê—longhorns, broad in the brow,

[10] She is a "true wife" because Zeus had adopted the disguise of her husband, Amphitrion, in order to lie with her; the offspring of this union was Heraklês (Hercules).

[11] More commonly known as *Jocasta*. She was mother and wife of the Theban ruler Oidipous (Oedipus). The story, in which he unwittingly kills his father and marries his mother, is best known through Sophocles' drama *Oedipus the King*. Jocasta committed suicide after learning that she had been guilty of incest.

so fierce that one man only, a diviner,[12]
offered to round them up. But bitter fate 320
saw him bound hand and foot by savage herdsmen.
Then days and months grew full and waned, the year
went wheeling round, the seasons came again,
before at last the power of Íphiklos,
relenting, freed the prisoner, who foretold
all things to him. So Zeus's will was done.

And I saw Lêda,[13] wife of Tyndareus,
upon whom Tyndareus had sired twins
indomitable: Kastor, tamer of horses,
and Polydeukês, best in the boxing ring. 330
Those two live still, though life-creating earth
embraces them: even in the underworld
honored as gods by Zeus, each day in turn
one comes alive, the other dies again.

Then after Lêda to my vision came
the wife of Aloeus, Iphimedeia,
proud that she once had held the flowing sea
and borne him sons, thunderers for a day,
the world-renowned Otos and Ephialtês.
Never were men on such a scale 340
bred on the plowlands and the grainlands, never
so magnificent any, after Orion.
At nine years old they towered nine fathoms tall,
nine cubits in the shoulders, and they promised
furor upon Olympos, heaven broken by battle cries,
the day they met the gods in arms.
With Ossa's
mountain peak they meant to crown Olympos
and over Ossa Pelion's[14] forest pile
for footholds up the sky. As giants grown
they might have done it, but the bright son[15] of Zeus 350
by Lêto of the smooth braid shot them down
while they were boys unbearded; no dark curls
clustered yet from temples to the chin.

[12] Melampous, who was gifted with prophetic power; the giant released him in return for his services as a prophet. In some versions of the myth, Melampous performs the described feats as a service to his brother Bias, who courts and eventually marries Pêro.

[13] Mother, by Zeus, of Helen of Troy. By her mortal husband, Tyndareus, she is also mother of Agamémnon's wife, Klytaimnéstra, and of the twins named Kastor and Polydeukês (better known in later myth and in astronomy as the "Gemini," Castor and Pollux). The twins are granted life after death but can never be both alive at the same time. In some versions of the myth the twins' father is Zeus.

[14] The mountains Ossa and Pelion are near Olympos, where Zeus and his generation of deities dwell.

[15] Apollo.

Then I saw Phaidra, Prokris; and Ariadnê,
daughter of Minos,[16] the grim king. Theseus took her
aboard with him from Krete for the terraced land
of ancient Athens; but he had no joy of her.
Artemis killed her on the Isle of Dia
at a word from Dionysos.
Maira, then,
and Klymênê, and that detested queen, 360
Eríphylê,[17] who betrayed her lord for gold . . .
but how name all the women I beheld there,
daughters and wives of kings? The starry night
wanes long before I close.
Here, or aboard ship,
amid the crew, the hour for sleep has come.
Our sailing is the gods' affair and yours."

Then he fell silent. Down the shadowy hall
the enchanted banqueters were still. Only
the queen with ivory pale arms, Arêtê, spoke,
saying to all the silent men:

"Phaiákians, 370
how does he stand, now, in your eyes, this captain,
the look and bulk of him, the inward poise?
He is my guest, but each one shares that honor.
Be in no haste to send him on his way
or scant your bounty in his need. Remember
how rich, by heaven's will, your possessions are."

Then Ekhenêos, the old soldier, eldest
of all Phaiákians, added his word:

"Friends, here was nothing but our own thought spoken,
the mark hit square. Our duties to her majesty. 380
For what is to be said and done,
we wait upon Alkínoös' command."

At this the king's voice rang:

"I so command—
as sure as it is I who, while I live,

[16] King of Krete (Crete), in some myths regarded as a just man who posthumously became a judge of the dead. In other myths he is a savage ruler who demanded that Athens provide victims for human sacrifice to the monstrous bull called the Minotaur. The Athenian ruler Theseus, husband of Phaidra (Phaedra), killed the Minotaur with the aid of Ariadnê, her sister. After eloping with Ariadnê, Theseus abandoned her on the island of Dia (Naxos). Ariadnê then incurred the anger of the god Dionysos, though in most versions of the myth she wedded him.

[17] Corrupted by Polyneices (son of Oidipous of Thebes) with the gift of a gold necklace, Eríphylê treacherously persuaded her husband, Amphiaraos, to take part in an ill-fated assault on Thebes in which he was killed.

rule the sea rovers of Phaiákia. Our friend
longs to put out for home, but let him be
content to rest here one more day, until
I see all gifts bestowed. And every man
will take thought for his launching and his voyage,
I most of all, for I am master here." 390

Odysseus, the great tactician, answered:

"Alkínoös, king and admiration of men,
even a year's delay, if you should urge it,
in loading gifts and furnishing for sea—
I too could wish it; better far that I
return with some largesse of wealth about me—
I shall be thought more worthy of love and courtesy
by every man who greets me home in Ithaka."

The king said:

"As to that, one word, Odysseus:
from all we see, we take you for no swindler— 400
though the dark earth be patient of so many,
scattered everywhere, baiting their traps with lies
of old times and of places no one knows.
You speak with art, but your intent is honest.
The Argive troubles, and your own troubles,
you told as a poet would, a man who knows the world.
But now come tell me this: among the dead
did you meet any of your peers, companions
who sailed with you and met their doom at Troy?
Here's a long night—an endless night—before us, 410
and no time yet for sleep, not in this hall.
Recall the past deeds and the strange adventures.
I could stay up until the sacred Dawn
as long as you might wish to tell your story."

Odysseus the great tactician answered:

"Alkínoös, king and admiration of men,
there is a time for story telling; there is
also a time for sleep. But even so,
if, indeed, listening be still your pleasure,
I must not grudge my part. Other and sadder 420
tales there are to tell, of my companions,
of some who came through all the Trojan spears,
clangor and groan of war,
only to find a brutal death at home—
and a bad wife behind it.

After Perséphonê,
icy and pale, dispersed the shades of women,
the soul of Agamémnon, son of Atreus,

came before me, sombre in the gloom,
and others gathered round, all who were with him
when death and doom struck in Aegísthos' hall. 430
Sipping the black blood, the tall shade perceived me,
and cried out sharply, breaking into tears;
then tried to stretch his hands toward me, but could not,
being bereft of all the reach and power
he once felt in the great torque of his arms.
Gazing at him, and stirred, I wept for pity,
and spoke across to him:

'O son of Atreus,
illustrious Lord Marshal, Agamémnon,
what was the doom that brought you low in death?
Were you at sea, aboard ship, and Poseidon 440
blew up a wicked squall to send you under,
or were you cattle-raiding on the mainland
or in a fight for some strongpoint, or women,
when the foe hit you to your mortal hurt?'

But he replied at once:

'Son of Laërtês,
Odysseus, master of land ways and sea ways,
neither did I go down with some good ship
in any gale Poseidon blew, nor die
upon the mainland, hurt by foes in battle.
It was Aigísthos who designed my death, 450
he and my heartless wife,[18] and killed me, after
feeding me, like an ox felled at the trough.
That was my miserable end—and with me
my fellows butchered, like so many swine
killed for some troop, or feast, or wedding banquet
in a great landholder's household. In your day
you have seen men, and hundreds, die in war,
in the bloody press, or downed in single combat,
but these were murders you would catch your breath at:
think of us fallen, all our throats cut, winebowl 460
brimming, tables laden on every side,
while blood ran smoking over the whole floor.
In my extremity I heard Kassandra,[19]
Priam's daughter, piteously crying
as the traitress Klytaimnéstra made to kill her
along with me. I heaved up from the ground
and got my hands around the blade, but she

[18] In Agamémnon's version here, his wife (as in Aeschylus' *Oresteia*) bears a greater responsibility for the murder than in the version outlined in Book IV.

[19] A Trojan princess and prophetess. Agamémnon brought her home from Troy as a slave. Also spelled *Cassandra.*

eluded me, that whore. Nor would she close
my two eyes[20] as my soul swam to the underworld
or shut my lips. There is no being more fell, 470
more bestial than a wife in such an action,
and what an action that one planned!
The murder of her husband and her lord.
Great god, I thought my children and my slaves
at least would give me welcome. But that woman,
plotting a thing so low, defiled herself
and all her sex, all women yet to come,
even those few who may be virtuous.'

He paused then, and I answered:

'Foul and dreadful.
That was the way that Zeus who views the wide world 480
vented his hatred on the sons of Atreus—
intrigues of women, even from the start.
Myriads
died by Helen's fault, and Klytaimnéstra
plotted against you half the world away.'

And he at once said:

'Let it be a warning
even to you. Indulge a woman never,
and never tell her all you know. Some things
a man may tell, some he should cover up.
Not that I see a risk for you, Odysseus,
of death at your wife's hands. She is too wise, 490
too clear-eyed, sees alternatives too well,
Penélopê, Ikários' daughter—
that young bride whom we left behind—think of it!—
when we sailed off to war. The baby boy
still cradled at her breast—now he must be
a grown man, and a lucky one. By heaven,
you'll see him yet, and he'll embrace his father
with old fashioned respect, and rightly.
My own
lady never let me glut my eyes
on my own son, but bled me to death first. 500
One thing I will advise, on second thought;
stow it away and ponder it.
Land your ship
in secret on your island; give no warning.
The day of faithful wives is gone forever.

[20] That is, she would not perform the customary funeral rites.

But tell me, have you any word at all
about my son's[21] life? Gone to Orkhómenos
or sandy Pylos, can he be? Or waiting
with Meneláos in the plain of Sparta?
Death on earth has not yet taken Orestês.'

But I could only answer:

'Son of Atreus 510
why do you ask these questions of me? Neither
news of home have I, nor news of him,
alive or dead. And empty words are evil.'

So we exchanged our speech, in bitterness,
weighed down by grief, and tears welled in our eyes,
when there appeared the spirit of Akhilleus,
son of Peleus; then Patróklos' shade,
and then Antílokhos, and then Aias,
first among all the Danaans in strength
and bodily beauty, next to prince Akhilleus. 520
Now that great runner, grandson of Aíakhos,
recognized me and called across to me:

'Son of Laërtês and the gods of old,
Odysseus, master mariner and soldier,
old knife, what next? What greater feat remains
for you to put your mind on, after this?
How did you find your way down to the dark
where these dimwitted dead are camped forever,
the after images of used-up men?'

I answered:

'Akhilleus, Peleus' son, strongest of all 530
among the Akhaians, I had need of foresight
such as Teirêsias alone could give
to help me, homeward bound for the crags of Ithaka.
I have not yet coasted Akhaia, not yet
touched my land; my life is all adversity.
But was there ever a man more blest by fortune
than you, Akhilleus? Can there ever be?
We ranked you with immortals in your lifetime,
we Argives did, and here your power is royal
among the dead men's shades. Think, then, Akhilleus: 540
you need not be so pained by death.'

To this

he answered swiftly:

[21] Agamémnon asks about Orestês, who avenged his father's murder.

'Let me hear no smooth talk
of death from you, Odysseus, light of councils.
Better, I say, to break sod as a farm hand
for some poor country man, on iron rations,
than lord it over all the exhausted dead.
Tell me, what news of the prince my son:[22] did he
come after me to make a name in battle
or could it be he did not? Do you know
if rank and honor still belong to Peleus[23] 550
in the towns of the Myrmidons? Or now, may be,
Hellas and Phthia[24] spurn him, seeing old age
fetters him, hand and foot. I cannot help him
under the sun's rays, cannot be that man
I was on Troy's wide seaboard, in those days
when I made bastion for the Argives
and put an army's best men in the dust.
Were I but whole again, could I go now
to my father's house, one hour would do to make
my passion and my hands no man could hold 560
hateful to any who shoulder him aside.'

Now when he paused I answered:

'Of all that—
of Peleus' life, that is—I know nothing;
but happily I can tell you the whole story
of Neoptólemos, as you require.
In my own ship I brought him out from Skyros
to join the Akhaians under arms.
And I can tell you,
in every council before Troy thereafter
your son spoke first and always to the point;
no one but Nestor and I could out-debate him. 570
And when we formed against the Trojan line
he never hung back in the mass, but ranged
far forward of his troops—no man could touch him
for gallantry. Aye, scores went down before him
in hard fights man to man. I shall not tell
all about each, or name them all—the long
roster of enemies he put out of action,
taking the shock of charges on the Argives.
But what a champion his lance ran through
in Eurýpulos[25] the son of Télephos! Keteians 580
in throngs around that captain also died—

[22] Neoptólemos, or Pyrrhus, who was brought to the Trojan War after his father's death and killed Priam, the Trojan king.

[23] Akhilleus' father.

[24] Greece and Peleus' kingdom.

[25] Leader of a force persuaded to join the war in support of the Trojans.

all because Priam's gifts had won his mother
to send the lad to battle; and I thought
Memnon alone in splendor ever outshone him.

But one fact more: while our picked Argive crew
still rode that hollow horse Epeios built,
and when the whole thing lay with me, to open
the trapdoor of the ambuscade or not,
at that point our Danaan lords and soldiers
wiped their eyes, and their knees began to quake, 590
all but Neoptólemos. I never saw
his tanned cheek change color or his hand
brush one tear away. Rather he prayed me,
hand on hilt, to sortie, and he gripped
his tough spear, bent on havoc for the Trojans.
And when we had pierced and sacked Priam's tall city
he loaded his choice plunder and embarked
with no scar on him; not a spear had grazed him
nor the sword's edge in close work—common wounds
one gets in war. Arês in his mad fits 600
knows no favorites.'

But I said no more,
for he had gone off striding the field of asphodel,[26]
the ghost of our great runner, Akhilleus Aiákidês,
glorying in what I told him of his son.

Now other souls of mournful dead stood by,
each with his troubled questioning, but one
remained alone, apart: the son of Télamon,
Aîas, it was—the great shade burning still[27]
because I had won favor on the beachhead
in rivalry over Akhilleus' arms. 610
The Lady Thetis, mother of Akhilleus,
laid out for us the dead man's battle gear,
and Trojan children, with Athena,
named the Danaan fittest to own them. Would
god I had not borne the palm that day!
For earth took Aîas then to hold forever,
the handsomest and, in all feats of war,
noblest of the Danaans after Akhilleus.
Gently therefore I called across to him:

'Aîas, dear son of royal Télamon, 620
you would not then forget, even in death,

[26] A flower, possibly a variety of narcissus.

[27] After the death of Akhilleus, the "greater" Aîas (Ajax) and Odysseus had been rival claimants for Akhilleus' weapons; when the arms were awarded to Odysseus, Aîas killed himself.

your fury with me over those accurst
calamitous arms?—and so they were, a bane
sent by the gods upon the Argive host.
For when you died by your own hand we lost
a tower, formidable in war. All we Akhaians
mourn you forever, as we do Akhilleus;
and no one bears the blame but Zeus.
He fixed that doom for you because he frowned
on the whole expedition of our spearmen. 630
My lord, come nearer, listen to our story!
Conquer your indignation and your pride.'

But he gave no reply, and turned away,
following other ghosts toward Erebos.
Who knows if in that darkness he might still
have spoken, and I answered?
But my heart
longed, after this, to see the dead elsewhere.

And now there came before my eyes Minos,
the son of Zeus, enthroned, holding a golden staff,
dealing out justice among ghostly pleaders 640
arrayed about the broad doorways of Death.

And then I glimpsed Orion, the huge hunter,
gripping his club, studded with bronze, unbreakable,
with wild beasts he had overpowered in life
on lonely mountainsides, now brought to bay
on fields of asphodel.
And I saw Títyos,
the son of Gaia, lying
abandoned over nine square rods of plain.
Vultures, hunched above him, left and right,
rifling his belly, stabbed into the liver, 650
and he could never push them off.
This hulk
had once committed rape of Zeus's mistress,
Lêto, in her glory, when she crossed
the open grass of Panopeus toward Pytho.

Then I saw Tántalos[28] put to the torture:
in a cool pond he stood, lapped round by water
clear to the chin, and being athirst he burned
to slake his dry weasand[29] with drink, though drink
he would not ever again. For when the old man

[28] The sin for which Tántalos (Tantalus) is being punished here is uncertain—possibly it is for revealing the gods' secrets, possibly for his serving his son's flesh to the gods (see the headnote to Aeschylus' *Oresteia*).
[29] Throat.

put his lips down to the sheet of water 660
it vanished round his feet, gulped underground,
and black mud baked there in a wind from hell.
Boughs, too, drooped low above him, big with fruit,
pear trees, pomegranates, brilliant apples,
luscious figs, and olives ripe and dark;
but if he stretched his hand for one, the wind
under the dark sky tossed the bough beyond him.

Then Sísyphos[30] in torment I beheld
being roustabout to a tremendous boulder.
Leaning with both arms braced and legs driving, 670
he heaved it toward a height, and almost over,
but then a Power spun him round and sent
the cruel boulder bounding again to the plain.
Whereon the man bent down again to toil,
dripping sweat, and the dust rose overhead.
Next I saw manifest the power of Heraklês—
a phantom,[31] this, for he himself has gone
feasting amid the gods, reclining soft
with Hêbê of the ravishing pale ankles,
daughter of Zeus and Hêra, shod in gold. 680
But, in my vision, all the dead around him
cried like affrighted birds; like Night itself
he loomed with naked bow and nocked arrow
and glances terrible as continual archery.
My hackles rose at the gold swordbelt he wore
sweeping across him: gorgeous intaglio
of savage bears, boars, lions with wildfire eyes,
swordfights, battle, slaughter, and sudden death—
the smith who had that belt in him, I hope
he never made, and never will make, another. 690
The eyes of the vast figure rested on me,
and of a sudden he said in kindly tones:

'Son of Laërtês and the gods of old,
Odysseus, master mariner and soldier,
under a cloud, you too? Destined to grinding
labors like my own in the sunny world?
Son of Kroníon Zeus or not, how many
days I sweated out, being bound in servitude
to a man far worse than I, a rough master![32]
He made me hunt this place one time 700
to get the watchdog of the dead: no more

[30] A Corinthian ruler, noted during his lifetime for cunning treachery. More commonly spelled *Sisyphus.*

[31] Heraklês, or Hercules, was taken to heaven after his death. He was thereafter wedded to the goddess Hêbê.

[32] Eurystheus, in whose service Heraklês was forced to perform many superhumanly difficult feats, including the capture of Cerberus, the dog who guarded the realm of the dead.

perilous task, he thought, could be; but I
brought back that beast, up from the underworld;
Hermês and grey-eyed Athena showed the way.'

And Heraklês, down the vistas of the dead,
faded from sight; but I stood fast, awaiting
other great souls who perished in times past.
I should have met, then, god-begotten Theseus
and Peirithoös,[33] whom both I longed to see,
but first came shades in thousands, rustling 710
in a pandemonium of whispers, blown together,
and the horror took me that Perséphonê
had brought from darker hell some saurian death's head.[34]
I whirled then, made for the ship, shouted to crewmen
to get aboard and cast off the stern hawsers,
an order soon obeyed. They took their thwarts,
and the ship went leaping toward the stream of Ocean
first under oars, then with a following wind.

BOOK TWELVE: SEA PERILS AND DEFEAT

The ship sailed on, out of the Ocean Stream,
riding a long swell on the open sea
for the Island of Aiaia.
Summering Dawn
has dancing grounds there, and the Sun his rising;[1]
but still by night we beached on a sand shelf
and waded in beyond the line of breakers
to fall asleep, awaiting the Day Star.

When the young Dawn with finger tips of rose
made heaven bright, I sent shipmates to bring
Elpênor's body from the house of Kirkê. 10
We others cut down timber on the foreland,
on a high point, and built his pyre of logs,
then stood by weeping while the flame burnt through
corse and equipment.
Then we heaped his barrow,
lifting a gravestone on the mound, and fixed
his light but unwarped oar against the sky.
These were our rites in memory of him. Soon, then,
knowing us back from the Dark Land, Kirkê came
freshly adorned for us, with handmaids bearing
loaves, roast meats, and ruby-colored wine. 20

[33] A friend of Theseus.
[34] Reptilian specter.
[1] Aiaia is distinguished from the sunless land of the dead which they have just left behind.

She stood among us in immortal beauty
jesting:

'Hearts of oak, did you go down
alive into the homes of Death? One visit
finishes all men but yourselves, twice mortal!
Come, here is meat and wine, enjoy your feasting
for one whole day; and in the dawn tomorrow
you shall put out to sea. Sailing directions,
landmarks, perils, I shall sketch for you, to keep you
from being caught by land or water
in some black sack of trouble.'

In high humor 30
and ready for carousal, we agreed;
so all that day until the sun went down
we feasted on roast meat and good red wine,
till after sunset, at the fall of night,
the men dropped off to sleep by the stern hawsers.
She took my hand then, silent in the hush,
drew me apart, made me sit down, and lay
beside me, softly questioning, as I told
all I had seen, from first to last.
Then said the Lady Kirkê:

'So: all those trials are over.
Listen with care 40
to this, now, and a god will arm your mind.
Square in your ship's path are Seirênês,[2] crying
beauty to bewitch men coasting by;
woe to the innocent who hears that sound!
He will not see his lady nor his children
in joy, crowding about him, home from sea;
the Seirênês will sing his mind away
on their sweet meadow lolling. There are bones
of dead men rotting in a pile beside them
and flayed skins shrivel around the spot.
Steer wide; 50
keep well to seaward; plug your oarsmen's ears
with beeswax kneaded soft; none of the rest
should hear that song.
But if you wish to listen,
let the men tie you in the lugger,[3] hand
and foot, back to the mast, lashed to the mast,
so you may hear those harpies'[4] thrilling voices;
shout as you will, begging to be untied,

[2] In Grecian fable, women who could lure men to their destruction through their entrancing song. Also spelled *Sirens*.

[3] A small boat.

[4] In this passage, the word "harpies" means "temptresses." They are not the obscene and filthy females who appear in Virgil's *Aeneid*, Book III.

your crew must only twist more line around you
and keep their stroke up, till the singers fade.
What then? One of two courses you may take, 60
and you yourself must weigh them. I shall not
plan the whole action for you now, but only
tell you of both.

Ahead are beetling rocks
and dark blue glancing Amphitritê,[5] surging,
roars around them. Prowling Rocks,[6] or Drifters,
the gods in bliss have named them—named them well.
Not even birds can pass them by, not even
the timorous doves that bear ambrosia
to Father Zeus; caught by downdrafts, they die
on rockwall smooth as ice.

Each time, the Father 70
wafts a new courier to make up his crew.
Still less can ships get searoom of these Drifters,
whose boiling surf, under high fiery winds,
carries tossing wreckage of ships and men.
Only one ocean-going craft, the far-famed
Argo,[7] made it, sailing from Aiêta;
but she, too, would have crashed on the big rocks
if Hêra had not pulled her through, for love
of Iêson, her captain.

A second course[8]
lies between headlands. One is a sharp mountain 80
piercing the sky, with stormcloud round the peak
dissolving never, not in the brightest summer,
to show heaven's azure there, nor in the fall.
No mortal man could scale it, nor so much
as land there, not with twenty hands and feet,
so sheer the cliffs are—as of polished stone.
Midway that height, a cavern full of mist
opens toward Erebos and evening. Skirting
this in the lugger, great Odysseus,
your master bowman, shooting from the deck, 90
would come short of the cavemouth with his shaft;
but that is the den of Skylla, where she yaps
abominably, a newborn whelp's cry,

[5] Sea nymph; consort of Poseidon. She is the female personification of the ocean.

[6] Possibly the Planctae, islands at the north end of what is now called the Strait of Messina, which divides Sicily from the Italian mainland.

[7] The fabled ship, manned by great heroes and captained by Iêson (Jason), that sailed to capture the Golden Fleece.

[8] The following lines describe the two fabled monsters Skylla (Scylla) and Kharybdis (Charybdis), who presumably personify the dangers of the Strait of Messina. Skylla is a treacherous reef, Kharybdis a whirlpool. The proverbial phrase "between Scylla and Charybdis" has come to mean a situation in which one has to choose between equally dreadful alternatives.

though she is huge and monstrous. God or man,
no one could look on her in joy. Her legs—
and there are twelve—are like great tentacles,
unjointed, and upon her serpent necks
are borne six heads like nightmares of ferocity,
with triple serried rows of fangs and deep
gullets of black death. Half her length, she sways 100
her heads in air, outside her horrid cleft,
hunting the sea around that promontory
for dolphins, dogfish, or what bigger game
thundering Amphitritê feeds in thousands.
And no ship's company can claim
to have passed her without loss and grief; she takes,
from every ship, one man for every gullet.

The opposite point seems more a tongue of land
you'd touch with a good bowshot, at the narrows.
A great wild fig, a shaggy mass of leaves, 110
grows on it, and Kharybdis lurks below
to swallow down the dark sea tide. Three times
from dawn to dusk she spews it up
and sucks it down again three times, a whirling
maelstrom; if you come upon her then
the god who makes earth tremble could not save you.
No, hug the cliff of Skylla, take your ship
through on a racing stroke. Better to mourn
six men than lose them all, and the ship, too.'

So her advice ran; but I faced her, saying: 120

'Only instruct me, goddess, if you will,
how, if possible, can I pass Kharybdis,
or fight off Skylla when she raids my crew?'

Swiftly that loveliest goddess answered me:

'Must you have battle in your heart forever?
The bloody toil of combat? Old contender,
will you not yield to the immortal gods?
That nightmare cannot die, being eternal
evil itself—horror, and pain, and chaos;
there is no fighting her, no power can fight her, 130
all that avails is flight.

Lose headway there
along that rockface while you break out arms,
and she'll swoop over you, I fear, once more,
taking one man again for every gullet.
No, no, put all your backs into it, row on;
invoke Blind Force, that bore this scourge of men,
to keep her from a second strike against you.

Then you will coast Thrinákia,[9] the island
where Hêlios' cattle graze, fine herds, and flocks
of goodly sheep. The herds and flocks are seven, 140
with fifty beasts in each.

No lambs are dropped,
or calves, and these fat cattle never die.
Immortal, too, their cowherds are—their shepherds—
Phaëthousa and Lampetía, sweetly braided
nymphs that divine Neaira bore
to the overlord of high noon, Hêlios.
These nymphs their gentle mother bred and placed
upon Thrinákia, the distant land,
in care of flocks and cattle for their father.

Now give those kine a wide berth, keep your thoughts 150
intent upon your course for home,
and hard seafaring brings you all to Ithaka.
But if you raid the beeves, I see destruction
for ship and crew.

Rough years then lie between
you and your homecoming, alone and old,
the one survivor, all companions lost.'

As Kirkê spoke, Dawn mounted her golden throne,
and on the first rays Kirkê left me, taking
her way like a great goddess up the island.
I made straight for the ship, roused up the men 160
to get aboard and cast off at the stern.
They scrambled to their places by the rowlocks
and all in line dipped oars in the grey sea.
But soon an off-shore breeze blew to our liking—
a canvas-bellying breeze, a lusty shipmate
sent by the singing nymph with sunbright hair.
So we made fast the braces, and we rested,
letting the wind and steersman work the ship.
The crew being now silent before me, I
addressed them, sore at heart:

'Dear friends, 170
more than one man, or two, should know those things
Kirkê foresaw for us and shared with me,
so let me tell her forecast: then we die
with our eyes open, if we are going to die,
or know what death we baffle if we can. Seirênês
weaving a haunting song over the sea
we are to shun, she said, and their green shore

[9] Sicily.

all sweet with clover; yet she urged that I
alone should listen to their song. Therefore
you are to tie me up, tight as a splint, 180
erect along the mast, lashed to the mast,
and if I shout and beg to be untied,
take more turns of the rope to muffle me.'

I rather dwelt on this part of the forecast,[10]
while our good ship made time, bound outward down
the wind for the strange island of Seirênês.
Then all at once the wind fell, and a calm
came over all the sea, as though some power
lulled the swell.

The crew were on their feet
briskly, to furl the sail, and stow it; then, 190
each in place, they poised the smooth oar blades
and sent the white foam scudding by. I carved
a massive cake of beeswax into bits
and rolled them in my hands until they softened—
no long task, for a burning heat came down
from Hêlios, lord of high noon. Going forward
I carried wax along the line, and laid it
thick on their ears. They tied me up, then, plumb
amidships, back to the mast, lashed to the mast,
and took themselves again to rowing. Soon, 200
as we came smartly within hailing distance,
the two Seirênês, noting our fast ship
off their point, made ready, and they sang:

This way, oh turn your bows,
Akhaia's glory,
As all the world allows—
Moor and be merry.

Sweet coupled airs we sing.
No lonely seafarer
Holds clear of entering 210
Our green mirror.

Pleased by each purling note
Like honey twining
From her throat and my throat,
Who lies a-pining?

[10] Odysseus shrewdly failed to mention the inevitable devouring of some of his men by Skylla.

Sea rovers here take joy
Voyaging onward,
As from our song of Troy
Greybeard and rower-boy
Goeth more learnèd. 220

All feats on that great field
In the long warfare,
Dark days the bright gods willed,
Wounds you bore there,

Argos' old soldiery
On Troy beach teeming,
Charmed out of time we see.
No life on earth can be
Hid from our dreaming.

The lovely voices in ardor appealing over the water 230
made me crave to listen, and I tried to say
'Untie me!' to the crew, jerking my brows;
but they bent steady to the oars. Then Perimêdês
got to his feet, he and Eurýlokhos,
and passed more line about, to hold me still.
So all rowed on, until the Seirênês
dropped under the sea rim, and their singing
dwindled away.

My faithful company
rested on their oars now, peeling off
the wax that I had laid thick on their ears; 240
then set me free.

But scarcely had that island
faded in blue air than I saw smoke
and white water, with sound of waves in tumult—
a sound the men heard, and it terrified them.
Oars flew from their hands; the blades went knocking
wild alongside till the ship lost way,
with no oarblades to drive her through the water.

Well, I walked up and down from bow to stern,
trying to put heart into them, standing over
every oarsman, saying gently,

'Friends, 250
have we never been in danger before this?
More fearsome, is it now, than when the Kyklops
penned us in his cave? What power he had!
Did I not keep my nerve, and use my wits
to find a way out for us?

Now I say
by hook or crook this peril too shall be
something that we remember.
Heads up, lads!
We must obey the orders as I give them.
Get the oarshafts in your hands, and lay back
hard on your benches; hit these breaking seas. 260
Zeus help us pull away before we founder.
You at the tiller, listen, and take in
all that I say—the rudders are your duty;
keep her out of the combers and the smoke;
steer for that headland; watch the drift, or we
fetch up in the smother, and you drown us.'

That was all, and it brought them round to action.
But as I sent them on toward Skylla, I
told them nothing, as they could do nothing.
They would have dropped their oars again, in panic, 270
to roll for cover under the decking. Kirkê's
bidding against arms had slipped my mind,
so I tied on my cuirass and took up
two heavy spears, then made my way along
to the foredeck—thinking to see her first from there,
the monster of the grey rock, harboring
torment for my friends. I strained my eyes
upon that cliffside veiled in cloud, but nowhere
could I catch sight of her.
And all this time,
in travail, sobbing, gaining on the current, 280
we rowed into the strait—Skylla to port
and on our starboard beam Kharybdis, dire
gorge of the salt sea tide. By heaven! when she
vomited, all the sea was like a cauldron
seething over intense fire, when the mixture
suddenly heaves and rises.
The shot spume
soared to the landside heights, and fell like rain.

But when she swallowed the sea water down
we saw the funnel of the maelstrom, heard
the rock bellowing all around, and dark 290
sand raged on the bottom far below.
My men all blanched against the gloom, our eyes
were fixed upon that yawning mouth in fear
of being devoured.
Then Skylla made her strike,
whisking six of my best men from the ship.
I happened to glance aft at ship and oarsmen
and caught sight of their arms and legs, dangling

high overhead. Voices came down to me
in anguish, calling my name for the last time.

A man surfcasting on a point of rock 300
for bass or mackerel, whipping his long rod
to drop the sinker and the bait far out,
will hook a fish and rip it from the surface
to dangle wriggling through the air:
so these
were borne aloft in spasms toward the cliff.

She ate them as they shrieked there, in her den,
in the dire grapple, reaching still for me—
and deathly pity ran me through
at that sight—far the worst I ever suffered,
questing the passes of the strange sea.
We rowed on. 310
The Rocks were now behind; Kharybdis, too,
and Skylla dropped astern.
Then we were coasting
the noble island of the god, where grazed
those cattle with wide brows, and bounteous flocks
of Hêlios, lord of noon, who rides high heaven.

From the black ship, far still at sea, I heard
the lowing of the cattle winding home
and sheep bleating; and heard, too, in my heart
the words of blind Teirêsias of Thebes
and Kirkê of Aiaia: both forbade me 320
the island of the world's delight, the Sun.
So I spoke out in gloom to my companions:

'Shipmates, grieving and weary though you are,
listen: I had forewarning from Teirêsias
and Kirkê, too; both told me I must shun
this island of the Sun, the world's delight.
Nothing but fatal trouble shall we find here.
Pull away, then, and put the land astern.'

That strained them to the breaking point, and, cursing,
Eurýlokhos cried out in bitterness: 330

'Are you flesh and blood, Odysseus, to endure
more than a man can? Do you never tire?
God, look at you, iron is what you're made of.
Here we all are, half dead with weariness,
falling asleep over the oars, and you
say "No landing"—no firm island earth
where we could make a quiet supper. No:
pull out to sea, you say, with night upon us—

just as before, but wandering now, and lost.
Sudden storms can rise at night and swamp 340
ships without a trace.
Where is your shelter
if some stiff gale blows up from south or west—
the winds that break up shipping every time
when seamen flout the lord gods' will? I say
do as the hour demands and go ashore
before black night comes down.
We'll make our supper
alongside, and at dawn put out to sea.'

Now when the rest said 'Aye' to this, I saw
the power of destiny devising ill.
Sharply I answered, without hesitation: 350

'Eurýlokhos, they are with you to a man.
I am alone, outmatched.
Let this whole company
swear me a great oath: Any herd of cattle
or flock of sheep here found shall go unharmed;
no one shall slaughter out of wantonness
ram or heifer; all shall be content
with what the goddess Kirkê put aboard.'

They fell at once to swearing as I ordered,
and when the round of oaths had ceased, we found
a halfmoon bay to beach and moor the ship in, 360
with a fresh spring nearby. All hands ashore
went about skillfully getting up a meal.
Then, after thirst and hunger, those besiegers,
were turned away, they mourned for their companions
plucked from the ship by Skylla and devoured,
and sleep came soft upon them as they mourned.

In the small hours of the third watch, when stars
that shone out in the first dusk of evening
had gone down to their setting, a giant wind
blew from heaven, and clouds driven by Zeus 370
shrouded land and sea in a night of storm;
so, just as Dawn with finger tips of rose
touched the windy world, we dragged our ship
to cover in a grotto, a sea cave
where nymphs had chairs of rock and sanded floors.
I mustered all the crew and said:

'Old shipmates,
our stores are in the ship's hold, food and drink;
the cattle here are not for our provision,
or we pay dearly for it.

Fierce the god is
who cherishes these heifers and these sheep: 380
Hêlios; and no man avoids his eye.'

To this my fighters nodded. Yes. But now
we had a month of onshore gales, blowing
day in, day out—south winds, or south by east.
As long as bread and good red wine remained
to keep the men up, and appease their craving,
they would not touch the cattle. But in the end,
when all the barley in the ship was gone,
hunger drove them to scour the wild shore
with angling hooks, for fishes and sea fowl, 390
whatever fell into their hands; and lean days
wore their bellies thin.
The storms continued.
So one day I withdrew to the interior
to pray the gods in solitude, for hope
that one might show me some way of salvation.
Slipping away, I struck across the island
to a sheltered spot, out of the driving gale.
I washed my hands there, and made supplication
to the gods who own Olympos, all the gods—
but they, for answer, only closed my eyes 400
under slow drops of sleep.
Now on the shore Eurýlokhos
made his insidious plea:
'Comrades,' he said,
'You've gone through everything; listen to what I say.
All deaths are hateful to us, mortal wretches,
but famine is the most pitiful, the worst
end that a man can come to.
Will you fight it?
Come, we'll cut out the noblest of these cattle
for sacrifice to the gods who own the sky;
and once at home, in the old country of Ithaka,
if ever that day comes— 410
we'll build a costly temple and adorn it
with every beauty for the Lord of Noon.
But if he flares up over his heifers lost,
wishing our ship destroyed, and if the gods
make cause with him, why, then I say: Better
open your lungs to a big sea once for all
than waste to skin and bones on a lonely island!'

Thus Eurýlokhos; and they murmured 'Aye!'
trooping away at once to round up heifers.
Now, that day tranquil cattle with broad brows 420

were grazing near, and soon the men drew up
around their chosen beasts in ceremony.
They plucked the leaves that shone on a tall oak—
having no barley meal—to strew the victims,
performed the prayers and ritual, knifed the kine
and flayed each carcass, cutting thighbones free
to wrap in double folds of fat. These offerings,
with strips of meat, were laid upon the fire.
Then, as they had no wine, they made libation
with clear spring water, broiling the entrails first; 430
and when the bones were burnt and tripes shared,
they spitted the carved meat.

Just then my slumber
left me in a rush, my eyes opened,
and I went down the seaward path. No sooner
had I caught sight of our black hull, than savory
odors of burnt fat eddied around me;
grief took hold of me, and I cried aloud:

'O Father Zeus and gods in bliss forever,
you made me sleep away this day of mischief!
O cruel drowsing, in the evil hour! 440
Here they sat, and a great work they contrived.'

Lampetía[11] in her long gown meanwhile
had borne swift word to the Overlord of Noon:

'They have killed your kine.'

And the Lord Hêlios
burst into angry speech amid the immortals:

'O Father Zeus and gods in bliss forever,
punish Odysseus' men! So overweening,
now they have killed my peaceful kine, my joy
at morning when I climbed the sky of stars,
and evening, when I bore westward from heaven. 450
Restitution or penalty they shall pay—
and pay in full—or I go down forever
to light the dead men in the underworld.'

Then Zeus who drives the stormcloud made reply:

'Peace, Hêlios: shine on among the gods,
shine over mortals in the fields of grain.
Let me throw down one white-hot bolt, and make
splinters of their ship in the winedark sea.'

[11]One of the nymphs who tended her father Hêlios' cattle.

—Kalypso later told me of this exchange,
as she declared that Hermês had told her. 460
Well, when I reached the sea cave and the ship,
I faced each man, and had it out; but where
could any remedy be found? There was none.
The silken beeves of Hêlios were dead.
The gods, moreover, made queer signs appear:
cowhides began to crawl, and beef, both raw
and roasted, lowed like kine upon the spits.

Now six full days my gallant crew could feast
upon the prime beef they had marked for slaughter
from Hêlios' herd; and Zeus, the son of Kronos, 470
added one fine morning.
All the gales
had ceased, blown out, and with an offshore breeze
we launched again, stepping the mast and sail,
to make for the open sea. Astern of us
the island coastline faded, and no land
showed anywhere, but only sea and heaven,
when Zeus Kroníon piled a thunderhead
above the ship, while gloom spread on the ocean.
We held our course, but briefly. Then the squall
struck whining from the west, with gale force, breaking 480
both forestays, and the mast came toppling aft
along the ship's length, so the running rigging
showered into the bilge.
On the after deck
the mast had hit the steersman a slant blow
bashing the skull in, knocking him overside,
as the brave soul fled the body, like a diver.
With crack on crack of thunder, Zeus let fly
a bolt against the ship, a direct hit,
so that she bucked, in reeking fumes of sulphur,
and all the men were flung into the sea. 490
They came up 'round the wreck, bobbing a while
like petrels[12] on the waves.
No more seafaring
homeward for these, no sweet day of return;
the god had turned his face from them.
I clambered
fore and aft my hulk until a comber
split her, keel from ribs, and the big timber
floated free; the mast, too, broke away.
A backstay floated dangling from it, stout
rawhide rope, and I used this for lashing
mast and keel together. These I straddled, 500
riding the frightful storm.

[12] Seabirds.

Nor had I yet
seen the worst of it: for now the west wind
dropped, and a southeast gale came on—one more
twist of the knife—taking me north again,
straight for Kharybdis. All that night I drifted,
and in the sunrise, sure enough, I lay
off Skylla mountain and Kharybdis deep.
There, as the whirlpool drank the tide, a billow
tossed me, and I sprang for the great fig tree,
catching on like a bat under a bough. 510
Nowhere had I to stand, no way of climbing,
the root and bole being far below, and far
above my head the branches and their leaves,
massed, overshadowing Kharybdis pool.
But I clung grimly, thinking my mast and keel
would come back to the surface when she spouted.
And ah! how long, with what desire, I waited!
till, at the twilight hour, when one who hears
and judges pleas in the marketplace all day
between contentious men, goes home to supper, 520
the long poles at last reared from the sea.

Now I let go with hands and feet, plunging
straight into the foam beside the timbers,
pulled astride, and rowed hard with my hands
to pass by Skylla. Never could I have passed her
had not the Father of gods and men, this time,
kept me from her eyes. Once through the strait,
nine days I drifted in the open sea
before I made shore, buoyed up by the gods,
upon Ogýgia Isle. The dangerous nymph 530
Kalypso lives and sings there, in her beauty,
and she received me, loved me.

But why tell
the same tale that I told last night in hall
to you and to your lady? Those adventures
made a long evening, and I do not hold
with tiresome repetition of a story."

BOOK THIRTEEN: ONE MORE STRANGE ISLAND

He ended it, and no one stirred or sighed
in the shadowy hall, spellbound as they all were,
until Alkínoös answered:

"When you came
here to my strong home, Odysseus, under
my tall roof, headwinds were left behind you.

Clear sailing shall you have now, homeward now,
however painful all the past.
My lords,
ever my company, sharing the wine of Council,
the songs of the blind harper, hear me further:
garments are folded for our guest and friend 10
in the smooth chest, and gold
in various shaping of adornment lies
with other gifts, and many, brought by our peers;
let each man add his tripod and deep-bellied
cauldron: we'll make levy upon the realm
to pay us for the loss each bears in this."

Alkínoös had voiced their own hearts' wish.
All gave assent, then home they went to rest;
but young Dawn's finger tips of rose, touching
the world, roused them to make haste to the ship, 20
each with his gift of noble bronze. Alkínoös,
their ardent king, stepping aboard himself,
directed the stowing under the cross planks,
not to cramp the long pull of the oarsmen.
Going then to the great hall, lords and crew
prepared for feasting.
As the gods' anointed,
Alkínoös made offering on their behalf—an ox
to Zeus beyond the stormcloud, Kronos' son,
who rules the world. They burnt the great thighbones
and feasted at their ease on fresh roast meat, 30
as in their midst the godlike harper sang—
Demódokos, honored by all that realm.
Only Odysseus
time and again turned craning toward the sun,
impatient for day's end, for the open sea.
Just as a farmer's hunger grows, behind
the bolted plow and share, all day afield,
drawn by his team of winedark oxen: sundown
is benison for him, sending him homeward
stiff in the knees from weariness, to dine;
just so, the light on the sea rim gladdened Odysseus, 40
and as it dipped he stood among the Phaiákians,
turned to Alkínoös, and said:

"O king and admiration of your people,
give me fare well, and stain the ground with wine;
my blessings on you all! This hour brings
fulfillment to the longing of my heart:
a ship for home, and gifts the gods of heaven
make so precious and so bountiful.
After this voyage
god grant I find my own wife in my hall
with everyone I love best, safe and sound! 50

And may you, settled in your land, give joy
to wives and children; may the gods reward you
every way, and your realm be free of woe."

Then all the voices rang out, "Be it so!"
and "Well spoken!" and "Let our friend make sail!"

Whereon Alkínoös gave command to his crier:

"Fill the winebowl, Pontónoös: mix and serve:
go the whole round, so may this company
invoke our Father Zeus, and bless our friend,
seaborne tonight and bound for his own country." 60

Pontónoös mixed the honey-hearted wine
and went from chair to chair, filling the cups;
then each man where he sat poured out his offering
to the gods in bliss who own the sweep of heaven.
With gentle bearing Odysseus rose, and placed
his double goblet in Arêtê's hands,
saying:

"Great Queen, farewell;
be blest through all your days till age comes on you,
and death, last end for mortals, after age.
Now I must go my way. Live in felicity, 70
and make this palace lovely for your children,
your countrymen, and your king, Alkínoös."

Royal Odysseus turned and crossed the door sill,
a herald at his right hand, sent by Alkínoös
to lead him to the sea beach and the ship.
Arêtê, too, sent maids in waiting after him,
one with a laundered great cloak and a tunic,
a second balancing the crammed sea chest,
a third one bearing loaves and good red wine.
As soon as they arrived alongside, crewmen 80
took these things for stowage under the planks,
their victualling and drink; then spread a rug
and linen cover on the after deck,
where Lord Odysseus might sleep in peace.
Now he himself embarked, lay down, lay still,
while oarsmen took their places at the rowlocks
all in order. They untied their hawser,
passing it through a drilled stone ring; then bent
forward at the oars and caught the sea
as one man, stroking.

Slumber, soft and deep 90
like the still sleep of death, weighed on his eyes
as the ship hove seaward.

How a four horse team

whipped into a run on a straightaway
consumes the road, surging and surging over it!
So ran that craft and showed her heels to the swell,
her bow wave riding after, and her wake
on the purple night-sea foaming.
Hour by hour
she held her pace; not even a falcon wheeling
downwind, swiftest bird, could stay abreast of her
in that most arrowy flight through open water, 100
with her great passenger—godlike in counsel,
he that in twenty years had borne such blows
in his deep heart, breaking through ranks in war
and waves on the bitter sea.
This night at last
he slept serene, his long-tried mind at rest.

When on the East the sheer bright star arose
that tells of coming Dawn, the ship made landfall
and came up islandward in the dim of night.
Phorkys, the old sea baron, has a cove
here in the realm of Ithaka; two points 110
of high rock, breaking sharply, hunch around it,
making a haven from the plunging surf
that gales at sea roll shoreward. Deep inside,
at mooring range, good ships can ride unmoored.
There, on the inmost shore, an olive tree
throws wide its boughs over the bay; nearby
a cave of dusky light is hidden
for those immortal girls, the Naiadês.[1]
Within are winebowls hollowed in the rock
and amphorai; bees bring their honey here; 120
and there are looms of stone, great looms, whereon
the weaving nymphs make tissues, richly dyed
as the deep sea is; and clear springs in the cavern
flow forever. Of two entrances,
one on the north allows descent of mortals,
but beings out of light alone, the undying,
can pass by the south slit; no men come there.

This cove the sailors knew. Here they drew in,
and the ship ran half her keel's length up the shore,
she had such way on her from those great oarsmen. 130
Then from their benches forward on dry ground
they disembarked. They hoisted up Odysseus
unruffled on his bed, under his cover,
handing him overside still fast asleep,

[1] Sea nymphs.

to lay him on the sand; and they unloaded
all those gifts the princes of Phaiákia
gave him, when by Athena's heart and will
he won his passage home. They bore this treasure
off the beach, and piled it close around
the roots of the olive tree, that no one passing 140
should steal Odysseus' gear before he woke.
That done, they pulled away on the homeward track.

But now the god that shakes the islands, brooding
over old threats of his against Odysseus,
approached Lord Zeus to learn his will. Said he:

"Father of gods, will the bright immortals ever
pay me respect again, if mortals do not?—
Phaiákians, too, my own blood kin?
I thought
Odysseus should in time regain his homeland;
I had no mind to rob him of that day— 150
no, no; you promised it, being so inclined;
only I thought he should be made to suffer
all the way.
But now these islanders
have shipped him homeward, sleeping soft, and put him
On Ithaka, with gifts untold
of bronze and gold, and fine cloth to his shoulder.
Never from Troy had he borne off such booty
if he had got home safe with all his share."

Then Zeus who drives the stormcloud answered, sighing:

"God of horizons, making earth's underbeam 160
tremble, why do you grumble so?
The immortal gods show you no less esteem,
and the rough consequence would make them slow
to let barbs fly at their eldest and most noble.
But if some mortal captain, overcome
by his own pride of strength, cuts or defies you,
are you not always free to take reprisal?
Act as your wrath requires and as you will."

Now said Poseidon, god of earthquake:

"Aye,
god of the stormy sky, I should have taken 170
vengeance, as you say, and on my own;
but I respect, and would avoid, your anger.
The sleek Phaiákian cutter, even now,
has carried out her mission and glides home
over the misty sea. Let me impale her,

end her voyage, and end all ocean-crossing
with passengers, then heave a mass of mountain
in a ring around the city."

Now Zeus who drives the stormcloud said benignly:

"Here is how I should do it, little brother: 180
when all who watch upon the wall have caught
sight of the ship, let her be turned to stone—
an island like a ship, just off the bay.
Mortals may gape at that for generations!
But throw no mountain round the sea port city."

When he heard this, Poseidon, god of earthquake,
departed for Skhería, where the Phaiákians
are born and dwell. Their ocean-going ship
he saw already near, heading for harbor;
so up behind her swam the island-shaker 190
and struck her into stone, rooted in stone, at one
blow of his palm,

then took to the open sea.

Those famous ship handlers, the Phaiákians,
gazed at each other, murmuring in wonder;
you could have heard one say:

"Now who in thunder
has anchored, moored that ship in the seaway,
when everyone could see her making harbor?"

The god had wrought a charm beyond their thought.
But soon Alkínoös made them hush, and told them:

"This present doom upon the ship—on me— 200
my father prophesied in the olden time.
If we gave safe conveyance to all passengers
we should incur Poseidon's wrath, he said,
whereby one day a fair ship, manned by Phaiákians,
would come to grief at the god's hands; and great
mountains would hide our city from the sea.
So my old father forecast.

Use your eyes:

these things are even now being brought to pass.
Let all here abide by my decree:

We make

an end henceforth of taking, in our ships, 210
castaways who may land upon Skhería;
and twelve choice bulls we dedicate at once
to Lord Poseidon, praying him of his mercy
not to heave up a mountain round our city."

In fearful awe they led the bulls to sacrifice

and stood about the altar stone, those captains,
peers of Phaiákia, led by their king in prayer
to Lord Poseidon.

Meanwhile, on his island,
his father's shore, that kingly man, Odysseus,
awoke, but could not tell what land it was 220
after so many years away; moreover,
Pallas Athena, Zeus's daughter, poured
a grey mist all around him, hiding him
from common sight—for she had things to tell him
and wished no one to know him, wife or townsmen,
before the suitors paid up for their crimes.

The landscape then looked strange, unearthly strange
to the Lord Odysseus: paths by hill and shore,
glimpses of harbors, cliffs, and summer trees.
He stood up, rubbed his eyes, gazed at his homeland, 230
and swore, slapping his thighs with both his palms,
then cried aloud:

"What am I in for now?
Whose country have I come to this time? Rough
savages and outlaws, are they, or
godfearing people, friendly to castaways?
Where shall I take these things? Where take myself,
with no guide, no directions? These should be
still in Phaiákian hands, and I uncumbered,
free to find some other openhearted
prince who might be kind and give me passage. 240
I have no notion where to store this treasure;
first-comer's trove it is, if I leave it here.
My lords and captains of Phaiákia
were not those decent men they seemed, not honorable,
landing me in this unknown country—no,
by god, they swore to take me home to Ithaka
and did not! Zeus attend to their reward,
Zeus, patron of petitioners, who holds
all other mortals under his eye; he takes
payment from betrayers!

I'll be busy. 250
I can look through my gear. I shouldn't wonder
if they pulled out with part of it on board."

He made a tally of his shining pile—
tripods, cauldrons, cloaks, and gold—and found
he lacked nothing at all.

And then he wept,
despairing, for his own land, trudging down
beside the endless wash of the wide, wide sea,

weary and desolate as the sea. But soon
Athena came to him from the nearby air,
putting a young man's figure on—a shepherd, 260
like a king's son, all delicately made.
She wore a cloak, in two folds off her shoulders,
and sandals bound upon her shining feet.
A hunting lance lay in her hands.
At sight of her
Odysseus took heart, and he went forward
to greet the lad, speaking out fair and clear:

"Friend, you are the first man I've laid eyes on
here in this cove. Greetings. Do not feel
alarmed or hostile, coming across me; only
receive me into safety with my stores. 270
Touching your knees I ask it, as I might
ask grace of a god.
O sir, advise me,
what is this land and realm, who are the people?
Is it an island all distinct, or part
of the fertile mainland, sloping to the sea?"

To this grey-eyed Athena answered:

"Stranger,
you must come from the other end of nowhere,
else you are a great booby, having to ask
what place this is. It is no nameless country.
Why, everyone has heard of it, the nations 280
over on the dawn side, toward the sun,
and westerners in cloudy lands of evening.
No one would use this ground for training horses,
it is too broken, has no breadth of meadow;
but there is nothing meager about the soil,
the yield of grain is wondrous, and wine, too,
with drenching rains and dewfall.
There's good pasture
for oxen and for goats, all kinds of timber,
and water all year long in the cattle ponds.
For these blessings, friend, the name of Ithaka 290
has made its way even as far as Troy—
and they say Troy lies far beyond Akhaia."

Now Lord Odysseus, the long-enduring,
laughed in his heart, hearing his land described
by Pallas Athena, daughter of Zeus who rules
the veering stormwind; and he answered her
with ready speech—not that he told the truth,

but, just as she did, held back what he knew,
weighing within himself at every step
what he made up to serve his turn.

Said he: 300

"Far away in Krete I learned of Ithaka—
in that broad island over the great ocean.
And here I am now, come myself to Ithaka!
Here is my fortune with me. I left my sons
an equal part, when I shipped out. I killed
Orsílokhos, the courier, son of Idómeneus.[2]
This man could beat the best cross country runners
in Krete, but he desired to take away
my Trojan plunder, all I had fought and bled for,
cutting through ranks in war and the cruel sea. 310
Confiscation is what he planned; he knew
I had not cared to win his father's favor
as a staff officer in the field at Troy,
but led my own command.

I acted: I
hit him with a spearcast from a roadside
as he came down from the open country. Murky
night shrouded all heaven and the stars.
I made that ambush with one man at arms.
We were unseen. I took his life in secret,
finished him off with my sharp sword. That night 320
I found asylum on a ship off shore
skippered by gentlemen of Phoinikia;[3] I gave
all they could wish, out of my store of plunder,
for passage, and for landing me at Pylos
or Elis Town, where the Epeioi are in power.
Contrary winds carried them willy-nilly
past that coast; they had no wish to cheat me,
but we were blown off course.

Here, then, by night
we came, and made this haven by hard rowing.
All famished, but too tired to think of food, 330
each man dropped in his tracks after the landing,
and I slept hard, being wearied out. Before
I woke today, they put my things ashore
on the sand here beside me where I lay,
then reimbarked for Sidon, that great city.
Now they are far at sea, while I am left
forsaken here."

At this the grey-eyed goddess
Athena smiled, and gave him a caress,
her looks being changed now, so she seemed a woman,
tall and beautiful and no doubt skilled 340
at weaving splendid things. She answered briskly:

[2] The king of Krete (Crete).

[3] Phoenicia; an area of the Syrian coast noted for commerce. Sidon was one of its principal cities.

"Whoever gets around you must be sharp
and guileful as a snake; even a god
might bow to you in ways of dissimulation.
You! You chameleon!
Bottomless bag of tricks! Here in your own country
would you not give your stratagems a rest
or stop spellbinding for an instant?
You play a part as if it were your own tough skin.

No more of this, though. Two of a kind, we are, 350
contrivers, both. Of all men now alive
you are the best in plots and story telling.
My own fame is for wisdom among the gods—
deceptions, too.
Would even you have guessed
that I am Pallas Athena, daughter of Zeus,
I that am always with you in times of trial,
a shield to you in battle, I who made
the Phaiákians befriend you, to a man?
Now I am here again to counsel with you—
but first to put away those gifts the Phaiákians 360
gave you at departure—I planned it so.
Then I can tell you of the gall and wormwood
it is your lot to drink in your own hall.
Patience, iron patience, you must show;
so give it out to neither man nor woman
that you are back from wandering. Be silent
under all injuries, even blows from men."

His mind ranging far, Odysseus answered:

"Can mortal man be sure of you on sight,
even a sage, O mistress of disguises? 370
Once you were fond of me—I am sure of that—
years ago, when we Akhaians made
war, in our generation, upon Troy.
But after we had sacked the shrines of Priam
and put to sea, God scattered the Akhaians;
I never saw you after that, never
knew you aboard with me, to act as shield
in grievous times—not till you gave me comfort
in the rich hinterland of the Phaiákians
and were yourself my guide into that city. 380

Hear me now in your father's name, for I
cannot believe that I have come to Ithaka.
It is some other land. You made that speech
only to mock me, and to take me in.
Have I come back in truth to my home island?"

To this the grey-eyed goddess Athena answered:

"Always the same detachment! That is why
I cannot fail you, in your evil fortune,
coolheaded, quick, well-spoken as you are!
Would not another wandering man, in joy, 390
make haste home to his wife and children? Not
you, not yet. Before you hear their story
you will have proof about your wife.

I tell you,
she still sits where you left her, and her days
and nights go by forlorn, in lonely weeping.
For my part, never had I despaired; I felt
sure or your coming home, though all your men
should perish; but I never cared to fight
Poseidon, Father's brother, in his baleful
rage with you for taking his son's eye. 400

Now I shall make you see the shape of Ithaka.
Here is the cove the sea lord Phorkys owns,
there is the olive spreading out her leaves
over the inner bay, and there the cavern
dusky and lovely, hallowed by the feet
of those immortal girls, the Naiadês—
the same wide cave under whose vault you came
to honor them with hekatombs—and there
Mount Neion, with his forest on his back!"

She had dispelled the mist, so all the island 410
stood out clearly. Then indeed Odysseus'
heart stirred with joy. He kissed the earth,
and lifting up his hands prayed to the nymphs:

"O slim shy Naiadês, young maids of Zeus,
I had not thought to see you ever again!

O listen smiling
to my gentle prayers, and we'll make offering
plentiful as in the old time, granted I
live, granted my son grows tall, by favor
of great Athena, Zeus's daughter,
who gives the winning fighter his reward!" 420

The grey-eyed goddess said directly:

"Courage;
and let the future trouble you no more.
We go to make a cache now, in the cave,
to keep your treasure hid. Then we'll consider
how best the present action may unfold."

The goddess turned and entered the dim cave,
exploring it for crannies, while Odysseus
carried up all the gold, the fire-hard bronze,
and well-made clothing the Phaiákians gave him.
Pallas Athena, daughter of Zeus the storm king, 430
placed them, and shut the cave mouth with a stone,
and under the old grey olive tree those two
sat down to work the suitors death and woe.
Grey-eyed Athena was the first to speak, saying:

"Son of Laërtês and the gods of old,
Odysseus, master of land ways and sea ways,
put your mind on a way to reach and strike
a crowd of brazen upstarts.
Three long years
they have played master in your house: three years
trying to win your lovely lady, making 440
gifts as though betrothed. And she? Forever
grieving for you, missing your return,
she has allowed them all to hope, and sent
messengers with promises to each—
though her true thoughts are fixed elsewhere."

At this
the man of ranging mind, Odysseus, cried:

"So hard beset! An end like Agamémnon's
might very likely have been mine, a bad end,
bleeding to death in my own hall. You forestalled it,
goddess, by telling me how the land lies. 450
Weave me a way to pay them back! And you, too,
take your place with me, breathe valor in me
the way you did that night when we Akhaians
unbound the bright veil from the brow of Troy!
O grey-eyed one, fire my heart and brace me!
I'll take on fighting men three hundred strong
if you fight at my back, immortal lady!"

The grey-eyed goddess Athena answered him:

"No fear but I shall be there; you'll go forward
under my arm when the crux comes at last. 460
And I foresee your vast floor stained with blood,
spattered with brains of this or that tall suitor
who fed upon your cattle.
Now, for a while,
I shall transform you; not a soul will know you,
the clear skin of your arms and legs shriveled,
your chestnut hair all gone, your body dressed
in sacking that a man would gag to see,
and the two eyes, that were so brilliant, dirtied—

contemptible, you shall seem to your enemies,
as to the wife and son you left behind. 470

But join the swineherd first—the overseer
of all your swine, a good soul now as ever,
devoted to Penélopê and your son.
He will be found near Raven's Rock and the well
of Arethousa,[4] where the swine are pastured,
rooting for acorns to their hearts' content,
drinking the dark still water. Boarflesh grows
pink and fat on that fresh diet. There
stay with him, and question him, while I
am off to the great beauty's land of Sparta, 480
to call your son Telémakhos home again—
for you should know, he went to the wide land
of Lakedaimon, Meneláos' country,
to learn if there were news of you abroad."

Odysseus answered:

"Why not tell him, knowing
my whole history, as you do? Must he
traverse the barren sea, he too, and live
in pain, while others feed on what is his?"

At this the grey-eyed goddess Athena said:

"No need for anguish on that lad's account. 490
I sent him off myself, to make his name
in foreign parts—no hardship in the bargain,
taking his ease in Meneláos' mansion,
lapped in gold.

The young bucks here, I know,
lie in wait for him in a cutter, bent
on murdering him before he reaches home.
I rather doubt they will. Cold earth instead
will take in her embrace a man or two
of those who fed so long on what is his."

Speaking no more, she touched him with her wand, 500
shriveled the clear skin of his arms and legs,
made all his hair fall out, cast over him
the wrinkled hide of an old man, and bleared
both his eyes, that were so bright. Then she
clapped an old tunic, a foul cloak, upon him,
tattered, filthy, stained by greasy smoke,
and over that a mangy big buck skin.

[4] The fountain identified with the water nymph Arethousa (Arethusa) is more often located in Sicily.

A staff she gave him, and a leaky knapsack
with no strap but a loop of string.
Now then,
their colloquy at an end, they went their ways— 510
Athena toward illustrious Lakedaimon
Far over sea, to join Odysseus' son.

BOOK FOURTEEN: HOSPITALITY IN THE FOREST

He went up from the cove through wooded ground,
taking a stony trail into the high hills, where
the swineherd lived, according to Athena.
Of all Odysseus' field hands in the old days
this forester cared most for the estate;
and now Odysseus found him
in a remote clearing, sitting inside the gate
of a stockade he built to keep the swine
while his great lord was gone.
Working alone,
far from Penélopê and old Laërtês, 10
he had put up a fieldstone hut and timbered it
with wild pear wood. Dark hearts of oak he split
and trimmed for a high palisade around it,
and built twelve sties adjoining in this yard
to hold the livestock. Fifty sows with farrows
were penned in each, bedded upon the earth,
while the boars lay outside—fewer by far,
as those well-fatted were for the suitors' table,
fine pork, sent by the swineherd every day.
Three hundred sixty now lay there at night, 20
guarded by dogs—four dogs like wolves, one each
for the four lads the swineherd reared and kept
as under-herdsmen.
When Odysseus came,
the good servant sat shaping to his feet
oxhide for sandals, cutting the well-cured leather.
Three of his young men were afield, pasturing
herds in other woods; one he had sent
with a fat boar for tribute into town,
the boy to serve while the suitors got their fill.

The watch dogs, when they caught sight of Odysseus, 30
faced him, a snarling troop, and pelted out
viciously after him. Like a tricky beggar
he sat down plump, and dropped his stick. No use.
They would have rolled him in the dust and torn him

there by his own steading[1] if the swineherd
had not sprung up and flung his leather down,
making a beeline for the open. Shouting,
throwing stone after stone,
he made them scatter; then turned to his lord
and said:

"You might have got a ripping, man! 40
Two shakes more and a pretty mess for me
you could have called it, if you had the breath.
As though I had not trouble enough already,
given me by the gods, my master gone,
true king that he was. I hang on here,
still mourning for him, raising pigs of his
to feed foreigners, and who knows where the man is,
in some far country among strangers! Aye—
if he is living still, if he still sees the light of day.

Come to the cabin. You're a wanderer too. 50
You must eat something, drink some wine, and tell me
where you are from and the hard times you've seen."

The forester now led him to his hut
and made a couch for him, with tips of fir
piled for a mattress under a wild goat skin,
shaggy and thick, his own bed covering.

Odysseus,
in pleasure at this courtesy, gently said:

"May Zeus and all the gods give you your heart's desire
for taking me in so kindly, friend."

Eumaios—
O my swineherd![2]—answered him:

"Tush, friend, 60
rudeness to a stranger is not decency,
poor though he may be, poorer than you.
All wanderers
and beggars come from Zeus. What we can give
is slight but well-meant—all we dare. You know
that is the way of slaves,[3] who live in dread
of masters—new ones like our own.

[1] Farmhouse or farm.

[2] This kind of direct address by the poet, expressing affection, is used in the *Odyssey* only for Eumaios.

[3] Though owned by masters as in modern forms of slavery, and often obtained by forced capture, "slaves" in the aristocratic Homeric times were often more like trusted and responsible servants than like maltreated property. Eumaios and Telémakhos' old nurse Eurýkleia, described elsewhere in the *Odyssey*, are representative examples.

I told you
the gods, long ago, hindered our lord's return.
He had a fondness for me, would have pensioned me
with acres of my own, a house, a wife
that other men admired and courted; all 70
gifts good-hearted kings bestow for service,
for a life work the bounty of god has prospered—
for it does prosper here, this work I do.
Had he grown old in his own house, my master
would have rewarded me. But the man's gone.
God curse the race of Helen and cut it down,
that wrung the strength out of the knees of many!
And he went, too—for the honor of Agamémnon
he took ship overseas for the wild horse country
of Troy, to fight the Trojans."

This being told, 80
he tucked his long shirt up inside his belt
and strode into the pens for two young porkers.
He slaughtered them and singed them at the fire,
flayed and quartered them, and skewered the meat
to broil it all; then gave it to Odysseus
hot on the spits. He shook out barley meal,
took a winebowl of ivy wood and filled it,
and sat down facing him, with a gesture, saying:

"There is your dinner, friend, the pork of slaves.
Our fat shoats are all eaten by the suitors, 90
cold-hearted men, who never spare a thought
for how they stand in the sight of Zeus. The gods
living in bliss are fond of no wrongdoing,
but honor discipline and right behavior.
Even the outcasts of the earth, who bring
piracy from the sea, and bear off plunder
given by Zeus in shiploads—even those men
deep in their hearts tremble for heaven's eye.
But the suitors, now, have heard some word, some oracle
of my lord's death, being so unconcerned 100
to pay court properly or to go about their business.
All they want is to prey on his estate,
proud dogs; they stop at nothing. Not a day
goes by, and not a night comes under Zeus,
but they make butchery of our beeves and swine—
not one or two beasts at a time, either.
As for swilling down wine, they drink us dry.
Only a great domain like his could stand it—
greater than any on the dusky mainland
or here in Ithaka. Not twenty heroes 110
in the whole world were as rich as he. I know:
I could count it all up; twelve herds in Elis,

as many flocks, as many herds of swine,
and twelve wide-ranging herds of goats, as well,
attended by his own men or by others—
out at the end of the island, eleven herds
are scattered now, with good men looking after them,
and every herdsman, every day, picks out
a prize ram to hand over to those fellows.
I too as overseer, keeper of swine, 120
must go through all my boars and send the best."

While he ran on, Odysseus with zeal
applied himself to the meat and wine, but inwardly
his thought shaped woe and ruin for the suitors.
When he had eaten all that he desired
and the cup he drank from had been filled again
with wine—a welcome sight—,
he spoke, and the words came light upon the air:

"Who is this lord who once acquired you,
so rich, so powerful, as you describe him? 130
You think he died for Agamémnon's honor.
Tell me his name: I may have met someone
of that description in my time. Who knows?
Perhaps only the immortal gods could say
if I should claim to have seen him: I have roamed
about the world so long."
The swineherd answered

as one who held a place of trust:

"Well, man,
his lady and his son will put no stock
in any news of him brought by a rover.
Wandering men tell lies for a night's lodging, 140
for fresh clothing; truth doesn't interest them.
Every time some traveller comes ashore
he has to tell my mistress his pretty tale,
and she receives him kindly, questions him,
remembering her prince, while the tears run
down her cheeks—and that is as it should be
when a woman's husband has been lost abroad.
I suppose you, too, can work your story up
at a moment's notice, given a shirt or cloak.
No: long ago wild dogs and carrion 150
birds, most like, laid bare his ribs on land
where life had left him. Or it may be, quick fishes
picked him clean in the deep sea, and his bones
lie mounded over in sand upon some shore.
One way or another, far from home he died,
a bitter loss, and pain, for everyone,
certainly for me. Never again shall I

have for my lot a master mild as he was
anywhere—not even with my parents
at home, where I was born and bred. I miss them 160
less than I do him—though a longing comes
to set my eyes on them in the old country.
No, it is the lost man I ache to think of—
Odysseus. And I speak the name respectfully,
even if he is not here. He loved me, cared for me.
I call him dear my lord, far though he be."

Now royal Odysseus, who had borne the long war,
spoke again:

"Friend, as you are so dead sure
he will not come—and so mistrustful, too—
let me not merely talk, as others talk, 170
but swear to it: your lord is now at hand.
And I expect a gift for this good news
when he enters his own hall. Till then I would not
take a rag, no matter what my need.
I hate as I hate Hell's own gate that weakness
that makes a poor man into a flatterer.
Zeus be my witness, and the table garnished
for true friends, and Odysseus' own hearth—
by heaven, all I say will come to pass!
He will return, and he will be avenged 180
on any who dishonor his wife and son."

Eumaios—O my swineherd!—answered him:

"I take you at your word, then: you shall have
no good news gift from me. Nor will Odysseus
enter his hall. But peace! drink up your wine.
Let us talk now of other things. No more
imaginings. It makes me heavy-hearted
when someone brings my master back to mind—
my own true master.

No, by heaven,
let us have no oaths! But if Odysseus 190
can come again god send he may! My wish
is that of Penélopê and old Laërtês
and Prince Telémakhos.

Ah, he's another
to be distressed about—Odysseus' child,
Telémakhos! By the gods' grace he grew
like a tough sapling, and I thought he'd be
no less a man than his great father—strong
and admirably made; but then someone,
god or man, upset him, made him rash,
so that he sailed away to sandy Pylos 200
to hear news of his father. Now the suitors

lie in ambush on his homeward track,
ready to cut away the last shoot of Arkêsios'[4]
line, the royal stock of Ithaka.
No good
dwelling on it. Either he'll be caught
or else Kroníon's[5] hand will take him through.

Tell me, now, of your own trials and troubles.
And tell me truly first, for I should know,
who are you, where do you hail from, where's your home
and family? What kind of ship was yours, 210
and what course brought you here? Who are your sailors?
I don't suppose you walked here on the sea."

To this the master of improvisation answered:

"I'll tell you all that, clearly as I may.
If we could sit here long enough, with meat
and good sweet wine, warm here, in peace and quiet
within doors, while the work of the world goes on—
I might take all this year to tell my story
and never end the tale of misadventures
that wore my heart out, by the gods' will. 220

My native land is the wide seaboard of Krete
where I grew up. I had a wealthy father,
and many other sons were born to him
of his true lady. My mother was a slave,
his concubine; but Kastor Hylákidês,
my father, treated me as a true born son.
High honor came to him in that part of Krete
for wealth and ease, and sons born for renown,
before the death-bearing Kêrês[6] drew him down
to the underworld. His avid sons thereafter 230
dividing up the property by lot
gave me a wretched portion, a poor house.
But my ability won me a wife
of rich family. Fool I was never called,
nor turn-tail in a fight.
My strength's all gone,
but from the husk you may divine the ear
that stood tall in the old days. Misery owns me
now, but then great Arês and Athena
gave me valor and man-breaking power,
whenever I made choice of men-at-arms 240
to set a trap with me for my enemies.

[4] Odysseus' paternal grandfather.
[5] Zeus, son of Kronos.
[6] That is, the forces of death.

Never, as I am a man, did I fear Death
ahead, but went in foremost in the charge,
putting a spear through any man whose legs
were not as fast as mine. That was my element,
war and battle. Farming I never cared for,
nor life at home, nor fathering fair children.
I reveled in long ships with oars; I loved
polished lances, arrows in the skirmish,
the shapes of doom that others shake to see. 250
Carnage suited me; heaven put those things
in me somehow. Each to his own pleasure!
Before we young Akhaians shipped for Troy
I led men on nine cruises in corsairs
to raid strange coasts, and had great luck, taking
rich spoils on the spot, and even more
in the division. So my house grew prosperous,
my standing therefore high among the Kretans.
Then came the day when Zeus who views the wide world
drew men's eyes upon that way accurst 260
that wrung the manhood from the knees of many!
Everyone pressed me, pressed King Idómeneus
to take command of ships for Ilion.
No way out; the country rang with talk of it.
So we Akhaians had nine years of war.
In the tenth year we sacked the inner city,
Priam's town, and sailed for home; but heaven
dispersed the Akhaians. Evil days for me
were stored up in the hidden mind of Zeus.
One month, no more, I stayed at home in joy 270
with children, wife, and treasure. Lust for action
drove me to go to sea then, in command
of ships and gallant seamen bound for Egypt.
Nine ships I fitted out; my men signed on
and came to feast with me, as good shipmates,
for six full days. Many a beast I slaughtered
in the gods' honor, for my friends to eat.
Embarking on the seventh, we hauled sail
and filled away from Krete on a fresh north wind
effortlessly, as boats will glide down stream. 280
All rigging whole and all hands well, we rested,
letting the wind and steersmen work the ships,
for five days; on the fifth we made the delta.[7]
I brought my squadron in to the river bank
with one turn of the sweeps. There, heaven knows,
I told the men to wait and guard the ships
while I sent out patrols to rising ground.

[7] The estuary of the Nile River. Though the entire present account by Odysseus of his past life is meant to deceive, many of his invented stories correspond to what in fact did happen to him.

But reckless greed carried them all away
to plunder the rich bottomlands; they bore off
wives and children, killed what men they found. 290

When this news reached the city, all who heard it
came at dawn. On foot they came, and horsemen,
filling the river plain with dazzle of bronze;
and Zeus lord of lightning
threw my men into blind panic: no one dared
stand against that host closing around us.
Their scything weapons left our dead in piles,
but some they took alive, into forced labor.
And I—ah, how I wish that I had died
in Egypt, on that field! So many blows 300
awaited me!—Well, Zeus himself inspired me;
I wrenched my dogskin helmet off my head,
dropped my spear, dodged out of my long shield,
ran for the king's chariot and swung on
to embrace and kiss his knees. He pulled me up,
took pity on me, placed me on the footboards,
and drove home with me crouching there in tears.
Aye—for the troops, in battle fury still,
made one pass at me after another, pricking me
with spears, hoping to kill me. But he saved me, 310
for fear of the great wrath of Zeus that comes
when men who ask asylum are given death.

Seven years, then, my sojourn lasted there,
and I amassed a fortune, going about
among the openhanded Egyptians.
But when the eighth came round, a certain
Phoinikian adventurer came too,
a plausible rat, who had already done
plenty of devilry in the world.

This fellow
took me in completely with his schemes, 320
and led me with him to Phoinikia,
where he had land and houses. One full year
I stayed there with him, to the month and day,
and when fair weather came around again
he took me in a deepsea ship for Libya,
pretending I could help in the cargo trade;
he meant, in fact, to trade me off, and get
a high price for me. I could guess the game
but had to follow him aboard. One day
on course due west, off central Krete, the ship 330
caught a fresh norther, and we ran southward
before the wind while Zeus piled ruin ahead.
When Krete was out of sight astern, no land

anywhere to be seen, but sky and ocean,
Kroníon put a dark cloud in the zenith
over the ship, and gloom spread on the sea.
With crack on crack of thunder, he let fly
a bolt against the ship, a direct hit,
so that she bucked, in sacred fumes of sulphur,
and all the men were flung into the water. 340
They came up round the wreck, bobbing a while
like petrels on the waves. No homecoming
for these, from whom the god had turned his face!
Stunned in the smother as I was, yet Zeus
put into my hands the great mast of the ship—
a way to keep from drowning. So I twined
my arms and legs around it in the gale
and stayed afloat nine days. On the tenth night,
a big surf cast me up in Thesprotia.[8]
Pheidon the king there gave me refuge, nobly, 350
with no talk of reward. His son discovered me
exhausted and half dead with cold, and gave me
a hand to bear me up till he reached home
where he could clothe me in a shirt and cloak.
In that king's house I heard news of Odysseus,
who lately was a guest there, passing by
on his way home, the king said; and he showed me
the treasure that Odysseus had brought:
bronze, gold, and iron wrought with heavy labor—
in that great room I saw enough to last 360
Odysseus' heirs for ten long generations.
The man himself had gone up to Dodona[9]
to ask the spelling leaves of the old oak
the will of God: how to return, that is,
to the rich realm of Ithaka, after so long
an absence—openly, or on the quiet.
And, tipping wine out, Pheidon swore to me
the ship was launched, the seamen standing by
to take Odysseus to his land at last.
But he had passage first for me: Thesprotians 370
were sailing, as luck had it, for Doulíkhion,[10]
the grain-growing island; there, he said,
they were to bring me to the king, Akastos.
Instead, that company saw fit to plot
foul play against me; in my wretched life
there was to be more suffering.

[8] In Epirus, on the northwest shore of Greece, somewhat north of Ithaka along the mainland coast.

[9] Site of the oldest oracle of Zeus, where the god's utterances were interpreted from the rustling of oak leaves.

[10] An island near Ithaka.

At sea, then,
when land lay far astern, they sprang their trap.
They'd make a slave of me that day, stripping
cloak and tunic off me, throwing around me
the dirty rags you see before you now. 380
At evening, off the fields of Ithaka,
they bound me, lashed me down under the decking
with stout ship's rope, while they all went ashore
in haste to make their supper on the beach.
The gods helped me to pry the lashing loose
until it fell away. I wound my rags
in a bundle round my head and eased myself
down the smooth lading plank into the water,
up to the chin, then swam an easy breast stroke
out and around, putting that crew behind, 390
and went ashore in underbrush, a thicket,
where I lay still, making myself small.
They raised a bitter yelling, and passed by
several times. When further groping seemed
useless to them, back to the ship they went
and out to sea again. The gods were with me,
keeping me hid; and with me when they brought me
here to the door of one who knows the world.
My destiny is yet to live awhile."

The swineherd bowed and said:

"Ah well, poor drifter, 400
you've made me sad for you, going back over it,
all your hard life and wandering. That tale
about Odysseus, though, you might have spared me;
you will not make me believe that.
Why must you lie, being the man you are,
and all for nothing?

I can see so well
what happened to my master, sailing home!
Surely the gods turned on him, to refuse him
death in the field, or in his friends' arms
after he wound up the great war at Troy. 410
They would have made a tomb for him, the Akhaians,
and paid all honor to his son thereafter. No,
stormwinds made off with him. No glory came to him.

I moved here to the mountain with my swine.
Never, now, do I go down to town
unless I am sent for by Penélopê
when news of some sort comes. But those who sit
around her go on asking the old questions—
a few who miss their master still,
and those who eat his house up, and go free. 420

For my part, I have had no heart for inquiry
since one year an Aitolian[11] made a fool of me.
Exiled from land to land after some killing,
he turned up at my door; I took him in.
My master he had seen in Krete, he said,
lodged with Idómeneus, while the long ships,
leaky from gales, were laid up for repairs.
But they were all to sail, he said, that summer,
or the first days of fall—hulls laden deep
with treasure, manned by crews of heroes.
This time 430
you are the derelict the Powers bring.
Well, give up trying to win me with false news
or flattery. If I receive and shelter you,
it is not for your tales but for your trouble,
and with an eye to Zeus, who guards a guest."

Then said that sly and guileful man, Odysseus:

"A black suspicious heart beats in you surely;
the man you are, not even an oath could change you.
Come then, we'll make a compact; let the gods
witness it from Olympos, where they dwell. 440
Upon your lord's homecoming, if he comes
here to this very hut, and soon—
then give me a new outfit, shirt and cloak,
and ship me to Doulíkhion—I thought it
a pleasant island. But if Odysseus
fails to appear as I predict, then Swish!
let the slaves pitch me down from some high rock,
so the next poor man who comes will watch his tongue."

The forester gave a snort and answered:

"Friend,
if I agreed to that, a great name 450
I should acquire in the world for goodness—
at one stroke and forever: your kind host
who gave you shelter and the hand of friendship,
only to take your life next day!
How confidently, after that, should I
address my prayers to Zeus, the son of Kronos!

It is time now for supper. My young herdsmen
should be arriving soon to set about it.
We'll make a quiet feast here at our hearth."

At this point in their talk the swine had come 460
up to the clearing, and the drovers followed
to pen them for the night—the porkers squealing

[11] Aitolia (or Aetolia) was part of the western Greek mainland, east of Ithaka.

to high heaven, milling around the yard.
The swineherd then gave orders to his men:

"Bring in our best pig for a stranger's dinner.
A feast will do our hearts good, too; we know
grief and pain, hard scrabbling with our swine,
while the outsiders live on our labor."

Bronze
axe in hand, he turned to split up kindling,
while they drove in a tall boar, prime and fat, 470
planting him square before the fire. The gods,
as ever, had their due in the swineherd's thought,
for he it was who tossed the forehead bristles
as a first offering on the flames, calling
upon the immortal gods to let Odysseus
reach his home once more.
Then he stood up
and brained the boar with split oak from the woodpile.
Life ebbed from the beast; they slaughtered him,
singed the carcass, and cut out the joints.
Eumaios, taking flesh from every quarter, 480
put lean strips on the fat of sacrifice,
floured each one with barley meal, and cast it
into the blaze. The rest they sliced and skewered,
roasted with care, then took it off the fire
and heaped it up on platters. Now their chief,
who knew best the amenities, rose to serve,
dividing all that meat in seven portions—
one to be set aside, with proper prayers,
for the wood nymphs and Hermês, Maia's son;
the others for the company. Odysseus 490
he honored with long slices from the chine—
warming the master's heart. Odysseus looked at him
and said:

"May you be dear to Zeus
as you are dear to me for this, Eumaios,
favoring with choice cuts a man like me."

And—O my swineherd!—you replied, Eumaios:

"Bless you, stranger, fall to and enjoy it
for what it is. Zeus grants us this or that,
or else refrains from granting, as he wills;
all things are in his power."

He cut and burnt 500
a morsel for the gods who are young forever,
tipped out some wine, then put it in the hands
of Odysseus, the old soldier, raider of cities,

who sat at ease now with his meat before him.
As for the loaves, Mesaúlios dealt them out,
a yard boy, bought by the swineherd on his own,
unaided by his mistress or Laërtês,
from Taphians,[12] while Odysseus was away.
Now all hands reached for that array of supper,
until, when hunger and thirst were turned away 510
Mesaúlios removed the bread and, heavy
with food and drink, they settled back to rest.

Now night had come on, rough, with no moon,
but a nightlong downpour setting in, the rainwind
blowing hard from the west. Odysseus
began to talk, to test the swineherd, trying
to put it in his head to take his cloak off
and lend it, or else urge the others to.
He knew the man's compassion.

"Listen," he said,
"Eumaios, and you others, here's a wishful 520
tale that I shall tell. The wine's behind it,
vaporing wine, that makes a serious man
break down and sing, kick up his heels and clown,
or tell some story that were best untold.
But now I'm launched, I can't stop now.

Would god I felt
the hot blood in me that I had at Troy!
Laying an ambush near the walls one time,
Odysseus and Meneláos were commanders
and I ranked third. I went at their request.
We worked in toward the bluffs and battlements 530
and, circling the town, got into canebrakes,[13]
thick and high, a marsh where we took cover,
hunched under arms.

The northwind dropped, and night
came black and wintry. A fine sleet descending
whitened the cane like hoarfrost, and clear ice
grew dense upon our shields. The other men,
all wrapt in blanket cloaks as well as tunics,
rested well, in shields up to their shoulders,
but I had left my cloak with friends in camp,
foolhardy as I was. No chance of freezing hard, 540
I thought, so I wore kilts and a shield only.
But in the small hours of the third watch, when stars
that rise at evening go down to their setting,
I nudged Odysseus, who lay close beside me;
he was alert then, listening, and I said:

[12] Inhabitants of western Greece. That Eumaios the slave himself acquired a servant is another sign that in Homeric times slavery was not always degrading serfdom.
[13] Thick growths of cane.

'Son of Laërtês and the gods of old,
Odysseus, master mariner and soldier,
I cannot hold on long among the living.
The cold is making a corpse of me. Some god
inveigled me to come without a cloak. 550
No help for it now; too late.'

Next thing I knew
he had a scheme all ready in his mind—
and what a man he was for schemes and battles!
Speaking under his breath to me, he murmured:

'Quiet; none of the rest should hear you.'

Then,
propping his head on his forearm, he said:

'Listen, lads, I had an ominous dream,
the point being how far forward from our ships
and lines we've come. Someone should volunteer
to tell the corps commander, Agamémnon; 560
he may reinforce us from the base.'

At this,
Thoas jumped up, the young son of Andraimon,
put down his crimson cloak and headed off,
running shoreward.

Wrapped in that man's cloak
how gratefully I lay in the bitter dark
until the dawn came stitched in gold! I wish
I had that sap and fiber in me now!"

Then—O my swineherd!—you replied, Eumaios:

"That was a fine story, and well told,
not a word out of place, not a pointless word. 570
No, you'll not sleep cold for lack of cover,
or any other comfort one should give
to a needy guest. However, in the morning,
you must go flapping in the same old clothes.
Shirts and cloaks are few here; every man
has one change only. When our prince arrives,
the son of Odysseus, he will make you gifts—
cloak, tunic, everything—and grant you passage
wherever you care to go."

On this he rose
and placed the bed of balsam near the fire, 580
strewing sheepskins on top, and skins of goats.
Odysseus lay down. His host threw over him
a heavy blanket cloak, his own reserve
against the winter wind when it came wild.

So there Odysseus dropped off to sleep,
while herdsmen slept nearby. But not the swineherd:
not in the hut could he lie down in peace,
but now equipped himself for the night outside;
and this rejoiced Odysseus' heart, to see him
care for the herd so, while his lord was gone. 590
He hung a sharp sword from his shoulder, gathered
a great cloak round him, close, to break the wind,
and pulled a shaggy goatskin on his head.
Then, to keep at a distance dogs or men,
he took a sharpened lance, and went to rest
under a hollow rock where swine were sleeping
out of the wind and rain.

BOOK FIFTEEN: HOW THEY CAME TO ITHAKA

South into Lakedaimon[1]
into the land where greens are wide for dancing
Athena went, to put in mind of home
her great-hearted hero's honored son,
rousing him to return.
And there she found him
with Nestor's lad in the late night at rest
under the portico of Meneláos,
the famous king. Stilled by the power of slumber
the son of Nestor lay, but honeyed sleep
had not yet taken in her arms Telémakhos. 10
All through the starlit night, with open eyes,
he pondered what he had heard about his father,
until at his bedside grey-eyed Athena
towered and said:
"The brave thing now, Telémakhos,
would be to end this journey far from home.
All that you own you left behind
with men so lost to honor in your house
they may devour it all, shared out among them.
How will your journey save you then?
Go quickly
to the lord of the great war cry, Meneláos; 20
press him to send you back. You may yet find
the queen your mother in her rooms alone.
It seems her father and her kinsmen say
Eurýmakhos is the man for her to marry.
He has outdone the suitors, all the rest,
in gifts to her, and made her pledges double.

[1] The story of Telémakhos, broken off after Book IV, is here resumed.

Check him, or he will have your lands and chattels
in spite of you.
You know a woman's pride
at bringing riches to the man she marries.
As to her girlhood husband, her first children, 30
he is forgotten, being dead—and they
no longer worry her.[2]
So act alone.
Go back; entrust your riches to the servant
worthiest in your eyes, until the gods
make known what beauty you yourself shall marry.

This too I have to tell you: now take heed:
the suitors' ringleaders are hot for murder,
waiting in the channel between Ithaka
and Samê's rocky side; they mean to kill you
before you can set foot ashore. I doubt 40
they'll bring it off. Dark earth instead
may take to her cold bed a few brave suitors
who preyed upon your cattle.
Bear well out
in your good ship, to eastward of the islands,
and sail again by night. Someone immortal
who cares for you will make a fair wind blow.
Touch at the first beach, go ashore, and send
your ship and crew around to port by sea,
while you go inland to the forester,
your old friend, loyal keeper of the swine. 50
Remain that night with him; send him to town
to tell your watchful mother Penélopê
that you are back from Pylos safe and sound."

With this Athena left him for Olympos.
He swung his foot across and gave a kick
and said to the son of Nestor:
"Open your eyes,
Peisístratos. Get our team into harness.
We have a long day's journey."

Nestor's son
turned over and answered him:
"It is still night,
and no moon. Can we drive now? We can not, 60
itch as we may for the road home. Dawn is near.
Allow the captain of spearmen, Meneláos,

[2] These last three lines are a comment on widows in general, not on Penélopê in particular. Athena assumes this cynical view in order to hasten Telémakhos' return.

time to pack our car with gifts and time
to speak a gracious word, sending us off.
A guest remembers all his days
that host who makes provision for him kindly."

The Dawn soon took her throne of gold, and Lord
Meneláos, clarion in battle,
rose from where he lay beside the beauty 70
of Helen with her shining hair. He strode
into the hall nearby.
Hearing him come,
Odysseus' son pulled on his snowy tunic
over the skin, gathered his long cape
about his breadth of shoulder like a captain,
the heir of King Odysseus. At the door
he stood and said:
"Lord Marshal, Meneláos,
send me home now to my own dear country:
longing has come upon me to go home."

The lord of the great war cry said at once: 80
"If you are longing to go home, Telémakhos,
I would not keep you for the world, not I.
I'd think myself or any other host
as ill-mannered for over-friendliness
as for hostility.
Measure is best in everything
To send a guest packing, or cling to him
when he's in haste—one sin equals the other.
'Good entertaining ends with no detaining.'
Only let me load your car with gifts
and fine ones, you shall see.
I'll bid the women 90
set out breakfast from the larder stores;
honor and appetite—we'll attend to both
before a long day's journey overland.
Or would you care to try the Argive midlands
and Hellas, in my company? I'll harness
my own team, and take you through the towns.
Guests like ourselves no lord will turn away;
each one will make one gift, at least,
to carry home with us: tripod or cauldron
wrought in bronze, mule team, or golden cup." 100

Clearheaded Telémakhos replied:
"Lord Marshal
Meneláos, royal son of Atreus,
I must return to my own hearth. I left
no one behind as guardian of my property.

This going abroad for news of a great father—
heaven forbid it be my own undoing,
or any precious thing be lost at home."

At this the tall king, clarion in battle,
called to his lady and her waiting women
to give them breakfast from the larder stores. 110
Eteóneus, the son of Boethoös, came
straight from bed, from where he lodged nearby,
and Meneláos ordered a fire lit
for broiling mutton. The king's man obeyed.
Then down to the cedar chamber Meneláos
walked with Helen and Prince Megapénthês.
Amid the gold he had in that place lying
the son of Atreus picked a wine cup, wrought
with handles left and right, and told his son
to take a silver winebowl.

Helen lingered 120
near the deep coffers filled with gowns, her own
handiwork.

Tall goddess among women,
she lifted out one robe of state so royal,
adorned and brilliant with embroidery,
deep in the chest it shimmered like a star.
Now all three turned back to the door to greet
Telémakhos. And red-haired Meneláos
cried out to him:

"O prince Telémakhos,
may Hêra's Lord of Thunder see you home
and bring you to the welcome you desire! 130
Here are your gifts—perfect and precious things
I wish to make your own, out of my treasure."

And gently the great captain, son of Atreus,
handed him the goblet. Megapénthês
carried the winebowl glinting silvery
to set before him, and the Lady Helen
drew near, so that he saw her cheek's pure line.
She held the gown and murmured:

"I, too,
bring you a gift, dear child, and here it is; 140
remember Helen's hands by this; keep it
for your own bride, your joyful wedding day;
let your dear mother guard it in her chamber.
My blessing: may you come soon to your island,
home to your timbered hall."

So she bestowed it,
and happily he took it. These fine things

Peisístratos packed well in the wicker carrier,
admiring every one. Then Meneláos
led the two guests in to take their seats
on thrones and easy chairs in the great hall. 150
Now came a maid to tip a golden jug
of water over a silver finger bowl,
and draw the polished tables up beside them;
the larder mistress brought her tray of loaves,
with many savories to lavish on them;
viands were served by Eteóneus, and wine
by Meneláos' son. Then every hand
reached out upon good meat and drink to take them,
driving away hunger and thirst. At last,
Telémakhos and Nestor's son led out 160
their team to harness, mounted their bright car,
and drove down under the echoing entrance way,
while red-haired Meneláos, Atreus' son,
walked alongside with a golden cup—
wine for the wayfarers to spill at parting.
Then by the tugging team he stood, and spoke
over the horses' heads:

"Farewell, my lads.
Homage to Nestor, the benevolent king;
in my time he was fatherly to me,
when the flower of Akhaia warred on Troy." 170

Telémakhos made this reply:

"No fear
but we shall bear at least as far as Nestor
your messages, great king. How I could wish
to bring them home to Ithaka! If only
Odysseus were there, if he could hear me tell
of all the courtesy I have had from you,
returning with your finery and your treasure."

Even as he spoke, a beat of wings went skyward
off to the right—a mountain eagle, grappling 180
a white goose in his talons, heavy prey
hooked from a farmyard. Women and men-at-arms
made hubbub, running up, as he flew over,
but then he wheeled hard right before the horses—
a sight that made the whole crowd cheer, with hearts
lifting in joy. Peisístratos called out:

"Read us the sign, O Meneláos, Lord
Marshal of armies! Was the god revealing
something thus to you, or to ourselves?"

At this the old friend of the god of battle 190

groped in his mind for the right thing to say,
but regal Helen put in quickly:

"Listen:
I can tell you—tell what the omen means,
as light is given me, and as I see it
point by point fulfilled. The beaked eagle
flew from the wild mountain of his fathers
to take for prey the tame house bird. Just so,
Odysseus, back from his hard trials and wandering,
will soon come down in fury on his house. 200
He may be there today, and a black hour
he brings upon the suitors."

Telémakhos
gazed and said:

"May Zeus, the lord of Hêra,
make it so! In far-off Ithaka, all my life,
I shall invoke you as a goddess, lady."

He let the whip fall, and the restive mares
broke forward at a canter through the town
into the open country.

All that day
they kept their harness shaking, side by side,
until at sundown when the roads grew dim 210
they made a halt at Pherai. There Dióklês
son of Ortílokhos whom Alpheios fathered,
welcomed the young men, and they slept the night.
Up when the young Dawn's finger tips of rose
opened in the east, they hitched the team
once more to the painted car
and steered out westward through the echoing gate,
whipping their fresh horses into a run.
Approaching Pylos Height at the day's end,
Telémakhos appealed to the son of Nestor: 220

"Could you, I wonder, do a thing I'll tell you,
supposing you agree?
We take ourselves to be true friends—in age
alike, and bound by ties between our fathers,
and now by partnership in this adventure.
Prince, do not take me roundabout,
but leave me at the ship, else the old king
your father will detain me overnight
for love of guests, when I should be at sea."

The son of Nestor nodded, thinking swiftly 230
how best he could oblige his friend.
Here was his choice: to pull the team hard over

along the beach till he could rein them in
beside the ship. Unloading Meneláos'
royal keepsakes into the stern sheets,
he sang out:

"Now for action! Get aboard,
and call your men, before I break the news
at home in hall to father. Who knows better
the old man's heart than I? If you delay,
he will not let you go, but he'll descend on you 240
in person and imperious; no turning
back with empty hands for him, believe me,
once his blood is up."

He shook the reins
to the lovely mares with long manes in the wind,
guiding them full tilt toward his father's hall.
Telémakhos called in the crew, and told them:

"Get everything shipshape aboard this craft;
we pull out now, and put sea miles behind us."

The listening men obeyed him, climbing in
to settle on their benches by the rowlocks, 250
while he stood watchful by the stern. He poured out
offerings there, and prayers to Athena.

Now a strange man came up to him, an easterner
fresh from spilling blood in distant Argos,
a hunted man. Gifted in prophecy,
he had as forebear that Melampous,[3] wizard
who lived of old in Pylos, mother city
of western flocks.

Melampous, a rich lord,
had owned a house unmatched among the Pylians,
until the day came when king Neleus, noblest 260
in that age, drove him from his native land.
And Neleus for a year's term sequestered
Melampous' fields and flocks, while he lay bound
hand and foot in the keep of Phylakos.
Beauty of Neleus' daughter put him there
and sombre folly the inbreaking Fury
thrust upon him. But he gave the slip
to death, and drove the bellowing herd of Iphiklos
from Phylakê to Pylos, there to claim
the bride that ordeal won him from the king. 270
He led her to his brother's house, and went on
eastward into another land, the bluegrass

[3] For the stories of Melampous and Amphiaraos, see Book XI and the notes to it.

plain of Argos. Destiny held for him
rule over many Argives. Here he married,
built a great manor house, fathered Antíphatês
and Mantios, commanders both, of whom
Antíphatês begot Oikleiês
and Oikleiês the firebrand Amphiaraos.
This champion the lord of stormcloud, Zeus,
and strong Apollo loved; nor had he ever 280
to cross the doorsill into dim old age.
A woman, bought by trinkets, gave him over
to be cut down in the assault on Thebes.
His sons were Alkmáon and Amphílokhos.
In the meantime Lord Mantios begot
Polypheidês, the prophet, and
Kleitos—famous name! For Dawn[4] in silks
of gold carried off Kleitos for his beauty
to live among the gods. But Polypheidês,
high-hearted and exalted by Apollo 290
above all men for prophecy, withdrew
to Hyperesia[5] when his father angered him.
He lived on there, foretelling to the world
the shape of things to come.
His son it was,
Theoklýmenos, who came upon Telémakhos
as he poured out the red wine in the sand
near his trim ship, with prayer to Athena;
and he called out, approaching:
"Friend, well met
here at libation before going to sea.
I pray you by the wine you spend, and by 300
your god, your own life, and your company;
enlighten me, and let the truth be known.
Who are you? Of what city and what parents?"

Telémakhos turned to him and replied:

"Stranger, as truly as may be, I'll tell you.
I am from Ithaka, where I was born;
my father is, or he once was, Odysseus.
But he's a long time gone, and dead, may be;
and that is what I took ship with my friends
to find out—for he left long years ago." 310

Said Theoklýmenos in reply:

"I too
have had to leave my home. I killed a cousin.

[4] Eos, goddess of the dawn.
[5] A town on the Corinthian bay; part of Agamémnon's kingdom.

In the wide grazing lands of Argos live
many kinsmen of his and friends in power,
great among the Akhaians. These I fled.
Death and vengeance at my back, as Fate
has turned now, I came wandering overland.
Give me a plank aboard your ship, I beg,
or they will kill me. They are on my track." 320

Telémakhos made answer:

"No two ways
about it. Will I pry you from our gunnel[6]
when you are desperate to get to sea?
Come aboard; share what we have, and welcome."

He took the bronze-shod lance from the man's hand
and laid it down full-length on deck; then swung
his own weight after it aboard the cutter,
taking position aft, making a place
for Theoklýmenos near him. The stern lines
were slacked off, and Telémakhos commanded: 330

"Rig the mast; make sail!" Nimbly they ran
to push the fir pole high and step it firm
amidships in the box, make fast the forestays,
and hoist aloft the white sail on its halyards.
A following wind came down from grey-eyed Athena,
blowing brisk through heaven, and so steady
the cutter lapped up miles of salt blue sea,
passing Krounoi[7] abeam and Khalkis estuary
at sundown when the sea ways all grew dark.
Then, by Athena's wind borne on, the ship 340
rounded Pheai by night and coasted Elis,
the green domain of the Epeioi; thence
he put her head north toward the running pack
of islets, wondering if by sailing wide
he sheered off Death, or would be caught.

That night
Odysseus and the swineherd supped again
with herdsmen in their mountain hut. At ease
when appetite and thirst were turned away,
Odysseus, while he talked, observed the swineherd
to see if he were hospitable still— 350
if yet again the man would make him stay
under his roof, or send him off to town.

[6] Gunwale; the top edge of the ship's side.
[7] The following lines describe the ship's northwest course along the southwest coast of Greece.

"Listen," he said, "Eumaios; listen, lads.
At daybreak I must go and try my luck
around the port. I burden you too long.
Direct me, put me on the road with someone.
Nothing else for it but to play the beggar
in populous parts. I'll get a cup or loaf,
maybe, from some householder. If I go
as far as the great hall of King Odysseus 360
I might tell Queen Penélopê my news.
Or I can drift inside among the suitors
to see what alms they give, rich as they are.
If they have whims, I'm deft in ways of service—
that I can say, and you may know for sure.
By grace of Hermês the Wayfinder, patron
of mortal tasks, the god who honors toil,
no man can do a chore better than I can.
Set me to build a fire, or chop wood,
cook or carve, mix wine and serve—or anything 370
inferior men attend to for the gentry."

Now you were furious at this, Eumaios,
and answered—O my swineherd!—

"Friend, friend,

how could this fantasy take hold of you?
You dally with your life, and nothing less,
if you feel drawn to mingle in that company—
reckless, violent, and famous for it
out to the rim of heaven. Slaves
they have, but not like you. No—theirs are boys
in fresh cloaks and tunics, with pomade 380
ever on their sleek heads, and pretty faces.
These are their minions, while their tables gleam
and groan under big roasts, with loaves and wine.
Stay with us here. No one is burdened by you,
neither myself nor any of my hands.
Wait here until Odysseus' son returns.
You shall have clothing from him, cloak and tunic,
and passage where your heart desires to go."

The noble and enduring man replied:

"May you be dear to Zeus for this, Eumaios, 390
even as you are to me. Respite from pain
you give me—and from homelessness. In life
there's nothing worse than knocking about the world,
no bitterness we vagabonds are spared
when the curst belly rages! Well, you master it
and me, making me wait for the king's son.
But now, come, tell me:

what of Odysseus' mother, and his father
whom he took leave of on the sill of age?
Are they under the sun's rays, living still, 400
or gone down long ago to lodge with Death?"

To this the rugged herdsman answered:

"Aye,
that I can tell you; it is briefly told.
Laërtês lives, but daily in his hall
prays for the end of life and soul's delivery,
heartbroken as he is for a son long gone
and for his lady. Sorrow, when she died,
aged and enfeebled him like a green tree stricken;
but pining for her son, her brilliant son, 410
wore out her life.
Would god no death so sad
might come to benefactors dear as she!
I loved always to ask and hear about her
while she lived, although she lived in sorrow.
For she had brought me up with her own daughter,
Princess Ktimenê, her youngest child.
We were alike in age and nursed as equals
nearly, till in the flower of our years
they gave her, married her, to a Samian prince,
taking his many gifts. For my own portion 420
her mother gave new clothing, cloak and sandals,
and sent me to the woodland. Well she loved me.
Ah, how I miss that family! It is true
the blissful gods prosper my work; I have
meat and drink to spare for those I prize;
but so removed I am, I have no speech
with my sweet mistress, now that evil days
and overbearing men darken her house.
Tenants all hanker for good talk and gossip
around their lady, and a snack in hall, 430
a cup or two before they take the road
to their home acres, each one bearing home
some gift to cheer his heart."

The great tactician
answered:

"You were still a child, I see,
when exiled somehow from your parents' land.
Tell me, had it been sacked in war, the city
of spacious ways in which they made their home,
your father and your gentle mother? Or
were you kidnapped alone, brought here by sea
huddled with sheep in some foul pirate squadron, 440
to this landowner's hall? He paid your ransom?"

The master of the woodland answered:

"Friend,
now that you show an interest in that matter,
attend me quietly, be at your ease,
and drink your wine. These autumn nights are long,
ample for story-telling and for sleep.
You need not go to bed before the hour;
sleeping from dusk to dawn's a dull affair.
Let any other here who wishes, though,
retire to rest. At daybreak let him breakfast 450
and take the king's own swine into the wilderness.
Here's a tight roof; we'll drink on, you and I,
and ease our hearts of hardships we remember,
sharing old times. In later days a man
can find a charm in old adversity,
exile and pain. As to your question, now:

A certain island, Syriê by name—
you may have heard the name—lies off Ortýgia[8]
due west, and holds the sunsets of the year.
Not very populous, but good for grazing 460
sheep and kine; rich too in wine and grain.
No dearth is ever known there, no disease
wars on the folk, of ills that plague mankind;
but when the townsmen reach old age, Apollo
with his longbow of silver comes, and Artemis,
showering arrows of mild death.

Two towns
divide the farmlands of that whole domain,
and both were ruled by Ktêsios, my father,
Orménos' heir, and a great godlike man.

Now one day some of those renowned seafaring 470
men, sea-dogs, Phoinikians, came ashore
with bags of gauds for trading. Father had
in our household a woman of Phoinikia,
a handsome one, and highly skilled. Well, she
gave in to the seductions of those rovers.
One of them found her washing near the mooring
and lay with her, making such love to her
as women in their frailty are confused by,
even the best of them.

In due course, then,
he asked her who she was and where she hailed from: 480
and nodding toward my father's roof, she said:

[8] Though there were actual places bearing the names of Syriê and Ortýgia, in the present context they refer vaguely to unidentifiable localities, probably in northwestern Greece, and possibly invented by the poet.

'I am of Sidon town, smithy of bronze
for all the East. Arubas Pasha's daughter.
Taphian pirates caught me in a byway
and sold me into slavery overseas
in this man's home. He could afford my ransom.'

The sailor who had lain with her replied:

'Why not ship out with us on the run homeward,
and see your father's high-roofed hall again,
your father and your mother? Still in Sidon 490
and still rich, they are said to be.'

She answered:

'It could be done, that, if you sailors take
oath I'll be given passage home unharmed.'

Well, soon she had them swearing it all pat
as she desired, repeating every syllable,
whereupon she warned them:

'Not a word
about our meeting here! Never call out to me
when any of you see me in the lane
or at the well. Some visitor might bear
tales to the old man. If he guessed the truth, 500
I'd be chained up, your lives would be in peril.
No: keep it secret. Hurry with your peddling,
and when your hold is filled with livestock, send
a message to me at the manor hall.
Gold I'll bring, whatever comes to hand,
and something else, too, as my passage fee—
the master's child, my charge: a boy so high,
bright for his age; he runs with me on errands.
I'd take him with me happily; his price
would be I know not what in sale abroad.' 510

Her bargain made, she went back to the manor.
But they were on the island all that year,
getting by trade a cargo of our cattle;
until, the ship at length being laden full,
ready for sea, they sent a messenger
to the Phoinikian woman. Shrewd he was,
this fellow who came round my father's hall,
showing a golden chain all strung with amber,
a necklace. Maids in waiting and my mother
passed it from hand to hand, admiring it, 520
engaging they would buy it. But that dodger,
as soon as he had caught the woman's eye
and nodded, slipped away to join the ship.

She took my hand and led me through the court
into the portico. There by luck she found
winecups and tables still in place—for Father's
attendant counselors had dined just now
before they went to the assembly. Quickly
she hid three goblets in her bellying dress
to carry with her, while I tagged along 530
in my bewilderment. The sun went down
and all the lanes grew dark as we descended,
skirting the harbor in our haste to where
those traders of Phoinikia held their ship.
All went aboard at once and put to sea,
taking the two of us. A favoring wind
blew from the power of heaven. We sailed on
six nights and days without event. Then Zeus
the son of Kronos added one more noon—and sudden
arrows from Artemis pierced the woman's heart. 540
Stone-dead she dropped
into the sloshing bilge the way a tern
plummets; and the sailors heaved her over
as tender pickings for the seals and fish.
Now I was left in dread, alone, while wind
and current bore them on to Ithaka.
Laërtês purchased me. That was the way
I first laid eyes upon this land."

Odysseus,
the kingly man, replied:

"You rouse my pity,
telling what you endured when you were young. 550
But surely Zeus put good alongside ill:
torn from your own far home, you had the luck
to come into a kind man's service, generous
with food and drink. And a good life you lead,
unlike my own, all spent in barren roaming
from one country to the next, till now."

So the two men talked on, into the night,
leaving few hours for sleep before the Dawn
stepped up to her bright chair.

The ship now drifting
under the island lee, Telémakhos' 560
companions took in sail and mast, unshipped
the oars and rowed ashore. They moored her stern
by the stout hawser lines, tossed out the bow stones,
and waded in beyond the wash of ripples
to mix their wine and cook their morning meal.
When they had turned back hunger and thirst, Telémakhos
arose to give the order of the day.

"Pull for the town," he said, "and berth our ship,
while I go inland across country. Later,
this evening, after looking at my farms, 570
I'll join you in the city. When day comes
I hope to celebrate our crossing, feasting
everyone on good red meat and wine."

His noble passenger, Theoklýmenos,
now asked:

"What as to me, my dear young fellow,
where shall I go? Will I find lodging here
with some one of the lords of stony Ithaka?
Or go straight to your mother's hall and yours?"

Telémakhos turned round to him and said:

"I should myself invite you to our hall 580
if things were otherwise; there'd be no lack
of entertainment for you. As it stands,
no place could be more wretched for a guest
while I'm away. Mother will never see you;
she almost never shows herself at home
to the suitors there, but stays in her high chamber
weaving upon her loom. No, let me name
another man for you to go to visit:
Eurýmakhos,[9] the honored son of Pólybos.
In Ithaka they are dazzled by him now— 590
the strongest of their princes, bent on making
mother and all Odysseus' wealth his own.
Zeus on Olympos only knows
if some dark hour for them will intervene."

The words were barely spoken, when a hawk,
Apollo's courier, flew up on the right,
clutching a dove and plucking her—so feathers
floated down to the ground between Telémakhos
and the moored cutter. Theoklýmenos
called him apart and gripped his hand, whispering: 600

"A god spoke in this bird-sign on the right.
I knew it when I saw the hawk fly over us.
There is no kinglier house than yours, Telémakhos,
here in the realm of Ithaka. Your family
will be in power forever."

[9] *Eurýmakhos.* Since he is one of Penélopê's principal suitors, it is odd that Eurýmakhos should be recommended by Telémakhos as a host for his passenger. Indeed, Telémakhos soon changes his mind and asks the trusted crewman Peiraios to house Theoklýmenos. Possibly Telémakhos, with something of his father's wariness, hesitates until he has some evidence of Theoklýmenos' goodwill.

The young prince,
clear in spirit, answered:

"Be it so,
friend, as you say. And may you know as well
the friendship of my house, and many gifts
from me, so everyone may call you fortunate."

He called a trusted crewman named Peiraios, 610
and said to him:

"Peiraios, son of Klýtios,
can I rely on you again as ever, most
of all the friends who sailed with me to Pylos?
Take this man home with you, take care of him,
treat him with honor, till I come."

To this
Peiraios the good spearman answered:

"Aye,
stay in the wild country while you will,
I shall be looking after him, Telémakhos.
He will not lack good lodging."

Down to the ship 620
he turned, and boarded her, and called the others
to cast off the stern lines and come aboard.
So men climbed in to sit beside the rowlocks.
Telémakhos now tied his sandals on
and lifted his tough spear from the ship's deck;
hawsers were taken in, and they shoved off
to reach the town by way of the open sea
as he commanded them—royal Odysseus'
own dear son, Telémakhos.

On foot
and swiftly he went up toward the stockade 630
where swine were penned in hundreds, and at night
the guardian of the swine, the forester,
slept under arms on duty for his masters.

BOOK SIXTEEN: FATHER AND SON

But there were two men in the mountain hut—
Odysseus and the swineherd. At first light
blowing their fire up, they cooked their breakfast
and sent their lads out, driving herds to root
in the tall timber.

When Telémakhos came,
the wolvish troop of watchdogs only fawned on him
as he advanced. Odysseus heard them go
and heard the light crunch of a man's footfall—
at which he turned quickly to say:

"Eumaios,
here is one of your crew come back, or maybe 10
another friend: the dogs are out there snuffling
belly down; not one has even growled.
I can hear footsteps—"

But before he finished
his tall son stood at the door.
The swineherd
rose in surprise, letting a bowl and jug
tumble from his fingers. Going forward,
he kissed the young man's head, his shining eyes
and both hands, while his own tears brimmed and fell.
Think of a man whose dear and only son,
born to him in exile, reared with labor, 20
has lived ten years abroad and now returns:
how would that man embrace his son! Just so
the herdsman clapped his arms around Telémakhos
and covered him with kisses—for he knew
the lad had got away from death. He said:

"Light of my days, Telémakhos,
you made it back! When you took ship for Pylos
I never thought to see you here again.
Come in, dear child, and let me feast my eyes;
here you are, home from the distant places! 30
How rarely, anyway, you visit us,
your own men, and your own woods and pastures!
Always in the town, a man would think
you loved the suitors' company, those dogs!"

Telémakhos with his clear candor said:

"I am with you, Uncle. See now, I have come
because I wanted to see you first, to hear from you
if Mother stayed at home—or is she married
off to someone, and Odysseus' bed
left empty for some gloomy spider's weaving?" 40

Gently the forester replied to this:

"At home indeed your mother is, poor lady,
still in the women's hall. Her nights and days
are wearied out with grieving."

Stepping back
he took the bronze-shod lance, and the young prince
entered the cabin over the worn door stone.
Odysseus moved aside, yielding his couch,
but from across the room Telémakhos checked him:

"Friend, sit down; we'll find another chair
in our own hut. Here is the man to make one!" 50

The swineherd, when the quiet man sank down,
built a new pile of evergreens and fleeces—
a couch for the dear son of great Odysseus—
then gave them trenchers of good meat, left over
from the roast pork of yesterday, and heaped up
willow baskets full of bread, and mixed
an ivy bowl of honey-hearted wine.
Then he in turn sat down, facing Odysseus,
their hands went out upon the meat and drink
as they fell to, ridding themselves of hunger, 60
until Telémakhos paused and said:

"Oh, Uncle,
what's your friend's home port? How did he come?
Who were the sailors brought him here to Ithaka?
I doubt if he came walking on the sea."

And you replied, Eumaios—O my swineherd—

"Son, the truth about him is soon told.
His home land, and a broad land, too, is Krete,
but he has knocked about the world, he says,
for years, as the Powers wove his life. Just now
he broke away from a shipload of Thesprotians 70
to reach my hut. I place him in your hands.
Act as you will. He wishes your protection."

The young man said:

"Eumaios, my protection!
The notion cuts me to the heart. How can I
receive your friend at home? I am not old enough
or trained in arms. Could I defend myself
if someone picked a fight with me?

Besides,
mother is in a quandary, whether to stay with me
as mistress of our household, honoring
her lord's bed, and opinion in the town, 80
or take the best Akhaian who comes her way—
the one who offers most.

I'll undertake,
at all events, to clothe your friend for winter,

now he is with you. Tunic and cloak of wool,
a good broadsword, and sandals—these are his.
I can arrange to send him where he likes
or you may keep him in your cabin here.
I shall have bread and wine sent up; you need not
feel any pinch on his behalf.

Impossible
to let him stay in hall, among the suitors. 90
They are drunk, drunk on impudence, they might
injure my guest—and how could I bear that?
How could a single man take on those odds?
Not even a hero could.

The suitors are too strong."

At this the noble and enduring man, Odysseus,
addressed his son:

"Kind prince, it may be fitting
for me to speak a word. All that you say
gives me an inward wound as I sit listening.
I mean this wanton game they play, these fellows,
riding roughshod over you in your own house, 100
admirable as you are. But tell me,
are you resigned to being bled? The townsmen,
stirred up against you, are they, by some oracle?
Your brothers—can you say your brothers fail you?
A man should feel his kin, at least, behind him
in any clash, when a real fight is coming.
If my heart were as young as yours, if I were
son to Odysseus, or the man himself,
I'd rather have my head cut from my shoulders
by some slashing adversary, if I 110
brought no hurt upon that crew! Suppose
I went down, being alone, before the lot,
better, I say, to die at home in battle
than see these insupportable things, day after
day the stranger cuffed, the women slaves
dragged here and there, shame in the lovely rooms,
the wine drunk up in rivers, sheer waste
of pointless feasting, never at an end!"

Telémakhos replied:

"Friend, I'll explain to you.
There is no rancor in the town against me, 120
no fault of brothers, whom a man should feel
behind him when a fight is in the making;
no, no—in our family the First Born
of Heaven, Zeus, made single sons the rule.
Arkeísios had but one, Laërtês; he
in turn fathered only one, Odysseus,

who left me in his hall alone, too young
to be of any use to him.
And so you see why enemies fill our house
in these days: all the princes of the islands, 130
Doulíkhion, Samê, wooded Zakýnthos,
Ithaka, too—lords of our island rock—
eating our house up as they court my mother.
She cannot put an end to it; she dare not
bar the marriage that she hates; and they
devour all my substance and my cattle,
and who knows when they'll slaughter me as well?
It rests upon the gods' great knees.
Uncle,
go down at once and tell the Lady Penélopê
that I am back from Pylos, safe and sound. 140
I stay here meanwhile. You will give your message
and then return. Let none of the Akhaians
hear it; they have a mind to do me harm."

To this, Eumaios, you replied:
"I know.
But make this clear, now—should I not likewise
call on Laërtês with your news? Hard hit
by sorrow though he was, mourning Odysseus,
he used to keep an eye upon his farm.
He had what meals he pleased, with his own folk.
But now no more, not since you sailed for Pylos; 150
he has not taken food or drink, I hear,
sitting all day, blind to the work of harvest,
groaning, while the skin shrinks on his bones."

Telémakhos answered:

"One more misery,
but we had better leave it so.
If men choose, and have their choice, in everything,
we'd have my father home.
Turn back
when you have done your errand, as you must,
not to be caught alone in the countryside.
But wait—you may tell Mother 160
to send our old housekeeper on the quiet
and quickly; she can tell the news to Grandfather."

The swineherd, roused, reached out to get his sandals,
tied them on, and took the road.

Who else
beheld this but Athena? From the air
she walked, taking the form of a tall woman,

handsome and clever at her craft, and stood
beyond the gate in plain sight of Odysseus,
unseen, though, by Telémakhos, unguessed,
for not to everyone will gods appear. 170
Odysseus noticed her; so did the dogs,
who cowered whimpering away from her. She only
nodded, signing to him with her brows,
a sign he recognized. Crossing the yard,
he passed out through the gate in the stockade
to face the goddess. There she said to him:

"Son of Laërtês and the gods of old,
Odysseus, master of land ways and sea ways,
dissemble to your son no longer now.
The time has come: tell him how you together 180
will bring doom on the suitors in the town.
I shall not be far distant then, for I
myself desire battle."

Saying no more,
she tipped her golden wand upon the man,
making his cloak pure white, and the knit tunic
fresh around him. Lithe and young she made him,
ruddy with sun, his jawline clean, the beard
no longer grey upon his chin. And she
withdrew when she had done.

Then Lord Odysseus
reappeared—and his son was thunderstruck. 190
Fear in his eyes, he looked down and away
as though it were a god, and whispered:

"Stranger,
you are no longer what you were just now!
Your cloak is new; even your skin! You are
one of the gods who rule the sweep of heaven!
Be kind to us, we'll make you fair oblation
and gifts of hammered gold. Have mercy on us!"

The noble and enduring man replied:

"No god. Why take me for a god? No, no.
I am that father whom your boyhood lacked 200
and suffered pain for lack of. I am he."

Held back too long, the tears ran down his cheeks
as he embraced his son.

Only Telémakhos,
uncomprehending, wild
with incredulity, cried out:

"You cannot
be my father Odysseus! Meddling spirits
conceived this trick to twist the knife in me!
No man of woman born could work these wonders
by his own craft, unless a god came into it 
with ease to turn him young or old at will. 210
I swear you were in rags and old,
and here you stand like one of the immortals!"

Odysseus brought his ranging mind to bear
and said:

"This is not princely, to be swept
away by wonder at your father's presence.
No other Odysseus will ever come,
for he and I are one, the same; his bitter 
fortune and his wanderings are mine.
Twenty years gone, and I am back again
on my own island.

As for my change of skin, 220
that is a charm Athena, Hope of Soldiers,
uses as she will; she has the knack
to make me seem a beggar man sometimes
and sometimes young, with finer clothes about me.
It is no hard thing for the gods of heaven
to glorify a man or bring him low."

When he had spoken, down he sat.

Then, throwing
his arms around this marvel of a father
Telémakhos began to weep. Salt tears
rose from the wells of longing in both men, 230
and cries burst from both as keen and fluttering
as those of the great taloned hawk,
whose nestlings farmers take before they fly.
So helplessly they cried, pouring out tears,
and might have gone on weeping so till sundown,
had not Telémakhos said:

"Dear father! Tell me
what kind of vessel put you here ashore
on Ithaka? Your sailors, who were they?
I doubt you made it, walking on the sea!"

Then said Odysseus, who had borne the barren sea: 240

"Only plain truth shall I tell you, child.
Great seafarers, the Phaiákians, gave me passage
as they give other wanderers. By night
over the open ocean, while I slept,

they brought me in their cutter, set me down
on Ithaka, with gifts of bronze and gold
and stores of woven things. By the gods' will
these lie all hidden in a cave. I came
to this wild place, directed by Athena,
so that we might lay plans to kill our enemies. 250
Count up the suitors for me, let me know
what men at arms are there, how many men.
I must put all my mind to it, to see
if we two by ourselves can take them on
or if we should look round for help."

Telémakhos
replied:

"O Father, all my life your fame
as a fighting man has echoed in my ears—
your skills with weapons and the tricks of war—
but what you speak of is a staggering thing,
beyond imagining, for me. How can two men 260
do battle with a houseful in their prime?
For I must tell you this is no affair
of ten or even twice ten men, but scores,
throngs of them. You shall see, here and now.
The number from Doulíkhion alone
is fifty-two, picked men, with armorers,
a half dozen; twenty-four came from Samê,
twenty from Zakýnthos; our own island
accounts for twelve, high-ranked, and their retainers,
Medôn the crier, and the Master Harper 270
besides a pair of handymen at feasts.
If we go in against all these
I fear we pay in salt blood for your vengeance.
You must think hard if you would conjure up
the fighting strength to take us through."

Odysseus
who had endured the long war and the sea
answered:

"I'll tell you now.
Suppose Athena's arm is over us, and Zeus
her father's, must I rack my brains for more?"

Clearheaded Telémakhos looked hard and said: 280

"Those two are great defenders, no one doubts it,
but throned in the serene clouds overhead;
other affairs of men and gods they have
to rule over."

And the hero answered:

"Before long they will stand to right and left of us
in combat, in the shouting, when the test comes—
our nerve against the suitors' in my hall.
Here is your part: at break of day tomorrow
home with you, go mingle with our princes.
The swineherd later on will take me down 290
the port-side trail—a beggar, by my looks,
hangdog and old. If they make fun of me
in my own courtyard, let your ribs cage up
your springing heart, no matter what I suffer,
no matter if they pull me by the heels
or practice shots at me, to drive me out.
Look on, hold down your anger. You may even
plead with them, by heaven! in gentle terms
to quit their horseplay—not that they will heed you,
rash as they are, facing their day of wrath. 300
Now fix the next step in your mind.

Athena,
counseling me, will give me word, and I
shall signal to you, nodding: at that point
round up all armor, lances, gear of war
left in our hall, and stow the lot away
back in the vaulted store room. When the suitors
miss those arms and question you, be soft
in what you say: answer:

'I thought I'd move them
out of the smoke. They seemed no longer those
bright arms Odysseus left us years ago 310
when he went off to Troy. Here where the fire's
hot breath came, they had grown black and drear.
One better reason, too, I had from Zeus:
suppose a brawl starts up when you are drunk,
you might be crazed and bloody one another,
and that would stain your feast, your courtship. Tempered
iron can magnetize a man.'

Say that.
But put aside two broadswords and two spears
for our own use, two oxhide shields nearby
when we go into action. Pallas Athena 320
and Zeus All Provident will see you through,
bemusing our young friends.

Now one thing more.
If son of mine you are and blood of mine,
let no one hear Odysseus is about.
Neither Laërtês, nor the swineherd here,
nor any slave, nor even Penélopê.
But you and I alone must learn how far

the women are corrupted; we should know
how to locate good men among our hands,
the loyal and respectful, and the shirkers 330
who take you lightly, as alone and young."

His admirable son replied:

"Ah, Father,
even when danger comes I think you'll find
courage in me. I am not scatterbrained.
But as to checking on the field hands now,
I see no gain for us in that. Reflect,
you make a long toil, that way, if you care
to look men in the eye at every farm,
while these gay devils in our hall at ease
eat up our flocks and herds, leaving us nothing. 340

As for the maids I say, Yes: make distinction
between good girls and those who shame your house;
all that I shy away from is a scrutiny
of cottagers just now. The time for that
comes later—if in truth you have a sign
from Zeus the Stormking."

So their talk ran on,
while down the coast, and round toward Ithaka,
hove the good ship that had gone out to Pylos
bearing Telémakhos and his companions.
Into the wide bay waters, on to the dark land, 350
they drove her, hauled her up, took out the oars
and the canvas for light-hearted squires to carry
homeward—as they carried, too, the gifts
of Meneláos round to Klýtios'[1] house.
But first they sped a runner to Penélopê.
They knew that quiet lady must be told
the prince her son had come ashore, and sent
his good ship round to port; not one soft tear
should their sweet queen let fall.

Both messengers,
crewman and swineherd—reached the outer gate 360
in the same instant, bearing the same news,
and went in side by side to the king's hall.
He of the ship burst out among the maids:

"Your son's ashore this morning, O my Queen!"

[1] Father of the trusty Peiraios; see the end of Book XV.

But the swineherd calmly stood near Penélopê
whispering what her son had bade him tell
and what he had enjoined on her. No more.
When he had done, he left the place and turned
back to his steading in the hills.

By now,
sullen confusion weighed upon the suitors. 370
Out of the house, out of the court they went,
beyond the wall and gate, to sit in council.
Eurýmakhos, the son of Pólybos,
opened discussion:

"Friends, face up to it;
that young pup, Telémakhos, has done it;
he made the round trip, though we said he could not.
Well—now to get the best craft we can find
afloat, with oarsmen who can drench her bows,
and tell those on the island to come home."

He was yet speaking when Amphínomos, 380
craning seaward, spotted the picket ship
already in the roadstead under oars
with canvas brailed up; and this fresh arrival
made him chuckle. Then he told his friends:

"Too late for messages. Look, here they come
along the bay. Some god has brought them news,
or else they saw the cutter pass—and could not
overtake her."

On their feet at once,
the suitors took the road to the sea beach,
where, meeting the black ship, they hauled her in. 390
Oars and gear they left for their light-hearted
squires to carry, and all in company
made off for the assembly ground. All others,
young and old alike, they barred from sitting.
Eupeithês' son, Antínoös, made the speech:

"How the gods let our man escape a boarding,
that is the wonder.

We had lookouts posted
up on the heights all day in the sea wind,
and every hour a fresh pair of eyes;
at night we never slept ashore 400
but after sundown cruised the open water
to the southeast, patrolling until Dawn.
We were prepared to cut him off and catch him,
squelch him for good and all. The power of heaven
steered him the long way home.

Well, let this company plan his destruction,
and leave him no way out, this time. I see
our business here unfinished while he lives.
He knows, now, and he's no fool. Besides,
his people are all tired of playing up to us. 410
I say, act now, before he brings the whole
body of Akhaians to assembly—
and he would leave no word unsaid, in righteous
anger speaking out before them all
of how we plotted murder, and then missed him.
Will they commend us for that pretty work?
Take action now, or we are in for trouble;
we might be exiled, driven off our lands.
Let the first blow be ours.
If we move first, and get our hands on him 420
far from the city's eye, on path or field,
then stores and livestock will be ours to share;
the house we may confer upon his mother—
and on the man who marries her. Decide
otherwise you may—but if, my friends,
you want that boy to live and have his patrimony,
then we should eat no more of his good mutton,
come to this place no more.
Let each from his own hall
court her with dower gifts. And let her marry
the destined one, the one who offers most." 430

He ended, and no sound was heard among them,
sitting all hushed, until at last the son
of Nísos Aretíadês arose—
Amphínomos.
He led the group of suitors
who came from grainlands on Doulíkhion,
and he had lightness in his talk that pleased
Penélopê, for he meant no ill.
Now, in concern for them, he spoke:
"O Friends
I should not like to kill Telémakhos.
It is a shivery thing to kill a prince 440
of royal blood.
We should consult the gods.
If Zeus hands down a ruling for that act,
then I shall say, 'Come one, come all,' and go
cut him down with my own hand—
but I say Halt, if gods are contrary."

Now this proposal won them, and it carried.
Breaking their session up, away they went
to take their smooth chairs in Odysseus' house.

Meanwhile Penélopê the Wise,
decided, for her part, to make appearance 450
before the valiant young men.
She knew now
they plotted her child's death in her own hall,
for once more Medôn, who had heard them, told her.
Into the hall that lovely lady came,
with maids attending, and approached the suitors,
till near a pillar of the well-wrought roof
she paused, her shining veil across her cheeks,
and spoke directly to Antínoös:

"Infatuate,
steeped in evil! Yet in Ithaka they say
you were the best one of your generation 460
in mind and speech. Not so, you never were.
Madman, why do you keep forever knitting
death for Telémakhos? Have you no piety
toward men dependent on another's mercy?
Before Lord Zeus, no sanction can be found
for one such man to plot against another!
Or are you not aware that your own father
fled to us when the realm was up in arms
against him? He had joined the Taphian pirates
in ravaging Thesprotian folk, our friends. 470
Our people would have raided *him*, then—breached
his heart, butchered his herds to feast upon—
only Odysseus took him in, and held
the furious townsmen off. It is Odysseus'
house you now consume, his wife you court,
his son you kill, or try to kill. And me
you ravage now, and grieve. I call upon you
to make an end of it!—and your friends too!"

The son of Pólybos it was, Eurýmakhos,
who answered her with ready speech:

"My lady 480
Penélopê, wise daughter of Ikários,
you must shake off these ugly thoughts. I say
that man does not exist, nor will, who dares
lay hands upon your son Telémakhos,
while I live, walk the earth, and use my eyes.
The man's life blood, I swear,
will spurt and run out black around my lancehead!
For it is true of me, too, that Odysseus,
raiders of cities, took me on his knees
and fed me often—tidbits and red wine. 490
Should not Telémakhos, therefore, be dear to me
above the rest of men? I tell the lad
he must not tremble for his life, at least

alone in the suitors' company. Heaven
deals death no man avoids."

Blasphemous lies
in earnest tones he told—the one who planned
the lad's destruction!

Silently the lady
made her way to her glowing upper chamber,
there to weep for her dear lord, Odysseus,
until grey-eyed Athena 500
cast sweet sleep upon her eyes.

At fall of dusk
Odysseus and his son heard the approach
of the good forester. They had been standing
over the fire with a spitted pig,
a yearling. And Athena coming near
with one rap of her wand made of Odysseus
an old old man again, with rags about him—
for if the swineherd knew his lord were there
he could not hold the news; Penélopê
would hear it from him.

Now Telémakhos 510
greeted him first:

"Eumaios, back again!
What was the talk in town? Are the tall suitors
home again, by this time, from their ambush,
or are they still on watch for my return?"

And you replied, Eumaios—O my swineherd:

"There was no time to ask or talk of that;
I hurried through the town. Even while I spoke
my message, I felt driven to return.
A runner from your friends turned up, a crier,
who gave the news first to your mother. Ah! 520
One thing I do know; with my own two eyes
I saw it. As I climbed above the town
to where the sky is cut by Hermês' ridge,
I saw a ship bound in for our own bay
with many oarsmen in it, laden down
with sea provisioning and two-edged spears,
and I surmised those were the men.

Who knows?"

Telémakhos, now strong with magic, smiled
across at his own father—but avoided
the swineherd's eye.

So when the pig was done, 530
the spit no longer to be turned, the table
garnished, everyone sat down to feast

on all the savory flesh he craved. And when
they had put off desire for meat and drink,
they turned to bed and took the gift of sleep.

BOOK SEVENTEEN: THE BEGGAR AT THE MANOR

When the young Dawn came bright into the East
spreading her finger tips of rose, Telémakhos
the king's son, tied on his rawhide sandals
and took the lance that bore his handgrip. Burning
to be away, and on the path to town,
he told the swineherd:

"Uncle, the truth is
I must go down myself into the city.
Mother must see me there, with her own eyes,
or she will weep and feel forsaken still,
and will not set her mind at rest. Your job 10
will be to lead this poor man down to beg.
Some householder may want to dole him out
a loaf and pint. I have my own troubles.
Am I to care for every last man who comes?
And if he takes it badly—well, so much
the worse for him. Plain truth is what I favor."

At once Odysseus the great tactician
spoke up briskly:

"Neither would I myself
care to be kept here, lad. A beggar man
fares better in the town. Let it be said 20
I am not yet so old I must lay up
indoors and mumble, 'Aye, Aye' to a master.[1]
Go on, then. As you say, my friend can lead me
as soon as I have had a bit of fire
and when the sun grows warmer. These old rags
could be my death, outside on a frosty morning,
and the town is distant, so they say."

Telémakhos
with no more words went out, and through the fence,
and down hill, going fast on the steep footing,
nursing woe for the suitors in his heart. 30

[1] Odysseus means that he is not yet so old that he must remain in one place, subject to a single master.

Before the manor hall, he leaned his lance
against a great porch pillar and stepped in
across the door stone.
Old Eurýkleia
saw him first, for that day she was covering
handsome chairs nearby with clean fleeces.
She ran to him at once, tears in her eyes;
and other maidservants of the old soldier
Odysseus gathered round to greet their prince,
kissing his head and shoulders.
Quickly, then,
Penélopê the Wise, tall in her beauty 40
as Artemis or pale-gold Aphroditê,
appeared from her high chamber and came down
to throw her arms around her son. In tears
she kissed his head, kissed both his shining eyes,
then cried out, and her words flew:
"Back with me!
Telémakhos, more sweet to me than sunlight!
I thought I should not see you again, ever,
after you took the ship that night to Pylos—
against my will, with not a word! you went
for news of your dear father. Tell me now 50
of everything you saw!"

But he made answer:

"Mother, not now. You make me weep. My heart
already aches—I came near death at sea.
You must bathe, first of all, and change your dress,
and take your maids to the highest room to pray.
Pray, and burn offerings to the gods of heaven,
that Zeus may put his hand to our revenge.

I am off now to bring home from the square
a guest, a passenger I had. I sent him
yesterday with all my crew to town. 60
Peiraios was to care for him, I said,
and keep him well, with honor, till I came."

She caught back the swift words upon her tongue.
Then softly she withdrew
to bathe and dress her body in fresh linen,
and make her offerings to the gods of heaven,
praying Almighty Zeus
to put his hand to their revenge.

Telémakhos
had left the hall, taken his lance, and gone
with two quick hounds at heel into the town, 70

Athena's grace in his long stride
making the people gaze as he came near.
And suitors gathered, primed with friendly words,
despite the deadly plotting in their hearts—
but these, and all their crowd, he kept away from.
Next he saw sitting some way off, apart,
Mentor, with Antiphos and Halithersês,
friends of his father's house in years gone by.
Near these men he sat down, and told his tale
under their questioning.

His crewman, young Peiraios, 80
guided through town, meanwhile, into the Square,
the Argive exile, Theoklýmenos.
Telémakhos lost no time in moving toward him;
but first Peiraios had his say:

Telémakhos,
you must send maids to me, at once, and let me
turn over to you those gifts from Meneláos!"

The prince had pondered it, and said:

"Peiraios,
none of us knows how this affair will end.
Say one day our fine suitors, without warning,
draw upon me, kill me in our hall, 90
and parcel out my patrimony—I wish
you, and no one of them, to have those things.
But if my hour comes, if I can bring down
bloody death on all that crew,
you will rejoice to send my gifts to me—
and so will I rejoice!"

Then he departed,
leading his guest, the lonely stranger, home.

Over chair-backs in hall they dropped their mantles
and passed in to the polished tubs, where maids
poured out warm baths for them, anointed them, 100
and pulled fresh tunics, fleecy cloaks around them.
Soon they were seated at their ease in hall.
A maid came by to tip a golden jug
over their fingers into a silver bowl
and draw a gleaming table up beside them.
The larder mistress brought her tray of loaves
and savories, dispensing each.

In silence
across the hall, beside a pillar, propped
in a long chair, Telémakhos' mother
spun a fine wool yarn.

The young men's hands 110
went out upon the good things placed before them,
and only when their hunger and thirst were gone
did she look up and say:

"Telémakhos,
what am I to do now? Return alone
and lie again on my forsaken bed—
sodden how often with my weeping
since that day when Odysseus put to sea
to join the Atreidai[2] before Troy?

Could you not
tell me, before the suitors fill our house,
what news you have of his return?"

He answered: 120

"Now that you ask a second time, dear Mother,
here is the truth.

We went ashore at Pylos
to Nestor, lord and guardian of the West,
who gave me welcome in his towering hall.
So kind he was, he might have been my father
and I his long-lost son—so truly kind,
taking me in with his own honored sons.
But as to Odysseus' bitter fate,
living or dead, he had no news at all
from anyone on earth, he said. He sent me 130
overland in a strong chariot
to Atreus' son, the captain, Meneláos.
And I saw Helen there, for whom the Argives
fought, and the Trojans fought, as the gods willed.
Then Meneláos of the great war cry
asked me my errand in that ancient land
of Lakedaimon. So I told our story,
and in reply he burst out:[3]

'Intolerable!
That feeble men, unfit as those men are,
should think to lie in that great captain's bed, 140
fawns in the lion's lair! As if a doe
put down her litter of sucklings there, while she
sniffed at the glen or grazed a grassy hollow.
Ha! Then the lord returns to his own bed
and deals out wretched doom on both alike.

So will Odysseus deal out doom on these.
O Father Zeus, Athena, and Apollo!
I pray he comes as once he was, in Lesbos,

[2] Sons of Atreus—Agamémnon and Meneláos.
[3] The following quotation of Meneláos' words summarizes his narrative in Book IV.

when he stood up to wrestle Philomeleidês—
champion and Island King— 150
and smashed him down. How the Akhaians cheered!
If that Odysseus could meet the suitors,
they'd have a quick reply, a stunning dowry!
Now for your questions, let me come to the point.
I would not misreport it for you; let me
tell you what the Ancient of the Sea,
that infallible seer, told me.
On an island
your father lies and grieves. The Ancient saw him
held by a nymph, Kalypso, in her hall;
no means of sailing home remained to him, 160
no ship with oars, and no ship's company
to pull him on the broad back of the sea.'

I had this from the lord marshal, Meneláos,
and when my errand in that place was done
I left for home. A fair breeze from the gods
brought me swiftly back to our dear island."

The boy's tale made her heart stir in her breast,
but this was not all. Mother and son now heard
Theoklýmenos, the diviner, say:

"He does not see it clear—
O gentle lady, 170
wife of Odysseus Laërtiadês,
listen to me, I can reveal this thing.
Zeus be my witness, and the table set
for strangers and the hearth to which I've come—
the lord Odysseus, I tell you
is present now, already, on this island!
Quartered somewhere, or going about, he knows
what evil is afoot. He has it in him
to bring a black hour on the suitors. Yesterday,
still at the ship, I saw this in a portent. 180
I read the sign aloud, I told Telémakhos!"

The prudent queen, for her part, said:
"Stranger,
if only this came true—
our love would go to you, with many gifts;
aye, every man who passed would call you happy!"

So ran the talk between these three.
Meanwhile,
swaggering before Odysseus' hall,
the suitors were competing at the discus throw
and javelin, on the level measured field.

But when the dinner hour drew on, and beasts 190
were being driven from the fields to slaughter—
as beasts were, every day—Medôn spoke out:
Medôn, the crier, whom the suitors liked;
he took his meat beside them.

"Men," he said,
"each one has had his work-out and his pleasure,
come in to Hall now; time to make our feast.
Are discus throws more admirable than a roast
when the proper hour comes?"

At this reminder
they all broke up their games, and trailed away
into the gracious, timbered hall. There, first, 200
they dropped their cloaks on chairs; then came their ritual:
putting great rams and fat goats to the knife—
pigs and a cow, too.

So they made their feast.

During these hours, Odysseus and the swineherd
were on their way out of the hills to town.
The forester had got them started, saying:

"Friend, you have hopes, I know, of your adventure
into the heart of town today. My lord
wishes it so, not I. No, I should rather
you stood by here as guardian of our steading. 210
But I owe reverence to my prince, and fear
he'll make my ears burn later if I fail.
A master's tongue has a rough edge. Off we go.
Part of the day is past; nightfall will be
early, and colder, too."

Odysseus,
who had it all timed in his head, replied:

"I know, as well as you do. Let's move on.
You lead the way—the whole way. Have you got
a staff, a lopped stick, you could let me use
to put my weight on when I slip? This path 220
is hard going, they said."

Over his shoulders
he slung his patched-up knapsack, an old bundle
tied with twine. Eumaios found a stick for him,
the kind he wanted, and the two set out,
leaving the boys and dogs to guard the place.
In this way good Eumaios led his lord
down to the city.

And it seemed to him
he led an old outcast, a beggar man,
leaning most painfully upon a stick,
his poor cloak, all in tatters, looped about him. 230

Down by the stony trail they made their way
as far as Clearwater, not far from town—
a spring house where the people filled their jars.
Ithakos, Nêritos, and Polýktor[4] built it,
and round it on the humid ground a grove,
a circular wood of poplars grew. Ice cold
in runnels from a high rock ran the spring,
and over it there stood an altar stone
to the cool nymphs, where all men going by
laid offerings.
Well, here the son of Dólios 240
crossed their path—Melánthios.[5]
He was driving
a string of choice goats for the evening meal,
with two goatherds beside him; and no sooner
had he laid eyes upon the wayfarers
than he began to growl and taunt them both
so grossly that Odysseus' heart grew hot:

"Here comes one scurvy type leading another!
God pairs them off together, every time.
Swineherd, where are you taking your new pig,
that stinking beggar there, licker of pots? 250
How many doorposts has he rubbed his back on
whining for garbage, where a noble guest
would rate a cauldron or a sword?
Hand him
over to me, I'll make a farmhand of him,
a stall scraper, a fodder carrier! Whey
for drink will put good muscle on his shank!
No chance: he learned his dodges long ago—
no honest sweat. He'd rather tramp the country
begging, to keep his hoggish belly full.
Well, I can tell you this for sure: 260
in King Odysseus' hall, if he goes there,
footstools will fly around his head—good shots
from strong hands. Back and side, his ribs will catch it
on the way out!"

[4] These three were the founding fathers of the island; Ithakos' name represents the island itself, Nêritos' name an important mountain on the island.

[5] Dólios was a trusty steward of Odysseus' father, Laërtês. As we learn later, Melánthios' sister Melántho, maid to Penélopê, is a mistress of the suitor Eurýmakhos, a fact that probably accounts for the intimacy of her goatherd brother with the suitors.

And like a drunken fool
he kicked at Odysseus' hip as he passed by.
Not even jogged off stride, or off the trail,
the Lord Odysseus walked along, debating
inwardly whether to whirl and beat
the life out of this fellow with his stick,
or toss him, brain him on the stony ground. 270
Then he controlled himself, and bore it quietly.
Not so the swineherd.
Seeing the man before him,
he raised his arms and cried:

"Nymphs of the spring,
daughters of Zeus, if ever Odysseus
burnt you a thighbone in rich fat—a ram's
or kid's thighbone, hear me, grant my prayer:
let our true lord come back, let heaven bring him
to rid the earth of these fine courtly ways
Melánthios picks up around the town—
all wine and wind! Bad shepherds ruin flocks!" 280

Melánthios the goatherd answered:

"Bless me!
The dog can snap: how he goes on! Some day
I'll take him in a slave ship overseas
and trade him for a herd!
Old Silverbow
Apollo, if he shot clean through Telémakhos[6]
in hall today, what luck! Or let the suitors
cut him down!
Odysseus died at sea;
no coming home for him."

He flung this out
and left the two behind to come on slowly,
while he went hurrying to the king's hall. 290
There he slipped in, and sat among the suitors,
beside the one he doted on—Eurýmakhos.
Then working servants helped him to his meat
and the mistress of the larder gave him bread.

Reaching the gate, Odysseus and the forester
halted and stood outside, for harp notes came
around them rippling on the air
as Phêmios picked out a song. Odysseus
caught his companion's arm and said:

[6] That is, if Telémakhos should drop dead.

"My friend,
here is the beautiful place—who could mistake it? 300
Here is Odysseus' hall: no hall like this!
See how one chamber grows out of another;
see how the court is tight with wall and coping;
no man at arms could break this gateway down!
Your banqueting young lords are here in force,
I gather, from the fumes of mutton roasting
and strum of harping—harping, which the gods
appoint sweet friend of feasts!"

And—O my swineherd!
you replied:

"That was quick recognition;
but you are no numbskull—in this or anything. 310
Now we must plan this action. Will you take
leave of me here, and go ahead alone
to make your entrance now among the suitors?
Or do you choose to wait?—Let me go forward
and go in first.
Do not delay too long;
someone might find you skulking here outside
and take a club to you, or heave a lance.
Bear this in mind, I say."

The patient hero
Odysseus answered:

"Just what I was thinking.
You go in first, and leave me here a little. 320
But as for blows and missiles,
I am no tyro[7] at these things. I learned
to keep my head in hardship—years of war
and years at sea. Let this new trial come.
The cruel belly, can you hide its ache?
How many bitter days it brings! Long ships
with good stout planks athwart—would fighters rig them
to ride the barren sea, except for hunger?
Seawolves—woe to their enemies!"

While he spoke
an old hound, lying near, pricked up his ears 330
and lifted up his muzzle. This was Argos,
trained as a puppy by Odysseus,
but never taken on a hunt before
his master sailed for Troy. The young men, afterward,

[7] Inexperienced beginner.

hunted wild goats with him, and hare, and deer,
but he had grown old in his master's absence.
Treated as rubbish now, he lay at last
upon a mass of dung before the gates—
manure of mules and cows, piled there until 
fieldhands could spread it on the king's estate. 340
Abandoned there, and half destroyed with flies,
old Argos lay.

But when he knew he heard
Odysseus' voice nearby, he did his best
to wag his tail, nose down, with flattened ears,
having no strength to move nearer his master.
And the man looked away, 
wiping a salt tear from his cheek; but he
hid this from Eumaios. Then he said:

"I marvel that they leave this hound to lie
here on the dung pile; 350
he would have been a fine dog, from the look of him,
though I can't say as to his power and speed
when he was young. You find the same good build 
in house dogs, table dogs landowners keep
all for style."

And you replied, Eumaios:

"A hunter owned him—but the man is dead
in some far place. If this old hound could show
the form he had when Lord Odysseus left him,
going to Troy, you'd see him swift and strong.
He never shrank from any savage thing 360
he'd brought to bay in the deep woods; on the scent
no other dog kept up with him. Now misery
has him in leash. His owner died abroad,
and here the women slaves will take no care of him. 
You know how servants are: without a master
they have no will to labor, or excel.
For Zeus who views the wide world takes away
half the manhood of a man, that day
he goes into captivity and slavery."

Eumaios crossed the court and went straight forward 370
into the mégaron[8] among the suitors;
but death and darkness in that instant closed
the eyes of Argos, who had seen his master, 
Odysseus, after twenty years.

[8] The great hall of the house.

Long before anyone else
Telémakhos caught sight of the grey woodsman
coming from the door, and called him over
with a quick jerk of his head. Eumaios'
narrowed eyes made out an empty bench
beside the one the carver used—that servant
who had no respite, carving for the suitors. 380
This bench he took possession of, and placed it
across the table from Telémakhos
for his own use. Then the two men were served
cuts from a roast and bread from a bread basket.

At no long interval, Odysseus came
through his own doorway as a mendicant,
humped like a bundle of rags over his stick.
He settled on the inner ash wood sill,
leaning against the door jamb—cypress timber
the skilled carpenter planed years ago 390
and set up with a plumbline.

Now Telémakhos
took an entire loaf and a double handful
of roast meat; then he said to the forester:

"Give these to the stranger there. But tell him
to go among the suitors, on his own;
he may beg all he wants. This hanging back
is no asset to a hungry man."

The swineherd rose at once, crossed to the door,
and halted by Odysseus.

"Friend," he said,
"Telémakhos is pleased to give you these, 400
but he commands you to approach the suitors;
you may ask all you want from them. He adds,
your shyness is no asset to a beggar."

The great tactician, lifting up his eyes,
cried:

"Zeus aloft! A blessing on Telémakhos!
Let all things come to pass as he desires!"

Palms held out, in the beggar's gesture, he
received the bread and meat and put it down
before him on his knapsack—lowly table!—
then he fell to, devouring it. Meanwhile 410
the harper in the great room sang a song.
Not till the man was fed did the sweet harper

end his singing—whereupon the company
made the walls ring again with talk.

Unseen,
Athena took her place beside Odysseus
whispering in his ear:

"Yes, try the suitors.
You may collect a few more loaves, and learn
who are the decent lads, and who are vicious—
although not one can be excused from death!"

So he appealed to them, one after another, 420
going from left to right, with open palm,
as though his life time had been spent in beggary.
And they gave bread, for pity—wondering, though,
at the strange man. Who could this beggar be,
where did he come from? each would ask his neighbor;
till in their midst the goatherd, Melánthios,
raised his voice:

"Hear just a word from me,
my lords who court our illustrious queen!
This man,
this foreigner, I saw him on the road;
the swineherd here was leading him this way; 430
who, what, or whence he claims to be, I could not
say for sure."

At this, Antínoös
turned on the swineherd brutally, saying:

"You famous
breeder of pigs, why bring this fellow here?
Are we not plagued enough with beggars,
foragers and such rats?
You find the company
too slow at eating up your lord's estate—
is that it? So you call this scarecrow in?"

The forester replied:

"Antínoös,

well born you are, but that was not well said. 440
Who would call in a foreigner?—unless
an artisan with skill to serve the realm,
a healer, or a prophet, or a builder,
or one whose harp and song might give us joy.
All these are sought for on the endless earth,
but when have beggars come by invitation?

Who puts a field mouse in his granary? My lord,
you are a hard man, and you always were,
more so than others of this company—hard
on all Odysseus' people and on me. 450
But this I can forget
as long as Penélopê lives on, the wise and tender
mistress of this hall; as long
as Prince Telémakhos—"

But he broke off
at a look from Telémakhos, who said:

"Be still.
Spare me a long-drawn answer to this gentleman.
With his unpleasantness, he will forever make
strife where he can—and goad the others on."

He turned and spoke out clearly to Antínoös:

"What fatherly concern you show me! Frighten 460
this unknown fellow, would you, from my hall
with words that promise blows—may God forbid it!
Give him a loaf. Am I a niggard? No,
I call on you to give. And spare your qualms
as to my mother's loss, or anyone's—
not that in truth you have such care at heart:
your heart is all in feeding, not in giving."

Antínoös replied:

"What high and mighty
talk, Telémakhos! No holding you!
If every suitor gave what I may give him, 470
he could be kept for months—kept out of sight!"

He reached under the table for the footstool
his shining feet had rested on—and this
he held up so that all could see his gift.

But all the rest gave alms,
enough to fill the beggar's pack with bread
and roast meat.

So it looked as though Odysseus
had had his taste of what these men were like
and could return scot free to his own doorway—
but halting now before Antínoös 480
he made a little speech to him. Said he:

"Give a mite, friend. I would not say, myself,
you are the worst man of the young Akhaians.
The noblest, rather; kingly, by your look;

therefore you'll give more bread than others do.
Let me speak well of you as I pass on
over the boundless earth!

I, too, you know,
had fortune once, lived well, stood well with men,
and gave alms, often, to poor wanderers
like this one that you see—aye, to all sorts, 490
no matter in what dire want. I owned
servants—many, god knows—and all the rest
that goes with being prosperous, as they say.
But Zeus the son of Kronos brought me down.

No telling
why he would have it, but he made me go
to Egypt with a company of rovers—
a long sail to the south—for my undoing.
Up the broad Nile and in to the river bank
I brought my dipping squadron. There, indeed, 500
I told the men to stand guard at the ships;
I sent patrols out—out to rising ground;
but reckless greed carried my crews away
to plunder the Egyptian farms; they bore off
wives and children, killed what men they found.
The news ran on the wind to the city, a night cry,
and sunrise brought both infantry and horsemen,
filling the river plain with dazzle of bronze;
then Zeus lord of lightning
threw my men into a blind panic; no one dared 510
stand against that host closing around us.
Their scything weapons left our dead in piles,
but some they took alive, into forced labor,
myself among them. And they gave me, then,
to one Dmêtor, a traveller, son of Iasos,
who ruled at Kypros.[9] He conveyed me there.
From that place, working northward, miserably—"

But here Antínoös broke in, shouting:

"God!
What evil wind blew in this pest?

Get over,
stand in the passage! Nudge my table, will you? 520
Egyptian whips are sweet
to what you'll come to here, you nosing rat,
making your pitch to everyone!
These men have bread to throw away on you
because it is not theirs. Who cares? Who spares
another's food, when he has more than plenty?"

[9] Cyprus, a large island off the Syrian coast.

With guile Odysseus drew away, then said:

"A pity that you have more looks than heart.
You'd grudge a pinch of salt from your own larder
to your own handy man. You sit here, fat 530
on others' meat, and cannot bring yourself
to rummage out a crust of bread for me!"

Then anger made Antínoös' heart beat hard,
and, glowering under his brows, he answered:

"Now!

You think you'll shuffle off and get away
after that impudence? Oh, no you don't!"

The stool he let fly hit the man's right shoulder
on the packed muscle under the shoulder blade—
like solid rock, for all the effect one saw.
Odysseus only shook his head, containing 540
thoughts of bloody work, as he walked on,
then sat, and dropped his loaded bag again
upon the door sill. Facing the whole crowd
he said, and eyed them all:

"One word only,
my lords, and suitors of the famous queen.
One thing I have to say.
There is no pain, no burden for the heart
when blows come to a man, and he defending
his own cattle—his own cows and lambs.
Here it was otherwise. Antínoös 550
hit me for being driven on by hunger—
how many bitter seas men cross for hunger!
If beggars interest the gods, if there are Furies
pent in the dark to avenge a poor man's wrong, then may
Antínoös meet his death before his wedding day!"

Then said Eupeithês' son, Antínoös:

"Enough.
Eat and be quiet where you are, or shamble elsewhere,
unless you want these lads to stop your mouth
pulling you by the heels, or hands and feet,
over the whole floor, till your back is peeled!" 560

But now the rest were mortified, and someone
spoke from the crowd of young bucks to rebuke him:

"A poor show, that—hitting this famished tramp—
bad business, if he happened to be a god.
You know they go in foreign guise, the gods do,
looking like strangers, turning up

in towns and settlements to keep an eye
on manners, good or bad."

But at this notion
Antínoös only shrugged.

Telémakhos,
after the blow his father bore, sat still
without a tear, though his heart felt the blow. 570
Slowly he shook his head from side to side,
containing murderous thoughts.

Penélopê
on the higher level of her room had heard
the blow, and knew who gave it. Now she murmured:

"Would god you could be hit yourself, Antínoös—
hit by Apollo's bowshot!"

And Eurýnomê
her housekeeper, put in:

"He and no other?
If all we pray for came to pass, not one
would live till dawn!"

Her gentle mistress said: 580

"Oh, Nan,[10] they are a bad lot; they intend
ruin for all of us; but Antínoös
appears a blacker-hearted hound than any.
Here is a poor man come, a wanderer,
driven by want to beg his bread, and everyone
in hall gave bits, to cram his bag—only
Antínoös threw a stool, and banged his shoulder!"

So she described it, sitting in her chamber
among her maids—while her true lord was eating.
Then she called in the forester and said: 590

"Go to that man on my behalf, Eumaios,
and send him here, so I can greet and question him.
Abroad in the great world, he may have heard
rumors about Odysseus—may have known him!"

Then you replied—O swineherd!

"Ah, my queen,
if these Akhaian sprigs would hush their babble
the man could tell you tales to charm your heart.
Three days and nights I kept him in my hut;
he came straight off a ship, you know, to me.

[10] Affectionate diminutive for an old woman.

There was no end to what he made me hear 600
of his hard roving; and I listened, eyes
upon him, as a man drinks in a tale
a minstrel sings—a minstrel taught by heaven
to touch the hearts of men. At such a song
the listener becomes rapt and still. Just so
I found myself enchanted by this man.
He claims an old tie with Odysseus, too—
in his home country, the Minoan[11] land
of Krete. From Krete he came, a rolling stone
washed by the gales of life this way and that 610
to our own beach.
If he can be believed
he has news of Odysseus near at hand
alive, in the rich country of Thesprotia,
bringing a mass of treasure home."

Then wise Penélopê said again:

"Go call him, let him come here, let him tell
that tale again for my own ears.
Our friends
can drink their cups outside or stay in hall,
being so carefree. And why not? Their stores
lie intact in their homes, both food and drink, 620
with only servants left to take a little.
But these men spend their days around our house
killing our beeves, our fat goats and our sheep,
carousing, drinking up our good dark wine;
sparing nothing, squandering everything.
No champion like Odysseus takes our part.
Ah, if he comes again, no falcon ever
struck more suddenly than he will, with his son,
to avenge this outrage!"

The great hall below
at this point rang with a tremendous sneeze[12]— 630
"kchaou!" from Telémakhos—like an acclamation.
And laughter seized Penélopê.
Then quickly,
lucidly she went on:

"Go call the stranger
straight to me. Did you hear that, Eumaios?
My son's thundering sneeze at what I said!
May death come of a sudden so; may death
relieve us, clean as that, of all the suitors!

[11] Minos, to whom the adjective *Minoan* refers, had been king of Krete (Crete).
[12] A sneeze was regarded as a sign of good luck.

Let me add one thing—do not overlook it—
if I can see this man has told the truth,
I promise him a warm new cloak and tunic." 640

With all this in his head, the forester
went down the hall, and halted near the beggar,
saying aloud:

"Good father, you are called
by the wise mother of Telémakhos,
Penélopê. The queen, despite her troubles,
is moved by a desire to hear your tales
about her lord—and if she finds them true,
she'll see you clothed in what you need, a cloak
and a fresh tunic.

You may have your belly
full each day you go about this realm 650
begging. For all may give, and all they wish."

Now said Odysseus, the old soldier:

"Friend,
I wish this instant I could tell my facts
to the wise daughter of Ikários, Penélopê—
and I have much to tell about her husband;
we went through much together.

But just now
this hard crowd worries me. They are, you said
infamous to the very rim of heaven
for violent acts: and here, just now, this fellow
gave me a bruise. What had I done to him? 660
But who would lift a hand for me? Telémakhos?
Anyone else?

No; bid the queen be patient,
Let her remain till sundown in her room,
and then—if she will seat me near the fire—
inquire tonight about her lord's return.
My rags are sorry cover; you know that;
I showed my sad condition first to you."

The woodsman heard him out, and then returned;
but the queen met him on her threshold, crying: 670
"Have you not brought him? Why? What is he thinking?
Has he some fear of overstepping? Shy
about these inner rooms? A hangdog beggar?"

To this you answered, friend Eumaios:

"No:
he reasons as another might, and well,

not to tempt any swordplay from these drunkards.
Be patient, wait—he says—till darkness falls.
And, O my queen, for you too that is better:
better to be alone with him, and question him, 680
and hear him out."

Penélopê replied:

"He is no fool; he sees how it could be.
Never were mortal men like these
for bullying and brainless arrogance!"

Thus she accepted what had been proposed,
so he went back into the crowd. He joined
Telémakhos, and said at once in whispers—
his head bent, so that no one else might hear:

"Dear prince, I must go home to keep good watch
on hut and swine, and look to my own affairs. 690
Everything here is in your hands. Consider
your own safety before the rest; take care
not to get hurt. Many are dangerous here.
May Zeus destroy them first, before we suffer!"

Telémakhos said:

"Your wish is mine, Uncle.
Go when your meal is finished. Then come back
at dawn, and bring good victims for a slaughter.
Everything here is in my hands indeed—
and in the disposition of the gods."

Taking his seat on the smooth bench again, 700
Eumaios ate and drank his fill, then rose
to climb the mountain trail back to his swine,
leaving the mégaron and court behind him
crowded with banqueters.

These had their joy
of dance and song, as day waned into evening.

BOOK EIGHTEEN: BLOWS AND A QUEEN'S BEAUTY

Now a true scavenger came in—a public tramp
who begged around the town of Ithaka,
a by-word for his insatiable swag-belly,
feeding and drinking, dawn to dark. No pith
was in him, and no nerve, huge as he looked.
Arnaios, as his gentle mother called him,

he had been nicknamed "Iros"[1] by the young
for being ready to take messages.
This fellow
thought he would rout Odysseus from his doorway,
growling at him:

"Clear out, grandfather, 10
or else be hauled out by the ankle bone.
See them all giving me the wink? That means,
'Go on and drag him out!' I hate to do it.
Up with you! Or would you like a fist fight?"

Odysseus only frowned and looked him over,
taking account of everything, then said:

"Master, I am no trouble to you here.
I offer no remarks. I grudge you nothing.
Take all you get, and welcome. Here is room
for two on this doorslab—or do you own it? 20
You are a tramp, I think, like me. Patience:
a windfall from the gods will come. But drop
that talk of using fists; it could annoy me.
Old as I am, I might just crack a rib
or split a lip for you. My life would go
even more peacefully, after tomorrow,
looking for no more visits here from you."

Iros the tramp grew red and hooted:

"Ho,
listen to him! The swine can talk your arm off, 30
like an old oven woman! With two punches
I'd knock him snoring, if I had a mind to—
and not a tooth left in his head, the same
as an old sow caught in the corn! Belt up!
And let this company see the way I do it
when we square off. Can you fight a fresher man?"

Under the lofty doorway, on the door sill
of wide smooth ash, they held this rough exchange.
And the tall full-blooded suitor, Antínoös,
overhearing, broke into happy laughter. 40
Then he said to the others:

"Oh, my friends,
no luck like this ever turned up before!
What a farce heaven has brought this house!
The stranger
and Iros have had words, they brag of boxing!
Into the ring they go, and no more talk!"

[1]A pun on Iris, goddess of the rainbow and a messenger of the gods.

All the young men got on their feet now, laughing,
to crowd around the ragged pair. Antínoös
called out:

"Gentlemen, quiet! One more thing:
here are goat stomachs ready on the fire
to stuff with blood and fat, good supper pudding. 50
The man who wins this gallant bout
may step up here and take the one he likes.
And let him feast with us from this day on:
no other beggar will be admitted here
when we are at our wine."

This pleased them all.
But now that wily man, Odysseus, muttered:

"An old man, an old hulk, has no business
fighting a young man, but my belly nags me;
nothing will do but I must take a beating.
Well, then, let every man here swear an oath 60
not to step in for Iros. No one throw
a punch for luck. I could be whipped that way."

So much the suitors were content to swear,
but after they reeled off their oaths, Telémakhos
put in a word to clinch it, saying:

"Friend,
if you will stand and fight, as pride requires,
don't worry about a foul blow from behind.
Whoever hits you will take on the crowd.
You have my word as host; you have the word
of these two kings, Antínoös and Eurýmakhos— 70
a pair of thinking men."

All shouted, "Aye!"
So now Odysseus made his shirt a belt
and roped his rags around his loins, baring
his hurdler's thighs and boxer's breadth of shoulder,
the dense rib-sheath and upper arms. Athena
stood nearby to give him bulk and power,
while the young suitors watched with narrowed eyes—
and comments went around:

"By god, old Iros now retiros."

"Aye,
he asked for it, he'll get it—bloody, too." 80

"The build this fellow had, under his rags!"

Panic made Iros' heart jump, but the yard-boys
hustled and got him belted by main force,

though all his blubber quivered now with dread.
Antínoös' angry voice rang in his ears:

"You sack of guts, you might as well be dead,
might as well never have seen the light of day,
if this man makes you tremble! Chicken-heart,
afraid of an old wreck, far gone in misery!
Well, here is what I say—and what I'll do. 90
If this ragpicker can outfight you, whip you,
I'll ship you out to that king in Epeíros,
Ékhetos[2]—he skins everyone alive.
Let him just cut your nose off and your ears
and pull your privy parts out by the roots
to feed raw to his hunting dogs!"

Poor Iros
felt a new fit of shaking take his knees.
But the yard-boys pushed him out. Now both contenders
put their hands up. Royal Odysseus
pondered if he should hit him with all he had 100
and drop the man dead on the spot, or only
spar, with force enough to knock him down.
Better that way, he thought—a gentle blow,
else he might give himself away.
The two
were at close quarters now, and Iros lunged
hitting the shoulder. Then Odysseus hooked him
under the ear and shattered his jaw bone,
so bright red blood came bubbling from his mouth,
as down he pitched into the dust, bleating,
kicking against the ground, his teeth stove in. 110
The suitors whooped and swung their arms, half dead
with pangs of laughter.
Then, by the ankle bone,
Odysseus hauled the fallen one outside,
crossing the courtyard to the gate, and piled him
against the wall. In his right hand he stuck
his begging staff, and said:
"Here, take your post.
Sit here to keep the dogs and pigs away.
You can give up your habit of command
over poor waifs and beggarmen—you swab.
Another time you may not know what hit you." 120

When he had slung his rucksack by the string
over his shoulder, like a wad of rags,
he sat down on the broad door sill again,

[2] Probably a nonhistorical tyrannical ruler whose name was a byword for cruelty. Epeíros (Epirus), in the preceding line, is the Grecian mainland north of Ithaka.

as laughing suitors came to flock inside;
and each young buck in passing gave him greeting,
saying, maybe,

"Zeus fill your pouch for this!
May the gods grant your heart's desire!"

"Well done
to put that walking famine out of business."

"We'll ship him out to that king in Epeíros,
Ékhetos—he skins everyone alive." 130

Odysseus found grim cheer in their good wishes—
his work had started well.

Now from the fire
his fat blood pudding came, deposited
before him by Antínoös—then, to boot,
two brown loaves from the basket, and some wine
in a fine cup of gold. These gifts Amphínomos
gave him. Then he said:

"Here's luck, grandfather;
a new day; may the worst be over now."

Odysseus answered, and his mind ranged far:

"Amphínomos, your head is clear, I'd say; 140
so was your father's—or at least I've heard
good things of Nísos the Doulíkhion,
whose son you are, they tell me—an easy man.
And you seem gently bred.

In view of that,
I have a word to say to you, so listen.

Of mortal creatures, all that breathe and move,
earth bears none frailer than mankind. What man
believes in woe to come, so long as valor
and tough knees are supplied him by the gods?
But when the gods in bliss bring miseries on, 150
then willy-nilly, blindly, he endures.
Our minds are as the days are, dark or bright,
blown over by the father of gods and men.

So I, too, in my time thought to be happy;
but far and rash I ventured, counting on
my own right arm, my father, and my kin;
behold me now.

No man should flout the law,
but keep in peace what gifts the gods may give.

I see you young blades living dangerously,
a household eaten up, a wife dishonored— 160

and yet the master will return, I tell you,
to his own place, and soon; for he is near.
So may some power take you out of this,
homeward, and softly, not to face that man
the hour he sets foot on his native ground.
Between him and the suitors I foretell
no quittance,[3] no way out, unless by blood,
once he shall stand beneath his own roof-beam."

Gravely, when he had done, he made libation
and took a sip of honey-hearted wine, 170
giving the cup, then, back into the hands
of the young nobleman. Amphínomos, for his part,
shaking his head, with chill and burdened breast,
turned in the great hall.
Now his heart foreknew
the wrath to come, but he could not take flight,
being by Athena bound there.
Death would have him
broken by a spear thrown by Telémakhos.
So he sat down where he had sat before.

And now heart-prompting from the grey-eyed goddess
came to the quiet queen, Penélopê: 180
a wish to show herself before the suitors;
for thus by fanning their desire again
Athena meant to set her beauty high
before her husband's eyes, before her son.
Knowing no reason, laughing confusedly,
she said:
"Eurýnomê, I have a craving
I never had at all—I would be seen
among those ruffians, hateful as they are.
I might well say a word, then, to my son,
for his own good—tell him to shun that crowd; 190
for all their gay talk, they are bent on evil."

Mistress Eurýnomê replied:
"Well said, child,
now is the time. Go down, and make it clear,
hold nothing back from him.
But you must bathe
and put a shine upon your cheeks—not this way,
streaked under your eyes and stained with tears.
You make it worse, being forever sad,
and now your boy's a bearded man! Remember
you prayed the gods to let you see him so."

[3] Repayment.

Penélopê replied:

"Eurýnomê, 200
it is a kind thought, but I will not hear it—
to bathe and sleek with perfumed oil. No, no,
the gods forever took my sheen away
when my lord sailed for Troy in the decked ships.
Only tell my Autonoë to come,
and Hippodameía; they should be attending me
in hall, if I appear there. I could not
enter alone into that crowd of men."

At this the good old woman left the chamber
to tell the maids her bidding. But now too 210
the grey-eyed goddess had her own designs.
Upon the quiet daughter of Ikários
she let clear drops of slumber fall, until
the queen lay back asleep, her limbs unstrung,
in her long chair. And while she slept the goddess
endowed her with immortal grace to hold
the eyes of the Akhaians. With ambrosia
she bathed her cheeks and throat and smoothed her brow—
ambrosia, used by flower-crowned Kythereia[4]
when she would join the rose-lipped Graces dancing. 220
Grandeur she gave her, too, in height and form,
and made her whiter than carved ivory.
Touching her so, the perfect one was gone.
Now came the maids, bare-armed and lovely, voices
breaking into the room. The queen awoke
and as she rubbed her cheek she sighed:

"Ah, soft
that drowse I lay embraced in, pain forgot!
If only Artemis the Pure would give me
death as mild, and soon! No heart-ache more,
no wearing out my lifetime with desire 230
and sorrow, mindful of my lord, good man
in all ways that he was, best of the Akhaians!"

She rose and left her glowing upper room,
and down the stairs, with her two maids in train,
this beautiful lady went before the suitors.
Then by a pillar of the solid roof
she paused, her shining veil across her cheek,
the two girls close to her and still;
and in that instant weakness took those men
in the knee joints, their hearts grew faint with lust; 240
not one but swore to god to lie beside her.

[4] Aphroditê, goddess of love.

But speaking for her dear son's ears alone
she said:

"Telémakhos, what has come over you?
Lightminded you were not, in all your boyhood.
Now you are full grown, come of age; a man
from foreign parts might take you for the son
of royalty, to go by your good looks;
and have you no more thoughtfulness or manners?
How could it happen in our hall that you
permit the stranger to be so abused? 250
Here, in our house, a guest, can any man
suffer indignity, come by such injury?
What can this be for you but public shame?"

Telémakhos looked in her eyes and answered,
with his clear head and his discretion:

"Mother,
I cannot take it ill that you are angry.
I know the meaning of these actions now,
both good and bad. I had been young and blind.
How can I always keep to what is fair 260
while these sit here to put fear in me?—princes
from near and far whose interest is my ruin;
are any on my side?

But you should know
the suitors did not have their way, matching
the stranger here and Iros—for the stranger
beat him to the ground.

O Father Zeus!
Athena and Apollo! could I see
the suitors whipped like that! Courtyard and hall
strewn with our friends, too weak-kneed to get up,
chapfallen to their collarbones, the way 270
old Iros rolls his head there by the gate
as though he were pig-drunk! No energy
to stagger on his homeward path; no fight
left in his numb legs!"

Thus Penélopê
reproached her son, and he replied. Now, interrupting,
Eurýmakhos called out to her:

"Penélopê,
deep-minded queen, daughter of Ikários,
if all Akhaians in the land of Argos
only saw you now! What hundreds more
would join your suitors here to feast tomorrow! 280
Beauty like yours no woman had before,
or majesty, or mastery."

She answered:

"Eurýmakhos, my qualities—I know—
my face, my figure, all were lost or blighted
when the Akhaians crossed the sea to Troy,
Odysseus my lord among the rest.
If he returned, if he were here to care for me,
I might be happily renowned!
But grief instead heaven sent me—years of pain.
Can I forget?—the day he left this island, 290
enfolding my right hand and wrist in his,
he said:

'My lady, the Akhaian troops
will not easily make it home again
full strength, unhurt, from Troy. They say the Trojans
are fighters too; good lances and good bowmen,
horsemen, charioteers—and those can be
decisive when a battle hangs in doubt.
So whether God will send me back, or whether
I'll be a captive there, I cannot tell.
Here, then, you must attend to everything. 300
My parents in our house will be a care for you
as they are now, or more, while I am gone.
Wait for the beard to darken our boy's cheek;
then marry whom you will, and move away.'

The years he spoke of are now past; the night
comes when a bitter marriage overtakes me,
desolate as I am, deprived by Zeus
of all the sweets of life.

How galling, too,
to see newfangled manners in my suitors!
Others who go to court a gentlewoman, 310
daughter of a rich house, if they are rivals,
bring their own beeves and sheep along; her friends
ought to be feasted, gifts are due to her;
would any dare to live at her expense?"

Odysseus' heart laughed when he heard all this—
her sweet tones charming gifts out of the suitors
with talk of marriage, though she intended none.
Eupeithês' son, Antínoös, now addressed her:

"Ikários' daughter, O deep-minded queen!
If someone cares to make you gifts, accept them! 320
It is no courtesy to turn gifts away.
But we go neither to our homes nor elsewhere
until of all Akhaians here you take
the best man for your lord."

Pleased at this answer,
every man sent a squire to fetch a gift—
Antínoös, a wide resplendent robe,
embroidered fine, and fastened with twelve brooches,
pins pressed into sheathing tubes of gold;
Eurýmakhos, a necklace, wrought in gold,
with sunray pieces of clear glinting amber. 330
Eurýdamas's men came back with pendants,
ear-drops in triple clusters of warm lights;
and from the hoard of Lord Polýktor's son,
Peisándros, came a band for her white throat,
jewelled adornment. Other wondrous things
were brought as gifts from the Akhaian princes.
Penélopê then mounted the stair again,
her maids behind, with treasure in their arms.

And now the suitors gave themselves to dancing,
to harp and haunting song, as night drew on; 340
black night indeed came on them at their pleasure.
But three torch fires were placed in the long hall
to give them light. On hand were stores of fuel,
dry seasoned chips of resinous wood, split up
by the bronze hatchet blade—these were mixed in
among the flames to keep them flaring bright;
each housemaid of Odysseus took her turn.

Now he himself, the shrewd and kingly man,
approached and told them:

"Housemaids of Odysseus,
your master so long absent in the world, 350
go to the women's chambers, to your queen.
Attend her, make the distaff whirl, divert her,
stay in her room, comb wool for her.

I stand here
ready to tend these flares and offer light
to everyone. They cannot tire me out,
even if they wish to drink till Dawn.
I am a patient man."

But the women giggled,
glancing back and forth—laughed in his face;
and one smooth girl, Melántho, spoke to him
most impudently. She was Dólios' daughter, 360
taken as ward in childhood by Penélopê
who gave her playthings to her heart's content
and raised her as her own. Yet the girl felt
nothing for her mistress, no compunction,
but slept and made love with Eurýmakhos.
Her bold voice rang now in Odysseus' ears:

"You must be crazy, punch drunk, you old goat.
Instead of going out to find a smithy
to sleep warm in—or a tavern bench—you stay
putting your oar in, amid all our men. 370
Numbskull, not to be scared! The wine you drank
has clogged your brain, or are you always this way,
boasting like a fool? Or have you lost
your mind because you beat that tramp, that Iros?
Look out, or someone better may get up
and give you a good knocking about the ears
to send you out all bloody."

But Odysseus
glared at her under his brows and said:

"One minute:
let me tell Telémakhos how you talk
in hall, you slut; he'll cut your arms and legs off!" 380

This hard shot took the women's breath away
and drove them quaking to their rooms, as though
knives were behind: they felt he spoke the truth.
So there he stood and kept the firelight high
and looked the suitors over, while his mind
roamed far ahead to what must be accomplished.

They, for their part, could not now be still
or drop their mockery—for Athena wished
Odysseus mortified still more.

Eurýmakhos,
the son of Pôlybos, took up the baiting, 390
angling for a laugh among his friends.

"Suitors of our distinguished queen," he said,
"hear what my heart would have me say.

This man
comes with a certain aura of divinity
into Odysseus' hall. He shines.

He shines
around the noggin, like a flashing light,
having no hair at all to dim his lustre."

Then turning to Odysseus, raider of cities,
he went on:

"Friend, you have a mind to work,
do you? Could I hire you to clear stones 400
from wasteland for me—you'll be paid enough—
collecting boundary walls and planting trees?
I'd give you a bread ration every day,
a cloak to wrap in, sandals for your feet.

Oh no: you learned your dodges long ago—
no honest sweat. You'd rather tramp the country
begging, to keep your hoggish belly full."

The master of many crafts replied:

"Eurýmakhos,
we two might try our hands against each other
in early summer when the days are long, 410
in meadow grass, with one good scythe for me
and one as good for you: we'd cut our way
down a deep hayfield, fasting to late evening.
Or we could try our hands behind a plow,
driving the best of oxen—fat, well-fed,
well-matched for age and pulling power, and say
four strips apiece of loam the share could break:
you'd see then if I cleft you a straight furrow.
Competition in arms? If Zeus Kroníon
roused up a scuffle now, give me a shield, 420
two spears, a dogskin cap with plates of bronze
to fit my temples, and you'd see me go
where the first rank of fighters lock in battle.
There would be no more jeers about my belly.
You thick-skinned menace to all courtesy!
You think you are a great man and a champion,
but up against few men, poor stuff, at that.
Just let Odysseus return, those doors
wide open as they are, you'd find too narrow
to suit you on your sudden journey out." 430

Now fury mounted in Eurýmakhos,
who scowled and shot back:

"Bundle of rags and lice!
By god, I'll make you suffer for your gall,
your insolent gabble before all our men."

He had his foot-stool out: but now Odysseus
took to his haunches by Amphínomos' knees,
fearing Eurýmakhos' missile, as it flew.
It clipped a wine steward on the serving hand,
so that his pitcher dropped with a loud clang
while he fell backward, cursing, in the dust. 440
In the shadowy hall a low sound rose—of suitors
murmuring to one another.

"Ai!" they said,
"This vagabond would have done well to perish
somewhere else, and make us no such rumpus.
Here we are, quarreling over tramps; good meat
and wine forgotten; good sense gone by the board."

Telémakhos, his young heart high, put in:

"Bright souls, alight with wine, you can no longer
hide the cups you've taken.[5] Aye, some god
is goading you. Why not go home to bed?— 450
I mean when you are moved to. No one jumps
at my command."

Struck by his blithe manner,
the young men's teeth grew fixed in their under lips,
but now the son of Nísos, Lord Amphínomos
of Aretíadês, addressed them all:

"O friends, no ruffling replies are called for;
that was fair counsel.

Hands off the stranger, now,
and hands off any other servant here
in the great house of King Odysseus. Come,
let my own herald wet our cups once more, 460
we'll make an offering, and then to bed.
The stranger can be left behind in hall;
Telémakhos may care for him; he came
to Telémakhos' door, not ours."

This won them over.
The soldier Moulios, Doulíkhion herald,
comrade in arms of Lord Amphínomos,
mixed the wine and served them all. They tipped out
drops for the blissful gods, and drank the rest,
and when they had drunk their thirst away
they trailed off homeward drowsily to bed. 470

BOOK NINETEEN: RECOGNITIONS AND A DREAM

Now by Athena's side in the quiet hall
studying the ground for slaughter, Lord Odysseus
turned to Telémakhos.

"The arms," he said.
"Harness and weapons must be out of sight
in the inner room. And if the suitors miss them,
be mild; just say 'I had a mind to move them
out of the smoke. They seemed no longer

[5] That is, they cannot hide the fact that they have drunk so much.

the bright arms that Odysseus left at home
when he went off to Troy. Here where the fire's
hot breath came, they had grown black and drear. 10
One better reason struck me, too:
suppose a brawl starts up when you've been drinking—
you might in madness let each other's blood,
and that would stain your feast, your courtship.
Iron
itself can draw men's hands.'"

Then he fell silent,
and Telémakhos obeyed his father's word.
He called Eurýkleia, the nurse, and told her:

"Nurse, go shut the women in their quarters
while I shift Father's armor back
to the inner rooms—these beautiful arms unburnished, 20
caked with black soot in his years abroad.
I was a child then. Well, I am not now.
I want them shielded from the draught and smoke."

And the old woman answered:

"It is time, child,
you took an interest in such things. I wish
you'd put your mind on all your house and chattels.[1]
But who will go along to hold a light?[2]
You said no maids, no torch-bearers."

Telémakhos
looked at her and replied:

"Our friend here.
A man who shares my meat can bear a hand, 30
no matter how far he is from home."

He spoke so soldierly
her own speech halted on her tongue. Straight back
she went to lock the doors of the women's hall.
And now the two men sprang to work—father
and princely son, loaded with round helms
and studded bucklers, lifting the long spears,
while in their path Pallas Athena
held up a golden lamp of purest light.
Telémakhos at last burst out:

[1] Possessions other than house and lands.
[2] Maids would normally have been the torchbearers.

"Oh, Father,
here is a marvel! All around I see 40
the walls and roof beams, pedestals and pillars,
lighted as though by white fire blazing near.
One of the gods of heaven is in this place!"

Then said Odysseus, the great tactician,

"Be still: keep still about it: just remember it.
The gods who rule Olympos make this light.
You may go off to bed now. Here I stay
to test your mother and her maids again.
Out of her long grief she will question me."

Telémakhos went across the hall and out 50
under the light of torches—crossed the court
to the tower chamber where he had always slept.
Here now again he lay, waiting for dawn,
while in the great hall by Athena's side
Odysseus waited with his mind on slaughter.

Presently Penélopê from her chamber
stepped in her thoughtful beauty.
So might Artemis
or golden Aphroditê have descended;
and maids drew to the hearth her own smooth chair
inlaid with silver whorls and ivory. The artisan 60
Ikmálios had made it, long before,
with a footrest in a single piece, and soft
upon the seat a heavy fleece was thrown.
Here by the fire the queen sat down. Her maids,
leaving their quarters, came with white arms bare
to clear the wine cups and the bread, and move
the trestle boards where men had lingered drinking.
Fiery ashes out of the pine-chip flares
they tossed, and piled on fuel for light and heat.
And now a second time Melántho's voice 70
rang brazen in Odysseus' ears:

"Ah, stranger,
are you still here, so creepy, late at night
hanging about, looking the women over?
You old goat, go outside, cuddle your supper;
get out, or a torch may kindle you behind!"

At this Odysseus glared under his brows
and said:

"Little devil, why pitch into me again?
Because I go unwashed and wear these rags,

and make the rounds? But so I must, being needy;
that is the way a vagabond must live. 80
And do not overlook this: in my time
I too had luck, lived well, stood well with men,
and gave alms, often, to poor wanderers
like him you see before you—aye, to all sorts,
no matter in what dire want. I owned
servants—many, I say—and all the rest
that goes with what men call prosperity.
But Zeus the son of Kronos brought me down.
Mistress, mend your ways, or you may lose
all this vivacity of yours. What if her ladyship 90
were stirred to anger? What if Odysseus came?—
and I can tell you, there is hope of that—
or if the man is done for, still his son
lives to be reckoned with, by Apollo's will.
None of you can go wantoning on the sly
and fool him now. He is too old for that."

Penélopê, being near enough to hear him,
spoke out sharply to her maid:

"Oh, shameless,
through and through! And do you think me blind,
blind to your conquest?[3] It will cost your life. 100
You knew I waited—for you heard me say it—
waited to see this man in hall and question him
about my lord; I am so hard beset."

She turned away and said to the housekeeper:

"Eurýnomê, a bench, a spread of sheepskin,
to put my guest at ease. Now he shall talk
and listen, and be questioned."

Willing hands
brought a smooth bench, and dropped a fleece upon it.
Here the adventurer and king sat down;
then carefully Penélopê began: 110

"Friend, let me ask you first of all:
who are you, where do you come from, of what nation
and parents were you born?"

And he replied:

"My lady, never a man in the wide world
should have a fault to find with you. Your name

[3] The reference is to Melántho's sexual dalliance with Eurýmakhos. The following words are probably less a threat than a warning that Melántho will have brought on her own punishment.

has gone out under heaven like the sweet
honor of some god-fearing king, who rules
in equity over the strong: his black lands bear
both wheat and barley, fruit trees laden bright,

new lambs at lambing time—and the deep sea 120
gives great hauls of fish by his good strategy,
so that his folk fare well.

O my dear lady,
this being so, let it suffice to ask me
of other matters—not my blood, my homeland.

Do not enforce me to recall my pain.
My heart is sore; but I must not be found
sitting in tears here, in another's house:
it is not well forever to be grieving.
One of the maids might say—or you might think—
I had got maudlin over cups of wine." 130

And Penélopê replied:

"Stranger, my looks,
my face, my carriage, were soon lost or faded
when the Akhaians crossed the sea to Troy,
Odysseus my lord among the rest.

If he returned, if he were here to care for me,
I might be happily renowned!
But grief instead heaven sent me—years of pain.
Sons of the noblest families on the islands,
Doulíkhion, Samê, wooded Zakýnthos,
with native Ithakans, are here to court me, 140
against my wish; and they consume this house.

Can I give proper heed to guest or suppliant
or herald on the realm's affairs?

How could I?
wasted with longing for Odysseus, while here
they press for marriage.

Ruses served my turn
to draw the time out—first a close-grained web
I had the happy thought to set up weaving
on my big loom in hall. I said, that day:
'Young men—my suitors, now my lord is dead,
let me finish my weaving before I marry, 150
or else my thread will have been spun in vain.

It is a shroud I weave for Lord Laërtês
when cold Death comes to lay him on his bier.
The country wives would hold me in dishonor
if he, with all his fortune, lay unshrouded.'
I reached their hearts that way, and they agreed.
So every day I wove on the great loom,
but every night by torchlight I unwove it;
and so for three years I deceived the Akhaians.

But when the seasons brought a fourth year on, 160
as long months waned, and the long days were spent,
through impudent folly in the slinking maids
they caught me—clamored up to me at night;
I had no choice then but to finish it.
And now, as matters stand at last,
I have no strength left to evade a marriage,
cannot find any further way; my parents
urge it upon me, and my son
will not stand by while they eat up his property.
He comprehends it, being a man full grown, 170
able to oversee the kind of house
Zeus would endow with honor.
But you too
confide in me, tell me your ancestry.
You were not born of mythic oak or stone."

And the great master of invention answered:

"O honorable wife of Lord Odysseus,
must you go on asking about my family?
Then I will tell you, though my pain
be doubled by it: and whose pain would not
if he had been away as long as I have 180
and had hard roving in the world of men?
But I will tell you even so, my lady.

One of the great islands of the world
in midsea, in the winedark sea, is Krete:
spacious and rich and populous, with ninety
cities and a mingling of tongues.
Akhaians there are found, along with Kretan
hillmen of the old stock, and Kydonians,
Dorians in three blood-lines, Pelasgians[4]—
and one among their ninety towns is Knossos. 190
Here lived King Minos[5] whom great Zeus received
every ninth year in private council—Minos,
the father of my father, Deukálion.
Two sons Deukálion had: Idómeneus,
who went to join the Atreidai before Troy
in the beaked ships of war; and then myself,
Aithôn by name—a stripling next my brother.
But I saw with my own eyes at Knossos once
Odysseus.

[4] Kydonians, Dorians, Pelasgians were various ethnic groups, natives of Krete or immigrants.

[5] Minos, sometimes represented as a cruel king (as in Book XI), is here represented as supremely honored. Knossos is on the north shore of Krete. In this version of his autobiography, Odysseus obviously departs from what he had told Eumaios (Book XIV) and Antínoös (Book XVII).

Gales had caught him off Cape Malea,
driven him southward on the coast of Krete, 200
when he was bound for Troy. At Ámnisos,
hard by the holy cave of Eileithuía,[6]
he lay to, and dropped anchor, in that open
and rough roadstead riding out the blow.
Meanwhile he came ashore, came inland, asking
after Idómeneus: dear friends he said they were;
but now ten mornings had already passed,
ten or eleven, since my brother sailed.
So I played host and took Odysseus home,
saw him well lodged and fed, for we had plenty; 210
then I made requisitions—barley, wine,
and beeves for sacrifice—to give his company
abundant fare along with him.

Twelve days
they stayed with us, the Akhaians, while that wind
out of the north shut everyone inside—
even on land you could not keep your feet,
such fury was abroad. On the thirteenth,
when the gale dropped, they put to sea."

Now all these lies he made appear so truthful
she wept as she sat listening. The skin 220
of her pale face grew moist the way pure snow
softens and glistens on the mountains, thawed
by Southwind after powdering from the West,
and, as the snow melts, mountain streams run full:
so her white cheeks were wetted by these tears
shed for her lord—and he close by her side.
Imagine how his heart ached for his lady,
his wife in tears; and yet he never blinked;
his eyes might have been made of horn or iron
for all that she could see. He had this trick— 230
wept, if he willed to, inwardly.

Well, then,
as soon as her relieving tears were shed
she spoke once more:

"I think that I shall say, friend,
give me some proof, if it is really true
that you were host in that place to my husband
with his brave men, as you declare. Come, tell me
the quality of his clothing, how he looked,
and some particular of his company."

[6] Ámnisos is an anchorage off Krete. Eileithuía was a goddess, daughter of Hêra, who controlled maternal labor and childbirth.

Odysseus answered, and his mind ranged far:

"Lady, so long a time now lies between, 240
it is hard to speak of it. Here is the twentieth year
since that man left the island of my father.
But I shall tell what memory calls to mind.
A purple cloak, and fleecy, he had on—
a double thick one. Then, he wore a brooch
made of pure gold with twin tubes for the prongs,
and on the face a work of art: a hunting dog
pinning a spotted fawn in agony
between his forepaws—wonderful to see
how being gold, and nothing more, he bit 250
the golden deer convulsed, with wild hooves flying.
Odysseus' shirt I noticed, too—a fine
closefitting tunic like dry onion skin,
so soft it was, and shiny.
Women there,
many of them, would cast their eyes on it.
But I might add, for your consideration,
whether he brought these things from home, or whether
a shipmate gave them to him, coming aboard,
I have no notion: some regardful host
in another port perhaps it was. Affection 260
followed him—there were few Akhaians like him.
And I too made him gifts: a good bronze blade,
a cloak with lining and a broidered shirt,
and sent him off in his trim ship with honor.
A herald, somewhat older than himself,
he kept beside him; I'll describe this man:
round-shouldered, dusky, woolly-headed;
Eurýbatês, his name was—and Odysseus
gave him preferment over the officers.
He had a shrewd head, like the captain's own." 270

Now hearing these details—minutely true—
she felt more strangely moved, and tears flowed
until she had tasted her salt grief again.
Then she found words to answer:

"Before this
you won my sympathy, but now indeed
you shall be our respected guest and friend.
With my own hands I put that cloak and tunic
upon him—took them folded from their place—
and the bright brooch for ornament.
Gone now,
I will not meet the man again 280
returning to his own home fields. Unkind
the fate that sent him young in the long ship
to see that misery at Ilion, unspeakable!"

And the master improviser answered:
"Honorable
wife of Odysseus Laërtiadês,
you need not stain your beauty with these tears,
nor wear yourself out grieving for your husband.
Not that I can blame you. Any wife
grieves for the man she married in her girlhood,
lay with in love, bore children to—though he 290
may be no prince like this Odysseus,
whom they compare even to the gods. But listen:
weep no more, and listen:
I have a thing to tell you, something true.
I heard but lately of your lord's return,
heard that he is alive, not far away,
among Thesprótians in their green land
amassing fortune to bring home. His company
went down in shipwreck in the winedark sea
off the coast of Thrinákia. Zeus and Hêlios 300
held it against him that his men had killed
the kine of Hêlios. The crew drowned for this.
He rode the ship's keel. Big seas cast him up
on the island of Phaiákians, godlike men
who took him to their hearts. They honored him
with many gifts and a safe passage home,
or so they wished. Long since he should have been here,
but he thought better to restore his fortune
playing the vagabond about the world;
and no adventurer could beat Odysseus 310
at living by his wits—no man alive.
I had this from King Phaidôn of Thesprótia;
and, tipping wine out, Phaidôn swore to me
the ship was launched, the seamen standing by
to bring Odysseus to his land at last,
but I got out to sea ahead of him
by the king's order—as it chanced a freighter
left port for the grain bins of Doulíkhion.
Phaidôn, however, showed me Odysseus' treasure.
Ten generations of his heirs or more 320
could live on what lay piled in that great room.
The man himself had gone up to Dodona
to ask the spelling leaves of the old oak
what Zeus would have him do—how to return to Ithaka
after so many years—by stealth or openly.
You see, then, he is alive and well, and headed
homeward now, no more to be abroad
far from his island, his dear wife and son.
Here is my sworn word for it. Witness this,
god of the zenith, noblest of the gods, 330
and Lord Odysseus' hearthfire, now before me:

I swear these things shall turn out as I say.
Between this present dark and one day's ebb,
after the wane, before the crescent moon,[7]
Odysseus will come."

Penélopê,
the attentive queen, replied to him:

"Ah, stranger,
if what you say could ever happen!
You would soon know our love! Our bounty, too:
men would turn after you to call you blessed.
But my heart tells me what must be. 340
Odysseus will not come to me; no ship
will be prepared for you. We have no master
quick to receive and furnish out a guest
as Lord Odysseus was.

Or did I dream him?

Maids, maids: come wash him, make a bed for him,
bedstead and colored rugs and coverlets
to let him lie warm into the gold of Dawn.
In morning light you'll bathe him and anoint him
so that he'll take his place beside Telémakhos
feasting in hall. If there be one man there 350
to bully or annoy him, that man wins
no further triumph here, burn though he may.
How will you understand me, friend, how find in me,
more than in common women, any courage
or gentleness, if you are kept in rags
and filthy at our feast? Men's lives are short.
The hard man and his cruelties will be
cursed behind his back, and mocked in death.
But one whose heart and ways are kind—of him
strangers will bear report to the wide world, 360
and distant men will praise him."

Warily
Odysseus answered:

"Honorable lady,
wife of Odysseus Laërtiadês,
a weight of rugs and cover? Not for me.
I've had none since the day I saw the mountains
of Krete, white with snow, low on the sea line
fading behind me as the long oars drove me north.

[7] Between now and the time of the new moon. As it happens, the day specified will be the morrow.

Let me lie down tonight as I've lain often,
many a night unsleeping, many a time
afield on hard ground waiting for pure Dawn. 370
No: and I have no longing for a footbath
either; none of these maids will touch my feet,
unless there is an old one, old and wise,
one who has lived through suffering as I have:
I would not mind letting my feet be touched
by that old servant."

And Penélopê said:

"Dear guest, no foreign man so sympathetic
ever came to my house, no guest more likeable,
so wry and humble are the things you say.
I have an old maidservant ripe with years, 380
one who in her time nursed my lord. She took him
into her arms the hour his mother bore him.
Let her, then, wash your feet, though she is frail.
Come here, stand by me, faithful Eurýkleia,
and bathe—bathe your master, I almost said,
for they are of an age, and now Odysseus'
feet and hands would be enseamed like his.
Men grow old soon in hardship."

Hearing this,
the old nurse hid her face between her hands
and wept hot tears, and murmured:

"Oh, my child! 390
I can do nothing for you! How Zeus hated you,
no other man so much! No use, great heart,
O faithful heart, the rich thighbones you burnt
to Zeus who plays in lightning—and no man
ever gave more to Zeus—with all your prayers
for a green age, a tall son reared to manhood.
There is no day of homecoming for you.
Stranger, some women in some far off place
perhaps have mocked my lord when he'd be home
as now these strumpets[8] mock you here. No wonder 400
you would keep clear of all their whorishness
and have no bath. But here am I. The queen
Penélopê, Ikários' daughter, bids me;
so let me bathe your feet to serve my lady—
to serve you, too.

My heart within me stirs,
mindful of something. Listen to what I say:
strangers have come here, many through the years,

[8] Whores.

but no one ever came, I swear, who seemed
so like Odysseus—body, voice and limbs—
as you do."

Ready for this, Odysseus answered: 410

"Old woman, that is what they say. All who have seen
the two of us remark how like we are,
as you yourself have said, and rightly, too."

Then he kept still, while the old nurse filled up
her basin glittering in firelight; she poured
cold water in, then hot.

But Lord Odysseus
whirled suddenly from the fire to face the dark.
The scar: he had forgotten that. She must not
handle his scarred thigh, or the game was up.
But when she bared her lord's leg, bending near, 420
she knew the groove at once.

An old wound
a boar's white tusk inflicted, on Parnassos[9]
years ago. He had gone hunting there
in company with his uncles and Autólykos,
his mother's father—a great thief and swindler
by Hermês'[10] favor, for Autólykos pleased him
with burnt offerings of sheep and kids. The god
acted as his accomplice. Well, Autólykos
on a trip to Ithaka
arrived just after his daughter's boy was born. 430
In fact, he had no sooner finished supper
than Nurse Eurýkleia put the baby down
in his own lap and said:

"It is for you, now,
to choose a name for him, your child's dear baby;
the answer to her prayers."

Autólykos replied:

"My son-in-law, my daughter, call the boy
by the name I tell you. Well you know, my hand
has been against the world of men and women;
odium and distrust I've won. Odysseus
should be his given name.[11] When he grows up, 440
when he comes visiting his mother's home

[9] The famous mountain near Delphi. Also spelled *Parnassus.*
[10] Noted for cleverness, Hermês was the patron god of thieves, though he is not usually presented in that role by Homer.
[11] *Odysseus* means something like "wrathful."

under Parnassos, where my treasures are,
I'll make him gifts and send him back rejoicing."

Odysseus in due course went for the gifts,
and old Autólykos and his sons embraced him
with welcoming sweet words; and Amphithéa,
his mother's mother, held him tight and kissed him,
kissed his head and his fine eyes.
The father
called on his noble sons to make a feast,
and going about it briskly they led in 450
an ox of five years, whom they killed and flayed
and cut in bits for roasting on the skewers
with skilled hands, with care; then shared it out.
So all the day until the sun went down
they feasted to their hearts' content. At evening,
after the sun was down and dusk had come,
they turned to bed and took the gift of sleep.

When the young Dawn spread in the eastern sky
her finger tips of rose, the men and dogs
went hunting, taking Odysseus. They climbed 460
Parnassos' rugged flank mantled in forest,
entering amid high windy folds at noon
when Hêlios beat upon the valley floor
and on the winding Ocean whence he came.
With hounds questing ahead, in open order,
the sons of Autólykos went down a glen,
Odysseus in the lead, behind the dogs,
pointing his long-shadowing spear.
Before them
a great boar lay hid in undergrowth,
in a green thicket proof against the wind 470
or sun's blaze, fine soever the needling sunlight,
impervious too to any rain, so dense
that cover was, heaped up with fallen leaves.
Patter of hounds' feet, men's feet, woke the boar
as they came up—and from his woody ambush
with razor back bristling and raging eyes
he trotted and stood at bay. Odysseus,
being on top of him, had the first shot,
lunging to stick him; but the boar
had already charged under the long spear. 480
He hooked aslant with one white tusk and ripped out
flesh above the knee, but missed the bone.
Odysseus' second thrust went home by luck,
his bright spear passing through the shoulder joint;
and the beast fell, moaning as life pulsed away.
Autólykos' tall sons took up the wounded,

working skillfully over the Prince Odysseus
to bind his gash, and with a rune[12] they stanched
the dark flow of blood. Then downhill swiftly
they all repaired to the father's house, and there 490
tended him well—so well they soon could send him,
with Grandfather Autólykos' magnificent gifts,
rejoicing, over sea to Ithaka.
His father and the Lady Antikleía
welcomed him, and wanted all the news
of how he got his wound; so he spun out
his tale, recalling how the boar's white tusk
caught him when he was hunting on Parnassos.

This was the scar the old nurse recognized;
she traced it under her spread hands, then let go, 500
and into the basin fell the lower leg
making the bronze clang, sloshing the water out.
Then joy and anguish seized her heart; her eyes
filled up with tears; her throat closed, and she whispered,
with hand held out to touch his chin:

"Oh yes!

You are Odysseus! Ah, dear child! I could not
see you until now—not till I knew
my master's very body with my hands!"

Her eyes turned to Penélopê with desire
to make her lord, her husband, known—in vain, 510
because Athena had bemused the queen,
so that she took no notice, paid no heed.
At the same time Odysseus' right hand
gripped the old throat; his left hand pulled her near,
and in her ear he said:

"Will you destroy me,

nurse, who gave me milk at your own breast?
Now with a hard lifetime behind I've come
in the twentieth year home to my father's island.
You found me out, as the chance was given you.
Be quiet; keep it from the others, else 520
I warn you, and I mean it, too,
if by my hand god brings the suitors down
I'll kill you, nurse or not, when the time comes—
when the time comes to kill the other women."

Eurýkleia kept her wits and answered him:

"Oh, what mad words are these you let escape you!
Child, you know my blood, my bones are yours;

[12] Magic spell or charm.

no one could whip this out of me. I'll be
a woman turned to stone, iron I'll be.
And let me tell you too—mind now—if god 530
cuts down the arrogant suitors by your hand,
I can report to you on all the maids,
those who dishonor you, and the innocent."

But in response the great tactician said:

"Nurse, no need to tell me tales of these.
I will have seen them, each one, for myself.
Trust in the gods, be quiet, hold your peace."

Silent, the old nurse went to fetch more water,
her basin being all spilt.
When she had washed
and rubbed his feet with golden oil, he turned, 540
dragging his bench again to the fire side
for warmth, and hid the scar under his rags.
Penélopê broke the silence, saying:

"Friend,
allow me one brief question more. You know,
the time for bed, sweet rest, is coming soon,
if only that warm luxury of slumber
would come to enfold us, in our trouble. But for me
my fate at night is anguish and no rest.
By day being busy, seeing to my work,
I find relief sometimes from loss and sorrow; 550
but when night comes and all the world's abed
I lie in mine alone, my heart thudding,
while bitter thoughts and fears crowd on my grief.
Think, how Pandáreos'[13] daughter, pale forever,
sings as the nightingale in the new leaves
through those long quiet hours of night,
on some thick-flowering orchard bough in spring;
how she rills out and tilts her note, high now, now low,
mourning for Itylos whom she killed in madness—
her child, and her lord Zêthos' only child. 560
My forlorn thought flows variable as her song,
wondering: shall I stay beside my son
and guard my own things here, my maids, my hall,
to honor my lord's bed and the common talk?
Or had I best join fortunes with a suitor,
the noblest one, most lavish in his gifts?
Is it now time for that?

[13] In this version of the nightingale myth, Aedon (daughter of Pandáreos and wife of Zêthos) was metamorphosed into a nightingale, through the compassion of Zeus, after she had killed her only son, Itylos, by mistake. She had intended to kill the eldest son of Niobe, her sister-in-law, who had aroused her jealousy by having so many children.

My son being still a callow boy forbade
marriage, or absence from my lord's domain;
but now the child is grown, grown up, a man, 570
he, too, begins to pray for my departure,
aghast at all the suitors gorge on.

Listen:

interpret me this dream: From a water's edge
twenty fat geese have come to feed on grain
beside my house. And I delight to see them.
But now a mountain eagle with great wings
and crooked beak storms in to break their necks
and strew their bodies here. Away he soars
into the bright sky; and I cry aloud—
all this in dream—I wail and round me gather 580
softly braided Akhaian women mourning
because the eagle killed my geese.

Then down

out of the sky he drops to a cornice beam
with mortal voice telling me not to weep.
'Be glad,' says he, 'renowned Ikários' daughter:
here is no dream but something real as day,
something about to happen. All those geese
were suitors, and the bird was I. See now,
I am no eagle but your lord come back
to bring inglorious death upon them all!' 590
As he said this, my honeyed slumber left me.
Peering through half-shut eyes, I saw the geese
in hall, still feeding at the self-same trough."

The master of subtle ways and straight replied:

"My dear, how can you choose to read the dream
differently? Has not Odysseus himself
shown you what is to come? Death to the suitors,
sure death, too. Not one escapes his doom."

Penélopê shook her head and answered:

"Friend,

many and many a dream is mere confusion, 600
a cobweb of no consequence at all.
Two gates for ghostly dreams there are: one gateway
of honest horn, and one of ivory.
Issuing by the ivory gate are dreams
of glimmering illusion, fantasies,
but those that come through solid polished horn
may be borne out, if mortals only know them.
I doubt it came by horn, my fearful dream—
too good to be true, that, for my son and me.
But one thing more I wish to tell you: listen 610
carefully. It is a black day, this that comes.

Odysseus' house and I are to be parted.
I shall decree a contest for the day.
We have twelve axe heads. In his time, my lord
could line them up, all twelve, at intervals
like a ship's ribbing; then he'd back away
a long way off and whip an arrow through.
Now I'll impose this trial on the suitors.
The one who easily handles and strings the bow
and shoots through all twelve axes I shall marry, 620
whoever he may be—then look my last
on this my first love's beautiful brimming house.
But I'll remember, though I dream it only."

Odysseus said:

"Dear honorable lady,
wife of Odysseus Laërtiadês,
let there be no postponement of the trial.
Odysseus, who knows the shifts of combat,
will be here: aye, he'll be here long before
one of these lads can stretch or string that bow
or shoot to thread the iron!"

Grave and wise, 630
Penélopê replied:

"If you were willing
to sit with me and comfort me, my friend,
no tide of sleep would ever close my eyes.
But mortals cannot go forever sleepless.
This the undying gods decree for all
who live and die on earth, kind furrowed earth.
Upstairs I go, then, to my single bed,
my sighing bed, wet with so many tears
after my Lord Odysseus took ship
to see that misery at Ilion, unspeakable. 640
Let me rest there, you here. You can stretch out
on the bare floor, or else command a bed."

So she went up to her chamber softly lit,
accompanied by her maids. Once there, she wept
for Odysseus, her husband, till Athena
cast sweet sleep upon her eyes.

BOOK TWENTY: SIGNS AND A VISION

Outside in the entry way he made his bed—
raw oxhide spread on level ground, and heaped up
fleeces, left from sheep the Akhaians killed.

And when he had lain down, Eurýnomê
flung out a robe to cover him. Unsleeping
the Lord Odysseus lay, and roved in thought
to the undoing of his enemies.

Now came a covey of women
laughing as they slipped out, arm in arm,
as many a night before, to the suitors' beds;
and anger took him like a wave to leap 10
into their midst and kill them, every one—
or should he let them all go hot to bed
one final night? His heart cried out within him
the way a brach[1] with whelps between her legs
would howl and bristle at a stranger—so
the hackles of his heart rose at that laughter.
Knocking his breast he muttered to himself:

"Down; be steady. You've seen worse, that time
the Kyklops like a rockslide ate your men
while you looked on. Nobody, only guile, 20
got you out of that cave alive."

His rage
held hard in leash, submitted to his mind,
while he himself rocked, rolling from side to side,
as a cook turns a sausage, big with blood
and fat, at a scorching blaze, without a pause,
to broil it quick: so he rolled left and right,
casting about to see how he, alone,
against the false outrageous crowd of suitors
could press the fight.

And out of the night sky
Athena came to him; out of the nearby dark 30
in body like a woman; came and stood
over his head to chide him:

"Why so wakeful,
most forlorn of men? Here is your home,
there lies your lady; and your son is here,
as fine as one could wish a son to be."

Odysseus looked up and answered:

"Aye,
goddess, that much is true; but still
I have some cause to fret in this affair.
I am one man; how can I whip those dogs? 40
They are always here in force. Neither
is that the end of it, there's more to come.

[1] Female dog; bitch.

If by the will of Zeus and by your will
I killed them all, where could I go for safety?
Tell me that!"

And the grey-eyed goddess said:

"Your touching faith! Another man would trust
some villainous mortal, with no brains—and what
am I? Your goddess-guardian to the end
in all your trials. Let it be plain as day:
if fifty bands of men surrounded us 50
and every sword sang for your blood,
you could make off still with their cows and sheep.
Now you, too, go to sleep. This all night vigil
wearies the flesh. You'll come out soon enough
on the other side of trouble."

Raining soft
sleep on his eyes, the beautiful one was gone
back to Olympos. Now at peace, the man
slumbered and lay still, but not his lady.
Wakeful again with all her cares, reclining
in the soft bed, she wept and cried aloud 60
until she had had her fill of tears, then spoke
in prayer first to Artemis:

"O gracious
divine lady Artemis, daughter of Zeus,
if you could only make an end now quickly,
let the arrow fly, stop my heart,
or if some wind could take me by the hair
up into running cloud, to plunge in tides of Ocean,
as hurricane winds took Pandáreos' daughters[2]
when they were left at home alone. The gods
had sapped their parents' lives. But Aphroditê 70
fed those children honey, cheese, and wine,
and Hêra gave them looks and wit, and Artemis,
pure Artemis, gave lovely height, and wise
Athena made them practised in her arts—
till Aphroditê in glory walked on Olympos,
begging for each a happy wedding day
from Zeus, the lightning's joyous king, who knows
all fate of mortals, fair and foul—
but even at that hour the cyclone winds
had ravished them away 80
to serve the loathsome Furies.

[2] Pandáreos stole a statue from a temple of Zeus; after the death of Pandáreos, his three daughters (Aedon and two of her sisters), though pitied by the greatest of the goddesses, were carried away by the Furies, the avengers of the father's wickedness. This story differs from the one in Book XIX, in which Aedon was changed into a nightingale.

Let me be
blown out by the Olympians! Shot by Artemis,
I still might go and see amid the shades
Odysseus in the rot of underworld.
No coward's eye should light by my consenting!
Evil may be endured when our days pass
in mourning, heavy-hearted, hard beset,
if only sleep reign over nighttime, blanketing
the world's good and evil from our eyes.
But not for me: dreams too my demon sends me. 90
Tonight the image of my lord came by
as I remember him with troops. O strange
exultation! I thought him real, and not a dream."

Now as the Dawn appeared all stitched in gold,
the queen's cry reached Odysseus at his waking,
so that he wondered, half asleep: it seemed
she knew him, and stood near him! Then he woke
and picked his bedding up to stow away
on a chair in the mégaron. The oxhide pad
he took outdoors. There, spreading wide his arms, 100
he prayed:

"O Father Zeus, if over land and water,
after adversity, you willed to bring me home,
let someone in the waking house give me good augury,
and a sign be shown, too, in the outer world."

He prayed thus, and the mind of Zeus in heaven
heard him. He thundered out of bright Olympos
down from above the cloudlands, in reply—
a rousing peal for Odysseus. Then a token
came to him from a woman grinding flour
in the court nearby. His own handmills were there, 110
and twelve maids had the job of grinding out
whole grain and barley meal, the pith of men.
Now all the rest, their bushels ground, were sleeping;
one only, frail and slow, kept at it still.
She stopped, stayed her hand, and her lord heard
the omen from her lips:

"Ah, Father Zeus
almighty over gods and men!
A great bang of thunder that was, surely,
out of the starry sky, and not a cloud in sight.
It is your nod to someone. Hear me, then, 120
make what I say come true:
let this day be the last the suitors feed
so dainty in Odysseus' hall!
They've made me work my heart out till I drop,
grinding barley. May they feast no more!"

The servant's prayer, after the cloudless thunder
of Zeus, Odysseus heard with lifting heart,
sure in his bones that vengeance was at hand.
Then other servants, wakening, came down
to build and light a fresh fire at the hearth. 130
Telémakhos, clear-eyed as a god, awoke,
put on his shirt and belted on his sword,
bound rawhide sandals under his smooth feet,
and took his bronze-shod lance. He came and stood
on the broad sill of the doorway, calling Eurýkleia:

"Nurse, dear Nurse, how did you treat our guest?
Had he a supper and a good bed? Has he lain
uncared for still? My mother is like that,
perverse for all her cleverness:
she'd entertain some riff-raff, and turn out 140
a solid man."

The old nurse answered him:

"I would not be so quick to accuse her, child.
He sat and drank here while he had a mind to;
food he no longer hungered for, he said—
for she did ask him. When he thought of sleeping,
she ordered them to make a bed. Poor soul!
Poor gentleman! So humble and so miserable,
he would accept no bed with rugs to lie on,
but slept on sheepskins and a raw oxhide
in the entry way. We covered him ourselves." 150

Telémakhos left the hall, hefting his lance,
with two swift flickering hounds for company,
to face the island Akhaians in the square;
and gently born Eurýkleia, the daughter
of Ops Peisenóridês, called to the maids:

"Bestir yourselves! you have your brooms, go sprinkle
the rooms and sweep them, robe the chairs in red,
sponge off the tables till they shine.
Wash out the winebowls and two-handled cups.
You others go fetch water from the spring; 160
no loitering; come straight back. Our company
will be here soon; morning is sure to bring them;
everyone has a holiday today."[3]

The women ran to obey her—twenty girls
off to the spring with jars for dusky water,
the rest at work inside. Then tall woodcutters
entered to split up logs for the hearth fire,

[3] The day is a special festival.

the water carriers returned; and on their heels
arrived the swineherd, driving three fat pigs,
chosen among his pens. In the wide court 170
he let them feed, and said to Odysseus kindly:

"Friend, are they more respectful of you now,
or still insulting you?"

Replied Odysseus:

"The young men, yes. And may the gods requite
those insolent puppies for the game they play
in a home not their own. They have no decency."

During this talk, Melánthios the goatherd
came in, driving goats for the suitors' feast,
with his two herdsmen. Under the portico
they tied the animals, and Melánthios 180
looked at Odysseus with a sneer. Said he:

"Stranger,
I see you mean to stay and turn our stomachs
begging in this hall. Clear out, why don't you?
Or will you have to taste a bloody beating
before you see the point? Your begging ways
nauseate everyone. There are feasts elsewhere."

Odysseus answered not a word, but grimly
shook his head over his murderous heart.
A third man came up now: Philoítios
the cattle foreman, with an ox behind him 190
and fat goats for the suitors. Ferrymen
had brought these from the mainland, as they bring
travellers, too—whoever comes along.
Philoítios tied the beasts under the portico
and joined the swineherd.

"Who is this," he said,
"Who is the new arrival at the manor?
Akhaian? or what else does he claim to be?
Where are his family and fields of home?
Down on his luck, all right: carries himself like a captain.
How the immortal gods can change and drag us down 200
once they begin to spin dark days for us!—
Kings and commanders, too."

Then he stepped over
and took Odysseus by the right hand, saying:

"Welcome, Sir. May good luck lie ahead
at the next turn. Hard times you're having, surely.

O Zeus! no god is more berserk in heaven
if gentle folk, whom you yourself begot,[4]
you plunge in grief and hardship without mercy!
Sir, I began to sweat when I first saw you,
and tears came to my eyes, remembering 210
Odysseus: rags like these he may be wearing
somewhere on his wanderings now—
I mean, if he's alive still under the sun.
But if he's dead and in the house of Death,
I mourn Odysseus. He entrusted cows to me
in Kephallênia,[5] when I was knee high,
and now his herds are numberless, no man else
ever had cattle multiply like grain.
But new men tell me I must bring my beeves
to feed them, who care nothing for our prince, 220
fear nothing from the watchful gods. They crave
partition of our lost king's land and wealth.
My own feelings keep going round and round
upon this tether: can I desert the boy
by moving, herds and all, to another country,
a new life among strangers? Yet it's worse
to stay here, in my old post, herding cattle
for upstarts.
I'd have gone long since,
gone, taken service with another king; this shame
is no more to be borne; but I keep thinking 230
my own lord, poor devil, still might come
and make a rout of suitors in his hall."

Odysseus, with his mind on action, answered:

"Herdsman, I make you out to be no coward
and no fool: I can see that for myself.
So let me tell you this. I swear by Zeus
all highest, by the table set for friends,
and by your king's hearthstone to which I've come,
Odysseus will return. You'll be on hand
to see, if you care to see it, 240
how those who lord it here will be cut down."

The cowman said:
"Would god it all came true!
You'd see the fight that's in me!"

Then Eumaios
echoed him, and invoked the gods, and prayed
that his great-minded master should return.

[4] To say that Zeus was their father was a way of describing great leaders.
[5] A large island near Ithaka; modern Cephalonia.

While these three talked, the suitors in the field
had come together plotting—what but death
for Telémakhos?—when from the left an eagle
crossed high with a rockdove in his claws.

Amphínomos got up. Said he, cutting them short: 250

"Friends, no luck lies in that plan for us,
no luck,[6] knifing the lad. Let's think of feasting."

A grateful thought, they felt, and walking on
entered the great hall of the hero Odysseus,
where they all dropped their cloaks on chairs or couches
and made a ritual slaughter, knifing sheep,
fat goats and pigs, knifing the grass-fed steer.
Then tripes were broiled and eaten. Mixing bowls
were filled with wine. The swineherd passed out cups,
Philoítios, chief cowherd, dealt the loaves 260
into the panniers, Melánthios poured wine,
and all their hands went out upon the feast.

Telémakhos placed his father to advantage
just at the door sill of the pillared hall,
setting a stool there and a sawed-off table,
gave him a share of tripes, poured out his wine
in a golden cup, and said:

"Stay here, sit down
to drink with our young friends. I stand between you
and any cutting word or cuffing hand
from any suitor. Here is no public house 270
but the old home of Odysseus, my inheritance.
Hold your tongues then, gentlemen, and your blows,
and let no wrangling start, no scuffle either."

The others, disconcerted, bit their lips
at the ring in the young man's voice. Antínoös,
Eupeithês' son, turned round to them and said:

"It goes against the grain, my lords, but still
I say we take this hectoring by Telémakhos.
You know Zeus balked at it, or else
we might have shut his mouth a long time past, 280
the silvery speaker."

But Telémakhos
paid no heed to what Antínoös said.

[6] The bird's appearance on the left is an ill omen.

Now public heralds wound through Ithaka
leading a file of beasts for sacrifice, and islanders
gathered under the shade trees of Apollo,
in the precinct of the Archer—while in hall
the suitors roasted mutton and fat beef
on skewers, pulling off the fragrant cuts;
and those who did the roasting served Odysseus
a portion equal to their own, for so 290
Telémakhos commanded.

But Athena
had no desire now to let the suitors
restrain themselves from wounding words and acts.
Laërtês' son again must be offended.
There was a scapegrace[7] fellow in the crowd
named Ktésippos, a Samian, rich beyond
all measure, arrogant with riches, early
and late a bidder for Odysseus' queen.
Now this one called attention to himself:

"Hear me, my lords, I have a thing to say. 300
Our friend has had his fair share from the start
and that's polite; it would be most improper
if we were cold to guests of Telémakhos—
no matter what tramp turns up. Well then, look here,
let me throw in my own small contribution.
He must have prizes to confer, himself,
on some brave bathman or another slave
here in Odysseus' house."

His hand went backward
and, fishing out a cow's foot from the basket,
he let it fly.

Odysseus rolled his head 310
to one side softly, ducking the blow, and smiled
a crooked smile with teeth clenched. On the wall
the cow's foot struck and fell. Telémakhos
blazed up:

"Ktésippos, lucky for you, by heaven,
not to have hit him! He took care of himself,
else you'd have had my lance-head in your belly;
no marriage, but a grave instead on Ithaka
for your father's pains.

You others, let me see
no more contemptible conduct in my house!
I've been awake to it for a long time—by now 320
I know what is honorable and what is not.

[7] Unprincipled.

Before, I was a child. I can endure it
while sheep are slaughtered, wine drunk up, and bread—
can one man check the greed of a hundred men?—
but I will suffer no more viciousness.
Granted you mean at last to cut me down:
I welcome that—better to die than have
humiliation always before my eyes,
the stranger buffeted, and the serving women
dragged about, abused in a noble house." 330

They quieted, grew still, under his lashing,
and after a long silence, Ageláos,
Damástor's son, spoke to them all:

"Friends, friends,
I hope no one will answer like a fishwife.
What has been said is true. Hands off this stranger,
he is no target, neither is any servant
here in the hall of King Odysseus.
Let me say a word, though, to Telémakhos
and to his mother, if it please them both:
as long as hope remained in you to see 340
Odysseus, that great gifted man, again,
you could not be reproached for obstinacy,
tying the suitors down here; better so,
if still your father fared the great sea homeward.
How plain it is, though, now, he'll come no more!
Go sit then by your mother, reason with her,
tell her to take the best man, highest bidder,
and you can have and hold your patrimony,
feed on it, drink it all, while she
adorns another's house."

Keeping his head, 350
Telémakhos replied:

"By Zeus Almighty,
Ageláos, and by my father's sufferings,
far from Ithaka, whether he's dead or lost,
I make no impediment to Mother's marriage.
'Take whom you wish,' I say, 'I'll add my dowry.'
But can I pack her off against her will
from her own home? Heaven forbid!"

At this,
Pallas Athena touched off in the suitors
a fit of laughter, uncontrollable.[8]
She drove them into nightmare, till they wheezed 360

[8] The laughter is a sign that the suitors are out of their right minds.

and neighed as though with jaws no longer theirs,
while blood defiled their meat,[9] and blurring tears
flooded their eyes, heart-sore with woe to come.
Then said the visionary, Theoklýmenos:

"O lost sad men, what terror is this you suffer?
Night shrouds you to the knees, your heads, your faces;
dry retch of death runs round like fire in sticks;
your cheeks are streaming; these fair walls and pedestals
are dripping crimson blood. And thick with shades
is the entry way, the courtyard thick with shades 370
passing athirst toward Érebos, into the dark,
the sun is quenched in heaven, foul mist hems us in . . ."

The young men greeted this with shouts of laughter,
and Eurýmakhos, the son of Pólybos, crowed:

"The mind of our new guest has gone astray.
Hustle him out of doors, lads, into the sunlight;
he finds it dark as night inside!"

The man of vision looked at him and said:

"When I need help, I'll ask for it, Eurýmakhos.
I have my eyes and ears, a pair of legs, 380
and a straight mind, still with me. These will do
to take me out. Damnation and black night
I see arriving for yourselves: no shelter,
no defence for any in this crowd—
fools and vipers in the king's own hall."

With this he left that handsome room and went
home to Peiraios, who received him kindly.
The suitors made wide eyes at one another
and set to work provoking Telémakhos
with jokes about his friends. One said, for instance: 390

"Telémakhos, no man is a luckier host
when it comes to what the cat dragged in. What burning
eyes your beggar had for bread and wine!
But not for labor, not for a single heave—
he'd be a deadweight on a field. Then comes
this other, with his mumbo-jumbo. Boy,
for your own good, I tell you, toss them both
into a slave ship for the Sikels.[10] That would pay you."

Telémakhos ignored the suitors' talk.
He kept his eyes in silence on his father, 400

[9] That is, in the eyes of Odysseus, Telémakhos, and Theoklýmenos.
[10] Sicilians.

awaiting the first blow. Meanwhile
the daughter of Ikários, Penélopê,
had placed her chair to look across and down
on father and son at bay; she heard the crowd,
and how they laughed as they resumed their dinner,
a fragrant feast, for many beasts were slain—
but as for supper, men supped never colder
than these, on what the goddess and the warrior
were even then preparing for the suitors,
whose treachery had filled that house with pain. 410

BOOK TWENTY-ONE: THE TEST OF THE BOW

Upon Penélopê, most worn in love and thought,
Athena cast a glance like a grey sea
lifting her. Now to bring the tough bow out and bring
the iron blades. Now try those dogs at archery
to usher bloody slaughter in.

So moving stairward
the queen took up a fine doorhook of bronze,
ivory-hafted, smooth in her clenched hand,
and led her maids down to a distant room,
a storeroom where the master's treasure lay:
bronze, bar gold, black iron forged and wrought. 10
In this place hung the double-torsion bow
and arrows in a quiver, a great sheaf—
quills of groaning.

In the old time in Lakedaimon[1]
her lord had got these arms from Íphitos,
Eurýtos'[2] son. The two met in Messenia[3]
at Ortílokhos' table, on the day
Odysseus claimed a debt owed by that realm—
sheep stolen by Messenians out of Ithaka
in their long ships, three hundred head, and herdsmen.
Seniors of Ithaka and his father sent him 20
on that far embassy when he was young.
But Íphitos had come there tracking strays,
twelve shy mares, with mule colts yet unweaned.
And a fatal chase they led him over prairies
into the hands of Heraklês. That massive
son of toil and mortal son of Zeus

[1] The region of Sparta, in southern Greece.
[2] A famous archer.
[3] A region down the coast from Ithaka, in southwestern Greece.

murdered his guest at wine[4] in his own house—
inhuman, shameless in the sight of heaven—
to keep the mares and colts in his own grange.
Now Íphitos, when he knew Odysseus, gave him 30
the master bowman's arm; for old Eurýtos
had left it on his deathbed to his son.
In fellowship Odysseus gave a lance
and a sharp sword. But Heraklês killed Íphitos
before one friend could play host to the other.
And Lord Odysseus would not take the bow
in the black ships to the great war at Troy.
As a keepsake he put it by:
it served him well at home in Ithaka.

Now the queen reached the storeroom door and halted. 40
Here was an oaken sill, cut long ago
and sanded clean and bedded true. Foursquare
the doorjambs and the shining doors were set
by the careful builder. Penélopê untied the strap
around the curving handle, pushed her hook
into the slit, aimed at the bolts inside
and shot them back. Then came a rasping sound
as those bright doors the key had sprung gave way—
a bellow like a bull's vaunt in a meadow—
followed by her light footfall entering 50
over the plank floor. Herb-scented robes
lay there in chests, but the lady's milkwhite arms
went up to lift the bow down from a peg
in its own polished bowcase.

Now Penélopê
sank down, holding the weapon on her knees,
and drew her husband's great bow out, and sobbed
and bit her lip and let the salt tears flow.
Then back she went to face the crowded hall
tremendous bow in hand, and on her shoulder hung
the quiver spiked with coughing death. Behind her 60
maids bore a basket full of axeheads, bronze
and iron implements for the master's game.
Thus in her beauty she approached the suitors,
and near a pillar of the solid roof
she paused, her shining veil across her cheeks,
her maids on either hand and still,
then spoke to the banqueters:

[4] Íphitos' pursuit of his lost mares brought him to Tiryns, the city of the great hero-adventurer Heraklês, who, according to certain versions of the story, had something to do with the mares' disappearance. By some accounts, Heraklês killed Íphitos by throwing him down from the city walls.

"My lords, hear me:
suitors indeed, you commandeered this house
to feast and drink in, day and night, my husband
being long gone, long out of mind. You found 70
no justification for yourselves—none
except your lust to marry me. Stand up, then:
we now declare a contest for that prize.
Here is my lord Odysseus' hunting bow.
Bend and string it if you can. Who sends an arrow
through iron axe-helve sockets,[5] twelve in line?
I join my life with his, and leave this place, my home,
my rich and beautiful bridal house, forever
to be remembered, though I dream it only."

Then to Eumaios:
"Carry the bow forward. 80
Carry the blades."

Tears came to the swineherd's eyes
as he reached out for the big bow. He laid it
down at the suitors' feet. Across the room
the cowherd sobbed, knowing the master's weapon.
Antínoös growled, with a glance at both:
"Clods.

They go to pieces over nothing.
You two, there,
why are you sniveling? To upset the woman
even more? Has she not pain enough
over her lost husband? *Sit down.*
Get on with dinner quietly, or cry about it 90
outside, if you must. Leave us the bow.
A clean-cut game, it looks to me.
Nobody bends that bowstave easily
in this company. Is there a man here
made like Odysseus? I remember him
from childhood: I can see him even now."

That was the way he played it, hoping inwardly
to span the great horn bow with corded gut
and drill the iron with his shot—he, Antínoös,
destined to be the first of all to savor 100
blood from a biting arrow at his throat,
a shaft drawn by the fingers of Odysseus
whom he had mocked and plundered, leading on

[5] The details of the feat to be performed have been much discussed and are not entirely clear; in any case, the archer had to send an arrow through twelve openings—notches, holes, or other apertures—in the handles or blades of the axes.

the rest, his boon companions. Now they heard
a gay snort of laughter from Telémakhos,
who said then brilliantly:

"A queer thing, that!
Has Zeus almighty made me a half-wit?
For all her spirit, Mother has given in,
promised to go off with someone—and
is that amusing? What am I cackling for? 110
Step up, my lords, contend now for your prize.
There is no woman like her in Akhaia,
not in old Argos, Pylos, or Mykênê,
neither in Ithaka nor on the mainland,
and you all know it without praise of mine.
Come on, no hanging back, no more delay
in getting the bow bent. Who's the winner?
I myself should like to try that bow.
Suppose I bend it and bring off the shot,
my heart will be less heavy, seeing the queen my mother 120
go for the last time from this house and hall,
if I who stay can do my father's feat."

He moved out quickly, dropping his crimson cloak,
and lifted sword and sword belt from his shoulders.
His preparation was to dig a trench,
heaping the earth in a long ridge beside it
to hold the blades half-bedded. A taut cord
aligned the socket rings. And no one there
but looked on wondering at his workmanship,
for the boy had never seen it done.

He took his stand then 130
on the broad door sill to attempt the bow.
Three times he put his back into it and sprang it,
three times he had to slack off. Still he meant
to string that bow and pull for the needle shot.
A fourth try, and he had it all but strung—
when a stiffening in Odysseus made him check.
Abruptly then he stopped and turned and said:

"Blast and damn it, must I be a milksop
all my life? Half-grown, all thumbs,
no strength or knack at arms, to defend myself 140
if someone picks a fight with me.

Take over,
O my elders and betters, try the bow,
run off the contest."

And he stood the weapon
upright against the massy-timbered door
with one arrow across the horn aslant,

then went back to his chair. Antínoös
gave the word:

"Now one man at a time
rise and go forward. Round the room in order;
left to right from where they dip the wine."

As this seemed fair enough, up stood Leódês 150
the son of Oinops. This man used to find
vision for them in the smoke of sacrifice.
He kept his chair well back, retired by the winebowl,
for he alone could not abide their manners
but sat in shame for all the rest. Now it was he
who had first to confront the bow,
standing up on the broad door sill. He failed.
The bow unbending made his thin hands yield,
no muscle in them. He gave up and said:

"Friends, I cannot. Let the next man handle it. 160
Here is a bow to break the heart and spirit
of many strong men. Aye. And death is less
bitter than to live on and never have
the beauty that we came here laying siege to
so many days. Resolute, are you still,
to win Odysseus' lady Penélopê?
Pit yourselves against the bow, and look
among Akhaians for another's daughter.
Gifts will be enough to court and take her.
Let the best offer win."

With this Leódês 170
thrust the bow away from him, and left it
upright against the massy-timbered door,
with one arrow aslant across the horn.
As he went down to his chair he heard Antínoös'
voice rising:

"What is that you say?
It makes me burn. You cannot string the weapon,
so 'Here is a bow to break the heart and spirit
of many strong men.' Crushing thought!
You were not born—you never had it in you—
to pull that bow or let an arrow fly. 180
But here are men who can and will."

He called out to the goatherd, Melánthios:

"Kindle a fire there, be quick about it,
draw up a big bench with a sheepskin on it,
and bring a cake of lard out of the stores.
Contenders from now on will heat and grease the bow.
We'll try it limber, and bring off the shot."

Melánthios darted out to light a blaze,
drew up a bench, threw a big sheepskin over it,
and brought a cake of lard. So one by one 190
the young men warmed and greased the bow for bending,
but not a man could string it. They were whipped.
Antínoös held off; so did Eurýmakhos,
suitors in chief, by far the ablest there.

Two men had meanwhile left the hall:
swineherd and cowherd, in companionship,
one downcast as the other. But Odysseus
followed them outdoors, outside the court,
and coming up said gently:

"You, herdsman
and you, too, swineherd, I could say a thing to you, 200
or should I keep it dark?

No, no; speak,
my heart tells me. Would you be men enough
to stand by Odysseus if he came back?
Suppose he dropped out of a clear sky, as I did?
Suppose some god should bring him?
Would you bear arms for him, or for the suitors?"

The cowherd said:

"Ah, let the master come!
Father Zeus, grant our old wish! Some courier
guide him back! Then judge what stuff is in me
and how I manage arms!"

Likewise Eumaios 210
fell to praying all heaven for his return,
so that Odysseus, sure at least of these,
told them:

"I am at home, for I am he.
I bore adversities, but in the twentieth year
I am ashore in my own land. I find
the two of you, alone among my people,
longed for my coming. Prayers I never heard
except your own that I might come again.
So now what is in store for you I'll tell you:
If Zeus brings down the suitors by my hand 220
I promise marriages to both, and cattle,
and houses built near mine. And you shall be
brothers-in-arms of my Telémakhos.
Here, let me show you something else, a sign
that I am he, that you can trust me, look:
this old scar from the tusk wound that I got
boar hunting on Parnassos—
Autólykos' sons and I."

Shifting his rags
he bared the long gash. Both men looked, and knew,
and threw their arms around the old soldier, weeping, 230
kissing his head and shoulders. He as well
took each man's head and hands to kiss, then said—
to cut it short, else they might weep till dark—

"Break off, no more of this.
Anyone at the door could see and tell them.
Drift back in, but separately at intervals
after me.
Now listen to your orders:
when the time comes, those gentlemen, to a man,
will be dead against giving me bow or quiver.
Defy them. Eumaios, bring the bow 240
and put it in my hands there at the door.
Tell the women to lock their own door tight.
Tell them if someone hears the shock of arms
or groans of men, in hall or court, not one
must show her face, but keep still at her weaving.
Philoítios, run to the outer gate and lock it.
Throw the cross bar and lash it."

He turned back
into the courtyard and the beautiful house
and took the stool he had before. They followed
one by one, the two hands loyal to him. 250

Eurýmakhos had now picked up the bow.
He turned it round, and turned it round
before the licking flame to warm it up,
but could not, even so, put stress upon it
to jam the loop over the tip
though his heart groaned to bursting.
Then he said grimly:

"Curse this day.
What gloom I feel, not for myself alone,
and not only because we lose that bride.
Women are not lacking in Akhaia,
in other towns, or on Ithaka. No, the worst 260
is humiliation—to be shown up for children
measured against Odysseus—we who cannot
even hitch the string over his bow.
What shame to be repeated of us, after us!"

Antínoös said:

"Come to yourself. You know
that is not the way this business ends.

Today the islanders held holiday, a holy day,[6]
no day to sweat over a bowstring.
Keep your head.
Postpone the bow. I say we leave the axes
planted where they are. No one will take them. 270
No one comes to Odysseus' hall tonight.
Break out good wine and brim our cups again,
we'll keep the crooked bow safe overnight,
order the fattest goats Melánthios has
brought down tomorrow noon, and offer thighbones burning
to Apollo, god of archers,
while we try out the bow and make the shot."

As this appealed to everyone, heralds came
pouring fresh water for their hands, and boys
filled up the winebowls. Joints of meat went round, 280
fresh cuts for all, while each man made his offering,
tilting the red wine to the gods, and drank his fill.
Then spoke Odysseus, all craft and gall:

"My lords, contenders for the queen, permit me:
a passion in me moves me to speak out.
I put it to Eurýmakhos above all
and to that brilliant prince, Antínoös. Just now
how wise his counsel was, to leave the trial
and turn your thoughts to the immortal gods! Apollo
will give power tomorrow to whom he wills. 290
But let me try my hand at the smooth bow!
Let me test my fingers and my pull
to see if any of the oldtime kick is there,
or if thin fare and roving took it out of me."

Now irritation beyond reason swept them all,
since they were nagged by fear that he could string it.
Antínoös answered, coldly and at length:

"You bleary vagabond, no rag of sense is left you.
Are you not coddled here enough, at table
taking meat with gentlemen, your betters, 300
denied nothing, and listening to our talk?
When have we let a tramp hear all our talk?
The sweet goad of wine has made you rave!
Here is the evil wine can do
to those who swig it down. Even the centaur
Eurýtion,[7] in Peiríthoös' hall

[6] With ironic appropriateness, a feast day of Apollo, god of archery; Antínoös makes this an excuse for putting off the present challenge.

[7] The centaurs were an uncivilized tribe (often represented in myth as having horses' trunks and legs and human torsos and heads), inhabitants of Thessaly, in northeastern Greece. They were invited to the wedding of Peiríthoös, king of the Lapíthai, a neighboring people, and at the wedding tried to carry off the bride; the present version tells the story in the singular, of Eurýtion. In the ensuing battle the centaurs were defeated.

among the Lapíthai, came to a bloody end
because of wine; wine ruined him: it crazed him,
drove him wild for rape in that great house.
The princes cornered him in fury, leaping on him 310
to drag him out and crop his ears and nose.
Drink had destroyed his mind, and so he ended
in that mutilation—fool that he was.
Centaurs and men made war for this,
but the drunkard first brought hurt upon himself.

The tale applies to you: I promise you
great trouble if you touch that bow. You'll come by
no indulgence in our house; kicked down
into a ship's bilge, out to sea you go,
and nothing saves you. Drink, but hold your tongue. 320
Make no contention here with younger men."

At this the watchful queen Penélopê
interposed:

"Antínoös, discourtesy
to a guest of Telémakhos—whatever guest—
that is not handsome. What are you afraid of?
Suppose this exile put his back into it
and drew the great bow of Odysseus—
could he then take me home to be his bride?
You know he does not imagine that! No one
need let that prospect weigh upon his dinner! 330
How very, very improbable it seems."

It was Eurýmakhos who answered her:

"Penélopê, O daughter of Ikários,
most subtle queen, we are not given to fantasy.
No, but our ears burn at what men might say
and women, too. We hear some jackal whispering:
'How far inferior to the great husband
her suitors are! Can't even budge his bow!
Think of it; and a beggar, out of nowhere,
strung it quick and made the needle shot!' 340
That kind of disrepute we would not care for."

Penélopê replied, steadfast and wary:

"Eurýmakhos, you have no good repute
in this realm, nor the faintest hope of it—
men who abused a prince's house for years,
consumed his wine and cattle. Shame enough.
Why hang your heads over a trifle now?
The stranger is a big man, well-compacted,
and claims to be of noble blood.

Ai! 350
Give him the bow, and let us have it out!
What I can promise him I will:
if by the kindness of Apollo he prevails
he shall be clothed well and equipped.
A fine shirt and a cloak I promise him;
a lance for keeping dogs at bay, or men;
a broadsword; sandals to protect his feet;
escort, and freedom to go where he will."

Telémakhos now faced her and said sharply:

"Mother, as to the bow and who may handle it 360
or not handle it, no man here
has more authority than I do—not one lord
of our own stony Ithaka nor the islands lying
east toward Elis: no one stops me if I choose
to give these weapons outright to my guest.
Return to your own hall. Tend your spindle.
Tend your loom. Direct your maids at work.
This question of the bow will be for men to settle,
most of all for me. I am master here."

She gazed in wonder, turned, and so withdrew, 370
her son's clearheaded bravery in her heart.
But when she had mounted to her rooms again
with all her women, then she fell to weeping
for Odysseus, her husband. Grey-eyed Athena
presently cast a sweet sleep on her eyes.

The swineherd had the horned bow in his hands
moving toward Odysseus, when the crowd
in the banquet hall broke into an ugly din,
shouts rising from the flushed young men:

"Ho! Where
do you think you are taking that, you smutty slave?" 380

"What is this dithering?"

"We'll toss you back alone
among the pigs, for your own dogs to eat,
if bright Apollo nods and the gods are kind!"

He faltered, all at once put down the bow, and stood
in panic, buffeted by waves of cries,
hearing Telémakhos from another quarter
shout:

"Go on, take him the bow!

Do you obey this pack?
You will be stoned back to your hills! Young as I am

my power is over you! I wish to God 390
I had as much the upper hand of these!
There would be suitors pitched like dead rats
through our gate, for the evil plotted here!"

Telémakhos' frenzy struck someone as funny,
and soon the whole room roared with laughter at him,
so that all tension passed. Eumaios picked up
bow and quiver, making for the door,
and there he placed them in Odysseus' hands.
Calling Eurýkleia to his side he said:

"Telémakhos
trusts you to take care of the women's doorway. 400
Lock it tight. If anyone inside
should hear the shock of arms or groans of men
in hall or court, not one must show her face,
but go on with her weaving."

The old woman
nodded and kept still. She disappeared
into the women's hall, bolting the door behind her.
Philoítios left the house now at one bound,
catlike, running to bolt the courtyard gate.
A coil of deck-rope of papyrus fiber
lay in the gateway; this he used for lashing, 410
and ran back to the same stool as before,
fastening his eyes upon Odysseus.

And Odysseus took his time,
turning the bow, tapping it, every inch,
for borings that termites might have made
while the master of the weapon was abroad.
The suitors were now watching him, and some
jested among themselves:

"A bow lover!"

"Dealer in old bows!"

"Maybe he has one like it
at home!"

"Or has an itch to make one for himself."

"See how he handles it, the sly old buzzard!" 420

And one disdainful suitor added this:

"May his fortune grow an inch for every inch he bends it!"

But the man skilled in all ways of contending,
satisfied by the great bow's look and heft,

like a musician, like a harper, when
with quiet hand upon his instrument
he draws between his thumb and forefinger
a sweet new string upon a peg: so effortlessly
Odysseus in one motion strung the bow.
Then slid his right hand down the cord and plucked it, 430
so the taut gut vibrating hummed and sang
a swallow's note.
In the hushed hall it smote the suitors
and all their faces changed. Then Zeus thundered
overhead, one loud crack for a sign.
And Odysseus laughed within him that the son
of crooked-minded Kronos had flung that omen down.
He picked one ready arrow from his table
where it lay bare: the rest were waiting still
in the quiver for the young men's turn to come.
He nocked it, let it rest across the handgrip, 440
and drew the string and grooved butt of the arrow,
aiming from where he sat upon the stool.
Now flashed
arrow from twanging bow clean as a whistle
through every socket ring, and grazed not one,
to thud with heavy brazen head beyond.
Then quietly
Odysseus said:

"Telémakhos, the stranger
you welcomed in your hall has not disgraced you.
I did not miss, neither did I take all day
stringing the bow. My hand and eye are sound,
not so contemptible as the young men say. 450
The hour has come to cook their lordships' mutton—
supper by daylight. Other amusements later,
with song and harping that adorn a feast."

He dropped his eyes and nodded, and the prince
Telémakhos, true son of King Odysseus,
belted his sword on, clapped hand to his spear,
and with a clink and glitter of keen bronze
stood by his chair, in the forefront near his father.

BOOK TWENTY-TWO: DEATH IN THE GREAT HALL

Now shrugging off his rags the wiliest fighter of the islands
leapt and stood on the broad door sill, his own bow in his hand.
He poured out at his feet a rain of arrows from the quiver
and spoke to the crowd:

"So much for that. Your clean-cut game is over.
Now watch me hit a target that no man has hit before,
if I can make this shot. Help me, Apollo."

He drew to his fist the cruel head of an arrow for Antínoös
just as the young man leaned to lift his beautiful drinking cup,
embossed, two-handled, golden: the cup was in his fingers:
the wine was even at his lips: and did he dream of death? 10
How could he? In that revelry amid his throng of friends
who would imagine a single foe—though a strong foe indeed—
could dare to bring death's pain on him and darkness on his eyes?
Odysseus' arrow hit him under the chin
and punched up to the feathers through his throat.

Backward and down he went, letting the winecup fall
from his shocked hand. Like pipes his nostrils jetted
crimson runnels, a river of mortal red,
and one last kick upset his table
knocking the bread and meat to soak in dusty blood. 20
Now as they craned to see their champion where he lay
the suitors jostled in uproar down the hall,
everyone on his feet. Wildly they turned and scanned
the walls in the long room for arms; but not a shield,
not a good ashen spear was there for a man to take and throw.
All they could do was yell in outrage at Odysseus:

"Foul! to shoot at a man! That was your last shot!"

"Your own throat will be slit for this!"

"Our finest lad is down!
You killed the best on Ithaka."

"Buzzards will tear your eyes out!"

For they imagined as they wished—that it was a wild shot, 30
an unintended killing—fools, not to comprehend
they were already in the grip of death.
But glaring under his brows Odysseus answered:

"You yellow dogs, you thought I'd never make it
home from the land of Troy. You took my house to plunder,
twisted my maids to serve your beds. You dared
bid for my wife while I was still alive.
Contempt was all you had for the gods who rule wide heaven,
contempt for what men say of you hereafter.
Your last hour has come. You die in blood." 40

As they all took this in, sickly green fear
pulled at their entrails, and their eyes flickered
looking for some hatch or hideaway from death.
Eurýmakhos alone could speak. He said:

"If you are Odysseus of Ithaka come back,
all that you say these men have done is true.
Rash actions, many here, more in the countryside.
But here he lies, the man who caused them all.
Antínoös was the ringleader, he whipped us on
to do these things. He cared less for a marriage 50
than for the power Kronion has denied him
as king of Ithaka. For that
he tried to trap your son and would have killed him.
He is dead now and has his portion. Spare
your own people. As for ourselves, we'll make
restitution of wine and meat consumed,
and add, each one, a tithe of twenty oxen
with gifts of bronze and gold to warm your heart.
Meanwhile we cannot blame you for your anger."

Odysseus glowered under his black brows 60
and said:

"Not for the whole treasure of your fathers,
all you enjoy, lands, flocks, or any gold
put up by others, would I hold my hand.
There will be killing till the score is paid.
You forced yourselves upon this house. Fight your way out,
or run for it, if you think you'll escape death.
I doubt one man of you skins by."

They felt their knees fail, and their hearts—but heard
Eurýmakhos for the last time rallying them.

"Friends," he said, "the man is implacable. 70
Now that he's got his hands on bow and quiver
he'll shoot from the big door stone there
until he kills us to the last man.
Fight, I say,
let's remember the joy of it. Swords out!
Hold up your tables to deflect his arrows.
After me, everyone: rush him where he stands.
If we can budge him from the door, if we can pass
into the town, we'll call out men to chase him.
This fellow with his bow will shoot no more."

He drew his own sword as he spoke, a broadsword of fine bronze, 80
honed like a razor on either edge. Then crying hoarse and loud
he hurled himself at Odysseus. But the kingly man let fly
an arrow at that instant, and the quivering feathered butt
sprang to the nipple of his breast as the barb stuck in his liver.
The bright broadsword clanged down. He lurched and fell aside,
pitching across his table. His cup, his bread and meat,
were spilt and scattered far and wide, and his head slammed on the
ground.

Revulsion, anguish in his heart, with both feet kicking out,
he downed his chair, while the shrouding wave of mist closed on his
eyes.

Amphínomos now came running at Odysseus, 90
broadsword naked in his hand. He thought to make
the great soldier give way at the door.
But with a spear throw from behind Telémakhos hit him
between the shoulders, and the lancehead drove
clear through his chest. He left his feet and fell
forward, thudding, forehead against the ground.
Telémakhos swerved around him, leaving the long dark spear
planted in Amphínomos. If he paused to yank it out
someone might jump him from behind or cut him down with a
sword
at the moment he bent over. So he ran—ran from the tables 100
to his father's side and halted, panting, saying:

"Father let me bring you a shield and spear,
a pair of spears, a helmet.
I can arm on the run myself; I'll give
outfits to Eumaios and this cowherd.
Better to have equipment."

Said Odysseus:

"Run then, while I hold them off with arrows
as long as the arrows last. When all are gone
if I'm alone they can dislodge me."

Quick
upon his father's word Telémakhos 110
ran to the room where spears and armor lay.
He caught up four light shields, four pairs of spears,
four helms of war high-plumed with flowing manes,
and ran back, loaded down, to his father's side.
He was the first to pull a helmet on
and slide his bare arm in a buckler strap.
The servants armed themselves, and all three took their stand
beside the master of battle.
While he had arrows
he aimed and shot, and every shot brought down
one of his huddling enemies. 120
But when all barbs had flown from the bowman's fist,
he leaned his bow in the bright entry way
beside the door, and armed: a four-ply shield
hard on his shoulder, and a crested helm,
horsetailed, nodding stormy upon his head,
then took his tough and bronze-shod spears.
The suitors
who held their feet, no longer under bowshot,

could see a window high in a recess of the wall,
a vent, lighting the passage to the storeroom.
This passage had one entry, with a door, 130
at the edge of the great hall's threshold, just outside.[1]

Odysseus told the swineherd to stand over
and guard this door and passage. As he did so,
a suitor named Ageláos asked the others:

"Who will get a leg up on that window
and run to alarm the town? One sharp attack
and this fellow will never shoot again."

His answer
came from the goatherd, Melánthios:

"No chance, my lord.
The exit into the courtyard is too near them,
too narrow. One good man could hold that portal 140
against a crowd. No: let me scale the wall
and bring you arms out of the storage chamber.
Odysseus and his son put them indoors,
I'm sure of it; not outside."

The goatish goatherd
clambered up the wall, toes in the chinks,
and slipped through to the storeroom. Twelve light shields,
twelve spears he took, and twelve thick-crested helms,
and handed all down quickly to the suitors.
Odysseus, when he saw his adversaries
girded and capped and long spears in their hands 150
shaken at him, felt his knees go slack,
his heart sink, for the fight was turning grim.
He spoke rapidly to his son:

"Telémakhos, one of the serving women
is tipping the scales against us in this fight,
or maybe Melánthios."

But sharp and clear
Telémakhos said:

"It is my own fault, Father,
mine alone. The storeroom door—I left it
wide open. They were more alert than I.
Eumaios, go and lock that door 160
and bring back word if a woman is doing this
or Melánthios, Dólios' son. More likely he."

[1] The window in the *mégaron,* or great hall, connects with an external corridor that runs to the rear of the house, past the women's chambers, to the storeroom; the only exit from the corridor to the outdoor courtyard is close to where Odysseus and his three allies have posted themselves. It is therefore, as Melánthios soon points out, not a safe escape route.

Even as they conferred, Melánthios
entered the storeroom for a second load,
and the swineherd at the passage entry saw him.
He cried out to his lord:

"Son of Laërtês,
Odysseus, master mariner and soldier,
there he goes, the monkey, as we thought,
there he goes into the storeroom.
Let me hear your will:
put a spear through him—I hope I am the stronger— 170
or drag him here to pay for his foul tricks
against your house?"

Odysseus said:

"Telémakhos and I
will keep these gentlemen in hall, for all their urge to leave.
You two go throw him into the storeroom, wrench his arms
and legs behind him, lash his hands and feet
to a plank, and hoist him up to the roof beams.
Let him live on there suffering at his leisure."

The two men heard him with appreciation
and ducked into the passage. Melánthios,
rummaging in the chamber, could not hear them 180
as they came up; nor could he see them freeze
like posts on either side the door.
He turned back with a handsome crested helmet
in one hand, in the other an old shield
coated with dust—a shield Laërtês bore
soldiering in his youth. It had lain there for years,
and the seams on strap and grip had rotted away.
As Melánthios came out the two men sprang,
jerked him backward by the hair, and threw him.
Hands and feet they tied with a cutting cord 190
behind him, so his bones ground in their sockets,
just as Laërtês' royal son commanded.
Then with a whip of rope they hoisted him
in agony up a pillar to the beams,
and—O my swineherd—you were the one to say:

"Watch through the night up there, Melánthios.
An airy bed is what you need.
You'll be awake to see the primrose Dawn
when she goes glowing from the streams of Ocean
to mount her golden throne.
No oversleeping 200
the hour for driving goats to feed the suitors."

They stooped for helm and shield and left him there
contorted, in his brutal sling,

and shut the doors, and went to join Odysseus,
whose mind moved through the combat now to come.
Breathing deep, and snorting hard, they stood
four at the entry, facing two score men.
But now into the gracious doorway stepped
Zeus's daughter Athena. She wore the guise of Mentor,
and Odysseus appealed to her in joy: 210

"O Mentor, join me in this fight! Remember
how all my life I've been devoted to you,
friend of my youth!"

For he guessed it was Athena,
Hope of Soldiers. Cries came from the suitors,
and Ageláos, Damástor's son, called out:

"Mentor, don't let Odysseus lead you astray
to fight against us on his side.
Think twice: we are resolved—and we will do it—
after we kill them, father and son,
you too will have your throat slit for your pains 220
if you make trouble for us here. It means your life.
Your life—and cutting throats will not be all.
Whatever wealth you have, at home, or elsewhere,
we'll mingle with Odysseus' wealth. Your sons
will be turned out, your wife and daughters
banished from the town of Ithaka."

Athena's anger grew like a storm wind as he spoke
until she flashed out at Odysseus:

"Ah, what a falling off!
Where is your valor, where is the iron hand
that fought at Troy for Helen, pearl of kings, 230
no respite and nine years of war? How many foes
your hand brought down in bloody play of spears!
What stratagem but yours took Priam's town?
How is it now that on your own door sill,
before the harriers[2] of your wife, you curse your luck
not to be stronger?

Come here, cousin, stand by me,
and you'll see action! In the enemies' teeth
learn how Mentor, son of Álkimos,
repays fair dealing!"

For all her fighting words
she gave no overpowering aid—not yet; 240
father and son must prove their mettle still.
Into the smoky air under the roof

[2] Predatory dogs or hawks.

the goddess merely darted to perch on a blackened beam—
no figure to be seen now but a swallow.

Command of the suitors had fallen to Ageláos.
With him were Eurýnomos, Amphímedon,
Demoptólemos, Peisándros, Pólybos,
the best of the lot who stood to fight for their lives
after the streaking arrows downed the rest.
Ageláos rallied them with his plan of battle: 250

"Friends, our killer has come to the end of his rope,
and much good Mentor did him, that blowhard, dropping in.
Look, only four are left to fight, in the light there at the door.
No scattering of shots, men, no throwing away good spears;
we six will aim a volley at Odysseus alone,
and may Zeus grant us the glory of a hit.
If he goes down, the others are no problem."

At his command, then, "Ho!" they all let fly
as one man. But Athena spoiled their shots.
One hit the doorpost of the hall, another 260
stuck in the door's thick timbering, still others
rang on the stone wall, shivering hafts[3] of ash.
Seeing his men unscathed, royal Odysseus
gave the word for action.

"Now I say, friends,
the time is overdue to let them have it.
Battlespoil they want from our dead bodies
to add to all they plundered here before."

Taking aim over the steadied lanceheads
they all let fly together. Odysseus killed
Demoptólemos; Telémakhos 270
killed Euryádes; the swineherd, Élatos;
and Peisándros went down before the cowherd.
As these lay dying, biting the central floor,
their friends gave way and broke for the inner wall.
The four attackers followed up with a rush
to take spears from the fallen men.

Re-forming,
the suitors threw again with all their strength,
but Athena turned their shots, or all but two.
One hit a doorpost in the hall, another
stuck in the door's thick timbering, still others 280
rang on the stone wall, shivering hafts of ash.
Amphímedon's point bloodied Telémakhos'
wrist, a superficial wound, and Ktésippos'
long spear passing over Eumaios' shield

[3] Shafts.

grazed his shoulder, hurtled on and fell.
No matter: with Odysseus the great soldier
the wounded threw again. And Odysseus raider of cities
struck Eurýdamas down. Telémakhos
hit Amphímedon, and the swineherd's shot
killed Pólybos. But Ktésippos, who had last evening thrown 290
a cow's hoof at Odysseus, got the cowherd's heavy cast
full in the chest—and dying heard him say:

"You arrogant joking bastard!
Clown, will you, like a fool, and parade your wit?
Leave jesting to the gods who do it better.
This will repay your cow's-foot courtesy
to a great wanderer come home."

The master
of the black herds had answered Ktésippos.
Odysseus, lunging at close quarters, put a spear
through Ageláos, Damástor's son. Telémakhos 300
hit Leókritos from behind and pierced him,
kidney to diaphragm. Speared off his feet,
he fell face downward on the ground.

At this moment that unmanning thunder cloud,
the aegis,[4] Athena's shield,
took form aloft in the great hall.
And the suitors mad with fear
at her great sign stampeded like stung cattle by a river
when the dread shimmering gadfly strikes in summer,
in the flowering season, in the long-drawn days.
After them the attackers wheeled, as terrible as falcons 310
from eyries in the mountains veering over and diving down
with talons wide unsheathed on flights of birds,
who cower down the sky in chutes and bursts along the valley—
but the pouncing falcons grip their prey, no frantic wing avails,
and farmers love to watch those beakèd hunters.
So these now fell upon the suitors in that hall,
turning, turning to strike and strike again,
while torn men moaned at death, and blood ran smoking
over the whole floor.
Now there was one
who turned and threw himself at Odysseus' knees— 320
Leódês, begging for his life:

"Mercy,
mercy on a suppliant, Odysseus!
Never by word or act of mine, I swear,
was any woman troubled here. I told the rest
to put an end to it. They would not listen,

[4] The shield of Zeus, lent by him to Athena.

would not keep their hands from brutishness,
and now they are all dying like dogs for it.
I had no part in what they did: my part
was visionary—reading the smoke of sacrifice.
Scruples go unrewarded if I die." 330

The shrewd fighter frowned over him and said:

"You were diviner to this crowd? How often
you must have prayed my sweet day of return
would never come, or not for years!—and prayed
to have my dear wife, and beget children on her.
No plea like yours could save you
from this hard bed of death. Death it shall be!"

He picked up Ageláos' broadsword
from where it lay, flung by the slain man,
and gave Leódês' neck a lopping blow 340
so that his head went down to mouth in dust.

One more who had avoided furious death
was the son of Terpis, Phêmios, the minstrel,
singer by compulsion to the suitors.
He stood now with his harp, holy and clear,
in the wall's recess, under the window, wondering
if he should flee that way to the courtyard altar,
sanctuary of Zeus, the Enclosure God.
Thighbones in hundreds had been offered there
by Laërtês and Odysseus. No, he thought; 350
the more direct way would be best—to go
humbly to his lord. But first to save
his murmuring instrument he laid it down
carefully between the winebowl and a chair,
then he betook himself to Lord Odysseus,
clung hard to his knees, and said:

"Mercy,
mercy on a suppliant, Odysseus!
My gift is song for men and for the gods undying.
My death will be remorse for you hereafter.
No one taught me: deep in my mind a god 360
shaped all the various ways of life in song.
And I am fit to make verse in your company
as in the god's. Put aside lust for blood.
Your own dear son Telémakhos can tell you,
never by my own will or for love
did I feast here or sing amid the suitors.
They were too strong, too many; they compelled me."

Telémakhos in the elation of battle
heard him. He at once called to his father:

"Wait: that one is innocent: don't hurt him. 370
And we should let our herald live—Medôn;
he cared for me from boyhood. Where is *he?*
Has he been killed already by Philoítios
or by the swineherd? Else he got an arrow
in that first gale of bowshots down the room."

Now this came to the ears of prudent Medôn
under the chair where he had gone to earth,
pulling a new-flayed bull's hide over him.
Quiet he lay while blinding death passed by.
Now heaving out from under 380
he scrambled for Telémakhos' knees and said:

"Here I am, dear prince; but rest your spear!
Tell your great father not to see in me
a suitor for the sword's edge—one of those
who laughed at you and ruined his property!"

The lord of all the tricks of war surveyed
this fugitive and smiled. He said:

"Courage: my son has dug you out and saved you.
Take it to heart, and pass the word along:
fair dealing brings more profit in the end. 390
Now leave this room. Go and sit down outdoors
where there's no carnage, in the court,
you and the poet with his many voices,
while I attend to certain chores inside."

At this the two men stirred and picked their way
to the door and out, and sat down at the altar,
looking around with wincing eyes
as though the sword's edge hovered still.
And Odysseus looked around him, narrow-eyed,
for any others who had lain hidden 400
while death's black fury passed.

In blood and dust
he saw that crowd all fallen, many and many slain.

Think of a catch that fishermen haul in to a halfmoon bay
in a fine-meshed net from the white-caps of the sea:
how all are poured out on the sand, in throes for the salt sea,
twitching their cold lives away in Hêlios' fiery air:
so lay the suitors heaped on one another.

Odysseus at length said to his son:

"Go tell old Nurse I'll have a word with her.
What's to be done now weighs on my mind." 410

Telémakhos knocked at the women's door and called:

"Eurýkleia, come out here! Move, old woman.
You kept your eye on all our servant girls.
Jump, my father is here and wants to see you."

His call brought no reply, only the doors
were opened, and she came. Telémakhos
led her forward. In the shadowy hall
full of dead men she found his father
spattered and caked with blood like a mountain lion
when he has gorged upon an ox, his kill— 420
with hot blood glistening over his whole chest,
smeared on his jaws, baleful and terrifying—
even so encrimsoned was Odysseus
up to his thighs and armpits. As she gazed
from all the corpses to the bloody man
she raised her head to cry over his triumph,
but felt his grip upon her, checking her.
Said the great soldier then:

"Rejoice
inwardly. No crowing aloud, old woman.
To glory over slain men is no piety. 430
Destiny and the gods' will vanquished these,
and their own hardness. They respected no one,
good or bad, who came their way.
For this, and folly, a bad end befell them.
Your part is now to tell me of the women,
those who dishonored me, and the innocent."

His own old nurse Eurýkleia said:

"I will, then.
Child, you know you'll have the truth from me.
Fifty all told they are, your female slaves,
trained by your lady and myself in service, 440
wool carding and the rest of it, and taught
to be submissive. Twelve went bad,
flouting me, flouting Penélopê, too.
Telémakhos being barely grown, his mother
would never let him rule the serving women—
but you must let me go to her lighted rooms
and tell her. Some god sent her a drift of sleep."

But in reply the great tactician said:

"Not yet. Do not awake her. Tell those women
who were the suitors' harlots to come here." 450

She went back on this mission through his hall.
Then he called Telémakhos to his side
and the two herdsmen. Sharply Odysseus said:

"These dead must be disposed of first of all.
Direct the women. Tables and chairs will be
scrubbed with sponges, rinsed and rinsed again.
When our great room is fresh and put in order,
take them outside, these women,
between the roundhouse[5] and the palisade,
and hack them with your swordblades till you cut 460
the life out of them, and every thought of sweet
Aphroditê under the rutting suitors,
when they lay down in secret."

As he spoke
here came the women in a bunch, all wailing,
soft tears on their cheeks. They fell to work
to lug the corpses out into the courtyard
under the gateway, propping one
against another as Odysseus ordered,
for he himself stood over them. In fear
these women bore the cold weight of the dead. 470
The next thing was to scrub off chairs and tables
and rinse them down. Telémakhos and the herdsman
scraped the packed earth floor with hoes, but made
the women carry out all blood and mire.
When the great room was cleaned up once again,
at swordpoint they forced them out, between
the roundhouse and the palisade, pell-mell
to huddle in that dead end without exit.
Telémakhos, who knew his mind,[6] said curtly:

"I would not give the clean death of a beast 480
to trulls[7] who made a mockery of my mother
and of me too—you sluts, who lay with suitors."

He tied one end of a hawser to a pillar
and passed the other about the roundhouse top,
taking the slack up, so that no one's toes
could touch the ground. They would be hung like doves
or larks in springes[8] triggered in a thicket,
where the birds think to rest—a cruel nesting.
So now in turn each woman thrust her head
into a noose and swung, yanked high in air, 490
to perish there most piteously.
Their feet danced for a little, but not long.

[5] A building, with a cone-shaped roof, near the wall surrounding the courtyard; probably a place for storing implements.

[6] Telémakhos departs from Odysseus' instructions; he gives the offending women a dishonorable death by hanging rather than death by the knife or sword, as in the ritual sacrifice of an innocent animal.

[7] Harlots.

[8] Nooses, attached to tied branches, used to trap birds and other small animals.

From storeroom to the court they brought Melánthios,
chopped with swords to cut his nose and ears off,
pulled off his genitals to feed the dogs
and raging hacked his hands and feet away.

As their own hands and feet called for a washing,
they went indoors to Odysseus again.
Their work was done. He told Eurýkleia:

"Bring me
brimstone[9] and a brazier—medicinal 500
fumes to purify my hall. Then tell
Penélopê to come, and bring her maids.
All servants round the house must be called in."

His own old nurse Eurýkleia replied:

"Aye, surely that is well said, child. But let me
find you a good clean shirt and cloak and dress you.
You must not wrap your shoulders' breadth again
in rags in your own hall. That would be shameful."

Odysseus answered:

"Let me have the fire.
The first thing is to purify this place." 510

With no more chat Eurýkleia obeyed
and fetched out fire and brimstone. Cleansing fumes
he sent through court and hall and storage chamber.
Then the old woman hurried off again
to the women's quarters to announce her news,
and all the servants came now, bearing torches
in twilight, crowding to embrace Odysseus,
taking his hands to kiss, his head and shoulders,
while he stood there, nodding to every one,
and overcome by longing and by tears. 520

BOOK TWENTY-THREE: THE TRUNK OF THE OLIVE TREE

The old nurse went upstairs exulting,
with knees toiling, and patter of slapping feet,
to tell the mistress of her lord's return,
and cried out by the lady's pillow:

[9] Sulfur.

"Wake,
wake up, dear child! Penélopê, come down,
see with your own eyes what all these years you longed for!
Odysseus is here! Oh, in the end, he came!
And he has killed your suitors, killed them all
who made his house a bordel[1] and ate his cattle
and raised their hands against his son!"

Penélopê said: 10

"Dear nurse . . . the gods have touched you.
They can put chaos into the clearest head
or bring a lunatic down to earth. Good sense
you always had. They've touched you. What is this
mockery you wake me up to tell me,
breaking in on my sweet spell of sleep?
I had not dozed away so tranquilly
since my lord went to war, on that ill wind
to Ilion.
Oh, leave me! Back down stairs!
If any other of my women came in babbling 20
things like these to startle me, I'd see her
flogged out of the house! Your old age spares you that."

Eurýkleia said:

"Would I play such a trick on you, dear child?
It is true, true, as I tell you, he has come!
That stranger they were baiting was Odysseus.
Telémakhos knew it days ago—
cool head, never to give his father away,
till he paid off those swollen dogs!"

The lady in her heart's joy now sprang up 30
with sudden dazzling tears, and hugged the old one,
crying out:

"But try to make it clear!
If he came home in secret, as you say,
could he engage them singlehanded? How?
They were all down there, still in the same crowd."

To this Eurýkleia said:

"I did not see it,
I knew nothing; only I heard the groans
of men dying. We sat still in the inner rooms
holding our breath, and marvelling, shut in,
until Telémakhos came to the door and called me— 40
your own dear son, sent this time by his father!

[1] Bordello; brothel.

So I went out, and found Odysseus
erect, with dead men littering the floor
this way and that. If you had only seen him!
It would have made your heart glow hot!—a lion
splashed with mire and blood.
But now the cold
corpses are all gathered at the gate,
and he has cleansed his hall with fire and brimstone,
a great blaze. Then he sent me here to you.
Come with me: you may both embark this time 50
for happiness together, after pain,
after long years. Here is your prayer, your passion,
granted: your own lord lives, he is at home,
he found you safe, he found his son. The suitors
abused his house, but he has brought them down."

The attentive lady said:

"Do not lose yourself
in this rejoicing: wait: you know
how splendid that return would be for us,
how dear to me, dear to his son and mine;
but no, it is not possible, your notion 60
must be wrong.
Some god has killed the suitors,
a god, sick of their arrogance and brutal
malice—for they honored no one living,
good or bad, who ever came their way.
Blind young fools, they've tasted death for it.
But the true person of Odysseus?
He lost his home, he died far from Akhaia."

The old nurse sighed:

"How queer, the way you talk!
Here he is, large as life, by his own fire,
and you deny he ever will get home! 70
Child, you always were mistrustful!
But there is one sure mark that I can tell you:
that scar left by the boar's tusk long ago.
I recognized it when I bathed his feet
and would have told you, but he stopped my mouth,
forbade me, in his craftiness.
Come down,
I stake my life on it, he's here!
Let me die in agony if I lie!"

Penélopê said:

"Nurse dear, though you have your wits about you,
still it is hard not to be taken in 80

by the immortals. Let us join my son, though,
and see the dead and that strange one who killed them."

She turned then to descend the stair, her heart
in tumult. Had she better keep her distance
and question him, her husband? Should she run 
up to him, take his hands, kiss him now?
Crossing the door sill she sat down at once
in firelight, against the nearest wall,
across the room from the lord Odysseus.
There
leaning against a pillar, sat the man 90
and never lifted up his eyes, but only waited
for what his wife would say when she had seen him.
And she, for a long time, sat deathly still
in wonderment—for sometimes as she gazed 
she found him—yes, clearly—like her husband,
but sometimes blood and rags were all she saw.
Telémakhos' voice came to her ears:

"Mother,
cruel mother, do you feel nothing,
drawing yourself apart this way from Father?
Will you not sit with him and talk and question him?  100
What other woman could remain so cold?
Who shuns her lord, and he come back to her
from wars and wandering, after twenty years?
Your heart is hard as flint and never changes!"

Penélopê answered:

"I am stunned, child.
I cannot speak to him. I cannot question him. 
I cannot keep my eyes upon his face.
If really he is Odysseus, truly home,
beyond all doubt we two shall know each other
better than you or anyone. There are 110
secret signs we know, we two."

A smile
came now to the lips of the patient hero, Odysseus,
who turned to Telémakhos and said:

"Peace: let your mother test me at her leisure.
Before long she will see and know me best.
These tatters, dirt—all that I'm caked with now—
make her look hard at me and doubt me still. 
As to this massacre, we must see the end.
Whoever kills one citizen, you know,
and has no force of armed men at his back, 120
had better take himself abroad by night 

and leave his kin. Well, we cut down the flower of Ithaka,
the mainstay of the town. Consider that."

Telémakhos replied respectfully:

"Dear Father,
enough that you yourself study the danger,
foresighted in combat as you are,
they say you have no rival.

We three stand
ready to follow you and fight. I say
for what our strength avails, we have the courage."

And the great tactician, Odysseus, answered:

"Good. 130
Here is our best maneuver, as I see it:
bathe, you three, and put fresh clothing on,
order the women to adorn themselves,
and let our admirable harper choose a tune
for dancing, some lighthearted air, and strum it.
Anyone going by, or any neighbor,
will think it is a wedding feast he hears.
These deaths must not be cried about the town
till we can slip away to our own woods. We'll see
what weapon, then, Zeus puts into our hands." 140

They listened attentively, and did his bidding,
bathed and dressed afresh; and all the maids
adorned themselves. Then Phêmios the harper
took his polished shell and plucked the strings,
moving the company to desire
for singing, for the sway and beat of dancing,
until they made the manor hall resound
with gaiety of men and grace of women.
Anyone passing on the road would say:

"Married at last, I see—the queen so many courted. 150
Sly, cattish wife! She would not keep—not she!—
the lord's estate until he came."

So travellers'
thoughts might run—but no one guessed the truth.

Greathearted Odysseus, home at last,
was being bathed now by Eurýnomê
and rubbed with golden oil, and clothed again
in a fresh tunic and a cloak. Athena
lent him beauty, head to foot. She made him
taller, and massive, too, with crisping hair
in curls like petals of wild hyacinth 160

but all red-golden. Think of gold infused
on silver by a craftsman, whose fine art
Hephaistos taught him, or Athena: one
whose work moves to delight: just so she lavished
beauty over Odysseus' head and shoulders.
He sat then in the same chair by the pillar,
facing his silent wife, and said:

"Strange woman,
the immortals of Olympos made you hard,
harder than any. Who else in the world
would keep aloof as you do from her husband 170
if he returned to her from years of trouble,
cast on his own land in the twentieth year?

Nurse, make up a bed for me to sleep on.
Her heart is iron in her breast."

Penélopê
spoke to Odysseus now. She said:

"Strange man,
if man you are . . . This is no pride on my part
nor scorn for you—not even wonder, merely.
I know so well how you—how he—appeared
boarding the ship for Troy. But all the same . . .

Make up his bed for him, Eurýkleia. 180
Place it outside the bedchamber my lord
built with his own hands. Pile the big bed
with fleeces, rugs, and sheets of purest linen."

With this she tried him to the breaking point,
and he turned on her in a flash raging:

"Woman, by heaven you've stung me now!
Who dared to move my bed?
No builder had the skill for that—unless
a god came down to turn the trick. No mortal
in his best days could budge it with a crowbar. 190
There is our pact and pledge, our secret sign,
built into that bed—my handiwork
and no one else's!

An old trunk of olive
grew like a pillar on the building plot,
and I laid out our bedroom round that tree,
lined up the stone walls, built the walls and roof,
gave it a doorway and smooth-fitting doors.
Then I lopped off the silvery leaves and branches,
hewed and shaped that stump from the roots up
into a bedpost, drilled it, let it serve 200

as model for the rest. I planed them all,[2]
inlaid them all with silver, gold and ivory,
and stretched a bed between—a pliant web
of oxhide thongs dyed crimson.
There's our sign!
I know no more. Could someone else's hand
have sawn that trunk and dragged the frame away?"

Their secret! as she heard it told, her knees
grew tremulous and weak, her heart failed her.
With eyes brimming tears she ran to him,
throwing her arms around his neck, and kissed him, 210
murmuring:

"Do not rage at me, Odysseus!
No one ever matched your caution! Think
what difficulty the gods gave: they denied us
life together in our prime and flowering years,
kept us from crossing into age together.
Forgive me, don't be angry. I could not
welcome you with love on sight! I armed myself
long ago against the frauds of men,
impostors who might come—and all those many
whose underhanded ways bring evil on! 220
Helen of Argos, daughter of Zeus and Leda,
would she have joined the stranger,[3] lain with him,
if she had known her destiny? known the Akhaians
in arms would bring her back to her own country?
Surely a goddess moved her to adultery,
her blood unchilled by war and evil coming,
the years, the desolation; ours, too.
But here and now, what sign could be so clear
as this of our own bed?
No other man has ever laid eyes on it— 230
only my own slave, Aktoris, that my father
sent with me as a gift—she kept our door.
You make my stiff heart know that I am yours."

Now from his breast into his eyes the ache
of longing mounted, and he wept at last,
his dear wife, clear and faithful, in his arms,
longed for
as the sunwarmed earth is longed for by a swimmer
spent in rough water where his ship went down
under Poseidon's blows, gale winds and tons of sea.
Few men can keep alive through a big surf 240

[2] That is, planed all the bedposts, of which one was the shaped tree trunk.
[3] Paris, the Trojan guest of Meneláos and Helen, with whom she ran away.

to crawl, clotted with brine, on kindly beaches
in joy, in joy, knowing the abyss behind:
and so she too rejoiced, her gaze upon her husband,
her white arms round him pressed as though forever.

The rose Dawn might have found them weeping still
had not grey-eyed Athena slowed the night
when night was most profound, and held the Dawn
under the Ocean of the East. That glossy team,
Firebright and Daybright, the Dawn's horses
that draw her heavenward for men—Athena 250
stayed their harnessing.
Then said Odysseus:

"My dear, we have not won through to the end.
One trial—I do not know how long—is left for me
to see fulfilled. Teirêsias' ghost forewarned me[4]
the night I stood upon the shore of Death, asking
about my friends' homecoming and my own.
But now the hour grows late, it is bed time,
rest will be sweet for us; let us lie down."

To this Penélopê replied:

"That bed,
that rest is yours whenever desire moves you, 260
now the kind powers have brought you home at last.
But as your thought has dwelt upon it, tell me:
what is the trial you face? I must know soon;
what does it matter if I learn tonight?"

The teller of many stories said:

"My strange one,
must you again, and even now,
urge me to talk? Here is a plodding tale;
no charm in it, no relish in the telling.
Teirêsias told me I must take an oar
and trudge the mainland, going from town to town, 270
until I discover men who have never known
the salt blue sea, nor flavor of salt meat—
strangers to painted prows, to watercraft
and oars like wings, dipping across the water.
The moment of revelation he foretold
was this, for you may share the prophecy:
some traveller falling in with me will say:
'A winnowing fan, that on your shoulder, sir?'

[4] See Book XI.

There I must plant my oar,[5] on the very spot,
with burnt offerings to Poseidon of the Waters: 280
a ram, a bull, a great buck boar. Thereafter
when I come home again, I am to slay
full hekatombs to the gods who own broad heaven,
one by one.
Then death will drift upon me
from seaward, mild as air, mild as your hand,
in my well-tended weariness of age,
contented folk around me on our island.
He said all this must come."

Penélopê said:

"If by the gods' grace age at least is kind,
we have that promise—trials will end in peace." 290

So he confided in her, and she answered.
Meanwhile Eurýnomê and the nurse together
laid soft coverlets on the master's bed,
working in haste by torchlight. Eurýkleia
retired to her quarters for the night,
and then Eurýnomê, as maid-in-waiting,
lighted her lord and lady to their chamber
with bright brands.

She vanished.
So they came
into that bed so steadfast, loved of old,
opening glad arms to one another. 300
Telémakhos by now had hushed the dancing,
hushed the women. In the darkened hall
he and the cowherd and the swineherd slept.

The royal pair mingled in love again
and afterward lay revelling in stories:
hers of the siege her beauty stood at home
from arrogant suitors, crowding on her sight,
and how they fed their courtship on his cattle,
oxen and fat sheep, and drank up rivers
of wine out of the vats.
Odysseus told 310
of what hard blows he had dealt out to others
and of what blows he had taken—all that story.
She could not close her eyes till all was told.

[5] The point of this gesture would be to appease the sea god by spreading his fame even into places where the sea is unknown. This excursion does not, in fact, take place in the *Odyssey.*

His raid on the Kikonês, first of all,
then how he visited the Lotos Eaters,
and what the Kyklops did, and how those shipmates,
pitilessly devoured, were avenged.
Then of his touching Aiolos's isle
and how that king refitted him for sailing
to Ithaka; all vain: gales blew him back 320
groaning over the fishcold sea. Then how
he reached the Laistrygonians' distant bay
and how they smashed his ships and his companions.
Kirkê, then: of her deceits and magic,
then of his voyage to the wide underworld
of dark, the house of Death, and questioning
Teirêsias, Theban spirit.
Dead companions,
many, he saw there, and his mother, too.
Of this he told his wife, and told how later
he heard the choir of maddening Seirênês, 330
coasted the Wandering Rocks, Kharybdis' pool
and the fiend Skylla who takes toll of men.
Then how his shipmates killed Lord Hêlios' cattle
and how Zeus thundering in towering heaven
split their fast ship with his fuming bolt,
so all hands perished.
He alone survived,
cast away on Kalypso's isle, Ogýgia.
He told, then, how that nymph detained him there
in her smooth caves, craving him for her husband,
and how in her devoted lust she swore 340
he should not die nor grow old, all his days,
but he held out against her.
Last of all
what sea-toil brought him to the Phaiákians;
their welcome; how they took him to their hearts
and gave him passage to his own dear island
with gifts of garments, gold and bronze . . .
Remembering,
he drowsed over the story's end. Sweet sleep
relaxed his limbs and his care-burdened breast.

Other affairs were in Athena's keeping.
Waiting until Odysseus had his pleasure 350
of love and sleep, the grey-eyed one bestirred
the fresh Dawn from her bed of paling Ocean
to bring up daylight to her golden chair,
and from his fleecy bed Odysseus
arose. He said to Penélopê:

"My lady,
what ordeals have we not endured! Here, waiting
you had your grief, while my return dragged out—

my hard adventures, pitting myself against
the gods' will, and Zeus, who pinned me down
far from home. But now our life resumes: 360
we've come together to our longed-for bed.
Take care of what is left me in our house;
as to the flocks that pack of wolves laid waste
they'll be replenished: scores I'll get on raids
and other scores our island friends will give me
till all the folds are full again.
This day
I'm off up country to the orchards. I must see
my noble father, for he missed me sorely.
And here is my command for you—a strict one,
though you may need none, clever as you are. 370
Word will get about as the sun goes higher
of how I killed those lads. Go to your rooms
on the upper floor, and take your women. Stay there
with never a glance outside or a word to anyone."

Fitting cuirass and swordbelt to his shoulders,
he woke his herdsmen, woke Telémakhos,
ordering all in arms. They dressed quickly,
and all in war gear sallied from the gate,
led by Odysseus.
Now it was broad day
but these three men Athena hid in darkness, 380
going before them swiftly from the town.

BOOK TWENTY-FOUR: WARRIORS, FAREWELL

Meanwhile the suitors' ghosts were called away
by Hermês of Kyllênê,[1] bearing the golden wand
with which he charms the eyes of men or wakens
whom he wills.
He waved them on, all squeaking
as bats will in a cavern's underworld,
all flitting, flitting criss-cross in the dark
if one falls and the rock-hung chain is broken.
So with faint cries the shades trailed after Hermês,
pure Deliverer.
He led them down dank ways,
over grey Ocean tides, the Snowy Rock, 10
past shores of Dream and narrows of the sunset,
in swift flight to where the Dead inhabit
wastes of asphodel at the world's end.

[1] Birthplace and home of Hermês, in Arcadia.

Crossing the plain they met Akhilleus'[2] ghost,
Patróklos and Antílokhos, then Aías,
noblest of Danaans after Akhilleus
in strength and beauty. Here the newly dead
drifted together, whispering. Then came
the soul of Agamémnon, son of Atreus,
in black pain forever, surrounded by men-at-arms 20
who perished with him in Aigísthos' hall.
Akhilleus greeted him:

"My lord Atreidês,
we held that Zeus who loves the play of lightning
would give you length of glory, you were king
over so great a host of soldiery
before Troy, where we suffered, we Akhaians.
But in the morning of your life
you met that doom that no man born avoids.
It should have found you in your day of victory,
marshal of the army, in Troy country; 30
then all Akhaia would have heaped your tomb
and saved your honor for your son. Instead
piteous death awaited you at home."

And Atreus' son replied:

"Fortunate hero,
son of Pêleus, godlike and glorious,
at Troy you died, across the sea from Argos,
and round you Trojan and Akhaian peers
fought for your corpse and died. A dustcloud wrought
by a whirlwind hid the greatness of you slain,
minding no more the mastery of horses. 40
All that day we might have toiled in battle
had not a storm from Zeus broken it off.
We carried you out of the field of war
down to the ships and bathed your comely body
with warm water and scented oil. We laid you
upon your long bed, and our officers
wept hot tears like rain and cropped their hair.
Then hearing of it in the sea, your mother, Thetis,[3]
came with nereids of the grey wave crying
unearthly lamentation over the water, 50
and trembling gripped the Akhaians to the bone.
They would have boarded ship that night and fled
except for one man's wisdom—venerable
Nestor, proven counselor in the past.

[2] The following passage mentions several heroes of the Trojan War. Patróklos and Antílokhos were especially close friends of Akhilleus.

[3] A nereid (sea nymph), mother of Akhilleus.

He stood and spoke to allay their fear: 'Hold fast,
sons of the Akhaians, lads of Argos.
His mother it must be, with nymphs her sisters,
come from the sea to mourn her son in death.'

Veteran hearts at this contained their dread
while at your side the daughters of the ancient 60
seagod wailed and wrapped ambrosial shrouding
around you.
Then we heard the Muses sing
a threnody[4] in nine immortal voices.
No Argive there but wept, such keening[5] rose
from that one Muse who led the song.
Now seven
days and ten, seven nights and ten, we mourned you,
we mortal men, with nymphs who know no death,
before we gave you to the flame, slaughtering
longhorned steers and fat sheep on your pyre.

Dressed by the nereids and embalmed with honey, 70
honey and unguent in the seething blaze,
you turned to ash. And past the pyre Akhaia's
captains paraded in review, in arms,
clattering chariot teams and infantry.
Like a forest fire the flame roared on, and burned
your flesh away. Next day at dawn, Akhilleus,
we picked your pale bones from the char to keep
in wine and oil. A golden amphora[6]
your mother gave for this—Hephaistos' work,
a gift from Dionysos.[7] In that vase, 80
Akhilleus, hero, lie your pale bones mixed
with mild Patróklos' bones, who died before you,
and nearby lie the bones of Antílokhos,
the one you cared for most of all companions
after Patróklos.
We of the Old Army,
we who were spearmen, heaped a tomb for these
upon a foreland over Hellê's waters,[8]
to be a mark against the sky for voyagers
in this generation and those to come.
Your mother sought from the gods magnificent trophies 90
and set them down midfield for our champions. Often

[4] Dirge; lament. The Muses are goddesses of song, literature, and the arts. Homer does not describe them elsewhere as being nine in number; this is one of several anomalies about the present scene in Hades that have caused certain commentators to reject it as unauthentic.

[5] Loud, shrill lamenting for the dead.

[6] A type of jar.

[7] God of wine and revelry.

[8] The Hellespont; the modern Dardanelles, the strait connecting the Aegean Sea with the Sea of Marmara; located just north of Troy.

at funeral games after the death of kings
when you yourself contended, you've seen athletes
cinch their belts when trophies went on view.
But these things would have made you stare—the treasures
Thetis on her silver-slippered feet
brought to your games—for the gods held you dear.
You perished, but your name will never die.
It lives to keep all men in mind of honor
forever, Akhilleus.
As for myself, what joy 100
is this, to have brought off the war? Foul death
Zeus held in store for me at my coming home;
Aigísthos and my vixen cut me down."

While they conversed, the Wayfinder[9] came near,
leading the shades of suitors overthrown
by Lord Odysseus. The two souls of heroes
advanced together, scrutinizing these.
Then Agamémnon recognized Amphímedon,
son of Meláneus—friends of his on Ithaka—
and called out to him:
"Amphímedon, 110
what ruin brought you into this undergloom?
All in a body, picked men, and so young?
One could not better choose the kingdom's pride.
Were you at sea, aboard ship, and Poseidon
blew up a dire wind and foundering waves,
or cattle-raiding, were you, on the mainland,
or in a fight for some stronghold, or women,
when the foe hit you to your mortal hurt?
Tell me, answer my question. Guest and friend
I say I am of yours—or do you not remember 120
I visited your family there? I came
with Prince Meneláos, urging Odysseus
to join us in the great sea raid on Troy.
One solid month we beat our way, breasting
south sea and west, resolved to bring him round,
the wily raider of cities."

The new shade said:

"O glory of commanders, Agamémnon,
all that you bring to mind I remember well.
As for the sudden manner of our death
I'll tell you of it clearly, first to last. 130
After Odysseus had been gone for years
we were all suitors of his queen. She never
quite refused, nor went through with a marriage,

[9] Hermês.

hating it, ever bent on our defeat.
Here is one of her tricks: she placed her loom,
her big loom, out for weaving in her hall,
and the fine warp of some vast fabric on it.
We were attending her, and she said to us:
'Young men, my suitors, now my lord is dead,
let me finish my weaving before I marry, 140
or else my thread will have been spun in vain.
This is a shroud I weave for Lord Laërtês
when cold Death comes to lay him on his bier.
The country wives would hold me in dishonor
if he, with all his fortune, lay unshrouded.'
We had men's hearts; she touched them; we agreed.
So every day she wove on the great loom—
but every night by torchlight she unwove it,
and so for three years she deceived the Akhaians.
But when the seasons brought the fourth around, 150
as long months waned, and the slow days were spent,
one of her maids, who knew the secret, told us.
We found her unraveling the splendid shroud,
and then she had to finish, willy nilly—
finish, and show the big loom woven tight
from beam to beam with cloth. She washed the shrouding
clean as sun or moonlight.
Then, heaven knows
from what quarter of the world, fatality
brought in Odysseus to the swineherd's wood
far up the island. There his son went too 160
when the black ship put him ashore from Pylos.
The two together planned our death-trap. Down
they came to the famous town—Telémakhos
long in advance: we had to wait for Odysseus.
The swineherd led him to the manor later
in rags like a foul beggar, old and broken,
propped on a stick. These tatters that he wore
hid him so well that none of us could know him
when he turned up, not even the older men.
We jeered at him, took potshots at him, cursed him. 170
Daylight and evening in his own great hall
he bore it, patient as a stone. That night
the mind of Zeus beyond the stormcloud stirred him
with Telémakhos at hand to shift his arms
from mégaron to storage room and lock it.
Then he assigned his wife her part: next day
she brought his bow and iron axeheads out
to make a contest. Contest there was none;
that move doomed us to slaughter. Not a man
could bend the stiff bow to his will or string it, 180
until it reached Odysseus. We shouted,
'Keep the royal bow from the beggar's hands

no matter how he begs!' Only Telémakhos
would not be denied.
So the great soldier
took his bow and bent it for the bowstring
effortlessly. He drilled the axeheads clean,
sprang, and decanted arrows on the door sill,
glared, and drew again. This time he killed
Antínoös.
There facing us he crouched
and shot his bolts of groaning at us, brought us 190
down like sheep. Then some god, his familiar,[10]
went into action with him round the hall,
after us in a massacre. Men lay groaning,
mortally wounded, and the floor smoked with blood.

That was the way our death came, Agamémnon.
Now in Odysseus' hall untended still
our bodies lie,[11] unknown to friends or kinsmen
who should have laid us out and washed our wounds
free of the clotted blood, and mourned our passing.
So much is due the dead."

But Agamémnon's 200
tall shade when he heard this cried aloud:

"O fortunate Odysseus, master mariner
and soldier, blessed son of old Laërtês!
The girl you brought home made a valiant wife!
True to her husband's honor and her own,
Penélopê, Ikários' faithful daughter!
The very gods themselves will sing her story
for men on earth—mistress of her own heart,
Penélopê!
Tyndáreus' daughter waited, too—how differently! 210
Klytaimnéstra, the adulteress,
waited to stab her lord and king. That song
will be forever hateful. A bad name
she gave to womankind, even the best."

These were the things they said to one another
under the rim of earth where Death is lord.

Leaving the town, Odysseus and his men
that morning reached Laërtês' garden lands,
long since won by his toil from wilderness—
his homestead, and the row of huts around it 220

[10] A friendly attendant spirit.
[11] It is unusual in Homer that the souls of unburied men should be admitted to Hades.

where fieldhands rested, ate and slept. Indoors
he had an old slave woman, a Sikel,[12] keeping
house for him in his secluded age.

Odysseus here took leave of his companions.

"Go make yourselves at home inside," he said.
"Roast the best porker and prepare a meal.
I'll go to try my father. Will he know me?
Can he imagine it, after twenty years?"

He handed spear and shield to the two herdsmen,
and in they went, Telémakhos too. Alone 230
Odysseus walked the orchard rows and vines.
He found no trace of Dólios and his sons
nor the other slaves—all being gone that day
to clear a distant field, and drag the stones
for a boundary wall.
But on a well-banked plot
Odysseus found his father in solitude
spading the earth around a young fruit tree.

He wore a tunic, patched and soiled, and leggings—
oxhide patches, bound below his knees
against the brambles; gauntlets[13] on his hands 240
and on his head a goatskin cowl of sorrow.[14]
This was the figure Prince Odysseus found—
wasted by years, racked, bowed under grief.
The son paused by a tall pear tree and wept,
then inwardly debated: should he run
forward and kiss his father, and pour out
his tale of war, adventure, and return,
or should he first interrogate him, test him?
Better that way, he thought—
first draw him out with sharp words, trouble him. 250
His mind made up, he walked ahead. Laërtês
went on digging, head down, by the sapling,
stamping the spade in. At his elbow then
his son spoke out:
"Old man, the orchard keeper
you work for is no townsman. A good eye
for growing things he has; there's not a nurseling,
fig tree, vine stock, olive tree or pear tree
or garden bed uncared for on this farm.
But I might add—don't take offense—your own
appearance could be tidier. Old age 260
yes—but why the squalor, and rags to boot?

[12] Sicilian. [13] Gloves with protective cuffs.
[14] The goatskin cap is an expression of his mourning.

It would not be for sloth, now, that your master
leaves you in this condition; neither at all
because there's any baseness in your self.
No, by your features, by the frame you have,
a man might call you kingly,
one who should bathe warm, sup well, and rest easy
in age's privilege. But tell me:
who are your masters? whose fruit trees are these
you tend here? Tell me if it's true this island 270
is Ithaka, as that fellow I fell in with
told me on the road just now? He had
a peg loose, that one: couldn't say a word
or listen when I asked about my friend,
my Ithakan friend. I asked if he were alive
or gone long since into the underworld.
I can describe him if you care to hear it:
I entertained the man in my own land
when he turned up there on a journey; never
had I a guest more welcome in my house. 280
He claimed his stock was Ithakan: Laërtês
Arkeísiadês, he said his father was.
I took him home, treated him well, grew fond of him—
though we had many guests—and gave him
gifts in keeping with his quality: seven
bars of measured gold, a silver winebowl
filigreed with flowers, twelve light cloaks,
twelve rugs, robes and tunics—not to mention
his own choice of women trained in service,
the four well-favored ones he wished to take." 290

His father's eyes had filled with tears. He said:

"You've come to that man's island, right enough,
but dangerous men and fools hold power now.
You gave your gifts in vain. If you could find him
here in Ithaka alive, he'd make
return of gifts and hospitality,
as custom is, when someone has been generous.
But tell me accurately—how many years
have now gone by since that man was your guest?
your guest, my son—if he indeed existed— 300
born to ill fortune as he was. Ah, far
from those who loved him, far from his native land,
in some sea-dingle[15] fish have picked his bones,
or else he made the vultures and wild beasts
a trove[16] ashore! His mother at his bier
never bewailed him, nor did I, his father,

[15] Dell; valley.
[16] A valuable find.

nor did his admirable wife, Penélopê,
who should have closed her husband's eyes in death
and cried aloud upon him as he lay.
So much is due the dead.
But speak out, tell me further: 310
who are you, of what city and family?
where have you moored the ship that brought you here,
where is your admirable crew? Are you a peddler
put ashore by the foreign ship you came on?"

Again Odysseus had a fable ready.

"Yes," he said, "I can tell you all those things.
I come from Rover's Passage where my home is,
and I'm King Allwoes' only son. My name
is Quarrelman.[17]
Heaven's power in the westwind
drove me this way from Sikania,[18] 320
off my course. My ship lies in a barren
cove beyond the town there. As for Odysseus,
now is the fifth year since he put to sea
and left my homeland—bound for death, you say.
Yet landbirds flying from starboard crossed his bow—
a lucky augury. So we parted joyously,
in hope of friendly days and gifts to come."

A cloud of pain had fallen on Laërtês.
Scooping up handfuls of the sunburnt dust
he sifted it over his grey head, and groaned, 330
and the groan went to the son's heart. A twinge
prickling up through his nostrils warned Odysseus
he could not watch this any longer.
He leaped and threw his arms around his father,
kissed him, and said:
"Oh, Father, I am he!
Twenty years gone, and here I've come again
to my own land!
Hold back your tears! No grieving!
I bring good news—though still we cannot rest.
I killed the suitors to the last man!
Outrage and injury have been avenged!" 340

Laërtês turned and found his voice to murmur:

"If you are Odysseus, my son, come back,
give me some proof, a sign to make me sure."

[17] Rover's Passage, Allwoes, and Quarrelman are imaginary assumed (though appropriate) names.
[18] Sicily, perhaps.

His son replied:

"The scar then, first of all.
Look, here the wild boar's flashing tusk
wounded me on Parnassos; do you see it?
You and my mother made me go, that time,
to visit Lord Autólykos, her father,
for gifts he promised years before on Ithaka.
Again—more proof—let's say the trees you gave me 350
on this revetted[19] plot of orchard once.
I was a small boy at your heels, wheedling
amid the young trees, while you named each one.
You gave me thirteen pear, ten apple trees,
and forty fig trees. Fifty rows of vines
were promised too, each one to bear in turn.
Bunches of every hue would hang there ripening,
weighed down by the god of summer days."

The old man's knees failed him, his heart grew faint,
recalling all that Odysseus calmly told. 360
He clutched his son. Odysseus held him swooning
until he got his breath back and his spirit
and spoke again:

"Zeus, Father! Gods above!—
you still hold pure Olympos, if the suitors
paid for their crimes indeed, and paid in blood!
But now the fear is in me that all Ithaka
will be upon us. They'll send messengers
to stir up every city of the islands."

Odysseus the great tactician answered:

"Courage, and leave the worrying to me. 370
We'll turn back to your homestead by the orchard.
I sent the cowherd, swineherd, and Telémakhos
ahead to make our noonday meal."

Conversing
in this vein they went home, the two together,
into the stone farmhouse. There Telémakhos
and the two herdsmen were already carving
roast young pork, and mixing amber wine.
During these preparations the Sikel woman
bathed Laërtês and anointed him,
and dressed him in a new cloak. Then Athena, 380
standing by, filled out his limbs again,
gave girth and stature to the old field captain
fresh from the bathing place. His son looked on

[19] Buttressed by stones.

in wonder at the godlike bloom upon him,
and called out happily:

"Oh, Father,
surely one of the gods who are young forever
has made you magnificent before my eyes!"

Clearheaded Laërtês faced him, saying:

"By Father Zeus, Athena and Apollo,
I wish I could be now as once I was, 390
commander of Kephallenians,[20] when I took
the walled town, Nérikos, on the promontory!
Would god I had been young again last night
with armor on me, standing in our hall
to fight the suitors at your side! How many
knees I could have crumpled, to your joy!"

While son and father spoke, cowherd and swineherd
attended, waiting, for the meal was ready.
Soon they were all seated, and their hands
picked up the meat and bread.

But now old Dólios 400
appeared in the bright doorway with his sons,
work-stained from the field. Laërtês' housekeeper,
who reared the boys and tended Dólios
in his bent age, had gone to fetch them in.
When it came over them who the stranger was
they halted in astonishment. Odysseus
hit an easy tone with them. Said he:

"Sit down and help yourselves. Shake off your wonder.
Here we've been waiting for you all this time,
and our mouths watering for good roast pig!" 410

But Dólios came forward, arms outstretched,
and kissed Odysseus' hand at the wrist bone,
crying out:

"Dear master, you returned!
You came to us again! How we had missed you!
We thought you lost. The gods themselves have brought you!
Welcome, welcome; health and blessings on you!
And tell me, now, just one thing more: Penélopê,
does she know yet that you are on the island?
or should we send a messenger?"

[20] Inhabitants of the large island (modern Cephalonia) near Ithaka. Nérikos is on a nearby island.

Odysseus gruffly said,

"Old man, she knows. 420
Is it for you to think of her?"

So Dólios
quietly took a smooth bench at the table
and in their turn his sons welcomed Odysseus,
kissing his hands; then each went to his chair
beside his father. Thus our friends
were occupied in Laërtês' house at noon.

Meanwhile to the four quarters of the town
the news ran: bloody death had caught the suitors;
and men and women in a murmuring crowd
gathered before Odysseus' hall. They gave 430
burial to the piteous dead, or bore
the bodies of young men from other islands
down to the port, thence to be ferried home.
Then all the men went grieving to assembly
and being seated, rank by rank, grew still,
as old Eupeithês rose to address them. Pain
lay in him like a brand for Antínoös,
the first man that Odysseus brought down,
and tears flowed for his son as he began:

"Heroic feats that fellow did for us 440
Akhaians, friends! Good spearmen by the shipload
he led to war and lost—lost ships and men,
and once ashore again killed these, who were
the islands' pride.

Up with you! After him!—
before he can take flight to Pylos town
or hide at Elis, under Epeian law!
We'd be disgraced forever! Mocked for generations
if we cannot avenge our sons' blood, and our brothers!
Life would turn to ashes—at least for me;
rather be dead and join the dead!

I say 450
we ought to follow now, or they'll gain time
and make the crossing."

His appeal, his tears,
moved all the gentry listening there;
but now they saw the crier and the minstrel
come from Odysseus' hall, where they had slept.
The two men stood before the curious crowd,
and Medôn said:

"Now hear me, men of Ithaka.
When these hard deeds were done by Lord Odysseus
the immortal gods were not far off. I saw

with my own eyes someone divine who fought 460
beside him, in the shape and dress of Mentor;
it was a god who shone before Odysseus,
a god who swept the suitors down the hall
dying in droves."

At this pale fear assailed them,
and next they heard again the old forecaster,
Halithérsês Mastóridês. Alone
he saw the field of time, past and to come.
In his anxiety for them he said:

"Ithakans, now listen to what I say.
Friends, by your own fault these deaths came to pass. 470
You would not heed me nor the captain, Mentor;
would not put down the riot of your sons.
Heroic feats they did!—all wantonly
raiding a great man's flocks, dishonoring
his queen, because they thought he'd come no more.
Let matters rest; do as I urge; no chase,
or he who wants a bloody end will find it."

The greater number stood up shouting "Aye!"
But many held fast, sitting all together
in no mind to agree with him. Eupeithês 480
had won them to his side. They ran for arms,
clapped on their bronze, and mustered
under Eupeithês at the town gate
for his mad foray.

Vengeance would be his,
he thought, for his son's murder; but that day
held bloody death for him and no return.

At this point, querying Zeus, Athena said:

"O Father of us all and king of kings,
enlighten me. What is your secret will?
War and battle, worse and more of it, 490
or can you not impose a pact on both?"

The summoner of cloud replied:

"My child,
why this formality of inquiry?
Did you not plan that action by yourself—
see to it that Odysseus, on his homecoming,
should have their blood?

Conclude it as you will.
There is one proper way, if I may say so:
Odysseus' honor being satisfied,

let him be king by a sworn pact forever,
and we, for our part, will blot out the memory 500
of sons and brothers slain. As in the old time
let men of Ithaka henceforth be friends;
prosperity enough, and peace attend them."

Athena needed no command, but down
in one spring she descended from Olympos
just as the company of Odysseus finished
wheat crust and honeyed wine, and heard him say:

"Go out, someone, and see if they are coming."

One of the boys went to the door as ordered
and saw the townsmen in the lane. He turned 510
swiftly to Odysseus.

"Here they come,"
he said, "best arm ourselves, and quickly."

All up at once, the men took helm and shield—
four fighting men, counting Odysseus,
with Dólios' half dozen sons. Laërtês
armed as well, and so did Dólios—
greybeards, they could be fighters in a pinch.
Fitting their plated helmets on their heads
they sallied out, Odysseus in the lead.

Now from the air Athena, Zeus's daughter, 520
appeared in Mentor's guise, with Mentor's voice,
making Odysseus' heart grow light. He said
to put cheer in his son:

"Telémakhos,
you are going into battle against pikemen
where hearts of men are tried. I count on you
to bring no shame upon your forefathers.
In fighting power we have excelled this lot
in every generation."

Said his son:

"If you are curious, Father, watch and see
the stuff that's in me. No more talk of shame." 530

And old Laërtês cried aloud:

"Ah, what a day for me, dear gods!
to see my son and grandson vie in courage!"

Athena halted near him, and her eyes
shone like the sea. She said:

"Arkeísiadês,
dearest of all my old brothers-in-arms,
invoke the grey-eyed one and Zeus her father,
heft your spear and make your throw."

Power flowed into him from Pallas Athena,
whom he invoked as Zeus's virgin child, 540
and he let fly his heavy spear.

It struck
Eupeithês on the cheek plate of his helmet,
and undeflected the bronze head punched through.
He toppled, and his armor clanged upon him.
Odysseus and his son now furiously
closed, laying on with broadswords, hand to hand,
and pikes: they would have cut the enemy down
to the last man, leaving not one survivor,
had not Athena raised a shout
that stopped all fighters in their tracks.

"Now hold!" 550
she cried, "Break off this bitter skirmish;
end your bloodshed, Ithakans, and make peace."

Their faces paled with dread before Athena,
and swords dropped from their hands unnerved, to lie
strewing the ground, at the great voice of the goddess.
Those from the town turned fleeing for their lives.
But with a cry to freeze their hearts
and ruffling like an eagle on the pounce,
the lord Odysseus reared himself to follow—
at which the son of Kronos dropped a thunderbolt 560
smoking at his daughter's feet.

Athena
cast a grey glance at her friend and said:

"Son of Laërtês and the gods of old,
Odysseus, master of land ways and sea ways,
command yourself. Call off this battle now,
or Zeus who views the wide world may be angry."

He yielded to her, and his heart was glad.
Both parties later swore to terms of peace
set by their arbiter, Athena, daughter
of Zeus who bears the stormcloud as a shield— 570
though still she kept the form and voice of Mentor.

Aesop

(Sixth Century B.C.)

Nowadays, fables are generally thought of as children's literature: little animal stories that culminate in simplistic "morals" ("Haste makes waste," or "Don't put off until tomorrow what you can do today"). Marcel Gutwirth, one of the shrewdest students of the fable, points out that it is commonly thought of as "the place where the archaic and the puerile meet." There are reasons for this modern link between fables and children. Renaissance educators used Aesop's fables to teach Greek and Latin, thus creating an association between childhood and fables. The link was further strengthened in the nineteenth century by teachers of the young who used translations of the fables to teach moral lessons (not noticing, perhaps, how flimsily the morals are sometimes linked to the stories or how the morals sometimes seem contradictory). The connection persists; "Aesop" is to be found in the children's sections of bookstores.

The infantilizing of Aesop is unfortunate insofar as it leads us to ignore a voice from classical Greece that is very different from the heroic, aristocratic ones of epic and tragedy: the voice of ordinary people. It is true that the voice is muffled in Aesop—the texts have gone through too many transmogrifications to be perfectly clear—but they express, however indistinctly, a view of Greece from the bottom up rather than from the top down. In Aesop, as in many later fabulists, the fable is, in the words of another fine critic, Annabel Patterson, "a medium of political analysis and communication, especially in the form of a communication from or on behalf of the politically powerless."

The serious student of Aesop is immediately confronted with two difficulties: We do not know who Aesop was (if, indeed, he really existed), and we do not know what he wrote. By the second half of the fifth century, his name was well-known in Greece as a writer of fables who had lived in the previous century. A book of his fables was in circulation at least by the time of Plato, and the Greek historian Herodotus, in his *Histories,* identified him as a sixth-century slave who lived on the island of Samos. References to him in a number of other writers—Aristophanes, Xenophon, Plato, Aristotle, and others—suggest that his name was generally recognizable as a writer of witty fables. There would be no reason to doubt Herodotus's facts (if they are facts) if it were not that over the years the figure of Aesop became the subject of fantastic legends. A fanciful "biography" of him was in circulation very early and for centuries was attached to collections of the fables. This biography asserted that he was hideously ugly and had a speech impediment, that he recurringly clashed with the philosopher Xanthus (always coming out on top, of course), and that his death came when the people of Delphi flung him from a rock into the sea while he recited his fable of "The Eagle and the Scarab Beetle." One version even asserted that after his death he revived in order to fight at the battle of Thermopylae. Perhaps it is appropriate that a fable-writer be given a life so fabulous, but the effect of the legend was to cast into doubt everything about Aesop, even his existence.

It is similarly impossible to determine what in "Aesop's fables" is genuinely Aesopian and what is not. There is no reason to believe that, if he existed, he ever wrote anything down; the legends present him as a teller rather than a writer. The collections that were in circulation in the fifth century, insofar as we know anything about them, seem to have been miscellaneous collections of tales from various sources, some of them demonstrably predating Aesop. Within a century after he was said to have lived, Aesop had become "Aesop," a generalized name that could be cited as the author of a large body of folk narrative gathered from oral as well as written tradition.

Several collections of Aesop's fables were apparently made in classical times; one we know of indirectly was made by someone named Demetrius in about 300 B.C. But modern versions of Aesop derive mainly from the two earliest collections to survive: a collection in Latin made by Phaedrus, a freed slave who lived in Rome during the first century A.D., and a collection in Greek verse by Babrius in the second century A.D. These early versions apparently lacked the "morals" now generally assumed to be a defining characteristic of fables; these were tacked onto the fables in medieval versions, probably less to inculcate morality than to serve as a quick guide for using the fables to make points in public speaking. The present translators, Olivia and Robert Temple, comment that the morals are "often silly and inferior in wit and interest to the fables themselves" and that "some of them are truly appalling, even idiotic." At least one modern translator, Lloyd W. Daly, has refused to print the morals and calls his version *Aesop Without Morals*. In some ironic modern versions—those of La Fontaine, for example—the disjuncture between fable and moral becomes significant in itself; a bland, innocuous moral sometimes becoming a device of concealment for the genuinely subversive content of the fable.

When we strip away the accretions of sentimentality and childishness that have gathered around Aesop's *Fables*, we glimpse a grim world indeed. The Temples describe it well when they write that "the fables are not the pretty purveyors of Victorian morals that we have been led to believe. They are instead savage, coarse, brutal, lacking in all mercy or compassion, and lacking also in any political system other than absolute monarchy. . . . This is largely a world of brutal, heartless men—and of cunning, of wickedness, of murder, of treachery and deceit, of laughter at the misfortune of others, of mockery and contempt. It is also a world of savage humor, of deft wit, of clever wordplay, of one-upmanship, of 'I told you so!'"

This bleak assessment of the Aesopian world is accurate, but it perhaps understates the variety of that world. The *Fables* are, among other things, a joke book, and many of them seem intended as harmless entertainment. Many of them, too, satirize common human foibles: conceit, laziness, drunkenness, gluttony, and avarice. A number of others, underrepresented here, are bawdy tales of sexual infidelity, often turning around an unfaithful wife and her gullible husband. The gallery of animals, too, that inhabit the fables are not undifferentiated predators. The lion and the wolf are always ferocious, but the smaller animals, the nightingales, lambs, and chickens, are always victims.

The pervasive theme of the *Fables*—insofar as so heterogeneous a collection can be said to have a theme—is power, the war of those who have it upon those who do not, the strategies that the powerful employ to dominate the powerless, and those that the powerless employ to resist that dominance. This theme is stated most nakedly in such fables as 12: "The Cat and the Cock," and 221: "The Wolf and the Lamb." In both, a powerful predator proposes to eat a powerless victim, and despite rational arguments against such an action, the predator eats the victim anyway. As the wolf says in "The Wolf and the Lamb," "Whatever you say to justify yourself, I will eat you all the same," and he does.

Plato, in his dialogue *Phaedo,* reports that Socrates had Aesop's fables very much on his mind during his last days in prison, awaiting execution by poisoning for religious heresy and "corrupting the youth." When Socrates' fetters were removed on the day of his death, he commented on how closely pleasure is linked with pain and wondered how Aesop would have composed a fable on the subject. Then he told his friend that he had spent much of his time in prison turning Aesop's fables into verse. A recurring dream had told him to turn from philosophy to music, and Socrates tells his auditors,

> I thought that it would be safer to acquit my conscience by creating poetry in obedience to the dream before I departed. So . . . I turned such fables of Aesop as I knew, and had ready to my hand, into verse . . . for I reflected that a man who means to be a poet has to use fiction and not facts for his poems; and I could not invent fiction myself.

Socrates may have been drawn to Aesop by something more than his ability to make up stories. A person sentenced by an authoritarian state to die for having told the truth may well have found a special wisdom and relevance in Aesop's fierce fables of power.

FURTHER READING: There is no such thing as an authoritative complete works of Aesop. As Olivia and Robert Temple, the present translators, comment, "The 'complete fables of Aesop' is whatever the editor of its Greek text chooses to say it is." There have three main twentieth-century attempts to establish the most reliable texts, by Emile Chambry (1925–1926), Ben Edwin Perry (1952), and A. Hausrath (1956–1959). The Temples' translation, 1998, of the 358 fables in Chambry's edition is the closest thing we have in English to a complete Aesop. Serious analyses of the fables are scarce. Marcel Gutwirth's *Fable,* 1980, is about the form in general, but he has some useful things to say about Aesop in particular. Perry's *Aesopica,* 1952, largely consists of Greek texts, but the introductory material contains some interesting commentary. Annabel Patterson's *Fables of Power: Aesopian Writing and Political History,* 1991, concentrates on political fables in England between 1575 and 1725, but her analysis of the fable form and its connection with censorship has wide applicability to the fable tradition in general.

FABLES

Translated by Olivia and Robert Temple

3

THE EAGLE AND THE FOX

An eagle and a fox, having become friends, decided to live near one another and be neighbors. They believed that this proximity would strengthen their friendship. So the eagle flew up and established herself on a very high branch of a tree, where she made her nest. And the fox, creeping about among the bushes which were at the foot of the same tree, made her den there, depositing her babies right beneath the eagle.

But, one day when the fox was out looking for food, the eagle, who was very short of food too, swooped down to the bushes and took the fox cubs up to her nest and feasted on them with her own young.

When the fox returned, she was less distressed at the death of her little ones than she was driven mad by frustration at the impossibility of ever effectively avenging herself. For she, a land animal [*chersaia*], could never hope to pursue a winged bird. She had no option but to content herself, in her powerlessness and feebleness, with cursing her enemy from afar.

Now it was not long afterwards that the eagle did actually receive her punishment for her crime against her friend.

Some men were sacrificing a goat in the countryside and the eagle swooped down on the altar, carrying off some burning entrails, which she took up to her nest. A strong wind arose which blew the fire from the burning entrails into some old straw that was in the nest. The eaglets were singed and, as they were not yet able to fly, when they leaped from the nest they fell to the ground. The fox rushed up and devoured them all in front of the eagle's eyes.

This story shows that if you betray friendship, you may evade the vengeance of those whom you wrong if they are weak, but ultimately you cannot escape the vengeance of heaven.[1]

8

THE NIGHTINGALE AND THE HAWK

A nightingale, perched on a tall oak, was singing as usual when a hawk saw her. He was very hungry, so he swooped down upon her and seized her. Seeing herself about to die, the nightingale pleaded to the hawk to let her go, saying she was not a sizeable enough meal and would never fill the stomach of a hawk, and that if he were hungry he ought to find some bigger birds. But the hawk replied:

"I would certainly be foolish if I let a meal go which I already have in my talons to run after something else which I haven't yet seen."

Men are foolish who, in hope of greater things, let those which they have in their grasp escape.[1]

[1]This fable is told in verse by the poet Archilochus (eighth or seventh century B.C.) and also referred to by Aristophanes in 414 B.C. in *The Birds* (651), where it is attributed to Aesop. (Notes to Aesop are by the translators.)

[1]A different fable of "The Hawk and the Nightingale" is related by the poet Hesiod (circa 700 B.C.) in his *Works and Days* (201–210). In that fable the hawk has seized the nightingale, and, as he carries her high up among the clouds, he tells the nightingale she should not cry out or resist his superior might, for: "He is a fool who tries to withstand the stronger, for he does not get the mastery and suffers pain besides his shame." The old fable clearly antedates the time of Aesop, and perhaps he or another wrote a fable with the same characters because they were familiar. Two points particularly noteworthy about the fable recounted by Hesiod are that it clearly preceded him and that it had a clear moral appended to it, showing that this practice of appending morals to animal fables was very ancient.

12

THE CAT AND THE COCK

A cat who had caught a cock wanted to give a plausible reason for devouring it. So she accused it of annoying people by crowing at night and disturbing their sleep.

The cock defended himself by saying that he did it to be helpful. For, if he woke people up, it was to summon them to their accustomed work.

Then the cat produced another grievance and accused the cock of insulting Nature by his relationship with his mother and sisters.

The cock replied that in this also he was serving his master's interests, since it was thanks to this that the chickens laid lots of eggs.

"Ah well!" cried the cat, "I'm not going to go without food just because you can produce a lot of justifications!" And she ate the cock.

This fable shows that someone with a wicked nature who is determined to do wrong, when he cannot do so in the guise of a good man, does his evil deeds openly.

20

THE TWO COCKS AND THE EAGLE

Two cockerels were fighting over some hens. One triumphed and saw the other off. The defeated one then withdrew into a thicket where he hid himself. The victor fluttered up into the air and sat atop a high wall, where he began to crow with a loud voice.

Straight away an eagle fell upon him and carried him off. And, from then on, the cockerel hidden in the shadows possessed all the hens at his leisure.

This fable shows that the Lord resisteth the proud but giveth grace unto the humble.[1]

21

THE COCKS AND THE PARTRIDGE

A man who kept some cocks at his house, having found a partridge for sale privately, bought it and took it back home with him to feed it along with the cocks. But, as the cocks pecked it and pursued it, the partridge, with heavy heart, imagined that this rejection was because she was of a foreign race.

[1]This moral, which calls the fable by the late term *mythos*, uses the term *Kyrios* (Lord) which, though it was used in inscriptions to Zeus and other Greek deities, is used as an epithet for both God and Jesus in the Christian gospels. S. A. Handford pointed out that the moral was the same as a passage in the New Testament Epistle to James (iv.6). We have accordingly quoted the relevant words from the King James Bible. Handford believed that this moral was appended by a Christian, which is probably more likely than that the Epistle to James was quoting a popular maxim derived from an edition of Aesop.

However, a little while later, having seen that the cocks fought among themselves as well and never stopped until they drew blood, she said to herself:

"I'm not going to complain at being attacked by these cocks any longer, because I see that they do not have any mercy on each other either."

This fable shows that sensible men easily tolerate the outrages of their neighbors when they see that the latter do not even spare their parents.

32

THE FOX AND THE BUNCH OF GRAPES

A famished fox, seeing some bunches of grapes hanging [from a vine which had grown] in a tree, wanted to take some, but could not reach them. So he went away saying to himself:

"Those are unripe."

Similarly, certain people, not being able to run their affairs well because of their inefficiency, blame the circumstances.[1]

40

THE FOX AND THE BILLY-GOAT

A fox, having fallen into a well, was faced with the prospect of being stuck there. But then a billy-goat came along to that same well because he was thirsty and saw the fox. He asked him if the water was good.

The fox decided to put a brave face on it and gave a tremendous speech about how wonderful the water was down there, so very excellent. So the billy-goat climbed down the well, thinking only of his thirst. When he had had a good drink, he asked the fox what he thought was the best way to get back up again.

The fox said:

"Well, I have a very good way to do that. Of course, it will mean our working together. If you just push your front feet up against the wall and hold your horns up in the air as high as you can, I will climb up on to them, get out, and then I can pull you up behind me."

The billy-goat willingly consented to this idea, and the fox briskly clambered up the legs, the shoulders, and finally the horns of his companion. He found himself at the mouth of the well, pulled himself out, and immediately scampered off. The billy-goat shouted after him, reproaching him for breaking their agreement of mutual assistance. The fox came back to the top of the well and shouted down to the billy-goat:

[1]This famous fable gave rise to the common English expression "sour grapes." *Omphakes* can mean "sour," but it is more accurate to translate it as "unripe," since the sourness was a result of the unripeness, and when Greeks used the word to describe grapes they were usually referring to their unripe state rather than to their taste. The same word was used to describe girls who had not yet reached sexual maturity.

"Ha! If you had as many brains as you have hairs on your chin, you wouldn't have got down there in the first place without thinking of how you were going to get out again."

It is thus that sensible men should not undertake any action without having first examined the end result.

52
THE MIDDLE-AGED MAN AND HIS MISTRESSES

A middle-aged man who was going gray had two mistresses, one young and the other old. Now she who was advanced in years had a sense of shame at having sexual intercourse with a lover younger than herself. And so she did not fail, each time that he came to her house, to pull out all of his black hairs.

The young mistress, on her part, recoiled from the idea of having an old lover, and so she pulled out his white hairs.

Thus it happened that, plucked in turn by the one and then the other, he became bald.

That which is ill-matched always gets into difficulties.[1]

53
THE SHIPWRECKED MAN

A rich Athenian was sailing with some other travellers. A violent tempest suddenly arose, and the boat capsized. Then, while the other passengers were trying to save themselves by swimming, the Athenian continually invoked the aid of the goddess Athena [patroness of his city], and promised offering after offering if only she would save him.

One of his shipwrecked companions, who swam beside him, said to him: "Appeal to Athena by all means, but also move your arms!"

We also invoke the gods, but we mustn't forget to put in our own efforts to save ourselves. We count ourselves lucky if, in making our own efforts, we obtain the protection of the gods. But if we abandon ourselves to our fate, the daimons alone can save us.[1]

[1]A *hetaira* was a "female companion," a courtesan or concubine, as opposed to a legal wife. The English word "mistress" does not adequately convey the full social meaning if we wish to be precise about ancient Greek society. Similarly, the man is described as a *mesopolios*, a form of *mesaipolios*, which means "half-gray" but is also the word used by association to mean "middle-aged" in Greek.

[1]The *daimons* were semidivine beings intermediate between men and the gods, who might come to the aid of men from time to time if whimsy took them, or they might even be persuaded by promises of offerings.

59
THE MAN AND THE LION TRAVELLING TOGETHER

A man and a lion were travelling along together one day when they began to argue about which of them was the stronger. Just then they passed a stone statue representing a man strangling a lion.

"There, you see, we are stronger than you," said the man, pointing it out to the lion.

But the lion smiled and replied:

"If lions could make statues, you would see plenty of men under the paws of lions."

Many people boast of how brave and fearless they are, but when put to the test are exposed as frauds.

65
THE ASTRONOMER

The astronomer was in the habit of going out every evening to look at the stars. Then, one night when he was in the suburbs absorbed in contemplating the sky, he accidentally fell into a well. A passer-by heard him moaning and calling out. When the man realized what had happened, he called down to him:

"Hey, you there! You are so keen to see what is up in the sky that you don't see what is down here on the ground!"

One could apply this fable to men who boast of doing wonders and who are incapable of carrying out the everyday things of life.

73
THE NORTH WIND AND THE SUN

The North Wind [*Boreas*] and the Sun had a contest of strength. They decided to allot the palm of victory to whichever of them could strip the clothes off a traveller.

The North Wind tried first. He blew violently. As the man clung on to his clothes, the North Wind attacked him with greater force. But the man, uncomfortable from the cold, put on more clothes. So, disheartened, the North Wind left him to the Sun.

The Sun now shone moderately, and the man removed his extra cloak [*himation*]. Then the Sun darted beams which were more scorching until the man, not being able to withstand the heat, took off his clothes and went to take a dip in a nearby river.

This fable shows that persuasion is often more effective than violence.[1]

76

THE HOUSE-FERRET AND APHRODITE

A house-ferret, having fallen in love with a handsome young man, begged Aphrodite, goddess of love, to change her into a human girl. The goddess took pity on this passion and changed her into a gracious young girl. The young man, when he saw her, fell in love with her and led her to his home. As they rested in the nuptial chamber [*thalamos*], Aphrodite, wanting to see if in changing body the house-ferret had also changed in character, released a mouse in the middle of the room. The house-ferret, forgetting her present condition, leapt up from the bed and chased the mouse in order to eat it. Then the indignant goddess changed her back to her former state.

Bad people who change their appearance do not change their character.[1]

96

THE ORATOR DEMADES

The orator Demades spoke one day to the people of Athens. As no one was taking much notice of what he was saying, someone asked if he could tell one of Aesop's fables. Agreeing to the request, he commenced thus:

"The goddess Demeter, the swallow, and the eel all took the same route. They arrived at the edge of a river. Then the swallow flew up into the air and the eel dived into the water."

At that point he stopped speaking.

"And Demeter?" someone asked. "What did she do?"

[1]This fable was cleverly utilized by the playwright Sophocles, according to Hieronymus of Rhodes in his lost work, *Historical Notes*, where he related a picaresque story of Sophocles seducing a young boy outside the city wall of Athens. They wrapped themselves in Sophocles's cape while they pursued their physical delights, and when he had consummated their act, the boy ran off with the playwright's cape, leaving him with his own boyish cloak. This story led to the ridicule of Sophocles by the townsmen, and his rival Euripides boasted that he had consorted with the same boy without having to pay any such price. Sophocles then used the fable to form an epigram, claiming that it was the Sun God, and not the boy, who had stripped him of his cape, whereas the North Wind blew when Euripides seduced another man's wife. See Athenaeus, *Deipnosophistae* (xiii, 604).

[1]Before cats came to Greece, or when they were still rare, the house-ferret, otherwise known as the domesticated polecat, was the chief household pet. The cat eventually usurped the polecat's position, so that people today no longer remember that polecats were once their intimate companions.

"She got angry with you," he replied, "who are neglecting the affairs of the state to listen to the fables of Aesop."

Thus men are unreasonable who neglect important things in preference to things which give them pleasure.[1]

135

THE KITE AND THE SNAKE

A kite swooped down and carried off a snake but the snake twisted round and bit the bird. So the two of them then hurtled down from a great height and the kite was killed by the fall.

The snake declaimed:

"Why were you so stupid as to harm me, who had done nothing against you? It serves you right to be punished for having carried me off."

People who give in to jealousy and hurt those who are weaker than themselves could fall into the same trap: they pay the price when all the harm they have done is unexpectedly revealed.

150

THE CRAB AND THE FOX

A crab, having climbed up out of the sea on to the shore, was pursuing his solitary life. A starving fox spotted him and, as he had not a scrap of food to put between his teeth, he ran up and pounced on the crab to devour him. As he was about to be eaten, the crab cried out:

"I deserve this fate! I, who lived in the sea, had the folly to imagine I could live on the land!"

It is thus with men also: those who abandon their own occupations to mix themselves up in affairs which don't concern them meet with misfortune as a natural consequence.

151

THE CRAB AND HER MOTHER

"Don't walk sideways," said a mother crab to her child, "and don't drag your sides against the wet rock."

[1]Demades was an Athenian of the fourth century B.C. who commenced life as a sailor but became one of the leading orators of the Athenian Assembly and a great favorite of King Philip of Macedon. Later in his career he became corrupt and was convicted of taking political bribes. Cicero says the wittiest orators were the Athenians, but the wittiest of them was Demades. He was renowned for devastatingly quick-witted sarcasm, and would demolish a long and carefully crafted speech by Demosthenes with an impromptu aside, which made him a favorite of the populace. It is even probable that this little tale, which has been preserved among the Aesop fables—since it contains a part of a fable otherwise unknown—is an excerpt from a lost historical work, and represents a true incident from the life of Demades.

"Mother," the young crab replied, "if you want to teach me, walk straight yourself. I will watch you and then I will copy you."

When one reproves others, it is just as well to live straight and walk straight oneself before starting to preach a lesson.

162

THE JACKDAW AND THE BIRDS

Wishing to establish a King of the Birds, Zeus set a date for summoning them all before him for comparison: he would choose the most beautiful one to reign over them. The birds went off then to the shallow water near the shore of a river to wash. Now the jackdaw, realizing his ugliness, went around gathering up the feathers which fell from the other birds, which he then arranged and attached to his own body. Thus he became the most handsome of all.

Then the big day arrived and all the birds presented themselves before Zeus. The jackdaw, with his motley adornment, was among them. And Zeus voted for him to be the royal bird on account of his beauty. But the other birds, outraged at this decision, each pulled out the feather that had come from him. The result was that the jackdaw was stripped and once again became just a jackdaw.

Likewise with men who have debts: as long as they possess the wealth of other people, they seem to be somebody. But when they have paid their debts they find that they are once again their old selves.[1]

165

THE RAVEN AND THE FOX

A raven stole a piece of meat and flew up and perched on a branch with it. A fox saw him there and determined to get the meat for himself. So he sat at the base of the tree and said to the raven:

"Of all the birds you are by far the most beautiful. You have such elegant proportions, are so stately and sleek. You were ideally made to be the king of all the birds. And if you only had a voice you would surely be the king."

The raven, wanting to demonstrate to him that there was nothing wrong with his voice, dropped the meat and uttered a great cry. The fox rushed forward, pounced on the meat, and said:

[1]This fable was doubtless suggested by the jackdaw's actual habit of collecting colorful bits, including other birds' feathers, for its nest.

"Oh, raven, if only you also had judgment, you would want for nothing to be the king of the birds."

This fable is a lesson to all fools.[1]

180

THE DOG, THE COCK, AND THE FOX

A dog and a cockerel, having made friends, were strolling along a road together. As evening fell, the cockerel flew up into a tree to sleep there, and the dog went to sleep at the foot of the tree, which was hollow.

According to his habit, the cockerel crowed just before daybreak. This alerted a fox nearby, who ran up to the tree and called up to the cockerel:

"Do come down, sir, for I dearly wish to embrace a creature who could have such a beautiful voice as you!"

The cockerel said:

"I shall come down as soon as you awaken the doorkeeper who is asleep at the foot of the tree."

Then, as the fox went to look for the "doorkeeper," the dog pounced briskly on him and tore him to pieces.

This fable teaches us that sensible men, when their enemies attack them, divert them to someone better able to defend them than they are themselves.

185

THE DOG WHO CARRIED THE MEAT

A dog was crossing a river holding a piece of meat in his mouth. Catching sight of his reflection in the water, he believed that it was another dog who was holding a bigger piece of meat. So, dropping his own piece, he leaped into the water to take the piece from the other dog. But the result was that he ended up with neither piece—one didn't even exist and the other was swept away by the current.

This fable applies to the covetous.

[1]Two versions of this fable occur in India. Both are preserved in the Buddhist collection of *Jataka* tales, many of which are pre-Buddhist. One version is number 294. In this version, a jackal persuades a crow to shake the branch of a fruit tree so that he can get some fruit. In the other version, number 295, the crow sees a jackal eating a carcass and devises flattery to try and get some meat from the jackal. Another *Jataka* tale, number 215, describes a tortoise being carried through the air while he bites on a stick and, by opening his mouth to speak, he falls and is killed; this motif is somewhat similar to the Aesop fable of being undone by opening one's mouth and letting go of something.

192

THE HARE AND THE FOX

The hare, wishing to ingratiate himself with the fox to avoid trouble, said:

"I know you are called wily. But I have heard it is really because you know how to while away the hours better than anybody else. Is that so?"

"If you have any doubts," replied the fox, "come to my place and I will entertain you to dinner and show you how I pass an evening."

The hare followed him home. Once inside, the fox had nothing for dinner but the hare. As it realized its fate, the hare bewailed:

"Oh, to learn by such misfortune! For I see that your name truly comes from your wiles."

Great misfortunes often happen to the curious who abandon themselves to a clumsy indiscretion.[1]

194

THE LIONESS AND THE VIXEN

A vixen criticized a lioness for only ever bearing one child.

"Only one," she said, "but a lion."

Do not judge merit by quantity, but by worth.

205

THE LION, THE WOLF, AND THE FOX

A very old lion lay ill in his cave. All of the animals came to pay their respects to their king except for the fox. The wolf, sensing an opportunity, accused the fox in front of the lion:

"The fox has no respect for you or your rule. That's why he hasn't even come to visit you."

Just as the wolf was saying this, the fox arrived, and he overheard these words. Then the lion roared in rage at him, but the fox managed to say in his own defense:

"And who, of all those who have gathered here, has rendered Your Majesty as much service as I have done? For I have travelled far and wide asking physicians for a remedy for your illness, and I have found one."

[1]The Greek original is based upon a nontranslatable pun using the word *kerdos,* which means both "profit" and "wily." We have substituted an English pun which, though the meaning is not exact, gives some impression of the fable. In the original the hare ingratiatingly says he thinks the fox is really called *wily* only because he knows how to make a *profit,* but discovers how wrong he is!

The lion demanded to know at once what cure he had found, and the fox said:

"It is necessary for you to flay a wolf alive, and then take his skin and wrap it around you while it is still warm."

The wolf was ordered to be taken away immediately and flayed alive. As he was carried off, the fox turned to him with a smile and said:

"You should have spoken well of me to His Majesty rather than ill."

This fable shows that if you speak ill of someone, you yourself will fall into a trap.

206

THE LION AND THE MOUSE WHO RETURNED A KINDNESS

Once, a lion was asleep and a mouse ran all along his body. The lion woke up with a start, seized the mouse and was about to eat him, when the mouse begged him to spare his life, promising that he would repay the favor.

The lion was so amused at this that he let the little fellow go.

Not very long afterwards, the mouse was able to return the favor. For, as a matter of fact, some hunters caught the lion and tied him to a tree with a rope. The mouse heard him groaning, ran up and gnawed through the rope until the lion was free.

"You see?" squeaked the mouse. "Not long ago you mocked me when I said I would return your favor. But now you can see that even mice are grateful!"

This fable shows how, through the changes of fortune, the strong can come to depend on the weak.[1]

209

THE LION, THE ASS, AND THE FOX

The lion, the ass, and the fox, having made an agreement together, went off hunting for game. When they had taken plenty of game, the lion asked the ass to divide the spoils between them. The ass divided the food into three equal parts and invited the lion to choose his portion. The lion became enraged, pounced on the ass, and devoured him.

Then the lion asked the fox to divide the spoils. The fox took all that they had accumulated and gathered it into one large heap, retaining only the tiniest possible morsel for himself. He then invited the lion to choose.

The lion then said:

[1]A version of this fable occurs in the Indian fable collection, the *Panchatantra*, in the "Winning of Friends" section (169), only there it is a large number of mice who gnawed the ropes tying the king-elephant in a trap and set him free. The probability is that the Indian version is an adaptation of the Greek fable done after the time of Alexander the Great.

"Well, my good fellow, who taught you to divide so well? You are excellent at it."

The fox replied:

"I learned this technique from the ass's misfortune."

This fable shows that we learn from the misfortunes of others.

221

THE WOLF AND THE LAMB

A wolf saw a lamb drinking at a stream and wanted to devise a suitable pretext for devouring it. So, although he was himself upstream, he accused the lamb of muddying the water and preventing him from drinking. The lamb replied that he only drank with the tip of his tongue and that, besides, being downstream he couldn't muddy the water upstream. The wolf's stratagem having collapsed, he replied:

"But last year you insulted my father."

"I wasn't even born then," replied the lamb.

So the wolf resumed:

"Whatever you say to justify yourself, I will eat you all the same."

This fable shows that when some people decide upon doing harm, the fairest defense has no effect whatever.

224

THE WOLF AND THE HERON

A wolf swallowed a bone and looked everywhere for relief from his predicament. He met a heron who, for a certain fee, agreed to retrieve the bone. So the heron lowered his head into the wolf's throat, pulled out the bone, and then claimed his promised fee.

"Listen, pal!" replied the wolf. "Isn't it enough to have pulled your head safe and sound from a wolf's throat? What more do you want?"

This fable shows that the most we can expect from bad people is that they won't commit an injury against us in addition to their lack of gratitude.

241

THE ANT AND THE SCARAB BEETLE

All summer an ant roamed the countryside gathering up grains of wheat and barley and storing them up for winter. Seeing this, a scarab beetle expressed surprise that she was working so hard at the time of year when most other animals rested from their labors and had a holiday. At the time the ant didn't reply. But when winter had come and rain soaked the dung, the scarab beetle was hungry. She asked the ant to lend her a bit of food. Then the ant replied:

"Oh, beetle! If you had worked when I took the trouble to, instead of mocking me, you would have plenty of food now too."

Similarly, in times of abundance we should plan ahead lest we suffer distress when times change.[1]

243

THE FIELD MOUSE AND THE TOWN MOUSE

A field mouse had a town mouse for a friend. The field mouse invited the town mouse to dinner in the country. When he saw that there was only barley and corn to eat, the town mouse said:

"Do you know, my friend, that you live like an ant? I, on the other hand, have an abundance of good things. Come home with me and I will share it all with you."

So they set off together. The house mouse showed his friend some beans and bread-flour, together with some dates, a cheese, honey, and fruit. And the field mouse was filled with wonder and blessed him with all his heart, cursing his own lot. Just as they were preparing to start their meal, a man suddenly opened the door. Alarmed by the noise, the mice rushed fearfully into the crevices. Then, as they crept out again to taste some dried figs, someone else came into the room and started looking for something. So they again rushed down the holes to hide. Then the field mouse, forgetting his hunger, sighed, and said to his friend:

"Farewell, my friend. You can eat your fill and be glad of heart, but at the price of a thousand fears and dangers. I, poor little thing, will go on living by nibbling barley and corn without fear or suspicion of anyone."

This fable shows that one should:

Live simply and free from passion
Instead of luxuriously in fear and dread.[1]

267

THE ASS CLOTHED IN THE SKIN OF A LION, AND THE FOX

As ass who had clothed himself in the skin of a lion went about the countryside frightening all the animals. He encountered a fox and tried to frighten him also. But the fox, who had heard his voice before, said to him:

[1]In later versions, the scarab beetle (which was sacred in Egypt) becomes a grasshopper. (Editor's note.)

[1]This fable, like several others, is in verse, but we have only rendered the moral in verse. Horace also did a version of this fable in *Satires* (II, 6, 79–117); it is a witty verse tale told to conclude Satire 6 of Book II, which hints that the story was a popular one in Rome at that time. Fontaine's fable of "The Town Mouse and the Country Mouse" derives only its title from Aesop and differs otherwise.

"You would have scared me too, there's no doubt about it, if I hadn't heard you bray."

Thus, uneducated people who put on airs betray themselves by their longing to speak.[1]

287

THE HEN THAT LAID THE GOLDEN EGGS

A man had a beautiful hen who laid golden eggs. Believing that she might have a lump of gold in her belly, the man killed her and found that she was just the same inside as other hens. He had hoped to find riches in one go, and was thus deprived of even the little profit that he had.

This fable shows that we should be content with our lot, and shun insatiable greed.

318

THE JOKING SHEPHERD

A shepherd who led his flock rather far from the village frequently indulged in the following practical joke. He called to the people of the village to help him, crying that wolves were attacking his sheep. Two or three times the villagers were alarmed and rushed forth, then returned home having been fooled. But, in the end, it happened that some wolves really did appear. While they ravaged the flock, the shepherd called out for help to the villagers. But they, imagining that he was hoaxing them as usual, didn't bother with him. So it was that he lost his sheep.

This fable shows that liars gain only one thing, which is not to be believed even when they tell the truth.

352

THE TORTOISE AND THE HARE

The tortoise and the hare argued over which was the swifter. So, as a result, they agreed on a fixed period of time and a place and parted company. Now the hare, trusting in his natural speed, didn't hurry to set out. He lay down at the side of the road and fell asleep. But the tortoise, well aware of his slowness, didn't stop running and, overtaking the sleeping hare, he arrived first and won the contest.

This fable shows that hard work often prevails over natural talents if they are neglected.

[1]A version of this fable is found in the "Loss or Gain" section of the Indian *Panchatantra* (44), but there a donkey is clothed in a tiger's skin by his owner so that he can browse in other people's barley fields safely and the farmers would be too frightened to drive him off. However, the donkey brays and the enraged farmers then kill him with stones, arrows, and blows with wooden staves. This is probably an adaptation of the Greek fable done after the time of Alexander the Great.

Aeschylus
(c. 525–456 B.C.)

The oldest of the three great Greek tragedians, Aeschylus was born around 525 B.C. in Eleusis, a town near Athens, and died in Sicily in 456. He fought in the Persian wars, taking part in the great Athenian victory at Marathon in 490 and later in other climactic victories over the invading Persians, including the naval battle of Salamis in 480. Earlier that year, the Persians had partially destroyed Athens. Aeschylus' sense of pride in his city's accomplishments and triumphant survival is expressed most directly in his play *The Persians* (472), the only surviving Greek tragedy based on history, but also in the Orestes trilogy, or *Oresteia.* Aeschylus is a definitive spokesman for central Athenian values during the noblest age of ancient Greece. It is probable, in fact, that the eminent political and civic leader Pericles was the "choregus" (roughly equivalent of "producer") for one of Aeschylus' plays.

Today, as was true in antiquity, Aeschylus is called the "Father of Tragedy." He earned the title not only by his achievements as an artist, as typified by the power and loftiness of his stories, themes, and style, but also by his technical innovations. He is said to have introduced the "second actor" (earlier there had been only one and a chorus), thus making possible more complex plots and interactions. (The addition of an actor multiplied the number of possible characters, since parts were regularly doubled and men played female as well as male roles.) At the same time, he preserved the major lyrical and dramatic role of the chorus, which both participates in and comments on the action—this in addition to its musical and choreographic function. His output was impressive: some eighty or ninety plays. Of these, seven have survived: *The Persians, Seven Against Thebes, The Suppliant Maidens, Prometheus Bound,* and the three plays that make up the *Oresteia.*

Greek tragedies were regularly written and performed as cycles of three, each cycle followed by a raucous "satyr play" designed to contrast with the emotional loftiness and intensity of the tragedies. Aeschylus' *Oresteia,* performed in 458 just two years before his death, is the only such cycle of tragedies to have survived in its entirety.

Much of the power of this awesome work lies in the universality of its theme. Like the Book of Job, Virgil's *Aeneid,* and Milton's *Paradise Lost,* the *Oresteia* explores the perennially urgent question of whether suffering and evil can be reconciled with cosmic justice—and, if it can be, how. The literal story, however, focuses on a concrete and practical form of the question: What is the relationship between strict justice and human welfare, individual and communal? Social order, even more obviously than cosmic justice, would seem to demand that evil acts be punished—especially when, as in Aeschylus' trilogy, these acts violate the most fundamental relationships, husband-wife and parent-child. Yet the act of punishment itself frequently seems an obscenity, at odds with our sense of what is noble in humanity and worth loving or emulating in the divine order, however we define it. In our own time the question, independent of theology, underlies the debate about the function of punishment, mercy, rehabilitation, and deterrence in the judicial and penal systems. It is not at all coincidental that the *Oresteia* ends with the establishment of a law court.

Aeschylus explores the question by dramatizing the events growing out of the curse on the lineage of Atreus. The family has been guilty of unspeakable atrocities for generations before the plays' action begins, culminating in Agamemnon's sacrifice of his daughter Iphigeneia and the excesses committed against the innocents of Troy. (See the Headnote to the *Oresteia.*) Within the plays themselves, the chain of violence is extended by two further acts: the murder of Agamemnon by his wife, Clytaemnestra, and the successful conspiracy of their children, Orestes and Electra, to kill their mother in the cause of justice. The main agency and symbol of retaliation are the Furies, repellent primitive beings who in their very unsophistication embody an uncompromising honesty in dealing with elemental evil, especially violations of blood kinship.

"Tragedy" seems hardly the right term for this superdrama, either for the whole or for its separate plays. In Aeschylus' early plays, such as the surviving *Persians* and *Seven Against Thebes,* he placed human affairs in the foreground, with the gods relegated to the background. But in the *Oresteia,* as apparently also in the late Prometheus and Danaid trilogies (now represented only in the surviving *Prometheus Bound* and *The Suppliant Maidens*), he brought the cosmos itself on stage as he dramatized the divisions within the universe and their ultimate reconciliation. The *Oresteia* is not so much a tragedy, in the Aristotelian sense, as it is a Divine Comedy, tracing the emergence of civilization out of darkness into light. This process is presented in terms of sexual conflict and its resolution, conflict which penetrates all levels of existence, from the psychological through the domestic and political to the cosmic. *Agamemnon* presents a world trapped in a net (a crucial image throughout the trilogy) of blood vengeance, a primitive code presided over by the conservative, irrational, female Furies. The nightmare world of *Agamemnon* is shot through with sexual conflict and confusion. The unwifely Clytaemnestra "maneuvers like a man," while Aegisthus is a womanly man, and the heart of Cassandra's premonitory vision (which no one understands) is, "What outrage—the woman kills the man!" Confusion of personal sexual identity is echoed on the domestic level in the marital hatred of Agamemnon and his queen and on the political level in the Trojan War, fought "all for another's woman." The Greek victory has been a rape—"for their mad outrage of a queen we raped their city"—and Agamemnon, who killed his own daughter, has been "the darling of all the golden girls who spread the gates of Troy."

The Libation Bearers introduces the title character of the trilogy, Orestes, who is to become the pivotal figure in the revolution of values the *Oresteia* traces. The law of blood vengeance still reigns, but the vengeance of Orestes and Electra, so reluctant and self-doubting, is very different from the self-confident exultation of Clytaemnestra's bloodletting. Sexual conflict and confusion here are translated into the agonized ambivalence of a son and daughter forced to choose between love for a mother and honor for a father. And by the end of the play, sexual conflicts on the familial and political levels have broadened to a cosmic level in the conflict of the embodied Furies with the male Olympian Apollo, who authorized Orestes' vengeance. This conflict is brought directly on stage as we move from the nightmarish mode of *Agamemnon* and the comparatively realistic and Sophoclean manner of *The Libation Bearers* to the allegorical theomachy of *The Eumenides.* The curiously bisexual Athena, female but motherless, since she sprang straight from the head of Zeus, becomes the instrument for the resolution of sexual conflict, personally for Orestes, politically for Athens, and cosmically, in the reconciliation of the gods. The male Olympians triumph, but the female Furies are honored too, as they are transformed into the Eumenides, the "Kindly Ones," watchers over the rain, sunshine, and fertility of nature. This "Divine Comedy" ends with a distinctly nontragic hymn of triumph to the Athenian balance between the claims of earth and sky, female and male, fertility and control, with an optimism unclouded by the darker visions of Sophocles and Euripides.

Aeschylus' poetic and dramatic style matches the grandeur of his theme. The language, with its daring metaphors and bold dislocations of syntax, mirrors an emotional and intellectual unrest perfectly in keeping with the dramatic excitement and the profundity of theme. Image patterns are used with dazzling skill to heighten effects and to convey nuances of theme and meaning. The patterns are many and omnipresent: of fire, light and darkness, nets, wealth, wind, storm, yokes, animals, hunting, lawsuits, wrestling and other sports, "threeness," and so on. These images are not a code, each image having a static meaning; their significance is always shaped by the immediate context. For example, a yoke can suggest enslavement but also the intimacy of a harmonious bond such as happy marriage. (The word "bond" itself has the same ambiguous meaning.) Moreover, the images evolve in parallel with the evolution of action and values; an example is the ominous torch flame that at the beginning of the *Agamemnon* signals the fall of Troy and the imminent fall of the returning general but at the end of *The Eumenides* symbolizes fertility and deep joy.

As a stage craftsman, Aeschylus is the most daring and flamboyant of the three Greek tragedians. His contemporaries called him the poet of "shock," and a persistent story insisted that he wrote his plays while drunk. He served both as composer and choreographer for his own plays, and the dances he arranged for his choruses were famous for their violence and extravagance: The Persian Lords, for example, in *The Persians,* howl and scrape at the earth to conjure up the ghost of Darius. Shock follows shock in the *Oresteia.* The entrance of Agamemnon and his army is an impressive spectacle, and the dark red carpet running out from the palace door like a stream of blood is one of the most brilliant uses of a stage property in Greek drama. A contemporary testified that the first appearance of the Furies in *The Eumenides,* moaning and dripping blood from their eye sockets, caused children in the audience to faint and women to miscarry. The comment is possibly an exercise of critical license, but it nevertheless captures the shock the scene must have created. And the final great procession of the entire cast out of the theater and up to the hill of the Areopagus, in full view of the audience, is an extraordinary dramatic effect that suddenly moves the timeless, legendary action of the plays into the here and now.

The *Oresteia* is an allusive work that, like Virgil's *Aeneid,* brings together the two wellsprings of Greek literature, the *Iliad* and the *Odyssey,* while also transforming them. The Trojan War is the immediate occasion of the acts that bring on Agamemnon's murder and the ensuing events of the three plays. But the Odyssean themes of the warrior's return to his wife and of the loyal son determined to preserve his father and his house from harm are also reworked by Aeschylus with penetrating irony and insight.

The trilogy makes a political and religious statement, through the medium of great art. But it is more than ideology or theology, and more than art in a narrow sense of the word. It is an emblem of the full range of human nature, one of those rare works—like Dante's *Comedy,* Shakespeare's last plays, Beethoven's last music—that can explore vastness and mystery without losing touch with the human, including the earthy and even the homely. Dante included jokes and personal reminiscences in his account of the cosmos; Beethoven in his last symphony inserted a grunting German-band episode into an Olympian, ecstatic hymn to joy. Aeschylus, in *The Libation Bearers,* reminds us through Orestes' old nurse that the agent and victim of large tragic and providential forces was once a baby who needed to have his diapers changed. The magnificence of the *Oresteia* is ultimately a product of its range, its clear understanding and respect for humanity as many-layered. "Beneath" us lie elemental forces like the Furies; "above" us beckon the Olympian forces of the sky; "around" us lie the familiar facts of our condition in the actual world. All three of these levels, though, are within us, needing to be humanized and synthesized if we are to realize our full potential, individually and communally.

FURTHER READING: John Herington, *Aeschylus,* 1986, is a clearly written introductory overview of the author's work, especially valuable for its attention to patterns of diction and theatrical effect. Helen Bacon's essay on Aeschylus in Volume I of *Ancient Writers: Greece and Rome,* ed. T. James Luce, 1982, and Oliver Taplin's *The Stagecraft of Aeschylus,* 1977, are also recommended. Gilbert Murray, in his classic *Aeschylus: The Creator of Tragedy,* 1940, deals not only with the extant works but also with Aeschylus' contribution to tragedy. Anthony J. Podlecki, *The Political Background of Aeschylean Tragedy,* 1966, comments on all seven plays. H. D. F. Kitto in *Form and Meaning in Drama,* 1956, is concerned mainly with the writings of Aeschylus and Sophocles; while Albin Lesky in *Greek Tragedy,* 1938, trans. H. A. Frankfort, 1965, presents material on all three tragedians. Stimulating essays on many aspects of Aeschylean drama are offered by Marsh H. McCall, ed., *Aeschylus: A Collection of Critical Essays,* 1972. Jon Mikalson, *Honor Thy Gods,* 1992, discusses conformity and rebellion in Aeschylus, Euripides, and Sophocles. The Greek text of the three plays, a translation, and general remarks are given by W. Headlam and George Thomson, ed., *The Oresteia of Aeschylus,* 1938, 2nd ed. 1966. Anne Lebeck, in *The Oresteia: A Study in Language and Structure,* 1971, shows how the imagery in the three dramas is interconnected. Hugh Lloyd-Jones's introductions in his translation of the *Oresteia,* 1979, are first-rate.

THE ORESTEIA

Translated by Robert Fagles

Before the action of the first play *(Agamemnon)* begins, a line of evil acts, each inciting an act of terrible retaliation, already extends back several generations. Tantalus, the mythical great-grandfather of Agamemnon, murdered his son Pelops and tried to deceive the gods by serving them his son's flesh at a banquet. The gods saw through his deception, however, restoring Pelops to life and punishing Tantalus in Hades in a manner expressed by the word "tantalize." (The sinner was immersed in water up to his neck, with fruit trees over his head, both the water and the fruit receding when he tried to drink or eat.) Pelops in his turn doublecrossed and then murdered Myrtilus, a conspirator with him in a plot to win a bride for Pelops.

Pelops had two sons, Atreus and Thyestes. Thyestes seduced his brother's wife; in revenge, Atreus first banished Thyestes and then, after luring him home again, served the flesh of Thyestes' children to him at a banquet. Thyestes cursed the house of Atreus and fled. Aegisthus, a surviving son of Thyestes, inherited his father's hatred of the line of Atreus.

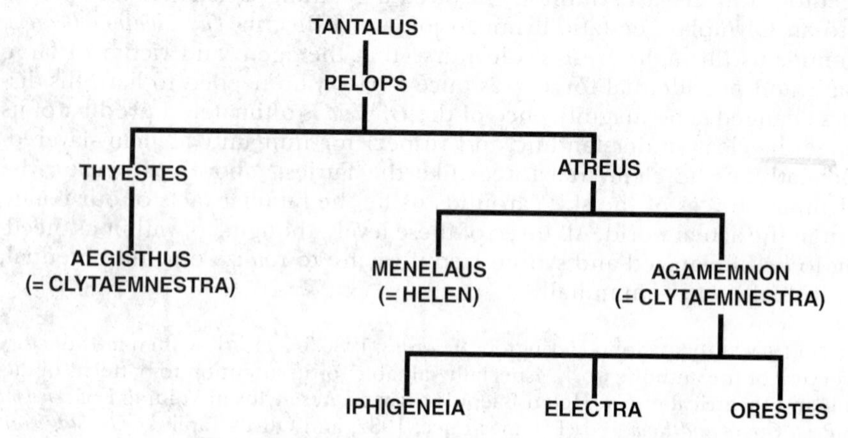

The genealogy of Orestes, according to Aeschylus.

Agamemnon and Menelaus are sons of Atreus. Menelaus married the beautiful Helen. She later eloped with Paris (son of King Priam of Troy), whom Menelaus had been entertaining as a guest. Agamemnon and Menelaus then organized a Greek coalition to recapture Helen from Troy and to take revenge on the Trojans. But the Greek fleet was threatened and detained at the port of Aulis by adverse winds and weather. In order to propitiate the gods, especially Artemis, and secure favorable winds, Agamemnon sacrificed the life of his daughter Iphigeneia, thereby extending the line of sacrilegious killings and incurring the hatred of his wife, Clytaemnestra (half-sister to Helen). During Agamemnon's absence at Troy, Clytaemnestra has entered into an adulterous union with Aegisthus, both of whom have a motive for killing Agamemnon. [*Editors' headnote.*]

AGAMEMNON

CHARACTERS

WATCHMAN	CHORUS, THE OLD MEN OF ARGOS AND THEIR LEADER
CLYTAEMNESTRA	*Attendants of Clytaemnestra and of Agamemnon, bodyguard of Aegisthus*
HERALD	
AGAMEMNON	
CASSANDRA	
AEGISTHUS	

TIME AND SCENE

A night in the tenth and final autumn of the Trojan war. The house of Atreus in Argos.[1] *Before it, an altar stands unlit; a watchman on the high roofs fights to stay awake.*

WATCHMAN.

Dear gods, set me free from all the pain,
the long watch I keep, one whole year awake . . .
propped on my arms, crouched on the roofs of Atreus
like a dog.
I know the stars by heart,
the armies of the night, and there in the lead 5
the ones that bring us snow or the crops of summer,
bring us all we have—
our great blazing kings of the sky,
I know them, when they rise and when they fall . . .
and now I watch for the light, the signal-fire 10
breaking out of Troy, shouting Troy is taken.
So she commands,[2] full of her high hopes.
That woman—she maneuvers like a man.

And when I keep to my bed, soaked in dew,
and the thoughts go groping through the night 15
and the good dreams that used to guard my sleep . . .
not here, it's the old comrade, terror at my neck.
I mustn't sleep, no—

[*Shaking himself awake.*]

Look alive, sentry.
And I try to pick out tunes, I hum a little,
a good cure for sleep, and the tears start, 20
I cry for the hard times come to the house,
no longer run like the great place of old.

Oh for a blessed end to all our pain,
some godsend burning through the dark—

[*Light appears slowly in the east;
he struggles to his feet and scans it.*]

I salute you!
You dawn of the darkness, you turn night to day— 25
I see the light at last.

[1]According to Homer, Agamemnon lived in Mycenae; Aeschylus changes the scene of the tragedy to Argos. Both cities were located in the plain of Argolis, in south-central Greece.
[2]Clytaemnestra, Agamemnon's queen, has established a chain of fire beacons that will relay quickly the news that Troy has fallen.

They'll be dancing in the streets of Argos
thanks to you, thanks to this new stroke of—
Aieeeeee!
There's your signal clear and true, my queen!
Rise up from bed—hurry, lift a cry of triumph 30
through the house, praise the gods for the beacon,
if they've taken Troy . . .
But there it burns,
fire all the way. I'm for the morning dances.
Master's luck is mine. A throw of the torch
has brought us triple-sixes[3]—we have won! 35
My move now—

[*Beginning to dance, then breaking off, lost in thought.*]

Just bring him home. My king,
I'll take your loving hand in mine and then . . .
the rest is silence. The ox is on my tongue.[4]
Aye, but the house and these old stones,
give them a voice and what a tale they'd tell. 40
And so would I, gladly . . .
I speak to those who know; to those who don't
my mind's a blank. I never say a word.

[*He climbs down from the roof and disappears into the palace through a side entrance. A* CHORUS, *the old men of Argos who have not learned the news, enters and marches around the altar.*]

CHORUS.
Ten years gone, ten to the day
our great avenger[5] went for Priam— 45
Menelaus and lord Agamemnon,
two kings with the power of Zeus,
the twin throne, twin scepter,
Atreus' sturdy yoke of sons
launched Greece in a thousand ships, 50
armadas cutting loose from the land,
armies massed for the cause, the rescue—

[*From within the palace* CLYTAEMNESTRA *raises a cry of triumph.*]

[3]A winning throw of the dice in a game related to backgammon.
[4]A proverbial phrase, the equivalent of "my lips are sealed." The watchman is probably thinking ominously of the guilty affair between Clytaemnestra and Aegisthus.
[5]Agamemnon and his brother Menelaus (whose wife Helen had run away with Paris, thus occasioning the war against Troy). Priam was the Trojan king.

the heart within them screamed for all-out war!
Like vultures robbed of their young,
   the agony sends them frenzied, 55
soaring high from the nest, round and
round they wheel, they row their wings,
stroke upon churning thrashing stroke,
but all the labor, the bed of pain,
   the young are lost forever. 60
Yet someone hears on high—Apollo,
Pan or Zeus[6]—the piercing wail
these guests of heaven raise,
and drives at the outlaws, late
but true to revenge, a stabbing Fury![7] 65

[CLYTAEMNESTRA *appears at the doors and pauses with her entourage.*]

So towering Zeus the god of guests[8]
drives Atreus' sons at Paris,
all for a woman manned by many[9]
the generations wrestle, knees
grinding the dust, the manhood drains, 70
the spear snaps in the first blood rites
   that marry Greece and Troy.
And now it goes as it goes
and where it ends is Fate.
And neither by singeing flesh 75
nor tipping cups of wine[10]
nor shedding burning tears can you
enchant away the rigid Fury.

[CLYTAEMNESTRA *lights the altar-fires.*]

We are the old, dishonored ones,
the broken husks of men. 80

[6]Apollo, Pan, and Zeus are, respectively, the god of prophecy, the god of nature, and the king of the gods.

[7]The Furies are female personifications and agents of vengeance for crime, especially crime against blood kin. In the last play of the trilogy they are redefined as "the Eumenides," or "Kindly Ones."

[8]One of the roles of Zeus. Paris had violated the laws of hospitality by stealing Helen away from the house of his host, Menelaus.

[9]Helen had been courted by innumerable suitors in addition to the man she married (Menelaus) and the man she ran away with (Paris).

[10]Ritual offerings to the gods included sacrificed animals and poured-out wine. The imagery here and the two following lines could refer to any of several persons in the play. Such ambiguity is recurrent in the trilogy.

Even then they cast us off,
the rescue mission[11] left us here
to prop a child's strength upon a stick.
What if the new sap rises in his chest?
He has no soldiery in him, 85
no more than we,
and we are aged past aging,
gloss of the leaf shriveled,
three legs at a time we falter on.
Old men are children once again, 90
a dream that sways and wavers
into the hard light of day.
But you,
daughter of Leda, queen Clytaemnestra,
what now, what news, what message
drives you through the citadel 95
burning victims? Look,
the city gods, the gods of Olympus,
gods of the earth and public markets—
all the altars blazing with your gifts!
Argos blazes! Torches 100
race the sunrise up her skies—
drugged by the lulling holy oils,
unadulterated,
run from the dark vaults of kings.
Tell us the news! 105
What you can, what is right—
Heal us, soothe our fears!
Now the darkness comes to the fore,
now the hope glows through your victims,
beating back this raw, relentless anguish 110
gnawing at the heart.

[CLYTAEMNESTRA *ignores them and pursues her rituals; they assemble for the opening chorus.*]

O but I still have power to sound the gods' command at the roads[12]
that launched the kings. The gods breathe power through my
song,
my fighting strength, Persuasion grows with the years—

[11] The naval and military expedition to bring Helen back from Troy.

[12] In lines 112–258 the chorus recalls fearfully the ominous beginning of the expedition against Troy. The eagles' devouring of the hare was understood by Calchas, the Greek soothsayer, to foreshadow the destruction of Troy. But Artemis, goddess of the hunt (and thus protector of pregnant animals) and of childbirth (thus offended by the anticipated slaughter of innocents at Troy) was angered. Unfavorable winds threatened the Greek fleet anchored at Aulis. Ironically, Artemis had to be appeased by the sacrificial killing at Aulis of Agamemnon's daughter Iphigeneia—an example of strict retribution in kind, a central theme in the Orestes trilogy.

I sing how the flight of fury hurled the twin command, 115
one will that hurled young Greece
and winged the spear of vengeance straight for Troy!
The kings of birds to kings of the beaking prows,[13] one black,
one with a blaze of silver
skimmed the palace spearhand right 120
and swooping lower, all could see,
plunged their claws in a hare, a mother
bursting with unborn young—the babies spilling,
quick spurts of blood—cut off the race just dashing into life!
Cry, cry for death, but good win out in glory in the end. 125

But the loyal seer[14] of the armies studied Atreus' sons,
two sons with warring hearts—he saw two eagle-kings
devour the hare and spoke the things to come,
"Years pass, and the long hunt nets the city of Priam,
the flocks beyond the walls, 130
a kingdom's life and soul—Fate stamps them out.
Just let no curse of the gods lour on us first,
shatter our giant armor
forged to strangle Troy. I see
pure Artemis bristle in pity— 135
yes, the flying hounds of the Father
slaughter for armies . . . their own victim . . . a woman
trembling young, all born to die—She loathes the eagles' feast!"[15]
Cry, cry for death, but good win out in glory in the end.

"Artemis, lovely Artemis, so kind 140
to the ravening lion's tender, helpless cubs,
the suckling young of beasts that stalk the wilds—
bring this sign for all its fortune,
all its brutal torment home to birth!
I beg you, Healing Apollo,[16] soothe her before 145
her crosswinds hold us down and moor the ships too long,
pressing us on to another victim . . .
nothing sacred, no
no feast to be eaten
the architect of vengeance 150

[*Turning to the palace.*]

growing strong in the house
with no fear of the husband
here she waits

[13] The kings of birds are eagles; the kings of the beaking prows are Agamemnon and Menelaus.
[14] Calchas.
[15] We are meant to recall also the abominable meal at which Thyestes was served his children's flesh by Atreus.
[16] Apollo, god of healing, is brother to Artemis.

the terror raging back and back in the future
the stealth, the law of the hearth, the mother— 155
Memory womb of Fury child-avenging Fury!"
So as the eagles wheeled at the crossroads,
Calchas clashed out the great good blessings mixed with doom
for the halls of kings and singing with our fate
we cry, cry for death, but good win out in glory in the end. 160

Zeus, great nameless all in all,
if that name will gain his favor,
I will call him Zeus.
I have no words to do him justice,
weighing all in the balance, 165
all I have is Zeus, Zeus—
Lift this weight, this torment from my spirit,
cast it once for all.

He who was so mighty once,[17]
storming for the wars of heaven, 170
he has had his day.
And then his son who came to power
met his match in the third fall
and he is gone. Zeus, Zeus—
raise your cries and sing him Zeus the Victor! 175
You will reach the truth:

Zeus has led us on to know,
the Helmsman lays it down as law
that we must suffer, suffer into truth.
We cannot sleep, and drop by drop at the heart 180
the pain of pain remembered comes again,
and we resist, but ripeness comes as well.
From the gods enthroned on the awesome rowing-bench
there comes a violent love.

So it was that day the king, 185
the steersman at the helm of Greece,
would never blame a word the prophet said—
swept away by the wrenching winds of fortune
he conspired! Weatherbound we could not sail,
our stores exhausted, fighting strength hard-pressed, 190
and the squadrons rode in the shallows off Chalkis[18]
where the riptide crashes, drags,

and winds from the north pinned down our hulls at Aulis,
port of anguish . . . head winds starving,

[17] The following lines describe the overthrow of Ouranos (Uranus) by his son Kronos (Saturn) and of the latter by his son Zeus, who now reigns as supreme god.
[18] Chalkis, on the island Euboea, faced the port of Aulis on the mainland.

sheets and the cables snapped 195
and the men's minds strayed,
the pride, the bloom of Greece
was raked as time ground on,
ground down, and then the cure for the storm
and it was harsher—Calchas cried, 200
"My captains, Artemis must have blood!"—
as harsh the sons of Atreus
dashed their scepters on the rocks,
could not hold back the tears,

and I still can hear the older warlord saying, 205
"Obey, obey, or a heavy doom will crush me—
Oh but doom *will* crush me
once I rend my child,
the glory of my house—
a father's hands are stained, 210
blood of a young girl streaks the altar.
Pain both ways and what is worse?
Desert the fleets, fail the alliance?
No, but stop the winds with a virgin's blood,
feed their lust, their fury?—feed their fury!— 215
Law is law!—
Let all go well."

And once he slipped his neck in the strap of Fate,
his spirit veering black, impure, unholy,
once he turned he stopped at nothing,
seized with the frenzy 220
blinding driving to outrage—
wretched frenzy, cause of all our grief!
Yes, he had the heart
to sacrifice his daughter!—
to bless the war that avenged a woman's loss, 225
a bridal rite that sped the men-of-war.

"My father, father!"—she might pray to the winds;
no innocence moves her judges mad for war.
Her father called his henchmen on,
on with a prayer, 230
"Hoist her over the altar
like a yearling, give it all your strength!
She's fainting—lift her,
sweep her robes around her,
but slip this strap in her gentle curving lips . . . 235
here, gag her hard, a sound will curse the house"—
and the bridle chokes her voice . . . her saffron[19] robes

[19]Orange-yellow, the traditional color of the bridal garment.

pouring over the sand
her glance like arrows showering
wounding every murderer through with pity
clear as a picture, live, 240
she strains to call their names . . .
I remember often the days with father's guests
when over the feast her voice unbroken,
pure as the hymn her loving father
bearing third libations, sang to Saving Zeus— 245
transfixed with joy, Atreus' offspring
throbbing out their love.

What comes next? I cannot see it, cannot say.
The strong techniques of Calchas do their work.

But Justice turns the balance scales, 250
sees that we suffer
and we suffer and we learn.
And we will know the future when it comes.
Greet it too early, weep too soon.
It all comes clear in the light of day. 255
Let all go well today, well as she could want,

[*Turning to* CLYTAEMNESTRA.]

our midnight watch, our lone defender,
single-minded queen.

LEADER.[20]
We've come,
Clytaemnestra. We respect your power.
Right it is to honor the warlord's woman 260
once he leaves the throne.
But why these fires?
Good news, or more good hopes? We're loyal,
we want to hear, but never blame your silence.

CLYTAEMNESTRA.
Let the new day shine, as the proverb says,
glorious from the womb of Mother Night.[21] 265

[*Lost in prayer, then turning to the* CHORUS.]

You will hear a joy beyond your hopes.
Priam's citadel—the Greeks have taken Troy!

LEADER.
No, what do you mean? I can't believe it.

[20] The principal spokesman for the chorus.
[21] Ironically, the avenging Furies are also offspring of the primeval Night.

CLYTAEMNESTRA.

Troy is ours. Is that clear enough?

LEADER.

The joy of it,

stealing over me, calling up my tears— 270

CLYTAEMNESTRA.

Yes, your eyes expose your loyal hearts.

LEADER.

And you have proof?

CLYTAEMNESTRA.

I do,

I must. Unless the god is lying.

LEADER.

That,

or a phantom spirit sends you into raptures.

CLYTAEMNESTRA.

No one takes me in with visions—senseless dreams. 275

LEADER.

Or giddy rumor, you haven't indulged yourself—

CLYTAEMNESTRA.

You treat me like a child, you mock me?

LEADER.

Then when did they storm the city?

CLYTAEMNESTRA.

Last night, I say, the mother of this morning.

LEADER.

And who on earth could run the news so fast? 280

CLYTAEMNESTRA.

The god of fire—rushing fire from Ida![22]
And beacon to beacon rushed it on to me,
my couriers riding home the torch.

From Troy

to the bare rock of Lemnos, Hermes' Spur,
and the Escort winged the great light west 285
to the Saving Father's face, Mount Athos hurled it
third in the chain and leaping Ocean's back
the blaze went dancing on to ecstasy—pitch-pine
streaming gold like a newborn sun—and brought
the word in flame to Mount Makistos' brow. 290
No time to waste, straining, fighting sleep,

[22]A mountain range near Troy. Clytaemnestra's description of the progress of the flame signal from Troy to Argos is filled with ironic overtones. Mount Athos, here associated with Zeus as "Saving Father," recalls by contrast Agamemnon's slaying of his daughter Iphigeneia; the "murderous" straits of Euripos are the location of her death; the "Black Widow" (Mount Arachnaion, or "Spider Mountain") suggests both Clytaemnestra herself and a web, one of the variants of the net imagery ubiquitous in the play; the "true son" of Ida suggests the causal link between Agamemnon's Trojan adventure and his fate at his homecoming, as well as foreshadowing the avenging role of his son Orestes.

that lookout heaved a torch glowing over
the murderous straits of Euripos to reach
Messapion's watchmen craning for the signal.
Fire for word of fire! tense with the heather 295
withered gray, they stack it, set it ablaze—
the hot force of the beacon never flags,
it springs the Plain of Asôpos, rears
like a harvest moon to hit Kithairon's crest
and drives new men to drive the fire on. 300
That relay pants for the farflung torch,
they swell its strength outstripping my commands
and the light inflames the marsh, the Gorgon's Eye,
it strikes the peak where the wild goats range—
my law, my fire whips that camp! 305
They spare nothing, eager to build its heat,
and a huge beard of flame overcomes the headland
beetling down the Saronic Gulf, and flaring south
it brings the dawn to the Black Widow's face—
the watch that looms above your heads—and now 310
the true son of the burning flanks of Ida
crashes on the roofs of Atreus' sons!

And I ordained it all.
Torch to torch, running for their lives,
one long succession racing home my fire.
One, 315
first in the laps and last,[23] wins out in triumph.
There you have my proof, *my* burning sign, I tell you—
the power my lord passed on from Troy to me.

LEADER.
We'll thank the gods, my lady—first this story,
let me lose myself in the wonder of it all! 320
Tell it start to finish, tell us all.

CLYTAEMNESTRA.
The city's ours—in our hands this very day!
I can hear the cries in crossfire rock the walls.
Pour oil and wine in the same bowl,
what have you, friendship? A struggle to the end. 325
So with the victors and the victims—outcries,
you can hear them clashing like their fates.

They are kneeling by the bodies of the dead,
embracing men and brothers, infants over
the aged loins that gave them life, and sobbing, 330
as the yoke constricts their last free breath,
for every dear one lost.

[23]A winning relay team ("first in the laps") achieves the victory when the runner of the anchor leg (the "last") crosses the finish line.

And the others,
there, plunging breakneck through the night—
the labor of battle sets them down, ravenous,
to breakfast on the last remains of Troy. 335
Not by rank but the lots of chance they draw,
they lodge in the houses captured by the spear,
settling in so soon, released from the open sky,
the frost and dew. Lucky men, off guard at last,
they sleep away their first good night in years. 340

If only they are revering the city's gods,
the shrines of the gods who love the conquered land,
no plunderer will be plundered in return.
Just let no lust, no mad desire seize the armies
to ravish what they must not touch— 345
overwhelmed by all they've won!
The run for home
and safety waits, the swerve at the post,[24]
the final lap of the grueling two-lap race.
And even if the men come back with no offense
to the gods, the avenging dead[25] may never rest— 350
Oh let no new disaster strike! And here
you have it, what a woman has to say.
Let the best win out, clear to see.
A small desire but all that I could want.

LEADER.
Spoken like a man, my lady, loyal, 355
full of self-command. I've heard your sign
and now your vision.

[*Reaching toward her as she turns and re-enters the palace.*]

Now to praise the gods.
The joy is worth the labor.

CHORUS.
O Zeus my king and Night, dear Night,[26]
queen of the house who covers us with glories, 360
you slung your net on the towers of Troy,
neither young nor strong could leap
the giant dredge net of slavery,
all-embracing ruin.

[24] The turning-post in a race, where the racers turn and head back for where they started.

[25] The chorus is meant to apply the phrase to the Trojan dead; Clytaemnestra also alludes cryptically to her dead daughter.

[26] The chorus in this passage concentrates on Paris as the evil man whom the gods punish, but much of what they say applies also to Agamemnon and the whole line of Atreus. In the latter part of the song (lines 426 ff.), the chorus begins to sense dimly this more general guilt.

I adore you, iron Zeus of the guests 365
and your revenge—you drew your longbow
year by year to a taut full draw
till one bolt, not falling short
or arching over the stars,
could split the mark of Paris! 370
The sky stroke of god!—it is all Troy's to tell,
but even I can trace it to its cause:
god does as god decrees.
And still some say
that heaven would never stoop to punish men 375
who trample the lovely grace of things
untouchable. How wrong they are!
A curse burns bright on crime—
full-blown, the father's crimes will blossom,
burst into the son's. 380
Let there be less suffering . . .
give us the sense to live on what we need.

Bastions of wealth
are no defense for the man
who treads the grand altar of Justice 385
down and out of sight.

Persuasion, maddening child of Ruin
overpowers him—Ruin plans it all.
And the wound will smolder on,
there is no cure, 390
a terrible brilliance kindles on the night.
He is bad bronze scraped on a touchstone:[27]
put to the test, the man goes black.
Like the boy who chases
a bird on the wing,[28] brands his city, 395
brings it down and prays,
but the gods are deaf
to the one who turns to crime, they tear him down.

So Paris learned:
he came to Atreus' house 400
and shamed the tables spread for guests,
he stole away the queen.

And she left her land *chaos,* clanging shields,
companions tramping, bronze prows, men in bronze,
and she came to Troy with a dowry, death, 405
strode through the gates
defiant in every stride,

[27]A stone that, rubbed against a metal, shows whether the metal is true or counterfeit.
[28]To chase a bird on the wing is foolishly to attempt the impossible.

as prophets of the house looked on and wept,
"Oh the halls and the lords of war,
the bed and the fresh prints of love. 410
I *see* him,[29] unavenging, unavenged,
the stun of his desolation is so clear—
he longs for the one who lies across the sea
until her phantom seems to sway the house.

Her curving images, 415
her beauty hurts her lord,
the eyes starve and the touch
of love is gone,

"and radiant dreams are passing in the night,
the memories throb with sorrow, joy with pain . . . 420
it is pain to dream and see desires
slip through the arms,
a vision lost forever
winging down the moving drifts of sleep."
So he grieves at the royal hearth 425
yet others' grief is worse, far worse.
All through Greece for those who flocked to war
they are holding back the anguish now,
you can feel it rising now in every house;
I tell you there is much to tear the heart. 430

They knew the men they sent,
but now in place of men
ashes and urns come back
to every hearth.

War, War, the great gold-broker of corpses 435
holds the balance of the battle on his spear!
Home from the pyres he sends them,
home from Troy to the loved ones,
weighted with tears, the urns brimmed full,
the heroes return in gold-dust, 440
dear, light ash for men; and they weep,
they praise them, "He had skill in the swordplay,"
"He went down so tall in the onslaught,"
"All for another's woman." So they mutter
in secret and the rancor steals 445
toward our staunch defenders, Atreus' sons.

And there they ring the walls, the young,
the lithe, the handsome hold the graves
they won in Troy; the enemy earth
rides over those who conquered. 450

[29] The primary reference is to Menelaus left alone without Helen.

The people's voice is heavy with hatred,
now the curses of the people must be paid,
and now I wait, I listen . . .
there—there is something breathing
under the night's shroud. God takes aim 455
at the ones who murder many;
the swarthy Furies stalk the man
gone rich beyond all rights—with a twist
of fortune grind him down, dissolve him
into the blurring dead—there is no help. 460
The reach for power can recoil,
the bolt of god can strike you at a glance.

Make me rich with no man's envy,
neither a raider of cities, no,
nor slave come face to face with life 465
overpowered by another.

[*Speaking singly.*]

—Fire comes and the news is good,
it races through the streets
but is it true? Who knows?
Or just another lie from heaven? 470

—Show us the man so childish, wonderstruck,
he's fired up with the first torch,
then when the message shifts
he's sick at heart.

—Just like a woman
to fill with thanks before the truth is clear. 475

—So gullible. Their stories spread like wildfire,
they fly fast and die faster;
rumors voiced by women come to nothing.

LEADER.
Soon we'll know her fires for what they are,
her relay race of torches hand-to-hand— 480
know if they're real or just a dream,
the hope of a morning here to take our senses.
I see a herald running from the beach
and a victor's spray of olive shades his eyes
and the dust he kicks, twin to the mud of Troy, 485
shows he has a voice—no kindling timber
on the cliffs, no signal-fires for him.
He can shout the news and give us joy,
or else . . . please, not that.
Bring it on,
good fuel to build the first good fires. 490

And if anyone calls down the worst on Argos
let him reap the rotten harvest of his mind.

[*The* HERALD *rushes in and kneels on the ground.*]

HERALD.
Good Greek earth, the soil of my fathers!
Ten years out, and a morning brings me back.
All hopes snapped but one—I'm home at last. 495
Never dreamed I'd die in Greece, assigned
the narrow plot I love the best.
And now
I salute the land, the light of the sun,
our high lord Zeus and the king of Pytho[30]—
no more arrows, master, raining on our heads! 500
At Scamander's banks we took our share,
your longbow brought us down like plague.
Now come, deliver us, heal us—lord Apollo!
Gods of the market, here, take my salute.

And you, my Hermes, Escort, 505
loving Herald, the herald's shield and prayer!—
And the shining dead of the land who launched the armies,
warm us home . . . we're all the spear has left.

You halls of the kings, you roofs I cherish,
sacred seats—you gods that catch the sun, 510
if your glances ever shone on him in the old days,
greet him well—so many years are lost.
He comes, he brings us light in the darkness,
free for every comrade, Agamemnon lord of men.

Give him the royal welcome he deserves! 515
He hoisted the pickax of Zeus who brings revenge,
he dug Troy down, he worked her soil down,
the shrines of her gods and the high altars, gone!—
and the seed of her wide earth he ground to bits.
That's the yoke he claps on Troy. The king, 520
the son of Atreus comes. The man is blest,
the one man alive to merit such rewards.

Neither Paris nor Troy, partners to the end,
can say their work outweighs their wages now.
Convicted of rapine, stripped of all his spoils, 525
and his father's house and the land that gave it life—
he's scythed them to the roots. The sons of Priam
pay the price twice over.

[30] The archer god Apollo, who had sided with the Trojans and launched the arrows of plague against the Greeks.

LEADER.

Welcome home
from the wars, herald, long live your joy.

HERALD.

Our joy—
now I could die gladly. Say the word, dear gods. 530

LEADER.

Longing for your country left you raw?

HERALD.

The tears fill my eyes, for joy.

LEADER.

You too,
down the sweet disease that kills a man
with kindness . . .

HERALD.

Go on, I don't see what you—

LEADER.

Love
for the ones who love you—that's what took you.

HERALD.

You mean 535
the land and the armies hungered for each other?

LEADER.

There were times I thought I'd faint with longing.

HERALD.

So anxious for the armies, why?

LEADER.

For years now,
only my silence kept me free from harm.

HERALD.

What,
with the kings gone did someone threaten you?

LEADER.

So much . . . 540
now as you say, it would be good to die.

HERALD.

True, we *have* done well.
Think back in the years and what have you?
A few runs of luck, a lot that's bad.
Who but a god can go through life unmarked? 545

A long, hard pull we had, if I would tell it all.
The iron rations, penned in the gangways
hock by jowl like sheep. Whatever miseries
break a man, our quota, every sunstarved day.

Then on the beaches it was worse. Dug in 550
under the enemy ramparts—deadly going.
Out of the sky, out of the marshy flats
the dews soaked us, turned the ruts we fought from

into gullies, made our gear, our scalps
crawl with lice.
And talk of the cold, 555
the sleet to freeze the gulls, and the big snows
come avalanching down from Ida. Oh but the heat,
the sea and the windless noons, the swells asleep,
dropped to a dead calm . . .

But why weep now? 560
It's over for us, over for them.
The dead can rest and never rise again;
no need to call their muster. We're alive,
do we have to go on raking up old wounds?
Good-by to all that. Glad I am to say it. 565

For us, the remains of the Greek contingents,
the good wins out, no pain can tip the scales,
not now. So shout this boast to the bright sun—
fitting it is—wing it over the seas and rolling earth:
"Once when an Argive expedition captured Troy 570
they hauled these spoils back to the gods of Greece,
they bolted them high across the temple doors,
the glory of the past!"
And hearing that,
men will applaud our city and our chiefs,
and Zeus will have the hero's share of fame— 575
he did the work.
That's all I have to say.

LEADER.
I'm convinced, glad that I was wrong.
Never too old to learn; it keeps me young.

[CLYTAEMNESTRA *enters with her women.*]

First the house and the queen, it's their affair,
but I can taste the riches.

CLYTAEMNESTRA.
I cried out long ago!— 580
for joy, when the first herald came burning
through the night and told the city's fall.
And there were some who smiled and said,
"A few fires persuade you Troy's in ashes.
Women, women, elated over nothing." 585

You made me seem deranged.
For all that I sacrificed—a woman's way,
you'll say—station to station on the walls
we lifted cries of triumph that resounded

in the temples of the gods. We lulled and blessed 590
the fires with myrrh and they consumed our victims.

[*Turning to the* HERALD.]

But enough. Why prolong the story?
From the king himself I'll gather all I need.
Now for the best way to welcome home
my lord, my good lord . . .
No time to lose! 595
What dawn can feast a woman's eyes like this?
I can see the light, the husband plucked from war
by the Saving God and open wide the gates.

Tell him that, and have him come with speed,
the people's darling—how they long for him. 600
And for his wife,
may he return and find her true at hall,
just as the day he left her, faithful to the last.
A watchdog gentle to him alone,

[*Glancing toward the palace.*]

savage
to those who cross his path. I have not changed. 605
The strains of time can never break our seal.
In love with a new lord, in ill repute I am
as practiced as I am in dyeing bronze.

That is my boast, teeming with the truth.
I am proud, a woman of my nobility— 610
I'd hurl it from the roofs!

[*She turns sharply, enters the palace.*]

LEADER.
She speaks well, but it takes no seer to know
she only says what's right.

[*The* HERALD *attempts to leave; the* LEADER *takes him by the arm.*]

Wait, one thing.
Menelaus, is he home too, safe with the men?
The power of the land—dear king. 615

HERALD.
I doubt that lies will help my friends,
in the lean months to come.

LEADER.
Help us somehow, tell the truth as well.

But when the two conflict it's hard to hide—
out with it.

HERALD.
He's lost, gone from the fleets! 620
He and his ship, it's true.

LEADER.
After you watched him
pull away from Troy? Or did some storm
attack you all and tear him off the line?

HERALD.
There,
like a marksman, the whole disaster cut to a word.

LEADER.
How do the escorts give him out—dead or alive? 625

HERALD.
No clear report. No one knows . . .
only the wheeling sun that heats the earth to life.

LEADER.
But then the storm—how did it reach the ships?
How did it end? Were the angry gods on hand?

HERALD.
This blessed day, ruin it with *them?* 630
Better to keep their trophies far apart.
When a runner comes, his face in tears,
saddled with what his city dreaded most,
the armies routed, two wounds in one,
one to the city, one to hearth and home . . . 635
our best men, droves of them, victims
herded from every house by the two-barb whip
that Ares[31] likes to crack,
that charioteer
who packs destruction shaft by shaft,
careening on with his brace of bloody mares— 640
When he comes in, I tell you, dragging that much pain,
wail your battle-hymn to the Furies, and high time!

But when he brings salvation home to a city
singing out her heart—
how can I mix the good with so much bad 645
and blurt out this?—
"Storms swept the Greeks,
and not without the anger of the gods!"

Those enemies for ages, fire and water,
sealed a pact and showed it to the world—
they crushed our wretched squadrons.
Night looming, 650
breakers lunging in for the kill

[31] God of war.

and the black gales come brawling out of the north—
ships ramming, prow into hooking prow, gored
by the rush-and-buck of hurricane pounding rain
by the cloudburst—
ships stampeding into the darkness, 655
lashed and spun by the savage shepherd's hand!

But when the sun comes up to light the skies
I see the Aegean heaving into a great bloom
of corpses . . . Greeks, the pick of a generation
scattered through the wrecks and broken spars. 660

But not us, not our ship, our hull untouched.
Someone stole us away or begged us off.
No mortal—a god, death grip on the tiller,
or lady luck herself, perched on the helm,
she pulled us through, she saved us. Aye, 665
we'll never battle the heavy surf at anchor,
never shipwreck up some rocky coast.

But once we cleared that sea-hell, not even
trusting luck in the cold light of day,
we battened on our troubles, they were fresh— 670
the armada punished, bludgeoned into nothing.

And now if one of them still has the breath
he's saying *we* are lost. Why not?
We say the same of him. Well,
here's to the best.
And Menelaus? 675
Look to it, he's come back, and yet . . .
if a shaft of the sun can track him down,
alive, and his eyes full of the old fire—
thanks to the strategies of Zeus, Zeus
would never tear the house out by the roots— 680
then there's hope our man will make it home.

You've heard it all. Now you have the truth.

[*Rushing out.*]

CHORUS.
Who—what power named the name that drove your fate?—[32]
what hidden brain could divine your future,

[32] The foregoing inquiries about Menelaus lead naturally to the theme of this choral passage: the significance of Helen, whom Menelaus was bringing home. The chorus, punning on the root meaning of Helen's name in Greek ("destruction," rendered here as "hell"), see her as an agent of ruin inflicted as just punishment for Paris and the Trojans. She is also, however, a scourge to Greece and to the house of Atreus.

steer that word to the mark, 685
to the bride of spears,
the whirlpool churning armies,
Oh for all the world a Helen!
Hell at the prows, hell at the gates
hell on the men-of-war, 690
from her lair's sheer veils she drifted
launched by the giant western wind,
and the long tall waves of men in armor,
huntsmen trailing the oarblades' dying spoor[33]
slipped into her moorings, 695
Simois'[34] mouth that chokes with foliage,
bayed for bloody strife,

for Troy's Blood Wedding Day—she drives her word,
her burning will to the birth, the Fury
late but true to the cause, 700
to the tables shamed
and Zeus who guards the hearth—
the Fury makes the Trojans pay!
Shouting their hymns, hymns for the bride
hymns for the kinsmen doomed 705
to the wedding march of Fate,
Troy changed her tune in her late age,
and I think I hear the dirges mourning
"Paris, born and groomed for the bed of Fate!"
They mourn with their life breath, 710
they sing their last, the sons of Priam
born for bloody slaughter.

So a man[35] once reared
a lion cub at hall, snatched
from the breast, still craving milk 715
in the first flush of life.
A captivating pet for the young,
and the old men adored it, pampered it
in their arms, day in, day out,
like an infant just born. 720
Its eyes on fire, little beggar,
fawning for its belly, slave to food.

But it came of age
and the parent strain broke out
and it paid its breeders back. 725

[33]The track of a wild animal. Having sailed from her home to Troy, Helen is pursued by the Greek fleet ("huntsmen") sailing to recover her.

[34]A river near Troy.

[35]Helen is compared to a lion cub reared as a household pet until, having grown, its latent nature asserts itself in bloodshed. The house can be the Trojans' or that of Agamemnon and Menelaus.

Grateful it was,[36] it went
through the flock to prepare a feast,
an illicit orgy—the house swam with blood,
none could resist that agony—
massacre vast and raw! 730
From god there came a priest of ruin,
adopted by the house to lend it warmth.

And the first sensation Helen brought to Troy . . .
call it a spirit
shimmer of winds dying 735
glory light as gold
shaft of the eyes dissolving, open bloom
that wounds the heart with love.
But veering wild in mid-flight
she whirled her wedding on to a stabbing end, 740
slashed at the sons of Priam—hearthmate, friend to the death,
sped by Zeus who speeds the guest,
a bride of tears, a Fury.

There's an ancient saying,[37] old as man himself:
men's prosperity 745
never will die childless,
once full-grown it breeds.
Sprung from the great good fortune in the race
comes bloom on bloom of pain—
insatiable wealth. But not I, 750
I alone say this. Only the reckless act
can breed impiety, multiplying crime on crime,
while the house kept straight and just
is blessed with radiant children.

But ancient Violence longs to breed, 755
new Violence comes
when its fatal hour comes, the demon comes
to take her toll—no war, no force, no prayer
can hinder the midnight Fury stamped
with parent Fury moving through the house. 760

But Justice shines in sooty hovels,
loves the decent life.
From proud halls crusted with gilt by filthy hands
she turns her eyes to find the pure in spirit—
spurning the wealth stamped counterfeit with praise, 765
she steers all things toward their destined end.

[36] Grim humor; the grown lion is like someone thankfully repaying parents for rearing him.
[37] In the following lines the chorus echoes the traditional belief that excess of prosperity in itself brings on punishment by the gods, but the old men go on to insist that the more important cause is evil deeds. Wealth acquired through evil combines both incitements to divine retribution.

[AGAMEMNON *enters in his chariot, his plunder borne before him by his entourage; behind him, half hidden, stands* CASSANDRA.[38] *The old men press toward him.*]

Come, my king, the scourge of Troy,
the true son of Atreus—
How to salute you, how to praise you
neither too high nor low, but hit 770
the note of praise that suits the hour?
So many prize some brave display,
they prefer some flaunt of honor
once they break the bounds.
When a man fails they share his grief, 775
but the pain can never cut them to the quick.
When a man succeeds they share his glory,
torturing their faces into smiles.
But the good shepherd[39] knows his flock.
When the eyes seem to brim with love 780
and it is only unction,
he will know, better than we can know.
That day you marshaled the armies
all for Helen—no hiding it now—
I drew you in my mind in black; 785
you seemed a menace at the helm,
sending men to the grave
to bring her home, that hell on earth.
But now from the depths of trust and love
I say Well fought, well won— 790
the end is worth the labor!
Search, my king, and learn at last
who stayed at home and kept their faith
and who betrayed the city.

AGAMEMNON.

First,
with justice I salute my Argos and my gods, 795
my accomplices who brought me home and won
my rights from Priam's Troy—the just gods.
No need to hear our pleas. Once for all
they consigned their lots to the urn[40] of blood,
they pitched on death for men, annihilation 800
for the city. Hope's hand, hovering
over the urn of mercy, left it empty.

[38]A prophetess, daughter of King Priam of Troy, taken captive by Agamemnon.
[39]Agamemnon, regarded as protector of his subjects.
[40]In deciding law cases, an Athenian juror cast his vote by dropping a pebble into one of two urns signifying conviction and acquittal.

Look for the smoke—it is the city's seamark,
building even now.
The storms of ruin live!
Her last dying breath, rising up from the ashes 805
send us gales of incense rich in gold.

For that we must thank the gods with a sacrifice
our sons will long remember. For their mad outrage
of a queen we raped their city—we were right.
The beast of Argos, foals of the wild mare,[41] 810
thousands massed in armor rose on the night
the Pleiades[42] went down, and crashing through
their walls our bloody lion lapped its fill,
gorging on the blood of kings.
Our thanks to the gods,
long drawn out, but it is just the prelude. 815

[CLYTAEMNESTRA *approaches with her women; they are carrying dark red tapestries.* AGAMEMNON *turns to the leader.*]

And your concern, old man, is on my mind.
I hear you and agree, I will support you.
How rare, men with the character to praise
a friend's success without a trace of envy,
poison to the heart—it deals a double blow. 820
Your own losses weigh you down but then,
look at your neighbor's fortune and you weep.
Well I know. I understand society,
the fawning mirror of the proud.
My comrades . . .
they're shadows, I tell you, ghosts of men 825
who swore they'd die for me. Only Odysseus:
I dragged that man to the wars but once in harness
he was a trace-horse, he gave his all for me.
Dead or alive, no matter, I can praise him.

And now this cause involving men and gods. 830
We must summon the city for a trial,
found a national tribunal. Whatever's healthy,
shore it up with law and help it flourish.
Wherever something calls for drastic cures
we make our noblest effort: amputate or wield 835
the healing iron, burn the cancer at the roots.

[41] Agamemnon refers to the Greek soldiers who, hidden inside the wooden horse, brought about the fall of Troy. The story is told in Virgil's *Aeneid,* Book II.

[42] The setting of this constellation is associated in the present context with the approach of winter and storms.

Now I go to my father's house—
I give the gods my right hand, my first salute.
The ones who sent me forth have brought me home.

[*He starts down from the chariot, looks at* CLYTAEMNESTRA, *stops, and offers up a prayer.*]

Victory, you have sped my way before, 840
now speed me to the last.

[CLYTAEMNESTRA *turns from the king to the* CHORUS.]

CLYTAEMNESTRA.
Old nobility of Argos
gathered here, I am not ashamed to tell you
how I love the man. I am older,
and the fear dies away . . . I am human.
Nothing I say was learned from others. 845
This is my life, my ordeal, long as the siege
he laid at Troy and more demanding.

First,
when a woman sits at home and the man is gone,
the loneliness is terrible,
unconscionable . . . 850
and the rumors spread and fester,
a runner comes with something dreadful,
close on his heels the next and his news worse,
and they shout it out and the whole house can hear;
and wounds—if he took one wound for each report 855
to penetrate these walls, he's gashed like a dragnet,
more, if he had only died . . .
for each death that swelled his record, he could boast
like a triple-bodied Geryon[43] risen from the grave,
"Three shrouds I dug from the earth, one for every body 860
that went down!"
The rumors broke like fever,
broke and then rose higher. There were times
they cut me down and eased my throat from the noose.
I wavered between the living and the dead.

[*Turning to* AGAMEMNON.]

And so
our child is gone, not standing by our side, 865

[43]A three-headed giant.

the bond of our dearest pledges, mine and yours;
by all rights our child should be here . . .
Orestes.[44] You seem startled.
You needn't be. Our loyal brother-in-arms
will take good care of him, Strophios the Phocian. 870
He warned from the start we court two griefs in one.
You risk all on the wars—and what if the people
rise up howling for the king, and anarchy
should dash our plans?
Men, it is their nature,
trampling on the fighter once he's down. 875
Our child is gone. That is my self-defense
and it is true.
For me, the tears that welled
like springs are dry. I have no tears to spare.
I'd watch till late at night, my eyes still burn,
I sobbed by the torch I lit for you alone. 880

[*Glancing toward the palace.*]

I never let it die . . . but in my dreams
the high thin wail of a gnat would rouse me,
piercing like a trumpet—I could see you
suffer more than all
the hours that slept with me could ever bear. 885

I endured it all. And now, free of grief,
I would salute that man the watchdog of the fold,
the mainroyal, saving stay[45] of the vessel,
rooted oak that thrusts the roof sky-high,
the father's one true heir. 890
Land at dawn to the shipwrecked past all hope,
light of the morning burning off the night of storm,
the cold clear spring to the parched horseman—
O the ecstasy, to flee the yoke of Fate!

It is right to use the titles he deserves. 895
Let envy keep her distance. We have suffered
long enough.

[*Reaching toward* AGAMEMNON.]

[44] One of the many ironies in Clytaemnestra's speech; the preceding lines suggest Orestes' dead sister Iphigeneia. Clytaemnestra has sent Orestes away to the city of Phocis, to clear the way for Aegisthus and herself, or to protect Orestes against civil mutiny while his father was away, or perhaps for both reasons.

[45] A cable that supports the mainroyal mast of a ship.

Come to me now, my dearest,
down from the car of war, but never set the foot
that stamped out Troy on earth again, my great one.

Women, why delay? You have your orders. 900
Pave his way with tapestries.

[*They begin to spread the crimson tapestries between the king and the palace doors.*]

Quickly.
Let the red stream flow and bear him home
to the home he never hoped to see[46]—Justice,
lead him in!
Leave all the rest to me.
The spirit within me never yields to sleep. 905
We will set things right, with the gods' help.
We will do whatever Fate requires.

AGAMEMNON.
There
is Leda's daughter,[47] the keeper of my house.
And the speech to suit my absence, much too long.
But the praise that does us justice, 910
let it come from others, then we prize it.
This—
You treat me like a woman, groveling, gaping up at me!
What am I, some barbarian peacocking out of Asia?
Never cross my path with robes and draw the lightning.
Never—only the gods deserve the pomps of honor 915
and the stiff brocades of fame. To walk on them . . .
I am human, and it makes my pulses stir
with dread.[48]
Give me the tributes of a man
and not a god, a little earth to walk on,
not this gorgeous work. 920
There is no need to sound my reputation.
I have a sense of right and wrong, what's more—
heaven's proudest gift. Call no man blest
until he ends his life in peace, fulfilled.
If I can live by what I say, I have no fear. 925

CLYTAEMNESTRA.
One thing more. Be true to your ideals and tell me—

[46]A grim pun: both "the home in Argos he had lost hope of seeing again" and "the home (death) he hoped never to see."

[47]Clytaemnestra; she and Helen are half-sisters, Leda being mother to both.

[48]Agamemnon feels (or perhaps feigns) reluctance to commit an act of *hubris*, the overweening pride of a man which will bring on angry retribution by the gods.

AGAMEMNON.

True to my ideals? Once I violate them I am lost.

CLYTAEMNESTRA.

Would you have sworn this act[49] to god in a time of terror?

AGAMEMNON.

Yes, if a prophet called for a last, drastic rite.

CLYTAEMNESTRA.

But Priam—can you see him if he had your success? 930

AGAMEMNON.

Striding on the tapestries of god, I see him now.

CLYTAEMNESTRA.

And *you* fear the reproach of common men?

AGAMEMNON.

The voice of the people—aye, they have enormous power.

CLYTAEMNESTRA.

Perhaps, but where's the glory without a little gall?[50]

AGAMEMNON.

And where's the woman in all this lust for glory? 935

CLYTAEMNESTRA.

But the great victor—it becomes him to give away.

AGAMEMNON.

Victory in this . . . war of ours, it means so much to you?

CLYTAEMNESTRA.

O give way! The power is yours[51] if you surrender
all of your own free will to me.

AGAMEMNON.

Enough.

If you are so determined— 940

[*Turning to the women, pointing to his boots.*]

Let someone help me off with these at least.
Old slaves, they've stood me well.

Hurry,

and while I tread his splendors dyed red in the sea,[52]
may no god watch and strike me down with envy
from on high. I feel such shame— 945
to tread the life of the house, a kingdom's worth
of silver in the weaving.

[49] Clytaemnestra refers to the act of walking on the splendid "red carpet." She also has in mind Agamemnon's willingness in the past to commit an outrage like the killing of his daughter when such an outrage served his purpose.

[50] Clytaemnestra implies that great men must be prepared to endure the "gall" of inferior men's envy.

[51] That is, "If you yield freely and magnanimously to my whim, it is you who will have overcome me" (in their little dispute, what Agamemnon calls "this . . . war of ours").

[52] The red dye of the tapestry-carpet was derived from a kind of sea snail.

[*He steps down from the chariot to the tapestries and reveals* CASSANDRA, *dressed in the sacred regalia, the fillets,*[53] *robes, and scepter of* APOLLO.]

Done is done.
Escort this stranger in, be gentle.
Conquer with compassion. Then the gods
shine down upon you, gently. No one chooses 950
the yoke of slavery, not of one's free will—
and she least of all. The gift of the armies,
flower and pride of all the wealth we won,
she follows me from Troy.
And now,
since you have brought me down with your insistence, 955
just this once I enter my father's house,
trampling royal crimson as I go.

[*He takes his first steps and pauses.*]

CLYTAEMNESTRA.
There is the sea
and who will drain it dry? Precious as silver,[54]
inexhaustible, ever-new, it breeds the more we reap it—
tides on tides of crimson dye our robes blood-red. 960
Our lives are based on wealth, my king,
the gods have seen to that.
Destitution, our house has never heard the word.
I would have sworn to tread on legacies of robes,
at one command from an oracle, deplete the house— 965
suffer the worst to bring that dear life back!

[*Encouraged,* AGAMEMNON *strides to the entrance.*]

When the root lives on, the new leaves come back,
spreading a dense shroud of shade across the house
to thwart the Dog Star's[55] fury. So you return
to the father's hearth, you bring us warmth in winter 970
like the sun—
And you are Zeus when Zeus
tramples the bitter virgin grape for new wine[56]
and the welcome chill steals through the halls, at last
the master moves among the shadows of his house, fulfilled.

[53] Ribbons. Cassandra had been wooed by Apollo, the god of prophecy, but because she resisted him, she had been cursed with the gift of prophesying to hearers who would always refuse to believe her.
[54] The red fabric had silver woven into it.
[55] The star Sirius, considered as a harbinger of killing heat, disease, and madness.
[56] An allusion to the shedding of the young Iphigeneia's blood.

[AGAMEMNON *goes over the threshold; the women gather up the tapestries while* CLYTAEMNESTRA *prays.*]

Zeus, Zeus, master of all fulfillment, now fulfill our prayers— 975
speed our rites to their fulfillment once for all!

[*She enters the palace, the doors close, the old men huddle in terror.*]

CHORUS.
Why, why does it rock me,[57] never stops,
this terror beating down my heart,
this seer that sees it all—
it beats its wings, uncalled unpaid 980
thrust on the lungs
the mercenary song beats on and on
singing a prophet's strain—
and I can't throw it off
like dreams that make no sense, 985
and the strength drains
that filled the mind with trust,
and the years drift by and the driven sand
has buried the mooring lines
that churned when the armored squadrons cut for Troy . . . 990
and now I believe it, I can prove he's home,
my own clear eyes for witness—
Agamemnon!
Still it's chanting, beating deep so deep in the heart
this dirge of the Furies, oh dear god,
not fit for the lyre,[58] its own master 995
it kills our spirit
kills our hopes
and it's real, true, no fantasy—
stark terror whirls the brain
and the end is coming 1000
Justice comes to birth—
I pray my fears prove false and fall
and die and never come to birth!
Even exultant health, well we know,
exceeds its limits,[59] comes so near disease 1005
it can breach the wall between them.

[57] The anguished choral song that follows expresses two levels of awareness by the chorus: (1) its consciousness of the old hereditary curse on the lineage of Atreus and (2) the more immediate suspicion of Clytaemnestra based on the knowledge of her adulterous relationship with Aegisthus.

[58] Not fit for joyous song.

[59] The principle of the golden mean, of steering between too little and too much, applies even to health, according to the Chorus.

Even a man's fate, held true on course,
in a blinding flash rams some hidden reef;
but if caution only casts the pick of the cargo[60]—
one well-balanced cast— 1010
the house will not go down, not outright;
laboring under its wealth of grief
the ship of state rides on.

Yes, and the great green bounty of god,
sown in the furrows year by year and reaped each fall 1015
can end the plague of famine.

But a man's lifeblood
is dark and mortal.
Once it wets the earth
what song can sing it back? 1020
Not even the master-healer[61]
who brought the dead to life—
Zeus stopped the man before he did more harm.

Oh, if only the gods had never forged
the chain that curbs our excess, 1025
one man's fate curbing the next man's fate,
my heart would outrace my song, I'd pour out all I feel—
but no, I choke with anguish,
mutter through the nights.
Never to ravel out a hope in time 1030
and the brain is swarming, burning—

[CLYTAEMNESTRA *emerges from the palace and goes to* CASSANDRA, *impassive in the chariot.*]

CLYTAEMNESTRA.

Won't you come inside? I mean you, Cassandra.
Zeus in all his mercy wants you to share
some victory libations[62] with the house.
The slaves are flocking. Come, lead them 1035
up to the altar of the god who guards
our dearest treasures.
Down from the chariot,
no time for pride. Why even Heracles,[63]
they say, was sold into bondage long ago,

[60] A ship in peril can be saved by jettisoning cargo so as to lighten it; similarly, a man may salvage his happiness and his "house" by forsaking his most prized wealth.

[61] Asclepios, a physician so gifted that he brought a dead man back to life. As punishment for thus violating the natural order, Zeus killed him with a thunderbolt.

[62] Ritual pourings of liquids.

[63] The heroic Heracles (Hercules) had served as a slave to Omphale, queen of Lydia in Asia Minor.

he had to endure the bitter bread of slaves. 1040
But if the yoke descends on you, be grateful
for a master born and reared in ancient wealth.
Those who reap a harvest past their hopes[64]
are merciless to their slaves.
From us
you will receive what custom says is right. 1045

[CASSANDRA *remains impassive.*]

LEADER.
It's *you* she is speaking to, it's all too clear.
You're caught in the nets of doom—obey
if you can obey, unless you cannot bear to.

CLYTAEMNESTRA.
Unless she's like a swallow, possessed
of her own barbaric song, strange, dark. 1050
I speak directly as I can—she must obey.

LEADER.
Go with her. Make the best of it, she's right.
Step down from the seat, obey her.

CLYTAEMNESTRA.
Do it *now*—
I have no time to spend outside. Already
the victims crowd the hearth, the Navelstone,[65] 1055
to bless this day of joy I never hoped to see!—
our victims[66] waiting for the fire and the knife,
and you,
if you want to taste our mystic rites, come now.
If my words can't reach you—

[*Turning to the* LEADER.]

Give her a sign, 1060
one of her exotic handsigns.

LEADER.
I think
the stranger needs an interpreter, someone clear.
She's like a wild creature, fresh caught.

CLYTAEMNESTRA.
She's mad,
her evil genius murmuring in her ears.
She comes from a *city* fresh caught. 1065
She must learn to take the cutting bridle

[64] Men whose wealth ("harvest") is not "ancient" but recent.

[65] Also the name of a stone at Apollo's shrine in Delphi; Orestes goes to that Navelstone, to be purged of his blood guilt, at the beginning of *The Eumenides*.

[66] The animals to be sacrificed in the ritual; but Clytaemnestra's statement has also a more sinister private meaning.

before she foams her spirit off in blood—
and that's the last I waste on her contempt!

[*Wheeling, re-entering the palace. The* LEADER *turns to* CASSANDRA, *who remains transfixed.*]

LEADER.
Not I, I pity her. I will be gentle.
Come, poor thing. Leave the empty chariot— 1070
Of your own free will try on the yoke of Fate.

CASSANDRA.
Aieeeeee! Earth—Mother—
Curse of the Earth—Apollo Apollo!

LEADER.
Why cry to Apollo?
He's not the god to call with sounds of mourning.

CASSANDRA.
Aieeeeee! Earth—Mother— 1075
Rape of the Earth—Apollo Apollo!

LEADER.
Again, it's a bad omen.
She cries for the god who wants no part of grief.[67]

[CASSANDRA *steps from the chariot, looks slowly toward the rooftops of the palace.*]

CASSANDRA.
God of the long road,
Apollo *Apollo* my destroyer—
you destroy me once, destroy me twice— 1080

LEADER.
She's about to sense her own ordeal, I think.
Slave that she is, the god lives on inside her.

CASSANDRA.
God of the iron marches,
Apollo *Apollo* my destroyer—
where, where have you led me now? what house— 1085

LEADER.
The house of Atreus and his sons. Really—
don't you know? It's true, see for yourself.

CASSANDRA.
No . . . the house that hates god,
an echoing womb of guilt, kinsmen
torturing kinsmen, severed heads, 1090
slaughterhouse of heroes, soil streaming blood—

[67]Apollo is more typically associated with joy.

LEADER.
A keen hound, this stranger.
Trailing murder, and murder she will find.
CASSANDRA.
See, my witnesses—
I trust to them, to the babies 1095
wailing, skewered on the sword,
their flesh charred, the father gorging on their parts—
LEADER.
We'd heard your fame as a seer,
but no one looks for seers in Argos.
CASSANDRA.
Oh no, what horror, what new plot, 1100
new agony this?—
it's growing, massing, deep in the house,
a plot, a monstrous—*thing*
to crush the loved ones, no,
there is no cure, and rescue's far away and— 1105
LEADER.
I can't read these signs; I knew the first,[68]
the city rings with them.
CASSANDRA.
You, you godforsaken—you'd do *this*?
The lord of your bed,
you bathe him . . . his body glistens, then— 1110
how to tell the climax?—
comes so quickly, see,
hand over hand shoots out, hauling ropes—
then lunge!
LEADER.
Still lost. Her riddles, her dark words of god—
I'm groping, helpless.
CASSANDRA.
No no, look *there!*— 1115
what's that? some net flung out of hell—
No, *she* is the snare,
the bedmate, deathmate, murder's strong right arm!
Let the insatiate discord in the race
rear up and shriek "Avenge the victim—stone them dead!" 1120
LEADER.
What Fury is this? Why rouse it, lift its wailing
through the house? I hear you and lose hope.
CHORUS.
Drop by drop at the heart, the gold of life ebbs out.
We are the old soldiers . . . wounds will come
with the crushing sunset of our lives. 1125
Death is close, and quick.

[68] The Leader had understood Cassandra's earlier reference to the familiar story of Thyestes' feast but does not understand her allusion to the imminent murder of Agamemnon.

CASSANDRA.

Look out! *look out!—*
Ai, drag the great bull from the mate!—
a thrash of robes, she traps him—
writhing—
black horn glints, twists—
she gores him through!
And now he buckles, look, the bath swirls red— 1130
There's stealth and murder in that caldron, do you hear?

LEADER.

I'm no judge, I've little skill with the oracles,
but even I know danger when I hear it.

CHORUS.

What good are the oracles to men? Words, more words,
and the hurt comes on us, endless words 1135
and a seer's techniques have brought us
terror and the truth.

CASSANDRA.

The agony—O I am breaking!—Fate's so hard,
and the pain that floods my voice is mine alone.
Why have you brought me here, tormented as I am? 1140
Why, unless to die with him, why else?

LEADER AND CHORUS.

Mad with the rapture—god speeds you on
to the song, the deathsong,
like the nightingale[69] that broods on sorrow,
mourns her son, her son, 1145
her life inspired with grief for him,
she lilts and shrills, dark bird that lives for night.

CASSANDRA.

The nightingale—O for a song, a fate like hers!
The gods gave her a life of ease, swathed her in wings,
no tears, no wailing. The knife waits for me. 1150
They'll splay me on the iron's double edge.

LEADER AND CHORUS.

Why?—what god hurls you on, stroke on stroke
to the long dying fall?
Why the horror clashing through your music,
terror struck to song?— 1155
why the anguish, the wild dance?
Where do your words of god and grief begin?

CASSANDRA.

Ai, the wedding, wedding of Paris,
death to the loved ones. Oh Scamander,[70]

[69] Tereus, husband of Procne, raped his wife's sister Philomela. In revenge, after being informed of the rape by her sister, Procne killed Itys, her son by Tereus, and served the son's flesh as a meal for the father. In some versions of the myth Procne was later metamorphosed into a nightingale, Philomela into a swallow. (In other versions the metamorphoses are reversed, Procne becoming the swallow and Philomela the nightingale.)

[70] A river at Troy.

you nursed my father . . . once at your banks 1160
I nursed and grew, and now at the banks
of Acheron,[71] the stream that carries sorrow,
it seems I'll chant my prophecies too soon.

LEADER AND CHORUS.
What are you saying? Wait, it's clear,
a child could see the truth, it wounds within, 1165
like a bloody fang it tears—
I hear your destiny—breaking sobs,
cries that stab the ears.

CASSANDRA.
Oh the grief, the grief of the city
ripped to oblivion. Oh the victims, 1170
the flocks my father burned at the wall,
rich herds in flames . . . no cure for the doom
that took the city after all, and I,
her last ember, I go down with her.

LEADER AND CHORUS.
You cannot stop, your song goes on— 1175
some spirit drops from the heights and treads you down
and the brutal strain grows—
your death-throes come and come and
I cannot see the end!

CASSANDRA.
Then off with the veils that hid the fresh young bride— 1180
we will see the truth.
Flare up once more, my oracle! Clear and sharp
as the wind that blows toward the rising sun,
I can feel a deeper swell now, gathering head
to break at last and bring the dawn of grief. 1185
No more riddles. I will teach you.
Come, bear witness, run and hunt with me.
We trail the old barbaric works of slaughter.

These roofs—look up—there is a dancing troupe
that never leaves. And they have their harmony 1190
but it is harsh, their words are harsh, they drink
beyond the limit. Flushed on the blood of men
their spirit grows and none can turn away
their revel breeding in the veins—the Furies!
They cling to the house for life. They sing, 1195
sing of the frenzy that began it all,
strain rising on strain, showering curses
on the man who tramples on his brother's bed.[72]

[71]A river in Hades, the underground world of the dead.

[72]Thyestes had provoked Atreus' anger by seducing his wife, thus bringing on Atreus' revenge and the lineal curse.

There. Have I hit the mark or not? Am I a fraud,
a fortune-teller babbling lies from door to door? 1200
Swear how well I know the ancient crimes
that live within this house.

LEADER.
And if I did?
Would an oath bind the wounds and heal us?
But you amaze me. Bred across the sea,
your language strange and still you sense the truth 1205
as if you had been here.

CASSANDRA.
Apollo the Prophet
introduced me to his gift.

LEADER.
A *god*—and moved with love?

CASSANDRA.
I was ashamed to tell this once,
but now . . .

LEADER.
We spoil ourselves with scruples, 1210
long as things go well.

CASSANDRA.
He came like a wrestler,
magnificent, took me down and breathed his fire
through me and—

LEADER.
You bore him a child?

CASSANDRA.
I yielded,
then at the climax I recoiled—I deceived Apollo!

LEADER.
But the god's skills—they seized you even then? 1215

CASSANDRA.
Even then I told my people all the grief to come.

LEADER.
And Apollo's anger never touched you?—is it possible?

CASSANDRA.
Once I betrayed him I could never be believed.

LEADER.
We believe you. Your visions seem so true.

CASSANDRA.
Aieeee!—
the pain, the terror! the birth-pang of the seer 1220
who tells the truth—
it whirls me, oh,
the storm comes again, the crashing chords!

Look, you see them nestling at the threshold?
Young, young in the darkness like a dream,

like children really, yes, and their loved ones 1225
brought them down . . .
their hands, they fill their hands
with their own flesh, they are serving it like food,
holding out their entrails . . . now it's clear,
I can see the armfuls of compassion, see the father
reach to taste and—
For so much suffering, 1230
I tell you, someone plots revenge.
A lion[73] who lacks a lion's heart,
he sprawled at home in the royal lair
and set a trap for the lord on his return.
My lord . . . I must wear his yoke, I am his slave. 1235
The lord of the men-of-war, he obliterated Troy—
he is so blind, so lost to that detestable hellhound[74]
who pricks her ears and fawns and her tongue draws out
her glittering words of welcome—
No, he cannot see
the stroke that Fury's hiding, stealth, murder. 1240
What outrage—the woman kills the man!
What to call
that . . . monster of Greece, and bring my quarry down?
Viper coiling back and forth?
Some sea-witch?—
Scylla[75] crouched in her rocky nest—nightmare of sailors?
Raging mother of death, storming deathless war against 1245
the ones she loves!
And how she howled in triumph,
boundless outrage. Just as the tide of battle
broke her way, she seems to rejoice that he
is safe at home from war, saved for her.

Believe me if you will. What will it matter 1250
if you won't? It comes when it comes,
and soon you'll see it face to face
and say the seer was all too true.
You will be moved with pity.

LEADER.
Thyestes' feast,
the children's flesh—that I know, 1255
and the fear shudders through me. It's true,
real, no dark signs about it. I hear the rest
but it throws me off the scent.

[73] The "lion" is Aegisthus.
[74] Clytaemnestra.
[75] A female monster, imagined as dwelling in a cave, personifying the dangerous rocks on one side of the strait of Messina, which separates Italy from Sicily. She is described in both Homer's *Odyssey* and Virgil's *Aeneid*.

CASSANDRA.

Agamemnon.

You will see him dead.

LEADER.

Peace, poor girl!

Put those words to sleep.

CASSANDRA.

No use, 1260

the Healer[76] has no hand in this affair.

LEADER.

Not if it's true—but god forbid it is!

CASSANDRA.

You pray, and they close in to kill!

LEADER.

What man prepares this, this dreadful—

CASSANDRA.

Man?

You *are* lost, to every word I've said.[77]

LEADER.

Yes— 1265

I don't see who can bring the evil off.

CASSANDRA.

And yet I know my Greek, too well.

LEADER.

So does the Delphic oracle,
but he's hard to understand.

CASSANDRA.

His *fire!*—

sears me, sweeps me again—the torture! 1270
Apollo Lord of the Light, you burn,
you blind me—

Agony!

She is the lioness,

she rears on her hind legs, she beds with the wolf
when her lion king goes ranging—

she will kill me—

Ai, the torture!

She is mixing her drugs, 1275

adding a measure more of hate for me.
She gloats as she whets the sword for him.
He brought me home and we will pay in carnage.

Why mock yourself with these—trappings, the rod,
the god's wreath, his yoke around my throat? 1280
Before I die I'll tread you—

[76]Apollo.

[77]Cassandra means that she has been referring to a woman, not a man.

[*Ripping off her regalia, stamping it into the ground.*]

Down, out,
die die die!
Now you're down. I've paid you back.
Look for another victim—I am free at last—
make her rich in all your curse and doom.

[*Staggering backward as if wrestling with a spirit tearing at her robes.*]

See, 1285
Apollo himself, his fiery hands—I feel him again,
he's stripping off my robes, the Seer's robes!
And after he looked down and saw me mocked,
even in these, his glories, mortified by friends[78]
I loved, and they hated me, they were so blind 1290
to their own demise—
I went from door to door,
I was wild with the god, I heard them call me
"Beggar! Wretch! Starve for bread in hell!"

And I endured it all, and now he will
extort me as his due. A seer for the Seer. 1295
He brings me here to die like this,
not to serve at my father's altar. No,
the block is waiting. The cleaver steams
with my life blood, the first blood drawn
for the king's last rites.

[*Regaining her composure and moving to the altar.*]

We will die, 1300
but not without some honor from the gods.
There will come another[79] to avenge us,
born to kill his mother, born
his father's champion. A wanderer, a fugitive
driven off his native land, he will come home 1305
to cope the stones of hate that menace all he loves.
The gods have sworn a monumental oath: as his father lies
upon the ground he draws him home with power like a prayer.

Then why so pitiful, why so many tears?
I have seen my city faring as she fared, 1310
and those who took her, judged by the gods,

[78] The Trojans; Cassandra's own people did not heed her.
[79] Orestes, son of Agamemnon and Clytaemnestra.

faring as they fare. I must be brave.
It is my turn to die.

[*Approaching the doors.*]

I address you as the Gates of Death.
I pray it comes with one clean stroke, 1315
no convulsions, the pulses ebbing out
in gentle death. I'll close my eyes and sleep.

LEADER.
So much pain, poor girl, and so much truth,
you've told so much. But if you *see* it coming,
clearly—how can you go to your own death, 1320
like a beast to the altar driven on by god,
and hold your head so high?

CASSANDRA.
No escape, my friends,
not now.

LEADER.
But the last hour should be savored.

CASSANDRA.
My time has come. Little to gain from flight.

LEADER.
You're brave, believe me, full of gallant heart. 1325

CASSANDRA.
Only the wretched go with praise like that.

LEADER.
But to go nobly lends a man some grace.

CASSANDRA.
My noble father—you and your noble children.

[*She nears the threshold and recoils, groaning in revulsion.*]

LEADER.
What now? what terror flings you back?
Why? Unless some horror in the brain—

CASSANDRA.
Murder. 1330
The house breathes with murder—bloody shambles![80]

LEADER.
No, no, only the victims at the hearth.

CASSANDRA.
I know that odor. I smell the open grave.

LEADER.
But the Syrian myrrh, it fills the halls with splendor,
can't you sense it?

[80]A place of bloodshed; a slaughterhouse.

CASSANDRA.

Well, I must go in now, 1335
mourning Agamemnon's death and mine.
Enough of life!

[*Approaching the doors again and crying out.*]

Friends—I cried out,
not from fear like a bird fresh caught,
but that you will testify to *how* I died.
When the queen, woman for woman, dies for me, 1340
and a man falls for the man who married grief.
That's all I ask, my friends. A stranger's gift
for one about to die.

LEADER.

Poor creature, you
and the end you see so clearly. I pity you.

CASSANDRA.

I'd like a few words more, a kind of dirge, 1345
it is my own. I pray to the sun,
the last light I'll see,
that when the avengers cut the assassins down
they will avenge me too, a slave who died,
an easy conquest.

Oh men, your destiny. 1350
When all is well a shadow can overturn it.
When trouble comes a stroke of the wet sponge,
and the picture's blotted out. And that,
I think that breaks the heart.

[*She goes through the doors.*]

CHORUS.

But the lust for power never dies— 1355
men cannot have enough.
No one will lift a hand to send it
from his door, to give it warning,
"Power, never come again!"
Take this man: the gods in glory 1360
gave him Priam's city to plunder,
brought him home in splendor like a god.
But now if he must pay for the blood
his fathers shed, and die for the deaths
he brought to pass, and bring more death 1365
to avenge his dying, show us one
who boasts himself born free
of the raging angel, once he hears—

[*Cries break out within the palace.*]

Agamemnon.

Aagh!

Struck deep—the death-blow, deep—

Leader.

Quiet. Cries,

but who? Someone's stabbed—

Agamemnon.

Aaagh, again . . . 1370

second blow—struck home.

Leader.

The work is done,
you can feel it. The king, and the great cries—
Close ranks now, find the right way out.

[*But the old men scatter, each speaks singly.*]

Chorus.

—I say send out heralds, muster the guard,
they'll save the house.

—And I say rush in now, 1375
catch them red-handed—butchery running on their blades.

—Right with you, do something—now or never!

—Look at them, beating the drum for insurrection.

—Yes,
we're wasting time. They rape the name of caution,
their hands will never sleep.

—Not a plan in sight. 1380
Let men of action do the planning too.

—I'm helpless. Who can raise the dead with words?

—What, drag out our lives? bow down to the tyrants,
the ruin of the house?

—Never, better to die
on your feet than live on your knees.

—Wait, 1385
do we take the cries for signs, prophesy like seers
and give him up for dead?

—No more suspicions,
not another word till we have proof.

—Confusion
on all sides—one thing to do. See how it stands
with Agamemnon, once and for all we'll see— 1390

[*He rushes at the doors. They open and reveal a silver caldron that holds the body of* AGAMEMNON *shrouded in bloody robes, with the body of* CASSANDRA *to his left and* CLYTAEMNESTRA *standing to his right, sword in hand. She strides toward the* CHORUS.]

CLYTAEMNESTRA.
Words, endless words I've said to serve the moment!
Now it makes me proud to tell the truth.
How else to prepare a death for deadly men
who seem to love you? How to rig the nets
of pain so high no man can overleap them? 1395

I brooded on this trial, this ancient blood feud
year by year. At last my hour came.
Here I stand and here I struck
and here my work is done.
I did it all. I don't deny it, no. 1400
He had no way to flee or fight his destiny—

[*Unwinding the robes from* AGAMEMNON*'s body, spreading them before the altar where the old men cluster around them, unified as a chorus once again.*]

our never-ending, all-embracing net, I cast it
wide for the royal haul, I coil him round and round
in the wealth, the robes of doom, and then I strike him
once, twice, and at each stroke he cries in agony— 1405
he buckles at the knees and crashes here!
And when he's down I add the third, last blow,
to the Zeus who saves the dead beneath the ground
I send that third blow home in homage like a prayer.

So he goes down, and the life is bursting out of him— 1410
great sprays of blood, and the murderous shower
wounds me, dyes me black and I, I revel
like the Earth when the spring rains come down,
the blessed gifts of god, and the new green spear
splits the sheath and rips to birth in glory! 1415

So it stands, elders of Argos gathered here.
Rejoice if you can rejoice—I glory.
And if I'd pour upon his body the libation
it deserves, what wine could match my words?
It is right and more than right. He flooded 1420
the vessel of our proud house with misery,
with the vintage of the curse and now
he drains the dregs. My lord is home at last.

LEADER.
You appall me, you, your brazen words—
exulting over your fallen king.

CLYTAEMNESTRA.
And you, 1425
you try me like some desperate woman.
My heart is steel, well you know. Praise me,
blame me as you choose. It's all one.
Here is Agamemnon, my husband made a corpse
by this right hand—a masterpiece of Justice. 1430
Done is done.

CHORUS.
Woman!—what poison cropped from the soil
or strained from the heaving sea, what nursed you,
drove you insane? You brave the curse of Greece.
You have cut away and flung away and now
the people cast you off to exile, 1435
broken with our hate.

CLYTAEMNESTRA.
And now you sentence me?—
you banish *me* from the city, curses breathing
down my neck? But *he*—
name one charge you brought against him then.
He thought no more of it than killing a beast, 1440
and his flocks were rich, teeming in their fleece,
but he sacrificed his own child, our daughter,
the agony I labored into love
to charm away the savage winds of Thrace.

Didn't the law demand you banish him?— 1445
hunt him from the land for all his guilt?
But now you witness what I've done
and you are ruthless judges.
Threaten away!
I'll meet you blow for blow. And if I fall
the throne is yours. If god decrees the reverse, 1450
late as it is, old men, you'll learn your place.

CHORUS.
Mad with ambition,
shrilling pride!—some Fury
crazed with the carnage rages through your brain—

I can see the flecks of blood inflame your eyes! 1455
But vengeance comes—you'll lose your loved ones,
stroke for painful stroke.

CLYTAEMNESTRA.

Then learn this too, the power of my oaths.
By the child's Rights I brought to birth,
by Ruin, by Fury—the three gods to whom 1460
I sacrificed this man—I swear my hopes
will never walk the halls of fear so long
as Aegisthus lights the fire on my hearth.
Loyal to me as always, no small shield
to buttress my defiance.
Here he lies. 1465
He brutalized me. The darling of all
the golden girls who spread the gates of Troy.
And here his spearprize . . . what wonders she beheld!—
the seer of Apollo shared my husband's bed,
his faithful mate who knelt at the rowing-benches, 1470
worked by every hand.
They have their rewards.
He as you know. And she, the swan[81] of the gods
who lived to sing her latest, dying song—
his lover lies beside him.
She brings a fresh, voluptuous relish to my bed! 1475

CHORUS.

Oh quickly, let me die—
no bed of labor, no, no wasting illness . . .
bear me off in the sleep that never ends,
now that he has fallen,
now that our dearest shield lies battered— 1480
Woman made him suffer,
woman struck him down.

Helen the wild, maddening Helen,
one for the many, the thousand lives
you murdered under Troy. Now you are crowned 1485
with this consummate wreath, the blood
that lives in memory, glistens age to age.
Once in the halls she walked and she was war,
angel of war, angel of agony, lighting men to death.

CLYTAEMNESTRA.

Pray no more for death, broken 1490
as you are. And never turn
your wrath on her, call her
the scourge of men, the one alone
who destroyed a myriad Greek lives—
Helen the grief that never heals. 1495

[81] In folklore, the swan sings for the first and last time just before its death.

CHORUS.

The *spirit!*—you who tread
the house and the twinborn sons[82] of Tantalus—
you empower the sisters, Fury's twins
whose power tears the heart!
Perched on the corpse your carrion raven 1500
glories in her hymn,
her screaming hymn of pride.

CLYTAEMNESTRA.

Now you set your judgment straight,
you summon *him!* Three generations
feed the spirit in the race. 1505
Deep in the veins he feeds our bloodlust—
aye, before the old wound dies
it ripens in another flow of blood.

CHORUS.

The great curse of the house, the spirit,
dead weight wrath—and you can praise it! 1510
Praise the insatiate doom that feeds
relentless on our future and our sons.
Oh all through the will of Zeus,
the cause of all, the one who works it all.
What comes to birth that is not Zeus? 1515
Our lives are pain, what part not come from god?

Oh my king, my captain,
how to salute you, how to mourn you?
What can I say with all my warmth and love?
Here in the black widow's web you lie, 1520
gasping out your life
in a sacrilegious death, dear god,
reduced to a slave's bed,
my king of men, yoked by stealth and Fate,
by the wife's hand that thrust the two-edged sword. 1525

CLYTAEMNESTRA.

You claim the work is mine, call me
Agamemnon's wife—you are so wrong.
Fleshed in the wife of this dead man,
the spirit lives within me,
our savage ancient spirit of revenge. 1530
In return for Atreus' brutal feast
he kills his perfect son—for every
murdered child, a crowning sacrifice.

CHORUS.

And *you*, innocent of his murder?
And who could swear to that? and how? . . . 1535

[82]"Sons" can refer either to Tantalus' grandsons, Thyestes and Atreus, or to his great-grandsons, Agamemnon and Menelaus, who married the sisters Clytaemnestra and Helen.

and still an avenger could arise,
bred by the fathers' crimes, and lend a hand.
He wades in the blood of brothers,
stream on mounting stream—black war erupts
and where he strides revenge will stride, 1540
clots will mass for the young who were devoured.

Oh my king, my captain,
how to salute you, how to mourn you?
What can I say with all my warmth and love?
Here in the black widow's web you lie, 1545
gasping out your life
in a sacrilegious death, dear god,
reduced to a slave's bed,
my king of men, yoked by stealth and Fate,
by the wife's hand that thrust the two-edged sword. 1550

CLYTAEMNESTRA.
No slave's death, I think—
no stealthier than the death he dealt
our house and the offspring of our loins,
Iphigeneia, girl of tears.
Act for act, wound for wound! 1555
Never exult in Hades, swordsman,
here you are repaid. By the sword
you did your work and by the sword you die.

CHORUS.
The mind reels—where to turn?
All plans dashed, all hope! I cannot think . . . 1560
the roofs are toppling, I dread the drumbeat thunder
the heavy rains of blood will crush the house
the first light rains are over—
Justice brings new acts of agony, yes,
on new grindstones Fate is grinding sharp the sword of Justice. 1565

Earth, dear Earth,
if only you'd drawn me under
long before I saw him huddled
in the beaten silver bath.
Who will bury him, lift his dirge? 1570

[*Turning to* CLYTAEMNESTRA.]

You, can you dare *this?*
To kill your lord with your own hand
then mourn his soul with tributes, terrible tributes—
do his enormous works a great dishonor.
This godlike man, this hero. Who at the grave 1575
will sing his praises, pour the wine of tears?
Who will labor there with truth of heart?

CLYTAEMNESTRA.

This is no concern of yours.
The hand that bore and cut him down
will hand him down to Mother Earth. 1580
This house will never mourn for him.
Only our daughter Iphigeneia,
by all rights, will rush to meet him
first at the churning straits,
the ferry[83] over tears— 1585
she'll fling her arms around her father,
pierce him with her love.

CHORUS.

Each charge meets countercharge.
None can judge between them. Justice.
The plunderer plundered, the killer pays the price. 1590
The truth still holds while Zeus still holds the throne:
the one who acts must suffer—
that is law. Who, who can tear from the veins
the bad seed, the curse? The race is welded to its ruin.

CLYTAEMNESTRA.

At last you see the future and the truth! 1595
But I will swear a pact with the spirit
born within us. I embrace his works,
cruel as they are but done at last,
if he will leave our house[84]
in the future, bleed another line 1600
with kinsmen murdering kinsmen.
Whatever he may ask. A few things
are all I need, once I have purged
our fury to destroy each other—
purged it from our halls.

[AEGISTHUS *has emerged from the palace with his bodyguard and stands triumphant over the body of* AGAMEMNON.]

AEGISTHUS.

O what a brilliant day 1605
it is for vengeance! Now I can say once more
there are gods in heaven avenging men,
blazing down on all the crimes of earth.
Now at last I see this man brought down
in the Furies' tangling robes. It feasts my eyes— 1610
he pays for the plot his father's hand contrived.

[83] The boat in which Charon ferried the dead across the river Styx to Hades.

[84] As the later plays of the triology show, there is sad irony in Clytaemnestra's hope that her deed of revenge will have ended the chain of retributive acts.

Atreus, this man's father, was king of Argos.
My father, Thyestes—let me make this clear—
Atreus' brother challenged him for the crown,
and Atreus drove him out of house and home 1615
then lured him back, and home Thyestes came,
poor man, a suppliant to his own hearth,
to pray that Fate might save him.
So it did.
There was no dying, no staining our native ground
with *his* blood. Thyestes was the guest, 1620
and this man's godless father—

[*Pointing to* AGAMEMNON.]

the zeal of the host outstripping a brother's love,
made my father a feast that seemed a feast for gods,
a love feast of his children's flesh.
He cuts
the extremities, feet and delicate hands 1625
into small pieces, scatters them over the dish
and serves it to Thyestes throned on high.
He picks at the flesh he cannot recognize,
the soul of innocence eating the food of ruin—
look,

[*Pointing to the bodies at his feet.*]

that feeds upon the house! And then, 1630
when he sees the monstrous thing he's done, he shrieks,
he reels back head first and vomits up that butchery,
tramples the feast—brings down the curse of Justice:
"Crash to ruin, all the race of Pleisthenes,[85] crash down!"

So you see him, down. And I, the weaver of Justice, 1635
plotted out the kill. Atreus drove us into exile,
my struggling father and I, a babe-in-arms,
his last son, but I became a man
and Justice brought me home. I was abroad
but I reached out and seized my man, 1640
link by link I clamped the fatal scheme
together. Now I could die gladly, even I—
now I see this monster in the nets of Justice.

LEADER.

Aegisthus, you revel in pain—you sicken me.
You say you killed the king in cold blood, 1645
singlehanded planned his pitiful death?
I say there's no escape. In the hour of judgment,

[85]Apparently an ancestor of Agamemnon, his exact identity is vague.

trust to this, your head will meet the people's
rocks and curses.

AEGISTHUS.

You say! you slaves at the oars—
while the master on the benches cracks the whip? 1650
You'll learn, in your late age, how much it hurts
to teach old bones their place. We have techniques—
chains and the pangs of hunger,
two effective teachers, excellent healers.
They can even cure old men of pride and gall. 1655
Look—can't you see? The more you kick
against the pricks, the more you suffer.

LEADER.

You, pathetic—
the king had just returned from battle.
You waited out the war and fouled his lair, 1660
you planned my great commander's fall.

AEGISTHUS.

Talk on—
you'll scream for every word, my little Orpheus.[86]
We'll see if the world comes dancing to your song,
your absurd barking—snarl your breath away!
I'll make you dance, I'll bring you all to heel. 1665

LEADER.

You rule Argos? You who schemed his death
but cringed to cut him down with your own hand?

AEGISTHUS.

The treachery was the woman's work, clearly.
I was a marked man, his enemy for ages.
But I will use his riches, stop at nothing 1670
to civilize his people. All but the rebel:
him I'll yoke and break—
no cornfed colt, running free in the traces.
Hunger, ruthless mate of the dark torture-chamber,
trains her eyes upon him till he drops! 1675

LEADER.

Coward, why not kill the man yourself?
Why did the woman, the corruption of Greece
and the gods of Greece, have to bring him down?
Orestes—

If he still sees the light of day,
bring him home, good Fates, home to kill 1680
this pair at last. Our champion in slaughter!

AEGISTHUS.

Bent on insolence? Well, you'll learn, quickly.
At them, men—you have your work at hand!

[86] The archetypal poet-musician whose song compelled even nature to listen. See, for example, Ovid's *Metamorphoses*, Book X.

[*His men draw swords; the old men take up their sticks.*]

LEADER.
At them, fist at the hilt, to the last man—
AEGISTHUS.
Fist at the hilt, I'm not afraid to die. 1685
LEADER.
It's death you want and death you'll have—
we'll make that word your last.

[CLYTAEMNESTRA *moves between them, restraining* AEGISTHUS.]

CLYTAEMNESTRA.
No more, my dearest,
no more grief. We have too much to reap
right here, our mighty harvest of despair.
Our lives are based on pain. No bloodshed now. 1690

Fathers of Argos, turn for home before you act
and suffer for it. What we did was destiny.
If we could end the suffering, how we would rejoice.
The spirit's brutal hoof has struck our heart.
And that is what a woman has to say. 1695
Can you accept the truth?

[CLYTAEMNESTRA *turns to leave.*]

AEGISTHUS.
But these . . . mouths
that bloom in filth—spitting insults in my teeth.
You tempt your fates, you insubordinate dogs—
to hurl abuse at me, your master!
LEADER.
No Greek
worth his salt would grovel at your feet. 1700
AEGISTHUS.
I—I'll stalk you all your days!
LEADER.
Not if the spirit brings Orestes home.
AEGISTHUS.
Exiles feed on hope—well I know.
LEADER.
More,
gorge yourself to bursting—soil justice, while you can.
AEGISTHUS.
I promise you, you'll pay, old fools—in good time too! 1705
LEADER.
Strut on your own dunghill, you cock beside your mate.

CLYTAEMNESTRA.
Let them howl—they're impotent. You and I have power now.
We will set the house in order once for all.

[*They enter the palace; the great doors close behind them; the old men disband and wander off.*]

THE LIBATION BEARERS

CHARACTERS

ORESTES, *son of Agamemnon and Clytaemnestra*
PYLADES, *his companion*
ELECTRA, *his sister*
CHORUS OF SLAVEWOMEN AND THEIR LEADER
CLYTAEMNESTRA
CILISSA, *Orestes' old nurse*
AEGISTHUS
A servant of Aegisthus
Attendants of Orestes, bodyguard of Aegisthus

TIME AND SCENE

Several years have passed since Agamemnon's death. At Argos, before the tomb of the king and his fathers, stands an altar; behind it looms the house of Atreus. ORESTES *and* PYLADES *enter, dressed as travelers.* ORESTES *kneels and prays.*

ORESTES.
Hermes,[1] lord of the dead, look down and guard
the fathers' power. Be my savior, I beg you,
be my comrade now.
I have come home
to my own soil, an exile home at last.
Here at the mounded grave I call my father, 5
Hear me—I am crying out to you . . .

[*He cuts two locks of hair*[2] *and lays them on the grave.*]

There is a lock for Inachos[3] who nursed me
into manhood, there is one for death.

[1] The messenger of the gods, patron of human messengers and heralds. He also guided the dead to Hades.
[2] The locks were customary ritual tributes to the dead.
[3] River at Argos; Orestes pays tribute to his original fatherland as well as to his dead father, Agamemnon.

I was not here to mourn you when you died,
my father, never gave the last salute 10
when they bore your corpse away.

[ELECTRA *and a chorus of slave-women enter in procession. They are dressed in black and bear libations, moving toward* ORESTES *at the grave.*]

What's this?
Look, a company moving toward us. Women,
robed in black . . . so clear in the early light.

I wonder what they mean, what turn of fate?—
some new wound to the house? 15
Or perhaps they come to honor you, my father,
bearing cups to soothe and still the dead.
That's right, it must be . . .
Electra, I think I see *her* coming, there,
my own sister, worn, radiant in her grief— 20
Dear god, let me avenge my father's murder—
fight beside me now with all your might!

Out of their way, Pylades.[4] I must know
what they mean, these women turning toward us,
what their prayers call forth. 25

[*They withdraw behind the tomb.*]

CHORUS.[5]
Rushed from the house we come
escorting cups for the dead,
in step with the hands' hard beat,
our cheeks glistening,
flushed where the nails have raked new furrows running blood; 30
and life beats on, and through it all
we nurse our lives with tears,
to the sound of ripping linen beat our robes in sorrow,
close to the breast the beats throb
and laughter's gone and fortune throbs and throbs. 35

Aie!—bristling Terror[6] struck—
Terror the seer of the house,

[4]Son of Strophios, with whom the exiled Orestes had lived in Phokis after Clytaemnestra sent him away (see the *Agamemnon*).

[5]The chorus consists of women brought back from Troy as slaves. In the lament that follows they express grief for both the house of Atreus and that of Troy.

[6]Clytaemnestra has been frightened by a nightmare; she has therefore sent the women to Agamemnon's tomb with propitiatory libations (mixtures of honey and wine).

the nightmare ringing clear
breathed its wrath in sleep,
in the midnight watch a cry!—the voice of Terror 40
deep in the house, bursting down
on the women's darkened chambers, yes,
and the old ones, skilled at dreams, swore oaths to god and called,
"The proud dead stir under earth,
they rage against the ones who took their lives." 45

But the gifts, the empty gifts
she hopes will ward them off—
good Mother Earth!—that godless woman sends me here . . .
I dread to say her prayer.
What can redeem the blood that wets the soil? 50
Oh for the hearthfire banked with grief,
the ramparts down, a fine house down—
dark, dark, and the sun, the life is curst,
and mist enshrouds the halls
where the lords of war went down. 55

And the ancient pride no war,
no storm, no force could tame,
ringing in all men's ears, in all men's hearts is gone.
They are afraid. Success,
they bow to success, more god than god himself. 60
But Justice waits and turns the scales:
a sudden blow for some at dawn,
for some in the no man's land of dusk
her torments grow with time,
and the lethal night takes others. 65

And the blood that Mother Earth consumes
clots hard, it won't seep through, it breeds revenge
and frenzy goes through the guilty,
seething like infection, swarming through the brain.

For the one who treads a virgin's bed 70
there is no cure. All the streams of the world,
all channels run into one
to cleanse a man's red hands will swell the bloody tide.

And I . . . Fate and the gods brought down their yoke,
they ringed our city, out of our fathers' halls 75
they led us here as slaves.
And the will breaks, we kneel at their command—
our masters right or wrong!
And we beat the tearing hatred down,
behind our veils we weep for her, 80

[*Turning to* ELECTRA.]

her senseless fate.
Sorrow turns the secret heart to ice.

ELECTRA.

Dear women,
you keep the house in order, best you can;
and now you've come to the grave to say a prayer
with me, my escorts. I'll need your help with this. 85
What to say when I pour the cup of sorrow?

[*Lifting her libation cup.*]

What kindness, what prayer can touch my father?
Shall I say I bring him love for love, a woman's
love for husband? My mother, love from her?
I've no taste for that, no words to say 90
as I run the honeyed oil on father's tomb.

Or try the salute we often use at graves?
"A wreath for a wreath. Now bring the givers
gifts to match" . . . no, give them pain for pain.[7]

Or silent, dishonored, just as father died, 95
empty it out for the soil to drink and then
retrace my steps, like a slave sent out with scourings
left from the purging of the halls, and throw
the cup behind me, looking straight ahead.

Help me decide, my friends. Join me here. 100
We nurse a common hatred in the house.
Don't hide your feelings—no, fear no one.
Destiny waits us all,

[*Looking toward the tomb.*]

born free,
or slaves who labor under another's hand.
Speak to me, please. Perhaps you've had 105
a glimpse of something better.

LEADER.

I revere
your father's death-mound like an altar.
I'll say a word, now that you ask,
that comes from deep within me.

ELECTRA.

Speak on,
with everything you feel for father's grave. 110

[7] Electra possibly means "pain for the murderers to match the pain they gave my father."

LEADER.
Say a blessing as you pour, for those who love you.
ELECTRA.
And of the loved ones, whom to call my friends?
LEADER.
First yourself, then all who hate Aegisthus.
ELECTRA.
I and you. I can say a prayer for us
and then for—
LEADER.
You know, try to say it. 115
ELECTRA.
There is someone else to rally to our side?
LEADER.
Remember Orestes, even abroad and gone.
ELECTRA.
Well said, the best advice I've had.
LEADER.
Now for the murderers. Remember them and—
ELECTRA.
What?
I'm so unseasoned, teach me what to say. 120
LEADER.
Let some god or man come down upon them.
ELECTRA.
Judge or avenger, which?
LEADER.
Just say "the one who murders in return!"
ELECTRA.
How can I ask the gods for that
and keep my conscience clear?
LEADER.
How not, 125
and pay the enemy back in kind?

[ELECTRA *kneels at the grave in prayer.*]

ELECTRA.
—Herald king
of the world above and the quiet world below,
lord of the dead, my Hermes, help me now.
Tell the spirits underground to hear my prayers,
and the high watch hovering over father's roofs, 130
and have her listen too, the Earth herself
who brings all things to life and makes them strong,
then gathers in the rising tide once more.

And I will tip libations to the dead.
I call out to my father, Pity me, 135
dear Orestes too.

Rekindle the light that saves our house!
We're auctioned off, drift like vagrants now.
Mother has pawned us for a husband, Aegisthus,
her partner in her murdering.
I go like a slave,
Orestes driven from his estates while they, 140
they roll in the fruits of all your labors,
magnificent and sleek. O bring Orestes home,
with a happy twist of fate, my father. Hear me,
make me far more self-possessed than mother,
make this hand more pure. 145

These prayers for us. For our enemies I say,
Raise up your avenger, into the light, my father—
kill the killers in return, with justice!
So in the midst of prayers for good I place
this curse for them. 150
Bring up your blessings,
up into the air, led by the gods and Earth
and all the rights that bring us triumph.

[*Pouring libations on the tomb and turning to the women.*]

These are my prayers. Over them I pour libations.
Yours to adorn them with laments, to make them bloom, 155
so custom says—sing out and praise the dead.

CHORUS.
Let the tears fall, ring out and die,
die with the warlord at this bank,
this bulwark of the good, defense against the bad,
the guilt, the curse we ward away 160
with prayer and all we pour. Hear me, majesty, hear me,
lord of glory, from the darkness of your heart.
Ohhhhhh!—
Dear god, let him come! Some man
with a strong spear, born to free the house,
with the torsion bow of Scythia[8] bent for slaughter, 165
splattering shafts like a god of war—sword in fist
for the slash-and-hack of battle!

[ELECTRA *remains at the grave, staring at the ground.*]

ELECTRA.
Father,
you have it now, the earth has drunk your wine.
Wait, friends, here's news. Come share it.

[8]A region in southwest Asia, noted for its archers and their powerful bows.

LEADER.

Speak on,

my heart's a dance of fear.

ELECTRA.

A lock of hair, 170

here on the grave . . .

LEADER.

Whose? A man's?

A growing girl's?

ELECTRA.

And it has the marks,

and anyone would think—

LEADER.

What?

We're old. You're young, now you teach us.

ELECTRA.

No one could have cut this lock but I and— 175

LEADER.

Callous they are, the ones who ought to shear

the hair and mourn.

ELECTRA.

Look at the texture, just like—

LEADER.

Whose? I want to know.

ELECTRA.

Like mine, identical,

can't you see?

LEADER.

Orestes . . . he brought a gift

in secret?

ELECTRA.

It's *his*—I can see his curls. 180

LEADER.

And how could he risk the journey here?

ELECTRA.

He sent it, true, a lock to honor father.

LEADER.

All the more cause for tears. You mean

he'll never set foot on native ground again.

ELECTRA.

Yes!

It's sweeping over me too—anguish 185

like a breaker—a sword ripping through my heart!

Tears come like the winter rains that flood the gates—

can't hold them back, when I see this strand of hair.

How could I think another Greek could play

the prince with this?

She'd never cut it, 190

the murderess, my mother. She insults the name,
she and her godless spirit preying on her children.

But how, how can I come right out and say it *is*
the glory of the dearest man I know, Orestes?
Stop, I'm fawning on hope.
Oh, if only 195
it had a herald's voice, kind and human—
I'm so shaken, torn—and told me clearly
to throw it away, they severed it from a head
that I detest. Or it could sorrow with me
like a brother, aye, 200
this splendor come to honor father's grave.

We call on the gods, and the gods well know
what storms torment us, sailors whirled to nothing.
But if we are to live and reach the haven,
one small seed could grow a mighty tree— 205
Look, tracks.
A new sign to tell us more.
Footmarks . . . pairs of them, like mine.
Two outlines, two prints, his own, and there,
a fellow traveler's.

[*Putting her foot into* ORESTES' *print.*]

The heel, the curve of the arch
like twins.

[*While* ORESTES *emerges from behind the grave, she follows cautiously in his steps until they come together.*]

Step by step, my step in his . . .
we meet— 210
Oh the pain, like pangs of labor—this is madness!

ORESTES.
Pray for the future. Tell the gods they've brought
your prayers to birth, and pray that we succeed.

[ELECTRA *draws back, struggling for composure.*]

ELECTRA.
The gods—why now? What have I ever won from them?

ORESTES.
The sight you prayed to see for many years. 215

ELECTRA.
And you know the one I call?

ORESTES.

I know Orestes,

know he moves you deeply.

ELECTRA.

Yes,

but now what's come to fill my prayers?

ORESTES.

Here I am. Look no further.

No one loves you more than I.

ELECTRA.

No, 220

it's a trap, stranger . . . a net you tie around me?

ORESTES.

Then I tie myself as well.

ELECTRA.

But the pain,

you're laughing at all—

ORESTES.

Your pain is mine.

If I laugh at yours, I only laugh at mine.

ELECTRA.

Orestes— 225

can I call you?—are you really—

ORESTES.

I am!

Open your eyes. So slow to learn.

You saw the lock of hair I cut in mourning.

You scanned my tracks, you could see my marks,

your breath leapt, you all but saw me in the flesh— 230

Look—

[*Holding the lock to his temple, then to* ELECTRA'*s*.]

put it where I cut it.

It's your brother's. Try, it matches yours.

[*Removing a strip of weaving from his clothing.*]

Work of your own hand, you tamped the loom,

look, there are wild creatures in the weaving.

[*She kneels beside him, weeping; he lifts her to her feet and they embrace.*]

No, no, control yourself—don't lose yourself in joy! 235

Our loved ones, well I know, would slit our throats.

LEADER.

Dearest, the darling of your father's house,

hope of the seed we nursed with tears—you save us.
Trust to your power, win your father's house once more!

ELECTRA.

You light to my eyes, four loves in one! 240
I have to call you father, it is fate;
and I turn to you the love I gave my mother—
I despise her, she deserves it, yes,
and the love I gave my sister,[9] sacrificed
on the cruel sword, I turn to you. 245
You were my faith, my brother—
you alone restore my self-respect.

[*Praying.*]

Power and Justice, Saving Zeus, Third Zeus,[10]
almighty all in all, be with us now.

ORESTES.

Zeus, Zeus, watch over all we do, 250
fledglings reft of the noble eagle father.
He died in the coils, the viper's dark embrace.
We are his orphans worn down with hunger,
weak, too young to haul the father's quarry
home to shelter.
Look down on us! 255
I and Electra too, I tell you, children
robbed of our father, both of us bound
in exile from our house.
And what a father—
a priest at sacrifice, he showered you
with honors. Put an end to his nestlings now 260
and who will serve you banquets rich as his?
Destroy the eagle's brood, you can never
send a sign that wins all men's belief.
Rot the stock of a proud dynastic tree—
it can never shore your altar steaming 265
with the oxen in the mornings.
Tend us—
we seem in ruins now, I know. Up from nothing
rear a house to greatness.

LEADER.

Softly, children,
white hopes of your father's hearth. Someone
might hear you, children, charmed with his own voice 270
blurt all this out to the masters. Oh, just once
to see them—live bones crackling in the fire
spitting pitch!

[9]Iphigeneia, sacrificed at Aulis. See headnote to the *Oresteia*.

[10]Zeus in his role as savior. Compare the more material and pragmatic emphasis in the following prayer to Zeus by Orestes.

ORESTES.

Apollo will never fail me, no,
his tremendous power, his oracle charges me
to see this trial through.
I can still hear the god— 275
a high voice ringing with winters of disaster,
piercing the heart within me, warm and strong,
unless I hunt my father's murderers, cut them down
in their own style—they destroyed my birthright.
"Gore them like a bull!" he called, "or pay their debt 280
with your own life, one long career of grief."

He revealed[11] so much about us,
told how the dead take root beneath the soil,
they grow with hate and plague the lives of men.
He told of the leprous boils that ride the flesh, 285
their wild teeth gnawing the mother tissue, aye,
and a white scurf spreads like cancer over these,
and worse, he told how assaults of Furies spring
to life on the father's blood . . .
You can *see* them—
the eyes burning, grim brows working over you in the dark— 290
the dark sword of the dead—your murdered kinsmen
pleading for revenge. And the madness haunts
the midnight watch, the empty terror shakes you,
harries, drives you on—an exile from your city—
a brazen whip will mutilate your back. 295

For such as us, no share in the winebowl,
no libations poured in love. You never see
your father's wrath but it pulls you from the altars.
There is no refuge, none to take you in.
A pariah, reviled, at long last you die, 300
withered in the grip of all this dying.

Such oracles are persuasive,
don't you think? And even if I am not convinced,
the rough work of the world is still to do.
So many yearnings meet and urge me on. 305
The god's commands. Mounting sorrow for father.
Besides, the lack of patrimony[12] presses hard;
and my compatriots, the glory of men
who toppled Troy with nerves of singing steel,
go at the beck and call of a brace of women. 310
Womanhearted he is[13]—if not, we'll soon see.

[11] In the following lines Orestes describes the physical, psychological, and social ills that, according to Apollo's oracle, Orestes will have to endure if he does not avenge his father's murder.

[12] What Orestes ought rightfully to inherit.

[13] That is, Aegisthus, who now rules Argos with Clytaemnestra.

[*The* LEADER *lights the altar fires.* ORESTES, ELECTRA, *and the* CHORUS *gather for the invocation at the grave.*]

CHORUS.
Powers of destiny, mighty queens of Fate!—
by the will of Zeus your will be done,
press on to the end now,
Justice turns the wheel. 315
"Word for word, curse for curse
be born now," Justice thunders,
hungry for retribution,
"stroke for bloody stroke be paid.
The one who acts must suffer." 320
Three generations strong the word resounds.

ORESTES.
Dear father, father of dread,
what can I do or say to reach you now?
What breath can reach from here
to the bank where you lie moored at anchor?[14] 325
What light can match your darkness? None,
but there is a kind of grace that comes
when the tears revive a proud old house
and Atreus' sons, the warlords lost and gone.

LEADER.
The ruthless jaws of the fire,[15] 330
my child, can never tame the dead,
his rage inflames his sons.
Men die and the voices rise, they light the guilty, true—
cries raised for the fathers, clear and just,
will hunt their killers harried to the end. 335

ELECTRA.
Then hear me now, my father,
it is my turn, my tears are welling now,
as child by child we come
to the tomb and raise the dirge, my father.
Your grave receives a girl in prayer 340
and a man in flight, and we are one,
and the pain is equal, whose is worse?
And who outwrestles death—what third last fall?[16]

CHORUS.
But still some god, if he desires,
may work our strains to a song of joy, 345

[14] In the world of the dead; but the phrase calls up also the memory of the Greek fleet at Aulis, where Agamemnon had committed the outrage on Iphigeneia that ultimately brought on his murder.

[15] The fire in which the dead are cremated.

[16] The deciding round in a wrestling match.

from the dirges chanted over the grave
may lift a hymn in the kings' halls
and warm the loving cup you stir this morning.

ORESTES.

If only at Troy
a Lycian[17] cut you down, my father— 350
gone, with an aura left at home behind you,
children to go their ways
and the eyes look on them bright with awe,
and the tomb you win on headlands seas away
would buoy up the house . . . 355

LEADER.

And loved by the men you loved
who died in glory, there you'd rule
beneath the earth—lord, prince,
stern aide to the giant kings who judge the shadows there.[18]
You were a king of kings when you drew breath; 360
the mace you held could make men kneel or die.

ELECTRA.

No, not under Troy!—
not dead and gone with them, my father,
hordes pierced by the spear Scamander[19] washes down.
Sooner the killers die 365
as they killed you—at the hands of friends,
and the news of death would come from far away,
we'd never know this grief.[20]

CHORUS.

You are dreaming, children,
dreams dearer than gold, more blest 370
than the Blest beyond the Northwind's raging.[21]
Dreams are easy, oh,
but the double lash is striking home.
Now our comrades group underground.
Our masters' reeking hands are doomed— 375
the children take the day!

ORESTES.

That thrills his ear,
that arrow lands!
Zeus, Zeus, force up from the earth
destruction, late but true to the mark, 380
to the reckless heart, the killing hand—
for parents of revenge revenge be done.

[17] The Lycians fought in aid of the Trojans.

[18] The giant kings are Minos, Rhadamanthus, and Aeacus, who were rewarded for their just lives by being made judges of the dead in Hades.

[19] The river Scamander, near Troy.

[20] Electra wishes that Clytaemnestra and Aegisthus had died before they killed Agamemnon.

[21] The chorus refers to the Hyperboreans, a mythical people supposed to live happily in the far north, beyond Boreas (the north wind). They had a special devotion to Apollo.

LEADER.
And the ripping cries of triumph mine
to sing when the man is stabbed,
the woman[22] dies— 385
why, why hide what's deep inside me,
black wings beating, storming the spirit's prow—
hurricane, slashing hatred!

ELECTRA.
Both fists at once
come down, come down—
Zeus, *crush* their skulls! Kill! Kill! 390
Now give the land some faith, I beg you,
from these ancient wrongs bring forth our rights.
Hear me, Earth, and all you lords of death.

CHORUS.
It is the law: when the blood of slaughter
wets the ground it wants more blood. 395
Slaughter cries for the Fury
of those long dead to bring destruction
on destruction churning in its wake!

ORESTES.
Sweet Earth, how long?—great lords of death, look on,
you mighty curses of the dead. Look on 400
the last of Atreus' children, here, the remnant—
helpless, cast from home . . . god, where to turn?

LEADER.
And again my pulses race and leap,
I can feel your sobs, and hope
becomes despair 405
and the heart goes dark to hear you—
then the anguish ebbs, I see you stronger,
hope and the light come on me.

ELECTRA.
What hope?—what force to summon, what can help?
What but the pain we suffer, bred by her? 410
So let her fawn. She can never soothe her young wolves—
Mother dear, you bred our wolves' raw fury.

LEADER AND CHORUS.
I beat and beat the dirge like a Persian mourner,[23]
hands clenched tight and the blows are coming thick and fast,
you can see the hands shoot out, 415
now hand over hand and down—the head pulsates,
blood at the temples pounding to explode!

[22]Aegisthus is "the man"; Clytaemnestra is "the woman."
[23]Noted for violent demonstrations of grief.

ELECTRA.
Reckless, brutal mother—oh dear god!—
The brutal, cruel cortege,[24]
the warlord stripped of his honor guard 420
and stripped of mourning rites—
you dared entomb your lord unwept, unsung.

ORESTES.
Shamed for all the world, you mean—
dear god, my father degraded so!
Oh she'll pay, 425
she'll pay, by the gods and these bare hands—
just let me take her life and *die*!

LEADER AND CHORUS.
Shamed? *Butchered,* I tell you—hands lopped,
strung to shackle his neck and arms!
So she worked, 430
she buried him, made your life a hell.
Your father mutilated—do you hear?

ELECTRA.
You tell him of father's death, but I was an outcast,
worthless, leashed like a vicious dog in a dark cell.
I wept—laughter died that day . . . 435
I wept, pouring out the tears behind my veils.
Hear *that,* my brother, carve it on your heart!

LEADER AND CHORUS.
Let it ring in your ears
but let your heart stand firm.
The outrage stands as it stands, 440
you burn to know the end,
but first be strong, be steel, then down and fight.

ORESTES.
I am calling you, my father—be with all you love!

ELECTRA.
I am with you, calling through my tears.

LEADER AND CHORUS.
We band together now, the call resounds— 445
hear us now, come back into the light.
Be with us, battle all you hate.

ORESTES.
Now force *clash* with force, right with right!

ELECTRA.
Dear gods, be just—win back our rights.

LEADER AND CHORUS.
The flesh crawls to hear them pray. 450
The hour of doom has waited long . . .
pray for it once, and oh my god, it comes.

[24]Followers of or ceremony at a funeral. Agamemnon's mutilated body had received no funeral rites.

CHORUS.

Oh, the torment bred in the race,
the grinding scream of death
and the stroke that hits the vein, 455
the hemorrhage none can stanch, the grief,
the curse no man can bear.

But there is a cure in the house
and not outside it, no,
not from others but from *them*, 460
their bloody strife. We sing to you,
dark gods beneath the earth.

Now hear, you blissful powers underground—
answer the call, send help.
Bless the children, give them triumph now. 465

[*They withdraw, while* ELECTRA *and* ORESTES *come to the altar.*]

ORESTES.
Father, king, no royal death you died—
give me the power now to rule our house.

ELECTRA.
I need you too, my father.
Help me kill her lover, then go free.

ORESTES.
Then men will extend the sacred feast to you. 470
Or else, when the steam and the rich savor burn
for Mother Earth, you will starve for honor.

ELECTRA.
And I will pour my birthright out to you—
the wine of the fathers' house, my bridal wine,[25]
and first of all the shrines revere your tomb. 475

ORESTES.
O Earth, bring father up to watch me fight.

ELECTRA.
O Persephone,[26] give us power—lovely, gorgeous power!

ORESTES.
Remember the bath—they stripped away your life, my father.

ELECTRA.
Remember the all-embracing net—they made it first for you.

ORESTES.
Chained like a beast—chains of hate, not bronze, my father! 480

ELECTRA.
Shamed in the schemes, the hoods they slung around you!

[25] Electra has been barred from marrying while Clytaemnestra and Aegisthus are alive, lest she bear a son to avenge Agamemnon.
[26] Queen of the land of the dead.

ORESTES.

Does our taunting wake you, oh my father?

ELECTRA.

Do you lift your beloved head?

ORESTES.

Send us justice, fight for all you love,
or help us pin them grip for grip. They threw you— 485
don't you long to throw them down in turn?

ELECTRA.

One last cry, father. Look at your nestlings
stationed at your tomb—pity
your son and daughter. We are all you have.

ORESTES.

Never blot out the seed of Pelops here. 490
Then in the face of death you cannot die.

[*The* LEADER *comes forward again.*]

LEADER.

The voices of children—salvation to the dead!
Corks[27] to the net, they rescue the linen meshes
from the depths. This line will never drown!

ELECTRA.

Hear us—the long wail we raise is all for you. 495
Honor our call and you will save yourself.

LEADER.

And a fine thing it is to lengthen out the dirge;
you adore a grave and fate they never mourned.
But now for action—now you're set on action,
put your stars to proof.

ORESTES.

So we will. 500
One thing first, I think it's on the track.
Why did she send libations? What possessed her,
so late, to salve a wound past healing?
To the unforgiving dead she sends this sop,
this . . . who am I to appreciate her gifts? 505
They fall so short of all her failings. True,
"pour out your all to atone an act of blood,
you work for nothing." So the saying goes.
I'm ready. Tell me what you know.

LEADER.

I know, my boy,
I was there. She had bad dreams. Some terror 510
came groping through the night—it shook her,
and she sent these cups, unholy woman.

[27] Floats to keep the net from sinking.

ORESTES.
And you know the dream, you can tell it clearly?
LEADER.
She dreamed she bore a snake, said so herself and . . .
ORESTES.
Come to the point—where does the story end? 515
LEADER.
. . . she swaddled it like a baby, laid it to rest.
ORESTES.
And food, what did the little monster want?
LEADER.
She gave it her breast to suck—she was dreaming.
ORESTES.
And didn't it tear her nipple, the brute inhuman—
LEADER.
Blood curdled the milk with each sharp tug . . . 520
ORESTES.
No empty dream. The vision of a man.
LEADER.
. . . and she woke with a scream, appalled,
and rows of torches, burning out of the blind dark,
flared across the halls to soothe the queen,
and then she sent the libations for the dead, 525
an easy cure she hopes will cut the pain.
ORESTES.
No,
I pray to the Earth and father's grave to bring
that dream to life in me. I'll play the seer—
it all fits together, watch!
If the serpent came from the same place as I, 530
and slept in the bands that swaddled me, and its jaws
spread wide for the breast that nursed me into life
and clots stained the milk, mother's milk,
and she cried in fear and agony—so be it.
As she bred this sign, this violent prodigy, 535
so she dies by violence. I turn serpent,
I kill her. So the vision says.
LEADER.
You are the seer for me, I like your reading.
Let it come! But now rehearse your friends.
Say do this, or don't do that— 540
ORESTES.
The plan is simple. My sister goes inside.
And I'd have her keep the bond with me a secret.
They killed an honored man by cunning, so
they die by cunning, caught in the same noose.
So he commands, 545
Apollo the Seer who's never lied before.

And I like a stranger, equipped for all events,
go to the outer gates with this man here,
Pylades, a friend, the house's friend-in-arms.
And we both will speak Parnassian, both try 550
for the native tones of Delphi.[28]
Now, say none
at the doors will give us a royal welcome
(after all the house is ridden by a curse),[29]
well then we wait . . . till a passer-by will stop
and puzzle and make insinuations at the house, 555
"Aegisthus shuts his door on the man who needs him.
Why, I wonder—does he know? Is he home?"
But once through the gates, across the threshold,
once I find that man on *my* father's throne,
or returning late to meet me face to face, 560
and his eyes shift and fall—
I promise you,
before he can ask me, "Stranger, who are you?"—
I drop him dead, a thrust of the sword, and twist!
Our Fury never wants for blood. *His* she drinks unmixed,
our third libation poured to Saving Zeus. 565

[*Turning to* ELECTRA.]

Keep a close watch inside, dear, be careful.
We must work together step by step.

[*To the* CHORUS.]

And you,
better hold your tongues, religiously.
Silence, friends, or speak when it will help.

[*Looking toward* PYLADES *and the death-mound and beyond.*]

For the rest, watch over me, I need you— 570
guide my sword through struggle, guide me home!

[*As* ORESTES, PYLADES *and* ELECTRA *leave, the women reassemble for the* CHORUS.]

[28] Delphi and Mount Parnassus, both associated with the god Apollo, are in the region (Phokis) where Orestes has lived in exile. He may mean that he will adopt the regional dialect of Delphi or that his words will be delphic (obscure but faithful to the commission given him by Apollo).

[29] The curse would cause the house's inhabitants to sin against the laws of hospitality and also to fear visitors.

CHORUS.

Marvels, the Earth breeds many marvels,
terrible marvels overwhelm us.
The heaving arms of the sea embrace and swarm
with savage life. And high in the no man's land of night 575
torches[30] hang like swords. The hawk on the wing,
the beast astride the fields
can tell of the whirlwind's fury roaring strong.

Oh but a man's high daring spirit,
who can account for that? Or woman's 580
desperate passion daring past all bounds?
She couples with every form of ruin known to mortals.
Woman, frenzied, driven wild with lust,
twists the dark warm harness
of wedded love—tortures man and beast. 585

Well you know, you with a sense of truth
recall Althaia,[31]
the heartless mother
who killed her son,
ai! what a scheme she had— 590
she rushed his destiny,
lit the bloody torch
preserved from the day he left her loins with a cry—
the life of the torch paced his,
burning on till Fate burned out his life. 595

There is one more in the tales of hate:
remember Scylla,[32]
the girl of slaughter
seduced by foes
to take her father's life. 600
The gift of Minos,
a choker forged in gold
turned her head and Nisos' immortal lock she cut
as he slept away his breath . . .
ruthless bitch, now Hermes takes her down. 605

[30] Strange celestial bodies, such as comets.

[31] The chorus in the following passage cites three examples of perverted parental, filial, or conjugal love, all of which in the present context are ironic or double-edged, like the matricide Orestes and Electra are planning. Althaia, in mythology, had been warned at the birth of her son Meleager that his life would end when a certain torch, or brand from the fire, was burnt out. She hid it away, but later her anger with her son, who had killed her brothers, impelled her to burn the torch, bringing on his death.

[32] This Scylla (not to be confused with the monster of the same name who threatened navigators of the straits of Messina) was in myth the daughter of Nisos, king of Megara, whose city was besieged by King Minos of Crete. In Aeschylus' version of her story she succumbed to bribery (in other versions her motive is love for Minos) and cut off a lock of her father's hair on which his life depended.

Now that I call to mind old wounds that never heal—
Stop, it's time for the wedded love-in-hate,
for the curse of the halls,
the woman's brazen cunning
bent on her lord in arms, 610
her warlord's power—
Do you respect such things?
I prize the hearthstone warmed by faith,
a woman's temper nothing bends to outrage.

First at the head of legendary crime stands Lemnos.[33]
People shudder and moan, and can't forget— 615
each new horror that comes
we call the hells of Lemnos.
Loathed by the gods for guilt,
cast off by men, disgraced, their line dies out.
Who could respect what god detests? 620
What of these tales have I not picked with justice?

The sword's at the lungs!—it stabs deep,
the edge cuts through and through
and Justice drives it—Outrage still lives on,
not trodden to pieces underfoot, not yet, 625
though the laws lie trampled down,
the majesty of Zeus.

The anvil of Justice stands fast
and Fate beats out her sword.
Tempered for glory, a child will wipe clean 630
the inveterate stain of blood shed long ago—
Fury brings him home at last,
the brooding mother Fury!

[*The women leave.* ORESTES *and* PYLADES *approach the house of* ATREUS.]

ORESTES.

Slave, the slave!—
where is he? Hear me pounding the gates?
Is there a man inside the house? 635
For the third time, come out of the halls!
If Aegisthus has them welcome friendly guests.

[*A voice from inside.*]

[33]An island in the Aegean. It is associated in mythology and legend with atrocities, the most notorious being the attempted slaughter of all husbands and other males by the women of the island, who were jealous of their mistresses.

PORTER.

All right, I hear you. . . .
Where do you come from, stranger? Who are you?

ORESTES.

Announce me to the masters of the house. 640
I've come for them, I bring them news.
Hurry,
the chariot of the night is rushing on the dark!
The hour falls, the traveler casts his anchor
in an inn where every stranger feels at home.
Come out!
Whoever rules the house. The woman in charge. 645
No, the man, better that way.
No scruples then. Say what you mean,
man to man launch in and prove your point,
make it clear, strong.

[CLYTAEMNESTRA *emerges*[34] *from the palace, attended by* ELECTRA.]

CLYTAEMNESTRA.

Strangers, please,
tell me what you would like and it is yours. 650
We've all you might expect in a house like ours.
We have warm baths and beds to charm away your pains
and the eyes of Justice[35] look on all we do.
But if you come for higher things, affairs
that touch the state, that is the men's concern 655
and I will stir them on.

ORESTES.

I am a stranger,
from Daulis, close to Delphi. I'd just set out,
packing my own burden bound for Argos
(here I'd put my burden down and rest),
when I met a perfect stranger, out of the blue, 660
who asks about my way and tells me his.
Strophios,
a Phocian, so I gathered in conversation.

[34] Orestes had hoped that Aegisthus, about whom he feels "no scruples," would encounter him first, but (by dramatic logic and the logic of the curse) he is brought immediately face-to-face with his mother, who is simultaneously his fundamental antagonist, a person whose intimate relationship to him causes the ambivalent human feelings in both of them, and the most recent carrier of the self-propagating retaliatory curse that lies on the lineage of Atreus.

[35] A typical specimen of the irony omnipresent in the trilogy. In extending the expected hospitable welcome to the guest, Clytaemnestra evokes her murder of her husband Agamemnon in his bath; the "eyes of Justice" are those that enforce the rites of hospitality and (for the audience) are the forces that punish an adulterous wife for murdering her husband. The dialogue here between Clytaemnestra and Orestes epitomizes the tragedy of the entire story: Clytaemnestra had killed her husband because he had murdered their daughter Iphigeneia at Aulis; now she is engaged in a life-or-death struggle with another of her own children.

"Well, my friend," he says, "out for Argos
in any case? Remember to tell the parents
he is dead, Orestes . . .
promise me please 665
(it's only right), it will not slip your mind.
Then whatever his people want, to bring him home
or bury him here, an alien, all outcast here
forever, won't you ferry back their wishes?
As it is, a bronze urn is armor to his embers. 670
The man's been mourned so well . . ."
I only tell you
what I heard. And am I speaking now
with guardians, kinsmen who will care?
It's hard to say. But a parent ought to know.[36]

CLYTAEMNESTRA.
I, I—
your words, you storm us, raze us to the roots, 675
you curse of the house so hard to wrestle down!
How you range—targets at peace, miles away,
and a shaft from your lookout brings them down.
You strip me bare of all I love, destroy me,
now—Orestes. 680

And he was trained so well, we'd been so careful,
kept his footsteps clear of the quicksand of death.
Just now, the hope of the halls, the surgeon to cure
our Furies' lovely revel—he seemed so close,
he's written off the rolls.

ORESTES.
If only I were . . . 685
my friends, with hosts as fortunate as you
if only I *could* be known for better news[37]
and welcomed like a brother. The tie between
the host and stranger, what is kinder?
But what an impiety, so it seemed to me, 690
not to bring this to a head for loved ones.

[36] This poignant line has at least three meanings: (a) "Shouldn't a mother know her own son?"; (b) "It is only right that this tragic message be delivered to a parent, not a more distant kinsman or guardian"; (c) "Any mother who killed her son's father should be told what has happened to the son she exiled so that she could commit her crimes." Clytaemnestra's reply, in her lines that follow, shows her mixed feelings as mother of the man she has most to fear.

[37] Messengers were frequently (if illogically) rewarded for bringing good news and were hated or punished for bringing bad news. Clytaemnestra's reply, that the messenger will "receive what you deserve," is another ambiguity; does she mean that he will be rewarded for bringing to Aegisthus (and perhaps to her) the good news that a potentially avenging son is dead, or that the news of this son's death, welcome or not, is a service to the dead son's family, or both? And does Clytaemnestra's reassurance that the messenger will be "as welcome in these halls as one of us" mean that he will be treated kindly or that he will be given the same kind of unnatural treatment that all the house of Atreus has given to its kindred?

I was bound by honor, bound by the rights
of hospitality.

CLYTAEMNESTRA.

Nothing has changed.
For all that you receive what you deserve,
as welcome in these halls as one of us. 695
Wouldn't another bear the message just as well?
But you must be worn from the long day's journey—
time for your rewards.

[*To* ELECTRA.]

Escort him in,
where the men who come are made to feel at home.
He and his retinue, and fellow travelers. 700
Let them taste the bounty of our house.
Do it, as if you depended on his welfare.

And we will rouse the powers in the house
and share the news. We never lack for loved ones,
we will probe this turn of fortune every way. 705

[ELECTRA *leads* ORESTES, PYLADES *and their retinue into the halls;* CLYTAEMNESTRA *follows, while the* CHORUS *reassembles.*]

LEADER.

Oh dear friends who serve the house,
when can we speak out, when
can the vigor of our voices serve Orestes?

CHORUS.

Queen of the Earth, rich mounded Earth,
breasting over the lord of ships, 710
the king's corpse at rest,
hear us now, now help us,
now the time is ripe—
Down to the pit Persuasion goes
with all her cunning. Hermes of Death, 715
the great shade patrols the ring
to guide the struggles, drive the tearing sword.

LEADER.

And I think our new friend is at his mischief.
Look, Orestes' nurse in tears.

[*Enter* CILISSA.]

Where now, old-timer, padding along the gates? 720
With pain a volunteer to go your way.

NURSE.

"Aegisthus,"[38]

your mistress calling, "hurry and meet your guests.
There's news. It's clearer man to man, you'll see."

And she looks at the maids and pulls that long face
and down deep her eyes are laughing over the work 725
that's done. Well and good for her. For the house
it's the curse all over—the strangers make that plain.
But let *him* hear, he'll revel once he knows.
Oh god,
the life is hard. The old griefs, the memories
mixing, cups of pain, so much pain in the halls, 730
the house of Atreus . . . I suffered, the heart within me
always breaking, oh, but I never shouldered
misery like this. So many blows, good slave,
I took my blows.
Now dear Orestes—
the sweetest, dearest plague of all our lives! 735

Red from your mother's womb I took you, reared you . . .
nights, the endless nights I paced, your wailing
kept me moving—led me a life of labor,
all for what?
And such care I gave it . . .
baby can't think for itself, poor creature. 740
You have to nurse it, don't you? Read its mind,
little devil's got no words, it's still swaddled.
Maybe it wants a bite or a sip of something,
or its bladder pinches—a baby's soft insides
have a will of their own. I had to be a prophet. 745
Oh I tried, and missed, believe you me, I missed,
and I'd scrub its pretty things until they sparkled.
Washerwoman and wetnurse shared the shop.
A jack of two trades, that's me,
and an old hand at both . . .
and so I nursed Orestes, 750
yes, from his father's arms I took him once,
and now they say he's dead,
I've suffered it all, and now I'll fetch that man,
the ruination of the house—give him the news,
he'll relish every word.

[38] In addition to revealing the nurse Cilissa's hatred for Aegisthus, her words introduce a poignantly human note. Like his mother, Clytaemnestra, Orestes is more, and less, than an instrument in a cosmic system of right and wrong; he was also a human baby who needed feeding and diaper changing. The nurse's comparison of herself to a "prophet" (line 745) in her dealings with a baby joins together the most cosmic, theological implications and the most homely, personal ones.

LEADER.

She tells him to come, 755

but how, prepared?

NURSE.

Prepared, how else?

I don't see . . .

LEADER.

With his men, I mean, or all alone?

NURSE.

Oh, she says to bring his bodyguard, his cutthroats.

LEADER.

No, not now, not if you hate our master—
tell him to come alone. 760
Nothing for him to fear then, when he hears.
Have him come quickly too, rejoicing all the way!
The teller sets the crooked message straight.

NURSE.

What,

you're *glad* for the news that's come?

LEADER.

Why not,

if Zeus will turn the evil wind to good? 765

NURSE.

But how? Orestes, the hope of the house is gone.

LEADER.

Not yet. It's a poor seer who'd say so.

NURSE.

What are you saying—something I don't know?

LEADER.

Go in with your message. Do as you're told.
May the gods take care of cares that come from them. 770

NURSE.

Well, I'm off. Do as I'm told.
And here's to the best . . .
some help, dear gods, some help.

[*Exit.*]

CHORUS.

O now bend to my prayer, Father Zeus,
lord of the gods astride the sky— 775
grant them all good fortune,
the lords of the house who strain to see
strict discipline return.
Our cry is the cry of Justice,
Zeus, safeguard it well.

Zeus, 780

set him against his enemies in the halls!

Do it, rear him to greatness—two, threefold
he will repay you freely, gladly.

Look now—watch the colt of a man you loved,
yoked to the chariot of pain. 785
Now the orphan needs you—
harness his racing, rein him in,
preserve his stride so we
can watch him surge in the homestretch,
storming for the goal. 790

And you who haunt the vaults
where the gold glows in the darkness,
hear us now, good spirits of the house,
conspire with us—come,
and wash old works of blood 795
in the fresh-drawn blood of Justice.
Let the gray retainer, murder, breed no more.

And you, Apollo, lord of the glorious masoned cavern,[39]
grant that this man's house lift up its head,
that we may see with loving eyes 800
the light of freedom burst from its dark veil!
And lend a hand and scheme
for the rights, my Hermes, help us,
sail the action on with all your breath.
Reveal what's hidden, please, 805
or say a baffling word
in the night and blind men's eyes—
when the morning comes your word is just as dark.

Soon, at last, in the dawn that frees the house,
we sea-widows wed to the winds 810
will beat our mourning looms of song
and sing, "Our ship's come in!
Mine, mine is the wealth that swells her holds—
those I love are home and free of death."

But you, when your turn in the action comes, be strong. 815
When she cries "Son!" cry out "My *father's* son!"
Go through with the murder—innocent at last.

Raise up the heart of Perseus[40] in your breast!
And for all you love under earth

[39]Apollo's temple at Delphi and the cleft in the earth over which it was built.

[40]The mythical hero Perseus, with the help of Pluto, Hermes, and Athena, killed Medusa, one of the three female monsters (the Gorgons) with snakes in their hair; anyone who looked at her was turned to stone. Athena gave Perseus a mirror so that he would not have to look directly at Medusa.

and all above its rim, now scarf your eyes
against the Gorgon's fury—
In, go in for the slaughter now! 820

[*Enter* AEGISTHUS, *alone.*]

The butcher comes. Wipe out death with death.

AEGISTHUS.
Coming, coming. Yes, I have my summons.
There's news, I gather, travelers here to tell it. 825
No joy in the telling though—Orestes dead.
Saddle the house with a bloody thing like that
and it might just collapse. It's still raw
from the last murders, galled and raw.

But how to take the story, for living truth? 830
Or work of a woman's panic, gossip starting up
in the night to flicker out and die?[41]

[*Turning to the* LEADER.]

Do you know?
Tell me, clear my mind.

LEADER.
We've heard a little.
But get it from the strangers, go inside.
Messengers have no power. Nothing like 835
a face-to-face encounter with the source.

AEGISTHUS.
—Must see him, test the messenger. Where was he
when the boy died, standing on the spot?
Or is he dazed with rumor, mouthing hearsay?
No, he'll never trap me open-eyed! 840

[*Striding through the doors.*]

CHORUS.
Zeus, Zeus, what can I say?—
how to begin this prayer, call down
the gods for help? what words
can reach the depth of all I feel?
Now they swing to the work, 845
the red edge of the cleaver
hacks at flesh and men go down.
Agamemnon's house goes down—
all-out disaster now,
or a son ignites the torch of freedom, 850

[41] Compare the chorus's skepticism about Clytaemnestra's report of the fall of Troy, in *Agamemnon.*

wins the throne, the citadel,
the fathers' realms of gold.
The last man on the bench,[42] a challenger
must come to grips with two. Up,
like a young god, Orestes, wrestle— 855
let it be to win.

[*A scream inside the palace.*]

—Listen!
—What's happening?
—The house,
what have they done to the house?

LEADER.
Back,
till the work is over! Stand back—
they'll count us clean of the dreadful business. 860

[*The women scatter; a wounded servant of* AEGISTHUS *enters.*]

Look, the die is cast, the battle's done.

SERVANT.
Ai,
Ai, all over, master's dead—Aie,
a third, last salute. Aegisthus is no more.

[*Rushing at a side door, struggling to work it open.*]

Open up, wrench the bolts on the women's doors.
Faster! A strong young arm it takes, 865
but not to save him now, he's finished.
What's the use?
Look—wake up!
No good,
I call to the deaf, to sleepers . . . a waste of breath.
Where are you, Clytaemnestra? What are you doing?

LEADER.
Her head is ripe for lopping on the block. 870
She's next, and justice wields the ax.

[*The door opens, and* CLYTAEMNESTRA *comes forth.*]

CLYTAEMNESTRA.
What now?
Why this shouting up and down the halls?

[42] The wrestler who must meet the winner of the earlier match or matches.

SERVANT.
The dead are killing the living,[43] I tell you!
CLYTAEMNESTRA.
Ah, a riddle. I do well at riddles.
By cunning we die, precisely as we killed. 875
Hand me the man-ax, someone, hurry!

[*The servant dashes out.*]

Now we will see. Win all or lose all,
we have come to this—the crisis of our lives.

[*The main doors open;* ORESTES, *sword in hand, is standing over the body of* AEGISTHUS, *with* PYLADES *close behind him.*]

ORESTES.
It's you I want. This one's had enough.
CLYTAEMNESTRA.
Gone, my violent one—Aegisthus, very dear. 880
ORESTES.
You love your man? Then lie in the same grave.
You can never be unfaithful to the dead.

[*Pulling her toward* AEGISTHUS' *body.*]

CLYTAEMNESTRA.
Wait, son—no feeling for this, my child?
The breast[44] you held, drowsing away the hours,
soft gums tugging the milk that made you grow? 885

[ORESTES *turns to* PYLADES.]

ORESTES.
What will I do, Pylades—I dread to kill my mother!
PYLADES.
What of the future? What of the Prophet God Apollo,
the Delphic voice, the faith and oaths we swear?
Make all mankind your enemy, not the gods.
ORESTES.
O you win me over—good advice.

[*Wheeling on* CLYTAEMNESTRA, *thrusting her toward* AEGISTHUS.]

[43] The line means (a) the supposedly dead Orestes is killing Aegisthus, and (b) all the dead victims of the curse on the house are taking revenge.
[44] Either Clytaemnestra has exposed her breast or Orestes has done so in his violence.

This way— 890
I want to butcher you—right across his body!
In life you thought he dwarfed my father—*Die!*—
go down with him forever!
You love this man,
the man you should have loved you hated.

CLYTAEMNESTRA.
I gave you life. Let me grow old with you. 895

ORESTES.
What—kill my father, then you'd live with me?

CLYTAEMNESTRA.
Destiny had a hand in that, my child.

ORESTES.
This too: destiny is handing you your death.

CLYTAEMNESTRA.
You have no fear of a mother's curse, my son?

ORESTES.
Mother? You flung me to a life of pain. 900

CLYTAEMNESTRA.
Never flung you, placed you in a comrade's house.

ORESTES.
—Disgraced me, sold me, a freeborn father's son.

CLYTAEMNESTRA.
Oh? then name the price I took for you.

ORESTES.
I am ashamed to mention it[45] in public.

CLYTAEMNESTRA.
Please, and tell your father's failings too. 905

ORESTES.
Never judge him—he suffered, you sat here at home.

CLYTAEMNESTRA.
It hurts women, being kept from men, my son.

ORESTES.
Perhaps . . . but the man slaves to keep them safe at home.

CLYTAEMNESTRA.
—I see murder in your eyes, my child—mother's murder!

ORESTES.
You are the murderer, not I—and you will kill yourself.[46] 910

CLYTAEMNESTRA.
Watch out—the hounds of a mother's curse will hunt you down.

ORESTES.
But how to escape a father's if I fail?

CLYTAEMNESTRA.
I must be spilling live tears on a tomb of stone.

[45] Orestes probably means both the killing of Agamemnon in the son's absence and his mother's adultery. Her reply in the next line balances these crimes against Agamemnon's killing of Iphigeneia and his adulteries with Trojan women such as his captive, Cassandra.
[46] That is, she will have brought on her own death through her evil acts.

ORESTES.
Yes, my father's destiny—it decrees your death.
CLYTAEMNESTRA.
Ai—you are the snake I bore—I gave you life!
ORESTES.
Yes! 915
That was the great seer, that terror in your dreams.
You killed and it was outrage—suffer outrage now.

[*He draws her over the threshold; the doors close behind them, and the* CHORUS *gathers at the altar.*]

LEADER.
I even mourn the victims' double fates.
But Orestes fought, he reached the summit
of bloodshed here—we'd rather have it so. 920
The bright eye of the halls must never die.
CHORUS.
Justice came at last to the sons of Priam,
late but crushing vengeance, yes,
but to Agamemnon's house returned
the double lion,[47] 925
the double onslaught
drove to the hilt—the exile sped by god,
by Delphi's just command that drove him home.

Lift the cry of triumph O! the master's house
wins free of grief, free of the ones 930
who bled its wealth, the couple stained with murder,
free of Fate's rough path.

He came back with a lust for secret combat,
stealthy, cunning vengeance, yes,
but his hand was steered in open fight 935
by god's true daughter,
Right, Right we call her,
we and our mortal voices aiming well—
she breathes her fury, shatters all she hates.

Lift the cry of triumph O! the master's house 940
wins free of grief, free of the ones
who bled its wealth, the couple stained with murder,
free of Fate's rough path.
Apollo wills it so!—

[47] Orestes and Pylades. The optimism expressed throughout this choral passage, the belief that the curse has finally been put to rest and that the chain of acts of revenge has been broken, is shortsighted and premature. Later, the chorus will become aware of this fact.

Apollo, clear from the Earth's deep cleft 945
his voice came shrill, "Now stealth will master stealth!"
And the pure god came down and healed our ancient wounds,
the heavens come, somehow, to lift our yoke of grief—
Now to praise the heavens' just command.

Look, the light is breaking! 950
The huge chain that curbed the halls gives way.
Rise up, proud house, long, too long
your walls lay fallen, strewn along the earth.

Time brings all to birth—
soon Time will stride through the gates with blessings, 955
once the hearth burns off corruption, once
the house drives off the Furies. Look, the dice of Fate
fall well for all to see. We sing how fortune smiles—
the aliens in the house are routed out at last!

Look, the light is breaking! 960
The huge chain that curbed the halls gives way.
Rise up, proud house, long, too long
your walls lay fallen, strewn along the earth.

[*The doors open. Torches light* PYLADES *and* ORESTES, *sword in hand, standing over the bodies of* CLYTAEMNESTRA *and* AEGISTHUS, *as* CLYTAEMNESTRA *stood over the bodies of* AGAMEMNON *and* CASSANDRA.]

ORESTES.
Behold the double tyranny of our land!
They killed my father, stormed my fathers' house. 965
They had their power when they held the throne.
Great lovers still, as you may read their fate.
True to their oath, hand in hand they swore
to kill my father, hand in hand to die.
Now they keep their word.

[*Unwinding from the bodies on the bier the robes that entangled* AGAMEMNON, *he displays them, as* CLYTAEMNESTRA *had displayed them, to the* CHORUS *at the altar.*]

Look once more on this, 970
you who gather here to attend our crimes—
the master-plot that bound my wretched father,

shackled his ankles, manacled his hands.
Spread it out! Stand in a ring around it,
a grand shroud for a man.
Here, unfurl it 975
so the Father—no, not mine but the One
who watches over all, the Sun can behold
my mother's godless work. So he may come,
my witness when the day of judgment comes,
that I pursued this bloody death with justice, 980
mother's death.
Aegisthus, why mention him?
The adulterer dies. An old custom, justice.

But she who plotted this horror against her husband,
she carried his children, growing in her womb
and she—I loved her once 985
and now I loathe, I have to loathe—
what is she?

[*Kneeling by the body of his mother.*]

Some moray eel, some viper born to rot her mate
with a single touch, no fang to strike him,
just the wrong, the reckless fury in her heart!

[*Glancing back and forth from* CLYTAEMNESTRA *to the robes.*]

This—how can I dignify this . . . snare for a beast?— 990
sheath for a corpse's feet?
This winding-sheet,
this tent for the bath of death!
No, a hunting net,
a coiling—what to call—?
Foot-trap—
woven of robes . . .
why, this is perfect gear for the highwayman 995
who entices guests and robs them blind and plies
the trade of thieves. With a sweet lure like this
he'd hoist a hundred lives and warm his heart,

Live with such a woman, marry *her*? Sooner
the gods destroy me—die without an heir! 1000

CHORUS.
Oh the dreadful work . . .
Death calls and she is gone.
But oh, for you, the survivor,
suffering is just about to bloom.

Orestes.
Did she do the work or not?—Here, come close— 1005
This shroud's my witness, dyed with Aegisthus' blade[48]—
Look, the blood ran here, conspired with time to blot
the swirling dyes, the handsome old brocade.

[*Clutching* Agamemnon*'s robes, burying his face in them and weeping.*]

Now I can praise you, now I am here to mourn.
You were my father's death, great robe, I hail you! 1010
Even if I must suffer the work and the agony
and all the race of man—
I embrace you . . . you,
my victory, are my guilt, my curse, and still—

Chorus.
No man can go through life
and reach the end unharmed. 1015
Aye, trouble is now,
and trouble still to come.

Orestes.
But *still,*
that you may know—
I see no end in sight,
I am a charioteer—the reins are flying, look,
the mares plunge off the track—
my bolting heart, 1020
it beats me down and terror beats the drum,
my dance-and-singing master pitched to fury—

And still, while I still have some self-control,
I say to my friends in public: I killed my mother,
not with a little justice. She was stained 1025
with father's murder, she was cursed by god.
And the magic spells that fired up my daring?
One comes first. The Seer of Delphi who declared,
"Go through with this and you go free of guilt.
Fail and—"
I can't repeat the punishment. 1030
What bow could hit the crest of so much pain?

[Pylades *gives* Orestes *a branch of olive and invests him in the robes of Apollo, the wreath and insignia of suppliants to Delphi.*][49]

[48] Presumably the blade used by Clytaemnestra to kill Agamemnon.
[49] Apollo has promised to purge Orestes from blood guilt after Orestes returns to the god's temple.

Now look on me, armed with the branch and wreath,
a suppliant bound for the Navelstone of Earth,
Apollo's sacred heights
where they say the fire of heaven can never die. 1035

[*Looking at his hand that still retains the sword.*]

I must escape this blood . . . it is my own.
—Must turn toward his hearth,
none but his, the Prophet God decreed.

I ask you, Argos and all my generations,
remember how these brutal things were done. 1040
Be my witness to Menelaus[50] when he comes.
And now I go, an outcast driven off the land,
in life, in death, I leave behind a name for—

LEADER.
But you've done well. Don't burden yourself
with bad omens, lash yourself with guilt. 1045
You've set us free, the whole city of Argos,
lopped the heads of these two serpents once for all.

[*Staring at the women and beyond,* ORESTES *screams in terror.*]

ORESTES.
No, no! Women[51]—look—like Gorgons,
shrouded in black, their heads wreathed,
swarming serpents!
—Cannot stay, I must move on. 1050

LEADER.
What dreams can whirl you so? You of all men,
you have your father's love. Steady,
nothing to fear with all you've won.

ORESTES.
No dreams,
these torments, not to me, they're clear, real—the hounds
of mother's hate.

LEADER.
The blood's still wet on your hands. 1055
It puts a kind of frenzy in you . . .

[50] Brother of Agamemnon and husband of Helen; he has not yet returned to Argos.
[51] The women are the Furies, avengers of blood guilt. In the final play of the trilogy they will confront Orestes; eventually they will be renamed "the Eumenides" ("Kindly Ones").

ORESTES.

God Apollo!

Here they come, thick and fast,
their eyes dripping hate—

LEADER.

One thing
will purge you. Apollo's touch will set you free
from all your . . . torments.

ORESTES.

You can't see them— 1060
I can, they drive me on! I must move on—

[*He rushes out;* PYLADES *follows close behind.*]

LEADER.

Farewell then. God look down on you with kindness,
guard you, grant you fortune.

CHORUS.

Here once more, for the third time,
the tempest in the race has struck 1065
the house of kings and run its course.
First the children eaten,
the cause of all our pain, the curse.
And next the kingly man's ordeal,
the bath where the proud commander, 1070
lord of Achaea's armies lost his life.
And now a third has come, but who?
A third like Saving Zeus?
Or should we call him death?
Where will it end?— 1075
where will it sink to sleep and rest,
this murderous hate, this Fury?

THE EUMENIDES

CHARACTERS

THE PYTHIA, *the priestess of Apollo*
APOLLO
ORESTES
HERMES
THE GHOST OF CLYTAEMNESTRA
CHORUS OF FURIES AND THEIR LEADER
ATHENA
Escorting Chorus of Athenian women
Men of the jury, herald, citizens

TIME AND SCENE

The FURIES *have pursued* ORESTES *to the temple of* APOLLO *at Delphi. It is morning. The priestess of the god appears at the great doors and offers up her prayer.*

PYTHIA.[1]

First of the gods I honor in my prayer is Mother Earth,
the first of the gods to prophesy, and next I praise
Tradition, second to hold her Mother's mantic seat,
so legend says, and third by the lots of destiny,
by Tradition's free will—no force to bear her down— 5
another Titan, child of the Earth, took her seat
and Phoebe passed it on as a birthday gift to Phoebus,
Phoebus a name for clear pure light derived from hers.
Leaving the marsh and razorback of Delos,[2] landing
at Pallas' headlands flocked by ships, here he came 10
to make his home Parnassus[3] and the heights.
And an escort filled with reverence brought him on,
the highway-builders, sons of the god of fire who tamed
the savage country, civilized the wilds—on he marched
and the people lined his way to cover him with praise, 15
led by Delphos,[4] lord, helm of the land, and Zeus
inspired his mind with the prophet's skill, with godhead,
made him fourth in the dynasty of seers to mount this throne,
but it is Zeus that Apollo speaks for, Father Zeus.
These I honor in the prelude of my prayers—these gods. 20
But Athena at the Forefront of the Temple[5] crowns our legends.
I revere the nymphs who keep the Corycian rock's[6] deep hollows,
loving haunt of birds where the spirits drift and hover.
And Great Dionysos rules the land. I never forget that day

[1] The name of the priestess derives from the Python, a dragon killed by Apollo when the god assumed power at Delphi. Omitting this incident, the priestess traces the history of the Delphic oracle (the "mantic," or prophetic, center of Greece) in terms of the successive powers or deities who prophesied there. The first was Earth, a primitive maternal being or principle, followed by Themis ("Tradition," associated with justice and custom), followed by Phoebe, a Titaness associated with the moon, followed by her grandson Phoebus, or Apollo, whom the priestess associates in her speech with highway building, the taming of savagery, and generally the advent of the civilized. But in fact, despite the Pythia's natural inclination toward the "Apollonian" values of reason and moderation, the play will be much more even-handed in its treatment of the conflicting claims of the primitive forces represented by the Furies, Mother Night, and Mother Earth, and on the other hand the more "civilized" forces Apollo represents.

[2] The island where Apollo was born.

[3] The mountain at Delphi; generally associated with Apollo, it actually had two peaks, one sacred to him and one to Dionysos, the god of wine who embodies the libidinal energies antithetical to Apollo's moderation. Dionysos rules the temple at Delphi during the winter, when Apollo is absent.

[4] The original king from whom Delphi was supposed to derive its name.

[5] Athena had a shrine near the temple's entrance.

[6] An area of Mount Parnassus; it contained a cave sacred to Pan, god of nature.

he marshaled his wild women in arms—he was all god, 25
he ripped Pentheus[7] down like a hare in the nets of doom.
And the rushing springs of Pleistos, Poseidon's[8] force I call,
and the king of the sky, the king of all fulfillment, Zeus.
Now the prophet goes to take her seat.[9] God speed me—
grant me a vision greater than all my embarkations past! 30

[*Turning to the audience.*]

Where are the Greeks among you? Draw your lots and enter.
It is the custom here. I will tell the future
only as the god will lead the way.

[*She goes through the doors and reappears in a moment, shaken, thrown to her knees by some terrific force.*]

Terrors—
terrors to tell, terrors all can see!—
they send me reeling back from Apollo's house. 35
The strength drains, it's very hard to stand,
crawling on all fours, no spring in the legs . . .
an old woman,[10] gripped by fear, is nothing,
a child, nothing more.

[*Struggling to her feet, trying to compose herself.*]

I'm on my way to the vault, 40
it's green with wreaths, and there at the Navelstone[11]
I see a man—an abomination to god—
he holds the seat where suppliants sit for purging;[12]
his hands dripping blood, and his sword just drawn,
and he holds a branch (it must have topped an olive) 45
wreathed with a fine tuft of wool, all piety,
fleece gleaming white. So far it's clear, I tell you.

[7] The rationalistic Pentheus, opposed to the orgiastic worship of Dionysos, was torn apart by his mother and other frenzied female worshipers of the god.

[8] God of the ocean.

[9] The seat is a tripod situated over the underground cleft beneath the temple. The Pythia's role was to relay the utterances of Apollo.

[10] The Pythia was always an elderly woman.

[11] The Omphalos, a cone-shaped rock near or in the temple. It was believed to be the center of the earth.

[12] Because he has taken his mother Clytaemnestra's life, Orestes must be ritually "purged" of the pollution of blood before he can be tried at law. Here he carries the emblems customary for those seeking purgation.

But there in a ring around the man, an amazing company—
women,[13] sleeping, nestling against the benches . . .
women? No, 50
Gorgons I'd call them; but then with Gorgons
you'd see the grim, inhuman . . .
I saw a picture
years ago, the creatures tearing the feast
away from Phineus—
These have no wings,
I looked. But black they are, and so repulsive. 55
Their heavy, rasping breathing makes me cringe.
And their eyes ooze a discharge, sickening,
and what they wear—to flaunt *that* at the gods,
the idols, sacrilege! even in the homes of men.
The tribe that produced that brood I never saw, 60
or a plot of ground to boast it nursed their kind
without some tears, some pain for all its labor.

Now for the outcome. This is his concern,
Apollo the master of this house, the mighty power.
Healer, prophet, diviner of signs, he purges 65
the halls of others—He must purge his own.

[*She leaves. The doors of the temple open and reveal* APOLLO *rising over* ORESTES; *he kneels in prayer at the Navelstone, surrounded by the* FURIES *who are sleeping.* HERMES *waits in the background.*]

APOLLO.
No, I will never fail you, through to the end
your guardian standing by your side or worlds away!
I will show no mercy to your enemies! Now
look at these—

[*Pointing to the* FURIES.]

these obscenities!—I've caught them, 70
beaten them down with sleep.
They disgust me.
These gray, ancient children never touched
by god, man or beast—the eternal virgins.
Born for destruction only, the dark pit,

[13] The Furies, who pursue Orestes in revenge for his act of matricide. Appropriately, the priestess of Apollo does not recognize these primitive beings; she guesses that they may be the Gorgons (female monsters the sight of whom turned gazers to stone) or Harpies (hideous bird women sent by Helios the sun god to punish the king Phineus by defiling his food; compare the description of the Harpies in Virgil's *Aeneid,* Book III).

they range the bowels of Earth, the world of death, 75
loathed by men and the gods who hold Olympus.[14]

Nevertheless keep racing on and never yield.
Deep in the endless heartland they will drive you,
striding horizons, feet pounding the earth forever,
on, on over seas and cities swept by tides! 80
Never surrender, never brood on the labor.

And once you reach the citadel of Pallas,[15] kneel
and embrace her ancient idol in your arms and there,
with judges of your case, with a magic spell—
with words—we will devise the master-stroke 85
that sets you free from torment once for all.
I persuaded you to take your mother's life.

ORESTES.
Lord Apollo, you know the rules of justice,
know them well. Now learn compassion too.
No one doubts your power to do great things. 90

APOLLO.
Remember that. No fear will overcome you.

[*Summoning* HERMES *from the shadows.*]

You, my brother, blood of our common Father,
Hermes, guard him well. Live up to your name,
good Escort. Shepherd him well, he is my suppliant,
and outlaws have their rights that Zeus reveres. 95
Lead him back to the world of men with all good speed.

[APOLLO *withdraws to his inner sanctuary;* ORESTES *leaves with* HERMES *in the lead.* THE GHOST OF CLYTAEMNESTRA *appears at the Navelstone, hovering over the* FURIES *as they sleep.*]

THE GHOST OF CLYTAEMNESTRA.
You—how can you *sleep?*
Awake, awake—what use are sleepers now?
I go stripped of honor, thanks to you,
alone among the dead. And for those I killed 100
the charges of the dead will never cease, never—

[14] There is a natural antipathy between the elemental and ancient force represented by the Furies and the modern, supposedly more advanced Olympian gods, especially Apollo.

[15] Athena; Apollo directs Orestes to her city, Athens. The "ancient idol" was a wooden statue of the goddess located there.

I wander in disgrace, I feel the guilt, I tell you,
withering guilt from all the outraged dead!

But I suffered too, terribly, from dear ones,
and none of my spirits rages to avenge me. 105
I was slaughtered by his matricidal hand.
See these gashes—

[*Seizing one of the* FURIES *weak with sleep.*]

Carve them in your heart!
The sleeping brain has eyes that give us light;
we can never see our destiny by day.

And after all my libations . . . how you lapped 110
the honey, the sober offerings poured to soothe you,
awesome midnight feasts I burned at the hearthfire,
your dread hour never shared with gods.
All those rites, I see them trampled down.
And he springs free like a fawn, one light leap 115
at that—he's through the thick of your nets,
he breaks away!
Mocking laughter twists across his face.
Hear me, I am pleading for my life.
Awake, my Furies, goddesses of the Earth! 120
A dream is calling—Clytaemnestra calls you now.

[*The* FURIES *mutter in their sleep.*]

Mutter on. Your man is gone, fled far away.
My son has friends to defend him, not like mine.

[*They mutter again.*]

You sleep too much, no pity for my ordeal.
Orestes murdered his mother—he is gone. 125

[*They begin to moan.*]

Moaning, sleeping—onto your feet, quickly.
What is your work? What but causing pain?
Sleep and toil, the two strong conspirators,
they sap the mother dragon's deadly fury—

[*The* FURIES *utter a sharp moan and moan again, but they are still asleep.*]

FURIES.
Get him, get him, get him, get him— 130
there he goes.

THE GHOST OF CLYTAEMNESTRA.

The prey you hunt is just a dream—
like hounds mad for the sport you bay him on,
you never leave the kill.
But what are you *doing?*
Up! don't yield to the labor, limp with sleep.
Never forget my anguish. 135
Let my charges hurt you, they are just;
deep in the righteous heart they prod like spurs.
You, blast him on with your gory breath,
the fire of your vitals—wither him, after him,
one last foray—waste him, burn him out!

[*She vanishes. The lead* FURY *urges on the pack.*]

LEADER.

Wake up! 140
I rouse you, you rouse her. Still asleep?
Onto your feet, kick off your stupor.
See if this prelude has some grain of truth.

[*The* FURIES *circle, pursuing the scent with hunting calls, and cry out singly when they find* ORESTES *gone.*]

FURIES.

—Aieeeeee—no, no, *no,* they do us wrong, dear sisters.

—The miles of pain, the pain I suffer . . . 145
and all for nothing, all for pain, more pain,
the anguish, oh, the grief too much to bear.

—The quarry's slipped from the nets, our quarry lost and gone.

—Sleep defeats me . . . I have lost the prey.

—You—child of Zeus[16]—*you,* a common thief! 150

—Young god, you have ridden down the powers
proud with age. You worship the suppliant,
the godless man who tears his parent's heart—

—The matricide, you steal him away, and you a god!

—Guilt both ways, and who can call it justice? 155

—Not I: her charges stalk my dreams,

[16]Apollo.

yes, the charioteer rides hard,
her spurs digging the vitals,
under the heart, under the heaving breast—

—I can feel the executioner's lash, it's searing 160
deeper, sharper, the knives of burning ice—

—Such is your triumph, you young gods,
world dominion past all rights.
Your throne is streaming blood,
blood at the foot, blood at the crowning head— 165

—I can see the Navelstone of the Earth, it's bleeding,
bristling corruption, oh, the guilt it has to bear—
Stains on the hearth! The Prophet stains the vault,
he cries it on, drives on the crime himself.
Breaking the god's first law, he rates men first, 170
destroys the old dominions of the Fates.

He wounds me too, yet *him* he'll never free,
plunging under the earth, no freedom then:
curst as he comes for purging, at his neck
he feels new murder springing from his blood. 175

[APOLLO *strides from his sanctuary in full armor, brandishing his bow and driving back the* FURIES.]

APOLLO.
Out, I tell you, out of these halls—fast!—
set the Prophet's chamber free!

[*Seizing one of the* FURIES, *shaking an arrow across her face.*]

Or take
the flash and stab of this, this flying viper
whipped from the golden cord that strings my bow!

Heave in torment, black froth erupting from your lungs, 180
vomit the clots of all the murders you have drained.
But never touch my halls, you have no right.

Go where heads are severed, eyes gouged out,
where Justice and bloody slaughter are the same . . .
castrations, wasted seed, young men's glories butchered, 185
extremities maimed, and huge stones at the chest,
and the victims wail for pity—
spikes inching up the spine, torsos stuck on spikes.

[*The* FURIES *close in on him.*]

So, you hear your love feast, yearn to have it all?
You revolt the gods. Your look, 190
your whole regalia gives you away—your kind
should infest a lion's cavern reeking blood.
But never rub your filth on the Prophet's shrine.
Out, you flock without a herdsman—out!
No god will ever shepherd you with love. 195

LEADER.
Lord Apollo, now it is your turn to listen.
You are no mere accomplice in this crime.
You did it all, and all the guilt is yours.

APOLLO.
No, how? Enlarge on that, and only that.

LEADER.
You commanded the guest to kill his mother. 200

APOLLO.
—Commanded him to avenge his father, what of it?

LEADER.
And then you dared embrace him, fresh from bloodshed.

APOLLO.
Yes, I ordered him on, to my house, for purging.

LEADER.
And we sped him on, and you revile us?

APOLLO.
Indeed, you are not fit to approach this house. 205

LEADER.
And yet we have our mission and our—

APOLLO.
Authority—you? Sound out your splendid power.

LEADER.
Matricides: we drive them from their houses.

APOLLO.
And what of the wife who strikes her husband down?

LEADER.
That murder would not destroy one's flesh and blood. 210

APOLLO.
Why, you'd disgrace—obliterate the bonds of Zeus
and Hera queen of brides! And the queen of love
you'd throw to the winds at a word, disgrace love,
the source of mankind's nearest, dearest ties.
Marriage of man and wife is Fate itself, 215
stronger than oaths, and Justice guards its life.
But if one destroys the other and you relent—
no revenge, not a glance in anger—then
I say your manhunt of Orestes is unjust.
Some things stir your rage, I see. Others, 220
atrocious crimes, lull your will to act.

Pallas
will oversee this trial. She is one of us.[17]

LEADER.
I will never let that man go free, never.

APOLLO.
Hound him then, and multiply your pains.

LEADER.
Never try to cut my power with your logic. 225

APOLLO.
I'd never touch it, not as a gift—your power.

LEADER.
Of course,
great as you are, they say, throned on high with Zeus.
But blood of the mother draws me on—must hunt
the man for Justice. Now I'm on his trail!

[*Rushing out, with the* FURIES *in full cry.*]

APOLLO.
And I will defend my suppliant and save him. 230
A terror to gods and men, the outcast's anger,
once I fail him, all of my own free will.

[APOLLO *leaves. The scene changes to the Acropolis in Athens. Escorted by* HERMES, ORESTES *enters and kneels, exhausted, before the ancient shrine and idol of* ATHENA.]

ORESTES.
Queen Athena,
under Apollo's orders I have come.
Receive me kindly. Curst and an outcast,
no suppliant for purging . . . my hands are clean. 235
My murderous edge is blunted now, worn down at last
on the outland homesteads, beaten paths of men.

On and out over seas and dry frontiers,
I kept alive the Prophet's strong commands.
Struggling toward your house, your idol—

[*Taking the knees of* ATHENA*'s idol in his arms.*]

Goddess, 240
here I keep my watch,
I await the consummation of my trial.

[17] One of the modern Olympian gods, whom the primitive Furies oppose.

[*The* FURIES *enter in pursuit but cannot find* ORESTES, *who is entwined around* ATHENA*'s idol. The* LEADER *sees the footprints.*]

LEADER.

At last!
The clear trail of the man. After it, silent
but it tracks his guilt to light. He's wounded—
go for the fawn, my hounds, the splash of blood, 245
hunt him, rake him down.
Oh, the labor,
the man-killing labor. My lungs are bursting . . .
over the wide rolling earth we've ranged in flock,
hurdling the waves in wingless flight and now we come,
all hot pursuit, outracing ships astern—and now 250
he's here, somewhere, cowering like a hare . . .
the reek of human blood—it's laughter to my heart!

[*Inciting a pair of* FURIES.]

Look, look again, you two,
scour the ground before he escapes—one dodge
and the matricide slips free.

[*Seeing* ORESTES, *one by one they press around him and* ATHENA*'s idol.*]

FURIES.

—There he is! 255
Clutching the knees of power once again,
twined in the deathless goddess' idol, look,
he wants to go on trial for his crimes.

—Never . . .
the mother's blood that wets the ground,
you can never bring it back, dear god, 260
the Earth drinks, and the running life is gone.

—No,
you'll give me blood for blood, you must!
Out of your living marrow I will drain
my red libation, out of your veins I suck my food,
my raw, brutal cups—

—Wither you alive, 265
drag you down and there you pay, agony
for mother-killing agony!

—And there you will see them all.

Every mortal who outraged god or guest or loving parent:
each receives the pain his pains exact.

—A mighty god is Hades. There 270
at the last reckoning underneath the earth
he scans all, he squares all men's accounts
and graves them on the tablets of his mind.

[ORESTES *remains impassive.*]

ORESTES.
I have suffered into truth. Well I know
the countless arts of purging, where to speak, 275
where silence is the rule.[18] In this ordeal
a compelling master urges me to speak.

[*Looking at his hands.*]

The blood sleeps, it is fading on my hands,
the stain of mother's murder washing clean.
It was still fresh at the god's hearth. Apollo 280
killed the swine[19] and the purges drove it off.
Mine is a long story
if I'd start with the many hosts I met,
I lived with, and I left them all unharmed.[20]
Time refines all things that age with time. 285

And now with pure, reverent lips I call
the queen of the land. Athena, help me!
Come without your spear—without a battle
you will win myself, my land, the Argive people[21]
true and just, your friends-in-arms forever. 290
Where are you now? The scorching wilds of Libya,
bathed by the Triton pool[22] where you were born?
Robes shrouding your feet
or shod and on the march to aid allies?
Or striding the Giants' Plain,[23] marshal of armies, 295
hero scanning, flashing through the ranks?
Come—
you can hear me from afar, you are a god.
Set me free from this!

[18] A person who had not been ritually purged might spread pollution merely by speaking.

[19] The animals normally sacrificed in rites of purgation.

[20] That he has not brought misfortune to his hosts indicates that Orestes has been successfully purged.

[21] Athens had contracted an alliance with Argos (the city where the action of the two earlier plays occurs) a few years before the *Oresteia* was performed.

[22] This lake in Libya, according to one version of the myth, was Athena's birthplace.

[23] The place where the Giants (offspring of Ouranos and Ge, the personification of Earth) unsuccessfully challenged the gods of Olympus. The present passage emphasizes Athena's role as warrior and guardian of her city, Athens.

LEADER.

Never—neither
Apollo's nor Athena's strength can save you.
Down you go, abandoned, 300
searching your soul for joy but joy is gone.
Bled white, gnawed by demons, a husk, a wraith—

[*She breaks off, waiting for reply, but* ORESTES *prays in silence.*]

No reply? you spit my challenge back?
You'll feast me alive, my fatted calf,
not cut on the altar first. Now hear my spell, 305
the chains of song I sing to bind you tight.

FURIES.

Come, Furies, dance!—
link arms for the dancing hand-to-hand,
now we long to reveal our art,
our terror, now to declare our right
to steer the lives of men, 310
we all conspire, we dance! we are
the just and upright, we maintain.
Hold out your hands, if they are clean
no fury of ours will stalk you,
you will go through life unscathed. 315
But show us the guilty—one like this
who hides his reeking hands,
and up from the outraged dead we rise,
witness bound to avenge their blood
we rise in flames against him to the end! 320

Mother who bore me,
O dear Mother Night,
to avenge the blinded dead
and those who see by day,
now hear me! The whelp Apollo 325
spurns my rights, he tears this trembling victim
from my grasp—the one to bleed,
to atone away the mother-blood at last.

Over the victim's burning head
this chant this frenzy striking frenzy 330
lightning crazing the mind
this hymn of Fury
chaining the senses, ripping cross the lyre,[24]
withering lives of men!

[24] The lyre was associated with Apollo in his role as god of song and of joyful poetry.

This, this is our right,
spun for us by the Fates,[25] 335
the ones who bind the world,
and none can shake our hold.
Show us the mortals overcome,
insane to murder kin—we track them down
till they go beneath the earth, 340
and the dead find little freedom in the end.

Over the victim's burning head
this chant this frenzy striking frenzy
lightning crazing the mind
this hymn of Fury 345
chaining the senses, ripping cross the lyre,
withering lives of men!

Even at birth, I say, our rights were so ordained.
The deathless gods must keep their hands far off—
no god may share our cups, our solemn feasts. 350
We want no part of their pious white robes—
the Fates who gave us power made us free.

Mine is the overthrow of houses, yes,
when warlust reared like a tame beast
seizes near and dear— 355
down on the man we swoop, aie!
for all his power black him out!—
for the blood still fresh from slaughter on his hands.

So now, striving to wrench our mandate from the gods,
we make ourselves exempt from their control, 360
we brook no trial—no god can be our judge.[26]

[*Reaching toward* ORESTES.]

His breed, worthy of loathing, streaked with blood,
Zeus slights, unworthy his contempt.

Mine is the overthrow of houses, yes,
when warlust reared like a tame beast 365
seizes near and dear—

[25] In mythology, the three sisters who control the "thread" of a human life. The first spins the thread, the second measures its length, and the third cuts it off at its destined end, the time of death.

[26] What the Furies are fighting for is not merely the punishment of Orestes as an individual. They also question the basic grounds of justice. How, they protest, can an Olympian—Athena, for example—be legally competent to decide the question of whether the Olympians or the more primeval powers should be the final court of appeal? And, even more fundamentally, should the primitive law of retaliation for crimes against kindred be subordinated to *any* court or technical legal system?

down on the man we swoop, aie!
for all his power black him out!—
for the blood still fresh from slaughter on his hands.

And all men's dreams of grandeur, 370
tempting the heavens,
all melt down, under earth their pride goes down—
lost in our onslaught, black robes swarming,
Furies throbbing, dancing out our rage.

Yes! leaping down from the heights, 375
dead weight in the crashing footfall
down we hurl on the runner
breakneck for the finish—
cut him down, our fury stamps him down!

Down he goes, sensing nothing, 380
blind with defilement . . .
darkness hovers over the man, dark guilt,
and a dense pall overhangs his house,
legend tells the story through her tears.

Yes! leaping down from the heights, 385
dead weight in the crashing footfall
down we hurl on the runner
breakneck for the finish—
cut him down, our fury stamps him down!

So the center holds. 390
We are the skilled, the masterful,
we the great fulfillers,
memories of grief, we awesome spirits
stern, unappeasable to man,
disgraced, degraded, drive our powers through; 395
banished far from god to a sunless, torchlit dusk,[27]
we drive men through their rugged passage,
blinded dead and those who see by day.

[27] These two lines, applicable to either the Furies or their victims, are a good gloss on the Furies. Both they and the punished sinners dwell in a dark underground world that is the polar opposite of the heaven and light where the newer gods dwell on Mount Olympus (above, not below, humanity). Since the Furies and the sinners inhabit the same dark place, the Furies can be understood not just as an external force of punishment but also as the internal force of guilty conscience; the sinner is ultimately his or her own avenger. The concept is akin to what Dante intimates in his *Inferno,* that the outer and internal forces that punish sin are not clearly separable. Intriguingly, then, the Furies can be interpreted as either a primitive force superseded by an advance in ethical understanding or—as a modern depth-psychologist might argue—the personification of a timeless fact about human psychology that has been obscured by the illusory progress of "civilization."

Then where is the man
not stirred with awe, not gripped by fear 400
to hear us tell the law that
Fate ordains, the gods concede the Furies,
absolute till the end of time?
And so it holds, our ancient power still holds.
We are not without our pride, though beneath the earth 405
our strict battalions form their lines,
groping through the mist and sunstarved night.

[*Enter* ATHENA, *armed for combat with her aegis*[28] *and her spear.*]

ATHENA.
From another world I heard a call for help.
I was on the Scamander's banks, just claiming Troy.[29]
The Achaean warlords chose the hero's share 410
of what their spear had won—they decreed that land,
root and branch all mine, for all time to be,
for Theseus' sons a rare, matchless gift.

Home from the wars I come, my pace unflagging,
wingless, flown on the whirring, breasting cape 415
that yokes my racing spirit in her prime.

[*Unfurling the aegis, seeing* ORESTES *and the* FURIES *at her shrine.*]

And I see some new companions on the land.
Not fear, a sense of wonder fills my eyes.

Who are you? I address you all as one:
you, the stranger seated at my idol, 420
and you, like no one born of the sown seed,
no goddess watched by the gods, no mortal either,
not to judge by your look at least, your features . . .
Wait, I call my neighbors into question.
They've done nothing wrong. It offends the rights, 425
it violates tradition.

LEADER.
You will learn it all,
young daughter of Zeus, cut to a few words.
We are the everlasting children of the Night.
Deep in the halls of Earth they call us Curses.

[28] Here, a cape worn by Athena.

[29] In Aeschylus' time the Athenians had a colony near Troy that they claimed had been given them by right after the Trojan War. "Theseus' sons" (line 413) are the Athenians; he was the legendary hero of their city.

ATHENA.
Now I know your birth, your rightful name— 430

LEADER.
But not our powers, and you will learn them quickly.

ATHENA.
I can accept the facts, just tell them clearly.

LEADER.
Destroyers of life: we drive them from their houses.

ATHENA.
And the murderer's flight, where does it all end?

LEADER.
Where there is no joy, the word is never used. 435

ATHENA.
Such flight for him? You shriek him on to that?

LEADER.
Yes,
he murdered his mother—called that murder just.

ATHENA.
And nothing forced him on, no fear of someone's anger?

LEADER.
What spur could force a man to kill his mother?

ATHENA.
Two sides are here, and only half is heard. 440

LEADER.
But the oath[30]—he will neither take the oath nor give it,
no, his will is set.

ATHENA.
And you are set
on the name of justice rather than the act.

LEADER.
How? Teach us. You have a genius for refinements.

ATHENA.
Injustice, I mean, should never triumph thanks to oaths. 445

LEADER.
Then examine him yourself, judge him fairly.

ATHENA.
You would turn over responsibility to me,
to reach the final verdict?

LEADER.
Certainly.[31]
We respect you. You show us respect.

[ATHENA *turns to* ORESTES.]

[30] The ritual oath of innocence. Orestes refuses it because the fact itself of matricide is for him not the main issue. A few lines later Athena argues that such rituals should not govern in legal contests.

[31] The Furies now agree to be bound by Athena's verdict.

ATHENA.

Your turn, stranger. What do you say to this? 450
Tell us your land, your birth, your fortunes.
Then defend yourself against their charge,
if trust in your rights has brought you here to guard
my hearth and idol, a suppliant for purging
like Ixion,[32] sacred. Speak to all this clearly, 455
speak to me.

ORESTES.

Queen Athena, first,
the misgiving in your final words is strong.
Let me remove it. I haven't come for purging.
Look, not a stain on the hands that touch your idol.
I have proof for all I say, and it is strong. 460

The law condemns the man of the violent hand
to silence, till a master trained at purging
slits the throat of a young suckling victim,
blood absolves his blood. Long ago
at the halls of others I was fully cleansed 465
in the cleansing springs, the blood of many victims.
Threat of pollution, sweep it from your mind.

Now for my birth. You will know at once.
I am from Argos. My father, well you ask,
was Agamemnon, sea-lord of the men-of-war, 470
your partisan when you made the city Troy
a city of the dead.

What an ignoble death he died
when he came home—Ai! my blackhearted mother
cut him down, enveloped him in her handsome net—
it still attests his murder in the bath. 475
But I came back, my years of exile weathered—
killed the one who bore me, I won't deny it,
killed her in revenge. I loved my father,
fiercely.

And Apollo shares the guilt—
he spurred me on, he warned of the pains I'd feel 480
unless I acted, brought the guilty down.
But were we just or not? Judge us now.
My fate is in your hands. Stand or fall
I shall accept your verdict.

ATHENA.

Too large a matter,
some may think, for mortal men to judge. 485

[32]After murdering his father-in-law, Ixion was absolved by Zeus. (Later, after trying to seduce Zeus's consort, Hera, Ixion was punished by being tied in the Underworld to an ever-revolving wheel.)

But by all rights not even I should decide
a case of murder—murder whets the passions.
Above all, the rites have tamed your wildness.
A suppliant, cleansed, you bring my house no harm.
If you are innocent, I'd adopt you for my city. 490

[*Turning to the* FURIES.]

But they have their destiny too, hard to dismiss,
and if they fail to win their day in court—
how it will spread, the venom of their pride,
plague everlasting blights our land, our future . . .

So it stands. A crisis either way. 495

[*Looking back and forth from* ORESTES *to the* FURIES.]

Embrace the one? expel the other? It defeats me.

But since the matter comes to rest on us,
I will appoint the judges of manslaughter,
swear them in, and found a tribunal here
for all time to come.[33]

[*To* ORESTES *and the* FURIES.]

My contestants, 500
summon your trusted witnesses and proofs,
your defenders under oath to help your cause.
And I will pick the finest men of Athens,
return and decide the issue fairly, truly—
bound to our oaths, our spirits bent on justice. 505

[ATHENA *leaves. The* FURIES *form their chorus.*]

FURIES.

Here, now,[34] is the overthrow
of every binding law—once his appeal,
his outrage wins the day,
his matricide! One act links all mankind,
hand to desperate hand in bloody license. 510
Over and over deathstrokes

[33] The court of the Areopagus, the main forum of the Athenian judicial system.

[34] In the following chorus, the Furies argue that the force they represent, of vengeance and fear of punishment, is the very foundation of social order; if Orestes is acquitted, the whole community will be engulfed by general chaos, since the distinction between good and evil will no longer govern human behavior.

dealt by children wait their parents,
mortal generations still unborn.

We are the Furies still, yes,
but now our rage that patrolled the crimes of men, 515
that stalked their rage dissolves—
we loose a lethal tide to sweep the world!
Man to man foresees his neighbor's torments,
groping to cure his own—
poor wretch, there is no cure, no use, 520
the drugs that ease him speed the next attack.

Now when the sudden blows come down,
let no one sound the call that once brought help,
"Justice, hear me—Furies throned in power!"
Oh I can hear the father now 525
or the mother sob with pain
at the pain's onset . . . hopeless now,
the house of Justice falls.

There is a time when terror helps,
the watchman must stand guard upon the heart. 530
It helps, at times, to suffer into truth.
Is there a man who knows no fear
in the brightness of his heart,
or a man's city, both are one,
that still reveres the rights? 535

Neither the life of anarchy
nor the life enslaved by tyrants, no,
worship neither.
Strike the balance all in all and god will give you power;
the laws of god may veer from north to south— 540
we Furies plead for Measure.
Violence is Impiety's child, true to its roots,
but the spirit's great good health breeds all we love
and all our prayers call down,
prosperity and peace. 545

All in all I tell you people,
bow before the altar of the rights,
revere it well.
Never trample it underfoot, your eyes set on spoils;
revenge will hunt the godless day and night— 550
the destined end awaits.
So honor your parents first with reverence, I say,
and the stranger guest you welcome to your house,
turn to attend his needs,
respect his sacred rights. 555

All of your own free will, all uncompelled,
be just and you will never want for joy,
you and your kin can never be uprooted from the earth.
The reckless one—I warn the marauder
dragging plunder, chaotic, rich beyond all rights: 560
he'll strike his sails,
harried at long last,
stunned when the squalls of torment break his spars to bits.

He cries to the deaf, he wrestles walls of sea
sheer whirlpools down, down, with the gods' laughter 565
breaking over the man's hot heart—they see him flailing, crushed.
The one who boasted never to shipwreck
now will never clear the cape and steer for home;
he lived for wealth,
golden his life long— 570
he rams on the reef of law and drowns unwept, unseen.

[*The scene has shifted to the Areopagus, the tribunal on the Crag of Ares.*[35] ATHENA *enters in procession with a herald and ten citizens she has chosen to be judges.*]

ATHENA.
Call for order, herald, marshal our good people.
Lift the Etruscan battle-trumpet,[36]
strain it to full pitch with human breath,
crash out a stabbing blast along the ranks. 575

[*The trumpet sounds. The judges take up positions between the audience and the actors.* ATHENA *separates the* FURIES *and* ORESTES, *directing him to the Stone of Outrage and the* LEADER *to the Stone of Unmercifulness, where the* FURIES *form their chorus. Then* ATHENA *takes her stand between two urns that will receive the ballots.*]

And while this court of judgment fills, my city,
silence will be best. So that you can learn
my everlasting laws. And you too,

[*To* ORESTES *and the* FURIES.]

[35]Ares, the god of war, had according to legend once been tried on the Areopagus (the "Crag of Ares" in Athens), for murder.
[36]Athena's battle trumpet, supposedly made in a region of northern Italy.

that our verdict may be well observed by all.

[APOLLO *enters suddenly and looms behind* ORESTES.]

Lord Apollo—rule it over your own sphere! 580
What part have you in this? Tell us.

APOLLO.

I come
as a witness. This man, according to custom,
this suppliant sought out my house and hearth.
I am the one who purged his bloody hands.
His champion too, I share responsibility 585
for his mother's execution.

Bring on the trial.
You know the rules, now turn them into justice.

[ATHENA *turns to the* FURIES.]

ATHENA.

The trial begins! Yours is the first word—
the prosecution opens. Start to finish,
set the facts before us, make them clear. 590

LEADER.

Numerous as we are, we will be brief.

[*To* ORESTES.]

Answer count for count, charge for charge.
First, tell us, did you kill your mother?

ORESTES.

I killed her. There's no denying that.

LEADER.

Three falls in the match. One is ours[37] already. 595

ORESTES.

You exult before your man is on his back.

LEADER.

But *how* did you kill her? You must tell us that.

ORESTES.

I will. I drew my sword—more, I cut her throat.

LEADER.

And who persuaded you? who led you on?

ORESTES.

This god and his command.

[*Indicating* APOLLO.]

[37] Three overthrows of the opponent were required to win a wrestling match; the Leader claims to have won the first.

He bears me witness. 600

LEADER.
The Seer? He drove you on to matricide?

ORESTES.
Yes,
and to this hour I have no regrets.

LEADER.
If the verdict
brings you down, you'll change your story quickly.

ORESTES.
I have my trust; my father will help me from the grave.

LEADER.
Trust to corpses now! You made your mother one. 605

ORESTES.
I do. She had two counts against her, deadly crimes.

LEADER.
How? Explain that to your judges.

ORESTES.
She killed her husband—killed my father too.

LEADER.
But murder set her free, and you live on for trial.

ORESTES.
She lived on. You never drove *her* into exile—why? 610

LEADER.
The blood of the man she killed was not her own.

ORESTES.
And I? Does mother's blood run in my veins?

LEADER.
How could she breed you in her body, murderer?
Disclaim your mother's blood? She gave you life.

[ORESTES *turns to* APOLLO.]

ORESTES.
Bear me witness—show me the way, Apollo! 615
Did I strike her down with justice?
Strike I did, I don't deny it, no.
But how does our bloody work impress you now?—
Just or not? Decide.
I must make my case to them.

[*Looking to the judges.*]

APOLLO.
Just, 620
I say, to you and your high court, Athena.
Seer that I am, I never lie. Not once
from the Prophet's thrones have I declared
a word that bears on man, woman or city
that Zeus did not command, the Olympian Father. 625

This is *his* justice—omnipotent, I warn you.
Bend to the will of Zeus. No oath can match
the power of the Father.

LEADER.

Zeus, you say,
gave that command to your oracle? He charged
Orestes here to avenge his father's death 630
and spurn his mother's rights?

APOLLO.

—Not the same
for a noble man to die, covered with praise,
his scepter the gift of god—murdered, at that,
by a woman's hand, no arrows whipping in
from a distance as an Amazon[38] would fight. 635
But as you will hear, Athena, and your people
poised to cast their lots and judge the case.
Home from the long campaign he came, more won
than lost on balance, home to her loyal, waiting arms,
the welcome bath . . .

he was just emerging at the edge, 640
and there she pitched her tent, her circling shroud—
she shackled her man in robes,
in her gorgeous never-ending web she chopped him down!

Such was the outrage of his death, I tell you,
the lord of the squadrons, that magnificent man. 645
Her I draw to the life to lash your people,
marshaled to reach a verdict.

LEADER.

Zeus, you say,
sets more store by a father's death? He shackled
his own father, Kronos[39] proud with age.
Doesn't that contradict you? 650

[*To the judges.*]

Mark it well. I call you all to witness.

APOLLO.

You grotesque, loathsome—the gods detest you!
Zeus can break chains, we've cures for that,
countless ingenious ways to set us free.
But once the dust drinks down a man's blood, 655
he is gone, once for all. No rising back,
no spell sung over the grave can sing him back—

[38] The Amazons were women warriors, noted especially as archers.

[39] Zeus had overcome his father Kronos (the Roman Saturn) and imprisoned him in the Underworld; Apollo will reply to this charge by arguing that imprisonment is not the same as irrevocable death.

not even Father can. Though all things else
he can overturn and never strain for breath.

LEADER.

So
you'd force this man's acquittal? Behold, Justice! 660

[*Exhibiting* APOLLO *and* ORESTES.]

Can a son spill his mother's blood on the ground,
then settle into his father's halls in Argos?
Where are the public altars he can use?
Can the kinsmen's holy water touch his hands?

APOLLO.

Here is the truth, I tell you—see how right I am. 665
The woman you call the mother of the child
is not the parent,[40] just a nurse to the seed,
the new-sown seed that grows and swells inside her.
The *man* is the source of life—the one who mounts.
She, like a stranger for a stranger, keeps 670
the shoot alive unless god hurts the roots.
I give you proof that all I say is true.
The father can father forth without a mother.
Here she stands, our living witness. Look—

[*Exhibiting* ATHENA.]

Child sprung full-blown from Olympian Zeus, 675
never bred in the darkness of the womb
but such a stock no goddess could conceive!

And I, Pallas, with all my strong techniques
will rear your host and battlements to glory.
So I dispatched this suppliant to your hearth 680
that he might be your trusted friend forever,
that you might win a new ally,[41] dear goddess.
He and his generations arm-in-arm with yours,
your bonds stand firm for all posterity—

ATHENA.

Now
have we heard enough? May I have them cast 685
their honest lots as conscience may decide?

LEADER.

For us, we have shot our arrows, every one.
I wait to hear how this ordeal will end.

[40] This genetic theory is proved, Apollo goes on to argue, by Athena herself, who was born from Zeus's head.

[41] The people of Argos; at the time of the *Oresteia*, Athens had recently concluded an alliance with them.

ATHENA.

Of course.

And what can I do to merit your respect?

APOLLO.

You have heard what you have heard. 690

[*To the judges.*]

Cast your lots, my friends,
strict to the oath that you have sworn.

ATHENA.

And now
if you would hear my law, you men of Greece,
you who will judge the first trial of bloodshed.
Now and forever more, for Aegeus' people[42] 695
this will be the court where judges reign.
This is the Crag of Ares, where the Amazons
pitched their tents when they came marching down
on Theseus, full tilt in their fury, erecting
a new city to overarch his city, towers thrust 700
against his towers—they sacrificed to Ares,
named this rock from that day onward Ares' Crag.
Here from the heights, terror and reverence,
my people's kindred powers
will hold them from injustice through the day 705
and through the mild night. Never pollute
our law with innovations. No, my citizens,
foul a clear well and you will suffer thirst.
Neither anarchy nor tyranny, my people.
Worship the Mean, I urge you, 710
shore it up with reverence and never
banish terror from the gates, not outright.[43]
Where is the righteous man who knows no fear?
The stronger your fear, your reverence for the just,
the stronger your country's wall and city's safety, 715
stronger by far than all men else possess
in Scythia's rugged steppes or Pelops' level plain.[44]
Untouched by lust for spoil, this court of law
majestic, swift to fury, rising above you
as you sleep, our night watch always wakeful, 720
guardian of our land—I found it here and now.

So I urge you, Athens. I have drawn this out
to rouse you to your future. You must rise,

[42] The Athenians; Aegeus was a legendary ruler of the city and father of Theseus.

[43] The phrase probably means two things: (a) maintain as part of your conscience a wholesome fear of committing evil, and (b) do not summarily turn away from your city a frightened stranger seeking asylum.

[44] That is, in the wild land of faraway Scythia or in the Grecian land of Pelops that included Argos.

each man must cast his lot and judge the case,
reverent to his oath. Now I have finished. 725

[*The judges come forward, pass between the urns and cast their lots.*]

LEADER.
Beware. Our united force can break your land.
Never wound our pride, I tell you, never.

APOLLO.
The oracles, not mine alone but Zeus's too—
dread them, I warn you, never spoil their fruit.

[*The* LEADER *turns to* APOLLO.]

LEADER.
You dabble in works of blood beyond your depth. 730
Oracles, your oracles will be stained forever.

APOLLO.
Oh, so the Father's judgment faltered when Ixion,
the first man-slayer came to him for purging?

LEADER.
Talk on, talk on. But if I lose this trial
I will return in force to crush the land. 735

APOLLO.
Never—among the gods, young and old,
you go disgraced. I will triumph over you!

LEADER.
Just as you triumphed in the house of Pheres,[45]
luring the Fates to set men free from death.

APOLLO.
What?—is it a crime to help the pious man, 740
above all, when his hour of need has come?

LEADER.
You brought them down, the oldest realms of order,
seduced the ancient goddesses with wine.

APOLLO.
You will fail this trial—in just a moment
spew your venom and never harm your enemies. 745

LEADER.
You'd ride me down, young god, for all my years?
Well here I stand, waiting to learn the verdict.
Torn with doubt . . . to rage against the city or—

[45] Father of Admetus, a favorite of Apollo, who preserved Admetus from destined death by overcoming "the ancient goddesses"—that is, the Fates—"with wine" (line 743) so that they agreed to accept an alternative victim. Admetus' wife Alcestis offered her own life instead of his. The story is told in Euripides' *Alcestis.*

ATHENA.
My work is here, to render the final judgment.
Orestes,

[*Raising her arm, her hand clenched as if holding a ballot-stone.*]

I will cast my lot for you. 750
No mother gave me birth.
I honor the male, in all things but marriage.
Yes, with all my heart I am my Father's child.
I cannot set more store by the woman's death—
she killed her husband, guardian of their house. 755
Even if the vote is equal, Orestes wins.[46]

Shake the lots from the urns. Quickly,
you of the jury charged to make the count.

[*Judges come forward, empty the urns, and count the ballot-stones.*]

ORESTES.
O God of the Light, Apollo, how will the verdict go?
LEADER.
O Night, dark mother, are you watching now? 760
ORESTES.
Now for the goal—the noose, or the new day!
LEADER.
Now we go down, or forge ahead in power.
APOLLO.
Shake out the lots and count them fairly, friends.
Honor Justice. An error in judgment now
can mean disaster. The cast of a single lot 765
restores a house to greatness.

[*Receiving the judges' count,* ATHENA *lifts her arm once more.*]

ATHENA.
The man goes free,
cleared of the charge of blood. The lots are equal.
ORESTES.
O Pallas Athena—you, you save my house!
I was shorn of the fatherland but you
reclaim it for me. Now any Greek will say, 770

[46] In interpreting Athena's decision here, we can accept her own explanation, that she is her father Zeus's child (an Olympian who is biased toward males). But these reasons seem incompatible with her evenhandedness elsewhere in the play. That she has not simply ignored the Furies' side of the case is proved by her later actions and words.

"He lives again, the man of Argos lives
on his fathers' great estates. Thanks to Pallas,
Apollo and Zeus, the lord of all fulfillment,
Third, Saving Zeus." He respected father's death,
looked down on mother's advocates—

[*Indicating the* FURIES.]

he saved me. 775

And now I journey home. But first I swear
to you, your land and assembled host, I swear
by the future years that bring their growing yield
that no man, no helmsman of Argos wars on Athens,
spears in the vanguard moving out for conquest. 780
We ourselves, even if we must rise up from the grave,
will deal with those who break the oath I take—
baffle them with disasters, curse their marches,
send them hawks aloft on the left[47] at every crossing—
make their pains recoil upon their heads. 785
But all who keep our oath, who uphold your rights
and citadel forever, comrade spear to spear,
we bless with all the kindness of our heart.
Now farewell, you and the people of your city.
Good wrestling—a grip no foe can break. 790
A saving hope, a spear to bring you triumph!

[*Exit* ORESTES, *followed by* APOLLO.
The FURIES *reel in wild confusion*
around ATHENA.]

FURIES.

You, you younger gods!—you have ridden down
the ancient laws, wrenched them from my grasp—
and I, robbed of my birthright, suffering, great with wrath,
I loose my poison over the soil, aieee!— 795
poison to match my grief comes pouring out my heart,
cursing the land to burn it sterile and now
rising up from its roots a cancer blasting leaf and child,
now for Justice, Justice!—cross the face of the earth
the bloody tide comes hurling, all mankind destroyed. 800
. . . Moaning, only moaning? What will I do?
The mockery of it, Oh unbearable,
mortified by Athens,
we the daughters of Night,
our power stripped, cast down.

[47] The left was the side on which ill omens supposedly appeared. Compare the eagles (mentioned in *Agamemnon,* lines 118 ff.) who appeared on the right before the sacrifice of Iphigeneia at Aulis.

ATHENA.

Yield to me. 805
No more heavy spirits. You were not defeated—
the vote was tied, a verdict fairly reached
with no disgrace to you, no, Zeus brought
luminous proof before us. He who spoke
god's oracle, he bore witness that Orestes 810
did the work but should not suffer harm.

And now you'd vent your anger, hurt the land?
Consider a moment. Calm yourself. Never
render us barren, raining your potent showers
down like spears, consuming every seed. 815
By all my rights I promise you your seat
in the depths of earth,[48] yours by all rights—
stationed at hearths equipped with glistening thrones,
covered with praise! My people will revere you.

FURIES.

You, you younger gods!—you have ridden down 820
the ancient laws, wrenched them from my grasp—
and I, robbed of my birthright, suffering, great with wrath,
I loose my poison over the soil, aieee!—
poison to match my grief comes pouring out my heart,
cursing the land to burn it sterile and now 825
rising up from its roots a cancer blasting leaf and child,
now for Justice, Justice!—cross the face of the earth
the bloody tide comes hurling, all mankind destroyed.
. . . Moaning, only moaning? What will I do?
The mockery of it, Oh unbearable, 830
mortified by Athens,
we the daughters of Night,
our power stripped, cast down.

ATHENA.

You have your power,
you are goddesses—but not to turn
on the world of men and ravage it past cure. 835
I put my trust in Zeus and . . . must I add this?
I am the only god who knows the keys
to the armory where his lightning-bolt is sealed.
No need of that, not here.

Let me persuade you.
The lethal spell of your voice, never cast it 840
down on the land and blight its harvest home.
Lull asleep that salt black wave of anger—
awesome, proud with reverence, live with me.
The land is rich, and more, when its first fruits,

[48]Appropriately, the Furies, who have been all along portrayed as forces of earth and night, will be given cave shrines at the Athenian Acropolis, where they will combine their old role as ministers of avenging justice with a new role as agents of fertility and the blessings symbolized by it.

offered for heirs and the marriage rites, are yours 845
to hold forever, you will praise my words.

FURIES.

But for me to suffer such disgrace . . . I,
the proud heart of the past, driven under the earth,
condemned, like so much filth,
and the fury in me breathing hatred— 850
O good Earth,
what is this stealing under the breast,
what agony racks the spirit? . . . Night, dear Mother Night!
All's lost, our ancient powers torn away by their cunning,
ruthless hands, the gods so hard to wrestle down 855
obliterate us all.

ATHENA.

I will bear with your anger.
You are older. The years have taught you more,
much more than I can know. But Zeus, I think,
gave me some insight too, that has its merits.
If you leave for an alien land and alien people, 860
you will come to love this land, I promise you.
As time flows on, the honors flow through all
my citizens, and you, throned in honor
before the house of Erechtheus,[49] will harvest
more from men and women moving in solemn file 865
than you can win throughout the mortal world.

Here in our homeland never cast the stones
that whet our bloodlust. Never waste our youth,
inflaming them with the burning wine of strife.
Never pluck the heart of the battle cock 870
and plant it in our people—intestine war
seething against themselves. Let our wars
rage on abroad, with all their force, to satisfy
our powerful lust for fame. But as for the bird
that fights at home—my curse on civil war. 875

This is the life I offer, it is yours to take.
Do great things, feel greatness, greatly honored.
Share this country cherished by the gods.

FURIES.

But for me to suffer such disgrace . . . I,
the proud heart of the past, driven under the earth, 880
condemned, like so much filth,
and the fury in me breathing hatred—
O good Earth,
what is this stealing under the breast,
what agony racks the spirit? . . . Night, dear Mother Night! 885

[49] A legendary ruler of Athens; a temple named for him (the Erechtheum) stood on the Acropolis.

All's lost, our ancient powers torn away by their cunning,
ruthless hands, the gods so hard to wrestle down
obliterate us all.

ATHENA.

No, I will never tire
of telling you your gifts. So that you,
the older gods, can never say that I, 890
a young god and the mortals of my city
drove you outcast, outlawed from the land.

But if you have any reverence for Persuasion,
the majesty of Persuasion,
the spell of my voice that would appease your fury— 895
Oh please stay . . .
and if you refuse to stay,
it would be wrong, unjust to afflict this city
with wrath, hatred, populations routed. Look,
it is all yours, a royal share of our land—
justly entitled, glorified forever.

LEADER.

Queen Athena, 900
where is the home you say is mine to hold?

ATHENA.

Where all the pain and anguish end. Accept it.

LEADER.

And if I do, what honor waits for me?

ATHENA.

No house can thrive without you.

LEADER.

You would do that—
grant me that much power?

ATHENA.

Whoever reveres us— 905
we will raise the fortunes of their lives.

LEADER.

And you will pledge me that, for all time to come?

ATHENA.

Yes—I must never promise things I cannot do.

LEADER.

Your magic is working . . . I can feel the hate,
the fury slip away.

ATHENA.

At last! And now take root 910
in the land and win yourself new friends.

LEADER.

A spell—
what spell to sing? to bind the land forever? Tell us.

ATHENA.

Nothing that strikes a note of brutal conquest. Only peace—
blessings, rising up from the earth and the heaving sea,

and down the vaulting sky let the wind-gods breathe 915
a wash of sunlight streaming through the land,
and the yield of soil and grazing cattle flood
our city's life with power and never flag
with time. Make the seed of men live on,
the more they worship you the more they thrive. 920
I love them as a gardener loves his plants,
these upright men, this breed fought free of grief.
All that is yours to give.
And I,
in the trials of war where fighters burn for fame,
will never endure the overthrow of Athens— 925
all will praise her, victor city, pride of man.

[*The* FURIES *assemble, dancing around* ATHENA, *who becomes their leader.*]

FURIES.

I will embrace
one home with you, Athena,
never fail the city
you and Zeus almighty, you and Ares 930
hold as the fortress of the gods, the shield
of the high Greek altars, glory of the powers.
Spirit of Athens, hear my words, my prayer
like a prophet's warm and kind,
that the rare good things of life 935
come rising crest on crest,
sprung from the rich black earth and
gleaming with the bursting flash of sun.

ATHENA.

These blessings I bestow on you, my people, gladly.
I enthrone these strong, implacable spirits here 940
and root them in our soil.
Theirs,
theirs to rule the lives of men,
it is their fated power.
But he who has never felt their weight,
or known the blows of life and how they fall, 945
the crimes of his fathers hale him toward their bar,
and there for all his boasts—destruction,
silent, majestic in anger,
crushes him to dust.

FURIES.

Yes and I ban
the winds that rock the olive— 950
hear my love, my blessing—
thwart their scorching heat that blinds the buds,
hold from our shores the killing icy gales,

and I ban the blight that creeps on fruit and withers—
God of creation, Pan, make flocks increase 955
and the ewes drop fine twin lambs
when the hour of labor falls.
And silver, child of Earth,
secret treasure of Hermes,
come to light and praise the gifts of god. 960

ATHENA.
Blessings—now do you hear, you guards of Athens,
all that she will do?
Fury the mighty queen, the dread
of the deathless gods and those beneath the earth,
deals with mortals clearly, once for all. 965
She delivers songs to some, to others
a blinding life of tears—
Fury works her will.

FURIES.
And the lightning stroke
that cuts men down before their prime, I curse,
but the lovely girl who finds a mate's embrace, 970
the deep joy of wedded life—O grant that gift, that prize,
you gods of wedlock, grant it, goddesses of Fate!
Sisters born of the Night our mother,
spirits steering law,
sharing at all our hearths, 975
at all times bearing down
to make our lives more just,
all realms exalt you highest of the gods.

ATHENA.
Behold, my land, what blessings Fury kindly,
gladly brings to pass— 980
I am in my glory! Yes, I love Persuasion;
she watched my words, she met their wild refusals.
Thanks to Zeus of the Councils who can turn
dispute to peace—he won the day.

[*To the* FURIES.]

Thanks to our duel for blessings; 985
we win through it all.

FURIES.
And the brutal strife,
the civil war devouring men, I pray
that it never rages through our city, no,
that the good Greek soil never drinks the blood of Greeks,
shed in an orgy of reprisal life for life— 990
that Fury like a beast will never
rampage through the land.
Give joy in return for joy,
one common will for love,

and hate with one strong heart: 995
such union heals a thousand ills of man.

ATHENA.

Do you *hear* how Fury sounds her blessings forth,
how Fury finds the way?
Shining out of the terror of their faces
I can see great gains for you, my people. 1000
Hold them kindly, kind as they are to you.
Exalt them always, you exalt your land,
your city straight and just—
its light goes through the world.

FURIES.

Rejoice,
rejoice in destined wealth, 1005
rejoice, Athena's people—
poised by the side of Zeus,
loved by the loving virgin girl,[50]
achieve humanity at last,
nestling under Pallas' wings 1010
and blessed with Father's love.

ATHENA.

You too rejoice! and I must lead the way
to your chambers by the holy light of these,
your escorts bearing fire.

[*Enter* ATHENA*'s entourage of women, bearing offerings and victims and torches still unlit.*]

Come, and sped beneath the earth 1015
by our awesome sacrifices,
keep destruction from the country,
bring prosperity home to Athens,
triumph sailing in its wake.
And you,
my people born of the Rock King,[51] 1020
lead on our guests for life, my city—
May they treat you with compassion,
compassionate as you will be to them.

FURIES.

Rejoice!—
rejoice—the joy resounds—
all those who dwell in Athens, 1025
spirits and mortals, come,
govern Athena's city well,

[50] The "virgin goddess" Athena; her kinship with the Furies, who are now also kindly Eumenides, ironically recalls Apollo's sneer at the Furies earlier as "the eternal virgins" (line 73).

[51] The primitive king of the Acropolis.

revere us well, we are your guests;
you will learn to praise your Furies,
you will praise the fortunes of your lives. 1030

ATHENA.
My thanks! and I will speed your prayers, your blessings—
lit by the torches breaking into flame
I send you home, home to the core of Earth,
escorted by these friends who guard my idol
duty-bound.

[ATHENA*'s entourage comes forward, bearing crimson robes.*[52]]

Bright eye of the land of Theseus, 1035
come forth, my splendid troupe. Girls and mothers,
trains of aged women grave in movement,
dress our Furies now in blood-red robes.
Praise them—let the torch move on!
So the love this family bears toward our land 1040
will bloom in human strength from age to age.

[*The women invest the* FURIES *and sing the final chorus. Torches blaze; a procession forms, including the actors and the judges and the audience.* ATHENA *leads them from the theater and escorts them through the city.*]

THE WOMEN OF THE CITY.
On, on, good spirits born for glory,
Daughters of Night, her children always young,
now under loyal escort—
Blessings, people of Athens, sing your blessings out. 1045

Deep, deep in the first dark vaults of Earth,
sped by the praise and victims we will bring,
reverence will attend you—
Blessings now, all people, sing your blessings out.

You great good Furies, bless the land with kindly hearts, 1050
you Awesome Spirits, come—exult in the blazing torch,
exultant in our fires, journey on.
Cry, cry in triumph, carry on the dancing on and on!

This peace between Athena's people and their guests
must never end. All-seeing Zeus and Fate embrace, 1055
down they come to urge our union on—
Cry, cry in triumph, carry on the dancing on and on!

[52] The red robes and torches recall and reverse the ominous symbolism of robes, blood, and torches in the *Agamemnon*.

Sophocles

(496–406 B.C.)

In more than one sense, Sophocles is the central figure among the three great Greek tragedians. He was born in 496 B.C. in Colonus, the suburb of Athens celebrated in his last play, *Oedipus at Colonus;* he died in 406. Much of his life span thus overlapped that of his predecessor, Aeschylus, who died when Sophocles was forty. The third of the great triumvirate, Euripides, was sixteen years younger than Sophocles but died slightly before him. As a dramatist, Sophocles was a consummate artist who combined the high ethical and religious concerns of Aeschylus with the intense interest in individual human psychology characteristic of Euripides. Sophocles' ninety years of life therefore coincided with the entire history—the rise and fall—of the golden age of Greek tragedy. His years also coincided with the rise and fall of the uniquely splendid—and historically tragic—Athenian culture of the fifth century. In 480, when Sophocles was sixteen years old, he took part in a public celebration of the naval victory over the Persians at Salamis, a victory that, coincidentally or not, raised the curtain on the awesome cultural and social achievements of the ensuing age. Sophocles' death occurred only two years before the definitive collapse of Athenian supremacy, when in 404 the city succumbed to Sparta and its allies.

By most accounts, Sophocles was a man comfortably at home in his world and at the center of its public life. He was enormously successful and popular as a man of the theater. His temperament was urbane, gregarious, balanced. He held several important public positions during the years of Athens' primacy—as treasurer, as a diplomatic and military policymaker, as an ambassador, even as a priest. In short, he was what we have come to call a member of the establishment. And yet, intriguingly, he wrote dramas that call into question—though they do not necessarily undermine—the values generally associated with that role. Oedipus, in *Oedipus the King,* is the model of a good ruler, a humanely intelligent and vigorously active leader, a man who earlier saved his adopted city Thebes from disaster. Yet Oedipus is finally driven to self-mutilation and self-imposed exile because he has committed, though unwittingly, the most horrendous crimes against the divine order, the natural order, and the polity: patricide, incest, and the pollution of his city. In *Antigone,* Oedipus' brave, lovable, headstrong daughter confronts her uncle Kreon, the new ruler of Thebes, over an issue—the conflicting demands of civic, familial, and religious principles—that few establishmentarians would press urgently. Probings of these themes, stories, and issues are not what one would normally expect of either a religious pietist or a politically complacent conservative.

That paradox, along with others, makes Sophocles an especially challenging artist and personality. Authorities disagree on how to interpret him, as man or playwright. He wrote more than 120 plays, of which only seven have survived intact: the two included in this volume plus *Ajax, Philoctetes, The Women of Trachis, Electra,* and *Oedipus at Colonus.* His artistic control of plot and other elements of the drama has helped identify Sophocles as the perfect "classicist," and the extravagant praise heaped on him by Aristotle in his *Poetics* has reinforced that image. Yet "classicist" is an inadequate term, and a seriously misleading one if we make the simple-minded but familiar identification of the classical with calm, serene detachment. Sophocles tends to represent in his characters general human types, an approach usually considered classical. Antigone is the archetype of the martyr to principle. Oedipus is the intelligent man brought low by the very intellectual gifts and compulsion to understand that make him admirable (not to mention the universality found in him by Sigmund Freud, who discerned in the "Oedipus complex" a fundamental law of filial and psychic experience). Yet at no time do we lose sight of these characters as individuals racked by conflict, pain, or both. Antigone is indeed a type, but, like Cordelia in Shakespeare's *King Lear,* who has a similar blend of vulnerability and toughness, she embodies that type in a distinct individual personality that includes a waspish streak. Her awareness of the sanctity of the family bond makes her compassionate toward her dead brother Polynices but incongruously contemptuous of her sister Ismene.

One of the pervading themes in Sophocles is the justice of the universe. We are to understand that, in some sense, cosmic justice ultimately prevails. But any cosmic justice that demands the blinding and exile of the essentially just Oedipus and the death of the heroic Antigone would seem ambiguous, indeed very frightening. Few authors of any age have rendered the experience of raw pain—psychological and physical—so compellingly. Significantly, the nineteenth-century poet Matthew Arnold described Sophocles as a man who "saw life steadily and saw it whole" but also as one who heard "the eternal note of sadness" and was preeminently sensitive to "the turbid ebb and flow of human misery."

Sophocles does not treat issues in a vacuum; he is above all a dramatist. The innovations he made in dramatic method and staging have the effect of making conflict more humanly immediate—if not necessarily more powerful—than in Aeschylus. By increasing the number of speaking actors from two to three, Sophocles made possible even more intricate interpersonal relationships than Aeschylus had portrayed; by reducing the lyrical role of the chorus (though he increased its size), Sophocles was able to focus more directly, and in a less stylized way, on complexities of character as conveyed in dialogue. He also expanded the use of stage machinery. The total effect is to intensify our awareness of conflict, both external and within individual characters.

Oedipus the King has a special place in literature; it may well be the most important and influential drama ever written. Aristotle seems to have considered it the definitive tragedy, just as he considered Homer's *Iliad* and *Odyssey* the definitive epics. The play is the best known and most frequently cited example of "dramatic irony," where the audience possesses information of which the main characters in the play are ignorant. The gradual revelation to Oedipus of his past history, an already familiar story the audience would have known from the very beginning of the play, makes for powerful suspense, especially since it is Oedipus himself who relentlessly investigates and puts together the case that—for all the elaborate precautions he has taken not to commit unspeakable crimes—will in the end damn him in his own eyes and in those of other people. The gigantic metaphor of eyes, of seeing and blindness, is worked with virtuoso skill. But the metaphor is not a mere "literary" device; it typifies Sophocles' view of humanity's place in the totality of things. Human beings in his plays are an integral part of a world order that can be only partially understood at best. The cosmic system includes, besides human beings and nature, those darkly inscrutable forces identified—inadequately—as the gods and fate.

Yet Sophocles is not a fatalist either. Despite the sense of inevitability his plays convey, human beings are considered responsible for their acts. But this belief in responsibility raises an even deeper question about necessity and human freedom, for if the lives of men and women are governed by themselves and not by their stars, are not these human beings themselves determined in their behavior by what they "are"? Character may be destiny, but to what extent is character itself an unchangeable given? Even more than such difficult but relatively concrete issues as the conflict between the person and polity, this mind-bending question makes Sophocles' plays touchstones for an appreciation of the human dilemma.

FURTHER READING: An excellent general introduction to Sophocles and to each of his plays is Ruth Scodel, *Sophocles,* 1984. Now available in English is the classic by Karl Reinhardt, *Sophocles,* 1947, trans. Hazel and David Harvey, 1979, which discusses all the extant plays. Other works dealing with all or some of the Sophoclean dramas are S. M. Adams, *Sophocles the Playwright,* 1957; William Nickerson Bates, *Sophocles: Poet and Dramatist,* 1940, repr. 1961; Bernard M. W. Knox, *The Heroic Temper: Studies in Sophoclean Tragedy,* 1964. Further critical works on the life and thought of Sophocles are T. B. L. Webster, *An Introduction to Sophocles,* 1936, repr. 1969; and H. D. F. Kitto, *Sophocles: Dramatist and Philosopher,* 1958, repr. 1981. A number of modern interpretations of Sophocles are edited by Thomas Marion Woodard, *Sophocles: A Collection of Critical Essays,* 1966. The theatrical production of Sophocles' plays is the subject of David Seale, *Vision and Stagecraft in Sophocles,* 1982; see also the discussion of Sophocles' theater in J. Michael Walton, *The Greek Sense of Theatre: Tragedy Reviewed,* 1985. A close analysis of the word patterns in *Antigone* is given by R. F. Goheen, *The Imagery of Sophocles' Antigone,* 1951. The staging of *Antigone* is discussed in Leo Aylen, *The Greek Theater,* 1985. Charles Segal, *Oedipus Tyrannus,* 1993, presents a succinct but searching analysis of the play. Frederick Ahl, *Sophocles' Oedipus,* 1992, explores the play's cultural complexities. Luci Berkowitz and Theodore F. Brunner, eds., *Sophocles: Oedipus Tyrannus,* 1970, includes both a translation and a number of essays by various scholars on themes such as religion and psychology. See further M. J. O'Brien, ed., *Twentieth Century Interpretations of Oedipus Rex: A Collection of Critical Essays,* 1968.

OEDIPUS THE KING

Translated by Stephen Berg and Diskin Clay

CHARACTERS

OEDIPUS, *king of Thebes*
PRIEST *of Zeus*
KREON, *Oedipus' brother-in-law*
CHORUS OF THEBAN ELDERS
LEADER OF THE CHORUS
TEIRESIAS, *prophet, servant to Apollo*
JOCASTA, *wife of Oedipus*
MESSENGER *from Corinth*
SHEPHERD, *member of Laios' household*
SERVANT, *household slave of Oedipus*
Delegation of Thebans, servants to lead Teiresias and Oedipus; attendants to Oedipus, Kreon, Jocasta; and Antigone and Ismene, the daughters of Oedipus

TIME AND SCENE

Dawn. Silence. The royal palace of Thebes. The altar of Apollo[1] *to the left of the central palace. A delegation of Thebans—old men, boys, young children—enters the orchestra*[2] *by the steps below the altar, assembles, and waits. They carry suppliant boughs—olive branches tied with strips of wool. Some climb the steps between the orchestra and the altar, place their branches on the altar, and return to the orchestra. A* PRIEST *stands apart from the suppliants at the foot of one of the two stairs. Silence. Waiting. The central doors open. From inside the palace, limping,*[3] OEDIPUS *comes through the palace doors and stands at the top of the steps leading down into the orchestra. He is dressed in gold and wears a golden crown.*

OEDIPUS. Why children,
why are you here, why
are you holding those branches tied with wool,
begging me for help? Children,
the whole city smolders with incense.[4]
Wherever I go I hear sobbing, praying. Groans fill the air.
Rumors, news from messengers, they are not enough for me.
Others cannot tell me what you need.
I am king, I had to come. As king,
I had to know. Know for myself, know for me. 10
Everybody everywhere knows who I am: Oedipus. King.
Priest of Zeus, we respect your age, your high office.
Speak.
Why are you kneeling? Are you afraid, old man?
What can I give you?
How can I help? Ask.
Ask me anything. Anything at all.
My heart would be a stone
if I felt no pity for these poor shattered people of mine
kneeling here, at my feet. 20

PRIEST. Oedipus, lord of Thebes, you see us, the people of Thebes, your people,
crowding in prayer around your altar,
these small children here, old men bent with age, priests, and I, the priest of Zeus,
and our noblest young men, the pride and strength of Thebes.
And there are more of us, lord Oedipus, more—gathered in the city, stunned,
kneeling, offering their branches, praying before the two great temples of Athena[5]

[1] The utterances of Apollo, god of prophecy, are central to the play's action. He was also god of healing and, conversely, of plague.

[2] In a Greek theater, the open space in front of the stage.

[3] In Greek, the name Oedipus means "swell-foot." The cause of his lameness is revealed later in the play.

[4] The city has been making religious offerings to appease the angry gods who have visited plague on Thebes.

[5] Goddess of wisdom and knowledge; also, the patron of Athens and of Greek cities in general.

or staring into the ashes of burnt offerings,[6] staring,
waiting, waiting for the god to speak.
Look,
look at it, 30
lord Oedipus—right there,
in front of your eyes—this city—
it reels under a wild storm of blood, wave after wave battering Thebes.
We cannot breathe or stand.
We hunger, our world shivers with hunger. A disease hungers,
nothing grows, wheat, fruit, nothing grows bigger than a seed.
Our women bear
dead things,
all they can do is grieve,
our cattle wither, stumble, drop to the ground, 40
flies simmer on their bloated tongues,
the plague spreads everywhere, a stain seeping through our streets,
our fields, our houses,
look—god's fire eating everyone, everything,
stroke after stroke of lightning, the god stabbing it alive—
it can't be put out, it can't be stopped,
its heat thickens the air, it glows like smoking metal,
this god of plague guts our city and fills the black world under us
where the dead go
with the shrieks of women,
living women, wailing.
You are a man, not a god—I know. 50
We all know this, the young kneeling here before you know it, too,
but we know how great you are, Oedipus, greater than any man.
When crisis struck, you saved us[7] here in Thebes,
you faced the mysterious, strange disasters hammered against us
by the gods.
This is our history—
we paid our own flesh to the Sphinx until you set us free.
You knew no more than anyone, but you knew.
There was a god in it, a god in you.

[*The* PRIEST *kneels.*]

Help us. Oedipus, we beg you, we all turn to you, kneeling to your
greatness.
Advice from the gods or advice from human beings—you will know
which is needed. 60

[6]Sacrifices to the gods; the inspection of the ashes, it was hoped, would reveal the gods' will.

[7]Thebes had earlier been ravaged by the Sphinx, a monster with a lion's body and a woman's head, who proposed a famous riddle, a wrong solution to which was punished by death. The question was, "What animal moves first on four legs, then on two, then on three, and is weakest when moving on four legs?" Oedipus correctly solved the riddle: Man, who first crawls, then walks, then goes with a walking stick. The solution of the riddle destroyed the Sphinx and established Oedipus in power as savior of Thebes.

But help us. Power and experience are yours, all yours.
Between thought and action, between
our plans and their results a distance opens.
Only a man like you, Oedipus, tested by experience,
can make them one. That much I know.
Oedipus, more like a god than any man alive,
deliver us, raise us to our feet. Remember who you are.
Remember your love for Thebes. Your skill was our salvation once
before.
For this Thebes calls you savior.
Don't let us remember you as the king—godlike in power— 70
who gave us back our life, then let us die.
Steady us forever. You broke the riddle for us then.
It was a sign. A god was in it. Be the man you were—
rule now as you ruled before.
Oh Oedipus,
how much better to rule a city of men than be king of empty earth.
A city is nothing, a ship is nothing
where no men live together, where no men work together.

OEDIPUS. Children, poor helpless children.
I know what brings you here, I know. 80
You suffer, this plague is agony for each of you,
but none of you, not one suffers as I do.
Each of you suffers for himself, only himself.
My whole being wails and breaks
for this city, for myself, for all of you,
old man, all of you.
Everything ends here, with me. I am the man.
You have not wakened me from some kind of sleep.
I have wept, struggled, wandered in this maze of thought,
tried every road, searched hard— 90
finally I found one cure, only one:
I sent my wife's brother, Kreon, to great Apollo's shrine at Delphi;[8]
I sent him to learn what I must say or do to save Thebes.
But his long absence troubles me. Why isn't he here? Where is he?
When he returns, what kind of man would I be
if I failed to do everything the god reveals?

[*Some of the suppliants by the steps to the orchestra stand to announce* KREON*'s arrival to the* PRIEST. KREON *comes in by the entrance to the audience's left with a garland on his head.*]

PRIEST. You speak of Kreon, and Kreon is here.

OEDIPUS. [*turning to the altar of Apollo, then to* KREON]
Lord Apollo, look at him—his head is crowned with laurel, his eyes
glitter.

[8] The most important center of prophecy in Greece; see the description at the beginning of Aeschylus' *The Eumenides*.

Let his words blaze, blaze like his eyes, and save us.
PRIEST. He looks calm, radiant, like a god. If he brought bad news, 100
would he be wearing that crown of sparkling leaves?
OEDIPUS. At last we will know.
Lord Kreon, what did the god Apollo say?
KREON. His words are hopeful.
Once everything is clear, exposed to the light,
we will see our suffering is blessing. All we need is luck.
OEDIPUS. What do you mean? What did Apollo say? What should we do?
Speak.
KREON. Here? Now? In front of all these people?
Or inside, privately? 110

[KREON *moves toward the palace.*]

OEDIPUS. Stop. Say it. Say it to the whole city.
I grieve for them, for their sorrow and loss, far more than I grieve for myself.
KREON. This is what I heard—there was no mistaking the god's meaning—
Apollo commands us:
Cleanse the city of Thebes, cleanse the plague from that city,
destroy the black stain spreading everywhere, spreading,
poisoning the earth, touching each house, each citizen,
sickening the hearts of the people of Thebes!
Cure this disease that wastes all of you, spreading, spreading,
before it grows so vast nothing can cure it. 120
OEDIPUS. What is this plague?
How can we purify the city?
KREON. A man must be banished. Banished or killed.
Blood for blood. The plague is blood,
blood, breaking over Thebes.
OEDIPUS. *Who* is the man? *Who* is Apollo's victim?
KREON. My lord, before you came to Thebes, before you came to power,
Laios was our king.
OEDIPUS. I know. But I never saw Laios.
KREON. Laios was murdered. Apollo's command was very clear: 130
Avenge the murderers of Laios. Whoever they are.
OEDIPUS. But where *are* his murderers?
The crime is old. How will we find their tracks?
The killers could be anywhere.
KREON. Apollo said the killers are still here, here in Thebes.
Pursue a thing, and you may catch it;
ignored, it slips away.
OEDIPUS. And Laios—where was he murdered?
At home? Or was he away from Thebes?
KREON. He told us before he left—he was on a mission to Delphi, 140
his last trip away from Thebes. He never returned.
OEDIPUS. Wasn't there a witness, someone with Laios who saw what happened?

KREON. They were all killed, except for one man. He escaped.
But he was so terrified he remembered only one thing.
OEDIPUS. What was it? One small clue might lead to others.
KREON. This is what he said: bandits ambushed Laios, not one man.
They attacked him like hail crushing a stalk of wheat.
OEDIPUS. How could a single bandit dare attack a king
unless he had supporters, people with money, here,
here in Thebes? 150
KREON. There were suspicions. But after Laios died we had no leader,
no king.
Our life was turmoil, uncertainty.
OEDIPUS. But once the throne was empty,
what threw you off the track, what kept you from searching
until you uncovered everything, knew every detail?
KREON. The intricate, hard song of the Sphinx
persuaded us the crime was not important, not then.
It seemed to say we should focus on what lay at our feet, in front
of us,
ignore what we could not see.
OEDIPUS. Now, *I* am here. 160
I will begin the search again, I
will reveal the truth, expose everything, let it all be seen.
Apollo and you were right to make us wonder about the dead man.
Like Apollo, I am your ally.
Justice and vengeance are what I want,
for Thebes, for the god.
Family, friends—I won't rid myself of this stain, this disease, for
them—
they're far from here.[9] I'll do it for myself, for me.
The man who killed Laios might take revenge on me
just as violently. 170
So by avenging Laios' death, I protect myself.
[*turning to the suppliants*] Rise, children,
pick up your branches,
let someone announce my decision to the whole city of Thebes.
[*to the* PRIEST] I will do everything. Everything.
And, with the god's help, we will be saved.
Bright Apollo, let your light help us see.
Our happiness is yours to give, our failure and ruin yours.
PRIEST. Rise. We have the help we came for, children.
The king himself has promised. 180
May Apollo, who gave these oracles, come as our savior now.
Apollo, heal us, save us from this plague!

[OEDIPUS *enters the palace. Its doors close.* KREON *leaves by a door to the*

[9]Oedipus means that his wife's first husband, Laios, is now far removed by time and death; in addition, at this point Oedipus wrongly believes that he is the son of parents who reside in another city (Corinth).

right on the wing of the stage. The PRIEST *and suppliants go down into the orchestra and leave by the entrance to the left as a chorus of fifteen Theban elders files into the orchestra by the entrance on the right, preceded by a flute player.*]

CHORUS. voice voice voice
voice who knows everything o god
glorious voice of Zeus[10]
how have you come from Delphi bathed in gold
what are you telling our bright city Thebes
what are you bringing me
health death fear
I know nothing 190
so frightened rooted here
awed by you
healer what have you sent
is it the sudden doom of grief
or the old curse the darkness
looming in the turning season

o holy immortal voice
hope golden seed of the future
listen be with me speak
these cries of mine rise 200
tell me
I call to you reach out to you first
holy Athena god's daughter who lives forever
and your sister Artemis[11]
who cradles the earth our earth
who sits on her great throne at the hub of the market place
and I call to Apollo who hurls light
from deep in the sky
o gods be with us now
shine on us your three shields[12] 210
blazing against the darkness
come in our suffering as you came once before
to Thebes o bright divinities
and threw your saving light against the god of grief
o gods
be with us now

pain pain my sorrows have no sound
no name no word no pain like this

[10]The message or communication from Zeus, king of the gods. More concretely, the "voice" is Apollo, the prophetic spokesman of the supreme god's will and knowledge.

[11]Athena was the daughter of Zeus, born directly without a mother from his head; Artemis, born of Zeus and Leto, is her half-sister and also Apollo's full sister.

[12]The protective power of the three deities invoked (Athena, Artemis, Apollo).

plague sears my people everywhere
everyone army citizens no one escapes 220
no spear of strong anxious thought protects us
great Thebes grows nothing
seeds rot in the ground
our women when they labor
cry Apollo Apollo but their children die
and lives one after another split the air
birds taking off
wingrush hungrier than fire
souls leaping away they fly
to the shore 230
of the cold god of evening[13]
west

the death stain spreads
so many corpses lie in the streets everywhere
nobody grieves for them
the city dies and young wives
and mothers gray-haired mothers wail
sob on the altar steps
they come from the city everywhere mourning their bitter days
prayers blaze to the Healer 240
grief cries a flute mingling
daughter of Zeus[14] o shining daughter show us
the warm bright face of peace of help
of our salvation

[*The doors of the palace open.*
OEDIPUS *enters.*]

and turn back the huge raging jaws of the death god Ares[15]
drive him back drive him away
his flames lash at me
this is his war these are his shields
shouts pierce us on all sides
turn him back lift him on a strong wind 250
rush him away
to the two seas[16] at the world's edge
the sea where the waters boil
the sea where no traveler can land
because if night leaves anything alive
day destroys it
o Zeus
god beyond all other gods

[13] Hades, god of the Underworld and of the dead.
[14] His daughter Athena.
[15] The god of war, often regarded as the personification of any kind of destruction.
[16] The Atlantic at the western edge of the world, the Black Sea at the eastern.

handler of the fire
father 260
make the god of our sickness
ashes

Apollo
great bowman of light draw back your bow
fire arrow after arrow
make them a wall circling us
shoot into our enemy's eyes
draw the string twined with gold
come goddess[17]
who dances on the mountains 270
sowing light where your feet brush the ground
blind our enemy come
god of golden hair
piled under your golden cap Bacchus
your face blazing like the sea when the sun falls on it
like sunlight on wine
god whose name is our name Bacchus[18]
god of joy god of terror
be with us now your bright face
like a pine torch roaring 280
thrust into the face of the slaughtering war god
blind him
drive him down from Olympos
drive him away from Thebes
forever

OEDIPUS. Every word of your prayers has touched me.
Listen. Follow me. Join me in fighting this sickness, this plague,
and all your sufferings may end, like a dark sky,
clear suddenly, blue, after a week of storms,
soothing the torn face of the sea, 290
soothing our fears.
Your fate looms in my words—
I heard nothing about Laios' death.
I know nothing about the murder,
I was alone, how could I have tracked the killer, without a clue,
I came to Thebes after the crime was done,
I was made a Theban after Laios' death. Listen carefully—
these words come from an innocent man.

[*Addressing the* CHORUS.]

One of *you* knows who killed Laios.
Where is that man? 300

[17]Artemis, goddess of the hunt.
[18]The god of wine, Bacchus or Dionysus, had special associations with Thebes.

Speak.
I command it. Fear is no excuse.
He must clear himself of the dangerous charge.
Who did this thing?
Was it a stranger?
Speak.
I will not harm him. The worst he will suffer is exile.
I will pay him well. He will have a king's thanks.
But if he will not speak because he fears me,
if he fears what I will do to him or to those he loves, 310
if he will not obey me,
I say to him:
My power is absolute in Thebes, my rule reaches everywhere,
my words will drive the guilty man, the man who *knows,*
out of this city, away from Thebes, forever.

Nothing.
My word for him is nothing.
Let him *be* nothing.
Give him nothing.
Let him touch nothing of yours, he is nothing to you. 320
Lock your doors when he approaches.
Say nothing to him, do not speak.
No prayers with him, no offerings with him.
No purifying water.
Nothing.
Drive him from your homes. Let him have no home, nothing.
No words, no food, shelter, warmth of hand, shared worship.
Let him have nothing. Drive him out, let him die.
He is our disease.
I know.
Apollo has made it clear.
Nothing can stop me, nothing can change my words. 330
I fight for Apollo, I fight for the dead man.
You see me, you hear me, moving against the killer.
My words are his doom.
Whether he did it alone, and escaped unseen,
whether others helped him kill, it makes no difference—
let my hatred burn out his life, hatred, always.
Make him an ember of suffering.
Make all his happiness
ashes.
If he eats at my side, sits at my sacred hearth, and I know these
things, 340
let every curse I spit out against him find *me,*
come home to *me.*
Carry out my orders. You must,
for me, for Apollo, and for Thebes, Thebes,
this poor wasted city,
deserted by its gods.

I know—the gods have given us this disease.
That makes no difference. You should have acted,
you should have done something long ago to purge our guilt.
The victim was noble, a king— 350
you should have done everything to track his murderer down.
And so,
because I rule now where he ruled;
because I share his bed, his wife;
because the same woman who mothered my children might have mothered his;
because fate swooped out of nowhere and cut him down;
because of all these things
I will fight for him as I would fight for my own murdered father.
Nothing will stop me.
No man, no place, nothing will escape my gaze. I will not stop 360
until I know it all, all, until everything is clear.
For every king, every king's son and his sons,
for every royal generation of Thebes, *my* Thebes,
I will expose the killer, I will reveal him
to the light.
Oh gods, gods,
destroy all those who will not listen, will not obey.
Freeze the ground until they starve.
Make their wives barren as stone.
Let this disease that shakes Thebes to its roots— 370
or any worse disease, if there is any worse than this—waste them,
crush everything they have, everything they are.
But you men of Thebes—
you, who know my words are right, who obey me—
may justice and the gods defend you, bless you,
graciously, forever.

LEADER. Your curse forces me to speak, Master.
I cannot escape it.
I did not murder the king, I cannot show you the man who did.
Apollo told us to search for the killer. 380
Apollo must name him.

OEDIPUS. No man can force the gods to speak.

LEADER. Then I will say the next best thing.

OEDIPUS. If there's a third best thing, say that too.

LEADER. Teiresias sees what the god Apollo sees.
Truth, truth.
If you heard the god speaking, heard his voice,
you might see more, more, and more.

OEDIPUS. Teiresias? I have seen to that already.
Kreon spoke of Teiresias, and I sent for him. Twice. 390
I find it strange he still hasn't come.

LEADER. And there's an old story, almost forgotten,
a dark, faded rumor.

OEDIPUS. What rumor? I must sift each story,
see it, understand it.

LEADER. Laios was killed by bandits.
OEDIPUS. I have heard that story: but who can show me the man who saw the murderer?
Has anyone seen him?
LEADER. If he knows the meaning of fear,
if he heard those curses you spoke against him, 400
those words still scorching the air,
you won't find him now, not in Thebes.
OEDIPUS. The man *murdered.* Why would words frighten him?

[TEIRESIAS *has appeared from the stage entrance to the right of the audience. He walks with a staff and is helped by a slave boy and attendants. He stops at some distance from center stage.*]

LEADER. Here is the man who can catch the criminal.
They're bringing him now—
the godlike prophet who speaks with the voice of god.
He, only he, knows truth.
The truth is rooted in his soul.
OEDIPUS. Teiresias, you understand all things,
what can be taught, what is locked in silence, 410
the distant things of heaven, and things that crawl the earth.
You cannot see, yet you know the nature of this plague infesting our city.
Only you, my lord, can save us, only you can defend us.
Apollo told our messenger—did you hear?—
that we could be saved only by tracking down Laios' killers,
only by killing them, or sending them into exile.
Help us, Teiresias.
Study the cries of birds, study their wild paths,
ponder the signs of fire, use all your skills of prophecy.
Rescue us, preserve us. 420
Rescue yourself, rescue Thebes, rescue me.
Cleanse every trace of the growing stain left by the dead man's blood.
We are in your hands, Teiresias.
No work is more nobly human than helping others,
helping with all the strength and skill we possess.
TEIRESIAS. Wisdom is a curse
when wisdom does nothing for the man who has it.
Once I knew this well, but I forgot.
I never should have come.
OEDIPUS. Never should have come? Why this reluctance, prophet? 430
TEIRESIAS. Let me go home.
That way is best, for you, for me.
Let me live my life, and you live yours.
OEDIPUS. Strange words, Teiresias, cruel to the city that gave you life.
Your holy knowledge could save Thebes. How can you keep silent?

TEIRESIAS. What have you said that helps Thebes? Your words are wasted.
I would rather be silent than waste my words.

OEDIPUS. Look at us, [OEDIPUS *stands, the* CHORUS *kneel.*]
kneeling to you, Teiresias, imploring you.
In the name of the gods, if you know— 440
help us, tell us what you know.

TEIRESIAS. You kneel because you do not understand.
But I will never let you see my grief. Never.
My grief is yours.

OEDIPUS. What? You know and won't speak?
You'd betray us all, you'd destroy the city of Thebes?

TEIRESIAS. I will do nothing to hurt myself, or you. Why insist?
I will not speak.

OEDIPUS. Stubborn old fool, you'd make a rock angry!
Tell me what you know! Say it! 450
Where are your feelings? Won't you ever speak?

TEIRESIAS. You call me cold, stubborn, unfeeling, you insult me. But *you,*
Oedipus, what do you know about yourself,
about your real feelings?
You don't see how much alike we are.

OEDIPUS. How can *I* restrain my anger when I see how little you care for Thebes.

TEIRESIAS. The truth will come, by itself,
the truth will come
no matter how I shroud it in silence.

OEDIPUS. All the more reason why you should speak. 460

TEIRESIAS. Not another word.
Rage away. You will never make me speak.

OEDIPUS. I'll rage, prophet, I'll give you all my anger.
I'll say it all—
Listen: I think you were involved in the murder of Laios,
you helped plan it, I think you
did everything in your power to kill Laios,
everything but strike him with your own hands,
and if you weren't blind, if you still had eyes to see with,
I'd say you, and *you* alone, did it all. 470

TEIRESIAS. Do you think so? Then obey your own words, obey
the curse everyone heard break from your own lips:
Never speak again to these men of Thebes,
never speak again to me.
You, it's
you.
What plagues the city is *you.*
The plague is *you.*

OEDIPUS. Do you know what you're saying?
Do you think I'll let you get away with these vile accusations?

TEIRESIAS. I am safe. 480
Truth lives in me, and the truth is strong.

OEDIPUS. Who taught you this truth of yours? Not your prophet's craft.

TEIRESIAS. You taught me. You forced me to speak.
OEDIPUS. Speak what? Explain. Teach me.
TEIRESIAS. Didn't you understand?
Are you trying to make me say the word?
OEDIPUS. What word? Say it. Spit it out.
TEIRESIAS. Murderer.
I say *you,*
you are the killer you're searching for. 490
OEDIPUS. You won't say *that* again to me and get away with it.
TEIRESIAS. Do you want more? Shall I make you really angry?
OEDIPUS. Say anything you like. Your words are wasted.
TEIRESIAS. I say you live in shame, and you do not know it,
do not know that you
and those you love most
wallow in shame,
you do not know
in what shame you live.
OEDIPUS. You'll pay for these insults, I swear it. 500
TEIRESIAS. Not if the truth is strong.
OEDIPUS. The truth *is* strong, but not your truth.
You have no truth. You're blind.
Blind in your eyes. Blind in your ears. Blind in your mind.
TEIRESIAS. And I pity you for mocking my blindness.
Soon everyone in Thebes will mock you, Oedipus. They'll mock you
as you have mocked me.
OEDIPUS. One endless night swaddles you in its unbroken black sky.
You can't hurt me, you can't hurt anyone who sees the light of day.
TEIRESIAS. True. Nothing I do will harm you. You, you 510
and your fate belong to Apollo.
Apollo will see to *you.*
OEDIPUS. Are these your own lies, prophet—or Kreon's?
TEIRESIAS. Kreon? Your plague is *you,* not Kreon.
OEDIPUS. Money, power, one great skill surpassing another,
if a man has these things, other men's envy grows and grows,
their greed and hunger are insatiable.
Most men would lust for a life like mine—but I did not demand my life,
Thebes gave me my life, and from the beginning, my good friend Kreon,
loyal, trusted Kreon, 520
was reaching for my power, wanted to ambush me, get rid of me by hiring this cheap wizard,
this crass, conniving priest, who sees nothing but profit,
whose prophecy is simple profit. *You,*
what did *you* ever do that proves you a real seer? What did you ever *see,* prophet?
And when the Sphinx who sang mysteriously
imprisoned us
why didn't you speak and set us free?

No ordinary man could have solved her riddle,
it took prophecy, prophecy and skill you clearly never had.
Even the paths of birds, even the gods' voices were useless. 530
But I showed up, I, Oedipus,
stupid, untutored Oedipus,
I silenced her, I destroyed her, I used my wits, not omens,
to sift the meaning of her song.
And this is the man you want to kill so you can get close to King Kreon,
weigh his affairs for him, advise him, influence him.
No, I think you and your master, Kreon, who contrived this plot,
will be whipped out of Thebes.
Look at you.
If you weren't so old, and weak, oh 540
I'd make you pay
for this conspiracy of yours.

LEADER. Oedipus, both of you spoke in anger.
Anger is not what we need.
We need all our wits, all our energy to interpret Apollo's words.
Then we will know what to do.

TEIRESIAS. Oedipus, you are king, but you must hear my reply.
My right to speak is just as valid as yours.
I am not your slave. Kreon is not my patron.
My master is Apollo. I can say what I please. 550
You insulted me. You mocked me. You called me blind.
Now hear *me* speak, Oedipus.
You have eyes to see with,
but you do not see yourself, you do not see
the horror shadowing every step of your life,
the blind shame in which you live,
you do not see where you live and who lives with you,
lives always at your side.
Tell me, Oedipus, who are your parents?
Do you know? 560
You do not even know
the shame and grief you have brought your family,
those still alive, those buried beneath the earth.
But the curse of your mother, the curse of your father
will whip you, whip you again and again, wherever you turn,
it will whip you out of Thebes forever,
your clear eyes flooded with darkness.
That day will come.
And then what scoured, homeless plain, what leafless tree,
what place on Kithairon,[19] 570
where no other humans are or ever will be,

[19]Also spelled *Cithaeron.* A mountain range near Thebes. Oedipus, as later events will reveal, was abandoned there as a child; it will also be his destination when he goes into exile later. Sophocles' audience knew this detail, and all the other significant elements of the story, at the outset of the play.

where the wind is the only thing that moves,
what raw track of thorns and stones, what rock, gulley,
or blind hill won't echo your screams, your howls of anguish
when you find out that the marriage song,
sung when you came to Thebes, heard in your house,
guided you to *this* shore, this wilderness
you thought was home, *your* home?
And you do not see
all the other awful things 580
that will show you who you really are, show you
to your children, face to face.
Go ahead! Call me quack, abuse Kreon, insult Apollo, the god
who speaks through me, whose words move on my lips.
No man will ever know worse suffering than you,
your life, your flesh, your happiness an ember of pain. Ashes.

OEDIPUS. [*to the* CHORUS] Must I stand here and listen to these attacks?

TEIRESIAS. [*beginning to move away*] I am here, Oedipus, because you sent for me.

OEDIPUS. You old fool,
I'd have thought twice before asking you to come 590
if I had known you'd spew out such idiocy.

TEIRESIAS. Call me fool, if you like, but your parents,
who gave you life, they respected my judgment.

OEDIPUS. Parents?
What do you mean?
Who are my mother and father?

TEIRESIAS. This day is your mother and father—this day will give you your birth,
it will destroy you too.

OEDIPUS. How you love mysterious, twisted words.

TEIRESIAS. Aren't you the great solver of riddles?
Aren't you Oedipus?

OEDIPUS. Taunt me for the gift of my brilliant mind. 600
That gift is what makes me great.

TEIRESIAS. That gift is your destiny. It made you everything you are,
and it has ruined you.

OEDIPUS. But if this gift of mine saved Thebes, who cares what happens to me?

TEIRESIAS. I'm leaving. Boy, take me home.

OEDIPUS. Good. Take him home. Here
I keep stumbling over you, here you're in my way.
Scuttle home, and leave us in peace!

TEIRESIAS. I'm going. I said what I came to say,
and that scowl, darkening your face, doesn't frighten me. How can you hurt me? 610
I tell you again:
the man you've been trying to expose—
with all your threats, with your inquest into Laios' murder—
that man is here, in Thebes.

Now people think he comes from Corinth, but later
they will see he was born in Thebes.
When they know, he'll have no pleasure in that news.
Now he has eyes to see with, but they will be slashed out;
rich and powerful now, he will be a beggar,
poking his way with a stick, feeling his way to a strange country. 620
And his children—the children he lives with—
will see him at last, see what he is, see who he really is:
their brother and their father; his wife's son, his mother's husband;
the lover who slept with his father's wife; the man who murdered
his father—
the man whose hands still drip with his father's blood.
These truths will be revealed.

Go inside and ponder *that* riddle, and if you find I've lied,
then call me a prophet who cannot see.

[OEDIPUS *turns and enters the palace.* TEIRESIAS *is led out through the stage entrance on the right.*]

CHORUS. who did crimes unnameable things
things words cringe at 630
which man did the rock of prophecy at Delphi say
did these things
his hands dripping with blood
he should run now flee
his strong feet swallowing the air
stronger than the horses of storm winds
their hooves slicing the air
now in his armor
Apollo lunges at him
his infinite branching fire reaches out 640
and the steady dread death-hungry Fates follow and never stop
their quick scissors[20] seeking the cloth of his life

just now
from high snowy Parnassus[21]
the god's voice exploded its blazing message
follow his track find the man
no one knows
a bull loose under wild bushes and trees
among caves and gray rocks
cut from the herd he runs and runs but runs nowhere 650
zigzagging desperate to get away

[20] The three Fates were spinners of the thread of human life; the third, Atropos, cut the thread at a point that determined the moment of death.
[21] The mountain near Apollo's oracle at Delphi.

birds of prophecy birds of death circling his head
forever
voices forged at the white stone core of the earth[22]
they go where he goes always

terror's in me flooding me
how can I judge
what the god Apollo says
trapped hoping confused
I do not see what is here now 660
when I look to the past I see nothing
I know nothing about a feud
wounding the families of Laios or Oedipus
no clue to the truth then or now
nothing to blacken his golden fame in Thebes
and help Laios' family
solve the mystery of his death

Zeus and Apollo know
they understand
only they see 670
the dark threads crossing beneath our life
but no man can say a prophet sees more than I
one man surpasses another
wisdom against wisdom skill against skill
but I will not blame Oedipus
whatever anyone says
until words are as real as things

one thing is clear
years back the Sphinx tested him
his answer was true 680
he was wise and sweet to the city
so he can never be evil
not to me

[KREON *enters through the stage entrance at right, and addresses the* CHORUS.]

KREON. Men of Thebes, I hear Oedipus, our king and master,
has brought terrible charges against me.
I have come to face those charges. I resent them bitterly.
If he imagines I have hurt him, spoken or acted against him
while our city dies, believe me—I have nothing left to live for.
His accusations pierce me, wound me mortally—
nothing they touch is trivial, private— 690

[22] The Omphalos, or Navelstone, at Delphi. It was believed to be the center of the earth.

if you, my family and friends,
think I'm a traitor, if all Thebes believes it, says it.
LEADER. Perhaps he spoke in anger, without thinking,
perhaps his anger made him accuse you.
KREON. Did he really say I persuaded Teiresias to lie?
LEADER. I heard him say these things,
but I don't know what they mean.
KREON. Did he look you in the eyes when he accused me?
Was he in his right mind?
LEADER. I do not know or see what great men do. 700

[*turning to* OEDIPUS, *who has emerged from the palace*]

But here he is—Oedipus.
OEDIPUS. What? *You* here? Murderer!
You dare come here, to my palace, when it's clear
you've been plotting to murder me and seize the throne of Thebes?
You're the bandit, *you're* the killer.
Answer me—
Did you think I was cowardly or stupid?
Is that why you betrayed me?
Did you really think I wouldn't see what you were plotting,
how you crept up on me like a cloud inching across the sun?
Did you think I wouldn't defend myself against you? 710
You thought I was a fool, but the fool was you, Kreon.
Thrones are won with money and men, you fool!
KREON. You have said enough, Oedipus. Now let me reply.
Weigh my words against your charges, then judge for yourself.
OEDIPUS. Eloquent, Kreon. But you won't convince me now.
Now that I know your hatred, your malice.
KREON. Let me explain.
OEDIPUS. Explain?
What could explain your treachery?
KREON. If you think this stubborn anger of yours, this perversity, 720
is something to be proud of, you're mad.
OEDIPUS. And if you think you can injure your sister's husband,
and not pay for it, *you're* mad.
KREON. I would be mad to hurt you. How have I hurt you?
OEDIPUS. Was it you who advised me to send for that great holy prophet?
KREON. Yes, and I'd do it again.
OEDIPUS. How long has it been since Laios disappeared?
KREON. Disappeared?
OEDIPUS. Died. Was murdered . . .
KREON. Many, many years. 730
OEDIPUS. And this prophet of yours—was he practicing his trade at the time?
KREON. With as much skill, wisdom and honor as ever.
OEDIPUS. Did he ever mention my name?
KREON. Not in my presence.

OEDIPUS. Was there an inquest? A formal inquiry?
KREON. Of course. Nothing was ever discovered.
OEDIPUS. Then why didn't our wonderful prophet, our Theban wizard,
denounce me as the murderer then?
KREON. I don't know. And when I don't know, I don't speak.
OEDIPUS. But you know this. You know it with perfect certainty. 740
KREON. What do you mean?
OEDIPUS. This: if you and Teiresias were not conspiring against me,
Teiresias would never have charged *me* with Laios' murder.
KREON. If he said that, you should know.
But now, Oedipus, it's my right, my turn to question you.
OEDIPUS. Ask anything. You'll never prove I killed Laios.
KREON. Did you marry my sister, Jocasta?
OEDIPUS. I married Jocasta.
KREON. And you gave her an equal share of the power in Thebes?
OEDIPUS. Whatever she wants is hers. 750
KREON. And I share that power equally with you and her?
OEDIPUS. Equally.
And that's precisely why it's clear you're false, treacherous.
KREON. No, Oedipus.
Consider it rationally, as I have. Reflect:
What man, what sane man, would prefer a king's power
with all its dangers and anxieties,
when he could enjoy that same power, without its cares,
and sleep in peace each night? Power?
I have no instinct for power, no hunger for it either. 760
It isn't royal power I want, but its advantages.
And any sensible man would want the same.
Look at the life I lead. Whatever I want, I get from you,
with your goodwill and blessing. I have nothing to fear.
If I were king, my life would be constant duty and constraint.
Why would I want your power or the throne of Thebes
more than what I enjoy now—the privilege of power
without its dangers? I would be a fool to want more
than what I have—the substance, not the show, of power.
As matters stand, no man envies me, I am courted 770
and admired by all. Men wear no smiling masks for Kreon.
And those who want something from you come to me
because the way to royal favor lies through me.
Tell me, Oedipus, why should I give these blessings up
to seize your throne and all the dangers it confers?
A man like me, who knows his mortal limits and accepts them,
cannot be vicious or treacherous by nature.
The love of power is not my nature, nor is treason
or the thoughts of treason that go with love of power.
I would never dare conspire against your life. 780

Do you want to test the truth of what I say?
Go to Delphi, put the question to the oracle,
ask if I have told you exactly what Apollo said.

Then if you find that Teiresias and I have plotted against you,
seize me and put me to death. Convict me
not by one vote alone, but two—yours *and* mine, Oedipus.
But don't convict me on the strength of your suspicions,
don't confuse friends with traitors, traitors with friends.
There's no justice in that.
To throw away a good and loyal friend 790
is to destroy what you love most—
your own life, and what makes life worth living.
Someday you will know the truth:
time, only time reveals the good man;
one day's light reveals the evil man.

LEADER. Good words
for someone careful, afraid he'll fall.
But a mind like lightning
stumbles.

OEDIPUS. When a clever man plots against me and moves swiftly 800
I must move just as swiftly, I must plan.
But if I wait, if I do nothing, he will win, win everything,
and I will lose.

KREON. What do you want? My exile?

OEDIPUS. No. Your death.

KREON. You won't change your mind? You won't believe me?

OEDIPUS. I'll believe you when you teach me the meaning of envy.

KREON. Envy? You talk about envy. You don't even know what sense is.
Can't you listen to me?

OEDIPUS. I *am* listening. To my own good sense. 810

KREON. Listen to *me*. I have sense on my side too.

OEDIPUS. You? You were born devious.

KREON. And if you're wrong?

OEDIPUS. I still must govern.

KREON. Not if you govern badly.

OEDIPUS. Oh Thebes, Thebes . . .

KREON. Thebes is mine too.

LEADER. [*turning to* JOCASTA, *who has entered from the palace, accompanied by a woman attendant*]
Stop. I see
Jocasta coming from the palace
just in time, my lords, to help you 820
settle this deep, bitter feud raging between you.
Listen to what she says.

JOCASTA. Oedipus! Kreon! Why this insane quarreling?
You should be ashamed, both of you. Forget yourselves.
This is no time for petty personal bickering.
Thebes is sick, dying.
—Come inside, Oedipus
—And you, Kreon, leave us.
Must you create all this misery over nothing, nothing?

KREON. Jocasta,
Oedipus has given me two impossible choices: 830

Either I must be banished from Thebes, my city, my home,
or be arrested and put to death.

OEDIPUS. That's right.
I caught him plotting against me, Jocasta.
Viciously, cunningly plotting against the king of Thebes.

KREON. Take every pleasure I have in life, curse me, let me die,
if I've done what you accuse me of, let the gods
destroy everything I have, let them do anything to me.
I stand here, exposed to their infinite power.

JOCASTA. Oedipus, in the name of the gods, believe him. 840
His prayer has made him holy, naked to the mysterious
whims of the gods, has taken him beyond what is human.
Respect his words, respect me, respect these men standing at your side.

CHORUS. [*beginning a dirge-like appeal to* OEDIPUS]
listen to her
think yield
we implore you

OEDIPUS. What do you want?

CHORUS. be generous to Kreon give him respect
he was never foolish before
now his prayer to the gods has made him great 850
great and frightening

OEDIPUS. Do you know what you're asking?

CHORUS. I know

OEDIPUS. Then say it.

CHORUS. don't ever cut him off
without rights or honor
blood binds you both
his prayer has made him sacred
don't accuse him
because some blind suspicion hounds you 860

OEDIPUS. Understand me:
when you ask for these things
you ask for my death or exile.

CHORUS. no
by the sun
the god who bathes us in his light
who sees all
I will die godless no family no friends
if what I ask means that
it is Thebes 870
Thebes dying wasting away life by life
this is the misery
that breaks my heart
and now this quarrel raging between you and Kreon
is more more than I can bear

OEDIPUS. Then let him go, if it means I must die
or be forced out of Thebes forever, stripped of all my rights, all my honors.

Your grief, *your* words touch me. Not his.
I pity you. But him,
my hatred will reach him wherever he goes. 880

KREON. It's clear you hate to yield, clear
you yield only under pressure, only
when you've worn out the fierceness of your anger.
Then all you can do is sit, and brood.
Natures like yours are a torment to themselves.

OEDIPUS. Leave. Go!

KREON. I'm going. Now I know
you do not know me.
But these men know I am the man I seem to be, a just man,
not devious, not a traitor. 890

[KREON *leaves.*]

CHORUS. woman why are you waiting
lead him inside comfort him

JOCASTA. Not before I know what has happened here.

CHORUS. blind ignorant words suspicion without proof
the injustice of it
gnaws at us

JOCASTA. From both men?

CHORUS. yes

JOCASTA. What caused it?

CHORUS. enough enough 900
no more words
Thebes is so tormented now
let it rest where it ended

OEDIPUS. Look where cooling my rage,
where all your decent, practical thoughts have led you.

CHORUS. Oedipus I have said this many times
I would be mad helpless to give advice
if I turned against you now
once
you took our city in her storm of pain 910
straightened her course found fair weather
o lead her to safety now
if you can

JOCASTA. If you love the gods, tell me, too, Oedipus—I implore you—
why are you still so angry, why can't you let it go?

OEDIPUS. I will tell you, Jocasta.
You mean more, far more to me than these men here.
Jocasta, it is Kreon—Kreon and his plots against me.

JOCASTA. What started your quarrel?

OEDIPUS. He said I murdered Laios. 920

JOCASTA. Does he know something? Or is it pure hearsay?

OEDIPUS. He sent me a vicious, trouble-making prophet
to avoid implicating himself. He did not say it to my face.

JOCASTA. Oedipus, forget all this. Listen to me:

no mortal can practice the art of prophecy; no man can see the future.
One experience of mine will show you why.
Long ago an oracle came to Laios.
It came not from Apollo himself but from his priests.
It said Laios was doomed to be murdered by a son, his son and mine.
But Laios, from what we heard, was murdered by bandits from a foreign country, 930
cut down at a crossroads. My poor baby
was only three days old when Laios had his feet pierced together behind the ankles
and gave orders to abandon our child on a mountain, leave him alone to die
in a wilderness of rocks and bare gray trees
where there were no roads, no people.
So you see—Apollo didn't make that child his father's killer,
Laios wasn't murdered by his son. That dreadful act which so terrified Laios—
it never happened.

All those oracular voices meant was nothing, nothing.
Ignore them. 940
Apollo creates. Apollo reveals. He needs no help from men.

OEDIPUS. [*who has been very still*]
While you were speaking, Jocasta, it flashed through my mind
like wind suddenly ruffling a stretch of calm sea.
It stuns me. I can almost see it—some memory, some image.
My heart races and swells—

JOCASTA. Why are you so strangely excited, Oedipus?

OEDIPUS. You said Laios was cut down *near* a crossroads?

JOCASTA. That was the story. It hasn't changed.

OEDIPUS. Where did it happen? Tell me. Where?

JOCASTA. In Phokis. Where the roads from Delphi and Daulia meet. 950

OEDIPUS. When?

JOCASTA. Just before you came to Thebes and assumed power.
Just before you were proclaimed King.

OEDIPUS. O Zeus, Zeus,
what are you doing with my life?

JOCASTA. Why are you so disturbed, Oedipus?

OEDIPUS. Don't ask me. Not yet.
Tell me about Laios.
How old was he? What did he look like?

JOCASTA. Streaks of gray were beginning to show in his black hair.
He was tall, strong—built something like you. 960

OEDIPUS. No! O gods, o
it seems each hard, arrogant curse
I spit out
was meant for me, and I

didn't
know it!
JOCASTA. Oedipus, what do you mean? Your face is so strange.
You frighten me.
OEDIPUS. It *is* frightening—can the blind prophet see, can he really see?
I would know if you told me . . . 970
JOCASTA. I'm afraid to ask, Oedipus.
Told you what?
OEDIPUS. Was Laios traveling with a small escort
or with many armed men, like a king?
JOCASTA. There were five, including a herald.
Laios was riding in his chariot.
OEDIPUS. Light, o light, light
now everything, everything is clear. All of it.
Who told you this? Who was it?
JOCASTA. A household slave. The only survivor. 980
OEDIPUS. Is he here, in Thebes?
JOCASTA. No. When he returned and saw that you were king
and learned Laios was dead, he came to me and clutched my hand,
begged me to send him to the mountains
where shepherds graze their flocks, far from the city,
so he could never see Thebes again.
I sent him, of course. He deserved that much, for a slave, and more.
OEDIPUS. Can he be called back? Now?
JOCASTA. Easily. But why?
OEDIPUS. I am afraid I may have said too much— 990
I *must* see him.
Now.
JOCASTA. Then he will come.
But surely I have a right to know what disturbs you, Oedipus.
OEDIPUS. Now that I've come this far, Jocasta,
hope torturing me, each step of mine heavy with fear,
I won't keep anything from you.
Wandering through the mazes of a fate like this,
how could I confide in anyone but you?

My father was Polybos, of Corinth. 1000
My mother, Merope, was Dorian.
Everyone in Corinth saw me as its first citizen,
but one day something happened,
something strange, puzzling. Puzzling, but nothing more.
Still, it worried me.
One night, I was at a banquet,
and a man—he was very drunk—said I wasn't my father's son,
called me "bastard." That stung me, I was shocked.
I could barely control my anger, I lay awake all night.
The next day I went to my father and mother, 1010
I questioned them about the man and what he said.

They were furious with him, outraged by his insult,
and I was reassured. But I kept hearing the word "bastard"
"bastard"—
I couldn't get it out of my head.
Without my parents' knowledge, I went to Delphi: I wanted the truth,
but Apollo refused to answer me.
And yet he did reveal other things, he did show me
a future dark with torment, evil, horror,
he made me *see*—
see myself, doomed to sleep with my own mother, doomed 1020
to bring children into this world where the sun pours down,
children no one could bear to see, doomed
to murder the man who gave me life, whose blood is *my* blood. My
father.
And after I heard all this, I fled Corinth,
measuring my progress by the stars, searching for a place
where I would never see those words, those dreadful predictions
come true. And on my way
I came to the place where you say King Laios was murdered.

Jocasta, the story I'm about to tell you is the truth:
I was on the road, near the crossroads you mentioned, 1030
when I met a herald, with an old man, just as you described him.
The man was riding in a chariot
and his driver tried to push me off the road
and when he shoved me I hit him. I hit him.
The old man stood quiet in the chariot until I passed under him,
then he leaned out and caught me on the head with an ugly goad[23]—
its two teeth wounded me—and with this hand of mine,
this hand clenched around my staff,
I struck him back even harder—so hard, so quick he couldn't
dodge it,
and he toppled out of the chariot and hit the ground, face up. 1040
I killed them. Every one of them. I still see them.

[*to the* CHORUS]

If this stranger and Laios
are somehow linked by blood,
tell me what man's torment equals mine?

Citizens, hear my curse again—
Give this man nothing. Let him touch nothing of yours.
Lock your doors when he approaches.
Say nothing to him when he approaches.
And these, these curses,
with my own mouth I
spoke these monstrous curses against myself. 1050

[23]A barbed stick used to prod animals.

[OEDIPUS *turns back to* JOCASTA]

These hands, these bloodstained hands made love to you in your dead husband's bed,
these hands murdered him.

If I must be exiled, never to see my family,
never to walk the soil of my country
so I will not sleep with my mother
and kill Polybos, my father, who raised me—his son!—
wasn't I born evil—answer me!—isn't every part of me
unclean? Oh
some unknown god, some savage venomous demon must have done this,
raging, swollen with hatred. Hatred 1060
for me.

Holiness, pure, radiant powers, o gods
don't let me see that day,
don't let it come, take me away
from men, men with their eyes, hide me
before I see
the filthy black stain reaching down over me, into me.

[*The* CHORUS *have moved away from the stage*]

LEADER. Your words make us shudder, Oedipus,
but hope, hope
until you hear more from the man who witnessed the murder. 1070
OEDIPUS. That is the only hope I have. Waiting.
Waiting for that man to come from the pastures.
JOCASTA. And when he finally comes, what do you hope to learn?
OEDIPUS. If his story matches yours, I am saved.
JOCASTA. What makes you say that?
OEDIPUS. Bandits—you said he told you bandits killed Laios.
So if he still talks about bandits,
more than one, I couldn't have killed Laios.
One man is not the same as many men.
But if he speaks of one man, traveling alone, 1080
then all the evidence points to me.
JOCASTA. Believe me, Oedipus, those were his words.
And he can't take them back: the whole city heard him, not only me.
And if he changes only the smallest detail of his story,
that still won't prove Laios was murdered as the oracle foretold.
Apollo was clear—it was Laios' fate to be killed by my son,
but my poor child died before his father died.
The future has no shape. The shapes of prophecy lie.
I see nothing in them, they are all illusions.
OEDIPUS. Even so, I want that shepherd summoned here. 1090
Now. Do it now.

JOCASTA. I'll send for him immediately. But come inside.
My only wish is to please you.

[JOCASTA *dispatches a servant.*]

CHORUS. fate[24]
be here let what I say be pure
let all my acts be pure
laws forged in the huge clear fields of heaven
rove the sky
shaping my words limiting what I do
Olympos[25] made those laws not men who live and die 1100
nothing lulls those laws to sleep
they cannot die
and the infinite god in them never ages

arrogance insatiable pride
breed the tyrant
feed him on thing after thing blindly
at the wrong time uselessly
and he grows reaches so high
nothing can stop his fall
his feet thrashing the air standing on nothing 1110
and nowhere to stand he plunges down
o god shatter the tyrant
but let men compete let self-perfection grow
let men sharpen their skills
soldiers citizens building the good city
Apollo
protect me always
always the god I will honor

if a man walks through his life arrogant
strutting proud 1120
says anything does anything
does not fear justice
fear the gods bow to their shining presences
let fate make him stumble in his tracks
for all his lecheries and headlong greed
if he takes whatever he wants right or wrong
if he touches forbidden things
what man who acts like this would boast

[24] The choral passage that follows seems central to the play, but its application is problematical. The chorus expresses a pious revulsion from the kind of evil acts that bring on divine punishment; it then proceeds to define *hubris,* the state of overweening pride that is especially dangerous in provoking divine wrath. The passage implies that if these ancient moral principles and the gods' oracles no longer can be depended on, all order has been lost. But no character in the play seems to have *deliberately* committed such acts of impiety as the chorus describes.

[25] The mountain home of the gods.

he can escape the anger of the gods
why should I join these sacred public dances 1130
if such acts are honored

no
I will never go to the holy untouchable stone
navel of the earth at Delphi
never again
go to the temples at Olympia at Abai[26]
if all these things are not joined
if past present future are not made one
made clear to mortal eyes
o Zeus if that is your name 1140
power above all immortal king
see these things look
those great prophecies are fading
men say they're nothing
nobody prays to the god of light no one believes
nothing of the gods stays

[JOCASTA *enters from the palace, carrying a branch tied with strands of wool, and a jar of incense. She is accompanied by a servant woman. She addresses the* CHORUS.]

JOCASTA. Lords of Thebes, I come to the temples of the god
with offerings—this incense and this branch.
So many thoughts torture Oedipus. He never rests.
He acts without reason. He is like a man 1150
who has lost everything he knows—the past
is useless to him; strange, new things baffle him.
And if someone talks disaster, it stuns him: he listens, he is afraid.
I have tried to reassure him, but nothing helps.
So I have come to you—
Apollo, close to my life, close to this house,
listen to my prayers: [*she kneels*]
help us purify ourselves of this disease,
help us survive the long night of our suffering,
protect us. We are afraid when we see Oedipus confused
and frightened—Oedipus, the only man who can pilot Thebes 1160
to safety.

[A MESSENGER *from Corinth has arrived by the entrance to the orchestra on the audience's left. He sees* JOCASTA *praying, then turns to address the* CHORUS.]

[26] Sites of oracles, of Apollo and Zeus respectively.

MESSENGER. Friends,
can you tell me where King Oedipus lives
or better still, where I can find him?
LEADER. Here, in this house.
This lady is his wife and mother
of his children.
MESSENGER. May you and your family prosper.
May you be happy always under this great roof.
JOCASTA. Happiness and prosperity to you, too, for your kind words. 1170
But why are you here? Do you bring news?
MESSENGER. Good news for your house, good news for King Oedipus.
JOCASTA. What is your news? Who sent you?
MESSENGER. I come from Corinth, and what I have to say I know will bring you joy.
And pain perhaps. . . . I do not know.
JOCASTA. Both joy and pain? What news could do that?
MESSENGER. The people of Corinth want Oedipus as their king.
That's what they're saying.
JOCASTA. But isn't old Polybos still king of Corinth?
MESSENGER. His kingdom is his grave. 1180
JOCASTA. Polybos is *dead?*
MESSENGER. If I'm lying, my lady, let me die for it.
JOCASTA. You. [*to a servant*] Go in and tell Oedipus.
O oracles of the gods, where are you now!
This man, the man Oedipus was afraid he would murder,
the man he feared, the man he fled from has died a natural death.
Oedipus didn't kill him, it was luck, luck.

[*She turns to greet* OEDIPUS *as he comes out of the palace.*]

OEDIPUS. Jocasta, why did you send for me? [*taking her gently by the arm*]
JOCASTA. Oedipus,
listen to this man, see what those ominous, holy predictions of Apollo mean now. 1190
OEDIPUS. Who is this man? What does he say?
JOCASTA. He comes from Corinth.
Your father is dead. Polybos is dead!
OEDIPUS. What?
Let me hear those words from your own mouth, stranger.
Tell me yourself, in your own words.
MESSENGER. If that's what you want to hear first, then I'll say it:
Polybos is dead.
OEDIPUS. How did he die? Assassination? Illness? How?
MESSENGER. An old man's life hangs by a fragile thread. Anything can snap it. 1200
OEDIPUS. That poor old man. It was illness then?
MESSENGER. Illness and old age.
OEDIPUS. Why, Jocasta,
why should men look to the great hearth at Delphi

or listen to birds shrieking and wheeling overhead—
cries meaning I was doomed to kill my father?
He is dead, gone, covered by the earth.
And here I am—my hands never even touched a spear—
I did not kill him,
unless he died from wanting me to come home. 1210
No. Polybos has bundled up all these oracles
and taken them with him to the world below.
They are only words now, lost in the air.

JOCASTA. Isn't that what I predicted?

OEDIPUS. You were right. My fears confused me.

JOCASTA. You have nothing to fear. Not now. Not ever.

OEDIPUS. But the oracle said I am doomed to sleep with my mother.
How can I live with that and not be afraid?

JOCASTA. Why should men be afraid of anything? Fortune rules our lives.
Luck is everything. Things happen. The future is darkness. 1220
No human mind can know it.
It's best to live in the moment, live for today, Oedipus.
Why should the thought of marrying your mother make you so afraid?
Many men have slept with their mothers in their dreams.
Why worry? See your dreams for what they are—nothing, nothing at all.
Be happy, Oedipus.

OEDIPUS. All that you say is right, Jocasta. I know it.
I should be happy,
but my mother is still living. As long as she's alive,
I live in fear. This fear is necessary. 1230
I have no choice.

JOCASTA. But Oedipus, your father's death is a sign, a great sign—
the sky has cleared, the sun's gaze holds us in its warm, hopeful light.

OEDIPUS. A great sign, I agree. But so long as my mother is alive,
my fear lives too.

MESSENGER. Who is this woman you fear so much?

OEDIPUS. Merope, King Polybos' wife.

MESSENGER. Why does Merope frighten you so much?

OEDIPUS. A harrowing oracle hurled down upon us by some great god.

MESSENGER. Can you tell me? Or did the god seal your lips? 1240

OEDIPUS. I can.
Long ago, Apollo told me I was doomed to sleep with my mother
and spill my father's blood, murder him
with these two hands of mine.
That's why I never returned to Corinth. Luckily, it would seem.
Still, nothing on earth is sweeter to a man's eyes
than the sight of his father and mother.

MESSENGER. And you left Corinth because of this prophecy?

OEDIPUS. Yes. And because of my father. To avoid killing my father.

MESSENGER. But didn't my news prove you have nothing to fear? 1250
I brought good news.

OEDIPUS. And I will reward you for your kindness.
MESSENGER. That's why I came, my lord. I knew you'd remember me when you returned to Corinth.
OEDIPUS. I will never return, never live with my parents again.
MESSENGER. Son, it's clear you don't know what you're doing.
OEDIPUS. What do you mean? In the name of the gods, speak.
MESSENGER. If you're afraid to go home because of your parents.
OEDIPUS. I *am* afraid, afraid
Apollo's prediction will come true, all of it, 1260
as god's sunlight grows brighter on a man's face at dawn
when he's in bed, still sleeping,
and reaches into his eyes and wakes him.
MESSENGER. Afraid of murdering your father, of having his blood on your hands?
OEDIPUS. Yes. His blood. The stain of his blood. That terror never leaves me.
MESSENGER. But Oedipus, then you have no reason to be afraid.
OEDIPUS. I'm their son, they're my parents, aren't they?
MESSENGER. Polybos is nothing to you.
OEDIPUS. Polybos is not my father? 1270
MESSENGER. No more than I am.
OEDIPUS. But you are nothing to me. Nothing.
MESSENGER. And Polybos is nothing to you either.
OEDIPUS. Then why did he call me his son?
MESSENGER. Because I gave you to him. With these hands
I gave you to him.
OEDIPUS. How could he have loved me like a father if I am not his son?
MESSENGER. He had no children. That opened his heart.
OEDIPUS. And what about you?
Did you buy me from someone? Or did you find me? 1280
MESSENGER. I found you squawling, left alone to die in the thickets of Kithairon.
OEDIPUS. Kithairon? What were you doing on Kithairon?
MESSENGER. Herding sheep in the high summer pastures.
OEDIPUS. You were a shepherd, a drifter looking for work?
MESSENGER. A drifter, yes, but it was I who saved you.
OEDIPUS. Saved me? Was I hurt when you picked me up?
MESSENGER. Ask your feet.
OEDIPUS. Why,
why did you bring up that childhood pain?
MESSENGER. I cut you free. Your feet were pierced, tied together at the ankles 1290
with leather thongs strung between the tendons and the bone.
OEDIPUS. That mark of my shame—I've worn it from the cradle.
MESSENGER. That mark is the meaning of your name:
Oedipus, Swollenfoot, Oedipus.
OEDIPUS. Oh gods
who did this to me?

My mother?
My father?
MESSENGER. I don't know. The man I took you from—he would know.
OEDIPUS. So you didn't find me? Somebody else gave me to you? 1300
MESSENGER. I got you from another shepherd.
OEDIPUS. What shepherd? Who was he? Do you know?
MESSENGER. As I recall, he worked for Laios.
OEDIPUS. The same Laios who was king of Thebes?
MESSENGER. The same Laios. The man was one of Laios' shepherds.
OEDIPUS. Is he still alive? I want to see this man.
MESSENGER. [*pointing to the* CHORUS] These people would know that better than I do.
OEDIPUS. Do any of you know this shepherd he's talking about?
Have you ever noticed him in the fields or in the city?
Answer, if you have. 1310
It is time everything came out, time everything was made clear.
Everything.
LEADER. I think he's the shepherd you sent for.
But Jocasta, she would know.
OEDIPUS. [*to* JOCASTA]
Jocasta, do you know this man?
Is he the man this shepherd here says worked for Laios?
JOCASTA. What man? Forget about him. Forget what was said.
It's not worth talking about.
OEDIPUS. How can I forget
with clues like these in my hands? 1320
With the secret of my birth staring me in the face?
JOCASTA. No, Oedipus!
No more questions.
For god's sake, for the sake of your own life!
Isn't my anguish enough—more than enough?
OEDIPUS. You have nothing to fear,[27] Jocasta.
Even if my mother
and her mother before her were both slaves,
that doesn't make *you* the daughter of slaves.
JOCASTA. Oedipus, you *must* stop.
I beg you—stop! 1330
OEDIPUS. Nothing can stop me now. I must know everything.
Everything!
JOCASTA. I implore you, Oedipus. For your own good.
OEDIPUS. Damn my own good!
JOCASTA. Oh, Oedipus, Oedipus,
I pray to god you never see who you are!
OEDIPUS. [*to one of the attendants, who hurries off through the exit stage left*]
You there, go find that shepherd, bring him here.
Let that woman bask in the glory of her noble birth.

[27] Oedipus believes Jocasta's anguish is caused by fears that he is of lowly birth and social station.

JOCASTA. God help you, Oedipus—
you were born to suffer, born 1340
to misery and grief.
These are the last words I will ever speak, ever
Oedipus.

[JOCASTA *rushes offstage into the palace. Long silence.*]

LEADER. Why did Jocasta rush away,
Oedipus, fleeing in such pain?
I fear disaster, or worse,
will break from this silence of hers.
OEDIPUS. Let it break! Let everything break!
I must discover who I am, know the secret of my birth,
no matter how humble, how vile. 1350
Perhaps Jocasta is ashamed of my low birth, ashamed to be my wife.
Like all women she's proud.
But Luck, goddess who gives men all that is good, made *me,*
and I won't be cheated of what is mine, nothing can dishonor me,
ever.
I am like the months, my brothers the months—they shaped me
when I was a baby in the cold hills of Kithairon,
they guided me, carved out my times of greatness,
and they still move their hands over my life.
I am the man I am. I will not stop
until I discover who my parents are. 1360
CHORUS. if I know if I see
if the dark force of prophecy is mine
Kithairon
when the full moon
rides over us tomorrow
listen listen to us sing to you
dance worship praise you
mountain where Oedipus was found
know Oedipus will praise you
praise his nurse country and mother 1370
who blessed our king
I call on you Apollo
let these visions please you
god Apollo
healer
Oedipus son
who was your mother
which of the deathless mountain nymphs who lay
with the great god Pan[28]
on the high peaks he runs across 1380
or with Apollo
who loves the high green pastures above

[28]God of the forest, of mountains, and of wild nature.

which one bore you
did the god of the bare windy peaks Hermes[29]
or the wild, dervish Dionysus
living in the cool air of the hills
take you
a foundling
from one of the nymphs he plays with
joyously lift you hold you in his arms 1390

OEDIPUS. Old men, I think the man coming toward us now
must be the shepherd we are looking for.
I have never seen him, but the years, chalking his face and hair, tell me
he's the man. And my men are with him. But you probably know him.

LEADER. I do know him. If Laios ever had a man he trusted,
this was the man.

OEDIPUS. [*to the* MESSENGER]
You—is this the man you told me about?

MESSENGER. That's him. You're looking at the man.

OEDIPUS. [*to the* SHEPHERD *who has been waiting, hanging back*]
You there, come closer.
Answer me, old man.
Did you work for Laios? 1400

SHEPHERD. I was born his slave, and grew up in his household.

OEDIPUS. What was your work?

SHEPHERD. Herding sheep, all my life.

OEDIPUS. Where?

SHEPHERD. Kithairon, mostly. And the country around Kithairon.

OEDIPUS. Do you remember ever seeing this man?

SHEPHERD. Which man?

OEDIPUS. [*pointing to the* MESSENGER]
This man standing here. Have you ever seen him before?

SHEPHERD. Not that I remember.

MESSENGER. No wonder, master. But I'll make him remember. 1410
He knows who I am. We used to graze our flocks together
in the pastures around Kithairon.
Every year, for six whole months, three years running.
From March until September, when the Dipper rose, signaling the harvest.
I had one flock, he had two.
And when the frost came, I drove my sheep back to their winter pens
and he drove his back to Laios' fold.
Remember, old man? Isn't that how it was?

SHEPHERD. Yes. But it was all so long ago.

MESSENGER. And do you remember giving me a baby boy at the time— 1420
to raise as my own son?

[29] Hermes was born on a mountain (Cyllene); he was also the god of shepherds.

SHEPHERD. What if I do? Why all these questions?
MESSENGER. That boy became King Oedipus, friend.
SHEPHERD. Damn you, can't you keep quiet.
OEDIPUS. Don't scold him, old man.
It's you who deserve to be punished, not him.
SHEPHERD. What did I say, good master?
OEDIPUS. You haven't answered his question about the boy.
SHEPHERD. He's making trouble, master. He doesn't know a thing.

[OEDIPUS *takes the* SHEPHERD *by the cloak*]

OEDIPUS. Tell me or you'll be sorry. 1430
SHEPHERD. For god's sake, don't hurt me, I'm an old man.
OEDIPUS. [*to one of his men*] You there, hold him. We'll make him talk.

[*The attendant pins the* SHEPHERD*'s arms behind his back*]

SHEPHERD. Oedipus, Oedipus,
god knows I pity you.
What more do you want to know?
OEDIPUS. Did you give the child to this man?
Speak. Yes or no?
SHEPHERD. Yes.
And I wish to god I'd died that day.
OEDIPUS. You *will* be dead unless you tell me the whole truth.
SHEPHERD. And worse than dead if I do. 1440
OEDIPUS. It seems our man won't answer.
SHEPHERD. No. I told you already. I gave him the boy.
OEDIPUS. Where did you get him? From Laios' household? Or where?
SHEPHERD. He wasn't *my* child. He was given to me.
OEDIPUS. [*turning to the* CHORUS *and the audience*]
By whom? Someone here in Thebes?
SHEPHERD. Master, please, in god's name, no more questions.
OEDIPUS. You're a dead man if I have to ask you once more.
SHEPHERD. He was one
of the children
from Laios' 1450
household.
OEDIPUS. A slave child? Or Laios' own?
SHEPHERD. I can't say it . . . it's
awful, the words
are awful . . . awful.
OEDIPUS. And I,
I am afraid to hear them . . .
but I must.
SHEPHERD. He was Laios' own child.
Your wife, inside the palace, she can explain it all. 1460
OEDIPUS. *She* gave you the child?
SHEPHERD. My lord . . . yes.

OEDIPUS. Why?
SHEPHERD. She wanted me to abandon the child on a mountain.
OEDIPUS. His own mother?
SHEPHERD. Yes. There were prophecies, horrible oracles. She was afraid.
OEDIPUS. What oracles?
SHEPHERD. Oracles predicting he would murder his own father.
OEDIPUS. But why did you give the boy to this old man?
SHEPHERD. Because I pitied him, master, because I 1470
thought the man would take the child away, take him to another country.
Instead he saved him. Saved him for—oh gods,
a fate so horrible, so awful, words can't describe it.
If you were the baby that man took from me, Oedipus,
what misery, what grief is yours!
OEDIPUS. [*looking up at the sun*]
LIGHT LIGHT LIGHT
never again flood these eyes with your white radiance, oh gods, my eyes. All, all
the oracles have proven true. I, Oedipus, I
am the child
of parents who should never have been mine—doomed, doomed! 1480
Now everything is clear—I
lived with a woman, she was my mother, I slept in my mother's bed, and I
murdered, murdered my father,
the man whose blood flows in these veins of mine,
whose blood stains these two hands red.

[OEDIPUS *raises his hands to the sun, then turns and walks into the palace.*]

CHORUS. man after man after man
o mortal generations
here once
almost not here
what are we 1490
dust ghosts images a rustling of air
nothing nothing
we breathe on the abyss
we are the abyss
our happiness no more than traces of a dream
the high noon sun sinking into the sea
the red spume of its wake raining behind it
we are you
we are you Oedipus
dragging your maimed foot 1500
in agony
and now that I see your life finally revealed
your life fused with the god

blazing out of the black nothingness of all we know
I say
no happiness lasts nothing human lasts

wherever you aimed you hit
no archer had your skill
you grew rich powerful great
everything came falling to your feet 1510
o Zeus
after he killed the Sphinx
whose claws curled under
whose weird song of the future[30] baffled and destroyed
he stood like a tower high above our country
warding off death
and from then on Oedipus we called you
king our king
draped you in gold
our highest honors were yours 1520
and you ruled this shining city
Thebes Thebes

now
your story is pain pity no story is worse
than yours Oedipus
ruined savage blind
as you struggle with your life
as your life changes
and breaks and shows you who you are
Oedipus Oedipus 1530
son father you harbored in the selfsame place[31]
the same place sheltered you both
bridegroom
how could the furrow your father plowed
not have cried out all this time
while you lay there unknowing
and saw the truth too late

time like the sun sees all things
and it sees you
you cannot hide from that light 1540
your own life opening itself to you
to all
married unmarried father son
for so long

[30]The Sphinx was a kind of oracle; specifically, her riddle about the three states of man reflects this play's focus on Oedipus' infancy, prime of manhood, and final weakness when, blinded, he must use a walking stick.

[31]Harbored sexually, with Jocasta; geographically, the place alluded to is the mountain Kithairon, where Laios died and to which Oedipus will flee.

justice comes like the dawn
always
and it shows the world your marriage now

I wish
o child of Laios
I wish I had never seen you 1550
I grieve for you
wail after wail fills me and pours out
because of you my breath came flowing back
but now
the darkness of your life
floods my eyes

[*The palace doors open. A* SERVANT *enters and approaches the* CHORUS *and audience.*]

SERVANT. Noble citizens, honored above all others in Thebes,
if you still care for the house of Laios
if you still can feel the spirit of those who ruled before, now
the horrors you will hear, the horrors you will see, will shake 1560
your hearts and shatter you with grief beyond enduring.
Not even the waters of those great rivers Ister and Phasis[32]
could wash away the blood
that now darkens every stone of this shining house,
this house that will reveal, soon, soon
the misery and evil two mortals,
both masters of this house, have brought upon themselves.

The griefs we cause ourselves cut deepest of all.[33]

LEADER. What we already know
has hurt us enough, 1570
has made us cry out in pain.
What more can you say?

SERVANT. This:
Jocasta is dead. The queen is dead.

LEADER. Ah, poor
unhappy Jocasta,
how did she die?

SERVANT. She killed herself. She did it.
But you did not see what happened there,
you were not there, in the palace. You did not see it. 1580
I did.
I will tell you how Queen Jocasta died,
the whole story, all of it. All I can remember.

[32]Ister is the Danube River; Phasis is a river flowing into the Black Sea.

[33]The reference may be to the acts of Laios and Oedipus in the distant past or to the recent suicide and self-blinding of Jocasta and Oedipus. The words "cut deepest of all" can also apply to the Thebans and to the theatrical audience.

After her last words to Oedipus
she rushed past us through the entrance hall, screaming,
raking her hair with both hands, and flew into the bedroom, *their* bedroom,
and slammed the doors shut as she lunged at her bridal bed,
crying "Laios" "Laios"—dead all these years—
remembering Laios—how his own son years ago
grew up and then killed him, leaving her to 1590
sleep with her own son, to have his children, *their* children,
children—not sons, not daughters, something else, monsters. . . .
Then she collapsed, sobbing, cursing the bed where she held both men in her arms,
got husband from husband, children from her child.
We heard it all, but suddenly, I couldn't tell what was happening.
Oedipus came crashing in, he was howling,
stalking up and down—we couldn't take our eyes off him—
and we stopped listening to her pitiful cries.
We stood there, watching him move like a bull, lurching, charging,
shouting at each of us to give him a sword, demanding we tell him 1600
where his wife was, that woman whose womb carried him,
him and his children, that wife who gave him birth.
Some god, some demon, led him to her, and he knew—
none of us showed him—
suddenly a mad, inhuman cry burst from his mouth
as if the wind rushed through his tortured body,
and he heaved against those bedroom doors so the hinges whined
and bent from their sockets and the bolts snapped,
and he stood in the room.
There she was— 1610
we could see her—his wife
dangling by her neck from a noose of braided, silken cords
tied to a rafter, still swaying.
And when he saw her he bellowed and stretched up and loosened the rope,
cradling her in one arm,
and slowly laid her body on the ground.
That's when it happened—he
ripped off the gold
brooches she was wearing—one on each shoulder of her gown—
and raised them over his head—you could see them flashing— 1620
and tilted his face up and
brought them right down into his eyes
and the long pins sank deep, all the way back into the sockets,
and he shouted at his eyes:
"Now you won't see me, you won't see
my agonies or my crimes,
but in endless darkness, always, there you'll see
those I never should have seen.
And those I should have known were my parents, father and mother—

these eyes will never see their faces in the light. 1630
These eyes will never see the light again, never."
Cursing his two blind eyes over and over, he
lifted the brooches again and drove their pins through his eyeballs
up
to the hilts until they were pulp, until the blood streamed out
soaking his beard and cheeks,
a black storm splashing its hail across his face.

Two mortals acted. Now grief tears their lives apart
as if that pain sprang from a single, sorrowing root
to curse each one, man and wife. For all those years
their happiness was truly happiness, but now, now 1640
wailing, madness, shame and death,
every evil men have given a name,
everything criminal and vile
that mankind suffers they suffer. Not one evil is missing.

LEADER. But now
does this torn, anguished man
have any rest from his pain?

SERVANT. No, no—
then he shouted at us to open the doors and show everyone in Thebes
his father's killer, his mother's—I cannot say it. 1650
Once we have seen him as he is
he will leave Thebes, lift the curse from his city—
banish himself, cursed by his own curses.
But his strength is gone, his whole life is pain,
more pain than any man can bear.
He needs help, someone to guide him.
He is alone, and blind. Look,
look—the palace doors are opening—now
a thing
so horrible will stand before you 1660
you will shudder with disgust and try to turn away
while your hearts will swell with pity for what you see.

[*The central doors open.* OEDIPUS *enters, led by his household servants. His mask is covered with blood. The* CHORUS *begin a dirge to which* OEDIPUS *responds antiphonally.*]

CHORUS. horror horror o what suffering
men see
but none is worse than this
Oedipus o
how could you have slashed out your eyes
what god leaped on you
from beyond that last border of space

what madness entered you 1670
clawing even more misery into you
I cannot look at you

but there are questions
so much I would know
so much that I would see
no no
the shape of your life makes me shudder

OEDIPUS. I I
this voice of agony
I am what place am I 1680
where? Not here, nowhere I know!
What force, what tide breaks over my life?
Pain, demon stabbing into me
leaving nothing, nothing, no man I know, not human,
fate howling out of nowhere what am I
fire a voice where where
is it being taken?

LEADER. Beyond everything to a place
so terrible nothing is seen there, nothing is heard.

OEDIPUS. [*reaching out, groping*]
Thing thing darkness 1690
spilling into me, my
black cloud smothering me forever,
nothing can stop you, nothing can escape,
I cannot push you away.

I am
nothing but my own cries breaking
again and again
the agony of those gold pins
the memory of what I did
stab me 1700
again
again.

LEADER. What can you feel but pain?
It all comes back, pain in remorse,
remorse in pain, to tear you apart with grief.

OEDIPUS. Dear, loyal friend
you, only you, are still here with me, still care
for this blind, tortured man.
Oh,
I know you are there, I know you, friend, 1710
even in this darkness, friend, touched by your voice.

LEADER. What you did was horrible,
but how could you quench the fire of your eyes,
what demon lifted your hands?

OEDIPUS. Apollo Apollo
it was Apollo, always Apollo,

who brought each of my agonies to birth,
but I,
nobody else, *I*,
I raised these two hands of mine, held them above my head, 1720
and plunged them down,
I stabbed out these eyes.
Why should I have eyes? Why,
when nothing I saw was worth seeing?
Nothing.

LEADER. Nothing. Nothing.

OEDIPUS. Oh friends. Nothing.
No one to see, no one to love,
no one to speak to, no one to hear!
Friends, friends, lead me away now.
Lead me away from Thebes—Oedipus, 1730
destroyer and destroyed,
the man whose life is hell
for others and for himself, the man
more hated by the gods than any other man, ever.

LEADER. Oh I pity you,
I weep for your fate
and for your mind,
for what it is to be you, Oedipus.
I wish you had never seen the man you are.

OEDIPUS. I hate 1740
the man who found me, cut the thongs from my feet,
snatched me from death, cared for me—
I wish he were dead!
I should have died up there on those wild, desolate slopes of Kithairon.
Then my pain and the pain
those I love suffer now
never would have been.

LEADER. These are my wishes too.

OEDIPUS. Then I never would have murdered my father,
never heard men call me my mother's husband. 1750

Now
I am
Oedipus!
Oedipus, who lay in that loathsome bed, made love there in that bed,
his father's and mother's bed, the bed
where he was born.

No gods anywhere now, not for me,[34] now,
unholy, broken man.
What man ever suffered grief like this?

[34]Oedipus means that he has been forsaken by the gods.

LEADER. How can I say that what you did was right? 1760
Better to be dead than live blind.
OEDIPUS. I did what I had to do. No more advice.
How could *my* eyes,
when I went down into that black, sightless place beneath the earth,
the place where the dead go down, how,
how could I have looked at anything,
with what human eyes could I have gazed
on my father, on my mother—
oh gods, my mother!
What I did against those two 1770
not even strangling could punish.

And my children, how would the sight of them, born as they were born,
be sweet? Not to these eyes of mine, never to these eyes.
Nothing, nothing is left me now—no city with its high walls,
no shining statues of the gods. I stripped all these things from myself—
I, Oedipus, fallen lower than any man now, born nobler than the best,
born the king of Thebes! Cursed with my own curses, I
commanded Thebes to drive out the killer.
I banished the royal son of Laios, the man the gods revealed
is stained with the awful stain. The secret stain 1780
that I myself revealed is *my* stain. And now, revealed at last,
how could I ever look men in the eyes?
Never. Never.

If I could, I would have walled my ears so they heard nothing,
I would have made this body of mine a wall.
I would have heard nothing, tasted nothing, smelled nothing, seen nothing.
No thought. No feeling. Nothing. Nothing.
So pain would never reach me any more.

O Kithairon,
why did you shelter me and take me in? 1790
Why did you let me live? Better to have died on that bare slope of yours
where no man would ever have seen me or known the secret of my birth!

Polybos, Corinth, that house I thought was my father's home,
how beautiful I was when you sheltered me as a child
and oh what disease festered beneath that beauty.
Now everyone knows the secret of my birth, knows
how vile I am.

O roads, secret valley, cluster of oaks,

O narrow place where two roads join a third,[35]
roads that drank my blood as it streamed from my hands, 1800
flowing from my dead father's body,
do you remember me now?
Do you remember what I did with my own two hands, there in your presence,
and what I did after that, when I came here to Thebes?
O marriage, marriage, you gave me my life, and then
from the same seed, *my* seed, spewed out
fathers, brothers, sisters, children, brides, wives—
nothing, no words can express the shame.
No more words. Men should not name what men should never do.

[*To the* CHORUS]

Gods, oh gods, gods, 1810
hide me, hide me
now
far away from Thebes,
kill me,
cast me into the sea,
drive me where you will never see me—never again.

[*Reaching out to the* CHORUS, *who back away*]

Touch this poor man, touch me,
don't be afraid to touch me. Believe me, nobody,
nobody but me can bear
this fire of anguish. 1820
It is mine. Mine.

LEADER. Kreon has come.
Now he, not you, is the sole guardian of Thebes,
and only he can grant you what you ask.

OEDIPUS. [*turning toward the palace*]
What can I say to him, how can anything I say
make him listen now?
I wronged him. I accused him, and now everything I said
proves I am vile.

KREON. [*enters from the entrance to the right. He is accompanied by men who gather around* OEDIPUS]

I have not come to mock you, Oedipus; I have not come to blame you for the past.

[*To attendants*]

You men, standing there, if you have no respect for human dignity, 1830
at least revere the master of life,

[35]Not only the crossroads where Oedipus killed his father but also the sexual "narrow place" where Oedipus, his father, and Jocasta conjoined.

the all-seeing sun whose light nourishes
every living thing on earth.
Come, cover this cursed, naked, holy thing,[36] hide him
from the earth and the sacred rain and the light,
you powers who cringe from his touch.
Take him. Do it now. Be reverent.
Only his family should see and hear his grief.
Their grief.

OEDIPUS. I beg you, Kreon, if you love the gods, 1840
grant me what I ask.
I have been vile to you, worse than vile.
I have hurt you, terribly, and yet
you have treated me with kindness, with nobility.
You have calmed my fear, you did not turn away from me.
Do what I ask. Do it for yourself, not for me.

KREON. What do you want from me, Oedipus?

OEDIPUS. Drive me out of Thebes, do it now, now—
drive me someplace where no man can speak to me,
where no man can see me anymore. 1850

KREON. Believe me, Oedipus, I would have done it long ago.
But I refuse to act until I know precisely what the god desires.

OEDIPUS. Apollo has revealed what he desires. Everything is clear.
I killed my father, I am polluted and unclean.
I must die.

KREON. That is what the god commanded, Oedipus.
But there are no precedents for what has happened.
We need to *know* before we act.

OEDIPUS. Do you care so much for me, enough to ask Apollo?
For *me,* Oedipus? 1860

KREON. Now even you will trust the god, I think.

OEDIPUS. I will. And I turn to you, I implore you, Kreon—
the woman lying dead inside, your sister,
give her whatever burial you think best.
As for me,
never let this city of my fathers see me here in Thebes.
Let me go and live on the mountain, on Kithairon—the mountain
my parents intended for my grave.
Let me die the way they wanted me to die: slowly, alone—
die *their* way.
And yet this much I know—
no sickness, 1870
no ordinary, natural death[37] is mine.

[36]Because he bears a burden of guilt that transforms ordinary human nature, Oedipus has, paradoxically, become a kind of sacred being.

[37]In his play *Oedipus at Colonus,* Sophocles continues the story of *Oedipus the King* (though the plays, along with the further continuation, *Antigone,* were written at different periods of Sophocles' life). Since Oedipus died at Colonus, a suburb of Athens that included a place sacred to the Furies, the personified forces of atonement celebrated in the last play of Aeschylus' Orestes trilogy, the present reference to Oedipus' mysterious and sacred death and resting place would have been important to Sophocles' Athenian audience as a sign of the redemptive value of Oedipus' wanderings and sufferings.

I have been saved, preserved, kept alive
for some strange fate, for something far more awful still.
When that thing comes, let it take me
where it will.

[OEDIPUS *turns, looking for something, waiting*]

As for my sons,[38] Kreon,
they are grown men, they can look out for themselves.
But my daughters, those two poor girls of mine,
who have never left their home before, never left their father's side,
who ate at my side every day, who shared whatever was mine, 1880
I beg you, Kreon,
care for them, love them.
But more than anything, Kreon,
I want to touch them,

[*he begins to lift his hands*]

let me touch them with these hands of mine,
let them come to me so we can grieve together.
My noble lord, if only I could touch them with my hands,
they would still be mine just as they were
when I had eyes that could still see.

[OEDIPUS' *two small daughters are brought out of the palace*]

O gods, gods, is it possible? Do I hear 1890
my two daughters crying? Has Kreon pitied me and brought me
what I love more than my life—
my daughters?

KREON. I brought them to you, knowing how much you love them, Oedipus,
knowing the joy you would feel if they were here.

OEDIPUS. May the gods who watch over the path of your life, Kreon,
prove kinder to you than they were to me.
Where are you, children?
Come, come to your brother's hands—

[*taking his daughters into his arms*]

his mother was your mother, too, 1900
come to these hands which made these eyes, bright clear eyes once,
sockets seeing nothing, the eyes
of the man who fathered you. Look . . . your father's eyes,
your father—

[38] Eteocles and Polyneices. Their enmity in a subsequent war for control of the city of Thebes, and the related ordeals of Oedipus' daughters Antigone and Ismene, are central to Sophocles' *Oedipus at Colonus* and *Antigone*.

who knew nothing until now, saw nothing until now, and became
the husband of the woman who gave him birth.
I weep for you
when I think how men will treat you, how bitter your lives will be.
What festivals will you attend, whose homes will you visit
and not be assailed by whispers and people's stares?
Where will you go and not leave in tears? 1910
And when the time comes for you to marry,
what men will take you as their brides, and risk the shame of marrying
the daughters of Oedipus?
What sorrow will not be yours?
Your father killed his father, made love
to the woman who gave birth to him. And he fathered you
in the same place where he was fathered.
That is what you will hear; that is what they will say.
Who will marry you then? You will never marry,
but grow hard and dry like wheat so far beyond harvest 1920
that the wind blows its white flakes into the winter sky.
Oh Kreon,
now you are the only father my daughters have.
Jocasta and I, their parents, are lost to them forever.
These poor girls are yours. Your blood.
Don't let them wander all their lives,
begging, alone, unmarried, helpless.
Don't let them suffer as their father has. Pity them, Kreon,
pity these girls, so young and helpless except for you.
Promise me this. Noble Kreon, 1930
touch me with your hand, give me a sign.

[KREON *takes his hands*]

Daughters,
daughters, if you were older, if you could understand,
there is so much more I would say to you.
But for now, I give you this prayer—
Live,
live your lives, live each day as best you can,
may your lives be happier than your father's was.

KREON. No more grief. Come in.
OEDIPUS. I must. But obedience comes hard.
KREON. Everything has its time.
OEDIPUS. First, promise me this. 1940
KREON. Name it.
OEDIPUS. Banish me from Thebes.
KREON. I cannot. Ask the gods for that.
OEDIPUS. The gods hate me.
KREON. Then you will have your wish.
OEDIPUS. You promise?
KREON. I say only what I mean.
OEDIPUS. Then lead me in.

[OEDIPUS *reaches out and touches his daughters, trying to take them with him*]

KREON. Oedipus, come with me. Let your daughters go. Come.
OEDIPUS. No. You will not take my daughters. I forbid it. 1950
KREON. You *forbid* me?
You have no power any more.
All the great power you once had is gone,
gone forever.

[*The* CHORUS *turn to face the audience.* KREON *leads* OEDIPUS *toward the palace. His daughters follow. He moves slowly, and disappears into the palace as the* CHORUS *ends.*]

CHORUS. O citizens of Thebes, this is Oedipus,
who solved the famous riddle, who held more power than any mortal.
See what he is: all men gazed on his fortunate life,
all men envied him, but look at him, look.
All he had, all this man was,
pulled down and swallowed by the storm of his own life, 1960
and by the god.
Keep your eyes on that last day, on your dying.
Happiness and peace, they were not yours
unless at death you can look back on your life and say
I lived, I did not suffer.

ANTIGONE

Translated by Robert Fagles

CHARACTERS

ANTIGONE *daughter of Oedipus and Jocasta*
ISMENE *sister of Antigone*
A CHORUS *of old Theban citizens and their* LEADER
CREON[1] *king of Thebes, uncle of Antigone and Ismene*
A SENTRY
HAEMON *son of Creon and Eurydice*
TIRESIAS *a blind prophet*
A MESSENGER
EURYDICE *wife of Creon*
Guards, attendants, and a boy

[1]The Kreon of *Oedipus the King.* The names in this translation sometimes are spelled differently.

TIME AND SCENE

The royal house of Thebes. It is still night, and the invading armies of Argos have just been driven from the city. Fighting on opposite sides, the sons of Oedipus, Eteocles and Polynices, have killed each other in combat. Their uncle, CREON, *is now king of Thebes.*

Enter ANTIGONE, *slipping through the central doors of the palace. She motions to her sister,* ISMENE, *who follows her cautiously toward an altar at the center of the stage.*

ANTIGONE.
My own flesh and blood—dear sister, dear Ismene,
how many griefs our father Oedipus handed down![2]
Do you know one, I ask you, one grief
that Zeus will not perfect for the two of us
while we still live and breathe? There's nothing,
no pain—our lives are pain—no private shame,
no public disgrace, nothing I haven't seen
in your griefs and mine. And now this:
an emergency decree, they say, the Commander
has just now declared for all of Thebes. 10
What, haven't you heard? Don't you see?
The doom reserved for enemies
marches on the ones we love the most.

ISMENE.
Not I, I haven't heard a word, Antigone.
Nothing of loved ones,
no joy or pain has come my way, not since
the two of us were robbed of our two brothers,[3]
both gone in a day, a double blow—
not since the armies of Argos vanished,
just this very night. I know nothing more, 20
whether our luck's improved or ruin's still to come.

ANTIGONE.
I thought so. That's why I brought you out here,
past the gates, so you could hear in private.

[2] The two sisters had accompanied their self-blinded father Oedipus in his wanderings and sufferings after his banishment from Thebes. (The banishment is described at the end of *Oedipus the King.*) Possibly we are to regard Oedipus' lineage as afflicted by an inherited curse. Oedipus' crimes, committed unwittingly, had been to kill his father, Laius, the king of Thebes, and to marry his mother.

[3] Oedipus' two sons, Eteocles and Polynices, had been rivals for the rulership of the city. After being exiled by Eteocles, Polynices had recruited a military force in Argos to attack Thebes. In the ensuing battle, the Thebans had defeated the Argives and the brothers Eteocles and Polynices had killed each other, leaving Creon to rule Thebes.

ISMENE.
What's the matter? Trouble, clearly . . .
you sound so dark, so grim.

ANTIGONE.
Why not? Our own brothers' burial![4]
Hasn't Creon graced one with all the rites,
disgraced the other? Eteocles, they say,
has been given full military honors,
rightly so—Creon has laid him in the earth 30
and he goes with glory down among the dead.
But the body of Polynices, who died miserably—
why, a city-wide proclamation, rumor has it,
forbids anyone to bury him, even mourn him.
He's to be left unwept, unburied, a lovely treasure
for birds that scan the field and feast to their heart's content.

Such, I hear, is the martial law our good Creon
lays down for you and me—yes, me, I tell you—
and he's coming here to alert the uninformed
in no uncertain terms, 40
and he won't treat the matter lightly. Whoever
disobeys in the least will die, his doom is sealed:
stoning to death inside the city walls!

There you have it. You'll soon show what you are,
worth your breeding, Ismene, or a coward—
for all your royal blood.

ISMENE.
My poor sister, if things have come to this,
who am I to make or mend them, tell me,
what good am I to you?

ANTIGONE.
Decide.
Will you share the labor, share the work? 50

ISMENE.
What work, what's the risk? What do you mean?

ANTIGONE.
[*Raising her hands.*]
Will you lift up his body with these bare hands
and lower it with me?

[4]It was believed that the unburied were treated with contempt in the underground realm of the dead. Moreover, to mourn and to prepare bodies for proper burial was the special duty of the women.

ISMENE.

What? You'd bury him—
when a law forbids the city?

ANTIGONE.

Yes!
He is my brother and—deny it as you will—
your brother too.
No one will ever convict me for a traitor.

ISMENE.
So desperate, and Creon has expressly—

ANTIGONE.

No,
he has no right to keep me from my own.

ISMENE.
Oh my sister, think—
think how our own father died,[5] hated, 60
his reputation in ruins, driven on
by the crimes he brought to light himself
to gouge out his eyes with his own hands—
then mother . . . his mother and wife, both in one,
mutilating her life in the twisted noose—
and last, our two brothers dead in a single day,
both shedding their own blood, poor suffering boys,
battling out their common destiny hand-to-hand.
Now look at the two of us, left so alone . . .
think what a death we'll die, the worst of all 70
if we violate the laws and override
the fixed decree of the throne, its power—
we must be sensible. Remember we are women,
we're not born to contend with men. Then too,
we're underlings, ruled by much stronger hands,
so we must submit in this, and things still worse.

I, for one, I'll beg the dead to forgive me—
I'm forced, I have no choice—I must obey
the ones who stand in power. Why rush to extremes? 80
It's madness, madness.

ANTIGONE.

I won't insist,
no, even if you should have a change of heart,

[5]The version in *Oedipus at Colonus* is that Oedipus, after long suffering, died a holy and mysterious death. The events Ismene describes here (her mother Jocasta's suicide and Oedipus' self-blinding) take place in *Oedipus the King*.

I'd never welcome you in the labor, not with me.
So, do as you like, whatever suits you best—
I will bury him myself.
And even if I die in the act, that death will be a glory.
I will lie with the one I love and loved by him—
an outrage sacred to the gods! I have longer
to please the dead than please the living here.
In the kingdom down below I'll lie forever. 90
Do as you like, dishonor the laws
the gods hold in honor.

ISMENE.
I'd do them no dishonor . . .
but defy the city? I have no strength for that.

ANTIGONE.
You have your excuses. I am on my way,
I will raise a mound for him, for my dear brother.

ISMENE.
Oh Antigone, you're so rash—I'm so afraid for you!

ANTIGONE.
Don't fear for me. Set your own life in order.

ISMENE.
Then don't, at least, blurt this out to anyone.
Keep it a secret. I'll join you in that, I promise.

ANTIGONE.
Dear god, shout it from the rooftops. I'll hate you 100
all the more for silence—tell the world!

ISMENE.
So fiery—and it ought to chill your heart.

ANTIGONE.
I know I please where I must please the most.

ISMENE.
Yes, if you can, but you're in love with impossibility.

ANTIGONE.
Very well, then, once my strength gives out
I will be done at last.

ISMENE.
You're wrong from the start,
you're off on a hopeless quest.

ANTIGONE.
If you say so, you will make me hate you,
and the hatred of the dead, by all rights,
will haunt you night and day. 110
But leave me to my own absurdity, leave me
to suffer this—dreadful thing. I will suffer
nothing as great as death without glory.
[*Exit to the side.*]

ISMENE.
Then go if you must, but rest assured,
wild, irrational as you are, my sister,
you are truly dear to the ones who love you.
[*Withdrawing to the palace. Enter a* CHORUS, *the old citizens of Thebes, chanting as the sun begins to rise.*]

CHORUS.
Glory!—great beam of the sun, brightest of all
that ever rose on the seven gates of Thebes,
you burn through night at last!
Great eye of the golden day, 120
mounting the Dirce's[6] banks you throw him back—
the enemy out of Argos, the white shield, the man of bronze—
he's flying headlong now
the bridle of fate stampeding him with pain!

And he had driven against our borders,
launched by the warring claims of Polynices—
like an eagle screaming, winging havoc
over the land, wings of armor
shielded white as snow,
a huge army massing, 130
crested helmets bristling for assault.

He hovered above our roofs, his vast maw gaping,
closing down around our seven gates,
his spears thirsting for the kill,
but now he's gone, look,
before he could glut his jaws with Theban blood
or the god of fire put our crown of towers to the torch.
He grappled the Dragon[7] none can master—Thebes—
the clang of our arms like thunder at his back!

Zeus hates with a vengeance all bravado, 140
the mighty boasts of men. He watched them

[6]A river near Thebes.
[7]According to myth, the Thebans were descendants of men metamorphosed from the teeth of a dragon killed by Cadmus, founder of the city.

coming on in a rising flood, the pride
of their golden armor ringing shrill—
and brandishing his lightning
blasted the fighter just at the goal,
rushing to shout his triumph from our walls.[8]
Down from the heights he crashed, pounding down on the earth!
And a moment ago, blazing torch in hand—
mad for attack, ecstatic
he breathed his rage, the storm 150
of his fury hurling at our heads!
But now his high hopes have laid him low
and down the enemy ranks the iron god of war
deals his rewards, his stunning blows—Ares[9]
rapture of battle, our right arm in the crisis.

Seven captains marshaled at seven gates
seven against their equals, gave
their brazen trophies up to Zeus,
god of the breaking rout of battle,
all but two: those blood brothers, 160
one father, one mother—matched in rage,
spears matched for the twin conquest—
clashed and won the common prize of death.

But now for Victory! Glorious in the morning,
joy in her eyes to meet our joy
she is winging down to Thebes,
our fleets of chariots wheeling in her wake—
Now let us win oblivion from the wars,
thronging the temples of the gods
in singing, dancing choirs through the night! 170
Lord Dionysus,[10] god of the dance
that shakes the land of Thebes, now lead the way!

[*Enter* CREON *from the palace, attended by his guard.*]

But look, the king of the realm is coming,
Creon, the new man for the new day,
whatever the gods are sending now . . .
what new plan will he launch?
Why this, this special session?
Why this sudden call to the old men
summoned at one command?

[8] The fighter is Capaneus. Having scaled the walls of Thebes, he boasted that not even Zeus, king of the gods, could stop him, but Zeus killed him with a thunderbolt.

[9] God of war and destruction.

[10] God of wine; his mother, Semele, who was ravished by Zeus in the form of lightning, was a Theban.

CREON.

My countrymen
the ship of state is safe. The gods who rocked her, 180
after a long, merciless pounding in the storm,
have righted her once more.

Out of the whole city
I have called you here alone. Well I know,
first, your undeviating respect
for the throne and royal power of King Laius.
Next, while Oedipus steered the land of Thebes,
and even after he died, your loyalty was unshakable,
you still stood by their children. Now then,
since the two sons are dead—two blows of fate
in the same day, cut down by each other's hands, 190
both killers, both brothers stained with blood—
as I am next in kin to the dead,[11]
I now possess the throne and all its powers.

Of course you cannot know a man completely,
his character, his principles, sense of judgment,
not till he's shown his colors, ruling the people,
making laws. Experience, there's the test.
As I see it, whoever assumes the task,
the awesome task of setting the city's course,
and refuses to adopt the soundest policies 200
but fearing someone, keeps his lips locked tight,
he's utterly worthless. So I rate him now,
I always have. And whoever places a friend
above the good of his own country, he is nothing:
I have no use for him.[12] Zeus my witness,
Zeus who sees all things, always—
I could never stand by silent, watching destruction
march against our city, putting safety to rout,
nor could I ever make that man a friend of mine
who menaces our country. Remember this: 210
our country *is* our safety.
Only while she voyages true on course
can we establish friendships, truer than blood itself.
Such are my standards. They make our city great.

Closely akin to them I have proclaimed,
just now, the following decree to our people
concerning the two sons of Oedipus.

[11] Creon is the brother of the dead rivals' mother, Jocasta; he is also a cousin of the former king Laius.

[12] Creon here states his side of the play's central moral and political issue. The word "friend" has also the meaning of "kindred."

Eteocles, who died fighting for Thebes,
excelling all in arms: he shall be buried,
crowned with a hero's honors, the cups we pour 220
to soak the earth and reach the famous dead.

But as for his blood brother, Polynices,
who returned from exile, home to his father-city
and the gods of his race, consumed with one desire—
to burn them roof to roots—who thirsted to drink
his kinsmen's blood and sell the rest to slavery:
that man—a proclamation has forbidden the city
to dignify him with burial, mourn him at all.
No, he must be left unburied, his corpse
carrion for the birds and dogs to tear, 230
an obscenity for the citizens to behold!

These are my principles. Never at my hands
will the traitor be honored above the patriot.
But whoever proves his loyalty to the state—
I'll prize that man in death as well as life.

LEADER.
If this is your pleasure, Creon, treating
our city's enemy and our friend this way . . .
The power is yours, I suppose, to enforce it
with the laws, both for the dead and all of us,
the living.

CREON.
Follow my orders closely then, 240
be on your guard.

LEADER.
We are too old.
Lay that burden on younger shoulders.

CREON.
No, no,
I don't mean the body—I've posted guards already.

LEADER.
What commands for us then? What other service?

CREON.
See that you never side with those who break my orders.

LEADER.
Never. Only a fool could be in love with death.

CREON.
Death is the price—you're right. But all too often
the mere hope of money has ruined many men.
[*A* SENTRY *enters from the side.*]

SENTRY.
My lord,
I can't say I'm winded from running, or set out
with any spring in my legs either—no sir, 250
I was lost in thought, and it made me stop, often,
dead in my tracks, wheeling, turning back,
and all the time a voice inside me muttering,
"Idiot, why? You're going straight to your death."
Then muttering, "Stopped again, poor fool?
If somebody gets the news to Creon first,
what's to save your neck?"
And so,
mulling it over, on I trudged, dragging my feet,
you can make a short road take forever . . .
but at last, look, common sense won out, 260
I'm here, and I'm all yours,
and even though I come empty-handed
I'll tell my story just the same, because
I've come with a good grip on one hope,
what will come will come, whatever fate—

CREON.
Come to the point!
What's wrong—why so afraid?

SENTRY.
First, myself, I've got to tell you,
I didn't do it, didn't see who did—
Be fair, don't take it out on me. 270

CREON.
You're playing it safe, soldier,
barricading yourself from any trouble.
It's obvious, you've something strange to tell.

SENTRY.
Dangerous too, and danger makes you delay
for all you're worth.

CREON.
Out with it—then dismiss!

SENTRY.
All right, here it comes. The body—

someone's just buried it, then run off . . .
sprinkled some dry dust on the flesh,
given it proper rites.

CREON.

What? 280
What man alive would dare—

SENTRY.

I've no idea, I swear it.
There was no mark of a spade, no pickaxe there,
no earth turned up, the ground packed hard and dry,
unbroken, no tracks, no wheelruts, nothing,
the workman left no trace. Just at sunup
the first watch of the day points it out—
it was a wonder! We were stunned . . .
a terrific burden too, for all of us, listen:
you can't see the corpse, not that it's buried,
really, just a light cover of road-dust on it, 290
as if someone meant to lay the dead to rest
and keep from getting cursed.
Not a sign in sight that dogs or wild beasts
had worried the body, even torn the skin.
But what came next! Rough talk flew thick and fast,
guard grilling guard—we'd have come to blows
at last, nothing to stop it; each man for himself
and each the culprit, no one caught red-handed,
all of us pleading ignorance, dodging the charges,
ready to take up red-hot iron in our fists, 300
go through fire, swear oaths to the gods—
"I didn't do it, I had no hand in it either,
not in the plotting, not the work itself!"

Finally, after all this wrangling came to nothing,
one man spoke out and made us stare at the ground,
hanging our heads in fear. No way to counter him,
no way to take his advice and come through
safe and sound. Here's what he said:
"Look, we've got to report the facts to Creon,
we can't keep this hidden." Well, that won out, 310
and the lot fell to me, condemned me,
unlucky as ever, I got the prize. So here I am,
against my will and yours too, well I know—
no one wants the man who brings bad news.

LEADER.

My king,
ever since he began I've been debating in my mind,
could this possibly be the work of the gods?

CREON.

Stop—
before you make me choke with anger—the gods![13]
You, you're senile, must you be insane?
You say—why it's intolerable—say the gods
could have the slightest concern for that corpse? 320
Tell me, was it for meritorious service
they proceeded to bury him, prized him so? The hero
who came to burn their temples ringed with pillars,
their golden treasures—scorch their hallowed earth
and fling their laws to the winds.
Exactly when did you last see the gods
celebrating traitors? Inconceivable!

No, from the first there were certain citizens
who could hardly stand the spirit of my regime,
grumbling against me in the dark, heads together, 330
tossing wildly, never keeping their necks beneath
the yoke, loyally submitting to their king.
These are the instigators, I'm convinced—
they've perverted my own guard, bribed them
to do their work.
Money! Nothing worse
in our lives, so current, rampant, so corrupting.
Money—you demolish cities, root men from their homes,
you train and twist good minds and set them on
to the most atrocious schemes. No limit,
you make them adept at every kind of outrage, 340
every godless crime—money!
Everyone—
the whole crew bribed to commit this crime,
they've made one thing sure at least:
sooner or later they will pay the price.
[*Wheeling on the* SENTRY.]
You—
I swear to Zeus as I still believe in Zeus,
if you don't find the man who buried that corpse,
the very man, and produce him before my eyes,
simple death won't be enough for you,
not till we string you up alive
and wring the immorality out of you. 350
Then you can steal the rest of your days,
better informed about where to make a killing.
You'll have learned, at last, it doesn't pay
to itch for rewards from every hand that beckons.

[13] The chorus's surmise about divine intervention in this first burial is conceivably true; the play is somewhat ambiguous on the matter.

Filthy profits wreck most men, you'll see—
they'll never save your life.

SENTRY.
Please,
may I say a word or two, or just turn and go?

CREON.
Can't you tell? Everything you say offends me.

SENTRY.
Where does it hurt you, in the ears or in the heart?

CREON.
And who are you to pinpoint my displeasure? 360

SENTRY.
The culprit grates on your feelings,
I just annoy your ears.

CREON.
Still talking?
You talk too much! A born nuisance—

SENTRY.
Maybe so,
but I never did this thing, so help me!

CREON.
Yes you did—
what's more, you squandered your life for silver!

SENTRY.
Oh it's terrible when the one who does the judging
judges things all wrong.

CREON.
Well now,
you just be clever about your judgments—
if you fail to produce the criminals for me,
you'll swear your dirty money brought you pain. 370
[*Turning sharply, reentering the palace.*]

SENTRY.
I hope he's found. Best thing by far.
But caught or not, that's in the lap of fortune:
I'll never come back, you've seen the last of me.
I'm saved, even now, and I never thought,

I never hoped—
dear gods, I owe you all my thanks!
[*Rushing out.*]

CHORUS.

Numberless wonders
terrible wonders walk the world but none the match for man—
that great wonder crossing the heaving gray sea,
driven on by the blasts of winter
on through breakers crashing left and right, 380
holds his steady course
and the oldest of the gods he wears away—
the Earth, the immortal, the inexhaustible—
as his plows go back and forth, year in, year out
with the breed of stallions turning up the furrows.

And the blithe, lightheaded race of birds he snares,
the tribes of savage beasts, the life that swarms the depths—
with one fling of his nets
woven and coiled tight, he takes them all,
man the skilled, the brilliant! 390
He conquers all, taming with his techniques
the prey that roams the cliffs and wild lairs,
training the stallion, clamping the yoke across
his shaggy neck, and the tireless mountain bull.

And speech and thought, quick as the wind
and the mood and mind for law that rules the city—
all these he has taught himself
and shelter from the arrows of the frost
when there's rough lodging under the cold clear sky
and the shafts of lashing rain— 400
ready, resourceful man!
Never without resources
never an impasse as he marches on the future—
only Death, from Death alone he will find no rescue
but from desperate plagues he has plotted his escapes.

Man the master, ingenious past all measure
past all dreams, the skills within his grasp—
he forges on, now to destruction
now again to greatness. When he weaves in
the laws of the land, and the justice of the gods 410
that binds his oaths together
he and his city rise high—
but the city casts out
that man who weds himself to inhumanity
thanks to reckless daring. Never share my hearth
never think my thoughts, whoever does such things.

[*Enter* ANTIGONE *from the side, accompanied by the* SENTRY.]

Here is a dark sign from the gods—
what to make of this? I know her,
how can I deny it? That young girl's Antigone!
Wretched, child of a wretched father, 420
Oedipus. Look, is it possible?
They bring you in like a prisoner—
why? Did you break the king's laws?
Did they take you in some act of mad defiance?

SENTRY.
She's the one, she did it single-handed—
we caught her burying the body. Where's Creon?
[*Enter* CREON *from the palace.*]

LEADER.
Back again, just in time when you need him.

CREON.
In time for what? What is it?

SENTRY.
My king,
there's nothing you can swear you'll never do—
second thoughts make liars of us all. 430
I could have sworn I wouldn't hurry back
(what with your threats, the buffeting I just took),
but a stroke of luck beyond our wildest hopes,
what a joy, there's nothing like it. So,
back I've come, breaking my oath, who cares?
I'm bringing in our prisoner—this young girl—
we took her giving the dead the last rites.
But no casting lots this time; this is *my* luck,
my prize, no one else's.
Now, my lord,
here she is. Take her, question her, 440
cross-examine her to your heart's content.
But set me free, it's only right—
I'm rid of this dreadful business once and for all.

CREON.
Prisoner! Her? You took her—where, doing what?

SENTRY.
Burying the man. That's the whole story.

CREON.
What?
You mean what you say, you're telling me the truth?

SENTRY.
She's the one. With my own eyes I saw her
bury the body, just what you've forbidden.
There. Is that plain and clear?

CREON.
What did you see? Did you catch her in the act? 450

SENTRY.
Here's what happened. We went back to our post,
those threats of yours breathing down our necks—
we brushed the corpse clean of the dust that covered it,
stripped it bare . . . it was slimy, going soft,
and we took to high ground, backs to the wind
so the stink of him couldn't hit us;
jostling, baiting each other to keep awake,
shouting back and forth—no napping on the job,
not this time. And so the hours dragged by
until the sun stood dead above our heads, 460
a huge white ball in the noon sky, beating,
blazing down, and then it happened—
suddenly, a whirlwind!
Twisting a great dust-storm up from the earth,
a black plague of the heavens, filling the plain,
ripping the leaves off every tree in sight,
choking the air and sky. We squinted hard
and took our whipping from the gods.

And after the storm passed—it seemed endless—
there, we saw the girl! 470
And she cried out a sharp, piercing cry,
like a bird come back to an empty nest,
peering into its bed, and all the babies gone . . .
Just so, when she sees the corpse bare
she bursts into a long, shattering wail
and calls down withering curses on the heads
of all who did the work. And she scoops up dry dust,
handfuls, quickly, and lifting a fine bronze urn,
lifting it high and pouring, she crowns the dead
with three full libations.[14]
Soon as we saw 480
we rushed her, closed on the kill like hunters,
and she, she didn't flinch. We interrogated her,
charging her with offenses past and present—
she stood up to it all, denied nothing. I tell you,
it made me ache and laugh in the same breath.
It's pure joy to escape the worst yourself,

[14] Ritual pourings of liquids.

it hurts a man to bring down his friends.
But all that, I'm afraid, means less to me
than my own skin. That's the way I'm made.

CREON.

[*Wheeling on* ANTIGONE.]
You,
with your eyes fixed on the ground—speak up. 490
Do you deny you did this, yes or no?

ANTIGONE.
I did it. I don't deny a thing.

CREON.

[*To the* SENTRY.]
You, get out, wherever you please—
you're clear of a very heavy charge.
[*He leaves;* CREON *turns back to* ANTIGONE.]
You, tell me briefly, no long speeches—
were you aware a decree had forbidden this?

ANTIGONE.
Well aware. How could I avoid it? It was public.

CREON.
And still you had the gall to break this law?

ANTIGONE.
Of course I did.[15] It wasn't Zeus, not in the least,
who made this proclamation—not to me. 500
Nor did that Justice, dwelling with the gods
beneath the earth, ordain such laws for men.
Nor did I think your edict had such force
that you, a mere mortal, could override the gods,
the great unwritten, unshakable traditions.
They are alive, not just today or yesterday:
they live forever, from the first of time,
and no one knows when they first saw the light.
These laws—I was not about to break them,
not out of fear of some man's wounded pride, 510
and face the retribution of the gods.
Die I must, I've known it all my life—
how could I keep from knowing?—even without
your death-sentence ringing in my ears.

[15] In the following lines Antigone states her creed; compare Creon's maxim in lines 203–205. Both antagonists can cite religious or political principles. A major question in the play is whether Antigone and Creon are actually governed by these large principles or by more personal motives (good or bad).

And if I am to die before my time
I consider that a gain. Who on earth,
alive in the midst of so much grief as I,
could fail to find his death a rich reward?
So for me, at least, to meet this doom of yours
is precious little pain. But if I had allowed 520
my own mother's son to rot, an unburied corpse—
that would have been an agony! This is nothing.
And if my present actions strike you as foolish,
let's just say I've been accused of folly
by a fool.

LEADER.
Like father like daughter,
passionate, wild . . .
she hasn't learned to bend before adversity.

CREON.
No? Believe me, the stiffest stubborn wills
fall the hardest; the toughest iron,
tempered strong in the white-hot fire, 530
you'll see it crack and shatter first of all.
And I've known spirited horses you can break
with a light bit—proud, rebellious horses.
There's no room for pride, not in a slave,[16]
not with the lord and master standing by.

This girl was an old hand at insolence
when she overrode the edicts we made public.
But once she had done it—the insolence,
twice over—to glory in it, laughing,
mocking us to our face with what she'd done. 540
I am not the man, not now: she is the man
if this victory goes to her and she goes free.

Never! Sister's child or closer in blood
than all my family clustered at my altar
worshiping Guardian Zeus—she'll never escape,
she and her blood sister, the most barbaric death.
Yes, I accuse her sister of an equal part
in scheming this, this burial.
[*To his attendants.*]
Bring her here!
I just saw her inside, hysterical, gone to pieces.
It never fails: the mind convicts itself 550
in advance, when scoundrels are up to no good,
plotting in the dark. Oh but I hate it more

[16] This is arrogantly false; Antigone is not in fact a slave.

when a traitor, caught red-handed,
tries to glorify his crimes.

ANTIGONE.
Creon, what more do you want
than my arrest and execution?

CREON.
Nothing. Then I have it all.

ANTIGONE.
Then why delay? Your moralizing repels me,
every word you say—pray god it always will.
So naturally all I say repels you too.
Enough. 560
Give me glory! What greater glory could I win
than to give my own brother decent burial?
These citizens here would all agree,
[*To the* CHORUS.]
they would praise me too
if their lips weren't locked in fear.
[*Pointing to* CREON.]
Lucky tyrants—the perquisites of power!
Ruthless power to do and say whatever pleases *them.*

CREON.
You alone, of all the people in Thebes,
see things that way.

ANTIGONE.
They see it just that way
but defer to you and keep their tongues in leash. 570

CREON.
And you, aren't you ashamed to differ so from them?
So disloyal!

ANTIGONE.
Not ashamed for a moment,
not to honor my brother, my own flesh and blood.

CREON.
Wasn't Eteocles a brother too—cut down, facing him?

ANTIGONE.
Brother, yes, by the same mother, the same father.

CREON.
Then how can you render his enemy such honors,
such impieties in his eyes?

ANTIGONE.
He will never testify to that,
Eteocles dead and buried.

CREON.
He will—
if you honor the traitor just as much as him. 580

ANTIGONE.
But it was his brother, not some slave that died—

CREON.
Ravaging our country!—
but Eteocles died fighting in our behalf.

ANTIGONE.
No matter—Death longs for the same rites for all.

CREON.
Never the same for the patriot and the traitor.

ANTIGONE.
Who, Creon, who on earth can say the ones below
don't find this pure and uncorrupt?

CREON.
Never. Once an enemy, never a friend,
not even after death.

ANTIGONE.
I was born to join in love, not hate— 590
that is my nature.

CREON.
Go down below and love,
if love you must—love the dead! While I'm alive,
no woman is going to lord it over me.
[*Enter* ISMENE *from the palace, under guard.*]

CHORUS.
Look,
Ismene's coming, weeping a sister's tears,
loving sister, under a cloud . . .
her face is flushed, her cheeks streaming.
Sorrow puts her lovely radiance in the dark.

CREON.
You—
in my own house, you viper, slinking undetected,

sucking my life-blood! I never knew
I was breeding twin disasters, the two of you 600
rising up against my throne. Come, tell me,
will you confess your part in the crime or not?
Answer me. Swear to me.

ISMENE.
I did it, yes—
if only she consents—I share the guilt,
the consequences too.

ANTIGONE.
No,
Justice will never suffer that—not you,
you were unwilling. I never brought you in.

ISMENE.
But now you face such dangers . . . I'm not ashamed
to sail through trouble with you,
make your troubles mine.

ANTIGONE.
Who did the work? 610
Let the dead and the god of death bear witness!
I have no love for a friend who loves in words alone.

ISMENE.
Oh no, my sister, don't reject me, please,
let me die beside you, consecrating
the dead together.

ANTIGONE.
Never share my dying,
don't lay claim to what you never touched.
My death will be enough.

ISMENE.
What do I care for life, cut off from you?

ANTIGONE.
Ask Creon. Your concern is all for him.

ISMENE.
Why abuse me so? It doesn't help you now.

ANTIGONE.
You're right— 620
if I mock you, I get no pleasure from it,
only pain.

ISMENE.
Tell me, dear one,
what can I do to help you, even now?

ANTIGONE.
Save yourself. I don't grudge you your survival.

ISMENE.
Oh no, no, denied my portion in your death?

ANTIGONE.
You chose to live, I chose to die.

ISMENE.
Not, at least,
without every kind of caution I could voice.

ANTIGONE.
Your wisdom appealed to one world—mine, another.

ISMENE.
But look, we're both guilty, both condemned to death.

ANTIGONE.
Courage! Live your life. I gave myself to death, 630
long ago, so I might serve the dead.

CREON.
They're both mad, I tell you, the two of them.
One's just shown it, the other's been that way
since she was born.

ISMENE.
True, my king,
the sense we were born with cannot last forever . . .
commit cruelty on a person long enough
and the mind begins to go.

CREON.
Yours did,
when you chose to commit your crimes with her.

ISMENE.
How can I live alone, without her?

CREON.
Her?
Don't even mention her—she no longer exists. 640

ISMENE.
What? You'd kill your own son's bride?

CREON.
Absolutely:
there are other fields for him to plow.

ISMENE.
Perhaps,
but never as true, as close a bond as theirs.

CREON.
A worthless woman for my son? It repels me.

ISMENE.
Dearest Haemon, your father wrongs you so![17]

CREON.
Enough, enough—you and your talk of marriage!

ISMENE.
Creon—you're really going to rob your son of Antigone?

CREON.
Death will do it for me—break their marriage off.

LEADER.
So, it's settled then? Antigone must die?

CREON.
Settled, yes—we both know that. 650
[*To the guards.*]
Stop wasting time. Take them in.
From now on they'll act like women.
Tie them up, no more running loose;
even the bravest will cut and run,
once they see Death coming for their lives.
[*The guards escort* ANTIGONE *and* ISMENE *into the palace.* CREON *remains while the old citizens form their* CHORUS.]

CHORUS.
Blest, they are the truly blest who all their lives
have never tasted devastation. For others, once
the gods have rocked a house to its foundations
the ruin will never cease, cresting on and on

[17] In some versions, this line is given to Antigone.

from one generation on throughout the race— 660
like a great mounting tide
driven on by savage northern gales,
surging over the dead black depths
roiling up from the bottom dark heaves of sand
and the headlands, taking the storm's onslaught full-force,
roar, and the low moaning
echoes on and on
and now
as in ancient times I see the sorrows of the house,[18]
the living heirs of the old ancestral kings,
piling on the sorrows of the dead
and one generation cannot free the next— 670
some god will bring them crashing down,
the race finds no release.
And now the light, the hope
springing up from the late last root
in the house of Oedipus, that hope's cut down in turn
by the long, bloody knife swung by the gods of death
by a senseless word
by fury at the heart.
Zeus,
yours is the power, Zeus, what man on earth
can override it, who can hold it back?
Power that neither Sleep, the all-ensnaring 680
no, nor the tireless months of heaven
can ever overmaster—young through all time,
mighty lord of power, you hold fast
the dazzling crystal mansions of Olympus.
And throughout the future, late and soon
as through the past, your law prevails:
no towering form of greatness
enters into the lives of mortals
free and clear of ruin.
True,
our dreams, our high hopes voyaging far and wide 690
bring sheer delight to many, to many others
delusion, blithe, mindless lusts
and the fraud steals on one slowly . . . unaware
till he trips and puts his foot into the fire.
He was a wise old man who coined
the famous saying: "Sooner or later
foul is fair, fair is foul
to the man the gods will ruin"—
He goes his way for a moment only
free of blinding ruin. 700

[18] The sorrows of the family extend farther into the past than to Oedipus' acts of patricide and incest; for example, his father, Laius, had been cursed by Pelops (the ancestor of the cursed family treated in Aeschylus' Orestes trilogy) after Laius had wronged Pelops, his protector during a period of exile, by stealing his son.

[*Enter* HAEMON *from the palace.*]

Here's Haemon now, the last of all your sons.[19]
Does he come in tears for his bride,
his doomed bride, Antigone—
bitter at being cheated of their marriage?

CREON.

We'll soon know, better than seers could tell us.
[*Turning to* HAEMON.]
Son, you've heard the final verdict on your bride?
Are you coming now, raving against your father?
Or do you love me, no matter what I do?

HAEMON.

Father, I'm your *son* . . . you in your wisdom
set my bearings for me—I obey you. 710
No marriage could ever mean more to me than you,
whatever good direction you may offer.

CREON.

Fine, Haemon.
That's how you ought to feel within your heart,
subordinate to your father's will in every way.
That's what a man prays for: to produce good sons—
a household full of them, dutiful and attentive,
so they can pay his enemy back with interest
and match the respect their father shows his friend.
But the man who rears a brood of useless children,
what has he brought into the world, I ask you? 720
Nothing but trouble for himself, and mockery
from his enemies laughing in his face.
Oh Haemon,
never lose your sense of judgment over a woman.
The warmth, the rush of pleasure, it all goes cold
in your arms, I warn you . . . a worthless woman
in your house, a misery in your bed.
What wound cuts deeper than a loved one
turned against you? Spit her out,
like a mortal enemy—let the girl go.
Let her find a husband down among the dead. 730
Imagine it: I caught her in naked rebellion,
the traitor, the only one in the whole city.
I'm not about to prove myself a liar,
not to my people, no, I'm going to kill her!
That's right—so let her cry for mercy, sing her hymns
to Zeus who defends all bonds of kindred blood.
Why, if I bring up my own kin to be rebels,

[19]According to one version of the Thebes saga, Haemon's brother Megareus had committed suicide in order to propitiate the war god Ares and thus save Thebes.

think what I'd suffer from the world at large.
Show me the man who rules his household well:
I'll show you someone fit to rule the state. 740
That good man, my son,
I have every confidence he and he alone
can give commands and take them too. Staunch
in the storm of spears he'll stand his ground,
a loyal, unflinching comrade at your side.

But whoever steps out of line, violates the laws
or presumes to hand out orders to his superiors,
he'll win no praise from me. But that man
the city places in authority, his orders
must be obeyed, large and small, 750
right and wrong.
Anarchy—
show me a greater crime in all the earth!
She, she destroys cities, rips up houses,
breaks the ranks of spearmen into headlong rout.
But the ones who last it out, the great mass of them
owe their lives to discipline. Therefore
we must defend the men who live by law,
never let some woman triumph over us.
Better to fall from power, if fall we must,
at the hands of a man—never be rated 760
inferior to a woman, never.

LEADER.
To us,
unless old age has robbed us of our wits,
you seem to say what you have to say with sense.

HAEMON.
Father, only the gods endow a man with reason,
the finest of all their gifts, a treasure.
Far be it from me—I haven't the skill,
and certainly no desire, to tell you when,
if ever, you make a slip in speech . . . though
someone else might have a good suggestion.

Of course it's not for you, 770
in the normal run of things, to watch
whatever men say or do, or find to criticize.
The man in the street, you know, dreads your glance,
he'd never say anything displeasing to your face.
But it's for me to catch the murmurs in the dark,
the way the city mourns for this young girl.
"No woman," they say, "ever deserved death less,
and such a brutal death for such a glorious action.

She, with her own dear brother lying in his blood—
she couldn't bear to leave him dead, unburied, 780
food for the wild dogs or wheeling vultures.
Death? She deserves a glowing crown of gold!"
So they say, and the rumor spreads in secret,
darkly . . .
I rejoice in your success, father—
nothing more precious to me in the world.
What medal of honor brighter to his children
than a father's growing glory? Or a child's
to his proud father? Now don't, please,
be quite so single-minded, self-involved,
or assume the world is wrong and you are right. 790
Whoever thinks that he alone possesses intelligence,
the gift of eloquence, he and no one else,
and character too . . . such men, I tell you,
spread them open—you will find them empty.
No,
it's no disgrace for a man, even a wise man,
to learn many things and not to be too rigid.
You've seen trees by a raging winter torrent,
how many sway with the flood and salvage every twig,
but not the stubborn—they're ripped out, roots and all.
Bend or break. The same when a man is sailing: 800
haul your sheets too taut, never give an inch,
you'll capsize, and go the rest of the voyage
keel up and the rowing-benches under.

Oh give way. Relax your anger—change!
I'm young, I know, but let me offer this:
it would be best by far, I admit,
if a man were born infallible, right by nature.
If not—and things don't often go that way,
it's best to learn from those with good advice.

LEADER.
You'd do well, my lord, if he's speaking to the point, 810
to learn from him,
[*Turning to* HAEMON.]
and you, my boy, from him.
You both are talking sense.

CREON.
So,
men our age, we're to be lectured, are we?—
schooled by a boy his age?

HAEMON.
Only in what is right. But if I seem young,
look less to my years and more to what I do.

CREON.
Do? Is admiring rebels an achievement?

HAEMON.
I'd never suggest that you admire treason.

CREON.
Oh?—
isn't that just the sickness that's attacked her?

HAEMON.
The whole city of Thebes denies it, to a man. 820

CREON.
And is Thebes about to tell me how to rule?

HAEMON.
Now, you see? Who's talking like a child?

CREON.
Am I to rule this land for others—or myself?

HAEMON.
It's no city at all, owned by one man alone.

CREON.
What? The city *is* the king's—that's the law!

HAEMON.
What a splendid king you'd make of a desert island—
you and you alone.

CREON.
[*To the* CHORUS.]
This boy, I do believe
is fighting on her side, the woman's side.

HAEMON.
If you are a woman, yes—
my concern is all for you. 830

CREON.
Why, you degenerate—bandying accusations,
threatening me with justice, your own father!

HAEMON.
I see my father offending justice—wrong.

CREON.
Wrong?
To protect my royal rights?

HAEMON.

Protect your rights?
When you trample down the honors of the gods?

CREON.
You, you soul of corruption, rotten through—
woman's accomplice!

HAEMON.

That may be,
but you will never find me accomplice to a criminal.

CREON.
That's what *she* is,
and every word you say is a blatant appeal for her— 840

HAEMON.
And you, and me, and the gods beneath the earth.

CREON.
You will never marry her, not while she's alive.

HAEMON.
Then she will die . . . but her death will kill another.

CREON.
What, brazen threats? You go too far!

HAEMON.

What threat?
Combating your empty, mindless judgments with a word?

CREON.
You'll suffer for your sermons, you and your empty wisdom!

HAEMON.
If you weren't my father, I'd say you were insane.

CREON.
Don't flatter me with Father—you woman's slave!

HAEMON.
You really expect to fling abuse at me
and not receive the same?

CREON.

Is that so! 850
Now, by heaven, I promise you, you'll pay—
taunting, insulting me! Bring her out,

that hateful—she'll die now, here,
in front of his eyes, beside her groom!

HAEMON.
No, no, she will never die beside me—
don't delude yourself. And you will never
see me, never set eyes on my face again.
Rage your heart out, rage with friends
who can stand the sight of you.
[*Rushing out.*]

LEADER.
Gone, my king, in a burst of anger. 860
A temper young as his . . . hurt him once,
he may do something violent.

CREON.
Let him do—
dream up something desperate, past all human limit!
Good riddance. Rest assured,
he'll never save those two young girls from death.

LEADER.
Both of them, you really intend to kill them both?

CREON.
No, not her, the one whose hands are clean—
you're quite right.

LEADER.
But Antigone—
what sort of death do you have in mind for her?

CREON.
I will take her down some wild, desolate path 870
never trod by men, and wall her up alive
in a rocky vault, and set out short rations,
just the measure piety demands
to keep the entire city free of defilement.[20]
There let her pray to the one god she worships:
Death[21]—who knows?—may just reprieve her from death.
Or she may learn at last, better late than never,
what a waste of breath it is to worship Death.

[20] This method of execution is inconsistent with the earlier passage that decrees death by stoning (lines 41–43). Creon apparently believes, legalistically, that he can avoid the crime of shedding kindred blood by merely shutting Antigone up alone and by providing her with food. Technically no act of execution will have been committed.
[21] Hades, king of the realm of the dead.

[*Exit to the palace.*]

CHORUS.
Love, never conquered in battle
Love the plunderer laying waste the rich! 880
Love standing the night-watch
guarding a girl's soft cheek,
you range the seas, the shepherds' steadings off in the wilds—
not even the deathless gods can flee your onset,
nothing human born for a day—
whoever feels your grip is driven mad.
Love!—
you wrench the minds of the righteous into outrage,
swerve them to their ruin—you have ignited this,
this kindred strife, father and son at war
and Love alone the victor— 890
warm glance of the bride triumphant, burning with desire!
Throned in power, side-by-side with the mighty laws!
Irresistible Aphrodite,[22] never conquered—
Love, you mock us for your sport.

[ANTIGONE *is brought from the palace under guard.*]

But now, even I would rebel against the king,
I would break all bounds when I see this—
I fill with tears, I cannot hold them back,
not any more . . . I see Antigone make her way
to the bridal vault where all are laid to rest.

ANTIGONE.
Look at me, men of my fatherland, 900
setting out on the last road
looking into the last light of day
the last I will ever see . . .
the god of death who puts us all to bed
takes me down to the banks of Acheron[23] alive—
denied my part in the wedding-songs,
no wedding-song in the dusk has crowned my marriage—
I go to wed the lord of the dark waters.

CHORUS.
Not crowned with glory or with a dirge,
you leave for the deep pit of the dead. 910
No withering illness laid you low,
no strokes of the sword—a law to yourself,
alone, no mortal like you, ever, you go down
to the halls of Death alive and breathing.

[22] Goddess of love.
[23] A river in the land of the dead.

ANTIGONE.
But think of Niobe[24]—well I know her story—
think what a living death she died,
Tantalus' daughter, stranger queen from the east:
there on the mountain heights, growing stone
binding as ivy, slowly walled her round
and the rains will never cease, the legends say 920
the snows will never leave her . . .
wasting away, under her brows the tears
showering down her breasting ridge and slopes—
a rocky death like hers puts me to sleep.

CHORUS.
But she was a god, born of gods,[25]
and we are only mortals born to die.
And yet, of course, it's a great thing
for a dying girl to hear, even to hear
she shares a destiny equal to the gods,
during life and later, once she's dead.

ANTIGONE.
O, you mock me! 930
Why, in the name of all my fathers' gods
why can't you wait till I am gone—
must you abuse me to my face?[26]
O my city, all your fine rich sons!
And you, you springs of the Dirce,
holy grove of Thebes where the chariots gather,
you at least, you'll bear me witness, look,
unmourned by friends and forced by such crude laws
I go to my rockbound prison, strange new tomb—
always a stranger, O dear god, 940
I have no home on earth and none below,
not with the living, not with the breathless dead.

CHORUS.
You went too far, the last limits of daring—
smashing against the high throne of Justice!
Your life's in ruins, child—I wonder . . .
do you pay for your father's terrible ordeal?

[24] Niobe, originally from Phrygia in Asia Minor, was the wife of Amphion, a former ruler of Thebes. Mother of fourteen children, she boasted of her superiority to the goddess Leto, who had only two, Apollo and Artemis. In revenge for her impiety, all of Niobe's children were killed and she was turned into a stone from which flowed a perpetual stream of her tears. There is an irony: Niobe was punished for flouting the gods, while Antigone is being killed for her piety.

[25] Niobe was the daughter of Tantalus, whose father was Zeus.

[26] Antigone's protest probably reflects her bitter reaction to the elders' implication that she is lucky in sharing the fate of the famed Niobe.

ANTIGONE.

There—at last you've touched it, the worst pain
the worst anguish! Raking up the grief for father
three times over, for all the doom
that's struck us down, the brilliant house of Laius. 950
O mother, your marriage-bed
the coiling horrors, the coupling there—
you with your own son, my father—doomstruck mother!
Such, such were my parents, and I their wretched child.
I go to them now, cursed, unwed, to share their home—
I am a stranger! O dear brother, doomed
in your marriage—your marriage murders mine,[27]
your dying drags me down to death alive!

[*Enter* CREON.]

CHORUS.

Reverence asks some reverence in return—
but attacks on power never go unchecked, 960
not by the man who holds the reins of power.
Your own blind will, your passion has destroyed you.

ANTIGONE.

No one to weep for me, my friends,
no wedding-song—they take me away
in all my pain . . . the road lies open, waiting.
Never again, the law forbids me to see
the sacred eye of day. I am agony!
No tears for the destiny that's mine,
no loved one mourns my death.

CREON.

Can't you see?
If a man could wail his own dirge *before* he dies, 970
he'd never finish.

[*To the guards.*]

Take her away, quickly!
Wall her up in the tomb, you have your orders.
Abandon her there, alone, and let her choose—
death or a buried life with a good roof for shelter.
As for myself, my hands are clean. This young girl—
dead or alive, she will be stripped of her rights,
her stranger's rights, here in the world above.

ANTIGONE.

O tomb, my bridal-bed—my house, my prison
cut in the hollow rock, my everlasting watch!

[27] Polynices, as part of his plan to enlist the aid of Argos in attacking Thebes, married a daughter of the Argive king. The war, and Polynices' death, have brought death to Antigone too.

I'll soon be there, soon embrace my own, 980
the great growing family of our dead
Persephone[28] has received among her ghosts.
I,
the last of them all, the most reviled by far,
go down before my destined time's run out.
But still I go, cherishing one good hope:
my arrival may be dear to father,
dear to you, my mother,
dear to you, my loving brother, Eteocles—
When you died I washed you with my hands,
I dressed you all, I poured the sacred cups 990
across your tombs. But now, Polynices,
because I laid your body out as well,
this, this is my reward. Nevertheless
I honored you—the decent will admit it—
well and wisely too.
Never, I tell you,
if I had been the mother of children
or if my husband died, exposed and rotting—
I'd never have taken this ordeal upon myself,
never defied our people's will. What law,
you ask, do I satisfy with what I say? 1000
A husband dead, there might have been another.
A child by another too, if I had lost the first.
But mother and father both lost in the halls of Death,
no brother could ever spring to light again.[29]
For this law alone I held you first in honor.
For this, Creon, the king, judges me a criminal
guilty of dreadful outrage, my dear brother!
And now he leads me off, a captive in his hands,
with no part in the bridal-song, the bridal-bed,
denied all joy of marriage, raising children— 1010
deserted so by loved ones, struck by fate,
I descend alive to the caverns of the dead.

What law of the mighty gods have I transgressed?
Why look to the heavens any more, tormented as I am?
Whom to call, what comrades now? Just think,
my reverence only brands me for irreverence!
Very well: if this is the pleasure of the gods,

[28] Consort of Hades, king of the dead.

[29] For various reasons, including the opinion that Antigone's fine distinctions and perhaps insensitivity here are inconsistent with the rest of the play, some editors and translators reject lines 995–1004. The appropriateness of the passage has been defended on grounds of dramatic psychology (e.g., the marital and maternal roles must be merely imagined by Antigone, while her role of sister is one she has experienced) and more technical grounds (e.g., the notion that the sibling bond is closer than either the marital one which involves no blood kinship or the "half-interest" bond of blood kinship that links a child with one of its two parents).

once I suffer I will know that I was wrong.
But if these men are wrong, let them suffer
nothing worse than they mete out to me— 1020
these masters of injustice!

LEADER.
Still the same rough winds, the wild passion
raging through the girl.

CREON.
[*To the guards.*]
Take her away.
You're wasting time—you'll pay for it too.

ANTIGONE.
Oh god, the voice of death. It's come, it's here.

CREON.
True. Not a word of hope—your doom is sealed.

ANTIGONE.
Land of Thebes, city of all my fathers—
O you gods, the first gods of the race![30]
They drag me away, now, no more delay.
Look on me, you noble sons of Thebes— 1030
the last of a great line of kings,
I alone, see what I suffer now
at the hands of what breed of men—
all for reverence, my reverence for the gods!
[*She leaves under guard: the* CHORUS *gathers.*]

CHORUS.
Danaë,[31] Danaë—
even she endured a fate like yours,
in all her lovely strength she traded
the light of day for the bolted brazen vault—
buried within her tomb, her bridal-chamber,
wed to the yoke and broken. 1040
But she was of glorious birth
my child, my child
and treasured the seed of Zeus within her womb,
and cloudburst streaming gold!
The power of fate is a wonder,
dark, terrible wonder—

[30]According to the myths, several of Antigone's forebears in the Theban dynasty were related to the gods by blood or marriage.

[31]Danaë's father Acrisius, a king of Argos, had imprisoned her because of a prophecy that she would bear a son who would kill him. Zeus came to her in a shower of golden rain, begetting Perseus, who did later kill Acrisius.

neither wealth nor armies
towered walls nor ships
black hulls lashed by the salt
can save us from that force. 1050

The yoke tamed him too
young Lycurgus[32] flaming in anger
king of Edonia, all for his mad taunts
Dionysus clamped him down, encased
in the chain-mail of rock
and there his rage
his terrible flowering rage burst—
sobbing, dying away . . . at last that madman
came to know his god—
the power he mocked, the power 1060
he taunted in all his frenzy
trying to stamp out
the women strong with the god—
the torch, the raving sacred cries—
enraging the Muses who adore the flute.
And far north where the Black Rocks[33]
cut the sea in half
and murderous straits
split the coast of Thrace
a forbidding city stands 1070
where once, hard by the walls
the savage Ares thrilled to watch
a king's new queen, a Fury rearing in rage
against his two royal sons—
her bloody hands, her dagger-shuttle
stabbing out their eyes—cursed, blinding wounds—
their eyes blind sockets screaming for revenge!

They wailed in agony, cries echoing cries
the princes doomed at birth . . .
and their mother doomed to chains, 1080
walled up in a tomb of stone—
but she traced her own birth back
to a proud Athenian line and the high gods
and off in caverns half the world away,
born of the wild North Wind
she sprang on her father's gales,
racing stallions up the leaping cliffs—

[32]Lycurgus, a legendary Thracian king, had been imprisoned after being driven to madness by the gods for opposing the worship of Bacchus (Dionysus). Maenads (line 1063) were orgiastic female worshipers of the god.

[33]The following lines allude to a third story of imprisonment; most interpreters have found the story itself and its application to Antigone obscure. Phineus, a king of Thrace, divorced his wife Cleopatra (daughter of Boreas, the north wind), who had borne him two sons, and cast her into prison; his second wife blinded the two children and entombed them.

child of the heavens. But even on her the Fates
the gray everlasting Fates rode hard
my child, my child.

[*Enter* TIRESIAS, *the blind prophet, led by a boy.*]

TIRESIAS.

Lords of Thebes, 1090
I and the boy have come together,
hand in hand. Two see with the eyes of one . . .
so the blind must go, with a guide to lead the way.

CREON.
What is it, old Tiresias? What news now?

TIRESIAS.
I will teach you. And you obey the seer.

CREON.

I will,
I've never wavered from your advice before.

TIRESIAS.
And so you kept the city straight on course.

CREON.
I owe you a great deal, I swear to that.

TIRESIAS.
Then reflect, my son: you are poised,
once more, on the razor-edge of fate. 1100

CREON.
What is it? I shudder to hear you.

TIRESIAS.

You will learn
when you listen to the warnings of my craft.
As I sat on the ancient seat of augury,
in the sanctuary where every bird I know
will hover at my hands—suddenly I heard it,
a strange voice in the wingbeats, unintelligible,
barbaric, a mad scream! Talons flashing, ripping,
they were killing each other—that much I knew—
the murderous fury whirring in those wings
made that much clear!

I was afraid, 1110
I turned quickly, tested the burnt-sacrifice,
ignited the altar at all points—but no fire,
the god in the fire never blazed.

Not from those offerings . . . over the embers
slid a heavy ooze from the long thighbones,
smoking, sputtering out, and the bladder
puffed and burst—spraying gall into the air—
and the fat wrapping the bones slithered off
and left them glistening white. No fire!
The rites failed that might have blazed the future 1120
with a sign. So I learned from the boy here:
he is my guide, as I am guide to others.
And it is you—
your high resolve that sets this plague on Thebes.
The public altars and sacred hearths are fouled,
one and all, by the birds and dogs with carrion
torn from the corpse, the doomstruck son of Oedipus!
And so the gods are deaf to our prayers, they spurn
the offerings in our hands, the flame of holy flesh.
No birds cry out an omen clear and true—
they're gorged with the murdered victim's blood and fat. 1130
Take these things to heart, my son, I warn you.
All men make mistakes, it is only human.
But once the wrong is done, a man
can turn his back on folly, misfortune too,
if he tries to make amends, however low he's fallen,
and stops his bullnecked ways. Stubbornness
brands you for stupidity—pride is a crime.
No, yield to the dead!
Never stab the fighter when he's down.
Where's the glory, killing the dead twice over? 1140

I mean you well. I give you sound advice.
It's best to learn from a good adviser
when he speaks for your own good:
it's pure gain.

CREON.

Old man—all of you! So,
you shoot your arrows at my head like archers at the target—
I even have *him* loosed on me, this fortune-teller.
Oh his ilk has tried to sell me short
and ship me off for years.[34] Well,
drive your bargains, traffic—much as you like—
in the gold of India, silver-gold of Sardis. 1150
You'll never bury that body in the grave,
not even if Zeus's eagles rip the corpse
and wing their rotten pickings off to the throne of god!
Never, not even in fear of such defilement
will I tolerate his burial, that traitor.

[34] Ironically, Oedipus (in *Oedipus the King*) had accused Tiresias and Creon himself of a similar, and equally imaginary, mercenary plot.

Well I know, we can't defile the gods—
no mortal has the power.
No,
reverend old Tiresias, all men fall,
it's only human, but the wisest fall obscenely
when they glorify obscene advice with rhetoric— 1160
all for their own gain.

TIRESIAS.
Oh god, is there a man alive
who knows, who actually believes . . .

CREON.
What now?
What earth-shattering truth are you about to utter?

TIRESIAS.
. . . just how much a sense of judgment, wisdom
is the greatest gift we have?

CREON.
Just as much, I'd say,
as a twisted mind is the worst affliction known.

TIRESIAS.
You are the one who's sick, Creon, sick to death.

CREON.
I am in no mood to trade insults with a seer.

TIRESIAS.
You have already, calling my prophecies a lie.

CREON.
Why not? 1170
You and the whole breed of seers are mad for money!

TIRESIAS.
And the whole race of tyrants lusts for filthy gain.

CREON.
This slander of yours—
are you aware you're speaking to the king?

TIRESIAS.
Well aware. Who helped you save the city?

CREON.
You—
you have your skills, old seer, but you lust for injustice!

TIRESIAS.
You will drive me to utter the dreadful secret in my heart.

CREON.
Spit it out! Just don't speak it out for profit.

TIRESIAS.
Profit? No, not a bit of profit, not for you.

CREON.
Know full well, you'll never buy off my resolve. 1180

TIRESIAS.
Then know this too, learn this by heart!
The chariot of the sun will not race through
so many circuits more, before you have surrendered
one born of your own loins, your own flesh and blood,
a corpse for corpses given in return, since you have thrust
to the world below a child sprung for the world above,
ruthlessly lodged a living soul within the grave—
then you've robbed the gods below the earth,
keeping a dead body here in the bright air,
unburied, unsung, unhallowed by the rites. 1190

You, you have no business with the dead,
nor do the gods above—this is violence
you have forced upon the heavens.
And so the avengers, the dark destroyers late
but true to the mark, now lie in wait for you,
the Furies[35] sent by the gods and the god of death
to strike you down with the pains that you perfected!

There. Reflect on that, tell me I've been bribed.
The day comes soon, no long test of time, not now,
when the mourning cries for men and women break 1200
throughout your halls. Great hatred rises against you—
cities in tumult,[36] all whose mutilated sons
the dogs have graced with burial, or the wild beasts
or a wheeling crow that wings the ungodly stench of carrion
back to each city, each warrior's hearth and home.

These arrows for your heart! Since you've raked me
I loose them like an archer in my anger,
arrows deadly true. You'll never escape
their burning, searing force.

[*Motioning to his escort.*]

Come, boy, take me home. 1210
So he can vent his rage on younger men,

[35] Primitive personifications of vengeance, especially for crimes against kindred.
[36] The cities that organized the army to attack Thebes.

and learn to keep a gentler tongue in his head
and better sense than what he carries now.
[*Exit to the side.*]

LEADER.
The old man's gone, my king—
terrible prophecies. Well I know,
since the hair on this old head went gray,
he's never lied to Thebes.

CREON.
I know it myself—I'm shaken, torn.
It's a dreadful thing to yield . . . but resist now?
Lay my pride bare to the blows of ruin? 1220
That's dreadful too.

LEADER.
But good advice,
Creon, take it now, you must.

CREON.
What should I do? Tell me . . . I'll obey.

LEADER.
Go! Free the girl from the rocky vault
and raise a mound for the body you exposed.

CREON.
That's your advice? You think I should give in?

LEADER.
Yes, my king, quickly. Disasters sent by the gods
cut short our follies in a flash.

CREON.
Oh it's hard,
giving up the heart's desire . . . but I will do it—
no more fighting a losing battle with necessity. 1230

LEADER.
Do it now, go, don't leave it to others.

CREON.
Now—I'm on my way! Come, each of you,
take up axes, make for the high ground,
over there, quickly! I and my better judgment
have come round to this—I shackled her,
I'll set her free myself. I am afraid . . .
it's best to keep the established laws
to the very day we die.

[*Rushing out, followed by his entourage. The* CHORUS *clusters around the altar.*]

CHORUS.

God of a hundred names![37]

Great Dionysus—

Son and glory of Semele! Pride of Thebes— 1240

Child of Zeus whose thunder rocks the clouds—

Lord of the famous lands of evening—

King of the Mysteries!

King of Eleusis,[38] Demeter's plain

her breasting hills that welcome in the world—

Great Dionysus!

Bacchus, living in Thebes

the mother-city of all your frenzied women—

Bacchus

living along the Ismenus' rippling waters

standing over the field sown with the Dragon's teeth!

You—we have seen you through the flaring smoky fires,

your torches blazing over the twin peaks[39] 1250

where nymphs of the hallowed cave climb onward

fired with you, your sacred rage—

we have seen you at Castalia's running spring[40]

and down from the heights of Nysa[41] crowned with ivy

the greening shore rioting vines and grapes

down you come in your storm of wild women

ecstatic, mystic cries—

Dionysus—

down to watch and ward the roads of Thebes!

First of all cities, Thebes you honor first

you and your mother, bride of the lightning— 1260

come, Dionysus! now your people lie

in the iron grip of plague,

come in your racing, healing stride

down Parnassus' slopes

or across the moaning straits.

Lord of the dancing—

dance, dance the constellations breathing fire!

Great master of the voices of the night!

[37]The chorus invokes Dionysus as the patron deity of Thebes.

[38]Eleusis, a town near Athens, was the center of the mysterious fertility rites of Demeter, goddess of the fields and harvest.

[39]Parnassus, a mountain near Apollo's shrine at Delphi; one of the peaks was sacred to Apollo, one to Bacchus (Dionysus).

[40]A spring and pool on Mount Parnassus.

[41]A mountain where Dionysus had been reared by nymphs.

Child of Zeus, God's offspring, come, come forth!
Lord, king, dance with your nymphs, swirling, raving
arm-in-arm in frenzy through the night 1270
they dance you, Iacchus—
Dance, Dionysus
giver of all good things!

[*Enter a* MESSENGER *from the side.*]

MESSENGER.

Neighbors,
friends of the house of Cadmus and the kings,
there's not a thing in this mortal life of ours
I'd praise or blame as settled once for all.
Fortune lifts and Fortune fells the lucky
and unlucky every day. No prophet on earth
can tell a man his fate. Take Creon:
there was a man to rouse your envy once,
as I see it. He saved the realm from enemies, 1280
taking power, he alone, the lord of the fatherland,
he set us true on course—he flourished like a tree
with the noble line of sons he bred and reared . . .
and now it's lost, all gone.
Believe me,
when a man has squandered his true joys,
he's good as dead, I tell you, a living corpse.
Pile up riches in your house, as much as you like—
live like a king with a huge show of pomp,
but if real delight is missing from the lot,
I wouldn't give you a wisp of smoke for it, 1290
not compared with joy.

LEADER.

What now?
What new grief do you bring the house of kings?

MESSENGER.
Dead, dead—and the living are guilty of their death!

LEADER.
Who's the murderer? Who is dead? Tell us.

MESSENGER.
Haemon's gone, his blood spilled by the very hand—

LEADER.
His father's or his own?

MESSENGER.

His own . . .
raging mad with his father for the death—

LEADER.

Oh great seer,
you saw it all, you brought your word to birth!

MESSENGER.

Those are the facts. Deal with them as you will.
[*As he turns to go,* EURYDICE *enters from the palace.*]

LEADER.

Look, Eurydice. Poor woman, Creon's wife, 1300
so close at hand. By chance perhaps,
unless she's heard the news about her son.

EURYDICE.

My countrymen,
all of you—I caught the sound of your words
as I was leaving to do my part,
to appeal to queen Athena with my prayers.
I was just loosing the bolts, opening the doors,
when a voice filled with sorrow, family sorrow,
struck my ears, and I fell back, terrified,
into the women's arms—everything went black.
Tell me the news, again, whatever it is . . . 1310
sorrow and I are hardly strangers.
I can bear the worst.

MESSENGER.

I—dear lady,
I'll speak as an eye-witness. I was there.
And I won't pass over one word of the truth.
Why should I try to soothe you with a story,
only to prove a liar in a moment?
Truth is always best.

So,
I escorted your lord, I guided him
to the edge of the plain where the body lay,
Polynices, torn by the dogs and still unmourned. 1320
And saying a prayer to Hecate of the Crossroads,
Pluto[42] too, to hold their anger and be kind,
we washed the dead in a bath of holy water
and plucking some fresh branches, gathering . . .
what was left of him, we burned them all together
and raised a high mound of native earth, and then
we turned and made for that rocky vault of hers,

[42] Hecate, associated with crossroads, was a goddess of night, magic, and the Underworld; Pluto is another name for Hades, god of the dead.

the hollow, empty bed of the bride of Death.
And far off, one of us heard a voice,
a long wail rising, echoing 1330
out of that unhallowed wedding-chamber,
he ran to alert the master and Creon pressed on,
closer—the strange, inscrutable cry came sharper,
throbbing around him now, and he let loose
a cry of his own, enough to wrench the heart,
"Oh god, am I the prophet now? going down
the darkest road I've ever gone? My son—
it's *his* dear voice, he greets me! Go, men,
closer, quickly! Go through the gap,
the rocks are dragged back— 1340
right to the tomb's very mouth—and look,
see if it's Haemon's voice I think I hear,
or the gods have robbed me of my senses."

The king was shattered. We took his orders,
went and searched, and there in the deepest,
dark recesses of the tomb we found her . . .
hanged by the neck in a fine linen noose,
strangled in her veils—and the boy,
his arms flung around her waist,
clinging to her, wailing for his bride, 1350
dead and down below, for his father's crimes
and the bed of his marriage blighted by misfortune.
When Creon saw him, he gave a deep sob,
he ran in, shouting, crying out to him,
"Oh my child—what have you done? what seized you,
what insanity? what disaster drove you mad?
Come out, my son! I beg you on my knees!"
But the boy gave him a wild burning glance,
spat in his face, not a word in reply,
he drew his sword—his father rushed out, 1360
running as Haemon lunged and missed!—
and then, doomed, desperate with himself,
suddenly leaning his full weight on the blade,
he buried it in his body, halfway to the hilt.
And still in his senses, pouring his arms around her,
he embraced the girl and breathing hard,
released a quick rush of blood,
bright red on her cheek glistening white.
And there he lies, body enfolding body . . .
he has won his bride at last, poor boy, 1370
not here but in the houses of the dead.

Creon shows the world that of all the ills
afflicting men the worst is lack of judgment.

[EURYDICE *turns and reenters the palace.*]

LEADER.
What do you make of that? The lady's gone,
without a word, good or bad.

MESSENGER.
I'm alarmed too
but here's my hope—faced with her son's death
she finds it unbecoming to mourn in public.
Inside, under her roof, she'll set her women
to the task and wail the sorrow of the house.
She's too discreet. She won't do something rash. 1380

LEADER.
I'm not so sure. To me, at least,
a long heavy silence promises danger,
just as much as a lot of empty outcries.

MESSENGER.
We'll see if she's holding something back,
hiding some passion in her heart.
I'm going in. You may be right—who knows?
Even too much silence has its dangers.
[*Exit to the palace. Enter* CREON *from the side, escorted by attendants carrying* HAEMON*'s body on a bier.*]

LEADER.
The king himself! Coming toward us,
look, holding the boy's head in his hands.
Clear, damning proof, if it's right to say so— 1390
proof of his own madness, no one else's,
no, his own blind wrongs.

CREON.
Ohhh,
so senseless, so insane . . . my crimes,
my stubborn, deadly—
Look at us, the killer, the killed,
father and son, the same blood—the misery!
My plans, my mad fanatic heart,
my son, cut off so young!
Ai, dead, lost to the world,
not through your stupidity, no, my own.

LEADER.
Too late, 1400
too late, you see what justice means.

CREON.
Oh I've learned

through blood and tears! Then, it was then,
when the god came down and struck me—a great weight
shattering, driving me down that wild savage path,
ruining, trampling down my joy. Oh the agony,
the heartbreaking agonies of our lives.

[*Enter the* MESSENGER *from the palace.*]

MESSENGER.

Master,
what a hoard of grief you have, and you'll have more.
The grief that lies to hand you've brought yourself—

[*Pointing to* HAEMON*'s body.*]

the rest, in the house, you'll see it all too soon.

CREON.

What now? What's worse than this?

MESSENGER.

The queen is dead. 1410
The mother of this dead boy . . . mother to the end—
poor thing, her wounds are fresh.

CREON.

No, no,
harbor of Death, so choked, so hard to cleanse!—
why me? why are you killing me?
Herald of pain, more words, more grief?
I died once, you kill me again and again!
What's the report, boy . . . some news for me?
My wife dead? O dear god!
Slaughter heaped on slaughter?

[*The doors open; the body of* EURYDICE *is brought out on her bier.*]

MESSENGER.

See for yourself:
now they bring her body from the palace.

CREON.

Oh no, 1420
another, a second loss to break the heart.
What next, what fate still waits for me?
I just held my son in my arms and now,
look, a new corpse rising before my eyes—
wretched, helpless mother—O my son!

MESSENGER.

She stabbed herself at the altar,
then her eyes went dark, after she'd raised

a cry for the noble fate of Megareus,[43] the hero
killed in the first assault, then for Haemon,
then with her dying breath she called down 1430
torments on your head—you killed her sons.

CREON.

Oh the dread,
I shudder with dread! Why not kill me too?—
run me through with a good sharp sword?
Oh god, the misery, anguish—
I, I'm churning with it, going under.

MESSENGER.
Yes, and the dead, the woman lying there,
piles the guilt of all their deaths on you.

CREON.
How did she end her life, what bloody stroke?

MESSENGER.
She drove home to the heart with her own hand,
once she learned her son was dead . . . that agony. 1440

CREON.
And the guilt is all mine—
can never be fixed on another man,
no escape for me. I killed you,
I, god help me, I admit it all!
[*To his attendants.*]
Take me away, quickly, out of sight.
I don't even exist—I'm no one. Nothing.

LEADER.
Good advice, if there's any good in suffering.
Quickest is best when troubles block the way.

CREON.
[*Kneeling in prayer.*]
Come, let it come!—that best of fates for me
that brings the final day, best fate of all. 1450
Oh quickly, now—
so I never have to see another sunrise.

LEADER.
That will come when it comes;
we must deal with all that lies before us.
The future rests with the ones who tend the future.

[43] The other son of Creon and Eurydice; he had bravely committed suicide to save Thebes.

CREON.
That prayer—I poured my heart into that prayer!

LEADER.
No more prayers now. For mortal men
there is no escape from the doom we must endure.

CREON.
Take me away, I beg you, out of sight.
A rash, indiscriminate fool! 1460
I murdered you, my son, against my will—
you too, my wife . . .
Wailing wreck of a man,
whom to look to? where to lean for support?
[*Desperately turning from* HAEMON *to* EURYDICE *on their biers.*]
Whatever I touch goes wrong—once more
a crushing fate's come down upon my head!
[*The* MESSENGER *and attendants lead* CREON *into the palace.*]

CHORUS.
Wisdom is by far the greatest part of joy,
and reverence toward the gods must be safeguarded.
The mighty words of the proud are paid in full
with mighty blows of fate, and at long last
those blows will teach us wisdom. 1470
[*The old citizens exit to the side.*]

Euripides
(c. 480–406 B.C.)

Aeschylus fought in the momentous Greek naval victory at Salamis in 480 B.C. The adolescent Sophocles helped to celebrate it publicly. Tradition has it that Euripides was born in Salamis on the very day of the battle. Even if, or especially if, the tradition is historically inaccurate (he may have been born a few years earlier), it symbolizes a desire by the ancients to link Euripides with his two mighty predecessors as the third definitive playwright of the greatest age of Greece.

Unlike Aeschylus and Sophocles, Euripides seems to have taken little active part in the official public life of Athens; he was not a social man by temperament. The size of his library indicates that he was extensively learned. From the year 455 on, he participated regularly in the dramatic contests held annually in Athens, but he won first prize less often than did Aeschylus or Sophocles, possibly because of the "irregularities" later alleged, by Aristotle and other critics, to exist in his work, or possibly because of his nonconformist attitude toward Greek religion and Athenian politics. His political dissidence intensified during the last two decades of his life as the tragic and misguided Peloponnesian War against Sparta and its allies moved inexorably toward a dismal conclusion. His play *The Trojan Women,* for example (produced in 415), exposes the brutality of "heroic" conquerors and, indirectly, shows Euripides' distaste for Athenian imperialism. He spent the last two years of his life in Macedonia where he died in 406, slightly earlier than Sophocles, who conducted a scene of public mourning for him in the theater. After his death, Euripides' plays were immensely popular; of the ninety he wrote, eighteen have survived, as compared with seven apiece by Aeschylus and Sophocles. Among these is *The Cyclops,* the only extant specimen of the grotesque "satyr play" that in Athenian dramatic practice regularly followed the set of three tragedies performed earlier in the same day.

Euripides' work as a whole illustrates several new departures. The formal structure is looser than in Aeschylus or Sophocles, though perhaps we ought, rather, to call it freer. He made extensive use of the Prologue and, at the end of his plays, was partial to the *deus ex machina* device, whereby a deity intervenes to impose an arbitrary resolution. The endings of his plays are frequently ambiguous or disturbing, as in Medea's escape to Athens. In Euripides, the chorus often sings magnificent lyrics, but they tend to be less integral to the dramatic action than in the plays of Aeschylus or Sophocles. Another recurrent device is the *agon,* a direct and usually hostile confrontation between two characters in which arguments or accusations are exchanged in rapid-fire fashion. Euripides also helped popularize the mode of drama we now call tragicomedy; his *Alcestis,* in which the dead heroine is reclaimed from the grave, is an example. To regard his innovations as regrettable departures from the kind of coherent unity Aristotle called for is unjust to Euripides, who created several powerful forms of drama that are best allowed to operate by their own organically functional rules, without being measured against arbitrary norms of what ancient drama, or tragedy, is supposed to be.

Some of these formal, or antiformal, elements, but more especially the ideas conveyed or implied in his plays, have earned Euripides a reputation as the most "romantic" of the three great tragedians. The alleged untidiness of his dramatic construction often parallels and indeed emphasizes the central Euripidean theme of irrationality, in people and in the cosmos. Throughout *Medea,* the heroine, like many other characters in Euripides, is overcome by passion (sometimes tender, more often violent in the extreme). As an exploration of human values, the play seems to many readers to present an almost maddening stalemate; it is equally impossible either to dismiss Medea's motives or to endorse them, not to mention her hair-raising acts. The same ambivalence informs his last play, *The Bacchae,* which addresses, not incidentally but head-on, the value of the irrational Dionysian drives. This tragedy has been interpreted both as a return by Euripides to religious piety and as profound skepticism; both as an indictment of rationality and as an indictment of irrational fanaticism.

According to the chorus in Aeschylus' *Oresteia*, humanity suffers into truth. In Sophocles much the same thing is true, though the theology is less explicit; for example, in *Oedipus at Colonus*, the unspeakable suffering endured by the blinded and exiled king is redeemed at his death, when he is mysteriously transfigured. In the last analysis, both these dramatists are optimists—though by no means facile ones. Euripides is more pessimistic. For him, an intellectual and a skeptic, whatever force governs the world—whether we call that force Fate, the divine will, Necessity, or by any other name—is amoral and entirely indifferent to humanity. As *Medea* shows, human acts of good and evil are thrown into a moral void. Certainly suffering is something humanity has to undergo alone, without much theological comfort. The world, for him, is both utterly unpredictable and also utterly predictable, in the sense that its operation is affected by neither piety nor virtue. Granted that it is dangerous to translate the values of an ancient Athenian into modern terms, it still seems tempting, if not inevitable, to read Euripides, as a quintessentially modern man, for better or worse. His view of the world, as in modern scientific determinism, posits a universe (in which laws cannot be changed by human moral acts) almost indistinguishable—from the human point of view—from one that is not governed at all. The universe most metaphysically determined is morally the most chaotic.

Euripides' attitude toward the sexes is another crucial topic. Legend surrounds his birth; at the other end, legend has it that at his death he was torn apart, by dogs or women. Again, the legend may be quaint but the fact remains that, beginning in his own time, Euripides has been charged with misogyny. Aristophanes, for one, gave weight to the charge in *Lysistrata* and in other comedies. It is easy to see how, superficially, the creator of a violent and male-threatening witch such as Medea could be regarded as defaming women. It is just as easy, however, and especially from the viewpoint of modern feminism, to see Euripides as a master psychologist and critic of the masculine and feminine mystiques that operate on a powerful thematic and symbolic level in Greek tragedy from Aeschylus' *Oresteia* on. At much the same time that Aristophanes was exploring these mystiques in a comic vein, Euripides was exploring them in a tragic vein, and as more intractable than in Aeschylus.

Euripides' free and often iconoclastic use of the Greek stage, his central concern with both the power and the limitations of reason, his philosophical skepticism, and his explorations of both the literal and symbolic meanings of gender are all well illustrated by *Medea* (which came in last in the tragic competition of 431 B.C.) and *Helen* (which was staged in 412 and mercilessly parodied by Aristophanes in his *Thesmophoriazusae* or *Women at a Religious Festival* the following year).

There is no way of knowing why *Medea* was ranked so low by the judges at its first production. It may have struck them as old-fashioned. It has almost no plot, just a series of confrontations leading up to the climactic action. Also, it makes no use of the variety of scenes made possible by Sophocles' introduction of a third speaking actor; it can be performed with only two actors, with its series of duologues (although Medea's confrontations with various individual men are thematically significant). The judges may have found the play morally repugnant, too. Medea is practically alone among tragedy's great felon-heroes to escape scot-free; at the end, she merely flies off to Athens behind her dragons, blithely thwarting any justice, poetic or otherwise. It is likely, though, that the original Athenian spectators may have found the play morally troubling in a quite different way. Its production in 431 coincided with the outbreak of the Peloponnesian War, the war between Athens and Sparta that was to drag on for twenty-seven years and end in Spartan victory. Corinth was on the Spartan side—the war began as a conflict between Athens and Corinth over their colonies—and anti-Corinthian feeling ran high in the Athens of 431. Aegeus's offer of safe haven to a Corinthian must have struck the original audience as deliberately provocative. It comes, moreover, as the culmination of the play's exploration of society's reaction to Otherness. When *Medea* was written, Athens was an exclusionary society; twenty years before, the great Athenian statesman Pericles had instituted a law denying citizen privileges to those who could not prove their descent from Athenian citizen-families. Suspicion of the "barbarian" ran high and was only heightened by war fever. A play that presented Jason and Medea and so sharply asked the question "Who is the barbarian?" could not have received an unmixed response.

Helen, written almost twenty years after *Medea*, is as shot through with Euripidean ironies as the earlier play but carries them much further, calling into question not only our readings of history and myth but even our ability to trust the evidence of our senses in a world riddled with incompatible opposites. Readers and especially spectators of the play must identify sympathetically with Menelaus in the second episode of the play when he exclaims:

> What does it mean? What can I think? This story of hers seems to alter the whole situation. Is it possible that I should capture my wife in Troy, bring her here and put her in a cave for safety, and now find another woman, with the same name as my wife, living in this palace? But she called this woman the daughter of Zeus! Can there be a man by the name of Zeus living on the banks of the Nile? There's only one Zeus, the one in heaven. And where in the world is there a Sparta, except on the reedy banks of the lovely Eurotas? Are there two men called Tyndareus? Is there another Lacedaemon, another Troy? I don't know what to say.

Euripides did not invent the conceit that the true Helen was spirited away to Egypt and that a false Helen was taken to Troy by Paris. The lyric poet Stesichorus had done that a century before, and his account had been elaborated by the historian Herodotus in his *History of the Persian Wars.*

But only Euripides saw the possibility of using the story of the two Helens as the basis of a philosophical comedy that uses the nature of theatrical illusion as a metaphor for our quest for metaphysical certitude. In this play, presided over by Helen's twin brothers Castor and Pollux, everything is twinned, not only the characters but history itself. Was the Trojan War a heroic engagement or a meaningless exercise driven by illusion? No wonder that modern critics have been tempted to call the play not a tragedy, a comedy, or even a tragicomedy but, anachronistically, a postmodern play or, as the critic Colin Leach calls it, "a remote prototype of Beckett's *Waiting for Godot* or Tom Stoppard's *Jumpers*."

But despite *Helen*'s high-spirited, light-hearted playing with self-referential themes of illusion and reality, the play does not represent a withdrawal from reality into metaphysics. As *Medea* was written as Greece was splintering into the Peloponnesian War, so *Helen* was written a year after the greatest Athenian disaster of that war, the Sicilian expedition, in which the entire Greek fleet and many thousands of lives were lost. In this context, Euripides' scathing debunking of the Trojan War, Greece's foundational myth of militarism; his ridicule of male *machismo* in the person of Theoclymenus; and his rehabilitation of the despised Helen as the embodiment of the "feminine" virtues of patience, loyalty, and resistance to tyranny link the fairy-tale world of *Helen* to the very real world of Athens in crisis.

FURTHER READING: Good general overviews of Euripidean drama, all with sections on *Medea* and *Helen*, include *Directions in Euripidean Criticism*, ed. Peter Burian, 1985; Christopher Collard, *Euripides*, 1981; D. J. Conacher, *Euripidean Drama: Myth, Theme, and Structure*, 1967; Helene Foley, *Ritual Irony: Poetry and Sacrifice in Euripides*, 1985; Michael Halleran, *Stagecraft in Euripides*, 1985; Philip Vellacott, *Ironic Drama: A Study of Euripides' Method and Meaning*, 1975; and Justina Gregory, *Euripides and the Instruction of the Athenians*, 1991. On the important topic of Euripides and women, see Nicole Loraux, *Tragic Ways of Killing a Woman*, 1987; *Euripides, Women, and Sexuality*, ed. Anton Powell, 1990; and Nancy Sorkin Rabinowitz, *Anxiety Veiled: Euripides and the Traffic in Women*, 1993. On Euripides and religion, see Harvey Yunis, *A New Creed: Fundamental Religious Beliefs in the Athenian Polis and Euripidean Drama*, 1988. Emily McDermott, *Euripides' "Medea": The Incarnation of Disorder*, 1989, is a detailed study of the play. Charles Segal's essay "The Two Worlds of Euripides' *Helen*," 1971, has become a classic; it is reprinted in his *Interpreting Greek Tragedy: Myth, Poetry, Text*, 1986. Erich Segal and Harold Bloom have edited collections of critical essays in the Twentieth Century Views and Modern Critical Views series, respectively.

MEDEA

Translated by Philip Vellacott

The kingship of the city of Iolcus (in Thessaly, the northeastern region of Greece) had been usurped by Pelias. Jason's father, Aeson, was half brother of Pelias and rightful ruler of Iolcus. After a period of protective exile under the tutelage of Chiron the Centaur, Jason returned to Iolcus. His usurper-uncle Pelias then sent Jason off to Colchis (on the Black Sea) to capture the magically potent Golden Fleece of a ram. Jason made the adventurous voyage, in company with some of the most famous and fabled Greek heroes, called the Argonauts after the name of their ship the *Argo*. When Jason reached Colchis, its king Aeetes (Medea's father) agreed to give up the Golden Fleece if Jason performed certain superhumanly difficult tasks. He was able to perform them with the help of Medea, who had fallen in love with him and who possessed magical arts. The heroes then returned with the Golden Fleece to Iolcus, along with Medea, who assisted their return by killing her brother so that her father Aeetes would be delayed in his pursuit. In Iolcus, Medea continued to aid Jason by using her witchcraft to cause the death of Pelias at the hands of his daughters. But Jason was unable to claim his throne, and he and Medea were banished from Iolcus. They settled in Corinth, the setting of the play *Medea*. After some time there, Jason has decided to cast off Medea and to marry Glauce, daughter of Creon, the king of Corinth. This Creon should not be confused with the Creon who, in Sophocles' Oedipus plays, rules Thebes. [*Editors' headnote.*]

CHARACTERS

NURSE
TUTOR *to Medea's sons*
MEDEA
CHORUS *of Corinthian women*
CREON, *king of Corinth*
JASON
AEGEUS, *king of Athens*
MESSENGER
MEDEA'S TWO CHILDREN

SCENE

Before JASON*'s house in Corinth*

NURSE. If only they had never gone! If the Argo's hull
Never had winged out through the grey-blue jaws of rock[1]
And on towards Colchis! If that pine on Pelion's[2] slopes
Had never felt the axe, and fallen, to put oars
Into those heroes' hands, who went at Pelias' bidding
To fetch the golden fleece! Then neither would Medea,

[1] The Symplegades, two mythical rocks at the north end of the strait of Bosporus, the entrance to the Black Sea. The rocks were supposed to crush ships that sailed between them.
[2] A mountain in Thessaly.

My mistress, ever have set sail for the walled town
Of Iolcus, mad with love for Jason; nor would she,
When Pelias' daughters, at her instance, killed their father,
Have come with Jason and her children to live here 10
In Corinth; where, coming as an exile, she has earned
The citizens' welcome; while to Jason she is all
Obedience—and in marriage that's the saving thing,
When a wife obediently accepts her husband's will.

But now her world has turned to enmity, and wounds her
Where her affection's deepest. Jason has betrayed
His own sons, and my mistress, for a royal bed,
For alliance with the king of Corinth. He has married
Glauce, Creon's daughter. Poor Medea! Scorned and shamed,
She raves, invoking every vow and solemn pledge 20
That Jason made her, and calls the gods as witnesses
What thanks she has received for her fidelity.
She will not eat; she lies collapsed in agony,
Dissolving the long hours in tears. Since first she heard
Of Jason's wickedness, she has not raised her eyes,
Or moved her cheek from the hard ground; and when her friends
Reason with her, she might be a rock or wave of the sea,
For all she hears—unless, maybe, she turns away
Her lovely head, speaks to herself alone, and wails
Aloud for her dear father, her own land and home, 30
Which she betrayed and left, to come here with this man
Who now spurns and insults her. Poor Medea! Now
She learns through pain what blessings they enjoy who are not
Uprooted from their native land. She hates her sons:
To see them is no pleasure to her. I am afraid
Some dreadful purpose is forming in her mind. She is
A frightening woman; no one who makes an enemy
Of her will carry off an easy victory.

Here come the boys, back from their running. They've no thought
Of this cruel blow that's fallen on their mother. Well, 40
They're young; young heads and painful thoughts don't go together.

[*Enter the* TUTOR *with* MEDEA'*s* TWO SONS.]

TUTOR. Old nurse and servant of my mistress's house, tell me,
What are you doing, standing out here by the door,
All alone, talking to yourself, harping on trouble?
Eh? What does Medea say to being left alone?

NURSE. Old friend, tutor of Jason's sons, an honest slave
Suffers in her own heart the blow that strikes her mistress.
It was too much, I couldn't bear it; I had to come
Out here and tell my mistress's wrongs to earth and heaven.

TUTOR. Poor woman! Has she not stopped crying yet? 50

NURSE. Stopped crying?
I envy you. Her grief's just born—not yet half-grown.
TUTOR. Poor fool—though she's my mistress and I shouldn't say it—
She had better save her tears. She has not heard the worst.
NURSE. The worst? What now? Don't keep it from me. What has happened?
TUTOR. Why, nothing's happened. I'm sorry I said anything.
NURSE. Look—we're both slaves together: don't keep me in the dark.
Is it so great a secret? I can hold my tongue.
TUTOR. I'd gone along to the benches where the old men play
At dice, next to the holy fountain of Peirene; 60
They thought I was not listening; and I heard one say
That Creon king of Corinth means to send these boys
Away from here—to banish them, and their mother too.
Whether the story's true I don't know. I hope not.
NURSE. But surely Jason won't stand by and see his sons
Banished, even if he has a quarrel with their mother?
TUTOR. Old love is ousted by new love. Jason's no friend
To this house.
NURSE. Then we're lost, if we must add new trouble
To old, before we're rid of what we had already.
TUTOR. But listen: it's no time to tell Medea this. 70
Keep quiet, say nothing about it.
NURSE. Children, do you hear
What sort of father Jason is to you? My curse
On—No! No curse; he is my master. All the same,
He is guilty: he has betrayed those near and dear to him.
TUTOR. What man's not guilty? It's taken you a long time to learn
That everybody loves himself more than his neighbour.
These boys are nothing to their father: he's in love.
NURSE. Run into the house, boys. Everything will be all right.

[*The children move away a little.*]

You do your best to keep them by themselves, as long
As she's in this dark mood; don't let them go to her. 80
I've watched her watching them, her eye like a wild bull's.
There's something that she means to do; and I know this:
She'll not relax her rage till it has found its victim.
God grant she strike her enemies and not her friends!

[MEDEA*'s voice is heard from inside the house.*]

MEDEA. Oh, oh! What misery, what wretchedness!
What shall I do? If only I were dead!
NURSE. There! You can hear; it is your mother
Racking her heart, racking her anger.
Quick, now, children, hurry indoors;
And don't go within sight of her, 90
Or anywhere near her; keep a safe distance.

Her mood is cruel, her nature dangerous,
Her will fierce and intractable.
Come on, now, in with you both at once.

[*The* CHILDREN *go in, and the* TUTOR *follows.*]

The dark cloud of her lamentations
Is just beginning. Soon, I know,
It will burst aflame as her anger rises.
Deep in passion and unrelenting,
What will she do now, stung with insult?

MEDEA [*indoors*]. Do I not suffer? Am I not wronged? Should I not weep? 100
Children, your mother is hated, and you are cursed:
Death take you, with your father, and perish his whole house!

NURSE. Oh, the pity of it! Poor Medea!
Your children—why, what have *they* to do
With their father's wickedness? Why hate *them?*
I am sick with fear for you, children, terror
Of what may happen. The mind of a queen
Is a thing to fear. A queen is used
To giving commands, not obeying them;
And her rage once roused is hard to appease. 110

To have learnt to live on the common level
Is better. No grand life for me,
Just peace and quiet as I grow old.
The middle way, neither great nor mean,
Is best by far, in name and practice.
To be rich and powerful brings no blessing;
Only more utterly
Is the prosperous house destroyed, when the gods are angry.

[*Enter the* CHORUS *of Corinthian women.*]

CHORUS.
I heard her voice, I heard
That unhappy woman from Colchis 120
Still crying, not calm yet.
Old Nurse, tell us about her.
As I stood by the door I heard her
Crying inside the palace.
And my own heart suffers too
When Jason's house is suffering;
For that is where my loyalty lies.

NURSE. Jason's house? It no longer exists; all that is finished.
Jason is a prisoner in a princess's bed;
And Medea is in her room 130
Melting her life away in tears;
No word from any friend can give her comfort.

MEDEA [*still from indoors*].

Come, flame of the sky,
Pierce through my head!
What do I gain from living any longer?
Oh, how I hate living! I want
To end my life, leave it behind, and die.

CHORUS.

O Zeus, and Earth, and Light,
Do you hear the chanted prayer
Of a wife in her anguish? 140

[*turning to the door and addressing* MEDEA]

What madness is this? The bed you long for—
Is it what others shrink from?
Is it death you demand?
Do not pray that prayer, Medea!
If your husband is won to a new love—
The thing is common; why let it anger you?
Zeus will plead your cause.
Check this passionate grief over your husband
Which wastes you away.

MEDEA. Mighty Themis! Dread Artemis![3] 150
Do you see how I am used—
In spite of those great oaths I bound him with—
By my accursed husband?
Oh, may I see Jason and his bride
Ground to pieces in their shattered palace
For the wrong they have dared to do to me, unprovoked!
O my father, my city, you I deserted;
My brother I shamefully murdered!

NURSE. Do you hear what my mistress is saying,
Clamouring to Themis, hearer of prayer, 160
And to Zeus, who is named guardian of men's oaths?
It is no trifling matter
That can end a rage like hers.

CHORUS. I wish she would come out here and let us see her
And talk to her; if she would listen
Perhaps she would drop this fierce resentful spirit,
This passionate indignation.
As a friend I am anxious to do whatever I can.
Go, nurse, persuade her to come out to us.
Tell her we are all on her side. 170
Hurry, before she does harm—to those in there;
This passion of hers is an irresistible flood.

[3] Themis is the personification of justice; Artemis is the virgin goddess of the hunt who protects young creatures and women in childbirth.

NURSE. I will. I fear I shall not persuade her;
Still, I am glad to do my best.
Yet as soon as any of us servants
Goes near to her, or tries to speak,
She glares at us like a mad bull
Or a lioness guarding her cubs.

[*The* NURSE *goes to the door, where she turns.*]

The men of old times had little sense;
If you called them fools you wouldn't be far wrong. 180
They invented songs, and all the sweetness of music,
To perform at feasts, banquets, and celebrations;
But no one thought of using
Songs and stringed instruments
To banish the bitterness and pain of life.
Sorrow is the real cause
Of deaths and disasters and families destroyed.
If music could cure sorrow it would be precious;
But after a good dinner why sing songs?
When people have fed full they're happy already. 190

[*The* NURSE *goes in.*]

CHORUS.
I heard her sobbing and wailing,
Shouting shrill, pitiful accusations
Against her husband who has betrayed her.
She invokes Themis, daughter of Zeus,
Who witnessed those promises which drew her
Across from Asia to Hellas, setting sail at night,
Threading the salt strait,
Key and barrier to the Pontic Sea.[4]

[MEDEA *comes out. She is not shaken with weeping, but cool and self-possessed.*]

MEDEA. Women of Corinth, I would not have you censure me,
So I have come. Many, I know, are proud at heart, 200
Indoors or out; but others are ill spoken of
As supercilious, just because their ways are quiet.
There is no justice in the world's censorious eyes.
They will not wait to learn a man's true character;
Though no wrong has been done them, one look—and they hate.
Of course a stranger must conform; even a Greek

[4] The Black Sea.

Should not annoy his fellows by crass stubbornness.
I accept my place; but this blow that has fallen on me
Was not to be expected. It has crushed my heart.
Life has no pleasure left, dear friends. I want to die. 210
Jason was my whole life; he knows that well. Now he
Has proved himself the most contemptible of men.

Surely, of all creatures that have life and will, we women
Are the most wretched. When, for an extravagant sum,
We have bought a husband,[5] we must then accept him as
Possessor of our body. This is to aggravate
Wrong with worse wrong. Then the great question: will the man
We get be bad or good? For women, divorce is not
Respectable; to repel the man, not possible.

Still more, a foreign woman, coming among new laws, 220
New customs, needs the skill of magic, to find out
What her home could not teach her, how to treat the man
Whose bed she shares. And if in this exacting toil
We are successful, and our husband does not struggle
Under the marriage yoke, our life is enviable.
Otherwise, death is better. If a man grows tired
Of the company at home, he can go out, and find
A cure for tediousness. We wives are forced to look
To one man only. And, they tell us, we at home
Live free from danger, they go out to battle: fools! 230
I'd rather stand three times in the front line than bear
One child.

But the same arguments do not apply
To you and me. You have this city, your father's home,
The enjoyment of your life, and your friends' company.
I am alone; I have no city; now my husband
Insults me. I was taken as plunder from a land
At the earth's edge. I have no mother, brother, nor any
Of my own blood to turn to in this extremity.
So, I make one request. If I can find a way
To work revenge on Jason for his wrongs to me, 240
Say nothing. A woman's weak and timid in most matters;
The noise of war, the look of steel, makes her a coward.
But touch her right in marriage, and there's no bloodier spirit.

CHORUS. I'll do as you ask. To punish Jason will be just.
I do not wonder that you take such wrongs to heart.

[CREON *approaches.*]

But look, Medea; I see Creon, King of Corinth;
He must have come to tell you of some new decision.

[5] The reference is to the dowry given with the bride in marriage.

CREON. You there, Medea, scowling rage against your husband!
I order you out of Corinth; take your sons and go
Into exile. Waste no time; I'm here to see this order 250
Enforced. And I'm not going back into my palace
Until I've put you safe outside my boundaries.

MEDEA. Oh! this is the cruel end of my accursed life!
My enemies have spread full sail; no welcoming shore
Waits to receive and save me. Ill-treated as I am,
Creon, I ask: for what offence do you banish me?

CREON. I fear you. Why wrap up the truth? I fear that you
May do my daughter some irreparable harm.
A number of things contribute to my anxiety.
You're a clever woman, skilled in many evil arts; 260
You're barred from Jason's bed, and that enrages you.
I learn too from reports, that you have uttered threats
Of revenge on Jason and his bride and his bride's father.
I'll act first, then, in self-defence. I'd rather make you
My enemy now, than weaken, and later pay with tears.

MEDEA. My reputation, yet again! Many times, Creon,
It has been my curse and ruin. A man of any shrewdness
Should never have his children taught to use their brains
More than their fellows. What do you gain by being clever?
You neglect your own affairs; and all your fellow citizens 270
Hate you. Those who are fools will call you ignorant
And useless, when you offer them unfamiliar knowledge.
As for those thought intelligent, if people rank
You above *them,* that is a thing they will not stand.
I know this from experience: because I am clever,
They are jealous; while the rest dislike me. After all,
I am not so clever as all that.

So you, Creon,
Are afraid—of what? Some harm that I might do to you?
Don't let *me* alarm you, Creon. I'm in no position—
A woman—to wrong a king. You have done me no wrong. 280
You've given your daughter to the man you chose. I hate
My husband—true; but you had every right to do
As you have done. So now I bear no grudge against
Your happiness: marry your daughter to him, and good luck
To you both. But let me live in Corinth. I will bear
My wrongs in silence, yielding to superior strength.

CREON. Your words are gentle: but my blood runs cold to think
What plots you may be nursing deep within your heart.
In fact, I trust you so much less now than before.
A woman of hot temper—and a man the same— 290
Is a less dangerous enemy than one quiet and clever.
So out you go, and quickly; no more arguing.
I've made my mind up; you're my enemy. No craft
Of yours will find a way of staying in my city.

MEDEA. I kneel to you, I beseech you by the young bride, your child.

CREON. You're wasting words; you'll never make me change my mind.

MEDEA. I beg you! Will you cast off pity, and banish me?
CREON. I will: I have more love for my family than for you.
MEDEA. My home, my country! How my thoughts turn to you now!
CREON. I love my country too—next only to my daughter. 300
MEDEA. Oh, what an evil power love has in people's lives!
CREON. That would depend on circumstances, I imagine.
MEDEA. Great Zeus, remember who caused all this suffering!
CREON. Go, you poor wretch, take all my troubles with you! Go!
MEDEA. I know what trouble is; I have no need of more.
CREON. In a moment you'll be thrown out neck and crop. Here, men!
MEDEA. No, no, not that! But, Creon, I have one thing to ask.
CREON. You seem inclined, Medea, to give me trouble still.
MEDEA. I'll go. [*She still clings to him.*] It was not *that* I begged.
CREON. Then why resist?
Why will you not get out?
MEDEA. This one day let me stay, 310
To settle some plan for my exile, make provision
For my two sons, since their own father is not concerned
To help them. Show some pity: you are a father too,
You should feel kindly towards them. For myself, exile
Is nothing. I weep for them; their fate is very hard.
CREON. I'm no tyrant by nature. My soft heart has often
Betrayed me; and I know it's foolish of me now;
Yet none the less, Medea, you shall have what you ask.
But take this warning: if tomorrow's holy sun
Finds you or them inside my boundaries, you die. 320
That is my solemn word. Now stay here, if you must,
This one day. You can hardly in one day accomplish
What I am afraid of.

[*Exit* CREON.]

CHORUS.
Medea, poor Medea!
Your grief touches our hearts.
A wanderer, where can you turn?
To what welcoming house?
To what protecting land?
How wild with dread and danger
Is the sea where the gods have set your course! 330
MEDEA. A bad predicament all round—yes, true enough;
But don't imagine things will end as they are now.
Trials are yet to come for this new-wedded pair;
Nor shall those nearest to them get off easily.

Do you think I would ever have fawned so on this man,
Except to gain my purpose, carry out my schemes?
Not one touch, not one word: yet he—oh, what a fool!

By banishing me at once he could have thwarted me
Utterly; instead, he allows me to remain one day.
Today three of my enemies I shall strike dead: 340
Father and daughter; and *my* husband.

I have in mind so many paths of death for them,
I don't know which to choose. Should I set fire to the house,
And burn the bridal chamber? Or creep up to their bed
And drive a sharp knife through their guts? There is one fear:
If I am caught entering the house, or in the act,
I die, and the last laugh goes to my enemies.
The best is the direct way, which most suits my bent:
To kill by poison.

So—say they are dead: what city will receive me then? 350
What friend will guarantee my safety, offer land
And home as sanctuary? None. I'll wait a little.
If some strong tower of help appears, I'll carry out
This murder cunningly and quietly. But if Fate
Banishes me without resource, I will myself
Take sword in hand, harden my heart to the uttermost,
And kill them both, even if I am to die for it.

For, by Queen Hecate,[6] whom above all divinities
I venerate, my chosen accomplice, to whose presence
My central hearth is dedicated, no one of them 360
Shall hurt me and not suffer for it! Let me work:
In bitterness and pain they shall repent this marriage,
Repent their houses joined, repent my banishment.

Come! Lay your plan, Medea; scheme with all your skill.
On to the deadly moment that shall test your nerve!
You see now where you stand. Your father was a king,
His father was the Sun-god:[7] you must not invite
Laughter from Jason and his new allies, the tribe
Of Sisyphus.[8] You know what you must do. Besides—

[*She turns to the* CHORUS.]

We were born women—useless for honest purposes, 370
But in all kinds of evil skilled practitioners.

CHORUS. Streams of the sacred rivers flow uphill;
Tradition, order, all things are reversed:
Deceit is *men's* device now,
Men's oaths are gods' dishonour.

[6]Goddess of witchcraft, though also in some contexts a protective deity.
[7]Helios, father of Aeetes.
[8]An earlier, legendary king of Corinth, noted for deceitfulness.

Legend will now reverse our reputation;
A time comes when the female sex is honoured;
That old discordant slander
Shall no more hold us subject.
Male poets of past ages, with their ballads 380
Of faithless women, shall go out of fashion;
For Phoebus,[9] Prince of Music,
Never bestowed the lyric inspiration
Through female understanding—
Or we'd find themes for poems,
We'd counter with our epics against man.
Oh, Time is old; and in his store of tales
Men figure no less famous
Or infamous than women.

So you, Medea, wild with love, 390
Set sail from your father's house,
Threading the Rocky Jaws of the eastern sea;
And here, living in a strange country,
Your marriage lost, your bed solitary,
You are driven beyond the borders,
An exile with no redress.
The grace of sworn oaths is gone;
Honour remains no more
In the wide Greek world, but is flown to the sky.
Where can you turn for shelter? 400
Your father's door is closed against you;
Another is now mistress of your husband's bed;
A new queen rules in your house.

[*Enter* JASON.]

JASON. I have noticed—this is not the first occasion—
What fatal results follow from ungoverned rage.
You could have stayed in Corinth, still lived in this house,
If you had quietly accepted the decisions
Of those in power. Instead, you talked like a fool; and now
You are banished. Well, your angry words don't upset *me;*
Go on as long as you like reciting Jason's crimes. 410
But after your abuse of the King and the princess
Think yourself lucky to be let off with banishment.
I have tried all the time to calm them down; but you
Would not give up your ridiculous tirades against
The royal family. So, you're banished. However, I
Will not desert a friend. I have carefully considered
Your problem, and come now, in spite of everything,
To see that you and the children are not sent away

[9] Apollo, god of music and poetry.

With an empty purse, or unprovided. Exile brings
With it a train of difficulties. You no doubt 420
Hate me: but I could never bear ill-will to you.

MEDEA. You filthy coward!—if I knew any worse name
For such unmanliness I'd use it—so, you've come!
You, my worst enemy, come to me! Oh, it's not courage,
This looking friends in the face after betraying them.
It is not even audacity; it's a disease,
The worst a man can have, pure shamelessness. However,
It is as well you came; to say what I have to say
Will ease my heart; to hear it said will make you wince.

I will begin at the beginning. When you were sent 430
To master the fire-breathing bulls, yoke them, and sow
The deadly furrow, then I saved your life; and that
Every Greek who sailed with you in the Argo knows.
The serpent that kept watch over the Golden Fleece,
Coiled round it fold on fold, unsleeping—it was I
Who killed it, and so lit the torch of your success.[10]
I willingly deceived my father; left my home;
With you I came to Iolcus by Mount Pelion,
Showing much love and little wisdom. There I put
King Pelias to the most horrible of deaths[11] 440
By his own daughters' hands, and ruined his whole house.
And in return for this you have the wickedness
To turn me out, to get yourself another wife,
Even after I had borne you sons! If you had still
Been childless I could have pardoned you for hankering
After this new marriage. But respect for oaths has gone
To the wind. Do you, I wonder, think that the old gods
No longer rule? Or that new laws are now in force?
You must know you are guilty of perjury to me.

My poor right hand, which you so often clasped! My knees 450
Which you then clung to! How we are besmirched and mocked
By this man's broken vows, and all our hopes deceived!

Come, I'll ask your advice as if you were a friend.
Not that I hope for any help from you; but still,
I'll ask you, and expose your infamy. Where now
Can I turn? Back to my country and my father's house,
Which I betrayed to come with you? Or to Iolcus,
To Pelias's wretched daughters? What a welcome they
Would offer me, who killed their father! Thus it stands:

[10] Medea refers in the preceding six lines to the difficult tasks Jason had to accomplish in Colchis to win the Golden Fleece.

[11] Medea had deceitfully persuaded Pelias' daughters that they could magically restore their father's youth by boiling him in a cauldron.

My friends at home now hate me; and in helping you 460
I have earned the enmity of those I had no right
To hurt. For my reward, you have made me the envy
Of Hellene women everywhere! A marvellous
Husband I have, and faithful too, in the name of pity;
When I'm banished, thrown out of the country without a friend,
Alone with my forlorn waifs. Yes, a shining shame
It will be to you, the new-made bridegroom, that your own sons,
And I who saved your life, are begging beside the road!

O Zeus! Why have you given us clear signs to tell
True gold from counterfeit; but when we need to know 470
Bad *men* from good, the flesh bears no revealing mark?

CHORUS. The fiercest anger of all, the most incurable,
Is that which rages in the place of dearest love.

JASON. I have to show myself a clever speaker, it seems.
This hurricane of recrimination and abuse
Calls for good seamanship: I'll furl all but an inch
Of sail, and ride it out. To begin with, since you build
To such a height your services to me, I hold
That credit for my successful voyage was solely due
To Aphrodite,[12] no one else divine or human. 480
I admit, you have intelligence; but, to recount
How helpless passion drove you then to save my life
Would be invidious; and I will not stress the point.
Your services, so far as they went, were well enough;
But in return for saving me you got far more
Than you gave. Allow me, in the first place, to point out
That you left a barbarous land to become a resident
Of Hellas;[13] here you have known justice; you have lived
In a society where force yields place to law.
Moreover, here your gifts are widely recognized, 490
You are famous; if you still lived at the ends of the earth
Your name would never be spoken. Personally, unless
Life brings me fame, I long neither for hoards of gold,
Nor for a voice sweeter than Orpheus![14]—Well, *you* began
The argument about my voyage; and that's my answer.

As for your scurrilous taunts against my marriage with
The royal family, I shall show you that my action
Was wise, not swayed by passion, and directed towards
Your interests and my children's.—No, keep quiet! When I
Came here from Iolcus as a stateless exile, dogged 500
And thwarted by misfortunes—why, what luckier chance
Could I have met, than marriage with the King's daughter?

[12]Goddess of love.

[13]Greece.

[14]A legendary poet and one of the Argonauts; his music was so wonderful that he could enchant nature itself. See the account in Ovid's *Metamorphoses,* Book X.

It was not, as you resentfully assume, that I
Found your attractions wearisome, and was smitten with
Desire for a new wife; nor did I specially want
To raise a numerous family—the sons we have
Are enough, I'm satisfied; but I wanted to ensure
First—and the most important—that we should live well
And not be poor; I know how a poor man is shunned
By all his friends. Next, that I could bring up my sons 510
In a manner worthy of my descent; have other sons,
Perhaps, as brothers to your children; give them all
An equal place, and so build up a closely-knit
And prosperous family. *You* need no more children, do you?
While *I* thought it worth while to ensure advantages
For those I have, by means of those I hope to have.

Was such a plan, then, wicked? Even you would approve
If you could govern your sex-jealousy. But you women
Have reached a state where, if all's well with your sex-life,
You've everything you wish for; but when *that* goes wrong, 520
At once all that is best and noblest turns to gall.
If only children could be got some other way,
Without the female sex! If women didn't exist,
Human life would be rid of all its miseries.

CHORUS. Jason, you have set your case forth very plausibly.
But to my mind—though you may be surprised at this—
You are acting wrongly in thus abandoning your wife.

MEDEA. No doubt I differ from many people in many ways.
To me, a wicked man who is also eloquent
Seems the most guilty of them all. He'll cut your throat 530
As bold as brass, because he knows he can dress up murder
In handsome words. He's not so clever after all.
You dare outface me now with glib high-mindedness!
One word will throw you: if you were honest, you ought first
To have won me over, not got married behind my back.

JASON. No doubt, if I had mentioned it, you would have proved
Most helpful. Why, even now you will not bring yourself
To calm this raging temper.

MEDEA. That was not the point;
But you're an ageing man, and an Asiatic wife
Was no longer respectable.

JASON. Understand this: 540
It's not for the sake of any woman that I have made
This royal marriage, but, as I've already said,
To ensure your future, and to give my children brothers
Of royal blood, and build security for us all.

MEDEA. I loathe your prosperous future; I'll have none of it,
Nor none of your security—it galls my heart.

JASON. You know—you'll change your mind and be more sensible.
You'll soon stop thinking good is bad, and striking these
Pathetic poses when in fact you're fortunate.

MEDEA. Go on, insult me: you have a roof over your head. 550
I am alone, an exile.
JASON. It was your own choice.
Blame no one but yourself.
MEDEA. *My* choice? What did I do?
Did I make you my wife and then abandon you?
JASON. You called wicked curses on the King and his house.
MEDEA. I did. On your house too Fate sends me as a curse.
JASON. I'll not pursue this further. If there's anything else
I can provide to meet the children's needs or yours,
Tell me: I'll gladly give whatever you want, or send
Letters of introduction, if you like, to friends
Who will help you.—Listen: to refuse such help is mad. 560
You've everything to gain if you give up this rage.
MEDEA. Nothing would induce me to have dealings with your friends,
Nor to take any gift of yours; so offer none.
A lying traitor's gifts carry no luck.
JASON. Very well.
I call the gods to witness that I have done my best
To help you and the children. You make no response
To kindness; friendly overtures you obstinately
Reject. So much the worse for you.
MEDEA. Go! You have spent
Too long out here. You are consumed with craving for
Your newly-won bride. Go, enjoy her.

[*Exit* JASON.]

It may be— 570
And God uphold my words—that this your marriage-day
Will end with marriage lost, loathing and horror left.
CHORUS.
Visitations of love that come
Raging and violent on a man
Bring him neither good repute nor goodness.
But if Aphrodite descends in gentleness
No other goddess brings such delight.
Never, Queen Aphrodite,
Loose against me from your golden bow,
Dipped in sweetness of desire, 580
Your inescapable arrow!

Let Innocence, the gods' loveliest gift,
Choose me for her own;
Never may the dread Cyprian[15]
Craze my heart to leave old love for new,
Sending to assault me

[15]Aphrodite, goddess of love. Born of the foam of the sea, she made her first appearance in Cyprus.

Angry disputes and feuds unending;
But let her judge shrewdly the loves of women
And respect the bed where no war rages.

O my country, my home! 590
May the gods save me from becoming
A stateless refugee
Dragging out an intolerable life
In desperate helplessness!
That is the most pitiful of all griefs;
Death is better. Should such a day come to me
I pray for death first.
Of all pains and hardships none is worse
Than to be deprived of your native land.

This is no mere reflection derived from hearsay; 600
It is something we have seen.
You, Medea, have suffered the most shattering of blows;
Yet neither the city of Corinth
Nor any friend has taken pity on you.
May dishonour and ruin fall on the man
Who, having unlocked the secrets
Of a friend's frank heart, can then disown him!
He shall be no friend of mine.

[*Enter* AEGEUS.[16]]

AEGEUS. All happiness to you, Medea! Between old friends
There is no better greeting.
MEDEA. All happiness to you, 610
Aegeus, son of Pandion the wise! Where have you come from?
AEGEUS. From Delphi, from the ancient oracle of Apollo.
MEDEA. The centre of the earth,[17] the home of prophecy:
Why did you go?
AEGEUS. To ask for children; that my seed
May become fertile.
MEDEA. Why, have you lived so many years
Childless?
AEGEUS. Childless I am; so some fate has ordained.
MEDEA. You have a wife, or not?
AEGEUS. I am married.
MEDEA. And what answer
Did Phoebus give you about children?
AEGEUS. His answer was
Too subtle for me or any human interpreter.
MEDEA. Is it lawful for me to hear it?

[16]In myth, the father of Theseus, the great Athenian ruler.
[17]The "Navelstone," believed to be the center of the earth, was located at Delphi. Compare the opening of Aeschylus' *The Eumenides*.

AEGEUS. Certainly; a brain 620
Like yours is what is needed.
MEDEA. Tell me, since you may.
AEGEUS. He commanded me 'not to unstop the wineskin's neck'—
MEDEA. Yes—until when?
AEGEUS. Until I came safe home again.
MEDEA. I see. And for what purpose have you sailed to Corinth?
AEGEUS. You know the King of Troezen, Pittheus, son of Pelops?
MEDEA. Yes, a most pious man.
AEGEUS. I want to ask his advice
About this oracle.
MEDEA. He is an expert in such matters.
AEGEUS. Yes, and my closest friend. We went to the wars together.
MEDEA. I hope you will get all you long for, and be happy.
AEGEUS. But you are looking pale and wasted: what is the matter? 630
MEDEA. Aegeus, my husband's the most evil man alive.
AEGEUS. Why, what's this? Tell me all about your unhappiness.
MEDEA. Jason has betrayed me, though I never did him wrong.
AEGEUS. What has he done? Explain exactly.
MEDEA. He has taken
Another wife, and made her mistress of *my* house.
AEGEUS. But such a thing is shameful! He has never dared—
MEDEA. It is so. Once he loved me; now I am disowned.
AEGEUS. Was he tired of you? Or did he fall in love elsewhere?
MEDEA. Oh, passionately. He's not a man his friends can trust.
AEGEUS. Well, if—as you say—he's a bad lot, let him go. 640
MEDEA. It's royalty and power he's fallen in love with.
AEGEUS. What?
Go on. Who's the girl's father?
MEDEA. Creon, King of Corinth.
AEGEUS. I see. Then you have every reason to be upset.
MEDEA. It is the end of everything! What's more, I'm banished.
AEGEUS. Worse still—extraordinary! Why, who has banished you?
MEDEA. Creon has banished me from Corinth.
AEGEUS. And does Jason
Accept this? How disgraceful!
MEDEA. Oh, no! He protests.
But he's resolved to bear it bravely.—Aegeus, see,
I touch your beard as a suppliant, embrace your knees,
Imploring you to have pity on my wretchedness. 650
Have pity! I am an exile; let me not be friendless.
Receive me in Athens;[18] give me a welcome in your house.
So may the gods grant you fertility, and bring
Your life to a happy close. You have not realized
What good luck chance has brought you. I know certain drugs
Whose power will put an end to your sterility.
I promise you shall beget children.

[18]Athens often boasted of its hospitality to aliens.

AEGEUS. I am anxious,
For many reasons, to help you in this way, Medea;
First, for the gods' sake, then this hope you've given me
Of children—for I've quite despaired of my own powers. 660
This then is what I'll do: once you can get to Athens
I'll keep my promise and protect you all I can.
But I must make this clear first: I do not intend
To take you with me away from Corinth. If you come
Yourself to Athens, you shall have sanctuary there;
I will not give you up to anyone. But first
Get clear of Corinth without help; the Corinthians too
Are friends of mine, and I don't wish to give offence.

MEDEA. So be it. Now confirm your promise with an oath,
And all is well between us.

AEGEUS. Why? Do you not trust me? 670
What troubles you?

MEDEA. I trust you; but I have enemies—
Not only Creon, but the house of Pelias.
Once you are bound by oaths you will not give me up
If they should try to take me out of your territory.
But if your promise is verbal, and not sworn to the gods,
Perhaps you will make friends with them, and agree to do
What they demand. I've no power on my side, while they
Have wealth and all the resources of a royal house.

AEGEUS. Your forethought is remarkable; but since you wish it
I've no objection. In fact, the taking of an oath 680
Safeguards me; since I can confront your enemies
With a clear excuse; while *you* have full security.
So name your gods.

MEDEA. Swear by the Earth under your feet,
By the Sun, my father's father, and the whole race of gods.

AEGEUS. Tell me what I shall swear to do or not to do.

MEDEA. Never yourself to expel me from your territory;
And, if my enemies want to take me away, never
Willingly, while you live, to give me up to them.

AEGEUS. I swear by Earth, and by the burning light of the Sun,
And all the gods, to keep the words you have just spoken. 690

MEDEA. I am satisfied. And if you break your oath, what then?

AEGEUS. Then may the gods do to me as to all guilty men.

MEDEA. Go now, and joy be with you. Everything is well.
I'll reach your city as quickly as I can, when I
Have carried out my purpose and achieved my wish.

[AEGEUS *clasps her hand and hurries off.*]

CHORUS. May Hermes, protector of travellers, bring you
Safe to your home, Aegeus; may you accomplish
All that you so earnestly desire;
For your noble heart wins our goodwill.

MEDEA. O Zeus! O Justice, daughter of Zeus! O glorious Sun! 700
Now I am on the road to victory; now there's hope!
I shall see my enemies punished as they deserve.
Just where my plot was weakest, at that very point
Help has appeared in this man Aegeus; he is a haven
Where I shall find safe mooring, once I reach the walls
Of the city of Athens. Now I'll tell you all my plans:
They'll not make pleasant hearing.

[*Medea's* NURSE *has entered; she listens in silence.*]

First I'll send a slave
To Jason, asking him to come to me; and then
I'll give him soft talk; tell him he has acted well,
Tell him I think this royal marriage which he has bought 710
With my betrayal is for the best and wisely planned.
But I shall beg that my children be allowed to stay.
Not that I would think of leaving sons of mine behind
On enemy soil for those who hate me to insult;
But in my plot to kill the princess they must help.
I'll send them to the palace bearing gifts, a dress
Of soft weave and a coronet of beaten gold.
If she takes and puts on this finery, both she
And all who touch her will expire in agony;
With such a deadly poison I'll anoint my gifts. 720

However, enough of that. What makes me cry with pain
Is the next thing I have to do. I will kill my sons.
No one shall take my children from me. When I have made
Jason's whole house a shambles,[19] I will leave Corinth
A murderess, flying from my darling children's blood.
Yes, I can endure guilt, however horrible;
The laughter of my enemies I will not endure.

Now let things take their course. What use is life to me?
I have no land, no home, no refuge from despair.
My folly was committed long ago, when I 730
Was ready to desert my father's house, won over
By eloquence from a Greek, whom with God's help I now
Will punish. He shall never see alive again
The sons he had from me. From his new bride he never
Shall breed a son; she by my poison, wretched girl,
Must die a hideous death. Let no one think of me
As humble or weak or passive; let them understand
I am of a different kind: dangerous to my enemies,
Loyal to my friends. To such a life glory belongs.

[19]A slaughterhouse.

CHORUS. Since you have told us everything, and since I want 740
To be your friend, and also to uphold the laws
Of human life—I tell you, you must not do this!
MEDEA. No other thing is possible. You have excuse
For speaking so: you have not been treated as I have.
CHORUS. But—to kill your own children! Can you steel your heart?
MEDEA. This is the way to deal Jason the deepest wound.
CHORUS. This way will bring you too the deepest misery.
MEDEA. Let be. Until it is done words are unnecessary.
Nurse! You are the one I use for messages of trust.
Go and bring Jason here. As you're a loyal servant, 750
And a woman, breathe no word about my purposes.

[*Exit* NURSE.]

CHORUS. The people of Athens, sons of Erechtheus, have enjoyed their prosperity
Since ancient times. Children of blessed gods,
They grew from holy soil unscorched by invasion.[20]
Among the glories of knowledge their souls are pastured;
They walk always with grace under the sparkling sky.
There long ago, they say, was born golden-haired Harmony,
Created by the nine virgin Muses[21] of Pieria.

They say that Aphrodite dips her cup
In the clear stream of the lovely Cephisus;[22] 760
It is she who breathes over the land the breath
Of gentle honey-laden winds; her flowing locks
She crowns with a diadem of sweet-scented roses,
And sends the Loves to be enthroned beside Knowledge,
And with her to create excellence in every art.

Then how will such a city,
Watered by sacred rivers,
A country giving protection to its friends—
How will Athens welcome
You, the child-killer 770
Whose presence is pollution?
Contemplate the blow struck at a child,
Weigh the blood you take upon you.
Medea, by your knees,
By every pledge or appeal we beseech you,
Do not slaughter your children!

[20]An irony and a significant phrase, for *Medea* was produced in 431, on the eve of the long Peloponnesian War between Athens and the confederacy headed by Sparta. The Athenians ultimately were conquered.
[21]The nine goddesses of the arts, worshiped at Pieria, on the slopes of Mount Olympus.
[22]The main river near Athens.

Where will you find hardness of purpose?
How will you build resolution in hand or heart
To face horror without flinching?
When the moment comes, and you look at them— 780
The moment for you to assume the role of murderess—
How will you do it?
When your sons kneel to you for pity,
Will you stain your fingers with their blood?
Your heart will melt; you will know you cannot.

[*Enter* JASON *from the palace. Two maids come from the house to attend* MEDEA.]

JASON. You sent for me: I have come. Although you hate me, I
Am ready to listen. You have some new request; what is it?

MEDEA. Jason, I ask you to forgive the things I said.
You must bear with my violent temper; you and I
Share many memories of love. I have been taking 790
Myself to task. 'You are a fool,' I've told myself,
'You're mad, when people try to plan things for the best,
To be resentful, and pick quarrels with the King
And with your husband; what he's doing will help us all.
His wife is royal; her sons will be my sons' brothers.
Why not throw off your anger? What is the matter, since
The gods are making kind provision? After all
I have two children still to care for; and I know
We came as exiles, and our friends are few enough.'
When I considered this, I saw my foolishness; 800
I saw how useless anger was. So now I welcome
What you have done; I think you are wise to gain for us
This new alliance, and the folly was all mine.
I should have helped you in your plans, made it my pleasure
To get ready your marriage-bed, attend your bride.
But we women—I won't say we are bad by nature,
But we are what we are. You, Jason, should not copy
Our bad example, or match yourself with us, showing
Folly for folly. I give in; I was wrong just now,
I admit. But I have thought more wisely of it since. 810
Children, children! Are you indoors? Come out here.

[*The* CHILDREN *come out. Their* TUTOR *follows.*]

Children,
Greet your father, as I do, and put your arms round him.
Forget our quarrel, and love him as your mother does.
We have made friends; we are not angry any more.
There, children; take his hand.

[*She turns away in a sudden flood of weeping.*]

Forgive me; I recalled
What pain the future hides from us.

[*After embracing* JASON, *the* CHILDREN *go back to* MEDEA.]

Oh children! Will you
All your lives long, stretch out your hands to me like this?
Oh, my tormented heart is full of tears and terrors.
After so long, I have ended my quarrel with your father;
And now, see! I have drenched this young face with my tears. 820

CHORUS. I too feel fresh tears fill my eyes. May the course of evil
Be checked now, go no further!

JASON. I am pleased, Medea,
That you have changed your mind; though indeed I do not blame
Your first resentment. Only naturally a woman
Is angry when her husband marries a second wife.
You have had wiser thoughts; and though it has taken time,
You have recognized the right decision. This is the act
Of a sensible woman. As for you, my boys, your father
Has taken careful thought, and, with the help of the gods,
Ensured a good life for you. Why, in time, I'm sure, 830
You with your brothers will be leading men in Corinth.
Only grow big and strong. Your father, and those gods
Who are his friends, have all the rest under control.
I want to see you, when you're strong, full-grown young men,
Tread down my enemies.

[*Again* MEDEA *breaks down and weeps.*]

What's this? Why these floods of tears?
Why are you pale? Did you not like what I was saying?
Why do you turn away?

MEDEA. It is nothing. I was thinking
About these children.

JASON. I'll provide for them. Cheer up.

MEDEA. I will. It is not that I mean to doubt your word.
But women—are women; tears come naturally to us. 840

JASON. Why do you grieve so over the children?

MEDEA. I'm their mother.
When you just now prayed for them to live long, I wondered
Whether it would be so; and grief came over me.
But I've said only part of what I had to say;
Here is the other thing. Since Creon has resolved
To send me out of Corinth, I fully recognize

That for me too this course is best. If I lived here
I should become a trouble both to you and him.
People believe I bear a grudge against you all.
So I must go. But the boys—I would like *them* to be 850
Brought up in your care. Beg Creon to let them stay.

JASON. I don't know if I can persuade him; but I'll try.

MEDEA. Then—get your wife to ask her father to let them stay.

JASON. Why, certainly; I'm pretty sure she'll win him over.

MEDEA. She will, if she's like other women. But I too
Can help in this. I'll send a present to your wife—
The loveliest things to be found anywhere on earth.
The boys shall take them.—One of you maids, go quickly, bring
The dress and golden coronet.—They will multiply
Her happiness many times, when she can call her own 860
A royal, noble husband, and these treasures, which
My father's father the Sun bequeathed to his descendants.

[*A slave has brought a casket, which* MEDEA *now hands to her sons.*]

Boys, hold these gifts. Now carry them to the happy bride,
The princess royal; give them into her own hands.
Go! She will find them all that such a gift should be.

JASON. But why deprive yourself of such things, foolish woman?
Do you think a royal palace is in want of dresses?
Or gold, do you suppose? Keep them, don't give them away.
If my wife values me at all she will yield to *me*
More than to costly presents, I am sure of that. 870

MEDEA. Don't stop me. Gifts, they say, persuade even the gods;
With mortals, gold outweighs a thousand arguments.
The day is hers; from now on *her* prosperity
Will rise to new heights. She is royal and young. To buy
My sons from exile I would give life, not just gold.
Come, children, go both of you into this rich palace;
Kneel down and beg your father's new wife, and my mistress,
That you may not be banished. And above all, see
That she receives my present into her own hands.
Go quickly; be successful, and bring good news back, 880
That what your mother longs for has been granted you.

[*Exit* JASON *followed by the* CHILDREN *and the* TUTOR.]

CHORUS.

Now I have no more hope,
No more hope that the children can live;
They are walking to murder at this moment.
The bride will receive the golden coronet,
Receive her merciless destroyer;

With her own hands she will carefully fit
The adornment of death round her golden hair.

She cannot resist such loveliness, such heavenly gleaming;
She will enfold herself 890
In the dress and the wreath of wrought gold,
Preparing her bridal beauty
To enter a new home—among the dead.
So fatal is the snare she will fall into,
So inevitable the death that awaits her;
From its cruelty there is no escape.

And you, unhappy Jason, ill-starred in marriage,
You, son-in-law of kings:
Little you know that the favour you ask
Will seal your sons' destruction 900
And fasten on your wife a hideous fate.
O wretched Jason!
So sure of destiny, and so ignorant!

Your sorrow next I weep for, pitiable mother;
You, for jealousy of your marriage-bed,
Will slaughter your children;
Since, disregarding right and loyalty,
Your husband has abandoned you
And lives with another wife.

[*The* TUTOR *returns from the palace with the two* CHILDREN.]

TUTOR. Mistress! These two boys are reprieved from banishment. 910
The princess took your gifts from them with her own hand,
And was delighted. They have no enemies in the palace.

[MEDEA *is silent.*]

Well, bless my soul!
Isn't that good news? Why do you stand there thunderstruck?
MEDEA [*to herself*]. How cruel, how cruel!
TUTOR. That's out of tune with the news I brought.
MEDEA. How cruel life is!
TUTOR. Have I, without knowing it,
Told something dreadful, then? I thought my news was good.
MEDEA. Your news is what it is. I am not blaming you.
TUTOR. Then why stand staring at the ground, with streaming eyes? 920
MEDEA. Strong reason forces me to weep, old friend. The gods,
And my own evil-hearted plots, have led to this.
TUTOR. Take heart, mistress; in time your sons will bring you home.
MEDEA. Before then, I have others to send home.—Oh, gods!

[*She weeps.*]

TUTOR. You're not the only mother parted from her sons.
We are all mortal; you must not bear grief so hard.
MEDEA. Yes, friend. I'll follow your advice. Now go indoors
And get things ready for them, as on other days.

[*Exit* TUTOR. *The* CHILDREN *come to* MEDEA.]

O children, children! You have a city, and a home;
And when we have parted, there you both will stay for ever, 930
You motherless, I miserable. And I must go
To exile in another land, before I have had
My joy of you, before I have seen you growing up,
Becoming prosperous. I shall never see your brides,
Adorn your bridal beds, and hold the torches high.
My misery is my own heart, which will not relent.
All was for nothing, then—these years of rearing you,
My care, my aching weariness, and the wild pains
When you were born. Oh, yes, I once built many hopes
On you; imagined, pitifully, that you would care 940
For my old age, and would yourselves wrap my dead body
For burial. How people would envy me my sons!
That sweet, sad thought has faded now. Parted from you,
My life will be all pain and anguish. You will not
Look at your mother any more with these dear eyes.
You will have moved into a different sphere of life.

Dear sons, why are you staring at me so? You smile
At me—your last smile: why?

[*She weeps. The* CHILDREN *go from her a little, and she turns to the* CHORUS.]

Oh, what am I to do?
Women, my courage is all gone. Their young, bright faces—
I can't do it. I'll think no more of it. I'll take them 950
Away from Corinth. Why should I hurt *them,* to make
Their father suffer, when I shall suffer twice as much
Myself? I won't do it. I won't think of it again.

What is the matter with me? Are my enemies
To laugh at me? Am I to let them off scot free?
I must steel myself to it. What a coward I am,
Even tempting my own resolution with soft talk.
Boys, go indoors.

[*The* CHILDREN *go to the door, but stay there watching her.*]

If there is any here who finds it
Not lawful to be present at my sacrifice,
Let him see to it. My hand shall not weaken. 960

Oh, my heart, don't, don't do it! Oh, miserable heart,
Let them be! Spare your children! We'll all live together
Safely in Athens; and they will make you happy. . . . No!
No! No! By all the fiends of hate in hell's depths, no!
I'll not leave sons of mine to be the victims of
My enemies' rage. In any case there is no escape,
The thing's done now. Yes, now—the golden coronet
Is on her head, the royal bride is in her dress,
Dying, I know it. So, since I have a sad road
To travel, and send these boys on a still sadder road, 970
I'll speak to them. Come, children; give me your hand, dear son;
Yours too. Now we must say goodbye. Oh, darling hand,
And darling mouth; your noble, childlike face and body!
Dear sons, my blessing on you both—but there, not here!
All blessing here your father has destroyed. How sweet
To hold you! And children's skin is soft, and their breath pure.
Go! Go away! I can't look at you any longer;
My pain is more than I can bear.

[*The* CHILDREN *go indoors.*]

I understand
The horror of what I am going to do; but anger,
The spring of all life's horror, masters my resolve. 980

[MEDEA *goes to stand looking towards the palace.*]

CHORUS.
I have often engaged in arguments,
And become more subtle, and perhaps more heated,
Than is suitable for women;
Though in fact women too have intelligence,
Which forms part of our nature and instructs us—
Not all of us, I admit; but a certain few
You might perhaps find, in a large number of women—
A few not incapable of reflection;

And this is my opinion: those men or women
Who never had children of their own at all 990
Enjoy the advantage in good fortune
Over those who are parents. Childless people

Have no means of knowing whether children are
A blessing or a burden; but being without them
They live exempt from many troubles.

While those who have growing up in their homes
The sweet gift of children I see always
Burdened and worn with incessant worry,
First, how to rear them in health and safety,
And bequeath them, in time, enough to live on; 1000
And then this further anxiety:
They can never know whether all their toil
Is spent for worthy or worthless children.

And beyond the common ills that attend
All human life there is one still worse:
Suppose at last they are pretty well off,
Their children have grown up, and, what's more,
Are kind and honest: then what happens?
A throw of chance—and there goes Death
Bearing off your child into the unknown. 1010

Then why should mortals thank the gods,
Who add to their load, already grievous,
This one more grief, for their children's sake,
Most grievous of all?

MEDEA. Friends, I have long been waiting for a message from the palace.
What is to happen next? I see a slave of Jason's
Coming, gasping for breath. He must bring fearful news.

[*Enter a* MESSENGER.]

MESSENGER. Medea! Get away, escape! Oh, what a thing to do!
What an unholy, horrible thing! Take ship, or chariot,
Any means you can, but escape!

MEDEA. Why should I escape? 1020

MESSENGER. She's dead—the princess, and her father Creon too,
They're both dead, by your poisons.

MEDEA. Your news is excellent.
I count you from today my friend and benefactor.

MESSENGER. What? Are you sane, or raving mad? When you've committed
This hideous crime against the royal house, you're glad
At hearing of it? Do you not tremble at such things?

MEDEA. I could make suitable reply to that, my friend.
But take your time now; tell me, how did they die? You'll give
Me double pleasure if their death was horrible.

MESSENGER. When your two little boys came hand in hand, and
entered 1030
The palace with their father, where the wedding was,
We servants were delighted. We had all felt sorry
To hear how you'd been treated; and now the word went round

From one to another, that you and Jason had made it up.
So we were glad to see the boys; one kissed their hand,
Another their fair hair. Myself, I was so pleased,
I followed with them to the princess's room. Our mistress—
The one we now call mistress in your place—before
She saw your pair of boys coming, had eyes only
For Jason; but seeing them she dropped her eyes, and turned 1040
Her lovely cheek away, upset that they should come
Into her room. Your husband then began to soothe
Her sulkiness, her girlish temper. 'You must not,'
He said, 'be unfriendly to our friends. Turn your head round,
And give up feeling angry. Those your husband loves
You must love too. Now take these gifts,' he said, 'and ask
Your father to revoke their exile for my sake.'
So, when she saw those lovely things, she was won over,
And agreed to all that Jason asked. At once, before
He and your sons were well out of the house, she took 1050
The embroidered gown and put it round her. Then she placed
Over her curls the golden coronet, and began
To arrange her hair in a bright mirror, smiling at
Her lifeless form reflected there. Then she stood up,
And to and fro stepped daintily about the room
On white bare feet, and many times she would twist back
To see how the dress fell in clear folds to the heel.

Then suddenly we saw a frightening thing. She changed
Colour; she staggered sideways, shook in every limb.
She was just able to collapse on to a chair, 1060
Or she would have fallen flat. Then one of her attendants,
An old woman, thinking that perhaps the anger of Pan[23]
Or some other god had struck her, chanted the cry of worship.
But then she saw, oozing from the girl's lips, white froth;
The pupils of her eyes were twisted out of sight;
The blood was drained from all her skin. The old woman knew
Her mistake, and changed her chant to a despairing howl.
One maid ran off quickly to fetch the King, another
To look for Jason and tell him what was happening
To his young bride; the whole palace was filled with a clatter 1070
Of people running here and there.
All this took place
In a few moments, perhaps while a fast runner might run
A hundred yards; and she lay speechless, with eyes closed.
Then she came to, poor girl, and gave a frightful scream,
As two torments made war on her together: first
The golden coronet round her head discharged a stream
Of unnatural devouring fire: while the fine dress

[23]The old woman at first suspects some attack of unreasonable terror such as was associated with the nature god Pan (from whose name the word "panic" derives).

Your children gave her—poor miserable girl!—the stuff
Was eating her clear flesh. She leapt up from her chair,
On fire, and ran, shaking her head and her long hair 1080
This way and that, trying to shake off the coronet.
The ring of gold was fitted close and would not move;
The more she shook her head the fiercer the flame burned.
At last, exhausted by agony, she fell to the ground;
Save to her father, she was unrecognizable.
Her eyes, her face, were one grotesque disfigurement;
Down from her head dripped blood mingled with flame; her flesh,
Attacked by the invisible fangs of poison, melted
From the bare bone, like gum-drops from a pine-tree's bark—
A ghastly sight. Not one among us dared to touch 1090
Her body. What we'd seen was lesson enough for us.

But suddenly her father came into the room.
He did not understand, poor man, what kind of death
Had struck his child. He threw himself down at her side,
And sobbed aloud, and kissed her, and took her in his arms,
And cried, 'Poor darling child, what god destroyed your life
So cruelly? Who robs me of my only child,
Old as I am, and near my grave? Oh, let me die
With you, my daughter!' Soon he ceased his tears and cries,
And tried to lift his aged body upright; and then, 1100
As ivy sticks to laurel-branches, so he stuck
Fast to the dress. A ghastly wrestling then began;
He struggled to raise up his knee, she tugged him down.
If he used force, he tore the old flesh off his bones.
At length the King gave up his pitiful attempts;
Weakened with pain, he yielded, and gasped out his life.
Now, joined in death, daughter and father—such a sight
As tears were made for—they lie there.
To you, Medea,
I have no more to say. You will yourself know best
How to evade reprisal. As for human life, 1110
It is a shadow, as I have long believed. And this
I say without hesitation: those whom most would call
Intelligent, the propounders of wise theories—
Their folly is of all men's the most culpable.
Happiness is a thing no man possesses. Fortune
May come now to one man, now to another, as
Prosperity increases; happiness never.

[*Exit* MESSENGER.]

CHORUS. Today we see the will of Heaven, blow after blow,
Bring down on Jason justice and calamity.
MEDEA. Friends, now my course is clear: as quickly as possible 1120
To kill the children and then fly from Corinth; not
Delay and so consign them to another hand

To murder with a better will. For they must die,
In any case; and since they must, then I who gave
Them birth will kill them. Arm yourself, my heart: the thing
That you must do is fearful, yet inevitable.
Why wait, then? My accursed hand, come, take the sword;
Take it, and forward to your frontier of despair.
No cowardice, no tender memories; forget
That you once loved them, that of your body they were born. 1130
For one short day forget your children; afterwards
Weep: though you kill them, they were your beloved sons.
Life has been cruel to me.

[MEDEA *goes into the house.*]

CHORUS. Earth, awake! Bright arrows of the Sun,
Look! Look down on the accursed woman
Before she lifts up a murderous hand
To pollute it with her children's blood!
For they are of your own golden race;
And for mortals to spill blood that grew
In the veins of gods is a fearful thing. 1140
Heaven-born brightness, hold her, stop her,
Purge the palace of her, this pitiable
Bloody-handed fiend of vengeance!

All your care for them lost! Your love
For the babes you bore, all wasted, wasted!
Why did you come from the blue Symplegades
That hold the gate of the barbarous sea?
Why must this rage devour your heart
To spend itself in slaughter of children?
Where kindred blood pollutes the ground 1150
A curse hangs over human lives;
And murder measures the doom that falls
By Heaven's law on the guilty house.

[*A child's scream is heard from inside the house.*]

CHORUS. Do you hear? The children are calling for help.
O cursed, miserable woman!
CHILDREN'S VOICES. Help, help! Mother, let me go!
Mother, don't kill us!
CHORUS. Shall we go in?
I am sure we ought to save the children's lives.
CHILDREN'S VOICES. Help, help, for the gods' sake! She is killing us! 1160
We can't escape from her sword!
CHORUS. O miserable mother, to destroy your own increase,
Murder the babes of your body!
Stone and iron you are, as you resolved to be.

There was but one in time past,
One woman that I have heard of,
Raised hand against her own children.
It was Ino,[24] sent out of her mind by a god,
When Hera, the wife of Zeus,
Drove her from her home to wander over the world. 1170
In her misery she plunged into the sea
Being defiled by the murder of her children;
From the steep cliff's edge she stretched out her foot,
And so ended,
Joined in death with her two sons.

What can be strange or terrible after this?
O bed of women, full of passion and pain,
What wickedness, what sorrow you have caused on the earth!

[*Enter* JASON, *running and breathless.*]

JASON. You women standing round the door there! Is Medea
Still in the house?—vile murderess!—or has she gone 1180
And escaped? I swear she must either hide in the deep earth
Or soar on wings into the sky's abyss, to escape
My vengeance for the royal house.—She has killed the King
And the princess! Does she expect to go unpunished?

Well, I am less concerned with her than with the children.
Those who have suffered at her hands will make her suffer;
I've come to save my sons, before Creon's family
Murder them in revenge for this unspeakable
Crime of their mother's.
CHORUS. Jason, you have yet to learn
How great your trouble is; or you would not have spoken so. 1190
JASON. What trouble? Is Medea trying to kill me too?
CHORUS. Your sons are dead. Their mother has killed both your sons.
JASON. What? Killed my sons? That word kills me.
CHORUS. They are both dead.
JASON. Where are they? Did she kill them out here, or indoors?
CHORUS. Open that door, and see them lying in their blood.
JASON. Slaves, there! Unbar the doors! Open, and let me see
Two horrors: my dead sons, and the woman I will kill.

[JASON *batters at the doors.* MEDEA *appears above the roof, sitting in a chariot drawn by dragons, with the bodies of the two children beside her.*]

[24]Ino had helped to bring up the god Dionysus, who was born of Zeus and Semele. Hera, Zeus' consort, drove Ino to madness in revenge for Zeus' begetting of Dionysus.

MEDEA. Jason! Why are you battering at these doors, seeking
The dead children and me who killed them? Stop! Be quiet.
If you have any business with me, say what you wish. 1200
Touch us you cannot, in this chariot which the Sun
Has sent to save us from the hands of enemies.

JASON. You abomination! Of all women most detested
By every god, by me, by the whole human race!
You could endure—a mother!—to lift sword against
Your own little ones; to leave me childless, my life wrecked.
After such murder do you outface both Sun and Earth—
Guilty of gross pollution? May the gods blast your life!
I am sane now; but I was mad before, when I
Brought you from your palace in a land of savages 1210
Into a Greek home—you, a living curse, already
A traitor both to your father and your native land.
The vengeance due for your sins the gods have cast on me.
You had already murdered your brother at his own hearth
When first you stepped on board my lovely Argo's hull.
That was your beginning. Then you became my wife, and bore
My children; now, out of mere sexual jealousy,
You murder them! In all Hellas there is not one woman
Who could have done it; yet in preference to them
I married you, chose hatred and murder for my wife— 1220
No woman, but a tiger; a Tuscan Scylla[25]—but more savage.
Ah, what's the use? If I cursed you all day, no remorse
Would touch you, for your heart's proof against feeling. Go!
Out of my sight, polluted fiend, child-murderer!
Leave me to mourn over my destiny: I have lost
My young bride; I have lost the two sons I begot
And brought up; I shall never see them alive again.

MEDEA. I would if necessary have answered at full length
Everything you have said; but Zeus the father of all
Knows well what service I once rendered you, and how 1230
You have repaid me. You were mistaken if you thought
You could dishonour my bed and live a pleasant life
And laugh at me. The princess was wrong too, and so
Was Creon, when he took you for his son-in-law
And thought he could exile me with impunity.
So now, am I a tiger, Scylla?—Hurl at me
What names you please! I've reached your heart; and that is right.

JASON. You suffer too; my loss is yours no less.

MEDEA. It is true;
But my pain's a fair price, to take away your smile.

JASON. O children, what a wicked mother Fate gave you! 1240

MEDEA. O sons, your father's treachery cost you your lives.

JASON. It was not my hand that killed my sons.

[25]A monster who attacked mariners sailing between Italy and Sicily through what is now called the strait of Messina.

MEDEA. No, not your hand;
But your insult to me, and your new-wedded wife.
JASON. You thought *that* reason enough to murder them, that I
No longer slept with you?
MEDEA. And is that injury
A slight one, do you imagine, to a woman?
JASON. Yes,
To a modest woman; but to you—the whole world lost.
MEDEA. I can stab too: your sons are dead!
JASON. Dead? No! They live
To haunt your life with vengeance.
MEDEA. Who began this feud?
The gods know.
JASON. Yes—they know the vileness of your heart. 1250
MEDEA. Loathe on! Your bitter voice—how I abhor the sound!
JASON. As I loathe yours. Let us make terms and part at once.
MEDEA. Most willingly. What terms? What do you bid me do?
JASON. Give me my sons for burial and mourning rites.
MEDEA. Oh, no! I will myself convey them to the temple
Of Hera[26] Acraea; there in the holy precinct I
Will bury them with my own hand, to ensure that none
Of my enemies shall violate or insult their graves.
And I will ordain an annual feast and sacrifice
To be solemnized for ever by the people of Corinth, 1260
To expiate this impious murder. I myself
Will go to Athens, city of Erechtheus,[27] to make my home
With Aegeus son of Pandion. You, as you deserve,
Shall die an unheroic death,[28] your head shattered
By a timber from the Argo's hull. Thus wretchedly
Your fate shall end the story of your love for me.
JASON. The curse of children's blood be on you!
Avenging Justice blast your being!
MEDEA. What god will hear your imprecation,
Oath-breaker, guest-deceiver, liar? 1270
JASON. Unclean, abhorrent child-destroyer!
MEDEA. Go home: your wife waits to be buried.
JASON. I go—a father once; now childless.
MEDEA. You grieve too soon. Old age is coming.
JASON. Children, how dear you were!
MEDEA. To their mother; not to you.
JASON. Dear—and you murdered them?
MEDEA. Yes, Jason, to break your heart.
JASON. I long to fold them in my arms;
To kiss their lips would comfort me. 1280

[26]The goddess was regarded as defender of wives and marriage.
[27]Legendary Athenian king.
[28]One version of Jason's death is that he died in this way, at Corinth, struck by a falling beam as he sat near his old ship, the *Argo*.

MEDEA. *Now* you have loving words, now kisses for them:
Then you disowned them, sent them into exile.
JASON. For God's sake, let me touch their gentle flesh.
MEDEA. You shall not. It is waste of breath to ask.
JASON.
Zeus, do you hear how I am mocked,
Rejected, by this savage beast
Polluted with her children's blood?

But now, as time and strength permit,
I will lament this grievous day,
And call the gods to witness, how 1290
You killed my sons, and now refuse
To let me touch or bury them.
Would God I had not bred them,
Or ever lived to see
Them dead, you their destroyer!

[*During this speech the chariot has moved out of sight.*]

CHORUS. Many are the Fates which Zeus in Olympus dispenses;
Many matters the gods bring to surprising ends.
The things we thought would happen do not happen;
The unexpected God makes possible;
And such is the conclusion of this story.[29] 1300

HELEN

Translated by Philip Vellacott

CHARACTERS

HELEN, *daughter of Zeus and Leda*
TEUCER, *a Greek*
CHORUS *of captive Spartan women*
MENELAUS, *husband of Helen and King of Sparta*
OLD WOMAN, *portress at the palace*
MESSENGER, *one of Menelaus' crew*
THEONOE, *sister of Theoclymenus*
THEOCLYMENUS, *King of Egypt*
MESSENGER, *servant of Theoclymenus*
THE DIOSCORI, *sons of Zeus and Leda, now deified*

SCENE

The scene is Egypt, before the royal palace, not far from the shore. On one side of the stage is a monument enshrining a stone sarcophagus, at which HELEN *has taken sanctuary.*

[29] The last five lines are a formulaic ending, used also at the conclusion of several other plays by Euripides, including *Alcestis, Andromache, Helen,* and *The Bacchae.*

HELEN. This is Egypt; here flows the virgin river, the lovely Nile, who brings down melted snow to slake the soil of the Egyptian plain with the moisture heaven denies. Proteus, while he lived, was King here, ruling the whole of Egypt from his palace on the island of Pharos. Now Proteus married Psamathe, one of the sea-nymphs, and formerly the wife of Aeacus. She bore Proteus two children: a son, Theoclymenus (a name contradicted by his impious life[1]) and a daughter, the apple of her mother's eye, called Eido when she was a child; when she grew up and was ripe for marriage they called her Theonoe, for she had divine knowledge of all things present and to come[2]—a gift inherited from her grandfather Nereus.

But I am not an Egyptian; my home country is a place of some note—Sparta; and my father was Tyndareus. There is—you know—a legend which says that Zeus took the feathered form of a swan, and that being pursued by an eagle, and flying for refuge to the bosom of my mother, Leda, he used this deceit to accomplish his desire upon her. That is the story of my origin—if it is true.[3] My name is Helen. Now let me tell you of my misfortunes.

The three goddesses, Hera, Aphrodite, and Athene, daughter of Zeus, came as rivals to the glen of Mount Ida, where Paris lived, each one eager to be judged the first in beauty. And *my* beauty—if so great a misfortune can be so named—was used by Aphrodite as the bribe by which she won the prize, promising Paris that he should marry me. So Paris left his dairy-farm on Mount Ida and came to Sparta to win me as his bride.

But Hera, balked of her victory over the other goddesses, in her resentment turned the substance of Aphrodite's promise into air. She gave the royal son of Priam for his bride—not me, but a living image compounded of the ether in my likeness. Paris believes that he possesses me: what he holds is nothing but an airy delusion.

And Zeus by his subsequent arrangements has added to my misfortune. He brought war upon Hellas and the unhappy Phrygians, to ease the swarming earth of her measureless burden of men and make Achilles famous among the fighters of Greece. The Helen who went to Phrygia as a prize for Troy to defend and the Greeks to fight for—that Helen was not I, only my name. Zeus did not forget me: I was taken by Hermes, wrapped in a cloud, borne through the secret places of the upper air, and set down here in the palace of Proteus, whom Zeus picked out as the most honorable of all men, so that I might preserve my chastity inviolate for Menelaus. So here I have lived, while my poor husband gathered an army and in pursuit of his stolen wife sailed to the fortress of Troy. Many souls of men perished for my sake by the river Scamander; and I, the center of these tragic events, am named with curses, as the betrayer of my husband, who brought upon Greece the pestilence of war.

Why do I still live? Because Hermes told me this: once my husband learns that I did not go to Troy to accept the embraces of a lover, I shall

[1]Theoclymenus means "famous because of a god."

[2]Theonoe means "she who knows about divine things." Nereus, Theonoe's grandfather, was an Old Man of the Sea with mystic powers.

[3]According to Helen, she has two fathers, the mortal Tyndareus and the divine Zeus, who, in the form of a swan, ravished her mother. Through the rest of the play, it is assumed that her father was Zeus.

once again live with him in the famous land of Sparta. As long as Proteus lived my marriage was not threatened; now he is in his dark grave, and his son Theoclymenus is pestering me to marry him. So in loyalty to my true husband I have come here as a suppliant to the tomb of Proteus, praying him to preserve me for Menelaus; so that even if my name is reviled in Hellas, here in Egypt I may keep my body free from reproach.

Enter TEUCER.[4]

TEUCER. Who is master of this imposing palace? These royal precincts, that magnificent pediment, suggest the very house of Plutus, the temple of Wealth. [*With a sudden cry he catches sight of* HELEN.] Ye gods! What do I see? It is the accursed woman—her very image! The murderess who blasted my life and ruined Greece! May the gods abhor you as the perfect copy of Helen! If I were not standing on foreign soil, with this good arrow I would take your life in payment for your likeness to the daughter of Zeus!

HELEN. What do you say? Poor soul, who are you? Why do you shrink from me? You say I am like Helen: why blame me for that? What hate me because of what happened to her?

TEUCER. I was wrong; I let anger get the better of me. The daughter of Zeus is hated all over Hellas. Forgive what I said.

HELEN. But who are you? Where have you come from?

TEUCER. I am one of those ruined Greeks.

HELEN. No wonder, then, that you hate Helen. But who are you? Of what country, what family?

TEUCER. My name is Teucer; my father is Telamon, and I was born and brought up in Salamis.

HELEN. Then what brings you here to the valley of the Nile?

TEUCER. I have been driven out of my father's land. I am an exile.

HELEN. That is hard. Who drove you out?

TEUCER. The man who should have loved me most: my own father, Telamon.

HELEN. Exiled you! There must have been some serious reason. What had happened?

TEUCER. I had a brother, Aias; his death at Troy was the cause of it.

HELEN. How? You did not kill him yourself?

TEUCER. No. He died by his own hand, his own sword.

HELEN. Was he mad? Surely no man in his right mind could do it?

TEUCER. I will tell you. You have heard of Achilles, son of Peleus?

HELEN. He was one of the suitors of Helen—so I have heard.

TEUCER. At his death he left his armor to be competed for by those who had fought with him.

HELEN. And how did that hurt Aias?

TEUCER. He ended his life because the armor was awarded to another man.

HELEN. And his troubles were the cause of your exile?

TEUCER. Yes, because I did not die at his side.

HELEN. So you too went to the famous city of Ilion?

TEUCER. I was in at the death—and lost my own life for my pains.

HELEN. Is the city now burned and destroyed?

TEUCER. Utterly. Not even the outline of the walls can be traced.

[4]Brother of the Greater Aias (Ajax) and the best archer among the Greeks at Troy. See *Iliad*, Book 8.

HELEN. Oh, Helen, Helen! It was for you Troy died!
TEUCER. Troy? Greece too! Untold harm has been done.
HELEN. How long is it since the city was sacked?
TEUCER. Seven harvests have been reaped since Troy lay barren.
HELEN. And before that, how long had you been there?
TEUCER. Months without number—ten interminable years.
HELEN. And did you capture the Spartan queen?
TEUCER. Menelaus took her—dragged her off by the hair.
HELEN. Poor woman! Did you see her? Or are you telling me what you heard?
TEUCER. I saw her as plainly as I see you now.
HELEN. Is it not possible that the gods made you all imagine this?
TEUCER. Talk about something else—that is enough of Helen.
HELEN. Then—you all really believed it was true?
TEUCER. Why, I saw her with my own eyes carried off by Menelaus.
HELEN. And is Menelaus now at home—with his wife?
TEUCER. Not in Argos, certainly; nor in Sparta.
HELEN. That is sad news—for those who hoped for better.
TEUCER. He is said to have vanished, and his wife with him.
HELEN. But surely all the Argives were sailing home together?
TEUCER. They were; but a storm scattered them in all directions.
HELEN. Where were they when the storm fell?
TEUCER. Cresting the rollers of the mid-Aegean.
HELEN. And since then—no one has news of his landing anywhere?
TEUCER. No one. He is generally reported as dead.
HELEN [*aside*]. Dead! What shall I do? [*To* TEUCER] And what of Leda? Is she alive?
TEUCER. No, Leda is dead and gone.
HELEN. Can it be that Helen's disgrace broke her heart?
TEUCER. So they say; she was of royal blood. She hanged herself.
HELEN. And her two sons by Tyndareus—are they alive or dead?
TEUCER. Dead and not dead; of them there are two different accounts.
HELEN. Tell me the truer. [*Aside*] My mother—how can I bear it?
TEUCER. It is said they were deified—in the form of stars.[5]
HELEN. That would be well. What was the other?
TEUCER. That shame for their sister drove them to end their lives with the sword. But enough of tales—I have wept for these things once already.

My reason for coming here to the king's palace was to see the prophetess Theonoe, and ask for divine help in getting a fair wind for Cyprus. Will you take me to her? An oracle of Apollo told me I was to settle in Cyprus, and give to my new home there the name of Salamis, in remembrance of that other island where I was born.

HELEN. From here to Cyprus is plain sailing; but you must get clear of land before Theoclymenus sees you. He is the king of this country, and at present he is away slaughtering wild beasts with the aid of hounds. Every Greek that he captures here he kills. Why? don't ask me—I won't tell you.[6] What good would it do you?

[5]The two sons of Tyndareus were the twins Castor and Pollux (Polydeuces). When they died, they were placed in heaven as the constellation Gemini (Twins) or the Dioscori.

[6]Theoclymenus is afraid that Menelaus will come to Egypt and find Helen.

TEUCER. Just as you say, my lady; and thank you for telling me. The gods reward you for your kindness! You are like Helen only in appearance; in heart you are utterly different. I pray she may never reach home, but come to a bad end. But you—good luck be with you always!

Exit TEUCER

HELEN:

Strong griefs ask strong lamenting. Who shall be
Pattern and partner to my crying soul?
What tearful song can match the toll
Of deep pain paid by silent misery?

Come, Seiren maidens[7], daughters of Earth, [*Strophe* I
Young and light of wing,
Come with Libyan flute, with pipe and string,
Bring music for my despair,
Share your tears to suit my sorrow,
Couple note with note, pain with my pain;
And when songs of death,
Solemn chants dear to departed souls,
Ring through the vaulted shades of death,
Hear and accept them, Queen Persephone,[8]
Echoes of my heart's agony,
Offerings to fill my tears' deficiency.

The CHORUS *begin to enter.*

CHORUS:

Where the spring grass grows rank beside blue water [*Antistrophe* I
I was at work, spreading
Purple clothes on the young reeds to dry
In golden heat of the sun;
When I heard my lady's voice, a pitiful cry,
A joyless clamor of pain,
An anguished wail of loss—
What could it be?—
Like the haunted scream of a woodland nymph
At bay in the echoing depths of a rocky cave,
Caught and spoiled by the lust of Pan.[9]

HELEN:

Women of Greece, victims of piracy! [*Strophe* 2
Listen: a Grecian sailor has been here
Bringing new tears to flow with those I had.
Great Troy lies dead: fire is her monument.
And I—my hated name—must bear the guilt
Of countless agonies and countless dead.
Leda is dead; for her, my name's disgrace
Fastened the noose. My husband's lost from sight,

[7]Sirens. The chorus is made up of Spartan slave women, but Helen here presents them as earth goddesses who watch over the grave of Proteus.

[8]Goddess of the underworld, married to Hades.

[9]God of shepherds and flocks. He was represented as a man above his waist and a goat below, usually in lascivious pursuit of a nymph.

His endless voyage ended in death. My brothers,
Their country's glory and pride, are seen no more
Riding like thunder through the reedy marsh,
Or wrestling with their fellows by the stream.

CHORUS:

Weep for Helen, victim of Destiny! [*Antistrophe* 2
Mocked cruelly with the gift of life, when Zeus
Swan-winged like snow swooping thro' dazzled air
Touched Leda's womb! Your single life has known
All sorrow, knows it still. Leda is dead;
Twin sons of Zeus, your brothers are no more;
Your eyes can never see your native land;
Rumor through every state and street in Greece
Gives you as paramour to a foreign prince;
Your husband's life is lost in the salt sea;
And you will no more gladden your dear home
Or thank Athene in her brazen temple.

HELEN:

Whose was the Trojan hand that felled [*Strophe* 3
The fateful pine whose timbers held
Tears for the Trojans, tears for Greece?
Thence the accursed ship was built
That brought to Sparta Priam's son
(A dark-skinned slave at each oar-hilt)
To seek my beauty, break my peace,
And tempt my heart with love and guilt.
With Paris, till his prize was won,
Came murderous Aphrodite, mistress of deceit—
  Goddess, what have you done?—
To prostrate Greece and Troy in slaughter at her feet.

Then Hera, loved of Zeus, who shares [*Antistrophe* 3
His golden throne and soothes his cares,
Sent the swift-footed Hermes[10] down.
He found me gathering in a glade
Fresh roses folded in my gown,
An offering for the Holy Maid;[11]
Carried me swiftly through the sky
Into this land of little joy,
To live accursed and know that I
Sent my own race to bloody war with Ilion.
  Now by the shores of Troy
My fair name is reviled for wrong I have not done.

CHORUS. You have cause for sorrow, I know; but it is best to bear what burdens life lays upon us as cheerfully as we can.

HELEN. Burdens! Look, what a millstone life has hung round my neck! From the moment my mother bore me I was pointed at for a freak. It's not usual in Hellas or anywhere else for a woman to produce her young enclosed in

[10]Messenger of the gods; he wore winged shoes.
[11]Athena.

a white shell—which is the way Leda is said to have borne me, with Zeus for my father![12] Since then every fresh misfortune—in fact my whole life has been a freak; partly through Hera's fault, partly because my very beauty led to my taking on an untrue and hideous appearance in the eyes of the world. Oh, if the picture could have been wiped out and painted over again, to give me my true beauty, so that the Greeks could forget the blemishes I now possess, and remember the good instead of the bad!

When a man broods on a single misfortune and feels the gods are against him, though his suffering is real, it can be borne; but I am crushed by innumerable blows at once. In the first place, though I am innocent, my name is a byword of reproach; and if there is any worse fate than suffering for real crimes, it is suffering for crimes that were never committed. Then, the gods have uprooted me from my home, and planted me among an outlandish race, where I am friendless, and degraded from nobility to slavery; for in a country like this all are slaves except one man. The sole anchor of hope that I cling to, that some day my husband would come and rescue me—that hope has gone, if he is dead. And my mother is dead, and men say I killed her—say it unjustly, but it is an injustice I must bear. My daughter,[13] the pride of her home, and of her mother, grows gray in virginity; and my two brothers, whom they call the sons of Zeus, are gone. Meanwhile, surrounded by so many disasters, in this make-believe situation I too am dead, though in fact I am alive. To crown all, even if I were to reach my home, Sparta would shut the door on me as a foreigner; for they all think the sea swallowed me together with Menelaus. For if he were alive, we would recognize each other by certain secrets known to us alone. But he is not alive; I shall never see him again.

Then why should I go on living? What is left to me now? To save my life I can choose to marry Theoclymenus, to live as a Egyptian wife, the lady of a great house. But an odious husband makes even wealth odious. The wisest course is—to die.

How can I do it well? A rope? No. I will not be seen dangling in a noose. Even slaves think it beneath them. To strike with a knife has a certain touch of royalty, of heroism. But that way of escape hurts, and I shrink from it. What a depth of desperation! Beauty is a blessing to other women: it reduces *me* to this!

CHORUS. Helen, you should not assume that this Greek, whoever he may be, told you nothing but the truth.
HELEN. He told me clearly enough that Menelaus was dead.
CHORUS. Many tales might be clear, and yet not true.
HELEN. Truth itself is often bewildering.
CHORUS. You dwell on the worst that may happen, instead of the best.
HELEN. Fear grips me and drives me to the thought that I dread.
CHORUS. Tell me—how much good-will have you in the palace?
HELEN. They are all my friends, except the man who is bent on marrying me.

[12]After Leda mated with Zeus in the guise of a swan, she was said to have produced two eggs. Helen and Castor were hatched from one, Clytemnestra and Pollux from the other. Euripides is making a little joke, imagining that the young Helen was teased by the other children because she was born from an egg.

[13]Hermione. (Teucer has not actually mentioned her.)

CHORUS. Then listen: this is what you must do: leave your sanctuary here and—

HELEN. Leave sanctuary? What are you suggesting?

CHORUS. Go to the house of Theonoe, daughter of the sea. She possesses all knowledge: inquire of her whether your husband is alive or dead; and when you have a clear answer you may rejoice or weep accordingly. Before you know for certain, what do you gain by grieving? Do as I suggest: leave this tomb, go to Theonoe, and you will know everything. When you have here in the palace one who can tell you the truth and is also your friend, why look further? I will willingly go myself and join with you in asking for a divine revelation. Women ought to help each other.

HELEN. Friends, I will do as you say.
Into the palace, quickly in,
To learn what I must lose or win!

CHORUS. We are ready now, at your word.

HELEN. I tremble! This is a day
Of fear: what answer waits to be heard?
What doom of tears?

CHORUS. But why
Be sure of the worst, and weep too soon?

HELEN. What bitter fate has my husband found?
Does he live to see the sun
Charioting the sky,
And the journeys of stars and moon?
Or has his soul begun
Its endless, lifeless exile under ground?

CHORUS. Whatever is to come,
Helen, accept and use for the best.

HELEN. Eurotas,[14] river of home,
With reedy banks of green,
If report of him is true,
If death holds him at rest,
Hear what I swear to do—!

CHORUS. This is folly! What do you mean?

HELEN. To die! I will swing high,
My throat in a choking rope,
Or the hand shall war on the wincing skin
And eager iron shall grope
And blood leap forth where the deadly blade passed in;
My death a sacrifice
To the three goddesses, and to Priam's son,[15]
The shepherd whose heart was won,
The judge whose word was brought
For Aphrodite's price.

CHORUS:
Hold to this happier thought,
That the clouds of fear my pass unshed.

[14]Principal river of Sparta.

[15]The three goddesses are Hera, Aphrodite, and Athena; Priam's son is Paris.

HELEN:

Weep for the tears of Troy!
For Troy, deeds without name have bred
Pain without end. Aphrodite, goddess of joy,
Gave, and I was her gift; thence without respite sprang
Anguish of blood and tears and deep despair;
Mothers of Troy wailed for their vanished sons;
Sisters knelt by Scamander's brims to hang
On new-made tombs locks of their virgin hair.

But listen! Loud and full
Through Hellas too the same river of weeping runs,
And hands are clasped over the stricken head,
And nerveless fingers clutch and pull
The unfeeling flesh till the nails are red.

Happy Arcadian girl,[16] who long ago
Lay in the bed of Zeus! For you, once fair,
Still in the rough pelt of a shambling bear
Made your shape gentle with your eyes' soft glow.
Beauty, that tortures me, to you was kind:
With it, you left the pangs of grief behind.

And Merops' daughter, happy too was she,
The Titan maid whom for her beauty's flower
Artemis drove out from her company
And turned her to a hind with horns of gold;[17]
But my curs'd beauty damned with deadly power
Trojan and wandering Greek to sufferings untold.

HELEN *and* CHORUS *exeunt into the palace. Enter* MENELAUS.

MENELAUS. O Pelops my grandfather, winner of your famous chariot-race against Oenomaus at Pisa! How I wish that on the same day when you were prepared as a banquet for the gods, you had ended your life forthwith between immortal teeth! Then you could never have begotten my father Atreus; who in his turn was father, by his wife Aerope, to Agamemnon and myself, a celebrated pair of sons.[18] In fact, my opinion is—I say this without any wish to boast—that, of the two of us, I took the larger part in the transporting of our armament by sea to Troy; a monarch owing his authority not to superior force, but to the willing obedience of the fighting men of Hellas.

Many of those men are dead; many others—the exact figure is ascertainable—rejoice in a happy escape from the perils of the sea, and have returned home bringing with them tokens and keepsakes of those who

[16]Callipso; Zeus raped her and then turned her into a she-bear.

[17]Merops is a Greek soothsayer in the *Iliad.* The story that his daughter was turned into a golden-horned deer by Artemis is otherwise unknown.

[18]Menelaus, on his entrance, summarizes the family history that has led to a curse on the house of Atreus. His great-grandfather, Tantalus, killed his own son, Pelops, and served him as a meal for the gods. The gods, horrified, restored Pelops to life. Pelops later won his wife Hippodamia from her father Oenomaus in a rigged chariot race.

died. But I, through all the years since I overthrew the towers of Troy, have been an unhappy wanderer upon the stormy wastes of the gray ocean. I long to reach my own country; but the gods have not thought me worthy. I have sailed into every desolate landing-place, every hostile port, on the Libyan coast. Every time I near the shores of my own country a storm drives me back; no favoring wind ever fills my sail to bring me home.

And now here I am on this coast, a wretched castaway, all my friends lost; our ship broken in a thousand pieces against the rocks. But a curiously-fitted keel remained intact, and on this, with much difficulty, and much to my surprise, I was able to get ashore, and with me Helen whom I dragged off from Troy. What country this is, what nation inhabits it I have no idea. I could have inquired; but I preferred not to meet people in my present embarrassing costume, which decency demands should be kept out of sight. A man accustomed to high position feels misfortune more than one who is inured to it. I am, in fact, exhausted: no food, no clothes—these rags I have on are what I could save from the wreck, as anyone can see. My usual clothes—rich cloaks, soft gowns—the sea has taken them all. But I have my wife—the source of all my sufferings; and before coming up here I hid her in a cave together with the survivors of my company, and ordered them to guard her for me. I have come alone to procure any supplies I can find for them. As soon as I saw this palace I approached it; the high surrounding wall, the imposing entrance, indicate a man of wealth. Sailors in need may hope for something from a well-stocked house; otherwise we shall die; for a whole ship's crew, if they can get no supplies, can give no help, however willing. [*He shouts*] Hallo, there! Porter! Come to the door, and take a message in for me. I need help.

An OLD WOMAN *answers from inside.*

OLD WOMAN. Who's that at the door? Go away, will you? Don't stand there in the porch disturbing my master! Or you'll get killed: you're a Greek, and we have no dealings with Greeks.

MENELAUS. Old woman, these are empty threats. I may speak bluntly, for I've no time to spare. Come on, undo the bolt!

She opens the door and appears.

OLD WOMAN. Go away! My orders are that no Greek shall come near the house.

MENELAUS. Look here, don't shake your finger at me or push me about.

OLD WOMAN. It's your fault; you won't do what I tell you.

MENELAUS. Go and tell your master I'm here.

OLD WOMAN. I wouldn't take the risk of delivering your message.

MENELAUS. I'm a shipwrecked man; he would not dare to harm me.[19]

OLD WOMAN. Now you go away from here to some other house.

MENELAUS. I won't. I'm coming in. Do as I tell you.

OLD WOMAN. I tell you you're troublesome. Before long you'll be thrown out.

MENELAUS. Ah! If only I had my army here!

OLD WOMAN. No doubt you were a great man in your army; here you're not.

MENELAUS. Gods! that I should suffer such indignity!

OLD WOMAN. Ha! Tears in your eyes! Who do you think is sorry for you?

[19]Menelaus appeals to the Greek laws of hospitality, apparently not observed in Egypt.

MENELAUS. The gods were once kind to me.
OLD WOMAN. Then go away and bestow your tears on your friends.
MENELAUS. What country is this? Whose is this palace?
OLD WOMAN. This is Proteus' palace; and the country is Egypt.
MENELAUS. Egypt! Could anything be worse? What a place to have reached!
OLD WOMAN. Why do you speak ill of the jewel of the Nile?
MENELAUS. I did not. I was groaning at my own misfortune.
OLD WOMAN. Many are unfortunate; you are not the only one.
MENELAUS. Is this king—whatever you called him—at home?
OLD WOMAN. This is his tomb. His son reigns now.
MENELAUS. Then where is his son, at home or away?
OLD WOMAN. He is not at home. And he is a bitter enemy of all Greeks.
MENELAUS. Why does he hate Greeks—so unhappily for me?
OLD WOMAN. Helen is in this palace, the daughter of Zeus.
MENELAUS. What? What did you say? Say that again.
OLD WOMAN. The daughter of Tyndareus, who used to live in Sparta.
MENELAUS. But where did she come from? What can this mean?
OLD WOMAN. Why, she came here from Lacedaemon.
MENELAUS. When? [*Aside*] Surely my wife can't have been kidnapped out of the cave.
OLD WOMAN. Before the Greeks went to Troy, my friend. But get away from this house. There's an extraordinary trouble that's upsetting us just now; you have come at a most unfortunate time. If my master catches you, your welcome will be death. I'm a friend to you Greeks, in spite of what I said; I spoke harshly for fear of my master.

Exit.

MENELAUS. What does it mean? What can I think? This story of hers seems to alter the whole situation. Is it possible that I should capture my wife in Troy, bring her here and put her in a cave for safety, and now find another woman, with the same name as my wife, living in this palace? But she called this woman the daughter of Zeus! Can there be a *man* by the name of Zeus living on the banks of the Nile? There's only one Zeus, the one in heaven. And where in the world is there a Sparta, except on the reedy banks of the lovely Eurotas? Are there two men called Tyndareus? Is there another Lacedaemon, another Troy? I don't know what to say.

Well, after all, the world's a big place: no doubt many women have the same names—many towns too. There's really nothing to wonder at. Nor is there anything to run away from in a slave's threats. No man could be so uncivilized as to refuse me food—once he heard my name. The fire of Troy is famous; so is the man who lit it—known all over the world: Menelaus!

I will wait for the master of the house. That means two things to look out for: if the man's a savage, I must first hide, then get back to the wreck; if he shows any softness, I must be sure to ask for the provisions we need.—This, then, was the final humiliation in store for me, that I should beseech a fellow-king for bread to keep me alive! Well, I must. *Nothing is stronger than necessity*—I did not invent that proverb, but it's true none the less, and very well known.

Re-enter CHORUS.

CHORUS. When in her need my lady Helen
Went to the royal palace to inquire,
I heard the virgin prophetess say
That King Menelaus has not vanished
To the land of shadows under the earth
Where light is dark, but lives, the sport
Of the stormy seas, and never yet
Has moored in the harbor of his own city;
But sick with travel, stripped of friends,
Has grounded keel, in his voyage from Troy,
On every shore between East and West.

Re-enter HELEN.

HELEN. Now, back to my place of sanctuary—but Theonoe's answer has warmed my heart! She knows everything, and it is true! She says openly that my husband is alive, alive! that he wanders endlessly from sea to sea, this way and that; but at last, when he is exhausted with travel, and reaches the appointed end of his sufferings, he will come!—One thing she did not tell me, whether after coming he will get safely away; but I was so overjoyed at hearing he was alive that I refrained from pressing her further. She says that he's somewhere near at hand, that he has been wrecked, and has landed with only a few companions. Oh, Menelaus, when will you come? How I long to see you! [*She sees him.*]

Oh! Who is that? He is lying in wait for me—this is some sacrilegious plot of Theoclymenus! Quick, to the tomb, fast as the wind, fast as frenzy! He means to capture me! What a wild look he has!

MENELAUS. Listen to me! Stop clutching so desperately at that tomb—those altar pillars—wait! Why run away? . . . Ah! now that you show me your face, you strike me speechless with astonishment.

HELEN. Friends, this is a cruel wrong! He is keeping me away from sanctuary! He is going to seize me, and give me as wife to the king, whom I hate!

MENELAUS. I'm not a criminal, nor has anyone sent me to commit any crime.

HELEN. Are you not? But you're dressed in rags!

MENELAUS [*returning from the tomb*]. Don't run away; there's nothing to be afraid of.

HELEN. Now that I can cling to the tomb, I'll stay.

MENELAUS. Who are you? Whose face am I looking at?

HELEN. But who are *you*? We are both in the same perplexity.

MENELAUS. I never saw anyone more exactly like—

HELEN. O gods! Yes, there is something godlike in recognition!

MENELAUS. Are you a Greek, or a native here?

HELEN. A Greek. I want to know your country too.

MENELAUS. To me you appear to be exactly like Helen!

HELEN. To me you look like Menelaus! I don't know what to think.

MENELAUS. You are right! I am Menelaus—to my sorrow.

HELEN [*stretching out her arms*]. Come to me—I am your wife! I have waited so long for you! [*She kneels, clasps his rags, and kisses them.*]

MENELAUS. Wife? What do you mean? Leave my clothes alone!

HELEN. I am! My father Tyndareus gave me to you!

MENELAUS. Hecate, bringer of light, send me good dreams![20]

[20]Hecate was the goddess of the night and of dreams.

HELEN. I am not a dream, Hecate has not sent me!
MENELAUS. But neither am I the husband of two women!
HELEN. What other woman's husband are you?
MENELAUS. I left her hidden in the cave—I was bringing her back from Troy.
HELEN. You have no wife other than me.
MENELAUS. I am not mad—can there be something wrong with my sight?
HELEN. There is nothing wrong! When you look at me do you not know that I am your wife?
MENELAUS. In appearance you are the same; but the mystery of it baffles me.
HELEN. Look at me! What plainer proof do you want?
MENELAUS. You are like her; that I don't deny.
HELEN. Then what evidence should you trust, if not your eyes?
MENELAUS. My difficulty is this: I have another wife!
HELEN. I did not go to Troy. That was a phantom.
MENELAUS. And who can make a phantom that lives and breathes?
HELEN. Air! It was the gods' work. That wife of yours is made—of air!
MENELAUS. Which of the gods made her? I never heard of such a thing!
HELEN. Hera made her as a substitute for me, so that Paris should not have me.
MENELAUS. What? Then you were here and in Troy at the same time?
HELEN. A name can be in any number of places: a person can only be in one place. [*She clasps his hand.*]
MENELAUS. Let go! I had enough to plague me before I came.
HELEN. Will you leave me, and go away with your phantom wife?
MENELAUS. Yes! You are too much like Helen; so good-bye!
HELEN. You kill me to say so. I have found you, my husband, and now I cannot keep you!
MENELAUS. The memory of what I went through at Troy is more convincing than you are.
HELEN [*weeping*]. Oh, oh! was anyone ever so miserable? My husband is leaving me once more; I shall never live in my own country or see my own home again!

Enter a MESSENGER, *one of* MENELAUS' *men.*

MESSENGER. Menelaus, here you are at last! I have been wandering all over this outlandish place, trying to find you. The others that you left behind sent me.
MENELAUS. What's the matter? You are not being robbed by natives, I hope?
MESSENGER. Something extraordinary—but the word doesn't describe it.
MENELAUS. Tell me. It's something strange, to judge by the state you're in.
MESSENGER. All your endless hardships—all suffered for nothing!
MENELAUS. That's no news to me. What has happened?
MESSENGER. Your wife has gone, vanished into the air! She just went up and disappeared! Now she's out of sight, in the sky, and the cave where we were guarding her is empty! But before she went she said this: "You poor pitiful Trojans and suffering Greeks, it was a trick of Hera's that sent you to your deaths on the banks of the Scamander. Paris did not possess Helen, as you thought. Now that I have stayed as long as I had to stay, I return, as Fate ordains, to the sky that formed me. The curses that men heap on the unhappy Helen are mistaken: she has done nothing wrong." [*He sees* HELEN.] Oh! *there* you are, daughter of Leda! So you were here all the time! I have just been reporting you as departed to the regions of the stars, being

unaware that you possessed wings. Now I'm not letting you play tricks on us a second time: you gave quite enough trouble to your husband and his friends when you were in Troy.

MENELAUS. It's true—this proves it! All she said is confirmed! Helen! [*He holds out his arms and* HELEN *runs to him; they embrace.*] How I have longed for this day, longed to take you in my arms! Now you are mine!

HELEN. O dearest love! year after endless year
Crept by: now joy has come, for you are here!
Women, I laugh for you:
My husband is mine once more,
And my arms are round his neck.
He comes like a flare of flame
Lighting my dark despair.

MENELAUS:
And you are mine. So much, since then, has passed—
What should I tell—what ask you—first or last?

HELEN. My hair wings wild in the wind for joy;
My eyes are brimming, while my hands
Feel your dear form, and taste
Pleasure so long denied!

MENELAUS:
No dearer sight than this! All grief forgotten!
Daughter of Zeus, you are mine to have and hold.
I claimed you once, when the Heavenly Twins your brothers
Rode their white horses under the torchlit night,[21]
And their shouts of blessing echoed, echoed again—
Once, long ago; and then
Hera stole you away, and my house was empty.

HELEN:
Now Heaven leads us on from this happy meeting
To a still happier day.

MENELAUS:
Good defeats ill once more; we are united.
Though joy was long on the way,
Now fortune smiles, and may blessing follow!

CHORUS:
Blessing indeed; we too pray the same prayer,
For your fate and hers are one:
You cannot suffer, and she be safe.

HELEN:
Dear friends, pain that is past has lost its sting;
My husband is mine, is mine!
He has come, and my long despair is over.

MENELAUS:
We have each other. In truth, I dimly guessed,
As the endless chain of tedious days went on,
That the Queen of Gods was at work.
There is more joy in my tears
Than all the sorrow of all the past.

[21]Castor and Pollux were often represented as horsemen riding white horses.

HELEN:
Bliss beyond words, sweeter than heart could hope—
I hold you close to my breast.

MENELAUS:
And you to mine—you who we thought were living
In the shadow of Mount Ida,
Behind the sad battlements of Troy.
—Helen, how did you steal from home that day?

HELEN. The story you seek began in pain,
Cruel to suffer, cruel to recount again.

MENELAUS. Tell me; for every mortal must
Accept Heaven's gifts as best he may.

HELEN. The words will choke me. How can I speak?

MENELAUS. Speak, for my sake.

HELEN. I felt no guilty lust;
I did not fly over the sea to seek
The unlawful bed of an Eastern prince.

MENELAUS. What god, what fate, then, stole you away?

HELEN. Hermes the son of Zeus conveyed me here
To the banks of the Nile.

MENELAUS. At whose command?
—The son of Zeus!

HELEN. I wept long since,
And now I weep again for fear—
My enemy is the Queen of Heaven.

MENELAUS. Hera! and how have *we* incurred her curse?

HELEN:
The cruel reproaches I have borne
Flowed from that fountain-source
Where the three bright immortals came to adorn
Their beauty on which the famous judgment then was given.

MENELAUS. But why must Hera's spite be vented
On you, for judgment she resented?[22]

HELEN. To despoil Paris of the bride
The Cyprian promised him—

MENELAUS. Of you!

HELEN. She sent me to this desert land,
Weeping—

MENELAUS. And in your place supplied
A phantom Helen—all too true!

HELEN. At home there is more sorrow yet:
My mother—

MENELAUS. What of her?

HELEN. Is dead.
She tied the noose with her own hand,
Believing I had shamed your bed.

[22]Hera, Aphrodite, and Athena each offered Paris bribes to award her the golden apple as most beautiful. Hera offered power (the rule of all Asia), Aphrodite offered him love (the hand of Helen), and Athena promised him wisdom. Hera became enraged when he chose Aphrodite.

MENELAUS. O gods!—What of Hermione?
HELEN. What joy has she? What hope to get
Husband or child, when all men point to me?

MENELAUS:
Paris! You who have murdered my whole house,
Your deed brought death to your city and to you,
And to ten thousand bronze-armed men of Greece.

HELEN:
And I, accursed, unhappy, not untrue,
Exiled perforce, guiltless of broken vows,
Was robbed of city, home, my husband, and my peace!

CHORUS. If only you meet with good luck for the future, it will compensate you for all that is past.

MESSENGER. Menelaus, I realize that something has made you happy, though I have not yet fully grasped what it is. Will you let me share your good news?

MENELAUS. Why, of course, you must share it, old fellow.

MESSENGER. Then is not this lady Helen, the prize of all we went through at Troy?

MENELAUS. This lady was never in Troy. We were tricked by the gods. The Helen we captured was a phantom to make fools of us.

MESSENGER. What? All our sweat and blood—spent for a ghost?

MENELAUS. Yes. Hera was in a rage because of the Judgment of Paris.

MESSENGER. Then the one who really is your wife is this lady here?

MENELAUS. She is. You must take my word for it.

MESSENGER [*to* HELEN]. My daughter! The ways of the gods are involved and mysterious; they send us good and bad fortune in turn, and all is for the best. One man suffers, but soon his suffering is over and he prospers beyond his hopes; another man does not suffer, but when his turn comes the luck he enjoyed so long deserts him, and he perishes miserably. So you and your husband had your share of suffering—you were ill spoken of, he was caught in the storm of battle. As long as he struggled for what he wanted, he gained nothing; now good fortune has come to him of its own accord, and he's a happy man. So, you did not disgrace your old father and your two brothers, as the world says you did.

How well I remember your wedding-day! I can see it all again now—the horses, four in a yoke, with me running beside them holding a torch, and you in the chariot with Menelaus, leaving your lovely home to be married! [*He wipes a tear.*] Excuse me. To a slave his master's affairs mean a great deal; he shares in joy and sorrow alike; if not, he's no true man. I'm a slave by birth, I know; but there are slaves who are noble, who have the mind of a free man, if not the name: I want to count as one of them. It's the best way; otherwise you've a double misfortune—you take orders from every one all around, and you *feel* like a slave as well.

MENELAUS. You're a good old man; you've borne your full share of hardship in my service on the field; and now that you're here to share in my good fortune, go back to the others and tell them what has happened. Explain the present position; warn them to wait on the shore and be ready in case I have to make a fight for it, as I expect; and if we should find any possible way of getting my wife out of this place, after meeting so miraculously, they must see to it that we aren't caught by the natives.

MESSENGER. I'll do it, my lord. And I'll tell you, this is my experience of prophets: you can expect nothing from them but silliness and lies. Shapes of sacrifices, cries of birds—there no truth in any of it, never was! Can birds do men any good? The very notion's foolish. Calchas saw his friends dying in battle for the sake of a phantom, yet he gave them neither word nor sign; no more did the Trojan Helenus—his city was sacked for nothing.[23] You may say it was because the gods did not wish them to speak. Then why do we consult prophets? Better ask the gods for blessing, after due offerings; and leave prophets alone. Prophecy was invented to entrap men with the promise of success; no one ever got wealth without labor by studying sacrifices. The best oracle is care and common sense.

CHORUS. I entirely agree with the old man about oracles. To make friends with the gods is better than all the skill of prophets.

Exit MESSENGER.

HELEN. So far, then, everything goes well. But tell me about your adventures on the voyage from Troy. I gain nothing by knowing it, but because you are dear to me I want to share in all you have suffered.

MENELAUS. You have asked me a hundred questions in one. There were shipwrecks in the Aegean; the false beacons that Nauplius lit on Euboea; cities in Crete and Libya were visited; the watch-tower of Perseus—why should I tell you all this?[24] I have endured it once in reality; the distress of telling you would make me endure it twice.

HELEN. I am sorry if I asked you things too painful to speak of. Leave the rest and tell me one thing: how long have you wandered over the ridges of the salt sea?

MENELAUS. We were at Troy ten years; since than I have been voyaging seven summers and seven winters.

HELEN. Seven years! What a terrible, weary time! And even now, after finding me, you must not stay. You must get away from this country as quickly as possible. You have escaped the war and the sea, but death waits for you here.

MENELAUS. What do you mean? Death? This is bad news.

HELEN. The man who owns this palace will kill you.

MENELAUS. What have I done to deserve that?

HELEN. He wants to marry me; your unexpected arrival will put a stop to that.

MENELAUS. What? A man was proposing to marry my wife?

HELEN. Yes, and to take me by force, if I had not escaped from him.

MENELAUS. How could he have the power? Is he a private person, or—is it the king?

HELEN. He is the king of Egypt, the son of Proteus.

MENELAUS. Oh! I see now what the old woman at the door meant.

HELEN. What door? Have you called at some house here in Egypt?

MENELAUS. This door, the king's. I was driven away as a beggar.

HELEN. You surely were not asking for food? Oh, how dreadful!

[23]Calchas and Helenus were prophets on the Greek and Trojan sides respectively.

[24]Nauplius's son Palamedes was unjustly stoned to death by the Greeks at Troy after Odysseus falsely denounced him. In revenge, Nauplius lighted false beacons to lure the returning Greek ships onto the rocks. The watch-tower of Perseus was near the mouth of the Nile, where Perseus saved the maiden Andromeda, later his wife, from a sea monster.

MENELAUS. I was in fact begging; but I didn't say so.
HELEN. Then no doubt you know all about his plans for marrying me.
MENELAUS. I do. What I don't know is whether you have managed to evade them.
HELEN. Be reassured: your wife's chastity is untouched.
MENELAUS. What deterred him? I should be most happy to believe you.
HELEN. You see this tomb where you found me sitting in despair?
MENELAUS. I see you have a mattress there; what was that for?
HELEN. I was a suppliant there, praying to escape this marriage.
MENELAUS. Was there no altar? Or do the Egyptians reverence a tomb?
HELEN. This was as strong a protection as any temple.
MENELAUS. Then can I not take you with me and sail for home?
HELEN. You are more likely to be killed than ever to have me for your wife again.
MENELAUS. Gods forbid such a cruel fate!
HELEN. Now, don't be ashamed to seek your own safety, but escape!
MENELAUS. And leave you here? I took Troy for your sake.
HELEN. Better leave me than be killed for my sake.
MENELAUS. You counsel me to be a coward—the man who took Troy!
HELEN. Perhaps you think of killing the king—you could not do it.
MENELAUS. Why not? Is his skin steel-proof?
HELEN. You will see. It is folly to attempt the impossible.
MENELAUS. Why, then, shall I meekly hold out my hands to be manacled?
HELEN. You're in a trap. We must contrive some way out.
MENELAUS. Certainly; I would rather be killed in action.
HELEN. There is one hope, one way of escape; and only one.
MENELAUS. What shall we use? Bribes, boldness, or persuasion?
HELEN. If the king could be prevented from knowing of your arrival—
MENELAUS. Who will tell him? At least he won't know who I am.
HELEN. He has an ally in his palace whose help is worth as much as a god's.
MENELAUS. Do you mean some divine voice that speaks inside his walls?
HELEN. No, I mean his sister; they call her Theonoe.
MENELAUS. Her name is prophetic.[25] What of her actions?
HELEN. She knows everything, and will tell her brother you are here.
MENELAUS. If she does we shall be killed. I've no way of hiding.
HELEN. If we both together appealed to her—
MENELAUS. Yes?
HELEN. Not to tell her brother about you—
MENELAUS. If she agreed, we could escape!
HELEN. Yes, easily, with her help; but no chance without telling her.
MENELAUS. *You* must persuade her; she will listen to a woman.
HELEN. At least she will let me approach her as suppliant.[26]
MENELAUS. Well; what if she rejects our appeal?
HELEN. You will be killed, and I shall be forced into marriage.
MENELAUS. To consent would prove you false. He could not force you—that is an excuse.

[25]See note 2.

[26]In Greek culture, to supplicate was to make a request of someone while touching the person's chin, knees, or both. The person supplicated was then under considerable pressure to honor the request.

HELEN. I swear solemnly by your life—
MENELAUS. You swear—to die, rather than to belong to another man.
HELEN. By the same sword that kills you. I will lie at your side.
MENELAUS. To seal that promise, take my hand.
HELEN [*taking his hand*]. I swear, if you die, to die too.
MENELAUS. And I swear that if I lose you I will take my own life.
HELEN. How shall we die so that our death brings us fame and honor?
MENELAUS. Here on this tomb. I will kill you, and afterwards myself. But first I will put up a mighty struggle to win you. Let them all come! I shall not disgrace the name I won at Troy; nor am I going back to Greece to be blackguarded as the man who robbed Thetis of Achilles, saw Ajax fall on his sword, and led Nestor's son to his death, but was not ready to die himself for his own wife's sake.[27] I am ready, with all my heart. If the gods have understanding, the earth of burial lies lightly on a brave man killed by his enemies; but to a coward his grave is a crushing rock.
CHORUS. O gods, let the house of Tantalus find good fortune at last, and be delivered from all their troubles!

Voices are heard in the palace, and the name of "Theonoe," and the sound of heavy bolts being moved.

HELEN. Oh! Gods have pity! What cruel fortune! Menelaus, we are caught. Here comes the priestess Theonoe. I hear them unbolting the door. You must fly!—yet, what is the use? She knows you're here whether she sees you or not. O Menelaus! this is my fate! You escaped the cruelty of Troy only to meet other cruel swords here.

Enter THEONOE.

THEONOE. Hold the lamp bright before me and lead on. Sanctify every corner of the air with pure ritual, that I may draw holy breath from heaven. If any man has polluted this place with unhallowed tread, purge my path with flame; wave the torch before me, that I may pass. Your sacred service done, carry back the fire to the central hearth.

Helen, I have news for you, divinely revealed. Your husband Menelaus has come: there he stands before you! He has lost both his ships and the phantom of yourself. Unhappy Menelaus! What sufferings, what escapes you have known! This was not, after all, your homeward voyage; not, at least, if you loiter here. For among the gods this day there is conference and dispute about you in the court of Zeus. Hera, who once hated you, is now your friend; she wishes to bring you both safely to your home, so that all Hellas may know Paris was deceived in the wife whom Aphrodite gave him. But Aphrodite hopes to frustrate your return, lest she be known to have bargained with Helen's beauty for an unlawful love, and men condemn her. Thus, in the event, it lies in my power either to destroy you, as Aphrodite desires, by telling my brother of your arrival, or to take Hera's part and save your life by deceiving my brother, who has ordered me to inform him immediately upon your appearance here.

[27]Thetis, a sea-goddess, was the mother of Achilles, killed at Troy. Ajax, son of Telemon, killed himself after Odysseus defeated him in contending for the armor of the dead Achilles. Nestor, the oldest of the Greek warriors, lost his son Antilochus at Troy. Menelaus thus mentions three parents whose sons lost their lives at Troy trying to regain Helen; they would be angry if Menelaus was not ready to die for her.

I will safeguard my own position. Go, one of you, and tell my brother that Menelaus has come.

HELEN. Maiden, I fall a suppliant at your feet, beseeching you in misery and humility for myself and for Menelaus. After many years I have found him: yet in this moment I must see him die. Now that my beloved husband has come, and I hold him in my arms, do not betray him to your brother, but spare him, I entreat you. Do not purchase the favor of tyranny, the gratitude of a wicked heart, by shaming your own piety. God hates violence, and bids us possess what we possess without robbery. What can only come by crime we must not touch. As the sky is a common grace to all mankind, so is the earth, where each may fill his house with goods but must not hold what is another's, nor take it by force. My coming here was timely, but has turned to misery. Hermes gave me to your father to keep safe for my husband; now my husband is here and wants to receive what is his. How can he, if they kill him? How can the king pay his just debt by bestowing the living on the dead? That debt was contracted between the god and your father, and it is their integrity, their wishes, that you must consider. Would they not have what belongs to another duly returned? You should not feel more bound to your impious brother than to your noble father. You are a seer, and believe in divine providence: if now you pervert your father's purpose, and take your unjust brother's part, is it not shameful that you who know the secrets of Heaven both now and to come, should not know right from wrong? Look at my husband and me, persecuted by misery and misfortune; pity us and save us. Use your power for this better purpose. I am Helen, hated by the whole world, infamous throughout Hellas as the wife who betrayed her husband for the sake of a wealthy home in Phrygia.[28] But if I return to Hellas and live again in Sparta, if their own ears and eyes prove to them that they were cruelly tricked by the goddess, and that I did not betray my husband, then they will give me back my good name: I shall see my daughter married, whom no man will take now; this hateful, homeless life that I live here will end, and I shall enjoy the comfort and splendor of my own home. If Menelaus had died across the sea, I should be weeping at the news, without even being able to see him; but he is alive, and here: must he be taken from me?

No, no, Theonoe! I implore you, be like your noble father, and grant what I ask. A good man's daughter can have no higher praise, than that her goodness equals his.

CHORUS. Your pleading words, Helen—and still more you yourself—move my pity. But Menelaus has yet to speak for his life: I long to hear what he will say.

MENELAUS. You need not expect me to fall at your feet in tears; such weakness now would make Troy blush for her conqueror. Certainly weeping is held no disgrace to a king when Fate is hard; though even if tears be a credit, I prefer courage.

If you intend to help, as in duty bound, a man who rightfully asks to receive back his own wife, give her to me, and further, ensure my escape. If not, I am already familiar with misfortune; and your reward will be infamy. But I will make my appeal for that just treatment which I claim to

[28]Troy.

deserve, my appeal for the sympathy of your inmost heart, as a suppliant here before the tomb of your father. [MENELAUS *moves to the tomb.*]

Aged Proteus, guardian spirit of this marble tomb! Restore to me my wife, whom Zeus sent here to you in trust for me. Death, I know, forbids that I should receive her from your own hands; but surely your daughter will not allow that men should call you from the dead to curse your once noble name. We are in her hands. [*He turns from the tomb and addresses the earth.*]

Lord of the lower world, you too I call upon for help. You have received countless bodies of men that fell by my sword: you have your payment. Either restore now those dead to life, or bid Theonoe prove herself more righteous than this impious king, by giving me my wife. [*He turns to* THEONOE *again.*]

But if you and the king steal my wife from me—I will tell you now what she has left unsaid. You must know, Theonoe, that I have bound myself by solemn oaths, first, to engage your brother in combat, till one of us kills the other: that is final. But if he will not meet me sword to sword, but besieges us with hunger here in our sanctuary, then I am resolved, first to kill Helen, afterwards to drive this two-edged sword into my own heart, here upon the slab of this monument, that our blood may stream down upon Proteus's grave; we shall lie both dead together upon this polished stone, to wring your heart and soil your father's name for ever. Neither your brother nor any other man shall have Helen: I shall take her myself, to my own home, if possible; if not, to the dead. [*His voice breaks, and he brushes a tear.*]

What is this—*tears*? Because my eyes are womanish you perhaps think me readier to sue than to do. Kill me, if that is your mind: the crime will brand you. But make the better choice; do what is just and right: let me have my wife.

CHORUS. You must judge, Theonoe, what each has said; make a decision that will satisfy everyone.

THEONOE. Both nature and inclination prompt me to piety. I love myself; I am anxious not to cloud my father's good name; while to my brother I must refuse any service that would turn to his dishonor. There is in my soul a great temple of righteousness, a gift that I have from my father Nereus.[29] So I will try to save Menelaus; and since Hera wishes to help him, I will cast my vote with hers. For Aphrodite—may she forgive me; but I have had no dealing with her in the past, and I will grow old a virgin as I am now. Your appeal to my father to vindicate his honor is one which I myself echo. To refuse to deliver you your wife would be to wrong him; for if he were living he would certainly restore you to each other. Right and wrong are rewarded in every country on earth, and not less among the dead. The mind of one departed may not have life; but it has become one with immortal spirit, and therefore has immortal understanding.

So, to be brief, I will, as you have asked, keep silence, and be no accomplice to my brother's wickedness. Indeed, what I do is a true service to him, turning his impious intent to righteousness.

[29]Actually grandfather. See note 2.

Now I will leave you to yourselves and say nothing; you must discover some way of escape. Let your first thought be of the gods: pray that Aphrodite may allow you a safe voyage home; and that Hera, who now intends the welfare of you both, may not change her mind.

She turns to the tomb.

Father, I make this promise to your departed soul: no deed of mine shall ever profane your pious memory.

Exit.

CHORUS. Wickedness never prospers; but goodness may hope for its reward.

HELEN. Menelaus, as far as she is concerned we are safe. For the rest—make some suggestion; together we must plot our escape.

MENELAUS. Listen then: you have lived in the palace a long time; you are intimate with the servants?

HELEN. Why do you ask? Yes, there might be a hope there. Tell me your plan.

MENELAUS. Could you persuade one of the stable-men to get us a four-horse chariot?

HELEN. I could; but how should we escape by land—over these endless plains, and with Egyptians all round us?

MENELAUS. No, it's impossible. Well, what if I hid in the palace—I have my sword—and killed the king?

HELEN. Theonoe would never allow her brother to be killed; she would warn him.

MENELAUS. Even if we reach the shore, there is no ship to escape in; mine is at the bottom of the sea.

HELEN. Listen, Menelaus—a woman's plan might succeed: will you let me invent a story that you are dead?

MENELAUS. It may invite ill-luck; but if there's something solid to be gained, I'm willing to die—in fiction.

HELEN. Good; then I will appear before this pagan king in mourning for you, and weeping—

MENELAUS. How will that help our escape? This plan of yours seems a bit old-fashioned.

HELEN. I will tell him you were drowned at sea, and ask his permission to make a cenotaph[30] for you.

MENELAUS. Suppose he agrees; giving me a cenotaph won't save our lives without a ship.

HELEN. I will ask him to provide us a ship, from which we may drop your burial-offerings into the lap of the sea.

MENELAUS. It's a good plan, except for this: if he tells you to perform the rites on land your story will be no use.

HELEN. But I'll tell him it's against Greek custom to bury on land those drowned at sea.

MENELAUS. Yes, that will do; then I'll go on board with you to help in the ritual.

HELEN. Yes, you, of course, chiefly; and all your sailors too who survived the wreck.

MENELAUS. Once I get hold of a ship at anchor, my men will be there, armed and disciplined.

[30]A monument in honor of one whose remains are elsewhere.

HELEN. You must see to that; I only pray for favoring winds and a fair voyage.

MENELAUS. We shall have them; the gods are going to be kind!—By the way, who will you say told you I was dead?

HELEN. You. Say that you are the sole survivor of Menelaus's crew, and that you saw him drown.

MENELAUS. Yes! And this strip of sail I've tied round me will confirm your story of the wreck.

HELEN. It was luckily found, though you at that moment were almost lost. You're a pitiful sight; and that is going to save us.

MENELAUS. Had I better come indoors with you, or shall I sit quietly here by the tomb?

HELEN. Stay here; if he tries violence with you, the tomb gives you sanctuary—and you have your sword. I will go in now, change this white dress for mourning black, cut my hair short and tear my face with my nails till the blood runs. [MENELAUS *begins to protest.*] I must indeed; everything is at stake—my safe home-coming and your life. There is no third way; if we fail, if the king discovers my deception, I must die.

We pray to you, Queen Hera, who lie in the bed of Zeus, stretching our hands towards heaven, where you live in the star-embroidered heights: have pity upon us both and deliver us!

We pray to you, child of Dione, Aphrodite, for whom the prize of beauty was won by the promise of my hand: do not destroy me! Did I not suffer enough before, when you gave my name to dishonor among my own people? Will you now give my body to death in a foreign land? If you wish for my death, let me die in the city of my fathers. Why are you never sated with mortal suffering?

You traffic in lust and falsehood; crooked intrigue and secret drugs are your instruments of death. Were there but measure in your power, no other gives gifts so sweet as yours. That is all I can say.

HELEN *goes into the palace;* MENELAUS *remains.*

CHORUS:

Shy nightingale,[31] mistress of woodland music, [*Strophe* I
Rapt votress, sweetening with each anguished note
The green leaf-curtained chambers of the forest,
Come to my call, and share my sorrow's burden
With shrill grief rippling from your russet throat.

Sharp was the pain of Helen, hot the tears
Troy's women shed, cursing the Hellene spears,
Since Trojan oars raced the rough Malean water,
And Paris, doomed in love, brought home from Sparta,
With mocking Aphrodite as his guide,
The phantom Helen for his fatal bride.

[31]The chorus appeals to Procne to help them tell Helen's story. Procne's husband Tereus raped her sister Philomela and cut her tongue out so she could not tell anyone. Philomela, however, told her sister of the rape by embroidering a picture of it. Procne took revenge by killing her son by Tereus and making the body into a stew which she fed to Tereus. When the enraged Tereus pursued the sisters, the gods saved them by changing Procne into a nightingale and Philomela into a swallow.

The sword played and the slung stone flew; and breath [*Antistrophe* I
Failed, and ten thousand Hellenes dwell with death,
Leaving heart-broken wives to mourn shorn-headed
In empty chambers. The lone sailor Nauplius
Lit his false fire on the Capherian Cape—[32]
A star turned liar, that lured ten thousand more
To ram the sunk rocks like fierce jaws agape;
And watched men die amidst the Aegean's roar.

Menelaus, wandering storm-swept leagues from Sparta,
From Malea's bare cliff, to this foreign water,
Clutched the sham prize of many a gory blade—
The phantom Helen, that mocking Hera made.

You who in earnest ignorance [*Strophe* 2
Would check the deeds of lawless men,
And in the clash of spear on spear
Gain honor—you are all stark mad!
If men, to settle each dispute,
Must needs compete in bloodshed, when
Shall violence vanish, hate be soothed,
Or men and cities live in peace?

Why have the sons of Priam
Received each his portion in chambers of quiet earth,
When reasonable words could have solved the quarrel for Helen?
Now they lie deep in the lap of Death;
And flames leaping like Zeus's thunderbolt
Have leveled their walls with dust;
Helen, your heart bears grief on grief;
And brave Menelaus wrings tears from every eye.

You who with learned patience plod [*Antistrophe* 2
Remotest realms of toilsome thought,
Can you by searching find out God,
Or bound his nature? Look at man!
From want to wealth, now forth, now back,
Now tossed from fame to infamy
By unforeseen, ambiguous chance!
Zeus was your father, Helen;
Winged like a swan he swooped to plant you in Leda's womb;
Yet, your name was shouted with execration
Through cities of Hellas, East to West:
Breaker of man's law and God's, breaker of faith!
So now I cannot tell
What mortal utterance may be called sure;
But truth is found in the mouth of God.

[32]See note 27.

Enter THEOCLYMENUS *from hunting, with attendants.*
He does not at first see MENELAUS, *but turns to pay respect to the tomb.*

THEOCLYMENUS. Proteus, my father, I salute your monument, which I placed here that I might greet you at my doorway. Always, going or coming, your son Theoclymenus thus pays you worship.

Men, take the hounds and all your hunting gear into the palace.

Attendants go in; THEOCLYMENUS *turns to the* CHORUS.

I've just been calling myself a fool. The trouble is, I don't punish slackness in servants with death. And now I discover that some Greek has landed here in broad daylight, and slipped past my scouts; come to reconnoitre for Helen, or even hoping to steal her away. Well, if we only catch him, he shall die.

He notices HELEN'S *absence.*

Why! By the gods, I'm too late; he seems to have done it. There's no one here. Helen's gone—she has been carried off, taken out of the country! Ho, there, open the doors! The woman I mean to marry shall not get clear of our shores if I can prevent it.

The doors open revealing HELEN; *she is dressed in mourning.*

Wait, wait! I see what I was looking for. She is here in the palace. She has not escaped.

Why, Helen! You have changed your white dress for mourning black; you have laid the shears to your proud head, and mown off your hair; your cheek is wet; you are weeping! Why is this? Is it some vivid dream that has made you sad? Or some rumor you have heard from Hellas, that has so changed your looks?

HELEN. My lord—now I may indeed call you "my lord"—I am in deep distress; all my hopes are lost; my life is over.

THEOCLYMENUS. But what is your trouble? What has happened?

HELEN. Menelaus—oh, how can I say it?—Menelaus is dead.

THEOCLYMENUS. Then I do not grudge you your tears, if my good fortune is so great. But how do you know? Did you hear this from Theonoe?

HELEN. Yes, from her; and from a man who witnessed his death.

THEOCLYMENUS. What? Has someone come who can vouch for this?

HELEN. Yes, he has come; and may he go where I would have him go!

THEOCLYMENUS. Who is he? Where is he? I want to hear more details.

HELEN. There he sits, crouching by the tomb.

THEOCLYMENUS. By Apollo, what a sight! The man's in rags.

HELEN [*weeping*]. Oh! My poor husband suffered as he does!

THEOCLYMENUS. What is his country? Where was he sailing from?

HELEN. He is a Greek; one of those who were sailing with Menelaus.

THEOCLYMENUS. How does he say Menelaus died?

HELEN. The most piteous of deaths: drowned in the salt sea.

THEOCLYMENUS. Where was he sailing at the time?

HELEN. He was wrecked on the steep rocks of the Libyan coast.

THEOCLYMENUS. If this man was on the same ship, how did he escape?

HELEN. A slave is sometimes luckier than a king.

THEOCLYMENUS. Where has he left his wrecked ship?

HELEN. At the bottom of the sea—my curse on it! If only Menelaus had escaped!

THEOCLYMENUS [*what a satisfaction he cannot resist*]. But Menelaus was drowned. What vessel brought this man here?

HELEN. Sailors found him and picked him up, so he says.
THEOCLYMENUS. And what of the phantom that was sent in your place to curse Troy?
HELEN. It has vanished into air.
THEOCLYMENUS. Then Priam and his people perished for nothing.
HELEN. And I was involved in their disaster—for nothing.
THEOCLYMENUS. Did he leave your husband's body unburied, or—
HELEN. Yes, unburied, unburied. [*She weeps.*]
THEOCLYMENUS. So this is why you have cut your golden locks.
HELEN. I loved him long ago when he was with me; I love him still.
THEOCLYMENUS. It is true, then? This is really what you are weeping for?
HELEN. Would it be easy for me to deceive your sister?
THEOCLYMENUS. It would not. Well: are you going to remain clinging to this tomb?
HELEN. I shrink from you—out of loyalty to my husband.
THEOCLYMENUS. Why tantalize me? Must you still remember him?
HELEN. I will not any more. Now you may begin preparing for our marriage.
THEOCLYMENUS. Your consent has been long in coming; but it makes me happy.
HELEN. You know what must be done. Let us forget the past.
THEOCLYMENUS. I must be gracious in return. What shall I do?
HELEN. Let us call a truce, and be friends.
THEOCLYMENUS. All my anger—I renounce it, fling it to the winds.
HELEN. Then, since you are my friend, I fall at your feet and beg you, I cling to you as a suppliant—
THEOCLYMENUS. What do you desire?
HELEN. I want to bury my husband who has died.
THEOCLYMENUS. Bury him? What, a grave without a body? Do you want to bury his ghost?
HELEN. It is the custom in Hellas, when a man is lost at sea, to prepare an empty winding-sheet and perform the rites of burial.
THEOCLYMENUS. True, the sons of Pelops are skilled in these matters.[33] Perform what is due; build a tomb for him anywhere you wish.
HELEN. We do not build tombs for men who go down with their ships.
THEOCLYMENUS. What, then? I know nothing of your customs.
HELEN. We lower into the sea the gifts that are due to the dead.
THEOCLYMENUS. What would you like me to provide for him?
HELEN. This man knows. I have no experience—such a loss is new to me.
THEOCLYMENUS [*to* MENELAUS]. Fellow, you have brought me happy news.
MENELAUS. Not happy for me; nor for the dead.
THEOCLYMENUS. How do you bury those who are drowned at sea?
MENELAUS. It varies according to the dead man's means.
THEOCLYMENUS. I will spare no expense, for Helen's sake. Tell me everything that should be done.
MENELAUS. First, an offering of blood to the powers of the earth.
THEOCLYMENUS. What beast should we offer? I will do as you say.
MENELAUS. You yourself must decide; whatever you give will be suitable.
THEOCLYMENUS. Our custom here is to kill a horse or a bull.
MENELAUS. But see that the beast you offer is without blemish.

[33]In other words, Spartans know Greek burial customs.

THEOCLYMENUS. My herds are large; we have perfect beasts in plenty.
MENELAUS. Next we bring rugs and coverlets, as it were for a bed.
THEOCLYMENUS. You shall have them. What else?
MENELAUS. Armor and weapons of bronze: he was a soldier.
THEOCLYMENUS. The arms I give you shall be fit for a son of Pelops.
MENELAUS. And last, an offering of fine fruit, of every sort your soil produces.
THEOCLYMENUS. Good. Then how do you lower these gifts into the sea?
MENELAUS. There must be a ship manned with rowers.
THEOCLYMENUS. And how far must the ship go from shore?
MENELAUS. Till her white wake is hardly visible.
THEOCLYMENUS. But why? What do you achieve with this observance?
MENELAUS. That the tide may not cast up our offerings again on land.
THEOCLYMENUS. You shall have a Phoenician barque, which will prove swift enough.
MENELAUS. That is well; you are generous to Menelaus.
THEOCLYMENUS. Cannot you perform these rites alone, without Helen?
MENELAUS. The dead must be buried by mother, or wife, or child.
THEOCLYMENUS. You mean, this observance is Helen's duty.
MENELAUS. Those who fear God do not scant the service of the dead.
THEOCLYMENUS. Let her go; I would wish my wife to be a god-fearing woman. Go indoors, choose what gifts you need, make all arrangements; and if Helen is pleased with your work, I shall not send you away empty-handed. Pitiable figure as you are, you have brought me welcome news; then you shall have clothes for your nakedness, and food, and a happy return to your own country. And you, Helen—do not wear yourself out with useless weeping. I am sorry for you; but Menelaus has met his fate, and the dead cannot come back to life.
MENELAUS. It is your duty to obey, my lady. You must accept the husband who stands before you, and forget the one whose claim is ended. In your present position this will be best for you. And if I come safely home to Hellas, I will put an end to evil tales about you; only be the wife you should be to your husband.
HELEN. I will; and you shall be there to witness that my husband will have no cause to blame me.

But now go indoors and have a bath, poor man, and change your clothes. I will give you your reward at once; after all, you are more likely to show real devotion in performing what is due to my beloved Menelaus, if you have found me properly grateful.

Exeunt into the palace THEOCLYMENUS *and* HELEN,
followed by Guards escorting MENELAUS

CHORUS:
There was a time, they say, when the Great Mother[34] [*Strophe* I
Ran to and fro frantic over the mountains,

[34]Demeter, mother of the gods and the mother goddess of the earth. Hades, god of the underworld, captured Demeter's daughter Persephone and dragged her down to the underworld. When Demeter learned what had happened, she abandoned her role as goddess of fertility, and the earth became sterile. The gods promised to let Persephone return to earth if she did not eat while in the underworld, but Persephone had eaten a pomegranate seed and so is compelled to return to Hades for part of each year (the winter season). In this chorus, Euripides suggests a close comparison between Demeter and Menelaus.

Through green glades of the forest,
Scanning the swirl of every river,
Scouring the deep-voiced swell of the salt ocean,
Searching in anguish for her lost Persephone,
Maiden of mysteries.

Then with a shrill shout
Sang out the ecstatic cymbals,
The Phrygian lions were yoked,
And in her gorgeous chariot the goddess rode
To seek Persephone, stolen from the dancing ring of girls.
Beside her swept like whirlwinds the virgin goddesses,
Artemis armed with invincible arrows,
Athene with spear and Gorgon shield.
But Zeus from the throne of heaven saw their purpose,
And the will of Zeus went a different way.

Now when, weary and bewildered, the Great Mother [*Antistrophe* I
Ceased her swift searching over the mountains,
In despair for her stolen daughter
She climbed the dazzling snow-bound summits
Sacred to nymphs of Ida; and at her command
The swollen torrents that leap down the mountain gorges
Were swallowed in the sink of the sea.

And cattle starved on the brown plains;
The sapless earth could bear no fruit;
The child died in the womb;
No lusty bud or curling tendril-spray
Burst from the vine; and on cities a deathly silence fell;
No pious thanksgiving thronged the temples,
No altar flamed with holy oil;
Even the shining springs the goddess forbade to flow,
In frenzy of grief for her lost child.

So when the Phrygian Mother had compelled [*Strophe* 2
Mortals and gods to cease from banqueting,
To soothe her, Zeus the King
Spoke to the Graces, those dread deities:
"Go to the goddess of Earth, who is angry still
For her stolen virgin child;
Charm her resentful heart with melodies,
And let the Muses lend their skill,
Dancing and singing." First of the immortals came
Glorious Aphrodite, and she held
High the bronze cymbals, voiced like subterranean flame,
And the leathern tabors rattling wild.
And the goddess-mother smiled,

And her hands received the flute of sonorous tone
Which filled her heart with music like its own.

But the maid had sinned, in childish innocence [*Antistrophe* 2
Breaking her fast in the dark rooms of earth.
The Mother of all birth
Saw her law slighted, and her anger rose.

A fearful power fills the bright dappled folds
Of a fawnskin cloak, fills the young ivy-shoot
Wreathed round a sacred fennel-wand;
Godhead itself is seen
In flash of an ecstatic hand that holds
High in the wind the whirling tambourine;
The toss of loose hair live with Bacchus' power;
Rapt vigil in the holy midnight hour.
And this dread deity who goes
Blazoned with glory on every hand—
She pardons none who taste the forbidden fruit.

HELEN *enters from the palace.*

HELEN. My dears, all goes well for us in the palace. The King questioned Theonoe; but she is on our side and told him nothing about my husband's arrival. Out of pure kindness to me she told him that Menelaus was dead. As for the equipment my husband needs, it was his own masterstroke that procured it. He asked for bronze weapons to throw into the sea: now he's bringing them himself, with his left hand firm on the grip of the shield, and his right holding the spear—all this by way of partaking in the ceremonies due to the dead. So he's ready armed for the fight; and once we're on board and under way, he'll settle accounts with any number of Egyptians. I have provided him with clothes instead of those rags from the wreck, and at last, after all these years, he has had a proper bath in fresh water.—I must be silent; here comes the man who thinks that marriage with me is in his grasp. I beg of you, be my friends; guard your tongues. It may be, if we escape, some day we could help you to escape too.

Enter THEOCLYMENUS, *attended.*

THEOCLYMENUS. Now, men, take these gifts consecrated to the sea, and pass on in due order, following this man's instructions. Helen: if I may suggest it, take my advice and stay here. You will honor your husband equally whether present at the ceremony or not. I am afraid some frenzy of grief or devotion may drive you to throw yourself into the sea. You are giving way to sorrow too much; especially since his body is not even here.

HELEN. My husband—to be, duty insists that I honor my first husband, and the memory of our marriage; and for love of him I would even die with him. But what pleasure could it give him, that I should share his death? No; let me go myself, and give my gifts to the dead; and may the gods grant to you everything that I wish; and to this man too, for his help in what I am doing. You shall find in me such a wife as your goodness to us both deserves; for all this leads to a happy end. Now, complete your generosity by commanding a ship to be given us, to carry these gifts.

THEOCLYMENUS [*to an attendant*]. Go; give them a fifty-oared Sidonian ship fully manned.

HELEN. As this man is arranging the burial, had he not better command the ship?

THEOCLYMENUS. Certainly; my men must take his orders.

HELEN. Repeat that command, to make sure your men understand you.

THEOCLYMENUS [*to the attendants*]. I repeat it: you take his orders. [*To* HELEN] I will say it a third time, if you wish.

HELEN. Blessings on you—and on my undertaking.

THEOCLYMENUS. Now, you must not spoil your beauty with too many tears.

HELEN. Today will show how grateful I am to you.

THEOCLYMENUS. This is wasted labor: the dead are nothing.

HELEN. I remember both the dead and the living.

THEOCLYMENUS. You will find in me as good a husband as Menelaus.

HELEN. You have been wonderful. All I pray for is good fortune.

THEOCLYMENUS. That lies with you. Only give me your heart.

HELEN. My heart knows now where its love belongs.

THEOCLYMENUS. Would you like my help? Shall I escort you myself?

HELEN. By no means; my lord must not serve his own servants.

THEOCLYMENUS. Away, then; your Greek ritual is nothing to me. My house is clean—it was not here that Menelaus died. Go, someone, tell my nobles to bring their wedding-gifts to the palace. Let the land ring aloud with music and songs of blessing, to celebrate the joy of my marriage with Helen.

[*To* MENELAUS] You, stranger, go and deliver these gifts into the arms of the sea, to honor him who was once her husband. When you have done it, bring my wife back with all speed to my palace. Then you shall share my table at our wedding-feast; and afterwards either sail for Hellas or live happily here.

Exit THEOCLYMENUS *to the palace.*

MENELAUS. O Zeus, named the Father of men, the compassionate, look upon us in our peril and save us. As we drag our hopeful fortunes up the steep hill, stretch out your hand and help us. One touch of your finger, and we shall reach the deliverance we long for. Are my past sufferings not enough for me to bear? Gods, I have blamed you foolishly, and I repent. I have not deserved perpetual misery; now my path should be straight. You have shown me one favor: grant me now a lasting joy.

MENELAUS, HELEN *and attendants move off towards the shore.*

CHORUS:

Oars of the East [*Strophe* I
Winged Sidonian[35] galley,
Flash through the foam-spray!
Darling of Nereus, dance,
While the dancing dolphins follow!
Now in the soft season,

[35]Phoenician. Phoenician ships had a high reputation.

The sea smoothed with the wind's caress,
When the voice of Calm, the grey-blue daughter of Ocean,
Quietly sings,
Now spread sails to the breeze,
Good-bye to the sheltering port,
Grip and pull on the pinewood sweep,
Crew of Menelaus, and carry in triumph
Helen to the harbors of home and the city that Perseus built.[36]

What will she see? [*Antistrophe* I
Perhaps the daughters of Leucippus[37]
By the rough Eurotas
Or before the temple of Pallas,
If she comes at the season of dances,
Or on the enchanted night
When the Spartans revel for Hyacinthus,[38]

Whom Apollo killed by chance with his discus-rim
In the game of throws;
For whose sake the son of Zeus
Appointed a holy day,
Slaughter of bulls and banqueting.
Perhaps she will see in the dancing ring
The child she left, long ago, at home—
Hermione, waiting still for the bridal torches' flame.

O for wings to tread the air [*Strophe* 2
Where the cranes in ordered flight
Shun the wintry rain-storm,
Seek their southern homeland;
Swift, obedient to their eldest leader's cry
Rising shrill, triumphant,
As they near the frontiers
Of this land, where rainless valleys teem with corn.

Turn, you long-necked travellers,
Who run winged races with the dancing clouds,
And while the Pleiads still are in mid-course
And Orion rides the darkened sky, swoop down,
Alight on Eurotas and proclaim your news
That the taker of Troy, Menelaus, is coming home.

[36]Perseus founded Mycenae, where Menelaus plans to land.
[37]Wives of Castor and Pollux.
[38]Hyacinthus was a youth whom Apollo loved but whom he accidentally killed while throwing the discus. The Spartans held an annual festival in his honor.

Speed along your airy path, [*Antistrophe* 2
Riding sons of Tyndareus,[39]
You whose home is heaven
And the stars' bright orbits!
Helen's brothers, Helen's rescuers, ride on,
Skim the green and foam-white ridges
On the dark face of the ocean,
Bring soft breath of welcome winds, the gift of Zeus.

Cleanse your sister's fame,
Slandered as paramour of a foreign prince.
Dearly she paid for that hot feud begun
When on Mount Ida goddesses came to trial;
Though never did Helen sail to the land of Troy
Or see the towers that Apollo built.[40]

Enter THEOCLYMENUS, *unannounced, from the palace; before he can speak, the* MESSENGER, *one of the attendants sent by* THEOCLYMENUS *to accompany the procession, arrives from the shore.*

MESSENGER. My lord! We know you were never one to harbor suspicion; and now listen to the terrible news I have to tell.

THEOCLYMENUS. What has happened?

MESSENGER. You must begin looking for another bride. Helen has gone—fled the country.

THEOCLYMENUS. Gone! Has she escaped on foot or taken wings?

MESSENGER. Menelaus has sailed clean away with her. It was Menelaus who came and told you the tale of his own death.

THEOCLYMENUS. Terrible news indeed; it is incredible! How could they get away by sea?

MESSENGER. In the ship you gave to that Greek. Briefly, he cleared your crew out, and sailed off with your ship.

THEOCLYMENUS. How? I want to know how! Was I to suppose he could overpower a whole crew single-handed? You were one of them!

MESSENGER. I will tell you all that took place after we left the palace. As soon as the daughter of Zeus reached the shore, with gestures and cries she made an accomplished pretense of mourning for her husband—who, so far from being dead, was there at her side. We entered the royal dock, and launched a Sidonian ship of the first line, with a full complement of fifty rowers. Everything was done in order: one man was setting the mast, another placing the oars, others knitting the line of them in a clean row, furling the white sails, dropping the rudders into position by the cords.

While we were busy, some Greek sailors, who had come with Menelaus and must have been watching for the right moment, came towards us on the shore. They were fine-looking men, but wild and unkempt and dressed in rags like castaways. As soon as Menelaus saw them, with a fine show of grief in his voice and face he spoke to them. "O you unlucky Greeks, what was your ship? How were you wrecked? We are going to pay funeral honors to Menelaus, son of Atreus; his body is lost, but this lady, his wife

[39]Helen's brothers, Caster and Pollux, who, as constellations, guide mariners.
[40]Apollo was said to have built the walls of Troy, with the assistance of Poseidon.

Helen, will perform the ceremonies. Will you come and join us?" So they, with pretended tears, and solemnly bringing their own sea-offerings, came on board. To us that seemed suspicious; and some of us remarked that they were too many for the ship. However, we kept your instructions and held our tongues; it was putting that Greek in command that caused the whole disaster.

Now most of the gear, being light, we hoisted on board easily enough; but the bull for sacrifice stuck in his heels and refused to set foot on the gangway. He bellowed, rolled his eyes, humped his back, looked down his horn and would not let anyone touch him. Then Helen's husband shouted, "Come on, you sackers of Troy, pick up that bull Greek-fashion! Get your shoulders under him and heave him on board; we'll offer him to the dead!" At the same time he drew his sword and held it high. The men came at his command, picked up the bull, carried him and set him down on deck. With the horse there was no trouble; Menelaus stroked his neck and forehead, and coaxed him on board.

At last, when everything was stowed, Helen set her lovely foot on the ship's ladder, and there she was, sitting near the stern, and Menelaus—the dead man—at her side. The rest of the Greeks were sitting along the gunwale, left and right, man for man, each with a sword hidden in his clothes; and the hull was full of our voices as we shouted the rowing-song.

When we were some way from shore—not too far, but well out—the helmsman called to Menelaus, "Tell us, are we to sail on further? You are in command; will this do?" Menelaus replied, "Far enough." Then he made his way, sword in hand, to the prow. And as he stood there to slaughter the bull, and as he cut its throat, instead of uttering any dead man's name, he prayed, "Poseidon, Lord of the sea, and you divine Nereids, bring my wife and me safe to the shores of Nauplia, home to a free land!" The blood streamed out in a long jet and fell into the sea—a good omen for the Greek. One of our men said, "There's treachery afoot; let's get back to shore. Make them pull on the right; put the helm over." Menelaus left the bull dead and stood and shouted to his men, "Now is the time! Make Hellas proud of you! Cut these Egyptians to pieces and throw them into the sea!" And our captain in reply shouted to your crew, "Up men, they are enemies! Get spars for weapons, smash benches, tear out rowlocks; at them and break their heads!"

Every man leapt to his feet. We had poles, they had swords; the ship was a welter of blood. We heard a voice from the stern cheering them on—it was Helen: "Show these Egyptians the way you fought at Troy!" she cried, and her eager voice whetted their spirits for the battle. Your men were falling, struggling to their feet again; some you could see lying still and dead. Menelaus, in full armor, wherever he saw his friends worsted, went to their help; his sword flashed among his enemies, and their bodies flew hurtling overboard, till he had cleared every one of your rowers from the ship. Then he went over to the steersman and told him to make course for Hellas. The Greeks hoisted sail, and the wind was in their favor.

So they have gone. I escaped being killed and lowered myself into the sea by the anchor. I was nearly exhausted when a fisherman picked me up and put me ashore to bring you the news.—Well, there is one thing every man has to learn: it is, not to be too trustful.

CHORUS. My lord, I could never have believed that Menelaus could come here, as he did, in person, without being recognized either by yourself or us.

THEOCLYMENUS. Oh! to be so miserably outwitted by a woman! That my chosen wife should slip from my hands! If there were any hope of overtaking them by ship, I would spare no effort to lay hands on them. As things are—it was my sister who betrayed me: she saw Menelaus in the palace and said nothing to me; then I will be revenged on her. She used her prophetic power to cheat me: it shall be the last time!

He turns to enter the palace; but the MESSENGER *has stepped between him and the palace door.*

MESSENGER. Now, my lord, where are you going? Do you mean to commit murder?

THEOCLYMENUS. Get out of my way. I am going to commit justice.

MESSENGER. It would be a terrible crime. I will not let you go.

THEOCLYMENUS. Am I to take orders from a slave?

MESSENGER. Yes, because I am right!

THEOCLYMENUS. You are doing me wrong, unless you let me go—

MESSENGER. I will not!

THEOCLYMENUS. My sister deserves death; she is a traitress.

MESSENGER. No, she is a woman who fears the gods; it was just and right to deceive you.

THEOCLYMENUS. She gave my wife to another man.

MESSENGER. She was his by right; her father gave her to Menelaus.

THEOCLYMENUS. Fortune gave her to me. Menelaus had no right to what was mine.

MESSENGER. Fate took her from you: it was to be.

THEOCLYMENUS. I can judge my own affairs.

MESSENGER. But I am a better judge than you.

THEOCLYMENUS. Who is king, you or I?

MESSENGER. It is for the king to do right, not wrong.

THEOCLYMENUS. You are in love with death, I think.

MESSENGER. Kill me! But you shall not kill your sister if I can prevent it. The noblest thing a slave can do is to die for his master.

The DIOSCORI *suddenly appear above the palace door.*[41]

DIOSCORI:

Control your sinful fury, Theoclymenus, King of Egypt!
We are the sons of Zeus and Leda, the Dioscori,
Brothers of this same Helen who has escaped from your palace.
Despite your rage, know that this marriage was not for you;
Theonoe your sister, the Nereid's daughter, did not wrong you,
But honored the will of Heaven and your father's just command.
Destiny ordained that Helen until this present day
Should live here in your palace; but now that Troy's strong walls
Are breached and blackened, no divine end is further served
By Helen's borrowed name; it is right that she once more
Be joined with her true husband and live in her own home.
Then sheathe that murderous sword drawn for your sister's blood;
Confess her wisdom. We, now raised by Zeus to godhead,

[41]Castor and Pollux, as "gods from the machine," either appear on the roof of the stage building or are swung in on a crane.

Would long ago have contrived to rescue her from your land,
But bowed to Fate, and the divine purpose thus fulfilled.

So much for you, Theoclymenus; next I speak to Helen:
Sail on with your true husband; fair winds shall speed you; and we
Your brothers, riding the waves, will escort you safely home.
And when your course is run, and your mortal term fulfilled,
You shall rise divine, and with us receive from the race of men
Worship and holy feasts; for such is the will of Zeus.
The island where Hermes first, running the sky from Sparta,
A thief with his spoil, your beauty, to cheat the ardent Paris—
Where Hermes hid his treasure, the straggling isle that lines
The Actaean coast, henceforth shall bear your name for
remembrance.
Menelaus the far-voyager wins by the will of Heaven
A home in the Isle of the Blest. For the noble and brave are not
Hated by the gods; but they meet more trouble than common men.

THEOCLYMENUS:
Sons of Leda and Zeus! I renounce my bitterness of heart
For my lost bride. Let her go to her home, since Heaven so wills.
Theonoe's life I spare. Immortal Twins, the sister
Your almighty Father gave you is perfect in faith and chastity.
Women, I wish you joy in the virtuous heart of Helen—
A joy which many women can have no hope to share!

CHORUS:
The gods reveal themselves in many forms,
Bring many matters to surprising ends.
The things we thought would happen do not happen;
The unexpected God makes possible:
And this is what has happened here today.[42]

Aristophanes

(c. 450–c. 386 B.C.)

Aristophanes was born around 450 B.C., and his death some time during the 380s marks the end of the great century of ancient Greek drama. The chronological sequence of the four preeminent playwrights—the tragedians Aeschylus, Sophocles, and Euripides and the comedian Aristophanes—coincides with two important trends in the theater. In aesthetic form, drama moved from the loftily stylized to the more realistic (as typified in the "New Comedy" of the fourth century, which stressed the individual actors and took away from the chorus its role in the action); in mood and attitude, there was a shift from idealistic optimism to disillusioned cynicism. These trends in the drama parallel trends in Athenian political, religious, and philosophical attitudes. In the epoch ending shortly before 400 B.C., Athens endured military,

[42]The stock ending of several of Euripides' plays. Compare *Medea*.

political, and cultural ordeals that culminated in the overthrow of Athenian democracy and independence. The period when Athens was the moral and political exemplar of what was best in ancient Greece was at an end.

Aristophanes is the only representative of the fifth-century "Old Comedy" whose works have survived. Since biographical information about him is scant, it is difficult to isolate what is distinctive in him from what is characteristic of the Old Comedy; the man and the movement are not clearly separable. If we are thinking about dramaturgy, neither can be called realistic, since the settings, costumes, and freewheeling plots of Aristophanes' plays are often fantastic to the point of surrealism. In *The Wasps* (a play about the Athenian judicial system; 422), in *The Frogs* (a literary satire pitting the deceased tragedians Aeschylus and Euripides against each other; 405), and in *The Birds* (a utopian fantasy-satire; 414), characters or chorus or both are costumed and portrayed grotesquely in the guise of the animals after which the plays are named.

Yet Aristophanes is a realist in his own way—in subject and theme, if not in theatrical style. His plays (of the forty he wrote, eleven have survived) repeatedly present unflattering portraits of actual people—people who may well have been in his audience—disguised thinly or not at all (they include Socrates, Euripides, and the Athenian political leader Cleon, whom Aristophanes despised). His favorite subjects were literary satire, particularly lampoons of Euripides and what Aristophanes chose to see as the other dramatist's hatred of women; intellectual satire of newfangled trends in education, philosophy, and moral values; and above all, political satire, directed mainly against the Athenian effort in the Peloponnesian War. Aristophanes consistently regarded the war as cruelty toward the enemies and allies of Athens and as suicidal folly from the vantage point of Athens itself. In fact, early in his career he was once prosecuted for disloyalty. He got off lightly and immediately resumed his role of political gadfly, which says something about Aristophanes and perhaps about Athenian political tolerance even in its days of militaristic jingoism. Spectators of Aristophanes' plays saw the world pictured not in the long vistas of myth and perennial archetypes about the human condition but in the context of what had happened yesterday and what was likely to happen tomorrow. For all his zany exuberance, Aristophanes was an intellectual, and one concerned intimately with current events.

Lysistrata (411) is one of his masterpieces. A witty specimen of antiwar propaganda, it includes also some of his typical wisecracks about tragedy, literature, and Euripides, though it does not demonstrate much if any of his concern with philosophical issues. The affection and respect Aristophanes felt for women as capable agents and as custodians of ultimate human sanity come across warmly and brilliantly. The same sympathy and admiration emerge in his plays *Thesmophoriazusae,* or *Ladies' Day* (411), in which women plot to avenge themselves on Euripides, and in *Ecclesiazusae,* or *Women in Parliament* (392).

Roman comedy, which established the model for subsequent comedy in Western theater, was modeled on the Greek New Comedy, a form that thrived after the accession of Alexander the Great, when Athens lost its political freedom. New Comedy abandoned the Aristophanic Old Comedy's freedom of structure and political comment in favor of comparatively realistic plots that usually turned around a young man's attempts to marry over his father's objections. But in many ways the spirit of comedy—laughter, irreverence, the celebration of sexuality, and a movement toward liberation from social and personal bonds—was already established in Old Comedy and was transmitted intact to New Comedy and thence to later dramatic history. In Aristophanes, as in comedy ever since, the action begins with a society constricted by authority, proceeds through a series of laughable irreverent events to dissolve that authority, and ends with a new, liberated society, reconstituted around the values of youth, vitality, and sexuality. Many of Aristophanes' plays end with a feast or a dance, forerunners of the boy-gets-girl celebrations of modern comedy. Sexuality triumphs, and as the modern critic Northrop Frye wittily puts it, "the plot usually moves toward an act which, like death in Greek tragedy, takes place offstage, and is symbolized by a closing embrace."

Lysistrata is not far removed from a fertility celebration, and its cheerful, innocent obscenity is basic to its meaning. Underlying its bawdy, topical jokes and its absurd, incredible plot is a serious confrontation of values. Aristophanes, like his epic and tragic predecessors, almost instinctively defines this confrontation along sexual lines. *Lysistrata* begins with a comic Athens in thrall to sterile, destructive "male" values, in pursuit of a war that Aristophanes regards as misguided and hopeless. "War's a man's affair," says Lysistrata; she is quoting Homer, but she gives the line an ironic twist very far from Homer's meaning. To the male thirst for glory and self-destructive competitiveness, Lysistrata opposes not only sexuality but also common sense and a respect for nonheroic ordinary life. In the most famous passage in the play, she compares the state to a ball of tangled yarn, which the housewife must untangle, wash, and weave together into a seamless unity. "It would take a woman," the Commissioner exclaims, "to reduce state questions to a matter of carding and weaving!"

Who "wins" in *Lysistrata?* Just as it is typically Greek to see the world as divided between "male" rationality and abstraction and "female" desire and vitality, so it is typically Greek to see the solution as a balance between the two forces. The women *do* stop the war (a bit of unhistorical wishful thinking on the part of Aristophanes), but the men's claims of honor are satisfied, too, in the peace negotiations. The real winner is "Reconciliation," a concept represented on stage by a statue under whose eyes the resolution is effected and given significance in the form of an enormous naked woman. We seem to be witnessing an earthy, comic echo of the sexual reconciliation and the hymn to Athens at the end of the *Oresteia* when Lysistrata says, "Each man be kind to his woman, and you, women, be equally kind," and the play ends with a joyous hymn to "Athena of the House of Brass."

FURTHER READING: On the festivals, staging and production of ancient comedy, see F. H. Sandbach, *The Comic Theatre of Greece and Rome,* 1977; Kenneth McLeish, *The Theatre of Aristophanes,* 1980; Leo Aylen, *The Greek Theater,* 1985 (with special attention to *The Frogs*); Katherine Lever, *The Art of Greek Comedy,* 1956; and C. W. Dearden, *The Stage of Aristophanes,* 1976. Useful general material on Aristophanes' life and writings may be found in K. J. Dover, *Aristophanic Comedy,* 1972; and Lois Spatz, *Aristophanes,* 1978. Victor Ehrenberg, *The People of Aristophanes: A Sociology of Old Attic Comedy,* 1943, 3rd ed. 1962, introduces the reader to the farmers, tradesmen, slaves, and family members of the late fifth century B.C. *Yale Classical Studies,* vol. XXVI (1980), is devoted to essays on the interpretation of Aristophanes. Gilbert Murray, in *Aristophanes: A Study,* 1933, in addition to presenting background material on Aristophanes and on comedy in general, devotes a chapter to *Lysistrata.*

LYSISTRATA

Translated by Dudley Fitts

The political and military background of the play is the Peloponnesian war, a series of conflicts between confederacies led by Athens and Sparta. The Peloponnese, of which Sparta was the capital, was a large peninsula that made up southern Greece. The period of the war, from 431 B.C. to 404, was a tragic era, especially for Athens, whose defeat in the latter year marked the end of its greatest political and cultural age. In 413, two years before *Lysistrata* was produced in Athens, the city's naval and military forces had suffered a calamitous defeat in connection with the ill-fated Sicilian expedition that Athenian patriots—or imperialists—had hoped would establish Athenian dominance of the Mediterranean. Through comedy that is sometimes caustic and sometimes good-humored, Aristophanes' play was intended to show the folly of both political power-lust and civil war among Greeks. As art, *Lysistrata* is a triumph; judged in the light of historical consequences, the play was a failure, since the war went on to its disastrous end.

Some of the jokes can be understood only if one keeps in mind that the usual costume in fifth-century Greek comedy included an exaggeratedly prominent leather phallus.

The characters' names are in many instances significant puns: for example, Lysistrata's name means "Dismisser of Armies" and "Myrrhine" puns on the word meaning female genitals. [*Editors' headnote.*]

PERSONS REPRESENTED

LYSISTRATA	COMMISSIONER
KALONIKE	KINESIAS
MYRRHINE	SPARTAN HERALD
LAMPITO	SPARTAN AMBASSADOR
CHORUS	A SENTRY

SCENE: *Athens. First, a public square; later, beneath the walls of the Akropolis; later, a courtyard within the Akropolis.*[1]

Until the *éxodos,* the CHORUS is divided into two hemichori: the first, of Old Men; the second, of Old Women. Each of these has its KORYPHAIOS. In the *éxodos,* the hemichori return as Athenians and Spartans.[2]

The supernumeraries include the BABY SON of Kinêsias; STRATYLLIS, a member of the hemichorus of Old Women; various individual speakers, both Spartan and Athenian.

[1]The hill upon which the main civic and religious centers of Athens were located.

[2]The *éxodus* is the last choral song of the play. The *koryphaios* is the principal spokesman for the chorus or, as here, for a division of it.

PROLOGUE

Athens; a public square; early morning; LYSISTRATA *sola.*

LYSISTRATA.
If someone had invited them to a festival—
of Bacchos, say; or to Pan's shrine, or to Aphroditê's
over at Kôlias[3]—, you couldn't get through the streets,
what with the drums and the dancing. But now,
not a woman in sight!
Except—oh, yes!

[*Enter* KALONIKE]

Here's one of my neighbors, at last. Good
morning, Kalonikê.

KALONIKE.
Good morning, Lysistrata.
Darling,
don't frown so! You'll ruin your face!

LYSISTRATA.
Never mind my face.
Kalonikê,
the way we women behave! Really, I don't blame the men 10
for what they say about us.

KALONIKE.
No; I imagine they're right.

LYSISTRATA.
For example: I call a meeting
to think out a most important matter—and what happens?
The women all stay in bed!

KALONIKE.
Oh, they'll be along.
It's hard to get away, you know: a husband, a cook,
a child . . . Home life can be *so* demanding!

LYSISTRATA.
What I have in mind is even more demanding.

KALONIKE.
Tell me: what is it?

LYSISTRATA.
It's big.

KALONIKE.
Goodness! *How* big?

LYSISTRATA.
Big enough for all of us.

KALONIKE.
But we're not all here!

LYSISTRATA.
We would be, if *that's* what was up!

[3]An area of the Greek coast where Aphroditê, goddess of love, had a temple.

No, Kalonikê, 20
this is something I've been turning over for nights,
long sleepless nights.

KALONIKE.

It must be getting worn down, then,
if you've spent so much time on it.

LYSISTRATA.

Worn down or not,
it comes to this: Only we women can save Greece!

KALONIKE.

Only we women? Poor Greece!

LYSISTRATA.

Just the same,
it's up to us. First, we must liquidate
the Peloponnesians—

KALONIKE.

Fun, fun!

LYSISTRATA.

—and then the Boiotians.[4]

KALONIKE.

Oh! But not those heavenly eels!

LYSISTRATA.

You needn't worry.
I'm not talking about eels.—But here's the point:
If we can get the women from those places— 30
all those Boiotians and Peloponnesians—
to join us women here, why, we can save
all Greece!

KALONIKE.

But dearest Lysistrata!
How can women do a thing so austere, so
political? We belong at home. Our only armor's
our perfumes, our saffron dresses and
our pretty little shoes!

LYSISTRATA.

Exactly. Those
transparent dresses, the saffron, the
perfume, those pretty shoes—

KALONIKE.

Oh?

LYSISTRATA.

Not a single man would lift
his spear—

KALONIKE.

I'll send my dress to the dyer's tomorrow! 40

LYSISTRATA.

—or grab a shield—

[4]Inhabitants of a region opposed to Athens in the war. The area was noted for its succulent eels and other seafood. Athenian sophisticates regarded Boiotia as a crude and backward place.

KALONIKE.
The sweetest little negligée—
LYSISTRATA.
—or haul out his sword.
KALONIKE.
I know where I can buy
the dreamiest sandals!
LYSISTRATA.
Well, so you see. Now, shouldn't
the women have come?
KALONIKE.
Come? They should have *flown!*
LYSISTRATA.
Athenians are always late.
But imagine!
There's no one here from the South Shore, or from Sálamis.[5]
KALONIKE.
Things are hard over in Sálamis, I swear.
They have to get going at dawn.
LYSISTRATA.
And nobody from Acharnai.[6]
I thought they'd be here hours ago.
KALONIKE.
Well, you'll get
that awful Theagenês woman;[7] she'll be 50
a sheet or so in the wind.
But look!
Someone at last! Can you see who they are?

[*Enter* MYRRHINE *and other women*]

LYSISTRATA.
They're from Anagyros.[8]
KALONIKE.
They certainly are.
You'd know them anywhere, by the scent.
MYRRHINE.
Sorry to be late, Lysistrata.
Oh come,
don't scowl so. Say something!
LYSISTRATA.
My dear Myrrhinê,
what is there to say? After all,
you've been pretty casual about the whole thing.

[5]An island south of Greece, site of the memorable Greek naval victory over the Persians in 480. Lysistrata (whose name means "dismisser of armies") intends to gather women from Greek cities, both allied with and opposed to Athens.
[6]A town near Athens.
[7]The wife of Theagenês, a notoriously superstitious man. The phrase "a sheet or so in the wind" means drunk.
[8]A malodorous marshland.

MYRRHINE.

Couldn't find
my girdle in the dark, that's all.
But what *is*
'the whole thing'?

KALONIKE.

No, we've got to wait 60
for those Boiotians and Peloponnesians.

LYSISTRATA.

That's more like it.—But, look!
Here's Lampitô!

[*Enter* LAMPITO *with women from Sparta*]

LYSISTRATA.

Darling Lampitô,
how pretty you are today! What a nice color!
Goodness, you look as though you could strangle a bull!

LAMPITO.

Ah think Ah could! It's the work-out
in the gym every day; and, of co'se that dance of ahs
where y' kick yo' own tail.[9]

KALONIKE.

What an adorable figure!

LAMPITO.

Lawdy, when y' touch me lahk that,
Ah feel lahk a heifer at the altar!

LYSISTRATA.

And this young lady? 70
Where is she from?

LAMPITO.

Boiotia. Social-Register type.

LYSISTRATA.

Ah. 'Boiotia of the fertile plain.'

KALONIKE.

And if you look,
you'll find the fertile plain has just been mowed.

LYSISTRATA.

And this lady?

LAMPITO.

Hagh, wahd, handsome. She comes from Korinth.

KALONIKE.

High and wide's the word for it.

LAMPITO.

Which one of you
called this heah meeting, and why?

[9] The Spartans were proverbially associated with discipline and the more austere virtues. Lampito here refers to a strenuous dance performed as exercise by Spartan females. The translator renders Spartan speech as backwoods southern American because the Athenians condescendingly viewed Spartans as unsophisticated.

LYSISTRATA.
I did.

LAMPITO.
Well, then, tell us:

What's up?

MYRRHINE.
Yes, darling, what *is* on your mind, after all?

LYSISTRATA.
I'll tell you.—But first, one little question.

MYRRHINE.
Well?

LYSISTRATA.
It's your husbands. Fathers of your children. Doesn't it bother you
that they're always off with the Army? I'll stake my life, 80
not one of you has a man in the house this minute!

KALONIKE.
Mine's been in Thrace the last five months, keeping an eye
on that General.[10]

MYRRHINE.
Mine's been in Pylos for seven.

LAMPITO.
And mahn,

whenever he gets a *dis*charge, he goes raht back
with that li'l ole shield of his, and enlists again!

LYSISTRATA.
And not the ghost of a lover to be found!
From the very day the war began—
those Milesians![11]

I could skin them alive!
—I've not seen so much, even,
as one of those leather consolation prizes.—
But there! What's important is: If I've found a way 90
to end the war, are you with me?

MYRRHINE.
I should *say* so!

Even if I have to pawn my best dress and
drink up the proceeds.

KALONIKE.
Me, too! Even if they split me

right up the middle, like a flounder.

LAMPITO.
Ah'm shorely with you.

Ah'd crawl up Taÿgetos[12] on mah knees
if that'd bring peace.

[10]Eukrates, an Athenian commander of doubtful loyalty.

[11]Former allies of Athens who had defected shortly before *Lysistrata* was produced. The Milesians reputedly manufactured a kind of dildo, or phallic substitute.

[12]A mountain range near Sparta.

LYSISTRATA.
All right, then; here it is:
Women! Sisters!
If we really want our men to make peace,
we must be ready to give up—

MYRRHINE.
Give up what!
Quick, tell us!

LYSISTRATA.
But *will* you?

MYRRHINE.
We will, even if it kills us. 100

LYSISTRATA.
Then we must give up going to bed with our men.

[*Long silence*]

Oh? So now you're sorry? Won't look at me?
Doubtful? Pale? All teary-eyed?
But come: be frank with me.
Will you do it, or not? Well? Will you do it?

MYRRHINE.
I couldn't. No.
Let the war go on.

KALONIKE.
Nor I. Let the war go on.

LYSISTRATA.
You, you little flounder,
ready to be split up the middle?

KALONIKE.
Lysistrata, no!
I'd walk through fire for you—you *know* I would!—but don't
ask us to give up *that!* Why, there's nothing like it!

LYSISTRATA.
And you?

BOIOTIAN.
No. I must say *I'd* rather walk through fire. 110

LYSISTRATA.
What an utterly perverted sex we women are!
No wonder poets write tragedies about us.
There's only one thing we can think of.
But you from Sparta:
if you stand by me, we may win yet! Will you?
It means so much!

LAMPITO.
Ah sweah, it means *too* much!
By the Two Goddesses,[13] it does! Asking a girl
to sleep—Heaven knows how long!—in a great big bed

[13] Demeter, goddess of the fields and fertility, and her daughter Persephone, who was associated with both death and fertility.

with nobody there but herself! But Ah'll stay with you!
Peace comes first!

LYSISTRATA.
Spoken like a true Spartan!

KALONIKE.
But if—
oh dear!
—if we give up what you tell us to, 120
will there *be* any peace?

LYSISTRATA.
Why, mercy, of course there will!
We'll just sit snug in our very thinnest gowns,
perfumed and powdered from top to bottom, and those men
simply won't stand still! And when we say No,
they'll go out of their minds! And there's your peace.
You can take my word for it.

LAMPITO.
Ah seem to remember
that Colonel Menelaos threw his sword away
when he saw Helen's breast[14] all bare.

KALONIKE.
But, goodness me!
What if they just get up and leave us?

LYSISTRATA.
In that case
we'll have to fall back on ourselves, I suppose. 130
But they won't.

KALONIKE.
I must say that's not much help. But
what if they drag us into the bedroom?

LYSISTRATA.
Hang on to the door.

KALONIKE.
What if they slap us?

LYSISTRATA.
If they do, you'd better give in.
But be sulky about it. Do I have to teach you how?
You know there's no fun for men when they have to force you.
There are millions of ways of getting them to see reason.
Don't you worry: a man
doesn't like it unless the girl co-operates.

KALONIKE.
I suppose so. Oh, all right. We'll go along.

LAMPITO.
Ah imagine us Spahtans can arrange a peace. But you 140
Athenians! Why, you're just war-mongerers!

[14] The reference is to Euripides' play *Andromache;* Menelaos (Menelaus), the cuckolded husband of Helen of Troy, is so struck with Helen's beauty that he abandons his plan to kill her in revenge.

LYSISTRATA.

Leave that to me.

I know how to make them listen.

LAMPITO.

Ah don't see how.

After all, they've got their boats; and there's lots of money[15]

piled up in the Akropolis.

LYSISTRATA.

The Akropolis? Darling,

we're taking over the Akropolis today!

That's the older women's job. All the rest of us

are going to the Citadel to sacrifice—you understand me?

And once there, we're in for good!

LAMPITO.

Whee! Up the rebels!

Ah can see you're a good strat*ee*gist.

LYSISTRATA.

Well, then, Lampitô,

what we have to do now is take a solemn oath.[16] 150

LAMPITO.

Say it. We'll sweah.

LYSISTRATA.

This is it.

—But where's our Inner Guard?

—Look, Guard: you see this shield?

Put it down here. Now bring me the victim's entrails.

KALONIKE.

But the oath?

LYSISTRATA.

You remember how in Aischylos' *Seven*

they killed a sheep and swore on a shield? Well, then?

KALONIKE.

But I don't see how you can swear for peace on a shield.

LYSISTRATA.

What else do you suggest?

KALONIKE.

Why not a white horse?[17]

We could swear by that.

LYSISTRATA.

And where will you get a white horse?

KALONIKE.

I never thought of that. *What* can we do?

[15]A fund stored on the Akropolis, designed to finance the war effort.

[16]What follows is a parody of a standard ritual sacrifice and oath of loyalty.

[17]In Aeschylus' tragedy *Seven Against Thebes,* the seven leaders attacking the city take an oath on a shield. (This war provides the background of Sophocles' *Antigone.*) The reference to the white horse is possibly some kind of sexual joke, but commentators are puzzled by the phrase.

LYSISTRATA.

I have it!

Let's set this big black wine-bowl on the ground 160
and pour in a gallon or so of Thasian,[18] and swear
not to add one drop of water.

LAMPITO.

Ah lahk *that* oath!

LYSISTRATA.

Bring the bowl and the wine-jug.

KALONIKE.

Oh, what a simply *huge* one!

LYSISTRATA.

Set it down. Girls, place your hands on the gift-offering.
O Goddess of Persuasion! And thou, O Loving-cup
Look upon this our sacrifice, and
be gracious!

KALONIKE.

See the blood spill out. How red and pretty it is!

LAMPITO.

And Ah must say it smells good.

MYRRHINE.

Let me swear first!

KALONIKE.

No, by Aphroditê, we'll match for it! 170

LYSISTRATA.

Lampitô: all of you women: come, touch the bowl,
and repeat after me—remember, this is an oath—:
I WILL HAVE NOTHING TO DO WITH MY HUSBAND OR MY LOVER

KALONIKE.

I will have nothing to do with my husband or my lover

LYSISTRATA.

THOUGH HE COME TO ME IN PITIABLE CONDITION

KALONIKE.

Though he come to me in pitiable condition
(Oh Lysistrata! This is killing me!)

LYSISTRATA.

IN MY HOUSE I WILL BE UNTOUCHABLE

KALONIKE.

In my house I will be untouchable

LYSISTRATA.

IN MY THINNEST SAFFRON SILK 180

KALONIKE.

In my thinnest saffron silk

LYSISTRATA.

AND MAKE HIM LONG FOR ME.

KALONIKE.

And make him long for me.

[18]A wine of high quality.

LYSISTRATA.
I WILL NOT GIVE MYSELF
KALONIKE.
I will not give myself
LYSISTRATA.
AND IF HE CONSTRAINS ME
KALONIKE.
And if he constrains me
LYSISTRATA.
I WILL BE COLD AS ICE AND NEVER MOVE
KALONIKE.
I will be cold as ice and never move
LYSISTRATA.
I WILL NOT LIFT MY SLIPPERS TOWARD THE CEILING 190
KALONIKE.
I will not lift my slippers toward the ceiling
LYSISTRATA.
OR CROUCH ON ALL FOURS LIKE THE LIONESS IN THE CARVING
KALONIKE.
Or crouch on all fours like the lioness in the carving
LYSISTRATA.
AND IF I KEEP THIS OATH LET ME DRINK FROM THIS BOWL
KALONIKE.
And if I keep this oath let me drink from this bowl
LYSISTRATA.
IF NOT, LET MY OWN BOWL BE FILLED WITH WATER.
KALONIKE.
If not, let my own bowl be filled with water.
LYSISTRATA.
You have all sworn?
MYRRHINE.
We have.
LYSISTRATA.
Then thus
I sacrifice the victim.

[*Drinks largely*]

KALONIKE.
Save some for us!
Here's to you, darling, and to you, and to you! 200

[*Loud cries off-stage*]

LAMPITO.
What's all *that* whoozy-goozy?
LYSISTRATA.
Just what I told you.
The older women have taken the Akropolis.

Now you, Lampitô,
rush back to Sparta. We'll take care of things here. Leave
these girls here for hostages.
The rest of you,
up to the Citadel: and mind you push in the bolts.

KALONIKE.
But the men? Won't they be after us?

LYSISTRATA.
Just you leave
the men to me. There's not fire enough in the world,
or threats either, to make me open these doors
except on my own terms.

KALONIKE.
I hope not, by Aphroditê! 210
After all,
we've got a reputation for bitchiness to live up to.

[*Exeunt*]

PÁRODOS:[19] CHORAL EPISODE

The hillside just under the Akropolis. Enter CHORUS OF OLD MEN *with burning torches and braziers; much puffing and coughing.*

KORYPHAIOS^{m}.
Forward march, Drakês, old friend: never you mind
that damn big log banging hell down on your back.

CHORUS^{m}.
There's this to be said for longevity: [STROPHE 1]
You see things you thought that you'd never see.
Look, Strymodôros, who would have thought it?
We've caught it—
the New Femininity!
The wives of our bosom, our board, our bed—
Now, by the gods, they've gone ahead 220
And taken the Citadel (Heaven knows why!),
Profanèd the sacred statuary,[20]
And barred the doors,
The subversive whores!

KORYPHAIOS^{m}.
Shake a leg there, Philûrgos, man: the Akropolis or bust!
Put the kindling around here. We'll build one almighty big
bonfire for the whole bunch of bitches, every last one;
and the first we fry will be old Lykôn's woman.[21]

[19] The song sung at the first entrance of the chorus. The superscripts *m* and *w* indicate division of the chorus into men and women.

[20] An old and revered wooden statue of Athêna in her role as protector of Athens.

[21] A woman noted for lax morality; here, as often elsewhere, Aristophanes refers to actual people of his time.

CHORUS[m].

[ANTISTROPHE 1]

They're not going to give me the old horse-laugh!
No, by Deméter, they won't pull this off! 230
Think of Kleómenés:[22] even he
Didn't go free
till he brought me his stuff.
A good man he was, all stinking and shaggy,
Bare as an eel except for the bag he
Covered his rear with. God, what a mess!
Never a bath in six years, I'd guess.
Pure Sparta, man!
He also ran.

KORYPHAIOS[m].

That was a siege, friends! Seventeen ranks strong
we slept at the Gate. And shall we not do as much 240
against these women, whom God and Euripides[23] hate?
If we don't, I'll turn in my medals from Marathon.

CHORUS[m].

[STROPHE 2]

Onward and upward! A little push,
And we're there.
Ouch, my shoulders! I could wish
For a pair
Of good strong oxen. Keep your eye
On the fire there, it mustn't die.
Akh! Akh!
The smoke would make a cadaver cough! 250

Holy Heraklês, a hot spark [ANTISTROPHE 2]
Bit my eye!
Damn this hellfire, damn this work!
So say I.
Onward and upward just the same.
(Lachês, remember the Goddess: for shame!)
Akh! Akh!
The smoke would make a cadaver cough!

KORYPHAIOS[m].

At last (and let us give suitable thanks to God
for his infinite mercies) I have managed to bring 260
my personal flame to the common goal. It breathes, it lives.
Now, gentlemen, let us consider. Shall we insert
the torch, say, into the brazier, and thus extract
a kindling brand? And shall we then, do you think,

[22]A Spartan king who, in 508, had occupied the Akropolis in aid of the aristocratic party during a civil conflict in Athens. His occupation was brief, not the six years the senile chorus remembers. The reference to this incident, like the following reminiscence of the great victory at Marathon (490), would make the members of the chorus a hundred or more years old—probably a joke by Aristophanes, designed to emphasize the old men's decrepitude.
[23]Often represented by Aristophanes, perhaps only half-seriously, as a misogynist.

push on to the gate like valiant sheep? On the whole, yes.
But I would have you consider this, too: if they—
I refer to the women—should refuse to open,
what then? Do we set the doors afire
and smoke them out? At ease, men. Meditate.
Akh, the smoke! Woof! What we really need 270
is the loan of a general or two from the Samos[24] Command.
At least we've got this lumber off our backs.
That's something. And now let's look to our fire.

O Pot, brave Brazier, touch my torch with flame!
Victory, Goddess, I invoke thy name!
Strike down these paradigms of female pride,
And we shall hang our trophies up inside.

[*Enter* CHORUS OF OLD WOMEN *on the walls of the Akropolis, carrying jars of water*]

KORYPHAIOS[W].
Smoke, girls, smoke! There's smoke all over the place!
Probably fire, too. Hurry, girls! Fire! Fire!

CHORUS[W].
Nikodikê, run! [STROPHE 1] 280
Or Kalyké's done
To a turn, and poor Kritylla's
Smoked like a ham.
Damn
These old men! Are we too late?
I nearly died down at the place
Where we fill our jars:
Slaves pushing and jostling—
Such a hustling
I never saw in all my days.

But here's water at last. [ANTISTROPHE 1] 290
Haste, sisters, haste!
Slosh it on them, slosh it down,
The silly old wrecks!
Sex
Almighty! What they want's
A hot bath? Good. Send one down.
Athêna of Athens town,
Trito-born![25] Helm of Gold!
Cripple the old
Firemen! Help us help them drown!

[24]An island near Asia Minor. At the time of the play it was the headquarters of Athenian forces.
[25]Athêna, by one account, was born near Tritonis, a lake in Libya.

[*The* OLD MEN *capture a woman,* STRATYLLIS]

STRATYLLIS.
Let me go! Let me go!

KORYPHAIOS^W^.
You walking corpses, 300
have you no shame?

KORYPHAIOS^m^.
I wouldn't have believed it!
An army of women in the Akropolis!

KORYPHAIOS^W^.
So we scare you, do we? Grandpa, you've seen
only our pickets yet!

KORYPHAIOS^m^.
Hey, Phaidrias!
Help me with the necks of these jabbering hens!

KORYPHAIOS^W^.
Down with your pots, girls! We'll need both hands
if these antiques attack us.

KORYPHAIOS^m^.
Want your face kicked in?

KORYPHAIOS^W^.
Want your balls chewed off?

KORYPHAIOS^m^.
Look out! I've got a stick!

KORYPHAIOS^W^.
You lay a half-inch of your stick on Stratyllis,
and you'll never stick again! 310

KORYPHAIOS^m^.
Fall apart!

KORYPHAIOS^W^.
I'll spit up your guts!

KORYPHAIOS^m^.
Euripides! Master!
How well you knew women!

KORYPHAIOS^W^.
Listen to him! Rhodippê,
up with the pots!

KORYPHAIOS^m^.
Demolition of God,
what good are your pots?

KORYPHAIOS^W^.
You refugee from the tomb,
what good is your fire?

KORYPHAIOS^m^.
Good enough to make a pyre
to barbecue you!

KORYPHAIOS^W^.
We'll squizzle your kindling!

KORYPHAIOS^{m}.
You think so?
KORYPHAIOS^{w}.
Yah! Just hang around a while!
KORYPHAIOS^{m}.
Want a touch of my torch?
KORYPHAIOS^{w}.
It needs a good soaping.
KORYPHAIOS^{m}.
How about you?
KORYPHAIOS^{w}.
Soap for a senile bridegroom!
KORYPHAIOS^{m}.
Senile? Hold your trap!
KORYPHAIOS^{w}.
Just *you* try to hold it! 320
KORYPHAIOS^{m}.
The yammer of women!
KORYPHAIOS^{w}.
Oh is that so?
You're not in the jury room[26] now, you know.
KORYPHAIOS^{m}.
Gentlemen, I beg you, burn off that woman's hair!
KORYPHAIOS^{w}.
Let it come down!

[*They empty their pots on the men*]

KORYPHAIOS^{m}.
What a way to drown!
KORYPHAIOS^{w}.
Hot, hey?
KORYPHAIOS^{m}.
Say,
enough!
KORYPHAIOS^{w}.
Dandruff
needs watering. I'll make you
nice and fresh.
KORYPHAIOS^{m}.
For God's sake, you,
hold off!

[26]Elderly Athenians frequently served as jurors in law cases.

SCENE I

[*Enter a* COMMISSIONER[27] *accompanied by four constables*]

COMMISSIONER.
These degenerate women! What a racket of little drums, 330
what a yapping for Adonis on every house-top!
It's like the time in the Assembly when I was listening
to a speech—out of order, as usual—by that fool
Demostratos,[28] all about troops for Sicily,
that kind of nonsense—
and there was his wife
trotting around in circles howling
Alas for Adonis!—
and Demostratos insisting
we must draft every last Zakynthian[29] that can walk—
and his wife up there on the roof,
drunk as an owl, yowling 340
Oh weep for Adonis!—
and that damned ox Demostratos
mooing away through the rumpus. That's what we get
for putting up with this wretched woman-business!

KORYPHAIOS[m].
Sir, you haven't heard the half of it. They laughed at us!
Insulted us! They took pitchers of water
and nearly drowned us! We're still wringing out our clothes,
for all the world like unhousebroken brats.

COMMISSIONER.
Serves you right, by Poseidon![30]
Whose fault is it if these women-folk of ours
get out of hand? We coddle them, 350
we teach them to be wasteful and loose. You'll see a husband
go into a jeweler's. 'Look,' he'll say,
'jeweler,' he'll say, 'you remember that gold choker
'you made for my wife? Well, she went to a dance last night
'and broke the clasp. Now, I've got to go to Sálamis,
'and can't be bothered. Run over to my house tonight,
'will you, and see if you can put it together for her.'
Or another one
goes to a cobbler—a good strong workman, too,
with an awl that was never meant for child's play. 'Here,' 360

[27]One of a group of men appointed to oversee the Athenian legislature after the defeat in Sicily.

[28]One of the most aggressive supporters of the recent disastrous campaign in Sicily. At the time the expedition set forth, the women were celebrating the rituals of Adonis, a god who represented the death-and-resurrection cycle in nature. The women's ritual laments for his death were interpreted as having put a hex on the military expedition.

[29]Dwellers on the island of Zakynthos; they were allies of Athens who, it had been hoped, would strengthen the Athenian forces in the Sicilian campaign.

[30]God of water and ocean.

he'll tell him, 'one of my wife's shoes is pinching
'her little toe. Could you come up about noon
'and stretch it out for her?'

Well, what do you expect?
Look at me, for example. I'm a Public Officer,
and it's one of my duties to pay off the sailors.
And where's the money? Up there in the Akropolis!
And those blasted women slam the door in my face!
But what are we waiting for?

—Look here, constable,
stop sniffing around for a tavern, and get us
some crowbars. We'll force their gates! As a matter of fact, 370
I'll do a little forcing myself.

[*Enter* LYSISTRATA, *above, with* MYRRHINE, KALONIKE, *and the* BOIOTIAN]

LYSISTRATA.

No need of forcing.
Here I am, of my own accord. And all this talk
about locked doors—! We don't need locked doors,
but just the least bit of common sense.

COMMISSIONER.

Is that so, ma'am!

—Where's my constable?

—Constable,
arrest that woman, and tie her hands behind her.

LYSISTRATA.

If he touches me, I swear by Artemis[31]
there'll be one scamp dropped from the public pay-roll tomorrow!

COMMISSIONER.

Well, constable? You're not afraid, I suppose? Grab her,
two of you, around the middle!

KALONIKE.

No, by Pándrosos![32] 380
Lay a hand on her, and I'll jump on you so hard
your guts will come out the back door!

COMMISSIONER.

That's what *you* think!
Where's the sergeant?—Here, you: tie up that trollop first,
the one with the pretty talk!

MYRRHINE.

By the Moon-Goddess,
just try! They'll have to scoop you up with a spoon!

[31] The virgin goddess of the hunt, the moon, and childbirth. In the following lines, she is referred to as "the Moon-Goddess" and "the Taurian."

[32] Daughter of a legendary ruler of Athens.

COMMISSIONER.
Another one!
Officer, seize that woman!
I swear
I'll put an end to this riot!
BOIOTIAN.
By the Taurian,
one inch closer, you'll be one screaming bald-head!
COMMISSIONER.
Lord, what a mess! And my constables seem ineffective.
But—women get the best of us? By God, no!
—Skythians![33] 390
Close ranks and forward march!
LYSISTRATA.
'Forward,' indeed!
By the Two Goddesses, what's the sense in *that?*
They're up against four companies of women
armed from top to bottom.
COMMISSIONER.
Forward, my Skythians!
LYSISTRATA.
Forward, yourselves, dear comrades!
You grainlettucebeanseedmarket girls!
You garlicandonionbreadbakery girls!
Give it to 'em! Knock 'em down! Scratch 'em!
Tell 'em what you think of 'em!

[*General mêlée; the Skythians yield*]

—Ah, that's enough!
Sound a retreat: good soldiers don't rob the dead. 400
COMMISSIONER.
A nice day *this* has been for the police!
LYSISTRATA.
Well, there you are.—Did you really think we women
would be driven like slaves? Maybe now you'll admit
that a woman knows something about spirit.
COMMISSIONER.
Spirit enough,
especially spirits in bottles! Dear Lord Apollo!
KORYPHAIOS^{m}.
Your Honor, there's no use talking to them. Words
mean nothing whatever to wild animals like these.
Think of the sousing they gave us! and the water
was not, I believe, of the purest.
KORYPHAIOS^{w}.
You shouldn't have come after us. And if you try it again, 410
you'll be one eye short!—Although, as a matter of fact,

[33]Archers from the north who made up much of the Athenian police force.

what I like best is just to stay at home and read,
like a sweet little bride: never hurting a soul, no,
never going out. But if you *must* shake hornets' nests,
look out for the hornets.

CHORUS[m].

Of all the beasts that God hath wrought [STROPHE 1]
What monster's worse than woman?
Who shall encompass with his thought
Their guile unending? No man.

They've seized the Heights, the Rock, the Shrine— 420
But to what end? I wot not.
Sure there's some clue to their design!
Have you the key? I thought not.

KORYPHAIOS[m].

We might question them, I suppose. But I warn you, sir,
don't believe anything you hear! It would be un-Athenian
not to get to the bottom of this plot.

COMMISSIONER.

Very well.
My first question is this: Why, so help you God,
did you bar the gates of the Akropolis?

LYSISTRATA.

Why?
To keep the money, of course. No money, no war.

COMMISSIONER.

You think that money's the cause of war?

LYSISTRATA.

I do. 430
Money brought about that Peisandros[34] business
and all the other attacks on the State. Well and good!
They'll not get another cent here!

COMMISSIONER.

And what will you do?

LYSISTRATA.

What a question! From now on, we intend
to control the Treasury.

COMMISSIONER.

Control the Treasury!

LYSISTRATA.

Why not? Does that seem strange? After all,
we control our household budgets.

COMMISSIONER.

But that's different!

LYSISTRATA.

'Different'? What do you mean?

[34]A corrupt and venal Athenian politician who plotted to overthrow the city's democratic regime.

COMMISSIONER.
I mean simply this:
it's the Treasury that pays for National Defense.
LYSISTRATA.
Unnecessary. We propose to abolish war. 440
COMMISSIONER.
Good God.—And National Security?
LYSISTRATA.
Leave that to us.
COMMISSIONER.
You?
LYSISTRATA.
Us.
COMMISSIONER.
We're done for, then!
LYSISTRATA.
Never mind.
We women will save you in spite of yourselves.
COMMISSIONER.
What nonsense!
LYSISTRATA.
If you like. But you must accept it, like it or not.
COMMISSIONER.
Why, this is downright subversion!
LYSISTRATA.
Maybe it is.
But we're going to save you, Judge.
COMMISSIONER.
I don't *want* to be saved.
LYSISTRATA.
Tut. The death-wish. All the more reason.
COMMISSIONER.
But the idea
of women bothering themselves about peace and war!
LYSISTRATA.
Will you listen to me?
COMMISSIONER.
Yes. But be brief, or I'll—
LYSISTRATA.
This is no time for stupid threats.
COMMISSIONER.
By the gods, 450
I can't stand any more!
AN OLD WOMAN.
Can't stand? Well, well.
COMMISSIONER.
That's enough out of you, you old buzzard!
Now, Lysistrata: tell me what you're thinking.
LYSISTRATA.
Glad to.
Ever since this war began

We women have been watching you men, agreeing with you,
keeping our thoughts to ourselves. That doesn't mean
we were happy: we *weren't,* for we saw how things were going;
but we'd listen to you at dinner
arguing this way and that.
—Oh you, and your big
Top Secrets!—
And then we'd grin like little patriots 460
(though goodness knows we didn't feel like grinning) and ask you:
'Dear, did the Armistice come up in Assembly today?'
And you'd say, 'None of your business! Pipe down!' you'd say.
And so we would.

AN OLD WOMAN.
I wouldn't have by God!

COMMISSIONER.
You'd have taken a beating, then!
—Go on.

LYSISTRATA.
Well, we'd be quiet. But then, you know, all at once
you men would think up something worse than ever.
Even *I* could see it was fatal. And, 'Darling,' I'd say,
'have you gone completely mad?' And my husband would look at me
and say, 'Wife, you've got your weaving to attend to. 470
'Mind your tongue, if you don't want a slap. "War's
"a man's affair"!'[35]

COMMISSIONER.
Good words, and well pronounced.

LYSISTRATA.
You're a fool if you think so.
It was hard enough
to put up with all this banquet-hall strategy.
But then we'd hear you out in the public square:
'Nobody left for the draft-quota here in Athens?'
you'd say; and, 'No,' someone else would say, 'not a man!'
And so we women decided to rescue Greece.
You might as well listen to us now: you'll have to, later.

COMMISSIONER.
You rescue Greece? Absurd.

LYSISTRATA.
You're the absurd one. 480

COMMISSIONER.
You expect me to take orders from a woman?
I'd die first!

[35]Hector addresses these last four words to his wife, Andromache, in Homer's *Iliad,* Book VI.

LYSISTRATA.
Heavens, if that's what's bothering you, take my veil,
here, and wrap it around your poor head.

KALONIKE.
Yes,
and you can have my market-basket, too.
Go home, tighten your girdle, do the washing, mind
your beans! 'War's
a woman's affair'!

KORYPHAIOS^W.
Ground pitchers! Close ranks!

CHORUS^W.
[ANTISTROPHE]

This is a dance that I know well.
My knees shall never yield.
Wobble and creak I may, but still 490
I'll keep the well-fought field.

Valor and grace march on before,
Love prods us from behind.
Our slogan is EXCELSIOR.[36]
Our watchword SAVE MANKIND.

KORYPHAIOS^W.
Women, remember your grandmothers! Remember
that little old mother of yours, what a stinger she was!
On, on, never slacken. There's a strong wind astern!

LYSISTRATA.
O Erôs of delight! O Aphroditê! Kyprian![37]
If ever desire has drenched our breasts or dreamed 500
in our thighs, let it work so now on the men of Hellas
that they shall tail us through the land, slaves, slaves
to Woman, Breaker of Armies!

COMMISSIONER.
And if we do?

LYSISTRATA.
Well, for one thing, we shan't have to watch you
going to market, a spear in one hand, and heaven knows
what in the other.

KALONIKE.
Nicely said, by Aphroditê!

LYSISTRATA.
As things stand now, you're neither men nor women.
Armor clanking with kitchen pans and pots—
you sound like a pack of Korybantês![38]

COMMISSIONER.
A man must do what a man must do.

[36]A Latin motto meaning, roughly, "On to nobler things," or, literally, "higher."
[37]Erôs, Aphroditê, and Kyprian are names for the god and goddess of love.
[38]Devotees of the earth goddess Cybele, whose rites included frenzied dancing and music.

LYSISTRATA.

So I'm told. 510

But to see a General, complete with Gorgon-shield,[39]
jingling along the dock to buy a couple of herrings!

KALONIKE.

I saw a Captain the other day—lovely fellow he was,
nice curly hair—sitting on his horse; and—can you believe it?—
he'd just bought some soup, and was pouring it into his helmet!
And there was a soldier from Thrace
swishing his lance like something out of Euripides,
and the poor fruit-store woman got so scared
that she ran away and let him have his figs free!

COMMISSIONER.

All this is beside the point.
Will you be so kind 520
as to tell me how you mean to save Greece?

LYSISTRATA.

Of course.

Nothing could be simpler.

COMMISSIONER.

I assure you, I'm all ears.

LYSISTRATA.

Do you know anything about weaving?
Say the yarn gets tangled: we thread it
this way and that through the skein, up and down,
until it's free. And it's like that with war.
We'll send our envoys
up and down, this way and that, all over Greece,
until it's finished.

COMMISSIONER.

Yarn? Thread? Skein?
Are you out of your mind? I tell you, 530
war is a serious business.

LYSISTRATA.

So serious
that I'd like to go on talking about weaving.

COMMISSIONER.

All right. Go ahead.

LYSISTRATA.

The first thing we have to do
is to wash our yarn, get the dirt out of it.
You see? Isn't there too much dirt here in Athens?
You must wash those men away.
Then our spoiled wool—
that's like your job-hunters, out for a life
of no work and big pay. Back to the basket,

[39] The Gorgon's head, in myth, turned gazers to stone; it was therefore a common design on warriors' shields.

citizens or not, allies or not,
or friendly immigrants.
And your colonies? 540
Hanks of wool lost in various places. Pull them
together, weave them into one great whole,
and our voters are clothed for ever.

COMMISSIONER.
It would take a woman
to reduce state questions to a matter of carding and weaving.

LYSISTRATA.
You fool! Who were the mothers whose sons sailed off
to fight for Athens in Sicily?

COMMISSIONER.
Enough!
I beg you, do not call back those memories.

LYSISTRATA.
And then,
instead of the love that every woman needs,
we have only our single beds, where we can dream
of our husbands off with the Army.
Bad enough for wives! 550
But what about our girls, getting older every day,
and older, and no kisses?

COMMISSIONER.
Men get older, too.

LYSISTRATA.
Not in the same sense.
A soldier's discharged,
and he may be bald and toothless, yet he'll find
a pretty young thing to go to bed with.
But a woman!
Her beauty is gone with the first grey hair.
She can spend her time
consulting the oracles and the fortune-tellers,
but they'll never send her a husband.

COMMISSIONER.
Still, if a man can rise to the occasion— 560

LYSISTRATA.
Rise? Rise, yourself!

[*Furiously*]

Go invest in a coffin!
You've money enough.
I'll bake you
a cake[40] for the Underworld.

[40]Part of the customary funeral ritual; a honey cake was the offering with which the dead person was to propitiate Cerberus, the monster dog who guarded the Underworld, or realm of the dead.

And here's your funeral
wreath!

[*She pours water upon him*]

MYRRHINE.
And here's another!

[*More water*]

KALONIKE.
And here's
my contribution!

[*More water*]

LYSISTRATA.
What are you waiting for?
All aboard Styx Ferry![41]
Charôn's calling for you!
It's sailing-time: don't disrupt the schedule!

COMMISSIONER.
The insolence of women! And to me!
No, by God, I'll go back to town and show 570
the rest of the Commission what might happen to them.

[*Exit* COMMISSIONER]

LYSISTRATA.
Really, I suppose we should have laid out his corpse
on the doorstep, in the usual way.
But never mind.
We'll give him the rites of the dead tomorrow morning.

[*Exit* LYSISTRATA *with* MYRRHINE *and* KALONIKE]

PARÁBASIS:[42] CHORAL EPISODE

KORYPHAIOS[m].

[ODE 1]

Sons of Liberty, awake! The day of glory is at hand.

CHORUS[m].
I smell tyranny afoot, I smell it rising from the land.
I scent a trace of Hippias,[43] I sniff upon the breeze
A dismal Spartan hogo that suggests King Kleisthenês.[44]

[41] The dead were ferried by the boatman Charôn across the river Styx to the Underworld.
[42] An address to the audience by the chorus.
[43] The last of the Athenian tyrants; he ruled about a century before the present action.
[44] A notoriously effeminate bisexual.

Strip, strip for action, brothers!
Our wives, aunts, sisters, mothers 580
Have sold us out: the streets are full of godless female rages.
Shall we stand by and let our women confiscate our wages?[45]

KORYPHAIOS^{m}.

[EPIRRHEMA[46] 1]

Gentlemen, it's a disgrace to Athens, a disgrace
to all that Athens stands for, if we allow these grandmas
to jabber about spears and shields and making friends
with the Spartans. What's a Spartan? Give me a wild wolf
any day. No. They want the Tyranny back, I suppose.
Are we going to take that? No. Let us look like
the innocent serpent, but be the flower under it,
as the poet sings. And just to begin with, 590
I propose to poke a number of teeth
down the gullet of that harridan[47] over there.

KORYPHAIOS^{w}.

[ANTODE 1]

Oh, is that so? When you get home, your own mammá won't know
you!

CHORUS^{w}.

Who do you think we are, you senile bravos? Well, I'll show you.
I bore the sacred vessels[48] in my eighth year, and at ten
I was pounding out the barley for Athêna Goddess; then
They made me Little Bear
At the Braunonian Fair;
I'd held the Holy Basket by the time I was of age,
The Blessed Dry Figs had adorned my plump décolletage. 600

KORYPHAIOS^{w}.

[ANTEPIRRHEMA 1]

A 'disgrace to Athens', am I, just at the moment
I'm giving Athens the best advice she ever had?
Don't I pay taxes to the State? Yes, I pay them
in baby boys. And what do you contribute,
you impotent horrors? Nothing but waste: all
our Treasury,[49] dating back to the Persian Wars,
gone! rifled! And not a penny out of your pockets!
Well, then? Can you cough up an answer to that?
Look out for your own gullet, or you'll get a crack
from this old brogan that'll make your teeth see stars! 610

[45]The fund from which the elderly jurors' fees were paid was kept at the Akropolis.

[46]Along with the following "Antode" and "Antepirrhema," this section is a choral song that customarily made a satiric comment on current events.

[47]A sharp-tongued old woman.

[48]In the following lines, the women describe various roles in the rites of Athêna and Artemis. Selected preadolescent Athenian girls of good family were privileged to perform these roles.

[49]A fund originally established in the days of Greek unity to finance the war against Persia; the money had since been misappropriated by unscrupulous politicians.

CHORUS[m].

Oh insolence! [ODE 2]
Am I unmanned?
Incontinence!
Shall my scarred hand
Strike never a blow
To curb this flow-
ing female curse?

Leipsydrion![50]
Shall I betray
The laurels won 620
On that great day?
Come, shake a leg,
Shed old age, beg
The years reverse!

KORYPHAIOS[m].

[EPIRRHEMA 2]

Give them an inch, and we're done for! We'll have them
launching boats next and planning naval strategy,
sailing down on us like so many Artemisias.[51]
Or maybe they have ideas about the cavalry.
That's fair enough, women are certainly good
in the saddle. Just look at Mikôn's paintings, 630
all those Amazons[52] wrestling with all those men!
On the whole, a straitjacket's their best uniform.

CHORUS[w].

Tangle with me, [ANTODE 2]
And you'll get cramps.
Ferocity
's no use now, Gramps!
By the Two,
I'll get through
To you wrecks yet!

I'll scramble your eggs, 640
I'll burn your beans,
With my two legs.
You'll see such scenes
As never yet
Your two eyes met.
A curse? You bet!

KORYPHAIOS[w].

[ANTEPIRRHEMA 2]

If Lampitô stands by me, and that delicious Theban girl,

[50]Another site of patriotic Athenian heroism from the great days (in this instance about a century earlier) of the city's fight against tyranny.

[51]A queen who had commanded a naval unit in the Persian war against Greece.

[52]Fabled women warriors; Mikôn was a famous contemporary painter.

Ismênia—what good are *you?* You and your seven
Resolutions! Resolutions? Rationing Boiotian eels
and making our girls go without them at Hekatê's Feast! 650
That was statesmanship! And we'll have to put up with it
and all the rest of your decrepit legislation
until some patriot—God give him strength!—
grabs you by the neck and kicks you off the Rock.

SCENE II

[*Re-enter* LYSISTRATA *and her lieutenants*]

KORYPHAIOS^{W} [*Tragic tone*].

Great Queen, fair Architect of our emprise,
Why lookst thou on us with foreboding eyes?

LYSISTRATA.

The behavior of these idiotic women!
There's something about the female temperament
that I can't bear!

KORYPHAIOS^{W}.

What in the world do you mean?

LYSISTRATA.

Exactly what I say.

KORYPHAIOS^{W}.

What dreadful thing has happened? 660
Come, tell us: we're all your friends.

LYSISTRATA.

It isn't easy
to say it; yet, God knows, we can't hush it up.

KORYPHAIOS^{W}.

Well, then? Out with it!

LYSISTRATA.

To put it bluntly,
we're dying to get laid.

KORYPHAIOS^{W}.

Almighty God!

LYSISTRATA.

Why bring God into it?—No, it's just as I say.
I can't manage them any longer: they've gone man-crazy,
they're all trying to get out.

Why, look:
one of them was sneaking out the back door
over there by Pan's cave; another
was sliding down the walls with rope and tackle; 670
another was climbing aboard a sparrow,[53] ready to take off
for the nearest brothel—I dragged *her* back by the hair!

[53] The bird was associated with Aphroditê, goddess of love.

They're all finding some reason to leave.
Look there!

There goes another one.
—Just a minute, you!

Where are you off to so fast?

FIRST WOMAN.
I've got to get home.

I've a lot of Milesian wool, and the worms are spoiling it.

LYSISTRATA.
Oh bother you and your worms! Get back inside!

FIRST WOMAN.
I'll be back right away, I swear I will.
I just want to get it stretched out on my bed.

LYSISTRATA.
You'll do no such thing. You'll stay right here.

FIRST WOMAN.
And my wool? 680

You want it ruined?

LYSISTRATA.
Yes, for all I care.

SECOND WOMAN.
Oh dear! My lovely new flax from Amorgos[54]—
I left it at home, all uncarded!

LYSISTRATA.
Another one!

And all she wants is someone to card her flax.
Get back in there!

SECOND WOMAN.
But I swear by the Moon-Goddess,

the minute I get it done, I'll be back!

LYSISTRATA.
I say No.

If you, why not all the other women as well?

THIRD WOMAN.
O Lady Eileithyia![55] Radiant goddess! Thou
intercessor for women in childbirth! Stay, I pray thee,
oh stay this parturition. Shall I pollute 690
a sacred spot?

LYSISTRATA.
And what's the matter with *you*?

THIRD WOMAN.
I'm having a baby—any minute now.

LYSISTRATA.
But you weren't pregnant yesterday.

[54]An Aegean island noted for the excellence of its flax.

[55]A goddess of childbirth. To give birth in the precincts of the Akropolis would be sacrilegious.

THIRD WOMAN.

Well, I am today.

Let me go home for a midwife, Lysistrata:
there's not much time.

LYSISTRATA.

I never heard such nonsense.

What's that bulging under your cloak?

THIRD WOMAN.

A little baby boy.

LYSISTRATA.

It certainly isn't. But it's something hollow,
like a basin or—Why, it's the helmet of Athêna!
And you said you were having a baby.

THIRD WOMAN.

Well, I am! So there!

LYSISTRATA.

Then why the helmet?

THIRD WOMAN.

I was afraid that my pains 700
might begin here in the Akropolis; and I wanted
to drop my chick into it, just as the dear doves do.

LYSISTRATA.

Lies! Evasions!—But at least one thing's clear:
you can't leave the place before your purification.

THIRD WOMAN.

But I can't stay here in the Akropolis! Last night I dreamed
of the Snake.[56]

FIRST WOMAN.

And those horrible owls,[57] the noise they make!

I can't get a bit of sleep; I'm just about dead.

LYSISTRATA.

You useless girls, that's enough: Let's have no more lying.
Of course you want your men. But don't you imagine
that they want you just as much? I'll give you my word, 710
their nights must be pretty hard.

Just stick it out!

A little patience, that's all, and our battle's won.
I have heard an Oracle. Should you like to hear it?

FIRST WOMAN.

An Oracle? Yes, tell us!

LYSISTRATA.

Here is what it says:

WHEN SWALLOWS SHALL THE HOOPOE[58] SHUN
AND SPURN HIS HOT DESIRE,
ZEUS WILL PERFECT WHAT THEY'VE BEGUN
AND SET THE LOWER HIGHER.

[56] Though never seen, this mythical snake was considered the guardian of Athêna's temple on the Akropolis.

[57] Birds sacred to Athena.

[58] A bird, here identified with the male sex.

FIRST WOMAN.
Does that mean we'll be on top?

LYSISTRATA.
BUT IF THE SWALLOWS SHALL FALL OUT 720
AND TAKE THE HOOPOE'S BAIT,
A CURSE MUST MARK THEIR HOUR OF DOUBT,
INFAMY SEAL THEIR FATE.

THIRD WOMAN.
I swear, *that* Oracle's all too clear.

FIRST WOMAN.
Oh the dear gods!

LYSISTRATA.
Let's not be downhearted, girls. Back to our places!
The god has spoken. How can we possibly fail him?

[*Exit* LYSISTRATA *with the dissident women*]

CHORAL EPISODE

CHORUS[m].

[STROPHE]

I know a little story that I learned way back in school
Goes like this:
Once upon a time there was a young man—and no fool—
Named Melanion;[59] and his 730
One aversion was marriage. He loathed the very thought.
So he ran off to the hills, and in a special grot
Raised a dog, and spent his days
Hunting rabbits. And it says
That he never never never did come home.
It might be called a refuge *from* the womb.
All right,
all right,
all right!
We're as bright as young Melanion, and we hate the very sight
Of you women!

A MAN.
How about a kiss, old lady? 740

A WOMAN.
Here's an onion for your eye!

A MAN.
A kick in the guts, then?

A WOMAN.
Try, old bristle-tail, just try!

[59]An obscure personage; in this context, he is a kind of male equivalent of Artemis, the determinedly virgin goddess of the hunt.

A MAN.
Yet they say Myronidês[60]
On hands and knees
Looked just as shaggy fore and aft as I!

CHORUS[W].

[ANTISTROPHE]

Well, *I* know a little story, and it's just as good as yours.
Goes like this:
Once there was a man named Timon[61]—a rough diamond, of course,
And that whiskery face of his 750
Looked like murder in the shrubbery. By God, he was a son
Of the Furies, let me tell you! And what did he do but run
From the world and all its ways,
Cursing mankind! And it says
That his choicest execrations as of then
Were leveled almost wholly at *old* men.
All right,
all right,
all right!
But there's one thing about Timon: he could always stand the sight
Of us women.

A WOMAN.
How about a crack in the jaw, Pop? 760

A MAN.
I can take it, Ma—no fear!

A WOMAN.
How about a kick in the face?

A MAN.
You'd reveal your old caboose?

A WOMAN.
What I'd show
I'll have you know,
Is an instrument you're too far gone to use.

SCENE III

[*Re-enter* LYSISTRATA]

LYSISTRATA.
Oh, quick, girls, quick! Come here!

A WOMAN.
What is it?

[60]An Athenian general.

[61]A noted misanthrope (the titular character of one of Shakespeare's plays). The women choose here to present him as an enemy to males rather than to humankind.

LYSISTRATA.

A man.

A man simply bulging with love.

O Kyprian Queen,[62]

O Paphian, O Kythereian! Hear us and aid us!

A WOMAN.

Where is this enemy?

LYSISTRATA.

Over there, by Demêter's shrine. 770

A WOMAN.

Damned if he isn't. But who *is* he?

MYRRHINE.

My husband.

Kinêsias.

LYSISTRATA.

Oh then, get busy! Tease him! Undermine him!

Wreck him! Give him everything—kissing, tickling, nudging,

whatever you generally torture him with—: give him everything

except what we swore on the wine we would not give.

MYRRHINE.

Trust me.

LYSISTRATA.

I do. But I'll help you get him started.

The rest of you women, stay back.

[*Enter* KINESIAS]

KINESIAS.

Oh God! Oh my God!

I'm stiff from lack of exercise. All I can do to stand up.

LYSISTRATA.

Halt! Who are you, approaching our lines?

KINESIAS.

Me? I.

LYSISTRATA.

A man?

KINESIAS.

You have eyes, haven't you?

LYSISTRATA.

Go away. 780

KINESIAS.

Who says so?

LYSISTRATA.

Officer of the Day.

KINESIAS.

Officer, I beg you,

by all the gods at once, bring Myrrhinê out.

[62] *Kyprian* and the names in the following line are epithets for Aphroditê, goddess of love.

LYSISTRATA.
Myrrhinê? And who, my good sir, are you?
KINESIAS.
Kinêsias. Last name's Pennison. Her husband.
LYSISTRATA.
Oh, of course. I beg your pardon. We're glad to see you.
We've heard so much about you. Dearest Myrrhinê
is always talking about 'Kinêsias'—never nibbles an egg
or an apple without saying
'Here's to Kinêsias!'
KINESIAS.
Do you really mean it?
LYSISTRATA.
I do.
When we're discussing men, she always says 790
'Well, after all, there's nobody like Kinêsias!'
KINESIAS.
Good God.—Well, then, please send her down here.
LYSISTRATA.
And what do *I* get out of it?
KINESIAS.
A standing promise.
LYSISTRATA.
I'll take it up with her.

[*Exit* LYSISTRATA]

KINESIAS.
But be quick about it!
Lord, what's life without a wife? Can't eat. Can't sleep.
Every time I go home, the place is so empty, so
insufferably sad. Love's killing me. Oh,
hurry!

[*Enter* MANES, *a slave, with* KINESIAS' *baby; the voice of* MYRRHINE *is heard off-stage.*]

MYRRHINE.
But of course I love him! Adore him!—But no,
he hates love. No. I won't go down.

[*Enter* MYRRHINE, *above*]

KINESIAS.
Myrrhinê!
Darlingest Myrrhinette! Come down quick! 800
MYRRHINE.
Certainly not.
KINESIAS.
Not? But why, Myrrhinê?

MYRRHINE.
Why? You don't need me.
KINESIAS.
Need you? My God, *look* at me!
MYRRHINE.
So long!

[*Turns to go*]

KINESIAS.
Myrrhinê, Myrrhinê, Myrrhinê!
If not for my sake, for our child!

[*Pinches* BABY]

—All right, you: pipe up!

BABY.
Mummie! Mummie! Mummie!
KINESIAS.
You hear that?
Pitiful, I call it. Six days now
with never a bath; no food; enough to break your heart!
MYRRHINE.
My darlingest child! What a father *you* acquired!
KINESIAS.
At least come down for his sake.
MYRRHINE.
I suppose I must.
Oh, this mother business!

[*Exit*]

KINESIAS.
How pretty she is! And younger! 810
The harder she treats me, the more bothered I get.

[MYRRHINE *enters, below*]

MYRRHINE.
Dearest child,
you're as sweet as your father's horrid. Give me a kiss.
KINESIAS.
Now don't you see how wrong it was to get involved
in this scheming League of women? It's bad
for us both.
MYRRHINE.
Keep your hands to yourself!
KINESIAS.
But our house
going to rack and ruin?
MYRRHINE.
I don't care.

KINESIAS.

And your knitting
all torn to pieces by the chickens? Don't you care?

MYRRHINE.

Not at all.

KINESIAS.

And our debt to Aphroditê?
Oh, *won't* you come back?

MYRRHINE.

No.—At least, not until you men
make a treaty and stop this war.

KINESIAS.

Why, I suppose 820
that might be arranged.

MYRRHINE.

Oh? Well, I suppose
I might come down then. But meanwhile,
I've sworn not to.

KINESIAS.

Don't worry.—Now, let's have fun.

MYRRHINE.

No! Stop it! I said no!
—Although, of course,
I *do* love you.

KINESIAS.

I know you do. Darling Myrrhinê:
come, shall we?

MYRRHINE.

Are you out of your mind? In front of the child?

KINESIAS.

Take him home, Manês.

[*Exit* MANÊS *with* BABY]

There. He's gone.
Come on!
There's nothing to stop us now.

MYRRHINE.

You devil! But where?

KINESIAS.

In Pan's cave. What could be snugger than that?

MYRRHINE.

But my purification before I go back to the Citadel? 830

KINESIAS.

Wash in the Klepsydra.[63]

MYRRHINE.

And my oath?

[63]A spring on the Akropolis.

KINESIAS.
Leave the oath to me.
After all, I'm the man.
MYRRHINE.
Well . . . if you say so.
I'll go find a bed.
KINESIAS.
Oh, bother a bed! The ground's good enough for me.
MYRRHINE.
No. You're a bad man, but you deserve something better than dirt.

[*Exit* MYRRHINE]

KINESIAS.
What a love she is! and how thoughtful!

[*Re-enter* MYRRHINE]

MYRRHINE.
Here's your bed.
Now let me get my clothes off.
But, good horrors!
We haven't a mattress.
KINESIAS.
Oh, forget the mattress!
MYRRHINE.
No.
Just lying on blankets? Too sordid.
KINESIAS.
Give me a kiss.
MYRRHINE.
Just a second.

[*Exit* MYRRHINE]

KINESIAS.
I swear, I'll explode!

[*Re-enter* MYRRHINE]

MYRRHINE.
Here's your mattress.
I'll just take my dress off.
But look— 840
where's our pillow?
KINESIAS.
I don't *need* a pillow!
MYRRHINE.
Well, *I* do.

[*Exit* MYRRHINE]

KINESIAS.
I don't suppose even Heraklês[64]
would stand for this!

[*Re-enter* MYRRHINE]

MYRRHINE.
There we are. Ups-a-daisy!

KINESIAS.
So we are. Well, come to bed.

MYRRHINE.
But I wonder:
is everything ready now?

KINESIAS.
I can swear to that. Come, darling!

MYRRHINE.
Just getting out of my girdle.
But remember, now,
what you promised about the treaty.

KINESIAS.
Yes, yes, yes!

MYRRHINE.
But no coverlet!

KINESIAS.
Damn it, I'll be
your coverlet!

MYRRHINE.
Be right back.

[*Exit* MYRRHINE]

KINESIAS.
This girl and her coverlets
will be the death of me.

[*Re-enter* MYRRHINE]

MYRRHINE.
Here we are. Up you go! 850

KINESIAS.
Up? I've been up for ages.

MYRRHINE.
Some perfume?

KINESIAS.
No, by Apollo!

MYRRHINE.
Yes, by Aphroditê!
I don't care whether you want it or not.

[64]A lustful womanizer, Heraklês (Hercules) could also be chivalrous and even self-abasing in his relations with women.

[*Exit* MYRRHINE]

KINESIAS.
For love's sake, hurry!

[*Re-enter* MYRRHINE]

MYRRHINE.
Here, in your hand. Rub it right in.
KINESIAS.
Never cared for perfume.

And this is particularly strong. Still, here goes.
MYRRHINE.
What a nitwit I am! I brought you the Rhodian bottle.
KINESIAS.
Forget it.
MYRRHINE.
No trouble at all. You just wait here.

[*Exit* MYRRHINE]

KINESIAS.
God damn the man who invented perfume!

[*Re-enter* MYRRHINE]

MYRRHINE.
At last! The right bottle!
KINESIAS.
I've got the rightest 860
bottle of all, and it's right here waiting for you.
Darling, forget everything else. Do come to bed.
MYRRHINE.
Just let me get my shoes off.
—And, by the way,

you'll vote for the treaty?
KINESIAS.
I'll think about it.

[MYRRHINE *runs away*]

There! That's done it! The damned woman,
she gets me all bothered, she half kills me,
and she runs! What'll I do? Where
can I get laid?
—And you, little prodding pal,
who's going to take care of *you?* No, you and I
had better get down to old Foxdog's[65] Nursing Clinic. 870

[65]A well-known pimp.

CHORUS^{m}.

Alas for the woes of man, alas
Specifically for you.
She's brought you to a pretty pass:
What are you going to do?
Split, heart! Sag, flesh! Proud spirit, crack!
Myrrhinê's got you on your back.

KINESIAS.

The agony, the protraction!

KORYPHAIOS^{m}.

Friend,
What woman's worth a damn?
They bitch us all, world without end.

KINESIAS.

Yet they're so damned sweet, man! 880

KORYPHAIOS^{m}.

Calamitous, that's what I say.
You should have learned that much today.

CHORUS^{m}.

O blessed Zeus, roll womankind
Up into one great ball;
Blast them aloft on a high wind,
And once there, let them fall.
Down, down they'll come, the pretty dears,
And split themselves on our thick spears.

[*Exit* KINESIAS]

SCENE IV

[*Enter a* SPARTAN HERALD]

HERALD.

Gentlemen, Ah beg you will be so kind
as to direct me to the Central Committee. 890
Ah have a communication.

[*Re-enter* COMMISSIONER]

COMMISSIONER.

Are you a man,
or a fertility symbol?

HERALD.

Ah refuse to answer that question!
Ah'm a certified herald from Spahta, and Ah've come
to talk about an ahmistice.

COMMISSIONER.

Then why
that spear under your cloak?

HERALD.

Ah have no speah!

COMMISSIONER.

You don't walk naturally, with your tunic
poked out so. You have a tumor, maybe,
or a hernia?

HERALD.

You lost yo' mahnd, man?

COMMISSIONER.

Well,
something's up, I can see that. And I don't like it.

HERALD.

Colonel, Ah resent this.

COMMISSIONER.

So I see. But what *is* it?

HERALD.

A staff 900
with a message from Spahta.

COMMISSIONER.

Oh. I know about those staffs.[66]
Well, then, man, speak out: How are things in Sparta?

HERALD.

Hahd, Colonel, hahd! We're at a standstill.
Cain't seem to think of anything but women.

COMMISSIONER.

How curious! Tell me, do you Spartans think
that maybe Pan's[67] to blame?

HERALD.

Pan? No. Lampitô and her little naked friends.
They won't let a man come nigh them.

COMMISSIONER.

How are you handling it?

HERALD.

Losing our mahnds,
if y' want to know, and walking around hunched over 910
lahk men carrying candles in a gale.
The women have swohn they'll have nothing to do with us
until we get a treaty.

COMMISSIONER.

Yes, I know.
It's a general uprising, sir, in all parts of Greece.
But as for the answer—
Sir: go back to Sparta
and have them send us your Armistice Commission.

[66] The pun alludes to a Spartan method of cryptography: a message was written on fabric wound around a staff (like an overlapping bandage). It was then unwound, despatched by messenger, and rewound on a staff identical in shape with the sender's. Only then could the scrambled lines of writing be realigned to make sense.

[67] The nature god Pan was held accountable for sudden and inexplicable fits of madness, or "panic." The god could also cause sexual excesses.

I'll arrange things in Athens.

And I may say

that my standing is good enough to make them listen.

HERALD.

A man after mah own haht! Seh, Ah thank you.

[*Exit* HERALD]

CHORAL EPISODE

CHORUS[m].

Oh these women! Where will you find [STROPHE] 920
A slavering beast that's more unkind?
Where a hotter fire?
Give me a panther, any day.
He's not so merciless as they,
And panthers don't conspire.

CHORUS[w].

We may be hard, you silly old ass, [ANTISTROPHE]
But who brought you to this stupid pass?
You're the ones to blame.
Fighting with us, your oldest friends,
Simply to serve your selfish ends— 930
Really, you have no shame!

KORYPHAIOS[m].

No, I'm through with women for ever.

KORYPHAIOS[w].

If you say so.

Still, you might put some clothes on. You look too absurd
standing around naked. Come, get into this cloak.

KORYPHAIOS[m].

Thank you; you're right. I merely took it off
because I was in such a temper.

KORYPHAIOS[w].

That's much better.

Now you resemble a man again.

Why have you been so horrid?

And look: there's some sort of insect in your eye.
Shall I take it out?

KORYPHAIOS[m].

An insect, is it? So that's

what's been bothering me. Lord, yes: take it out! 940

KORYPHAIOS[w].

You might be more polite.

—But, heavens!

What an enormous mosquito!

KORYPHAIOS[m].

You've saved my life.

That mosquito was drilling an artesian well
In my left eye.

KORYPHAIOS^{w}.

Let me wipe
those tears away.—And now: one little kiss?

KORYPHAIOS^{m}.

No, no kisses.

KORYPHAIOS^{w}.

You're so difficult.

KORYPHAIOS^{m}.

You impossible women! How you do get around us!
The poet was right: Can't live with you, or without you.
But let's be friends.
And to celebrate, you might join us in an Ode. 950

CHORUS$^{m \text{ and } w}$.

Let it never be said [STROPHE 1]
That my tongue is malicious:
Both by word and by deed
I would set an example that's noble and gracious.
We've had sorrow and care
Till we're sick of the tune.
Is there anyone here
Who would like a small loan?
My purse is crammed,
As you'll soon find; 960
And you needn't pay me back if the Peace gets signed.

I've invited to lunch [STROPHE 2]
Some Karystian rips[68]—
An esurient bunch,
But I've ordered a menu to water their lips.
I can still make soup
And slaughter a pig.
You're all coming, I hope?
But a bath first, I beg!
Walk right up 970
As though you owned the place,
And you'll get the front door slammed to in your face.

SCENE V

[*Enter* SPARTAN AMBASSADOR, *with entourage*]

KORYPHAIOS^{m}.

The Commission has arrived from Sparta.
How oddly
they're walking!

[68] People from Karystos, allied with Athens. They were considered uninhibited and morally loose.

Gentlemen, welcome to Athens!
How is life in Lakonia?[69]

AMBASSADOR.
Need we discuss that?
Simply use your eyes.

CHORUS^{m}.
The poor man's right:
What a sight!

AMBASSADOR.
Words fail me.
But come, gentlemen, call in your Commissioners,
and let's get down to a Peace.

CHORAGOS^{m}.
The state we're in! Can't bear
a stitch below the waist. It's a kind of pelvic 980
paralysis.

COMMISSIONER.
Won't somebody call Lysistrata?—Gentlemen,
we're no better off than you.

AMBASSADOR.
So I see.

A SPARTAN.
Seh, do y'all feel a certain strain
early in the morning?

AN ATHENIAN.
I do, sir. It's worse than a strain.
A few more days, and there's nothing for us but Kleisthenês,
that broken blossom.

CHORAGOS^{m}.
But you'd better get dressed again.
You know these people going around Athens with chisels,
looking for statues of Hermês.[70]

ATHENIAN.
Sir, you are right.

SPARTAN.
He certainly is! Ah'll put mah own clothes back on.

[*Enter* ATHENIAN COMMISSIONERS]

COMMISSIONER.
Gentlemen from Sparta, welcome. This is a sorry business. 990

SPARTAN. [*To one of his own group*]:
Colonel, we got dressed just in time. Ah sweah,
if they'd seen us the way we were, there'd have been a new wah
between the states.

[69] The southern area of Greece. Sparta was its most important city.

[70] Opponents of the expedition to Sicily had mutilated these phallic statues (commonly located in front of homes) just before the fleet set sail. Some Athenians believed that the vandalism had jinxed the Sicilian campaign.

COMMISSIONER.
Shall we call the meeting to order?
Now, Lakonians,
what's your proposal?

AMBASSADOR.
We propose to consider peace.

COMMISSIONER.
Good. That's on our minds, too.
—Summon Lysistrata.
We'll never get anywhere without her.

AMBASSADOR.
Lysistrata?
Summon Lysis-*any*body! Only, summon!

KORYPHAIOS[m].
No need to summon:
here she is, herself.

[*Enter* LYSISTRATA]

COMMISSIONER.
Lysistrata! Lion of women!
This is your hour to be 1000
hard and yielding, outspoken and shy, austere and
gentle. You see here
the best brains of Hellas (confused, I admit,
by your devious charming) met as one man
to turn the future over to you.

LYSISTRATA.
That's fair enough,
unless you men take it into your heads
to turn to each other instead of to us. But I'd know
soon enough if you did.
—Where is Reconciliation?
Go, some of you: bring her here.

[*Exeunt two women*]

And now, women,
lead the Spartan delegates to me: not roughly 1010
or insultingly, as our men handle them, but gently,
politely, as ladies should. Take them by the hand,
or by anything else if they won't give you their hands.

[*The* SPARTANS *are escorted over*]

There.—The Athenians next, by any convenient handle.

[*The* ATHENIANS *are escorted*]

Stand there, please.—Now, all of you, listen to me.

[*During the following speech the two women re-enter, carrying an enormous statue of a naked girl; this is* RECONCILIATION.]

I'm only a woman, I know; but I've a mind,
and, I think, not a bad one: I owe it to my father
and to listening to the local politicians.
So much for that.
Now, gentlemen,
since I have you here, I intend to give you a scolding. 1020
We are all Greeks.
Must I remind you of Thermopylai, of Olympia,
of Delphoi?[71] names deep in all our hearts?
Are they not a common heritage?
Yet you men
go raiding through the country from both sides,
Greek killing Greek, storming down Greek cities—
and all the time the Barbarian[72] across the sea
is waiting for his chance!
—That's my first point.

AN ATHENIAN.
Lord! I can hardly contain myself.

LYSISTRATA.
As for you Spartans:
Was it so long ago that Perikleidês[73] 1030
came here to beg our help? I can see him still,
his grey face, his sombre gown. And what did he want?
An army from Athens. All Messênê
was hot at your heels, and the sea-god splitting your land.
Well, Kimôn and his men,
four thousand strong, marched out and saved all Sparta.
And what thanks do we get? You come back to murder us.

AN ATHENIAN.
They're aggressors, Lysistrata!

A SPARTAN.
Ah Admit it.
When Ah look at those laigs, Ah sweah Ah'll aggress mahself!

LYSISTRATA.
And you, Athenians: do you think you're blameless? 1040
Remember that bad time when we were helpless,
and an army came from Sparta,

[71] The place-names evoke the former days of Greek unity and glory before the tragic civil war.

[72] Foreign; non-Greek.

[73] An emissary sent from Sparta, earlier in the fifth century, to request help from Athens in putting down civil war in Sparta and rebellion by Spartan-controlled Messênê. Athens responded by sending a rescue force led by Kimôn.

and that was the end of the Thessalian menace,
the end of Hippias[74] and his allies.
And that was Sparta,
and only Sparta; but for Sparta, we'd be
cringing slaves today, not free Athenians.

[*From this point, the male responses are less to* LYSISTRATA *than to the statue*]

A SPARTAN.
A well shaped speech.

AN ATHENIAN.
Certainly it has its points.

LYSISTRATA.
Why are we fighting each other? With all this history
of favors given and taken, what stands in the way
of making peace?

AMBASSADOR.
Spahta is ready, ma'am, 1050
so long as we get that place back.

LYSISTRATA.
What place, man?

AMBASSADOR.
Ah refer to Pylos.[75]

COMMISSIONER.
Not a chance, by God!

LYSISTRATA.
Give it to them, friend.

COMMISSIONER.
But—what shall we have to bargain with?

LYSISTRATA.
Demand something in exchange.

COMMISSIONER.
Good idea.—Well, then:
Cockeville first, and the Happy Hills, and the country
between the Legs of Mêgara.

AMBASSADOR.
Mah government objects.

LYSISTRATA.
Over-ruled. Why fuss about a pair of legs?

[*General assent. The statue is removed.*]

[74] The Spartans had helped Athens to overthrow and expel the tyrant Hippias.

[75] A town; the root meaning of its name is "flank." This and the following lines make a series of puns referring both to control of geographic areas and to portions of the female body as visible in the statue of the nude "Reconciliation." Conventional diplomatic bargaining for territory is thus blended with the sexual diplomacy employed by the women in the play.

AN ATHENIAN.
I want to get out of these clothes and start my plowing.
A SPARTAN.
Ah'll fertilize mahn first, by the Heavenly Twins!
LYSISTRATA.
And so you shall, 1060
once you've made peace. If you are serious,
go, both of you, and talk with your allies.
COMMISSIONER.
Too much talk already. No, we'll stand together.
We've only one end in view. All that we want
is our women; and I speak for our allies.
AMBASSADOR.
Mah government concurs.
AN ATHENIAN.
So does Karystos.
LYSISTRATA.
Good.—But before you come inside
to join your wives at supper, you must perform
the usual lustration.[76] Then we'll open
our baskets for you, and all that we have is yours. 1070
But you must promise upright good behavior
from this day on. Then each man home with his woman!
AN ATHENIAN.
Let's get it over with.
A SPARTAN.
Lead on. Ah follow.
AN ATHENIAN.
Quick as a cat can wink!

[*Exeunt all but the* CHORUSES]

CHORUS[W].
Embroideries ánd [ANTISTROPHE 1]
Twinkling ornaments ánd
Pretty dresses—I hand
Them all over to you, and with never a qualm.
They'll be nice for your daughters
On festival days 1080
When the girls bring the Goddess
The ritual prize.
Come in, one and all:
Take what you will.
I've nothing here so tightly corked that you can't make it spill.

[76]Ceremonial purification.

You may search my house, [ANTISTROPHE 2]
But you'll not find
The least thing of use,
Unless your two eyes are keener than mine.
Your numberless brats 1090
Are half starved? and your slaves?
Courage, grandpa! I've lots
Of grain left, and big loaves.
I'll fill your guts
I'll go the whole hog;
But if you come too close to me, remember: 'ware the dog!

[*Exeunt* CHORUSES]

ÉXODOS

[*A* DRUNKEN CITIZEN *enters, approaches the gate, and is halted by a* SENTRY]

CITIZEN.
Open. The. Door.
SENTRY.
Now, friend, just shove along!
—So you want to sit down. If it weren't such an old joke,
I'd tickle your tail with this torch. Just the sort of gag
this audience appreciates.
CITIZEN.
I. Stay. Right. Here. 1100
SENTRY.
Get away from there, or I'll scalp you! The gentlemen from Sparta
are just coming back from dinner.

[*Exit* CITIZEN; *the general company re-enters; the two* CHORUSES *now represent* SPARTANS *and* ATHENIANS.]

A SPARTAN.
Ah must say,
Ah never tasted better grub.
AN ATHENIAN.
And those Lakonians!
They're gentlemen, by the Lord! Just goes to show,
a drink to the wise is sufficient.

COMMISSIONER.

And why not?

A sober man's an ass.
Men of Athens, mark my words: the only efficient
Ambassador's a drunk Ambassador. Is that clear?
Look: we go to Sparta,
and when we get there we're dead sober. The result? 1110
Everyone cackling at everyone else. They make speeches;
and even if we understand, we get it all wrong
when we file our reports in Athens. But today—!
Everybody's happy. Couldn't tell the difference
between *Drink to Me Only* and
The Star-Spangled Athens.

What's a few lies,

washed down in good strong drink?

[*Re-enter the* DRUNKEN CITIZEN]

SENTRY.

God almighty,

he's back again!

CITIZEN.

I. Resume. My. Place.

[*To an* ATHENIAN]

A SPARTAN.

Ah beg yo', seh,
take yo' instrument in yo' hand and play for us. 1120
Ah'm told
yo' understand the in*tri*cacies of the floot?
Ah'd lahk to execute a song and dance
in honor of Athens,

and, of cohse, of Spahta.

CITIZEN.

Toot. On. Your. Flute.

[*The following song is a solo—an aria—accompanied by the flute. The* CHORUS OF SPARTANS *begins a slow dance.*]

A SPARTAN.

O Memory,
Let the Muse speak once more
In my young voice. Sing glory.

Sing Artemision's shore,[77]
Where Athens fluttered the Persians. *Alalaí,* 1130
Sing glory, that great
Victory! Sing also
Our Leonidas and his men,
Those wild boars, sweat and blood
Down in a red drench. Then, then
The barbarians broke, though they had stood
Numberless as the sands before!
O Artemis,
Virgin Goddess, whose darts
Flash in our forests: approve 1140
This pact of peace and join our hearts,
From this day on, in love.
Huntress, descend!

LYSISTRATA.
All that will come in time.
But now, Lakonians,
take home your wives. Athenians, take yours.
Each man be kind to his woman; and you, women,
be equally kind. Never again, pray God,
shall we lose our way in such madness.

KORYPHAIOS[a].
And now
let's dance our joy.

[*From this point the dance becomes general*]

CHORUS[a].
Dance, you Graces
Artemis, dance 1150
Dance, Phoibos, Lord of dancing
Dance
In a scurry of Maenads, Lord Dionysus
Dance, Zeus Thunderer
Dance, Lady Hêra
Queen of the Sky
Dance, dance, all you gods
Dance witness everlasting of our pact
Evohí Evohé

[77]In the former days of Grecian unity, the Athenian fleet had fought against the Persians near Artemision while the Spartans, led by the hero Leonidas, had bravely fought the Persians on land, at Thermopylae. *Alalaí* is a battle cry.

Dance for the dearest
the Bringer of Peace
Deathless Aphroditê!

COMMISSIONER.
Now let us have another song from Sparta. 1160

CHORUS[s].
From Taÿgetos, from Taÿgetos,
Lakonian Muse, come down.
Sing to the Lord Apollo
Who rules Amyklai[78] Town.

Sing Athêna of the House of Brass![79]

Sing Lêda's Twins,[80] that chivalry
Respondent on the shore
Of our Eurôtas;[81] sing the girls
That dance along before:

Sparkling in dust their gleaming feet, 1170
Their hair a Bacchant[82] fire,
And Lêda's daughter,[83] thyrsos raised,
Leads their triumphant choir.

CHORUSES[s and a]
Evohé!
Evohaí!
Evohé!
We pass
Dancing
dancing
to greet
Athêna of the House of Brass.

[78]A town, associated with Apollo, in the Spartan region.
[79]The temple of Athêna in Sparta.
[80]The "Heavenly Twins," Castor and Pollux, protectors of their sister, Helen of Troy.
[81]The river of Sparta.
[82]Associated with the Bacchantes, female worshipers of Bacchus (Dionysus), the god of wine, sex, and revelry.
[83]Helen of Troy, symbol of woman as cause of war but here of woman as reconciler. The thyrsos is a staff carried by worshipers of Dionysus/Bacchus.

Virgil
(70 B.C.–19 B.C.)

Because of the nobility of his conceptions and his poetic genius, Virgil has had a more continuous and profound impact on European culture, antique and Christian, than any other single classical author. Since his own day his works have been the fare of schoolchildren and of connoisseurs of poetry alike. He has been regarded not only as a prototype of the consummate artist but also as a sage, a religious prophet, and even a sorcerer. Perhaps his most distinctive achievement is to have defined heroism, and its costs, in a context not of primitive social conditions but of a sophisticated, intricately organized civilization and its values.

Like several other great Roman poets, notably Catullus, Horace, and Ovid, Virgil came from the provinces. He was born, like Catullus, in the part of northern Italy called Cisalpine Gaul, in 70 B.C. There he learned the deep love of rural nature that would later shine through his poetry. His father seems to have been a man of humble stock who acquired farmland near Mantua. Virgil nevertheless got a very good education—especially in language and literature, science, and philosophy—at Cremona, Milan, and finally Rome, where he arrived at the age of seventeen. He is said to have contemplated a career in law but to have lacked the quickness and hardihood necessary for success in it. Although he was amiable and made influential friends in the political and cultural circles of Rome, he was a shy, studious person who never married and who took no direct part in public life. A professional poet, he devoted almost all his time to his art and the studies ancillary to it.

His three principal works were the *Eclogues* (written between 42 and 37), the *Georgics* (36–29), and the *Aeneid* (29–19). The *Eclogues* are pastoral poems, in the tradition of the Greek poet Theocritus, depicting the idyllic life of shepherds, but Virgil intriguingly combines with the escapist setting references to actual persons and current topics. Two of the *Eclogues* deal with dispossession from one's land—a poignant, typically Virgilian theme—and are believed to refer to the expropriation of Virgil's family farm for the benefit of soldiers in the army of Mark Antony and Octavian after they defeated the assassins of Julius Caesar at Philippi. (The property was apparently returned to Virgil at a later date.) The *Fourth Eclogue,* which prophesies the birth of a wondrous child who is to restore the Golden Age, was later interpreted by Christians as a prophecy of Jesus; hence its name the "Messianic eclogue." The *Georgics* too has a rural theme and setting; in fact, it is largely a practical handbook for farmers, though the work also has a broad patriotic theme in keeping with Virgil's desire to help restore Italian agriculture and the moral values associated with it. It counterpoints dream and reality, tragedy and comedy, pessimism and optimism. The *Georgics,* composed slowly and carefully, at the rate of less than one line a day, is often praised as the most perfect of all Latin poems. After completing it, Virgil turned to his greatest work, the *Aeneid,* to which he devoted his remaining years. At the time of his death in 19 B.C. he had not quite perfected it and asked that it be burned. Octavian (the emperor Caesar Augustus) is said to have rescued it.

Despite his retiring temperament, Virgil lived at a time when it was not easy for any Roman to avoid the impact of public events. The wars of Roman against Roman had begun decades before Virgil's birth. During his boyhood the republican form of Roman government was proving less and less capable of curbing the ambitions of powerful men. Pompey the Great, one of the two consuls (chief magistrates) in 70, the year Virgil was born, had a meteoric career as general and legislator. In 55, as Virgil reached the traditional age of manhood, Pompey was consul a second time, and in 52 the leader assumed the unprecedented office of sole consul to deal with the gang warfare and street disorders which were racking the life of the capital. Cicero, the eminent Roman thinker and statesman, dreamed that in some such central and autocratic figure as Pompey Rome might find salvation from the ills that were too widespread for its traditional government to control.

In fact, Rome's first autocracy in almost five centuries was to be established not by Pompey but by Julius Caesar, who, at first simply a popular politician from an impoverished noble family, gradually had begun to emerge as an unmatched leader and a strategist of ruthless brilliance. Caesar defeated Pompey in 48 at the Battle of Pharsalus, and during four breathless years he attempted to reshape Roman government as a centralized monarchy on the model of Alexander the Great. But Caesar's audacity went too far. In 44 a group of conspirators led by Brutus assassinated him in Pompey's Theater at Rome. The conspirators had no clear plan of action. It looked as if Rome would collapse under the sheer size of its own problems, when out of the welter of confusion and carnage emerged Caesar's ailing nineteen-year-old grandnephew Octavian. A skilled politician driven by an extraordinary genius, Octavian maneuvered his way through the labyrinth of Roman power politics over the next thirteen years, winning at length the general support of Rome. His most formidable rival, his brother-in-law Mark Antony, had become infatuated with Cleopatra, the queen of Egypt, and even planned to yield her part of the Roman domain. In the climactic naval battle of Actium in 31 (an event foreshadowed in Book III and described in Book VIII of the *Aeneid*), Octavian defeated Antony and Cleopatra. Their subsequent suicide left Octavian supreme in authority, and in 23 he became known as Caesar Augustus. His regime aimed at several goals: the civic renewal of Rome, the revival of traditional religious devotion, and the fostering of a new patriotism. The arts were to be important vehicles for these ideals, all of which are reflected in the *Aeneid.*

For Virgil, as for many other Romans, the restoration of peace was in itself a blessed achievement, an occasion and opportunity for Roman national glory. In Book I of the *Aeneid* Jupiter prophesies a time when

> wars will cease, and a rough age grow gentler,
> White Faith and Vesta, Romulus and Remus,
> Give law to nations. War's grim gates will close,
> Tight-shut with bars of iron, and inside them
> The wickedness of war sit bound and silent,
> The red mouth straining and the hands held tight
> In fastenings of bronze, a hundred hundred.
>
> *(I. 305–311)*

To "give law to nations"—this, and not mere narrow chauvinism, is the distinctive Roman mission. The shade of Anchises tells his son Aeneas in Book VI:

> Others, no doubt, will better mould the bronze
> To the semblance of soft breathing, draw, from marble,
> The living countenance; and others plead
> With greater eloquence, or learn to measure,
> Better than we, the pathways of the heaven,
> The risings of the stars: remember, Roman,
> To rule the people under law, to establish
> The way of peace, to battle down the haughty,
> To spare the meek. Our fine arts, these, forever.
>
> *(VI. 888–896)*

Although Anchises is historically right in conceding superiority in the fine arts to other nations, specifically Greece, and identifying government as the epitome of Roman greatness, it is somewhat ironic that his exhortation, at once modest and proud, should appear in a poem that is one of the world's aesthetic masterpieces.

The *Aeneid* is, then, a eulogy of Roman values. But it also puts those values in perspective by showing insistently the great cost at which they are achieved and sustained. The poem, particularly in the second half, treats political negotiation and war at length, but war is presented there as a moral tragedy, however necessary, and even admirable, martial prowess and courage may be. Aeneas is no Homeric hero, free to demonstrate valor and prowess for their own sake, with no social obligation beyond himself, his family, and the cohorts banded together under him. The distinctively Virgilian melancholy, combined inextricably with tones of triumph, arises largely from the poet's awareness that public duty requires again and again the sacrifice of personal fulfillment. Aeneas, the mirror of Augustus and of Roman potential, must be educated in suffering before he can perform his mission and become a worthy embodiment of the Roman ideal. His affair with Dido is a personal tragedy on both sides. Since Carthage, the city she rules, was to become an inveterate enemy of Rome in three major wars during the two centuries before Virgil, it would have been easy for him to present this African queen as merely ignoble, a focus for propaganda. That instead he portrays her sympathetically, indeed creating in her the most memorable character in Latin literature, both enhances her own tragic stature and underlines Aeneas' tragic dilemma in having to renounce her in the name of duty.

For the formal vehicle of his story and message, Virgil chose the epic, a literary genre he had aspired to since early in his life. His handling of epic owes something to the Greek Alexandrians, but his primary models are the two Homeric epics. Books I to VI are, like the *Odyssey,* a tale of wandering; Books VII to XII are a war story, like the *Iliad.* But those general correspondences are, in themselves, only the most superficial marks of Homeric influence, and there are ironic differences too. The journey of Homer's Odysseus is a true homecoming; Aeneas' odyssey, despite the ancestral roots the Trojans have in Italy, is a leavetaking, a deracination. Virgil's echoing of Homer is intricate but also intricately varied, so that the echoing is less imitative than expressive. Virgil's synthesizing tour de force overlies a radical originality of the utmost importance in the history of epic. Aristotle, in his *Poetics,* had praised Homer for his objectivity, his effacement of himself, and had identified such self-effacement as the epic poet's proper role. In his own way, of course, Virgil too is objective; that is, he combines with his didacticism flexibility of sympathy with individual human beings, realistic insight into human psychology, and a sense that there is often right on both sides. Yet the *Aeneid* is, after all, a subjective poem—in the sense that the author's presence can be felt everywhere, in the ideas and in the characteristic Virgilian tone of pathos, introspectiveness, and poignancy.

An even more important innovation is Virgil's imaginative redefinition of the role of history in epic. Rather than narrating and directly celebrating modern Roman history, which is ultimately his main concern, he chooses to return to the legendary roots of the Roman experience nearly a millennium earlier, in the wanderings and wars of the Trojans after the fall of their city. In treating the seeds of later Roman history, Roman religious ritual, Roman character traits as having been sown in that era of the dim past, the *Aeneid,* unlike the Homeric models, envisions time and history as a meaningful linear movement toward goals ordained by a mysterious but purposeful providence. Understood in this way, the fall of Troy is ultimately a fortunate fall. In ancient literature the closest thing we have to this is not in pagan literature but in the Bible, especially in the Exodus saga. Both there and in the *Aeneid* we see a guiding providence operating through divinely appointed, half-reluctant heroes, Moses and Aeneas, both of whom must grow into their roles but then rest content not quite to reach the ultimate goal of their people. In both works the journey is out of a disastrous past toward a new promised land that is also an ancestral homeland. Both leaders must mediate between the exigencies of providence and the weariness and backslidings of their followers. It is no wonder that poets in the Judeo-Christian tradition could retrospectively claim Virgil as one of their own.

Except for the Bible, the *Aeneid* may well be the most highly revered book in European literary history, especially before the reemergence of the Greek classics in Europe during the Renaissance. Like the Bible, Virgil's works were used by people seeking supernatural guidance; they opened a copy at random and found wisdom in the first passage their eyes struck. That practice (the *Sortes Vergilianae*) reflects the moral sententiousness of the *Aeneid,* but it also reflects the poem's style. To translate Virgil is especially challenging, for almost every line is dense with meaning, nuance, implication. That is partly owing to the nature of classical Latin, which can produce special effects because the word order is freer than in modern English, and partly to Virgil's painstaking method of composition, which is utterly different from the essentially oral manner of Homer's verse (though Virgil did sometimes read his poetry aloud). The meter is the standard epic meter, dactylic hexameter—each of the six feet made up of a long syllable and two short ones (*dactyl*) or of two long ones (*spondee*). But in addition to this quantitative meter, based on the actual time duration of syllables, Virgil's verse recognizes the stress accents that words possessed in spoken Latin as they do in English, and this stress-accent pattern is played against the quantitative pattern in ways from which Virgil elicits enormously varied expressive effects. It should be noted too that, in the last two feet of Virgil's hexameter line, the stress-accent pattern and the quantitative pattern coincide, so that each line sustains rhythmic tensions that are resolved in the last two feet. The first seven lines of the *Aeneid,* quoted below, are given as a sample; the slash marks indicate the divisions into feet; the long and short syllables are indicated, respectively, by the marks — and ˘; and the normal spoken stress accents are indicated by italics:

> *Ā*rmă vī/*rūm* quĕ *că*/nō, Trō/iāe quī / *prī* mŭs ăb / *ō*rĭs
> Ī*tă* lĭ/ām, *fā*/tō *prŏ* fŭ/gŭs, Lā/*vīn* iăquĕ / *vē* nĭt
> *lī* tŏră, / *mūl* tum *īl*/le ēt *tēr*/rīs iāc/*tā* tŭs ĕt / *āl* tō
> *vī sŭ* pĕ/rūm, *sāe*/vāe *mĕ* mŏ/rēm Īu/*nō* nĭs ŏb / *ī* răm,
> *mūl* tă *quŏ*/que ēt *bēl*/lō *pās*/sūs, dūm / *cōn* dĕrĕt / *ūr* bēm,
> īnfēr/*rēt* quĕ *dĕ*/ōs *Lă* tĭ/ō, *gĕ* nŭs / *ūn* dĕ Lă/*tī* nūm,
> Ālbā/*nī* quĕ *pă*/trēs, *āt*/que *āl* tāe / *mōe* nĭă / *Rō* māe.

In his poem "To Virgil," composed in 1882 for the 1,900th anniversary of Virgil's death, Tennyson paid tribute to what he called Virgil's "ocean-roll of rhythm":

I salute thee, Mantovano [Mantuan], I that loved thee since my day began,
Wielder of the stateliest measure ever molded by the lips of man.

FURTHER READING: W. F. Jackson Knight, *Roman Vergil,* 1944, 2nd ed. 1966, is especially useful on Virgil's language and style. For a comprehensive treatment of Virgil's work and his debt to Homer and to the Alexandrians, see Brooks Otis, *Virgil: A Study in Civilized Poetry,* 1964. Also valuable on the Alexandrian background to Augustan poetry is J. K. Newman, *Augustus and the New Poetry,* 1967. Lively and stimulating twentieth-century interpretations are presented by Steele Commager, ed., *Virgil: A Collection of Critical Essays,* 1966; by Donald R. Dudley, ed., *Virgil,* 1969; and by John D. Bernard, ed., *Vergil at 2000: Commemorative Essays on the Poet and His Influence,* 1986. A more recent collection, centered on the *Aeneid,* is Harold Bloom, ed., *Modern Critical Interpretations of the Aeneid,* 1987. A useful introduction to the poem is K. W. Grandsen's *Virgil: The Aeneid,* 1990. Viktor Pöschl, *The Art of Vergil: Image and Symbol in the Aeneid,* 1950, trans. Gerda Seligson, 1962, shows how the epic is unified thematically, symbolically, and artistically. Kenneth Quinn, *Virgil's "Aeneid": A Critical Description,* 1968, brings twentieth-century critical methods to bear on traditional material. Also helpful and incisive are W. A. Camps, *An Introduction to Virgil's Aeneid,* 1969, and the Introduction to R. D. Williams's commentary *The Aeneid of Virgil,* 1973. Gordon Williams, *Technique and Ideas in the "Aeneid,"* 1983, is excellent, though intellectually demanding. A more accessible recent work, Jasper Griffin's *Virgil,* 1986, can be strongly recommended.

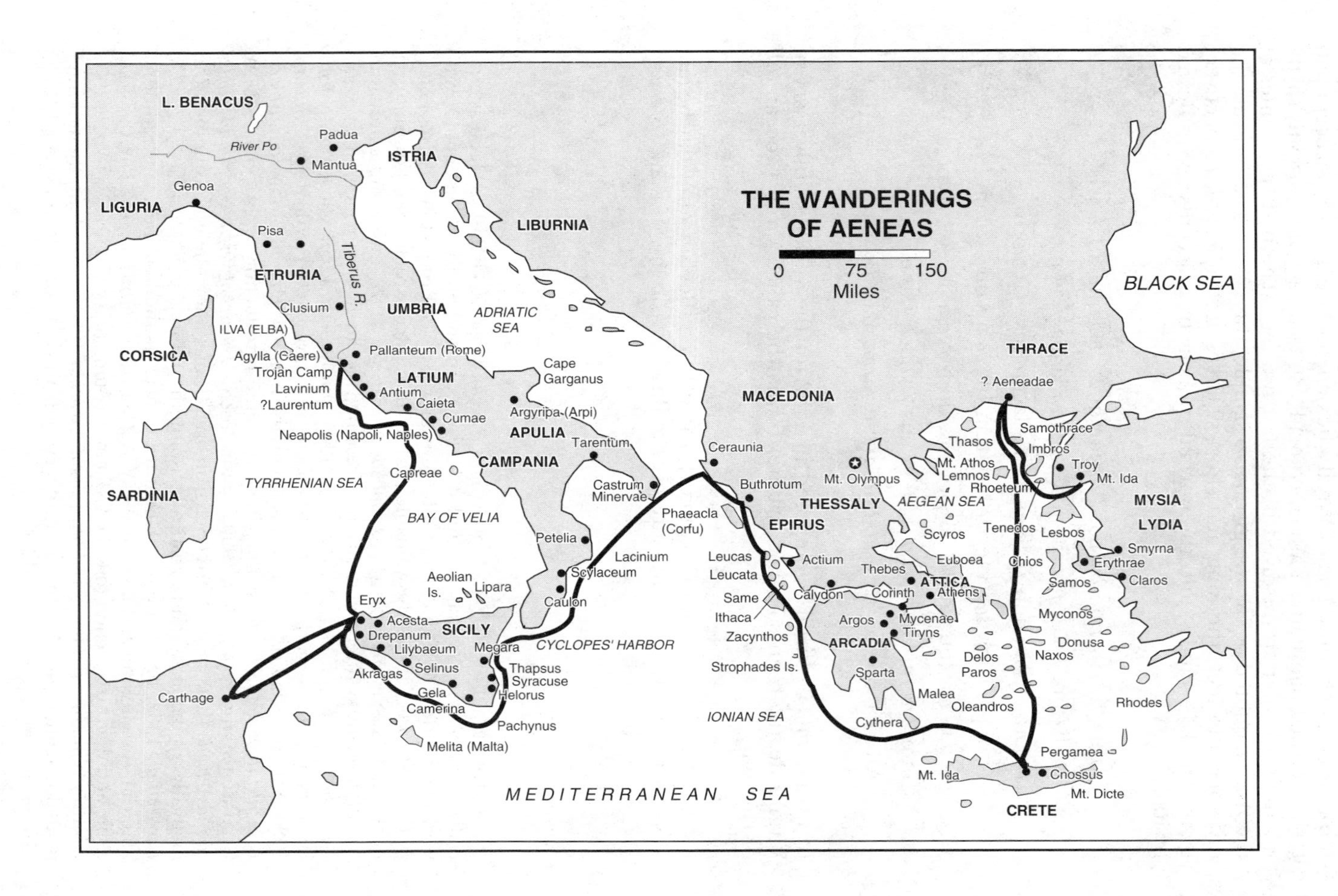
THE WANDERINGS OF AENEAS
0
75
150
Miles
L. BENACUS
Padua
River Po
Mantua
ISTRIA
Genoa
LIGURIA
LIBURNIA
Pisa
Tiberus R.
ETRURIA
Clusium
UMBRIA
ADRIATIC SEA
ILVA (ELBA)
CORSICA
Agylla (Caere)
Trojan Camp
Lavinium
?Laurentum
Pallanteum (Rome)
LATIUM
Antium
Caieta
Cumae
Cape Garganus
Argyripa-(Arpi)
APULIA
Neapolis (Napoli, Naples)
Tarentum
CAMPANIA
Capreae
TYRRHENIAN SEA
SARDINIA
Castrum Minervae
BAY OF VELIA
Petelia
Lacinium
Scylaceum
Caulon
Aeolian Is.
Lipara
Eryx
Acesta
Drepanum
SICILY
Lilybaeum
Megara
CYCLOPES' HARBOR
Selinus
Akragas
Thapsus
Syracuse
Helorus
Gela
Camerina
Pachynus
Melita (Malta)
Carthage
MEDITERRANEAN SEA
BLACK SEA
THRACE
? Aeneadae
MACEDONIA
Samothrace
Thasos
Imbros
Troy
Mt. Ida
Ceraunia
Mt. Athos
Lemnos
Rhoeteum
Mt. Olympus
Buthrotum
MYSIA
THESSALY
AEGEAN SEA
Phaeacia (Corfu)
EPIRUS
Scyros
Tenedos
Lesbos
LYDIA
Smyrna
Leucas
Actium
Euboea
Chios
Erythrae
Leucata
Thebes
ATTICA
Samos
Claros
Same
Calydon
Corinth
Athens
Ithaca
Argos
Mycenae
Myconos
Zacynthos
Tiryns
Donusa
ARCADIA
Naxos
Strophades Is.
Delos
Paros
Sparta
Malea
Oleandros
Rhodes
IONIAN SEA
Cythera
Pergamea
Mt. Ida
Cnossus
Mt. Dicte
CRETE

from *THE AENEID*

Translated by Rolfe Humphries

BOOK I: THE LANDING NEAR CARTHAGE

Arms and the man I sing,[1] the first who came,
Compelled by fate, an exile out of Troy,
To Italy and the Lavinian coast,[2]
Much buffeted on land and on the deep
By violence of the gods, through that long rage,
That lasting hate, of Juno's. And he suffered
Much, also, in war, till he should build his town
And bring his gods to Latium,[3] whence, in time,
The Latin race, the Alban[4] fathers, rose
And the great walls of everlasting Rome. 10
Help me, O Muse, recall the reasons: why,
Why did the queen of heaven[5] drive a man
So known for goodness, for devotion, through
So many toils and perils? Was there slight,
Affront, or outrage? Is vindictiveness
An attribute of the celestial mind?
There was an ancient city, Carthage, once
Founded by Tyrians,[6] facing Italy
And Tiber's[7] mouth, far-off, a wealthy town,
War-loving, and aggressive; and Juno held 20
Even her precious Samos[8] in less regard.
Here were her arms, her chariot, and here,
Should fate at all permit, the goddess burned
To found the empire of the world forever.
But, she had heard, a Trojan race would come,
Some day, to overthrow the Tyrian towers,
A race would come, imperious people,[9] proud
In war, with wide dominion, bringing doom
For Libya. Fate willed it so. And Juno
Feared, and remembered: there was the old war 30

[1] Lines 1–16 use the standard epic "opening formula," including the identification of the hero, the proclamation of the theme and of its significance, and the invocation of the inspiring Muse.

[2] The west coast of Italy.

[3] The area of Italy destined to be settled by the Trojans.

[4] The city Alba Longa was founded by Ascanius, Aeneas' son. It produced Romulus, who was, according to legend, the founder of Rome.

[5] Juno, queen of the gods and inveterate enemy of the Trojans.

[6] People from Tyre, a city on the Syrian coast, noted for commerce.

[7] The river of Rome. The epithet *War-loving* refers to the fact that Rome and Carthage fought three wars against each other during the third and second centuries B.C.

[8] An island in the Aegean Sea, site of the great temple of Juno.

[9] The Romans.

She fought at Troy for her dear Greeks; her mind
Still fed on hurt and anger; deep in her heart
Paris' decision[10] rankled, and the wrong
Offered her slighted beauty; and the hatred
Of the whole race; and Ganymede's[11] honors—
All that was fuel to fire; she tossed and harried
All over the seas, wherever she could, those Trojans
Who had survived the Greeks and fierce Achilles,
And so they wandered over many an ocean,
Through many a year, fate-hounded. Such a struggle 40
It was to found the race of Rome!

They were happy
Spreading the sail, rushing the foam with bronze,
And Sicily hardly out of sight, when Juno,
Still nourishing the everlasting wound,
Raged to herself: "I am beaten, I suppose;
It seems I cannot keep this Trojan king
From Italy. The fates, no doubt, forbid me.[12]
Pallas, of course, could burn the Argive ships,
Could drown the sailors, all for one man's guilt,
The crazy acts of Ajax.[13] Her own hand 50
Hurled from the cloud Jove's thunderbolt, and shattered
Their ships all over the sea; she raised up storm
And tempest; she spiked Ajax on the rocks,
Whirled him in wind, blasted his heart with fire.
And I, who walk my way as queen of the gods,
Sister of Jove, and wife of Jove, keep warring
With one tribe through the long, long years. Who cares
For Juno's godhead? Who brings sacrifice
Devoutly to her altars?"

Brooding, burning,
She sought Aeolia, the storm-clouds' dwelling, 60
A land that sweeps and swarms with the winds' fury,
Whose monarch, Aeolus, in his deep cave rules
Imperious, weighing down with bolt and prison
Those boisterous struggling roarers, who go raging
Around their bars, under the moan of the mountain.
High over them their sceptered lord sits watching,
Soothing, restraining, their passionate proud spirit,
Lest, uncontrolled, they seize, in their wild keeping,
The land, the sea, the arch of sky, in ruin
Sweeping through space. This Jupiter feared; he hid them 70

[10] Paris, one of the sons of King Priam of Troy, had been asked to judge which of the three goddesses Juno, Minerva, and Venus was most beautiful. He chose Venus, who rewarded him with Helen; Helen's abduction by Paris from her husband, Menelaus, then ignited the Trojan War.

[11] Promoted over Juno's daughter Hebe as cupbearer to the gods.

[12] Even the gods were considered subject to the superior power of Fate.

[13] Pallas, or Athena (the Greek equivalent of Minerva, goddess of wisdom), had inflicted the punishment described in revenge for the rape by Ajax of the prophetess Cassandra.

Deep in dark caverns, with a mass of mountain
Piled over above them, and a king to give them
Most certain regulation, with a knowledge
When to hold in, when to let go. Him Juno
Approached in supplication:—"Aeolus,
Given by Jove the power to still the waters,
Or raise them with a gale, a tribe I hate
Is on its way to Italy, and they carry
Troy with them, and their household gods, once beaten.
Shake anger into those winds of yours, turn over 80
Their ships, and drown them; drive them in all directions,
Litter the sea with bodies! For such service
The loveliest nymph I have, Deiopea,
Shall be your bride forever, and you will father
Fair children on her fairness." Aeolus
Made answer: "Yours, O Queen, the task of seeking
Whatever it is you will; and mine the duty
To follow with performance. All my empire,
My sceptre, Jove's indulgence, are beholden
To Juno's favor, by whose blessing I 90
Attend the feasts of the gods and rule this storm-land."
His spear-butt struck the hollow mountain-side,
And the winds, wherever they could, came sweeping forth,
Whirled over the land, swooped down upon the ocean.
East, South, Southwest, they heave the billows, howl,
Storm, roll the giant combers toward the shore.
Men cry; the rigging creaks and strains; the clouds
Darken, and men see nothing; a weight of darkness
Broods over the deep; the heavy thunder rumbles
From pole to pole; the lightning rips and dazzles; 100
There is no way out but death. Aeneas shudders
In the chill shock, and lifts both hands to heaven:—
"O happy men, thrice happy, four times happy,
Who had the luck to die, with their fathers watching
Below the walls of Troy! Ah, Diomedes,
Bravest of Greeks, why could I not have fallen,
Bleeding my life away on plains of Ilium[14]
In our encounter there, where mighty Hector
Went down before Achilles'[15] spear, and huge
Sarpedon[16] lay in dust, and Simois river 110
Rolled to the sea so many noble heroes,
All drowned in all their armor?" And the gale
Howls from the north, striking the sail, head on;
The waves are lifted to the stars; the oars

[14] Troy.

[15] Hector and Achilles were the chief warriors of the Trojans and Greeks, respectively. The slaying of Hector by Achilles is described in Homer's *Iliad,* Book XXII.

[16] King of Lycia, killed while fighting on the side of the Trojans. The Simois was a river at the battlefield of Troy.

Are broken, and the prow slews round; the ship
Lies broadside on; a wall of water, a mountain,
Looms up, comes pouring down; some ride the crest,
Some, in the trough, can see the boil of the sand.
The South wind hurls three ships on the hidden rocks,
That sea-reef which Italians call the Altars; 120
The West takes three, sweeping them from the deep
On shoal and quicksand; over the stern of one,
Before Aeneas' eyes, a great sea falls,
Washing the helmsman overboard; the ship
Whirls thrice in the suck of the water and goes down
In the devouring gulf; and here and there
A few survivors swim, the Lycian men
Whose captain was Orontes; now their arms,
Their Trojan treasures, float with the broken timbers
On the swing and slide of the waves. The storm, triumphant, 130
Rides down more boats, and more; there goes Achates;
Abas, Aletes, Ilioneus,
Receive the hostile water; the walls are broken;
The enemy pours in.
But meanwhile Neptune[17]
Saw ocean in a welter of confusion,
The roar of storm, and deep and surface mingled.
Troublesome business, this; he rose, majestic,
From under the waves, and saw the Trojan vessels
Scattered all over the sea by the might of the waves
And the wreck of sky; he recognized the anger 140
And cunning of his sister, and he summoned
The winds by name:—"What arrogance is this,
What pride of birth, you winds, to meddle here
Without my sanction, raising all this trouble?
I'll—No, the waves come first: but listen to me,
You are going to pay for this! Get out of here!
Go tell your king the lordship of the ocean,
The trident, are not his, but mine. His realm
Reaches no further than the rocks and caverns
You brawlers dwell in; let him rule that palace, 150
Big as he pleases, shut you in, and stay there!"
This said, he calmed the swollen sea and cloud,
Brought back the sun; Cymothoe and Triton,[18]
Heaving together, pulled the ships from the reef,
As Neptune used his trident for a lever,
Opened the quicksand, made the water smooth,
And the flying chariot skimmed the level surface.
Sometimes, in a great nation, there are riots
With the rabble out of hand, and firebrands fly
And cobblestones; whatever they lay their hands on 160

[17] God of the ocean.
[18] Cymothoe and Triton were, respectively, a sea nymph and a sea god.

Is a weapon for their fury, but should they see
One man of noble presence, they fall silent,
Obedient dogs, with ears pricked up, and waiting,
Waiting his word, and he knows how to bring them
Back to good sense again. So ocean, roaring,
Subsided into stillness, as the sea-god
Looked forth upon the waters, and clear weather
Shone over him as he drove his flying horses.
Aeneas' weary children make for harbor,
Whichever lies most near, and the prows are turned 170
To Libya's coast-line. In a bay's deep curve
They find a haven, where the water lies
With never a ripple. A little island keeps
The sea-swell off, and the waves break on its sides
And slide back harmless. The great cliffs come down
Steep to deep water, and the background shimmers,
Darkens and shines, the tremulous aspen moving
And the dark fir pointing still. And there is a cave
Under the overhanging rocks, alive
With water running fresh, a home of the Nymphs, 180
With benches for them, cut from the living stone.
No anchor is needed here for weary ships,
No mooring-cable. Aeneas brings them in,
Seven weary vessels, and the men are glad
To be ashore again, to feel dry sand
Under the salt-stained limbs. Achates[19] strikes
The spark from the flint, catches the fire on leaves,
Adds chips and kindling, blows and fans the flame,
And they bring out the soaked and salty corn,
The hand-mills, stone and mortar, and make ready, 190
As best they can, for bread.
Meanwhile Aeneas
Climbs to a look-out, for a view of the ocean,
Hoping for some good luck; the Phrygian galleys
Might meet his gaze, or Capys' boats, or a pennon
On a far-off mast-head flying. There is nothing,
Nothing to see out yonder, but near the water
Three stags are grazing, with a herd behind them,
A long line browsing through the peaceful valley.
He reaches for the bow and the swift arrows
Borne by Achates, and he shoots the leaders, 200
High-antlered, routs the common herd, and ceases
Only when seven are slain, a number equal
To the ships' tally, and then he seeks the harbor,
Divides the spoil, broaches the wine Acestes
Had stowed for them at Drepanum on their leaving,
A kingly present, and he calms their trouble,

[19] Aeneas' most faithful companion.

Saying: "O comrades, we have been through evil
Together before this; we have been through worse,
Scylla, Charybdis, and the Cyclops' dwelling,[20]
The sounding rocks. This, too, the god will end. 210
Call the nerve back; dismiss the fear, the sadness.
Some day, perhaps, remembering even this
Will be a pleasure. We are going on
Through whatsoever chance and change, until
We come to Latium, where the fates point out
A quiet dwelling-place, and Troy recovered.
Endure, and keep yourself for better days."
He kept to himself the sorrow in the heart,
Wearing, for them, a mask of hopefulness.
They were ready for the feasting. Part lay bare 220
The flesh from the torn hides, part cut the meat
Impaling it, still quivering, on spits,
Setting the kettles, keeping the water boiling,
And strong with food again, sprawling stretched out
On comfortable grass, they take their fill
Of bread and wine and venison, till hunger
Is gone, and the board cleared. And then they talk
For a long time, of where their comrades are,
Are, or may be, hopeful and doubtful both.
Could they believe them living? or would a cry 230
Fall on deaf ears forever? All those captains,
Brave Gyas, brave Cloanthus, Amycus,
Lycus, Orontes—in his secret heart
Aeneas mourns them.

Meanwhile, from the heaven
Jupiter watched the lands below, and the seas
With the white points of sails, and far-off people,
Turning his gaze toward Libya. And Venus
Came to him then, a little sadly, tears
Brimming in those bright eyes of hers. "Great father,"
She said, "Great ruler of the world 240
Of men and gods, great wielder of the lightning,
What has my poor Aeneas[21] done? what outrage
Could Trojans perpetrate, so that the world
Rejects them everywhere, and many a death
Inflicted on them over Italy?
There was a promise once, that as the years
Rolled onward, they would father Rome and rulers
Of Roman stock, to hold dominion over
All sea and land. That was a promise, father;
What changed it? Once that promise was my comfort; 250
Troy fell; I weighed one fate against another

[20] These perils are described in Book III.
[21] Venus is Aeneas' mother; Anchises, his father, is a mortal.

And found some consolation. But disaster
Keeps on; the same ill-fortune follows after.
What end of it all, great king? One man, Antenor,
Escaped the Greeks, came through Illyrian waters
Safe to Liburnian regions, where Timavus[22]
Roars underground, comes up nine times, and reaches
The floodland near the seas. One man, Antenor,
Founded a city, Padua, a dwelling
For Trojan men, a resting-place from labor, 260
And shares their quietude. But we, your children,
To whom heaven's height is granted, we are betrayed,
We have lost our ships, we are kept from Italy,
Kept far away. One enemy—I tell you
This is a shameful thing! Do we deserve it?
Is this our rise to power?"
He smiled, in answer,
The kind of smile that clears the air, and kissed her.
"Fear not, my daughter; fate remains unmoved
For the Roman generations. You will witness
Lavinium's rise, her walls fulfill the promise; 270
You will bring to heaven lofty-souled Aeneas.
There has been no change in me whatever. Listen!
To ease this care, I will prophesy a little,
I will open the book of fate. Your son Aeneas
Will wage a mighty war in Italy,[23]
Beat down proud nations, give his people laws,
Found them a city, a matter of three years
From victory to settlement. His son,
The boy Ascanius, named Ilus once,
When Troy was standing, and now called Iulus, 280
Shall reign for thirty years, and great in power
Forsake Lavinium, transfer the kingdom
To Alba Longa, new-built capital.
Here, for three hundred years, the line of Hector
Shall govern, till a royal priestess bears
Twin sons to Mars, and Romulus, rejoicing
In the brown wolf-skin[24] of his foster-mother,
Takes up the tribe, and builds the martial walls
And calls the people, after himself, the Romans.
To these I set no bounds in space or time; 290
They shall rule forever. Even bitter Juno
Whose fear now harries earth and sea and heaven
Will change to better counsels, and will cherish
The race that wears the toga, Roman masters

[22] The river Timavus flows into the Adriatic Sea (east of Italy); Liburnia is part of the Adriatic coast.

[23] The war is described in the second half of the poem, Books VII to XII.

[24] Romulus and his twin, Remus, were supposed to have been suckled by a she-wolf.

Of all the world. It is decreed. The time
Will come, as holy years wheel on, when Troy
Will subjugate Mycenae, vanquish Phthia,
Be lord of Argos.[25] And from this great line
Will come a Trojan, Caesar, to establish
The limit of his empire at the ocean, 300
His glory at the stars, a man called Julius
Whose name recalls Iulus. Welcome waits
For him in heaven; all the spoils of Asia
Will weight him down, and prayer be made before him.
Then wars will cease, and a rough age grow gentler,
White Faith and Vesta,[26] Romulus and Remus,
Give law to nations. War's grim gates will close,
Tight-shut with bars of iron, and inside them
The wickedness of war sit bound and silent,
The red mouth straining and the hands held tight 310
In fastenings of bronze, a hundred hundred."

With that, he sent down Mercury[27] from heaven
That Carthage might be kindly, and her land
And new-built towers receive them with a welcome,
And their queen, Dido, knowing the will of fate,
Swing wide her doors. On the oarage of his wings
He flies through the wide sweep of air to Libya,
Where, at the will of the god, the folk make ready
In kindliness of heart, and their queen's purpose
Is gracious and gentle.

All night long Aeneas 320
Had pondered many a care, and with bright morning
Resolved to reconnoiter; the winds have brought him
To a new country: who lives in it, men
Or only beasts? The fields appear untended.
The fleet lies under a hollow cliff, surrounded
By spikes of shade, and groves arch overhead,
Ample concealment. Aeneas and Achates
Went forth together, armed, down the trail in the forest,
And there his mother met him, a girl, it seemed,
From Thrace or Sparta, trim as any huntress 330
Who rides her horses hard, or outspeeds rivers
In her swift going. A bow hung over her shoulder,
Her hair blew free, her knees were bare, her garments
Tucked at the waist and knotted. As she saw them,
"Ho there, young men," she cried, "have you seen my sister
Around here anywhere? She wears a quiver,
And a spotted lynx-hide; maybe you have heard her
Hunting the boar and shouting?"

[25] Cities associated with the Trojans' Greek conquerors: Phthia with Achilles, Mycenae and Argos with Agamemnon, the Greek commander.

[26] Goddess of the hearth.

[27] Messenger of the gods.

But her son
Responded: "No; we have heard no sounds of hunting,
We have seen no one here. But tell me, maiden, 340
What name to call you by? In voice and feature
You are, I think, no mortal; a goddess, surely,—
Nymph, or Apollo's sister?[28] Whoever you are,
Be kind to us, lighten our trouble, tell us
Under what sky, along what coast of the world,
We wander, knowing neither land nor people,
Driven by gales and billows. Many a victim
We shall make ready for your altar." Venus
Answered: "I have no title to such honor.
The Tyrian girls all wear these crimson leggings 350
Like mine, and carry quivers. Tyrian folk
Live here; their city is Carthage; over the border
Lies Libya, warlike people. Our queen, Dido,
Came here from Tyre; she was fleeing from her brother,—
A long and complicated story; outrage,—
No matter, here it is, in brief. Her husband
Was Sychaeus, wealthiest of all Phoenicians,
At least in land, and Dido loved him dearly
Since first her father gave her to him, virgin,
And then unlucky bride. She had a brother, 360
Pygmalion, king of Tyre, a monster, evil
In wickedness, and madness came between
Those men, the two of them. Pygmalion murdered
Sychaeus at the altar; he was crazy
And blind for gold and crafty; what did he care
About his sister's love? And he kept it quiet
For a long time, kept telling Dido something
To fool her with false comfort, but Sychaeus
Came to her in a dream, a ghost, unburied,
With the wounds in his breast, the story of the altar, 370
The pale lips blurting out the secret horror,
The crime in the dark of the household. *Flee,* he told her,
Forsake this land; and he told her where the treasure
Lay hidden in earth, uncounted gold and silver.
Dido was moved to flight, secured companions,
All those possessed by fear, all those whom hatred
Had made relentless; ships were standing ready,
As it so happened; they put the gold aboard,
And over the sea the greedy tyrant's treasure
Went sailing, with a woman for a captain. 380
They came here; you will see the walls arising
And the great citadel of the town called Carthage.
Here they bought ground; they used to call it Byrsa,
That being a word for bull's hide; they bought only

[28] Diana, goddess of the hunt.

What a bull's hide could cover. And now tell me
Who you might be yourselves? what land do you come from,
Bound for what coast?"
And he began his answer
With a long sigh: "O goddess, if I told you
All from the first beginning, if you had leisure
To listen to the record of our trouble, 390
It would take me all day long. From ancient Troy,
In case that name means anything, we come
Driven over many seas, and now a storm
Has whipped us on this coast. I am Aeneas,
A good, devoted man; I carry with me
My household gods, saved from the Greeks; I am known
In heaven; it is Italy I seek,
A homeland for me there, and a race descended
From lofty Jove. With a score of ships we started
Over the Phrygian ocean, following fate 400
And the way my mother pointed. Only seven
Are left us now, battered survivors, after
The rage of wind and wave. And here I wander
The wastes of Libya, unknown and needy,
Driven from Europe and Asia." And his mother
Broke in on his complaining:—"Whoever you are,
Some god must care for you, I think, to bring you
Here to the city of Carthage. Follow on,
Go to the royal palace. For, I tell you,
Your comrades have returned, your fleet is safe, 410
Brought to good haven by the turn of the winds,
Unless the augury my parents taught me
Was foolish nonsense. In the heaven yonder
You see twelve swans, rejoicing in long column,
Scattered, a little while ago, and driven
By the swooping eagle, over all the sky,
But now, it seems, they light on land, or watch
Those who came down before them; as they circle
In company, and make a cheerful sound
With whir of wing or song, so, let me tell you, 420
Your ships and men already enter harbor
Or near it under full sail. Keep on, go forward
Where the path leads."
And as she turned, her shoulders
Shone with a radiant light; her hair shed fragrance,
Her robes slipped to her feet, and the true goddess
Walked in divinity.[29] He knew his mother,
And his voice pursued her flight: "Cruel again!
Why mock your son so often with false phantoms?

[29] A goddess could be distinguished from a mortal by her gait and carriage.

Why may not hand be joined to hand, and words
Exchanged in truthfulness?" So, still reproachful, 430
He went on toward the city, with Achates,
But Venus cast dark air around their going,
A veil of mist, so that no man might see them
Or lay a hand on them, or halt them, asking
The reasons of their coming. She soared upward
To Paphos, happily home to temple and altars
Steaming with incense, redolent with garlands.
And they went on, where the little pathway led them
To rising ground; below them lay the city,
Majestic buildings now, where once were hovels, 440
A wonder to Aeneas, gates and bustle
And well-paved streets, the busy Tyrians toiling
With stones for walls and citadel, or marking
Foundations for their homes, drainage and furrow,
All under ordered process. They dredge harbors,
Set cornerstones, quarry the rock, where someday
Their theater will tower. They are like bees
In early summer over the country flowers
When the sun is warm, and the young of the hive emerge,
And they pack the molten honey, bulge the cells 450
With the sweet nectar, add new loads, and harry
The drones away from the hive, and the work glows,
And the air is sweet with bergamot and clover.
"Happy the men whose walls already rise!"
Exclaims Aeneas, gazing on the city,
And enters there, still veiled in cloud—a marvel!—
And walks among the people, and no one sees him.
There was a grove in the middle of the city,
Most happy in its shade; this was the place
Where first the Tyrians, tossed by storm and whirlwind, 460
Dug up the symbol royal Juno showed them,
The skull of a war-horse, a sign the race to come
Would be supreme in war and wealth, for ages,
And Dido here was building a great temple
In Juno's honor, rich in gifts, and blessed
With the presence of the goddess. Lintel and rafter
Were bronze above bronze stairways, and bronze portals
Swung on bronze hinges. Here Aeneas first
Dared hope for safety, find some reassurance
In hope of better days: a strange sight met him, 470
To take his fear away. Waiting the queen,
He stood there watching, under the great temple,
Letting his eyes survey the city's fortune,
The artist's workmanship, the craftsman's labor,
And there, with more than wonder, he sees the battles
Fought around Troy, and the wars whose fame had travelled
The whole world over; there is Agamemnon,

Priam, and Menelaus,[30] and Achilles,
A menace to them all. He is moved to tears.
"What place in all the world," he asks Achates, 480
"Is empty of our sorrow? There is Priam!
Look! even here there are rewards for praise,
There are tears for things, and what men suffer touches
The human heart. Dismiss your fear; this story
Will bring some safety to you." Sighing often,
He could not turn his gaze away; it was only
A picture on a wall, but the sight afforded
Food for the spirit's need. He saw the Greeks,
Hard-pressed, in flight, and Trojans coming after,
Or, on another panel, the scene reversed, 490
Achilles in pursuit, his own men fleeing;
He saw, and tears came into his eyes again,
The tents of Rhesus,[31] snowy-white, betrayed
In their first sleep by bloody Diomedes
With many a death, and the fiery horses driven
Into the camp, before they ever tasted
The grass of Troy, or drank from Xanthus' river.
Another scene showed Troilus, poor youngster,
Running away, his arms flung down; Achilles
Was much too good for him; he had fallen backward 500
Out of his car, but held the reins, and the horses
Dragged him along the ground, his hair and shoulders
Bounding in dust, and the spear making a scribble.
And there were Trojan women, all in mourning,
With streaming hair, on their way to Pallas' temple,
Bearing, as gift, a robe, but the stern goddess[32]
Kept her gaze on the ground. Three times Achilles
Had dragged the body of Hector around the walls,
And was selling it for money. What a groan
Came from Aeneas' heart, seeing that spoil, 510
That chariot, and helpless Priam reaching
His hands, unarmed, across the broken body!
And he saw himself there, too, fighting in battle
Against Greek leaders, he saw the Eastern columns,
And swarthy Memnon's[33] arms. Penthesilea,
The Amazon, blazes in fury, leading
Her crescent-shielded thousands, a golden buckle
Below her naked breast, a soldieress
Fighting with men.

[30] Priam was the patriarchal king of Troy, Menelaus was the cuckolded husband of Helen, brother of Agamemnon and co-commander of the Greek forces at Troy.

[31] Rhesus supported the Trojans against the Greeks. Troy could not fall, it was believed, if his horses tasted Troy's grass or drank from its river Xanthus. But before they could do either, Diomedes and Ulysses carried the horses off.

[32] Pallas (the Greek Athena or Roman Minerva) sided with the Greeks against the Trojans.

[33] Ethiopian king who sided with the Trojans.

And as he watched these marvels
In one long fascinated stare of wonder, 520
Dido, the queen, drew near; she came to the temple
With a great train, all majesty, all beauty,
As on Eurotas' riverside, or where
Mount Cynthus[34] towers high, Diana leads
Her bands of dancers, and the Oreads follow
In thousands, right and left, the taller goddess,
The quiver-bearing maiden, and Latona
Is filled with secret happiness, so Dido
Moved in her company, a queen, rejoicing,
Ordering on her kingdom's rising glory. 530
At Juno's portal, under the arch of the temple,
She took her throne, a giver of law and justice,
A fair partitioner of toil and duty,
And suddenly Aeneas, from the crowd,
Saw Trojan men approaching, brave Cloanthus,
Sergestus, Antheus, and all those others
Whom the black storm had driven here and yonder.
This he cannot believe, nor can Achates,
Torn between fear and joy. They burn with ardor
To seek their comrades' handclasp, but confusion 540
Still holds them in the cloud: what can have happened?
They watch from the cover of mist: men still were coming
From all the ships, chosen, it seemed, as pleaders
For graciousness before the temple, calling
Aloud: what fortune had been theirs, he wonders,
Where had they left the ships; why were they coming?
They were given audience; Ilioneus,
Senior to all, began: "O Queen, whom Jove
Has given the founding of a great new city,
Has given to bridle haughty tribes with justice, 550
We, pitiful Trojans, over every ocean
Driven by storm, make our appeal: keep from us
The terrible doom of fire; protect our vessels;
Have mercy on a decent race; consider
Our lot with closer interest. We have not come
To ravish Libyan homes, or carry plunder
Down to the shore. We lack the arrogance
Of conquerors; there is no aggression in us.
There is a place which Greeks have given a name,
The Land in the West; it is powerful in arms, 560
Rich in its soil; Oenotrians used to live there,
And now, the story goes, a younger people
Inhabit it, calling themselves Italians
After their leader's name.[35] We were going there

[34] Birthplace of Diana, goddess of the hunt. In the passage following, *Oreads* are mountain nymphs, *the taller goddess* refers to Diana, *Latona* was another name for Leto, mother of Diana.

[35] Italus, a legendary ruler.

When, big with storm and cloud, Orion[36] rising
Drove us on hidden quicksands, and wild winds
Scattered us over the waves, by pathless rocks
And the swell of the surge. A few of us have drifted
Here to your shores. What kind of men are these,
What barbarous land permits such attitudes? 570
We have been denied the welcome of the beach,
Forbidden to set foot on land; they rouse
All kinds of war against us. You despise,
It may be, human brotherhood, and arms
Wielded by men. But there are gods, remember,
Who care for right and wrong. Our king Aeneas
May be alive; no man was ever more just,
More decent ever, or greater in war and arms.
If fate preserves him still, if he still breathes
The welcome air, above the world of shadows, 580
Fear not; to have treated us with kindly service
Need bring you no repentance. We have cities
In Sicily as well, and King Acestes
Is one of us, from Trojan blood. We ask you
To let us beach our battered fleet, make ready
Beams from the forest timber, mend our oarage,
Seek Italy and Latium, glad at knowing
Our king and comrades rescued. But if safety
Is hopeless for him now, and Libyan water
Has been his grave, and if his son Iulus 590
Is desperate, or lost, grant us permission
At least to make for Sicily, whence we came here,
Where king Acestes has a dwelling for us."
The Trojans, as he ended, all were shouting,
And Dido, looking down, made a brief answer:
"I am sorry, Trojans; put aside your care,
Have no more fear. The newness of the kingdom
And our strict need compel me to such measures—
Sentries on every border, far and wide.
But who so ignorant as not to know 600
The nation of Aeneas, manly both
In deeds and people, and the city of Troy?
We are not as dull as that, we folk from Carthage;
The sun shines on us here. Whether you seek
The land in the west, the sometime fields of Saturn,[37]
Or the Sicilian realms and king Acestes,
I will help you to the limit; should you wish
To settle here and share this kingdom with me,
The city I found is yours; draw up your ships;

[36] The constellation was believed to presage storms.
[37] Italy, where Saturn dwelt after his dethronement by Jupiter and his new generation of gods. Saturn's reign is associated with an ancient "golden age" of simplicity.

Trojan and Tyrian I treat alike. 610
Would, also, that your king were here, Aeneas,
Driven by that same wind. I will send good men
Along the coast to seek him, under orders
To scour all Libya; he may be wandering
Somewhere, in woods or town, surviving shipwreck."
Aeneas and Achates both were eager
To break the cloud; the queen inspired their spirit
With her address. Achates asked Aeneas:—
"What do we do now, goddess-born? You see
They all are safe, our vessels and our comrades, 620
Only one missing, and we saw him drowning,
Ourselves, beneath the waves; all other things
Confirm what Venus told us." And as he finished,
The cloud around them broke, dissolved in air,
Illumining Aeneas, like a god,
Light radiant around his face and shoulders,
And Venus gave him all the bloom of youth,
Its glow, its liveliness, as the artist adds
Luster to ivory, or sets in gold
Silver or marble. No one saw him coming 630
Until he spoke:—"You seek me; here I am,
Trojan Aeneas, saved from the Libyan waves.
Worn out by all the perils of land and sea,
In need of everything, blown over the great world,
A remnant left by the Greeks, Dido, we lack
The means to thank our only pitier
For offer of a city and a home.
If there is justice anywhere, if goodness
Means anything to any power, if gods
At all regard good people, may they give 640
The great rewards you merit. Happy the age,
Happy the parents who have brought you forth!
While rivers run to sea, while shadows move
Over the mountains, while the stars burn on,
Always, your praise, your honor, and your name,
Whatever land I go to, will endure."[38]
His hand went out to greet his men, Serestus,
Gyas, Cloanthus, Ilioneus,
The others in their turn. And Dido marvelled
At his appearance, first, and all that trouble 650
He had borne up under; there was a moment's silence
Before she spoke: "What chance, what violence,
O goddess-born, has driven you through danger,
From grief to grief? Are you indeed that son
Whom Venus bore Anchises? I remember

[38]Aeneas' words are ironic in the light of later events in the poem and in history.

When Teucer came to Sidon,[39] as an exile
Seeking new kingdoms, and my father helped him,
My father, Belus, conqueror of Cyprus.
From that time on I have known about your city,
Your name, and the Greek kings, and the fall of Troy. 660
Even their enemies would praise the Trojans,
Or claim descent from Teucer's line. I bid you
Enter my house. I, too, am fortune-driven
Through many sufferings; this land at last
Has brought me rest. Not ignorant of evil,
I know one thing, at least,—to help the wretched."
And so she led Aeneas to the palace,
Proclaiming sacrifice at all the temples
In honor of his welcome, and sent presents
To his comrades at the shore, a score of bullocks, 670
A hundred swine, a hundred ewes and lambs
In honor of the joyous day. The palace,
Within, is made most bright with pomp and splendor,
The halls prepared for feasting. Crimson covers
Are laid, with fine embroidery, and silver
Is heavy on the tables; gold, engraven,
Recalls ancestral prowess, a tale of heroes
From the race's first beginnings.
And Aeneas,
Being a thoughtful father, speeds Achates
Back to the ships, with tidings for Iulus, 680
He is to join them; all the father's fondness
Is centered on the son. Orders are given
To bring gifts with him, saved from the Trojan ruins,
A mantle stiff with figures worked in gold;
A veil with gold acanthus running through it,
Once worn by Helen, when she sailed from Sparta
Toward that forbidden marriage, a wondrous gift
Made by her mother Leda; and the sceptre
That Ilione, Priam's eldest daughter,
Had carried once; a necklace hung with pearls; 690
A crown of gold and jewels. Toward the ships
Achates sped the message.
Meanwhile Venus
Plotted new stratagems, that Cupid, changed
In form and feature, should appear instead
Of young Ascanius,[40] and by his gifts
Inspire the queen to passion, with his fire
Burning her very bones. She feared the house
Held dubious intentions; men of Tyre

[39] Teucer was a Greek exiled by his father; he is not to be confused with the Teucer who was the legendary ancestor of the Trojans (who are therefore sometimes called Teucrians). Sidon was a city near Tyre, Dido's former home.

[40] Aeneas' son is sometimes called Ascanius, sometimes Iulus.

Were always two-faced people, and Juno's anger
Vexed her by night. She spoke to her wingèd son:— 700
"O my one strength and source of power, my son,
Disdainful of Jove's thunderbolt, to you
I come in prayer for help. You know that Juno
Is hateful toward Aeneas, keeping him tossing
All over the seas in bitterness; you have often
Grieved with me for your brother. And now Dido
Holds him with flattering words; I do not trust
Juno's ideas of welcome; she will never
Pause at a point like this. Therefore I purpose
To take the queen by cunning, put around her 710
A wall of flame, so that no power can change her,
So that a blazing passion for Aeneas
Will bind her to us. Listen! I will tell you
How you can manage this. The royal boy,
My greatest care, has heard his father's summons
To come to the city, bringing presents, rescued
From the flames of Troy and the sea; and he is ready.
But I will make him drowsy, carry him off
In slumber over Cythera, or hide him
Deep on Idalium[41] in a secret bower 720
Before he learns the scheme or interrupts it.
You, for one night, no more, assume his features,
The boy's familiar guise, yourself a boy,
So that when Dido takes you to her bosom
During the royal feast, with the wine flowing,
And happiness abounding, you, receiving
The sweetness of her kiss, will overcome her
With secret fire and poison."
For his mother
Cupid put off his wings, and went rejoicing
With young Iulus' stride; the real Iulus 730
Venus had lulled in soft repose, and borne him
Warm in her bosom to Idalian groves,
Where the soft marjoram cradled him with blossom
Exhaling shadowy sweetness over his slumber.
And, with Achates leading, Cupid came
Obedient to his mother, bringing gifts.
The queen receives them, on a golden couch
Below the royal tapestries, where spreads
Of crimson wait Aeneas and his Trojans.
Servants bring water for their hands, and bread 740
In baskets, and fine napkins. At the fire
Are fifty serving-maids, to set the feast,
A hundred more, girls, and a hundred boys
To load the tables, and bring the goblets round,

[41] Cythera was the island associated with Venus' birth; Idalium was a part of Cyprus associated with worship of her.

As through the happy halls the Tyrians throng,
Admire the Trojan gifts, admire Iulus,
The young god with the glowing countenance,
The charming words, the robe, the saffron veil
Edged with acanthus. More than all the rest,
Disaster-bound, the unhappy queen takes fire, 750
And cannot have enough of looking, moved
Alike by boy and gifts. She watches him
Cling to his father's neck, or come to her
For fondling, and her eyes, her heart, receive him,
Alas, poor queen, not knowing what a god
Is plotting for her sorrow. He remembers
What Venus told him; she forgets a little
About Sychaeus; the heart unused to love
Stirs with a living passion.
When the first quiet settled over the tables, 760
And the boards were cleared, they set the great bowls down,
Crowning the wine with garlands. A great hum
Runs through the halls, the voices reach the rafters,
The burning lamps below the fretted gold,
The torches flaring, put the night to rout.
The queen commands the loving-cup of Belus,
Heavy with gems and gold, and fills it full,
And silence fills the halls before her prayer:—
"Jupiter, giver of laws for host and guest,
Grant this to be a happy day for all, 770
Both Tyrians and travellers from Troy,
And something for our children to remember!
May Bacchus,[42] giver of joy, attend, and Juno
Be kind, and all my Tyrians be friendly!"
She poured libation on the table, touched
The gold rim with her lips, passed on the bowl
To Bitias, who dove deep, and other lords
Took up the challenge. And a minstrel played
A golden lyre, Iopas, taught by Atlas:[43]
Of the sun's labors and the wandering moon 780
He sang, whence came the race of beasts and man,
Whence rain and fire, the stars and constellations,
Why suns in winter hasten to the sea,
Or what delay draws out the dawdling nights.
The Tyrians roar, applauding, and the Trojans
Rejoice no less, and the poor queen prolongs
The night with conversation, drinking deep
Of her long love, and asking many questions
Of Priam, Hector; of the arms of Memnon;
How big Achilles was; and Diomedes, 790

[42] God of wine.

[43] The bard Iopas sings of astronomical science, which is associated with Atlas, the gigantic being who in mythology supports the heavens on his shoulders.

What were his horses like? "Tell us, my guest,"
She pleads, "from the beginning, all the story,
The treachery of the Greeks, the wanderings,
The perils of the seven tiresome years."

BOOK II: THE FALL OF TROY

They all were silent, watching. From his couch
Aeneas spoke: "A terrible grief, O Queen,
You bid me live again, how Troy went down
Before the Greeks, her wealth, her pitiful kingdom,
Sorrowful things I saw myself, wherein
I had my share and more. Even Ulysses,[1]
Even his toughest soldiery might grieve
At such a story. And the hour is late
Already; night is sliding down the sky
And setting stars urge slumber. But if you long 10
To learn our downfall, to hear the final chapter
Of Troy, no matter how I shrink, remembering,
And turn away in grief, let me begin it.[2]

Broken in war, set back by fate, the leaders
Of the Greek host, as years went by, contrived,
With Pallas' help, a horse as big as a mountain.
They wove its sides with planks of fir, pretending
This was an offering for their safe return,
At least, so rumor had it. But inside
They packed, in secret, into the hollow sides 20
The fittest warriors; the belly's cavern,
Huge as it was, was filled with men in armor.
There is an island, Tenedos, well-known,
Rich in the days of Priam; now it is only
A bay, and not too good an anchorage
For any ship to trust. They sailed there, hid
On the deserted shore. We thought they had gone,
Bound for Mycenae,[3] and Troy was very happy,
Shaking off grief, throwing the gates wide open.
It was a pleasure, for a change, to go 30
See the Greek camp, station and shore abandoned;
Why, this was where Achilles camped, his minions,
The Dolopes, were here; and the fleet just yonder,
And that was the plain where we used to meet in battle.
Some of us stared in wonder at the horse,

[1] The Latin name for Odysseus, the Greek hero.

[2] Typically, epic poems begin in the middle of the story, the earlier events being supplied in a flashback narrative like that of Aeneas in Books II and III.

[3] City in Greece ruled by Agamemnon, the Greek commander.

Astounded by its vastness, Minerva's gift,
Death from the virgin goddess, had we known it.
Thymoetes, whether in treachery, or because
The fates of Troy so ordered, was the first one
To urge us bring it in to the heart of the city, 40
But Capys, and some others, knowing better,
Suspicious of Greek plotting, said to throw it
Into the sea, to burn it up with fire,
To cut it open, see what there was inside it.
The wavering crowd could not make up its mind.

And, at that point, Laocoön came running,
With a great throng at his heels, down from the hilltop
As fast as ever he could, and before he reached us,
Cried in alarm: 'Are you crazy, wretched people?
Do you think they have gone, the foe? Do you think that any 50
Gifts of the Greeks lack treachery? Ulysses,—
What was his reputation? Let me tell you,
Either the Greeks are hiding in this monster,
Or it's some trick of war, a spy, or engine,
To come down on the city. Tricky business
Is hiding in it. Do not trust it, Trojans,
Do not believe this horse. Whatever it may be,
I fear the Greeks, even when bringing presents.'
With that, he hurled the great spear at the side
With all the strength he had. It fastened, trembling, 60
And the struck womb rang hollow, a moaning sound.
He had driven us, almost, to let the light in
With the point of the steel, to probe, to tear, but something
Got in his way, the gods, or fate, or counsel,
Ill-omened, in our hearts; or Troy would be standing
And Priam's lofty citadel unshaken.

Meanwhile, some Trojan shepherds, pulling and hauling,
Had a young fellow, with his hands behind him,
Tied up, and they were dragging him to Priam.
He had let himself be taken so, on purpose, 70
To open Troy to the Greeks, a stranger, ready
For death or shifty cunning, a cool intriguer,
Let come what may. They crowd around to see him,
Take turns in making fun of him, that captive.
Listen, and learn Greek trickiness; learn all
Their crimes from one.
He stopped in the middle, frightened and defenceless,
Looked at the Trojan ranks,—'What land, what waters,
Can take me now?' he cried, 'There is nothing, nothing
Left for me any more, no place with the Greeks, 80
And here are the Trojans howling for my blood!'
Our mood was changed. We pitied him, poor fellow,
Sobbing his heart out. We bade him tell his story,

His lineage, his news: what can he count on,
The captive that he is? His fear had gone
As he began: 'O King, whatever happens,
I will tell the truth, tell all of it; to start with,
I own I am a Greek. Sinon is wretched,
Fortune has made him so, but she will never
Make him a liar. You may perhaps have heard 90
Rumors of Palamedes, son of Belus,[4]
A man of glorious fame. But the Greeks killed him,—
He was against the war, and so they killed him,
An innocent man, by perjury and lying
False witness. Now that he is dead they mourn him.
My father, his poor relative, had sent me
To soldier in his company; I was then
Scarcely beyond my boyhood. Palamedes
Held, for some time, some influence and standing
In royal councils, and we shared his glory, 100
But, and all men know this, Ulysses' hatred,
His cunning malice, pulled him down; thereafter
I lived in darkness, dragging out a lifetime
In sorrow for my innocent lord, and anger,
And in my anger I was very foolish,
I talked; I vowed, if I got home to Argos,
I would have vengeance: so I roused Ulysses
To hate me in his turn, and that began it,
Downfall and evil, Ulysses always trying
To frighten me with hint and accusation, 110
With rumors planted where the crowd would listen;
Oh yes, Ulysses knew what he was doing,
He never stopped, until with Calchas[5] working
Hand in glove with him—why am I telling this,
And what's the use? I am stalling. All the Greeks,
You think, are all alike; what more do you want?
Inflict the punishment. That would be something
Ulysses would rejoice in, and some others
Pay handsome money for!'

But we were all on fire to hear him further. 120
Pelasgian[6] craft meant nothing to our folly.
Trembling and nervous, he resumed his lying:
'The Greeks were tired of the long war; they often
Wanted to sail from Troy for home. Oh, would
That they had only done it! But a storm
Would cut them off, or the wrong wind terrify them.
Especially, just after the horse was finished,

[4] Not to be confused with Dido's father Belus, mentioned in Book I.

[5] As a Greek priest and prophet, Calchas' task was to discover and reveal the will of the gods.

[6] Here a synonym for "Greek."

With the joined planks of maple, all the heaven
Roared loud with storm-clouds. In suspense and terror
We sent Eurypylus to ask Apollo 130
What could be done; the oracle was gloomy,
Foreboding: "Blood, O Greeks, and a slain virgin[7]
Appeased the winds when first you came here; blood
Must pay for your return, a life be given,
An Argive life." The word came to our ears
With terror in it, our blood ran cold in our veins,
For whom was fate preparing? who would be
The victim of Apollo? Then Ulysses
Dragged Calchas into our midst, with a great uproar,
Trying his best to make the prophet tell us 140
What the gods wanted. And there were many then
Who told me what was coming, or kept silent
Because they saw, and all too well, the scheme
Ulysses had in mind. For ten days Calchas
Said nothing at all, hid in his tent, refusing
To have a word of his pronounce the sentence,
And all the time Ulysses kept on shouting,
Till Calchas broke, and doomed me to the altar.
And all assented; what each man had feared
In his own case, he bore with great composure 150
When turned another way.
The terrible day was almost on me; fillets
Were ready for my temples, the salted meal
Prepared, the altars standing. But I fled,
I tore myself away from death, I admit it,
I hid all night in sedge and muddy water
At the edge of the lake, hoping, forever hoping,
They might set sail. And now I hope no longer
To see my home, my parents, or my children,
Poor things, whom they will kill because I fled them, 160
Whom they will murder for my sacrilege.
But oh, by the gods above, by any power
That values truth, by any uncorrupted
Remnant of faith in all the world, have pity,
Have pity on a soul that bears such sorrow,
More than I ever deserved.'
He had no need to ask us. Priam said,
Untie him, and we did so with a promise
To spare his life. Our king, with friendly words,
Addressed him, saying, 'Whoever you are, forget 170
The Greeks, from now on. You are ours; but tell me
Why they have built this monstrous horse? who made it,
Who thought of it? What is it, war-machine,

[7] Iphigenia, daughter of Agamemnon; her life had been sacrificed to appease the gods and thus gain for the Greeks favorable winds for their expedition against Troy.

Religious offering?' And he, instructed
In every trick and artifice, made answer,
Lifting his hands, now free: 'Eternal fires,
Inviolable godhead, be my witness,
You altars, you accursèd swords, you fillets
Which I as victim wore, I had the right
To break those solemn bonds, I had the right 180
To hate those men, to bring whatever they hide
Into the light and air; I am bound no longer
To any country, any laws, but, Trojans,
Keep to the promise, if I tell the truth,
If I pay back with interest.
All the Greek hope, since first the war began,
Rested in Pallas, always. But Ulysses,
The crime-contriver, and the son of Tydeus[8]
Attacked Minerva's temple, stole her image
Out of the holy shrine, and slew the guards, 190
And laid their bloody hands upon the goddess,
And from that time the Danaan[9] hopes were broken,
Faltered and failed. It was no doubtful anger
Pallas revealed; she gave them signs and portents.
From her image in the camp the upraised eyes
Shot fire, and sweat ran salty down the limbs,
Thrice from the ground she seemed to flash and leap
With vibrant spear and clashing shield. The priest,
Calchas, made prophecy: they must take to flight
Over the sea, and Troy could not be taken 200
Without new omens; they must go to Argos,
Bring back the goddess again, whom they have taken
In curved ships over the sea. And if they have gone,
They are bound for home, Mycenae, for new arms,
New gods, new soldiers; they will be here again
When least expected. Calchas' message warned them,
And so they built this image, to replace
The one they had stolen, a gigantic offering
For a tremendous sacrilege. It was Calchas,
Again, who bade them build a mass so mighty 210
It almost reached the stars, too big to enter
Through any gate, or be brought inside the walls.
For if your hands should damage it, destruction,
(May God avert it) would come upon the city,
But if your hands helped bring it home, then Asia
Would be invading Greece, and doom await
Our children's children.'
We believed him, we
Whom neither Diomede nor great Achilles
Had taken, nor ten years, nor that armada,

[8]His son was Diomedes, one of the greatest of the Greek warriors.
[9]Greek.

A thousand ships of war. But Sinon did it 220
By perjury and guile.
Then something else,
Much greater and more terrible, was forced
Upon us, troubling our unseeing spirits.
Laocoön, allotted priest of Neptune,
Was slaying a great bull beside the altars,
When suddenly, over the tranquil deep
From Tenedos,—I shudder even now,
Recalling it—there came a pair of serpents
With monstrous coils, breasting the sea, and aiming
Together for the shore. Their heads and shoulders 230
Rose over the waves, upright, with bloody crests,
The rest of them trailing along the water,
Looping in giant spirals; the foaming sea
Hissed under their motion. And they reached the land,
Their burning eyes suffused with blood and fire,
Their darting tongues licking the hissing mouths.
Pale at the sight, we fled. But they went on
Straight toward Laocoön, and first each serpent
Seized in its coils his two young sons, and fastened
The fangs in those poor bodies. And the priest 240
Struggled to help them, weapons in his hand.
They seized him, bound him with their mighty coils,
Twice round his waist, twice round his neck, they squeezed
With scaly pressure, and still towered above him.
Straining his hands to tear the knots apart,
His chaplets[10] stained with blood and the black poison,
He uttered horrible cries, not even human,
More like the bellowing of a bull when, wounded,
It flees the altar, shaking from the shoulder
The ill-aimed axe. And on the pair went gliding 250
To the highest shrine, the citadel of Pallas,
And vanished underneath the feet of the goddess
And the circle of her shield.
The people trembled
Again; they said Laocoön deserved it,
Having, with spear, profaned the sacred image.
It must be brought to its place, they cried, the goddess
Must be appeased. We broke the walls, exposing
The city's battlements, and all were busy
Helping the work, with rollers underfoot
And ropes around the neck. It climbed our walls, 260
The deadly engine. Boys, unwedded girls
Sang alleluias round it, all rejoicing
To have a hand on the tow-rope. It came nearer,
Threatening, gliding, into the very city.

[10] Garlands for the head.

O motherland! O Ilium, home of gods,
O walls of Troy! Four times it stopped, four times
The sound of arms came from it, and we pressed on,
Unheedful, blind in madness, till we set it,
Ill-omened thing, on the citadel we worshipped.
And even when Cassandra[11] gave us warning, 270
We never believed her; so a god had ordered.
That day, our last, poor wretches, we were happy,
Garlanding the temples of the gods
All through the town.
And the sky turned, and darkness
Came from the ocean, the great shade covering earth
And heaven, and the trickery of the Greeks.
Sprawling along the walls, the Trojans slumbered,
Sleep holding their weary limbs, and the Greek armada,
From Tenedos, under the friendly silence
Of a still moon, came surely on. The flagship 280
Blazed at the masthead with a sudden signal,
And Sinon, guarded by the fates, the hostile
Will of the gods, swung loose the bolts; the Greeks
Came out of the wooden womb. The air received them,
The happy captains, Sthenelus, Ulysses,
Thessandrus, Acamas, Achilles' son
Called Neoptolemus, Thoas, Machaon,
Epeos, who designed the thing,—they all
Came sliding down the rope, and Menelaus
Was with them in the storming of a city 290
Buried in sleep and wine. The watch was murdered,
The open doors welcome the rush of comrades,
They marshal the determined ranks for battle.
It was the time when the first sleep begins
For weary mortals, heaven's most welcome gift.
In sleep, before my eyes, I seemed to see
Hector, most sorrowful, black with bloody dust,
Torn, as he had been, by Achilles' car,
The thong-marks on his swollen feet. How changed
He was from that great Hector who came, once, 300
Triumphant in Achilles' spoil, from hurling
Fire at the Grecian ships. With ragged beard,
Hair matted with his blood, wearing the wounds
He earned around the walls of Troy, he stood there.
It seemed that I spoke first:—'O light of Troy,
Our surest hope, we have long been waiting for you,
What shores have kept you from us? Many deaths,
Much suffering, have visited our city,
And we are tired. Why do I see these wounds?

[11] A daughter of the royal family of Troy; gifted with prophecy, she was nevertheless doomed always to have her true prophecies disbelieved.

What shame has caused them?' Those were foolish questions; 310
He made no answer but a sigh or a groan,
And then: 'Alas, O goddess-born! Take flight,
Escape these flames! The enemy has the walls,
Troy topples from her lofty height; enough
Has been paid out to Priam and to country.
Could any hand have saved them, Hector's would have.
Troy trusts to you her household gods, commending
Her holy things to you; take them, companions
Of destiny; seek walls for them, and a city
To be established, a long sea-wandering over.' 320
From the inner shrine he carried Vesta's chaplets
In his own hands, and her undying fire.

Meanwhile, the city is all confusion and sorrow;
My father Anchises' house, remote and sheltered
Among its trees, was not so far away
But I could hear the noises, always clearer,
The thickening din of war. Breaking from sleep,
I climb to the roof-top, listening and straining
The way a shepherd does on the top of a mountain
When fire goes over the corn, and the winds are roaring, 330
Or the rush of a mountain torrent drowns the fields
And the happy crops and the work of men and oxen
And even drags great trees over. And then I knew
The truth indeed; the craft of the Greeks was hidden
No longer from my sight. The house of a neighbor,
Deiphobus, went up in flames; next door,
Ucalegon was burning. Sigeum's[12] water
Gave back the glow. Men shouted, and the trumpets
Blared loud. I grab my arms, with little purpose,
There was no sense in it, but my heart was burning 340
To mass a band for war, rush to the hilltop
With comrades at my side. Anger and frenzy
Hurry me on. A decent death in battle
Is a helpful thought, sometimes.

And here came Panthus, running from the weapons,
Priest of Apollo, and a son of Othrys,
With holy relics in his hands, and dragging
His little grandson, here came Panthus, running
In madness to my door. 'How goes it, Panthus?
What stronghold still is ours?' I had hardly spoken, 350
When he began, with a groan: 'It has come, this day
Will be our last, and we can not escape it.
Trojans we have been, Troy has been, and glory
Is ours no more. Fierce Jupiter has taken

[12] A cape near Troy.

Everything off to Argos, and Greeks lord it
In a town on fire. The horse, high in the city,
Pours out armed men, and Sinon, arrogant victor,
Lights up more fires. The gates are standing open,
And men are there by the thousands, ever as many
As came once from Mycenae; others block 360
The narrow streets, with weapons drawn; the blades
Flash in the dark; the point is set for murder.
A few of the guards are trying, striking blindly,
For all the good it does.'

His words, or the gods' purpose, swept me on
Toward fire and arms, where the grim furies call,
And the clamor and confusion, reaching heaven.
Ripheus joined me, Epytus, mighty in arms,
Came to my side in the moonlight, Hypanis, Dymas,
And young Coroebus, Mygdon's son, poor youngster, 370
Mad with a hopeless passion for Cassandra,
He wanted to help Priam, but never heeded
The warnings of his loved one.
As they ranged
Themselves for battle, eager, I addressed them:
'O brave young hearts, it will do no good; no matter.
Even if your will is fixed, to follow a leader
Taking the final risk, you can't help seeing
The fortune of our state. The gods have gone,
They have left their shrines and altars, and the power
They once upheld is fallen. You are helping 380
A town already burnt. So let us die,
Rush into arms. One safety for the vanquished
Is to have hope of none.'
They were young, and angry.
Like wolves, marauders in black mist, whom hunger
Drives blindly on, whose whelps, abandoned, wait them
Dry-jawed, so we went on, through foes, through weapons,
To certain death; we made for the heart of the city,
Black night around us with its hollow shadow.
Who could explain that night's destruction, equal
Its agony with tears? The ancient city, 390
A power for many years, comes down, and corpses
Lie littering the streets and homes and altars.
Not only Trojans die. The old-time valor
Returns to the vanquished heart, and the Greek victors
Know what it is to fall. Everywhere sorrow,
Everywhere panic, everywhere the image
Of death, made manifold.

Out of a crowd of Greeks comes one Androgeos,
Thinking us allies, hailing us as friendly:
'Why men, where have you been, you dawdling fellows? 400

Hurry along! Here is plunder for the taking,
Others are busy at it, and you just coming
From the high ships!' And then he knew he had blundered;
He had fallen in with foes, who gave no answer.
He stopped, stepped back, like a man who treads on a serpent
Unseen in the rough brush, and then in panic
Draws back as the purple neck swells out in anger.
Even so, Androgeos pulled away in terror.
We rush them, swarm all over them; they are frightened,
They do not know their ground, and fortune favors 410
Our first endeavor. Coroebus, a little crazy
With nerve and luck, cries out: 'Comrades, where fortune
First shows the way and sides with us, we follow.
Let us change our shields, put on the Grecian emblems!
All's fair in war: we lick them or we trick them,
And what's the odds?' He takes Androgeos' helmet,
Whose plume streams over his head, takes up the shield
With proud device, and fits the sword to his side.
And Ripheus does the same, and so does Dymas,
And all the others, happily being armed 420
With spoil, new-won. We join the Greeks, all going
Under no gods of ours, in the night's darkness
Wade into many a fight, and Greeks by the dozens
We send to hell. And some of them in panic
Speed to the ships; they know that shore, and trust it,
And some of them—these were the abject cowards—
Climb scrambling up the horse's sides, again
Take refuge in the womb.

It is not for men to trust unwilling gods.
Cassandra was being dragged from Pallas' temple, 430
Her hair loosed to the wind, her eyes turned upward
To heaven for mercy; they had bound her hands.
Coroebus could not bear that sight; in madness
He threw himself upon them, and he died.
We followed, all of us, into the thick of it,
And were cut down, not only by Greeks; the rooftops,
Held by our friends, rained weapons: we were wearing
Greek crests and armor, and they did not know us.
And the Greeks came on, shouting with anger, burning
To foil that rescue; there was Menelaus, 440
And Agamemnon, and the savage Ajax,
And a whole army of them. Hurricanes
Rage the same way, when winds from different quarters
Clash in the sky, and the forest groans, and Neptune
Storms underneath the ocean. Those we routed
Once in the dark came back again from the byways
And alleys of the town; they mark our shields,
Our lying weapons, and our foreign voices.
Of course we are outnumbered. Peneleus

It was, who slew Coroebus, at the altar 450
Sacred to Pallas. Ripheus fell, a man
Most just of all the Trojans, most fair-minded.
The gods thought otherwise. Hypanis, Dymas,
Were slain by their own men, and Panthus' goodness
Was no protection, nor his priestly office.
I call to witness Troy, her fires, her ashes,
And the last agonies of all our people
That in that hour I ran from no encounter
With any Greek, and if the fates had been
For me to fall in battle, there I earned it. 460
The current swept me off, with two companions,
One, Iphitus, too slow with age, the other,
Pelias, limping from Ulysses' wound.
The noise kept calling us to Priam's palace.

There might have been no fighting and no dying
Through all the city, such a battle raged
Here, from the ground to roof-top. At the threshold
Waves of assault were breaking, and the Greeks
Were climbing, rung by rung, along the ladders,
Using one hand, the right one up and forward 470
Over the battlements, the left one thrust
In the protecting shield. And over their heads
The Trojans pried up towers and planking, wrecking
The building; gilded beams, the spoils of their fathers,
Were ample weapons for the final moment.
Some had the doorways blocked, others, behind them,
Were ready with drawn swords. We had a moment
When help seemed possible; new reinforcement
Might yet relieve the palace.
There was a secret entrance there, a passage 480
All the way through the building, a postern gate,
Where, while the kingdom stood, Andromache[13]
Would go, alone, or bring the little boy,
Astyanax, to Hector's father and mother.
I climbed to the top of the roof, where the poor Trojans
Were hurling down their unavailing darts.
A tower stood on the very edge, a look-out
Over all Troy, the ships and camp of the Greeks.
This we attacked with steel, where the joints were weakest,
And pried it up, and shoved it over. It crashed, 490
A noisy ruin, over the hostile columns;
But more kept coming up; the shower of stones
And darts continued raining.
Before the entrance, at the very threshold

[13] Wife of Hector and mother of Astyanax. Hector's parents are Priam and Hecuba, king and queen of Troy.

Stood Pyrrhus,[14] flashing proudly in bronze light,
Sleek as a serpent coming into the open,
Fed on rank herbs, wintering under the ground,
The old slough cast, the new skin shining, rolling
His slippery length, reaching his neck to the sun,
While the forked tongue darts from the mouth. Automedon 500
Was with him, Periphas, Achilles' driver,
A giant of a man, and the host from Scyros,[15]
All closing in on the palace, and hurling flames.
Among the foremost, Pyrrhus, swinging an axe,
Burst through, wrenched the bronze doors out of their hinges,
Smashed through the panelling, turned it into a window.
The long halls came to view, the inner chambers
Of Priam and the older kings; they see
Armed warriors at the threshold.
Within, it is all confusion, women wailing, 510
Pitiful noise, groaning, and blows; the din
Reaches the golden stars. The trembling mothers
Wander, not knowing where, or find a spot
To cling to; they would hold and kiss the doors.
Pyrrhus comes on, aggressive as his father;
No barrier holds him back; the gate is battered
As the ram[16] smashes at it; the doors come down.
Force finds a way; the Greeks pour in, they slaughter
The first one in their path; they fill the courtyard
With soldiery, wilder than any river 520
In flood over the banks and dikes and ploughland.
I saw them, Pyrrhus, going mad with murder,
And Atreus' twin sons,[17] and Hecuba
I saw, and all her daughters, and poor old Priam,
His blood polluting the altars he had hallowed.
The fifty marriage-chambers,[18] the proud hope
Of an everlasting line, are violated,
The doors with the golden spoil are turned to splinters.
Whatever the fire has spared the Greeks take over.
You would ask, perhaps, about the fate of Priam? 530
When he saw the city fall, and the doors of the palace
Ripped from the hinge, and the enemy pouring in,
Old as he was, he went and found his armor,
Unused so many years, and his old shoulders
Shook as he put it on. He took his sword,
A useless weapon, and, doomed to die, went rushing
Into the midst of the foe. There was an altar
In the open court-yard, shaded by a laurel
Whose shadow darkened the household gods, and here
Hecuba and her daughters had come thronging, 540

[14] Achilles' son, fierce like his war-loving father. [15] Birthplace of Pyrrhus.
[16] The battering ram. [17] Agamemnon and Menelaus.
[18] The quarters of Priam's fifty sons and their wives; Priam also had fifty daughters.

Like doves by a black storm driven. They were praying
Here at the altar, and clinging to the gods,
Whatever image was left. And the queen saw Priam
In the arms of his youth. 'O my unhappy husband,'
She cried, 'have you gone mad, to dress yourself
For battle, so? It is all no use; the time
Needs better help than yours; not even my Hector
Could help us now. Come to me, come to the altar;
It will protect us, or at least will let us
Die all together.' And she drew him to her. 550
  Just then through darts, through weapons, came Polites,
A son of Priam, fleeing deadly Pyrrhus,
Down the long colonnades and empty hallways,
Wounded, and Pyrrhus after him, vicious, eager
For the last spear-thrust, and he drives it home;
Polites falls, and his life goes out with his blood,
Father and mother watching. And then Priam,
In the very grip of death, cried out in anger:—
'If there is any righteousness in heaven,
To care about such wickedness, the gods 560
Will have the right reward and thanks to offer
A man like this, who has made a father witness
The murder of his son, the worst pollution!
You claim to be Achilles' son. You liar!
Achilles had some reverence, respected
A suppliant's right and trust; he gave me back
My Hector's lifeless body[19] for the tomb,
And let me go to my kingdom.' With the word
He flung a feeble spear, which dropped, deflected
From the rough bronze; it had hung there for a moment. 570
And Pyrrhus sneered: 'So, go and tell my father
The latest news: do not forget to mention,
Old messenger-boy, my villainous behavior,
And what a bastard Pyrrhus is. Now die!'
He dragged the old man, trembling, to the altar,
Slipping in his son's blood; he grabbed his hair
With the left hand, and the right drove home the sword
Deep in the side, to the hilt. And so fell Priam,
Who had seen Troy burn and her walls come down, once monarch,
Proud ruler over the peoples and lands of Asia. 580
He lies, a nameless body, on the shore,
Dismembered, huge, the head torn from the shoulders.
  Grim horror, then, came home to me. I saw
My father when I saw the king, the life
Going out with the cruel wound. I saw Creusa[20]

[19] After killing Hector, Achilles agreed to return the corpse to Hector's father, Priam (see Homer's *Iliad*, Book XXIV). Achilles himself has since been slain, struck in the heel (his one vulnerable spot) by an arrow from Paris's bow.

[20] Aeneas' wife.

Forsaken, my abandoned home, Iulus,
My little son. I looked around. They all
Had gone, exhausted, flung down from the walls,
Or dead in the fire, and I was left alone.
And I saw Helen, hiding, of all places, 590
At Vesta's shrine, and clinging there in silence,
But the bright flames lit the scene. That hated woman,
Fearing both Trojan anger and Greek vengeance,
A common fury to both lands, was crouching
Beside the altar. Anger flared up in me
For punishment and vengeance. Should she then,
I thought, come home to Sparta safe, uninjured
Walk through Mycenae,[21] a triumphant queen?
See husband, home, parents and children, tended
By Trojan slave-girls? This, with Priam fallen 600
And Troy burnt down, and the shore soaked in blood?
Never! No memorable name, I knew,
Was won by punishing women, yet, for me,
There might be praise for the just abolition
Of this unholiness, and satisfaction
In vengeance for the ashes of my people.
All this I may have said aloud, in frenzy,
As I rushed on, when to my sight there came
A vision of my lovely mother, radiant
In the dark night, a goddess manifest, 610
As tall and fair as when she walks in heaven.
She caught me by the hand and stopped me:[22]—'Son,
What sorrow rouses this relentless anger,
This violence? Do you care for me no longer?
Consider others first, your aged father,
Anchises; is your wife Creusa living?
Where is Iulus? Greeks are all around them,
Only my love between them, fire and sword.
It is not for you to blame the Spartan woman,
Daughter of Tyndareus, or even Paris. 620
The gods are the ones, the high gods are relentless;
It is they who bring this power down, who topple
Troy from the high foundation. Look! Your vision
Is mortal dull, I will take the cloud away,—
Fear not a mother's counsel. Where you see
Rock torn from rock, and smoke and dust in billows,
Neptune is working, plying the trident, prying
The walls from their foundations. And see Juno,
Fiercest of all, holding the Scaean gates,
Girt with the steel, and calling from the ships 630

[21] The meaning is "Greece" (from the home city of Agamemnon, the Greek commander). Helen's actual home city was Sparta.

[22] Though she is Aeneas' mother, Venus as goddess of love naturally protects Helen, the most beautiful of all women.

Implacable companions. On the towers,—
Turn, and be certain—Pallas takes command
Gleaming with Gorgon and storm-cloud. Even Jove,
Our father, nerves the Greeks with fire and spirit,
And spurs the other gods against the Trojans.
Hasten the flight, my son; no other labor
Waits for accomplishment. I promise safety
Until you reach your father's house.' She had spoken
And vanished in the thickening night of shadows.
Dread shapes come into vision, mighty powers, 640
Great gods at war with Troy, which, so it seemed,
Was sinking as I watched, with the same feeling
As when on mountain-tops you see the loggers
Hacking an ash-tree down, and it always threatens
To topple, nodding a little, and the leaves
Trembling when no wind stirs, and dies of its wounds
With one long loud last groan, and dirt from the ridges
Heaves up as it goes down with roots in air.
Divinity my guide, I leave the roof-top,
I pass unharmed through enemies and blazing, 650
Weapons give place to me, and flames retire.

At last I reached the house, I found my father,
The first one that I looked for. I meant to take him
To the safety of the hills, but he was stubborn,
Refusing longer life or barren exile,
Since Troy was dead. 'You have the strength,' he told me,
'You are young enough, take flight. For me, had heaven
Wanted to save my life, they would have spared
This home for me. We have seen enough destruction,
More than enough, survived a captured city. 660
Speak to me as a corpse laid out for burial,
A quick farewell, and go. Death I shall find
With my own hand; the enemy will pity,
Or look for spoil. The loss of burial[23]
Is nothing at all. I have been living too long
Hated by gods and useless, since the time
Jove blasted me[24] with lightning wind and fire.'
He would not move, however we wept, Creusa,
Ascanius, all the house, insistent, pleading
That he should not bring all to ruin with him. 670
He would not move, he would not listen. Again
I rush to arms, I pray for death; what else
Was left to me? 'Dear father, were you thinking
I could abandon you, and go? what son
Could bear a thought so monstrous? If the gods
Want nothing to be left of so great a city,

[23] Failure to receive proper burial was a grievous misfortune. See Book VI.
[24] The god took revenge because Anchises boasted of Venus' love for him.

If you are bound, or pleased, to add us all
To the wreck of Troy, the way is open for it—
Pyrrhus will soon be here; from the blood of Priam
He comes; he slays the son before the father, 680
The sire at the altar-stone; O my dear mother,
Was it for this you saved me, brought me through
The fire and sword, to see our enemies
Here in the very house, and wife and son
And father murdered in each other's blood?
Bring me my arms; the last light calls the conquered.
Let me go back to the Greeks, renew the battle,
We shall not all of us die unavenged.'
　　Sword at my side, I was on the point of going,
Working the left arm into the shield. Creusa 690
Clung to me on the threshold, held my feet,
And made me see my little son:—'Dear husband,
If you are bent on dying, take us with you,
But if you think there is any hope in fighting,
And you should know, stay and defend the house!
To whom are we abandoned, your father and son,
And I, once called your wife?' She filled the house
With moaning outcry. And then something happened,
A wonderful portent. Over Iulus' head,
Between our hands and faces, there appeared 700
A blaze of gentle light; a tongue of flame,
Harmless and innocent, was playing over
The softness of his hair, around his temples.
We were afraid, we did our best to quench it
With our own hands, or water, but my father
Raised joyous eyes to heaven, and prayed aloud:—
'Almighty Jupiter, if any prayer
Of ours has power to move you, look upon us,
Grant only this, if we have ever deserved it,
Grant us a sign, and ratify the omen!' 710
He had hardly spoken, when thunder on the left
Resounded, and a shooting star from heaven
Drew a long trail of light across the shadows.
We saw it cross above the house, and vanish
In the woods of Ida,[25] a wake of gleaming light
Where it had sped, and a trail of sulphurous odor.
This was a victory: my father rose
In worship of the gods and the holy star,
Crying: 'I follow, son, wherever you lead;
There is no delay, not now; Gods of my fathers, 720
Preserve my house, my grandson; yours the omen,
And Troy is in your keeping. O my son,
I yield, I am ready to follow.' But the fire
Came louder over the walls, the flames rolled nearer

[25] A mountain and mountain range near Troy.

Their burning tide. 'Climb to my shoulders, father,
It will be no burden, so we are together,
Meeting a common danger or salvation.
Iulus, take my hand; Creusa, follow
A little way behind. Listen, you servants!
You will find, when you leave the city, an old temple 730
That once belonged to Ceres;[26] it has been tended
For many years with the worship of our fathers.
There's a little hill there, and a cypress tree;
And that's where we shall meet, one way or another.
And one thing more: you, father, are to carry
The holy objects and the gods of the household,
My hands are foul with battle and blood, I could not
Touch them without pollution.'

I bent down
And over my neck and shoulders spread the cover
Of a tawny lion-skin, took up my burden; 740
Little Iulus held my hand, and trotted,
As best he could, beside me; Creusa followed.
We went on through the shadows. I had been
Brave, so I thought, before, in the rain of weapons
And the cloud of massing Greeks. But now I trembled
At every breath of air, shook at a whisper,
Fearful for both my burden and companion.

I was near the gates, and thinking we had made it,
But there was a sound, the tramp of marching feet,
And many of them, it seemed; my father, peering 750
Through the thick gloom, cried out:—'Son, they are coming!
Flee, flee! I see their shields, their gleaming bronze.'
Something or other took my senses from me
In that confusion. I turned aside from the path,
I do not know what happened then. Creusa
Was lost;[27] she had missed the road, or halted, weary,
For a brief rest. I do not know what happened,
She was not seen again; I had not looked back,
Nor even thought about her, till we came
To Ceres' hallowed home. The count was perfect, 760
Only one missing there, the wife and mother.
Whom did I not accuse, of gods and mortals,
Then in my frenzy? What worse thing had happened
In the city overthrown? I left Anchises,
My son, my household gods, to my companions,
In a hiding-place in the valley; and I went back
Into the city again, wearing my armor,
Ready, still one more time, for any danger.

[26] Goddess of the fields and harvest.

[27] The loss, literally, of Creusa (exactly what happens to her is not clear) may indicate something about Aeneas' priorities, but it is providentially necessary that Aeneas be free to marry Lavinia as part of the Trojans' later establishment of themselves in Italy.

I found the walls again, the gate's dark portals,
I followed my own footsteps back, but terror, 770
Terror and silence were all I found. I went
On to my house. She might, just might, have gone there.
Only the Greeks were there, and fire devouring
The very pinnacles. I tried Priam's palace;
In the empty courtyards Phoenix and Ulysses
Guarded the spoils piled up at Juno's altar.
They had Trojan treasure there, loot from the altars,
Great drinking-bowls of gold, and stolen garments,
And human beings. A line of boys and women
Stood trembling there. 780
I took the risk of crying through the shadows,
Over and over, 'Creusa!' I kept calling,
'Creusa!' and 'Creusa!' but no answer.
No sense, no limit, to my endless rushing
All through the town; and then at last I saw her,
Or thought I did, her shadow a little taller
Than I remembered. And she spoke to me
Beside myself with terror:—'O dear husband,
What good is all this frantic grief? The gods
Have willed it so, Creusa may not join you 790
Out of this city; Jupiter denies it.
Long exile lies ahead, and vast sea-reaches
The ships must furrow, till you come to land
Far in the West; rich fields are there, and a river
Flowing with gentle current; its name is Tiber.
And happy days await you there, a kingdom,
A royal wife. Banish the tears of sorrow
Over Creusa lost. I shall never see
The arrogant houses of the Myrmidons,[28]
Nor be a slave to any Grecian woman; 800
I am a Dardan woman; I am the wife
Of Venus' son; it is Cybele[29] who keeps me
Here on these shores. And now farewell, and love
Our son.' I wept, there was more to say; she left me,
Vanishing into empty air. Three times
I reached out toward her, and three times her image
Fled like the breath of a wind or a dream on wings.
The night was over; I went back to my comrades.
I was surprised to find so many more
Had joined us, ready for exile, pitiful people, 810
Mothers, and men, and children, streaming in
From everywhere, looking for me to lead them
Wherever I would. Over the hills of Ida

[28] The Greek soldiers who had been led by Achilles.

[29] A goddess identified with Rhea, consort of Saturn during the reign of the older gods. It is possible that Creusa has not died but rather has been mysteriously inducted into the service of Cybele.

The morning-star was rising; in the town
The Danaans held the gates, and help was hopeless.
I gave it up, I lifted up my father,
Together we sought the hills.

BOOK III: THE WANDERINGS OF AENEAS

"After the gods' decision to overthrow
The Asian world, the innocent house of Priam,
And the proud city, built by Neptune, smoked
From the ruined ground, we were driven, different ways,
By heaven's auguries, seeking lands forsaken.
Below Antandros,[1] under Phrygian Ida,
We built a fleet, and gathered men, uncertain
Of either direction or settlement. The summer
Had scarce begun, when at my father's orders,
We spread our sails. I wept as I left the harbor, 10
The fields where Troy had been. I was borne, an exile
Over the deep, with son, companions, household,
And household gods.
Far off there lies a land,
Sacred to Mars; the Thracians[2] used to till it,
Whose king was fierce Lycurgus; they were friendly,
Of old, to Troy, when we were prosperous. Hither
I sailed, and on its curving shore established
A city site; Aeneadae, I called it.
This I began, not knowing fate was adverse.

I was offering my mother proper homage, 20
And other gods, to bless the new beginnings,
I had a white bull ready as a victim
To the king of the gods. There was a mound nearby,
Bristling with myrtle and with cornel-bushes.
I needed greenery to veil the altar,
But as I struggled with the leafy branches,
A fearful portent met my gaze. Black drops
Dripped from the ends of the roots, black blood was falling
On the torn ground, and a cold chill went through me.
I tried again; the shoot resisted; blood 30
Followed again. Troubled, I prayed to the Nymphs,
To the father of the fields, to bless the vision,
Remove the curse; and down on my knees I wrestled
Once more against the stubborn ground, and heard
A groan from under the hillock, and voice crying:

[1] A town near Troy.
[2] Inhabitants of Thrace, an area north of the Aegean Sea, northwest of the Hellespont strait (the modern Dardanelles).

'Why mangle a poor wretch, Aeneas? Spare me,
Here in the tomb, and save your hands pollution.
You know me, I am Trojan-born, no stranger,
This is familiar blood. Alas! Take flight,
Leave this remorseless land; the curse of greed 40
Lies heavy on it. I am Polydorus,
Pierced by an iron harvest; out of my body
Rise javelins and lances.' I was speechless,
Stunned, in my terror.
Priam, forever unfortunate, had sent
This Polydorus on a secret mission,
Once, to the king of Thrace, with gold for hiding
When the king despaired of the siege and the city's fortune.
And when Troy fell, and Fortune failed, the Thracian
Took Agamemnon's side, broke off his duty, 50
Slew Polydorus, took the gold. There is nothing
To which men are not driven by that hunger.
Once over my fear, I summoned all the leaders,
My father, too; I told them of the portent,
Asked for their counsel. All agreed, a land
So stained with violence and violation
Was not for us to dwell in. Southward ho!
For Polydorus we made restoration
With funeral rites anew; earth rose again
Above his outraged mound; dark fillets made 60
The altar sorrowful, and cypress boughs,
And the Trojan women loosed their hair in mourning.
We offered milk in foaming bowls, and blood
Warm from the victims, so to rest the spirit,
And cry aloud the voice of valediction.
Then, when we trust the sea again, and the wind
Calls with a gentle whisper, we crowd the shores,
Launch ship again, leave port, the lands and cities
Fade out of sight once more.
There is an island[3]
In the middle of the sea; the Nereids' mother[4] 70
And Neptune hold it sacred. It used to wander
By various coasts and shores, until Apollo,
In grateful memory, bound it fast, unmoving,
Unfearful of winds, between two other islands
Called Myconos and Gyaros. I sailed there;
Our band was weary, and the calmest harbor
Gave us safe haven. This was Apollo's city;
We worshipped it on landing. And their king,
Priest of Apollo also, came to meet us,
His temples bound with holy fillets, and laurel. 80

[3] Delos, an island in the Aegean, was the birthplace of Apollo.
[4] Doris; Nereids are sea nymphs.

His name was Anius; he knew Anchises
As an old friend, and gave us joyful welcome.
Apollo's temple was built of ancient rock,
And there I prayed: 'Grant us a home, Apollo,
Give walls to weary men, a race, a city
That will abide; preserve Troy's other fortress,
The remnant left by the Greeks and hard Achilles.
Whom do we follow? where are we bidden to go
To find our settlement? An omen, father!'
I had scarcely spoken, when suddenly all things trembled, 90
The doors, and the laurel, and the whole mountain moved,
And the shrine was opened, and a rumbling sound
Was heard. We knelt, most humbly; and a voice
Came to our ears: 'The land which brought you forth,
Men of endurance, will receive you home.
Seek out your ancient mother. There your house
Will rule above all lands, your children's children,
For countless generations.' Apollo spoke,
And we were joyful and confused, together:
What walls were those, calling the wanderers home? 100
My father, pondering history, made answer:
'Hear, leaders; learn your hopes. There is a land
Called Crete, an island in the midst of the sea,
The cradle of our race; it has a mountain,
Ida, like ours, a hundred mighty cities,
Abounding wealth; if I recall correctly,
Teucer, our greatest father, came from there
To the Rhoetean[5] shores to found his kingdom.
Ilium was nothing then, the towers of Troy
Undreamed of; men lived in the lowly valleys. 110
And Cybele, the Great Mother, came from Crete
With her clashing cymbals, and her grove of Ida
Was named from that original; the silence
Of her mysterious rites, the harnessed lions
Before her chariot wheels, all testify
To Cretan legend. Come, then, let us follow
Where the gods lead, and seek the Cretan kingdom.
It is not far; with Jupiter to favor,
Three days will see us there. With prayer, he made
Most solemn sacrifice, a bull to Neptune, 120
One to Apollo, to Winter a black heifer,
A white one for fair winds.
The story ran
That no one lived in Crete, Idomeneus[6]
Having left his father's kingdom, that the houses
Were empty now, dwellings vacated for us.

[5] Trojan.
[6] Former king of Crete who fought against Troy. In fulfillment of a vow to kill the first living thing he saw after returning to Crete, he murdered his son. His people thereafter banished him, the gods having visited a plague on Crete as punishment.

We sailed from Delos, flying over the water
Past Naxos, on whose heights the Bacchae revel,
Past green Donysa, snowy Paros,[7] skimming
The passages between the sea-sown islands.
No crew would yield to another; there is shouting, 130
And the cheer goes up, 'To Crete, and the land of our fathers!'
A stern wind follows, and we reach the land.
I am glad to be there; I lay out the walls
For the chosen city, name it Pergamea,[8]
And the people are happy. *Love your hearths,* I told them,
Build high the citadel. The ships were steadied
On the dry beach, the young were busy ploughing,
Or planning marriage, and I was giving laws,
Assigning homes. But the weather turned, the sky
Grew sick, and from the tainted heaven came 140
Pestilence and pollution, a deadly year
For people and harvest. Those who were not dying
Dragged weary bodies around; the Dog-Star[9] scorched
The fields to barrenness; grass withered, corn
Refused to ripen. 'Over the sea again!'
My father said, 'let us return to Delos,
Consult the oracle, implore Apollo
To show us kindliness; what end awaits
Our weary destiny, where does he bid us turn
For help in trouble?' 150
Sleep held all creatures over the earth at rest;
In my own darkness visions came, the sacred
Images of the household gods I had carried
With me from Troy, out of the burning city.
I saw them plain, in the flood of light, where the moon
Streamed through the dormers. And they eased me, saying:
'Apollo would tell you this, if you went over
The sea again to Delos; from him we come
To you, with willing spirit. We came with you
From the burnt city, we have followed still 160
The swollen sea in the ships; in time to come
We shall raise your sons to heaven, and dominion
Shall crown their city. Prepare to build them walls,
Great homes for greatness; do not flee the labor,
The long, long toil of flight. Crete, says Apollo,
Is not the place. There is a land in the West,
Called by the Greeks, Hesperia:[10] anciency
And might in arms and wealth enrich its soil.
The Oenotrians lived there once; now, rumor has it,

[7] Naxos, Donysa, and Paros are islands in the south Aegean, passed during the southward voyage to Crete.
[8] Named for Pergamus, the citadel of Troy.
[9] Sirius, the brightest star in the sky, first visible in the hot days of late summer.
[10] The western region of the world, associated with Hesperus, the evening star.

A younger race has called it Italy 170
After the name of a leader, Italus.
Dardanus came from there, our ancestor,
As Iasius[11] was. There is our dwelling-place.
Be happy, then, waken, and tell Anchises
Our certain message: seek the land in the West.
Crete is forbidden country.'
The vision shook me, and the voice of the gods;
(It was not a dream, exactly; I seemed to know them,
Their features, the veiled hair, the living presence.)
I woke in a sweat, held out my hands to heaven, 180
And poured the pure libation for the altar,
Then, gladly, to Anchises. He acknowledged
His own mistake, a natural confusion,
Our stock was double, of course; no need saying
We had more ancestors than one. 'Cassandra,'
Anchises said, 'alone, now I remember,
Foretold this fate; it seemed she was always talking
Of a land in the West, and Italian kingdoms, always.
But who would ever have thought that any Trojans
Would reach the shores in the West? Or, for that matter, 190
Who ever believed Cassandra? Let us yield
To the warning of Apollo, and at his bidding
Seek better fortunes.' So we obeyed him,
Leaving this place, where a few stayed, and sailing
The hollow keels over the mighty ocean.
We were in deep water, and the land no longer
Was visible, sky and ocean everywhere.
A cloud, black-blue, loomed overhead, with night
And tempest in it, and the water roughened
In shadow; winds piled up the sea, the billows 200
Rose higher; we were scattered in the surges.
Clouds took away the daylight, and the night
Was dark and wet in the sky, with lightning flashing.
We wandered, off our course, in the dark of ocean,
And our pilot, Palinurus, swore he could not
Tell day from night, nor the way among the waters.
For three lost days, three starless nights, we rode it,
Saw land on the fourth, mountains and smoke arising.
The sails came down, we bent to the oars; the sailors
Made the foam fly, sweeping the dark blue water. 210
I was saved from the waves; the Strophades received me,
(The word means Turning-point in the Greek language),[12]

[11]Brother of Dardanus.

[12]The Strophades are islands west of Greece, in the Ionian Sea. The Trojans have rounded the southwest corner of Greece; from this time until shortly after they leave Helenus and Andromache, their course will be northwest, along the shore and among the islands of Greece that face Sicily and southern Italy.

Ionian islands where the dire Celaeno
And other Harpies[13] live, since Phineus' house
Was closed to them, and they feared their former tables.
No fiercer plague of the gods' anger ever
Rose out of hell, girls with the look of birds,
Their bellies fouled, incontinent, their hands
Like talons, and their faces pale with hunger.
We sailed into the harbor, happy to see 220
Good herds of cattle grazing over the grass
And goats, unshepherded. We cut them down
And made our prayer and offering to Jove,
Set trestles on the curving shore for feasting.
Down from the mountains with a fearful rush
And a sound of wings like metal came the Harpies,
To seize our banquet, smearing dirtiness
Over it all, with a hideous kind of screaming
And a stinking smell. We found a secret hollow
Enclosed by trees, under a ledge of rock, 230
Where shade played over; there we moved the tables
And lit the fire again; the noisy Harpies
Came out of somewhere, sky, or rock, and harried
The feast again, the filthy talons grabbing,
The taint all through the air. *Take arms,* I ordered,
We have to fight them. And my comrades, hiding
Their shields in the grass, lay with their swords beside them,
And when the birds swooped screaming, and Misenus
Sounded the trumpet-signal, they rose to charge them,
A curious kind of battle, men with sword-blades 240
Against the winged obscenities of ocean.
Their feathers felt no blow, their backs no wound,
They rose to the sky as rapidly as ever,
Leaving the souvenirs of their foul traces
Over the ruined feast. And one, Celaeno,
Perched on a lofty rock, squawked out a warning:—
'Is it war you want, for slaughtered goats and bullocks,
Is it war you bring, you sons of liars, driving
The innocent Harpies from their father's kingdom?
Take notice, then, and let my words forever 250
Stick in your hearts; what Jove has told Apollo,
Apollo told me, and I, the greatest fury,
Shove down your throats; it is Italy you are after,
And the winds will help you, Italy and her harbors
You will reach, all right; but you will not wall the city
Till, for the wrong you have done us, deadly hunger
Will make you gnaw and crunch your very tables!'[14]

[13] Foul creatures sent originally by Jove to punish Phineus, king of Thrace, whence the Harpies have emigrated. Celaeno is their leader.

[14] This prophecy will be fulfilled, in an unexpectedly casual way, in Book VII, when the hungry Trojans eat the wheaten platters on which they have placed fruit.

She flew back to the forest. My companions
Were chilled with sudden fear; their spirit wavered,
They call on me, to beg for peace, not now 260
With arms, but vows and praying, filthy birds
Or ill-foreboding goddesses, no matter.
Anchises prayed with outstretched hands, appeasing
The mighty gods with sacrifice:—'Be gracious,
Great gods, ward off the threats, spare the devoted!'
He bade us tear the cable from the shore,
Shake loose the sails. And a wind sprang up behind us,
Driving us northward; we passed many islands,
Zacynthus, wooded, Dulichium, and Same,
The cliffs of Neritus, Laertes' kingdom, 270
With a curse as we went by for Ithaca,
Land of Ulysses. Soon Leucate's headland
Came into view, a dreadful place for sailors,
Where Apollo had a shrine. We were very weary
As we drew near the little town; the anchor
Was thrown from the prow, the sterns pulled up on the beaches.
This was unhoped-for land; we offered Jove
Our purifying rites, and had the altars
Burning with sacrifice. We thronged the shore
With games of Ilium. Naked, oiled for wrestling, 280
The young held bouts, glad that so many islands
Held by the Greeks were safely passed. A year
Went by, and icy winter roughened the waves
With gales from the north. A shield of hollow bronze,
Borne once by Abas,[15] I fastened to the door-posts,
And set a verse below it: *Aeneas won*
These arms from the Greek victors. I gave the order
To man the thwarts and leave this harbor; all
Obeyed, swept oars in rivalry. We left
Phaeacia's airy heights, coasting Epirus, 290
Drawn to Buthrotum, a Chaonian harbor.
And here we met strange news, that Helenus,
The son of Priam, was ruling Grecian cities,
Having won the wife of Pyrrhus and his crown,
And that Andromache once more had married
A lord of her own race. Amazed, I burn
With a strange longing to seek out that hero,
To learn his great adventures. It so happened,
Just as I left the landing, that was the day
Andromache, in a grove before the city, 300
By the waters of a river that resembled
The Simois at home, was offering homage,

[15] Not the Trojan mentioned in the storm scene of Book I, but rather a Greek killed at Troy. The present scene takes place at the site of the future naval battle of Actium, where in 31 B.C. Octavian defeated Mark Antony and Cleopatra; see the Introduction to Virgil.

Her annual mourning-gift to Hector's ashes,
Calling his ghost to the place which she had hallowed
With double altars, a green and empty tomb.
I found her weeping there, and she was startled
At the sight of me, and Trojan arms, a shock
Too great to bear: she was rigid for a moment,
And then lost consciousness, and a long time later
Managed to speak: 'Is it real, then, goddess-born? 310
What are you, living messenger or phantom,
Mortal or ghost? If the dear light has left you,
Tell me where Hector is.' I was moved, so deeply
I found it hard to answer to her tears
And through my own, but I did say a little:—
'I am alive; I seem to keep on living
Through all extremes of trouble; do not doubt me,
I am no apparition. And what has happened
To you, dear wife of Hector? Could any gain
Atone for such a loss? Has fortune tried 320
To even matters at all? Does Pyrrhus still
Presume on you as husband?' With lowered gaze
And quiet voice she answered:—'Happy the maiden
Slain at the foeman's tomb, at the foot of the walls;
Happy the daughter of Priam, who never knew
The drawing of the lots,[16] nor came to the bed
Of a conqueror, his captive. After the fire
I travelled different seas, endured the pride
Achilles filled his son with, bore him children
In bondage, till he tired of me and left me 330
For Leda's daughter and a Spartan marriage.
He passed me on to Helenus, fair enough,
Slave-woman to slave-man; but then Orestes,[17]
Inflamed with passion for his stolen bride,
And maddened by the Furies of his vengeance,
Caught Pyrrhus off-guard, and slew him at the altar
In his ancestral home. And Pyrrhus dying,
Part of the kingdom came to Helenus,
Who named the fields Chaonian, the land
Chaonia, after a man from Troy, 340
And filled the heights, as best he could, with buildings
To look like those we knew. But what of yourself?
What winds, what fate, have brought you here, or was it
Some god? did you know you were on our coast? How is
The boy Ascanius, living still, whom Troy
Might have—does he ever think about his mother?

[16] For the division of the women among the conquerors.

[17] Pyrrhus married Hermione (daughter of Menelaus and Helen and thus Leda's granddaughter, not her daughter), to whom Orestes had been betrothed.

Does he want to be a hero, a manly spirit,
Such as his father was, and his uncle Hector?'
She was in tears again, when the son of Priam,
Helenus, with an escort, came from the city, 350
Happy to recognize us, bringing us in
With tears and greeting mingled. I went on,
Seeing a little Troy, low walls that copied
The old majestic ramparts, a tiny river
In a dry bed, trying to be the Xanthus,
I found the Scaean gates, to hold and cling to.
My Trojans, too, were fond of the friendly town,
Whose king received them in wide halls; libations
Were poured to the gods, and feasts set on gold dishes.
Day after day went by, and the winds were calling 360
And the sails filling with a good south-wester.
I put my questions to the king and prophet:
'O son of Troy, the god's interpreter,
Familiar with the tripod and the laurel
Of great Apollo, versed in stars and omens,
Bird-song and flying wing, be gracious to me,
Tell me,—for heaven has prophesied a journey
Without mischance, and all the gods have sent me
The counsel of their oracles, to follow
Italy and a far-off country; one, 370
But one, Celaeno, prophesied misfortune,
Wrath and revolting hunger,—tell me, prophet,
What dangers first to avoid, what presence follow
To overcome disaster?'
Bullocks slain
With proper covenant, and the chaplets loosened,
He led me to the temple of Apollo,
The very gates, where the god's presence awed me,
And where he spoke, with eloquent inspiration:—
'O goddess-born, the journey over the sea
Holds a clear sanction for you, under Jove, 380
Who draws the lots and turns the wheel of Fate.
I will tell you some few things, not all, that safely
You may go through friendly waters, and in time
Come to Ausonian[18] harborage; the rest
Helenus does not know, or, if he did,
Juno would stop his speaking. First of all,
Italy, which you think is near, too fondly
Ready to enter her nearest port, is distant,
Divided from you by a pathless journey
And longer lands between. The oar must bend 390
In the Sicilian ocean, and the ships

[18] Italian.

Sail on a farther coast, beyond the lakes
Of an infernal world, beyond the isles
Where dwells Aeaean Circe,[19] not till then
Can the built city rise on friendly ground.
Keep in the mind the sign I give you now:
One day, when you are anxious and alone
At the wave of a hidden river, you will find
Under the oaks on the shore, a sow, a white one,
Immense, with a new-born litter, thirty young 400
At the old one's udders; that will be the place,
The site of the city, the certain rest from labor.
And do not fear the eating of the tables,
The fates will find a way, Apollo answer.
Avoid this coast of Italy,[20] the lands
Just westward of our own; behind those walls
Dwell evil Greeks, Narycian Locri, soldiers
Of the Cretan king, Idomeneus; the plains
Are full of them; a Meliboean captain
Governs Petelia, a tiny town 410
Relying on her fortress! Philoctetes
Commands her walls. And furthermore, remember,
Even when the ships have crossed the sea and anchored,
When the altars stand on the shore, and the vows are paid,
Keep the hair veiled, and the robe of crimson drawn
Across the eyes, so that no hostile visage
May interfere, to gaze on the holy fire
Or spoil the sacred omens. This rite observe[21]
Through all the generations; keep it holy.
From that first landing, when the wind brings you down 420
To Sicily's coast, and narrow Pelorus widens
The waters of her strait, keep to the left,
Land on the left, and water on the left,
The long way round; the right is dangerous.
Avoid it. There's a story that this land
Once broke apart—(time brings so many changes)—
By some immense convulsion, though the lands
Had been one country once. But now between them
The sea comes in, and now the waters bound
Italian coast, Sicilian coast; the tide 430
Washes on severed shores, their fields, their cities.
Scylla keeps guard on the right; on the left Charybdis,

[19] A sorceress who, during Odysseus' wanderings as described in Homer's *Odyssey,* Book X, changed his men into swine. Aeaea is her home island.

[20] In the following lines, Helenus advises Aeneas to avoid the eastern coast of Italy (infested with people hostile to the Trojans) and to sail around Sicily rather than through the narrow passage (the modern straits of Messina) dividing Sicily from the Italian mainland. The straits are guarded on both sides, by a rock and whirlpool mythologized as, respectively, Scylla and Charybdis.

[21] As often in the poem, Virgil ascribes an ancient origin to Roman religious ritual of later times.

The unappeasable; from the deep gulf she sucks
The great waves down, three times; three times she belches
Them high up into the air, and sprays the stars.
Scylla is held in a cave, a den of darkness,
From where she thrusts her huge jaws out, and draws
Ships to her jagged rocks. She looks like a girl
Fair-breasted to the waist, from there, all monster,
Shapeless, with dolphins' tails, and a wolf's belly. 440
Better to go the long way round, make turning
Beyond Pachynus,[22] than to catch one glimpse
Of Scylla the misshapen, in her cavern,
And the rocks resounding with the dark-blue sea-hounds.
And one thing more than any, goddess-born,
I tell you over and over: pray to Juno,
Give Juno vows and gifts and overcome her
With everlasting worship. So you will come
Past Sicily and reach Italian beaches.
You will come to a town called Cumae,[23] haunted lakes, 450
And a forest called Avernus, where the leaves
Rustle and stir in the great woods, and there
You will find a priestess, in her wildness singing
Prophetic verses under the stones, and keeping
Symbols and signs on leaves. She files and stores them
In the depth of the cave; there they remain unmoving,
Keeping their order, but if a light wind stirs
At the turn of a hinge, and the door's draft disturbs them,
The priestess never cares to catch them fluttering
Around the halls of rock, put them in order, 460
Or give them rearrangement. Men who have come there
For guidance leave uncounselled, and they hate
The Sibyl's dwelling. Let no loss of time,
However comrades chide and chafe, however
The wind's voice calls the sail, postpone the visit
To this great priestess; plead with her to tell you
With her own lips the song of the oracles.
She will predict the wars to come, the nations
Of Italy, the toils to face, or flee from;
Meet her with reverence, and she, propitious, 470
Will grant a happy course. My voice can tell you
No more than this. Farewell; raise Troy to heaven.'
After the friendly counsel, other gifts
Were sent to our ships, carved ivory, and gold,
And heavy silver, cauldrons from Dodona,
A triple breastplate linked with gold, a helmet
Shining with crested plume, the arms of Pyrrhus.

[22] The southeastern corner of Sicily, which is triangular.

[23] The meeting with the Sibyl of Cumae, in preparation for Aeneas' descent into the Lower World, occurs in Book VI.

My father, too, has gifts; horses and guides
Are added, and sailing-men, and arms for my comrades.
Anchises bade the fleet prepare; the wind 480
Was rising, why delay? But Helenus
Spoke to Anchises, in compliment and honor:—
'Anchises, worthy of Venus' couch, and the blessing
Of other gods, twice saved from Trojan ruins,
Yonder behold Ausonia! Near, and far,
It lies, Apollo's offering; sail westward.
Farewell, made blest by a son's goodness. I
Am a nuisance with my talking.'
And his queen,
Sad at the final parting, was bringing gifts,
Robes woven with a golden thread, a Trojan 490
Scarf for Ascanius, all courteous honor
Given with these:—'Take them, my child; these are
The work of my own hands, memorials
Of Hector's wife Andromache, and her love.
Receive these farewell gifts; they are for one
Who brings my own son back to me; your hands,
Your face, your eyes, remind me of him so,—
He would be just your age.'
I, also, wept,
As I spoke my words of parting: 'Now farewell;
Your lot is finished, and your rest is won, 500
No ocean fields to plough, no fleeing fields
To follow, you have your Xanthus and your Troy,
Built by your hands, and blest by happier omens,
Far from the path of the Greeks. But we are called
From fate to fate; if ever I enter Tiber
And Tiber's neighboring lands, if ever I see
The walls vouchsafed my people, I pray these shores,
Italy and Epirus, shall be one,
The life of Troy restored, with friendly towns
And allied people. A common origin, 510
A common fall, was ours. Let us remember,
And our children keep the faith.'
Over the sea we rode, the shortest run
To Italy, past the Ceraunian rocks.[24]
The sun went down; the hills were dark with shadow.
The oars assigned, we drew in to the land
For a little welcome rest; sleep overcame us,
But it was not yet midnight when our pilot
Sprang from his blanket, studying the winds,
Alert and listening, noting the stars 520
Wheeling the silent heaven, the twin Oxen,

[24] After this point, the Trojan fleet changes its course; hereafter, until the storm that beaches it at Carthage, the fleet will sail southwest past the heel along the sole of the "boot" of southern Italy, then clockwise around Sicily.

Arcturus and the rainy Kids. All calm,
He saw, and roused us; camp was broken; the sail
Spread to the rushing breeze, and as day reddened
And the stars faded, we saw a coast, low-lying,
And made out hills. 'Italy!', cried Achates,
'Italy!' all the happy sailors shouted.
Anchises wreathed a royal wine-bowl, stood
On the high stern, calling:—'Gods of earth and ocean
And wind and storm, help us along, propitious 530
With favoring breath!' And the breeze sprang up, and freshened;
We saw a harbor open, and a temple
Shone on Minerva's headland. The sails came down,
We headed toward the land. Like the curve of a bow
The port turned in from the Eastern waves; its cliffs
Foamed with the salty spray, and towering rocks
Came down to the sea, on both sides, double walls,
And the temple fled the shore. Here, our first omen,
I saw four horses grazing, white as snow,
And father Anchises cried:—'It is war you bring us, 540
Welcoming land, horses are armed for war,
It is war these herds portend. But there is hope
Of peace as well. Horses will bend to the yoke
And bear the bridle tamely.' Then we worshipped
The holy power of Pallas, first to hear us,
Kept our heads veiled before the solemn altar,
And following Helenus' injunction, offered
Our deepest prayer to Juno.
And sailed on,
With some misgiving, past the homes of Greeks;
Saw, next, a bay, Tarentum, and a town 550
That rumor said was Hercules'; against it,
The towers of Caulon rose, and Scylaceum,[25]
Most dangerous to ships, and a temple of Juno.
Far off, Sicilian Etna[26] rose from the waves,
And we heard the loud sea roar, and the rocks resounding,
And voices broken on the coast; the shoals
Leaped at us, and the tide boiled sand. My father
Cried in alarm:—'This must be that Charybdis
Helenus warned us of. Rise to the oars,
O comrades, pull from the danger!' They responded 560
As they did, always, Palinurus swinging
The prow to the waves on the left, and all our effort
Strained to the left, with oars and sail. One moment
We were in the clouds, the next in the gulf of Hell;
Three times the hollow rocks and reefs roared at us,
Three times we saw spray shower the very stars,

[25] Tarentum, Caulon, and Scylaceum were cities lying along the sole of the "boot" of Italy.
[26] A volcano.

And the wind went down at sunset; we were weary,
Drifting, in ignorance, to the Cyclops[27] shores.
    There is a harbor, safe enough from wind,
But Etna thunders near it, crashing and roaring, 570
Throwing black clouds up to the sky, and smoking
With swirling pitchy color, and white-hot ashes,
With balls of flame puffed to the stars, and boulders,
The mountain's guts, belched out, or molten rock
Boiling below the ground, roaring above it.
The story goes that Enceladus, a giant,
Struck by a bolt of lightning, lies here buried
Beneath all Etna's weight, with the flames pouring
Through the broken furnace-flues; he shifts his body,
Every so often, to rest his weariness, 580
And then all Sicily seems to moan and tremble
And fill the sky with smoke. We spent the night here,
Hiding in woods, enduring monstrous portents,
Unable to learn the cause. There were no stars,
No light or fire in the sky; the dead of the night,
The thick of the cloud, obscured the moon.
                                                            And day
Arrived, at last, and the shadows left the heaven,
And a man came out of the woods, a sorry figure,
In hunger's final stages, reaching toward us
His outstretched hands. We looked again. His beard 590
Unshorn, his rags pinned up with thorns, and dirty,
He was, beyond all doubt of it, a Greek,
And one of those who had been at Troy in the fighting.
He saw, far off, the Trojan dress and armor,
Stopped short, for a moment, almost started back
In panic, then, with a wild rush, came on,
Pleading and crying:—'By the stars I beg you,
By the gods above, the air we breathe, ah Trojans,
Take me away from here, carry me off
To any land whatever; that will be plenty. 600
I know I am one of the Greeks, I know I sailed
With them, I warred against the gods of Ilium,
I admit all that; drown me for evil-doing,
Cut me to pieces, scatter me over the waves.
Kill me. If I must die, it will be a pleasure
To perish at the hands of men.' He held
Our knees and clung there, grovelling before us.
We urged him tell his story, his race, his fortune.
My father gave him his hand, a pledge of safety,
And his fear died down a little.

[27] One-eyed giants.

'I come,' he said, 610
'From Ithaca, a companion of Ulysses;
My name is Achaemenides;[28] my father,
His name was Adamastus, was a poor man,
And that was why I came to Troy. My comrades
Left me behind here, in their terrible hurry,
To leave these cruel thresholds. The Cyclops live here
In a dark cave, a house of gore, and banquets
Soaking with blood. It is dark inside there, monstrous.
He hits the stars with his head—Dear gods, abolish
This creature from the world!—he is not easy 620
To look at; he is terrible to talk to.
His food is the flesh of men, his drink their blood.
I saw him once myself, with two of our men
In that huge fist of his; he lay on his back
In the midst of the cave, and smashed them on a rock,
And the whole place swam with blood; I watched him chew them
The limbs with black clots dripping, the muscles, warm,
Quivering as he bit them. But we got him!
Ulysses did not stand for this; he kept
His wits about him, never mind the danger. 630
The giant was gorged with food, and drunk, and lolling
With sagging neck, sprawling all over the cavern
Belching and drooling blood-clots, bits of flesh,
And wine all mixed together. And we stood
Around him, praying, and drew lots,—we had found a stake
And sharpened it at the end,—and so we bored
His big eye out; it glowered under his forehead
The size of a shield, or a sun. So we got vengeance
For the souls of our companions. But flee, I tell you,
Get out of here, poor wretches, cut the cables, 640
Forsake this shore. There are a hundred others
As big as he is, and just like him, keeping
Sheep in the caves of the rocks, a hundred others
Wander around this coast and these high mountains.
I have managed for three months, hiding in forests,
In the caves of beasts, on a rocky look-out, watching
The Cyclops, horribly frightened at their cries
And the tramp of their feet. I have lived on plants and berries,
Gnawed roots and bark. I saw this fleet come in,
And I did not care; whatever it was, I gladly 650
Gave myself up. At least, I have escaped them.
Whatever death you give is more than welcome.'
And as he finished, we saw that very giant,
The shepherd Polyphemus, looming huge
Over his tiny flock; he was trying to find

[28]One of Ulysses', or Odysseus', sailors. The story he summarizes here is told in Homer's *Odyssey,* Book IX.

His way to the shore he knew, a shapeless monster,
Lumbering, clumping, blind in the dark, with a stumble,
And the step held up with trunk of a pine. No comfort
For him, except in the sheep. He reached the sand,
Wading into the sea, and scooped up water 660
To wash the ooze of blood from the socket's hollow,
Grinding his teeth against the pain, and roaring,
And striding into the water, but even so
The waves were hardly up to his sides. We fled
Taking on board our Greek; we cut the cable,
Strained every nerve at the oars. He heard, and struggled
Toward the splash of the wave, but of course he could not catch us,
And then he howled in a rage, and the sea was frightened,
Italy deeply shaken, and all Etna
Rumbled in echoing terror in her caverns. 670
Out of the woods and the thicket of the mountains
The Cyclops came, the others, toward the harbor,
Along the coast-line. We could see them standing
In impotent anger, the wild eye-ball glaring,
A grim assortment, brothers, tall as mountains
Where oak and cypress tower, in the groves
Of Jove or great Diana. In our speed
And terror, we sailed anywhere, forgetting
What Helenus had said: Scylla, Charybdis,
Were nothing to us then. But we remembered 680
In time, and a north wind came from strait Pelorus,
We passed Pantagia,[29] and the harbor-mouth
Set in the living-rock, Thapsus, low-lying,
The bay called Megara: all these were places
That Achaemenides knew well, recalling
The scenes of former wanderings with Ulysses.
An island faces the Sicanian bay
Against Plemyrium, washed by waves; this island
Has an old name, Ortygia. The story
Tells of a river, Alpheus, come from Elis,[30] 690
By a secret channel undersea, to join
The Arethusan fountains, mingling here
With the Sicilian waters. Here we worshipped
The land's great gods; went on, to pass Helorus,
A rich and marshy land; and then Pachynus
Where the cliffs rose sharp and high; and Camerina,
With firm foundation; the Geloan plains,
And Gela, named for a river; then Acragas,

[29] The places named in the following lines are located on the east and south coasts of Sicily; Drepanum lies directly opposite Carthage, across a narrow part of the Mediterranean, and is thus approximately where the action of Book I begins.

[30] Part of Greece; thus the river Alpheus must flow under the Ionian and Mediterranean seas to join the fountain Arethusa. According to the myth, Alpheus was a river god in love with the nymph Arethusa.

A towering town, high-walled, and sometime famous
For its breed of horses; the city of palms, Selinus; 700
The shoals of Lilybaeum, where the rocks
Are a hidden danger; so at last we came
To Drepanum, a harbor and a shoreline
That I could not rejoice in, a survivor
Of all those storms of the sea. For here I lost
My comforter in all my care and trouble,
My father Anchises. All the storms and perils,
All of the weariness endured, seemed nothing
Compared with this disaster; and I had
No warning of it; neither Helenus, 710
Though he foretold much trouble, nor Celaeno,
That evil harpy, prophesied this sorrow.
There was nothing more to bear; the long roads ended
At that unhappy goal; and when I left there,
Some god or other brought me to your shores.'

And so he told the story, a lonely man
To eager listeners, destiny and voyage,
And made an end of it here, ceased, and was quiet.

BOOK IV: AENEAS AND DIDO

But the queen finds no rest. Deep in her veins
The wound is fed; she burns with hidden fire.
His manhood, and the glory of his race
Are an obsession with her, like his voice,
Gesture and countenance. On the next morning,
After a restless night, she sought her sister:
"I am troubled, Anna, doubtful, terrified,
Or am I dreaming? What new guest is this
Come to our shores? How well he talks, how brave
He seems in heart and action! I suppose 10
It must be true; he does come from the gods.
Fear proves a bastard spirit. He has been
So buffeted by fate. What endless wars
He told of! Sister, I must tell you something:
Were not my mind made up, once and for all,
Never again to marry, having been
So lost when Sychaeus left me for the grave,
Slain by my murderous brother at the altar,
Were I not sick forever of the torch[1]
And bridal bed, here is the only man 20
Who has moved my spirit, shaken my weak will.

[1] Carried in wedding processions; an emblem of marriage.

I might have yielded to him. I recognize
The marks of an old fire. But I pray, rather,
That earth engulf me, lightning strike me down
To the pale shades and everlasting night
Before I break the laws of decency.[2]
My love has gone with Sychaeus; let him keep it,
Keep it with him forever in the grave."
She ended with a burst of tears. "Dear sister,
Dearer than life," Anna replied, "why must you 30
Grieve all your youth away in loneliness,
Not know sweet children, or the joys of love?
Is that what dust demands, and buried shadows?
So be it. You have kept your resolution
From Tyre to Libya, proved it by denying
Iarbas and a thousand other suitors
From Africa's rich kingdoms. Think a little.
Whose lands are these you settle in? Getulians,
Invincible in war, the wild Numidians,
Unfriendly Syrtes, ring us round, and a desert 40
Barren with drought, and the Barcaean rangers.
Why should I mention Tyre, and wars arising
Out of Pygmalion's threats? And you, my sister,
Why should you fight against a pleasing passion?
I think the gods have willed it so, and Juno
Has helped to bring the Trojan ships to Carthage.
What a great city, sister, what a kingdom
This might become, rising on such a marriage!
Carthage and Troy together in arms, what glory
Might not be ours? Only invoke the blessing 50
Of the great gods, make sacrifice, be lavish
In welcome, keep them here while the fierce winter
Rages at sea, and cloud and sky are stormy,
And ships still wrecked and broken."
So she fanned
The flame of the burning heart; the doubtful mind
Was given hope, and the sense of guilt was lessened.
And first of all they go to shrine and altar
Imploring peace; they sacrifice to Ceres,
Giver of law, to Bacchus, to Apollo,
And most of all to Juno, in whose keeping 60
The bonds of marriage rest. In all her beauty
Dido lifts up the goblet, pours libation
Between the horns of a white heifer, slowly,
Or, slowly, moves to the rich altars, noting
The proper gifts to mark the day, or studies
The sacrificial entrails for the omens.
Alas, poor blind interpreters! What woman
In love is helped by offerings or altars?

[2] Dido had sworn to remain faithful to her dead husband.

Soft fire consumes the marrow-bones, the silent
Wound grows, deep in the heart. 70
Unhappy Dido burns, and wanders, burning,
All up and down the city, the way a deer
With a hunter's careless arrow in her flank
Ranges the uplands, with the shaft still clinging
To the hurt side. She takes Aeneas with her
All through the town, displays the wealth of Sidon,
Buildings projected; she starts to speak, and falters,
And at the end of the day renews the banquet,
Is wild to hear the story, over and over,
Hangs on each word, until the late moon, sinking, 80
Sends them all home. The stars die out, but Dido
Lies brooding in the empty hall, alone,
Abandoned on a lonely couch. She hears him,
Sees him, or sees and hears him in Iulus,[3]
Fondles the boy, as if that ruse might fool her,
Deceived by his resemblance to his father.
The towers no longer rise, the youth are slack
In drill for arms, the cranes and derricks rusting,
Walls halt halfway to heaven.

And Juno saw it,
The queen held fast by this disease, this passion 90
Which made her good name meaningless. In anger
She rushed to Venus:—"Wonderful!—the trophies,
The praise, you and that boy of yours are winning!
Two gods outwit one woman—splendid, splendid!
What glory for Olympus! I know you fear me,
Fear Carthage, and suspect us. To what purpose?
What good does all this do? Is there no limit?
Would we not both be better off, to sanction
A bond of peace forever, a formal marriage?
You have your dearest wish; Dido is burning 100
With love, infected to her very marrow.
Let us—why not?—conspire to rule one people
On equal terms; let her serve a Trojan husband;
Let her yield her Tyrian people as her dowry."

This, Venus knew, was spoken with a purpose,
A guileful one, to turn Italian empire
To Libyan shores: not without reservation
She spoke in answer: "Who would be so foolish
As to refuse such terms, preferring warfare,
If only fortune follows that proposal? 110
I do not know, I am more than a little troubled
What fate permits: will Jupiter allow it,
One city for the Tyrians and Trojans,
This covenant, this mixture? You can fathom
His mind, and ask him, being his wife. I follow

[3]The actual Iulus, not Cupid, who had been substituted for him in Book I.

Wherever you lead." And royal Juno answered:
"That I will tend to. Listen to me, and learn
How to achieve the urgent need. They plan,
Aeneas, and poor Dido, to go hunting
When sunlight floods the world to-morrow morning. 120
While the rush of the hunt is on, and the forest shaken
With beaters and their nets, I will pour down
Dark rain and hail, and make the whole sky rumble
With thunder and threat. The company will scatter,
Hidden or hiding in the night and shadow,
And Dido and the Trojan come for shelter
To the same cave. I will be there and join them
In lasting wedlock; she will be his own,
His bride, forever; this will be their marriage."
Venus assented,[4] smiling, not ungracious— 130
The trick was in the open.
Dawn, rising, left the ocean, and the youth
Come forth from all the gates, prepared for hunting,
Nets, toils, wide spears, keen-scented coursing hounds.
And Dido keeps them waiting; her own charger
Stands bright in gold and crimson; the bit foams,
The impatient head is tossed. At last she comes,
With a great train attending, gold and crimson,
Quiver of gold, and combs of gold, and mantle
Crimson with golden buckle. A Trojan escort 140
Attends her, with Iulus, and Aeneas
Comes to her side, more lordly than Apollo
Bright along Delos' ridges in the springtime
With laurel in his hair and golden weapons
Shining across his shoulders. Equal radiance
Is all around Aeneas, equal splendor.
They reach the mountain heights, the hiding-places
Where no trail runs; wild goats from the rocks are started,
Run down the ridges; elsewhere, in the open
Deer cross the dusty plain, away from the mountains. 150
The boy Ascanius, in the midst of the valley,
Is glad he has so good a horse, rides, dashing
Past one group or another: deer are cowards
And wild goats tame; he prays for some excitement,
A tawny lion coming down the mountain
Or a great boar with foaming mouth.
The heaven
Darkens, and thunder rolls, and rain and hail
Come down in torrents. The hunt is all for shelter,
Trojans and Tyrians and Ascanius dashing
Wherever they can; the streams pour down the mountains. 160
To the same cave go Dido and Aeneas,

[4] Having been told by Jove (in Book I) of the destined future of Trojans and Romans, Venus is aware that Juno's plan will fail.

Where Juno, as a bridesmaid, gives the signal,
And mountain nymphs wail high their incantations,
First day of death, first cause of evil. Dido
Is unconcerned with fame, with reputation,
With how it seems to others. This is marriage
For her, not hole-and-corner guilt; she covers
Her folly with this name.
Rumor goes flying
At once, through all the Libyan cities, Rumor
Than whom no other evil was ever swifter. 170
She thrives on motion and her own momentum;
Tiny at first in fear, she swells, colossal
In no time, walks on earth, but her head is hidden
Among the clouds. Her mother, Earth, was angry,
Once, at the gods, and out of spite produced her,
The Titans' youngest sister, swift of foot,
Deadly of wing, a huge and terrible monster,
With an eye below each feather in her body,
A tongue, a mouth, for every eye, and ears
Double that number; in the night she flies 180
Above the earth, below the sky, in shadow
Noisy and shrill; her eyes are never closed
In slumber; and by day she perches, watching
From tower or battlement, frightening great cities.
She heralds truth, and clings to lies and falsehood,
It is all the same to her. And now she was going
Happy about her business, filling people
With truth and lies: Aeneas, Trojan-born,
Has come, she says, and Dido, lovely woman,
Sees fit to mate with him, one way or another, 190
And now the couple wanton out the winter,
Heedless of ruling, prisoners of passion.
They were dirty stories, but the goddess gave them
To the common ear, then went to King Iarbas[5]
With words that fired the fuel of his anger.
This king was Ammon's son, a child of rape
Begotten on a nymph from Garamantia;
He owned wide kingdoms, had a hundred altars
Blazing with fires to Jove, eternal outposts
In the gods' honor; the ground was fat with blood, 200
The temple portals blossoming with garlands.
He heard the bitter stories, and went crazy,
Before the presences of many altars
Beseeching and imploring:—"Jove Almighty,
To whom the Moorish race on colored couches
Pours festive wine, do you see these things, or are we
A pack of idiots, shaking at the lightning

[5]A rejected African suitor of Dido, Iarbas is a son of Jove (identified here with Ammon).

We think you brandish, when it is really only
An aimless flash of light, and silly noises?
Do you see these things? A woman, who used to wander 210
Around my lands, who bought a little city,
To whom we gave some ploughland and a contract,
Disdains me as a husband, takes Aeneas
To be her lord and master, in her kingdom,
And now that second Paris, with his lackeys,
Half-men, I call them, his chin tied up with ribbons,
With millinery on his perfumed tresses,
Takes over what he stole, and we keep bringing
Gifts to your temples, we, devout believers
Forsooth, in idle legend."
And Jove heard him 220
Making his prayer and clinging to the altars,
And turned his eyes to Carthage and the lovers
Forgetful of their better reputation.
He summoned Mercury:—"Go forth, my son,
Descend on wing and wind to Tyrian Carthage,
Speak to the Trojan leader, loitering there
Unheedful of the cities given by fate.
Take him my orders through the rapid winds:
It was not for this his lovely mother saved him
Twice[6] from Greek arms; she promised he would be 230
A ruler, in a country loud with war,
Pregnant with empire; he would sire a race
From Teucer's noble line; he would ordain
Law for the world. If no such glory moves him,
If his own fame and fortune count as nothing,
Does he, a father, grudge his son the towers
Of Rome to be? What is the fellow doing?
With what ambition wasting time in Libya?
Let him set sail. That's all; convey the message."
Before he ended, Mercury made ready 240
To carry out the orders of his father;
He strapped the golden sandals on, the pinions
To bear him over sea and land, as swift
As the breath of the wind; he took the wand, which summons
Pale ghosts from Hell, or sends them there, denying
Or giving sleep, unsealing dead men's eyes,
Useful in flight through wind and stormy cloud,
And so came flying till he saw the summit
And towering sides of Atlas,[7] rugged giant
With heaven on his neck, whose head and shoulders 250
Are dark with fir, ringed with black cloud, and beaten
With wind and rain, and laden with the whiteness
Of falling snow, with rivers running over

[6] First in a combat with Diomede, then during the sack of Troy.
[7] The mountain in Africa, here personified as the giant.

His agèd chin, and the rough beard ice-stiffened.
Here first on level wing the god paused briefly,
Poised, plummeted to ocean, like a bird
That skims the water's surface, flying low
By shore and fishes' rocky breeding-ground,
So Mercury darted between earth and heaven
To Libya's sandy shore, cutting the wind 260
From the home of Maia's[8] father.
Soon as the winged sandals skim the rooftops,
He sees Aeneas founding towers, building
New homes for Tyrians; his sword is studded
With yellow jasper; he wears across his shoulders
A cloak of burning crimson, and golden threads
Run through it, the royal gift of the rich queen.
Mercury wastes no time:—"What are you doing,
Forgetful of your kingdom and your fortunes,
Building for Carthage? Woman-crazy fellow, 270
The ruler of the gods, the great compeller
Of heaven and earth, has sent me from Olympus
With no more word than this: what are you doing,
With what ambition wasting time in Libya?
If your own fame and fortune count as nothing,
Think of Ascanius at least, whose kingdom
In Italy, whose Roman land, are waiting
As promise justly due." He spoke, and vanished
Into thin air. Appalled, amazed, Aeneas
Is stricken dumb; his hair stands up in terror, 280
His voice sticks in his throat. He is more than eager
To flee that pleasant land, awed by the warning
Of the divine command. But how to do it?
How get around that passionate queen? What opening
Try first? His mind runs out in all directions,
Shifting and veering. Finally, he has it,
Or thinks he has: he calls his comrades to him,
The leaders, bids them quietly prepare
The fleet for voyage, meanwhile saying nothing
About the new activity; since Dido 290
Is unaware, has no idea that passion
As strong as theirs is on the verge of breaking,
He will see what he can do, find the right moment
To let her know, all in good time. Rejoicing,
The captains move to carry out the orders.
    Who can deceive a woman in love? The queen
Anticipates each move, is fearful even
While everything is safe, foresees this cunning,
And the same trouble-making goddess, Rumor,
Tells her the fleet is being armed, made ready 300

[8] Daughter of Atlas and mother of Mercury.

For voyaging. She rages through the city
Like a woman mad, or drunk, the way the Maenads
Go howling through the night-time on Cithaeron[9]
When Bacchus' cymbals summon with their clashing.
She waits no explanation from Aeneas;
She is the first to speak: "And so, betrayer,
You hoped to hide your wickedness, go sneaking
Out of my land without a word? Our love
Means nothing to you, our exchange of vows,
And even the death of Dido could not hold you. 310
The season is dead of winter, and you labor
Over the fleet; the northern gales are nothing—
You must be cruel, must you not? Why, even,
If ancient Troy remained, and you were seeking
Not unknown homes and lands, but Troy again,
Would you be venturing Troyward in this weather?
I am the one you flee from: true? I beg you
By my own tears, and your right hand—(I have nothing
Else left my wretchedness)—by the beginnings
Of marriage, wedlock, what we had, if ever 320
I served you well, if anything of mine
Was ever sweet to you, I beg you, pity
A falling house; if there is room for pleading
As late as this, I plead, put off that purpose.
You are the reason I am hated; Libyans,
Numidians, Tyrians, hate me; and my honor
Is lost, and the fame I had, that almost brought me
High as the stars, is gone. To whom, O guest—
I must not call you husband any longer—
To whom do you leave me? I am a dying woman; 330
Why do I linger on? Until Pygmalion,
My brother, brings destruction to this city?
Until the prince Iarbas leads me captive?
At least if there had been some hope of children
Before your flight, a little Aeneas playing
Around my courts, to bring you back, in feature
At least, I would seem less taken and deserted."

There was nothing he could say. Jove bade him keep
Affection from his eyes, and grief in his heart
With never a sign. At last, he managed something:— 340
'Never, O Queen, will I deny you merit
Whatever you have strength to claim; I will not
Regret remembering Dido, while I have
Breath in my body, or consciousness of spirit.
I have a point or two to make. I did not,
Believe me, hope to hide my flight by cunning;
I did not, ever, claim to be a husband,

[9] A mountain where the Maenads (female worshipers of Bacchus) conducted their orgiastic rites.

Made no such vows. If I had fate's permission
To live my life my way, to settle my troubles
At my own will, I would be watching over 350
The city of Troy, and caring for my people,
Those whom the Greeks had spared, and Priam's palace
Would still be standing; for the vanquished people
I would have built the town again. But now
It is Italy I must seek, great Italy,
Apollo orders, and his oracles
Call me to Italy. There is my love,
There is my country. If the towers of Carthage,
The Libyan citadels, can please a woman
Who came from Tyre, why must you grudge the Trojans 360
Ausonian land? It is proper for us also
To seek a foreign kingdom. I am warned
Of this in dreams: when the earth is veiled in shadow
And the fiery stars are burning, I see my father,
Anchises, or his ghost, and I am frightened;
I am troubled for the wrong I do my son,
Cheating him out of his kingdom in the west,
And lands that fate assigns him. And a herald,
Jove's messenger—I call them both to witness—
Has brought me, through the rush of air, his orders; 370
I saw the god myself, in the full daylight,
Enter these walls, I heard the words he brought me.
Cease to inflame us both with your complainings;
I follow Italy not because I want to."

Out of the corner of her eye she watched him
During the first of this, and her gaze was turning
Now here, now there; and then, in bitter silence,
She looked him up and down; then blazed out at him:—
"You treacherous liar! No goddess was your mother,
No Dardanus the founder of your tribe, 380
Son of the stony mountain-crags, begotten
On cruel rocks, with a tigress for a wet-nurse!
Why fool myself, why make pretense? what is there
To save myself for now? When I was weeping
Did he so much as sigh? Did he turn his eyes,
Ever so little, toward me? Did he break at all,
Or weep, or give his lover a word of pity?
What first, what next? Neither Jupiter nor Juno
Looks at these things with any sense of fairness.
Faith has no haven anywhere in the world. 390
He was an outcast on my shore, a beggar,
I took him in, and, like a fool, I gave him
Part of my kingdom; his fleet was lost, I found it,
His comrades dying, I brought them back to life.
I am maddened, burning, burning: now Apollo
The prophesying god, the oracles
Of Lycia, and Jove's herald, sent from heaven,

Come flying through the air with fearful orders,—
Fine business for the gods, the kind of trouble
That keeps them from their sleep. I do not hold you, 400
I do not argue, either. Go. And follow
Italy on the wind, and seek the kingdom
Across the water. But if any gods
Who care for decency have any power,
They will land you on the rocks; I hope for vengeance,
I hope to hear you calling the name of Dido
Over and over, in vain. Oh, I will follow
In blackest fire, and when cold death has taken
Spirit from body, I will be there to haunt you,
A shade, all over the world. I will have vengeance, 410
And hear about it; the news will be my comfort
In the deep world below." She broke it off,
Leaving the words unfinished; even light
Was unendurable; sick at heart, she turned
And left him, stammering, afraid, attempting
To make some kind of answer. And her servants
Support her to her room, that bower of marble,
A marriage-chamber once; here they attend her,
Help her lie down.
And good Aeneas, longing
To ease her grief with comfort, to say something 420
To turn her pain and hurt away, sighs often,
His heart being moved by this great love, most deeply,
And still—the gods give orders, he obeys them;
He goes back to the fleet. And then the Trojans
Bend, really, to their work, launching the vessels
All down the shore. The tarred keel swims in the water,
The green wood comes from the forest, the poles are lopped
For oars, with leaves still on them. All are eager
For flight; all over the city you see them streaming,
Bustling about their business, a black line moving 430
The way ants do when they remember winter
And raid a hill of grain, to haul and store it
At home, across the plain, the column moving
In thin black line through grass, part of them shoving
Great seeds on little shoulders, and part bossing
The job, rebuking laggards, and all the pathway
Hot with the stream of work.
And Dido saw them
With who knows what emotion: there she stood
On the high citadel, and saw, below her,
The whole beach boiling, and the water littered 440
With one ship after another, and men yelling,
Excited over their work, and there was nothing
For her to do but sob or choke with anguish.
There is nothing to which the hearts of men and women
Cannot be driven by love. Break into tears,

Try prayers again, humble the pride, leave nothing
Untried, and die in vain:—"Anna, you see them
Coming from everywhere; they push and bustle
All up and down the shore: the sails are swelling,
The happy sailors garlanding the vessels. 450
If I could hope for grief like this, my sister,
I shall be able to bear it. But one service
Do for me first, dear Anna, out of pity.
You were the only one that traitor trusted,
Confided in; you know the way to reach him,
The proper time and place. Give him this message,
Our arrogant enemy: tell him I never
Swore with the Greeks at Aulis to abolish
The Trojan race, I never sent a fleet
To Pergamus, I never desecrated 460
The ashes or the spirit of Anchises:
Why does he, then, refuse to listen to me?
What is the hurry? Let him give his lover
The one last favor: only wait a little,
Only a little while, for better weather
And easy flight. He has betrayed the marriage,
I do not ask for that again; I do not
Ask him to give up Latium and his kingdom.
Mere time is all I am asking, a breathing-space,
A brief reprieve, until my luck has taught me 470
To reconcile defeat and sorrow. This
Is all I ask for, sister; pity and help me:
If he grants me this, I will pay it ten times over
After my death." And Anna, most unhappy,
Over and over, told her tears, her pleading;
No tears, no pleading, move him; no man can yield
When a god stops his ears. As northern winds
Sweep over Alpine mountains, in their fury
Fighting each other to uproot an oak-tree
Whose ancient strength endures against their roaring 480
And the trunk shudders and the leaves come down
Strewing the ground, but the old tree clings to the mountain,
Its roots as deep toward hell as its crest toward heaven,
And still holds on—even so, Aeneas, shaken
By storm-blasts of appeal, by voices calling
From every side, is tossed and torn, and steady.
His will stays motionless, and tears are vain.

Then Dido prays for death at last; the fates
Are terrible, her luck is out, she is tired
Of gazing at the everlasting heaven. 490
The more to goad her will to die, she sees—
Oh terrible!—the holy water blacken,
Libations turn to blood, on ground and altar,
When she makes offerings. But she tells no one,
Not even her sister. From the marble shrine,

Memorial to her former lord, attended,
Always, by her, with honor, fleece and garland,
She hears his voice, his words, her husband calling
When darkness holds the world, and from the house-top
An owl sends out a long funereal wailing, 500
And she remembers warnings of old seers,
Fearful, foreboding. In her dreams Aeneas
Appears to hunt her down; or she is going
Alone in a lost country, wandering
Trying to find her Tyrians, mad as Pentheus,
Or frenzied as Orestes, when his mother
Is after him with whips of snakes, or firebrands,
While the Avengers menace at the threshold.[10]
She was beaten, harboring madness, and resolved
On dying; alone, she plotted time and method; 510
Keeping the knowledge from her sorrowing sister,
She spoke with calm composure:—"I have found
A way (wish me good luck) to bring him to me
Or set me free from loving him forever.
Near Ocean[11] and the west there is a country,
The Ethiopian land, far-off, where Atlas
Turns on his shoulders the star-studded world;
I know a priestess there; she guards the temple
Of the daughters of the Evening Star; she feeds
The dragon there, and guards the sacred branches, 520
She sprinkles honey-dew, strews drowsy poppies,
And she knows charms to free the hearts of lovers
When she so wills it, or to trouble others;
She can reverse the wheeling of the planets,
Halt rivers in their flowing; she can summon
The ghosts of night-time; you will see earth shaking
Under her tread, and trees come down from mountains.
Dear sister mine, as heaven is my witness,
I hate to take these arts of magic on me!
Be secret, then; but in the inner courtyard, 530
Raise up a funeral-pyre, to hold the armor
Left hanging in the bower, by that hero,
That good devoted man, and all his raiment,
And add the bridal bed, my doom: the priestess
Said to do this, and it will be a pleasure
To see the end of all of it, every token
Of that unspeakable knave."
And so, thought Anna,
Things are no worse than when Sychaeus perished.
She did not know the death these rites portended,
Had no suspicion, and carried out her orders. 540

[10] Pentheus was driven to madness by Bacchus for opposing worship of him. Orestes was pursued by the Furies ("Avengers") in revenge for the murder of his mother; see Aeschylus' *Oresteia*.

[11] The waters believed to surround the world.

The pyre is raised in the court; it towers high
With pine and holm-oak, it is hung with garlands
And funeral wreaths, and on the couch she places
Aeneas' sword, his garments, and his image,
Knowing the outcome. Round about are altars,
Where, with her hair unbound, the priestess calls
On thrice a hundred gods, Erebus, Chaos,
Hecate, queen of Hell, triple Diana.
Water is sprinkled, from Avernus[12] fountain,
Or said to be, and herbs are sought, by moonlight 550
Mown with bronze sickles, and the stem-ends running
With a black milk, and the caul of a colt, new-born.
Dido, with holy meal and holy hands,
Stands at the altar, with one sandal loosened
And robes unfastened, calls the gods to witness,
Prays to the stars that know her doom, invoking,
Beyond them, any powers, if there are any,
Who care for lovers in unequal bondage.
Night: and tired creatures over all the world
Were seeking slumber; the woods and the wild waters 560
Were quiet, and the silent stars were wheeling
Their course half over; every field was still;
The beasts of the field, the brightly colored birds,
Dwellers in lake and pool, in thorn and thicket,
Slept through the tranquil night, their sorrows over,
Their troubles soothed. But no such blessèd darkness
Closes the eyes of Dido; no repose
Comes to her anxious heart. Her pangs redouble,
Her love swells up, surging, a great tide rising 570
Of wrath and doubt and passion. "What do I do?
What now? Go back to my Numidian suitors,
Be scorned by those I scorned? Pursue the Trojans?
Obey their orders? They were grateful to me,
Once, I remember. But who would let them take me?
Suppose I went. They hate me now; they were always
Deceivers: is Laomedon[13] forgotten,
Whose blood runs through their veins? What then? Attend them,
Alone, be their companion, the loud-mouthed sailors? 580
Or with my own armada follow after,
Wear out my sea-worn Tyrians once more
With vengeance and adventure? Better die.
Die; you deserve to; end the hurt with the sword.
It is your fault, Anna; you were sorry for me,
Won over by my tears; you put this load
Of evil on me. It was not permitted,
It seems, for me to live apart from wedlock,
A blameless life. An animal does better.
I vowed Sychaeus faith. I have been faithless." 590

[12] *Erebus . . . Avernus* were all associated with death or the Lower World.
[13] King of Troy before Priam; he was noted for deceitfulness.

So, through the night, she tossed in restless torment.
Meanwhile Aeneas, on the lofty stern,
All things prepared, sure of his going, slumbers
As Mercury comes down once more to warn him,
Familiar blond young god: "O son of Venus,
Is this a time for sleep? The wind blows fair,
And danger rises all around you. Dido,
Certain to die, however else uncertain,
Plots treachery, harbors evil. Seize the moment
While it can still be seized, and hurry, hurry! 600
The sea will swarm with ships, the fiery torches
Blaze, and the shore rankle with fire by morning.
Shove off, be gone! A shifty, fickle object
Is woman, always." He vanished into the night.
And, frightened by that sudden apparition,
Aeneas started from sleep, and urged his comrades:—
"Hurry, men, hurry; get to the sails and benches,
Get the ships under way. A god from heaven
Again has come to speed our flight, to sever
The mooring-ropes. O holy one, we follow, 610
Whoever you are, we are happy in obeying.
Be with us, be propitious; let the stars
Be right in heaven!" He drew his sword; the blade
Flashed, shining, at the hawser; and all the men
Were seized in the same restlessness and rushing.
They have left the shore, they have hidden the sea-water
With the hulls of the ships; the white foam flies, the oars
Dip down in dark-blue water.
And Aurora[14]
Came from Tithonus' saffron couch to freshen
The world with rising light, and from her watch-tower 620
The queen saw day grow whiter, and the fleet
Go moving over the sea, keep pace together
To the even spread of the sail; she knew the harbors
Were empty of sailors now; she struck her breast
Three times, four times; she tore her golden hair,
Crying, "God help me, will he go, this stranger,
Treating our kingdom as a joke? Bring arms,
Bring arms, and hurry! follow from all the city,
Haul the ships off the ways, some of you! Others,
Get fire as fast as you can, give out the weapons, 630
Pull oars! What am I saying? O where am I?
I must be going mad. Unhappy Dido,
Is it only now your wickedness strikes home?
The time it should have was when you gave him power.
Well, here it is, look at it now, the honor,
The faith of the hero who, they tell me, carries
With him his household gods, who bore on his shoulders

[14] Goddess of the dawn, mate of Tithonus.

His agèd father! Could I not have seized him,
Torn him to pieces, scattered him over the waves?
What was the matter? Could I not have murdered 640
His comrades, and Iulus, and served the son
For a dainty at the table of his father?
But fight would have a doubtful fortune. It might have,
What then? I was going to die; whom did I fear?
I would have, should have, set his camp on fire,
Filled everything with flame, choked off the father,
The son, the accursèd race, and myself with them.
Great Sun, surveyor of all the works of earth,
Juno, to whom my sorrows are committed,
Hecate,[15] whom the cross-roads of the cities 650
Wail to by night, avenging Furies, hear me,
Grant me divine protection, take my prayer.
If he must come to harbor, then he must,
If Jove ordains it, however vile he is,
False, and unspeakable. If Jove ordains,
The goal is fixed. So be it. Take my prayer.[16]
Let him be driven by arms and war, an exile,
Let him be taken from his son Iulus,
Let him beg for aid, let him see his people dying
Unworthy deaths, let him accept surrender 660
On unfair terms, let him never enjoy the kingdom,
The hoped-for light, let him fall and die, untimely,
Let him lie unburied on the sand. Oh, hear me,
Hear the last prayer, poured out with my last blood!
And you, O Tyrians, hate, and hate forever
The Trojan stock. Offer my dust this homage.
No love, no peace, between these nations, ever!
Rise from my bones, O great unknown avenger,
Hunt them with fire and sword, the Dardan settlers,
Now, then, here, there, wherever strength is given. 670
Shore against shore, wave against wave, and war,
War after war, for all the generations."

She spoke, and turned her purpose to accomplish
The quickest end to the life she hated. Briefly
She spoke to Barce, Sychaeus' nurse; her own
Was dust and ashes in her native country:—
"Dear nurse, bring me my sister, tell her to hurry,
Tell her to sprinkle her body with river water,
To bring the sacrificial beast and offerings,
And both of you cover your temples with holy fillets. 680
I have a vow to keep; I have made beginning
Of rites to Stygian[17] Jove, to end my sorrows,

[15] A goddess associated with the Lower World, worshiped at crossways.

[16] Much of the curse that follows is fulfilled (though the poem does not describe the death of Aeneas).

[17] Associated with Styx, a river in the Lower World. The "Stygian Jove" was Hades (also called Dis, Pluto, and Orcus).

To burn the litter of that Trojan leader."
Barce, with an old woman's fuss and bustle,
Went hurrying out of sight; but Dido, trembling,
Wild with her project, the blood-shot eyeballs rolling,
Pale at the death to come, and hectic color
Burning the quivering cheeks, broke into the court,
Mounted the pyre in madness, drew the sword,
The Trojan gift, bestowed for no such purpose, 690
And she saw the Trojan garments, and the bed
She knew so well, and paused a little, weeping,
Weeping, and thinking, and flung herself down on it,
Uttering her last words:—
"Spoils that were sweet while gods and fate permitted,
Receive my spirit, set me free from suffering.
I have lived, I have run the course that fortune gave me,
And now my shade, a great one, will be going
Below the earth. I have built a noble city,
I have seen my walls, I have avenged a husband, 700
Punished a hostile brother. I have been
Happy, I might have been too happy, only
The Trojans made their landing." She broke off,
Pressed her face to the couch, cried:—"So, we shall die,
Die unavenged; but let us die. So, so,—
I am glad to meet the darkness. Let his eyes
Behold this fire across the sea, an omen
Of my death going with him."
As she spoke,
Her handmaids saw her, fallen on the sword,
The foam of blood on the blade, and blood on the hands. 710
A scream rings through the house; Rumor goes reeling,
Rioting, through the shaken town; the palace
Is loud with lamentation, women sobbing,
Wailing and howling, and the vaults of heaven
Echo the outcry, as if Tyre or Carthage
Had fallen to invaders, and the fury
Of fire came rolling over homes and temples.
Anna, half lifeless, heard in panic terror,
Came rushing through them all, beating her bosom,
Clawing her face:—"Was it for this, my sister? 720
To trick me so? The funeral pyre, the altars,
Prepared this for me? I have, indeed, a grievance,
Being forsaken; you would not let your sister
Companion you in death? You might have called me
To the same fate; we might have both been taken,
One sword, one hour. I was the one who built it,
This pyre, with my own hands; it was my voice
That called our fathers' gods, for what?—to fail you
When you were lying here. You have killed me, sister,
Not only yourself, you have killed us all, the people, 730
The town. Let me wash the wounds with water,

Let my lips catch what fluttering breath still lingers."
She climbed the lofty steps, and held her sister,
A dying woman, close; she used her robe
To try to stop the bleeding. And Dido tried
In vain to raise her heavy eyes, fell back,
And her wound made a gurgling hissing sound.
Three times she tried to lift herself; three times
Fell back; her rolling eyes went searching heaven
And the light hurt when she found it, and she moaned. 740
At last all-powerful Juno, taking pity,
Sent Iris[18] from Olympus, in compassion
For the long racking agony, to free her
From the limbs' writhing and the struggle of spirit.
She had not earned this death, she had only sought it
Before her time, driven by sudden madness,
Therefore, the queen of Hades had not taken
The golden lock, consigning her to Orcus.[19]
So Iris, dewy on saffron wings, descending,
Trailing a thousand colors through the brightness 750
Comes down the sky, poises above her, saying,
"This lock I take as bidden, and from the body
Release the soul," and cuts the lock; and cold
Takes over, and the winds receive the spirit.

from BOOK V: THE FUNERAL GAMES FOR ANCHISES

The Trojans return to Sicily, where they solemnize the anniversary of Anchises' death through religious ritual and athletic contests. During the games some of the women, weary of travel and incited by Juno, try to burn the ships, but Jove sends a rainstorm that extinguishes the flames. Aeneas decides to leave the less hardy and zealous of the Trojans behind in Sicily, under the friendly ruler Acestes. The fleet then departs for Italy.

The masts are raised, and sail
Stretched from the halyards; right and left they bend
The canvas to fair winds: at the head of the fleet
Rides Palinurus, and the others follow,
As ordered, close behind him; dewy night
Has reached mid-heaven, while the sailors, sleeping,
Relax on the hard benches under the oars, 800
All calm, all quiet. And the god of Sleep
Parting the shadowy air, comes gently down,
Looking for Palinurus, bringing him,
A guiltless man, ill-omened dreams. He settles
On the high stern, a god disguised as a man,
Speaking in Phorbas'[1] guise, "O Palinurus,

[18] Goddess of the rainbow, Juno's messenger.
[19] The queen of Hades, or the Lower World, was Proserpina.
[1] A friend of the helmsman Palinurus.

The fleet rides smoothly in the even weather,
The hour is given for rest. Lay down the head,
Rest the tired eyes from toil. I will take over
A little while." But Palinurus, barely 810
Lifting his eyes, made answer: "Trust the waves,
However quiet? trust a peaceful ocean?
Put faith in such a monster? Never! I
Have been too often fooled by the clear stars
To trust Aeneas to their faithless keeping."
And so he clung to the tiller, never loosed
His hand from the wood, his eyes from the fair heaven.
But lo, the god over his temples shook
A bough that dripped with dew from Lethe, steeped
With Stygian magic,[2] so the swimming eyes, 820
Against his effort, close, blink open, close
Again, and slumber takes the drowsy limbs.
Bending above him, leaning over, the god
Shoves him, still clinging to the tiller, calling
His comrades vainly, into the clear waves.
And the god is gone like a bird to the clear air,
And the fleet is going safely over its journey
As Neptune promised.[3] But the rocks were near,
The Siren-cliffs, most perilous of old,
White with the bones of many mariners, 830
Loud with their hoarse eternal warning sound.[4]
Aeneas starts from sleep, aware, somehow,
Of a lost pilot, and a vessel drifting,
Himself takes over guidance, with a sigh
And heartache for a friend's mishap, "Alas,
Too trustful in the calm of sea and sky,
O Palinurus, on an unknown shore,
You will be lying, naked."

BOOK VI: THE LOWER WORLD

Mourning for Palinurus, he drives the fleet
To Cumae's[1] coast-line; the prows are turned, the anchors
Let down, the beach is covered by the vessels.
Young in their eagerness for the land in the west,

[2] Lethe, the river of forgetfulness, and Styx, the river of death, are part of the landscape of the Lower World, described in Book VI.

[3] In response to Venus' pleas, the ocean god Neptune had promised her that the Trojan fleet should reach Italy in safety, but he had also stipulated that one sailor should be drowned.

[4] The Sirens, as described in Homer's *Odyssey*, Book XII, were females who enchanted sailors with their beautiful songs, luring them to destruction. Virgil associates this peril with certain actual rocks in the sea near modern Naples.

[1] A city, near the modern Naples, where Aeneas is to visit the Sybil named Deiphobe, mythical prophet and priestess of Apollo, in preparation for his visit to the Lower World.

They flash ashore; some seek the seeds of flame
Hidden in veins of flint, and others spoil
The woods of tinder, and show where water runs.
Aeneas, in devotion, seeks the heights
Where stands Apollo's temple, and the cave
Where the dread Sibyl dwells, Apollo's priestess, 10
With the great mind and heart, inspired revealer
Of things to come. They enter Diana's grove,
Pass underneath the roof of gold.[2]
The story
Has it that Daedalus fled from Minos' kingdom,
Trusting himself to wings he made, and travelled
A course unknown to man, to the cold north,
Descending on this very summit; here,
Earth-bound again, he built a mighty temple,
Paying Apollo homage, the dedication
Of the oarage of his wings. On the temple doors 20
He carved, in bronze, Androgeos' death, and the payment
Enforced on Cecrops' children, seven sons
For sacrifice each year: there stands the urn,
The lots are drawn—facing this, over the sea,
Rises the land of Crete: the scene portrays
Pasiphae in cruel love, the bull
She took to her by cunning, and their offspring,
The mongrel Minotaur, half man, half monster,
The proof of lust unspeakable; and the toil
Of the house is shown, the labyrinthine maze 30
Which no one could have solved, but Daedalus
Pitied a princess' love, loosened the tangle,
Gave her a skein to guide her way. His boy,
Icarus, might have been here, in the picture,
And almost was—his father had made the effort
Once, and once more, and dropped his hands; he could not
Master his grief that much.[3] The story held them;

[2] The temple and its environs were sacred to both Apollo and Diana, his sister. In her alter ego as Hecate, she was goddess of the Lower World and was sometimes associated with witchcraft.

[3] Minos was king of Crete. His wife, Pasiphae, in a bovine disguise fabricated by the craftsman Daedalus, made love with a bull and then gave birth to the Minotaur, half bull and half human. Minos then forced Daedalus to construct a labyrinth to contain the Minotaur. After the Athenians killed Androgeos, the son of Minos, the king in revenge forced them (the "children" of Cecrops, an early king of Athens) to sacrifice to the Minotaur, each year, the lives of seven young men and seven young women, chosen by lots drawn from an urn. The Athenian hero Theseus went to Crete and succeeded in killing the monster that was devouring his compatriots. In this enterprise he was helped by Daedalus and the love-smitten Ariadne, Minos' daughter, who gave Theseus a thread to guide him back out of the labyrinth. Imprisoned for his part in this feat, Daedalus with his son Icarus escaped from Crete on wings the father had constructed; Icarus, however, died when he flew too close to the sun, which melted the wax fastenings of his wings. Daedalus, after reaching Italy, built the temple and executed the carvings that Aeneas is examining, though Virgil represents the artist as having been incapable, in his grief, of representing his son's tragic story.

They would have studied it longer, but Achates[4]
Came from his mission; with him the priestess,
Deiphobe, daughter of Glaucus,[5] who tends the temple 40
For Phoebus and Diana; she warned Aeneas:
"It is no such sights the time demands; far better
To offer sacrifice, seven chosen bullocks,
Seven chosen ewes, a herd without corruption."
They were prompt in their obedience, and the priestess
Summoned the Trojans to the lofty temple.

The rock's vast side is hollowed into a cavern,
With a hundred mouths, a hundred open portals,
Whence voices rush, the answers of the Sibyl.
They had reached the threshold, and the virgin cried: 50
"It is time to seek the fates; the god is here,
The god is here, behold him." And as she spoke
Before the entrance, her countenance and color
Changed, and her hair tossed loose, and her heart was heaving,
Her bosom swollen with frenzy; she seemed taller,
Her voice not human at all, as the god's presence
Drew nearer, and took hold on her. "Aeneas,"
She cried, "Aeneas, are you praying?
Are you being swift in prayer? Until you are,
The house of the gods will not be moved, nor open 60
Its mighty portals." More than her speech, her silence
Made the Trojans cold with terror, and Aeneas
Prayed from the depth of his heart: "Phoebus Apollo,
Compassionate ever, slayer of Achilles
Through aim of Paris' arrow,[6] helper and guide
Over the seas, over the lands, the deserts,
The shoals and quicksands, now at last we have come
To Italy, we hold the lands which fled us:
Grant that thus far, no farther, a Trojan fortune
Attend our wandering. And spare us now, 70
All of you, gods and goddesses, who hated
Troy in the past, and Trojan glory. I beg you,
Most holy prophetess, in whose foreknowing
The future stands revealed, grant that the Trojans—
I ask with fate's permission—rest in Latium
Their wandering storm-tossed gods. I will build a temple,
In honor of Apollo and Diana,
Out of eternal marble, and ordain
Festivals in their honor, and for the Sibyl
A great shrine in our kingdom, and I will place there 80
The lots and mystic oracles for my people

[4] Aeneas' most faithful friend.
[5] Glaucus was a sea god gifted with prophetic powers.
[6] Apollo, patron of archers, helped Paris to slay Achilles by shooting him in the heel, the only part of his body not supernaturally protected.

With chosen priests to tend them.[7] Only, priestess,
This once, I pray you, chant the sacred verses
With your own lips; do not trust them to the leaves,
The mockery of the rushing wind's disorder."[8]
  But the priestess, not yet subject to Apollo,
Went reeling through the cavern, wild, and storming
To throw the god, who presses, like a rider,
With bit and bridle and weight, tames her wild spirit,
Shapes her to his control. The doors fly open, 90
The hundred doors, of their own will, fly open,
And through the air the answer comes:—"O Trojans,
At last the dangers of the sea are over;
That course is run, but graver ones are waiting
On land. The sons of Dardanus will reach
The kingdom of Lavinia—be easy
On that account—the sons of Dardanus, also,
Will wish they had not come there. War, I see,
Terrible war, and the river Tiber foaming
With streams of blood. There will be another Xanthus, 100
Another Simois, and Greek encampment,
Even another Achilles, born in Latium,
Himself a goddess' son. And Juno further
Will always be there: you will beg for mercy,
Be poor, turn everywhere for help. A woman
Will be the cause once more of so much evil,
A foreign bride, receptive to the Trojans,
A foreign marriage.[9] Do not yield to evil,
Attack, attack, more boldly even than fortune
Seems to permit. An offering of safety,— 110
Incredible!—will come from a Greek city."[10]
  So, through the amplifiers of her cavern,
The hollow vaults, the Sibyl cast her warnings,
Riddles confused with truth; and Apollo rode her,
Reining her rage, and shaking her, and spurring
The fierceness of her heart. The frenzy dwindled,
A little, and her lips were still. Aeneas
Began:—"For me, no form of trouble, maiden,
Is new, or unexpected; all of this
I have known long since, lived in imagination. 120
One thing I ask: this is the gate of the kingdom,

[7] The Sibylline books, venerated in Virgil's day, were supposed to contain prophetic oracles important to the guidance of Rome.

[8] See Helenus' instructions to Aeneas in III.455–463, 466–467.

[9] In short, it will be the Trojan War all over again. Xanthus and Simois were rivers at Troy. The second Achilles will be the Italian hero Turnus (son of the nymph Venilia as Achilles had been the son of the nymph Thetis), who will become Aeneas' rival for the princess Lavinia. Thus, according to the prophecy, woman will again be at the root of the troubles, as with Helen and (it may be implied) Dido.

[10] Pallanteum, a city on the site of the future Rome; it had been founded by Evander, king of Arcadia (in Greece), who had emigrated to Italy.

So it is said, where Pluto reigns, the gloomy
Marsh where the water of Acheron[11] runs over.
Teach me the way from here, open the portals
That I may go to my belovèd father,
Stand in his presence, talk with him. I brought him,
Once, on these shoulders, through a thousand weapons
And following fire, and foemen. He shared with me
The road, the sea, the menaces of heaven,
Things that an old man should not bear; he bore them, 130
Tired as he was. And he it was who told me
To come to you in humbleness. I beg you
Pity the son, the father. You have power,
Great priestess, over all; it is not for nothing
Hecate gave you this dominion over
Avernus' groves. If Orpheus could summon
Eurydice from the shadows with his music,
If Pollux could save his brother, coming, going,
Along this path,—why should I mention Theseus,
Why mention Hercules?[12] I, too, descended 140
From the line of Jupiter." He clasped the altar,
Making his prayer, and she made answer to him:
"Son of Anchises, born of godly lineage,
By night, by day, the portals of dark Dis
Stand open: it is easy, the descending
Down to Avernus.[13] But to climb again,
To trace the footsteps back to the air above,
There lies the task, the toil. A few, beloved
By Jupiter, descended from the gods,
A few, in whom exalting virtue burned, 150
Have been permitted. Around the central woods
The black Cocytus glides, a sullen river;
But if such love is in your heart, such longing
For double crossing of the Stygian lake,[14]
For double sight of Tartarus,[15] learn first
What must be done. In a dark tree there hides

[11] One of the rivers of the Lower World.

[12] The legendary musician Orpheus was allowed to lead his dead wife, Eurydice, out of the Lower World (though he lost her after all, being unable to obey the command not to look back as she followed him). Pollux, an immortal who was half-brother to the mortal Castor, wished to die with him but could not; Jupiter, however, agreed to let them exchange places daily, each living alternately in the heavens and in the world of the dead. Theseus and Pirithous had tried to abduct Proserpine, queen of the dead. (She is also called Proserpina and Persephone.) The most difficult of Hercules' famous "labors" was the theft of Cerberus, the three-headed dog guarding the Lower World. (See lines 415–421.)

[13] Dis, like Hades (Greek) and Orcus, is another name for the god Pluto, and also for his realm, the Lower World. Avernus in this passage also means the Lower World, named for a sulfurous volcanic lake near Cumae. See also line 136.

[14] The four rivers of the Lower World (besides Lethe, the river of forgetfulness) were Styx, Acheron, Cocytus, and Phlegethon.

[15] The place in the Lower World where evil was punished. Aeneas actually sees only the walls of Tartarus, but it is described in lines 573–660. *Tartarus* can also mean the Lower World in general.

A bough, all golden, leaf and pliant stem,
Sacred to Proserpine. This all the grove
Protects, and shadows cover it with darkness.
Until this bough, this bloom of light, is found, 160
No one receives his passport to the darkness
Whose queen requires this tribute. In succession,
After the bough is plucked, another grows,
Gold-green with the same metal. Raise the eyes,
Look up, reach up the hand, and it will follow
With ease, if fate is calling; otherwise,
No power, no steel, can loose it. Furthermore,
(Alas, you do not know this!), one of your men
Lies on the shore, unburied, a pollution
To all the fleet, while you have come for counsel 170
Here to our threshold.[16] Bury him with honor;
Black cattle slain in expiation for him
Must fall before you see the Stygian kingdoms,
The groves denied to living men."
Aeneas,
With sadness in his eyes, and downcast heart,
Turned from the cave, and at his side Achates
Accompanied his anxious meditations.
They talked together: who could be the comrade
Named by the priestess, lying there unburied?
And they found him on dry sand; it was Misenus, 180
Aeolus' son, none better with the trumpet
To make men burn for warfare. He had been
Great Hector's man-at-arms; he was good in battle
With spear as well as horn, and after Hector
Had fallen to Achilles, he had followed
Aeneas, entering no meaner service.
Some foolishness came over him; he made
The ocean echo to the blare of his trumpet
That day, and challenged the sea-gods to a contest
In martial music, and Triton, jealous, caught him, 190
However unbelievable the story,
And held him down between the rocks, and drowned him
Under the foaming waves.[17] His comrades mourned,
Aeneas most of all, and in their sorrow
They carry out, in haste, the Sibyl's orders,
Construct the funeral altar, high as heaven,
They go to an old wood, and the pine-trees fall
Where wild beasts have their dens, and holm-oak rings
To the stroke of the axe, and oak and ash are riven

[16]An unburied corpse was offensive for religious reasons. See the meeting with Palinurus later in Book VI.

[17]Triton was a sea deity, son of Neptune, and was often portrayed as blowing a conch-shell trumpet. The classical gods did not like to be challenged at their own specialties. Appropriately, the father of the trumpeter Misenus (line 181) is the namesake of the god of the winds, Aeolus.

By the splitting wedge, and rowan-trees come rolling 200
Down the steep mountain-side. Aeneas helps them,
And cheers them on; studies the endless forest,
Takes thought, and prays: "If only we might see it,
That golden bough, here in the depth of the forest,
Bright on some tree. She told the truth, our priestess,
Too much, too bitter truth, about Misenus."
No sooner had he spoken than twin doves
Came flying down before him, and alighted
On the green ground. He knew his mother's birds,
And made his prayer, rejoicing,—"Oh, be leaders, 210
Wherever the way, and guide me to the grove
Where the rich bough makes rich the shaded ground.
Help me, O goddess-mother!" And he paused,
Watching what sign they gave, what course they set.
The birds flew on a little, just ahead
Of the pursuing vision; when they came
To the jaws of dank Avernus, evil-smelling,
They rose aloft, then swooped down the bright air,
Perched on the double tree, where the off-color
Of gold was gleaming golden through the branches. 220
As mistletoe, in the cold winter, blossoms
With its strange foliage on an alien tree,
The yellow berry gilding the smooth branches,[18]
Such was the vision of the gold in leaf
On the dark holm-oak, so the foil was rustling,
Rattling, almost, the bract[19] in the soft wind
Stirring like metal. Aeneas broke it off
With eager grasp, and bore it to the Sibyl.
Meanwhile, along the shore, the Trojans mourned,
Paying Misenus' dust the final honors. 230
A mighty pyre was raised, of pine and oak,
The sides hung with dark leaves, and somber cypress
Along the front, and gleaming arms above.
Some made the water hot, and some made ready
Bronze caldrons, shimmering over fire, and others
Lave and anoint the body, and with weeping
Lay on the bier his limbs, and place above them
Familiar garments, crimson color; and some
Take up the heavy burden, a sad office,
And, as their fathers did, they kept their eyes 240
Averted, as they brought the torches nearer.
They burn gifts with him, bowls of oil, and viands,
And frankincense; and when the flame is quiet
And the ashes settle to earth, they wash the embers
With wine, and slake the thirsty dust. The bones

[18] Mistletoe is a parasite with hardly visible roots, so that in winter it contrasts in appearance with the tree it grows on and seems to live a strange, self-sustaining life.

[19] A botanical term translating *brattea,* a thin metallic leaf.

Are placed in a bronze urn by Corynaeus,
Who, with pure water, thrice around his comrades
Made lustral cleansing, shaking gentle dew
From the fruitful branch of olive; and they said
Hail and farewell! And over him Aeneas 250
Erects a mighty tomb, with the hero's arms,
His oar and trumpet, where the mountain rises
Memorial for ever, and named Misenus.[20]
These rites performed, he hastened to the Sibyl.
There was a cavern, yawning wide and deep,
Jagged, below the darkness of the trees,
Beside the darkness of the lake. No bird
Could fly above it safely, with the vapor
Pouring from the black gulf (the Greeks have named it
Avernus, or A-Ornos, meaning *birdless*),[21] 260
And here the priestess for the slaughter set
Four bullocks, black ones, poured the holy wine
Between the horns, and plucked the topmost bristles
For the first offering to the sacred fire,
Calling on Hecate, a power in heaven,
A power in hell. Knives to the throat were driven,
The warm blood caught in bowls. Aeneas offered
A lamb, black-fleeced, to Night and her great sister,
A sterile heifer for the queen;[22] for Dis
An altar in the night, and on the flames 270
The weight of heavy bulls, the fat oil pouring
Over the burning entrails. And at dawn,
Under their feet, earth seemed to shake and rumble,
The ridges move, and bitches bay in darkness,
As the presence neared. The Sibyl cried a warning,
"Keep off, keep off, whatever is unholy,
Depart from here![23] Courage, Aeneas; enter
The path, unsheathe the sword. The time is ready
For the brave heart." She strode out boldly, leading
Into the open cavern, and he followed. 280
Gods of the world of spirit, silent shadows,
Chaos and Phlegethon, areas of silence,
Wide realms of dark, may it be right and proper
To tell what I have heard, this revelation
Of matters buried deep in earth and darkness!
Vague forms in lonely darkness, they were going
Through void and shadow, through the empty realm
Like people in a forest, when the moonlight

[20] The promontory at the southwestern end of the Bay of Naples is still called Cape Miseno.
[21] Most authoritative manuscripts of the *Aeneid* omit this parenthetical statement.
[22] The sister of Night (Nox) was Earth (Tellus). The "queen" is Proserpine.
[23] At Roman religious ceremonies, the ritual dismissal of the uninitiated; here applied to Aeneas' companions, who must now leave him. The approaching "presence" (line 275) is that of the goddess Hecate, accompanied by her hounds.

Shifts with a baleful glimmer, and shadow covers
The sky, and all the colors turn to blackness. 290
At the first threshold, on the jaws of Orcus,
Grief and avenging Cares have set their couches,
And pale Diseases dwell, and sad Old Age,
Fear, evil-counselling Hunger, wretched Need,
Forms terrible to see, and Death, and Toil,
And Death's own brother, Sleep, and evil Joys,
Fantasies of the mind, and deadly War,
The Furies' iron chambers, Discord, raving,
Her snaky hair entwined in bloody bands.
An elm-tree loomed there, shadowy and huge, 300
The aged boughs outspread, beneath whose leaves,
Men say, the false dreams cling, thousands on thousands.
And there are monsters in the dooryard, Centaurs,
Scyllas, of double shape, the beast of Lerna,
Hissing most horribly, Briareus,
The hundred-handed giant, a Chimaera
Whose armament is fire, Harpies, and Gorgons,
A triple-bodied giant.[24] In sudden panic
Aeneas drew his sword, the edge held forward,
Ready to rush and flail, however blindly, 310
Save that his wise companion warned him, saying
They had no substance, they were only phantoms
Flitting about, illusions without body.

From here, the road turns off to Acheron,
River of Hell; here, thick with muddy whirling,
Cocytus boils with sand. Charon is here,
The guardian of these mingling waters, Charon,
Uncouth and filthy, on whose chin the hair
Is a tangled mat, whose eyes protrude, are burning,
Whose dirty cloak is knotted at the shoulder. 320
He poles a boat, tends to the sail, unaided,
Ferrying bodies in his rust-hued vessel.
Old, but a god's senility is awful
In its raw greenness. To the bank come thronging
Mothers and men, bodies of great-souled heroes,
Their life-time over, boys, unwedded maidens,
Young men whose fathers saw their pyres burning,
Thick as the forest leaves that fall in autumn
With early frost, thick as the birds to landfall

[24] These lines are a catalog of many of the most famous or fearsome monsters of ancient fable. Centaurs were half man, half horse; Scylla was a six-headed monster (described in III.432–444) who devoured sailors in the straits of Messina; the beast of Lerna was the Hydra, a gigantic many-headed serpent; Briareus, as the text states, was a giant with a hundred hands; the fire-breathing Chimaera was a combination of lion, goat, and serpent; the Harpies were foul bird women (described in III.213–257); the Gorgons (Medusa and her two sisters) were snake-haired female monsters who literally petrified men who gazed on them; the triple-bodied giant was named Geryon.

From over the seas, when the chill of the year compels them 330
To sunlight. There they stand, a host, imploring
To be taken over first. Their hands, in longing,
Reach out for the farther shore. But the gloomy boatman
Makes choice among them, taking some, and keeping
Others far back from the stream's edge. Aeneas,
Wondering, asks the Sibyl, "Why the crowding?
What are the spirits seeking? What distinction
Brings some across the livid stream, while others
Stay on the farther bank?" She answers, briefly:
"Son of Anchises, this is the awful river, 340
The Styx, by which the gods take oath; the boatman
Charon; those he takes with him are the buried,
Those he rejects, whose luck is out, the graveless.
It is not permitted him to take them over
The dreadful banks and hoarse-resounding waters
Till earth is cast upon their bones. They haunt
These shores a hundred restless years of waiting
Before they end postponement of the crossing."
Aeneas paused, in thoughtful mood, with pity
Over their lot's unevenness; and saw there, 350
Wanting the honor given the dead, and grieving,
Leucaspis, and Orontes, the Lycian captain,
Who had sailed from Troy across the stormy waters,
And drowned off Africa, with crew and vessel,
And there was Palinurus, once his pilot,
Who, not so long ago, had been swept over,
Watching the stars on the journey north from Carthage.
The murk was thick; Aeneas hardly knew him,
Sorrowful in that darkness, but made question:
"What god, O Palinurus, took you from us? 360
Who drowned you in the deep? Tell me. Apollo
Never before was false, and yet he told me
You would be safe across the seas, and come
Unharmed to Italy; what kind of promise
Was this, to fool me with?" But Palinurus
Gave him assurance:—"It was no god who drowned me,[25]
No falsehood on Apollo's part, my captain,
But as I clung to the tiller, holding fast
To keep the course, as I should do, I felt it
Wrenched from the ship, and I fell with it, headlong. 370
By those rough seas I swear, I had less fear
On my account than for the ship, with rudder
And helmsman overboard, to drift at the mercy
Of rising seas. Three nights I rode the waters,
Three nights of storm, and from the crest of a wave,

[25] Palinurus is ignorant of the role of the god of Sleep in casting him overboard. Apollo's promise is not mentioned elsewhere in the poem.

On the fourth morning, sighted Italy,
I was swimming to land, I had almost reached it, heavy
In soaking garments; my cramped fingers struggled
To grasp the top of the rock, when barbarous people,
Ignorant men, mistaking me for booty,[26]
Struck me with swords; waves hold me now, or winds 380
Roll me along the shore. By the light of heaven,
The lovely air, I beg you, by your father,
Your hope of young Iulus, bring me rescue
Out of these evils, my unconquered leader!
Cast over my body earth—you have the power—
Return to Velia's[27] harbor,—or there may be
Some other way—your mother is a goddess,
Else how would you be crossing this great river,
This Stygian swamp?—help a poor fellow, take me 390
Over the water with you, give a dead man
At least a place to rest in." But the Sibyl
Broke in upon him sternly:—"Palinurus,
Whence comes this mad desire? No man, unburied,
May see the Stygian waters, or Cocytus,
The Furies' dreadful river; no man may come
Unbidden to this bank. Give up the hope
That fate is changed by praying, but hear this,
A little comfort in your harsh misfortune:
Those neighboring people will make expiation, 400
Driven by signs from heaven, through their cities
And through their countryside; they will build a tomb,
Thereto bring offerings yearly, and the place
Shall take its name from you, Cape Palinurus."[28]
So he was comforted a little, finding
Some happiness in the promise.
And they went on,
Nearing the river, and from the stream the boatman
Beheld them cross the silent forest, nearer,
Turning their footsteps toward the bank. He challenged:—
"Whoever you are, O man in armor, coming 410
In this direction, halt where you are, and tell me
The reason why you come. This is the region
Of shadows, and of Sleep and drowsy Night;
I am not allowed to carry living bodies
In the Stygian boat; and I must say I was sorry
I ever accepted Hercules and Theseus
And Pirithous, and rowed them over the lake,
Though they were sons of gods and great in courage.

[26]A man carrying valuable goods.
[27]A town near Cumae.
[28]As with Misenus and modern Cape Miseno (line 253), Palinurus' name is still given today to a promontory on the Italian coast (Point Palinuro).

One of them dared to drag the guard of Hell,
Enchained, from Pluto's throne, shaking in terror, 420
The others to snatch our queen from Pluto's chamber."
The Sibyl answered briefly: "No such cunning
Is plotted here; our weapons bring no danger.
Be undisturbed: the hell-hound in his cavern
May bark forever, to keep the bloodless shadows
Frightened away from trespass; Proserpine,
Untouched, in pureness guard her uncle's[29] threshold.
Trojan Aeneas, a man renowned for goodness,
Renowned for nerve in battle, is descending
To the lowest shades; he comes to find his father. 430
If such devotion has no meaning to you,
Look on this branch at least, and recognize it!"
And with the word she drew from under her mantle
The golden bough; his swollen wrath subsided.
No more was said; he saw the bough, and marvelled
At the holy gift, so long unseen; came sculling
The dark-blue boat to the shore, and drove the spirits,
Lining the thwarts, ashore, and cleared the gangway,
And took Aeneas aboard; as that big man
Stepped in, the leaky skiff groaned under the weight, 440
And the strained seams let in the muddy water,
But they made the crossing safely, seer and soldier,
To the far margin, colorless and shapeless,
Grey sedge and dark-brown ooze. They heard the baying
Of Cerberus, that great hound, in his cavern crouching,
Making the shore resound, as all three throats
Belled horribly; and serpents rose and bristled
Along the triple neck. The priestess threw him
A sop with honey and drugged meal; he opened
The ravenous throat, gulped, and subsided, filling 450
The den with his huge bulk. Aeneas, crossing,
Passed on beyond the bank of the dread river
Whence none return.
A wailing of thin voices
Came to their ears, the souls of infants crying,
Those whom the day of darkness took from the breast
Before their share of living. And there were many
Whom some false sentence brought to death. Here Minos[30]
Judges them once again; a silent jury
Reviews the evidence. And there are others,
Guilty of nothing, but who hated living, 460
The suicides. How gladly, now, they would suffer
Poverty, hardship, in the world of light!

[29] Proserpine's father, Jove, was Pluto's brother.

[30] King of Crete, who had ordered the famous labyrinth built; he later was made judge of the dead.

But this is not permitted; they are bound
Nine times around by the black unlovely river;
Styx holds them fast.
They came to the Fields of Mourning,
So-called, where those whom cruel love had wasted
Hid in secluded pathways, under myrtle,
And even in death were anxious. Procris, Phaedra,
Eriphyle, displaying wounds her son
Had given her, Caeneus, Laodamia, 470
Caeneus, a young man once, and now again
A young man, after having been a woman.[31]
And here, new come from her own wound, was Dido,
Wandering in the wood. The Trojan hero,
Standing near by, saw her, or thought he saw her,
Dim in the shadows, like the slender crescent
Of moon when cloud drifts over. Weeping, he greets her:—
"Unhappy Dido, so they told me truly
That your own hand had brought you death. Was I—
Alas!—the cause? I swear by all the stars, 480
By the world above, by everything held sacred
Here under the earth, unwillingly, O queen,
I left your kingdom. But the gods' commands,
Driving me now through these forsaken places,
This utter night, compelled me on. I could not
Believe my loss would cause so great a sorrow.
Linger a moment, do not leave me; whither,
Whom, are you fleeing? I am permitted only
This last word with you."
But the queen, unmoving
As flint or marble, turned away, her eyes 490
Fixed on the ground: the tears were vain, the words,
Meant to be soothing, foolish; she turned away,
His enemy forever, to the shadows
Where Sychaeus, her former husband, took her
With love for love, and sorrow for her sorrow.
And still Aeneas wept for her, being troubled
By the injustice of her doom; his pity
Followed her going.
They went on. They came
To the farthest fields, whose tenants are the warriors,
Illustrious throng. Here Tydeus came to meet him, 500
Parthenopaeus came, and pale Adrastus,[32]
A fighter's ghost, and many, many others,

[31] Some of these figures (all women) were evil, some admirable. Procris' jealousy of her husband led to his killing her by accident; Phaedra nursed a guilty, unrequited love for her stepson; Eriphyle, having been bribed, sent her husband to his death in war and was then, in return, killed by her son; Laodamia, on the other hand, was the faithful wife of the first man to die at Troy and gave up her life to be with him after his death. The sex-changed Caeneus had been seduced, as a maiden named Caenis, by Neptune.

[32] Three of the seven heroes who led a famous siege of the city of Thebes.

Mourned in the world above, and doomed in battle,
Leaders of Troy, in long array; Aeneas
Sighed as he saw them: Medon; Polyboetes,
The priest of Ceres; Glaucus; and Idaeus
Still keeping arms and chariot;[33] three brothers,
Antenor's sons; Thersilochus; a host
To right and left of him, and when they see him,
One sight is not enough; they crowd around him, 510
Linger, and ask the reasons for his coming.
But Agamemnon's men, the Greek battalions,
Seeing him there, and his arms in shadow gleaming,
Tremble in panic, turn to flee for refuge,
As once they used to, toward their ships, but where
Are the ships now? They try to shout, in terror;
But only a thin and piping treble issues
To mock their mouths, wide-open.
One he knew
Was here, Deiphobus, a son of Priam,
With his whole body mangled, and his features 520
Cruelly slashed, and both hands cut, and ears
Torn from his temples, and his nostrils slit
By shameful wounds. Aeneas hardly knew him,
Shivering there, and doing his best to hide
His marks of punishment; unhailed, he hailed him:—
"Deiphobus, great warrior, son of Teucer,
Whose cruel punishment was this? Whose license
Abused you so? I heard, it seems, a story
Of that last night, how you had fallen, weary
With killing Greeks at last; I built a tomb, 530
Although no body lay there, in your honor,
Three times I cried, aloud, over your spirit,
Where now your name and arms keep guard. I could not,
Leaving my country, find my friend, to give him
Proper interment in the earth he came from."
And Priam's son replied:—"Nothing, dear comrade,
Was left undone; the dead man's shade was given
All ceremony due. It was my own fortune
And a Spartan woman's[34] deadliness that sunk me
Under these evils; she it was who left me 540
These souvenirs. You know how falsely happy
We were on that last night; I need not tell you.
When that dread horse came leaping over our walls,
Pregnant with soldiery, she led the dancing,
A solemn rite, she called it, with Trojan women
Screaming their bacchanals;[35] she raised the torches

[33] Idaeus had been charioteer to Priam, king of Troy.

[34] Helen, who had left her husband, Menelaus, and run off to Troy with Paris; after Paris's death she had become the wife of Deiphobus.

[35] Wild revels in honor of Bacchus, god of wine. Helen carried one of the torches customary in such revels but used it treacherously, as a signal to the Greeks.

High on the citadel; she called the Greeks.
Then—I was worn with trouble, drugged in slumber,
Resting in our ill-omened bridal chamber,
With sleep as deep and sweet as death upon me— 550
Then she, that paragon of helpmates, deftly
Moved all the weapons from the house; my sword,
Even, she stole from underneath my pillow,
Opened the door, and called in Menelaus,
Hoping, no doubt, to please her loving husband,
To win forgetfulness of her old sinning.
It is quickly told: they broke into the chamber,
The two of them, and with them, as accomplice,
Ulysses came, the crime-contriving bastard.[36]
O gods, pay back the Greeks; grant the petition 560
If goodness asks for vengeance! But you, Aeneas,
A living man—what chance has brought you here?
Vagrant of ocean, god-inspired,—which are you?
What chance has worn you down, to come, in sadness,
To these confusing sunless dwelling-places?"
While they were talking, Aurora's rosy car
Had halfway crossed the heaven; all their time
Might have been spent in converse, but the Sibyl
Hurried them forward:—"Night comes on, Aeneas;
We waste the hours with tears. We are at the cross-road, 570
Now; here we turn to the right, where the pathway leads
On to Elysium, under Pluto's ramparts.
Leftward is Tartarus, and retribution,
The terminal of the wicked, and their dungeon."
Deiphobus left them, saying, "O great priestess,
Do not be angry with me; I am going;
I shall not fail the roll-call of the shadows.
Pride of our race, go on; may better fortune
Attend you!" and, upon the word, he vanished.
As he looked back, Aeneas saw, to his left, 580
Wide walls beneath a cliff, a triple rampart,
A river running fire, Phlegethon's torrent,
Rocks roaring in its course, a gate, tremendous,
Pillars of adamant, a tower of iron,
Too strong for men, too strong for even gods
To batter down in warfare, and behind them
A Fury, sentinel in bloody garments,
Always on watch, by day, by night. He heard
Sobbing and groaning there, the crack of the lash,
The clank of iron, the sound of dragging shackles. 590
The noise was terrible; Aeneas halted,
Asking, "What forms of crime are these, O maiden?
What harrying punishment, what horrible outcry?"
She answered:—"O great leader of the Trojans,

[36] The insult is meant literally by Deiphobus, suggesting actual infidelity by Ulysses' mother.

I have never crossed that threshold of the wicked;
No pure soul is permitted entrance thither,
But Hecate, by whose order I was given
Charge of Avernus' groves, my guide, my teacher,
Told me how gods exact the toll of vengeance.
The monarch here, merciless Rhadamanthus,[37] 600
Punishes guilt, and hears confession; he forces
Acknowledgment of crime; no man in the world,
No matter how cleverly he hides his evil,
No matter how much he smiles at his own slyness,
Can fend atonement off; the hour of death
Begins his sentence. Tisiphone, the Fury,
Leaps at the guilty with her scourge; her serpents
Are whips of menace as she calls her sisters.
Imagine the gates, on jarring hinge, rasp open,
You would see her in the doorway, a shape, a sentry, 610
Savage, implacable. Beyond, still fiercer,
The monstrous Hydra dwells; her fifty throats
Are black, and open wide, and Tartarus
Is black, and open wide, and it goes down
To darkness, sheer deep down, and twice the distance
That earth is from Olympus.[38] At the bottom
The Titans crawl, Earth's oldest breed, hurled under
By thunderbolts; here lie the giant twins,
Aloeus' sons, who laid their hands on heaven
And tried to pull down Jove; Salmoneus here 620
Atones for high presumption,—it was he
Who aped Jove's noise and fire, wheeling his horses
Triumphant through his city in Elis, cheering
And shaking the torch, and claiming divine homage,
The arrogant fool, to think his brass was lightning,
His horny-footed horses beat out thunder!
Jove showed him what real thunder was, what lightning
Spoke from immortal cloud, what whirlwind fury
Came sweeping from the heaven to overtake him.
Here Tityos, Earth's giant son, lies sprawling 630
Over nine acres, with a monstrous vulture
Gnawing, with crooked beak, vitals and liver
That grow as they are eaten; eternal anguish,
Eternal feast.[39] Over another hangs
A rock, about to fall; and there are tables
Set for a banquet, gold with royal splendor,

[37] Brother of Minos and, like him, a judge in the Lower World.

[38] The dwelling place of the gods.

[39] The Titans, giant offspring of Heaven and Earth, fought alongside Saturn in his unsuccessful struggle against his son Jupiter. The sons of Aloeus, Otus and Ephialtes, were giants who tried to assault the gods by piling the mountains Ossa and Pelion on top of Olympus. Salmoneus imitated Jove's thunder, in a city sacred to Jove, by driving a brass chariot over a brass bridge. Tityos had sexually assaulted the goddess Latona, who was avenged by her children Apollo and Diana.

But if a hand goes out to touch the viands,
The Fury drives it back with fire and yelling.
Why name them all, Pirithous, the Lapiths,
Ixion?[40] The roll of crime would take forever. 640
Whoever, in his lifetime, hated his brother,
Or struck his father down; whoever cheated
A client, or was miserly—how many
Of these there seem to be!—whoever went
To treasonable war, or broke a promise
Made to his lord, whoever perished, slain
Over adultery, all these, walled in,
Wait here their punishment. Seek not to know
Too much about their doom. The stone is rolled,
The wheel keeps turning; Theseus forever 650
Sits in dejection; Phlegyas, accursed,
Cries through the halls forever: *Being warned,*
Learn justice; reverence the gods![41] The man
Who sold his country is here in hell; the man
Who altered laws for money; and a father
Who knew his daughter's bed. All of them dared,
And more than dared, achieved, unspeakable
Ambitions. If I had a hundred tongues,
A hundred iron throats, I could not tell
The fullness of their crime and punishment." 660
And then she added:—"Come: resume the journey,
Fulfill the mission; let us hurry onward.
I see the walls the Cyclops[42] made, the portals
Under the archway, where, the orders tell us,
Our tribute must be set." They went together
Through the way's darkness, came to the doors, and halted,
And at the entrance Aeneas, having sprinkled
His body with fresh water, placed the bough
Golden before the threshold. The will of the goddess
Had been performed, the proper task completed. 670
They came to happy places, the joyful dwelling,
The lovely greenery of the groves of the blessèd.
Here ampler air invests the fields with light,
Rose-colored, with familiar stars and sun.
Some grapple on the grassy wrestling-ground
In exercise and sport, and some are dancing,
And others singing; in his trailing robe
Orpheus[43] strums the lyre; the seven clear notes
Accompany the dance, the song. And heroes
Are there, great-souled, born in the happier years, 680

[40] Ixion, king of the Lapiths, had attempted a sexual assault on Juno; for Pirithous (son of Ixion), see lines 139–140 and note and lines 415–421.

[41] Theseus was punished, perhaps, for his attempt to abduct Proserpina. Phlegyas had burned Apollo's temple at Delphi.

[42] The laborers in the forge of Vulcan, the blacksmith god of fire.

[43] In myth, the prototype of poets and musicians. See note to lines 136–140.

Ilus, Assaracus; the city's founder,
Prince Dardanus.[44] Far off, Aeneas wonders,
Seeing the phantom arms, the chariots,
The spears fixed in the ground, the chargers browsing,
Unharnessed, over the plain. Whatever, living,
The men delighted in, whatever pleasure
Was theirs in horse and chariot, still holds them
Here under the world. To right and left, they banquet
In the green meadows, and a joyful chorus
Rises through groves of laurel, whence the river 690
Runs to the upper world.[45] The band of heroes
Dwell here, all those whose mortal wounds were suffered
In fighting for the fatherland; and poets,
The good, the pure, the worthy of Apollo;
Those who discovered truth and made life nobler;
Those who served others—all, with snowy fillets
Binding their temples, throng the lovely valley.
And these the Sibyl questioned, most of all
Musaeus,[46] for he towered above the center
Of that great throng:—"O happy souls, O poet, 700
Where does Anchises dwell? For him we come here.
For him we have traversed Erebus'[47] great rivers."
And he replied:—"It is all our home, the shady
Groves, and the streaming meadows, and the softness
Along the river-banks. No fixed abode
Is ours at all; but if it is your pleasure,
Cross over the ridge with me; I will guide you there
By easy going." And so Musaeus led them
And from the summit showed them fields, all shining,
And they went on over and down. 710

Deep in a valley of green, father Anchises
Was watching, with deep earnestness, the spirits
Whose destiny was light, and counting them over,
All of his race to come, his dear descendants,
Their fates and fortunes and their works and ways,
And as he saw Aeneas coming toward him
Over the meadow, his hands reached out with yearning,
He was moved to tears, and called:—"At last, my son,—
Have you really come, at last? and the long road nothing
To a son who loves his father? Do I, truly, 720
See you, and hear your voice? I was thinking so,
I was hoping so, I was counting off the days,
And I was right about it. O my son!
What a long journey, over land and water,
Yours must have been! What buffeting of danger!

[44] Three illustrious ancestors of the Trojans.
[45] The river is Eridanus, believed in fable to be the underground source of the river Po.
[46] Legendary poet, taught by Orpheus.
[47] The god of darkness; more generally, the Lower World itself.

I feared, so much, the Libyan realm would hurt you."
And his son answered:—"It was your spirit, father,
Your sorrowful shade, so often met, that led me
To find these portals. The ships ride safe at anchor,
Safe in the Tuscan sea. Embrace me, father; 730
Let hand join hand in love; do not forsake me."
And as he spoke, the tears streamed down. Three times
He reached out toward him, and three times the image
Fled like the breath of the wind or a dream on wings.
He saw, in a far valley, a separate grove
Where the woods stir and rustle, and a river,
The Lethe,[48] gliding past the peaceful places,
And tribes of people thronging, hovering over,
Innumerable as the bees in summer
Working the bright-hued flowers, and the shining 740
Of the white lilies, murmuring and humming.
Aeneas, filled with wonder, asks the reason
For what he does not know, who are the people
In such a host, and to what river coming?
Anchises answers:—"These are spirits, ready
Once more for life; they drink of Lethe's water
The soothing potion of forgetfulness.
I have longed, for long, to show them to you, name them,
Our children's children; Italy discovered,
So much the greater happiness, my son." 750
"But, O my father, is it thinkable
That souls would leave this blessedness, be willing
A second time to bear the sluggish body,
Trade Paradise for earth? Alas, poor wretches,
Why such a mad desire for light?" Anchises
Gives detailed answer: "First, my son, a spirit
Sustains all matter, heaven and earth and ocean,
The moon, the stars; mind quickens mass, and moves it.
Hence comes the race of man, of beast, of wingèd
Creatures of air, of the strange shapes which ocean 760
Bears down below his mottled marble surface.
All these are blessed with energy from heaven;
The seed of life is a spark of fire, but the body
A clod of earth, a clog, a mortal burden.
Hence humans fear, desire, grieve, and are joyful,
And even when life is over, all the evil
Ingrained so long, the adulterated mixture,
The plagues and pestilences of the body
Remain, persist. So there must be a cleansing,
By penalty, by punishment, by fire, 770
By sweep of wind, by water's absolution,

[48] River of forgetfulness.

Before the guilt is gone. Each of us suffers
His own peculiar ghost.[49] But the day comes
When we are sent through wide Elysium,
The Fields of the Blessed, a few of us, to linger
Until the turn of time, the wheel of ages,
Wears off the taint, and leaves the core of spirit
Pure sense, pure flame.[50] A thousand years pass over
And the god calls the countless host to Lethe
Where memory is annulled, and souls are willing 780
Once more to enter into mortal bodies."
The discourse ended; the father drew his son
And his companion toward the hum, the center
Of the full host; they came to rising ground
Where all the long array was visible,
Anchises watching, noting, every comer.
"Glory to come, my son, illustrious spirits
Of Dardan lineage, Italian offspring,
Heirs of our name, begetters of our future!
These I will name for you and tell our fortunes:[51] 790
First, leaning on a headless spear, and standing
Nearest the light, that youth, the first to rise
To the world above, is Silvius; his name
Is Alban; in his veins Italian blood
Will run with Trojan; he will be the son
Of your late age; Lavinia will bear him,
A king and sire of kings; from him our race
Will rule in Alba Longa. Near him, Procas,
A glory to the Trojan race; and Capys,
And Numitor, and Silvius Aeneas, 800
Resembling you in name, in arms, in goodness,
If ever he wins the Alban kingdom over.
What fine young men they are! What strength, what prowess!
The civic oak already shades their foreheads.
These will found cities, Gabii, Fidenae,
Nomentum; they will crown the hills with towers
Above Collatia, Inuus fortress, Bola,
Cora, all names to be, thus far ungiven.
"And there will be a son of Mars; his mother

[49] This notoriously elusive aphorism, typical of the difficulties in translating Virgil, probably means something like "Each endures his own penance and lives with his own purgatorial consciousness" (though other meanings have been suggested).

[50] Certain rare and noble spirits remain in Elysian bliss rather than being reincarnated. Anchises is one of these.

[51] In lines 791–808, Anchises describes the Trojan lineage in Italy up to the time of Romulus, legendary founder (in 753 B.C., several centuries after Aeneas) of Rome proper. Alba Longa, forerunner of Rome, was the city founded by Ascanius (as we are told in I.278–283). Silvius was third in the line to rule after Aeneas and Ascanius/Iulus. The persons listed in lines 798–800 were subsequent Alban kings (one of whom, Silvius Aeneas, was denied the throne for a long time). The aboriginal towns mentioned in lines 805–808 were near Rome.

Is Ilia, and his name is Romulus, 810
Assaracus' descendant. On his helmet
See, even now, twin plumes; his father's honor
Confers distinction on him for the world.
Under his auspices Rome, that glorious city,
Will bound her power by earth, her pride by heaven,
Happy in hero sons, one wall surrounding
Her seven hills, even as Cybele, riding
Through Phrygian cities, wears her crown of towers,
Rejoicing in her offspring, and embracing
A hundred children of the gods, her children, 820
Celestials, all of them, at home in heaven.[52]
Turn the eyes now this way; behold the Romans,
Your very own. These are Iulus' children,[53]
The race to come. One promise you have heard
Over and over: here is its fulfillment,
The son of a god, Augustus Caesar, founder
Of a new age of gold, in lands where Saturn
Ruled long ago;[54] he will extend his empire
Beyond the Indies, beyond the normal measure
Of years and constellations, where high Atlas 830
Turns on his shoulders the star-studded world.[55]
Maeotia[56] and the Caspian seas are trembling
As heaven's oracles predict his coming,
And all the seven mouths of Nile are troubled.
Not even Hercules, in all his travels,
Covered so much of the world, from Erymanthus
To Lerna; nor did Bacchus, driving his tigers
From Nysa's summit.[57] How can hesitation
Keep us from deeds to make our prowess greater?
What fear can block us from Ausonian[58] land? 840
"And who is that one yonder, wearing the olive,
Holding the sacrifice? I recognize him,
That white-haired king of Rome, who comes from Cures,
A poor land, to a mighty empire, giver
Of law to the young town. His name is Numa.

[52] Cybele, a Phrygian (Trojan) deity, considered the mother of the gods, was associated with the building and fortifying of cities.

[53] Iulus, Aeneas' son, was regarded as the progenitor of the Julian clan of Virgil's time, and thus of the line of Caesars.

[54] Augustus was "son of a god" because Julius Caesar, of whom Augustus was the adopted son, was deified at his death. Saturn, after being deposed by his son Jupiter, was supposed to have reigned in Italy during the mythical Age of Gold.

[55] The giant Atlas (sometimes identified with the north African mountain) was imagined as supporting the heavens on his shoulders.

[56] Region north of the Black Sea.

[57] Erymanthus, a mountain range, and Lerna, a lake, were in Greece; among the Twelve Labors of Hercules were victories over monsters inhabiting these places. The mountain Nysa (located in India, according to one tradition) was the boyhood home of Bacchus, the god of wine, whose chariot was drawn by tigers.

[58] Italian.

Near him is Tullus; he will rouse to arms
A race grown sluggish, little used to triumph.
Beyond him Ancus, even now too boastful,
Too fond of popular favor.[59] And then the Tarquins,
And the avenger Brutus, proud of spirit, 850
Restorer of the balance. He shall be
First holder of the consular power; his children
Will stir up wars again, and he, for freedom
And her sweet sake, will calm down judgment on them,
Unhappy, however future men may praise him,
In love of country and intense ambition.[60]
"There are the Decii, and there the Drusi,
A little farther off, and stern Torquatus,
The man with the axe, and Camillus, the regainer
Of standards lost. And see those two, resplendent 860
In equal arms, harmonious friendly spirits
Now, in the shadow of night, but if they ever
Come to the world of light, alas, what warfare,
What battle-lines, what slaughter they will fashion,
Each for the other, one from Alpine ramparts
Descending, and the other ranged against him
With armies from the east, father and son
Through marriage, Pompey and Caesar.[61] O my children,
Cast out the thoughts of war, and do not murder
The flower of our country. O my son, 870
Whose line descends from heaven, let the sword
Fall from the hand, be leader in forbearing!
"Yonder is one who, victor over Corinth,
Will ride in triumph home, famous for carnage
Inflicted on the Greeks; near him another,
Destroyer of old Argos and Mycenae
Where Agamemnon ruled; he will strike down
A king descended from Achilles; Pydna
Shall be revenge for Pallas' ruined temple,
For Trojan ancestors. Who would pass over, 880
Without a word, Cossus, or noble Cato,
The Gracchi, or those thunderbolts of warfare,
The Scipios, Libya's ruin, or Fabricius
Mighty with little, or Serranus, ploughing

[59] The religious and civic lawgiver Numa Pompilius, the warlike Tullus, and Ancus (according to Virgil, a demagogue) were, respectively, the second, third, and fourth kings of Rome (Romulus having been the first).

[60] Brutus (not to be confused with the Brutus who assassinated Julius Caesar centuries later) expelled the last (seventh) of the Roman kings, Tarquinius Superbus, and founded the Roman republic in 509 B.C. He had his sons executed for attempting to restore the old monarchical line.

[61] The Decii, Torquatus, and Camillus were military or civic heroes of the fourth and third centuries B.C. The Drusi were ancestors of Livia, wife of Caesar Augustus. The civil war (49–45 B.C.) between the forces of Julius Caesar and those of his son-in-law Pompey, in Virgil's own lifetime, had been part of the chain of events culminating in the accession of Augustus.

The humble furrow? My tale must hurry on:
I see the Fabii next, and their great Quintus
Who brought us back an empire by delaying.[62]
Others, no doubt, will better mould the bronze
To the semblance of soft breathing, draw, from marble,
The living countenance; and others plead 890
With greater eloquence, or learn to measure,
Better than we, the pathways of the heaven,
The risings of the stars; remember, Roman,
To rule the people under law, to establish
The way of peace, to battle down the haughty,
To spare the meek. Our fine arts, these, forever."[63]
 Anchises paused a moment, and they marvelled,
And he went on:—"See, how Marcellus[64] triumphs,
Glorious over all, with the great trophies
Won when he slew the captain of the Gauls, 900
Leader victorious over leading foeman.
When Rome is in great trouble and confusion
He will establish order, Gaul and Carthage
Go down before his sword, and triple trophies
Be given Romulus in dedication."
 There was a young man going with Marcellus,
Brilliant in shining armor, bright in beauty,
But sorrowful, with downcast eyes. Aeneas
Broke in, to ask his father: "Who is this youth[65]
Attendant on the hero? A son of his? 910
One of his children's children? How the crowd
Murmurs and hums around him! what distinction,
What presence, in his person! But dark night
Hovers around his head with mournful shadow.
Who is he, father?" And Anchises answered:—
"Great sorrow for our people! O my son,
Ask not to know it. This one fate will only
Show to the world; he will not be permitted
Any long sojourn. Rome would be too mighty,

[62] The "victor over Corinth" (line 873) was Mummius; the "another" of line 875 was probably Paullus (both second century B.C.). The latter, by defeating a Greek opponent, descended from Achilles, at the battle of Pydna, avenged Greek desecration of the Trojan temple of Pallas Athena during the Trojan War; see I.48–50, II.430–432 These two heroes, along with the other men named in lines 881–887, were among the greatest of the Roman military and political figures from the fifth through the second centuries B.C. The legacy of the episode with Dido is hinted at through the mention of the two Scipios and Quintus Fabius Maximus ("Cunctator," or "Delayer," famous for his drawn-out avoidance tactics), all three of whom won victories over Carthage in the Punic Wars (third and second centuries B.C.).

[63] In these memorable lines, one of the most famous passages in all of literature, the "Others" (line 888), with whose accomplishments Anchises is comparing those of the Romans, are primarily the Greeks. In oratory the Greeks were not in fact superior, but Anchises concedes even this area, so as to keep the distinction between the two peoples clean and emphatic.

[64] Roman general of the third century B.C.

[65] The Younger Marcellus—descendant of the Marcellus just described, nephew and son-in-law of Caesar Augustus, and presumed successor to him—died of malaria in 23 B.C. at the age of nineteen.

Too great in the gods' sight, were this gift hers. 920
What lamentation will the field of Mars[66]
Raise to the city! Tiber, gliding by
The new-built tomb, the funeral state, bear witness!
No youth from Trojan stock will ever raise
His ancestors so high in hope, no Roman
Be such a cause for pride. Alas for goodness,
Alas for old-time honor, and the arm
Invincible in war! Against him no one,
Whether on foot or foaming horse, would come
In battle and depart unscathed. Poor boy, 930
If you should break the cruel fates; if only—
You are to be Marcellus. Let me scatter
Lilies, or dark-red flowers, bringing honor
To my descendant's shade; let the gift be offered,
However vain the tribute."
So through the whole wide realm they went together,
Anchises and his son, from fields of air
Learning and teaching of the fame and glory,
The wars to come, the toils to face, or flee from,
Latinus' city and the Latin peoples, 940
The love of what would be.
There are two portals,
Twin gates of Sleep, one made of horn, where easy
Release is given true shades, the other gleaming
White ivory, whereby the false dreams issue
To the upper air. Aeneas and the Sibyl
Part from Anchises at the second portal.[67]
He goes to the ships, again, rejoins his comrades,
Sails to Caieta's[68] harbor, and the vessels
Rest on their mooring-lines.

SUMMARY OF BOOKS VII–VIII

The Trojans continue their northward voyage along the western coast of Italy. They land and, while eating their meal off bread platters, suddenly realize that their acts fulfill the prophecy of hunger and that they are at the destined place. On the following day they reach the river Tiber and the city of King Latinus. He recognizes in Aeneas the realization of a prophecy that his daughter Lavinia would marry a stranger. At Juno's instigation, the Italian hero Turnus, a suitor of Lavinia who is jealous of Aeneas, stirs up opposition to the Trojans, and Aeneas prepares for war with him. Guided by a dream, Aeneas enlists the support of Evander, whose city lies on the future site of Rome. Aeneas' mother Venus presents him with a shield, made by the god Vulcan, on which important events in the future history of Rome have been carved, a history that culminates in the victory of Augustus over Antony and Cleopatra at Actium:

[66] The Campus Martius, site of Marcellus' tomb.

[67] Why Aeneas should emerge through the gate of falsehood is one of the most mystifying problems in the entire poem. Virgil may mean no more than that Aeneas ends his visit to the Lower World early in the night, since dreams dreamt at that time were considered deceiving. (The reliable dreams were those dreamt just before waking.) But the apparently deliberate effect of high-solemn mystery suggests some weightier meaning.

[68] A town about thirty-five miles up the coast from Cumae and the modern Naples.

from BOOK VIII: AENEAS AT THE SITE OF ROME

And the bright goddess through the clouds of heaven
Came bringing gifts, seeing her son alone
By the cold river in the quiet valley,
And spoke to him:—"Behold, the gifts made ready
By Vulcan's promised skill. Fear not, my son,
To face the wars with Turnus and the Latins!"
After the word, the embrace. She placed the armor,
All shining in his sight, against an oak-tree; 630
Rejoicing in the gift, the honor, he turned
His eyes to these, over and over again,
Could not be satisfied, took in his hands
The helmet with the terrible plumes and flame,
The fatal sword, the breastplate, made of bronze,
Fire-colored, huge, shining the way a cloud,
Dark-blue, turns crimson under the slanting sun,
The greaves of gold refined and smooth electrum,[1]
The spear, the final masterpiece, the shield.
Hereon the great prophetic Lord of Fire 640
Had carved the story out, the stock to come,
The wars, each one in order, all the tale
Of Italy and Roman triumph.[2] Here
In Mars' green cave the she-wolf gives her udders
To the twin boys, turning half round to lick them,
And neither is afraid, and both are playing.[3]
Another scene presents the Circus-games,
When Romans took their Sabine brides, and war
Broke out between old Tatius and the sons
Of Romulus, and was ended, monarchs pledging 650
Peace at the altars over sacrifice.[4]
Mettus, the false, by the wild horses drawn
And quartered, sheds his life-blood over the brambles;[5]
Porsena, the besieger, rings the city
For Tarquin's sake, exile and tyrant; Romans

[1] Greaves were armor for the shins. Electrum was an alloy of gold and silver.

[2] The divinely made shield of Achilles in Homer's *Iliad*, Book XVIII, contains in pictures a synopsis of the ways of human life, in fairly universal terms. Virgil's equivalent, for Aeneas, is a vision of the glories of Roman history to come and of the Roman character.

[3] To make his usurped power secure, Amulius attempted to have his great-nephews, the infant Romulus and his twin brother, Remus, drowned in the Tiber, but they survived, being suckled by a she-wolf in the cave of the Lupercal on the site of Rome. Romulus grew up to found the city and establish its line of kings.

[4] The men of the newly founded city, having no women, seized them from Sabines who had come to watch the games in honor of Neptune being celebrated in the Circus, or amphitheater, of Rome. The seizing of the women caused war between the Romans and Sabines (ruled by Tatius), but it was halted through the intervention of the women, and the two peoples became allies.

[5] Mettus Fufetius was executed in the way described when, after having promised to fight for Rome during one of its early regional conflicts, he treacherously withdrew his troops from battle.

Rush on the steel for freedom; Clelia breaks
Her bonds to swim the river; and Horatius
Breaks down the bridge.[6] The guardian Manlius
Holds the high capitol and that crude palace
Fresh with the straw of Romulus; the goose 660
Flutters in silver through the colonnades
Shrieking alarm; the Gauls are near in darkness,
Golden their hair, their clothing, and their necks
Gleam white in collars of gold, and each one carries
Two Alpine javelins; they have long shields.
Near them, the Fire-god sets the priests with caps
Of wool, the miracle of the shields from heaven,
The Salii dancing, the Luperci naked,
And the chaste matrons riding through the city
In cushioned chariots.[7] Far off, he adds 670
The seats of Hell, the lofty gates of Pluto,
Penance for sin: Catiline, with the Furies
Making him cower; farther off, the good,
With Cato giving laws.[8] And all this scene
Bound with the likeness of the swelling ocean,
Blue water and whitecap, where the dolphins playing
Leap with a curve of silver. In the center
Actium,[9] the ships of bronze, Leucate[10] burning
Hot with the glow of war, and waves on fire
With molten gold. Augustus Caesar stands 680
High on the lofty stern; his temples flame
With double fire, and over his head there dawns

[6] After the Romans expelled their savage and tyrannical king Tarquinius Superbus, the Etrurian king Lars Porsena of Clusium attacked Rome in an attempt to restore Tarquinius to the throne. In the face of the enemy, Horatius held a bridge over the Tiber until it could be destroyed. This helped save the newborn (509 B.C.) Roman republic. Clelia was a young Roman woman who, having been taken hostage by Porsena, escaped by swimming the Tiber, was then returned to Porsena by the Romans, and finally was freed by Porsena, along with other prisoners, because he admired her courage.

[7] When Gauls from the Alps threatened the citadel of Rome in 390 B.C., the Roman consul Manlius was alerted to their night attack by the cackling of the sacred geese kept at the Capitol, where the early thatched hut of the founder Romulus was also preserved. Lines 666–670 describe religious celebrations of Roman victory and also acknowledge the Roman matrons, whose right to ride in luxury was earned by earlier contributions of their gold and jewels to the state.

[8] We see scenes of contrasted evil and good: Catiline, who in 63 B.C. plotted against the Roman government and is now punished in Hell by the Furies, and Cato the Younger (95–46 B.C.), the model of old-fashioned Roman virtue.

[9] The climactic scene, at the center of the shield, shows the naval victory by the forces of Octavian (later Caesar Augustus) over the combined forces of Mark Antony, his rival for power, and Cleopatra, the Egyptian queen who had become Antony's consort. The great battle took place at Actium, off western Greece, in 31 B.C.; it ended decades of Roman civil war. Virgil presents this battle as a conflict between Roman virtue and Eastern luxury, decadence, and religious barbarism. Antony's and Cleopatra's fleets returned to Egypt, after she panicked, and a year later both he and she died defeated, leaving Octavian in sole power and bringing peace to Rome.

[10] A promontory near Actium that served as base for Octavian's fleet.

His father's star.[11] Agrippa[12] leads a column
With favoring wind and god, the naval garland
Wreathing his temples. Antony assembles
Egypt and all the East; Antony, victor
Over the lands of dawn and the Red Sea,
Marshals the foes of Rome, himself a Roman,
With—horror!—an Egyptian wife. The surge
Boils under keel, the oar-blades churn the waters, 690
The triple-pointed beaks drive through the billows,
You would think that mountains swam and battled mountains,
That islands were uprooted in their anger.
Fireballs and shafts of steel are slanting showers,
The fields of Neptune redden with the slaughter.
The queen drives on her warriors, unseeing
The double snakes of death;[13] rattle and cymbals
Compete with bugle and trumpet. Monstrous gods,
Of every form and fashion, one, Anubis,
Shaped like a dog, wield their outrageous weapons 700
In wrath at Venus, Neptune, and Minerva.
Mars, all in steel, storms through the fray; the Furies
Swoop from the sky; Discord exults; Bellona,[14]
With bloody scourge, comes lashing; and Apollo
From Actium bends his bow. Egypt and India,
Sabaeans and Arabians, flee in terror.
And the contagion takes the queen, who loosens
The sheets to slackness, courts the wind, in terror,
Pale at the menace of death. And the Nile comes
To meet her, a protecting god, his mantle 710
Spread wide, to bring a beaten woman home.
And Caesar enters Rome triumphant, bringing
Immortal offerings, three times a hundred
New altars through the city. Streets are loud
With gladness, games, rejoicing; all the temples
Are filled with matrons praying at the altars,
Are heaped with solemn sacrifice. And Caesar,
Seated before Apollo's shining threshold,
Reviews the gifts, and hangs them on the portals.
In long array the conquered file, their garments, 720
Their speech, as various as their arms, the Nomads,
The naked Africans, Leleges, Carians,
Gelonians with quivers, the Morini,

[11] A comet representing the spirit of the late Julius Caesar was supposed to have appeared in 43 B.C. in honor of Octavian, his adopted son; thereafter Octavian wore a star on his helmet.

[12] War minister and commander of Octavian's forces at Actium.

[13] The ill-omened double snakes are especially appropriate to Cleopatra because she afterward committed suicide by allowing herself to be bitten by asps.

[14] Goddess of war.

Of mortals most remote, Euphrates moving
With humbler waves, the two-mouthed Rhine, Araxes,
Chafing beneath his bridge.[15]
All this Aeneas
Sees on his mother's gift, the shield of Vulcan,
And, without understanding, is proud and happy
As he lifts to his shoulder all that fortune,
The fame and glory of his children's children. 730

SUMMARY OF BOOKS IX–XII

Turnus' army has been laying siege to the Trojan camp in Aeneas' absence. Aeneas returns to the battlefield with new allies, including Evander's forces under the command of his young son Pallas. A general battle ensues. Evander's troops are nearly defeated when Pallas rallies them, but Pallas is then killed by Turnus, who savagely exults over the defeated youth and callously strips him of his armor. Aeneas is enraged and grief-stricken, all the more because he had been entrusted by Evander with the care of his dear son. Aeneas seeks Turnus in order to avenge Pallas' death, but Juno lures Turnus away from the battlefield. With great ceremony, Aeneas sends Pallas' body back to his father, and a twelve-day truce is declared.

An agreement is reached under which Aeneas and Turnus will settle the war through single combat. But the agreement is violated by the Latins and general fighting breaks out again:

from BOOK XII: THE FINAL COMBAT

And now his goddess-mother sent Aeneas
A change of purpose, to direct his column
More quickly toward the town, confuse the Latins 610
With sudden onslaught.[1] He was tracking Turnus
Here, there, all up and down the columns, watching,
Shifting his gaze, and so he saw that city
Immune from that fierce warfare, calm and peaceful.
The vision of a greater fight comes to him:
He calls Sergestus, Mnestheus, brave Serestus,
And takes position on a mound; the Trojans
Come massing toward him, shield and spear held ready.
And as he stands above them, he gives the orders:—
"Let there be no delay: great Jove is with us. 620
Let no man go more slackly, though this venture
Is new and unexpected. That city yonder,
The cause of war, the kingdom of Latinus,
Unless they own our mastery, acknowledge
Defeat, declare obedience, I will topple,

[15] The list of names is primarily geographic symbolism honoring Caesar Augustus and Rome. The wandering Nomads (Numidians) were from Africa, the Leleges and Carians from Asia, the Gelonians and Morini from eastern and northern Europe. The Araxes is the river Aras, in Armenia.

[1] Aeneas decides to assault Latinus' city directly rather than engage the enemy troops on the field outside the city.

Level its smoking roof-tops to the ground.
Or should I wait until it suits prince Turnus
To face the duel with me, and, once beaten,
Consent to fight again? This[2] is the head,
O citizens, this the evil crown of warfare. 630
Hurry, bring firebrands, win from fire the treaty!"
His words inflame their zeal, and, all together
They form a wedge; a great mass moves to the wall,
Ladders and sudden fire appear from nowhere;
The guards at the gate are butchered; steel is flying,
The sky is dark with arrows. Toward the city
Aeneas lifts his hand, rebukes Latinus,
Calling the gods to witness that his will
Was not for battle, it was forced upon him
By the Italians, double treaty-breakers, 640
His foes for now the second time.[3] The townsmen
Quarrel among themselves: "Open the town!"
Cry some, "Admit the Trojans!" and would drag
The king himself to the ramparts. Others hurry
With arms, man the defenses. When a shepherd
Trails bees to their hive in the cleft of a rock and fills it
With smarting smoke, there is fright and noise and fury
Within the waxen camp, and anger sharpened
With buzzing noises, and a black smell rises
With a blind sound, inside the rock, and rolling 650
Smoke lifts to empty air.
Now a new sorrow
Came to the weary Latins, shook the city
To its foundations, utterly. The queen
Had seen the Trojans coming and the walls
Under attack and fire along the gables
And no Rutulian column, nowhere Turnus
Coming to help. He had been killed, her hero,
She knew at last.[4] Her mind was gone; she cried
Over and over:—"I am the guilty one,
I am the cause, the source of all these evils!" 660
And other wilder words. And then she tore
Her crimson robes, and slung a noose and fastened
The knot of an ugly death to the high rafter.
The women learned it first, and then Lavinia:
The wide hall rings with grief and lamentation;
Nails scratch at lovely faces, beautiful hair
Is torn from the head. And Rumor spreads the story

[2] This city.

[3] The Italians, or Latins, had first violated a treaty of alliance with the Trojans, including a plan for Aeneas to marry Latinus' daughter Lavinia, then violated the single-combat treaty.

[4] Latinus' queen, Amata, had favored Turnus and bitterly opposed Aeneas as suitor for her daughter Lavinia's hand. The Rutulians were Turnus' people.

All up and down the town, and poor Latinus,
Rending his garments, comes and stares,—wife gone,
And city falling, an old man's hoary hair 670
Greyer with bloody dust.
And meanwhile Turnus
Out on the plain pursues the stragglers, slower
And slower now, and less and less exultant
In his triumphant car. From the city comes
A wind that bears a cry confused with terror,
Half heard, but known,—confusion, darkness, sorrow,
An uproar in the town. He checks the horses,
Pauses and listens. And his sister prompts him:[5]—
"This way, this way! The Trojans run, we follow
Where victory shows the path. Let others guard 680
The houses with their valor. The Italians
Fall in the fight before Aeneas. Let us
Send death to the Trojans, in our turn. You will not
Come off the worse, in numbers or in honor."
Turnus replies:—"O sister, I have known,
A long while since, that you were no Metiscus,
Since first you broke the treaty and joined the battle.
No use pretending you are not a goddess.
But who, from high Olympus, sent you down
To bear such labors? Was it to see your brother 690
In pitiful cruel death? What am I doing,
What chance will fortune grant me? I have seen
A man I loved more than the rest, Murranus,
A big man, slain by a big wound, go down.
Ufens is fallen, lucky or unlucky,
In that he never saw our shame; the Trojans
Have won his body and arms. Our homes are burning,
The one thing lacking up to now,—and shall I
Endure this, not refute the words of Drances
With this right hand?[6] Shall I turn my back upon them? 700
Is it so grim to die? Be kind, O shadows,[7]
Since the high gods have turned their favor from me.
A decent spirit, undisgraced, no coward,
I shall descend to you, never unworthy
Of all my ancient line."
He had hardly spoken
When a warrior, on foaming steed, came riding

[5] Turnus' sister Juturna, seduced by Jupiter and granted immortality as a water nymph in recompense, has disguised herself as Metiscus, her brother's charioteer, steering the chariot away from Aeneas in the hope of postponing Turnus' fated death.

[6] Drances, in an assembly of the Latins, had denounced Turnus and (unjustly) accused him of cowardice.

[7] The gods of the Lower World. They are contrasted with the "high gods," mentioned in the following line.

Through all the enemy. His name was Saces,
And his face was badly wounded by an arrow.
He called the name of Turnus, and implored him:—
"We have no other hope; pity your people! 710
Aeneas is a lightning-bolt; he threatens
Italy's topmost towers; he will bring them down
In ruins; even now the brands[8] are flying
Along the roof-tops. They look to you, the Latins,
They look for you; and king Latinus mumbles
In doubt—who are his sons, who are his allies?[9]
The queen, who trusted you the most, has perished
By her own hand, has fled the light in terror.
Alone before the gates the brave Atinas
And Messapus hold the line. Around them, squadrons 720
Crowd close on either side, and the steel harvest
Bristles with pointed swords. And here is Turnus
Wheeling his car across a plain deserted."
Bewildered by disaster's shifting image,
Turnus is silent, staring; shame and sadness
Boil up in that great heart, and grief and love
Driven by frenzy. He shakes off the shadows;
The light comes back to his mind. His eyes turn, blazing,
From the wheels of the car to the walls of that great city
Where the flame billowed upward, the roaring blast 730
Catching a tower, one he himself had fashioned
With jointed beams and rollers and high gangways.
"Fate is the winner now; keep out of my way,
My sister: now I follow god and fortune.
I am ready for Aeneas, ready to bear
Whatever is bitter in death. No longer, sister,
Shall I be shamed, and you behold me. Let me,
Before the final madness, be a madman!"
He bounded from the chariot, came rushing
Through spears, through enemies; his grieving sister 740
He left behind, forgotten. As a boulder
Torn from a mountain-top rolls headlong downward,
Impelled by wind, or washed by storm, or loosened
By time's erosion, and comes down the hillside
A mass possessed of evil, leaping and bounding,
And rolling with it men and trees and cattle,
So, through the broken columns, Turnus rushes
On to the city, where the blood goes deepest
Into the muddy ground, and the air whistles
With flying spears. He makes a sudden gesture, 750
Crying aloud:—"No more, no more, Rutulians!

[8] Firebrands; flaming missiles.
[9] Latinus wonders whether the women among his people are to marry Trojans or Latins.

Hold back your weapons, Latins! Whatever fortune
There may be here is mine. I am the one,
Not you, to make the treaty good, to settle
The issue with the sword. That will be better."
They all made way and gave him room.
Aeneas,
Hearing the name of Turnus, leaves the city,
Forsakes the lofty walls; he has no patience
With any more delay, breaks off all projects,
Exults, a terrible thunderer in armor, 760
As huge as Athos, or as huge as Eryx,
Or even father Apennine, that mountain
Roaring above the oaks, and lifting high
His crown of shimmering trees and snowy crest.[10]
Now all men turned their eyes, Rutulians, Trojans,
Italians, those who held the lofty ramparts,
Those battering at the wall below; their shoulders
Were eased of armor now. And king Latinus
Could hardly, in amazement, trust his senses
Seeing these two big men, born worlds apart, 770
Meeting to make decision with the sword.
The plain was cleared, and they came rushing forward,
Hurling, far off, their spears; the fight is on,
The bronze shields clang and ring. Earth gives a groan.
The swords strike hard and often; luck and courage
Are blent in one. And as on mighty Sila
Or on Taburnus' mountain,[11] when two bullocks
Charge into fight head-on, and trembling herdsmen
Fall back in fear, and the herd is dumb with terror,
And heifers, hardly lowing, stare and wonder 780
Which one will rule the woodland, which one the herd
Will follow meekly after, and all the time
They gore each other with savage horns, and shoulders
And necks and ribs run streams of blood, and bellowing
Fills all the woodland,—even so, Aeneas
And Daunus' son[12] clash shield on shield; the clamor
Fills heaven. And Jupiter holds the scales in balance
With each man's destiny as weight and counter,
And one the heavier under the doom of death.
Confident, Turnus, rising to the sword 790
Full height, is a flash of light; he strikes. The Trojans,
The Latins, cry aloud and come up standing.
But the sword is treacherous; it is broken off

[10] Athos and Eryx were mountains in, respectively, northern Greece and Sicily. The Apennines were the mountains forming the geographic backbone of Italy.

[11] Sila was a mountain range and forest in southern Italy, Taburnus a mountain in central Italy.

[12] Turnus was the son of Daunus and the nymph Venilia.

With the blow half spent: the fire of Turnus finds
No help except in flight. Swift as the wind
He goes, and stares at a broken blade, a hand
Unarmed. The story is that in that hurry,
That rush of his, to arms, when the steeds were harnessed,
He took Metiscus' sword, not the one Daunus
Had left him.[13] For a while it served its purpose 800
While the Trojans ran away, but when it met
The armor Vulcan forged, the mortal blade
Split off, like brittle ice, with glittering splinters
Like ice on the yellow sand. So Turnus flies
Madly across the plain in devious circles:
The Trojans ring him round, and a swamp on one side,
High walls on the other.

Aeneas, the pursuer,
Is none too swift: the arrow has left him hurt;[14]
His knees give way, but he keeps on, keeps coming
After the panting enemy, as a hound, 810
Running a stag to bay, at the edge of the water
Or hedged by crimson plumes,[15] darts in, and barks,
And snaps his jaws, closes and grips, is shaken
Off from the flanks again, and once more closes,
And a great noise goes up the air; the waters
Resound, and the whole sky thunders with the clamor.
Turnus has time, even in flight, for calling
Loud to Rutulians, each by name, demanding,
In terrible rage, the sword, the sword, the good one,
The one he knows. Let anybody bring it, 820
Aeneas threatens, and death and doom await him,
And the town will be a ruin. Wounded, still
He presses on. They go in five great circles,
Around and back: no game, with silly prizes,
Are they playing now; the life and blood of Turnus
Go to the winner.

A wild olive-tree
Stood here, with bitter leaves, sacred to Faunus,[16]
Revered by rescued sailors, who used to offer
Ex-votos[17] to the native gods, their garments
In token of gratitude. For this the Trojans 830
Cared nothing, lopped the branches off to clear
The run of the field. Aeneas' spear had fastened
Deep in the trunk where the force of the cast had brought it,

[13] Like Aeneas' armor, the sword Turnus inherited from Daunus had been made by the god Vulcan.

[14] Earlier in the day, Aeneas had been put temporarily out of action when he was wounded by an anonymous archer. His mother, Venus, had helped heal his wound.

[15] In hunting, barriers made of colorful feathers were used to scare game animals and keep them inside the hunting precincts.

[16] King Latinus' father, a rustic god.

[17] Offerings made in fulfillment of a vow or in acknowledgment of a prayer answered.

Stuck in the grip of the root. Aeneas, stooping,
Yanks at the shaft; he cannot equal Turnus
In speed of foot, but the javelin is wingèd.
And Turnus, in a terrible moment of panic,
Cries:—"Faunus, pity me, and Earth, most kindly,
If ever I was reverent, as Aeneas
And those he leads have not been, hold the steel, 840
Do not let go!" He prayed, and he was answered.
Aeneas tugged and wrestled, pulled and hauled,
But the wood held on. And, while he strained, Juturna
Rushed forward, once again Metiscus' double,
With the good sword for her brother. Then Venus, angry
Over such wanton interference, enters
And the root yields. The warriors, towering high,
Each one renewed in spirit, one with sword,
One with the spear, both breathing hard, are ready
For what Mars[18] has to send.
And Juno, gazing 850
From a golden cloud to earth, watching the duel,
Heard the all-powerful king of high Olympus:—
"What will the end be now, O wife? What else
Remains? You know, and you admit you know it,
Aeneas is heaven-destined, the native hero
Become a god,[19] raised by the fates, exalted.
What are you planning? with what hope lingering on
In the cold clouds? Was it proper that a mortal
Should wound a god?[20] that the sword, once lost, be given
Turnus again?—Juturna, of course, is nothing 860
Without your help—was it proper that the beaten
Increase in violence? Stop it now, I tell you;
Listen to my entreaties: I would not have you
Devoured by grief in silence; I would not have you
Bring me, again, anxiety and sorrow,
However sweet the voice. The end has come.
To harry the Trojans over land and ocean,
To light up war unspeakable, to defile
A home with grief, to mingle bridal and sorrow,—
All this you were permitted. Go no farther! 870
That is an absolute order." And Juno, downcast
In gaze, replied:—"Great Jove, I knew your pleasure:
And therefore, much against my will, left Turnus,
Left earth. Were it not so, you would not see me
Lonely upon my airy throne in heaven,
Enduring things both worthy and unworthy,

[18] The god of war.
[19] In the future, Aeneas will be deified and regarded as their own hero by the natives of Italy.
[20] The "god" is Aeneas; the "mortal" is the anonymous bowsman who wounded Aeneas earlier.

But I would be down there, by flame surrounded,
Fighting in the front ranks, and hauling Trojans
To battle with their enemies. Juturna,
I urged, I own, to help her wretched brother, 880
And I approved, I own, her greater daring
For his life's sake, but I did not approve,
And this I swear by Styx, that river whose name
Binds all the gods to truth, her taking weapons,
Aiming the bow.[21] I give up now, I leave
These battles, though I hate to. I ask one favor
For Latium, for the greatness of your people,
And this no law of fate forbids: when, later,
And be it so, they join in peace, and settle
Their laws, their treaties, in a blessèd marriage, 890
Do not command the Latins, native-born,
To change their language, to be known as Trojans,
To alter speech or garb; let them be Latium,
Let Alban kings endure through all the ages,[22]
Let Roman stock, strong in Italian valor,
Prevail: since Troy has fallen, let her name
Perish and be forgotten." Smiling on her,
The great creator answered:—"You are truly
True sister of Jove and child of Saturn, nursing
Such tides of anger in the heart![23] Forget it! 900
Abate the rise of passion. The wish is granted.
I yield, and more than that,—I share your purpose.
Ausonians[24] shall keep their old tradition,
Their fathers' speech and ways; their name shall be
Even as now it is. Their sacred laws,
Their ritual, I shall add, and make all Latins
Men of a common tongue. A race shall rise
All-powerful, of mingled blood; you will see them
By virtue of devotion rise to glories
Not men nor gods have known, and no race ever 910
Will pay you equal honor."[25] And the goddess
Gave her assent, was happy, changed her purpose,
Left heaven and quit the cloud.
This done, the father
Formed yet another purpose, that Juturna
Should leave her fighting brother. There are, men say,

[21] Juturna, in a different disguise, had been instrumental in the violation of the single-combat pact.

[22] Latium was the region in west-central Italy where the action of the second half of the poem has been taking place. The royal line of Alba Longa, the city Iulus/Ascanius will found, was prophetically described by Anchises in VI.787–808.

[23] The Greek god Cronus, identified by the Romans with Saturn, was notoriously violent, fiercely devouring almost all his children.

[24] Italians.

[25] Juno was one of the three deities worshiped in the great Roman temple at the Capitol (the other two being Jupiter and Minerva).

Twin fiends, or triple, sisters named the Furies,
Daughters of Night, with snaky coils, and pinions[26]
Like those of wind. They are attendant spirits
Before the throne of Jove and whet the fears
Of sickly mortals, when the king of heaven 920
Contrives disease or dreadful death, or frightens
The guilty towns in war. Now he dispatches
One of the three to earth, to meet Juturna,
An omen visible; and so from heaven
She flew with whirlwind swiftness, like an arrow
Through cloud from bowstring, armed with gall or poison,
Loosed from a Parthian quiver,[27] cleaving shadows
Swifter than man may know, a shaft no power
Has power of healing over:—so Night's daughter
Came down to earth, and when she saw the Trojans 930
And Turnus' columns, she dwindled, all of a sudden,
To the shape of that small bird, which, in the night-time,
Shrills its late song, ill-omened, on the roof-tops
Or over tombs, insistent through the darkness.
And so the fiend, the little screech-owl, flying
At Turnus, over and over, shrilled in warning,
Beating the wings against the shield, and Turnus
Felt a strange torpor seize his limbs, and terror
Made his hair rise, and his voice could find no utterance.
    But when, far off, Juturna knew the Fury 940
By whir of those dread wings, she tore her tresses,
Clawed at her face, and beat her breast, all anguish
Over her brother:—"What can a sister do
To help you now, poor Turnus? What remains
For me to bear? I have borne so much already.
What skill of mine can make the daylight longer
In your dark hour? Can I face such a portent?[28]
Now, now, I leave the battle-line forever.
Foul birds, I fear enough; haunt me no further,
I know that beat of the wings, that deadly whirring; 950
I recognize, too well, Jove's arrogant orders,
His payment for my maidenhood. He gave me
Eternal life, but why? Why has he taken
The right of death away from me? I might have
Ended my anguish, surely, with my brother's,
Gone, at his side, among the fearful shadows,
But, no,—I am immortal. What is left me
Of any possible joy, without my brother?
What earth can open deep enough to take me,
A goddess, to the lowest shades?" The mantle, 960

[26] Wings.
[27] Parthia, in what is now Iran, was noted for skill in archery.
[28] Bad omen. The appearance here of one of the Furies, agents of retribution and punishing fate, gives the ending of the poem an effect like that of Greek tragedy.

Grey-colored, veiled her head, and the goddess, sighing,
Sank deep from sight to the greyness of the river.
And on Aeneas presses: the flashing spear,
Brandished, is big as a tree; his anger cries:—
"Why put it off forever, Turnus, hang-dog?
We must fight with arms, not running. Take what shape
You will, gather your strength or craft; fly up
To the high stars, or bury yourself in earth!"
And Turnus shook his head and answered:—"Jove,
Being my enemy, scares me, and the gods, 970
Not your hot words, fierce fellow." And his vision,
Glancing about, beheld a mighty boulder,
A boundary-mark, in days of old, so huge
A dozen men in our degenerate era
Could hardly pry it loose from earth, but Turnus
Lifts it full height, hurls it full speed and, acting,
Seems not to recognize himself, in running,
Or moving, or lifting his hands, or letting the stone
Fly into space; he shakes at the knees, his blood
Runs chill in the veins, and the stone, through wide air going, 980
Falls short, falls spent. As in our dreams at night-time,
When sleep weighs down our eyes, we seem to be running,
Or trying to run, and cannot, and we falter,
Sick in our failure, and the tongue is thick
And the words we try to utter come to nothing,
No voice, no speech,—so Turnus finds the way
Blocked off, wherever he turns, however bravely.
All sorts of things go through his mind: he stares
At the Rutulians, at the town; he trembles,
Quails at the threat of the lance; he cannot see 990
Any way out, any way forward. Nothing.
The chariot is gone, and the charioteer,
Juturna or Metiscus, nowhere near him.
The spear, flung by Aeneas, comes with a whir
Louder than stone from any engine, louder
Than thunderbolt; like a black wind it flies,
Bringing destruction with it, through the shield-rim,
Its sevenfold strength, through armor, through the thigh.
Turnus is down, on hands and knees, huge Turnus
Struck to the earth. Groaning, the stunned Rutulians 1000
Rise to their feet, and the whole hill resounds,
The wooded heights give echo. A suppliant, beaten,
Humbled at last, his hands reach out, his voice
Is low in pleading:—"I have deserved it, surely,
And I do not beg off. Use the advantage.
But if a parent's grief has any power
To touch the spirit, I pray you, pity Daunus,
(I would Anchises), send him back my body.
You have won; I am beaten, and these hands go out
In supplication: everyone has seen it. 1010

No more. I have lost Lavinia. Let hatred
Proceed no further."
Fierce in his arms, with darting glance, Aeneas
Paused for a moment, and he might have weakened,
For the words had moved him, when, high on the shoulder,
He saw the belt of Pallas, slain by Turnus,
Saw Pallas on the ground, and Turnus wearing
That belt with the bright studs, of evil omen
Not only to Pallas now, a sad reminder,
A deadly provocation. Terrible 1020
In wrath, Aeneas cries:—"Clad in this treasure,
This trophy of a comrade, can you cherish
Hope that my hands would let you go? Now Pallas,
Pallas exacts his vengeance, and the blow
Is Pallas, making sacrifice!" He struck
Before he finished speaking: the blade went deep
And Turnus' limbs were cold in death; the spirit
Went with a moan indignant to the shadows.

Ovid

(43 B.C.–17 A.D.)

Ovid and Virgil have been the two most influential Latin narrative poets—though for very different reasons. Ovid was born into an old established family in the town now called Sulmona, about a hundred miles east of Rome, in 43 B.C.—one year after the assassination of Julius Caesar. He died in A.D. 17, during the reign of Tiberius, Augustus's successor as emperor. Significantly, even symbolically, the twelve-year-old Ovid was sent to Rome, to be educated for the law, at very nearly the same time Augustus defeated Antony and Cleopatra in the battle of Actium. The victory brought order and peace—if also efficient autocracy—to the Roman state for the first time in generations. (See the Introduction to Virgil.) Virgil's values and sensibilities, shaped and indeed scarred by the experience of civil war, were essentially conservative. Ovid was a decade too young to have known that trauma; his formative years were not shadowed by harrowing memories of iron, blood, and strife. Like a Parisian boulevardier of the 1920s too young to have known the trenches, Ovid frequented a somewhat younger set of artists less closely associated than Virgil's circle was with the Augustan establishment.

After a few routine assignments in the Roman civil service and some travel in Greece, Ovid abandoned the law to become a professional poet. Although the tradition that he was a dissipated playboy may or may not be true, there is no doubt that, as poet, Ovid was witty, skeptical, and irreverent toward the austere official Augustan values. For example, his *Ars Amatoria,* or *Art of Love* (completed about 1 B.C.), a manual on how to conduct love affairs, is an amusingly amoral, worldly, though also psychologically sensitive treatment of men and women in love.

Predictably, the poem—and doubtless other poems treating love—got Ovid in serious trouble. In A.D. 8, though he was now the leading poet of Rome, he was summoned before Augustus, tried summarily, and banished to Tomis (in modern Romania), an outpost of the Roman Empire, and indeed of civilization. One reason for Ovid's exile is known: his authorship of *The Art of Love,* a work incompatible with Augustus's program for Roman piety. There was also a second reason, never explicitly identified by Ovid, that remains mysterious despite much detective work by scholars. Apparently it too was some personal or political offense against Augustus or his official code of values.

This most urban and urbane of men now had to endure not just the absence of metropolitan society and amenities but also real danger from hostile border tribes. From Tomis the poet wrote a number of poignant works in verse, directly or indirectly pleading for permission to return to the city and to the people he knew and loved. But Augustus did not relent, nor, after his death, did Tiberius. Ovid was still in exile when he died. All this is ironic; whatever real or imaginary excesses Ovid may have been guilty of, they can hardly have rivaled the enormities that Roman historians have attributed to Tiberius, Nero, and their ages.

Besides *The Art of Love* and a sequel to it, *Remedia Amoris* ("Cures for Love"), Ovid's love poetry includes the *Amores* ("Loves") and the *Heroides* ("Heroines' Letters").The *Amores* was his earliest major work, first published around 20 B.C. The version that has come down to us is not the one Ovid first published but, rather, a three-book revision of the original, five-book poem. Stylistically, therefore, what we have is not novice work. Even as revised, the poem retains a sassy impudence, aimed in several directions: toward official, puritanical sexual morality; toward traditional, stoic Roman values, and especially Augustus's version of them; toward a number of literary traditions; toward women, who are unabashedly treated as sexual prey, though also with affection and an almost cowed admiration. Not least, the irreverence is directed at the poet himself, who appears in various guises: as the smooth amatory expert; as the frustrated male, no match for women at the game of love; as the hardened cynic; as the helplessly enamored, bedazzled swain; as the vulnerable victim who ultimately pays a high price for playing with fire. It seems significant that the Ovid who, in the *Amores,* puts himself at the center of the erotic action will retreat from that personal, starring role in *The Art of Love,* where he becomes the disengaged coach instructing lovers and egging them on from the sidelines.

In the *Amores,* Ovid is particularly amusing, and intriguing, in his capacity as artist magnanimously bestowing poetic immortality on those women lucky enough to become his creative material by playing the game of love with him. This role—the lover as artist—is a key element in the *Amores.* Sometimes it is hilarious, as Ovid irritably tries to shoo away the high-serious Muse, swathed in the ceremonious garb of epic hexameters, so that he can have his frivolous fun, epitomized in the less dignified meter of elegiac couplets (the meter of almost all Ovid's poetry). But this is not mere fooling around. Implicit (and sometimes explicit) in the conflict between literary forms is a rejection by Ovid of the "hexameter values": all the stuffy and stoic "Roman" obsessions, including a high-serious, epic glorification of war. In the *Amores* I.9, Ovid elaborately compares the lover to the soldier in terms of their strategies, ways of life, and triumphs. The comparison is farcical but also makes a serious point and points a serious contrast: There are arenas of human challenge and fulfillment as important as the battlefield, and they have the advantage of giving pleasure rather than inflicting death. To be a poet and lover is to be soft in one sense but not in another.

Some experts construe the Ovid of the *Amores* as more interested in literature than in life, totally inventing the persona, the women, and the situations in the poem in order to satirize or otherwise comment on the literary conventions governing the traditions of love poetry. It is obvious that Ovid is, among other things, writing literary satire. But to see that as his whole, or even main, intent seems unconvincing. If we read the *Amores* as merely a literary game, for an audience of sophisticates in belles lettres, both the vividness of Ovid's comedy and the urgency of his ethical priorities are largely drained off. Ovid sounds like a man who means just what he says: that he likes to chase women and genuinely prefers that kind of campaign to its military alternative.

There is more, then, to Ovid's value system than the playboy philosophy. All the same, it remains true that most of his love poetry is emphatically male-centered. The *Heroides* is a major exception. The viewpoints in this work, written just before and after the turn of the century, are entirely feminine, except in the three sets where the women's letters are paired with those of their male correspondents, as with Paris and Helen. (That these paired sets are authentically by Ovid has sometimes been challenged, but the trend in recent years has been to reinstate them as his work.) All the women represented, drawn from legend and literature, have been abducted, abandoned, betrayed, or otherwise manipulated by men, though the women are not always blameless themselves.

One of the most interesting things about the *Heroides* is the counterpoint in the letters between standard legendary details and circumstances, as handed down from the traditional, heroic-age myths (to which Ovid is generally faithful) and the new tone imparted by Ovid, which can be banally modern. Because heroics are combined with soap opera, the psychological portraiture is often rich and suggestive. The mythic facts about Paris, for example, blend with modern modes of characterization (largely unconscious self-revelation on Paris's part) so as to develop and refine his ancient reputation as unheroic while also suggesting a commonplace, rather silly personal style of naivete and foppish vanity. Helen's ancient reputation for glamour is overlaid with a more modern, bourgeois concern on her part with respectability, reputation, "honor." I'm not that kind of girl, she suggests, though we know she is. The effect is ludicrous—both amusing and repellent.

The *Metamorphoses,* composed in the years immediately preceding Ovid's exile, belongs to his middle period, between the naughty early love poetry and the sad poetry of exile. The title suggests miraculous transformations, although this theme sometimes has only perfunctory importance in the tales. Few poems of any age or language have shaped so much later literature. There are many reasons for this influence. For one thing, the poem is an almost exhaustive handbook of the best-known classical myths; it is thus a treasury of good stories and indeed a reference work. It is also a rhetorical tour de force, a model illustrating a great variety of poetic, linguistic, and stylistic tricks. (Ovid's training in the law and public speaking did not go to waste.)

It is a wonderfully comic work. The characterizations of deities are sometimes amusingly casual, and both they and human beings are portrayed with complexity and sensitivity. It is also, in places, a tragic work, especially if one defines tragedy so as to include painful conflicts within individual persons independent of historical, public, and other grand consequences.

This interest in the idiosyncrasies, sometimes in the pathology, of feeling, especially of people in love, puts Ovid in somewhat the same relationship to Virgil that Euripides held to Aeschylus. Perhaps the nearest modern equivalent of the *Metamorphoses* is Byron's *Don Juan* (1818–1823); defending his poem through a sneer at his brother Romantics' overintensity, Byron once wrote, "You have so many 'divine' poems; is it nothing to have written a human one?" Like *Don Juan,* the *Metamorphoses* is a seriocomic poem, simultaneously a spoof of the heroic tradition and a searching critique of it. In writing the poem, Ovid abandoned his usual poetic meter, the elegiac couplet, and chose instead the six-foot dactylic line used in the *Iliad,* the *Odyssey,* and the *Aeneid.* The meter is one of many indications that Ovid meant his poem to be compared with Virgil's epic. Sometimes the relationship is that of mock-epic diminution: Virgil's grand vision of origins, which finds the seeds of history and empire in the past, becomes for Ovid an account of the origin of such things as flowers and trees—rather like modern nursery tales about how the tiger got his stripes. Yet there is a saucy implication that Ovid can beat Virgil at his own game; if Virgil's epic could span a thousand years of legend and history, Ovid will outdo him by beginning, not with the fall of Troy, but with the aboriginal creation of the cosmos itself.

Ovid repeatedly undermines Virgil's moralism. And yet, as with Byron, his technique of deflation is itself a kind of moral statement. In treating the gods and goddesses not religiously but as recognizable human beings, Ovid satirizes Virgil's religious piety and his implication that the universe, though mysterious, is just.

From the late Middle Ages on, Ovid's poetry has never lost its appeal, for readers and for authors both minor and great. A number of attempts have been made to rehabilitate Ovid's moral values, mainly by treating him allegorically. And his strategies can be adapted to serious purposes, as Kafka demonstrates in our century in his novella *The Metamorphosis.* But the most typical attitude of later authors toward Ovid is not reverence but affection. His poetry is, above all, good entertainment, whether we define that term as diversion or as the deeper pleasure that comes from recognizing his wide range of sympathy and his understanding of human psychology.

FURTHER READING: Concise introductory material can be found in the pertinent sections of the *Latin Literature* volume, ed. E. J. Kenney and W. V. Clausen, 1982, of *The Cambridge History of Classical Literature,* and in Michael Grant, *Greek and Latin Authors, 800 B.C.–A.D. 1000,* 1980. Sara Mack, *Ovid,* 1988, is a good comprehensive introduction to Ovid, his narrative methods, and other aspects of his work. In the influential book by Brooks Otis, *Ovid as an Epic Poet,* 1966, 2nd ed. 1970, a number of individual passages from Ovid are discussed, arranged according to topic. Ovid's life and literary art are treated by L. P. Wilkinson in *Ovid Recalled,* 1955, and in his shortened version *Ovid Surveyed,* 1962. Essays edited by J. W. Binns in *Ovid,* 1973, deal with a number of works by Ovid, and with the influence these works have had throughout the centuries. Peter Green's extensive introduction, very full notes, and detailed commentary in his translation *Ovid: The Erotic Poems,*

1982, are an excellent guide to the *Amores,* the *Ars Amatoria,* and the *Remedia Amoris.* The *Metamorphoses* is treated in Charles P. Segal, *Landscape in Ovid's Metamorphoses: A Study in the Transformations of* a *Literary Symbol,* 1969, which is useful on symbol, unity, tradition, and the motif of moral order; and in Otto Steen Due, *Changing Forms: Studies in the Metamorphoses of Ovid,* 1974. Frederick Ahl, *Metaformations,* 1985, is highly recommended for advanced undergraduates.

from *AMORES*

Translated by Peter Green

from BOOK I

I

Arms, warfare, violence—I was winding up to produce a
  Regular epic, with verse-form to match—
Hexameters, naturally. But Cupid[1] (they say) with a snicker
  Lopped off one foot from each alternate line.[2]
"Nasty young brat," I told him, "who made *you* Inspector of Metres?
  We poets come under the Muses,[3] we're not in your mob.
What if Venus took over the weapons of blonde Minerva,
  While blonde Minerva began fanning passion's flame?[4]
Who'd stand for Our Lady of Wheatfields looking after rides and
    forests?
  Who'd trust the Virgin Huntress[5] to safeguard crops? 10
Imagine long-haired Apollo on parade with a pikestaff
  While the War-God fumbled tunes from Apollo's lyre![6]
Look, boy, you've got your own empire, and a sight too much
    influence
  As it is. Don't get ambitious, quit playing for more.
Or is your fief[7] universal? Is Helicon[8] yours? Can't even
  Apollo call his lyre his own these days?
I'd got off to a flying start, clean paper, one magnificent
  Opening line. Number two brought me down
With a bump. I haven't the theme to suit your frivolous metre:

[1] The child god Cupid is the son of Venus (the Greeks' Aphrodite), goddess of beauty, love, and sex.

[2] The hexameter line, used in high-serious poetry such as epic, consists of six feet, each foot either a dactyl (a long syllable followed by two short ones) or a spondee (two long syllables). The elegiac couplet, used in lightweight amatory poems such as the *Amores,* consists of one hexameter line followed by a five-foot line, broken into halves each having two and a half feet. *Arma,* the first word of this poem, is the first word also of Virgil's epic the *Aeneid.*

[3] Goddesses of inspiration.

[4] The virgin goddess Minerva (the Greeks' Athena) is the antithesis of Venus.

[5] Respectively, Ceres (the Greeks' Demeter), goddess of grain, harvest, and fertility; and Diana (the Greeks' Artemis), chaste goddess of the hunt.

[6] Apollo was god of (among other things) music; the War-God is Mars (the Greeks' Ares).

[7] Dominion; territory.

[8] The mountain of the Muses, source of the fountain of poetic inspiration.

No boyfriend, no girl with a mane of coiffured hair—" 20
When I'd got so far, presto, he opened his quiver, selected
An arrow to lay me low,
Then bent the springy bow in a crescent against his knee, and
Let fly. "Hey, poet!" he called, "you want a theme? Take *that!*"
His shafts—worse luck for me—never miss their target:
I'm on fire now, Love owns the freehold[9] of my heart.
So let my verse rise with six stresses, drop to five on the downbeat—
Goodbye to martial epic, and epic metre too!
Come on then, my Muse, bind your blonde hair with a wreath of
Sea-myrtle, and lead me off in the six-five groove! 30

2

What's wrong with me nowadays, how explain why my mattress
Feels so hard, and the bedclothes will *never* stay in place?
Why am I kept awake all night by insomnia, thrashing around till
Every weary bone in my body aches?
If Love were my assailant, surely I'd know it—unless he's
Craftily gone under cover, slipped past my guard?
Yes, that must be it; heart skewered by shafts of desire, the raging
Beast, passion, out at prowl in my breast.
Shall I give in? To resist might just bank up the furnace—
All right, I give in. A well-squared load lies light. 10
Flourish a torch, it burns fiercer. I know, I've seen it. Stop the
Motion, and pouf! it's out.
Yoke-shy rebellious oxen collect more blows and curses
Than a team that's inured to the plough.
Your restive horse earns a wolf-curb, his mouth's all bruises;
A harness-broken nag scarcely feels the reins.
It's the same with Love. Play stubborn, you get a far more thorough
Going-over than those who admit they're hooked.
So I'm coming clean, Cupid: here I am, your latest victim,
Hands raised in surrender. Do what you like with me. 20
No need for military action. I want terms, an armistice—
You wouldn't look good defeating an unarmed foe.
Put on a wreath of myrtle, yoke up your mother's pigeons—[10]
Your stepfather[11] himself will lend you a fine
Chariot: mount it, drive in triumph through the cheering
Rabble, skilfully whipping your birds ahead,
With your train of prisoners behind you, besotted youths and maidens,
Such pomp, such magnificence, your very own
Triumph: and I'll be there too, fresh-wounded, your latest
Prisoner—displaying my captive mind— 30

[9] Permanent ownership.

[10] The myrtle was associated with Venus, as were doves.

[11] Probably Mars, who had an adulterous affair with Venus. The parade described in the following lines is based on the Roman "triumph," the procession through the city of a conquering hero, his chariot surrounded by defeated or enslaved captives.

With Conscience, hands bound behind her, and Modesty, and all Love's
Other enemies, whipped into line.
You'll have them all scared cold, while the populace goes crazy,
Waves to its conquering hero, splits its lungs.
And what an escort—the Blandishment Corps, the Illusion
And Passion Brigade, your regular bodyguard:
These are the troops you employ to conquer men and immortals—
Without them, why, you're nothing, a snail unshelled.
How proudly your mother will applaud your triumphal progress
From high Olympus,[12] shower roses on your head; 40
Wings bright-bejewelled, jewels starring your hair, you'll
Ride in a car of gold, all gold yourself.
What's more, if I know you, even on this occasion
You'll burn the crowd up, break hearts galore all round:
With the best will in the world, dear, you can't keep your arrows idle—
They're so hot, they scorch the crowd as you go by.
Your procession will match that of Bacchus, after he'd won the Ganges
Basin (though *he* was drawn by tigers, not birds).[13]
So then, since I am doomed to be part of your—*sacré* [14] triumph,
Why waste victorious troops on me now? 50
Take a hint from the campaign record of your cousin, Augustus
Caesar[15]—*his* conquests became protectorates.

3

Fair's fair now, Venus. This girl's got me hooked. All I'm asking from her
Is love—or at least some future hope for my own
Eternal devotion. No, even that's too much—hell, just let me love her!
(*Listen*, Venus: I've asked you so often now.)
Say yes, pet. I'd be your slave for years, for a lifetime.
Say yes—unswerving fidelity's my strong suit.
I may not have top-drawer connections, I can't produce blue-blooded
Ancestors to impress you, my father's plain middle-class,
And there aren't any squads of ploughmen to deal with *my* broad acres—
My parents are both pretty thrifty, and need to be. 10

[12] The mountain home of the gods.

[13] Bacchus, god of wine (the Greeks' Dionysus), was reared in India, the location of the river Ganges.

[14] Literally, *sacré* (French) means "sacred" but in effect means "damned" or "confounded."

[15] Augustus, Roman emperor in Ovid's day, tried to foster in his subjects an austere morality (though Augustus was far from exemplifying it himself). He later banished Ovid from Rome, partly because of the poet's irreverent writings.

What *have* I got on my side, then? Poetic genius, sweetheart,
  Divine inspiration. And love. I'm yours to command—
Unswerving faithfulness, morals above suspicion,
  Naked simplicity, a born-to-the-purple blush.
I don't chase thousands of girls, I'm no sexual circus-rider;[16]
  Honestly, all I want is to look after you
Till death do us part, have the two of us living together
  All my time, and know you'll cry for me when I'm gone.
Besides, when you give me yourself, what you'll be providing
  Is creative material. My art will rise to the theme 20
And immortalize *you*. Look, why do you think we remember
  The swan-upping of Leda, or Io's life as a cow,
Or poor virgin Europa whisked off overseas, clutching
  That so-called bull by the—horn?[17] Through poems, of course.
So you and I, love, will enjoy the same world-wide publicity,
  And our names will be linked, for ever, with the gods.

4

"So your man's going to be present at this dinner-party?
  I hope he drops down dead before the dessert!
Does this mean no hands, just eyes (any chance guest's privilege)—
  Just to *look* at my darling, while *he*
Lies there with you beside him, in licensed embracement
  And paws your bosom or neck as he feels inclined?
I'm no longer surprised at those Centaurs for horsing around over
  Some cute little filly when they were full of wine[18]—
I may not live in the forest, or be semi-equipped as a stallion,
  But still *I* can hardly keep my hands to myself 10
When you're around. Now listen, I've got some instructions for you,
  And don't let the first breeze blow them out of your head!
Arrive before your escort. I don't see what can be managed
  If you do—but anyway, get there first.
When he pats the couch, put on your Respectable Wife expression,
  And take your place beside him—but nudge my foot
As you're passing by. Watch out for my nods and eye-talk,
  Pick up my stealthy messages, send replies.
I shall speak whole silent volumes with one raised eyebrow,
  Words will spring from my fingers, words traced in wine. 20
When you're thinking about the last time we made love together,
  Touch your rosy cheek with one elegant thumb.
If you're cross with me, and can't say so, then pinch the bottom
  Of your earlobe. But when I do or say

[16] Here, one who jumps from one running horse to another.

[17] Jove (the Greeks' Zeus), king of the gods, took many forms for his sexual adventures with human women, coming as a swan to Leda and to Europa as a bull. Jove changed Io into a heifer after Juno (the Greeks' Hera) became jealous of her.

[18] While attending the wedding feast of Perithous and Hippodamia, the Centaurs (who had horses' bodies and human heads) ran amok and tried to carry off the women.

Something that gives you especial pleasure, my darling,
  Keep turning the ring on your finger to and fro.
When you yearn for your man to suffer some well-merited misfortune
  Place your hands on the table as though in prayer.
If he mixes wine specially for you, watch out, make him drink it
  Himself. Ask the waiter for what *you* want 30
As you hand back the goblet. I'll be the first to seize it
  And drink from the place your lips have touched.
If *he* offers you tit-bits out of some dish he's tasted,
  Refuse what's been near his mouth.
Don't let him put his arms round your neck, and oh, don't lay that
  Darling head of yours on *his* coarse breast.
Don't let his fingers roam down your dress to touch up
  Those responsive nipples. Above all, don't you dare
Kiss him, not once. If you do, I'll proclaim myself your lover,
  Lay hand upon you, claim those kisses as mine. 40
So much for what I can see. But there's plenty goes on under
  A long evening wrap. The mere thought worries me stiff.
Don't start rubbing your thigh against his, don't go playing
  Footsy under the table, keep smooth from rough."
(I'm scared all right, and no wonder—I've been too successful
  An operator myself, it's my own
Example I find so unnerving. I've often petted to climax
  With my darling at a party, hand hidden under her cloak—)
"—Well, *you* won't do *that.* But still, to avoid the least suspicion,
  Remove such natural protection when you sit down. 50
Keep pressing fresh drinks—but no kisses—on your husband,
  Slip neat wine in his glass if you get the chance.
If he passes out comfortably, drowned in sleep and liquor,
  We must improvise as occasion dictates.
When we all (you too) get up and leave, remember
  To stick in the middle of the crowd—
That's where you'll find me, or I you: whenever
  There's a chance to touch me, please do!"
(Yet the most I can win myself is a few hours' respite:
  At nightfall my mistress and I must part.) 60
"At nightfall he'll lock you inside, and I'll be left weeping
  On that cold front doorstep—the nearest I can come
To your longed-for embraces, while *he's* enjoying, under license,
  The kisses, and more, that you give me on the sly.
What you *can* do is show unwilling, behave as though you're frigid,
  Begrudge him endearments, make sex a dead loss."
(Grant my prayer, Venus. Don't let either of them get pleasure
  Out of the act—*and certainly not her!*)
"But whatever the outcome tonight, when you see me tomorrow
  Just swear, through thick and thin, that you told him No." 70

8

There's a certain—well: any reader in need of a procuress? Listen,
  Try Dipsas. A certain bitch, snake, hag.

Dipsas, dipso, well-named. If *she* ever saw pink horses
At sunrise, they weren't the Dawn's.[19]
She's a witch, mutters magical cantrips,[20] can make rivers
Run uphill, knows the best aphrodisiacs—
When to use herbal brews, or the whirring bullroarer,[21]
How to extract that stuff from a mare in heat.
She can control the weather, make a day overcast with
Cloud at will, or brilliant and clear; 10
I've known times (believe it or not) when the moon turned bloody,
And blood dripped from the stars.
It wouldn't surprise me if the old bitch grew feathers at nightfall
And went flapping round like an owl—
I've heard rumours, it's possible. What's more, she's got double
Pupils, a twin light glinting from each eye.
She conjures up long-dead souls from their crumbling sepulchres
And has incantations to split the solid earth.
Well: this old hag undertook to suborn[22] *our* relationship,
And a glibly poisonous tongue she had for the job. 20
By pure chance I overheard her. The big double doors stood open.
Here, then, is what she said: "You know,
Dearie, you made a great hit with that rich young gentleman
Yesterday. He'd got eyes for nobody else—
And why should he have? There's no girl more beautiful. Such a pity
Your turn-out doesn't match your face.
I'd like to see you become as wealthy as you're good-looking—
Once get you in the money, I shan't ever starve.
The stars were against you, dearie, Mars stood in opposition,
But now Mars has wheeled off, and today 30
Venus is in the ascendant. Look how her rising favours
Your lot: a rich suitor, and anxious to oblige!
Dead handsome, too, just about as pretty as you are—if he wasn't
Bidding himself, why, people would bid for *him*.
Ah, that got a blush! Pale faces need colour, but Nature's method
Is so unpredictable. Safer to stick to Art.[23]
Keep your eyes on your lap. Look demure, scale your responses
To the size of each lover's gifts.
In the old days it was different. Those Sabine women stuck to
One husband apiece. But then *they* didn't wash.[24] 40
Today Mars is so taken up with foreign campaigning
That Venus has made a clean sweep of Rome,

[19] The reference is to the horse-drawn chariot of Aurora (the Greeks' Eos), goddess of the dawn.

[20] Spells.

[21] A wooden slat, attached to a string; when whirled, it made a roaring noise. It was part of a witch's stock in trade.

[22] Underhandedly corrupt.

[23] Cosmetics.

[24] The men of Rome in its primitive days got themselves wives by seizing the neighboring Sabine women, who had come to Rome to observe games being celebrated there. The women insisted on monogamy.

Her own Aeneas' city.[25] Pretty girls have a ball. No virgins
Except the unasked—and a smart kid asks for herself.
Prissy-faced women are worth close scrutiny: you'll discover
A frown can hide a multitude of sins.
Bending that bow made trial of Penelope's young wooers,
A good stiff horn proved too much for them.[26]
Volatile time slips past us without our knowledge
Like a swift-gliding river. Brass shines 50
With constant usage, a beautiful dress needs wearing,
Leave a house empty, it rots.
Lack of exercise withers your beauty, you need to take lovers—
And the treatment calls for more than one or two.
Run a string, take your pick. It's safer, less troublesome:
Wolves that raid flocks eat best.
That poet of yours, now, what does he give you, except his latest
Verses? Find the right lover, you'd scoop the pool.
Why isn't he richer? The patron god of poets[27]
Wears gold, plays a gilded lyre. 60
Look, dear, stop worshipping genius, try generosity
Just for a change. To give is a fine art.
And don't you look down your nose at some slave who's purchased
His freedom. Chalked feet are no crime.[28]
Don't let yourself be fooled by ancestral portraits. Your lover's
Broke? Then give him the boot, and his pedigree too.
When he asks for a night on the house because he's so handsome
Tell him No. His boyfriend can foot the bill.
While you're spreading your net, go easy. Don't show too rapacious
Or your bird may fly off. Once you've caught him, anything goes. 70
Some show of love does no harm: let him fancy himself your darling,
But take good care you collect a *quid pro quo*.[29]
Don't say Yes every night. Pretend that you have a headache,
Or make Isis your excuse, then you can plead
Religious abstention.[30] Enough's enough, though—he may get
accustomed
To going without, over-frequent rebuffs may cool
His passion off. Take gifts, but be deaf to entreaties—
Let the lucky man hear his rival cursing outside.
You've hurt him? *He* started it. Throw a quick tantrum. This kind of
Counter-attack will very soon choke him off. 80
But never stay angry too long. A festering quarrel
Can make permanent enemies.

[25] Aeneas, legendary hero of Virgil's *Aeneid* and aboriginal forebear of the Romans, led the survivors of defeated Troy to Italy.

[26] In Homer's *Odyssey*, Book XXI, the suitors of Penelope, wife of the supposedly dead Odysseus, are unable to perform the feat she assigns them, of stringing Odysseus' bow.

[27] Apollo.

[28] The feet of newly imported slaves were marked with chalk.

[29] (Latin): something valuable in return.

[30] Ceremonial sexual abstinence in preparation for a feast of the goddess Isis.

Another trick you must learn is control of the tear-ducts,
  How to weep buckets at will—
And when you're deceiving someone, don't let perjury scare you:
  Venus ensures that her fellow-gods
Turn a deaf ear to such gambits. You must get yourself a houseboy
  And a well-trained maid, who can hint
What gifts will be welcome. Don't let them demand exorbitant
  Tips for themselves. Little presents soon add up. 90
Your sister and mother, your nurse, these can all help fleece a lover—
  Many hands make quick loot.
When you've run through all other excuses for getting presents
  Say it's your birthday, show him the cake.
Don't let him get cocksure, without any rivals:
  Love minus competition never wears well.
Leave the bed suspiciously rumpled, make sure he sees it,
  Flaunt a few sexy bruises on your neck—
Above all, show him his rival's presents (if none are forthcoming
  Order some yourself, from a good shop). 100
When you've dug enough gold, then protest he's being far too
    generous
  And ask him for a *loan*—which you'll never repay.
Beguile with sweet words, and blandish while you despoil him:
  A taste of honey will mask the nastiest dose.
These tactics are guaranteed by a lifetime's experience,
  So don't ignore them. Follow my advice.
And you'll never regret it. Ah, many's the time you'll bless me
  While I'm alive, and pray that my old bones
Lie easy after I'm gone—"
        At this point my shadow
  Betrayed me. I was dying to get my hands 110
On those sparse white locks, to tear at the old hag's raddled[31]
  Cheeks and drink-bleary eyes.
May the gods strip the roof from her head, end her days in poverty,
  Send her horrible winters and an eternal thirst!

9

Every lover's on active service, my friend, active service, believe me,
  And Cupid has his headquarters in the field.
Fighting and love-making belong to the same age-group—
  In bed as in war, old men are out of place.
A commander looks to his troops for gallant conduct,
  A mistress expects no less.
Soldier and lover both keep night-long vigil,
  Lying rough outside their captain's (or lady's) door.
The military life brings long route-marches—but just let his mistress
  Be somewhere ahead, and the lover too 10

[31] Withered.

Will trudge on for ever, scale mountains, ford swollen rivers,
  Thrust his way through deep snow.
Come embarkation-time *he* won't talk of "strong north-easters,"
  Or say it's "too late in the season" to put to sea.
Who but a soldier or lover would put up with freezing
  Nights—rain, snow, sleet? The first
Goes out on patrol to observe the enemy's movements,
  The other watches his rival, an equal foe.
A soldier lays siege to cities, a lover to girls' houses,
  The one assaults city gates, the other front doors. 20
Night attacks are a great thing. Catch your opponents sleeping
  And unarmed. Just slaughter them where they lie.
That's how the Greeks dealt with Rhesus and his wild Thracians
  While rustling those famous mares.[32]
Lovers, too, will take advantage of slumber (her husband's),
  Strike home while the enemy sleeps: getting past
Night patrols and eluding sentries are games both soldiers
  And lovers need to learn.
Love, like war, is a toss-up. The defeated can recover,
  While some you might think invincible collapse; 30
So if you've got love written off as an easy option
  You'd better think twice. Love calls
For guts and initiative. Great Achilles sulks for Briseis—
  Quick, Trojans, smash through the Argive wall!
Hector went into battle from Andromache's embraces
  Helmeted by his wife.
Agamemnon himself, the Supremo, was struck into raptures
  At the sight of Cassandra's tumbled hair;[33]
Even Mars was caught on the job, felt the blacksmith's meshes—
  Heaven's best scandal in years.[34] Then take 40
My own case. I was idle, born to leisure *en déshabillé*,[35]
  Mind softened by lazy scribbling in the shade.
But love for a pretty girl soon drove the sluggard
  To action, made him join up.
And just look at me now—fighting fit, dead keen on night exercises:
  If you want a cure for slackness, fall in love!

[32] In Homer's *Iliad,* Book X, the Greek heroes Odysseus and Diomedes raid the camp where the soldiers of Rhesus, newly arrived to support the Trojans, are sleeping. The two Greeks carry off Rhesus's fabulous horses.

[33] The references, again, are to the Trojan War. The Greeks' foremost warrior, Achilles, and the commander-in-chief, Agamemnon, quarreled over possession of Briseis, a woman Achilles had taken captive. The resentful Achilles remained for a time on the sidelines, allowing the Trojans some success in battle. After winning the war, Agamemnon took home with him the captive Trojan princess and prophet Cassandra. In Book VI of Homer's *Iliad,* the Trojan hero Hector takes his last farewell of his wife, after having temporarily removed his helmet because it frightened their infant son.

[34] Vulcan (the Greeks' Hephaestus), god of metalworking, having learned of the adulterous affair between his wife, Venus, and the god Mars, trapped them in bed together with a fine-meshed net that the cuckolded husband had crafted. See Homer's *Odyssey,* Book VIII.

[35] In semi-undress (French)—in a bathrobe, for example.

14

I *told* you to stop using rinses—and now just look at you!
No hair worth mentioning left to dye.
Why couldn't you let well alone? It grew so luxuriantly,
Right down to below your hips,
And fine—so fine you were scared to set it, like silken
Threads in a vivid Chinese screen,
Or the filament spun by a spider, the subtle creation
That she hangs beneath some deserted beam.
It was neither dark nor blonde, but a brindled[36] auburn,
A mixture of both, like some tall cedar when 10
The outer bark's stripped off, in a dew-wet precipitous
Valley of Ida.[37] Not to mention the fact
That it was so tractable, could be dressed in a hundred styles, and
Never made you get cross. With no pins
Or curlers to make it go brittle, no bristling side-combs,
Your maid could relax. I've been there
Often enough while she fixed it, but never once saw you
Pick up a hairpin and stick it in her arm.
If it was early morning, you'd be propped up among lilac
Pillows and coverlets, your hair 20
Not yet combed out. Yet even in tangled disorder
It still became you. You looked like a wild
Exhausted Maenad, *al fresco*.[38]
Poor down-fine tresses,
What torture they had to endure!
You decided on corkscrew ringlets. The irons were heated,
Your poor hair crimped and racked
Into spiralling curls "It's a crime," I told you, "a downright
Crime to singe it like that. Why on earth
Can't you leave well alone? You'll *wreck* it, you obstinate creature,
It's *not for burning*. Why, in its natural state 30
It'd make the best perm look silly—" No good. Her crowning
Glory, that any mod god might well
Have envied, sleek tresses like those that sea-wet naked
Dione holds up in the picture—gone, all gone.[39]
Why complain of the loss? You silly girl, you detested
That waist-length tangle, so stop
Making sad *moues* [40] in your mirror. You must get accustomed
To your own New Look, and forget
Yourself if you aim to attract. No rival's incantations
Or tisanes[41] have harmed you, no witch 40

[36] Light with darker streaks.

[37] A mountainous region near Troy.

[38] The reference is to the streaming hair of the Maenads, frenzied worshipers of the wine god Bacchus. *Al fresco* (Italian) means out-of-doors.

[39] Dione is another name for Venus. The famous picture referred to, by the Greek artist Apelles (fourth century B.C.), shows Venus wringing out her wet hair.

[40] Pouts; grimaces.

[41] Medicinal broths (here, potions prepared by a witch).

Has hexed your rinse, you haven't—touch wood—had an illness;
  If your hair's fallen out, it's not
Any envious tongue that's to blame. You applied that concoction
  Yourself. It was you that did it. *All your fault.*
Still, after our German conquests a wig is easily come by—
  A captive Mädchen's tresses will see you through.
You'll blush, it's true, when your borrowed plumage elicits
  Admiration galore. You'll feel that the praise (like the hair)
Has been bought. Once you really deserved it. Now each compliment
  Belongs to some Rhine maiden, not to you. 50
Poor sweet—she's shielding her face to hide those ladylike
  Blushes, and making a brave effort not to cry
As she stares at the ruined hair in her lap, a keepsake
  Unhappily out of place. Don't worry, love,
Just put on your makeup. This loss is by no means irreparable—
  Give it time, and your hair will grow back as good as new.

15

Why, gnawing Envy, impute an idler's existence to me?
  Why dismiss the poet as a drone?
What's your complaint? That I've failed (though young and healthy) to follow
  Tradition, or chase the dusty rewards
Of a soldier's career? That I haven't mugged up dull lawsuits,
  Or sold my eloquence like a whore
In the courts and Forum?[42] Such labours are soon forgotten.
  What *I* seek is perennial fame,
Undying world-wide remembrance. While Ida and Tenedos
  Still stand, while Simois still runs swift to the sea,[43] 10
Old Homer will live. While clustering grapes still ripen
  And wheat still falls to the scythe
Hesiod's works will be studied. The verse of Callimachus—
  Weak in imagination, strong on technique—
Has a worldwide readership. Sophoclean tragedy
  Is safe from Time's ravages. While sun and moon
Survive, so will Aratus. While the world holds one devious servant,
  Stern father, blandishing whore, or ponce[44] on the make
Menander's immortal. Rough Ennius, spirited Accius
  Have names time will never destroy. What age 20
Will not cherish great Varro's epic of Argo's voyage,
  Jason's quest for the Golden Fleece?
The work of sublime Lucretius will prove immortal
  While the world itself endures;

[42] Ovid means that he has not gone into politics. The Forum was the Roman civic center.

[43] Places associated with the Trojan War, the subject of Homer's *Iliad.* The writers mentioned in lines 11–30 (all dead at the time when Ovid is writing) include both Greek (lines 11–19) and Latin (lines 19–30) poets. For some of them Ovid tries to capture briefly their typical subject matter or achievement.

[44] British slang for a pimp or a gaudily effeminate male.

And so long as Rome's empire holds sway over the nations,
Virgil's country poems,[45] his *Aeneid*, will be read.
While Cupid's armoury still consists of torch and arrows
Tibullus' elegant verse
Will always be quoted. From lands of sunset to sunrise, Gallus,
Gallus and his Lycoris, will be renowned. 30
Though Time, in time, can consume the enduring ploughshare,
Though flint itself will perish, poetry lives—
Deathless, unfading, triumphant over kings and their triumphs,
Richer than Spanish river-gold. Let the crowd
Gape after baubles. To me may golden Apollo proffer
A cup, brimming over, from the Castalian spring[46]
And a wreath of sun-loving myrtle.[47] May my audience always
Consist of star-crossed lovers. Never forget
It's the living that Envy feeds on. After death the pressure
Is taken off. All men get their due in the end. 40
So when the final flames have devoured my body, I shall
Survive, and my better part live on.

from BOOK 2

I

A second batch of verses by that naughty provincial poet,
Naso,[1] the chronicler of his own
Wanton frivolities; another of Love's commissions (warning
To puritans: *This volume is not for you*).
I want my works to be read by the far-from-frigid virgin
On fire for her sweetheart, by the boy
In love for the very first time. May some fellow-sufferer,
Perusing my anatomy of desire,
See his own passion reflected there, cry in amazement:
"Who told this scribbler about my private affairs?" 10
One time, I recall, I got started on an inflated epic
About War in Heaven, with all
Those hundred-handed monsters, and Earth's fell vengeance, and towering
Ossa piled on Olympus (plus Pelion too).[2]
But while I was setting up Jove—stormclouds and thunderbolts gathered
Ready to hand, a superb defensive barrage—

[45] Virgil's "country," or pastoral, poems are the *Eclogues* and *Georgics*.

[46] A spring on Mount Parnassus, which was sacred to Apollo and the Muses.

[47] Myrtle wreaths or garlands were used to honor poets.

[1] Ovid's full name was Publius Ovidius Naso. He was "provincial" in that he came from a region about a hundred miles east of Rome.

[2] A standard subject for high-serious poetry was the war of the Giants (sons of Earth) against the Olympian gods, during which the Giants assaulted Mount Olympus by piling mountains atop one another. The Giants were overcome by thunderbolts, invented by Minerva, made by Vulcan, and wielded by Jove.

My mistress staged a lock-out. I dropped Jupiter[3] and his lightnings
That instant, didn't give him another thought.
Forgive me, good Lord, if I found your armoury useless—
Her shut door ran to larger bolts 20
Than any *you* wielded. I went back to verses and compliments,
My natural weapons. Soft words
Remove harsh door-chains. There's magic in poetry, its power
Can pull down the bloody moon,
Turn back the sun, make serpents burst asunder
Or rivers flow upstream.
Doors are no match for such spellbinding, the toughest
Locks can be open-sesamed by its charms.[4]
But epic's a dead loss for me. I'll get nowhere with swift-footed
Achilles, or with either of Atreus' sons. 30
Old what's-his-name wasting twenty years on war and travel,
Poor Hector dragged in the dust—
No good.[5] But lavish fine words on some young girl's profile
And sooner or later she'll tender herself as the fee,
An ample reward for your labours. So farewell, heroic
Figures of legend—the *quid*
Pro quo[6] you offer won't tempt me. A bevy of beauties
All swooning over my love-songs—that's what *I* want.

9B

If I heard a voice from heaven say "Live without loving,"
I'd beg off. Girls are such exquisite hell.
When desire's slaked, when I'm sick of the whole business,
Some kink in my wretched nature drives me back.
It's like riding a hard-mouthed horse, that bolts headlong, foam flying
From his bit, and won't answer the rein—
Or being aboard a ship, on the point of docking, in harbour,
When a sudden squall blows you back out to sea:
That's how the veering winds of desire so often catch me—
Hot Love up to his lethal tricks again. 10
All right, boy,[7] skewer me. I've dropped my defences,
I'm an easy victim. Why, by now
Your arrows practically know their own way to the target
And feel less at home in their quiver than in me.

[3]Another name for Jove.

[4]Ovid puns on the Latin word *carmen*, which can mean both poem and magic spell. With the supernatural powers ascribed to poetry in lines 23–28 compare the powers attributed to the witch Dipsas in I.8.

[5]The heroes mentioned in lines 29–32 are all from Homer's epics: Achilles, Atreus' sons (Agamemnon and Menelaus, husband of the abducted Helen), and the Trojan leader Hector are in the *Iliad*; "old what's-his-name" is Odysseus, who is described in the Odyssey as taking ten years to return home after ten years of fighting at Troy.

[6]Return payment.

[7]Cupid (the Greeks' Eros, thus called "Love" in line 10).

I'm sorry for any fool who rates sleep a prime blessing
  And enjoys it from dusk to dawn
Night in, night out. What's sleep but cold death's reflection?
  Plenty of time for rest when you're in the grave.
My mistress deceives me—so what? I'd rather be lied to
  Than ignored. I can live on hope. Today 20
She'll be all endearments, tomorrow throw screaming tantrums,
  Envelop me one night, lock me out the next.
War, like love, is a toss-up. If Mars is inconstant, he gets that
  From you, his stepson.[8] You're quite
Unpredictable, Cupid, with your lucky-dip favours,
  And more volatile than your own wings.
Maybe you'll hear my appeal, though—your delectable mother[9]
  Might help there—and settle in as king of my heart?
Then admit the flighty sex *en masse* to your dominions
  And you'd have guaranteed popularity all round. 30

19

You may not feel any need (and more fool you) to guard that
  Girl of yours—but it sharpens *my* desire,
So would you oblige? What's allowed is a bore, it's what isn't
  That turns me on. What cold clod
Could woo with his rival's approval? We lovers need hope and
    despair in
  Alternate doses. An intermittent rebuff
Makes us promise the earth. Who wants a beautiful woman
  When she never deceives him? I can't
Love a girl who's not intermittently bitchy. Corinna[10] spotted
  My weakness (full marks!) and saw how 10
To use it against me. The times she invented a headache,
  And when I still hung around, just threw me out,
Or pretended she'd had an affair, looking horribly guilty
  When in fact she'd done nothing at all—
And having thus quickly rekindled my cooling ardour
  Would suddenly switch her mood
To the ultra-compliant. Her compliments, her sweet nothings,
  Her kisses—oh God, her kisses! So you too,
My latest eye-ravisher, must ensnare me at times by pretending
  To be frightened: must—on occasion—say No, 20
And leave me there, prostrate on your doorstep, to suffer
  Long hours of frosty cold, the whole night through.
Act thus, and my love will endure, grow stronger with each passing
  Year—that's the way I like it, that feeds the flame,
Love too indulged, too compliant, will turn your stomach
  Like a surfeit of sweet rich food.

[8] See I.2.24 and note.
[9] The goddess Venus.
[10] In most other poems in the *Amores,* Corinna is the name of the woman Ovid is in love with.

Had Danaë never been locked in that brazen turret, would Jupiter
 Ever have got her with child?
When Juno transmogrified Io into a horned heifer
 She increased the girl's sex-appeal.[11] 30
If you're after what's lawful and easy, then why not gather
 Leaves from the trees, or drink
Water out of the Tiber?[12] To prolong your dominion over
 Your lover calls for deception. (I hope I won't
Have cause to regret that statement.) Yet come what may, indulgence
 Irks me. I flee the eager, pursue the coy.
And as for *you*, man, so careless of your good lady,
 Why not start locking up at night?
Why not ask who it is comes tapping, ever so softly,
 On your front door—or why it is the dogs 40
Start barking at midnight? What about all those to-and-fro missives
 The maid delivers? How come your wife now sleeps
Alone so often? Why can't you get really worried just
 Once in a while, allow me to display
My skill at deception? To covet the wife of a dummy
 Is like stealing sand off the beach.
I'm warning you: put your foot down, play the heavy husband,
 Or I'll start going cold on your wife!
I've stood it quite long enough, always hoping you'd lock her
 Away out of sight, so that I 50
Could outwit you. But no. You clod, you put up with things no husband
 Should stand for a moment. Let me have the girl
And there's an end to my passion. Won't you *ever* deny me
 Entry, won't you beat me up one night?
Can't I ever feel scared? have insomnia? sigh in frustration?
 Won't you give me some good excuse
To wish you dead? I've no time for complaisant, pimping husbands—
 Their kinkiness spoils my fun.
Find someone else, who *likes* your easy-going habits, or if you
 Must have me as a rival, then *get tough!* 60

from BOOK 3

I

There's this ancient wood—no axe has thinned it for ages,
 It might well be some spirit's home.
At its centre, a sacred spring, an arched limestone grotto,
 And sweet birdsong all around.
While I was strolling here, through an overwoven
 Dapple of shade, and wondering just what task

[11] Jupiter came to Danaê in a shower of gold, after her father had locked her in a tower lest she bear a son who, as had been prophesied, would slay him. In most versions of the Io myth, it is Jupiter who changes her into a heifer, in order to foil his jealous wife Juno.

[12] The river of Rome.

My Muse should embark on next, there appeared before me
  Elegy, perfumed hair caught up in a knot,
And short—I think—in one foot: good figure, nice dress, a loving
  Expression.[1] Even her lameness looked chic. 10
Behind her stalked barnstorming Tragedy, fraught brow hidden
  By flowing hair, mantle atrail in the dust,
Left hand waving a royal sceptre, high Lydian[2]
  Boots encasing her calves.
"Won't you *ever*," she asked me, "have done with love as a subject?
  Why get stuck in the same old poetic rut?
Your efforts to shock make gossip for drunken parties, a buzz at
  Every street-corner. As you walk by
Fingers point, people whisper: "Look, there goes that poet
  With the ultra-combustible heart." 20
All this shameless parade of your sexual activities makes you
  The talk of the whole town—and what do *you* care?
It's high time your inspiration chose a loftier model:
  You've idled enough. Start on some major work.
Your present theme cramps your style. Try the deeds of heroes—
  A subject (you'll find) more worthy of your art.
You've been playing at poetry—ballads for girl-adolescents,
  Juvenile stuff, the eternal *enfant terrible*.[3]
Now why not turn *my* way, make Roman tragedy famous,
  Give me the inspiration that I need?" 30
With that she nodded three or four times, her scarlet buskins[4]
  Holding her upright against the weight of her hair.
At this point, or so I recall, a mischievous expression
  Crept over Elegy's face. (Had she got
A myrtle-wand[5] In her hand? I think so.) "You posturing
  Windbag," she cried," do you *have* to be such a bore?
Can't you *ever* stop your pomposity? At least you condescended
  To attack me in elegiacs, you turned my own
Metre against me—not that I'd ever dream of comparing
  Your high palatial vein with my own 40
Minuscule talent. Besides, I'm frivolous, like my subject,
  And equally unheroic. All the same,
Without me Our Lady of Passion[6] would be plain vulgar—
  She needs my help as adviser and go-between.
The door your tough buskin can't break down flies open
  At one flattering word of mine;
Corinna took lessons from me, how to hoodwink porters
  Or spring the most foolproof lock,

[1] The elegiac couplet, the meter used in this and Ovid's other love poems, has a six-foot line followed by a five-foot line. See the note to the *Amores*, I.i.4.

[2] Lydia was a region in Asia Minor.

[3] A shockingly unconventional person (literally, French for "terrible child").

[4] The heavy-soled laced boots worn by actors in ancient tragic drama.

[5] The myrtle was sacred to Venus, goddess of love.

[6] Venus.

How to slip out of bed in her nightdress and move with unerring
  Feet, like a cat, through the night. 50
Yet I've earned my advantage. I've beaten you by submitting
  To indignities which your pride
Would recoil from in horror. The times I've been nailed to indifferent
  Front doors, for any passer-by to read!
Why, I even remember lying snug in a maid's bosom
  Till some crusty chaperone took off—
Not to mention the time I was sent as a birthday present
  To that frightful girl who just tore me into shreds
And flushed me away. It was I who awakened your dormant
  Poetic genius. If *she's* after you now 60
It's me you should thank for it." "Ladies, please listen," I told them
  Nervously, "don't take offence—
One of you honours me with sceptre and buskins: high-flown
  Utterance springs to my lips at her touch.
But the other offers my passions undying glory: come then,
  Short foot and limping metre, it's you I choose!
I'm sorry, Tragedy. Just be patient awhile. Your service
  Demands a lifetime. *Her* needs are quickly met."
The goddess forgave me. I'd better get on with this little volume
  While I may—my subconscious is hatching a masterpiece. 70

3

Gods exist? Don't tell me. She went back on her sworn word—yet
  Her face looks no whit less pretty than before
That act of gross perfidy, her long hair has got no shorter
  Since she spat in divinity's eye. Her fair
Peaches-and-cream complexion is just as it was, the same delicate
  Flush warms her ivory cheek.
Those sweet little feet of hers are as tiny as ever; graceful
  And tall she was—graceful and tall she remains.
Bright eyes she had—they still shine like stars. Yet how many
  Times did the treacherous creature invoke 10
Them falsely to my deceit? Oh, I know the gods in heaven
  Forgive a girl's lies; true beauty enjoys divine
Status as such. Why, she swore an oath only the other
  Day, by the eyes of us both—but mine
Were the ones that suffered.[7] Come clean, Gods—if she bamboozled
  You with impunity, why should *I* have to pay
For another's offences? Isn't it bad enough that you ordered
  Andromeda to be sacrificed for her mama's
Crime of excessive beauty?[8] Worse still, that I find you puffball
  Witnesses, so that she fools 20

[7] She swore to the gods by both her own eyes and Ovid's, but only he came down with the eye ailment inflicted as divine punishment for the false oath.

[8] Cassiopeia incurred the wrath of the sea god Neptune when she boasted that she was more beautiful than the sea nymphs; as punishment, her daughter, Andromeda, was bound to a rock near the sea. (She was eventually rescued by Perseus.)

Us both with a laugh, unpunished. To redeem her perjury
Must *I* pay the price, be stuck with a double con?
Either God is a word without substance, an empty bogey
To play on the dumb credulity of the mob,
Or if he exists he's besotted by girls, allows them
Exclusive rights, carte blanche.
We men aren't so lucky. Mars girds on his deadly broadsword
Against us, Pallas Athene wields her spear
In unconquered might. Against us the bow of Apollo
Is bent, and Jupiter poises his bolt, 30
Arm upflung—yet these same gods are scared of chastising
A pretty blasphemer, they fear
Those who don't fear *them.* Then why bother to burn incense
On their altars? We men should display
More courage. Jupiter's bolts blast his own high places and sacred
Groves—but he's careful never to hit
A perjured lady. So many deserved it, yet only wretched
Semele died, burnt up by her own zeal.
What, pray, would have happened if she'd resisted her lover's
Advances? No motherly stint for divine Papa 40
Delivering Bacchus![9] Oh, what's the point of bombarding
The sky with complaints? Gods have eyes, have hearts—
If *I* was divine, I'd legitimize ladies' barefaced
Whoppers, let them take my godhead in vain.
Why, I'd even swear it was truth the little darlings were telling—
I wouldn't be one of those mean old gods.
Still, darling, I'd be glad if you strained their forbearance
A little less often—or left my eyes out of it.

11A

I've stood enough, for too long. Heart and patience are both exhausted
By this fickle obsession. So—*out!*
That's right, I've slipped the chain, achieved emancipation,
Can blush—now—for what I once
Bore so unblushingly. Triumph: passion spurned and trodden
Under my feet. A tardy access of horn-
Stiff will. Keep it up, stand firm. Such suffering's bound to
Pay off in the end. Nasty medicine does you good.
How *could* I have swallowed such insults? The times I was driven
Away from your door, to grovel on the bare 10
Pavement—*me,* a gentleman! The times I stood guard, slave-like,
Outside your shuttered house (while you
Made love to God knows who) and was forced to watch your lover
Lurch home exhausted, done in!

[9] Semele, seduced by Jove and made pregnant with the god Bacchus, was maliciously persuaded by Juno to request a direct vision of Jove. Semele was destroyed by the sight as though by lightning. Zeus rescued the fetal Bacchus from the dead Semele's womb and continued the gestation in his thigh.

Yet even this hurt less than *him* seeing *me*—I could wish my
  Bitterest enemy no worse a fate.
Was there ever a day when I failed to act as your personal
  Watchdog, companion, shadow, lover, friend?
And wasn't it our relationship made you a public sweetheart,
  One love-affair generating so many more? 20
Why remind you of all your sordid lies, those broken
  Promises, worthless oaths
You swore to my undoing, the young men who gave you private
  Signals at parties, coded exchanges? "She's sick,"
They told me: at once I hurried back like a madman, found you
  The picture of health—and in my rival's arms.
Such incidents (there were others I'd sooner omit) have hardened
  My heart at long last. So go find
Some other more willing victim. My vessel lies safe in harbour,
  Garlanded,[10] indifferent to the swelling storm outside. 30
Leave off your blandishments. The old line's lost its magic
  Hold on my senses. I'm not the fool I was.

11B

My capricious heart's a cockpit for conflicting emotions,
  Love versus hate—but love, I think, will win.
I'll hate if I can. If not, I'll play the reluctant lover:
  No ox loves the yoke—he's just stuck with what he hates.
A fugitive from your vices, I'm lured back by your beauty:
  Your morals turn me off, your body on.
So I can live neither with nor without you, I don't seem
  To know my own mind. I wish you were
Either less beautiful or more faithful: such a good figure
  Doesn't go with your bad ways. 10
The facts demand censure, the face begs for love—and gets it,
  Eclipsing (to my cost) its owner's crimes.
By the bed we shared, by all those gods who so often
  Let you take their names in vain,
By your face, that image for me of high divinity,
  By those eyes which captivated mine,
Spare me! And mine you'll always remain, whatever your nature;
  Just choose—would you rather I loved
Freely or by constraint? Let me spread sail, cruise with a following
  Breeze—make me want what I can't resist! 20

15

Mother of tender loves, you must find another poet:
  My elegies are homing on their final lap.
Postscript concerning the author: of Paelignian extraction,
  A man whose delights have never let him down,
Heir—for what that's worth—to an ancient family,
  No brand-new knight jumped up

[10] Ships that reached port safely were draped with garlands.

Through the maelstrom fortunes of war.[11] Mantua boasts her Virgil,
  The Veronese their Catullus.[12] *I* shall become the pride
Of my fellow-Paelignians—a race who fought for freedom,
  Freedom with honour, in the Italian wars 10
That scared Rome witless. I can see some visitor to Sulmona
  Taking in its tiny scale, the streams and walls,
And saying: "Any township, however small, that could breed so
  Splendid a poet, I call great." Boy-god,
And you, Cyprian goddess,[13] his mother, remove your golden
  Standards from my terrain—
Horned Bacchus is goading me on to weightier efforts, bigger
  Horses, a really ambitious trip.[14]
So farewell, congenial Muse, unheroic elegiacs—
  Work born to live on when its maker's dead! 20

from *HEROIDES*

Translated by Daryl Hine

Ovid's *Heroides* ("Heroines") is a set of twenty-one fictional letters written either by legendary women or to them. Fifteen of the letters are freestanding solos; three others are paired with letters written to the women by their respective men. Among this latter set are an epistle from Paris to Helen and hers replying to him. On the upshot of these letters, we are to understand, will depend the eruption of the Trojan War.

Hecuba and Priam were king and queen of Troy, the enormously opulent city in Asia Minor. While pregnant with Paris, Hecuba dreamed that she would give birth to a firebrand. Frightened at the ill omen, the royal couple disowned Paris, who grew up as a simple shepherd. One day the young man was commanded by the gods to judge a divine beauty contest, the three contestants being Juno, queen of the gods (the Greeks' Hera); Minerva, or Pallas, goddess of wisdom (the Greeks' Athena); and Venus, goddess of love and beauty (the Greeks' Aphrodite). Each goddess tried to bribe the young judge, but the winning bribe was from Venus: In return for choosing her, Paris would be awarded Helen, the most beautiful of mortal women, wife of Menelaus of Sparta in Greece. Leaving behind the lovelorn wood nymph Oenone whose lover he had been in his days as a shepherd, Paris sailed for Greece with the intent of meeting and abducting Helen, his allotted prize.

In her early youth, Helen had been carried off by Theseus, ruler of Athens, but brought home again by her brothers, Castor and Pollux. When she became marriageable, and before she married Menelaus, the competition for Helen among her

[11] Ovid came originally from the town of Sulmona, in the Paelignian region, in east-central Italy (known today as the Abruzzi). The Paeligni had fought for freedom against Rome early in the first century B.C. but later were granted Roman citizenship. Ovid's family was an old, respected one, Roman citizens for generations, not one of the new-rich families spawned by the mid-century civil wars.

[12] The poets Virgil and Catullus (both first century B.C.) were also from the provinces—in their cases, northern Italy.

[13] Venus was especially venerated on the island of Cyprus.

[14] Bacchus was the patron god of drama. Ovid went on to write a tragedy, *Medea*, much admired in antiquity but now lost. He continued, though, to write much irreverent love poetry in the elegiac meter, including such works as *The Art of Love*.

countless suitors had been bitterly intense. A treaty, therefore, was made in advance: Helen's wooers agreed not only to respect her union with whoever won her but also to act in concert against any man who interfered with the resultant marriage. Their commitment to this pledge would, after Helen eloped with Paris, bring the Greeks together to fight the Trojans. The outcome of the divine beauty contest still rankling, Juno and Minerva would assist the Greeks in the war, Venus the Trojans.

Both Paris and Helen were descendants of Jupiter, Helen more directly, since she had been begotten by the god when, in the form of a swan, he ravished Leda, Helen's mother. [*Editors' headnote.*]

PARIS TO HELEN (XVI)

From Priam's son, whom nothing can avail
But Leda's daughter's salutation: hail!
Shall I speak out? Or is my love so well
Known that it would be tedious to tell?
Is my desire more obvious than I
Desire? You know that secrecy was my
Strong preference, until the day when we're
Free to enjoy each other without fear.
But I dissemble badly: who could hide
A fire whose brilliance cannot be denied? 10
If you insist that I articulate
The matter, *ardent* would describe my state.
Forgive my frankness, please, and read the rest
Not with a frowning face and lips compressed,
But with that air which suits your beauty best.
Your kind reception of this billet-doux[1]
Fills me with hopes you'll treat me kindly, too,
And that the queen of love made no mistake
About this quest she bade me undertake—
For, just in case you didn't know, divine 20
Protection of the highest kind is mine,
And I am brought here by a god's design.

The prize is great, but no more than my due.
Venus herself has promised me to you.
She aided me to trace the mazy way
Across the broad seas from the Trojan bay,
And furnished favorable winds, for she,
Born of the sea, is mistress of the sea.[2]
Just as she lulled the stormy waves to rest,
May she assuage the tumult in my breast 30
And give my hopes safe harbor as your guest.

[1] Love letter.

[2] By one account, Venus was born of sea foam gathering around the genitals of the ancient god Uranus, castrated by his usurping son, Cronus (the Romans' Saturn).

I brought with me what I did not discover
Here: my raison d'être as a lover.
Neither by storm nor error was I brought
Hither: this was the shore my vessel sought.
Don't think I sail the seas with goods for sale
(Heaven protect my tiny capital!)
Or that as a tourist I have come
(For we have bigger towns than yours at home!).
It's you I seek, whom Venus, don't forget, 40
Made mine. I yearned for you before we met;
Before I saw you, my soul recognized
The face that fame at first had advertised;
Nor is it strange if Cupid's arrows are
Equally fatal when shot from afar.
So fate decreed; don't try to topple fate.
Believe the tale I faithfully relate.

While in my mother's womb I lingered too
Late, my delivery long overdue,
She dreamt that from her swollen belly came 50
Forth an enormous firebrand all aflame.
Hecuba leapt up terrified, and told
Her nightmare to her husband, and the old
King asked his augurs what the dream foretold.
They prophesied that I'd set Troy on fire,
(Meaning, by this incendiary desire).
Exposed at birth, I was adopted by
Shepherds who raised me as a shepherd. My
Good looks seemed to belie my humble birth,
My spirit, too, proclaimed my hidden worth. 60
In Ida's[3] wooded vales there is a lone-
Some spot with oaks and pine trees overgrown,
Where neither placid sheep nor lazy cows
Nor goats that love a craggy landscape browse.
From there I glimpsed, when I had climbed a tree,
Beyond the walls and roofs of Troy, the sea.
Once, suddenly the earth was shaken by
Footsteps—it sounds incredible, but I
Speak truth: before my eyes on winged feet
Hermes[4] alighted. (Let me just repeat 70
The things I was permitted to behold.)
His godly fingers held a wand of gold.
Then on the greensward Juno, Pallas, and
Venus appeared with dainty feet to stand.
Sheer stupefaction and dumb terror made
My hair stand on end. "Don't be afraid,

[3] Ida was a mountain and mountainous region near Troy.
[4] Messenger god (the Romans' Mercury).

Just judge this beauty contest," Hermes said,
"Resolve these beauties' quarrel, and advise
Which of the three is worthy of first prize."
Then, Jove's command conveyed, without delay 80
Lest I refuse, he went his airy way.
Gradually I felt my nerve recover
Till I was not afraid to look them over.
They looked so lovely that I, to begin
With, wished that every one of them could win.
One nonetheless appealed to me above
The others—she, you know, who stirs both love
And rivalry. The bribes with which each tried
To influence the way I should decide!
Minerva courage, Juno power vaunted, 90
But I could not determine what I wanted,
Till Venus laughed, "Don't let such gifts affect
Your judgment, Paris. Dire is their effect.
I'll give you love. Though Leda's daughter's charms
Are unsurpassed, she'll fall into your arms."
Beauty's bribe proved irresistible,
And Venus returned to heaven invincible.

Meanwhile at last my fortunes had improved.
By certain signs my royal birth was proved;
Priam received his long-lost son with joy, 100
Decreeing a public holiday for Troy.
Girls yearned for me just as I yearn for you,
Thus you alone possess what not a few
Sighed for; not only dames of high degree
But dryads,[5] even, fell in love with me,
And if to Oenone I prefer
Yourself, no paramour is worthier.
I'm bound all other women to disparage
Now that I hope to win your hand in marriage.
My imagination used to keep 110
Your image before me, waking or asleep.
What will your presence do, whom I desire
Unseen? I burn before I touch the fire.

Not one to harbor hopes too long in vain,
I tried my luck upon the bounding main.
First to my hatchet Asian pine trees fell,
Or any kind of wood that floated well;
The slopes of Gargara[6] were stripped for timber,
And lofty Ida furnished me much lumber.

[5] Wood nymphs.
[6] A town and region on a bay south of Troy.

Curving hulls were built with oak keels, bent 120
And covered with a wooden tegument.
The rigging, masts and sails were added now,
And icons of the gods hung from the prow—
Venus on mine, who'd promised me a bride,
Full-length, with little Cupid at her side.
Soon all these preparations were complete,
And I could hardly wait to launch my fleet;
But, with my parents begging me to stay,
My undertaking suffered more delay.
Sister Cassandra[7] then began to wail 130
Just as the ships were ready to set sail,
"Why all this rush to fetch home fire and slaughter
Worse than you can guess across the water?"
True seer! the flames she prophesied are real,
For in my heart a raging fire I feel.

So I set out, and making use of most
Favorable winds, approached the Grecian coast.
Your husband made me welcome, not without
Discreet divine encouragement, no doubt;
Undoubtedly he showed me everything 140
In Sparta he deemed worth exhibiting.
So keen to see your famous charms was I
That nothing else at all could catch my eye;
And when I saw you, even as I held
My breath, my heart with new emotions swelled.
The face and form of Venus when she came
To judgment, I recall, looked much the same;
Had you competed in that contest, she
Might not have won the prize so easily.
Both far and wide extends your beauty's fame: 150
There is no land that does not praise your name;
Your loveliness has its equivalent
Nowhere from orient to occident.
Believe me, fame depreciates your true
Beauty, and rumour almost slanders you.
I find more here than hearsay promised me;
Legend falls short of your reality.

No wonder Theseus esteemed your charms
In toto worthy of a hero's arms!
You illustrated Spartan mores when 160
You wrestled nude in public with nude men.[8]
Well, who could blame him? Why return you, though?

[7] A Trojan princess and seer, whose prophecies always went unheeded.
[8] Spartans were noted for rigorous physical exercises (and an ascetic lifestyle).

A prize like you should never be let go.
I think that I would sooner lose my head
Than see somebody steal you from my bed;
Willingly these arms will never give
You up, or let you leave me while you live.
I'd not have sent you back before I got
Something venereal,[9] no matter what;
You would have given me your maidenhead, 170
Or that which may be sacrificed instead.
But simply give yourself, and you'll discover
In Paris a completely faithful lover,
For only in the ashes of my pyre[10]
Will my enflamed concupiscence[11] expire.

You I preferred to those great realms with which
Jove's wife and sister[12] promised to enrich
Me; if I could embrace you I'd despise
Minerva's promises to make me wise.
I don't regret my choice as foolish now; 180
My mind is made up once for all, I vow.
I beg you not to bring my hopes to nought,
Worthy of being with such trouble sought!
No base-born suitor for your noble hand
Am I; you shan't wed badly, understand.
You'll find a member of the Pleiades
And Jove himself among our family's
Forebears, and few mere mediocrities.[13]
My father rules the Asian continent,
Infinite in resources and extent; 190
There countless cities, gilded domes you'll see,
And temples worthy of their deity.
The towered walls of Troy you shall behold,
Walls which Apollo's music built of old.[14]
What can I tell you of the populace,
Who seem for earth almost too numerous?
Matrons of Troy will welcome you, for whom
The royal palace scarcely can find room.
You'll frequently exclaim, "How poor is Greece,
Whose cities have one wealthy house apiece!" 200

[9] Having to do with Venus, or sexual love.

[10] Cremating funeral fire.

[11] Carnal desire.

[12] Jove and Juno were son and daughter of Cronus.

[13] The Pleiades were seven daughters of Atlas, a primeval Titan. One of the daughters, Maia, was the mother of Hermes/Mercury by Jupiter. Dardanus, a son of Jupiter, was the aboriginal forebear of the Trojan line.

[14] Along with Neptune, Apollo had built the walls of Troy. (Both were defrauded of the wages due them for this work.)

I shouldn't sneer at Sparta, though in jest:
The land that bore you I consider blest.
Yet Sparta's stingy. You deserve to dress
Richly; that spot ill suits your loveliness.
With such a face you should spare no expense
On novel and exotic ornaments.
(Seeing the getup of our men of war,
You'll wonder what the Trojan women wore!)
Come, daughter of the Spartan countryside,
Do not disdain to be a Trojan's bride. 210
Trojan he was, and of our royal line,
Who now dilutes the gods' ambrosial wine;[15]
Trojan, Aurora's husband, snatched away
By the divine precursor of the day;[16]
Trojan, Anchises, whom the mother of
The wingèd Loves on Ida loved to love.[17]
You will not say your husband can compare
To me in youth and beauty, that I'll swear.
I do not have a relative, at least,
Who caused a blackout with his bloody feast. 220
Did Priam's father's bloody treachery
Give a bad name to the Myrtoan sea?
Among my ancestors, none vainly craves
For food and drink amid the Stygian waves.[18]
Yet, notwithstanding his descent, your spouse
Can boast of Jove's connection with his house.
And every night and all night long, this cad
Embraces you. It really is too bad!

I barely see you when we meat at meal-
Times—and then what agonies I feel! 230
I only wish that my worse enemies
Might all partake of banquets such as these!
Seeing that boor, his arm about your bare
Shoulders, I truly wish I weren't there.

[15] Ganymede, a beautiful young prince of early Trojan days, swept up into heaven by Jupiter to be the gods' cupbearer.

[16] Tithonus, another early Trojan prince, was so beautiful that Aurora, goddess of the dawn, took him for her lover and even granted him immortality (though, fatefully, she forget to exempt him from the process of aging).

[17] Anchises, beloved of Venus, was father by her of Aeneas, the Trojan hero of Virgil's *Aeneid*.

[18] The ancestors of Menelaus (and of his brother Agamemnon) perpetrated many atrocities. Atreus, their father, served his brother Thyestes' children to him as a dish at dinner. Their grandfather, Pelops, conspired with Myrtilus (for whom the Myrtoan Sea, part of the Aegean, was named) to kill a king by sabotaging his chariot, after which Pelops double-crossed Myrtilus and drowned him. Their great-grandfather, Tantalus, committed various crimes, for which he was punished in hell (the "Stygian" realm) by the "tantalizing" proximity of water and food he could not quite reach.

I burst with envy, watching him caress
Your lovely body underneath your dress.
In drink, when tenderly you kiss him right
In front of me, I drown the horrid sight,
Lowering my eyes if he holds you too tight.
In short, revolted by the things I saw, 240
The food I didn't want stuck in my craw.
Often I groaned aloud, and heard soon after
How my groans provoked your giddy laughter.
But when with wine I tried to quench desire,
Intoxication added fire to fire.
To see no more, I turned my head away,
But constantly my looks would stray your way.
The sight was painful, but what could I do?
My torment would be worse away from you.
I try to hide my state, I do my best, 250
But still my secret love is manifest,
Not just by word of mouth: my wounds are known
To you as well as if they were your own—
I wish that they were known to you alone!
How often tearfully I turned aside,
Lest Menelaus wonder why I cried.
Sometimes when drunk, recounting some romance,
I lent a personal significance
To every word, encountering your glance.
Who guessed that under a fictitious name 260
Myself and each true lover was the same?
At times, that I might speak more saucily,
I simulated inebriety.
Your dress, if it fell open, might lay bare
Your breasts, at which I could not help but stare:
Whiter than snow or milk they are, or than
Jove when he lay with Leda as a swan.
Astonished at this vision, I let slip
The goblet's twisted handle from my grip.
Each time you kissed your daughter, I would take 270
Your kisses from her lips for your sweet sake.
Singing old lays of love I'd sprawl supine,
Or with a nod send you a secret sign.
Your maids of honor recently I dared
Approach with winning words, but they declared
Only that they were scared, and left me there
Without an answer, halfway through my prayer.

I wish the gods would make you the reward
Of him who won your favors by the sword!
Like Atalanta, cunningly outrun, 280
Or Hippodameia once by Pelops won,
Like Deianira, carried off by force

By Hercules, who changed a river's course.[19]
In such case, my bravado might succeed,
And you would know that you'd been won indeed!
But now there's nothing else for me to do
But kiss your feet, if you'll allow me to,
And press my suit respectfully with you.
Sister of the Dioscuri,[20] your worth
Makes you their representative on earth. 290
Glorious beauty, who, had you not been
Jupiter's daughter, would have been his queen,
Either I'll take you home to be my wife
Or here in exile I shall end my life.
Love's arrow did not merely graze my heart
But penetrated to the deepest part;
Transfixed by that celestial dart, I guess
My sister[21] really was a prophetess!
Helen, this fateful love do not deride,
If you would have the gods upon your side. 300
So we may speak more privately, invite
Me to your bedroom at the dead of night.
Are you afraid to shame your marriage bed
And to betray the royal oaf you wed?
Poor, simpleminded Helen! To believe
Your looks innocuous—that *is* naive!
Alter your face, or else become more kind:
A modest loveliness is hard to find.
Venus and Jove enjoy the furtive act—
Like that in which he fathered you, in fact. 310
With parentage like yours, how could you be
Chaste? Is there nothing in heredity?
Behave yourself at Troy when we get there:
I want to be your only love affair!
Sin now, our wedding day will put it right—
If Venus' promises turn out alright!

So much your husband's actions seem to say:
To give me a free hand he stays away.

[19] Paris cites an odd assortment of examples to illustrate his point about winning brides by the sword. The swift runner Atalanta, a determined virgin who would marry only a man who defeated her in a foot race, was won when her suitor Hippomanes distracted her by throwing golden apples on the track. Hippodameia was the daughter of the king treacherously killed by Pelops and Myrtilus (see the preceding note); she was to be given in marriage only to someone who defeated her father in a chariot race. To win his wife Deianira, Hercules had to outwrestle the river god Achelous; she later inadvertently caused Hercules' death.

[20] Castor and Pollux, Helen's heroic brothers, who were raised to the heavens as the constellation Gemini.

[21] Cassandra; see lines 130–135 and note.

No better time (he says) to visit Crete.
Oh, what a man! So prudent and discreet! 320
He left with this hospitable request:
"Take care for my sake of our Trojan guest."
But his commandment you neglect, I swear,
For of your guest you do not take good care.
If you think your god-given beauty can
Be rightly appreciated by that man,
You're wrong; for if he knew your value, would
He trust a stranger with his greatest good?
Even if you do not believe me, we
Should profit from such blind complicity, 330
Or we'd be stupider than he, to miss
A golden opportunity like this.
He all but ties the knot with his own hands,
So let's do what the simpleton demands.
Now all night long alone in bed you lie,
Night after endless night, and so do I.
Why not anticipate our honeymoon,
When night will be more radiant than noon?
I'll swear, in any formula that you
Suggest, and by your gods, that I'll be true. 340
If confidence is not misplaced, I hope
In person to persuade you to elope.
Afraid the deed will cover you with shame?
Well, don't be; I alone shall take the blame.
I'll merely follow Theseus' and your brothers'
Examples, as more pertinent than others';
For weren't you carried off by Theseus,
And weren't your brothers just as amorous?
The same old story will be told of us.
The Trojan fleet lies ready in the bay, 350
And wind and oar will speed our getaway.
You'll disembark at Troy like royalty;
The throng will hail a new divinity;
Along your route will clouds of incense rise
As at each step a sacred victim dies.
To every gift the house of Priam brings
You, Troy will add resplendent offerings.
But I can only hint at how much better
Your life will be in future, in this letter.

Don't worry, your abduction won't incite 360
Mayhem, with Greece arrayed in all its might.
How many women have been snatched before
Now, whose recovery provoked no war?
Believe me, Helen, there's no reason for
That fear. The Thracians were immune from slaughter
Although they took the king of Athens' daughter,

And Jason's homeland was not made to pay
When Jason with Medea ran away.
The very hero who abducted you
Once, abducted Ariadne too, 370
Yet Minos did not make a great to-do.[22]
Anxiety exceeds real danger here;
We fear what we should be ashamed to fear.
But say a great war does break out: I'm tough,
My weapons are injurious enough.[23]
The wealth of Asia, rich in men and horses,
Is more than equal to this land's resources.
Nor is your husband any braver than
Your lover, or a better fighting man.
Why, even as a lad I would attack 380
Our enemies to get our cattle back,
From which I got my nickname, Alexander,
Meaning "the best of men" or "the defender."
I beat the adolescent flower of Troy
In different competitions when a boy,
As an opponent formidable not
Only hand to hand, but a good shot.
You can't pretend that Menelaus ever
Struck you as precocious, skilled, and clever,
Nor can you give him what is worth another 390
Battalion, namely, Hector for a brother.[24]
Do you appreciate how brave and strong
This hero is to whom you will belong?
So, either the Greeks will not create a fuss
To get you back, or they will yield to us.
I don't mind taking arms for such a wife:
Magnificent prizes do promote some strife,
And if the whole world strove for you, your name
In times to come might gain undying fame.
Don't be afraid to hope. In recompense 400
The gods will favor your departure hence,
So claim your just deserts with confidence.

[22]Again, the examples Paris adduces are sinister. The first of these references may be to Procne (daughter of the legendary Athenian king Pandion), who married Tereus, king of Thrace. Tereus, Procne, and her sister Philomena suffered and committed several atrocities. Jason captured the Golden Fleece at Colchis, with the help of the king's daughter Medea, but she later committed several murders out of jealousy when Jason tired of her. Theseus, with the help of the princess Ariadne, killed the Minotaur, a predatory monster of Crete; Theseus later abandoned her, on the island of Naxos.

[23]Homer's *Iliad* shows Paris as a weakling in war, whom Helen treats with some contempt. According to tradition, though, he did kill the great Grecian warrior Achilles, with an arrow launched at long range.

[24]In the *Iliad*, Hector, the greatest of the Trojan warriors, treats Paris with forbearance but also expresses exasperation with his weakness. Helen will come to have something of a crush on Hector.

HELEN TO PARIS (XVII)

Now that your letter's thrust itself on my
Attention, politeness dictates a reply.
Profaning hospitality, you tried
To tempt your host's completely faithful bride.
Was it for this that our snug harbor gave
You shelter, tempest-tossed by wind and wave?
And though you were a total stranger, too,
Our palace portals opened wide to you?
O how could you repay our kindness so,
Intruding thus? And were you friend, or foe? 10
But you no doubt consider my complaint,
However justified, absurdly quaint:
Well, so be it! Better quaint than shameless,
Provided my behavior is blameless.
Although I don't affect a gloomy frown,
Sitting with knitted brows and eyes cast down,
My reputation and my pastimes are
Above reproach, and I do not, so far,
Condone adultery. I wonder at
Your confidence: what made you so sure that 20
I'd sleep with you? that, once a victim, I'm
Ripe for ravishment a second time?[1]
Had he seduced me, I might feel remorse,
But how was I to counter force with force?
Yet Theseus got no pleasure from his act;
I came back sacred, virginity intact.
I struggled so, that if he snatched a kiss
Or two, he got no more from me than this,
With which your lust would not have been content.
Theseus—thank god!—was different, 30
His self-restraint diminished his offense,
Nor did his youth prevent his penitence,
And your success would add to his regret.
How notorious can a woman get!

Still, I might be kind enough to hear
Your suit—who can object if love's sincere?
Which I doubt, although I'm not suspicious.
I can't pretend my face is not delicious,
But trust has led so many girls astray,
And your sweet talk is insincere, they say. 40
"Chaste wives are not exactly numerous":
But why should my name not be cited thus?
Perhaps you think the precedent of my
Mother was one I could be ruined by?

[1] Helen is referring to her earlier abduction by Theseus. See the Headnote to the *Heroides*.

But Leda was deluded into sin:
A feathery seducer took her in.
If I succumb, it will be with my eyes
Open, my fall no "error" will disguise.
Her sin was blest, her partner was divine,
But where's the Jupiter to sanction mine? 50
Boast about your high descent, do you?
My family is quite distinguished too.
My father-in-law's remote forefather is
Jupiter, the grandfather of his
Father, Pelops, son of Tantalus—
But what has his descent to do with us?
Jove's my father; by a bird misled,
Credulous Leda took him to her bed.
Go tell the world about this tribe of yours,
And Priam, and your other ancestors, 60
Whom I respect—but you are fifth in line
From Jove, while my conception was divine.
Your empire is extensive, I admit,
But ours is not inferior to it,
Which, if more populous and richer than
Ours, is nonetheless barbarian.
Such promises your lavish letter made,
Even a goddess would, I'm sure, be swayed.
Your self is (were I tempted to transgress)
A better argument for wantonness. 70
If I don't keep my honor clear of stain,
It will be for your sake and not for gain.
And, though your gifts are precious to me, for
The giver's sake, your love means so much more
To me, and all the trouble that you take,
And all the miles you've voyaged for my sake.

I note your bold behavior, wretch, at table,
Dissembling just as far as I am able:
You look at me so naughtily that I
Find it difficult to meet your eye. 80
Sighing, you pick up the nearest cup
To me, and where I lately sipped you sup,
And neither your covert sign language nor
Your too expressive winks can I ignore,
Till, dreading lest my husband see the same,
Your blatant signals make me blush for shame.
"Nothing fazes him!" I whisper low,
And heaven only knows that this is so!
Scribbled on the tabletop in wine
I spotted your initials twined with mine; 90
Though I dismissed this then as poppycock,
I since have learned the meaning of such talk.

If I were going to sin, such blandishments
Might possibly exert some influence.
You have, I must admit, a pretty face,
And any girl might welcome your embrace.
Let others enjoy themselves in innocence!
My sense of married decency prevents
My sharing their amorous experience.
Learn from me how to dispense with beauty; 100
Abstinence from pleasure is a duty.
How many youths with your desires are wise,
Do you suppose? Do you alone have eyes?
The rest were less persistent, that is all.
You haven't got more heart: you've got more gall.

I wish you'd come in your swift vessel when
My maidenhood was sought by many men,
From whom I would have picked you at first sight—
My husband himself would overlook the slight.
Too late you've come to share preempted pleasures, 110
For what you hope to take, another treasures.
I might have liked to be your wife, but still
No husband holds me here against my will.
Stop using words to cause the downfall of
This tender heart which you affect to love.
Let me be faithful to my destiny—
You'll get no medal for seducing me.
Yet wasn't that the promise Venus made
When she and her sister goddesses displayed
Themselves before you in the Idaean glade? 120
One offered power, another martial pride,
But, "Helen," said the third, "will be your bride."
I can't believe those heavenly bodies lent
Their loveliness to your arbitrament,
But if they did, it surely is a lie
That your reward, and Venus' bribe, was I.
I am not so conceited I believe
Myself the greatest boon she could conceive.
Enough that men approve the way I look—
The praise of Venus only brings bad luck. 130
I shan't repudiate your homage, though:
How could I question what I wish were so?
If I was slow to credit you, I'm sorry:
In vital matters trust is dilatory.
I'm glad if what found favor in the eyes
Of Venus seems to you a worthy prize.
My beauty she had only to describe
And you rejected every other bribe,
So I'm your honor and your kingdom too.
I must be iron not to care for you. 140

Well, iron I'm not, and yet I think it wrong
To love someone to whom I can't belong.
Why should I try to till the seashore and
Pin false hopes upon the sterile sand?
Heaven knows that I am not so clever
As to deceive my doting husband ever!
In writing this clandestine letter, I'm
Abusing the alphabet for the first time.
Happy the skilled adulteress! I guess
How tricky are the paths of wickedness. 150
Confused, tormented by anxiety,
I think that every eye is fixed on me—
With reason: tittle-tattle I have heard,
Low talk, of which my handmaid brings me word.
Dissemble—or perhaps you'd rather go
Home? Why go, when you dissemble so?
In Menelaus' absence be discreet;
Our freedom is enlarged but not complete.
My husband was called suddenly away
On urgent business brooking no delay— 160
At least I thought it urgent anyway,
And when he stalled encouraged him to pack:
"The sooner you leave, the sooner you'll get back."
Reassured, he left with one request:
"Take care of Sparta—and our Trojan guest."
I had to laugh, and struggling to repress
My ribald giggles, answered merely, "Yes."
But now he's gone off on this Cretan jaunt
Don't think you can do anything you want,
For though he's absent I can feel his eyes 170
On us—have you forgotten kings have spies?
Rumor aggravating our position,
Your constant praise confirms his worst suspicion.
Renown, however pleasant, will be my
Ruin; better to give fame the lie.
You think it odd he leaves you with his wife?
He trusts my conduct and my blameless life.
He thinks that he can count, although my beauty
Makes him nervous, on my sense of duty.
"Do not overlook," you're telling me, 180
"This heaven-given opportunity
To profit by such dumb complacency."
Your opposition tempts me, but I'm scared;
I can't decide, my mind is unprepared.
My husband's gone, and you are lonely too,
Your looks please me as much as mine please you;
Long nights in the same house, and your discourse
Too sweet for purely verbal intercourse—
Everything is tempting me to stray,
Only some secret scruple blocks my way. 190

Where persuasion failed, may force succeed!
The only cure for backwardness indeed!
Victims sometimes don't find rape so bad:
I wish someone would force me to be glad.
It's easier to quell a new desire;
A little water quenches a fresh fire.
No stranger's love can be depended on;
Just when you think it's here to stay, it's gone.
Hypsipyle and Ariadne were
Each tricked into sleeping with a traveler,[2] 200
And did you not quite cavalierly wrong
Poor Oenone whom you liked so long?
You can't deny it! I have studied, so
To find out all about you, don't you know.
You could not, if you wanted, keep your word,
For your departure cannot be deferred.
Even as you're talking to me, and
While our night of bliss is being planned,
A western wind will waft you to your land;
Yes, in the midst of our debaucheries 210
You'll leave, and love will vanish on the breeze.
Shall I come too, as you are urging me
To do, your celebrated Troy to see
And marry into Priam's family?
No, am I so indifferent to fame
That I should fill the world with my bad name?
How will Sparta, how will Greece react?
And all of Asia—Troy itself, in fact?
What will Priam think, and Hecuba,
And all your brothers and your sisters-in-law? 220
How can you ever think me innocent
Again when you provide this precedent?
Every chance newcomer to appear
In Troy will fill you with dismay and fear;
Often in anger will you call me whore
While your own fault you're willing to ignore,
At once the scourge and prompter of my crime.
I pray that I'll be dead before that time!
And yet the splendid opulence of Troy,
Surpassing all you promised, I'd enjoy, 230
Purple and precious raiment, gold of which
There would be heaps enough to make me rich.

[2] During their voyage to seek the Golden Fleece, the Argonauts stopped for a time at Lemnos, where their leader, Jason, seduced Hypsipyle and then later abandoned her. On Ariadne, see the note to Paris's letter, lines 369–371.

Forgive me, but your gifts are not so grand.
Something still keeps me in my native land.
What help, if on your coast I should be wrecked,
From brother or father could I then expect?
Although false-hearted Jason promised all
She wanted to Medea, after all
Wasn't she driven from his father's hall?
How could she return, so much maligned, 240
To the family she left behind?[3]
I'm not afraid—nor was her ladyship,
But between cup and lip there's many a slip,
And many a ship with which the waves make sport,
You'll find, that had no trouble leaving port.
That bloody brand alarms me, which before
Your birth was due your mother dreamt she bore,
That prophecy as well, that Greece will come
And fire the topless towers of Ilium.[4]
Of course you're Venus' favorite, for she 250
Owes to you a twofold victory:
I fear the losing pair whom, if your boast
Is true, you robbed of what they wanted most.
No doubt if I eloped with you, a war
Would follow. Is our love worth fighting for?
Did not Hippodamia incite
The centaurs and the Lapiths once to fight?[5]
And do you think the justice of their cause
Will for a moment give my menfolk pause?
Although you vaunt your valor to the skies, 260
Such boastful words your countenance belies.
Your face and form are better fashioned for
Venus than Mars; her service suits you more;
Let strong men fight, while you make love not war.
Ask Hector, whom you laud, to fight for you:
Other fields deserve your derring-do,
And there I'd join you, were I not afraid,
And so would any knowledgeable maid.
Perhaps I shall, my honor laid aside,
And offer you my hands, which time has tied. 270
As for that tête-à-tête, I know what kind
Of private interview you have in mind!
Not so fast—your plans are immature
As yet—but time is on your side, I'm sure.

[3]On Medea, see Paris's letter, lines 367–368 and note. By helping Jason get the Golden Fleece at Colchis, Medea alienated her people there. After fleeing with Jason to his home city, Iolcus, Medea caused the death of that city's king, Pelias, so that she and Jason had to flee once more, this time to Corinth, from Pelias' enraged subjects.

[4]Another name for Troy.

[5]At the feast celebrating the wedding of Hippodamia to Pirithous, one of the Lapiths, general violence broke out after a drunken Centaur assaulted the bride.

It's time that this clandestine letter, penned
With furtive, flagging fingers, had an end.
Further communication will be through
My maids, companions, and advisers too.

METAMORPHOSES

Translated by Rolfe Humphries

from BOOK I

My intention is to tell of bodies changed
To different forms; the gods, who made the changes,
Will help me—or I hope so—with a poem
That runs from the world's beginning to our own days.[1]

THE CREATION[2]

Before the ocean was, or earth, or heaven,
Nature was all alike, a shapelessness,
Chaos, so-called, all rude and lumpy matter,
Nothing but bulk, inert, in whose confusion
Discordant atoms warred: there was no sun
To light the universe; there was no moon 10
With slender silver crescents filling slowly;
No earth hung balanced in surrounding air;
No sea reached far along the fringe of shore.
Land, to be sure, there was, and air, and ocean,
But land on which no man could stand, and water
No man could swim in, air no man could breathe,
Air without light, substance forever changing,
Forever at war: within a single body
Heat fought with cold, wet fought with dry, the hard
Fought with the soft, things having weight contended 20
With weightless things.
Till God, or kindlier Nature,[3]
Settled all argument, and separated
Heaven from earth, water from land, our air
From the high stratosphere, a liberation;

[1] The full fifteen-book poem ends with the transformations of Julius Caesar into a star and of Augustus, after his death (still in the future), into a god.

[2] The primordial transformation of chaos to order was itself a "metamorphosis." Compare the biblical account of creation in Genesis.

[3] The citing of two possible causes is a reflection of Ovid's wry religious skepticism.

So things evolved, and out of blind confusion
Found each its place, bound in eternal order.
The force of fire, that weightless element,
Leaped up and claimed the highest place in heaven;
Below it, air; and under them the earth
Sank with its grosser portions; and the water, 30
Lowest of all, held up, held in, the land.[4]

Whatever god it was, who out of chaos
Brought order to the universe, and gave it
Division, subdivision, he molded earth,
In the beginning, into a great globe,
Even on every side, and bade the waters
To spread and rise, under the rushing winds,
Surrounding earth; he added ponds and marshes,
He banked the river-channels, and the waters
Feed earth or run to sea, and that great flood 40
Washes on shores, not banks. He made the plains
Spread wide, the valleys settle, and the forest
Be dressed in leaves; he made the rocky mountains
Rise to full height, and as the vault of Heaven
Has two zones, left and right, and one between them
Hotter than these, the Lord of all Creation
Marked on the earth the same design and pattern.
The torrid zone too hot for men to live in,
The north and south too cold, but in the middle
Varying climate, temperature and season. 50
Above all things the air, lighter than earth,
Lighter than water, heavier than fire,
Towers and spreads; there mist and cloud assemble,
And fearful thunder and lightning and cold winds,
But these, by the Creator's order, held
No general dominion; even as it is,
These brothers brawl and quarrel; though each one
Has his own quarter, still, they come near tearing
The universe apart. Eurus is monarch
Of the lands of dawn, the realms of Araby, 60
The Persian ridges under the rays of morning.
Zephyrus holds the west that glows at sunset,
Boreas, who makes men shiver, holds the north,
Warm Auster governs in the misty southland,
And over them all presides the weightless ether,[5]
Pure without taint of earth.
These boundaries given,
Behold, the stars, long hidden under darkness,
Broke through and shone, all over the spangled heaven,

[4] The four primal elements were believed to be fire, air, earth, and water.
[5] The element of fire.

Their home forever, and the gods lived there,
And shining fish were given the waves for dwelling 70
And beasts the earth, and birds the moving air.

But something else was needed, a finer being,
More capable of mind, a sage, a ruler,
So Man was born, it may be, in God's image,
Or Earth, perhaps, so newly separated
From the old fire of Heaven, still retained
Some seed of the celestial force which fashioned
Gods out of living clay and running water.
All other animals look downward; Man,
Alone, erect, can raise his face toward Heaven. 80

THE FOUR AGES

The Golden Age was first, a time that cherished
Of its own will, justice and right; no law,
No punishment, was called for; fearfulness
Was quite unknown, and the bronze tablets[6] held
No legal threatening; no suppliant throng
Studied a judge's face; there were no judges,
There did not need to be. Trees had not yet
Been cut and hollowed, to visit other shores.
Men were content at home, and had no towns
With moats and walls around them; and no trumpets 90
Blared out alarums;[7] things like swords and helmets
Had not been heard of. No one needed soldiers.
People were unaggressive, and unanxious;
The years went by in peace. And Earth, untroubled,
Unharried by hoe or plowshare, brought forth all
That men had need for, and those men were happy,
Gathering berries from the mountain sides,
Cherries, or blackcaps, and the edible acorns.
Spring was forever, with a west wind blowing
Softly across the flowers no man had planted, 100
And Earth, unplowed, brought forth rich grain; the field,
Unfallowed, whitened with wheat, and there were rivers
Of milk, and rivers of honey, and golden nectar
Dripped from the dark-green oak-trees,
After Saturn[8]
Was driven to the shadowy land of death,
And the world was under Jove, the Age of Silver
Came in, lower than gold, better than bronze.

[6] The Roman laws were written and publicly displayed on such tablets.
[7] Calls to battle.
[8] Chief of the gods in the older generation of divinities. He reigned during the Golden Age, until he was deposed by Jove and his dynasty.

Jove made the springtime shorter, added winter,
Summer, and autumn, the seasons as we know them.
That was the first time when the burnt air glowed 110
White-hot, or icicles hung down in winter.
And men built houses for themselves; the caverns,
The woodland thickets, and the bark-bound shelters
No longer served; and the seeds of grain were planted
In the long furrows, and the oxen struggled
Groaning and laboring under the heavy yoke.

Then came the Age of Bronze, and dispositions
Took on aggressive instincts, quick to arm,
Yet not entirely evil. And last of all
The Iron Age succeeded, whose base vein 120
Let loose all evil: modesty and truth
And righteousness fled earth, and in their place
Came trickery and slyness, plotting, swindling,
Violence and the damned desire of having.
Men spread their sails to winds unknown to sailors,
The pines came down their mountain-sides, to revel
And leap in the deep waters, and the ground,
Free, once, to everyone, like air and sunshine,
Was stepped off by surveyors. The rich earth,
Good giver of all the bounty of the harvest, 130
Was asked for more; they dug into her vitals,
Pried out the wealth a kinder lord had hidden
In Stygian[9] shadow, all that precious metal,
The root of evil. They found the guilt of iron,
And gold, more guilty still. And War came forth
That uses both to fight with; bloody hands
Brandished the clashing weapons. Men lived on plunder.
Guest was not safe from host, nor brother from brother,
A man would kill his wife, a wife her husband,
Stepmothers, dire and dreadful, stirred their brews 140
With poisonous aconite,[10] and sons would hustle
Fathers to death, and Piety lay vanquished,
And the maiden Justice, last of all immortals,
Fled from the bloody earth.
Heaven was no safer.
Giants[11] attacked the very throne of Heaven,
Piled Pelion on Ossa, mountain on mountain
Up to the very stars. Jove struck them down
With thunderbolts, and the bulk of those huge bodies
Lay on the earth, and bled, and Mother Earth,

[9] Pertaining to the underground world.
[10] A plant related to monkshood, often poisonous.
[11] The Giants were offspring of Earth and Heaven; Ossa and Pelion are mountains in Thessaly, a region of Greece.

Made pregnant by that blood, brought forth new bodies, 150
And gave them, to recall her older offspring,
The forms of men. And this new stock was also
Contemptuous of gods, and murder-hungry
And violent. You would know they were sons of blood.

JOVE'S INTERVENTION

And Jove was witness from his lofty throne
Of all this evil, and groaned as he remembered
The wicked revels of Lycaon's table,
The latest guilt, a story still unknown
To the high gods. In awful indignation
He summoned them to council. No one dawdled. 160
Easily seen when the night skies are clear,
The Milky Way shines white. Along this road
The gods move toward the palace of the Thunderer,[12]
His royal halls, and, right and left, the dwellings
Of other gods are open, and guests come thronging.
The lesser gods live in a meaner section,
An area not reserved, as this one is,
For the illustrious Great Wheels of Heaven.
(Their Palatine Hill,[13] if I might call it so.)

They took their places in the marble chamber 170
Where high above them all their king was seated,
Holding his ivory sceptre, shaking out
Thrice, and again, his awful locks, the sign
That made the earth and stars and ocean tremble,
And then he spoke, in outrage: "I was troubled
Less for the sovereignty of all the world
In that old time when the snake-footed[14] giants
Laid each his hundred hands on captive Heaven.
Monstrous they were, and hostile, but their warfare
Sprung from one source, one body. Now, wherever 180
The sea-gods roar around the earth, a race
Must be destroyed, the race of men. I swear it!
I swear by all the Stygian rivers[15] gliding
Under the world, I have tried all other measures.
The knife must cut the cancer out, infection
Averted while it can be, from our numbers.
Those demigods, those rustic presences,
Nymphs, fauns, and satyrs, wood and mountain dwellers,
We have not yet honored with a place in Heaven,

[12] Jove.
[13] In the Rome of Ovid's time, the site of Caesar Augustus's dwelling.
[14] The lower part of the Giants' body was serpentine.
[15] To swear by the river Styx was the most solemn and binding oath a god could take.

But they should have some decent place to dwell in, 190
In peace and safety. Safety? Do you reckon
They will be safe, when I, who wield the thunder,
Who rule you all as subjects, am subjected
To the plottings of the barbarous Lycaon?"

They burned, they trembled. Who was this Lycaon,
Guilty of such rank infamy? They shuddered
In horror, with a fear of sudden ruin,
As the whole world did later, when assassins
Struck Julius Caesar down, and Prince Augustus[16]
Found satisfaction in the great devotion 200
That cried for vengeance, even as Jove took pleasure,
Then, in the gods' response. By word and gesture
He calmed them down, awed them again to silence,
And spoke once more:

THE STORY OF LYCAON

"He has indeed been punished.
On that score have no worry. But what he did,
And how he paid, are things that I must tell you.
I had heard the age was desperately wicked,
I had heard, or so I hoped, a lie, a falsehood,
So I came down, as man, from high Olympus,
Wandered about the world. It would take too long 210
To tell you how widespread was all that evil.
All I had heard was grievous understatement!
I had crossed Maenala, a country bristling
With dens of animals, and crossed Cyllene,
And cold Lycaeus'[17] pine woods. Then I came
At evening, with the shadows growing longer,
To an Arcadian palace, where the tyrant
Was anything but royal in his welcome.
I gave a sign that a god had come, and people
Began to worship, and Lycaon mocked them, 220
Laughed at their prayers, and said: 'Watch me find out
Whether this fellow is a god or mortal,
I can tell quickly, and no doubt about it.'
He planned, that night, to kill me while I slumbered;
That was his way to test the truth. Moreover,
And not content with that, he took a hostage,
One sent by the Molossians,[18] cut his throat,
Boiled pieces of his flesh, still warm with life,

[16]A glance ahead to the very end of the poem, which celebrates the metamorphoses of these two Caesars.

[17]Maenala, Cyllene, Lycaeus are mountains in Arcadia, a rustic region in Greece.

[18]Inhabitants of Molossus, a city in Crete.

Broiled others, and set them before me on the table.
That was enough. I struck, and the bolt of lightning 230
Blasted the household of that guilty monarch.
He fled in terror, reached the silent fields,
And howled, and tried to speak. No use at all!
Foam dripped from his mouth; bloodthirsty still, he turned
Against the sheep, delighting still in slaughter,
And his arms were legs, and his robes were shaggy hair,
Yet he is still Lycaon, the same grayness,
The same fierce face, the same red eyes, a picture
Of bestial savagery. One house has fallen,
But more than one deserves to. Fury reigns 240
Over all the fields of Earth. They are sworn to evil,
Believe it. Let them pay for it, and quickly!
So stands my purpose."
Part of them approved
With words and added fuel to his anger,
And part approved with silence, and yet all
Were grieving at the loss of humankind,
Were asking what the world would be, bereft
Of mortals: who would bring their altars incense?
Would earth be given the beasts, to spoil and ravage?
Jove told them not to worry; he would give them 250
Another race, unlike the first, created
Out of a miracle; he would see to it.

He was about to hurl his thunderbolts
At the whole world, but halted, fearing Heaven
Would burn from fire so vast, and pole to pole
Break out in flame and smoke, and he remembered
The fates had said that some day land and ocean,
The vault of Heaven, the whole world's mighty fortress,
Besieged by fire, would perish. He put aside
The bolts made in Cyclopean[19] workshops; better, 260
He thought, to drown the world by flooding water.

THE FLOOD

So, in the cave of Aeolus,[20] he prisoned
The North-wind, and the West-wind, and such others
As ever banish cloud, and he turned loose
The South-wind, and the South-wind came out streaming
With dripping wings, and pitch-black darkness veiling
His terrible countenance. His beard is heavy
With rain-cloud, and his hoary locks a torrent,

[19] The Cyclops were workers under Vulcan, the blacksmith god of fire.
[20] God of the winds; with the following lines compare the storm at the beginning of Virgil's *Aeneid,* Book I.

Mists are his chaplet,[21] and his wings and garments
Run with the rain. His broad hands squeeze together 270
Low-hanging clouds, and crash and rumble follow
Before the cloudburst, and the rainbow, Iris,
Draws water from the teeming earth, and feeds it
Into the clouds again. The crops are ruined,
The farmers' prayers all wasted, all the labor
Of a long year comes to nothing.
And Jove's anger,
Unbounded by his own domain, was given
Help by his dark-blue brother. Neptune called
His rivers all, and told them, very briefly,
To loose their violence, open their houses, 280
Pour over embankments, let the river horses
Run wild as ever they would. And they obeyed him.
His trident[22] struck the shuddering earth; it opened
Way for the rush of waters. The leaping rivers
Flood over the great plains. Not only orchards
Are swept away, not only grain and cattle,
Not only men and houses, but altars, temples,
And shrines with holy fires. If any building
Stands firm, the waves keep rising over its roof-top,
Its towers are under water, and land and ocean 290
Are all alike, and everything is ocean,
An ocean with no shore-line.
Some poor fellow
Seizes a hill-top; another, in a dinghy,
Rows where he used to plough, and one goes sailing
Over his fields of grain or over the chimney
Of what was once his cottage. Someone catches
Fish in the top of an elm-tree, or an anchor
Drags in green meadow-land, or the curved keel brushes
Grape-arbors under water. Ugly sea-cows
Float where the slender she-goats used to nibble 300
The tender grass, and the Nereids[23] come swimming
With curious wonder, looking, under water,
At houses, cities, parks, and groves. The dolphins
Invade the woods and brush against the oak-trees;
The wolf swims with the lamb; lion and tiger
Are borne along together; the wild boar
Finds all his strength is useless, and the deer
Cannot outspeed that torrent; wandering birds
Look long, in vain, for landing-place, and tumble,

[21] A garland for the head.
[22] The three-pronged spear wielded by the sea god Neptune.
[23] Sea nymphs.

Exhausted, into the sea. The deep's great license 310
Has buried all the hills, and new waves thunder
Against the mountain-tops. The flood has taken
All things, or nearly all, and those whom water,
By chance, has spared, starvation slowly conquers.

DEUCALION AND PYRRHA

Phocis,[24] a fertile land, while there was land,
Marked off Oetean from Boeotian fields.
It was ocean now, a plain of sudden waters.
There Mount Parnassus lifts its twin peaks skyward,
High, steep, cloud-piercing. And Deucalion came there
Rowing his wife. There was no other land, 320
The sea had drowned it all. And here they worshipped
First the Corycian[25] nymphs and native powers,
Then Themis, oracle and fate-revealer.
There was no better man than this Deucalion,
No one more fond of right; there was no woman
More scrupulously reverent than Pyrrha.
So, when Jove saw the world was one great ocean,
Only one woman left of all those thousands,
And only one man left of all those thousands,
Both innocent and worshipful, he parted 330
The clouds, turned loose the North-wind, swept them off,
Showed earth to heaven again, and sky to land,
And the sea's anger dwindled, and King Neptune
Put down his trident, calmed the waves, and Triton,[26]
Summoned from far down under, with his shoulders
Barnacle-strewn, loomed up above the waters,
The blue-green sea god, whose resounding horn
Is heard from shore to shore. Wet-bearded, Triton
Set lip to that great shell, as Neptune ordered,
Sounding retreat, and all the lands and waters 340
Heard and obeyed. The sea has shores; the rivers,
Still running high, have channels; the floods dwindle,
Hill-tops are seen again; the trees, long buried,
Rise with their leaves still muddy. The world returns.

Deucalion saw that world, all desolation,
All emptiness, all silence, and his tears
Rose as he spoke to Pyrrha: "O my wife,
The only woman, now, on all this earth,

[24]A mountainous region separating Boeotia from Oeta, a mountain range on the border of Thessaly.

[25]Of Corycus, a sacred grotto. Themis, in the next line, was a goddess of justice who controlled the oracle of Delphi before it became associated with Apollo.

[26]A merman, son of Neptune.

My consort and my cousin and my partner
In these immediate dangers, look! Of all the lands 350
To East or West, we two, we two alone,
Are all the population. Ocean holds
Everything else; our foothold, our assurance,
Are small as they can be, the clouds still frightful.
Poor woman—well, we are not all alone—
Suppose you had been, how would you bear your fear?
Who would console your grief? My wife, believe me,
Had the sea taken you, I would have followed.
If only I had the power, I would restore
The nations as my father[27] did, bring clay 360
To life with breathing. As it is, we two
Are all the human race, so Heaven has willed it,
Samples of men, mere specimens."
They wept,
And prayed together, and having wept and prayed,
Resolved to make petition to the goddess
To seek her aid through oracles. Together
They went to the river-water, the stream Cephisus,
Still far from clear, but flowing down its channel,
And they took river-water, sprinkled foreheads,
Sprinkled their garments, and they turned their steps 370
To the temple of the goddess, where the altars
Stood with the fires gone dead, and ugly moss
Stained pediment and column. At the stairs
They both fell prone, kissed the chill stone in prayer:
"If the gods' anger ever listens
To righteous prayers, O Themis, we implore you,
Tell us by what device our wreck and ruin
May be repaired. Bring aid, most gentle goddess,
To sunken circumstance."
And Themis heard them,
And gave this oracle: "Go from the temple, 380
Cover your heads, loosen your robes, and throw
Your mother's bones behind you!" Dumb, they stood
In blank amazement, a long silence, broken
By Pyrrha, finally: she would not do it!
With trembling lips she prays whatever pardon
Her disobedience might merit, but this outrage
She dare not risk, insult her mother's spirit
By throwing her bones around. In utter darkness
They voice the cryptic saying over and over,
What can it mean? They wonder. At last Deucalion 390
Finds the way out: "I might be wrong, but surely
The holy oracles would never counsel

[27] Prometheus, who made man from clay and also stole fire from heaven for human use.

A guilty act. The earth is our great mother,
And I suppose those bones the goddess mentions
Are the stones of earth; the order means to throw them,
The stones, behind us."
She was still uncertain,
And he by no means sure, and both distrustful
Of that command from Heaven; but what damage,
What harm, would there be in trying? They descended,
Covered their heads, loosened their garments, threw 400
The stones behind them as the goddess ordered.
The stones—who would believe it, had we not
The unimpeachable witness of Tradition?—
Began to lose their hardness, to soften, slowly,
To take on form, to grow in size, a little,
Become less rough, to look like human beings,
Or anyway as much like human beings
As statues do, when the sculptor is only starting,
Images half blocked out. The earthy portion,
Damp with some moisture, turned to flesh, the solid 410
Was bone, the veins were as they always had been.
The stones the man had thrown turned into men,
The stones the woman threw turned into women,
Such being the will of God. Hence we derive
The hardness that we have, and our endurance
Gives proof of what we have come from.
Other forms
Of life came into being, generated
Out of the earth: the sun burnt off the dampness,
Heat made the slimy marshes swell; as seed
Swells in a mother's womb to shape and substance, 420
So new forms came to life. When the Nile river
Floods and recedes and the mud is warmed by sunshine,
Men, turning over the earth, find living things,
And some not living, but nearly so, imperfect,
On the verge of life, and often the same substance
Is part alive, part only clay. When moisture
Unites with heat, life is conceived; all things
Come from this union. Fire may fight with water,
But heat and moisture generate all things,
Their discord being productive. So when earth, 430
After that flood, still muddy, took the heat,
Felt the warm fire of sunlight, she conceived,
Brought forth, after their fashion, all the creatures,
Some old, some strange and monstrous.

* * *

The New Testament

(First and Second Centuries A.D.)

The name given to the distinctively Christian part of the Bible, the *New Testament,* can also be rendered as *New Covenant,* a term that has the advantage of underlining the intimate relationship, of kinship and separation, between it and what Christians call the Old Testament. The old covenant, sealed at Mount Sinai, was essentially a contract between God and the people of Israel. It was the culmination of a series of lesser covenants established between God and humanity, then between God and the Hebrew patriarchs. The contract spelled out the provisions by which God, on the occasion of the deliverance of the Hebrews from Egypt, revealed Himself to them and singled them out for special obligations and a special mission. Although the Exodus story, as told in the first six books of the Old Testament (the Hexateuch), has mythic content that links it to universal human religious insights, it nevertheless solemnizes a preeminently *historical* event, the establishment of the nation of Israel.

In later Old Testament times, written and popular traditions grew up stating that a divinely appointed Messiah would arise among the Jews to deliver them from their national tribulations and usher in a new era of triumph and glory. The Christians of the first century believed that this Messiah had in fact appeared, in the historical figure of Jesus of Nazareth. Through him God had established a new covenant, this time with a body of believers extending beyond the Jews. As the old covenant had been sealed with the ritual sprinkling of blood (Exodus 24:6–8), so had the new covenant, for this Messiah was—unexpectedly—a sacrificial victim. But he had risen from the dead as a pledge of an imminent second coming, or *Parousia,* that would vindicate God's newly adopted people. The doctrine of the Resurrection and the concomitant belief in the Parousia and final Judgment lay at the heart of Christian faith during the first century.

The canonical books of the New Testament, as finally defined several centuries after Jesus, number twenty-seven, all written in Greek: the four Gospels, some of unknown authorship but named Matthew, Mark, Luke, and John; a history of the early Church written by the author of Luke and called Acts of the Apostles; twenty-one letters, or Epistles, the most important of which are by St. Paul; and a visionary, allegorical work of prophecy named Revelation, or the Apocalypse. The earliest of these books are the Pauline letters, which were written mainly over the sixth decade of the first century; the other books were written at various dates extending through the end of the first century into the early part of the second century. Most of the New Testament books are statements of doctrine and church discipline; the more biographical ones are Acts and the four Gospels that center on the life and teaching of Jesus.

Although the four Gospels contain substantially similar accounts of the trial, sufferings, and execution of Jesus (the Passion), and all present an empty tomb that points to his resurrection, their portrayals of the earlier phases of Jesus' life are significantly different from one another. John, on the one hand, has its own distinctive material. Matthew, Mark, and Luke (the "synoptic" Gospels), on the other hand, contain a common fund of different material, and many passages have almost identical wording. In fact, approximately 99 percent of Mark, and much of its ordering of material, are paralleled (although sometimes recast) in Matthew and Luke. An enormous scholarly literature attempts to explain the significant overlap when these Gospels are "seen together" (the meaning of *synoptic*), and a consensus, called the two-document hypothesis, has dominated the field of interpretation during this century. The hypothesis proposes that Mark is the earliest Gospel (written around 65–70) and that Matthew and Luke, although written independently of each other (between about 80 and 95), are based partly on a direct knowledge of Mark. The shared but non-Markan material in Matthew and Luke is derived from a now lost collection, largely of sayings of Jesus, called *Q* (from German *Quelle,* "source"). Some authorities postulate that both Matthew and Luke also used other sources, called *M* and *L,* respectively. The synoptic problem is of course important in itself, but it has also intrigued scholars because it bears on the possibility of recovering facts about the historical Jesus from the earliest accounts. This search for the "real" Jesus, independent of later tendentious biases of the Gospel authors (the "evangelists"), was especially urgent in the nineteenth century. This search continues today, often from outside the distinctively Christian source materials—from archaeology, for example, or ancient history in general. The results, however, are often fanciful or farfetched. Scholars have attained some confidence concerning the typical teaching and activity of Jesus from the earliest form of sayings and stories, but they are doubtful that any of the evangelists, even the earliest, has provided an account either of Jesus' acts or of the sequence of his acts that is free from substantial interpretation.

That view may unsettle or puzzle readers accustomed to the goals of modern biography and historiography. But to the earliest Christians it was the overwhelming fact of the Messiah's death, resurrection, and imminent Parousia that was centrally important, not the circumstantial details of his life. (It is significant that the word translated as "gospel"—*good news*—did not originally refer as it usually does now to the formal genre represented by Matthew, Mark, Luke, and John but rather to the essential *message* just outlined.) Moreover, the tradition of both Jewish and pagan historiography assumed that the truth about any event or person could best be revealed by a respect for tradition and sources in the setting of the author's own creative intuition. This combination operates even in the author of Luke and Acts, the New Testament works governed most by the classical rules for writing history. The interest among Christians in what Jesus had said and done during his life as a whole arose only secondarily, and even then less from a modern need for historical accuracy in itself than from a sense of Jesus as an enduring, living presence and a desire to explore and authenticate the current doctrine and discipline of his living Church. The earliest Christians did not feel that the circumstantial data were of value apart from their significance.

It is important to recognize that each of the four Gospels has its own special intention and effect. They contain basic stories about Jesus' life and death that create an impression of coherence in the New Testament (some apocryphal Gospels written later do not cohere with these accounts), but the portraits differ unmistakably in their overtones: In Mark, Jesus is presented earthily, almost naturalistically; in Luke, beautifully and heroically; in John, with a supernal serenity; in Matthew, as compassionate but magisterial. More careful study reveals also differences between the Gospels in their doctrinal emphases, their views of the timing and nature of the coming apocalyptic Parousia, their definitions of ethical and communal duties of Christians, and their notions of worship. Each Gospel addresses the needs of a different group of early Christians in its own place and set of circumstances.

Matthew was probably written in Syria, as a manual of instruction for a well-established Christian community, containing both Jewish and Gentile converts, that was competing with Pharisaic Judaism after the destruction of the Jerusalem Temple in 70 A.D. The author is concerned to define the Church as the New Israel, replacing the old one by means of a way of righteousness surpassing the righteousness of the Pharisees (a difficult goal, because the Pharisees were the most fervently religious Jews within first-century Jewish society). Events of Jesus' life—especially healings, exorcisms, and other miraculous manifestations of messianic power—are integrated into a careful, five-fold structure culminating five times in authoritative, didactic discourses—a structure possibly designed deliberately to parallel the five books of Torah or Mosaic law. The first of these discourses is the Sermon on the Mount (chapters 5–7), which outlines Christian ethics and its spiritual premises. Much of the Sermon contrasts traditional teaching with the new Christian version of such teaching. The implication, it might seem, is that a new dispensation has replaced the old Law. At the same time, paradoxically, Jesus insists that the old Law remains in force: "Till heaven and earth pass, one jot or one tittle shall in no wise pass from the law, till all be fulfilled" (Matthew 5:18). The paradox can be partially resolved if we understand "fulfilled" to mean "brought to fruition" rather than "superseded": The Christian code is a living outgrowth of the Law, and it no more negates its origin than the fruit of a tree negates the tree's earlier history of bud and leaf. Accordingly, Matthew also has a strong sense of continuity with the Old Testament, including its iconography, symbolism, and settings. It is no coincidence that the Sermon in Matthew 5–7 takes place on a "mount" (actually, a hill), for this setting bears witness to its awesome earlier archetype, the Mount Sinai where God originally promulgated His teachings. In many ways, Matthew is the most "Jewish" of the gospels, despite the evident tensions between it and traditional Judaism.

FURTHER READING: *Harper's Bible Dictionary,* general ed. Paul J. Achtemeier, 1985, is scholarly but accessible to general readers and contains articles of manageable length on such topics as "Jesus" and "Jerusalem." The 1975 revision, by Allen C. Myers et al., of *The Eerdmans Bible Dictionary,* rep. 1987, is an excellent one-volume comprehensive reference work on the Bible, arranged alphabetically. Another excellent work of reference, containing general articles on the New Testament, introductions, exegesis, and expositions for individual books, is *The Interpreter's Bible,* ed. George A. Buttrick, 12 vols., 1952. Also very helpful is *The Interpreter's Dictionary of the Bible: An Illustrated Encyclopedia,* ed. George A. Buttrick, 4 vols., 1962, and its *Supplementary Volume,* ed. Keith Crim, 1976. For further useful articles, see John E. Steinmueller and Kathryn Sullivan, eds., *Catholic Biblical Encyclopedia: New Testament,* 1950. Werner Jaeger, *Early Christianity and Greek Paideia,* 1961, shows the influence of Greek civilization on Christianity; David Daube, *The New Testament and Rabbinic Judaism,* 1956, explores the relationship between Christianity and Judaism; and Howard Clark Kee, Franklin W. Young, and Karlfried Froehlich, *Understanding the New Testament,* 1957, 3rd ed. 1973, assembles excellent material on both the Hellenistic and the Jewish background to the Gospel narratives. Exegetical treatments of the individual books are given by A. E. Harvey, *The New English Bible: Companion to the New Testament,* 1970; and by Raymond E. Brown, Joseph A. Fitzmyer, and Roland E. Murphy, *The Jerome Biblical Commentary,* 1968. Early Christian beliefs, the expansion of the early Church, and its consolidation are discussed by James L. Price, *Interpreting the New Testament,* 1961. Anthony J. Tambasco, *In the Days of Jesus: The Jewish Background and Unique Teaching of Jesus,* 1983, is a short book capsulizing recent research on the Gospels and placing Jesus in the historical setting. Gerhard Lohfink, *Jesus and Community: The Social Dimension of Christian Faith,* trans. John P. Galvin, 1984, examines the life and mission of Jesus in the context of contemporary Judaism. David E. Aune, *Prophecy in Early Christianity and the Ancient Mediterranean World,* 1983, views the teaching of Jesus in the light of Jewish and Greco-Roman prophetic traditions. *The Literary Guide to the Bible,* eds. Robert Alter and Frank Kermode, 1987, includes introductions to both Testaments and essays on almost all the biblical books; Kermode writes on Matthew.

THE NEW TESTAMENT

King James Version (1611)

from THE GOSPEL ACCORDING TO SAINT MATTHEW

THE SERMON ON THE MOUNT

And seeing the multitudes, he went up into a mountain: and when he was set, his disciples came unto him: and he opened his mouth, and taught them, saying,[1]

Blessed are the poor in spirit: for theirs is the kingdom of heaven.
Blessed are they that mourn: for they shall be comforted.
Blessed are the meek: for they shall inherit the earth.
Blessed are they which do hunger and thirst after righteousness: for they shall be filled.
Blessed are the merciful: for they shall obtain mercy.
Blessed are the pure in heart: for they shall see God.
Blessed are the peacemakers: for they shall be called the children of God.
Blessed are they which are persecuted for righteousness' sake: for theirs is the kingdom of heaven.
Blessed are ye, when men shall revile you, and persecute you, and shall say all manner of evil against you falsely, for my sake. Rejoice, and be exceeding glad: for great is your reward in heaven: for so persecuted they the prophets which were before you. (5:1–12)

Ye are the salt of the earth: but if the salt have lost his savor, wherewith shall it be salted? it is thenceforth good for nothing, but to be cast out, and to be trodden under foot of men. Ye are the light of the world. A city that

[1] The Sermon on the Mount is often regarded as the quintessence of Christian ethical teaching. That it is given from a hill (or "mountain") underlines a basic theme in what follows: the relationship of the new teaching to the law of Moses, also delivered from a mountain (Sinai).

is set on an hill cannot be hid. Neither do men light a candle, and put it under a bushel,[2] but on a candlestick; and it giveth light unto all that are in the house. Let your light so shine before men, that they may see your good works, and glorify your Father which is in heaven. (5:13–16)

Think not that I am come to destroy the law, or the prophets: I am not come to destroy, but to fulfill. For verily I say unto you, Till heaven and earth pass, one jot or one tittle shall in no wise pass from the law, till all be fulfilled. Whosoever therefore shall break one of these least commandments, and shall teach men so, he shall be called the least in the kingdom of heaven: but whosoever shall do and teach them, the same shall be called great in the kingdom of heaven. For I say unto you, That except your righteousness shall exceed the righteousness of the scribes and Pharisees, ye shall in no case enter into the kingdom of heaven. (5:17–20)

Ye have heard that it was said by them of old time, 'Thou shalt not kill'; and 'whosoever shall kill shall be in danger of the judgment':[3] but I say unto you, That whosoever is angry with his brother without a cause shall be in danger of the judgment: and whosoever shall say to his brother, 'Raca,'[4] shall be in danger of the council:[5] but whosoever shall say, 'Thou fool,' shall be in danger of hell fire. Therefore if thou bring thy gift to the altar, and there rememberest that thy brother hath ought against thee; leave there thy gift before the altar, and go thy way; first be reconciled to thy brother, and then come and offer thy gift. Agree with thine adversary quickly, whiles thou art in the way with him;[6] lest at any time the adversary deliver thee to the judge, and the judge deliver thee to the officer, and thou be cast into prison. Verily I say unto thee, Thou shalt by no means come out thence, till thou hast paid the uttermost farthing.[7] (5:21–26)

Ye have heard that it was said by them of old time, 'Thou shalt not commit adultery': but I say unto you, That whosoever looketh on a woman to lust after her hath committed adultery with her already in his heart. And if thy right eye offend thee, pluck it out, and cast it from thee: for it is profitable for thee that one of thy members should perish, and not that thy whole body should be cast into hell. And if thy right hand offend thee, cut it off, and cast it from thee: for it is profitable for thee that one of thy members should perish, and not that thy whole body should be cast into hell. It hath been said, 'Whosoever shall put away his wife, let him give her a writing of divorcement': but I say unto you, That whosoever shall put away his wife, saving for the cause of fornication, causeth her to commit adultery: and whosoever shall marry her that is divorced committeth adultery. (5:27–32)

Again, ye have heard that it hath been said by them of old time, 'Thou shalt not forswear thyself, but shalt perform unto the Lord thine oaths': but I say unto you, Swear not at all; neither by heaven; for it is God's throne: nor by the earth; for it is his footstool: neither by Jerusalem; for it is the city of the great King. Neither shalt thou swear by thy head,[8] because thou canst

[2] A measuring tub for meal.

[3] Prosecutable in court. Jesus goes on to say that even anger should be similarly prosecutable, like actual murder.

[4] Blockhead or idiot. [5] The Sanhedrin, the highest Jewish law court.

[6] On the way to court.

[7] The last penny of the money owed for which one is being sued.

[8] By one's self.

not make one hair white or black. But let your communication be, 'Yea, yea'; 'Nay, nay': for whatsoever is more than these cometh of evil. (5:33–37)

Ye have heard that it hath been said, 'An eye for an eye, and a tooth for a tooth': but I say unto you, That ye resist not evil: but whosoever shall smite thee on thy right cheek, turn to him the other also. And if any man will sue thee at the law, and take away thy coat, let him have thy cloak also. And whosoever shall compel thee to go a mile, go with him twain.[9] Give to him that asketh thee, and from him that would borrow of thee turn not thou away. (5:38–42)

Ye have heard that it hath been said, 'Thou shalt love thy neighbor, and hate thine enemy.'[10] But I say unto you, Love your enemies, bless them that curse you, do good to them that hate you, and pray for them which despitefully use you, and persecute you; that ye may be the children of your Father which is in heaven: for he maketh his sun to rise on the evil and on the good, and sendeth rain on the just and on the unjust. For if ye love them which love you, what reward have ye? do not even the publicans[11] the same? And if ye salute your brethren only, what do ye more than others? do not even the publicans so? Be ye therefore perfect, even as your Father which is in heaven is perfect. (5:43–48)

Take heed that ye do not your alms before men, to be seen of them: otherwise ye have no reward of your Father which is in heaven. Therefore when thou doest thine alms, do not sound a trumpet before thee, as the hypocrites do in the synagogues and in the streets, that they may have glory of men. Verily I say unto you, They have their reward. But when thou doest alms, let not thy left hand know what thy right hand doeth: that thine alms may be in secret: and thy Father which seeth in secret himself shall reward thee openly. (6:1–4)

And when thou prayest, thou shalt not be as the hypocrites are: for they love to pray standing in the synagogues and in the corners of the streets, that they may be seen of men. Verily I say unto you, They have their reward. But thou, when thou prayest, enter into thy closet,[12] and when thou hast shut thy door, pray to thy Father which is in secret; and thy Father which seeth in secret shall reward thee openly. But when ye pray, use not vain repetitions, as the heathen do: for they think that they shall be heard for their much speaking. Be not ye therefore like unto them: for your Father knoweth what things ye have need of, before ye ask him. After this manner therefore pray ye:

Our Father which art in heaven,
Hallowed be thy name.
Thy kingdom come.
Thy will be done
in earth as it is in heaven.

[9] Two.

[10] The Old Testament enjoins love of one's neighbor but not explicitly hatred of enemies. That was, however, a popular inference from the former.

[11] Tax collectors, a generally despised group; elsewhere in the Gospels they are usually mentioned more sympathetically.

[12] Private room. Jesus is not condemning, however, congregational prayer in the temple or synagogue.

Give us this day our daily bread.
And forgive us our debts,
as we forgive our debtors.[13]
And lead us not into temptation,
but deliver us from evil:[14]
For thine is the kingdom, and the power, and the glory, for ever.
Amen.

For if ye forgive men their trespasses, your heavenly Father will also forgive you: but if ye forgive not men their trespasses, neither will your Father forgive your trespasses. (6:5–15)

Moreover when ye fast, be not, as the hypocrites, of a sad countenance: for they disfigure their faces, that they may appear unto men to fast. Verily I say unto you, They have their reward. But thou, when thou fastest, anoint thine head, and wash thy face;[15] that thou appear not unto men to fast, but unto thy Father which is in secret: and thy Father, which seeth in secret, shall reward thee openly. (6:16–18)

Lay not up for yourselves treasures upon earth, where moth and rust doth corrupt, and where thieves break through and steal: but lay up for yourselves treasures in heaven, where neither moth nor rust doth corrupt, and where thieves do not break through nor steal: for where your treasure is, there will your heart be also. The light of the body is the eye: if therefore thine eye be single,[16] thy whole body shall be full of light. But if thine eye be evil, thy whole body shall be full of darkness. If therefore the light that is in thee be darkness, how great is that darkness! (6:19–23)

No man can serve two masters: for either he will hate the one, and love the other; or else he will hold to the one, and despise the other. Ye cannot serve God and mammon.[17] Therefore I say unto you, Take no thought for your life, what ye shall eat, or what ye shall drink; nor yet for your body, what ye shall put on. Is not the life more than meat, and the body than raiment? Behold the fowls of the air: for they sow not, neither do they reap, nor gather into barns; yet your heavenly Father feedeth them. Are ye not much better than they? Which of you by taking thought can add one cubit[18] unto his stature? And why take ye thought for raiment? Consider the lilies of the field, how they grow; they toil not, neither do they spin: and yet I say unto you, That even Solomon in all his glory was not arrayed like one of these. Wherefore, if God so clothe the grass of the field, which today is, and tomorrow is cast into the oven,[19] shall he not much more clothe you, O ye of little faith? Therefore take no thought, saying, 'What shall we eat?' or, 'What shall we drink?' or, 'Wherewithal shall we be clothed?' (for after all these things do the Gentiles seek:) for your heavenly Father knoweth that ye have need of all these things. But seek ye first the kingdom of God, and

[13] The words *debts* and *debtors* can be rendered as, respectively, the wrongs we have committed and those that have been committed against us.

[14] In most of the earliest manuscripts, the Lord's Prayer ends here.

[15] Anointing and washing were part of preparing for a banquet.

[16] Healthy, as opposed to the "evil" (diseased) eye.

[17] Material possessions and money. [18] About 20 inches.

[19] As fuel.

his righteousness; and all these things shall be added unto you. Take therefore no thought for the morrow: for the morrow shall take thought for the things of itself. Sufficient unto the day is the evil thereof.[20] (6:24–34)

Judge not, that ye be not judged. For with what judgment ye judge, ye shall be judged: and with what measure ye mete, it shall be measured to you again. And why beholdest thou the mote[21] that is in thy brother's eye, but considerest not the beam that is in thine own eye? Or how wilt thou say to thy brother, 'Let me pull out the mote out of thine eye'; and, behold, a beam is in thine own eye? Thou hypocrite, first cast out the beam out of thine own eye; and then shalt thou see clearly to cast out the mote out of thy brother's eye. (7:1–5)

Give not that which is holy unto the dogs, neither cast ye your pearls before swine, lest they trample them under their feet, and turn again and rend you. (7:6)

Ask, and it shall be given you; seek, and ye shall find; knock, and it shall be opened unto you: for every one that asketh receiveth; and he that seeketh findeth; and to him that knocketh it shall be opened. Or what man is there of you, whom if his son ask bread, will he give him a stone? Or if he ask a fish, will he give him a serpent? If ye then, being evil, know how to give good gifts unto your children, how much more shall your Father which is in heaven give good things to them that ask him? (7:7–11)

Therefore all things whatsoever ye would that men should do to you, do ye even so to them: for this is the law and the prophets. (7:12)

Enter ye in at the strait gate: for wide is the gate, and broad is the way, that leadeth to destruction, and many there be which go in thereat: because strait is the gate, and narrow is the way, which leadeth unto life, and few there be that find it. (7:13–14)

Beware of false prophets,[22] which come to you in sheep's clothing, but inwardly they are ravening wolves. Ye shall know them by their fruits. Do men gather grapes of thorns, or figs of thistles? Even so every good tree bringeth forth good fruit; but a corrupt tree bringeth forth evil fruit. A good tree cannot bring forth evil fruit, neither can a corrupt tree bring forth good fruit. Every tree that bringeth not forth good fruit is hewn down and cast into the fire. Wherefore by their fruits ye shall know them. (7:15–20)

Not every one that saith unto me, 'Lord, Lord,' shall enter into the kingdom of heaven; but he that doeth the will of my Father which is in heaven. Many will say to me in that day, 'Lord, Lord, have we not prophesied in thy name? and in thy name have cast out devils? and in thy name done many wonderful works?' And then will I profess unto them, 'I never knew you: depart from me, ye that work iniquity.' (7:21–23)

Therefore whosoever heareth these sayings of mine, and doeth them, I will liken him unto a wise man, which built his house upon a rock: and the rain descended, and the floods came, and the winds blew, and beat upon that house; and it fell not: for it was founded upon a rock. And every one

[20] Each day has anxieties enough of its own; one need not add to them worries about the future.

[21] A tiny speck of wood, as contrasted with a "beam," or large board.

[22] The caution against false prophets and that in the following passage against those who say "Lord, Lord" are less applicable to Jesus' own time than to the problems the early Church faced a half-century later (when Matthew was written).

that heareth these sayings of mine, and doeth them not, shall be likened unto a foolish man, which built his house upon the sand: and the rain descended, and the floods came, and the winds blew, and beat upon that house; and it fell: and great was the fall of it. (7:24–27)

And it came to pass, when Jesus had ended these sayings, the people were astonished at his doctrine: for he taught them as one having authority, and not as the scribes.[23] (7:28–29)

Greek and Latin Lyric Poetry

(Seventh Century B.C to Second Century A.D.)

Just as Homer invented the epic for the Western world and Aeschylus, Sophocles, Euripides, and Aristophanes invented drama, so a number of Greek and Roman poets invented a form of lyric poetry practiced for a thousand years or so. Modern lyric poets do not merely follow classical conventions, of course, any more than novelists march in step with Homer or playwrights reproduce Greek tragedy. Modern western lyric poetry draws on the indigenous traditions of its respective national literatures as well. But the Greeks and the Romans created a powerful set of forms and practices in poetry, as in epic and drama, to which more recent writers, including those of the twentieth century, have periodically turned for inspiration.

The study of Greek lyric poetry takes us back to the etymological meaning of lyric: "sung to the lyre" (a stringed, harp-like instrument). Greek poems are performance texts, meant for the ears rather than the eyes, at least in the early centuries of its recorded history. Historians now believe that early Greek poetry belongs to a tradition that sketches back at least to the Bronze Age civilization of the Mycenaeans, which ended about 1100 B.C. and perhaps back as far as 2000 B.C., the age of the Indian Vedas whose rhythms are echoed in the Aeolic meters of Sappho and Alcaeus. The development of an alphabet for Greek in the eighth century did not coincide with the beginning of Greek poetry; it merely permitted the written transcription of poems from a centuries-old tradition.

When we read Greek poetry, then, we should imagine not a solitary artist bent over his or her manuscript but a singer performing before a group, whether a few friends or a large crowd assembled in a stadium. Performance considerations determined the main division in Greek poetry between solo songs and choric songs. Some poetry, such as that of Sappho, was clearly meant for solo singing to the accompaniment of a lyre, while other poetry, like that of Pindar, was meant for choral singing before a substantial audience.

Within this broad distinction, the Greeks recognized particular forms. Elegiac poetry was written in dactyls that alternated lines of six feet (hexameters) with lines of five feet (pentameter); each line ended with an extra

[23] He did not teach with a cautious conformity to tradition, like the scribes, but rather like the prophets.

stressed syllable. It did not necessarily deal with death, as modern elegies do, but nevertheless had relatively lofty, dignified subject matter. It was accompanied not by the lyre but by the *aulus,* an oboe-like wind instrument. (An *aulus*-player played two at a time.) Iambic poems, as the term implies, used iambic feet, usually in trimeter lines. Their subject matter was less formal and more personal, and they were not sung but recited. "Melic" poetry merely meant "musical" poetry. (The Greek *melos* could mean a melody, the sound of a musical instrument, or the human voice.) Melic poetry was made up of solo lyrics; it was sung to the lyre and corresponds most closely to what we call lyric poetry: short, personal, and song-like.

Lyric poetry was amateur poetry for the Greeks, at least in the early days. Epics were performed by professional bards, and when drama came along it, too, was performed by professionals. But all cultivated people were expected to be able to compose and perform lyric poetry. In Athens at least, and presumably other places as well, after-dinner singing was common. A myrtle branch was circulated, and each guest was expected to take the lyre and perform an original poem when the branch was passed to him. (Such drinking parties were generally all male.) A distinction was sometimes drawn between such ordinary party pieces and the work of the more talented, but poetry remained for a long time a participatory art with no separation between performers and audiences.

The watershed mark for classical poetry was the spread of writing in the seventh century B.C. Once poems were written down, a steady move began that loosened the link between an oral culture in which poetry and performance were almost synonymous and a written one in which that link was broken. The link still held in the fourth century. Plato, in *Ion,* describes performances of epic poetry at religious festivals before audiences of twenty thousand or so, and in the *Republic* he describes lyric poetry (*melos*) as made up not only of words (*logos*) but also of melody (*harmonia*) and rhythm (*rhuthmos*). Aristotle lists the same elements in the *Poetics.* Neither Plato nor Aristotle seems to know much about music, and their comments on lyric poetry concentrate almost exclusively on the words. The Hellenistic scholars who tried to create an archive of the literature of Greece's golden age completed the process; their editions presented the poems as words on a page with no acknowledgment of their musical and performative dimensions. As one scholar has commented, they filtered out the *melos* from the melic poets.

To try to recover the musicality of Greek poetry after two millennia is a daunting task. Despite strenuous efforts at recovery, we know almost nothing about Greek music; it remains, in Keats's words, "unheard melodies." But at least we can read the poems aloud and imagine them with our ears and vocal cords as well as with our eyes.

Early Greek poetry flourished especially in four regions, each identified with a certain kind of poetry. Ionia (across the Aegean Sea from Greece, on the western coast of present-day Turkey, along with the islands of Chios, Samos, and the Cyclades) was thought to be the place where Homer lived and wrote; the dactyllic hexameter, the most important of all Greek verse forms, was said to have originated there. Lesbos, an island in the Aegean off the northwest coast of Turkey, was famed for the brilliance of its solo lyrics, largely because of the reputations of Sappho and Alcaeus. Sparta, on the southern tip of the Greek peninsula, was famous for its choral lyrics, performed in competitions at annual festivals; its principal poet was Alcman (second half of the seventh century B.C.). Boeotia, in central Greece, was honored as the home of Hesiod who, around the beginning of the seventh century, wrote his Homerically inflected works of cultural lore, the origin and history of the Greek gods (the *Theogony*), the history of the Greek heroic families (the *Ehoiai*), and the rules of ordinary life (*Works and Days*).

The two centuries between about 650 B.C. and about 450 B.C. are sometimes called the Lyric Age of Greece, when lyric poetry flourished most vigorously. The fifth century saw the precipitous decline of both solo and choral lyrics and the simultaneous rise of tragedy, which subsumed some of the earlier forms within its structure, especially the choric ode. The fourth century is remembered for its prose, especially the works of Plato and Aristotle, and the poetry of the Hellenistic Age (ca. 300–31 B.C.) is remembered principally for its pallid imitations of earlier glories. By the time Greece fell to Rome in 31 B.C., the torch of the Greek poetic tradition had long since been passed to Rome.

In poetry, Rome's relation to Greece was as complex and troubled as in other areas. The career of the first significant Roman writer, Quintus Ennius (239–169 B.C.) exemplifies the divided energies of early Latin literature. On the one hand, he produced a great body of tragedies, comedies, didactic poems, and epigrams in the Greek manner; on the other, his major work was the *Annals*, an epic chronicle of Roman history from the beginning down to his own day. Both the impulse to pay homage to the superior culture of Greece and the contrary one to glorify his own country were to reappear many times in Latin literature.

It appears, for example, in the comedies of Plautus (250–184 B.C.) and Terence (ca. 185–ca. 159 B.C.). Plautus adapted a number of the plays of the Greek New Comedy into Latin but incorporated in the process elements of his own rough native tradition, producing a successful, energetic kind of farce. A generation later, Terence wrote a series of comedies similarly based on Greek and Roman traditions but blended them and polished them so as to appeal to a learned, elite audience. Similar meldings of Greek and Roman elements directed to a sophisticated audience appear in the long didactic poem *On the Nature of Things* by Lucretius (ca. 99–ca. 55 B.C.) and in the poems of Catullus (ca. 84–c. 54 B.C.). The fusion of Greek and Roman elements that troubled early Latin poetry was triumphantly achieved by Virgil (70–19 B.C.) in the *Aeneid*, which in its blend of Greek elements (epic form and stylistic polish) and Roman ones (patriotism and didacticism) in effect created the myth of Roman national culture.

The six poets represented here, three Greek and three Roman, are selected not only for their chronological spread but also for their range of lyric genres, which have cast a long shadow through western poetry.

FURTHER READING: Good commentaries on Greek lyric poetry are David A. Campbell, *Greek Lyric Poetry*, 2nd ed. 1981; and Anthony J. Podlecki, *The Early Greek Poets and Their Times*, 1984. For Latin lyricists, see R. O. A. M. Lyne, *The Latin Love Poets from Catullus to Horace*, 1980; and Jasper Griffin, *Latin Poets and Roman Life*, 1985. Women poets of both Greece and Rome are given attention in Jane McIntosh Snyder, *The Woman and the Lyre: Women Writers in Classical Greece and Rome*, 1988. On individual poets, see Anne Pippin Burnett, *Three Archaic Poets: Archilochus, Alcaeus, and Sappho*, 1983; Richard H. A. Jenkyns, *Three Classical Poets: Sappho, Catullus, Juvenal*, 1982; D.

S. Carne-Ross, *Pindar*, 1985; John K. Newman, *Roman Catullus*, 1990; David West, *Reading Horace*, 1967; and Margaret Hubbard, *Propertius*, 1974.

Sappho

(Early Sixth Century B.C.)

The poems of Sappho provide our best window on the solo songs, or monodies, of early Greek poetry. Sappho's life is encrusted by legend, but it is clear that she lived on the island of Lesbos, that she was surrounded by a circle of young female companions, that she was a skilled performer on the lyre, and that she wrote passionate, homoerotically-tinged lyric poetry. The textual history of Sappho's poetry is complex. She may not have written her poems down; the earliest manuscripts date from centuries after her death and seem to be derived from oral transmission. Her lesbianism made her anathema to the medieval church, which burned many of the manuscripts of her poems. Renaissance scholars attempted to recover her work by assembling quotations from it in other Greek and Roman writings, but the results were pitifully scanty. And then, incredibly, in 1879 new poems by Sappho were discovered in an ancient rubbish heap in Egypt, and further manuscripts came to light in a series of archaeological digs in the 1890s. Papyrus scrolls upon which the poems had been copied had been torn into strips, lengthwise, and used as mummy wrappings. Others had been used to stuff mummified crocodiles. As a result of this shredding, the new texts of Sappho, while valuable, include many partial lines. Reconstructing what Sappho wrote involves a great deal of guesswork. We now have about seven hundred intelligible lines of Sappho's voluminous verse.

Sappho left her mark on Greek prosody. A "sapphic stanza" consists of three "sapphic lines" (dactylic pentameter) followed by an "adonic" (dactylic dimeter). It is not well adapted to English, and the present translator has not attempted to reproduce it.

POEMS[1]

30

We drink your health

Lucky bridegroom!
Now the wedding you
asked for is over

[1]Translated by Mary Barnard.

and your wife is the 5
girl you asked for;
she's a bride who is

charming to look at,
with eyes as soft as
honey, and a face 10

that Love has lighted
with his own beauty.
Aphrodite[1] has surely

outdone herself in
doing honor to you! 15

34

Lament for a maidenhead

FIRST VOICE
Like a quince-apple
ripening on a top
branch in a tree top

not once noticed by 5
harvesters or if
not unnoticed, not reached

SECOND VOICE
Like a hyacinth in
the mountains, trampled
by shepherds until 10
only a purple stain
remains on the ground

37

You[1] know the place: then

Leave Crete and come to us
waiting where the grove is
pleasantest, by precincts

sacred to you; incense 5
smokes on the altar, cold
streams murmur through the

[1] Goddess of love, as well as of the sea and of beauty, flowers, and seasons.
[1] The poem is addressed to Aphrodite (the "Cyprian" of line 14).

apple branches, a young
rose thicket shades the ground
and quivering leaves pour 10

down deep sleep; in meadows
where horses have grown sleek
among spring flowers, dill

scents the air. Queen! Cyprian!
Fill our gold cups with love 15
stirred into clear nectar

38

Prayer to my lady of Paphos[1]

Dapple-throned Aphrodite,
eternal daughter of God,
snare-knitter! Don't, I beg you,

cow my heart with grief! Come, 5
as once when you heard my far-
off cry and, listening, stepped

from your father's house to your
gold car, to yoke the pair whose
beautiful thick-feathered wings[2] 10

oaring down mid-air from heaven
carried you to light swiftly
on dark earth; then, blissful one,

smiling your immortal smile
you asked, What ailed me now that 15
made me call you again? What

was it that my distracted
heart most wanted? "Whom has
Persuasion to bring round now

to your love? Who, Sappho, is 20
unfair to you? For, let her
run, she will soon run after;

[1]Aphrodite, who was born of the sea foam and washed ashore at Paphos.
[2]The sparrows that drew Aphrodite's chariot.

if she won't accept gifts, she
will one day give them; and if
he won't love you—she soon will 25

love, although unwillingly. . . ."
If ever—come now! Relieve
this intolerable pain!

What my heart most hopes will
happen, make happen; you yourself join forces on my side! 30

39

He is more than a hero

He is a god in my eyes—
the man who is allowed
to sit beside you—he

who listens intimately 5
to the sweet murmur of
your voice, the enticing

laughter that makes my own
heart beat fast. If I meet
you suddenly, I can't 10

speak—my tongue is broken;
a thin flame runs under
my skin; seeing nothing,

hearing only my own ears
drumming, I drip with sweat; 15
trembling shakes my body

and I turn paler than
dry grass. At such times
death isn't far from me

40

Yes, Atthis,[1] you may be sure

Even in Sardis

Anactoria will think often of us

[1] Atthis and Anactoria were two of the girls in Sappho's circle.

of the life we shared here, when you seemed
the Goddess incarnate 5
to her and your singing pleased her best

Now among Lydian women she in her
turn stands first as the red-
fingered moon rising at sunset takes

precedence over stars around her; 10
her light spreads equally
on the salt sea and fields thick with bloom

Delicious dew pours down to freshen
roses, delicate thyme
and blossoming sweet clover; she wanders 15

aimlessly, thinking of gentle
Atthis, her heart hanging
heavy with longing in her little breast

She shouts aloud, Come! we know it;
thousand-eared night repeats that cry 20
across the sea shining between us

41

To an army wife, in Sardis:

Some say a cavalry corps,
some infantry, some, again,
will maintain that the swift oars

of our fleet are the finest 5
sight on dark earth; but I say
that whatever one loves, is.

This is easily proved: did
not Helen[1]—she who had scanned
the flower of the world's manhood— 10

choose as first among men one
who laid Troy's honor in ruin?
warped to his will, forgetting

[1]Helen of Troy, whose choice of Paris as a lover and subsequent flight with him to Troy began the Trojan War.

love due her own blood, her own
child, she wandered far with him. 15
So Anactoria, although you

being far away forget us,
the dear sound of your footstep
and light glancing in your eyes

would move me more than glitter 20
of Lydian horse or armored
tread of mainland infantry

42

I have had not one word from her

Frankly I wish I were dead.
When she left, she wept

a great deal; she said to
me, "This parting must be 5
endured, Sappho. I go unwillingly."

I said, "Go, and be happy
but remember (you know
well) whom you leave shackled by love

"If you forget me, think 10
of our gifts to Aphrodite
and all the loveliness that we shared

"all the violet tiaras,
braided rosebuds, dill and
crocus twined around your young neck 15

"myrrh poured on your head
and on soft mats girls with
all that they most wished for beside them

"while no voices chanted
choruses without ours, 20
no woodlot bloomed in spring without song . . ."

43

It was you, Atthis, who said

"Sappho, if you will not get
up and let us look at you
I shall never love you again!

"Get up, unleash your suppleness, 5
lift off your Chian nightdress[1]
and, like a lily leaning into

"a spring, bathe in the water.
Cleis[2] is bringing your best
purple frock and the yellow 10

"tunic down from the clothes chest;
you will have a cloak thrown over
you and flowers crowning your hair . . .

"Praxinoa, my child, will you please
roast nuts for our breakfast? One 15
of the gods is being good to us:

"today we are going at last
into Mitylene, our favorite
city, with Sappho, loveliest

"of its women; she will walk 20
among us like a mother with
all her daughters around her

"when she comes home from exile . . ."

But you forget everything

97

I have often asked you
not to come now
Hermes,[1] Lord, you
who lead the ghosts
home: 5
But this time
I am not happy; I
want to die, to see
the moist lotus open
along Acheron[2] 10

[1]From the island of Chios, off the coast of Asia Minor.
[2]Sappho's daughter.
[1]The god who guided the dead to the underworld.
[2]The river of Death.

Pindar
(518–438 B.C.)

The poetry of Pindar exemplifies another genre of Greek lyric and another function it served in Greek culture. A native of Thebes, in mainland Greece, Pindar wrote in a number of forms. Ancient collections of his works included hymns, paeans, dithyrambs, processional songs, maiden-songs, encomia, and dirges (all forms of choric songs). His surviving works, however, are all epinician odes, or victory songs, written to honor the victors of athletic events at the various games that were held around Greece, at Nemea in the Peloponnese, at the Isthmus of Corinth, at Delphi, and at Olympia. The Pindaric odes are thus classified as Nemean, Isthmian, Pythian, or Olympian. The odes, written to be sung by a chorus on the occasion of the victor's return home, are structured as series of parallel strophes (or stanzas) or in triads of stanzas, each made up of a strophe, an antistrophe, and an epode (or, in the terminology of the present translator, turn, counterturn, and stand). Pindar's odes are heavily mythic; in most of them he retells a myth, inserting moral maxims, praise of the gods, and accounts of the victor's achievements.

"Olympian I," the ode included here, is an interesting example of Pindar's practice. The myth he chooses to use in celebrating the victory of Hiero of Syracuse in 476 B.C. in the race for single horse is that of Pelops, the hero who was said to have founded the Olympian games (and who gave his name to Peloponnesus, the main land mass of southern Greece). The traditional form of the story is that Pelops's father Tantalus, king of Lydia, dared to invite the gods to dine at his table. Rashly wanting to test the gods' perception and wisdom, he killed his son Pelops and served his flesh to the gods. The only one deceived was Demeter, god of the harvest; she swallowed Pelops's shoulder. Enraged, the other gods brought Pelops back to life, providing an ivory shoulder to replace the one Demeter had eaten. They condemned Tantalus to eternal punishment in Hades, forever "tantalized" by food and drink that receded whenever he reached for it.

Pindar rejects this barbaric myth and constructs an alternative one; "Pelops," he writes, "I will tell your story / differently from the men of old." In Pindar's version, the story begins with Poseidon's abduction of Pelops to be his lover. When he could not be found, neighbors started a rumor that the gods had cooked and eaten him. Tantalus displeased the gods not by serving his son as food but by stealing ambrosia and nectar, the food and drink of the gods, to serve to mortals. For this they returned Pelops to mortality and condemned his father to lie forever beneath a tottering boulder. (Pindar explains Pelops's famous ivory shoulder by having him born with it; it was there when Klotho, one of the three Fates who presided over births, took him out of the "pure cauldron.") He also adds an episode from Pelops's later history, his winning of Hippodamea. Her father, King Oenomaus of Pisa, did not want her to marry and so decreed that all her suitors had to compete with him in a chariot race. If a suitor won, he could have the hand of Hippodamea; if not, he was killed. Pelops, with the help of Posidon, won the race. He married Hippodamea and became king, since Oenomaus had been killed in the race.

Pindar's use of the (revised) Pelops story is graceful and ingenious. It allows him to connect Hiero with a heroic horseman of the past and to provide hope that divine power will help him achieve further honor: victory in the four-horse chariot race. At the same time, it allows him to warn Hiero of the dangers of *hubris,* through the story of Pelops's father, Tantalus.

The Pindaric ode has inspired a great many poems in modern European languages. In some, the Pindaric form of strophe, antistrophe, and epode has been followed. In others, "Pindaric" has been taken to mean free and unstructured, as in Wordsworth's "Ode on Imitations of Immortality."

ODES

OLYMPIAN I: HIERON OF SYRACUSE, RACE FOR SINGLE HORSE, 476 B.C.[1]

Turn 1

Water is preeminent and gold, like a fire
burning in the night, outshines
all possessions that magnify men's pride.[2]
But if, my soul, you yearn
to celebrate great games, 5
look no further
for another star
shining through the deserted ether
brighter than the sun, or for a contest
mightier than Olympia—
where the song 10
has taken its coronal
design of glory, plaited
in the minds of poets
as they come, calling on Zeus' name,
to the rich radiant hall of Hieron 15

Counterturn 1

who wields the scepter of justice in Sicily,
reaping the prime of every distinction.
And he delights in the flare of music,
the brightness of song circling
his table from man to man. 20
then take the Dorian lyre
down from its peg
if the beauty of Pisa[3]
and of Pherenikos[4]

[1]Translated by Frank Nisetich.

[2]The theme that in every sphere there is one thing that is preeminent runs throughout the poems. Water is the best of the elements, while among valuable possessions gold shines like a fire in the night. Similarly, a victory at Olympus is the greatest one.

[3]The district where Olympia was located.

[4]The name of Hieron's horse; it means "victory bringer."

somehow 25
cast your mind
under a gracious spell,
when by the stream
of Alpheos, keeping his flanks
ungrazed by the spur, he sped 30
and put his lord in the embrace of power—

Stand 1

Syracusan knight and king, blazoned
with glory in the land of Pelops:
Pelops, whom earth-cradling Poseidon loved,
since Klotho had taken him 35
out of the pure cauldron, his ivory shoulder
gleaming in the hearth-light.
Yes! marvels are many, stories
starting from mortals somehow
stretch truth to deception 40
woven cunningly on the loom of lies.

Turn 2

Grace, the very one who fashions every delight
for mortal men, by lending her sheen
to what is unbelievable, often makes it believed.
But the days to come 45
are the wisest witness.
It is proper for a man
to speak well of the gods—
the blame will be less.
Pelops, I will tell your story 50
differently from the men of old.
Your father Tantalos
had invited the gods to banquet
in his beloved Sipylos, providing
a stately feast in return 55
for the feast they had given him.
It was then Poseidon seized you,

Counterturn 2

overwhelmed in his mind with desire, and swept you
on golden mares to Zeus' glorious palace
on Olympos, where, at another time, Ganymede came also 60
for the same passion in Zeus.
But after you had disappeared
and searchers
again and again
returned to your mother 65
without you, then one of the neighbors,
invidious, whispered
that the gods had sliced you
limb by limb into the fury
of boiling water, 70
and then they passed

morsels of your flesh
    around the table, and ate them.

Stand 2 No! I cannot call any of the blessed gods
    a savage: I stand apart. 75
Disaster has often claimed the slanderer.
If ever the watchlords of Olympos
honored a man, this was Tantalos.
    But he could not digest
his great bliss—in his fullness he earned the doom 80
that the father poised above him, the looming
    boulder which, in eternal
distraction, he strains to heave from his brow.

Turn 3 Such is the misery upon him, a fourth affliction
    among three others, because he robbed 85
the immortals—their nektar and ambrosia,
    which had made him deathless,
        he stole and gave
            to his drinking companions.
        But a man who hopes 90
    to hide his doings from the gods
  is deluded.
For this they hurled his son Pelops
                back among the short-lived
generations of men. 95
But when he grew
toward the time of bloom
  and black down curled on his cheeks,
    he thought of a marriage there for his seeking—

Counterturn 3 to win from her Pisan father the girl Hippodameia. 100
    Going down by the dim sea,
alone in the dark, he called on the god
    of the trident, loud pounding
        Poseidon, who appeared
            and stood close by. 105
        "If in any way,"
    Pelops said to him,
  "the gifts of Aphrodite
count in my favor,
            shackle the bronze spar of Oinomaos, 110
bring me on the swiftest chariot
to Elis, and put me
within the reach
  of power, for he has slain
    thirteen suitors now, and so he delays 115

Stand 3 his daughter's marriage. Great danger
    does not come upon
the spineless man, and yet, if we must die,

why squat in the shadows, coddling a bland
old age, with no nobility, for nothing? 120
As for me, I will undertake this exploit.
And you—I beseech you: let me achieve it."
He spoke, and his words found fulfillment:
the god made him glow with gifts—
a golden chariot and winged horses never weary. 125

Turn 4

He tore the strength from Oinomaos and took
the maiden to his bed.
She bore him six sons, leaders of the people,
intent on prowess.
Now in the bright blood rituals 130
Pelops has his share, reclining
by the ford of Alpheos.
Men gather at his tomb, near the crowded altar.
The glory of the Olympiads
shoots its rays afar 135
in his races, where speed
and strength are matched
in the bruise of toil.
But the victor,
for the rest of his life, 140
enjoys days of contentment,

Counterturn 4

as far as contests can assure them.
A single day's blessing
is the highest good a mortal knows.
I must crown him now 145
to the horseman's tune,
in Aiolian rhythms,
for I believe
the shimmering folds of my song
shall never embrace 150
a host more lordly in power
or perception of beauty.
Hieron, a god is overseer
to your ambitions, keeping watch,
cherishing them as his own. 155
If he does not abandon you soon,
still sweeter the triumph I hope

Stand 4

will fall to your speeding chariot,
and may I be the one to praise it,
riding up the sunny Hill of Kronos! 160
The Muse is tempering her mightiest arrow for me.
Men are great in various ways, but in kingship
the ultimate crest is attained.
Peer no farther into the beyond.
For the time we have, may you continue to walk on high, 165
and may I for as long consort with victors,
conspicuous for my skill among Greeks everywhere.

Theocritus

(Third Century B.C.)

Theocritus (third century B.C.) was an Alexandrian poet in two senses: He spent the most productive part of his career in Alexandria and his work is marked by the characteristics of the Alexandrian age (ca. 300–31 B.C.). Born in Syracuse, a Greek city in Sicily, he spent the early part of his life on Cos, an island in the southeastern Aegean Sea. In his twenties he moved to the large Greek city of Alexandria, in Egypt. The conquests of Alexander the Great in the fourth century B.C. had extended Greek power and the Greek language into the Near and Middle East, where Greek cities sprang up, the largest being Alexandria. Greek poets of the Alexandrian (or Hellenistic) period sought to carry on the poetic tradition by using the ancient forms. On the other hand, the social conditions and cultural practices—the festivals and ceremonies—that had produced those forms no longer existed. As a result, Greek Alexandrian poetry often seems polished but bloodless, finished exercises in nostalgia.

The only original poetic genre practiced by the Alexandrian poets was the pastoral, of which Theocritus was the acknowledged master. Pastoral, or bucolic, poetry is poetry about shepherds. Its aim, though, is not the realistic treatment of rural life, but the evocation of a stylized, idealized world of natural innocence. Thelma Sargent, Theocritus's translator, sums up the appeal of pastoral in this way: "The world of shepherds and music and love and beauty struck a responsive chord in the human heart that has reverberated down through the ages—a longing for escape, for the simple life close to nature, free of the complexities of civilization and the tribulations of daily life."

Theocritus's reputation rests on a single collection of thirty poems, the *Idylls.* (*Idyll* simply means "short poem" in Greek.) Eight of the thirty are probably not by Theocritus, and of the remaining twenty-two, not all are pastorals. But it was the pastorals that established a poetic idiom that has persisted through the later literary history of the West, imitated by Virgil in the *Eclogues* and by Dante in his Latin idylls, adopted by Shakespeare in *As You Like It* and other plays, by Edmund Spenser in his *Shepheards Calender,* and by Milton in "Lycidas," and leaving its mark even on such modern poets as Robert Frost and Seamus Heaney.

IDYLL I: SONG OF THYRSIS[1]

THYRSIS

Sweet is the whisper of wind as it plays in that pine
Near the spring, O goatherd, and sweet, too, is your piping;
In a contest with Pan[2] you would win second prize.

[1]Translated by Thelma Sargent.

[2]God of woods, fields, and flocks. He was depicted as having a human torso, with goat's legs, horns, and ears.

If he took the horned he-goat, you'd win the dam,
But should his prize be the dam, the kid would be yours, 5
And a kid before it gives milk is delectable eating.

GOATHERD

Sweeter, O shepherd, pours forth the song from your lips
Than the water tumbling down from those rocks overhead.
Should the Muses bear away a ewe as their gift,
The cosset lamb would be your prize; but if the lamb 10
Should content them, you next would be awarded the ewe.

THYRSIS

By the nymphs, goatherd, would it please you to sit down
On this sloping hillock here where the tamarisks grow
And play your syrinx,[3] while I meanwhile look after your goats?

GOATHERD

Custom forbids, O shepherd, that at noontime we play on the
syrinx, 15
For we go in fear of great Pan. At this time of day,
Weary, he rests from the chase. He has an irascible temper,
And bitter gall perches forever over his nostrils.
But you, Thyrsis, sing of the sorrows of Daphnis[4]
And are skilled in the pastoral song of the Muses. 20
Let us sit down here under the elm tree facing Priapos[5]
And the nymphs of the spring, where stand the oaks
And the bench of the shepherds, and if you sing as you did
When vying in song once with Chromis of Libya,
I will let you have a twin-bearing goat for three milkings, 25
Who, besides feeding two kids, yields up to two milk pails,
And a deep ivywood drinking cup coated with sweet-scented wax,
Two-handled and newly wrought, and from the chisel still fragrant.[6]
Ivy twines high along the lip of the cup,
And scattered among the ivy leaves are helichryse[7] blossoms, 30
And the spiraling tendrils below are glorious with golden fruit.
Inside the cup is a woman, carved as by one of the gods,
Wearing a peplos[8] and headband; two men stand beside her
With fine long hair, contending with speeches, first one,
Then the other in turn, but they cannot kindle her heart. 35
At one moment, laughing, she looks on this man,
The next moment turns her mind to the other, while they,
Long heavy-eyed from love's suffering, labor in vain.
Near them is engraved a fisherman on a rough rock,

[3]The panpipe, a series of pipes or reeds bound together and played by blowing across the open ends. Different pitches are produced by cutting the reeds to different lengths or stopping them with wax at different points.

[4]A legendary Sicilian shepherd who was credited with the invention of pastoral poetry. His sorrows were that a naiad to whom he had been unfaithful punished him with blindness. Hermes changed him to a god.

[5]God of male sexuality as well as of vineyards, gardens, bees, herds, and fish.

[6]The detailed description of the wine cup that follows is a familiar setpiece in Greek pastoral poetry. Compare Keats's "Ode on a Grecian Urn."

[7]Marigold or a similar flower.

[8]A woman's full outer garment.

An old man who visibly strains as he gathers up 40
His great net for a cast, like a man worn out with hard work.
You might say he was fishing with all the strength of his limbs
From the swollen sinews that stand out all over his neck,
But gray-haired though he is, his strength is that of a youth.
And not far away from this seaworn old man is a vineyard 45
Heavily laden with ripening clusters of grapes,
Where on a dry-stone wall a small boy sits on guard.
Two foxes flank him: one prowls up and down the vine rows,
Pilfering the already ripe fruit, while the other
Directs all her cunning toward the boy's wallet, and vows not to
rest 50
Until she has left him lean fare for his breakfast.
But he, plaiting with asphodel[9] stalks a fine cage for locusts,
Fits in a reed and thinks not at all of his wallet
Or of the vines, so great is his joy in his weaving.
And all over the cup is spread the wavy acanthus— 55
A sight for goatherds! The marvelous thing will amaze you!
I gave the Calydnian[10] boatman a she-goat in payment
And a great wheel of white cheese. Never so far
Has it been touched by my lips, but still lies unsullied.
It would be a pleasure indeed, my friend, to give it to you 60
If you would sing for me that beautiful song.
I do not mock you. Come, sir, for to hoard it
Will not serve you at all in Hades' realm where all is forgotten.

THYRSIS

Begin the pastoral song, dear Muses, begin the song.

Thyrsis of Etna am I, and this is the sweet voice of Thyrsis. 65
Where were you, nymphs, where were you when Daphnis was
wasting?
In Tempe, the lovely vale of Peneois, or off on the slopes of the
Pindos?
For not then did you haunt the great stream of the river Anapos
Or Etna's high peak or the holy waters of Acis.[11]

Begin the pastoral song, dear Muses, begin the song. 70

For him the jackals lamented, for him the wolves howled,
For him, dead, the lion mourned in the oak wood.

Begin the pastoral song, dear Muses, begin the song.

Around him cows without number and bulls made lament,
Many a heifer and many a calf too bewailed him. 75

[9]A flowering plant, possibly the narcissus. The asphodel, like the helichryse and the acanthus (a prickly flowering herb), were stock flower names in pastoral poetry.

[10]From Calydon, an ancient Greek city. The reference is an exotic touch.

[11]*Tempe*: a beautiful valley between Mt. Olympus and Mt. Ossa in Thessaly, regarded as sacred to Apollo. The river *Peneios* ran through it. *Pindos*: mountain system in northern Greece. *Etna*: mountain named after a Sicilian nymph. *Acis*: lover of Galatea. When his rival, Polyphemus, crushed him with a rock, the gods transformed him into a river that rises from Mt. Etna. Such place-names with mythological associations are stock elements in pastoral poetry.

Begin the pastoral song, dear Muses, begin the song.
Hermes[12] came from the hill first of all and said, "Daphnis,
Who wastes away your life thus? For whom, good man, such desire?"
Begin the pastoral song, dear Muses, begin the song.
The cowherds came, the shepherds came, and the goatherds, 80
And all of them asked why he suffered. Priapos came too
And said, "Daphnis, poor wretch, why are you pining? The girl
On hastening feet goes to every spring, every grove searching.
Begin the pastoral song, dear Muses, begin the song.
"A laggard in love are you and helpless indeed! 85
Cowherd you were called, but now you resemble a goatherd—
A goatherd, forsooth, who when he sees nannies mounted
Pines, teary-eyed, because he was not born a he-goat.
Begin the pastoral song, dear Muses, begin the song.
"And you, whenever you chance to see maidens laughing, 90
Pine, teary-eyed, because you cannot dance among them."
To all of this the herdsman made no reply,
But endured his bitter love, bore it out to the end preordained.
Begin the song, Muses, begin again the pastoral song.
Cypris came too, sweetly laughing but laughing falsely, 95
Holding back the wrath deep in her heart,
And said, "Daphnis, you vowed to wrestle Love to a fall,
But have not you yourself been thrown by mischievous Eros?"
Begin the song, Muses, begin again the pastoral song.
And to her then Daphnis replied, "Hardhearted Cypris,[13] 100
Cypris the terrible, Cypris hateful to mortals,
Are you so sure that all my suns have already set?
Even in Hades will Daphnis be bitter trouble for Eros.
Begin the song, Muses, begin again the pastoral song.
"Is it not said that with Cypris a cowherd once—? Creep off to
Ida, 105
Crawl to Anchises[14]; oak trees grow there and galingale,[15]
And bees murmurously hum in swarms round the hives.
Begin the song, Muses, begin again the pastoral song.
"Adonis,[16] too, in the prime of his youth pastures his flocks,
And shoots hares and hunts every wild beast in the chase. 110
Begin the song, Muses, begin again the pastoral song.

[12]Messenger of the gods. Also the god of commerce, invention, cunning, and theft.

[13]Aphrodite, goddess of love, who was supposed to have risen from the seafoam near the island of Cyprus.

[14]Mountain named for the mortal Anchises, whose liaison with Aphrodite produced Aeneas, hero of the *Aeneid*.

[15]An aromatic plant related to ginger. Another stock pastoral plant.

[16]Mortal lover of Aphrodite. He was torn to pieces by a wild boar, and from his blood sprang the anemone flower.

"Or go take up your stand again before Diomedes[17]
And say, 'I overcame Daphnis the herdsman, but come on and fight me.'
Begin the song, Muses, begin again the pastoral song.
"O wolves, O jackals, O bears lurking in dens in the mountains, 115
Farewell. No more will I, Daphnis the herdsman, pass through your forest,
No more through your oak woods or groves. Farewell, Arethusa,[18]
And rivers whose rushing water pours down from Thybris.
Begin the song, Muses, begin again the pastoral song.
"I, that Daphnis who here pastured his cattle, 120
The Daphnis who here watered his bulls and his calves.
Begin the song, Muses, begin again the pastoral song.
"O Pan, Pan, whether you range the lofty peaks of Lycaios
Or busy yourself on high Mainalos, come to the island
Of Sicily, leaving Helike's mound and the tall tomb 125
Of the son of Lycaon's daughter,[19] at which even the blessed ones marvel.
Cease the song, Muses, cease now the pastoral song.
"Come, lord, and take this sweet-breathing syrinx smelling of honey
And beeswax, and bound securely around the fine lip,
For now, defeated by Eros, I go down to Hades. 130
Cease the song, Muses, cease now the pastoral song.
"Now you brambles, you thornbushes, may you bear violets,
May the lovely narcissus on junipers bloom,
Let all be confounded, and pears grow on pine trees,
Since Daphnis is dying; may deer drag down dogs, 135
And may owls from the mountains to nightingales sing."
Cease the song, Muses, cease now the pastoral song.
So much he said, then was silent. Willingly would Aphrodite
Have spared him but the whole thread of his fate had run out,
And Daphnis went to the stream.[20] The swirling waters washed over 140
The man dear to the Muses, the man not abhorred by the nymphs.
Cease the song, Muses, cease now the pastoral song.
Now give me the goat and the cup, so I may milk her
And pour out to the Muses an offering. Muses, farewell,
Many times farewell, but I will sing you a sweeter song later. 145

[17]Probably the hero of the Trojan War, second only to Achilles. He was a favorite of Athena, but when he wounded Aeneas, Aeneas's mother Aphrodite saved him. The reference continues the theme of mortals loved by gods.

[18]River named for a wood nymph. Fleeing from the river-god Alpheus, she was changed into a stream by Artemis.

[19]Lycaon's daughter was Callisto, mother of Arcas, ancestor of the Arcadians.

[20]Acheron, river of Hades.

GOATHERD

May your lovely mouth be filled with honey, Thyrsis,
Filled too with honeycomb, and may you munch the sweet figs
Of Aigilia, for you sing to surpass the cicada.
See, here is the cup; notice, my friend, its fine fragrance.
It would make you think it was dipped in the spring of the
Hours. 150
Come here, Cissaitha!—you milk her. Don't frisk around,
You other nannies! Calm down lest the billy goat mount you.

Catullus

(c. 84–c. 54 B.C.)

With Catullus, we make the leap from Greece to Rome and from the Greek language to Latin. Gaius Valerius Catullus was born in Verona, in a northern Italian province (Cisalpine Gaul) that was controlled by Rome but whose citizens did not enjoy the rights of full Roman citizenship. He moved to Rome when he was about twenty and divided the rest of his short life between that city and Verona. In Rome, he fell in with a group of young poets called the Neoterics or "new poets" who rejected the Roman tradition of high seriousness in favor of more personal and private topics. The Neoterics concentrated on short poems, marked by the elegance of form, the learned allusions, and the fastidious taste of the Alexandrian Greek poet-scholars.

Catullus wrote poems on a variety of themes, but the most memorable ones are the Lesbia poems. It seems virtually certain that Lesbia was in real life a woman named Clodia, seven to ten years older than Catullus. (Catullus called her "Lesbia" in tribute to Sappho of Lesbos, whose poetry was in some respects a model for his.) Lesbia was married but scarcely bound to a rather pompous husband. She was an aristocrat, probably, the center of a set of political adventurers, a woman of brilliance, beauty, and strong sexual appetites, and, if the gossip of the time was accurate, the lover of her brother and the poisoner of her husband. Something is known of her from a hostile portrait in a speech by Cicero defending one of her former lovers against a charge of attempting to poison her. Her husband, Metellus Celer, was governor of Cisalpine Gaul in the year 62, and if Catullus met Clodia then (which is possible though not certain), he would have been twenty-two at the time the affair began. The twenty-five poems that depict it can be arranged to form a dramatic sequence (which does not necessarily reflect their order of composition), beginning in idealism and fire (see Poem 51, a close paraphrase of Sappho's "He is more than a hero") and progressing through disillusionment, reconciliation, jealousy, anger, self-pity, and brooding resolution to shake off his passion, to his final dismissal of Lesbia in the elaborately contemptuous Poem 11, where Catullus ironically returns to the verse form named for Sappho. The first ten poems reprinted here are arranged in narrative sequence of the affair with Lesbia; the last two are outside the Lesbia story.

Catullus's influence on ancient literature was great, extending even to poets very dissimilar to him like Virgil and Horace. All the same, his poetry came precariously close to disappearing as almost all of Sappho's has done. Poem 62 exists in a ninth-century manuscript; Catullus would else be unknown (except for brief fragments) without the discovery around 1300 of a manuscript of the other 115 or so poems of his that we have. Even this manuscript was soon lost again, but fortunately not before it had been copied. To these lucky accidents we owe the survival of a voice expressive of the passion and dissipation that coexisted with Roman austerity.

POEMS

Translated by Horace Gregory

1[1]

Who shall receive my new-born book,
my poems, elegant and shy,
neatly dressed and polished?[2]

You, Cornelius,
shall be my single patron, 5
for, long ago, you praised
my slender lines and stanzas;

You, the only man in Italy
whose genius had the vigour
to write the history of the world 10
in three sturdy volumes;

These were books, by Jupiter,
that showed a learned mind and
the strength for heavy labour.

Then, take this little book 15
for what it is, my friend.

Patroness and Muse,
keep these poems green for
a day or so beyond a hundred years,
O Virgin![3] 20

[1] This dedicatory poem was written to introduce a collection of Catullus' poems; his surviving work would take up more than one book (that is, scroll), and so it is uncertain which poems the dedication applies to. The addressee is Cornelius Nepos, who had written a history of the world in three scrolls and who, like Catullus, came from Cisalpine Gaul, south of the Alps in northern Italy.

[2] Polished with pumice (volcanic rock), used to smooth the ends of the papyrus and give the volume elegance.

[3] *Virgin.* The Muse.

51[1]

He is changed to a god he who looks on her,
godlike he shines when he's seated beside her,
immortal joy to gaze and hear the fall of
her sweet laughter.

All of my senses are lost and confounded; 5
Lesbia rises before me and trembling
I sink into earth and swift dissolution
seizes my body.

Limbs are pierced with fire and the heavy tongue fails,
ears resound with noise of distant storms shaking 10
this earth, eyes gaze on stars that fall forever
into deep midnight.

* * *

This languid madness destroys you Catullus,
long day and night shall be desolate, broken,
as long ago ancient kings and rich cities 15
fell into ruin.

* * *

3

Dress now in sorrow, O all
you shades of Venus,
and your little cupids weep.

My girl has lost her darling sparrow;
he is dead, her precious toy 5
that she loved more than her two eyes,
O, honeyed sparrow following her
as a girl follows her mother,

[1] This poem, the first in the "Lesbia" sequence, records the poet's feelings at or near the beginning of his relationship with the woman usually identified as Clodia, a fashionable and emancipated beauty. (The numbering of Catullus' poems does not correspond to the order of their composition or of the events recorded.) The first three stanzas are a near-translation from a poem by Sappho of Lesbos, part of which survives ("He is more than a hero"). Authorities do not agree on whether the last four lines of Catullus's poem are really part of it or represent instead an error in the manuscript. The Latin meter ("sapphics") is also derived from Sappho and, as far as we know, was used only twice by Catullus: once here and once in his bitter farewell to Lesbia (Poem 11). "He" in line one is presumably a rival, possibly Clodia's husband.

never to leave her breast, but tripping
now here, now there, and always singing 10
his sweet falsetto
song to her alone.

Now he is gone; poor creature,
lost in darkness,
to a sad place 15
from which no one returns.

O ravenous hell!
My evil hatred rises against your power,
you that devour
all things beautiful; 20
and now this pitiful, broken sparrow,
who is the cause of my girl's grief,
making her eyes weary and red with sorrow.

5

Come, Lesbia, let us live and love,
nor give a damn what sour old men say.
The sun that sets may rise again
but when our light has sunk into the earth,
it is gone forever. 5
Give me a thousand kisses,
then a hundred, another thousand,
another hundred
and in one breath
still kiss another thousand, 10
another hundred.
O then with lips and bodies joined
many deep thousands;
confuse
their number, 15
so that poor fools and cuckolds (envious
even now) shall never
learn our wealth and curse us
with their
evil eyes. 20

85

I hate and love.
And if you ask me why,
I have no answer, but I discern,
can feel, my senses rooted in eternal torture.

109

My life, my love, you say our love will last forever;
O gods remember
her pledge, convert the words of her avowal into a prophecy.
Now let her blood speak, let sincerity govern each syllable fallen
from her lips, so that the long years of our lives shall be 5
a contract of true love inviolate
against time itself, a symbol of eternity.

39[1]

Egnatius has white teeth and therefore always pleasant, always smiling;
and if a lawyer is telling a sad tale for the defense[2] (a pitiful client),
Egnatius is there with his eternal smile.
If there's a funeral with the mother weeping
over the body of her only son, 5
Egnatius arrives gleaming with his happy smile:
no matter where he is or who he sees or what he does,
he is forever smiling.
O what a foul disease,
this smile, 10
not sweet nor gracious,
nor a sign of social charm.
Listen to me, my dear,
good, fine Egnatius,
if you were Roman, Sabine, Tibertine, 15
or a starved greedy pig from Umbria,
or an Etruscan, short and round, or a dark Lanuvian
with glittering teeth or a man from my own province,[3]
or anybody at all who scrubs his teeth with good clean water daily—
your smile would still offend me; nothing is worse 20
than senseless laughter from a foolish face. But you're a Spaniard,
and we already know the Spanish custom:
how Spaniards clean their teeth
and scour their gums with the same water that issues
from their bladders. 25
So if your teeth are clean, my friend, we know how
you have used your urine.

[1]Egnatius, a Spaniard, was one of Clodia/Lesbia's lovers.

[2]Egnatius is pictured as sitting among the defendant's supporters, where sadness and concern would be fitting.

[3]Six non-Roman peoples who were nevertheless socially accepted. The people of Catullus' own province, in northern Italy south of the Alps, had still not acquired full Roman citizenship in Catullus' lifetime.

8

Poor damned Catullus, here's no time for nonsense,
open your eyes, O idiot, innocent boy, look at what has happened:
once there were sunlit days when you followed after
where ever a girl would go, she loved with greater
love than any woman knew. 5
Then you took your pleasure
and the girl was not unwilling. Those were the bright days, gone;
now she's no longer yielding; you must be, poor idiot,
more like a man! not running after
her your mind all tears; stand firm, insensitive. 10
Say with a smile, voice steady, "Good-bye, my girl," Catullus
strong and manly no longer follows you, nor comes when you are calling
him at night and you shall need him.
You whore! Where's your man to cling to, who will praise your beauty,
where's the man that you love and who will call you his, 15
and when you fall to kissing, whose lips will you devour?
But always, your Catullus will be as firm as rock is.

76

If man can find rich consolation, remembering his good deeds and
all he has done,
if he remembers his loyalty to others, nor abuses his religion by heartless betrayal
of friends to the anger of powerful gods,[1]
then, my Catullus, the long years before you shall not sink in darkness with all hope gone,
wandering, dismayed, through the ruins of love. 5
All the devotion that man gives to man, you have given, Catullus,
your heart and your brain flowed into a love that was desolate, wasted,
nor can it return.
But why, why do you crucify love and yourself through the years?
Take what the gods have to offer and standing serene, rise forth as a
rock against darkening skies;
and yet you do nothing but grieve, sunken deep in your sorrow, Catullus, 10
for it is hard, hard to throw aside years lived in poisonous love that
has tainted your brain
and must end.
If this seems impossible now, you must rise
to salvation. O gods of pity and mercy, descend and witness my sorrow, if ever
you have looked upon man in his hour of death, see me now in despair. 15

[1] That is, does not make dishonest oaths.

Tear this loathsome disease from my brain. Look, a subtle corruption has entered my bones,[2]
no longer shall happiness flow through my veins like a river. No longer I pray
that she love me again, that her body be chaste, mine forever.
Cleanse my soul of this sickness of love, give me power to rise, resurrected, to thrust love aside,
I have given my heart to the gods, O hear me, omnipotent heaven, 20
and ease me of love and its pain.

11[1]

Furius, Aurelius, bound to Catullus
though he marches piercing farthest India
where echoing waves of the Eastern Oceans
break upon the shores:

Under Caspian seas, to mild Arabia, 5
east of Parthia,[2] dark with savage bowmen,
or where the Nile, sevenfold and uprising,
stains its leveled sands,—

Even though he marches over Alps to gaze on
great Caesar's monuments:[3] the Gallic Rhine and 10
Britons who live beyond torn seas, remotest
men of distant lands—

Friends who defy with me all things, whatever
gods may send us, go now, friends, deliver
these words to my lady, nor sweet—flattering, 15
nor kind nor gentle:

Live[4] well and sleep with adulterous lovers,
three hundred men between your thighs, embracing
all love turned false, again, again, and breaking
their strength, now sterile. 20

[2] These words echo and contrast with the description of ardent love in Poem 51: "swift dissolution/seizes my body./Limbs are pierced with fire."

[1] This poem marks the final contemptuous farewell to Lesbia/Clodia. In the original Latin, Catullus uses for the second and last time the sapphic verse form used in Poem 51, the overture to the love affair. Furius and Aurelius have apparently been sent as envoys from Lesbia to seek a reconciliation; since they were not in fact friends of Catullus, his address to them as fellow comrades-in-arms is perhaps heavily sarcastic. Before getting to the point—his message to Lesbia—the poet surveys the entire known world, from India in the east to Britain in the west.

[2] A country in what is now northeastern Iran.

[3] Reminders of Julius Caesar's exploits. Caesar crossed the Rhine in the summer of 55 B.C., and later in that year he crossed the English Channel to Britain.

[4] The word recalls its use in the first line of the rapturous Poem 5.

She will not find my love (once hers) returning;
she it was who caused love, this lonely flower,[5]
tossed aside, to fall by the plow dividing
blossoming meadows.

62[1]

BOYS

Twilight and star we hope to see arise, pouring bright rain from Mount Olympus[2] down
over the wedding feast, have now arrived, we sing our praise to the advancing bride,
rise now to greet her singing:
O Hymen, Hymenaee, come now, O Hymen.[3]

GIRLS

And is it true that Hesperus is here? Witness this company of boys now standing 5
facing us and the star of night flames with the fire of Mount Oeta,[4]
O hear them sing and see their ritual, wonder and joy for us to gaze upon
O Hymen, Hymenaee, come now, O Hymen.

BOYS

Hear how the girls have set their song in perfect measures, and each word recited
sounds from an infallible memory, surely their minds were rooted 10
deep in memorable music while we (our minds and ears distracted) wandered, and we shall be outdone;
O victory shall fall to those who sing in perfect rhythm, we must equal them and what they say must find
our words a perfect complement.
O Hymen, Hymenaee, come now, O Hymen.

[5] The image is another reminiscence of Sappho, who uses a similar image of a damaged flower in "Lament for a maidenhead."

[1] This epithalamium, or wedding song, was not written for any particular wedding. Influenced strongly by Greek poetry, it describes a mixture of Greek and Roman nuptial ceremonies. The setting is the end of an evening feast in the house of the bride's parents; the form is that of a choral competition between the young male and female guests, who are seated apart from each other. The bride makes her appearance in the course of the poem.

[2] That is, the sky; Mount Olympus was the dwelling place of the gods.

[3] A ritual refrain at weddings. (Later, Hymen was personified as the god of marriage.) The refrain is probably an interjection by the poet, not by the singers.

[4] There may have been a cult of Hesperus, the evening star, on Oeta, a mountain in central Greece.

GIRLS

What are these flames that roll against the skies, divorcing mother and child, more terrible 15
than earthly fires? These flames of Hesperus that seize a daughter from her mother's arms
delivering the girl into the quick embrace of a young husband—here is destruction greater
than a tall city given to its enemies.
O Hymen, Hymenaee, come now, O Hymen.

BOYS

What is more beautiful than this rich fire, the crown of heaven rising, 20
the fire that joins the marriage a true contract spoken by husband and parents of the bride,
and yet does not disclose its vital power until the marriage bed is made. What a gift from heaven
greater than this gift from gods to man in a superlative hour of happiness?
O Hymen, Hymenaee, come now, O Hymen.

* * *

GIRLS

O friends who love us, Hesperus has taken one of us, our sister, taken. . . .[5] 25

BOYS

O Hesperus when you rise, our guardian, eyes open the night long,
you come, disguised as dawn star now disclosing thieves hidden under night's vast shadow
but virgins cry against you, a false lamentation against him who is desire
coiled in their brains, a secret never spoken.
O Hymen, Hymenaee, come now, O Hymen. 30

GIRLS

We are as flowers[6] in a garden hidden from all men's eyes, no creature of the field walks in this place,
no plow divides us; only the gentlest wind, rain from a soft warm cloud and the quickening sun to nourish us.
We are the treasure that many girls and boys desire; but once deflowered (the flower stained and torn)
the virgin's body rancid, neither boys nor girls will turn to her again
nor can she wake their passion. 35

[5]Most of the young women's words here and the beginning of the men's reply have been lost. The women apparently charge Hesperus, herald of night, with being the ally of thieves. The men answer that, besides alerting the night police to be on guard, Hesperus as morning star also brings daylight and thus catches thieves (Venus can be either a morning or an evening star).

[6]The following flower simile, like the one in Catullus's Poem 11, is probably a reminiscence of Sappho's "Lament for a maidenhead."

BOYS

You are as a vine in a barren field that cannot climb by its own strength
nor its fruit prosper (the vine driven downward with its own weight
neither the ox nor plowman shall teach it how
to grow, but if its body twined round an elm, gives promise of fruit,
then by this marriage
many a farmer and his beast will wait upon it). So is it with you O
virgins.
The virgin, perfect, wastes until she ripens in the marriage bed and
there receives 40
her father's blessing and her husband's love.
Never resist the power of this union made, O virgin; father and mother
have given you to him, this man, your husband
your maidenhead by this division is not yours alone, you hold one third
of that which is the treasure
of parents and your husband—this is the lawful contract given to him
whose hands receive your dowry.
O Hymen, Hymenaee, come now, O Hymen. 45

101[1]

Dear brother, I have come these many miles, through strange lands
to this Eastern Continent
to see your grave, a poor sad monument of what you were, O brother.
And I have come too late; you cannot hear me; alone now I must speak
to these few ashes that were once your body and expect no answer.
I shall perform an ancient ritual over your remains, weeping, 5
(this plate of lentils for dead men to feast upon, wet with my tears)
O brother, here's my greeting: here's my hand forever welcoming you
and I forever saying: good-bye, good-bye.

Horace

(65–8 B.C.)

Horace (Quintus Horatius Flaccus), along with Virgil, brought Roman poetry to its pinnacle. In his urbane, polished verses, the Greek spirit is thoroughly integrated with the Roman, the rhythms of Greek lyric are fully translated into Latin, and the Greek reverence for beauty is harmonized with the Roman concern with duty. He was born in Venusia, in south-central Italy. He called himself the son of a freedman, an ex-slave who dealt in real estate, but the

[1] Catullus' brother had died young, in Asia Minor near the site of ancient Troy. In 57 B.C., during a term of service abroad, in nearby Bithynia, Catullus visited his brother's grave. He offers ritual gifts to the dead.

family was evidently prosperous. They were able to send Horace to Rome and to Athens to study Greek language and philosophy. When he was twenty-one, he was recruited as an officer in the army that Brutus raised to fight Antony and Octavian. When the army was defeated at Philippi, Horace returned to Rome where he obtained a government post. In 38 B.C., when he was twenty-seven, he was introduced to Maecenas, a wealthy friend and advisor to Octavian; Maecenas became his lifelong friend and patron. Horace thus moved in the highest circles in Rome, a position even more exalted when Octavian defeated his rivals Antony and Cleopatra at the battle of Actium in 31 B.C. and shortly thereafter took the title of Caesar Augustus.

His first book of *Satires*, modelled after the Greek satires of Lucillius, appeared in 35 B.C.; a second collection of satires and a book of *Epodes*, iambic poems based on the Greek Archilochus, were published five years later. Horace's finest achievement, though, was the three books of *Odes* that he published in 23 B.C., graceful short poems in the meters of Sappho and Alcaeus. His later work included two collections of *Epistles*; a fourth book of *Odes*; *The Art of Poetry*, which versified the principles of a Greek critic named Neoptolemus; and a Roman centennial ode.

The first nine poems in the first book of *Odes* provide a good sampling of Horace's style and themes. He wrote each of them in a different meter, derived from Greek, in a bravura display of technique. (The effect cannot be captured in English.) He also varied them thematically, as if to demonstrate his range of subjects as well. For these reasons, these nine poems have been called the "Parade Odes."

No classical poet figured more prominently in the neoclassical movement in Europe in the seventeenth and eighteenth centuries than Horace. He was translated repeatedly in the major European languages and was imitated so frequently that he became as great an influence on the modern European literatures as native writers were. The nine Parades Odes are included here both in a modern scholarly translation by David West and in a range of earlier translations, many by well-known poets.

ODES, BOOK I

ODE 1.1[1]

Maecenas, sprung from an ancient line of kings,
my stronghold, my pride, and my delight,
some like to collect Olympic dust
on their chariots, and if their scorching wheels

[1]Translated by David West. Ode 1.1, sometimes given such names as "Vocations" or "Ways of Life," surveys nine pursuits, the last of which is poetry. Addressed to Maecenas, Horace's patron, the poem asserts Horace's commitment to poetry and, implicitly, his wish to be added to the list of nine canonical Greek lyric poets: Alcman, Sappho, Alcaeus, Pindar, Bacchylides, Anacreon, Simonides, Stesichorus, and Ibycus. (The nine ways of life may echo this number.) Pindar's victory odes are alluded to in lines 3–6, the poetry of Sappho and Alcaeus in line 34.

graze the turning-post and they win the palm of glory, 5
they become lords of the earth and rise to the gods;
one man is pleased if the fickle mob of Roman citizens
competes to lift him up to triple honors;[2]

another, if he stores away in his own granary
the sweepings from all the threshing-floors of Libya; 10
the man who enjoys cleaving his ancestral fields
with the mattock, you could never move, not with the legacy

of Attalus,[3] to become a frightened sailor
cutting the Myrtoan sea with Cyprian timbers;
the merchant, terrified at the brawl of African gale 15
with Icarian waves,[4] is all for leisure and the countryside

round his own home town, but he is soon rebuilding
his shattered ships—he cannot learn to endure poverty;
there is a man who sees no objection to drinking
old Massic wine or taking time out of the day, 20

stretched out sometimes under the green arbutus,
sometimes by a gently welling spring of sacred water;
many enjoy the camp, the sound of the trumpet merged
in the bugle, the wars that mothers

abhor; the huntsman stays out under a cold sky, 25
and forgets his tender wife the moment
his faithful dogs catch sight of a hind
or a Marsian boar bursts his delicate nets.

As for me, it is ivy, the reward of learned brows,
that puts me among the gods above. As for me, 30
the cold grove and the light-footed choruses of Nymphs
and Satyrs set me apart from the people

if Euterpe[5] lets me play her pipes, and Polyhymnia[6]
does not withhold the lyre of Lesbos.
But if you enroll me among the lyric bards 35
my soaring head will touch the stars.

[2]The three honors were to be named quaestor, praetor, and consul.

[3]Attalus's legacy was the kingdom of Pergamum, which he bequeathed to the Roman people in 133 B.C.

[4]The Myrtoan sea is east of the Peloponnese, the Icarian sea is in the Aegean around the island of Icaria. Both were known for their fierce storms.

[5]Muse of music and lyric poetry.

[6]Muse of sacred long, oratory, and rhetoric.

ODE 1.1[1]

Application for a Grant

Noble executors of the munificent testament
Of the late John Simon Guggenheim,[2] distinguished bunch
Of benefactors, there are certain kinds of men
Who set their hearts on being bartenders,
For whom a life upon duck-boards,[3] among fifths, 5
Tapped kegs and lemon twists, crowded with lushes

Who can master neither their bladders nor consonants,
Is the only life, greatly to be desired.
There's the man who yearns for the White House, there to compose
Rhythmical lists of enemies, while someone else 10
Wants to be known to the *Tour d'Argent*'s head waiter.[4]
As the Sibyl of Cumae[5] said: It takes all kinds.
Nothing could bribe your Timon,[6] your charter member
Of the Fraternal Order of Grizzly Bears, to love
His fellow, whereas it's just the opposite 15
With interior decorators; that's what makes horse races.
One man may have a sharp nose for tax shelters,
Screwing the IRS with mirth and profit;
Another devote himself to his shell collection,
Deaf to his offspring, indifferent to the feast 20
With which his wife hopes to attract his notice.
Some at the Health Club sweating under bar bells
Labor away like grunting troglodytes,
Smelly and thick and inarticulate,
Their brains squeezed out through their pores by sheer exertion. 25
As for me, the prize for poets, the simple gift
For amphibrachs[7] strewn by a kind Euterpe,[8]
With perhaps a laurel crown of the evergreen
Imperishable of your fine endowment
Would supply my modest wants, who dream of nothing 30
But a pad on Eighth Street and your approbation.

[1]Translated by Anthony Hecht (1979). Hecht's imitation of Horace is a witty updating to the present.

[2]The John Simon Guggenheim Memorial Foundation annually awards substantial grants to scholars, writers, and artists.

[3]Boards placed behind bars so workers will not slip on wet floors.

[4]The *Tour d'Argent* (Gold Tower) is a fashionable New York restaurant.

[5]The most famous prophetess in Greek mythology. She was given the gift of prophecy and a thousand years of life by Apollo. She forgot to ask for continuing youth; Apollo refused to give it because she spurned his advances, and so she aged steadily for a thousand years. She lived in a cave at Cumae.

[6]Legendary Athenian misanthrope, subject of Shakespeare's *Timon of Athens.*

[7]Greek metrical feet consisting of one accented syllable between two unaccented ones, as in the word "remember."

[8]Muse of music and lyric poetry.

ODE 1.2[1]

Father Jupiter has already sent enough fierce hail
and snow, and his red right arm
has struck his holy citadel bringing
  fear to the city

and fear to the nations. The cruel age of Pyrrha[2] seemed 5
to be returning and the strange sights she had to bewail—
Proteus[3] driving his herds to visit
  the high mountains,

shoals of fishes sticking in the tops of elms
where once the doves had nested, 10
and frightened deer swimming in seas hurled down
  upon the earth.

We have seen yellow Tiber wrench back his waves
from the Tuscan shore and rush
to throw down king Numa's memorials 15
  and Vesta's temple,[4]

eager to avenge the shrill grievances
of Ilia his wife.[5] Without the blessing of Jupiter
this doting husband left his course and flooded
  his left bank. 20

Young men will hear that citizen sharpened against citizen
swords that should have slain our Persian enemies.[6] They will hear—
what few there are, thanks to the sins of their fathers—
  of the battles we fought.

[1]Translated by David West. Ode 1.2, sometimes known as "To Augustus," has the dramatic date of 27 B.C., a year when two disasters struck Rome: The Tiber flooded, and Caesar Augustus gave up his extraordinary constitutional powers and proposed to return to private life. Horace uses the first as a metaphor for the second.

[2]Pyrra and her husband Deucalion were the only survivors of the Flood that Jupiter sent to punish the human race.

[3]A sea deity with the power to assume different shapes. Here, as a herdsman, he is driving his waves to the mountain tops.

[4]Numa, the second king of Rome, built several memorial buildings and the temple of Vesta.

[5]The legendary Ilia was raped by Mars; gave birth to Romulus and Remus, the founders of Rome; and later became wife of the River Tiber. This section may contain buried references to Julius Caesar, Augustus's predecessor. Julius, as Chief Priest, lived in the Regia, built by Numa, and Ilia was his legendary ancestor. Horace is praying that the flood does not portend Augustus's overthrow as similar portents foreshadowed Julius Caesar's assassination.

[6]The Parthians. Parthia, part of the Persian Empire, defeated the Romans in 53 B.C. but was defeated by them in 39–38 B.C.

What god can the people call upon to shore up 25
their crumbling empire?[7] What prayer can the Virgins
din into the ears of Vesta[8] who does not listen
to their chanting?

To whom will Jupiter give the task of expiating
our crime? Come at long last, we pray, 30
your white shoulders veiled in cloud,
augur Apollo;

or you come if you prefer, smiling Venus of Eryx,[9]
with Jest and Cupid hovering round you;
or, if you take thought for the race you founded 35
and your neglected descendants,

come, god of war,[10] sated with your long sport,
exulting in the battle cry, in polished helmets,
in the face of the Marsian foot soldier showing no pity
for his bleeding enemy; 40

or if you, Mercury, winged son of bountiful Maia,
have changed shape and are imitating
a young man on the earth, accepting the name
of Caesar's avenger,[11]

do not return too soon to the sky. For long years 45
be pleased to stay with the people of Romulus,
and may no breeze come and snatch you up too soon,
angered by our sins.[12]

Here rather celebrate your triumphs.
Here delight to be hailed as Father and Princeps[13] 50
and do not allow the Medes to ride unavenged
while you, Caesar, are our leader.

[7]From this point on, the Ode takes the form of a hymn, including an address to a god; praise of the god's attributes, names, and parentage; and a final request.

[8]Goddess of the hearth and the home.

[9]Eryx, on the northwest tip of Sicily, was the site of a shrine to Venus, mother of Aeneas. It is also the location of the grave of Anchises, father of Aeneas and thus ancestor of both Julius Caesar and Augustus Caesar.

[10]Mars.

[11]Octavian, heir of Julius Caesar, had sworn to avenge him.

[12]Romulus was said to have been snatched up by the wind and never seen again.

[13]Augustus had been named *Princeps Senatus*, Leader of the Senate.

ODE 1.2[1]

Since Jove decreed in storms to vent
 The winter of his discontent,
Thundering o'er Rome impenitent
 With red right hand,
The flood-gates of the firmament 5
 Have drenched the land!

Terror hath seized the minds of men,
Who deemed the days had come again
When Proteus led, up mount and glen,
 And verdant lawn, 10
Of teeming ocean's darksome den
 The monstrous spawn.

When Pyrrha saw the ringdove's nest
Harbour a strange unbidden guest,
And, by the deluge dispossest 15
 Of glade and grove
Deers down the tide, with antler'd crest,
 Affrighted drove.

We saw the yellow Tiber, sped
Back to his Tuscan fountain-head, 20
O'erwhelm the sacred and the dead
 In one fell doom,
And Vesta's pile in ruins spread,
 And Numa's tomb.

Dreaming of days that once had been, 25
He deemed that wild disastrous scene
Might soothe his Ilia, injured queen!
 And comfort give her,
Reckless though Jove should intervene,
 Uxorious river! 30

Our sons will ask, why men of Rome
Drew against kindred, friends, and home,
Swords that a Persian hecatomb
 Might best imbue—
Sons, by their fathers' feuds become 35
 Feeble and few!

[1]Translated by Francis Sylvester Mahony (1804–1866). Mahony was an Irish humorist and journalist who wrote under the name "Father Prout."

Whom can our country call in aid?
Where must the patriot's vow be paid?
With orisons shall vestal maid
  Fatigue the skies? 40
Or will not Vesta's frown upbraid
  Her votaries?

Augur Apollo! shall we kneel
To *thee*, and for our commonweal
With humbled consciousness appeal? 45
  Oh, quell the storm!
Come, though a silver vapour veil
  Thy radiant form!

Will Venus from Mount Eryx stoop,
And to our succour hie, with troop 50
Of laughing Graces, and a group
  Of Cupids round her?
Or comest *thou* with wild war-whoop,
  Dread Mars! our founder?

Whose voice so long bade peace avaunt; 55
Whose war-dogs still for slaughter pant;
The tented field thy chosen haunt,
  Thy child the Roman,
Fierce legioner, whose visage gaunt
  Scowls on the foeman. 60

Or hath young Hermes, Maia's son,
The graceful guise and form put on
Of thee, Augustus? and begun
  (Celestial stranger!)
To wear the name which *thou* has won— 65
  "Caesar's Avenger"?

Blest be the days of thy sojourn,
Distant the hour when Rome shall mourn
The fatal sight of they return
  To Heaven again, 70
Forced by a guilty age to spurn
  The haunts of men.

Rather remain, beloved, adored,
Since Rome, reliant on thy sword,
To thee of Julius hath restored 75
  The rich reversion;
Baffle Assyria's hovering horde,
  And smite the Persian!

ODE 1.3[1]

O ship, to whom Virgil has been entrusted
and who has to repay that debt, may the goddess
who rules over Cyprus, may Helen's brothers,
those shining stars, and the father of the winds,[2]

shutting them all up except the nor'wester Iapyx, 5
govern your sailing, if only you deliver Virgil safe,
I pray you, to the boundaries of Attica,
and preserve half of my soul.

Oak and triple bronze
were round the breast of the man who first committed 10
a fragile ship to the truculent sea.
He was not afraid of the swooping sou'western

battling it out with the winds of the north,
nor the weeping Hyades,[3] nor the madness of the south wind,
the supreme judge of when to raise 15
and when to lay the Adriatic sea.

He did not fear the approaching step of death,
but looked with dry eyes on monsters swimming,
on ocean boiling, and on
the ill-famed Acroceraunian rocks.[4] 20

In vain in his wise foresight did God sever
the lands of the earth by means of the dividing sea,
if impious ships yet leap
across waters which they should not touch.

Boldly enduring everything, 25
the human race rushes to forbidden sin.
Boldly the offspring of Iapetus brought down fire
by wicked deceit to the peoples of the earth.[5]

[1]Translated by David West. Ode 1:3 is sometimes given an editorial title such as "Prayer for Safety at Sea." Like Horace's other odes, it has a quite specific dramatic situation: the departure of his friend Virgil on a ship for Greece. Horace turns the *bon voyage* into a meditation on the human race's *hubris* in trying to overcome nature.

[2]The goddess who rules over Cyprus is Venus. Helen's brothers are the Dioscuri, Castor and Pollux, who were believed to calm storms at sea when they appeared among the masts of ships in the form of St. Elmo's fire. The father of the winds is Aeolus.

[3]A constellation. It is "weeping" because it brings rains when it rises or sets.

[4]A rocky promontory on the northwest coast of Greece. It is ill-famed because Octavian's ship was damaged there after the battle of Actium.

[5]The son of Iapetus was Prometheus.

After the theft of fire from its home
in the heavens, wasting disease and a cohort 30
of new fevers fell upon the earth
and the slow necessity of death, once so remote,

speeded its step.
Daedalus ventured upon the empty air
with wings not meant for man.[6] 35
The labor of Hercules burst through Acheron.[7]

For mortals no height is too steep:
in our stupidity we try to scale the very heavens
and by our wickedness we do not allow
Jupiter to lay down his angry thunderbolts.[8] 40

ODE 1.3[1]

Inscrib'd to the Earl of Roscommon, on his intended Voyage to Ireland

So may th' auspitious Queen of Love,
And the twin stars (the Seed of Jove,)
And he, who rules the rageing wind
To thee, O sacred Ship, be kind,
And gentle Breezes fill thy Sails, 5
Supply soft Etesian Gales,[2]
As thou to whom the Muse commends,
The best of Poets and of Friends,
Dost thy committed Pledge restore:
And land him safely on the shore: 10
And save the better part of me,
From perishing with him at Sea.
Sure he, who first the passage try'd,
In harden'd Oak his heart did hide,
And ribs of Iron arm'd his side! 15

[6]Ovid, in the *Metamorphoses*, tells the story of how Daedalus and his son Icarus escaped from the Cretan labyrinth by building wings of wax and feathers. Icarus flew too near the sun; the wax melted and he was drowned.

[7]The last and the most dangerous of the Twelve Labors of Hercules was to go to the Underworld and bring back Cerberus, the guardian dog.

[8]Horace associates Jupiter's thunderbolts with civil war. See the first lines of Ode 1:2.

[1]Translated by John Dryden (1631–1700). Like many other translators of Horace, Dryden adapts his version to a contemporary event. Wentworth Dillon, Earl of Roscommon (1633?–1685), an English lord with estates in Ireland, was a friend and patron of Dryden. He died before making the planned trip to Ireland that occasioned the translation.

[2]Summer winds out of the northeast. Dryden substitutes them for Horace's winds out of the northwest as suiting better a trip from England to Ireland.

Or his at least, in hollow wood,
Who tempted first the briny Floud:
Nor fear'd the winds contending roar,
Nor billows beating on the shore;
Nor all the Tyrants of the Main. 20
What form of death cou'd him affright,
Who unconcern'd with stedfast sight,
Cou'd view the Surges mounting steep,
And monsters rolling in the deep?
Cou'd thro' the ranks of ruin go, 25
With Storms above, and Rocks below!
In vain did Natures[3] wise command,
Divide the Waters from the Land,
If daring Ships, and Men prophane,
Invade th' inviolable Main: 30
Th' eternal Fences over leap;
And pass at will the boundless deep.
No toyl, no hardship can restrain
Ambitious Man inur'd to pain;
The more confin'd, the more he tries, 35
And at forbidden quarry flies.
Thus bold Prometheus did aspire,
And stole from heaven the seed of Fire:
A train of Ills, a ghastly crew,
The Robbers blazing track persue; 40
Fierce Famine, with her Meagre face,
And Feavours of the fiery Race,
In swarms th' offending Wretch surround,
All brooding on the blasted ground:
And limping Death, lash'd on by Fate, 45
Comes up to shorten half our date.
This made not Dedalus beware,
With borrow'd wings to sail in Air:
To Hell Alcides forc'd this way,
Plung'd thro' the Lake, and snatch'd the Prey 50
Nay scarce the Gods, or heav'nly Climes
Are safe from our audacious Crimes;
We reach at Jove's Imperial Crown,
And pull the unwilling thunder down.

[3]In Horace, it is God (deus) who separated the sea from the land; Dryden changes it to Nature.

ODE 1.4[1]

Harsh winter is melting away in the welcome change to spring
and zephyrs,
winches are pulling down dry-bottomed ships,
the cattle no longer like the steading, the plowman does not
hug the fire,
and meadows are not white with hoar-frost.

Venus of Cythera leads on the dance beneath a hanging moon, 5
and the lovely Graces linking arms with Nymphs,
shake the ground with alternate feet, while burning Vulcan
visits the grim foundries of the Cyclopes.[2]

Now is the time to oil the hair and bind the head with green myrtle
or flowers born of the earth now freed from frost; 10
now too is the time to sacrifice to Faunus[3] in shady groves
whether he asks a lamb or prefers a kid.

Pale death kicks with impartial foot at the hovels of the poor
and the towers of kings. O fortunate Sestius,[4]
the brief sum of life does not allow us to start on long hopes. 15
You will soon be kept close by Night and the fabled shades

in Pluto's meagre house.[5] When you go there
you will no longer cast lots to rule the wine,
nor admire tender Lycidas,[6] whom all the young men
now burn for and for whom the girls will soon be warm. 20

[1]Translated by David West. Ode 1:4, sometimes titled "Spring" or something similar, makes a surprising connection between spring and human mortality. Its theme is *carpe diem* ("seize the day"), advising Sestius to enjoy life's pleasures before death comes.

[2]*Venus of Cythera*: goddess of love. *Graces*: the *charities* (Aglaia, Euphrosyne, and Thalia): personifications of gracefulness who attended Venus. *Vulcan*: Roman name for the Greek Hephaestus, god of fire and metalworking. His forge was in the heart of Mt. Aetna; he held it in partnership with the *Cyclopes*, one-eyed giants.

[3]Another name for Pan, god of agriculture, crops, prophecy, fertility, and country life.

[4]Lucius Sestius was a member of a Roman family that had made a great fortune in their potteries. Sestius was also a powerful politician who had taken over the consulship from Augustus in 23 B.C.

[5]The Roman name for the Greek Hades, god of the dead.

[6]Although Horace may have had a particular youth in mind, "Lycidas" is a stock pastoral name.

ODE 1.4[1]

*To Sextius, a person of consular dignity**

By describing the delightfulness of spring, and urging the common lot of mortality, he exhorts Sextius, as an Epicurean, to a life of voluptuousness.

A grateful change! Favonius,[2] and the spring
 To the sharp winter's keener blasts succeed,
Along the beach, with ropes, the ships they bring,
 And launch again, their watry way to speed.
No more the plowmen in their cots delight, 5
 Nor cattle are contented in the stall;
No more the fields with hoary frosts ware white,
 But Cytherean Venus leads the ball.
She, while the moon attends upon the scene,
 The Nymphs and decent Graces in the set, 10
Shakes with alternate feet the shaven green,
 While Vulcan's Cyclops at the anvil sweat.
Now we with myrtle shou'd adorn our brows,
 Or any flow'r that decks the lossen'd sod;
In shady groves to Faunus pay our vows, 15
 Whether a lamb or kid delight the God.
Pale death alike knocks at the poor man's door,
 O happy Sextius, and the royal dome,
The whole of life forbids our hope to soar,
 Death and the shades anon shall press thee home. 20
And when into the shallow grave you run,
 You cannot win the monarchy of wine,
Nor doat on Lycidas, as on a son,
 Whom for their spouse all little maids design.

ODE 1.4[1]

Sharp winter now dissolved, the linnets sing,
The grateful breath of pleasing Zephyrs bring
The welcome joys of long desired spring.

The gallies now for open sea prepare,
The herds forsake their stalls for balmy air, 5
The fields adorn'd with green th' approaching sun declare.

[1]Translated by Christopher Smart (1722–1771). Smart published a translation of Horace's complete *Odes* in 1767. His iambic pentameter quatrains and "poetic diction" ("watry way," "shaven green," etc.) give a neoclassic neatness to Horace's lines.

[2]Roman name for Zephyrus, the west wind.

[1]Translated by Lady Mary Wortley Montagu (1689–1762). Montagu's pentameter triplets, like her contemporary Smart's quatrains, are an attempt to find an English equivalent for Horatian meters. The last line introduces a female point of view of Lycidas.

In shining nights the charming Venus leads
Her troop of Graces, and her lovely maids
Who gaily trip the ground in myrtle shades.

The blazing forge her husband Vulcan heats, 10
And thunderlike the labouring hammer beats,
While toiling Cyclops every stroke repeats.

Of myrtle new the chearful wreath compose,
Or various flowers which opening spring bestows,
Till coming June presents the blushing rose. 15

Pay your vow'd offering to God Faunus' bower!
Then, happy Sestius, seize the present hour,
'Tis all that nature leaves to mortal power.

The equal hand of strong impartial fate,
Levels the peasant and th' imperious great, 20
Nor will that doom on human projects wait.

To the dark mansions of the senseless dead,
With daily steps our destined path we tread,
Realms still unknown, of which so much is said.

Ended your schemes of pleasure and of pride, 25
In joyous feasts no one will there preside,
Torn from your Lycidas' beloved side;

Whose tender youth does now our eyes engage,
And soon will give in his maturer age,
Sighs to our virgins—to our matrons rage. 30

ODE 1.5[1]

What slim youngster soaked in perfumes
is hugging you now, Pyrrha, on a bed of roses
deep in your lovely cave? For whom
are you tying up your blonde hair?

[1]Translated by David West. This is the most famous and the most translated of all Horace's odes. Ronald Storrs has collected 451 translations of it in twenty-one languages (and published 144 of them in 1959). It has been given such editorial titles as "To Pyrrha," "One More Unfortunate," and "Speaking from Experience," none of which quite captures the delicate tone of the poem and its witty development of the interplay between sea storms and love storms. The last stanza of the poem refers to a religious ceremony in which a survivor of a shipwreck would hang a picture or a description of the event on a temple wall and dedicate his wet clothes to Neptune, god of the sea. Surviving an affair with Pyrrha is like surviving a shipwreck.

You're so elegant and so simple. Many's the time 5
he'll weep at your faithlessness and the changing gods,
and be amazed at seas
roughened by black winds,

but now in all innocence he enjoys your golden beauty
and imagines you always available, always lovable, 10
not knowing about treacherous breezes—
I pity poor devils who have no experience of you

and are dazzled by your radiance. As for me,
the table on the temple wall announces
that I have dedicated my dripping clothes 15
to the god who rules the sea.

ODE 1.5[1]

What slender Youth bedew'd with liquid odours
Courts thee on Roses in some pleasant Cave,
Pyrrha for whom bindst thou
In wreaths thy golden Hair,
Plain in thy neatness; O how oft shall he 5
On Faith and changed Gods complain: and Seas
Rough with black winds and storms
Unwonted shall admire:
Who now enjoyes thee credulous, all Gold,
Who alwayes vacant alwayes amiable 10
Hopes thee; of flattering gales
Unmindfull. Hapless they
To whom thou untry'd seem'st fair. Me in my vow'd
Picture the sacred wall declares t' have hung
My dank and dropping weeds 15
To the stern God of Sea.

ODE 1.5[1]

I

What mean those Amorous Curles of Jet?
For what heart-Ravisht Maid
Dost thou thy Hair in order set,
Thy Wanton Tresses Braid?
And thy vast Store of Beauties open lay, 5
That the deluded Fancy leads astray.

[1]Translated by John Milton (1608–1674).
[1]Translated by Aphra Behn (1640–1689). Behn's "imitation" reverses the sexes and thus questions the *femme fatale* stereotype implicit in the original.

II

For pitty hide thy Starry eyes,
Whose Languishments destroy
And look not on the Slave that dyes
With an excess of Joy. 10
Defend thy Coral Lips, thy Amber Breath;
To taste these Sweets lets in a Certain Death.

III

Forbear, fond Charming Youth, forbear,
Thy words of Melting Love:
Thy Eyes thy Language well may spare, 15
One Dart enough can move.
And she that hears thy voice and sees thy Eyes
With too much Pleasure, too much Softness dies.

IV

Cease, Cease, with Sighs to warm my Soul,
Or press me with thy Hand: 20
Who can the kindling fire controul,
The tender force withstand?
Thy Sighs and Touches like wing'd Lightning fly,
And are the Gods of Loves Artillery.

ODE 1.5[1]

For whom are now your Airs put on?
And what new Beauty doom'd to be undone?
That careless Elegance of Dress,
This Essence that perfumes the Wind,
Your every motion does confess 5
Some secret Conquest is design'd.

Alas the poor unhappy Maid,
To what a train of ills betraid!
What fears! what pangs shall rend her Breast!
How will her eyes disolve in Tears! 10
That now with glowing Joy is blest,
Charm'd with the faithless vows she hears.

[1]Translated by Lady Mary Wortley Montagu (1689–1762). Montagu, like Behn a century before, reverses the sexes but, unlike Behn, introduces a stereotype of her own, the innocent maiden "snatch'd from Ruin."

So the young Sailor on the Summer Sea
Gaily pursues his destin'd way,
Fearless and careless on the deck he stands 15
Till sudden storms arise, and Thunders rowl,
In vain he casts his Eye to distant Lands,
Distracting Terror tears his timerous Soul.

For me, secure I view the raging Main,
Past are my Dangers, and forgot my Pain, 20
My Votive Tablet in the temple shews
The Monument of Folly past,
I paid the bounteous God my gratefull vows
Who snatch'd from Ruin sav'd me at the last.

ODE 1.6[1]

Varius, the eagle of Homeric song, will write
of your valour and your victories, all the feats
of formidable soldiers fighting under your command
on ship or on horseback.

We do not attempt, Agrippa, to speak of these things, 5
nor of the bad temper of Peleus' son who did not know
how to yield, nor of the voyages of Ulixes the double-dealer,
nor of the savage house of Pelops.[2]

We are too slight for these large themes. Modesty
and the Muse who commands the unwarlike lyre forbid us 10
to diminish the praise of glorious Caesar and yourself
by our imperfect talent.

Who could write worthily of Mars girt in adamantine tunic,
or Meriones, black with the dust of Troy,
or the son of Tydeus, who with the help of Pallas Athene 15
was the equal of the gods?[3]

What we sing of is drinking parties, of battles fought
by fierce virgins with nails cut sharp to wound young men.
Sometimes we are fancy free, sometimes a little moved,
cheerfully, after our fashion. 20

[1]Translated by David West. Ode 1:6 belongs to the genre of *recusatio,* or "refusal to praise." Horace's tongue-in-cheek refusal to praise Caesar Augustus and his great admiral Marcus Agrippa on the grounds that he is only a love poet and his recommendation of the epic poet and tragedian Varius instead manages to compliment three people: Augustus, Agrippa, and Varius.

[2]Peleus' son was Achilles, hero of the *Iliad*; Ulixes is Ulysses or Odysseus, hero of the *Odyssey*; and the house of Pelops is the house of Atreus, the subject of the *Oresteia.* Horace trivializes these subjects as a comic "proof" of his inadequacy for heroic themes.

[3]*Mars*: god of war. *Meriones*: Greek warrior at Troy; mentioned in the *Iliad,* Book 2. *Son of Tydeus*: Diomedes: Greek warrior at Troy, mentioned in the *Iliad,* Book 4. Diomedes figures in one of the grislier episodes of the Trojan War. He offended the gods by managing, though mortally wounded himself, to kill his opponent Melanippus, behead him, and eat his brains. Horace's reference to him as "the equal of the gods" pokes a bit of fun at the heroic tradition.

ODE 1.6[1]

To a Roman Admiral

On Homer's wing let Varius sing
  Agrippa, good and brave;
With what his warriors, conquering,
  Have done by land or wave:
But nor to strains like these aspire 5
Our warblings, nor Pelides' ire
  Can we sublimely tell,
Nor how across old ocean's roar
His course the wise Ulysses bore,
Nor how, defiled with kindred gore, 10
  The house of Pelops fell.

Nor may our Muse, unwarlike, mar
  With coldly creeping line
The praise of Caesar famed so far,
  Or, great Agrippa, thine! 15
And who *can* sing the God of war
With bright arms blazing from afar;
  Or Merion famed in fight,
With blackened front and bloody blade;
Or Diomede, by Pallas' aid 20
  Equal to Gods in might?

No, feasts and frolics be our theme,
  And brimming bowls of wine,
And pleasure's laugh, and beauty's beam,
  And dance and song divine: 25
We'll sing of virgins' wanton wiles,
Who fight with rage disclosed in smiles,
  And *tempt* the foe to try;
Ourself, as wont, of careless frame,
Whether we feel the general flame, 30
  Or coldly smile it by.

ODE 1.7[1]

Others will praise bright Rhodes or Mytilene or Ephesus
  or the walls of Corinth with its two seas,
Thebes famous for Bacchus or Delphi for Apollo
  or Thessalian Tempe;

[1]Translated by Patrick Branwell Brontë (1847–1848), brother of Charlotte, Emily, and Anne Brontë. Brontë uses the iambic tetrameter lines and the heavy, jingling rhymes of Victorian comic verse to approximate Horace's light tone.

[1]Translated by David West. In Ode 1.7, Horace continues the display of the range of his talents in the nine Parade Odes by writing a poem in praise of a city. As in the previous eight odes, however, he personalizes and deepens his theme by turning it into a meditation on the respective claims of being at home and away.

there are those whose one task is to celebrate the city 5
of chaste Pallas in unbroken song,
and to sport on their brows a crown of olive plucked wherever
they find it; in honor of Juno many a one

will speak of wealthy Mycenae and horse-rearing Argos.
As for me, I am not so struck 10
by much-enduring Lacedaemon or the fat plain of Larisa,[3]
as by Albunea's sounding home

and the plunging Anio, by the grove of Tiburnus and its orchards
watered by swiftly flowing streams.[4]
The bright south wind will often wipe the clouds from the dark sky 15
It is not always pregnant with rain.

So you too, Plancus,[5] would be wise to remember to put a stop
to sadness and the labors of life
with mellow, undiluted wine, whether you are in camp among
the gleaming standards or whether you will be 20

in the deep shade of your beloved Tibur. When Teucer[6] was on the run
from Salamis and his father, they say that nevertheless,
awash with wine, he bound his brow with a crown of poplar leaves[7]
and spoke these words to his grieving friends:

"Allies and comrades, Fortune is kinder than a father. 25
Wherever she takes us, there shall we go. Do not despair
while Teucer takes the auspices and Teucer is your leader.
Apollo does not err and he has promised

that in a new land we shall find a second Salamis.[8]
You are brave men and have often suffered worse 30
with me. Drive away your cares with wine. Tomorrow
we shall set out again upon the broad sea."

[2]The virgin goddess Pallas Athena was the patron of Athens, to which she gave the olive tree as a gift.

[3]The place-names in this section allude to the heroes of the Trojan War. Mycenae was the home of Agamemnon, Argos the home of Diomede, Lacedaemon (Sparta) the home of Menelaus, and Larisa the home of Achilles.

[4]Tibur (modern name: Tivoli) was about thirty miles east of Rome. Albunea was the Sibyl, or prophetess, of Tibur, the Anio its river, and Tiburnus its founder.

[5]Titus Munatius Plancus, governor of Asia Minor, fought against Antony and with Octavian at the Battle of Actium. Plancus's homelessness at the time parallels Teucer's.

[6]The Greek hero Teucer was exiled by his father, Telamon, when he returned from the war to his native Salamis.

[7]The poplar was sacred to Hercules, patron of both Salamis and Tibur.

[8]Teucer founded a new Salamis on the island of Cyprus.

ODE 1.7[1]

To Munatius Plancus, a person of consular dignity

Some writers praise one city or region, and some another. Horace prefers Tibur to all the world, in which place Plancus was born, whom he exhorts to the washing away of care by wine.

Let others sing the praise of famous Rhodes
 Or Mytilene, or th' Ephesian pride,
Or chant the walls of Corinth in their odes,
 Wash'd by a different sea on either side,
Or Thebes for Bacchus, Delphi justly fam'd 5
 For Phœbus, or Thessalian Tempe's vale;
Some make the seat of Pallas, nymph unblam'd,
 The theme of one uninterrupted tale,
And run all lengths to wear an olive-crown—
 Many for Juno, with poetic zeal, 10
Argus so apt for cavalry renown,
 And, rich Mycenæ, boast thy public weal.
With me nor patient Sparta, nor the plains
 Of high-manur'd Larissa e'er cou'd take,
As where Albunea's tinkling fount remains, 15
 Or Anio roaring down into the lake.
And old Tiburnus' grove for ever green,
 Where flow'ring orchards give a strong perfume,
Where marshal'd trees upon the stream are seen,
 And in the waggling waters wave their bloom. 20
As the white south at times serenes the skies,
 Nor are his gathring show'rs for ever rife;
So thou, O Plancus, 'gainst thy cares be wise,
 With mellow wine dismiss the toils of life,
Whether the camp, with shining standards gay, 25
 Detain you ready for the hour of fight,
Or in your native Tibur you shall stay,
 And in the dense embow'ring shades delight.
When Teucer by his father was oppress'd,
 And driv'n away from Salamis he fled, 30
He thus his weeping company address'd,
 As, wet with wine, the poplar bound his head.
"Sped on by fortune, kinder than my sire,
 O my co-mates, we'll go where'er she please;
Despair of nothing and to all aspire— 35
 By Teucer's guidance Teucer's auspices.
For Phœbus has of certainty foretold,
 That in a land to us advent'rers new,

[1]Translated by Christopher Smart (1722–1771).

Fair Salamis a doubtful name shall hold,
O brave companions, O my faithful few! 40
Ye that with me have harder things endur'd,
Than all the evils which ye now sustain,
This day your grief and care with wine be cur'd,
To-morrow sends us to the depth again."

ODE 1.8[1]

Tell me, Lydia, by all the gods I beg you,
why you are in such a hurry to destroy Sybaris with your love.
And why is he deserting the sunny Campus?[2]
He never used to complain about dust or heat.

Why is he not on horseback and training 5
for war with his young friends? Why is he not disciplining
Gallic mouths with jagged bits?
Why is he afraid to put his toe in the yellow Tiber?

Why does he avoid athletes' oil
like vipers' blood and why are his arms no longer bruised 10
with weapons, this champion of the discus,
champion of the javelin, so often throwing beyond the mark?

Why does he hide as the son of Thetis
the sea-goddess hid, so they say, before the tears and deaths
of Troy, in case his man's clothes 15
should send him off to the killing and the Lycian cohorts?[3]

ODE 1.8[1]

WHY INDEED?

Lydia, in Heavens Name
Why melts yong Sybaris in thy Flame?
Why doth he bed-rid lie
That can indure th' intemp'rate Skie?

[1]Translated by David West. Ode 1:8 is a dramatic monologue that vividly expresses the tension between love and duty, Epicureanism and Stoicism, self and country that runs throughout Horace's work.

[2]The Campus Martius, or Field of Mars, the military training ground in Rome.

[3]The sea goddess Thetis is said to have dressed her son Achilles in women's clothes and hidden him on the island of Scyros in order to prevent him from going to the Trojan War, where she knew he would be killed.

[1]Translated by Sir Richard Fanshawe (1608–1666). Fanshawe was a prolific Renaissance translator of classical texts as well as of non-English poetry of his own day. His punchy couplets, each made up of a trimeter and a tetrameter line, do a good job of carrying Horace's immediacy and colloquialism over into seventeenth-century English.

Why rides he not and twits 5
The French great Horse with wringled bits?
Why shuns he Tybur's Flood,
And wrastlers Oyle like vipers Blood?
Nor hath His Flesh made soft
With bruising Arms; having so oft 10
Been prais'd for shooting farre
And clean delivered of the Barre?
For shame, why lies he hid
As at Troy's Siege Achilles did,
For fear lest Mans Array 15
Should Him to Manly Deeds betray?

ODE 1.9[1]

You see Soracte[2] standing white and deep
with snow, the woods in trouble, hardly able
to carry their burden, and the rivers
halted by sharp ice.

Thaw out the cold, pile up the logs 5
on the hearth and be more generous, Thaliarchus,[3]
as you draw the four-year-old Sabine[4]
from its two-eared cask.

Leave everything else to the gods. As soon as
they still the winds battling it out 10
on the boiling sea, the cypresses stop waving
and the old ash trees.

Don't ask what will happen tomorrow.
Whatever day Fortune gives you, enter it
as profit, and don't look down on love 15
and dancing while you're still a lad,

while the gloomy gray keeps away from the green.
Now is the time for the Campus and the squares
and soft sighs at the time arranged
as darkness falls. 20

Now is the time for the lovely laugh from the secret corner
giving away the girl in her hiding-place,
and for the token snatched from her arm
or finger feebly resisting.[5]

[1]Translated by David West. Many of Horace's characteristic features come together in this final poem of the Parade Odes: his keen sense of landscape and weather, his urbane epicureanism, his tendency to philosophize, and his mild naughtiness.

[2]A mountain north of Rome.

[3]*Thaliarchus* means, in Greek, "banquet-master." He is presumably Horace's slave, cupbearer, and boy lover.

[4]Wine.

[5]If Thaliarchus is Horace's boy lover, the ending of the poem suggests that he is making the expected transition from adolescent homosexuality to adult heterosexuality.

ODE 1.9[1]

See! how Soracte's hoary brow
  And melancholy crags uprear
Their weight of venerable snow:
  And scarce the groaning forests bear
The burthen of the gloomy year 5
  And motionless the stream remains
  Beneath the weight of icy chains.
Thou of the social banquet King,
Now store of welcome faggots bring,
  Now bid a brighter flame arise, 10
Now let the rich and rosy wine
Within the joyful goblets shine,
That wine whose age hath seen the ray
Of four long summers roll away
  Along yon wintry skies. 15
Leave to the Gods the rest—whose force
Can stay the whirlwind's wasting course;
When they have soothed the maddening jar
Of mingled elemental war,
Nor those tall ash-trees dread the storm 20
Nor cypress bows his shadowy form.
Why should we fear tomorrow's woe?
  Whatever day the Powers above
Have given, rejoice: nor, while the flow
  Of joy and golden youth delight 25
  Thy soul—while age avoids thee—slight
The mazy dance—the power of love.

Propertius

(c. 50 B.C.–after 16 B.C.)

The classicist Palmer Bovie has written rather paradoxically of a "classical tradition of romantic poetry" that flourished in Rome in the last three decades of the first century B.C. and that consisted of the work of seven love poets: Catullus, Gallus, Propertius, Tibullus, Virgil, Horace, and Ovid. In their love poems, we hear a voice of "individual feeling and direct self-expression" that can fairly be called "romantic." Of these poets, the most passionate and extreme

[1]Translated by Alfred, Lord Tennyson (1909–1892). Tennyson was both a good Latinist and one of the best metricists in the history of English poetry. His translation of Ode 1:9 captures most of the qualities of the poem except one, its strong sexual undercurrent. Tennyson's Victorian sensibility leads him to omit Thaliarchus's tell-tale name and to collapse into tangled constructions that are barely grammatically coherent at the sensual ending. Horace's blunt eroticism becomes in Tennyson's hands a general endorsement of "the power of love."

is perhaps Propertius. For him, love is the most important thing in the world, and he focuses single-mindedly on exploring its dimensions, especially its extremes of ecstasy and misery.

Little is known of his life. He was born in the Umbrian region of central Italy. He received a good education but was left with little else when his parents died and the state confiscated his inheritance. He gravitated to Rome, resolved to become a poet. He published Book 1 of his *Elegies* when he was about twenty-six; it brought him immediate fame and the patronage of the same Maecenas who supported Horace. Three more collections of elegies followed at intervals; Book 4 may have been published posthumously.

The elegiac form had been identified with love poetry, first in Greek and then in Latin, since at least the seventh century B.C. Metrically, it consists of couplets made up of one line of dactyllic hexameter followed by one of dactyllic pentameter. It was used for patriotic verse, for mourning poems, and for various sorts of topical or descriptive verse. But love was its primary theme, and Propertius makes it almost the exclusive one of *Elegies 1,* tracing the progress of his relationship with "Cynthia," its joys and sorrows. ("Cynthia" is a conventionalized Greek name, like Catullus's Lesbia and Ovid's Corinna, but like Lesbia and unlike Corinna, she seems to be a real woman with whom Propertius had a real affair.) In the three volumes of elegies that followed Book 1, Propertius took up other themes, but Cynthia poems appear in them all, even after Propertius finally rejects her at the end of Book 2; number 7 in Book 4 is devoted to Cynthia's ghost.

Propertius was regarded in his own day as a challenging, difficult poet, but the difficulties lie chiefly in the unexpected dramatic situations he sets up: an agonized conversation with a friend, an interior monologue into which the presence of Cynthia sometimes intrudes, the moment of receiving an urgent summons from Cynthia, a revery in which Cynthia speaks from beyond the grave. Such unexpected situations, combined with psychological complexity, have made Propertius especially attractive to modern poets. Of the four elegies included here, two are close, scholarly translations by Constance Carrier; the other two are looser versions "after Propertius" by the distinguished poets Ezra Pound and Robert Lowell.

ELEGIES

BOOK I, NO. 6: "I AM NO ORDINARY COWARD"[1]

I am no ordinary coward, Tullus;
I do not fear the dangers of the seas.
I'd climb the Alps with you as my companion,
or voyage past the far Hesperides.
It's Cynthia's arms have robbed me of my valor; 5
I hear her weep, I watch her as she pales,

[1]Translated by Constance Carrier.

swearing the gods will leave her all forsaken—
I watch, I listen, and my courage fails.
Though she is mine, she will not let me take her;
she screams that if I leave her she will die. 10
Refusals, threats and tears—these are her weapons.
You could not face them, Tullus, nor can I.
What heart have I for Athens or for Asia?
I'd hear her words, shrieked out, half-heard, wind-snatched
across the widening waters, and I'd see her, 15
her face all bloodied where her nails have scratched.
You have your uncle's record to surpass, now—
like him the governor, you must seek the good.
You've never loved a woman. What you cherish
is patriotism, justice, brotherhood. 20
O but that's wise, that's safe, that's as it should be!
Never let loving make a fool of you.
I would not wish an enemy, much less Tullus,
the agonies that Cynthia puts me through.
Fortune has willed it so, that I should suffer, 25
obedient to the worst she may demand.
Well, men have died for love, they say, and gladly.
I shall be one of that immortal band.
I am not fit for warfare and its glories;
love's is the only war that I can wage. 30
But you, whatever fortune may befall you,
whatever honors come to you with age—
sea-captain or explorer, merchant, ruler
beloved by all his subjects near and far—
if, in those days, you think of me, remember: 35
I was born under an unlucky star.

BOOK II, NO. 15: "NO MAN MORE BLEST!"[1]

No man more blest! O night, not dark for me,
beloved bed, scene of such dear delight!
To lie and talk there in the lamp's soft flickering,
and then to learn ourselves by touch, not sight—
to have her hold me with her breasts uncovered, 5
or, slipping on her tunic, balk my hand;
to have her kiss my eyes awake and murmur,
Why must you sleep? and make her sweet demand.
Shifting our arms, moving to new embraces,
we kissed a thousand kisses multiplied; 10

[1]Translated by Constance Carrier.

then, with the lamp rekindled, fed our senses
on new delights—the eye is love's best guide.
For Paris himself, they say, seeing Helen naked
on Menelaus' bed, loved at first sight;[2]
Endymion, naked, roused the cold Diana, 15
naked to lie with her throughout the night.[3]
Put on your tunic if you will, my Cynthia;
these furious hands will rip it into shreds.
You'll have bruised arms to show your mother, sweetheart;
when did frustration ever cool hot heads? 20
Youth's in those light ripe breasts, not yet gone flabby
as women's do when they have borne a child.
O let us love until we are each other—
we on whom Fate these few swift hours has smiled.
It will not be for long. A night will take us 25
which must refuse to brighten into dawn.
Strain closer to me, lock me in a nearness
that will not fail when time would have it gone.
Remember doves, how they are one in passion,
yoked, as we are, the male and female one? 30
Love is a frenzy, and it has no limit:
no love, if it is true, is ever done.
Let earth bear winter fruit and shock the farmer,
or let the sun god drive the steeds of night,
rivers run backward, or the seas be shrivelled, 35
fish dead in unaccustomed air and light—
these things will chance before I love another.
Living, I'll praise her; dead, dream of no other.

A single year of such nights, should she grant it—
for this I'd give up all three-score-and-ten. 40
If there were many, I would be immortal;
if there were even one, a god again.
Ah, men are fools who do not pass their life so,
limbs languorous and heavy with much wine.
Did they, there'd be no need for swords and warships, 45
for sailors' bones to steep in Actium's brine;[4]
no need for Rome to break her heart when Romans
die in the shambles of a civil war.
No god was ever outraged by our wine cups—
men can say this for us, if nothing more. 50
Do not renounce life while its light is in you.
Given all your kisses, still I'd have too few.

[2]The Trojan Paris abducted Helen, wife of Menelaus of Sparta, beginning the Trojan War.

[3]Diana, goddess of the moon, saw the shepherd Endymion sleeping naked, came down to earth, and made love to him in his dreams. Endymion begged Zeus for immortality, perpetual youth, and perpetual sleep so he could prolong his dream forever.

[4]Actium was the naval battle in which Octavian (later Caesar Augustus) defeated the forces of Antony and Cleopatra.

See how the withering wreath lets fall its petals
to float within the cup—O Cynthia, you
and I are lovers blest and hopeful, but 55
who knows what day may see that last door shut?

BOOK III, NO. 16: "MIDNIGHT, AND A LETTER COMES TO ME"[1]

Midnight, and a letter comes to me from our mistress:
Telling me to come to Tibur[2]:
At once!!
"Bright tips reach up from twin towers,
"Anienan spring water falls into flat-spread pools."

What *is* to be done about it? 5
Shall I entrust myself to entangled shadows,
Where bold hands may do violence to my person?

Yet if I postpone my obedience
because of this respectable terror,
I shall be prey to lamentations worse than a nocturnal assailant. 10
And I shall be in the wrong,
and it will last a twelve month,
For her hands have no kindness me-ward,

Nor is there anyone to whom lovers are not sacred at midnight
And in the Via Sciro.[3]
If any man would be a lover 15
he may walk on the Scythian coast,[4]
No barbarism would go to the extent of doing him harm,
The moon will carry his candle,
the stars will point out the stumbles,
Cupid will carry lighted torches before him 20
and keep mad dogs off his ankles.
Thus all roads are perfectly safe
and at any hour;
Who so indecorous as to shed the pure gore of a suitor?!
Cypris is his cicerone.[5]
What if undertakers follow my track, 25
such a death is worth dying.

[1]Translated by Ezra Pound. Pound translated twelve of Propertius's elegies in *Homage to Sextus Propertius* (1917).
[2]Tibur (now Tivoli) was about thirty miles east of Rome.
[3]A street in Rome.
[4]The Scythians occupied a large region of what is now eastern Europe and southern Russia. To the Romans, "Scythian" was synonymous with "barbarian."
[5]Cypris is Venus, the goddess of love (who came from Cyprus). A cicerone is a guide or protector.

She would bring frankincense and wreaths to my tomb,
  She would sit like an ornament on my pyre.

Gods' aid, let not my bones lie in a public location
With crowds too assiduous in their crossing of it; 30
For thus are tombs of lovers most desecrated.

May a woody and sequestered place cover me with its foliage
Or may I inter beneath the hummock
    of some as yet uncatalogued sand;
At any rate I shall not have my epitaph in a high road. 35

BOOK IV, NO. 7: "A GHOST IS SOMEONE"[1]

THE GHOST

(After Sextus Propertius)

A ghost is someone: death has left a hole
For the lead-colored soul to beat the fire:
  Cynthia leaves her dirty pyre
  And seems to coil herself and roll
    Under my canopy, 5
Love's stale and public playground, where I lie
And fill the run-down empire of my bed.
I see the street, her potter's field, is red
And lively with the ashes of the dead;

But she no longer sparkles off in smoke: 10
It is the body carted to the gate
  Last Friday, when the sizzling gate
  Left its charred furrows on her smock
    And ate into her hip.
A black nail dangles from a finger-tip 15
And Lethe[2] oozes from her nether lip.
Her thumb-bones rattle on her brittle hands,
As Cynthia stamps and hisses and demands:

[1]Translated by Robert Lowell in *Lord Weary's Castle* (1946). Lowell described the poem as "not a translation but an imitation which should be read as though it were an original English poem."
[2]River of forgetfulness in the Underworld; hence, death.

"Sextus, has sleep already washed away
Your manhood? You forget the window-sill 20
My sliding wore to slivers? Day
Would break before the Seven Hills[3]
Saw Cynthia retreat
And climb your shoulders to the knotted sheet.
You shouldered me and galloped on bare feet 25
To lay me by the crossroads. Have no fear:
Notus, who snatched your promise, has no ear.
"But why did no one call in my deaf ear?
Your calling would have gained me one more day.
Sextus, although you ran away 30
You might have called and stopped my bier
A second by your door.
No tears drenched a black toga for your whore
When broken tilestones bruised her face before
The Capitol. Would it have strained your purse 35
To scatter ten cheap roses on my hearse?

"The State will make Pompilia's Chloris burn:
I knew her secret when I kissed the skull
Of Pluto in the tainted bowl.
Let Nomas burn her books and turn 40
Her poisons into gold;
The finger-prints upon the potsherd told
Her love. You let a slut, whose body sold
To Thracians, liquefy my golden bust
In the coarse flame that crinkled me to dust.[4] 45

"If Chloris' bed has left you with your head,
Lover, I think you'll answer my arrears:
My nurse is getting on in years,
See that she gets a little bread—
She never clutched your purse; 50
See that my little humpback hears no curse
From her close-fisted friend. But burn the verse
You bellowed half a lifetime in my name:
Why should you feed me to the fires of fame?
"I will not hound you, much as you have earned 55
It, Sextus: I shall reign in your four books—
I swear this by the Hag who looks
Into my heart where it was burned:

[3]A Roman landmark.

[4]Cynthia suspects that Chloris (Propertius's new lover) paid Nomas (Cynthia's servant) to poison her (the "tainted bowl"). She also accuses Chloris of melting down her gold image.

Propertius, I kept faith;
If not, may serpents suck my ghost to death 60
And spit it with their forked and killing breath
Into the Styx where Agamemnon's wife
Founders in the green circles of her life.[5]

"Beat the sycophant ivy from my urn,
That twists its binding shoots about my bones 65
Where apple-sweetened Anio[6] drones
through orchards that will never burn
While honest Herakles,
My patron, watches. Anio, you will please
Me if you whisper upon sliding knees: 70
'Propertius, Cynthia is here:
She shakes her blossoms when my waters clear.'

"You cannot turn your back upon a dream,
For phantoms have their reasons when they come:
We wander midnights: then the numb 75
Ghost wades from the Lethean stream;
Even the foolish dog
Stops its hell-raising mouths and casts its clog;
At cock-crow Charon checks us in his log.[7]
Others can have you, Sextus; I alone 80
Hold: and I grind your manhood bone on bone."

[5]Clytaemnestra murdered her husband Agamemnon when he returned from the Trojan War. Cynthia says that she is condemned to spend eternity in the Styx, the boundary river of the Underworld.

[6]The river that runs through Tibur, where Cynthia is buried.

[7]Cynthia says that at midnight the ghosts of the Underworld walk: They wade through the river Lethe, and Cerberus ("the foolish dog") does not bark. At dawn, Charon, the gatekeeper and ferryman of Hades, checks them back in.

Cultural Texts of the Ancient World

Plato

(427–341 B.C.)

from *THE REPUBLIC*[1]

BOOK VII

THE PARABLE OF THE CAVE

And now, I said,[2] let me show in a figure how far our nature is enlightened or unenlightened:—Behold! human beings living in an underground den, which has a mouth open towards the light and reaching all along the den; here they have been from their childhood, and have their legs and necks chained so that they cannot move, and can only see before them, being prevented by the chains from turning round their heads. Above and behind them a fire is blazing at a distance, and between the fire and the prisoners there is a raised way; and you will see, if you look, a low wall built along the way, like the screen which marionette players have in front of them, over which they show the puppets.

I see.

And do you see, I said, men passing along the wall carrying all sorts of vessels, and statues and figures of animals made of wood and stone and various materials, which appear over the wall? Some of them are talking, others silent.

You have shown me a strange image, and they are strange prisoners.

Like ourselves, I replied; and they see only their own shadows, or the shadows of one another, which the fire throws on the opposite wall of the cave?

True, he said; how could they see anything but the shadows if they were never allowed to move their heads?

And of the objects which are being carried in like manner they would only see the shadows?

Yes, he said.

And if they were able to converse with one another, would they not suppose that they were naming what was actually before them?

Very true.

And suppose further that the prison had an echo which came from the

[1]Translated by Benjamin Jowett. *The Republic,* the second-longest (after *The Laws*) of Plato's works, is an inquiry into the nature of justice. The inquiry leads, in turn, to an attempt to define the ideal state. The form is that of a dialogue between Socrates and six other speakers. Book VII begins with the famous Parable of the Cave (or Den), in which Socrates, addressing an older brother of Plato named Glaucon, illustrates the difference between unenlightened people and enlightened philosophers. The parable also suggests the difficulty philosophers will have in returning to the sphere of practical affairs after having envisioned the ideal, supra-earthly form of the good. (Nevertheless, in the just commonwealth such civic service will be the duty of philosopher-rulers.)

[2]The entire dialogue is related, by Socrates, on the day after it is supposed to have occurred.

other side, would they not be sure to fancy when one of the passers-by spoke that the voice which they heard came from the passing shadow?

No question, he replied.

To them, I said, the truth would be literally nothing but the shadows of the images.

That is certain.

And now look again, and see what will naturally follow if the prisoners are released and disabused of their error. At first, when any of them is liberated and compelled suddenly to stand up and turn his neck round and walk and look towards the light, he will suffer sharp pains; the glare will distress him, and he will be unable to see the realities of which in his former state he had seen the shadows; and then conceive some one saying to him, that what he saw before was an illusion, but that now, when he is approaching nearer to being and his eye is turned towards more real existence, he has a clearer vision,—what will be his reply? And you may further imagine that his instructor is pointing to the objects as they pass and requiring him to name them,—will he not be perplexed? Will he not fancy that the shadows which he formerly saw are truer than the objects which are now shown to him?

Far truer.

And if he is compelled to look straight at the light, will he not have a pain in his eyes which will make him turn away to take refuge in the objects of vision which he can see, and which he will conceive to be in reality clearer than the things which are now being shown to him?

True, he said.

And suppose once more, that he is reluctantly dragged up a steep and rugged ascent, and held fast until he is forced into the presence of the sun himself, is he not likely to be pained and irritated? When he approaches the light his eyes will be dazzled, and he will not be able to see anything at all of what are now called realities.

Not all in a moment, he said.

He will require to grow accustomed to the sight of the upper world. And first he will see the shadows best, next the reflections of men and other objects in the water, and then the objects themselves; then he will gaze upon the light of the moon and the stars and the spangled heaven; and he will see the sky and the stars by night better than the sun or the light of the sun by day?

Certainly.

Last of all he will be able to see the sun, and not mere reflections of him in the water, but he will see him in his own proper place, and not in another; and he will contemplate him as he is.

Certainly.

He will then proceed to argue that this is he who gives the season and the years, and is the guardian of all that is in the visible world, and in a certain way the cause of all things which he and his fellows have been accustomed to behold?

Clearly, he said, he would first see the sun and then reason about him.

And when he remembered his old habitation, and the wisdom of the den and his fellow-prisoners, do you not suppose that he would felicitate himself on the change, and pity them?

Certainly, he would.

And if they were in the habit of conferring honors among themselves on those who were quickest to observe the passing shadows and to remark which of them went before, and which followed after, and which were together; and who were therefore best able to draw conclusions as to the future, do you think that he would care for such honors and glories, or envy the possessors of them? Would he not say with Homer,

"Better to be the poor servant of a poor master,"[3]

and to endure anything, rather than think as they do and live after their manner?

Yes, he said, I think that he would rather suffer anything than entertain these false notions and live in this miserable manner.

Imagine once more, I said, such a one coming suddenly out of the sun to be replaced in his old situation; would he not be certain to have his eyes full of darkness?

To be sure, he said.

And if there were a contest, and he had to compete in measuring the shadows with the prisoners who had never moved out of the den, while his sight was still weak, and before his eyes had become steady (and the time which would be needed to acquire this new habit of sight might be very considerable), would he not be ridiculous? Men would say of him that up he went and down he came without his eyes; and that it was better not even to think of ascending; and if any one tried to loose another and lead him up to the light, let them only catch the offender, and they would put him to death.

No question, he said.

This entire allegory, I said, you may now append, dear Glaucon, to the previous argument; the prison-house is the world of sight, the light of the fire is the sun, and you will not misapprehend me if you interpret the journey upwards to be the ascent of the soul into the intellectual world according to my poor belief, which, at your desire, I have expressed—whether rightly or wrongly God knows. But, whether true or false, my opinion is that in the world of knowledge the idea of good appears last of all, and is seen only with an effort; and, when seen, is also inferred to be the universal author of all things beautiful and right, parent of light and of the lord of light in this visible world, and the immediate source of reason and truth in the intellectual; and that this is the power upon which he who would act rationally either in public or private life must have his eye fixed.

I agree, he said, as far as I am able to understand you.

Moreover, I said, you must not wonder that those who attain to this beatific vision are unwilling to descend to human affairs; for their souls are ever hastening into the upper world where they desire to dwell; which desire of theirs is very natural, if our allegory may be trusted.

Yes, very natural.

And is there anything surprising in one who passes from divine contemplations to the evil state of man, misbehaving himself in a ridiculous manner; if, while his eyes are blinking and before he has become accustomed to the surrounding darkness, he is compelled to fight in courts of law, or in other places, about

[3]In the dim underworld of Hades visited by Odysseus in the *Odyssey*, Book XI, the shade of the great warrior Achilles says that he would rather be alive as the lowliest servant than reign as king of the Underworld.

the images or the shadows of images of justice, and is endeavoring to meet the conceptions of those who have never yet seen absolute justice?

Anything but surprising, he replied.

Any one who has common sense will remember that the bewilderments of the eyes are of two kinds, and arise from two causes, either from coming out of the light or from going into the light, which is true of the mind's eye, quite as much as of the bodily eye; and he who remembers this when he sees any one whose vision is perplexed and weak, will not be too ready to laugh; he will first ask whether that soul of man has come out of the brighter life, and is unable to see because unaccustomed to the dark, or having turned from darkness to the day is dazzled by excess of light. And he will count the one happy in his condition and state of being, and he will pity the other; or, if he have a mind to laugh at the soul which comes from below into the light, there will be more reason in this than in the laugh which greets him who returns from above out of the light into the den.

That, he said, is a very just distinction.

But then, if I am right, certain professors of education must be wrong when they say that they can put a knowledge into the soul which was not there before, like sight into blind eyes.

They undoubtedly say this, he replied.

Whereas, our argument shows that the power and capacity of learning exists in the soul already; and that just as the eye was unable to turn from darkness to light without the whole body, so too the instrument of knowledge can only by the movement of the whole soul be turned from the world of becoming into that of being, and learn by degrees to endure the sight of being, and of the brightest and best of being, or in other words, of the good. . . .

THE APOLOGY[1]

How you, O Athenians, have been affected by my accusers, I cannot tell; but I know that they almost made me forget who I was—so persuasively did they speak; and yet they have hardly uttered a word of truth. But of the many

[1]Translated by Benjamin Jowett. In 399 B.C., the seventy-year-old Socrates had made enemies of certain prominent Athenians to the extent that he was brought to trial, on two counts: for atheism and for the corruption of Athenian youth. The *Apology* is Socrates' defense of himself against the charges, both the immediate and specific ones on which he was arraigned and those brought against him during his entire life and career. If the word *apology* is mistakenly understood in its ordinary modern sense, the title of this work will be puzzling, for Socrates' speech is not a confession of guilt or error; it is quite the contrary. Socrates' words are an "apology" in the older sense of *apologia,* meaning an aggressive vindication of himself and of his principles. In keeping with his distinctive style of behavior, Socrates conducts his defense in an utterly personal way, with little regard for expediency or for legal forms and procedures.

Plato himself, then in his late twenties, is mentioned in the *Apology* as among the followers of Socrates present at the trial. If he was indeed present, Plato was in a position to record Socrates' words accurately. To what extent he actually did so, we cannot be sure; as with other Socratic dialogues, we must assume that the *Apology* is a combination of Socrates' ideas and his pupil Plato's own emphases and artistry. But the image of Socrates that emerges is so compelling that it conveys a strong impression of historical and even reportorial accuracy.

For many centuries readers have been irresistibly drawn to compare Socrates and Jesus. The accounts of their trials and executions are especially worthy of comparison—for both the similarities and the differences. See, for example, Matthew 26–27 and John 18–19.

falsehoods told by them, there was one which quite amazed me;—I mean when they said that you should be upon your guard and not allow yourselves to be deceived by the force of my eloquence. To say this, when they were certain to be detected as soon as I opened my lips and proved myself to be anything but a great speaker, did indeed appear to me most shameless—unless by the force of eloquence they mean the force of truth; for if such is their meaning, I admit that I am eloquent. But in how different a way from theirs! Well, as I was saying, they have scarcely spoken the truth at all; but from me you shall hear the whole truth: not, however, delivered after their manner in a set oration duly ornamented with words and phrases. No, by heaven! but I shall use the words and arguments which occur to me at the moment; for I am confident in the justice of my cause: at my time of life I ought not to be appearing before you, O men of Athens, in the character of a juvenile orator—let no one expect it of me. And I must beg of you to grant me a favor:—If I defend myself in my accustomed manner, and you hear me using the words which I have been in the habit of using in the agora,[2] at the tables of the money-changers, or anywhere else, I would ask you not to be surprised, and not to interrupt me on this account. For I am more than seventy years of age, and appearing now for the first time in a court of law, I am quite a stranger to the language of the place; and therefore I would have you regard me as if I were really a stranger,[3] whom you would excuse if he spoke in his native tongue, and after the fashion of his country:—Am I making an unfair request of you? Never mind the manner, which may or may not be good; but think only of the truth of my words, and give heed to that: let the speaker speak truly and the judge decide justly.

And first, I have to reply to the older charges and to my first accusers, and then I will go on to the later ones. For of old I have had many accusers, who have accused me falsely to you during many years; and I am more afraid of them than of Anytus and his associates,[4] who are dangerous, too, in their own way. But far more dangerous are the others, who began when you were children, and took possession of your minds with their falsehoods, telling of one Socrates, a wise man, who speculated about the heaven above, and searched into the earth beneath, and made the worse appear the better cause.[5] The disseminators of this tale are the accusers whom I dread; for their hearers are apt to fancy that such enquirers do not believe in the

[2]The public marketplace where citizens congregated.

[3]A noncitizen of Athens, whose dialect would have sounded uncouth to Athenians. Socrates' ironic point is that, though he is a genuine and lifelong Athenian, his manner of discourse will sound unconventional, like that of a "stranger" or foreigner.

[4]The three men who pressed charges against Socrates were Anytus, Meletus, and Lycon. Anytus was a wealthy leather merchant who disliked Socrates partly on political grounds and partly because Socrates had tried to persuade Anytus to let his son pursue a career different from his father's. Meletus (cross-examined by Socrates later in the *Apology*) may have been a poet (poets were both adulated and despised by Socrates/Plato). Of Lycon little is known; he may have been a professional orator.

[5]Socrates was almost entirely concerned with ethical human values, as distinguished from both natural science and the tricks of logic and language associated with the Sophists (professional teachers of rhetoric and logic or pseudo-logic). Nevertheless, his dexterity in discourse and his subtleties of argument caused some people to believe that he was a Sophist.

existence of the gods. And they are many, and their charges against me are of ancient date, and they were made by them in the days when you were more impressible than you are now—in childhood, or it may have been in youth—and the cause when heard went by default, for there was none to answer. And hardest of all, I do not know and cannot tell the names of my accusers; unless in the chance case of a Comic poet.[6] All who from envy and malice have persuaded you—some of them having first convinced themselves—all this class of men are most difficult to deal with; for I cannot have them up here, and cross-examine them, and therefore I must simply fight with shadows in my own defense, and argue when there is no one who answers. I will ask you then to assume with me, as I was saying, that my opponents are of two kinds; one recent, the other ancient: and I hope that you will see the propriety of my answering the latter first, for these accusations you heard long before the others, and much oftener.

Well, then, I must make my defense, and endeavor to clear away in a short time, a slander which has lasted a long time. May I succeed, if to succeed be for my good and yours, or likely to avail me in my cause! The task is not an easy one; I quite understand the nature of it. And so leaving the event with God, in obedience to the law I will now make my defense.

I will begin at the beginning, and ask what is the accusation which has given rise to the slander of me, and in fact has encouraged Meletus to prefer this charge against me. Well, what do the slanderers say? They shall be my prosecutors, and I will sum up their words in an affidavit: 'Socrates is an evil-doer, and a curious person, who searches into things under the earth and in heaven, and he makes the worse appear the better cause; and he teaches the aforesaid doctrines to others.' Such is the nature of the accusation: it is just what you have yourselves seen in the comedy of Aristophanes, who has introduced a man whom he calls Socrates, going about and saying that he walks in air, and talking a deal of nonsense concerning matters of which I do not pretend to know either much or little—not that I mean to speak disparagingly of any one who is a student of natural philosophy. I should be very sorry if Meletus could bring so grave a charge against me. But the simple truth is, O Athenians, that I have nothing to do with physical speculations. Very many of those here present are witnesses to the truth of this, and to them I appeal. Speak then, you who have heard me, and tell your neighbors whether any of you have ever known me hold forth in few words or in many upon such matters. . . . You hear their answer. And from what they say of this part of the charge you will be able to judge of the truth of the rest.

As little foundation is there for the report that I am a teacher, and take money; this accusation has no more truth in it than the other. Although, if a man were really able to instruct mankind, to receive money

[6]Aristophanes, who in his play *The Clouds* represented Socrates unfavorably, as a pretender to miraculous powers.

for giving instruction would, in my opinion, be an honor to him. There is Gorgias of Leontium, and Prodicus of Ceos, and Hippias of Elis,[7] who go the round of the cities, and are able to persuade the young men to leave their own citizens by whom they might be taught for nothing, and come to them whom they not only pay, but are thankful if they may be allowed to pay them. There is at this time a Parian philosopher residing in Athens, of whom I have heard; and I came to hear of him in this way:—I came across a man who has spent a world of money on the Sophists, Callias, the son of Hipponicus, and knowing that he had sons, I asked him: 'Callias,' I said, 'if your two sons were foals or calves, there would be no difficulty in finding some one to put over them; we should hire a trainer of horses, or a farmer probably, who would improve and perfect them in their own proper virtue and excellence; but as they are human beings, whom are you thinking of placing over them? Is there any one who understands human and political virtue? You must have thought about the matter, for you have sons; is there any one?' 'There is,' he said. 'Who is he?' said I, 'and of what country? and what does he charge?' 'Evenus[8] the Parian,' he replied; 'he is the man, and his charge is five minae.' Happy is Evenus, I said to myself, if he really has this wisdom, and teaches at such a moderate charge. Had I the same, I should have been very proud and conceited; but the truth is that I have no knowledge of the kind.

I dare say, Athenians, that some one among you will reply, 'Yes, Socrates, but what is the origin of these accusations which are brought against you; there must have been something strange which you have been doing? All these rumors and this talk about you would never have arisen if you had been like other men: tell us, then, what is the cause of them, for we should be sorry to judge hastily of you.' Now I regard this as a fair challenge, and I will endeavor to explain to you the reason why I am called wise and have such an evil fame. Please to attend then. And although some of you may think that I am joking, I declare that I will tell you the entire truth. Men of Athens, this reputation of mine has come of a certain sort of wisdom which I possess. If you ask me what kind of wisdom, I reply, wisdom such as may perhaps be attained by man, for to that extent I am inclined to believe that I am wise; whereas the persons of whom I was speaking have a superhuman wisdom, which I may fail to describe, because I have it not myself; and he who says that I have, speaks falsely, and is taking away my character. And here, O men of Athens, I must beg you not to interrupt me, even if I seem to say something extravagant. For the word which I will speak is not mine. I will refer you to a witness who is worthy of credit; that witness shall be the God of Delphi[9]—he will tell you about my wisdom, if I have any, and of what sort it is. You must have known Chaerephon; he was early a friend of mine,

[7]Noted Sophists and teachers, mainly of rhetoric and logic.

[8]A poet and teacher of oratory, from the island of Paros. The low sum he charged may indicate his low repute as a teacher. A mina was worth about forty dollars.

[9]Site of the most famous temple of Apollo; the god's oracles were pronounced there by the Pythia, his priestess.

and also a friend of yours, for he shared in the recent exile of the people,[10] and returned with you. Well, Chaerephon, as you know, was very impetuous in all his doings, and he went to Delphi and boldly asked the oracle to tell him whether—as I was saying, I must beg you not to interrupt—he asked the oracle to tell him whether any one was wiser than I was, and the Pythian prophetess answered, that there was no man wiser. Chaerephon is dead himself; but his brother, who is in court, will confirm the truth of what I am saying.

Why do I mention this? Because I am going to explain to you why I have such an evil name. When I heard the answer, I said to myself, What can the god mean? and what is the interpretation of his riddle? for I know that I have no wisdom, small or great. What then can he mean when he says that I am the wisest of men? And yet he is a god, and cannot lie; that would be against his nature. After long consideration, I thought of a method of trying the question. I reflected that if I could only find a man wiser than myself, then I might go to the god with a refutation in my hand. I should say to him, 'Here is a man who is wiser than I am; but you said that I was the wisest.' Accordingly I went to one who had the reputation of wisdom, and observed him—his name I need not mention; he was a politician whom I selected for examination—and the result was as follows: When I began to talk with him, I could not help thinking that he was not really wise, although he was thought wise by many, and still wiser by himself; and thereupon I tried to explain to him that he thought himself wise, but was not really wise; and the consequence was that he hated me, and his enmity was shared by several who were present and heard me. So I left him, saying to myself, as I went away: Well, although I do not suppose that either of us knows anything really beautiful and good, I am better off than he is,—for he knows nothing, and thinks that he knows; I neither know nor think that I know. In this latter particular, then, I seem to have slightly the advantage of him. Then I went to another who had still higher pretensions to wisdom, and my conclusion was exactly the same. Whereupon I made another enemy of him, and of many others beside him.

Then I went to one man after another, being not unconscious of the enmity which I provoked, and I lamented and feared this: but necessity was laid upon me,—the word of God, I thought, ought to be considered first. And I said to myself, Go I must to all who appear to know, and find out the meaning of the oracle. And I swear to you, Athenians, by the dog I swear!—for I must tell you the truth—the result of my mission was just this: I found that the men most in repute were all but the most foolish; and that others less esteemed were really wiser and better. I will tell you the tale of my wanderings and of the 'Herculean'[11] labors, as I may call them, which I endured only to find at last the oracle irrefutable. After the politicians, I went to the poets; tragic, dithyrambic, and all sorts. And there, I said to myself, you will be instantly detected; now you will find out that you are more ignorant than they are.

[10]Five years earlier, after the defeat of Athens by Sparta in 404, the "Thirty Tyrants" had temporarily ruled and terrorized Athens, driving the democratic leaders (who included Socrates' friend Chaerephon) into temporary exile. The democracy had been reestablished in 403.

[11]The legendary hero Hercules had been forced to undertake a series of superhumanly difficult tasks.

Accordingly, I took them some of the most elaborate passages in their own writings, and asked what was the meaning of them—thinking that they would teach me something. Will you believe me? I am almost ashamed to confess the truth, but I must say that there is hardly a person present who would not have talked better about their poetry than they did themselves. Then I knew that not by wisdom do poets write poetry, but by a sort of genius and inspiration; they are like diviners or soothsayers who also say many fine things, but do not understand the meaning of them.[12] The poets appeared to me to be much in the same case; and I further observed that upon the strength of their poetry they believed themselves to be the wisest of men in other things in which they were not wise. So I departed, conceiving myself to be superior to them for the same reason that I was superior to the politicians.

At last I went to the artisans,[13] for I was conscious that I knew nothing at all, as I may say, and I was sure that they knew many fine things; and here I was not mistaken, for they did know many things of which I was ignorant, and in this they certainly were wiser than I was. But I observed that even the good artisans fell into the same error as the poets;—because they were good workmen they thought that they also knew all sorts of high matters, and this defect in them overshadowed their wisdom; and therefore I asked myself on behalf of the oracle, whether I would like to be as I was, neither having their knowledge nor their ignorance, or like them in both; and I made answer to myself and to the oracle that I was better off as I was.

This inquisition has led to my having many enemies of the worst and most dangerous kind, and has given occasion also to many calumnies. And I am called wise, for my hearers always imagine that I myself possess the wisdom which I find wanting in others: but the truth is, O men of Athens, that God only is wise; and by his answer he intends to show that the wisdom of men is worth little or nothing; he is not speaking of Socrates, he is only using my name by way of illustration, as if he said, He, O men, is the wisest, who, like Socrates, knows that his wisdom is in truth worth nothing. And so I go about the world, obedient to the god, and search and make enquiry into the wisdom of any one, whether citizen or stranger, who appears to be wise; and if he is not wise, then in vindication of the oracle I show him that he is not wise; and my occupation quite absorbs me, and I have no time to give either to any public matter of interest or to any concern of my own, but I am in utter poverty by reason of my devotion to the god.

There is another thing:—young men of the richer classes, who have not much to do, come about me of their own accord; they like to hear the pretenders examined, and they often imitate me, and proceed to examine others; there are plenty of persons, as they quickly discover, who think that they know something, but really know little or nothing; and then those who are examined by them instead of being angry with themselves are angry with me: This confounded Socrates, they say; this villainous misleader of youth!—and then if somebody asks them, Why, what evil does he practice or teach?

[12]This view of poets and of their interpreters is elaborated, half-playfully, by Socrates in Plato's *Ion*.

[13]Craftsmen.

they do not know, and cannot tell; but in order that they may not appear to be at a loss, they repeat the ready-made charges which are used against all philosophers about teaching things up in the clouds and under the earth, and having no gods, and making the worse appear the better cause; for they do not like to confess that their pretense of knowledge has been detected—which is the truth; and as they are numerous and ambitious and energetic, and are drawn up in battle array and have persuasive tongues, they have filled your ears with their loud and inveterate calumnies. And this is the reason why my three accusers, Meletus and Anytus and Lycon, have set upon me; Meletus, who has a quarrel with me on behalf of the poets; Anytus, on behalf of the craftsmen and politicians; Lycon, on behalf of the rhetoricians: and as I said at the beginning, I cannot expect to get rid of such a mass of calumny all in a moment. And this, O men of Athens, is the truth and the whole truth; I have concealed nothing, I have dissembled nothing. And yet, I know that my plainness of speech makes them hate me, and what is their hatred but a proof that I am speaking the truth?—Hence has arisen the prejudice against me; and this is the reason of it, as you will find out either in this or in any future enquiry.

I have said enough in my defense against the first class of my accusers; I turn to the second class. They are headed by Meletus, that good man and true lover of his country, as he calls himself. Against these, too, I must try to make a defense:—Let their affidavit be read: it contains something of this kind: It says that Socrates is a doer of evil, who corrupts the youth; and who does not believe in the gods of the state, but has other new divinities of his own. Such is the charge; and now let us examine the particular counts. He says that I am a doer of evil, and corrupt the youth; but I say, O men of Athens, that Meletus is a doer of evil, in that he pretends to be in earnest when he is only in jest, and is so eager to bring men to trial from a pretended zeal and interest about matters in which he really never had the smallest interest. And the truth of this I will endeavor to prove to you.

Come hither, Meletus, and let me ask a question of you. You think a great deal about the improvement of youth?

Yes, I do.

Tell the judges, then, who is their improver; for you must know, as you have taken the pains to discover their corrupter, and are citing and accusing me before them. Speak, then, and tell the judges who their improver is.—Observe, Meletus, that you are silent, and have nothing to say. But is not this rather disgraceful, and a very considerable proof of what I was saying, that you have no interest in the matter? Speak up, friend, and tell us who their improver is.

The laws.

But that, my good sir, is not my meaning. I want to know who the person is, who, in the first place, knows the laws.[14]

[14]In the following lines, Socrates calls into play his notorious talent for reducing his opponent's view to foolishness. The half-defiant, half-squirming Meletus is forced to define the non-corrupters of youth first as the "judges" (that is, the men empowered to render the verdict), then the entire audience, then the "senators" (the five hundred select members of the assembly who constituted the Athenian civic council), then the whole "assembly," which in law included the entire adult citizenry of Athens.

The judges, Socrates, who are present in court.

What, do you mean to say, Meletus, that they are able to instruct and improve youth?

Certainly they are.

What, all of them, or some only and not others?

All of them.

By the goddess Herè,[15] that is good news! There are plenty of improvers, then. And what do you say of the audience,—do they improve them?

Yes, they do.

And the senators?

Yes, the senators improve them.

But perhaps the members of the assembly corrupt them?—or do they too improve them?

They improve them.

Then every Athenian improves and elevates them; all with the exception of myself; and I alone am their corrupter? Is that what you affirm?

That is what I stoutly affirm.

I am very unfortunate if you are right. But suppose I ask you a question: How about horses? Does one man do them harm and all the world good? Is not the exact opposite the truth? One man is able to do them good, or at least not many;—the trainer of horses, that is to say, does them good, and others who have to do with them rather injure them? Is not that true, Meletus, of horses, or of any other animals? Most assuredly it is; whether you and Anytus say yes or no. Happy indeed would be the condition of youth if they had one corrupter only, and all the rest of the world were their improvers. But you, Meletus, have sufficiently shown that you never had a thought about the young: your carelessness is seen in your not caring about the very things which you bring against me.

And now, Meletus, I will ask you another question—by Zeus I will: Which is better, to live among bad citizens, or among good ones? Answer, friend, I say; the question is one which may be easily answered. Do not the good do their neighbors good, and the bad do them evil?

Certainly.

And is there any one who would rather be injured than benefited by those who live with him? Answer, my good friend, the law requires you to answer—does any one like to be injured?

Certainly not.

And when you accuse me of corrupting and deteriorating the youth, do you allege that I corrupt them intentionally or unintentionally?

Intentionally, I say.

But you have just admitted that the good do their neighbors good, and the evil do them evil. Now, is that a truth which your superior wisdom has recognized thus early in life, and am I, at my age, in such darkness and ignorance as not to know that if a man with whom I have to live is corrupted by me, I am very likely to be harmed by him; and yet I corrupt him, and intentionally, too—so you say, although neither I nor any other human being is

[15]Hera, queen of the gods; this oath is often used by Socrates.

ever likely to be convinced by you. But either I do not corrupt them, or I corrupt them unintentionally; and on either view of the case you lie. If my offense is unintentional, the law has no cognizance of unintentional offenses: you ought to have taken me privately, and warned and admonished me; for if I had been better advised, I should have left off doing what I only did unintentionally—no doubt I should; but you would have nothing to say to me and refused to teach me. And now you bring me up in this court, which is a place not of instruction, but of punishment.

It will be very clear to you, Athenians, as I was saying, that Meletus has no care at all, great or small, about the matter. But still I should like to know, Meletus, in what I am affirmed to corrupt the young. I suppose you mean, as I infer from your indictment, that I teach them not to acknowledge the gods which the state acknowledges, but some other new divinities or spiritual agencies in their stead. These are the lessons by which I corrupt the youth, as you say.

Yes, that I say emphatically.

Then, by the gods, Meletus, of whom we are speaking, tell me and the court, in somewhat plainer terms, what you mean! for I do not as yet understand whether you affirm that I teach other men to acknowledge some gods, and therefore that I do believe in gods, and am not an entire atheist—this you do not lay to my charge,—but only you say that they are not the same gods which the city recognizes—the charge is that they are different gods. Or, do you mean that I am an atheist simply, and a teacher of atheism?

I mean the latter—that you are a complete atheist.

What an extraordinary statement! Why do you think so, Meletus? Do you mean that I do not believe in the godhead of the sun or moon,[16] like other men?

I assure you, judges, that he does not: for he says that the sun is stone, and the moon earth.

Friend Meletus, you think that you are accusing Anaxagoras:[17] and you have but a bad opinion of the judges, if you fancy them illiterate to such a degree as not to know that these doctrines are found in the books of Anaxagoras the Clazomenian, which are full of them. And so, forsooth, the youth are said to be taught them by Socrates, when there are not unfrequently exhibitions of them at the theater (price of admission one drachma at the most); and they might pay their money, and laugh at Socrates if he pretends to father these extraordinary views. And so, Meletus, you really think that I do not believe in any god?

I swear by Zeus that you believe absolutely in none at all.

[16]Apollo was the god of the sun, Artemis the goddess of the moon; but, whether the sun and moon were literally identified with these deities or not, reverence for the two great celestial bodies was a hallmark of religious piety for the Greeks. Socrates did, in fact, hold the sun and moon in awe, as is shown in Plato's *Symposium.*

[17]A philosopher-scientist, born around 500 B.C. Socrates, concerned almost entirely with ethics, would have resisted such materialist astrophysical theories. The reference to the theater a few lines later may mean that Anaxagoras' ideas were explored by the playwrights (particularly Euripides and Aristophanes) or that the philosopher's writings could be purchased there (or in some similar public place). In any event, Socrates' point is that such religiously heterodox ideas were freely available to the public apart from anything he might have taught.

Nobody will believe you, Meletus, and I am pretty sure that you do not believe yourself. I cannot help thinking, men of Athens, that Meletus is reckless and impudent, and that he has written this indictment in a spirit of mere wantonness and youthful bravado. Has he not compounded a riddle, thinking to try me? He said to himself:—I shall see whether the wise Socrates will discover my facetious contradiction, or whether I shall be able to deceive him and the rest of them. For he certainly does appear to me to contradict himself in the indictment as much as if he said that Socrates is guilty of not believing in the gods, and yet of believing in them—but this is not like a person who is in earnest.

I should like you, O men of Athens, to join me in examining what I conceive to be his inconsistency; and do you, Meletus, answer. And I must remind the audience of my request that they would not make a disturbance if I speak in my accustomed manner:

Did ever man, Meletus, believe in the existence of human things, and not of human beings? . . . I wish, men of Athens, that he would answer, and not be always trying to get up an interruption. Did ever any man believe in horsemanship, and not in horses? or in flute-playing, and not in flute-players? No, my friend; I will answer to you and to the court, as you refuse to answer for yourself. There is no man who ever did. But now please to answer the next question: Can a man believe in spiritual and divine agencies, and not in spirits or in demigods?[18]

He cannot.

How lucky I am to have extracted that answer, by the assistance of the court! But then you swear in the indictment that I teach and believe in divine or spiritual agencies (new or old, no matter for that); at any rate, I believe in spiritual agencies,—so you say and swear in the affidavit; and yet if I believe in divine beings, how can I help believing in spirits or demigods;—must I not? To be sure I must; and therefore I may assume that your silence gives consent. Now what are spirits or demigods? are they not either gods or the sons of gods?

Certainly they are.

But this is what I call the facetious riddle invented by you: the demigods or spirits are gods, and you say first that I do not believe in gods, and then again that I do believe in gods; that is, if I believe in demigods. For if the demigods are the illegitimate sons of gods, whether by the nymphs or by any other mothers, of whom they are said to be the sons—what human being will ever believe that there are no gods if they are the sons of gods? You might as well affirm the existence of mules,[19] and deny that of horses and asses. Such nonsense, Meletus, could only have been intended by you to make trial of me. You have put this into the indictment because you had nothing real of which to accuse me. But no one who has a particle of understanding will ever be convinced by you that the same men can believe in divine and superhuman things, and yet not believe that there are gods and demigods and heroes.

[18]The ensuing cross-examination of Meletus, logically sound or not, should probably be understood as an attempt by Socrates to prove contemptuously that he could easily defeat his opponents at their legalistic game if he did not have more substantial arguments to make (the ones that emerge in the following parts of his speech).

[19]A mule is a sterile animal produced by the union of a jackass with a mare.

I have said enough in answer to the charge of Meletus: any elaborate defense is unnecessary; but I know only too well how many are the enmities which I have incurred, and this is what will be my destruction if I am destroyed;—not Meletus, nor yet Anytus, but the envy and detraction of the world, which has been the death of many good men, and will probably be the death of many more; there is no danger of my being the last of them.

Some one will say: And are you not ashamed, Socrates, of a course of life which is likely to bring you to an untimely end? To him I may fairly answer: There you are mistaken: a man who is good for anything ought not to calculate the chance of living or dying; he ought only to consider whether in doing anything he is doing right or wrong—acting the part of a good man or of a bad. Whereas, upon your view, the heroes who fell at Troy were not good for much, and the son of Thetis[20] above all, who altogether despised danger in comparison with disgrace; and when he was so eager to slay Hector, his goddess mother said to him, that if he avenged his companion Patroclus, and slew Hector, he would die himself—'Fate,' she said, in these or the like words, 'waits for you next after Hector;' he, receiving this warning, utterly despised danger and death, and instead of fearing them, feared rather to live in dishonor, and not to avenge his friend. 'Let me die forthwith,' he replies, 'and be avenged of my enemy, rather than abide here by the beaked ships, a laughing-stock and a burden of the earth.' Had Achilles any thought of death and danger? For wherever a man's place is, whether the place which he has chosen or that in which he has been placed by a commander, there he ought to remain in the hour of danger; he should not think of death or of anything but of disgrace. And this, O men of Athens, is a true saying.

Strange, indeed, would be my conduct, O men of Athens, if I who, when I was ordered by the generals whom you chose to command me at Potidaea and Amphipolis and Delium,[21] remained where they placed me, like any other man, facing death—if now, when, as I conceive and imagine, God orders me to fulfil the philosopher's mission of searching into myself and other men, I were to desert my post through fear of death, or any other fear; that would indeed be strange, and I might justly be arraigned in court for denying the existence of the gods, if I disobeyed the oracle because I was afraid of death, fancying that I was wise when I was not wise. For the fear of death is indeed the pretense of wisdom, and not real wisdom, being a pretense of knowing the unknown; and no one knows whether death, which men in their fear apprehend to be the greatest evil, may not be the greatest good. Is not this ignorance of a disgraceful sort, the ignorance which is the conceit that a man knows what he does not know? And in this respect only I believe myself to differ from men in general, and may perhaps claim to be wiser than they

[20]A sea nymph, mother of Achilles, the hero of Homer's *Iliad*. The Trojan prince and hero Hector had killed Achilles' best friend, Patroclus, an event that brought Achilles back into the battle after a period of sulky neutrality occasioned by his quarrel with the Greek commander Agamemnon. The dialogue cited here, between Achilles and Thetis, occurs in Book XVIII of the *Iliad*.

[21]Sites of battles (fought, respectively, in 432, 422, and 424) in which Socrates had served bravely as a soldier. At Potidaea Socrates had saved the life of the Athenian soldier-playboy Alcibiades; see Plato's *Symposium*.

are:—that whereas I know but little of the world below, I do not suppose that I know: but I do know that injustice and disobedience to a better, whether God or man, is evil and dishonorable, and I will never fear or avoid a possible good rather than a certain evil. And therefore if you let me go now, and are not convinced by Anytus, who said that since I had been prosecuted I must be put to death; (or if not that I ought never to have been prosecuted at all); and that if I escape now, your sons will all be utterly ruined by listening to my words—if you say to me, Socrates, this time we will not mind Anytus, and you shall be let off, but upon one condition, that you are not to enquire and speculate in this way any more, and that if you are caught doing so again you shall die;—if this was the condition on which you let me go, I should reply: Men of Athens, I honor and love you; but I shall obey God rather than you, and while I have life and strength I shall never cease from the practice and teaching of philosophy, exhorting any one whom I meet and saying to him after my manner: You, my friend,—a citizen of the great and mighty and wise city of Athens,—are you not ashamed of heaping up the greatest amount of money and honor and reputation, and caring so little about wisdom and truth and the greatest improvement of the soul, which you never regard or heed at all? And if the person with whom I am arguing, says: Yes, but I do care; then I do not leave him or let him go at once; but I proceed to interrogate and examine and cross-examine him, and if I think that he has no virtue in him, but only says that he has, I reproach him with undervaluing the greater, and overvaluing the less. And I shall repeat the same words to every one whom I meet, young and old, citizen and alien, but especially to the citizens, inasmuch as they are my brethren. For know that this is the command of God; and I believe that no greater good has ever happened in the state than my service to the God. For I do nothing but go about persuading you all, old and young alike, not to take thought for your persons or your properties, but first and chiefly to care about the greatest improvement of the soul. I tell you that virtue is not given by money, but that from virtue comes money and every other good of man, public as well as private. This is my teaching, and if this is the doctrine which corrupts the youth, I am a mischievous person. But if any one says that this is not my teaching, he is speaking an untruth. Wherefore, O men of Athens, I say to you, do as Anytus bids or not as Anytus bids, and either acquit me or not; but whichever you do, understand that I shall never alter my ways, not even if I have to die many times.

Men of Athens, do not interrupt, but hear me; there was an understanding between us that you should hear me to the end: I have something more to say, at which you may be inclined to cry out; but I believe that to hear me will be good for you, and therefore I beg that you will not cry out. I would have you know, that if you kill such an one as I am, you will injure yourselves more than you will injure me. Nothing will injure me, not Meletus nor yet Anytus—they cannot, for a bad man is not permitted to injure a better than himself. I do not deny that Anytus may, perhaps, kill him, or drive him into exile, or deprive him of civil rights; and he may imagine, and others may imagine, that he is inflicting a great injury upon him: but there I do not agree. For the evil of doing as he is doing—the evil of unjustly taking away the life of another—is greater far.

And now, Athenians, I am not going to argue for my own sake, as you may think, but for yours, that you may not sin against the God by condemning me, who am his gift to you. For if you kill me you will not easily find a successor to me, who, if I may use such a ludicrous figure of speech, am a sort of gadfly, given to the state by God; and the state is a great and noble steed who is tardy in his motions owing to his very size, and requires to be stirred into life. I am that gadfly which God has attached to the state, and all day long and in all places am always fastening upon you, arousing and persuading and reproaching you. You will not easily find another like me, and therefore I would advise you to spare me. I dare say that you may feel out of temper (like a person who is suddenly awakened from sleep), and you think that you might easily strike me dead as Anytus advises, and then you would sleep on for the remainder of your lives, unless God in his care of you sent you another gadfly. When I say that I am given to you by God, the proof of my mission is this:—if I had been like other men, I should not have neglected all my own concerns or patiently seen the neglect of them during all these years, and have been doing yours, coming to you individually like a father or elder brother, exhorting you to regard virtue; such conduct, I say, would be unlike human nature. If I had gained anything, or if my exhortations had been paid, there would have been some sense in my doing so; but now, as you will perceive, not even the impudence of my accusers dares to say that I have ever exacted or sought pay of any one; of that they have no witness. And I have a sufficient witness to the truth of what I say—my poverty.

Some one may wonder why I go about in private giving advice and busying myself with the concerns of others, but do not venture to come forward in public and advise the state. I will tell you why. You have heard me speak at sundry times and in divers places of an oracle or sign which comes to me, and is the divinity which Meletus ridicules in the indictment. This sign, which is a kind of voice, first began to come to me when I was a child; it always forbids but never commands me to do anything which I am going to do. This is what deters me from being a politician. And rightly, as I think. For I am certain, O men of Athens, that if I had engaged in politics, I should have perished long ago, and done no good either to you or to myself. And do not be offended at my telling you the truth: for the truth is, that no man who goes to war with you or any other multitude, honestly striving against the many lawless and unrighteous deeds which are done in a state, will save his life; he who will fight for the right, if he would live even for a brief space, must have a private station and not a public one.

I can give you convincing evidence of what I say, not words only, but what you value far more—actions. Let me relate to you a passage of my own life which will prove to you that I should never have yielded to injustice from any fear of death, and that 'as I should have refused to yield' I must have died at once. I will tell you a tale of the courts, not very interesting perhaps, but nevertheless true. The only office of state which I ever held, O men of Athens, was that of senator: the tribe Antiochis, which is my tribe, had the presidency at the trial of the generals who had not taken up the bodies of the slain after the battle of Arginusae; and you proposed to try them in a body, contrary to law, as you all thought afterwards; but at the time I was the only one of the Prytanes who was opposed to the illegality, and I gave my vote against you; and when the orators threatened to impeach and arrest me, and you called and shouted, I made up my mind that I would run the risk, having law and justice with me, rather than take part in your injustice because I feared imprisonment and death. This happened in the days of the democracy.[22] But when the oligarchy of the Thirty was in power, they sent for me and four others into the rotunda, and bade us bring Leon[23] the Salaminian from Salamis, as they wanted to put him to death. This was a specimen of the sort of commands which they were always giving with the view of implicating as many as possible in their crimes; and then I showed, not in word only but in deed, that, if I may be allowed to use such an expression, I cared not a straw for death, and that my great and only care was lest I should do an unrighteous or unholy thing. For the strong arm of that oppressive power did not frighten me into doing wrong; and when we came out of the rotunda the other four went to Salamis and fetched Leon, but I went quietly home. For which I might have lost my life, had not the power of the Thirty shortly afterwards come to an end. And many will witness to my words.

Now do you really imagine that I could have survived all these years, if I had led a public life, supposing that like a good man I had always maintained the right and had made justice, as I ought, the first thing? No indeed, men of Athens, neither I nor any other man. But I have been always the same in all my actions, public as well as private, and never have I yielded any base compliance to those who are slanderously termed my disciples, or to any other. Not that I have any regular disciples. But if anyone likes to come and hear me while I am pursuing my mission, whether he be young or old, he is not excluded. Nor do I converse only with those who pay; but any one, whether he be rich or poor, may ask and answer me and listen to my words; and whether he turns out to be a bad man or a good one, neither result can be justly imputed to me; for I never taught or professed to teach him anything. And if any one says that he has ever learned or heard anything from me in private which all the world has not heard, let me tell you that he is lying.

But I shall be asked, Why do people delight in continually conversing with you? I have told you already, Athenians, the whole truth about this matter: they like to hear the cross-examination of the pretenders to wisdom; there is amusement in it. Now this duty of cross-examining other men has been imposed upon me by God; and has been signified to me by oracles, visions, and in every way in which the will of divine power was ever intimated to any one. This is true, O Athenians; or, if not true, would be soon refuted. If I am or have been corrupting the youth, those of them who are now grown up and have become sensible that I gave them bad advice in the days of their youth should come forward as accusers, and take their revenge; or if they do not like to come themselves, some of their relatives, fathers, brothers, or

[22]The Athenian senate consisted of five hundred members, fifty from each of the ten phylae, or "tribes." Socrates belonged to a tribe named for the mythical figure Antiochus. Each tribe served for one-tenth of the year as the executive body of the senate; during that period they were called "Prytanes." While Socrates was serving in that capacity, certain Athenian commanders were indicted for allegedly neglecting the dead after the naval battle of Arginusae in 406. Socrates refused to participate in the trial, which violated due process of Athenian law in a number of ways.

[23]As he had defied the authority of the democratic state, Socrates also defied the tyrannical "Thirty" who ruled in 404, by refusing to extradite Leon from Salamis after he had fled there to escape the despotic regime.

other kinsmen, should say what evil their families have suffered at my hands. Now is their time. Many of them I see in the court. There is Crito, who is of the same age and of the same deme[24] with myself, and there is Critobulus his son, whom I also see. Then again there is Lysanias of Sphettus, who is the father of Aeschines—he is present; and also there is Antiphon of Cephisus, who is the father of Epigenes; and there are the brothers of several who have associated with me. There is Nicostratus the son of Theosdotides, and the brother of Theodotus (now Theodotus himself is dead, and therefore he, at any rate, will not seek to stop him); and there is Paralus the son of Demodocus, who had a brother Theages; and Adeimantus the son of Ariston, whose brother Plato[25] is present; and Aeantodorus, who is the brother of Apollodorus, whom I also see. I might mention a great many others, some of whom Meletus should have produced as witnesses in the course of his speech; and let him still produce them, if he has forgotten—I will make way for him. And let him say, if he has any testimony of the sort which he can produce. Nay, Athenians, the very opposite is the truth. For all these are ready to witness on behalf of the corrupter, of the injurer of their kindred, as Meletus and Anytus call me; not the corrupted youth only—there might have been a motive for that—but their uncorrupted elder relatives. Why should they too support me with their testimony? Why, indeed, except for the sake of truth and justice, and because they know that I am speaking the truth, and that Meletus is a liar.

Well, Athenians, this and the like of this is all the defense which I have to offer. Yet a word more. Perhaps there may be some one who is offended at me, when he calls to mind how he himself on a similar, or even a less serious occasion, prayed and entreated the judges with many tears, and how he produced children in court, which was a moving spectacle, together with a host of relations and friends; whereas I, who am probably in danger of my life, will do none of these things. The contrast may occur to his mind, and he may be set against me, and vote in anger because he is displeased at me on this account. Now if there be such a person among you,—mind, I do not say that there is,—to him I may fairly reply: My friend, I am a man, and like other men, a creature of flesh and blood, and not 'of wood or stone,' as Homer says;[26] and I have a family, yes, and sons, O Athenians, three in number, one almost a man, and two others who are still young; and yet I will not bring any of them hither in order to petition you for an acquittal. And why not? Not from any self-assertion or want of respect for you. Whether I am or am not afraid of death is another question, of which I will not now speak. But, having regard to public opinion, I feel that such conduct would be discreditable to myself, and to you, and to the whole state. One who has reached my years, and who has a name for wisdom, ought not to demean himself. Whether this opinion of me be deserved or not, at any rate the world has decided that Socrates is in some way superior to other men. And if those among you who are said to be superior in wisdom and courage, and any other virtue, demean themselves in this way, how shameful is their conduct! I have seen men of reputation, when they have been condemned, behaving in the

[24]District.

[25]The author of the present work. Several of the persons mentioned appear in other works by Plato.

[26]The words are addressed to the disguised Odysseus by his wife, Penelope, in Book XIX of Homer's *Odyssey.*

strangest manner: they seemed to fancy that they were going to suffer something dreadful if they died, and that they could be immortal if you only allowed them to live; and I think that such are a dishonor to the state, and that any stranger coming in would have said of them that the most eminent men of Athens, to whom the Athenians themselves give honor and command, are no better than women. And I say that these things ought not to be done by those of us who have a reputation; and if they are done, you ought not to permit them; you ought rather to show that you are far more disposed to condemn the man who gets up a doleful scene and makes the city ridiculous, than him who holds his peace.

But, setting aside the question of public opinion, there seems to be something wrong in asking a favor of a judge, and thus procuring an acquittal, instead of informing and convincing him. For his duty is, not to make a present of justice, but to give judgment; and he has sworn that he will judge according to the laws, and not according to his own good pleasure; and we ought not to encourage you, nor should you allow yourselves to be encouraged, in this habit of perjury—there can be no piety in that. Do not then require me to do what I consider dishonorable and impious and wrong, especially now, when I am being tried for impiety on the indictment of Meletus. For if, O men of Athens, by force of persuasion and entreaty I could overpower your oaths, then I should be teaching you to believe that there are no gods, and in defending should simply convict myself of the charge of not believing in them. But that is not so—far otherwise. For I do believe that there are gods, and in a sense higher than that in which any of my accusers believe in them. And to you and to God I commit my cause, to be determined by you as is best for you and me.[27]

There are many reasons why I am not grieved, O men of Athens, at the vote of condemnation. I expected it, and am only surprised that the votes are so nearly equal; for I had thought that the majority against me would have been far larger; but now, had thirty votes gone over to the other side, I should have been acquitted. And I may say, I think, that I have escaped Meletus. I may say more, for without the assistance of Anytus and Lycon, any one may see that he would not have had a fifth part of the votes, as the law requires, in which case he would have incurred a fine of a thousand drachmae.[28]

And so he proposes death as the penalty. And what shall I propose on my part, O men of Athens? Clearly that which is my due. And what is my due? What return shall be made to the man who has never had the wit to be idle during his whole life; but has been careless of what the many care for—wealth, and family interests, and military offices, and speaking in the assembly, and magistracies, and plots, and parties. Reflecting that I was really too honest a man to be a politician and live, I did not go where I could do

[27]At this point the jurors cast their votes; about 280 vote for conviction, 220 for acquittal. (Plato does not describe these deliberations; there has been no omission from the text.) The next decision is on the sentence.

[28]Socrates ironically intimates that each of his three accusers has captured a third of the vote cast against him—approximately ninety-three apiece, a number lower than the one-fifth (about one hundred) necessary for an accuser to avoid paying a fine. The fine was intended to discourage capricious prosecutions.

no good to you or to myself; but where I could do the greatest good privately to every one of you, thither I went, and sought to persuade every man among you that he must look to himself, and seek virtue and wisdom before he looks to his private interests, and look to the state before he looks to the interests of the state; and that this should be the order which he observes in all his actions. What shall be done to such an one? Doubtless some good thing, O men of Athens, if he has his reward; and the good should be of a kind suitable to him. What would be a reward suitable to a poor man who is your benefactor, and who desires leisure that he may instruct you? There can be no reward so fitting as maintenance in the Prytaneum,[29] O men of Athens, a reward which he deserves far more than the citizen who has won the prize at Olympia in the horse or chariot race, whether the chariots were drawn by two horses or by many. For I am in want, and he has enough; and he only gives you the appearance of happiness, and I give you the reality. And if I am to estimate the penalty fairly, I should say that maintenance in the Prytaneum is the just return.

Perhaps you think that I am braving you in what I am saying now, as in what I said before about the tears and prayers. But this is not so. I speak rather because I am convinced that I never intentionally wronged any one, although I cannot convince you—the time has been too short; if there were a law in Athens, as there is in other cities, that a capital cause should not be decided in one day, then I believe that I should have convinced you. But I cannot in a moment refute great slanders; and, as I am convinced that I never wronged another, I will assuredly not wrong myself. I will not say of myself that I deserve any evil, or propose any penalty. Why should I? Because I am afraid of the penalty of death which Meletus proposes? When I do not know whether death is a good or an evil, why should I propose a penalty which would certainly be an evil? Shall I say imprisonment? And why should I live in prison, and be the slave of the magistrates of the year—of the Eleven?[30] Or shall the penalty be a fine, and imprisonment until the fine is paid? There is the same objection. I should have to lie in prison, for money I have none, and cannot pay. And if I say exile (and this may possibly be the penalty which you will affix), I must indeed be blinded by the love of life, if I am so irrational as to expect that when you, who are my own citizens, cannot endure my discourses and words, and have found them so grievous and odious that you will have no more of them, others are likely to endure me. No indeed, men of Athens, that is not very likely. And what a life should I lead, at my age, wandering from city to city, ever changing my place of exile, and always being driven out! For I am quite sure that wherever I go, there, as here, the young men will flock to me; and if I drive them away, their elders will drive me out at their request; and if I let them come, their fathers and friends will drive me out for their sakes.

Some one will say: Yes, Socrates, but cannot you hold your tongue, and then you may go into a foreign city, and no one will interfere with you? Now I have great difficulty in making you understand my answer to this. For if I

[29]A place on the Acropolis where benefactors of Athens were honored. Olympia, in southwestern Greece, was the site of a great festival, held every four years, featuring athletic contests. The modern Olympic Games are named for this festival.

[30]A public committee that enforced and supervised criminal penalties, including executions. It was made up of a representative from each of the ten "tribes," plus a secretary.

tell you that to do as you say would be a disobedience to the God, and therefore that I cannot hold my tongue, you will not believe that I am serious; and if I say again that daily to discourse about virtue, and of those other things about which you hear me examining myself and others, is the greatest good of man, and that the unexamined life is not worth living,[31] you are still less likely to believe me. Yet I say what is true, although a thing of which it is hard for me to persuade you. Also, I have never been accustomed to think that I deserve to suffer any harm. Had I money I might have estimated the offense at what I was able to pay, and not have been much the worse. But I have none, and therefore I must ask you to proportion the fine to my means. Well, perhaps I could afford a mina, and therefore I propose that penalty:[32] Plato, Crito, Critobulus, and Apollodorus, my friends here, bid me say thirty minae, and they will be the sureties. Let thirty minae be the penalty; for which sum they will be ample security to you.[33]

Not much time will be gained, O Athenians, in return for the evil name which you will get from the detractors of the city, who will say that you killed Socrates, a wise man; for they will call me wise, even although I am not wise, when they want to reproach you. If you had waited a little while, your desire would have been fulfilled in the course of nature. For I am far advanced in years, as you may perceive, and not far from death. I am speaking now not to all of you, but only to those who have condemned me to death. And I have another thing to say to them: You think that I was convicted because I had no words of the sort which would have procured my acquittal—I mean, if I had thought fit to leave nothing undone or unsaid. Not so; the deficiency which led to my conviction was not of words—certainly not. But I had not the boldness or impudence or inclination to address you as you would have liked me to do, weeping and wailing and lamenting, and saying and doing many things which you have been accustomed to hear from others, and which, as I maintain, are unworthy of me. I thought at the time that I ought not to do anything common or mean when in danger: nor do I now repent of the style of my defense; I would rather die having spoken after my manner, than speak in your manner and live. For neither in war nor yet at law ought I or any man to use every way of escaping death. Often in battle there can be no doubt that if a man will throw away his arms, and fall on his knees before his pursuers, he may escape death; and in other dangers there are other ways of escaping death, if a man is willing to say and do anything. The difficulty, my friends, is not to avoid death, but to avoid unrighteousness; for that runs faster than death. I am old and move slowly, and the slower runner has overtaken me, and my accusers are keen and quick, and the faster runner, who is unrighteousness, has overtaken them. And now I depart hence condemned by you to suffer the penalty of death,—they too go their ways condemned by the truth to suffer the penalty of villainy and wrong; and I must abide by my award—let them abide by theirs. I suppose that these things may be regarded as fated,—and I think that they are well.

[31]One of Socrates' most memorable axioms.

[32]Socrates' decision to propose a monetary penalty is not mercenary but just the opposite: it is a dramatization of his contempt for money as a measure of life and values.

[33]At this point, the five hundred judges cast another split vote, for the death penalty. (Again, Plato does not describe these deliberations; the text given here is complete.)

And now, O men who have condemned me, I would fain prophesy to you; for I am about to die, and in the hour of death men are gifted with prophetic power. And I prophesy to you who are my murderers, that immediately after my departure punishment far heavier than you have inflicted on me will surely await you. Me you have killed because you wanted to escape the accuser, and not to give an account of your lives. But that will not be as you suppose: far otherwise. For I say that there will be more accusers of you than there are now; accusers whom hitherto I have restrained: and as they are younger they will be more inconsiderate with you, and you will be more offended at them. If you think that by killing men you can prevent some one from censuring your evil lives, you are mistaken; that is not a way of escape which is either possible or honorable; the easiest and the noblest way is not to be disabling others, but to be improving yourselves. This is the prophecy which I utter before my departure to the judges who have condemned me.

Friends, who would have acquitted me, I would like also to talk with you about the thing which has come to pass, while the magistrates are busy, and before I go to the place at which I must die. Stay then a little, for we may as well talk with one another while there is time. You are my friends, and I should like to show you the meaning of this event which has happened to me. O my judges—for you I may truly call judges—I should like to tell you of a wonderful circumstance. Hitherto the divine faculty of which the internal oracle is the source has constantly been in the habit of opposing me even about trifles, if I was going to make a slip or error in any matter; and now as you see there has come upon me that which may be thought, and is generally believed to be, the last and worst evil. But the oracle made no sign of opposition, either when I was leaving my house in the morning, or when I was on my way to the court, or while I was speaking, at anything which I was going to say; and yet I have often been stopped in the middle of a speech, but now in nothing I either said or did touching the matter in hand has the oracle opposed me. What do I take to be the explanation of this silence? I will tell you. It is an intimation that what has happened to me is a good, and that those of us who think that death is an evil are in error. For the customary sign would surely have opposed me had I been going to evil and not to good.

Let us reflect in another way, and we shall see that there is great reason to hope that death is a good; for one of two things—either death is a state of nothingness and utter unconsciousness, or, as men say, there is a change and migration of the soul from this world to another. Now if you suppose that there is no consciousness, but a sleep like the sleep of him who is undisturbed even by dreams, death will be an unspeakable gain. For if a person were to select the night in which his sleep was undisturbed even by dreams, and were to compare with this the other days and nights of his life, and then were to tell us how many days and nights he had passed in the course of his life better and more pleasantly than this one, I think that any man, I will not say a private man, but even the great king will not find many such days or nights, when compared with the others. Now if death be of such a nature, I say that to die is gain; for eternity is then only a single night. But if death is the journey to another place, and there, as men say, all the dead abide, what good, O my friends and judges, can be greater than this? If indeed when the pilgrim arrives in the world below, he is delivered from the professors of justice in this world, and finds the true judges who are said to give judgment there, Minos and Rhadamanthus and Aeacus and Triptolemus,[34] and other sons of God who were righteous in their own life, that pilgrimage will be worth making. What would not a man give if he might converse with Orpheus and Musaeus and Hesiod and Homer?[35] Nay, if this be true, let me die again and again. I myself, too, shall have a wonderful interest in there meeting and conversing with Palamedes, and Ajax[36] the son of Telamon, and any other ancient hero who has suffered death through an unjust judgment; and there will be no small pleasure, as I think, in comparing my own sufferings with theirs. Above all, I shall then be able to continue my search into true and false knowledge; as in this world, so also in the next; and I shall find out who is wise, and who pretends to be wise, and is not. What would not a man give, O judges, to be able to examine the leader of the great Trojan expedition; or Odysseus or Sisyphus,[37] or numberless others, men and women too! What infinite delight would there be in conversing with them and asking them questions! In another world they do not put a man to death for asking questions: assuredly not. For besides being happier than we are, they will be immortal, if what is said is true.

Wherefore, O judges, be of good cheer about death, and know of a certainty, that no evil can happen to a good man, either in life or after death. He and his are not neglected by the gods; nor has my own approaching end happened by mere chance. But I see clearly that the time had arrived when it was better for me to die and be released from trouble; wherefore the oracle gave no sign. For which reason, also, I am not angry with my condemners, or with my accusers; they have done me no harm, although they did not mean to do me any good; and for this I may gently blame them.

Still I have a favor to ask of them. When my sons are grown up, I would ask you, O my friends, to punish them; and I would have you trouble them, as I have troubled you, if they seem to care about riches, or anything, more than about virtue; or if they pretend to be something when they are really nothing,—then reprove them, as I have reproved you, for not caring about that for which they ought to care, and thinking that they are something when they are really nothing. And if you do this, both I and my sons will have received justice at your hands.

The hour of departure has arrived, and we go our ways—I to die, and you to live. Which is better God only knows.[38]

[34]The four judges of the dead in the afterlife.

[35]Great poets, legendary and real.

[36]Two victims of unjust or dubious trials or verdicts.

[37]Both were noted for their cunning. In mentioning them here, Socrates is anticipating a meeting not merely with eminent men but with adversaries whose mental agility will put his powers to a real test.

[38]In two other dialogues, the *Crito* and the *Phaedo,* the story of Socrates' last days is concluded. In the former, his friend Crito pleads with Socrates to accept an opportunity to escape from Athens, to which Socrates replies (in his usual style of reasoned argument) that such a course would be wrong, since to defy the Athenian laws that have condemned him is the equivalent of rejecting parents who have nurtured him and whose authority he has implicitly accepted throughout his life. The *Phaedo* includes Socrates' argument for the immortality and inviolability of the soul and narrates his serene death, imposed by his drinking of the poison liquid called hemlock.

Aristotle

(384–322 B.C.)

from *NICOMACHEAN ETHICS*[1]

[THE GOLDEN MEAN]

We must, however, not only describe virtue as a state of character, but also say what sort of state it is. We may remark, then, that every virtue or excellence both brings into good condition the thing of which it is the excellence and makes the work of that thing be done well; e.g., the excellence of the eye makes both the eye and its work good; for it is by the excellence of the eye that we see well. Similarly the excellence of the horse makes a horse both good in itself and good at running and at carrying its rider and at awaiting the attack of the enemy. Therefore, if this is true in every case, the virtue of man also will be the state of character which makes a man good and which makes him do his own work well.

How this is to happen we have stated already, but it will be made plain also by the following consideration of the specific nature of virtue. In everything that is continuous and divisible it is possible to take more, less, or an equal amount, and that either in terms of the thing itself or relatively to us; and the equal is an intermediate between excess and defect. By the intermediate in the object I mean that which is equidistant from each of the extremes, which is one and the same for all men; by the intermediate relatively to us that which is neither too much nor too little—and this is not one, nor the same for all. For instance, if ten is many and two is few, six is the intermediate, taken in terms of the object; for it exceeds and is exceeded by an equal amount; this is intermediate according to arithmetical proportion. But the intermediate relatively to us is not to be taken so; if ten pounds are too much for a particular person to eat and two too little, it does not follow that the trainer will order six pounds; for this also is perhaps too much for the person who is to take it, or too little—too little for Milo,[2] too much for the beginner in athletic exercises. The same is true of running and wrestling. Thus a master of any art avoids excess and defect, but seeks the intermediate and chooses this—the intermediate not in the object but relatively to us.

[1]Translated by W. D. Ross. Aristotle studied at the Athenian Academy with Plato; he inherited the Platonic tradition but pointed it in important new directions. The common view of Plato and Aristotle as polar contrasts—Plato being an idealist and Aristotle a materialist—is misleading, though it is true that Aristotle was considerably more empirical in his thought than Plato was. His range was great; he wrote on the natural sciences including zoology, embryology, physics, meteorology, astronomy, and chemistry; mathematics; psychology; politics and ethics; and the language arts, including rhetoric and poetics. The *Nicomachean Ethics*, like most of his surviving works, was not written for publication but was instead notes for teaching, prepared by others later for publication. The title derives from the fact that he wrote it for his son Nicomachus, who was believed to have edited the work for publication. The *Nicomachean Ethics* expresses an Aristotelean version of the familiar Greek doctrine of moderation in all things. (The editorial subtitle "The Golden Mean" derives not from Aristotle but from Horace, *Odes* II.10.5.)

[2]A famous wrestler.

If it is thus, then, that every art does its work well—by looking to the intermediate and judging its works by this standard (so that we often say of good works of art that it is not possible either to take away or to add anything, implying that excess and defect destroy the goodness of works of art, while the mean preserves it; and good artists, as we say, look to this in their work), and if, further, virtue is more exact and better than any art, as nature also is, then virtue must have the quality of aiming at the intermediate. I mean moral virtue; for it is this that is concerned with passions and actions, and in these there is excess, defect, and the intermediate. For instance, both fear and confidence and appetite and anger and pity and in general pleasure and pain may be felt both too much and too little, and in both cases not well; but to feel them at the right times, with reference to the right objects, towards the right people, with the right motive, and in the right way, is what is both intermediate and best, and this is characteristic of virtue. Similarly with regard to actions also there is excess, defect, and the intermediate. Now virtue is concerned with passions and actions, in which excess is a form of failure, and so is defect, while the intermediate is praised and is a form of success; and being praised and being successful are both characteristics of virtue. Therefore virtue is a kind of mean, since, as we have seen, it aims at what is intermediate.

Again, it is possible to fail in many ways (for evil belongs to the class of the unlimited, as the Pythagoreans conjecture,[3] and good to that of the limited), while to succeed is possible only in one way (for which reason also one is easy and the other difficult—to miss the mark easy, to hit it difficult); for these reasons also, then, excess and defect are characteristic of vice, and the mean of virtue;

For men are good in but one way, but bad in many.

Virtue, then, is a state of character concerned with choice, lying in a mean, i.e., the mean relative to us, this being determined by a rational principle, and by that principle by which the man of practical wisdom would determine it. Now it is a mean between two vices, that which depends on excess and that which depends on defect; and again it is a mean because the vices respectively fall short of or exceed what is right in both passions and actions, while virtue both finds and chooses that which is intermediate. Hence in respect of its substance and the definition which states its essence virtue is a mean, with regard to what is best and right an extreme.

But not every action nor every passion admits of a mean; for some have names that already imply badness, e.g., spite, shamelessness, envy, and in the case of actions adultery, theft, murder; for all of these and such like things imply by their names that they are themselves bad, and not the excesses or deficiencies of them. It is not possible, then, ever to be right with regard to them; one must always be wrong. Nor does goodness or badness with regard to such things depend on committing adultery with the right woman, at the right time, and in the right way, but simply to do any of them is to go wrong. It would be equally absurd, then, to expect that in unjust, cowardly, and voluptuous action there should be a mean, an excess, and a deficiency; for at that

[3]The Pythagoreans were followers of Pythagoras, a sixty-century B.C. Greek philosopher. They were skilled mathematicians who believed that the essence of all things was number and that even moral concepts such as good and evil could be expressed numerically.

rate there would be a mean of excess and of deficiency, an excess of excess, and a deficiency of deficiency. But as there is no excess and deficiency of temperance and courage because what is intermediate is in a sense an extreme, so too of the actions we have mentioned there is no mean nor any excess and deficiency, but however they are done they are wrong; for in general there is neither a mean of excess and deficiency, nor excess and deficiency of a mean.

We must, however, not only make this general statement, but also apply it to the individual facts. For among statements about conduct those which are general apply more widely, but those which are particular are more genuine, since conduct has to do with individual cases, and our statements must harmonize with the facts in these cases. We may take these cases from our table. With regard to feelings of fear and confidence courage is the mean; of the people who exceed, he who exceeds in fearlessness has no name (many of the states have no name), while the man who exceeds in confidence is rash, and he who exceeds in fear and falls short in confidence is a coward. With regard to pleasures and pains—not all of them, and not so much with regard to the pains—the mean is temperance, the excess self-indulgence. Persons deficient with regard to the pleasures are not often found; hence such persons also have received no name. But let us call them "insensible."

With regard to giving and taking of money the mean is liberality, the excess and the defect prodigality and meanness. In these actions people exceed and fall short in contrary ways; the prodigal exceeds in spending and falls short in taking, while the mean man exceeds in taking and falls short in spending. (At present we are giving a mere outline or summary, and are satisfied with this; later these states will be more exactly determined.) With regard to money there are also other dispositions—a mean, magnificence (for the magnificent man differs from the liberal man; the former deals with large sums, the latter with small ones), an excess, tastelessness and vulgarity, and a deficiency, niggardliness; these differ from the states opposed to liberality, and the mode of their difference will be stated later.

With regard to honor and dishonor the mean is proper pride, the excess is known as a sort of "empty vanity," and the deficiency is undue humility; and as we said liberality was related to magnificence, differing from it by dealing with small sums, so there is a state similarly related to proper pride, being concerned with small honors while that is concerned with great. For it is possible to desire honor as one ought, and more than one ought, and less, and the man who exceeds in his desires is called ambitious, the man who falls short unambitious, while the intermediate person has no name. The dispositions also are nameless, except that that of the ambitious man is called ambition. Hence the people who are at the extremes lay claim to the middle place; and we ourselves sometimes call the intermediate person ambitious and sometimes unambitious, and sometimes praise the ambitious man and sometimes the unambitious. The reason of our doing this will be stated in what follows; but now let us speak of the remaining states according to the method which has been indicated.

With regard to anger also there is an excess, a deficiency, and a mean. Although they can scarcely be said to have names, yet since we call the intermediate person good-tempered let us call the mean good temper; of the persons at the extremes let the one who exceeds be called irascible, and his vice irascibility, and the man who falls short an inirascible sort of person, and the deficiency inirascibility.

There are also three other means, which have a certain likeness to one another, but differ from one another: for they are all concerned with intercourse in words and actions, but differ in that one is concerned with truth in this sphere, the other two with pleasantness; and of this one kind is exhibited in giving amusement, the other in all the circumstances of life. We must therefore speak of these too, that we may the better see that in all things the mean is praiseworthy, and the extremes neither praiseworthy nor right, but worthy of blame. Now most of these states also have no names ourselves so that we may be clear and easy to follow. With regard to truth, then, the intermediate is a truthful sort of person and the mean may be called truthfulness, while the pretence which exaggerates is boastfulness and the person characterized by it a boaster, and that which understates is mock modesty and the person characterized by it mock-modest. With regard to pleasantness in the giving of amusement the intermediate person is ready-witted and the disposition ready wit, the excess is buffoonery and the person characterized by it a buffoon, while the man who falls short is a sort of boor and his state is boorishness. With regard to the remaining kind of pleasantness, that which is exhibited in life in general, the man who is pleasant in the right way is friendly and the mean is friendliness, while the man who exceeds is an obsequious person if he has no end in view, a flatterer if he is aiming at his own advantage, and the man who falls short and is unpleasant in all circumstances is a quarrelsome and surly sort of person.

There are also means in the passions and concerned with the passions; since shame is not a virtue, and yet praise is extended to the modest man. For even in these matters one man is said to be intermediate, and another to exceed, as for instance the bashful man who is ashamed of everything; while he who falls short or is not ashamed of anything at all is shameless, and the intermediate person is modest. Righteous indignation is a mean between envy and spite, and these states are concerned with the pain and pleasure that are felt at the fortunes of our neighbors; the man who is characterized by righteous indignation is pained at undeserved good fortune, the envious man, going beyond him, is pained at all good fortune, and the spiteful man falls so far short of being pained that he even rejoices. But these states there will be an opportunity of describing elsewhere; with regard to justice, since it has not one simple meaning, we shall, after describing the other states, distinguish its two kinds and say how each of them is a mean; and similarly we shall treat also of the rational virtues.

There are three kinds of disposition, then, two of them vices, involving excess and deficiency respectively, and one a virtue, viz. the mean, and all are in a sense opposed to all; for the extreme states are contrary both to the intermediate state and to each other, and the intermediate to the extremes; as the equal is greater relatively to the less, less relatively to the greater, so the middle states are excessive relatively to the deficiencies, deficient relatively to the excesses, both in passions and in actions. For the brave man appears rash relatively to the coward, and cowardly relatively to the rash man; and similarly the temperate man appears self-indulgent relatively to the insensible man, insensible relatively to the self-indulgent, and the liberal man prodigal relatively to the mean man, mean relatively to the prodigal. Hence also the people at the extremes push the intermediate man each over to the other, and the brave man is called rash by the coward, cowardly by the rash man, and correspondingly in the other cases.

These states being thus opposed to one another, the greatest contrariety is that of the extremes to each other, rather than to the intermediate; for these are further from each other than from the intermediate, as the great is further from the small and the small from the great than both are from the equal. Again, to the intermediate some extremes show a certain likeness, as that of rashness to courage and that of prodigality to liberality; but the extremes show the greatest unlikeness to each other; now contraries are defined as the things that are furthest from each other, so that things that are further apart are more contrary.

To the mean in some cases the deficiency, in some the excess is more opposed; e.g., it is not rashness, which is an excess, but cowardice, which is a deficiency, that is more opposed to courage, and not insensibility, which is a deficiency, but self-indulgence, which is an excess, that is more opposed to temperance. This happens from two reasons, one being drawn from the thing itself; for because one extreme is nearer and liker to the intermediate, we oppose not this but rather its contrary to the intermediate. E.g., since rashness is thought liker and nearer to courage, and cowardice more unlike, we oppose rather the latter to courage; for things that are further from the intermediate are thought more contrary to it. This, then, is one cause, drawn from the thing itself; another is drawn from ourselves; for the things to which we ourselves more naturally tend seem more contrary to the intermediate. For instance, we ourselves tend more naturally to pleasures, and hence are more easily carried away towards self-indulgence than towards propriety. We describe as contrary to the mean, then, rather the directions in which we more often go to great lengths; and therefore self-indulgence, which is an excess, is the more contrary to temperance.

That moral virtue is a mean, then, and in what sense it is so, and that it is a mean between two vices, the one involving excess, the other deficiency, and that it is such because its character is to aim at what is intermediate in passions and in actions, has been sufficiently stated. Hence also it is no easy task to be good. For in everything it is no easy task to find the middle, e.g., to find the middle of a circle is not for every one but for him who knows; so, too, any one can get angry—that is easy—or give or spend money; but to do this to the right person, to the right extent, at the right time, with the right motive, and in the right way, *that* is not for every one, nor is it easy; wherefore goodness is both rare and laudable and noble.

Hence he who aims at the intermediate must first depart from what is the more contrary to it, as Calypso advises—

> Hold the ship out beyond that surf and spray.[4]

For of the extremes one is more erroneous, one less so; therefore, since to hit the mean is hard in the extreme, we must as a second best, as people say, take the least of the evils; and this will be done best in the way we describe.

[4]See Homer, *Odyssey* Book 12, II. 264–266. Odysseus is telling his steersman how to avoid Scylla and Charybdis; he is passing on Circe's advice, not Calypso's.

But we must consider the things towards which we ourselves also are easily carried away; for some of us tend to one thing, some to another; and this will be recognizable from the pleasure and the pain we feel. We must drag ourselves away to the contrary extreme; for we shall get into the intermediate state by drawing well away from error, as people do in straightening sticks that are bent.

Now in everything the pleasant or pleasure is most to be guarded against; for we do not judge it impartially. We ought, then, to feel towards pleasure as the elders of the people felt towards Helen, and in all circumstances repeat their saying;[5] for if we dismiss pleasure thus we are less likely to go astray. It is by doing this, then (to sum the matter up), that we shall best be able to hit the mean.

But this is no doubt difficult, and especially in individual cases; for it is not easy to determine both how and with whom and on what provocation and how long one should be angry; for we too sometimes praise those who fall short and call them good-tempered, but sometimes we praise those who get angry and call them manly. The main, however, who deviates little from goodness is not blamed, whether he do so in the direction of the more or of the less, but only the man who deviates more widely; for *he* does not fail to be noticed. But up to what point and to what extent a man must deviate before he becomes blameworthy it is not easy to determine by reasoning, any more than anything else that is perceived by the senses; such things depend on particular facts, and the decision rests with perception. So much, then, is plain, that the intermediate state is in all things to be praised, but that we must incline sometimes towards the excess, sometimes towards the deficiency; for so shall we most easily hit the mean and what is right.

from *POETICS*[1]

I

I propose to treat of Poetry in itself and of its various kinds, noting the essential quality of each; to inquire into the structure of the plot required for a good poem; into the number and nature of the parts of which a poem is

[5]In Homer's *Iliad* Book 3, II. 156–160, the elders of Troy admire Helen's beauty but wish that she would sail away and not be the ruin of the city.

[1]Translated by Samuel Henry Butcher, revised and annotated by Louise Ropes Loomis. The *Poetics* is undoubtedly the most influential work of literary criticism in the history of Western literature. It has shaped the way we read not only Greek tragedy but also other literature, even contemporary works. Aristotle's method is analytical; that is, he characteristically divides a subject into its parts and considers each separately. Thus tragedy is divided into its six component parts, and the tragic hero is considered in terms of separate character traits. The *Poetics* contributed a number of key ideas to literary criticism, including the division of literature into lyric, narrative, and dramatic; the idea of *mimesis* or imitation; the concept of *catharsis* as the purpose of tragedy; the identification of the mixed or complex character as the best; and the emphasis on *mythos* or plot, along with ways of discriminating between good and bad plots. Aristotle's ideas may be tested against the models of Greek tragedy; they fit the plays of Sophocles (his favorite playwright) better than they do those of Aeschylus or Euripides.

composed; and similarly into whatever else falls within the same inquiry. Following, then, the order of nature, let us begin with the principles which come first.

Epic poetry and tragedy, comedy also and dithyrambic[2] poetry, and the music of the flute and of the lyre in most of their forms, are all in their general conception modes of imitation. They differ, however, from one another in three respects—their mediums, their objects, their manner or mode of imitation being in each case distinct.

For as there are persons who, by conscious art or mere habit, imitate and represent various objects through the medium of color and form, or, again, by the voice; so in the group of arts above mentioned, taken as a whole, the imitation is produced by rhythm, language, or harmony, either singly or combined.

Thus in the music of the flute and of the lyre, harmony and rhythm alone are employed; also in other arts, such as that of the shepherd's pipe, which are essentially similar to these. In dancing, rhythm alone is used without harmony; for even dancing imitates character, emotion, and action, by rhythmical movement. . . .

There are, again, some arts which employ all the means above mentioned—namely, rhythm, tune, and meter. Such are dithyrambic and nomic[3] poetry, and also tragedy and comedy; but between them the difference is that in the first two cases these means are all employed in combination, in the latter, now one means is employed, now another.

Such, then, are the differences of the arts with respect to the medium of imitation.

II

Since the objects of imitation are men in action, and these men must be either of a high or a low type (for moral character mainly answers to this division, goodness and badness being the distinguishing marks of moral differences), it follows that we must represent men either as better than in real life, or as worse, or as they are. It is the same in painting. Polygnotus depicted men as nobler than they are, Pauson as less noble, Dionysius drew them true to life.[4]

Now it is evident that each of the arts of imitation above mentioned will exhibit these differences, and itself become a distinct kind in imitating objects that are thus distinct. Such diversities may be found even in dancing, flute playing, and lyre playing. So again in language, whether prose or verse, unaccompanied by music. Homer, for example, makes men

[2]For dithyrambic poetry the ordinary English reader may understand what we call lyric poetry. More strictly defined, the dithyramb was a hymn or ode in rapturous style, such as were sung at the festivals of the god Dionysus.

[3]Nomic poetry is instructive poetry, maxims or wise sayings in the form of verse.

[4]Unfortunately no work by any of these famous Greek painters has come down to us.

better than they are; Cleophon as they are; Hegemon of Thasos, the inventor of parodies, worse than they are.[5] The same distinction marks off tragedy from comedy; for comedy aims at representing men as worse, tragedy as better than in actual life.

III

There is still a third difference—the manner in which each of these objects may be imitated. For the medium being the same, the objects the same, the poet may imitate by narration—in which case he can either take another personality as Homer does, or speak in his own person, unchanged—or he may present all his characters as living and moving before us.

These, then, as we said at the beginning, are the three differences which distinguish artistic imitation—the medium, the objects, and the manner. So that from one point of view, Sophocles[6] is an imitator of the same kind as Homer—for both imitate higher types of character; from another point of view, he is of the same kind as Aristophanes[7]—for both imitate persons acting and doing. Hence, some say, the name of "drama" is given to such plays, as representing action. . . .

IV

Poetry in general seems to have sprung from two sources, each of them lying deep in our nature. First, the instinct of imitation is implanted in man from childhood, one difference between him and other animals being that he is the most imitative of living creatures, and through imitation learns his earliest lessons. And no less universal is the pleasure he takes in seeing things imitated. We have evidence of this in the facts of experience. Objects which in themselves we view with pain, we delight to contemplate when reproduced with minute fidelity: such as the forms of the most ignoble animals and of dead bodies. The cause of this, again, is that to learn gives the liveliest pleasure, not only to philosophers but to men in general, although their capacity of learning is more limited. Thus the reason why men enjoy seeing a likeness is that in contemplating it they find themselves learning or inferring, and saying perhaps, "Ah, that is he." If they happen not to have seen the original, their pleasure will be due not to the imitation as such, but to the execution, the coloring, or some such other cause.

[5]The writings of Cleophon and Hegemon are also lost.

[6]Sophocles was one of the great trio of fifth-century Athenian tragedians, the other two being Aeschylus and Euripides. Seven of Sophocles' tragedies have been preserved.

[7]The famous satirical comedy writer of the end of the fifth century B.C.

Imitation, then, is one instinct of our nature. Next there is the instinct for harmony and rhythm, meters being manifestly sections of rhythm. Persons, therefore, starting with this natural gift developed by degrees their special aptitudes, until their rude improvisations gave birth to poetry.

Poetry now diverged in two directions, according to the individual character of the writers. The graver spirits imitated noble actions and the actions of good men. The more trivial sort imitated the actions of meaner persons, at first composing satires, as the former did hymns to the gods and praises of famous men. A poem of the satirical kind cannot indeed be put down to any author earlier than Homer; though there were probably many such writers. But from Homer onward, instances can be cited—his own *Margites,*[8] for example, and other similar compositions. The appropriate meter was also here introduced; hence the measure is still called the iambic[9] or lampooning measure, being that in which people lampooned one another. Thus the older poets were distinguished as writers either of heroic or of lampooning verse.

As in the serious style Homer is pre-eminent among poets, for he alone combined dramatic form with excellence of imitation, so he too first laid down the main lines of comedy, by dramatizing the ludicrous instead of writing personal satire. His *Margites* bears the same relation to comedy that the *Iliad* and *Odyssey* do to tragedy. And when tragedy and comedy appeared, the two classes of poets still followed their natural bent: the lampooners became writers of comedy, and the epic poets were succeeded by tragedians, since the drama was a larger and higher form of art. . . . Tragedy advanced by slow degrees; each new element that showed itself was in turn developed. Having passed through many changes, it found its natural form, and there it stopped.

Aeschylus first introduced a second actor;[10] he diminished the importance of the chorus, and assigned the leading part to the dialogue. Sophocles raised the number of actors to three, and added scene painting. It was not till late that the short plot was discarded for one of greater compass, and the grotesque diction of the earlier satiric form for the stately manner of tragedy.

V

Comedy is, as we have said, an imitation of characters of a lower type—not, however, in the full sense of the word bad, the ludicrous being merely a subdivision of the ugly. It consists of some defect or ugliness which is not painful

[8]The mock battle epic that went by the name of *Margites* has long been lost. Whether it was really the work of the author of the *Iliad,* as Aristotle thought, we cannot judge.

[9]The pattern of the iambic meter was a line composed of a series of pairs of syllables, a short syllable, followed by a long one. We in English still use its equivalent, an unaccented syllable followed by an accented, both in comic verse, such as

"O oysters, come and walk with us,
The walrus did beseech,"

and also in grand and serious poetry, such as *Paradise Lost.*

[10]Before Aeschylus' time the embryonic Greek tragedy consisted of speeches by a single actor or narrator telling the chorus what had happened and a series of songs, dances, and responses by the chorus, expressing their wonder, joy, or grief at the news.

or destructive. To take an obvious example, the comic mask is ugly and distorted, but does not imply pain.

The successive changes through which tragedy passed, and the authors of these changes, are well known, whereas comedy has had no history, because it was not at first treated seriously. . . .

Epic poetry agrees with tragedy in so far as it is an imitation in verse of characters of a higher type. They differ in that epic poetry admits but one kind of meter[11] and is narrative in form. They differ, again, in their length: for tragedy endeavors, as far as possible, to confine itself to a single circuit of the sun, or but slightly to exceed this limit; whereas the epic action has no limits of time. This, then, is a second point of difference; though at first the same freedom was admitted in tragedy as in epic poetry. . . .

VI

Tragedy, then, is an imitation of an action that is serious, complete, and of a certain magnitude; in language embellished with every kind of artistic ornament, the several kinds being found in separate parts of the play; in the form of dramatic action, not of narrative; through pity and fear effecting the proper purification of these emotions.[12] By "language embellished," I mean language into which rhythm, harmony, and song enter. By "the several kinds in separate parts," I mean that some parts are rendered through the medium of verse alone, others again with the aid of song.

Now as tragic imitation implies persons acting, it necessarily follows, in the first place, that spectacular equipment will be a part of tragedy. Next, song and diction, for these are the medium of imitation. By diction, I mean the metrical arrangement of the words: as for song, it is a term whose sense everyone understands.

Again, tragedy is the imitation of an action, and an action implies personal actors, who necessarily possess certain distinctive qualities of character and thought; for it is by these that we form our estimate of their actions and these two—thought and character—are the natural causes from which their actions spring, and on their actions all success or failure depends. Now, the imitation of the action is the plot; by plot I here mean the arrangement of the incidents. By character I mean that because of which we ascribe certain qualities to the actors. Thought is needed whenever they speak to prove a statement or declare a general truth. Every tragedy, therefore, must have six parts, which parts determine its quality—namely, plot, character, diction, thought, spectacle, song. . . .

But most important of all is the structure of the incidents. For tragedy is an imitation, not of men, but of action and life, of happiness and misery.

Plot = most important

[11] To a Greek the only meter admissible in an epic poem was the meter of the *Iliad* and the *Odyssey*, or what was called hexameter verse. Virgil used the same meter for the *Aeneid*. In English a well known example of hexameter verse is Longfellow's *Evangeline:*

"This is the forest primeval: the murmuring pines and the hemlocks"—

[12] Note that an unhappy or what we call a tragic ending was not one of the Greek requirements for a tragedy, though Aristotle thought it the perfect ending. See XIII. Many tragedies ended with a solemn reconciliation after a conflict or quiet after pain, to please the audience, Aristotle says.

And life consists of action, and its end is a mode of activity,[13] not a quality. Now character determines men's qualities, but it is their actions that make them happy or wretched. The purpose of action in the tragedy, therefore, is not the representation of character: character comes in as contributing to the action. Hence the incidents and the plot are the end of the tragedy; and the end is the chief thing of all. So without action there cannot be a tragedy; there may be one without character. . . .

Again, you may string together a set of speeches expressive of character, and well finished in point of diction and thought, and not produce the essential tragic effect nearly so well as with a play which, however deficient in these respects, yet has a plot and artistically constructed incidents. Besides which, the most powerful elements of emotional interest in tragedy—reversal of the situation and recognition scenes[14]—are parts of the plot. A further proof is that novices in the art attain to finish of diction and precision of portraiture before they can construct the plot. It is the same with almost all the early poets.

The plot, then, is the first principle, and, as it were, the soul of a tragedy: character holds the second place. A similar statement is true of painting. The most beautiful colors, laid on confusedly, will not give as much pleasure as a simple chalk outline of a portrait. Thus tragedy is the imitation of an action, and of actors mainly with a view to the action. . . .

The spectacle is, indeed, an attraction in itself, but of all the parts it is the least artistic, and connected least with the art of poetry. For the power of tragedy is felt even apart from representation and actors. Besides, the production of scenic effects is more a matter for the property man than for the poet.

VII

These principles being established, let us now discuss the proper structure of the plot, since this is the first and most important thing in tragedy.

Now, according to our definition, tragedy is an imitation of an action that is complete and whole and of a certain magnitude; for there may be a whole that is wanting in magnitude. A whole is that which has a beginning, a middle, and an end. A beginning is that which does not have to follow anything else, but after which something else naturally takes place. An end, on the contrary, is that which itself naturally follows something else, either by necessity or as a general rule, but has nothing coming after it. A middle is that which follows something else as some other thing follows it. A well-constructed plot must neither begin nor end at haphazard, but conform to these principles.

Again, a beautiful object, whether it be a living organism or any whole composed of parts, must not only have an orderly arrangement of parts, but must also be of a certain magnitude; for beauty depends on magnitude and order. Hence a very tiny creature cannot be beautiful; for the view of it is confused, the object being seen in an almost imperceptible moment of time. Nor, again, can one of vast size be beautiful; for as the eye cannot take it all

[13]See the *Ethics,* Book I, Chapter 6.

[14]These two admired features of many old dramatic plots Aristotle explains further on.

in at once, the unity and sense of the whole is lost for the spectator; as it would be if there were a creature a thousand miles long. As, therefore, in the case of living bodies and organisms, a certain magnitude is necessary, and a magnitude which may be easily embraced in one view; so in the plot, a certain length is necessary, and a length which can be easily embraced by the memory. . . . And to state the matter roughly, we may say that the proper length is such as to allow for a sequence of necessary or probable events that will bring about a change from calamity to good fortune, or from good fortune to calamity.

VIII

Unity of plot does not, as some persons think, consist of having a single man as the hero. For infinitely various are the incidents in one man's life which cannot be reduced to unity; and so, too, there are many actions of one man out of which we cannot make one action. Hence the error, as it appears, of all poets who have composed a Heracleid, a Theseid,[15] or other poems of the kind. They imagine that as Heracles was one man, the story of Heracles must also be a unity. But Homer, as in all else he is of surpassing merit, here too—whether from art or natural genius—seems to have happily discerned the truth. In composing the *Odyssey* he did not include all the adventures of Odysseus—such as his wound on Parnassus, or his feigned madness at the mustering of the host[16]—incidents between which there was no necessary or probable connection: but he made the *Odyssey* and likewise the *Iliad* center around an action that in our sense of the word is one. As therefore, in the other imitative arts, the imitation is one when the object imitated is one, so the plot, being an imitation of an action, must imitate one action and that a whole, the structural union of the parts being such that, if any one of them is displaced or removed, the whole will be disjointed and disturbed. For a thing whose presence or absence makes no visible difference is not an organic part of the whole.

IX

It is, moreover, evident from what has been said that it is not the function of the poet to relate what has happened but what may happen—what is possible according to the law of probability or necessity. The poet and the historian differ not by writing in verse or in prose. The work of Herodotus[17] might be put into verse, and it would still be a species of history, with meter no less than without it. The true difference is that one relates what has happened, the other what may happen. Poetry, therefore, is a more philosophical and a higher thing than history: for poetry tends to express the universal, history the particular. . . .

[15]That is, a long-drawn narrative of all the exploits of a Heracles or a Theseus.
[16]Incidents said to have occurred before the opening of the *Iliad*.
[17]The first of the great Greek historians, who wrote the story of the world, as he knew it, down through the Persian wars.

But even if a poet chances to take an historical subject, he is nonetheless a poet; for there is no reason why some events that have actually happened should not conform to the law of the probable and the possible, and in virtue of that aspect of them he is their poet or maker.

Of all plots and actions the episodic are the worst. I call a plot "episodic" in which the episodes or acts succeed one another without probable or necessary sequence. Bad poets compose such pieces by their own fault, good poets, to please the players; for, as they write show pieces for competition, they stretch the plot beyond its capacity, and are often forced to break the natural continuity.

But again, tragedy is an imitation not only of a complete action, but of events inspiring fear or pity. Such an effect is best produced when the events come on us by surprise and when, at the same time, they follow as cause and effect. The wonder will then be greater than if they happened of themselves or merely by accident; for coincidences too are most marvelous when they have a look of design. We may instance the statue of Mitys at Argos, which fell upon his murderer while he was watching a festival, and killed him. Such events seem the result of more than chance. Plots, therefore, constructed on these principles are necessarily the best.

X

Plots are either simple or complex, for the actions in real life, of which they are an imitation, are obviously either one or the other. An action which is one and continuous in the sense above defined, I call simple, when the change in the hero's fortune takes place without reversal of the situation and without recognition.

A complex action is one in which the change is accompanied by such a reversal, or by recognition, or by both. These all should arise from the internal structure of the plot, so that what follows should be the necessary or probable result of what went before. It makes a great difference whether the event is caused by or simply happens after the previous action.

XI

Reversal of the situation is a change by which conditions in the play are transformed into their opposite, keeping always to our rule of probability or necessity. Thus in the Oedipus,[18] the messenger comes to cheer Oedipus and free him from his alarms about his mother, but by revealing who Oedipus really is produces the opposite effect. . . .

[18]The *Oedipus Tyrannus* [*Oedipus the King*] of Sophocles is a tragedy which Aristotle much admired and which happily has come down to us. At its opening, Oedipus is the prosperous king of Thebes, with a wife, Jocasta, whom he dearly loves. In the course of the play he discovers that . . . he is the child of Jocasta and her former husband, the late King of Thebes, exposed to die in infancy because of an ominous prophecy and rescued by [a shepherd]. He learns also that an arrogant old man he killed in a roadside quarrel was the late king, his father. He is therefore the unwitting murderer of his own father and for years has lived in incest with his own mother. At the news, Jocasta hangs herself and Oedipus puts out his eyes and goes blinded and accursed into banishment.

Recognition, as the name indicates, is a change from ignorance to knowledge, producing love or hate between the persons destined by the poet for good or bad fortune. The best form of recognition is coincident with a reversal of the situation, as in the Oedipus.[19]

Even inanimate things of the most trivial kind may in a sense be objects of recognition. Again, we may recognize or discover whether a person has done a thing or not. But the recognition which is most intimately connected with the plot and action is, as we have said, the recognition of persons. This recognition, combined with a reversal, will produce either pity or fear; and actions producing these effects are those which, by our definition, tragedy represents. Moreover, it is upon such situations that the issue of good or bad fortune will depend. Recognition, then, being between persons, it may happen that one person only is recognized by the other—when the latter is already known—or it may be necessary that the recognition should be on both sides. Thus Iphigenia is revealed to Orestes by the sending of the letter; but another act of recognition is required to make Orestes known to Iphigenia.[20]

Two parts, then, of the plot—reversal of the situation and recognition—turn upon surprises. A third part is the scene of suffering. The scene of suffering is a destructive or painful action, such as a death on the stage, bodily agony, wounds, and the like. . . .

XIII

As a sequel to what has already been said, we must proceed to consider what the poet should aim at, and what he should avoid in constructing his plots; and by what means the specific effect of tragedy will be produced.

A perfect tragedy should, as we have seen, be arranged not on the simple but on the complex plan. It should, moreover, imitate actions which excite pity and fear, this being the distinctive mark of tragic imitation. It follows plainly, in the first place, that the change of fortune presented must not be the spectacle of a virtuous man brought from prosperity to adversity: for this moves neither pity nor fear: it merely shocks us. Nor, again, that of a bad man passing from adversity to prosperity: for nothing can be more alien to the spirit of tragedy; it possesses no single tragic quality; it neither satisfies

[19]Shakespeare frequently uses these classical dramatic devices of reversal of situation and recognition. The tragedy of *King Lear* is an outstanding illustration of the first. The themes of disguise, mistaken identity, and revelation or recognition occur again and again, notably in *As You Like It, Twelfth Night, Winter's Tale,* and *The Tempest.*

[20]The reference here is to Euripides' play *Iphigenia in Tauris.* Aristotle summarizes briefly the story of Iphigenia in XVII. As the young daughter of King Agamemnon, she was brought from her home to the port of Aulis to be sacrificed, that her father and his fleet might have a favorable wind to sail to Troy. She was snatched from the altar by the goddess Artemis and disappeared. Years later she is a priestess serving in the savage country of Tauris. Her brother Orestes, whom she left at home, a little child, is now a maddened wanderer, seeking absolution for his crime of killing his mother, Clytemnestra, in revenge for her murder of his father, Agamemnon. When Iphigenia finds Orestes on the shore at Tauris, neither, of course, knows the other. In fact, he has no idea that his long lost sister is alive. Through a letter which she gives him he learns who she is, but meanwhile by a law of the country he is condemned to die as a sacrilegious intruder. Through some words of his at the last moment she discovers that he is Orestes and saves him.

the moral sense nor calls forth pity or fear. Nor, again, should the downfall of an utter villain be exhibited. A plot of this kind would, doubtless, satisfy the moral sense, but it would inspire neither pity nor fear;[21] for pity is aroused by unmerited misfortune, fear by the misfortune of a man like ourselves. Such an event, therefore, will be neither pitiful nor terrible.

There remains, then, the character between these two extremes—that of a man extraordinarily good and just, who yet brings misfortune on himself not by vice or depravity, but by some error or frailty.[22] He must be one who is highly renowned and prosperous, a personage like Oedipus, Thyestes, or other illustrious men of great families.

The best constructed plot should, therefore, be single in its issue, rather than double, as some maintain. The change of fortune should be not from bad to good, but, reversely, from good to bad. It should come about as the result not of vice, but of some great error or frailty, in a character either such as we have described, or better rather than worse. . . . A tragedy, to be perfect according to the rules of art, should be of this construction. Hence they are in error who censure Euripides just because he follows this principle in his plays, many of which end unhappily. It is, as we have said, the right ending. The best proof is that on the stage and in dramatic competition, such plays, if well worked out, are the most tragic in effect; and Euripides, faulty though he may be in the general management of his subject, yet is felt to be the most tragic of the poets.

In the second rank comes the kind of tragedy which some place first. Like the Odyssey, it has a double thread of plot, and also an opposite ending for the good and for the bad actors. It is accounted the best only because of the weakness of the spectators; for the poet is guided in what he writes by the wishes of his audience. The pleasure, however, thence derived is not the true tragic pleasure. It is proper rather to comedy, where those who, in the piece, are the deadliest enemies—like Orestes and Aegisthus[23]—quit the stage as friends at the close, and no one slays or is slain.

XIV

Fear and pity may be aroused by spectacular means; but they may also result from the inner structure of the piece, which is the better way, and indicates a superior poet. For the plot ought to be so constructed that, even without the aid of the eye, he who hears the tale told will thrill with horror and melt to pity at what takes place. This is the impression we should receive from hearing the story of Oedipus. But to produce this effect by the mere spectacle is a less artistic method, and dependent on extraneous aids. Those who

[21]Shakespeare's tragedy of *Richard III* is sometimes cited in disproof of this statement. Richard is an "utter villain" but we take a keen interest in his bold struggle to master fate.

[22]Two notably brave and generous tragic heroes, whose downfall is due to one shortcoming in character or judgment, are, of course, Lear and Othello. Some readers would include Hamlet.

[23]In the tragic story of Agamemnon and his son Orestes, Aegisthus is the paramour of Agamemnon's wife, Clytemnestra, who influences her to murder her husband on his return from Troy. Orestes, her son, kills Aegisthus as well as his mother when he finally avenges his father. [See Aeschylus' *Oresteia—Editors' note.*]

employ spectacular means to create a sense not of the terrible but of the merely monstrous are strangers to the purpose of tragedy; for we must not demand of tragedy any and every kind of pleasure, but only that which is proper to it. And since the pleasure the tragic poet should offer is that which comes from pity and fear through imitation, it is evident that this quality must be impressed on the incidents.

Let us then determine what circumstances strike us as terrible or pitiful.

Actions of this sort must happen between persons who are either friends or enemies or indifferent to one another. If an enemy kills an enemy, there is nothing to excite pity either in the act or the intention—except in so far as the suffering itself is pitiful. So too with indifferent persons. But when the tragic incident occurs between those who are near or dear to one another—if, for example, a brother kills, or intends to kill, a brother, a son his father, a mother her son, a son his mother, or any other deed of the kind is done—these are situations to be looked for by the poet. He may not indeed destroy the framework of the received legends—the fact, for instance, that Clytemnestra was slain by Orestes . . . but he ought to show invention of his own, and skillfully handle the traditional material. . . .

Enough has now been said concerning the structure of the incidents and the right kind of plot.

XV

With regard to the characters there are four things to be aimed at. First, and most important, they must be good. Now any speech or action that manifests some kind of moral purpose will be expressive of character: the character will be good if the purpose is good. The goodness is possible in every class of persons. Even a woman may be good, and also a slave, though the one is liable to be an inferior being, and the other quite worthless. The second thing to aim at is appropriateness. There is a type of manly valor, but manliness in a woman, or unscrupulous cleverness, is inappropriate. Thirdly, a character must be true to life: which is something different from goodness and appropriateness, as here described. The fourth point is consistency: for even though the person being imitated, who suggested the type, is inconsistent, still he must be consistently inconsistent.

As in the structure of the plot, so too in the portraiture of character, the poet should always aim at either the necessary or the probable. Thus a person of a given character should speak or act as it is necessary or probable that he would; just as this event should follow that as a necessary or probable consequence. It is therefore evident that the unraveling of the plot, no less than the complication, must arise out of the plot itself; it must not be brought about by supernatural interference—as in the *Medea*.[24] The supernatural should be employed only for events outside the drama—for past or

[24]In Euripides' play *Medea,* the heroine, who out of indignation at her wrongs has killed her two children and brought about the death of her husband's new bride, escapes from his fury into the sky in a magic chariot.

future events, beyond the range of human knowledge, which need to be reported or foretold; for to the gods we ascribe the power of seeing all things. Within the action there must be nothing improbable. If the improbable cannot be excluded, it should be outside the field of the tragedy, as is the improbable element in the *Oedipus* of Sophocles.

Again, since tragedy is an imitation of persons above the common level, the example of good portrait painters should be followed. They, while reproducing the distinctive features of the original, make a likeness true to life and yet more beautiful. So too the poet, in representing men hot tempered or indolent or with other defects of character, should preserve the type and yet ennoble it. In this way Agathon and Homer have portrayed Achilles.[25]

These, then, are rules the poet should observe. Nor should he neglect those appeals to the eye, which, though not among the essentials, are the concomitants of poetry; for here too there is much room for error. But of this enough has been said in our published treatise. . . .[26]

XVII

In constructing the plot and working it out with the proper diction, the poet should put the scene, as far as possible, before his eyes. In this way, seeing everything with the utmost vividness, as if he were an actual eyewitness, he will discover what is in keeping with it, and be most unlikely to overlook inconsistencies. . . .

Again, the poet should act out his own play to the best of his power, with the gestures that go with it; for those with a sympathetic nature, who themselves feel the emotion, are most convincing; and one who is grieved himself despairs, one who is angry rages with the most lifelike reality. Hence poetry implies either a special gift of nature or a strain of madness. In the one case a man can take the mold of any character; in the other, he is lifted out of his proper self.

As for the story, whether the poet takes it ready-made or constructs it for himself, he should first sketch its general outline and then fill in the episodes and amplify in detail. The general plan may be illustrated by the *Iphigenia*.[27] A young girl is sacrificed; she disappears mysteriously from the eyes of those who sacrificed her; she is transported to another country, where the custom is to offer up all strangers to the goddess. To this ministry she is appointed. Some time later her own brother chances to arrive. The fact that the oracle for some reason ordered him to go there is outside the general plan of the play. The purpose, again, of his coming is outside the action proper. However, he comes, he is seized, and, when on the point of being sacrificed,

[25]We have nothing left of any work by Agathon. We know only that he was a playwright who promised to rival Euripides but who left Athens for some reason at the age of forty and died disappointed in a foreign land. At the banquet celebrated in Plato's dialogue of the *Symposium* he was the happy and admired host. For Homer's noble treatment of Achilles, see especially the *Iliad,* Books IX, XIX, XXIV.

[26]Aristotle wrote a dialogue *On Poets,* now lost.

[27]On the story of Iphigenia see XI, note.

reveals who he is. The mode of recognition may be either that of Euripides or of Polyidus,[28] in whose play he exclaims very naturally: "So it was not my sister only, but I too who was doomed to be sacrificed"; and by that remark he is saved.

After this, the names being once given, it remains to fill in the episodes. We must see, however, that they are relevant to the action. In the case of Orestes, for example, there is the madness which led to his capture and his deliverance by means of the purificatory rite. In a play the episodes are short, but in epic poetry they lengthen out the tale. Thus the story of the *Odyssey* can be stated briefly. A certain man is absent from home for many years; he is jealously watched by Poseidon, and quite alone. Meanwhile his home is in a wretched plight—suitors are wasting his substance and plotting against his son. At length, tempest-tossed, he arrives and makes himself known; he attacks the suitors with his own hand, and is himself preserved while he destroys them. This is the essence of the plot; the rest is episode.

XVIII

Every tragedy falls into two parts—complication and unraveling or *dénouement.* Incidents before the play opens and often others within the play itself form the complication; the rest is the unraveling. By the complication I mean all that extends from the beginning of the action to the part which marks the turning point to good or bad fortune. The unraveling is that which extends from the beginning of the change to the end. . . .

Again, the poet should remember what has been often said, and not make an epic structure into a tragedy. By an epic structure I mean one with a multiplicity of plots—as if, for instance, you were to make a tragedy out of the entire story of the *Iliad.* In the epic poem, owing to its length, each part can assume its proper magnitude. In the drama the result is far from answering to the poet's expectation. The proof is that the poets who have dramatized the whole story of the fall of Troy, instead of selecting portions like Euripides; or who have taken the whole tale of Niobe, and not a part of her story, like Aeschylus, either fail utterly or meet with poor success on the stage. . . .

XXIII

As for that poetry which is narrative in form and imitates in meter, the plot manifestly ought, as in a tragedy, to be constructed on dramatic principles. It should have for its subject a single action, whole and complete, with a beginning, a middle, and an end. It will thus resemble a living organism in all its unity, and produce the pleasure proper to it. It will differ in structure from historical compositions, which of necessity present not a single action, but a single period, and all that happened within that period to one person or to many, however little connected together the events may be. For as the sea fight at Salamis and the battle with the Carthaginians in Sicily took place

[28] We have no plays of Polyidus.

at the same time but did not tend to any one result, so in the ordinary course of events one thing sometimes follows another, and yet no single end is thereby produced. Such is the way, we may say, most poets write.

Here again, then, as has been already observed, the transcendent excellence of Homer is manifest. He never attempts to make the whole war of Troy the subject of his poem, though that war had a beginning and an end. It would have been too vast a theme, and not easily embraced in a single view. If not that, it would have been overcomplicated by the variety of the incidents in it. As it is, he detaches a single portion, though he admits as episodes many events from the general story of the war—such as the Catalogue of Ships[29] and others—thus diversifying the poem. . . . For this reason the *Iliad* and the *Odyssey* each furnish the subject of but one tragedy, or, at most, of two. . . .

XXIV

Again, epic poetry may have as many kinds as tragedy: it may be simple, or complex, a tale of character or of suffering. The parts also, with the exception of song and spectacle, are the same; for it requires reversals of the situation, recognitions, and scenes of suffering. Moreover, the thought and the diction must be artistic. In all these respects, Homer is our earliest and sufficient model. Indeed each of his poems has a twofold character. The *Iliad* is at once simple and a tale of suffering, and the *Odyssey* complex (for recognition scenes run through it), and at the same time a tale of character. Moreover, in diction and thought they are supreme.

Epic poetry differs from tragedy in the scale on which it is constructed, and in its meter. As regards scale or length, we have already laid down an adequate limit: the beginning and the end must be capable of being brought within a single view. This condition will be satisfied by poems on a smaller scale than the old epics, and answering in length to the group of tragedies presented at a single sitting.[30]

Epic poetry has, however, a great—a special—capacity for enlarging its dimensions, and we can see the reason. In tragedy we cannot imitate several lines of action carried on at one and the same time; we must confine ourselves to the action on the stage and the part taken by the players. But in epic poetry, owing to the narrative form, many events simultaneously transacted can be presented; and these, if relevant to the subject, add mass and dignity to the poem. The epic has here an advantage, and one that conduces to grandeur of effect, to diverting the mind of the hearer, and relieving the story with varying episodes. For sameness of incident soon produces satiety, and makes tragedies fail on the stage. . . .

Homer, admirable in all respects, has the special merit of being the only poet who rightly appreciates the part he should take himself. The poet should

[29]In the second half of Book II of the *Iliad,* Homer interrupts the course of his story to insert a catalog of the ships that came to Troy and their leaders.

[30]Greek dramatists of the great period used to produce their plays in groups of four, three more or less connected tragedies followed by a comic or satiric play, all seen by the audience in one sitting.

speak as little as possible in his own person, for it is not this that makes him an imitator. Other poets appear themselves upon the scene throughout, and imitate but little and rarely. Homer, after a few prefatory words, at once brings in a man or woman or other personage, none of them wanting in characteristic qualities, but each with a character of his own.

The element of the wonderful is required in tragedy. But the improbable, on which the wonderful depends for its chief effects, has wider scope in epic poetry, because there the person acting is not seen. Thus, the pursuit of Hector would be ludicrous if placed upon the stage—the Greeks standing still and not joining in the pursuit, and Achilles waving them back.[31] But in the epic poem the absurdity passes unnoticed. Now the wonderful is pleasing, as may be inferred from the fact that everyone tells a story with some addition of his own, knowing that his hearers like it. . . .

But the poet should prefer probable impossibilities to improbable possibilities. The tragic plot must not be composed of improbable parts. Everything improbable should, if possible, be excluded; or, at all events, it should lie outside the action of the play itself. . . .

But once the improbable has been introduced and an air of likelihood imparted to it, we must accept it in spite of the absurdity. Take even the incidents in the *Odyssey* where Odysseus is left upon the shore of Ithaca.[32] How intolerable even these might have been would be apparent if an inferior poet were to treat the subject! As it is, the absurdity is veiled by the poetic charm with which the poet invests it.

The diction should be elaborated in the pauses of the action where there is no expression of character or thought. For, conversely, character and thought are merely obscured by a diction that is over brilliant.

XXV

With respect to problems and their solutions, the number and nature of the sources from which they spring may be thus set forth.

The poet being an imitator, like a painter or any other artist, must of necessity imitate one of three objects: things as they were or are, things as they are said or thought to be, or things as they ought to be. This he does in language—using either current expressions or, it may be, rare words or metaphors. There are also many modifications of language, which we concede to the poets. Add to this, that the standard of correctness is not the same in poetry and in politics, any more than in poetry and in any other art. Within the art of poetry itself there are two kinds of faults—those which touch its essence, and those which are accidental. If the poet intended to describe something right, but described it incorrectly through lack of ability to express himself, his art is faulty. But if his failure was due to a wrong intention—if, for instance, he represented a horse as throwing out both his off legs at once, or introduced technical inaccuracies in medicine, or some other science—the error was not in the essentials of his art. These are the

[31] Achilles' pursuit of Hector is described in the *Iliad*, Book XXII.
[32] *Odyssey*, Book XIII.

points of view from which we should consider and answer the questions raised in the problems.

First as to questions which concern the poet's own art. If he describes the impossible, he is guilty of an error; but the error may be justified, if the end of the art be thereby attained (the end being that already mentioned)—if, that is, the effect of this or any other part of the poem is thus rendered more striking. A case in point is the pursuit of Hector. If, however, the end might have been as well or better attained without violating the rules of poetic correctness, the error is not justified; for every kind of error should, if possible, be avoided.

Again, does the error touch the essentials of the poetic art or some accident of it? For example, not to know that a hind has no horns is a less serious matter than to paint it inartistically.

Further, if it be objected that a description is not true to fact, the poet may perhaps reply, "But the objects are as they ought to be"; just as Sophocles said that he drew men as they ought to be, Euripides as they are. In this way the objection may be met. If, however, the description is neither true nor of the thing as it should be, the poet may answer, "This is how men say the thing is." This dictum applies to the tales about the gods. It may well be that these stories are not loftier than the facts nor yet true to fact; they are, very possibly, what Xenophanes[33] says of them. But anyhow, "this is what is said."

XXVI

The question may be raised whether the epic or tragic form of imitation is the higher. If the more refined art is the higher, and the more refined in every case is that which appeals to the better sort of audience, the art which addresses itself to any and everyone is manifestly most unrefined. The audience then is supposed to be too dull to comprehend unless the performers throw in something of their own, who therefore indulge in perpetual movements.

So we are told that epic poetry is addressed to a cultivated audience, who do not need gestures, tragedy to an inferior public. Being then unrefined, it is evidently the lower of the two.

Now, in the first place, this censure attaches not to the poetic but to the actors' art; for gesticulation may be equally overdone in epic recitation. . . . Next, all action is not to be condemned—any more than all dancing—but only that of bad performers. . . . Again, tragedy, like epic poetry, produces its effect even without action; it reveals its power by mere reading. If, then, in all other respects it is superior, this fault, we say, is not inherent in it.

And superior it is, because it has all the epic elements—it may even use the epic meter, with music and spectacular effects as important accessories; and these produce the most lively of pleasures. Further, it creates a vivid impression when read as well as when acted. Moreover, the art in it attains its end

[33]Xenophanes of Colophon, who lived almost two hundred years before Aristotle, seems to have been remembered largely for his attacks on and ridicule of the popular polytheism of Greece.

within narrower limits; and the concentrated effect is more pleasurable than one which is spread over a long time and so diluted. What, for example, would be the effect of the *Oedipus* of Sophocles, if it were cast into a form as long as the *Iliad?* Once more, the epic imitation has less unity; as is shown by this, that any epic poem will furnish subjects for several tragedies. . . .

If, then, tragedy is superior to epic poetry in all these respects and, moreover, fulfills its specific function better as an art—for each art ought to produce, not any chance pleasure, but the pleasure proper to it, as already stated—it plainly follows that tragedy is the higher art, as attaining its end more perfectly.

Thus much may suffice concerning tragic and epic poetry in general; their several kinds and parts, with the number of each and their differences; the causes that make a poem good or bad; the objections of the critics and the answer to their objections.

Herodotus

(490–c. 425 B.C.)

from *THE HISTORY*[1]

[CANDAULES AND GYGES]

There was a certain king of Sardis,[2] Candaules by name, whom the Greeks call Myrsilus. He was a descendant of Alcaeus, son of Heracles. The first king of this dynasty was Agron, son of Ninus, grandson of Belus, and great-grandson of Alcaeus; Candaules, son of Myrsus, was the last. The kings who reigned before Agron sprang from Lydus, son of Atys, from whom the people of the land, called previously Maeonians, received the name of Lydians. The Heraclidae, descended from Heracles and the slave-girl of Jardanus, having

[1]Translated by George Rawlinson. Herodotus is generally credited with initiating the discipline of history, as his fifth-century Greek contemporaries initiated a number of other scientific and humanistic disciplines. His *History* tells the story of the Persian Wars (500–449 B.C.), during which the Persian Empire attempted to conquer Greece, only to be defeated. In the telling, however, Herodotus ranges back to mythical times and across the known world to explore all conflicts between Greeks and non-Greeks. Lacking substantial written records and relying principally on oral traditions, Herodotus produced a heterogeneous work that presents fairly reliable accounts of recent events alongside myths, legends, and fanciful accounts of remote places. Much of the book is devoted to the stories of individuals. The stories of Candaules and Gyges and of Solon and Croesus, from early in the *History*, demonstrate both Herodotus's gift for storytelling and the extent to which his accounts of the past are shaped by Greek conceptions of vice and virtue.

[2]Sardis was the capital of the ancient kingdom of Lydia, in Asia Minor. Herodotus is thus telling a story about the "barbarians."

been entrusted by these princes with the management of affairs, obtained the kingdom by an oracle. Their rule endured for twenty-two generations of men, a space of 505 years, during the whole of which period, from Agron to Candaules, the crown descended in the direct line from father to son.

Now it happened that this Candaules was in love with his own wife; and not only so, but thought her the fairest woman in the whole world. This fancy had strange consequences. There was in his bodyguard a man whom he specially favored, Gyges, the son of Dascylus. All affairs of greatest moment were entrusted by Candaules to this person, and to him he was wont to extol the surpassing beauty of his wife. So matters went on for a while. At length, one day, Candaules, for he was fated to end ill, thus addressed his follower, "I see you do not credit what I tell you of my lady's loveliness; but come now, since men's ears are less credulous than their eyes, contrive some means whereby you may behold her naked." At this the other loudly exclaimed, saying, "What most unwise speech is this, master, which you have uttered? Would you have me behold my mistress when she is naked? Remember that a woman, with her clothes, puts off her bashfulness. Our fathers, in time past, distinguished right and wrong plainly enough, and it is our wisdom to submit to be taught by them. There is an old saying, 'Let each look on his own.' I hold your wife for the fairest of all womankind. Only, I beseech you, ask me not to do wickedly."

Gyges thus endeavored to decline the king's proposal, trembling lest some dreadful evil should befall him through it. But the king replied to him, "Courage, friend; suspect me not of the design to prove you by this discourse; nor dread your mistress, lest mischief befall you at her hands. Be sure I will so manage that she shall not even know that you have looked upon her. I will place you behind the open door of the chamber in which we sleep. When I enter to go to rest she will follow me. There stands a chair close to the entrance, on which she will lay her clothes one by one as she takes them off. You will be able thus at your leisure to peruse her person. Then, when she is moving from the chair towards the bed, and her back is turned on you, be it your care that she see you not as you pass through the door-way."

Gyges, unable to escape, could but declare his readiness. Then Candaules, when night came, led Gyges into his sleeping-chamber, and a moment after the queen followed. She came in, and laid her garments on the chair, and Gyges gazed on her. After a while she moved towards the bed, and her back being then turned, he glided stealthily from the apartment. As he was passing out, however, she saw him, and instantly divining what had happened, she neither screamed as her shame impelled her, nor even appeared to have noticed anything, purposing to take vengeance upon the husband who had so affronted her. For among the Lydians, and indeed among the barbarians generally, it is reckoned a deep disgrace, even to a man, to be seen naked.

No sound or sign of intelligence escaped her at the time. But in the morning, as soon as day broke, she hastened to choose from among her retinue, such as she knew to be most faithful to her, and preparing them for what was to ensue, summoned Gyges into her presence. Now it had often happened before that the queen had desired to confer with him, and he was accustomed to come to her at her call. He therefore obeyed the summons, not suspecting that she knew what had occurred. Then she addressed these words to him, "Take your choice, Gyges, of two courses which are open to you. Slay Candaules, and thereby become my lord, and obtain the Lydian throne, or die this moment in his room. So you will not again, obeying all behests of your master, behold what is not lawful for you. It must needs be, that either he perish by whose counsel this thing was done, or you, who saw me naked, and so did break our usages." At these words Gyges stood awhile in mute astonishment; recovering after a time, he earnestly besought the queen that she would not compel him to so hard a choice. But finding he implored in vain, and that necessity was indeed laid on him to kill or to be killed, he made choice of life for himself, and replied by this inquiry, "If it must be so, and you compel me against my will to put my lord to death, come, let me hear how you will have me set on him." "Let him be attacked," she answered, "on that spot where I was by him shown naked to you, and let the assault be made when he is asleep."

All was then prepared for the attack, and when night fell, Gyges, seeing that he had no retreat or escape, but must absolutely either slay Candaules, or himself be slain, followed his mistress into the sleeping-room. She placed a dagger in his hand, and hid him carefully behind the self-same door. Then Gyges, when the king was fallen asleep, entered privily into the chamber and struck him dead. Thus did the wife and kingdom of Candaules pass into the possession of his follower Gyges, of whom Archilochus the Parian, who lived about the same time, made mention in a poem written in Iambic trimeter verse.

Gyges was afterwards confirmed in the possession of the throne by an answer of the Delphic oracle. Enraged at the murder of their king, the people flew to arms, but after a while the partisans of Gyges came to terms with them, and it was agreed that if the Delphic oracle declared him king of the Lydians, he should reign; if otherwise, he should yield the throne to he Heraclidae. As the oracle was given in his favor he became king. The Pythian priestess, however, added that, in the fifth generation from Gyges, vengeance should come for the Heraclidae; a prophecy of which neither the Lydians nor their princes took any account till it was fulfilled. Such was the way in which the Mermnadae deposed the Heraclidae, and themselves obtained the sovereignty.

[SOLON]

Croesus[3] afterwards, in the course of many years, brought under his sway almost all the nations to the west of the Halys. The Lycians and Cilicians alone continued free; all the other tribes he reduced and held in subjection. They were the following: the Lydians, Phrygians, Mysians, Mariandynians, Chalybians, Paphlagonians, Thynian and Bithynian Thracians, Carians, Ionians, Dorians, Aeolians, and Pamphylians.

When all these conquests had been added to the Lydian empire, and the prosperity of Sardis was now at its height, there came thither, one after another, all the sages of Greece living at the time, and among them Solon, the Athenian.[4] He was on his travels, having left Athens to be absent ten years, under the pretence of wishing to see the world, but really to avoid being forced to repeal any of the laws which, at the request of the Athenians, he had made for them.

[3]Croesus, King of Lydia, was legendarily the richest man in the world.

[4]Solon (c. 639–c. 559 B.C.) was an Athenian statesman who introduced a number of constitutional reforms that became the basis of the Athenian state. There is no evidence that he ever visited Lydia; he is treated by Herodotus as a strictly legendary character, like Croesus.

Without his sanction the Athenians could not repeal them, as they had bound themselves under a heavy curse to be governed for ten years by the laws which should be imposed on them by Solon.

On this account, as well as to see the world, Solon set out upon his travels, in the course of which he went to Egypt to the court of Amasis, and also came on a visit to Croesus at Sardis. Croesus received him as the guest, and lodged him in the royal palace. On the third or fourth day after, he bade his servants conduct Solon over his treasuries, and show him all their greatness and magnificence. When he had seen them all, and, so far as time allowed, inspected them, Croesus addressed this question to him, "Stranger of Athens, we have heard much of your wisdom and of your travels through many lands, from love of knowledge and a wish to see the world. I am curious therefore to inquire of you, whom, of all the men that you have seen, you consider the most happy?" This he asked because he thought himself the happiest of mortals: but Solon answered him without flattery, according to his true sentiments, "Tellus of Athens, sire." Full of astonishment at what he heard, Croesus demanded sharply, "And wherefore do you deem Tellus happiest?" To which the other replied, "First, because his country was flourishing in his days, and he himself had sons both beautiful and good, and he lived to see children born to each of them, and these children all grew up; and further because, after a life spent in what our people look upon as comfort, his end was surpassingly glorious. In a battle between the Athenians and their neighbors near Eleusis, he came to the assistance of his countrymen, routed the foe, and died upon the field most gallantly. The Athenians gave him a public funeral on the spot where he fell, and paid him the highest honors."

Thus did Solon admonish Croesus by the example of Tellus, enumerating the manifold particulars of his happiness. When he had ended, Croesus inquired a second time, who after Tellus seemed to him the happiest, expecting that, at any rate, he would be given the second place. "Cleobis and Bito," Solon answered, "they were of Argive race: their fortune was enough for their wants, and they were besides endowed with so much bodily strength that they had both gained prizes at the Games. Also this tale is told of them: There was a great festival in honor of the goddess Hera at Argos, to which their mother must needs be taken in a car. Now the oxen did not come home from the field in time: so the youths, fearful of being too late, put the yoke on their own necks, and themselves drew the car in which their mother rode. Five miles they drew her, and stopped before the temple. This deed of theirs was witnessed by the whole assembly of worshippers, and then their life closed in the best possible way. Herein, too, God showed forth most evidently, how much better a thing for man death is than life. For the Argive men stood thick around the car and extolled the vast strength of the youths; and the Argive women extolled the mother who was blessed with such a pair of sons; and the mother herself, overjoyed at the deed and at the praises it had won, stranding straight before the image, besought the goddess to bestow on Cleobis and Bito, the sons who had so mightily honored her, the highest blessing to which mortals can attain. Her prayer ended, they offered sacrifice, and partook of the holy banquet, after which the two youths fell asleep in the temple. They never woke more, but so passed from the earth. The Argives, looking on them as among the best of men, caused statues of them to be made, which they gave to the shrine at Delphi."

When Solon had thus assigned these youths the second place, Croesus broke in angrily, "What, stranger of Athens, is my happiness, then, valued so little by you, that you do not even put me on a level with private men?"

"Croesus," replied the other, "you asked a question concerning the condition of man, of one who knows that the power above us is full of jealousy, and fond of troubling our lot. A long life gives one to witness much, and experience much oneself, that one would not choose. Seventy years I regard as the limit of the life of man. In these seventy years are contained, without reckoning intercalary months, 25,200 days. Add an intercalary month to every other year, that the seasons may come round at the right time, and there will be, besides the seventy years, thirty-five such months, making an addition of 1,050 days. The whole number of the days contained in the seventy years will thus be 26,250, whereof not one but will produce events unlike the rest. Hence man is wholly accident. For yourself, Croesus, I see that you are wonderfully rich, and the lord of many nations; but with respect to your question, I have no answer to give, until I hear that you have closed your life happily. For assuredly he who possesses great store of riches is no nearer happiness than he who has what suffices for his daily needs, unless luck attend upon him, and so he continue in the enjoyment of all his good things to the end of life. For many of the wealthiest men have been unfavored of fortune, and many whose means were moderate, have had excellent luck. Men of the former class excel those of the latter but in two respects; these last excel the former in many. The wealthy man is better able to content his desires, and to bear up against a sudden buffet of calamity. The other has less ability to withstand these evils (from which, however, his good luck keeps him clear), but he enjoys all these following blessings: he is whole of limb, a stranger to disease, free from misfortune, happy in his children, and comely to look upon. If, in addition to all this, he end his life well, he is of a truth the man of whom you are in search, the man who may rightly be termed happy. Call him, however, until he die, not happy but fortunate. Scarcely, indeed, can any man unite all these advantages: as there is no country which contains within it all that it needs, but each, while it possesses some things, lacks others, and the best country is that which contains the most; so no single human being is complete in every respect—something is always lacking. He who unites the greatest number of advantages, and retaining them to the day of his death, then dies peaceably, that man alone, sire, is, in my judgment, entitled to bear the name of 'happy.' But in every matter we must mark well the end; for oftentimes God gives men a gleam of happiness, and then plunges them into ruin."

Such was the speech which Solon addressed to Croesus, a speech which brought him neither largess nor honor. The king saw him depart with much indifference, since he thought that a man must be an arrant fool who made no account of present good, but bade men always wait and mark the end.

After Solon had gone away a dreadful vengeance, sent of God, came upon Croesus, to punish him, it is likely, for considering himself the happiest of men. First he had a dream in the night, which foreshowed him truly the evils that were about to befall him in the person of his son. For Croesus had two sons, one blasted by a natural defect, being deaf and dumb; the other, distinguished far above all his mates in every pursuit. The name of the last was Atys.[5] It was this son concerning whom he dreamed a dream, that he would die by the blow of an iron weapon. When he woke, he considered earnestly with himself, and, greatly alarmed at the dream, instantly made his son take a wife, and whereas in former years the youth had been wont to command the Lydian forces in the field, he now would not suffer him to accompany them. All the spears and javelins, and weapons used in the wars, he removed out of the male apartments, and laid them in heaps in the chambers of the women, fearing lest perhaps one of the weapons that hung against the wall might fall and strike him.

Now it chanced that while he was making arrangements for the wedding, there came to Sardis a man under a misfortune, who had upon him the stain of blood. He was by race a Phrygian, and belonged to the family of the king. Presenting himself at the palace of Croesus, he prayed to be admitted to purification according to the customs of the country. Now the Lydian method of purifying is very nearly the same as the Greek. Croesus granted the request, and went through all the customary rites, after which he asked the suppliant of his birth and country, addressing him as follows, "Who are you, stranger, and from what part of Phyrgia did you flee to take refuge at my hearth? And whom, moreover, what man or what woman, have you slain?" "O king," replied the Phrygian, "I am the son of Gordias, son of Midas. I am named Adrastus.[6] The man I unintentionally slew was my own brother. For this my father drove me from the land, and I lost all. Then fled I here to you." "You are the offspring," Croesus rejoined, "of a house friendly to mine, and you have come to friends. You shall want for nothing so long as you stay in my dominions. Bear your misfortune as easily as you may, so will it go best with you." Thenceforth Adrastus lived in the palace of the king.

It chanced that at this very same time there was in the Mysian Olympus[7] a huge monster of a boar, which went forth often from this mountain-country, and wasted the corn-fields of the Mysians. Many a time had the Mysians collected to hunt the beast, but instead of doing him any hurt, they came off always with some loss to themselves. At length they sent ambassadors to Croesus, who delivered their message to him in these words, "O king, a mighty monster of a boar has appeared in our parts, and destroys the labor of our hands. We do our best to take him, but in vain. Now therefore we beseech you to let your son accompany us back, with some chosen youths and hounds, that we may rid our country of the animal." Such was the tenor of their prayer.

But Croesus thought of his dream, and answered, "Say no more of my son going with you; that may not be in any wise. He is but just joined in wedlock, and is busy enough with that. I will grant you a picked band of Lydians, and all my hunting array, and I will charge those whom I send to use all zeal in aiding you to rid your country of the brute."

With this reply the Mysians were content; but the king's son, hearing what the prayer of the Mysians was, came suddenly in, and on the refusal of Croesus to let him go with them, thus addressed his father, "Formerly, my father, it

[5]*Atys* means "the youth under the influence of Até," that is, "the youth ruled by Fate."
[6]*Adrastus* means "the doomed" or "the man unable to escape."
[7]The mountainous region of Mysia in Asia Minor, part of Croesus's kingdom.

was considered the noblest and most suitable thing for me to frequent the wars and hunting-parties, and win myself glory in them; but now you keep me away from both, although you have never beheld in me either cowardice or lack of spirit. What face meanwhile must I wear as I walk to the agora[8] or return from it? What must the citizens, what must my young bride think of me? What sort of man will she suppose her husband to be? Either, therefore, let me go to the chase of this boar, or give me a reason why it is best for me to do according to your wishes."

Then Croesus answered, "My son, it is not because I have seen in you either cowardice or anything else which has displeased me that I keep you back; but because a vision, which came before me in a dream as I slept, warned me that you were doomed to die young, pierced by an iron weapon. It was this which first led me to hasten on your wedding, and now it hinders me from sending you upon this enterprise. I would like to keep watch over you, if by any means I may cheat fate of you during my own lifetime. For you are the one and only son that I possess; the other, whose hearing is destroyed, I regard as if he were not."

"Ah father," returned the youth, "I blame you not for keeping watch over me after a dream so terrible; but if you are mistaken, if you do not apprehend the dream rightly, it is no blame for me to show you your error. Now the dream, you said, foretold that I should die stricken by an iron weapon. But what hands has a boar to strike with? What iron weapon does he wield? Yet this is what you fear for me. Had the dream said that I should die pierced by a tusk, then you would have done well to keep me away; but it said a weapon. Now here we do not combat men, but a wild animal. I pray you, therefore, let me go with them."

"There you have me, my son," said Croesus, "your interpretation is better than mine. I yield to it, and change my mind, and consent to let you go."

Then the king sent for Adrastus the Phrygian, and said to him, "Adrastus, when you were smitten with the rod of affliction—no reproach, my friend—I purified you, and have taken you to live with me in my palace, and have been at every charge. Now, therefore, you should requite the good offices you have received at my hands by consenting to go with my son on this hunting-party, and to watch over him, in case you should be attacked upon the road by some band of daring robbers. Even apart from this, it were right for you to go where you may make yourself famous by noble deeds. They are the heritage of your family, and you too are stalwart and strong."

Adrastus answered, "Except for your request, O king, I would rather have kept away from this hunt, for it ill beseems a man under a misfortune such as mine to consort with his happier compeers, and besides, I have no heart to it. On many grounds I had stayed behind, but, as you urge it, and I am bound to pleasure you (for truly it does behoove me to requite your good offices), I am content to do as you wish. For your son, whom you give into my charge, be sure you shall receive him back safe and sound, so far as depends upon a guardian's carefulness."

[8]Place of assembly, usually in the market place, of an ancient Greek city.

Thus assured, Croesus let them depart, accompanied by a band of picked youths, and well provided with dogs of chase. When they reached Olympus, they scattered in quest of the animal; he was soon found, and the hunters, drawing round him in a circle, hurled their weapons at him. Then the stranger, the man who had been purified of blood, whose name was Adrastus, he also hurled his spear at the boar, but missed his aim, and struck Atys. Thus was the son of Croesus slain by the point of an iron weapon, and the warning of the vision was fulfilled. Then one ran to Sardis to bear the tidings to the king, and he came and informed him of the combat, and of the fate that had befallen his son.

If it was a heavy blow to the father to learn that his child was dead, it yet more strongly affected him to think that the very man whom he himself once purified had done the deed. In the violence of his grief he called aloud on Zeus the Purifier, to be a witness of what he had suffered at the stranger's hands. Afterwards he invoked the same god as Zeus the Protector of hearths and friendships, using the one term because he had unwittingly harbored in his house the man who had now slain his son; and the other, because the stranger, who had been sent as his child's guardian, had turned out his most cruel enemy.

Presently the Lydians arrived, bearing the body of the youth, and behind them followed the homicide. He took his stand in front of the corpse, and, stretching forth his hands to Croesus, delivered himself into his power with earnest entreaties that he would sacrifice him upon the body of his son, "his former misfortune was burden enough; now that he had added to it a second, and had brought ruin on the man who purified him, he could not bear to live." Then Croesus, when he heard these words, was moved with pity towards Adrastus, notwithstanding the bitterness of his own calamity; and so he answered, "Enough, my friend; I have all the revenge that I require, since you give sentence of death against yourself. But indeed it is not you who have injured me, except so far as you accidentally dealt the blow. Some god is the author of my misfortune, and I was forewarned of it a long time ago." Croesus after this buried the body of his son, with such honors as fitted the occasion. Adrastus, son of Gordias, son of Midas, the destroyer of his brother in time past, the destroyer now of his purifier, regarding himself as the most unfortunate wretch whom he had ever known, as soon as all was quiet about the place, slew himself upon the tomb. Croesus, bereft of his son, gave himself up to mourning for two full years. . . .

Sardis [was] taken by the Persians, and Croesus himself fell into their hands, after having reigned fourteen years, and been besieged in his capital fourteen days; thus too did Croesus fulfil the oracle, which said that he should destroy a mighty empire, by destroying his own. Then the Persians who had made Croesus prisoner brought him before Cyrus. Now a vast pile had been raised by his orders, and Croesus, laden with fetters, was placed upon it, and with him twice seven of the sons of the Lydians. I know not whether Cyrus was minded to make an offering of the first-fruits to some god or other, or whether he had vowed a vow and was performing it, or whether, as may well be, he had heard that Croesus was a holy man, and so wished to see if any of the heavenly powers would appear to save him from being burned alive. However it might be, Cyrus was thus engaged, and Croesus was already on the pile, when it entered his mind in the depth of his woe that there was a divine warning in the words which had come to him from the lips of Solon, "No one while he lives is happy." When this thought smote him he fetched a long breath, and breaking his deep silence, groaned out aloud, thrice uttering the name of Solon. Cyrus caught the sounds, and bade the interpreters inquire of Croesus who it was he called on. They drew near and asked him, but he held his peace, and for a long-time made no answer to their questionings, until at length, forced to say something, he exclaimed, "One I would give much to see converse with every monarch." Not knowing what he meant by this reply, the interpreters begged him to explain himself; and as they pressed for an answer, and grew to be troublesome, he told them how, a long time before, Solon, an Athenian, had come and seen all his splendor, and made light of it; and how whatever he had said to him had fallen out exactly as he foreshowed, although it was nothing that especially concerned him, but applied to all mankind alike, and most to those who seemed to themselves happy. Meanwhile, as he thus spoke, the pile was lighted, and the outer portion began to blaze. Then Cyrus, hearing from the interpreters what Croesus had said, relented, bethinking himself that he too was a man, and that it was a fellow-man, and one who had once been as blessed by fortune as himself, that he was burning alive; afraid, moreover, of retribution, and full of the thought that whatever is human is insecure. So he bade them quench the blazing fire as quickly as they could, and take down Croesus and the other Lydians, which they tried to do, but the flames were not to be mastered.

Then, the Lydians say that Croesus, perceiving by the efforts made to quench the fire that Cyrus had relented, and seeing also that all was in vain, and that the men could not get the fire under, called with a loud voice upon the god Apollo, and prayed him, if he had ever received at his hands any acceptable gift, to come to his aid, and deliver him from his present danger. As thus with tears he besought the god, suddenly, though up to that time the sky had been clear and the day without a breath of wind, dark clouds gathered, and the storm burst over their heads with rain of such violence, that the flames were speedily extinguished. Cyrus, convinced by this that Croesus was a good man and a favorite of heaven, asked him after he was taken off the pile, "Who it was that had persuaded him to lead an army into his country, and so become his foe rather than continue his friend?" To which Croesus made answer as follows, "What I did, O king, was to thy advantage and to my own loss. If there be blame, it rests with the god of the Greeks, who encouraged me to begin the war. No one is so foolish as to prefer to peace war, in which, instead of sons burying their fathers, fathers bury their sons. But the gods willed it so."

Thus did Croesus speak. Cyrus then ordered his fetters to be taken off, and made him sit down near himself, and paid him much respect, looking upon him, as did also the courtiers, with a sort of wonder.

Thucydides

(Middle Fifth Century–399 B.C.?)

from *THE PELOPONNESIAN WARS*[1]

[PERICLES' FUNERAL SPEECH]

During the same winter, in accordance with an ancestral custom, the funeral of those who first fell in this war was celebrated by the Athenians at the public charge. The ceremony is as follows: Three days before the celebration they erect a tent in which the bones of the dead are laid out, and every one brings to his own dead any offering which he pleases. At the time of the funeral the bones are placed in chests of cypress wood, which are conveyed on wagons; there is one chest for each tribe. They also carry a single empty litter decked with a pall for all whose bodies are missing, and cannot be recovered after the battle. The procession is accompanied by any one who chooses, whether citizen or stranger, and the female relatives of the deceased are present at the place of interment and make lamentation. The public sepulchre is situated in the most beautiful spot outside the walls; there they always bury those who fall in war; only after the battle of Marathon the dead, in recognition of their pre-eminent valour, were interred on the field. When the remains have been laid in the earth, some man of known ability and high reputation, chosen by the city, delivers a suitable oration over them; after which the people depart. Such is the manner of interment; and the ceremony was repeated from time to time throughout the war. Over those who were the

[1]Translated by Benjamin Jowett. As Herodotus's history of the Persian Wars chronicles the war that ushered in the golden age of Athens, so Thucydides' history tells the story of the disastrous war that marked the end of that age. The Peloponnesian War (431–404 B.C.) ended in the defeat of Athens and the passing of power to Sparta. The lives of Herodotus and Thucydides overlapped, and by the time Herodotus finished his history, the opening battles of the Peloponnesian War were being fought. Despite their closeness in time, though, their histories differ sharply. Herodotus has been called a "romantic" historian, Thucydides a "realistic" one, and the labels have some truth, though modern critics have found more reality in Herodotus and more romance in Thucydides than their contemporaries did. Thucydides lived through and even participated in the events he describes; hence he had better access to accurate information about his subject than Herodotus did. Beyond this, he seems temperamentally different. Herodotus seeks the causes of historical events in divine fate; Thucydides seeks them in human actions. Herodotus tends to express his views of history through exemplary anecdotes of individuals struck down by Nemesis; Thucydides expresses his through reports of speeches and debates. Two such passages are Pericles' famous funeral speech in Book II and the Melian Dialogue in Book V. Thucydides did not claim that his reports of what was said were verbatim. He rather took the opportunity to express in these passages what he took to be the underlying themes of his history; in Pericles's funeral speech, the high ideals of Athenian life, and in the Melian Dialogue, the amoral realities of power that underlay those ideals, realities expressed by the Athenians in the cynical aphorism "The powerful exact what they can, and the weak grant what they must."

first buried Pericles[2] was chosen to speak. At the fitting moment he advanced from the sepulchre to a lofty platform, which had been erected in order that he might be heard as far as possible by the multitude, and spoke as follows:

"Most of those who have spoken here before me have commended the lawgiver who added this oration to our other funeral customs; it seemed to them a worthy thing that such an honor should be given at their burial to the dead who have fallen on the field of battle. But I should have preferred that, when men's deeds have been brave, they should be honored in deed only, and with such an honor as this public funeral, which you are now witnessing. Then the reputation of many would not have been imperilled on the eloquence or want of eloquence of one, and their virtues believed or not as he spoke well or ill. For it is difficult to say neither too little nor too much; and even moderation is apt not to give the impression of truthfulness. The friend of the dead who knows the facts is likely to think that the words of the speaker fall short of his knowledge and of his wishes; another who is not so well informed, when he hears of anything which surpasses his own powers, will be envious and will suspect exaggeration. Mankind are tolerant of the praises of others so long as each hearer thinks that he can do as well or nearly as well himself, but, when the deed is beyond him, jealousy is aroused and he begins to be incredulous. However, since our ancestors have set the seal of their approval upon the practice, I must obey, and to the utmost of my power shall endeavor to satisfy the wishes and beliefs of all who hear me.

"I will speak first of our ancestors, for it is right and becoming that now, when we are lamenting the dead, a tribute should be paid to their memory. There has never been a time when they did not inhabit this land, which by their valor they have handed down from generation to generation, and we have received from them a free state. But if they were worthy of praise, still more were our fathers, who added to their inheritance, and after many a struggle transmitted to us their sons this great empire. And we ourselves assembled here to-day, who are still most of us in the vigor of life, have chiefly done the work of improvement, and have richly endowed our city with all things, so that she is sufficient for herself both in peace and war. Of the military exploits by which our various possessions were acquired, or of the energy with which we or our fathers drove back the tide of war, Hellenic or barbarian, I will not speak; for the tale would be long and is familiar to you. But before I praise the dead, I should like to point out by what principles of action we rose to power, and under what institutions and through what manner of life our empire became great. For I conceive that such thoughts are not unsuited to the occasion, and that this numerous assembly of citizens and strangers may profitably listen to them.

"Our form of government does not enter into rivalry with the institutions of others. We do not copy our neighbors, but are an example to them. It is true that we are called a democracy, for the administration is in the hands of the many and not of the few. But while the law secures equal justice to

[2]Pericles was the chief statesman and general of Athens. He presided over the flowering of Athens in the mid-fifth century. Controversy over the Peloponnesian War drove him from office in 430 B.C. He was restored to office the following year but died six months later.

all alike in their private disputes, the claim of excellence is also recognized; and when a citizen is in any way distinguished, he is preferred to the public service, not as a matter of privilege, but as the reward of merit. Neither is poverty a bar, but a man may benefit his country whatever be the obscurity of his condition. There is no exclusiveness in our public life, and in our private intercourse we are not suspicious of one another, nor angry with our neighbor if he does what he likes; we do not put on sour looks at him which, though harmless, are not pleasant. While we are thus unconstrained in our private intercourse, a spirit of reverence pervades our public acts; we are prevented from doing wrong by respect for authority and for the laws, having an especial regard to those which are ordained for the protection of the injured as well as to those unwritten laws which bring upon the transgressor of them the reprobation of the general sentiment.

"And we have not forgotten to provide for our weary spirits many relaxations from toil; we have regular games and sacrifices throughout the year; at home the style of our life is refined; and the delight which we daily feel in all these things helps to banish melancholy. Because of the greatness of our city the fruits of the whole earth flow in upon us; so that we enjoy the goods of other countries as freely as of our own.

"Then, again, our military training is in many respects superior to that of our adversaries. Our city is thrown open to the world, and we never expel a foreigner or prevent him from seeing or learning anything of which the secret if revealed to any enemy might profit him. We rely not upon management or trickery, but upon our own hearts and hands. And in the matter of education, whereas they from early youth are always undergoing laborious exercises which are to make them brave, we live at ease, and yet are equally ready to face the perils which they face. And here is the proof. The Lacedaemonians[3] come into Attica not by themselves, but with their whole confederacy following; we go alone into a neighbor's country; and although our opponents are fighting for their homes and we on a foreign soil, we have seldom any difficulty in overcoming them. Our enemies have never yet felt our united strength; the care of a navy divides our attention, and on land we are obliged to send our own citizens everywhere. But they, if they meet and defeat a part of our army, are as proud as if they had routed us all, and when defeated they pretend to have been vanquished by us all.

"If then we prefer to meet danger with a light heart but without laborious training, and with a courage which is gained by habit and not enforced by law, are we not greatly the gainers? Since we do not anticipate the pain, although, when the hour comes, we can be as brave as those who never allow themselves to rest; and thus too our city is equally admirable in peace and in war.

"For we are lovers of the beautiful, yet with economy, and we cultivate the mind without loss of manliness. Wealth we employ, not for talk and ostentation, but when there is a real use for it. To avow poverty with us is no disgrace; the true disgrace is in doing nothing to avoid it. An Athenian citizen does not neglect the state because he takes care of his own household; and even those of us who are engaged in business have a very fair idea of politics. We alone regard a man who takes no interest in public affairs, not as

[3]Spartans.

a harmless, but as a useless character; and if few of us are originators, we are all sound judges of a policy. The great impediment to action is, in our opinion, not discussion, but the want of that knowledge which is gained by discussion preparatory to action. For we have a peculiar power of thinking before we act and of acting too, whereas other men are courageous from ignorance but hesitate upon reflection. And they are surely to be esteemed the bravest spirits who, having the clearest sense both of the pains and pleasures of life, do not on that count shrink from danger. In doing good, again, we are unlike others; we make our friends by conferring, not by receiving favors. Now he who confers a favor is the firmer friend, because he would fain by kindness keep alive the memory of an obligation; but the recipient is colder in his feelings, because he knows that in requiting another's generosity he will not be winning gratitude but only paying a debt. We alone do good to our neighbors not upon a calculation of interest, but in the confidence of freedom and in a frank and fearless spirit.

"To sum up: I say that Athens is the school of Hellas, and that the individual Athenian in his own person seems to have the power of adapting himself to the most varied forms of action with the utmost versatility and grace. This is no passing and idle word, but truth and fact; and the assertion is verified by the position to which these qualities have raised the state. For in the hour of trial Athens alone among her contemporaries is superior to the report of her. No enemy who comes against her is indignant at the reverses which he sustains at the hands of such a city; no subject complains that his masters are unworthy of him. And we shall assuredly not be without witnesses; there are mighty monuments of our power which will make us the wonder of this and of succeeding ages; we shall not need the praises of Homer or of any other panegyrist whose poetry may please for the moment, although his representation of the facts will not bear the light of day. For we have compelled every land and every sea to open a path for our valor, and have everywhere planted eternal memorials of our friendship and of our enmity. Such is the city for whose sake these men nobly fought and died; they could not bear the thought that she might be taken from them; and every one of us who survive should gladly toil on her behalf.

"I have dwelt upon the greatness of Athens because I want to show you that we are contending for a higher prize than those who enjoy none of these privileges, and to establish by manifest proof the merit of these men whom I am now commemorating. Their loftiest praise has been already spoken. For in magnifying the city I have magnified them, and men like them whose virtues made her glorious. And of how few Hellenes can it be said as of them, that their deeds when weighed in the balance have been found equal to their fame! It seems to me that a death such as theirs has been gives the true measure of a man's worth; it may be the first revelation of his virtues, but is at any rate their final seal. For even those who come short in other ways may justly plead the valor with which they have fought for their country; they have blotted out the evil with the good, and have benefited the state more by their public services than they have injured her by their private actions. None of these men were enervated by wealth or hesitated to resign the pleasures of life; none of them put off the evil day in the hope, natural to poverty, that a man, though poor, may one day become rich. But, deeming that the punishment of their enemies was sweeter than any of these things, and that they could fall in no nobler cause, they determined at the hazard of their lives to be honorably avenged, and to leave the rest. They resigned to hope their unknown chance of happiness; but in the face of death they resolved to rely upon themselves alone. And when the moment came they were minded to resist and suffer, rather than to fly and save their lives; they ran away from the word of dishonor, but on the battle-field their feet stood fast, and in an instant, at the height of their fortune, they passed away from the scene, not of their fear, but of their glory.

"Such was the end of these men; they were worthy of Athens, and the living need not desire to have a more heroic spirit, although they may pray for a less fatal issue. The value of such a spirit is not to be expressed in words. Any one can discourse to you for ever about the advantages of a brave defense which you know already. But instead of listening to him I would have you day by day fix your eyes upon the greatness of Athens, until you become filled with the love of her; and when you are impressed by the spectacle of her glory, reflect that this empire has been acquired by men who knew their duty and had the courage to do it, who in the hour of conflict had the fear of dishonor always present to them, and who, if ever they failed in an enterprise, would not allow their virtues to be lost to their country, but freely gave their lives to her as the fairest offering which they could present at her feast. The sacrifice which they collectively made was individually repaid to them; for they received again each one for himself a praise which grows not old, and the noblest of all sepulchres—I speak not of that in which their remains are laid, but of that in which their glory survives, and is proclaimed always and on every fitting occasion both in word and deed. For the whole earth is the sepulchre of famous men; not only are they commemorated by columns and inscriptions in their own country, but in foreign lands there dwells also an unwritten memorial of them, graven not on stone but in the hearts of men. Make them your examples, and esteeming courage to be freedom and freedom to be happiness, do not weigh too nicely the perils of war. The unfortunate who has no hope of a change for the better has less reason to throw away his life than the prosperous who, if he survive, is always liable to a change for the worse, and to whom any accidental fall makes the most serious difference. To a man of spirit, cowardice and disaster coming together are far more bitter than death striking him unperceived at a time when he is full of courage and animated by the general hope.

"Wherefore I do not now commiserate the parents of the dead who stand here; I would rather comfort them. You know that your life has been passed amid manifold vicissitudes; and that they may be deemed fortunate who have gained most honor, whether an honorable death like theirs, or an honorable sorrow like yours, and whose days have been so ordered that the term of their happiness is likewise the term of their life. I know how hard it is to make you feel this, when the good fortune of others will too often remind you of the gladness which once lightened your hearts. And sorrow is felt at the want of those blessings, not which a man never knew, but which were a part of his life before they were taken from him. Some of you are of an age at which they may hope to have other children, and they ought to bear their sorrow better; not only will the children who may hereafter be born make them forget their own lost ones, but the city will be doubly a gainer. She will not be left desolate, and she will be safer. For a man's counsel cannot have equal weight or worth, when he alone has no children to risk in the general danger. To those of you who have passed their prime, I say, 'Congratulate yourselves that you have been happy during the greater part of your days; remember that your life of sorrow will not last long, and be comforted by the glory of those who are gone. For the love of honor alone is ever young, and not riches, as some say, but honor is the delight of men when they are old and useless.'

"To you who are the sons and brothers of the departed, I see that the struggle to emulate them will be an arduous one. For all men praise the dead, and however pre-eminent your virtue may be, hardly will you be thought, I do not say to equal, but even to approach them. The living have their rivals and detractors, but when a man is out of the way, the honor and good-will which he receives is unalloyed. And, if I am to speak of womanly virtues to those of you who will henceforth be widows, let me sum them up in one short admonition: To a woman not to show more weakness than is natural to her sex is a great glory, and not to be talked about for good or for evil among men.

"I have paid the required tribute, in obedience to the law, making use of such fitting words as I had. The tribute of deeds has been paid in part; for the dead have been honorably interred, and it remains only that their children should be maintained at the public charge until they are grown up: this is the solid prize with which, as with a garland, Athens crowns her sons living and dead, after a struggle like theirs. For where the rewards of virtue are greatest, there the noblest citizens are enlisted in the service of the state. And now, when you have duly lamented, every one his own dead, you may depart."

Such was the order of the funeral celebrated in this winter, with the end of which ended the first year of the Peloponnesian War.

[THE MELIAN DIALOGUE]

The Athenians next made an expedition against the island of Melos with thirty ships of their own, six Chian, and two Lesbian, 1,200 hoplites and 300 archers besides twenty mounted archers of their own, and about 1,500 hoplites furnished by their allies in the islands. The Melians are colonists of the Lacedaemonians who would not submit to Athens like the other islanders. At first they were neutral and took no part. But when the Athenians tried to coerce them by ravaging their lands, they were driven into open hostilities. The generals, Cleomedes the son of Lycomedes and Tisias the son of Tisimachus, encamped with the Athenian forces on the island. But before they did the country any harm they sent envoys to negotiate with the Melians. Instead of bringing these envoys before the people, the Melians desired them to explain their errand to the magistrates and to the chief men. They spoke as follows:

"Since we are not allowed to speak to the people, lest, forsooth, they should be deceived by seductive and unanswerable arguments which they should hear set forth in a single uninterrupted oration (for we are perfectly aware that this is what you mean in bringing us before a select few), you who are sitting here may as well make assurance yet surer. Let us have no set speeches at all, but do you reply to each several statement of which you disapprove, and criticise it at once. Say first of all how you like this mode of proceeding."

The Melian representatives answered: "The quiet interchange of explanations is a reasonable thing, and we do not object to that. But your warlike movements, which are present not only to our fears but to our eyes, seem to belie your words. We see that, although you may reason with us, you mean to be our judges; and that at the end of the discussion, if the justice of our cause prevail and we therefore refuse to yield, we may expect war; if we are convinced by you, slavery."

Athenians: Nay, but if you are only going to argue from fancies about the future, or if you meet us with any other purpose than that of looking your circumstances in the face and saving your city, we have done; but if this is your intention we will proceed.

Melians: It is an excusable and natural thing that men in our position should have much to say and should indulge in many fancies. But we admit that this conference has met to consider the question of our preservation; and therefore let the argument proceed in the manner which you propose.

Athenians: Well, then, we Athenians will use no fine words; we will not go out of our way to prove at length that we have a right to rule, because we overthrew the Persians; or that we attack you now because we are suffering any injury at your hands. We should not convince you if we did; nor must you expect to convince us by arguing that, although a colony of the Lacedaemonians, you have taken no part in their expeditions, or that you have never done us any wrong. But you and we should say what we really think, and aim only at what is possible, for we both alike know that into the discussion of human affairs the question of justice only enters where the pressure of necessity is equal, and that the powerful exact what they can, and the weak grant what they must.

Melians: Well, then, since you set aside justice and invite us to speak of expediency, in our judgment it is certainly expedient that you should respect a principle which is for the common good; and that to every man when in peril a reasonable claim should be accounted a claim of right, and any plea which he is disposed to urge, even if failing of the point a little, should help his cause. Your interest in this principle is quite as great as ours, inasmuch as you, if you fall, will incur the heaviest vengeance, and will be the most terrible example to mankind.

Athenians: The fall of our empire, if it should fall, is not an event to which we look forward with dismay; for ruling states such as Lacedaemon are not cruel to their vanquished enemies. And we are fighting not so much against the Lacedaemonians, as against our own subjects who may some day rise up and overcome their former masters. But this is a danger which you may leave to us. And we will now endeavor to show that we have come in the interests of our empire, and that in what we are about to say we are only seeking the preservation of your city. For we want to make you ours with the least trouble to ourselves, and it is for the interests of us both that you should not be destroyed.

Melians: It may be your interest to be our masters, but how can it be ours to be your slaves?

Athenians: To you the gain will be that by submission you will avert the worst; and we shall be all the richer for your preservation.

Melians: But must we be your enemies? Will you not receive us as friends if we are neutral and remain at peace with you?

Athenians: No, your enmity is not half so mischievous to us as your friendship; for the one is in the eyes of our subjects an argument of our power, the other of our weakness.

Melians: But are your subjects really unable to distinguish between states in which you have no concern, and those which are chiefly your own colonies, and in some cases have revolted and been subdued by you?

Athenians: Why, they do not doubt that both of them have a good deal to say for themselves on the score of justice, but they think that states like yours are left free because they are able to defend themselves, and that we do not attack them because we dare not. So that your subject will give us an increase of security, as well as an extension of empire. For we are masters of the sea, and you who are islanders, and insignificant islanders too, must not be allowed to escape us.

Melians: But do you not recognize another danger? For, once more, since you drive us from the plea of justice and press upon us your doctrine of expediency, we must show you what is for our interest, and, if it be for yours also, may hope to convince you: Will you not be making enemies of all who are now neutrals? When they see how you are treating us they will expect you some day to turn against them; and if so, are you not strengthening the enemies whom you already have, and bringing upon you others who, if they could help, would never dream of being your enemies at all?

Athenians: We do not consider our really dangerous enemies to be any of the peoples inhabiting the mainland who, secure in their freedom, may defer indefinitely any measures of precaution which they take against us, but islanders who, like you, happen to be under no control, and all who may be already irritated by the necessity of submission to our empire—these are our real enemies, for they are the most reckless and most likely to bring themselves as well as us into a danger which they cannot but foresee.

Melians: Surely then, if you and your subjects will brave all this risk, you to preserve your empire and they to be quit of it, how base and cowardly would it be in us, who retain our freedom, not to do and suffer anything rather than be your slaves.

Athenians: Not so, if you calmly reflect: for you are not fighting against equals to whom you cannot yield without disgrace, but you are taking counsel whether or no you shall resist an overwhelming force. The question is not one of honor but of prudence.

Melians: But we know that the fortune of war is sometimes impartial, and not always on the side of numbers. If we yield now, all is over; but if we fight, there is yet a hope that we may stand upright.

Athenians: Hope is a good comforter in the hour of danger, and when men have something else to depend upon, although hurtful, she is not ruinous. But when her spendthrift nature has induced them to stake their all, they see her as she is in the moment of their fall, and not till then. While the knowledge of her might enable them to beware of her, she never fails. You are weak and a single turn of the scale might be your ruin. Do not you be thus deluded; avoid the error of which so many are guilty, who, although they might still be saved if they would take the natural means, when visible grounds of confidence forsake them, have recourse to the invisible, to prophecies and oracles and the like, which ruin men by the hopes which they inspire in them.

Melians: We know only too well how hard the struggle must be against your power, and against fortune, if she does not mean to be impartial. Nevertheless we do not despair of fortune; for we hope to stand as high as you in the favor of heaven, because we are righteous, and you against whom we contend are unrighteous; and we are satisfied that our deficiency in power will be compensated by the aid of our allies the Lacedaemonians; they cannot refuse to help us, if only because we are their kinsmen, and for the sake of their own honor. And therefore our confidence is not so utterly blind as you suppose.

Athenians: As for the gods, we expect to have quite as much of their favor as you: for we are not doing or claiming anything which goes beyond common opinion about divine or men's desires about human things. Of the gods we believe, and of men we know, that by a law of their nature wherever they can rule they will. This law was not made by us, and we are not the first who have acted upon it; we did but inherit it, and shall bequeath it to all time, and we know that you and all mankind, if you were as strong as we are, would do as we do. So much for the gods; we have told you why we expect to stand as high in their good opinion as you. And then as to the Lacedaemonians—when you imagine that out of very shame they will assist you, we admire the simplicity of your idea, but we do not envy you the folly of it. The Lacedaemonians are exceedingly virtuous among themselves, and according to their national standard of morality. But, in respect of their dealings with others, although many things might be said, a word is enough to describe them, of all men whom we know they are the most notorious for identifying what is pleasant with what is honorable, and what is expedient with what is just. But how inconsistent is such a character with your present blind hope of deliverance!

Melians: That is the very reason why we trust them; they will look to their interest, and therefore will not be willing to betray the Melians, who are their own colonists, lest they should be distrusted by their friends in Hellas, and play into the hands of their enemies.

Athenians: But do you not see that the path of expediency is safe, whereas justice and honor involve danger in practice, and such dangers the Lacedaemonians seldom care to face?

Melians: On the other hand, we think that whatever perils there may be, they will be ready to face them for our sakes, and will consider danger less dangerous where we are concerned. For if they need to act we are close at hand, and they can better trust our loyal feeling because we are their kinsmen.

Athenians: Yes, but what encourages men who are invited to join in a conflict is clearly not the good-will of those who summon them to their side, but a decided superiority in real power. To this no men look more keenly than the Lacedaemonians; so little confidence have they in their own resources, and they only attack their neighbors when they have numerous allies, and therefore they are not likely to find their way by themselves to an island, when we are masters of the sea.

Melians: But they may send their allies: the Cretan sea is a large place;

and the masters of the sea will have more difficulty in overtaking vessels which want to escape than the pursued in escaping. If the attempt should fail they may invade Attica itself, and find their way to allies of yours whom Brasidas did not reach: and then you will have to fight, not for the conquest of a land in which you have no concern, but nearer home, for the preservation of your confederacy and of your own territory.

Athenians: Help may come from Lacedaemon to you as it has come to others, and should you ever have actual experience of it, then you will know that never once have the Athenians retired from a siege through fear of a foe elsewhere. You told us that the safety of your city would be your first care, but we remark that, in this long discussion, not a word has been uttered by you which would give a reasonable man expectation of deliverance. Your strongest grounds are hopes deferred, and what power you have is not to be compared with that which is already arrayed against you. Unless after we have withdrawn you mean to come, as even now you may, to a wider conclusion, you are showing a great want of sense. For surely you cannot dream of flying to that false sense of honor which has been the ruin of so many when danger and dishonor were staring them in the face. Many men with their eyes still open to the consequences have found the word honor too much for them, and have suffered a mere name to lure them on, until it has drawn down upon them real and irretrievable calamities; through their own folly they have incurred a worse dishonor than fortune would have inflicted upon them. If you are wise you will not run this risk; you ought to see that there can be no disgrace in yielding to a great city which invites you to become her ally on reasonable terms, keeping your own land, and merely paying tribute; and that you will certainly gain no honor if, having to choose between two alternatives, safety and war, you obstinately prefer the worse. To maintain our rights against equals, to be politics with superiors, and to be moderate towards inferiors is the path of safety. Reflect once more when we have withdrawn, and say to yourselves over and over again that you are deliberating about your one and only country, which may be saved or may be destroyed by a single decision.

The Athenians left the conference: the Melians, after consulting among themselves, resolved to persevere in their refusal, and answered as follows, "Men of Athens, our resolution is unchanged; and we will not in a moment surrender that liberty which our city, founded 700 years ago, still enjoys; we will trust to the good-fortune which, by the favor of the gods, has hitherto preserved us, and for human help to the Lacedaemonians, and endeavor to save ourselves. We are ready however to be your friends, and the enemies neither of you nor of the Lacedaemonians, and we ask you to leave our country when you have made such a peace as may appear to be in the interest of both parties."

Such was the answer of the Melians; the Athenians, as they quitted the conference, spoke as follows, "Well, we must say, judging from the decision at which you have arrived, that you are the only men who deem the future to be more certain than the present, and regard things unseen as already realized in your fond anticipation, and that the more you cast yourselves upon the Lacedaemonians and fortune, and hope, and trust them, the more complete will be your ruin."

Livy

(59 B.C.–A.D. 17)

from *THE HISTORY OF ROME*[1]

[INTRODUCTION]

Whether in tracing the history of the Roman people, from the foundation of the city, I shall employ myself to a useful purpose, I am neither very certain, or, if I were, dare I say: inasmuch as I observe, that it is both an old and hackneyed practice, later authors always supposing that they will either adduce something more authentic in the facts, or, that they will excel the less polished ancients in their style of writing.

Be that as it may, it will, all events, be a satisfaction to me, that I too have contributed my share to perpetuate the achievements of a people, the lords of the world; and if, amidst so great a number of historians, my reputation should remain in obscurity, I may console myself with the celebrity and luster of those who shall stand in the way of my fame. Moreover, the subject is both of immense labor, as being one which must be traced back for more than seven hundred years, and which, having set out from small beginnings, has increased to such a degree that it is now distressed by its own magnitude.

And, to most readers, I doubt not but that the first origin and the events immediately succeeding, will afford but little pleasure, while they will be hastening to these later times, in which the strength of this overgrown people has for a long period been working its own destruction. I, on the contrary, shall seek this, as a reward of my labor, viz. to withdraw myself from the view of the calamities, which our age has witnessed for so many years, so long as I am reviewing with my whole attention these ancient times, being free from every care that may distract a writer's mind, though it cannot warp it from the truth.

The traditions which have come down to us of what happened before the building of the city, or before its building was contemplated, as being suitable rather to the fictions of poetry than to the genuine records of history, I have no intention either to affirm or refute. This indulgence is conceded

[1]Translated by Daniel Spillan. Livy (Titus Livius) wrote his massive *History of Rome* in a frank attempt to do for Rome what Herodotus and Thucydides had done for Greece, to honor his country with a comprehensive account of its history. But whereas Herodotus and Thucydides had striven for historical accuracy (according to their own lights), Livy virtually ignores factual truth in favor of a moral urgency. Writing when both public and private morals in Rome had become thoroughly corrupt, Livy offers his book in support of the reforms of his friend the Emperor Augustus. Often misread as an uncritical celebration of Rome, the *History* is actually a narrative of decline, as Livy makes clear in his introduction. He calls on his readers to contemplate, first, the high morality of the early Romans, and, then, to consider that of the present, when "we can neither endure our vices, nor their remedies." The stories of Lucretia and the father of Titus Manlius, presented in this selection, illustrate the Roman morality that Livy held up as an example to his fallen contemporaries.

to antiquity, that by blending things human with divine, it may make the origin of cities appear more venerable; and if any people might be allowed to consecrate their origin, and to ascribe it to the gods as its authors, such is the renown of the Roman people in war, that when they represent Mars,[2] in particular, as their own parent and that of their founder, the nations of the world may submit to this as patiently as they submit to their sovereignty.

But in whatever way these and such like matters shall be attended to, or judged of, I shall not deem of great importance. I would have every man apply his mind seriously to consider these points, viz. what their life and what their manners were; through what men and by what measures, both in peace and in war, their empire was acquired and extended; then, as discipline gradually declined, let him follow in his thoughts their morals, at first as slightly giving way, anon how they sunk more and more, then began to fall headlong, until he reaches the present times, when we can neither endure our vices, nor their remedies. This it is which is particularly salutary and profitable in the study of history, that you behold instances of every variety of conduct displayed on a conspicuous monument; that from thence you may select for yourself and for your country that which you may imitate; thence *note* what is shameful in the undertaking, and shameful in the result, which you may avoid. But either a fond partiality for the task I have undertaken deceives me, or there never was any state either greater, or more moral, or richer in good examples, nor one into which luxury and avarice made their entrance so late, and where poverty and frugality were so much and so long honored; so that the less wealth there was, the less desire was there. Of late, riches have introduced avarice, and excessive pleasures a longing for them, amidst luxury and a passion for ruining ourselves and destroying everything else. But let complaints, which will not be agreeable even then, when perhaps they will be also necessary, be kept aloof at least from the first stage of commencing so great a work. We should rather, if it was usual with us (historians) as it is with poets, begin with good omens, vows and prayers to the gods and goddesses to vouchsafe good success to our efforts in so arduous an undertaking.

In my opinion, the origin of so great a city, and the establishment of an empire next in power to that of the gods, was due to the Fates. The vestal Rhea,[3] being deflowered by force, when she had brought forth twins, declares Mars to be the father of her illegitimate offspring, either because she believed it to be so, or because a god was a more creditable author of her offense. But neither gods nor men protect her or her children from the king's cruelty: the priestess is bound and thrown into prison; the children he commands to be thrown into the current of the river. By some interposition of providence, the Tiber having overflowed its banks in stagnant pools, did not admit of any access to the regular bed of the river; and the bearers supposed that the infants could be drowned in water however still; thus, as if they had effectually executed the king's orders, they expose the boys in the nearest

[2]The Romans, as the following section explains, regarded Mars, the god of war and the reputated father of Romulus and Remus, as their divine parent.

[3]The Vestal Virgins were priestesses consecrated to the service of Vesta, goddess of hearth and home, in the oldest temple in Rome. Aeneas was said to have chosen the first Vestals. Violation of her vows of chastity by a Vestal Virgin was a capital offense.

land-flood, where now stands the ficus Ruminalis[4] (they say that it was called Romularis).

The country thereabout was then a vast wilderness. The tradition is, that when the water, subsiding, had left the floating trough, in which the children had been exposed, on dry ground, a thirsty she-wolf, coming from the neighboring mountains, directed her course to the cries of the infants, and that she held down her dugs to them with so much gentleness, that the keeper of the king's flock found her licking the boys with her tongue. It is said his name was Faustus; and that they were carried by him to his homestead to be nursed by his wife Laurentia. Some are of opinion that she was called Lupa among the shepherds, from her being a common prostitute, and that this gave rise to the surprising story. The children thus born and thus brought up, when arrived at the years of manhood, did not loiter away their time in tending the folds or following the flocks, but roamed and hunted in the forests. Having by this exercise improved their strength and courage, they not only encountered wild beasts, but even attacked robbers laden with plunder, and afterwards divided the spoil among the shepherds. And in company with these, the number of their young associates daily increasing, they carried on their business and their sports.

They say that the festival of the lupercal, as now celebrated, was even at that time solemnized on the Palatine hill[5] . . . in such manner, that young men ran about naked in sport and wantonness, doing honour to Pan Lycaeus, whom the Romans afterwards called Inuus. That the robbers, through rage at the loss of their booty, having lain in wait for them whilst intent on this sport, as the festival was now well known, while Romulus vigorously defended himself, took Remus prisoner; that they delivered him up, when taken, to King Amulius, accusing him with the utmost effrontery. They principally alleged it as a charge against them that they had made incursions upon Numitor's[6] lands, and plundered them in a hostile manner, having assembled a band of young men for the purpose. Upon this Remus was delivered to Numitor to be punished.

Now, from the very first, Faustulus had entertained hopes that the boys whom he was bringing up were of the blood royal; for he both knew that the children had been exposed by the king's orders, and that the time at which he had taken them up agreed exactly with that period; but he had been unwilling that the matter, as not being yet ripe for discovery, should be disclosed, till either a fit opportunity or necessity should arise. Necessity came first; accordingly, compelled by fear, he reveals the whole affair to Romulus. By accident also, while he had Remus in custody, and had heard that the brothers were twins, on comparing their age, and observing their turn of mind entirely free from servility, the recollection of his grandchildren struck Numitor; and on making inquires he arrived at the same conclusion, so that he was well-nigh recognizing Remus. Thus a plot is formed against the king on all sides. Romulus, not accompanied by a body of young men (for he was unequal to open force) but having commanded

[4]A fig tree still standing in Rome in Livy's time. It was said to be the tree under which Romulus and Remus were found.

[5]One of the Seven Hills of Rome.

[6]Numitor, as father of the Vestal Virgin Rhea, was grandfather of Romulus and Remus. His throne had been usurped by the present king, Amulius.

the shepherds to come to the palace by different roads at a fixed time, forces his way to the king; and Remus, with another party from Numitor's house, assists his brother, and so they kill the king.[7]

Numitor . . . when he saw the young men, after they had killed the king, advancing to congratulate him, immediately called an assembly of the people, and represented to them the unnatural behavior of his brother towards him, the ancestry of his grandchildren, the manner of their birth and education, and how they came to be discovered; then he informed them of the king's death, and that he was killed by his orders. When the young princes, coming up with their band through the middle of the assembly, saluted their grandfather king, an approving shout, following from all the people present, ratified to him both that title and the sovereignty.

Thus the government of Alba[8] being committed to Numitor, a desire seized Romulus and Remus to build a city on the spot where they had been exposed and brought up. And there was an overflowing population of Albans and of Latins. The shepherds too had come into that design, and all these readily inspired hopes, that Alba and Lavinium would be but petty places in comparison with the city which they intended to build. But ambition of the sovereignty, the bane of their grandfather, interrupted these designs, and thence arose a shameful quarrel from a beginning sufficiently amicable. For as they were twins, and the respect due to seniority could not determine the point, they agreed to leave to the tutelary gods of the place to choose, by augury, which should give a name to the new city, which govern it when built.

Romulus chose the Palatine and Remus the Aventine hill as their stands to make their observations. It is said, that to Remus an omen came first, six vultures; and now, the omen having been declared, when double the number presented itself to Romulus, his own party saluted each king; the former claimed the kingdom on the ground of priority of time, the latter on account of the number of birds. Upon this, having met in an altercation, from the contest of angry feelings they turn to bloodshed; there Remus fell from a blow received in the crowd. A more common account is, that Remus, in derision of his brother, leaped over his new-built wall, and was, for that reason, slain by Romulus in a passion; who, after sharply chiding him, added words to this effect: "So shall every one fare, who shall dare to leap over my fortifications." Thus Romulus got the sovereignty to himself; the city, when built, was called after the name of its founder.

[THE SABINE WOMEN]

And now the Roman state had become so powerful, that it was a match for any of the neighboring nations in war, but, from the paucity of women, its greatness could only last for one age of man; for they had no hope of issue at home, nor had they any intermarriages with their neighbors. Therefore, by the advice of the Fathers,[9] Romulus sent ambassadors to the neighboring

[7]Amulius.

[8]Alba Longa was the town founded by Aeneas Sylvia, son of Aeneas, that was later renamed Rome.

[9]The Senators.

states to solicit an alliance and the privilege of intermarriage for his new subjects. . . .

Nowhere did the embassy obtain a favorable hearing: so much did they at the same time despise, and dread for themselves and their posterity, so great a power growing up in the midst of them. They were dismissed by the great part with the repeated question, "Whether they had opened any asylum for women also, for that such a plan only could obtain them suitable matches?"

The Roman youth resented this conduct bitterly, and the matter unquestionably began to point towards violence. Romulus, in order that he might afford a favorable time and place for this, dissembling his resentment, purposely prepares games in honor of Neptunus Equestris; he calls them Consualia. He then orders the spectacle to be proclaimed among their neighbors; and they prepare for the celebration with all the magnificence they were then acquainted with, or were capable of doing, that they might render the matter famous, and an object of expectation. Great numbers assembled, from a desire also of seeing the new city; especially their nearest neighbors, the Caeninenses, Crustumini, and Antemnates. Moreover the whole multitude of the Sabines came, with their wives and children. Having been hospitably invited to the different houses, when they had seen the situation, and fortifications, and the city crowded with houses, they became astonished that the Roman power had increased so rapidly.

When the time of the spectacle came on, and while their minds and eyes were intent upon it, according to plan a tumult began, and upon a signal given the Roman youth ran different ways to carry off the virgins by force. A great number were carried off haphazardly, according as they fell into their hands. Persons from the common people, who had been charged with the task, conveyed to their houses some women of surpassing beauty, destined for the leading senators. . . .

The festival being disturbed by this alarm, the parents of the young women retire in grief, appealing to the compact of violated hospitality, and invoking the god, to whose festival and games they had come, deceived by the pretence of religion and good faith. Neither had the ravished virgins better hopes of their condition, or less indignation. But Romulus in person went about and declared, "That what was done was owing to the pride of their fathers, who had refused to grant the privilege of marriage to their neighbors; but notwithstanding, they should be joined in lawful wedlock, participate in all their possessions and civil privileges, and than which nothing can be dearer to the human heart, in their common children. He begged them only to assuage the fierceness of their anger, and cheerfully surrender their affections to those to whom fortune had consigned their persons." [He added,] "That from injuries love and friendship often arise; and that they should find them kinder husbands on this account, because each of them, besides the performance of his conjugal duty, would endeavor to the utmost of his power to make up for the want of their parents and native country." To this the caresses of the husbands were added, excusing what they had done on the plea of passion and love, arguments that work most successfully on women's hearts.

[TARQUIN]

After this period Tarquin[10] began his reign, whose actions procured him the surname of the Proud. . . . He surrounded his person with armed men, for he had no claim to the kingdom except force, inasmuch as he reigned without either the order of the people or the sanction of the senate. To this was added the fact that, as he reposed no hope in the affection of his subjects, he found it necessary to secure his kingdom by terror; and in order to strike this into the greater number, he took cognizance of capital cases solely by himself without assessors; and under that pretext he had it in his power to put to death, banish, or fine, not only those who were suspected or hated, but those also from whom he could obtain nothing else but plunder. The number of the fathers more especially being thus diminished, he determined to elect none into the senate, in order that the order might become contemptible by their very paucity, and that they might feel the less resentment at no business being transacted by them. For he was the first king who violated the custom derived from his predecessors of consulting the senate on all subjects; he administered the public business by family councils. War, peace, treaties, alliances, he contracted and dissolved with whomsoever he pleased, without the sanction of the people and senate. The nation of the Latins in particular he wished to attach to him, so that by foreign influence also he might be more secure among his own subjects; and he contracted not only ties of hospitality but affinities also with their leading men.

. . .

Then he turned his thoughts to the business of the city. The chief whereof was that of leaving behind him the temple of Jupiter[11] on the Tarpeian mount, as a monument of his name and reign. . . . It is reported that the head of a man, with the face entire, appeared to the workmen when digging the foundation of the temple. The sight of this phenomenon unequivocally presaged that this temple should be the metropolis of the empire, and the head of the world; and so declared the soothsayers, both those who were in the city, and those whom they had sent for from Etruria, to consult on this subject. . . .

Tarquin, intent upon finishing this temple, having sent for workmen from all parts of Etruria, employed on it not only the public money, but the manual labor of the people; and when this labor, by no means inconsiderable in itself, was added to their military service, still the people murmured less at their building the temples of the gods with their own hands; they were afterwards transferred to other works, which, while less in show, required still greater toil: such as erecting benches in the circus, and conducting under ground the principal sewer, the receptacle of all the filth of the city; to which two works even modern splendor can scarcely produce any thing equal. . . .

[10]Lucius Tarquinius Superbus was a legendary king of early Rome. He was said to have murdered his father-in-law, Servius Tullius, to get the throne. He was the father of Sixtus Tarquinius, who raped Lucretia.

[11]The Roman name for Zeus, father of the gods. His temple on the Tarpeian Rock was a Roman landmark.

While he was thus employed a frightful prodigy appeared to him. A serpent sliding out of a wooden pillar, after causing dismay and a run into the palace, not so much struck the king's heart with sudden terror, as filled him with anxious solicitude. Accordingly . . . he determined on sending persons to Delphi to the most celebrated oracle in the world; and not venturing to entrust the responses of the oracle to any other person, he despatched his two sons to Greece through lands unknown at that time, and seas still more so. Titus and Aruns were the two who went. To them were added, as a companion, L. Junius Brutus, the son of Tarquinia, sister to the king, a youth of an entirely different quality of mind from that of the disguise which he had assumed.

Brutus, on hearing that the chief men of the city, and among others his own brother, had been put to death by his uncle, resolved to leave nothing in his intellects that might be dreaded by the king, nor any thing in his fortune to be coveted, and thus to be secure in contempt, where there was but little protection in justice. Therefore designedly fashioning himself to the semblance of foolishness, after he suffered himself and his whole estate to become a prey to the king, he did not refuse to take even the surname of Brutus, that, concealed under the cover of such a cognomen, that genius that was to liberate the Roman people might await its proper time. He, being brought to Delphi by the Tarquinii[12] rather as a subject of sport than as a companion, is said to have brought with him as an offering to Apollo a golden rod, enclosed in a staff of cornel-wood hollowed out for the purpose, a mystical emblem of his own mind.

When they arrived there, their father's commission being executed, a desire seized the young men of inquiring on which of them the sovereignty of Rome should devolve. They say that a voice was returned from the bottom of the cave, "Young men, whichever of you shall first kiss his mother shall enjoy the sovereign power at Rome." The Tarquinii order the matter to be kept secret with the utmost care, that Sextus, who had been left behind at Rome, might be ignorant of the response, and have no share in the kingdom; they cast lots among themselves, as to which of them should first kiss his mother, after they had returned to Rome. Brutus, thinking that the Delphic response had another meaning, as if he had stumbled and fallen, touched the ground with his lips; she being, forsooth, the common mother of all mankind. After this they all returned to Rome, where preparations were being made with the greatest vigor for a war against the Rutulians.[13]

The Rutulians, a nation very wealthy, considering the country and age they lived in, were at that time in possession of Ardea. Their riches gave occasion to the war; for the king of the Romans, being exhausted of money by the magnificence of his public works, was desirous both to enrich himself, and by a large booty to soothe the minds of his subjects, who, besides other instances of his tyranny, were incensed against his government, because they were indignant that they had been kept so long a time by the king in the employments of mechanics, and in labor fit for slaves.

An attempt was made to take Ardea by storm; when that did not succeed,

[12]The two sons of Tarquin, Titus and Aruns.

[13]Residents of a kingdom next to Rome. Their founder Turnus was a rival of Aeneas for Lavinia and fought against him and the Trojans when they came to Italy.

the enemy began to be distressed by a blockade, and by works raised around them. As it commonly happens in standing camps, the war being rather tedious than violent, furloughs were easily obtained, more so by the officers, however, than the common soldiers. The young princes sometimes spent their leisure hours in feasting and entertainments. One day as they were drinking in the tent of Sextus Tarquin, where Collatinus Tarquinius, the son of Egerius, was also at supper, mention was made of wives. Every one commended his own in an extravagant manner, till a dispute arising about it, Collatinus said, "There is no occasion for words; it might be known in a few hours how far Lucretia excels all the rest. If then we have any share of the vigor of youth, let us mount our horses and examine the behavior of our wives; that must be most satisfactory to every one, what shall meet his eyes on the unexpected arrival of the husband." They were heated with wine; "Come on, then," say all. They immediately galloped to Rome, where they arrived in the dusk of the evening. From thence they went to Collatia,[14] where they find Lucretia, not like the king's daughters-in-law, whom they had seen spending their time in luxurious entertainments with their equals, but though at an advanced time of night, employed at her wool, sitting in the middle of the house amid her maids working around her. The merit of the contest regarding the ladies was assigned to Lucretia. Her husband on his arrival, and the Tarquinii, were kindly received; the husband, proud of his victory, gives the young princes a polite invitation. There the villainous passion for violating Lucretia by force seizes Sextus Tarquin; both her beauty, and her approved purity, act as incentives. And then, after this youthful frolic of the night, they return to the camp.

A few days after, without the knowledge of Collatinus, Sextus came to Collatia with one attendant only; where, being kindly received by them, as not being aware of his intention, after he had been conducted after supper into the guests' chamber, burning with passion, when every thing around seem sufficiently secure, and all fast asleep, he comes to Lucretia, as she lay asleep, with a naked sword, and with his left hand pressing down the woman's breast, he says, "Be silent, Lucretia; I am Sextus Tarquin; I have a sword in my hand; you shall die, if you utter a word." When awaking terrified from sleep, the woman beheld no aid, impending death nigh at hand; then Tarquin acknowledged his passion, entreated, mixed threats with entreaties, tried the female's mind in every possible way. When he saw her inflexible, and that she was not moved even by the terror of death, he added to terror the threat of dishonor; he says that he will lay a murdered slave naked by her side when dead, so that she may be said to have been slain in infamous adultery.

When by the terror of this disgrace his lust, as it were victorious, had overcome her inflexible chastity, and Tarquin had departed, exulting in having triumphed over a lady's honor, Lucretia, in melancholy distress at so dreadful a misfortune, despatches the same messenger to Rome to her father, and to Ardea to her husband, that they would come each with one trusted friend; that it was necessary to do so, and that quickly. Sp. Lucretius comes with P. Valerius, the son of Volesus, Collatinus with L. Junius Brutus, with whom, as he was returning to Rome, he happened to be met by this wife's messenger. They find Lucretia sitting in her chamber in sorrowful dejection. On the arrival of her friends the tears burst from her eyes; and to her husband, on

[14]A village near Rome.

his inquiry "whether all was right," she says, "By no means, for what can be right with a woman who has lost her honor? The traces of another man are on your bed, Collatinus. But the body only has been violated, the mind is guiltless; death shall be my witness. But give me your right hands, and your honor, that the adulterer shall not come off unpunished. It is Sextus Tarquin, who, an enemy in the guise of a guest, has borne away hence a triumph fatal to me, and to himself, if you are men."

They all pledge their honor; they attempt to console her, distracted as she was in mind, by turning away the guilt from her, constrained by force, on the perpetrator of the crime; that it is the mind sins, not the body; and that where intention was wanting guilt could not be. "It is for you to see," says she, "what is due to him. As for me, though I acquit myself of guilt, from punishment I do not discharge myself; nor shall any woman survive her dishonor pleading the example of Lucretia." The knife, which she kept concealed beneath her garment, she plunges into her heart, and falling forward on the wound, she dropped down expiring. The husband and father shriek aloud.

Brutus, while they were overpowered with grief, having drawn the knife out of the wound, and holding it up before him reeking with blood, said, "By this blood, most pure before the pollution of royal villainy, I swear, and I call you, O gods, to witness my oath, that I shall pursue Lucius Tarquin the Proud, his wicked wife, and all their race, with fire, sword, and all other means in my power; nor shall I ever suffer them or any other to reign at Rome." Then he gave the knife to Collatinus, and after him to Lucretius and Valerius, who were surprised at such extraordinary mind in the breast of Brutus. However, they all take the oath as they were directed, and converting their sorrow into rage, follow Brutus as their leader, who from that time ceased not to solicit them to abolish the regal power. . . .

Nor does the heinousness of the circumstance excite less violent emotions at Rome than it had done at Collatia; accordingly they run from all parts of the city into the forum, whither, when they came, the public crier summoned them to attend the tribune of the celeres, with which office Brutus happened to be at that time vested. There an harangue was delivered by him, by no means of that feeling and capacity which had been counterfeited up to that day, concerning the violence and lust of Sextus Tarquin, the horrid violation of Lucretia and her lamentable death, the bereavement of Tricipitinus, to whom the cause of his daughter's death was more exasperating and deplorable than the death itself. To this was added the haughty insolence of the king himself, and the sufferings and toils of the people, buried in the earth in cleansing sinks and sewers; that the Romans, the conquerors of all the surrounding states, instead of warriors had become laborers and stone-cutters. . . .

By stating these and other, I suppose, more exasperating circumstances, which though by no means easily detailed by writers, the heinousness of the case suggested at the time, he persuaded the multitude, already incensed, to deprive the king of his authority, and to order the banishment of L. Tarquin with his wife and children. He himself having selected and armed some of the young men, who readily gave in their names, set out for Ardea to the camp to excite the army against the king. . . .

News of these transactions reached the camp when the king, alarmed at this sudden revolution, was going to Rome to quell the commotions. Brutus, for he had notice of his approach, turned out of the way, that he might not meet him; and much about the same time Brutus and Tarquin arrived by different routes, the one at Ardea, the other at Rome. The gates were shut against Tarquin, and an act of banishment passed against him; the deliverer of the state the camp received with great joy, and the king's sons were expelled. Two of them followed their father, and went into banishment to Caere, a city of Etruria. Sextus Tarquin, having gone to Gabii, as to his own kingdom, was slain by the avengers of the old feuds, which he had raised against himself by his rapines and murders.

Lucius Tarquin the Proud reigned twenty-five years; the regal form of government had lasted from the building of the city to this period of its deliverance, two hundred and forty-four years. Two consuls, viz. Lucius Junius Brutus and Lucius Tarquinius Collatinus, were elected by the prefect of the city at the comitia by centuries,[15] according to the commentaries of Servius Tullius.

[TITUS MANLIUS]

The consuls, after raising two armies, marched into the territories of the Marsians and Pelignians, the army of the Samnites having joined them, and pitched their camp near Capua, where the Latins and their allies had now assembled. . . .

What excited their attention particularly was, that they had to contend against Latins, who coincided with themselves in language, manners, in the same kind of arms, and more especially in military institutions; soldiers had been mixed with soldiers, centurions with centurions, tribunes with tribunes, as comrades and colleagues, in the same armies, and often in the same companies. Lest in consequence of this the soldiers should be involved in any mistake, the consuls issue orders that no one should fight against an enemy out of his post.[16]

It happened that among the other prefects[17] of the troops, who had been sent out in all directions to reconnoitre, Titus Manlius, the consul's son, came with his troop to the back of the enemy's camp, so near that he was scarcely distant a dart's throw from the next post. In that place were some Tusculan cavalry; they were commanded by Geminus Metius, a man distinguished among his countrymen both by birth and exploits. When he recognised the Roman cavalry, and conspicuous among them the consul's son marching at their head (for they were all known to each other, especially the men of note), "Romans, are ye going to wage war with the Latins and allies with a single troop? What in the interim will the consuls, what will the two consular armies be doing?" "They will be here in good time," says Manlius, "and with them will be Jupiter himself, as a witness of the treaties violated by you, who is

[15]The *Comitia Centuriata* (Assembly of Centuries) was a proto-democratic citizen assembly. It was made up of one representative for each hundred citizens (century).

[16]That is, away from the Roman camp.

[17]Commanders.

stronger and more powerful. If we fought at the lake Regillus until you had quite enough, here also we shall so act, that a line of battle and an encounter with us may afford you no very great gratification." In reply to this, Geminus, advancing some distance from his own party, says, "Do you choose then, until that day arrives on which you are to put your armies in motion with such mighty labor, to enter the lists with me, that from the result of a contest between us both, it may be seen how much a Latin excels a Roman horseman?"

Either resentment, or shame at declining the contest, or the invincible power of fate, arouses the determined spirit of the youth. Forgetful therefore of his father's command, and the consul's edict, he is driven headlong to that contest, in which it made not much difference whether he conquered or was conquered. The other horsemen being removed to a distance as if to witness the sight, in the space of clear ground which lay between them they spurred on their horses against each other; and when they were together in fierce encounter, the spear of Manlius passed over the helmet of his antagonist, that of Metius across the neck of the other's horse. Then wheeling round their horses, when Manlius arose to repeat the blow, he fixed his javelin between the ears of his opponent's horse. When, by the pain of this wound, the horse, having raised his fore-feet on high, tossed his head with great violence, he shook off his rider, whom, when he was raising himself from the severe fall, by leaning on his spear and buckler, Manlius pierced through the throat, so that the steel passed out through the ribs, and pinned him to the earth; and having collected the spoils, he returned to his own party, and with his troop, who were exulting with joy. He proceeds to the camp, and thence to the general's tent to his father, ignorant of what awaited him, whether praise or punishment had been merited. "Father," says he, "that all may truly represent me as sprung from your blood; when challenged, I slew my adversary, and have taken from him these equestrian spoils."

When the consul heard this, immediately turning away from his son, he ordered an assembly to be summoned by sound of trumpet. When these assembled in great numbers, "Since you, Titus Manlius," says he, "revering neither the consular power nor a father's majesty, have fought against the enemy out of your post contrary to our orders, and, as far as in you lay, have subverted military discipline, by which the Roman power has stood to this day, and have brought me to this necessity, that I must either forget the republic, or myself and mine; we shall expiate our own transgressions rather than the republic should sustain so serious a loss for our misdeeds. We shall be a melancholy example, but a profitable one, to the youth of future ages. As for me, both the natural affection for my children, as well as that instance of bravery which has led you astray by the false notion of honor, affects me for you. But since either the authority of consuls is to be established by your death, or by your forgiveness to be for ever annulled; I do not think that even you, if you have any of our blood in you, will refuse to restore, by your punishment, the military discipline which has been subverted by your misconduct. Go, lictor,[18] bind him to the stake." All became motionless, more

[18]An official who bore the *fasces*, a bundle of sticks with an axe-head protruding from it, as a symbol of his office. His duties were to attend a magistrate and to apprehend and punish criminals.

through fear than discipline, astounded by so cruel an order, each looking on the axe as if drawn against himself. Therefore when they stood in profound silence, suddenly, when the blood spouted from his severed neck, their minds recovering, as it were, from a state of stupefaction, then their voices arose together in free expressions of complaint, so that they spared neither lamentations nor execrations; and the body of the youth, being covered with the spoils, was burned on a pile erected outside the rampart, with all the military zeal with which any funeral could be celebrated; and Manlian orders were considered with horror, not only for the present, but of the most austere severity for future times.

The severity of the punishment, however, rendered the soldiers more obedient to the general; the guards and watches and the regulation of the posts were everywhere more strictly attended to, and such severity was also profitable in the final struggle when they came into the field of battle.

Marcus Aurelius

(121–180)

from *MEDITATIONS*[1]

[HIS FATHER]

In my father[2] I observed mildness of temper, and unchangeable resolution in the things which he had determined after due deliberation; and no vainglory in those things which men call honors; and a love of labor

[1]Translated by George Long. Marcus Aurelius was Emperor of Rome from A.D. 161 to 189. The Empire was in decline by the time he took the throne, and much of his reign was spent repressing rebellions by the Parthians, Germans, and Britons. His *Meditations* are perhaps the fullest and most moving expression of Stoic philosophy. It has been said (with considerable oversimplification) that the Roman worldview alternated between Epicureanism and Stoicism. Epicureanism (named for its founder Epicurus, 341–270 B.C.) held that pleasure was the highest and only good; defining pleasure, however, not as mere self-indulgence but as serenity or absence of pain, achieved through prudence, honesty, and justice. Stoicism (founded by Zeno of Citium, c. 300 B.C.) placed the emphasis not on pleasure but on duty, defining duty as subduing passion and self-indulgence and placing oneself in harmony with the divine order. The *Meditations* seem to have been written over a long period of time for Marcus Aurelius's own use, rather than for publication (though it may have been intended as advice for his son Commodus). The twelve short books that make it up contain notations on where each was written, in Rome, on various battlefields, etc. Text of the *Meditations* all derive, apparently, from a manuscript found after his death.

[2]Marcus refers not to his biological father but to the Emperor Antonius Pius, who adopted him and groomed him as his successor.

and perseverance; and a readiness to listen to those who had anything to propose for the common weal; and undeviating firmness in giving to every man according to his deserts; and a knowledge derived from experience of the occasions for vigorous action and for remission. And I observed that he had overcome all passion for boys[3]; and he considered himself no more than any other citizen; and he released his friends from all obligation to sup with him or to attend him of necessity when he went abroad, and those who had failed to accompany him, by reason of any urgent circumstances, always found him the same. I observed too his habit of careful inquiry in all matters of deliberation, and his persistency, and that he never stopped his investigation through being satisfied with appearances which first present themselves; and that his disposition was to keep his friends, and not to be soon tired of them, nor yet to be extravagant in his affection; and to be satisfied on all occasions, and cheerful; and to foresee things a long way off, and to provide for the smallest without display; and to check immediately popular applause and all flattery; and to be ever watchful over the things which were necessary for the administration of the empire, and to be a good manager of the expenditure, and patiently to endure the blame which he got for such conduct; and he was neither superstitious with respect to the gods, nor did he court men by gifts or by trying to please them, or by flattering the populace; but he showed sobriety in all things and firmness, and never any mean thoughts or action, nor love of novelty. And the things which conduce in any way to the commodity of life, and of which fortune gives an abundant supply, he used without arrogance and without excusing himself; so that when he had them, he enjoyed them without affectation, and when he had them not, he did not want them. No one could ever say of him that he was either a sophist or a [home-bred] flippant slave or a pedant; but every one acknowledged him to be a man ripe, perfect, above flattery, able to manage his own and other men's affairs. Besides this, he honored those who were true philosophers, and he did not reproach those who pretended to be philosophers, nor yet was he easily led by them. He was also easy in conversation, and he made himself agreeable without any offensive affectation. He took a reasonable care of his body's health, not as one who was greatly attached to life, nor out of regard to personal appearance, nor yet in a careless way, but so that, through his own attention, he very seldom stood in need of the physician's art or of medicine or external applications. He was most ready to give way without envy to those who possessed any particular faculty, such as that of eloquence or knowledge of the law or of morals, or of anything else; and he gave them his help, that each might enjoy reputation according to his deserts; and he always acted conformably to the institutions of his country, without showing any affectation of doing so. Further, he was not fond of change nor unsteady, but he loved to stay in the same places, and to employ himself about the same things; and after his paroxysms

[3]Upper-class Roman men were encouraged to form homosexual liaisons in adolescence. On achieving manhood, they were expected to become heterosexual.

of headache he came immediately fresh and vigorous to his usual occupations. His secrets were not many, but very few and very rare, and these only about public matters; and he showed prudence and economy in the exhibition of the public spectacles and the construction of public buildings, his donations to the people, and in such things, for he was a man who looked to what ought to be done, not to the reputation which is got by a man's acts. He did not take the bath at unseasonable hours; he was not fond of building houses, nor curious about what he ate, nor about the texture and color of his clothes, nor about the beauty of his slaves. His dress came from Lorium, his villa on the coast, and from Lanuvium generally. We know how he behaved to the toll-collector at Tusculum who asked his pardon; and such was all his behavior. There was in him nothing harsh, nor implacable, nor violent, nor, as one may say, anything carried to the sweating point; but he examined all things severally, as if he had abundance of time, and without confusion, in an orderly way, vigorously and consistently. And that might be applied to him which is recorded of Socrates that he was able both to abstain from, and to enjoy, those things which many are too weak to abstain from, and cannot enjoy without excess. But to be strong enough both to bear the one and to be sober in the other is the mark of a man who has a perfect and invincible soul, such as he showed in the illness of Maximus.

To the gods I am indebted for having good grandfathers, good parents, a good sister, good teachers, good associates, good kinsmen and friends, nearly everything good. Further, I owe it to the gods that I was not hurried into any offense against any of them, though I had a disposition which, if opportunity had offered, might have led me to do something of this kind; but, through their favor, there never was such a concurrence of circumstances as put me to the trial. Further, I am thankful to the gods that I was not longer brought up with my grandfather's concubine, and that I preserved the flower of my youth, and that I did not make proof of my virility before the proper season, but even deferred the time; that I was subjected to a ruler and a father who was able to take away all pride from me, and to bring me to the knowledge that it is possible for a man to live in a palace without wanting either guards or embroidered dresses, or torches and statues, and such-like show; but that it is in such a man's power to bring himself very near to the fashion of a private person, without being for this reason either meaner in thought, or more remiss in action, with respect to the things which must be done for the public interest in a manner that befits a ruler. I thank the gods for giving me such a brother,[4] who was able by his moral character to rouse me to vigilance over myself, and who, at the same time, pleased me by his respect and affection; that my children have not been stupid nor deformed in body; that I did not make more proficiency in rhetoric, poetry, and the other studies, in which I should perhaps have been completely engaged, if I had seen that I was making progress in

[4]Marcus refers to his adoptive brother, Lucius Verus, who shared the throne with him for the first eight years of his reign.

them; that I made haste to place those who brought me up in the station of honor, which they seemed to desire, without putting them off with hope of my doing it some time after, because they were then still young; that I knew Apollonius, Rusticus, Maximus; that I received clear and frequent impressions about living according to nature, and what kind of a life that is, so that, so far as depended on the gods, and their gifts, and help, and inspirations, nothing hindered me from forthwith living according to nature, though I still fall short of it through my own fault, and through not observing the admonitions of the gods, and, I may almost say, their direct instructions; that my body has held out so long in such a kind of life; that I never touched either Benedicta or Theodotus, and that, after having fallen into amatory passions, I was cured; and, though I was often out of humor with Rusticus, I never did anything of which I had occasion to repent; that, though it was my mother's fate to die young, she spent the last years of her life with me; that, whenever I wished to help any man in his need, or on any other occasion, I was never told that I had not the means of doing it; and that to myself the same necessity never happened, to receive anything from another; that I have such a wife, so obedient, and so affectionate, and so simple; that I had abundance of good masters for my children; and that remedies have been shown to me by dreams, both others, and against bloodspitting and giddiness . . .. . .; and that, when I had an inclination to philosophy, I did not fall into the hands of any sophist, and that I did not waste my time on writers [of histories], or in the resolution of syllogisms, or occupy myself about the investigation of appearances in the heavens; for all these things require the help of the gods and fortune.

[THE STOIC MIND]

Begin the morning by saying to thyself, I shall meet with the busybody, the ungrateful, arrogant, deceitful, envious, unsocial. All these things happen to them by reason of their ignorance of what is good and evil. But I who have seen the nature of the good that it is beautiful, and of the bad that it is ugly, and the nature of him who does wrong, that it is akin to me, not [only] of the same blood or seed, but that it participates in [the same] intelligence and [the same] portion of the divinity, I can neither be injured by any of them, for no one can fix on me what is ugly, nor can I be angry with my kinsman, nor hate him. For we are made for co-operation, like feet, like hands, like eyelids, like the rows of the upper and lower teeth. To act against one another then is contrary to nature; and it is acting against one another to be vexed and to turn away.

Whatever this is that I am, it is a little flesh and breath, and the ruling part. Throw away thy books; no longer distract thyself: it is not allowed; but as if thou wast now dying, despise the flesh; it is blood and bones and a network, a contexture of nerves, veins, and arteries. See the breath also, what kind of a thing it is, air, and not always the same, but every moment sent out and again sucked in. The third then is the ruling part: consider thus: Thou art an old man; no longer let this be a slave, no longer be pulled by the strings like a puppet to unsocial movements, no longer be either dissatisfied with thy present lot, or shrink from the future.

All that is from the gods is full of providence. That which is from fortune is not separated from nature or without an interweaving and involution with the things which are ordered by providence. From thence all things flow; and there is besides necessity, and that which is for the advantage of the whole universe, of which thou art a part. But that is good for every part of nature which the nature of the whole brings, and what serves to maintain this nature. Now the universe is preserved, as by the changes of the elements so by the changes of things compounded of the elements. Let these principles be enough for thee, let them always be fixed opinions. But cast away the thirst after books, that thou mayest not die murmuring, but cheerfully, truly, and from thy heart thankful to the gods.

Remember how long thou hast been putting off these things, and how often thou hast received an opportunity from the gods, and yet dost not use it. Thou must now at last perceive of what universe thou art a part, and of what administrator of the universe thy existence is an efflux, and that a limit of time is fixed for thee, which if thou dost not use for clearing away the clouds from thy mind, it will go and thou wilt go, and it will never return.

Every moment think steadily as a Roman and a man to do what thou hast in hand with perfect and simple dignity, and feeling of affection, and freedom, and justice; and to give thyself relief from all other thoughts. And thou wilt give thyself relief, if thou doest every act of thy life as if it were the last, laying aside all carelessness and passionate aversion from the commands of reason, and all hypocrisy, and self-love, and discontent with the portion which has been given to thee. Thou seest how few the things are, the which if a man lays hold of, he is able to live a life which flows in quiet, and is like the existence of the gods; for the gods on their part will require nothing more from him who observes these things.

Thou art doing violence to thyself my soul; but thou wilt no longer have the opportunity of honoring thyself. Every man's life is sufficient. But thine is nearly finished, though thy soul reverences not itself, but places thy felicity in the souls of others.

Do the things external which fall upon thee distract thee? Give thyself time to learn something new and good, and cease to be whirled around. But then thou must also avoid being carried about the other way. For those too are triflers who have wearied themselves in life by their activity, and yet have no object to which to direct every movement, and, in a word, all their thoughts.

Through not observing what is in the mind of another a man has seldom been seen to be unhappy; but those who do not observe the movements of their own minds must of necessity be unhappy.

This thou must always bear in mind, what is the nature of the whole, and what is my nature, and how this is related to that, and what kind of a part it is of what kind of a whole; and that there is no one who hinders thee from always doing and saying the things which are according to the nature of which thou art a part.

Theophrastus,[5] in his comparison of bad acts—such a comparison as one would make in accordance with the common notions of mankind—says, like a true philosopher, that the offenses which are committed through desire are more blameable than those which are committed through anger. For he who is excited by anger seems to turn away from reason with a certain pain and unconscious contraction; but he who offends through desire, being overpowered by pleasure, seems to be in a manner more intemperate and more womanish in his offenses. Rightly then, and in a way worthy of philosophy, he said that the offense which is committed with pleasure is more blameable than that which is committed with pain; and on the whole the one is more like a person who has been first wronged and through pain is compelled to be angry; but the other is moved by his own impulse to do wrong, being carried towards doing something by desire.

Since it is possible that thou mayest depart from life this very moment, regulate every act and thought accordingly. But to go away from among men, if there are gods, is not a thing to be afraid of, for the gods will not involve thee in evil; but if indeed they do not exist, or if they have no concern about human affairs, what is it to me to live in a universe devoid of gods or devoid of providence? But in truth they do exist, and they do care for human things, and they have put all the means in man's power to enable him not to fall into real evils. And as to the rest, if there was anything evil, they would have provided for this also, that it should be altogether in a man's power not to fall into it. Now that which does not make a man worse, how can it make a man's life worse? But neither through ignorance, nor having the knowledge, but not the power to guard against or correct these things, is it possible that the nature of the universe has overlooked them; nor is it possible that it has made so great a mistake, either through want of power or want of skill, that good and evil should happen indiscriminately to the good and the bad. But death certainly, and life, honor and dishonor, pain and pleasure, all these things equally happen to good men and bad, being things which make us neither better nor worse. Therefore they are neither good nor evil.

How quickly all things disappear, in the universe the bodies themselves, but in time the remembrance of them; what is the nature of all sensible things, and particularly those which attract with the bait of pleasure or terrify by pain, or are noised abroad by vapory fame; how worthless, and contemptible, and sordid, and perishable, and dead they are—all this it is the part of the intellectual faculty to observe. To observe too who these are whose opinions and voices give reputation; what death is, and the fact that, if a man looks at it in itself, and by the abstractive power of reflection resolves into their parts all the things which present

[5]Greek philosopher (371–287 B.C.) and author of the *Characters.*

themselves to the imagination in it, he will then consider it to be nothing else than an operation of nature; and if any one is afraid of an operation of nature, he is a child. This, however, is not only an operation of nature, but it is also a thing which conduces to the purposes of nature. To observe too how man comes near to the deity, and by what part of him, and when this part of man is so disposed.

Nothing is more wretched than a man who traverses everything in a round, and pries into the things beneath the earth, as the poet[6] says, and seeks by conjecture what is in the minds of his neighbors, without perceiving that it is sufficient to attend to the daemon within him, and to reverence it sincerely. And reverence of the daemon consists in keeping it pure from passion and thoughtlessness, and dissatisfaction with what comes from gods and men. For the things from the gods merit veneration for their excellence; and the things from men should be dear to us by reason of kinship; and sometimes even, in a manner, they move our pity by reason of men's ignorance of good and bad; this defect being not less than that which deprives us of the power of distinguishing things that are white and black.

Though thou shouldest be going to live three thousand years, and as many times ten thousand years, still remember that no man loses any other life than this which he now lives, nor lives any other than this which he now loses. The longest and shortest are thus brought to the same. For the present is the same to all, though that which perishes is not the same; and so that which is lost appears to be a mere moment. For a man cannot lose either the past or the future: for what a man has not, how can any one take this from him? These two things then thou must bear in mind; the one, that all things from eternity are of like forms and come round in a circle, and that it makes no difference whether a man shall see the same things during a hundred years or two hundred, or an infinite time; and the second, that the longest liver and he who will die soonest lose just the same. For the present is the only thing of which a man can be deprived, if it is true that this is the only thing which he has, and that a man cannot lose a thing if he has it not.

Remember that all is opinion. For what was said by the Cynic Monimus is manifest: and manifest too is the use of what was said, if a man receives what may be got out of it as far as it is true.

The soul of man does violence to itself, first of all, when it becomes an abscess and, as it were, a tumor on the universe, so far as it can. For to be vexed at anything which happens is a separation of ourselves from nature, in some part of which the natures of all other things are contained. In the next place, the soul does violence to itself when it turns away from any man, or even moves towards him with the intention of injuring, such as are the souls of those who are angry. In the third place, the soul does violence to itself when it is overpowered by pleasure or by pain. Fourthly, when it plays a part, and does or says anything insincerely and untruly. Fifthly, when it allows any act of its own and any movement

[6]Pindar, in the *Theaetetus of Plato.*

to be without an aim, and does anything thoughtlessly and without considering what it is, it being right that even the smallest things be done with reference to an end; and the end of rational animals is to follow the reason and the law of the most ancient city and polity.

Of human life the time is a point, and the substance is in a flux, and the perception dull, and the composition of the whole body subject to putrefaction, and the soul a whirl, and fortune hard to divine, and fame a thing devoid of judgment. And, to say all in a word, everything which belongs to the body is a stream, and what belongs to the soul is a dream and vapor, and life is a warfare and a stranger's sojourn, and after-fame is oblivion. What then is that which is able to conduct a man? One thing and only one, philosophy. But this consists in keeping the daemon within a man free from violence and unharmed, superior to pains and pleasures, doing nothing without a purpose, nor yet falsely and with hypocrisy, not feeling the need of another man's doing or not doing anything; and besides, accepting all that happens, and all that is allotted, as coming from thence, wherever it is, from whence he himself came; and, finally, waiting for death with a cheerful mind, as being nothing else than a dissolution of the elements of which every living being is compounded. But if there is no harm to the elements themselves in each continually changing into another, why should a man have any apprehension about the change and dissolution of all the elements? For it is according to nature and nothing is evil which is according to nature.

The Middle Ages

The term *Middle Ages* as a description of the thousand-year period between the fifth and the fifteenth centuries—between the end of the Roman Empire and the Renaissance—is at once an oversimplification and a distortion of a long and complex period of European history. Coined by Renaissance and Enlightenment thinkers, the label *Middle Ages* (or its Latin form, the *Medieval* period) implies a mere transitional era, a long interruption in the continuity of Western history during which the classical culture of Greece and Rome, waiting to be revived in the Renaissance, lay dormant or dead.

From our perspective, we can see the Middle Ages in more positive terms, not as an interruption but as a fertile and dynamic period that produced a distinctive and permanently valuable culture of its own. It was more varied than a single, reductive label would imply. There is a certain unity in this long span of history that justifies our considering it as a single period, but within this unity is enormous diversity. Only the very early Middle Ages, from the sixth to the ninth centuries, were characterized by the cultural inertia often attributed to the whole period. The collapse of the Roman Empire left Europe for a time in chaos, with its economy, its social organization, and its culture brought almost to a halt. But even these "Dark Ages" were not without their rays of light, especially in areas where survivals of the Roman heritage or the Church preserved pockets of culture. In retrospect, we can see forces working during this fallow period that were to emerge later in a new and vital form of social organization. The new organization began to take shape in about the tenth century and led by the thirteenth century to a flowering of art and culture that anticipated and rivaled the Renaissance without forfeiting its own distinctively medieval character.

The formidable challenge to the early Middle Ages was to find a mode of social organization to replace the Roman Empire and to weave together the various threads of European culture: the remnants of Latin civilization, Christianity, and the northern, Germanic, "barbarian" tradition. The solution that gradually emerged over a period of several centuries lay in two institutions, the Roman Church and feudalism.

By the time of the Empire's final collapse, the Church had made great strides toward becoming a universal institution. Paul, the "Apostle of the Gentiles," was the chief architect in the conversion of Christianity from a parochial, nationalistic cult among dissident Jews to a universal religion. During the fourth century, Christianity gradually became the state religion of Rome; the emperor Theodosius at the end of the century formally proclaimed it as such, closed heathen temples, and forbade heathen sacrifices. Within a few years, pagans were actively persecuted as the Christians had been persecuted earlier.

At the beginning of the fifth century, the centralizing forces in Christianity culminated in the claim by Pope Innocent I to jurisdiction over all Christendom. The centrally organized Church was to a large extent modeled on the Empire. As the Empire gradually wasted away, the Church emerged more and more clearly as its spiritual heir and as a universal source of authority. It also became, for a thousand years, the heir and the chief custodian of Latin culture. It preserved much of the classic Roman literature and over the centuries fostered a rich body of medieval Latin writing, largely ecclesiastical in nature. This work included philosophy such as that of St. Augustine, St. Anselm, and St. Thomas Aquinas; rhetoric, such as Geoffrey of Vinsauf's; chronicles and compilations of legendary history, such as the *Gesta Romanorum* and the Venerable Bede's *Ecclesiastical History of the English Nation;* a rich body of Latin religious poetry, especially hymns; and many other works.

The power of the medieval church was based upon two propositions, which it inculcated almost universally: that the visible scene of human life was a perpetual conflict between the Kingdom of God and the Kingdom of the Devil, and that salvation for the individual was available only through the offices of the Church. This world was seen as secondary to the world to come, a testing ground determining whether the individual would spend eternity in Heaven or Hell. Because participation in the sacraments of the Church was a requirement for salvation, the Church vitally affected the individual's fate through all eternity, a fate that at its worst was regarded with a fearful literalness.

The elaborate bureaucracy of the Roman Empire was reflected in the detailed hierarchy through which the Church performed its functions and which, in its meticulous emphasis upon rank and degree, expressed one of the deepest and most pervasive habits of medieval thought. The individual was linked to God through an elaborate chain of hierarchical relationships. Above the individual believer was the priest; above the priest were, in succession, bishop, archbishop, cardinal, and pope. The ranks rose, beyond the earthly Church, above the pope through the intricate orders of angels to God Himself. The pope was thus, in this minutely detailed scheme of things, the direct representative of God on earth, with absolute power to "bind and loose."

Quite apart from its religious function, the medieval Church was a vitally important social institution in the Middle Ages. In an era full of political disorder and conflict, it provided a slight check upon secular warfare, by asserting an authority that transcended political boundaries. It tempered social oppression by opening Church offices to commoners and upholding the doctrine of the equality of all men before God. It also helped unify and stabilize European culture by defining a broadly accepted system of values and beliefs.

The fixed hierarchy of the medieval Church was mirrored in feudalism, the secular social and economic system that gradually emerged to replace the fallen Empire. Feudalism originated in the human need to band together for mutual protection in a lawless and chaotic age. Inhabitants of a particular region placed themselves under the protection of the most powerful local lord and in return for his military protection pledged certain services. Like the Church, feudalism echoed certain aspects of the Roman Empire, notably the custom of clients gathering around wealthy patrons, but it also drew heavily upon the Germanic social organization, in which warriors gathered around a powerful chieftain, to whom they were bound by a complex system of obligations and rewards.

In its fully developed form, feudalism was, like the Church, a pyramidal structure encompassing all of society and organized by an intricate code of privileges and mutual commitments. The medieval king was the secular counterpart of the pope, subordinate to him only in matters of faith. The feudal system placed literal ownership of all the king's domain (except that controlled by the Church) in his hands. These lands, or "fiefs," were, in effect, leased and subleased down through hierarchical orders of nobility to the level of the individual manor, the basic social and economic unit of feudalism. Each nobleman became the "vassal" of his immediate superior and owed him, in return for the lands he was granted, money payments and, when demanded, military service. The exact terms of feudal obligations were never standardized across Europe. They depended on local custom, but they were quite precise and were ritualized in the ceremony of homage and investiture, in which the vassal knelt before his lord and, placing his hands between his lord's hands, vowed to fulfill the terms of his obligation. At the bottom of the feudal pyramid was the serf, bound to the land he worked and obliged to cultivate his lord's land as well, in a sort of peonage or sharecropper arrangement.

Feudal society thus consisted of only two classes, the people and the nobility, which included the orders of the Church as well as the secular feudal orders. There was no socially mobile middle class; such a class, outside the rigid ordering of rank, would have been incompatible with the idea of feudalism, and when it did begin to emerge late in the Middle Ages, it marked the beginning of the collapse of the whole system.

The first comparatively stable kingdom to be established after the fall of Rome was that of the Franks, founded by Clovis (465–511). Charlemagne (742–814), a descendant of Clovis, embarked upon a series of campaigns against the Saxons and Bavarians, the Moors of northeast Spain, and the Lombards in northern Italy, building an immense empire to rival that of the Caesars. He was crowned "Holy Roman Emperor" by Pope Leo III on Christmas Day, 800. Charlemagne's victories became the stuff of legend, and his deeds, along with those of his twelve "peers," were celebrated in a number of medieval works of which the *Song of Roland* is the most famous. The imperial court was also a great center of art and learning, the focal point of the "Carolingian renaissance." Charlemagne brought the learned monk Alcuin from England to found a palace school of theology and literature, imported architects from Italy to build a number of cathedrals, and encouraged the study of Latin literature as well as Germanic epics.

Another nucleus of culture in the early Middle Ages, the Benedictine monastic order, was founded in the late sixth century by St. Benedict of

Nursia with the encouragement of the great medieval pope Gregory I (540–604), who launched a series of missions to Christianize the northern Germanic peoples. Within a century, the Benedictine monasteries had spread across Europe, succeeding the Roman schools as centers of learning. In these monasteries libraries were collected and copied, instruction was carried on, and medieval architecture was born, with many of the monks working as master masons in the construction of early cathedrals.

Charlemagne's empire was short-lived, crumbling under the impact of invasions from the north. The Vikings, seafaring warriors from Scandinavia, swept into England and northern France in the ninth century and established the kingdom of Normandy in 885. The result, however, was not a new age of barbarism. The Danish Vikings were gradually assimilated in England, where the reign of Alfred the Great of Wessex (871–899) accompanied a genuine revival of art and learning. The Vikings in Normandy were likewise assimilated with the Franks, and a similar revival of learning took place; when these Normans conquered England in 1066, they brought with them a culture superior to that of the Anglo-Saxons.

The eleventh and twelfth centuries were a time of explosive intellectual and cultural development. The Crusades, launched by Pope Urban II in 1095, were eventually a dismal failure as attempts to capture the Holy Lands from the "Saracens," but they had the unforeseen effect of bringing Europeans into contact with the riches of Muslim culture, literature, mathematics, and science. Industry and commerce began to revive across Europe, and a number of universities were founded: Oxford in 1167, Paris in 1170, Cambridge in 1209. Provence in southern France was a particularly fertile ground; a vigorous economic and cultural atmosphere brought the development of chivalry and a rich tradition of *troubadour* literature expressing chivalric values, a tradition paralleled in northern France by the poetry of the *trouvères.*

This rapid development culminated in the thirteenth century, the high point, in many ways, of medieval culture. Both the medieval papacy and the medieval monarchy reached the height of their power in the thirteenth century, the papacy under Innocent III, Gregory IX, and Nicholas III, the monarchy under such kings as Edward I of England, Louis IX of France, and Ferdinand III of Spain. The greatest of the Gothic cathedrals were built—Notre Dame de Paris, Mont-Saint-Michel, Rheims, Amiens, Chartres. The period also marked the golden age of Scholasticism, the philosophical project of reconciling the teachings of the Church with the logic of Aristotle, or faith with reason; St. Thomas Aquinas's *Summa Theologica,* the masterpiece of Scholasticism, was completed in 1273.

But already, at the peak of its triumph, the medieval system was beginning to show signs of its ultimate decline. The medieval monarchy received an ominous blow when the English barons forced King John to sign Magna Charta in 1215. The strains upon the medieval papacy surfaced in such conflicts as the prolonged struggles between the Guelphs (supporters of the Pope) and the Ghibellines (supporters of the Holy Roman Emperor) in the city-states of Italy. The rise in the thirteenth century of the guilds, organizations of skilled craftsmen, also heralded the rise of a middle class incompatible with the rigid categories of the feudal system and prophetic of its ultimate collapse.

These fragmenting tendencies gained momentum in the turbulent fourteenth century. The papacy was split, for most of the century, by the so-called Babylonian Captivity, 1305–1376, during which the papal see was removed to Avignon in France, and by the following Great Schism (1378–1417), when there were two, and sometimes even three, rival popes. The chaos that followed the Black Death in mid-century further weakened the feudal system. The second half of the century was shaken by people's revolutions: the French Jacquerie in 1358 and the English Peasants' Revolt in 1381. These and other uprisings were put down, with great cruelty, but they foreshadowed the end of economic serfdom.

The greatest imaginative writers of medieval Europe emerged during its decline. The medieval worldview is perhaps best expressed by such writers as Thomas Aquinas and John of Salisbury, but the masterpieces of medieval literature date from the fourteenth century: the *Divine Comedy,* the *Decameron,* the *Rhymes* of Petrarch, the *Canterbury Tales.* Paradoxically, none of these works is wholly medieval in spirit. The tension apparent in all of them between the passing medieval world and the emerging Renaissance world provides much of their energy.

That we can distinguish the "medieval" and the "modern" in such works, however tentatively, suggests that, despite the span and variety of the Middle Ages, there is a certain consistency in its worldview. At the risk of overgeneralizing, it is possible to point to three qualities pervasive enough to define the age: authoritarianism, comprehensiveness, and otherworldliness. The cathedral, often cited as the quintessential expression of the medieval spirit, illustrates all three tendencies. The system of communal engineering that made the building of cathedrals possible implies the subordination of individual creativity to collective authority. If one values the occasional evidences of individual personality, in the playful elaboration of a gargoyle carving, for instance, it is because such features are exceptions. Medieval literature, too, is often anonymous, and when we begin to hear, as in Petrarch, the sound of an individual voice, we know that a new element has entered the medieval literary world.

As for comprehensiveness, the cathedral was also a microcosm of an all-inclusive vision of life. Not only did it represent a synthesis of social values, art, and religion, but its art characteristically undertook to represent the whole Christian revelation, the divine plan from Creation to the Day of Judgment. The literary analogues were the compendiums, ambitious works that attempted a total view of human life, its individual parts placed in relation to a whole, as in Aquinas's *Summa Theologica* or Dante's *Divine Comedy.* And finally, the very shape of the cathedral, its great spires pointing away from the earth toward Heaven, suggests the pervasive otherworldliness of medieval life. This tendency made empirical science impossible but also, at its best, gave a hope and dignity to human life in an age when life was too often bleak and short. Medieval literature has its own distinctive form of earthiness, but it almost always provides a view of eternity too, whether in brief glimpses or in visionary panoramas.

The Middle Ages have a claim to the label the following age preempted; they were not merely a hiatus between the classic and modern worlds but in some ways themselves a renaissance, a rebirth after the collapse of Roman civilization. Much of the modern world has medieval origins: the modern state and the modern city, modern languages, and a large body of collective myth, including the idea of romantic love, are rooted in the Middle Ages. But the major medieval achievement was the welding together of the separate strands of Western culture—Hebrew, Greek, Roman, and Christian—into a single culture. This culture has been greatly amplified and modified by succeeding ages, but it still retains the general shape the Middle Ages gave it.

The literature of the Middle Ages is as varied as the time that produced it. Its characteristic forms are the epic, the romance, the allegory, the folktale, the lyric, and the drama.

The Germanic and Celtic tribes had a body of heroic legend as rich as that which Homer drew upon for the *Iliad* and the *Odyssey.* There is good reason to believe that this material was in oral circulation for centuries before Christian monks, in about the eighth century, began to write it down. The earliest of the folk epics is the English *Beowulf,* which may have been based upon the exploits of a sixth-century Scandinavian warrior but acquired a heavy overlay of folklore before an eighth-century English monk put it in written form. (The poem as we know it dates from a tenth-century manuscript.) Although *Beowulf,* like the *Iliad* and the *Aeneid,* celebrates the virtues of its culture's heroic past, these virtues are not precisely the same as those of Greece and Rome. The poem provides a fascinating glimpse into an ancient Germanic courtly culture held together by the complex, ritualized mutual obligations of the *comitatus* relationship, the bond between Germanic warriors and their lord. Magnanimity, loyalty, and the willingness to fight to the death to fulfill an obligation are the virtues celebrated, all against the background of a tragic belief in fate and eventual, inevitable defeat. This ethical system blends in *Beowulf* with other elements derived from Christianity and classical culture. Beowulf has a Christian gentleness; his monstrous antagonists are identified with Cain and the Devil himself, and in the end he, Christlike, lays down his life for his people. The *Beowulf* poet also apparently knew the *Aeneid.* Although he never alludes directly to Virgil's work, its influence is apparent in the poem's sophistication of organization and in the epic conception of Beowulf's character.

The other early medieval folk epics, in various ways, also depict the confrontation of pagan heroic ethics with the ethics of classical culture and Christianity. The *Elder,* or *Poetic, Edda,* composed in the ninth century but written down in the twelfth century, preserves the heroic legends of Iceland; the *Hildebrandslied* (ninth century) and *Nibelungenlied* (early thirteenth century) record German heroic tales; the Irish sagas of Cu Chulainn and Conchubar (eighth to tenth centuries) and the Welsh *Mabinogion* (eleventh century) preserve the heroic tales of the Celts. In France, the epic spirit was expressed in the *chansons de geste;* the greatest of these was the *Song of Roland* (twelfth century), which, like most of the *chansons de geste,* deals with legends of Charlemagne and his knights. The *Poem of My Cid* (twelfth century) presents a Spanish hero to rival Roland and Cu Chulainn. The Icelandic sagas, dealing with events in Iceland between about 930 and 1030 but written down several centuries later, represent a late survival of the epic impulse, perhaps because of the relative cultural isolation of Iceland.

In general, however, epic yielded some ground to romance in the eleventh and twelfth centuries. The term *romance* was originally applied to the Old French language as distinguished from the parent language, Latin or "Roman." In time, however, it came to refer to any work in the French language and ultimately to the most common form of French works, the tale of chivalric adventure. France remained preeminent in the romance form throughout the Middle Ages. Romances were fundamentally epics in which the center of interest had shifted from warfare to love, especially the elaborately ritualized cult of "courtly love," which first developed among the *troubadours* of Provence and the *trouvères* of northern France. Originally half-facetious, it transferred the homage the epic hero owed to his lord to the romance hero's lady, developing an elaborate code to govern the relation between the sexes. The idealization inherent in courtly love was probably, in part, a sublimation of youthful ungratified fervor; it arose in castles where numbers of young, unmarried knights surrounded their lords and the lords' remote, unattainable ladies. The revival of interest in Greek romances and in Ovid's *Art of Love* was also a factor, as was the growing cult of the Virgin Mary beginning in the second half of the tenth century.

The favorite subjects of medieval romance derived from the Matter of Britain (the Celtic sagas, especially those of King Arthur), the Matter of France (the Charlemagne legends), and the Matter of Rome the Great (Greek and Roman stories). Popular and widely circulated romances included those of Chrétien de Troyes, who wrote the first extant French romance, *Eric and Enid* (twelfth century) and a number of other Arthurian romances; Gottfried von Strassburg's *Tristan* (c. 1200); Wolfram von Eschenbach's *Parzival* (c. 1200); *Floris and Blanchefleur* (c. 1250); *Amis and Amiloun* (before 1300); and *Ipomedon* (fourteenth century). Among the most readable of these romances today are the twelve short *lais* of the twelfth-century Marie de France, sophisticated probings into the psychology of love within magical, "Breton" settings.

By the thirteenth century, the worldliness and sensuality of the romances had led the Church to regard them as detrimental to faith. Following its regular policy of assimilation and incorporation, however, the Church did not ban romances but rather encouraged the writing of a new kind, the "moral romance," which advanced Christian ideals while staying within the narrative conventions of the genre. The romances of the Holy Grail, the thirteenth-century French *Romance of the Rose,* and the fourteenth-century English *Sir Gawain and the Green Knight* all belong to this second phase. By the fifteenth century, the romance had become stale and formulaic, and after a period of rambling, inflated prose romances, uneasy blends of chivalric and moral elements, the genre was transformed and blended with new emphases in the Renaissance.

The *Romance of the Rose* also illustrates another major genre of medieval literature, the allegory. One of the most influential works of the Middle Ages, the *Romance of the Rose* is a dream poem in which the poet visits the Garden of Delight, where he sees the Rose, which symbolizes his sweetheart. Major characters in the story are personified qualities: Idleness, Pleasure, Fair Welcome, Danger, Shame, and Evil Tongue. Primarily an allegory of courtly love, the poem is also a satire directed at a number of targets (including sexual infatuation, superstition, and the celibacy of the clergy) and a compendium of miscellaneous medieval lore. The work became immensely popular in France, England (where it was at least partly translated by Chaucer), and Italy (where it was translated into sonnet form, possibly by Dante). The use of a dream to introduce an allegorical narrative and of the dream-allegory structure to hold together a wide range of material was widely imitated for three hundred years. Chaucer's *Book of the Duchess, House of Fame,* and *Parliament of Fowls* are all dream allegories; even the *Canterbury Tales* exhibits some features of the genre, including the pilgrimage motif, the use of representative characters, and the inclusion of varied tales within a generally symbolic framework. The fourteenth-century *Confessio Amantis,* by Chaucer's contemporary John Gower, and *Piers Plowman,* by William Langland, both continue to use the form. Christine de Pizan's *Book of the City of Ladies* is a fascinating feminist dream allegory, a refutation of the misogynistic *Romance of the Rose* which uses its own techniques to confound it. The supreme masterpiece of the genre is Dante's *Divine Comedy.* Allegory was also an important element in medieval drama. It survived vigorously into later ages, in such works as Edmund Spenser's *Faerie Queene* (1596) and John Bunyan's *Pilgrim's Progress* (1675). In fact, allegory has never died out.

Epic, romance, and allegory were all aristocratic narrative forms, written and read (or listened to) by the medieval aristocracy and gentry. There was also throughout the Middle Ages a flourishing body of popular oral narrative: folktales, beast fables, bawdy anecdotes called *fabliaux,* and folk ballads. These popular works were occasionally collected and written down; there are several collections of versified *fabliaux;* beast fables are the basis of several beast epics, the most famous of which is the French *Romance of Reynard* (twelfth century); and many popular ballads survive, though in versions dating from long after the Middle Ages. The importance of the oral folk tradition lies less in directly surviving texts than in the pervasive influence it exerted upon written literature—as sources, for example, of the stories in the *Decameron* and the *Canterbury Tales.*

Among medieval literary forms, the lyric is second in importance only to romance. There was a rich tradition of Latin lyric poetry that included Latin hymns; praises of rulers or patrons; nature songs; and "Goliardic" poetry (light occasional secular poetry, often satiric, written mainly by clerics in pretended praise of the fictional "Bishop Golias"). Vernacular poetry flowered earliest in twelfth-century Provence in southern France among the *troubadours.* The *troubadours* (or "finders" of treasure) were courtly singers who composed and sang elaborate, highly wrought poems, transmitting them orally to professional minstrels called *jongleurs,* who in turn spread them from place to place. Their major form was the *canzone,* an expression of idealized love written in a complex and rigid rhyme scheme, although they developed a number of other forms as well. The Provençal lyric influenced the *trouvères* of northern France and the *Minnesingers* of Germany. (*Trouvère* also means "finder," and *Minnesinger* means "singer of romantic love.") But its most vigorous influence was in Italy, which traveling *troubadours* visited in the early thirteenth century. There they inspired a school of imitators some of whom wrote in Provençal themselves, as a tribute to their mentors. Florence became the birthplace of the *dolce stil novo*—a "sweet new style"—that combined the forms of the *troubadours* with a grave, philosophical content derived from Scholastic philosophy.

It is one of the more surprising facts about literary history that the very idea of drama had to be reinvented beginning in the tenth century. The plays of Plautus and Terence were read throughout the Middle Ages, and the tenth-century German nun Hroswitha of Gandersheim wrote several plays about saints' lives, imitating the form of Terence though not his ribald content. Medieval readers seem to have thought that the Roman plays were merely monologues or dialogues to be declaimed, not acted, and Hroswitha apparently had no notion of actual performance. There was a live tradition of popular entertainment—mimes, jugglers, and clowns, as well as a body of pagan fertility plays—but no conception of the sustained acting of a dramatic text.

Drama was reborn out of the liturgy of the Church, beginning in the tenth century with brief dramatized episodes (tropes) inserted into the Mass and then developed over several centuries into increasingly elaborate plays. The plays were separated from the Church in the thirteenth century and came to be performed outdoors at the spring Corpus Christi festivals. The major forms (which overlap considerably) were the mystery play, based on scripture and performed at the festivals by "mysteries," or trade guilds; the miracle play, based on a saint's life and staged on his or her feast day; and the morality play, a moral allegory dramatizing the spiritual life of the typical man. Secular forms included the folk play, which was independent of the religious drama and dramatized the deeds of a popular hero such as Robin Hood or St. George; the farce, a genre derived from popular and classical rather than religious models; and the secular interlude, a short play for performance between the parts of a banquet or other celebration.

Medieval drama, like most medieval art, was an international phenomenon, flourishing in England, France, Germany, Spain, and Italy. Although it produced few masterpieces—*Everyman* is one—it made possible the flowering of drama in the Renaissance, which built not only upon the rediscovered drama of Greece and Rome but upon native traditions as well.

Medieval literature, like the age that produced it, was rich and diverse. And, again like the age itself, it was not merely a prelude to what followed but, in many respects, the matrix of the future. Fiction, poetry, and drama since the Renaissance have drawn heavily upon the classical heritage, but the forms in which they developed were established in the Middle Ages.

FURTHER READING: C.W. Previté-Orton's *Shorter Cambridge Medieval History,* 2 vols., 1952, is a standard history of the Middle Ages. See also Denys Hay, *The Medieval Centuries,* 1965; Friedrich Heer, *The Medieval World,* 1962; Johan Huizinga, *The Waning of the Middle Ages,* 1924; and R. W. Southern, *The Making of the Middle Ages,* 1953. The rise of the individual is a key subject in Norman F. Cantor, *The Civilization of the Middle Ages,* 1993. An authoritative overview of medieval literature is J. A. Burrow's *Medieval Writers and Their Work,* 1982. *European Writers: The Middle Ages and the Renaissance,* ed. William T. H. Jackson and George Stade, 2 vols. (the second beginning with Petrarch), 1983, is a work of sound scholarship understandable by nonexperts. E. R. Curtius's *European Literature and the Latin Middle Ages,* trans. Willard Trask, 1953, is challenging but rewarding. C. S. Lewis's *The Discarded Image,* 1964, is a very readable description of the popular worldview that underlay medieval literature and culture. For aspects of medieval culture closely related to literature, see Henri Pirenne, *Mohammed and Charlemagne,* 1939; T. H. White, *The Book of Beasts,* 1956; Emile Male, *The Gothic Image,* trans. Dora Nussey, 1958; Erwin Panofsky, *Gothic Architecture and Scholasticism,* 1951; David C. Fowler, *The Bible in Early English Literature,* 1976 (a broader treatment of cultural contexts than the title would suggest); and John Cummins, *The Hound and the Hawk,* 1989 (on hunting). Two readable and fairly concise books on medieval philosophy are John Marenbon, *Early Medieval Philosophy, 480–1150: An Introduction,* 1983; and Michael Haren, *Medieval Thought: The Western Intellectual Tradition from Antiquity to the Thirteenth Century,* 1985; both address the relationship between philosophy and religion. Especially interesting, on the subject the title announces, are the essays collected in *Women in the Middle Ages and the Renaissance: Literary and Historical Perspectives,* ed. Mary Beth Rose, 1986. On particular genres, see, for lyric poetry, Maurice Valency's *In Praise of Love,* 1958 (on Provençal and Italian poetry); James J. Wilhelm, *Medieval Song,* 1971; and Frederick Goldin, *Lyrics of the Troubadours and Trouvères,* 1973. On epic and romance, W. P. Ker's *Epic and Romance,* 1897, is, despite its date, still valuable. See also *Arthurian Literature in the Middle Ages,* ed. R. S. Loomis, 1959, and Eugene Vinaver, *The Rise of Romance,* 1971. Various aspects of courtly life are discussed in Joachim Bumke, *Courtly Culture,* 1991. Good on medieval drama are V. A. Kolve, *The Play Called Corpus Christi,* 1966, and Rosemary Woolf, *The English Mystery Plays,* 1972.

The Koran (Qur'an)

(Seventh Century)

Sometime around the year 610, a forty-year-old Arab merchant named Muhammad, who lived in Mecca and who occasionally retreated to a hill cave for nights of meditation, had a vision of an angelic figure (later identified as the angel Gabriel) and heard a voice saying to him, "You are the Messenger of God. Recite!" Muhammad, who in some accounts was unlettered, replied, "I cannot recite." The angel repeated, "Recite in the name of the Lord!" Muhammad then recited spontaneously some lines of verse in praise of God. From this time until his death, twenty-two years later, Muhammad received periodic revelations. He committed the messages to memory and passed them on to followers, and they were sometimes written down. About 650, several years after Muhammad's death, they were gathered together to form the Koran, the sacred book of Islam, the religion that Muhammad founded. Islam is the youngest of the three great monotheistic world religions, the others being Judaism and Christianity. There are now about 935 million Muslims, many concentrated in North Africa, the Middle East, and Central Asia but others disseminated worldwide. There are about six million Muslims in the United States, for example.

Muhammad was born in Mecca in about 570. His father died before he was born, he lost his mother when he was six, and his grandfather, into whose care he had been placed, died when Muhammad was eight. He then came under the care of an uncle, who was a trader and the head of the Hashem clan in the tribe of Quraysh to which Muhammad belonged. When Muhammad was about twenty-five, Khadijah, a successful business woman for whom he worked, asked for his hand in marriage. She had four daughters and three sons from previous marriages, and she bore Muhammad six children, two sons who died young and four daughters, the best known of whom was Fatima. After Khadijah's death, Muhammad married several other women from other tribes.

The revelations began about 610, and Muhammad soon became regarded as a prophet and religious leader by a steadily increasing band of followers. The new religion came to be known as Islam, which means "surrender" in Arabic (that is, to the will of God), and adherents were known as Muslims ("those who have surrendered").

Opposition rose in Mecca to Muhammad and his teachings from those who resented his implicit criticism of the wealthy merchant class and feared his potential political power. There were rumors of plots to kill Muhammad, and in 622 he and about seventy followers in small groups slipped out of Mecca and moved to a town called Yathrib, subsequently renamed Medina ("city of the Prophet"). This journey is called the *hijrah* (Latin "hegira"), and the date on which it began is the beginning of the Islamic calendar; the first day of the Islamic Era (AH or Anno Hegirae) is July 16, 622 by Western reckoning. Muhammad spent the rest of his life in Medina, consolidating his rapidly increasing political and religious power. By 630, he had built a powerful federation of Arab tribes, destined as the Arab Muslim empire to spread across a large part of the globe, an area extending from Spain across Central Asia to India. Muhammad, however, did not live to see this great conquest; he died in 632.

The book that was derived from the revelations made to Muhammad is the Koran (Arabic: "recitation"). The texts of the revelations were preserved in oral traditions; followers memorized them and used them in ritual prayers. There is also a tradition that Muhammad had them written down soon after each revelation. They were not brought together into a book, though, until 651–52, when Uthman, the third caliph (successor to the Prophet), commissioned scholars to make an authoritative compilation.

The Koran is about the same length as the New Testament. It is divided into 114 chapters, or *suras. Sura* means "unit of revelation"; the more familiar term "chapter" is used in our selections here. Each chapter is divided into verses. The chapters, after the brief Opening (*Fatihah*), are arranged roughly in descending order of length. Each chapter has a traditional name derived from some characteristic word or phrase in the chapter ("The Cow," "The Bee," "The Night Journey"). In modern times, chapters and verses have been assigned numbers, and passages are often cited by number, as with the Bible. From the beginning of the Koran's history, chapters have been identified as Meccan or Medinan, depending on where they were revealed. Every chapter except the ninth begins with the invocation "In the name of God, the Merciful, the Compassionate." Twenty-nine of the chapters follow this invocation with one or more Arabic letters. (See the beginning of "Ya Sin," for example, in this book.) Muslim scholars insist that these mysterious letters are part of the original revelations, but there is no agreement on what they mean.

The arrangement of the Koranic chapters by length means that there is no chronological order to the collection. Nor is there any clear logical arrangement. Passages on similar topics are not discussed together but are scattered throughout the entire text, and there is no obvious sense of a gradually unfolding argument. These characteristics are perhaps inevitable in a book that originated in a series of separate revelations. The Koran is probably best read as a series of separate impassioned and prophetic utterances about how to construct an ideal, unified community.

Christians and Jews who approach the Koran for the first time are likely to be surprised by the amount of overlap with the Hebrew and Christian scriptures. As the Christian New Testament confirms the Hebrew Old Testament, so the Koran confirms them both. Muhammad did not see himself as negating the Hebrew and Christian revelations but as extending them, and he expected to be well received by Jews and Christians, the other "peoples of the book," an expectation that was, of course, not fulfilled. Muhammad appears in the Koran not as the Messiah but as the culminating figure in a series of prophets through whom God has communicated with humankind, including Abraham, Moses, David, and Jesus.

The teachings of the Koran form the core of Islam. Central among them is the doctrine of a single unified and unifying God. Islam has been compared to Judaism in its absolute insistence on monotheism and in its distrust of the Trinity as potentially polytheistic. More importantly, Islam is a worldly religion that insists on the unity of the sacred and the earthly, of faith and the practice of building a good society. Whereas Christianity originally defined itself by posing the church against the Roman state, Islam has no church and no priests. Muslims can pray in any place so long as they direct their prayers geographically toward Mecca, rather paradoxically, since that city where Muhammad grew up later rebelled, riven by clan and tribal warfare, against his revolutionary and egalitarian teachings.

In the early days of Islam, becoming a Muslim meant becoming part of a community ruled by social and divine laws of equality, justice, and fraternity to which the Muslim had to submit. The politics of Islam ("surrender") meant that Muslims would no longer be torn apart by clan and feudal rivalries and by hierarchies governed by the rich and powerful ruling class in Mecca.

Although the eschatology (the doctrine of last things, the Day of Judgement, and Hell and Heaven) of Islam and many of its narratives are similar to those of Christianity, Islam differs in its beginnings as a political rebellion against the existing social order. Historians who see it as a "revolutionary" religion do so because Muhammad's teachings required him to flee the anger of the rulers in Mecca in order to conduct guerrilla warfare against the old ways of running a society. The early struggles against social injustice continue in current fundamentalist justifications of *jihad* or "holy war." Koranic laws insisted on the defeat of the more than three hundred idols worshipped in Mecca in favor of one God and on the need to submit to new laws about such things as marriage, the spoils of war, slavery, inheritance, and the rights of women. The common practice of killing newborn girls was outlawed. The Koran also addresses matters of everyday life such as the disciplines of washing, eating, daily prayer, pilgrimage, fasting, and giving alms.

In Islam, as in Christianity, "in the beginning was the Word." Islamic history begins with Gabriel's command to "Recite!" and Islam's first mystery is how the untutored Muhammad produced the beautiful poetry and wisdom of the Koran. For Muslims even more than for Jews and Christians, God's presence is bound up in the words of their sacred book, since those words are literally God's, delivered to Muhammad through his intermediary Gabriel and taken from a parallel book in Heaven, a "guarded tablet" that is "the mother of the book." Muslims are therefore reluctant to have the Koran translated, and translators often refer to their work as interpretations or paraphrases rather than translations. Nevertheless, the book has been translated into different languages from the ninth century to the present. In the brief selections presented here, the emphasis has been placed on especially eloquent and poetic passages that play an important role in ordinary Muslim life, rather than on the central doctrinal passages.

FURTHER READING: A comprehensive survey of Islam is the *Cambridge History of Islam,* ed. Peter Malcolm Holt et al., 1970. A more concise introduction is Fazlur Rahman, *Islam,* 2nd ed., 1979. *Islam and the Arab World,* ed. Bernard Lewis, 1976, is a useful collection of essays on various aspects of Islamic culture. A standard biography of Muhammad is W. Montgomery Watt, *Muhammad at Mecca,* 1953, and *Muhammad at Medina,* 1956, summarized in one volume, *Muhammad: Prophet and Statesman,* 1961. See also Maxime Rodinson, *Mohammad,* 1971. On the Koran, Abdullah Yusef Ali, *The Holy Qur'an: Text, Translation, Commentary,* 1978, is a comprehensive and valuable work. Other good introductions are Richard Bell, *Introduction to the Qur'an,* new ed., rev. and enl. W. Montgomery Watt, 1970; and Muhammad Abdel Haleem, *Understanding the Qur'an,* 1996. *The Essential Koran: The Heart of Islam: An Introductory Selection of Readings from the Qur'an,* translated and presented by Thomas Cleary, 1993, is helpful; "presented" in this case means offering quite poetic translations of selected passages, with a short but pithy introduction and ample notes directed toward the non-Muslim

from *THE KORAN*

Translated by Arthur J. Arberry

THE OPENING[1]

In the Name of God, the Merciful, the Compassionate[2]

Praise belongs to God, the Lord of all Being,
the All-merciful, the All-compassionate,
the Master of the Day of Doom.

Thee only we serve; to Thee alone we pray for succour. 5
Guide us in the straight path,
the path of those whom Thou hast blessed,
not of those against whom Thou art wrathful,
nor of those who are astray.

from THE COW[3]

It is not piety, that you turn your faces[4] 177
to the East and to the West.
True piety is this:
to believe in God, and the Last Day,
the angels, the Book, and the Prophets,
to give of one's substance, however cherished,
to kinsmen, and orphans,
the needy, the traveller, beggars,
and to ransom the slave,
to perform the prayer, to pay the alms.
And they who fulfil their covenant
when they have engaged in a covenant,
and endure with fortitude
misfortune, hardship and peril,

[1] This short opening chapter (called the *Fatihah*) was revealed at Mecca. Perhaps the best-known passage in the Koran, it is used as a short, general prayer on any occasion. (The marginal numbers here and throughout the Koran refer not to line numbers but to the verse numbers in the Arabic original.)

[2] Each *surah,* or chapter, in the Koran (except for the ninth one, "Repentance") begins with this invocation, called the Basmalah, after the Arabic *Bismillah al-rahman al-rahim.*

[3] "The Cow," the second chapter of the Koran, is also the longest. It was revealed in Medina. As with most of the chapters, the traditional title is drawn from an identifying word or passage in the chapter, in this case a passage in which Moses commands his people to sacrifice a cow. Only two short, lyric sections are given here from this long chapter.

[4] Verse 177 beautifully summarizes Islamic beliefs.

these are they who are true in their faith,
these are the truly godfearing.

* * *

God 255
there is no god but He, the
Living, the Everlasting.[5]
Slumber seizes Him not, neither sleep;
to Him belongs
all that is in the heavens and the earth.
Who is there that shall intercede with Him
save by His leave?
He knows what lies before them
and what is after them,
and they comprehend not anything of His knowledge
save such as He wills.
His Throne comprises the heavens and earth;
the preserving of them oppresses Him not;
He is the All-high, the All-glorious.

LIGHT[6]

* * *

God is the Light of the heavens and the earth; 35
the likeness of His Light is as a niche
wherein is a lamp
(the lamp in a glass,
the glass as it were a glittering star)
kindled from a Blessed Tree,
an olive that is neither of the East nor of the West
whose oil wellnigh would shine, even if no fire touched it;
Light upon Light;
(God guides to His Light whom He will.)
(And God strikes similitudes for men,
and God has knowledge of everything.)
in temples God has allowed to be raised up,
and His Name to be commemorated therein;
therein glorifying Him, in the mornings and the evenings,
are men whom neither commerce nor trafficking

[5] Verse 255 is the famous "Throne Verse," a passage, like the *Fatihah* and "Sincere Religion" (Chapter 112), often recited by Muslims at moments of special reverence or crisis.

[6] "Light," the twenty-fourth chapter of the Koran, was revealed at Medina. The first verses of the chapter, omitted here, deal with chastity and gossip. Verse 35, called the Light Verse, is one of the most exalted and poetic sections of the Koran.

diverts from the remembrance of God
and to perform the prayer, and to pay the alms,
fearing a day when hearts and eyes shall be turned about,
that God may recompense them for their fairest works
and give them increase of His bounty;
and God provides whomsoever He will, without reckoning.

And as for the unbelievers,
their works are as a mirage in a spacious plain
which the man athirst supposes to be water,
till, when he comes to it, he finds it is nothing;
there indeed he finds God,
and He pays him his account in full; (and God is swift
at the reckoning.)
or they are as shadows upon a sea obscure 40
covered by a billow
above which is a billow
above which are clouds,
shadows piled one upon another;
when he puts forth his hand, wellnigh he cannot see it.
And to whomsoever God assigns no light,
no light has he.

Hast thou not seen how that whatsoever is in the heavens
and in the earth extols God,
and the birds spreading their wings?
Each—He knows its prayer and its extolling; and God knows
the things they do.
To God belongs the Kingdom of the heavens and the earth,
and to Him is the homecoming.
Hast thou not seen how God drives the clouds, then composes them,
then converts them into a mass,
then thou seest the rain issuing out of the midst of them?
And He sends down out of heaven mountains, wherein is hail,
so that He smites whom He will with it, and turns it aside
from whom He will;
wellnigh the gleam of His lightning snatches away the sight.
God turns about the day and the night;
surely in that is a lesson for those who have eyes.
God has created every beast of water,
and some of them go upon their bellies,
and some of them go upon two feet,
and some of them go upon four; God
creates whatever He will; God is powerful
over everything.

Now We have sent down signs making all 45
clear; God guides whomsoever He will
to a straight path.

They say, 'We believe in God and the
Messenger, and we obey.' Then after that
a party of them turn away; those—
they are not believers.
When they are called to God and His Messenger
that he may judge between them, lo, a party of them
are swerving aside;
but if they are in the right, they will come to
him submissively.
What, is there sickness in their hearts,
or are they in doubt, or do they fear
that God may be unjust towards them
and His Messenger? Nay, but those—
they are the evildoers.
All that the believers say, when they 50
are called to God and His Messenger, that he
may judge between them, is that they say,
'We hear, and we obey'; those—
they are the prosperers.
Whoso obeys God and His Messenger,
and fears God and has awe of Him, those—
they are the triumphant.
They have sworn by God the most earnest oaths,
if thou commandest them they will go forth.
Say: 'Do not swear; honourable obedience
is sufficient. Surely God is aware of
the things you do.'
Say: 'Obey God, and obey the Messenger;
then, if you turn away, only upon
him rests what is laid on him, and
upon you rests what is laid on you.
If you obey him, you will be guided.
It is only for the Messenger to deliver
the manifest Message.'

God has promised those of you who believe
and do righteous deeds that He will surely
make you successors in the land, even as He
made those who were before them successors,
and that He will surely establish their
religion for them that He has approved for them,
and will give them in exchange, after
their fear, security: 'They shall serve Me,
not associating with Me anything.'
Whoso disbelieves after that, those—
they are the ungodly.
Perform the prayer, and pay the alms, 55
and obey the Messenger—haply so
you will find mercy.

Think not the unbelievers able to frustrate
God in the earth; their refuge is the Fire—
an evil homecoming.

O believers, let those your right hands own
and those of you who have not reached puberty[7]
ask leave of you three times—before
the prayer of dawn, and when you put off
your garments at the noon, and after
the evening prayer—three times of nakedness
for you. There is no fault in you or them, apart
from these, that you go about one to the other.
So God makes clear to you the signs; and God is
All-knowing, All-wise.
When your children reach puberty, let them
ask leave, as those before them asked leave.
So God makes clear to you His signs; and God is
All-knowing, All-wise.
Such women as are past child-bearing
and have no hope of marriage—there is no
fault in them that they put off their clothes,
so be it that they flaunt no ornament;
but to abstain is better for them; and God is
All-hearing, All-knowing.

There is no fault in the blind, and there is 60
no fault in the lame, and there is no fault
in the sick, neither in yourselves, that you
eat of your houses, or your fathers' houses,
or your mothers' houses, or your brothers' houses,
or your sisters' houses, or the houses of
your uncles or your aunts paternal, or
the houses of your uncles or your aunts
maternal, or that whereof you own the keys,
or of your friend; there is no fault in you
that you eat all together, or in groups
separately.
But when you enter houses, greet one another
with a greeting from God, blessed and good.
So God makes clear to you the signs; haply
you will understand.

Those only are believers, who believe
in God and His Messenger and who, when they
are with him upon a common matter,
go not away until they ask his leave.
Surely those who ask thy leave—those are

[7] That is, slaves and children. This section of the chapter moves from exaltation of the power and goodness of God to matters of proper conduct in domestic life, particularly of modesty and privacy.

they that believe in God and His Messenger;
so, when they ask thy leave for some affair
of their own, give leave to whom thou wilt
of them, and ask God's forgiveness
for them; surely God is All-forgiving,
All-compassionate.
Make not the calling of the Messenger
among yourselves like your calling
one of another. God knows those of you
who slip away surreptitiously; so let those
who go against His command beware, lest
a trial befall them, or there befall them
a painful chastisement.

Why, surely to God belongs whatsoever is in the heavens
and the earth; He ever knows what state you are upon;
and the day when they shall be returned to Him, then He
will tell them of what they did; and God knows everything.

YA SIN[8]

In the Name of God, the Merciful, the Compassionate

Ya Sin

By the Wise Koran,
thou[9] art truly among the Envoys
on a straight path;
the sending down of the All-mighty, the All-wise,
that thou mayest warn a people whose fathers were 5
never warned, so they are heedless.
The Word has been realised against most of them,
yet they do not believe.
Surely We have put on their necks fetters
up to the chin, so their heads are raised;
and We have put before them a barrier and
behind them a barrier; and We have covered
them, so they do not see.
Alike it is to them whether thou hast warned them
or thou hast not warned them, they do not believe.
Thou only warnest him who follows the Remembrance 10
and who fears the All-merciful in the Unseen; so
give him the good tidings of forgiveness
and a generous wage.

[8] "Ya Sin," the thirty-sixth chapter of the Koran, revealed at Mecca, is named after the two mystical letters that precede it. Muhammed is said to have called it "the heart of the Koran." It has a special significance in Islam and is often recited to the dying and on ceremonial occasions.

[9] That is, Muhammed.

Surely it is We who bring the dead to life
and write down what they have forwarded
and what they have left behind; everything
We have numbered in a clear register.

Strike for them a similitude—
the inhabitants of the city,[10] when
the Envoys came to it;
when We sent unto them two men,
but they cried them lies, so We
sent a third as reinforcement.
They said, 'We are assuredly
Envoys unto you.'
They said, 'You are naught but
mortals like us; the All-merciful
has not sent down anything. You
are speaking only lies.'
They said, 'Our Lord knows we are 15
Envoys unto you;
and it is only for us to deliver
the Manifest Message.'
They said, 'We augur ill of you. If
you give not over, we will stone you
and there shall visit you from us
a painful chastisement.'
They said, 'Your augury is with you;
if you are reminded? But you are a
prodigal people.'
Then came a man from the furthest part of
the city, running; he said, 'My people,
follow the Envoys!
Follow such as ask no wage of you, 20
that are right-guided.
And why should I not serve Him who
originated me, and unto whom
you shall be returned?
What, shall I take, apart from Him, gods
whose intercession, if the All-merciful
desires affliction for me, shall not
avail me anything, and who will
never deliver me?
Surely in that case I should be in
manifest error.
Behold, I believe in your Lord;
therefore hear me!'

[10] The city referred to in this exemplary story is generally held to be Antioch, to which Jesus sent first two disciples and then Simon Peter. The story is told in the Christian Bible in Acts 13.

It was said, 'Enter Paradise!' 25
He said, 'Ah, would that my people
had knowledge
that my Lord has forgiven me
and that He has placed me
among the honoured.'
And We sent not down upon his
people, after him, any host
out of heaven; neither would We
send any down.
It was only one Cry and lo, they were
silent and still.
Ah, woe for those servants! Never
comes unto them a Messenger, but
they mock at him.
What, have they not seen how many 30
generations We have destroyed
before them,
and that it is not unto them
that they return?
They shall every one of them be arraigned
before Us.

And a sign for them is the dead land, that We quickened
and brought forth from it grain, whereof they eat;
and We made therein gardens of palms and vines,
and therein We caused fountains to gush forth,
that they might eat of its fruits and their hands' labour. 35
What, will they not be thankful?
Glory be to Him, who created all the pairs
of what the earth produces, and of themselves,
and of what they know not.
And a sign for them is the night; We strip it of the
day and lo, they are in darkness.
And the sun—it runs to a fixed resting-place;
that is the ordaining of the All-mighty, the All-knowing.
And the moon—We have determined it by stations,
till it returns like an aged palm-bough.
It behoves not the sun to overtake the moon, neither 40
does the night outstrip the day,
each swimming in a sky.
And a sign for them is that We carried their seed
in the laden ship,
and We have created for them the like of it
whereon they ride;
and if We will, We drown them,
then none have they to cry to,
neither are they delivered,
save as a mercy from Us, and enjoyment
for a while.

And when it is said to them, 'Fear what is before you 45
and what is behind you; haply you will find mercy'—
yet never any sign of the signs of their Lord
comes to them, but they are turning away from it.
And when it is said to them, 'Expend of that God has
provided you,' the unbelievers say to the believers,
'What, shall we feed such a one whom, if God willed,
He would feed? You are only in manifest error!'

They also say, 'When shall this promise come to
pass, if you speak truly?'
They are awaiting only for one Cry to seize them
while they are yet disputing,
then they will not be able to make any testament, 50
nor will they return to their people.
And the Trumpet shall be blown; then behold, they are sliding down
from their tombs unto their Lord.
They say, 'Alas for us! Who roused us out of our sleeping place?
This is what the All-merciful promised, and the Envoys spoke truly.'
'It was only one Cry; then behold, they are all arraigned before Us.
So today no soul shall be wronged anything, and you shall not be
recompensed, except according to what you have been doing.
See, the inhabitants of Paradise today are busy in their rejoicing, 55
they and their spouses, reclining upon couches in the shade;
therein they have fruits, and they have all that they call for.
'Peace!'—such is the greeting, from a Lord All-compassionate.
'Now keep yourselves apart, you sinners, upon this day!
Made I not covenant with you, Children of Adam, that you 60
should not serve Satan—surely he is a manifest foe to you—
and that you should serve Me? This is a straight path.
He led astray many a throng of you; did you not understand?
This is Gehenna, then, the same that you were promised;
roast well in it today, for that you were unbelievers!'
Today We set a seal on their mouths, and their hands speak to Us, 65
and their feet bear witness as to what they have been earning.

Did We will, We would have obliterated
their eyes, then they would race to the path,
but how would they see?
Did We will, We would have changed them
where they were, then they could not go on,
nor could they return.
And to whomsoever We give long life,
We bend him over in His constitution; what,
do they not understand?

We have not taught him poetry; it is not
seemly for him. It is only a Remembrance
and a Clear Koran,
that he may warn whosoever is living, 70

and that the Word may be realized against
the unbelievers.

Have they not seen how that We have created for them
of that Our hands wrought cattle that they own?
We have subdued them to them, and some of them they ride,
and some they eat;
other uses also they have in them, and beverages.
What, will they not be thankful?
Yet they have taken, apart from God, gods;
haply they might be helped.
They cannot help them, though they be hosts 75
made ready for them.
So do not let their saying grieve thee;
assuredly We know what they keep secret
and what they publish.

Has not man regarded how that We created him
of a sperm-drop?
Then lo, he is a manifest adversary.
And he has struck for Us a similitude
and forgotten his creation;
he says, 'Who shall quicken the bones
when they are decayed?'
Say: 'He shall quicken them, who originated them
the first time; He knows all creation,
who has made for you out of the green tree 80
fire and lo, from it you kindle.'
Is not He, who created the heavens and earth,
able to create the like of them? Yes indeed;
He is the All-creator, the All-knowing.
His command, when He desires a thing, is to say to it
'Be,' and it is.
So glory be to Him, in whose hand is the dominion
of everything,
and unto whom you shall be returned.

SINCERE RELIGION[11]

In the Name of God, the Merciful, the Compassionate

Say: 'He is God, One,
God, the Everlasting Refuge,
who has not begotten, and has not been begotten,
and equal to Him is not any one.'

[11] "Sincere Religion," the one-hundred-and-twelfth chapter, holds, like the *Fatihah* and the Throne Verse, a special place in Islamic life. It is generally held to contain the essence of the Koran and of Islam, and Muhammed is said to have recommended reciting it a hundred times a day if possible. It was revealed at Mecca.

The Cattle Raid of Cooley

(Seventh–Eighth Centuries)

The eleventh-century legendary history of Ireland is called *The Book of Invasions.* As history it is fanciful, a myth of origins that traces a series of invasions going back before the Flood. As metaphor, even prophecy, it is better, for the history of Ireland, before and since, has been a series of invasions, from the first emigration of fishermen and food-gatherers from Europe about 8000 B.C., to the arrival of a different group of Stone Age people (whose marks remain in the great stone "passage graves" still visible in Ireland) around 3000 B.C., the gradual invasion of the Celts during the first century B.C., the incursions of the Vikings beginning late in the eighth century, the Norman invasion of the twelfth century, and—most relevant for our own time—the hegemony of the English from the sixteenth century to early in our own century, and, in Northern Ireland, to our own day. The Irish, through this history of change and especially in modern times, have drawn heavily upon a rich body of heroic saga, the earliest recorded and among the richest in Europe, for a sense of cultural identity.

Christianity, and hence writing, came to Ireland in the fifth century, and although no surviving manuscript in the Irish language dates from earlier than the twelfth century, there is evidence that the earliest manuscripts lie at the end of a series of copies that go back to a pre-Christian Gaelic oral tradition. Indeed the action of many of the Irish tales seems to be set in the early days of the Celtic invasion, in the first century before Christ. There are five large groups of tales. One consists of mythological tales, "Tales of the Tuatha De Danaan" (or peoples of the goddess Donu), which deal, sometimes in a veiled way, with the gods of the Celts. Another is the so-called Ulster Cycle, which deals with the exploits of Cu Chulainn, the major Celtic hero. The centerpiece of the Ulster Cycle is *The Cattle-Raid of Cooley*, the story of a heroic struggle between Cu Chulainn's men of Ulster and Queen Maeve's men of Connacht over possession of a marvelous bull. *The Cattle-Raid of Cooley* is the Irish national epic. A third group, the King Tales, contains tales, often delightfully fanciful, about traditional kings of Ireland. The most famous of them, "The Madness of Sweeney," tells of an eastern-Ulster king who went mad through the curse of a saint and lived in the wilderness among wild animals. The mythological tales, the Ulster Cycle, and the King Tales date from very early in Irish history. The Finn Cycle and a group of romantic tales were developed later. The Finn Cycle, represented most fully in thirteenth-century manuscripts, concerns the exploits of Finn Mac Cumhaill, his son Oisin, and his grandson Oscar. And finally a group of fourteenth- and fifteenth-century tales reflect the spirit of romance, often through the retelling of earlier stories.

Perhaps the most famous of all Irish tales is the story of Deirdre, or Derdriu, as it is told in the "Exile of the Sons of Uisliu." This tale is one of the "pre-tales" attached to *The Cattle-Raid of Cooley* in the Ulster Cycle, tales that provide the background of the action. In this case, the tale is intended to explain how such Ulster heroes as Fergus, Dubthach, and Cormac came to fight with Connacht against Ulster in the battles of the cattle-raid. But this purpose recedes into insignificance before the force of the story's central character and its swift, tragic action. Derdriu is both an Irish Helen, whose beauty disrupts a kingdom, and an Irish Isolde, a king's intended bride who elopes with one of his warriors.

The "Exile of the Sons of Uisliu" gives us a brief but vivid glimpse into the world of the Irish saga. Conchobar, a king of Ulster, rules absolutely over a province not yet subordinated to a "high king." His house, in which the action begins, is, like Hrothgar's mead-hall Heorot in *Beowulf*, a large, bare hall where his warriors gather to carouse. These warriors are bound to Conchobar and to one another by an elaborate system of blood-ties and obligations, which Derdriu and Noisiu violate when they elope. The court itself is a charming combination of sophistication and simplicity. Named among Conchobar's entourage are an official storyteller, a seer, and a satirist, and yet his world is a pastoral one, never far from the realities of raising and slaughtering cattle.

Irish saga has taken on an added interest since the rise of the nationalist movement in the late nineteenth century through the number of Irish writers who have drawn upon traditional materials for their work. Long before the modern period, the tales of Finn and Oisin were revived in James MacPherson's *Fingal* (1762) and *Temora* (1763). MacPherson claimed that his poems were translations from "Ossian" (the Scottish form of Oisin); even after his claim was exploded, his "Ossianic" poems continued to seize the imagination of Romantic Europe. Cu Chulainn was revived much later in such retellings of the Ulster Cycle as Standish James O'Grady's *Cuculain: An Epic* (1882) and Lady Augusta Gregory's *Cuchulain of Muirthemne* (1902). The shadowy figure of Cu Chulainn became the embodiment of the heroic aspirations of the leaders of the 1916 Easter Rising. As William Butler Yeats wrote of the heroes of the Rising:

Who thought Cuchulainn till it seemed
He stood where they had stood?

And to this day a statue of the dying Cu Chulainn stands in the lobby of the Dublin General Post Office. Throughout his career, Yeats himself wrote poems and plays about the old heroes, and James Joyce, in one of the most personal treatments, wove the legends of Finn Mac Cumhaill into the complex fabric of *Finnegans Wake* (1939). More recently, the Irish poet Seamus Heaney has reworked the old King Tale of Mad Sweeney as *Sweeney Astray* (1983).

No Irish tale has been treated more frequently by modern writers, though, than the "Exile of the Sons of Uisliu." Yeats took the tale as the basis for his 1906 play *Deirdre* (see Volume II); another famous dramatic treatment is John Millington Synge's *Deirdre of the Sorrows* (1910). The novelist James Stephens based his novel *Deirdre* (1923) on the story. And there have been a number of other retellings. Something in this ancient story—the representation of Ireland as a strong, defiant woman, the power of the love between Derdriu and Noisiu, even the charm of a story about a bewitching woman who picks a lover by pulling his ears—has spoken to readers and writers across a thousand years.

PRONUNCIATION OF NAMES

Uisliu:	*ish*-lu
Conchobor:	*kon*-chov-or / *kon*-chor
Fedlimid:	*fedh*-lim-idh / *fe*-lim-i
Cathbad:	*kath*-vadh / *kaff*-a
Derdriu:	*der*-dru
Emain:	*ev*-in
Leborcham:	*le*-vor-cham
Noisiu:	*noy*-shu
Dubthach:	*duv*-thach / *duff*-ach
Medb:	medhv / mayv
Ailill:	*al*-il
Táin:	toyn

FURTHER READING: The best contribution to the study of Irish saga in recent years has been Thomas Kinsella's fine translation of *The Táin*, 1969, magnificently illustrated by Louis le Brocquy. Kinsella, an accomplished poet, makes *The Cattle-Raid of Cooley*, along with its "pre-tales," available to modern readers in a way that makes its artistry clear. Proinsias Mac Cana's *Celtic Mythology*, rev. ed. 1983, not only surveys the literature but places it in its historical context. Tom Peete Cross and Clark Harris Slover, eds., *Ancient Irish Tales*, rev. ed., 1969, and Jeffrey Gantz, ed., *Early Irish Myths and Sagas*, 1981, are convenient collections. Myles Dillon's *Early Irish Literature*, 1948, remains an authoritative critical account. On the place of Irish heroic legends in the modern nationalist movement, see John Wilson Foster, *Fictions of the Irish Literary Revival: A Changeling Art*, 1987.

EXILE OF THE SONS OF UISLIU

Translated by Thomas Kinsella

What caused the exile of the sons of Uisliu?

It is soon told.

The men of Ulster were drinking in the house of Conchobor's storyteller, Fedlimid mac Daill. Fedlimid's wife was overseeing everything and looking after them all. She was full with child. Meat and drink were passed round, and a drunken uproar shook the place. When they were ready to sleep the woman went to her bed. As she crossed the floor of the house the child screamed in her womb and was heard all over the enclosure. At that scream everyone in the house started up, ready to kill. Sencha mac Ailella said:

"No one move! Bring the woman here. We'll see what caused this noise."

So the woman was brought before them. Her husband Fedlimid said:

"Woman,
what was that fierce shuddering sound
furious in your troubled womb?
The weird uproar at your waist

hurts the ears of all who hear it.
My heart trembles at some great error
or some cruel injury."

She turned distracted to the seer Cathbad:

"Fair-faced Cathbad, hear me
—prince, pure, precious crown,
grown huge in druid spells.
I can't find the fair words
that would shed the light of knowledge
for my husband Fedlimid,
even though it was the hollow
of my own womb that howled.
No woman knows what her womb bears."

Then Cathbad said:

"A woman with twisted yellow tresses,
green-irised eyes of great beauty
and cheeks flushed like the foxglove
howled in the hollow of your womb.
I say that whiter than the snow
is the white treasure of her teeth;
Parthian-red,[1] her lip's lustre.
Ulster's chariot-warriors
will deal many a blow for her.
There howled in your troubled womb
a tall, lovely, long-haired woman.
Heroes will contend for her,
high kings beseech on her account;
then, west of Conchobor's kingdom
a heavy harvest of fighting men.
High queens will ache with envy
to see those lips of Parthian-red
opening on her pearly teeth,
and see her pure perfect body."

Cathbad placed his hand on the woman's belly and the baby wriggled under it.

"Yes," he said, "there is a girl there. Derdriu shall be her name. She will bring evil."

Then the daughter was born and Cathbad said:

"Much damage, Derdriu, will follow
your high fame and fair visage:
Ulster in your time tormented,
demure daughter of Fedlimid.

[1]Leather from Parthia, an ancient country in Asia, was traditionally dyed a bright red.

And later, too, jealousy
will dog you, woman like a flame,
and later still—listen well—
the three sons of Uisliu exiled.

Then again, in your lifetime,
a bitter blow struck in Emain.
Remorse later for that ruin
wrought by the great son of Roech;[2]

Fergus exiled out of Ulster
through your fault, fatal woman,
and the much-wept deadly wound
of Fiachna, Conchobor's son.

Your fault also, fatal woman,
Gerrce felled, Illadan's son,
and a crime that no less cries out,
the son of Durthacht, Eogan, struck.

Harsh, hideous deeds done
in anger at Ulster's high king,
and little graves everywhere
—a famous tale, Derdriu."

"Kill the child!" the warriors said.

"No," Conchobor said. "The girl will be taken away tomorrow. I'll have her reared for me. This woman I'll keep to myself."

The men of Ulster didn't dare speak against him.

And so it was done. She was reared by Conchobor and grew into the loveliest woman in all Ireland. She was kept in a place set apart, so that no Ulsterman might see her until she was ready for Conchobor's bed. No one was allowed in the enclosure but her foster-father and her foster-mother, and Leborcham, tall and crooked, a satirist, who couldn't be kept out.

One day in winter, the girl's foster-father was skinning a milk-fed calf on the snow outside, to cook it for her. She saw a raven drinking the blood on the snow. She said to Leborcham:

"I could desire a man who had those three colours there: hair like the raven, cheeks like blood and his body like snow."

"Good luck and success to you!" Leborcham said. "He isn't too far away, but close at hand—Noisiu, Uisliu's son."

"I'll be ill in that case," she said, "until I see him."

This man Noisiu was chanting by himself one time near Emain, on the rampart of the stronghold. The chanting of the sons of Uisliu was very sweet. Every cow or beast that heard it gave two thirds more milk. Any person hearing it was filled with peace and music. Their deeds in war were great also: if the whole province of Ulster came at them at once, they could put their

[2]Fergus.

three backs together and not be beaten, their parrying and defense were so fine. Beside this they were swift as hounds in the chase, killing the wild beasts in flight.

While Noisiu was out there alone, therefore, she slipped out quickly to him and made as though to pass him and not recognize him.

"That is a fine heifer going by," he said.

"As well it might," she said. "The heifers grow big where there are no bulls."

"You have the bull of this province all to yourself," he said, "the king of Ulster."

"Of the two," she said, "I'd pick a game young bull like you."

"You couldn't," he said. "There is Cathbad's prophecy."

"Are you rejecting me?"

"I am," he said.

Then she rushed at him and caught the two ears of his head.

"Two ears of shame and mockery," she said, "if you don't take me with you."

"Woman, leave me alone!" he said.

"You will do it," she said, binding him.[3]

A shrill cry escaped him at that. The men of Ulster nearby, when they heard it, started up ready to kill. Uisliu's other sons went out to quieten their brother.

"What is wrong?" they said. "Whatever it is, Ulstermen shouldn't kill each other for it."

He told them what had happened.

"Evil will come of this," the warriors said. "But even so, you won't be shamed as long as we live. We can bring her with us to some other place. There's no king in Ireland who would deny us a welcome."

They decided on that. They left that night, with three times fifty warriors and three times fifty women and the same of hounds and menials. Derdriu was among them, mingling with the rest.

They travelled about Ireland for a long time, under protection. Conchobor tried to destroy them often with ambushes and treachery. They went round southwestward from the red cataract at Es Ruaid, and to the promontory at Benn Etair, northeastward. But still the men of Ulster pursued them until they crossed the sea to the land of Alba.[4]

They settled there in the waste places. When the mountain game failed them they turned to take the people's cattle. A day came when the people of Alba went out to destroy them. Then they offered themselves to the king of Alba, who accepted them among his people as hired soldiers. They set their houses on the green. They built their houses so that no one could see in at the girl in case there might be killing on her account.

It happened that a steward came looking around their house early one morning. He saw the couple sleeping. Then he went and woke the king:

[3]The words translated here as "binding him" mean that Derdriu places Noisiu under a formal bond, or *geasa*, to do her will.

[4]Britain. Es Ruaid was near modern Ballyshannon in western Ireland; Benn Etair is the Hill of Howth, north of Dublin Bay.

"I never found a woman fit for you until today," he said. "There is a woman with Noisiu mac Uislenn who is fit for a king over the Western World. If you have Noisiu killed, you can have the woman to sleep with," the steward said.

"No," the king said, "but go and ask her every day in secret."

He did this, but every day he came she told Noisiu about it that night. Since nothing could be done with her, the sons of Uisliu were ordered into all kinds of traps and dangerous battles to have them killed. But they were so hard in the carnage that nothing came of it.

They tried her one last time. Then the men of Alba were called together to kill them. She told Noisiu this.

"Go away from here," she said. "If you don't leave here this night, you will be dead tomorrow."

So they left that night and reached an island in the sea.

This news reached Ulster.

"Conchobor," everyone said, "it would be shameful if the sons of Uisliu fell in enemy lands by the fault of a bad woman. Better to forgive and protect them—to save their lives and let them come home—than for enemies to lay them low."

"Let them come," Conchobor said. "Send for them, with guarantees of safety."

This news was brought to them.

"It is welcome," they said. "We'll go if Fergus comes as a pledge of safety, and Dubthach and Conchobor's son Cormac."

Then they went down with the messengers to the sea.

So they were brought back to Ireland. But Fergus was stopped through Conchobor's cunning. He was invited to a number of ale feasts and, by an old oath, couldn't refuse. The sons of Uisliu had sworn they would eat no food in Ireland until they ate Conchobor's food first, so they were bound to go on. Fiacha, Fergus's son, went on with them, while Fergus and Dubthach stayed behind. The sons of Uisliu came to the green at Emain. Eogan mac Durthacht, king of Fernmag, was there: he had come to make peace with Conchobor, with whom he had long been at enmity. He had been chosen to kill them. Conchobor's hired soldiers gathered around him so that the sons of Uisliu couldn't reach him. They stood in the middle of the green. The women settled on the ramparts of Emain.

Eogan crossed the green with his men. Fergus's son came and stood at Noisiu's side. Eogan welcomed Noisiu with the hard thrust of a great spear that broke his back. Fergus's son grasped Noisiu in his two arms and pulled him down and threw himself across him, and Noisiu was finished off through Fergus's son's body. Then the slaughter broke out all over the green. No one left except by spike of spear or slash of sword. Derdriu was brought over to Conchobor and stood beside him with her hands bound at her back.

Fergus was told of this, and Dubthach and Cormac. They came at once and did mighty deeds. Dubthach killed Maine, Conchobor's son. Fiachna, son of Conchobor's daughter Fedelm, was killed with a single thrust. Fergus killed Traigthrén, Traiglethan's son, and his brother. Conchobor was outraged, and on a day soon afterward battle was joined between them, and three hundred among the men of Ulster fell. Before morning Dubthach had massacred the girls of Ulster and Fergus had burned Emain.

Then they went to Connacht, to Ailill and Medb—not that this was a home from home for Ulstermen, but that they knew these two would protect them. A full three thousand the exiles numbered. For sixteen years they made sure that weeping and trembling never died away in Ulster; there was weeping and trembling at their hands every single night.

She was kept a year by Conchobor. In that time she never gave one smile, nor took enough food or sleep, nor lifted up her head from her knees. If they sent musicians to her, she would say this following poem:

"Sweet in your sight the fiery stride
of raiding men returned to Emain.
More nobly strode the three proud
sons of Uisliu toward their home:

Noisiu bearing the best mead
—I would wash him by the fire—
Ardán, with a stag or a boar,
Anle, shouldering his load.

The son of Nes, battle-proud,
drinks, you say, the choicest mead.
Choicer still—a brimming sea—
I have taken frequently.

Modest Noisiu would prepare
a cooking-pit in the forest floor.
Sweeter then than any meat
the son of Uisliu's, honey-sweet.

Though for you the times are sweet
with pipers and with trumpeters,
I swear today I can't forget
that I have known far sweeter airs.

Conchobor your king may take delight
in pipers and in trumpeters
—I have known a sweeter thing,
the three sons' triumphant song.

Noisiu's voice a wave roar,
a sweet sound to hear forever;
Ardán's bright baritone;
Anle, the hunter's, high tenor.

Noisiu: his grave-mound is made
and mournfully accompanied.
The highest hero—and I poured
the deadly drink when he died.

His cropped gold fleece I loved,
and fine form—a tall tree.
Alas, I needn't watch today,
nor wait for the son of Uisliu.

I loved the modest, mighty warrior,
loved his fitting, firm desire,
loved him at daybreak as he dressed
by the margin of the forest.

Those blue eyes that melted women,
and menaced enemies, I loved;
then, with our forest journey done,
his chanting through the dark woods.

I don't sleep now,
nor redden my fingernails.
What have I to do with welcomes?
The son of Indel[5] will not come.

I can't sleep,
lying there half the night.
These crowds—I am driven out of my mind.
I can neither eat nor smile.

What use for welcome have I now
with all these nobles crowding Emain?
Comfortless, no peace nor joy,
nor mansion nor pleasant ornament."

If Conchobor tried to soothe her, she would chant this following poem:

"Conchobor, what are you thinking, you
that piled up sorrow over woe?
Truly, however long I live,
I can't spare you much love.

The thing most dear to me in the world,
the very thing I most loved,
your harsh crime took from me.
I won't see him till I die.

I feel his lack, wearily,
the son of Uisliu. All I see—
black boulders on fair flesh
so bright once among the others.

[5]Mother of the three sons.

Red-cheeked, sweet as the river-brink;
red-lipped; brows beetle-black;
pearly teeth gleaming bright
with a noble snowy light.

His figure easiest to find,
bright among Alba's fighting-men
—a border made of red gold
matched his handsome crimson cloak.

A soft multitude of jewels
in the satin tunic—itself a jewel:
for decoration, all told, fifty ounces of light gold.

He carried a gold-hilted sword
and two javelins sharply tipped,
a shield rimmed with yellow gold
with a knob of silver at the middle.

Fergus did an injury
bringing us over the great sea.
How his deeds of valor shrank
when he sold honor for a drink!

If all Ulster's warriors
were gathered on this plain, Conchobor,
I would gladly give them all
for Noisiu, son of Uisliu.

Break my heart no more today.
In a short while I'll be no more.
Grief is heavier than the sea,
if you were but wise, Conchobor."

"What do you see that you hate most?" Conchobor said.

"You, of course," she said, "and Eogan mac Durthacht!"

"Go and live for a year with Eogan, then," Conchobor said.

Then he sent her over to Eogan.

They set out the next day for the fair of Macha. She was behind Eogan in the chariot. She had sworn that two men alive in the world together would never have her.

"This is good, Derdriu," Conchobor said. "Between me and Eogan you are a sheep eyeing two rams."

A big block of stone was in front of her. She let her head be driven against the stone, and made a mass of fragments of it, and she was dead.

Hrafnkel the Priest of Frey
(Twelfth–Fourteenth Centuries)

The prose sagas of Iceland are a vital part of medieval literature. The term *saga,* which literally means no more than "a saying," covers a wide range of narratives. Some of the Icelandic sagas are fairly literal histories—for example, the *Book of the Settlements,* which deals with the first settlers of Iceland, and Snorri Sturluson's *Heimskringla,* which chronicles the kings of Norway. Others—the "lying sagas"—are frankly fictional; these include the Icelandic versions of stories about Gawain, the Trojan War, and other favorite subjects of medieval romances.

The most interesting sagas, however, are the "Sagas of Icelanders" or the "Family Sagas." These were written for the most part in the twelfth and thirteenth centuries, but they deal with people and events dating from about 930, when the settlement of Iceland was substantially complete, to about 1030. (This century overlaps with the first generation of Icelandic Christianity, which was adopted as the official religion in the year 1000.) The Family Sagas are poised between fact and fiction. The anonymous authors based their work upon historical tales and legends two or three centuries old, but they exercised a fairly free hand in reshaping their material into artistic narratives.

The world the sagas evoke is stark and dramatic, as harsh and lonely as the Icelandic landscape. The settlers of Iceland—mostly Norwegians, Norsemen, and Celts from Ireland and other parts of the British Isles—brought Norse values and customs with them. Political and social organization was loose and turned around family estates. The head of a large estate was, by virtue of his position, a *godi*—both a priest (since he was responsible for maintaining the local temples of Thor, Frey, and the other Norse gods) and a secular chieftain who distributed land and favors to his followers, exacting from them in return allegiance and military aid. The *godi's* authority was called his *godord,* and his followers were called *thingmen.* This system depended strongly on family ties and other personal bonds of obligation and allegiance.

The only centralizing institution was the *Thing,* a public assembly for deliberation and decision attended by all freemen. At first a regional forum, it became after 925 a national one. This institution, common in ancient Germanic countries, was carried to Iceland from the settlers' native Norway. The *Thing* was both a legislative body and a law court, ruling for or against individual plaintiffs through the general vote of the assembly. It was primarily a deliberative body, however, with little power to enforce its verdicts. Execution of the law therefore remained primarily in the hands of the individuals concerned and was carried out in accordance with the ancient code: either direct vengeance or *wergeld* (blood money, or compensation).

Such social and political conditions naturally emphasized individual character—an emphasis further sharpened in the religious context of the sagas. Their Christian authors were dealing with pre-Christian men and women subject neither to the Christian God nor to the gods of the Norse pantheon, so that their fortunes depended on their own characters. The code of personal conduct in the sagas is an extension of the ancient Germanic heroic code. The world is ruled by an inexorable fate; man's duty is to face this fate with courage, even defiance. The central ethic is a man's personal and family honor; when that honor is impeached, it must be fully and publicly vindicated. This imperative lies behind most of the bloody and violent deeds of the sagas. The violence is redeemed to some extent, however, by another ideal of conduct: the notion of *drengskapr. Drengskapr* means something like "magnanimity" or "largeness of soul." The saga hero not only meets his fate with a stoical acceptance but also treats his enemy with respect and even admiration, avoiding meanness or pettiness of word or deed.

The style of the sagas is austere, like the heroic code they embody. For the most part, the stories are told with a dramatic objectivity. The narrator seldom intrudes his own interpretations or explores the characters' inner thoughts and feelings. The emphasis is upon bare, unadorned narrative, action rather than emotion. We find out what the characters are like by what they do, and we are left on our own to discover the meaning of the story. Great care is taken with the overall structure of the narrative; frequently the meaning is implied by careful balancing and repetition of elements.

Hrafnkel the Priest of Frey is one of the shorter sagas, but also one of the most effective. Its violent action unfolds swiftly in a series of short, economical episodes, told objectively and in terse dialogue. Hrafnkel is a complex figure, one of the few saga protagonists who change in the course of their stories. The balancing of his story with that of Sam raises basic questions of character, religious faith, and heroic conduct.

FURTHER READING: An excellent introduction to the Family Sagas is Theodore M. Anderson's *The Icelandic Family Saga: An Analytical Reading,* 1967. The first part of this work deals with structure, rhetoric, and the heroic legacy. The second part analyzes several individual sagas, including *Hrafnkel.* Peter Hallberg's *The Icelandic Saga,* trans. by Paul Schach, 1962, examines the centrally important question of the historical reliability of *Hrafnkel,* a matter also explored by E. V. Gordon in *Medium Aevun,* 8 (1939), 1–32. Sigurour Nordal's *Hrafnkels Saga Freysgoda,* 1949, trans. by R. George Thomas, 1958, is indispensable; it analyzes, among other things, the work's historical reliability, theme, and characterization. *Scandinavian Studies,* 47, No. 4 (1975) consists largely of four critical articles on *Hrafnkel* by Frederick J. Heinemann and Peter Hallberg.

HRAFNKEL THE PRIEST OF FREY

Translated by Gwyn Jones

1

It was in the days of king Harald Fairhair, son of Halfdan the Black, son of Gudrod the Hunting King, son of Halfdan the Freehanded but Foodstingy, son of Eystein Fret, son of Olaf Woodcutter the Swedish king,[1] that a man by the name of Hallfred brought his ship out to Iceland to Breiddal, which lies east of Fljotsdalsheid. On board were his wife and a son by the name of Hrafnkel, who was fifteen years old at the time, handsome and enterprising. Hallfred built himself a house to live in; then, during the winter, a foreign bondwoman died whose name was Arnthrud, which is why the place has been known as Arnthrudarstadir ever since.

In the spring Hallfred moved house northwards over the heath, and built himself a new home at a place called Geitdal. One night he dreamt how a man appeared to him, saying: "There you lie, Hallfred—and rashly, to be sure! Move your home away from here, west across Lagarfljot. All your good luck lies there." After this he awoke and moved house out over the Ranga river into Tunga, to the place now known as Hallfredarstadir, where he lived till he was an old man. But a goat and she-goat got left behind him, and the very day Hallfred moved out a landslide crashed on to the farm, and those fine animals perished there—which is why the place has been called Geitdal ever since.

2

Hrafnkel made it his practice to go riding over the heath in summer. By this time Jokulsdal had been fully settled right up to the rock-bridges. Hrafnkel went riding up along Fljotsdalsheid and saw where an empty valley branched off from Jokulsdal, which looked to him a better place to settle in than any other valley he had seen up to then; so when he got back home he asked his father for what was due to him of their property, and announced that he had a mind to make his home there. His father gave him his head over this, and he built himself a home in the valley and called it Adalbol, or Manor. Hrafnkel married Oddbjorg, Skjalduf's daughter from Laxardal, and they had two sons, the older called Thorir and the younger Asbjorn.

Once Hrafnkel had taken possession of the land at Adalbol he went in a lot for sacrifices and had a big temple built. Hrafnkel loved no other god more than Frey,[2] on whom he bestowed a half share in all his best treasures. He occupied the entire valley and apportioned men their land, but was determined to be their master even so, and took the priesthood over them, for which reason his name was lengthened and he was called Frey's Priest. He

[1]Genealogies of this kind are common in Icelandic sagas. *Hrafnkel the Priest of Frey* contains fewer than most, substituting detailed lists of place names. Harald Fairhair was the famous king of Norway who reigned in the last part of the ninth century and the first part of the tenth and unified Norway under a single rule. His victories in Norway drove out many of his enemies—a major cause of the settlement of Iceland.

[2]The Scandinavian god of earth's fruitfulness and the dispenser of wealth.

was a very overbearing, if talented, man, and compelled the Jokulsdalers to become his retainers. To his own people Hrafnkel was kindly and pleasant, but toward those of Jokulsdal he proved harsh and hard-headed, and they had a rough time of it at his hands. Hrafnkel took part in numerous single combats, and paid no one so much as a penny, so that nobody got any redress from him, whatever it was he did.

Fljotsdalsheid is a hard place to get about in, being very stony and boggy, but despite this father and son were always riding on visits one to the other, for their relationship was very real to them. Hallfred found the road troublesome, and cast about for a route over the high ground which stands in Fljotsdalsheid, where he found a drier if longer road, the one known as Hallfredargata. They alone use this road who really know their way about in Fljotsdalsheid.

3

Living at a farm called Laugarhus, in Hrafnkelsdal, was a man by the name of Bjarni. He was married, and had two sons by his wife, the one called Sam[3] and the other Eyvind—handsome, promising men. Eyvind lived at home wit his father, but Sam was married and living in the northern end of the valley at a farm by the name of Leikskalar. He was quite well-to-do. Sam was a highly contentious man and clever at the law, but Eyvind became a merchant and returned to Norway, where he spent the winter. From there he travelled into foreign parts, coming to a halt at Constantinople, where he won the favor of the Greek king and stayed on for a while.

Hrafnkel had one particular treasure in his possession which he prized higher than anything else. This was a stallion, dark mouse-grey in color and with a black stripe the length of his spine, which he called his Freyfaxi. He gave his friend Frey a half share in this stallion. He was so besotted with this stallion that he swore a great oath that he would be the death of any man who rode him without his express permission.

Bjarni's brother Thorbjorn was living in Hrafnkelsdal, at a farm called Holar, opposite Adalbol to the east. Thorbjorn had few assets and many dependants. His eldest son was a big, handy lad by the name of Einar, and it happened one spring that Thorbjorn had a word with Einar, how he should be looking round for some employment—"For I cannot use more labor than this household here can provide, while you are such a handy man you will easily get a good place. This is not a case of lack of affection making me get rid of you, for you mean much more to me than my other children. No, it is rather my lack of means that causes it, and my poverty. My other children are growing into workmen, but you will find a good job more easily than they."

"You have told me about this too late," replied Einar, "for by now every one will have his hands on the best jobs, and I don't much fancy having the leavings."

One day Einar caught his horse and rode to Adalbol. Hrafnkel was sitting in the living-room and gave him a warm and cheerful welcome. He asked Hrafnkel for a job.

"Why are you so late asking this," was his reply, "for I would have taken

[3]*Sam* is not the diminutive of *Samuel*, but a Scandinavian name in its own right, pronounced with a broad *a*, as in "art."

you on the very first? But by now I have engaged all my hands, except for the one job you will not care to have."

Einar asked what this might be. Hrafnkel explained that he had not yet engaged anyone for sheep-tending, and admitted he needed a good man for this. Einar said that he was not much concerned what he did, whether it was that or anything else. He stressed that what he needed was a job with full keep both winter and summer.

"Then I will give you a quick choice," said Hrafnkel. "You shall drive home the fifty ewes at the shieling[4] and fetch in all the summer firewood, and that shall be your work for the two seasons. But I must get one thing straight with you as with my other shepherds. Freyfaxi roams the upper end of the valley with his stud. You must look after him winter and summer, and I warn you against one thing: it is my will that you never get on his back, however great may be your need, for I have sworn a great oath about this, how I would be the death of any man who rides him. Twelve mares run with him, and whichever of these you want to ride, night or day, shall be at your disposal. Now do as I tell you, for it is an old saying: 'His hands are clean who warns another.' Bear in mind now what I have been talking about."

Einar said he would not be so bent on trouble as to ride this horse which was forbidden him—all the more so since there were plenty of others. With that he went home for his clothes, removed back to Adalbol, and later on they went to the shieling in the upper reaches of Hrafnkelsdal at the place called Grjotteigssel. Everything went well for Einar that summer, so that there was never a sheep lost right up till midsummer, but then there were nearly thirty ewes missing in a single night. He searched all over the pastures without finding them, and the sheep were missing nearly a week. One morning it happened that Einar went out early, and all the southern mist and drizzle had cleared away. He took a staff in his hand, a bridle, and saddle-cloth, and walked up across the river Grjotteigsa, which falls away there from the shieling, and there on the tongue of land lay the sheep which had been at home overnight. He headed these back to the shieling and went to look for those others which had been lost earlier. He could see the mares farther out on the tongue and wondered about catching a horse to ride, feeling that he would get along faster if he rode than if he walked. When he reached the mares he stalked them, but these, which never used to run away from man, were now hard to approach—except for Freyfaxi alone. He was as still as if he had taken root.

Einar realized that the morning was wearing on, and judged that Hrafnkel would not know even if he did ride the stallion. He now laid hold of him and bridled him, fixed the saddle-cloth under him on the horse's back, and rode up beside Grjotargil, so up to the glaciers and west alongside the glaciers where the river Jokulsa falls away, and so down along the river to Reykjasel. He asked all the shepherds at the Reykjasel shieling whether any of them had seen the sheep, but nobody could say that he had. Einar rode Freyfaxi from dawn right to mid-evening, the stallion covering a lot of ground with him in a short time, he was such a fine horse. It now occurred to Einar that it would be time for him to get back and drive in the sheep that were at home, even if he failed to find the others, so he rode east over the ridges into Hrafnkelsdal. As he came down to Grjotteig he heard the bleating of

[4]Summer shed.

sheep from higher up the very ravine he had ridden by before. He turned that way and saw thirty ewes running towards him, the very ones he had lost the week before, and he headed for home with the sheep.

The stallion was all running with sweat, so that it dripped from every hair he had. He was caked with mud and utterly spent. He went rolling over and over a dozen times, and after that set up a loud neighing; then away he went at a great gallop down along the pathway. Einar turned after him, meaning to head him off, catch him, and lead him back to his mares, but this time he was so shy that Einar could get nowhere near him. He went tearing down the valley without halt or pause till he reached Adalbol, where Hrafnkel was sitting at table. As soon as the horse came in front of the door he neighed shrilly. Hrafnkel spoke to a woman who was serving at table, telling her to go to the door—"Because a horse neighed, and it sounded to me like the neighing of Freyfaxi." She walked out into the doorway, where she saw Freyfaxi in sorry plight, and told Hrafnkel that it was indeed Freyfaxi outside the door, as filthy as could be.

"What can my brave lad want, that he has come home?" asked Hrafnkel. "This can bode no good."

With that he went outside and took a look at Freyfaxi. "I do not like it," he told him, "that they are treating you this way, foster-son, but you had your wits about you when you told me of it. It shall be avenged, so off with you to your stud!"

With no more ado he trotted back up the valley to his mares.

Hrafnkel went to bed that evening and slept through the night. In the morning he had his horse caught and saddled and rode up to the shieling. He rode in blue clothes, had an axe in his hand, but no further weapons.[5] Einar had just driven the sheep into the fold wall, counting the sheep, and the women were busy milking. They greeted Hrafnkel. He asked how they were getting on.

"I have had a bad time of it," confessed Einar, "for there were thirty sheep missing the best part of a week. They are found now though."

Hrafnkel said he had no quarrel with this or its like. "But has not something worse taken place? It has not happened as often as one would expect that the sheep have got lost, but did you not maybe ride my Freyfaxi yesterday?"

Einar said he could not deny it.

"But why did you ride this horse which was forbidden you, when there were any number of others at your disposal? I would have forgiven you a first offense, had I not sworn so great an oath in the matter. And yet you have owned up to it like a man."

But in the belief that nothing goes right for those men who draw down on themselves the curse for a broken oath, he dismounted, ran at him, and struck him his death-blow. After this he rode back to Adalbol without more ado, told his news, and later sent another man to the sheep at the shieling. He had Einar carried west from the shieling to the hillside, and raised a cairn there to mark his grave. The place is called Einarsvarda, and is mid-eve mark[6] from the shieling.

[5]Men wore blue clothes when they intended to kill someone. The axe is a battle-axe.

[6]"Mid-eve mark" means that the cairn is at a point where at "mid-eve" (about 6 P.M.) it is on a straight line between the sun and the shed.

Thorbjorn heard tell over at Holar of the killing of Einar his son, and took the news hard. He caught his horse, rode over to Adalbol, and asked Hrafnkel to make redress for killing his son.

Hrafnkel retorted that he had killed more men than this one. "And it can be no news to you that I am unwilling to make anyone reparation, and folk have to put up with it just the same. Even so, I admit that this deed of mine strikes me as among the very worst killings I have committed. You have been my neighbor a long while now, I have liked you, and each of us the other. No small matter would have made trouble between me and Einar, had he not ridden the stallion. Well, we must often regret opening our mouths too wide—and seldom repent speaking too little rather than too much. I am now going to make it clear that I regard this deed of mine as worse than anything else I have done. I shall provide your household with milk cows in summer and with meat in the autumn, and I shall do this for you season by season as long as you want to keep on your farm. Under my management your sons and daughters shall be taken off your hands, and so endowed that they can make good matches as a result; while anything at all you know to be in my possession that you have need of from now on, you must tell me and never again go short of whatever it is you need. You shall keep your farm as long as you please, but come here to me as soon as you grow tired of it, whereupon I will look after you to the day of your death; and we shall then be atoned. I shall expect this too, that most people are going to say the man was pretty dear."

"I'll not take this offer," said Thorbjorn.

"What do you want then?" Hrafnkel asked him.

"I want us to appoint men to arbitrate between us."

"Then you consider yourself my equal," replied Hrafnkel, "and we shall never be atoned on those terms."[7]

At this Thorbjorn rode away and down along Hrafnkelsdal until he reached Laugarhus and met Bjarni his brother, to whom he told his news, with a request that he should play some part in the affair. But Bjarni held that it was no fair match if Hrafnkel came into it. "For while we have lots of money we cannot possibly tackle Hrafnkel. It's a good saying too that a wise man knows his limits. He has tied up plenty in lawsuits who have more bone in their fists than we. As I see it, you behaved like a fool in refusing so good an offer. I want neither part nor parcel of it."

At this Thorbjorn spoke many bitter words to Bjarni his brother, maintaining that the more there lay at stake the more gutless he proved. Then he rode away, and they parted with little kindness. He made no stay till he came down to Leikskalar, where he knocked and they answered the door. Thorbjorn asked Sam to step outside. Sam had a warm welcome for his kinsman and invited him to put up there, an offer which Thorbjorn accepted without much eagerness. Sam could see that Thorbjorn was heavy-hearted; he asked what had happened, and Thorbjorn told him of the killing of Einar his son.

"It is no great news," commented Sam, "though Hrafnkel kills a man."

[7]Thorbjorn, as the relative of the murdered man, has three choices under Icelandic law. He can (1) avenge the murder directly; (2) accept compensation, arranged either directly or through arbitrators; or (3) bring a formal suit against Hrafnkel. Here he rejects Hrafnkel's liberal offer and demands arbitration. The arrogant Hrafnkel refuses, because arbitration would imply that the parties were equal.

Thorbjorn asked whether Sam was prepared to help him in any way. "The case stands thus, that though the dead man is closest to me, the blow has landed not so very far from you either."

"Have you by any chance tried for redress from Hrafnkel?" asked Sam.

Thorbjorn told him the whole truth, how things had gone between the two of them.

"I have never heard tell before," said Sam, "that Hrafnkel has made such offers to anyone as to you now. So I am prepared to ride with you up to Adalbol, and let us approach him humbly and see if he will stand by the same offer. He is sure to behave well one way or another."

"For one thing," answered Thorbjorn, "he will no longer be willing for it; and for another, it is no more to my liking now than when I rode away."

"It is heavy work," said Sam, "I fancy, to bring a lawsuit against Hrafnkel."

"You young men," scolded Thorbjorn, "you will never get anywhere, the way you make mountains out of molehills. I cannot believe anybody has such wretches for kinsmen as I. This strikes me as the height of meanness in a man like you, who consider yourself so smart at law and go falling over yourself in petty suits, but are unwilling to take on this case which is so glaringly clear. It will be a reproach to you, right enough, for you are the biggest boaster in the whole of our family. Well, I see now how the affair will turn out."

"What better off are you than before," asked Sam, "though I do take on the case, and we are both of us thrown out of court?"

"Just the same," said Thorbjorn, "It will be a great comfort to me if you take it on, come of it what may."

"I shall be going into this against my will," Sam warned him. "It is mainly for our kinship's sake that I am doing it. And you may as well know, I think I am helping a fool in helping you."

Then Sam reached out his hand and took over the case from Thorbjorn.

Next Sam had his horse caught and rode up along the valley to a farm where (he had already enlisted men for the purpose) he gave notice of the killing against Hrafnkel. This reached Hrafnkel's ears, and he thought it a great joke that Sam had started a lawsuit against him. The winter wore away, and in spring, when the summons-days came round, Sam rode from home up to Adalbol and summoned Hrafnkel for killing Einar. Afterwards Sam rode down through the valley and summoned the neighbors to ride to the Assembly, and thereafter kept quiet till men made ready for their journey there.[8]

At this point Hrafnkel sent down through the valley to summon his men together. He set off from his territory with seventy men. With this troop he rode east across Fljotsdalsheid, and so past the head of the lake, and across the pass to Skridudal, up along Skridudal and south to Oxarheid, to Berufjord, where he took the direct road of all riders to the Assembly to Sida. South from Fljotsdal it is a seventeen days' journey to the Assembly at Thingvellir.

Once he had ridden away from the district Sam assembled his men. For the most part he got masterless men to ride with him, in addition to those

[8]Icelandic law was largely taken over from Norway. In a case such as the one against Hrafnkel, the plaintiff had to give notice to the defendant and the witnesses by the "summons-days." The case was then presented before the Thing, the national assembly and court. Icelandic law, however, did not provide for enforcement; that is why Sam must give the summons himself and win the support of powerful chieftains for his case, as well as carry out the decision of the court if his suit is successful.

he had called up before. All these too he provided with weapons, clothes, and victuals. Sam left the valley by a different route, proceeding north to the rock-bridges, where he made his crossing, and from there over Modrudalsheid, to spend the night in Modrudal. From there they rode to Herdibreidstunga, and so inland of Blafjoll, on again to Kroksdal, and so south to Sprengisand, making down for Sandafell, and from there to Thingvellir, where Hrafnkel had not yet arrived. He was making slower time because he had the longer road. Sam pitched a booth for his men well away from where the Eastfirthers usually encamp, and somewhat later Hrafnkel reached the Assembly, to pitch his booth where he normally did. He heard that Sam was at the Assembly and thought the whole thing a great joke.

This Assembly was very crowded. Almost all the chieftains who were in Iceland were present there. Sam approached all these chieftains and asked them for help and assistance, but all answered the same way; not one of them could say he was under such obligation to Sam that he was prepared to get into a fight with Hrafnkel the Priest and so imperil his good name; they added further that it had gone one way for most of those who had dealings with Hrafnkel at the Assembly, in that he had driven everyone who had tackled him headlong from their lawsuits. Sam returned to his booth, and the kinsmen were heavy-hearted indeed, fearing that their case would so fall through that they would win nothing but shame and dishonor, and such great dismay filled uncle and nephew that they could neither eat nor sleep; for all the chieftains hung back from helping them, including those they had fully expected to lend them a hand.

4

Early one morning old Thorbjorn awoke. He roused Sam and told him to get up.

"I can't sleep."

Sam rose and got into his clothes. They went outside, down to the Oxara river below the bridge, where they washed themselves.

"It is my counsel," said Thorbjorn to Sam, "that you have our horses driven in, and let us make ready for home. It is clear by now that nothing lies ahead of us except humiliation."

"And fair enough too," replied Sam, "for you wanted nothing in the world except to fight this out with Hrafnkel, and were unwilling to accept an offer which so many would have been glad to accept who had to claim redress for a near kinsman. You cast a great slur on my courage and everybody else's who didn't want to get into this lawsuit with you, and now I will never give up till I think it beyond all hope that I get something or other to show for it."

At this Thorbjorn was so moved that he wept.

It was then that they saw how, a little lower down than where they were seated, five men came walking together from a booth and east towards the river. He was a tallish man, and very thickly built, who walked at their head, in a leaf-green kirtle[9] and with a mounted sword in his hand, his features regular, and his coloring ruddy, of distinguished appearance, and with a fine head of chestnut hair on him. He was a man easy to recognize, for he had a whitish lock of hair on the left side.

"Up we get," said Sam "and let us cross west of the river to meet these men."

[9]Tunic.

They walked down alongside the river, and this man who was walking in front got in first with a greeting. He asked who they might be, and they told him.

Sam asked the man his name. He said his name was Thorkel, adding that he was the son of Thjostar.

Sam asked what might his origins be, and where was his home.

He was a Westfirther, he said, by birth and descent, and had a home in Thorskafjord.

"Are you a man with a priesthood?" Sam asked him.

"Far from it," he replied.

"Are you a farmer then?"

No, he said, he was not.

"What sort of man are you then?"

"I am a footloose sort of man. I came out to Iceland last winter. I have spent seven years abroad, and went out to Constantinople, where I became a liegeman of the emperor; but at the moment I am lodging with a brother of mine named Thorgeir."

"Is he a man with a priesthood?" asked Sam.

"To be sure he is, with a priesthood the length and breadth of Thorskafjord, and wider still throughout the Westfirths."

"Is he here at the Assembly?" asked Sam.

"To be sure he is."

"And how is he off for men?"

"He has seventy," said Thorkel.

"Have you any more brothers?" asked Sam.

"There is a third," Thorkel admitted.

"And who is he?"

"His name is Thormod. He lives at Gardar on Alptanes. He married Thordis, Thorolf Skallagrimsson's daughter, from Borg."

"Would you care to lend us a hand?" asked Sam.

"Why, what do you need?"

"The help and strength of chieftains," replied Sam, "for we have a lawsuit to thrash out with Hrafnkel the Priest for the killing of Einar Thorbjorn's son. And we could safely trust to our pleading with support from you."

"It's as I said," Thorkel pointed out. "I hold no priesthood."

"But why are you pushed aside so," demanded Sam, "since you are as much a chieftain's son as your brothers are?"

"I did not tell you," said Thorkel, "that I had no stake in such, but I handed over my authority to Thorgeir my brother before I went abroad. Nor have I taken it back since, for it strikes me as being in very good keeping however long he looks after it. Go and have a word with him, and ask him to help you. He is a man in a thousand, a splendid fellow and in every respect outstanding, youngish still and eager to distinguish himself. In short, the likeliest kind of man to lend you a hand."

"We shall get nothing out of him," said Sam, "unless you put in a word for us."

"I will promise this much," said Thorkel, "to be for you rather than against, for it seems to me a man's plain duty to take up the bloodsuit for his close kinsman. Now get along to the booth, and make your way inside. The men are still asleep there. You will see where two hammocks extend across the innermost side of the booth. I got up from one of them, and in the other Thorgeir my brother lies resting. He has had a big boil on his foot ever since he came to the Assembly, and as a result has had little sleep of nights, but last night the foot broke and the core is out of the boil. He has been sleeping since, and has stuck his foot out from under the bedclothes on to the foot-board, because of the excessive heat which is in the foot. Let the old man lead the way on into the booth. He seems to me very infirm both in sight and years. And, friend," Thorkel went on, "when you reach the hammock, you must stumble heavily, and fall on to the foot-board, catch hold of the toe which is tied up, wrench it towards you—and find out how he takes it."

"You are going to be a great help to us," said Sam, "but this does not sound a good plan to me."

"You can do one or the other," replied Thorkel. "do as I suggest or seek no advice of mine."

"Then what he advises," announced Sam, "shall be done."

Thorkel said he would be coming along later. "For I am waiting for my men."

So now Sam and Thorbjorn set off and arrived inside the booth. All the men there were asleep. They soon saw where Thorgeir was lying. Old Thorbjorn went in front, stumbling awkwardly, and when he reached the hammock he went sprawling on to the foot-board, grabbed at the afflicted toe, and wrenched it towards him. This roused Thorgeir, who shot up in bed, demanding to know who could be dashing about the place so headlong as to go falling over people's feet, which were bad enough before. But Sam and Thorbjorn had nothing really to say for themselves.

Then Thorkel stepped briskly into the booth to speak to Thorgeir his brother. "Don't be in such a flurry and panic over this, brother. It won't hurt you. Many a man acts worse than he intends, and it happens every day that a man cannot attend with equal care to everything when he had a great deal on his mind. Yet it is your excuse, kinsman, that your foot is painful, and, indeed, has suffered great affliction; and you yourself will be the one to feel it most. Now it may also be the case that to this old man his son's death is no less painful, yet he can obtain no cure or redress, and nothing goes right for him. He will be the one to feel this most, and it is only to be expected that a man with so much on his mind will not pay due heed to everything."

"I had no idea he could quarrel with me over it," Thorgeir retorted. "For I didn't kill his son, and by the same token he cannot avenge it on me."

"He didn't mean to avenge it on you," said Thorkel. "He came at you harder than he intended, and paid the penalty for his failing sight. In fact he was looking for some help from you, and what a fine thing it would be now to help a man so old and needy! For this is duty in him, not greed, when he takes up the bloodsuit after his son. But now the chieftains hang back from helping these men, and in so doing show great cowardice."

"Whom are they accusing, these men?" Thorgeir asked.

"Hrafnkel the Priest has killed Thorbjorn's son without cause," explained Thorkel. "He commits crime after crime, and will pay recompense to nobody."

"I must stand with the rest," said Thorgeir. "I do not find myself so obligated to these men that I want a fight with Hrafnkel on my hands. It seems to me he sets to work in such a way every summer against those men who have lawsuits to settle with him that most of them win little or no honor before it ends, and as I see it, it goes one and the same way with the lot of them. That, I fancy, is why most men who have no duty in that matter feel no desire to meddle with it."

"It may be," Thorkel replied, "that if I were a chieftain myself I should act the same way, and think it a bad business to clash with Hrafnkel. But the way things are, I just do not see it in that light, for I should think it best to pit myself against the very man from whom all took a tumble before; and I believe that mine or any other chieftain's fame would increase greatly who could out-row Hrafnkel, yet now grow less though I went the same road as the others, because what happens to the rest can happen to me, and, 'Nothing venture, nothing gain.'"

"I see how you are inclined," said Thorgeir. "You would like to help these men. I am now going to hand over to you my priesthood and authority; you hold it on just such terms as I have held it before, and from there on let us share it equally—and then you help anybody you want to."

"It appears to me," said Thorkel, "that our priesthood is in the safest keeping the longer you hold on to it. I should not care for anyone to hold it as I do you, for you have many talents beyond all us brothers. Nor am I just now settled what I intend to do with myself. Besides you know, kinsman, how I have kept very much to myself since I came to Iceland. However, I can see now what my advice is worth. I have pleaded as much as I will for the present. Maybe Thorkel Lock will come where his word has more weight!"

"I see now the way the wind blows, brother," replied Thorgeir. "You are offended, and I cannot have that, so we will help these men, come of it what may, if you want to."

"I ask only such things," said Thorkel, "as I think will be better granted."

"What do these two reckon themselves capable of," asked Thorgeir, "so that their case may have a happy ending?"

"Even as I said today" (this was Sam speaking), "our need is for the strength of chieftains, but I can manage the pleading of the suit myself."

Thorgeir told him that in that case he was easy to help. "And what is now necessary is to prepare the case as accurately as can be. I fancy too that Thorkel would like you to let him know before the courts go into procession. You will then get some return for your pains, some comfort or shame even greater than before, and anguish and humiliation. Now, go home and be cheerful, for if you are proposing to tackle Hrafnkel the Priest you need to bear up well in the meantime. But let no one know we have promised you aid."

They now returned to their booth and were in high spirits. Everyone was astonished at this, why they had so quickly changed their mood, for they were quite downcast when they left their booth.

They waited there till the courts went into procession, when Sam called out his men and marched to the Lawhill, where the court was by this time in session. Sam went boldly into court, at once began naming his witnesses, and presented his case against Hrafnkel the Priest according to the true law of the land, without error and with distinguished pleading. Hot on his heels came the sons of Thjostar with a strong force of men. Everybody from the west country stood behind them, and it was clear that the sons of Thjostar were well off for friends. Sam prosecuted his case in court to the point where Hrafnkel was called on for the defense, unless some man was present there who desired to put forward a defense on his behalf. There was loud applause for Sam's case, and no one offered to produce any legal defense for Hrafnkel. Men ran to his booth to tell him what was happening. He was quickly on the move, collected his men, and marched towards the court, expecting to find the coast all clear. It was his intention to give such small fry their bellyful of bringing lawsuits against him: he meant to wreck the court for Sam and drive him from his case. But by now there was no chance of this. There was such a press of men in front of him that he could get nowhere near the place. He was crowded away by sheer force, so that he might not hear his prosecutor's case, which made it rather a problem for him to bring forward his defense. So Sam drove his suit to the full limit of the law, till Hrafnkel was declared an outlaw at this Assembly.

5

Hrafnkel returned to his booth at once, had his horses caught, and rode away from the Assembly, profoundly dissatisfied with his end of the case, for nothing of the kind had ever happened to him before. He rode east to Lyngdalsheid, and so eastwards to Sida, and made no stay till he arrived in Hrafnkelsdal and settled in at Adalbol, where he acted as though nothing had happened. But Sam stayed on at the Assembly, strutting about with his tail up. A lot of people were well pleased that it had turned out this way, that Hrafnkel had suffered this blow to his self-esteem; and they now called to mind how he had shown injustice to many.

Sam waited till the Assembly was dissolved and men made ready for home. He thanked the brothers for all they had done, and Thorgeir, laughing, asked Sam how he thought things were going.

It had gone off very well, he maintained.

"You think yourself any better off now than before?" asked Thorgeir.

"I think Hrafnkel has suffered a humiliation which will be remembered for a long time," replied Sam, "and that is worth a lot of money."

"The man is not outlawed so long as the court of execution[10] is not held," quoted Thorgeir, "and that must needs be done at his own domicile, and take place fourteen nights after the weapontake." They call it the weapontake, or recovery of weapons, when the gathering rides from the Assembly. "Now it is my guess," Thorgeir went on, "that Hrafnkel will have arrived home, intending to sit firm in the saddle at Adalbol. It is my further guess that, for anything you can do, he will maintain his position there. So you will be reckoning to ride home and at best remain on your farm—always supposing you can manage it. I guess you have this much from your lawsuit that you can call him a forest outlaw, but he will hold the same old helm of terror over most as before, with the exception (so I guess) that you must needs crawl somewhat lower."

"I have never been frightened of that," said Sam.

"You are a bold fellow," Thorgeir assured him, "but I fancy brother Thorkel is not thinking to leave you in the lurch. He now wants to go on backing you till all is concluded between you and Hrafnkel, and you can rest easy. You must feel that we are bound to stand by you, for we have taken the biggest part in this so far, so we are going to help you this once in the Eastfirths. Do you know any road to the Eastfirths which is not a frequented way?"

Sam said he would follow the same route he had travelled from the east, and was all cock-a-hoop[11] at this.

[10]The "court of execution" was the ceremony carrying out the decision of the court.
[11]Delighted.

Thorgeir picked his following and had forty men ride with him. Sam too had forty men, and the entire company was well equipped with weapons and horses.

After this they all followed the same route till they reached Jokulsdal just before dawn. They crossed the river at the bridge; and it was the very morning they had to hold the court of execution. Thorgeir asked how they might best take them by surprise. Sam reckoned he would know a plan for this, and without more ado turned from the path up to the bluff, and so along the ridge between Hrafnkelsdal and Jokulsdal, till they came out from under the mountain beneath which stands the farmstead at Adalbol. Grassy clefts ran up on to the heath there, and there was a steep slope down to the valley, and there below stood the farmstead.

Here Sam dismounted. "Let us leave our horses here, with twenty men to watch them," he suggested, "and the other sixty of us will make a dash for the farm. I feel sure there will be few up and doing there."

They did this, and the place has been called Hrossageilar, Horselanes, ever since. They raced swiftly for the farmstead. The hour for rising was past, but the people had not got up. They dashed a beam against the door and rushed inside. Hrafnkel was lying in his bed. They dragged him out of it, together with every man of his household who could use arms. The women and children were driven into a building on their own. In the home-field stood a storehouse, and from this back to the wall of the main building there extended a beam for the washing. They led Hrafnkel that way along with his men. He made many offers for himself and his followers, and when these served no purpose pleaded for the lives of his men.

"For they have done nothing to offend against you, while it is no discredit to me though you kill me. I am not asking to be spared that, but I do ask to be spared humiliation. There is no credit to you in that."

"We have heard tell," said Thorkel, "that you have proved hardmouthed in harness for your enemies. It is just as well that you are today made to feel this in your turn."

They laid hold of Hrafnkel and his men and tied their hands behind their backs. After that they broke into a storehouse and took a rope down off the hooks. They next took their knives and pierced holes through their hough sinews,[12] threaded the rope through, swung them up so over the beam, and secured them so, eight together.

"So it has come to this, Hrafnkel," said Thorgeir, "that you have got your deserts at last. And how unlikely you must have thought it that you would come by such shame at anyone's hands as is now the case. Which will you do now, Thorkel: stay here with Hrafnkel and keep an eye on them, or will you go with Sam away out of the yard, yet within arrow-shot of the house, and hold the court of execution on some rocky mound where there is neither meadow nor furrow?"

This should be done at the time when the sun is full south.

"I'll stay here with Hrafnkel," replied Thorkel. "That looks to me the less bothersome."

Thorgeir and Sam then went and held the court of execution, after which they walked back, took down Hrafnkel and his men, and laid them out in the home-field. By this time the blood had started into their eyes.

[12]The Achilles tendons in their heels.

Thorgeir told Sam that he could do just as he pleased with Hrafnkel. "He seems to me to present no problem now."

"I am offering you a choice of two things, Hrafnkel," said Sam to that. "One is that you shall be led away from the house with such men as I please and be killed. However, because you have so many dependent on you, I am prepared to let you go on looking after them. But if you choose to live, then leave Adalbol with all your household, and have only those assets I assign you—which will be precious little. For I shall take over this homestead and all your authority too. You shall never lay claim to these, you nor your heirs; nor shall you ever again live nearer than east of Fljotsdalsheid. You can now strike hands on our bargain, if you can bring yourself to accept it."

"To many," said Hrafnkel, "a quick death would seem better than such disgrace. But I shall take the same course as most others: my choice is life, if choice there be. I do it mainly for my sons' sake, for theirs is a poor prospect if I die and leave them."

Hrafnkel was then loosed, and he gave Sam the right to make his own award. He allotted Hrafnkel such goods as he pleased, and this was painfully little. Hrafnkel had his spear with him but no further weapon. That same day Hrafnkel took himself off from Adalbol, and all his people with him.

"I cannot think why you are doing this," Thorgeir told Sam. "You will live to regret it more than anyone that you are giving Hrafnkel his life."

That was how it would have to be then, said Sam.

Hrafnkel now removed to a home east of Fljotsdalsheid and across Fljotsdal to eastwards of Lagarfljot. At the end of the lake stood a little farm, Likhilla by name, where he bought land on credit, for he had no money beyond what he needed for his farm things. There was a lot of talk about this, how his haughtiness had been humbled, and there were many to call to mind the old proverb—"Pride goes before a fall." This was fine, extensive forest-land, but sadly off for buildings, and that was why he bought the land cheap. Hrafnkel spared no expense; he felled the timber because it was big, and raised a stately farm there which has ever since been called Hrafnkelsstadir, and from that day to this reputed a good farm. He lived there in great hardship that first winter. He had a lavish yield from the fisheries. He went hard at work while the farm was building. That first year he kept calf and kid for feeding through the winter, and all the animals he took that risk with he looked after so well that nearly all of them lived; so that it could just about be said that there were two heads to each of his beasts. That same summer there was a big run of fish in Lagarfljot, which proved a great help towards housekeeping in the district, and that held good every summer.

6

Sam started housekeeping at Adalbol after Hrafnkel, and later held a splendid feast, to which he invited all those who had been retainers of Hrafnkel, offering himself to be their leader in his place. They agreed to this, but were not without misgivings all the same.

The sons of Thjostar advised him to be cheerful, liberal, and kindly to his men, a helper to everyone who had need of him. "Then they are no men if they do not stand firmly by you, whatever your need. We give you this advice because we would like you to make a success of things, for we take you to be a gallant sort of fellow. Now, keep your eyes open and look out for yourself, for 'It is warm work watching out for the wicked.'"

The sons of Thjostar sent after Freyfaxi and his stud, saying that they wanted to see these precious creatures about whom there had been such great tales told. The horses were fetched in and the brothers looked them over.

"These mares appear to me useful for farmwork," said Thorgeir. "It is my advice that they perform such useful tasks as they may, till they can no longer keep going for old age. As for the stallion, he strikes me as no better than other stallions—indeed, rather worse, in that so much evil has come about because of him. I have no desire that further killings come about through him than have arisen already. It is only right that he who owns him should now take him."

They led the stallion down along the level ground. A crag stands below by the river, and underneath it a deep pool. They led the stallion out on to the crag there. The sons of Thjostar drew a bag over his head, tied a stone round his neck, then took long poles and pushed the horse over the edge, so making an end of him. Since then the place has been known as Freyfaxahamar.

Lower down stood the temple which had belonged to Hrafnkel. Thorkel wanted to have a look at it. He had all the gods plundered, and then set fire to the temple, and burnt the whole lot together. Later the guests made ready to leave. Sam chose splendid treasures by way of gifts for both the brothers. They vowed everlasting friendship between them and parted on the most cordial terms. They rode the quickest road west to the Firths and came home to Thorskafjord with honor. Sam established old Thorbjorn at Leikskalar (he was to live there), but Sam's wife went to live with him at Adalbol, and Sam dwelt there for a while.

7

East in Fljotsdal Hrafnkel heard how the sons of Thjostar had destroyed Freyfaxi and burnt the temple. "I think it folly," he said, "to believe in gods," and announced that from then on he never would believe in gods, and he kept to what he said, so that he never again offered up a sacrifice.

Hrafnkel sat tight at Hrafnkelsstadir and raked money together. He quickly won great honor in the district, and everyone showed willingness to sit or stand as he decided for them. At this time ship after ship came sailing from Norway to Iceland (most of the land in the district was settled in Hrafnkel's day), but no one was allowed to settle there in peace unless he asked Hrafnkel's permission. They all had to promise him their backing, and he promised his support in return. He brought under his authority the whole countryside east of Lagarfljot. This territory was soon much bigger and better blessed with men than the one he had ruled before, reaching up around Skridudal, and the whole way along Lagarfljot. And now a change had come over his temper. He was much more popular than before. He had the same mind to be helpful and hospitable, but was now altogether more reasonable than before and gentler in every way. Sam and Hrafnkel often met at various gatherings, but they never made mention of their dealings together. In this fashion six years went by. Sam was well liked by his followers, for he was quiet and easy-going and always ready to help in time of trouble, and bore in mind what those brothers had advised him. Sam was a great man for show.

8

The story goes on to tell how a ship put into Reydarfjord from the open sea whose skipper was Eyvind Bjarnason. He had been abroad for seven years. Eyvind was a much improved man in style and breeding, and had grown into the gallantest person. He was soon informed of what had happened, but he made little or no comment on it. He was a rather reserved sort of man.

As soon as Sam heard the news he rode to the ship, and there was now a great and joyful meeting between the brothers. Sam invited him home out west, and Eyvind accepted eagerly, requesting Sam to ride on home and send horses for his cargo, while he hauled his ship ashore and made it ready for the winter. Sam did as he was asked, went home, and had horses driven to meet Eyvind; and once Eyvind had made arrangements about his cargo he made ready for his journey to Hrafnkelsdal and started up along Reydarfjord. There were five men in the party. The sixth was Eyvind's servant lad, an Icelander by birth, and related to him. Eyvind had plucked this lad from destitution, and carried him abroad with him, and looked after him as himself. This deed of his had become quite famous, and it was the general opinion that there were few to equal him.

They now rode up Thorisdalsheid and were driving sixteen packhorses in front of them. There were two of Sam's housecarles[13] there and three sailors. They were all dressed in colored clothes and rode with gay shields. They rode across Skirdudal and over the ridge of Fljotsdal, at a place called Bulungarvellir, then down to Gilsareyr, where the gravel bank runs west to the river between Hallormsstadir and Hrafnkelsstadir. Then they rode up along Lagarfljot, below the meadow at Hrafnkelsstadir, so past the head of the lake, and forded the Jokulsa at Skalavad. The time was about 7:30 in the morning.

There was a woman by the lake doing her day's wash, and she saw the men passing. The servant woman swept her linen together and ran home, where she flung it down outside near the woodpile and went scurrying indoors. Hrafnkel had not yet got up. Some of the more favored men were lying about the hall, but the workmen had departed about their tasks. It was haymaking time.

The woman burst into speech the moment she came inside. "Aye, true it is," she cried, "that old proverb—'Grow old and grow afraid.' Small grows that honor which is acquired early, if later a man grows shamefully slack and wants for courage ever to exact his dues—and such is very strange in a man who in his day showed spirit. How different is their way of life who grow up in their fathers' homes and seem to you mere nobodies compared with yourselves; but no sooner are they out of their childhood than they go travelling from land to land and are thought of great weight wherever they come, and so they return home again, counting themselves greater than chieftains. Eyvind Bjarnason has just ridden through the river here at Skalavad with so gay a shield that the light came sparkling off it. He is a good enough man to reap a good vengeance on."

The servant woman really let herself go. Hrafnkel got up and gave her this answer. "No doubt you are babbling what is only too true, yet not out of any good will either. It is just as well then for you to bear some of the load. Hurry south to Vidivellir for Sighvat and Snorri, the sons of Hallstein. Tell them to come to me instantly with any men there who can use arms."

He sent a second woman servant out to Hrolfsstadir for Thord and Halli,

[13]Personal servants.

the sons of Hrolf, and any there who could use arms. Both sets of brothers were able and worthy men. Hrafnkel also sent after his housecarles, so that they were eighteen all told. They took up their weapons in earnest, and rode through the river as the others had done before.

By now Eyvind and his men had got up on to the heath. He kept riding west till he reached Bersagotur in the middle of the heath. There is a turfless swamp there—it is like riding through nothing but ooze, and one is sinking all the time to the knee or thigh, and on occasion to the horse's belly, while below the surface it is as hard as a slab of rock. Next comes a great waste of stony ground to the west of it, and as they reached this waste the boy looked back and said to Eyvind: "There are men riding after us, no fewer than eighteen of them, with a big man riding in blue clothes. He looks to me like Hrafnkel the Priest, though it is a long time since last I saw him."

"What business is that of ours?" replied Eyvind. "I cannot imagine I have anything to fear from a gallop of Hrafnkel's. I have done nothing against him. He must have an errand west to the Dale to meet his friends."

"I have a feeling it is you he wants to meet," the lad replied.

"I am not aware," said Eyvind, "that anything has happened between him and Sam my brother since they came to terms."

"I should like you to ride off west to the Dale," replied the lad. "Then you will be safe. I know Hrafnkel's temper, how he will do nothing to us if he fails to get at you. Everything is taken care of so long as you are all right. The game is not in the toils then, so all is well, whatever happens to us."

Eyvind said he would not ride off quite so fast. "I don't know who they are, and there would be plenty to laugh at me if I took to my heels with nothing proved."

They now rode west from the stony ground. Ahead of them lay a second swamp, called Oxamyr. This one is very grassy. There are soft patches, so that it is wellnigh impassable, which was why old Hallfred established the higher way round, even though it proved longer.

Eyvind now rode west into the swamp. Their horses sank deep into the mire and they were seriously delayed. The others, who rode unhampered, were overhauling them fast. Hrafnkel and his men were now riding up to the swamp while Eyvind's company were just coming out of it. They recognized Hrafnkel and both his sons, and begged Eyvind to make his escape.

"All the bad places are now past. You will get to Adalbol while the swamp stands between you."

"I'll not run from men to whom I have done no wrong," replied Eyvind.

They then rode up on to the ridge. Hillocks stand on the ridge, and on the slope of the mountain is a turf knoll much denuded by the wind, with high banks surrounding it. Eyvind rode to this knoll, where he dismounted and awaited them.

"We shall soon know their errand now," said Eyvind.

After that they climbed up on to the knoll and tore up some stones for missiles.

At the same time Hrafnkel turned from the path and south to the knoll. He had never a word for Eyvind, but instantly made the assault. Eyvind defended himself skillfully and like a brave man. Eyvind's lad judged himself not strong enough for the fray, got hold of his horse and rode westward over the ridge to Adalbol to tell Sam what game was afoot. Sam moved quickly and sent for his men. They were twenty all told, and a well-equipped company, and with these he rode east to the heath to the scene of action. But by this time the battle was over. Hrafnkel was riding eastward from his work, while Eyvind had fallen and all his men with him. The first thing Sam did was to look for life in his brother, but the job had been thoroughly done: they were all dead, the five of them together. Twelve of Hrafnkel's men had fallen too, and six were riding away.

Sam made short stay there, but bade his men instantly give chase. They rode off after them, but their horses were flagging.

"We may be able to catch them," said Sam, "for their horses are tired, while ours are all fresh. Still, it will be a close thing whether we catch them or not before they get down off the heath."

Hrafnkel had by now put himself east of Oxamyr. Pursued and pursuers kept riding till Sam reached the brow of the heath, where he saw how Hrafnkel had come a long way down the slope. He saw too that he would escape away down into his own territory.

"This is where we turn back," he told his men. "It will be easy now for Hrafnkel to collect all the men he wants."

So Sam turned back with that for his pains. He came to where Eyvind was lying, and threw up a mound over him and his mates. The place-names there are now Eyvindartorfa, Eyvindarfjoll, and Eyvindardal.

Then Sam returned to Adalbol with all Eyvind's goods. When he reached home he sent word to his retainers that they should muster there in the morning before breakfast. He had made up his mind to ride east over the heath—"Be our outing as it may," said he. In the evening he went to bed, and a lot of men had gathered there.

9

Hrafnkel rode home and told what had happened. He ate his food and after that gathered a force together, so that he set out with seventy men, and riding with that band westward over the heath, came unawares to Adalbol, seized Sam in his bed, and led him out.

"Now, Sam," said Hrafnkel, "your plight has become such as must have seemed unlikely to you even a short while since, in that I have your life in my hands. I must not now prove a worse fellow to you than you were to me, so I am giving you your choice of two things: to be killed, or the other, that I alone shall shear and shape[14] between us."

Sam said he would rather choose to live, adding that he thought even so either way would be hard.

Hrafnkel said he could expect that. "For we have that to repay you; whereas I would have treated you twice as well, had you deserved it. You shall move away from Adalbol down to Leikskalar and settle there on your own farm. You shall take with you the goods that Eyvind owned. But you shall not carry away any more in the way of property than what you brought here—all that, though, you shall carry away in full. I shall take back my priesthood, the farm, and homestead likewise. I see that there has been a big increase in my holdings, but you shall not benefit by that. No payment shall be made for Eyvind your brother, because you followed up the bloodsuit too ruthlessly for your former kinsman; while for your kinsman Einar you have had redress enough in that you have enjoyed power and wealth these six winters. Not that, in

[14]A proverbial term meaning "settle everything."

any case, I consider the killing of Eyvind and his comrades worth more than the maiming of me and my men. You made me a fugitive from my own country-side, but I am content for you to remain at Leikskalar. At the same time it will prove as well for you if you do not puff yourself up to your own hurt. You shall stay my underling as long as we live; and you can count on this too, that the worse we get on together, the worse you will find things."

Sam now went away with his household down to Leikskalar, and there he stayed, on his farm.

10

Hrafnkel organized the household at Adalbol with his men, and put his son Thorir in charge at Hrafnkelsstadir. He now held the priesthood over the entire country-side. Asbjorn stayed with his father, because he was the younger son.

Sam remained at Leikskalar that winter. He was taciturn and kept much to himself, and it was obvious to many that he was disgruntled with his lot. But the winter over, once the days grew longer, Sam with one other man and three horses set out over the bridge, and from there across Modrudalsheid, so over the Jokulsa river (the one up on the mountain), and on to Myvatn, and from there over Fljotsheid and Ljosavatnsskard, making no real break in his journey till he arrived west in Thorskafjord, where he was made most welcome. Thorkel had just got home after a sea-voyage, and had been abroad for four years. Sam spent a week there, resting himself, and then he told them what had now happened between him and Hrafnkel, and asked the brothers for help and backing this time as before.

Thorgeir did more of the answering for the brothers this time. He would be keeping out of it, he said. "There is a great distance between us. We thought we had put things right for you before we came away, so that it would be easy for you to hold on to; but things have turned out as I felt sure they would when you gave Hrafnkel his life, that you would live to regret it most. We begged you to take his life, but, no, you had to have your own way. And how obvious it has become what a difference of judgment lay between you, when he let you live in peace and made his attack only when he had removed from his path him who, in his opinion, was a better man than you. We cannot burden ourselves with this lucklessness of yours, nor have we such great eagerness to quarrel with Hrafnkel that we feel tempted to endanger our good name all over again. But we should like to invite you here in under our lee with all your household, if you consider it less galling here than alongside Hrafnkel."

Sam said he had no wish for that. He told them he wanted to get back home, and asked them to change horses with him, a thing that was quickly put right. The brothers wanted to give him fine gifts, but he would accept nothing, arguing that it would show a mean spirit. With so much for his pains Sam rode back home, and there he remained till old age. He never achieved anything against Hrafnkel to the end of his days.

But Hrafnkel lived on his farm and kept his honors. He died of a sickness, and his burial mound stands in Hrafnkelsdal, down the valley from Adalbol. Great riches were laid in the mound alongside him, all his armor and that good spear of his. His sons succeeded to his authority, Thorir living at Hrafnkelsstadir and Asbjorn at Adalbol. They shared the priesthood between them, and were reckoned very able men.

And that is the end of Hrafnkel's Saga.

Marie de France

(Late Twelfth Century)

"The first woman novelist of our era"; that is the contemporary novelist John Fowles's description of Marie de France. The phrase is deliberately playful and paradoxical, especially in calling the author of twelve very brief verse romances a "novelist." Yet it is precise; Marie's gifts are those of a fiction writer rather than a poet. She excels in storytelling: in shaping often simple, apparently naive stories so as to make them powerfully evocative and anything but naive. Her characters are memorable, lightly sketched and yet psychologically convincing, even when they are engaged in fabulous actions. And she creates a highly distinctive fictional world, an imaginative "Brittany" that is simultaneously the world of fairy tales and a dreamlike version of her own courtly circle. Fowles's emphasis upon her femininity seems right, too. Marie works on a small scale—Fowles calls her "a laborer on two inches of ivory"—but within her miniature would she has a feminine eye for the nuances and often the absurdities of human emotions. After eight centuries, we can still recognize Marie's charming fictions as belonging to "our era."

The historical Marie is a shadowy figure. She is thought to be the author of three surviving works, the *Lais*, a collection of *Fables*, and a didactic, supernatural tale called *St. Patrick's Purgatory*. All three date from the second half of the twelfth century, and all three contain statements that they were written by someone named "Marie." At the end of the *Fables*, she also gives her nationality: "I'll give my name, for memory: / I am from France, my name's Marie." She also tells us in a Prologue to the *Lais* that she wrote them for a "noble king." Scholars have concluded that Marie must have been born in France but at some point went to England and wrote for the English court, heavily French in the years following the Norman Conquest. The noble king is probably Henry II, whose queen was Eleanor of Aquitaine, a sophisticated patron of literature. It is even possible that Marie was Henry II's half-sister. Henry's father, Geoffrey Plantagenet, had an illegitimate daughter named Marie, who became abbess of Shaftesbury about 1180, and some scholars have identified her with the evidently well-educated, apparently highly placed Frenchwoman who wrote under the name "Marie de France."

Whoever Marie was, her work is one of the finest literary expressions of the twelfth-century renaissance in European culture that marked the end of the so-called "dark ages." The preoccupation with military prowess that marked earlier medieval narrative gave way to an overwhelming interest in love as a literary subject, as the new class of courtly aristocrats who clustered around the great courts of England and France sought to define and mythologize their class values. Ovid's *Metamorphoses* and especially his *Art of Love* and *Remedy for Love* were translated and endlessly studied as a guide to the psychology of refined love. Classical stories were translated and adapted to emphasize their romantic elements, as in the *Romance of Aeneas* and the *Romance of Thebes*. Legendary histories such as William of Malmesbury's *Deeds of the English Kings* (about 1125) and Geoffrey of Monmouth's *History of the Kings of Britain* (about 1135) introduced Arthurian material soon to be worked into romances. During Marie's lifetime, Chrétien de Troyes, across the Channel, wrote the first account of the love of Lancelot and Guinevere.

Marie's special interest, in the *Lais*, was the "matter of Britain," Celtic or "Breton" stories. At the beginning of the first of the twelve *Lais*, "Guigemar," she writes, "The tales—and I know they're true— / from which the Bretons made their *lais* / I'll now recount for you briefly," and repeatedly through the collection, she refers to her "Breton" sources. Many of the stories do seem to be from Celtic folklore, but Marie perhaps reset even those from written French sources in a fairy-tale-like Wales or Brittany as a result of a literary vogue for Celtic material.

A certain amount of controversy centers around Marie's conception of a *lai*. Generally speaking, it is a short romance in rhyme that fuses supernatural elements, a fairy-tale "Celtic" setting, and a treatment of courtly love, originally performed by Breton minstrels to the accompaniment of a harp or a kind of lyre called a *rote*. Sometimes, Marie seems to use the term to refer to her sources, as in the prologue to "Guigemar"; at other times, she seems to use it to refer to her own work (although we are not sure that she gave her collection the title that the manuscript bears). Perhaps it is best to think of her poems as "literary *lais*," sophisticated adaptations of folk *lais*, probably intended to be read rather than chanted or sung.

Marie's twelve *lais* are enormously varied in length, form, and subject matter. But all of them center around the subject of love, like an elaborate set of variations on a single theme. The variations are so great that it is difficult to generalize about her view of love. It is remarkably open-minded; adulterous love is not ruled out, though generally she celebrates the possibilities for happiness within a loving marriage. She also celebrates sensuality, though she emphasizes the necessity for spiritual and emotional union as well. There is often tension in the *lais* between private ecstasy and public acknowledgment of love; love cannot survive the claustrophobia of secrecy and yet the world is often ranged against lovers who seek the endorsement of society. A recurring theme is what Marie calls *desmesure*, the passionate excess or loss of restraint characteristic of genuine love. This excess is one of the glories of love, but it carries within it the chief threat to continued love. Over and over in the stories, disaster ensues when one or the other of the lovers gives way to *desmesure* and oversteps the bounds of discretion and restraint.

The twelve stories in the *Lais* are so intricately interconnected by parallels, balances, and echoes that only a reading of the entire collection can convey the full range of Marie's variations on her theme. But *Bisclavret* and *Yonec* make a good pairing, partly because the first shows a false, disloyal love that is ultimately punished, while the other presents a genuine love that is ended by violence but is finally vindicated. Ironically, the false love is within marriage, the true one outside it. The two *lais* present a sharp contrast structurally as well. *Bisclavret*, like many of Marie's shorter *lais*, is centered around a single climactic scene, with the earlier part of the poem devoted to preparing for that scene. *Yonec*, on the other hand, covers a long span of time, with the emphasis upon the earlier scenes and the final scene only a sort of coda to the main action. Both illustrate Marie's fondness for organizing her work around a central symbolic creature or object that suggests the nature of the love and its moral problems. Marie takes the primitive figures of the werewolf in *Bisclavret* and turns it into an ironic and suggestive symbol of the central theme of the story, the conflict of bestiality and civilization in human nature. The bird-lover of *Yonec* is similarly suggestive as a representation of the story's themes of imprisonment and freedom, a symbol of love's power to enable us to liberate ourselves.

Nowadays, we think of Marie primarily as the author of the *Lais.* In her own day, she was probably better known for the *Fables*; only five manuscripts of the *Lais* survive, as opposed to twenty-three of the *Fables.* Scholars believe (admittedly on very flimsy evidence) that Marie wrote the *Lais* first (around 1155–1160), then the *Fables,* and finally *St. Patrick's Purgatory,* thus moving from tales of love and romance to tales of social and political satire and then to religious matters. However this may be, it is certainly true that the thematic emphasis shifts in the *Fables.* Love and romance are seldom mentioned (although there is some mild satire on marriage); instead, Marie is primarily concerned in the *Fables* in the workings of society as a whole and especially in the nature of good and bad governments.

The question of the originality of the *Fables* is a matter of some debate. They are often referred to as a "translation." Marie herself in her prologue and epilogue says that she is responding to the request of a noble lord named "Count William" that she translate Aesop, and references to "the book," an English translation of Aesop by King Alfred the Great from which she is taking her stories, are scattered through the collection. On the other hand, of her one hundred and three fables, only the first forty can be found in Aesopian collections; the other sixty-three either derive from sources now lost or are her own original contributions to the fable genre. We can perhaps take her insistence that she is merely translating with a grain of salt; citing sources and authorities was a familiar ploy for medieval writers.

Whether translated or original, Marie's fables are quite different from classical Aesopian fables. The classical fables, for the most part, present a Hobbsian world of naked power in which wolves always eat sheep. Marie's fable-world is far more complex. In effect, she "medievalizes" the Aesopian fables. The bestial and the predatory are still there, but so is the possibility of an orderly society in which both rulers and ruled abide by their duties and obligations within a society ruled by law. "The Frogs Who Asked for a King" and "The Wolf King," for example, both explore the natures of good and bad kings and wise and foolish subjects, while "The Peasant and His Jackdaw" is a lighthearted but serious treatment of the consequences of a corrupt legal system. Marie is certainly no democrat—she never questions the hierarchical nature of medieval society and indeed "The Vole Who Sought a Wife" is a cautionary tale about an animal who wants to move out of his "natural" place in the hierarchy—but in her sympathy for those on the bottom of the ladder and her insistence on the responsibilities of rulers, she reveals the same generosity of spirit and psychological insight in the *Fables* that she does in the *Lais.*

FURTHER READING: Two good introductory surveys of Marie's life and work are Paula Clifford's *Marie de France: Lais,* 1982, a volume in the *Critical Guides to French Texts* series, and Emanuel J. Mickel, Jr.'s *Marie de France,* 1974, in the *Twayne's World Authors* series. Recent critical essays are collected in *In Quest of Marie de France, a Twelfth-Century Poet,* ed. Chantal A. Marechal, 1992. Glyn Burgess's *Marie de France,* 1977, is an annotated bibliography of scholarship up to its date. On the *lais,* see the present translators' *The Lais of Marie de France,* 1978; it contains a short appreciative foreword by John Fowles, a lengthy critical and historical introduction by the translators, translations of all the *lais,* and a short critical commentary on each. Similarly, *The Fables of Marie de France,* trans. Mary Lou Martin, 1984; and *Marie de France, Fables,* ed. and trans. Harriet Spiegel, 1987, offer useful commentaries on the *Fables.* In the title novella of *The Ebony Tower,*

1974, the novelist John Fowles gives a modern treatment of some of Marie's themes, followed by a short "Personal Note" on Marie and a translation of "Eliduc"—all of which makes for a dazzling "metafictional" improvisation and a provocative interpretation of Marie. Readers interested in women's writing in general during the Middle Ages can find fifteen authors, including Marie de France, excerpted and succinctly discussed in *Medieval Women Writers,* ed. and with an introduction by Katharina M. Wilson, 1984; the section on Marie is by Joan M. Ferrante.

LAIS

Translated by Robert Hanning and Joan Ferrante

BISCLAVRET (THE WEREWOLF)

Since I am undertaking to compose *lais,*
I don't want to forget Bisclavret;
In Breton, the *lai's* name is *Bisclavret*—
the Normans call it *Garwaf [The Werewolf].*
In the old days, people used to say—
and it often actually happened—
that some men turned into werewolves
and lived in the woods.
A werewolf is a savage beast;
while his fury is on him 10
he eats men, does much harm,
goes deep in the forest to live.
But that's enough of this for now:
I want to tell you about the Bisclavret.

In Brittany there lived a nobleman
whom I've heard marvelously praised;
a fine, handsome knight
who behaved nobly.
He was close to his lord,
and loved by all his neighbors. 20
He had an estimable wife,
one of lovely appearance;
he loved her and she him,
but one thing was very vexing to her:
during the week he would be missing
for three whole days, and she didn't know
what happened to him or where he went.
Nor did any of his men know anything about it.
One day he returned home
happy and delighted; 30
she asked him about it.
"My lord," she said, "and dear love,
I'd very much like to ask you one thing—
if I dared;

but I'm so afraid of your anger
that nothing frightens me more."
When he heard that, he embraced her,
drew her to him and kissed her.
"My lady," he said, "go ahead and ask!
There's nothing you could want to know, 40
that, if I knew the answer, I wouldn't tell you."
"By God," she replied, "now I'm cured!
My lord, on the days when you go away from me
I'm in such a state—
so sad at heart,
so afraid I'll lose you—
that if I don't get quick relief
I could die of this very soon.
Please, tell me where you go,
where you have been staying. 50
I think you must have a lover,
and if that's so, you're doing wrong."
"My dear," he said, "have mercy on me, for God's sake!
Harm will come to me if I tell you about this,
because I'd lose your love
and even my very self."
When the lady heard this
she didn't take it lightly;
she kept asking him,
coaxed and flattered him so much, 60
that he finally told her what happened to him—
he hid nothing from her.
"My dear, I become a werewolf:
I go off into the great forest,
in the thickest part of the woods,
and I live on the prey I hunt down."
When he had told her everything,
she asked further
whether he undressed or kept his clothes on [when he became a
werewolf].
"Wife," he replied, "I go stark naked." 70
"Tell me, then, for God's sake, where your clothes are."
"That I won't tell you;
for if I were to lose them,
and then be discovered,
I'd stay a werewolf forever.
I'd be helpless
until I got them back.
That's why I don't want their hiding place to be known."
"My lord," the lady answered,
"I love you more than all the world; 80
you mustn't hide anything from me
or fear me in any way:
that doesn't seem like love to me.

What wrong have I done? For what sin of mine
do you mistrust me about anything?
Do the right thing and tell me!"
She harassed and bedeviled him so,
that he had no choice but to tell her.
"Lady," he said, "near the woods,
beside the road that I use to get there, 90
there's an old chapel
that has often done me good service;
under a bush there is a big stone,
hollowed out inside;
I hide my clothes right there
until I'm ready to come home."
The lady heard this wonder
and turned scarlet from fear;
she was terrified of the whole adventure.
Over and over she considered 100
how she might get rid of him;
she never wanted to sleep with him again.
There was a knight of that region
who had loved her for a long time,
who begged for her love,
and dedicated himself to serving her.
She'd never loved him at all,
nor pledged her love to him,
but now she sent a messenger for him,
and told him her intention. 110
"My dear," she said, "cheer up!
I shall now grant you without delay
what you have suffered for;
you'll meet with no more refusals—
I offer you my love and my body;
make me your mistress!"
He thanked her graciously
and accepted her promise,
and she bound him to her by an oath.
Then she told him 120
how her husband went away and what happened to him;
she also taught him the precise path
her husband took into the forest,
and then she sent the knight to get her husband's clothes.
So Bisclavret[1] was betrayed,
ruined by his own wife.
Since people knew he was often away from home
they all thought
this time he'd gone away forever.
They searched for him and made inquiries 130

[1] Until this point, "Bisclavret" is a common noun; hereafter it is used as the werewolf's name.

but could never find him,
so they had to let matters stand.
The wife later married the other knight,
who had loved her for so long.
A whole year passed
until one day the king went hunting;
he headed right for the forest
where Bisclavret was.
When the hounds were unleashed,
they ran across Bisclavret; 140
the hunters and the dogs
chased him all day,
until they were just about to take him
and tear him apart,
at which point he saw the king
and ran to him, pleading for mercy.
He took hold of the king's stirrup,
kissed his leg and his foot.
The king saw this and was terrified;
he called his companions. 150
"My lords," he said, "come quickly!
Look at this marvel—
this beast is humbling itself to me.
It has the mind of a man, and it's begging me for mercy!
Chase the dogs away,
and make sure no one strikes it.
This beast is rational—he has a mind.
Hurry up: let's get out of here.
I'll extend my peace to the creature;
indeed, I'll hunt no more today!" 160
Thereupon the king turned away.
Bisclavret followed him;
he stayed close to the king, and wouldn't go away;
he'd no intention of leaving him.
The king led him to his castle;
he was delighted with this turn of events,
for he'd never seen anything like it.
He considered the beast a great wonder
and held him very dear.
He commanded all his followers, 170
for the sake of their love for him, to guard Bisclavret well,
and under no circumstances to do him harm;
none of them should strike him;
rather, he should be well fed and watered.
They willingly guarded the creature;
every day he went to sleep
among the knights, near the king.
Everyone was fond of him;
he was so noble and well behaved
that he never wished to do anything wrong. 180

Regardless of where the king might go,
Bisclavret never wanted to be separated from him;
he always accompanied the king.
The king became very much aware that the creature loved him.
Now listen to what happened next.
The king held a court;
to help him celebrate his feast
and to serve him as handsomely as possible,
he summoned all the barons
who held fiefs from him. 190
Among the knights who went,
and all dressed up in his best attire,
was the one who had married Bisclavret's wife.
He neither knew nor suspected
that he would find Bisclavret so close by.
As soon as he came to the palace
Bisclavret saw him,
ran toward him at full speed,
sank his teeth into him, and started to drag him down.
He would have done him great damage 200
if the king hadn't called him off,
and threatened him with a stick.
Twice that day he tried to bite the knight.
Everyone was extremely surprised,
since the beast had never acted that way
toward any other man he had seen.
All over the palace people said
that he wouldn't act that way without a reason:
that somehow or other, the knight had mistreated Bisclavret,
and now he wanted his revenge. 210
And so the matter rested
until the feast was over
and until the barons took their leave of the king
and started home.
The very first to leave,
to the best of my knowledge,
was the knight whom Bisclavret had attacked.
It's no wonder the creature hated him.
Not long afterward,
as the story leads me to believe, 220
the king, who was so wise and noble,
went back to the forest
where he had found Bisclavret,
and the creature went with him.
That night, when he finished hunting,
he sought lodging out in the countryside.
The wife of Bisclavret heard about it,
dressed herself elegantly,
and went the next day to speak with the king,
bringing rich presents for him. 230

When Bisclavret saw her coming,
no one could hold him back;
he ran toward her in a rage.
Now listen to how well he avenged himself!
He tore the nose off her face.
What worse thing could he have done to her?
Now men closed in on him from all sides;
they were about to tear him apart,
when a wise man said to the king,
"My lord, listen to me! 240
This beast has stayed with you,
and there's not one of us
who hasn't watched him closely,
hasn't traveled with him often.
He's never touched anyone,
or shown any wickedness,
except to this woman.
By the faith that I owe you,
he has some grudge against her,
and against her husband as well. 250
This is the wife of the knight
whom you used to like so much,
and who's been missing for so long—
we don't know what became of him.
Why not put this woman to torture
and see if she'll tell you
why the beast hates her?
Make her tell what she knows!
We've seen many strange things
happen in Brittany!" 260
The king took his advice;
he detained the knight.
At the same time he took the wife
and subjected her to torture;
out of fear and pain
she told all about her husband:
how she had betrayed him
and taken away his clothes;
the story he had told her
about what happened to him and where he went; 270
and how after she had taken his clothes
he'd never been seen in his land again.
She was quite certain
that this beast was Bisclavret.
The king demanded the clothes;
whether she wanted to or not
she sent home for them,
and had them brought to Bisclavret.
When they were put down in front of him
he didn't even seem to notice them; 280
the king's wise man—

the one who had advised him earlier—
said to him, "My lord, you're not doing it right.
This beast wouldn't, under any circumstances,
in order to get rid of his animal form,
put on his clothes in front of you;
you don't understand what this means:
he's just too ashamed to do it here.
Have him led to your chambers
and bring the clothes with him; 290
then we'll leave him alone for a while.
If he turns into a man, we'll know about it."
The king himself led the way
and closed all the doors on him.
After a while he went back,
taking two barons with him;
all three entered the king's chamber.
On the king's royal bed
they found the knight asleep.
The king ran to embrace him. 300
He hugged and kissed him again and again.
As soon as he had the chance,
the king gave him back all his lands;
he gave him more than I can tell.
He banished his wife,
chased her out of the country.
She went into exile with the knight
with whom she had betrayed her lord.
She had several children
who were widely known 310
for their appearance:
several women of the family
were actually born without noses,
and lived out their lives noseless.

The adventure that you have heard
really happened, no doubt about it.
The *lai* of Bisclavret was made
so it would be remembered forever.

YONEC

Now that I've begun these *lais*
the effort will not stop me;
every adventure that I know
I shall relate in rhyme.
My intention and my desire

is to tell you next of Yonec,
how he was born and how his father
first came to his mother.
The man who fathered Yonec
was called Muldumarec. 10

There once lived in Brittany
a rich man, old and ancient.
At Caerwent, he was acknowledged
and accepted as lord of the land.
The city sits on the Duelas,
which at one time was open to boats.
The man was very far along in years
but because he possessed a large fortune
he took a wife in order to have children,
who would come after him and be his heirs. 20
The girl who was given to the rich man
came from a good family;
she was wise and gracious and very beautiful—
for her beauty he loved her very much.
Because she was beautiful and noble
he made every effort to guard her.
He locked her inside his tower
in a great paved chamber.
A sister of his,
who was also old and a widow, without her own lord, 30
he stationed with his lady
to guard her even more closely.
There were other women, I believe,
in another chamber by themselves,
but the lady never spoke to them
unless the old woman gave her permission.
So he kept her more than seven years—
they never had any children;
she never left that tower,
neither for family nor for friends. 40
When the lord came to sleep there
no chamberlain or porter
dared enter that room,
not even to carry a candle before the lord.
The lady lived in great sorrow,
with tears and sighs and weeping;
she lost her beauty,
as one does who cares nothing for it.
She would have preferred
death to take her quickly. 50

It was the beginning of April
when the birds begin their songs.
The lord arose in the morning

and made ready to go to the woods.
He had the old woman get up
and close the door behind him—
she followed his command.
The lord went off with his men.
The old woman carried a psalter
from which she intended to read the psalms. 60
The lady, awake and in tears,
saw the light of the sun.
She noticed that the old woman
had left the chamber.
She grieved and sighed
and wept and raged:
"I should never have been born!
My fate is very harsh.
I'm imprisoned in this tower
and I'll never leave it unless I die. 70
What is this jealous old man afraid of
that he keeps me so imprisoned?
He's mad, out of his senses;
always afraid of being deceived.
I can't even go to church
or hear God's service.
If I could speak to people
and enjoy myself with them
I'd be very gracious to my lord
even if I didn't want to be. 80
A curse on my family,
and on all the others
who gave me to this jealous man,
who married me to his body.
It's a rough rope that I pull and draw.
He'll never die—
when he should have been baptized
he was plunged instead in the river of hell;
his sinews are hard, his veins are hard,
filled with living blood. 90
I've often heard
that one could once find
adventures in this land
that brought relief to the unhappy.
Knights might find young girls
to their desire, noble and lovely;
and ladies find lovers
so handsome, courtly, brave, and valiant
that they could not be blamed,
and no one else would see them. 100
If that might be or ever was,
if that has ever happened to anyone,
God, who has power over everything,

grant me my wish in this."
When she'd finished her lament,
she saw, through a narrow window,
the shadow of a great bird.
She didn't know what it was.
It flew into the chamber;
its feet were banded; it looked like a hawk
of five or six moultings. 110
It alighted before the lady.
When it had been there awhile
and she'd stared hard at it,
it became a handsome and noble knight.
The lady was astonished;
her blood went cold, she trembled,
she was frightened—she covered her head.
The knight was very courteous,
he spoke first:
"Lady," he said, "don't be afraid. 120
The hawk is a noble bird,
although its secrets are unknown to you.
Be reassured
and accept me as your love.
That," he said, "is why I came here.
I have loved you for a long time,
I've desired you in my heart.
Never have I loved any woman but you
nor shall I ever love another,
yet I couldn't have come to you 130
or left my own land
had you not asked for me.
But now I can be your love."
The lady was reassured;
she uncovered her head and spoke.
She answered the knight,
saying she would take him as her lover
if he believed in God,
and if their love was really possible.
For he was of great beauty. 140
Never in her life
had she seen so handsome a knight—
nor would she ever.
"My lady," he said, "you are right.
I wouldn't want you to feel
guilt because of me,
or doubt or suspicion.
I do believe in the creator
who freed us from the grief
that Adam, our father, led us into 150
when he bit into the bitter apple.

He is, will be, and always was
the life and light of sinners.
If you don't believe me
send for your chaplain.
Say that you've suddenly been taken ill
and that you desire the service
that God established in this world
for the healing of sinners. 160
I shall take on your appearance
to receive the body of our lord God,
and I'll recite my whole credo for you.
You will never doubt my faith again."
She answered that she was satisfied.
He lay beside her on the bed
but he didn't try to touch her,
to embrace her or to kiss her.
Meanwhile, the old woman had returned.
She found the lady awake 170
and told her it was time to get up,
she would bring her clothes.
The lady said she was ill,
that the old woman should send for the chaplain
and bring him to her quickly—
she very much feared she was dying.
The old woman said, "Be patient,
my lord has gone to the woods.
No one may come in here but me."
The lady was very upset; 180
she pretended to faint.
When the other saw her, she was frightened;
she unlocked the door of the chamber
and sent for the priest.
He came as quickly as he could,
bringing the *corpus domini.*[1]
The knight received it,
drank the wine from the chalice.
Then the chaplain left
and the old woman closed the doors. 190
The lady lay beside her love—
there was never a more beautiful couple.
When they had laughed and played
and spoken intimately,
the knight took his leave
to return to his land.
She gently begged him
to come back often.
"Lady," he said, "whenever you please,

[1] The "body of the Lord," bread for Communion.

I will be here within the hour. 200
But you must make certain
that we're not discovered.
This old woman will betray us,
night and day she will spy on us.
She will perceive our love,
and tell her lord about it.
If that happens,
if we are betrayed,
I won't be able to escape.
I shall die." 210
With that the knight departed,
leaving his love in great joy.
In the morning she rose restored;
she was happy all week.
Her body had now become precious to her,
she completely recovered her beauty.
Now she would rather remain here
than look for pleasure elsewhere.
She wanted to see her love all the time
and enjoy herself with him. 220
As soon as her lord departed,
night or day, early or late,
she had him all to her pleasure.
God, let their joy endure!
Because of the great joy she felt,
because she could see her love so often,
her whole appearance changed.
But her lord was clever.
In his heart he sensed
that she was not what she had been. 230
He suspected his sister.
He questioned her one day,
saying he was astonished
that the lady now dressed with care.
He asked her what it meant.
The old woman said she didn't know—
no one could have spoken to her,
she had no lover or friend—
it was only that she was now more willing
to be alone than before. 240
His sister, too, had noticed the change.
Her lord answered:
"By my faith," he said, "I think that's so.
But you must do something for me.
In the morning, when I've gotten up
and you have shut the doors,
pretend you are going out
and leave her lying there alone.
Then hide yourself in a safe place,

watch her and find out 250
what it is, and where it comes from,
that gives her such great joy."
With that plan they separated.
Alas, how hard it is to protect yourself
from someone who wants to trap you,
to betray and deceive you!

Three days later, as I heard the story,
the lord pretended to go away.
He told his wife the story
that the king had sent for him by letter 260
but that he would return quickly.
He left the chamber and shut the door.
The old woman got up,
went behind a curtain;
from there she could hear and see
whatever she wanted to know.
The lady lay in bed but did not sleep,
she longed for her love.
He came without delay,
before any time had passed. 270
They gave each other great joy
with word and look
until it was time to rise—
he had to go.
But the old woman watched him,
saw how he came and went.
She was quite frightened
when she saw him first a man and then a bird.
When the lord returned—
he hadn't gone very far— 280
she told him and revealed
the truth about the knight
and the lord was troubled by it.
But he was quick to invent
a way to kill the knight.
He had great spikes of iron forged,
their tips sharpened—
no razor on earth could cut better.
When he had them all prepared
and pronged on all sides, 290
he set them in the window—
close together and firmly placed—
through which the knight passed
when he visited the lady.
God, he doesn't know what treachery
the villains are preparing.
The next day in the morning
the lord rose before dawn

and said he was going hunting.
The old woman saw him to the door 300
and then went back to bed
for day was not yet visible.
The lady awoke and waited
for the one she loved faithfully;
she said he might well come now
and be with her at leisure.
As soon as she asked,
he came without delay.
He flew into the window,
but the spikes were there. 310
One wounded him in his breast—
out rushed the red blood.
He knew he was fatally wounded;
he pulled himself free and entered the room.
He alighted on the bed, in front of the lady,
staining the bedclothes with blood.
She saw the blood and the wound
in anguish and horror.
He said, "My sweet love,
I lose my life for love of you. 320
I told you it would happen,
that your appearance would kill us."
When she heard that, she fainted;
for a short while she lay as if dead.
He comforted her gently,
said that grief would do no good,
but that she was pregnant with his child.
She would have a son, brave and strong,
who would comfort her;
she would call him Yonec. 330
He would avenge both of them
and kill their enemy.
But he could remain no longer
for his wound was bleeding badly.
He left in great sorrow.
She followed him with loud cries.
She leapt out a window—
it's a wonder that she wasn't killed,
for it was at least twenty feet high
where she made her leap, 340
naked beneath her gown.
She followed the traces of blood
that flowed from the knight
onto the road.
She followed that road and kept to it
until she came to a hill.
In the hill there was an opening,
red with his blood.

She couldn't see anything beyond it
but she was sure 350
that her love had gone in there.
She entered quickly.
She found no light
but she kept to the right road
until it emerged from the hill
into a beautiful meadow.
When she found the grass there wet with blood,
she was frightened.
She followed the traces through the meadow
and saw a city not far away. 360
The city was completely surrounded by walls.
There was no house, no hall or tower,
that didn't seem entirely of silver.
The buildings were very rich.
Going toward the town there were marshes,
forests, and enclosed fields.
On the other side, toward the castle,
a stream flowed all around,
where ships arrived—
there were more than three hundred sails. 370
The lower gate was open;
the lady entered the city,
still following the fresh blood
through the town to the castle.
No one spoke to her,
she met neither man nor woman.
When she came to the palace courtyard,
she found it covered with blood.
She entered a lovely chamber
where she found a knight sleeping. 380
She did not know him, so she went on
into another larger chamber.
There she found nothing but a bed
with a knight sleeping on it;
she kept going.
She entered the third chamber
and on that bed she found her love.
The feet of the bed were all of polished gold,
I couldn't guess the value of the bedclothes;
the candles and the chandeliers, 390
which were lit night and day,
were worth the gold of an entire city.
As soon as she saw him
she recognized the knight.
She approached, frightened,
and fell fainting over him.
He, who greatly loved her, embraced her,
lamenting his misfortune again and again.

When she recovered from her faint
he comforted her gently. 400
"Sweet friend, for God's sake, I beg you,
go away! Leave this place!
I shall die within the day,
there will be great sorrow here,
and if you are found
you will be hurt.
Among my people it will be well known
that they have lost me because of my love for you.
I am disturbed and troubled for you."
The lady answered: "Love, 410
I would rather die with you
than suffer with my lord.
If I go back to him he'll kill me."
The knight reassured her,
gave her a ring,
and explained to her
that, as long as she kept it,
her lord would not remember
anything that had happened—
he would imprison her no longer. 420
He gave her his sword
and then made her swear
no man would ever possess it,
that she'd keep it for their son.
When the son had grown and become
a brave and valiant knight,
she would go to a festival,
taking him and her lord with her.
They would come to an abbey.
There, beside a tomb, 430
they would hear the story of his death,
how he was wrongfully killed.
There she would give her son the sword.
The adventure would be recited to him,
how he was born and who his father was;
then they'd see what he would do.
When he'd told her and shown her everything,
he gave her a precious robe
and told her to put it on.
Then he sent her away. 440
She left carrying the ring
and the sword—they comforted her.
She had not gone half a mile
from the gate of the city
when she heard the bells ring
and the mourning begin in the castle,
and in her sorrow
she fainted four times.

When she recovered from the faints
she made her way to the hill. 450
She entered it, passed through it,
and returned to her country.
There with her lord
she lived many days and years.
He never accused her of that deed,
never insulted or abused her.
Her son was born and nourished,
protected and cherished.
They named him Yonec.
In all the kingdom you couldn't find 460
one so handsome, brave, or strong,
so generous, so munificent.
When he reached the proper age,
he was made a knight.
Hear now what happened
in that very year.

To the feast of St. Aaron,
celebrated in Caerleon
and in many other cities,
the lord had been summoned 470
to come with his friends,
according to the custom of the land,
and to bring his wife and his son,
all richly attired.
So it was; they went.
But they didn't know the way;
they had a boy with them
who guided them along the right road
until they came to a castle—
none more beautiful in all the world. 480
Inside, there was an abbey
of very religious people.
The boy who was guiding them to the festival
housed them there.
In the abbot's chamber
they were well served and honored.
Next day they went to hear Mass
before they departed,
but the abbot went to speak to them
to beg them to stay 490
so he could show them the dormitory,
the chapter house, and the refectory.
And since they were comfortable there,
the lord agreed to stay.
That day, after they had dined,
they went to the workshops.
On their way, they passed the chapter house,

where they found a huge tomb
covered with a cloth of embroidered silk,
a band of precious gold running from one side to the other. 500
At the head, the feet, and at the sides
burned twenty candles.
The chandeliers were pure gold,
the censers amethyst,
which through the day perfumed
that tomb, to its great honor.
They asked and inquired
of people from that land
whose tomb it was,
what man lay there. 510
The people began to weep
and, weeping, to recount
that it was the best knight,
the strongest, the most fierce,
the most handsome and the best loved,
that had ever lived.
"He was king of this land;
no one was ever so courtly.
At Caerwent he was discovered
and killed for the love of a lady. 520
Since then we have had no lord,
but have waited many days,
just as he told and commanded us,
for the son the lady bore him."
When the lady heard that news,
she called aloud to her son.
"Fair son," she said, "you hear
how God has led us to this spot.
Your father, whom this old man murdered,
lies here in this tomb. 530
Now I give and commend his sword to you.
I have kept it a long time for you."
Then she revealed, for all to hear,
that the man in the tomb was the father and this was his son,
and how he used to come to her,
how her lord had betrayed him—
she told the truth.
Then she fainted over the tomb
and, in her faint, she died.
She never spoke again. 540
When her son saw that she had died,
he cut off his stepfather's head.
Thus with his father's sword
he avenged his mother's sorrow.
When all this had happened,
when it became known through the city,
they took the lady with great honor
and placed her in the coffin.

Before they departed
they made Yonec their lord. 550

Long after, those who heard this adventure
composed a lay about it,
about the pain and the grief
that they suffered for love.

FABLES

Translated by Harriet Spiegel

THE MOUSE AND THE FROG

Now following the written text,
About a mouse I'll tell you next
Who by her cleverness and skill
Had made her household at a mill. 4
I'll show you, through this tale, her way:
The mouse sat on her stoop one day;
She smoothed her whiskers, made them neat,
And combed them out with tiny feet. 8
And now a frog came up to her—
As if by chance she did appear.
The frog, in mouse-talk, asked the mouse
If she were lady of this house 12
Where she'd assumed the mastery,
And how she lived from day to day.
The mouse then answered her, 'My dear,
Some time I've been landlady here. 16
And all is under my control
When I'm protected by my hole.
Here I have shelter day and night
To play and follow my delight. 20
Why don't you spend the night with me!
I'll show you, most assuredly,
The mill and its amenities—
There's nothing here that will not please. 24
Here ample grain and wheat you'll find
In what the peasants leave behind.'
To this request the frog came round;
Upon the stone they both sat down. 28
And there they found much nourishment,
No peril and no argument.

Most lovingly the mouse then asked
The frog concerning her repast: 32
How was it, in all honesty?
'I will not lie to you,' said she,
'Though you've prepared a splendid meal,
Some water now would help, I feel. 36
Oh, how I wish we could go romp
Across the field to that fine swamp—
It's there that I have made my home.
Dear friend, let's go there now—do come! 40
There you'll have such delight, such bliss
That I believe you'll have no wish
Ever to come back to this mill.'
Such promises and crafty skill 44
And flattery went to her head.
She trusted frog—but was misled.
So off together went the two.
The meadow was awash with dew; 48
And thus the mouse got wet all 'round
And thought for certain she'd be drowned.
She must return now, go back home,
She knew she could no farther roam. 52
But then once more the frog addressed her;
Against the mouse's will, she pressed her.
She urged her onward, praised her so,
Until the mouse had reached the flow. 56
The mouse now saw no point in trying.
She tried to speak, though she was crying:
'I'm sure I cannot get across—
For I can't swim! I'm at a loss!' 60
'Now take and tie this little thread
Around your knees,' the frog then said,
'And I'll attach it thus to mine—
We'll cross the river then just fine.' 64
So with this plan the mouse complied,
With string both frog and mouse were tied;
And thus attached they made their start.
But when they reached the deepest part, 68
The frog intended mouse to drown,
And so she started plunging down.
The mouse let out a peeping cry,
She was convinced that she would die. 72
High overhead there soared a kite
Who heard her peeps and saw her plight.
He closed his wings, flew down to get her,
And grabbed the frog and mouse together— 76
For to each other they'd been tied.
The frog was plump and stout and wide;
The kite ignored the mouse, for greed
Told him the frog was better feed. 80

The kite devoured the frog quite fast,
And thus the mouse was free at last.
With cunning villains this is clear:
They never will have friends so dear 84
That they, in honor of their friend,
Could bear a single penny spend.
Without compunction, they are glad
If they can trick their good comrade. 88
And yet it happens every day:
Those folk who torment in this way
And think that others they'll ensnare, will
Find that they place themselves in peril. 92

THE FROGS WHO ASKED FOR A KING

Once, in a pond, it came to pass,
Around the banks and the morass,
There lived great frog confederations
Who had been there for generations. 4
They hated staying in the pond
And wished to move to solid ground.
So they cried out to Destiny—
Repeatedly they made their plea— 8
That she might send to them a king;
They needed not another thing.
When many times the frogs had prayed,
Then Destiny to them conveyed 12
Right in the pond, a sturdy log
Which caused great fear in every frog.
The frog close by the log observed,
Since it had come, it had not stirred. 16
He to his friends a summons croaked;
The log together they approached.
They greeted it as their king royal,
And each one promised to be loyal. 20
The frogs all thought of it as lord,
Thus was it honoured and adored.
But when the log stayed motionless,
They saw that it was fixed in place, 24
Lying so still there in the water.
They climbed upon it all together.
Such dirty deeds performed each frog
That to the depths they sank the log. 28
They then to Destiny went back
And begged a king; they felt the lack:
The one she'd given them was bad.

So Destiny then sent that crowd 32
An adder powerful and great—
Death to the frogs he seized and ate.
Those left were all in great distress.
They cried out with much bitterness 36
For mercy now from Destiny
To rid them of their enemy.
Responding, Destiny avowed,
'Oh no! Oh no! You've been allowed 40
All of the things which you desired.
A lord good-natured you acquired.
You shamed churlishly that seignior,
And now you have what you asked for!' 44
This is what many folks have done
To a good lord (should they have one):
They always want to stamp their lord;
His honour they don't know to guard. 48
If they're not kept in stressful plight,
They'll do him neither wrong nor right.
To him they cling who them destroys;
With what they have, he makes his noise. 52
Then for their good seignior they long
To whom they have done shameful wrong.

THE WOLF KING

It's said that once a lion planned
To go live in another land.
Then all the beasts held a convention.
He told them all of his intention, 4
And that they should select a king:
He thought he'd not be back again.
The beasts requested, every one,
That he provide another lion. 8
He answered that he had no heir:
He had not raised one—did not dare.
Among themselves must be their quest
To find the one who'd govern best. 12
And thus it was they chose the wolf,
For no one else was bold enough
To dare take anyone but him

(Though all thought wolf a villain grim). 16
Yet he assured them all, and swore
He'd love them best forevermore.
They went to lion next and stated
That wolf had now been designated. 20
He said to doubt not in the least
That they had picked a clever beast,
Extremely fast and versatile,
Provided that his heart and will 24
Were as they ought to be: sincere.
But one thing caused the lion fear—
That wolf for counsellor would pick
The fox who knew well how to trick; 28
Both are insidious and base.
If from the wolf they wanted peace,
On holy relics he must swear
That he'd touch no beast anywhere 32
And that forever he would not
Eat any meat, no matter what.
The wolf most willingly then swore
To more than they had asked him for. 36
But when he had been bound by oath,
And when the lion had set out,
Such craving wolf had for some meat,
That he made plans to use deceit 40
To get the beasts all to agree
And give him leave accordingly.
The wolf then summoned a roe deer,
And secretly he questioned her 44
If for his love the truth she'd tell
About wolf's breath: How did it smell?
She said it smelled so terrible
It was almost unbearable. 48
The wolf was very angry then.
He sent a summons to his men.
He questioned all those who had come:
What kind of sentence they'd give one 52
Who spoke such things to his lord's face,
Such words of shame, slur, and disgrace.
This one should die, they all attested.
The wolf then had the deer arrested. 56
While they all watched, he killed the deer
And ate the better part of her.
His crime to cover—he proclaimed
He'd portion to them what remained. 60
After his hunger pains had ceased,
He called for yet another beast.
He questioned her in the same way—
How smelled his breath—what would she say? 64

The poor thing would much rather lie
Than for truth's sake suffer and die.
So she replied she knew no scent
So fragrant and so excellent. 68
The wolf summoned his cabinet;
He asked his barons, when they met,
What punishment he should decree
To one who'd lied deceitfully. 72
All judged that she must die. When caught,
She thus before the wolf was brought.
He killed her, tore her limb from limb,
And ate her up in front of them. 76
After a little time passed by,
The wolf, observing, chanced to spy
A monkey fat and quite well fed—
How he that monkey coveted! 80
To eat, devour him, he desired.
One day wolf went to him, inquired
About his breath—now did it stink
Or smell quite sweet—what did he think? 84
The monkey was extremely sly:
He'd be no way condemned to die.
Thus he replied, he did not know.
Now wolf did not know what to do. 88
The monkey could not be condemned
Because he did no harm intend.
Wolf went to bed; illness he feigned.
To all the beasts he then complained; 92
He thought he never would get well.
They came in turn to pay a call.
They sent out for some doctors then
To know if he'd be well again. 96
The doctors all were at a loss.
None saw a thing, nor found a cause,
No injury which brought this mood.
If only he'd desire some food! 100
'I have,' he said, 'no other wish
Except to eat some monkey flesh.
Of course, to touch a beast I'm loath!—
I must, you know, keep my sworn oath— 104
Unless I can well justify it;
My barons then could ratify it.'
They met together, gave this view,
That that is just what he must do. 108
Against his heart's desire, no cure—
Their remedies could not be sure.
When he heard what they advocated,
He seized the monkey and he ate it. 112
On all in turn was sentence passed:
His oath to none of them was fast.

Thus by the wise man we are taught
That we, no matter what, must not 116
A wicked man e'er make seignior,
Nor show to such a one honour.
His loyalty's as much pretence
With strangers as with his close friends. 120
And toward his people he will act
As did the wolf, with his sworn pact.

THE PEASANT AND HIS JACKDAW

There was a peasant, as I've heard,
Who once brought up a jackdaw bird.
The bird could speak, so well he'd raised her.
Then she was murdered by a neighbour. 4
Our man complained about his daw
In court, and told the judge there how
His bird was wont to talk away
And, in the mornings, sing each day. 8
The neighbour, said the judge, was wrong;
He summoned him to trial ere long.
The neighbour got a leather hide,
Put it beneath his cloak, inside, 12
And then he let hang down an end
So that the judge could comprehend
That it was brought as bribery
If he would help him in his plea. 16
His cloak he opened frequently
Until the hide this judge did see.
He called the other man amain,
The one who'd come there to complain. 20
The judge asked, in his questioning,
What songs the daw was wont to sing
And what great words she'd say also.
The man replied he did not know. 24
'If you,' he said, 'don't know a thing,
Don't understand her chattering,
And if her songs you do not know,
To you my judgment should not go.' 28
Without his due the man went out—
Thanks to the bribe; the judge took that.
And thus it is, a king or prince
Should not his law or ordinance 32
Entrust to people covetous:
Destroyed will be all righteousness.

THE VOLE WHO SOUGHT A WIFE

There once was so vainglorious
A vole (which is a kind of mouse)
That he'd not of his lineage,
Of his own kind or heritage, 4
Look for or choose a wife to wed.
He'd never have a wife, he said,
Unless he found one very pleasing—
The daughter of a most high being 8
Was what the vole thought he should seek.
So to the sun he went to speak:
The sun, highest of all, he guessed,
Hottest in summer, mightiest. 12
Vole wished to wed sun's daughter now;
He'd gone as high as he knew how.
If he looked further, said the sun,
He'd find an even stronger one— 16
The cloud—who shades and makes a cover—
Sun can't come out when cloud takes over.
The vole went to the cloud erelong
And said that since she seemed so strong, 20
Her daughter he would like to wed.
He'd better look some more, she said,
For she would like to demonstrate
That he'd find someone stronger yet: 24
It was the wind, she did believe;
Whene'er wind blew, he made cloud leave.
'I'll go to him.' thus vole did speak,
'Your daughter's hand I will not seek!' 28
On to the wind the vole went now.
Addressing him, the vole told how
By cloud he'd been directed there.
The wind in answer made it clear 32
He was, indeed, the strongest creature,
His power was beyond all measure.
He'd force all other things to scatter
Whene'er he blew—destroy all matter. 36
Vole sought his daughter's hand, therefore;
He'd had enough, would hear no more,
For he had heard what people say:
That no one dared get in wind's way. 40
The wind replied, 'You are misled—
'There's no wife for you here,' he said.
'There is an even stronger one
That I find very bothersome. 44
She put up such a strong defence,
My force was of no consequence.
I'm talking of the great stone wall
Who stands so strong and sound through all. 48

The wall no force can devastate,
Nor all my wind debilitate.
She hurls me back so powerfully—
Another visit won't please me!' 52
The vole replied to him just this:
'Your daughter's hand I do not wish.
I'll choose no wife of lesser station—
That would not suit my situation! 56
I'll have a wife of quality!
So now the wall I must go see.'
He went to wall and sought to wed
Her daughter; eyeing him, wall said, 60
'You certainly do misconstrue—
It seems that nothing's clear to you.
Whoever sent you on your way
Has made a fool of you. I'd say. 64
Today one stronger yet than I
You'll see—one whom I can't defy.'
The vole responded, 'Who is this?
The strongest in the world, I guess!' 68
'You're right, and that's the mouse,' said she,
'Who makes her nest inside of me.
There's no mortar—with which I'm made—
So strong that she cannot invade. 72
She digs below and runs through me;
Nought hinders her activity.'
The vole replied, 'What's this? Oh dear!
Oh this is dreadful news to hear! 76
The mouse and I are family!
My mission's ruined utterly!
I thought that I would rise so high,
But now I must turn back, so I 80
Can bow to my own kind,' said he.
Said wall, 'That's what your lot must be.
Go home, and keep in mind for aye,
That you should never, come what may, 84
Your nature ever again despise.
Whoever thinks that he can rise
Beyond his rightful situation
Must come back to a lower station. 88
Never should one his birthright scorn,
Whate'er he knows (unless baseborn).
Because so far you cannot go
To find yourself a wife, you know, 92
Who would be better in your house
Than this—the little lady mouse.'
  With prideful folks it's often thus—
Those arrogant and envious— 96
Who seek what they should not; for they
End back where they don't want to be.

EPILOGUE

To end these tales I've here narrated
And into Romance tongue translated,
I'll give my name, for memory:
I am from France, my name's Marie. 4
And it may hap that many a clerk
Will claim as his what is my work.
But such pronouncements I want not!
It's folly to become forgot! 8
Out of my love for Count William,
The doughtiest in any realm,
This volume was by me created,
From English to Romance translated. 12
This book's called Aesop for this reason:
He translated and had it written
In Latin from the Greek, to wit.
King Alfred, who was fond of it, 16
Translated it to English hence,
And I have rhymed it now in French
As well as I was competent.
I pray to God omnipotent 20
To let me to such work attend
And thus to Him my soul commend.

Renard the Fox

(Twelfth and Thirteenth Centuries)

It is tempting sometimes to think that the surviving literature of the Middle Ages represents medieval life fully and accurately, that medieval people thought of war in the heroic terms of *The Song of Roland*, of love in the moralistic terms of *Sir Gawain and the Green Knight*, and of God in the cosmic terms of *The Divine Comedy*. But only a tiny fraction of the population could read and write, almost exclusively the aristocracy and the clergy, and the texts that they produced inevitably reflect aristocratic and clerical points of view. But what of the points of view of the foot soldiers in Roland's army or of the women who cooked the feasts for the knights of the Round Table? For these, we have to comb through evidence of a tradition of oral literature, what we might call the literature of the unliterary. Even this reaches us in a heavily mediated form, written down by literate collectors sometimes centuries after its supposed origin. *Renard the Fox* is one of the most effective (and one of the funniest) such oppositional texts, and despite its problems of transcription and transmission it can fairly be read as a skeptical view from below of the chivalric ideology of the ruling class.

The first adventures of Renard were written down in French (there were German versions as well) by Pierre de Saint-Cloud in about 1170. Pierre's general source was the large body of animal fables that had circulated in Europe since Aesop. The nineteenth-century folklorist Leopold Sudre found precedents for the cast of characters and their stock traits (the fox as trickster, the cock as boaster, the bear as a lover of honey) throughout the folklore of Europe and even India. Pierre had written sources as well, including Marie de France's verse translations of Aesop's fables, her original ones, and a long Latin poem by Nivard named *Ysengrimus* (1148). It is Pierre, however, who is credited with drawing these materials together in an extended satirical "beast epic."

Pierre wrote two fragments, developing the central plot element of *Renard*—the triangle of Renard the fox, Ysengrin the wolf, and the wolf's wife, Hersent. Over the next three decades, other writers contributed episodes, generally called "branches," to form what one critic has called a "rather ramshackle epic." The most gifted of these writers, including Pierre himself, was an anonymous writer who wrote the episode of the trial of Renard about five years after Pierre had begun the story. Other branches told of Renard's adventures on pilgrimage. The epic was essentially complete by 1200, though other writers continued to write related stories for another fifty or so years.

Renard the Fox was one of the most widely read books of the Middle Ages and was often imitated. One of the best versions of Renard's story was by the late twelfth-century German writer Heinrich der Glichezaere. Chaucer's "Nun's Priest's Tale" in the *Canterbury Tales* (1387–1400) is essentially a Renard story; one of the first books printed in English by William Caxton was a translation of a Flemish version of *Renard.* Ben Jonson's play *Volpone* (1605) draws on Renard, though Volpone is a foxy human, and Johann Wolfgang von Goethe wrote his own version of the tale, *Reineke Fuchs* (1792), with the politics updated to his own time.

The first-time reader of *Renard* might pay special attention to the successive descriptions of Renard's home, Maupertuis. It is regularly described as an imposing medieval castle with a number of towers with banners flying from them. But without warning, in the middle of an idealized description, Maupertuis turns into a realistic fox's den. (*Maupertuis* means "evil den.") When Grinbert the badger, for example, visits Renard, he first crosses the moat and then walks along spacious passageways, but then is suddenly sliding feet-first down a hole into the fox's foul-smelling den. (Renard sees and recognized Grinbert's rump before he sees his face.)

The author maintains the same double vision throughout the tale. Because the animals are aristocratic members of King Noble's court, they must ride horses wherever they go. But at the same time they are animals, for whom horsebackriding presents certain logistical problems. How could Tibert the cat, with his short legs, straddle a horse? (The answer, of course, is that he doesn't; he rides sidesaddle.)

The duality of the characters as both humans and animals extends to larger issues. On the one hand, the characters obey their animal natures: The fox is a wily predator, the rooster is vain, the bear will forget everything when he detects honey. On the other hand, they are aristocratic humans, judged by human standards of morality, subject to human laws, and bound by the practices of a complex courtly society. This juxtaposition of animal and human natures suggests a pervasive undercutting of chivalric pretensions. Knightly martial exploits are reduced to the level of a fox stealing chickens, and chivalric romance is reduced to the lusty adulteries of Hersent the female wolf.

But there is even more to *Renard* than this. Its world is more complex than that of the Aesopian fables upon which it drew. Aesopian nature is nature red in tooth and claw; the wolf always eats the lamb, the lion wins every argument. But King Noble in *Renard*, it could be argued, really is noble. Confronted with the depredations of a rogue subject, he really does try to act justly, observing such principles as the right of the accused to confront his accusers and even commuting a death sentence when he can find a reason to do so. *Renard* is about power, both that of the vulpine aristocrat who preys upon his vassals and that of the wise king whose power may be absolute but who uses it generously and benevolently. Its themes, even draped in the protective coverings of the beast fable, are a useful corrective to the dominant courtly and ecclesiastical literature of the Middle Ages.

FURTHER READING: The most useful commentaries on *Renard* are all in French. For an introductory bibliography, see Jean-Pierre de Beaumarchais, Daniel Conty, and Alain Rey, *Dictionnaire des Litteratures de Langue Francais*, 1994. Patricia Terry's introduction to her translation, *Renard the Fox*, 1983, usefully sums up the history and interpretation of the work, as does D. D. R. Owen's introduction to his translation, *The Romance of Reynard the Fox*, 1994. Erich Auerbach, *Mimesis*, 1957, and C. S. Lewis's *The Discarded Image*, 1979, both contain short but suggestive treatments. For the iconography, see Kenneth Varty, *Reynard the Fox: A Study of the Fox in Medieval English Art*, 1967.

from *RENARD THE FOX*

THE TRIAL OF RENARD

Translated by Patricia Terry

Though his wit and talent did not fail
When Perrot[1] set out to rhyme the tale
Of Renard and Ysengrin, his friend,
He left out the best part and the end:
The prosecution and defense
As to the guilt or innocence
Of Renard, dragged out, despite his guile,
To Noble's court where he stood trial
For having vilely fornicated
With Hersent, as her husband stated.[2] 10
The author tells us, in line one,[3]
That winter had passed, and in the sun

[1]Pierre de Saint-Cloud, the first to write about Renard.

[2]The husband is Ysengrin, the wolf. Elsewhere in the Renard cycle he and Renard are said to be cousins. They are, in any case, friends and collaborators.

[3]The "author" here is not Saint-Cloud but the fictitious author to which medieval writers liked to attribute their work. The author seems to be parodying the convention here, as he parodies the invocation of spring in romances. See the Prologue to the *Canterbury Tales*, for example.

Roses were opening, and bright
Hawthorn flowers, shining white.
The king announced his firm intention,[4]
Close to the Feast of the Ascension,
That all the animals report
To the palace where he held his court.
Not one would dare let anything
Keep him from promptly answering 20
The lion's urgent proclamation,
Except for Sir Renard, damnation
Take him for a lying thief!
Whom the others said, in their belief,
The king should punish for his pride,
And for the crimes he hoped to hide.
Ysengrin had no objection,
Viewing Renard without affection;
Loudest of all he expressed his ire:
"Your majesty, dear gracious Sire, 30
Grant me justice! Madame Hersent,
Held by Renard with foul intent
In his domain at Maupertuis,
Was forced to commit adultery,
And he pissed on my poor cubs as well!
That's the latest woe I have to tell.
All of this Renard denied,
And in order that the case be tried
He chose the day when he would swear
On holy relics, as is fair. 40
But somehow he was warned, and when
We came, retreated to his den.
Why I'm so angry must be clear."
Then said the king, so all could hear:
"Forget about it, Ysengrin—
The only thing that you can win
Is more dishonor to your name.
Counts and kings will play that game,
And nowadays one sees all sorts
Of cuckolds, even ruling courts![5] 50
You have little cause, it seems to us,
For making such an awful fuss.
This woe you bring to our attention
Doesn't deserve the slightest mention."

[4]A springtime convocation of vassals at the king's court is another convention of medieval romance. Several of the King Arthur romances, for example, begin this way.

[5]Perhaps a reference to the rather colorful sexual life of Eleanor of Aquitaine (1122–1204), who married Louis VII of France, had the marriage annulled, and then married Henry II of England. Guinevere, the errant queen in the Arthurian romances, is also paralleled to Fiere, King Noble's queen.

"Most gracious Sire," said Bruin the bear,
"Is such an answer really fair?
Ysengrin is alive and free,
And if Renard's his enemy,
To seek revenge would not be wrong.
You know that Ysengrin is strong; 60
If Renard lived close to his domain,
And if your sworn peace[6] did not restrain
All ruled by you from acts of war,
Renard would get what he's asking for!
Of all this kingdom you are lord—
Why don't you put an end to discord,
Put an end to your vassals' fray!
We will hate anyone you say.
Count on us to defend your side!
If Ysengrin's dissatisfied 70
About Renard, let the case be tried;
Let it be judged as you decide.
If one wronged the other, what is due
For that misdeed must be paid to you.[7]
Send for Renard at Maupertuis;
If you'll entrust that task to me,
And I can find him, there's no doubt
He'll learn what a royal court's about."
As soon as he'd finished, Clamor[8] roared,
"Sir Bruin, a curse on any lord— 80
Saving your presence—who would say
That the king should let a fine repay
Adultery! Make Renard repent
The shame he inflicted on Hersent!
For other beasts so many times
Have suffered from his filthy crimes,
No one should help him in his need.
Why should Ysengrin have to plead
For justice when Renard attacked
His wife so openly the fact 90
Is known to all? Believe you me,
If he behaved so villainously
And it was my wife he molested,
However strongly she protested,
As far as Maupertuis let him run
But I would make him pay for his fun—
Deep in a muddy ditch he'd groan
Without a sex to call his own!
How could you dream of it, Hersent?

[6]Louis VII imposed a truce on the warring factions within his kingdom in 1155; it lasted for ten years.

[7]Under medieval laws, offenders owed compensation to their lords as well as their victims, since crime was a breaking of the peace.

[8]The loud-mouthed Clamor is a bull.

Surely it's something to lament 100
When Renard who lives without a care
Can boast of mounting you like a mare!"
The badger[9] said, "Before it's too late,
Sir Clamor, let us end this debate
Which will otherwise get worse and worse
And beyond our power to reverse.
A malicious tale will soon expand
Until it's entirely out of hand.
And since this case involves no use
Of force, no broken door or truce,[10] 110
And Renard was prompted by affection,
Why do you make such strong objection?
For a long time he has loved Hersent.
This complaint was never her intent,
And Ysengrin, with little wit,
Is making much too much of it.
Let King Noble and his lords decide
How Ysengrin should be satisfied!
If the baron really has good cause
To accuse Renard of breaking laws, 120
If he took a walnut not his own,
Then certainly he must atone—
But not until he is here to face
This court for judgment on his case.
However, I think Madame Hersent
Is very far from innocent.
Alas, it does you honor indeed
When your husband has to come and plead
His case where all of us can hear.
Truly, if you still hold him dear, 130
You have already lived too long!
He fears you not, and you were wrong
To let him give you a lover's name."
Hersent blushed; she felt such great shame
Her fur stood on end, as with a sigh
She made the badger this reply:[11]
"My lord Grinbert, I can bear no more.
All my desire is to end the war
Between my husband and Renard
Whose conduct has in no way marred 140
My honor. Here and now I'd appeal
For the right to prove this by ordeal—

[9]Grinbert the badger, Renard's only real defender, is his cousin.
[10]Breaking and entering was a capital offense.
[11]Hersent's heartrending (and comical speech) parodies the pleas of a number of Romantic heroines, especially those of Isolde in the Tristain and Isolde romances. Like Isolde, she offers to submit to an ordeal in order to prove her innocence and indirectly reveals her guilt while directly denying it.

Boiling water, red iron would fail
To burn me—but truth would not prevail.
Alas! I'm doomed to a life of woe.
Why does my lord distrust me so?
I swear by the holy saints above,
And as I hope to deserve God's love,
Renard has had from me no other
Kindness than if I'd been his mother. 150
Don't think I say this to win support
For Sir Renard when he comes to court;
I care for him, and it's simply stated,
Whether he may be loved or hated,
Lose his case or win its dismissal,
As you care for a donkey's thistle.
But jealousy took my husband's wits,
And he thinks the name of cuckold fits!
On Easter day—April first, this year[12]—
As I hold Pinsard, my young son, dear, 160
For a decade I had lived my life
As Ysengrin's devoted wife.
Everyone came to celebrate
When we were married, a crowd so great,
Such a multitude in den and lair,
That truly you might look everywhere
And not find even so much space
As a goose needs for a nesting place.
Since Ysengrin took me for his own,
I have kept my love for him alone— 170
I'm wronged by this scandalous affair!
So, once again now, I will swear—
And if you don't take me at my word,
At least I will know that you have heard—
By the faith I owe to Saint Marie,
I'm guiltless of debauchery,
And there is nothing I've ever done
That would disgrace a holy nun."

When they had listened to Hersent
Claiming that she was innocent, 180
Bernard the donkey took the floor.
He believed everything she swore,
Rejoicing to take as proven fact
That Ysengrin's honor was intact.
"Ah me!" he said, "most noble dame,
Would that my spouse were just the same
For loyalty—and everyone,
Dogs, wolves, and women, under the sun!
For, as I hope God will be kind,

[12]Easter fell on April 1 in 1179, perhaps evidence for dating the poem. Of course, April Fool's Day is an appropriate date, given the context.

Forgive my sins and let me find 190
Tender thistles where I graze,
So sure am I that it's not false praise
To say that you would in no measure
Care for Renard or give him pleasure,
Or to his love pay any heed.
But these are wicked times indeed;
The stink of slander fills the air
And people cheerfully will swear
To what was never in their sight,
And blame what they should say is right. 200
Wild Renard, you won't be believed!
In an evil hour were you conceived
And born. The entire world's persuaded
That you improperly invaded
Madame Hersent. And she'll appeal
For your acquittal by her ordeal.
Say, most noble, gracious king,
Why not put an end to this hateful thing?
On poor Renard bestow your grace!
Give me leave to go to his place 210
And bring him, by safe conduct, back
To answer Ysengrin's attack.
Renard will pay whatever fee
Your court in its wisdom may decree,
And if they find that lack of respect
Caused him to so long neglect
Your summons,[13] for that too he'll pay
Before you let him go away."
"Sire!" the angry lords protest,
"May Saint Giles deny your least request 220
If you favor Renard to that extent!
Don't have another message sent
To summon him! Let's wait right here
Two more days; if he doesn't appear,
Then have him brought back under guard,
And let his punishment be hard,
Something that he'll remember long."
Noble the king said, "You are wrong
To condemn Renard so out of hand.
I have forces at my command. 230
If I am threatened by your pride,
There will be nowhere you can hide!
Renard has a place in my heart still,
Whether you wish him well or ill.
I won't agree to your shameful plan,
If he still wants to be my man.

[13]In addition to his adultery, Renard is guilty of failing to answer Noble's summons for all his vassals to appear at court.

Ysengrin, as your wife suggested,
Let her innocence be tested,
Or else forget the whole affair."
"Don't say that, Sire! It isn't fair! 240
What if the red-hot iron is shown
To have burned her fingers to the bone?
Some will learn what they now don't know.
Joy will come to my every foe.
I'll hear their voices loud and clear
Shouting, 'The jealous cuckold's here!'
Let Renard think he's won the game.
I will live with my grief and shame
Until I can do what must be done.
But before the harvest has begun 250
He'll find himself in such a war
No wall or moat or bolted door
Will save him—I will strike him dead!"
"To Hell with that!" King Noble said;
"By Christ's bones, my lord Ysengrin,
Is that a war you think you'll win?
Can you really do as you have claimed?
Will Renard be either dead or maimed?
By the faith I owe to Saint Lenard,
With all the tricks known to Renard, 260
It's much more likely he won't fail
To do you in than you prevail.
Anyway, what can be the use
Of discussing it? We've sworn a truce,
And all the land has been brought to peace.
Woe to the guilty if that should cease!"
  Ysengrin, when the king had spoken
Of his concern lest the truce be broken,
Was so upset and in such dismay
He didn't know to what saint to pray. 270
He sat near the benches on the ground;
Between his legs his tail was wound.
Renard would have much to celebrate
If God had meant him for that fate:
With the king determined to achieve
The peace whoever that might grieve,
Renard and Ysengrin could no more
Incite each other to make war.
But Chanteclere and Pinte his hen
Were arriving at the court just then 280
With three others all of whom
Want justice for their sister's doom.
Now the fat is in the fire,
For Chanteclere, that noble sire,
And Pinte, whose eggs have such a span,
And Blacky, Whitey, and Roseanne,

Had brought with them a little cart
With curtains that they drew apart.
The others saw, as they came near,
A little on which, as on a bier, 290
A hen was lying. She'd been caught
By Renard whose cruel teeth had wrought
Such harm her leg was a splintered shred,
And one of her wings hung by a thread.
  King Noble felt that he had earned
A rest, and court should be adjourned;
But all at once the hens appear,
Wringing their hands, and Chanteclere.
First of all Pinte begins to plead,
And the others loudly take her lead: 300
"Most gracious beasts, for God's sweet sake,
You dogs and wolves, do not forsake
A poor creature so forlorn!
I curse the day that I was born!
Oh come, make haste and take me, Death,
Since Renard won't let me draw a breath
In peace. I had, on my father's side,
Five brothers—every one supplied
A dinner for Renard, the thief
Who has brought me to such bitter grief. 310
Not counting me, my mother gave birth
To five young virgin hens whose worth
For Gonbert del Frenne[14] would well repay
His fattening them to make them lay.
Oh! How I wish he'd kept his grain!
He fed them well, and yet the gain
Went to Renard, for all but one
Had passed through his throat when he was done.
And you who are lying in the bier,
My sister sweet, my friend so dear, 320
So tender and so plump, alas!
How wearily the days will pass
Without you—in sorrow I must dwell.
Renard, I hope you burn in Hell!
Not a moment can we turn our backs
Without the fear of your attacks—
Chased and mauled, your victim's pressed
Against the wall as you rip her vest!
I came out yesterday and found
My poor dead sister hurled to the ground, 330
And Renard so far away from the place
That Gonbert could not have given chase
On foot, and he has no swift horse.

[14]The farmer who owned the hens.

That's why I've come here. But no force
Can bring to justice one who grins
At threats, and doesn't care two pins
For anyone's wrath." She said no more,
Poor Pinte, but fell straight down on the floor.
They saw she had fainted dead away,
And next to her the other three lay.[15] 340
To get the ladies up on their feet,
Each dog and wolf rises from his seat,
And helped by the other beasts, they pour
Buckets of water on all four.
Just as soon as they'd recovered,
As in my source book I discovered,
They went where King Nobel had his seat
And fell on their faces at his feet.
Meanwhile the kneeling Chanteclere
Wet the king's feet with many a tear. 350
When Noble saw Chanteclere, in truth
He felt such pity for the youth,
That nothing on earth could make him hide
His feelings; from his depths he sighed,
Then raging, lifted up his head.
The bravest beast could not have said—
Not even the mighty bear or boar—
He felt no fear at the lion's roar.
Coward the hare heard it and quivered,
Two whole days in a fever shivered. 360
All the courtiers shook as one.
By their terror they were quite undone.
King Noble, lifting his tail up high,
In rage and anguish gave a cry
So loud that the house walls nearly broke,
And when the echoes died he spoke:
"My lady Pinte," the emperor said,
"I swear on my dead father's head—
His daily alms from me are still due—
I feel great sympathy for you, 370
And wish somehow to relieve your woe.
Renard shall come if he will or no!
By what you shall see with your own eyes,
Hear with your ears, you'll realize
How truly justice has been done.
Vengeance I'll have on anyone
For breaking the peace and murdering!"
Ysengrin, when he heard the king,
Leaped to his feet exclaiming, "Sire!
Actions of valor must inspire 380

[15]The simultaneous swooning of the four hens parodies similar collective fainting scenes in medieval epics and romances. At one point in *The Song of Roland*, for example, 20,000 men faint simultaneously (*Iaisse* CLXXVII).

Great praise. It will be a noble deed
If you can help poor Pinte in her need,
And get revenge for Madame Copee,
Mangled and butchered as we see.
I do not say it because I hate
Renard, but in sorrow for her fate;
Not out of hatred, but I resent
The slaughter of the innocent."
The emperor replied, "My friend,
My heart is heavy. Times without end 390
Renard's misdeeds have cost us dear.
To you and to the strangers here
I say the adulterer can't hide
From the consequences of his pride;
He broke the peace that I proclaimed,
And by his actions I am shamed.
But now there is another affair
We must attend to. Bruin the bear,
I ask you to put on your stole,[16]
Commend to God the poor hen's soul! 400
And you, Lord Clamor, by my command,
Shall dig a grave in that ploughed land."
"As you will, Sire," replied the bear,
And he went quickly to prepare
The several things that he would need.
Meanwhile, their ruler in the lead,
The other council members started
The vigil for the dear departed.
They heard Lord Slow the snail intone
Three whole lessons all on his own, 410
Bricemer the stag and the dog Roenel
Sang verse and responses very well.
The service lasted through the night,
But when the sun gave its first light,
The burial could not be delayed.
First, in a casket that was made
Fit for a king, and all of lead,
They reverently placed the dead.
They buried her beneath a tree
With a marble stone in memory 420
Of Madame Copee and to extol
Her deeds and to God commend her soul.
Carved with a chisel or else a knife,
This epitaph summed up her life:
"Here on this plain, beneath this tree,
Lies Pinte's sister, Madame Copee.
Renard, who pursues his evil ways,
With cruel teeth cut short her days."

[16]Priest's vestment.

Whoever witnessed poor Pinte's crying,
Cursing Renard for her sister's dying, 430
And Chanteclere with his feet stretched out,[17]
Would pity them, I have no doubt.
When grief had lost its violence
And mourning was not quite so intense,
The lords cried, "Emperor, it's time
That you made that thief pay for his crime!
We're tired of his tricks, and it's no use
Hoping that he'll respect a truce."
"Yes," says the king, "that's all too true.
Brother Bruin, here's a task for you— 440
There's nothing at all for you to fear—
Tell Renard that I have been here
Waiting for him three whole days."
"Gladly," says Bruin. He delays
Not for a moment but mounts and rides
Toward the forest where Renard resides,
And, never stopping, on he went.
Meanwhile there was a great event,
As through the valley Bruin rode,
Back at the court, and it would bode 450
Ill for Renard. Sir Coward the hare,
Who'd caught such a fever from his scare
(Two days he was in a shivering fit),
Had now, thank God, been cured of it.
Here's how he found the remedy:
Not wanting to leave Madame Copee,
Above the martyr's grave he lay,
Fell fast asleep, and was cured that way.
Ysengrin, when he heard the story
Of the new martyr's proven glory, 460
Said that he had an awful earache,
And then, deciding he would take
Roenel's advice, he put his head
Upon the grave and was cured, he said.
Were it not good doctrine that about
A miracle one can have no doubt—
And there was Roenel to provide
A witness—they would have thought he lied.
When they listened to this new report,
Some were happy at the court, 470
But Grinbert thought it bad indeed.
He and Tibert the cat, who plead
On Renard's behalf, fear that the news
Means that without a mighty ruse
Renard's in a bad way if he's caught.
And a shortcut had already brought
Lord Bruin through the depths of the wood

[17]The rooster has apparently fainted along with the hens.

To where Renard's great fortress stood.
Bruin would have to shrink before
He found a way inside the door— 480
At the barbican he has to stay.[18]
Renard, who takes the world for his prey,
Had his inner lair dug very deep,
And just then he was fast asleep.
He had provisions in his den:
There was a beautiful plump hen;
And two chicken legs down to the feet
That morning had left him quite replete.
Now, as if he meant to ruin
Renard's sweet slumber, here comes Bruin! 490
"Renard," he says, "it's Bruin the bear,
Sent by the king. Come out of there!
Come out and talk to me where I stand,
And I will tell you the king's command."
Renard saw enough to recognize
Bruin the bear by his great size,
And, in an instant, he had planned
A way to get the upper hand.
"Good Bruin, as I hold you dear,
I'm sorry they sent you way down here 500
On a useless errand—it's a shame.
I would have left before you came
Except that I was disinclined
To leave a good French meal behind.
You know how a wealthy man is treated:
'Sir, will you wash?' is the way he's greeted
When he comes to court; everyone believes
It's an honor just to hold his sleeves.
They serve him beef cooked with vinegar,
Then ask him which he would prefer 510
Among the many other dishes.
Who listens to a poor man's wishes?
They think he's made of a devil's shit.
Not by the fireside does he sit;
For a table he must use his lap
As the housedogs crowd around and snap,
Snatching the bread out of his fingers.
Over a single drink he lingers,
Knowing they won't refill his glass,
And once will the serving platter pass. 520
Boys will shower him with bones
Drier than red-hot burning stones.
Each holds his bread clutched in his hand.
The tables of the lords of the land
Miss what seneschals and cooks withhold,
All of them cut form the self-same mold.

[18]A barbican is the gate-tower of a castle. The description of Renard's home, Maupertuis, comically blends romantic elements of a castle with realistic ones of a fox's den.

Would they were burned and their ashes blown!
Whatever they want they take for their own;
Meat and bread from the master's stores
Go to make dinner for their whores. 530
All this is why I wouldn't have cared,
Good my lord, to travel unprepared,
And this noon I have not only dined
On good peas and bacon well combined,
But ate every bit I had at home
Of fresh new honey in the comb."
"*Nomini Dame, file Christom!*"[19]
The bear said, "Honeycomb! Where's it from?
By the bones of Giles the blessed saint,
My belly so craves it I feel faint! 540
God's heart! Dear gracious lord, please say,
Mea culpa![20] that you'll show the way!"
Renard sticks his tongue out with a look
That says the bear is on the hook,
And, all unknown to the poor Bruin,
Prepares to bring his victim in,
Carefully coiling his long line:
"Bruin, if you were a friend of mine,"
Renard said, "if I only knew
That I really could depend on you, 550
Then, by my son Rovel, I swear
This very day I'd take you there.
You'd be standing at the honeyed site,
Filling your belly with delight.
In Lanfroi the forester's domain,
Not far from here, rich combs remain.
But near or far, what does it matter?
All this is only idle chatter.
You, if I served you as a guide,
Would take it out of my poor hide." 560
"Renard, how can you distrust me so!"
"I do." "But why?" "What I know I know.
There's an evil purpose in your heart."
"Renard, it must be the devil's art
That makes you think I could be so vile."
"All right. I'll give your good faith a trial.
I would not wrong you, nor you me."
"That's the truth! For by the fealty
I swore to Noble, our gracious king,
Never would I do anything 570
To harm you; never do I intend
To treat you other than as my friend."
"Those are the words I wanted to hear,
Bruin, and now I have no fear."

[19]Garbled Latin for "in the name of our Lady, daughter of Christ."
[20]"My fault" (Latin), a mild exclamation.

When they had come to this agreement,
Happy for both, away they went
On their good chargers, the two abreast,
And galloped, never taking a rest,
So urgently did they wish to gain
Lanfroi's forest, where they drew rein. 580
There an enormous oak tree stood.
Lanfroi, who wanted to sell the wood,
Had driven in two mighty wedges,
Making a slit between their edges.
Renard said, "Bruin, my dear friend,
We have come to our journey's end.
The honey's inside there. Eat it first,
Then we will go and quench our thirst;
You shall have what you've always loved."
Standing on his hind legs, Bruin shoved 590
His muzzle and his two front paws
Into the hole. To help his cause,
Renard keeps pushing him from below,
Shouting he hasn't far to go:
"Open your mouth, you son of a whore!
You're almost there! Just a little more!
Only unlock your teeth, you scum!"
Now Renard's great moment has come;
For Bruin, though, it's not so funny—
He didn't find a drop of honey 600
However hard and long he tried,
And, while his mouth was opened wide,
Renard, damn his soul! with a mighty clout,
Suddenly knocked both wedges out!
In the space where the oak tree had been split,
A third of Bruin was tightly fit—
Not a good way to take a rest!
The poor bear really is hard-pressed,
Held a captive by the tree,
While Renard (not known for charity, 610
And let his confession not be made)[21]
Shouts that it's he who's been betrayed:
"Bruin, I always did believe
That you had something up your sleeve!
You're at the honey and won't stop
Until you've left me not a drop!
Next time I'll beat you at your game!
But don't you feel the slightest shame
At eating all that lovely honey?
And then, I suppose, I'll get no money! 620
I can imagine the kind of trick
You'd have played on me had I fallen sick—

[21]In other words, "Let him go to hell."

You'd have brought rotten pears for a treat!"
But Renard knew he had better retreat
When he looked up just in time to see
That Lanfroi was coming toward the tree.
The peasant could not believe his luck—
There was Bruin so tightly stuck!
Off to the village Lanfroi sped,
Shouting, "Come help and the bear is dead! 630
We've got him now but hurry! hurry!"
You should have seen the peasants scurry,
Swarm through the trees with bloodthirsty looks!
Some carry clubs, some pruning hooks,
Flails and axes raised to attack!
Bruin shivers, fears for his back.
Hearing the mob's ferocious voice,
He knows in his heart he has no choice—
Better, no doubt, to sacrifice
His muzzle, held as in a vice, 640
Than to wait there for Lanfroi to seize.
So Bruin starts to push and squeeze
And pull, no matter how it hurts,
Stretching his skin while blood spurts
In bright streams from his broken veins.
His skin gives way—not enough remains
On his mangled head to make a purse—
Never did any beast look worse!
From all his dreadful wounds the blood
Comes pouring in a crimson flood; 650
There's no skin at all on his front feet.
Much has he suffered to retreat!
But now at last poor Bruin could
Run away through the depths of the wood.
And the shouting peasants are not slow:
The son of Lord Billin, called Bertot,
And with him Hardoin Hit and Run,
Gonbert and with him Gallon's son
(Falcon's nephew) and Count Ortrands
Who strangled his wife with his own hands; 660
Tygers, who baked the village's bread—
(Black Cornelia he took to bed).
And Aymery the Sickle Breaker,
And Rocelin the son of Shaker.
Ogier's son, not there to relax,
Held in his hand a battle-axe;
And there was my lord Hubert Grosset
And the son of Faucher Galopet.
The war party was increased
By the presence of the parish priest, 670
Father of Martin de la Tour.

He had just finished spreading manure
And took up the pitchfork he had plied
To plant it deep in Bruin's side
As the bear in pain and anguish fled—
A little deeper and he was dead.
Catching Bruin against an oak,
Another of those peasant folk,
A comb and lantern maker by trade,
Struck at him, not with a blade, 680
But with a steer's horn, wrenching his back.
Besides all these, there is no lack
Of peasants beating him with flails—
The wonder is that he prevails.
Renard, who knows his prospects are grim
If Bruin gets a chance at him,
Hears the bear at a distance, free,
And takes a shortcut to Maupertuis,
That mighty fortress where he knows
He'll be safe from his strongest foes. 690
Seeing Bruin close to his door,
Renard gibes at him once more:
"Bruin, I hope you're satisfied!
I know you never meant to divide
Lanfroi's honey. Those who pretend
Good faith will come to a bitter end,
And don't think a priest will see you through!
But tell me, are you aspiring to
A monastic order? What's this red
Hood-like thing that's on your head?" 700
But Bruin, too far gone for banter,
Left at an energetic canter,
Still in terror at the thought
Of what would happen if he were caught.
So he spurred on, so fast that soon,
Just as the bells were rung at noon,
The bear was riding through the gate
To where the lion sat in state.
Bruin fell fainting on the floor,
His face entirely covered with gore. 710
As his friends come running, it appears
The bear has arrived without his ears.
The king said, "Bruin, who did that?
Who so foully ripped off your hat
And left your legs in such a state?"
His loss of blood had been so great
That Bruin's voice was very weak:
"King," he said, "I went out to seek
Renard, and found him, as you can tell."
Then at King Noble's feet he fell. 720

You should have heard the lion roar,
Tearing his mane out as he swore
On Christ's pure heart what he would do!
"Bruin," he says, "I think you're through.
You've been murdered, but it won't be long,
By the death of Christ, before this wrong
Is avenged. Renard will pay so dear
No one in France will fail to hear!
Where are you, Tibert? Be on your way
To Maupertuis, and with no delay! 730
Tell that red-haired bastard I command
That before the nobles of this land
He make the reparation due.
And that won't be accomplished through
Gold and silver, nor is there hope
That words will cut down the gallows rope
Waiting for the killer we accuse!"
Tibert, could he have dared refuse,
Would still not have come to Maupertuis,
But there's no way out; he must agree 740
With what the king and council decide.
So the cat, who doesn't ride astride,
Gallops along the valley floor,
Spurring his mule—and there's the door
Behind which he will find Renard.
He prays to God and to Saint Lenard,
Who oftentimes has captives freed,
That he, by his prayers, would intercede
And keep Tibert safe from his old friend,
For he is sure Renard would contend 750
With the devil to do an evil deed,
So dear to him is the holy creed!
Something increased his consternation
Just as he reached his destination:
Between an ash tree and a pine
He saw a buzzard. He made a sign,
And said to it, "Go right! Go right!"
But the bird kept on its left-hand flight.
For quite some moments Tibert paused.
It was most of all the bird that caused 760
The cat to think he'd be defeated,
Shamed and very badly treated.
Tibert, by gloomy thoughts inspired,
Felt that he was not required
To ask if he could go inside.
He went just up to the door and tried
To do his errand tactfully;
No good came of it, as you shall see.
"Renard," he said, "as I hold you dear,
Tell me, at least, if you are here." 770

Renard seemed not to reply at first;
Out of sight, between his teeth, he cursed:
"Tibert, my friend, you'll rue the day
You ever put yourself in my way!
I'll have your hide right down to the bone!"
Then he said, in a normal tone:
"*Welcomme*, good Tibert, to my home!
If you were on your way from Rome
Or from Compostela,[22] I'd hold you dear
And be as glad to see you here 780
As to welcome the Pentecostal feast!"
It doesn't hurt Renard in the least
To offer greetings of that sort.
Tibert's reply is rather short:
"Renard, please understand one thing:
I'm only here to speak for the eking—
It's certainly not the way I feel—
And he condemns you without appeal.
Grinbert, your cousin, takes your side,
But with no one else are you allied— 790
What the others feel for you is hate."
Renard is not inclined to debate:
"How I deal with threats you shall see,
And those who'd sharpen their teeth on me.
While I can I will live my life!
I'll go to court and settle this strife,
If they dare accuse me to my face."
"That will be very wise, your Grace;
For this, as always, you have my praise.
But I've had nothing to eat for days— 800
My spine is bent just like a bow.
Haven't you something down below,
A hen or a rooster I could taste?"
Renard said, "That would be a waste.
Everyone knows the way you steal
Plump mice and rats to make a meal—
Poultry is not the thing for you!"
"Oh yes it is!" "That can't be true."
"I'll eat until the last hen's gone."
"All right. Tomorrow, before the dawn, 810
You'll be full where you now are hollow.
I'll go first, and you just follow."
With that Renard came out of his lair.
Tibert followed him, unaware
That he as already caught by guile.
They saw a village after a while

[22]Both Rome and the shrine of Saint-Jacques de Compostela in Spain were favorite destinations for pilgrims.

Where for sure you'd be hard-put to find
A coop where Renard had never dined.
"Tibert," he says, "you're in for a treat.
In one of the houses on that street, 820
Lucky for us, there lives a priest—
I know him well, to say the least.
His oats and barley would well suffice
Except that he is plagued by mice
Who take such pleasure in that fare
It was nearly gone when I was there.
I set out to capture a hen—
Before I knew it, I'd taken ten!
Five of them I ate today;
The others I put safely away. 830
Just inside is the hiding-place,
So go right in and stuff your face!"
That treacherous master of deceit
Was lying. Neither oats nor wheat
Were kept in the place where Tibert went,
A fact the priest did much lament.
The whole village used to deplore
The way the priest's light-fingered whore,
The mother of Martin de la Tour,
Took all he owned. I am quite sure 840
He had no oxen, not a cow—
His barnyard was reduced by now
To just two chickens and a cock.
Young Martin, who later wore the frock,
And then would choose monkish robes to wear,
Had closed the entrance with a snare,
Hoping to catch the foxy beast.
God had most greatly blessed the priest
With a son to think of tricks like that,
And so outwit a fox or cat! 850
Renard says, "Tibert, my dear fellow,
Go help yourself, unless you're yellow!
I'll be waiting for you right outside."
Tibert sets forth in a running stride
And then his neck is in the noose—
There seems no way to get it loose!
He knows he's done a stupid thing—
The more he pulls, the tighter the string.
He struggles—surely something can be done!
But here comes Martin on the run 860
Yelling, "Father! Oh, make haste!
Help me, Mother! There's no time to waste!
Come to the hole and bring a light—
We'll have some sport with the fox tonight!"

At this young Martin's mother awakes,
Jumps up, lights a candle, and she takes
Her spindle with her. At Martin's calls
The priest, holding on to his balls,
Leaps out of bed, and runs still faster.
For Tibert it's a real disaster: 870
He carries more than a hundred blows
Away with him when at last he goes.
The priest strikes, and his concubine,
And both of them are doing fine
When Tibert, in his struggle, spies
What's dangling between the priest's thin thighs,
And grabs—this is told in all the books—
With teeth and claws like grappling hooks,
And hangs on until it is off for good.
As soon as the woman understood 880
The full extent of the tragedy,
Three times she cried, "Alas for me!"
And when she would have made it four,
She swooned and fell down upon the floor.
This gave young Martin such a scare
That the cat, who'd bitten through the snare,
Could take advantage of the uproar
And run until he was safe once more.
Tibert has had some satisfaction—
Ah! could he now go into action 890
Against the cause of his rage and pain!
But Renard hadn't chosen to remain.
When he saw Tibert in the snare,
He was on his way right out of there,
Having no desire to come to harm;
He heard young Martin sound the alarm
And went home—he didn't even wait
To see what would be poor Tibert's fate.
"Ah! Renard, Renard," Tibert said,
"May God not take you when you're dead! 900
But I deserve to be badly treated,
Having so often been defeated
By that lying cheat, Renard the Red!
May the cuckold priest have little bread
And a wretched place to lay his head,
He and the whore he takes to bed,
For what they've done to me today!
But at least he won't be able to play
The parish music very well
Since he's been left with just one bell. 910
And as for Martin de la Tour,
I hope he'll be forever poor

And that, for giving me such blows,
His lifetime will not come to a close
Before he's a monk with no relief
Until he's hanged for a proven thief!"
  So in a rage at his disgrace,
He came through the valley to the place
Where the king sat in his judgment seat.
Tibert saw him, fell at his feet, 920
And told him his fantastic tale.
"God!" said the king, "My powers fail.
My lords, I am extremely shocked
To find my dignity so mocked.
And where's the champion I need
To take revenge for Renard's foul deed?
My lord Grinbert, I'm half-inclined
To see your influence behind
The way Renard despises me."
"I swear, Sire, that could never be!" 930
"Then go and bring Renard to court.
If you fail, don't bother to report."
"Sire," said Grinbert, "it can't be done.
That bastard would just think it fun—
He'd never yield to my desire,
Unless I had a letter, Sire.
By Saint Israel, no appeal
Would move him, but if he saw your seal,
He'd know, whatever pretext he used,
There's no way for him to be excused." 940
"My dear Sir, that makes very good sense."
Noble then dictated the contents
While Baucent wrote down everything;
He sealed the letter for the king.
  Then Grinbert, with the king's permission,
Started out to perform his mission.
Through meadow and wood he went; no lack
Of sweat was pouring off his back,
And still he had far to go before
He would be close to Renard's front door. 950
At vespers he came upon a lane,
And at nightfall found Renard's domain.
The walls rose high above his head;
There were narrow passageways that led
To where he found a low-vaulted door
Into a courtyard. Then, still more
Afraid of what Renard would do
If he should hear him coming through,
He hugged the walls and waited to see—
That was Grinbert at Maupertuis. 960

As soon as his visitor had stepped
Onto the turning bridge[23] and crept
Along the passageways—even then,
Before Grinbert came into his den,
Hindquarters first and head to the rear,
Renard knew who was coming near.
He welcomed Grinbert with warm delight,
Wrapped both arms around him tight,
And two soft pillows behind him pressed,
Because his cousin was his guest. 970
I think Grinbert was very wise
To keep his message for a surprise
Until he'd had enough to eat,
But after dinner, feeling replete,
"My lord," he said, "everyone knows
The way you lie and cheat—it shows.
I'm here to tell you the king demands,
No, not demands—the king commands
That at his palace you submit
To whatever sentence he deems fit. 980
Why wage a war you cannot win?
What did you want of Ysengrin?
Why harm Tibert? Why hurt Bruin?
You have betrayed them to your ruin.
I'd like to offer you some cheer,
But I think your time to die is near,
And all your children will share your fate.
Break this seal and you'll get it straight.
Just read the words that are written here."
Renard listens, and shakes with fear. 990
He trembles, as he breaks the seal,
For what that gesture may reveal.
He reads the first few words and sighs,
Well understanding what meets his eyes.
"Noble the lion, whose majesty
Prevails throughout these lands where he
Over all the beasts is king and lord,
Promises Renard he cannot afford
To ignore this summons: he'll pay dear
If tomorrow he does not appear 1000
To make amends for his misdeeds.
Not silver and not gold he needs,
And let no champion give him hope;
He'll pay his debt with a hangman's rope."
A terrible message for Renard!

[23]Drawbridge (over the moat).

Inside his chest his heart beat hard,
His face took on a somber hue.
"For God's sake, Grinbert, what shall I do?
Pity a poor defenseless captive!
Alas that I have this hour to live 1010
If I must hang until I'm dead
Tomorrow. I wish I'd been instead
A monk at Cluny or Citeaux!
But many of them are false, and so
I'd soon have wanted to depart;
In that case better not to start."
"You've other things to worry about!"
Said Grinbert. "And while you're here without
People around you, I suggest
That it would be well if you confessed. 1020
Confess your sins to me at least—
Since I don't see any closer priest."
"My lord Grinbert," Renard replies,
I think your counsel very wise;
I'm close to death for my transgression,
And if you hear my true confession
I've nothing at all to lose thereby,
And I am saved if I have to die.
Listen! I heartily repent
For what I did with Dame Hersent 1030
Who is the wife of Ysengrin.
She tried to cover up that sin
But no one believed her—that was shrewd
For she was well and truly screwed.
My God preserve my soul from Hell,
So many times I rang her bell—
Mea culpa!—if I have to face
Ysengrin, I'll lose the case.
How to deny that he's been cheated,
Three times imprisoned and defeated! 1040
Now I will tell you all about it.
I made him fall into the pit
Just as he carried off a sheep.
Lucky for him he got to keep
Any skin at all, for it was shed
In a hundred blows before he fled.
When I had trapped him as I planned,
There were three shepherds close at hand
Who beat him like a balky ass.
Another time I helped him to pass 1050
Through an entrance to a rich man's larder,
But getting out was a great deal harder,
For his belly swelled still more with each
Of three hams he found within his reach.

I set him to fishing through the ice;
His tail was caught as in a vise.
I made him fish in a pool one night
When the full moon was very bright,
And its reflection, white and round,
Looked like a lovely cheese he'd found. 1060
So once again I had my wish—
He ended up on a load of fish.
A hundred times I took him in
With the guileful schemes my wits can spin.
Thanks to me he had a tonsured head.[24]
Then he saw how well the canons fed
And thought their life wouldn't be so hard;
Those fools gave him their sheep to guard!
I could talk all day and not be done
Telling you how I had my fun. 1070
There's not one beast in Noble's court
Who wouldn't give me a bad report.
When I led Tibert into the net
He thought that it was rats he'd get.
In all Pinte's family there lives
One aunt; her other relatives,
Cocks and hens alike, were able
To fill a place at my dinner table.
When a cow and ox and the mighty boar
With other beasts stood at my door 1080
Well armed, Ysengrin, in the lead,
Was sure that he had all he'd need
To win. There were on his side as well,
With the watchdog, Loudmouth Roenel,
Seven times twenty dogs and bitches
All of whom soon needed stitches,
Having most foully been betrayed—
I'd gotten to everyone they paid.
I certainly have no cause to boast
Of how I routed that great host— 1090
Only by guile were they defeated.
I watched as long as they retreated
And in salute stuck out my tongue.
God! What I did when I was young!
But now, *mea culpa!* true remorse
Turns my life from its sinful course."
"Renard, Renard," Grinbert begins,
"I've heard the confession of your sins
And all the evil you have done.

[24]The shaved crown of a monk. In another episode of *Renard*, the fox pours boiling water over the wolf's head.

Your trial, by God's will, may yet be won. 1100
Take care from now on to do no wrong."
"My God not let me live so long."
Renard replied, "that all my ways
Are not deserving of His praise."
he shows a pious resolution,
Kneels, and Grinbert gives absolution
In French and in the tongue of Rome.
Next morning, before Renard left home,
He kissed his children and his wife,
All of them fearing for his life. 1110
When the time of separation came,
"My sons," he said, "defend our name!
However this misadventure goes,
Protect my castles against our foes.
Against a count, against a king,
For months you won't need to fear a thing—
No count or baron, no lord would dare
Rob your head of a single hair.
You'll never be so much as grazed,
If you keep every drawbridge raised 1120
And are well provisioned—for seven years
You'll stand them off and have no fears.
What more is there for me to say?
I commend you now to God, and pray
That He will bring me back once more."
With that he knelt down on the floor;
Because he would have to leave his lair,
Renard began to say a prayer.
"God, King, in your omnipotence,
Let my craft and my common sense 1130
Not be lost to me out of fear
When before the king I must appear
To answer Ysengrin in court.
Whatever he chooses to report
Let me make it harmless to admit,
Or find some way of denying it;
And let me come back to Maupertuis
Alive and well, so that I may be
Avenged on those who seek my disgrace."
Renard fell down upon his face, 1140
Then, beating his breast for what he'd done,
Made the sign against the evil one.
And now the noble lords will go
To court; on their way swift rivers flow;
There are narrow trails to follow past
High mountain ridges until at last
They ride across a level plain.
Renard is really feeling the strain;

That's why, in the woods, they go astray
And find no footpath, road or way 1150
Until, where farmland had been cleared,
A barn that belonged to nuns appeared.
Surely one would find inside
The best of what the world can provide:
Cheese and milk and lambs they keep,
Geese and oxen, cows and sheep,
And young ones they fatten up to eat.
"Come one!" said Renard. "Don't drag your feet!
Now I can see where we went wrong.
There's underbrush to follow along 1160
To the henyard, then it's straight ahead."
"Renard, Renard," the badger said,
"Does God not know what you say that for?
Foul unbelieving son of a whore,
Stinking glutton—I thought you craved,
Pleading for mercy, to be saved!
I heard your confession, did I not?"
Replied Renard, "I quite forgot.
I'm ready now. Let's go on like friends."
"Renard, Renard, it never ends! 1170
God himself you will try to trick!
On you repentance can never stick.
How you came to be so mad, God knows!
Your life may be coming to a close,
And scarcely have you confessed before
You turn around and sin once more.
Evil has marked you out as prey.
Let's go now. A curse upon the day
When you were severed from your mother!"
"You do very well to say so, brother! 1180
But now let's go our way in peace."
To make his cousin's scolding cease
Renard was keeping very quiet
As to the farm—he dared not try it,
But he craned his neck a little when
He caught a sight of a lovely hen,
Sadly thinking he'd rather have fed
And paid the price, though it were his head!
As the two lords proceed with their ride,
Grinbert's mule has a mighty stride, 1190
But fear of his master's wrath so grips
Renard's horse that he constantly trips;
Beneath his skin the blood pounds hard,
So greatly does he fear Renard.
They run through fields, through woods they scramble,
Galloping or at an amble,
Over the mountain pass they ride

To the valley on the other side
Where those accused are called to account;
In front of the great hall they dismount. 1200
  As soon as it's known Renard is there
Everyone hastens to prepare
An accusation or defense.
Renard's discomfort is intense.
He'll suffer whether or not he hangs;
Ysengrin's sharpening his fangs,
Tibert the cat is thinking hard,
And Bruin whose face is red and scarred.
But regardless of their love or hate,
Renard's courage does not abate. 1210
He makes his speech with his head held high,
Looking the king straight in the eye.
  "Sire, I've come to meet you here[25]
Knowing that you should hold me dear
Above all other lords of this land.
You have been wronged by those who planned
To injure me. Perhaps it's just
My bad luck, but I could never trust
Your love, not for a single day—
That's about as long as I've been away. 1220
You know that there was no ill will
Between us, no dispute, and still,
When I left in peace and by your leave,
You were all ready to believe
Slander about me from my foes.
That is the way a kingdom goes
To ruin—when the king will treat
Without suspicion those who cheat,
And loyalty cannot prevail:
He throws out the head and keeps the tail. 1230
Those who should be serfs by station
Don't know the wisdom of moderation.
They'll go to any lengths to gain
Favor by someone else's pain.
They'll do evil of any sort
Providing they can rise at court,
Fleecing others as their hearts desire.
And now allow me to inquire
Why Tibert and Bruin complain of me.
Although, should it please Your Majesty, 1240
I can tell you what it's all about.
If I harmed them it was not without
Their help, as they both are well aware.
Who ate the honey if not the bear?

[25]Renard's self-serving speech parodies heroic speeches in medieval epics and romances, especially Roland's in *The Song of Roland* (in *Laisses* LIX–LXIII, for example).

If Lanfroi defends his property,
Should Bruin take it out on me?
Look what he has for legs and paws,
Enormous feet, with enormous claws.
And if Tibert here, my lord the cat,
Was eating a meal of mouse or rat 1250
When he was caught in nets and shamed,
God's heart! I don't see why I am blamed.
As for Ysengrin—what can I say?
His accusation's true, in a way,
For certainly I have loved Hersent.
But that had to be with her consent—
Did she ever come here to protest?
Is it right, at a jealous fool's request,
That I be hanged until I'm dead?
God forbid, Sire! Recognize instead 1260
The good faith and true fidelity
I have always shown Your Majesty:
Your kingdom, so deserving praise,
Is what I've lived for all my days.
But now my muzzle has gone gray;
There is no game left that I can play,
By God and Saint George, I'm much too weak.
It's a sin to drag me here to speak,
Old as I am, before this court.
When the king commands that I report, 1270
I do his will, as I hold him dear,
And now I stand in his presence here.
I could hang or perish at the stake;
There is no protest I can make
Against the king—I am not so strong.
But to get revenge that way is wrong.
To hang me will be called a disgrace,
If there's no real judgment on my case."[26]
"Renard," the emperor begins,
"May your father suffer for his sins! 1280
May the whore who bore you be accursed
Because she didn't abort you first!
Treacherous thief, can you explain
Why you have such a scheming brain?
You know how to argue and to plead,
But to that my court will give no heed.
There's no way for you to leave this place;
You shall hear my verdict on your case!
Your bravado won't be any use;
Your scheming will find you no excuse. 1290
Though you are as slippery as an eel,
There's no escape and no appeal—

[26]Twelfth-century French law guaranteed the right to a trial. The principle was cited in some romances in reference to Lancelot's adultery with Guinevere, which never came to trial.

Your fate was predicted long ago,
And now its coming won't be slow.
My noble lords are in court to say
Just what a thief who's caught must pay,
And to sentence a traitor for his crime.
You'll feel the weight of their wrath this time!
Unless you can find a hiding-place,
They'll say what they think right to your face." 1300
Then spoke Grinbert the badger: "Sire,
With the deference that you inspire,
We give you, and rightly, our full trust.
But that doesn't mean that you can just
Do what you want to—it is vile
To deny a lord his rightful trial.
You may not like it, but it's clear
Renard had safe conduct to come here.
Let those who accuse him state their case,
And then allow him, by your grace, 1310
With your court as witness, to be tried
As justice and the law provide."
he could not say all he intended.
Before the badger's speech had ended,
Up on his feet was Ysengrin,
And the sheep as well, my lord Belin,
And my lord Tiecelin, the crow,
Chanteclere, Dame Pinte, and also
The three other hens who support their claim.
The hedgehog, Spikey was his name, 1320
And the peacock, Petipas, step out,
And Frobert the cricket—he, no doubt,
Has the loudest voice of those who shout.
Then one with much to complain about:
The squirrel, called my lord Roxat,
And Roenel and Tibert the cat.
Coward the hare, who's very fleet,
Hurries through courtyards, from street to street;
He has very good cause to pray
That justice should be done that day. 1330
Renard is sure if he had to cope
With these he'd have very little hope.
But the king commands that they be still—
Vengeance is subject to his will.
King Noble's voice, which is very loud,
Carries through the assembled crowd:
"Hear me, my lords," he says in a roar,
"Renard can be trusted like a whore!
What punishment should I decree
To avenge what he has done to me?" 1340
"Sire," they answered, "as you said before,
Renard has the virtue of a whore.

The only thing that's of any use
To reform him is a hangman's noose."
The king replied, "I like what you say!
Let's do it, and without delay!
He's a menace, and I don't know how
We'd get him back if we lost him now.
We'll suffer for it, should he leave:
Some who think they are safe will grieve." 1350
On a hilltop, by the king's command,
In a rocky place, the gallows stand,
Set up to end the fox's career—
Death, it would seem, is very near.
A monkey, mocking Renard's disgrace,
Is answered by a slap in the face.
Renard looks behind him; he can see
His foes approaching, more than three.
One gives him a kick and one a shove—
He has plenty to be fearful of. 1360
From a good distance—he wouldn't dare
Come any closer—Coward the hare
Did his part too: he threw a stone,
Hit Renard's head, and broke the bone.
But that gave Coward such a fright
That henceforth he stayed out of sight.
One look from Renard put him on edge;
He ran to take shelter in a hedge.
From there, he thought, he could watch and wait
Till Renard had finally met his fate. 1370
But hiding was, I think, a mistake,
He'll have, this day, good cause to shake.
Renard, with stout ropes securing him,
Felt his prospects were growing dim,
He couldn't think of a thing that might
Rescue him from his dreadful plight.
No doubt you'd have to be a master
To walk away from this disaster.
When he saw the gallows standing there
Renard was reduced to real despair. 1380
He said, "Most gracious lord and king,
Allow me to mention just one thing:
You have had me brought out here and tied,
And want to hang me before I'm tried;
But there are sinful things I've done,
And God's forgiveness could still be won,
Were I allowed, for my soul's defense,
To take the cross in penitence,
And obedient to God's command,
Cross the sea to the Holy Land. 1390
If I die there my soul will rise,
But if I'm hanged I'm the devil's prize—

More honor to you if you relent.
All I want now is to repent."
At the king's feet he lay his head.
Noble was moved by what he'd said.
And then Grinbert came forward to plead
That Renard, repentant, should be freed:
"Before you answer, Sire, think twice!
For God's sake listen to my advice! 1400
Renard's not afraid of any foe.
If he stays away five months you'll know
That your kingdom really can't afford
To lose so fine and valiant a lord."
The king replied, "I'll be more than glad
To lose him, and he'd be twice as bad
Should he return. The best ones trade
Virtue for evil on crusade.
If Renard survives, there is no doubt
That all of us had better look out!" 1410
"If he doesn't get his conscience clear,
Never again will you see him here."
"Then he shall be, by my command,
Forever in the Holy Land."
Renard hears that with a joyful heart.
He may not do any more than start
His journey, so it's no great loss.
On his right shoulder he wears a cross;
They bring him a pilgrim's purse and staff.
Some do not feel inclined to laugh, 1420
Though they kicked and taunted him before;
They fear he will even up the score.
  Behold Renard, ashwood staff in hand,
A pilgrim bound for the Holy Land!
He must forgive them, says the king
In the name of all, for everything;
And if he abandons tricks and lies,
He'll win salvation when he dies.
Whatever Renard may have in mind,
He seems not in the least inclined 1430
To turn away from piety.
He leaves, as he tells His Majesty,
With peace and forgiveness in his heart;
Just after noon he's ready to start.
To no else does he say farewell—
He wishes each one of them in Hell!
He'd have revenge on that whole crowd
Except for the king and Fiere the proud,
His courteous and lovely queen
Whose parting words show her far from mean: 1440
"Renard," she says, "we'll pray for you,
And remember us in your prayers too."

"My lady, I will do my best
To show how I honor your request;
And who would not be joyful indeed
To have your prayers in his soul's great need!
But even better would I fare
If I could have that ring you wear.
If you allow me that great boon,
You shall be well rewarded soon: 1450
I have jewels[27] that I will bring
And they're worth a hundred times one ring."
Renard takes the ring that he is handed—
No need for him to be commanded!
Between his teeth he says very low:
"If there is someone who doesn't know
This ring, I have only to appear
For that to cost him very dear."
Renard puts the ring upon his finger,
Bows to the king, and does not linger. 1460
His spurs strike at his horse's sides;
At a racing trot away he rides.
Presently, close at hand, he found
The hedge where Coward went to ground.
It was so long since Renard ate last
He had a headache from his fast.
Coward, seeing Renard so near,
Is just about overcome with fear.
He jumps right up, and in his fright
Greets him, sounding very polite: 1470
"I can hardly tell you what delight
It gives me to see that you're all right!
I have felt weighed down by my dismay
At the way they treated you today."
Replies Renard from his crafty brain,
"If my misfortune gives you pain,
And you see my person so disgraced,
Let's make sure that yours won't go to waste!"
Every word that Coward hears
Seems to justify his gravest fears. 1480
It would be better if he fled
(If he stays he thinks he'll soon be dead),
And he would have headed for the plain
Had Renard not grabbed his horse's rein.
"Ha! Coward, my lord, by God's heart
I swear you shall not so soon depart!
Did you think your horse had so much speed
That you wouldn't be the one to feed
My hungry cubs at home today?"
With his staff he prods him on his way. 1490

[27]"Jewels" had a sexual double meaning in medieval French, as it does in modern English.

King Noble, his barons and their men
Were passing through a valley just then
Whose walls towered very high
To four huge rocks set against the sky.
At the top Renard pursues his course
With Coward slung beneath his horse,
Face downward to his bitter shame.
Renard, well deserving his bad name,
Intends, and very soon, to greet
His cubs with a delicious treat. 1500
They'll have Coward for their dinner—
God save him from the crafty sinner!
Renard looks downward through the trees.
There, with the king and queen, he sees
So many beasts and barons swarm
That the woods are shaking as in a storm.
They talk of Renard, quite unaware
Of what is happening to the hare,
Dragged off, like a convicted thief,
To a prison where he'll come to grief. 1510
Renard tears his cross off, holds it high,
And summons them with a mighty cry:
"My lord king, behold your flag!
I'm giving back the lousy rag!
Those who weighed me down with staff and purse
My God in His own true wisdom curse!"
He wipes himself in a filthy place,
And throws the cross at Noble's face.
Then once again he shouts to the king,
"Listen to me, my lord! I bring 1520
The greetings Noradin[28] has sent
When I, as a worthy pilgrim, went
To where the pagans across the sea
At the very thought of you will flee."
Renard was so busy having fun
That Coward got his ropes undone,
With a mighty leap was on his horse,
And had set off on a headlong course
Before Renard could realize
That he was about to lose his prize. 1530
Soon Coward, going very fast,
Reached his friends and was safe at last.
His sides had lost quite a lot of skin
Where Renard had stuck his staff right in;
With both his hands and his feet stripped bare—
He really needed a doctor's care.
Just barely able to complete
His journey, he fell at Noble's feet
And told how his life had been at stake.

[28]the Sultan Noradin, prince of the Muslims ("Saracens"), who held the Holy Land.

"Help me, my lord, for God's sweet sake!" 1540
"Oh God, I'm betrayed!" King Noble mourned;
"How utterly is my power scorned!
It's all too easy now to see
How much Renard despises me.
But, my lords, make no mistake—
We know what route Renard will take;
If he makes it home there's not a thing
Can save your necks—you all shall swing!
But whoever captures him shall win
Nobility for all his kin." 1550
You should have seen the race begin!
There's Belin the sheep and Ysengrin,
Bruin the bear and Bald the rat,
As well as my lord Tibert the cat.
Dame Pinte and her three good friends appear
And with them, of course, Lord Chanteclere,
Ferran, the horse who carries packs,
Roenel, the watchdog who attacks.
After him comes Frobert the cricket
And then the ferret, Little Sticket, 1560
Followed by the boar Baucent
Whose teeth can make a mighty dent,
And of course the raging bull won't lag,
Nor, at a gallop, Bricemer the stag.
The flag is carried by the snail
Who's first in line as they take the trail.
Renard, looking back, can see their haste,
And knows he has little time to waste.
There, first in the field, goes Slow—
The wind is making his banner blow. 1570
What should he do? He can't decide;
Renard jumps out of the path to hide
In the underbrush, and finds a ditch—
But close behind is Short the bitch
With the others at her heels. They swear
That Renard will never reach his lair,
That their attack will not be stayed
By castle wall or palisade;
The widest moat, the strongest tower,
Thickets, burrows, have no power 1580
To save Renard from the king this time—
On a rope he'll end his life of crime!
Renard feels that his strength has ended.
Flee or go on as he intended,
He knows he'll never reach his home.
His mouth is dripping, white with foam.
And they've very nearly plucked him bare!
Tufts of his robe fly through the air.
His sides are totally abraded—
How can his capture be evaded? 1590

It's a miracle if, nearly in their grip
Renard gives his enemies the slip!
Yet twisting and turning he breaks free,
And is on his way to Maupertuis,
His palace, fortress, mighty tower,
Home and citadel, seat of power,
The one place in all the world he knows
Will keep him safe from his strongest foes.
Let them love or hate him, once he's there
He will wait for them without a care. 1600
His wife embraced him even before
He had a foot inside the door.
Three sons had that noble lady,
One was Malebranche, one Shady,
The third was named Rovel, and he
Was the handsomest among the three.
They all came running out in haste,
To clasp their arms around his waist,
And seeing his wounds—they were very deep—
Began to comfort him and weep. 1610
They washed his injuries with white wine,
Placed a pillow so that he'd recline;
Then they were ready to serve a meal.
But Renard was too worn out to feel
Like swallowing much of anything
But a chicken leg and half a wing.
He lay in a bath his wife had filled,
And then she bled him. She was skilled
At leechcraft, and before too long
Renard, once again, was feeling strong. 1620

Dante Alighieri
(1265–1321)

The reputation of Dante Alighieri, already high in the time immediately following his death, is today such as to rank him with Homer and Shakespeare at the summit of world literature and his *Divine Comedy* as perhaps the greatest single work of literary art. Dante's simple title was the *Commedia* (the epithet *Divina* was added on title pages beginning in the sixteenth century). The work was called a comedy because its style was a middle one beneath the high-serious tone of tragedy and because its movement was from sadness to joy. The *Comedy* is often described as the quintessence of the medieval worldview, a codification of the values of the high Middle Ages in art, science, theology, and philosophy. This view has considerable truth. It is not without its ironies, however; Dante felt nostalgia for the past and entertained hopes for the future, but he considered his own age vicious, corrupt, and benighted. The circumstances of his life and its public backdrop bear out his judgment in many respects.

Dante was born in 1265 in the independent, republican city-state of Florence, which in its commercial prosperity and its culture was beginning to rank with the leading cities of Europe. For decades before his birth an appallingly bloody feud had divided Florence into two factions: the Ghibellines, a feudal and military class allied with the Holy Roman Emperor, and the Guelfs, a middle-class party that tended to side with the papacy in its struggle against the empire. Dante's family were Guelfs. After an alternation of victories by one side over the other, the Guelfs triumphed decisively when Dante was a year old. But by the end of the century the Guelfs themselves had split into factions: the Blacks, who represented the nobility and were willing to tolerate papal political influence, and the Whites, who represented the commercial bourgeoisie and wanted political independence. Dante was a moderate White. After some military service, he held in his early thirties a succession of increasingly prominent political offices, becoming one of the chief magistrates of Florence in 1300, the year in which the events of the *Divine Comedy* are imagined to take place. Fighting broke out in the streets. Dante's solution was to help banish the leaders of both factions, including his brother-in-law and also Guido Cavalcanti, one of his best friends and a fellow poet. But the Blacks conspired with Dante's detested Pope Boniface VIII, who wished to establish his power in Florence and the surrounding region of Tuscany, and with the help of a foreign army the Whites were ousted, while Dante was absent on a diplomatic mission to Rome. In 1302 he was unjustly accused of barratry (graft), tried *in absentia,* fined the large sum of 5,000 florins, and banished for two years. When he refused to pay the fine and thus admit guilt, the banishment was ruled perpetual, under penalty of being burned alive. Dante never saw his beloved—and henceforth also hated—Florence again, or his wife, Gemma, whom he had married in his mid-twenties. The *Divine Comedy* refers often to this century-long saga of bloody and sleazy politics.

For a time Dante nourished the hope that the Whites would regain control of Florence, but these hopes remained unfulfilled, and gradually Dante became a party of one, disillusioned with all the factions. He was thereafter dependent on a series of patrons who gave him asylum in various Italian cities, mainly in the north. Tradition has it that he spent some time in France and possibly in England, at Oxford. In 1308 his hopes for the regeneration, reordering, and pacification of Italy, including Florence, were rekindled by the election of a new, idealistic Holy Roman Emperor, Henry VII. Dante believed that most of the political evils of his country, and some of the spiritual ones too, sprang from a lack of guidance by an enlightened emperor such as Rome had had in its best ancient days. But Henry's expedition to Italy failed, thwarted by party conflicts, the opposition of the Pope, and finally by Henry's death in 1313. Dante's hopes were once more disappointed. His very last years, however, were relatively serene; he had already circulated the first two parts of his *Comedy,* the *Inferno* and *Purgatory,* the fame of which helped sustain him, and his children were again with him. His last patron, in Ravenna, was a nephew of the Francesca da Rimini whose story Dante had told so movingly in *Inferno* canto V. Dante died in 1321, not long after he completed the *Paradise* and with it the entire *Comedy.*

As references in that work show, Dante's political vicissitudes are reflected in his art. Yet he lived another inner and creative life independent of public traumas. He seems to have had a happy childhood and a good education, probably under Dominican and Franciscan priests. He studied rhetoric under the philosopher-poet Brunetto Latini whom he honors in *Inferno* XV. He was early influenced by French Provençal poetry and by the Italian vernacular poetry that had only recently begun to flourish. A protégé of Guido Cavalcanti, Dante developed a *dolce stil nuovo* ("sweet new style"), rejecting elegant artifice for its own sake and emphasizing instead sincerity of feeling and substance in ideas. The central event of his earlier spiritual life is narrated in the *Vita Nuova* ("New Life"), an amatory and spiritual autobiography with allegorical overtones, which he composed in Italian in 1292. It records, in a mixture of lyric verse and prose commentary, Dante's first love, inspired in him at the age of nine by the sight of Beatrice Portinari, a girl one year younger. He immediately conceived for her a lifelong, intensely idealistic passion that owes much to the medieval tradition of worship of woman, to which Dante adds a moral and philosophical dimension. Nine years later Dante and Beatrice greeted each other. There followed episodes of alienation and psychological distress (apparently idealized, for Dante seems not to have had much close contact with Beatrice). After she died in 1290, he turned to a compassionate lady who later became an emblem of the philosophical pursuits that occupied him after Beatrice's death. The composition of the *Vita Nuova,* when Dante was twenty-seven, marks the end of the third nine-year period, the number symbolism foreshadowing an even more elaborate dependence in the *Divine Comedy* on threes and nines. In all this it is difficult to separate fact from idealization, but perhaps such a symbol-making mind as Dante's would reject the distinction. The *Vita Nuova* ends with the mention of a wondrous vision and with the determination by Dante that he will write no more of Beatrice until he can write of her "what has not before been written of any woman." This decision is one seed of the *Divine Comedy,* in which Beatrice ("giver of blessings") reappears, the Florentine girl transfigured as the heavenly lady who, having helped rescue Dante from his dark night, conducts him through the spheres of the celestial paradise. She becomes both a symbol and vehicle of God's love and revelation.

The study of philosophy and literature that Dante embarked on after the death of Beatrice was continued and deepened in later years until he had mastered most of the important ancient and medieval writers accessible in that time before the Renaissance revival of classical Greek. Indeed, he became one of the most learned men in Europe. He was indebted philosophically to Aristotle, by way of St. Thomas Aquinas. Poetically, he was immensely indebted to Virgil, whom he echoes again and again in the *Comedy* and chooses to represent as his guide through Hell and most of Purgatory, the realms that can be largely understood by the human reason that (among other things) Virgil represents. Dante claimed to know the *Aeneid* by heart. His erudition led him to attempt several ambitious works. Much of what he had learned by 1305 or so he tried to put into a philosophically encyclopedic work called the *Convivio* ("Banquet"), which was to contain fifteen treatises in alternating prose and verse, like the *Vita Nuova.* The *Convivio,* although abandoned by Dante in about 1308, is a landmark in its use of Italian prose instead of Latin for serious philosophical purposes, anticipating the choice of Italian for the *Comedy*. Conversely, Dante explored the general and practical principles involved in creating a worthy Italian language and literature in a Latin work of the same period, *De Vulgari Eloquentia* ("Of Eloquence in the Vernacular Tongue"), which he also left incomplete. Somewhat later, at the time Dante's hero Henry VII was in Italy, he wrote the Latin *De Monarchia,* in which, picking up a theme treated in the *Convivio,* Dante argued the bold thesis that the rightful powers of emperor and pope, respectively temporal and spiritual, were both derived directly from God. The implication was that in a Christian state the two should be separate but equal authorities and should limit themselves to their own mutually exclusive spheres. This idea influences not just the thematic content of the *Divine Comedy* but its very rationale and symbolism; for example, at the end of the *Inferno,* at the bottom and center of Hell, the place of supreme dishonor in the jaws of Satan, the author of all evil, is shared by the spiritual traitor Judas and imperial traitors Brutus and Cassius.

Dante wrote the *Comedy* between 1308 and 1321, completing the *Inferno* by 1312 and the *Purgatory* by 1315. Literally, it is an account of a privileged journey taken by Dante the character (who should be distinguished from the Dante who writes the poem after the fact) into the world of the afterlife. On this level the *Comedy* is a theological work. The damned are those who, each in his or her own way, have definitively rebelled against God's law and defied or ignored His mercy; these include pagans, Jews, and Christians. The saved are those who, having repented and been forgiven by God, dwell with Him in the celestial paradise. Also among the saved are those who, having died at peace with God, are still spiritually imperfect and must refine away their potential for evil in Purgatory, which Dante locates on a mountain in the southern ocean. The Christian faith is a prerequisite for beatitude, although the righteous Jews of the Old Testament period are saved by their implicit faith in Christ to come; moreover, Jewish infants and baptized Christian infants are also among the saved. The virtuous pagans of antiquity and of more modern times cannot enter Heaven; instead they dwell in Limbo, the uppermost circle of Hell, where their only suffering is to live without hope of redemption. These righteous pagans include even Virgil. Dante shows, especially in the *Paradise,* that he is troubled by the lot of these blameless persons, and in fact in *Paradise* XX he opens a loophole, revealing that at least some good pagans can finally be saved. But this is only a loophole, a faint gleam of mysterious hope, and much pathos arises in the *Inferno* and *Purgatory* from the assumption that the magisterial and fatherlike Virgil is inexorably excluded from eternal bliss.

Theologically, Purgatory is the most distinctively Catholic realm, reflecting one fundamental difference in belief between the Catholic and Protestant faiths. The basic Protestant position, as formulated two centuries later during the Reformation, is that human beings are saved by faith in God's mercy and grace; Catholics believe that we are saved by a combination of such faith and "works" (acts of goodness and remedial suffering). This latter view can make God seem a niggardly taskmaster, forgiving only grudgingly. But the Catholic view, if we can extrapolate from Dante's idea of the Redemption in *Paradise* VII, is that God is like a generous creditor who might have forgiven a debt outright but instead asks that part be repaid so as to salvage the self-respect and elevate the dignity of the sinner-debtor.

Dante's purgatorians thus suffer, in a discipline of compensation, but joyfully and willingly. Because they can rise to a higher slope of the mountain as soon as they feel ready and worthy, their own wills are the essential ministers of the purgatorial process.

An awareness of such theological fundamentals is important for an understanding of the *Comedy,* but the modern appeal of the work, even for believers, is not primarily theological but rather ethical and artistic. The *Comedy* is intended to be a picture of the world we live in; the journey into the afterlife is also the struggle in this life of every person who confronts evil, conquers it, and rises above it. Dante most obviously makes us aware of the temporal life by portraying known persons, great and commonplace, antique and modern, dead and living, and by commenting frequently on immediate, local issues, especially politics. In describing the three great realms and making clear his own emotional states, he draws vivid comparisons with the scenes and landscapes of recognizable life—the breaking of a gambler's lucky streak, the shipyards at Venice, a tailor's squint, fireflies on a summer evening, windmills seen through mist.

Above all, Dante comments on earthly life through the descriptions of the punishments in Hell. These are not merely imposed from outside and after the fact; rather, they are symbols of the sins when they are truly understood and realized in imaginative fullness. Someone once said that the motto of the *Inferno* might well be "They got what they wanted." Or, in Gerard Manley Hopkins's words, "The lost are like this, and their scourge [is] to be . . . their sweating selves." Thus the adulterous lovers Francesca and Paolo will be united forever, airborne on the winds of passion; the suicides who separated soul from body will remain so divided even after the Last Judgment, when other creatures have reassumed their flesh; the heretics who denied the immortality of the soul lie forever in sarcophagi, which will be sealed at the Judgment just as, in effect, they predicted; the popes who desecrated their office for money are all crammed, upside down and head to foot, into a single hole, in a parody of the apostolic succession and the laying on of hands by which the episcopal office is transmitted; the grafters continue their life of concealment and trickery.

Moreover, the scheme of punishments in Hell reflects a theory of human nature and a rather complex scheme of ethics. (The divisions of Hell and of Purgatory are outlined by Virgil in *Inferno* XI and *Purgatory* XVII.) The merely sensual sinners are the least guilty, and of them the sexual sinners least of all, possibly because sex retains some touch of the love that, properly understood, is God. The next most guilty are the violent. But the worst sinners are those who pervert the divine plan of creation by misusing the specifically human power of reason—that is, the fraudulent. But even fraud has gradations, and it is worst when it is treacherous. And the worst form of treachery is that shown to lords and benefactors. God as understood by Dante is associated with motion and energy and it is therefore appropriate that the punishment for treacherous fraud is not the hellfire of popular imagination but complete entropy in the form of a lake of ice. The Limbo and the circle of the heretics are conceived in the light of distinctively Christian beliefs, but the remainder of the Inferno is defined in terms of nearly universal human insights and values. Theologically, it may strike some people as arbitrary that in Dante salvation and damnation depend on the state of the human soul at the moment when, perhaps by sudden accident, death occurs, although in fact that notion is not uniquely Dantean or Christian. But from a moral rather than theological perspective, the idea suggests in the most powerful way possible that all actions in life are of incalculable consequence, each containing in itself the essence of utter good or utter evil. Perhaps it is Dante's sense of this urgency that makes him consign the contemptible trimmers, who were neither good nor evil, to the outer vestibule of Hell, lest their presence in Hell proper make "the wicked gain pride by comparison" (*Inferno* III.42).

Probably no great work of literature has a structure so precisely articulated as the *Divine Comedy*. It is governed, texturally and architecturally, by the numbers 3, 9, and 10. The entire *Comedy* has 100 cantos, the square of the perfect number 10. Each of the three great divisions has 33 cantos (the first of the 34 cantos in the *Inferno* serving as a prelude to the entire work). There are 9 (3 times 3) circles or spheres in each of the three realms, to which is added another region of a different order (the vestibule of Hell, the Garden of Eden, the empyrean Heaven), making a total of 10. The entire poem is written in tercets, three-line stanzas, and the Italian rhyme scheme is *terza rima* ("third rhyme"), a system of interlocking rhymes in the pattern *aba bcb cdc,* each end rhyme thus sounding three times. The tercet is the normal syntactical unit of statement, producing along with the rhyme scheme an effect of powerful but deliberate forward movement. The symbolism of threes is an ever-present acknowledgment of the divine Trinity. Dante's mind, like others in the Middle Ages, could imagine a God who is both love and mathematical order.

But the synthesizing imagination of Dante is best revealed not in such number symbolism but in the poem's total mode of understanding the structure of reality. Time is boldly conflated and twisted, sinners who have been in Hell for millennia coexist in an eternal now with those who have been dead for only a few years. The period of Dante's journey through Hell, from Good Friday to Easter Sunday, corresponds mythically to the time Jesus spent in the tomb. Cultures that were distinct on earth are homogenized in the hereafter, classical monsters and Christian demons reduced to a common denominator of allegorical and moral values. The boundaries between science, theology, philosophy, geography, history, and other branches of knowledge are virtually nonexistent; Dante hears lectures on politics and lunar astrophysics even in Paradise. Physical gravitation is closely identified with the spiritual operation of love, which is the motive power alike of the astronomical heavens and of every human act, good or bad. Evil and suffering, symbolized in *Inferno* XIV by the tears of a gigantic Cretan statue weeping for the sorrows and sins of human history, move ever downward, channeled by Hell's four rivers to the motionless center of the universe; in the meantime, from the mountain of Purgatory on the other side of the globe the river of Lethe flows down to join the others in the same place, carrying with it the dead memories of the vices of the saved. Conversely, as the repentant move up the slopes of Purgatory, the burden of their evil propensities is quite literally lightened, so that like modern astronauts they feel the ascent easier and easier until, made perfect again in Eden, they rise to Heaven as naturally as flames fly upward.

The ultimate goal of Dante the pilgrim and of the poem is the direct vision of God in the uncircumscribed empyrean heaven. In describing this experience, the last cantos of the *Paradise* achieve a sublimity unsurpassed in literature. There Dante must realize for us what is utterly suprasensory and beyond speech without relinquishing the poetic tools of language and sense imagery that are the poet's only means of communication. His imagistic media, as throughout the *Paradise,* are mainly light, color, and nearly abstract patterns. His subject is not only the Deity but the relationship of Deity to the immensely variegated, differentiated world of things, places, and people so much of which the *Comedy* has revealed:

> In its depths I saw contained, bound with love
> in one volume, what is scattered
> on leaves throughout the world. . . . [*Paradise* XXXIII.85–87]

The paradox, fundamental to any theistic vision, is that a God who is one and changeless created and sustains the teeming variety of our world.

It is impossible for translation to capture the exquisite sound effects of Dante's Italian, particularly the incantatory echoing of consonant and vowel sounds in lines such as *Dei remi facemmo ali al folle volo* ("we made wings of our oars for the mad flight"—*Inferno* XXVI.125). But in many other respects Dante's style and manner are unusually translatable. Although convoluted passages do occur, the hallmarks of Dante's usual style are directness and economy. He prefers verbs and nouns, using adjectives sparingly, and then more for utilitarian description than for atmosphere or ornament. (As an example, see Ulysses' famous speech in *Inferno* XXVI.91–142.) Exactly because he is describing what none of us has seen, he is compelled, as a good technical writer is, to furnish lucid visual descriptions and analogies. His method is eminently dramatic, realized in the overt gestures and speech of his characters. The characterizations are masterful; the most memorable—Francesca, Farinata, Brunetto Latini, Ulysses, Ugolino—are accomplished in a few dozen lines. Much of this can be captured by a literal translator who, renouncing the hopeless effort to compete with Dante's versification, lets this most literal of poets speak directly to us in language as nearly unclouded as his own.

FURTHER READING: A fine biography for the general reader is Monroe Stearns's *Dante: Poet of Love,* 1965, which is also a good introduction to *The Divine Comedy.* Carlo Golino's *Dante Alighieri,* 1979, which also provides both biographical information and criticism, has good discussions of works other than *The Divine Comedy.* Background material for the study of Dante's *Comedy,* a canto-by-canto summary, and critical analysis are combined in Aldo S. Bernardo and Anthony L. Pellegrini, *A Critical Study Guide to Dante's "Divine Comedy,"* 1968. The visual aids in this work are particularly useful. Especially accessible and helpful are Wallace Fowlie, *A Reading of Dante's "Inferno,"* 1981; and *Approaches to Teaching Dante's "Divine Comedy,"* ed. Carole Slande and Giovanni Cecchetti, 1982. The notes and running commentary in Mark Musa's translation of *The Divine Comedy,* completed in 1984, are extremely helpful. Uberto Limentani's *Dante's Comedy: Introductory Readings of Selected Cantos,* 1985, provides an excellent model of how to read the poem as a whole. Joan M. Ferrante's *The Political Vision of the Divine Comedy,* 1984, is another excellent study, even broader in its critical scope than the title implies. A general appreciation of the *Comedy* is offered in Thomas Goddard Bergin's *Dante's "Divine Comedy,"* 1971, which is also good on the cosmology. George

Holmes's *Dante,* 1980, in the Past Masters series, is a good introductory overview, of manageable length. For a historical introduction to the *Comedy,* see Erich Auerbach's *Dante, Poet of the Secular World,* 1929, trans. Ralph Manheim, 1961. Auerbach's analysis of structure in the *Comedy* is also particularly readable and rewarding. *Dante: A Collection of Critical Essays,* ed. J. Freccero, 1965, contains thirteen articles by Auerbach, Pirandello, and others. Selected cantos are interpreted in Mark Musa's *Advent at the Gates,* 1974. Musa's discussion of ambiguity in the characterization of Francesca is especially interesting. Marianne Shapiro's *Woman, Earthly and Divine in the "Comedy" of Dante,* 1975, emphasizes the poet's relationship with Beatrice and offers a provocative discussion of Virgil's maternal and paternal aspects in the *Inferno.* Also valuable are David Nolan, ed., *Dante Commentaries: Eight Studies of "The Divine Comedy,"* 1977, and its companion volume, *Dante Soundings,* 1981. For clear explanations of Dante's Aristotelian ideas, see Patrick Boyde, *Perception and Passion in Dante's Comedy,* 1993.

THE DIVINE COMEDY

Translated, with interpolated summaries and bracketed glosses, by H. R. Huse.

INFERNO

A SAMPLE OF THE ORIGINAL VERSE

The opening tercets from Canto I will give readers an idea of the language and form of the original work.

Nel mezzo del cammin di nostra vita
  mi ritrovai per una selva oscura,
  chè la diritta via era smarrita.

Ah quanto a dir qual era è cosa dura
  esta selva selvaggia e aspra e forte
  che nel pensier rinnova la paura!

Tant'è amara che poco è più morte;
  ma per trattar del ben ch'io vi trovai,
  dirò dell'altre cose ch' i' v'ho scorte.

Io non so ben ridir com'io v'entrai,
  tant'era pieno di sonno a quel punto
  che la verace via abbandonai. 12

Ma poi ch'i' fui al piè d'un colle giunto,
  là dove terminava quella valle
  che m'avea di paura il cor compunto,

guardai in alto, e vidi le sue spalle
  vestite già de' raggi del pianeta
  che mena dritto altrui per ogni calle.

A diagram of the earth in the center of the universe.

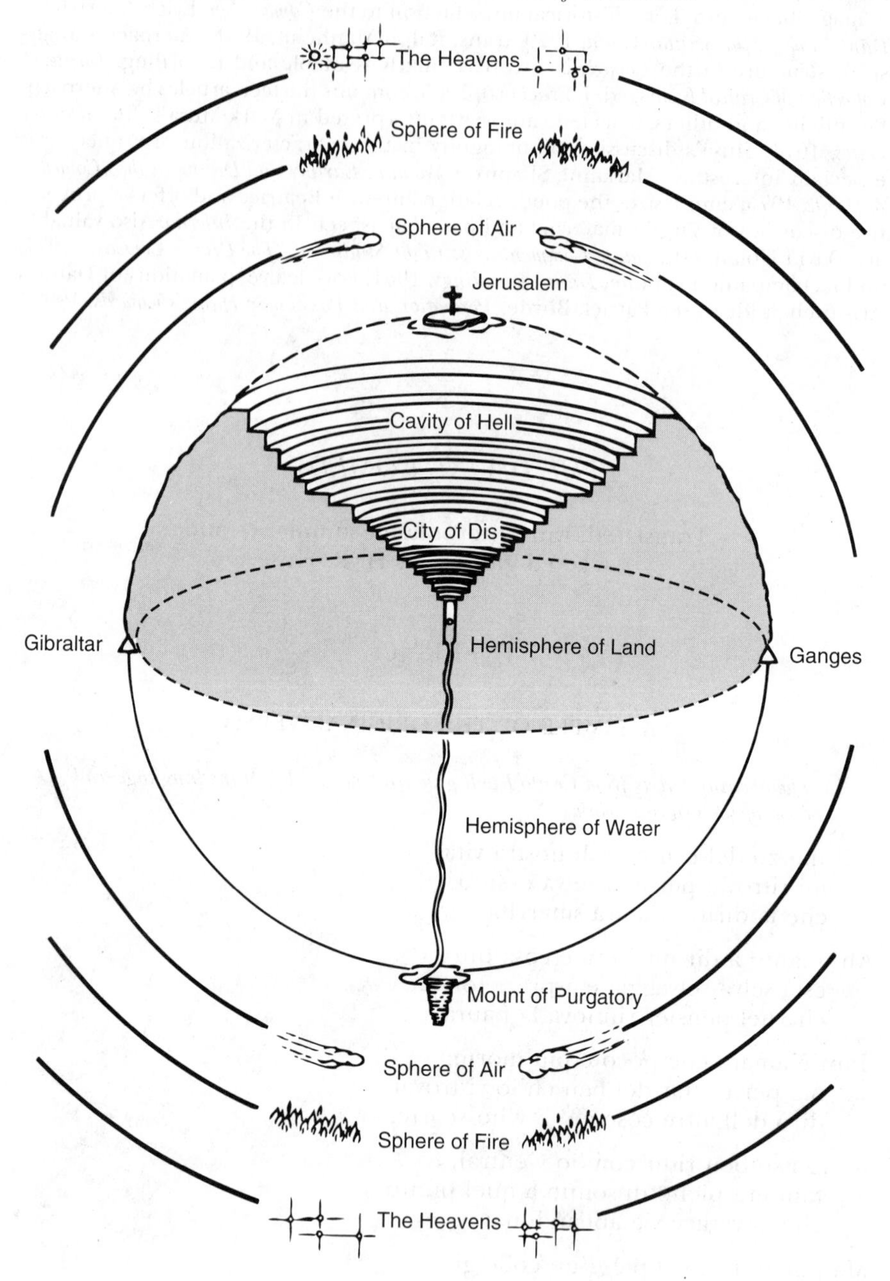

Allor fu la paura un poco queta
che nel lago del cor m'era durata
la notte chi'i' passai con tanta pièta.

E come quei che con lena affannata
uscito fuor del pelago alla riva
si volge all'acqua perigliosa e guata, 24

così l'animo mio, ch'ancor fuggiva,
si volse a retro a rimirar lo passo
che non lasciò già mai persona viva.

OUTLINE OF THE INFERNO

Upper Hell, Incontinence

REGION	SINNERS	PUNISHMENTS
Vestibule	Trimmers, neutrals	Stung by insects, run after banners
Circle I	[Virtuous pagans, unbaptized infants]	Melancholy, desire without hope
Circle II	The lustful	Blown forever by storm winds
Circle III	The gluttons	Discomfort, all senses punished
Circle IV	The avaricious and the prodigal	Pushing rocks, useless labor
Circle V	The angry and the sullen	The angry thrashing about helplessly; the sullen submerged, emitting bubbles

Lower Hell, Malice (Violence and Fraud)

REGION	SINNERS	PUNISHMENTS
Circle VI	[Heretics]	In burning tombs
Circle VII	The violent	
Round 1	against neighbors, fellow men	Submerged in hot blood
Round 2	against self (suicides)	Enclosed in new bodies, as trees and bushes
Round 3	against God (blasphemers, sodomites, usurers)	On burning sand in rain of fire
Circle VIII	Fraud against those who have no special trust	
Bolgia 1	Panders and seducers	Whipped by devils
Bolgia 2	Flatterers	Covered with filth
Bolgia 3	Simonists	Upside down in holes, feet on fire
Bolgia 4	Soothsayers	Heads twisted, turned backward
Bolgia 5	Barrators	Covered by boiling pitch
Bolgia 6	Hypocrites	Wearing leaden mantles
Bolgia 7	Thieves	In snake pit, transformations
Bolgia 8	Evil counselors	Concealed in flames

OUTLINE OF THE INFERNO *(continued)*

Lower Hell, Malice (Violence and Fraud)

Bolgia 9	Sowers of discord	Wounds, mutilations
Bolgia 10	Falsifiers (alchemists, impersonators, counterfeiters, liars)	Diseases (leprosy, madness, dropsy, high fever)
Circle IX	Fraudulent against those who have special trust	
Caïna	Murderers of kindred	In ice to necks, heads bent forward
Antenora	Traitors to party or country	In ice to necks
Tolomea	Murderers of guests	In ice to necks, heads bent backward
Giudecca	Traitors to lords and benefactors	Completely submerged in ice

At the Center of the Earth (Universe)

Lucifer with Judas, Brutus, and Cassius in his three mouths, with three sets of wings sending forth a freezing blast of impotence, ignorance, and hatred.

NOTE: The souls in Circle I and Circle VI are outside of the classifications of Incontinence and Malice. They are guilty only from a Christian viewpoint, and Dante has to fit them as well as he can into the Aristotelian classification.

CANTO I

VIRGIL

The story begins on Thursday night, April 7, 1300. Dante, at the age of thirty-five, having completed half of man's traditional three-score years and ten, awakens to find himself in the forest of worldliness or sin. He cannot recall how he entered it: he had sunk, as men do, gradually and imperceptibly into sinful habits.

The night passes, and the sun (Divine Enlightenment or Righteous Choice) rises behind the Mount of Rectitude.

In the middle of the journey of our life
 I came to my senses in a dark forest,
 for I had lost the straight path.

Oh, how hard it is to tell
 what a dense, wild, and tangled wood this was,
 the thought of which renews my fear!

So terrible it is that death is hardly worse.
 But to reveal the good that I found there,
 I will speak first of other things.

I cannot tell how I entered it,
 so heavy with slumber was I at the moment
 when I abandoned the true way.

But when I had reached the foot of a hill,
there where the valley ended
which had filled my heart with fear,

I looked up, and saw its shoulders
clothed already with the rays of the planet
which leads men straight on every path.

Then the fear was somewhat quieted
which had lasted in the lake of my heart
during the night I had passed so piteously.

And as a seafarer, who has escaped from the storm
to the shore, turns with wearied breath
to the turbulent waters and gazes, 24

so I, still fleeing in my mind,
turned back to look at the pass
which no one before had ever left alive.

As Dante starts to climb the hill, a leopard, the symbol of luxury or lust, appears. It offers some opposition, but the early hour and the buoyant influence of Spring, the season when the universe was supposed to have been created, give him hope. Then a lion (Pride) assails him, rushing on with such fury that the very air around seems to tremble. And finally a she-wolf, the symbol of avarice or greed, the most widespread of vices. Dante (Mankind) feels that he could overcome the others, but at the sight of the wolf, he despairs.[1]

After I had rested a little my weary body,
I took my way over the lonely slope
[climbing][2] so that the firm foot always was the lower.

And behold! almost at the beginning of the rise,
a leopard, light, and very nimble,
which was covered with a spotted hide!

It did not move from in front of me,
but instead so blocked my way
that several times I turned to go back. 36

The time was the beginning of the morning,
and the sun was rising with those stars
that were with it when Divine Love

first set those beautiful things in motion,
so that I found cause for good hope
concerning the beast with the gaily spotted hide

in the hour of the day and in the sweet season;
but even so I feared again
at the sight of a lion that confronted me.

[1] This is a traditional interpretation of the allegory of the three beasts. Other explanations are possible—for example, that the leopard is Fraud, the lion Violence, and the wolf Incontinence. These three evils would correspond to the tripartite classification of sins in Dante's Hell.

[2] The words within square brackets, here and later in *The Divine Comedy*, are explanations inserted by the translator.

It appeared to be coming at me
with head erect and with ravenous hunger,
so that the air seemed afraid of it, 48

and a she-wolf came also, burdened
in her leanness with all cravings,
and which has indeed made many live in sorrow.

The sight of her brought such fear
and such distress upon me
that I lost hope of the ascent.

And as a gambler who gladly wins,
but when the time comes for him to lose,
weeps and is saddened in all his thoughts,

so I changed as the restless beast advanced
against me, and little by little
drove me down to where the sun is silent. 60

At this critical moment, Virgil (Reason, Philosophy), whose voice has long been unheard, appears. Dante forgets for a moment his despair, and bends reverently before his master. Then he mentions the wolf which has blocked his (and mankind's) reform. Virgil explains the nature of the greed for which the wolf stands: it is an element in nearly all the crimes men commit. But a "hound," a redeemer (variously identified), possibly from between the towns of Feltro and Montefeltro, will ultimately come.

While I was falling back to a lower place
someone appeared before me whose voice
from long silence seemed faint.

When I saw him in that desolation,
"Have pity on me!" I cried to him,
"whoever you are, whether a shade or a real man."

He answered, "Not a man now,
a man once I was, and both my parents
were Lombards, Mantuans by city.

I was born *sub Julio*[3] although late,
and I lived in Rome under the good Augustus
at the time of the false and lying gods. 72

I was a poet and sang of [Aeneas] that just son
of Anchises who came from Troy
after proud Ilion had been burned.

But why do you return to such misery?
Why not climb the delightful mountain
which is the beginning and the source of all joy?"

[3]"Under Julius Caesar."

"Now are you that Virgil, that spring
which pours forth so broad a stream of speech?"
I answered him with bashful brow,

"Oh, honor and light of other poets,
may the long study and great love help me
which made me search through your volume! 84

You are my master and my author;
you alone are the one from whom I took
the style which has done me honor.

See the beast because of which I turned;
save me from her, famous sage,
for she makes my whole body tremble!"

"You must take another road," he answered
after he had seen me weep,
"if you want to escape from this wild place;

for the animal of which you complain
lets no one pass along her way,
but so hinders that she kills, 96

and she has a nature so vicious and perverse
that she never satisfies her greedy desires,
and after feeding is hungrier than before.

Many are the animals with which she mates,
and there will be still more until the Hound comes
that will make her die in pain.

He will not feed on earth or pelf,
but on wisdom, love and virtue,
and his nation will be between Feltro and Feltro.

He will be the savior of that humbled Italy
for whom the virgin Camilla,
Euryalus, Turnus, and Nisus[4] died of wounds. 108

He will hunt her through every town
until he has driven her back to Hell,
whence Envy [of man's happiness] first released her.

Now Virgil proposes to lead Dante through Hell and Purgatory, and outlines the course of the journey. In Heaven, Beatrice (Revelation, Theology) will be the guide.

In his humble submission to the mystery of Divine Justice, Virgil accuses himself of "rebellion" against God's law. There is a note of sadness in his words, condemned as he is, for having lived before Christ, to an eternity of longing. Dante generously suggests his apology by a reference to the God the ancient poet did not and, of course, could not know.

[4]Characters in the second half of Virgil's *Aeneid,* which describes war in Italy.

Therefore I think it best for you
  to follow me, and I will be your guide
  to take you through an eternal place [Hell]

where you will hear despairing cries
  and will see the tormented spirits
  each of whom proclaims the second death [damnation],

and you will see [in Purgatory] those who are contented
  in the fire, because they hope to come,
  whenever it may be, among the blessed, 120

to whom, then, if you wish to ascend,
  a guide worthier than I will take you:
  to her I will entrust you when I leave,

for that Emperor who reigns up there,
  because I was rebellious to His law,
  does not want me as a guide to His city.

Everywhere He reigns and there He rules;
  there is His seat and His high throne,
  O happy are those whom He chooses!"

And I to him, "Poet, I beg you
  by that God you did not know, in order
  that I may flee from this evil and worse, 132

take me where you have said,
  so that I may see St. Peter's gate
  and those you proclaim so sad."

Then he moved on, and I followed him.

CANTO II

Beatrice

It is now the evening of Good Friday. The sun which had cheered Dante is going down, and the animals on earth (all workers in God's universe) are returning home from their labors of the day. In this dark moment, Dante's courage fails, and he wonders about the advisability of the journey. It is true, he reflects, that both Aeneas and St. Paul, the "Chosen Vessel," visited the future world; but Aeneas' visit led to the founding of the Roman Empire, divinely ordained to be the seat of the papacy, and St. Paul brought from Heaven a confirmation of the true faith. Dante disclaims any such mission.

The day was departing, and the darkening air
  was taking the creatures that are on earth
  from their daily toil, and I alone

was preparing to endure the hardship
  both of the journey and of the pity
  which unerring memory will relate.

O Muses, O lofty genius, aid me now!
    O mind which inscribed what I saw,
    here your worth will be revealed.

I began, "Poet, you who guide me,
    consider my strength, whether it is great enough
    before you commit me to the arduous journey. 12

You say that [Aeneas] the father of Sylvius,
    still subject to corruption,
    went bodily to the eternal world;

but that the Adversary of all Evil [God]
    should be gracious to him, thinking of the result
    and of who and what he was,

does not seem unreasonable to a thoughtful man;
    for he was chosen in the Empyrean heaven
    to be father of glorious Rome

and of her empire, both of which
    were established for the holy place
    where the successors of St. Peter sit. 24

On this journey through which you honor him,
    he heard things which led to his victory
    and to the papal mantle.

Afterward the Chosen Vessel [St. Paul] went there
    to bring comfort to the faith
    which is the beginning of the way of salvation.

But why should I go? Who grants it?
    I am not Aeneas, nor am I Paul;
    for that neither I nor others believe me worthy.

Therefore, if I allow myself to go,
    I fear the journey may be folly: you are wise
    and understand better than I can speak." 36

And, as a person unwills what he wills,
    and with new thoughts changes purpose,
    holding back from what he has started,

so I became on that dark slope,
    for, by thinking, I delayed the undertaking
    that I had begun so quickly.

Not deceived by this rationalizing, Virgil reproves Dante for being afraid. Then, to reassure him, he describes the occasion of his coming, a scene in the first circle of Hell where the souls of the virtuous pagans are "in suspense," longing for an understanding of God and of the mystery of life, with the realization that they can never attain it.

"If I have understood your words rightly,"
answered that magnanimous shade,
"your resolution is dulled by cowardice

which often distracts a man
and turns him away from honorable deeds,
as imperfect sight causes an animal to shy. 48

To free you from this fear, I will tell
why I came and what I heard
when I first took pity on you.

I was among those who are in suspense,
and a lady [Beatrice] called to me
so blessed and beautiful that I asked her to command.

Her eyes shone more than the stars,
and with an angelic voice,
softly and sweetly she spoke to me,

'O courteous Mantuan soul whose fame
still lasts on the earth, and will last
as long as the world, 60

my friend, but not the friend of Fortune,
is so impeded on the deserted slope
that in fear he has turned back,

and, from what I have heard in Heaven,
I am afraid he is already so lost
that I have come too late for his relief.

Now go to him, and with your eloquent speech
and with all else needful for his escape
help him, so that I may be consoled.

I am Beatrice, bidding you to go;
I come from a place to which I would return;
Love moved me and makes me speak. 72

When I am in the presence of my Lord
I will praise you often to Him.'
She was silent then and I began,

'O lady of virtue [Revelation] through whom alone
the human race excels all creatures contained
within the heaven of the smallest orbit [all on earth],

your command so pleases me that complying
if already begun would seem slow;
you need only to reveal your desire;

but tell me why you do not shrink
from descending to this depth from the broad expanse
to which you are eager to return.' 84

Beatrice explains how, although pitying Dante, she can feel no distress at the working of Divine Justice.

The formal allegory of the scene in Heaven she then describes is as follows: Mary (Divine Mercy) sends Lucia (Illuminating Grace) to prepare the way for Beatrice (Revelation) whom Dante (Mankind) will perceive when Virgil (Reason) makes him ready to behold her.

'Since you wish to know so much
I will tell you briefly,' she answered,
'why I do not fear to come here.

We should be afraid only of things
which can harm, not of others,
since they are not fearful.

Through God's grace I am formed in such a way
that your misery does not touch me,
nor does a flame of this burning hurt me.

There is a gentle lady in Heaven [Mary]
whose pity is aroused by the distress of him
to whom I send you, and who tempers harsh judgment. 96

She called upon Lucia and said in her request,
"Your faithful one now has need of you,
and I recommend him to you."

Lucia, the enemy of all cruelty,
arose and came to where I was
seated by the ancient Rachel.

She said, "Beatrice, true praise of God,
why do you not help him who loved you so much
that through you he arose above the common crowd?

Do you not hear the pity of his cries?
Do you not see Death struggling with him
on the river [of evil] not less terrible than the sea?" 108

On earth men were never so swift
to seek gain and flee from harm
as I was after these words were spoken

to come here from my blessed seat,
trusting in your noble speech
which honors you and those who have heard it.'

After she said this to me
she turned away her shining eyes in tears,
which made me still readier to go,

and to you I came as she desired.
I freed you from the beast
which had cut off the short way up the fair mount. 120

So what is it? Why, why do you hold back?
Why keep such cowardice in your heart?
Why are you not bold and free,

since three such holy ladies
care for you in the court of Heaven,
and my words promise you so much good?"

As little flowers, bent down and closed by the frost of night,
stand up, all open on their stems,
when the sun comes back to warm and brighten them,

so I revived my failing strength,
and so much boldness rushed into my heart
that I began like one set free, 132

"O compassionate lady who gave aid to me!
O courteous shade who obeyed so quickly
the true words she spoke to you!

You have disposed my heart
with such desire for going by your account
that I have regained my first intent.

Now go, for one wish is in both of us,
you my leader [guide], my lord [superior], my master [teacher]!"
Thus I spoke to him, and when he started

I followed on the deep and wild way.

CANTO III

THE ENTRANCE

In the faint light of the evening of Good Friday, the anniversary of the Crucifixion when, according to the Creed, Christ "entered into Hell," the two travelers move on to the gate over which appears a fearful inscription pointing out the woe within, the eternal pain, the people lost even to hope. Divine Justice (incomprehensible to reason alone) moved God in his three-fold attributes of Power, Wisdom, and Love to create Hell. It was made when only eternal things (the elements, the heavens, and the angels) existed, and it also will last and function eternally.

On reading these words Dante begins again to doubt, but, ashamed to confess his fear, he seeks delay or assurance by asking about their meaning which, incidentally, is painfully explicit. Virgil, undeceived, reproves Dante for his weakness.

THROUGH ME YOU GO INTO THE CITY OF GRIEF,
THROUGH ME YOU GO INTO THE PAIN THAT IS ETERNAL,
THROUGH ME YOU GO AMONG PEOPLE LOST.

JUSTICE MOVED MY EXALTED CREATOR;
THE DIVINE POWER MADE ME,
THE SUPREME WISDOM, AND THE PRIMAL LOVE.

BEFORE ME ALL CREATED THINGS WERE ETERNAL,
AND ETERNAL I WILL LAST.
ABANDON EVERY HOPE, YOU WHO ENTER HERE.

These words of a dark coloring
I saw written above a gate; whereupon I said,
"Master, their meaning is hard for me." 12

Then he spoke like one who understands:
"Here you must give up all distrust,
here all cowardice must end.

We have come to the place where I said
that you would see the woeful people
who have lost the good of the intellect.

And after he had taken me by the hand,
with a cheerful look which comforted me,
he drew me within the secret place [the eternal world].

On entering, Dante sees little because of the darkness, but hears sounds which he distinguishes gradually as cries, languages, words, accents, voices, and finally as the dull noise of blows. Virgil contemptuously refuses to waste words on the souls here. They are the trimmers, the mediocre, the poor in spirit, the neutrals, joined with the angels who refused to take sides in the revolt against God. They are in a kind of vestibule, outside of Hell proper. Their punishment is slight compared to those which come later, yet they are envious of every other lot.

There, sighs, lamentations, and deep wailings
resounded through the starless air,
so that at first I began to weep. 24

Diverse tongues, horrible languages,
words of pain, accents of rage,
voices loud and hoarse, and the sounds of blows

made a tumult which moved forever
in that air unchanged by time,
as sand eddies in a whirlwind.

And I said, my head girt with horror,
"Master, what is it that I hear,
and who are these people so overcome by pain?"

Then he to me, "This miserable fate
afflicts the wretched souls of those
who lived without infamy and without praise. 36

They are joined with that choir of wicked angels
who were neither rebellious
nor faithful to God, but for themselves.

The heavens, to remain beautiful, drove them out,
nor would deep Hell receive them
lest the wicked gain pride by comparison."

And I, "Master, what is so burdensome
that it makes them lament loudly?"
He answered, "Briefly I will tell you.

They have no hope of death,
and their blind life is so debased
that they are envious of every other lot. 48

The world does not grant them any fame;
pity [of Heaven] and justice [of Hell] alike disdain them.
Let us not speak of them, but look and pass on."

Some of these souls, neutral and perhaps sedentary in life, are condemned now to active partisanship. The poet recognizes one, but will not distinguish him with a name. Most commentators have identified him as Celestine V, a pope who, by his refusal to keep his office, allowed Dante's great enemy, Boniface VIII, to rise to power. There are less scandalous interpretations, however, notably as Pontius Pilate, who refused justice to Christ and who offers a better motivation for the extreme contempt shown here.

And I, looking, saw a banner
which, circling, moved so fast
that it seemed to scorn all rest,

and behind it came such a throng of people
that I never would have believed
that death could have undone so many.

After I had recognized some of them,
I saw and knew the shade of him
who, through cowardice, made the great refusal. 60

At once I understood and was certain
that this was the sect of the wicked
displeasing both to God and to His enemies.

These wretches, who had never really lived,
were naked and stung constantly
by hornets and wasps that were there.

These made their faces stream with blood
which, mixed with tears, was consumed
by loathsome maggots at their feet.

When Dante asks about a crowd in the distance, Virgil tells him to wait and see. Taking this as a reproach, our poet remains silent for a long time.

As the travelers move on, Charon appears, the ancient boatman of the Styx, who prophesies Dante's ultimate salvation and whom Virgil appeases with a kind of conjuring formula.

When I began to look farther on
I saw people on the shore of a great river;
whereupon I said, "Master, now grant 72

that I should know who they are
and what makes them so ready to pass over,
as I discern through the faint light."

And he to me, "These things will be known to you
when we stay our steps
on the sad bank of the Acheron."

Then with eyes ashamed and lowered,
fearing that my words might have offended him,
I kept from speaking until we reached the stream.

And behold! coming toward us in a skiff
an old man, white with ancient locks,
shouting, "Woe to you, depraved spirits; 84

hope not ever to see Heaven.
I come to take you to the other shore
into eternal darkness, into heat and cold.

And you there, living soul,
get away from these who are dead."
But when he saw that I did not leave,

"By another way, at other ports," he said,
"you will come ashore, not here;
a lighter boat will carry you."

And my guide, "Charon, do not be disturbed;
this is wished for where the power is
to do what is wished; and ask no more." 96

Then were quieted the woolly cheeks
of the boatman of the livid marsh
who, around his eyes, had rings of flame.

The souls are impelled by a kind of instinct to seek their proper place, since sin leads inevitably to its own results, its own suffering.

We are not told how Dante crosses the river. There is a flash, an earthquake, and he falls unconscious. On awakening he is on the other bank.

But those weary and naked souls
changed color and gnashed their teeth
as soon as they heard the cruel words.

They cursed God and their parents,
the human race, and the place, time, and seed
of their begetting and of their birth.

Then, all together they withdrew,
weeping loudly, to the accursed shore
which awaits every man without fear of God. 108

Charon the demon, with eyes like glowing coals,
beckoning to them, gathered them in,
and hit with an oar any who delayed.

As in autumn the leaves fall
one after the other, until the branch
sees all its spoils upon the ground,

so, the evil seed of Adam
fell to that shore, one by one, and at signals,
as the falcon does at its recall.

Thus they go over the dark water,
and before they have landed on the other shore,
again on this side a new crowd assembles. 120

"My son," said the courteous master,
"those who die in the wrath of God
gather here from every country,

and they are ready to pass the river,
for Divine Justice so spurs them
that fear is changed into desire.

Along here no good spirit ever passes;
therefore, if Charon complains of you,
you can understand what his words imply."

When he had ended, the dark country
trembled so that from fright
my memory bathes me still with sweat. 132

The tearful land produced a blast
which flashed a crimson light
conquering all my senses;

and I fell, like one overcome by sleep.

CANTO IV

LIMBO

When Dante awakens from his swoon he is in Limbo, the first circle of Hell. He interprets Virgil's pallor as due to fear, but learns that it comes from pity for those in the ancient poet's own circle. Although Dante still refrains from questioning, Virgil is anxious to point out that the shades here committed no sin, but died unbaptized or lived before Christ. Their damnation is an article of faith, beyond man's understanding. Here there is no torment other than a sense of unfulfillment, a feeling that expresses itself in melancholy, in suspense, in a vague longing for knowledge of God and for a solution of the mystery of life without hope of ever having either.

The deep sleep into which I fell was broken
by heavy thunder, so that I started,
like one awakened by force,

and having risen, I glanced around
and looked intently with rested eyes
to discover where I was.

In truth, I found myself on the brink
of the dolorous valley of the abyss
which resounds with the sound of countless cries.

It was so dark, deep, and cloudy
that in looking toward the bottom
I could discern nothing. 12

"Now, let us go into the blind world,"
the poet began all pale,
"I will be first and you second."

And I, noticing his color, said,
"How shall I come if you are afraid,
you who always comfort me in my doubt?"

And he to me, "The anguish
of the people down there paints on my face
the pity which you mistake for fear.

Let us go, for the long way impels us."
Thus he moved on and made me enter
the first circle which girds the abyss. 24

Here, so far as one could tell by listening,
there was no lament, but only sighs
which made the eternal air tremble.

They came from the sadness without torment
felt by the great crowd
of children and of women and of men.

My good master said to me, "You do not ask
what spirits these are. Now,
I want you to know before you go farther

that they did not sin, but having merit
was not enough, for they lacked baptism,
which is a portal of the faith you hold; 36

and if they lived before Christianity
they did not worship God rightly;
among such as these am I myself.

For such defects, not for other faults,
are we lost, and afflicted only
in that we live in longing without hope."

Great grief gripped my heart when I heard this,
for I knew that people of much worth
were in that Limbo in suspense.

Dante now risks a timid question. He wants to know about the "Harrowing of Hell," when Christ was supposed to have gone to Limbo to release the ancient Hebrews who had believed in His coming. After the explanation the poets move on to a special region reserved for the great men of the past. Virgil (as Reason) approves the recognition of Dante as the sixth in rank of the world's poets.

"Tell me, Master, tell me, sir," I began,
wishing to be assured of the faith
that destroys every error, 48

"did any ever through his own merit
or another's leave here to be blessed?"
And he, understanding my veiled speech, answered,

"I was new in this condition
when I saw a Powerful One [Christ]
crowned with the sign of victory [the cross as an aureole].

He took from here our first parent,
Abel his son, and Noah,
obedient Moses, the lawgiver,

the patriarch Abraham, and David, the king,
Israel [Jacob] with his father and his sons,
and Rachel for whom he [Jacob] did so much, 60

and many others, and he made them blessed,
and I wish you to know that before then
no human souls were ever saved."

We did not stop because of his remarks,
but kept passing through the forest—
the forest, I mean, of crowded spirits.

Our way had not yet taken us far
after my slumber when I saw a light
which dispelled a hemisphere of darkness.

We were still distant from the glow
but not too far for me to discern
that notable people occupied that place. 72

"O you who honor every science and art," I said,
"who are these whose great merit
separates them from the others?"

And he answered, "The deserved fame
which still honors them in your life
gains favor in Heaven, and thus promotes them."

Meanwhile a voice was heard, saying,
"Honor the greatest poet;
his shade which had left is returning."

When this voice was silent
I saw four great figures come to us,
their faces neither sad nor gay. 84

My good master began to speak:
"See that one with sword in hand,
coming ahead of the others as their lord.

He is Homer, the sovereign poet;
the other. following, is Horace, the satirist;
Ovid is the third, and Lucan the last.

Since each shares with me the title 'poet'
which the single voice pronounced,
they do me honor, and in doing this do well."

Thus I saw assembled the school
of that lord of the lofty song who soars
above the others like an eagle. 96

After they had talked together a little
they turned to me with signs of greeting,
and my master smiled at that.

And still more honor they showed me
by making me one of their group,
so that I was the sixth among such sages.

The poets now come to the Castle of Wisdom or Fame, surrounded by the walls of the cardinal and speculative virtues and defended by a moat which may represent eloquence or desire for knowledge. They pass through the gates of the seven liberal arts. On a kind of enameled meadow within, the great spirits of the past appear: first the Trojans, Greeks, and legendary figures of early Rome; then philosophers, scientists, mathematicians, and doctors; and finally the Moorish scholar Averroës.

Thus we continued toward the light,
speaking of matters concerning which silence
is as fitting now as speech was then,

and we arrived at the foot of a noble castle,
seven times encircled by high walls,
defended all around by a fair rivulet. 108

This we crossed as if on solid ground.
Through seven gates I passed with these sages
and we arrived on a meadow of fresh verdure.

There we saw people dignified and grave,
of great authority in their semblance;
they spoke seldom, and with soft voices.

Afterward we withdrew to one side
to an open place, luminous and high,
from which all could be seen.

There, standing on the green enamel,
the great spirits were shown to me,
to have seen whom I feel exalted. 120

I saw Electra[5] with many companions,
among whom I recognized Hector and Aeneas,
and Caesar clad in arms, with hawklike eyes.

[5] Not the daughter of Agamemnon and Clytemnestra but rather the mother of Dardanus, founder of Troy.

I saw Camilla and Penthesilea
    on the other side, and I saw the Latian king,
    sitting with Lavinia, his daughter.

I saw that Brutus[6] who expelled the Tarquin,
    Lucretia, Julia, Marcia, and Cornelia;
    and alone, to one side, the Saladin.

When I had raised my eyes a little higher
    I saw the Master of the Knowing [Aristotle]
    sitting with his philosophic family. 132

All looked at him, all did him honor;
    there I saw Socrates and Plato
    who stood ahead of the others closest to him:

Democritus, who thought the world due to chance;
    Diogenes, Anaxagoras, and Thales,
    Empedocles, Heraclitus, and Zeno;

and I saw the good compiler of the qualities [of plants],
    Dioscorides, I mean; and Orpheus,
    Tully [Cicero], Linus, and Seneca, the moralist;

Euclid the geometer, and Ptolemy,
    Hippocrates, Avicenna, and Galen,
    and Averroës who made the great commentary [on Aristotle]. 144

I cannot enumerate them all fully;
    my long theme so drives me on that many times
    my words fall short of the facts.

The sixfold company diminished to two [Virgil and Dante];
    by another way my wise guide took me,
    out of the quiet into the trembling air,

and I came to a place where no light shines.

CANTO V

Francesca da Rimini

Since Hell is like an inverted cone, the circumference of each succeeding circle diminishes.

The guardian of the second ring is Minos, the ancient judge of the dead, represented by Dante as having some of the characteristics of a medieval demon. Like Charon, Minos offers a slight opposition which is overcome by the conjuring formula.

Thus I descended from the first circle
    down to the second which encloses less space
    but so much more pain that it moves to tears.

[6] This is not the assassin of Julius Caesar; that Brutus appears at the center of Hell in Canto XXXIV. The Brutus referred to here founded the ancient Roman republic.

There Minos stands, horrible and snarling,
examining the offenses, judging,
and sending down as he girds himself—

I mean that when an ill-born soul
comes before him, it confesses wholly,
and that discerner of sin,

seeing what place in Hell belongs to it,
encircles himself with his tail as many times
as the degrees he wants it to descend. 12

Always many stand in front of him;
they come in turns to their judgment,
confess and hear, and then are hurled below.

"O you who come to the painful refuge,"
Minos said when he saw me,
interrupting the work of his great office,

"consider how you entered and in whom you trust;
do not let the breadth of the entrance deceive you."
And my guide to him, "Why do you cry out?

Do not impede his fated going.
It is wished for where the power is
to do what is wished; so ask no more." 24

The poets hear and see the shades guilty of lust. A landslide caused by an earthquake at the time of the Crucifixion perhaps reminds the restless souls as they pass of the impossibility of their redemption. Dante pities more than blames these victims of the flesh and of the imagination. They pass like birds in autumn flight.

Now I begin to hear the sad notes of pain,
now I have come to where
loud cries beat upon my ears.

I have reached a place mute of all light
which roars like the sea in a tempest
when beaten by conflicting winds.

The infernal storm which never stops
drives the spirits in its blast;
whirling and beating, it torments them.

When they come in front of the landslide,
they utter laments, moans, and shrieks;
there they curse the Divine Power. 36

I learned that to such a torment
carnal sinners are condemned
who subject their reason to desire.

And, as starlings are borne by their wings
in the cold season, in a broad and dense flock,
so that blast carries the evil spirits.

Here, there, up, and down, it blows them;
no hope ever comforts them
of rest or even of less pain.

And as cranes go chanting their lays,
making a long line of themselves in the air,
so I saw coming, uttering laments, 48

shades born by that strife of winds.

Dante is eager to know who is punished here. No vulgar examples are cited but only glamorous figures of the ancient and medieval past whom love too completely mastered. Perhaps our poet suspects already that Francesca da Rimini and her lover are here. In any case he asks to speak to two who seem unusually light and is told to address them in the name of love, to which, in a nobler form, all his own life was a dedication. The real appeal, however, is in the sympathy expressed by the words, "O wearied souls!" Like doves borne on by desire, Francesca and Paolo leave their company, so responsive are they still to the slightest note of affection.

I asked, "Master, who are these people
whom the black air so punishes?"

"The first of those about whom
you want to know," he said to me,
"was an empress over many peoples,

by the vice of luxury so subdued
that she made lust lawful in her decrees
to take away the blame she had incurred.

She is Semiramis who, we read,
succeeded Ninus, her spouse;
she held the land that now the Sultan rules. 60

The other is she [Dido] who killed herself
after breaking faith with the ashes of Sichaeus;
next comes luxurious Cleopatra.

See Helen [of Troy] for whom
so many bad years revolved, and the great Achilles
whose last battle was with love.[7]

See Paris, Tristan,"—and he pointed out and named
more than a thousand shades
whom love had taken from our life.

After I had heard my teacher
name the knights and ladies of olden times,
pity overcame me, and I felt dismayed. 72

[7] Dante knew a medieval tradition according to which Achilles, as a result of love for a Trojan princess, was ambushed and killed.

I began, "Poet, willingly would I speak
with those two who go together
and seem so light upon the wind."

And he to me, "Wait until they come closer,
then entreat them by the love
which impels them and they will come."

As soon as the wind brought them to us,
I raised my voice, "O wearied souls,
come speak to us if it is not forbidden."

As doves summoned by their desire,
with wings raised and firm, sail through the air,
borne on to their sweet nest by their will alone, 84

so those spirits moved from the band where Dido is,
coming to us through the malignant air,
so responsive were they to my affectionate cry.

Now Francesca speaks, and her first words are an implied prayer to God whose mysterious justice has condemned her beyond remission, an unselfish prayer for this living soul who has shown them pity. It is a prayer for the "peace" which romantic and illicit love can never know. In her heart's response to Dante's simple words, she treats him already as "gracious" and "benign" and exaggerates her own misdoing. Her story is a mere outline, told partly in terms of the maxims of courtly love. With ladylike reticence she does not name herself or Paolo, her brother-in-law and lover, or even the city where she was born. Death itself would not have been so tragic: one moment for repentance might have permitted her to be saved; it was the suddenness of her and Paolo's death that was so cruel. Caïna, at the bottom of Hell, where traitors to kindred are punished, awaits her husband who surprised and killed them.

"O living creature, gracious and benign,
going through the dark air
visiting us who stained the earth with blood,

if the King of the universe were friendly to us
we would pray to Him for your peace,
since you pity our perverse evil.

Whatever you are pleased to hear from us or say
we will relate and listen to,
while the wind, as now, is silent. 96

The city [Ravenna] where I was born
lies on the shore where the Po descends
with all its tributaries to find peace.

Love which flames quickly in noble hearts
was kindled in this soul by the fair body
taken from me; the manner [of that taking] still offends.

Love that exempts no one beloved from loving
caught me so strongly with his charm
that, as you see, it still does not leave me.

Love led us to one death together.
Caïna waits for him who quenched our lives."
These words were borne from them to us. 108

On hearing this delicate outline of the tragedy, Dante bows his head, perhaps recalling who the speaker is, and then naming Francesca, he asks, in words as respectful and delicate as her own, about the immediate cause and occasion of her sin. Although she dislikes to recall the intimate details, she speaks, unable to refuse an affectionate appeal. There was no premeditation in her sin. She and Paolo had been reading a love story without suspecting the effect it might have. One moment of weakness overcame them, a moment which ended their reading and their lives and which stands now in contrast to eternity.

When I heard those afflicted souls
I bent down my face, and held it low so long
that the poet said, "Of what are you thinking?"

When I answered I began, "Alas!
how many sweet thoughts, what desire
led them to the woeful pass!"

Then I turned to them and said,
"Francesca, your suffering
makes me weep with sorrow and with pity,

But tell me, at the time of the sweet sighs,
by what means and how love permitted you
to know the dubious desires." 120

And she to me, "There is no greater pain
than to recall a happy time in misery
and this your teacher knows;

but if to learn the first root of our love
you have such desire, I will answer
like one who speaks and weeps.

One day for our delight we were reading
about Lancelot, how love constrained him;
alone we were and without any suspicion.

Several times that reading made our glances meet
and changed the color of our faces;
but one moment alone overcame us. 132

When we read how the fond smile [of Guinevere]
was kissed by such a lover,
he, who never will be separated from me,

kissed me, on my lips. all trembling.
    A Gallehaut [pander] was the book and he who wrote it.
    That day we read no farther."

While one spirit was saying this
    the other wept, so that from pity
    I fainted, as if I had been dying,

and I fell, as a dead body falls.

CANTO VI

THE GLUTTONS

On recovering my senses, which were stunned
    by pity for the two kinsfolk
    who overwhelmed me with sadness,

new torments and new tormented shades
    I see around me, wherever I move
    and wherever I turn to gaze.

The poets are now among the gluttons who are lying like pigs in a sty under a constant, unvarying rain. Although the punishments here are relatively mild, they are particularly distasteful to the luxury-loving. All the senses are afflicted: sight by the dismal setting, touch by the cold rain, smell and taste by the stench, and hearing by the loud barking of Cerberus, the three-headed dog, the bestial guardian of this circle. Cerberus is appeased, not by a honey cake, as in the Aeneid, *but by dirt, to emphasize further the filthiness of gluttony.*

I am in the third circle of the rain,
    eternal, accursed, cold, and heavy;
    its amount and kind never change.

Large hailstones, dirty water, and snow
    pour down through the dark air;
    the ground that receives them stinks. 12

Cerberus, the fierce and cruel beast,
    barks doglike with three throats
    over those submerged there.

His eyes are red, his beard greasy and black,
    his belly large, his paws armed with claws;
    grasping the spirits, he flays and tears them.

The rain makes them howl like dogs;
    they use one side to shelter the other;
    often they turn, the profane wretches.

When Cerberus, the monster, saw us,
    he opened his mouths and showed his teeth,
    trembling in all his limbs. 24

And my leader, opening his hands,
took some earth and threw handfuls
into the ravenous gullets.

As a barking dog, longing for food,
grows quiet after he has seized it,
since he thinks only of eating,

so did those filthy heads of the demon Cerberus
who thunders over the shades,
making them wish they were deaf.

A soul nicknamed "Ciacco" (the pig) recognizes Dante but is himself unrecognizable since the bestial vice of gluttony disfigures. To spare the feelings of this shade Dante suggests that perhaps Ciacco's pain prevented the recognition.

We passed over the spirits subdued
by the heavy rain, placing our feet
on their nothingness which appears as flesh. 36

They were all lying on the ground
except one who sat up quickly
as soon as he saw us pass in front of him.

"O you, led through this Hell,"
he said to me, "recognize me if you can;
you were made [born] before I was unmade [died]."

And I to him, "The anguish that you feel
perhaps takes you from my memory
so that I do not seem ever to have seen you,

but tell me who you are, placed here
in such punishment that, if others
are greater, none is so displeasing." 48

And he to me, "Your city [Florence] so full of envy
that it can hold no more
kept me in the bright life.

The citizens called me Ciacco;
for the damning sin of gluttony,
as you see, I lie helpless in the rain.

And I, sad spirit, am not alone,
for all of these are in similar pain
for a like sin,"—and he said no more.

I answered, "Ciacco, your distress weighs upon me
so that it moves to tears;
but tell me, if you can, the fate 60

of the citizens of the divided city;
if any one of them is just, and tell me
why such discord has assailed it."

Then he to me, "After long dispute
they will come to blows, and the rustic party [the Whites]
Will drive out the other with much offense.

Afterward that faction will fall
within three suns [years], and the other rise
through one [Boniface VIII] who now is moving carefully.

For a long time it will hold high its head,
keeping the other under heavy burdens,
however much it may weep and be put to shame. 72

Two men are just, but are not listened to.
Pride, envy, and avarice are the sparks
which have enflamed all hearts."

Here he put an end to his sad words,
and I said to him, "I wish to learn more,
and beg you to grant me the gift of further speech.

Farinata and Tegghiaio, who were so worthy,
Jacopo Rusticucci, Arrigo, and Mosca,
and the others who set their minds to doing good,

tell me where they are, let me know about them,
for a great desire urges me to find out
if Heaven soothes or Hell embitters them." 84

And he, "They are among the blackest spirits;
different sins weigh them to the bottom;
if you go down so far, you will see them.

But when you are again in the sweet world,
I beg you to recall me to the memory of others.
More I will not say; this is all I answer."

He twisted his straight eyes asquint,
looked at me a little, then bent his head,
and fell to the level of the other blind ones.

My guide said to me, "No more will he awaken
until the angelic trumpet sounds [on Judgment Day]
when the hostile Power [hostile to sinners] will come. 96

Each then will find his sad tomb,
will resume his flesh and form,
and will hear what resounds to all eternity."

Thus we passed over the filthy mixture of the shades
and of the rain, with slow steps,
touching a little on the future life.

I asked, "Master, will these torments increase
after the great judgment,
or will they be less or equally painful?"

He answered, "Recall your science
which maintains that the more perfect a thing is,
the more bliss or pain it feels. 108

Although these accursed people
never come to true perfection,
they will be more complete after than before."

We bent our course along that way,
saying much more than I relate,
and came to a place for descending.

There we found Plutus, the great enemy.

CANTO VII

The Avaricious and the Prodigal

Plutus, the ancient god of wealth and here the guardian of the circle of the avaricious and the prodigal, is represented as an inflated monster. He speaks in a high voice, like certain fat men, and his words are not clearly comprehensible. A reference to the Power through which the archangel Michael defeated the revolt of Satan easily deflates this weak, unhealthy, and puffy creature, who collapses suddenly, without resistance.

"*Papè Satàn, Papè Satàn, aleppe,*"[8]
Plutus began with a clucking voice,
and that noble sage [Virgil], who understood,

said to comfort me, "Do not fear,
for whatever power he may have,
he cannot prevent our descending this rock."

Then he turned to that inflated visage
and said, "Keep still, accursed wolf;
consume yourself inwardly with your rage.

Not without reason is our going to the depth.
It is decreed on high where Michael
took vengeance for the proud revolt." 12

As sails swelled by the wind
fall entangled when the mast breaks,
so the cruel monster fell to the ground.

The avaricious on one side and the prodigal on the other push great weights around their respective semicircles. At the two points where they clash, like the waves between Scylla and Charybdis, they exchange insults and turn, going to the opposite point. Thus they work hard, like the avaricious on earth, but uselessly, missing the spiritual pleasures which make this life and the next worth while. All are alike, without distinction, and unrecognizable as individuals.

[8]These words are not clearly understandable; perhaps a threat and a warning to Satan. (Translator's note.)

Thus we descended into the fourth cavity,
taking in more of the dismal bank
which holds all the evil of the universe.

Ah, Justice of God! Who can combine
so many new pains and torments,
and why does our sin so waste us?

As the waves above Charybdis break
against each other as they meet,
so in this place the souls must clash. 24

Here I saw more people than elsewhere
on one side and the other, shouting loudly
and pushing weights with their chests.

They bump against each other and then all turn,
pushing back the load and crying,
"Why do you hoard?" or "Why do you squander?"

Thus they go on each side
of the dark circle to the opposite point,
shouting their insulting refrains.

When they reach that place, they turn again
through their half circles to the other clash.
And I, my heart oppressed, said, 36

"Master, now tell me who these are
and if all the tonsured ones
on the left are of the clergy?"

And he to me, "In the first life
all were so twisted mentally
that they could not spend with moderation.

Quite clearly their voices bark this out
when they come to the two points of the circle
where contrary faults divide them.

Those whose heads are tonsured, as you see,
were clerics and popes and cardinals
in whom avarice shows its strength." 48

And I, "Master, among such as these
I must surely recognize some
who were defiled by these vices."

And he to me, "You conceive a vain thought;
the undiscerning life which made them sordid
now leaves them too obscure for recognition.

Throughout eternity they will clash;
some will arise from the grave with fists closed,
and the others [the prodigal] with their hair shorn.

Bad giving and bad keeping have taken from them
the fair world and placed them in this strife
which words of mine will not glorify. 60

Wealth, according to Dante, is in the hands of a special divinity, Fortune, who performs her functions as the angels guide and direct the various heavens. No reason or moral order is discernible in the distribution of wealth among individuals, families, and nations.

Now, my son, you can see how wealth,
committed to Fortune, and for which
the human race struggles, mocks us.

All the gold that is under the moon
or ever was, could not give rest
to one of these weary souls."

"Master," I asked, "now tell me,
who is this Fortune
with the world's riches in her hands?"

And he to me, "Oh foolish creatures,
how deep is the ignorance that blinds you!
Now I want you to hear my judgment. 72

He [God] whose understanding transcends all
made the heavens and gave them guides,
so that each part shines on all the others,

distributing the light equally.
Likewise, for mundane splendors,
He ordained a general minister and guide

to transfer vain wealth in due time
from people to people, and from one to another family,
beyond the intervention of human intelligence.

Thus one people rules and another languishes,
according to her judgment, which is hidden from us,
like a snake in the grass. 84

Your knowledge is of no avail against her;
she foresees, judges, and rules her province
as the other gods [angels] do theirs.

Her activity has no truce;
necessity makes her quick to act,
so that changes [in fortune] come often.

She is the one so reviled
even by those who should praise her
but who, instead, give her ill repute.

Yet she is blessed and does not hear;
happy with the other primal [angelic] creatures
she rules her sphere and rejoices in her bliss. 96

It is now a little after midnight of Good Friday. In a swamp the poets see the bemired souls of the angry and the bubbles made by the sullen beneath the surface. The travelers make a long detour to the left, which indicates an approach to worse things.

Now let us descend to greater misery;
already each star that was rising when I started
is falling, and staying too long is forbidden."

We crossed the circle to the inner bank
along a stream which bubbled and flowed
through a channel it had formed.

The water was darker than purplish-black;
and, accompanying the murky waves,
on a rough path, we reached the place below.

This dreary stream forms a marsh, the Styx,
when it has reached the foot
of the gray, malignant banks. 108

And I, who remained intent on looking,
saw muddy people in that bog,
naked, and with angry looks.

They struck each other not only with their hands,
but with their heads, chests, and feet,
and tore each other with their teeth, bit by bit.

My good master said, "Son, now see
the souls of those whom anger overcame;
I wish you to believe also

that under the water there are people sighing
and making bubbles on the surface
as your eyes tell you wherever you look. 120

Fixed in the slime they say, 'Sullen were we
in the sweet air gladdened by the sun,
keeping within us the fumes of spite;

now we are sullen in the black mire.'
This hymn is gurgled in their throats,
for they cannot speak in clear words."

Thus we covered a wide arc around the filthy slough
between the dry bank and the swamp,
with eyes turned to those swallowing the mire.

At last we came to the foot of a tower.

CANTO VIII

The Angry and the Sullen

Continuing the account of the fifth circle, Dante anxiously inquires about the meaning of certain signals. These are explained by the coming of a boat guided by Phlegyas,[9] the guardian of this round.

I say, continuing, that long before we reached
the foot of the high tower
our eyes were drawn to its top

by two little flames placed there;
and another gave back a signal from so far
that our eyes could hardly catch it.

Turning to the sea of all wisdom, I asked,
"What does this mean? what does the other flame
answer? and who are they who light it?"

And he to me, "Over the foul waters
already you can see what is expected
if the mist of the marsh does not hide it from you." 12

Never did a bowstring drive an arrow
which sped so quickly through the air
as a little boat I saw then

coming through the water toward us
under the guidance of a single boatman
who cried, "Now you are caught, fell spirit!"

"Phlegyas, Phlegyas, this time you cry out
in vain," said my lord, "you will keep us
only while crossing the slough."

As one who learns of a great trick
played on him and who resents it,
so Phlegyas became in his pent-up rage. 24

My guide stepped down into the boat,
making me get in after him,
and only then did it appear burdened.

As soon as my master and I had embarked,
the ancient prow moved on,
cleaving more of the water than it does with others.

Dante becomes angry at one of the shades, apparently incurring the very sin punished here, but is commended for it by Virgil. The episode is intended to show that righteous indignation is permissible. We cannot love gentleness and politeness intensely without disliking arrogance and incivility with equal intensity.

[9] Enraged with Apollo for raping his daughter, Phlegyas set the god's temple on fire and was killed by him.

While we were going through the stagnant channel,
a shade covered with mud rose up, saying [insolently],
"Who are you, coming before your time?"

I answered, "If I come, I do not stay,
but who are you, now so dirty?"
And he, "You see I am one who weeps." 36

Then I to him, "With tears and grief
stay here, damned spirit,
for I recognize you for all your filth."

Then the shade stretched both hands toward the boat,
but my wary master pushed him off, saying,
"Get over there with the other dogs!"

And embracing me with both arms
he kissed my face and said, "Indignant soul,
may she be blessed who bore you!

In the world he was an arrogant person;
no kindness adorned his memory,
so his shade is furious here. 48

How many think themselves great kings
who will lie like swine in the mire,
leaving behind horrible censure."

And I, "Master, I would be glad
to see him soused in this soup [muddy water]
before we leave the pond."

He answered, "Before you see the shore
you will be satisfied;
it is proper that such a wish be granted."

In a little while I saw the muddy crowd
wreak such havoc on him
that I still praise and thank God for it. 60

All cried, "At Filippo Argenti!"
and the raging Florentine spirit
turned with his teeth upon himself.

Here we left him, and of him I say no more.
A wailing now struck my ears,
so that I looked ahead intently.

My good master said, "Now son,
the City of Dis [Satan] draws near,
with its grave citizens, its great garrison."

And I, "Master, already I discern its mosques
clearly there within the valley,
red, as if they had come out of fire." 72

He continued, "The eternal flames
enkindling them make them glow
as you see in this lower Hell."

We now arrived within the moats
which surround the disconsolate city,
the walls of which seemed of iron.

Not without making a wide circuit [to the left]
did we come to where the boatman loudly cried,
"Get out, here is the entrance!"

Above the gates more than a thousand [rebellious angels],
rained down from Heaven, cried angrily,
"Who is this one, without death, 84

going through the kingdom of the dead?"
And my wise master signaled
that he wished to speak with them secretly.

Then they held back their great anger
and said, "You come alone and let him go
who so boldly entered this kingdom.

Let him return by himself on the mad path;
let him see if he can; for you will stay here,
you who have led him through so dark a country."

Threatened with the loss of Virgil (Reason), Dante begs not to be left alone. His guide tries to reassure him, but, as an intellectual rather than a suggestive force, he can do that only imperfectly. As Virgil leaves, Dante wonders whether the answer to a question about the success of the mission will be "yes," or "no." Virgil also is not sure, but, on returning, tries to comfort Dante by passing off his doubt and dismay as anger. He hopes, with the limited confidence reason gives, that an angel will bring divine aid.

Think, Reader, if I was frightened
at the sound of the accursed words,
for I did not believe I could ever return. 96

"O my dear guide, you who many times
have made me safe and drawn me
through deep peril confronting me,

do not leave me so undone," I said,
"and if going farther is denied us,
let us retrace our steps together rapidly."

Then that lord who had brought me there replied,
"Do not fear, for no one can prevent our journey;
by Such a One it has been granted.

Wait for me here, and with good hope
comfort and feed your weary spirit,
for I will not leave you in the lower world." 108

Thus my dear father went away
and abandoned me, and I remained in doubt,
for "yes" and "no" struggled within my mind.

I could not hear what he said to our adversaries,
but he did not stay long with them
before each of them raced back.

They closed the gates in the face
of my lord, who remained outside
and then came toward me with slow steps,

his eyes upon the ground and with a face
shorn of all boldness. He asked, sighing,
"Who has denied us the abode of woe?" 120

Then to me he said, "Although I may get angry,
do not fear, for I will win the fight,
whatever is contrived within.

This insolence of theirs is not new;
they showed it once at a less secret gate
which is now without a fastening.

Over it you saw the deadly inscription;[10]
and already on this side of it,
passing through the circles without escort,

someone descends who will open the city for us."

CANTO IX

THE CITY OF DIS

The hue that cowardice put on my face
when I saw my guide come back
made him repress more quickly his dismay.

He stopped, attentive, like a man listening;
for sight could not go far
through the dark air and thick mist.

"Still we must win the fight," he began,
"if not . . . such help was offered us;
oh, how I long for someone to come!"

I noticed how he covered up
his first words with those that followed
which expressed a different thought, 12

and his remark made me afraid
because I drew the words cut off
into a meaning perhaps worse than he intended.

[10] The words written over Hell's gate, III.1–9. Dante and Virgil are now about to enter the lower hell, where the sins of malice (violence and fraud) are punished.

Dante asks indirectly if Virgil really knows the way.

"To this depth of the dismal hole
does any ever descend from the first circle
where hope cut off is the only punishment?"

This question I asked, and he answered,
"It seldom happens that one of us
makes the journey on which I am going.

It is true that I was down here once before,
conjured by that cruel Erichtho [a sorceress],
who brought shades back to their bodies. 24

Not for long had my flesh been without me
when she made me go within those walls
to bring out a spirit from Judas' circle.[11]

That is the lowest and darkest place, the one
farthest removed from the heaven that encircles all.
I know the road well; therefore be reassured.

This swamp exhaling the great stench
surrounds the woeful city
which we cannot enter now peacefully."

Three Furies, handmaidens of Hecate, the ancient queen of Hell, symbols of madness or remorseful terror, rise up, citing their error in letting Theseus enter their region to rescue Persephone. Dante clings to Virgil with desperation. The Furies then call upon the Gorgon (Medusa, Despair) to turn the intruder to stone. Virgil warns his charge with great urgency not to look at her.

The allegorical meaning is perhaps as follows: the reforming Christian (Dante), when confronted by remorseful terror (the Furies), may lose his reason (Virgil), but as long as hope remains, he can appeal for divine aid. Only despair (Medusa) cuts off irremediably the path to salvation.

And more he said, but I do not recall it
because my eyes drew all my thoughts
to the glowing summit of the high tower 36

where suddenly three infernal Furies,
with the shape and features of women,
and stained with blood, stood upright.

They were girded with green hydras[12]
and had serpents and horned snakes for hair
with which their wild heads were bound.

And he who knew well the handmaidens
of the Queen of eternal lamentation
said to me, "Behold! the fierce Erinyes [Furies].

[11] The very lowest and innermost circle of Hell, described in Canto XXXIV.
[12] Monsters with several heads.

The one on the left is Megaera;
she on the right, weeping, is Alecto;
Tisiphone is in the middle,"—and with that he was silent. 48

They were tearing their breasts with their nails,
beating themselves with their hands, and shouting
so loudly that in fear I drew close to my master.

"Let Medusa come, and we will change him to stone,"
they all said, looking down,
"badly did we avenge the assault of Theseus."

"Turn back and keep your eyes closed,
for if the Gorgon [Medusa] shows herself
and you see her, there will be no returning."

Thus my master spoke, and he himself
turned me around, not trusting my hands,
but with his also covered my eyes. 60

O you who have sound understanding,
observe the meaning hidden
beneath the veil of the strange verses.

And now over the turbid waters
came a crash full of terror
at which both the shores trembled,

a sound like that of a whirlwind
made violent by conflicting currents
which hits the forest without restraint,

shatters, beats down, and sweeps away the boughs.
Behind a cloud of dust it moves on fiercely,
and makes the beasts and shepherds flee. 72

My master freed my eyes and said,
"Now direct your sight over that ancient foam
to where the mist is thickest."

As frogs before their enemy the snake
scatter through the water
until each squats on the bottom,

so I saw more than a thousand ruined spirits
fleeing before one [an angel] who,
with dry feet, passed over the Styx.

From his face he fanned that gross air,
moving his left hand in front of it,
and only with that effort seemed weary. 84

I saw at once that he was sent from Heaven,
and I turned to my master, who made a sign
that I should keep quiet and bow to him.

How full of scorn he seemed to me!
Coming to the gate, he opened it
with a wand, for there was no resistance.

"O outcasts from Heaven, despised creatures!"
he began, on the horrible threshold,
"why do you harbor this insolence?

Why do you oppose that will
whose purpose can never be hindered,
and which has several times increased your pain? 96

Of what use is it to butt against fate?
Your Cerberus [chained by Hercules] because of this
still has a chin and throat without hair."[13]

Then he turned back over the filthy road
and said no word to us, but seemed
like one intent on other cares

than those of the people near him;
and we moved on toward the city,
safe, after the holy words.

On entering, Dante sees open tombs, hotter than iron in a blacksmith's forge. Each contains the leader of a heretical sect with his followers. Here, contrary to their custom, the travelers turn to the right, perhaps to indicate that heresy can be incurred honestly, although persistence in it is a sin of pride.

We entered without any strife,
and I, wanting to see what punishments
such a fortress enclosed, 108

as soon as within glanced around
and saw on every side a great plain
full of grief and torment.

As at Arles where the Rhone spreads out
or at Pola near [the bay of] Quarnero
which encloses Italy and bathes her boundaries,

the tombs make the land uneven,
so they did here, on all sides,
except that these graves were more terrible;

for among the tombs flames spread
by which they were so heated
that no trade needs iron hotter. 120

[13]Theseus of Athens (line 54) tried to carry off Persephone (Hecate), queen of the Underworld, but was himself held prisoner until he was rescued by Hercules, who in chaining the dog Cerberus tore the skin from its neck.

All their lids were open,
and such harsh laments came from them
as from the wretched and the suffering.

And I, "Master, who are the people
buried within the tombs,
making themselves heard by their painful sighs?"

And he to me, "Here are the archheretics[14]
with their followers of every sect;
and the tombs are laden much more than you think.

Like with like is buried,
and the monuments are more and less hot."
Then, after we had turned to the right, 132

we passed between the torments and the high battlements.

CANTO X

FARINATA DEGLI UBERTI

Now along a solitary path
between the city wall and the torments,
my master makes his way, and I behind him.

"O supreme genius, you who through the impious circles
turn me [to the left or right] as you please," I began,
"speak to me and satisfy my wishes.

The people lying in the sepulchres,
might they be seen?—all the lids
are raised and no one guards them."

And he to me, "All will be locked in
when they return from Jehoshaphat [on Judgment Day]
with the bodies they have left above. 12

Epicurus is with the heretics of Christian times since he, almost alone among ancient philosophers, denied the immortality of the soul.

Still hesitant about asking questions, Dante represses his desire to see certain Florentines.

On this side is the burial place
of Epicurus and of all his followers
who hold that the soul dies with the body.

[14]This circle of the heretics, like Limbo, is a special case, heresy being a mental or spiritual condition rather than one of the sins of behavior (Incontinence, Violence, Fraud) punished in the overall threefold scheme of Dante's Hell. Moreover, heresy, like failure to be baptized, is a fault defined not by universal ethics but from a specifically Christian point of view.

But concerning the question you ask
you will soon be satisfied,
and also as to the wish you keep silent."[15]

And I, "Good guide, I hide my thought
only to speak little; not long ago
you disposed me to do that."

A deep voice sounds amid the silence of the graves. It is that of Farinata degli Uberti, a Ghibelline leader who, in 1260, won the bloody battle of Montaperti over the Florentine Guelfs, to which party Dante's family belonged. In recalling the bloodshed, Farinata has a moment of spontaneous repentance. Dante timidly draws closer to his guide who then directs him toward this proud, towering figure.

"O Tuscan, you who through the city of fire
go alive, speaking thus modestly,
may it please you to remain in this place. 24

Your speech shows you a native
of that noble fatherland
to which, perhaps, I was too harmful."

Suddenly this sound came
from one of the tombs, so that, startled,
I drew closer to my guide.

He said to me, "Turn around! what are you doing?
See Farinata, who has stood erect;
from the waist upward, wholly, you can see him!"

I had already fixed my eyes on his,
and he lifted up his chest and head,
as if he had scorn for Hell, 36

and the bold and ready hands of my guide
pushed me among the sepulchres to him,
saying, "Let your words be well chosen."

Disappointed in not seeing someone of his own generation, Farinata asks about Dante's ancestors. On hearing the names of these former enemies, he tells angrily how he had scattered them. Now Dante's partisan spirit is aroused. He points out that his party has been able to return to Florence, whereas Farinata's has not learned the art of getting back. Dante's remark is an unexpected blow for the Ghibelline captain, who is unaware of all the events and who remains silent, trying to recover and to collect his thoughts.

When I was at the foot of his tomb
he looked at me a little; then, almost disdainfully,
he asked, "Who were your ancestors?"

[15] Possibly a wish to see Farinata.

I, desirous to obey, did not hide them,
but revealed them all,
whereupon he raised his brows a little

and said, "Fiercely were they adverse
to me and to my ancestors and to my party,
so that twice I scattered them." 48

"If they were driven out, they came back from every side,"
I answered him, "both the first and the second time,
but yours did not learn well that art!"

Now the shade of the father of Guido Cavalcanti, the latter a leading poet and Dante's best friend, rises beside the great Ghibelline leader. He too is not interested in Dante. He assumes that our poet is allowed to visit Hell because of some peculiar merit, and since he cannot conceive of greater nobility of mind than that of his son, he wonders why Guido is not there also. Dante is perplexed, not knowing that the shades are ignorant of immediate happenings on earth, and replies ambiguously, implying lack of devotion on Guido's part to Virgil. The important point, however, is the past tense of the verb he uses. Cavalcante assumes from it that his son is dead, and from the embarrassed tone of Dante's remarks, suspects that Guido may have had a fate somewhat like his own. Dante's delay in answering confirms his fear, and he falls back into his tomb.

Now beside him there arose to sight
a shade visible down to his chin;
I believe he had risen on his knees.

He looked around me as if anxious
to see if someone else were with me,
but when this expectation was wholly spent,

weeping he said, "If through this blind prison
you go because of the greatness of your mind,
where is my son? why is he not with you?" 60

And I to him, "By myself I do not come;
Virgil, waiting there, guides me,
whom perhaps your Guido held in disdain."

His words and the manner of his punishment
had already revealed his name to me;
therefore my reply was so complete.

Rising suddenly he cried, "What did you say?
he *held?* Does he not live still?
Does not the sweet light strike his eyes?"

When he was aware of some delay
before I answered, he fell back supine
and showed himself no more. 72

Meanwhile Farinata has been pondering over Dante's remark and, without transition, oblivious to the drama enacted at his feet, he returns the verbal blow by predicting the poet's exile within four years. Relieved by this aggression, he asks in a more kindly tone why the Florentines have persecuted his family, and he points out proudly how, after the battle, when the Ghibelline leaders proposed razing Florence to the ground, he alone defended and saved her. Now Dante's partisan spirit is likewise softened, and in the conversation that follows he learns that the shades remember the past and can predict the future, but, like farsighted people, cannot see what is close at hand. This accounts for the misunderstanding between him and Cavalcante, and he asks to have his error corrected.

But that other magnanimous one, at whose instance
I had stopped, did not change his expression,
nor move his head, nor bend his body.

"And if," he said, continuing his first remark,
"they have badly learned that art,
it torments me more than this bed.

But not fifty times will be rekindled
the face of her [Hecate, the moon] who rules here
before you will know the hardness of that art!

And—so may you return sometime to the sweet world—
tell me why the people are so fierce
against my kindred in all their laws." 84

Then I to him, "The slaughter and havoc
which dyed the [river] Arbia red
cause such prayers to rise in our temple."

Sighing he shook his head and said,
"In that I was not alone, nor certainly
would I and the others have moved without cause,

but I was alone when all the rest
agreed to wipe out Florence:
I defended her openly before all."

"So may your descendants sometime have rest,"
I replied, "please solve for me this puzzle
which has now entangled my judgment. 96

It seems that you see, if I hear rightly,
what the future brings,
but for the present have a different vision."

"Like those with imperfect sight,
we see things far from us," he said,
"so much light the Supreme ruler still allows,

but when they come close, or exist, our minds
do not perceive them, and, without news from others,
we know nothing of your human state.

Therefore you can understand that our knowledge [gained from others]
will be wholly dead after that moment [Judgment Day]
when the gates of the future are closed." 108

Then, as if sorry for my fault,
I said, "Now please tell that fallen one
that his son is still joined with the living,

and if I was silent at his question,
let him know it was because my thoughts
were confused by the error you have corrected."

Before moving on, Virgil declares emphatically that Beatrice will reveal to Dante the course of his life. This is a mistake on Virgil's part: Cacciaguida, not Beatrice, makes the prophecy.[16]

(The treatment of the heretics is a comedy of errors which illustrates the fallibility of human reason. The Epicureans, in their tombs, erred in thinking that the grave ended all; Farinata is deceived in several ways; Cavalcante makes a series of false assumptions; Dante likewise is bewildered. Finally Virgil [Reason itself] is emphatically wrong.)

Already my master was calling me back,
so that I begged the spirit more hastily
to tell me who was with him.

He said, "With more than a thousand I lie:
here is the second Frederick [of Sicily]
and the Cardinal [Ubaldino]; of the others I am silent." 120

Then he hid himself, and toward the ancient poet
I turned my steps, meditating
about the prophecy hostile to me.

My guide moved on and, as we were going,
he said to me, "Why are you so bewildered?"
and I satisfied his request.

"Let your mind retain what you have heard
against you," that sage commanded me,
"and now listen to this," and he raised his finger:

"When you face the sweet light
of her [Beatrice] whose fair eyes see everything
you will learn from her the journey of your life." 132

Then he turned his steps to the left;
we went from the wall toward the center
along a path which goes into a valley

which even up there stifled us with its stench.

[16]This occurs in *Paradise,* Canto XVII, where the exile of Dante, separated from the places and people he cherished most, is poignantly outlined by Cacciaguida, Dante's great-great-grandfather.

CANTO XI

THE CLASSIFICATION OF SINS

As the poets proceed toward the inner edge of the sixth circle, they observe a tomb inscribed with the name of Anastasius. There was confusion in Dante's time between a pope and a heretical Byzantine emperor of that name.

While waiting to become accustomed to the smell which rises from a river of hot blood below, Virgil explains the various divisions of Hell.

To explain why usurers are classed with blasphemers and sodomites as doing violence to God, Virgil points out that Nature, which offers man its bounty, derives from God; that men's art (industry) gives further value to the products of Nature and, in a sense, derives also from God; that man was intended to earn his living through the bounty of Nature and by the sweat of his brow, and that usurers violate this divine plan.

At the end of the canto we learn by the position of the stars that it is about three hours after midnight, Saturday, April 9, 1300.

On the edge of a high bank
    formed by a circle of broken rocks
    we stood above a more cruel pack;

and here because of the horrible stench
    which the deep abyss exhales
    we approached behind the cover of a great tomb

on which I saw an inscription saying,
    "I hold Anastasius, the pope,
    whom Photinus drew from the straight path."

"Our descent must be slow, so that our sense of smell
    may get used to the foul breath,
    and then we will not heed it." 12

Thus my master spoke, and I, "Please find compensation,
    so that time will not be wasted."
    And he, "That is what I have been thinking of.

My son," he then continued,
    "below us are three smaller circles
    like those you are leaving,

full of accursed spirits. In order
    that sight alone may suffice henceforth,
    observe how and why they are confined.

The malice which Heaven reproves
    causes injury and grief to others
    either by violence or by fraud, 24

but because fraud is peculiar to man
    it displeases God more; therefore
    the fraudulent are placed lower and have more pain.

The next circle [seventh] is for the violent,
  and, since force can be used
  against God, oneself, and one's fellow men—

I mean against them or their property—
  it is divided into three bands
  as you will clearly hear.

Death and painful wounds may be inflicted
  on one's fellows, and plunder, arson,
  and extortion on their property. 36

Thus the first round torments, in various groups,
  assassins, plunderers, and robbers,
  and all who strike maliciously.

A man may commit violence against himself
  and against his property; therefore, in the second round,
  all who deprive themselves of your world

or gamble and dissipate their wealth
  must unavailingly repent
  and weep instead of being happy.

Violence is committed against the Deity
  by cursing Him and denying Him in one's heart;
  and by scorning Nature and her bounty; 48

therefore the smallest band stamps with its seal
  both Sodom [the sodomites] and Cahors [the usurers]
  and those [the blasphemers] who speak disdaining God.

Fraud which hurts man's conscience
  can be used against those who trust
  and against those who have no special confidence.

In the latter case, only the love that Nature makes
  [the natural brotherhood of man] is violated;
  thus, in the following [eighth] circle are nested

hypocrisy, flattery, sorcery,
  falsifying, theft, and simony,
  panders, barrators, and similar filth. 60

The other fraud violates
  both the love Nature creates and that
  which implies a special trust.

Therefore, in the smallest circle
  at the center of the universe where Dis [Satan] holds forth
  whoever betrays is eternally consumed."

And I, "Master, your account proceeds clearly
  and makes plain the division
  of this abyss and those who are in it,

but tell me, the souls [above] in the slimy bog,
those whom the wind blows, and those the rain beats,
and those who meet with such sharp tongues, 72

why are they not inside the ruddy city
if God is angry with them,
and if not, why are they in such a plight?"

He answered, "Why does your mind
go astray more than usual?
or are you thinking of something else?

Do you not remember those words
with which your *Ethics* [of Aristotle] treats
the three dispositions Heaven does not admit—

incontinence, malice, and mad bestiality—
and how incontinence offends God less
and incurs less blame? 84

If you consider this teaching
and recall who is being punished
outside of the city,

you will see why they are separated
from these and why, less angrily,
Divine Justice torments them."

"O Sun, you who heal every troubled vision,
I am so glad to hear you explain
that to question pleases me no less than knowing;

but go back a little," I said,
"to where you say that usury offends
divine goodness, and solve the puzzle." 96

"Philosophy," he said,
"states in more than one place
that Nature takes her course

from the Divine Intellect and from Its operation,
and if you note well your *Physics*,
you will find after not many pages

that your activity follows the divine plan,
as the pupil does his master, so that your art [industry]
is, as it were, a grandchild of God.

From these two [Nature and Industry], if you recall
the early part of Genesis,
man should earn his living and prosper. 108

And because the usurer takes another way,
he scorns Nature in itself and in its follower [Industry],
since he places his hope in something else.

But follow me now, for I wish to go.
The Fishes [Pisces] are quivering on the horizon
and the Chariot [Big Dipper] lies wholly over Caurus [the north-west],

and the cliff we descend is far over there.

CANTO XII

THE VIOLENT

Near a break in the cliff, a landslide caused by the revulsion of the earth at the Crucifixion, is the Minotaur, a creature with a man's body and a bull's head, the bestial guardian of the circle of the violent. To get around this monster, Virgil puts him in a blind rage by mentioning the circumstances of his death, how his half sister, Ariadne, had guided Theseus through the labyrinth to him.

The place where we came to descend the bank
was craggy and, because of what was there [the Minotaur],
such that every eye would shun it.

As the landslide which, on this side of Trento,
struck the Adige, either because of an earthquake
or from being undermined—

for, from the top of the mountain
to the plain, the cliff has so fallen
that it provides a path for one above—

such was the descent into this ravine;
and on the edge of the broken chasm,
the infamy of Crete [the Minotaur], conceived 12

in the false [wooden] cow,[17] was stretched out.
On seeing us the monster bit himself
like one subdued by anger.

My sage cried to him, "Perhaps you think
the Duke of Athens [Theseus] is here
who killed you in the world.

Get away, beast, for this man does not come
instructed by your sister,
but journeys on to see your punishments."

As a bull that breaks loose at the moment
when it receives a mortal blow
and cannot go straight, but plunges here and there, 24

so I saw the Minotaur stagger,
and my wary guide shouted, "Run to the pass;
while he is raging it is well for you to go down."

[17]The Minotaur was born of Pasiphae, wife of Minos, king of Crete, after she hid herself inside a wooden cow in order to have intercourse with a bull.

Thus we made our way over the loose rocks
which often moved under my feet
because of the unusual burden.

As I went on, thinking, my guide said,
"Perhaps you are wondering about this landslide
guarded by the bestial wrath I outwitted.

Now I want you to know that the other time
I went down here into deep Hell
this cliff had not yet been broken, 36

but, if I discern correctly, shortly before
He [Christ] came to the first circle
to remove the great prey from Dis [at the "harrowing"]

the loathsome pit trembled on all sides
so that I thought the universe felt love
because of which some [philosophers] believed

the world has many times reverted to chaos [a fusion
of the elements]; and at that moment these old rocks
here and elsewhere fell down.

But look below, for the river of blood
is near, in which are boiled
those who through violence harm others." 48

On the banks of the river are centaurs, creatures with horses' bodies, but whose heads (unlike that of the Minotaur) are human.

O blind greed, wicked and foolish,
which so spurs us in the brief life,
and in the eternal condemns to such pain!

I saw a wide moat making a bend
surrounding the level ground [of the circle]
like the one my escort had mentioned,

and between the foot of the bank and the ditch
centaurs, armed with arrows, were running, in single file,
as they used to go hunting in our world.

Seeing us descend all stopped,
and three came from the band,
having armed themselves with bows and arrows. 60

One shouted from afar, "To what punishment
are you coming? Tell us from there;
if not, I'll draw the bow!"

My master answered, "We will reply
to Chiron over there; unfortunately,
you were always quick to act."

Then he touched me and said, "That is Nessus
who died for the beautiful Dejanira
and by himself took vengeance for himself.[18]

The one in the middle, looking at his breast,
is the great Chiron, the teacher of Achilles,
and the other is Pholus, who was so full of rage. 72

Around the ditch they go by thousands
shooting shades that rise from the blood
farther than their sins allow."

As we drew near those rapid beasts
Chiron took an arrow, and with the notch
combed back the beard on his jaws,

and when he had uncovered his great mouth
he said to his companions, "Did you notice
that the one behind moves what he touches?

The feet of the dead do not do this."
And my good guide, already close to the breast
where the two natures were joined, answered, 84

"He is indeed alive, and thus alone
I must show him the dark valley.
Necessity brings him here, not pleasure.

A lady [Beatrice] who came from singing hallelujah
entrusted this mission to me;
he is no robber nor am I a thief.

Therefore, by that power through which
I move my feet over so rough a road,
give us one of your band to be with us,

to show us where the ford is, and to carry
this man on his back, for he is not a spirit
that can go through the air." 96

Chiron, turning to his better side, appoints Nessus as the leader. The party see first various Greek and Italian tyrants, sunk to their eyebrows in the blood; then assassins, among whom, shunned by the others, is the first Englishman mentioned, Guy of Montfort who in a church at Viterbo killed Prince Henry. Henry's heart, it was said, was placed in a golden urn in Westminster Abbey.

Chiron turned to his right
and said to Nessus, "Go back and guide them,
and if you meet another band, make it give way."

[18]While trying to abduct Dejanira, the centaur Nessus was killed by an arrow from her husband, Hercules. As he was dying, Nessus gave Dejanira a robe, stained with his blood, that would supposedly preserve Hercules' love for her. But the robe killed Hercules, after which she committed suicide.

We started with our trusted escort
    along the bank of the vermilion stream
    in which those boiled uttered loud cries.

I saw shades in it up to their eyebrows;
    and the great centaur said, "These are tyrants
    who engaged in bloodshed and in plunder.

Now they weep for their pitiless crimes.
    Here are Alexander and fierce Dionysius[19]
    who gave Italy years of woe, 108

and that head with such black hair
    is Azzolino; and the blond one,
    Opizzo da Este, who, in truth,

was killed by his stepson in the world above."
    Then I turned to the poet, who said,
    "Let him go first now and me second."

A little farther on the centaur stopped
    above a group who down to their throats
    appeared above the boiling stream.

Then he showed us a shade to one side, alone, saying,
    "That one, in God's bosom, pierced the heart
    that still is honored on the Thames." 120

Afterward I saw some who kept their heads
    and chests out of the stream,
    and of those I recognized many.

Thus, little by little, the blood grew shallow
    until it cooked only the feet,
    and there was our passage over the moat.

"As on this side you see the boiling river
    grow shallow," said the centaur,
    "so I wish you to believe

that on the other its bottom gets deeper
    until it reaches the place
    where tyrants must groan. 132

There Divine Justice torments
    that Attila who was a scourge on earth,
    and Pyrrhus and Sextus; and eternally it milks

the tears, which the boiling releases,
    from Rinieri da Corneto and Rinieri Pazzo
    who waged such warfare on the highways."

Then Nessus turned back and repassed the ford.

[19]Either Alexander the Great or another Alexander (of Pherae); Dionysius was tyrant of Syracuse (fourth century B.C.).

CANTO XIII

PIER DELLE VIGNE

The poets enter the wood of the Christian suicides. This wild forest represents the world as it would be if all revolted against life. It is infested by the Harpies, loathsome creatures, half human, half birds, which stand for the storm winds of human passions.

In every way the suicides, now changed into trees or saplings, are frustrated. They have used their power of movement to deprive themselves of what distinguished them from plants; but they have not found death. The Harpies they tried to escape go with them, and the old agony is pent up in their new embodiments.

Nessus had not yet reached the other side
when we entered a wood
that was marked by no path.

No green foliage was there, but of a dark color,
no smooth branches, but knotty and twisted,
no fruit, but poisonous thorns.

The wild beasts that shun cultivated places
do not have such dense and tangled thickets
[in the Maremma] between Cecina and Corneto.[20]

Here the ugly Harpies make their nests
who with sad predictions of future harm
drove the Trojans from the Strophades.[21] 12

They have wide wings and human necks and faces,
feet with claws, and great feathered bellies;
they utter laments on the strange trees.

My good master began to speak, saying,
"Before you go any farther, know
that you are in the second round and will be

until you come to the horrible sand.
Therefore look closely and you will see
what would seem incredible in my speech."

I heard moans on every side
and saw no one to make them,
so that I stopped, all bewildered. 24

I believe he believed that I believed
that so many voices came from people
hidden from us among the trees;

[20] Two towns, at the northern and southern edges of the Maremma, a swamp near Florence.

[21] Islands visited by Aeneas and the other Trojans in their wanderings after the fall of Troy. This incident and one involving a bleeding shrub (referred to in line 48) occur in Virgil's *Aeneid,* Book III.

therefore he said, "If you break
a twig of one of these woody plants
the thoughts you have will be corrected."

Then I stretched forth my hand
and plucked a small branch from a great thorn tree,
and its trunk cried, "Why do you break me?"

After it had grown dark with blood,
it began again to lament, "Why do you tear me?
have you no trace of pity? 36

We were men, and now are turned to wood;
your hand should have been more merciful
if we had been the souls of serpents."

As a green log, burning at one end,
drips from the other and hisses
with the steam that escapes,

so from the broken branch words and blood
came out together; and I let the twig fall
and stood like one afraid.

The tree whose branch Dante has broken is that of Pier delle Vigne, a famous statesman, scholar, and poet at the court of Frederick II of Sicily. (In several curious, repetitious lines Dante imitates the style of the Frederician poets.) Frederick accused him of treason, had him blinded and led in derision on an ass from town to town. To escape this dishonor, Pier is said to have beaten his head against the walls of his prison. Dante presents him as innocent, as the model of a devoted public servant. He is proud of the office he once held and still loyal to the king who could do no wrong. It was Envy, he says, the harlot at every court, who caused his death. And he swears by his new body that he was never unfaithful.

"If he [Dante] could have believed, offended soul,"
my master answered,
"what he has seen only in my verse, 48

he would not have raised his hand against you,
but the incredible thing made me prompt him
to do what grieves me.

Now tell him who you were, so that
to make amends, he may refresh your fame
in the world above to which he is permitted to return."

Then the tree, "You so allure me with kind words
that I cannot keep silent, and may you
not be wearied if I grow sticky talking.

I am the one who held both keys [of consent and denial]
to Frederick's heart, and who turned them,
locking and unlocking so softly 60

that I kept almost everyone from his secrets.
Such trust I bore to the glorious office
that I lost sleep and strength.

The harlot [Envy] who never from Caesar's dwelling
has turned aside her shameless eyes,
the common bane and vice of courts,

inflamed all minds against me,
and the inflamed so inflamed Augustus [Frederick]
that my joyous honors changed to dismal sorrow.

My soul with disgust and scorn,
hoping to escape disdain,
made me unjust to my just self. 72

By the new roots of this tree, I swear to you
that I never broke faith with my lord
who was so worthy of honor.

And if either of you return to the world,
comfort my memory which still lies crushed
by the blow that Envy gave it."

Pier tells how the souls fall and become trees and bushes.

After Judgment Day, the bodies the suicides could not endure for a few brief years will hang on their branches forever. This is the final frustration.

The poet waited a little and then said,
"Since he is silent, do not lose the chance,
but question him if you want to hear more."

And I answered, "*You* ask what you think
will satisfy me, for I could not;
such pity saddens me." 84

Then he began, "So may this man
do freely for you what you ask,
please tell us, imprisoned spirit,

how the soul becomes bound in these branches,
and let us know if you can
if any ever frees himself from them."

The tree blew loudly, and soon
the wind changed into these sounds:
"Briefly will you be answered.

When the fierce soul leaves the body
from which it has torn itself,
Minos sends it to the seventh depth. 96

It falls into the wood; no place is chosen for it,
but where chance throws it
it sprouts, like a grain of wheat.

It grows into a sapling and a wild tree;
the Harpies, feeding then upon its leaves,
give pain and to the pain an outlet.

Like the others we will come for our bodies,
but not to be clothed again with them,
for it is not right to get back what is rejected.

Here we will drag them, and
in the sad wood our bodies will be hung
on the branches of our injurious souls." 108

Two spirits rush by, chased by the hounds of ruin and crying for a second death they can never have. These are souls of reckless squanderers, destroyers of their estates and indirectly of themselves. One, Lano, in desperate circumstances, allowed himself to be killed in the battle of Toppo.

We were still attentive to the tree,
believing that it wished to say more,
when a loud sound startled us

as it does the hunter who sees the boar and chase
approach his post and who hears the beast
and the crash of the branches.

And behold! two on the left,
naked and scratched, fleeing so fast
that they broke the brambles of the wood.

The one in the front cried, "Now come, now come, O Death!"
and the other who saw himself outdistanced, called,
"Lano, your legs were not so nimble 120

at the tournament of Toppo." And, perhaps
because his breath had failed, he plunged
into a bush, making a tangle of it and of himself.

Behind them the wood was full of black bitches,
ravenous and running fast,
like greyhounds just freed from the leash.

They fixed their teeth in the one who squatted
and tore him to pieces,
then carried off the suffering members.

My guide then took me by the hand
and led me to the bush, which lamented vainly
through its bleeding wounds. 132

"O Giacomo da Sant'Andrea," it cried,
"what do you gain by making me a screen?
what blame have I for your wicked life?"

My master had stopped beside it and asked,
"Who were you, you who through so many breaks
blow forth your woeful blood and words?"

The soul in the bush deplores the situation in Florence where martial virtue has been sacrificed for money-making (represented by John the Baptist whose image was stamped on Florentine coins); then he identifies himself briefly, not by a name but by an act: he desecrated his own home by making a gallows in it.

And the bush to us, "O souls coming
to see the shameful ravage
that has so separated my leaves from me,

gather them together at the foot of the poor plant.
I was of the city which changed its first patron [Mars]
for the Baptist, because of which 144

that god will always sadden it with his art,
and if, at the bridge over the Arno
there did not remain a trace of him [the ruins of a statue],

those citizens who rebuilt the city
on the ashes left by Attila[22]
would have done their work in vain.

I made a gibbet for myself of my own house."

CANTO XIV

THE VIOLENT AGAINST GOD

The round of the violent against God or Nature is characterized by sterility. On the hot sand the blasphemers are lying supine, the sodomites are running, the usurers sitting. Over all is falling a rain of fire which, here and elsewhere, symbolizes the direct wrath of God.

Because love for my native city moved me,
I gathered the scattered leaves and gave them back
to him whose voice was already faint.

Then we came to where the second round [the wood]
is divided from the third [the plain]
and where is seen a fearful kind of justice.

To make the new place manifest,
I say that we reached a desert
which repels every plant from its bed.

The doleful wood forms a garland around it,
just as the dismal moat does to the wood.
Here, at the very edge, we stopped. 12

[22]Attila the Hun, fifth-century invader of Europe, was supposed to have sacked Florence. See also XII.134.

The ground was of dry, thick sand,
not different from that [of the Libyan desert]
once trod by Cato's feet.[23]

O how greatly the vengeance of God
should be feared by everyone who reads
what was apparent to my eyes!

I saw many groups of naked souls,
all of whom wept miserably,
but different positions were imposed on them.

Some were lying supine upon the ground,
some were sitting, bent over,
and others were running continually. 24

Those that kept moving were most numerous
and those fewest who were lying in the torment,
but their tongues were loosened by greater pain.

Over all the plain, falling slowly,
dilated flakes of fire came down,
like snow in Alps without a wind.

As Alexander in those hot parts
of India saw flames fall on his host
intact as far as to the ground,

and made his legions trample
on the soil, since the fire
could be extinguished better before it spread; 36

so fell the eternal heat
by which the sand was kindled
like tinder under flint, to double the pain.

Ever without rest was the dance
of the miserable hands, now here, now there,
brushing off the fresh burning.

Dante notices a shade still untamed, bold, indomitable, defying Jove and the thunderbolts which defeated the giants. Virgil has more contempt for this apparent superman than for anyone else in Hell. Flat on his back, feeling hour after hour eternally the power of the God he is defying, his attitude seems stupid rather than courageous, and is peculiarly disgusting to Reason.

I began, "Master, you who have overcome everything
except the fierce demons who rushed out against us
at the entrance to the City,

[23] In 47 B.C., during the Roman civil war between Julius Caesar and Pompey, Cato led part of Pompey's army across Libya.

who is that great shade not heeding the fire,
lying scornful and contorted,
whom the rain does not seem to ripen?" 48

And he, aware that I was asking my guide
about him, shouted loudly,
"As I was alive, so am I dead.

Though Jove exhaust his smith from whom,
angrily, he took the sharp thunderbolt
by which I was struck on my last day,

and though he weary the others [the Cyclops] one by one
in Mongibello [Mt. Etna] at the black forge,
crying, 'Help, help, good Vulcan!'—

as he did in the battle of Phlegra [against the giants]—
and hit me with all his strength,
he could not have the joy of vengeance." 60

Then my guide spoke with such feeling
that I had never heard his voice so loud,
"O Capaneus, since your pride

remains untamed you are punished more.
No torture except your rage itself
would be adequate for your fury."

Then he turned to me with a better look, saying,
"This was one of the seven kings
who besieged Thebes; he held and still seems

to hold God in contempt, and to fear Him little;
but, as I told him, his blasphemy
is a fitting ornament for his breast. 72

The travelers come to where the overflow from Phlegethon, the river of blood, crosses the plain. The water of this little stream is like the Bulicame, a hot spring near Viterbo, where special bathhouses were provided for prostitutes. Its sterile banks offer a passageway, since over the blood-stained water the fire is quenched, a confirmation or symbol of atonement, the appeasing of God's wrath by human suffering.

Now follow me and be careful
not to put your feet on the burning sand,
but always keep them close to the wood."

In silence we came to where, out of
the forest, a little rivulet gushes,
the redness of which still makes me shudder.

As from the Bulicame a stream flows
which sinful women share among themselves,
so this one flowed across the sand.

Its bottom and both its sides
were made of stone and also the banks
on which I perceived that our way led. 84

"Among all the things I have shown you
since we entered the gate
whose threshold is denied to none,

nothing has been seen by your eyes
as notable as the present stream
which quenches all the flames above it."

These words were spoken by my guide,
and I asked him to grant the food
for which he had given me an appetite.

With elaborate symbolism, Virgil now tells of man's fall from grace and the consequences. On Mount Ida, in Crete, the center of the ancient world and the supposed cradle of the human race, there is a statue which represents the history of mankind. Its back is turned toward the East, its face in the direction of the course of empire. Its head, representing the Golden Age of the Ancients or the period of the Garden of Eden, is of gold; other parts, according to the various ages, are of different metals. One foot is of iron (the Roman Empire), the other of clay (the Papacy), and the weight of the statue bears too heavily on the latter, the cause, in Dante's view, of much of the anarchy and disorder in the world. The whole statue except the head has been cracked by man's sin. From this fissure tears drip. They flow down to Hell, form the waters of the Acheron, the Styx, the Phlegethon, and ultimately the frozen Cocytus. Thus, by a kind of conservation of sorrow, the tears shed through cruelty are not lost, but flow down to punish those who cause them.

Another river, the Lethe, descends to Hell from Purgatory carrying with it the last trace, that is, the very memory, of sin.

"In the middle of the sea," he said then,
"lies a waste land, called Crete,
under whose kings the world once was chaste. 96

A mountain there, named Ida,
was joyous with water and with leaves;
now it is deserted, like a thing worn out.

Rhea chose it for the safe cradle
of her son [Jupiter]; and to hide him better
when he cried, she had a clamor made.[24]

On the mountain stands a great old man [a statue]
with back turned toward Damietta [in the East]
and looking toward Rome as in a mirror.

His head is formed of fine gold,
his arms and breast are of pure silver;
then he is of brass as far as to the fork. 108

[24]Rhea was the wife of Saturn, who devoured most of his sons. To save their son Jupiter, she had his protectors, the Curetes, make loud noises to drown out the infant's crying.

From there down he is made of fine iron,
except that the right foot is of baked clay,
and he stands on that more than on the other.

Every part except the gold is broken
by a fissure which drips tears
and these, joining, cut through that bank,

flow down to this pit, and form the Acheron,
the Styx, and the Phlegethon;
then, moving on through this narrow channel,

go down to where there can be no further descent.
They form Cocytus; and since you will see
how that lake is, I do not describe it." 120

And I to him, "If the present stream
comes thus from our world,
why does it appear only here?"

And he, "You know that the place is round,
and, although you have come far
always descending to the left,

you have not yet completed the circle;
therefore, if something new appears,
it should not cause marveling."

Then I asked, "Master, where are the Phlegethon
and Lethe, for you are silent about one [Lethe]
and say that this rain forms the other." 132

"In all your questions you please me,"
he replied, "but the boiling red water
ought to answer one [about the Phlegethon].

You will see Lethe outside of this pit
where souls go to wash themselves
when guilt, repented, is removed.

Now it is time to leave the wood;
see that you come behind me;
the banks, not burned, offer a way,

and over them all fire is extinguished."

CANTO XV

BRUNETTO LATINI

The banks of the rivulet are like the dikes built by the Flemings or those made along the Brenta before the snow melts in the Chiarentana mountains. As the poets pass, they are eyed intently by a band of sodomites. Dante recognizes one as Brunetto Latini, a famous author and scholar, some of whose lectures Dante evidently heard. Dante extends his hand with reverence and, using the polite (voi) *form of address, tells of his surprise at meeting him in this place.*

Now one of the hard banks offers us a way,
and the vapor of the stream makes a shelter
which protects the shores and water from the fire.

As the Flemings between Wissant and Bruges,
fearing the flood which rushes toward them,
make a bulwark to repel the sea,

and as the Paduans do along the Brenta
to defend their cities and their castles,
before Chiarentana feels the heat,

in such a manner those banks were formed,
although their builder, whoever he was,
made them not so high nor so thick. 12

Already we were so far from the wood
that I could not have seen where it was
if I had turned back

when we met a band of spirits
coming along the banks, and each gazed at us
as, at dusk, under a new moon,

men are wont to look at each other,
sharpening their eyes at us
as an old tailor does at his needle's eye.

Thus gazed at by such a group,
I was recognized by one who grasped my skirt
and cried, "What a marvel!" 24

And as he held out his arm toward me
I fixed my glance on his baked aspect
so that his burned face did not prevent

the recognition of him by my memory.
Lowering my hand toward his face,
I asked, "Are *you* here, *ser* Brunetto?"

Brunetto proposes to accompany Dante by walking along below him. He must keep moving: restlessness is common to the punishment of all sexual sinners. Dante shows the greatest affection for his old master, a feeling reciprocated by Brunetto, who prophesies Dante's quarrel with the Florentines. They, according to legend, represent a fusion of the descendants of a Roman colony and of the rough hill people from Fiesole. Dante wishes that Brunetto had not been banished in a double sense from human nature, and pays him the supreme tribute to a teacher: he taught, not the minutiae of scholarship and pedantry, but the important things, how man, through fame, can make himself eternal.

And he, "O my son, may it not displease you
if Brunetto Latini goes back with you a little,
letting his company move on."

I said to him, "As much as I can I beg you to,
and if you want me to sit down with you,
I will do so, if he with whom I go permits." 36

"O son," he said, "whoever of this flock
stops one instant, lies afterward a hundred years
without brushing off the fire that strikes him;

therefore, go on; I will follow at your skirts
and then I will rejoin my band
which goes lamenting its eternal punishment."

I did not dare go down from the path
to be with him, but I held my head low
like one who walks with reverence.

He began, "What chance or destiny
brings you here before your last day,
and who is this one showing you the road?" 48

"Up there in the serene life," I answered,
"I went astray in a valley,
before my allotted time was spent.

Yesterday morning I turned my back on it;
then, as I was falling into it again, this shade appeared
who is taking me home by this road."

And he to me, "If you follow your star
you cannot fail to reach a glorious port
if I discerned rightly in the fair life.

And if I had not died so early,
seeing the heavens so gracious to you,
I would have cheered you in your work. 60

That ungrateful, malignant people who of old
came down from Fiesole and still keep
the roughness of the mountains and the rocks

will become your enemies because of your good deeds.
And that is right, for among the bitter sorb trees
it is not fitting that the sweet fig bear fruit.

Old report in the world calls them blind,
an avaricious, envious, haughty people:
see that you cleanse yourself from their ways.

Your fate reserves such honor
that both parties will be hungry for you;
but far from the goat will be the grass! 72

Let the beasts of Fiesole make fodder
of themselves and not touch the plant
if one grows on their dung heap

in whom the holy virtues are revived
of those Romans who remained there
when it was made the nest of such wickedness."

"If my request could be fully granted,"
I answered him, "you would not yet
be exiled from human nature;

for in my mind is fixed and my heart knows
the dear and kindly image of you
as a father when, from hour to hour, 84

you taught how man makes himself eternal;
and while I am alive, it is fitting
that my tongue show how grateful I am.

What you say about my life I write down
and keep to be explained with another text
by a lady [Beatrice] who can do this if I see her.

This much I would have plain to you—
so may my conscience not chide me—
I am prepared for Fortune as she wills.

Such warnings are not new to my ears;
therefore, as they please, 'Let Fortune
turn her wheel, and the churl his mattock.'" 96

My master turned to the right
and looked at me, then said,
"He listens well who notes what is told."

Among the many famous and infamous men guilty of sodomy was Dante's bishop, whom Boniface VIII, instead of punishing severely, merely transferred to another see. Thus the two men whose duty was to teach Dante how to become eternal on earth and in Heaven are together.

Brunetto hurriedly commends his work, The Treasury, *to Dante and then leaves, running fast, his loss of dignity showing the effect of one vice on an otherwise venerable character.*

Nonetheless I continued talking
to *ser* Brunetto, and I asked
who were his most noted companions.

And he to me, "It is well to know of some;
of the others it is more laudable to keep silent,
for time would be short for so much speech.

Know briefly that all were clerks[25]
and scholars and of great fame,
by the same sin defiled on earth. 108

[25]Clerics.

Priscian goes with that wretched crowd,
and Francesco d'Accorso; moreover,
if you had a hankering for such filth,

you might see him who by the Servant of the Servants
was transferred from the Arno to the Bacchiglione,
where he left his ill-strained muscles.

I would say more, but my going and my speech
must not continue longer, since I see new smoke
rising over there from the sand.

People are coming with whom I must not be.
Let my *Treasury*, in which I live
be commended to you; more I do not ask." 120

Then he turned, and seemed like one of those
who, at Verona, through the fields, run races
for a green cloth; and of these he appeared to move

like the one who wins, and not like the one who loses.

CANTO XVI

THE WATERFALL

Already I had reached a place where the roar
of the water falling into the next circle
could be heard, like the hum of a beehive,

when three shades running together
left a troop passing through the rain
of the fiery torment.

They came toward us and each cried,
"Stop, you who by your dress seem to us
to come from our perverse city!"

Ah! what wounds I saw on their bodies,
old and recent, burnt in by the flames!
I still grieve whenever I recall it. 12

My teacher listened to their cries,
then turned his face toward me and said,
"Now wait, to these we must be courteous,

and if it were not for the fire
which the nature of this place lets fall,
I should say that haste befitted you more than them."

Since the edge of the precipice is not far off, the shades propose to keep moving by circling around one spot.

As we stopped they began again their old lament,
and when they had reached us
all three made of themselves a circle,

as wrestlers, naked and oiled, are wont to do,
watching for a hold and an advantage,
before the tugs and blows begin. 24

Thus circling, all kept their eyes on me,
so that their heads and necks,
together with their feet, moved continually.

And one of them began, "If the misery of this sandy place
and our scorched and burned faces
cause scorn for us and for our prayers,

may our fame incline you to tell us
who you are, you who move so securely
your living feet through Hell.

The man in whose footsteps you see me tread,
although he goes now bare and hairless,
was of a higher rank than you might believe. 36

He was a grandson of the good Gualdrada;
Guido Guerra was his name, and in his life
he did much with counsel and with sword.

The other who treads the sand behind me
is Tegghiaio Aldobrandi, whose voice
should have been heeded in the world.

And I, placed on the cross with them,
am Jacopo Rusticucci; and certainly my fierce wife
troubles me more than anything else."

If I had been sheltered from the fire,
I would have thrown myself down among them,
and I believe my master would have permitted; 48

but since I would have been burned and cooked,
fear overcame the good will
which made me eager to embrace them.

Then I began, "Not contempt, but such grief
as will not soon leave me,
your condition caused in me

as soon as my lord spoke words
through which I inferred
that people like you were coming.

I am from your city; and always
I have heard and told with affection
of your honored deeds and names. 60

I leave the gall and go for the sweet fruit
promised me by my truthful guide,
but first I must descend to the center."

"So may your soul long guide your body,"
he answered then,
"and so may your fame shine after you,

tell us if courtesy and valor dwell
in our city as they were wont
or whether they have gone entirely,

for Guglielmo Borsiere who has suffered with us
only a little while and is over there with his companions
grieves us much with his remarks." 72

"New people and sudden gains, O Florence,
have generated pride and excess in you
so that already you are weeping!"

This I cried with my face raised, and the three
who understood my words as a reply, glanced at each other
as people do when the truth is spoken.

"If, at other times, it costs you so little
to satisfy others," they all replied,
"you are fortunate, speaking thus at will;

therefore, if you escape from this dark place
and return to see the beautiful stars,
when you can delight in saying 'I was there . . . ' 84

see that you speak to others about us."
Then they broke the wheel, and in their flight
their nimble legs seemed wings.

An "amen" could not have been said
so quickly as they disappeared;
whereupon my master thought it best to go on.

I followed him, and we had not gone far
before the waterfall was so near
that we could hardly hear each other speak.

As the river which has its own channel at first
from Monte Veso toward the east,
on the left slope of the Apennines— 96

which is called Acquacheta up above
before it flows to its lower bed,
and at Forlì loses that name—

resounds there above San Benedetto dell'Alpe,
because of falling in one single leap
instead of being broken by a thousand,

so, down from a steep bank
we found the colored water roaring so loudly
that it soon would have hurt our ears.

A cord around Dante's waist probably stands for self-confidence, useful in combating incontinence, but worse than useless in dealing with the fraud ahead. He gives it to Virgil who throws it over the precipice as a signal. Dante waits anxiously to see what will happen.

I had a cord around my waist
with which I had thought once
to catch the leopard with the painted hide. 108

After I had loosened it from my body
as my leader had ordered me,
I handed it to him, coiled and knotted.

Then he turned to the right side,
and threw it far from the bank
down into that deep abyss.

"Surely," I said within myself, "something strange
must respond to this new signal
which my master so follows with his eyes."

Ah, how cautious we must be
with those who see not only what we do
but look also within our thoughts! 120

He said to me, "Soon what I am waiting for
will come up, and what you are thinking about
will be revealed to your eyes."

To the truth which appears to be a lie
we should close our lips as long as we can,
not to incur blamelessly a reproach;

but here I cannot keep silent and, Reader,
by the notes of this Comedy, I swear to you—
so may it not lack long favor—

that I saw, through that thick and dark air,
a form marvelous to every steadfast heart
come swimming up 132

as a swimmer rises after going down
to loosen an anchor caught by a rock
or something else hidden in the sea,

who stretches forth his arms and draws up his feet.

CANTO XVII

Geryon

The monster coming up is Geryon, a symbol of the fraud which is universal and more powerful than arms. His face has an honest look, but his body is reptile-like and covered with devious and intricate patterns, like oriental tapestries. He lies with his head on the bank as beavers were supposed to do when using their tails to throw their prey on the shore.

"Behold the beast with the pointed tail
that can cross mountains and break through walls;
behold the one that infects the whole world!"

Thus my guide began to speak to me
and signaled to the beast to come ashore
near the end of the stone banks we had walked on;

and that foul image of fraud came up
and landed his head and breast,
but did not put his tail upon the bank.

His face was that of an honest man,
so kind an aspect it had outwardly,
but all the rest was like a reptile. 12

He had two paws, hairy to the armpits;
his back and breast and both sides
were decorated with loops and circles;

never did Tartars nor Turks make cloth
with more colors in groundwork and in pattern,
nor did Arachne[26] ever put such webs on her loom.

As skiffs sometimes lie along the shore
partly in the water and partly on land,
and as up there among the gluttonous Germans

the beaver sits to carry on his war,
so that worst of wild beasts lay
on the edge which binds the sand with stone. 24

He darted his tail in the empty space,
twisting up its venomous tip
which was armed like that of a scorpion.

The usurers (the remaining group of the violent against God) are crouching near the edge where it is easy to fall into the circle of fraud below. Dante treats them with the utmost contempt, as he does all mercenary souls. They are unrecognizable except by the coats of arms on their now empty purses.

Virgil has warned Dante not to waste words on them: our poet does not speak at all. The usurers are still competing, quarreling, rivaling, and envying each other, without honor, courage, good manners, artistic or intellectual distinction.

My leader said, "We must now bend our course
a little as far as to the wicked beast
that is lying over there."

We descended to the right
and took ten steps on the extreme edge
in order to avoid the sand and the flames.

[26]A skilled weaver who challenged the goddess Minerva to a competition; Minerva later changed her into a spider.

After we had reached the monster,
I saw a little farther on some people on the sand
sitting close to the empty space. 36

My master said, "So that you may take with you
complete experience of this round,
go and see their ways.

Let your talk with them be brief;
until you return I will speak with this one
so that he may lend us his strong shoulders."

Thus I advanced along the extreme edge
of the seventh circle all alone
to where the sad souls were sitting.

Through their eyes their grief burst forth;
on this side and that they used their hands,
brushing off the fire and lifting themselves from the hot ground; 48

not otherwise are dogs busy in summer,
now with their muzzles and now with their paws,
when bitten by gadflies or fleas.

In looking at the faces of some
on whom the painful fire was falling,
I could recognize none, but I noticed

that from the necks of each a purse hung
which had a certain color and design
and on which it seemed that their eyes feasted.

As I came looking at them,
on a yellow purse I saw in azure
the head and the form of a lion. 60

Then continuing the course of my glances,
I saw another, red as blood,
showing a goose whiter than butter.

And one who had a white sack marked
with an azure pregnant sow,
said to me, "What are you doing in this hole?

Now go away and, since you are still alive,
know that my neighbor Vitaliano
will sit here on my left side.

With these Florentines I am a Paduan;
many times they deafen my ears,
shouting, 'Let the sovereign knight come 72

who will bring the pouch marked by three goats.'"
Then he twisted his mouth and stuck out his tongue
as an ox does to lick its nose.

And I, fearing that to stay longer
might annoy my master, who had admonished me
to be brief, turned my back on those wearied souls.

When Dante climbs on Geryon's back over the immense void, he is so frightened he cannot speak.

The transition from violence to deliberate, premeditated fraud is shown by the long and slow descent.

I found my leader already mounted
on the back of the fierce animal.
He said to me, "Now be strong and bold;

we descend here by such stairs.
Mount in front, for I wish to be placed
so that the tail cannot hurt you." 84

As one who has the chill of the quartan fever
so close that his nails are already blue,
and who shivers merely at the sight of shade,

so I became on hearing these words,
but Virgil's admonition caused the shame
which, in sight of his master, makes a servant strong.

I placed myself on those big shoulders.
"See that you hold me," I wished to say,
but my voice did not come out as I thought.

And he who at other times helped me
in other fears, as soon as I had mounted,
embraced and held me with his arms; 96

then said, "Geryon, move now;
let the circles be large and the descent slow;
think of the new burden that you have."

As a little ship moves from its berth,
back, back, thus Geryon moved off,
and when he felt his whole body clear,

he turned his tail to where his breast had been,
and stretching it out, moved it like an eel,
and with his paws drew in the air.

I do not believe there was greater fear when Phaëthon[27]
let loose the reins [of the sun's chariot] so that the sky
as still appears [by the Milky Way] was scorched, 108

[27]Son of Apollo, the charioteer of the sun. Entrusted with his father's chariot, Phaëthon lost control of it so that it burned the sky.

nor when poor Icarus[28] [while flying] felt his loins unfeathered
because of the melting of the wax,
his father shouting to him, "The wrong way you're taking!"

than was mine when I saw myself in the air
on every side and with every view hidden
except that of the beast.

It went on swimming slowly, slowly,
circled and descended, but I was aware of the movement
only by the wind blowing in my face and from below.

Already I heard the torrent on the right
roaring horribly beneath us,
so that I stretched out my head to look down. 120

Then I was still more afraid,
for I saw fires and heard laments,
at which I crouched back, all trembling.

I noticed then the descending and the circling
which I had not seen before
by the torments drawing near on every side.

As a falcon that has long been on the wing
without seeing a bird or lure, and that makes the falconer cry,
"Alas, you are coming down!"

descends wearily, after many circles,
to where it had swiftly started out,
and lands far from its master, sullen and angry, 132

so Geryon set us down on the bottom,
at the foot of the jagged rock;
then freed of the weight of our bodies,

he darted off, like an arrow-notch from the string.

CANTO XVIII

PANDERS, SEDUCERS, AND FLATTERERS

The matter-of-fact description of Malebolge contrasts with the deviousness of the fraud it harbors. The term means "evil pouches" or "purses," perhaps with some reference to the greed which motivates most fraud. Those who sinned through violence are in the open. The fraudulent, appropriately, are hidden in dark ditches. Over the moats are "scogli," rocky bridges, which come together at the center like spokes of a wheel.

There is a place in Hell called Malebolge,
all of stone and of an iron color
like the bank which surrounds it.

[28] Icarus, for whom his father Daedalus made wings cemented with wax, flew too near the sun and fell when it melted the wax.

Right in the middle of the baleful space
a well, rather wide and deep, opens up
whose features I will describe in their place.

The belt that remains, then,
between the well and the high, hard bank,
had its bottom divided into ten valleys.

As the ground appears
where several moats surround a castle
as a protection for the walls, 12

such was the design these made.
And, as from the thresholds of fortresses
little bridges extend to the outer banks,

so from the bottom of the wall, rough spans
crossed the ditches and the banks down to the well
which brings them all together and cuts them off.

In this place, shaken from the back of Geryon,
we found ourselves, and the poet started
to the left, and I moved on behind him.

The souls in the first bolgia or ditch are guided by traffic regulations as was the crowd at the jubilee in Rome in 1300, the panders on the outside going to the right, the seducers on the inside to the left.

We now meet the first devils. These, appropriately, wear the horns associated with adultery. We find also the first shade who is ashamed. When recognized, he tells how he sold his sister to the Marquis of Este. He confesses also for the other Bolognese panders, more numerous than the little children learning the dialect word for "yes" within the boundaries of their province.

Here, as elsewhere, movement characterizes punishments for sins related to sexuality. Where the activity was natural, the agent of punishment is wind, a natural force; where unnatural, as on the plain, a supernatural fire is falling. Here, among the fraudulent, a devil plies the whip.

On the right I saw new misery,
new torments, and new tormentors
with which the first ditch was filled. 24

The sinners along the bottom of the ditch were naked,
coming on this side facing us, on the other
moving with us, but with longer steps.

Thus the Romans because of the great throng
in the year of the jubilee, chose a way
to divide the traffic on the bridge,

so that on one side all had their faces
toward the Castle [of Sant' Angelo], and went to St. Peter's,
on the other side they advanced toward the Mount [Giordano].

On both sides of the dark rock
I saw horned demons with great whips
beating the shades fiercely from behind. 36

Ah, how they made them lift their legs
at the first stroke! Indeed,
none waited for the second or for the third.

While I was going on, my eyes fell on one;
whereupon immediately I said,
"I am not fasting for the sight of him!"[29]

Therefore I delayed advancing to look;
and my dear leader stopped with me
and consented that I go back a little.

The whipped shade thought he could hide
by lowering his face, but it availed him little,
for I said, "You who cast your eyes on the ground, 48

if the features you wear are not false,
are Venedico Caccianemico;
but what brings you into such a pickle?"

And he to me, "Unwillingly I say it,
but I am compelled by your clear speech
which makes me recall the world.

I am the one who led Ghisolabella [his sister]
to do the Marquis' [of Este's] will,
however the vile tale may sound,

and I am not the only Bolognese weeping here;
on the contrary the place is so full of them
that as many tongues are not now being taught 60

to say 'sipa' between the Savena and the Reno;
and if you want assurance of that,
recall to your mind our avaricious hearts."

While he was speaking thus, a demon struck him
with his whip, saying, "Away, pander!
Here are no women to turn into cash!"

To see the seducers, who have been going to the left, the poets mount to the top of the bridge. They observe Jason, a dignified figure, but whipped, like the others. His principal crime, besides robbing the Colchians of the Golden Fleece and deserting Medea, was the seduction of Hypsipyle. The latter, according to the legend, had already shown her weakness by saving her father's life when the disgusted women of Lemnos tried to kill off all the men.

[29] "I have seen this person before."

I rejoined my escort; then,
after a few steps, we came
to where a rough bridge projects from the bank.

Quite easily we climbed it,
and turning to the right over its ridge
we moved away from that eternal bank. 72

When we reached the point below which the bridge opens
to give passage for those whipped,
my leader said, "Stop, and let your sight

fall on these other ill-born souls
whose faces you have not yet seen,
since they have been going with us."

From the old bridge we looked at the file
coming toward us on the other side
and whom the whip likewise drove on.

And my good master, without my asking, said,
"Look at that great one coming,
who, for his pain, sheds no tears; 84

what a regal bearing he still has!
That is Jason who through courage and slyness
deprived the Colchians of their ram [Golden Fleece].

He passed through the island of Lemnos
after the bold and pitiless women
had given up to death all their men.

There, with gifts and fine words,
he deceived Hypsipyle, the young girl
who first had deceived all the others.[30]

He abandoned her pregnant and forlorn.
Such guilt condemns him to this punishment;
and vengeance is taken also for Medea. 96

With him go all those who deceive in this way:
let this knowledge suffice for the first vale
and for those it holds in its grip."

The poets proceed to where they can see the flatterers in the second ditch. Dante chooses the elegant Thaïs as his ancient example, perhaps to emphasize the essential filthiness of these sinners who, like dogs, lick the sores of those they exploit. The contrast is all the more striking because the charge against her seems trivial. Moreover, Dante had misread the incident in Cicero; the guilty one was Gnatho, not Thaïs. But the lesson is clear: even Thaïs could not make flattery clean.

[30] Hypsipyle spared her father and told the other women of Lemnos that he had been killed along with the other males. For a version of the Jason-Medea story, see Euripides' *Medea.*

We had already come to where the narrow road
crosses the second bank and makes of it
an abutment for another arch.

Here we heard people moaning in the next ditch
and puffing with their snouts
and hitting themselves with their hands.

The banks were encrusted with a mold
condensed from the vapor from below
which offends both the eyes and nose. 108

The bottom was so deep it could be seen
only by mounting to the summit of the arch
where the bridge stands highest.

We reached that place, and down in the ditch
I saw people plunged in excrement
which seemed to have come from human privies.

And while I was searching down there with my eyes,
I saw one with his head so smeared with filth
that you could not tell if he were a layman or a clerk.

He bawled to me, "Why are you so eager
to look at me more than at the other ugly ones?"
And I to him, "Because, if I remember well, 120

I saw you once with dry hair;
you are Alessio Interminei da Lucca;
therefore, I eye you more than all the rest."

Then beating on his pate, he said,
"The flatteries with which my tongue
was never cloyed have put me down here."

After that my guide said to me,
"See that you extend your gaze
so that your eyes may reach the face

of that filthy and disheveled wench
who is scratching herself with her dirty nails
and now squats and now is standing on her feet. 132

Thaïs,[31] she is, the harlot
who answered her paramour when he said,
'Have I *great* favor with you?' 'No, *marvelous!*'

And with this let our sight be satisfied."

[31] This is not the famous courtesan but a whore in a play by Terence, the Roman dramatist (second century B.C.).

CANTO XIX

THE SIMONISTS

Dante's objectivity ceases when we come to the simonists who by trafficking in church offices and enriching themselves tend to destroy the Church itself. Their fat feeds the fire which now punishes them.

O Simon Magus![32] O rapacious followers,
you who should be wedded to righteousness
and instead prostitute the things of God

for gold and silver, now for you
it is necessary that the trumpet sound,
since you are in the third ditch.

Already we had mounted to that part
of the following bridge
which hangs over the middle of the moat.

O Supreme Wisdom, how great is the art Thou showest
in Heaven, on earth, and in the evil world,
and how justly Thy power rewards! 12

I saw the livid stone covered with holes
on the sides and on the bottom,
all round, and of one breadth.

They appeared neither larger nor smaller
than those in my beautiful San Giovanni
made for the baptizers to stand in,

one of which, not many years ago, I broke
to save a drowning child—and let this
be my seal [on the truth] to undeceive all men.[33]

From the mouth of each a sinner's feet protruded
and his legs up to the calf,
and the rest remained within. 24

The soles of the feet of all were on fire,
and their legs above the joints writhed so sharply
that they would have broken withes or ropes.

As flames on oily things are wont
to move only over the outer surface,
so they did here from heel to toe.

"Who is that one, Master, who writhes so,
twitching more than the others, his companions,
and who feeds a ruddier flame?" I asked.

[32]Simon "the Magician," who, according to Acts of the Apostles 8, was rebuked by Peter for attempting to buy the powers of the apostles that only God could give. The word *simony* is derived from his name.

[33]Untrue rumors apparently had circulated about this incident, but what they were is not known.

And he to me, "If you want me to carry you down there
over the [inner] bank which slopes less steeply,
you will learn from him about himself and his misdeeds." 36

And I, "Whatever you want is good for me;
you are my lord, and you know that my will
is like your own, and you know also what I keep silent."

Then we came to the fourth bank
where we turned and descended on the left
down into the narrow and pitted bottom.

My kind master still did not put me down,
but carried me to the hole of the one
who was so lamenting with his shanks.

The inverted shade, Pope Nicholas III, mistakes Dante for Boniface VIII (still living in 1300) who, after outraging the Church (the "Bride of Christ"), is to follow him here. Nicholas belonged to the Orsini family (orso, *bear), and used his office to advance the cubs. In this mockery of the apostolic succession, Boniface will be succeeded by Clement V, who, as the tool of Philip the Fair of France, transferred the papacy to Avignon. A certain vulgarity characterizes the speech of all mercenary sinners and the terms used to describe them.*

"O, whoever you are, sad spirit,
upside down, planted like a stake,"
I began to say, "if you can, speak." 48

I stood like the friar confessing a treacherous assassin
who, after being put in the hole [to be buried alive],
calls the confessor back to delay his death,

and he shouted, "Are you already standing there,
are you already there, O Boniface?—
The writing [Book of Fate] lied to me by several years.

Are you so quickly sated with the wealth
for which you were not afraid to seize the beautiful lady
through guile and then to outrage her?"

I became like those who wonder
if they are mocked, not understanding the words
said to them, and who are unable to reply. 60

Then Virgil said, "Tell him quickly
'I am not, I am not the one you think,'"
and I answered as I had been bidden.

At that the spirit twisted both his feet,
then sighing and with a tearful voice
he said, "What do you ask of me?

If you want so much to learn who I am
that you have come down the bank to hear,
know that I was clothed with the great mantle,

and truly I was a son of the she-bear
so covetous to advance the cubs
that on earth I put wealth, and here myself, in a sack. 72

Below, under my head, the others[34]
who preceded me in simony are compressed,
squeezed into the fissures of the rock.

Down there I also will be pressed
when he comes for whom I took you
when I asked the sudden question.

But I have already been roasted
and have stood thus upside down longer
than he will stay planted with reddened feet,

for after him, out of the West, will come
a shepherd without law, of uglier deed,
fit to cover both him and me. 84

He will be like the Jason[35] of whom we read in Maccabees,
and as to Jason a king dealt gently,
so will the ruler of France treat him."

Dante addresses Nicholas with intense feeling, restrained only by reverence for this sinner's past office. He mentions the Scarlet Woman, as the symbol of the corrupt Church.

In this bolgia things are generally upside down. The clergy inverted their duties and are now inverted themselves; Dante, a layman, hears a confession, like a friar, and then preaches a sermon to an ex-pope.

I do not know if I was now too bold,
but I answered him in this strain:
"Alas, now tell me, how much treasure

did our Lord ask of St. Peter
before he put the keys in his hands?
Surely he demanded only, 'Follow me!'

Nor did Peter and the others ask Matthias
for gold or silver when he was chosen
for the place the guilty soul [Judas] had lost.[36] 96

Therefore, stay there, for you are well punished,
and keep securely the ill-got money
which made you so bold against Charles [of Anjou].

[34]That is, the other simoniacal popes, all of whom are thrust into the same hole.

[35]In 2 Maccabees 4–5 (a book of the Roman Catholic Bible), the unworthy Jason obtains from the king of Syria by bribery the office of Jewish high priest.

[36]In Acts 1, Matthias is chosen by prayer and the casting of lots as successor to Judas as one of the twelve apostles.

And if I were still not prevented
by reverence for the holy keys
which you kept in the happy life,

I would use words still heavier;
for your avarice afflicts the world,
crushing the good and lifting up the bad.

The Evangelist [St. John] had shepherds like you in mind
when she [the Scarlet Woman][37] that sitteth upon many waters
was seen by him fornicating with kings, 108

she who was born with seven heads [virtues]
and from ten horns [commandments] gained strength
as long as virtue pleased the bridegroom [the papacy].

You have made a god of gold and silver,
and how do you differ from the idolater,
except that he worships one thing of gold, and you a hundred?

The papal claims to temporal power were based in part on the supposed gift of the Western Empire to St. Sylvester by Constantine. The document confirming this transfer was not recognized as a forgery until after Dante's time, but our poet held that the emperor had no power to make such a gift nor the pope to receive it.

Virgil, as the representative of the Roman Empire in the political allegory, is so delighted with Dante's sermon that he carries his pupil out of the ditch and to the top of the next bridge.

Ah, Constantine,[38] to how much ill gave birth
not your conversion, but that dowry
which the first rich father took from you!"

While I sang these notes to him,
whether anger or conscience stung him,
he kicked hard with both his feet. 120

I believe my leader was pleased,
with such a contented look he listened
to the true words I had expressed.

With both arms he took hold of me,
and when he had me quite upon his breast,
he remounted by the way we had come down,

nor did he tire of holding me tightly,
but carried me to the top of the arch
which crosses from the fourth to the fifth bank.

[37] The details Dante gives are from Revelation 17; the passage refers to Rome.
[38] Roman emperor from 306 to 337, a convert to Christianity who moved the capital of the empire to Constantinople.

There, softly, he put down his burden—
softly because of the rough and steep rocks
which would have been a hard road even for goats. 132

From there another valley was disclosed.

CANTO XX

THE DIVINERS

The sight of the soothsayers, diviners, and magicians, with their heads twisted around and walking backward, makes Dante weep. He had previously shown pity for the victims of our human defects, but now he is sorry for the punishment itself. This is a kind of protest against the divine order, and he is severely rebuked by Virgil. The scolding is most striking since Virgil had been considered a diviner, a master of magic art, and the sin punished here often tempted men of learning like Dante himself.

For new punishments I must make verses
and provide matter for the twentieth canto
of the first book, which is about the damned.

I was already placed where I could see
into the uncovered depth
which was bathed with tears of anguish,

and I saw people move silent and weeping
through the circular valley, at the pace of those
who chant litanies in this world.

When my eyes saw them more clearly
each appeared to be twisted marvelously
between the chin and the beginning of the chest, 12

for their faces were turned to the rear,
and each was obliged to move backward,
since seeing ahead was denied them.

Perhaps by the force of paralysis
someone might be wholly twisted thus,
but I have never seen the case nor believe it exists.

Reader, so may God let you profit
by your reading, now think for yourself
how I could keep my face dry

when I saw our [human] image, close at hand,
so twisted that the tears from the eyes
bathed the buttocks along the cleft. 24

Certainly I wept, leaning on a rock
of the hard bridge, so that my escort said to me,
"Are you, too, like the other fools?

Here pity lives when it is completely dead.
Who is more impious than that one
who feels sorrow for God's judgment?

Virgil now points out certain soothsayers of antiquity, characters chosen from various epic poems. The accounts of them are incorrect in some respects, perhaps to show once more the fallibility of men's minds. In discussing Manto, Virgil gives an account of the founding of Mantua different from one in the Aeneid. *Moreover, in the* Purgatory, *Manto is mentioned as in a different circle. The digression interests even Dante only slightly.*

Lift up your head and see him [an augur] for whom
the earth opened in the sight of the Thebans
so that they cried, 'Where are you falling,

O Amphiaraus? why are you giving up the war?'
and he did not stop rushing headlong
down to Minos who seizes everyone; 36

observe how he has made a breast of his shoulders;
because he wished to see too far ahead,
he looks behind, and goes backward.

See Tiresias [a soothsayer] who changed his semblance
when he became from man, a woman,
transforming all his members,

and before he could regain his manly hair
it was necessary for him to strike again
the two entwined serpents with his wand.[39]

The one backing up to his belly
is Aruns who, in the Luni mountains
beneath which the Carrarese live and plow, 48

had a cave in the white marble for a dwelling
from which no obstacle cut off
a view of the sea or of the stars.

And she who covers her breasts
which you do not see, with her loose tresses,
and has on the other side all hairy skin,

was Manto, who sought through many lands
before she settled where I was born
and of her I would like for you to hear.

After her father had given up his life
and Bacchus' city [Thebes] was enslaved
she wandered a long time through the world. 60

[39] Tiresias had first been changed from a man into a woman when he struck two entwined serpents with his wand; years later he saw and struck them again, whereupon he was changed back into a man. Manto, mentioned later, was his daughter.

In beautiful Italy, above the Tyrol,
at the foot of the Alps which enclose Germany,
lies a lake named Benaco.

A thousand brooks and more bathe the Apennino
from Guarda to Val Canonica
whose waters come to rest in this lake.

In the middle is a point where the pastors
of Trento, Brescia, and Verona
could give a blessing if they went that way.

Peschiera lies as a fair and powerful rampart
to face the Brescians and the Bergamese
where the shore is lowest. 72

There, all that the lap of Benaco
cannot hold must overflow
through green pastures and make a river.

When the water begins to flow,
it is no longer called Benaco, but Mincio
as far as Governo, where it falls into the Po.

After a short course it finds a flat region
over which it spreads and forms a marsh
which in summer is wont to be noisome.

While passing there, the cruel virgin
saw land in the middle of the fen
uncultivated and devoid of inhabitants. 84

There, to shun all human intercourse,
she, with her servants, stayed to practice her art,
and lived, and left there her empty body.

Later the people scattered around
gathered in that place which was strong
because of the marsh on all sides.

They built the city on her bones
and for her who first chose the place
they called it Mantua, without other augury.

Once its people were more numerous
before the madness of Casalodi [its ruler]
was deceived by Pinamonte. 96

Therefore I warn you, that if you ever hear
of another origin for my city,
let no falsehood defraud the truth."

And I, "Master, your account is so certain
and takes such hold on my belief
that others would be like dead coals.

But tell me about the people passing by,
whether you see any worthy of note,
for to that alone my mind reverts."

The account of Eurypylus at the time of the Trojan wars differs also from its source in Virgil, a slip all the more striking since Dante implies that he knew the Aeneid *by heart.*

Among the modern soothsayers is Michael Scott who lived at the court of Frederick II of Sicily. His legend survived in Scotland down to modern times. Other minor figures include Guido Bonatti, an astrologer of Forlì, Asdente, the cobbler of Parma, and various fortune-tellers and witches.

In Italian folklore, the Man in the Moon is Cain. He is mentioned in indicating the time. It is about six o'clock on Saturday morning, April 9, 1300.

Then he said, "That one who from his cheeks
lets his beard fall on his dark shoulders
was an augur [during the Trojan War] when Greece was so empty of males 108

that scarcely any remained for the cradles,
and in Aulis, together with Calchas,
he set the time for setting sail for Troy.

Eurypylus was his name, and my lofty tragedy
sings of him in one place,
as you know well, since you know it all.

The other, so slender in the flanks,
was Michael Scott, who really knew
the game of magic frauds.

See also Guido Bonatti, see Asdente
who now wishes he had attended
to his leather and his thread, but too late repents. 120

See the poor women who left the needle,
the shuttle, and the spindle, and became fortunetellers;
they wrought magic with herbs and images.

But come now, for Cain with his thorns
is already on the confines of both hemispheres
and below Seville is sinking in the sea,

and last night the moon was round;
you must remember, since it was not unwelcome
at times in the deep wood."

Thus he spoke as we moved on.

CANTO XXI

The Barrators (Grafters)

Thus we went from bridge to bridge, talking of things
my Comedy does not care to mention,
and reached the top of the next arch

where we stopped to see the ditch
and to hear the other vain laments;
and I found it marvelously dark.

As in the shipyards of the Venetians,
in winter, the tenacious pitch boils
to calk their damaged ships,

since the sailors cannot navigate, and instead
some build new boats, some strengthen the ribs
of one that has made many voyages; 12

some hammer at the prow and some at the stern;
some make oars, and some twist ropes;
some mend the jib and mainsail,

so, not by fire, but through divine art
a dense tar boils down there
which coats the banks on each side.

I saw the pitch, but did not see in it
anything except the bubbles which rise,
swell up, and then collapse.

While I was looking fixedly down there
my guide drew me from where I was,
saying, "Look! look!" 24

Then I turned like one suddenly dismayed,
striving to see something
from which he must escape

and who, to see, does not delay his start;
and I noticed behind us a black devil
coming at a run over the bridge.

Ah, how fierce he was in aspect,
and how ferocious he seemed in act,
with wings open, and light upon his feet!

His shoulders which were high and sharp
were burdened by the haunches of a sinner
the sinews of whose feet he clutched. 36

From our bridge he cried, "O Malebranche [devils],
here is one of the elders[40] of Santa Zita [Lucca],
put him under while I go back for more

to that city I have so well furnished with them.
Everyone is a barrator there, except Bonturo;[41]
there, for money, a 'no' becomes a 'yes.'"

Down he hurled him, and turned back
over the rough bridge, and never was a mastiff
in such haste to follow a thief.

[40] Public officials of Lucca, of which Zita was the patron saint.
[41] This is ironic; Bonturo was an especially notorious grafter.

The sinner plunged in, then rose doubled up,
but the demons hiding under the bridge shouted,
"Here there is no Holy Face [as at Lucca] to pray to! 48

Here you do not swim as in the Serchio!
So, unless you want to feel our hooks,
don't show yourself above the pitch!"

Then they struck him with more than a hundred prongs,
saying, "Here you must dance under cover
and pilfer secretly if you can!"

Not otherwise do cooks have their scullions
dip the meat in the middle of the boiler
with forks, so that it will not float.

Virgil holds a parley with the demons below the bridge. Then Dante rejoins his master, keeping as close to him (Reason) as he can, but using his eyes as well. The entire episode with the devils beginning here (a concession to the popular spirit of the Middle Ages) symbolizes incidentally Dante's narrow escape from Florence, where one of the false charges against him was barratry.

My good master said, "So that it may not appear
that you are here, crouch down
behind a rock and remain hidden, 60

and whatever outrage is done to me
do not be afraid, for I know about this business;
once before I was in a like affray."

Then he went to the head of the bridge,
and as he arrived on the sixth bank
he needed a steadfast heart.

With that fury and that uproar
with which dogs run out at a beggar
who suddenly stops and begs from where he is,

those devils rushed out from under the bridge,
turning against him all their hooks.
But he cried, "Let none of you be headstrong. 72

Before your grapples touch me,
let one of you come forward to hear me
and then decide about hooking me."

All shouted, "Let Malacoda go"; whereupon one
stepped forward while the others stood firm,
and came to him saying, "What good will it do him?"

"Do you think, Malacoda,
that you see me here," my master said,
"safe from all your opposition,

without divine will and propitious fate?
Let me go on, for it is willed in Heaven
that I should show another this wild way." 84

Then Malacoda's pride collapsed so suddenly
that he let his hook fall at his feet
and said to the others, "Do not strike him."

And my guide called to me, "O you, crouching quietly
behind the rocks of the bridge,
you may come now securely."

I started out and went quickly to him,
and all the devils pressed forward,
so that I feared they might not keep their pact.

Thus I once saw foot soldiers afraid
on leaving Caprona under safe conduct,
when they saw themselves among so many enemies. 96

I drew close to my guide with my whole body,
but did not take my eyes
from the devils' looks, which were not good.

They lowered their hooks, one saying to another,
"Should I nick him on the rump?"
and being answered, "Yes, let him have it!"

But the demon who had held the parley
with my leader turned instantly,
and said, "Quiet, quiet, Scarmiglione!"

Malacoda proposes that a squad accompany the travelers to the next "unbroken" bridge. Since all the bridges over the next bolgia are broken, the devils understand that a trick is to be played on Virgil. To be more convincing in his fraud, Malacoda cites some statistics to show how much time has passed since the Crucifixion and the resultant earthquake. Dante, using his senses and intuition, would prefer to go on alone, but Virgil (Reason), taken in, tries to reassure him; and the grotesque company moves on.

Then he said to us, "You cannot go farther
on this bridge, since the sixth arch
lies all broken on the bottom, 108

but if you still want to go ahead,
keep advancing along this bank;
nearby is another bridge that provides a way.

Yesterday, five hours later than this hour
a thousand two hundred and sixty-six years[42]
were completed since the bridge here was broken.

I am sending some of my men over there
to see if any are airing themselves;
go with them, since they won't be harmful.

[42] Christ died at the age of thirty-three, and the present year is 1300, but Dante is presumably dating from Christ's conception, not his birth.

Step forward, Alichino and Calcabrina,"
he then began to say, "and Cagnazzo,
and you, Barbariccia, guide the squad. 120

Let Libicocco come and Draghignazzo,
Ciriatto with his tusks, and Graffiacane,
and Farfarello, and mad Rubicante.

Look around the boiling glue;
let these be safe as far as to the bridge
which *all unbroken* passes over the dens."

"Oh, Master, what is this I see?"
I exclaimed. "Ah, without escort, let us go alone
if you know the way; as for me, I ask for none.

If you are as wary as usual,
don't you see that they are gnashing their teeth,
and with their frowns threaten grief to us?" 132

And he to me, "Do not be afraid,
let them grind away as they like,
because they do that for the wretches in the pitch."

The devils turned to the left on the bank,
but first each pressed his tongue between his teeth,
as a signal to their leader,

and he, for a trumpet, used his rump.[43]

CANTO XXII

Ciampolo of Navarre

I have seen horsemen move camp
and launch an attack, and hold their muster,
and sometimes turn back to escape;

I have seen scouting parties in your land,
O Aretines! and foragers start out,
tournaments begin and races run,

sometimes at the sound of trumpets or of bells,
with drums and with castle signals,
and with familiar and strange devices,

but never yet did I see horse or footmen move
to so strange a bugle call,
or a ship at a sign on land or in the sky. 12

We went along with the ten demons;
ah, fierce company! but "in church with saints,
and in the tavern with the gluttons!"

[43]Farted.

I was attentive to the pitch to see
what the bolgia contained
and the people burning in it.

As dolphins make signs to sailors
by the arching of their backs
to prepare to save their ship,

so now and then, to relieve the pain,
some of the sinners showed their backs
and hid again as fast as lightning flashes; 24

and, as at the edge of the water of a ditch,
frogs lie with just their muzzles out,
hiding their feet and bodies,

so, on every side, the sinners lay;
but when Barbariccia came near,
they withdrew within the boiling.

I saw, and still my heart shudders at it,
a soul waiting thus, just as it happens
that one frog may remain when the others dart away,

and Graffiacane who was closest to him
hooked his pitchy locks, and pulled him out
so that he looked like an otter. 36

I already knew the names of all the demons
so well did I note them when they were chosen,
and as they called each other I noticed how.

"O Rubicante, see that you get your claws
on him and skin him alive,"
the accursed ones shouted all together,

and I, "Master, find out if you can
who the unfortunate wretch is
that has fallen into the hands of his enemies."

My guide went close to him and asked
whence he came, and he replied,
"I was born in the kingdom of Navarre. 48

My mother placed me as a servant to a lord,
for she had borne me to a spendthrift,
a destroyer of himself and of his property.

Then I was in the service of good King Thibault;
there I began to commit barratry
for which I give reckoning in this heat."

And Ciriatto from each side of whose mouth
a tusk issued, as from a boar's,
made him feel how one of them could rip.

The mouse had fallen among vicious cats;
but Barbariccia took him in his arms
and said, "Stand over there while I grip him." 60

And turning his face to my master,
"Ask, if you want to hear more about him,"
he said, "before the others mangle him."

My guide then said, "Now tell me, do you know
any others under the pitch who are Italians?"
And he answered, "A little while ago

I left one from a nearby island—
(might I still be covered with him,
for then I would fear neither claw nor hook!").

And Libicocco cried, "Too much have we endured,"
and with his prong seized his arm
and tearing it, carried off a sinew. 72

Draghignazzo also tried to lay hold
of his legs, whereupon their corporal
turned around with wicked looks.

When they were somewhat pacified
my guide without delay addressed the sinner
who was still looking at his wounds.

"Who is the one you say you left
unluckily in order to come ashore?"
and he replied, "It was Friar Gomita,

from Gallura, a vessel of every fraud
who had his master's enemies in his hands
and dealt with them so [gently] that all praise him. 84

Money he took, and let them off quietly
as he says; and in other offices also
he was not a little barrator, but a supreme one.

With him Don Michel Zanche of Logodoro
keeps company, and their tongues
are never tired of talking about Sardinia.

O me! see that one grinding his teeth;
I would say more, but I am afraid
he is getting ready to scratch my sticky coat!"

And their commander in chief, turning to Farfarello,
who was rolling his eyes on the point of striking,
said, "Get over there, vile bird!" 96

"If you wish to see or hear,"
the frightened one [Ciampolo] then began,
"some Tuscans or Lombards, I will have some come,

but let the Malebranche stand back a little
so that their vengeance will not be feared,
and I, sitting in this very place,

for one that I am, will make many come
when I whistle, as it is our custom
to do when any of us gets out."

Cagnazzo at these words raised his snout,
shaking his head, and said, "Listen to the trick
he has thought of to plunge down." 108

Then he [Ciampolo], who had a wealth of guile,
answered, "I am too tricky indeed
when I get greater sorrow for my friends!"

Alichino could hold back no longer
and contrary to the others said,
"If you plunge, I'll not gallop after you,

but will beat my wings above the pitch!
Let the ridge be left and the bank made a screen
to see if you can get the best of us."

O you who read will now hear new sport.
All turned their eyes to the other side,
and he first who had been most unwilling. 120

The Navarese chose well his time,
steadied his feet upon the ground, and in an instant
leaped, and from the marshal freed himself.

At that each was stung with guilt, and that one most
who had been the cause of the mistake.
He, swooping down, cried, "You're caught!"

but it availed little, for wings
could not outstrip terror. The sinner went under,
and his pursuer, flying, turned up his breast.

Not otherwise does the wild duck plunge
when the falcon comes near
which, defeated and angry, flies up again. 132

Calcabrina, furious at the trick,
also went after him, eager for the sinner to escape
so that he could start a quarrel.

And when the barrator had disappeared,
he turned his claws on his companion
and grappled with him above the ditch.

But Alichino was a full-grown hawk
for clawing him back, and both fell
into the middle of the boiling pond.

The heat at once broke their grip,
but there was no way for them to rise,
since their wings were so beglued. 144

Barbariccia, complaining with the rest,
had four fly to the other bank
with all their hooks, and quickly

on this side and that they went to their places
and reached with their grapples to those stuck
and already partly cooked within the crust;

and while they were embarrassed in this way we left them.

CANTO XXIII

THE HYPOCRITES

The devils' fight over the pitch has reminded Dante of a fable which tells how a frog offers to tow a mouse tied to himself over a stream, intending to pull the rodent under. A kite, seeing their struggle, swoops down and carries off both.

Silent, alone, and without company
we went on, one in front of the other,
as minor friars go along their way.

My thought was turned to Aesop's fable
by the present quarrel, where he speaks
of the frog and of the mouse;

for "mo" and "issa" [synonyms for "now"] are not more alike
if one compares with close attention
the beginning and the end of each case.

And, as one thought bursts from another,
there arose from that one a second
which caused my first fear to be doubled. 12

I reflected thus: "Those devils through us
are mocked with such scorn and damage
as, I believe, must enrage them.

If anger is added to ill will,
they will rush after us more fiercely
than a hound after the rabbit he snaps up."

Already I felt my hair stand on end from fear,
and I looked back intently and said,
"Master, if you do not quickly hide

yourself and me, I fear the Malebranche;
we already have them right behind us,
I so imagine it that I can feel them now." 24

And he, "If I were leaded glass [a mirror]
I would not reflect your outer image
more quickly than I do your inner feelings.

Just now your thoughts were coming among mine
similar to them in force and in meaning,
so that of them all I made one resolve.

If it happens that the right bank lies
so that we can go into the next ditch,
we will escape the dreaded chase."

He had not finished giving this counsel
when I saw the demons not far away
coming with wings extended to seize us. 36

My guide suddenly took hold of me and,
as a mother who is awakened by a noise
and sees close to her the burning flames,

who takes her son and flees, caring more for him
than for herself, and who does not stop
even long enough to put on any clothes,

so, down from the edge of the hard bank,
lying on his back, my guide slid over the rock
which walls one side of the ditch.

Water never ran so fast through a sluice
to turn a millwheel, at the moment
when it is closest to the paddles, 48

as my master went down over the bank,
carrying me upon his breast,
not as a companion, but as a son.

Scarcely had his feet touched the bottom
when the devils reached the height above us,
but there was nothing to fear,

for High Providence, which wished to put them
as ministers of the fifth ditch,
took from all of them the power to leave.

The hypocrites whom the travelers now see wear gowns brilliant outwardly but of lead, like those Frederick II was supposed to have had melted on the backs of offenders against the throne. Like all who affect a pose, they must carry the weight of it forever. They move slowly, watching their steps. A kind of whining reproach sounds in their affected reference to Dante's and Virgil's clothes and to their "running." Not willing to commit themselves, they qualify the slightest promise with a "perhaps."

Down there we found a painted people
who moved around the circle with slow steps,
weeping, and, in countenance, wearied and overcome. 60

They wore capes with low hoods coming down
in front of their eyes, cut in the style
of those worn by the monks of Cluny,

outwardly gilded, so that they dazzled,
but within of lead, and so heavy
that [in comparison] those Frederick used were of straw.

O mantle eternally tiring! We turned once more
to the left, moving with the sinners
and listening to their sad lament;

but, because of their loads, those weary people
came so slowly that at every step we took
we found ourselves in new company. 72

Therefore I said to my guide, "Try to find someone
who by name or deed might be recognized,
and look around as we move on."

And one who understood the Tuscan speech
shouted from behind us, "Stay your steps,
you who are running so through the dark air;

perhaps you will hear from me what you ask for."
My guide turned around and said,
"Wait, and then come on at his pace."

I stopped and saw two showing by their looks
great eagerness to be with me,
but their burden and the narrow way delayed them. 84

When they came up, with sidelong glances
they looked at me, without saying a word,
then turned to each other and remarked,

"This man, by the movement of his throat, seems alive,
and if they are both dead, by what privilege
do they go divested of the heavy gown?"

Then they addressed me, "O Tuscan, you who have come
to the college of the sad hypocrites,
do not disdain to tell us who you are."

And I to them, "I was born and grew up
by the beautiful Arno river, in the great city,
and I am in the body I have always had. 96

But who are you whose distilled grief
drips down over your cheeks,
and what punishment glitters so on you?"

The two shades had been chosen as arbiters in the party strife of Florence instead of the usual one man. Far from being neutral, they favored the Guelfs. As a result certain houses of Ghibelline leaders near the old Gardingo fortress were destroyed and the site was made into a public square.

One shade, new to Virgil, naked, like Christ at the Crucifixion, is lying on the ground. This is Caiaphas, the high priest who, with others of the council of the Jews, favored sacrificing Christ.

And one answered, "The orange-colored mantles
are of lead, so thick that their weight
would make any scales creak.

We are Jolly Friars, and Bolognese,
I Catalano, and he, Loderingo,
appointed together by your city

(as a single man usually is taken)
to preserve the peace, and what we did
can still be seen around the Gardingo. 108

I began, "O Brothers, your evil . . ."
but I said no more, for the sight of a shade on the ground,
crucified with three stakes, caught my eye.

When he saw me he writhed all his body,
breathing into his beard with sighs,
and Friar Catalano who noticed that

said to me, "The transfixed one at whom you are looking
counseled the Pharisees that it was fitting
to torture one man for the people.[44]

Now he is lying crosswise and naked on the road,
as you see; and he must feel
the weight of each one who passes. 120

In a similar way his father-in-law is tortured
in this ditch, and the others of the Council
which was a seed of evil for the Jews."

Then I saw Virgil marveling
over the one stretched out so basely,
like a cross, in the eternal exile.

Virgil learns of the humiliating trick played on him by the devils of the fifth bolgia. The hypocrites are more expert in perceiving this deception than Reason itself. In his usual indirect manner, not committing himself, Catalano points out that the Devil tells lies. Virgil, angry at the trick and disgusted with Catalano, moves on contemptuously, without a word.

Afterward he addressed to the friar these words,
"Please tell us, if you can,
whether there is a gap on the right side

by which we two can get out of here
without constraining the black angels
to come and extricate us from this bottom." 132

[44]For the roles of Caiaphas and his father-in-law Annas in Jesus' passion, see John 11 and 18.

He answered, "Nearer than you expect
is a bridge which begins at the outer circle
and covers all the cruel valleys,

except that over this one it is broken.
You will be able to climb up on its ruins
which slope down the side and pile up on the bottom."

My guide stood a moment with his head lowered,
then said, "Falsely did the one up there
who hooks the sinners explain the matter."

And the friar added, "I once heard someone say at Bologna
that the Devil has many vices, among which I heard
that he is a liar and the father of lies." 144

Then with long steps my guide went on,
a little disturbed in his looks by anger,
and I also departed from the burdened ones,

following the imprints of the beloved feet.

CANTO XXIV

Vanni Fucci

A dainty comparison takes us for a moment into the fresh air of late winter when the nights are beginning to get shorter and when the frost resembles for a while the snow.

The poets struggle laboriously to get out of the ditch of hypocrisy.

In that part of the young year
when the sun warms his locks beneath Aquarius
and the long nights are moving toward the south,

when the frost copies on the ground
the image of her white sister
although the point of her pen lasts but little,

the poor peasant whose fodder is getting low
rises, looks out, and sees the fields all white;
whereupon he strikes his thigh,

turns back and, lamenting, walks up and down
like a wretch who does not know what to do.
Later he looks out again and recovers hope 12

on seeing that the world, in a little while,
has changed appearance; and he takes his crook
and drives forth the lambs to feed.

Thus my master made me disheartened
when I saw his face so troubled,
and thus quickly to the sore the plaster came.

For, when we reached the ruins of the bridge
    my guide turned to me with that pleasant look
    which I saw first at the foot of the mountain.

He opened his arms, after having made a plan
    within his mind, and looking carefully
    at the rocks he took hold of me, 24

and like one who calculates while working,
    who always seems to provide ahead of time,
    on lifting me toward the top of one rock

examined another crag, saying,
    "Afterward catch hold of that,
    but see first if it will bear your weight."

It was not a way for one clothed in a leaden cloak,
    for we, he a shade and I pushed,
    could hardly mount from jag to jag.

And were it not that on this side
    the slope was shorter than on the other,
    I do not know about him, but I would have been exhausted; 36

but, since Malebolge slopes wholly
    toward the edge of the lowest well,
    the position of each ditch demands

that one side be higher than the other.
    We came finally to the place
    where the last stone is broken off.

The breath had been so pumped from my lungs
    as I went up that at the top
    I could go no farther, and sat down at once.

"Now you must free yourself from sloth,"
    my master said, "for, sitting on down
    or lying under covers, no one comes to fame, 48

without which whoever consumes his life
    leaves such vestige of himself on earth
    as smoke in air or foam on water.

Therefore get up, overcome your panting
    with the spirit which wins every battle
    if it does not sink with its heavy body.

A longer stairs must be climbed;
    it is not enough to have left this one;
    if you understand, act so that it may profit you."

I then got up showing myself better furnished
    with breath than I was, and I said,
    "Go on, for I am strong and bold." 60

The travelers now come to the ditch of the thieves.

We made our way up over the bridge
which was rocky, narrow, and difficult,
and much steeper than the previous ones.

I kept talking in order not to appear faint;
whereupon from the next ditch a voice issued
unsuited for forming words.

I do not know what it said, although I was already
on top of the arch that crosses there,
but whoever spoke seemed moved to anger.

I had turned to look down, but my living eyes
could not penetrate to the bottom
through the darkness; therefore I said, 72

"Master, let us try to reach the next bank,
for, just as I hear, but do not understand,
so I look, and can distinguish nothing."

"No reply do I make except by an act,"
he said, "for a modest request
should be followed silently by the deed."

We went down the bridge to the place
where it joins the eighth bank,
and then the ditch was revealed to me.

I saw in it a terrible pack of serpents
of such diverse appearance
that the memory of it still chills my blood. 84

Let Libya with its sands boast no longer,
for if it produced chelydri, jaculi, and phareae,
and cencri with amphisbaena [fabulous snakes],

it has never shown so many plagues
or such bad ones, together with all of Ethiopia
and the land [Arabia] which lies above the Red Sea.

Amid this cruel and dismal swarm, I saw people running,
naked and terrified, without hope of hiding place
or of heliotrope [to make themselves invisible].

Their hands were tied behind them by serpents
which stuck their heads and tails through their backs,
and were knotted together in front. 96

And behold! at one that was near our bank
a serpent sprang and transfixed him
right where the neck meets the shoulders.

Neither I nor O was ever written so quickly
as he took fire and burned and fell
like a cinder to the ground.

Then when he was thus destroyed
the ashes came together of themselves
and took on instantly the previous form.

Thus it is maintained by great sages
that the Phoenix[45] dies and then is reborn
when the five-hundredth year approaches. 108

During its life it feeds on neither grain
nor herb, but on incense and amomum,
and nard and myrrh make up its shroud.

And like one [an epileptic] who falls not knowing how,
through the force of a demon pulling him to the ground
or through some obstruction that paralyzes him,

and who, when he gets up, looks around, all bewildered
by the great anguish he has suffered,
and while looking sighs,

such was the sinner after he arose.
O Power of God, how severe it is
in showering down such blows of vengeance! 120

The stricken soul is Vanni Fucci, one of Dante's former political enemies, whom the poet had known, not as a thief, but only as hotheaded and violent. Vanni predicts obscurely and maliciously certain events which will lead to the defeat of the Florentine Whites.

My guide then asked the sinner who he was;
whereupon he answered, "I rained down from
Tuscany into this gullet a little while ago.

A bestial, not human life, I liked,
mule [of irregular birth] that I was; I am Vanni Fucci,
a beast, and Pistoia was a den worthy of me."

I said to my guide, "Tell him not to slip away
and ask what sin thrusts him down here,
for I saw him once a man of blood and rage."

And the soul, having heard, did not dissemble,
but directed toward me his face
and his attention with a look of dismal shame. 132

Then he said, "It grieves me more
that you have caught me in this misery
than when I was taken from the other world.

I cannot deny what you ask for;
I have been put down this far for the theft
of the fine ornaments of the sacristy,

[45] The mythical bird that was consumed in fire every 500 years and then arose to new life from the ashes of its dead self.

for which another was falsely accused.
But to keep you from enjoying this sight,
if you ever get out of this dark place,

open your ears to my prophecy and hear:
Pistoia first is thinned of Blacks,
then Florence renews her masters and her ways; 144

Mars draws a fiery vapor [thunderbolt] from Val di Magra
which is wrapped in turbid clouds,
and in an impetuous and angry storm

a battle will be fought on the Piceno field;
then the blast will pierce the mist
so that every White will be wounded by it.

And I have told you this so that you may grieve."

CANTO XXV

The Metamorphosis of Thieves

At the end of his remarks the thief
raised both hands, making the [obscene] sign of the fig,
and shouting, "Take that, God, for at Thee I point them!"

From then on the serpents were my friends,
for one coiled around his neck, as if saying,
"I will not have you speak any more,"

and another encircled his arms and bound them,
so clinching itself in front
that he could not make a move with those members.

Ah, Pistoia, why do you not resolve to burn
so that you will last no longer, since you surpass
your own founders [followers of Catiline] in wickedness? 12

Through all the dark circles of Hell
I saw no spirit so bold against God,
not even him [Capaneus] who fell from the walls of Thebes.

The thief fled, saying nothing further.
Then I saw a centaur, full of wrath, come calling,
"Where is he? Where is the impious one?"

I do not believe Maremma has as many snakes
as the centaur had on its back
up to where our human form begins.

Upon his shoulders, behind his neck,
a dragon was lying with open wings
which set on fire all it met. 24

My master said, "That is Cacus [a fire-breathing monster]
who, under the rocks of Mount Aventine,
many times made a lake of blood.

He does not go on the same road as his brothers [the other centaurs]
because of the theft he slyly made
of the great herd [of cattle] kept near him,

which led to the end of his wicked life
under the club of Hercules, who gave him
perhaps a hundred blows, although hardly ten were felt."

While Virgil was saying this, the centaur ran off,
and three spirits [Agnello, Buoso, and Puccio] came below us
whom neither my master nor I had noticed 36

until they cried, "Who are you?"
Whereupon our talking ceased,
and we gave heed to them alone.

I did not recognize them, but it happened
as sometimes occurs by chance
that one needed to name the other,

saying, "Where can Cianfa [now a serpent] have remained?"
In order to make my guide attentive,
I held my finger against my mouth from chin to nose.

If you are slow, Reader, to believe
what I am to relate, it will be no wonder,
for I who saw it scarcely admit it to myself. 48

As I kept my eyes on them, a serpent [Cianfa]
with six legs darted in front of one
and fastened itself wholly to him.

With its middle feet it clasped his belly
and with those in front seized his arms;
then it set its fangs in both his cheeks.

It spread its hind feet over his thighs
and thrust its tail between them
drawing it up along his back.

Ivy never clung to a tree so tightly
as the horrible beast
entwined the other's members in its own; 60

then they grew together and exchanged their color
as if they had been hot wax,
nor did either one or the other appear as before.

Thus a dark hue moves ahead of a flame
over a sheet of paper, as the whiteness
dies away before it becomes black.

The other two [Buoso and Puccio] watched and shouted,
"O me, Agnello, how you are changing!
Behold! You are now neither two nor one."

The two heads had already fused into one,
and the shapes of two faces appeared blended
in the one in which the others had disappeared. 72

The two arms were formed of four strips;
the thighs with the legs, the belly and the chest,
became such members as were never seen.

All the former features were blotted out;
the perverse image seemed two and none,
and thus went away with slow steps.

As a lizard, under the great scourge
of the dog days, passing from hedge to hedge,
seems a flash as it crosses the path,

so appeared, making for the bellies
of the remaining two, a small, fiery serpent,
livid and black as a peppercorn, 84

and pierced that part in one of them
where we first receive our nourishment;
then fell, stretched out, in front of him.

The one transfixed [Buoso] looked at it, silently,
and with feet motionless, yawned,
as if sleep or a fever had come upon him.

He eyed the reptile, and the reptile him;
from the wound of one and mouth of the other
thick smoke issued and combined.

Let Lucan be silent now where he tells
of poor Sabellus and of Nasidius [transformed by serpents],
and wait to hear what is announced. 96

Let Ovid keep still concerning Cadmus and Arethusa,
for if he changes one into a serpent in his verse
and the other into a spring, I do not envy him,

since he never changed two natures
face to face so that both forms
were ready to exchange their substance.

The two responded to each other in such a way
that the serpent made a fork of its tail,
and the wounded shade drew its feet together.

The legs and the thighs united,
so that in a little while there was no sign
you could see of the joining. 108

The split tail took on the shape
lost in the other; the skin of one became soft
and that of the other hard.

I saw the arms withdraw through the armpits
  and the short legs of the reptile
  lengthen as much as the other's arms were shortened.

Then the hind feet, twisted together,
  became the member man hides,
  and the shade from his made two legs project.

As the smoke covered both with a new color
  it brought out hair on one
  and removed it from the other. 120

One got up and the other fell,
  neither, however, turning aside his gaze
  under which each had changed faces.

The one standing drew his snout toward his temples,
  and with the flesh left over
  ears were formed on the smooth cheeks.

What was not drawn back and remained
  in excess made a nose for the face
  and thickened the lips to a fit size.

The one on the ground stretched forth his nose,
  withdrew his ears within his head,
  as a snail does its horns, 132

and his tongue which had been undivided
  and apt for speech, split; and the forked tongue
  united; then the smoke stopped.

The soul that had become a brute
  fled hissing through the ditch,
  and after it the other, talking and sputtering.

Then he turned his new back to the reptile
  and said, "I want Buoso to run
  as I have, crawling over the way."

Thus I saw the seventh ballast change
  and interchange, and let the strangeness of it
  be my excuse if my pen has gone astray. 144

Although my eyes were somewhat confused
  and my mind bewildered, those shades
  could not slip away so secretly

that I did not recognize easily
  Puccio Sciancato, who was the only one
  of the three companions left unchanged.

The unidentified figure (originally the second snake) was Francesco de' Cavalcanti, killed by the people of Gaville. The town mourns because of the vengeance taken for him.

The other was he because of whom you, Gaville, weep.

CANTO XXVI

Ulysses

The bitter tone of the beginning lines of an apostrophe to Florence ends quickly when Dante thinks of the misfortune certain to come to his city, a disaster wished for by neighboring towns, like Prato, not to mention enemies. Here, as elsewhere, the invective expresses deep concern, a kind of inverted love.

Rejoice, Florence, since you are so great
that over land and over sea you beat your wings,
and your name is famous in Hell!

Among the thieves I found five citizens of yours,
such that shame comes over me;
and you do not rise through them to great honor.

But if the truth is dreamed of near the morning,
you will soon feel what Prato,
not to mention others, craves for you.

And if that had already happened, it would not be
too soon; so were it, since it has to be!
for it will weigh heavier on me as I grow older. 12

The poets reach the summit of the bridge over the bolgia where evil counseling is punished. This sin, incurred mainly by those of superior intelligence, offered constant temptations to Dante, an exile dependent upon patronage.

In the ditch below, lights appear, like fireflies at dusk on a summer evening. And just as Elisha saw Elijah rise up, enveloped in a cloud of flame, so here the fire concealed the spirits. Dante asks about a double flame, like that on the funeral pyre of Eteocles and Polynices, two brothers who had killed each other.

We departed, and over the steps
which stones had made for our descent,
my guide remounted, and drew me up,

and continuing our solitary way
over the stones and rocks of the bridge,
feet did not advance without help from hands.

I grieved then, and now I grieve again
when I direct my thought to what I saw,
and I control my mind more than usual

so that virtue alone may guide it.
Thus, if a kindly star or something better [Divine Grace]
has given an advantage, it may not be harmful through abuse. 24

As a peasant who is resting on a slope
in the season when the sun that lights the world
keeps his face least hidden from us—

at the hour when gnats take the place of flies—
sees fireflies down below in the valley,
perhaps where he gathers grapes or plows;

so, with as many flames the eighth bolgia
was all resplendent, as I noticed
when I came to where I could see the bottom.

And, as he [Elisha] who avenged himself with the bears
saw the chariot of Elijah depart
when the horses rose erect to Heaven[46]— 36

for he could not follow so closely with his eyes
that he could see anything except the flame itself,
like a little cloud rising upward—

so each light moved through the ditch,
none revealing what it hid,
and yet each concealed a sinner.

I was standing on the bridge leaning out to see,
so that if I had not held to a rock,
without being pushed I would have fallen,

and my guide, who saw me so attentive, said,
"Within the fires are the spirits;
each is wrapped in what is burning him." 48

"Master," I answered, "through hearing you
I am more certain, but already I was aware
that this was so, and wished to ask

who is in the fire which comes so divided at the top
that it seems to rise from the pyre
on which Eteocles was placed with his brother."

Ulysses and Diomed, in the double flame, are guilty on three counts: (1) the trick of the Trojan horse, which led to the destruction of Troy and the founding of Rome; (2) enticing Achilles to abandon Deidamia and to leave for the Trojan wars, and (3) the theft of the Palladium, a statue of Pallas on which the fate of Troy depended.

He answered, "In that flame Ulysses and Diomed
are tortured, and thus they go together
in punishment as in their battles.

They groan within their flame for the ambush
of the horse which was the portal
through which came the noble ancestors of the Romans.[47] 60

Also they weep for the art on account of which
Deidamia still grieves for Achilles,
and they suffer too for the Palladium."

[46] For the ascent of Elijah to Heaven and the story of Elisha's revenge on some children who taunted him for his baldness (they were attacked by bears), see 2 Kings 2.

[47] The story of the Trojan horse is told in Virgil's *Aeneid*, Book II. The Greeks besieging Troy built a large wooden horse and concealed a band of troops inside it; the deluded Trojans brought it into their city, which was then destroyed by the Greeks. The exiled Trojans wandered to Italy, where their descendants founded Rome.

"If they can speak within those fires," I said,
"Master, I beg you earnestly, and beg again
(and may my prayer be worth a thousand),

that you do not deny our waiting
until the horned flame comes here;
you see how my desire bends me toward it!"

And he to me, "Your request is worthy
of praise; therefore I grant it,
but see that your tongue keeps silent. 72

Let me speak, for I have conceived
what you want to know. Since they were Greeks,
they might shy away from your words."

When Virgil, who had celebrated Ulysses in the Aeneid, *asks about his death, the latter, the representative of the spirit of adventure and of scientific discovery, answers with great dignity and relevance, pointing out how compelling was his desire for knowledge of the two worlds of things and of men. In the story Dante invents, instead of returning to Penelope and the comforts of home, Ulysses sails westward through the Mediterranean, then past Gibraltar, and out on the vast and terrifying Atlantic. His course, like that of Columbus almost two centuries after Dante, is west-southwest. Five months pass; the crew of old men see the constellations of the other hemisphere; then land (probably the island of Purgatory) appears. But a storm arises, and Ulysses ends his life in the glory of a last adventure.*

When the flame had come to where
time and place seemed best to my guide,
I heard him speak in these terms:

"O you two within one fire,
if I merited thanks from you while I lived,
if I deserved much or little

when in the world I wrote the lofty verses,[48]
do not move, but let one of you tell
where, lost, he went to die." 84

The greater horn of the ancient flame
began to shake, murmuring like a fire
struggling in the wind,

then moving the tip here and there,
as if it were a tongue speaking,
it formed words, and said:

"When I left Circe who detained me
more than a year near Gaeta
before Aeneas had named it thus,

[48] Dante had not read Homer's *Odyssey.* (Ulysses is the Latin name for Odysseus.)

neither fondness for my son, nor pity
    for an old father, nor the love for Penelope
    which should have made her happy, 96

could overcome in me the desire I had
    to gain experience of the world
    and of the vices and the worth of men.

I set out on the high, open sea,
    with only one ship, and with that little company
    by which I was not deserted.

Both coasts I saw as far as Spain,
    down to Morocco and the island of Sardinia
    and the others that are bathed in that sea.

I and my companions were old and slow
    when we came to that narrow pass [Gibraltar]
    where Hercules set up his landmarks 108

so that men should not venture beyond.
    On the right I left Seville,
    and on the other side had already passed Ceuta.

'O brothers,' I said, 'you who
    through a thousand perils have come to the West,
    to the brief vigil of our senses

which is left, do not deny
    experience of the unpeopled world
    to be discovered by following the sun.

Consider what origin you had;
    you were not created to live like brutes,
    but to seek virtue and knowledge.' 120

With this little speech I made my companions
    so eager for the journey
    that scarcely then could I have held them back,

and, having turned our stern to the morning,
    we made wings of our oars for the mad flight,
    always gaining on the left.

The night already saw the stars
    of the other pole, and ours [the North Star] so low
    it did not rise from the ocean floor.

Five times the light upon the moon
    had shone and been extinguished
    since we started on the deep way, 132

when a mount appeared to us,
    dim in the distance, and which seemed
    higher than any I had ever seen.

We rejoiced; but soon our joy changed to sorrow,
for, from the new land a whirlwind arose
which struck the prow of our ship.

Three times it made it whirl with all the water;
the fourth time it lifted high the stern
and made the prow go down as pleased Another [God],

until at last the sea closed over us."

CANTO XXVII

Guido da Montefeltro

A second flame roars like the brass statue of a bull in which prisoners were burned alive. This instrument of torture was made for a tyrant of Agrigentum and was tried out first on its inventor. The flame contains the soul of Guido da Montefeltro, a famous Ghibelline leader referred to in the Convivio *as "our most noble Italian." Guido enquires about Romagna, and Dante outlines briefly the conditions in that region, designating the various rulers by their armorial bearings.*

Already the flame was erect and quiet,
having ended its speech, and was going from us
with the leave of the dear Poet,

when another flame that came behind it
made us turn our eyes to its tip
because of a confused sound issuing from it.

As the Sicilian bull which roared first
with the groans of the one who made it
with his tools (and that was right)

bellowed with the voice of the tortured
in such a way that, although it was of brass,
it seemed transfixed with pain, 12

not having any opening or outlet
from their source in the fire,
the doleful words were transformed into its language.

After they had found their way
up through the tip, giving it the vibration
the tongue had imparted to them,

we heard it say, "O you to whom I direct my voice,
and who were speaking Lombard just now,
saying, 'Now go, further I do not urge you,'

although I have perhaps arrived somewhat late,
do not be displeased to speak with me;
you see it does not irk me, and I burn! 24

If you have just now fallen into this blind world
from that sweet Latin land
from which I bring all my sin,

tell me if the Romagnuols have peace or war,
for I was from the mountains there
between Urbino and the peak from which the Tiber comes."

I was still attentive and bent down
when my leader nudged me, saying,
"*You* speak, this is an Italian."

And I, having already prepared my reply,
began without delay, "O soul,
you who are hidden down there, 36

your Romagna is not and never was
without strife in the hearts of its tyrants,
but no open warfare did I leave there just now.

Ravenna stands as it has for many years,
the eagle of Polenta brooding over it,
and covering Cervia with its pinions.

The city [Forlì] which once bore the long siege,
and made a bloody heap of the French,
finds itself under the green claws [the Ordelaffi family].

The old and young mastiffs of Verrucchio [the Malatestas]
who disposed badly of Mantagna [their prisoner],
as usual, make an auger of their teeth. 48

The cities on the Lamone and the Santerno
are ruled by the young lion in the white lair [Maghinardo da Susinana]
who, from summer to winter, changes party.

And the city [Cesena] whose side the Savio bathes,
as it lies between the mountain and the plain,
lives [under party bosses] between tyranny and freedom.

Now I beg you to tell us who you are;
do not be more reluctant than another has been;
so may your name stay proudly in the world."

After a successful military career, Guido da Montefeltro withdrew from the world and joined the Franciscan order, hoping to make amends for the sins inseparable from military life and to prepare securely for the future world. His plan might have succeeded except for the pope, Boniface VIII, who asked him by what faithless stratagem he might defeat his enemies, offering absolution in advance for the evil counsel. Obliged either to comply or to disobey his superior, Guido chose what seemed (to a soldier) the lesser evil, and told how the pope might, through treachery, secure Palestrina, the stronghold of his enemies.

After the flame had roared a while in its manner,
the sharp tip moved to and fro,
and breathed forth this sound: 60

"If I believed that my reply were to anyone
who would ever return to the world,
this flame would remain quiet,

but since no one from this ditch
has ever returned alive, if I hear the truth,
I will answer without fear of infamy.

I was a man of arms, and then a Cordelier,
believing, thus girt, to make amends;
and certainly my intent would have been realized

except for the Great Priest (may ill befall him!)
who put me back into my former sins;
and how and why I want you to hear. 72

While I had the form of the flesh and bones
my mother gave me, my deeds
were not lionlike, but those of a fox.

The tricks and the secret ways,
I knew them all, and so carried on their art
that my fame spread to the ends of the earth.

When I saw that I had reached
that point in life when everyone
should lower sail and coil his ropes,

what first had pleased me became repugnant
and, having repented and confessed, I gave myself to God,
and alas! that should have availed. 84

The Prince of the new Pharisees [Boniface VIII],
waging war close to the Lateran—
and not with Saracens or with Jews,

for every enemy of his was a Christian,
and none had been a renegade at Acre
or a merchant in the Sultan's land—

considered neither his high office
and sacred orders, nor in me that cord I wore
which used to make those bound with it thinner.

But, as Constantine called upon Sylvester[49]
in Soracte to cure him of his leprosy,
so he called me, as his physician, 96

to cure the fever of his pride.
He asked advice of me, and I kept silent,
because his words seemed drunken,

[49]For Constantine and Sylvester, see XIX.115–117, the translator's gloss, and the note. Sylvester, according to legend, cured Constantine by baptizing him, in return for which Constantine yielded up the western part of the Roman Empire.

and then he said, "Do not let your heart mistrust,
right now I absolve you; let me know
how to cast Palestrina to the ground.

I can open and close Heaven,
as you know, since two are the keys
that my predecessor [Celestine V] did not hold dear."[50]

The heavy arguments brought me to where
silence seemed worse to me than complying,
and I said, 'Father, since you wash away 108

the sin into which I now must fall,
long promise with short fulfillment
will make you triumph on your lofty seat.'

At Guido's death, St. Francis came for him, but a "black Cherub" from the eighth circle of Hell, the counterpart of those of the eighth heaven who likewise operate through intelligence, objected, and pointed out the impossibility of absolution in advance.

Dante uses this extreme example to emphasize the point that salvation depends on the state of the soul at the moment of death. A similar contest, related in Purgatory, occurs in the case of Guido's son, but in almost exactly opposite circumstances.

When I was dead, Francis came for me,
but one of the black Cherubim said to him,
'Don't take him, don't wrong me.

He must come down among my minions
because he gave the fraudulent advice,
since when I have been lurking to grasp his hair.

For one who does not repent cannot be absolved,
nor can *repenting* and *willing* go together
because the contradiction does not allow it.' 120

Ah, wretched me, how I shuddered
when he seized me, saying,
'Perhaps you did not think I was a logician!'

To Minos he brought me, who twisted his tail
eight times around his stiff back,
and after he had bitten it in his rage, he said,

'This is one for the thievish fire.'
Therefore I am lost here as you see,
and while moving, clothed in fire, I grieve."

When he had finished speaking
the sorrowing spirit went on
twisting and shaking his sharp flame. 132

[50]For Celestine V, see III.59–60 and translator's gloss.

My guide and I passed over the bridge
to the top of the next arch
which crosses the ditch in which a fee is paid

by those who get a burden by dividing [sowing discord].

CANTO XXVIII

The Sowers of Discord

If it were possible to bring together the wounded on the battlegrounds of southern Italy in the long series of wars from ancient times down to the Norman invasions and the wars of Charles of Anjou against Manfred, the scene would be similar to that of the ninth bolgia.

Who even in unrhymed words [prose]
could ever fully tell in many narrations
of the blood and of the wounds I now saw?

Every tongue certainly would fail
because our language and our memories
are insufficient to contain so much.

If all the soldiers were assembled
who, on the stormy fields of Apulia,
have groaned for their blood

shed by Trojans, and in the long [Punic] war
which made so vast a spoil of rings [from fingers of dead Romans],
as Livy writes, who does not err, 12

together with those who suffered painful wounds
by opposing Robert Guiscard [the Norman conqueror]
and others whose bones are still piled up

at Ceperano, where every Apulian [allied with Manfred]
was a traitor, and at Tagliacozzo
where old Alardo conquered without arms [by strategy],

and were one to show his limbs pierced,
another his cut off, the view would not equal
the awful sight of the ninth ditch.

Mahomet, the first shade recognized, had been considered as originally a Christian and as the deliberate cause of the separation of the world into two monotheistic faiths. Mahomet mentions prophetically and with malicious pleasure Fra Dolcino, the leader of a heretical sect who, besieged in 1306, was forced by hunger to surrender.

Indeed, a cask without a stave or endboard
looks less mutilated than one I saw
split from his chin down to where wind is broken. 24

His entrails hung between his legs,
the vital parts appeared with the foul sack
which makes excrement of what is swallowed.

While I was intently looking at him,
he gazed at me, and with his hands opened his breast,
saying, "Now see how I tear myself,

see how mangled Mahomet is!
In front of me Ali [a son-in-law] goes weeping,
his head split from chin to forelock;

and all the others you see here
while alive were sowers of scandal and of schism
and therefore are split like this. 36

A devil is here behind us who cuts us
thus cruelly with the edge of his sword,
reopening all the wounds

when we have gone around the doleful road,
since they are healed
before we come again before him.

But who are you, dallying on the bridge,
perhaps to delay going to your punishment
decreed upon your own confession?"

"Not yet has death come to him, nor does guilt
bring him to torment," my master said,
"but to give him complete experience, 48

I, who am dead, must take him
down here from round to round, and this
is as true as that I am speaking to you."

More than a hundred in the ditch,
when they heard this, stopped to look at me,
forgetting their pain in their marveling.

"Now tell Fra Dolcino, you who perhaps
will soon see the sun again, that unless he wants
to follow me he had better provide himself

with food, so that the snow
will not bring victory to the Novarese,
which otherwise would be hard for them to gain." 60

After he had lifted one foot to go
Mahomet said these words to me,
then placed it on the ground, moving on.

Pier da Medicina, another schismatic of whom little is known, adds the prophecy of the death of two citizens of Fano who will be called to a parley and treacherously thrown overboard. They will not need the usual protection from the squalls of Focara, since they will never reach that place. Then Curio is mentioned who from private motives urged Caesar to cross the Rubicon and begin the civil war. He wishes now he had never seen the town of Rimini near that river. Another sower of discord, Mosca, according to tradition advised the killing of an opponent to settle a feud rather than a milder punishment, since that, he thought, would end the matter. Instead, the murder led to the first conflict between the Guelfs and Ghibellines in Florence. On seeing Mosca, Dante's Florentine spirit flares up, and he tells him of the banishment of his family, the Lamberti, from the city.

Another who had his throat cut
  and his nose severed up to his eyebrows,
  and who had only a single ear,

having stopped to look with wonder,
  before the others cleared his windpipe
  which was all red outside, and said,

"O you whom sin does not condemn
  and whom I have seen in the Latin land,
  if too much resemblance does not deceive me, 72

recall to mind Pier da Medicina
  if ever you go back to see the sweet plain
  which from Vercelli slopes to Marcabò,

and make known to the two best men of Fano,
  to Messer Guido and to Angiolello,
  that, unless foresight here is vain,

they will be thrown from their ship
  and drowned near La Cattolica
  through the treachery of a base tyrant.

Between the islands of Cyprus and Majorca,
  Neptune has never seen so great a crime
  of pirates or of Argolic people [Greeks]. 84

That traitor who sees with one eye only [Malatestino]
  and holds the city [Rimini] which someone here [Curio]
  would wish never to have seen,

will have them come for a parley with him,
  and will act so that to allay Focara's wind,
  they will need neither vow nor prayer."

And I to him, "Point out and tell me
  if you want me to take news of you above,
  who found the sight of that city bitter?"

Then he laid his hand on the jaw
  of one of his companions, and opened his mouth,
  saying, "This is he, and he does not speak. 96

While exiled, he quieted Caesar's fears,
  affirming that a man well prepared
  always loses by any delay."

Oh, how dismayed he seemed to me
  with his tongue cut in his throat,
  Curio, who before spoke so boldly!

And one who had both hands cut off,
lifting the stumps in the dark air
so that the blood dirtied his face,

cried, "Remember also Mosca
who said, alas, 'A thing done has an end,'
which was a seed of evil for the Tuscans." 108

And I added, "And death to your kindred,"
whereupon he, heaping grief on grief,
went off like one maddened by sorrow.

The last example is that of the Provençal poet Bertran de Born, who, Dante believed, had fomented a quarrel between Henry, the "young English king," and his father.

But I remained to look at the throng,
and I saw a thing I would fear
to tell about without more proof,

except that conscience reassures me,
the good companion which emboldens man
under the breastplate of conscious innocence.

I saw certainly, and I still seem to see
a body without a head, going on
like the others of the sad troop. 120

It held by the hair its severed head
dangling from its hand like a lantern,
which looked at us and said, "Woe is me!"

Of itself it made a lamp for itself,
and they were two in one and one in two;
how this can be He knows who so ordains.

When it was at the foot of the bridge,
it lifted the head high with its arm
to bring the words closer to me,

which were, "Now see my terrible penalty,
you who, breathing, are visiting the dead;
judge if any is as great as this. 132

And, that you may take news of me,
know that I am Bertran de Born, the one
who gave the young king the evil encouragement.

I made father and son rebellious to each other;
Ahithophel did not do worse to Absalom
and to David with his wicked plots.[51]

[51] For Absalom's rebellion, incited by Ahithophel (or Achitophel), against his father King David, see 2 Samuel 14–18.

Because I separated persons thus joined,
I now carry my brain, alas,
detached from its source in this body.

Thus retribution is observed in me."

CANTO XXIX

The Falsifiers

Fascinated by the sight of the horrible wounds, Dante keeps looking at them and incurs a reproach. He excuses himself (he is growing up in his relationship with his master) by mentioning that he believed that a relative was there, Geri del Bello, whose violent death had not been avenged. Dante pities Geri, perhaps for the latter's obvious adherence even here to the code of family vengeance.

The time, as usual in Hell, is indicated by the position of the moon: it is now shortly after noon on Saturday.

The great crowd and the diverse wounds
had made my eyes so inebriated
that they were eager to remain and weep.

But Virgil said, "What are you looking at?
Why does your sight still rest down there
on the sad, mutilated shades?

You have not done so at the other ditches.
Consider, if you wish to count them,
that the valley circles for twenty-two miles;

already the moon is under our feet;
the time granted to us now is short,
and there is much more to see." 12

"If you had taken note," I answered then,
"of the cause that made me look,
perhaps you would have granted me a longer stay."

Meanwhile my guide kept going on
and I followed, making my reply
and adding, "Within that hollow

on which I kept my eyes fixed so closely
I believe a spirit of my own blood
laments the sin that costs so much down here."

Then my master said, "From now on
do not let your thoughts be distracted by him;
attend to something else and let him stay there, 24

for I saw him at the foot of the little bridge
pointing you out and threatening you with his finger,
and I heard him called Geri del Bello.

You were then so completely occupied
with him [Bertran de Born] who once held Altaforte
that you did not look over there, and he departed."

"O my guide, his death by violence
which has not yet been avenged," I said,
"by [relatives] the partners of his shame,

made him indignant; therefore he went off
without speaking to me, as I judge,
and by that he has made me pity him the more." 36

The shades in the tenth bolgia are divided into four groups: falsifiers (1) of metals (alchemists), punished by leprosy and paralysis; (2) of persons (impersonators), punished by delirium or madness; (3) of coins (counterfeiters), afflicted with dropsy; and (4) of words (liars), suffering from high fever. Dante treats them with mild and amused contempt.

Thus we talked as far as to the point
which would have shown the next ditch
to the bottom if there had been more light.

Then, when we were above
the last cloister of Malebolge, so that
its lay brothers could be observed by us,

diverse laments kept striking me
which had their arrows barbed with such pity
that I covered my ears with my hands.

Such suffering as there would be if the sick
in the hospitals of Valdichiana, Maremma, and Sardinia
[malarious regions] between July and September 48

were all together in one ditch,
was here; and such stench issued
as comes from festered limbs.

We descended to the last bank of the long bridge,
still keeping to the left,
and then my sight was clearer

down toward the bottom, where the minister
of the Supreme Lord, Infallible Justice,
punishes the falsifiers registered here.

I do not believe there was greater sadness
to see all the people of Aegina sick
when the air was so full of pestilence 60

that the animals, even to the little worm,
fell dead—and then the ancient people,
as the poets hold as true,

were restored by the seed of ants[52]—
than it was to see in the dark ditch
the spirits languish in diverse heaps.

One lay upon the belly and one upon the shoulders
of another, and one on all fours
was crawling along the dismal path.

Step by step we went without speaking,
observing and listening to the sick,
who could not lift their bodies. 72

I saw two sitting, leaning on each other
as stewpan is propped against stewpan to warm,
spotted with scabs from head to foot,

and never have I seen a currycomb handled so quickly
by a stable boy whose master was waiting for him
or by one staying up against his will

as each of these plied the clawing of his nails
on himself, because of the great rage
of itching that had no other help;

and the nails scraped off the scabs
as a knife does the scales from bream
or some other fish that has them larger. 84

"O you who disarm yourself with your fingers,
at times making pincers of them,"
my guide began to say to one of them,

"tell us if any Latin is among those
who are here; so may your nails
suffice eternally for this work!"

"We are both Latins whom you see
so disfigured here," one answered, weeping,
"but who are you, asking about us?"

My guide replied, "I am one descending
with this *live* man from ledge to ledge,
and I intend to show Hell to him." 96

Then the mutual support broke,
and each of them, trembling, turned to me,
with others who had overheard the words.

My good master drew close to me, saying,
"Ask them what you want to know."
And I began to speak as he desired:

[52]Juno inflicted on Aegina a plague that destroyed all living creatures except one man, Aeacus, at whose prayer Jupiter repopulated the island by changing ants into human beings. The story is told by Ovid.

"So may your memory not fade
from human minds in the first world,
but may it live on for many suns,

tell me who you are, and of what people;
let not your ugly and annoying punishment
make you afraid to reveal yourselves to me." 108

Griffolino, a fraudulent alchemist, tells how he was burned by the presumptive father of the simple-minded Albero da Siena, who had taken seriously his remarks about flying. This prompts Dante to speak of the Sienese whose sometimes aristocratic folly was a standing joke in the bourgeois atmosphere of Florence. Dante is helped in his gibes by Capocchio, who mentions ironically the notorious spendthrift Stricca and the "Spendthrifts' Club," a group of young Sienese who deliberately ruined themselves by extravagance.

"I was of Arezzo," one answered,
"and Albero da Siena had me burned at the stake;
but what I died for does not bring me here.

It is true that I told him, speaking in jest,
that I could rise in the air in flight,
and he who had the desire but little sense

wanted me to show him the art, and because
I did not make him a Daedalus [a flyer], he had me burned
by one who considered him as a son.

But to the last ditch of the ten,
Minos, who cannot err, condemned me
for the alchemy that I practiced in the world." 120

And I said to the poet, "Now was there ever
a people as silly as the Sienese?
Certainly the French are not so by far."

Thereupon the other leper who heard me
answered my question and said, "Except Stricca
who knew how to spend with moderation,

and Niccolò who first discovered
the expensive use of the clove
in the garden[53] where such seed takes root,

and except the company in which
Caccia d'Ascian squandered vineyard and forest
and the Abbagliato displayed his wit. 132

But that you may know who seconds your remarks
against the Sienese, sharpen your eyes toward me,
so that my face may give the right response.

[53] The "garden" is Siena.

Then you will see that I am the shade of Capocchio
who falsified the metals by alchemy,
and you must recall, if I see you correctly,

how good an ape of nature I became."

CANTO XXX

Master Adam and the False Greek

Two terrible examples of insanity are cited at the beginning of this canto, the hallucination of Athamas and the hysterical grief of Hecuba. Two impersonators show a similar mania. One, Gianni Schicchi, had been engaged by Buoso Donati's son to impersonate his father and dictate a more favorable will. The commission was well performed except that the testator included himself in the legacy as the heir of the "queen of the herd," a valuable mare. The other example is that of Myrrha.

At the time when Juno because of Semele
was angry at the Theban royal family,
as she had shown already more than once,

Athamas was stricken with such madness
that on seeing his wife coming
burdened with two sons, one on either hand,

he shouted, "Let us spread the net, so that I
may catch the lioness and cubs as they pass";
then he stretched out his pitiless claws,

and seizing one, whose name was Learchus,
whirled him around and dashed him on a rock;
and she, with her other burden, drowned herself.[54] 12

And when Fortune had brought low
the bold pride of the Trojans
so that both king and kingdom were blotted out,

sad Hecuba, miserable and captive,[55]
after she had seen her [daughter] Polyxena slain
and, forlorn, recognized the body of [her son] Polydorus

on the shore of the sea, in her madness
barked like a dog, so greatly
had grief wrenched her mind.

But neither Theban nor Trojan Furies
were ever seen anywhere so cruel
in goading beasts, much less human bodies, 24

[54] Juno, angered at her consort Jupiter's love for Semele, a Theban princess who bore his son Bacchus, avenged herself on Semele's whole family. These included Semele's sister Ino, Ino's husband Athamas, and their children.

[55] Hecuba, queen of Troy, was carried off by the Greeks after they destroyed the city.

as those I saw in two spirits, pale and naked,
who ran biting as a hungry boar does
when just released from the sty.

One rushed on Capocchio and seized him
by the neck, then dragging him,
made his belly scrape on the hard bottom.

And the Aretine [Griffolino], who remained trembling,
said to me, "That mad one is Gianni Schicchi,
and he goes thus tearing others."

"Oh," I said to him, "so may the other
not bite you, please tell us
who it is before it gets away." 36

And he to me, "That is the ancient spirit
of wicked Myrrha;[56] who was devoted to her father
beyond the bounds of lawful love.

She came thus to sin with him,
changing herself into another's form,
just as the other who is running off

undertook, to gain the mistress of the herd,
to impersonate Buoso Donati,
making a will and giving it a legal form."

After the two mad ones on whom
I had kept my eyes had passed,
I turned to look at the other ill-born shades. 48

The counterfeiters are swollen with dropsy. One, a master of the art, had served the counts of Romena in one of the coolest, best watered of mountain regions, and the image of the place where he had worked increases the torture of his thirst. Amused at the size of Master Adam's belly, Dante asks about two shades on his boundaries. One, Sinon, suffering now from high fever, had pretended to be a fugitive from the Greeks, and had persuaded the Trojans to take in the wooden horse. The other liar is Potiphar's wife. Sinon objects to being called a "Greek from Troy," and we have a quarrel, the pot calling the kettle black. Sinon, considering each counterfeit coin as a separate indictment, charges Master Adam with the commission of more sins than any other demon. His opponent, in rebuttal, mentions the infamous notoriety Sinon has gained through the works of Homer and Virgil. Dante is scolded for listening to the quarrel. He tries to reply, but is so ashamed that he cannot, and excuses himself by this embarrassment more effectively than if he had been able to speak.

I saw one who would have looked like a lute
if only he had had his legs cut off
at the groin, where they join the body.

[56] The story of Myrrha's incestuous passion is told in Ovid's *Metamorphoses,* Book X.

The heavy dropsy, disproportioning him thus
with humors badly absorbed,
left his head too small for his belly,

and made him hold his lips apart
as the hectic does who, for thirst,
has one turned up, the other down.

"O you who are without any punishment
in this wretched world, and I don't know why,"
he said to us, "see and take note 60

of the misery of Master Adam!
When alive I had enough of what I wanted,
and now, alas! I long for a little drop of water.

The streams which from the green hills
of Casentino flow down to the Arno,
making their beds cool and soft,

always stand before my eyes and not in vain,
for the vision of them dries me up
more than the disease which wastes my features.

The rigid Justice which goads me
takes advantage of the place where I sinned
to put my sighs to quicker flight. 72

There is Romena where I counterfeited
the [Florentine] currency sealed with the Baptist's image,
for which I left my body burned above.

But if I could see the miserable soul
of Guido or of Alessandro or their brother [his employers]
I would not trade the sight for Fonte Branda [a spring].

One is already in, if the mad shades
that move around tell the truth,
but of what avail is it, if my limbs are tied?

Yet, if I were still nimble enough
to make an inch in a hundred years,
I would already have started out 84

to find them among these disgusting people,
although the ditch circles for eleven miles,
and is not less than half a mile across.

Because of them I am in such a household;
they induced me to stamp the florins
which had indeed *three* carats of alloy!"

And I to him, "Who are the two wretches,
steaming like wet hands in winter,
lying close to your right frontier?"

"Here I found them on raining down in this ditch,"
he answered, "since when they have not turned over,
nor will they, I believe, in eternity. 96

One is the lying woman who accused Joseph;[57]
the other is false Sinon, the Greek from Troy;
because of their fever they emit such stench."

And one of them [Sinon] who perhaps
took badly being named thus darkly,
with his fist struck the vile belly

which sounded like a drum, and Master Adam
struck him back in the face with his arm
which did not seem less hard,

saying to him, "Although locomotion is impossible
because of my heavy limbs,
I have an arm free for such business!" 108

Whereupon the other answered, "When you went
to the fire, you were not so quick,
but you were still quicker when you made the coins."

And he of the dropsy, "You tell the truth about this,
but you were not so good a witness
at Troy when the truth was asked of you."

"If I spoke falsely, you falsified the coins,"
said Sinon, "and I am here for one fault,
and you for more than any other demon."

"Remember, perjurer, the horse!" he of the swollen belly
answered, "and let it be a plague to you
that the whole world knows of it." 120

"And may the thirst that cracks your tongue
be a curse to you," said the Greek, "and the foul water
which makes a hedge before your eyes."

Then the counterfeiter, "Thus your mouth
still opens to your harm, as usual,
for, if I am thirsty and humor stuffs me up,

you have the burning and the headache,
and to lick the mirror[58] of Narcissus
you would not need a second invitation."

I was wholly intent on listening to them
when my master said to me, "Now keep on gazing!
a little more, and I will quarrel with you." 132

[57]After Joseph, son of Jacob, was sold into Egypt, the wife of Potiphar, an officer of Pharaoh, made sexual advances to Joseph. Rebuffed by him, she then accused him of making the advances. See Genesis 39.

[58]Water. Narcissus fell in love with his own reflected image.

When I heard him speak to me with anger,
I turned to him with such shame
that the memory of it still haunts me.

As one who dreams of a misfortune
and, while dreaming, hopes it is a dream,
so that he longs for what is as if it were not,

so I became, not being able to speak
although I wanted to excuse myself and did so,
without knowing that I was doing it.

"Less shame washes away a greater fault,"
said my master, "than yours has been;
therefore, free yourself of all sadness 144

and take note that I am at your side
if it happens again that chance catches you
where people are in a similar wrangle,

for wishing to overhear it is a low desire."

CANTO XXXI

The Giants

The same tongue first stung me
so that it tinted both my cheeks,
then offered me its cure.

Thus I hear that the lance of Achilles
and of his father was wont first
to wound and then to heal.

We turned our backs on the miserable ditch,
going up without speaking
over the bank which surrounds it.

Here it was less than night and less than day,
so that my sight did not go far;
but I heard a horn sound so loudly 12

that it would have made any thunder faint;
and retracing the course the sound took
I directed my eyes to one spot.

After the doleful rout,
when Charlemagne lost his holy company,
Roland did not blow so terribly.[59]

[59] See *The Song of Roland.* When Charlemagne's army returned from Spain toward France, Roland commanded the elite rear guard. Set upon by the pagans and defeated, Roland refused to blow his great horn to call for help until it was too late.

Only a short while did my eyes look toward the sound
when I seemed to see many high towers,
and I asked, "Master, tell me, what city is this?"

And he to me, "Since you are looking
through the darkness from too far off
your imagination leads you astray. 24

You will see when you arrive there
how the senses are deceived by distance;
therefore move a little faster."

Then he took me tenderly by the hand
and said, "Before we go farther,
to make the event seem less strange,

know that these are not towers, but giants,
and they are in the well around the bank
from the navel down, all of them."

As, when a mist has cleared somewhat,
our eyes little by little make out
what the vapor in the air had hidden, 36

so, piercing through the thick gloom
on approaching closer and closer to the bank,
my error fled, and my fear increased.

As, on the circle of its walls,
Montereggione [a fortress] is crowned with towers,
so, above the bank which surrounds the pit,

the horrible giants, whom Jove still threatens[60]
when he thunders in the heavens,
towered above us with half their bodies.

Already I saw the face, shoulders, and chest
of one, and a large part of his belly,
and both his arms down by his side. 48

Certainly when Nature gave up the art
of producing these creatures she did well
to deprive Mars of such agents;

and if she does not repent for elephants
and whales, whoever looks closely
will hold her more discreet and just,

for where the force of intellect [as in the giants]
is added to ill will and strength,
mankind can have no defense.

[60]Ovid's *Metamorphoses,* Book I, describes an attack on the gods by giants who piled mountains atop one another.

His face seemed to me as long and wide
as the pine cone[61] at St. Peter's in Rome,
and his other features were in proportion. 60

Thus the bank which was an apron
from his middle down, showed so much of him
that three Frieslanders [tall men] would have boasted

in vain to reach up to his hair.
I saw, indeed, thirty great spans[62] of him
down from [the neck] where a man buckles on his cloak.

Nimrod, the builder of the Tower of Babel, a "mighty hunter before the Lord," is with the giants who revolted against Jove. His words are meaningless. Virgil apostrophizes him for Dante's benefit. Then the travelers come to Antaeus, who was not present at the battle of the giants against the gods, and therefore is not bound like the others. Flattered by Virgil, who understands his fatuous character, Antaeus extends his hand and places the two poets on the bottom of the pit in the ninth and last circle.

"Raphèl maỳ amèch zabì almì"
the savage mouth for which sweeter
hymns were unfitting began to say.

And my guide to him, "Stupid soul,
keep to your horn, and with it express yourself
when anger or some other passion moves you. 72

Search around your neck and you will find the strap
which holds it, O confused spirit;
see it curving across your great chest."

Then he said to me, "He accuses himself.
This is Nimrod, through whose evil thought
a single tongue is not used in the world.[63]

Let us leave him and not speak in vain,
for, as the language of others is to him,
so is his to them, and is understood by none."

We kept on still to the left
and at the distance of a crossbow shot
we found another giant larger and fiercer. 84

Who the master was to bind him
I cannot say, but his right arm
at his back and the other in front

[61] A pine cone made of bronze, about ten feet high, is still visible in the Vatican.
[62] Hand spans.
[63] For the story of the Tower of Babel and the consequent confusion of tongues in the world, see Genesis 11.

were bound by a chain, which held him tied
from the neck down, so that over his exposed part
it encircled him five times.

"This haughty creature wished to make trial
of his power against supreme Jove,"
said my master; "therefore, he has such a reward.

Ephialtes is his name; he fought in the great battle
when the giants frightened the gods:
the arms he used once, he never moves." 96

Then I to my guide, "If possible
I should like for my eyes
to gain experience of the immense Briareus."

Whereupon he answered, "You will see Antaeus
nearby, who speaks and is unbound
and who will put us in the lowest depth of guilt.

The one you wish to see is farther on
and is bound and built like this one
except that he looks more ferocious."

Never did an earthquake jar
so violently a massive tower
as Ephialtes suddenly shook himself. 108

Then I feared death more than ever,
and fright alone would have caused it,
if I had not seen the chains.

We went on then and came to Antaeus
who protruded above the bank
fully five ells,[64] not counting his head.

"O you who in the fateful valley
which made Scipio an heir of glory,
when Hannibal and his army turned back,[65]

you who once brought a thousand lions as prey—
and, if you had fought in the great war,
with your brothers, it seems that some believe 120

the sons of Earth [the giants] might have conquered—
put us down, do not disdain to do so,
to where cold locks up Cocytus.

Do not make us go to Tityus or to Typhon;
this man can give what is longed for here;
therefore bend over and do not scornfully refuse.

[64]An ell is about four or five feet.
[65]Scipio and Hannibal were, respectively, Roman and Carthaginian generals.

He can revive your fame in the world,
for he lives and expects a long life, if Divine Grace
does not call him to herself ahead of time."

Thus my master spoke, and Antaeus
hurriedly held out the hand whose grip
Hercules once felt, and took hold of my master. 132

When Virgil felt himself grasped,
he said to me, "Come, let me take hold of you."
Then, of himself and me he made one bundle.

As the Garisenda tower seems to fall
if looked at under its leaning side
when a cloud passes over it in the opposite direction,

so Antaeus appeared to me as I watched
while he bent over; and he was such
that I would have wished to go by another way.

But lightly in the depth which swallows
Lucifer with Judas he placed us,
nor did he delay long bent over 144

but rose like a mast set in a ship.

CANTO XXXII

The Traitors

The tone of the Comedy now becomes harsh, scornful, vindictive. Dante again calls upon the Muses, but this time on those who helped to build Thebes, "the ancient home of crime."

If I had rhymes rough and harsh enough
to be fitting for the dismal hole
on which all the other circles weigh,

I would press out the substance of my conception
more fully; but since I do not have them,
not without fear do I bring myself to speak.

For, to describe the bottom of the whole universe
is not an enterprise to take up in jest,
nor for a tongue that still cries "mamma" and "papa."

But may those ladies who helped Amphion
to enclose Thebes aid my verse,
so that words and facts will not differ. 12

O rabble, miscreated above all others,
in this place to speak of which is hard,
here [on earth] you would better have been sheep or goats!

When we were down in the dark well
beyond the feet of the giant and much lower,
and as I was still looking at the high wall,

I heard someone say, "Watch how you step!
Move so you won't trample with your feet
on the heads of the weary, miserable brothers."

Then I turned and saw a lake in front of me
and under my feet which, frozen,
had the appearance of glass and not of water. 24

The Danube in Austria never made in winter
so thick a veil for its current,
nor the Don up there under its cold skies,

as this did; for if Tambernicchi [a mountain]
had fallen on it, or Pietrapana,
it would not have given a creak even at the edge.

And as a frog lies croaking
with just its muzzle out, in the season
when the peasant woman thinks of gleaning,

so the shades were lying in the ice,
livid up to where shame appears,
their teeth chattering like storks' bills. 36

Each held his face down; their mouths
gave evidence of the cold,
and their eyes of their sad hearts.

Caïna, the first division of the ninth circle, contains traitors to kindred, among whom are the counts of Mangona, who killed each other in a quarrel over an inheritance. Other minor figures also are mentioned.

When I had looked around a little,
I glanced at my feet and saw two so bound together
that the hair on their heads was intermingled.

"Tell me, you who press your chests so close together,
who you are," I asked, and they bent their necks,
and after they had lifted their faces to me,

their eyes, which previously were wet only within,
gushed through the lids, and the cold
froze their tears and locked them up again. 48

A clamp never bound wood to wood so strongly.
Then they, like two goats,
butted each other, such anger overcame them.

And one who had lost both ears from the cold,
with his face still downward, said,
"Why do you look at us so much?

If you want to know who these two are,
the valley from which the Bisenzio flows
belonged to them and to their father, Albert.

They came from one body, and you might search
through all Caïna[66] without finding a shade
more worthy to be preserved in ice, 60

not him [Mordred] whose breast and shadow
were laid open by a single blow from Arthur's hand,[67]
not Focaccia; not this one who covers me

with his head, so that I cannot see beyond
and whose name was Sassol Mascheroni,—
if you are a Tuscan you know now who he was.

And, so that you will not put me to further speech,
know that I was Camicion de' Pazzi, and am waiting
for Carlino to make me [by comparison] seem innocent."

Afterward I saw a thousand faces made doglike
by the cold; so that a shudder comes to me
and always will at the sight of frozen pools. 72

Passing on to Antenora, the second division of the ninth circle, where traitors to party and country are kept, Dante accidentally kicks one shade who mentions Montaperti, the scene of a defeat of the Florentine Guelfs. Dante's suspicion is immediately aroused, and he tries by force to make the shade name himself. Another, however, treacherously gives him away as Bocca degli Abati who, at a critical moment in the battle, cut off the hand of the Florentine standardbearer, an act which was thought to have caused the defeat. Dante's violence incurs no reproach: the implication is that ordinary rules of conduct are inapplicable to the completely depraved: one must keep away from them or act according to the code they establish. This is the realistic Gresham's law of competitive behavior. Bocca in turn mentions others, including Buoso da Duera, who had been bribed by Charles of Anjou, and Ganelon, the traitor in the Song of Roland.

And while we were moving toward the center
to which all weights are drawn
and I was shivering in the eternal chill,

whether it was destiny or chance, I know not,
but while walking among the heads
my foot struck hard against the face of one.

Weeping it cried, "Why do you kick me?
Unless you come to increase the vengeance
for Montaperti, why do you molest me?"

And I, "Master, now wait for me here
until this one relieves me of a doubt,
then you can make me hurry as you wish." 84

[66] Named for Cain, who murdered his brother Abel (Genesis 4). All the treacherous sinners punished in this and the other three divisions of the ninth circle happen also to be involved in murder.

[67] Mordred was the evil nephew of King Arthur and a would-be usurper. Arthur killed him with a blow that penetrated his whole body.

My guide stood still, and I said to the shade
who was still cursing loudly,
"Who are you complaining thus of others?"

"Now who are you, going through Antenora[68]
kicking others' cheeks," he answered,
"harder than if you were alive?"

"I am alive," was my response,
"and it may be dear to you, if you want fame,
that I should include your name in my notes."

And he to me, "The contrary is what I want,
get away from here; do not bother me,
for you know badly how to flatter in this bottom." 96

Then I seized him by the scalp and said,
"You will name yourself
or not a hair will be left on your head."

And he to me, "Even if you tear it out
and fall on my head a thousand times,
I will not tell or show you who I am."

I had already twisted his hair in my hand
and had pulled out more than one tuft,
he howling with eyes cast down,

when another shouted, "What's the matter with you, Bocca?
Isn't it enough to chatter with your jaws
but you must bark?—What devil is after you?" 108

"Now," I said, "I do not want you to speak,
damned traitor, for to your shame
I will carry off true news of you."

"Go," he answered, "and tell what you want,
but if you get out of here, don't keep silent
about him who has his tongue so ready.

He is weeping here for the money of the French.
'I saw,' you can say, 'him of Duera,
down there where sinners are put to cool.'

If any one asks about the others here,
you have beside you the one of Beccheria
whose throat was cut by Florence. 120

Gianni de' Soldanier, I believe,
is farther on, with Ganelon, and Tebaldello
who opened Faenza while it was sleeping."

[68]Antenor was a Trojan who, according to medieval legend, betrayed his city to the Greeks. He is treated favorably in Homer's *Iliad*.

We now see a bestial example of hatred. One shade is gnawing the head of another, as Tydeus, after being mortally wounded by Menalippus whom he in turn killed, called for the head of his enemy and chewed on it. Aghast at such a sight, Dante wonders what could motivate such hatred and offers to help in the vengeance by making the reason for it known in case there is just cause.

We had already departed from him
when I saw two frozen in one hole,
so that the head of one was a hood for the other,

and as bread is chewed from hunger,
so the one on top set his teeth in the other
where the brain joins the neck.

Not otherwise did Tydeus gnaw
in his rage the temples of Menalippus
than he did this one's skull and flesh. 132

"O you who show by such bestial signs
hatred of him whom you are chewing,
tell me why," I said, "on this condition

that if you rightfully complain of him,
knowing who you are and his sin,
I may repay you up in the world

if that [tongue] with which I speak is not dried up [by death]."

CANTO XXXIII

COUNT UGOLINO

Count Ugolino, a Pisan, had allied himself with the Florentine Guelfs and in 1285 was in control of his city. Perhaps he is among the traitors because of this change of party and because of the transfer of certain castles. In that year the Ghibellines, led by the Archbishop Ruggieri, revolted. Ugolino was called treacherously to a parley, then imprisoned with two sons and two grandsons in what was later known as the "Tower of Hunger." After some months the door of the prison was nailed shut, and the five were left to die of starvation. The bodies, on their removal, appeared mutilated, perhaps rat-bitten. Ugolino recognizes Dante as a Florentine, therefore a Guelf, and explains why he is violating so terribly the obligations of a neighbor.

The sinner raised his mouth from his fierce repast,
wiping it on the hair of the head
the back of which he had despoiled,

and then began, "You wish that I renew
desperate grief, which wrings my heart,
merely in thinking of it, before I speak.

But if my words can be seeds to bear infamy
to the traitor I am gnawing,
you will see me both speak and weep.

I do not know who you are, nor by what means
you have come down here, but certainly
you seem a Florentine when I hear you. 12

You must understand that I was Count Ugolino,
and this is the Archbishop Ruggieri;
now I will tell you why I am such a neighbor.

How, as the result of his evil thoughts,
I was seized, trusting in him,
and put to death, there is no need to tell,

but what you cannot have learned, that is,
how cruel my death was, you will hear
and know if he has offended me.

As in the Francesca episode, so here Dante reconstructs what could not be known, that is, the lonely, unwitnessed death of the five in prison. In the tower (compared to a "mew" in which falcons were kept while molting) several months had passed when a symbolic and prophetic dream revealed to the prisoners their fate. In describing it, Ugolino's fierce memory gets ahead of his words: the wolf becomes "a father" and the whelps "sons," and he turns on Dante, reproaching the poet for lack of feeling before he has told what happened.

A little loophole in the mew which
because of me was called the 'Tower of Hunger'
and in which others will be imprisoned 24

had shown through its opening several moons already
when I had the evil dream
which tore away the veil of the future.

This one seemed the lord and master of the hunt,
chasing the wolf and whelps on the mountain
which prevents the Pisans from seeing Lucca.

With lean, eager, and well-trained hounds [the mob],
he had placed the Gualandi, Sismondi,
and Lanfranchi [as leaders] in front of him.

After a short course, the father and the sons
seemed to me weary, and I thought I saw
their bodies torn by the sharp teeth. 36

When I had awakened before the dawn
I heard my children who were with me
weeping in their sleep and asking for bread.

You are cruel indeed not to grieve already
in thinking of what my heart foreboded;
and if you do not weep now, by what are you ever moved?

The drama passes in silence: almost nothing is said. On the first day Anselm, the smallest, showed concern for his father. On the second, Ugolino bit his hands from grief. That and the third day passed in complete silence. On the fourth,

Gaddo weakened and died, and on the fifth and sixth, the others. On the seventh, Ugolino crawled over the bodies, and on the eighth, he succumbed, hunger having accomplished what grief could not do.

The hatred of Ugolino is communicated to Dante who bursts out in an invective against Pisa.

They were now awake, and the hour drew near
when our food used to be brought to us,
and each was afraid because of his dream;

and below I heard the door of the horrible tower
nailed up; whereupon, without saying a word,
I looked into the faces of my sons. 48

I did not weep, so stony did I become within.
They cried, and my little Anselm said,
'You look so [hard], father, what ails you?'

Still I shed no tears nor did I answer
during all that day and the night after,
until another sun came forth upon the world.

When a little light had entered
the awful prison, and I saw
on four faces my own aspect,

I bit both my hands from grief,
and they, thinking I did it from hunger,
suddenly got up and said, 60

'Father, it will be much less painful
if you eat of us; you clothed us
with this poor flesh; may you take it from us!'

I became quiet then not to make them more sad.
That day and the next we all remained mute.
Ah, hard earth, why did you not open!

After we had reached the fourth day,
Gaddo fell stretched out at my feet, saying,
'Father, why don't you help me?'

There he died; and as you see me
I saw the three of them fall one by one
between the fifth day and the sixth; then I began, 72

already blind, to crawl over each, and for two days
I called them after they were dead.
Then fasting did more than grief."[69]

When he had said this, with eyes awry,
he seized again the wretched head with his teeth
which gnawed upon the bone, like a dog's.

[69] This line can mean that hunger could make him die as grief could not or else that Ugolino was driven to cannibalism.

Ah, Pisa! shame of the people.
of the beautiful land [Italy] where "si" ["yes"] is heard,
since your neighbors are slow to punish you,

may the Capraia and Gorgona [islands] move
and make a dam for the Arno at its mouth,[70]
so that it may drown everyone in you; 84

for if Count Ugolino was reputed
to have betrayed you of the castle,
you should not have put his sons on such a cross.

Their young age made Uguccione
and Brigata innocent, you modern Thebes![71]
and the other two named by my song.

The poets move on to Tolomea, the third division, where traitors to guests are punished. The heads of these sinners are thrown back, so that the tears, freezing in the cups of their eyes, cause a painful pressure.

We went farther on to where the frost
roughly binds another people
with faces thrown back, not turned down.

Weeping there prevents them from weeping:
the tears which find a barrier in the eyes
turn inward to increase the pain, 96

since they form a solid mass,
and like visors of crystal fill
the whole cavity beneath the eyebrows.

And, although, as in a callused spot,
every feeling had gone from my face
because of the intense cold,

already I seemed to notice a wind,
so that I said, "Master, what causes this?
Is not all vapor [atmospheric change] absent down here?"

And he to me, "Soon you will be
where your eyes will see the cause
of the blast and will give you the answer." 108

And one of the wretches in the cold crust
shouted at us, "O souls so cruel
that the last place is assigned to you,

take from my eyes the hard veils,
so that I may relieve the pain a little
that stuffs my heart before the tears freeze again."

To induce this soul to speak, Dante makes a promise with false intent, that is, he commits fraud, as previously in this circle he had committed violence. Our

[70] Pisa is at the mouth of the river Arno.
[71] Thebes was considered the most wicked of the ancient cities.

poet is emphasizing again, in opposition to certain idealists, that golden rules and codes of honor presuppose a certain uniformity in the social group. To apply them without discrimination is merely to favor and give superior survival value to the fraudulent and dishonorable.

The soul whom Dante has tricked had had guests murdered at a banquet, the signal for the execution being, "Bring on the fruit." He is now getting expensive dates for cheap figs, that is, being repaid with interest. His soul, apparently, has descended "quick" into Hell, and is replaced in his body by a demon.

And I to him, "If you want me to help you,
tell me who you are, and if I do not relieve you,
may I go to the bottom of the ice!"[72]

He answered then, "I am Friar Alberigo,
he of the fruit of the evil garden,
and am getting here dates for my figs." 120

"Oh," I said to him, "are you dead already?"
And he to me, "How my body fares
in the world above, I have no knowledge.

Such an advantage this Tolomea[73] has
that often a soul falls into it
before Atropos [a Fate] has thrust it forth.

And—so may you remove more willingly
the frozen tears from my face—
know that when a soul betrays as I did,

its body is taken from it by a demon
who afterward controls the flesh
until its allotted years have passed. 132

It falls into such a cistern as this,
and perhaps the body of the shade
wintering behind me appears on earth.

You must know him if you have just come down;
He is Ser Branca d'Oria [a Genoese], and many years
have passed since he was thus locked up."

"I believe that you are deceiving me,"
I said to him, "for Branca d'Oria has not died,
but eats and sleeps and puts on clothes."

"In the ditch of the Malebranche above,"
he said, "where the tenacious pitch is boiling,
Michel Zanche [his victim] had not yet arrived 144

when a devil took over his body
and that of a close relative
who did the treacherous act with him.

[72] Dante must in any event go beneath the ice, because that is the way out of Hell; see the next canto.

[73] Probably named for Ptolemy, a soldier of Jericho who in 1 Maccabees 16 murders several of his relatives whom he invited to a banquet.

But reach out your hand, open my eyes";
and I did not open them for him;
and to be rude to him was fitting.

Ah, Genoese, men who are estranged
from all good ways and full of all corruption,
why are you not scattered from the earth,

for, with the worst spirit of Romagna [Alberigo],
I found one of you whose soul
for his deeds already bathes in Cocytus, 156

and in body seems still alive on earth!

CANTO XXXIV

SATAN

To the first words of a Latin hymn to the cross, "The banners of the Lord come forth, . . ." Dante adds the word inferni, *applying them thus to Satan, the lord of Hell. Dante is now in Giudecca where traitors to benefactors are completely submerged in the ice.*

Satan is represented as the counterpart of the Trinity, with heads of three colors, yellow, black, and red, standing for impotence, ignorance, and hate, and corresponding to the divine power, wisdom, and love. His three pairs of wings send forth a threefold blast which freezes Cocytus. In the mouths of Lucifer are Judas, the traitor to Christ, and Brutus and Cassius, traitors to the Roman Empire. The poets reach Satan at six o'clock on Saturday evening, having spent twenty-four hours on the journey.

"*Vexilla Regis prodeunt inferni*
toward us, therefore, look ahead,"
my master said, "and try to discern him."

As, when a thick mist covers the land
or when night darkens our hemisphere,
a windmill, turning, appears from afar,

so now I seemed to see such a structure;
then because of the wind, I drew back
behind my guide, for there was no other protection.

Already—and with fear I put it into verse—
I was where the shades are covered in the ice
and show through like bits of straw in glass. 12

Some were lying, some standing erect,
some on their heads, others on their feet,
still others like a bow bent face to toes.

When we had gone so far ahead
that my master was pleased to show me
the creature [Lucifer] that once had been so fair,

he stood from in front of me, and made me stop,
saying, "Behold, Dis![74] Here is the place
where you must arm yourself with courage."

How faint and frozen I then became,
do not ask, Reader, for I do not write it down,
since all words would be inadequate. 24

I did not die and did not stay alive:
think now for yourself, if you have the wit
how I became, without life or death.

The emperor of the dolorous realm
from mid-breast protruded from the ice,
and I compare better in size

with the giants than they do with his arms.
Consider how big the whole must be,
proportioned as it is to such a part.

If he were once as handsome as he is ugly now,
and still presumed to lift his hand against his Maker,
all affliction must indeed come from him. 36

Oh, how great a marvel appeared to me
when I saw three faces on his head!
The one in front [hatred] was fiery red;

the two others which were joined to it
over the middle of each shoulder
were fused together at the top.

The right one [impotence] seemed between white and yellow;
the left [ignorance] was in color like those
who come from where the Nile rises.

Under each two great wings spread
of a size fitting to such a bird;
I have never seen such sails on the sea. 48

They had no feathers, and seemed
like those of a bat, and they flapped,
so that three blasts came from them.

Thence all Cocytus was frozen.
With six eyes he wept, and over his three chins
he let tears drip and bloody foam.

In each mouth he chewed a sinner with his teeth
in the manner of a hemp brake,[75]
so that he kept three in pain.

[74] Satan. (Dis, or Pluto, was the ancient god of the Underworld.)
[75] A machine for crushing stalks of hemp.

To the one in front the biting was nothing
compared to the scratching, for at times,
his back was stripped of skin. 60

"The soul up there with the greatest punishment,"
said my master, "is Judas Iscariot. His head
is inside the mouth, and he kicks with his legs.

Of the other two whose heads are down,
the one hanging from the black face is Brutus;
see how he twists and says nothing.

The other who seems so heavy set is Cassius.[76]
But night is rising again now,
and it is time to leave, for we have seen all."

At the center of the earth, also the center of gravity, the poets turn and begin climbing laboriously, the effort symbolizing the difficulty of getting rid of bad habits even when their ugliness is known. Lucifer now appears upside down, and the time changes to Saturday morning, since the travelers gain twelve hours in passing from Jerusalem time to that of Purgatory, directly opposite.

Through the passage made by Lucifer as he fell, the poets reach the foot of Purgatory just before dawn on Easter Sunday.

Each part of the Comedy ends with the word "stars," which stand for the goal of the journey, the objects farthest removed from Satan and the materialism of the earth, and whose beauty is most ethereal.

When my guide was ready, I embraced his neck,
and he took advantage of the time and place
so that when the wings were wide open 72

he caught hold of the shaggy sides
and descended from tuft to tuft
between the tangled hair and the frozen crust.

When we were at the place where the thigh
revolves on the swelling of the haunches,
my guide, with effort and with difficulty,

turned his head to where he had had his feet,
and grappled the hair, like one mounting,
so that I thought he was returning into Hell.

"Hold fast, for by such stairs,"
my master said, panting like one weary,
"we must depart from so much evil." 84

Then he came through the opening in a rock
and put me on its edge, sitting,
and climbed toward me with wary steps.

[76] The place of Brutus and Cassius, the assassins of Julius Caesar, at the center of Hell is a surprise to modern readers accustomed to think of them as heroic opponents of tyranny. But to Dante they were traitors to the Roman Empire (in the person of Caesar), the agency of earthly rule that properly counterweighs spiritual authority (Christ through the papacy).

I raised my eyes and thought
that I would find Lucifer as I had left him,
but saw him holding up his legs,

and if I then became perplexed,
let dull people imagine who do not see
what the point was that I had passed.

"Get up on your feet," said my master,
"the road is long and the path rough, and already
the sun has returned to mid-tierce [at 7:30 A.M.]." 96

The place where we were
was no palace hall, but a natural dungeon,
dark and with an uneven floor.

"Before I uproot myself from the abyss, Master,"
I said when I was standing,
"speak to me a little to dispel my error.

Where is the ice? and how is Satan planted
so upside down? and how in such a short time
has the sun made its way from evening to morning?"

And he to me, "You still imagine you are
on the other side of the center where I grasped the hair
of the wicked monster that pierces the world. 108

You were over there as long as I descended;
when I turned, you passed the point
to which all weights are drawn.

Now you have arrived in the hemisphere
opposite that which dry land covers
and at whose summit [Jerusalem] was consumed

the man [Christ] who was born and lived without sin.
You have your feet on a little circle
which forms the other face of Giudecca.[77]

Here it is morning when it is evening there,
and Satan who made a ladder for us
with his hair is still as he was before. 120

On this side he fell from Heaven, and the earth here,
through fear, made a veil for itself
of the sea, and came to our hemisphere,

and perhaps the land [Purgatory] which shows on this side,
to flee from him, rushed up
and left this passageway empty."[78]

[77] The innermost ring of the plain of ice; named for Judas.

[78] When Satan fell from Heaven into the southern hemisphere, the land there recoiled from him into the northern hemisphere; also, the land within the earth rushed back from him to form the island of Purgatory in the southern ocean, leaving empty the cavern through which Virgil and Dante emerge from Hell.

There is a place as remote
from Beelzebub[79] as his tomb extends,
not known by sight, but by the sound

of a little stream which descends in it
along the hollow of a rock which it has eaten out
with a slow and winding course."[80] 132

My guide and I started on that hidden way
to return to the bright world,
and, without caring for any rest,

we climbed, he first and I second,
until I saw, through a round opening,
the beautiful things that heaven bears,

and came forth to see again the stars.

OUTLINE OF PURGATORY

REGION	VICES	METHOD OF SUGGESTION	DISCIPLINES
Shore	[Excommunicated]		Waiting
Below gate	[Negligent]		Waiting
Ledge 1	Pride	Sculptures	Bending necks under heavy weights
Ledge 2	Envy	Voices	Practice in using other senses besides sight
Ledge 3	Anger	Visual and auditory imagery	Satiation with blindness of wrath
Ledge 4	Sloth	Recitation	Developing habit of speedy activity
Ledge 5	Avarice and Prodigality	Recitation	Satiation with living close to the ground
Ledge 6	Gluttony	Voices	Practice in abnegation
Ledge 7	Lust	Recitation	Purification by fire
The Earthly Paradise (Garden of Eden).			

NOTE: The suggestive treatment consists of constant contemplation of the "goads" and "checks," that is, beautiful examples of the opposite virtue and repulsive illustrations of the vice itself.

The first three vices are due to love of a bad object, the fourth to insufficient love, and the last three to disproportionate love.

[79] Here, another name for Satan.

[80] The stream is the river Lethe, which from Eden atop the mountain of Purgatory flows down to the center of the earth to join the four rivers of Hell, carrying with it the memory of the vices expiated in Purgatory. All evil, committed by the saved and the damned, thus comes to rest as dead weight, frozen and immobile, at the point of the universe farthest removed from God.

A diagram of Purgatory.

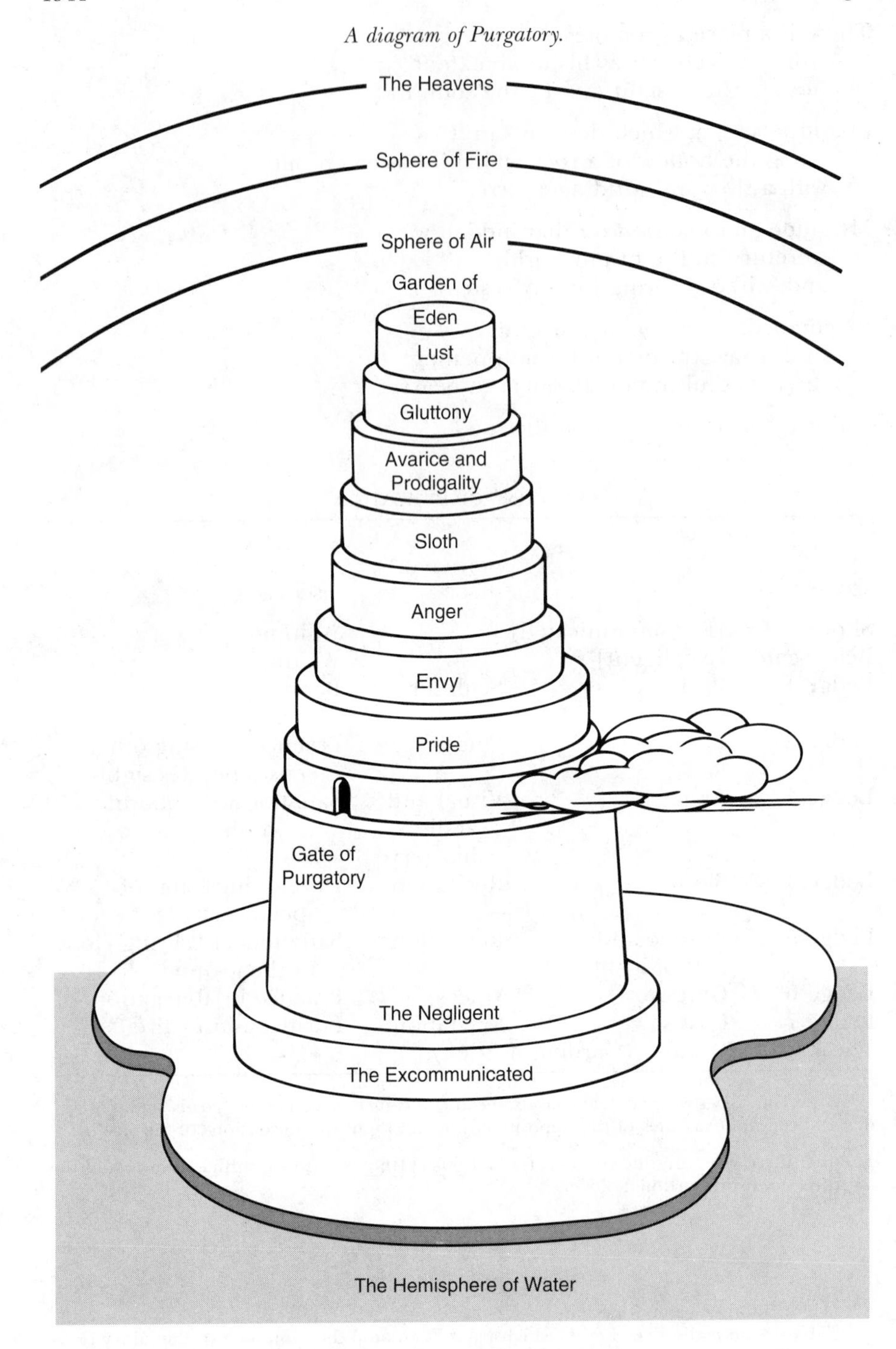

from PURGATORY

CANTO I

CATO

Dante indicates his new subject and invokes the "holy" Muses, especially Calliope, the inspirer of epic poetry whom the daughters of King Pieros once challenged in song, for which boldness they were changed into magpies. It is just before sunrise on Easter, April 10, 1300. The morning star, Venus, is obscuring with its light the constellation of the Fishes. In the new sky are four stars representing the cardinal virtues—Prudence, Temperance, Fortitude, and Justice[1]*—previously seen only by Adam and Eve.*

To move over better waters now hoists sail
the little vessel of my mind
which leaves behind so rough a sea;

and I will sing of the second realm
where the human spirit is cleansed
and becomes worthy to rise to Heaven.

Here, O holy Muses, since I am yours,
let dead poetry be revived
and let Calliope arise a while,

accompanying my song with the music
which struck the ears of the wretched magpies
so that they despaired of pardon. 12

A sweet color of oriental sapphire
which was forming in the clear sky,
pure from the zenith to the horizon,

restored delight to my eyes
as soon as I came out of the dead air
that had afflicted both my eyes and lungs.

The beautiful planet which prompts to love
made the whole east smile,
veiling the Fishes that escorted her.

I turned to the right and set my mind
on the other pole, and I noticed four stars
never seen except by the first people. 24

The heavens seemed to rejoice in their light.
O region of the north, widowed!
since you are denied that view.

Cato, Dante's favorite hero of antiquity and the symbol of Free Will, appears, his face shining with the light of the four virtues. Rather than submit to Caesar, he had committed suicide, a Christian but not a pagan sin. For this devotion

[1]Also called the "natural virtues" or "moral virtues."

to freedom and for other merits he is made the guardian of Purgatory and will be saved on Judgment Day.[2]

When I had withdrawn my eyes from them,
turning for a moment to the north
where the Great Bear [Dipper] had already disappeared,

I saw a solitary old man near me,
in semblance worthy of so much reverence
than no son owes more to his father.

The beard he wore was long
and streaked with white, like his hair
of which two tresses fell upon his breast. 36

The rays of the four holy lights
so brightened his face that he appeared
as if the sun were shining on him.

"Who are you who, moving up the dark stream,
have fled from the eternal prison?"
he asked, shaking his plumelike beard.

"Who has guided you or given you a light
to issue from the black night
which darkens the infernal depth?

Are the laws of the abyss thus broken,
or have decrees been changed in Heaven
so that the damned may come to my cliffs?" 48

My guide then took hold of me,
and with words and hands and gestures
made reverent my knees and brow.

Then he answered, "By myself I do not come;
a lady descended from Heaven, at whose prayers
I helped this man with my companionship.

But, since it is your will that more
of our present condition be explained,
my will is not able to refuse you.

The man has not seen his last hour,
but through his folly was so close to it
that there was little time left. 60

I was sent to him, as I said,
to rescue him, and there was no other way
than this one on which I have started.

I have shown him all the wicked people
and now propose to reveal those spirits
who are purging themselves under your charge.

[2] There were two famous Romans named Cato. This one is Cato the Younger (95–46 B.C.).

How I have brought him here would take long to tell;
a Power from above has helped me
to bring him to see and to hear you.

May it please you to welcome his coming;
he is seeking freedom, which is precious,
as one who gives up life for it knows. 72

You understand, since death for you was not bitter
in Utica where you left the clothing of your flesh
which, on the great day, will be so bright.

The eternal laws are not broken by us,
for this man lives, and Minos does not condemn me.
I am from the circle where the chaste eyes

of your Marcia still seem to supplicate,
O holy breast! that you hold her for your own.
For love of her, then, incline toward us;

let us go through your seven kingdoms;
I will tell her of your grace
if you deign to be mentioned down there." 84

Cato states plainly his indifference to the fate of his wife, Marcia: the felicity of Heaven would be impaired if earthly relationships were not ended and if sorrow could be felt for the damned. He directs Virgil to gird Dante with a reed (Humility) and to wash his face, so that he can appear properly before the guardians of the ledges of Purgatory. The sun (Righteous Choice, Enlightenment) must be their guide henceforth.

The two poets descend to the sea which Ulysses alone had sailed. There, the reed which Virgil plucks for Dante replaces itself. Humility cannot be defeated: the more it is crushed the more it grows.

"Marcia pleased my eyes so much
while I was yonder," he said then,
"that I granted all the favors she asked.

Now that she dwells beyond the evil stream
she cannot move me because of the law
which was made when I came from there.

But if a lady from Heaven sends and commands you,
as you say, there is no need for coaxing;
it is enough that you ask me for her sake.

Go then and see that you gird this man
with a slender rush, and that you bathe his face,
so that all stains are washed from it, 96

for it would not be fitting that eyes
darkened by any mist should meet
the first minister of those in Paradise.

This little island, around its very base,
where the waves beat upon it,
bears reeds upon the soft mud.

No other plant which brings forth leaves
or grows hard could exist there,
since it would not yield to the waves.

Afterward do not return along here;
the sun which is rising now will show you
the easiest way to climb the mount." 108

Then he disappeared, and I got up
without speaking and drew close
to my guide, my eyes fixed on him.

He began, "My son, follow my steps,
let us turn back, for from here
the plain slopes down to its low bounds."

The dawn was dispelling the morning hour
which fled before it, so that from afar
I recognized the trembling of the sea.

We went over the solitary plain
like men returning to the road they have lost
who, until they get there, seem to walk in vain. 120

When we reached the place where the dew
contends with the sun and
in shaded spots had dried but little,

my master softly placed both hands
spread out on the wet grass,
and I, aware of his purpose,

held toward him my tear-stained cheeks
on which he wholly restored the color
which the smoke of Hell had hidden.

We came then to the deserted shore
whose waters had never been sailed
by anyone who afterward was able to return. 132

There he girded me, as another [Cato] wished.
O marvel! for, as he plucked the humble plant,
it was suddenly reborn as it was

in the place from which he had torn it.

CANTO II. *As a beautiful day dawns, a boat arrives at the island (the counterpart of Charon's boat at the border of Hell), bearing souls of the saved. One of the new arrivals is the musician Casella, an old friend of Dante's. Casella performs for Dante a song Dante himself had written, a fact that shows the survival among the saved of personal attributes they had in their former lives on earth. Cato rebukes the company for this delay, and they hasten toward the mountain of Purgatory.*

CANTO III. *At the foot of the mountain, unable to begin their ascent as yet, though they are eager to do so, are persons who died in the state of excommunication from the Church. This ecclesiastical penalty is observed in Purgatory but limited in its effect: the souls in question must delay their cleansing on the mount for a period thirty times as long as they lived excommunicated.*

CANTO IV. *Dante and Virgil pass through a fissure in the rock and make the arduous climb to the lowermost slope of the mountain. Dante is startled to see the sun to the north rather than (as in the northern hemisphere) to the south. Virgil comforts the exhausted Dante by telling him that the ascent becomes progressively easier as they climb the mountain. (This is because the burden of inclination to sin is progressively lightened.) They come upon another group of souls debarred as yet from Purgatory proper; these are the persons who repented only at the last minute, and they must delay their purgation for a period as long as they remained unrepentant in life.*

CANTO V. *Continuing up and around the mountain (which they must ascend counterclockwise), Dante and Virgil meet a group of late-repentant souls who were violently slain, including Jacopo del Cassero and a woman named Pia, who tells in a mere half-dozen lines a poignant story of death at her husband's hands. Here, as elsewhere in Purgatory, the souls are eager that the living pray for them, thus making their purgatorial process quicker and easier. Such mutual assistance and communication between the living and dead are part of the Dantean and Catholic understanding of the "communion of saints" mentioned in the Apostles' Creed.*

CANTO VI. *Virgil explains to Dante the nature of prayer—the fact, for example, that it does not deflect the divine will—but adds that a full explanation can come only from Christian revelation as embodied in Beatrice. At the mention of his beloved lady, Dante is excitedly eager to ascend. A cordial meeting between Virgil and Sordello, another man from Mantua, leads Dante to a sad comparison with the hatred and division that afflict the present cities of Italy, especially Florence.*

CANTO VII. *Virgil explains to Sordello, in a poignant passage, his own exclusion from salvation. Sordello explains to the two pilgrims that after sunset no one can ascend the mountain. He leads them to a peaceful valley where former monarchs who neglected the spiritual side of life must now delay their desired purgatorial discipline. In their fraternal amity, the rulers make a striking contrast with their former selves and many among the current generation of rulers.*

CANTO VIII. *Dante converses with some of the rulers, who, like other souls on the mountain, are astounded to learn that he still lives. The Valley, because it is outside Purgatory proper and therefore not immune to evil, is guarded by angels, who drive off an evil serpent that approaches. In the night sky are shining the three stars representing the "theological virtues" of faith, hope, and love. It is only during the day, however, when the four stars representing the moral virtues—prudence, justice, temperance, and fortitude—are above, that souls can ascend. This is a way of saying that the Purgatorial process leads essentially to natural rather than supernatural perfection.*

CANTO IX. *In sleep (his first since before the descent to Hell), Dante is borne upward by St. Lucia, to the outside of the gate of Purgatory proper. It is now morning, when ascent can take place. After ceremonially re-enacting the sacrament of Penance, or confession, Dante is admitted through the gate by the angel who guards it. On Dante's forehead the angel engraves seven P's standing for the seven capital sins* (peccata). *These will be erased, one by one, as Dante moves through the seven corresponding mountain ledges of Purgatory.*

CANTO X. *Being careful to observe the angel's command not to look back, Dante enters Purgatory proper and climbs upward with Virgil. They emerge on a terrace, some eighteen feet wide, its outer edge exposed dizzyingly to the sheer drop of the mountain wall. Here the vice of pride, which underlies all the others, is punished. The purgatorians must bend low under the weight of great stones they are carrying on their backs. On each terrace, "checks" and "goads" will appear, drawn from sacred and secular history. The checks are warnings about the vice punished; the goads are examples of the opposing virtue. On the terrace of pride, the goads consist of scenes, illustrating humility, carved on the inner wall.*

CANTO XI. *Dante must stoop down to converse with the proud souls. Thus, here as elsewhere in Purgatory, he participates in the discipline of suffering rather than simply observing it. Among the prideful is the painter Oderisi, who outlines the process by which new schools of painting and poetry (including Dante's own school) succeed one another. All will be superseded in turn, and therefore artists ought to feel no prideful sense of triumph. The same is true of military glory.*

CANTO XII. *On the ground the pilgrims walk upon are carved the checks: instances of proud behavior. The proud are thus brought low in contrast with the humble whose deeds are carved on the vertical inner wall. Before leaving the Terrace of Pride and climbing the stairs to the next terrace, Dante and Virgil meet an angel, who erases the first of the seven P's from Dante's brow, the incision of the other six P's thereby becoming shallower. The ascent will now become easier. A voice is heard quoting, from the gospel Beatitudes, the blessing on the poor in spirit. A corresponding angelic absolution and scriptural acclamation will recur on the other six terraces.*

CANTO XIII. *On the second terrace, of Envy, Dante meets souls whose eyelids are stitched shut, removing their perception of the beautiful and good things that they had once begrudged to others. They lean on one another in mutual dependency, and voices acclaim the virtue of generosity. Dante, in conversing with Sapia, one of the penitents, indicates that he too, after his death, will have to undergo this punishment, but only slightly compared with what he will have to suffer below, on the Terrace of Pride.*

CANTO XIV. *Another penitent, Guido del Duca, in response to Dante's apologetic reference to his birthplace on the Arno river, utters a scathing denunciation of the evil places the river passes through, notably Florence and Pisa. Voices sound in warning against the vice of envy.*

CANTO XV. *Guido had condemned humankind for fixing its attention on the things incompatible with partnership. Virgil explains to Dante the meaning of this cryptic statement: that, by being shared, material goods are diminished but spiritual goods are multiplied. The two reach the third terrace, of Wrath, where the souls are enveloped in smoke. In a vision that stuns him, Dante beholds instances of meekness.*

CANTO XVI. *As Virgil leads him, blinded, through the smoke, Dante hears the formerly wrathful souls singing harmoniously in praise of the Lamb of God. Dante meets Marco Lombardo, one of several purgatorians who condemn the degeneracy of the present world. In reply to Dante's question whether this degeneracy is due to stellar influence, or to the intrinsic degradation of life on earth, Marco indignantly rejects the determinism that those explanations would imply. He blames the evils of the times, rather, on the perversion of earthly rule caused by the Church's usurpation of temporal authority in addition to the spiritual authority that it rightfully exercises. Virgil and Dante approach the stair leading to the fourth terrace, of Sloth.*

CANTO XVII. *Dante and Virgil ascend the stairs to the circle of the Slothful, where silence reigns. Night falls, a time when ascent of the mountain is not allowed. Virgil takes this opportunity to outline for Dante the scheme of Purgatory. Both the Creator and His creatures,*

Virgil explains, are moved by love. Sin arises when human reason distorts or misuses love. We cannot sin when we love what is inherently good, nor when we love secondary good in proper measure. When love takes the distorted form of rejoicing in our neighbor's ills, the results are pride, envy, and anger, the vices punished on the lower slopes of Purgatory. When we fail to pursue the highest good with sufficient zeal, the result is sloth, the vice punished on the fourth terrace. When we pursue in excessive or disproportionate ways the things that, while innocent, are not the supreme goods, the results are avarice (along with its twin opposite, prodigality), gluttony, and lust, which are purged on the three uppermost slopes. (This explanation takes place at the very midpoint of the poem, halfway through its middle section.)

CANTO XVIII. *In reply to Dante's further questioning, Virgil explains that love is the motive power of acts both good and evil. The mind is drawn toward a loved object, inclines toward it, and desires the fruition of desire through union with what is loved. No determinism is involved, since human reason has the power to reject specious good. Dante, about to fall asleep, is startled by a band of slothful spirits rushing by, eager to redeem their slothfulness even at night, when other creatures are at rest. Dante finally falls asleep.*

CANTO XIX. *In the night Dante has another dream, this time of the Siren who represents the excessive indulgence in sensory pleasure. In accord with the scheme Virgil has outlined, the sensual vices will be cleansed on the next three terraces. Virgil, in the dream, strips the Siren, revealing the vileness that underlies her attractions. He and Dante climb to the fifth terrace, of the avaricious and prodigal. Penitents afflicted with these vices are lying face down, forced thus to confront their overattachment to the earth-bound senses. Dante now learns, from Pope Adrian V, that souls in Purgatory can skip terraces if they are free from the vices punished there. Dante kneels in reverence to the pope but is told by him not to do so; such earthly honors are no longer payable to individuals in the afterlife.*

CANTO XX. *Dante hears praises of generosity and poverty from one of the souls lying prone, who proves to be the progenitor of the line of French kings. (The contrary warnings against avarice are recited at night.) The many evils perpetrated by this royal house are denounced. Dante is frightened into haste by a sudden violent tremor, as of an earthquake, and from the whole mountain rises a loud cry in praise of God.*

CANTO XXI. *The explanation for the loud noise is provided by a spirit traveling upward whom the two pilgrims meet: it is a cry of exultation, given by the spirits on the mountain when one of their number has completed his or her penance and is ready to ascend to the earthly paradise atop the mountain. Each soul judges for itself, he explains, when it has sufficiently completed its purgation on the mount, that is, when impulse and desire coincide. The newcomer proves to be the ancient Roman poet Statius, who speaks with great admiration of Virgil, who had influenced him. He has not yet recognized that he is in the very presence of that Virgil, but the truth comes out when Dante's amusement prompts Statius's curiosity. When Statius learns the truth, he tries to kiss his poetic master's feet, spirits though they both are.*

CANTO XXII. *As the three men leave the fifth terrace, Virgil expresses surprise that so noble a soul as Statius should have been guilty of avarice but is informed by Statius that he was guilty rather of prodigality, which is punished in the same circle. Statius adds that he owes his freedom from avarice, and indeed his very salvation, to his having read Virgil, who, through his eclogue prophesying the birth of a wondrous child, led Statius to the Christian faith. Virgil is compared to a man who walks in darkness, carrying a lantern that lights the way for those who follow but not for himself. Virgil, in turn, describes the position, in Limbo, of himself and of other ancient poets and worthies. Entering the Terrace of Gluttony, the travelers see a great fruit tree, sprayed with water from a fall nearby. From the tree comes a voice citing examples of abstinence.*

CANTO XXIII. *Dante sees the formerly gluttonous purgatorians, now emaciated by the tantalizing prospect of the tree and of others like it around the ledge. Their penitential suffering brings them joy, however. Dante meets his old friend Forese Donati, who condemns the immoral dress of the Florentine women. Dante explains how he was delivered by Beatrice and Virgil from the worldliness in which he and Forese had formerly been immersed.*

CANTO XXIV. *Among the emaciated souls is Bonagiunta da Lucca, a poet from the old school superseded by that of Dante, with its* dolce stil nuovo, *"sweet new style." Dante explains its principle as stressing the truth in beautiful things rather than beautiful expression for its own sake. Bonagiunta approves this advance over the earlier poetic manner. From within another tree resembling the first one, a growth from the fatal tree in Eden, voices proclaim warnings against gluttony. Passing the angel of the circle, who emits a dazzling brightness and sweet odor, the three pilgrims leave the sixth terrace.*

CANTO XXV. *Dante is puzzled by the fact that bodily emaciation can be suffered by the souls they have just seen, although these souls have left their earthly bodies behind them. Virgil hints at an answer but must defer to Statius, who outlines to Dante the process of human embryology and God's inbreathing of the soul into the developing human being after it has passed the stages of lower plant and animal life. At death, this soul survives and renews its capacity for sense experience by projecting from itself an immaterial body. The travelers have now reached the seventh terrace, of the lustful; here fires burn around the terrace, forcing the three men to walk at its extreme outer edge. From within the flames are heard voices praising chastity.*

CANTO XXVI. *A group of purgatorians moving in the same direction as the pilgrims encounters another group, this one made up of former sodomites, moving in the other direction; both groups cry out warning examples of lust. All these sufferers remain within the flames, but Dante is able to talk with Guido Guinicelli, to whom he pays ardent tribute as the founder of his school of poetry. The troubador poet Arnaut Daniel, the foremost of the Provençal poets, is also honored and introduced. The implication is that poets, as singers of love, are especially prone to the vice of lust purged away on this terrace.*

CANTO XXVII. *Dante, Virgil, and Statius must now pass through a band of fire in the circle of the lustful. Dante is terrified, but Virgil gives him strength and courage by reminding Dante of his beloved, Beatrice. After they pass through the fire, night falls and takes away their power to move on. In his sleep Dante has a visionary dream, of Leah (symbol of the active life) and Rachel (symbol of contemplation). Virgil announces to Dante that he, Dante, has now reascended to the state of human perfection represented by Eden; his will is now purified and he has attained the condition of perfect freedom, no longer in need of direction from without. No longer subject to institutions, Dante is crowned and mitered, made his own king and bishop.*

CANTO XXVIII. *Dante now enters the fresh and fragrant Garden of Eden. On the other side of a stream he sees a beautiful young woman, Matilda, who embodies the spirit of the place. The dazzle of her laughing eyes as she looks at Dante are a voucher of the sweet and innocent love of Eden. She explains that Eden is above and free from earthly weather and that its two streams are derived directly from God, not from ordinary sources. One of the streams, Lethe, makes humans forget their past sins; the other stream, Eunoë, makes them remember their good deeds. Matilda suggests that the reality of Eden was the source of the pagan poets' half-true conceptions about a Golden Age. Virgil and Statius, themselves poets of antiquity, respond smilingly.*

CANTO XXIX. *Witnessing the landscape of Eden, Dante feels indignation at the sin that deprived humanity of so blissful a state. He sees approach a magnificent allegorical pageant, which Virgil is no longer capable of elucidating: seven candlesticks streaming colors (the gifts of the spirit); twenty-four elders (books of the Old Testament); four beasts (the Gospels); the Chariot of the Church, drawn by a griffon (Christ, with his two natures, human and divine); seven dancers (the three theological, or evangelical, virtues and the four cardinal, or moral, virtues); seven more elders (the remaining New Testament sources, namely Paul and the author of Acts; the four authors of other epistles; and the author of Revelation). The procession halts as a peal of thunder rings out.*

CANTO XXX

THE COMING OF BEATRICE (REVELATION)

The candlesticks are compared to the Septentrion, the constellation that contains the North Star. When they stop, all those in the procession turn expectantly toward the chariot of the Church which is to bring Beatrice (Revelation) to Dante (Mankind). At a call, angels hover over it, and within a rain of flowers that veil her, Beatrice appears, dressed in the colors of the three evangelical virtues. At this climactic moment, Latin phrases occur frequently, among them a line from the Aeneid (Manibus o date lilia plenis!), *spoken by an angel as the last and supreme compliment to Virgil, who must now disappear, eclipsed. Dante feels the effect of Beatrice's presence as he had on earth, and in his distress turns to Virgil. But his former guide, denied the sight of Revelation, has already disappeared, and Dante is left alone before the overwhelming spectacle to accomplish the painful but necessary rites of contrition, confession, and satisfaction (penance).*

When the Septentrion of the first heaven—
which never knew rising or setting
nor the veil of any mist except of sin

and which made everyone there aware
of his duty, as the lower star does
him who turns the helm to come to port—

had stopped, the true people who had come
between it and the griffon[3]
turned to the chariot as to their peace.

And one of them, as if sent from Heaven,
cried three times in song *"Veni, sponsa, de Libano,"*[4]
and all the others sang after him. 12

As the blessed, at the last trumpet call,
will rise quickly from their graves,
singing with regained voices "Hallelujah,"

so, above the divine vehicle
a hundred [angels] rose *(ad vocem tanti senis)*[5]
the ministers and messengers of eternal life.

[3]A beast with an eagle's head and wings and a lion's body.

[4]"Come with me from Lebanon, my spouse" (Song of Solomon 4:8). Allegorically, the line represents Christ's greeting to the Church.

[5]"At the voice of so great an elder."

All cried, *"Benedictus qui venis,"*[6]
and scattering flowers above and around,
"Manibus o date lilia plenis!"[7]

I have often seen at the beginning of the day
the eastern sky all rosy, the rest
of the heavens beautifully clear, 24

and the sun's face appear veiled,
so that, through the tempering of the vapors,
the eyes could look steadily at it.

Thus, within a cloud of flowers,
thrown by angelic hands, which rose
and fell on and around the chariot,

underneath a white veil, crowned with olive,
a lady appeared to me, under a green mantle,
dressed in the color of living flame.

And my spirit which already had spent
so long a time without the trembling
from awe which her presence caused, 36

without seeing her more clearly,
through a hidden influence which came from her,
felt the great power of its old love.

As soon as on my eyes the great virtue fell
which already had pierced me
before I was out of childhood,[8]

I turned to the left with the expectation
which a child has who runs to its mother
when afraid or afflicted,

to say to Virgil, "Not a drop of blood
unmoved is left in me;
I recognize the signs of the old love!"[9] 48

But Virgil had left me without his company,
Virgil, my beloved father, Virgil,
to whom I gave myself up for my salvation;

nor could all that our ancient mother lost [Eden]
keep my cheeks, cleaned with dew,
from being darkened again by tears.

[6] "Blessed are you who come" (cf. Matthew 21:9). This is a slight variation on the acclamation of Christ at his entrance into Jerusalem.

[7] "Oh, give lilies with full hands!"

[8] When Dante first saw the earthly Beatrice, he was less than nine years old. She died in 1290, when she was twenty-four, Dante twenty-five.

[9] This line is translated from Virgil's *Aeneid,* Book IV, where Dido tells her sister Anna that Aeneas has reawakened in her the symptoms of love after she thought she had banished it from her life.

Now Beatrice speaks, not in her role as a tender friend, but severely, as a minister of the sacraments, calling Dante by his name (which appears here only), since the confession to follow must be personal and, in a manner, signed. Dante is paralyzed by this reception, but when the angels show sympathy for him, his awakened self-pity and his distress grow until he bursts into tears. Thus the first stage of the sacrament is accomplished.

"Dante, although Virgil is leaving,
do not weep yet, do not weep yet,
for you must cry for another wound!"

As an admiral, at the prow or stern,
looks at those who man the other ships,
and heartens them to their work, 60

so—when I turned at the sound of my name,
which is recorded here from necessity—
at the left side of the chariot

I saw the lady who at first appeared
veiled under the angelic shower
directing her eyes at me from beyond the stream,

although the veil descending from her head,
wreathed with Minerva's leaves [the olive],
kept her from being completely manifest.

Queenlike, stern in her bearing,
she continued, like one who speaks
while holding back the sharpest words. 72

"Look at me! I am indeed, I am indeed Beatrice.
How did you dare to approach the mount?
Did you not know that here man is happy?"

My glances fell down to the clear stream;
but seeing myself in it, I turned them
to the grass, such shame burdened my face.

As a mother at times seems cruel
to her son, so she appeared to me,
since the taste of stern pity is bitter.

Then she was silent, and the angels sang
at once, *"In te, Domine, speravi,"*[10]
but did not go beyond *pedes meos.*[11] 84

As snow on the living rafters [trees]
of the back of Italy [the Apennines] congeals
when blown and packed by Slavic winds,

[10]"In thee, O Lord, do I put my trust" (Psalm 31:1).

[11]"My feet." These words occur in verse 8 of the psalm; after this verse the tone changes from trust and assurance to despondency.

then, melted, trickles down, if a breath comes
from the land [Africa] without shadows,
like fire melting a candle,

so was I without tears or sighs
before those [angels] whose song is accompanied
by the melodies of the eternal spheres;

but when I heard in their sweet notes
their pity for me, more than if they had said,
"Lady, why do you shame him so?" 96

the frost which had gripped my heart
became breath and water, and with anguish
through mouth and eyes came from my breast.

To prepare for the next stage, Beatrice tells how Dante, after her death, had devoted himself to the donna pietosa *of the* Vita Nuova[12] *(profane philosophy), and to worldliness.*

She, still standing at the side
of the chariot, then turned to address
the angels who had shown pity for me.

"You watch in the eternal day,
so that neither night nor sleep hides from you
a step taken on the ways of the world;

therefore, my answer takes greater care
that he, weeping over there, should understand,
and that his sin and sorrow should be equal. 108

Not only by the operation of the great spheres
which direct each seed to some end,
according as the stars are conjoined,

but through the bounty of Divine Grace
which has such high vapors for its rain
that our sight cannot come close to them,

this man was such, potentially, in his young life
that every good disposition
might have come to marvelous fruition;

but the more vigor there is in the soil
the more malignant and rank it becomes
if uncultivated or sown with bad seed. 120

For a while I sustained him with my countenance,
and showing my youthful eyes to him,
I led him with me in the right direction.

[12] The *New Life,* a quasi-allegorical work by Dante in which his spiritual autobiography is traced in terms of his various loves. *Donna pietosa* means "compassionate lady."

As soon as I was on the threshold
of my second age, and changed life,
he abandoned me, and gave himself to others.

When I had risen from flesh to spirit
and beauty and virtue had increased in me,
I was less dear to him and less esteemed,

and he turned his steps on an evil path,
following false images of good
which never fulfill their promise. 132

Nor did it avail me to invoke inspirations
by which, in dreams and otherwise,
I recalled him, so little did he care.

He fell so low that all means
for his salvation would have been unavailing
except to show him the lost people.

Therefore, I visited the portal of the dead,
and to the one who brought him here,
in sorrow I addressed my request.

The high decrees of God would be broken
if Lethe were crossed and such a draught
were tasted without any payment 144

of the penance that causes tears to flow."

CANTO XXXI

CONFESSION AND SATISFACTION

Beatrice now addresses Dante directly.

"O you beyond the sacred stream,"
she continued without pausing,
directing the point of her speech toward me

which even with the edge had seemed sharp,
"say, say if this is true; to this accusation
your confession must be joined."

My senses were so confused
that my words began and were spent
before released from their organs.

She waited a moment, then, "What are you thinking?"
she questioned. "Answer me, for your sad memories
are not yet impaired by the water [of Lethe]!" 12

Confusion and fear joined together
sent forth such a "yes" from my mouth,
that eyes were needed to hear it.

As a crossbow under too great a tension
breaks both the string and the bow,
so that the shaft hits its mark with less force,

so I burst under my heavy burden,
pouring forth tears and sighs,
and my voice died away on its passage.

Then she said, "In your desires for me [Revelation]
which led you to love the good
above which there is none to aspire to, 24

what chains or what hindering pitfalls
did you find that you should lose
the hope of going onward?

And what comforts or what advantages
were displayed in the aspect of another good
that you should seek it?"

After heaving a bitter sigh,
scarcely had I voice for an answer,
and my lips only with effort formed it.

Sobbing I said, "The present things,
with their false pleasures, turned my steps away
as soon as your face was hidden." 36

And she, "If you were silent or denied
what you confess, your sin would not be concealed,
known as it is by such a judge.

But when confession bursts
from one's own mouth, the grindstone in our court
turns back against the edge [of the sword of Justice].

Still to make you bear more shame
for your error, and to make you stronger
another time if you hear the sirens,

put aside your sowing of tears and listen,
and you will hear how, when my flesh was buried,
I should have led you in the opposite direction. 48

Beatrice refers again to the pargoletta *(young girl). Then, by telling Dante to lift his "beard" instead of "chin," she points out indirectly that he is no child and should know better. Overcome by remorse, Dante falls in a faint, in this way giving "satisfaction," and accomplishing the last stage of the sacrament.*

Never did nature or art offer such delight
as the fair members in which I was once enclosed
and which are now in dust and scattered,

and if the supreme pleasure failed you
at my death, what mortal thing
should have drawn you with desire?

At the first shaft of fallacious things
you should have lifted yourself up,
following me, no longer [fallacious] like them.

No young girl or other vanity of such brief use
should have weighed down your wings
and exposed you to more blows. 60

A young bird takes two or three chances;
but before the eyes of a full-grown one,
the net is spread and the arrow shot in vain."

As children mute from shame stand listening,
with their eyes on the ground,
conscience-stricken and repentant,

so I stood; and she continued, "Since by hearing
you suffer, lift up your beard,
and you will have greater grief in looking."

With less effort a sturdy oak
is uprooted by a wind of ours
or by one from Iarbas' land [Libya] 72

than my chin was lifted at her command;
and when by "beard" she meant my chin,
I knew the venom of the argument.

Then when my face was raised,
I saw the primal creatures [angels]
resting from their scattering of flowers.

And my eyes, still insecure,
saw Beatrice turned toward the beast
which is one in two natures.

Under her veil and beyond the stream
she seemed to surpass her former self
more than she did others when on earth. 84

The thorn of repentance so pierced me then
that of all things, those that had made me
love them most now became most hateful to me.

Such remorse stung my heart
that I fell, vanquished; and what became of me,
she knows who caused this.

When my heart gave back a sense
of outward things, I saw the lady [Matilda]
above me, saying, "Hold to me, hold to me!"

She had drawn me into the river up to my throat,
and pulling me behind her, moved on
as lightly as a little boat over the water. 96

When I was near the sacred shore, *"Asperges me,"*[13]
I heard so sweetly that I cannot keep the sound
in mind, much less describe it.

The fair lady opened her arms,
took my head, and held it down
until I swallowed the water.

Matilda now takes Dante to the four nymphs (Prudence, Temperance, Fortitude, and Justice). These point out the deeper vision of the evangelical virtues (Faith, Hope, and Love) and bring Dante to the griffon (Christ), which he sees reflected in its twofold unity in the eyes of Revelation.

Then she drew me forth, and led me, bathed,
to the dance of the four nymphs,
each of whom covered me with her arms.

"Here we are nymphs, and in Heaven stars.
Before Beatrice came to the world
we were ordained for her as handmaids. 108

We will lead you to her eyes; but the three
over there who gaze more deeply
will sharpen yours better for the light in them."

Thus they began to sing, and then took me
with them to the breast of the griffon
where Beatrice stood, turned toward us.

They said, "See that you do not spare your eyes;
we have placed you before the jewels
from which Love once shot his arrows."

A thousand desires hotter than flames
bound my sight to the shining eyes
which still were fixed upon the griffon. 120

As the sun in a mirror, not otherwise
did the twofold creature shine in them,
now with one, now with the other nature.

Think, Reader, if I marveled
when I saw the object remain still
and yet change in its image.

While full of joy and wonder, my soul
tasted that [spiritual] food which,
satisfying, gives hunger for itself;

showing themselves of a higher order
by their actions, the other three [Virtues] advanced,
dancing to their angelic measure. 132

[13]"Thou shalt sprinkle me" (King James Version "purge me") "with hyssop, and I shall be clean" (Psalm 51:7).

"Turn, Beatrice, turn your holy eyes,"
was their song, "to your faithful one
who, to see you, has taken so many steps!

Do us the favor of unveiling for him
your smile, so that he may discern
the second beauty which you conceal."

O splendor of the living, eternal light [of Beatrice]!
who has become so pale in the shade of Parnassus,[14]
or drunk so deeply at its well,

that he would not seem to have a clouded mind
in trying to describe you as you appeared
when the harmonious heavens alone veiled you, 144

and you disclosed yourself in the open air?

CANTO XXXII. *Dante is temporarily blinded by the sight of Beatrice. When he recovers, he and Statius follow as the procession moves to the tree of the knowledge of good and evil, which represents civic obedience and the authority of the Empire, or civil state. The griffon pays tribute to the tree, and, in a gesture symbolic of the ideal fraternal equality of ecclesiastical and civil authority, the pole of the chariot of the Church is bound to the tree. Dante is overcome by sleep; when he awakens, the pageant has disappeared, leaving him with Beatrice and the representatives of the seven virtues. He is granted a vision of the tragic perversions that will afflict the church and the state.*

CANTO XXXIII. *Beatrice hints at the coming of a political savior, but Dante fails to understand her. In consideration of his still-darkened mind, she promises to speak henceforth less enigmatically. Dante, with Statius, drinks from the fountain of Eunoè, which restores the memory of all good things as Lethe had obliterated the memory of evil ones. Now, in the full brightness of noonday, Dante is ready to leave Earth and ascend to the stars.*

OUTLINE OF PARADISE

The Correspondences

PLANETS, HEAVENS	LIGHT	POSITION	PHYSICAL CHARACTERISTICS	WEAKNESS OR STRENGTH
1. Moon	Pearly	Within shadow of earth	Changing phases, spots	Weakness in Faith
2. Mercury	Veiled, eclipsed by sun	Within shadow of earth	Smallness	Weakness in Hope
3. Venus	Color of flame	Within shadow of earth	Double center of motion	Weakness in Love
4. Sun	White	Beyond shadow of earth	Brightness	Strength in Prudence
5. Mars	Red	Beyond shadow of earth	Redness	Strength in Fortitude
6. Jupiter	Silvery	Beyond shadow of earth	Temperate quality	Strength in Justice

[14] The mountain sacred to Apollo and the Muses.

Outline of Paradise *(continued)*

The Correspondences

7. Saturn	Crystal (cold)	Along Golden Ladder	Cold, ascetic	Strength in Temperance
8. Fixed Stars	Various		Variable	
9. Primum Mobile	Diaphanous		Diaphanous	
10. Empyrean				

The Correspondences

PLANETS, HEAVENS	SOULS REPRESENTED	SUBJECTS DISCUSSED	DENUNCIATIONS
1. Moon	Inconstant nuns	Vows	Ill-advised vows
2. Mercury	Lovers of earthly fame	Incarnation, atonement	Guelfs and Ghibellines
3. Venus	Sensual lovers	Heredity	Mercenary ecclesiastics
4. Sun	Theologians	God expounded in his creatures	Mendicant orders
5. Mars	Warriors of Faith	Decay of virility	Effeminacy of Florence
6. Jupiter	Just Rulers	Justice	Unjust rulers
7. Saturn	Monks	Predestination	Luxury and pomp of prelates
8. Fixed Stars	Apostles	Faith, Hope, Love	Unworthy popes
9. Primum Mobile		Angels	Popular preachers
10. Empyrean		[Beatific Vision]	Rejection of Henry VII

The Correspondences

PLANETS, HEAVENS	ANGELS	ANGELIC FUNCTION	HIERARCHIES	EARTHLY REPRESEN-ATIVES
1. Moon	Angels	Messengers to individuals	Purifying	Deacons
2. Mercury	Archangels	Messengers to nations		
3. Venus	Principalities	Guides of princes		
4. Sun	Powers	Subject to God	Illuminating	Priests
5. Mars	Virtues	Divine motion		
6. Jupiter	Dominations	Dominion		

OUTLINE OF PARADISE *(continued)*

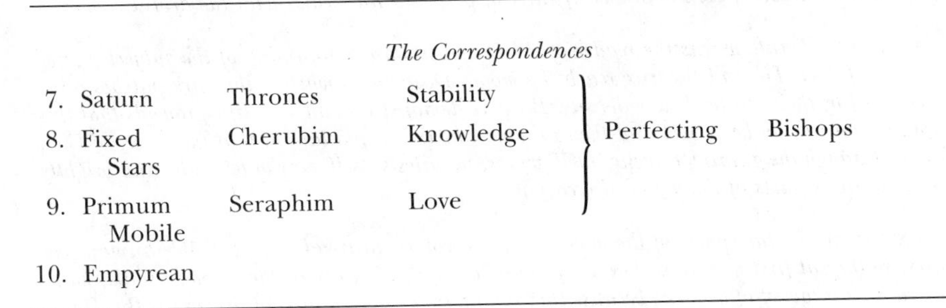

The Correspondences

7. Saturn	Thrones	Stability	Perfecting	Bishops
8. Fixed Stars	Cherubim	Knowledge		
9. Primum Mobile	Seraphim	Love		
10. Empyrean				

The Heavens.

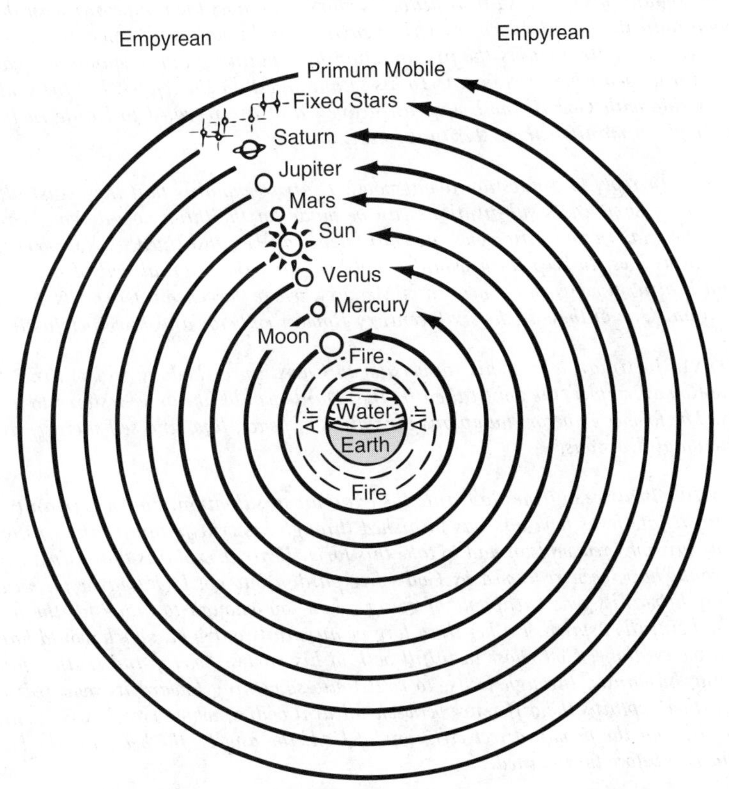

from PARADISE

CANTO I. *Dante prays for inspiration at the outset of his account of the third, celestial region. Following Beatrice's example, he gazes at the sun, so that his earthly nature is mystically transformed. Enrapt, he rises and hears the harmonies of heaven. Puzzled that he and Beatrice have left the earth and equally puzzled how they can ascend against gravity, Dante learns from his guide that they have now reached the point where ascent is the natural mode of motion, in accord with the proper affinity of perfected humanity with the divine.*

CANTO II. *Dante warns the reader of the immensity and profundity of the subject matter that is to follow. He and Beatrice reach the moon. Dante asks whether the dark patches on it are caused by their relatively low density. Beatrice demonstrates on scientific grounds that this explanation cannot be correct and then provides the true explanation: that the power of God, filtered through the guiding angelic intelligences, manifests itself more or less fully and brightly in the various parts of the material creation.*

CANTO III. *In the sphere of the moon, Dante becomes aware of faintly visible human features, so that at first he thinks they are mere reflections. They are in fact human souls, manifested in this lowest of heavens because they belong to the lowest order of the saved. But Dante learns from one of them, Piccarda, that "in His will is our peace"; every soul is perfectly happy to accept the lot accorded it by God.*

CANTO IV. *Dante is puzzled by two things: since the inconstant nuns were forced into inconstancy, why should this diminish their heavenly glory? and does their appearance in the sphere of the moon indicate that Plato was correct in saying that human souls come from and return to the planets? Beatrice answers the first question by explaining that acquiescence cannot be fully exonerated even when it is forced. To his second question she replies that the souls of the saved all reside with God in the Empyrean heaven and are revealed to Dante in the lower heavens simply to manifest their spiritual conditions.*

CANTO V. *In reply to a question about vows, Beatrice explains that they must always be kept but that in some cases substitutions can be made for the thing vowed. Vows can never be altered where, as in monastic vows, no equivalent can be substituted. As for vows that are wrong in themselves, to keep them would simply magnify the original evil of making them. Dante and Beatrice now reach the heaven of Mercury, where they encounter spirits once tainted with ambition. One of these is the sixth-century Roman emperor and lawgiver Justinian.*

CANTO VI. *Justinian tells of his conversion to Christian orthodoxy and outlines the history of the Roman empire, the political entity that Dante would like to see restored to its proper authority. The former emperor champions the values of peace, law, and self-sacrifice and condemns factional divisions.*

CANTO VII. *Beatrice outlines to Dante the dynamic of salvation. Fallen humanity, whose form the incarnate Jesus took on, was punished through his crucifixion for the sins of Eden. Dante is unsure why redemption had to take this form. Beatrice explains that humanity, after the Fall, could have been redeemed by God's free pardon but not by human efforts in themselves, since humanity was incapable of going down low enough to atone for the height to which it had sinfully aspired. Rather than forgive humanity outright, which would have been the way of mercy alone, God chose to fulfill both of his modes, "mercy and truth," forgiving but allowing humanity, through Jesus, to contribute something toward its own redemption. Beatrice further explains the difference between natural bodies, whose creation God entrusted to the angels, and the primal direct creations of God: the angels, the heavens, the bodies of Adam and Eve before they sinned.*

CANTO VIII. *In the heaven of Venus, Dante and Beatrice encounter souls who in life were especially given to amorous pursuits but have converted their carnal impulses to heavenly love. Carlo Martello, who was king of Hungary and whom Dante knew, speaks with him. Dante asks him why it is that noble family lines sometimes produce base offspring. Carlo replies that all human capacities are fitted for some valuable function in the world and that these capacities are not inherited but instilled by the heavens. Society brings out the worst in people by assigning roles according to hereditary station that ought to be assigned according to inherent merit.*

CANTO IX. *In other conversations with souls in the heaven of Venus, Dante hears further denunciations of corruption, especially in Florence and the Papacy. He learns too that after reaching Heaven the saved feel no repentance for past sins, which are now seen to have been occasions for God's saving forgiveness. But we are given to understand that the degree of bliss enjoyed by the souls in these lower heavens is limited owing to the vices that stained them on earth.*

CANTO X. *Dante and Beatrice rise to the fourth heaven, of the Sun, where the theologians are manifested. The sun being now near the equinox, Dante points out to the reader that the degree of tilt of the earth's axis in relation to the ecliptic is divinely ordained for the best effect. The theologians, rejoicing in the doctrine of the Trinity, stand out in their brightness even against the sun. Dante raptly contemplates the idea of God, but his trance is broken by his awareness of the enhanced beauty of Beatrice's smile (which becomes more and more dazzling as they ascend). From a circling crown of twelve theologians who surround Dante, St. Thomas Aquinas, the greatest of medieval theologians, emerges to talk with him and introduce the other souls.*

CANTO XI. *St. Thomas, who belonged to the Dominican religious order, recites the history of and praises St. Francis of Assisi, founder of the other great medieval order, dwelling especially on Francis' marriage with poverty. Thomas deplores the degeneracy of the monks.*

CANTO XII. *A second circle surrounds the first one, circling it in an effect like that of twin rainbows. From this second circle St. Bonaventure, a Franciscan, emerges to reciprocate St. Thomas' gesture and praise St. Dominic, upholder of truth and orthodoxy and founder of the Dominicans. Bonaventure too deplores the deterioration of monastic orders.*

CANTO XIII. *Thomas Aquinas solves a problem of interpretation for Dante, namely how to reconcile the attribution of supreme wisdom to Solomon with the attribution of perfect knowledge to the new-created Adam and to Christ. After outlining the way in which God's creative power is manifested diversely in His creatures, Thomas distinguishes royal wisdom—the kind Solomon possessed—from wisdom and knowledge in general. Thomas warns Dante, through this example, of the dangers of facile inferences, a danger to which philosophy and theology are all too prone.*

CANTO XIV. *Even before he puts it into words, Beatrice becomes aware of a problem puzzling Dante: will not the restoration of the body to the souls of the saved after the Last Judgment reimpose on them the burdens of flesh? The answer is given by Solomon: the complete human being includes body as well as soul, and when the two are ultimately united, the saved will both feel greater joy and be better able to love and serve God. The perfected body will not suffer from the limitations it now endures in earthly life. Dante and Beatrice pass into the sphere of Mars, where a white cross appears against the background of the red planet. Souls move rapidly along the surface of the cross, joyfully singing. These are the warriors of the faith.*

CANTO XV. *From the warriors appearing as lights on the cross in the heaven of Mars, one moves from it quickly and joyfully to accost Dante. He greets him with the joy Anchises, in the Sixth Book of Virgil's* Aeneid, *showed his son Aeneas when the latter visited Anchises in the realm of the dead. He identifies himself as Dante's great-great-grandfather, Cacciaguida, and describes the small town Florence was in earlier times. There he was born and lived before becoming a Crusader.*

CANTO XVI. *Dante is overcome both by humility toward his ancestor and by pride in his lineage. Cacciaguida contrasts the small and still-uncorrupted Florence of his day with what it has since become, describing in detail the vicissitudes of the old families and mourning the afflictions of the city.*

CANTO XVII. *On several occasions earlier in the* Comedy, *Dante had heard dire hints of calamity in his future. Cacciaguida, after explaining how his foreknowledge is consistent with free will, spells out plainly the sad future Dante has in store: his false indictment by Florence for the very acts of treachery that the city itself is guilty of; his impoverished and increasingly isolated exile; the hospitality that he will receive and be dependent on. But Cacciaguida bids Dante to have hopeful courage, to believe in his eventual vindication, and to publish his vision with unmitigated truthfulness.*

CANTO XVIII. *Dante, after musing on what his ancestor has told him, is recalled to awareness by Beatrice's beauty. Cacciaguida identifies some of the warriors appearing on the cross, after which Dante and his guide ascend to the heaven of Jupiter, the keynote of which is justice. Here spirits arrange themselves so as to spell out an appropriate biblical verse; the last letter re-forms as the eagle symbolic of Roman law. The perversion of law and justice in the world, especially by the Papacy, is lamented.*

CANTO XIX. *The souls that form the eagle are the just monarchs, who speak in unison. The heaven of justice seems the fitting place for Dante to explore his troubled doubts about the justice of excluding the righteous pagans from salvation. The kings answer by praising the justice of God, the Being who gives meaning to the very notion of justice, as beyond the comprehension and judgmental capacity of His creatures. They reaffirm that faith in Christ is necessary for salvation but then, intriguingly, declare that many heathens will be closer to God after the Last Judgment than some of those who are nominally Christians.*

CANTO XX. *The voice of the eagle names certain of the greatest souls there represented. Among those named are Ripheus the Trojan, a minor character whom Virgil, in the* Aeneid, *had praised as eminently just; and the pagan Roman emperor Trajan. That these pagans should have been saved, apparently in contravention of the doctrine that such is impossible, astonishes Dante and causes him to rejoice. Ripheus and Trajan, it is explained, were given visions of Christ to come or Christ having come in the past. The implication is that such revelations may have been made to others who are ordinarily considered outside the pale of salvation. Only God, it is revealed, knows which human beings are saved.*

CANTO XXI. *Beatrice and Dante rise to the heaven of Saturn, the realm of mystical contemplation. A replica of Jacob's ladder in Genesis extends down from above, and on it descend souls in light. Approached by one of them, the monk Peter Damiani, Dante inquires why Peter in particular has been singled out by God to address him. Peter replies that such individual particularities of Providence constitute a mystery even to the spirits in heaven. A former cardinal, Peter denounces the worldliness of high-ranking Church officials.*

CANTO XXII. *Dante has heard an outcry from the spirits, which, Beatrice explains to him, is a harbinger of divine vengeance. St. Benedict, the founder of Western monasticism, approaches Dante, who asks if he may see the saint in his full glory. Benedict replies that that will be accomplished in the Empyrean heaven beyond the realm of space and time. He too denounces the corruption of the monastic orders but holds out hope for their regeneration. The souls are swept up again out of sight, after which Dante and Beatrice rise to the heaven of the fixed stars. He gazes down at the heavens he has passed and at Earth, which appears tiny and insignificant.*

CANTO XXIII. *Dante experiences the stupendous vision of Christ amid the saved, a vision that stuns him into unconsciousness. When he comes to himself, however, his vision has been fortified by the sight, so that he is empowered to see the full beauty of Beatrice also, which is inexpressible in words. Christ having withdrawn in consideration of Dante's vulnerability, Dante gazes on the Virgin Mary and the Apostles. Mary is crowned by the angel Gabriel, and she too is lifted up beyond Dante's sight.*

CANTO XXIV. *As part of his preparation for the ultimate visions, Dante is examined, by St. Peter, on the nature and content of faith. As the foundation of faith, and of the existence of faith within him, Dante cites Scripture and the historical occurrence of miracles. He defines God first in terms of Aristotelian metaphysics and then in terms of the Trinity of which humankind learns by divine revelation.*

CANTO XXV. *Having passed the examination in faith, Dante is examined on hope, by St. James the Apostle. Beatrice vouches for the presence of hope in Dante, as the very virtue that has brought him to the vision of the heavens. To James' direct queries about the nature of hope Dante replies in terms of Scriptural definition; the content of his hope he centers on the resurrection of the body and the immortality of the soul. Dante having passed this second test, St. John appears in the midst of impenetrable light. Dante is told that he cannot see John's body, since only Jesus and his mother Mary have been bodily assumed into Heaven.*

CANTO XXVI. *Blinded by the glory of John, Dante is examined by him on the third of the theological virtues: love. After testifying to the power of love instilled in him by Beatrice, he declares God to be the comprehensive object of all love. Dante identifies the love of good with the love of God, citing both Aristotle and Scripture. He declares that God is to be loved both in Himself and because of His goodness to humankind. His sight restored after passing the third test, Dante converses with Adam, who lovingly answers his questions about the Garden of Eden and the Fall.*

CANTO XXVII. *St. Peter angrily denounces the corruption of the Papacy, the office he was the first to hold, and the corrupt Pope Boniface VIII, charging Dante to relay this message of indignation to those on Earth. The spirits soar above, beyond sight. Dante again looks down toward Earth, seeing it lighted like a gibbous moon. He and Beatrice rise to the Primum Mobile (First Mover), the outermost of the spherical heavens and the realm from which everything spatial and temporal takes its origin. Beyond the Primum Mobile exists the unlocalized, timeless abode of God and the saved in eternity.*

CANTO XXVIII. *Dante now sees a vision of the adoration of God by the nine orders of angels. The vision consists of a single point of intense light, surrounded by nine revolving concentric circles, of which the innermost is both the brightest and the swiftest—that is to say, a model directly opposed to that of the nine physical heavens, of which the outermost is the most excellent. The unsearchable relationship of God to His creations can, then, be understood and represented through either of these opposite models.*

CANTO XXIX. *Beatrice explains to Dante that God created other beings not so as to enhance Himself but so that joyful consciousness might exist outside of His own consciousness. She explains some metaphysical truths about Creation—for example, that the question what God did before Creation is meaningless, since time itself is meaningful only in connection with created reality. She narrates briefly the fall of the Satanic party and, among other truths about the angels, declares that each of these innumerable beings is wholly individualized.*

CANTO XXX. *The angelic spectacle fades away. Now, as Beatrice attains an indescribable new intensity of beauty, she and Dante leave behind the world of time and space and enter the Empyrean heaven, where they will behold the eternal forms of the angels and of the human saved. A great flash of light strengthens Dante to see the vision of the blessed who are gazing on God Himself.*

CANTO XXXI. *The saved are seated in a vast amphitheater, in the form of a rose, their gazes fixed on God. Angels fly in the space between them and God but without blocking divine or human vision. Dante is overwhelmed by the contrast with the troubled life of people on earth. Turning to look at the transfigured Beatrice, Dante finds that she has left him, as Virgil did earlier, and has been replaced by St. Bernard, the representative of contemplative, or immediately intuitive, vision. Bernard will help Dante attain the ultimate vision of God. Dante pours out his love and gratitude toward Beatrice, now in her place among the blessed; she smiles at him once more and then turns toward God. Dante is given a vision of the glory of the Virgin Mary.*

CANTO XXXII. *Bernard explains to Dante the arrangement here of the saved. Dividing the rose-amphitheater into two facing halves is a vertical line or plane separating the saved who lived before Christ (Hebrews) from the saved who lived after him (Christians). Mary has the highest place among the Hebrews. The two sides of the rose will have equal numbers when the half reserved for the Christian era is finally filled. The lower ranks, in each half, consist of saved infants who did not live long enough to help earn their own salvation. Dante is instructed to look toward Mary, to prepare himself for the final, divine vision.*

CANTO XXXIII

The Beatific Vision

A prayer to the Blessed Virgin, later copied in great part by Chaucer, opens the final canto.

The stages of the Beatific Vision are, in ascending order, a comprehension of the world, a vision of the Trinity, and, as a final revelation, a view of the Incarnation.

"Virgin mother, daughter of thy son,
humble and exalted more than any creature,
goal established by Eternal Counsel,

thou art the one by whom human nature
was so ennobled that its Maker
did not disdain to become its creature.

Within thy womb was rekindled the love
through whose warmth this flower
has blossomed in eternal peace.

Here thou art for us a noonday torch
of charity, and down below, among mortals,
a living fount of hope. 12

My lady, thou art so great and so triumphant
that whoever wants and does not turn to thee
would have his desire fly without wings.

Thy benignity succors not only those
who ask, but many times
freely anticipates the request.

In thee is mercy, in thee pity,
in thee magnificence, in thee whatever goodness
can be found in creatures is resumed.

Now, this man who from the deep well
of the universe up to here
has seen the spiritual lives, one after another, 24

begs thee of thy grace for strength,
so that he may lift his eyes
still higher toward the ultimate salvation.

And I who never for my own sight longed more
than I do for his, offer thee all my prayers,
and may they not be insufficient,

in order that thou, through thine, mayst dispel
every cloud of his mortality, so that
the Supreme Pleasure may reveal Itself to him.

I pray thee further, O Queen! thou who canst do
what thou wilt, that thou keepest
his affection sound after so great a vision. 36

May thy protection overcome his human impulses.
Behold Beatrice with so many of the blessed
clasping their hands to aid my prayer."

The eyes [of Mary] venerated and beloved
by God, fixed on him who prayed, showed
how gratefully devout prayers are heard.

Then they turned to the Eternal Light into which
we must not think any mortal vision,
however clear, can ever penetrate so deeply.

And I who drew near to the goal
of all desires, ended, as I ought,
within myself, the ardor of my longing. 48

Bernard signaled to me and smiled
so that I might look up, but I
already had made myself as he wished.

For my sight, growing pure, penetrated
ever deeper into the rays
of the Light which is true in Itself.

From then on my vision was greater
than our speech which fails at such a sight,
just as memory is overcome by the excess.

As one who in a dream sees clearly,
and the feeling impressed remains afterward,
although nothing else comes back to mind, 60

so am I; for my vision disappears
almost wholly, and yet the sweetness
caused by it is still distilled within my heart.

Thus, in sunlight, the snow melts away;
thus the sayings of the Sibyl,[1] written
on light leaves, were lost in the wind.

[1]A prophetess (Virgil, *Aeneid,* Books III, VI) who inscribed her prophecies on the leaves of trees which were then scattered by the wind.

O Supreme Light that risest so high
above mortal concepts, give back to my mind
a little of what Thou didst appear,

and make my tongue strong,
so that it may leave to future peoples
at least a spark of Thy glory! 72

For, by returning to my memory
and by sounding a little in these verses
more of Thy victory will be conceived.

By the keenness of the living ray I endured
I believe I would have been dazed
if my eyes had turned away from it;

and I remember that I was bolder
because of that to sustain the view
until my sight *attained* the Infinite Worth.

O abundant grace through which I presumed
to fix my eyes on the Eternal Light
so long that I consumed my vision on it! 84

In its depths I saw contained, bound with love
in one volume, what is scattered
on leaves throughout the world—

substances [things] and accidents [qualities] and their modes
as if fused together in such a way
that what I speak of is a single light.

The universal form [principle] of this unity
I believe I saw, because more abundantly
in saying this I feel that I rejoice.

One moment obscures more for me than twenty-five centuries
have clouded since the adventure which made Neptune
wonder at the shadow of the Argo [the first ship].[2] 96

Thus my mind with rapt attention
gazed fixedly, motionless and attentive,
continually enflamed by its very gazing.

In that light we become such
that we can never consent
to turn from it for another sight,

inasmuch as the good which is the object
of the will is all in it, and outside of it
whatever is perfect there is defective.

[2]The voyage of Jason and the Argonauts was considered to have taken place in the thirteenth century B.C. Dante means that the world has forgotten since then less than he has forgotten of the divine vision.

Now my speech, even for what I remember,
will be shorter than that of an infant
who still bathes his tongue at the breast. 108

Not that more than a single semblance
was in the living light I gazed upon
(for it is always as it was before),

but in my vision which gained strength
as I looked the single appearance,
through a change in me, was transformed.

Within the deep and clear subsistence
of the great light three circles of three colors
and of one dimension [the Trinity] appeared to me,

and one [the Son] seemed reflected from the other [the Father]
as Iris by Iris,[3] and the third [the Holy Spirit]
seemed fire emanating equally from both. 120

O how poor our speech is and how feeble
for my conception! Compared to what I saw
to say its power is "little" is to say too much.

O Eternal Light [Father], abiding in Thyself alone,
Thou [Son] alone understanding Thyself, and Thou [Holy Spirit]
understood only by Thee, Thou dost love and smile!

The circle which appeared in Thee
as a reflected light [the Son]
when contemplated a while

seemed depicted with our image within itself
and of its own [the Circle's] color,
so that my eyes were wholly fixed on it. 132

Like the geometer who strives
to square the circle and cannot find
by thinking the principle he needs

I was at that new sight. I wanted to see
how the [human] image was conformed
to the [divine] circle and has a place in it,

but my own wings were not enough for that—
except that my mind was illumined by a flash
[of Grace] through which its wish was realized.

For the great imagination here power failed;
but already my desire and will [in harmony]
were turning like a wheel moved evenly 144

by the Love which turns the sun and the other stars.

[3] Twin rainbows (Iris being the goddess of the rainbow).

The Thousand and One Nights
(Fourteenth Century)

When Salman Rushdie, the brilliant contemporary Anglo-Indian novelist, appeared a few years ago on a BBC radio program called "Desert Island Discs," he was asked, as all the program's guests are, what book, apart from the Bible and Shakespeare's plays, he would choose if he were marooned on a desert island. His reply was *The Thousand and One Nights.* The careful reader of Rushdie's books could have anticipated the answer. In *Midnight's Children* (1981), Saleem Sinai, one of a thousand and one children born on the stroke of the midnight in 1947 when India became independent, reads avidly the stories of Sindbad, Aladdin, and Ali Baba before setting out on the series of magical adventures that make up the book's plot. *The Thousand and One Nights* is, if anything, more pervasive in *The Satanic Verses* (1988), in which the wonderful adventures of the protagonists, Gibreel Farishta and Saladin Chamcha, weave in and out of their sources in the *Nights.* The children's book, *Haroun and the Sea of Stories* (1990) is a frank homage to the *Nights.* Rushdie's love of *The Thousand and One Nights* might seem more eccentric if he did not share it with a number of his postmodern contemporaries who have found in its "sea of stories" an inspiration in the very old for the very new.

The Thousand and One Nights belongs to the popular medieval genre of the collection of tales held together by a frame story; Chaucer's *Canterbury Tales,* Boccaccio's *Decameron,* and Marguerite de Navarre's *Heptameron* are other examples. The frame tale of *The Thousand and One Nights* concerns a King Shahriyar who discovers his queen having sex with a palace servant. He has her put to death and thereafter takes a virgin to bed each night and has her beheaded the following morning, thus avoiding further betrayals. When the supply of virgins runs low, Sheherazade, the daughter of his chief officer, volunteers to take her place in the King's bed, stipulating only that her sister Dunyazade attend her. After Shahriyar has deflowered Sheherazade, Dunyazade, as arranged, asks Sheherazade to tell a story, and Sheherazade begins the first story, "The Story of the Merchant and the Demon," timing it so that it is still unfinished when day breaks. Shahriyar, eager to hear the end, postpones Sheherazade's execution for a day, but when Sheherazade finishes "The Merchant and the Demons" she begins another tale, breaking off again before she finishes it. This pattern continues, if we are to take the thousand and one nights literally, for two years and 271 days. By the time Sheherazade exhausts her repertoire of stories, she has borne Shahriyar three children, he has been healed of his mad obsession, and he abandons any intention of executing her.

The frame story of *The Thousand and One Nights* is provocative in itself, but it also makes possible further complexities of structure. Sometimes characters in Sheherazade's stories tell stories themselves, and in turn, their characters tell stories, in a process called "nesting" or "boxing." Sheherazade's own stories and those nested within them (like the nested dolls sold in Russia) recurringly reflect on and illuminate one another. The outcome of an embedded story may determine the outcome of the story in which it is embedded, as the success of Sheherazade's stories determines the outcome of the frame story. (The sequence of Hunchback stories is a good example of this recursivity.)

The origins of this dazzling collection are obscure. The frame story seems to have been written and the core stories assembled in Persia sometime before the eighth century. The oldest stories in the collection have been traced to Persia and India, and the names in the frame story are Persian; *Shahriyar* (or *Shahrayar*) means "king," *Sheherazade* (or *Shahrazade*) means "noblewoman," and *Dunyazade* (or *Dinarzad*) means "the goddess exalted by Denis" in Middle Persian. The *Nights* was translated into Arabic in the eighth century, and, over the next five centuries, the core stories were augmented by Arab stories and the entire collection revised to give it an Arabic tone and atmosphere. The composition and transmission history of *The Thousand and One Nights* precludes the possibility of establishing a definitive text. The presumed Persian original vanished early, and even if it were recovered it was itself undoubtedly based on earlier texts, both oral and written. The *Thousand and One Nights* is, for better or worse, a collective, cumulative work that exists in many versions.

No translation before the eighteenth century of the *Nights* into either Latin or a modern European language has been traced. Nevertheless, some influence of the collection, perhaps transmitted orally, has been identified. Both "The Squire's Tale" and "The Merchant's Tale" in Chaucer's *Canterbury Tales* have close parallels with tales in the *Nights*, as do stories in Boccaccio's *Decameron*. The Spanish playwright Calderon de la Barca's play *Life Is a Dream* draws on "The Sleeper and The Waker" in the *Nights*; the frame story of Shakespeare's *Taming of the Shrew* echoes the same tale, though Shakespeare drew directly on a sixteenth-century English collection that includes versions of several *Nights* tales.

The Thousand and One Nights was not generally available in Europe, however, until 1704–1717, when a French Arabist named Antoine Galland published a twelve-volume French translation, working from an Arab manuscript he had found in Syria. The *Nights* took Europe by storm. Even before the publication of Galland's last volumes, sections of it had been translated into English and published in cheap, popular editions. The book triggered a vogue for "Oriental" tales that lasted for more than a century. Voltaire's philosophical romance *Zadig*, Samuel Johnson's *Rasselas: Prince of Abyssinia*, Lord Byron's "The Giaour" and "The Corsair," and Thomas Moore's *Lalla Rookh* are only a few examples of the better-known Oriental tales of eighteenth and early nineteenth-century Europe. The European vogue for *The Thousand and One Nights*, in England and America at least, perhaps climaxed with the publication of Sir Richard Francis Burton's translation, *The Arabian Nights' Entertainments; or, The Book of a Thousand Nights and One Night*, 12 volumes (1885–1888), a version that emphasized bawdy and violent elements and employed a bizarre quasi-Biblical, quasi-medieval style that thoroughly exoticized and Orientalized the book. Nevertheless, it is often regarded as an original contribution to English literature and has been highly praised by the great Argentinian writer Jorge Luis Borges.

In the twentieth century, *The Thousand and One Nights* underwent a curious double movement in its place in world literature. On the one hand, it slipped down the literary hierarchy to become established as a children's book, mostly read in abbreviated, sanitized versions or, more often, encountered in animated films such as the Walt Disney *Aladdin* (1992). On the other hand, it had a deep influence on a number of major twentieth-century writers. "The

Voyage of Sindbad the Sailor" is a major subtext, along with the *Odyssey*, for James Joyce's *Ulysses*, as Leopold Bloom's last thoughts as he drifts off to sleep indicate: "Sinbad the Sailor and Tinbad the Tailor and Jinbad the Jailor and Whinbad the Whaler," etc. The *Nights* provides not only a number of motifs for *Finnegans Wake* but also one of several precedents for the book's all-inclusive structure ("this scherzarade of one's thousand and one nightinesses"). *The Thousand and One Nights* functions similarly in Marcel Proust's *Remembrance of Things Past.* One of the narrator's earliest memories is of a set of cake plates in his childhood home that were decorated with scenes from the *Nights*; throughout the long novel, memories of those plates serve, like the famous madeleine, to guide the narrator back to his lost past. The *Nights* also serves, as it does in *Finnegans Wake*, as a structural analogue for the book. The narrator broods over the challenge of finishing his memoir before his death and wonders whether "the master of my destiny might not prove less indulgent than the Sultan Shahriyar, whether in the morning, when I broke off my story, he would consent to a further reprieve and permit me to resume my narrative the following evening." For the narrator, as for Sheherazade, life itself hangs upon story-telling.

Postmodernist fiction writers have drawn, if anything, even more heavily on *The Thousand and One Nights* than their modernist predecessors did, finding in its fantastic elements, its endless self-referentiality, and its profusion of pure narrative models for their own work. It is the explicit inspiration for the American postmodernist John Barth, for example, especially in *Chimera* (1974) and *The Last Voyage of Somebody the Sailor* (1991); it is similarly central to the short, haunting, metafictional tales of the Argentinian Jorge Luis Borges; and, as noted before, it pervades the work of Salman Rushdie.

"The Story of Sindbad the Sailor" belongs to the "greater" *Thousand and One Nights*—the total body of stories that have come to be known by that name—rather than to the "lesser" one—the small nucleus of stories in the thirteenth-century collection around which the others accreted. Galland did not include it in his version of the *Nights* but rather translated and published it separately; it was only later that it became swallowed up in the *Nights'* "sea of story." Nevertheless, there is good evidence that "Sindbad" originated in eighth-century Baghdad, when Basra was Baghdad's port on the Persian Gulf. The accounts of Sindbad's seven voyages have been shown to be based on Arab mariners' accounts of their experiences sailing the seas of India and China. But, in the telling, Sindbad's story becomes far more than a string of jaw-dropping extravagances. Like all great sea-stories, it is an account of an inner voyage as well as an outer one. Sindbad's outer voyage leads him into progressively more dangerous adventures; his inner one leads him to a healing of the division of his "Sailor" and "Porter" selves.

FURTHER READING: No better introduction to the *Nights* exists than Robert Irwin's readable and informative *The Arabian Nights: A Companion*, 1994. Irwin surveys, in graceful chapters, the history of the book, its translators, comparable collections, the Middle Eastern storytelling tradition, such themes as sex, marvels, and crime, the criticism of the *Nights*, and its influence on Western literature. Ferial J. Ghazoul's *Nocturnal Poetics: "The Arabian Nights" in Comparative Context*, 1996, offers a sophisticated structuralist analysis of the *Nights*, followed by a series of chapters relating the book to other literary works. A separate chapter is devoted to "The Story of Sindbad the Sailor." Mia I. Gerhardt's *The Art of Story-Telling: A Literary Study of the "Thousand*

and One Nights," 1963, is an insightful, somewhat more traditional reading of the *Nights.* Peter L. Caracciolo, ed., *"The Arabian Nights" in English Literature: Studies in the Reception of "The Thousand and One Nights" into British Culture,* 1988, is authoritative on its subject; the introduction is especially valuable. Richard G. Hovannisian et al, eds. *"The Thousand and One Nights" in Arabic Literature and Society,* 1997, presents well the Middle Eastern contexts.

THE STORY OF SINDBAD THE SAILOR

Translated by Husain Haddawy

There lived in Baghdad, in the time of the Commander of the Faithful, the Caliph Harun al-Rashid, a man called Sindbad the Porter, who was poor and who carried loads on his head for hire. One day, he was carrying a heavy load, and as it was very hot, he became weary and began to perspire under the burden and the intense heat. Soon he came to the door of a merchant's house, before which the ground was swept and watered, and the air was cool, and as there was a wide bench beside the door, he set his load on the bench to rest and take a breath. As he did so, there came out of the door a pleasant breeze and a lovely fragrance; so he remained sitting on the edge of the bench to enjoy this and heard from within the melodious sounds of lutes and other string instruments accompanying delightful voices singing all kinds of eloquent verses. He also heard the sounds of birds warbling and glorifying the Almighty God, in various voices and tongues, turtledoves, nightingales, thrushes, doves, and curlews. At that he marveled to himself and felt a great delight. He went to the door and saw inside the house a great garden and saw pages, servants, slaves, and attendants, the likes of whom are found only with kings and sultans. And through the door came the aromas of all kinds of fine delicious foods and delicious wine.

He raised his eyes to heaven and said, "Glory be to You, o God, Creator and Provider! You bestow riches on whomever You wish, without reckoning. O Lord, I ask Your forgiveness of all sins and repent to You of all faults. O Lord, there is no argument with Your judgment or Your power. You are not to be questioned on what You do, for You are omnipotent in every thing. Glory be to You! You enrich whomever You wish and impoverish whomever You wish. You exalt whomever You wish and humble whomever You wish. There is no god but You. How great is Your majesty, how mighty Your dominion, and how excellent Your government! You have bestowed favors on one you have chosen of your servants, for the owner of this place is in the height of comfort, enjoying all kinds of pleasant perfumes, delicious foods, and fine beverages. You have foreordained and apportioned to Your creatures what You wish, so that among them some are weary, some comfortable, and some enjoy life, while some, like me, suffer extreme toil and misery." Then he recited the following verses:

> How many wretched men toil without rest,
> And how many enjoy life in the shade!
> My weariness increases every day;
> 'Tis strange, how heavy is the burden on me laid!
> Others are prosperous and live in ease,
> Having never my heavy burden known,

Living in luxury throughout their life,
Enjoying food and drink and pleasure and renown.
Yet all God's creatures are of the same species;
My soul is like this one's and his like mine,
And yet we are so different, one from one,
As different as is vinegar from wine.
And yet, o Lord, I impugn not Thy ways,
For Thou art wise and just, and all judgment is Thine.

When the porter finished reciting his verses and was about to carry his load and continue on his way, a young page with a handsome face, fine build, and rich clothes, came out of the door, took his hand, and said, "Come in and speak with my master, for he is asking for you." The porter wanted to refuse but could not. He left his load with the doorkeeper in the hallway and went into the house with the page. He found it to be a handsome mansion, stately but cheerful. Then he came to a great hall in which he saw noblemen and great lords and saw all kinds of flowers and fresh and dried fruits and a great variety of exquisite foods and wines of the finest vintage. And he saw musical instruments and all kinds of beautiful slave-girls, all arranged in the proper order. At the upper end of that hall sat a venerable and majestic man whose beard was turning gray on the sides. He had a handsome appearance and a comely face, and he had an aspect of dignity, reverence, nobility, and majesty. When Sindbad the Porter saw all this, he was confounded and said to himself, "By God, this place is one of the spots of Paradise, or else it is the palace of a king or a sultan." Then he assumed a respectful posture, saluted the assembly, invoked a blessing on them, kissed the ground before them, and stood with his head bowed in humility. The master of the house asked him to sit near him, welcomed him, and spoke kindly to him. Then he set before Sindbad the Porter various kinds of fine, exquisite, and delicious foods. Sindbad the Porter invoked God, then ate until he was satisfied and said, "Praise be to God." Then he washed his hands and thanked the company.

The master of the house then said, "You are welcome, and your day is blessed. What is your name, and what do you do for a living?" The porter answered him, "Sir, my name is Sindbad the Porter, and I carry on my head people's goods for hire." The master of the house smiled and said to him, "Porter, your name is like mine, for I am called Sindbad the Sailor. I would like you to let me hear the verses you were reciting when you were at the door." The porter was ashamed and said, "For God's sake, don't reproach me, for fatigue, hardship, and poverty teach a man ill manners and impudence." The host said to him, "Do not be ashamed, for you have become a brother to me. Recite the verses, for they pleased me when you recited them at the door." The porter recited to him those verses, and when he heard them, he was pleased and delighted. Then he said, "Porter, my story is astonishing, and I will relate to you all that happened to me before I attained this prosperity and came to sit in this place, where you now see me, for I did not attain this good fortune and this place save after severe toil, great hardships, and many perils. How much toil and trouble I have endured at the beginning! I embarked on seven voyages, and each voyage is a wonderful tale that confounds the mind, and everything happened by fate and divine decree, and there is no escape nor refuge from that which is foreordained."

THE FIRST VOYAGE OF SINDBAD

Gentlemen, my father was one of the most prominent men and richest merchants, who possessed abundant wealth and property. When I was a little boy, he died and left me many buildings and fields. When I grew up, I seized everything and began to eat and drink freely, associated with young friends, wore nice clothes, and passed my life with my friends and companions, believing that this way of life would last forever and that it would benefit me. I lived in this way for a length of time but finally returned to my senses and awoke from my heedlessness and found that my wealth had gone and my condition had changed. When I came to myself and found that I had lost everything, I was stricken with fear and dismay, and I remembered a saying I had heard before, a saying of our Lord Solomon, the son of David, that three things are better than three: the day of death is better than the day of birth; a living dog is better than a dead lion; and the grave is better than the palace. Then I gathered all I had of effects and clothes and sold them, together with what was left of my buildings and property and netted three thousand dirhams, thinking that I might travel abroad and recalling what some poet said:

> A man must labor hard to scale the heights,
> And to seek greatness must spend sleepless nights,
> And to find pearls must plunge into the sea
> And so attains good fortune and eminent be.
> For he who seeks success without labor
> Wastes all his life in a futile endeavor.

I made my resolve and, having been inclined to take a sea voyage, I bought goods and merchandise, as well as provisions and whatever is needed for travel, and embarked with a group of merchants on a boat bound downstream for Basra. From there, we sailed for many days and nights from sea to sea and from island to island, and sold, bought, and bartered until we came to an island that seemed like one of the gardens of Paradise. There the captain docked, cast anchor, and put forth the landing plank. Then all those who were on the ship landed on that island. They set up wood stoves, lighted fires in them, and busied themselves with various tasks, some cooking, some washing, some sightseeing. I myself was among those who went to explore the place, while the passengers assembled to eat and drink and play games and amuse themselves.

While we were thus engaged, the captain, standing on the side of the ship, cried out at the top of his voice, "O passengers, may God preserve you! Run for your lives, leave your gear, and hurry back to the ship to save yourselves from destruction. For this island where you are is not really an island but a great fish that has settled in the middle of the sea, and the sand has accumulated on it, making it look like an island, and the trees have grown on it a long time. When you lighted the fire on it, it felt the heat and began to move, and it will soon descend with you into the sea, and you will all drown. Save yourselves before you perish."

When the passengers heard the captain's warning, they hurried to get into the ship, leaving behind their woodstoves, copper cooking pots, and their other gear, together with their goods. Some made it to the ship, but some did not. The island had moved and sunk to the bottom of the sea with everything that was on it, and the roaring sea with its clashing waves closed over it. I, being one of those left behind on the island, sank in the sea with those who sank, but God the Almighty saved me from drowning and provided me with a large wooden tub that the passengers had been using for washing. I held on to it for dear life, got on it, and began to paddle with my feet, while the waves tossed me to the right and left. Meanwhile, the captain spread the sails and pursued his voyage with those who had made it to the ship, without regard for those who were drowning. I kept looking at the ship until it disappeared from my sight, and as night descended, I became sure of perdition. I remained in this condition for a day and a night, but with the help of the wind and the waves, the tub landed me under a high island, with trees overhanging the water. I seized a branch of a tall tree, clung to it, after I had been on the verge of death, and climbed it to the land. I found my feet numb and my soles bore the marks of the nibbling of fish, something of which I had been unaware because of my extreme exhaustion and distress.

I threw myself on the ground like a dead man and, overcome by stupefaction, lost consciousness till the next day, when the sun rose and I woke up on the island. I found that my feet were swollen and that I was reduced to a helpless condition. So I began to move, sometimes dragging myself in a sitting position, sometimes crawling on my knees, and found that the island had abundant fruits and springs of sweet water. I ate those fruits, and after several days I recovered my strength, felt refreshed, and was able to move about. I reflected and, having made myself a crutch from a tree branch, walked along the shores of the island, enjoying the trees and what the Almighty God had created.

I lived in this manner until one day, as I walked along the shore, I saw an indistinct figure in the distance and thought it a wild beast or one of the creatures of the sea. I walked toward it, without ceasing to look at it, and found that it was a magnificent mare tethered by the seashore. I approached her, but she cried at me with a loud cry, and I was terrified, and as I was about to retreat, a man emerged suddenly from the ground, called to me and pursued me, saying, "Who are you, where do you come from, and what brings you here?" I said to him, "Sir, I am a stranger, and I was on a ship and sank in the sea with some other passengers, but God provided me with a wooden tub, and I got on it and floated until the waves cast me on this island." When he heard my words, he took me by the hand and said, "Come with me." I went with him, and he descended with me to a subterranean vault. We entered a large chamber, and he seated me at the upper end of the chamber and brought me food. I was hungry, and I ate until I was satisfied and felt good. Then he inquired about my situation and what had happened to me. I told him my story from beginning to end, and he marveled at it.

When I finished my story, I said to him, "Sir, I have told you all the particulars of my situation and all that has happened to me. For God's sake, pardon me, for I would like you to tell me who you are, why you live in this subterranean chamber, and why is the mare tethered by the seashore?" He said to me, "I am one of a group of men scattered on this island. We are the grooms of King Mihrajan, in charge of all the horses. Every month, at the new moon, we bring the best mares that have not been bred before and hide in the subterranean chamber, so that no one may see us. Then one of the sea horses comes out to the shore after the scent of the mares and, looking and seeing no one around, mounts one of them. When he finishes with her and dismounts her, he wishes to take her with him, but she cannot follow him, because she it tethered. Then he begins to cry out at her and batter her with his head and hoofs. When we hear his cries, we know that he has dismounted, and we run out, shouting at him, and frighten him back into the sea. Then the mare conceives and bears a mare or a filly worth a fortune, one whose like is not to be found on the face of the earth. This is the time of the coming of the sea horse and, God the Almighty willing, I will take you to King Mihrajan and show you our country. Had you not met us, you would not have found anyone else on this island, and you would have died miserably, and no one would have known of you, but I will save your life and return you to your country." I invoked a blessing on him and thanked him for his help and kindness.

While were in conversation, a sea horse suddenly came out of the sea and, letting out a great cry, leapt on the mare. When he finished with her, he dismounted and tried to take her with him but could not, as she resisted, neighing at him. The groom took a sword and buckler and ran out, shouting to his companions, "Run to the sea horse," as he hit the buckler with the sword. Then a group of them came out, shouting and brandishing spears. The sea horse, frightened by them, ran away, plunged into the water like a buffalo, and disappeared. As the groom sat down to rest for a while, his companions came, each leading a mare. When they saw me with him, they inquired about my situation, and I repeated to them what I had told him. Then they drew near me and, spreading the table, ate and invited me to eat; so I ate with them. Then they rode the mares and gave me one to ride, and we traveled until we reached the city of King Mihrajan.

Then they went in to see him and acquainted him with my story, and he sent for me, and they led me in and made me stand before him. I saluted him, and he returned my salutation, welcomed me, greeted me in a courteous manner, and inquired about my situation. I related to him what had happened to me and what I had seen from beginning to end, and he marveled at my story, saying, "By God, my son, you have had an extraordinary escape, and had you not been destined to a long life, you would not have escaped from these difficulties, but God be praised for your safety." Then he treated me kindly and honored me and, seating me near him, engaged me in friendly conversation. Then he made me his agent to the port and registrar of all the ships that landed. I stood in his presence to transact his affairs, and he treated me generously, bestowed a fine, rich suit on me, and rewarded me in every way. I became a person of high esteem with him, interceding for the people and facilitating their business.

I remained with him for a long time, but whenever I went to the port, I used to ask the merchants and the sailors about the direction of the city of Baghdad, hoping that someone might inform me and I go with him and return to my country, but no one knew it, nor knew anyone who went there. I was perplexed, and I had grown weary of my long absence from home, and I continued to feel this way for some time.

One day I went in to see King Mihrajan and found with him a group of Indians. I saluted them and they returned my salutation, welcomed me, and asked me about my country. Then I asked them about theirs, and they told me that they consisted of various races. One is called the Kshatriyas, who are the noblest of their races and who oppress no one, nor inflict violence on anyone. Another is called the Brahmans, who abstain from wine but live in joy, sport, merriment, and prosperity, possessing horses, camels, and cattle. They told me, moreover, that the Indians consist of seventy-two castes, and I marveled at that.

Among other things, I saw in the dominion of King Mihrajan an island called Kabil, on which the beating of drums and tambourines is heard all night long and whose inhabitants are reported by travelers and neighboring islanders to be people of judgment and serious pursuits. I saw in the sea a fish four hundred feet long and saw fish with faces that resembled the faces of owls. During that voyage, I saw many strange and wonderful things, which would take too long to relate to you.

I continued to divert myself with the sights of those islands until one day, as I stood in the port, with a staff in my hand, as was my custom, a large ship approached, carrying many merchants. When it entered the harbor and reached the pier, the captain furled the sails, cast anchor, and put forth the landing plank. Then the crew brought out to shore everything that was in the ship and took a long time in doing so, while I stood writing their account. I said to the captain, "Is there anything left in the ship?" He replied, "Yes, sir, I have some goods in the hold of the ship, but their owner drowned at one of the islands during our voyage here; so his goods remained in our charge, and our intention is to sell them and keep a record, so that we may give the money to his family in the city of Baghdad, the Abode of Peace." I asked the captain, "What was the name of the merchant, the owner of the goods?" He said, "His name was Sindbad the Sailor." When I heard these words, I looked carefully at him and, recognizing him, cried out loudly, saying, "Captain, I am the owner of the goods; I am that Sindbad who landed from the ship on the island, with the other merchants, and when the fish moved, and you called out to us, some of us got into the ship, and the rest sank. I was among those who sank, but God the Almighty preserved me and saved me from drowning by means of a wooden tub that the passengers had used for washing. I got on the tub and paddled with my feet, and the wind and the waves brought me to this island, where I landed and where, with the help of the Almighty God, I met the grooms of King Mihrajan, who brought me with them to this city and took me to the king, to whom I related my story, and he treated me generously and made me clerk of the harbor of this city, and he appreciated my services and rewarded me accordingly. These goods in your charge are my goods and possessions."

The captain said, "There is no power and no strength, save in God, the Almighty, the Magnificent. There is neither conscience nor trust left among men." I said to him, "Captain, why those words, after you heard me telling you my story?" The captain replied, "Because you heard me say that I have with me goods whose owner has drowned, you are trying to take them without any rightful claim, and this is unlawful. We saw the owner drown with many other passengers, none of whom escaped. How can you claim that you are the owner of the goods?" I said to him, "Captain, listen to my story and try to understand, and you will discover my veracity, for lying is the mark of a hypocrite." Then I enumerated to him everything I had with me, from the time I left Baghdad with him until we reached that island, where we sank in the sea, and I mentioned to him some incidents that had occurred between him and me. The captain and the other merchants then became convinced of my veracity, and they recognized me and congratulated me on my safety. All of them said, "We never believed that you had escaped from drowning, but God has granted you a new life." Then they gave me my goods, and we found my name written on them, and nothing was missing. Then I opened them and took out something precious and costly, and the crew of the ship carried it with me to the king as a gift. I told him that this ship is the one in which I had been a passenger and that all my goods were intact and in perfect order and that this present was a part of them. The king was amazed and was even more convinced of my truthfulness in everything I had told him. He felt a deep affection for me, treated me with great generosity, and gave me many presents in return for mine.

Then I sold my goods and all my other property and made a great profit. Then I bought goods, gear, and provisions from that city, and when the merchants were about to depart, I loaded everything I had on the ship and went in to see the king. I thanked him for his kindness and generosity and asked his permission to return to my country and family. He bade me farewell and gave me a great many of the products of that country for my voyage. I bade him farewell and embarked. Then we set sail with the permission of the Almighty God, and fortune served us and fate favored us, as we journeyed day and night until we reached Basra safely.

After staying in Basra for a short time rejoicing in my return to my country, I headed for Baghdad, the Abode of Peace, carrying with me an abundance of merchandise, provisions, and gear of great value. I went to my quarter and entered my house, and all my relatives and friends came to see me. Then I acquired a great number of servants and attendants and concubines and bought slaves, both black and white. Then I bought houses and other properties that exceeded what I had had before. And I associated with friends and companions, exceeding my former habits, and forgot all I had suffered of toil, exile, hardship, and perils, indulging for a long time in amusements and pleasures and delicious food and fine drink. This was my first voyage. Tomorrow, the Almighty God willing, I will tell you the story of the second of my seven voyages.

Then Sindbad the Sailor had Sindbad the Porter dine with him and gave him a hundred pieces of gold, saying to him, "You have cheered us today." The porter thanked him, took his present, and went on his way, meditating and marveling at the events that befall mankind. He spent that night at home, and as soon as it was morning, he went to the house of Sindbad the Sailor, who welcomed him, spoke courteously to him, and asked him to sit. When the rest of his companions arrived, he set food and drink before them, and when they were cheerful and merry, he said to them:

THE SECOND VOYAGE OF SINDBAD

Friends, as I told you yesterday, I lived a most enjoyable life of unalloyed pleasure until it occurred to me one day to travel abroad, and I felt a longing for trading, seeing other countries and islands, and making profit. Having made my resolve, I took out a large sum of money and bought goods and travel gear, packed them up, and went down to the shore. There I found a fine new ship, with sails of good cloth, numerous crewmen, and abundant equipment. I loaded my bales on it, as did a group of other merchants, and we sailed on the same day. We sailed under fair weather and journeyed from sea to sea and from island to island, and wherever we landed, we met merchants, high officials, and sellers and buyers, and we sold, bought, and bartered.

We continued in this fashion until fate brought us to a beautiful island abounding with trees, ripe fruits, fragrant flowers, singing birds, and clear streams, but there was not a single inhabitant nor a breathing soul around. The captain anchored the ship at the island, and the merchants and other passengers landed there, to divert themselves with the sight of the trees and birds and to glorify the One Omnipotent God and wonder at the power of the Almighty King. I landed with the rest and sat down by a spring of pure water among the trees. I had with me some food, and I sat there eating what the Almighty God had allotted me. The breeze was cool, and the place was pleasant; so I dozed off and rested there until the sweetness of the breeze and fragrance of the flowers lulled me into a deep sleep.

When I awoke, I did not find a single soul around, neither man nor demon. The ship had sailed with all the passengers and left me behind, none of the merchants or the crew taking any notice of me. I searched right and left, but found no one but myself. I felt extremely unhappy and outraged, and my spleen was about to burst from the severity of my anxiety, grief, and fatigue, for I was all alone with nothing of worldly goods and without food or drink. I felt desolate and despaired of life, saying to myself, "Not every time the jar is saved in time. If I escaped safely the first time, by finding someone who took me with him from the shore of that island to the inhabited part, this time I am very far from the prospect of finding someone who will deliver me out of here." Then I began to weep and wail for myself until I was completely overcome by grief, blaming myself for what I had done and for having embarked on the hardships of travel, after I had been reposing peacefully in my own house and in my own country, happily enjoying good food and good drink and good clothes, without need for money or goods. I regretted leaving Baghdad on this sea journey, especially after the hardships I had endured on the first and after my narrow escape from destruction, saying, "We are God's and to God we return." I felt like a madman.

At last, I arose and began to walk on the island, turning right and left, for I was unable to sit still in any one place. Then I climbed a tall tree and looked to the right and left but saw nothing but sky and water and trees and birds and islands and sands. Then I looked closely and saw a large, white object. I climbed down and walked in its direction until I reached it and found it to be a huge white dome of great height and circumference. I drew closer and walked around it but found that it had no door, and because of its extreme smoothness, I had neither the power nor the nimbleness to climb it. I marked the spot where I stood and went around the dome to measure its circumference and found it to be a good fifty paces. I stood, thinking of a way to get inside, as the day was about to end and the sun was about to set. Suddenly, the sun disappeared, and it grew dark. I therefore thought that a cloud had come over the sun, but since it was summer, I wondered at that. I raised my head to look at the object and saw that it was a great bird, with a huge body and outspread wings, flying in the air and veiling the sun from the island. My wonder increased, and I recalled a story I heard from tourists and travelers that there is on certain islands an enormous bird, called the Rukh, with feeds its young on elephants, and I became certain that the dome I saw was one of the Rukh's eggs and wondered at the works of God the Almighty.

While I was in this state, the bird alighted on the egg and brooded over it with its wing and, stretching its legs behind on the ground, went to sleep. Glory be to Him who never sleeps! I unwound my turban, twisted it with a rope and, girding my waist with it, tied it fast to the bird's feet, saying to myself, "Perhaps, this bird will carry me to a land where there are cities and people. That will be better than staying on this island." I spent that night without sleep, fearing that the bird might fly with me while I was unaware. When dawn broke and it was light, the bird rose from its egg, uttered a loud cry, and flew with me up into the sky. It soared higher and higher until I thought that it had reached the pinnacle of heaven. Then it began to descend gradually until it alighted with me on the ground, resting on a high place. As soon as I reached the ground, I hastened to unbind myself, and, loosening my turban from its feet, while shaking with fear, although it was unaware and took no notice of me, I walked away. Then it picked up something with its talon from the ground and flew high into the sky. When I looked at it carefully, I saw that it was an enormous serpent, which the bird had taken and flown with toward the sea. And I wondered at that.

Then I walked about the place and found myself on a crest overlooking a large, wide, and deep valley at the foot of a huge and lofty mountain that was so high no one could see the top nor climb to it, so I blamed myself for what I had done, saying, "I wish that I had stayed on the island, which is better than this desolate place, for there I might at least have eaten of its various fruits and drunk from its streams, whereas this place has neither trees nor fruits nor streams. There is no power and no strength save in God the Almighty, the Magnificent. Every time I escape from a calamity, I fall into one that is greater and more perilous." Then I arose and, gathering my strength, walked in that valley and saw that its ground was composed of diamonds, with which they perforate minerals and jewels, as well as porcelain and onyx, which is such a hard and dense stone that neither stone nor steel has any effect on it and which nobody can cut or break except with the leadstone. Moreover, the valley was full of serpents and snakes, each as big as a palm tree, indeed so huge that it could swallow an elephant. These serpents came out at night and hid themselves during the day, fearing that the Rukh or eagles might carry them away and cut them in pieces, for a reason of which I was unaware. I stood there, regretting what I had done and saying to myself, "By God, I have hastened my own destruction."

As the day was waning, I walked in that valley and began looking for a place to spend the night, being afraid of the serpents, forgetting my food and drink and subsistence, and thinking only of saving my life. Soon I saw a cave nearby. It had a narrow entrance, and when I went in I saw a big stone lying by that entrance. I pushed the stone and closed the entrance from the inside, saying to myself, "I am safe here now, and as soon as it is day, I will go out and see what fate will bring." But when I took a look inside, I saw a huge snake brooding over its eggs. My hair stood on end, and I raised my head, committing myself to fate and divine decree. I spent the entire night without sleep, and as soon as it was dawn, I removed the stone with which I had closed the entrance of the cave and went out, like a drunken man, feeling dizzy from excessive hunger, sleeplessness, and fear.

I walked in the valley in this condition, when suddenly a big slaughtered sheep fell before me, but when I saw no one else around, I was amazed, and I recalled a story I used to hear a long time ago from some merchants, tourists, and travelers that the mountains of the diamonds are so perilous that no one can gain access to them, but that the merchants who deal in diamonds employ a device to get them. They take a sheep, slaughter it, skin it, cut up the meat, and throw it from the top of the mountain into the valley. When the meat falls, still fresh, the diamonds stick to it. Then they leave it there till midday, when the eagles and vultures swoop down on it, pick it up with their talons, and fly with it to the top of the mountain. The merchants then rush, shouting at them, and scare them away from the meat. Then the merchants come to the meat, take the diamonds sticking to it, and carry them back to their country. No one can obtain diamonds except by this method.

When I saw that slaughtered sleep and recalled that story, I approached the carcass and began to pick a great number of diamonds and to put them into my pockets and the folds of my clothes, and I continued to fill my pockets, my clothes, my belt, and my turban. While I was thus engaged, another carcass suddenly fell before me. I bound myself to it with my turban and, lying on my back, placed it on my chest and held on to it. Thus it was raised above the ground. Suddenly, an eagle swooped down on it, caught it with his talons, and flew up into the air with it and with me clinging to it. The eagle continued to soar until it reached the top of the mountain and, alighting there, was about to tear off a piece of meat, when suddenly a loud cry and the sound of clattering with a piece of wood came from behind the eagle, who took fright and flew away.

I unbound myself from the carcass, with my clothes stained with its blood, and stood by its side. Suddenly, the merchant, who had shouted at the eagle, approached the carcass and saw me standing there, but he did not utter a word, for he was frightened of me. Then he came closer to the carcass, and when he turned it over and found nothing on it, he uttered a loud cry and said, "What a disappointment! There is no power and no strength, save in God the Almighty, the Magnificent. May God save us from Satan the accursed," and he kept expressing regret, wringing his hands and saying, "What a pity! How did this happen?" I went to him, and he said to me, "Who are you, and what brings you to this place?" I said to him, "Don't be afraid, for I am a human being, and one of the best men. I was a merchant, and I have a strange and extraordinary tale to tell, and the reason for my coming to this valley and the mountain is marvelous to relate. Don't worry, for you will receive from me what will please you. I have with me a great deal of diamonds, each one better than what you would have gotten, and I will give you a portion that will satisfy you. Don't fear and don't worry." When he heard this, he thanked me and invoked a blessing on me, and we began to converse.

When the other merchants, each of whom had thrown down a slaughtered sheep, heard me conversing with their companion, they came to meet me. They saluted me, congratulated me on my safety, and took me with them. I told them my whole story, relating to them what I had suffered on this voyage and the cause of my coming to this valley. Then I gave the merchant, to whose slaughtered sheep I had attached myself, a large portion of diamonds, and that made him happy, and he thanked me and invoked a blessing on me, and the merchants said to me, "By God, you have been granted a new life, for no one has come to this place before and escaped from it, but God be praised for your safety." They spent the night in a pleasant and safe place, and I spent the night with them, extremely happy for my safe escape from the Valley of Serpents and my arrival in an inhabited place.

When it was morning, we arose and journeyed along the ridge of the high mountain, seeing many snakes in the valley below, and we continued walking until we came to a large and pleasant island with a grove of camphor trees, each of which might provide a hundred men with shade. When someone wishes to obtain some camphor, he makes a perforation in the upper part of the tree with a piercing rod and catches what descends from it. The liquid camphor, which is the juice of that tree, flows and later hardens, like gum. Afterwards, the tree dries and becomes firewood. We also saw in that island, besides cattle, a kind of beast called the rhinoceros, which pastures as cows and buffaloes do in our country, and feeds on the leaves of trees, but the body of that beast is bigger than that of a camel. It is a huge beast, with a single horn in the middle of its head, thick and twenty feet long and resembling the figure of a man. Travelers and tourists on land and in the mountains report that this beast called the rhinoceros carries a huge elephant on its horn and grazes with it in the island and on the shores, without feeling its weight, and when the elephant dies on the horn, its fat melts under the heat of the sun and flows on the head of the rhinoceros and, entering his eyes, blinds it. Then it lies down by the shore, and the Rukh picks it up with its talons and carries it together with the elephant to feed to its young. I also saw in that island a great number of a certain kind of buffalo, the like of which is not seen among us.

The merchants exchanged goods and provisions with me and paid me money for some of the diamonds I carried in my pockets from the valley. They carried my goods for me, and I journeyed with them, from town to town and from valley to valley, buying and selling and viewing foreign countries and what God has created until we reached Basra, where I stayed for a few days, then headed for Baghdad. When I reached my quarter and entered my home, with a great quantity of diamonds and a considerable amount of goods and provisions, I met with my family and other relatives and gave alms and distributed presents to all my relatives and friends. Then I began to eat and drink well and wear handsome clothes, associating with friends and companions and forgetting all I had suffered, and I continued to lead a happy, merry, and carefree life of sport and merriment. And all who heard of my return came to me and inquired about my voyage and the countries I saw, and I told them, relating to them what I had seen and what I had suffered, and they were amazed at the extent of my hardships and congratulated me on my safety. That was the end of the second voyage. Tomorrow, the Almighty God willing, I will tell you the story of my third voyage.

When Sindbad the Sailor finished telling his story to Sindbad the Porter and the other guests, they all marveled at it. After they had supper, he gave Sindbad the Porter a hundred pieces of gold, which he took and, after thanking Sindbad the Sailor and invoking a blessing on him, went on his way, marveling at what Sindbad had suffered. The following day, as soon as it was light, the porter arose, and after performing his morning prayer, came to the house of Sindbad, as he had bidden him. The porter went in, wished him good morning, and Sindbad welcomed him and sat with him until the rest of his friends and companions arrived. After they had eaten and drunk and enjoyed themselves and felt relaxed and merry, Sindbad the Sailor began his story.

THE THIRD VOYAGE OF SINDBAD

Friends, the story of my third voyage is more amazing than the two you have already heard, and God in His wisdom knows best what He keeps hidden. When I returned from my second voyage, I led a life of ease and happiness, rejoicing in my safety, having gained great wealth, for God had compensated me for everything I had lost, as I had related to you yesterday. I lived in Baghdad for some time, in prosperity and peace and happiness, until my soul began to long for travel and sightseeing and commerce and profit, and the soul is naturally prone to evil. Having made my resolve, I bought a great quantity of goods suited for a sea voyage, packed them up, and journeyed with them from Baghdad to Basra. Then I went to the seashore where I found a large ship in which there were many merchants and other passengers who seemed to be good people—men of rectitude, piety, and kindness. I embarked with them on that ship, and we sailed, relying on the blessing and aid and favor of the Almighty God, feeling happy in the expectation of a safe and prosperous voyage. We sailed from sea to sea and from island to island and from city to city, buying and selling and diverting ourselves with the sights and feeling exceedingly content and happy until one day we found ourselves in the middle of a roaring, raging sea. The captain stood at the side of the ship and examined the sea in all directions. Then he slapped his face, furled the sails, cast the anchors, plucked his beard, tore his clothes, and uttered aloud cry. When we asked him, "Captain, what is the matter?" he said, "O fellows, may God preserve you. The wind has prevailed against us and forced us into the middle of the sea, and fate and our ill fortune have brought us to the Mountain of the Apes. No one has ever come here and escaped safely." I was sure that we were all going to perish, and no sooner had the captain finished his speech than the ship was surrounded by ape-like creatures who came in great number, like locusts, and swarmed on the boat and on the shore. We were afraid that if we killed, struck, or chased away any of them, they would easily kill us because of their number, for numbers prevail over courage. We also feared that they would plunder our goods and provisions. They are the ugliest of beasts, with a terrifying appearance, covered with hair like black felt. They have black faces, yellow eyes, and small size, no more than four spans. No one understands their language nor knows who they are, for they shun the society of men. They climbed up the anchor cables of the ship, on every side, and cut them with their teeth, and they cut likewise all the ropes; so the ship swerved with the wind and stopped on the shore, below the mountain. They seized all the merchants and the other passengers and, landing us on the island, took the ship with everything in it and disappeared into an unknown place, leaving us behind.

We stayed on the island, eating of its vegetables and fruits and drinking of its streams until one day we saw a stately mansion, situated in the middle of the island. We walked in its direction, and when we reached it, we found it to be a strong castle, with high walls and a gate of ebony, with two leaves, both of which were open. We entered and found inside a large courtyard, around which there were many high doors, and at the upper end of which there was a large, high bench, on which rested stoves and copper cooking pots hanging above. Around the bench lay many scattered bones. But we saw no one and were very much surprised. Then we sat down in the courtyard for a while and soon fell asleep and slept from mid-morning till sundown, when suddenly we felt the earth trembling under us, heard a rumbling noise in the air, and saw descending on us from the top of the castle a huge figure in the likeness of a man, black in color and tall in stature, as if he were a huge palm-tree, with eyes like torches; fangs like the tusks of a boar; a big mouth, like the mouth of a whale; lips like the lips of a camel, hanging down on his breast; ears like two barges, hanging down on his shoulders; and nails like the claws of a lion. When we saw him, we fainted, like men stricken dead with anxiety and terror.

When he descended, he sat on the bench for a while, then he got up and, coming to us, grabbed my hand from among my fellow merchants and, lifting me up in the air, turned me over, as I dangled from his hand like a little morsel, and felt my body as a butcher feels a sheep for the slaughter. But finding me feeble from grief, lean from the toil of the journey, and without much meat, he let me go and picked up on of my companions, turned him over, felt him, as he had done with me, and released him. He kept turning us over and feeling us, one after one, until he came to the captain of our ship, who was a fat, stout, and broad-shouldered man, a man of vigor and vitality. He was pleased by the captain, and he seized him, as a butcher seizes an animal he is about to slaughter, and, throwing him on the ground, set his foot on his neck and broke it. Then he fetched a long spit and thrust it through the captain's mouth until it came out from his posterior. Then he lit a big fire and set over it the spit on which the captain was spitted, turning it over the coal, until the flesh was roasted. Then he took the spit off the fire and, placing the body before him, separated the joints, as one separates the joints of a chicken, and proceeded to tear the flesh with his nails and eat it until he devoured all the flesh and gnawed the bones, and nothing was left of the captain except some bones, which he threw on one side. Then he sat on the bench for a while and fell asleep, snoring like a slaughtered sheep or cow, and slept till morning, when he got up and went on his way.

When we were sure that he was gone, we began to talk with one another, weeping for ourselves and saying, "We wish that we had drowned in the sea or been eaten by the apes, for that would have been better than being roasted on the coals. By God, this is a vile death, but what God wills comes to pass, and there is no power and no strength save in God the Almighty, the Magnificent. We will die miserably, and no one will know, for there is no escape from this place." We got up and walked in the island to look for a means of escape or a place to hide, feeling that death was lighter to bear than being roasted on the fire. But we failed to find a hiding place, and as the evening overtook us, we returned to the castle, driven by great fear.

No sooner had we sat down than the earth began to tremble under us, and that black creature approached us and began to turn us over and feel us, one after one, as he had done the first time, until he found one he liked, seized him, and did to him what he had done to the captain, on the first day. Then he roasted him and, after eating him, lay down on the bench and slept, snoring all night, like a slaughtered beast. In the morning, he got up and went on his way, leaving us, as usual.

We drew together and said to one another, "By God, if we throw ourselves into the sea and drown, it will be better than dying by fire, for this is a horrible death." One of us said, "Listen to me! Let us find a way to kill him and rid ourselves of this affliction and relieve all Muslims of his aggression and tyranny." I said to them, "Listen, friends! If we have to kill him, let us transport these planks of wood and some of the firewood and make for ourselves a raft and, after we find a way to kill him, embark on the raft and let the sea take us wherever God wishes. Then we will sit there until a ship passes by and picks us up. And if we fail to kill him, we can still embark on the raft and set out in the sea, even though we may drown, in order that we may escape from being slaughtered and roasted on the fire. If we escape, we escape, and if we drown, we die like martyrs." They all replied, "By God, this is a good plan," and we agreed to carry it out; so we carried the wood out of the castle, built a raft, tied it to the seashore and, after putting some food on it, returned to the castle.

When it was evening, the earth trembled under us, and in came the black creature, like a raging dog. He proceeded to turn us over and to feel us, one after one, until he picked one of us and did to him what he had done to his predecessors. Then he ate him and lay to sleep on the bench, snoring like thunder. We got up, took two of the iron spits of those set up there, and put them in the blazing fire until they became red-hot, like burning coals. Then, gripping the spits tightly, we went to the black creature, who was fast asleep, snoring, and pushing the spits with all our united strength and determination, thrust them deep into his eyes. He uttered a great, terrifying cry. Then he got up resolutely from the bench and began to search for us, while we fled from him to the right and left, in unspeakable terror, sure of destruction and despairing of escape. But being blind, he was unable to see us, and he groped his way to the door, and went out, as his screams made the ground tremble under us and made us quake with terror. When he went out, we followed him, as he went searching for us. Then he returned with a female, even bigger than he and more hideous in appearance. When we saw him and saw that his female companion was more horrible than he, we were in utmost terror. When the female saw us, we hurried to the raft, untied it and, embarking on it, pushed it into the sea, while the two stood, throwing big rocks on us until most of us died, except for three, I and two companions.

The raft conveyed us to another island. There, we walked till the end of the day, and, when it was night, we went to sleep. We were barely asleep when we were aroused by an enormous serpent with a wide belly. It surrounded us and, approaching one of us, swallowed him to his shoulders, then swallowed the rest of him, and we heard his ribs crack inside its belly. Then it went on its way, leaving us in utter amazement and grief for our companion and fear for our lives, thinking to ourselves, "By God, this is amazing, for each death is more terrible than the preceding one. We rejoiced at our escape from the black creature, but our joy did not last. There is no power and no strength, save in God. By God, we have escaped from the black creature and from drowning, but how shall we escape from this accursed monster?"

Then we walked in the island, eating of its fruits and drinking of its streams, and when it was evening, we found a huge, tall tree, climbed it, and went to sleep there, I myself being on the highest branch. As soon as it was dark, the serpent came and, looking right and left, headed for the tree on which we were, and climbed until it reached my companion. Then it swallowed him to his shoulders, coiled with him around the tree, as I heard his bones crack in its belly, then swallowed him whole, while I looked on. Then it slid down from the tree and went on its way.

I stayed on the tree for the rest of the night, and when it was daylight, I climbed down, like a man stricken dead with terror. I thought of throwing myself into the sea and delivering myself from the world. But I could not bring myself to do it, for life is dear. So I tied a wide piece of wood crosswise to my feet, tied two similar ones to my right side, to my left side, and to my chest, and tied another, very wide and long, crosswise to my head. Thus I was in the middle of these pieces of wood which surrounded me and, having fastened them tightly to my body, I threw myself on the ground and lay, with the wood enclosing me like a closet.

When it was dark, the serpent came, as usual, saw me, and headed for me, but it could not swallow me with the wood surrounding me. Then it began to circle around me, while I looked on, like a man stricken dead with terror. Then the serpent began to turn away from me and come back to me, and every time it tried to swallow me it was prevented by the wood that was tied to me on every side, and it continued in this fashion from sunset to sunrise. When it was light, it went its way, in the utmost vexation and rage. Then I moved my hands and untied myself from the pieces of wood, feeling almost dead from what I had suffered from that serpent.

I then walked in the island until I reached the shore and, happening to look toward the sea, saw a ship on the waves, in the distance. I took a big branch and began to make signs with it and call out the passengers. When they saw me, they said to each other, "We must see what this is, for it may be a man." They came closer, and when they heard my cries for help, they came to me and took me with them in the ship. Then they inquired about my situation, and I related to them what had happened to me, from beginning to end, and what hardships I had suffered, and they marveled at that. Then they gave me some of their clothes to make myself decent and offered me some food and some cool sweet water. I ate and drank until I had enough, and I felt refreshed, relaxed, and very comfortable, and my vigor returned. God the Almighty had brought me to life after death, and I thanked Him and praised Him for his abundant blessings, after I had been certain of destruction, thinking that I was in a dream.

We sailed, with God's permission, with a fair wind, until we came to an island called the Salahita Island. The captain cast anchor there, and all the merchants and other passengers landed with their goods to sell and buy. Then the captain turned to me and said, "Listen to me! You are a poor stranger who has, as you told us, suffered many horrors, and I wish to benefit you with something that will help you to return to your country, so that you will pray for me." I replied, "Very well, you will have my prayers." He said, "There was a passenger with us whom we lost, and we don't know whether he is alive or dead, for he has left no trace. I would like to give you his goods, and you will take charge of them to sell them in this island, and we will pay you an amount commensurate with your work and trouble and take the rest with us back to Baghdad, find his family, and give it to them, together with the proceeds of the sale. Will you receive the goods and take them to the island to sell them, like the other merchants?" I replied, "Sir, I hear and obey, with gratitude and thanks," and I invoked a blessing on him and thanked him. He then ordered the porters and sailors to carry the goods to the island and deliver them to me. The ship's clerk said to him, "What are those bales that the porters and sailors are carrying out and in whose merchant's name shall I register them?" The captain replied, "Register them in the name of Sindbad the Sailor, who was with us on that island and who drowned, without leaving any trace. I wish this stranger to sell these goods, and I will give him an amount commensurate with his work and trouble and keep the rest of the money with us until we reach Baghdad and, if we find Sindbad, give it to him and, if we don't, give it to his family." The clerk replied, "This is a good and wise plan." When I heard the captain mention that the goods were in my name, I said to myself, "By God, I am Sindbad the Sailor who was lost on that island!"

Then I controlled myself and waited patiently until the merchants came back to the ship and assembled to chat and consult on the affairs of buying and selling. I approached the captain and said to him, "Sir, do you know anything about the man whose goods you gave me to sell?" The captain replied, "I know nothing about him, except that he was a man from Baghdad, called Sindbad the Sailor. We cast anchor at one of the islands, and he was lost, and we have not heard anything about him to this day." I uttered a great cry and said, "O captain, may God preserve you! I am Sindbad the Sailor. When you cast anchor at that island, and the merchants and the rest of the passengers landed, I landed with them. I took with me something to eat, and sat in a place, enjoying myself; then I dozed off and fell into a deep sleep." When the merchants and the other passengers heard my words, they gathered around me, some believing me, some disbelieving. Soon, one of the merchants, hearing me mention the valley of diamonds approached me and said to them, "Listen to what I have to say, fellows! When I related to you the most extraordinary events that I encountered in my travels and how the merchants threw the slaughtered sheep into the valley of diamonds, and I threw mine with theirs, as was my habit, and how I found a man attached to my slaughtered sheep, you did not believe me and thought that I was lying." They said, "Yes, you did tell us that story, and we did not believe you." The merchant said, "This is the very man who gave me the unmatched expensive diamonds, compensating me with more than I would have gotten from my slaughtered sheep, and who traveled with me as my companion until we reached Basra, where he bade us farewell and headed to his city, while we returned to ours. This is the very man who told us that his name was Sindbad the Sailor and related to us how the ship had left, while he was sitting in that island. This man has come to us, in order that you may believe my story. All those goods are his property, for he informed us of them when he first met us, and the truth of his words is evident." When the captain heard the merchant's words, he stood up and, coming up to me, stared at me for a while and asked me, "What is the mark on your bales?" I said, "The mark is such and such," and when I informed him of a matter that had occurred between us when I embarked in the ship, in Basra, he became convinced that I was indeed Sindbad the Sailor, and he embraced me, saluted me, and congratulated me on my safety, saying, "By God, sir, your story is extraordinary and wonderful. God be praised for reuniting you with us and returning your goods and property to you."

Afterwards, I disposed of my goods, according to the best of my skill, and made a great deal of profit, and I felt exceedingly happy and congratulated myself on my safety and the recovery of my property. We continued to sell and buy in the islands until we reached the Indus Valley, where we likewise sold and bought and enjoyed the sights. I saw in the sea there many wonders and strange things. Among the things I saw was a fish in the form of a cow and a creature in the form of an ass. I also saw a bird that comes out of a seashell, lays its eggs on the surface of the water, and hatches them there but never comes up from the sea to the land.

Then we continued our voyage, with God's permission, until, with the aid of a fair wind, we reached Basra, where I stayed for a short time and headed for Baghdad. I went to my house, where I greeted my family and my friends and companions, rejoicing in my safe return to my country and city and home and family. I gave alms and gifts and clothed the widows and the orphans. Then I gathered around me my friends and companions and began to enjoy myself with them, eating well and drinking well, and diverting and entertaining myself, and I forgot all that had happened to me and all the hardships and perils I had suffered. On that voyage, I gained what cannot be numbered or calculated. These then were the most extraordinary events of that voyage. Tomorrow, God willing, come to me, and I will tell you the story of the fourth voyage, which is more wonderful than those of the preceding voyages.

Then Sindbad the Sailor gave the porter a hundred pieces of gold, as usual, and ordered that the table be spread. After the table was spread, and the guests dined, still marveling at that story and its events, the porter took the money and went on his way, marveling at what he had heard. The porter spent the night in his house, and as soon as it was morning, he performed his morning prayer and headed to Sindbad the Sailor. He went in and saluted him, and Sindbad received him with gladness and cheer and sat with him until the rest of his companions arrived. When food was served, and they ate and drank and felt merry, Sindbad began his story, saying:

THE FOURTH VOYAGE OF SINDBAD

Friends, when I returned to Baghdad and to the society of my family and friends and companions, I lived in the utmost happiness, pleasure, and ease and forgot what I had experienced, because of my great profit and my immersion in sport and mirth in the society of friends and companions. Thus I lived a most delightful life until my wicked soul suggested to me to travel to foreign countries, and I felt a longing for meeting other races and for selling and gain. Having made my resolve, I purchased precious goods, suited for a sea voyage, and having packed up more bales than usual, journeyed from Baghdad to Basra, where I loaded my bales in a ship and embarked with some of the chief merchants of the town.

We set out on our voyage and sailed, with the blessing of the Almighty God, in the sea, and the journey was pleasant, as we sailed, for many nights and days, from sea to sea and island to island until one day a contrary wind rose against us. So the captain cast the ship's anchors and brought it to a standstill, fearing that it would sink in midocean. While we were praying and imploring the Almighty God, a violent storm suddenly blew against us, tore the sails to pieces, and threw the people, with all their bales, provisions, and possessions, into the sea. I too was submerged like the rest. I kept myself afloat half the day, and when I was about to give up, the Almighty God provided me with one of the wooden planks of the ship, and I and some other merchants climbed on it, and we paddled with our feet, with the aid of the wind and the waves, for a day and a night. On the midmorning of the following day, a squall blew, and the waves rose, casting us on an island, almost dead from lack of sleep, exhaustion, hunger, thirst, and fear.

We walked along the shores of that island and found abundant vegetation, of which we ate a little to stay our hunger and to sustain ourselves. We spent the night on the shore, and when it was daylight, we arose and wandered in the island to the right and left until we saw a building in the distance. We walked toward that building and kept walking until we stood at its door. While we stood there, out came a group of naked men, who, without speaking to us, seized us and took us to their king. He ordered us to sit, and we sat. Then they brought us some strange food, the like of which we had never seen in our lives. My stomach revolted from it, and unlike my companions, I refrained from eating it, and my refraining was, by the favor of the Almighty God, the cause of my being alive till now. For when my companions ate of that food, they were dazed and began to eat like madmen, and their states changed. Then the people brought them coconut oil, and gave them to drink from it and anointed them with it. When they drank of that oil, their eyes rolled in their heads, and they proceeded to devour an unusual amount of food. When I saw them in that condition, I was puzzled and felt sorry for them, and I became extremely anxious and fearful for myself from these naked men. I looked at them carefully and realized that they were Magians and that the king of their city was a demon. Whenever someone came to their country, or they spotted him or chanced to meet him in the valley or on the roads, they brought him to their king, gave him of that food to eat and anointed him with that oil, so that his belly would expand and he would overeat, feeling stupefied, losing judgment, and becoming like an idiot. Then they gave him more and more of that food to eat and of that oil to drink, and when he became fat and stocky, they slaughtered him, roasted him, and gave him to their king to eat, while they themselves ate the flesh without roasting it or cooking it.

When I realized the situation, I was extremely anxious for myself and my companions, who, in their stupefaction, did not know what was being done to them. They were committed to a man who took them out every day and let them pasture on that island, like cattle. In the meantime, I wasted away and became emaciated from hunger and fear, and my skin shriveled on my bones. When the Magians saw me in this condition, they left me alone and forgot me, not one of them taking any notice of me, until one day I found a way to slip out of the building and walked away. Then I saw a herdsman sitting on something elevated in the middle of the sea, and when I looked at him, I realized that he was the man to whom they had committed my companions to be taken out to pasture. With him there were many men like them. As soon as the man saw me, he knew that I was in possession of my reason and that I was not afflicted like my companions. He signed to me from afar, saying, "Turn back, and take the road on your right, and it will lead you into the king's highway." I turned back, as he had told me and, finding a road on my right, began to follow it, sometimes running from fear, sometimes walking slowly, in order to catch my breath, and I kept following the road until I disappeared from the sight of the man who had directed me to it, and we were no longer able to see each other.

By then, the sun had set, and it had become dark. I sat down to rest and tried to sleep, but I could not sleep that night because of my extreme fear, hunger, and fatigue. When the night was half spent, I rose and walked in the island until it was daylight, and the sun rose over the tops of the hills and over the plains. I was tired, hungry, and thirsty; so I ate of the herbs and the plants that were on that island until I had enough to allay my hunger. Then I walked the whole day and the next night, and whenever I felt hungry, I ate of the plants to stay my stomach, and I walked on like this for seven days and nights.

On the morning of the eighth day, I happened to cast a glance and saw a vague object in the distance. I walked toward it and kept walking until I reached it, after sunset. I stood scrutinizing it from a distance, still fearful because of what I had suffered the first and the second time, and found that it was a group of men gathering peppercorn. When I approached them, and they saw me, they hastened to me and, surrounding me on all sides, asked me, "Who are you, and from where do you come?" I said to them, "Fellows, I am a poor stranger," and I informed them of my case and how I had suffered hardships and horrors. When they heard my words, they said, "By God, this is extraordinary, but tell us how you escaped from these black men and how you slipped by them, when they are so numerous on this island, and they eat people?" So I related to them what had happened to me with them and how they had given my companions the food I refrained from eating. They congratulated me on my safety and marveled at my story.

They seated me among them until they finished their work. Then they brought me some good food, which I ate, being hungry, and rested for a while. Then they took me and embarked with me in a ship and went to their island and their homes. There, they presented me to their king, and I saluted him, and he welcomed me, treated me with respect, and asked me about my case. I related to him all that had happened to me, from the day I left Baghdad until I came to him, and he, as well as all those present in his assembly, marveled greatly at my story. Then he asked me to sit and gave orders to bring the food, and I ate until I had enough, washed my hands, and offered thanks to the Almighty God and praised him for His favor. Then I left the presence of the king and went sightseeing in his city and found it flourishing, populous, and prosperous, abounding with food, markets, and buyers and sellers. I rejoiced in my arrival in that city and felt at ease there, as I made friends with its people who, together with their king, favored me and honored me more than even the chief men of that city.

I saw that all the men, great and small, rode fine horses, but without saddles, and wondered at that, so I said to the king, "My lord, why don't you ride on a saddle, for it offers the rider comfort and greater control?" He asked, "What kind of thing is a saddle, for I have never seen nor used one in all my life." I said to him, "Will you permit me to make you a saddle to ride on and experience its quality?" He said, "Very well." I said, "Let them fetch me some wood," and he gave orders to bring me everything I required. Then I asked for a skilled carpenter and sat with him and showed him the construction of the saddle and how to make it. Then I took some wool, carded it, and made a felt pad out of it. Then I brought leather and, covering the saddle with it, polished it and attached the straps and the girth. Afterwards, I brought a blacksmith and showed him how to make the stirrups, and he forged a great pair of stirrups which I filed and plated with tin and to which I attached fringes of silk. Then I brought one of the best of the king's horses, saddled him, attaching the stirrups to the saddle; bridled him; and led him to the king, who was pleased by the saddle and received it with approval and thanks. He seated himself on the saddle and was greatly pleased with it and gave me a large reward for it.

When his vizier saw that I had made the saddle, he asked me for one, and I made one like it. Moreover, all the leading men and high officials began to order saddles, and I kept making them and selling them, having taught the carpenter and blacksmith how to make saddles and stirrups. Thus I amassed a great deal of money, and was highly esteemed and greatly loved, and I continued to enjoy a high status with the king and his entourage, as well as the leading men of the city and the lords of the state.

One day, I sat with the king, in the utmost happiness and honor, when he said to me, "You are honored and loved among us, and you have become one of us, and we cannot part from you, nor can we bear your departure from our city. I wish you to obey me in a certain matter, without contradicting me." I said to him, "What does your majesty desire of me, for I cannot deny you, since I am indebted to you for your favors, benefits, and kindness, and, praise be to God, I have become one of your servants." He said, "I wish to marry you among us to a lovely, elegant, and charming woman, a woman of beauty and wealth, and you shall reside with us and live with me in my palace. Therefore, do not deny me or argue with me." When I heard the king's words, I remained silent, for I was too embarrassed to say anything. He said, "Son, why don't you answer me?" I replied, "My lord and king of the age, the command is yours." So he immediately summoned the judge and the witnesses and married me to a fine lady of high rank, noble birth, great lineage, surpassing beauty, and abundant wealth, possessing a great many buildings and dwellings. Then he gave me a great, beautiful house, standing alone, and gave me servants and attendants, and assigned me stipends and supplies. So I lived in the utmost ease, contentment, and happiness and forgot all the weariness, trouble, and hardship I had suffered. I said to myself, "If I ever go back to my country, I will take her with me. But whatever is predestined to happen will happen, and no one knows what will befall him," for I loved her and she loved me very much, and we lived in harmony, enjoying great prosperity and happiness.

One day, God the Almighty caused the wife of my neighbor, who was one of my companions, to die, and I went to see him to offer my condolences for the loss of his wife and found him in a sorry plight, anxious, weary, and distracted. I offered my condolences and began to comfort him, saying, "Don't mourn for your wife. God the Almighty will compensate you with a better wife and will grant you a long life, if it be His will." He wept bitterly, saying, "O my friend, how will God compensate me with a better wife, when I have only one day to live?" I said, "Friend, be rational and do not prophecy your own death, for you are well and in good health." He said, "By your life, brother, tomorrow you will lose me and never in your life will you see me again." I asked, "How so?" He said, "Today, they will bury my wife and bury me with her in the tomb, for it is the custom of our country, when the wife dies, to bury the husband alive with her, and when the husband dies, to bury the wife alive with him, in order that neither of them may enjoy life after the other." I said to him, "By God, this is a most vile custom, and no one should endure it."

While we were conversing, most of the people of the city came, offered their condolences for the death of my friend's wife and his own death, and began to prepare her, according to their custom. They brought a coffin and, placing the woman in it, carried her and took her husband with them, outside the city, until they reached a place in the side of a mountain by the sea. They advanced to a spot and lifted from it a large stone, revealing a stone-lined well. They threw the woman down into that well, which seemed to lead into a vast cavern beneath the mountain. Then they brought the husband and, tying a rope of palm fibers under his armpits, let him down the well, with a jug of sweet water and seven loaves of bread. When he was down, he undid the rope, and they drew it up, covered the mouth of the well with that large stone as it was before, and went on their way, leaving my friend with his wife in the cavern.

I said to myself, "By God, this death is worse than the first." Then I went to the king and said to him, "O my lord, why do you bury the living with the dead in your country?" He replied, "It is the custom of our country, when the husband dies, to bury his wife alive with him, and when the wife dies, to bury her husband alive with her, so that they may always be together, in life and in death. This custom we have received from our forefathers." I asked him, "O king of the age, will you do to a foreigner like me as you have done to that man, if his wife dies?" He replied, "Yes, we bury him and do to him as you have seen." When I heard his words, I was galled, dismayed, stricken with grief for myself, and dazed with fear that my wife might die before me and they bury me alive with her. Then I tried to divert my mind, by keeping busy, and to console myself, thinking, "Maybe I will die before her, for no one knows who will go first and who will follow."

But a short time later, my wife fell ill, and a few days later died. Most of the people of the city came to offer their condolences for her death to me and to her relatives. The king too came to offer his condolences, as was their custom. Then they brought a woman to wash her, and they washed her and arrayed her in her richest clothes and gold ornaments, necklaces, and jewels. Then they put her in the coffin and carried her to the side of the mountain and, removing the stone from the mouth of the well, they threw her in. Then all my friends and my wife's relatives turned to me to bid me the last farewell, while I was crying out among them, "I am a foreigner, and I cannot endure your custom." They did not pay any attention to my words, but, seizing me, they bound me by force and let me down the well into the large cavern beneath the mountain, with seven loaves of bread and a jug of sweet water, as was their custom. Then they said to me, "Untie yourself from the ropes," but I refused, and they threw the ropes down on me, covered the opening of the well, and departed.

I saw in that cavern many dead bodies that exhaled a putrid and loathsome smell, and I blamed myself for what I had done, saying to myself, "By God, I deserve everything that has happened to me." I could not distinguish night from day, and I sustained myself with very little food, not eating until I felt the pangs of hunger, nor drinking until I became extremely thirsty, fearing that my food and water would be exhausted. I said to myself, "There is no power and no strength, save in God the Almighty, the Magnificent. What possessed me to marry in this city? Every time I say to myself that I have escaped one calamity, I fall into a worse one. By God, this death is a vile death. I wish that I had drowned in the sea or died on the mountain; that would have been better than this horrible death." And I continued to blame myself. Then I threw myself down on the bones of the dead, begging, in the extremity of my despair, the Almighty God for a speedy death, but found it not, and I continued in this state until my stomach was lacerated by hunger, and my throat was inflamed with thirst. So I sat up and, groping for the bread, ate a little morsel and drank a mouthful of water. Then I stood up and began to explore that cavern. I found that it was wide and empty, except that its floor was covered with dead bodies and rotten bones from long ago. I made myself a place in the side of the cavern, far from the fresh bodies, and went to sleep there. Eventually my provisions dwindled until I had only a very little left. During each day, or more than a day, I had eaten only a morsel and drunk only a mouthful, fearing that the food and water would run out before my death.

I remained in this situation until one day, while I sat wondering what I would do when I ran out of food and water, the rock was suddenly removed from its place, and the light beamed on me. I said to myself, "I wonder what is happening," and saw people standing at the opening of the well who let down a dead man and a living woman, weeping and wailing for herself, and they let down with her food and water. I kept staring at the woman, without being seen by her, while they covered the mouth of the well with the stones and went on their way. Then I took the shinbone of a dead man and, going to the woman, struck her on the crown of the head, and she fell down unconscious. I struck her a second and a third time until she died. She had on her plenty of apparel, ornaments, necklaces, jewels, and precious metals, and I took all she had, together with the bread and water, and sat in the place I had made for myself in the side of the cavern where I used to sleep, and continued to eat only a little of that food, just enough to sustain me, for fear that it would be exhausted quickly and I would die of hunger and thirst.

I remained in the cavern for sometime, and whenever they buried a dead person, I killed the living one who was buried with him and took his food and water to sustain myself until one day I woke up from my sleep and heard something rummaging in the side of the cavern. I said to myself, "What can it be?" Then I got up and, with a shinbone in my hand, I walked toward the noise and found out that it was a wild beast which, when it became aware of me, ran away and fled from me. I followed it to the far end of the cavern and saw a spot of light, like a star, now appearing, now disappearing. When I saw it, I walked toward it, and the closer I got to it, the larger and brighter it became until I was certain that it was an opening in the cavern leading to the open air. I said to myself, "There must be an explanation for this. Either it is a second opening, like the one from which they let me down, or it is a fissure in the rock." I stood reflecting for a while; then I advanced toward the light and found that it was a hole in the side of the mountain which the wild beasts had made and through which they entered the cavern and ate of the dead bodies until they had their fill and went out as they came.

When I saw the hole, I felt relieved from my anxiety and worry, certain of life, after having been on the verge of death, and as happy as if I had been in a dream. Then I tried until I succeeded to climb out of the hole, finding myself on the side of a great mountain overlooking the sea and acting as a barrier between the sea, on the one side, and the island and the city, on the other, so that none could come to that part of the city. I praised and thanked the Almighty God, feeling extremely happy and regaining my courage. Then I returned through the hole to the cavern and brought out all the food and water I had saved. Then I changed my clothes, putting on some of the clothes of the dead, and gathered a great many of all kinds of necklaces of pearls and precious stones, ornaments of gold and silver set with gems, and other valuables I found on the corpses and, using the clothes of the dead to pack the jewelry in bundles, carried them out through the hole to the side of the mountain and stood on the seashore.

Every day I went into the cavern and explored it, and whenever they buried someone alive, I killed him, whether he was male or female, took his food and water and, coming out of the cavern, sat on the seashore to wait for deliverance by the Almighty God, by means of a passing ship. For some time, I kept gathering all the jewelry I could find, tying it up in bundles in the clothes of the dead, and carrying it out of the cavern.

One day, as I was sitting on the seashore, thinking about my situation, I saw a ship passing in the middle of a roaring, surging sea. I took a white shirt that I had taken from one of the dead, tied it to a stick, and ran along the seashore, making with it signals to the people on the ship, until, happening to glance in my direction, they saw me and turned toward me, and when they heard my cries, they sent a boat with a group of men. When they came close to me, they said, "Who are you, and why are you sitting in this place, and how did you reach this mountain, for in all our lives we have never known anyone who has reached it?" I said, "I am a merchant, who had been shipwrecked, and I saved myself by getting on a wooden plank, together with my belongings, and, with God's help and by my own exertions, skill, and great toil, I landed at this place, with my belongings." They took me with them in the boat, carrying all I had taken from the cavern, bundled in the clothes and shrouds of the dead, embarked in the ship, and took me with all my belongings to the captain.

The captain said to me, "Fellow, how did you reach this great mountain, which bars the shore from the great city behind it, for I have been sailing in this sea and passing by this mountain all my life, but I have never seen anyone here, except the birds and the wild beasts?" I replied, "I was a merchant on a large ship that was wrecked, and I was thrown into the sea with all my merchandise, which consisted of the fabrics and clothes that you see. But I placed them on one of the wide wooden planks of the ship, and fate and fortune aided me, and I landed on the mountain, where I have been waiting for someone to pass by and take me with him." I did not tell them, however, about what had happened to me in the city or in the cavern, for fear that they might have with them on the ship someone from that city. Then I took out a good portion of my property and presented it to the captain, saying, "Sir, you are the cause of my rescue from this mountain. Take this gift in gratitude for what you have done." But he refused my gift, saying, "We take nothing from anyone, and when we see a shipwrecked man on the seashore or on an island, we take him with us, feed him and give him to drink, and if he is naked, clothe him, and, when we reach a safe harbor treat him with kindness and charity and give him a present, for the sake of the Almighty God." When I heard his words, I offered prayers, wishing him a long life.

We sailed from sea to sea and from island to island, while I anticipated my deliverance and rejoiced in my safety, but every time I recalled my stay with my dead wife in that cavern, I almost lost my mind. At last, with the help of the Almighty God, we arrived safely in Basra, where I stayed for a few days, then headed for Baghdad. There, I came to my quarter, entered my house, and met my relatives and friends, inquiring about their condition, and they rejoiced and congratulated me on my safe return. Then I stored all I had brought with me in my storerooms, gave alms and clothed the widows and the orphans, and bestowed gifts. I felt extremely joyful and happy and returned to my former habit of associating with friends and companions and indulging in sport and pleasure. These, then, are the most extraordinary events of my fourth voyage. Dine with me now, brother, and come back tomorrow, as usual, and I will tell you the story of what happened to me on the fifth voyage, for it is more extraordinary and more wonderful than the preceding one.

Then Sindbad the Sailor gave the porter a hundred pieces of gold and ordered that the table be spread, and after the guests dined, they went their way, in great amazement, for each story was more extraordinary than the preceding one. Sindbad the Porter went to his house, where he spent the night in the utmost joy, happiness, and wonder. As soon as it was daylight, he got up, performed his morning prayer, and walked until he came to Sindbad the Sailor. He walked in, wished him good morning, and Sindbad welcomed him and asked him to sit with him until the rest of his companions arrived. They ate and drank, enjoyed themselves, and felt merry, and when they turned to conversation, Sindbad the Sailor began his story saying:

THE FIFTH VOYAGE OF SINDBAD

Friends, when I returned from the fourth voyage, I indulged in sport, pleasure, and delight, rejoicing greatly in my gains, profits, and benefits, and forgot all I have experienced and suffered until I began to think again of traveling to see foreign countries and islands. Having made my resolve, I bought valuable merchandise suited to a sea voyage, packed up my bales, and journeyed from Baghdad to Basra. I walked along the shore and saw a large, tall, and goodly ship, newly fitted. It pleased me and I bought it. Then I hired a captain and crew, over whom I set some of my slaves and pages as superintendents, and loaded my bales on the ship. Then a group of merchants joined me, loaded their bales on the ship, and paid me the freight. We set out in all joy and cheerfulness, rejoicing in the prospect of a safe and prosperous voyage, and sailed from sea to sea and from island to island, landing to see the sights of the islands and towns and to sell and buy.

We continued in this fashion until one day we came to a large uninhabited island, waste and desolate, except for a vast white dome. The merchants landed to look at the dome, which was in reality a huge Rukh's egg, but, not knowing what it was, they struck it with stones, and when they broke it, much fluid ran out of it, and the young Rukh appeared inside. They drew it out of the shell, slaughtered it, and took from it a great deal of meat. While this was going on, I was on the ship, uninformed and unaware of it until one of the passengers came to me and said, "Sir, go and look at that egg, which we thought to be a dome." I went to look at the egg and arrived just when the merchants were striking it. I cried out to them, "Don't do this, for the Rukh will come, demolish our ship, and destroy us all." But they did not heed my words.

While they were thus engaged, the sun suddenly disappeared, and the day great dark, as if a dark cloud was passing above us. We raised our heads to see that had veiled the sun and saw that it was the Rukh's wings that had blocked the sunlight and made the day dark, for when the Rukh came and saw its egg broken, it cried out at us, and its mate came, and they circled above the ship, shrieking with voices louder than thunder. I called out to the captain and the sailors, saying, "Push off the ship, and let us escape before we perish." The captain hurried and, as soon as the merchants embarked, unfastened the ship and sailed away from the island. When the Rukhs saw that we were on the open sea, they disappeared for a while.

We sailed, making speed, in the desire to leave their land behind and escape from them, but suddenly they caught up with us, each carrying in its talons a huge rock from a mountain. Then the male bird threw its rock on us, but the captain steered the ship aside, and the rock missed it by a little distance, and fell into the water with such force that we saw the bottom of the sea, and the ship went up and down, almost out of control. Then the female bird threw on us its rock, which was smaller than the first, but as it had been ordained, it fell on the stern of the ship, smashed it, sent the rudder flying in twenty pieces, and threw all the passengers into the sea.

I struggled for dear life to save myself until the Almighty God provided me with one of the wooden planks of the ship, to which I clung and, getting on it, began to paddle with my feet, while the wind and the waves helped me forward. The ship had sunk near an island in the middle of the sea, and fate cast me, according to God's will, on that island, where I landed, like a dead man, on my last breath from extreme hardship and fatigue and hunger and thirst. I threw myself on the seashore and lay for a while until I began to recover myself and feel better. Then I walked in the island and found that it was like one of the gardens of Paradise. Its trees were laden with fruits, its streams flowing, and its birds singing the glory of the Omnipotent, Everlasting One. There was an abundance of trees, fruits, and all kinds of flowers. So I ate of the fruits until I satisfied my hunger and drank of the streams until I quenched my thirst, and I thanked the Almighty God and praised Him.

I sat in the island until it was evening, and night approached, without seeing anyone or hearing any voice. I was still feeling almost dead from fatigue and fear; so I lay down and slept till the morning. Then I got up and walked among the trees until I came to a spring of running water, beside which sat a comely old man clad with a waistcloth made of tree leaves. I said to myself, "Perhaps the old man has landed on the island, being one of those who have been shipwrecked." I drew near him and saluted him, and he returned my salutation with a sign but remained silent. I said to him, "Old man, why are you sitting here?" He removed his head mournfully and motioned with his hand, meaning to say, "Carry me on your shoulders, and take me to the other side of the stream." I said to myself, "I will do this old man a favor and transport him to the other side of the stream, for God may reward me for it." I went to him, carried him on my shoulders, and took him to the place to which he had pointed. I said to him, "Get down at your ease," but he did not get off my shoulders. Instead, he wrapped his legs around my neck, and when I saw that their hide was as black and rough as that of a buffalo, I was frightened and tried to throw him off. But he pressed his legs around my neck and choked my throat until I blacked out and fell unconscious to the ground, like a dead man. He raised his legs and beat me on the back and shoulders, causing me intense pain. I got up, feeling tired from the burden, and he kept riding on my shoulders and motioning me with his hand to take him among the trees to the best of the fruits, and whenever I disobeyed him, he gave me, with his feet, blows more painful than the blows of the whip. He continued to direct me with his hand to any place he wished to go, and I continued to take him to it until we made our way among the trees to the middle of the island. Whenever I loitered or went leisurely, he beat me, for he held me like a captive. He nevr got off my shoulders, day or night, urinating and defecating on me, and whenever he wished to sleep, he would wrap his legs around my neck and sleep a little, then arise and beat me, and I would get up quickly, unable to disobey him because of the severity of the pain I suffered from him. I continued with him in this condition, suffering from extreme exhaustion and blaming myself for having taken pity on him and carried him on my shoulders. I said to myself, "I have done this person a good deed, and it has turned evil to myself. By God, I will never do good to anyone, as long as I live," and I began to beg, at every turn and every step, the Almighty God for death, because of the severity of my fatigue and distress.

I continued in this situation for some time until one day I came with him to a place in the island where there was an abundance of gourds, many of which were dry. I selected one that was large and dry, cut it at the neck and cleansed it. Then I went with it to a grapevine and filled it with the juice of the grapes. Then I plugged the gourd, placed in it the sun, and left it there several days until the juice turned into wine, from which I began to drink every day in order to find some relief from the exhausting burden of that obstinate devil, for I felt invigorated whenever I was intoxicated.

One day he saw me drinking and signed to me with his hand, meaning to say, "What is this?" I said to him, "This is an excellent drink that invigorates and delights." Then I ran with him and danced among the trees, clapping my hands and singing and enjoying myself, in the exhilaration of intoxication. When he saw me in that state, he motioned to me to give him the gourd, in order that he might drink from it. Being afraid of him, I gave it to him, and he drank all that was in it and threw it to the ground. Then he became enraptured and began to shake on my shoulders, and as he became extremely intoxicated and sank into torpor, all his limbs and muscles relaxed, and he began to sway back and forth on my shoulders. When I realized that he was drunk and that he was unconscious, I held his feet and loosened them from my neck and, stooping with him, I sat down and threw him to the ground, hardly believing that I had delivered myself from him. But, fearing that he might recover from his drunkenness and harm me, I took a huge stone from among the trees, came to him, struck him on the head as he lay asleep, mingling his flesh with his blood, and killed him. May God have no mercy on him!

Then I walked in the island, feeling relieved, until I came back to the spot on the seashore where I had been before. I remained there for some time, eating of the fruits of the island and drinking of its water and waiting for a ship to pass by, until one day, as I sat thinking about what had happened to me and reflecting on my situation, saying to myself, "I wonder whether God will preserve me and I will return to my country and be reunited with my relatives and friends," a ship suddenly approached from the middle of the roaring, raging sea and continued until it set anchor at the island, and its passengers landed. I walked toward them, and when they saw me, they all quickly hurried to me and gathered around me, inquiring about my situation and the reason for my coming to that island. I told them about my situation and what had happened to me, and they were amazed and said, "The man who rode on your shoulders is called the Old Man of the Sea, and no one was ever beneath his limbs and escaped safely, except yourself. God be praised for your safety." Then they brought me some food, and I ate until I had enough, and they gave me some clothes, which I wore to make myself decent. Then they took me with them in the ship, and we journeyed many days and nights until fate drove us to a city of tall buildings, all of which overlooked the sea. This city is called the City of the Apes, and when night comes, the inhabitants come out of the gates overlooking the sea and, embarking in boats and ships, spend the night there, for fear that the apes may descend on them from the mountains.

I landed, and while I was enjoying the sights of the city, the ship sailed, without my knowledge. I regretted having disembarked in that city, remembering my companions and what had happened to us with the apes the first and the second time, and I sat down, weeping and mourning. Then one of the inhabitants came to me and said, "Sir, you seem to be a stranger in this place." I replied, "Yes, I am a poor stranger. I was in a ship that anchored here, and I landed to see the sights of the city, and when I went back, I could not find the ship." He said, "Come with us and get into the boat, for if you spend the night here, the apes will destroy you." I said, "I hear and obey," and I got up immediately and embarked with them in the boat, and they pushed it off from the shore until we were a mile away. We spent the night in the boat, and when it was morning, they returned to the city, landed, and each of them went to his business. Such has been their habit every night, and whoever remains behind in the city at night, the apes come and destroy him. During the day, the apes go outside the city and eat of the fruits in the orchards and sleep in the mountains until the evening, at which time they return to the city.

This city is located in the farthest parts of the land of the blacks. One of the strangest things I experienced in the inhabitants' treatment of me was as follows. One of those with whom I spent the night in the boat said to me, "Sir, you are a stranger here. Do you have any craft you can work at?" I replied, "No, by God, my friend, I have no trade and no handicraft, for I was a merchant, a man of property and wealth, and I owned a ship laden with abundant goods, but it was wrecked in the sea, and everything in it sank. I escaped from drowning only by the grace of God, for He provided me with a plank of wood on which I floated and saved myself." When he heard my words, he got up and brought me a cotton bag and said, "Take this bag, fill it with pebbles from the shore, and go with a group of the inhabitants, whom I will help you join and to whom I will commend you, and do as they do, and perhaps you will gain what will help you to return to your country."

Then he took me with him until we came outside the city, where I picked small pebbles until the bag was filled. Soon a group of men emerged from the city, and he put me in their charge and commended me to them, saying, "This man is a stranger. Take him with you and teach him how to pick, so that he may gain his living and God may reward you." They said, "We hear and obey," and they welcomed me and took me with them, and proceeded, each carrying a cotton bag like mine, filled with pebbles. We walked until we came to a spacious valley, full of trees so tall that no one could climb them. The valley was also full of apes, which, when they saw us, fled and climbed up into the trees. The men began to pelt the apes with the pebbles from the bags, and the apes began to pluck the fruits of those trees and to throw them at the men, and as I looked at the fruits the apes were throwing, I found that they were coconuts.

When I saw what the men were doing, I chose a huge tree full of apes and, advancing to it, began to pelt them, while they plucked the nuts and threw them at me. I began to collect the nuts as the men did, and before my bag was empty of pebbles I had collected plenty of nuts. When the men finished the work, they gathered together all the nuts, and each of them carried as many as he could, and we returned to the city, arriving before the end of the day. Then I went to my friend, who had helped me join the group, and gave him all the nuts I had gathered, thanking him for his kindness, but he said to me, "Take the nuts, sell them, and use the money." Then he gave me a key to a room in his house, saying, "Keep there whatever is left of the nuts, and go out every day with the men, as you did today, and of what you bring with you separate the bad and sell them, and use the money, but keep the best in that room, so that you may gather enough to help you with your voyage." I said to him, "May the Almighty God reward you," and did as he told me, going out daily to gather pebbles, join the men, and do as they did, while they commended me to each other and guided me to the trees bearing the most nuts. I continued in this manner for some time, during which I gathered a great store of excellent coconuts and sold a great many, making a good deal of money, with which I bought whatever I saw and liked. So I thrived and felt happy in that city.

One day, as I was standing on the seashore, a ship arrived, cast anchor, and landed a group of merchants, who proceeded to sell and buy and exchange goods for coconuts and other commodities. I went to my friend and told him about the ship that had arrived and said that I would like to return to my country. He said, "It is for you to decide." So I thanked him for his kindness and bade him farewell. Then I went to the ship, met the captain, and, booking a passage, loaded my store of coconuts on the ship. We set out and continued to sail from sea to sea and from island to island, and at every island we landed, I sold and traded with coconuts until God compensated me with more than I had possessed before and lost.

Among other places we visited, we came to an island abounding in cinnamon and pepper. Some people told us that they had seen on every cluster of peppers a large leaf that shades it and protects it from the rain, and when the rain stops, the leaf flips over and assumes its place at its side. From that island I took with me a large quantity of pepper and cinnamon, in exchange for coconuts. Then we passed by the Island of the 'Usrat, from which comes the Comorin aloewood, and by another island, which is a five-day journey in length and from which comes the Chinese aloewood, which is superior to the Comorin. But the inhabitants of this island are inferior to those of the first, both in their religion and in their way of life, for they are given to lewdness and wine drinking and know no prayer nor the call to prayer. Then we came to the island of the pearl fishers, where I gave the divers some coconuts and asked them to dive, and try my luck for me. They dived in the bay and brought up a great number of large and valuable pearls, saying, "O master, by God, you are very lucky," and I took everything they brought up with me to the ship.

Then we sailed until we reached Basra, where I stayed for a few days, then headed for Baghdad. I came to my quarter, entered my house, and saluted my relatives and friends, and they congratulated me on my safety. Then I stored all the goods and gear I had brought with me, clothed the widows and the orphans, gave alms, and bestowed gifts on my relatives, friends, and all those dear to me. God had given me fourfold what I had lost, and because of my gains and the great profit I had made, I forgot what had happened to me and the toil I had suffered, and resumed my association with my friends and companions. These then are the most extraordinary events of my fifth voyage. Let us have supper now, and tomorrow, come, and I will tell you the story of my sixth voyage, for it is more wonderful than this.

They spread the table, and the guests dined, and when they finished Sindbad gave the porter a hundred pieces of gold, which he took and went on his way, marveling at what he had heard. He spent the night in his house, and as soon as it was morning, he got up, performed his morning prayer, and went to the house of Sindbad the Sailor. He went in and wished him good morning and Sindbad the Sailor asked him to sit and talked to him until the rest of his friends arrived. They talked for a while, then the table was spread, and they ate and drank and enjoyed themselves and felt merry. The Sindbad the Sailor began the story of the sixth voyage, saying:

THE SIXTH VOYAGE OF SINDBAD

Dear friends, after I returned from my fifth voyage, I forgot what I had suffered, indulging in sport, play, and merriment and leading a life of the utmost joy and happiness until one day a group of merchants came by, showing signs of travel. Their sight reminded me of the days of my return from my travels and my joy at seeing my country again and reuniting with my relatives and friends and dear ones. So I felt a longing for travel and trade, and I resolved to undertake another voyage. I bought valuable, rich merchandise suited to a sea voyage, packed it up in bales, and traveled from Baghdad to Basra. There, I found a large ship, full of prominent people and merchants with valuable goods, and I loaded my bales in the ship, and we departed from Basra peacefully.

We sailed from place to place and from city to city, selling and buying, seeing the sights of the different countries and enjoying our voyage and our good luck and profit. We continued in this way until one day the captain suddenly cried out, screaming, threw down his turban, slapped his face, plucked his beard, and fell down in the hold of the ship, in extreme anguish and grief. All the merchants and other passengers gathered around him and asked, "Captain, what is the matter?" He said, "We have strayed from our course and entered a sea of which we don't know the routes. If God does not provide us with a means of escape from this sea, we will all perish. Pray to the Almighty God to save us from this predicament." Then he climbed the mast, in order to loosen the sails, but a strong wind blew against the ship, driving it backward, and the rudder broke, near a high mountain. The captain came down from the mast and said, "There is no power and no strength save in God the Almighty, the Magnificent, and no one can prevent that which has been decreed. By God, we have fallen into a great peril, from which there is no escape." The passengers wept for themselves and bade each other farewell, having given themselves up for lost. Soon the ship veered toward the mountain and smashed against it, so that its planks scattered, and all that was in it sank into the sea. The merchants fell into the sea, and some of them drowned, while others held onto the mountain and landed on it. I was among those who landed.

That mountain was on a large island whose shores were strewn with wrecked ships and an abundance of goods, gear, and wealth that dazzled the mind, cast there by the sea from the ships that had been destroyed and whose passengers had drowned. I climbed to the upper part of the island, began to explore, and saw a stream of sweet water that issued from one side of the mountain and entered from the other. Then all the other passengers climbed to the upper part and wandered in the island, like madmen, for their minds were confounded by the profusion or goods and wealth they saw strewn on the shores.

I saw in that stream a great many rubies and royal pearls and all kinds of jewels and precious stones, which covered the bed of the stream like gravel, so that all the channels, which ran through the fields, glittered from their profusion. I saw also in that island an abundance of the best Chinese as well as Comorin aloewood. Moreover, in that island there is a gushing spring of some sort of crude ambergris, which flows like wax under the intense heat of the sun, and flows in a stream down to the seashore, where the sea beasts come up, swallow it, and return with it into the sea. When it gets hot in their stomachs, they eject it from their mouths into the water, and it rises to the surface, where it congeals and changes its color. Then the waves throw it on the shore, and the travelers and merchants who know it take it and sell it. As for the crude ambergris that is not swallowed, it flows over the side of that spring and congeals on the ground. When the sun rises, it flows, and its scent fills the whole valley with a musk-like fragrance, and when the sun sets, it congeals again. But that place where the ambergris is found, no one can reach, for the mountains surround the whole island, and no one can climb them.

We continued to wander in that island, marveling at the riches that the Almighty God had created there, but feeling perplexed in our predicament and sorely afraid. We had collected on the shore of the island a small amount of food, which we used sparingly, eating only every day or two, worried that the food would run out and we would die of starvation and fear. Whenever one of us died, we washed him, wrapped him in a shroud from the clothes cast on the shore by the sea, and buried him until most of us had died, except for a few who were weakened by a stomach ailment contracted from the sea. It was not long before all my friends and companions died, one by one.

I was left all alone in the island, with very little food. I wept for myself, thinking, "I wish that I had died before my companions, for they would have at least washed me and buried me. There is no power and no strength save in God the Almighty, the Magnificent." A little while later, I arose and dug for myself a deep hole on the shore, saying to myself, "When I grow weak and feel that I am about to die, I will lie in this grave and die in it, and the wind will blow the sand on me and cover me, and I will have my burial." I blamed myself for my lack of sense in leaving my country and city and traveling to foreign countries, after all I had suffered during the first, the second, the third, the fourth, and the fifth voyages, each marked by greater perils and horrors than the preceding one, each time hardly believing in my narrow escape. And I repented and renounced the sea and all travel in the sea, especially since I had no need of money, of which I had enough and, indeed, so much more that I could not spend or exhaust even half of it for the rest of my life.

After a while, however, I reflected and said to myself, "By God, the stream must have a beginning and an end, and it must lead to an inhabited part. The best plan will be to make a little raft, big enough to sit in, take it down, launch it on the stream, and drift with the current. If I find a way out, I will escape safely, the Almighty God permitting, and if I don't, it is better to die in the stream than in this place," and I sighed for myself.

Then I got up and proceeded to gather pieces of Comorin and Chinese aloewood from the island and tied them together on the shore with the ropes of wrecked ships. Then I took from the ships planks of even size and fixed them firmly on the wood. In this way, I made me a raft, which was a little narrower in width than the width of the stream. Then I attached a piece of wood on each side, to serve as oars, and launched it on the stream. Then I took some of the jewels, precious stones, and pearls that were as large as gravel and some of the best crude, pure ambergris, as well as other goods, together with whatever was left of the food, loaded everything on the raft, and did what the poet said:

> If you suffer injustice, save yourself
> And leave the house behind to mourn its builder.
> Your country you'll replace by another,
> But for yourself, you'll find no other self.
> Nor be too fretful at the blows of fate,
> For every misfortune begins and ends,

And he who in a certain place his death impends,
Will in no other place suffer that fate.
Nor for your mission trust another man,
For none is as loyal as you yourself.

I drifted with the stream, wondering what would happen to me, until I came to the place where the stream entered beneath the mountain and took the raft with it. I found myself in intense darkness, and the raft bore me with the current through a narrow tunnel beneath the mountain, and the sides of the raft began to rub against the sides of the tunnel, and my head began to rub against the roof. I was unable to go back, and I blamed myself for what I had done to myself and said, "If this tunnel becomes any narrower, the raft will not pass through, and since it cannot go back, I will inevitably perish miserably there." I prostrated myself on the raft, because of the narrowness of the channel, and continued to drift, not knowing night from day, because of the darkness beneath the mountain, and feeling concerned for myself and terrified that I might perish. In this condition, I continued my course along the stream, which sometimes widened and sometimes narrowed, until the intensity of the darkness and distress wearied me, and I fell asleep as I lay prostrate on the raft, which drifted, while I slept in utter oblivion.

When I awoke and opened my eyes, I found myself in the light, in the open air, and found the raft moored to an island, in the middle of a group of Indians and blacks. As soon as they saw me rise, they approached me and spoke to me in their language, but I did not understand what they said and kept thinking that I was still asleep and that this was a dream occasioned by my grief and distress. When they spoke to me, and I did not reply, not knowing their language, one of them came to me and said in Arabic, "Peace be on you, friend! Who are you, from where do you come, and what is the reason for your coming here? We are the owners of these lands and fields, which we came to irrigate, and we found you asleep on the raft. So we held it and moored it here, waiting for you to rise at your leisure. Tell us what is the reason for your coming here?" I said, "For God's sake, sir, bring me some food, for I am hungry. After that ask me what you wish." He hastened and brought me food, and I ate my fill until I felt satisfied and relaxed, and my spirit revived. I praised the Almighty God and rejoiced in my escape from that stream and in my finding them. Then I told them my story from beginning to end and how I had suffered from the narrowness of that stream.

They talked among themselves, saying, "We must take him with us and present him to our king, so that he may tell him his story." Then they took me, together with the raft and all that was on it of goods, jewels, precious stones, and gold ornaments, presented me to their king, and acquainted him with what had happened. He saluted me, welcomed me, and inquired about my condition and what I had experienced. I told him my story from beginning to end, at which he marveled exceedingly and congratulated me on my safety. Then I fetched from the raft a large quantity of jewels, precious stones, ambergris, and aloewood and presented them to the king, who accepted them, treated me very courteously, and gave me a lodging in his palace, where I stayed permanently. I associated with the best and most prominent people, who treated me with great respect. The visitors to that island came to me and questioned me about the affairs of my country, and I told them, and I, in turn, questioned them and was informed about the affairs in their own countries. One day the King himself questioned me about the conditions in my country and the way the caliph governs in Baghdad, and I told him about the caliph's just rule. The king marveled at that and said, "By God, the caliph's methods are wise and his ways praiseworthy, and you have made me love him. Therefore, I would like to prepare a present and send it with you to him." I said, "I hear and obey, my lord. I will convey the present to him and inform him that you are his sincere friend."

I continued to live with the king in great honor, consideration, and contentment for some time until one day, sitting in the king's palace, I heard that a group of people from the city had prepared for themselves a ship, with the intention of sailing to the environs of Basra. I said to myself, "I cannot do better than to travel with these people." I arose at once and, kissing the king's hand, informed him of my wish to travel with that group in the ship they had prepared, for I longed for my country and my family. The king said, "The decision is yours, yet if you wish to stay with us, we will be very glad, for we have enjoyed your company." I said, "By God, my lord, you have overwhelmed me with your kindness and your favors, but I long for my country and my family and friends." When he heard my reply, he summoned the merchants who had prepared the ship, commended me to them, paid my fare, and bestowed on me a great many gifts. He also entrusted me with a magnificent gift for the Caliph Harun al-Rashid in Baghdad. Then I bade the king, as well as my frequent companions, farewell and embarked with the merchants in the ship.

We sailed with a fair wind, committing ourselves to the care of the Almighty and Glorious God, and continued to travel from sea to sea and from island to island until, with the permission of the Almighty God, we reached Basra safely. I disembarked and spent a few days there to equip myself and pack up my goods. Then I headed for Baghdad, the Abode of Peace, and went to the Caliph Harun al-Rashid and conveyed the king's gift to him. Then I came to my quarter, entered my house, and stored my goods and gear. Soon my relatives and friends came to see me, and I bestowed gifts on all, and gave alms.

A little while later, the caliph summoned me and asked me the reason for the gift and from where it came. I said, "By God, O Commander of the Faithful, I do not know the name of the city from which this gift came, nor do I know the way to it. When the ship I was in was wrecked, I landed on an island, where I made me a raft and launched it on a stream in the middle of that island." Then I related to him what had happened to me on my journey and how I had escaped from the stream and reached that city safely. I also related to him what had happened to me in that city and explained the reason for the gift. The caliph marveled exceedingly, and he ordered the historians to record my story and deposit it in his library, so that whoever reads it might be edified by it, and he treated me very generously.

I resumed my former way of life in Baghdad and forgot all that I had experienced and suffered, living a life of sport, play, and pleasure. This, then, friends, is the story of my sixth voyage. Tomorrow, God the Almighty willing, I will tell you the story of my seventh voyage, for it is stranger and more wonderful than all the others.

Sindbad ordered that the table be spread, and the guests dined with him.

Then Sindbad the Sailor gave Sindbad the Porter a hundred pieces of gold, and the porter took the money and went on his way, as did the rest of the company, all marveling exceedingly at that story. Sindbad the Porter spent the night at his house, and as soon as he performed his morning prayer, he went to the house of Sindbad the Sailor. Then the rest of the group began to arrive, and when they were all assembled, Sindbad the Sailor began to tell them the story of his seventh voyage, saying,

THE SEVENTH VOYAGE OF SINDBAD

Fellows, after I returned from my sixth voyage, I resumed my former way of life and continued to lead a life of contentment and happiness, indulging day and night in play, diversion, and pleasure, having secured great gains and profits, until I began to long again to sail the seas, associate with fellow merchants, see foreign countries, and hear new things. I made my resolve and, packing up a quantity of precious goods suited to a sea voyage, carried them from Baghdad to Basra, where I found a ship ready to set sail, with a group of prominent merchants. I embarked with them, and we became friends, as we sailed with a fair wind in peace and good health until we passed by a city called the City of China, and while we were in the utmost joy and happiness, talking among ourselves about travel and commerce, a violent head wind blew suddenly, and a heavy rain began to fall on us until we and our bales were drenched. So we covered the bales with felt and canvas, fearing that the goods would be spoiled by the rain, and began to pray and implore God the Almighty to deliver us from the peril we were in. Then the captain, girding his waist and tucking up his clothes, climbed up the mast and began to look to the right and left. Then he looked at the people in the ship and began to slap his face and pluck his beard. We asked him, "Captain, what is the matter?" And he said, "Implore the Almighty God for deliverance from the peril we are in, and weep for yourselves and bid each other farewell, for the wind has prevailed against us and driven us into the farthest of the seas of the world." He then descended from the mast, opened a chest, and took out of it a cotton bag. Then he untied the bag, took out of it some dust, like ashes, wetted it with water, and, waiting a little, smelled it. Then he took out of the chest a small book and began to read in it. Then he said to us, "Passengers, in this book there is an amazing statement that whoever comes to this place will never leave it safely and will surely perish, for this region is called the Province of the Kings, and in it is the tomb of our Lord Solomon, the son of David (peace be on him), and there are huge, horrible-looking whales, and whenever a ship enters this region, one of them rises from the sea and swallows it with everything in it."

When we heard the captain's explanation, we were dumbfounded, and hardly had he finished his words when the ship suddenly began to rise out of the water and drop again, and we heard a great cry, like a peel of thunder, at which we were struck almost dead with terror, sure of our destruction. Suddenly we saw a whale heading for the boat, like a towering mountain, and we were terrified and wept bitterly for ourselves and prepared for death. We kept looking at that whale, marveling at its terrible shape, when suddenly another whale, the most huge and most terrible we had ever seen, approached us, and while we bade each other farewell and wept for ourselves, a third whale, even greater than the other two, approached, and we were stupefied and driven mad with terror. Then the three whales began to circle the ship, and the third whale lunged at the ship to swallow it, when suddenly a violent gust of wind blew, and the ship rose and fell on a massive reef, breaking in pieces, and all the merchants and the other passengers and the bales sank in the sea.

I took off all my clothes, except for a shirt, and swam until I caught a plank of wood from the ship and hung on to it. Then I got on it and held on to it, while the wind and the waves toyed with me on the surface of the water, carrying me up and down. I was in the worst of plights, with fear and distress and hunger and thirst. I blamed myself for what I had done and for incurring more hardships, after a life of ease, and said to myself, "O Sinbad the Sailor, you don't learn, for every time you suffer hardships and weariness, yet you don't repent and renounce travel in the sea, and when you renounce, you lie to yourself. I deserve my plight, which had been decreed by God the Almighty to cure me of my greed, which is the root of all my suffering, for I have abundant wealth." I returned to my reason and said to myself, "In this voyage, I repent to the Almighty God with a sincere repentance, and I will never again embark on travel, nor mention it, nor even think of it, for the rest of my life." I continued to implore the Almighty God and to weep, recalling my former days of play and pleasure and cheer and contentment and happiness.

I continued in this condition for a whole day and a second, at the end of which I came to a large island abounding in trees and streams. I landed and ate of the fruits of those trees and drank of the waters of those streams until I felt refreshed and regained my strength and recovered my spirit. Then I walked in the island and found on the other side a great river of sweet water, running with a strong current, and I remembered the raft I had made last time and said to myself, "I must make me a raft like that one; perhaps I will get out of here. If I get out safely, I will have my wish and vow to the Almighty God to foreswear travel, and if I perish, I will find rest from toil and misery."

Then I gathered many pieces of wood from the trees, which were of the finest sandalwood, the like of which does not exist anywhere else, although I did not know it at the time. Then I found a way to twist grasses and twigs into a kind of rope, with which I bound the raft, saying to myself, "If I escape safely, it will be by the grace of God." Then I got on the raft and proceeded along the river, leaving that part of the island behind. I lay on the raft for three days. I did not eat, but I drank from the water of the river, to quench my thirst, until I was giddy like a young bird from extreme weariness, hunger, and fear.

At the end of this time, the raft brought me to a high mountain, beneath which ran the river. When I saw this, I was frightened, recalling what I had suffered from the narrowness of that other stream during my preceding voyage. I tried to stop the raft and get off on the side of the mountain, but the current overpowered me and drew the raft, with me on it, beneath the mountain. I was sure that I would perish and said, "There is no power and no strength save in God the Almighty, the Magnificent," but after a short distance, the raft emerged in a wide space, a great valley, through which the river roared with a noise like thunder and ran with a swiftness like that of the wind. I held on to the raft, for fear of falling, while the waves tossed it to the right and left in the middle of the river. The raft continued to descend with the current, along the valley, while I was unable to stop or steer it toward the bank, until it brought me to a large, well-built, and populous city. When the people saw me on the raft, descending in the middle of the river with the current, they cast a net and ropes on the raft and drew it ashore.

I fell among them like a dead man, from extreme hunger, lack of sleep, and fear. Soon there approached me from among the people a venerable old man, who welcomed me and threw over me an abundance of handsome clothes, which I put on to make myself decent. Then he took me to the bath and brought me refreshing cordials and sweet perfumes. After the bath, he took me to his house, and his family received me joyfully. Then he seated me in a pleasant place and prepared sumptuous food for me, and I ate my fill and thanked the Almighty God for my safety. Then his pages brought me hot water, with which I washed my hands, and his maids brought me silk towels, with which I dried them and wiped my mouth. Then he prepared for me a private apartment in a part of his house and charged his pages and maids to wait on me and fulfill my needs, and they served me attentively. I stayed in the guest apartment for three days, enjoying delicious food and drink and sweet scents, until my fear subsided, my energy returned, and I felt at ease.

On the fourth day, the old man came to me and said, "Son, we have enjoyed your company, and God be praised for your safety. Would you like now to go down with me to the bank of the river and sell your goods in the market? Perhaps with the money you get, you will buy something with which to traffic." I remained silent for a while, thinking to myself, "What goods do I have, and what does he mean?" He added, "Son, don't worry and don't think too much about it. Let us go to the market, and if we find anyone who will offer a price that will content you, I will receive the money for you, and if we don't, I will keep them for you in my storerooms until the days of buying and selling arrive." I though about it and said to myself, "Let me do what he asks and see what these goods are." Then I said to him, "Uncle, I hear and obey. I cannot contradict you in anything, for what you do has God's blessing." So I went with him to the market and found out that he had taken the raft apart and delivered the sandalwood, of which it was made, to the broker who was announcing it for sale. The merchants came and opened the bidding, and they increased their offers until the bidding stopped at one thousand dinars. Then the old man turned to me and said, "Listen, son, this is the price of your goods at the present time. Would you like to sell them at this price, or would you like to wait and let me keep them for you in my storerooms to sell them for a higher price at the right time?" I replied, "Sir, I leave it to you; do as you wish." He said, "Son, will you sell me this wood for a hundred dinars above what the merchants have offered?" I said, "Yes, it is done." Then he ordered his servants to carry the wood to his storerooms, and we returned to his house, where we sat, and he counted the money in payment for the wood and, fetching bags, put the money in them, locked them up with an iron lock, and gave me the key.

Some days later, the old man said to me, "Son, I would like to propose something to you, and I hope that you will comply." I said, "What is it?" He replied, "Son, I am a very old man, and I am without a son, but I do have a daughter who is young and charming and endowed with great wealth and beauty. I would like to marry her to you, so that you may live with her here in our country. Then I will give you all I have, for I have become an old man, and you will take my place." I remained silent, and he added, "Son, accept my proposal, for I wish you good. If you obey me, I will marry my daughter to you, and you will be as my son and will possess all I have. If you wish to travel to your country and engage in trade, no one will prevent you. This is your property, at your disposal, to do with it what you wish and choose." I said to him, "By God, uncle, you have become as a father to me. I have suffered many horrors that have rendered me bewildered and lacking in judgment. It is for you to decide as you wish." Then he ordered his pages to bring the judge and witnesses, and when they came, he married me to his daughter, celebrating with a great entertainment and a great feast. When I went in to my wife, I found her extremely beautiful, with a graceful figure and a lovely gait, clad in rich apparel and covered with gold ornaments, necklaces, jewels, and precious stones, worth thousands of thousands of dinars and beyond the means of anyone. When I saw her, she pleased me, and we loved one another. I lived with her for some time, leading an extremely happy and joyful life. Soon her father died and was admitted to the mercy of God. We prepared him and buried him, and I took possession of all his property, and his servants became my servants to serve me at my bidding. Then the merchants appointed me to his office, for he was their chief, and that meant that none of them purchased anything without his knowledge and permission.

When I mingled with the people of the city, I noticed that they were transformed at the beginning of each month, in that they grew wings with which they flew to the upper region of the sky, and no one remained in the city except women and children. I said to myself, "When the first day of the month comes, I will ask some of them to carry me with them to where they go." When the day came, and their colors and shapes changed, I went to one of them and said, "For God's sake, carry me with you, so that I may divert myself and then return." He said, "This is not possible," but I pressed him until he granted me the favor. So I went with them, without telling any of my family or servants or friends, and he took me on his back and flew with me up into the air and kept flying upward until we were so high that I heard the angels glorifying God in the vault of heaven. I marveled at that and exclaimed, "Glory be to God, and His is the praise."

Hardly had I finished my prayer when a fire came out of heaven and almost consumed us. They flew down and, dropping me on a high mountain, departed, feeling very angry with me, and left me alone. I blamed myself for what I had done and said to myself, "There is no power and no strength, save in God the Almighty, the Magnificent. Every time I escape from a calamity, I fall into a worse one."

I sat on the mountain, not knowing where to go, when suddenly two young men passed by. They were like twin moons, each holding a walking staff of red gold. I approached them and saluted them, and they returned my salutation. Then I asked them, "For God's sake, tell me who and what you are." They replied, "We are servants of the Almighty God," and, giving me a walking staff of gold, like the ones they had with them, went on their way and left me. I walked along the ridge of the mountain, leaning on the staff and wondering about the two young men, when suddenly a serpent emerged from beneath the mountain, with a man in its mouth, whom it had swallowed to his navel, while he was screaming and crying out, "Whoever delivers me, God will deliver him from every difficulty." I went close to the serpent and struck it on its head with the gold staff, and it threw the man from its mouth. Then he approached me and said, "Since you have saved me from this serpent, I will never leave you, and you have become my companion on this mountain."

Soon a group of people approached us, and when I looked, I saw among them the man who had carried me on his shoulders and flew up with me. I approached him and, speaking courteously to him, offered my apologies and said, "Friend, this is not the way friends treat friends." He replied, "It was you who almost destroyed us by glorifying God on my back." I said, "Excuse me, for I had no knowledge of this, and I will never utter another word again." Finally, he consented to take me with him, on condition that I would refrain from mentioning the name of God or glorifying Him on his back. Then he carried me and flew up with me, as he had done before, until he brought me to my house.

My wife met me, greeted me, and, congratulating me on my safety, said, "Beware of going out again or associating with those people, for they are brothers of the devils and do not worship God." I asked her, "But how did your father then get along with them?" She replied, "My father was not one of them, nor did he as they did. Now that he is dead, I think that you should sell all our possessions, buy goods with the money, and go back to your country and family, and I will go with you, for I have no reason to stay in this city, since both my father and mother are dead." So I sold my father-in-law's property, little by little, and waited to find someone who would go to Baghdad, so that I might go with him.

Soon, a group of men in the city decided to travel and, failing to find a ship, bought wood and built for themselves a large one. I booked passage with them, paying them the fare in full, and embarked with my wife and all we could carry of our property, leaving our land and buildings behind. We set out and sailed with a fair wind from sea to sea and from island to island until we reached Basra, where, without tarrying, I booked passage on a boat and, loading our belongings, headed for Baghdad. Then I came to my quarter, entered my house, and met my family and friends and loved ones, and stored in my storerooms all the goods I had brought with me. My family had given up hope of my return, for when they calculated the time of my absence during the seventh voyage, they found that it was twenty-seven years. When I related to them all my experiences, they marveled exceedingly and congratulated me on my safety.

Then I vowed to the Almighty God never to travel again by land or sea, after the seventh voyage, which was the one to end all voyages. I also refrained from indulging my appetites and thanked the Almighty and Glorious God and praised Him and glorified Him for having brought me back to my native country and to my family. Consider, O Sindbad the Porter, what I had gone through.

Sindbad the Porter said to Sindbad the Sailor, "For God's sake, pardon me the wrong I did you," and they continued to enjoy their fellowship and friendship, in all cheer and joy, until there came to them death, the destroyer of delights, sunderer of companies, wrecker of palaces, and builder of tombs.

Sir Gawain and the Green Knight

(Late Fourteenth Century)

Romance, as a literary term, refers today to a kind of formulaic fiction about love affairs, written quickly, sold cheaply, and consumed thoughtlessly, as a pleasantly erotic diversion. It originally referred to something considerably less humble. The word *romance* was coined in the early Middle Ages to mean anything written in the popular languages (that is, the *Romance* languages). It soon narrowed, however, to refer to a particular kind of work in a popular language: a long narrative in prose or verse telling of the adventures of chivalric heroes, usually involving courtly love affairs and fanciful or supernatural creatures and incidents. The form persisted in England through the Elizabethan period, but in the seventeenth century, rationalistic critics began to regard it as a survival of a barbarous past, and the term began a slow slide into disreputability. That slide has continued, despite a brief rehabilitation during the Romantic period, until today a "romance" is generally a vulgar, subliterary work. Gradually, through this long history, the word *romance* divided and came to refer to love affairs as well as the books that described them, and so today we can have romances as well as read them. This process is perhaps a case of life imitating art; undoubtedly people would have fallen in love even if romances had never been written, but they probably would not have understood and described their feelings in the same way without the model of the romance.

Sir Gawain and the Green Knight marks the highest achievement in the romance tradition in England, at least among the romances that have survived. It is preserved in a single manuscript, along with three religious poems, *Pearl, Patience,* and *Purity,* in the same style and probably by the same anonymous poet, generally referred to as the *Pearl* poet or the *Gawain* poet. The poem was forgotten for more than four centuries, until it was rediscovered in the 1830s in the British Library. It was in a tiny manuscript measuring five by seven inches in what had once been the library of an Elizabethan book collector named Sir Robert Cotton.

The author of *Gawain, Pearl, Patience,* and *Purity* (and possibly another poem, a life of St. Erkenwald) was, on the evidence of the language and content of his poems, a contemporary of Chaucer. But while Chaucer was living and writing in London, the *Gawain* poet was working in the West Midlands, perhaps in Cheshire, about a hundred and fifty miles northwest of London. He (or conceivably she) wrote in a style very different from Chaucer's comparatively simple, straightforward mode, a style that preserved, or perhaps revived, the old alliterative style of Old English poetry. The basic line of *Sir Gawain* has four stressed syllables and a variable number of unstressed ones, divided by a caesura between the second and third stresses and linked by three identical initial sounds (*alliterations*), either identical consonants or any vowels. These lines are grouped in stanzas with varying numbers of lines, and each stanza ends with a "bob and wheel": a word or phrase of two syllables (the "bob") and a quatrain (the "wheel") rhyming *abab* with the bob (which establishes the *b* rhyme).

Thus *Gawain* begins (in Banks's translation, which uses the same verse form as the original):

> When the siege and assault / / ceased at Troy, and the city
> Was broken, and burned / / all to brands and to ashes,
> The warrior who wove there / / the web of his treachery
> Tried was for treason, / / the truest on earth.

After fourteen lines of this kind, the stanza is brought to an end with a bob and wheel:

> Doth found.
> War, waste, and wonder there
> Have dwelt within its bound;
> And bliss has changed to care
> In quick and shifting round.

The effect of this highly wrought, old-fashioned verse form is a combination of primitive simplicity (the stresses and alliterations recalling songs chanted to the harp) and a sophisticated complexity (the combination of alliteration and rhyme creating a high level of self-consciousness).

The story of *Sir Gawain and the Green Knight* exhibits the same sort of successful blending of seemingly disparate elements. It is made up of a combination of three ancient and widespread folk motifs: the Beheading Game, the Temptation by the Hostess, and the Exchange of Winnings. No precedent has been discovered for the ingenious combination of these three elements into a single plot.

A further and even more complex blending is the combination of the simple folk elements with a sophisticated and courtly code of chivalric ethics. Gawain, and by extension Arthur's court, are being tested in the romance for the degree to which they exemplify the quality of *courtesy. Courtesy* (and its adjectival form *courteous*) chime like a bell throughout the poem, in dozens of repetitions, and evoke the basic moral code of the story. It is a complex word and concept in its fourteenth-century context, very far from its trivial modern sense of "politeness" or "manners." *Courtesy* derives from *court* and refers to the values of the court. These are not merely aristocratic "courtliness" but amount, as D. S. Brewer has explained in a fine essay on "Courtesy and the Gawain-Poet," to an inclusive ideal of personal integrity, realized in benevolent speech and actions toward other people. It refers not only to moral virtues such as self-control, bravery, and cleanliness (although those are certainly included) but also to such matters as physical beauty, eloquence, politeness, and wit. For the *Gawain* poet, such qualities are not "natural," no matter how gentle one's birth, but the result of education, and Gawain at one point is tellingly referred to as "nurture's fine father" (l. 919). *Courtesy,* then, is nearly synonymous with "civilization," what people can achieve given the leisure and the opportunity.

The action of *Sir Gawain and the Green Knight* is, in a sense, a testing of courtesy. Arthur's court is famed as the flower of chivalric courtesy, but we have a sense at the beginning of the romance that the knights have become complacent and self-indulgent. The emphasis is much more on the fifteen-day feast—"All meat and all mirth that a man might devise"—than on the sterner virtues, and there is something of a sneer in the Green Knight's voice when he announces that "here, I have heard, is the highest of courtesy" (l. 262). And indeed only Arthur responds to the giant's challenge until the youthful Gawain saves the honor of the court by stepping forth. The encounter with the Green Knight, which seems at first to test only Gawain's courage, turns out to test his courtesy in ways he could never have foreseen. (Gawain's version of courtesy, though, it should be noted, does not include the often associated codes of "courtly love." He, unlike courtly lovers, respects the marriage vows, a fact that, literally, saves his neck.)

Ranged against the power of Gawain's courtesy, the product of civilization, is that of the Green Knight, who seems allied to nature in its more sinister aspects. Descending upon Arthur's court in the dead of winter, on New Year's Day, all green and carrying a holly bush, the Knight seems to embody the fertile powers of nature, especially when we later learn that his chapel is a mere hole in the ground. But if the Knight embodies nature, he does not do so in any simple or obvious way. He himself can mimic "courtesy" and charm us as well as Gawain does. It is not until we realize the unequal bargain that he has made with the mortal Gawain and his apparent motives for doing so, in collaboration with the inimical Morgan le Fay, that we remember that, charming or not, he is a demon out to discredit the Round Table and destroy its principal hero.

Sir Gawain and the Green Knight, of course, makes no claim to present medieval England as it really was. But as a charming fantasy of a chivalric ideal that never was, akin in its polished artificiality to contemporary manuscript illumination, it is one of the most accomplished literary achievements of medieval England.

FURTHER READING: For background on the author of *Gawain,* see the introduction to *The "Pearl"-Poet: His Complete Works,* ed. and trans. Margaret Williams, 1967; on genre, see Gillian Beer, *The Romance,* 1970; and for the historical context, see Thorlac Turville-Petre, *The Alliterative Revival,* 1977. Charles Moorman has a good critical analysis of *Gawain,* along with ones of *Pearl, Patience,* and *Purity,* in *The "Pearl"-Poet,* 1968. Useful book-length studies include Larry D. Benson, *Art and Tradition in "Sir Gawain and the Green Knight,"* 1965, and Marie Borroff, *"Sir Gawain and the Green Knight": A Stylistic and Metrical Study,* 1962. Collections of critical essays include *"Sir Gawain" and "Pearl": Critical Essays,* ed. Robert J. Blanch, 1966; *Critical Studies of "Sir Gawain and the Green Knight,"* ed. Donald R. Howard and Christian K. Zacher, 1968; and *Twentieth-Century Interpretations of "Sir Gawain and the Green Knight,"* ed. Denton Fox, 1968. A good guide to criticism is *"Sir Gawain and the Green Knight": A Reference Guide,* comp. Robert J. Blanch, 1984.

SIR GAWAIN AND THE GREEN KNIGHT

Translated by Theodore Howard Banks, Jr.

I

When the siege and assault ceased at Troy, and the city
Was broken, and burned all to brands and to ashes,
The warrior who wove there the web of his treachery

Tried was for treason, the truest on earth.[1]
'T was Æneas, who later with lords of his lineage
Provinces quelled, and became the possessors
Of well-nigh the whole of the wealth of the West Isles.[2]
Then swiftly to Rome rich Romulus[3] journeyed,
And soon with great splendor builded that city,
Named with his own name, as now we still know it. 10
Ticius to Tuscany turns for his dwellings;
In Lombardy Langobard lifts up his homes;[4]
And far o'er the French flood fortunate Brutus
With happiness Britain on hillsides full broad
Doth found.[5]
War, waste, and wonder there
Have dwelt within its bound;
And bliss has changed to care
In quick and shifting round.

And after this famous knight founded his Britain, 20
Bold lords were bred there, delighting in battle,
Who many times dealt in destruction. More marvels
Befell in those fields since the days of their finding
Than anywhere else upon earth that I know of.
Yet of all kings who came there was Arthur most comely;
My intention is, therefore, to tell an adventure
Strange and surprising, as some men consider,
A strange thing among all the marvels of Arthur.
And if you will list to the lay for a little,
Forthwith I shall tell it, as I in the town 30
Heard it told
As it doth fast endure
In story brave and bold,
Whose words are fixed and sure,
Known in the land of old.

In Camelot[6] Arthur the King lay at Christmas,
With many a peerless lord princely companioned,
The whole noble number of knights of the Round Table;[7]
Here right royally held his high revels,

[1] Aeneas, the prince of Troy who is the hero of the *Aeneid.* He is said to have been tried for treason because the Greeks tried him for refusing to hand over his sister Polyxena to them.

[2] The countries of Western Europe. The poet imagines descendants of Aeneas founding a series of European nations.

[3] Romulus, legendary founder of Rome, is not ordinarily said to be of Trojan ancestry.

[4] Ticius is apparently a descendant of Aeneas who founded Tuscany; he is not mentioned elsewhere. Langobard is the legendary founder of Lombardy.

[5] Brutus, the great-grandson of Aeneas, is the legendary founder of Britain, the westernmost of the European nations supposedly founded by Aeneas and the "lords of his lineage."

[6] The legendary seat of Arthur's kingdom, sometimes said to have been near Winchester or in Wales.

[7] The table Arthur had built to accommodate one hundred knights, made round to avoid a hierarchy among the knights. Oddly enough, the table described in the poem is not round.

Care-free and mirthful. Now much of the company, 40
Knightly born gentlemen, joyously jousted,
Now came to the court to make caroles; so kept they
For full fifteen days this fashion of feasting,
All meat and all mirth that a man might devise.
Glorious to hear was the glad-hearted gaiety,
Dancing at night, merry din in the daytime;
So found in the courts and the chambers the fortunate
Ladies and lords the delights they best loved.
In greatest well-being abode they together:
The knights whose renown was next to the Savior's, 50
The loveliest ladies who ever were living,
And he who held court, the most comely of kings.
For these fine folk were yet in their first flush of youth
Seated there,
The happiest of their kind,
With a king beyond compare.
It would be hard to find
A company so fair.

And now while the New Year was young were the nobles
Doubly served as they sat on the dais, 60
When Arthur had come to the hall with his court,
In the chapel had ceased the singing of mass;
Loud shouts were there uttered by priests and by others,
Anew praising Noel, naming it often.
Then hastened the lords to give handsel,[8] cried loudly
These gifts of the New Year, and gave them in person;
Debated about them busily, briskly.
Even though they were losers, the ladies laughed loudly,
Nor wroth was the winner, as well ye may know.[9]
All this manner of mirth they made till meat time, 70
Then when they had washed, they went to be seated,
Were placed in the way that appeared most proper,
The best men above. And Guinevere, beautiful,
Was in the midst of the merriment seated
Upon the rich dais, adorned all about:
Fine silks on all sides, and spread as a canopy
Tapestries treasured of Tars and Toulouse,[10]
Embroidered and set with stones most splendid—
They'd prove of great price if ye pence gave to buy them
Some day. 80
The comeliest was the Queen,
With dancing eyes of grey.
That a fairer he had seen
No man might truly say.

[8] Token gifts given for luck on New Year's.
[9] Handsels were accompanied by kisses.
[10] Tars (Turkestan) and Toulouse (in southern France) were famous for their weavings.

But Arthur would eat not till all were attended;
Youthfully mirthful and merry in manner,
He loved well his life, and little it pleased him
Or long to be seated, or long to lie down,
His young blood and wild brain were so busy and brisk.
Moreover, the King was moved by a custom 90
He once had assumed in a spirit of splendor:
Never to fall to his feast on a festival
Till a strange story of something eventful
Was told him, some marvel that merited credence
Of kings, or of arms, or all kinds of adventures;
Or some one besought him to send a true knight
To join him in proving the perils of jousting,
Life against life, each leaving the other
To have, as fortune would help him, the fairer lot.
This, when the King held his court, was his custom 100
At every fine feast 'mid his followers, freemen,
In hall.
And so with countenance clear
He stands there strong and tall,
Alert on that New Year,
And makes much mirth with all.

At his place the strong King stands in person, full courtly
Talking of trifles before the high table.
There sat the good Gawain by Guinevere's side,
And Sir Agravain, he of the Hard Hand, also, 110
True knights, and sons of the sister of Arthur.
At the top, Bishop Baldwin the table begins,
And Ywain beside him ate, Urien's son.
On the dais these sat, and were served with distinction;
Then many a staunch, trusty man at the side tables.[11]
The first course was served to the sharp sound of trumpets,
With numerous banners beneath hanging brightly.
Then newly the kettledrums sounded and noble pipes;
Wild and loud warbles awakened such echoes
That many a heart leaped on high at their melody. 120
Came then the choice meats, cates rare and costly,
Of fair and fresh food such profusion of dishes
'T was hard to find place to put by the people
The silver that carried the various stews
On the cloth.
Each to his best loved fare
Himself helps, nothing loth;
Each two, twelve dishes share,
Good beer and bright wine both.

[11] The high table is on a raised platform at one end of the room, and the side tables are on the main floor along the walls at right angles to the high table.

And now I will say nothing more of their service, 130
For well one may know that naught there was wanted.
Now another new noise drew nigh of a sudden,
To let all the folk take their fill of the feast.
And scarcely the music had ceased for a moment,
The first course been suitably served in the court,
When a being most dreadful burst through the hall door,
Among the most mighty of men in his measure.
From his throat to his thighs so thick were his sinews,
His loins and his limbs so large and so long,
That I hold him half-giant, the hugest of men, 140
And the handsomest, too, in his height, upon horseback.
Though stalwart in breast and in back was his body,
His waist and his belly were worthily small;
Fashioned fairly he was in his form, and in features
Cut clean.
Men wondered at the hue
That in his face was seen.
A splendid man to view
He came, entirely green.

All green was the man, and green were garments: 150
A coat, straight and close, that clung to his sides,
A bright mantle on top of this, trimmed on the inside
With closely-cut fur, right fair, that showed clearly,
The lining with white fur most lovely, and hood too,
Caught back from his locks, and laid on his shoulders,
Neat stockings that clung to his calves, tightly stretched,
Of the same green, and under them spurs of gold shining
Brightly on bands of fine silk, richly barred;
And under his legs, where he rides, guards of leather.
His vesture was verily color of verdure: 160
Both bars of his belt and other stones, beautiful,
Richly arranged in his splendid array
On himself and his saddle, on silken designs.
'T would be truly too hard to tell half the trifles
Embroidered about it with birds and with flies
In gay, verdant green with gold in the middle;
The bit-studs, the crupper, the breast-trappings' pendants,
And everything metal enamelled in emerald.
The stirrups he stood on the same way were colored,
His saddle-bows too, and the studded nails splendid, 170
That all with green gems ever glimmered and glinted.
The horse he bestrode was in hue still the same,
Indeed;
Green, thick, and of great height,
And hard to curb, a steed
In broidered bridle bright
That such a man would need.

This hero in green was habited gaily,
And likewise the hair on the head of his good horse;
Fair, flowing tresses enfolded his shoulders, 180
And big as a bush a beard hung on his breast.
This, and the hair from his head hanging splendid,
Was clipped off evenly over his elbows,
In cut like a king's hood, covering the neck,
So that half of his arms were held underneath it.
The mane of the mighty horse much this resembled,
Well curled and combed, and with many knots covered,
Braided with gold threads about the fair green,
Now a strand made of hair, now a second of gold.
The forelock and tail were twined in this fashion, 190
And both of them bound with a band of bright green.
For the dock's length the tail was decked with stones dearly,
And then was tied with a thong in a tight knot,
Where many bright bells of burnished gold rang.
In the hall not one single man's seen before this
Such a horse here on earth, such a hero as on him
Goes.
That his look was lightning bright
Right certain were all those
Who saw. It seemed none might 200
Endure beneath his blows.

Yet the hero carried nor helmet nor hauberk,[12]
But bare was of armor, breastplate or gorget,[13]
Spear-shaft or shield, to thrust or to smite.
But in one hand he bore a bough of bright holly,
That grows most greenly when bare are the groves,
In the other an axe, gigantic, awful,
A terrible weapon, wondrous to tell of.
Large was the head, in length a whole ell-yard,[14]
The blade of green steel and beaten gold both; 210
The bit had a broad edge, and brightly was burnished,
As suitably shaped as sharp razors for shearing.
This steel by its strong shaft the stern hero gripped:
With iron it was wound to the end of the wood,
And in work green and graceful was everywhere graven.
About it a fair thong was folded, made fast
At the head, and oft looped down the length of the handle.
To this were attached many splendid tassels,
On buttons of bright green richly embroidered.
Thus into the hall came the hero, and hastened 220
Direct to the dais, fearing no danger.
He gave no one greeting, but haughtily gazed,

[12] A long tunic of chain mail.
[13] A piece of armor defending the throat.
[14] An English ell-yard was forty-five inches.

And his first words were, "Where can I find him who governs
This goodly assemblage? for gladly that man
I would see and have speech with." So saying, from toe
To crown
On the knights his look he threw,
And rolled it up and down;
He stopped to take note who
Had there the most renown. 230

There sat all the lords, looking long at the stranger,
Each man of them marvelling what it might mean
For a horse and a hero to have such a hue.
It seemed to them green as the grown grass, or greener,
Gleaming more bright than on gold green enamel.
The nobles who stood there, astonished, drew nearer,
And deeply they wondered what deed he would do.
Since never a marvel they'd met with like this one,
The folk all felt it was magic or phantasy.
Many great lords then were loth to give answer, 240
And sat stone-still, at his speaking astounded,
In swooning silence that spread through the hall.
As their speech on a sudden was stilled, fast asleep
They did seem.
They felt not only fright
But courtesy, I deem.
Let him address the knight,
Him whom they all esteem.

This happening the King, ever keen and courageous,
Saw from on high, and saluted the stranger 250
Suitably, saying, "Sir, you are welcome.
I, the head of this household, am Arthur;
In courtesy light,[15] and linger, I pray you,
And later, my lord, we shall learn your desire."
"Nay, so help me He seated on high," quoth the hero,
"My mission was not to remain here a moment;
But, sir, since thy name is so nobly renowned,
Since thy city the best is considered, thy barons
The stoutest in steel gear that ride upon steeds,
Of all men in the world the most worthy and brave, 260
Right valiant to play with in other pure pastimes,
Since here, I have heard, is the highest of courtesy—
Truly, all these things have brought me at this time.
Sure ye may be by this branch that I bear
That I pass as in peace, proposing no fight.
If I'd come with comrades, equipped for a quarrel,
I have at my home both hauberk and helmet,

[15] Alight.

Shield and sharp spear, brightly shining, and other
Weapons to wield, full well I know also.
Yet softer my weeds are, since warfare I wished not; 270
But art thou as bold as is bruited[16] by all,
Thou wilt graciously grant me the game that I ask for
By right."
Arthur good answer gave,
And said, "Sir courteous knight,
If battle here you crave,
You shall not lack a fight."

"Nay, I ask for no fight; in faith, now I tell thee
But beardless babes are about on this bench.
Were I hasped in my armor, and high on a horse, 280
Here is no man to match me, your might is so feeble.
So I crave but a Christmas game in this court;
Yule and New Year are come, and here men have courage;
If one in this house himself holds so hardy,
So bold in his blood, in his brain so unbalanced
To dare stiffly strike one stroke for another,
I give this gisarme,[17] this rich axe, as a gift to him,
Heavy enough, to handle as pleases him;
Bare as I sit, I shall bide the first blow.
If a knight be so tough as to try what I tell, 290
Let him leap to me lightly; I leave him this weapon,
Quitclaim it forever, to keep as his own;
And his stroke here, firm on this floor, I shall suffer,
This boon if thou grant'st me, the blow with another
To pay;
Yet let his respite be
A twelvemonth and a day.
Come, let us quickly see
If one here aught dare say."

If at first he had startled them, stiller then sat there 300
The whole of the court, low and high, in the hall.
The knight on his steed turned himself in his saddle,
And fiercely his red eyes he rolled all around,
Bent his bristling brows, with green gleaming brightly,
And waved his beard, waiting for one there to rise.
And when none of the knights spoke, he coughed right noisily,
Straightened up proudly, and started to speak:
"What!" quoth the hero, "Is this Arthur's household,
The fame of whose fellowship fills many kingdoms?
Now where is your vainglory? Where are your victories? 310
Where is your grimness, your great words, your anger?

[16] Rumored.
[17] A medieval weapon consisting of an axhead on a long shaft, carried by foot soldiers.

For now the Round Table's renown and its revel
Is worsted by one word of one person's speech,
For all shiver with fear before a stroke's shown."
Then so loudly he laughed that the lord was grieved greatly,
And into his fair face his blood shot up fiercely
For shame.
As wroth as wind he grew,
And all there did the same.
The King that no fear knew 320
Then to that stout man came.

And said, "Sir, by heaven, strange thy request is;
As folly thou soughtest, so shouldest thou find it.
I know that not one of the knights is aghast
Of thy great words. Give me thy weapon, for God's sake,
And gladly the boon thou hast begged I shall grant thee."
He leaped to him quickly, caught at his hand,
And fiercely the other lord lights on his feet.
Now Arthur lays hold of the axe by the handle,
As if he would strike with it, swings it round sternly. 330
Before him the strong man stood, in stature
A head and more higher than all in the house.
Stroking his beard, he stood with stern bearing,
And with a calm countenance drew down his coat,
No more frightened or stunned by the axe Arthur flourished
Than if on the bench some one brought him a flagon
Of wine.
Gawain by Guinevere
Did to the King incline:
"I pray in accents clear 340
To let this fray be mine."

"If you now, honored lord," said this knight to King Arthur,
"Would bid me to step from this bench, and to stand there
Beside you—so could I with courtesy quit then
The table, unless my liege lady disliked it—
I'd come to your aid before all your great court.
For truly I think it a thing most unseemly
So boldly to beg such a boon in your hall here,
Though you in person are pleased to fulfil it,
While here on the benches such brave ones are seated, 350
Than whom under heaven, I think, none are higher
In spirit, none better in body for battle.
I am weakest and feeblest in wit, I know well,
And my life, to say truth, would be least loss of any.
I only since you are my uncle have honor;
Your blood the sole virtue I bear in my body.
Unfit is this foolish affair for you. Give it
To me who soonest have sought it, and let
All this court if my speech is not seemly, decide

Without blame." 360
The nobles gather round,
And all advise the same:
To free the King that's crowned,
And Gawain give the game.

The King then commanded his kinsman to rise,
And quickly he rose up and came to him courteously,
Kneeled by the King, and caught the weapon,
He left it graciously, lifted his hand,
And gave him God's blessing, and gladly bade him
Be sure that his heart and his hand both were hardy. 370
"Take care," quoth the King, "how you start, coz,[18] your cutting,
And truly, I think, if rightly you treat him,
That blow you'll endure that he deals you after."
Weapon in hand, Gawain goes to the hero,
Who boldly remains there, dismayed none the more.
Then the knight in the green thus greeted Sir Gawain,
"Let us state our agreement again ere proceeding.
And now first, sir knight, what your name is I beg
That you truly will tell, so in that I may trust."
"In truth," said the good knight, "I'm called Sir Gawain, 380
Who fetch you this blow, whatsoever befalls,
And another will take in return, this time twelvemonth,
From you, with what weapon you will; with no other
I'll go."
The other made reply:
"By my life here below,
Gawain, right glad am I
To have you strike this blow.

By God," said the Green Knight, "Sir Gawain, it pleases me—
Here, at thy hand, I shall have what I sought. 390
Thou hast rightly rehearsed to me, truly and readily,
All of the covenant asked of King Arthur;
Except that thou shalt, by thy troth, sir, assure me
Thyself and none other shalt seek me, wherever
Thou thinkest to find me, and fetch thee what wages
Are due for the stroke that to-day thou dost deal me
Before all this splendid assembly." "Where should I,"
Said Gawain, "go look for the land where thou livest?
The realm where thy home is, by Him who hath wrought me,
I know not, nor thee, sir, thy court nor thy name. 400
Truly tell me thy title, and teach me the road,
And I'll use all my wit to win my way thither,
And so by my sure word truly I swear."
" 'T is enough; No more now at New Year is needed,"
The knight in the green said to Gawain the courteous:

[18] "Cousin," a term of endearment.

"If truly I tell when I've taken your tap
And softly you've struck me, if swiftly I tell you
My name and my house and my home, you may then
Of my conduct make trial, and your covenant keep;
And if no speech I speak, you speed all the better: 410
No longer need look, but may stay in your land.
But ho!
Take your grim tool with speed,
And let us see your blow."
Stroking his axe, "Indeed,"
Said Gawain, "gladly so."

With speed then the Green Knight took up his stand,
Inclined his head forward, uncovering the flesh,
And laid o'er his crown his locks long and lovely,
And bare left the nape of his neck for the business. 420
His axe Gawain seized, and swung it on high;
On the floor his left foot he planted before him,
And swiftly the naked flesh smote with his weapon.
The sharp edge severed the bones of the stranger,
Cut through the clear flesh and cleft it in twain,
So the blade of the brown steel bit the ground deeply.
The fair head fell from the neck to the floor,
So that where it rolled forth with their feet many spurned it.
The blood on the green glistened, burst from the body;
And yet neither fell nor faltered the hero, 430
But stoutly he started forth, strong in his stride;
Fiercely he rushed 'mid the ranks of the Round Table,
Seized and uplifted his lovely head straightway;
Then back to his horse went, laid hold of the bridle,
Stepped into the stirrup and strode up aloft,
His head holding fast in his hand by the hair.
And the man as soberly sat in his saddle
As if he unharmed were, although now headless,
Instead.
His trunk around he spun, 440
That ugly body that bled.
Frightened was many a one
When he his words had said.

For upright he holds the head in his hand,
And confronts with the face the fine folk on the dais.
It lifted its lids, and looked forth directly,
Speaking this much with its mouth, as ye hear:
"Gawain, look that to go as agreed you are ready,
And seek for me faithfully, sir, till you find me,
As, heard by these heroes, you vowed in this hall. 450
To the Green Chapel go you, I charge you, to get
Such a stroke as you struck. You are surely deserving,
Sir knight, to be promptly repaid at the New Year.

As Knight of the Green Chapel many men know me;
If therefore to find me you try, you will fail not;
Then come, or be recreant[19] called as befits thee."
With furious wrench of the reins he turned round,
And rushed from the hall-door, his head in his hands,
So the fire of the flint flew out from the foal's hoofs.
Not one of the lords knew the land where he went to, 460
No more than the realm whence he rushed in among them.
What then?
The King and Gawain there
At the Green Knight laughed again;
Yet this the name did bear
Of wonder among men.

Though much in his mind did the courtly King marvel,
He let not a semblance be seen, but said loudly
With courteous speech to the Queen, most comely:
"To-day, my dear lady, be never alarmed; 470
Such affairs are for Christmas well fitted to sing of
And gaily to laugh at when giving an interlude,
'Mid all the company's caroles, most courtly.
None the less I may go now to get my meat;
For I needs must admit I have met with a marvel."
He glanced at Sir Gawain, and gladsomely said:
"Now sir, hang up thine axe; enough it has hewn."
O'er the dais 't was placed, to hang on the dosser,
That men might remark it there as a marvel,
And truly describing, might tell of the wonder. 480
Together these two then turned to the table,
The sovereign and good knight, and swiftly men served them
With dainties twofold, as indeed was most fitting,
All manner of meat and of minstrelsy both.
So the whole day in pleasure they passed till night fell
O'er the land.
Now take heed Gawain lest,
Fearing the Green Knight's brand,
Thou shrinkest from the quest
That thou hast ta'en in hand. 490

II

This sample had Arthur of strange things right early,
When young was the year, for he yearned to hear boasts.
Though such words when they went to be seated were wanting,
Yet stocked are they now with hand-fulls of stern work.
In the hall glad was Gawain those games to begin,
But not strange it would seem if sad were the ending;
For though men having drunk much are merry in mind,
Full swift flies a year, never yielding the same,

[19] Coward or traitor.

The start and the close very seldom according.
So past went this Yule, and the year followed after, 500
Each season in turn succeeding the other.
There came after Christmas the crabbed Lenten,
With fish and with plainer food trying the flesh;
But then the world's weather with winter contends;
Down to earth shrinks the cold, the clouds are uplifted;
In showers full warm descends the bright rain,
And falls on the fair fields. Flowers unfold;
The ground and the groves are green in their garments;
Birds hasten to build, blithesomely singing
For soft summer's solace ensuing on slopes 510
Everywhere.
The blossoms swell and blow,
In hedge-rows rich and rare,
And notes most lovely flow
From out the forest fair.

After this comes the season of soft winds of summer,
When Zephyrus sighs on the seeds and the green plants.
The herb that then grows in the ground is right happy,
When down from the leaves drops the dampening dew
To abide the bright sun that is blissfully shining. 520
But autumn comes speeding, soon grows severe,
And warns it to wax full ripe for the winter.
With drought then the dust is driven to rise,
From the face of the fields to fly to the heaven.
With the sun the wild wind of the welkin[20] is struggling;
The leaves from the limbs drop, and light on the ground;
And withers the grass that grew once so greenly.
Then all ripens that formerly flourished, and rots;
And thus passes the year in yesterdays many,
And winter, in truth, as the way of the world is, 530
Draws near,
Till comes the Michaelmas[21] moon
With pledge of winter sere.
Then thinks Sir Gawain soon
Of his dread voyage drear.

Till the tide of Allhallows[22] with Arthur he tarried;
The King made ado on that day for his sake
With rich and rare revel of all of the Round Table,
Knights most courteous, comely ladies,
All of them heavy at heart for the hero. 540
Yet nothing but mirth was uttered, though many
Joyless made jests for that gentleman's sake.

[20] Sky.
[21] Feast of the archangel Michael, celebrated on September 29.
[22] All Saints' Day, November 1.

After meat, with sorrow he speaks to his uncle,
And openly talks of his travel, saying:
"Liege lord[23] of my life, now I ask of you leave.
You know my case and condition, nor care I
To tell of its troubles even a trifle.
I must, for the blow I am bound to, to-morrow
Go seek as God guides me the man in the green."
Then came there together the best in the castle: 550
Ywain, Eric, and others full many,
Sir Dodinel de Sauvage, the Duke of Clarence,
Lancelot, Lyonel, Lucan the good,
Sir Bors and Sir Bedevere, both of them big men,
Mador de la Port, and many more nobles.
All these knights of the court came near to the King
With care in their hearts to counsel the hero;
Heavy and deep was the dole in the hall
That one worthy as Gawain should go on that errand,
To suffer an onerous stroke, and his own sword 560
To stay.
The knight was of good cheer:
"Why should I shrink away
From a fate stern and drear?
A man can but essay."

He remained there that day; in the morning made ready.
Early he asked for his arms; all were brought him.
And first a fine carpet was laid on the floor,
And much was the gilt gear that glittered upon it.
Thereon stepped the strong man, and handled the steel, 570
Dressed in a doublet of Tars that cost dearly,
A hood made craftily, closed at the top,
And about on the lining bound with a bright fur.
Then they set on his feet shoes fashioned of steel,
And with fine greaves of steel encircled his legs.
Knee-pieces to these were connected, well polished,
Secured round his knees with knots of gold.
Then came goodly cuisses, with cunning enclosing
His thick, brawny thighs; with thongs they attached them.
Then the man was encased in a coat of fine mail, 580
With rings of bright steel on a rich stuff woven,
Braces well burnished on both of his arms,
Elbow-pieces gay, good, and gloves of plate,
All the goodliest gear that would give him most succor
That tide:
Coat armor richly made,
His gold spurs fixed with pride,
Girt his unfailing blade
By a silk sash to his side.

[23]A lord to whom one is bound to allegiance and service, under the feudal system.

When in arms he was clasped, his costume was costly; 590
The least of the lacings or loops gleamed with gold.
And armed in this manner, the man heard mass,
At the altar adored and made offering, and afterward
Came to the King and all of his courtiers,
Gently took leave of the ladies and lords;
Him they kissed and escorted, to Christ him commending.
Then was Gringolet ready, girt with a saddle
That gaily with many a gold fringe was gleaming,
With nails studded newly, prepared for the nonce.
The bridle was bound about, barred with bright gold; 600
With the bow of the saddle, the breastplate, the splendid skirts,
Crupper, and cloth in adornment accorded,
With gold nails arrayed on a groundwork of red,
That glittered and glinted like gleams of the sun.
Then he caught up his helm, and hastily kissed it;
It stoutly was stapled and stuffed well within,
High on his head, and hasped well behind,
With a light linen veil laid over the visor,
Embroidered and bound with the brightest of gems
On a silken border; with birds on the seams 610
Like painted parroquets preening; true love-knots
As thickly with turtle doves tangled as though
Many women had been at the work seven winters
In town.
Great was the circle's price
Encompassing his crown;
Of diamonds its device,
That were both bright and brown.

Then they showed him his shield, sheer gules, whereon shone
The pentangle[24] painted in pure golden hue. 620
On his baldric he caught, and about his neck cast it;
And fairly the hero's form it befitted.
And why that great prince the pentangle suited
Intend I to tell, in my tale though I tarry.
'T is a sign that Solomon formerly set
As a token, for so it doth symbol, of truth.
A figure it is that with five points is furnished;
Each line overlaps and locks in another,
Nor comes to an end; and Englishmen call it
Everywhere, hear I, the endless knot. 630
It became then the knight and his noble arms also,
In five ways, and five times each way still faithful.
Sir Gawain was known as the good, refined gold,
Graced with virtues of castle, of villainy void,

[24] Pentacle, or five-pointed star, with magical or symbolic meaning.

Made clean.
So the pentangle new
On shield and coat was seen,
As man of speech most true,
And gentlest knight of mien.

First, in his five wits he faultless was found; 640
In his five fingers too the man never failed;
And on earth all his faith was fixed on the five wounds
That Christ, as the creed tells, endured on the cross.
Wheresoever this man was midmost in battle,
His thought above everything else was in this,
To draw all his fire from the fivefold joys[25]
That the fair Queen of Heaven felt in her child.
And because of this fitly he carried her image
Displayed on his shield, on its larger part,
That whenever he saw it his spirit should sink not. 650
The fifth five the hero made use of, I find,
More than all were his liberalness, love of his fellows,
His courtesy, chasteness, unchangeable ever,
And pity, all further traits passing. These five
In this hero more surely were set than in any.
In truth now, fivefold they were fixed in the knight,
Linked each to the other without any end,
And all of them fastened on five points unfailing;
Each side they neither united nor sundered,
Evermore endless at every angle, 660
Where equally either they ended or started.
And so his fair shield was adorned with this symbol,
Thus richly with red gold wrought on red gules,
So by people the pentangle perfect 't was called,
As it ought.
Gawain in arms is gay;
Right there his lance he caught,
And gave them all good-day
For ever, as he thought.

He set spurs to his steed, and sprang on his way 670
So swiftly that sparks from the stone flew behind him.
All who saw him, so seemly, sighed, sad at heart;
The same thing, in sooth, each said to the other,
Concerned for that comely man: "Christ, 't is a shame
Thou, sir knight, must be lost whose life is so noble!
To find, faith! his equal on earth is not easy.
'T would wiser have been to have acted more warily,
Dubbed yonder dear one a duke. He seems clearly
To be in the land here a brilliant leader:

[25] The "joys of Mary" were the Annunciation, Nativity, Resurrection, Ascension, and Assumption.

So better had been than brought thus to naught, 680
By an elf-man[26] beheaded for haughty boasting.
Who e'er knew any king such counsel to take,
As foolish as one in a Christmas frolic?"
Much was the warm water welling from eyes
When the seemly hero set out from the city
That day.
Nowhere he abode,
But swiftly went his way;
By devious paths he rode,
As I the book heard say. 690

Through the realm of Logres[27] now rides this lord,
Sir Gawain, for God's sake, no game though he thought it.
Oft alone, uncompanioned he lodges at night
Where he finds not the fare that he likes set before him.
Save his foal, he 'd no fellow by forests and hills;
On the way, no soul but the Savior to speak to.
At length he drew nigh unto North Wales, and leaving
To left of him all of the islands of Anglesey,
Fared by the forelands and over the fords
Near the Holy Head; hastening hence to the mainland, 700
In Wyral he went through the wilderness.[28] There,
Lived but few who loved God or their fellows with good heart.
And always he asked of any he met,
As he journeyed, if nearby a giant they knew of,
A green knight, known as the Knight of the Green Chapel.
All denied it with nay, in their lives they had never
Once seen any hero who had such a hue
Of green.
The knight takes roadways strange
In many a wild terrene;[29] 710
Often his feelings change
Before that chapel 's seen.

Over many cliffs climbed he in foreign countries;
From friends far sundered, he fared as a stranger;
And wondrous it were, at each water or shore
That he passed, if he found not before him a foe,
So foul too and fell that to fight he could fail not.
The marvels he met with amount to so many
Too tedious were it to tell of the tenth part.
For sometimes with serpents he struggled and wolves too, 720
With wood-trolls sometimes in stony steeps dwelling,

[26] Supernatural being.
[27] One of the names for Arthur's kingdom.
[28] Gawain's route may be followed on a map: north to the coast of north Wales, near the islands of Anglesey, then east across the River Dee to the forest of Wirral in Cheshire.
[29] Terrain.

And sometimes with bulls and with bears and with boars;
And giants from high fells hunted and harassed him.
If he'd been not enduring and doughty, and served God,
These doubtless would often have done him to death.
Though warfare was grievous, worse was the winter,
When cold, clear water was shed from the clouds
That froze ere it fell to the earth, all faded.
With sleet nearly slain, he slept in his armor
More nights than enough on the naked rocks, 730
Where splashing the cold stream sprang from the summit,
And hung in hard icicles high o'er his head.
Thus in peril and pain and desperate plights,
Till Christmas Eve wanders this wight through the country
Alone.
Truly the knight that tide
To Mary made his moan,
That she direct his ride
To where some hearth-fire shone.

By a mount on the morn he merrily rides 740
To a wood dense and deep that was wondrously wild;
High hills on each hand, with forests of hoar oaks
Beneath them most huge, a hundred together.
Thickly the hazel and hawthorn were tangled,
Everywhere mantled with moss rough and ragged,
With many a bird on the bare twigs, mournful,
That piteously piped for pain of the cold.
Sir Gawain on Gringolet goes underneath them
Through many a marsh and many a mire,
Unfriended, fearing to fail in devotion, 750
And see not His service, that Sire's, on that very night
Born of a Virgin to vanquish our pain.
And so sighing he said: "Lord, I beseech Thee,
And Mary, the mildest mother so dear,
For some lodging wherein to hear mass full lowly,
And matins, meekly I ask it, to-morrow;
So promptly I pray my pater and ave
And creed."
Thus rode he as he prayed,
Lamenting each misdeed; 760
Often the sign he made,
And said, "Christ's cross me speed."

He scarcely had signed himself thrice, ere he saw
In the wood on a mound a moated mansion,
Above a fair field, enfolded in branches
Of many a huge tree hard by the ditches:
The comeliest castle that knight ever kept.
In a meadow 't was placed, with a park all about,

And a palisade, spiked and pointed, set stoutly
Round many a tree for more than two miles. 770
The lord on that one side looked at the stronghold
That shimmered and shone through the shapely oak trees;
Then duly his helm doffed, and gave his thanks humbly
To Jesus and Julian,[30] both of them gentle,
For showing him courtesy, hearing his cry.
"Now good lodging," quoth Gawain, "I beg you to grant me."
Then with spurs in his gilt heels he Gringolet strikes,
Who chooses the chief path by chance that conducted
The man to the bridge-end ere many a minute
Had passed. 780
The bridge secure was made,
Upraised; the gates shut fast;
The walls were well arrayed.
It feared no tempest's blast.

The hero abode on his horse by the bank
Of the deep, double ditch that surrounded the dwelling.
The wall stood wonderfully deep in the water,
And again to a huge height sprang overhead;
Of hard, hewn rock that reached to the cornices,
Built up with outworks under the battlements 790
Finely; at intervals, turrets fair fashioned,
With many good loopholes that shut tight; this lord
Had ne'er looked at a barbican[31] better than this one.
Further in he beheld the high hall; here and there
Towers were stationed set thickly with spires,
With finials wondrously long and fair fitting,
Whose points were cunningly carven, and craftily.
There numerous chalk-white chimneys he noticed
That bright from the tops of the towers were gleaming.
Such pinnacles painted, so placed about everywhere, 800
Clustering so thick 'mid the crenels, the castle
Surely appeared to be shaped to cut paper.[32]
The knight on his foal it fair enough fancies
If into the court he may manage to come,
In that lodging to live while the holiday lasts
With delight.
A porter came at call,
His mission learned, and right
Civilly from the wall
Greeted the errant knight. 810

[30] Patron saint of hospitality.

[31] A defensive tower built by the gate of a castle.

[32] That is, it looked as if it were made of cut paper. Paper constructions were often used as table decorations.

Quoth Gawain: "Good sir, will you go on my errand,
Harbor to crave of this house's high lord?"
"Yea, by Peter. I know well, sir knight," said the porter,
"You're welcome as long as you list here to tarry."
Then went the man quickly, and with him, to welcome
The knight to the castle, a courteous company.
Down the great drawbridge they dropped, and went eagerly
Forth; on the frozen earth fell on their knees
To welcome this knight in the way they thought worthy;
Threw wide the great gate for Gawain to enter. 820
He bid them rise promptly, and rode o'er the bridge.
His saddle several seized as he lighted,
And stout men in plenty stabled his steed.
And next there descended knights and esquires
To lead to the hall with delight this hero.
When he raised his helmet, many made haste
From his hand to catch it, to care for the courtly man.
Some of them took then his sword and his shield both.
Then Gawain graciously greeted each knight;
Many proud men pressing to honor that prince, 830
To the hall they led him, all hasped in his harness,
Where fiercely a fair fire flamed on the hearth.
Then came the lord of this land from his chamber
To fittingly meet the man on the floor,
And said: "You are welcome to do what your will is;
To hold as your own, you have all that is here
In this place."
"Thank you," said Gawain then,
"May Christ reward this grace."
The two like joyful men 840
Each other then embrace.

Gawain gazed at the man who so graciously greeted him;
Doughty he looked, the lord of that dwelling,
A hero indeed huge, hale, in his prime;
His beard broad and bright, its hue all of beaver;
Stern, and on stalwart shanks steadily standing;
Fell[33] faced as the fire, in speech fair and free.
In sooth, well suited he seemed, thought Gawain,
To govern as prince of a goodly people.
To his steward the lord turned, and strictly commanded 850
To send men to Gawain to give him good service;
And prompt at his bidding were people in plenty.
To a bright room they brought him, the bed nobly decked
With hangings of pure silk with clear golden hems.
And curious coverings with comely panels,
Embroidered with bright fur above at the edges;
On cords curtains running with rings of red gold;

[33] Fierce.

From Tars and Toulouse were the tapestries covering
The walls; under foot on the floor more to match.
There he soon, with mirthful speeches, was stripped 860
Of his coat of linked mail and his armor; and quickly
Men ran, and brought him rich robes, that the best
He might pick out and choose as his change of apparel.
When lapped was the lord in the one he selected,
That fitted him fairly with flowing skirts,
The fur by his face, in faith it seemed made,
To the company there, entirely of colors,
Glowing and lovely; beneath all his limbs were.
That never made Christ a comelier knight
They thought. 870
On earth, or far or near,
It seemed as if he ought
To be a prince sans peer
In fields where fierce men fought.

A chair by the chimney where charcoal was burning
For Gawain was fitted most finely with cloths,
Both cushions and coverlets, cunningly made.
Then a comely mantle was cast on the man,
Of a brown, silken fabric bravely embroidered,
Within fairly furred with the finest of skins, 880
Made lovely with ermine, his hood fashioned likewise.
He sat on that settle in clothes rich and seemly;
His mood, when well he was warmed, quickly mended.
Soon was set up a table on trestles most fair;
With a clean cloth that showed a clear white it was covered,
With top-cloth and salt-cellar, spoons too of silver.
When he would the man washed, and went to his meat,
And seemly enough men served him with several
Excellent stews in the best manner seasoned,
Twofold as was fitting, and various fishes; 890
In bread some were baked, some broiled on the coals,
Some seethed, some in stews that were savored with spices;
And ever such subtly made sauces as pleased him.
He freely and frequently called it a feast,
Most courtly; the company there all acclaimed him
Well-bred.
"But now this penance take,[34]
And soon 't will mend," they said.
That man much mirth did make,
As wine went to his head. 900

They enquired then and queried in guarded questions
Tactfully put to the prince himself,

[34] The lords and ladies jocularly say that Gawain has been doing penance because the elaborate meal has consisted only of fish dishes, as for a fast-day.

Till he courteously owned he came of the court
The lord Arthur, gracious and goodly, alone holds,
Who rich is and royal, the Round Table's King;
And that Gawain himself in that dwelling was seated,
For Christmas come, as the case had befallen.
When he learned that he had that hero, the lord
Laughed loudly thereat so delightful he thought it.
Much merriment made all the men in that castle 910
By promptly appearing then in his presence;
For all prowess and worth and pure polished manners
Pertain to his person. He ever is praised;
Of all heroes on earth his fame is the highest.
Each knight full softly said to his neighbor,
"We now shall see, happily, knightly behavior,
And faultless terms of talking most noble;
What profit 's in speech we may learn without seeking,
For nurture's fine father has found here a welcome;
In truth God has graciously given His grace 920
Who grants us to have such a guest as Gawain
When men for His birth's sake sit merry and sing.
To each
Of us this hero now
Will noble manners teach;
Who hear him will learn how
To utter loving speech."

When at length the dinner was done, and the lords
Had risen, the night-time nearly was come.
The chaplains went their way to the chapels 930
And rang right joyfully, just as they should do,
For evensong solemn this festival season.
To this goes the lord, and the lady likewise;
She comes in with grace to the pew closed and comely,
And straightway Gawain goes thither right gaily;
The lord by his robe took him, led to a seat,
Acknowledged him kindly and called him by name,
Saying none in the world was as welcome as he was.
He heartily thanked him; the heroes embraced,
And together they soberly sat through the service. 940
Then longed the lady to look on the knight,
And emerged from her pew with many fair maidens;
In face she was fairest of all, and in figure,
In skin and in color, all bodily qualities;
Lovelier, Gawain thought, even than Guinevere.
He goes through the chancel[35] to greet her, so gracious.
By the left hand another was leading her, older
Than she, a lady who looked as if aged,
By heroes around her reverenced highly.

[35] The portion of a church set off for the use of the clergy.

The ladies, however, unlike were to look on: 950
If fresh was the younger, the other was yellow;
Rich red on the one was rioting everywhere,
Rough wrinkled cheeks hung in rolls on the other;
One's kerchiefs, with clear pearls covered and many,
Displayed both her breast and her bright throat all bare,
Shining fairer than snow on the hillsides falling;
The second her neck in a neck-cloth enswathed,
That enveloped in chalk-white veils her black chin;
Her forehead in silk was wrapped and enfolded
Adorned and tricked with trifles about it 960
Till nothing was bare but the lady's black brows,
Her two eyes, her nose, and her lips, all naked,
And those were bleared strangely, and ugly to see.
A goodly lady, so men before God
Might decide!
Her body thick and short,
Her hips were round and wide;
One of more pleasant sort
She led there by her side.

When Gawain had gazed on that gay one so gracious 970
In look, he took leave of the lord and went toward them,
Saluted the elder, bowing full lowly,
The lovelier lapped in his two arms a little,
And knightly and comely greeted and kissed her.
They craved his acquaintance, and quickly he asked
To be truly their servant if so they desired it.
They took him between them, and led him with talk
To the sitting-room's hearth; then straightway for spices
They called, which men sped to unsparingly bring,
And with them as well pleasant wine at each coming. 980
Up leaped right often the courteous lord,
Urged many a time that the men should make merry,
Snatched off his hood, on a spear gaily hung it,
And waved it, that one for a prize might win it
Who caused the most mirth on that Christmas season.
"I shall try, by my faith, to contend with the finest
Ere hoodless I find myself, helped by my friends."
Thus with laughing speeches the lord makes merry
That night, to gladden Sir Gawain with games.
So they spent 990
The evening in the hall.
The king for lights then sent,
And taking leave of all
To bed Sir Gawain went.

On the morn when the Lord, as men all remember,
Was born, who would die for our doom, in each dwelling
On earth grows happiness greater for His sake;

So it did on that day there with many a dainty:
With dishes cunningly cooked at meal-times,
With doughty men dressed in their best on the dais. 1000
The old lady was seated the highest; beside her
Politely the lord took his place, I believe;
The gay lady and Gawain together sat, mid-most,
Where fitly the food came, and afterward fairly
Was served through the hall as beseemed them the best,
Of the company each in accord with his station.
There was meat and mirth, there was much joy, too troublous
To tell, though I tried in detail to describe it;
Yet I know both the lovely lady and Gawain
So sweet found each other's society (pleasant 1010
And polished their converse, courtly and private;
Unfailing their courtesy, free from offence)
That surpassing, in truth, any play of a prince was
Their game.
There trumpets, drums and airs
Of piping loudly came.
Each minded his affairs,
And those two did the same.

Much mirth was that day and the day after made,
And the third followed fast, as full of delight. 1020
Sweet was the joy of St. John's day[36] to hear of,
The last, as the folk there believed, of the festival.
Guests were to go in the grey dawn, and therefore
They wondrously late were awake with their wine,
And danced delightful, long lasting caroles.
At length when 't was late they took their leave,
Each strong man among them to start on his way.
Gawain gave him good-day; then the good man laid hold of him,
Led to the hearth in his own room the hero;
There took him aside, and gave suitable thanks 1030
For the gracious distinction that Gawain had given
In honoring his house that holiday season,
And gracing his castle with courteous company.
"I'll truly as long as I live be the better
That Gawain at God's own feast was my guest."
"Gramercy,"[37] said Gawain, "by God, sir, not mine
Is the worth, but your own; may the high King reward you.
I am here at your will to work your behest,
As in high and low it behooves me to do
By right." 1040
The lord intently tries
Longer to hold the knight;
Gawain to him replies
That he in no way might.

[36] December 27. [37] "Thank you."

Then the man with courteous question enquired
What dark deed that feast time had driven him forth,
From the King's court to journey alone with such courage,
Ere fully in homes was the festival finished.
"In sooth," said the knight, "sir, ye say but the truth;
From these hearths a high and a hasty task took me. 1050
Myself, I am summoned to seek such a place
As to find it I know not whither to fare.
I'd not fail to have reached it the first of the New Year,
So help me our Lord, for the whole land of Logres;
And therefore, I beg this boon of you here, sir;
Tell me, in truth, if you ever heard tale
Of the Chapel of Green, of the ground where it stands,
And the knight, green colored, who keeps it. By solemn
Agreement a tryst was established between us,
That man at that landmark to meet if I lived. 1060
And now there lacks of New Year but little;
I'd look at that lord, if God would but let me,
More gladly than own any good thing, by God's Son.
And hence, by your leave, it behooves me to go;
I now have but barely three days to be busy.
As fain would I fall dead as fail of my mission."
Then laughing the lord said: "You longer must stay,
For I'll point out the way to that place ere the time's end,
The ground of the Green Chapel. Grieve no further;
For, sir, you shall be in your bed at your ease 1070
Until late, and fare forth the first of the year,
To your meeting place come by mid-morning, to do there
Your pleasure.
Tarry till New Year's day,
Then rise and go at leisure.
I'll set you on your way;
Not two miles is the measure."

Then was Gawain right glad, and gleefully laughed.
"Now for this more than anything else, sir, I thank you.
I have come to the end of my quest; at your will 1080
I shall bide, and in all things act as you bid me."
The lord then seized him, and set him beside him,
And sent for the ladies to better delight him.
Seemly the pleasure among them in private.
So gay were the speeches he spoke, and so friendly,
The host seemed a man well-nigh mad in behavior.
He called to the knight there, crying aloud:
"Ye have bound you to do the deed that I bid you.
Here, and at once, will you hold to your word sir?"
"Yes, certainly sir," the true hero said; 1090
"While I bide in your house I obey your behest."
"You have toiled," said the lord; "from afar have travelled,
And here have caroused, nor are wholly recovered

In sleep or in nourishment, know I for certain.
In your room you shall linger, and lie at your ease
To-morrow till mass-time, and go to your meat
When you will, and with you my wife to amuse you
With company, till to the court I return.
You stay
And I shall early rise, 1100
And hunting go my way."
Bowing in courteous wise,
Gawain grants all this play.

"And more," said the man, "let us make an agreement:
Whatever I win in the wood shall be yours;
And what chance you shall meet shall be mine in exchange.
Sir, let's so strike our bargain and swear to tell truly
Whate'er fortune brings, whether bad, sir, or better."
Quoth Gawain the good: "By God, I do grant it.
What pastime you please appears to me pleasant." 1110
"On the beverage brought us the bargain is made,"
So the lord of the land said. All of them laughed,
And drank, and light-heartedly revelled and dallied,
Those ladies and lords, as long as they liked.
Then they rose with elaborate politeness, and lingered,
With many fair speeches spoke softly together,
Right lovingly kissed, and took leave of each other.
Gay troops of attendants with glimmering torches
In comfort escorted each man to his couch
To rest. 1120
Yet ere they left the board
Their promise they professed
Often. That people's lord
Could well maintain a jest.

III

Betimes rose the folk ere the first of the day;
The guests that were going then summoned their grooms,
Who hastily sprang up to saddle their horses,
Packed their bags and prepared all their gear.
The nobles made ready, to ride all arrayed;
And quickly they leaped and caught up their bridles, 1130
And started, each wight on the way that well pleased him.
The land's beloved lord not last was equipped
For riding, with many a man too. A morsel
He hurriedly ate when mass he had heard,
And promptly with horn to the hunting field hastened.
And ere any daylight had dawned upon earth,
Both he and his knights were high on their horses.
The dog-grooms, accomplished, the hounds then coupled,
The door of the kennel unclosed, called them out,
On the bugle mightily blew three single notes; 1140

Whereupon bayed with a wild noise the brachets,[38]
And some they turned back that went straying, and punished.
The hunters, I heard, were a hundred. To station
They go,
The keepers of the hounds,
And off the leashes throw.
With noise the wood resounds
From the good blasts they blow.

At the first sound of questing, the wild creatures quaked;
The deer fled, foolish from fright, in the dale, 1150
To the high ground hastened, but quickly were halted
By beaters, loud shouting, stationed about
In a circle. The harts were let pass with their high heads,
And also the bucks, broad-antlered and bold;
For the generous lord by law had forbidden
All men with the male deer to meddle in close season.
The hinds were hemmed in with hey! and ware!
The does to the deep valleys driven with great din.
You might see as they loosed them the shafts swiftly soar—
At each turn of the forest their feathers went flying— 1160
That deep into brown hides bit with their broad heads;
Lo! they brayed on the hill-sides, bled there, and died,
And hounds, fleet-footed, followed them headlong.
And hunters after them hastened with horns
So loud in their sharp burst of sound as to sunder
The cliffs. What creatures escaped from the shooters,
Hunted and harried from heights to the waters,
Were pulled down and rent at the places there ready;
Such skill the men showed at these low-lying stations,
So great were the greyhounds that quickly they got them 1170
And dragged them down, fast as the folk there might look
At the sight.
Carried with bliss away,
The lord did oft alight,
Oft gallop; so that day
He passed till the dark night.

Thus frolicked the lord on the fringe of the forest,
And Gawain the good in his gay bed reposed,
Lying snugly, till sunlight shone on the walls,
'Neath a coverlet bright with curtains about it. 1180
As softly he slumbered, a slight sound he heard
At his door, made with caution, and quickly it opened.
The hero heaved up his head from the clothes;
By a corner he caught up the curtain a little,
And glanced out with heed to behold what had happened.

[38] Dogs that hunt by scent.

The lady it was, most lovely to look at,
Who shut the door after her stealthily, slyly,
And turned toward the bed. Then the brave man, embarrassed,
Lay down again subtly to seem as if sleeping;
And stilly she stepped, and stole to his bed, 1190
There cast up the curtain, and creeping within it,
Seated herself on the bedside right softly,
And waited a long while to watch when he woke.
And the lord too, lurking, lay there a long while,
Wondering at heart what might come of this happening,
Or what it might mean—a marvel he thought it.
Yet he said to himself, "'T would be surely more seemly
By speaking at once to see what she wishes."
Then roused he from sleep, and stretching turned toward her,
His eyelids unlocked, made believe that he wondered, 1200
And signed himself so by his prayers to be safer
From fall.
Right sweet in chin and cheek,
Both white and red withal,
Full fairly she did speak
With laughing lips and small.

"Good morrow, Sir Gawain," that gay lady said,
"You're a sleeper unwary, since so one may steal in.
In a trice you are ta'en! If we make not a truce,
In your bed, be you certain of this, I shall bind you." 1210
All laughing, the lady delivered those jests.
"Good morrow, fair lady," said Gawain the merry,
"You may do what you will, and well it doth please me,
For quickly I yield me, crying for mercy;
This method to me seems the best—for I must!"
So the lord in turn jested with laughter right joyous.
"But if, lovely lady, you would, give me leave,
Your prisoner release and pray him to rise,
And I'd come from this bed and clothe myself better;
So could I converse with you then with more comfort." 1220
"Indeed no, fair sir," that sweet lady said,
"You'll not move from your bed; I shall manage you better;
For here—and on that side too—I shall hold you,
And next I shall talk with the knight I have taken.
For well do I know that your name is Sir Gawain,
By everyone honored wherever you ride;
Most highly acclaimed is your courtly behavior
With lords and ladies and all who are living.
And now you're here, truly, and none but we two;
My lord and his followers far off have fared; 1230
Other men remain in their beds, and my maidens;
The door is closed, and secured with a strong hasp;
Since him who delights all I have in my house,
My time, as long as it lasts, I with talking

Shall fill.
My body's gladly yours;
Upon me work your will.
Your servant I, perforce,
Am now, and shall be still."

"In faith," quoth Sir Gawain, "a favor I think it, 1240
Although I am now not the knight you speak of;
To reach to such fame as here you set forth,
I am one, as I well know myself, most unworthy.
By God, should you think it were good, I'd be glad
If I could or in word or action accomplish
Your ladyship's pleasure—a pure joy 't would prove."
"In good faith, Sir Gawain," the gay lady said,
"Ill-bred I should be if I blamed or belittled
The worth and prowess that please all others.
There are ladies enough who'd be now more delighted 1250
To have you in thraldom, as here, sir, I have you,
To trifle gaily in talk most engaging,
To give themselves comfort and quiet their cares,
Than have much of the gold and the goods they command.
But to Him I give praise that ruleth the heavens,
That wholly I have in my hand what all wish."
So she
Gave him good cheer that day,
She who was fair to see.
To what she chanced to say 1260
With pure speech answered he.

Quoth the merry man, "Madam, Mary reward you,
For noble, in faith, I've found you, and generous.
People by others pattern their actions,
But more than I merit to me they give praise;
'T is your courteous self who can show naught but kindness."
"By Mary," said she, "to me it seems other!
Were I worth all the host of women now living,
And had I the wealth of the world in my hands,
Should I chaffer[39] and choose to get me a champion, 1270
Sir, from the signs I've seen in you here
Of courtesy, merry demeanor, and beauty,
From what I have heard, and hold to be true,
Before you no lord now alive would be chosen."
"A better choice, madam, you truly have made;
Yet I'm proud of the value you put now upon me.
Your servant as seemly, I hold you my sovereign,
Become your knight, and Christ give you quittance."
Thus of much they talked till mid-morning was past.

[39] Bargain; haggle.

The lady behaved as if greatly she loved him, 1280
But Gawain, on guard, right gracefully acted.
"Though I were the most lovely of ladies," she thought,
"The less would he take with him love." He was seeking,
With speed,
Grief that must be: the stroke
That him should stun indeed.
She then of leaving spoke,
And promptly he agreed.

Then she gave him good-day, and glanced at him, laughing,
And startled him, speaking sharp words as she stood: 1290
"He who blesses all words reward this reception!
I doubt if indeed I may dub you Gawain."
"Wherefore?" he queried, quickly enquiring,
Afraid that he'd failed in his fashion of speech.
But the fair lady blessed him, speaking as follows:
"One as good as is Gawain the gracious considered,
(And courtly behavior's found wholly in him)
Not lightly so long could remain with a lady
Without, in courtesy, craving a kiss
At some slight subtle hint at the end of a story." 1300
"Let it be as you like, lovely lady," said Gawain;
"As a knight is so bound, I'll kiss at your bidding,
And lest he displease you, so plead no longer."
Then closer she comes, and catches the knight
In her arms, and salutes him, leaning down affably.
Kindly each other to Christ they commend.
She goes forth at the door without further ado,
And he quickly makes ready to rise, and hastens,
Calls to his chamberlain, chooses his clothes,
And merrily marches, when ready, to mass. 1310
Then he fared to his meat, and fitly he feasted,
Made merry all day with amusements till moonrise.
None knew
A knight to better fare
With dames so worthy, two:
One old, one younger. There
Much mirth did then ensue.

Still was absent the lord of that land on his pleasure,
To hunt barren hinds in wood and in heath.
By the set of the sun he had slain such a number 1320
Of does and different deer that 't was wondrous.
Eagerly flocked in the folk at the finish,
And quickly made of the killed deer a quarry;
To this went the nobles with numerous men;
The game whose flesh was the fattest they gathered;
With care, as the case required, cut them open.

And some the deer searched at the spot of assay,[40]
And two fingers of fat they found in the poorest.
They slit at the base of the throat, seized the stomach,
Scraped it away with a sharp knife and sewed it; 1330
Next slit the four limbs and stripped off the hide;
Then opened the belly and took out the bowels
And flesh of the knot, quickly flinging them out.
They laid hold of the throat, made haste to divide, then,
The windpipe and gullet, and tossed out the guts;
With their sharp knives carved out the shoulders and carried them
Held through a small hole to have the sides perfect.
The breast they sliced, and split it in two;
And then they began once again at the throat,
And quickly as far as its fork they cut it; 1340
Pulled out the pluck,[41] and promptly thereafter
Beside the ribs swiftly severed the fillets,
Cleared them off readily right by the back-bone,
Straight down to the haunch, all hanging together.
They heaved it up whole, and hewed it off there,
And the rest by the name of the numbles[42]—and rightly—
They knew.
Then where divide the thighs,
The folds behind they hew,
Hasten to cut the prize 1350
Along the spine in two.

And next both the head and the neck off they hewed;
The sides from the backbone swiftly they sundered;
The fee of the ravens[43] they flung in the branches.
They ran through each thick side a hole by the ribs,
And hung up both by the hocks of the haunches,
Each fellow to have the fee that was fitting.
On the fair beast's hide, they fed their hounds
With the liver and lights and the paunch's lining,
Among which bread steeped in blood was mingled. 1360
They blew boldly the blast for the prize; the hounds barked.
Then the venison took they and turned toward home,
And stoutly many a shrill note they sounded.
Ere close of the daylight, the company came
To the comely castle where Gawain in comfort
Sojourned.
And when he met the knight
As thither he returned,
Joy had they and delight,
Where the fire brightly burned. 1370

[40] Place to test the thickness of the fat.
[41] Tender meat taken from the throat.
[42] Edible organs. [43] Bits of scrap meat flung to the birds.

In the hall the lord bade all his household to gather,
And both of the dames to come down with their damsels.
In the room there before all the folk he ordered
His followers, truly, to fetch him his venison.
Gawain he called with courteous gaiety,
Asked him to notice the number of nimble beasts,
Showed him the fairness of flesh on the ribs.
"Are you pleased with this play? Have I won your praise?
Have I thoroughly earned your thanks through my cunning?"
"In faith," said Sir Gawain, "this game is the fairest 1380
I've seen in the season of winter these seven years."
"The whole of it, Gawain, I give you," the host said;
"Because of our compact, as yours you may claim it."
"That is true," the knight said, "and I tell you the same:
That this I have worthily won within doors,
And surely to you with as good will I yield it."
With both of his arms his fair neck he embraced,
And the hero as courteously kissed as he could.
"I give you my gains. I got nothing further;
I freely would grant it, although it were greater." 1390
"It is good," said the good man; "I give you my thanks.
Yet things so may be that you'd think it better
To tell where you won this same wealth by your wit."
" 'T was no part of our pact," said he; "press me no more;
For trust entirely in this, that you've taken
Your due."
With laughing merriment
And knightly speech and true,
To supper soon they went
With store of dainties new, 1400

In a chamber they sat, by the side of the chimney,
Where men right frequently fetched them mulled wine.
In their jesting, again they agreed on the morrow
To keep the same compact they came to before:
That whatever should chance, they'd exchange at evening,
When greeting again, the new things they had gotten.
Before all the court they agreed to the covenant;
Then was the beverage brought forth in jest.
At last they politely took leave of each other,
And quickly each hero made haste to his couch. 1410
When the cock but three times had crowed and cackled,
The lord and his men had leaped from their beds.
So that duly their meal was dealt with, and mass,
And ere daylight they'd fared toward the forest, on hunting
Intent.
The huntsmen with loud horns
Through level fields soon went,
Uncoupling 'mid the thorns
The hounds swift on the scent.

Soon they cry for a search by the side of a swamp. 1420
The huntsmen encourage the hounds that first catch there
The scent, and sharp words they shout at them loudly;
And thither the hounds that heard them hastened,
And fast to the trail fell, forty at once.
Then such clamor and din from the dogs that had come there
Arose that the rocks all around them rang.
With horn and with mouth the hunters heartened them;
They gathered together then, all in a group,
'Twixt a pool in that copse and a crag most forbidding.
At a stone-heap, beside the swamp, by a cliff, 1430
Where the rough rock had fallen in rugged confusion,
They fared to the finding, the folk coming after.
Around both the crag and the rubble-heap searched
The hunters, sure that within them was hidden
The beast whose presence was bayed by the bloodhounds.
Then they beat on the bushes, and bade him rise up,
And wildly he made for the men in his way,
Rushing suddenly forth, of swine the most splendid.
Apart from the herd he'd grown hoary with age,
For fierce was the beast, the biggest of boars. 1440
Then many men grieved, full grim when he grunted,
For three at his first thrust he threw to the earth,
And then hurtled forth swiftly, no harm doing further.
They shrilly cried hi! and shouted hey! hey!
Put bugles to mouth, loudly blew the recall.
The men and dogs merry in voice were and many;
With outcry they all hurry after this boar
To slay.
He maims the pack when, fell,
He often stands at bay. 1450
Loudly they howl and yell,
Sore wounded in the fray.

Then to shoot at him came up the company quickly.
Arrows that hit him right often they aimed,
But their sharp points failed that fell on his shoulders'
Tough skin, and the barbs would not bite in his flesh;
But the smooth-shaven shafts were shivered in pieces,
The heads wherever they hit him rebounding.
But when hurt by the strength of the strokes they struck,
Then mad for the fray he falls on the men, 1460
And deeply he wounds them as forward he dashes.
Then many were frightened, and drew back in fear;
But the lord galloped off on a light horse after him,
Blew like a huntsman right bold the recall
On his bugle, and rode through the thick of the bushes,
Pursuing this swine till the sun shone clearly.
Thus the day they passed in doing these deeds,
While bides our gracious knight Gawain in bed,

With bed-clothes in color right rich, at the castle
Behind. 1470
The dame did not forget
To give him greetings kind.
She soon upon him set,
To make him change his mind.

Approaching the curtain, she peeps at the prince,
And at once Sir Gawain welcomes her worthily.
Promptly the lady makes her reply.
By his side she seats herself softly, heartily
Laughs, and with lovely look these words delivers:
"If you, sir, are Gawain, greatly I wonder 1480
That one so given at all times to goodness
Should be not well versed in social conventions,
Or, made once to know, should dismiss them from mind.
You have promptly forgotten what I in the plainest
Of talk that I knew of yesterday taught you."
"What is that?" said the knight. "For truly I know not;
If it be as you say, I am surely to blame."
"Yet I taught you," quoth the fair lady, "of kissing;
When clearly he's favored, quickly to claim one
Becomes each knight who practices courtesy." 1490
"Cease, dear lady, such speech," said the strong man;
"I dare not for fear of refusal do that.
'T would be wrong to proffer and then be repulsed."
"In faith, you may not be refused," said the fair one;
"Sir, if you pleased, you have strength to compel it,
Should one be so rude as to wish to deny you."
"By God, yes," said Gawain, "good is your speech;
But unlucky is force in the land I live in,
And every gift that with good will's not given.
Your word I await to embrace when you wish; 1500
You may start when you please, and stop at your pleasure."
With grace
The lady, bending low,
Most sweetly kissed his face.
Of joy in love and woe
They talked for a long space.

"I should like," said the lady, "from you, sir, to learn,
If I roused not your anger by asking, the reason
Why you, who are now so young and valiant,
So known far and wide as knightly and courteous 1510
(And principally, picked from all knighthood, is praised
The sport of true love and the science of arms;
For to tell of these true knights' toil, it is surely
The title inscribed and the text of their deeds,

How men their lives for their leal[44] love adventured,
Endured for their passion doleful days,
Then themselves with valor avenged, and their sorrow
Cast off, and brought bliss into bowers by their virtues),
Why you, thought the noblest knight of your time,
Whose renown and honor are everywhere noted, 1520
Have so let me sit on two separate occasions
Beside you, and hear proceed from your head
Not one word relating to love, less or more.
You so goodly in vowing your service and gracious
Ought gladly to give to a young thing your guidance,
And show me some sign of the sleights of true love.
What! know you nothing, and have all renown?
Or else do you deem me too dull, for your talking
Unfit?
For shame! Alone I come; 1530
To learn some sport I sit;
My lord is far from home;
Now, teach me by your wit."

"In good faith," said Gawain, "God you reward;
For great is the happiness, huge the gladness
That one so worthy should want to come hither,
And pains for so poor a man take, as in play
With your knight with looks of regard; it delights me.
But to take up the task of telling of true love,
To touch on those themes, and on tales of arms 1540
To you who've more skill in that art, I am certain,
By half than a hundred men have such as I,
Or ever shall have while here upon earth,
By my faith, 't would be, madam, a manifold folly.
Your bidding I'll do, as in duty bound,
To the height of my power, and will hold myself ever
Your ladyship's servant, so save me the Lord."
Thus the fair lady tempted and tested him often
To make the man sin—what'er more she'd in mind;
But so fair his defence was, no fault was apparent, 1550
Nor evil on either side; each knew but joy
On that day.
At last she kissed him lightly,
After long mirth and play,
And took her leave politely,
And went upon her way.

The man bestirs himself, springs up for mass.
Then made ready and splendidly served was their dinner;
In sport with the ladies he spent all the day.

[44] True.

But the lord through fields oft dashed as he followed 1560
The savage swine, that sped o'er the slopes,
And in two bit the backs of the best of his hounds
Where he stood at bay; till 't was broken by bowmen,
Who made him, despite himself, move to the open,
The shafts flew so thick when the throng had assembled.
Yet sometimes he forced the stoutest to flinch,
Till at last too weary he was to run longer,
But came with such haste as he could to a hole
In a mound, by a rock whence the rivulet runs out.
He started to scrape the soil, backed by the slope, 1570
While froth from his mouth's ugly corners came foaming.
White were the tushes he whetted, The bold men
Who stood round grew tired of trying from far
To annoy him, but dared not for danger draw nearer.
Before,
So many he did pierce
That all were loth a boar
So frenzied and so fierce
Should tear with tusks once more,

Till the hero himself came, spurring his horse, 1580
Saw him standing at bay, the hunters beside him.
He leaped down right lordly, leaving his courser,
Unsheathed a bright sword and strode forth stoutly,
Made haste through the ford where that fierce one was waiting.
Aware of the hero with weapon in hand,
So savagely, bristling his back up, he snorted
All feared for the wight lest the worst befall him.
Then rushed out the boar directly upon him,
And man was mingled with beast in the midst
Of the wildest water. The boar had the worse, 1590
For the man aimed a blow at the beast as he met him,
And surely with sharp blade struck o'er his breast bone,
That smote to the hilt, and his heart cleft asunder.
He squealing gave way, and swift through the water
Went back.
By a hundred hounds he's caught,
Who fiercely him attack;
To open ground he's brought,
And killed there by the pack.

The blast for the beast's death was blown on sharp horns, 1600
And the lords there loudly and clearly hallooed.
At the beast bayed the brachets, as bid by their masters,
The chief, in that hard, long chase, of the hunters.
Then one who was wise in woodcraft began
To slice up this swine in the seemliest manner.
First he hews off his head, and sets it on high;
Then along the back roughly rends him apart.

He hales out the bowels, and broils them on hot coals,
With these mixed with bread, rewarding his brachets.
Then slices the flesh in fine, broad slabs, 1610
And pulls out the edible entrails properly.
Whole, though, he gathers the halves together,
And proudly upon a stout pole he places them.
Homeward they now with this very swine hasten,
Bearing in front of the hero the boar's head,
Since him at the ford by the force of his strong hand
He slew.
It seemed long till he met
In hall Sir Gawain, who
Hastened, when called, to get 1620
The payment that was due.

The lord called out loudly, merrily laughed
When Gawain he saw, and gladsomely spoke.
The good ladies were sent for, the household assembled;
He shows them the slices of flesh, and the story
He tells of his largeness and length, and how fierce
Was the war in the woods where the wild swine had fled.
Sir Gawain commended his deeds right graciously,
Praised them as giving a proof of great prowess.
Such brawn on a beast, the bold man declared, 1630
And such sides on a swine he had ne'er before seen.
Then they handled the huge head; the courteous hero
Praised it, horror-struck, honoring his host.
Quoth the good man, "Now Gawain yours is this game
By our covenant, fast and firm, you know truly."
"It is so," said the knight; "and as certain and sure
All I get I'll give you again as I pledged you."
He about the neck caught, with courtesy kissed him,
And soon a second time served him the same way.
Said Gawain, "We've fairly fulfilled the agreement 1640
This evening we entered on, each to the other
Most true."
"I, by Saint Giles, have met
None," said the lord, "like you.
Riches you soon will get,
If you such business do."

And then the tables they raised upon trestles,
And laid on them cloths; the light leaped up clearly
Along by the walls, where the waxen torches
Were set by the henchmen who served in the hall. 1650
A great sound of sport and merriment sprang up
Close by the fire, and on frequent occasions
At supper and afterward, many a splendid song,
Conduits of Christmas, new carols, all kinds
Of mannerly mirth that a man may tell of.

Our seemly knight ever sat at the side
Of the lady, who made so agreeable her manner,
With sly, secret glances to glad him, so stalwart,
That greatly astonished was Gawain, and wroth
With himself; he in courtesy could not refuse her, 1660
But acted becomingly, courtly, whatever
The end, good or bad, of his action might be.
When quite
Done was their play at last,
The host called to the knight,
And to his room they passed
To where the fire burned bright.

The men there make merry and drink, and once more
The same pact for New Year's Eve is proposed;
But the knight craved permission to mount on the morrow: 1670
The appointment approached where he had to appear.
But the lord him persuaded to stay and linger,
And said, "On my word as a knight I assure you
You'll get to the Green Chapel, Gawain, on New Year's,
And far before prime,[45] to finish your business.
Remain in your room then, and take your rest.
I shall hunt in the wood and exchange with you winnings,
As bound by our bargain, when back I return,
For twice I've found you were faithful when tried:
In the morning 'best be the third time,' remember. 1680
Let's be mindful of mirth while we may, and make merry,
For care when one wants it is quickly encountered."
At once this was granted, and Gawain is stayed;
Drink blithely was brought him; to bed they were lighted.
The guest
In quiet and comfort spent
The night, and took his rest.
On his affairs intent,
The host was early dressed.

After mass a morsel he took with his men. 1690
The morning was merry; his mount he demanded.
The knights who'd ride in his train were in readiness,
Dressed and horsed at the door of the hall.
Wondrous fair were the fields, for the frost was clinging;
Bright red in the cloud-rack rises the sun,
And full clear sails close past the clouds in the sky.
The hunters unleashed all the hounds by a woodside:
The rocks with the blast of their bugles were ringing.
Some dogs there fall on the scent where the fox is,
And trail oft a traitoress using her tricks. 1700

[45] The canonical office for the first hour of the day, that is, 6:00 A.M.

A hound gives tongue at it; huntsmen call to him;
Hastens the pack to the hound sniffing hard,
And right on his track run off in a rabble,
He scampering before them. They started the fox soon;
When finally they saw him, they followed fast,
Denouncing him clearly with clamorous anger.
Through many a dense grove he dodges and twists,
Doubling back and harkening at hedges right often;
At last by a little ditch leaps o'er a thorn-hedge,
Steals out stealthily, skirting a thicket 1710
In thought from the wood to escape by his wiles
From the hounds; then, unknowing, drew near to a hunting-stand.
There hurled themselves, three at once, on him strong hounds,
All gray.
With quick swerve he doth start
Afresh without dismay.
With great grief in his heart
To the wood he goes away.

Huge was the joy then to hark to the hounds,
When the pack all met him, mingled together, 1720
Such curses they heaped on his head at the sight
That the clustering cliffs seemed to clatter down round them
In heaps. The men, when they met him, hailed him,
And loudly with chiding speeches hallooed him;
Threats were oft thrown at him, thief he was called;
At his tail were the greyhounds, that tarry he might not.
They rushed at him oft when he raced for the open,
And ran to the wood again, Reynard the wily.
Thus he led them, all muddied, the lord and his men,
In this manner along through the hills until midday. 1730
At home, the noble knight wholesomely slept
In the cold of the morn within comely curtains.
But the lady, for love, did not let herself sleep,
Or fail in the purpose fixed in her heart;
But quickly she roused herself, came there quickly,
Arrayed in a gay robe that reached to the ground,
The skins of the splendid fur skillfully trimmed close.
On her head no colors save jewels, well-cut,
That were twined in her hair-fret in clusters of twenty.
Her fair face was completely exposed, and her throat; 1740
In front her breast too was bare, and her back.
She comes through the chamber-door, closes it after her,
Swings wide a window, speaks to the wight,
And rallies him soon in speech full of sport
And good cheer.
"Ah! man, how can you sleep?
The morning is so clear."
He was in sorrow deep,
Yet her he then did hear.

In a dream muttered Gawain, deep in its gloom, 1750
Like a man by a throng of sad thoughts sorely moved
Of how fate was to deal out his destiny to him
That morn, when he met the man at the Green Chapel,
Bound to abide his blow, unresisting.
But as soon as that comely one came to his senses,
Started from slumber and speedily answered,
The lovely lady came near, sweetly laughing,
Bent down o'er his fair face and daintily kissed him.
And well, in a worthy manner, he welcomed her.
Seeing her glorious, gaily attired, 1760
Without fault in her features, most fine in her color,
Deep joy came welling up, warming his heart.
With sweet, gentle smiling they straightway grew merry;
So passed naught between them but pleasure, joy,
And delight.
Goodly was their debate,
Nor was their gladness slight.
Their peril had been great
Had Mary quit her knight.

For that noble princess pressed him so closely, 1770
Brought him so near the last bound, that her love
He was forced to accept, or, offending, refuse her:
Concerned for his courtesy not to prove caitiff,[46]
And more for his ruin if wrong he committed,
Betraying the hero, the head of that house.
"God forbid," said the knight; "that never shall be";
And lovingly laughing a little, he parried
The words of fondness that fell from her mouth.
She said to him, "Sir, you are surely to blame
If you love not the lady beside whom you're lying, 1780
Of all the world's women most wounded in heart,
Unless you've one dearer, a lover you like more,
Your faith to her plighted, so firmly made fast
You desire not to loosen it—so I believe.
Now tell me truly I pray you; the truth,
By all of the loves that in life are, conceal not
Through guile."
The knight said, "By Saint John,"
And pleasantly to smile
Began, "In faith I've none, 1790
Nor will have for a while."

"Such words," said the lady, "the worst are of all;
But in sooth I am answered, and sad it seems to me.
Kiss me now kindly, and quickly I'll go;

[46]A base, despicable person.

I on earth may but mourn, as a much loving mortal."
Sighing she stoops down, and kisses him seemly;
Then starting away from him, says as she stands,
"Now, my dear, at parting, do me this pleasure:
Give me some gift, thy glove if it might be,
To bring you to mind, sir, my mourning to lessen." 1800
"On my word," quoth the hero, "I would that I had here,
For thy sake, the thing that I think the dearest
I own, for in sooth you've deserved very often
A greater reward than one I could give.
But a pledge of love would profit but little;
'T would help not your honor to have at this time
For a keepsake a glove, as a gift of Gawain.
I've come on a mission to countries most strange;
I've no servants with splendid things filling their sacks:
That displeases me, lady, for love's sake, at present; 1810
Yet each man without murmur must do what he may
Nor repine."
"Nay, lord of honors high,
Though I have naught of thine,"
Quoth the lovely lady, "I
Shall give you gift of mine."

She offered a rich ring, wrought in red gold,
With a blazing stone that stood out above it,
And shot forth brilliant rays bright as the sun;
Wit you well that wealth right huge it was worth. 1820
But promptly the hero replied, refusing it,
"Madam, I care not for gifts now to keep;
I have none to tender and naught will I take."
Thus he ever declined her offer right earnest,
And swore on his word that he would not accept it;
And, sad he declined, she thereupon said,
"If my ring you refuse, since it seems too rich,
If you would not so highly to me be beholden,
My girdle, that profits you less, I'll give you."
She swiftly removed the belt circling her sides, 1830
Round her tunic knotted, beneath her bright mantle;
'T was fashioned of green silk, and fair made with gold,
With gold, too, the borders embellished and beautiful.
To Gawain she gave it, and gaily besought him
To take it, although he thought it but trifling.
He swore by no manner of means he'd accept
Either gold or treasure ere God gave him grace
To attain the adventure he'd there undertaken.
"And, therefore, I pray, let it prove not displeasing,
But give up your suit, for to grant it I'll never 1840
Agree.
I'm deeply in your debt
For your kind ways to me.

In hot and cold I yet
Will your true servant be."

"Refuse ye this silk," the lady then said,
"As slight in itself? Truly it seems so.
Lo! it is little, and less is its worth;
But one knowing the nature knit up within it,
Would give it a value more great, peradventure; 1850
For no man girt with this girdle of green,
And bearing it fairly made fast about him,
Might ever be cut down by any on earth,
For his life in no way in the world could be taken."
Then mused the man, and it came to his mind
In the peril appointed him precious 't would prove,
When he'd found the chapel, to face there his fortune.
The device, might he slaying evade, would be splendid.
Her suit then he suffered, and let her speak;
And the belt she offered him, earnestly urging it 1860
(And Gawain consented), and gave it with good will,
And prayed him for her sake ne'er to display it,
But, true, from her husband to hide it. The hero
Agreed that no one should know of it ever.
Then he
Thanked her with all his might
Of heart and thought; and she
By then to this stout knight
Had given kisses three.

Then the lady departs, there leaving the lord, 1870
For more pleasure she could not procure from that prince.
When she's gone, then quickly Sir Gawain clothes himself,
Rises and dresses in noble array,
Lays by the love-lace the lady had left him,
Faithfully hides it where later he'd find it.
At once then went on his way to the chapel,
Approached in private a priest, and prayed him
To make his life purer, more plainly him teach
How his soul, when he had to go hence, should be saved.
He declared his faults, confessing them fully, 1880
The more and the less, and mercy besought,
And then of the priest implored absolution.
He surely absolved him, and made him as spotless,
Indeed, as if doomsday were due on the morrow.
Then among the fair ladies he made more merry
With lovely caroles, all kinds of delights,
That day than before, until darkness fell.
All there
Were treated courteously,
"And never," they declare, 1890

"Has Gawain shown such glee
Since hither he did fare."

In that nook where his lot may be love let him linger!
The lord's in the meadow still, leading his men.
He has slain this fox that he followed so long;
As he vaulted a hedge to get view of the villain,
Hearing the hounds that hastened hard after him,
Reynard from out a rough thicket came running,
And right at his heels in a rush all the rabble.
He, seeing that wild thing, wary, awaits him, 1900
Unsheaths his bright brand and strikes at the beast.
And he swerved from its sharpness and back would have started;
A hound, ere he could, came hurrying up to him;
All of them fell on him fast by the horse's feet,
Worried that sly one with wrathful sound.
And quickly the lord alights, and catches him,
Takes him in haste from the teeth of the hounds,
And over his head holds him high, loudly shouting,
Where brachets, many and fierce, at him barked.
Thither huntsmen made haste with many a horn, 1910
The recall, till they saw him, sounding right clearly.
As soon as his splendid troop had assembled,
All bearing a bugle blew them together,
The others having no horns all hallooed.
'T was the merriest baying that man ever heard
That was raised for the soul of Reynard with sounding
Din.
They fondle each dog's head
Who his reward did win.
Then take they Reynard dead 1920
And strip him of his skin.

And now, since near was the night, they turned homeward,
Strongly and sturdily sounding their horns.
At last at his loved home the lord alighted,
A fire on the hearth found, the hero beside it,
Sir Gawain the good, who glad was withal,
For he had 'mong the ladies in love much delight.
A blue robe that fell to the floor he was wearing;
His surcoat, that softly was furred, well beseemed him;
A hood of the same hue hung on his shoulders, 1930
And both were bordered with white all about.
He, mid-most, met the good man in the hall,
And greeted him gladly, graciously saying:
"Now shall I first fulfil our agreement
We struck to good purpose, when drink was not spared."
Then Gawain embraced him, gave him three kisses,
The sweetest and soundest a man could bestow.

"By Christ, you'd great happiness," quoth then the host,
"In getting these wares, if good were your bargains."
"Take no care for the cost," the other said quickly, 1940
"Since plainly the debt that is due I have paid."
Said the other, "By Mary, mine's of less worth.
The whole of the day I have hunted, and gotten
The skin of this fox—the fiend take its foulness!—
Right poor to pay for things of such price
As you've pressed on me here so heartily, kisses
So good."
"Say no more," Gawain saith;
"I thank you, by the rood!"
How the fox met his death 1950
He told him as they stood.

With mirth and minstrelsy, meat at their pleasure
They made as merry as any men might
(With ladies' laughter, and launching of jests
Right glad were they both, the good man and Gawain)
Unless they had doted or else had been drunken.
Both the man and the company make many jokes,
Till the time is come when the two must be parted,
When finally the knights are forced to go bedward.
And first of the lord his respectful leave 1960
This goodly man took, and graciously thanked him:
"May God you reward for the welcome you gave me
This high feast, the splendid sojourn I've had here.
I give you myself, if you'd like it, to serve you.
I must, as you know, on the morrow move on;
Give me some one to show me the path, as you said,
To the Green Chapel, there, as God will allow me,
On New Year the fate that is fixed to perform."
"With a good will, indeed," said the good man; "whatever
I promised to do I deem myself ready." 1970
He a servant assigns on his way to set him,
To take him by hills that no trouble he'd have,
And through grove and wood by the way most direct
Might repair.
The lord he thanked again
For the honor done him there.
The knight his farewell then
Took of those ladies fair.

To them with sorrow and kissing he spoke,
And besought them his thanks most sincere to accept; 1980
And they, replying, promptly returned them,
With sighings full sore to the Savior commended him.
Then he with courtesy quitted the company,
Giving each man that he met his thanks

For kindness, for trouble he'd taken, for care
Whereby each had sought to serve him right eagerly.
Pained was each person to part with him then,
As if long they in honor had lived with that noble.
With people and lights he was led to his chamber,
To bed gaily brought there to be at his rest; 1990
Yet I dare not say whether soundly he slept,
For much, if he would, on the morn to remember
Had he.
Let him lie stilly there
Near what he sought to see.
What happened I'll declare,
If you will silent be.

IV

The New Year draws near, and the nighttime now passes;
The day, as the Lord bids, drives on to darkness.
Outside, there sprang up wild storms in the world; 2000
The clouds cast keenly the cold to the earth
With enough of the north sting to trouble the naked;
Down shivered the snow, nipping sharply the wild beasts;
The wind from the heights, shrilly howling, came rushing,
And heaped up each dale full of drifts right huge.
Full well the man listened who lay in his bed.
Though he shut tight his lids, he slept but a little;
He knew by each cock that crowed 't was the tryst time,
And swiftly ere dawn of the day he arose,
For there shone then the light of a lamp in his room; 2010
To his chamberlain called, who answered him quickly,
And bade him his saddle to bring and his mailshirt.
The other man roused up and fetched him his raiment,
Arrayed then that knight in a fashion right noble.
First he clad him in clothes to ward off the cold,
Then his other equipment, carefully kept:
His pieces of plate armor, polished right cleanly,
The rings of his rich mail burnished from rust.
All was fresh as at first; he was fain to give thanks
To the men. 2020
He had on every piece
Full brightly burnished then.
He, gayest from here to Greece,
Ordered his steed again.

He garbed himself there in the loveliest garments
(His coat had its blazon of beautiful needlework
Stitched upon velvet for show, its rich stones
Set about it and studded, its seams all embroidered,
Its lovely fur in the fairest of linings),
Yet he left not the lace, the gift of the lady: 2030

That, Gawain did not, for his own sake, forget.
When the brand[47] on his rounded thighs he had belted,
He twisted his love-token two times about him.
That lord round his waist with delight quickly wound
The girdle of green silk, that seemed very gay
Upon royal red cloth that was rich to behold.
But Gawain the girdle wore not for its great price,
Or pride in its pendants although they were polished,
Though glittering gold there gleamed on the ends,
But himself to save when he needs must suffer 2040
The death, nor could stroke then of sword or of knife
Him defend.
Then was the bold man dressed;
Quickly his way did wend;
To all the court expressed
His great thanks without end.

Then was Gringolet ready that great was and huge,
Who had safely, as seemed to him pleasant, been stabled;
That proud horse pranced, in the pink of condition.
The lord then comes to him, looks at his coat, 2050
And soberly says, and swears on his word,
"In this castle's a company mindful of courtesy,
Led by this hero. Delight may they have;
And may love the dear lady betide all her lifetime.
If they for charity cherish a guest,
And give so great welcome, may God reward them,
Who rules the heaven on high, and the rest of you.
Might I for long live my life on the earth,
Some repayment with pleasure I'd make, if 't were possible."
He steps in the stirrup, strides into the saddle, 2060
Receives on his shoulder the shield his man brings him,
And spurs into Gringolet strikes with his gilt heels;
Who leaps on the stones and lingers no longer
To prance.
The knight on his horse sits,
Who bears his spear and lance,
The house to Christ commits,
And wishes it good chance.

Then down the drawbridge they dropped, the broad gates
Unbarred, and on both sides bore them wide open. 2070
He blessed them quickly, and crossed o'er the planks there
(He praises the porter, who knelt by the prince
Begging God to save Gawain, and gave him goodday),
And went on his way with but one man attended

[47] Sword.

To show him the turns to that sorrowful spot
Where he must to that onerous onset submit.
By hillsides where branches were bare they both journeyed;
They climbed over cliffs where the cold was clinging.
The clouds hung aloft, but 't was lowering beneath them.
On the moor dripped the mist, on the mountains melted; 2080
Each hill had a hat, a mist-cloak right huge.
The brooks foamed and bubbled on hillsides about them,
And brightly broke on their banks as they rushed down.
Full wandering the way was they went through the wood,
Until soon it was time for the sun to be springing.
Then they
Were on a hill full high;
White snow beside them lay.
The servant who rode nigh
Then bade his master stay. 2090

"I have led you hither, my lord, at this time,
And not far are you now from that famous place
You have sought for, and asked so especially after.
Yet, sir, to you surely I'll say, since I know you,
A man in this world whom I love right well,
If you'd follow my judgment, the better you'd fare.
You make haste to a place that is held full of peril;
One dwells, the worst in the world, in that waste,
For he's strong and stern, and takes pleasure in striking.
No man on the earth can equal his might; 2100
He is bigger in body than four of the best men
In Arthur's own household, Hector or others.
And thus he brings it about at the chapel:
That place no one passes so proud in his arms
That he smites him not dead with a stroke of his hand.
He's a man most immoderate, showing no mercy;
Be it chaplain or churl that rides by the chapel,
Monk or priest, any manner of man,
Him to slay seems as sweet as to still live himself.
So I say, as sure as you sit in your saddle 2110
You're killed, should the knight so choose, if you come here;
That take as the truth, though you twenty lives had
To spend.
He's lived in this place long
In battles without end.
Against his strokes right strong
You cannot you defend.

"So let him alone, good Sir Gawain, and leave
By a different road, for God's sake, and ride
To some other country where Christ may reward you. 2120
And homeward again I will hie me, and promise

To swear by the Lord and all his good saints
(So help me the oaths on God's halidom[48] sworn)
That I'll guard well your secret, and give out no story
You hastened to flee any hero I've heard of."
"Thank you," said Gawain, and grudgingly added,
"Good fortune go with you for wishing me well.
And truly I think you'd not tell; yet though never
So surely you hid it, if hence I should hasten,
Fearful, to fly in the fashion you tell of, 2130
A coward I'd prove, and could not be pardoned.
The chapel I'll find whatsoever befalls,
And talk with that wight the way that I want to,
Let weal or woe follow as fate may wish.
Though the knave,
Hard to subdue and fell,
Should stand there with a stave,
Yet still the Lord knows well
His servants how to save."

Quoth the man, "By Mary, you've said now this much: 2140
That you wish to bring down your own doom on your head.
Since you'd lose your life, I will stay you no longer.
Put your helm on your head, take your spear in your hand,
And ride down this road by the side of that rock
Till it brings you down to the dale's rugged bottom;
Then look at the glade on the left hand a little:
You'll see in the valley that self-same chapel,
And near it the great-limbed knight who is guarding it.
Gawain the noble, farewell now, in God's name!
I would not go with thee for all the world's wealth, 2150
Nor in fellowship ride one more foot through the forest."
The man in the trees there then turns his bridle,
As hard as he can hits his horse with his heels,
And across the fields gallops, there leaving Sir Gawain
Alone.
"By God," the knight said, "now
I'll neither weep nor groan.
Unto God's will I bow,
And make myself his own."

He strikes spurs into Gringolet, starts on the path; 2160
By a bank at the side of a small wood he pushes in,
Rides down the rugged slope right to the dale.
Then about him he looks, and the land seems wild,
And nowhere he sees any sign of a shelter,
But slopes on each side of him, high and steep,
And rocks, gnarled and rough, and stones right rugged.

[48] Holiness or holy relics.

The clouds there seemed to him scraped by the crags.
Then he halted and held back his horse at that time,
And spied on all sides in search of the chapel;
Such nowhere he saw, but soon, what seemed strange, 2170
In the midst of a glade a mound, as it might be,
A smooth, swelling knoll by the side of the water,
The falls of a rivulet running close by;
In its banks the brook bubbled as though it were boiling.
The knight urged on Gringolet, came to the glade,
There leaped down lightly and tied to the limb
Of a tree, right rugged, the reins of his noble steed,
Went to the mound, and walked all about it,
Debating what manner of thing it might be:
On the end and on each side an opening; everywhere 2180
Over it grass was growing in patches,
All hollow inside, it seemed an old cave
Or a crag's old cleft: which, he could not decide.
Said the knight,
"Is this the chapel here?
Alas, dear Lord! here might
The fiend, when midnight's near,
His matin prayers recite.

"Of a truth," said Gawain, "the glade here is gloomy;
The Green Chapel's ugly, with herbs overgrown. 2190
It greatly becomes here that hero, green-clad,
To perform in the devil's own fashion his worship.
I feel in my five senses this is the fiend
Who has made me come to this meeting to kill me.
Destruction fall on this church of ill-fortune!
The cursedest chapel that ever I came to!"
With helm on his head and lance in his hand
He went right to the rock of that rugged abode.
From that high hill he heard, from a hard rock over
The stream, on the hillside, a sound wondrous loud. 2200
Lo! it clattered on cliffs fit to cleave them, as though
A scythe on a grindstone some one were grinding.
It whirred, lo! and whizzed like a water-mill's wheel;
Lo! it ground and it grated, grievous to hear.
"By God, this thing, as I think," then said Gawain,
"Is done now for me, since my due turn to meet it
Is near.
God's will be done! 'Ah woe!'
No whit doth aid me here.
Though I my life forego 2210
No sound shall make me fear."

And then the man there commenced to call loudly,
"Who here is the master, with me to hold tryst?
For Gawain the good now is going right near.

He who craves aught of me let him come hither quickly;
'T is now or never; he needs to make haste."
Said somebody, "Stop," from the slope up above him,
"And promptly you'll get what I promised to give you."
Yet he kept up the whirring noise quickly a while,
Turned to finish his sharpening before he'd descend. 2220
Then he came by a crag, from a cavern emerging,
Whirled out of a den with a dreadful weapon,
A new Danish axe to answer the blow with;
Its blade right heavy, curved back to the handle,
Sharp filed with the filing tool, four feet in length,
'T was no less, by the reach of that lace gleaming brightly.
The fellow in green was garbed as at first,
Both his face and his legs, his locks and his beard,
Save that fast o'er the earth on his feet he went fairly,
The shaft on the stone set, and stalked on beside it. 2230
On reaching the water, he would not wade it;
On his axe he hopped over, and hastily strode,
Very fierce, through the broad field filled all about him
With snow.
Sir Gawain met the man,
And bowed by no means low,
Who said, "Good sir, men can
Trust you to tryst to go."

Said the green man, "Gawain, may God you guard!
You are welcome indeed, sir knight, at my dwelling. 2240
Your travel you've timed as a true man should,
And you know the compact we came to between us;
A twelvemonth ago you took what chance gave,
And I promptly at New Year was pledged to repay you.
In truth, we are down in this dale all alone;
Though we fight as we please, here there's no one to part us.
Put your helm from your head, and have here your payment;
Debate no further than I did before,
When you slashed off my head with a single stroke."
"Nay," quoth Gawain, "by God who gave me my spirit, 2250
I'll harbor no grudge whatever harm happens.
Exceed not one stroke and still I shall stand;
You may do as you please, I'll in no way oppose
The blow."
He left the flesh all bare,
Bending his neck down low
As if he feared naught there,
For fear he would not show.

Then the man in green raiment quickly made ready,
Uplifted his grim tool Sir Gawain to smite; 2260
With the whole of his strength he heaved it on high,
As threateningly swung it as though he would slay him.

Had it fallen again with the force he intended
That lord, ever-brave, from the blow had been lifeless.
But Gawain a side glance gave at the weapon
As down it came gliding to do him to death;
With his shoulders shrank from the sharp iron a little.
The other with sudden jerk stayed the bright axe,
And reproved then that prince with proud words in plenty:
"Not Gawain thou art who so good is considered, 2270
Ne'er daunted by host in hill or in dale;
Now in fear, ere thou feelest a hurt, thou art flinching;
Such cowardice never I knew of that knight.
When you swung at me, sir, I fled not nor started;
No cavil I offered in King Arthur's castle.
My head at my feet fell, yet never I flinched,
And thy heart is afraid ere a hurt thou feelest,
And therefore thy better I'm bound to be thought
On that score."
"I shrank once," Gawain said, 2280
"And I will shrink no more;
Yet cannot I my head,
If it fall down, restore.

"But make ready, sir, quickly, and come to the point;
My destiny deal me, and do it forthwith;
For a stroke I will suffer, and start no further
Till hit with thy weapon; have here my pledged word."
Quoth the other, heaving it high, "Have at thee!"
As fierce in his manner as if he were mad,
He mightily swung but struck not the man, 2290
Withheld on a sudden his hand ere it hurt him.
And firmly he waited and flinched in no member,
But stood there as still as a stone or a stump
In rocky ground held by a hundred roots.
Then the Green Knight again began to speak gaily:
"It behooves me to hit, now that whole is thy heart.
Thy high hood that Arthur once gave you now hold back,
Take care that your neck at this cut may recover."
And Gawain full fiercely said in a fury,
"Come! lay on, thou dread man; too long thou art threatening. 2300
I think that afraid of your own self you feel."
"In sooth," said the other, "thy speech is so savage
No more will I hinder thy mission nor have it
Delayed."
With puckered lips and brow
He stands with ready blade.
Not strange 't is hateful now
To him past hope of aid.

He lifts his axe lightly, and lets it down deftly,
The blade's edge next to the naked neck. 2310

Though he mightily hammered he hurt him no more
Than to give him a slight nick that severed the skin there.
Through fair skin the keen axe so cut to the flesh
That shining blood shot to the earth o'er his shoulders.
As soon as he saw his blood gleam on the snow
He sprang forth in one leap, for more than a spear length;
His helm fiercely caught up and clapped on his head;
With his shoulders his fair shield shot round in front of him,
Pulled out his bright sword, and said in a passion
(And since he was mortal man born of his mother 2320
The hero was never so happy by half),
"Cease thy violence, man; no more to me offer,
For here I've received, unresisting, a stroke.
If a second thou strikest I soon will requite thee,
And swiftly and fiercely, be certain of that,
Will repay.
One stroke on me might fall
By bargain struck that way,
Arranged in Arthur's hall;
Therefore, sir knight, now stay!" 2330

The man turned away, on his weapon rested,
The shaft on the ground set, leaned on the sharp edge,
And gazed at Sir Gawain there in the glade;
Saw that bold man, unblenching, standing right bravely,
Full-harnessed and gallant; at heart he was glad.
Then gaily the Green Knight spoke in a great voice,
And said to the man in speech that resounded,
"Now be not so savage, bold sir, for towards you
None here has acted unhandsomely, save
In accord with the compact arranged in the King's court. 2340
I promised the stroke you've received, so hold you
Well payed. I free you from all duties further.
If brisk I had been, peradventure a buffet
I'd harshly have dealt that harm would have done you.
In mirth, with a feint I menaced you first,
With no direful wound rent you; right was my deed,
By the bargain that bound us both on the first night,
When, faithful and true, you fulfilled our agreement,
And gave me your gain as a good man ought to.
The second I struck at you, sir, for the morning 2350
You kissed my fair wife and the kisses accorded me.
Two mere feints for both times I made at you, man,
Without woe.
True men restore by right,
One fears no danger so;
You failed the third time, knight,
And therefore took that blow.

" 'T is my garment you're wearing, that woven girdle,
Bestowed by my wife, as in truth I know well.

I know also your kisses and all of your acts 2360
And my wife's advances; myself, I devised them.
I sent her to try you, and truly you seem
The most faultless of men that e'er fared on his feet.
As a pearl compared to white peas is more precious,
So next to the other gay knights is Sir Gawain.
But a little you lacked, and loyalty wanted,
Yet truly 't was not for intrigue or for wooing,
But love of your life; the less do I blame you."
Sir Gawain stood in a study a great while,
So sunk in disgrace that in spirit he groaned; 2370
To his face all the blood in his body was flowing;
For shame, as the other was talking, he shrank.
And these were the first words that fell from his lips:
"Be cowardice cursed, and coveting! In you
Are vice and villainy, virtue destroying."
The lace he then seized, and loosened the strands,
And fiercely the girdle flung at the Green Knight.
"Lo! there is faith-breaking! evil befall it.
To coveting came I, for cowardice caused me
From fear of your stroke to forsake in myself 2380
What belongs to a knight: munificence, loyalty.
I'm faulty and false, who've been ever afraid
Of untruth and treachery; sorrow betide both
And care!
Here I confess my sin;
All faulty did I fare.
Your good will let me win,
And then I will beware."

Then the Green Knight laughed, and right graciously said,
"I am sure that the harm is healed that I suffered. 2390
So clean you're confessed, so cleared of your faults,
Having had the point of my weapon's plain penance,
I hold you now purged of offence, and as perfectly
Spotless as though you'd ne'er sinned in your life.
And I give to you, sir, the golden-hemmed girdle,
As green as my gown. Sir Gawain, when going
Forth on your way among famous princes,
Think still of our strife and this token right splendid,
'Mid chivalrous knights, of the chapel's adventure.
This New Year you'll come to my castle again, 2400
And the rest of this feast in revel most pleasant
Will go."
Then pressed him hard the lord:
"My wife and you, I know
We surely will accord,
Who was your bitter foe."

"No indeed," quoth the hero, his helm seized and doffed it
Graciously, thanking the Green Knight; "I've stayed

Long enough. May good fortune befall you; may He
Who all fame doth confer give it fully to you, sir. 2410
To your lady, gracious and lovely, commend me,
To her and that other, my honored ladies,
That so with their sleights deceived their knight subtly.
But no marvel it is for a fool to act madly,
Through woman's wiles to be brought to woe.
So for certain was Adam deceived by some woman,
By several Solomon, Samson besides;
Delilah dealt him his doom; and David
Was duped by Bath-sheba, enduring much sorrow.
Since these were grieved by their guile, 't would be great gain 2420
To love them yet never believe them, if knights could.
For formerly these were most noble and fortunate,
More than all others who lived on the earth;

And these few

By women's wiles were caught
With whom they had to do.
Though I'm beguiled, I ought
To be excused now too.

"But your girdle," said Gawain, "may God you reward!
With a good will I'll use it, yet not for the gold, 2430
The sash or the silk, or the sweeping pendants,
Or fame, or its workmanship wondrous, or cost,
But in sign of my sin I shall see it oft.
When in glory I move, with remorse I'll remember
The frailty and fault of the stubborn flesh,
How soon 't is infected with stains of defilement;
And thus when I'm proud of my prowess in arms,
The sight of this sash shall humble my spirit.
But one thing I pray, if it prove not displeasing;
Because you are lord of the land where I stayed 2440
In your house with great worship (may He now reward you
Who sitteth on high and upholdeth the heavens),
What name do you bear? No more would I know."
And then "That truly I'll tell," said the other;
"Bercilak de Hautdesert here am I called.
Through her might who lives with me, Morgan le Fay,[49]
Well-versed in the crafts and cunning of magic
(Many of Merlin's[50] arts she has mastered,
For long since she dealt in the dalliance of love
With him whom your heroes at home know, that sage 2450

Without blame.

'Morgan the goddess,' so
She's rightly known by name.
No one so proud doth go
That him she cannot tame),

[49] King Arthur's half-sister.
[50] The magician of Arthur's court, who helped him become king.

"I was sent in this way to your splendid hall
To make trial of your pride, and to see if the people's
Tales were true of the Table's great glory.
This wonder she sent to unsettle your wits,
And to daunt so the Queen as to cause her to die 2460
From fear at the sight of that phantom speaker
Holding his head in his hand at the high table.
Lives she at home there, that ancient lady;
She's even thine aunt, King Arthur's half-sister,
Tyntagel's duchess's daughter, whom Uther
Made later the mother of mighty Lord Arthur.[51]
I beg thee, sir, therefore, come back to thine aunt;
In my castle make merry. My company love thee,
And I, sir, wish thee as well, on my word,
As any on earth for thy high sense of honor." 2470
He said to him, nay, this he'd never consent to.
The men kiss, embrace, and each other commend
To the Prince of Paradise; there they part
In the cold.
Gawain on his fair horse
To Arthur hastens bold;
The bright Green Knight his course
Doth at his pleasure hold.

Through the wood now goes Sir Gawain by wild ways
On Gringolet, given by God's grace his life. 2480
Oft in houses, and oft in the open he lodged,
Met many adventures, won many a victory:
These I intend not to tell in this tale.
Now whole was the hurt he had in his neck,
And about it the glimmering belt he was bearing,
Bound to his side like a baldric obliquely,
Tied under his left arm, that lace, with a knot
As a sign that with stain of sin he'd been found.
And thus to the court he comes all securely.
Delight in that dwelling arose when its lord knew 2490
That Gawain had come; a good thing he thought it.
The King kissed the lord, and the Queen did likewise,
And next many knights drew near him to greet him
And ask how he'd fared; and he wondrously answered,
Confessed all the hardships that him had befallen,
The happenings at chapel, the hero's behavior,
The lady's love, and lastly the lace.
He showed them the nick in his neck all naked
The blow that the Green Knight gave for deceit
Him to blame. 2500
In torment this he owned;
Blood in his face did flame;

[51] Igraine, duchess of Tintagel. Morgan le Fay was her daughter by her husband the duke. King Arthur was her son by Uther, who slept with her under the magical influence of Merlin.

With wrath and grief he groaned,
When showing it with shame.

Laying hold of the lace, quoth the hero, "Lo! lord!
The band of this fault I bear on my neck;
And this is the scathe and damage I've suffered,
For cowardice caught there, and coveting also,
The badge of untruth in which I was taken.
And this for as long as I live I must wear, 2510
For his fault none may hide without meeting misfortune,
For once it is fixed, it can ne'er be unfastened."
To the knight then the King gave comfort; the court too
Laughed greatly, and made this gracious agreement:
That ladies and lords to the Table belonging,
All of the brotherhood, baldrics should bear
Obliquely about them, bands of bright green,
Thus following suit for the sake of the hero.
For the Round Table's glory was granted that lace,
And he held himself honored who had it thereafter, 2520
As told in the book, the best of romances,
In the days of King Arthur this deed was done
Whereof witness is borne by Brutus's book.
Since Brutus, that bold man, first came here to Britain,
When ceased, indeed, had the siege and assault
At Troy's wall,
Full many feats ere now
Like this one did befall.
May He with thorn-crowned brow
To His bliss bring us all. Amen. 2530

HONY SOYT QUI MAL PENCE.[52]

Geoffrey Chaucer

(1340?–1400)

One of the most versatile of English and of medieval poets, Chaucer was born in 1340 or a little later, the son of a London wine merchant. The comfortable middle-class family had been rising socially, and young Geoffrey served as a page in the household of the Countess of Ulster, where as an intimate of a noble family he was well educated and early acclimated to aristocratic values and manners. In 1359 he served on the Continent during one of the military campaigns of the Hundred Years' War, waged in the fourteenth and

[52] "Shame be to him who evil thinks," the motto of the Order of the Garter, founded in the fourteenth century. Whoever added the motto to the end of *Sir Gawain* apparently associated the wearing of the green girdle to honor Gawain with the wearing of the Garter.

fifteenth centuries for control of disputed territories in France. He was captured and then ransomed with the help of King Edward III—an episode that marks the beginning of a series of favors, positions, and preferments (interrupted by some tribulations in the 1380s) that Chaucer received from English kings throughout his life. Besides serving again later in the army, he filled several high posts in the country's service: customs supervisor, director of public works, king's forester, and Member of Parliament. He undertook for the crown a number of important diplomatic missions to France, the Low Countries, Spain, and Italy. During his sojourns in Italy he was exposed to the work of the three fourteenth-century Italian masters, Dante, Boccaccio, and Petrarch; their influence on his later work is strong. Chaucer died in 1400, a year after the dethronement of Richard II by Henry IV, and was buried in what is now called the Poets' Corner of Westminster Abbey. That in a turbulent era he enjoyed the favor of three rulers says something about Chaucer as man and civil servant.

Chaucer's lifelong close association with public affairs and men of high station helps explain his urbanity and his wide-ranging knowledge of the world. The often mordant portraits of moral delinquents and, conversely, of saintly types in *The Canterbury Tales* testify that in his own way Chaucer is a social critic. But political matters do not play a large part in his works as they do in Dante's. Although he succeeded in portraying definitively the England of his time, Chaucer did so through the gifts he shares with the greatest storytellers: a sure and shrewd power of characterization, a keen eye for the quality of *things,* subtle and penetrating psychology, and an unfailing ear for good dialogue, which, like Shakespeare, he was able to accommodate naturally to a wide variety of verse forms, not to mention prose.

Chaucer's narrative genius is in many ways best exemplified in *Troilus and Criseyde* (1380s), one of his two supreme masterpieces. This poem of more than 8,000 lines, set during the Trojan War, allowed him to develop at book length a single story and to explore exhaustively the psychology of the characters, of whom the heroine Criseyde is the most complex. In *Troilus,* Chaucer also develops one of his favorite themes: the nature of love as it reveals the conflicting values of this world and the next.

The fullest range of Chaucer's powers emerges in his most popular work, *The Canterbury Tales,* which he wrote in the late 1380s and early 1390s. The work is unfinished; the plan outlined in the General Prologue calls for four stories from each of thirty or so travelers, but we have only one tale apiece from twenty-four of them. Moreover, the work exists in ten fragments, the order of which has had to be reconstructed by scholarly detective work. Nevertheless, enough was completed and joined together to give the impression of a whole, although not a fully assembled or finally polished one.

Like Boccaccio's *Decameron* (which Chaucer apparently did not know), *The Canterbury Tales* is framed by an agreement among the principals to tell stories to one another. Chaucer's scheme, in which the characters are drawn from all vocations and social classes and the tales usually are emphatically appropriate to the tellers and their stations in life, allows him to achieve a variety at least as wide as Boccaccio's and at the same time to join the tales organically to the basic story of the pilgrimage. That Chaucer's framework is a *religious* pilgrimage is not insignificant; the pilgrims and the characters in their stories are revealed in the light both of the world with which so many of them are preoccupied and also of eternity. The variety of the pilgrims and of their moral conditions has a similar effect; the depravity of characters such as the Pardoner, the integrity of the Knight and sanctity of the Parson, the more ambiguous status of such figures as the fastidious Prioress and the worldly Monk imply, taken together, a moral concern almost as profound as Dante's, if less insistent.

Chaucer is a distinctively English poet in many ways, but he also illustrates the characteristic internationalism of medieval culture and literature. Medieval authors were not expected to invent their own material, and Chaucer's tales, along with the frequent allusions and illustrations within them, are drawn mainly from non-English sources: French and Italian authors, classical legend and literature (notably Ovid), and the Bible (which Chaucer knew thoroughly). Chaucer reworks such materials in his own vein, infusing them with his distinctive qualities of drama, pathos, and wit. The media of the tales include an assortment of skillfully managed verse forms and genres. The Miller relates *a fabliau,* a comically bawdy tale of ordinary or "low" life; the Wife of Bath relates a folktale; the Pardoner delivers a sermon and a morally pointed "exemplum"; the Nun's Priest's tale is a mock-heroic beast fable. *The Canterbury Tales* includes also specimens of romance, saint's legend, "tragedy" (defined simply as an account of the downfall of an eminent personage), and other narrative genres.

Perhaps the most distinctive of Chaucer's gifts as storyteller is his ability to delineate characters and put them in realistic motion. They come most patently alive in the prologues to the individual tales and in the narrative links, but most of his people are realized three-dimensionally in the General Prologue as well. The pilgrims make up a human encyclopedia—comprehensive and universal but composed of unique individuals. Interpreting them can be problematical. The Wife of Bath, for example, projects to some readers an attractively earthy personality and to others a sinister moral obliquity. The Pardoner, unquestionably one of the most unsavory characters in world literature, raises questions too, most obviously about his motives in revealing his cynical duplicity so frankly to the company.

After the Normans conquered England in 1066, French became the language of polite society, while Latin continued to be the language of the learned. To a great extent this was still true in Chaucer's day. His decision to write in English at a time when the language was in a state of flux is a significant milestone in the development of English, like Dante's decision to write his *Divine Comedy* in Italian. But English continued to change radically for a long time after Chaucer, and it was not until the late seventeenth century that the evolution so slowed that the average modern reader can understand the language of the time without elaborate glossing. Chaucer's language, Middle English, is thus very different from the English of today. It is not so different, however, that modern readers should be discouraged from trying Chaucer in a good Middle English edition. The following is the beginning of the General Prologue:

> Whan that Aprille with his shoures soote
> The droghte of March hath perced to the rote,
> And bathed every veyne in swich licour

Of which vertu engendred is the flour;
Whan Zephirus eek with his swete breeth
Inspired hath in every holt and heeth
The tendre croppes, and the yonge sonne
Hath in the Ram his halve cours yronne,
And smale foweles maken melodye,
That slepen al the nyght with open ye 10
(So priketh hem nature in hir corages):
Than longen folk to goon on pilgrymages,
And palmers for to seken straunge strondes,
To ferne halwes, kouthe in sondry londes;
And specially from every shires ende
Of Engelond to Caunterbury they wende,
The holy blisful martir for to seke,
That hem hath holpen whan that they were seke.

FURTHER READING: George Kane's *Chaucer,* 1984, in the Past Masters series, is a short general introduction to the poet's life and work, particularly interesting on the division between the poet and narrator. Biographies of Chaucer that discuss his life and work in depth include Derek Pearsall, *The Life of Geoffrey Chaucer: A Critical Biography,* 1992; and Donald R. Howard, *Chaucer: His Life, His Works, His World,* 1987. Velma Bourgeois Richmond, *Geoffrey Chaucer,* 1992, treats incisively Chaucer's vision as a writer. Two works by Derek Stanley Brewer provide vivid sketches of Chaucer and his England: Brewer's *Chaucer,* 1953, is intended for the new student of Chaucer; his *Chaucer and His World,* 1978, contains a generous selection of illustrations. D. W. Robertson, Jr., *A Preface to Chaucer,* 1962, is an important work in Chaucer scholarship, taking a deductive approach to Chaucer's work through an extensive analysis of background material. Robertson's work is noted for its many unconventional interpretations. Muriel Bowden's *A Reader's Guide to Geoffrey Chaucer,* 1964, takes a more centrist approach. This book offers a biographical sketch and a long section on *The Canterbury Tales* that discusses various influences on Chaucer's writing. George Lyman Kittredge's *Chaucer and His Poetry,* 1915, reprinted in 1970, based on lectures delivered in 1914, remains fresh and instructive. Derek Albert Pearsall's *The Canterbury Tales,* 1985, includes a historical survey of the main critical issues raised by the work. David Aers, *Chaucer,* 1986, invites readers to examine the poet's work from modern perspectives, as does Stephen Thomas Knight, *Geoffrey Chaucer,* 1986, in the Rereading Literature series. Women and women's issues in Chaucer are treated in Jill Mann, *Geoffrey Chaucer,* 1991; Priscilla Martin, *Chaucer's Women: Nuns, Wives, and Amazons,* 1990; Margaret Hallissy, *Clean Maids, True Wives, Steadfast Widows: Chaucer's Women and Medieval Codes of Conduct,* 1993; and Elaine Tuttle Hansen, *Chaucer and the Fictions of Gender,* 1992. C. David Benson's *Chaucer's Drama of Style: Poetic Variety and Contrast in the "Canterbury Tales,"* 1986, discusses the topics mentioned in its title. One of the best essays on Chaucer's fabliaux can be found in Derek Brewer, *Chaucer: The Poet as Storyteller,* 1984, which also contains an essay on "The Nun's Priest's Tale" and another on Chaucer's place in European and English tradition. Critical perspectives from several centuries are represented in *Chaucer: "The Canterbury Tales": A Casebook,* ed. by J. J. Anderson, 1974. This volume includes Paul Ruggier's interesting "Irony in 'The Wife of Bath's Tale.'" Twenty-six essays, balanced between historical scholarship and literary criticism, are collected in *Chaucer: Modern Essays in Criticism,* ed. by Edward Wagenknecht, 1959. The emphasis is on *The Canterbury Tales,* including "The Pardoner's Tale" and "The Wife of Bath's Tale."

from *THE CANTERBURY TALES*

Translated by Theodore Morrison

PROLOGUE

As soon as April pierces to the root
The drought of March, and bathes each bud and shoot
Through every vein of sap with gentle showers
From whose engendering liquor spring the flowers;
When zephyrs have breathed softly all about
Inspiring every wood and field to sprout,
And in the zodiac the youthful sun
His journey halfway through the Ram[1] has run;
When little birds are busy with their song
Who sleep with open eyes the whole night long 10
Life stirs their hearts and tingles in them so,
Then off as pilgrims people long to go,
And palmers[2] to set out for distant strands
And foreign shrines renowned in many lands.
And specially in England people ride
To Canterbury[3] from every countryside
To visit there the blessed martyred saint
Who gave them strength when they were sick and faint.
In Southwark at the Tabard[4] one spring day
It happened, as I stopped there on my way, 20
Myself a pilgrim with a heart devout
Ready for Canterbury to set out,
At night came all of twenty-nine assorted
Travelers, and to that same inn resorted,
Who by a turn of fortune chanced to fall
In fellowship together, and they were all
Pilgrims who had it in their minds to ride
Toward Canterbury. The stable doors were wide,
The rooms were large, and we enjoyed the best,
And shortly, when the sun had gone to rest, 30
I had so talked with each that presently
I was a member of their company
And promised to rise early the next day
To start, as I shall show, upon our way.
But none the less, while I have time and space,
Before this tale has gone a further pace,

[1] The sun is in Aries (the Ram) during late March and early April.
[2] Zealous pilgrims who traveled to far-distant places.
[3] A city about sixty miles southeast of London. In Canterbury Cathedral was located the shrine of St. Thomas à Becket, murdered there in 1170.
[4] An inn in Southwark, a suburb of London on the south bank of the Thames.

I should in reason tell you the condition
Of each of them, his rank and his position,
And also what array they all were in;
And so then, with a knight I will begin. 40
A Knight was with us, and an excellent man,
Who from the earliest moment he began
To follow his career loved chivalry,
Truth, openhandedness, and courtesy.
He was a stout man in the king's campaigns
And in that cause had gripped his horse's reins
In Christian lands and pagan through the earth,
None farther, and always honored for his worth.
He was on hand at Alexandria's fall.[5]
He had often sat in precedence to all 50
The nations at the banquet board in Prussia.
He had fought in Lithuania and in Russia,
No Christian knight more often; he had been
In Moorish Africa at Benmarin,
At the siege of Algeciras in Granada,
And sailed in many a glorious armada
In the Mediterranean, and fought as well
At Ayas and Attalia when they fell
In Armenia and on Asia Minor's coast.
Of fifteen deadly battles he could boast, 60
And in Algeria, at Tremessen,
Fought for the faith and killed three separate men
In single combat. He had done good work
Joining against another pagan Turk
With the king of Palathia. And he was wise,
Despite his prowess, honored in men's eyes,
Meek as a girl and gentle in his ways.
He had never spoken ignobly all his days
To any man by even a rude inflection.
He was a knight in all things to perfection. 70
He rode a good horse, but his gear was plain,
For he had lately served on a campaign.
His tunic was still spattered by the rust
Left by his coat of mail, for he had just
Returned and set out on his pilgrimage.
His son was with him, a young Squire, in age
Some twenty years as near as I could guess.
His hair curled as if taken from a press.[6]
He was a lover and would become a knight.
In stature he was of a moderate height 80
But powerful and wonderfully quick.

[5]The places mentioned in the following lines were sites of battles, mostly fought against Muslims and other so-called pagans.
[6]Curlers.

He had been in Flanders, riding in the thick
Of forays in Artois and Picardy,
And bore up well for one so young as he,
Still hoping by his exploits in such places
To stand the better in his lady's graces.
He wore embroidered flowers, red and white,
And blazed like a spring meadow to the sight.
He sang or played his flute the livelong day.
He was as lusty as the month of May. 90
His coat was short, its sleeves were long and wide.
He sat his horse well, and knew how to ride,
And how to make a song and use his lance,
And he could write and draw well, too, and dance.
So hot his love that when the moon rose pale
He got no more sleep than a nightingale.
He was modest, and helped whomever he was able,
And carved as his father's squire at the table.
But one more servant had the Knight beside,
Choosing thus simply for the time to ride: 100
A Yeoman, in a coat and hood of green.
His peacock-feathered arrows, bright and keen,
He carried under his belt in tidy fashion.
For well-kept gear he had a yeoman's passion.
No draggled feather might his arrows show,
And in his hand he held a mighty bow.
He kept his hair close-cropped, his face was brown.
He knew the lore of woodcraft up and down.
His arm was guarded from the bowstring's whip
By a bracer, gaily trimmed. He had at hip 110
A sword and buckler, and at his other side
A dagger whose fine mounting was his pride,
Sharp-pointed as a spear. His horn he bore
In a sling of green, and on his chest he wore
A silver image of St. Christopher,
His patron, since he was a forester.
There was also a Nun, a Prioress,[7]
Whose smile was gentle and full of guilelessness.
"By St. Loy!"[8] was the worst oath she would say.
She sang mass well, in a becoming way, 120
Intoning through her nose the words divine,
And she was known as Madame Eglantine.
She spoke good French, as taught at Stratford-Bow,[9]
For the Parisian French she did not know.
She was schooled to eat so primly and so well
That from her lips no morsel ever fell.

[7] The head of a convent.
[8] A minor saint, popular with women at the royal court in Chaucer's day.
[9] A convent near London, where a dialect of French was spoken.

She wet her fingers lightly in the dish
Of sauce, for courtesy was her first wish.
With every bite she did her skillful best
To see that no drop fell upon her breast. 130
She always wiped her upper lip so clean
That in her cup was never to be seen
A hint of grease when she had drunk her share.
She reached out for her meat with comely air.
She was a great delight, and always tried
To imitate court ways, and had her pride,
Both amiable and gracious in her dealings.
As for her charity and tender feelings,
She melted at whatever was piteous.
She would weep if she but came upon a mouse 140
Caught in a trap, if it were dead or bleeding.
Some little dogs that she took pleasure feeding
On roasted meat or milk or good wheat bread
She had, but how she wept to find one dead
Or yelping from a blow that made it smart,
And all was sympathy and loving heart.
Neat was her wimple[10] in its every plait,
Her nose well formed, her eyes as gray as slate.
Her mouth was very small and soft and red.
She had so wide a brow I think her head 150
Was nearly a span[11] broad, for certainly
She was not undergrown, as all could see.
She wore her cloak with dignity and charm,
And had her rosary about her arm,
The small beads coral and the larger green,
And from them hung a brooch of golden sheen,
On it a large A and a crown above;
Beneath, "All things are subject unto love."
A Priest accompanied her toward Canterbury,
And an attendant Nun, her secretary. 160
There was a Monk, and nowhere was his peer,
A hunter, and a roving overseer.[12]
He was a manly man, and fully able
To be an abbot. He kept a hunting stable,
And when he rode the neighborhood could hear
His bridle jingling in the wind as clear
And loud as if it were a chapel bell.
Wherever he was master of a cell
The principles of good St. Benedict,[13]
For being a little old and somewhat strict, 170

[10]A cloth worn around the face; part of a nun's habit. [11]A hand span.
[12]An "outrider," a person who supervised monastic property at some distance from the monastery.
[13]Sixth-century author of a famous rule, or code, laying down strict regulations for monastic life.

Were honored in the breach, as past their prime.
He lived by the fashion of a newer time.
He would have swapped that text for a plucked hen
Which says that hunters are not holy men,
Or a monk outside his discipline and rule
Is too much like a fish outside his pool;
That is to say, a monk outside his cloister.
But such a text he deemed not worth an oyster.
I told him his opinion made me glad.
Why should he study always and go mad, 180
Mewed[14] in his cell with only a book for neighbor?
Or why, as Augustine commanded, labor
And sweat his hands? How shall the world be served?
To Augustine be all such toil reserved!
And so he hunted, as was only right.
He had greyhounds as swift as birds in flight.
His taste was all for tracking down the hare,
And what his sport might cost he did not care.
His sleeves I noticed, where they met his hand,
Trimmed with gray fur, the finest in the land. 190
His hood was fastened with a curious pin
Made of wrought gold and clasped beneath his chin,
A love knot at the tip. His head might pass,
Bald as it was, for a lump of shining glass,
And his face was glistening as if anointed.
Fat as a lord he was, and well appointed.
His eyes were large, and rolled inside his head
As if they gleamed from a furnace of hot lead.
His boots were supple, his horse superbly kept.
He was a prelate to dream of while you slept. 200
He was not pale nor peaked like a ghost.
He relished a plump swan as his favorite roast.
He rode a palfrey brown as a ripe berry.

A Friar was with us, a gay dog and a merry,
Who begged his district[15] with a jolly air.
No friar in all four orders[16] could compare
With him for gallantry; his tongue was wooing.
Many a girl was married by his doing,
And at his own cost it was often done.
He was a pillar, and a noble one, 210
To his whole order. In his neighborhood
Rich franklins[17] knew him well, who served good food,
And worthy women welcomed him to town;
For the license that his order handed down,
He said himself, conferred on him possession

[14] Caged.
[15] The friar is a "limiter," assigned a territory (limits) within which he can beg.
[16] The Franciscans, Dominicans, Carmelites, and Augustinians.
[17] Country gentlemen.

Of more than a curate's[18] power of confession.
Sweetly the list of frailties he heard,
Assigning penance[19] with a pleasant word.
He was an easy man for absolution
Where he looked forward to a contribution, 220
For if to a poor order a man has given
It signifies that he has been well shriven,[20]
And if a sinner let his purse be dented
The Friar would stake his oath he had repented.
For many men become so hard of heart
They cannot weep, though conscience makes them smart.
Instead of tears and prayers, then, let the sinner
Supply the poor friars with the price of dinner.
For pretty women he had more than shrift.
His cape was stuffed with many a little gift, 230
As knives and pins and suchlike. He could sing
A merry note, and pluck a tender string,
And had no rival at all in balladry.
His neck was whiter than a fleur-de-lis,[21]
And yet he could have knocked a strong man down.
He knew the taverns well in every town.
The barmaids and innkeepers pleased his mind
Better than beggars and lepers and their kind.
In his position it was unbecoming
Among the wretched lepers to go slumming. 240
It mocks all decency, it sews no stitch
To deal with such riffraff; but with the rich,
With sellers of victuals, that's another thing.
Wherever he saw some hope of profiting,
None so polite, so humble. He was good,
The champion beggar of his brotherhood.
Should a woman have no shoes against the snow,
So pleasant was his "*In principio*"[22]
He would have her widow's mite[23] before he went.
He took in far more than he paid in rent 250
For his right of begging within certain bounds.
None of his brethren trespassed on his grounds!
He loved as freely as a half-grown whelp.
On arbitration-days[24] he gave great help,
For his cloak was never shiny nor threadbare
Like a poor cloistered scholar's. He had an air

[18] Parish priest.

[19] After a sinner confesses to the priest, he is granted absolution (forgiveness of his sins), provided he does the assigned penance.

[20] Given shrift (absolution) in the sacrament of confession.

[21] Lily.

[22] Latin for "in the beginning," the opening words of St. John's gospel. The friar uses Latin to show off.

[23] A tiny sum of money.

[24] "Love-days," when people settled their disputes, friars sometimes serving as judges.

As if he were a doctor or a pope.
It took stout wool to make his semicope[25]
That plumped out like a bell for portliness.
He lisped a little in his rakishness 260
To make his English sweeter on his tongue,
And twanging his harp to end some song he'd sung
His eyes would twinkle in his head as bright
As the stars twinkle on a frosty night.
Hubert this gallant Friar was by name.
Among the rest a Merchant also came.
He wore a forked beard and a beaver hat
From Flanders. High up in the saddle he sat,
In figured cloth, his boots clasped handsomely,
Delivering his opinions pompously, 270
Always on how his gains might be increased.
At all costs he desired the sea policed[26]
From Middleburg in Holland to Orwell.
He knew the exchange rates, and the time to sell
French currency, and there was never yet
A man who could have told he was in debt
So grave he seemed and hid so well his feelings
With all his shrewd engagements and close dealings.
You'd find no better man at any turn;
But what his name was I could never learn. 280
There was an Oxford Student too, it chanced,
Already in his logic well advanced.
He rode a mount as skinny as a rake,
And he was hardly fat. For learning's sake
He let himself look hollow and sober enough.
He wore an outer coat of threadbare stuff,
For he had no benefice[27] for his enjoyment
And was too unworldly for some lay[28] employment.
He much preferred to have beside his bed
His twenty volumes bound in black or red 290
All packed with Aristotle from end to middle
Than a sumptuous wardrobe or a merry fiddle.
For though he knew what learning had to offer
There was little coin to jingle in his coffer.
Whatever he got by touching up a friend
On books and learning he would promptly spend
And busily pray for the soul of anybody
Who furnished him the wherewithal for study.
His scholarship was what he truly heeded.
He never spoke a word more than was needed, 300
And that was said with dignity and force,
And quick and brief. He was of grave discourse,

[25]Jacket. [26]That is, kept free of pirates.
[27]Position at a church.
[28]Secular. The student, or clerk, is preparing for a career in the Church.

Giving new weight to virtue by his speech,
And gladly would he learn and gladly teach.
 There was a Lawyer, cunning and discreet,
Who had often been to St. Paul's porch to meet
His clients. He was a Sergeant of the Law,
A man deserving to be held in awe,
Or so he seemed, his manner was so wise.
He had often served as Justice of Assize[29] 310
By the king's appointment, with a broad commission,
For his knowledge and his eminent position.
He had many a handsome gift by way of fee.
There was no buyer of land as shrewd as he.
All ownership to him became fee simple.[30]
His titles were never faulty by a pimple.
None was so busy as he with case and cause,
And yet he seemed much busier than he was.
In all cases and decisions he was schooled
That were of record since King William[31] ruled. 320
No one could pick a loophole or a flaw
In any lease or contract he might draw.
Each statute on the books he knew by rote.
He traveled in a plain, silk-belted coat.
 A Franklin[32] traveled in his company.
Whiter could never daisy petal be
Than was his beard. His ruddy face gave sign
He liked his morning sop of toast in wine.
He lived in comfort, as he would assure us,
For he was a true son of Epicurus[33] 330
Who held the opinion that the only measure
Of perfect happiness was simply pleasure.
Such hospitality did he provide,
He was St. Julian[34] to his countryside.
His bread and ale were always up to scratch.
He had a cellar[35] none on earth could match.
There was no lack of pasties in his house,
Both fish and flesh, and that so plenteous
That where he lived it snowed of meat and drink.
With every dish of which a man can think, 340
After the various seasons of the year,
He changed his diet for his better cheer.
He had coops of partridges as fat as cream,
He had a fishpond stocked with pike and bream.
Woe to his cook for an unready pot
Or a sauce that wasn't seasoned and spiced hot!

[29] Law court. [30] Unqualified ownership.
[31] King William the Conqueror (ruled 1066–1087).
[32] Country gentleman.
[33] Ancient Greek philosopher, often associated with love of pleasure, although this is an oversimplification of his teaching.
[34] Patron saint of hospitality. [35] Wine cellar.

A table in his hall stood on display
Prepared and covered through the livelong day.
He presided at court sessions for his bounty
And sat in Parliament often for his county. 350
A well-wrought dagger and a purse of silk
Hung at his belt, as white as morning milk.
He had been a sheriff and county auditor.
On earth was no such rich proprietor!
There were five Guildsmen, in the livery
Of one august and great fraternity,[36]
A Weaver, a Dyer, and a Carpenter,
A Tapestry-maker and a Haberdasher.
Their gear was furbished new and clean as glass.
The mountings of their knives were not of brass 360
But silver. Their pouches were well made and neat,
And each of them, it seemed, deserved a seat
On the platform at the Guildhall, for each one
Was likely timber to make an alderman.
They had goods enough, and money to be spent,
Also their wives would willingly consent
And would have been at fault if they had not.
For to be "Madamed" is a pleasant lot,
And to march in first at feasts for being well married,
And royally to have their mantles carried. 370
For the pilgrimage these Guildsmen brought their own
Cook to boil their chicken and marrow bone
With seasoning powder and capers and sharp spice.
In judging London ale his taste was nice.
He well knew how to roast and broil and fry,
To mix a stew, and bake a good meat pie,
Or capon creamed with almond, rice, and egg.
Pity he had an ulcer on his leg!
A Skipper was with us, his home far in the west.
He came from the port of Dartmouth, as I guessed. 380
He sat his carthorse pretty much at sea
In a coarse smock that joggled on his knee.
From his neck a dagger on a string hung down
Under his arm. His face was burnished brown
By the summer sun. He was a true good fellow.
Many a time he had tapped a wine cask mellow
Sailing from Bordeaux while the owner slept.
Too nice a point of honor he never kept.
In a sea fight, if he got the upper hand,
Drowned prisoners floated home to every land. 390
But in navigation, whether reckoning tides,
Currents, or what might threaten him besides,
Harborage, pilotage, or the moon's demeanor,
None was his like from Hull to Cartagena.

[36]Perhaps a religious lodge, since they all wear the same "livery," or uniform dress.

He knew each harbor and the anchorage there
From Gotland to the Cape of Finisterre
And every creek in Brittany and Spain,
And he had called his ship the *Madeleine.*
With us came also an astute Physician.
There was none like him for a disquisition 400
On the art of medicine or surgery,
For he was grounded in astrology.[37]
He kept his patient long in observation,
Choosing the proper hour for application
Of charms and images by intuition
Of magic, and the planets' best position.
For he was one who understood the laws
That rule the humors,[38] and could tell the cause
That brought on every human malady,
Whether of hot or cold, or moist or dry. 410
He was a perfect medico, for sure.
The cause once known, he would prescribe the cure,
For he had his druggists ready at a motion
To provide the sick man with some pill or potion—
A game of mutual aid, with each one winning.
Their partnership was hardly just beginning!
He was well versed in his authorities,
Old Aesculapius, Dioscorides,
Rufus, and old Hippocrates, and Galen,
Haly, and Rhazes, and Serapion, 420
Averroës, Bernard, Johannes Damascenus,
Avicenna, Gilbert, Gaddesden, Constantinus.[39]
He urged a moderate fare on principle,
But rich in nourishment, digestible;
Of nothing in excess would he admit.
He gave but little heed to Holy Writ.
His clothes were lined with taffeta; their hue
Was all of blood red and of Persian blue,
Yet he was far from careless of expense.
He saved his fees from times of pestilence, 430
For gold is a cordial,[40] as physicians hold,
And so he had a special love for gold.
A worthy woman there was from near the city
Of Bath, but somewhat deaf, and more's the pity.
For weaving she possessed so great a bent
She outdid the people of Ypres and of Ghent.[41]

[37] It was common for physicians in Chaucer's day to be guided by the position of the heavenly bodies.

[38] The relative proportion in a person of the four "humors" (blood, black bile, phlegm, yellow bile) was believed to influence character as well as health.

[39] Famous ancient and medieval medical authorities.

[40] A medical stimulant. Gold was sometimes used as an ingredient.

[41] Centers of the weaving industry in Flanders.

No other woman dreamed of such a thing
As to precede her at the offering,[42]
Or if any did, she fell in such a wrath
She dried up all the charity in Bath. 440
She wore fine kerchiefs of old-fashioned air,
And on a Sunday morning, I could swear,
She had ten pounds of linen on her head.
Her stockings were of finest scarlet-red,
Laced tightly, and her shoes were soft and new.
Bold was her face, and fair, and red in hue.
She had been an excellent woman all her life.
Five men in turn had taken her to wife,
Omitting other youthful company—
But let that pass for now! Over the sea 450
She had traveled freely; many a distant stream
She crossed, and visited Jerusalem
Three times. She had been at Rome and at Boulogne,
At the shrine of Compostella, and at Cologne.
She had wandered by the way through many a scene.
Her teeth were set with little gaps between.[43]
Easily on her ambling horse she sat.
She was well wimpled, and she wore a hat
As wide in circuit as a shield or targe.[44]
A skirt swathed up her hips, and they were large. 460
Upon her feet she wore sharp-roweled spurs.
She was a good fellow; a ready tongue was hers.
All remedies of love she knew by name,
For she had all the tricks of that old game.
There was a good man of the priest's vocation,
A poor town Parson of true consecration,
But he was rich in holy thought and work.
Learned he was, in the truest sense a clerk[45]
Who meant Christ's gospel faithfully to preach
And truly his parishioners to teach. 470
He was a kind man, fully of industry,
Many times tested by adversity
And always patient. If tithes[46] were in arrears,
He was loth to threaten any man with fears
Of excommunication;[47] past a doubt
He would rather spread his offering about
To his poor flock, or spend his property.
To him a little meant sufficiency.

[42] Offering at church.
[43] For a woman to be gap-toothed was considered a sign of being highly sexed.
[44] A type of shield.
[45] A clergyman-scholar.
[46] One tenth of one's earnings, the sum due to the Church.
[47] Barring of a person from the church and sacraments—a serious penalty.

Wide was his parish, with houses far asunder,
But he would not be kept by rain or thunder, 480
If any had suffered a sickness or a blow,
From visiting the farthest, high or low,
Plodding his way on foot, his staff in hand.
He was a model his flock could understand,
For first he did and afterward he taught.
That precept from the Gospel he had caught,
And he added as a metaphor thereto,
"If the gold rusts, what will the iron do?"
For if a priest is foul, in whom we trust,
No wonder a layman shows a little rust. 490
A priest should take to heart the shameful scene
Of shepherds filthy while the sheep are clean.
By his own purity a priest should give
The example to his sheep, how they should live.
He did not rent his benefice[48] for hire,
Leaving his flock to flounder in the mire,
And run to London, happiest of goals,
To sing paid masses in St. Paul's for souls,
Or as chaplain from some rich guild take his keep,
But dwelt at home and guarded well his sheep 500
So that no wolf should make his flock miscarry.
He was a shepherd, and not a mercenary.
And though himself a man of strict vocation
He was not harsh to weak souls in temptation,
Not overbearing nor haughty in his speech,
But wise and kind in all he tried to teach.
By good example and just words to turn
Sinners to heaven was his whole concern.
But should a man in truth prove obstinate,
Whoever he was, of rich or mean estate, 510
The Parson would give him a snub to meet the case.
I doubt there was a priest in any place
His better. He did not stand on dignity
Nor affect in conscience too much nicety,
But Christ's and his disciples' word he sought
To teach, and first he followed what he taught.
There was a Plowman with him on the road,
His brother, who had forked up many a load
Of good manure. A hearty worker he,
Living in peace and perfect charity. 520
Whether his fortune made him smart or smile,
He loved God with his whole heart all the while
And his neighbor as himself. He would undertake,
For every luckless poor man, for the sake
Of Christ to thresh and ditch and dig by the hour
And with no wage, if it was in his power.

[48]Hire out his position as pastor of his church.

His tithes on goods and earnings he paid fair.
He wore a coarse, rough coat and rode a mare.
There also were a Manciple,[49] a Miller,
A Reeve, a Summoner, and a Pardoner,[50] 530
And I—this makes our company complete.
As tough a yokel as you care to meet
The Miller was. His big-beefed arms and thighs
Took many a ram put up as wrestling prize.
He was a thick, squat-shouldered lump of sins.
No door but he could heave it off its pins
Or break it running at it with his head.
His beard was broader than a shovel, and red
As a fat sow or fox. A wart stood clear
Atop his nose, and red as a pig's ear 540
A tuft of bristles on it. Black and wide
His nostrils were. He carried at his side
A sword and buckler. His mouth would open out
Like a great furnace, and he would sing and shout
His ballads and jokes of harlotries and crimes.
He could steal corn[51] and charge for it three times,
And yet was honest enough, as millers come,
For a miller, as they say, has a golden thumb.
In white coat and blue hood this lusty clown,
Blowing his bagpipes, brought us out of town. 550
The Manciple was of a lawyers' college,
And other buyers might have used his knowledge
How to be shrewd provisioners, for whether
He bought on cash or credit, altogether
He managed that the end should be the same:
He came out more than even with the game.
Now isn't it an instance of God's grace
How a man of little knowledge can keep pace
In wit with a whole school of learned men?
He had masters to the number of three times ten 560
Who knew each twist of equity and tort;
A dozen in that very Inn of Court
Were worthy to be steward of the estate
To any of England's lords, however great,
And keep him to his income well confined
And free from debt, unless he lost his mind,
Or let him scrimp, if he were mean in bounty;
They could have given help to a whole county
In any sort of case that might befall;
And yet this Manciple could cheat them all! 570

[49]A steward.

[50]A reeve was an overseer for an estate; a summoner summoned to the ecclesiastical court persons charged with offenses against the Church; a pardoner distributed or sold pardons for sins in the name of the Pope.

[51]Grain.

The Reeve was a slender, fiery-tempered man.
He shaved as closely as a razor can.
His hair was cropped about his ears, and shorn
Above his forehead as a priest's is worn.
His legs were very long and very lean.
No calf on his lank spindles could be seen.
But he knew how to keep a barn or bin,
He could play the game with auditors and win.
He knew well how to judge by drought and rain
The harvest of his seed and of his grain. 580
His master's cattle, swine, and poultry flock,
Horses and sheep and dairy, all his stock,
Were altogether in this Reeve's control.
And by agreement, he had given the sole
Accounting since his lord reached twenty years.
No man could ever catch him in arrears.
There wasn't a bailiff, shepherd, or farmer working
But the Reeve knew all his tricks of cheating and shirking.
He would not let him draw an easy breath.
They feared him as they feared the very death. 590
He lived in a good house on an open space,
Well shaded by green trees, a pleasant place.
He was shrewder in acquisition than his lord.
With private riches he was amply stored.
He had learned a good trade young by work and will.
He was a carpenter of first-rate skill.
On a fine mount, a stallion, dappled gray,
Whose name was Scot, he rode along the way.
He wore a long blue coat hitched up and tied
As if it were a friar's, and at his side 600
A sword with rusty blade was hanging down.
He came from Norfolk, from nearby the town
That men call Bawdswell. As we rode the while,
The Reeve kept always hindmost in our file.
A Summoner in our company had his place.
Red as the fiery cherubim his face.
He was pocked and pimpled, and his eyes were narrow.
He was lecherous and hot as a cock sparrow.
His brows were scabby and black, and thin his beard.
His was a face that little children feared. 610
Brimstone or litharge bought in any quarter,
Quicksilver, ceruse, borax, oil of tartar,[52]
No salve nor ointment that will cleanse or bite
Could cure him of his blotches, livid white,
Or the nobs and nubbins sitting on his cheeks.
He loved his garlic, his onions, and his leeks.
He loved to drink the strong wine down blood-red.

[52] Remedies for skin diseases.

Then would he bellow as if he had lost his head,
And when he had drunk enough to parch his drouth,
Nothing but Latin issued from his mouth. 620
He had smattered up a few terms, two or three,
That he had gathered out of some decree—
No wonder; he heard law Latin all the day,
And everyone knows a parrot or a jay
Can cry out "Wat" or "Poll" as well as the pope;
But give him a strange term, he began to grope.
His little store of learning was paid out,
So "*Questio quod juris*"[53] he would shout.
He was a goodhearted bastard and a kind one.
If there were better, it was hard to find one. 630
He would let a good fellow, for a quart of wine,
The whole year round enjoy his concubine
Scot-free from summons, hearing, fine, or bail,
And on the sly he too could flush a quail.
If he liked a scoundrel, no matter for church law.
He would teach him that he need not stand in awe
If the archdeacon threatened with his curse—
That is, unless his soul was in his purse,
For in his purse he would be punished well.
"The purse," he said, "is the archdeacon's hell." 640
Of course I know he lied in what he said.
There is nothing a guilty man should so much dread
As the curse that damns his soul, when, without fail,
The church can save him, or send him off to jail.
He had the young men and girls in his control
Throughout the diocese; he knew the soul
Of youth, and heard their every last design.
A garland big enough to be the sign
Above an alehouse balanced on his head,
And he made a shield of a great round loaf of bread. 650
There was a Pardoner of Rouncivalle[54]
With him, of the blessed Mary's hospital,
But now come straight from Rome (or so said he).
Loudly he sang, "Come hither, love, to me,"
While the Summoner's counterbass trolled out profound—
No trumpet blew with half so vast a sound.
This Pardoner had hair as yellow as wax,
But it hung as smoothly as a hank of flax.
His locks trailed down in bunches from his head,
And he let the ends about his shoulders spread, 660
But in thin clusters, lying one by one.
Of hood, for rakishness, he would have none,
For in his wallet[55] he kept it safely stowed.

[53]Latin for "What law governs this case?"—a phrase picked up in courtrooms.
[54]A hospital just outside London. [55]Bag.

He traveled, as he thought, in the latest mode,
Disheveled. Save for his cap, his head was bare,
And in his eyes he glittered like a hare.
A Veronica[56] was stitched upon his cap,
His wallet lay before him in his lap
Brimful of pardons from the very seat
In Rome. He had a voice like a goat's bleat. 670
He was beardless and would never have a beard.
His cheek was always smooth as if just sheared.
I think he was a gelding or a mare;
But in his trade, from Berwick down to Ware,
No pardoner could beat him in the race,
For in his wallet he had a pillow case
Which he represented as Our Lady's veil;
He said he had a piece of the very sail
St. Peter, when he fished in Galilee
Before Christ caught him, used upon the sea. 680
He had a latten[57] cross embossed with stones
And in a glass he carried some pig's bones,
And with these holy relics, when he found
Some village parson grubbing his poor ground,
He would get more money in a single day
Than in two months would come the parson's way.
Thus with his flattery and his trumped-up stock
He made dupes of the parson and his flock.
But though his conscience was a little plastic
He was in church a noble ecclesiastic. 690
Well could he read the Scripture or saint's story,
But best of all he sang the offertory,[58]
For he understood that when this song was sung,
Then he must preach, and sharpen up his tongue
To rake in cash, as well he knew the art,
And so he sang out gaily, with full heart.

Now I have set down briefly, as it was,
Our rank, our dress, our number, and the cause
That made our sundry fellowship begin
In Southwark, at this hospitable inn 700
Known as the Tabard, not far from the Bell.[59]
But what we did that night I ought to tell,
And after that our journey, stage by stage,
And the whole story of our pilgrimage.
But first, in justice, do not look askance
I plead, nor lay it to my ignorance
If in this matter I should use plain speech

[56]An image of Christ's features supposed to have been made on the veil of St. Veronica after she let him wipe his face on it before the Crucifixion.

[57]Made of a brasslike metal.

[58]Part of the Catholic Mass.

[59]Another tavern.

And tell you just the words and style of each
Reporting all their language faithfully.
For it must be known to you as well as me 710
That whoever tells a story after a man
Must follow him as closely as he can.
If he takes the tale in charge, he must be true
To every word, unless he would find new
Or else invent a thing or falsify.
Better some breadth of language than a lie!
He may not spare the truth to save his brother.
He might as well use one word as another.
In Holy Writ Christ spoke in a broad sense,
And surely his word is without offense. 720
Plato, if his are pages you can read,
Says let the word be cousin to the deed.
So I petition your indulgence for it
If I have cut the cloth just as men wore it,
Here in this tale, and shown its very weave.
My wits are none too sharp, you must believe.
Our Host gave each of us a cheerful greeting
And promptly of our supper had us eating.
The victuals that he served us were his best.
The wine was potent, and we drank with zest. 730
Our Host cut such a figure, all in all,
He might have been a marshal in a hall.[60]
He was a big man, and his eyes bulged wide.
No sturdier citizen lived in all Cheapside,[61]
Lacking no trace of manhood, bold in speech,
Prudent, and well versed in what life can teach,
And with all this he was a jovial man.
And so when supper ended he began
To jolly us, when all our debts were clear.
"Welcome," he said. "I have not seen this year 740
So merry a company in this tavern as now,
And I would give you pleasure if I knew how.
And just this very minute a plan has crossed
My mind that might amuse you at no cost.
"You go to Canterbury—may the Lord
Speed you, and may the martyred saint reward
Your journey! And to while the time away
You mean to talk and pass the time of day,
For you would be as cheerful all alone
As riding on your journey dumb as stone. 750
Therefore, if you'll abide by what I say,
Tomorrow, when you ride off on your way,
Now, by my father's soul, and he is dead,

[60]Managing official in a great medieval house.
[61]A commercial street in London.

If you don't enjoy yourselves, cut off my head!
Hold up your hands, if you accept my speech."
 Our counsel did not take us long to reach.
We bade him give his orders at his will.
"Well, sirs," he said, "then do not take it ill,
But hear me in good part, and for your sport,
Each one of you, to make our journey short, 760
Shall tell two stories, as we ride, I mean,
Toward Canterbury; and coming home again
Shall tell two other tales he may have heard
Of happenings that some time have occurred.
And the one of you whose stories please us most,
Here in this tavern, sitting by this post
Shall sup at our expense while we make merry
When we come riding home from Canterbury.
And to cheer you still the more, I too will ride
With you at my own cost, and be your guide. 770
And if anyone my judgment shall gainsay
He must pay for all we spend along the way.
If you agree, no need to stand and reason.
Tell me, and I'll be stirring in good season."
 This thing was granted, and we swore our pledge
To take his judgment on our pilgrimage,
His verdict on our tales, and his advice.
He was to plan a supper at a price
Agreed upon: and so we all assented
To this command, and we were well contented. 780
The wine was fetched; we drank, and went to rest.
 Next morning, when the dawn was in the east,
Up sprang our Host, who acted as our cock,
And gathered us together in a flock,
And off we rode, till presently our pace
Had brought us to St. Thomas' watering place.
And there our Host began to check his horse.
"Good sirs," he said, "you know your promise, of course.
Shall I remind you what it was about?
If evensong and matins don't fall out,[62] 790
We'll soon find who shall tell us the first tale.
But as I hope to drink my wine and ale,
Whoever won't accept what I decide
Pays everything we spend along the ride.
Draw lots, before we're farther from the Inn.
Whoever draws the shortest shall begin.
Sir Knight," said he, "my master, choose your straw.
Come here, my lady Prioress, and draw,
And you, Sir Scholar, don't look thoughtful, man!

[62] That is, if you feel this morning as you did last evening. Evensong and matins are evening and morning prayers.

Pitch in now, everyone!" So all began 800
To draw the lots, and as the luck would fall
The draw went to the Knight, which pleased us all.
And when this excellent man saw how it stood,
Ready to keep his promise, he said, "Good!
Since it appears that I must start the game,
Why then, the draw is welcome, in God's name.
Now let's ride on, and listen, what I say."
And with that word we rode forth on our way,
And he, with his courteous manner and good cheer,
Began to tell his tale, as you shall hear. 810

PROLOGUE TO THE MILLER'S TALE

When the Knight had finished,[1] no one, young or old,
In the whole company, but said he had told
A noble story, one that ought to be
Preserved and kept alive in memory,
Especially the gentlefolk, each one.
Our good Host laughed, and swore, "The game's begun,
The ball is rolling! This is going well.
Let's see who has another tale to tell.
Come, match the Knight's tale if you can, Sir Monk!"
The Miller, who by this time was so drunk 10
He looked quite bloodless, and who hardly sat
His horse, he was never one to doff his hat
Or stand on courtesy for any man.
Like Pilate in the Church plays[2] he began
To bellow. "Arms and blood and bones," he swore,
"I know a yarn that will even up the score,
A noble one, I'll pay off the Knight's tale!"
Our Host could see that he was drunk on ale.
"Robin," he said, "hold on a minute, brother.
Some better man shall come first with another. 20
Let's do this right. You tell yours by and by."
"God's soul," the Miller told him, "that won't I!
Either I'll speak, or go on my own way."
"The devil with you! Say what you have to say,"
Answered our Host. "You are a fool. Your head
Is overpowered."
"Now," the Miller said,
"Everyone listen! But first I will propound
That I am drunk, I know it by my sound.

[1] The Knight had led off the program of storytelling on the way to Canterbury; see the General Prologue, lines 745–810.
[2] The "mystery plays," based on the Bible, especially the Gospels.

If I can't get my words out, put the blame
On Southwark ale,[3] I ask you, in God's name! 30
For I'll tell a golden legend[4] and a life
Both of a carpenter and of his wife,
How a student put horns on the fellow's head."
"Shut up and stop your racket," the Reeve said.[5]
"Forget your ignorant drunken bawdiness.
It is a sin and a great foolishness
To injure any man by defamation
And to give women such a reputation.
Tell us of other things; you'll find no lack."
Promptly this drunken Miller answered back: 40
"Oswald, my brother, true as babes are suckled,
The man who has no wife, he is no cuckold.
I don't say for this reason that you are.
There are plenty of faithful wives, both near and far,
Always a thousand good for every bad,
And you know this yourself, unless you're mad.
I see you are angry with my tale, but why?
You have a wife; no less, by God, do I.
But I wouldn't, for the oxen in my plow,
Shoulder more than I need by thinking how 50
I may myself, for aught I know, be one.
I'll certainly believe that I am none.
A husband mustn't be curious, for his life,
About God's secrets or about his wife.
If she gives him plenty and he's in the clover,
No need to worry about what's left over."
The Miller, to make the best of it I can,
Refused to hold his tongue for any man,
But told his tale like any low-born clown.
I am sorry that I have to set it down, 60
And all you people, for God's love, I pray,
Whose taste is higher, do not think I say
A word with evil purpose; I must rehearse
Their stories one and all, both better and worse,
Or play false with my matter, that is clear.
Whoever, therefore, may not wish to hear,
Turn over the page and choose another tale;
For small and great, he'll find enough, no fail,
Of things from history, touching courtliness,
And virtue too, and also holiness. 70
If you choose wrong, don't lay it on my head.
You know the Miller couldn't be called well bred.

[3]Ale from the Host's inn, in the Southwark district of London, from which the pilgrimage had set out.
[4]A saint's life.
[5]The Reeve was a carpenter by trade; see the General Prologue, line 596.

So with the Reeve, and many more as well,
And both of them had bawdy tales to tell.
Reflect a little, and don't hold me to blame.
There's no sense making earnest out of game.

THE MILLER'S TALE

There used to be a rich old oaf who made
His home at Oxford, a carpenter by trade,
And took in boarders. With him used to dwell
A student who had done his studies well,
But he was poor; for all that he had learned,
It was toward astrology his fancy turned.
He knew a number of figures and constructions
By which he could supply men with deductions
If they should ask him at a given hour
Whether to look for sunshine or for shower, 10
Or want to know whatever might befall,
Events of all sorts, I can't count them all.
He was known as handy[1] Nicholas, this student.
Well versed in love, he knew how to be prudent,
Going about unnoticed, sly, and sure.
In looks no girl was ever more demure.
Lodged at this carpenter's, he lived alone;
He had a room there that he made his own,
Festooned with herbs, and he was sweet himself
As licorice or ginger. On a shelf 20
Above his bed's head, neatly stowed apart,
He kept the trappings that went with his art,
His astrolabe,[2] his books—among the rest,
Thick ones and thin ones, lay his *Almagest*[3]—
And the counters for his abacus as well.
Over his cupboard a red curtain fell
And up above a pretty zither lay
On which at night so sweetly would he play
That with the music the whole room would ring.
"Angelus to the Virgin" he would sing 30
And then the song that's known as "The King's Note."[4]
Blessings were called down on his merry throat!
So this sweet scholar passed his time, his end
Being to eat and live upon his friend.

[1] "Chaucer's word is *hendë,* implying, I take it, both *ready to hand* and *ingratiating.* Nicholas was a Johnny-on-the-spot and also had a way with him."—Translator's note.
[2] An astronomical instrument, used to measure celestial altitudes.
[3] Handbook of the stars; from the treatise on astronomy by Ptolemy (2nd century A.D.).
[4] That is, both sacred and secular music.

This carpenter had newly wed a wife
And loved her better than he loved his life.
He was jealous, for she was eighteen in age;
He tried to keep her close as in a cage,
For she was wild and young, and old was he
And guessed that he might smack of cuckoldry. 40
His ignorant wits had never chanced to strike
On Cato's word, that man should wed his like;[5]
Men ought to wed where their conditions point,
For youth and age are often out of joint.
But now, since he had fallen in the snare,
He must, like other men, endure his care.
Fair this young woman was, her body trim
As any mink, so graceful and so slim.
She wore a striped belt that was all of silk;
A piece-work apron, white as morning milk, 50
About her loins and down her lap she wore.
White was her smock, her collar both before
And on the back embroidered all about
In coal-black silk, inside as well as out.
And like her collar, her white-laundered bonnet
Had ribbons of the same embroidery on it.
Wide was her silken fillet,[6] worn up high,
And for a fact she had a willing eye.
She plucked each brow into a little bow,
And each one was as black as any sloe.[7] 60
She was a prettier sight to see by far
Than the blossoms of the early pear tree are,
And softer than the wool of an old wether.[8]
Down from her belt there hung a purse of leather
With silken tassels and with studs of brass.
No man so wise, wherever people pass,
Who could imagine in this world at all
A wench like her, the pretty little doll!
Far brighter was the dazzle of her hue
Than a coin struck in the Tower,[9] fresh and new. 70
As for her song, it twittered from her head
Sharp as a swallow perching on a shed.
And she could skip and sport as a young ram
Or calf will gambol, following his dam.
Her mouth was sweet as honey-ale or mead
Or apples in the hay, stored up for need.
She was as skittish as an untrained colt,
Slim as a mast and straighter than a bolt.

[5] The *Distichs*, a book of Latin maxims used in schools, was attributed to Dionysius Cato (4th century A.D.).
[6] Headband.
[7] A small black fruit resembling a plum.
[8] Sheep.
[9] The Tower of London, where coins were minted.

On her simple collar she wore a big brooch-pin
Wide as a shield's boss underneath her chin. 80
High up along her legs she laced her shoes.
She was a pigsney,[10] she was a primrose
For any lord to tumble in his bed
Or a good yeoman honestly to wed.
Now sir, and again sir, this is how it was:
A day came round when handy Nicholas,
While her husband was at Oseney,[11] well away,
Began to fool with this young wife, and play.
These students always have a wily head.
He caught her in between the legs, and said, 90
"Sweetheart, unless I have my will with you
I'll die for stifled love, by all that's true,"
And held her by the haunches, hard. "I vow
I'll die unless you love me here and now,
Sure as my soul," he said, "is God's to save."
She shied just as a colt does in the trave,[12]
And turned her head hard from him, this young wife,
And said, "I will not kiss you, on my life.
Why, stop it now," she said, "stop, Nicholas,
Or I will cry out 'Help, help,' and 'Alas!' 100
Be good enough to take your hands away."
"Mercy," this Nicholas began to pray,
And spoke so well and poured it on so fast
She promised she would be his love at last,
And swore by Thomas à Becket, saint of Kent,[13]
That she would serve him when she could invent
Or spy out some good opportunity.
"My husband is so full of jealousy
You must be watchful and take care," she said,
"Or well I know I'll be as good as dead. 110
You must go secretly about this business."
"Don't give a thought to that," said Nicholas.
"A student has been wasting time at school
If he can't make a carpenter a fool."
And so they were agreed, these two, and swore
To watch their chance, as I have said before.
When Nicholas had spanked her haunches neatly
And done all I have spoken of, he sweetly
Gave her a kiss, and then he took his zither
And loudly played, and sang his music with her. 120
Now in her Christian duty, one saint's day,
To the parish church this good wife made her way,

[10] Cuckoo-flower; a term of endearment.
[11] A town near Oxford, site of an abbey where the carpenter performed jobs.
[12] A frame used by blacksmiths to immobilize horses being shod.
[13] The saint whose shrine at Canterbury was the goal of Chaucer's pilgrims.

And as she went her forehead cast a glow
As bright as noon, for she had washed it so
It glistened when she finished with her work.
   Serving this church there was a parish clerk
Whose name was Absolom, a ruddy man
With goose-gray eyes and curls like a great fan
That shone like gold on his neatly parted head.
His tunic was light blue and his nose red, 130
And he had patterns that had been cut through
Like the windows of St. Paul's in either shoe.
He wore above his tunic, fresh and gay,
A surplice white as a blossom on a spray.
A merry devil, as true as God can save,
He knew how to let blood, trim hair, and shave,
Or write a deed of land in proper phrase,
And he could dance in twenty different ways
In the Oxford fashion, and sometimes he would sing
A loud falsetto to his fiddle string 140
Or his guitar. No tavern anywhere
But he had furnished entertainment there.
Yet his speech was delicate, and for his part
He was a little squeamish toward a fart.
   This Absolom, so jolly and so gay,
With a censer[14] went about on the saint's day
Censing the parish women one and all.
Many the doting look that he let fall,
And specially on this carpenter's young wife.
To look at her, he thought, was a good life, 150
She was so trim, so sweetly lecherous.
I dare say that if she had been a mouse
And he a cat, he would have made short work
Of catching her. This jolly parish clerk
Had such a heartful of love-hankerings
He would not take the women's offerings;
No, no, he said, it would not be polite.
   The moon, when darkness fell, shone full and bright,
And Absolom was ready for love's sake
With his guitar to be up and awake, 160
And toward the carpenter's, brisk and amorous,
He made his way until he reached the house
A little after the cocks began to crow.
Under a casement he sang sweet and low,
"Dear lady, by your will, be kind to me,"
And strummed on his guitar in harmony.
This lovelorn singing woke the carpenter
Who said to his wife, "What, Alison, don't you hear
Absolom singing under our bedroom wall?"

[14] The vessel used in church to waft incense fumes.

"Yes, God knows, John," she answered, "I hear it all." 170
What would you like? In this way things went on
Till jolly Absolom was woebegone
For wooing her, awake all night and day.
He combed his curls and made himself look gay.
He swore to be her slave and used all means
To court her with his gifts and go-betweens.
He sang and quavered like a nightingale.
He sent her sweet spiced wine and seasoned ale,
Cakes that were piping hot, mead sweet with honey,
And since she was town-bred, he proffered money. 180
For some are won by wealth, and some no less
By blows, and others yet by gentleness.
Sometimes, to keep his talents in her gaze,
He acted Herod in the mystery plays
High on the stage. But what can help his case?
For she so loves this handy Nicholas
That Absolom is living in a bubble.
He has nothing but a laugh for all his trouble.
She leaves his earnestness for scorn to cool
And makes this Absolom her proper fool. 190
For this is a true proverb, and no lie:
"It always happens that the nigh and sly
Will let the absent suffer." So 'tis said,
And Absolom may rage or lose his head
But just because he was farther from her sight
This nearby Nicholas got in his light.
Now hold your chin up, handy Nicholas,
For Absolom may wail and sing "Alas!"
One Saturday when the carpenter had gone
To Oseney, Nicholas and Alison 200
Agreed that he should use his wit and guile
This simple jealous husband to beguile.
And if it happened that the game went right
She would sleep in his arms the livelong night,
For this was his desire and hers as well.
At once, with no more words, this Nicholas fell
To working out his plan. He would not tarry,
But quietly to his room began to carry
Both food and drink to last him out a day,
Or more than one, and told her what to say 210
If her husband asked her about Nicholas.
She must say she had no notion where he was;
She hadn't laid eyes on him all day long;
He must be sick, or something must be wrong;
No matter how her maid had called and cried
He wouldn't answer, whatever might betide.
This was the plan, and Nicholas kept away,
Shut in his room, for that whole Saturday.

He ate and slept or did as he thought best
Till Sunday, when the sun was going to rest, 220
This carpenter began to wonder greatly
Where Nicholas was and what might ail him lately.
"Now, by St. Thomas, I begin to dread
All isn't right with Nicholas," he said.
"He hasn't, God forbid, died suddenly!
The world is ticklish these days, certainly.
Today I saw a corpse to church go past,
A man that I saw working Monday last!
Go up," he told his chore-boy, "call and shout,
Knock with a stone, find what it's all about 230
And let me know."
The boy went up and pounded
And yelled as if his wits had been confounded.
"What, how, what's doing, Master Nicholas?
How can you sleep all day?" But all his fuss
Was wasted, for he could not hear a word.
He noticed at the bottom of a board
A hole the cat used when she wished to creep
Into the room, and through it looked in deep
And finally of Nicholas caught sight.
This Nicholas sat gaping there upright 240
As though his wits were addled by the moon
When it was new. The boy went down, and soon
Had told his master how he had seen the man.
The carpenter, when he heard this news, began
To cross himself. "Help us, St. Frideswide![15]
Little can we foresee what may betide!
The man's astronomy has turned his wit,
Or else he's in some agonizing fit.
I always knew that it would turn out so.
What God has hidden is not for men to know. 250
Aye, blessed is the ignorant man indeed,
Blessed is he that only knows his creed!
So fared another scholar of the sky,
For walking in the meadows once to spy
Upon the stars and what they might foretell,
Down in a clay-pit suddenly he fell!
He overlooked that! By St. Thomas, though,
I'm sorry for handy Nicholas. I'll go
And scold him roundly for his studying
If so I may, by Jesus, heaven's king! 260
Give me a staff, I'll pry up from the floor
While you, Robin, are heaving at the door.
He'll quit his books, I think."

[15]Eighth-century saint; she was the patron of Oxford, both city and university.

He took his stand
Outside the room. The boy had a strong hand
And by the hasp he heaved it off at once.
The door fell flat. With gaping countenance
This Nicholas sat studying the air
As still as stone. He was in black despair,
The carpenter believed, and hard about
The shoulders caught and shook him, and cried out 270
Rudely, "What, how! What is it? Look down at us!
Wake up, think of Christ's passion, Nicholas!
I'll sign you with the cross to keep away
These elves and things!" And he began to say,
Facing the quarters of the house, each side,
And on the threshold of the door outside,
The night-spell: "Jesu and St. Benedict[16]
From every wicked thing this house protect . . ."
Choosing his time, this handy Nicholas
Produced a dreadful sigh, and said, "Alas, 280
This world, must it be all destroyed straightway?"
"What," asked the carpenter, "what's that you say?
Do as we do, we working men, and think
Of God."
Nicholas answered, "Get me a drink,
And afterwards I'll tell you privately
Of something that concerns us, you and me.
I'll tell you only, you among all men."
This carpenter went down and came again
With a draught of mighty ale, a generous quart.
As soon as each of them had drunk his part 290
Nicholas shut the door and made it fast
And sat down by the carpenter at last
And spoke to him. "My host," he said, "John dear,
You must swear by all that you hold sacred here
That not to any man will you betray
My confidence. What I'm about to say
Is Christ's own secret. If you tell a soul
You are undone, and this will be the toll:
If you betray me, you shall go stark mad."
"Now Christ forbid it, by His holy blood," 300
Answered this simple man. "I don't go blabbing.
If I say it myself, I have no taste for gabbing.
Speak up just as you like, I'll never tell
Not wife nor child, by Him that harrowed hell."[17]
"Now, John," said Nicholas, "this is no lie.
I have discovered through astrology
And studying the moon that shines so bright

[16]Italian monk; founder, c. 529, of the first Western monastic order.
[17]The Harrowing of Hell was Jesus' descent into Hell (more exactly, into Limbo) after the Crucifixion, to liberate the souls of the pre-Christian just.

That Monday next, a quarter through the night,
A rain will fall, and such a mad, wild spate
That Noah's flood was never half so great. 310
This world," he said, "in less time than an hour
Shall drown entirely in that hideous shower.
Yes, every man shall drown and lose his life."
"Alas," the carpenter answered, "for my wife!
Alas, my Alison! And shall she drown?"
For grief at this he nearly tumbled down,
And said, "But is there nothing to be done?"
"Why, happily there is, for anyone
Who will take advice," this handy Nicholas said.
"You mustn't expect to follow your own head. 320
For what said Solomon, whose words were true?
'Proceed by counsel, and you'll never rue.'[18]
If you will act on good advice, no fail,
I'll promise, and without a mast or sail,
To see that she's preserved, and you and I.
Haven't you heard how Noah was kept dry
When, warned by Christ beforehand, he discovered
That the whole earth with water should be covered?"
"Yes," said the carpenter, "long, long ago."
"And then again," said Nicholas, "don't you know 330
The grief they all had trying to embark
Till Noah could get his wife into the Ark?[19]
That was a time when Noah, I dare say,
Would gladly have given his best black wethers away
If she could have had a ship herself alone.
And therefore do you know what must be done?
This demands haste, and with a hasty thing
People can't stop for talk and tarrying.
"Start out and get into the house right off
For each of us a tub or kneading-trough,[20] 340
Above all making sure that they are large,
In which we'll float away as in a barge.
And put in food enough to last a day.
Beyond won't matter; the flood will fall away
Early next morning. Take care not to spill
A word to your boy Robin, nor to Jill
Your maid. I cannot save her, don't ask why.
I will not tell God's secrets, no, not I.
Let it be enough, unless your wits are mad,
To have as good a grace as Noah had. 350
I'll save your wife for certain, never doubt it.
Now go along, and make good time about it.

[18]Ecclesiasticus 32:19. This book of proverbs was canonical in the Roman Catholic Bible.
[19]"A stock comic scene in the mystery plays, of which the carpenter would have been an avid spectator."—Translator's note.
[20]A wooden tub for kneading dough.

"But when you have, for her and you and me,
Brought to the house these kneading-tubs, all three,
Then you must hang them under the roof, up high,
To keep our plans from any watchful eye.
When you have done exactly as I've said,
And put in snug our victuals and our bread,
Also an ax to cut the ropes apart
So when the rain comes we can make our start, 360
And when you've broken a hole high in the gable
Facing the garden plot, above the stable,
To give us a free passage out, each one,
Then, soon as the great fall of rain is done,
You'll swim as merrily, I undertake,
As the white duck paddles along behind her drake.
Then I shall call, 'How, Alison! How, John!
Be cheerful, for the flood will soon be gone.'
And 'Master Nicholas, what ho!' you'll say.
'Good morning, I see you clearly, for it's day.' 370
Then we shall lord it for the rest of life
Over the world, like Noah and his wife.
"But one thing I must warn you of downright.
Use every care that on that selfsame night
When we have taken ship and climbed aboard,
No one of us must speak a single word,
Nor call, nor cry, but pray with all his heart.
It is God's will. You must hang far apart,
You and your wife, for there must be no sin
Between you, no more in a look than in 380
The very deed. Go now, the plans are drawn.
Go, set to work, and may God spur you on!
Tomorrow night when all men are asleep
Into our kneading-troughs we three shall creep
And sit there waiting, and abide God's grace.
Go along now, this isn't the time or place
For me to talk at length or sermonize.
The proverb says, 'Don't waste words on the wise.'
You are so wise there is no need to teach you.
Go, save our lives—that's all that I beseech you!" 390
This simple carpenter went on his way.
Many a time he said, "Alack the day,"
And to his wife he laid the secret bare.
She knew it better than he; she was aware
What this quaint bargain was designed to buy.
She carried on as if about to die,
And said, "Alas, go get this business done.
Help us escape, or we are dead, each one.
I am your true, your faithful wedded wife.
Go, my dear husband, save us, limb and life!" 400
Great things, in all truth, can the emotions be!
A man can perish through credulity

So deep the print imagination makes.
This simple carpenter, he quails and quakes.
He really sees, according to his notion,
Noah's flood come wallowing like an ocean
To drown his Alison, his pet, his dear.
He weeps and wails, and gone is his good cheer,
And wretchedly he sighs. But he goes off
And gets himself a tub, a kneading-trough, 410
Another tub, and has them on the sly
Sent home, and there in secret hangs them high
Beneath the roof. He made three ladders, these
With his own hands, and stowed in bread and cheese
And a jug of good ale, plenty for a day.
Before all this was done, he sent away
His chore-boy Robin and his wench likewise
To London on some trumped-up enterprise,
And so on Monday, when it drew toward night,
He shut the door without a candlelight 420
And saw that all was just as it should be,
And shortly they went clambering up, all three.
They sat there still, and let a moment pass.
"Now then, 'Our Father,' mum!" said Nicholas,
And "Mum!" said John, and "Mum!" said Alison,
And piously this carpenter went on
Saying his prayers. He sat there still and straining,
Trying to make out whether he heard it raining.
The dead of sleep, for very weariness,
Fell on this carpenter, as I should guess, 430
At about curfew time,[21] or little more.
His head was twisted, and that made him snore.
His spirit groaned in its uneasiness.
Down from his ladder slipped this Nicholas,
And Alison too, downward she softly sped
And without further word they went to bed
Where the carpenter himself slept other nights.
There were the revels, there were the delights!
And so this Alison and Nicholas lay
Busy about their solace and their play 440
Until the bell for lauds[22] began to ring
And in the chancel[23] friars began to sing.
Now on this Monday, woebegone and glum
For love, this parish clerk, this Absolom
Was with some friends at Oseney, and while there
Inquired after John the carpenter.
A member of the cloister drew him away
Out of the church, and told him, "I can't say.

[21]About 8 or 9 P.M.
[22]The earliest of the canonical hours, celebrated in monasteries around 3 or 4 A.M.
[23]The railed-in area of a church near the altar.

I haven't seen him working hereabout
Since Saturday. The abbot sent him out 450
For timber, I suppose. He'll often go
And stay at the granary[24] a day or so.
Or else he's at his own house, possibly.
I can't for certain say where he may be."
Absolom at once felt jolly and light,
And thought, "Time now to be awake all night,
For certainly I haven't seen him making
A stir about his door since day was breaking.
Don't call me a man if when I hear the cock
Begin to crow[25] I don't slip up and knock 460
On the low window by his bedroom wall.
To Alison at last I'll pour out all
My love-pangs, for at this point I can't miss,
Whatever happens, at the least a kiss.
Some comfort, by my word, will come my way.
I've felt my mouth itch the whole livelong day,
And that's a sign of kissing at the least.
I dreamed all night that I was at a feast.
So now I'll go and sleep an hour or two,
And then I'll wake and play the whole night through." 470
When the first cockcrow through the dark had come
Up rose this jolly lover Absolom
And dressed up smartly. He was not remiss
About the least point. He chewed licorice
And cardamom to smell sweet, even before
He combed his hair. Beneath his tongue he bore
A sprig of Paris like a truelove knot.[26]
He strolled off to the carpenter's house, and got
Beneath the window. It came so near the ground
It reached his chest. Softly, with half a sound, 480
He coughed, "My honeycomb, sweet Alison,
What are you doing, my sweet cinnamon?
Awake, my sweetheart and my pretty bird,
Awake, and give me from your lips a word!
Little enough you care for all my woe,
How for your love I sweat wherever I go!
No wonder I sweat and faint and cannot eat
More than a girl; as a lamb does for the teat
I pine. Yes, truly, I so long for love
I mourn as if I were a turtledove." 490
Said she, "You jack-fool, get away from here!
So help me God, I won't sing 'Kiss me, dear!'
I love another more than you. Get on,

[24]A barn, or perhaps farm, belonging to the abbey.
[25]The cock crowed around midnight and 3 A.M., and just before daybreak.
[26]A sprig of paris-herb, clover-shaped like a "truelove knot" and supposed to aid lovers.

For Christ's sake, Absolom, or I'll throw a stone.
The devil with you! Go and let me sleep."
"Ah, that true love should ever have to reap
So evil a fortune," Absolom said. "A kiss,
At least, if it can be no more than this,
Give me, for love of Jesus and of me."
"And will you go away for that?" said she. 500
"Yes, truly, sweetheart," answered Absolom.
"Get ready then," she said, "for here I come,"
And softly said to Nicholas, "Keep still,
And in a minute you can laugh your fill."
This Absolom got down upon his knee
And said, "I am a lord of pure degree,[27]
For after this, I hope, comes more to savor.
Sweetheart, your grace, and pretty bird, your favor!"
She undid the window quickly. "That will do,"
She said. "Be quick about it, and get through, 510
For fear the neighbors will look out and spy."
Absolom wiped his mouth to make it dry.
The night was pitch dark, coal-black all about.
Her rear end through the window she thrust out.
He got no better or worse, did Absolom,
Than to kiss her with his mouth on the bare bum
Before he had caught on, a smacking kiss.
He jumped back, thinking something was amiss.
A woman has no beard, he was well aware,
But what he felt was rough and had long hair. 520
"Alas," he cried, "what have you made me do?"
"Te-hee!" she said, and banged the window to.
Absolom backed away a sorry pace.
"You've bearded him!" said handy Nicholas.
"God's body, this is going fair and fit!"
This luckless Absolom heard every bit,
And gnawed his mouth, so angry he became.
He said to himself, "I'll square you, all the same."
But who now scrubs and rubs, who chafes his lips
With dust, with sand, with straw, with cloth and chips, 530
If not this Absolom? "The devil," says he,
"Welcome my soul if I wouldn't rather be
Revenged than have the whole town in a sack!
Alas," he cries, "if only I'd held back!"
His hot love had become all cold and ashen.
He didn't have a curse to spare for passion
From the moment when he kissed her on the ass.
That was the cure to make his sickness pass!
He cried as a child does after being whipped;
He railed at love. Then quietly he slipped 540

[27] In every way.

Across the street to a smith who was forging out
Parts that the farmers needed round about.
He was busy sharpening colter and plowshare[28]
When Absolom knocked as though without a care.
"Undo the door, Jervice, and let me come."
"What? Who are you?"
"It is I, Absolom."
"Absolom, is it! By Christ's precious tree,[29]
Why are you up so early? Lord bless me,
What's ailing you? Some gay girl has the power
To bring you out, God knows, at such an hour! 550
Yes, by St. Neot,[30] you know well what I mean!"
Absolom thought his jokes not worth a bean.
Without a word he let them all go by.
He had another kind of fish to fry
Than Jervice guessed. "Lend me this colter here
That's hot in the chimney, friend," he said. "Don't fear,
I'll bring it back right off when I am through.
I need it for a job I have to do."
"Of course," said Jervice. "Why, if it were gold
Or coins in a sack, uncounted and untold, 560
As I'm a rightful smith, I wouldn't refuse it.
But, Christ's foot! how on earth do you mean to use it?"
"Let that," said Absolom, "be as it may.
I'll let you know tomorrow or next day,"
And took the colter where the steel was cold
And slipped out with it safely in his hold
And softly over to the carpenter's wall.
He coughed and then he rapped the window, all
As he had done before.
"Who's knocking there?"
Said Alison. "It is a thief, I swear." 570
"No, no," said he. "God knows, my sugarplum,
My bird, my darling, it's your Absolom.
I've brought a golden ring my mother gave me,
Fine and well cut, as I hope that God will save me.
It's yours, if you will let me have a kiss."
Nicholas had got up to take a piss
And thought he would improve the whole affair.
This clerk, before he got away from there,
Should give *his* ass a smack; and hastily
He opened the window, and thrust out quietly, 580
Buttocks and haunches, all the way, his bum.
Up spoke this clerk, this jolly Absolom:
"Speak, for I don't know where you are, sweetheart."

[28] The colter was the vertical cutting blade of the plowshare. It was customary for blacksmiths to begin work long before dawn.
[29] The Cross.
[30] Ninth-century saint.

Nicholas promptly let fly with a fart
As loud as if a clap of thunder broke,
So great he was nearly blinded by the stroke,
And ready with his hot iron to make a pass,
Absolom caught him fairly on the ass.
Off flew the skin, a good handbreadth of fat
Lay bare, the iron so scorched him where he sat. 590
As for the pain, he thought that he would die,
And like a madman he began to cry,
"Help! Water! Water! Help, for God's own heart!"
At this the carpenter came to with a start.
He heard a man cry "Water!" as if mad.
"It's coming now," was the first thought he had.
"It's Noah's flood, alas, God be our hope!"
He sat up with his ax and chopped the rope
And down at once the whole contraption fell.
He didn't take time out to buy or sell 600
Till he hit the floor and lay there in a swoon.
Then up jumped Nicholas and Alison
And in the street began to cry, "Help, ho!"
The neighbors all came running, high and low,
And poured into the house to see the sight.
The man still lay there, passed out cold and white,
For in his tumble he had broken an arm.
But he himself brought on his greatest harm,
For when he spoke he was at once outdone
By handy Nicholas and Alison 610
Who told them one and all that he was mad.
So great a fear of Noah's flood he had,
By some delusion, that in his vanity[31]
He had bought himself these kneading-troughs, all three,
And hung them from the roof there, up above,
And he had pleaded with them, for God's love,
To sit there in the loft for company.
The neighbors laughed at such a fantasy,
And round the loft began to pry and poke
And turned his whole disaster to a joke. 620
He found it was no use to say a word.
Whatever reason he offered, no one heard.
With oaths and curses people swore him down
Until he passed for mad in the whole town.
Wit, clerk, and student all stood by each other.
They said, "It's clear the man is crazy, brother."
Everyone had his laugh about this feud.
So Alison, the carpenter's wife, got screwed
For all the jealous watching he could try,
And Absolom, he kissed her nether eye, 630
And Nicholas got his bottom roasted well.
God save this troop! That's all I have to tell.

[31] Folly.

PROLOGUE TO THE WIFE OF BATH'S TALE

"Experience,[1] though all authority
Was lacking in the world, confers on me
The right to speak of marriage, and unfold
Its woes. For, lords, since I was twelve years old
—Thanks to eternal God in heaven alive—
I have married at church door no less than five
Husbands, provided that I can have been
So often wed,[2] and all were worthy men.
But I was told, indeed, and not long since,
That Christ went to a wedding only once 10
At Cana, in the land of Galilee.[3]
By this example he instructed me
To wed once only—that's what I have heard!
Again, consider now what a sharp word,
Beside a well, Jesus, both God and man,
Spoke in reproving the Samaritan:
'Thou hast had five husbands'—this for a certainty
He said to her—'and the man that now hath thee
Is not thy husband.' True, he spoke this way,
But what he meant is more than I can say 20
Except that I would ask why the fifth man
Was not a husband to the Samaritan?
To just how many could she be a wife?
I have never heard this number all my life
Determined up to now. For round and round
Scholars may gloze, interpret, and expound,
But plainly, this I know without a lie,
God told us to increase and multiply.[4]
That noble text I can well understand.
My husband—this too I have well in hand— 30
Should leave both father and mother and cleave to me.[5]
Number God never mentioned, bigamy,
No, nor even octogamy; why do men
Talk of it as a sin and scandal, then?
"Think of that monarch, wise King Solomon.[6]
It strikes me that *he* had more wives than one!

[1] The Wife's appeal to experience is somewhat unorthodox, since written works were supposed to have stronger authority. She shows, however, that she can cite them too (though not always accurately).

[2] The Wife is not sure that all her marriages were valid.

[3] For the wedding at Cana, where Christ changed water to wine, see the gospel of John, 2:1–11. For Jesus' meeting with the sinful Samaritan woman, mentioned a few lines later, see John 4:3–30.

[4] God's command to humankind at the creation; Genesis 1:28.

[5] Adam's words about Eve, Genesis 2:24: "Therefore shall a man leave his father and his mother, and shall cleave unto his wife: and they shall be one flesh."

[6] The Old Testament king had 700 wives and 300 concubines.

To be refreshed, God willing, would please me
If I got it half as many times as he!
What a gift he had, a gift of God's own giving,
For all his wives! There isn't a man now living 40
Who has the like. By all that I make out
This king had many a merry first-night bout
With each, he was so thoroughly alive.
Blessed be God that I have married five,
And always, for the money in his chest
And for his nether purse, I picked the best.
In divers[7] schools ripe scholarship is made,
And various practice in all kinds of trade
Makes perfect workmen, as the world can see.
Five husbands have had turns at schooling me. 50
Welcome the sixth, whenever I am faced
With yet another. I don't mean to be chaste
At all costs. When a spouse of mine is gone,
Some other Christian man shall take me on,
For then, says the Apostle, I'll be free
To wed, in God's name, where it pleases me.
To marry is no sin, as we can learn
From him; better to marry than to burn,[8]
He says. Why should I care what obloquy
Men heap on Lamech and his bigamy? 60
Abraham was, by all that I can tell,
A holy man; so Jacob was as well,
And each of them took more than two as brides,
And many another holy man besides.
Where, may I ask, in any period,
Can you show in plain words that Almighty God
Forbade us marriage? Point it out to me!
Or where did he command virginity?
The Apostle, when he speaks of maidenhood,
Lays down no law. This I have understood 70
As well as you, milords, for it is plain.
Men may advise a woman to abstain
From marriage, but mere counsels aren't commands.
He left it to our judgment, where it stands.
Had God enjoined us all to maidenhood
Then marriage would have been condemned for good.
But truth is, if no seed were ever sown,
In what soil could virginity be grown?
Paul did not dare command a thing at best
On which his Master left us no behest. 80

[7] Various.

[8] In 1 Corinthians 7:8–9, Paul recommends celibacy to the unmarried and widows, and then adds, "But if they cannot contain, let them marry: for it is better to marry than to burn."

"But now the prize goes to virginity.
Seize it whoever can, and let us see
What manner of man shall run best in the race!
But not all men receive this form of grace
Except where God bestows it by his will.
The Apostle was a maid, I know; but still,
Although he wished all men were such as he,
It was only *counsel* toward virginity.
To be a wife he gave me his permission,
And so it is no blot on my condition 90
Nor slander of bigamy upon my state
If when my husband dies I take a mate.
A man does virtuously, St. Paul has said,
To touch no woman—meaning in his bed.
For fire and fat are dangerous friends at best.
You know what this example should suggest.
Here is the nub: he held virginity
Superior to wedded frailty,
And frailty I call it unless man
And woman both are chaste for their whole span. 100
"I am not jealous if maidenhood outweighs
My marriages; I grant it all the praise.
It pleases them, these virgins, flesh and soul
To be immaculate. I won't extol
My own condition. In a lord's household
You know that every vessel can't be gold.
Some are of wood, and serve their master still.
God calls us variously to do his will.
Each has his proper gift, of all who live,
Some this, some that, as it pleases God to give. 110
"To be virgin is a high and perfect course,
And continence is holy. But the source
Of all perfection, Jesus, never bade
Each one of us to go sell all he had
And give it to the poor; he did not say
That all should follow him in this one way.
He spoke to those who would live perfectly,
And by your leave, lords, that is not for me!
The flower of my best years I find it suits
To spend on the acts of marriage and its fruits. 120
"Tell me this also: why at our creation
Were organs given us for generation,
And for what profit were we creatures made?
Believe me, not for nothing! Ply his trade
Of twisting texts who will, and let him urge
That they were only given us to purge
Our urine; say without them we should fail
To tell a female rightly from a male
And that's their only object—say you so?
It won't work, as experience will show. 130

Without offense to scholars, I say this,
They were given us for both these purposes,
That we may both be cleansed, I mean, and eased
Through intercourse, where God is not displeased.
Why else in books is this opinion met,
That every man should pay his wife his debt?
Tell me with what a man should hope to pay
Unless he put his instrument in play?
They were supplied us, then, for our purgation,
But they were also meant for generation. 140
"But none the less I do not mean to say
That all those who are furnished in this way
Are bound to go and practice intercourse.
The world would then grant chastity no force.
Christ was a maid, yet he was formed a man,
And many a saint, too, since the world began,
And yet they lived in perfect chastity.
I am not spiteful toward virginity.
Let virgins be white bread of pure wheat-seed.
Barley we wives are called, and yet I read 150
In Mark, and tell the tale in truth he can,
That Christ with barley bread cheered many a man.[9]
In the state that God assigned to each of us
I'll persevere. I'm not fastidious.
In wifehood I will use my instrument
As freely by my Maker it was lent.
If I hold back with it, God give me sorrow!
My husband shall enjoy it night and morrow
When it pleases him to come and pay his debt.
But a husband, and I've not been thwarted yet, 160
Shall always be my debtor and my slave.
From tribulation he shall never save
His flesh, not for as long as I'm his wife!
I have the power, during all my life,
Over his very body, and not he.
For so the Apostle has instructed me,[10]
Who bade men love their wives for better or worse.
It pleases me from end to end, that verse!"
The Pardoner, before she could go on,
Jumped up and cried, "By God and by St. John, 170
Upon this topic you preach nobly, Dame!
I was about to wed, but now, for shame,
Why should my body pay a price so dear?
I'd rather not be married all this year!"

[9] The Wife alludes to the miracle in which Jesus fed 5,000 people with five barley loaves and two fishes.

[10] The Wife cites only the second half of the Apostle's (Paul's) statement (1 Corinthians 7:4): "The wife hath not power of her own body, but the husband: and likewise also the husband hath not power of his own body, but the wife."

"Hold on," she said. "I haven't yet begun.
You'll drink a keg of this before I'm done,
I promise you, and it won't taste like ale!
And after I have told you my whole tale
Of marriage, with its fund of tribulation—
And I'm the expert of my generation, 180
For I myself, I mean, have been the whip—
You can decide then if you want a sip
Out of the barrel that I mean to broach.
Before you come too close in your approach,
Think twice. I have examples, more than ten!
'The man who won't be warned by other men,
To other men a warning he shall be.'
These are the words we find in Ptolemy.
You can read them right there in his *Almagest*."[11]
"Now, Madame, if you're willing, I suggest," 190
Answered the Pardoner, "as you began,
Continue with your tale, and spare no man.
Teach us your practice—we young men need a guide."
"Gladly, if it will please you," she replied.
"But first I ask you, if I speak my mind,
That all this company may be well inclined,
And will not take offense at what I say.
I only mean it, after all, in play.
"Now, sirs, I will get onward with my tale.
If ever I hope to drink good wine or ale, 200
I'm speaking truth: the husbands I have had,
Three of them have been good, and two were bad.
The three were kindly men, and rich, and old.
But they were hardly able to uphold
The statute which had made them fast to me.
You know well what I mean by this, I see!
So help me God, I can't help laughing yet
When I think of how at night I made them sweat,
And I thought nothing of it, on my word!
Their land and wealth they had by then conferred 210
On me, and so I safely could neglect
Tending their love or showing them respect.
So well they loved me that by God above
I hardly set a value on their love.
A woman who is wise is never done
Busily winning love when she has none,
But since I had them wholly in my hand
And they had given me their wealth and land,
Why task myself to spoil them or to please
Unless for my own profit and my ease? 220
I set them working so that many a night

[11] The saying is not in the *Almagest*, although it was attributed to Ptolemy by a translator of the work. The same is true of the Wife's later citation of Ptolemy.

They sang a dirge, so grievous was their plight!
They never got the bacon, well I know,
Offered as prize to couples at Dunmow[12]
Who live a year in peace, without repentance!
So well I ruled them, by my law and sentence,
They were glad to bring me fine things from the fair
And happy when I spoke with a mild air,
For God knows I could chide outrageously.
"Now judge if I could do it properly! 230
You wives who understand and who are wise,
This is the way to throw dust in their eyes.
There isn't on the earth so bold a man
He can swear false or lie as a woman can.
I do not urge this course in every case,
Just when a prudent wife is caught off base;
Then she should swear the parrot's mad who tattled
Her indiscretions, and when she's once embattled
Should call her maid as witness, by collusion.
But listen, how I threw them in confusion: 240
"'Sir dotard,[13] this is how you live?' I'd say.
'How can my neighbor's wife be dressed so gay?
She carries off the honors everywhere.
I sit at home. I've nothing fit to wear.
What were you doing at my neighbor's house?
Is she so handsome? Are you so amorous?
What do you whisper to our maid? God bless me,
Give up your jokes, old lecher. They depress me.
When I have a harmless friend myself, you balk
And scold me like a devil if I walk 250
For innocent amusement to his house.
You drink and come home reeling like a souse
And sit down on your bench, worse luck, and preach.
Taking a wife who's poor—this is the speech
That you regale me with—costs grievously,
And if she's rich and of good family,
It is a constant torment, you decide,
To suffer her ill humor and her pride.
And if she's fair, you scoundrel, you destroy her
By saying that every lecher will enjoy her; 260
For chastity at best has frail protections
If a woman is assailed from all directions.
"'Some want us for our wealth, so you declare,
Some for our figure, some think we are fair,
Some want a woman who can dance or sing,
Some want kindness, and some philandering,
Some look for hands and arms well turned and small.

[12]A town in Essex, in southeastern England. Such a prize for peaceable couples was in fact given.
[13]A senile person.

Thus, by your tale, the devil may take us all!
Men cannot keep a castle or redoubt[14]
Longer, you tell me, than it can hold out. 270
Or if a woman's plain, you say that she
Is one who covets each man she may see,
For at him like a spaniel she will fly
Until she finds some man that she can buy.
Down to the lake goes never a goose so gray
But it will have a mate, I've heard you say.
It's hard to fasten—this too I've been told—
A thing that no man willingly will hold.
Wise men, you tell me as you go to bed,
And those who hope for heaven should never wed. 280
I hope wild lightning and a thunderstroke
Will break your wizened neck! You say that smoke
And falling timbers and a railing wife
Drive a man from his house. Lord bless my life!
What ails an old man, so to make him chide?
We cover our vices till the knot is tied,
We wives, you say, and then we trot them out.
Here's a fit proverb for a doddering lout!
An ox or ass, you say, a hound or horse,
These we examine as a matter of course. 290
Basins and also bowls, before we buy them,
Spoons, spools, and such utensils, first we try them,
And so with pots and clothes, beyond denial;
But of their wives men never make a trial
Until they are married. After that, you say,
Old fool, we put our vices on display.
"'I am in a pique if you forget your duty
And fail, you tell me, to praise me for my beauty,
Or unless you are always doting on my face
And calling me "fair dame" in every place, 300
Or unless you give a feast on my birthday
To keep me in good spirits, fresh and gay,
Or unless all proper courtesies are paid
To my nurse and also to my chambermaid,
And my father's kin with all their family ties—
You say so, you old barrelful of lies!
"'Yet just because he has a head of hair
Like shining gold, and squires me everywhere,
You have a false suspicion in your heart
Of Jenkin, our apprentice. For my part 310
I wouldn't have him if you died tomorrow!
But tell me this, or go and live in sorrow:
That chest of yours, why do you hide the keys
Away from me? It's my wealth, if you please,

[14]A small fort or defensive hiding place.

As much as yours. Will you make a fool of me,
The mistress of our house? You shall not be
Lord of my body and my wealth at once!
No, by St. James himself, you must renounce
One or the other, if it drives you mad!
Does it help to spy on me? You would be glad 320
To lock me up, I think, inside your chest.
"Enjoy yourself, and go where you think best,"
You ought to say; "I won't hear tales of malice.
I know you for a faithful wife, Dame Alice."
A woman loves no man who keeps close charge
Of where she goes. We want to be at large.
Blessed above all other men was he,
The wise astrologer, Don Ptolemy,
Who has this proverb in his *Almagest:*
"Of all wise men his wisdom is the best 330
Who does not care who has the world in hand."
Now by this proverb you should understand,
Since you have plenty, it isn't yours to care
Or fret how richly other people fare,
For by your leave, old dotard, you for one
Can have all you can take when day is done.
The man's a niggard to the point of scandal
Who will not lend his lamp to light a candle;
His lamp won't lose although the candle gain.
If you have enough, you ought not to complain. 340
"'You say, too, if we make ourselves look smart,
Put on expensive clothes and dress the part,
We lay our virtue open to disgrace.
And then you try to reinforce your case
By saying these words in the Apostle's name:
"In chaste apparel, with modesty and shame,
So shall you women clothe yourselves," said he,
"And not in rich coiffure or jewelry,
Pearls or the like, or gold, or costly wear."[15]
Now both your text and rubric, I declare, 350
I will not follow as I would a gnat!
"'You told me once that I was like a cat,
For singe her skin and she will stay at home,
But if her skin is smooth, the cat will roam.
No dawn but finds her on the neighbors calling
To show her skin, and go off caterwauling.
If I am looking smart, you mean to say,
I'm off to put my finery on display.
"'What do you gain, old fool, by setting spies?
Though you beg Argus[16] with his hundred eyes 360

[15] See St. Paul's First Epistle to Timothy 2:9.
[16] In mythology, a hundred-eyed giant who served as a guard.

To be my bodyguard, for all his skill
He'll keep me only by my own free will.
I know enough to blind him, as I live!
"'There are three things,[17] you also say, that give
Vexation to this world both south and north,
And you add that no one can endure the fourth.
Of these catastrophes a hateful wife—
You precious wretch, may Christ cut short your life!—
Is always reckoned, as you say, for one.
Is this your whole stock of comparison, 370
And why in all your parables of contempt
Can a luckless helpmate never be exempt?
You also liken woman's love to hell,
To barren land where water will not dwell.
I've heard you call it an unruly fire;
The more it burns, the hotter its desire
To burn up everything that burned will be.
You say that just as worms destroy a tree
A wife destroys her spouse, as they have found
Who get themselves in holy wedlock bound.' 380
"By these devices, lords, as you perceive,
I got my three old husbands to believe
That in their cups they said things of this sort,
And all of it was false; but for support
Jenkin bore witness, and my niece did too.
These innocents, Lord, what I put them through!
God's precious pains! And they had no recourse,
For I could bite and whinny like a horse.
Though in the wrong, I kept them well annoyed,
Or oftentimes I would have been destroyed! 390
First to the mill is first to grind his grain.
I was always the first one to complain,
And so our peace was made; they gladly bid
For terms to settle things they never did!
"For wenching I would scold them out of hand
When they were hardly well enough to stand.
But this would tickle a man; it would restore him
To think I had so great a fondness for him!
I'd vow when darkness came and out I stepped,
It was to see the girls with whom he slept. 400
Under this pretext I had plenty of mirth!
Such wit as this is given us at our birth.
Lies, tears, and needlework the Lord will give
In kindness to us women while we live.
And thus in one point I can take just pride:
In the end I showed myself the stronger side.

[17]Several of the examples of unpleasantness in the following lines are from Proverbs, chapter 30.

By sleight or strength I kept them in restraint,
And chiefly by continual complaint.
In bed they met their grief in fullest measure.
There I would scold; I would not do their pleasure. 410
Bed was a place where I would not abide
If I felt my husband's arm across my side
Till he agreed to square accounts and pay,
And after that I'd let him have his way.
To every man, therefore, I tell this tale:
Win where you're able, all is up for sale.
No falcon by an empty hand is lured.
For victory their cravings I endured
And even feigned a show of appetite.
And yet in old meat I have no delight; 420
It made me always rail at them and chide them,
For though the pope himself sat down beside them
I would not give them peace at their own board.
No, on my honor, I paid them word for word.
Almighty God so help me, if right now
I had to make my last will, I can vow
For every word they said to me, we're quits.
For I so handled the contest by my wits
That they gave up, and took it for the best,
Or otherwise we should have had no rest. 430
Like a mad lion let my husband glare,
In the end he got the worst of the affair.
"Then I would say, 'My dear, you ought to keep
In mind how gentle Wilkin looks, our sheep.
Come here, my husband, let me kiss your cheek!
You should be patient, too; you should be meek.
Of Job and of his patience when you prate
Your conscience ought to show a cleaner slate.
He should be patient who so well can preach.
If not, then it will fall on me to teach 440
The beauty of a peaceful wedded life.
For one of us must give in, man or wife,
And since men are more reasonable creatures
Than women are, it follows that *your* features
Ought to exhibit patience. Why do you groan?
You want my body yours, and yours alone?
Why, take it all! Welcome to every bit!
But curse you, Peter, unless you cherish it!
Were I inclined to peddle my *belle chose,*[18]
I could go about dressed freshly as a rose. 450
But I will keep it for your own sweet tooth.
It's your fault if we fight. By God, that's truth!'

[18] Literally, "beautiful thing" (French).

"This was the way I talked when I had need.
But now to my fourth husband I'll proceed.
"This fourth I married was a roisterer.
He had a mistress, and my passions were,
Although I say it, strong; and altogether
I was young and stubborn, pert in every feather.
If anyone took up his harp to play,
How I could dance! I sang as merry a lay 460
As any nightingale when of sweet wine
I had drunk my draft. Metellius,[19] the foul swine,
Who beat his spouse until he took her life
For drinking wine, had I only been his wife,
He'd never have frightened me away from drinking!
But after a drink, Venus gets in my thinking,
For just as true as cold engenders hail
A thirsty mouth goes with a thirsty tail.
Drinking destroys a woman's last defense
As lechers well know by experience. 470
"But, Lord Christ, when it all comes back to me,
Remembering my youth and jollity,
It tickles me to the roots. It does me good
Down to this very day that while I could
I took my world, my time, and had my fling.
But age, alas, that poisons everything
Has robbed me of my beauty and my pith.
Well, let it go! Good-by! The devil with
What cannot last! There's only this to tell:
The flour is gone, I've only chaff to sell. 480
Yet I'll contrive to keep a merry cheek!
But now of my fourth husband I will speak.
"My heart was, I can tell you, full of spite
That in another he should find delight.
I paid him for this debt; I made it good.
I furnished him a cross of the same wood,
By God and by St. Joce—in no foul fashion,
Not with my flesh; but I put on such passion
And rendered him so jealous, I'll engage
I made him fry in his own grease for rage! 490
On earth, God knows, I was his purgatory;
I only hope his soul is now in glory.
God knows it was a sad song that he sung
When the shoe pinched him; sorely was he wrung!
Only he knew, and God, the devious system
By which outrageously I used to twist him.
He died when I came home from Jerusalem.
He is buried near the chancel, under the beam

[19] The source of the story of Metellius is Valerius Maximus, one of Chaucer's favorite sources.

That holds the cross. His tomb is less ornate
Than the sepulcher where Darius[20] lies in state 500
And which the paintings of Appelles graced
With subtle work. It would have been a waste
To bury him lavishly. Farewell! God save
His soul and give him rest! He's in his grave.
"And now of my fifth husband let me tell.
God never let his soul go down to hell
Though he of all five was my scourge and flail!
I feel it on my ribs, right down the scale,
And ever shall until my dying day.
And yet he was so full of life and gay 510
In bed, and could so melt me and cajole me
When on my back he had a mind to roll me,
What matter if on every bone he'd beaten me!
He'd have my love, so quickly he could sweeten me.
I loved him best, in fact; for as you see,
His love was a more arduous prize for me.
We women, if I'm not to tell a lie,
Are quaint in this regard. Put in our eye
A thing we cannot easily obtain,
All day we'll cry about it and complain. 520
Forbid a thing, we want it bitterly,
But urge it on us, then we turn and flee.
We are chary of what we hope that men will buy.
A throng at market makes the prices high;
Men set no value on cheap merchandise,
A truth all women know if they are wise.
"My fifth, may God forgive his every sin,
I took for love, not money. He had been
An Oxford student once, but in our town
Was boarding with my good friend, Alison. 530
She knew each secret that I had to give
More than our parish priest did, as I live!
I told her my full mind, I shared it all.
For if my husband pissed against a wall
Or did a thing that might have cost his life,
To her, and to another neighbor's wife,
And to my niece, a girl whom I loved well,
His every thought I wouldn't blush to tell.
And often enough I told them, be it said.
God knows I made his face turn hot and red 540
For secrets he confided to his shame.
He knew he only had himself to blame.
"And so it happened once that during Lent,
As I often did, to Alison's I went,

[20]According to legend, Darius, king of the ancient Persians, had a lavish tomb.

For I have loved my life long to be gay
And to walk out in April or in May
To hear the talk and seek a favorite haunt.
Jenkin the student, Alice, my confidante,
And I myself into the country went.
My husband was in London all that Lent. 550
I had the greater liberty to see
And to be seen by jolly company.
How could I tell beforehand in what place
Luck might be waiting with a stroke of grace?
And so I went to every merrymaking.
No pilgrimage was past my undertaking.
I was at festivals, and marriages,
Processions, preachings, and at miracle plays,[21]
And in my scarlet clothes I made a sight.
Upon that costume neither moth nor mite 560
Nor any worm with ravening hunger fell.
And why, you ask? It was kept in use too well.
"Now for what happened. In the fields we walked,
The three of us, and gallantly we talked,
The student and I, until I told him he,
If I became a widow, should marry me.
For I can say, and not with empty pride,
I have never failed for marriage to provide
Or other things as well. Let mice be meek;
A mouse's heart I hold not worth a leek. 570
He has one hole to scurry to, just one,
And if that fails him, he is quite undone.
"I let this student think he had bewitched me.
(My mother with this piece of guile enriched me!)
All night I dreamed of him—this too I said;
He was killing me as I lay flat in bed;
My very bed in fact was full of blood;
But still I hoped it would result in good,
For blood betokens gold, as I have heard.
It was a fiction, dream and every word, 580
But I was following my mother's lore
In all this matter, as in many more.
"Sirs—let me see; what did I mean to say?
Aha! By God, I have it! When he lay,
My fourth, of whom I've spoken, on his bier,
I wept of course; I showed but little cheer,
As wives must do, since custom has its place,
And with my kerchief covered up my face.
But since I had provided for a mate,
I did not cry for long, I'll freely state. 590
And so to church my husband on the morrow
Was borne away by neighbors in their sorrow.

[21] Plays based on the lives of the saints.

Jenkin, the student, was among the crowd,
And when I saw him walk, so help me God,
Behind the bier, I thought he had a pair
Of legs and feet so cleanly turned and fair
I put my heart completely in his hold.
He was in fact some twenty winters old
And I was forty, to confess the truth;
But all my life I've still had a colt's tooth. 600
My teeth were spaced apart;[22] that was the seal
St. Venus printed, and became me well.
So help me God, I was a lusty one,
Pretty and young and rich, and full of fun.
And truly, as my husbands have all said,
I was the best thing there could be in bed.
For I belong to Venus in my feelings,
Though I bring the heart of Mars to all my dealings.
From Venus come my lust and appetite,
From Mars I get my courage and my might, 610
Born under Taurus, while Mars stood therein.
Alas, alas, that ever love was sin!
I yielded to my every inclination
Through the predominance of my constellation;
This made me so I never could withhold
My chamber of Venus, if the truth be told,
From a good fellow; yet upon my face
Mars left his mark, and in another place.
For never, so may Christ grant me intercession,
Have I yet loved a fellow with discretion, 620
But always I have followed appetite,
Let him be long or short or dark or light.
I never cared, as long as he liked me,
What his rank was or how poor he might be.
"What should I say, but when the month ran out,
This jolly student, always much about,
This Jenkin married me in solemn state.
To him I gave land, titles, the whole slate
Of goods that had been given me before;
But my repentance afterward was sore! 630
He wouldn't endure the pleasures I held dear.
By God, he gave me a lick once on the ear,
When from a book of his I tore a leaf,
So hard that from the blow my ear grew deaf.
I was stubborn as a lioness with young,
And by the truth I had a rattling tongue,
And I would visit, as I'd done before,
No matter what forbidding oath he swore.
Against this habit he would sit and preach me
Sermons enough, and he would try to teach me 640

[22]A sign of lustiness.

Old Roman stories,[23] how for his whole life
The man Sulpicius Gallus left his wife
Only because he saw her look one day
Bareheaded down the street from his doorway.
"Another Roman he told me of by name
Who, since his wife was at a summer's game
Without his knowledge, thereupon forsook
The woman. In his Bible he would look
And find that proverb of the Ecclesiast
Where he enjoins and makes the stricture fast 650
That men forbid their wives to rove about.
Then he would quote me this, you needn't doubt:
'Build a foundation over sands or shallows,
Or gallop a blind horse across the fallows,
Let a wife traipse to shrines that some saint hallows,
And you are fit to swing upon the gallows.'
Talk as he would, I didn't care two haws
For his proverbs or his venerable saws.
Set right by him I never meant to be.
I hate the man who tells my faults to me, 660
And more of us than I do, by your pleasure.
This made him mad with me beyond all measure.
Under his yoke in no case would I go.
"Now, by St. Thomas, I will let you know
Why from that book of his I tore a leaf,
For which I got the blow that made me deaf.
"He had a book, *Valerius*, he called it,
And Theophrastus, and he always hauled it
From where it lay to read both day and night
And laughed hard at it, such was his delight. 670
There was another scholar, too, at Rome
A cardinal, whose name was St. Jerome;
He wrote a book against Jovinian.
In the same book also were Tertullian,
Chrysippus, Trotula, Abbess Héloïse
Who lived near Paris; it contained all these,
Bound in a single volume, and many a one
Besides; the Parables of Solomon
And Ovid's *Art of Love.* On such vacation
As he could snatch from worldly occupation 680
He dredged this book for tales of wicked wives.[24]
He knew more stories of their wretched lives
Than are told about good women in the Bible.
No scholar ever lived who did not libel

[23] The following two stories are from Valerius Maximus.
[24] Jenkin's collection of anti-feminine literature is wide ranging, including the Bible; ancient classical authors such as Theophrastus and Ovid; early Christian authors such as Tertullian and Jerome; and medieval writers such as the twelfth-century Héloïse (loved by Abelard).

Women, believe me; to speak well of wives
Is quite beyond them, unless it be in lives
Of holy saints; no woman else will do.
Who was it painted the lion,[25] tell me who?
By God, if women had only written stories
Like wits and scholars in their oratories,[26] 690
They would have pinned on men more wickedness
Than the whole breed of Adam can redress.
Venus's children clash with Mercury's;
The two work evermore by contraries.
Knowledge and wisdom are of Mercury's giving,
Venus loves revelry and riotous living,
And with these clashing dispositions gifted
Each of them sinks when the other is uplifted.
Thus Mercury falls, God knows, in desolation
In the sign of Pisces, Venus's exaltation, 700
And Venus falls when Mercury is raised.
Thus by a scholar no woman can be praised.
The scholar, when he's old and cannot do
The work of Venus more than his old shoe,
Then sits he down, and in his dotage fond
Writes that no woman keeps her marriage bond!
"But now for the story that I undertook—
To tell how I was beaten for a book.
"Jenkin, one night, who never seemed to tire
Of reading in his book, sat by the fire 710
And first he read of Eve, whose wickedness
Delivered all mankind to wretchedness
For which in his own person Christ was slain
Who with his heart's blood bought us all again.
'By this,' he said, 'expressly you may find
That woman was the loss of all mankind.'
"He read me next how Samson lost his hair.
Sleeping, his mistress clipped it off for fair;
Through this betrayal he lost both his eyes.[27]
He read me then—and I'm not telling lies— 720
How Deianeira, wife of Hercules,
Caused him to set himself on fire.[28] With these
He did not overlook the sad to-do
Of Socrates with *his* wives—he had two.
Xantippe emptied the pisspot on his head.
This good man sat as patient as if dead.

[25] In a fable of Aesop, a lion who sees a picture of a man killing a lion says that if lions could paint, the roles in the picture might be reversed.

[26] Private chapels.

[27] Judges, chapter 16. Samson confided to his beloved, Delilah, that his strength lay in his hair; she betrayed him by having it cut off while he was sleeping. Thus weakened, he was enslaved by the Philistines.

[28] In her jealousy she gave Hercules a poisoned robe, which caused him such agony that to escape the pain he had himself cremated.

He wiped his scalp; he did not dare complain
Except to say 'With thunder must come rain.'
"Pasiphaë,[29] who was the queen of Crete,
For wickedness he thought her story sweet. 730
Ugh! That's enough, it was a grisly thing,
About her lust and filthy hankering!
And Clytemnestra[30] in her lechery
Who took her husband's life feloniously,
He grew devout in reading of her treason.
And then he told me also for what reason
Unhappy Amphiaraus lost his life.
My husband had the story of *his* wife,
Eriphyle, who for a clasp of gold
Went to his Grecian enemies and told 740
The secret of her husband's hiding place,
For which at Thebes he met an evil grace.[31]
Livia and Lucilia, he went through
Their tale as well; they killed their husbands, too.
One killed for love, the other killed for hate.
At evening Livia, when the hour was late,
Poisoned her husband, for she was his foe.
Lucilia doted on her husband so
That in her lust, hoping to make him think
Ever of her, she gave him a love-drink 750
Of such a sort he died before the morrow.[32]
And so at all turns husbands come to sorrow!
"He told me then how one Latumius,
Complaining to a friend named Arrius,
Told him that in his garden grew a tree
On which his wives had hanged themselves, all three,
Merely for spite against their partnership.
'Brother,' said Arrius, 'let me have a slip
From this miraculous tree, for, begging pardon,
I want to go and plant it in my garden.' 760
"Then about wives in recent times he read,
How some had murdered husbands lying abed
And all night long had let a paramour
Enjoy them with the corpse flat on the floor;
Or driven a nail into a husband's brain
While he was sleeping, and thus he had been slain;
And some had given them poison in their drink.
He told more harm than anyone can think,

[29] She fell in love with a bull and gave birth to a monster, half bull and half human.

[30] Wife of Agamemnon, commander of the Greeks against Troy. On his return from the war, she and her paramour killed him.

[31] In mythology, Amphiaraus was tricked by his wife (who had been bribed) into joining an expedition against Thebes from which it was known that he would not return alive.

[32] In ancient Roman history there were two Livias, each of whom killed her husband. Lucilia was married to the great Roman poet Lucretius (first century B.C.); the story of the love potion is from St. Jerome.

And seasoned his wretched stories with proverbs
Outnumbering all the blades of grass and herbs 770
On earth. 'Better a dragon for a mate,
Better,' he said, 'on a lion's whims to wait
Than on a wife whose way it is to chide.
Better,' he said, 'high in the loft to bide
Than with a railing wife down in the house.
They always, they are so contrarious,
Hate what their husbands like,' so he would say.
'A woman,' he said, 'throws all her shame away
When she takes off her smock.' And on he'd go:
'A pretty woman, unless she's chaste also, 780
Is like a gold ring stuck in a sow's nose.'
Who could imagine, who would half suppose
The gall my heart drank, raging at each drop?
"And when I saw that he would never stop
Reading all night from his accursed book,
Suddenly, in the midst of it, I took
Three leaves and tore them out in a great pique,
And with my fist I caught him on the cheek
So hard he tumbled backward in the fire.
And up he jumped, he was as mad for ire 790
As a mad lion, and caught me on the head
With such a blow I fell down as if dead.
And seeing me on the floor, how still I lay,
He was aghast, and would have fled away,
Till I came to at length, and gave a cry.
'Have you killed me for my lands? Before I die,
False thief,' I said, 'I'll give you a last kiss!'
"He came to me and knelt down close at this,
And said, 'So help me God, dear Alison,
I'll never strike you. For this thing I have done 800
You are to blame. Forgive me, I implore.'
So then I hit him on the cheek once more
And said, 'Thus far I am avenged, you thief.
I cannot speak. Now I shall die for grief.'
But finally, with much care and ado,
We reconciled our differences, we two.
He let me have the bridle in my hand
For management of both our house and land.
To curb his tongue he also undertook,
And on the spot I made him burn his book. 810
And when I had secured in full degree
By right of triumph the whole sovereignty,
And he had said, 'My dear, my own true wife,
Do as you will as long as you have life;
Preserve your honor and keep my estate,'
From that day on we had settled our debate.
I was as kind, God help me, day and dark
As any wife from India to Denmark,

And also true, and so he was to me.
I pray the Lord who sits in majesty 820
To bless his soul for Christ's own mercy dear.
And now I'll tell my tale, if you will hear."
"Dame," laughed the Friar, "as I hope for bliss,
It was a long preamble to a tale, all this!"
"God's arms!" the Summoner said, "it is a sin,
Good people, how friars are always butting in!
A fly and a friar will fall in every dish
And every question, whatever people wish.
What do you know, with your talk about 'preambling'?
Amble or trot or keep still or go scrambling, 830
You interrupt our pleasure."
"You think so,
Sir Summoner?" said the Friar. "Before I go,
I'll give the people here a chance or two
For a laugh at summoners, I promise you."
"Curse on your face," the Summoner said, "curse me,
If I don't tell some stories, two or three,
On friars, before I get to Sittingborne,[33]
With which I'll twist your heart and make it mourn,
For you have lost your temper, I can see."
"Be quiet," cried our Host, "immediately," 840
And ordered, "Let the woman tell her tale.
You act like people who've got drunk on ale.
Do, Madame, tell us. That is the best measure."
"All ready, sir," she answered "at your pleasure,
With the license of this worthy Friar here."
"Madame, tell on," he said. "You have my ear."

THE WIFE OF BATH'S TALE

In the old days when King Arthur ruled the nation,
Whom Welshmen speak of with such veneration,
This realm we live in was a fairy land.
The fairy queen danced with her jolly band
On the green meadows where they held dominion.
This was, as I have read, the old opinion;
I speak of many hundred years ago.
But no one sees an elf now, as you know,
For in our time the charity and prayers
And all the begging of these holy friars 10
Who swarm through every nook and every stream
Thicker than motes of dust in a sunbeam,
Blessing our chambers, kitchens, halls, and bowers,
Our cities, towns, and castles, our high towers,

[33]About forty miles from London.

Our villages, our stables, barns, and dairies,
They keep us all from seeing any fairies,
For where you might have come upon an elf
There now you find the holy friar himself
Working his district on industrious legs
And saying his devotions while he begs. 20
Women are safe now under every tree.
No incubus[1] is there unless it's he,
And all they have to fear from him is shame.
  It chanced that Arthur had a knight who came
Lustily riding home one day from hawking,
And in his path he saw a maiden walking
Before him, stark alone, right in his course.
This young knight took her maidenhead by force,
A crime at which the outcry was so keen
It would have cost his neck, but that the queen, 30
With other ladies, begged the king so long
That Arthur spared his life, for right or wrong,
And gave him to the queen, at her own will,
According to her choice, to save or kill.
  She thanked the king, and later told this knight,
Choosing her time, "You are still in such a plight
Your very life has no security.
I grant your life, if you can answer me
This question: what is the thing that most of all
Women desire? Think, or your neck will fall 40
Under the ax! If you cannot let me know
Immediately, I give you leave to go
A twelvemonth and a day, no more, in quest
Of such an answer as will meet the test.
But you must pledge your honor to return
And yield your body, whatever you may learn."
  The knight sighed; he was rueful beyond measure.
But what! He could not follow his own pleasure.
He chose at last upon his way to ride
And with such answer as God might provide 50
To come back when the year was at the close.
And so he takes his leave, and off he goes.
  He seeks out every house and every place
Where he has any hope, by luck or grace,
Of learning what thing women covet most.
But it seemed he could not light on any coast
Where on this point two people would agree,
For some said wealth and some said jollity,
Some said position, some said sport in bed
And often to be widowed, often wed. 60
Some said that to a woman's heart what mattered
Above all else was to be pleased and flattered.

[1]An evil spirit believed to have intercourse with women, in their sleep.

That shaft, to tell the truth, was a close hit.
Men win us best by flattery, I admit,
And by attention. Some say our greatest ease
Is to be free and do just as we please,
And not to have our faults thrown in our eyes,
But always to be praised for being wise.
And true enough, there's not one of us all
Who will not kick if you rub us on a gall. 70
Whatever vices we may have within,
We won't be taxed with any fault or sin.
Some say that women are delighted well
If it is thought that they will never tell
A secret they are trusted with, or scandal.
But that tale isn't worth an old rake handle!
We women, for a fact, can never hold
A secret. Will you hear a story told?
Then witness Midas! For it can be read
In Ovid that he had upon his head 80
Two ass's ears that he kept out of sight
Beneath his long hair with such skill and sleight
That no one else besides his wife could guess.
He loved her well, and trusted her no less.
He begged her not to make his blemish known,
But keep her knowledge to herself alone.
She swore that never, though to save her skin,
Would she be guilty of so mean a sin,
And yet it seemed to her she nearly died
Keeping a secret locked so long inside. 90
It swelled about her heart so hard and deep
She was afraid some word was bound to leap
Out of her mouth, and since there was no man
She dared to tell, down to a swamp she ran—
Her heart, until she got there, all agog—
And like a bittern booming in the bog
She put her mouth close to the watery ground:
"Water, do not betray me with your sound!
I speak to you, and you alone," she said.
"Two ass's ears grow on my husband's head! 100
And now my heart is whole, now it is out.
I'd burst if I held it longer, past all doubt."
Safely, you see, awhile you may confide
In us, but it will out; we cannot hide
A secret. Look in Ovid if you care
To learn what followed; the whole tale is there.[2]
This knight, when he perceived he could not find
What women covet most, was low in mind;

[2] See Ovid, *Metamorphoses,* Book XI. In Ovid, however, it is Midas's barber, not his wife, who reveals the secret.

But the day had come when homeward he must ride,
And as he crossed a wooded countryside 110
Some four and twenty ladies there by chance
He saw, all circling in a woodland dance,
And toward this dance he eagerly drew near
In hope of any counsel he might hear.
But the truth was, he had not reached the place
When dance and all, they vanished into space.
No living soul remained there to be seen
Save an old woman sitting on the green,
As ugly a witch as fancy could devise.
As he approached her she began to rise 120
And said, "Sir knight, here runs no thoroughfare.
What are you seeking with such anxious air?
Tell me! The better may your fortune be.
We old folk know a lot of things," said she.
"Good mother," said the knight, "my life's to pay,
That's all too certain, if I cannot say
What women covet most. If you could tell
That secret to me, I'd requite you well."
"Give me your hand," she answered. "Swear me true
That whatsoever I next ask of you, 130
You'll do it if it lies within your might
And I'll enlighten you before the night."
"Granted, upon my honor," he replied.
"Then I dare boast, and with no empty pride,
Your life is safe," she told him. "Let me die
If the queen herself won't say the same as I.
Let's learn if the haughtiest of all who wear
A net or coverchief upon their hair
Will be so forward as to answer 'no'
To what I'll teach you. No more; let us go." 140
With that she whispered something in his ear,
And told him to be glad and have no fear.
When they had reached the court, the knight declared
That he had kept his day, and was prepared
To give his answer, standing for his life.
Many the wise widow, many the wife,
Many the maid who rallied to the scene,
And at the head as justice sat the queen.
Then silence was enjoined; the knight was told
In open court to say what women hold 150
Precious above all else. He did not stand
Dumb like a beast, but spoke up at command
And plainly offered them his answering word
In manly voice, so that the whole court heard.
"My liege and lady, most of all," said he,
"Women desire to have the sovereignty
And sit in rule and government above
Their husbands, and to have their way in love.

That is what most you want. Spare me or kill
As you may like; I stand here by your will." 160
  No widow, wife, or maid gave any token
Of contradicting what the knight had spoken.
He should not die; he should be spared instead;
He was worthy of his life, the whole court said.
  The old woman whom the knight met on the green
Sprang up at this. "My sovereign lady queen,
Before your court has risen, do me right!
It was I who taught this answer to the knight,
For which he pledged his honor in my hand,
Solemnly, that the first thing I demand, 170
He would do it, if it lay within his might.
Before the court I ask you, then, sir knight,
To take me," said the woman, "as your wife,
For well you know that I have saved your life.
Deny me, on your honor, if you can."
  "Alas," replied this miserable man,
"That was my promise, it must be confessed.
For the love of God, though, choose a new request!
Take all my wealth, and let my body be."
  "If that's your tune, then curse both you and me," 180
She said. "Though I am ugly, old, and poor,
I'll have, for all the metal and the ore
That under earth is hidden or lies above,
Nothing, except to be your wife and love."
  "My love? No, my damnation, if you can!
Alas," he said, "that any of my clan
Should be so miserably misallied!"
  All to no good; force overruled his pride,
And in the end he is constrained to wed,
And marries his old wife and goes to bed. 190
  Now some will charge me with an oversight
In failing to describe the day's delight,
The merriment, the food, the dress at least.
But I reply, there was no joy nor feast;
There was only sorrow and sharp misery.
He married her in private, secretly,
And all day after, such was his distress,
Hid like an owl from his wife's ugliness.
  Great was the woe this knight had in his head
When in due time they both were brought to bed. 200
He shuddered, tossed, and turned, and all the while
His old wife lay and waited with a smile.
"Is every knight so backward with a spouse?
Is it," she said, "a law in Arthur's house?
I am your love, your own, your wedded wife,
I am the woman who has saved your life.
I have never done you anything but right.
Why do you treat me this way the first night?

You must be mad, the way that you behave!
Tell me my fault, and as God's love can save, 210
I will amend it, truly, if I can."
"Amend it?" answered this unhappy man.
"It can never be amended, truth to tell.
You are so loathsome and so old as well,
And your low birth besides is such a cross
It is no wonder that I turn and toss.
God take my woeful spirit from my breast!"
"Is this," she said, "the cause of your unrest?"
"No wonder!" said the knight. "It truly is."
"Now sir," she said, "I could amend all this 220
Within three days, if it should please me to,
And if you deal with me as you should do.
"But since you speak of that nobility
That comes from ancient wealth and pedigree,
As if *that* constituted gentlemen,
I hold such arrogance not worth a hen!
The man whose virtue is pre-eminent,
In public and alone, always intent
On doing every generous act he can,
Take him—he is the greatest gentleman! 230
Christ wills that we should claim nobility
From him, not from old wealth or family.
Our elders left us all that they were worth
And through their wealth and blood we claim high birth,
But never, since it was beyond their giving,
Could they bequeath to us their virtuous living;
Although it first conferred on them the name
Of gentlemen, they could not leave that claim!
"Dante the Florentine on this was wise:
'Frail is the branch on which man's virtues rise'— 240
Thus runs his rhyme—'God's goodness wills that we
Should claim from him alone nobility.'[3]
Thus from our elders we can only claim
Such temporal things as men may hurt and maim.
"It is clear enough that true nobility
Is not bequeathed along with property,
For many a lord's son does a deed of shame
And yet, God knows, enjoys his noble name.
But though descended from a noble house
And elders who were wise and virtuous, 250
If he will not follow his elders, who are dead,
But leads, himself, a shameful life instead,
He is not noble, be he duke or earl.
It is the churlish deed that makes the churl.
And therefore, my dear husband, I conclude
That though my ancestors were rough and rude,

[3]*Purgatory,* Canto VII.

Yet may Almighty God confer on me
The grace to live, as I hope, virtuously.
Call me of noble blood when I begin
To live in virtue and to cast out sin. 260
"As for my poverty, at which you grieve,
Almighty God in whom we all believe
In willful poverty chose to lead his life,
And surely every man and maid and wife
Can understand that Jesus, heaven's king,
Would never choose a low or vicious thing.
A poor and cheerful life is nobly led;
So Seneca and others have well said.
The man so poor he doesn't have a stitch,
If he thinks himself repaid, I count him rich. 270
He that is covetous, he is the poor man,
Pining to have the things he never can.
It is of cheerful mind, true poverty.
Juvenal[4] says about it happily:
'The poor man as he goes along his way
And passes thieves is free to sing and play.'
Poverty is a good we loathe, a great
Reliever of our busy worldly state,
A great amender also of our minds
As he that patiently will bear it finds. 280
And poverty, for all it seems distressed,
Is a possession no one will contest.
Poverty, too, by bringing a man low,
Helps him the better both God and self to know.
Poverty is a glass where we can see
Which are our true friends, as it seems to me.
So, sir, I do not wrong you on this score;
Reproach me with my poverty no more.
"Now, sir, you tax me with my age; but, sir,
You gentlemen of breeding all aver 290
That men should not despise old age, but rather
Grant an old man respect, and call him 'father.'
"If I am old and ugly, as you have said,
You have less fear of being cuckolded,
For ugliness and age, as all agree,
Are notable guardians of chastity.
But since I know in what you take delight,
I'll gratify your worldly appetite.
"Choose now, which of two courses you will try:
To have me old and ugly till I die 300
But evermore your true and humble wife,
Never displeasing you in all my life,
Or will you have me rather young and fair
And take your chances on who may repair

[4]Roman poet (about 60–140 A.D.). The reference is to his *Satires,* X.

Either to your house on account of me
Or to some other place, it well may be.
Now make your choice, whichever you prefer."
  The knight took thought, and sighed, and said to her
At last, "My love and lady, my dear wife,
In your wise government I put my life. 310
Choose for yourself which course will best agree
With pleasure and honor, both for you and me.
I do not care, choose either of the two;
I am content, whatever pleases you."
  "Then have I won from you the sovereignty,
Since I may choose and rule at will?" said she.
  He answered, "That is best, I think, dear wife."
  "Kiss me," she said. "Now we are done with strife,
For on my word, I will be both to you,
That is to say, fair, yes, and faithful too. 320
May I die mad unless I am as true
As ever wife was since the world was new.
Unless I am as lovely to be seen
By morning as an empress or a queen
Or any lady between east and west,
Do with my life or death as you think best.
Lift up the curtain, see what you may see."
  And when the knight saw what had come to be
And knew her as she was, so young, so fair,
His joy was such that it was past compare. 330
He took her in his arms and gave her kisses
A thousand times on end; he bathed in blisses.
And she obeyed him also in full measure
In everything that tended to his pleasure.
  And so they lived in full joy to the end.
And now to all us women may Christ send
Submissive husbands, full of youth in bed,
And grace to outlive all the men we wed.
And I pray Jesus to cut short the lives
Of those who won't be governed by their wives; 340
And old, ill-tempered niggards who hate expense,
God promptly bring them down with pestilence!

WORDS OF THE HOST TO THE PARDONER

"Now my fine friend," he said, "you Pardoner,
Be quick, tell us a tale of mirth or fun."[1]
  "By St. Ninian," he said, "it shall be done,
But at this tavern here, before my tale,
I'll just go in and have some bread and ale."

[1] The Host, having heard a sad tale from the Physician, wants the Pardoner to tell a merrier one. The travelers are at a tavern.

The proper pilgrims in our company
Cried quickly, "Let him speak no ribaldry!
Tell us a moral tale, one to make clear
Some lesson to us, and we'll gladly hear."
"Just as you wish," he said. "But I must think
Of something edifying while I drink."

PROLOGUE TO THE PARDONER'S TALE

"In churches," said the Pardoner, "when I preach,
I use, milords, a lofty style of speech
And ring it out as roundly as a bell,
Knowing by rote all that I have to tell.
My text is ever the same, and ever was:
Radix malorum est cupiditas.[2]
"First I inform them whence I come; that done,
I then display my papal bulls,[3] each one.
I show my license first, my body's warrant,
Sealed by the bishop, for it would be abhorrent 10
If any man made bold, though priest or clerk,
To interrupt me in Christ's holy work.
And after that I give myself full scope.
Bulls in the name of cardinal and pope,
Of bishops and of patriarchs I show.
I say in Latin some few words or so
To spice my sermon; it flavors my appeal
And stirs my listeners to greater zeal.
Then I display my cases made of glass
Crammed to the top with rags and bones. They pass 20
For relics[4] with all the people in the place.
I have a shoulder bone in a metal case,
Part of a sheep owned by a holy Jew.
'Good men,' I say, 'heed what I'm telling you:
Just let this bone be dipped in any well
And if cow, calf, or sheep, or ox should swell
From eating a worm, or by a worm be stung,
Take water from this well and wash its tongue
And it is healed at once. And furthermore
Of scab and ulcers and of every sore 30
Shall every sheep be cured, and that straightway,
That drinks from the same well. Heed what I say:
If the good man who owns the beasts will go,
Fasting, each week, and drink before cockcrow
Out of this well, his cattle shall be brought
To multiply—that holy Jew so taught

[2] "Greed is the root of all evil," adapted from 1 Timothy 6:10.
[3] Documents. [4] That is, of saints or biblical personages.

Our elders—and his property increase.
"'Moreover, sirs, this bone cures jealousies.
Though into a jealous madness a man fell,
Let him cook his soup in water from this well, 40
He'll never, though for truth he knew her sin,
Suspect his wife again, though she took in
A priest, or even two of them or three.
"'Now here's a mitten that you all can see.
Whoever puts his hand in it shall gain,
When he sows his land, increasing crops of grain,
Be it wheat or oats, provided that he bring
His penny or so to make his offering.
"'There is one word of warning I must say,
Good men and women. If any here today 50
Has done a sin so horrible to name
He daren't be shriven[5] of it for the shame,
Or if any woman, young or old, is here
Who has cuckolded her husband, be it clear
They may not make an offering in that case
To these my relics; they have no power nor grace.
But any who is free of such dire blame,
Let him come up and offer in God's name
And I'll absolve him through the authority
That by the pope's bull has been granted me.' 60
"By such hornswoggling I've won, year by year,
A hundred marks[6] since being a pardoner.
I stand in my pulpit like a true divine,
And when the people sit I preach my line
To ignorant souls, as you have heard before,
And tell skullduggeries by the hundred more.
Then I take care to stretch my neck well out
And over the people I nod and peer about
Just like a pigeon perching on a shed.
My hands fly and my tongue wags in my head 70
So busily that to watch me is a joy.
Avarice is the theme that I employ
In all my sermons, to make the people free
In giving pennies—especially to me.
My mind is fixed on what I stand to win
And not at all upon correcting sin.
I do not care, when they are in the grave,
If souls go berry-picking that I could save.
Truth is that evil purposes determine,
And many a time, the origin of a sermon: 80
Some to please people and by flattery
To gain advancement through hypocrisy,

[5]Absolved of sins in the confessional.
[6]The equivalent today of thousands of dollars.

Some for vainglory, some again for hate.
For when I daren't fight otherwise, I wait
And give him a tongue-lashing when I preach.
No man escapes or gets beyond the reach
Of my defaming tongue, supposing he
Has done a wrong to my brethren or to me.
For though I do not tell his proper name,
People will recognize him all the same. 90
By sign and circumstance I let them learn.
Thus I serve those who have done us an ill turn.
Thus I spit out my venom under hue
Of sanctity, and seem devout and true!
"But to put my purpose briefly, I confess
I preach for nothing but for covetousness.
That's why my text is still and ever was
Radix malorum est cupiditas.
For by this text I can denounce, indeed,
The very vice I practice, which is greed. 100
But though that sin is lodged in my own heart,
I am able to make other people part
From avarice, and sorely to repent,
Though that is not my principal intent.
"Then I bring in examples, many a one,
And tell them many a tale of days long done.
Plain folk love tales that come down from of old.
Such things their minds can well report and hold.
Do you think that while I have the power to preach
And take in silver and gold for what I teach 110
I shall ever live in willful poverty?
No, no, that never was my thought, certainly.
I mean to preach and beg in sundry lands.
I won't do any labor with my hands,
Nor live by making baskets. I don't intend
To beg for nothing; that is not my end.
I won't ape the apostles; I must eat,
I must have money, wool, and cheese, and wheat,
Though I took it from the meanest wretch's tillage
Or from the poorest widow in a village, 120
Yes, though her children starved for want. In fine,
I mean to drink the liquor of the vine
And have a jolly wench in every town.
But, in conclusion, lords, I will get down
To business: you would have me tell a tale.
Now that I've had a drink of corny ale,
By God, I hope the thing I'm going to tell
Is one that you'll have reason to like well.
For though myself a very sinful man,
I can tell a moral tale, indeed I can, 130
One that I use to bring the profits in
While preaching. Now be still, and I'll begin."

THE PARDONER'S TALE

There was a company of young folk living
One time in Flanders, who were bent on giving
Their lives to follies and extravagances,
Brothels and taverns, where they held their dances
With lutes, harps, and guitars, diced at all hours,
And also ate and drank beyond their powers,
Through which they paid the devil sacrifice
In the devil's temple with their drink and dice,
Their abominable excess and dissipation.
They swore oaths that were worthy of damnation; 10
It was grisly to be listening when they swore.
The blessed body of our Lord they tore—
The Jews, it seemed to them, had failed to rend
His body enough—and each laughed at his friend
And fellow in sin. To encourage their pursuits
Came comely dancing girls, peddlers of fruits,
Singers with harps, bawds and confectioners
Who are the very devil's officers
To kindle and blow the fire of lechery
That is the follower of gluttony. 20
Witness the Bible, if licentiousness
Does not reside in wine and drunkenness!
Recall how drunken Lot, unnaturally,
With his two daughters lay unwittingly,
So drunk he had no notion what he did.[1]
Herod, the stories tell us, God forbid,
When full of liquor at his banquet board
Right at his very table gave the word
To kill the Baptist, John, though guiltless he.[2]
Seneca[3] says a good word, certainly. 30
He says there is no difference he can find
Between a man who has gone out of his mind
And one who carries drinking to excess,
Only that madness outlasts drunkenness.
O gluttony, first cause of mankind's fall,[4]
Of our damnation the cursed original
Until Christ bought us with his blood again!
How dearly paid for by the race of men
Was this detestable iniquity!
This whole world was destroyed through gluttony. 40
Adam our father and his wife also
From paradise to labor and to woe

[1] See Genesis 19:30–36.
[2] See the versions of the story in the gospels of Matthew (chapter 14) and Mark (chapter 6).
[3] A Roman writer of the first century.
[4] Because Adam and Eve sinned by eating a forbidden fruit.

Were driven for that selfsame vice, indeed.
As long as Adam fasted—so I read—
He was in heaven; but as soon as he
Devoured the fruit of that forbidden tree
Then he was driven out in sorrow and pain.
Of gluttony well ought we to complain!
Could a man know how many maladies
Follow indulgences and gluttonies 50
He would keep his diet under stricter measure
And sit at table with more temperate pleasure.
The throat is short and tender is the mouth,
And hence men toil east, west, and north, and south,
In earth, and air, and water—alas to think—
Fetching a glutton dainty meat and drink.
This is a theme, O Paul, that you well treat:
"Meat unto belly, and belly unto meat,
God shall destroy them both," as Paul has said.[5]
When a man drinks the white wine and the red— 60
This is a foul word, by my soul, to say,
And fouler is the deed in every way—
He makes his throat his privy through excess.
The Apostle[6] says, weeping for piteousness,
"There are many of whom I told you—at a loss
I say it, weeping—enemies of Christ's cross,
Whose belly is their god; their end is death."
O cursed belly! Sack of stinking breath
In which corruption lodges, dung abounds!
At either end of you come forth foul sounds. 70
Great cost it is to fill you, and great pain!
These cooks, how they must grind and pound and strain
And transform substance into accident[7]
To please your cravings, though exorbitant!
From the hard bones they knock the marrow out.
They'll find a use for everything, past doubt,
That down the gullet sweet and soft will glide.
The spiceries of leaf and root provide
Sauces that are concocted for delight,
To give a man a second appetite. 80
But truly, he whom gluttonies entice
Is dead, while he continues in that vice.
O drunken man, disfigured is your face,
Sour is your breath, foul are you to embrace!
You seem to mutter through your drunken nose
The sound of "Samson, Samson," yet God knows

[5] See 1 Corinthians 6:13.
[6] St. Paul. See Philippians 3:18–19.
[7] Philosophical terms; "substance" is what a thing really is, "accident" is a nonessential quality or property of it.

That Samson[8] never indulged himself in wine.
Your tongue is lost, you fall like a stuck swine,
And all the self-respect that you possess
Is gone, for of man's judgment, drunkenness 90
Is the very sepulcher and annihilation.
A man whom drink has under domination
Can never keep a secret in his head.
Now steer away from both the white and red,
And most of all from that white wine keep wide
That comes from Lepe. They sell it in Cheapside
And Fish Street.[9] It's a Spanish wine, and sly
To creep in other wines[10] that grow nearby,
And such a vapor it has that with three drinks
It takes a man to Spain; although he thinks 100
He is home in Cheapside, he is far away
At Lepe. Then "Samson, Samson" will he say!
By God himself, who is omnipotent,
All the great exploits in the Old Testament
Were done in abstinence, I say, and prayer.
Look in the Bible, you may learn it there.
Attila,[11] conqueror of many a place,
Died in his sleep in shame and in disgrace
Bleeding out of his nose in drunkenness.
A captain ought to live in temperateness! 110
And more than this, I say, remember well
The injunction that was laid on Lemuel—
Not Samuel, but Lemuel, I say!
Read in the Bible; in the plainest way
Wine is forbidden to judges and to kings.[12]
This will suffice; no more upon these things.
Now that I've shown what gluttony will do,
Now I will warn you against gambling, too;
Gambling, the very mother of low scheming,
Of lying and forswearing and blaspheming 120
Against Christ's name, of murder and waste as well
Alike of goods and time; and, truth to tell,
With honor and renown it cannot suit
To be held a common gambler by repute.
The higher a gambler stands in power and place,
The more his name is lowered in disgrace.
If a prince gambles, whatever his kingdom be,
In his whole government and policy
He is, in all the general estimation,
Considered so much less in reputation. 130

[8] The Old Testament hero. His story is told in Judges, chapters 13–16.
[9] Main streets in London.
[10] Be mixed with other wines.
[11] Attila the Hun, fifth-century invader of Europe.
[12] In Proverbs, 31:4, Lemuel's mother admonishes him, "It is not for kings to drink wine." Not to be confused, the Pardoner insists, with Samuel, another Old Testament figure.

Stilbon,[13] who was a wise ambassador,
From Lacedaemon once to Corinth bore
A mission of alliance. When he came
It happened that he found there at a game
Of hazard all the great ones of the land,
And so, as quickly as it could be planned,
He stole back, saying, "I will not lose my name
Nor have my reputation put to shame
Allying you with gamblers. You may send
Other wise emissaries to gain your end, 140
For by my honor, rather than ally
My countrymen to gamblers, I will die.
For you that are so gloriously renowned
Shall never with this gambling race be bound
By will of mine or treaty I prepare."
Thus did this wise philosopher declare.
Remember also how the Parthians'[14] lord
Sent King Demetrius, as the books record,
A pair of golden dice, by this proclaiming
His scorn, because that king was known for gaming, 150
And the king of Parthia therefore held his crown
Devoid of glory, value, or renown.
Lords can discover other means of play
More suitable to while the time away.
Now about oaths I'll say a word or two,
Great oaths and false oaths, as the old books do.
Great swearing is a thing abominable,
And false oaths yet more reprehensible.
Almighty God forbade swearing at all,
Matthew be witness; but specially I call 160
The holy Jeremiah on this head.
"Swear thine oaths truly, do not lie," he said.
"Swear under judgment, and in righteousness."[15]
But idle swearing is a great wickedness.
Consult and see, and he that understands
In the first table of the Lord's commands
Will find the second of his commandments this:
"Take not the Lord's name idly or amiss."
If a man's oaths and curses are extreme,
Vengeance shall find his house, both roof and beam. 170
"By the precious heart of God," and "By his nails"—
"My chance is seven, by Christ's blood at Hailes,[16]

[13] This story and the following one about Demetrius are from a book by John of Salisbury, a learned English scholar of the twelfth century. Lacedaemon (Sparta) and Corinth were city-states of ancient Greece.

[14] Parthia was an ancient region in what is now Iran.

[15] In the gospel of Matthew, 5:34 (part of the Sermon on the Mount), Christ says, "Swear not at all." See also Jeremiah 4:2.

[16] In the dice game of hazard, a player's "chance" was roughly the equivalent of his "point" in modern craps. Hailes was an English abbey supposed to possess a relic of Christ's blood.

Yours five and three." "Cheat me, and if you do,
By God's arms, with this knife I'll run you through!"—
Such fruit comes from the bones, that pair of bitches:
Oaths broken, treachery, murder. For the riches
Of Christ's love, give up curses, without fail,
Both great and small!—Now, sirs, I'll tell my tale.
These three young roisterers of whom I tell
Long before prime[17] had rung from any bell 180
Were seated in a tavern at their drinking,
And as they sat, they heard a bell go clinking
Before a corpse being carried to his grave.
One of these roisterers, when he heard it, gave
An order to his boy: "Go out and try
To learn whose corpse is being carried by.
Get me his name, and get it right. Take heed."
"Sir," said the boy, "there isn't any need.
I learned before you came here, by two hours.
He was, it happens, an old friend of yours, 190
And all at once, there on his bench upright
As he was sitting drunk, he was killed last night.
A sly thief, Death men call him, who deprives
All the people in this country of their lives,
Came with his spear and smiting his heart in two
Went on his business with no more ado.
A thousand have been slaughtered by his hand
During this plague. And, sir, before you stand
Within his presence, it should be necessary,
It seems to me, to know your adversary. 200
Be evermore prepared to meet this foe.
My mother taught me thus; that's all I know."
"Now by St. Mary," said the innkeeper,
"This child speaks truth. Man, woman, laborer,
Servant, and child the thief has slain this year
In a big village a mile or more from here.
I think it is his place of habitation.
It would be wise to make some preparation
Before he brought a man into disgrace."
"God's arms!" this roisterer said. "So that's the case! 210
Is it so dangerous with this thief to meet?
I'll look for him by every path and street,
I vow it, by God's holy bones! Hear me,
Fellows of mine, we are all one, we three.
Let each of us hold up his hand to the other
And each of us become his fellow's brother.
We'll slay this Death, who slaughters and betrays.
He shall be slain whose hand so many slays,
By the dignity of God, before tonight!"
The three together set about to plight 220

[17]An early morning hour, between seven and nine.

Their oaths to live and die each for the other
Just as though each had been to each born brother.
And in their drunken frenzy up they get
And toward the village off at once they set
Which the innkeeper had spoken of before,
And many were the grisly oaths they swore.
They rent Christ's precious body limb from limb—
Death shall be dead, if they lay hands on him!
When they had hardly gone the first half mile,
Just as they were about to cross a stile, 230
An old man, poor and humble, met them there.
The old man greeted them with a meek air
And said, "God bless you, lords, and be your guide."
"What's this?" the proudest of the three replied.
"Old beggar, I hope you meet with evil grace!
Why are you all wrapped up except your face?
What are you doing alive so many a year?"
The old man at these words began to peer
Into this gambler's face. "Because I can,
Though I should walk to India, find no man," 240
He said, "in any village or any town,
Who for my age is willing to lay down
His youth. So I must keep my old age still
For as long a time as it may be God's will.
Nor will Death take my life from me, alas!
Thus like a restless prisoner I pass
And on the ground, which is my mother's gate,
I walk and with my staff both early and late
I knock and say, 'Dear mother, let me in!
See how I vanish, flesh, and blood, and skin! 250
Alas, when shall my bones be laid to rest?
I would exchange with you my clothing chest,
Mother, that in my chamber long has been
For an old haircloth rag to wrap me in.'
And yet she still refuses me that grace.
All white, therefore, and withered is my face.
"But, sirs, you do yourselves no courtesy
To speak to an old man so churlishly
Unless he had wronged you either in word or deed.
As you yourselves in Holy Writ may read, 260
'Before an aged man whose head is hoar
Men ought to rise.'[18] I counsel you, therefore,
No harm nor wrong here to an old man do,
No more than you would have men do to you
In your old age, if you so long abide.
And God be with you, whether you walk or ride!
I must go yonder where I have to go."

[18]See Leviticus 19:32.

"No, you old beggar, by St. John, not so,"
Said another of these gamblers. "As for me,
By God, you won't get off so easily! 270
You spoke just now of that false traitor, Death,
Who in this land robs all our friends of breath.
Tell where he is, since you must be his spy,
Or you will suffer for it, so say I
By God and by the holy sacrament.
You are in league with him, false thief, and bent
On killing us young folk, that's clear to my mind."
"If you are so impatient, sirs, to find
Death," he replied, "turn up this crooked way,
For in that grove I left him, truth to say, 280
Beneath a tree, and there he will abide.
No boast of yours will make him run and hide.
Do you see that oak tree? Just there you will find
This Death, and God, who bought again mankind,
Save and amend you!" So said this old man;
And promptly each of these three gamblers ran
Until he reached the tree, and there they found
Florins of fine gold, minted bright and round,
Nearly eight bushels of them, as they thought.
And after Death no longer then they sought. 290
Each of them was so ravished at the sight,
So fair the florins glittered and so bright,
That down they sat beside the precious hoard.
The worst of them, he uttered the first word.
"Brothers," he told them, "listen to what I say.
My head is sharp, for all I joke and play.
Fortune has given us this pile of treasure
To set us up in lives of ease and pleasure.
Lightly it comes, lightly we'll make it go.
God's precious dignity! Who was to know 300
We'd ever tumble on such luck today?
If we could only carry this gold away,
Home to my house, or either one of yours—
For well you know that all this gold is ours—
We'd touch the summit of felicity.
But still, by daylight that can hardly be.
People would call us thieves, too bold for stealth,
And they would have us hanged for our own wealth.
It must be done by night, that's our best plan,
As prudently and slyly as we can. 310
Hence my proposal is that we should all
Draw lots, and let's see where the lot will fall,
And the one of us who draws the shortest stick
Shall run back to the town, and make it quick,
And bring us bread and wine here on the sly,
And two of us will keep a watchful eye

Over this gold; and if he doesn't stay
Too long in town, we'll carry this gold away
By night, wherever we all agree it's best."
One of them held the cut out in his fist 320
And had them draw to see where it would fall,
And the cut fell on the youngest of them all.
At once he set off on his way to town,
And the very moment after he was gone
The one who urged this plan said to the other:
"You know that by sworn oath you are my brother.
I'll tell you something you can profit by.
Our friend has gone, that's clear to any eye,
And here is gold, abundant as can be,
That we propose to share alike, we three. 330
But if I worked it out, as I could do,
So that it could be shared between us two,
Wouldn't that be a favor, a friendly one?"
The other answered, "How that can be done,
I don't quite see. He knows we have the gold.
What shall we do, or what shall he be told?"
"Will you keep the secret tucked inside your head?
And in a few words," the first scoundrel said,
"I'll tell you how to bring this end about."
"Granted," the other told him. "Never doubt, 340
I won't betray you, that you can believe."
"Now," said the first, "we are two, as you perceive,
And two of us must have more strength than one.
When he sits down, get up as if in fun
And wrestle with him. While you play this game
I'll run him through the ribs. You do the same
With your dagger there, and then this gold shall be
Divided, dear friend, between you and me.
Then all that we desire we can fulfill,
And both of us can roll the dice at will." 350
Thus in agreement these two scoundrels fell
To slay the third, as you have heard me tell.
The youngest, who had started off to town,
Within his heart kept rolling up and down
The beauty of these florins, new and bright.
"O Lord," he thought, "were there some way I might
Have all this treasure to myself alone,
There isn't a man who dwells beneath God's throne
Could live a life as merry as mine should be!"
And so at last the fiend, our enemy, 360
Put in his head that he could gain his ends
If he bought poison to kill off his friends.
Finding his life in such a sinful state,
The devil was allowed to seal his fate.
For it was altogether his intent
To kill his friends, and never to repent.

So off he set, no longer would he tarry,
Into the town, to an apothecary,
And begged for poison; he wanted it because
He meant to kill his rats; besides, there was 370
A polecat living in his hedge, he said,
Who killed his capons; and when he went to bed
He wanted to take vengeance, if he might,
On vermin that devoured him by night.
The apothecary answered, "You shall have
A drug that as I hope the Lord will save
My soul, no living thing in all creation,
Eating or drinking of this preparation
A dose no bigger than a grain of wheat,
But promptly with his death-stroke he shall meet. 380
Die, that he will, and in a briefer while
Than you can walk the distance of a mile,
This poison is so strong and virulent."
Taking the poison, off the scoundrel went,
Holding it in a box, and next he ran
To the neighboring street, and borrowed from a man
Three generous flagons. He emptied out his drug
In two of them, and kept the other jug
For his own drink; he let no poison lurk
In that! And so all night he meant to work 390
Carrying off the gold. Such was his plan,
And when he had filled them, this accursed man
Retraced his path, still following his design,
Back to his friends with his three jugs of wine.
But why dilate upon it any more?
For just as they had planned his death before,
Just so they killed him, and with no delay.
When it was finished, one spoke up to say:
"Now let's sit down and drink, and we can bury
His body later on. First we'll be merry," 400
And as he said the words, he took the jug
That, as it happened, held the poisonous drug,
And drank, and gave his friend a drink as well,
And promptly they both died. But truth to tell,
In all that Avicenna[19] ever wrote
He never described in chapter, rule, or note
More marvelous signs of poisoning, I suppose,
Than appeared in these two wretches at the close.
Thus they both perished for their homicide,
And thus the traitorous poisoner also died. 410
O sin accursed above all cursedness,
O treacherous murder, O foul wickedness,

[19]Arab philosopher, physician, and author of a medical textbook of the early eleventh century.

O gambling, lustfulness, and gluttony,
Traducer of Christ's name by blasphemy
And monstrous oaths, through habit and through pride!
Alas, mankind! Ah, how may it betide
That you to your Creator, he that wrought you
And even with his precious heart's blood bought you,
So falsely and ungratefully can live?
And now, good men, your sins may God forgive 420
And keep you specially from avarice!
My holy pardon will avail in this,
For it can heal each one of you that brings
His pennies, silver brooches, spoons, or rings.
Come, bow your head under this holy bull!
You wives, come offer up your cloth or wool!
I write your names here in my roll, just so.
Into the bliss of heaven you shall go!
I will absolve you here by my high power,
You that will offer, as clean as in the hour 430
When you were born. —Sirs, thus I preach. And now
Christ Jesus, our souls' healer, show you how
Within his pardon evermore to rest,
For that, I will not lie to you, is best.
But in my tale, sirs, I forgot one thing.
The relics and the pardons that I bring
Here in my pouch, no man in the whole land
Has finer, given me by the pope's own hand.
If any of you devoutly wants to offer
And have my absolution, come and proffer 440
Whatever you have to give. Kneel down right here,
Humbly, and take my pardon, full and clear,
Or have a new, fresh pardon if you like
At the end of every mile of road we strike,
As long as you keep offering ever newly
Good coins, not counterfeit, but minted truly.
Indeed it is an honor I confer
On each of you, an authentic pardoner
Going along to absolve you as you ride.
For in the country mishaps may betide— 450
One or another of you in due course
May break his neck by falling from his horse.
Think what security it gives you all
That in this company I chanced to fall
Who can absolve you each, both low and high,
When the soul, alas, shall from the body fly!
By my advice, our Host here shall begin,
For he's the man enveloped most by sin.
Come, offer first, Sir Host, and once that's done,
Then you shall kiss the relics, every one, 460
Yes, for a penny! Come, undo your purse!

"No, no," said he. "Then I should have Christ's curse!
I'll do nothing of the sort, for love or riches!
You'd make me kiss a piece of your old britches
And for a saintly relic make it pass
Although it had the tincture of your ass.
By the cross St. Helen[20] found in the Holy Land,
I wish I had your balls here in my hand
For relics! Cut'em off, and I'll be bound
If I don't help you carry them around. 470
I'll have the things enshrined in a hog's turd!"
The Pardoner did not answer; not a word,
He was so angry, could he find to say.
"Now," said our Host, "I will not try to play
With you, nor any other angry man."
Immediately the worthy Knight began,
When he saw that all the people laughed, "No more,
This has gone far enough. Now as before,
Sir Pardoner, be gay, look cheerfully,
And you, Sir Host, who are so dear to me, 480
Come, kiss the Pardoner, I beg of you,
And Pardoner, draw near, and let us do
As we've been doing, let us laugh and play."
And so they kissed, and rode along their way.

THE KNIGHT'S INTERRUPTION OF THE MONK'S TALE

"Stop!" cried the Knight.[1] "No more of this, good sir!
You have said plenty, and much more, for sure,
For only a little such lugubriousness
Is plenty for a lot of folk, I guess.
I say for me it is a great displeasure,
When men have wealth and comfort in good measure,
To hear how they have tumbled down the slope,
And the opposite is a solace and a hope,
As when a man begins in low estate
And climbs the ladder and grows fortunate, 10
And stands there firm in his prosperity.
That is a welcome thing, it seems to me,
And of such things it would be good to tell."
"Well said," our Host declared. "By St. Paul's bell,
You speak the truth; this Monk's tongue is too loud.
He told how fortune covered with a cloud—
I don't know what-all; and of tragedy
You heard just now, and it's no remedy,

[20] She was believed to have discovered the cross of Jesus about 200 years after the Crucifixion.

[1] The Monk, whom the Knight interrupts, has been narrating a long series of "tragedies," tales about the fall of eminent personages.

When things are over and done with, to complain.
Besides, as you have said, it is a pain 20
To hear of misery; it is distressing.
Sir Monk, no more, as you would have God's blessing.
This company is all one weary sigh.
Such talking isn't worth a butterfly,
For where's the amusement in it, or the game?
And so, Sir Monk, or Don Pierce by your name,
I beg you heartily, tell us something else.
Truly, but for the jingling of your bells
That from your bridle hang on every side,
By Heaven's King, who was born for us and died, 30
I should long since have tumbled down in sleep,
Although the mud had never been so deep,
And then you would have told your tale in vain;
For certainly, as these learned men explain,
When his audience have turned their backs away,
It doesn't matter what a man may say.
I know well I shall have the essence of it
If anything is told here for our profit.
A tale of hunting, sir, pray share with us."
"No," said the Monk, "I'll not be frivolous. 40
Let another tell a tale, as I have told."
Then spoke our Host, with a rude voice and bold,
And said to the Nun's Priest, "Come over here,
You priest, come hither, you Sir John, draw near!
Tell us a thing to make our spirits glad.
Be cheerful, though the jade you ride is bad.
What if your horse is miserable and lean?
If he will carry you, don't care a bean!
Keep up a joyful heart, and look alive."
"Yes, Host," he answered, "as I hope to thrive, 50
If I weren't merry, I know I'd be reproached."
And with no more ado his tale he broached,
And this is what he told us, every one,
This precious priest, this goodly man, Sir John.

THE NUN'S PRIEST'S TALE

Once a poor widow, aging year by year,
Lived in a tiny cottage that stood near
A clump of shade trees rising in a dale.
This widow, of whom I tell you in my tale,
Since the last day that she had been a wife
Had led a very patient, simple life.
She had but few possessions to content her.
By thrift and husbandry of what God sent her
She and two daughters found the means to dine.
She had no more than three well-fattened swine, 10

As many cows, and one sheep, Moll by name.
Her bower and hall were black from the hearth-flame
Where she had eaten many a slender meal.
No dainty morsel did her palate feel
And no sharp sauce was needed with her pottage.
Her table was in keeping with her cottage.
Excess had never given her disquiet.
Her only doctor was a moderate diet,
And exercise, and a heart that was contented.
If she did not dance, at least no gout prevented; 20
No apoplexy had destroyed her head.
She never drank wine, whether white or red.
She served brown bread and milk, loaves white or black,
Singed bacon, all this with no sense of lack,
And now and then an egg or two. In short,
She was a dairy woman of a sort.
She had a yard, on the inside fenced about
With hedges, and an empty ditch without,
In which she kept a cock, called Chanticleer.
In all the realm of crowing he had no peer. 30
His voice was merrier than the merry sound
Of the church organ grumbling out its ground
Upon a saint's day. Stouter was this cock
In crowing than the loudest abbey clock.
Of astronomy instinctively aware,
He kept the sun's hours with celestial care,
For when through each fifteen degrees it moved,
He crowed so that it couldn't be improved.
His comb, like a crenelated[1] castle wall,
Red as fine coral, stood up proud and tall. 40
His bill was black; like polished jet it glowed,
And he was azure-legged and azure-toed.
As lilies were his nails, they were so white;
Like burnished gold his hue, it shone so bright.
This cock had in his princely sway and measure
Seven hens to satisfy his every pleasure,
Who were his sisters and his sweethearts true,
Each wonderfully like him in her hue,
Of whom the fairest-feathered throat to see
Was fair Dame Partlet. Courteous was she, 50
Discreet, and always acted debonairly.
She was sociable, and bore herself so fairly,
Since the very time that she was seven nights old,
The heart of Chanticleer was in her hold
As if she had him locked up, every limb.
He loved her so that all was well with him.
It was a joy, when up the sun would spring,
To hear them both together sweetly sing,

[1]Having walls with notched openings at the top.

"My love has gone to the country, far away!"
For as I understand it, in that day 60
The animals and birds could sing and speak.
  Now as this cock, one morning at daybreak,
With each of the seven hens that he called spouse,
Sat on his perch inside the widow's house,
And next him fair Dame Partlet, in his throat
This Chanticleer produced a hideous note
And groaned like a man who is having a bad dream;
And Partlet, when she heard her husband scream,
Was all aghast, and said, "Soul of my passion,
What ails you that you groan in such a fashion? 70
You are always a sound sleeper. Fie, for shame!"
  And Chanticleer awoke and answered, "Dame,
Take no offense, I beg you, on this score.
I dreamt, by God, I was in a plight so sore
Just now, my heart still quivers from the fright.
Now God see that my dream turns out all right
And keep my flesh and body from foul seizure!
I dreamed I was strutting in our yard at leisure
When there I saw, among the weeds and vines,
A beast, he was like a hound, and had designs 80
Upon my person, and would have killed me dead.
His coat was not quite yellow, not quite red,
And both his ears and tail were tipped with black
Unlike the fur along his sides and back.
He had a small snout and a fiery eye.
His look for fear still makes me almost die.
This is what made me groan, I have no doubt."
  "For shame! Fie on you, faint heart!" she burst out.
"Alas," she said, "by the great God above,
Now you have lost my heart and all my love! 90
I cannot love a coward, as I'm blest!
Whatever any woman may protest,
We all want, could it be so, for our part,
Husbands who are wise and stout of heart,
No blabber, and no niggard, and no fool,
Nor afraid of every weapon or sharp tool,
No braggart either, by the God above!
How dare you say, for shame, to your true love
That there is anything you ever feared?
Have you no man's heart, when you have a beard? 100
Alas, and can a nightmare set you screaming?
God knows there's only vanity in dreaming!
Dreams are produced by such unseemly capers
As overeating; they come from stomach vapors
When a man's humors[2] aren't behaving right
From some excess. This dream you had tonight,

[2] The four substances in the body believed to determine personality types and states of health. Dame Partlet discusses two: choler (bile) and melancholy (black bile).

It comes straight from the superfluity
Of your red choler, certain as can be,
That causes people terror in their dreams
Of darts and arrows, and fire in red streams, 110
And of red beasts, for fear that they will bite,
Of little dogs, or of being in a fight;
As in the humor of melancholy lies
The reason why so many a sleeper cries
For fear of a black bull or a black bear
Or that black devils have him by the hair.
Through other humors also I could go
That visit many a sleeping man with woe,
But I will finish as quickly as I can.
"Cato, that has been thought so wise a man, 120
Didn't he tell us, 'Put no stock in dreams'?
Now, sir," she said, "when we fly down from our beams,
For God's sake, go and take a laxative!
On my salvation, as I hope to live,
I give you good advice, and no mere folly:
Purge both your choler and your melancholy!
You mustn't wait or let yourself bog down,
And since there is no druggist in this town
I shall myself prescribe for what disturbs
Your humors, and instruct you in the herbs 130
That will be good for you. For I shall find
Here in our yard herbs of the proper kind
For purging you both under and above.
Don't let this slip your mind, for God's own love!
Yours is a very choleric complexion.
When the sun is in the ascendant, my direction
Is to beware those humors that are hot.
Avoid excess of them; if you should not,
I'll bet a penny, as a true believer,
You'll die of ague, or a tertian fever. 140
A day or so, if you do as I am urging,
You shall have worm-digestives, before purging
With fumitory or with hellebore
Or other herbs that grow here by the score;
With caper-spurge, or with the goat-tree berry
Or the ground-ivy, found in our yard so merry.
Peck 'em up just as they grow, and eat 'em in!
Be cheerful, husband, by your father's kin!
Don't worry about a dream. I say no more."
"Madame," he answered, "thanks for all your lore. 150
But still, to speak of Cato, though his name
For wisdom has enjoyed so great a fame,
And though he counseled us there was no need
To be afraid of dreams, by God, men read
Of many a man of more authority
Than this Don Cato could pretend to be

Who in old books declare the opposite,
And by experience they have settled it,
That dreams are omens and prefigurations
Both of good fortune and of tribulations 160
That life and its vicissitudes present.
This question leaves no room for argument.
The very upshot makes it plain, indeed.
"One of the greatest authors that men read
Informs us that two fellow travelers went,
Once on a time, and with the best intent,
Upon a pilgrimage, and it fell out
They reached a town where there was such a rout
Of people, and so little lodging space,
They could not find even the smallest place 170
Where they could both put up. So, for that night,
These pilgrims had to do as best they might,
And since they must, they parted company.
Each of them went off to his hostelry
And took his lodging as his luck might fall.
Among plow oxen in a farmyard stall
One of them found a place, though it was rough.
His friend and fellow was lodged well enough
As his luck would have it, or his destiny
That governs all us creatures equally. 180
And so it happened, long before the day,
He had a dream as in his bed he lay.
He dreamed that his parted friend began to call
And said, 'Alas, for in an ox's stall
This night I shall be murdered where I lie.
Come to my aid, dear brother, or I die.
Come to me quickly, come in haste!' he said.
He started from his sleep, this man, for dread,
But when he had wakened, he rolled back once more
And on this dream of his he set no store. 190
As a vain thing he dismissed it, unconcerned.
Twice as he slept that night the dream returned,
And still another and third time his friend
Came in a dream and said, 'I have met my end!
Look on my wounds! They are bloody, deep, and wide.
Now rise up early in the morningtide
And at the west gate of the town,' said he,
'A wagon with a load of dung you'll see.
Have it arrested boldly. Do as bidden,
For underneath you'll find my body hidden. 200
My money caused my murder, truth to tell,'
And told him each detail of how he fell,
With piteous face, and with a bloodless hue.
And do not doubt it, he found the dream was true,
For on the morrow, as soon as it was day,
To the place where his friend had lodged he made his way,

And no sooner did he reach this ox's stall
Than for his fellow he began to call.
"Promptly the stableman replied, and said,
'Your friend is gone, sir. He got out of bed 210
And left the town as soon as day began.'
"At last suspicion overtook this man.
Remembering his dreams, he would not wait,
But quickly went and found at the west gate,
Being driven to manure a farmer's land
As it might seem, a dung cart close at hand
That answered the description every way,
As you yourself have heard the dead man say.
And he began to shout courageously
For law and vengeance on this felony. 220
'My friend was killed this very night! He lies
Flat in this load of dung, with staring eyes.
I call on those who should keep rule and head,
The magistrates and governors here,' he said.
'Alas! Here lies my fellow, done to death!'
"Why on this tale should I waste further breath?
The people sprang and flung the cart to ground
And in the middle of the dung they found
The dead man, while his murder was still new.
"O blessed God, thou art so just and true, 230
Murder, though secret, ever thou wilt betray!
Murder will out, we see it day by day.
Murder so loathsome and abominable
To God is, who is just and reasonable,
That he will never suffer it to be
Concealed, though it hide a year, or two, or three.
Murder will out; to this point it comes down.
"Promptly the magistrates who ruled that town
Have seized the driver, and put him to such pain,
And the stableman as well, that under strain 240
Of torture they were both led to confess
And hanged by the neck-bone for their wickedness.
"Here's proof enough that dreams are things to dread!
And in the same book I have also read,
In the very chapter that comes right after this—
I don't speak idly, by my hopes of bliss—
Two travelers who for some reason planned
To cross the ocean to a distant land
Found that the wind, by an opposing fate,
Blew contrary, and forced them both to wait 250
In a fair city by a harborside.
But one day the wind changed, toward eventide,
And blew just as it suited them instead.
Cheerfully these travelers went to bed
And planned to sail the first thing in the morning.
But to one of them befell a strange forewarning

And a great marvel. While asleep he lay,
He dreamed a curious dream along toward day.
He dreamed that a man appeared at his bedside
And told him not to sail, but wait and bide.
'Tomorrow,' he told the man, 'if you set sail, 260
You shall be drowned. I have told you my whole tale.'
He woke, and of this warning he had met
He told his friend, and begged him to forget
His voyage, and to wait that day and bide.
His friend, who was lying close at his bedside,
Began to laugh, and told him in derision,
'I am not so flabbergasted by a vision
As to put off my business for such cause.
I do not think your dream is worth two straws!
For dreams are but a vain absurdity. 270
Of apes and owls and many a mystery
People are always dreaming, in a maze
Of things that never were seen in all their days
And never shall be. But I see it's clear
You mean to waste your time by waiting here.
I'm sorry for that, God knows; and so good day.'
With this he took his leave and went his way.
But not the half his course had this man sailed—
I don't know why, nor what it was that failed—
When by an accident the hull was rent 280
And ship and man under the water went
In full view of the vessels alongside
That had put out with them on the same tide.
Now then, fair Partlet, whom I love so well,
From old examples such as these I tell
You may see that none should give too little heed
To dreams; for I say seriously, indeed,
That many a dream is too well worth our dread.
"Yes, in St. Kenelm's life I have also read—
He was the son of Cynewulf, the king 290
Of Mercia—how this Kenelm dreamed a thing.
One day, as the time when he was killed drew near,
He saw his murder in a dream appear.
His nurse explained his dream in each detail,
And warned him to be wary without fail
Of treason; yet he was but seven years old,
And therefore any dream he could but hold
Of little weight, in heart he was so pure.
I'd give my shirt, by God, you may be sure,
If you had read his story through like me! 300
"Moreover, Partlet, I tell you truthfully,
Macrobius[3] writes—and by his book we know
The African vision of great Scipio—
Confirming dreams, and holds that they may be

[3]A fifth-century author of a commentary on Cicero's *Dream of Scipio.*

Forewarnings of events that men shall see.
Again, I beg, look well at what is meant
By the Book of Daniel in the Old Testament,
Whether *he* held that dreams are vanity!
Read also about Joseph. You shall see 310
That dreams, or some of them—I don't say all—
Warn us of things that afterward befall.
Think of the king of Egypt, Don Pharaoh;
Of his butler and his baker think also,
Whether they found that dreams have no result.[4]
Whoever will search through kingdoms and consult
Their histories reads many a wondrous thing
Of dreams. What about Croesus, Lydian king—
Didn't he dream he was sitting on a tree,
Which meant he would be hanged? Andromache, 320
The woman who was once great Hector's wife,
On the day that Hector was to lose his life,
The very night before his blood was spilled
She dreamed of how her husband would be killed
If he went out to battle on that day.
She warned him; but he would not heed nor stay.
In spite of her he rode out on the plain,
And by Achilles he was promptly slain.
But all that story is too long to tell,
And it is nearly day. I must not dwell 330
Upon this matter. Briefly, in conclusion,
I say this dream will bring me to confusion
And mischief of some sort. And furthermore,
On laxatives, I say, I set no store,
For they are poisonous, I'm sure of it.
I do not trust them! I like them not one bit!
"Now let's talk cheerfully, and forget all this.
My pretty Partlet, by my hope of bliss,
In one thing God has sent me ample grace
For when I see the beauty of your face, 340
You are so scarlet-red about the eye,
It is enough to make my terrors die.
For just as true as *In principio*
Mulier est hominis confusio—[5]
And Madame, what this Latin means is this:
'Woman is man's whole comfort and true bliss'—
When I feel you soft at night, and I beside you,
Although it's true, alas, I cannot ride you
Because our perch is built so narrowly,
I am then so full of pure felicity 350
That I defy whatever sort of dream!"

[4] See Genesis, chapters 40–41. Joseph, imprisoned in Egypt, won his freedom by interpreting accurately the dreams of Pharaoh's butler and baker and later Pharaoh's own dreams.
[5] Literally, "In the beginning, woman is the ruin of man."

And day being come, he flew down from the beam,
And with him his hens fluttered, one and all;
And with a "cluck, cluck" he began to call
His wives to where a kernel had been tossed.
He was a prince, his fears entirely lost.
The morning had not passed the hour of prime
When he treaded Partlet for the twentieth time.
Grim as a lion he strolled to and fro,
And strutted only on his either toe.
He would not deign to set foot on the ground. 360
"Cluck, cluck," he said, whenever he had found
A kernel, and his wives came running all.
Thus royal as a monarch in his hall
I leave to his delights this Chanticleer,
And presently the sequel you shall hear.
After the month in which the world began,[6]
The month of March, when God created man,
Had passed, and when the season had run through
Since March began just thirty days and two, 370
It happened that Chanticleer, in all his pride,
While his seven hens were walking by his side,
Lifted his eyes, beholding the bright sun,
Which in the sign of Taurus had then run
Twenty and one degrees and somewhat more,
And knew by instinct, not by learned lore,
It was the hour of prime. He raised his head
And crowed with lordly voice. "The sun," he said,
"Forty and one degrees and more in height
Has climbed the sky. Partlet, my world's delight, 380
Hear all these birds, how happily they sing,
And see the pretty flowers, how they spring.
With solace and with joy my spirits dance!"
But suddenly he met a sore mischance,
For in the end joys ever turn to woes.
Quickly the joys of earth are gone, God knows,
And could a rhetorician's art indite it,
He would be on solid ground if he should write it,
In a chronicle, as true notoriously!
Now every wise man, listen well to me. 390
This story is as true, I undertake,
As the very book of Lancelot of the Lake
On which the women set so great a store.
Now to my matter I will turn once more.
A sly iniquitous fox, with black-tipped ears,
Who had lived in the neighboring wood for some three years,
His fated fancy swollen to a height,
Had broken through the hedges that same night
Into the yard where in his pride sublime

[6]According to tradition, the creation occurred at the beginning of spring.

Chanticleer with his seven wives passed the time. 400
Quietly in a bed of herbs he lay
Till it was past the middle of the day,
Waiting his hour on Chanticleer to fall
As gladly do these murderers, one and all,
Who lie in wait, concealed, to murder men.
O murderer, lurking traitorous in your den!
O new Iscariot, second Ganelon,
False hypocrite, Greek Sinon,[7] who brought on
The utter woe of Troy and all her sorrow!
O Chanticleer, accursed be that morrow 410
When to the yard you flew down from the beams!
That day, as you were well warned in your dreams,
Would threaten you with dire catastrophe.
But that which God foresees must come to be,
As there are certain scholars who aver.
Bear witness, any true philosopher,
That in the schools there has been great altercation
Upon this question, and much disputation
By a hundred thousand scholars, man for man.
I cannot sift it down to the pure bran 420
As can the sacred Doctor, Augustine,
Or Boëthius, or Bishop Bradwardine,[8]
Whether God's high foreknowledge so enchains me
I needs must do a thing as it constrains me—
"Needs must"—that is, by plain necessity;
Or whether a free choice is granted me
To do it or not do it, either one,
Though God must know all things before they are done;
Or whether his foresight nowise can constrain
Except contingently, as some explain; 430
I will not labor such a high concern.
My tale is of a cock, as you shall learn,
Who took his wife's advice, to his own sorrow,
And walked out in the yard that fatal morrow.
Women have many times, as wise men hold,
Offered advice that left men in the cold.
A woman's counsel brought us first to woe
And out of Paradise made Adam go
Where he lived a merry life and one of ease.
But since I don't know whom I may displease 440
By giving women's words an ill report,
Pass over it; I only spoke in sport.

[7]Judas Iscariot betrayed Jesus; Ganelon is the traitor in *The Song of Roland;* Sinon, by means of the Trojan horse, betrayed the Trojans to the besieging Greeks (see Virgil's *Aeneid,* Book II).

[8]All three had discussed the notoriously difficult matter of reconciling God's foreknowledge with man's free will. Augustine (353–430), author of the *Confessions,* was one of the greatest Christian theologians; Boëthius (about 475–524) was a Roman who wrote *The Consolation of Philosophy,* one of the most influential works in the Middle Ages; Bradwardine was a theologian of Chaucer's own century.

There are books about it you can read or skim in,
And you'll discover what they say of women.
I'm telling you the cock's words, and not mine.
Harm in no woman at all can I divine.
  Merrily bathing where the sand was dry
Lay Partlet, with her sisters all near by,
And Chanticleer, as regal as could be,
Sang merrily as the mermaid in the sea; 450
For the *Physiologus*[9] itself declares
That they know how to sing the merriest airs.
And so it happened that as he fixed his eye
Among the herbs upon a butterfly,
He caught sight of this fox who crouched there low.
He felt no impulse then to strut or crow,
But cried "cucock!" and gave a fearful start
Like a man who has been frightened to the heart.
For instinctively, if he should chance to see
His opposite, a beast desires to flee, 460
Even the first time that it meets his eye.
  This Chanticleer, no sooner did he spy
The fox than promptly enough he would have fled.
But "Where are you going, kind sir?" the fox said.
"Are you afraid of me, who am your friend?
Truly, I'd be a devil from end to end
If I meant you any harm or villainy.
I have not come to invade your privacy.
In truth, the only reason that could bring
This visit of mine was just to hear you sing. 470
Beyond a doubt, you have as fine a voice
As any angel who makes heaven rejoice.
Also you have more feeling in your note
Than Boëthius,[10] or any tuneful throat.
Milord your father once—and may God bless
His soul—your noble mother too, no less,
Have been inside my house, to my great ease.
And verily, sir, I should be glad to please
You also. But for singing, I declare,
As I enjoy my eyes, that precious pair, 480
Save you, I never heard a man so sing
As your father did when night was on the wing.
Straight from the heart, in truth, came all his song,
And to make his voice more resonant and strong
He would strain until he shut his either eye,
So loud and lordly would he make his cry,
And stand up on his tiptoes therewithal
And stretch his neck till it grew long and small.
He had such excellent discretion, too,
That whether his singing, all the region through, 490

[9]A book about animals, including legendary ones.
[10]Boëthius, along with his other works, wrote a treatise on music.

Or his wisdom, there was no one to surpass.
I read in that old book, *Don Burnel the Ass,*[11]
Among his verses once about a cock
Hit on the leg by a priest who threw a rock
When he was young and foolish; and for this
He caused the priest to lose his benefice.
But no comparison, in all truth, lies
Between your father, so prudent and so wise,
And this other cock, for all his subtlety.
Sing, sir! Show me, for holy charity, 500
Can you imitate your father, that wise man?"
Blind to all treachery, Chanticleer began
To beat his wings, like one who cannot see
The traitor, ravished by his flattery.
Alas, you lords, about your court there slips
Many a flatterer with deceiving lips
Who can please you more abundantly, I fear,
Than he who speaks the plain truth to your ear.
Read in Ecclesiastes,[12] you will see
What flatterers are. Lords, heed their treachery! 510
This Chanticleer stood tiptoe at full height.
He stretched his neck, he shut his eyelids tight,
And he began to crow a lordly note.
The fox, Don Russell, seized him by the throat
At once, and on his back bore Chanticleer
Off toward his den that in the grove stood near,
For no one yet had threatened to pursue.
O destiny, that no man may eschew!
Alas, that he left his safe perch on the beams!
Alas, that Partlet took no stock in dreams! 520
And on a Friday happened this mischance!
Venus, whose pleasures make the whole world dance,
Since Chanticleer was ever your true servant,
And of your rites will all his power observant
For pleasure rather than to multiply,
Would you on Friday[13] suffer him to die?
Geoffrey,[14] dear master of the poet's art,
Who when your Richard perished by a dart
Made for your king an elegy so burning,
Why have I not your eloquence and learning 530
To chide, as you did, with a heart so filled,
Fridays? For on a Friday he was killed.

[11]A twelfth-century poem by Nigel Wireker. The cock took his revenge by crowing late, thus causing the priest to oversleep on the day when he was to have been ordained.

[12]The intended reference is apparently not to Ecclesiastes but to Ecclesiasticus (a book of the Roman Catholic Bible), 12:10ff, 27:26.

[13]Friday is Venus's day. (Compare the French for *Friday, vendredi.*)

[14]Geoffrey of Vinsauf, a twelfth-century author of a book on poetry. It includes as an example a poem, written in an elaborate style, about the death of King Richard the Lion-Hearted (Richard I).

Then should I show you how I could complain
For Chanticleer in all his fright and pain!
In truth, no lamentation ever rose,
No shriek of ladies when before its foes
Ilium fell, and Pyrrhus with drawn blade
Had seized King Priam by the beard and made
An end of him—the *Aeneid* tells the tale—[15]
Such as the hens made with their piteous wail 540
In their enclosure, seeing the dread sight
Of Chanticleer. But at the shrillest height
Shrieked Partlet. She shrieked louder than the wife
Of Hasdrubal, when her husband lost his life
And the Romans burned down Carthage; for her state
Of torment and of frenzy was so great
She willfully chose the fire for her part,
Leaped in, and burned herself with steadfast heart.
Unhappy hens, you shrieked as when for pity,
While the tyrant Nero put to flames the city 550
Of Rome, rang out the shriek of senators' wives
Because their husbands had all lost their lives;
This Nero put to death these innocent men.
But I will come back to my tale again.
Now this good widow and her two daughters heard
These woeful hens shriek when the crime occurred,
And sprang outdoors as quickly as they could
And saw the fox, who was making for the wood
Bearing this Chanticleer across his back.
"Help, help!" they cried. They cried, "Alas! Alack! 560
The fox, the fox!" and after him they ran,
And armed with clubs came running many a man.
Ran Coll the dog, and led a yelping band;
Ran Malkyn, with a distaff[16] in her hand;
Ran cow and calf, and even the very hogs,
By the yelping and the barking of the dogs
And men's and women's shouts so terrified
They ran till it seemed their hearts would burst inside;
They squealed like fiends in the pit, with none to still them.
The ducks quacked as if men were going to kill them. 570
The geese for very fear flew over the trees.
Out of the beehive came the swarm of bees.
Ah! Bless my soul, the noise, by all that's true,
So hideous was that Jack Straw's[17] retinue

[15]See Book II of Virgil's *Aeneid.* When the Greeks took Troy (Ilium), Pyrrhus, the son of Achilles, killed Priam, the Trojan king. The Nun's Priest goes on to compare the hens' lament over Chanticleer to the wailing when the Romans destroyed Carthage (second century B.C.) and when the emperor Nero supposedly burned Rome (A.D. 64).

[16]A long staff; part of a spinning wheel.

[17]In 1381, Jack Straw led into London a mob intent on killing foreigners.

Made never a hubbub that was half so shrill
Over a Fleming they were going to kill
As the clamor made that day over the fox.
They brought brass trumpets, and trumpets made of box,
Of horn, of bone, on which they blew and squeaked,
And those who were not blowing whooped and shrieked. 580
It seemed as if the very heavens would fall!
  Now hear me, you good people, one and all!
Fortune, I say, will suddenly override
Her enemy in his very hope and pride!
This cock, as on the fox's back he lay,
Plucked up his courage to speak to him and say,
"God be my help, sir, but I'd tell them all,
That is, if I were you, 'Plague on you fall!
Go back, proud fools! Now that I've reached the wood,
I'll eat the cock at once, for all the good 590
Your noise can do. Here Chanticleer shall stay.'"
  "Fine!" said the fox. "I'll do just what you say."
But the cock, as he was speaking, suddenly
Out of his jaws lurched expeditiously,
And flew at once high up into a tree.
And when the fox saw that the cock was free,
"Alas," he said, "alas, O Chanticleer!
Inasmuch as I have given you cause for fear
By seizing you and bearing you away,
I have done you wrong, I am prepared to say. 600
But, sir, I did it with no ill intent.
Come down, and I shall tell you what I meant.
So help me God, it's truth I'll offer you!"
  "No, no," said he. "We're both fools, through and through.
But curse my blood and bones for the chief dunce
If you deceive me oftener than once!
You shall never again by flattery persuade me
To sing and wink my eyes, by him that made me.
For he that willfully winks when he should see,
God never bless him with prosperity!" 610
  "Ah," said the fox, "with mischief may God greet
The man ungoverned, rash, and indiscreet
Who babbles when to hold his tongue were needful!"
  Such is it to be reckless and unheedful
And trust in flattery. But you who hold
That this is a mere trifle I have told,
Concerning only a fox, or a cock and hen,
Think twice, and take the moral, my good men!
For truly, of whatever is written, all
Is written for our doctrine, says St. Paul. 620
Then take the fruit, and let the chaff lie still.
Now, gracious God, if it should be your will,
As my Lord teaches, make us all good men
And bring us to your holy bliss! Amen.

Christine de Pizan

(1364–1430?)

"Who was it painted the lion, tell me who?" asks the Wife of Bath in Chaucer's *Canterbury Tales.* The Wife is thinking of an Aesopian fable in which a lion looks at a picture of a man killing a lion and remarks that if lions painted pictures, the roles might be reversed. Her point is that if books were written by women instead of elderly celibate clerics, the monotonous misogyny of medieval literature (of the sort that Jenkin, her fifth husband, infuriatingly read aloud) might be reversed. "By God," she goes on, "if women had only written stories / Like wits and scholars in their oratories, / They would have pinned on men more wickedness / Than the whole breed of Adam can redress."

It is a sentiment that Christine de Pizan, Chaucer's slightly younger contemporary, would have heartily endorsed. Only a few years after Chaucer wrote the Wife of Bath's Prologue, Christine was stung by her reading of a book by a dreary woman-hater named Mathéolus into breaking the long silence of medieval women and undertaking a sweeping universal history of women, defending her sex against the calumnies of the patriarchal tradition. *The Book of the City of Ladies* is an extraordinary production. It is both quintessentially of its age—in its allegorizing, cataloguing, and universalizing tendencies—and startlingly fresh in its tough, realistic treatment of feminist issues. After five centuries, it still has much to teach us.

Christine de Pizan was born in Venice. Both parents were from prominent Italian families. Her father was a noted physician and astrologer named Tommaso di Benvenuto da Pizzano (astrology was a respectable science in Christine's day, not very clearly differentiated from astronomy); her mother was a member of a well-known family named Mondino. When Christine was four, her family moved to Paris, where her father had accepted a position as court astrologer to King Charles V. Christine spent the rest of her life in France and thought of herself as a French writer.

Christine received some education from her father, against the wishes of her mother, apparently. When she was fifteen, she was married to a young man of her father's choosing, as was the custom. Her husband, about twenty-five years old, was Etienne de Castel, a young courtier who became secretary and notary to the king. The match was a happy one and produced three children. In 1390, however, after ten years of marriage, Castel suddenly died of a contagious disease. Pizzano had died three years before, after losing much of his fortune and suffering a long illness. The twenty-five-year-old widow was thus left with three children, a mother, and a niece to support. What money was left from her father's and husband's estates was tied up in litigation; it took fourteen years and large sums of money to settle her lawsuits.

Christine apparently resolved to earn her living by her pen. She launched into an intensive program of self-education, "like a child," she later wrote, "that one puts at first to studying his ABCs." She read ancient and then modern history, science, and finally poetry. During this period, in the early 1390s, she may also have worked in the book trade, as a manuscript copyist, according to a recent biographer. Throughout her life, she took an active interest in the physical format of her books, commissioning and overseeing their reproduction and illustration.

She had her first success as a writer around 1393, and by the end of the decade she was earning a dependable income from her work. She is thus often said to be the "first professional writer in Europe." Her writing falls into three periods. Between 1393 and 1400, she wrote mostly lyric poetry in the highly conventionalized forms popular at the time; these were eventually organized into three cycles of *ballades.* By 1400, she had turned her attention to longer, narrative poems. Several of these were fashionable "love debates," which described various lovers' dilemmas that were to be presented to a "court of love" for settlement. Others were more serious. *The Long Road of Learning* (1403) is a utopian dream-vision in which Christine visits the Court of Reason to learn who should rule a better world. *The Mutation of Fortune* (also 1403) traces the role of Fortune through universal history. Also around 1400, Christine began to turn more frequently to prose; the output of her last period consists almost exclusively of long prose works. These include a commissioned biography of King Charles V (1404), *The Book of the City of Ladies* (1405), *The Book of the Three Virtues* (1405), and a strange, semiautobiographical dream-vision called *Christine's Vision* (1405).

France was in turmoil during Christine's later years. Charles VI was mentally unstable, and several powerful nobles competed for control of the kingdom. War with England also threatened. Faced with such dangers, Christine entered a convent, apparently around 1418, and turned her attention to government and advice to princes: *The Book of the Body Politic* (1406–1407), *Feats of Arms and of Chivalry* (1410), and *The Book of Peace* (1414). For her last work, she returned to poetry in *The Tale of Joan of Arc* to celebrate Joan's victory at Orléans in 1429. Joan's miraculous career seemed to vindicate not only Christine's faith in France but her faith in heroic women as well. Apparently, Christine died before Joan was captured by the English and burned at the stake in 1431.

Christine de Pizan's masterpiece, among her voluminous writings, is *The Book of the City of Ladies.* It perhaps had its origins in an interesting literary controversy she engaged in between 1399 and 1403 called the "Debate of *The Romance of the Rose.*" *The Romance of the Rose* was an immensely long, immensely popular poem begun by Guillaume de Lorris around 1230 and completed by Jean de Meun in 1275–1280. It tells the story of the attempt of Amant ("lover") to pick a beautiful Rose, guarded by various allegorical figures: Danger, Jealousy, and the like. Guillaume de Lorris's section is innocuous enough, but Jean de Meun's continuation is full of attacks on women. Christine had objected to Jean de Meun's slanders in *Cupid's Letter* (1399), but the debate really started in 1401, when one of the king's secretaries named Jean de Montreuil wrote an open letter to Christine praising Jean de Meun and rejecting her criticism. Christine replied, and before the debate ended more than twenty letters had been exchanged and several other people had entered the debate, including Jean Gerson, the chancellor of the University of Paris (on Christine's side) and Gontier Gol, another of the king's secretaries (on Jean de Montreuil's). The terms of the controversy were fairly complex, involving the literary merits of Jean de Meun's poem and its effect on public morality as well as its treatment of women, but it was the issue of misogyny that most interested Christine and that was to concern her two years later in *The Book of the City of Ladies.*

The Book of the City of Ladies is cast in one of the Middle Ages' favorite forms: the dream-vision. After a short prologue, in which Christine broods about an attack on women she has just read, a strange light appears in her room. Shuddering, "as if wakened from sleep," she lifts her head to see three crowned ladies standing before her: Reason, Rectitude, and Justice. The rest of the book is devoted to the building of the City of Ladies under the instruction of these three ladies. Or perhaps the book is an anti-dream-vision. Christine says that she felt "*as if* wakened from sleep," not that she *was* wakened. (In dream-visions, falling asleep is ordinarily described as "waking" into a dream.) She may thus be distinguishing her work from *The Romance of the Rose,* in which Amant does wake into his dream of the Rose, and suggesting that her book is truer than the *Romance.* The basic metaphor of the book—the building of a verbal, conceptual city—derives from St. Augustine's *City of God.* The City of Ladies is not meant to rival the City of God, of course, but the echo of Augustine's title and the personifications of virtue that preside over the building of the city are probably meant to place the whole enterprise within a Christian context. Christine echoes, too, the most famous dream-vision of the Middle Ages, the *Divine Comedy,* which she was among the first to introduce into France. The visionary experience, like Dante's, is presented as a response to confusion and discouragement, and the three feminine guides may owe something to the three ladies who watch over Dante's pilgrimage.

The most immediate source for *The Book of the City of Ladies,* however, is Boccaccio's *Concerning Famous Women,* a compendium of sketches of famous women, both good and bad, starting with Eve and ending with Boccaccio's contemporary, Johanna of Naples, Queen of Sicily, but principally drawn from mythology and antiquity. Christine draws about three-fourths of her examples from Boccaccio. Her treatment of them, however, is completely different. For one thing, she treats only good women; for another, she goes out of her way to present pagan and Christian, ancient and contemporary women together, whereas Boccaccio kept them sharply separate.

The third part of *The Book of the City of Ladies,* presided over by Justice, is given over to a series of lives of female saints, climaxed by the life of Christine's own name-saint. It is given here as an example of a very widespread and popular medieval literary form.

Christine, it hardly need be pointed out, is not a typical feminist in the modern sense. She never questions the medieval hierarchical social order; she merely wants women to hold an honored place within it. She also, as the climactic inclusion of the life of St. Christine demonstrates, remains firmly within a religious frame of reference. But she clearly is a feminist, if a medieval one. In her work, and preeminently in *The Book of the City of Ladies,* we hear a voice otherwise largely silenced in medieval literature: the voice of a woman.

FURTHER READING: Much the fullest and best modern treatment in English of Christine de Pizan is Charity Cannon Willard's critical biography, *Christine de Pizan: Her Life and Works,* 1984. A more popularly written biography is Enid McLeod, *The Order of the Rose: The Life and Ideas of Christine de Pizan,* 1976. An excellent short critical overview is Earl Jeffrey Richards' introduction to his translation of *The Book of the City of Ladies,* 1982. A thoughtful treatment of Christine's feminism is F. Douglas

Kelly, "Reflections on the Role of Christine de Pisan as a Feminist Writer," *Sub-Stances* 2 (1972), 63–71. A good collection of essays on the same topic is *Ideals for Women in the Works of Christine de Pizan,* ed. Diane Bornstein, 1981. Bibliographies include Edith Yenal, *Christine de Pisan: A Bibliography of Writings by Her and About Her,* 1982; and Angus J. Kennedy, *Christine de Pizan: A Bibliographical Guide,* 1984. For a survey of fifteen women authors of the Middle Ages, including excerpts from their works and succinct discussions of them, see *Medieval Women Writers,* ed. with Introduction by Katharina M. Wilson, 1984; the section on Christine de Pizan is by Charity Cannon Willard. Also illuminating is Maureen Quilligan, *The Allegory of Female Authority: Christine de Pizan's Cité des Dames,* 1991.

from *THE BOOK OF THE CITY OF LADIES*

Translated by Earl Jeffrey Richards

HERE BEGINS THE BOOK OF THE CITY OF LADIES, WHOSE FIRST CHAPTER TELLS WHY AND FOR WHAT PURPOSE THIS BOOK WAS WRITTEN.

One day as I was sitting alone in my study surrounded by books on all kinds of subjects, devoting myself to literary studies, my usual habit, my mind dwelt at length on the weighty opinions of various authors whom I had studied for a long time. I looked up from my book, having decided to leave such subtle questions in peace and to relax by reading some light poetry. With this in mind, I searched for some small book. By chance a strange volume came into my hands, not one of my own, but one which had been given to me along with some others. When I held it open and saw from its title page that it was by Mathéolus,[1] I smiled, for though I had never seen it before, I had often heard that like other books it discussed respect for women. I thought I would browse through it to amuse myself. I had not been reading for very long when my good mother called me to refresh myself with some supper, for it was evening. Intending to look at it the next day, I put it down. The next morning, again seated in my study as was my habit, I remembered wanting to examine this book by Mathéolus. I started to read it and went on for a little while. Because the subject seemed to me not very pleasant for people who do not enjoy lies, and of no use in developing virtue or manners, given its lack of integrity in diction and theme, and after browsing here and there and reading the end, I put it down in order to turn my attention to more elevated and useful study. But just the sight of this book, even though it was of no authority, made me wonder how it happened that so many different men—and learned men among them—have been and are so inclined to express both in speaking and in their treatises and writings so many wicked insults about women and their behavior. Not only one or two and not even just this Mathéolus (for this book had a bad name anyway and was intended as a satire) but, more generally, judging from the treatises of all philosophers and poets and from all the orators—it would take too long to mention their

[1]The book is *The Book of the Lamentations of Mathéolus,* a long verse diatribe against women, written in Latin about 1300 and translated into French during Christine's lifetime.

names—it seems that they all speak from one and the same mouth. They all concur in one conclusion: that the behavior of women is inclined to and full of every vice. Thinking deeply about these matters, I began to examine my character and conduct as a natural woman[2] and, similarly, I considered other women whose company I frequently kept, princesses, great ladies, women of the middle and lower classes, who had graciously told me of their most private and intimate thoughts, hoping that I could judge impartially and in good conscience whether the testimony of so many notable men could be true. To the best of my knowledge, no matter how long I confronted or dissected the problem, I could not see or realize how their claims could be true when compared to the natural behavior and character of women. Yet I still argued vehemently against women, saying that it would be impossible that so many famous men—such solemn scholars, possessed of such deep and great understanding, so clear-sighted in all things, as it seemed—could have spoken falsely on so many occasions that I could hardly find a book on morals where, even before I had read it in its entirety, I did not find several chapters or certain sections attacking women, no matter who the author was. This reason alone, in short, made me conclude that, although my intellect did not perceive my own great faults and, likewise, those of other women because of its simpleness and ignorance, it was however truly fitting that such was the case. And so I relied more on the judgment of others than on what I myself felt and knew. I was so transfixed in this line of thinking for such a long time that it seemed as if I were in a stupor. Like a gushing fountain, a series of authorities, whom I recalled one after another, came to mind, along with their opinions on this topic. And I finally decided that God formed a vile creature when He made woman, and I wondered how such a worthy artisan could have deigned to make such an abominable work which, from what they say, is the vessel as well as the refuge and abode of every evil and vice. As I was thinking this, a great unhappiness and sadness welled up in my heart, for I detested myself and the entire feminine sex, as though we were monstrosities in nature. And in my lament I spoke these words:

"Oh, God, how can this be? For unless I stray from my faith, I must never doubt that Your infinite wisdom and most perfect goodness ever created anything which was not good. Did You yourself not create woman in a very special way and since that time did You not give her all those inclinations which it pleased You for her to have? And how could it be that You could go wrong in anything? Yet look at all these accusations which have been judged, decided, and concluded against women. I do not know how to understand this repugnance. If it is so, fair Lord God, that in fact so many abominations abound in the female sex, for You Yourself say that the testimony of two or three witnesses lends credence, why shall I not doubt that this is true? Alas, God, why did You not let me be born in the world as a man, so that all my inclinations would be to serve You better, and so that I would not stray in anything and would be as perfect as a man is said to be? But since Your kindness has not been extended to me, then forgive my negligence in Your service, most fair Lord God, and may it not displease You, for the servant who receives

[2]The phrase "natural woman" recalls *The Romance of the Rose,* in which the allegorical figure Nature argues that women are "naturally" unchaste.

fewer gifts from his lord is less obliged in his service." I spoke these words to God in my lament and a great deal more for a very long time in sad reflection, and in my folly I considered myself most unfortunate because God had made me inhabit a female body in this world.

HERE CHRISTINE DESCRIBES HOW THREE LADIES APPEARED TO HER AND HOW THE ONE WHO WAS IN FRONT SPOKE FIRST AND COMFORTED HER IN HER PAIN

So occupied with these painful thoughts, my head bowed in shame, my eyes filled with tears, leaning on the pommel of my chair's armrest, I suddenly saw a ray of light fall on my lap, as though it were the sun. I shuddered then, as if wakened from sleep, for I was sitting in a shadow where the sun could not have shone at that hour. And as I lifted my head to see where this light was coming from, I saw three crowned ladies standing before me, and the splendor of their bright faces shone on me and throughout the entire room. Now no one would ask whether I was surprised, for my doors were shut and they had still entered. Fearing that some phantom had come to tempt me and filled with great fright, I made the Sign of the Cross on my forehead.

Then she who was the first of the three smiled and began to speak, "Dear daughter, do not be afraid, for we have not come here to harm or trouble you but to console you, for we have taken pity on your distress, and we have come to bring you out of the ignorance which so blinds your own intellect that you shun what you know for a certainty and believe what you do not know or see or recognize except by virtue of many strange opinions. You resemble the fool in the prank who was dressed in women's clothes while he slept; because those who were making fun of him repeatedly told him he was a woman, he believed their false testimony more readily than the certainty of his own identity. Fair daughter, have you lost all sense? Have you forgotten that when fine gold is tested in the furnace, it does not change or vary in strength but becomes purer the more it is hammered and handled in different ways? Do you not know that the best things are the most debated and the most discussed? If you wish to consider the question of the highest form of reality, which consists in ideas or celestial substances, consider whether the greatest philosophers who have lived and whom you support against your own sex have ever resolved whether ideas are false and contrary to the truth. Notice how these same philosophers contradict and criticize one another, just as you have seen in the *Metaphysics* where Aristotle takes their opinions to task and speaks similarly of Plato and other philosophers. And note, moreover, how even Saint Augustine and the Doctors of the Church have criticized Aristotle in certain passages, although he is known as the prince of philosophers in whom both natural and moral philosophy attained their highest level. It also seems that you think that all the words of the philosophers are articles of faith, that they could never be wrong. As far as the poets of whom you speak are concerned, do you not know that they spoke on many subjects in a fictional way and that often they mean the contrary of what their words openly say? One can interpret them according to the grammatical figure of *antiphrasis,* which means, as you know, that if you call something bad, in fact, it is good, and also vice versa. Thus I advise you to profit from their works and to interpret them in the manner in which they are intended in those passages where they attack women. Perhaps this man, who called himself Mathéolus in his own book, intended it in such a way, for there are many things which, if taken literally, would be pure heresy. As for the attack against the estate of marriage—which is a holy estate, worthy and ordained by God—made not only by Mathéolus but also by others and even by the *Romance of the Rose* where greater credibility is averred because of the authority of its author, it is evident and proven by experience that the contrary of the evil which they posit and claim to be found in this estate through the obligation and fault of women is true. For where has the husband ever been found who would allow his wife to have authority to abuse and insult him as a matter of course, as these authorities maintain? I believe that, regardless of what you might have read, you will never see such a husband with your own eyes, so badly colored are these lies. Thus, in conclusion, I tell you, dear friend, that simplemindedness has prompted you to hold such an opinion. Come back to yourself, recover your senses, and do not trouble yourself anymore over such absurdities. For you know that any evil spoken of women so generally only hurts those who say it, not women themselves."

Here Christine Tells How the Lady Who Had Said This Showed Her Who She Was and What Her Character and Function Were and Told Her How She Would Construct a City with the Help of These Same Three Ladies.

The famous lady spoke these words to me, in whose presence I do not know which one of my senses was more overwhelmed: my hearing from having listened to such worthy words or my sight from having seen her radiant beauty, her attire, her reverent comportment, and her most honored countenance. The same was true of the others, so that I did not know which one to look at, for the three ladies resembled each other so much that they could be told apart only with difficulty, except for the last one, for although she was of no less authority than the others, she had so fierce a visage that whoever, no matter how daring, looked in her eyes would be afraid to commit a crime, for it seemed that she threatened criminals unceasingly. Having stood up out of respect, I looked at them without saying a word, like someone too overwhelmed to utter a syllable. Reflecting on who these beings could be, I felt much admiration in my heart and, if I could have dared, I would have immediately asked their names and identities and what was the meaning of the different scepters which each one carried in her right hand, which were of fabulous richness, and why they had come here. But since I considered myself unworthy to address these questions to such high ladies as they appeared to me, I did not dare to, but continued to keep my gaze fixed on them, half-afraid and half-reassured by the words which I had heard, which had made me reject my first impression. But the most wise lady who had spoken to me and who knew in her mind what I was thinking, as one who has insight into everything, addressed my reflections, saying:

"Dear daughter, know that God's providence, which leaves nothing void or empty, has ordained that we, though celestial beings, remain and circulate among the people of the world here below, in order to bring order and maintain in balance those institutions we created according to the will of

God in the fulfillment of various offices, that God whose daughters we three all are and from whom we were born. Thus it is my duty to straighten out men and women when they go astray and to put them back on the right path. And when they stray, if they have enough understanding to see me, I come to them quietly in spirit and preach to them, showing them their error and how they have failed, I assign them the causes, and then I teach them what to do and what to avoid. Since I serve to demonstrate clearly and to show both in thought and deed to each man and woman his or her own special qualities and faults, you see me holding this shiny mirror which I carry in my right hand in place of a scepter. I would thus have you know truly that no one can look into this mirror, no matter what kind of creature, without achieving clear self-knowledge. My mirror has such great dignity that not without reason is it surrounded by rich and precious gems, so that you see, thanks to this mirror, the essences, qualities, proportions, and measures of all things are known, nor can anything be done well without it. And because, similarly, you wish to know what are the offices of my other sisters whom you see here, each will reply in her own person about her name and character, and this way our testimony will be all the more certain to you. But now I myself will declare the reason for our coming. I must assure you, as we do nothing without good cause, that our appearance here is not at all in vain. For, although we are not common to many places and our knowledge does not come to all people, nevertheless you, for your great love of investigating the truth through long and continual study, for which you come here, solitary and separated from the world, you have deserved and deserve, our devoted friend, to be visited and consoled by us in your agitation and sadness, so that you might also see clearly, in the midst of the darkness of your thoughts, those things which taint and trouble your heart.

"There is another greater and even more special reason for our coming which you will learn from our speeches: in fact we have come to vanquish from the world the same error into which you had fallen, so that from now on, ladies and all valiant women may have a refuge and defense against the various assailants, those ladies who have been abandoned for so long, exposed like a field without a surrounding hedge, without finding a champion to afford them an adequate defense, notwithstanding those noble men who are required by order of law to protect them, who by negligence and apathy have allowed them to be mistreated. It is no wonder then that their jealous enemies, those outrageous villains who have assailed them with various weapons, have been victorious in a war in which women have had no defense. Where is there a city so strong which could not be taken immediately if no resistance were forthcoming, or the law case, no matter how unjust, which was not won through the obstinance of someone pleading without opposition? And the simple, noble ladies, following the example of suffering which God commands, have cheerfully suffered the great attacks which, both in the spoken and the written word, have been wrongfully and sinfully perpetrated against women by men who all the while appealed to God for the right to do so. Now it is time for their just cause to be taken from Pharaoh's hands, and for this reason, we three ladies whom you see here, moved by pity, have come to you to announce a particular edifice built like a city wall, strongly constructed and well founded, which has been predestined and established by our aid and counsel for you to build, where no one will reside except all ladies of fame and women worthy of praise, for the walls of the city will be closed to those women who lack virtue."

Here the Lady Explains to Christine the City Which She Has Been Commissioned to Build and How She Was Charged to Help Christine Build the Wall and Enclosure, and Then Gives Her Name.

"Thus, fair daughter, the prerogative among women has been bestowed on you to establish and build the City of Ladies. For the foundation and completion of this City you will draw fresh waters from us as from clear fountains, and we will bring you sufficient building stone, stronger and more durable than any marble with cement could be. Thus your City will be extremely beautiful, without equal, and of perpetual duration in the world.

"Have you not read that King Tros founded the great city of Troy with the aid of Apollo, Minerva, and Neptune, whom the people of that time considered gods, and also how Cadmus founded the city of Thebes with the admonition of the gods?[3] And yet over time these cities fell and have fallen into ruin. But I prophesy to you, as a true sybil, that this City, which you will found with our help, will never be destroyed, nor will it ever fall, but will remain prosperous forever, regardless of all its jealous enemies. Although it will be stormed by numerous assaults, it will never be taken or conquered.

"Long ago the Amazon kingdom was begun through the arrangement and enterprise of several ladies of great courage who despised servitude, just as history books have testified.[4] For a long time afterward they maintained it under the rule of several queens, very noble ladies whom they elected themselves, who governed them well and maintained their dominion with great strength. Yet, although they were strong and powerful and had conquered a large part of the entire Orient in the course of their rule and terrified all the neighboring lands (even the Greeks, who were then the flower of all countries in the world, feared them), nevertheless, after a time, the power of this kingdom declined, so that as with all earthly kingdoms, nothing but its name has survived to the present. But the edifice erected by you in this City which you must construct will be far stronger, and for its founding I was commissioned, in the course of our common deliberation, to supply you with durable and pure mortar to lay the sturdy foundations and to raise the lofty walls all around, high and thick, with mighty towers and strong bastions, surrounded by moats with firm blockhouses, just as is fitting for a city with a strong and lasting defense. Following our plan, you will set the foundations deep to last all the longer, and then you will raise the walls so high that they will not fear anyone. Daughter, now that I have told you the reason for our coming and so that you will more certainly believe my words, I want you to learn my name, by whose sound alone you will be able to learn

[3] In connecting her City of Ladies with Thebes and Troy, Christine is following a commonplace of her time, which held that France was the natural heir to the culture of Greece and Rome. Legendary history held that the French kings were descended from Franco, the son of Hector of Troy.

[4] In Greek legend, the Amazons were a tribe of women who spent their time in hunting and warfare. In the Trojan War, they were supposed to have fought against the Greeks.

and know that, if you wish to follow my commands, you have in me an administrator so that you may do your work flawlessly. I am called Lady Reason; you see that you are in good hands. For the time being then, I will say no more."

HERE CHRISTINE TELLS HOW THE SECOND LADY TOLD HER NAME AND WHAT SHE SERVED AS AND HOW SHE WOULD AID HER IN BUILDING THE CITY OF LADIES

When the lady above finished her speech, before I could resume, the second lady began as follows: "I am called Rectitude and reside more in Heaven than on Earth, but as the radiance and splendor of God and messenger of His goodness, I often visit the just and exhort them to do what is right, to give to each person what is his according to his capacity, to say and uphold the truth, to defend the rights of the poor and the innocent, not to hurt anyone through usurpation, to uphold the reputation of those unjustly accused. I am the shield and defense of the servants of God. I resist the power and might of evil-doers. I give rest to workers and reward those who act well. Through me, God reveals to His friends His secrets; I am their advocate in Heaven. This shining ruler which you see me carry in my right hand instead of a scepter is the straight ruler which separates right from wrong and shows the difference between good and evil: who follows it does not go astray. It is the rod of peace which reconciles the good and where they find support and which beats and strikes down evil. What should I tell you about this? All things are measured by this ruler, for its powers are infinite. It will serve you to measure the edifice of the City which you have been commissioned to build, and you will need it for constructing the façade, for erecting the high temples, for measuring the palaces, houses, and all public buildings, the streets and squares, and all things proper to help populate the City. I have come as your assistant, and this will be my duty. Do not be uneasy about the breadth and long circuit of the walls, for with God's help and our assistance you will build fair and sturdy mansions and inns without leaving anything vague; and you will people the City with no trouble."

HERE CHRISTINE TELLS HOW THE THIRD LADY TOLD HER WHO SHE WAS AND HER FUNCTION AND HOW SHE WOULD HELP BUILD THE HIGH ROOFS OF THE TOWERS AND PALACES AND WOULD BRING TO HER THE QUEEN, ACCOMPANIED BY NOBLE LADIES.

Afterward, the third lady spoke and said, "My friend Christine, I am Justice, the most singular daughter of God, and my nature proceeds purely from His person. My residence is found in Heaven, on Earth, or in Hell: in Heaven, for the glory of the saints and blessed souls; on Earth, for the apportionment to each man of the good or evil which he has deserved; in Hell, for the punishment of the evil. I do not bend anywhere, for I have not friend nor enemy nor changeable will; pity cannot persuade me nor cruelty move me. My duty is only to judge, to decide, and to dispense according to each man's just deserts. I sustain all things in their condition, nothing could be stable without me. I am in God and God is in me, and we are as one and the same. Who follows me cannot fail, and my way is sure. I teach men and women of sound mind who want to believe in me to chastise, know, and correct themselves, and to do to others what they wish to have done to themselves, to distribute wealth without favor, to speak the truth, to flee and hate lies, to reject all viciousness. This vessel of fine gold which you see me hold in my right hand, made like a generous measure, God, my Father, gave me, and it serves to measure out to each his rightful portion. It carries the sign of the fleur-de-lis of the Trinity,[5] and in all portions it measures true, nor can any man complain about my measure. Yet the men of the Earth have other measures which they claim depend upon and derive from mine, but they are mistaken. Often they measure in my shadow, and their measure is not always true but sometimes too much for some and too little for others. I could give a rather long account of the duties of my office, but, put briefly, I have a special place among the Virtues, for they are all based on me. And of the three noble ladies whom you see here, we are as one and the same, we could not exist without one another; and what the first disposes, the second orders and initiates, and then I, the third, finish and terminate it. Thus I have been appointed by the will of us three ladies to perfect and complete your City, and my job will be to construct the high roofs of the towers and of the lofty mansions and inns which will all be made of fine shining gold. Then I will populate the City for you with worthy ladies and the mighty Queen whom I will bring to you. Hers will be the honor and prerogative among all other women, as well as among the most excellent women. And in this condition I will turn the City over to you, completed with your help, fortified and closed off with strong gates which I will search for in Heaven, and then I will place the keys in your hands."

Here Christine Tells How She Spoke to the Three Ladies

When the speeches of all three ladies were over—to which I had listened intently and which had completely taken away the unhappiness which I had felt before their coming—I threw myself at their feet, not just on my knees but completely prostrate because of their great excellence. Kissing the earth around their feet, adoring them as goddesses of glory, I began my prayer to them:

"Oh ladies of supreme dignity, radiance of the heavens and light of the earth, fountains of Paradise and joy of the blessed, where did such humility come from to Your Highnesses that you have deigned to come down from your pontifical seats and shining thrones to visit the troubled and dark tabernacle of this simple and ignorant student? Who could give fitting thanks for such a boon? With the rain and dew of your sweet words, you have penetrated and moistened the dryness of my mind, so that it now feels ready to germinate and send forth new branches capable of bearing fruits of profitable virtue and sweet savor. How will such grace be bestowed on me that I will receive the boon, as you have said, to build and construct in the world from now on a new city? I am not Saint Thomas the Apostle, who through divine grace built a rich palace in Heaven for the king of India,[6] and my feeble sense does not know the craft, or the measures, or the study, or the

[5] The fleur-de-lis, or lily, the symbol of France, also symbolized the Trinity, because of its three petals in one flower.

[6] Thomas, one of the Twelve Apostles, was traditionally an apostle to Asia.

science, or the practice of construction. And if, thanks to learning, these things were within my ken, where would I find enough physical strength in my weak feminine body to realize such an enormous task? But nevertheless, my most respected ladies, although the awesomeness of this news seems strange to me, I know well that nothing is impossible for God. Nor do I doubt that anything undertaken with your counsel and help will not be completed well. Thus, with all my strength, I praise God and you, my ladies, who have so honored me by assigning me such a noble commission, which I most happily accept. Behold your handmaiden ready to serve. Command and I will obey, and may it be unto me according to your words."

HERE CHRISTINE TELLS HOW, UNDER REASON'S COMMAND AND ASSISTANCE, SHE BEGAN TO EXCAVATE THE EARTH AND LAY THE FOUNDATION.

Then Lady Reason responded and said, "Get up, daughter! Without waiting any longer, let us go to the Field of Letters. There the City of Ladies will be founded on a flat and fertile plain, where all fruits and freshwater rivers are found and where the earth abounds in all good things. Take the pick of your understanding and dig and clear out a great ditch wherever you see the marks of my ruler, and I will help you carry away the earth on my own shoulders."

I immediately stood up to obey her commands and, thanks to these three ladies, I felt stronger and lighter than before. She went ahead, and I followed behind, and after we had arrived at this field I began to excavate and dig, following her marks with the pick of cross-examination. . . .

CHRISTINE ASKS REASON WHETHER GOD HAS EVER WISHED TO ENNOBLE THE MIND OF WOMAN WITH THE LOFTINESS OF THE SCIENCES; AND REASON'S ANSWER.

[I, Christine, spoke: "I would like to know whether it has ever pleased God, who has bestowed so many favors] on women, to honor the feminine sex with the privilege of the virtue of high understanding and great learning, and whether women ever have a clever enough mind for this. I wish very much to know this because men maintain that the mind of women can learn only a little."

She answered, "My daughter, since I told you before, you know quite well that the opposite of their opinion is true, and to show you this even more clearly, I will give you proof through examples. I tell you again—and don't doubt the contrary—if it were customary to send daughters to school like sons, and if they were then taught the natural sciences, they would learn as thoroughly and understand the subtleties of all the arts and sciences as well as sons. And by chance there happen to be such women, for, as I touched on before, just as women have more delicate bodies than men, weaker and less able to perform many tasks, so do they have minds that are freer and sharper whenever they apply themselves."

"My lady, what are you saying? With all due respect, could you dwell longer on this point, please. Certainly men would never admit this answer is true, unless it is explained more plainly, for they believe that one normally sees that men know more than women do."

She answered, "Do you know why women know less?"

"Not unless you tell me, my lady."

"Without the slightest doubt, it is because they are not involved in many different things, but stay at home, where it is enough for them to run the household, and there is nothing which so instructs a reasonable creature as the exercise and experience of many different things."

"My lady, since they have minds skilled in conceptualizing and learning, just like men, why don't women learn more?"

She replied, "Because, my daughter, the public does not require them to get involved in the affairs which men are commissioned to execute, just as I told you before. It is enough for women to perform the usual duties to which they are ordained. As for judging from experience, since one sees that women usually know less than men, that therefore their capacity for understanding is less, look at men who farm the flatlands or who live in the mountains. You will find that in many countries they seem completely savage because they are so simpleminded. All the same, there is no doubt that Nature provided them with the qualities of body and mind found in the wisest and most learned men. All of this stems from a failure to learn, though, just as I told you, among men and women, some possess better minds than others. Let me tell you about women who have possessed great learning and profound understanding and treat the question of the similarity of women's minds to men's."

She Begins to Discuss Several Ladies Who Were Enlightened with Great Learning, and First Speaks About the Noble Maiden Cornificia.

"Cornificia, the noble maiden, was sent to school by her parents along with her brother Cornificius when they were both children, thanks to deception and trickery.[7] This little girl so devoted herself to study and with such marvelous intelligence that she began to savor the sweet taste of knowledge acquired through study. Nor was it easy to take her away from this joy to which she more and more applied herself, neglecting all other feminine activities. She occupied herself with this for such a long period of time that she became a consummate poet, and she was not only extremely brilliant and expert in the learnedness and craft of poetry but also seemed to have been nourished with the very milk and teaching of perfect philosophy, for she wanted to hear and know about every branch of learning, which she then mastered so thoroughly that she surpassed her brother, who was also a very great poet, and excelled in every field of learning. Knowledge was not enough for her unless she could put her mind to work and her pen to paper in the compilation of several very famous books. These works, as well as her poems, were much prized during the time of Saint Gregory and he himself mentions them. The Italian, Boccaccio, who was a great poet,[8] discusses this fact in his work and at the same time praises this woman: 'O most great honor for a woman who abandoned all feminine activities and applied and devoted

[7] Cornificia, a first-century B.C. Roman aristocrat, was the sister of Cornificius, a Roman general. Both were poets.

[8] The book referred to is Boccaccio's *Concerning Famous Women* (1360–1374), which was translated into French about 1401. It is Christine's principal source for *The Book of the City of Ladies*.

her mind to the study of the greatest scholars!' As further proof of what I am telling you, Boccaccio also talks about the attitude of women who despise themselves and their own minds, and who, as though they were born in the mountains totally ignorant of virtue and honor, turn disconsolate and say that they are good and useful only for embracing men and carrying and feeding children. God has given them such beautiful minds to apply themselves, if they want to, in any of the fields where glorious and excellent men are active, which are neither more nor less accessible to them as compared to men if they wished to study them, and they can thereby acquire a lasting name, whose possession is fitting for most excellent men. My dear daughter, you can see how this author Boccaccio testifies to what I have told you and how he praises and approves learning in women." . . .

HERE SHE SPEAKS OF SAPPHO, THAT MOST SUBTLE WOMAN, POET, AND PHILOSOPHER.

"The wise Sappho,[9] who was from the city of Mytilene, was no less learned. . . . This Sappho had a beautiful body and face and was agreeable and pleasant in appearance, conduct, and speech. But the charm of her profound understanding surpassed all the other charms with which she was endowed, for she was expert and learned in several arts and sciences, and she was not only well-educated in the works and writings composed by others but also discovered many new things herself and wrote many books and poems. Concerning her, Boccaccio has offered these fair words couched in the sweetness of poetic language: 'Sappho, possessed of sharp wit and burning desire for constant study in the midst of bestial and ignorant men, frequented the heights of Mount Parnassus, that is, of perfect study. Thanks to her fortunate boldness and daring, she kept company with the Muses, that is, the arts and sciences, without being turned away. She entered the forest of laurel trees filled with May boughs, greenery, and different colored flowers, soft fragrances and various aromatic spices, where Grammar, Logic, noble Rhetoric, Geometry, and Arithmetic live and take their leisure. She went on her way until she came to the deep grotto of Apollo, god of learning, and found the brook and conduit of the fountain of Castalia, and took up the plectrum and quill of the harp and played sweet melodies, with the nymphs all the while leading the dance, that is, following the rules of harmony and musical accord.' From what Boccaccio says about her, it should be inferred that the profundity of both her understanding and of her learned books can only be known and understood by men of great perception and learning, according to the testimony of the ancients. Her writings and poems have survived to this day, most remarkably constructed and composed, and they serve as illumination and models of consummate poetic craft and composition to those who have come afterward. She invented different genres of lyric and poetry, short narratives, tearful laments and strange lamentations about love and other emotions, and these were so well made and so well

[9] Sappho was a Greek poet of the seventh to sixth centuries B.C. Christine's semilegendary account of her is taken from Boccaccio. Christine could not have known Sappho's works directly, since by the fourteenth century, Sappho's ten volumes of collected works had long since been destroyed by clerical censors. A few of the poems were reconstructed, from scraps of papyrus and quotations by other authors, in the nineteenth century.

ordered that they were named 'Sapphic' after her. Horace recounts, concerning her poems, that when Plato, the great philosopher who was Aristotle's teacher, died, a book of Sappho's poems was found under his pillow.

"In brief this lady was so outstanding in learning that in the city where she resided a statue of bronze in her image was dedicated in her name and erected in a prominent place so that she would be honored by all and be remembered forever. This lady was placed and counted among the greatest and most famous poets, and, according to Boccaccio, the honors of the diadems and crowns of kings and the miters of bishops are not any greater, nor are the crowns of laurel and victor's palm.

"I could tell you a great deal about women of great learning. Leontium was a Greek woman and also such a great philosopher that she dared, for impartial and serious reasons, to correct and attack the philosopher Theophrastus,[10] who was quite famous in her time." . . .

Against Those Men Who Claim It Is Not Good for Women to Be Educated.

Following these remarks, I, Christine, spoke [to Lady Rectitude], "My lady, I realize that women have accomplished many good things and that even if evil women have done evil, it seems to me, nevertheless, that the benefits accrued and still accruing because of good women—particularly the wise and literary ones and those educated in the natural sciences whom I mentioned above—outweigh the evil. Therefore, I am amazed by the opinion of some men who claim that they do not want their daughters, wives, or kinswomen to be educated because their mores would be ruined as a result."

She responded, "Here you can clearly see that not all opinions of men are based on reason and that these men are wrong. For it must not be presumed that mores necessarily grow worse from knowing the moral sciences, which teach the virtues, indeed, there is not the slightest doubt that moral education amends and ennobles them. How could anyone think or believe that whoever follows good teaching or doctrine is the worse for it? Such an opinion cannot be expressed or maintained. I do not mean that it would be good for a man or a woman to study the art of divination or those fields of learning which are forbidden—for the holy Church did not remove them from common use without good reason—but it should not be believed that women are the worse for knowing what is good.

"Quintus Hortensius,[11] a great rhetorician and consummately skilled orator in Rome, did not share this opinion. He had a daughter, named Hortensia, whom he greatly loved for the subtlety of her wit. He had her learn letters and study the science of rhetoric, which she mastered so thoroughly that she resembled her father Hortensius not only in wit and lively memory but also in her excellent delivery and order of speech—in fact, he surpassed her in nothing. As for the subject discussed above, concerning the good which comes about through women, the benefits realized by this woman and her

[10] Theophrastus (third century B.C.) was a Greek Peripatetic philosopher and pupil of Aristotle. Leontium is known only in connection with this anecdote.

[11] Roman orator (114–50 B.C.). A leader of the aristocratic party, he was defeated (70 B.C.) by Cicero in the trial of Verres. His daughter Hortensia was as well educated and well known as Christine says she was.

learning were, among others, exceptionally remarkable. That is, during the time when Rome was governed by three men, this Hortensia began to support the cause of women and to undertake what no man dared to undertake. There was a question whether certain taxes should be levied on women and on their jewelry during a needy period in Rome. This woman's eloquence was so compelling that she was listened to, no less readily than her father would have been, and she won her case.

"Similarly, to speak of more recent times, without searching for examples in ancient history, Giovanni Andrea, a solemn law professor in Bologna not quite sixty years ago, was not of the opinion that it was bad for women to be educated. He had a fair and good daughter, named Novella, who was educated in the law to such an advanced degree that when he was occupied by some task and not at leisure to present his lectures to his students, he would send Novella, his daughter, in his place to lecture to the students from his chair. And to prevent her beauty from distracting the concentration of her audience, she had a little curtain drawn in front of her. In this manner she could on occasion supplement and lighten her father's occupation. He loved her so much that, to commemorate her name, he wrote a book of remarkable lectures on the law which he entitled *Novella super Decretalium,* after his daughter's name.[12]

"Thus, not all men (and especially the wisest) share the opinion that it is bad for women to be educated. But it is very true that many foolish men have claimed this because it displeased them that women knew more than they did. Your father, who was a great scientist and philosopher, did not believe that women were worth less by knowing science; rather, as you know, he took great pleasure from seeing your inclination to learning. The feminine opinion of your mother, however, who wished to keep you busy with spinning and silly girlishness, following the common custom of women, was the major obstacle to your being more involved in the sciences. But just as the proverb already mentioned above says, 'No one can take away what Nature has given,' your mother could not hinder in you the feeling for the sciences which you, through natural inclination, had nevertheless gathered together in little droplets. I am sure that, on account of these things, you do not think you are worth less but rather that you consider it a great treasure for yourself; and you doubtless have reason to."

And I, Christine, replied to all of this, "Indeed, my lady, what you say is as true as the Lord's Prayer."

HERE CHRISTINE SPEAKS TO RECTITUDE, WHO ARGUES AGAINST THOSE MEN WHO SAY THAT THERE ARE FEW CHASTE WOMEN, AND SHE TELLS OF SUSANNA.

"From what I see, my lady, all good and virtuous things are found in women. Where does the opinion that there are so few chaste women come from? Were this so, then all their other virtues would be nothing, since chastity is the supreme virtue in women. But from what I have heard you say, the complete opposite of what those men claim seems to be the case."

[12] Christine could have learned the story of Novella from her father, who was a colleague of Giovanni Andrea at the University of Bologna.

She replied, "From what I have already actually told you and from what you know about this, the contrary is quite obvious to you, and I could tell you more about this and then some. How many valiant and chaste ladies does Holy Scripture mention who chose death rather than transgress against the chastity and purity of their bodies and thoughts, just like the beautiful and good Susanna, wife of Joachim, a rich man of great authority among the Jews?[13] Once when this valiant lady Susanna was alone relaxing in her garden, two old men, false priests, entered the garden, approached her, and demanded that she sin with them. She refused them totally, whereupon, seeing their request denied, they threatened to denounce her to the authorities and to claim that they had discovered her with a young man. Hearing their threats and knowing that women in such a case were customarily stoned, she said, 'I am completely overwhelmed with anguish, for if I do not do what these men require of me, I risk the death of my body, and if I do it, I will sin before my Creator. However, it is far better for me, in my innocence, to die than to incur the wrath of my God because of sin.' So Susanna cried out, and the servants came out of the house, and, to put the matter briefly, with their disloyal testimony, these false priests managed to have Susanna condemned to death. Yet God who always provides for those dear to Him, opened the mouth of the prophet Daniel, who was a little child in his mother's arms and who, as Susanna was being led to her execution, with a great procession of people in tears following her, cried out that the innocent Susanna had been condemned because of a very grave mistake. So she was led back, and the false priests were thoroughly interrogated and found guilty by their own confessions. The innocent Susanna was freed and these men executed." . . .

Refuting Those Men Who Claim Women Want to Be Raped, Rectitude Gives Several Examples, and First of All, Lucretia.[14]

Then I, Christine, spoke as follows, "My lady, I truly believe what you are saying, and I am certain that there are plenty of beautiful women who are virtuous and chaste and who know how to protect themselves well from the entrapments of deceitful men. I am therefore troubled and grieved when men argue that many women want to be raped and that it does not bother them at all to be raped by men even when they verbally protest. It would be hard to believe that such great villainy is actually pleasant for them."

She answered, "Rest assured, dear friend, chaste ladies who live honestly take absolutely no pleasure in being raped. Indeed, rape is the greatest possible sorrow for them. Many upright women have demonstrated that this is true with their own credible examples, just like Lucretia, the noblest Roman woman, supreme in chastity among Roman women, wife of a nobleman named Tarquin Collatinus. Now, when another man, Tarquin the Proud, son of King Tarquin, was greatly taken with love for this noble Lucretia, he did not dare to tell her because of the great chastity he saw in her, and, despairing of achieving his goal with presents or entreaties, he considered how he could

[13] The story of Susanna and the Elders is told in Daniel 13.

[14] The story of Lucretia and her rape by Tarquin the Proud is legendary history, set at the court of Tarquinius Superbus, traditionally the seventh and last king of Rome (sixth century B.C.).

have her through ruse. Claiming to be a close friend of her husband, he managed to gain entrance into her house whenever he wished, and once, knowing her husband was not at home, he went there and the noble lady received him with the honors due to someone whom she thought to be a close friend of her husband. However, Tarquin, who had something altogether different on his mind, succeeded in entering Lucretia's bedroom and frightened her terribly. Put briefly, after trying to coax her for a long time with promises, gifts, and favors, he saw that entreaties were getting him nowhere. He drew his sword and threatened to kill her if she made a sound and did not submit to his will. She answered that he should go ahead and kill her, for she would rather die than consent. Tarquin, realizing that nothing would help him, concocted a great malice, saying that he would publicly declare that he had found her with one of his sergeants. In brief, he so scared her with this threat (for she thought that people would believe him) that finally she suffered his rape. Lucretia, however, could not patiently endure this great pain, so that when daylight came she sent for her husband, her father, and her close relatives who were among the most powerful people in Rome, and, weeping and sobbing, confessed to them what had happened to her. Then, as her husband and relatives, who saw that she was overwhelmed with grief, were comforting her, she drew a knife from under her robe and said, 'This is how I absolve myself of sin and show my innocence. Yet I cannot free myself from the torment nor extricate myself from the pain. From now on no woman will ever live shamed and disgraced by Lucretia's example.' Having said this, she forcibly plunged the knife into her breast and collapsed dead before her husband and friends. They rushed like madmen to attack Tarquin. All Rome was moved to this cause, and they drove out the king and would have killed his son if they had found him. Never again was there a king in Rome. And because of this outrage perpetrated on Lucretia, so some claim, a law was enacted whereby a man would be executed for raping a woman, a law which is fitting, just, and holy." . . .

Here [Justice] Speaks of Saint Christine, Virgin.[15]

"If you want me to tell you about all the holy virgins who are in Heaven because of their constancy during martyrdom, it would require a long history, including Saint Cecilia, Saint Agnes, Saint Agatha, and countless others. If you want more examples, you need only look at the *Speculum historiale* of Vincent de Beauvais, and there you will find a great many.[16] However, I will tell you about Saint Christine, both because she is your patron and because she is a virgin of great dignity. Let me tell you at greater length about her beautiful and pious life.

"The blessed Saint Christine, virgin, was from the city of Tyre and was the daughter of Urban, master of the knights. Her father shut her up in a

[15] There were two Saint Christines in the medieval church: Saint Christine of Tyre, whose story Justice tells, and Saint Christine of Bolsena. The two became confused and came to share the same legendary history. Saint Christine of Tyre probably never existed; Saint Christine of Bolsena seems to have been a genuine martyr of the fourth century A.D. but was probably not named Christine. Her history, as Justice tells it, is of course purely legendary.

[16] Vincent of Beauvais was a thirteenth-century French Dominican friar whose *Mirror of History* was a compendium of knowledge, including many saints' lives.

tower because of her great beauty, and she had twelve maids with her. Her father also had a very beautiful chapel with idols built near Christine's chamber so that she could worship them. She, however, even as a twelve-year-old child, had already been inspired by the faith of Jesus Christ and did not pay any attention to the idols, so that her maids were astonished and repeatedly urged her to sacrifice. Yet when she took the incense, as if to sacrifice to the idols, she knelt at a window facing east, looked up to Heaven, and offered her incense to the immortal God. She spent the greater part of the night at this window, watching the stars, and sighing, piously praying to God to help her against her enemies. The maids, clearly aware her heart was in Jesus Christ, would often kneel before her, their hands clasped together, begging her not to place her trust in a strange God but to worship her parents' gods, for if she were discovered they would all be killed. Christine would answer that the Devil was deceiving them by urging them to worship so many gods and that there was but one God. When her father at last realized that his daughter refused to worship his idols, he was terribly grieved and upbraided her a great deal. She replied that she would gladly worship the God of Heaven. He thought she meant Jupiter and he was overjoyed and wanted to kiss her, but she cried out, 'Do not touch my mouth, for I wish to offer a pure offering to the celestial God.' The father was even happy with this. She returned to her chamber and nailed the door shut, then she knelt down and offered a holy prayer to God, weeping all the while. And the angel of the Lord descended and comforted her and brought her white bread and meat which she ate, for she had not tasted food for three days. Once, afterward, when Christine saw from her window several poor Christians begging at the foot of her tower, seeing that she had nothing to give them, she searched for her father's idols which were made of gold and silver, and she smashed them all and gave the fragments to the poor. When her father learned of this, he beat her cruelly. She openly declared he was deceived to worship these false images and that there was but a single God in the Trinity and that her father should worship Him whom she confessed, and she refused to worship any other in order to escape death. Thereupon her enraged father had her tied up with chains and led from square to square to be beaten and then thrown into prison. He himself wanted to be the judge of this dispute, so on the following day he had her brought before him and threatened her with every conceivable torture if she would not worship his idols. After he realized that he could not convince her with entreaties or threats, he had her sprawled completely nude and beaten so much that twelve men wearied at the task. And the father kept asking her what she thought and he said to her, 'Daughter, natural affection wrings my heart terribly to torment you who are my own flesh, but the reverence I have for my gods forces me to do this because you scorn them.' And the holy virgin replied, 'Tyrant who should not be called my father but rather enemy of my happiness, you boldly torture the flesh which you engendered, for you can easily do this, but as for my soul created by my Father in Heaven, you have no power to touch it with the slightest temptation, for it is protected by my Savior, Jesus Christ.' The cruel father, all the more enraged, had a wheel brought in, which he had ordered built, and ordered her tied to it and a fire built below it, and then he had rivers of boiling oil poured over her body. The wheel turned and completely crushed her. But God, the Father of all mercies, took pity on His servant and dispatched His angel to wreck the torture machines and to extinguish the fire, delivering the virgin, healthy and whole, and killing more than a thousand treacherous spectators who had been watching her without pity and who blasphemed the name of God. And her father asked her, 'Tell me who taught you these evil practices!' She replied, 'Pitiless despot, have I not told you that my Father, Jesus Christ, taught me this long-suffering as well as every right thing in the faith of the Living God? Because of this, I scorn your tortures and will repel all the Devil's assaults with God's strength!' Beaten and confounded, he ordered her thrown into a horrible, dark prison. While she was there, contemplating the extraordinary mysteries of God, three angels came to her in great radiance and brought her food and comforted her. Urban did not know what to do with her but could not stop devising new tortures for her. Finally, fed up completely and wishing to be free of her, he had a great stone tied around her neck and had her thrown into the sea. But as she was being thrown in, the angels took her, and she walked on the water with them. Then, raising her eyes to heaven, Christine prayed to Jesus Christ, that it please Him for her to receive in this water the holy sacrament of baptism which she greatly desired to have; whereupon Jesus Christ descended in His own person with a large company of angels and baptized her and named her Christine, from His own name, and He crowned her and placed a shining star on her forehead and set her on dry land. That night Urban was tortured by the Devil and died. The blessed Christine, whom God wanted to receive through martyrdom (which she also desired), was led back to prison by these criminals. The new judge, named Dyon, knowing what had been done to her, summoned her to appear before him, and he lusted after her because of her beauty. When he saw that his alluring words were of no use, he had her tortured again. He ordered that a large cauldron be filled with oil and that a roaring fire be built beneath it; he had her thrown in, upside down, and four men used iron hooks to rotate her. And the holy virgin sang melodiously to God, mocking her torturers and threatening them with the pains of Hell. When this enraged criminal of a judge realized that nothing was of any avail, he ordered her to be hanged by her long golden hair in the square, in front of all. The women rushed up to her, and, wailing out of pity that such a young girl be so cruelly tortured, they cried out to the judge, saying, 'Cruel felon, crueler than a savage beast, how could a man's heart conceive such monstrous cruelty against such a beautiful and tender maiden?' And all the women tried to mob him. Then the judge, who was afraid, said to her, 'Christine, friend, do not let yourself be tortured anymore, but come with me and we will go worship the supreme God who has upheld you.' He meant Jupiter, who was considered the supreme god, but she understood him in a completely different way and so she replied, 'You have spoken well, so I consent.' He had her taken down and brought up to the temple, and a large crowd followed them. Then he led her before the idols, thinking she would worship them, and she knelt down, looked up at Heaven, and prayed to God. Thereupon she stood up and, turning toward the idol, said, 'I command you in the name of Jesus Christ, oh evil spirit residing in this idol, to come out.' Whereupon the Devil immediately came out and made a loud and frightening din which scared all the spectators, who fell to the ground in fear. When the judge stood up again, he said, 'Christine, you have moved our omnipotent god, and, out of pity for you, he came out to see his creature.' This remark angered her, and she reproached him harshly for being too blind to recognize divine virtue, so she prayed to God to overturn the idol and reduce it to dust, which was done. And more than three thousand men were converted through the words and signs of this virgin. The terrified judge exclaimed, 'If the king finds out what this Christine has done against our god, he will utterly destroy me.' Thereupon, full of anguish, he went out of his mind and died. A third judge, named Julian, appeared, and he ordered Christine seized, boasting that he would make her worship the idols. In spite of all the force he could apply, he was unable physically to move her from the spot where she was standing, so he ordered a large fire built around her. She remained in the fire for three days, and from inside the flames were heard sweet melodies. Her tormentors were terrified by the amazing signs they saw. When the fire had burned out, she emerged fully healthy. The judge commanded that snakes be brought to him and had two asps (with their deadly poisonous bite) and two adders released upon her. But these snakes dropped down at her feet, their heads bowed, and did not harm her at all. Two horrible vipers were let loose, and they hung from her breasts and licked her. And Christine looked to Heaven and said, 'I give You thanks, Lord God, Jesus Christ, who have deigned to grant through Your holy virtues that these horrible serpents would come to know in me Your dignity.' The obstinate Julian, seeing these wonders, yelled at the snake-tender, 'Have you too been enchanted by Christine, so that you have no power to rouse the snakes against her?' Fearing the judge, he then tried to provoke the snakes into biting her, but they rushed at him and killed him. Since everyone was afraid of these serpents and no one dared approach, Christine commanded them in God's name to return to their cages without harming anyone, and they did so. She revived the dead man, who immediately threw himself at her feet and was converted. The judge, blinded by the Devil so that he was unable to perceive the divine mystery, said to Christine, 'You have sufficiently demonstrated your magic arts.' Infuriated, she replied, 'If your eyes would see the virtues of God, you would believe in them.' Then in his rage he ordered her breasts ripped off, whereupon milk rather than blood flowed out. And because she unceasingly pronounced the name of Jesus Christ, he had her tongue cut out, but then she spoke even better and more clearly than before of divine things and of the one blessed God, thanking Him for the bounties which He had given to her. She prayed that it please Him to receive her in His company and that the crown of her martyrdom be finally granted to her. Then a voice was heard from Heaven, saying, 'Christine, pure and radiant, the heavens are opened to you and the eternal kingdom waits, prepared for you, and the entire company of saints blesses God for your sake, for you have upheld the name of Your Christ from childhood on.' And she glorified God, turning her eyes to Heaven. The voice was heard saying, 'Come, Christine, my most beloved and elect daughter, receive the palm and everlasting crown and the reward for your life spent suffering to confess My name.' The treacherous Julian, who heard this voice, castigated the executioners and said they had not cut Christine's tongue short enough and ordered them to cut it so short that she could not speak to her Christ, whereupon they ripped out her tongue and cut it off at the root. She spat this cut-off piece of her tongue into the tyrant's face, putting out one of his eyes. She then said to him, speaking as clearly as ever, 'Tyrant, what does it profit you to have my tongue cut out so that it cannot bless God, when my soul will bless Him forever while yours languishes forever in eternal damnation? And because you did not heed my words, my tongue has blinded you, with good reason.' She ended her martyrdom then, having already seen Jesus Christ sitting on the right hand of His Father, when two arrows were shot at her, one in her side and the other in her heart. One of her relatives whom she had converted buried her body and wrote out her glorious legend."

O blessed Christine, worthy virgin favored of God, most elect and glorious martyr, in the holiness with which God has made you worthy, pray for me, a sinner, named with your name, and be my kind and merciful guardian. Behold my joy at being able to make use of your holy legend and to include it in my writings, which I have recorded here at such length out of reverence for you. May this be ever pleasing to you! Pray for all women, for whom your holy life may serve as an example for ending their lives well. Amen.

Everyman

(Late Fifteenth Century)

Everyman was written in England by an anonymous clerical playwright in about 1475. There is a similar Dutch play of the same period named *Elckerlyc*. *Everyman* may be a translation of the Dutch play, or both may be derived independently from a Latin work named *Homulus*. Current scholarly opinion tends to conclude, however, that the English play is the original. Nothing is known of the author, and although the play was apparently produced with some frequency in the seventy-five years following its composition, no production records survive.

Everyman is the best example of the medieval "morality play," characterized by an allegorical plot that deals with some archetypal action in human spiritual life and by characters who personify abstract ideas, such as Fellowship, Wealth, or Knowledge. Morality plays were only one genre in a rich body of drama that flourished in Europe from the tenth to the sixteenth century, fascinating both in its own right and as background to the flowering of an even richer and more varied drama in the Renaissance.

By the time of the fall of Rome, classical drama had already declined to the level of crude entertainment, and the collapse of the Roman Empire ended dramatic performance altogether for more than five centuries. When drama began to reemerge in the tenth century, it was again from religious roots. As classical drama had begun in the worship of Dionysus, so medieval drama was born in the Christian liturgy. The earliest bits of medieval drama were *tropes*, brief exchanges of dialogue introduced into the chanted liturgy. These tropes were gradually elaborated until by the twelfth century practically all the narrative portions of the Bible had been dramatized in short, often crude, but vivid plays presented in the churches at Christmas and Easter.

By the fourteenth century, these liturgical plays had attracted such large and unruly audiences that they were removed from the churches and presented in village streets, usually on Corpus Christi Day, in late May or early June. Production of the plays was taken over by the craft and trade guilds, although the clergy continued to play an active role, especially in writing the plays. By the end of the fourteenth century, every town of any size in England had its own cycle of religious plays. Some idea of the numbers of plays involved is suggested by the four cycles that survive: the York cycle of forty-eight plays, the Wakefield cycle of thirty-two plays, the Chester cycle of twenty-five plays, and the Coventry cycle of forty-two plays. The subject matter was quite varied, ranging from authentic biblical material to various folk accretions upon that material to saints' lives. (Scholars used to discriminate clearly between mystery plays, based on the Bible, and miracle plays dealing with the lives of saints, but the distinction is so blurry in practice that they are now sometimes grouped together as liturgical plays.)

The morality play was the last of the medieval dramatic genres to emerge, in the middle of the fourteenth century, although there were many precedents for such didactic, allegorical works in nondramatic literature. The recurring subjects of morality plays are suggested by the titles of some of those that preceded *Everyman: The Pride of Life, The Castle of Perseverance,* and *The Debate of the Body and the Soul.*

Medieval plays were produced in several different ways. When they were still performed inside churches, they were staged on platforms distributed around the church, with a different platform, or *mansion,* for each locale. When they moved outside the churches, they were performed on large, two-decker pageant wagons. A curtained-off lower level was used as a dressing room, and a platform on the second level, reached by a ladder, was used as a stage. Sometimes the action spilled off the wagon-stage and into an open area in front of the wagon, the *platea.* These pageant wagons moved from one stopping place in the town to another on performance days, the actors performing their play at each stop. Spectators could station themselves in one place and see the successive plays in the cycle performed in sequence.

By the time *Everyman* was performed, however, a somewhat different production method had been adopted for the longer morality plays. These were performed not as part of a cycle by members of a guild but independently by troupes of traveling players performing in town squares and on village greens. The original setting for *Everyman* was probably a stationary version of pageant-wagon staging: a two-story scaffold stage with an open space in front of it and probably two smaller sets, one on each side of the scaffold, for Goods and Good Deeds. This simple theater presented an elementary model of the medieval world view. God undoubtedly appeared on the "Heaven" of the top level, Death entered from the "Hell" of the covered lower level, and Everyman's main action was played on the "Earth" of the *platea.* In other respects as well, the theater and the conventions of staging allowed every element of the play to be translated into concrete, dramatic terms. The idea that earthly possessions weigh one down in the quest for salvation is vividly and amusingly presented by the immobilized Goods, unable to stir because of the chests and bags full of gold lying upon and around him. Similarly, the "scourge of penance" that Knowledge gives Everyman is no metaphor, but an actual whip.

The hasty reader of *Everyman* may dismiss it as crude and obvious, interesting only historically. It is true that the message of the play is presented with a crude directness and that its rhymed doggerel is naive, sometimes monotonous. But upon a closer reading, and especially after seeing a good performance, one's respect for the skill and artistry of the nameless playwright is likely to increase. The play presents a generalized, archetypal action, a sort of X ray of human experience, but this generalizing tendency is everywhere in tension with a robust and earthy specificity. Everyman is not only all men, but a very particular man, economically but tellingly characterized. He is a fundamentally good-hearted but superficial sensualist who, at the existential moment when he must confront the reality of his impending death, undergoes a radical and convincing psychological transformation. The secondary characters are handled with a similar economical skill and frequently with a mordant, ironic comic touch. Fellowship, Kindred and Cousin, Goods, and the rest are not mere walking abstractions but vivid embodiments of the qualities they represent. Fellowship, for example, within his short scene, is presented as hail-fellow-well-met, blustery, effusive, and full of reminiscences of drinking bouts, but quick to take his leave when he discovers that something more serious than a party is about to occur. The action, too, is poised on a delicate line between the general and the particular. The plot is often described as an archetypal journey through life, but it is actually not quite so general; it suggests the whole of life through focusing sharply upon its end. The story becomes not only a parable of all human lives but a moving and personal study in one man's experience. Even the jogtrot language, at first distracting, comes to have a crude, direct power that is very moving.

Paradoxically, *Everyman*, which seems so quintessentially of its age, has had a long and prominent history on the modern stage and has exercised a considerable influence upon modern drama. William Poel restaged the play in London in 1901 in the medieval manner; the revival attracted much favorable attention and was repeated a number of times during the following fifteen years. The great German director Max Reinhardt was inspired by Poel's production to present his own version, adapted by the poet and playwright Hugo von Hofmannsthal. Reinhardt's *Jedermann* (German for *Everyman*) was first performed in 1911 in an elaborate production in an old Berlin circus building. In 1920, Reinhardt restaged his version of the play in front of the Salzburg Cathedral as part of the Salzburg Festival. The play was enormously successful and has been repeated every year since then to enormous festival crowds, except for a nine-year dark period between 1937 and 1946, when Hitler banned it as "Jewish." The Dutch version of the play has a similar annual production at the Holland Festival in the city of Delft.

Everyman, along with other pre-realistic plays, has had a strong influence on the development of the postrealistic modern drama, especially as a model for dramatizing inner, psychological action. Its influence is especially clear in two modern plays that also deal with approaching death: Eugene Ionesco's *Exit the King* and Samuel Beckett's *Endgame*.

FURTHER READING: A discussion of medieval drama, by Joseph A. Dane, is included in *European Writers: Medieval and Renaissance,* Vol. I, ed. George Stade, 1984. A thorough background study of miracle, mystery, and morality plays is Hardin Craig's *English Religious Drama of the Middle Ages,* 1955. In A. P. Rossiter's *English Drama from Early*

Times to the Elizabethans, 1950, morality plays are divided into two classes, those that view human life from cradle to grave and those that deal with a more specific situation. *The Castle of Perseverance* and *Everyman,* respectively, are discussed as representatives of these two classes, along with several other specimens. Glynne Wickham's *Shakespeare's Dramatic Heritage,* 1969, discusses the 1964 London production of *Everyman,* in which Everyman drifted onto stage wearing jeans and listening to music from the musical *Bye-bye Birdie.* Wickham discusses the persistence of the play's appeal and its ability to survive when transposed to a new setting. The first chapter of W. Roy MacKenzie's *The English Moralities from the Point of View of Allegory,* 1966, discusses the nature of the morality play, specifically considering *Everyman* as its best representative. Two complementary essays on the play's structure, a somewhat neglected topic, are Lawrence V. Ryan's "Doctrine and Dramatic Structure in *Everyman,*" *Speculum,* 32 (1957), 722–735, and Thomas F. Van Laan's "*Everyman:* A Structural Analysis," *PMLA,* 78 (1963), 465–475. Ryan discusses the relationship between structure and doctrinal content, arguing that the play's moral lessons are a natural outgrowth of the action.

EVERYMAN

MESSENGER	KNOWLEDGE
GOD: *Adonai*[1]	CONFESSION
DEATH	BEAUTY
EVERYMAN	STRENGTH
FELLOWSHIP	DISCRETION
COUSIN	FIVE WITS
KINDRED	ANGEL
GOODS	DOCTOR
GOOD DEEDS	

Here beginneth a treatise how the High Father of Heaven sendeth Death to summon every creature to come and give account of their lives in this world, and is in manner of a moral play.

MESSENGER. I pray you all give your audience,
And hear this matter with reverence,
By figure[2] a moral play—
The *Summoning of Everyman* called it is,
That of our lives and ending shows 5
How transitory we be all our day.
This matter is wondrous precious,
But the intent of it is more gracious,[3]
And sweet to bear away.
The story saith:—Man, in the beginning, 10
Look well, and take good heed to the ending,
Be you never so gay!
Ye think sin in the beginning full sweet,

[1]Hebrew name for God. [2]In form. [3]Having to do with God's grace.

Which in the end causeth the soul to weep,
When the body lieth in clay. 15
Here shall you see how Fellowship and Jollity,
Both Strength, Pleasure, and Beauty,
Will fade from thee as flower in May.
For ye shall hear how our Heaven King
Calleth Everyman to a general reckoning. 20
Give audience, and hear what he doth say. [*Exit.*]

[GOD *speaketh from above.*]

GOD. I perceive, here in my majesty,
How that all creatures be to me unkind,
Living without dread in worldly prosperity.
Of ghostly sight[4] the people be so blind, 25
Drowned in sin, they know me not for their God.
In worldly riches is all their mind,
They fear not my rightwiseness,[5] the sharp rod;
My love that I showed when I for them died
They forget clean, and shedding of my blood red; 30
I hanged between two, it cannot be denied;
To get them life I suffered to be dead;
I healed their feet, with thorns hurt was my head.
I could do no more than I did, truly;
And now I see the people do clean forsake me. 35
They use the seven deadly sins damnable;
As pride, covetise, wrath, and lechery,
Now in the world be made commendable;
And thus they leave of angels the heavenly company.
Every man liveth so after his own pleasure, 40
And yet of their life they be nothing sure.
I see the more that I them forbear
The worse they be from year to year;
All that liveth appaireth[6] fast.
Therefore I will, in all the haste, 45
Have a reckoning of every man's person;
For, and[7] I leave the people thus alone
In their life and wicked tempests,
Verily they will become much worse than beasts;
For now one would by envy another up eat; 50
Charity they all do clean forget.
I hoped well that every man
In my glory should make his mansion,
And thereto I had them all elect;
But now I see, like traitors deject,[8] 55
They thank me not for the pleasure that I to them meant,
Nor yet for their being that I them have lent.

[4]Spiritual insight. [5]Righteousness. [6]Degenerates.
[7]If (frequently throughout the play). [8]Abject.

I proffered the people great multitude of mercy,
And few there be that asketh it heartily;
They be so cumbered with worldly riches, 60
That needs on them I must do justice,
On every man living, without fear.
Where art thou, Death, thou mighty messenger?

[*Enter* DEATH.]

DEATH. Almighty God, I am here at your will,
Your commandment to fulfil. 65
GOD. Go thou to Everyman,
And show him, in my name,
A pilgrimage he must on him take,
Which he in no wise[9] may escape;
And that he bring with him a sure reckoning 70
Without delay or any tarrying.
DEATH. Lord, I will in the world go run over all,
And cruelly out search both great and small. [GOD *withdraws.*]
Every man will I beset that liveth beastly
Out of God's laws, and dreadeth not folly. 75
He that loveth riches I will strike with my dart,
His sight to blind, and from heaven to depart,
Except that alms be his good friend,
In hell for to dwell, world without end.
Lo, yonder I see Everyman walking; 80
Full little he thinketh on my coming;
His mind is on fleshly lusts and his treasure;
And great pain it shall cause him to endure
Before the Lord, Heaven King.
Everyman, stand still! Whither art thou going 85
Thus gaily? Hast thou thy Maker forgot?
EVERYMAN. Why askest thou?
Wouldst thou wete?[10]
DEATH. Yea, sir, I will show you;
In great haste I am sent to thee 90
From God out of his Majesty.
EVERYMAN. What, sent to me?
DEATH. Yea, certainly.
Though thou have forgot him here,
He thinketh on thee in the heavenly sphere, 95
As, ere we depart, thou shalt know.
EVERYMAN. What desireth God of me?
DEATH. That shall I show thee;
A reckoning he will needs have
Without any longer respite. 100
EVERYMAN. To give a reckoning longer leisure I crave;
This blind matter troubleth my wit.

[9] In no way (frequently throughout the play). [10] Know.

DEATH. On thee thou must take a long journey;
Therefore thy book of count[11] with thee thou bring;
For turn again thou can not by no way. 105
And look thou be sure of thy reckoning,
For before God thou shalt answer and show
Thy many bad deeds, and good but a few,
How thou hast spent thy life, and in what wise,
Before the Chief Lord of paradise. 110
Have ado[12] that we were in that way,
For, wete thou well, thou shalt make none attorney.[13]
EVERYMAN. Full unready I am such reckoning to give.
I know thee not. What messenger art thou?
DEATH. I am Death, that no man dreadeth. 115
For every man I 'rest, and no man spareth;
For it is God's commandment
That all to me should be obedient.
EVERYMAN. O Death! thou comest when I had thee least in mind!
In thy power it lieth me to save, 120
Yet of my goods will I give thee, if thou will be kind;
Yea, a thousand pound shalt thou have,
If thou defer this matter till another day.
DEATH. Everyman, it may not be, by no way!
I set not by gold, silver, nor riches, 125
Nor by pope, emperor, king, duke, nor princes.
For, and I would receive gifts great,
All the world I might get;
But my custom is clean contrary.
I give thee no respite. Come hence, and not tarry. 130
EVERYMAN. Alas! shall I have no longer respite?
I may say Death giveth no warning.
To think on thee, it maketh my heart sick,
For all unready is my book of reckoning.
But twelve year and I might have abiding, 135
My counting-book I would make so clear,
That my reckoning I should not need to fear.
Wherefore, Death, I pray thee, for God's mercy,
Spare me till I be provided of remedy.
DEATH. Thee availeth not to cry, weep, and pray; 140
But haste thee lightly that thou were gone that journey,
And prove thy friends if thou can.
For wete thou well the tide abideth no man;
And in the world each living creature
For Adam's sin must die of nature. 145
EVERYMAN. Death, if I should this pilgrimage take,
And my reckoning surely make,
Show me, for saint charity,
Should I not come again shortly?

[11]Accounts. [12]Get ready. [13]You cannot make anyone your representative.

DEATH. No, Everyman; and thou be once there, 150
Thou mayst never more come here,
Trust me verily.
EVERYMAN. O gracious God, in the high seat celestial,
Have mercy on me in this most need!
Shall I have no company from this vale terrestrial 155
Of mine acquaintance that way me to lead?
DEATH. Yea, if any be so hardy,
That would go with thee and bear thee company.
Hie thee that thou were gone[14] to God's magnificence,
Thy reckoning to give before his presence. 160
What! weenest[15] thou thy life is given thee,
And thy worldly goods also?
EVERYMAN. I had weened so, verily.
DEATH. Nay, nay; it was but lent thee;
For, as soon as thou art gone, 165
Another a while shall have it, and then go therefrom
Even as thou hast done.
Everyman, thou art mad! Thou hast thy wits[16] five,
And here on earth will not amend thy life;
For suddenly I do come. 170
EVERYMAN. O wretched caitiff![17] whither shall I flee,
That I might 'scape endless sorrow?
Now, gentle Death, spare me till tomorrow,
That I may amend me
With good advisement. 175
DEATH. Nay, thereto I will not consent,
Nor no man will I respite,
But to the heart suddenly I shall smite
Without any advisement.
And now out of thy sight I will me hie; 180
See thou make thee ready shortly,
For thou mayst say this is the day
That no man living may 'scape away. [*Exit* DEATH.]
EVERYMAN. Alas! I may well weep with sighs deep.
Now have I no manner of company 185
To help me in my journey and me to keep;
And also my writing is full unready.
How shall I do now for to excuse me?
I would to God I had never been gete![18]
To my soul a full great profit it had be; 190
For now I fear pains huge and great.
The time passeth; Lord, help, that all wrought.
For though I mourn it availeth naught.
The day passeth, and is almost a-go;[19]
I wot[20] not well what for to do. 195

[14]Hasten to be gone. [15]Thinkest. [16]Senses. [17]Knave.
[18]Born. [19]Gone. [20]Know.

To whom were I best my complaint to make?
What if I to Fellowship thereof spake,
And showed him of this sudden chance?
For in him is all mine affiance,[21]
We have in the world so many a day 200
Been good friends in sport and play.
I see him yonder, certainly;
I trust that he will bear me company;
Therefore to him will I speak to ease my sorrow.
Well met, good Fellowship, and good morrow! 205

[FELLOWSHIP *speaketh.*]

FELLOWSHIP. Everyman, good morrow, by this day!
Sir, why lookest thou so piteously?
If any thing be amiss, I pray thee me say,
That I may help to remedy.
EVERYMAN. Yea, good Fellowship, yea, 210
I am in great jeopardy.
FELLOWSHIP. My true friend, show to me your mind;
I will not forsake thee to my life's end
In the way of good company.
EVERYMAN. That was well spoken, and lovingly. 215
FELLOWSHIP. Sir, I must needs know your heaviness;
I have pity to see you in any distress;
If any have you wronged, ye shall revenged be,
Though I on the ground be slain for thee,
Though that I know before that I should die. 220
EVERYMAN. Verily, Fellowship, gramercy.[22]
FELLOWSHIP. Tush! by thy thanks I set not a straw!
Show me your grief, and say no more.
EVERYMAN. If I my heart should to you break,
And then you to turn your mind from me, 225
And would not me comfort when you hear me speak,
Then should I ten times sorrier be.
FELLOWSHIP. Sir, I say as I will do, indeed.
EVERYMAN. Then be you a good friend at need;
I have found you true here before. 230
FELLOWSHIP. And so ye shall evermore;
For, in faith, and thou go to hell,
I will not forsake thee by the way!
EVERYMAN. Ye speak like a good friend. I believe you well;
I shall deserve it, and I may. 235
FELLOWSHIP. I speak of no deserving, by this day!
For he that will say and nothing do
Is not worthy with good company to go;
Therefore show me the grief of your mind,
As to your friend most loving and kind. 240

[21] Trust. [22] Thank you.

EVERYMAN. I shall show you how it is:
Commanded I am to go a journey,
A long way, hard and dangerous,
And give a strict count without delay
Before the high judge, Adonai. 245
Wherefore, I pray you, bear me company,
As ye have promised, in this journey.
FELLOWSHIP. That is matter indeed! Promise is duty;
But, and I should take such a voyage on me,
I know it well, it should be to my pain. 250
Also it maketh me afeared, certain.
But let us take counsel here as well as we can,
For your words would fright a strong man.
EVERYMAN. Why, ye said if I had need,
Ye would me never forsake, quick nor dead, 255
Though it were to hell, truly.
FELLOWSHIP. So I said, certainly,
But such pleasures be set aside, the sooth[23] to say.
And also, if we took such a journey,
When should we come again? 260
EVERYMAN. Nay, never again till the day of doom.
FELLOWSHIP. In faith, then will not I come there!
Who hath you these tidings brought?
EVERYMAN. Indeed, Death was with me here.
FELLOWSHIP. Now, by God that all hath bought, 265
If Death were the messenger,
For no man that is living today
I will not go that loath journey—
Nor for the father that begat me!
EVERYMAN. Ye promised otherwise, pardie.[24] 270
FELLOWSHIP. I wot well I said so, truly;
And yet if thou wilt eat, and drink, and make good cheer,
Or haunt to women the lusty company,
I would not forsake you while the day is clear,
Trust me verily! 275
EVERYMAN. Yea, thereto ye would be ready;
To go to mirth, solace, and play,
Your mind will sooner apply
Than to bear me company in my long journey.
FELLOWSHIP. Now, in good faith, I will not that way. 280
But and thou wilt murder, or any man kill,
In that I will help thee with a good will!
EVERYMAN. O, that is a simple advice indeed!
Gentle fellow, help me in my necessity;
We have loved long, and now I need, 285
And now, gentle Fellowship, remember me!
FELLOWSHIP. Whether ye have loved me or no,
By Saint John, I will not with thee go.

[23]Truth. [24]*Par dieu:* indeed. (Literally, "by God.")

EVERYMAN. Yet, I pray thee, take the labor, and do so much for me
To bring me forward, for saint charity, 290
And comfort me till I come without the town.
FELLOWSHIP. Nay, and thou would give me a new gown,
I will not a foot with thee go;
But, and thou had tarried, I would not have left thee so.
And as now God speed thee in thy journey, 295
For from thee I will depart as fast as I may.
EVERYMAN. Whither away, Fellowship? Will you forsake me?
FELLOWSHIP. Yea, by my fay,[25] to God I betake[26] thee.
EVERYMAN. Farewell, good Fellowship! For thee my heart is sore;
Adieu for ever! I shall see thee no more. 300
FELLOWSHIP. In faith, Everyman, farewell now at the end!
For you I will remember that parting is mourning.

[*Exit* FELLOWSHIP.]

EVERYMAN. Alack! shall we thus depart indeed
(Ah, Lady, help!) without any more comfort?
Lo, Fellowship forsaketh me in my most need. 305
For help in this world whither shall I resort?
Fellowship here before with me would merry make,
And now little sorrow for me doth he take.
It is said, "In prosperity men friends may find,
Which in adversity be full unkind." 310
Now whither for succor shall I flee,
Sith that[27] Fellowship hath forsaken me?
To my kinsmen I will, truly,
Praying them to help me in my necessity;
I believe that they will do so, 315
For "kind will creep where it may not go."[28]
I will go say,[29] for yonder I see them go.
Where be ye now, my friends and kinsmen?

[*Enter* KINDRED *and* COUSIN.]

KINDRED. Here be we now, at your commandment.
Cousin, I pray you show us your intent 320
In any wise, and do not spare.
COUSIN. Yea, Everyman, and to us declare
If ye be disposed to go any whither,
For, wete you well, we will live and die together.
KINDRED. In wealth and woe we will with you hold, 325
For over his kin a man may be bold.
EVERYMAN. Gramercy, my friends and kinsmen kind.
Now shall I show you the grief of my mind.
I was commanded by a messenger
That is a high king's chief officer; 330
He bade me go a pilgrimage, to my pain,

[25]Faith. [26]Commit. [27]Since. [28]Walk. [29]Try.

And I know well I shall never come again;
Also I must give a reckoning straight,
For I have a great enemy that hath me in wait,[30]
Which intendeth me for to hinder. 335

KINDRED. What account is that which ye must render?
That would I know.

EVERYMAN. Of all my works I must show
How I have lived, and my days spent;
Also of ill deeds that I have used 340
In my time, sith life was me lent;
And of all virtues that I have refused.
Therefore I pray you go thither with me,
To help to make mine account, for saint charity.

COUSIN. What, to go thither? Is that the matter? 345
Nay, Everyman, I had liefer fast bread and water
All this five year and more.

EVERYMAN. Alas, that ever I was bore!
For now shall I never be merry
If that you forsake me. 350

KINDRED. Ah, sir, what! Ye be a merry man!
Take good heart to you, and make no moan.
But one thing I warn you, by Saint Anne,
As for me, ye shall go alone.

EVERYMAN. My Cousin, will you not with me go? 355

COUSIN. No, by our Lady! I have the cramp in my toe.
Trust not to me; for, so God me speed,
I will deceive you in your most need.

KINDRED. It availeth not us to tice.[31]
Ye shall have my maid with all my heart; 360
She loveth to go to feasts, there to be nice,[32]
And to dance, and abroad to start;
I will give her leave to help you in that journey,
If that you and she may agree.

EVERYMAN. Now show me the very effect of your mind. 365
Will you go with me, or abide behind?

KINDRED. Abide behind? Yea, that will I, and I may!
Therefore farewell till another day. [*Exit* KINDRED.]

EVERYMAN. How should I be merry or glad?
For fair promises men to me make, 370
But when I have most need, they me forsake.
I am deceived; that maketh me sad.

COUSIN. Cousin Everyman, farewell now,
For verily I will not go with you;
Also of mine own life an unready reckoning 375
I have to account; therefore I make tarrying.
Now, God keep thee, for now I go. [*Exit* COUSIN.]

EVERYMAN. Ah, Jesus! is all come hereto?

[30] Lies in wait for me. [31] Entice. [32] Wanton.

Lo, fair words maketh fools fain;[33]
They promise and nothing will do certain. 380
My kinsmen promised me faithfully
For to abide with me steadfastly,
And now fast away do they flee.
Even so Fellowship promised me.
What friend were best me of to provide? 385
I lose my time here longer to abide.
Yet in my mind a thing there is:
All my life I have loved riches;
If that my Goods now help me might,
He would make my heart full light. 390
I will speak to him in this distress.
Where art thou, my Goods and riches?

GOODS [*from within*]. Who calleth me? Everyman? What, hast thou haste?
I lie here in corners, trussed and piled so high,
And in chests I am locked so fast, 395
Also sacked in bags—thou mayst see with thine eye—
I cannot stir; in packs low I lie.
What would ye have? Lightly me say.

EVERYMAN. Come hither, Goods, in all the haste thou may.
For of counsel I must desire thee. 400

[*Enter* GOODS.]

GOODS. Sir, and ye in the world have sorrow or adversity,
That can I help you to remedy shortly.

EVERYMAN. It is another disease that grieveth me;
In this world it is not, I tell thee so.
I am sent for another way to go, 405
To give a strict count general
Before the highest Jupiter of all;
And all my life I have had joy and pleasure in thee;
Therefore I pray thee go with me,
For, peradventure,[34] thou mayst before God Almighty 410
My reckoning help to clean and purify;
For it is said ever among,
That "money maketh all right that is wrong."

GOODS. Nay, Everyman; I sing another song,
I follow no man in such voyages; 415
For, and I went with thee,
Thou shouldst fare much the worse for me;
For because on me thou did set thy mind,
Thy reckoning I have made blotted and blind,
That thine account thou cannot make truly; 420
And that hast thou for the love of me.

[33] Glad. [34] Perhaps.

EVERYMAN. That would grieve me full sore,
When I should come to that fearful answer.
Up, let us go thither together.
GOODS. Nay, not so! I am too brittle, I may not endure; 425
I will follow no man one foot, be ye sure.
EVERYMAN. Alas! I have thee loved, and had great pleasure
All my life-days on goods and treasure.
GOODS. That is to thy damnation, without lesing![35]
For my love is contrary to the love everlasting. 430
But if thou had me loved moderately during,
As to the poor to give part of me,
Then shouldst thou not in this dolor be,
Nor in this great sorrow and care.
EVERYMAN. Lo, now was I deceived ere I was ware, 435
And all I may wyte[36] my spending of time.
GOODS. What, weenest thou that I am thine?
EVERYMAN. I had weened so.
GOODS. Nay, Everyman, I say no;
As for a while I was lent thee, 440
A season thou hast had me in prosperity.
My condition is man's soul to kill;
If I save one, a thousand I do spill;[37]
Weenest thou that I will follow thee
From this world? Nay, verily. 445
EVERYMAN. I had weened otherwise.
GOODS. Therefore to thy soul Goods is a thief;
For when thou art dead, this is my guise—[38]
Another to deceive in the same wise
As I have done thee, and all to his soul's reprief.[39] 450
EVERYMAN. O false Goods, cursèd thou be!
Thou traitor to God, that hast deceived me
And caught me in thy snare.
GOODS. Marry! thou brought thyself in care,
Whereof I am right glad. 455
I must needs laugh, I cannot be sad.
EVERYMAN. Ah, Goods, thou hast had long my heartly love;
I gave thee that which should be the Lord's above.
But wilt thou not go with me indeed?
I pray thee truth to say. 460
GOODS. No, so God me speed!
Therefore farewell, and have good day. [*Exit* GOODS.]
EVERYMAN. O, to whom shall I make my moan
For to go with me in that heavy journey?
First Fellowship said he would with me gone; 465
His words were very pleasant and gay,
But afterward he left me alone.
Then spake I to my kinsmen, all in despair,
And also they gave me words fair,

[35] Lying. [36] Blame upon. [37] Ruin. [38] Practice; trick. [39] Reproof.

They lacked no fair speaking, 470
But all forsook me in the ending.
Then went I to my Goods, that I loved best,
In hope to have comfort, but there had I least;
For my Goods sharply did me tell
That he bringeth many into hell. 475
Then of myself I was ashamed,
And so I am worthy to be blamed;
Thus may I well myself hate.
Of whom shall I now counsel take?
I think that I shall never speed 480
Till that I go to my Good Deeds.
But alas! she is so weak
That she can neither go nor speak.
Yet will I venture on her now.
My Good Deeds, where be you? 485

[GOOD DEEDS *speaks from the ground.*]

GOOD DEEDS. Here I lie, cold in the ground.
Thy sins hath me sore bound,
That I cannot stir.
EVERYMAN. O Good Deeds! I stand in fear;
I must you pray of counsel, 490
For help now should come right well.
GOOD DEEDS. Everyman, I have understanding
That ye be summoned account to make
Before Messias, of Jerusalem King;
And you do by me,[40] that journey with you will I take. 495
EVERYMAN. Therefore I come to you my moan to make;
I pray you that ye will go with me.
GOOD DEEDS. I would full fain, but I cannot stand, verily.
EVERYMAN. Why, is there anything on you fall?
GOOD DEEDS. Yea, sir, I may thank you of all; 500
If ye had perfectly cheered[41] me,
Your book of count full ready had be.
Look, the books of your works and deeds eke;[42]
Ah, see how they lie under the feet,
To your soul's heaviness. 505
EVERYMAN. Our Lord Jesus help me!
For one letter here I can not see.
GOOD DEEDS. There is a blind reckoning in time of distress!
EVERYMAN. Good Deeds, I pray you, help me in this need,
Or else I am for ever damned indeed; 510
Therefore help me to make my reckoning
Before the Redeemer of all thing,
That King is, and was, and ever shall.
GOOD DEEDS. Everyman, I am sorry of your fall,
And fain would I help you, and I were able. 515
EVERYMAN. Good Deeds, your counsel I pray you give me.

[40] If you take my advice. [41] Cherished. [42] Also.

GOOD DEEDS. That shall I do verily;
Though that on my feet I may not go,
I have a sister that shall with you also,
Called Knowledge, which shall with you abide, 520
To help you to make that dreadful reckoning.

[*Enter* KNOWLEDGE.]

KNOWLEDGE. Everyman, I will go with thee, and be thy guide
In thy most need to go by thy side.
EVERYMAN. In good condition I am now in every thing,
And am wholly content with this good thing; 525
Thanked be God my Creator.
GOOD DEEDS. And when he hath brought thee there,
Where thou shalt heal thee of thy smart,
Then go you with your reckoning and your Good Deeds together
For to make you joyful at heart 530
Before the blessèd Trinity.
EVERYMAN. My Good Deeds, gramercy!
I am well content, certainly,
With your words sweet.
KNOWLEDGE. Now go we together lovingly 535
To Confession, that cleansing river.
EVERYMAN. For joy I weep; I would we were there!
But, I pray you, give my cognition
Where dwelleth that holy man, Confession.
KNOWLEDGE. In the house of salvation; 540
We shall find him in that place,
That shall us comfort, by God's grace.

[KNOWLEDGE *leads* EVERYMAN *to* CONFESSION.]

Lo, this is Confession. Kneel down and ask mercy,
For he is in good conceit[43] with God almighty.
EVERYMAN [*kneeling*]. O glorious fountain, that all uncleanness doth
clarify, 545
Wash from me the spots of vice unclean,
That on me no sin may be seen.
I come, with Knowledge, for my redemption,
Redempt with hearty and full contrition;
For I am commanded a pilgrimage to take, 550
And great accounts before God to make.
Now, I pray you, Shrift,[44] mother of salvation.
Help my Good Deeds for my piteous exclamation.
CONFESSION. I know your sorrow well, Everyman.
Because with Knowledge ye come to me, 555
I will you comfort as well as I can,
And a precious jewel I will give thee,
Called penance, voider of adversity;

[43]Esteem. [44]The sacrament of confession.

Therewith shall your body chastised be,
With abstinence, and perseverance in God's service. 560
Here shall you receive that scourge of me.

[*Gives* EVERYMAN *a scourge.*]

Which is penance strong, that ye must endure
To remember thy Savior was scourged for thee
With sharp scourges, and suffered it patiently;
So must thou ere thou 'scape that painful pilgrimage. 565
Knowledge, keep him in this voyage,
And by that time Good Deeds will be with thee.
But in any wise be seeker of mercy,
For your time draweth fast, and ye will saved be;
Ask God mercy, and He will grant truly; 570
When with the scourge of penance man doth him bind,
The oil of forgiveness then shall he find. [*Exit* CONFESSION.]

EVERYMAN. Thanked be God for his gracious work!
For now I will my penance begin;
This hath rejoiced and lighted my heart, 575
Though the knots be painful and hard within.

KNOWLEDGE. Everyman, look your penance that ye fulfil,
What pain that ever it to you be,
And Knowledge shall give you counsel at will
How your account ye shall make clearly. 580

[EVERYMAN *kneels.*]

EVERYMAN. O eternal God! O heavenly figure!
O way of rightwiseness! O goodly vision!
Which descended down in a virgin pure
Because he would Everyman redeem,
Which Adam forfeited by his disobedience. 585
O blesséd Godhead! elect and high divine,
Forgive me my grievous offence;
Here I cry thee mercy in this presence.
O ghostly treasure! O ransomer and redeemer!
Of all the world hope and conductor, 590
Mirror of joy, and founder of mercy,
Which illumineth heaven and earth thereby,
Hear my clamorous complaint, though it late be.
Receive my prayers; unworthy in this heavy life.
Though I be a sinner most abominable, 595
Yet let my name be written in Moses' table.
O Mary! pray to the Maker of all thing,
Me for to help at my ending,
And save me from the power of my enemy,
For Death assaileth me strongly. 600
And, Lady, that I may by means of thy prayer
Of your Son's glory to be partner,
By the means of his passion I it crave;
I beseech you, help my soul to save. [*He rises.*]

Knowledge, give me the scourge of penance. 605
My flesh therewith shall give a quittance.
I will now begin, if God give me grace.
KNOWLEDGE. Everyman, God give you time and space.
Thus I bequeath you in the hands of our Savior,
Now may you make your reckoning sure. 610
EVERYMAN. In the name of the Holy Trinity,
My body sore punished shall be. [*Scourges himself.*]
Take this, body, for the sin of the flesh;
Also thou delightest to go gay and fresh,
And in the way of damnation thou did me bring; 615
Therefore suffer now strokes of punishing.
Now of penance I will wade the water clear,
To save me from purgatory, that sharp fire.

[GOOD DEEDS *rises from floor.*]

GOOD DEEDS. I thank God, now I can walk and go,
And am delivered of my sickness and woe. 620
Therefore with Everyman I will go, and not spare;
His good works I will help him to declare.
KNOWLEDGE. Now, Everyman, be merry and glad!
Your Good Deeds cometh now, ye may not be sad;
Now is your Good Deeds whole and sound, 625
Going upright upon the ground.
EVERYMAN. My heart is light, and shall be evermore.
Now will I smite faster than I did before.
GOOD DEEDS. Everyman, pilgrim, my special friend,
Blesséd be thou without end. 630
For thee is prepared the eternal glory.
Ye have me made whole and sound,
Therefore I will bide by thee in every stound.[45]
EVERYMAN. Welcome, my Good Deeds; now I hear thy voice,
I weep for very sweetness of love. 635
KNOWLEDGE. Be no more sad, but ever rejoice;
God seeth thy living in his throne above.
Put on this garment to thy behoof,
Which is wet with your tears,
Or else before God you may it miss, 640
When you to your journey's end come shall.
EVERYMAN. Gentle Knowledge, what do ye it call?
KNOWLEDGE. It is the garment of sorrow;
From pain it will you borrow;
Contrition it is 645
That getteth forgiveness;
It pleaseth God passing well.
GOOD DEEDS. Everyman, will you wear it for your heal?

[45] In every situation; always.

[EVERYMAN *puts on garment of contrition.*]

EVERYMAN. Now blesséd be Jesu, Mary's Son,
For now have I on true contrition. 650
And let us go now without tarrying;
Good Deeds, have we clear our reckoning?
GOOD DEEDS. Yea, indeed I have it here.
EVERYMAN. Then I trust we need not fear.
Now, friends, let us not part in twain. 655
KNOWLEDGE. Nay, Everyman, that will we not, certain.
GOOD DEEDS. Yet must thou lead with thee
Three persons of great might.
EVERYMAN. Who should they be?
GOOD DEEDS. Discretion and Strength they hight,[46] 660
And thy Beauty may not abide behind.
KNOWLEDGE. Also ye must call to mind
Your Five Wits as for your counselors.
GOOD DEEDS. You must have them ready at all hours.
EVERYMAN. How shall I get them hither? 665
KNOWLEDGE. You must call them all together,
And they will hear you incontinent.[47]
EVERYMAN. My friends, come hither and be present;
Discretion, Strength, my Five Wits, and Beauty.

[*Enter* DISCRETION, STRENGTH, FIVE WITS, *and* BEAUTY.]

BEAUTY. Here at your will we be all ready. 670
What will ye that we should do?
GOOD DEEDS. That ye would with Everyman go,
And help him in his pilgrimage.
Advise you, will ye with him or not in that voyage?
STRENGTH. We will bring him all thither, 675
To his help and comfort, ye may believe me.
DISCRETION. So will we go with him all together.
EVERYMAN. Almighty God, lovéd may thou be!
I give thee laud that I have hither brought
Strength, Discretion, Beauty, and Five Wits. Lack I naught; 680
And my Good Deeds, with Knowledge clear,
All be in company at my will here.
I desire no more to my business.
STRENGTH. And I, Strength, will by you stand in distress,
Though thou would in battle fight on the ground. 685
FIVE WITS. And though it were through the world round,
We will not depart for sweet nor sour.
BEAUTY. No more will I, unto death's hour,
Whatsoever thereof befall.

[46]Are called. [47]At once.

DISCRETION. Everyman, advise you first of all; 690
Go with a good advisement and deliberation.
We all give you virtuous monition
That all shall be well.

EVERYMAN. My friends, hearken what I will tell:
I pray God reward you in his heavenly sphere. 695
Now hearken, all that be here,
For I will make my testament
Here before you all present:
In alms half my goods I will give with my hands twain
In the way of charity, with good intent, 700
And the other half still shall remain;
I it bequeath to be returned there it ought to be.
This I do in despite of the fiend of hell,
To go quite out of his peril
Ever after and this day. 705

KNOWLEDGE. Everyman, hearken what I say;
Go to Priesthood, I you advise,
And receive of him in any wise
The holy sacrament and ointment together;
Then shortly see ye turn again hither; 710
We will all abide you here.

FIVE WITS. Yea, Everyman, hie you that ye ready were.
There is no emperor, king, duke, nor baron,
That of God hath commission
As hath the least priest in the world being; 715
For of the blesséd sacraments pure and benign
He beareth the keys, and thereof hath the cure
For man's redemption—it is ever sure—
Which God for our soul's medicine
Gave us out of his heart with great pain, 720
Here in this transitory life, for thee and me.
The blesséd sacraments seven there be:
Baptism, confirmation, with priesthood good,
And the sacrament of God's precious flesh and blood,
Marriage, the holy extreme unction, and penance. 725
These seven be good to have in remembrance,
Gracious sacraments of high divinity.

EVERYMAN. Fain would I receive that holy body
And meekly to my ghostly[48] father I will go.

FIVE WITS. Everyman, that is the best that ye can do. 730
God will you to salvation bring,
For priesthood exceedeth all other thing;
To us Holy Scripture they do teach,
And converteth man from sin, heaven to reach;
God hath to them more power given, 735
Than to any angel that is in heaven.

[48] Spiritual.

With five words[49] he may consecrate
God's body in flesh and blood to make,
And handleth his Maker between his hands.
The priest bindeth and unbindeth all bands, 740
Both in earth and in heaven;
Thou ministers all the sacraments seven;
Though we kissed thy feet, thou wert worthy;
Thou art the surgeon that cureth sin deadly:
No remedy we find under God 745
But all only priesthood.
Everyman, God gave priests that dignity,
And setteth them in his stead among us to be;
Thus be they above angels, in degree.

[*Exit* EVERYMAN.]

KNOWLEDGE. If priests be good, it is so, surely. 750
But when Jesus hanged on the cross with great smart,
There he gave out of his blessèd heart
The same sacrament in great torment.
He sold them not to us, that Lord omnipotent.
Therefore Saint Peter the Apostle doth say 755
That Jesus' curse hath all they
Which God their Savior do buy or sell,
Or they for any money do take or tell.
Sinful priests giveth the sinners example bad;
Their children sitteth by other men's fires, I have heard; 760
And some haunteth women's company
With unclean life, as lusts of lechery.
These be with sin made blind.
FIVE WITS. I trust to God no such may we find.
Therefore let us priesthood honor, 765
And follow their doctrine for our souls' succor.
We be their sheep, and they shepherds be
By whom we all be kept in surety.
Peace! for yonder I see Everyman come,
Which hath made true satisfaction. 770
GOOD DEEDS. Methinketh it is he indeed.

[*Re-enter* EVERYMAN.]

EVERYMAN. Now Jesu be your alder speed.[50]
I have received the sacrament for my redemption,
And then mine extreme unction.
Blessèd be all they that counseled me to take it! 775
And now, friends, let us go without longer respite.
I thank God that ye have tarried so long.

[49] The five words are *Hoc est enim corpus meum:* "For this is my body."
[50] Jesus be the succor of all of you.

Now set each of you on this rod[51] your hand,
And shortly follow me.
I go before, there I would be. God be our guide. 780
STRENGTH. Everyman, we will not from you go,
Till ye have done this voyage long.
DISCRETION. I, Discretion, will bide by you also.
KNOWLEDGE. And though this pilgrimage be never so strong,
I will never part you fro. 785
Everyman, I will be as sure by thee
As ever I did by Judas Maccabee.[52]

[*They go together to the grave.*]

EVERYMAN. Alas! I am so faint I may not stand,
My limbs under me do fold.
Friends, let us not turn again to this land, 790
Not for all the world's gold;
For into this cave must I creep
And turn to earth, and there to sleep.
BEAUTY. What, into this grave? Alas!
EVERYMAN. Yea, there shall you consume, more and less. 795
BEAUTY. And what, should I smother here?
EVERYMAN. Yea, by my faith, and never more appear.
In this world live no more we shall,
But in heaven before the highest Lord of all.
BEAUTY. I cross out all this; adieu, by Saint John! 800
I take my cap in my lap and am gone.
EVERYMAN. What, Beauty, whither will ye?
BEAUTY. Peace! I am deaf. I look not behind me,
Not and thou would give me all the gold in thy chest. [*Exit* BEAUTY.]
EVERYMAN. Alas, whereto may I trust? 805
Beauty goeth fast away from me;
She promised with me to live and die.
STRENGTH. Everyman, I will thee also forsake and deny.
Thy game liketh me not at all.[53]
EVERYMAN. Why, then ye will forsake me all? 810
Sweet Strength, tarry a little space.
STRENGTH. Nay, sir, by the rood[54] of grace,
I will hie me from thee fast,
Though thou weep till thy heart to-brast.[55]
EVERYMAN. Ye would ever bide by me, ye said. 815
STRENGTH. Yea, I have you far enough conveyed.
Ye be old enough, I understand,
Your pilgrimage to take on hand.
I repent me that I hither came.
EVERYMAN. Strength, you to displease I am to blame; 820
Yet promise is debt, this ye well wot.

[51]Cross. [52]Jewish patriot, second century B.C.
[53]I do not like this game at all. [54]Cross. [55]Break into pieces.

STRENGTH. In faith, I care not!
Thou are but a fool to complain.
You spend your speech and waste your brain;
Go, thrust thee into the ground. [*Exit* STRENGTH.] 825
EVERYMAN. I had weened surer I should you have found.
He that trusteth in his Strength
She him deceiveth at the length.
Both Strength and Beauty forsaketh me,
Yet they promised me fair and lovingly. 830
DISCRETION. Everyman, I will after Strength be gone;
As for me I will leave you alone.
EVERYMAN. Why, Discretion, will ye forsake me?
DISCRETION. Yea, in faith, I will go from thee;
For when Strength goeth before 835
I follow after evermore.
EVERYMAN. Yet, I pray thee, for the love of the Trinity,
Look in my grave once piteously.
DISCRETION. Nay, so nigh will I not come.
Farewell, every one! [*Exit* DISCRETION.] 840
EVERYMAN. O all thing faileth, save God alone—
Beauty, Strength, and Discretion;
For when Death bloweth his blast,
They all run from me full fast.
FIVE WITS. Everyman, my leave now of thee I take; 845
I will follow the other, for here I thee forsake.
EVERYMAN. Alas! then may I wail and weep,
For I took you for my best friend.
FIVE WITS. I will no longer thee keep;
Now farewell, and there an end. [*Exit* FIVE WITS.] 850
EVERYMAN. O Jesu, help! All hath forsaken me!
GOOD DEEDS. Nay, Everyman; I will bide with thee,
I will not forsake thee indeed;
Thou shalt find me a good friend at need.
EVERYMAN. Gramercy, Good Deeds! Now may I true friends see. 855
They have forsaken me, every one;
I loved them better than my Good Deeds alone.
Knowledge, will ye forsake me also?
KNOWLEDGE. Yea, Everyman, when ye to death shall go;
But not yet, for no manner of danger. 860
EVERYMAN. Gramercy, Knowledge, with all my heart.
KNOWLEDGE. Nay, yet I will not from hence depart
Till I see where ye shall be come.
EVERYMAN. Methink, alas, that I must be gone
To make my reckoning and my debts pay, 865
For I see my time is nigh spent away.
Take example, all ye that this do hear or see,
How they that I loved best do forsake me,
Except my Good Deeds that bideth truly.
GOOD DEEDS. All earthly things is but vanity. 870
Beauty, Strength, and Discretion do man forsake,

Foolish friends and kinsmen, that fair spake,
All fleeth save Good Deeds, and that am I.
EVERYMAN. Have mercy on me, God most mighty;
And stand by me, thou Mother and Maid, holy Mary! 875
GOOD DEEDS. Fear not, I will speak for thee.
EVERYMAN. Here I cry God mercy!
GOOD DEEDS. Short our end, and 'minish our pain.
Let us go and never come again.
EVERYMAN. Into thy hands, Lord, my soul I commend. 880
Receive it, Lord, that it be not lost.
As thou me boughtest, so me defend,
And save me from the fiend's boast,
That I may appear with that blesséd host
That shall be saved at the day of doom. 885
In manus tuas—of might's most
For ever—*commendo spiritum meum.*[56]

[EVERYMAN *and* GOOD DEEDS *descend into the grave.*]

KNOWLEDGE. Now hath he suffered that we all shall endure;
The Good Deeds shall make all sure.
Now hath he made ending. 890
Methinketh that I hear angels sing
And make great joy and melody
Where Everyman's soul received shall be.
ANGEL [*within*]. Come, excellent elect spouse to Jesu!
Here above thou shalt go 895
Because of thy singular virtue.
Now the soul is taken the body fro,
Thy reckoning is crystal clear.
Now shalt thou into the heavenly sphere,
Unto the which all ye shall come 900
That liveth well before the day of doom.

[*Exit* KNOWLEDGE. *Enter* DOCTOR[57] *for Epilogue.*]

DOCTOR. This moral men may have in mind:
Ye hearers, take it of worth, old and young,
And forsake Pride, for he deceiveth you in the end,
And remember Beauty, Five Wits, Strength, and Discretion, 905
They all at the last do Everyman forsake,
Save his Good Deeds there doth he take.
But beware, and they be small

[56] "Into thy hands I commend my spirit."
[57] Theologian.

Before God he hath no help at all.
None excuse may be there for Everyman. 910
Alas, how shall he do then?
For, after death, amends may no man make,
For then mercy and pity doth him forsake.
If his reckoning be not clear when he doth come,
God will say, "*Ite, maledicti, in ignem aeternum.*"[58] 915
And he that hath his account whole and sound,
High in heaven he shall be crowned.
Unto which place God bring us all thither,
That we may live body and soul together.
Thereto help the Trinity! 920
Amen, say ye, for saint charity.

THUS ENDETH THIS MORAL PLAY OF EVERYMAN.

[58] "Go, cursed ones, into eternal fire."

John of Salisbury
(1115?–1180)

from *POLYCRATICUS*[1]

[THE BODY POLITIC]

A commonwealth, according to Plutarch,[2] is a certain body which is endowed with life by the benefit of divine favor, which acts at the prompting of the highest equity, and is ruled by what may be called the moderating power of reason. Those things which establish and implant in us the practice of religion, and transmit to us the worship of God (here I do not follow Plutarch, who says "of the Gods") fill the place of the soul in the body of the commonwealth. And therefore those who preside over the practice of religion should be looked up to and venerated as the soul of the body. For who doubts that the ministers of God's holiness are His representatives? Furthermore, since the soul is, as it were, the prince of the body, and has rulership over the whole thereof, so those whom our author calls the prefects of religion preside over the entire body. Augustus Cæsar was to such a degree subject to the priestly power of the pontiffs that in order to set himself free from this subjection and have no one at all over him, he caused himself to be created a pontiff of Vesta, and thereafter had himself promoted to be one of the gods during his own life-time. The place of the head in the body of the commonwealth is filled by the prince, who is subject only to God and to those who exercise His office and represent Him on earth, even as in the human body the head is quickened and governed by the soul. The place of the heart is filled by the Senate, from which proceeds the initiation of good works and ill. The duties of eyes, ears, and tongue are claimed by the judges and the

[1]Translated by John Dickinson. John of Salisbury was a French-educated English cleric who was secretary to two Archbishops of Canterbury and who later became bishop of Chartres. The *Polycraticus* ["The Statesman's Book"] (1159) is one of the most important books of political theory in the Middle Ages. It holds up an ideal of government based on classical and patristic principles against the practices of courtiers and administrators under King Henry II. In the passage printed here, John develops the familiar medieval analogy between the human body and human society, most famously repeated by Shakespeare in the first scene of *Coriolanus*.

[2]Greek essayist and biographer (46?–120? A.D.). John is citing an apocryphal work by Plutarch called "The Instruction of Trajan."

governors of provinces. Officials and soldiers correspond to the hands. Those who always attend upon the prince are likened to the sides. Financial officers and keepers (I speak now not of those who are in charge of the prisons, but of those who are keepers of the privy chest) may be compared with the stomach and intestines, and retain too tenaciously their accumulations, generate innumerable and incurable diseases, so that through their ailment the whole body is threatened with destruction. The husbandmen correspond to the feet, which always cleave to the soil, and need the more especially the care and foresight of the head, since while they walk upon the earth doing service with their bodies, they meet the more often with stones of stumbling, and therefore deserve aid and protection all the more justly since it is they who raise, sustain, and move forward the weight of the entire body. Take away the support of the feet from the strongest body, and it cannot move forward by its own power, but must creep painfully and shamefully on its hands, or else be moved by means of brute animals. . . .

Those are called the feet who discharge the humbler offices, and by whose services the members of the whole commonwealth walk upon solid earth. Among these are to be counted the husbandmen, who always cleave to the soil, busied about their plough-lands or vineyards or pastures or flower-gardens. To these must be added the many species of cloth-making, and the mechanic arts, which work in wood, iron, bronze and the different metals; also the menial occupations, and the manifold forms of getting a livelihood and sustaining life, or increasing household property, all of which, while they do not pertain to the authority of the governing power, are yet in the highest degree useful and profitable to the corporate whole of the commonwealth. All these different occupations are so numerous that the commonwealth in the number of its feet exceeds not only the eight-footed crab but even the centipede, and because of their very multitude they cannot be enumerated; for while they are not infinite by nature, they are yet of so many different varieties that no writer on the subject of offices or duties has ever laid down particular precepts for each special variety. But it applies generally to each and all of them that in their exercise they should not transgress the limits of the law, and should in all things observe constant reference to the public utility. For inferiors owe it to their superiors to provide them with service, just as the superiors in their turn owe it to their inferiors to provide them with all things needful for their protection and succor. Therefore Plutarch says that that course is to be pursued in all things which is of advantage to the humbler classes, that is to say to the multitude; for small numbers always yield to great. Indeed the reason for the institution of magistrates was to the end that subjects might be protected from wrongs, and that the commonwealth itself might be "shod," so to speak, by means of their services. For it is as it were "unshod" when it is exposed to wrongs,—than which there can be no more disgraceful pass of affairs to those who fill the magistracies. For an afflicted people is a sign and proof of the goutiness, so to speak, of the prince. Then and then only will the health of the commonwealth be sound and flourishing when the higher members shield the lower, and the lower respond faithfully and fully in like measure to the just demands of their superiors, so that each and all are as it were members one of another by a sort of reciprocity, and each regards his own interest as best served by that which he knows to be most advantageous for the others.

Pope Eugene III
(d. 1153)

GENERAL SUMMONS TO A CRUSADE[1]

Bishop Eugene, servant of the servants of God, to his most beloved son in Christ Louis, the illustrious and glorious king of the French, and to his beloved sons the princes, and to all the faithful ones of God who are established throughout Gaul,—greeting and apostolic benediction. How much our predecessors the Roman pontiffs did labor for the deliverance of the oriental church, we have learned from the accounts of the ancients and have found it written in their acts. For our predecessor of blessed memory, pope Urban, did sound, as it were, a celestial trump and did take care to arouse for its deliverance the sons of the holy Roman church from the different parts of the earth. At his voice, indeed, those beyond the mountain and especially the bravest and strongest warriors of the French kingdom, and also those of Italy, inflamed by the ardor of love did come together, and, congregating a very great army, not without much shedding of their own blood, the divine aid being with them, did free from the filth of the pagans that city where our Savior willed to suffer for us, and where He left His glorious sepulchre to us as a memorial of His passion,—and many others which, avoiding prolixity, we refrain from mentioning.

Which, by the grace of God, and the zeal of your fathers, who at intervals of time have striven to the extent of their power to defend them and to spread the name of Christ in those parts, have been retained by the Christians up to this day; and other cities of the infidels have by them been manfully stormed. But now, our sins and those of the people themselves requiring it, a thing which we can not relate without great grief and wailing, the city of Edessa which in our tongue is called Rohais,—which also, as is said, once when the whole land in the east was held by the pagans, alone by herself served God under the power of the Christians—has been taken and many of the castle of the Christians occupied by them (the pagans).[2] The archbishop, moreover, of this same city, together with his clergy and many other Christians, have there been slain, and the relics of the saints have been given over to the trampling under foot of the infidels, and dispersed. Whereby how great a danger threatens the church of God and the whole of Christianity, we both know ourselves and do not believe it to be hid from your prudence. For it is known that it will be the greatest proof of nobility and probity, if those things which the bravery of your fathers acquired be bravely defended by you the sons. But if it should happen otherwise, which God forbid, the valor of the fathers will be found to have diminished in the case of the sons.

[1]Translated by Ernest F. Henderson. Eugene III was Pope from 1145 to 1153. The crusade announced in this summons was the Second Crusade, in which the Christians were badly beaten by the Muslims.

[2]The city of Edessa (now Urfa, Turkey) was captured by Crusaders in 1097 but was recaptured by Muslims in 1144.

We exhort therefore all of you in God, we ask and command, and, for the remission of sins enjoin: that those who are of God, and, above all, the greater men and the nobles, do manfully gird themselves; and that you strive so to oppose the multitude of the infidels, who rejoice at the time in a victory gained over us, and so to defend the oriental church—freed from their tyranny by so great an outpouring of the blood of your fathers, as we have said,—and to snatch many thousands of your captive brothers from their hands,—that the dignity of the Christian name may be increased in your time, and that your valor which is praised throughout the whole world, may remain intact and unshaken. May that good Matthias be an example to you, who, to preserve the laws of his fathers, did not in the least doubt to expose himself with his sons and relations to death, and to leave whatever he possessed in the world; and who at length, by the help of the divine aid, after many labors however, did, as well as his progeny, manfully triumph over his enemies.[3]

We, moreover, providing with paternal solicitude for your tranquillity and for the destitution of that same church, do grant and confirm by the authority conceded to us of God, to those who by the promptings of devotion do decide to undertake and to carry through so holy and so necessary a work and labor, that remission of sins which our aforesaid predecessor pope Urban did institute; and do decree that their wives and sons, their goods also and possessions shall remain under the protection of ourselves and of the archbishops, bishops and other prelates of the church of God. By the apostolic authority, moreover, we forbid that, in the case of any thing which they possessed in peace when they took the cross, any suit be brought hereafter until most certain news has been obtained concerning their return or their death. Moreover since those who war for the Lord should by no means prepare themselves with precious garments, nor with provision for their personal appearance, nor with dogs or hawks or other things which portend licentiousness: we exhort your prudence in the Lord that those who have decided to undertake so holy a work shall not strive after these things, but shall show zeal and diligence with all their strength in the matter of arms, horses and other things with which they may fight the infidels. But those who are oppressed by debt and begin so holy a journey with a pure heart, shall not pay interest for the time past, and if they or others for them are bound by an oath or pledge in the matter of interest, we absolve them by apostolic authority. It is allowed to them also when their relations, being warned, or the lords to whose fee they belong, are either unwilling or unable to advance them the money, to freely pledge without any reclamation, their lands or other possessions to churches, or ecclesiastical persons, or to any other of the faithful. According to the institution of our aforesaid predecessor, by the authority of almighty God and by that of St. Peter the chief of the apostles, conceded to us by God, we grant such remission and absolution of sins, that he who shall devoutly begin so sacred a journey and shall accomplish it, or shall die during it, shall obtain absolution for all his sins which with a humble and contrite heart he shall confess, and shall receive the fruit of eternal retribution from the Remunerator of all. Given at Vetralle on the Calends of December.

[3]Matthias (or Mattathias) was a member of the Maccabees, a Jewish family that carried on a guerrilla war against the Syrian ruler Antiochus in the second century B.C. See First and Second Maccabees.

Usāmah Ibn-Munqidh
(1095–1188)

from *MEMOIRS*[1]

[AN ARAB VIEW OF THE CRUSADERS]

[THE FRANKS]

Their lack of sense.—Mysterious are the works of the Creator, the author of all things! When one comes to recount cases regarding the Franks, he cannot but glorify Allah (exalted is he!) and sanctify him, for he sees them as animals possessing the virtues of courage and fighting, but nothing else; just as animals have only the virtues of strength and carrying loads. I shall now give some instances of their doings and their curious mentality.

In the army of King Fulk, son of Fulk, was a Frankish reverend knight who had just arrived from their land in order to make the holy pilgrimage and then return home. He was of my intimate fellowship and kept such constant company with me that he began to call me "my brother." Between us were mutual bonds of amity and friendship. When he resolved to return by sea to his homeland, he said to me:

> My brother, I am leaving for my country and I want thee to send with me thy son (my son, who was then fourteen years old, was at that time in my company) to our country, where he can see the knights and learn wisdom and chivalry. When he returns, he will be like a wise man.

Thus there fell upon my ears words which would never come out of the head of a sensible man; for even if my son were to be taken captive, his captivity could not bring him a worse misfortune than carrying him into the lands of the Franks. However, I said to the man:

> By thy life, this has exactly been my idea. But the only thing that prevented me from carrying it out was the fact that his grandmother, my mother, is so fond of him and did not this time let him come out with me until she exacted an oath from me to the effect that I would return him to her.

Thereupon he asked, "Is thy mother still alive?" "Yes." I replied. "Well," said he, "disobey her not."

[1]Translated by Philip K. Hitti. Usāmah was a Syrian Arab who distinguished himself both as a warrior and as a poet. Exiled from his native Shayzar, in Syria, he spent much of his life in the Islamic capitals of Damascus, Jerusalem, and Cairo and ended his life as a distinguished member of the court of Saladin, sultan of Egypt and the great opponent of the Crusades. He dictated his *Memoirs* (*Kitāb al-I'tibār*) when he was ninety.

Their curious medication.—A case illustrating their curious medicine is the following:

The lord of al-Munayṭirah wrote to my uncle asking him to dispatch a physician to treat certain sick persons among his people. My uncle sent him a Christian physician named Thābit. Thābit was absent but ten days when he returned. So we said to him, "How quickly hast thou healed thy patients!" He said:

> They brought before me a knight in whose leg an abscess had grown; and a woman afflicted with imbecility. To the knight I applied a small poultice until the abscess opened and became well; and the woman I put on diet and made her humor wet. Then a Frankish physician came to them and said, "This man knows nothing about treating them." He then said to the knight, "Which wouldst thou prefer, living with one leg or dying with two?" The latter replied, "Living with one leg." The physician said, "Bring me a strong knight and a sharp ax." A knight came with the ax. And I was standing by. Then the physician laid the leg of the patient on a block of wood and bade the knight strike his leg with the ax and chop it off at one blow. Accordingly he struck it—while I was looking on—one blow, but the leg was not severed. He dealt another blow, upon which the marrow of the leg flowed out and the patient died on the spot. He then examined the woman and said, "This is a woman in whose head there is a devil which has possessed her. Shave off her hair." Accordingly they shaved it off and the woman began once more to eat their ordinary diet—garlic and mustard. Her imbecility took a turn for the worse. The physician then said, "The devil has penetrated through her head." He therefore took a razor, made a deep cruciform incision on it, peeled off the skin at the middle of the incision until the bone of the skull was exposed and rubbed it with salt. The woman also expired instantly. Thereupon I asked them whether my services were needed any longer, and when they replied in the negative I returned home, having learned of their medicine what I knew not before.

I have, however, witnessed a case of their medicine which was quite different from that.

The king of the Franks had for treasurer a knight named Bernard, who (may Allah's curse be upon him!) was one of the most accursed and wicked among the Franks. A horse kicked him in the leg, which was subsequently infected and which opened in fourteen different places. Every time one of these cuts would close in one place, another would open in another place. All this happened while I was praying for his perdition. Then came to him a Frankish physician and removed from the leg all the ointments which were on it and began to wash it with very strong vinegar. By this treatment all the cuts were healed and the man became well again. He was up again like a devil.

Another case illustrating their curious medicine is the following:

In Shayzar we had an artisan named abu-al-Fatḥ, who had a boy whose neck was afflicted with scrofula. Every time a part of it would close, another part would open. This man happened to go to Antioch on business of his, accompanied by his son. A Frank noticed the boy and asked his father about him. Abu-al-Fatḥ replied, "This is my son." The Frank said to him, "Wilt thou swear by thy religion that if I prescribe to thee a medicine which will cure thy boy, thou wilt charge nobody fees for prescribing it thyself? In that case, I shall prescribe to thee a medicine which will cure the boy." The man took the oath and the Frank said:

> Take uncrushed leaves of glasswort, burn them, then soak the ashes in olive oil and sharp vinegar. Treat the scrofula with them until the spot on which it is growing is eaten up. Then take burnt lead, soak it in ghee butter and treat him with it. That will cure him.

The father treated the boy accordingly, and the boy was cured. The sores closed and the boy returned to his normal condition of health.

I have myself treated with this medicine many who were afflicted with such disease, and the treatment was successful in removing the cause of the complaint.

Newly arrived Franks are especially rough: One insists that Usāmah should pray eastward.—Everyone who is a fresh emigrant from the Frankish lands is ruder in character than those who have become acclimatized and have held long association with the Moslems. Here is an illustration of their rude character.

Whenever I visited Jerusalem I always entered the Aqṣa Mosque, beside which stood a small mosque which the Franks had converted into a church. When I used to enter the Aqṣa Mosque, which was occupied by the Templars, who were my friends, the Templars would evacuate the little adjoining mosque so that I might pray in it. One day I entered this mosque, repeated the first formula, "Allah is great," and stood up in the act of praying, upon which one of the Franks rushed on me, got hold of me and turned my face eastward saying, "This is the way thou shouldst pray!" A group of Templars hastened to him, seized him and repelled him from me. I resumed my prayer. The same man, while the others were otherwise busy, rushed once more on me and turned my face eastward, saying, "This is the way thou shouldst pray!" The Templars again came in to him and expelled him. They apologized to me, saying, "This is a stranger who has only recently arrived from the land of the Franks and he has never before seen anyone praying except eastward." Thereupon I said to myself, "I have had enough prayer." So I went out and have ever been surprised at the conduct of this devil of a man, at the change in the color of his face, his trembling and his sentiment at the sight of one praying towards the *qiblah.*[2]

Another wants to show to a Moslem God as a child.—I saw one of the Franks come to al-Amir Mu'in-al-Din (may Allah's mercy rest upon his soul!) when he was in the Dome of the Rock[3] and say to him, "Dost thou want to see God as a child?" Mu'in-al-Din said, "yes." The Frank walked ahead of us until he showed us the picture of Mary with Christ (may peace be upon him!) as an infant in her lap. He then said, "This is God as a child." But Allah is exalted far above what the infidels say about him!

[2]The *kaaba,* the most sacred Muslim sanctuary, in Mecca.

[3]Famous sanctuary in Jerusalem, sacred to both Christians and Muslims.

Franks lack jealousy in sex affairs.—The Franks are void of all zeal and jealousy. One of them may be walking along with his wife. He meets another man who takes the wife by the hand and steps aside to converse with her while the husband is standing on one side waiting for his wife to conclude the conversation. If she lingers too long for him, he leaves her alone with the conversant and goes away.

Here is an illustration which I myself witnessed:

When I used to visit Nāblus, I always took lodging with a man named Mu'izz, whose home was a lodging house for the Moslems. The house had windows which opened to the road, and there stood opposite to it on the other side of the road a house belonging to a Frank who sold wine for the merchants. He would take some wine in a bottle and go around announcing it by shouting, "So and so, the merchant, has just opened a cask full of this wine. He who wants to buy some of it will find it in such and such a place." The Frank's pay for the announcement made would be the wine in that bottle. One day this Frank went home and found a man with his wife in the same bed. He asked him, "What could have made thee enter into my wife's room?" The man replied, "I was tired, so I went in to rest." "But how," asked he, "didst thou get into my bed?" The other replied, "I found a bed that was spread, so I slept in it." "But," said he, "my wife was sleeping together with thee!" The other replied, "Well, the bed is hers. How could I therefore have prevented her from using her own bed?" "By the truth of my religion," said the husband, "if thou shouldst do it again, thou and I would have a quarrel." Such was for the Frank the entire expression of his disapproval and the limit of his jealousy.

Another illustration:

We had with us a bath-keeper named Sālim, originally an inhabitant of al-Ma'arrah, who had charge of the bath of my father (may Allah's mercy rest upon his soul!). This man related the following story:

> I once opened a bath in al-Ma'arrah in order to earn my living. To this bath there came a Frankish knight. The Franks disapprove of girding a cover around one's waist while in the bath. So this Frank stretched out his arm and pulled off my cover from my waist and threw it away. He looked and saw that I had recently shaved off my pubes. So he shouted, "Sālim!" As I drew near him he stretched his hand over my pubes and said, "Sālim, good! By the truth of my religion, do the same for me." Saying this, he lay on his back and I found that in that place the hair was like his beard. So I shaved it off. Then he passed his hand over the place and, finding it smooth, he said, "Sālim, by the truth of my religion, do the same to madame," referring to his wife. He then said to a servant of his, "Tell madame to come here." Accordingly the servant went and brought her and made her enter the bath. She also lay on her back. The knight repeated, "Do what thou hast done to me." So I shaved all that hair while her husband was sitting looking at me. At last he thanked me and handed me the pay for my service.

Consider now this great contradiction! They have neither jealousy nor zeal but they have great courage, although courage is nothing but the product of zeal and ambition to be above ill repute.

Here is a story analogous to the one related above:

I entered the public bath in Ṣūr [Tyre] and took my place in a secluded part. One of my servants thereupon said to me, "There is with us in the bath a woman." When I went out, I sat on one of the stone benches and behold! the woman who was in the bath had come out all dressed and was standing with her father just opposite me. But I could not be sure that she was a woman. So I said to one of my companions, "By Allah, see if this is a woman," by which I meant that he should ask about her. But he went, as I was looking at him, lifted the end of her robe and looked carefully at her. Thereupon her father turned toward me and said, "This is my daughter. Her mother is dead and she has nobody to wash her hair. So I took her in with me to the bath and washed her head." I replied, "Thou hast well done! This is something for which thou shalt be rewarded [by Allah]!"

Another curious case of medication.—A curious case relating to their medicine is the following, which was related to me by William of Bures, the lord of Ṭabarayyah [Tiberias], who was one of the principal chiefs among the Franks. It happened that William had accompanied al-Amir Mu'in-al-Din (may Allah's mercy rest upon his soul!) from 'Akka to Ṭabarayyah when I was in his company too. On the way William related to us the following story in these words:

> We had in our country a highly esteemed knight who was taken ill and was on the point of death. We thereupon came to one of our great priests and said to him, "Come with us and examine so and so, the knight." "I will," he replied, and walked along with us while we were assured in ourselves that if he would only lay his hand on him the patient would recover. When the priest saw the patient, he said, "Bring me some wax." We fetched him a little wax, which he softened and shaped like the knuckles of fingers, and he stuck one in each nostril. The knight died on the spot. We said to him, "He is dead." "Yes," he replied, "he was suffering great pain, so I closed up his nose that he might die and get relief."

A funny race between two aged women.—We shall now leave the discussion of their treatment of the orifices of the body to something else.

I found myself in Ṭabarayyah at the time the Franks were celebrating one of their feasts. The cavaliers went out to exercise with lances. With them went out two decrepit, aged women whom they stationed at one end of the race course. At the other end of the field they left a pig which they had scalded and laid on a rock. They then made the two aged women run a race while each one of them was accompanied by a detachment of horsemen urging her on. At every step they took, the women would fall down and rise again, while the spectators would laugh. Finally one of them got ahead of the other and won that pig for a prize.

Their judicial trials: A duel.—I attended one day a duel in Nāblus between two Franks. The reason for this was that certain Moslem thieves took by surprise one of the villages of Nāblus. One of the peasants of that village was charged with having acted as guide for the thieves when they fell upon the village. So he fled away. The king sent and arrested his children. The peasant thereupon came back to the king and said, "Let justice be done in my case. I challenge to a duel the man who claimed that I guided the thieves to the village." The king then said to the tenant who held the village in fief, "Bring forth someone to fight the duel with him." The tenant went to his village, where a blacksmith lived, took hold of him and ordered him to fight the duel. The tenant became thus sure of the safety of his own peasants, none of whom would be killed and his estate ruined.

I saw this blacksmith. He was a physically strong young man, but his heart failed him. He would walk a few steps and then sit down and ask for a drink. The one who had made the challenge was an old man, but he was strong in spirit and he would rub the nail of his thumb against that of the forefinger in defiance, as if he was not worrying over the duel. Then came the viscount, i.e., the seignior of the town, and gave each one of the two contestants a cudgel and a shield and arranged the people in a circle around them.

The two met. The old man would press the blacksmith backward until he would get him as far as the circle, then he would come back to the middle of the arena. They went on exchanging blows until they looked like pillars smeared with blood. The contest was prolonged and the viscount began to urge them to hurry, saying, "Hurry on." The fact that the smith was given to the use of the hammer proved now of great advantage to him. The old man was worn out and the smith gave him a blow which made him fall. His cudgel fell under his back. The smith knelt down over him and tried to stick his fingers into the eyes of his adversary, but could not do it because of the great quantity of blood flowing out. Then he rose up and hit his head with the cudgel until he killed him. They then fastened a rope around the neck of the dead person, dragged him away and hanged him. The lord who brought the smith now came, gave the smith his own mantle, made him mount the horse behind him and rode off with him. This case illustrates the kind of jurisprudence and legal decisions the Franks have—may Allah's curse be upon them!

Ordeal by water.—I once went in the company of al-Amir Mu'in-al-Din (may Allah's mercy rest upon his soul!) to Jerusalem. We stopped at Nāblus. There a blind man, a Moslem, who was still young and was well dressed, presented himself before al-Amir carrying fruits for him and asked permission to be admitted into his service in Damascus. The amir consented. I inquired about this man and was informed that his mother had been married to a Frank whom she had killed. Her son used to practice ruses against the Frankish pilgrims and coöperate with his mother in assassinating them. They finally brought charges against him and tried his case according to the Frankish way of procedure.

They installed a huge cask and filled it with water. Across it they set a board of wood. They then bound the arms of the man charged with the act, tied a rope around his shoulders and dropped him into the cask, their idea being that in case he was innocent, he would sink in the water and they would then lift him up with the rope so that he might not die in the water; and in case he was guilty, he would not sink in the water. This man did his best to sink when they dropped him into the water, but he could not do it. So he had to submit to their sentence against him—may Allah's curse be upon them! They pierced his eyeballs with red-hot awls.

Later this same man arrived in Damascus. Al-Amir Mu'in-al-Din (may Allah's mercy rest upon his soul!) assigned him a stipend large enough to meet all his needs and said to a slave of his, "Conduct him to Burhān-al-Din al-Balkhi (may Allah's mercy rest upon his soul!) and ask him on my behalf to order somebody to teach this man the Koran and something of Moslem jurisprudence." Hearing that, the blind man remarked, "May triumph and victory be thine! But this was never my thought." "What didst thou think I was going to do for thee?" asked Mu'in-al-Din. The blind man replied, "I thought thou wouldst give me a horse, a mule and a suit of armor and make me a knight." Mu'in-al-Din then said, "I never thought that a blind man could become a knight."

A Frank domesticated in Syria abstains from eating pork.—Among the Franks are those who have become acclimatized and have associated long with the Moslems. These are much better than the recent comers from the Frankish lands. But they constitute the exception and cannot be treated as a rule.

Here is an illustration. I dispatched one of my men to Antioch on business. There was in Antioch at that time al-Ra'is Theodoros Sophianos, to whom I was bound by mutual ties of amity. His influence in Antioch was supreme. One day he said to my man, "I am invited by a friend of mine who is a Frank. Thou shouldst come with me so that thou mayest see their fashions." My man related the story in the following words:

> I went along with him and we came to the home of a knight who belonged to the old category of knights who came with the early expeditions of the Franks. He had been by that time stricken off the register and exempted from service, and possessed in Antioch an estate on the income of which he lived. The knight presented an excellent table, with food extraordinarily clean and delicious. Seeing me abstaining from food, he said, "Eat, be of good cheer! I never eat Frankish dishes, but I have Egyptian women cooks and never eat except their cooking. Besides, pork never enters my home." I ate, but guardedly, and after that we departed.
>
> As I was passing in the market place, a Frankish woman all of a sudden hung to my clothes and began to mutter words in their language, and I could not understand what she was saying. This made me immediately the center of a big crowd of Franks. I was convinced that death was at hand. But all of a sudden that same knight approached. On seeing me, he came and said to that woman, "What is the matter between thee and this Moslem?" She replied, "This is he who has killed my brother Hurso." This Hurso was a knight of Afāmiyah who was killed by someone of the army of Hamāh. The Christian knight shouted at her, saying, "This is a bourgeois (i.e., a merchant) who neither fights nor attends a fight." He also yelled at the people who had assembled, and they all dispersed. Then he took me by the hand and went away. Thus the effect of that meal was my deliverance from certain death.

Andreas Capellanus
(Late Twelfth Century)

from *THE ART OF COURTLY LOVE*[1]

[THE RULES OF LOVE]

Let us come now to the rules of love, and I shall try to present to you very briefly those rules which the King of Love is said to have proclaimed with his own mouth and to have given in writing to all lovers.

One of the knights of Britain was riding alone through the royal forest, going to see Arthur,[2] and when he had got well into the interior of this forest he came unexpectedly upon a young girl of marvellous beauty, sitting on a fine horse and binding up her hair. The knight lost no time in saluting her, and she answered him courteously and said, "Briton, no matter how hard you try you can't succeed in your quest unless you have our help." When he had heard these words he quickly asked the girl to tell him what he had come for, and then after that he would believe what she said to him. The young girl said to him, "When you asked for the love of a certain British lady, she told you that you could never obtain it unless you first brought back that victorious hawk which, men say, is on a golden perch in Arthur's court." The Briton admitted that all this was true, and the girl went on, "You can't get this hawk that you are seeking unless you prove, by a combat in Arthur's palace, that you enjoy the love of a more beautiful lady than any man at Arthur's court has; you can't even enter the palace until you show the guards the hawk's gauntlet,[3] and you can't get this gauntlet except by overcoming two mighty knights in a double combat."

The Briton answered, "I know that I cannot accomplish this task without your aid, and so I will submit myself to your direction, humbly beseeching you to give me your help in the matter and to permit me to claim, in view of the fact that you are directing me, that I enjoy the love of the more beautiful lady."

The young girl said to him, "If your heart is so stout that you are not afraid to carry out those things of which we have spoken, you may have from us what you ask." The Briton answered, "If you will grant my request, I know that I shall succeed in all that I hope for."

The young girl said to him, "Then let what you request be freely granted to you." Then she gave him the kiss of love and said, indicating the horse

[1]Translated by John Jay Perry. Andreas Capellanus ("Andreas the Chaplain") wrote *The Art of Courtly Love* (in Latin) in about 1185, at the request, apparently, of Marie, Countess of Champagne and daughter of Eleanor of Aquitaine. Marie probably provided the content of the treatise as well as its occasion. It was taken in its own day, and has been since, as the definitive statement of the doctrine and practice of "courtly love."

[2]The legendary king of Britain; hero of the Round Table.

[3]Armored glove.

on which she was sitting, "This horse will take you everywhere you want to go; but you must go forward without any fear and oppose with the highest courage all those who try to stop you. But bear in mind that after you have gained the victory over the first two who defend the gauntlet you must not accept it from them, but must take it for yourself from the golden pillar where it hangs; otherwise you cannot prevail in the combat at the palace or accomplish what you desire."

When she finished speaking, the Briton put on his arms and, after she had given him leave to depart, began to go at a walk through the wood. At length, as he was passing through a wild and lonely place, he came to a certain river of marvellous breadth and depth, with great waves in it, and because of the great height of its banks it was impossible for anyone to reach it. But as he rode along the edge of the bank he came to a bridge which was of gold and had one end fastened to each bank; the middle of it, however, rested in the water, and he could see that it was so shaken that great waves often covered it. At that end of it which the Briton was approaching there was a knight of a ferocious aspect who was sitting on a horse. The Briton greeted him courteously enough, but the knight scorned to return the greeting and said, "Armed Briton, who come from such distant regions, what are you seeking?"

The Briton answered, "I am trying to cross the river by the bridge"; and the bridge keeper said, "Then you must be seeking death, which no stranger here has been able to escape. But if you want to go back home and leave all your arms here, I will take pity on your youth which has led you so rashly and so foolishly into other men's countries and into strange realms."

The Briton replied, "If I were to lay down my arms, you would gain little credit for the victory of a man in arms over an unarmed man; but if you can keep an armed man from going along the public way, then you may consider that your victory has won you glory. If you do not make way peaceably for me to go across the bridge, I shall simply try to force a passage with my sword."

When the bridge keeper heard that the young man was trying to force a passage with his sword, he began to gnash his teeth, and he fell into a great rage and said, "Young man, Britain sent you here in an evil hour, since you shall perish by the sword in this wilderness, and you will never be able to bring back news of the country to your lady. Woe to you, wretched Briton, who have not been afraid to seek the place of your death at the persuasion of a woman!" Then spurring his horse against the Briton he began to attack him with his sharp sword and to hammer him so cruelly that one stroke, glancing off his shield, cut through two folds of his hauberk[4] and into the flesh of his side so that the blood commenced to flow in abundance from the wound. The young man, stung by the pain of his wound, directed the point of his lance at the knight of the bridge, and with a mighty thrust pierced him through, bore him from his horse, and stretched him shamefully upon the ground. But when the Briton was about to smite off his head, the bridge keeper, by the most humble entreaties, sought and obtained mercy.

But on the other side of the river there stood a man of tremendous size, who, seeing the bridge keeper overcome by the Briton and this same Briton

[4]Coat of chain mail.

starting to cross the golden bridge, began to shake it so violently that much of the time it was hidden by the waves. But the Briton, having great confidence in the excellence of his horse, did not cease to press forward manfully over the bridge, and at length, after great difficulty and many duckings, he arrived at the farther end of it by virtue of his horse's efforts; there he drowned beneath the water the man who had been shaking the bridge and bound up the wound in his own side as well as he could.

After this the Briton began to ride through very beautiful fields, and after he had ridden for about a mile the path came out into a pleasant meadow, fragrant with all sorts of flowers. In this meadow was a palace, marvellously built in a circular form and very beautifully decorated. He could not find a door anywhere in the palace, nor could he see any inhabitants; but in the fields he found silver tables, and on them were all sorts of food and drink set among snow-white napkins. In the same pleasant meadow was a shell of the purest silver in which there was sufficient food and drink for a horse. He therefore drove his horse off to feed, and he himself walked completely around the palace; but finding no sign of any entrance to the dwelling or any evidence that the place was inhabited, he drew near to the table and, driven by his hunger, began ravenously to devour the food he found there. A very little while after he had begun to eat, a door of the palace opened quickly with such violence that the shock of it resounded like near-by thunder, and suddenly out of this door came a man of gigantic size, brandishing in his hands a copper club of immense weight, which he shook like a straw without the least effort. To the youth at the table he said, "What sort of man are you, so presumptuous that you were not afraid to come to this royal place and so cooly and disrespectfully to eat the food on the royal table of the knights?"

The Briton answered, "The royal table should be freely open to everybody, and it is not proper that anybody should be refused the royal food and drink. Moreover it is right for me to partake of the rations prepared for the knights, since knighthood is my sole care and a knightly task has brought me to this place. You are therefore doubly discourteous in trying to forbid me the royal table."

To this the doorkeeper replied, "Although this is the royal table, it is not proper for anyone to eat at it except those who are assigned to this palace, and they allow no one to go beyond this point unless he fights with the palace guards and defeats them. And if anyone is beaten by them, there is no hope for him. Therefore get up from the table and hurry back to where you belong, or tell me that you want to fight your way onward and why you have come this far."

The Briton said to him, "I am seeking the hawk's gauntlet; that is why I came. When I get it I shall try to go further and as victor in Arthur's court take the hawk. Where is this palace guard you mention who will keep me from going on?"

The doorkeeper replied, "You fool! What madness possesses you, Briton! It would be easier for you to die and come to life again ten times than to get those things you mention. I am the palace guard who will deprive you of your reputation and spoil Britain of your youth. I am so strong that when I am angry two hundred of the best knights of Britain can hardly withstand me."

The Briton answered, "Although you say you are very powerful, I would like to fight with you to show you what sort of men Britain produces; however, it isn't proper for a knight to fight with a footman."

The doorkeeper said to him, "I see that your bad luck has brought you to death in this place where my right hand has felled more than a thousand. And although I am not reckoned among the knights, I would like to fight with you while you are on horseback, because then if you yield to the valor of a footman you will have good reason to know what sort of person would be overcome by the boldness of a man like me if I were on horseback."

To this the Briton answered, "God forbid that I should ever fight on horseback against a man on foot, for against a foot soldier every man should fight on foot," and grasping his arms he rushed bravely at the enemy before him and with a blow of his sword slightly damaged the latter's shield. The guardian of the palace, greatly enraged at this and contemptuous of the Briton's small size, shook his brazen club so furiously that the Briton's shield was almost shattered by the concussion, and he himself was greatly terrified. Thinking that a second blow would finish the Briton, the guard raised his hand to strike again, but before the blow could fall the other quickly feinted and with his sword caught him on the arm, so that the right hand, still holding the club, fell to the ground. But as he was about to put an end to him, the guard cried out, "Are you the one discourteous knight that sweet Britain has produced, you who would slay a wounded man? If you will spare my life I can easily get for you what you want, but without me you can gain nothing."

The Briton said, "Porter, I will spare your life if you will do what you promise."

The guard said, "Wait a bit and I will quickly get you the hawk's gauntlet."

The Briton answered, "You robber and deceiver of men! Now I see plainly that you are trying to cheat me. If you want to save your life just show me the place where the gauntlet of yours is kept."

The guard then led the Briton into the innermost part of the palace where there was a very beautiful golden column that held up the whole weight of the palace, and on this column hung the gauntlet he was seeking. As he grasped it boldly and held it firmly in his left hand he heard a great noise, and although he saw nobody, a wailing began to resound throughout the palace, and a cry, "Woe! woe! in spite of us the victor enemy is carrying away the spoil."

He left the palace and, mounting his horse which was already saddled, continued his journey until he came to a delightful place where there were more of those beautiful fields filled with flowers, and in the fields was a palace finely built of gold. Its length was six hundred cubits, and its width two hundred. The roof and all the outer walls were of silver, and the inside was all of gold set with precious stones. The palace was divided into a great many rooms, and in the hall of state King Arthur was sitting on a golden throne surrounded by beautiful women, more than I could count, and before him stood many splendid knights. In this palace was a beautifully fashioned golden perch on which was the hawk he was seeking, and chained near by lay two hawking dogs. But before he could get to the palace his way was blocked by a heavily fortified barbican,[5] raised to protect the palace, and to the defense of it were assigned twelve very strong knights who permitted no one to pass

[5]Defensive fortification at a gate or drawbridge.

unless he showed them the gauntlet for the hawk or forced his way sword in hand.

When the Briton saw them, he quickly showed them the gauntlet and they fell back, saying, "Your life isn't safe if you go on this way; it will lead you to great trouble." But the Briton continued on to the interior of the palace and saluted King Arthur. When the knights pressed him to know why he had come there, he replied that he had come to carry off the hawk. One of the knights of the court asked him, "Why are you trying to get the hawk?" and he replied, "Because I enjoy the love of a more beautiful woman than any knight in this court has." The other answered him, "Before you can take away the hawk you will have to fight to prove that statement." "Gladly!" said the Briton. After a suitable shield had been given him both took their places armed within the lists;[6] setting spurs to their horses, they rushed together violently, shattering each other's shields and splintering their lances; then with their swords they smote each other and hewed to pieces the iron armor. After they had fought in this fashion for a long time, the vision of the knight of the palace, whom the Briton had struck on the head with two shrewd[7] blows in rapid succession, began to be so disturbed that he could see almost nothing. When the Briton perceived this, he leapt boldly upon him and quickly struck him, beaten, from his horse. Then he seized the hawk, and, glancing as he did so at the two dogs, he saw a written parchment, which was fastened to the perch with a little gold chain. When he inquired carefully concerning this, he was told, "This is the parchment on which are written the rules of love which the King of Love himself, with his own mouth, pronounced for lovers. You should take it with you and make these rules known to lovers if you want to take away the hawk peaceably." He took the parchment, and after he had been given courteous permission to depart, quickly returned, without any opposition, to the lady of the wood, whom he found in the same place in the grove where she was when he first came upon her as he was riding along. She rejoiced greatly over the victory he had gained and dismissed him with these words, "Dearest friend, go with my permission, since sweet Britain desires you. But, that your departure may not seem too grievous to you, I ask you to come here sometimes alone, and you can always have me with you." He kissed her thirteen times over and went joyfully back to Britain. Afterward he looked over the rules which he had found written in the parchment, and then, in accordance with the answer he had previously received, he made them known to all lovers. These are the rules.

I. Marriage is no real excuse for not loving.
II. He who is not jealous cannot love.
III. No one can be bound by a double love.
IV. It is well known that love is always increasing or decreasing.
V. That which a lover takes against the will of his beloved has no relish.
VI. Boys do not love until they arrive at the age of maturity.
VII. When one lover dies, a widowhood of two years is required of the survivor.

[6]Arena for knightly combats.
[7]Sharp; penetrating.

VIII. No one should be deprived of love without the very best of reasons.
IX. No one can love unless he is impelled by the persuasion of love.
X. Love is always a stranger in the home of avarice.
XI. It is not proper to love any woman whom one would be ashamed to seek to marry.
XII. A true lover does not desire to embrace in love anyone except his beloved.
XIII. When made public love rarely endures.
XIV. The easy attainment of love makes it of little value; difficulty of attainment makes it prized.
XV. Every lover regularly turns pale in the presence of his beloved.
XVI. When a lover suddenly catches sight of his beloved his heart palpitates.
XVII. A new love puts to flight an old one.
XVIII. Good character alone makes any man worthy of love.
XIX. If love diminishes, it quickly fails and rarely revives.
XX. A man in love is always apprehensive.
XXI. Real jealousy always increases the feeling of love.
XXII. Jealousy, and therefore love, are increased when one suspects his beloved.
XXIII. He whom the thought of love vexes eats and sleeps very little.
XXIV. Every act of a lover ends in the thought of his beloved.
XXV. A true lover considers nothing good except what he thinks will please his beloved.
XXVI. Love can deny nothing to love.
XXVII. A lover can never have enough of the solaces of his beloved.
XXVIII. A slight presumption causes a lover to suspect his beloved.
XXIX. A man who is vexed by too much passion usually does not love.
XXX. A true lover is constantly and without intermission possessed by the thought of his beloved.
XXXI. Nothing forbids one woman being loved by two men or one man by two women.

These rules, as I have said, the Briton brought back with him on behalf of the King of Love to the lady for whose sake he endured so many perils when he brought her back the hawk. When she was convinced of the complete faithfulness of this knight and understood better how boldly he had striven, she rewarded him with her love. Then she called together a court of a great many ladies and knights and laid before them these rules of Love, and bade every lover keep them faithfully under threat of punishment by the King of Love. These laws the whole court received in their entirety and promised forever to obey in order to avoid punishment by Love. Every person who had been summoned and had come to the court took home a written copy of the rules and gave them out to all lovers in all parts of the world.

Giraldus Cambrensis
(c. 1146–1223)

from *THE TOPOGRAPHY OF IRELAND*[1]

OF THE CHARACTER, CUSTOMS, AND HABITS OF THIS PEOPLE.

I have considered it not superfluous to give a short account of the condition of this nation, both bodily and mentally; I mean their state of cultivation, both interior and exterior. This people are not tenderly nursed from their birth, as others are; for besides the rude fare they receive from their parents, which is only just sufficient for their sustenance, as to the rest, almost all is left to nature. They are not placed in cradles, or swathed, nor are their tender limbs either fomented by constant bathings, or adjusted with art. For the midwives make no use of warm water, nor raise their noses, nor depress the face, nor stretch the legs; but nature alone, with very slight aids from art, disposes and adjusts the limbs to which she has given birth, just as she pleases. As if to prove that what she is able to form she does not cease to shape also, she gives growth and proportions to these people, until they arrive at perfect vigor, tall and handsome in person, and with agreeable and ruddy countenances. But although they are richly endowed with the gifts of nature, their want of civilization, shown both in their dress and mental culture, makes them a barbarous people. For they wear but little woollen, and nearly all they use is black, that being the color of the sheep in this country. Their clothes are also made after a barbarous fashion.

Their custom is to wear small, close-fitting hoods, hanging below the shoulders a cubit's length, and generally made of parti-coloured strips sewn together. Under these, they use woollen rugs instead of cloaks, with breeches and hose of one piece, or hose and breeches joined together, which are usually dyed of some color.[2] Likewise, in riding, they neither use saddles, nor boots, nor spurs, but only carry a rod in their hand, having a crook at the upper end, with which they both urge forward and guide their horses. They use reins which serve the purpose both of a bridle and a bit, and do not prevent the horses from feeding, as they always live on grass. Moreover, they go to battle without armor, considering it a burden, and esteeming it brave and honorable to fight without it.

[1]Translated by Thomas Wright. Giraldus Cambrensis [Gerald of Wales] was an Anglo-Norman cleric related to the Fitzgerald family ("Geraldines") who held estates in Ireland. A strong advocate of English rule of Ireland, he visited Ireland twice, in 1182 and 1185–1186, and wrote two books (in Latin) about the country, *The Topography of Ireland* (1188) and *The Conquest of Ireland* (1189). Giraldus's gullibility and hostility toward the Irish exemplify the combination of curiosity and fear with which those in the centers of medieval European power regarded "exotic" cultures.

[2]The Irish national dress, consisting of a long cloak or mantle, close-fitting trousers, and leather boots or "brogues," was a source of national pride and was forbidden by English laws passed by Edward IV, Henry VII, and Henry VIII.

But they are armed with three kinds of weapons—namely, short spears, and two darts; in which they follow the customs of the Basclenses (Basques); and they also carry heavy battle-axes of iron, exceedingly well wrought and tempered. These they borrowed from the Norwegians and Ostmen,[3] of whom we shall speak hereafter. But in striking with the battle-axe they use only one hand, instead of both, clasping the haft firmly, and raising it above the head, so as to direct the blow with such force that neither the helmets which protect our heads, nor the plaiting of the coat of mail which defends the rest of our bodies, can resist the stroke. Thus it has happened, in my own time, that one blow of the axe has cut off a knight's thigh, although it was encased in iron, the thigh and leg falling on one side of his horse, and the body of the dying horseman on the other. When other weapons fail, they hurl stones against the enemy in battle with such quickness and dexterity, that they do more execution than the slingers of any other nation.

The Irish are a rude people, subsisting on the produce of their cattle only, and living themselves like beasts—a people that has not yet departed from the primitive habits of pastoral life. In the common course of things, mankind progresses from the forest to the field, from the field to the town, and to the social condition of citizens, but this nation, holding agricultural labor in contempt, and little coveting the wealth of towns, as well as being exceedingly averse to civil institutions—lead the same life their fathers did in the woods and open pastures, neither willing to abandon their old habits or learn anything new. They, therefore, only make patches of tillage; their pastures are short of herbage; cultivation is very rare, and there is scarcely any land sown. This want of tilled fields arises from the neglect of those who should cultivate them; for there are large tracts which are naturally fertile and productive. The whole habits of the people are contrary to agricultural pursuits, so that the rich glebe is barren for want of husbandmen, the fields demanding labor which is not forthcoming.

Very few sorts of fruit-trees are found in this country, a defect arising not from the nature of the soil, but from want of industry in planting them; for the lazy husbandman does not take the trouble to plant the foreign sorts which would grow very well here. There are four kinds of trees indigenous in Britain which are wanting here. Two of them are fruit-bearing trees, the chestnut and beech; the other two, the *arulus*[4] and the box, though they bear no fruit, are serviceable for making cups and handles. Yews, with their bitter sap, are more frequently to be found in this country than in any other I have visited; but you will see them principally in old cemeteries and sacred places, where they were planted in ancient times by the hands of holy men, to give them what ornament and beauty they could. The forests of Ireland also abound with fir-trees, producing frankincense and incense.[5] There are also veins of various kinds of metals ramifying in the bowels of the earth, which, from the same idle habits, are not worked and turned to account. Even gold, which the people require in large quantities, and still covet in a way that speaks their Spanish origin, is brought here by the merchants who traverse the ocean for the purposes of commerce. They neither employ

[3]Vikings.
[4]It is unclear what tree is referred to by this Latin name.
[5]Giraldus seems to mean resin and pitch.

themselves in the manufacture of flax or wool, or in any kind of trade or mechanical art; but abandoning themselves to idleness, and immersed in sloth, their greatest delight is to be exempt from toil, their richest possession the enjoyment of liberty.

This people, then, is truly barbarous, being not only barbarous in their dress, but suffering their hair and beards to grow enormously in an uncouth manner, just like the modern fashion recently introduced;[6] indeed, all their habits are barbarisms. But habits are formed by mutual intercourse; and as this people inhabit a country so remote from the rest of the world, and lying at its furthest extremity, forming, as it were, another world, and are thus secluded from civilized nations, they learn nothing, and practise nothing but the barbarism in which they are born and bred, and which sticks to them like a second nature. Whatever natural gifts they possess are excellent, in whatever requires industry they are worthless.

Saint Francis of Assisi
(1182?–1226)

THE CANTICLE OF THE SUN[1]

HERE BEGIN THE PRAISES OF THE CREATURES WHICH THE BLESSED FRANCIS MADE TO THE PRAISE AND HONOR OF GOD WHILE HE WAS ILL AT ST. DAMIAN'S:

Most high, omnipotent, good Lord,
Praise, glory and honor and benediction all, are Thine.
To Thee alone do they belong, most High,
And there is no man fit to mention Thee.

Praise be to Thee, my Lord, with all Thy creatures, 5
Especially to my worshipful brother sun,
The which lights up the day, and through him dost Thou brightness
give;
And beautiful is he and radiant with splendor great;
Of Thee, most High, signification gives.

Praised be my Lord, for sister moon and for the stars, 10
In heaven Thou hast formed them clear and precious and fair.

[6]Long hair had become fashionable in England during the reign of Henry I; it was much denounced by the Church.

[1]Translated by Paschal Robinson. Saint Francis of Assisi, founder of the Franciscan order, was among the most popular of the medieval saints for his simplicity, humility, joyful piety, and love of nature. Stories about him were collected in *The Little Flowers of Saint Francis.*

Praised be my Lord for brother wind
And for the air and clouds and fair and every kind of weather,
By the which Thou givest to Thy creatures nourishment.
Praised be my Lord for sister water, 15
The which is greatly helpful and humble and precious and pure.

Praised be my Lord for brother fire,
By the which Thou lightest up the dark.
And fair is he and gay and mighty and strong.

Praised be my Lord for our sister, mother earth, 20
The which sustains and keeps us
And brings forth diverse fruits with grass and flowers bright.

Praised be my Lord for those who for Thy love forgive
And weakness bear and tribulation.
Blessed those who shall in peace endure, 25
For by Thee, most High, shall they be crowned.

Praised be my Lord for our sister, the bodily death,
From the which no living man can flee.
Woe to them who die in mortal sin;
Blessed those who shall find themselves in Thy most holy will, 30
For the second death shall do them no ill.

Praise ye and bless ye my Lord, and give Him thanks,
And be subject unto Him with great humility.

Roger Bacon

(c. 1214–1294?)

from *OPUS MAJUS*[1]

[EXPERIMENTAL SCIENCE]

I now wish to unfold the principles of experimental science, since without experience nothing can be sufficiently known. For there are two modes of acquiring knowledge, namely, by reasoning and experience. Reasoning draws

[1]Translated by Robert Belle Burke. Roger Bacon, a Franciscan brother, was a scholastic philosopher and scientist who taught at Oxford University. He combined religious faith with a scientific bent far ahead of his time. He summarized his studies in three books written for Pope Clement I: *Major Work, Minor Work,* and *Third Work.* His uncomprehending contemporaries credited him with great accomplishments as a magician.

a conclusion and makes us grant the conclusion, but does not make the conclusion certain, nor does it remove doubt so that the mind may rest on the intuition of truth, unless the mind discovers it by the path of experience; since many have the arguments relating to what can be known, but because they lack experience they neglect the arguments, and neither avoid what is harmful nor follow what is good. For if a man who has never seen fire should prove by adequate reasoning that fire burns and injures things and destroys them, his mind would not be satisfied thereby, nor would he avoid fire, until he placed his hand or some combustible substance in the fire, so that he might prove by experience that which reasoning taught. But when he has had actual experience of combustion his mind is made certain and rests in the full light of truth. Therefore reasoning does not suffice, but experience does.

This is also evident in mathematics, where proof is most convincing. But the mind of one who has the most convincing proof in regard to the equilateral triangle will never cleave to the conclusion without experience, nor will he heed it, but will disregard it until experience is offered him by the intersection of two circles, from either intersection of which two lines may be drawn to the extremities of the given line; but then the man accepts the conclusion without any question. Aristotle's statement, then, that proof is reasoning that causes us to know is to be understood with the proviso that the proof is accompanied by its appropriate experience, and is not to be understood of the bare proof. . . .

He therefore who wishes to rejoice without doubt in regard to the truths underlying phenomena must know how to devote himself to experiment. For authors write many statements, and people believe them through reasoning which they formulate without experience. Their reasoning is wholly false. For it is generally believed that the diamond cannot be broken except by goat's blood, and philosophers and theologians misuse this idea. But fracture by means of blood of this kind has never been verified, although the effort has been made; and without that blood it can be broken easily. For I have seen this with my own eyes, and this is necessary, because gems cannot be carved except by fragments of this stone. Similarly it is generally believed that the castors[2] employed by physicians are the testicles of the male animal. But this is not true, because the beaver has these under its breast, and both the male and female produce testicles of this kind. Besides these castors the male beaver has its testicles in their natural place; and therefore what is subjoined is a dreadful lie, namely, that when the hunters pursue the beaver, he himself knowing what they are seeking cuts out with his teeth these glands. Moreover, it is generally believed that hot water freezes more quickly than cold water in vessels, and the argument in support of this is advanced that contrary is excited by contrary, just like enemies meeting each other. But it is certain that cold water freezes more quickly for any one who makes the experiment. People attribute this to Aristotle in the second book of the *Meteorologics*; but he certainly does not make this statement, but he does make one like it, by which they have been deceived, namely, that if cold water and hot water are poured on a cold place, as upon ice, the hot

[2]Dried animal glands used by medieval physicians.

water freezes more quickly, and this is true. But if hot water and cold are placed in two vessels, the cold will freeze more quickly. Therefore all things must be verified by experience.

But experience is of two kinds; one is gained through our external senses, and in this way we gain our experience of those things that are in the heavens by instruments made for this purpose, and of those things here below by means attested by our vision. Things that do not belong in our part of the world we know through other scientists who have had experience of them. As, for example, Aristotle on the authority of Alexander sent two thousand men through different parts of the world to gain experimental knowledge of all things that are on the surface of the earth, as Pliny bears witness in his *Natural History*. This experience is both human and philosophical, as far as man can act in accordance with the grace given him; but this experience does not suffice him, because it does not give full attestation in regard to things corporeal owing to its difficulty, and does not touch at all on things spiritual. It is necessary, therefore, that the intellect of man should be otherwise aided, and for this reason the holy patriarchs and prophets, who first gave sciences to the world, received illumination within and were not dependent on sense alone. The same is true of many believers since the time of Christ. For the grace of faith illuminates greatly, as also do divine inspirations, not only in things spiritual, but in things corporeal and in the sciences of philosophy; as Ptolemy states in the *Centilogium*, namely, that there are two roads by which we arrive at the knowledge of facts, one through the experience of philosophy, the other through divine inspiration, which is far the better way, as he says. . . .

Since this experimental science is wholly unknown to the rank and file of students, I am therefore unable to convince people of its utility unless at the same time I disclose its excellence and its proper signification. This science alone, therefore, knows how to test perfectly what can be done by nature, what by the effort of art, what by trickery, what the incantations, conjurations, invocations, deprecations, sacrifices, that belong to magic, mean and dream of, and what is in them, so that all falsity may be removed and the truth alone of art and nature may be retained. This science alone teaches us how to view the mad acts of magicians, that they may not be ratified but shunned, just as logic considers sophistical reasoning.

This science has three leading characteristics with respect to other sciences. The first is that it investigates by experiment the notable conclusions of all those sciences. For the other sciences know how to discover their principles by experiments, but their conclusions are reached by reasoning drawn from the principles discovered. But if they should have a particular and complete experience of their own conclusions, they must have it with the aid of this noble science. For it is true that mathematics has general experiments as regards its conclusions in its figures and calculations, which also are applied to all sciences and to this kind of experiment, because no science can be known without mathematics. But if we give our attention to particular and complete experiments and such as are attested wholly by the proper method, we must employ the principles of this science which is called experimental. I give as an example the rainbow and phenomena connected with it, of which nature are the circle around the sun and the stars, the streak also lying at the side of the sun or of a star, which is apparent to the eye in a straight line, and is called by Aristotle in the third book of the *Meteorologics* a perpendicular, but by Seneca a streak, and the circle is called a corona, phenomena which frequently have the colors of the rainbow. The natural philosopher discusses these phenomena, and the writer on perspective has much to add pertaining to the mode of vision that is necessary in this case. But neither Aristotle nor Avicenna in their natural histories has given us a knowledge of phenomena of this kind, nor has Seneca, who composed a special book on them. But experimental science attests them.

Let the experimenter first, then, examine visible objects, in order that he may find colors arranged as in the phenomena mentioned above and also the same figure. For let him take hexagonal stones[3] from Ireland or from India, which are called rainbows in Solinus on the *Wonders of the World*, and let him hold these in a solar ray falling through the window, so that he may find all the colors of the rainbow, arranged as in it, in the shadow near the ray. And further let the same experimenter turn to a somewhat dark place and apply the stone to one of his eyes which is almost closed, and he will see the colors of the rainbow clearly arranged just as in the bow. And since many employing these stones think that the phenomenon is due to the special virtue of those stones and to their hexagonal shape, therefore let the experimenter proceed further, and he will find this same peculiarity in crystalline stones correctly shaped, and in other transparent stones. Moreover, he will find this not only in white stones like the Irish crystals, but also in black ones, as is evident in the dark crystal and in all stones of similar transparency. He will find it besides in crystals of a shape differing from the hexagonal, provided they have a roughened surface, like the Irish crystals, neither altogether smooth, nor rougher than they are. Nature produces some that have surfaces like the Irish crystals. For a difference in the corrugations causes a difference in the colors. And further let him observe rowers, and in the drops falling from the raised oars he finds the same colors when the solar rays penetrate drops of this kind. The same phenomenon is seen in water falling from the wheels of a mill; and likewise when one sees on a summer's morning the drops of dew on the grass in meadow or field, he will observe the colors. Likewise when it is raining, if he stands in a dark place and the rays beyond it pass through the falling rain, the colors will appear in the shadow near by; and frequently at night colors appear around a candle. Moreover, if a man in summer, when he rises from sleep and has his eyes only partly open, suddenly looks at a hole through which a ray of the sun enters, he will see colors. Moreover, if seated beyond the sun he draws his cap beyond his eyes, he will see colors; and similarly if he closes an eye the same thing happens under the shade of the eyebrows; and again the same phenomenon appears through a glass vessel filled with water and placed in the sun's rays. Or similarly if one having water in his mouth sprinkles it vigorously into the rays and stands at the side of the rays. So, too, if rays in the required position pass through an oil lamp hanging in the air so that

[3]Prisms.

the light falls on the surface of the oil, colors will be produced. Thus in an infinite number of ways colors of this kind appear, which the diligent experimenter knows how to discover. . . .

Another example can be given in the field of medicine in regard to the prolongation of human life, for which the medical art has nothing to offer except the regimen of health. But a far longer extension of life is possible. . . .

Not only are remedies possible against the conditions of old age coming at the time of one's prime and before the time of old age, but also if the regimen of old age should be completed, the conditions of old age and senility can still be retarded, so that they do not arrive at their ordinary time, and when they do come they can be mitigated and moderated, so that both by retarding and mitigating them life may be prolonged beyond the limit, which according to the full regimen of health depends on the six articles mentioned. And there is another farther limit, which has been set by God and nature, in accordance with the property of the remedies retarding the accidents of old age and senility and mitigating their evil. The first limit can be passed but the second cannot be. . . .

Therefore the excellent experimenter in the book on the *Regimen of the Aged* says that if what is tempered in the fourth degree, and what swims in the sea, and what grows in the air, and what is cast up by the sea, and a plant of India, and what is found in the vitals of a long-lived animal, and the two snakes which are the food of Tyrians and Aethiopians, be prepared and used in the proper way, and the *minera* [blood?] of the noble animal be present, the life of man could be greatly prolonged and the conditions of old age and senility could be retarded and mitigated. But that which is tempered in the fourth degree is gold, as is stated in the book on *Spirits and Bodies,* which among all things is most friendly to nature. And if by a certain experiment gold should be made the best possible, or at any rate far better than nature and the art of alchemy can make it, as was the vessel found by the rustic, and it should be dissolved in such water as the ploughman drank, it would then produce a wonderful action on the body of man. And if there is added that which swims in the sea, namely, the pearl, which is a thing most efficacious for preserving life, and there is added also the thing that grows in the air. This last is an *anthos* [flower] and is the flower of seadew, which possesses an ineffable virtue against the condition of old age. But the *dianthos* that is put in an electuary[4] is not a flower, but is a mixture of leaves and fragments of wood and a small portion of flower. For the pure flower should be gathered in its proper season, and in many ways it is used in foods and drinks and electuaries. To these must be added what is cast up by the sea. This last is ambergris, which is spermaceti, a thing of wondrous virtue in this matter.[5] The plant of India is similar to these, and is the excellent wood of the aloe, fresh and not seasoned. To these ingredients there is added that which is in

[4]A medicinal paste made of powders mixed with honey or syrup.

[5]Ambergris and spermaceti are both waxy substances obtained from sperm whales.

the heart of a long-lived animal, namely, the stag. This is a bone growing in the stag's heart, which possesses great power against premature old age. The snake which is the food of the Tyrians is the Tyrian snake from which Tyriaca is made, and whose flesh is properly prepared and eaten with spices. This is an excellent remedy for the condition of old age and for all the corruptions of the constitution, if it is taken with things suitable to one's constitution and condition, as we are taught in the book on the *Regimen of the Aged.* Aristotle, moreover, in the book of *Secrets* recommends strongly the flesh of the Tyrian snake for our ills. The snake that is the food of the Aethiopians is the dragon, as David says in the Psalm, "Thou hast given it as food to the tribes of the Aethiopians." For it is certain that wise men of Aethiopia have come to Italy, Spain, France, England, and those lands of the Christians in which there are good flying dragons, and by the secret art they possess lure the dragons from their caverns. They have saddles and bridles in readiness, and they ride on these dragons and drive them in the air at high speed, so that the rigidity of their flesh may be overcome and its hardness tempered, just as in the case of boars and bears and bulls that are driven about by dogs and beaten in various ways before they are killed for food. After they have domesticated them in this way they have the art of preparing their flesh, similar to the art of preparing the flesh of the Tyrian snake, and they use the flesh against the accidents of old age, and they prolong life and sharpen their intellect beyond all conception. For no instruction that can be given by man can produce such wisdom as the eating of this flesh, as we have learned through men of proved reliability on whose word no doubt can be cast.

If the elements should be prepared and purified in some mixture, so that there would be no action of one element on another, but so that they would be reduced to pure simplicity, the wisest have judged that they would have the most perfect medicine. . . .

But owing to the difficulty of this very great experiment, and because few take an interest in experiments, since the labor involved is complicated and the expense very great, and because men pay no heed to the secrets of nature and the possibilities of art, it happens that very few have labored on this very great secret of science, and still fewer have reached a laudable end. . . .

The formation of judgments, as I have said, is a function of this science, in regard to what can happen by nature or be effected in art, and what not. This science, moreover, knows how to separate the illusions of magic and to detect all their errors in incantations, invocations, conjurations, sacrifices, and cults. But unbelievers busy themselves in these mad acts and trust in them, and have believed that the Christians used such means in working their miracles. Wherefore this science is of the greatest advantage in persuading men to accept the faith, since this branch alone of philosophy happens to proceed in this way, because this is the only branch that considers matters of this kind, and is able to overcome all falsehood and superstition and error of unbelievers in regard to magic, such as incantations and the like already mentioned. How far, moreover, it may serve to reprobate obstinate unbelievers is already shown by the violent means that have just been touched upon, and therefore I pass on.

Saint Thomas Aquinas
(1225–1274)

from *SUMMA CONTRA GENTILES*[1]

[THE END OF MAN]

We have shown in the preceding books that there is one First Being, possessing the full perfection of all being, whom we call God, and who of the abundance of His perfection, bestows being on all that exists, so that He is proved to be not only the first of beings, but also the beginning of all. Moreover He bestows being on others, not through natural necessity, but according to the decree of His will, as we have shown above. Hence it follows that He is the Lord of the things made by Him: since we dominate over those things that are subject to our will. And this is a perfect dominion that He exercises over things made by Him, forasmuch as in their making He needs neither the help of an extrinsic agent, nor matter as the foundation of His work: since He is the universal efficient cause of all being.

Now everything that is produced through the will of an agent is directed to an end by that agent: because the good and the end are the proper object of the will, wherefore whatever proceeds from a will must needs be directed to an end. And each thing attains its end by its own action, which action needs to be directed by him who endowed things with the principles whereby they act.

Consequently God, who in Himself is perfect in every way, and by His power endows all things with being, must needs be the Ruler of all, Himself ruled by none: nor is anything to be excepted from His ruling, as neither is there anything that does not owe its being to Him. Therefore as He is perfect in being and causing, so is He perfect in ruling.

The effect of this ruling is seen to differ in different things, according to the difference of natures. For some things are so produced by God that, being intelligent, they bear a resemblance to Him and reflect His image: wherefore not only are they directed, but they direct themselves to their appointed end by their own actions. And if in thus directing themselves they be subject to the divine ruling, they are admitted by that divine ruling to the attainment of their last end; but are excluded therefrom if they direct themselves otherwise.

[1]Translated by English Dominican Fathers. Saint Thomas Aquinas, a Dominican monk, was born in Italy and spent most of his life teaching in Paris and various Italian cities. *Summa Contra Gentiles* [Summation Against the Infidels] (c. 1259–1264), along with *Summa Theologica* [Summation of Theology] (1265–1274), epitomizes his thought, which achieves a synthesis among various far-flung philosophical traditions: ancient (especially Aristotle's), Neoplatonic (especially St. Augustine's), Islamic (especially Avicenna's), and Jewish (especially Maimonides').

Others there are, bereft of intelligence, which do not direct themselves to their end, but are directed by another. Of these some being incorruptible, even as they are not patient of defects in their natural being, so neither do they wander, in their own action, from the direction to their appointed end, but are subject, without fail, to the ruling of the Supreme Ruler; such are the heavenly bodies, whose movements are invariable. Others, however, being corruptible, are patient of defects in their natural being; yet this defect is supplied to the advantage of another: since when one thing is corrupted, another is generated. Likewise, they fail from their natural direction in their own actions, yet this failing is compensated by some resultant good. Whence it is clear that not even those things which are seen to wander from the direction of the supreme ruling, escape from the power of the Supreme Ruler: because also these corruptible bodies, even as they are created by God, so too are they perfectly subject to Him. . . .

Since then in the First Book we have treated of the perfection of the divine nature, and, in the Second, of the perfection of the divine power, inasmuch as He is the Creator and Lord of all: it remains for us in this Third Book to treat of His perfect authority or dignity, inasmuch as He is the end and Governor of all. We must therefore proceed in this wise, so as first to treat of Him as the end of all things; secondly of His universal government, inasmuch as He governs every creature: thirdly, of that special government, whereby He governs creatures endowed with intelligence.

Accordingly we must first show that every agent, by its action, intends an end.

For in those things which clearly act for an end, we declare the end to be that towards which the movement of the agent tends: for when this is reached, the end is said to be reached, and to fail in this is to fail in the end intended; as may be seen in the physician who aims at health, and in a man who runs towards an appointed goal. Nor does it matter, as to this, whether that which tends to an end be cognitive or not: for just as the target is the end of the archer, so is it the end of the arrow's flight. Now the movement of every agent tends to something determinate: since it is not from any force that any action proceeds, but heating proceeds from heat, and cooling from cold; wherefore actions are differentiated by their active principles. Action sometimes terminates in something made, for instance, building terminates in a house, healing ends in health: while sometimes it does not so terminate, for instance, understanding and sensation. And if action terminate in something made, the movement of the agent tends by that action towards that thing made: while if it does not terminate in something made, the movement of the agent tends to the action itself. It follows therefore that every agent intends an end while acting, which end is sometimes the action itself, sometimes a thing made by the action.

Again. In all things that act for an end, that is said to be the last end, beyond which the agent seeks nothing further: thus the physician's action goes as far as health, and this being attained, his efforts cease. but in the action of every agent, a point can be reached beyond which the agent does not desire to go; else actions would tend to infinity, which is impossible, for since *it is not possible to pass through an infinite medium*, the agent would never begin to act, because nothing moves towards what it cannot reach. Therefore every agent acts for an end. . . .

Again. Every agent acts either by nature or by intelligence. Now there can be no doubt that those which act by intelligence act for an end; since they act with an intellectual preconception of what they attain by their action, and act through such preconception, for this is to act by intelligence. Now just as in the preconceiving intellect there exists the entire likeness of the effect that is attained by the action of the intellectual being, so in the natural agent there pre-exists the similitude of the natural effect, by virtue of which similitude its action is determined to the appointed effect: for fire begets fire, and an olive produces an olive. Wherefore even as that which acts by intelligence tends by its action to a definite end, so also does that which acts by nature. Therefore every agent acts for an end.

Moreover. Fault is not found save in those things which are for an end: for we do not find fault with one who fails in that to which he is not appointed; thus we find fault with a physician if he fails to heal, but not with a builder or a grammarian. But we find fault in things done according to art, as when a grammarian fails to speak correctly; and in things that are ruled by nature, as in the case of monstrosities. Therefore every agent, whether according to nature, or according to art, or acting of set purpose, acts for an end. . . .

There are, however, certain actions which would seem not to be for an end, such as playful and contemplative actions, and those which are done without attention, such as scratching one's beard, and the like: whence some might be led to think that there is an agent that acts not for an end. But we must observe that contemplative actions are not for another end, but are themselves an end. Playful actions are sometimes an end, when one plays for the mere pleasure of play; and sometimes they are for an end, as when we play that afterwards we may study better. Actions done without attention do not proceed from the intellect, but from some sudden act of the imagination, or some natural principle: thus a disordered humor produces an itching sensation and is the cause of a man scratching his beard, which he does without his mind attending to it. Such actions do tend to an end, although outside the order of the intellect. Hereby is excluded the error of certain natural philosophers of old, who maintained that all things happen by natural necessity, thus utterly banishing the final cause from things.

Hence we must go on to prove that every agent acts for a good.

For that every agent acts for an end clearly follows from the fact that every agent tends to something definite. Now that to which an agent tends definitely must needs be befitting to that agent: since the latter would not tend to it save on account of some fittingness thereto. But that which is befitting to a thing is good for it. Therefore every agent acts for a good.

Further. The end is that wherein the appetite of the agent or mover is at rest, as also the appetite of that which is moved. Now it is the very notion of good to be the term of appetite, since *good is the object of every appetite.* Therefore all action and movement is for a good.

Again. All action and movement would seem to be directed in some way to being: either for the preservation of being in the species or in the individual; or for the acquisition of being. Now this itself, being, to wit, is a good: and for this reason all things desire being. Therefore all action and movement is for a good.

Furthermore. All action and movement is for some perfection. For if the action itself be the end, it is clearly a second perfection of the agent. And if the action consist in the transformation of external matter, clearly the mover intends to induce some perfection into the thing moved: towards which perfection the movable tends, if the movement be natural. Now when we say a thing is perfect, we mean that it is good. Therefore every action and movement is for a good. . . .

Moreover. The intellectual agent acts for an end, as determining on its end: whereas the natural agent, though it acts for an end, as proved above, does not determine on its end, since it knows not the ratio of end, but is moved to the end determined for it by another. Now an intellectual agent does not determine the end for itself except under the aspect of good; for the intelligible object does not move except it be considered as a good, which is the object of the will. Therefore also the natural agent is not moved, nor does it act for an end, except in so far as this end is a good: since the end is determined for the natural agent by an appetite. Therefore every agent acts for a good. . . .

Moreover. Whatever is moved is brought to the term of movement by the mover and agent. Therefore mover and moved tend to the same term. Now that which is moved, since it is in potentiality, tends to an act, and consequently to perfection and goodness: for by its movement it passes from potentiality to act. Therefore mover and agent by moving and acting always intend a good.

Hence the philosophers in defining the good said: "The good is the object of every appetite," and Dionysius (*De Div. Nom.*, IV) says that "all things desire the good and the best." . . .

From the foregoing it is clear that all things are directed to one good as their last end.

For if nothing tends to something as its end, except in so far as this is good, it follows that good, as such, is an end. Consequently that which is the supreme good is supremely the end of all. Now there is but one supreme good, namely God, as we have shown in the First Book. Therefore all things are directed to the supreme good, namely God, as their end. . . .

Further. In every series of causes, the first cause is more a cause than the second cause: since the second cause is not a cause save through the first. Therefore that which is the first cause in the series of final causes, must needs be more the final cause of each thing, than the proximate final cause. Now God is the first cause in the series of final causes: for He is supreme in the order of good things. Therefore He is the end of each thing more even than any proximate end. . . .

Furthermore. The particular good is directed to the common good as its end: for the being of the part is on account of the whole: wherefore *the good of the nation is more godlike than the good of one man.* Now the supreme good, namely God, is the common good, since the good of all things depends on Him: and the good whereby each thing is good, is the particular good of that thing, and of those that depend thereon. Therefore all things are directed to one good, God, to wit, as their end. . . .

Furthermore. In all mutually subordinate agents and movers, the end of the first agent must be the end of all; even as the end of the commander-in-chief is the end of all who are soldiering under him. Now of all the parts of man, the intellect is the highest mover: for it moves the appetite, by proposing its object to it; and the intellective appetite, or will, moves the sensitive appetites, namely the irascible and concupiscible, so that we do not obey the concupiscence, unless the will command; and the sensitive appetite, the will consenting, moves the body. Therefore the end of the intellect is the end of all human actions. *Now the intellect's end and good are the true*; and its last end is the first truth. Therefore the last end of all man and of all his deeds and desires, is to know the first truth, namely God.

Moreover. Man has a natural desire to know the causes of whatever he sees; wherefore through wondering at what they saw, and ignoring its cause, men first began to philosophize, and when they had discovered the cause they were at rest. Nor do they cease inquiring until they come to the first cause; and *then do we deem ourselves to know perfectly when we know the first cause.* Therefore man naturally desires, as his last end, to know the first cause. But God is the first cause of all. Therefore man's last end is to know God. . . .

Now the last end of man and of any intelligent substance is called happiness or beatitude; for it is this that every intelligent substance desires as its last end, and for its own sake alone. Therefore the last beatitude or happiness of any intelligent substance is to know God.

Hence it is said (Matthew v, 8): "Blessed are the clean of heart, for they shall see God": and (John XVII, 3): "This is eternal life: that they may know Thee, the only true God." Aristotle agrees with this statement (10 *Ethic,* VII) when he says that man's ultimate happiness is "contemplative, in regard to his contemplating the highest object of contemplation." . . .

It remains for us to inquire in what kind of knowledge of God the ultimate happiness of the intellectual substance consists. For there is a certain general and confused knowledge of God, which is in almost all men, whether from the fact that, as some think, the existence of God, like other principles of demonstration, is self-evident, as we have stated in the First Book: or, as seems nearer to the truth, because by his natural reason, man is able at once to arrive at some knowledge of God. For seeing that natural things are arranged in a certain order—since there cannot be order without a cause of order—men, for the most part, perceive that there is one who arranges in order the things that we see. But who or of what kind this cause of order may be, or whether there be but one, cannot be gathered from this general consideration: even, so, when we see a man in motion, and performing other works, we perceive that in him there is a cause of these operations, which is not in other things, and we give this cause the name of "soul," but without knowing yet what the soul is, whether it be a body, or how it brings about operations in question.

Now, this knowledge of God cannot possibly suffice for happiness. . . .

There is yet another knowledge of God, in one respect superior to the knowledge we have been discussing, namely that whereby God is known to men through demonstration, because by faith we know certain things about God, which are so sublime that reason cannot reach them by means of demonstration, as we have stated at the beginning of this work. But not even in this knowledge of God can man's ultimate happiness consist.

For happiness is the intellect's perfect operation, as already declared. But in knowledge by faith the operation of the intellect is found to be most imperfect as regards that which is on the part of the intellect: although it is the most perfect on the part of the object: for the intellect in believing does not grasp the object of its assent. Therefore neither does man's happiness consist in this knowledge of God.

Again. It has been shown that ultimate happiness does not consist chiefly in an act of will. Now in knowledge by faith the will has the leading place: for the intellect assents by faith to things proposed to it, because it wills, and not through being constrained by the evidence of their truth. Therefore man's final happiness does not consist in this knowledge. . . .

Seeing that man's ultimate happiness does not consist in that knowledge of God whereby He is known by all or many in a vague kind of opinion, nor again in that knowledge of God whereby He is known in science through demonstration; nor in that knowledge whereby He is known through faith, as we have proved above: and seeing that it is not possible in this life to arrive at a higher knowledge of God in His essence, or at least so that we understand other separate substances, and thus know God through that which is nearest to Him, so to say, as we have proved; and since we must place our ultimate happiness in some kind of knowledge of God, as we have shown; it is impossible for man's happiness to be in this life.

Again. Man's last end is the term of his natural appetite, so that when he has obtained it, he desires nothing more: because if he still has a movement towards something, he has not yet reached an end wherein to be at rest. Now, this cannot happen in this life: since the more man understands, the more is the desire to understand increased in him—this being natural to man—unless perhaps someone there be who understands all things: and in this life this never did nor can happen to anyone that was a mere man; seeing that in this life we are unable to know separate substances which in themselves are most intelligible, as we have proved. Therefore man's ultimate happiness cannot possibly be in this life.

Besides. Whatever is in motion towards an end has a natural desire to be established and at rest therein: hence a body does not move away from the place towards which it has a natural movement, except by a violent movement which is contrary to that appetite. Now happiness is the last end which man desires naturally. Therefore it is his natural desire to be established in happiness. Consequently unless together with happiness he acquires a state of immobility, he is not yet happy, since his natural desire is not yet at rest. When therefore a man acquires happiness, he also acquires stability and rest; so that all agree in conceiving stability as a necessary condition of happiness: hence the philosopher says (1 *Ethic*, X): "We do not look upon the happy man as a kind of chameleon." Now, in this life there is no sure stability; since, however happy a man may be, sickness and misfortune may come upon him, so that he is hindered in the operation, whatever it be, in which his happiness consists. Therefore man's ultimate happiness cannot be in this life. . . .

Further. All admit that happiness is a perfect good: else it would not bring rest to the appetite. Now perfect good is that which is wholly free from any admixture of evil: just as that which is perfectly white is that which is entirely free from any admixture of black. but man cannot be wholly free from evils in this state of life; not only from evils of the body, such as hunger, thirst, heat, cold, and the like, but also from evils of the soul. For no one is there who at times is not disturbed by inordinate passion; who sometimes does not go beyond the mean, wherein virtue consists, either in excess or in deficiency; who is not deceived in some thing or another; or at least ignores what he would wish to know, or feels doubtful about an opinion of which he would like to be certain. Therefore no man is happy in this life.

Again. Man naturally shuns death, and is sad about it: not only shunning it now when he feels its presence, but also when he thinks about it. But man, in this life, cannot obtain not to die. Therefore it is not possible for man to be happy in this life. . . .

Again. The natural desire cannot be void; since *nature does nothing in vain.* But nature's desire would be void if it could never be fulfilled. Therefore man's natural desire can be fulfilled. But not in this life, as we have shown. Therefore it must be fulfilled after this life. Therefore man's ultimate happiness is after this life.

Besides. As long as a thing is in motion towards perfection it has not reached its last end. Now in the knowledge of truth all men are ever in motion and tending towards perfection: because those who follow, make discoveries in addition to those made by their predecessors, as stated in 2 *Metaph.* Therefore in the knowledge of truth man is not situated as though he had arrived at his last end. Since then as Aristotle himself shows (10 *Ethic,* VII) man's ultimate happiness in this life consists apparently in speculation, whereby he seeks the knowledge of truth, we cannot possibly allow that man obtains his last end in this life. . . .

For these and like reasons Alexander and Averroes held that man's ultimate happiness does not consist in human knowledge obtained through speculative sciences, but in that which results from conjunction with a separate substance, which conjunction they deemed possible to man in this life. But as Aristotle realized that man has no knowledge in this life other than that which he obtains through speculative sciences, he maintained that man attains to happiness, not perfect, but proportionate to his capacity.

Hence it becomes sufficiently clear how these great minds suffered from being so straitened on every side. We, however, will avoid these straits if we suppose, in accordance with the foregoing arguments, that man is able to reach perfect happiness after this life, since man has an immortal soul; and that in that state his soul will understand in the same way as separate substances understand, as we proved in the Second Book.

Therefore man's ultimate happiness will consist in that knowledge of God which he possesses after this life; a knowledge similar to that by which separate substances know him. Hence our Lord promises us a "reward . . . in heaven" (Matthew v, 12) and (Matthew XXII, 30) states that the saints "shall be as the angels": who always see God in heaven (Matthew XVIII, 10).

Pope Boniface VIII
(1235–1301)

THE BULL "UNUM SANCTUM"[1]

We are compelled, our faith urging us, to believe and to hold—and we do firmly believe and simply confess—that there is one holy catholic and apostolic church, outside of which there is neither salvation nor remission of sins; her Spouse proclaiming it in the canticles: "My dove, my undefiled is but one, she is the choice one of her that bare her;" which represents one mystic body, of which body the head is Christ; but of Christ, God. In this church there is one Lord, one faith and one baptism. There was one ark of Noah, indeed, at the time of the flood, symbolizing one church; and this being finished in one cubit had, namely, one Noah as helmsman and commander. And, with the exception of this ark, all things existing upon the earth were, as we read, destroyed. This church, moreover, we venerate as the only one, the Lord saying through His prophet: "Deliver my soul from the sword, my darling from the power of the dog." He prayed at the same time for His soul—that is, for Himself the Head—and for His body,—which body, namely, he called the one and only church on account of the unity of the faith promised, of the sacraments, and of the love of the church. She is that seamless garment of the Lord which was not cut but which fell by lot. Therefore of this one and only church there is one body and one head—not two heads as if it were a monster:—Christ, namely, and the vicar of Christ, St. Peter, and the successor of Peter. For the Lord Himself said to Peter, Feed my sheep. My sheep, He said, using a general term, and not designating these or those particular sheep; from which it is plain that He committed to Him *all* His sheep. If, then, the Greeks or others say that they were not committed to the care of Peter and his successors, they necessarily confess that they are not of the sheep of Christ; for the Lord says, in John, that there is one fold, one shepherd and one only. We are told by the word of the gospel that in this His fold there are two swords,—a spiritual, namely, and a temporal. For when the apostles said "Behold there are two swords"—when, namely, the apostles were speaking in the church—the Lord did not reply that this was too much, but enough. Surely he who denies that the temporal sword is in the power of Peter wrongly interprets the word of the Lord when He says: "Put up thy sword in its scabbard." Both swords, the spiritual and

[1]Translated by Ernest F. Henderson. Boniface VIII became Pope in 1294, when conflict between Church and State in Europe had reached a crisis. Boniface spent his papacy trying to assert ecclesiastical authority, especially against Philip IV of France, who had levied taxes against the Church that it regarded as illegal. Boniface issued the papal bull "Unam Sanctum" [One Church] in 1302 in an attempt to assert the duty of princes to submit to the authority of the Church. He died the following year, the conflict still unresolved.

the material, therefore, are in the power of the church; the one, indeed, to be wielded for the church, the other by the church; the one by the hand of the priest, the other by the hand of kings and knights, but at the will and sufferance of the priest. One sword, moreover, ought to be under the other, and the temporal authority to be subjected to the spiritual. For when the apostle says "there is not power but of God, and the powers that are of God are ordained," they would not be ordained unless sword were under sword and the lesser one, as it were, were led by the other to great deeds. For according to St. Dionysius the law of divinity is to lead the lowest through the intermediate to the highest things. Not therefore, according to the law of the universe, are all things reduced to order equally and immediately; but the lowest through the intermediate, the intermediate through the higher. But that the spiritual exceeds any earthly power in dignity and nobility we ought the more openly to confess the more spiritual things excel temporal ones. This also is made plain to our eyes from the giving of tithes, and the benediction and the sanctification; from the acceptation of this same power, from the control over those same things. For, the truth bearing witness, the spiritual power has to establish the earthly power, and to judge it if it be not good. Thus concerning the church and the ecclesiastical power is verified the prophecy of Jeremiah: "See, I have this day set thee over the nations and over the kingdoms," and the other things which follow Therefore if the earthly power err it shall be judged by the spiritual power; but if the lesser spiritual power err, by the greater. But if the greatest, it can be judged by God alone, not by man, the apostle bearing witness. A spiritual man judges all things, but he himself is judged by no one. This authority, moreover, even though it is given to man and exercised through man, is not human but rather divine, being given by divine lips to Peter and founded on a rock for him and his successors through Christ himself whom he has confessed; the Lord himself saying to Peter: "Whatsoever thou shalt bind," etc. Whoever, therefore, resists this power thus ordained by God, resists the ordination of God, unless he makes believe, like the Manichean, that there are two beginnings. This we consider false and heretical, since by the testimony of Moses, not "in the beginnings," but "in the beginning" God created the Heavens and the earth. *Indeed we declare, announce and define, that it is altogether necessary to salvation for every human creature to be subject to the Roman pontiff.* The Lateran, Nov. 14, in our 8th year. As a perpetual memorial of this matter.

"The Goodman of Paris"
(Fourteenth Century)

from *THE GOODMAN OF PARIS*[1]

Dear Sister,

You being the age of fifteen years and in the week that you and I were wed, did pray me to be indulgent to your youth and to your small and ignorant service, until you had seen and learned more; to this end you promised me to give all heed and to set all care and diligence to keep my peace and my love, as you spoke full wisely, and as I well believe, with other wisdom than your own, beseeching me humbly in our bed, as I remember, for the love of God not to correct your harshly before strangers nor before our own folk, but rather each night, or from day to day, in our chamber, to remind you of the unseemly or foolish things done in the day or days past, and chastise you, if it pleased me, and then you would strive to amend yourself according to my teaching and correction, and to serve my will in all things, as you said. And your words were pleasing to me, and won my praise and thanks, and I have often remembered them since. And know, dear sister, that all that I know you have done since we were wed until now and all that you shall do hereafter with good intent, was and is to my liking, pleaseth me, and has well pleased me, and will please me. For your youth excuses your unwisdom and will still excuse you in all things as long as all you do is with good intent and not displeasing to me. And know that I am pleased rather than displeased that you tend rose-trees, and care for violets, and make chaplets, and dance, and sing: nor would I have you cease to do so among our friends and equals, and it is but good and seemly so to pass the time of your youth, so long as you neither seek nor try to go to the feasts and dances of lords of too high rank, for that does not become you, nor does it sort with your estate, nor mine. And as for the greater service that you say you would

[1]Translated by Eileen Power. "The Goodman of Paris" [*Le Ménagier de Paris*] is the name assigned by editors to a prosperous but anonymous middle-class Parisian who in 1392–1394 wrote a manual of housekeeping that is also known by that name. The Goodman was in his sixties, his wife only fifteen when they married, an orphan girl from the provinces who was from a higher class than himself. The book is crammed with miscellaneous material. The first part, from which this selection is taken, deals with a wife's duty to obey her husband and offers several exemplary tales, including those of Patient Griselda and of Melibeus and Prudence, both included by Chaucer in *The Canterbury Tales.* Part two is an exhaustive manual of housekeeping and included an extensive collection of medieval recipes. Part three, never finished, was to consist of a collection of parlor games, a treatise on hawking, and a section of jokes and riddles. The book gives us one of our most detailed accounts of medieval domestic life and especially the lives of women.

willingly do for me, if you were able and I taught it you, know dear sister, that I am well content that you should do me such service as your good neighbors of like estate do for their husbands, and as your kinswomen do unto their husbands. Take cousel privily of them, and then follow it either more or less as you please. For I am not so overweening in my attitude to you and your good intent that I am not satisfied with what you do for me therein, nor with all other services, provided there be no disorder or scorn or disdain, and that you are careful. For although I know well that you are of gentler birth than I, nathless that would not protect you, for by God, the women of your lineage be good enough to correct you harshly themselves, if I did not, an they learned of your error from me or from another source; but in you I have no fear, I have confidence in your good intent. Yet although, as I have said, to me belongs only the lesser service, I would that you know how to give good will and honor and service in great measure and abundance more than is fit for me, either to serve another husband, if you have one, after me, or to teach greater wisdom to your daughters, friends or others, if you list and have such need. For the more you know the greater honor will be yours and the greater praise will therefore be unto your parents and to me and to others about you, by whom you have been nurtured. And for your honor and love, and not for my service (for to me belongs but the common service, or less,) since I had pity and loving compassion on you who for long have had neither father nor mother, nor any of your kinswomen near you to whom you might turn for counsel in your private needs, save me alone, for whom you were brought from your kin and the country of your birth, I have often wondered how I might find a simple general introduction to teach you the which, without the aforesaid difficulties, you might of yourself introduce into your work and care. And lastly, me-seems that if your love is as it has appeared in your good words, it can be accomplished in this way, namely in a general instruction that I will write for you and present to you, in three sections containing nineteen principal articles.

* * *

The seventh article of the first section showeth how you should be careful and thoughtful of your husband's person. Wherefore, fair sister, if you have another husband after me, know that you should think much of his person, for after that a woman has lost her first husband and marriage, she commonly findeth it hard to find a second to her liking, according to her estate, and she remaineth long while all lonely and disconsolate and the more so still if she lose the second. Wherefore love your husband's person carefully, and I pray you keep him in clean linen, for that is your business, and because the trouble and care of outside affairs lieth with men, so must husbands take heed, and go and come, and journey hither and thither, in rain and wind, in snow and hail, now drenched, now dry, now sweating, now shivering, ill-fed, ill-lodged, ill-warmed and ill-bedded. And naught harmeth him, because he is upheld by the hope that he hath of the care which his wife will take of him on his return, and of the ease, the joys and the pleasures which she will do him, or cause to be done to him in her presence; to be unshod before a good fire, to have his feet washed and fresh shoes and hose, to be given good food and drink, to be well served and well looked after, well bedded in white sheets and nightcaps, well covered with good furs, and assuaged with other joys and desports, privities, loves and secrets whereof I am silent. And the next day fresh shirts and garments.

Certes, fair sister, such services make a man love and desire to return to his home and to see his goodwife, and to be distant with others. Wherefore I counsel you to make such cheer to your husband at all his comings and stayings, and to persevere therein; and also be peaceable with him, and remember the rustic proverb, which saith that there be three things which drive the goodman from home, to wit a leaking roof, a smoky chimney and a scolding woman. And therefore, fair sister, I beseech you that, to keep yourself in the love and good favor of your husband, you be unto him gentle, and amiable, and debonair. Do unto him what the good simple women of our country say hath been done to their sons, when these have set their love elsewhere and their mothers cannot wean them therefrom. Sure it is that when fathers and mothers be dead and stepfathers and stepmothers that have stepsons rail at them and scold them and repulse them and take no thought for their sleeping, nor for their food and drink, their hose and their shirts, nor for their other needs or affairs, and these same children find elsewhere a good refuge and counsel from some other woman, that receiveth them unto herself and taketh thought to warm them by some poor gruel with her, to give them a bed and keep them clean and mend their hosen, breeches, shirts and other clothes, then do these same children follow her and desire to be with her and to sleep and be warmed between her breasts, and they be altogether estranged from their mothers and fathers, that before took no heed of them, and now be fain to get them back and have them again; but it may not be, for these children hold more dear the company of strangers that think and care for them, than of their kinsfolk that care no whit for them. Then they lament and cry and say that these same women have bewitched their children and that the lads be spell bound and cannot leave them, and are never at ease save when they are with them. But, whatever they may say, it is no witchcraft, but it is for the sake of the love, the care, the intimacies, joys and pleasures that these women show unto them in all things and, on my soul, there is none other enchantment. For whoever giveth all its pleasure to a bear, a wolf, or a lion, that same bear, wolf, or lion will follow after him, and so the other beasts might say, could they but speak, that those thus tamed must be bewitched. And, on my soul, I trow that there is none other witchcraft than well doing, and no man can be better bewitched than by giving him what pleaseth him.

Wherefore, dear sister, I beseech you thus to bewitch and bewitch again your husband that shall be, and beware of roofless house and of smoky fire, and scold him not, but be unto him gentle and amiable and peaceable. Have a care that in winter he have a good fire and smokeless and let him rest well and be well covered between your breasts, and thus bewitch him. And in summer take heed that there be no fleas in your chamber, nor in your bed, the which you may do in six ways, as I have heard tell. For I have heard from several that if the room be strewn with alder leaves, the fleas will be caught thereon. Item, I have heard tell that if you have at night one or two trenchers [of bread] slimed with glue or turpentine and set about the room, with a lighted candle in the midst of each trencher, they will come and be stuck thereto. The other way that I have tried and 'tis true: take a rough cloth and spread it about your room and over your bed, and all the fleas that shall hop thereon will be caught, so that you may carry them away with the cloth wheresoe'er you will. Item, sheepskins. Item, I have seen blanchets [of white wool] set on the straw and on the bed, and when the black fleas hopped thereon, they were the sooner found upon the white, and killed. But the best way is to guard oneself against those that be within the coverlets and the furs, and the stuff of the dresses wherewith one is covered. For know that I have tried this, and when the coverlets, furs or dresses, wherein there be fleas, be folded and shut tightly up, as in a chest tightly corded with straps, or in a bag well tied up and pressed, or otherwise put and pressed to that the aforesaid fleas be without light and air and kept imprisoned, then will they perish forthwith and die. Item, I have sometimes seen in divers chambers, that when one had gone to bed they were full of mosquitoes, which at the smoke of the breath came to sit on the faces of those that slept, and stung them so hard, that they were fain to get up and light a fire of hay, in order to make a smoke so that they had to fly away or die, and this may be done by day if they be suspected, and likewise he that hath a mosquito net may protect himself therewith.

And if you have a chamber or a passage where there is great resort of flies, take little sprigs of fern and tie them to threads like to tassels, and hang them up and all the flies will settle on them at eventide; then take down the tassels and throw them out. Item, shut up your chamber closely in the evening, but let there be a little opening in the wall towards the east, and as soon as the dawn breaketh, all the flies will go forth through this opening, and then let it be stopped up. Item, take a bowl of milk and a hare's gall and mix them one with another and then set two or three bowls thereof in places where the flies gather and all that taste thereof will die. Item, otherwise, have a linen rag tied at the bottom of a pot with an opening in the neck, and set that pot in the place where the flies gather and smear it within with honey, or apples, or pears; when it is full of flies, set a trencher over the mouth and then shake it. Item, otherwise, take raw red onions and bray[2] them and pour the juice into a bowl and set it where the flies gather and all that taste thereof will die. Item, have whisks wherewith to slay them by hand. Item, have little twigs covered with glue on a basin of water. Item, have your windows shut full tight with oiled or other cloth, or with parchment or something else, so tightly that no fly

[2]Pound or grind.

may enter, and let the flies that be within be slain with the whisk or otherwise as above, and no others will come in. Item, have a string hanging soaked in honey, and the flies will come and settle thereon and at eventide let them be taken in a bag. Finally meseemeth that flies will not stop in a room wherein there be no standing tables, forms, dressers or other things whereon they can settle and rest, for if they have naught but straight walls whereon to settle and cling, they will not settle, nor will they in a shady or damp place. Wherefore meseemeth that if the room be well watered and well closed and shut up, and if nought be left lying on the floor, no fly will settle there.

And thus shall you preserve and keep your husband from all discomforts and give him all the comforts whereof you can bethink you, and serve him and have him served in your house, and you shall look to him for outside things, for if he be good he will take even more pains and labor therein than you wish, and by doing what I have said, you will cause him ever to miss you and have his heart with you and your loving service and he will shun all other houses, all other women, all other services and households. All will be as naught to him save you, who think for him as is aforesaid, and who ought so to do, by the ensample that you see of horsemen riding abroad, for you see that as soon as they be come home to their house from a journey, they cause their horses to be given fresh litter up to their bellies; these horses be unharnessed and made comfortable, they be given honey and picked hay and sifted oats, and they be better looked after in their own stables on their return than anywhere else. And if the horses be thus made comfortable, so much the more ought the persons, to wit the lords, to be so at their own expense on their return. Hounds returning from the woods and from the chase be littered before their master and he maketh their fresh litter himself before the fire; their feet be greased at the fire with soft grease, they be given sops and be well eased, for pity of their labor; and likewise, if women do thus unto their husbands, as men do unto their horses, dogs, asses, mules, and other beasts, certes all other houses, where they have been served, will seem to them but dark prisons and strange places, compared with their own, which will be then a paradise of rest unto them. And so on the road husbands will think of their wives, and no trouble will be a burden to them for the hope and love they will have of their wives, whom they will be fain to see again with as great longing as poor hermits and penitents are fain to see the face of Jesus Christ; and these husbands, that be thus looked after, will never be fain to abide elsewhere nor in other company, but they will withhold, withdraw and abstain therefrom; all the rest will seem unto them but a bed of stones compared with their home; but let it be unceasing, and with a good heart and without pretence.

But there be certain old hags, which be sly and play the wise woman and feign great love by way of showing their heart's great service, and naught else; and wot you, fair sister, that the husbands be fools if they perceive it not; and when they perceive it, if the husband and wife be silent and pretend one with another, it is an ill beginning and will lead to a worse end. And some women there be, that in the beginning serve their husbands full well, and they trow well that their husbands be then so amorous of them and so debonair that, trow they, those husbands will scarce dare to be wroth with them, if they do less, so they slacken and little by little they try to show less respect and service and obedience, but—what is more—they take upon themselves authority, command and lordship, at first in a small thing, then in a larger, and a little more every day. Thus they essay and advance and rise, as they think, and they trow that their husbands, the which because they be debonair or peradventure because they set a trap, say nought thereof, see it not because they suffer it thus. And certes, it is an ill thought and deed, for when the husbands see that they cease their service, and mount unto domination, and that they do it too much and that by suffering ill good may come, then those women be all at once, by their husband's rightful will, cast down even as Lucifer was, that was the chief of the angels of Paradise, and that our Lord so loved that He allowed and suffered him to do his will, and he grew puffed up with overweening pride. He did and undertook so much that he went too far, and displeased our Lord that long had dissimulated and suffered him without a word, and then all at once He bethought him of all. So He cast him forth into the nethermost depths of hell, because that he continued not the service whereunto he was ordained and for the which he had in the beginning won the full great love of our Lord. Wherefore you should be obedient in the beginning and ever persevere therein, by this ensample.

The Renaissance

The word *renaissance* means *rebirth. Renaissance* purports to describe a movement in European intellectual, cultural, and political history that first flourished in Italy, mainly from the mid-fourteenth to the sixteenth centuries, and then in other parts of Europe during an overlapping but generally later period that ended in the mid-seventeenth century. The origin of the Renaissance, both the concept and the term, is of considerable interest in exploring the question, much debated in the twentieth century, whether there was any genuine rebirth in the Renaissance and whether the movement so labeled really had a distinctive existence.

To many people in the vanguard of Renaissance literature, art, and thought, the age did in fact seem new. The first major spokesman for this view was Petrarch (1304–1374), who believed that the thousand years separating his age from the fall of ancient Roman civilization had been a dark night and that the first priority of his contemporaries should be to restore ancient literature, for its own sake and in the interests of human virtue. His followers, the humanists of Italy and later of northern Europe, extended Petrarch's primarily literary emphasis to include important new directions in the fine arts, religious studies, philosophy, mathematics, and political theory. When the new heliocentric astronomy was developed (or rediscovered) by Copernicus (1473–1543), the new Protestant movement was launched in 1517 by Luther (1483–1546), and maritime exploration in the fifteenth and sixteenth centuries revealed to Europeans the existence of the western hemisphere, the age necessarily became aware that changes of awesome momentousness, for better or worse, were in process. But for the most part the consciousness by the age of its own novelty remained limited and was primarily a matter of high culture. The term *rebirth* was popularized during the Renaissance by the eminent art historian Giorgio Vasari in his *Lives of the Most Eminent Italian Painters, Sculptors, and Architects* (1550), in which Vasari acclaimed the new artists for having revived classical aesthetic values and recovered the faculty to see and depict nature.

The modern, much broader, concept of a Renaissance is largely the creation not of the age itself but of retrospect. To eighteenth-century Enlightenment thinkers the Renaissance was the age when medieval "superstition," especially revealed religion, was overthrown. But it was not until the nineteenth century that there emerged the model of the Renaissance familiar today, along with its mystique. The landmarks of this new model were Jules Michelet's volume on the Renaissance in his *History of France* (1855) and Jacob Burckhardt's *The Civilization of the Renaissance in Italy* (1860), in combination with the work of Burckhardt's followers who broadened his model of the early Italian Renaissance to include later periods, other parts of Europe, and fields such as economic life that Burckhardt had not treated in depth. For these scholars and their intellectual heirs the Renaissance was not only or even primarily a revival of learning and the arts but a period with its own organic coherence, a sudden and radical break with the Middle Ages, and the point of departure for the modern world. In Michelet's phrase, it marked "the discovery of the world and of man." Above all, the Renaissance was an age of individual personalities, liberated from the political constraints of Holy Roman Emperor and Pope, free to understand and express themselves for good or evil. The state, for Burckhardt, had become a "work of art," the product of events working through human personalities rather than something imposed by an external sanction such as tradition or the will of God. The age had a pagan vitality.

This view of the Renaissance has the obvious appeal of glamour, and it survives, as not only the popular model but also that of scholars, even when they feel they must reject or modify it as many of them have done. Medievalists especially have bridled. They insist that many of the supposedly new departures in the Renaissance—the revival of classical learning, the emergence of an urban culture that fostered the arts and a capitalist economy, exploration of distant lands, the development of the rationalist scientific mentality, the growth of a lay rather than clerical culture, and the rise of national states—were actually continuations of trends that began centuries before Petrarch. It is also highly questionable, according to champions of the Middle Ages, that the most typical Renaissance trends were advances for humankind. For the most skeptical among them, the Renaissance was not a rebirth but the twilight of the great medieval era.

The conviction remains that the concept of a Renaissance (whether that is the right word or not) is useful and represents something real. But it can no longer be argued easily that the discontinuity with the Middle Ages was radical or that a single spirit dominated all of southern and western Europe for three centuries or that the Renaissance is simply an early stage of modernism. The tendency in Renaissance studies today is to examine different places and stages of it closely, discriminating and qualifying conscientiously in accord with concrete evidence rather than broad formulas, however exhilarating. In this brief essay there is not enough space to record all the qualifications and exceptions that the complexity of the Renaissance age and culture calls for. Almost all the generalizations that follow are challengeable. Even so, they may be helpful, especially because many of them originate in the Renaissance view of itself. Moreover, they provide an index to the history of sensibility. In the last century or so readers have developed the habit, when reading Renaissance literature, of isolating and responding selectively to those qualities in it that have the expansiveness of spirit which, accurately or not, has been understood as distinctively Renaissance.

We can begin with humanism, an aspect of the Renaissance that touches on virtually all the others. In a broad sense, the term *humanism* can be defined as any view of the world that places humankind at the center of things. It is as old as Greek antiquity but also quite modern, numbering among its adherents a wide variety of groups ranging from Marxists to existentialists (religious, atheistic, and agnostic) to educators who insist on the primacy of the liberal arts and humanities. In a more restricted though still rather elastic sense, humanism refers to a distinctive habit of thought that pervades Renaissance art and philosophy. Beginning roughly in the latter fourteenth century, with such men as Petrarch, it spread over the following centuries throughout Europe; in the north it reached its zenith of creative expression in the first decades of the sixteenth century in the great Dutch scholar, theologian, and satirist Desiderius Erasmus (1466?–1536) and in his English colleague Thomas More (1478–1535), the author of *Utopia*.

The humanists tended to think of themselves as a new breed, and they do represent at least a striking shift in emphasis. They accorded human beings a high degree of autonomy, an extreme form of which was expressed by the Italian humanist Pico della Mirandola (1463–1494) in his *Oration on the Dignity of Man*. In a famous passage from that work God addresses man: "I have given you, Adam, neither a predetermined place nor a particular aspect nor any special prerogatives in order that you may take and possess these through your own decision and choice. The limitations on the nature of other creatures are contained within my prescribed laws. You shall determine your own nature without constraint from any barrier, by means of the freedom to whose power I have entrusted you. . . . I have made you neither heavenly nor earthly, neither mortal nor immortal so that, like a free and sovereign artificer, you might mold and fashion yourself into that form you yourself shall have chosen." Asceticism was no longer necessarily the hallmark of sanctity, and pleasure became more respectable, whether celebrated riotously as in Rabelais or in the more spiritualized form it usually took for the northern humanists. (It must be stated, however, that the stereotype of Italian humanists as pagan rather than Christian is a misleading caricature.) The world and the life of the body were to be accepted and rejoiced in, regarded not as signs that man is alienated from his higher self but as avenues that, in parallel with the soul, humanity can use for its fulfillment. In "The Godly Feast," one of Erasmus's *Colloquies,* the host Eusebius urges his dinner guests: "But while we feast our minds plenteously, let us not neglect their partners." Asked who these partners are, he replies, "Our bodies; aren't they partners of our minds? For I prefer 'partners' to 'instruments' or 'dwellings' or 'tombs.'" The honorific status given in the Middle Ages to clerical authority and to the ideal of celibacy was considerably modified.

The vehicle for realizing the humanists' ideals was to be reason—more concretely, education of the most comprehensive kind: physical, moral, literary, philosophical. The ancient classics became major and indispensable tools of this education; without them the truly good life could not be envisioned in its wholeness. The humanists were therefore earnestly committed to the recovery and editing of ancient texts (which were not so much discovered as unearthed from churches and monasteries). The texts included both the secular and (especially for the northern humanists) the religious; Erasmus, most notably, did a landmark Greek edition of the New Testament. Moreover, this philological scholarship was not regarded as fastidious purism or as intellectual escapism; quite the contrary, for the humanists had as prime goals both the perfection of individual human character and the reform of public evils, in church and state. They were activist social scientists. In their educational systems, they wished to substitute for the medieval concern with elaborate formal logic an ideal of practical and moral wisdom instilled through a curriculum dominated by poetry, history, moral philosophy, and—in lieu of medieval theology—the Bible itself. Although they were in one way elitists, aiming to train a special educated cadre of reforming leaders, they were also egalitarian to the extent that they prized feudal nobility of birth less than a moral and intellectual nobility, the signs of which were rhetorical eloquence, refined diction, and urbane wit, all these combined with rectitude of conduct.

Humanist thought, elusive and ambiguous though it sometimes seems, was fundamentally concerned with wholeness, of the human personality and of world view. The clearest example is in their religious thought. Most of them were firm believers in Christianity (such occasional puzzles as Rabelais and Montaigne notwithstanding), which they did not regard as a system in rivalry with pagan antiquity. Nor did they regard antiquity as a mere allegorizing of Christian revelation (as often in Dante); the achievement of a genuinely historical point of view, by which the events and ideas of classical times could be understood as they really were in themselves, was another of their prime goals, akin to their passion for rejecting spurious literary texts and traditions. Rather, they saw Christianity and paganism as organic parts of total truth. In "The Godly Feast," Eusebius says, "whatever is devout and contributes to good morals should not be called profane. Sacred Scripture is of course the basic authority in everything; yet I sometimes run across ancient sayings or pagan writings—even the poets'—so purely and reverently and admirably expressed that I can't help believing their authors' hearts were moved by some divine power. And perhaps the spirit of Christ is more widespread than we understand, and the company of saints includes many not in our calendar. Speaking frankly among friends, I can't read [certain of Cicero's works] without sometimes kissing the book and blessing that pure heart, divinely inspired as it was. . . . So that I would much rather let all of Scotus [the medieval philosopher] and others of his sort perish than the books of a single Cicero or Plutarch." Some of the humanists went so far as to envisage a primal religious revelation of which all the world's creeds are reflections.

The complexity of the Renaissance age is well illustrated in the ambiguous relationship between humanism and the religious currents of the time, especially the Protestant Reformation, customarily dated from Luther's definitive rebellion against the Catholic Church in 1517. The papacy had been in dire trouble in the fourteenth and fifteenth centuries, sorely tried by its "Babylonian captivity" when the seat of the papacy was moved to Avignon in France, then weakened by a period of schism when there were rival popes, and after that by a period when a council laid claim to ecclesiastical authority. In the meantime, skeptical and heretical movements that had grown out of the late Middle Ages were flourishing, and powerful movements stressing mystical experience and simple piety were spreading rapidly among both clergy and laity. The last half of the fifteenth century and the first two decades of the sixteenth, immediately before Luther's revolt, saw a reinvigorated papacy at its height of cultural glory: The renowned Vatican Library was created, and Popes Julius II and Leo X, reigning from 1503 to 1521, patronized the work of great artists, including Michelangelo and Raphael. But many of the popes of the time were concerned more with political and personal aggrandizement than with the spiritual welfare of the European church. Out of this background the Reformation emerged, claiming to reassert the values of authentic early Christianity, drawing for theological support on epistles by St. Paul and the writings of early Church Fathers like Augustine (and of course on the Gospels as the Reformers understood them), preaching that humanity was saved not by its own efforts ("works") but by faith. The Protestant opposition to indulgences (remissions of punishment in Purgatory) was therefore not merely a moral rebellion against the venal selling of them by Rome but a theological stance that rejected the whole idea of Purgatory, with its implication that human beings can satisfy divine justice through their own merits rather than exclusively in Christ.

The Reformation is in different ways an expression of humanist ideals and a contradiction of them. The Protestant attempt to recover the ancient text and meaning of the Bible and to spread them widely, free of medieval theological overlays, is akin to and indeed part of the humanist movement, which conservative Catholic churchmen distrusted. Both Protestants and humanists agreed also in their contempt for medieval scholasticism in general, in pressing for institutional reform in the church, and in encouraging the active role of the laity in intellectual and religious life. Both put a high value on simple piety in contrast with elaborate formal liturgy and complicated systems of devotion such as the veneration of saints and their relics and the earning of indulgences. On the other hand, the two movements differed in some fundamental ways. The humanists were essentially optimistic about human nature, asserting the crucial role of free will. This emphasis contradicted the view, held by John Calvin (1509–1564) and the Protestant radicals who followed him, that humanity is weak in its fallen state ("totally depraved," to use the technical term) and therefore dependent on God's free gift of grace rather than its own spiritual exertions. Humanists tended not to be interested in sectarian dogma as such, except—as with Erasmus and More—to resist divisive innovations that threatened Church unity. Moreover, though the humanists scorned most things medieval, their essential internationalism, typified in the insistence by Erasmus and More that the Church remain unified, is closer to the medieval model than to the new localism and nationalism that evolved in parallel with the Protestant churches. And the advocacy of religious tolerance by humanists like Erasmus is antithetical to the intense sectarian partisanship expressed both in Protestantism and in the Catholic Counter-Reformation. (The latter is best exemplified in the militant Society of Jesus, or Jesuits, founded on a military model in 1534 by the Spanish saint and former soldier Ignatius Loyola. In the literature of Protestant countries like England, the Jesuits generally appear not only as agents of "papist" religion but as unscrupulous, subversive machiavels working in the interest of foreign political powers. It is interesting, then, that Ignatius himself exhibited a kind of practical mysticism that owes something to the devotional trends, fostered by humanists, that had helped produce the Reformation.) Finally, the humanists' willingness to envisage the world in terms of classical models that might be compatible with Christianity but also existed independent of it did not square with the impulse in radical Protestantism to reject everything that was religiously neutral as pagan worldliness. The humanists were thus in a curious position after the Reformation, distrusted as sowers of heresy by many Catholics (despite his Catholicism, some of Erasmus's works were put on the *Index* of prohibited books) and rejected by many Protestants as fainthearted, worldly temporizers, the lukewarm whom God, in the biblical phrase, would spew out of His mouth.

The role of the Renaissance and of humanism in the evolution of modern science is also ambivalent. The discovery of the world and the discovery of the human that Michelet found in the Renaissance age are not necessarily parallel endeavors. It is true that the recovery of ancient authors made available to thinkers models of the cosmos not available in the Middle Ages, including the heliocentric astronomy with which Copernicus replaced the old Ptolemaic model, and some unknown works by ancient scientists like Archimedes were revived. Humanists encouraged the study of algebra and geometry, the latter overlapping with experiments by painters in visual perspective. Thus the way was prepared for the incomparable mathematical developments of the seventeenth century that provided the language of modern science. But the human-centeredness of the humanists, as is still true of some of their modern counterparts, sometimes took the form of an antagonism or at least indifference to science.

For modern science to develop, another radical change had also to occur: The medieval picture of the universe, with its beautiful model of correspondences between matter on one hand and theology and human psychology on the other, had to be replaced by a more objective view of nature as having its own autonomy independent of its roles of revealing God and reflecting the human. The medieval correlation between the four humors in the human body and their corresponding psychological dispositions, and between the humors and the four elements in material nature; the systematic linking of the heavenly spheres with the hierarchical orders of angels; the notion that an apple falls from a tree because it loves the earth—such ideas had to go. (E. M. W. Tillyard argues in *The Elizabethan World Picture,* 1946, that assumptions like these continued to dominate much of Renaissance thought and art.) The trend in the Renaissance to study nature more objectively appears, for example, in the concern for accurate anatomy—systematically in the work of Vesalius (1514–1564) and aesthetically in the proportions and musculature of painted or sculpted nudes. The dogmatic medieval reverence for Galen in medicine and for Aristotle in general was weakened.

The new empirical direction was, however, more an extrapolation of late medieval thought than a bold Renaissance innovation. Furthermore, although empiricism is fundamental to experimental method, it is probably less essential to pure science than the mental discipline of abstraction: One must learn, in accounting for the trajectory of the falling apple, to ignore certain quite objective facts about it—that it is a Winesap, is overripe, and has a worm in it—and concentrate exclusively on the abstract properties (mass, distance from other objects) it shares with all other gravitationally attracted bodies. It can be argued convincingly that this abstract habit of thinking is much closer than the humanists' practical wisdom to the medieval scholastic discipline.

In pure science, then, the Renaissance is probably best understood as a transition period. Technologically, however, there were some epochal advances. The most important by far was the invention in the late fifteenth century, by Johann Gutenberg (1400?–1468?) and others, of printing by movable type. In the last few decades of the century, several million books were printed, multiplying by an incalculable factor the impact of all the religious, intellectual, and literary trends in the later Renaissance. It is true that this invention too depended on earlier discoveries—in papermaking, for example—but the practical culmination of the technology of printing in the Renaissance itself marks one of the few unquestionable differences, not only from the Middle Ages but from all previous world history.

The new technology included also the navigational tools—again, drawing on pre-Renaissance and non-European cultures—that made possible the Renaissance age of geographic exploration. At the end of the fifteenth century Bartholomeu Dias and Vasco da Gama opened the route to India around the Cape of Good Hope and Columbus reached the New World; in the sixteenth century Magellan's crew and Francis Drake sailed around the globe. Such voyages had an enormous impact on the European imagination, influencing works like More's *Utopia* and Luiz Vaz de Camoëns' (1524–1580) Portuguese epic *The Lusiads,* which celebrates Vasco da Gama and vaunts his superiority to those mere Mediterranean sailors Odysseus and Aeneas. The new geographic discoveries also affected the politics and economics of Europe in important ways, accelerating the trends toward nationalism, middle-class power, economic capitalism, urbanization, and the shift of money and power from the Mediterranean to the countries on the Atlantic and the North Sea.

It is precisely in such sociological, political, and economic areas, however, that the nineteenth-century model of the Renaissance as a separate and distinct, organically whole age breaks down most seriously. It is beyond question that by the sixteenth century rulers such as Philip II in Spain and the Netherlands, Francis I in France, and Henry VIII in England had achieved unprecedented authority in their realms, built on their predecessors' consolidation of royal power, territory, and wealth in the fifteenth century. Because in many respects the feudal nobility was the greatest obstacle to royal authority, the monarchs' new power was wielded increasingly through complex bureaucracies staffed largely by a new kind of middle-class men distinguished less by birth than by talent or money. (Italy, with its city-states, was dominated by outside powers in the sixteenth century and was not unified as a nation until the nineteenth.) It is also true that these new national regimes, along with the Italian city-states, had begun to define themselves and their goals in increasingly secular and local terms, less dominated than in the past by the transnational authority of Pope or Holy Roman Emperor or by the model of European Christendom as a unity. Populations boomed; banking flourished as money came to replace payment in kind and services; cities grew dramatically in size and importance, along with the intellectual and artistic activity that urban centers help foster. But the roots of all these movements go back, in some cases several centuries, into the medieval period. Moreover, the Renaissance is ridden by a great political-cultural paradox: While medieval internationalism was losing ground to the more local autonomy of city-state and national monarchy, in accordance with an ideal of patriotic citizenship that the humanists encouraged, the different parts of Europe were at the same time becoming more intellectually and culturally interdependent—a trend, greatly reinforced by the printing press, that also owes much to the humanists. A roughly similar paradox exists in the twentieth century: The breakup of the international colonial systems into scores of autonomous new states has coincided with the internationalist movement represented politically in the United Nations and with developments in technology and communication that have helped transform the world into a "global village."

Just as the humanists reacted contemptuously against things medieval in the name of a revived antiquity, so their classicizing counterparts in the visual arts often rejected medieval art, in theory at least. The Italians coined for it the pejorative term *Gothic* with a glance at the barbarians who overran ancient Rome. Today that term survives, but the accompanying value judgment has changed vastly. The Gothic style, alive from the twelfth to the fifteenth centuries (in some parts of Europe into the sixteenth), is now regarded as the expression of one of the great ages of world art. Much of its painting has disappeared, although a good deal is known about how it used two-dimensional media from tapestries, stained glass, and glorious color illuminations in manuscripts. Above all, its public architecture survives in the great European cathedrals, which embody an organic unity and a fusion with sculpture and other arts scarcely to be paralleled since the age of the Parthenon in ancient Greece.

The transition from Gothic to Renaissance art is problematical, like so many other aspects of the period when it happened. Compared with the Gothic, Renaissance art is more concerned with classical forms and subjects, with secular themes directed to a more secular clientele, with landscape and other aspects of nature, with the illusion of depth, with individual portraiture, and generally with greater representational realism. All these trends are also observable, however, in late medieval Gothic art as it developed from the Romanesque style that prevailed between the tenth and twelfth centuries. Further complications arise when one distinguishes between different parts of Europe, different stages of the Renaissance, and different art media. There remains nevertheless an immense difference between the Gothic and Renaissance periods in degree and also in consciousness, for the new trends were pursued with a programmatic deliberateness in the Renaissance that one does not find in the earlier era.

The most comprehensive of these trends was the revival of antiquity. Architectural models still existed, especially in Italy, and could be imitated directly. The spirituality implicit in the vertical-line composition and pointed arches of the Gothic cathedral yielded to the essentially horizontal classical emphasis. (Another way of looking at this shift is to see the cutting edge of architectural innovation as having shifted south to Italy, since the great Gothic cathedrals, with their mystically soaring vertical lines and spaces and their walls opened up with stained glass, had been an almost exclusively northern phenomenon.) The dome was revived by Filippo

Brunelleschi in his design for the Florence cathedral (1420), a landmark of the new style, and was used climactically by Michelangelo for St. Peter's in Rome. Classical columns, with their distinctive capitals marking the intersection of vertical with horizontal, took priority over the less clearly end-stopped Gothic pillars. In sculpture and painting, there were greater difficulties, since few antique models existed, especially in the early Renaissance before the discovery of statues such as the Apollo Belvedere. But artists in these media too did their enthusiastic best to classicize. Donatello (1386?–1466) pioneered in the revival of the freestanding nude and the equestrian statue. Painters, besides espousing the classical ideals of proportion and harmony, turned to ancient historical and mythological subjects—although the most frequent ones were still derived from the Bible and the lives of the saints.

The renewed interest in nature by Renaissance artists took many forms. The most obvious was an increased emphasis on landscape, though still almost always integrated with a human subject. The basic medieval worldview had regarded the physical creation as sacramental and symbolic, and the Renaissance did not by any means discard that view; Renaissance pictures continued to be expressions of ideas, often retaining a system of symbols and icons inherited from the Middle Ages, as myriad Renaissance "emblem books" attest. At the same time, Renaissance art suggests also that, apart from its human or divine analogies, the world "out there" can be reproduced for what it is in itself. The picture frame became a window through which one glimpsed the living world. (According to Vasari, Leonardo da Vinci once played a practical joke on his father by creating a terrifying picture so lifelike that it was mistaken for reality.) Anatomy became a formal study for artists; drawing from nude models became commonplace, and the nude as a subject became ubiquitous. Color effects were perfected, especially by Titian and other Venetians. Portraits of individuals became an important genre, as exemplified in the masterfully realistic ones done by Hans Holbein the Younger (1497?–1543) of Erasmus, More, and Henry VIII. This individualism of subject reinforces the general motif of individualism ascribed to the Renaissance in the nineteenth-century model.

Even more to the point is the new individualistic role of the artist. The greatest medieval works of art, the cathedrals, had been collective, indeed communal achievements, a union of large vision with the painstaking efforts of hundreds of skilled artists and craftsmen who remained anonymous. Many of the best medieval artists are identified today only by the word *Master* linked to the name of his city or one of his masterpieces. But in the Renaissance, artists, often working for individual patrons whom they glorified as individuals, came to think of themselves also as unique persons expressing their own unique visions and values. Some of them took to signing their canvases, a new practice, and even when they did not do so their works were figuratively signed by the unmistakable presence of their own personal styles. The medieval artist had been a maker and a servant of God; the Renaissance artist was a creator and, as such, God's rival.

Because it was essentially a literary movement, humanism naturally had its most direct impact on literature. Classical modes were revitalized—for example, the ode, the dialogue, and the pastoral, a form popular in Renaissance literary genres ranging from song to prose romance to drama.

Besides serving as midwives of the revived classicism, some of the humanists created literary masterpieces themselves. They were at their best in the nonfictional or semifictional forms wherein inventiveness could be combined with the expression of ideas and opinions: letters, orations, dialogues, and treatises. Their admiration of Plato appears in the writings of Marsilio Ficino (1433–1499) and Pico della Mirandola, whose *Oration on the Dignity of Man* (1486) has already been mentioned. Dialogues included Erasmus's *Colloquies* (1519), More's *Utopia* (1516), and Baldassare Castiglione's *Book of the Courtier* (1514; published 1528), a vastly influential exposition of the ideal of the Renaissance gentleman. Erasmus's *Praise of Folly* (1509) is a many-sided ironic masterpiece that, like *Utopia,* shows the reformist side of humanism.

The most fundamental development in Renaissance literature was the growth of literary nationalism. All the important medieval vernacular languages of Europe had produced important literature, but it lived in the shadow of Latin, the international language, and the vernacular literatures themselves had typically reflected international rather than local traditions. In the Renaissance, political and personal allegiances to patrons, city-states, or national monarchies helped foster literary ambitions linked to the writers' own distinctive languages. Latin continued to thrive; among many other writers, More and Erasmus used it, in the works just mentioned, and into the seventeenth and eighteenth centuries it continued to be the normal vehicle for scientific discourse, including such monumental works as Isaac Newton's *Principia* (1687). It also remained the language of Roman Catholic liturgy and church government into the twentieth century. But the new Latin of the humanists was based on classical models such as Cicero's prose, and the concentration on such models helped to kill medieval Latin as a living language—a real loss, since in its spare directness medieval Latin had a beauty and functionality that the humanists did not properly appreciate. Their adulation for the classical tongues was also in some respects a roadblock to the development of the vernacular literatures; for example, humanism may have retarded for a time the development of Italian literature in the fifteenth century.

For the most part, though, the humanist impulse had the contrary effect: Local patriotic feelings, reinforced by the humanist ideal of dedicated citizenship, inspired a desire to assert national identity while emulating in the national languages the achievements of antiquity. A notable example was the formation of the *Pléiade,* a group of sixteenth-century French writers that included Pierre de Ronsard (1524–1585), the greatest French poet of the Renaissance, and Joachim du Bellay (1522?–1560). Du Bellay, in his *Defense and Glorification of the French Language* (1549), produced the group's manifesto, calling for a French language and literature to rival that of Italy and antiquity in genres including tragedy, the ode, and the sonnet. The emergence of modern Italian vernacular literature had begun much earlier when Dante chose the Tuscan dialect for *The Divine Comedy,* supporting his program for Italian in a Latin treatise *On Eloquence in the Vernacular Tongue* (1304–1305), and later in the fourteenth century Petrarch and Boccaccio lent the weight of their prestige to Tuscan Italian. In Portugal, the achievements of Camoëns (1524–1580) in lyric and epic went a long way toward defining the Portuguese language. In the Protestant countries such as Germany, Holland, and England where the movement to translate the Bible into the vernacular could thrive, these translations were formative, especially Luther's German version (the New Testament in 1522, the Old Testament in 1534).

The most conscious and comprehensive assertions of Renaissance values appear in the long narrative works of the period, especially epics or works touched by the epic impulse. This is natural enough; the epic has always been a vehicle for communal ideas. If we did not know any of the great Renaissance epics and had to create a theoretical model for them on the basis of other tendencies of the time and clichés about it, we might arrive at something like this: a story of imposing events, written in a classical unrhymed verse, scornful of the outgrown medieval heritage, celebrating a modernist theme such as the recent achievements of the poet's own nation, and centered on a heroic but mentally elevated "Renaissance man" aglow with confidence and optimism. But, although virtually every Renaissance epic illustrates one or more of these motifs, what we most often find is a mixture, seemingly incongruous, of the modern, classical, and medieval, accompanied often by ambivalent value judgments. Some of these incongruities are attributable to the epic tradition itself, which since Virgil has tended to combine nationalist modernism with nostalgia, usually intimating a desire to keep alive what was best in the past and, on the other hand, a consciousness of having progressed beyond it.

Rabelais' *Gargantua and Pantagruel* (1532–1552), Cervantes' *Don Quixote* (1605, 1615), and Shakespeare's English history plays (1591–1599) are not epics in a strict formal sense, but they have the scale, comprehensiveness, and national flavor of epic. Rabelais' work is perhaps the showcase example of worldly Renaissance exuberance; yet it also recalls the medieval "goliardic," a student tradition of wining and wenching. The searching complexities of *Don Quixote* build from a direct confrontation between an idealism symbolized by the medieval romances and a contrasting pragmatism, and which set of values Cervantes endorses is not a question to answer simply. The *Quixote* is among other things an examination of the Spanish national character, but in the spirit of a sensitive critique rather than of panegyric. Of Shakespeare's ten English history plays, eight span the period from the end of the fourteenth century to the emergence in 1485 of the Tudor dynasty still reigning in Shakespeare's time, and these plays have been taken sometimes to constitute Shakespeare's epic. In it he celebrates the emergence of peace and order from a fragmented, dying medieval feudalism, but he also portrays the noble beauty of the chivalric code. None of these three authors, then, is simply heralding the glories of a new civilization unrooted in the medieval past.

When we turn to works more strictly describable as epics (almost all of them, interestingly, written in rhymed rather than in classical verse forms), we find the same mixture of allegiances. Perhaps the closest thing to our hypothetical national and modernist model is Camoëns' *Lusiad* (1572), a poem that intricately imitates Virgil's *Aeneid* and acclaims triumphantly the unprecedented Portuguese voyages around the Cape to the Far East for the glory of the nation and of Catholic Christianity. Here the sense of a vast new world in contrast to the constricted Mediterranean world of epic memory accords well enough with the nineteenth-century vision of an expansive Renaissance spirit. Iberian interest in the new explorations is also reflected in several sixteenth-century Spanish epics by authors including Alonso de Ercilla y Zúñga (1534–1594) and the great dramatist Lope de Vega (1562–1635).

The definitive Italian Renaissance epics are quite another matter. They consist of a series of poems written in Ferrara under the patronage of the Este family: the *Orlando in Love* (1483) of Matteo Boiardo, the *Orlando Driven Mad* (1516) of Ludovico Ariosto, and the *Jerusalem Delivered* (1575) of Torquato Tasso. (Boiardo and Ariosto built from an earlier work, *Morgante the Giant,* written about 1480 by Luigi Pulci.) All these authors belong unmistakably to the Renaissance; Ariosto especially, with his gaiety, sophistication, and sensuousness, and his theme of the impossible quest, expresses something quintessential to his time and place. But, like Pulci and Boiardo, he treats medieval matter and heroes derived from the traditions of King Arthur, Charlemagne, and Roland, although the hero of the great, austere *chanson de geste* is scarcely recognizable in this new Orlando ("Roland," in Italian). These poems are much closer to the magical atmosphere and free form of medieval romance than to the classical epic. Tasso's poem conforms more nearly to the ancient models, but it too has a medieval subject (the first Crusade) and owes much to the romance genre and atmosphere; moreover, the ideal it celebrates is a united Christian Europe that in the days of the Counter-Reformation had become no more than a wistful memory.

Edmund Spenser (1552?–1599), although a fervent Renaissance Protestant, wrote in this tradition of Italianate medievalism. In *The Faerie Queene* (published 1590–1595) he attempted a portrait of the ideal human being based on a scheme of Aristotelian ethical virtues that medieval authors like Dante would probably have found congenial, and he chose for his vehicle a blend of romance, allegory, and archaic diction that also have strong medieval associations. On the other hand, Spenser's political allegory is modern and militantly Protestant, pitting Queen Elizabeth (Gloriana, the fairy queen) and her champions against evil popes and Catholic monarchs who serve as agents of the Satanic.

The culmination of Renaissance epic was achieved by Milton, who inherited many of Spenser's values but wrote an utterly different kind of poem. His *Paradise Lost,* influenced by *La Semaine* (*The Week,* 1578), an epic account of the creation by the French Protestant poet Guillaume du Bartas, treats the fall of humankind, a universal theme sanctioned by the divine truth of the Bible rather than the mere fictions of medieval legend or classic fable. In his close textural and structural use of Homer and Virgil, his antimedievalism (reflected in a scornful passage abusing the monastic orders), his contemptuous rejection of rhyme as medieval barbarism, his deliberate disavowal of medieval romance as an epic mode ("fabled knights / In battles feigned")—in all these respects Milton adopts the humanist stance. Even more fundamentally, *Paradise Lost* is humanist in its relative freedom from sectarian factionalism (the passage about the monks notwithstanding) and in its ultimate theme: freedom, more specifically human free will. In rising above the doctrinaire polemics for his nation and theology that he reserved for his Puritan prose tracts, Milton may well have achieved in *Paradise Lost,* more than any other major Renaissance epic poet and at the very end of the Renaissance, the humanist goals that in so many ways define the age.

Renaissance values appear in the epics as broad, comprehensive visions, but equally characteristic is a new kind of literary intimacy and particularity akin to the vogue of portrait painting and the new self-expressive role of the artist. The best literary portraits are the characters in Shakespeare's plays; although they often owe something to earlier literary and dramatic traditions such as the morality play, scores of them are fully realized individuals. It may seem paradoxical, then, that Shakespeare reveals very little of himself. For the epitome of Renaissance self-revelation we can go to Montaigne (1533–1592), whose *Essays* (1580–1588) combine far-reaching speculation with the minutest factual details of his personal life and the quirks of his mind, all colored by his distinctive personality and voice.

But the principal medium for self-expression was the lyric. The prototype, once more, is Petrarch, whose lyrics focus so insistently on the poet himself. His Laura is clearly in the line of Dante's Beatrice, but, without denying that Beatrice is a real woman or that Laura is idealized, one senses that the latter is far more fully a unique individual. In the sonnet especially, Petrarch started a Renaissance fashion taken up by almost all the lyric poets of Europe, including Camoëns, Ronsard, Spenser, Sir Philip Sidney (1554–1586), Shakespeare, and Milton. It became the confessional love poem *par excellence,* but even when the subject was not inherently private or amatory (Shakespeare on time, Donne on religious experience), the viewpoint on these more universal matters was still usually subjective. This is not to say that the sonnets were reliably autobiographical; in fact, the genre became one of the most artificial, convention-ridden of forms, full of stylized sighing lovers, cruel but idealized mistresses (sometimes quite fictional), and other stock devices of the courtly love apparatus whose roots extend back beyond Petrarch into the Middle Ages. But even the most conventional of the sonnets reflect the vogue of self-expression, since the sonneteer had at least to assume the guise of a man revealing his intimate thoughts or feelings. "Fool," says Sidney's muse to him, "look in thy heart and write." (Ultimately the Petrarchan tradition of courtly praise fell by its own weight of artificiality; Donne in his lyrics scrutinizes the conventions ironically, and Shakespeare could satirize them as he does in his Sonnet 130: "My mistress' eyes are nothing like the sun; / Coral is far more red than her lips' red . . . .") Often, too, the sonneteers' self-consciousness took the form of commentary on their own work; poetry and the poets' ability to give immortality to their addressees were frequent themes, and beneath the overlays of this convention is an authentic new sense of the power of art that is characteristic of the Renaissance.

The heightened interest during the Renaissance in objectifying the world, portraying individuals, and exploring the complexities of human psychology as it is reflected in behavior—all these were favorable conditions for a resurgent interest in drama, which, especially in England and Spain, flourished as it had not done since Greek antiquity. The exact origins of this new dramatic impulse are hard to untangle from one another. The classical revival was unquestionably important: The plays of Terence, Plautus, and Seneca known to the Middle Ages were now approached less exclusively as rhetorical models and more as literary theater; the Greek dramatists were rediscovered along with some plays by Plautus that had disappeared; at schools and universities plays were studied avidly, and scholars began to write classically inspired dramas of their own, in both Latin and the vernacular. The printing press helped immeasurably; in the half-century or so after it came into use, the plays of all the great ancient dramatists—Aeschylus, Sophocles, Euripides, Aristophanes, Plautus, Terence, and Seneca—were published. The same period saw the publication of Aristotle's *Poetics,* and with it came a new consciousness of classical "rules" such as the preservation of the unities. Tragedians learned from Seneca how to write a long play that held together; comic playwrights learned the intricacies of tight plotting from Plautus and Terence. When the public theaters of London began to thrive in the 1580s and 1590s, the first important plays were written by men who, like Thomas Kyd (1557?–1595) and Christopher Marlowe (1564–1593), had learned their craft in the schools or universities.

Nevertheless, many of the greatest Renaissance plays are not in any obvious way classical. In both Spain and England, the most vital sources of the new drama were in native popular theatrical traditions which, in turn, had their ultimate roots in the medieval church. Shakespeare's friend and fellow playwright Ben Jonson (1572–1637), an aggressive advocate of classical form, felt himself to be in that role an enlightened exception among his formally footloose contemporaries. In Spain, the enormously prolific Lope de Vega (1562–1635) wrote a manifesto in 1609 rejecting classical rules; this anticlassical position was later modified by Calderón de la Barca (1600–1681), but he too in his more intellectual and theological vein was thoroughly Spanish in his religious preoccupations. Both Lope de Vega and Shakespeare blended the comic and the serious in a fashion closer to medievalism than to classicism. Even the staging of their plays, despite immense advances in professionalism and sophistication, recalls certain medieval features; for example, in the Elizabethan theater the areas below and above the main acting platform continued to be referred to as the "hell" and the "heaven," as in the three-level stage of the medieval period. (See the Introductions to *Everyman* and Shakespeare.)

The fact is that, although the Renaissance drama of England and Spain is unimaginable apart from either its medieval origins or the classical revival, it achieved expressive heights and explored human experience in ways not always clearly attributable to either strain. Religious themes continued to be immensely popular in Spain, but so were secular ones. In England these completely supplanted the overt devotional emphasis of the miracle, mystery, and morality plays. A Christian norm might be present, but, like the classicist goal of coherent unity, it was there organically and implicitly rather than texturally and explicitly. The history play perfected by Marlowe, Shakespeare, and Lope de Vega was an almost wholly new genre. Comedy owed something to medieval farce and to the stock characters of the Roman comedians (the "wily slave" transformed into the clowns and other clever "low" characters of playwrights such as Shakespeare), but in its highest reaches it became something new to the stage. In the Shakespearean comedies *Twelfth Night, As You Like It,* and *A Midsummer Night's Dream* (set, ludicrously, in ancient Athens but really in fairyland), laughter is combined with a warm and sympathetic insight into the romantic feelings of men and women, articulating a distinctive definition of love. Tragedy became both intimate and cosmic. The medieval notion of tragedy was simply the fall of a great personage from prosperous eminence (a strain vestigially recognizable in Shakespearean tragedies like *Macbeth*). The classical impulse in the Renaissance transformed this model radically—for example, Senecan models added a dimension of melodrama and a stoic sense of fatality, and from Aristotle came the notion of the hero's "tragic flaw." But no such formulas can define the great English tragedies of Marlowe, Shakespeare, or John Webster (1580?–1625). In Shakespeare's *Hamlet, King Lear, Othello,* and *Macbeth,* it is not only the hero's life and happiness but the entire vision of a morally ordered universe that is at stake, threatened by a demonic principle of evil that seems to have escaped human or divine control. Whether or not the principle of righteousness prevails in the end is a question that can be answered differently about different plays (opinion is notoriously divided about *King Lear*), but even when it does reassert itself, a terrible price has been paid in the suffering or destruction of precious, noble individuals. There is at the least a heartrending sense of human waste. But this sense is also mitigated by the very existence of human goodness, whether it triumphs or not. The integrity and love of Lear's daughter Cordelia are realities that in their nature cannot be denied or annulled, even by death. For dramatic visions so vast as these one must go back to Greek tragedy, and it might be argued that Shakespeare goes beyond the Greeks by combining with his cosmic themes a more intimate concern for the unique human person.

Italy, the original center of the humanist movement and the revival of antiquity, did not produce a great dramatic literature in the Renaissance, although some of its distinguished authors, including Ariosto and Tasso, produced notable plays, and there were occasional masterpieces such as Machiavelli's *Mandragola* (about 1518). Italy contributed influentially to post-Renaissance stagecraft, however; as in painting, it pioneered in the development of illusional perspective in stage settings, and it helped develop important architectural features like the proscenium arch. Such elements look past the Renaissance to the "picture-frame" stage that became the principal model for theater from the late seventeenth century until well into the twentieth. (Much of this new stagecraft reached other countries by way of Italian opera, a new art form developed around 1600 in rivalry with the integration of the arts in ancient Greek drama and crowned with immediate greatness in the works of Claudio Monteverdi [1567–1643].) The modern picture-frame stage, typically opening into someone's living room, is itself an emblem for the kind of realistically intimate drama often enacted on it, and the emblem represented by the physical theater is applicable to earlier dramatic traditions as well. The essentially public action of classical Greek drama took place before an unchanging background, the *skene* that typically represented a palace and concealed from the audience the merely domestic private scenes imagined to take place behind it. The medieval stage presented simultaneously to the audience three levels—heaven, earth, and hell—representing a constant awareness of the relationship between here and hereafter. The Renaissance stage of England and Spain was the vehicle for complete fluidity and variety, capable of representing, with the indispensable help of poetic language, any conceivable setting and of shifting from one to another instantaneously. The ceremonial and casual, the public and intimate, the lofty and low, the violent and serene, the realistic and romantic—all these manners and moods, in any combination, were at the service of the playwright and actors. It is therefore not surprising that Renaissance drama could encompass more of the world and of life than has been possible in the theater of any other age.

FURTHER READING: One entry into the Renaissance is by way of Jacob Burckhardt's epoch-making and controversial study *The Civilization of the Renaissance in Italy,* first published in 1860 (discussed in the preceding Introduction), which emphasizes Renaissance individualism. More concise is J. H. Plumb's *The Italian Renaissance,* 1961, which in surveying the period refers often to Dante, Boccaccio, Petrarch, and Machiavelli. E. M. W. Tillyard's *The Elizabethan World Picture,* 1946, another historically influential study, identifies three models by which the cosmos was envisaged: as a chain, a set of correspondences, and a dance. Tillyard's *The English Renaissance: Fact or Fiction?,* 1952, identifies and discusses essential differences between medieval and Renaissance thought in order to answer the question posed by the title; see also the excellent discussions in *The Renaissance: A Reconsideration of the Theories and Interpretations of the Age,* ed. Tinsley Helton, 1961. Two of the essays in this volume warrant special mention: Harry Levin's "English Literature of the Renaissance" and Paul Oskar Kristeller's "Changing Views of the Renaissance Since Jacob Burckhardt." The principles and attitudes reflected in Renaissance literature are treated in Douglas Bush's *Prefaces to Renaissance Literature,* 1965. Paul Oskar Kristeller's *Renaissance Thought and Its Sources,* ed. Michael Mooney, 1979, and Ernst Cassirer's *The Individual and the Cosmos in Renaissance Philosophy,* 1927, trans. Mario Domadi, 1963, are both careful and incisive; Kristeller begins with humanism and proceeds to study the classical forerunners of Renaissance thought, Renaissance attitudes toward the individual, and other topics; Cassirer's classic examines the Renaissance as a systematic unity. Surveys of literature and literary history include *The Continental Renaissance, 1500–1600,* by W. A. Coupe, A. J. Krailsheimer, J. A. Scott, and R. W. Truman, 1971, 1978; and A. C. Spearing, *Medieval to Renaissance in English Poetry,* 1985. Recently, progress toward understanding the Renaissance has been made through the study of a number of specific topics. One of the most important of these has been the role of women in the period, addressed in *Women in the Middle Ages and the Renaissance,* ed. Mary Beth Rose, 1986; Margaret L. King, *Women of the Renaissance,* 1991; *The Women's Sharp Revenge: Five Women's Pamphlets from the Renaissance,* ed. Simon Shepherd, 1985; and Angeline Goreau, *The Whole Duty of a Woman: Female Writers in Seventeenth-Century England,* 1985. Unconventional sexuality in the era is treated in Bruce R. Smith, *Homosexual Desire in Shakespeare's England,* 1991. Other works with large social implications include the collection of essays *Science and the Arts in the Renaissance,* ed. John W. Shirley and F. David Hoeniger, 1985; and J. R. Hale, *War and Society in Renaissance Europe, 1450–1620,* 1985. Derrick Henry, *The Listener's Guide to Medieval and Renaissance Music,* 1983, is largely a discography, but it serves also as a brief musical history of the periods. Complementing older studies of the humanist movement such as Douglas Bush, *The Renaissance and English Humanism,* 1939, and Myron P. Gilmore, *The World of Humanism, 1453–1517,* 1952, are such works as Donald R. Kelley, *Renaissance Humanism,* 1991; Charles Trinkaus, *The Scope of Renaissance Humanism,* 1983; and Benjamin G. Kohl, *Renaissance Humanism, 1300–1550: A Bibliography of Materials in English,* 1985.

Francis Petrarch
(1304–1374)

Possibly the greatest love poet in Western literature was Francis Petrarch, the fourteenth-century Italian classicist, humanist, and literary arbiter. Born in Arezzo in 1304, Petrarch was set to the study of law, first at Montpellier and then at Bologna. When his father died, the twenty-two-year-old Petrarch renounced law and moved to the lively city of Avignon, the seat of the papacy during its "Babylonian captivity" from 1309 to 1378. After briefly considering the Church, he entered instead the service of the wealthy and powerful Colonna family, the first of a series of patrons who made it possible for Petrarch to devote his life exclusively to literature. He has thus been called the first modern man of letters. By 1341 his reputation was so high that he received a laurel crown as poet laureate from the Roman Senate, an honor Petrarch always treasured as symbolizing not only his own achievement but his spiritual links with the great poets of classical Rome. For the rest of his life, Petrarch continued to be a celebrated public man, an intimate and counselor of princes as well as an arbiter of literary taste. During his mature years, he moved from one residence to another, to Milan as guest of the Visconti, to Venice as guest of the Republic, and finally to Arqua, near Padua, where he spent the last four years of his life in a country retreat. He died in 1374, just before his seventieth birthday, his copy of Virgil open before him on his desk.

In his own day and his own estimation, Petrarch's major achievement was in his Latin works, which far outnumbered his Italian ones. In a letter to Boccaccio, written in his later years, he told of his decision, sometime in his thirties, to use Latin rather than Italian in his major literary work. He had, he said, already begun "a great work" in Italian but had given it up for fear that his words would be "mangled by the public." (Dante, who had visited Petrarch's family when Petrarch was seven, had completed *The Divine Comedy* in Italian in 1321, about fifteen years before Petrarch decided in favor of Latin.) The most important of Petrarch's many Latin works are *Africa,* an unfinished epic poem about Scipio Africanus, the third-century B.C. conqueror of Hannibal; the *Secretum Meum* (My Secret), a spiritual autobiography in the form of three imaginary dialogues between Petrarch and St. Augustine; and his *Letters,* both in verse and prose, which Petrarch himself carefully edited and collected into a number of volumes. The humane and liberal spirit of Petrarch's classical studies was to be a major influence in the development of Renaissance humanism throughout Europe.

Later ages have known Petrarch less as a classicist, however, than as the author of the collection of poems in Italian which he called the *Rerum vulgarium fragmenta* (Poetic Fragments in the Vernacular) and which is now generally known either as the *Canzoniere* (Lyric Poems) or simply the *Rhymes.* This collection of poems was gradually built up through Petrarch's mature life. At least three times Petrarch arranged them in systematic collections, and he was still polishing and rearranging them when he died; the final version of the sequence contains 366 poems, intended to be read, like the Breviary, over the course of a year.

The inspiration for the poems was Petrarch's crucial meeting, on April 6, 1327, with "Laura," in the church of St. Clare in Avignon. (Petrarch never revealed Laura's identity, but she is believed to have been Laurette de Noves, who had been married for two years when Petrarch met her and who had a number of children by the time of her death in 1348.) Petrarch adored her, hopelessly and from afar, until her death twenty-one years later and continued to cherish her memory in his poetry for another ten years, after which he professed to renounce earthly love and turn his thoughts only to God.

There is something faintly absurd to the modern reader about this protracted and self-conscious cultivation of a hopeless love (especially, perhaps, when one learns that Petrarch had two illegitimate children by different mothers during the time of his idealization of Laura). But there is more than a little of the conventional in Petrarch's adoration of Laura. By the time he wrote, there was already a long tradition of sequences of love poems addressed to an unattainable woman. Originating in the poems of the twelfth- and thirteenth-century *troubadours* of southern France, the tradition had found its most notable expression before Petrarch in Dante's *La Vita Nuova* (The New Life), devoted to the transformation of the real Beatrice Portinari into "Beatrice," a symbol of Christian salvation (Latin *beata,* "blessed"). A friend of Petrarch, Giacomo Colonna, even suggested that Laura was not a real person but an invented symbol of the poetic "laurel." Petrarch replied with some vehemence that Laura was indeed real and that no one could counterfeit the "weariness and pallor" that his hopeless love had given him. But real passion for a real woman does not preclude making her also into a conventional poetic figure.

What raised the *Rhymes* above the level of its predecessors and made it one of the most widely read and imitated collections of poems in literary history was the wealth of classical learning in the poems, their scope and variety, their arrangement into a developing structure, and their sheer beauty. The classicism of the *Rhymes* is not obtrusive, but it is the more powerful for being so thoroughly assimilated. Virgil, Horace, Catullus, and especially Ovid are echoed throughout the *Rhymes.* One realizes with something of a shock, for example, that the poem "Upon the breeze she spread her golden hair" (XC), personal as it seems, is a close reworking of a passage from the *Aeneid.* Ovid is a pervasive presence in the *Rhymes,* not the Ovid of the *Art of Love* or the moralized, allegorical Ovid of the medieval interpreters, but the Ovid of the *Metamorphoses;* Ovid's Daphne, who, pursued by Apollo, was changed into a laurel tree, is one of the most important classical analogues for the Laura in Petrarch's sequence. The *Rhymes* are quite varied both in form and content. Sonnets predominate; 317 of the 366 poems in the collection are in this form. But there are also a number of *canzoni* (poems made up of five or six stanzas of equal length, followed by a shorter *envoy,* such as CXXVI and CXXIX), and several other forms appear. Most of the poems are about Laura, but a significant number have nothing to do with her, dealing instead with politics, moral problems, friendship, and other topics. The sequence begins and ends with a renunciation of the poet's passion for Laura. The poems between fall most obviously into two groups: Part One, consisting of 265 poems that deal with the living Laura, and Part Two, consisting of 99 poems devoted to the memory of the dead Laura. The poems are arranged in loose chronology, but more important than chronology is the range of moods of the speaker, a range that includes every emotion from spiritual ecstasy to agonized self-laceration and melancholy resignation, every mood associated with love, perhaps, except the joy of physical consummation.

Laura comes to mean many things for Petrarch in the course of the poems; as Thomas G. Bergin has pointed out, they reveal at least four Lauras. One is the Laura of the poet's "laurel," his poetic ambitions which he pursues as Apollo pursued his Daphne. Another is Laura as a virtuous guide to Heaven, like Dante's Beatrice; this view of Laura comes to dominate the second part of the sequence, after Laura's death. A third Laura represents beauty itself, especially as a fascinating temptation that draws the poet away from his proper pursuit of salvation; this Laura appears most explicitly in the sonnets of recantation: I and CCCLXV. And finally, Laura is, of course, merely a young woman with whom the poet fell in love on a spring day in 1327; many of the poems do not emphasize any metaphoric meanings for Laura but present her as a real human presence.

It is not Laura, however, but the poet who is the protagonist of the *Rhymes.* His lady is described in loving detail, but always from outside, from the poet's point of view; Petrarch has no interest in the workings of Laura's mind or in her attitudes toward such subjects as, say, her husband or her children. The personality we remember after reading the poems is Petrarch's—nostalgic, melancholy, passionate and yet always curiously removed from life, an observer rather than a participant.

The deeply personal and introspective quality of the *Rhymes* and their brilliant technique established a vogue that endured for at least three centuries and left a permanent impression on Western poetry, especially love poetry. "Petrarchism" offered a way of portraying the loved one, as a fascinating combination of earthly and divine qualities; a characteristic stance for the lover; and a repertory of devices that could be endlessly imitated, sometimes well, sometimes clumsily and mechanically. These included a repertory of stock images—stormy seas, beautiful landscapes, marble tombs, battles—and a liberal use of antithesis (strong contrasts), oxymoron (contradictory terms), and hyperbole (exaggeration). (See Poem CXXXIV for examples of Petrarch's own use of such devices.) Exaggerated Petrarchan catalogues of the features of a stock, composite mistress had become so common by Shakespeare's time that he could parody them in his Sonnet 130:

> My mistress' eyes are nothing like the sun;
> Coral is far more red than her lips' red:
> If snow be white, why then her breasts are dun;
> If hairs be wires, black wires grow on her head.

But pervasive as Petrarch's literary influence was, his influence upon attitudes toward love was probably even greater; even today, lovers who never heard of Petrarch tend to adopt Petrarchan attitudes. "The amatory attitudes of the *Rhymes* have in fact been built into our culture," Thomas G. Bergin writes. "It is possible, of course, that some day there may be a revolution in human emotions, whether it be a new morality or a new erotic, but until that day comes we shall live by the code that Petrarch elaborated with such instinctive perception and such compelling sophistication." We may be somewhat more skeptical than Bergin about the desirability of some aspects of

Petrarchan love, such as the radical split between the physical and the spiritual; the "revolution in human emotions" he mentions may now be taking place. But until it is completed, we must agree that lovers' meetings "will take place in the kingdom that Petrarch has explored for them."

FURTHER READING: Thomas G. Bergin s *Petrarch,* 1970, is an excellent introduction to the study of Petrarch. Bergin provides a concise survey of Petrarch's life and a clear and substantial commentary on the *Triumphs* and the *Rhymes.* Ernest Hatch Wilkins's *Life of Petrarch,* 1961, is a more detailed biography of the poet. Morris Bishop's *Petrarch and His World,* 1963, analyzes Petrarch and his times in great detail, but it is nonetheless suited for the new student of the poet. Nicholas Mann, *Petrarch,* 1984, in the Past Masters series, is a short book on Petrarch's life and mind, emphasizing especially Petrarch's self-consciousness and image of himself. Kenelm Foster, *Petrarch, Poet and Humanist,* 1984, is a comprehensive biographical and critical study, especially valuable on the relationship between the classical and religious sides of Petrarch. Petrarch's Italian poetry is discussed with critical acumen and a sense of the historical context in Peter Hainsworth, *Petrarch the Poet; An Introduction to the Rerum Vulgarium Fragmenta,* 1988. Marjorie O'Rourke Boyle, *Petrarch's Genius: Pentimento and Prophecy,* 1991, is notably fresh and original. A Nobel Prize poet's thoughts on Petrarch are recorded in Salvatore Quasimodo's *The Poet and the Politician,* 1960, translated by Thomas G. Bergin, 1964. The second essay in this volume contains sections on both Petrarch's solitude and Dante's reputation. Stephen Minta's *Petrarch and Petrarchism: The English and French Traditions,* 1980, is an excellent anthology of poems by Petrarch and by English and French poets influenced by him. On the Renaissance humanists in general, see the Further Reading section of the Introduction to the Renaissance in the present book.

RHYMES

Translation and notes by Anthony Mortimer

I

All you that hear in scattered rhymes[1] the sound
of sighs on which I used to feed my heart
in my first youthful error when, in part,
I was another man, now left behind;

for the vain hopes, vain sorrows of my mind, 5
the tears and discourse of my varied art,
in any who have played a lover's part
pardon and pity too I hope to find.

[1] The poet regards his "scattered rhymes" as a collection of fragments *(Rerum vulgarium fragmenta),* but there is also the possibility that they are scattered through the world. The whole sonnet is, indeed, indicative of Petrarch's ambiguous attitude towards the *Canzoniere:* he deplores it as evidence of a "youthful error," but he still hopes to find readers. (Notes, unless otherwise indicated, are by the translator.)

But now I see too well how I became
a tale for common gossip everywhere, 10
so that I grow ashamed of what I am;

and of my raving still the fruit is shame
and penitence, and last the knowledge clear
that all the world loves is a passing dream.

III

It was that very day on which the sun
in awe of his creator dimmed the ray,[1]
when I was captured, with my guard astray,
for your fine eyes, my lady, bound me then.

It hardly seemed the time for me to plan 5
defence against Love's stroke; I went my way
secure, unwary; so upon that day
of general sorrow all my pains began.

Love found me with no armour for the fight,
my eyes an open highway to the heart, 10
eyes that are now a vent for tears to flow.

And yet he played no honourable part,
wounding me with his shaft in such a state;
he saw you armed and dared not lift the bow.

XC

Upon the breeze she spread her golden hair[1]
that in a thousand gentle knots was turned,
and the sweet light beyond all measure burned
in eyes where now that radiance is rare;

and in her face there seemed to come an air 5
of pity, true or false, that I discerned:
I had love's tinder in my breast unburned,
was it a wonder if it kindled there?

[1] Petrarch first saw Laura at matins in the church of Saint Clare in Avignon on April 6, 1327. This was not the moveable feast of Good Friday, but, according to medieval calculations, the exact calendar anniversary of Christ's death.

[1] This sonnet is inspired by a description of Venus appearing to Aeneas in Virgil's *Aeneid,* Book I. (Editors' note.)

She moved not like a mortal, but as though
she bore an angel's form, her words had then 10
a sound that simple human voices lack;

a heavenly spirit, a living sun
was what I saw; now, if it is not so,
the wound's not healed because the bow grows slack.

CXXVI

Waters[1] fresh and sweet and clear
where the fair limbs reclined
of the one creature who to me seems woman;
and gentle tree-trunk where,
with sighs I call to mind, 5
the leaning side once loved to find a column;
flowers and grass that often
the light gown hid from sight
with the angelic breast;[2]
airs breathing holy rest 10
where Love with those fair eyes opened my heart:
come, and together grant
a hearing to my last lament.

If it be destiny,
and heaven works for this, 15
that Love should close these weeping eyes of mine,
then may some kindness lay
the body in your midst
and the soul naked to its home return;
death shall become less stern 20
if such a hope I bear
into that fearful pass,
for the soul's weariness
could find no calmer haven anywhere,
nor could it ever leave 25
the troubled flesh in a more quiet grave.

A time may come again
when she perhaps will stray
to the old haunt, untamed, yet fair and meek,

[1] The waters of the Sorgue in Vaucluse.

[2] Commentators have been unnecessarily puzzled here. The poet, in fact, recalls Laura in a number of different attitudes: bathing in the river, leaning against a tree, and sitting on the ground so that the gown which covers her breast also covers the grass and flowers.

and where she saw me then 30
upon that blessed day
will turn an eager and a happy look,
and there, O pity! seek
and find me turned to dust amid the stones:
at this may Love arise, 35
inspiring her with sighs
so sweet she forces heaven[3] and obtains
its mercy for my soul,
drying her eyes upon the lovely veil.

From the fair boughs there fell, 40
sweet in the memory,
upon her lap a rain of every flower,
and she sat there and still
was humble in such glory,
already covered by the loving shower; 45
upon the hem lay flowers,
and some the tresses crowned
which seemed that day to hold
both pearls and polished gold;
some rested on the waves, some on the ground; 50
some, sweetly turning through the air,
seemed in their drift to whisper: "Love reigns here."

How often I exclaimed,
seized by a sudden fear:
"For certain she was born in Paradise!" 55
Such deep oblivion came
from her celestial air,
the words, the gentle smiling, and the eyes,
so faintly did I seize
the image truth would show, 60
that I said sighing then:
"How came I here, or when?"
thinking myself in heaven, not here below.
And ever since I've loved this place
so much that elsewhere I can find no peace. 65

Song, had you beauty as you have desire,
intrepidly you could
go out among the crowd and leave this wood.

[3] Bosco [a modern Italian critic] points out that heaven will be impressed not by Laura's sorrow or piety, but by the sweetness of her sighs and the elegance of her gestures. Even the intercession of the living for the dead is seen in aesthetic terms.

CXXIX

From thought to thought, from mountainside to mountain
Love leads me on, since every beaten trail
I feel as hostile to my peace of mind.
If some deserted heath has stream or fountain,
or if two hills should hide a shadowed vale, 5
the spirit sees its suffering decline,
and there, as Love designs,
now laughs and weeps, now fears and learns to trust;
the face that follows where the spirit leads
grows clear and overclouds, 10
and no condition ever seems to last:
so, at the sight, a man who knew that life
would say: "He burns, and stands in doubtful strife."

Among high mountains and wild woods I find
some kind of rest; but each frequented place 15
becomes an enemy that my eyes abhor.
At every step a new thought comes to mind
of my dear lady, often bringing gladness
out of the torment that I feel for her;
and hardly would I prefer 20
to change the sweet and bitter life I bear
when I reflect: "Perhaps Love keeps in view
a better time for you;
you hate yourself, but she may hold you dear."
And with this thought sighing I change again: 25
"Can it be ever true? but how? and when?"

Where a tall pine-tree or a hill gives shade
sometimes I stop, and on the nearest stone
my mind will draw her face. At last I find,
on coming to myself, my breast is bathed 30
with that emotion; then "alas," I groan,
"where are you now? what have you left behind?"
But while my wandering mind
can be kept steadfastly on that first thought
and I forget myself and gaze on her, 35
then I feel Love so near
the soul is sated with its own deceit:
I see her in so many things, so fair,
that if the illusion lasts I ask no more.

Often I've seen (who will believe me now?) 40
on the green grass or in transparent water
her living self, in beech-trees or the face

of a white cloud, and ever fashioned so
that Leda[1] would have surely said her daughter
fades like a star outshone by the sun's rays; 45
and the more wild the place
I come upon, the lonelier the shore
the fairer does thought shadow forth[2] my love.
Then, when the truth removes
that sweet illusion, I sit as before, 50
cold and stone-dead upon the living stone,[3]
like one who thinks and weeps and writes alone.

To where the mountain shadows never lie,
towards the highest and best vantage-point,
a fierce desire often makes me start. 55
There I begin to measure with the eye
my sufferings, and tearfully give vent
to the sad mists that thicken in my heart,
when both my gaze and thought
span all that lies between me and the fair 60
face that is still so near and far away;
then, whispering to myself, I say:
"What can you know? this moment over there
perhaps your absence makes her sigh for you;"
and in this thought the spirit breathes anew. 65

My song, beyond this alp,
where skies are happier and clear above,
you'll find me sitting by a stream that flows
where gentle aura blows
in from a fresh and fragrant laurel-grove: 70
there is my heart and she that stole it from me;
and here my image all that you can see.[4]

[1] Leda, seduced by Zeus in the form of a swan, was the mother of Helen of Troy. (Editors' note.)

[2] The Italian word is *adombra.* More than "shadow forth" this suggests the conscious chiaroscuro of the painter, thus continuing the artist metaphor introduced in the previous stanza.

[3] The contrast is probably between the stone effigy on a tomb *(pietra morta)* and the natural stone *(pietra viva)* upon which the poet sits. Having transformed so many shapes into Laura's image, the poet now becomes an image himself. This reading is confirmed by the last line of the poem.

[4] The envoi sends the poem to join the poet's heart which is with Laura beyond the Alps. For once I have attempted to translate the pun on Laura's name.

CXXXIV

I find no peace, and have no arms for war,
and fear and hope, and burn and yet I freeze,
and fly to heaven, lying on earth's floor,
and nothing hold, and all the world I seize.

My jailer opens not, nor locks the door, 5
nor binds me to her, nor will loose my ties;
Love kills me not, nor breaks the chains I wear,
nor wants me living, nor will grant me ease.

I have no tongue, and shout; eyeless, I see;
I long to perish, and I beg for aid; 10
I love another, and myself I hate.

Weeping I laugh, I feed on misery,
by death and life so equally dismayed:
for you, my lady, am I in this state.

CCLXV

Fierce heart and bitter, and most cruel will,
sweet, humble, and angelic to the sight,
if this first rigor last throughout the fight,
the honour of their trophies will be small;

for when grass, leaf, and flower spring and fall, 5
when daylight comes, and in the dark of night,
always I weep. Indeed I have the right
on Love, my fate, my lady thus to call.

I live on hope alone, remembering
how I have seen a little moisture prove 10
to wear down marble and the solid stone:

there cannot be a heart so hard that weeping,
praying, and loving sometime will not move,
nor yet a will so cold it cannot burn.

CCXCII

The eyes I spoke of once in words that burn,
the arms and hands and feet and lovely face

that took me from myself for such a space
of time and marked me out from other men;

the waving hair of unmixed gold that shone, 5
the smile that flashed with the angelic rays
that used to make this earth a paradise,
are now a little dust, all feeling gone;

and yet I live, grief and disdain to me,
left where the light I cherished never shows, 10
in fragile bark on the tempestuous sea.

Here let my loving song come to a close,
the vein of my accustomed art is dry,
and this, my lyre, turned at last to tears.[1]

CCCLXV[1]

I keep lamenting over days gone by,
the time I spent loving a mortal thing,
with no attempt to soar, although my wing
might give no mean example in the sky.[2]

You that my foul unworthy sins descry, 5
unseen and everlasting, heaven's King,
succour my soul, infirm and wandering,
and what is lacking let your grace supply;

so if I lived in tempest and in war,
I die in port and peace; however vain 10
the stay, at least the parting may be fair.

Now in the little life that still remains
and at my death may your quick hand be near:
in others, you well know, my hope is gone.

[1] See Job, 30:31, "My lyre is turned to mourning."

[1] The last sonnet, but not the last poem in the *Canzoniere,* which concludes with a canzone to the Virgin.

[2] The humility of the recantation is rendered more poignant by this lingering touch of human pride. Love for the "mortal thing" has been an obstacle to salvation, but there is also the explicit regret that it has prevented him from demonstrating his true worth in the eyes of the world.

Giovanni Boccaccio
(1313–1375)

The great triumvirate of Italian literature in the fourteenth century consists of Dante, Petrarch, and Boccaccio. Boccaccio, the youngest, was born in 1313, the illegitimate son of a merchant-banker who had family roots in or near Florence. The legend, nurtured by Boccaccio, that he was born in Paris of an aristocratic mother is now regarded skeptically. He spent his childhood, not very happily, in Florence, moving with his businessman father to Naples when Boccaccio was about fourteen. His father gave him twelve years of education, first in commerce and then in church law, but Boccaccio wanted above all else to be a poet. His contact with the aristocracy of Naples, who had banking connections with his father's firm, gave Boccaccio the opportunity to develop as both writer and gentleman, since the Neapolitan court was highly cultivated and intellectual in tone. At the same time, his connection with commerce, in Naples and later in Florence, taught him about the life of middle-class people. It was in Naples too that Boccaccio is supposed to have met "Fiammetta," the object of his passionate love—the equivalent for Boccaccio of Dante's Beatrice and Petrarch's Laura. The identity of Fiammetta in real life is uncertain, and her very existence has been questioned. Real or fictitious, however, she was the occasion or focus for much of Boccaccio's early work. In this period, he wrote mainly in Italian rather than in the traditional learned language, Latin.

In 1340, Boccaccio reluctantly left Naples, where he had been very happy, and returned to Florence, where his literary art reached its full flower, culminating in *The Decameron* (completed by 1353), or "Work of Ten Days." Boccaccio's earlier writing had been distinctly medieval in its concern with chivalric themes and its use of the genres of romance and allegory. Certain of his early works had revealed his gift of keen insight into human psychology, but nothing quite prepares us for *The Decameron,* with its brilliant dramatic and narrative styles and its rich variety of tones, from the wholly serious and tragic to the raucously farcical. Boccaccio had seen at first hand in Florence the ravages of the plague (the Black Death), and his vividly gruesome account of it at the beginning of *The Decameron* throws into relief the idyllic life led by the seven women and three men who tell the stories. The tone of their life in their country refuge is witty, refined, decorous, but relaxedly sensuous, in sharp contrast with the horrors they have escaped. The reader is aware, however, at some level of consciousness, of the terrible background. The most broadly comic parts of the work can be experienced as a reflex response to the plague, by characters and readers alike.

The Decameron served as a model for Italian prose writers and had an enormous influence on later European literature. But Boccaccio wrote no later works in the same vein. In 1350, he met Petrarch (of whom he had already written a biography), and the two men enjoyed a close friendship for the rest of their lives. Petrarch influenced Boccaccio in some important ways, turning him toward the Latin tongue and various scholarly projects (for example, compendia of ancient myths, of famous men and women, and of place names in classical literature). Petrarch seems also to have been one cause, though not the only one, of an increasingly moral and religious tone in Boccaccio's later years. On the other hand, it was Petrarch who, when Boccaccio contemplated burning his earlier works, persuaded him not to do so. Having proved himself, in *The Decameron,* to be a humanist in the modern, popular sense, the older Boccaccio proved himself a humanist in the more technical sense that has to do with the revival of ancient classical learning and literature. He was instrumental, for example, in encouraging the translation of the epics of Homer. He also wrote, in Italian, a treatise on Dante and a commentary on the first half of Dante's *Inferno.* Despite the honor of public offices and of several ambassadorships, the last decades of Boccaccio's life were unsettled, often overshadowed by poverty. He died in 1375, a year later than Petrarch.

The much discussed question whether Boccaccio belongs to the Middle Ages or to the Renaissance is for some scholars a pseudo-question, implying an overly simple view of the Middle Ages as piously ascetic and of the Renaissance as exclusively secular. Even if one allows for the distortions of stereotyping, however, it is difficult not to see in Boccaccio's work, or at least *The Decameron,* something distinctively modern. Much of his work looks backward to medieval chivalric values and beyond them to antiquity. But the worldly pragmatism of *The Decameron,* with its almost exclusive emphasis on human ingenuity and resourcefulness, is something genuinely new. Heaven and divine grace play almost no role in *The Decameron.* In the hundred tales, people are what the vicissitudes of life and their own characters make them, whether shrewd or gullible, high-minded or unscrupulous. Moreover, *The Decameron* also represents a transition to social realism; the ten storytellers have the manners of aristocrats, but many of the stories involve people of the lower and especially the middle classes. The essence of *The Decameron* is its variety—of subject matter, of tone, and of source (Boccaccio invented few, if any, of the tales *in toto*). The sense of a broad social and literary spectrum is one of the several parallels between Boccaccio and Chaucer, who was influenced by him.

Part of the worldliness of *The Decameron* is its notorious bawdiness, which is sometimes very explicit. Boccaccio's defensiveness on the matter shows that in his own time, and not only in later more prudish eras, some of the stories gave offense. Boccaccio tries to vindicate himself in his conclusion, advancing arguments that the reader may or may not find convincing. To them one may add the obvious: that the governing theme of *The Decameron* is love, and any comprehensive treatment of it must include the carnal as well as the psychological and spiritual. To many readers the main justification for the bawdiness will be the sparkling wit that characterizes many of the sexual episodes. It must be added too that the sexuality of *The Decameron* is intimately connected with its treatment of the sexes, particularly the very modern portrayal of women not as etherealized ideals but as realistic creatures of flesh and blood who are driven as much by desire as men are. The controversially patient Griselda is the exception that dramatizes the rule.

FURTHER READING: Thomas Bergin's *Boccaccio,* 1982, is a comprehensive introduction to the author's life and writings. Valuable as a general introduction is Judith Powers Serafini-Sauli, *Giovanni Boccaccio,* 1982. Vittore Branca's *Boccaccio: The Man and His Works,* trans. Richard Monges, 1976, provides a brief biographical sketch. Book II is devoted to *The Decameron,* with discussions of the medieval tradition in Boccaccio's work, his narrative art, and other topics. Stephen A. McKnight, *Sacralizing the Secular,* 1989, throws light on the Renaissance understanding of the secular and Boccaccio's relation to it. On style, see *An Anatomy of Boccaccio's Style,* ed. Marga Cottino-Jones, 1968. Critical approaches in this volume range from linguistic to archetypal. The first essay offers an overview of Boccaccio criticism. Joan M. Ferrante's "Narrative Patterns in the *Decameron,*" *Romance Philology,* 31 (1978), 585–604, looks at the entire *Decameron,* seeking to clarify the meaning of narrative themes. "The Worlds of the *Decameron,*" Chapter Two in Yvonne Rodax's *The Real and the Ideal in the Novella of Italy, France and England,* 1968, discusses the achievement of vigorous reality in Boccaccio's tales, with a particular emphasis on medieval values. The first and third chapters in this work, on the novella and on *The Canterbury Tales,* are also of interest. Shirley S. Allen's "The Griselda Tale and the Portrayal of Women in the *Decameron,*" *Philological Quarterly,* 56 (1977), 1–13, considers previous interpretations of the tale of "patient Griselda" and argues that viewing the tale as an ironic plea for women's rights is in accord with the overall unity of *The Decameron.* Marga Cottino-Jones' "Comic Modalities in the *Decameron,*" in *Versions of Medieval Comedy,* ed. Paul G. Ruggiers, 1977, investigates the varying comic tones and makes some general observations on the nature of Boccaccio's comedy. Cormac Cuilleanáin's "Man and Beast in the *Decameron,*" *Modern Language Review,* 75 (1980), 86–93, studies animal imagery and symbolism as it reveals Boccaccio's principal theme of man's existence in a social community. Demanding but exciting is Giuseppe Mazzotta, *The World at Play in Boccaccio's "Decameron,"* 1986, which relates the work in incisive ways to the culture of its time.

THE DECAMERON

Translated by Richard Aldington

THE FIRST DAY

Here begins the first day of the Decameron, *wherein, after the author has showed the reasons why certain persons gathered to tell tales, they treat of any subject pleasing to them, under the rule of Pampinea.*

Most gracious ladies, knowing that you are all by nature pitiful, I know that in your judgment this work will seem to have a painful and sad origin. For it brings to mind the unhappy recollection of that late dreadful plague,[1] so pernicious to all who saw or heard of it. But I would not have this frighten you from reading further, as though you were to pass through nothing but sighs and tears in your reading. This dreary opening will be like climbing a steep mountain side to a most beautiful and delightful valley, which appears the more pleasant in proportion to the difficulty of the ascent. The end of happiness is pain, and in like manner misery ends in unexpected happiness.

This brief fatigue (I say brief, because it occupies only a few words) is quickly followed by pleasantness and delight, as I promised you above;

[1] The "Black Death," probably bubonic plague, killed millions in Europe and Asia in the mid-fourteenth century.

which, if I had not promised, you would not expect perhaps from this opening. Indeed, if I could have taken you by any other way than this, which I know to be rough, I would gladly have done so; but since I cannot otherwise tell you how the tales you are about to read came to be told, I am forced by necessity to write in this manner.

In the year 1348 after the fruitful incarnation of the Son of God, that most beautiful of Italian cities, noble Florence, was attacked by deadly plague. It started in the East either through the influence of the heavenly bodies or because God's just anger with our wicked deeds sent it as a punishment to mortal men; and in a few years killed an innumerable quantity of people. Ceaselessly passing from place to place, it extended its miserable length over the West. Against this plague all human wisdom and foresight were vain. Orders had been given to cleanse the city of filth, the entry of any sick person was forbidden, much advice was given for keeping healthy; at the same time humble supplications were made to God by pious persons in processions and otherwise. And yet, in the beginning of the spring of the year mentioned, its horrible results began to appear, and in a miraculous manner. The symptoms were not the same as in the East, where a gush of blood from the nose was the plain sign of inevitable death; but it began both in men and women with certain swellings in the groin or under the armpit. They grew to the size of a small apple or an egg, more or less, and were vulgarly called tumors. In a short space of time these tumors spread from the two parts named all over the body. Soon after this the symptoms changed and black or purple spots appeared on the arms or thighs or any other part of the body, sometimes a few large ones, sometimes many little ones. These spots were a certain sign of death, just as the original tumor had been and still remained.

No doctor's advice, no medicine could overcome or alleviate this disease. An enormous number of ignorant men and women set up as doctors in addition to those who were trained. Either the disease was such that no treatment was possible or the doctors were so ignorant that they did not know what caused it, and consequently could not administer the proper remedy. In any case very few recovered; most people died within about three days of the appearance of the tumors described above, most of them without any fever or other symptoms.

The violence of this disease was such that the sick communicated it to the healthy who came near them, just as a fire catches anything dry or oily near it. And it even went further. To speak to or go near the sick brought infection and a common death to the living; and moreover, to touch the clothes or anything else the sick had touched or worn gave the disease to the person touching.

What I am about to tell now is a marvelous thing to hear; and if I and others had not seen it with our own eyes I would not dare to write it, however much I was willing to believe and whatever the good faith of the person from whom I heard it. So violent was the malignancy of this plague that it was communicated, not only from one man to another, but from the garments of a sick or dead man to animals of another species, which caught the disease in that way and very quickly died of it. One day among other occasions I saw with my own eyes (as I said just now) the rags left lying in the street of a poor man who had died of the plague; two pigs came along and, as their habit is, turned the clothes over with their snouts and then munched at them, with the result that they both fell dead almost at once on the rags, as if they had been poisoned.

From these and similar or greater occurrences, such fear and fanciful notions took possession of the living that almost all of them adopted the same cruel policy, which was entirely to avoid the sick and everything belonging to them. By so doing, each one thought he would secure his own safety.

Some thought that moderate living and the avoidance of all superfluity would preserve them from the epidemic. They formed small communities, living entirely separate from everybody else. They shut themselves up in houses where there were no sick, eating the finest food and drinking the best wine very temperately, avoiding all excess, allowing no news or discussion of death and sickness, and passing the time in music and suchlike pleasures. Others thought just the opposite. They thought the sure cure for the plague was to drink and be merry, to go about singing and amusing themselves, satisfying every appetite they could, laughing and jesting at what happened. They put their words into practice, spent day and night going from tavern to tavern, drinking immoderately, or went into other people's houses, doing only those things which pleased them. This they could easily do because everyone felt doomed and had abandoned his property, so that most houses became common property and any stranger who went in made use of them as if he had owned them. And with all this bestial behavior, they avoided the sick as much as possible.

In this suffering and misery of our city, the authority of human and divine laws almost disappeared, for, like other men, the ministers and the executors of the laws were all dead or sick or shut up with their families, so that no duties were carried out. Every man was therefore able to do as he pleased.

Many others adopted a course of life midway between the two just described. They did not restrict their victuals so much as the former, nor allow themselves to be drunken and dissolute like the latter, but satisfied their appetites moderately. They did not shut themselves up, but went about, carrying flowers or scented herbs or perfumes in their hands, in the belief that it was an excellent thing to comfort the brain with such odors; for the whole air was infected with the smell of dead bodies, of sick persons and medicines.

Others again held a still more cruel opinion, which they thought would keep them safe. They said that the only medicine against the plague-stricken was to go right away from them. Men and women, convinced of this and caring about nothing but themselves, abandoned their own city, their own houses, their dwellings, their relatives, their property, and went abroad or at least to the country round Florence, as if God's wrath in punishing men's wickedness with this plague would not follow them but strike only those who remained within the walls of the city, or as if they thought nobody in the city would remain alive and that its last hour had come.

Not everyone who adopted any of these various opinions died, nor did all escape. Some when they were still healthy had set the example of avoiding the sick, and, falling ill themselves, died untended.

One citizen avoided another, hardly any neighbor troubled about others, relatives never or hardly ever visited each other. Moreover, such terror was struck into the hearts of men and women by this calamity, that brother abandoned brother, and the uncle his nephew, and the sister her brother, and very often the wife her husband. What is even worse and nearly incredible is that fathers and mothers refused to see and tend their children, as if they had not been theirs.

Thus, a multitude of sick men and women were left without any care except from the charity of friends (but these were few), or the greed of servants, though not many of these could be had even for high wages. Moreover, most of them were coarse-minded men and women, who did little more than bring the sick what they asked for or watch over them when they were dying. And very often these servants lost their lives and their earnings. Since the sick were thus abandoned by neighbors, relatives and friends, while servants were scarce, a habit sprang up which had never been heard of before. Beautiful and noble women, when they fell sick, did not scruple to take a young or old manservant, whoever he might be, and with no sort of shame, expose every part of their bodies to these men as if they had been women, for they were compelled by the necessity of their sickness to do so. This, perhaps, was a cause of looser morals in those women who survived.

In this way many people died who might have been saved if they had been looked after. Owing to the lack of attendants for the sick and the violence of the plague, such a multitude of people in the city died day and night that it was stupefying to hear of, let alone to see. From sheer necessity, then, several ancient customs were quite altered among the survivors.

The custom had been (as we still see it today) that women relatives and neighbors should gather at the house of the deceased, and there lament with the family. At the same time the men would gather at the door with the male neighbors and other citizens. Then came the clergy, few or many according to the dead person's rank; the coffin was placed on the shoulders of his friends and carried with funeral pomp of lighted candles and dirges to the church which the deceased had chosen before dying. But as the fury of the plague increased, this custom wholly or nearly disappeared, and new customs arose. Thus, people died, not only without having a number of women near them, but without a single witness. Very few indeed were honored with the piteous laments and bitter tears of their relatives, who, on the contrary, spent their time in mirth, feasting and jesting. Even the women abandoned womanly pity and adopted this custom for their own safety. Few were they whose bodies were accompanied to church by more than ten or a dozen neighbors. Nor were these grave and honorable citizens but grave-diggers from the lowest of the people who got themselves called sextons, and performed the task for money. They took up the bier and hurried it off, not to the church chosen by the deceased but the church nearest, preceded by four or six of the clergy with few candles and often none at all. With the aid of the grave-diggers, the clergy huddled the bodies away in any grave they could find, without giving themselves the trouble of a long or solemn burial service.

The plight of the lower and most of the middle classes was even more pitiful to behold. Most of them remained in their houses, either through poverty or in hopes of safety, and fell sick by thousands. Since they received no care and attention, almost all of them died. Many ended their lives in the streets both at night and during the day; and many others who died in their houses were only known to be dead because the neighbors smelled their decaying bodies. Dead bodies filled every corner. Most of them were treated in the same manner by the survivors, who were more concerned to get rid of their rotting bodies than moved by charity towards the dead. With the aid of porters, if they could get them, they carried the bodies out of the houses and laid them at the doors, where every morning quantities of the dead might be seen. They then were laid on biers, or, as these were often lacking, on tables.

Often a single bier carried two or three bodies, and it happened frequently that a husband and wife, two or three brothers, or father and son were taken off on the same bier. It frequently happened that two priests, each carrying a cross, would go out followed by three or four biers carried by porters; and where the priests thought there was one person to bury, there would be six or eight, and often, even more. Nor were these dead honored by tears and lighted candles and mourners, for things had reached such a pass that people cared no more for dead men than we care for dead goats. Thus it plainly appeared that what the wise had not learned to endure with patience through the few calamities of ordinary life, became a matter of indifference even to the most ignorant people through the greatness of this misfortune.

Such was the multitude of corpses brought to the churches every day and almost every hour that there was not enough consecrated ground to give them burial, especially since they wanted to bury each person in the family grave, according to the old custom. Although the cemeteries were full they were forced to dig huge trenches, where they buried the bodies by hundreds. Here they stowed them away like bales in the hold of a ship and covered them with a little earth, until the whole trench was full.

Not to pry any further into all the details of the miseries which afflicted our city, I shall add that the surrounding country was spared nothing of what befell Florence. The villages on a smaller scale were like the city; in the fields and isolated farms the poor wretched peasants and their families were without doctors and any assistance, and perished in the highways, in their fields and houses, night and day, more like beasts than men. Just as the townsmen became dissolute and indifferent to their work and property, so the peasants, when they saw that death was upon them, entirely neglected the future fruits of their past labors both from the earth and from cattle, and thought only of enjoying what they had. Thus it happened that cows, asses, sheep, goats, pigs, fowls and even dogs, those faithful companions of man, left the farms and wandered at their will through the fields, where the wheat crops stood abandoned, unreaped and ungarnered. Many of these animals seemed endowed with reason, for, after they had pastured all day, they returned to the farms for the night of their own free will, without being driven.

Returning from the country to the city, it may be said that such was the cruelty of Heaven, and perhaps in part of men, that between March and July more than one hundred thousand persons died within the walls of Florence, what between the violence of the plague and the abandonment in which the sick were left by the cowardice of the healthy. And before the plague it was not thought that the whole city held so many people.

Oh, what great palaces, how many fair houses and noble dwellings, once filled with attendants and nobles and ladies, were emptied to the meanest servant! How many famous names and vast possessions and renowned estates were left without an heir! How many gallant men and fair ladies and handsome youths, whom Galen, Hippocrates and Aesculapius[2] themselves would have said were in perfect health, at noon dined with their relatives and friends, and at night supped with their ancestors in the next world!

But it fills me with sorrow to go over so many miseries. Therefore, since I want to pass over all I can leave out, I shall go on to say that when our city was in this condition and almost emptied of inhabitants, one Tuesday morning the venerable church of Santa Maria Novella had scarcely any congregation for divine service except (as I have heard from a person worthy of belief) seven young women in the mourning garments suitable to the times, who were all related by ties of blood, friendship or neighborship. None of them was older than twenty-eight or younger than eighteen; all were educated and of noble blood, fair to look upon, well-mannered and of graceful modesty.

I should tell you their real names if I had not a good reason for not doing so, which is that I would not have any of them blush in the future for the things they say and hearken to in the following pages. The laws are now strict again, whereas then, for the reasons already shown, they were very lax, not only for persons of their age but for those much older. Nor would I give an opportunity to the envious (always ready to sneer at every praiseworthy life) to attack the virtue of these modest ladies with vulgar speech. But so that you may understand without confusion what each one says, I intend to give them names wholly or partly suitable to the qualities of each.

The first and eldest I shall call Pampinea, the second Fiammetta, the third Filomena, the fourth Emilia, the fifth Lauretta, the sixth Neifile, and the last Elisa[3] (or "the virgin") for a very good reason. They met, not by arrangement, but by chance, in the same part of the church, and sat down in a circle. After many sighs they ceased to pray and began to talk about the state of affairs and other things. After a short space of silence, Pampinea said:

"Dear ladies, you must often have heard, as I have, that to make a sensible use of one's reason harms nobody. It is natural for everybody to aid, preserve and defend his life as far as possible. And this is so far admitted that to save their own lives men often kill others who have done no harm. If this is permitted by the laws which are concerned with the general good, it must certainly be lawful for us to take any reasonable means for the preservation of our lives. When I think of what we have been doing this morning and still more on former days, when I remember what we have been saying, I perceive and you must perceive that each of us goes in fear of her life. I do not wonder at this, but, since each of us has a woman's judgment, I do wonder that we do not seek some remedy against what we dread.

"In my opinion we remain here for no other purpose than to witness how many bodies are buried, or listen whether the friars here (themselves reduced

[2] The first two were ancient Greek physicians; Aesculapius was a Greco-Roman god of medicine.

[3] Most of the names are derived from Greek and have something to do with love. The qualities or roles associated with the seven women are probably as follows: Pampinea (the eldest) is a leader and adviser; Fiammetta is loving and beloved; Filomena (related to "nightingale") is a lover of music; Emilia has pleasant manners; Lauretta (related to *laurel*) is learned; Neifile is young and naive; Elisa, who is also young, recalls *Elissa*, a name for Dido, the passionate Carthaginian queen in Virgil's *Aeneid*.

almost to nothing) sing their offices at the canonical hours,[4] or to display by our clothes the quantity and quality of our miseries to anyone who comes here. If we leave this church we see the bodies of the dead and the sick being carried about. Or we see those who had been exiled from the city by the authority of the laws for their crimes, deriding this authority because they know the guardians of the law are sick or dead, and running loose about the place. Or we see the dregs of the city battening on our blood and calling themselves sextons, riding about on horseback in every direction and insulting our calamities with vile songs. On every side we hear nothing but 'So-and-so is dead' or 'So-and-so is dying.' And if there were anyone left to weep we should hear nothing but piteous lamentations. I do not know if it is the same in your homes as in mine. But if I go home there is nobody left there but one of my maids, which fills me with such horror that the hair stands upon my head. Wherever I go or sit at home I seem to see the ghosts of the departed, not with the faces as I knew them but with dreadful looks which terrify me.

"I am ill at ease here and outside of here and at home; the more so since nobody who has the strength and ability to go away (as we have) now remains here, except ourselves. The few that remain (if there are any), according to what I see and hear, do anything which gives them pleasure or pleases their appetites, both by day and night, whether they are alone or in company, making no distinction between right and wrong. Not only laymen, but those cloistered in convents have broken their oaths and given themselves up to the delights of the flesh, and thus in trying to escape the plague by doing what they please, they have become lascivious and dissolute.

"If this is so (and we may plainly see it is) what are we doing here? What are we waiting for? What are we dreaming about? Are we less eager and active than other citizens in saving our lives? Are they less dear to us than to others? Or do we think that our lives are bound to our bodies with stronger chains than other people's, and so believe that we need fear nothing which might harm us? We were and are deceived. How stupid we should be to believe such a thing! We may see the plainest proofs from the number of young men and women who have died of this cruel plague.

"I do not know if you think as I do, but in my opinion if we, through carelessness, do not want to fall into this calamity when we can escape it, I think we should do well to leave this town, just as many others have done and are doing. Let us avoid the wicked examples of others like death itself, and go and live virtuously in our country houses, of which each of us possesses several. There let us take what happiness and pleasure we can, without ever breaking the rules of reason in any manner.

"There we shall hear the birds sing, we shall see the green hills and valleys, the wheat-fields rolling like a sea, and all kinds of trees. We shall see the open Heavens which, although now angered against man, do not withhold from us their eternal beauties that are so much fairer to look upon than the empty walls of our city. The air will be fresher there, we shall find a greater plenty of those things necessary to life at this time, and fewer troubles. Although the peasants are dying like the townsmen, still, since the houses

[4] Chant their prayers at the times of day specified by the Church.

and inhabitants are fewer, we shall see less of them and feel less misery. On the other hand I believe we are not abandoning anybody here. Indeed we can truthfully say that we are abandoned, since our relatives have either died or fled from death and have left us alone in this calamity as if we were nothing to them.

"If we do what I suggest, no blame can fall upon us; if we fail to do it, the result may be pain, trouble and perhaps death. Therefore I think that we should do well to take our servants and all things necessary, and go from one house to another, enjoying whatever merriment and pleasure these times allow. Let us live in this way (unless death comes upon us) until we see what end Heaven decrees to this plague. And remember that going away virtuously will not harm us so much as staying here in wickedness will harm others."

The other ladies listened to what Pampinea said, praised her advice, and in their eagerness to follow it began to discuss details, as if they were going to leave at once. But Filomena, who was a most prudent young woman, said:

"Ladies, although what Pampinea says is excellent advice, we must not rush off at once, as you seem to wish. Remember we are all women; and any girl can tell you how women behave together and conduct themselves without the direction of some man. We are fickle, wayward, suspicious, faint-hearted and cowardly. So if we have no guide but ourselves I greatly suspect that this company will very soon break up, without much honor to ourselves. Let us settle this matter before we start."

Elisa then broke in:

"Indeed men are a woman's head and we can rarely succeed in anything without their help; but how can we find any men? Each of us knows that most of her menfolk are dead, while the others are away, we know not where, flying with their companions from the end we wish to escape. To ask strangers would be unbecoming; for, if we mean to go away to save our lives we must take care that scandal and annoyance do not follow us where we are seeking rest and amusement."

While the ladies were thus arguing, three young men came into the church, the youngest of whom was not less than twenty-five. They were lovers whose love could not be quenched or even cooled by the horror of the times, the loss of relatives and friends, or even fear for themselves. The first was named Pamfilo, the second Filostrato, the third Dioneo.[5] They were pleasant, well-mannered men, and in this public calamity they sought the consolation of looking upon the ladies they loved. These ladies happened to be among our seven, while some of the others were related to one or other of the three men. They no sooner came into sight than the ladies saw them; whereupon Pampinea said with a smile:

"See how Fortune favors our plan at once by sending us these valiant and discreet young men, who will gladly act as our guides and servants if we do not refuse to accept them for such duties."

Neifile then became crimson, for she was one of the ladies beloved by one of the young men, and said:

[5] The name *Pamphilo* means "loving all"; *Filostrato* means "lover of strife" (perhaps the strife of being in love) and also "victim of love"; *Dioneo* is related to one of the names of Venus, goddess of sexual love.

"For God's sake, Pampinea, be careful what you are saying. I know quite well that nothing but good can be said of any of them and I am sure they could achieve greater things than this. I also think that their company would be fitting and pleasant, not only to us, but to ladies far more beautiful and charming than we are. But it is known to everyone that they are in love with some of us women here; and so, if we take them with us, I am afraid that blame and infamy will fall upon us, through no fault of ours or theirs."

Then said Filomena:

"What does that matter? If I live virtuously, my conscience never pricks me, whatever people may say. God and the truth will fight for me. If these men would come with us, then indeed, as Pampinea said, fortune would be favorable to our plan of going away."

The others not only refrained from censuring what she said, but agreed by common consent that the men should be spoken to, told their plan, and asked if they would accompany the ladies on their expedition. Without more ado, Pampinea, who was related to one of them, arose and went towards them where they stood looking at the ladies, saluted them cheerfully, told them the plan, and begged them in the name of all the ladies to accompany them out of pure and fraternal affection.

At first the young men thought this was a jest. But when they saw the lady was speaking seriously, they said they were willing to go. And in order to start without delay they at once gave the orders necessary for departure. Everything necessary was made ready, and word was sent on ahead to the place they were going. At dawn next morning, which was Wednesday, the ladies with some of their servants, and the young men with a man servant each, left the city and set out. They had not gone more than two miles when they came to the first place where they were to stay.

This estate was on slightly raised ground, at some distance from any main road, with many trees and plants, fair to look upon. At the top of the rise was a country mansion with a large inner courtyard. It had open colonnades, galleries and rooms, all beautiful in themselves and ornamented with gay paintings. Roundabout were lawns and marvelous gardens and wells of cool water. There were cellars of fine wines, more suitable to wine connoisseurs than to sober and virtuous ladies. The whole house had been cleaned, the beds were prepared in the rooms, and every corner was strewn with the flowers of the season and fresh rushes. All of which the company beheld with no little pleasure.

They all sat down to discuss plans, and Dioneo, who was a most amusing young man and full of witticisms, remarked:

"Ladies, your good sense, rather than our foresight, has brought us here. I do not know what you are thinking of doing with your troubles here, but I dropped mine inside the gates of the city when I left it with you a little time ago. Therefore, either you must make up your minds to laugh and sing and amuse yourselves with me (that is, to the extent your dignity allows), or you must let me go back to my troubles and stay in the afflicted city."

Pampinea, who had driven away her woes in the same way, cheerfully replied:

"Dioneo, you speak well, let us amuse ourselves, for that was the reason why we fled from our sorrows. But when things are not organized they cannot long continue. And, since I began the discussion which brought this fair company together and since I wish our happiness to continue, I think it necessary that one of us should be made chief, whom the others will honor and obey, and whose duty shall be to regulate our pleasures. Now, so that everyone—both man and woman—may experience the cares as well as the pleasures of ruling and no one feel any envy at not sharing them, I think the weight and honor should be given to each of us in turn for one day. The first shall be elected by all of us. At vespers[6] he or she shall choose the ruler for the next day, and so on. While their reigns last these rulers shall arrange where and how we are to spend our time."

These words pleased them all and they unanimously elected her for the first day. Filomena ran to a laurel bush, whose leaves she had always heard were most honorable in themselves and did great honor to anyone crowned with them, plucked off a few small branches and wove them into a fair garland of honor. When this was placed on the head of any one of them, it was a symbol of rule and authority over the rest so long as the party remained together.

Pampinea, thus elected queen, ordered silence. She then sent for the three servants of the young men and the four women servants the ladies had brought, and said:

"To set a first example to you all which may be bettered and thus allow our gathering to live pleasantly and orderly and without shame and to last as long as we desire, I appoint Dioneo's servant Parmeno as my steward, and hand over to him the care of the whole family and of everything connected with the dining hall. Pamfilo's servant Sirisco shall be our treasurer and buyer, and carry out Parmeno's instructions. Tindaro shall wait on Filostrato and Dioneo and Pamfilo in their rooms, when the other two servants are occupied with their new duties. Filomena's servant Licisca and my own servant Misia shall remain permanently in the kitchen and carefully prepare the food which Parmeno sends them. Lauretta's Chimera and Fiammetta's Stratilia shall take care of the ladies' rooms and see that the whole house is clean. Moreover we will and command that everyone who values our good grace shall bring back only cheerful news, wherever he may go or return from, and whatever he may hear or see."

Having given these orders, which were approved by everyone, she jumped gaily to her feet and said:

"Here are gardens and lawns and other delicious places, where each of us can wander and enjoy them at will. But let everyone be here at the hour of Tierce[7] so that we can eat together while it is still cool."

The company of gay young men and women, thus given the queen's permission, went off together slowly through the gardens, talking of pleasant matters, weaving garlands of different leaves, and singing love songs. After the time allotted by the queen had elapsed they returned to the house and found that Parmeno had carefully carried out the duties of his office. Entering a ground floor room decorated everywhere with broom[8] blossoms, they found tables covered with white cloths and set with glasses which shone like silver.

[6]One of the canonical hours; about 6 P.M.
[7]A canonical hour; 9 A.M. [8]A shrub.

They washed their hands and, at the queen's command, all sat down in the places allotted them by Parmeno. Delicately cooked food was brought, exquisite wines were at hand, and the three men servants waited at table. Everyone was delighted to see things so handsome and well arranged, and they ate merrily with much happy talk.

All the ladies and young men could dance and many of them could play and sing; so, when the tables were cleared, the queen called for musical instruments. At her command Dioneo took a lute and Fiammetta a viol, and began to play a dance tune. The queen sent the servants to their meal, and then with slow steps danced with the two young men and the other ladies. After that, they began to sing gay and charming songs.

In this way they amused themselves until the queen thought it was time for the siesta. So, at the queen's bidding, the three young men went off to their rooms (which were separated from the ladies') and found them filled with flowers as the dining hall had been. And similarly with the women. So they all undressed and went to sleep.

Not long after the hour of Nones,[9] the queen arose and made the other women and the young men also get up, saying that it was harmful to sleep too long during the daytime. Then they went out to a lawn of thick green grass entirely shaded from the sun. A soft breeze came to them there. The queen made them sit down in a circle on the grass, and said:

"As you see, the sun is high and the heat great, and nothing can be heard but the cicadas in the olive trees. To walk about at this hour would be foolish. Here it is cool and lovely, and, as you see, there are games of chess and draughts which everyone can amuse himself with, as he chooses. But, if my opinion is followed, we shall not play games, because in games the mind of one of the players must necessarily be distressed without any great pleasure to the other player or the onlookers. Let us rather spend this hot part of the day in telling tales, for thus one person can give pleasure to the whole company. When each of us has told a story, the sun will be going down and the heat less, and we can then go walking anywhere we choose for our amusement. If this pleases you (for here I am ready to follow your pleasure) let us do it. If it does not please you, let everyone do as he likes until evening."

The women and men all favored the telling of stories.

"Then if it pleases you," said the queen, "on this first day I order that everyone shall tell his tale about any subject he likes."

She then turned to Pamfilo, who was seated on her right, and ordered him to begin with a tale. Hearing this command, Pamfilo at once began as follows, while all listened.[10]

THIRD DAY, TENTH TALE

Alibech becomes a hermit, and the monk Rustico teaches her how to put the devil in Hell. She is afterwards taken away and becomes the wife of Neerbale.

[9]A canonical hour; about 3 P.M.

[10]Here the series of a hundred tales, ten each day, begins. After the first day, when the choice of tales is unrestricted, each day has a prescribed theme.

Dioneo had listened closely to the queen's story, and, when it was over and only he remained to tell a story, he did not wait to be commanded, but smilingly began as follows:

Most gracious ladies, perhaps you have never heard how the devil is put into hell; and so, without departing far from the theme[1] upon which you have all spoken today, I shall tell you about it. Perhaps when you have learned it, you also will be able to save your souls, and you may also discover that although love prefers to dwell in gay palaces and lovely rooms rather than in poor huts, yet he sometimes makes his power felt among thick woods and rugged mountains and desert caves. Whereby we may well perceive that all of us are subject to his power.

Now, to come to my story—in the city of Capsa[2] in Barbery there lived a very rich man who possessed among other children a pretty and charming daughter, named Alibech. She was not a Christian, but she heard many Christians in her native town crying up the Christian Faith and service to God, and one day she asked one of them how a person could most effectively serve God. The reply was that those best serve God who fly furthest from the things of this world, like the hermits who had departed to the solitudes of the Thebaid[3] Desert.

The girl was about fourteen and very simple minded. Urged by a mere childish enthusiasm and not by a well ordered desire, she secretly set out next morning quite alone, without saying a word to anyone, to find the Thebaid Desert. Her enthusiasm lasted several days and enabled her with great fatigue to reach those solitudes. In the distance she saw a little hut with a holy man standing at its entrance. He was amazed to see her there, and asked her what she was seeking. She replied that by God's inspiration she was seeking to serve Him, and begged the hermit to show her the right way to do so. But the holy man saw she was young and pretty, and feared that if he kept her with him he might be tempted of the devil. So he praised her good intentions, gave her some roots and wild apples to eat and some water to drink, and said:

"Daughter, not far from here dwells a holy man who is a far greater master of what you are seeking than I am; go to him."

And so he put her on the way. When she reached him, she was received with much the same words, and passing further on came to the cell of a young hermit named Rustico, to whom she made the same request as to the others. To test his spiritual strength, Rustico did not send her away, but took her into his cell. And when night came, he made her a bed of palm leaves and told her to sleep there.

Almost immediately after this, temptation began the struggle with his spiritual strength, and the hermit found that he had greatly over-estimated his powers of resistance. After a few assaults of the demon he shrugged his shoulders and surrendered. Putting aside holy thoughts and prayers and macerations,[4] he began to think of her beauty and youth, and then pondered how he should proceed with her so that she should not perceive that he obtained

[1] The stories told on the third day (ruled by Neifile) concern people who by cleverness gained or regained something desirable.
[2] A city in Tunisia; Barbery is in northern Africa.
[3] Near Thebes, in Egypt. [4] Starvation diets.

what he wanted from her like a dissolute man. First of all he sounded her by certain questions, and discovered that she had never lain with a man and appeared to be very simple minded. He then saw how he could bring her to his desire under pretext of serving God. He began by eloquently showing how the devil is the enemy of the Lord God, and then gave her to understand that the service most pleasing to God is to put the devil back into hell, to which the Lord God has condemned him. The girl asked how this was done, and Rustico replied:

"You shall soon know. Do what you see me do."

He then threw off the few clothes he had and remained stark naked, and the girl imitated him. He kneeled down as if to pray and made her kneel exactly opposite him. As he gazed at her beauty, Rustico's desire became so great that the resurrection of the flesh occurred. Alibech looked at it with amazement, and said:

"Rustico, what is that thing I see sticking out in front of you which I haven't got?"

"My daughter," said Rustico, "that is the devil I spoke of. Do you see? He gives me so much trouble at this moment that I can scarcely endure him."

Said the girl:

"Praised be God! I see I am better off than you are, since I haven't such a devil."

"You speak truly," said Rustico, "but instead of this devil you have something else which I haven't."

"What's that?" said Alibech.

"You've got hell," replied Rustico, "and I believe God sent you here for the salvation of my soul, because this devil gives me great trouble, and if you will take pity upon me and let me put him into hell, you will give me the greatest comfort and at the same time will serve God and please Him, since, as you say, you came here for that purpose."

In all good faith the girl replied: "Father, since I have hell in me, let it be whenever you please."

Said Rustico: "Blessings upon you, my daughter. Let us put him in now so that he will afterwards depart from me."

So saying, he took the girl to one of their beds, and showed her how to lie so as to imprison the thing accursed of God. The girl had never before put any devil into her hell and at first felt a little pain, and exclaimed to Rustico:

"O father! This devil must certainly be wicked and the enemy of God, for even when he is put back into hell he hurts it."

"Daughter," said Rustico, "it will not always be so."

To prevent this from happening, Rustico put it into hell six times, before he got off the bed, and so purged the devil's pride that he was glad to rest a little. Thereafter he returned often and the obedient girl was always glad to take him in; and then the game began to give her pleasure, and she said to Rustico:

"I see that the good men of Capsa spoke the truth when they told me how sweet a thing is the service of God. I certainly do not remember that I ever did anything which gave me so much delight and pleasure as I get from putting the devil into hell. I think that everyone is a fool who does anything but serve God."

Thus it happened that she would often go to Rustico, and say:

"Father, I came here to serve God and not to remain in idleness. Let us put the devil in hell."

And once as they were doing it, she said:

"Rustico, I don't know why the devil ever goes out of hell. If he liked to remain there as much as hell likes to receive and hold him, he would never leave it."

The girl's frequent invitations to Rustico and their mutual pleasures in the service of God so took the stuffing out of his doublet[5] that he now felt chilly where another man would have been in a sweat. So he told the girl that the devil must not be chastened or put into hell except when pride made him lift his head. "And we," he said, "have so quelled his rage that he prays God to be left in peace." And in this way he silenced the girl for a time. But when she found that Rustico no longer asked her to put the devil in hell, she said one day:

"Rustico, your devil may be chastened and give you no more trouble, but my hell is not. You should therefore quench the raging of my hell with your devil, as I helped you to quell the pride of your devil with my hell."

Rustico, who lived on nothing but roots and water, made a poor response to this invitation. He told her that many devils would be needed to soothe her hell, but that he would do what he could. In this way he satisfied her hell a few times, but so seldom that it was like throwing a bean in a lion's mouth. And the girl, who thought they were not serving God as much as she wanted, kept murmuring.

Now, while there was this debate between the excess of desire in Alibech's hell and the lack of potency in Rustico's devil, a fire broke out in Capsa, and burned Alibech's father with all his children and servants. So Alibech became heir to all his property. A young man named Neerbale, who had spent all his money in riotous living, heard that she was still alive and set out to find her, which he succeeded in doing before the Court took over her father's property as that of a man who had died without heirs. To Rustico's great relief, but against her will, Neerbale brought her back to Capsa and married her, and together they inherited her large patrimony. But before Neerbale had lain with her, certain ladies one day asked her how she had served God in the desert. She replied that her service was to put the devil in hell, and that Neerbale had committed a great sin by taking her away from such service. The ladies asked:

"And how do you put the devil in hell?"

Partly in words and partly by gestures, the girl told them. At this they laughed so much that they are still laughing, and said:

"Be not cast down, my child, they know how to do that here, and Neerbale will serve the Lord God with you in that way."

As they told it up and down the city, it passed into a proverb that the service most pleasing to God is to put the devil into hell. And this proverb crossed the seas and remains until this day.

Therefore, young ladies, when you seek God's favor, learn to put the devil in hell, because this is most pleasing to God and to all parties concerned, and much good may come of it.

[5]Jacket.

Dioneo's tale moved the chaste ladies to laughter hundreds of times, so apt and amusing did they find his words. When he had finished, the queen knew that the end of her reign had come, and therefore took the laurel wreath from her head and placed it upon Filostrato's, saying pleasantly:

"We shall soon find out if the wolf can guide the flock, as well as the flock has guided the wolves."

Filostrato laughingly replied:

"If my advice were followed, the wolves would have showed the flock how to put the devil in hell, as Rustico taught Alibech; and so they would not be called wolves, where you would not be the flock. However, since the rule now falls to me, I shall begin my reign."

Said Neifile:

"Filostrato, in trying to teach us, you might have learned wisdom, as Masetto da Lamporecchio learned it from the nuns,[6] and you might have regained your speech when your bones were rattling together from exhaustion!"

Filostrato, finding the ladies' sickles were as good as his shafts, ceased jesting, and occupied himself with the government of his kingdom. Calling the steward, he made enquiries into everything, and gave orders to ensure the well being and satisfaction of the band during his kingship. He then turned to the ladies and said:

"Amorous ladies, to my own misfortune—although I was quite aware of my disease—I have always been one of Love's subjects owing to the beauty of one of you. To be humble and obedient to her and to follow all her whims as closely as I could, was all of no avail to me, and I was soon abandoned for another. Thus I go from bad to worse, and believe I shall until I die. Tomorrow then it is my pleasure that we tell tales on a theme in conformity with my own fate—that is, about those persons whose love ended unhappily. In the long run I expect a most unhappy end for myself, and the person who gave me the nickname of Filostrato, or the Victim of Love, knew what she was doing."

So saying, he rose to his feet, and gave them all leave to depart until supper time.

The garden was so delightful and so beautiful that they all chose to remain there, since no greater pleasure could be found elsewhere. The sun was now not so hot, and therefore some of them began to chase the deer and rabbits and other animals which had annoyed them scores of times by leaping in among them while they were seated. Dioneo and Fiammetta began to sing the song of Messer Guglielmo and the Lady of Vergiu. Filomena and Pamfilo played chess. Thus, with one thing and another, time passed so quickly that supper time arrived long before they expected. The tables were set round the fountain, and there they ate their evening meal with the utmost pleasure.

When they rose from table, Filostrato would not depart from the path followed by the preceding queens, and so ordered Lauretta to dance and sing a song. And she said:

"My lord, I do not know any songs of other persons, and I do not remember any of my own which are fitting for this merry band. But if you wish to have one of those I remember, I will gladly sing it."

[6]A reference to another tale told earlier on the third day.

"Nothing of yours could be anything but fair and pleasing," said the king, "so sing it just as it is."

Then to the accompaniment of the others, Lauretta sang as follows in a sweet but rather plaintive voice:

No helpless lady has such cause to weep as I, who vainly sigh, alas, for love.

He who moves the heavens and all the stars[7] *made me for His delight so fair, so sweet, so gracious and so lovely that I might show to every lofty mind some trace of that high Beauty which ever dwells within His presence. But a weak man, who knew not Beauty, found me undelightful and scorned me.*

Once there was one who held me dear, and in my early years took me into his arms and to his thoughts, being quite conquered by my eyes. And time, that flies so swiftly, he spent in serving me; and I in courtesy made him worthy of me. But now, alas, he is taken from me.

Then came a proud presumptuous man, who thought himself both noble and valorous, and made me his, but through false belief became most jealous of me. And then, alas, I came near to despair, for I saw that I, who came into the world to pleasure many, was possessed by one alone.

I curse my luckless fate that ever I said "yes" to man, and changed to a wife's garb. I was so gay in my old plain maiden's dress! Now in these finer clothes I lead so sad a life, reputed less than chaste. O hapless wedding feast! Would I had died before I knew the fate it held for me!

O my first love, with whom I was so happy, who now in Heaven do stand before Him who created it, have pity on me. I cannot forget you for another. Let me feel that the flame wherewith you burned for me is not extinct, and pray that I may soon return to you.

Here ended Lauretta's song, which was noted carefully by them all, but interpreted differently. Some understood it in the Milanese sense—that it is better to be a good pig than a pretty girl.[8] Others were of a better, more sublime and truer understanding, but of this I shall not now speak.

After this the king had many torches brought and made them sing other songs as they sat on the grass and flowers, until the rising stars began to turn towards the west. Then, thinking it time for sleep, he said good night and sent each one to his room.

END OF THE THIRD DAY

[7] The mover is God; the line is a close paraphrase of the last line of Dante's *Divine Comedy.*
[8] That is, it is better to be an unhappy wife and alive than happily married and dead.

FOURTH DAY, SECOND TALE

Frate Alberto persuades a lady that the Angel Gabriel is in love with her and thus manages to lie with her several times. From fear of her relatives he flies from her house and takes refuge in the house of a poor man, who next day takes him to the Piazza as a wild man of the woods. He is recognized, arrested, and imprisoned.

The tale told by Fiammetta many times drew tears from her companions' eyes, but when it was ended the king said with a stern face:

"I should value my life little in comparison with half the joy Ghismonda had with Guiscardo.[1] Nor should you marvel at this, since while I am alive I suffer a thousand deaths hourly, and yet not one particle of delight is granted me. But, putting aside my life and its fate, it is my will that Pampinea should continue with a tale in part similar to my own fate. If she continues as Fiammetta has begun, doubtless some drops of dew will fall upon my amorous fire, and I shall feel them."

Pampinea felt the wishes of the company more through her own affection than through the king's words, and, being more willing to amuse them than to please the king, she determined to tell an amusing tale without departing from the subject given, and so began:

They say commonly in proverbial style: A wicked man who is thought to be good can do evil and yet not have it believed. This gives me ample material to speak on the subject proposed, and at the same time to show the hypocrisy of the monks. Their gowns are long and wide, their faces artificially pale, their voices humble and pleading when they ask something, loud and rude when they denounce their own vices in others, and when they declare how they obtain salvation of themselves and others by their gift. Not as men who seek Paradise, like ourselves, but as if they were its owners and lords, they allot a more or less eminent place there to everyone who dies, in accordance with the amount of money he leaves them; and thereby they first deceive themselves—if they really believe it—and then deceive those who put faith in their words. If I were permitted to do so, I could soon show many simple minded persons what is hidden in their ample gowns. Would to God that all their lies had the same fate as befell a minor friar,[2] who was no paltry fellow, but was considered one of the best casuists of Venice. It gives me the greatest pleasure to tell this tale, so that perhaps I may divert your minds with laughter and amusement from the pity you feel for Ghismonda's fate.

In Imola, most worthy ladies, there lived a man of wicked and corrupt life, named Berto della Massa. His evil deeds were so well known to many people of Imola that no one in Imola would believe him when he spoke truth, let alone when he lied. Seeing, then, that his tricks were useless there, he moved in despair to Venice, that welcomer of all wickedness, thinking that in that town he might make a different use of his vices than he had done before. As if conscience-stricken for his wicked deeds, he gave signs of the greatest humility. He became not only the most Catholic of men, but made

[1] Characters in the sad story with which Fiammetta had begun the fourth day's storytelling. The theme for the day, under Filostrato's rule, is love that ends unhappily.

[2] A member of the Franciscan religious order (Order of Friars Minor).

himself a minor friar, and took the name of Friar Alberto da Imola. In this guise he began to pretend to a severe life, praising penitence and abstinence, and never eating flesh or drinking wine when he could not get them good enough for him.

Never before had a thief, a ruffian, a forger, a murderer turned into a great preacher without having abandoned those vices, even when he had practiced them secretly. And after he had become a priest, whenever he was celebrating Mass at the altar in the presence of a large congregation, he always wept over the Saviour's Passion, for he was a man who could shed tears whenever he pleased. In short, what with his sermons and his tears, he so beguiled the Venetians that he was trustee and guardian of nearly everyone's will, the keeper of many people's money, the confessor and adviser of most men and women. Thus, from wolf he became shepherd, and in those parts the fame of his sanctity was greater than San Francesco's[3] ever was at Assisi.

Now, it happened that a silly stupid young woman, named Madonna Lisetta da ca Quirino, the wife of a merchant who was away in Flanders with the galleys, went with other women to confess to this holy friar. As she knelt at his feet like the Venetian she was—and they are all fools—he asked her half way through her confession if she had a lover. And she tartly replied:

"Why, messer friar, have you no eyes in your head? Do you think my beauties are no more than these other women's? I could have as many lovers as I wanted. But my beauty is not to be yielded to the love of anybody. How many beauties do you see like mine, for I should be beautiful in Paradise?"

And she went on to say so many things about her beauties that it was tedious to listen to her. Friar Alberto at once saw her weakness, and, feeling that she was ready made to his hand, he fell in love with her. But, reserving his flatteries for another time, he put on his saintly air and began to reprove her, and to say this was vain-glory and other things of the kind. So the lady told him he was a fool, and did not know how to distinguish one beauty from another. And Friar Alberto, not wanting to anger her too much, finished off the confession and let her go with the others.

A few days later he went with a trusted friend to Madonna Lisetta's house and took her aside into a room where they could not be seen. There he fell on his knees before her, and said:

"Madonna, I beseech you for God's sake to forgive me for what I said to you on Sunday when you spoke of your beauty, because I was so severely punished that night I have not been able to get up until today."

Then said Madonna Pot-stick: "And who punished you?"

"I will tell you," said Friar Alberto. "While I was praying that night, as I always do, I suddenly saw a bright light in my cell. Before I could turn to see what it was, I beheld a most beautiful young man with a large stick in his hand, who took me by the cowl, dragged me to my feet and beat me as if to break my bones. I asked him why he did this, and he replied: 'Because you presumed today to reprove the heavenly beauty of Madonna Lisetta whom I love more than anything except God himself.' And I asked: 'Who are you?' And he said he was the Angel Gabriel. 'O my lord,' said I, 'I beg you will

[3] Saint Francis of Assisi (1182?–1226), of whose piety many stories were told. He is eulogized in Dante's *Paradiso,* canto XI.

pardon me.' And he said: 'I will pardon you on condition that you go to her as soon as you can and obtain her forgiveness. And if she does not forgive you I shall return here, and so deal with you that you will be miserable for the rest of your days.' What he afterwards said to me I dare not tell you until you have pardoned me."

Donna Windy-noddle, who was as sweet as salt, was enchanted at these words, and thought them all true.

"I told you, Friar Alberto," said she, "that mine were heavenly beauties. But, so help me God, I am sorry for you, and to spare you any further trouble I forgive you, if only you will tell me truly what the Angel then said."

"Madonna," replied Friar Alberto, "since you have pardoned me, I will tell you willingly. But, you must not repeat a word of what I tell you to anyone in the world, if you do not want to destroy your happiness, you who are the luckiest woman in the world.

"The Angel Gabriel told me to tell you that he loves you so much he would often have come to spend the night with you, but for his fear of terrifying you. He now sends you a message through me to say that he wants to come to you one night and to spend part of it with you. But he is an Angel, and if he came to you in the form of an Angel you could not touch him; and so he says that for your delight he will come in a man's shape and bids you tell him when you want him to come and in whose shape, and he will come. And so you ought to think yourself more blessed than any other woman living."

Madonna Silly then said she was very glad to have the Angel Gabriel in love with her, because she loved him and always put up a fourpenny candle to him wherever she saw him painted. Whenever he liked to come to her he would be welcome and he would find her alone in her room, on one condition, which was that he would not abandon her for the Virgin Mary whom he was said to be very fond of; and she was inclined to believe this since whenever she saw his picture he was kneeling before the Virgin.[4] In addition, she said that the Angel should come in any shape he pleased—she would not be afraid.

Then said Friar Alberto:

"Madonna, you speak wisely, and I will arrange with him as you say. But you can do me a great favor, which will cost you nothing. The favor is that you will allow him to come in my body. This will be a very great favor because he will take the soul from my body and put it in Heaven, and he will enter into me, and my soul will be in Paradise as long as he remains with you."

Then said Madonna Littlewit:

"I am content. I want you to have this consolation for the stripes[5] you received on my account."

Said Friar Alberto:

"Tonight leave the door of your house open, so that he can come in. Since he is coming in a human body, he can only enter by the door."

The lady replied that this should be done. Friar Alberto departed, and she remained in such a state of delight that her chemise did not touch her

[4]The Annunciation, in which the angel Gabriel tells the Virgin Mary that she will be the mother of God, was a perennial subject of religious paintings.

[5]Blows.

backside, and the time she had to wait for the Angel Gabriel seemed like a thousand years.

Friar Alberto thought it better to be a good horseman than an Angel that night, so he fortified himself with all sorts of good cheer, in order not to be unhorsed too easily. He obtained permission to be out that night, and went with his trusted friend to the house of a woman friend, which he had made his starting point more than once before when he was going to ride the mare. From there he went in disguise to the lady's house, and having transformed himself into an Angel with the fripperies[6] he had brought with him, he went upstairs into the lady's bedroom. When she saw something white come in, she kneeled down. The Angel gave her his benediction, raised her to her feet, and signed to her to get into bed. She did so immediately in her willingness to obey, and the Angel got into bed with his devotee.

Friar Alberto was a robust and handsome man and in excellent health. Donna Lisetta was fresh and pretty and found him a very different person from her husband to lie with. That night he flew many times with her without wings, which made her call herself blessed; and in addition he told her a great many things about heavenly glory. Just before dawn, he collected his trappings and returned to his friend, who had kept friendly company with the other woman so that she should not feel afraid by sleeping alone.

After the lady had dined, she went with a woman friend to see Friar Alberto, and gave him news of the Angel Gabriel, telling him how the Angel looked and what he had said about the glory of eternal life, to which she added all sorts of marvelous fables.

"Madonna," said Friar Alberto, "I know not how you were with him, all I know is that last night he came to me, and when I had delivered him your message, he suddenly took my soul to a place where there were more flowers and roses than ever I saw, one of the most delicious places that ever existed, where my soul remained until dawn this morning. But what happened to my body I do not know."

"Didn't I tell you?" said the lady. "Your body lay all night in my arms with the Angel Gabriel. And if you don't believe me, look under your left breast, where I gave the Angel such a kiss that the mark will remain for several days."

Then said Friar Alberto:

"I will do something today which I have not done for a very long time. I shall undress myself to see if what you say is true."

After a lot more chatter, the lady returned home. And Friar Alberto thereafter visited her many times in the guise of an Angel, without the slightest difficulty. But one day Madonna Lisetta was with one of her gossips,[7] and as they were discussing their beauties, she said like the empty-pated fool she was, in order to show off:

"If you knew who was in love with my beauty you would not speak of anyone else's."

The gossip was anxious to hear about it, and knowing Lisetta well, said:

"Madonna, you may be right, but as I do not know whom you mean I shall not change my opinion so easily."

The lady, who had very little sense, then said:

[6] Gaudy costumes. [7] Intimate friends.

"Gossip, he does not want it talked about, but the person I mean is the Angel Gabriel, who loves me more than himself, so he says, because I am the most beautiful person in the world or the Maremma."[8]

The gossip felt like laughing outright, but restrained herself to keep the conversation going, and said:

"God's faith, Madonna, if you mean the Angel Gabriel and say so, it must be true, but I did not think the angels did such things."

"Gossip," said the lady, "you are wrong. By God's favor, he does it better than my husband, and he tells me they do it up above. But, because he thinks me more beautiful than anyone in Heaven, he has fallen in love with me, and often spends a night with me. So you see!"

As soon as the gossip had left Madonna Lisetta, it seemed like a thousand years to her before she had got into a company where she could laugh at all this. She went to a gathering of women, and told them the whole tale. These women told their husbands and other women, and they told others, and so in less than two days the story was all over Venice. Among others who heard it were the lady's cousins, and, without saying anything to her, they made up their minds to find this Angel and see whether he could fly. So they watched for him every night.

Some rumors of all this came to the ears of Friar Alberto, who went to the lady one night to scold her for it. He was scarcely undressed when her cousins, who had seen him come in, were at the door. Friar Alberto heard them, and guessed what they were. He jumped up, and, having no other means of escape, opened a window overlooking the Grand Canal,[9] from which he threw himself into the water.

The water there was deep; he was a good swimmer, and so did himself no harm. He swam to the other side of the canal and immediately entered an open house there, begging the goodman[10] for the love of God to save his life, and told him all sorts of lies to explain why he was there naked at that hour of night.

The goodman, who was just setting off on his business, pitied Friar Alberto and put him into bed, telling him to stop there until he came back. He then locked the friar in, and went about his business.

When the lady's cousins entered her room, they found the Angel Gabriel had left his wings behind and flown away. They abused the lady indignantly, and, leaving her very disconsolate, returned home with the Angel's trappings.

Meanwhile, soon after dawn, the goodman was on the Rialto[11] and heard how the Angel Gabriel had gone to lie with Madonna Lisetta the night before, how he had been discovered by her relatives and had thrown himself into the canal, and nobody knew what had become of him. So he immediately realized that this was the man in his own house. He went home and after much discussion arranged that the Friar should pay him fifty ducats not to hand him over to the cousins; and this was done. Friar Alberto then wanted to leave, but the goodman said:

[8]A marshy region near Florence. The boast is ludicrous, since the Maremma is a mere local district.

[9]The famous canals of Venice serve in lieu of streets.

[10]A title of respect for a man below the rank of gentry.

[11]The commercial center of Venice.

"There is only one way of doing this. There is a festival today where one man leads another dressed like a bear or a wild man of the woods or one thing or another, and then there is a hunt in the Piazza di San Marco,[12] and when that is over the festival ends. Then everyone goes off where he pleases with the person he has brought in disguise. Now, you may be spied out here, and so, if you like, I will lead you along in some disguise and can take you wherever you like. Otherwise I don't see how you can leave here without being recognized. The lady's relatives know you must be in some house in the neighborhood, and have posted guards everywhere to catch you."

Friar Alberto did not at all like the idea, but he was so much afraid of the lady's relatives that he agreed to it, and told the man where he wanted to go, and how he should be led along. The goodman smeared him all over with honey and then covered him with feathers, put a chain round his neck and a mask on his face. In one hand he gave him a large stick and in the other two great dogs which he had brought from the butcher; and then he sent someone to the Rialto who announced that everyone who wanted to see the Angel Gabriel should go to the Piazza di San Marco. That was true Venetian good faith!

Having done this, he took the Friar out, and, walking before him, led him along on a chain; and everybody came round saying: "What's this? What's this?" And thus he took the Friar to the Piazza, where there was a great crowd of people, made up of those who had followed them and those who had come from the Rialto on hearing the announcement. He then led his wild man of the woods to a column in a conspicuous and elevated place, pretending that he was waiting for the hunt. The poor friar was greatly plagued by flies and gad-flies, because he was smeared all over with honey. And when the goodman saw that the Piazza was full of people, he pretended that he was going to unchain his wild man; but instead he took off Friar Alberto's mask, and shouted:

"Gentlemen, since the pig has not come to the hunt and since the hunt is off, I don't want you to have gathered here for nothing, and so I want you to see the Angel Gabriel who came down from Heaven to earth last night to console the ladies of Venice."

As soon as the mask was off, Friar Alberto was recognized by everybody, and there went up a great shout against him, everybody saying the most insulting things that ever were said to any scoundrel. And first one and then another threw all sorts of filth in his face. There he was kept a long time until the news reached the other friars of his convent. Six of them came down to the Piazza, threw a gown on his back and bound him, and then in the midst of a great tumult took him back to the monastery, where he was imprisoned. And it is believed that he soon died there after a life of misery.

Thus a man who was thought to be good and acted evilly without being suspected, tried to be the Angel Gabriel and was turned into a wild man of the woods; and, in the long run, was insulted as he deserved and came to weep in vain for the sins he had committed. Please God that this may happen to all like him.

[12] The principal public square of Venice; St. Mark is the city's patron saint.

FIFTH DAY, TENTH TALE

Pietro di Vinciolo goes out to sup. His wife brings a lover into the house; Pietro returns, and she hides the lover under a chicken coop. Pietro tells her how, while he was supping with Ercolano, a young man whom the wife had hidden was discovered. She blames Ercolano's wife, but an ass unhappily treads on the lover's finger as he is under the coop, and he gives a shriek; Pietro runs out, sees him, and perceives how his wife has tricked him; but in the end he pardons her fault.

The queen finished her tale, and they all praised God for having worthily rewarded Federigo; and then Dioneo began, without waiting to be ordered.[1]

I know not whether it be an accidental vice and the result of the corruption of men's manners, or whether it be a natural failing to laugh at bad things rather than at good deeds, especially when we are not directly concerned. Now since the task I undertook before and am about to carry out again, has no other object but to drive away melancholy from you and to raise mirth and merriment, I shall tell you this tale, enamored ladies, although its matter in part be less than chaste, because it may amuse you. While you listen to it, do as you do when you enter a garden and, stretching out your delicate hands, pluck the roses and avoid the thorns. In so doing, leave the bad man in his misfortune with his woes, and laugh at the amorous tricks of the wife, and feel compassion for the misfortunes of others, where it is needed.

Not long ago in Perugia there was a rich man named Pietro di Vinciolo, who took a wife, more to deceive others and to avoid the general opinion of himself among the Perugians, than for any desire he had of her. And Fortune was so far conformable to his wish that the wife he took was a robust wench with lively red hair, who would rather have had two husbands than one, whereas she had chanced upon a man who would rather have had to do with another man than with her.

In process of time she found this out. And since she was fresh and pretty, and felt herself friskish and robust, she got angry and often exchanged sharp words with her husband; and they led a miserable life together. But, seeing that this exhausted her without improving her husband, she said to herself:

"This man leaves me in sorrow and goes off in his vice in wooden shoes through the dry, while I am trying to carry someone else in a ship through the rain.[2] I took him as my husband and gave him a good large dowry, knowing him to be a man, and thinking he wanted what men do and ought to want; and if I had not thought he was a man, I would never have taken him. He knew I was a woman; why did he marry me if he didn't like women? This is unendurable. If I had not wanted to live the life of the world, I should have become a nun. If I wait for delight and pleasure from him, I might perhaps wait in vain until I am an old woman, and then vainly regret my lost youth. He himself is an example to me, that I should find some consolation, and some pleasure as he does. In me this pleasure will be commendable, whereas in him it is blameworthy; for I only offend the laws, whereas he offends the laws and Nature too."

[1] The theme of the stories on the fifth day, under Fiammetta's rule, is love transformed from grief to happiness.

[2] She means that sexually her husband goes against nature whereas she conforms to it.

Having thought this over a good many times, the good woman, with an idea of carrying out her plan secretly, became familiar with an old woman, who yet seemed more like a pious old thing than a bawd, always going to church services with beads in her hand and never talking about anything but the lives of the Fathers or the stigmata of St. Francis,[3] so that almost everybody thought she was a saint. And when she thought it a fitting time, the wife told her everything she intended.

"My child," said the old woman, "God, who knows everything, knows that in this you will do well. And if you did it for no other reason, yet you and every other young woman should do it, in order not to waste the time of your youth, because to those who have any understanding there is no grief like having wasted time. What the devil good are we when we are old, except to watch the supper on the hearth? If anyone knows it and can bear witness to it, I can. Now I am an old woman I realize with bitter soulprickings how I wasted my time. And although I did not lose it all (for I don't want you to think I was a simpleton), still I did not do what I could have done. When I remember it, and see what I now am, and think how nobody would kindle up a spark of desire for me, God knows what grief I feel.

"The same thing does not happen to men. They are born fitted for a thousand things and not for this only, while the larger number of them are much better old than young. But women are only born to do it and make children, and so are esteemed. And if you haven't noticed anything else, you ought to have noticed this—that we are always ready for it, which does not happen with men. Moreover, one woman would tire out many men, whereas many men cannot tire one woman. Now, since we are born for this, I say once more you will be doing well to give your husband tit for tat, so that in your old age your mind will not have any reproach to bring against your flesh.

"Everyone gets from this world what he takes from it, especially women, who have far more necessity to make use of time while they have it than men, because, as you can see for yourself, when we get old, neither husband nor anyone else wants to see us, so we're chased in the kitchen to tell tales to the cat, and scour the pots and pans. Worse than that even, they make songs about us, saying: 'The best morsels for the girls, and quinsies[4] to the old women'; and they say lots of other similar things.

"To keep you no longer in talk, I say now that you could not have spoken to anyone in the world who can be more useful to you than me; for however haughty a man may be I am not afraid to say what is necessary to him, and however harsh or boorish, I can smooth him down and bring him to the point I want. Tell me the one you want, and leave the rest to me. But remember, my child, that I am poor, and that you will be remembered in all my church-goings and all the paternosters I say; and I shall pray God for the souls of all your departed dead."

Thus ended the old woman. And the young woman came to an agreement with the old one that, if she saw him, she was to bring her a young man who often passed through the district; and she described him in such a way that the old woman knew who he was. Then she gave her a piece of salt meat, and sent her away.

[3] The Fathers were religious authorities in the ancient Christian church. St. Francis of Assisi was believed to have received in his own body the marks ("stigmata") of Christ's wounds.

[4] Inflammations of the throat; the literal meaning in the Italian is "things to choke on."

Not many days afterwards the old woman brought the young man described to her room, and soon afterwards another, according as the young woman wanted. And, although in fear of her husband, she did not miss the opportunity.

One evening her husband was going out to supper with a friend of his, named Ercolano, and so the girl arranged with the old woman to bring her a young man, who was one of the handsomest and pleasantest in Perugia. Which was quickly done. The young woman and the young man were just sitting down to supper, when they heard Pietro at the door, shouting to her to open it. When she heard it, the wife gave herself up for dead. Wanting to hide the young man if she could, and not having the cunning to get him out of the house or hide him elsewhere, she hid him under a chicken coop in a shed next to the room in which they were supping, and threw over it a piece of straw sacking she had emptied that day. After which, she quickly opened the door to her husband. When he came into the house, she said:

"You've guzzled up that supper pretty quickly."

"We never even tasted it," said Pietro.

"How did that happen?" asked his wife.

"I'll tell you," said Pietro. "Ercolano and his wife and I were sitting down to table when we heard somebody sneeze near us, to which we paid no attention the first and second times. But the person sneezed a third, a fourth, a fifth and many other times, which greatly surprised us. Ercolano was already a little annoyed with his wife because she had kept him waiting a long time at the door, and said to her in a rage: 'What does this mean? Who is it sneezing like this?' He got up from the table, and went to the staircase near at hand, under which was a cupboard to store things away, as we see arranged in houses every day.

"It seemed to him that the sound of the sneezing came from this cupboard, so he opened a little door in it, and as soon as this was opened there suddenly came out the worst stink of sulphur imaginable, which he had noticed before and had complained of, whereupon his wife had said: 'I am whitening my veils in there with sulphur, and the pots too, which I sprinkled with sulphur so that they would get the fumes, and put them under the staircase, and the smell still comes from them.' And after Ercolano had opened the door and the fumes had cleared off a little, he looked inside and saw the person who had sneezed and was still sneezing owing to the sulphur fumes. And as he sneezed, the sulphur had got such a hold on his chest, that he was not far from never sneezing or doing anything else again.

"As soon as Ercolano saw him, he shouted: 'Now I see, wife, the man for whose sake you kept us waiting at the door so long without opening when we came. But may I never have anything please me again, if I don't make you pay for this!' The wife, hearing this and seeing that her fault was discovered, fled from the table without attempting any excuse; and I don't know where she went. Ercolano, not noticing that his wife had fled, told the sneezing man to come out; but he was beyond all power of moving, and did not stir for anything Ercolano said.

"Thereupon Ercolano took him by one of his feet and dragged him out, and ran for a knife to kill him. But, fearing the police on my own account, I jumped up and prevented him from killing the man or doing him any harm. My shouting and defending him aroused the neighbors who came in and took the almost swooning young man, and carried him somewhere—I don't know where—out of the house. So our supper was quite spoiled by all this, and I not only haven't guzzled it but never even tasted it, as I said."

At this tale the wife perceived that there were others who knew as much as she did, although some had bad luck. She would have been glad to defend Ercolano's wife with words, but as blaming the faults of others seemed to her to make things easier for her own, she said:

"Here's fine doings! Here's a good and saintly woman! Here's the faith of a modest woman, who seemed to me so saintly that I would have confessed my sins to her. And, what's worse, she gives a mighty good example to the young, since she's getting old already. Cursed be the hour when she came into the world and the hour which allowed her to live, the wicked deceitful woman that she must be, the universal shame and scorn of all women on this earth! Curse her for leaving her chastity and the faith promised to her husband and the honor of the world, he that is such a good man and an honorable citizen and treated her so well, for another man, and not being ashamed to bring him to scorn and herself with him! So help me God, I'd have no pity on such women. They ought to be killed. They ought to be thrown into the fire and burned to ashes."

Then, recollecting that her lover was near at hand, hidden under the hen-coop, she began to urge Pietro to go to bed, as it was then bedtime. But Pietro was more anxious to have something to eat than to go to bed, and asked if there were not something for supper.

"Ah!" said the wife, "yes, indeed, there's supper! We're quite accustomed to have supper when you're not here! Yes, I'm Ercolano's wife, am I? Why don't you go to bed? Go to sleep this evening!"

Now, it happened that during the evening some of Pietro's workmen had brought certain things in from the country, and had stalled their asses without giving them any water to drink, in a little stable next to the shed. One of the asses was very thirsty indeed, and, managing to get his head out of the halter, walked out of the stable and went snuffing at everything, trying to find some water. And so he came up to the hen-coop where the young man was hidden.

He was on his hands and knees, and one of his fingers was outside the hen-coop. Now, as luck or ill luck would have it, the ass trod on his finger; whereupon, in his anguish, he uttered a yell. Pietro was astonished to hear it, and knew that someone must be in the house. He went out of the room and heard the young man moaning, for the ass had not yet taken its hoof off his finger and was still pressing heavily on it. Said Pietro: "Who's there?" He ran to the hen-coop, lifted it up, and saw the young man who, in addition to the pain he felt from the ass treading on his finger, was trembling with fear lest Pietro should do him an injury.

Pietro recognized him as a young man he had long been prowling after for his vicious pleasures, and asked him: "What are you doing here?" but the youth made no answer, and only begged him for the love of God to do him no harm.

"Get up," said Pietro, "I won't do you any harm; but tell me, how do you happen to be here, and why?"

The young man confessed everything. Pietro, no less joyous than his wife was distressed at the discovery, took him by the hand and led him into the room, where the wife was waiting in the greatest terror imaginable. Pietro made her sit down opposite and said:

"So you cursed so hard Ercolano's wife, and you said she ought to be burned and that she was the shame of you all—why didn't you say it of yourself? Or, if you didn't want to confess that, how could your conscience endure to say it of her, when you knew you had done the same thing as she had? Nothing, indeed, induced you to do it, except that all you women are alike, and you hope to hide your own sins under the failings of others. May fire come down from heaven and burn you all, vile generation that you are!"

The wife, seeing that at the first onslaught he had hurt her with nothing worse than words, and noticing that he was in high glee at holding such a handsome youth by the hand, plucked up heart and said:

"I am very sure that you would like fire to come from heaven and burn up all us women, since you are as fond of us as a dog is of sticks. But, God's Cross! You won't see it happen. I should like to have a little discussion with you, to find out what you complain of. It is indeed well to compare me with Ercolano's wife, a hypocritical, snivelling old woman, who gets what she wants out of him, and he treats her as well as a wife can be treated, which doesn't happen to me. For, granted that I am well clad and shod, you know how I fare in other matters and how long it is since you lay with me. I'd go with rags on my back and broken shoes and be well treated by you in bed, rather than have all these things and be treated as you treat me. Understand plainly, Pietro, I'm a woman like other women, and I want what they want. So, if I go seeking for what I can't get from you, there's no need to abuse me. At least I do you so much honor that I don't go with boys and scrubby fellows."

Pietro saw that she could go on talking all night, and so, as he cared nothing about her, he said:

"That's enough, wife. I'll be content with that. Will you be so gracious as to get us some supper, for I rather fancy this boy has had no more supper than I have."

"No, indeed," said the wife, "he has had no supper; for when you arrived in an ill hour, we were just sitting down to table to sup."

"Go along then," said Pietro, "and get us some supper, and afterwards I will arrange this affair in such a way that you will have nothing to complain of."

Finding her husband so agreeable, the wife jumped up and re-laid the table, brought out the supper she had prepared, and supped merrily with her bad husband and the young man. What Pietro arranged after supper to satisfy all three of them has entirely gone out of my head. But I know that next morning the young man found himself in the piazza, not quite knowing whether the night before he had been with the wife or the husband. And so, dear ladies, I want to tell you: "He who does it to you, you do it to him." And if you can't, keep it in mind while you can, so that the ass may receive what he gets at home.

Dioneo's tale was now ended, and the ladies' laughter was restrained less from lack of amusement than from shame. The queen, seeing that the end of her reign was at hand, stood up and took off her garland, and gracefully placed it on Elisa's head, saying:

"Madonna, it is now for you to give orders."

Having received the honor, Elisa followed the adopted routine and first arranged with the steward for what was needed during the period of her rule; after which she said to the satisfaction of the company:

"We have already heard how many people by means of good sayings and prompt retorts and quick wits have been able to turn the teeth of others on themselves with a sharp nip or have averted threatened dangers. And since this is a good topic and may be useful, my will is that tomorrow, with God's help, we tell tales within these limits—that is, of such persons who have retorted a witticism directed at them, or with a quick retort or piece of shrewdness have escaped destruction, danger or contempt."

This was highly commended by them all. Whereupon the queen rose to her feet, and gave them all to do as they chose until supper time. The merry company arose as the queen arose, and according to custom, each of them gave himself up to what pleased him most. But when the cicadas ceased their song, everyone was called, and they all went to supper. After this had been festively served, they went to singing and music. Emilia danced at the queen's command, and then Dioneo was ordered to sing a song. He immediately began: "Old mother Hale, lift up your tail, and see the good news I bring you." Whereat all the ladies burst out laughing, especially the queen, who ordered him to abandon that song and start another.

"Madonna," said Dioneo, "if I had cymbals, I would sing: 'Up with your petties, Monna Lapa,' or 'Under the olive tree springs the grass,' or would you like me to sing: 'The waves of the ocean make me ill with their motion'? But then I haven't any cymbals, so see which of these others you would like. Do you like: 'Out you go to be chopped to shreds, like a melon down in the garden beds'?"

"No," said the queen, "sing something else."

"Well," said Dioneo, "shall I sing: 'Monna Simona, put it up in the cask, it isn't the month of October'?"

"No, no," said the queen laughing, "sing a nice song, if you like, but not that one."

"Don't get angry, madonna," said Dioneo. "Which do you like best? I know over a thousand. Would you like: 'If I don't tickle my little prickle,' or 'Gently, gently, husband dear,' or 'I'll buy a cock for a hundred dollars'?"

"Dioneo," said the queen rather angrily, although all the others were laughing, "cease joking, and sing a pleasant song. If you don't, you will discover how angry I can be."

At this Dioneo left his jests, and began to sing as follows:

Love, the fair light that issues from her eyes has made me slave to thee and her.

The splendor of her lovely eyes, passing through mine, moved me before your flame was kindled in my heart. However great your worth, I learned it through her beauteous face; imagining which, I found my self gathering every virtue and yielding them to her—another cause of sighs in me.

Now, dear my Lord, I have become one among your followers, and in obedience await your grace; but yet I know not if the high desire which you have set within my breast and my unshaken faith are wholly known to her, who so possesses all my mind that save from her I would not and I do not hope for peace.

Therefore I pray you, sweet my love, to show them to her, and make her feel a little of your flame, in grace to me who, as you see, am all consumed with love, and bit by bit worn down with pain. And then, when it is time, commend me to her, as you should, and gladly would I come with you to do it.

When Dioneo by his silence showed that his song was ended, the queen, after having highly praised it, had others sung. And when part of the night was spent and the queen felt that the heat of day was quenched in night's coolness, she ordered everyone to rest as he chose until the following day.

HERE ENDS THE FIFTH DAY

TENTH DAY, TENTH TALE

The Marquess of Saluzzo is urged by his subjects to take a wife and, to choose in his own way, takes the daughter of a peasant. He has two children by her and pretends to her that he has killed them. He then pretends that he is tired of her and that he has taken another wife and so brings their own daughter to the house as if she were his new wife, after driving her away in her shift. She endures it all patiently. He brings her back home, more beloved by him than ever, shows her their grown children, honors her and makes others honor her as Marchioness.

When the king[1] had ended his long tale, which, to judge by their looks, had greatly pleased everyone, Dioneo said, laughing:

"The good man who was waiting to bring down the ghost's stiff tail that night would not have given two cents for all the praise you give Messer Torello![2]

Then, knowing that he was the only one left to tell a tale, he began:

Gracious ladies, as far as I can see, today has been given up to Kings, Sultans and such like persons; so, not to wander away too far from you, I shall tell you about a Marquess, but not of his munificence. It will be about his silly brutality, although good came of it in the end. I do not advise anyone to imitate him, for it was a great pity that good did come to him.

A long time ago the eldest son of the Marquess of Saluzzo was a young man named Gualtieri. He was wifeless and childless, spent his time hunting and hawking, and never thought about marrying or having children, wherein he was probably very wise. This displeased his subjects, who several times begged him to take a wife, so that he might not die without an heir and leave them without a ruler, offering to find him a wife born of such a father and mother as would give him good hopes of her and content him. To which Gualtieri replied:

"My friends, you urge me to do something I was determined never to do, seeing how hard it is to find a woman of suitable character, and how many of the opposite sort there are, and how wretched is the life of a man who takes a wife unsuitable to him. It is foolishness of you to think you can judge a girl by the characters of her father and mother (from which you

[1] Pamfilo, who rules over the tenth day. The theme of the day is liberal and munificent behavior.

[2] A reference to the immediately preceding story and to the first story of Day Seven.

argue that you can find me one to please me), for I do not see how you can really know the fathers' or the mothers' secrets. And even if you did know them, daughters are often quite different from their fathers and mothers.

"But you want me to take these chains, and I am content to do so. If it turns out badly I want to have no one to complain of but myself, and so I shall choose for myself. And I tell you that if you do not honor the wife I choose as your lady you will find out to your cost how serious a thing it is to have compelled me by your entreaties to take a wife against my will."

They replied that they were content, if only he would take a wife.

For some time Gualtieri had been pleased by the character of a poor girl in a hamlet near his house. He thought her beautiful, and that he might live comfortably enough with her. So he decided that he would marry her without seeking any further, and, having sent for her father, who was a very poor man, he arranged to marry her. Having done this, Gualtieri called together all his friends from the surrounding country, and said:

"My friends, it has pleased you to desire that I should marry, and I am ready to do so, more to please you than from any desire I have of taking a wife. You know you promised me that you would honor anyone I chose as your lady. The time has now come for me to keep my promise to you and you to keep yours to me. I have found a girl after my heart quite near here; I intend to marry her and to bring her home in a few days. So take thought to make a handsome marriage feast and how you can honorably receive her, so that I may consider myself content with your promise as you may be with mine."

The good men cheerfully replied that they were glad of it, and that they would consider her their lady and honor her as their lady in all things. After which, they all set about preparing a great and handsome wedding feast, and so did Gualtieri. He prepared a great and fine banquet, and invited many friends and relatives and noblemen and others. Moreover, he had rich and beautiful dresses cut out and fitted on a girl, who seemed to him about the same build as the girl he proposed to marry. And he also purchased girdles and rings and a rich and beautiful crown, and everything necessary to a bride.

When the day appointed for the wedding arrived, Gualtieri about the middle of Terce[3] mounted his horse, and so did those who had come to honor him. Everything being arranged, he said:

"Gentlemen, it is time to go for the bride."

Setting out with all his company he came to the hamlet and the house of the girl's father, where he found her drawing water in great haste, so that she could go with the other women to see Gualtieri's bride. And when Gualtieri saw her, he called her by her name, Griselda, and asked where her father was. She blushed and said:

"He is in the house, my lord."

Gualtieri dismounted, told everyone to wait for him, entered the poor little house where he found the girl's father (who was named Giannucole), and said to him:

"I have come to marry Griselda, but first I want to ask her a few things in your presence."

[3] 7:30 A.M.

He then asked her whether, if he married her, she would try to please him, and never be angry at anything he said or did, and if she would be obedient, and several other things, to all of which she said "Yes." Gualtieri then took her by the hand and led her forth. In the presence of all his company he had her stripped naked, and then the clothes he had prepared were brought, and she was immediately dressed and shod, and he had a crown put on her hair, all unkempt as it was. Everyone marveled at this, and he said:

"Gentlemen, I intend to take this girl as my wife, if she will take me as her husband."

He then turned to her, as she stood blushing and irresolute, and said:

"Griselda, will you take me as your husband?"

"Yes, my lord," she replied.

"And I will take you as my wife," said he.

Then in the presence of them all he pledged his faith to her; and they set her on a palfrey and honorably conducted her to his house. The wedding feast was great and handsome, and the rejoicing no less than if he had married the daughter of the King of France.

The girl seemed to have changed her soul and manners with her clothes. As I said, she was beautiful of face and body, and she became so agreeable, so pleasant, so well-behaved that she seemed like the daughter of a nobleman, and not Giannucole's child and a cattle herder; which surprised everyone who had known her before. Moreover, she was so obedient and so ready to serve her husband that he felt himself to be the happiest and best matched man in the world. And she was so gracious and kindly to her husband's subjects that there was not one of them but loved her and gladly honored her, while all prayed for her good and her prosperity and advancement. Whereas they had said that Gualtieri had showed little wisdom in marrying her, they now said that he was the wisest and shrewdest man in the world, because no one else would have known the lofty virtue hidden under her poor clothes and village garb.

In short, before long she acted so well that not only in the marquisate but everywhere people were talking of her virtues and good actions; and whatever had been said against her husband for having married her was now turned to the opposite. She had not long been with Gualtieri when she became pregnant, and in due time gave birth to a daughter, at which Gualtieri rejoiced greatly.

Soon after this the idea came to him to test her patience with a long trial and intolerable things. He said unkind things to her, seemed to be angry, and said that his subjects were most discontented with her on account of her low birth, and especially when they saw that she bore children. He said they were very angry at the birth of a daughter and did nothing but murmur. When the lady heard these words, she did not change countenance or cheerfulness, but said to him:

"My lord, you may do with me what you think most to your honor and satisfaction. I shall be content, for I know that I am less than they and unworthy of the honor to which you have raised me by your courtesy."

Gualtieri liked this reply and saw that no pride had risen up in her from the honor done her by him and others.

Soon after, he informed his wife in general terms that his subjects could not endure the daughter she had borne. He then gave orders to one of his servants whom he sent to her. The man, with a dolorous visage, said:

"Madonna, if I am to avoid death I must do what my lord bids me. He tells me I am to take your daughter and . . ."

He said no more, but the lady, hearing these words and seeing the servant's face, and remembering what had been said to her, guessed that he had been ordered to kill the child. She went straight to the cradle, kissed and blessed the child, and although she felt great anguish in her heart, put the child in the servant's arms without changing her countenance, and said:

"Do what my lord and yours has ordered you to do. But do not leave her for the birds and animals to devour her body, unless you were ordered to do so."

The servant took the child and told Gualtieri what the lady had said. He marveled at her constancy, and sent the servant with the child to a relative at Bologna, begging her to bring her up and educate her carefully, but without ever saying whose daughter she was.

After this the lady again became pregnant, and in due time brought forth a male child, which delighted Gualtieri. But what he had already done was not enough for him. He pierced the lady with a worse wound, and one day said to her in pretended anger:

"Since you have borne this male child, I cannot live at peace with my subjects, who complain bitterly that a grandson of Giannucole must be their lord after me. If I am not to be driven out, I fear I must do now as I did before, and in the end abandon you and take another wife."

The lady listened to him patiently, and her only reply was:

"My lord, content yourself and do what is pleasing to you. Do not think about me, for nothing pleases me except as it pleases you."

Not many days afterwards Gualtieri sent for his son in the same way that he had sent for his daughter, and while pretending in the same way to kill the child, sent it to be brought up in Bologna, as he had sent the girl. And his wife said no more and looked no worse than she had done about the daughter. Gualtieri marveled at this and said to himself that no other woman could have done what she did; and if he had not seen that she loved her children while she had them, he would have thought she did it to get rid of them, whereas he saw it was from obedience to him.

His subjects thought he had killed his children, blamed him severely and thought him a cruel man, while they felt great pity for his wife. And when the women condoled with her on the death of her children, she never said anything except that it was not her wish but the wish of him who begot them.

Several years after his daughter's birth, Gualtieri thought the time had come for the last test of his wife's patience. He kept saying that he could no longer endure to have Griselda as his wife, that he knew he had acted childishly and wrongly when he married her, that he therefore meant to solicit the Pope for a dispensation to marry another woman and abandon Griselda; for all of which he was reproved by many good men. But his only reply was that it was fitting this should be done.

Hearing of these things, the lady felt she must expect to return to her father's house and perhaps watch cattle as she had done in the past, and see another woman take the man she loved; at which she grieved deeply. But she prepared herself to endure this with a firm countenance, as she had endured the other wrongs of Fortune.

Not long afterwards Gualtieri received forged letters from Rome, which he showed to his subjects, pretending that the Pope by these letters gave him a dispensation to take another wife and leave Griselda. So, calling her before him, he said to her in the presence of many of his subjects:

"Wife, the Pope has granted me a dispensation to leave you and to take another wife. Now, since my ancestors were great gentlemen and lords of this country while yours were always laborers, I intend that you shall no longer be my wife, but return to Giannucole's house with the dowry you brought me, while I shall bring home another wife I have found more suitable for me."

At these words the lady could only restrain her tears by a great effort, beyond that of women's nature, and replied:

"My lord, I always knew that my lowly rank was in no wise suitable to your nobility; and the rank I have had with you I always recognized as coming from God and you, and never looked upon it as given to me, but only lent. You are pleased to take it back, and it must and does please me to return it to you. Here is the ring with which you wedded me; take it. You tell me to take the dowry I brought you; to do this there is no need for you to pay anything nor shall I need a purse or a sumpter horse,[4] for I have not forgotten that I came to you naked. If you think it right that the body which has borne your children should be seen by everyone, I will go away naked. But in exchange for my virginity, which I brought here and cannot carry away, I beg you will at least be pleased to let me take away one shift[5] over and above my dowry."

Gualtieri, who was nearer to tears than anyone else present, managed to keep his countenance stern, and said:

"You shall have a shift."

Those who were present urged him to give her a dress, so that she who had been his wife for thirteen years should not be seen to leave his house so poorly and insultingly as it would be for her to leave it in a shift. But their entreaties were vain. So the lady, clad only in her shift, unshod and with nothing on her head, commended him to God, left his house, and returned to her father accompanied by the tears and lamentation of all who saw her.

Giannucole (who had never believed it was true that Gualtieri would keep his daughter as a wife and had always expected this event), had kept the clothes she had taken off on the morning when Gualtieri married her. So she took them and put them on, and devoted herself to drudgery in her father's house, enduring the assaults of hostile Fortune with a brave spirit.

After Gualtieri had done this, he told his subjects that he was to marry the daughter of one of the Counts of Panago. He therefore made great preparations for the wedding, and sent for Griselda to come to him; and when she came, he said:

"I am bringing home the lady I have just married, and I intend to do her honor at her arrival. You know there is not a woman in the house who can prepare the rooms and do many other things needed for such a feast. You know everything connected with the house better than anyone, so you

[4] Packhorse. [5] Loose undergarment; slip.

must arrange everything that is to be done, and invite all the women you think fit and receive them as if you were mistress of the house. Then, when the marriage feast is over, you can return home."

These words were a dagger in Griselda's heart, for she had not been able to dispense with the love she felt for him as she had her good fortune, but she said:

"My lord, I am ready."

So, in her coarse peasant dress, she entered the house she had left a little before in her shift, and had the rooms cleaned and arranged, put out hangings and carpets in the halls, looked to the kitchen, and set her hand to everything as if she had been a scullery wench of the house. And she never paused until everything was ready and properly arranged.

After this she invited all the ladies of the surrounding country in Gualtieri's name, and then awaited the feast. On the wedding day, dressed in her poor clothes, she received all the ladies with a cheerful visage and a womanly manner.

Gualtieri had had his children carefully brought up in Bologna by his relative, who was married into the family of the Counts of Panago. The daughter was now twelve years old, the most beautiful thing ever seen, and the boy was seven. He sent to her and asked her to come to Saluzzo with his son and daughter, to bring an honorable company with her, and to tell everyone that she was bringing the girl as his wife, and never to let anyone know that the girl was anything else. Her husband did what the Marquess asked, and set out. In a few days he reached Saluzzo about dinner time, with the girl and boy and his noble company; and all the peasants of the country were there to see Gualtieri's new wife.

The girl was received by the ladies and taken to the hall where the tables were spread, and Griselda went cheerfully to meet her, saying:

"Lady, you are welcome."

The ladies had begged Gualtieri, but in vain, to allow Griselda to stay in her room or to lend her one of her own dresses, so that she might not have to meet strangers in such a guise. They all sat down to table and began the meal. Every man looked at the girl and said that Gualtieri had made a good exchange, and Griselda above all praised her and her little brother.

Gualtieri now felt that he had tested his wife's patience as far as he desired. He saw that the strangeness of all this did not alter her and he was certain it was not the result of stupidity, for he knew her to be an intelligent woman. He thought it now time to take her from the bitterness which he felt she must be hiding behind a smiling face. So he called her to him, and in everyone's presence said to her smilingly:

"What do you think of my new wife?"

"My lord," replied Griselda, "I see nothing but good in her. If she is as virtuous as she is beautiful, as I well believe, I have no doubt that you will live with her the happiest lord in the world. But I beg you as earnestly as I can not to give her the wounds you gave the other woman who was your wife. I think she could hardly endure them, because she is younger and because she has been brought up delicately, whereas the other labored continually from her childhood."

Gualtieri saw that she really believed he was to marry the other, and yet spoke nothing but good of her. He made her sit down beside him, and said:

"Griselda, it is now time that you should reap the reward of your long patience, and that those who have thought me cruel and wicked and brutal should know that what I have done was directed towards a pre-determined end, which was to teach you to be a wife, then how to choose and keep a wife, and to procure me perpetual peace so long as I live with you. When I came and took you to wife, I greatly feared that this would not happen to me; and so, to test you, I have given you the trials and sufferings you know. I have never perceived that you thwarted my wishes by word or deed, and I think that in you I have the comfort I desire. I mean to give you back now what I deprived you of for a long time, and to heal the wounds I gave you with the greatest delight. Therefore, with a glad spirit, take her whom you think to be my wife and her brother as your children and mine. They are the children whom you and many others have long thought that I had cruelly murdered. And I am your husband, who loves you above all things, believing I can boast that no man exists who can so rejoice in his wife as I in you."

He then embraced and kissed her. She was weeping with happiness. They both arose and went to where their daughter was sitting, quite stupefied by what she had heard, and tenderly embraced her and her brother, thus undeceiving them and many of those present.

The ladies arose merrily from table and went with Griselda to her room. With better hopes they took off her old clothes and dressed her in one of her noble robes, and brought her back to the hall a lady, which she had looked even in her rags.

They rejoiced over their children, and everyone was glad at what had happened. The feasting and merrymaking were prolonged for several days, and Gualtieri was held to be a wise man, although they thought the testing of his wife harsh and intolerable. But above all they esteemed the virtue of Griselda.

The Count of Panago soon afterwards returned to Bologna. Gualtieri took Giannucole away from his labor and installed him as his father-in-law, so that he ended his days honorably and in great content. He afterwards married off his daughter to a nobleman of great wealth and distinction, and lived long and happily with Griselda, always honoring her as much as he could.

What more is to be said, save that divine souls are sometimes rained down from Heaven into poor houses, while in royal palaces are born those who are better fitted to herd swine than to rule over men? Who but Griselda could have endured with a face not only tearless but cheerful, the stern and unheard-of tests imposed on her by Gualtieri? It would perhaps not have been such a bad thing if he had chosen one of those women who, if she had been driven out of her home in a shift, would have let another man so shake her fur that a new dress would have come from it.

Dioneo's tale was over, and the ladies talked about it, taking first one part and then another, blaming some things and praising others. The king looked up at the sky and saw that the sun was already sinking towards the hour of Vespers,[6] and so, without rising, he spoke thus:

[6] 6 P.M.

"Beautiful ladies, as I think you know, human wisdom does not wholly consist in remembering past things and knowing the present; but grave men esteem it the highest wisdom to be able to foresee the future from a knowledge of both.

"As you know, it will be a fortnight tomorrow since we left Florence to find some amusement to support our health and vitality, and to escape the melancholy, agony and woes which have continued in our city since the beginning of the plague. In my opinion we have virtuously performed this. We have told merry tales, which perhaps might incline to concupiscence; we have eaten and drunk well, played and sung music, all of which things incite weak minds to things less than virtuous; but so far as I have seen there has not been one word or one act on your part or on ours which could be blamed. I have noticed only continual virtue, concord and fraternal familiarity; which is certainly most pleasing to me in your honor and in mine. Now, through too long a habit something might arise which would turn to annoyance, and if we stay away too long an opportunity for scandal might occur; and moreover each of us has now for one day exercised the honor which now dwells in me. I therefore think, if you agree, that it would be well for us to return to the place from which we set out. And, if you consider the matter, our being together is already known round about, and so our company might be increased in such a way as to destroy our pleasure. If you approve my advice, I shall retain the crown until we leave, which I think should be tomorrow. If you decide otherwise, I am quite ready to crown someone for tomorrow."

The discussion between the ladies and young men was long, but at last the king's advice was adopted as wise and virtuous, and they determined to do as he had said. So, having called the steward, he discussed with him what should be done next morning, and then, standing up, gave the company their freedom until supper time.

The ladies and the rest arose, and as usual amused themselves in different ways. They came to supper merrily, and after that began to sing and dance and play music. After Lauretta had danced, the king ordered Fiammetta to sing a song, and she began pleasantly as follows:

If Love came to us without jealousy, no woman living—whoever she might be—would be so glad as I!

And if a woman should be pleased to find in her lover gay youth, the very pinnacle of virtue, eagerness and prowess, wisdom, manners, eloquent speech and perfect grace—I should be pleased, who love them all and see them in my hope.

But since I see that other ladies are as wise as I, I tremble with my fears and dread the worst—which is that others may desire the man I love; and so my wondrous fortune turns to woe and sighing, and all life seems ill.

If my lover were but as faithful as he is valiant, I should feel no jealousy. But now so many ladies seek for lovers that I think all men are faithless. This stabs my heart and makes me wish to die; I dread each woman who looks at him, and fear I may be robbed of him.

Therefore in God's name I beg all ladies not to work this wrong on me; for should any seek to do me harm by word or sign or flattery, either I shall turn fool at learning it or she shall weep her bitter foolishness!

When Fiammetta had ended her song, Dioneo, who was sitting beside her, said laughingly:

"Madonna, you would be very courteous to let all women know this, so that no one in ignorance may deprive you of a possession, whose loss would make you so angry!"

After this, they sang several other songs, and when it was nearly midnight, the king commanded that they should all go to bed.

Next morning they arose after the steward had already sent off all their baggage, and returned to Florence under the guidance of their prudent king. The three young men left the seven ladies in Santa Maria Novella, where they had met; and after taking leave of them went about their business. And the ladies returned home.

END OF THE TENTH AND LAST DAY

from CONCLUSION

Most noble ladies, for whose delight I have given myself over to this long task, I believe that with the aid of divine grace it is more through your pious prayers than any merit of mine that I have carried out what I promised to do at the beginning of this work. So now, after giving thanks, first to God and then to you, I shall rest my pen and weary hand. I know that these tales can expect no more immunity than any others, as I think I showed in the beginning of the Fourth Day;[1] and so before I rest, I mean to reply to certain objections which might be made by you or others.

Some of you may say that in writing these tales I have taken too much license, by making ladies sometimes say and often listen to matters which are not proper to be said or heard by virtuous ladies. This I deny, for there is nothing so unchaste but may be said chastely if modest words are used; and this I think I have done.

But suppose it to be true—and I shall not strive with you, for you are certain to win—I reply that I have many arguments ready. First, if there is any license in some of them, the nature of the stories demanded it; and if any understanding person looks at them with a reasonable eye he will see that they could not be related otherwise, unless I had altered them entirely. And if there are a few words rather freer than suits the prudes, who weigh words more than deeds and take more pains to appear than to be good, I say that I should no more be reproved for having written them than

[1]At the beginning of Day Four, Boccaccio had defended himself against detractors who had charged him, among other things, with too great a fondness for women. He replied that love for them was almost irresistibly natural.

other men and women are reproved for daily saying "hole," "peg," "mortar," "pestle," "sausage," "Bologna sausage," and the like things.[2] My pen should be allowed no less power than is permitted the painter's brush; the painters are not censured for allowing Saint Michele to slay the serpent with a sword or lance and Saint Giorgio to kill the dragon as he pleases. They make Christ male and Eve female, and they fasten sometimes with one nail, sometimes with two, the feet of Him who died for the human race on the Cross.

In addition, anyone can see that these things were not told in church, where everything should be treated with reverent words and minds (although you will find plenty of license in the stories of the church); nor were they told in a school of philosophers, where virtue is as much required as anywhere else; nor among churchmen or other philosophers in any place; but they were told in gardens, in pleasure places, by young people who were old enough not to be led astray by stories, and at a time when everyone threw his cap over the mill and the most virtuous were not reproved for it.

But, such as they are, they may be amusing or harmful, like everything else, according to the persons who listen to them. Who does not know that wine is a most excellent thing, if we may believe Cinciglione and Scolaio,[3] while it is harmful to a man with a fever? Are we to say wine is wicked because it is bad for those who are feverish? Who does not know that fire is most useful and even necessary to mankind? And because it sometimes destroys houses, villages and towns, shall we say it is bad? Weapons defend the safety of those who wish to live in peace, but they also kill men, not through any wrong in them but through the wickedness of those who use them ill.

No corrupt mind ever understands words healthily. And just as such people do not enjoy virtuous words, so the well-disposed cannot be harmed by words which are somewhat less than virtuous, any more than mud can sully sunlight or earthy filth the beauty of the skies.

What books, what words, what letters are more holy, more worthy, more to be revered than those of the divine Scripture? Yet many people by perversely interpreting them have sent themselves and others to perdition. Everything in itself is good for something, and if wrongly used may be harmful in many ways; and I say the same of my tales. Whoever wants to turn them to bad counsel or bad ends will not be forbidden by the tales themselves, if by any chance they contain such things and are twisted and turned to produce them. Those who want utility and good fruits from them, will not find them denied; nor will the tales ever be thought anything but useful and virtuous if they are read at the times and to the persons for which they are intended. . . .

[2] Words that can be used literally and innocently or with sexual meanings. Boccaccio goes on to cite paintings in which images that might be considered phallic can be used for pious purposes.

[3] Names used to represent drinkers.

Marguerite de Navarre
(1492–1549)

A very few periods in history have witnessed a wholesale reexamination and redefinition of fundamental values. The twentieth century, it seems certain, will be remembered as one of these periods. Another such period was the sixteenth century in Europe. Whether the spiritual life demanded immersion in the world or withdrawal from it; whether society was best served by the principle of authority or the principle of independence; what it meant to be a Christian; what the distinctive roles (if there were distinctive roles) of men and women should be; how the institution of marriage could best promote individual happiness and social order—these questions are woven deep into sixteenth-century literature. The writings of Marguerite de Navarre are a good case in point. They are particularly instructive in that Marguerite combined firm convictions and the temperament of a believer with a profound openmindedness.

The marvel is that Marguerite, sister of the king of France and queen of a neighboring country, had time in her life for any such spiritual and psychological concerns, occupied as she was almost constantly with some of the key public events of an especially momentous period of European history. She was born in 1492, the daughter of Charles d'Orléans, Count of Angoulême, and his wife Louise de Savoie (often identified with Oisille in *The Heptameron*). The family was related to the reigning French royal house of Valois but lived on the outskirts of its favor and seemed unlikely to improve in fortunes. But the birth two years later of a son, François (Francis), kept dynastic hopes alive, and unexpected deaths among heirs to the throne made him king of France in 1515.

Meanwhile Marguerite had received a thorough education, as a by-product of her mother's attention to the rearing of the royal heir. (The father had died in 1496.) As a girl Marguerite read widely in the family's excellent library of ancient and modern writers. A stimulating life in her mother's cultivated circle ended for six years when in 1509 Marguerite entered into an arranged marriage with Charles, Duke of Alençon, a soldier with none of the mental or other attractions calculated to win his bride's love. This period of eclipse ended when her brother acceded to the throne, as King Francis I, and called Marguerite to share with him in the splendors of the royal court. The king and his sister proceeded, virtually, to introduce the Italian Renaissance into France, inaugurating a brilliant new era of art, literature, and social elegance. Marguerite, far more than Francis's queen, and almost as much as he, was the central figure in this vibrant new society.

She also exercised considerable administrative and diplomatic authority, as an adviser to her brother and in implementing plans of military preparedness throughout the country. When, in 1524, Francis led his army into Italy against the Spanish Holy Roman Emperor, Charles V, Marguerite and her mother governed France in the king's absence. In the following year they had to cope with a major crisis when, the king having been taken prisoner abroad, France witnessed widespread insurrection by local governments, nobles, and merchants. By traveling to Spain to bargain for her brother's freedom, Marguerite was instrumental in ending the war.

She also had to nurse her ailing husband through part of this period; he died in 1525. Two years later Marguerite was married again, to Henri d'Albret, King of Navarre, a coastal kingdom at the west end of the Pyrenees Mountains separating France from Spain. This time Marguerite gave her heart with her hand, though for his part Henri felt much less bound by the canons of marital fidelity. (The couple were later to appear, in *The Heptameron,* as Parlamente and Hircan.) For a time she continued to serve as a skilled diplomat on behalf of France. But increasingly her energies were occupied with the plight of her own new kingdom, largely under the control of Spain and, in its geographic position, symbolic of the new, ambiguous position she found herself in, as party to the complicated and not always edifying machinations of her husband, her brother, and the king of Spain. From that time on, until Francis died in 1547, Marguerite continued to act as a vitally important political agent for him, although the relationship was sometimes strained—notably by his high-handed treatment of her daughter Jeanne as an instrument, through marriage, of diplomatic policy. In her very last years Marguerite was able to spend a relatively (but only relatively) quiet life in Navarre. After two years of declining health, she died in 1549.

All this might sound like enough for one person, but there was in fact much more to Marguerite's life. In addition to her political and diplomatic activity, she invested enormous, and effective, energies in what today we would call social work. She reformed monasteries and convents; she established hospitals. Her artistic and intellectual patronage was likewise very widespread—in commissioning new works and in gathering under her protection advocates of all sorts of new ideas, sometimes dangerous ones. She never allied herself with the Protestants who broke with the Catholic Church, but she was strongly caught up in several movements that, to conservatives, seemed tarred with the same brush—the evangelical and humanist reform movements of the time—and she associated with suspect people such as Calvin and Rabelais. Like Rabelais, she got into serious trouble with the Sorbonne, the militantly conservative university in Paris that represented everything in the old scholastic intellectual culture that was repellent to both the new reformers and the humanist sponsors of the New Learning. In 1533, the Sorbonne condemned as heretical Marguerite's then-recent devotional poem *The Mirror of the Sinful Soul.* (It is ironic that, at exactly the same time, Thomas More, in many ways one of Marguerite's brothers in spirit, was adhering to the Roman church and thus digging his grave in Henry VIII's newly Protestant England.)

Thus far, a severely abridged account of Marguerite as a public figure has managed almost to avoid mentioning that she was an important writer. She is one of the very few authors to have distinguished themselves in all three of the major media of creative writing—prose fiction, in *The Heptameron;* drama, such as her late allegorical play *The Comedy of Mont-de-Marsan* (1548); and verse, notably her near-epic *Prisons* (of about the same date), concerning the ascent of the soul through the successive prisons of mundane love, ambition, and learning. Her works reveal a mind of considerable versatility, subtlety, tolerance, and complexity—in short, fineness of grain. This last quality is particularly striking, in light of the widespread assumption that immersion in political and other public affairs coarsens the sensibilities and fosters reductionist, simpleminded views. (Plato's Socrates came close to believing as much—another irony, in light of Marguerite's deep devotion to Plato.) Her mind illustrates a quality missing even in some of the best minds: an ability to rise above, or surprisingly invert, some of its own firmest convictions, in the interests of a more comprehensive view of reality. Jules Gelernt, in a book about Marguerite, shows how this operates in, for example, *The Comedy of Mont-de-Marsan.* In the play, the Wise Woman, a character who speaks for Marguerite's own cherished beliefs in the humanist New Learning and enlightened piety, is ultimately overshadowed by another character, the Woman Ravished with Love of God, who exists on a plane of spiritual experience that transcends both learning and piety.

In her last years Marguerite wrote (or so most scholars think) the work that became known, after its posthumous publication, as *The Heptameron.* Only seventy-odd of the projected hundred stories were completed (or have survived). It is modeled, as the Prologue indicates, on Boccaccio's *Decameron,* and in some ways it clearly imitates that work—in the lush meadow setting, in the device of common flight from danger (a flood rather than the plague as in Boccaccio), in the conversational framework surrounding the ten tales told each day, in the recurrent themes (the wickedness of the friars, sexual plotting and trickery, and others), in the occasional bawdiness, and, not least, in the exploration of male-female relationships.

The Heptameron is, however, a very different kind of work, especially in its sustained concern with spiritual and ethical issues. Boccaccio's battle-of-the-sexes motif is much deepened and expanded, and the stakes are raised. (This may explain why Marguerite shapes her cast for a fair fight, with five men and five women instead of Boccaccio's three men and seven women.) The sexual sparring in Boccaccio is usually, by comparison, decorous and flirtatious, and feelings are seldom seriously ruffled. Marguerite's characters, however, often quarrel like undomesticated cats and dogs over the sex-related issues. The range of sensibilities and values is about as wide as it can possibly be. Among the women, Oisille is a model of otherworldliness; her male antithetical opposite is the brutally cynical Saffredent, who—for instance—sees rape as merely one method of seduction among others.

This milieu and atmosphere would seem likelier to produce a shouting match (which, in fact, does occur at times) than to foster searching moral explorations and bring out psychological fine points, and yet these are what *The Heptameron* is all about. One reason is that the author is willing to entertain, and apparently sometimes empathize with, viewpoints that go against the fundamental grain of her temperament. It is clear, for example, that a kind of lofty Platonism (or Neoplatonism) is close to Marguerite's heart; Parlamente, her stand-in, delivers a memorable exposition of it at the end of Story Nineteen. It is also clear that the author, like other Renaissance humanists, connects Platonism with a Christian loftiness of vision, reflected—for example—by Simontaut's citation, in the same episode, of the First Epistle of John. But the spiritual "marriage" of the two lovers in Story Nineteen, with its subdued but lingering flavor of carnality, is likely to have disturbed some readers a little bit at least, and their misgivings are indeed expressed in the later postmortem, not decorously but in terms of the roundest ridicule.

As for the quotation from John, it too reappears, in a less reverent vein, after Story Thirty-six. Among the males, Dagoucin is the most uncompromising spokesman for platonic love (in the modern as well as the classic sense), an attitude for which he has to pay dearly by way of the quite raw, mocking incredulity expressed by certain of his hearers. The author is entirely capable of seeing the comedy in Dagoucin, a man so serenely determined to create a hermetic seal around his uncontaminated love that he would never risk revealing it even to his lady, who thus, for practical purposes, might as well not exist.

The fine grain of Marguerite's mind is reflected by the complexity of her vision, which in turn is reflected by the way in which different sets of values modify and interlock with one another. We get to appreciate this cumulatively, by reading various stories and noting more and more interconnections between matters that at first seem not to have much to do with one another. Take, for example, the very brief Story Fifty-five, about a Spanish widow commissioned to carry out her late husband's dying bequest of the proceeds from the sale of a fine horse. The point of the story might seem a simple one: the widow's amusing cleverness in adhering to the letter of the testator's instructions while also preserving his wealth for herself and her children. The ensuing discussion, however, explicitly raises a number of controversial issues and suggests some others implicitly. One of them is the greed of the Franciscan friars, whom Marguerite also treats in certain of the stories as lustful sexual predators. (P. A. Chilton, in the Introduction to the translation used in this anthology, provides an especially illuminating discussion of this sexual aggression.) The witheringly unfavorable attitude toward the Franciscans was not, in fact, something new in literature; one finds it also in Boccaccio and Chaucer. But in *The Heptameron* the friars are the focus for a whole complex of sociological, moral, and theological issues. For one thing, they stand for the old religious regime that the evangelical and humanist reformers found so benighted. They also stand for the monastic system, with its implicit hostility toward women and low valuation of marriage, which are central concerns in *The Heptameron* and were burning issues with the reformers and humanists, who fairly consistently attacked the enshrinement of the ideal of celibacy. As for deathbed bequests to the religious orders, the issue was not merely venal corruption in the Church but also the theological issue of belief in Purgatory, the concomitant belief in indulgences (remissions of punishment in Purgatory), and the notion that monetary gifts were one form of the "good works" that could earn indulgences. Behind that node of issues looms a still broader issue, the main theological battleground of the Reformation period: salvation by grace versus salvation by works. And even beyond that, at least for Marguerite, lies the problem of translating such theological concerns into a dynamic of love that can light up the heart with spiritual peace without ignoring the needs of a human society. Thus the feminist strands, for example, in Marguerite's work are part of a rich fabric of ideas and speculations. The intensity of the arguments that follow the stories is partly explained by the momentousness of such issues, far deeper-seated ones than those raised by, say, Boccaccio.

The discussions following the stories also have a bearing on the artistry of *The Heptameron*. Some of the stories—including the one about the horse—

are elegantly crafted in themselves, but many of them are not. Some of them simply trail off or are otherwise knocked askew. The key here is to take the ensuing discussion not just as commentary but as integral to the tale. The result is a new psychological complexity, reminding us that life is usually less tidy than invented art and epitomized in the discussion that, as often for Marguerite, is the climax of the narrative, not a mere appendage to it. The assertion made in the Prologue that the stories in *The Heptameron* are to be factual, not invented, may not always be literally true, but it is true at least in the sense that the barrier protecting the purity of literature from the unsettledness of life is often breached, in the interests of an urgent search, among many confusing options, for the most nearly comprehensive truth.

A Note on the Text

The Heptameron was first published some years after Marguerite's death, in printed editions significantly different from one another. Moreover, a large number of surviving manuscripts further complicate the problem of producing an authoritative text. The P. A. Chilton translation used in the present anthology prints certain manuscript variants in square brackets which, in the interests of smoother reading, have been removed in the pages that follow here. Readers interested in these textual discriminations should consult Chilton's volume in the Penguin Classics.

FURTHER READING: One of the most useful general introductions to Marguerite's life and the general tendencies of her mind and work can be found in the opening chapter of Jules Gelernt's *World of Many Loves: The Heptameron of Marguerite de Navarre,* 1966. Samuel Putnam's *Marguerite of Navarre,* 1935, is a clear, accurate account of both life and works. P. A. Chilton's introduction to his translation of the complete *Heptameron,* 1984, lays out the basic critical issues economically and thoughtfully and touches on textual complications and the merits of earlier translations. Brief, stimulating discussions of several facets of Marguerite's work are included in I. D. McFarlane, *A Literary History of France: Renaissance France 1470–1589,* 1974. C. J. Blaisdell, "Marguerite de Navarre and Her Circle," in *Female Scholars: A Tradition of Learned Women Before 1800,* 1980, places Marguerite in the tradition so identified. Three book-length studies in English of *The Heptameron* are Jules Gelernt's book already cited; Marcel Tetel, *Marguerite de Navarre's "Heptameron": Themes, Language, and Structure,* 1973; and Betty J. Davis, *The Storytellers in Marguerite de Navarre's "Heptameron,"* 1978. Gelernt explores the versions of love in the stories and Marguerite's Neoplatonism, Tetel emphasizes figurative language and structure, and Davis looks at the characters in the frame-story and their interrelationships. Another good study of the framing is Glyn P. Norton, "Narrative Function in the *Heptameron* Frame-Story," in *La Nouvelle française à la Renaissance,* ed. Lionello Sozzi, 1981. On the relation to the Boccaccio model, see Donald Stone, "Boccaccio's *Decameron* and the *Heptameron,*" in his *From Tales to Truth: Essays on French Fiction in the Sixteenth Century,* 1973. Recent criticism has tended to concentrate on the feminist themes of the collection. Two good treatments of this subject are Paula Sommers, "Feminine Authority in the *Heptameron:* A Reading of Oysille," in *Modern Language Studies* 13 (1983), 52–59; and Robert W. Bernard, "Feminist Rhetoric for the Renaissance Woman in Marguerite de Navarre's *Heptameron,*" *Chimères* 15 (1982), 73–98. Patricia Francis Cholakian, *Rape and Writing in the Heptameron of Marguerite de Navarre,* 1991, provides a book-length feminist analysis.

THE HEPTAMERON

Translated by P. A. Chilton

The Heptameron is a series of tales told by ten persons of aristocratic birth who, owing to several misadventures, are marooned together at the abbey of Our Lady of Sarrance, in the Pyrenees Mountains in southern France. All of them have been cut off, while returning from the mineral-spring town of Cauterets, by torrential floods. Although they are thrown together mostly by chance, they have known one another for some time.

The sage among the group is Oisille, a pious elderly widow interested in seeing the abbey for its own sake. The others take shelter there out of necessity and a desire to spend their time with friends and acquaintances.

The group includes a subgroup made up of two women named Parlamente and Longarine and three men named Hircan, Dagoucin, and Saffredent. Parlamente and her husband, Hircan, along with young Longarine and her husband, had been traveling together, followed at a discreet distance by Dagoucin and Saffredent, two young devotees of Parlamente and Longarine. (Which man loves which woman is not explicitly stated.) The two married couples, while staying overnight as the unwitting guests of a bandit, became embroiled in a fight between their host and certain of his partners in crime. Dagoucin and Saffredent came to the rescue, but not before Longarine's husband was killed.

Two other young women, Nomerfide and Ennasuite, were driven to shelter while fleeing on horseback from a bear.

The two other men are Geburon, who narrowly escaped from a house where armed attackers had beset him, and Simontaut, who also narrowly escaped with his life, after rashly trying to ford the floodwaters on horseback. Simontaut is secretly devoted to Parlamente. (There is also a hint that Parlamente's husband, Hircan may be in love with an unidentified woman of the party.)

The travelers commission the building of a footbridge over a nearby river but find that the construction will take ten or twelve days. Anticipating boredom, they cast about for a way to pass the time. Oisille suggests scriptural readings and other pious exercises, but most of the travelers feel the need for more secular diversion also. Being informed by Parlamente that the French royal family have wanted a French equivalent of the hundred tales told in Boccaccio's *Decameron,* of which a translation from Italian has recently appeared, the travelers undertake to further the royal project by relating tales themselves, ten each day. Unlike those in Boccaccio, however, these tales are all to be based on actual fact. To tell their stories, the ten ladies and gentlemen assemble each afternoon in the lush grass and ample shade of a beautiful meadow adjoining the abbey.

(The work was completed only through the first seven days; it therefore never became a French Decameron but remained a "Heptameron" or "Work of Seven Days.") [*Editors' headnote.*]

"Since you speak so strongly in favor of women who get suspected wrongly, Longarine," said Hircan, "I choose you to tell us the eighth story, on condition that you don't make us all weep, like Madame Oisille did, with her excessive zeal for stories in praise of virtuous women."

Longarine broke into a hearty laugh, and said: "Since you want me to make you laugh, in my usual fashion, it won't be at the expense of women. Yet I *shall* tell you something to show how easy they are to deceive when they fill their heads with jealous thoughts, and pride themselves on their good sense for wanting to deceive their husbands."

STORY EIGHT

In the county of Alès[1] there was once a man by the name of Bornet, who had married a very decent and respectable woman. He held her honor and reputation very dear, as I am sure all husbands here hold the honor and reputation of *their* wives dear. He wanted her to be faithful to him, but was not so keen on having the rule applied to them both equally. He had become enamoured of his chambermaid, though the only benefit he got from transferring his affections in this way was the sort of pleasure one gets from varying one's diet. He had a neighbor called Sendras, who was of similar station and temperament to himself—he was a tailor and a drummer. These two were such close friends that, with the exception of the wife, there was nothing that they did not share between them. Naturally he told him that he had designs on the chambermaid.

Not only did his friend wholeheartedly approve of this, but did his best to help him, in the hope that he too might get a share in the spoils.

The chambermaid herself refused to have anything to do with him, although he was constantly pestering her, and in the end she went to tell her mistress about it. She told her that she could not stand being badgered by him any longer, and asked permission to go home to her parents. Now the good lady of the house, who was really very much in love with her husband, had often had occasion to suspect him, and was therefore rather pleased to be one up on him, and to be able to show him that she had found out what he was up to. So she said to her maid: "Be nice to him, dear, encourage him a little bit, and then make a date to go to bed with him in my dressing-room. Don't forget to tell me which night he's supposed to be coming, and make sure you don't tell anyone else."

The maid did exactly as her mistress had instructed. As for her master, he was so pleased with himself that he went off to tell his friend about his stroke of luck, whereupon the friend insisted on taking his share afterwards, since he had been in on the business from the beginning. When the appointed time came, off went the master, as had been agreed, to get into bed, as he thought, with his little chambermaid. But his wife, having abandoned her position of authority in order to serve in a more pleasurable one, had taken her maid's place in the bed. When he got in with her, she did not act like a wife, but like a bashful young girl, and he was not in the slightest suspicious. It would be impossible to say which of them enjoyed themselves more—the wife deceiving her husband, or the husband who thought he was deceiving his wife. He stayed in bed with her for some time, not as long as he might have wished (many years of marriage were beginning to tell on him), but as long as he could manage. Then he went out to rejoin his accomplice, and tell him what a good time he had had. The lustiest piece of goods he had ever come across, he declared. His friend who was younger and more active than he was, said: "Remember what you promised?"

"Hurry up, then," replied the master, "in case she gets up, or my wife wants her for something."

[1]A town in the Languedoc region of southern France. The theme of Stories 1–10, told on the first day, is dirty tricks played by women on men and vice versa.

Off he went and climbed into bed with the supposed chambermaid his friend had just failed to recognize as his wife. *She* thought it was her husband again, and did not refuse anything he asked for (I say "asked," but "took" would be nearer the mark, because he did not dare open his mouth). He made a much longer business of it than the husband, to the surprise of the wife, who was not used to these long nights of pleasure. However, she did not complain, and looked forward to what she was planning to say to him in the morning, and the fun she would have teasing him. When dawn came, the man got up, and fondling her as he got out of bed, pulled off a ring she wore on her finger, a ring that her husband had given her at their marriage. Now the women in this part of the world are very superstitious about such things. They have great respect for women who hang on to their wedding rings till the day they die, and if a woman loses her ring, she is dishonored, and is looked upon as having given her faith to another man. But she did not mind him taking it, because she thought it would be sure evidence against her husband of the way she had hoodwinked him.

The husband was waiting outside for his friend, and asked him how he had got on. The man said he shared the husband's opinion, and added that he would have stayed longer, had he not been afraid of getting caught by the daylight. The pair of them then went off to get as much sleep as they could. When morning came, and they were getting dressed together, the husband noticed that his friend had on his finger a ring that was identical to the one he had given his wife on their wedding day. He asked him where he had got it, and when he was told it had come from the chambermaid the night before, he was aghast. He began banging his head against the wall, and shouted: "Oh my God! Have I gone and made myself a cuckold without my wife even knowing about it?"

His friend tried to calm him down. "Perhaps your wife had given the ring to the girl to look after before going to bed?" he suggested. The husband made no reply, but marched straight out and went back to his house.

There he found his wife looking unusually gay and attractive. Had she not saved her chambermaid from staining her conscience, and had she not put her husband to the ultimate test, without any more cost to herself than a night's sleep? Seeing her in such good spirits, the husband thought to himself: "She wouldn't be greeting me so cheerfully if she knew what I'd been up to."

As they chatted, he took hold of her hand and saw that the ring, which normally never left her finger, had disappeared. Horrified, he stammered: "What have you done with your ring?"

She was pleased that he was giving her the opportunity to say what she had to say.

"Oh! You're the most dreadful man I ever met! Who do you think you got it from? You think you got it from the chambermaid, don't you? You think you got it from that girl you're so much in love with, the girl who gets more out of you than I've ever had! The first time you got into bed you were so passionate that I thought you must be about as madly in love with her as it was possible for any man to be! But when you came back the *second* time, after getting up, you were an absolute devil! Completely uncontrolled you were, didn't know when to stop! You miserable man! You must have been blinded by desire to pay such tribute to my body—after all you've had me long enough without showing much appreciation for my figure. So it wasn't because that young girl is so pretty and so shapely that you were enjoying yourself so much. Oh no! You enjoyed it so much because you were seething with some depraved pent-up lust—in short the sin of concupiscence was raging within you, and your senses were dulled as a result. In fact you'd worked yourself up into such a state that I think any old nanny-goat would have done for you, pretty or otherwise! Well, my dear, it's time you mended your ways. It's high time you were content with me for what I am—your own wife and an honest woman, and it's high time that you found *that* just as satisfying as when you thought I was a poor little erring chambermaid. I did what I did in order to save you from your wicked ways, so that when you get old, we can live happily and peacefully together without anything on our consciences. Because if you go on in the way you have been, I'd rather leave you altogether than see you destroying your soul day by day, and at the same time destroying your physical health and squandering everything you have before my very eyes! But if you will acknowledge that you've been in the wrong, and make up your mind to live according to the ways of God and His commandments, then I'll overlook all your past misbehavior, even as I hope God will forgive me *my* ingratitude to Him, and failure to love Him as I ought."

If there was ever a man who was dumbfounded and despairing, it was this poor husband. There was his wife, looking so pretty, and yet so sensible and so chaste, and he had gone and left her for a girl who did not love him. What was worse, he had had the misfortune to have gone and made her do something wicked without her even realizing what was happening. He had gone and let another man share pleasures which, rightly, were his alone to enjoy. He had gone and given himself cuckold's horns and made himself look ridiculous for evermore. But he could see she was already angry enough about the chambermaid, and he did not dare tell her about the other dirty trick he had played. So he promised that he would leave his wicked ways behind him, asked her to forgive him and gave her the ring back. He told his friend not to breathe a word to anybody, but secrets of this sort nearly always end up being proclaimed from the roof-tops, and it was not long before the facts became public knowledge. The husband was branded as a cuckold without his wife having done a single thing to disgrace herself.

* * *

"Ladies, it strikes me that if all the men who offend their wives like that got a punishment like that, then Hircan and Saffredent ought to be feeling a bit nervous."

"Come now, Longarine," said Saffredent, "Hircan and I aren't the only married men here, you know."

"True," she replied, "but you're the only two who'd play a trick like that."

"And just when have you heard of us chasing our wives' maids?" he retorted.

"If the ladies in question were to tell us the facts," Longarine said, "then you'd soon find plenty of maids who'd been dismissed before their payday!"

"Really," intervened Geburon, "a fine one you are! You promise to make us all laugh, and you end up making these two gentlemen annoyed."

"It comes to the same thing," said Longarine. "As long as they don't get their swords out, their getting angry makes it all the more amusing."

"But the fact remains," said Hircan, "that if our wives were to listen to what this lady here has to say, she'd make trouble for every married couple here!"

"I know what I'm saying, and who I'm saying it to," Longarine replied. "Your wives are so good, and they love you so much, that even if you gave them horns like a stag's, they'd still convince themselves, and everybody else, that they were garlands of roses!"

Everyone found this remark highly amusing, even the people it was aimed at, and the subject was brought to a close. Dagoucin, however, who had not yet said a word, could not resist saying: "When a man already has everything he needs in order to be contented, it is very unreasonable of him to go off and seek satisfaction elsewhere. It has often struck me that when people are not satisfied with what they already have, and think they can find something better, then they only make themselves worse off. And they do not get any sympathy, because inconstancy is one thing that is universally condemned."

"But what about people who have not yet found their 'other half'?" asked Simontaut. "Would you still say it was inconstancy if they seek her wherever she may be found?"

"No man can know," replied Dagoucin, "where his other half is to be found, this other half with whom he may find a union so equal that between the parts there is no difference; which being so, a man must hold fast where Love constrains him and, whatever may befall him, he must remain steadfast in heart and will. For if she whom you love is your true likeness, if she is of the same will, then it will be your own self that you love, and not her alone."[2]

"Dagoucin, I think you're adopting a position that is completely wrong," said Hircan. "You make it sound as if we ought to love women without being loved in return."

"What I mean, Hircan, is this. If love is based on a woman's beauty, charm and favors, and if our aim is merely pleasure, ambition or profit, then such love can never last. For if the whole foundation on which our love is based should collapse, then love will fly from us and there will be no love left in us. But I am utterly convinced that if a man loves with no other aim, no other desire, than to love truly, he will abandon his soul in death rather than allow his love to abandon his heart."

"Quite honestly, Dagoucin, I don't think you've ever really been in love," said Simontaut, "because if you had felt the fire of passion, as the rest of us have, you wouldn't have been doing what you've just been doing—describing Plato's republic,[3] which sounds all very fine in writing, but is hardly true to experience."

"If I have loved," he replied, "I love still, and shall love till the day I die. But my love is a perfect love, and I fear lest showing it openly should betray it. So greatly do I fear this, that I shrink to make it known to the lady whose love and friendship I cannot but desire to be equal to my own. I scarcely

[2]The allusion is to the fable related by Aristophanes in the *Symposium* of Plato, the ultimate ancient spokesman for the philosophy of idealism. According to the fable, each person is half of a primordial unified being, divided by the vindictive gods, and can find happiness only by being united with his or her separated soulmate.

[3]In another major dialogue, *The Republic,* Plato envisions the ideal society.

dare think my own thoughts, lest something should be revealed in my eyes, for the longer I conceal the fire of my love, the stronger grows the pleasure in knowing that it is indeed a perfect love."

"Ah, but all the same," said Geburon, "I don't think you'd be sorry if she did return your love!"

"I do not deny it. But even if I were loved as deeply as I myself love, my love could not possibly increase, just as it could not possibly decrease if I were loved less deeply than I love."

At this point, Parlamente, who was suspicious of these flights of fancy, said: "Watch your step, Dagoucin. I've seen plenty of men who've died rather than speak what's in their minds."

"Such men as those," he replied, "I would count happy indeed."

"Indeed," said Saffredent, "and worthy to be placed among the ranks of the Innocents—of whom the Church chants *'Non loquendo, sed moriendo confessi sunt'!*[4] I've heard a lot of talk about these languishing lovers, but I've never seen a single one actually die. I've suffered enough from such torture, but I got over it in the end, and that's why I've always assumed that nobody else ever really dies from it either."

"Ah! Saffredent, the trouble is that you desire your love to be returned," Dagoucin replied, "and men of your opinions never die for love. But I know of many who *have* died, and died for no other cause than that they have loved, and loved perfectly."

* * *

"I think," said Oisille, turning to Hircan, "that you are so fond of speaking ill of women, that you wouldn't have great difficulty in finding something good to say about men. So will you tell us the next story?"

"That's easy," he replied. "Not long ago I was told a tale that was very much to the credit of a certain gentleman. This was a man whose love, long-suffering and loyalty were so praiseworthy that I believe it my duty to prevent them sinking into oblivion."

STORY EIGHTEEN

My story is about a noble lord of excellent family.[1] He was living in one of the important towns in the kingdom of France, and was studying at the schools there. His desire was to attain that knowledge which is the key to honor and virtue among men of worth. At the age of seventeen or eighteen he was so knowledgeable that one would have thought him a shining example, fit to instruct his fellow-students. However, he was also to become a pupil in the School of Love. Now Love is a subtle teacher, and to ensure that his lessons would be heard and taken to heart, he concealed himself behind

[4] From the Collect for the mass on the feast of the Holy Innocents: "not by speaking, but by dying have they confessed." This feast, celebrated on December 28, honors the infants slaughtered by Herod in his attempt to kill the newborn Jesus.

[1] Stories 11–20, told on the second day, do not have a prescribed subject.

the fair eyes and face of a certain lady. She was the most beautiful lady in all the land, and as chance would have it, was in the town at that time for some lawsuit. But before setting about the conquest of the heart of the noble young lord, Love first vanquished the heart of the lady herself, by bringing all his manly perfections before her eyes. For he was indeed so fair of face, so fair of speech, so fair in all his ways that there was not a man in all the land, whatever his station, who could surpass him. Those of you who know how quickly the fire of love spreads when it starts to smoulder in the heart and in the imagination will understand that once Love enters two such perfect subjects, he never stops until he has rendered them obedient to his commands, until indeed he has filled them both so full of his clear light that all their thoughts, all their desires and all their speech are nothing but the blazing forth of his flame. With the timidity of youth, the young lord pursued his desires with the utmost caution. But already the lady was conquered. There was no need of force. Yet Modesty, that persistent companion of ladies, prevented her for a while from showing her feelings. But in the end, the fortress of the heart where Honor dwells was destroyed, and the poor lady gave herself up to that which she had never wished to resist.

In order to test the long-suffering, constancy and love of her servant, she acceded to his demands on one exceedingly difficult condition. If he was able to keep this condition, then she would love him perfectly for evermore. If, however, he were to fail, then he would not possess her for as long as he should live. The condition was this. She would be happy to go to bed with him and to talk with him there. But they were both to keep their nightshirts on, and he was to demand nothing more than her discourse and chaste kisses! The young man, who felt that there was no joy in the world to be compared with that which she was promising him, agreed. Evening came, and the promise was kept. However much she encouraged him, however much he was tempted, he refused to break his word. Purgatory itself could not, he felt, be worse than what he went through that night. Yet so great was his love, so firm was his hope, that he was happy to wait in patience, for he was sure that the eternal love which it had cost him so much to win would in the end be his. So he left her bed without once asking of her anything that would have gone against his promise. But the lady was, I think, more astonished than pleased by his upright behavior, and began to think that either he did not love her as much as he had said, or that he had found her less attractive than he had expected. Completely disregarding his demonstration of honor, chastity, patience and fidelity, she decided to put the young man's love to another test before keeping her own promise. To this end, she asked him to approach one of the girls in her entourage, a girl who was extremely attractive and somewhat younger than herself. The idea was that he should make amorous overtures to this young girl, so that people would think it was because of her that he came to the house so often. The young lord, quite certain that his lady loved him as much as he loved her, carried out to the letter everything she ordered him to do. He forced himself for her sake to pursue her young companion, who, seeing what a handsome, gently spoken young man he was, believed his lies rather than the truth, and promptly fell in love with him, thinking he loved her. When the lady realized things had gone as far as this, she decided at last to permit the young man, who was still pressing her to fulfil her promise, to come to her room at one hour after midnight.

She had, she told him, tried out his love and tested his obedience so thoroughly that it was only right that she should reward his long and patient wait. There can be no doubt about the joy which her loving and devoted servant experienced.

At the appointed hour he went to his lady's room. But she still wanted to test the strength of his love. So before he arrived, she took the young girl on one side, and said to her: "I know that there's a certain young gentleman who's in love with you, and I think you are no less passionately in love with him. Well, I feel so sorry for you both, that I've decided to give you the opportunity to talk on your own together for as long as you like."

The girl was so transported, that she could scarcely conceal the love she felt, and said that she could never refuse such a proposal. Following her mistress's advice, indeed her orders, she went to the appointed bedroom, undressed and lay down on the magnificent bed. The door was left half open, and all the candles lit, so that the girl and all her charms could be clearly seen. Then, pretending to go away, the lady herself hid near the bed in a spot where she could not be seen. It was not long before her poor devoted servant arrived, prompt at the appointed hour and fully expecting to find his beloved waiting for him as promised. In he crept, closed the door behind him, took off his gown and his fur-lined shoes, and went over to the bed, thinking to find there his heart's desire. No sooner did he stretch out his arms to embrace the recumbent figure he took to be his lady, than the poor girl, thinking he was all hers, flung her arms around his neck. The expression in her eyes and the passionate words she murmured would have been enough to put the holiest hermit off his paternosters![2] But prompted by his great love for his lady, the young man recognized both the voice and the face, and jumped out of the bed even faster than he had jumped in, when he realized that this was not the woman for whom he had suffered so long and so deeply!

Angry not only with the girl herself, but also with her mistress, he said: "I shall not be made other than I am either by your wild desires or by the wicked one who put you here! Seek to be an honest woman, for by no act of mine shall your good name be lost!"

Beside himself with rage, he marched out, and for a long time he did not come back to see his lady. However, Love, who never abandons hope, assured the young gentleman that the longer his constancy was tried and tested, the longer and pleasanter would be the enjoyment in the end. For her part, the lady, who had seen and heard everything, was surprised at the depth and constancy of his love, but it pleased her too, and she was anxious to see him again to ask his forgiveness for the pain she had inflicted in testing him. So at the earliest opportunity she addressed him in tones of such gracious tenderness that he not only forgot all his past torments, but even began to think of them with pleasure. For after all, it was through them that his constancy was honored at last, and through them that his lady was convinced of his love. From that hour on there were no more obstacles and no more trials, and from his lady he received all that his heart could desire.

* * *

[2] "Our Fathers"; recitations of the Lord's Prayer.

"Now, Ladies, can you tell me of a woman as constant, as patient and as faithful in love as the man in this story? Anyone who's been through such temptations will find the temptations we are shown in pictures of St. Anthony[3] as nothing by comparison. Anyone who can remain patient and chaste when beautiful women offer not only their beauty and their love, but also time, place and opportunity, will surely be virtuous enough to resist every single devil in Hell!"

"It is a great shame," said Oisille, "that he did not address himself to a woman who had the same resources of virtue as he. We should then have had the most perfect example of pure and perfect love that has ever been heard of."

"Tell me," said Geburon, "which of the two trials do you think was the most difficult for the young man to bear?"

"I think the second," Parlamente said, "because disappointment and resentment are the strongest temptations of all."

Longarine, however, felt that the first trial was the hardest, "since he had to overcome Love as well as overcome himself, in order to keep his promise."

"It is easy for you to talk," said Simontaut, "but those of us who know the truth in such matters ought to say what they think. As far as I'm concerned, he acted like an idiot the first time, and like a madman the second. You see, I think that by keeping his promise he only made his lady suffer as much as, or more than, he himself suffered. The only reason she made him make such a promise in the first place was so that she could make herself look more virtuous than she really was. She knew perfectly well that desperate love can't be held back by orders or oaths or by anything else in the whole world. But she wanted to make her vice look virtuous, and to make it appear that she could be won only by acts of virtue nothing less than heroic. The second time, he showed that he was mad to let the girl go, when she was so obviously in love with him and was certainly worth more than the woman he'd made his promise to. What is more, he had a good excuse, given the bitter disappointment he had just experienced."

Dagoucin objected to this, saying that his opinion was exactly the opposite, and that on the first occasion the young man had shown himself patient, constant and true to his word, while the second occasion showed that in his love he was perfect, true and faithful.

"And how do we know," said Saffredent, "that he wasn't one of those referred to in a certain chapter headed *De frigidis et maleficiatis?*[4] If Hircan had really wanted to sing this man's praises, he should have gone on to tell us how he acquitted himself once he got what he wanted. Then we could judge whether it was his virtue or his impotence that made him so well-behaved!"

"You may be quite sure," said Hircan, "that if he'd told me, I wouldn't have kept it back, any more than I have the rest of the story. But knowing him as well as I do, and knowing what his temperament is like, I shall always take the view that he acted the way he did because of the power of his love rather than because of frigidity or impotence."

[3] Egyptian saint (251–356) and ascetic, the first monk. His sexual temptations during a sojourn in the desert were proverbial and were frequently portrayed by painters.

[4] Latin: "On persons rendered frigid by magic spells," a papal document issued in the thirteenth century.

"Well," Simontaut replied, "if he was the kind of man you say, then he ought to have broken his oath. After all, even if she had got annoyed at a little thing like that, it wouldn't have been too difficult to calm her down again!"

"But perhaps she didn't want him to do it just then?" said Ennasuite.

"So what? Wasn't he strong enough to force her," Saffredent said, "seeing that she led him on?"

"Holy Mary!" exclaimed Nomerfide. "That's a fine way to talk! Do you think that's the way to win the favor of a lady you believe to be chaste and virtuous?"

"In my opinion," said Saffredent, "when a man desires that sort of thing from a woman, the greatest honor he can do her is to take her by force. Because, however humble a girl may be, she will want you to beg and beseech over and over again. There are others who have to be given a lot of presents before you can win them round. Others are so stupid that they let themselves go at the slightest trick or guile, and with them it's merely a matter of finding the right method. But when you're faced with one that's too sensible and good to be tricked, and too well-behaved to be won round by presents and talk, is one not justified in trying every possible means of conquering her? Whenever you hear that a man's taken a woman by force, you can take it from me that the woman in question must have deprived him of all hope of success by other means. You shouldn't think the worse of a man who risks his life like that in order to give vent to his love."

Geburon started to laugh. "I've often seen places besieged and taken by storm," he said, "because neither threats nor offers of money could persuade the defending forces to parley, for they say that once you engage in talks, you're already half defeated!"

"It would seem that all the love-affairs in the world are based on the kind of wicked passion that Simontaut and Saffredent have just been talking about!" said Ennasuite. "But there *are* people who have been in love, and loved long and constantly, without having those motives."

"If you know a story about somebody like that," said Hircan, "then I hand over to you for the next one."

"I do know such a story," she replied, "and shall be only too happy to tell it to you."

STORY NINETEEN

In the time of the Marquis of Mantua, who had married the sister of the Duke of Ferrara,[1] there was in the Duchess's household a lady-in-waiting by the name of Paulina. She was deeply beloved of a certain gentleman in the service of the Marquis. People marvelled at his attachment to Paulina, for, though poor, he was a man of valor, and one would have expected him, in view of his master's great liking for him, to have sought a match with a lady of means. But in his eyes Paulina was worth all the treasure in the world,

[1] This marriage took place in 1490. Mantua and Ferrara are in northern Italy.

and it was she alone whom he desired to marry and make his own. The Marchioness wanted to use her influence to bring about a better marriage for Paulina and did her best to deter her from marrying the gentleman who loved her so much, and often stopped them talking together. They would, she warned them, be the poorest and most miserable wretches in the whole of Italy if their marriage took place. But the gentleman could not be convinced by such arguments as these. For her part Paulina disguised her love as best she could—but dreamt about it none the less. Thus they continued in their love, living in the hope that one day their fortunes would improve.

During this time war broke out, and the gentleman was taken prisoner along with a Frenchman, who had left his love at home in France, just as he had left his in Italy. Finding that they were companions in the same misfortune, the two men began to tell one another their secrets. The Frenchman confessed that his heart too was captive, though he did not name its captor. He knew already that his comrade was in love with Paulina, for he too was in the service of the Marquis, and he urged him, as a friend concerned for his interests and well-being, to abandon this infatuation. The Italian gentleman of course swore that it was not within his power to do so. He said that if the Marchioness did not let him marry his beloved in recompense for his sufferings in captivity and all his other services, then he would become a Franciscan friar and serve no other master than God. His comrade could not believe this, for, apart from his devotion to Paulina, the Italian gentleman did not seem to him to show the slightest sign of monastic piety. Nine months later the Frenchman was set free, and succeeded in obtaining the subsequent release of his comrade, who then immediately approached the Marquis and Marchioness and pursued the matter of his marriage to Paulina for all he was worth. But he had no success. They constantly reminded him that if he and Paulina were to marry they would have to live in poverty. Moreover, neither his family nor hers were in favor of the match, and they forbade him to speak to her in the hope that his infatuation would vanish if he was deprived of all means of meeting her. He realized that he had no alternative but to obey. So he asked the Marchioness if he might say farewell to Paulina, promising that he would never thereafter speak to her again. Permission was granted, and he immediately went to Paulina and began the following speech:

"I can see, Paulina, that both Heaven and earth are against us and desire not only that we should not marry, but that we should not even see one another and talk together. The orders of our master and our mistress are harsh indeed. Well might they boast that by uttering one word they have wounded two hearts, two hearts in two bodies that cannot now but languish unto death, and thus do our cruel master and our cruel mistress show that neither Love nor Pity ever entered their breasts. Their wish, I know, is that we should make rich marriages elsewhere, for they do not know that true riches are to be found in happiness alone. So badly have they treated me, so much grief have they caused me, it is impossible that I should any more do them service with a cheerful heart. If I had not mentioned marriage, I believe they are not so scrupulous that they would have prevented me meeting and talking with you. But I would sooner die than demean my love and, after having loved you with a love that is noble and good, seek to have that which I would defend against all others. Therefore, since to continue to be able to see you would be a penance too hard to bear, and since not to see you would fill my heart, which can never stay empty, with a despair that would bring me to a miserable end, I have resolved, and my resolve has long been firm, that I shall enter the religious life. It is not that I do not know well enough that all men can be saved, whatever their condition, but my wish is to have leisure to contemplate the divine Goodness, who will I hope take pity on my youthful faults and change my heart, that I may come to love spiritual things as I have loved those which are temporal. If God grants me this grace, it shall be my continual occupation to pray for you. And I beg you, in the name of this true and faithful love that is ours, to remember me in your devotions and to pray to Our Lord that He will give me as much constancy when I cease to see you as He gave me contentment when I was able to look upon you. My whole life I have lived in the hope that one day I would through marriage to you have that which honor and conscience allow, but now that I give up that hope, now that I can never expect that you will treat me as a wife treats a husband, I beseech you that you treat me as a brother, and permit me to kiss you."

Perceiving how deeply he was suffering, and yet how honorably even in the midst of such despair he contented himself with such a modest request, poor Paulina, who had always been severe, answered nothing, but threw her arms about his neck, weeping bitterly. So violent were her tears, that her voice, her faculty of speech and all her strength left her, and she fell into a faint in his arms. He, filled as he was with love and sorrow, was so overcome that he too fell in a faint. One of Paulina's companions, seeing them both collapse on the ground, called for help, and they were given medicaments which revived them.

When Paulina realized that she had revealed the strength of her feelings, she was overcome with shame, for she had always sought to disguise her love. But she was able to excuse herself on the grounds that she had been overwhelmed by compassion for the gentleman's plight. He, unable to bear the pain of uttering his final adieu, hastily left the scene, his face set, as he fought back the emotion that welled in his heart. No sooner had he returned home than he collapsed on his bed, a lifeless corpse. Throughout that night he lamented aloud, and his cries were so heart-rending that his servants thought he must have lost parents, friends and everything he had. The next day he commended himself to Our Lord, and shared out among his servants what little he possessed, taking only a small sum of money for himself. Then, forbidding anyone to follow him, he wended his way alone to the convent of the Observant Friars,[2] where, in the firm resolve never again to leave those walls, he requested the friar's habit.[3] The Superior, who had seen him in the past, thought at first that he must be dreaming or that it must be some sort of a joke. Indeed there could hardly have been a man in the whole land who was less endowed with the qualities and gifts required of a friar, for his gifts were the solid virtues of a gentleman of honor. But once the good father had heard the words he had to speak, once he had seen the tears pouring in torrents down his face, though he did not know their cause, he had compassion on him and took him in. It was not long afterwards that he acknowledged the gentleman's perseverance and granted him the habit, which the gentleman received with due devotion.

[2]A reformed branch of the Franciscan order.

[3]The robe worn as the uniform of the order.

When the Marquis and Marchioness heard of this, they found it so strange that they could scarcely believe it. Paulina, desiring to show that she was not in any way subject to the dictates of love, covered up as best she was able the sorrow she felt at the gentleman's departure. So complete was her dissimulation that all those around her said that she had at last forgotten the feelings she had once had for her faithful and devoted servant. Five or six months passed by, and still she revealed nothing. One day during this time a monk visited her and showed her a song that had been composed by her faithful servant shortly after he had taken the habit. The tune was Italian and is quite well-known, but I have translated the words as closely as possible. They go like this:

What will she say,
My Lady, pray,
What will she do, when her fair eyes
See me thus dressed in monkish guise?

Dear one, my own,
Sweet one alone,
Long speechless, wond'ring will she be,
Troubled and torn
Lady forlorn.
Strange will it seem, then presently
Her thoughts they will begin to dwell
On convent close and holy cell,
There to reside, eternally.
What will she say, etc.

What will they do,
Who from us two
Our love and joy did cause to go,
Seeing that love
Howe'er they strove
They yet more perfect caused to grow?
When they do look into our heart
They surely will repent their part
And bitter tears will surely flow.
What will she say, etc.

And if they say,
Oh come away!
And seek our souls so to divert,
Then you and I
Shall say, we'll die!
Far rather that than ever part,
For since we must their harshness bear,
We two do now the long robe wear
That we shall wear perpetually.
What will she say, etc.

And if again
With marriage then
They seek our souls to taunt and tempt,
While they relate
That pleasant state
And how we should be thus content,
Our soul, we'll say, is at God's side,
His holy spouse, His heavenly bride,
So shall it be, eternally.
What will she say, etc.

O love so great,
That through this gate
I have perforce for sorrow passed,
Ah! in this place
Grant me the grace
Without regret to pray and fast,
For this our love, our mutual love,
Shall rise so high, and dwell above
That God will be well pleased at last.
What will she say, etc.

Then put behind
The joys that bind
In iron bonds so dire and fell!
Quit worldly fame
That leads in shame
Black souls through pride to depths of Hell!
Let us shun lust and vanity,
And take that love which in mercy
Lord Jesus gives, with Him to dwell.
What will she say, etc.

Come then away,
Make no delay,
And with your best beloved go,
Fear not, I pray,
The habit gray,
Nor yet to flee this world below.
For with that love that's live and strong
From ashes must arise ere long
The phoenix true, enduringly.[4]
What will she say, etc.

Just as on earth
Our love had birth,
Pure and perfect, noble, rare,

[4] In myth, the phoenix was a single beautiful bird that was consumed in fire after living five hundred years in the desert but rose again to life from its own ashes.

It may appear,
Hidden here
In cloistered cell, beyond compare.
For loyal love that's true and sure
And endlessly shall e'er endure
Must lead to heav'n, eventually.
What will she say, etc.

She was sitting in a chapel as she read the song through, and when she had finished she wept bitterly, sprinkling the paper with the tears as they fell. Had it not been for her anxiety to avoid showing herself more moved than was becoming, she would even at that very moment have transported herself to some hermitage and shut herself away from all living creatures for evermore. But imbued as she was with the virtue of prudence, she was constrained to disguise her feelings for some little time longer. In her heart she was resolved to leave the world for ever, but in her outward appearance it was the very opposite she showed, for when in company she wore an expression that revealed nothing of her true self. For five or six months more she kept her intentions secret, appearing to the world gayer and happier even than she had used to be.

Then, one day, she went with her mistress to the Observant convent to hear high mass. As the priest, deacon and subdeacon came out of the sacristy[5] and made their way to the high altar, she beheld her poor suitor, who had still not completed his one year of novitiate.[6] He was serving as acolyte[7] and walked with eyes bent to the ground, bearing in his hands the altarcruets[8] covered in their white silk cloth. When she saw him attired thus in his vestments, his looks enhanced rather than diminished, she was so overcome with emotion that she made herself cough in order to cover up the color that had risen to her cheeks. Her poor servant could not fail to recognize the sound of her voice, a sound better known to him by far than the cloister bell. He dared not turn his head, yet as he passed by her, he could not prevent his eyes from turning in the direction that they had so long been accustomed to take. As he gazed sorrowfully upon her, he was so overwhelmed by the fire he believed almost extinct that in his desire to conceal it more than was in his power he fell to the ground at her feet. Fear lest the true cause be known led him to say that he had fallen over a broken pavingstone. But when Paulina realized that his change of habit could not change his heart, and that it was so long since he had entered the monastery that everyone would think she had forgotten him, she decided to carry out her long resolve. It was her desire that at the last their love should bring them together, that they should be alike in habit, condition and manner of life, just as at the beginning they had lived under the same roof, under the same master and under the same mistress. She had already more than four months previously made all the arrangements necessary for her entry into a convent, and one

[5]The deacon and subdeacon were the priest's assistants in celebrating mass. The sacristy was the room where the priest's vestments and the sacred vessels were stored.

[6]The trial period before becoming a full member of the order.

[7]Altar boy.

[8]The vessels containing the wine, water, and oil used by the priest in the mass.

morning she asked the Marchioness for permission to go and hear mass at the convent of Saint Clare.[9] Permission was granted, although the Marchioness was ignorant of the true reason for the request. As Paulina went past the Franciscan house, she stopped and asked the Father Superior to send her devoted servant, who, she said, was a relative, to speak to her. They met in a quiet chapel, and she addressed him thus:

"If my honor had allowed me to dare to enter the cloister as soon as you did, I should not have waited till now. But I have waited patiently, and now that my waiting has thwarted those who prefer to think ill of others than to think well, I am resolved to adopt the same condition of life and the same robes as you have adopted. I do not ask what people will say. For if your chosen way has brought you joy, I shall have my part therein. If it has brought you suffering, I have no wish to be spared. Whatever path you tread to Paradise, I wish to follow in your steps. For I believe that He who alone is worthy to be called true and perfect Love has drawn us to His service through a love that is reasonable and good, a love that through His Holy Spirit He will turn wholly unto Himself. And I beg you that we may put away the flesh of the old Adam that perisheth, and accept and put on that of Jesus Christ our Spouse."

Paulina's devoted servant, now a servant of God, was so filled with joy when he heard her express this sacred wish that, weeping tears of happiness, he strove to strengthen her resolve. Since he could have nothing of her but the enjoyment of the words she spoke, he held his lot happy indeed, for henceforth he would always be able to hear her, and her words would be such that both he and she would profit by them, living as they would in one love, one heart and one spirit, drawn and guided by the goodness of God. And he prayed that God would hold them in His hand, for in His hands no man can perish. As he spoke, he shed tears of love and joy. Then he bent to kiss her hand, but Paulina lowered her face to his, and in true charity they exchanged the holy kiss of love. Her soul thus filled with happiness, Paulina departed and went to the sister convent of Saint Clare, where after being received she took the veil.

Later she had the news conveyed to the Marchioness, who was so surprised she could not believe it, and went the very next day to try to make her change her mind. But Paulina's reply was firm. The Marchioness might have the power to remove her fleshly husband, the one in the world whom she had loved above all others, but that being so, she should now be satisfied and not seek to separate her from Him who was immortal and invisible, for neither the Marchioness nor any creature on earth had such power. Seeing that Paulina was resolute, the Marchioness kissed her, and filled with sorrow and regret, went on her way. From that time on Paulina and her servant lived devout and holy lives in their Observant houses. So devout and so holy were they, one cannot doubt that He whose law has its end in charity would tell them at their lives' end, even as He told Mary Magdalen, that their sins were forgiven, for they had loved much,[10] and that He would transport them in peace to the place whose recompenses surpass all human merits.

* * *

[9] St. Clare (1193–1253) founded the order of Franciscan nuns known as the Poor Clares.
[10] See Luke 7:47. Mary Magdalen was often interpreted to be a reformed harlot.

"Now you can't deny, Ladies, that the man's love was clearly the stronger. But it was so well repaid, that I only wish that everybody who fell in love had the same recompense."

"If that were the case," said Hircan, "there'd be more self-declared fools around than ever!"

"Do you call it folly if one loves with an honorable love in one's youth, and then converts this love entirely unto God?" asked Oisille.

"If melancholy and despair deserve praise," he replied laughing, "then Paulina and her devoted servant certainly deserve praise!"

"Yet God has many ways of drawing us to Him," said Geburon, "ways whose beginnings may seem bad, but whose end is good."

"Furthermore," said Parlamente, "I hold the view that no man will ever perfectly love God, unless he has perfectly loved some creature in this world."

"What do you mean by perfectly loved?" said Saffredent. "Is a perfect lover for you one of those paralytic individuals who adore their ladies from afar and never dare to bring their desires out into the open?"

"Those whom I call perfect lovers," replied Parlamente, "are those who seek in what they love some perfection, whether it be beauty, goodness or grace, those whose constant goal is virtue and whose hearts are so lofty and so pure that they would die rather than make their goal that which is low and condemned by honor and conscience. For the soul, which was created solely that it might return to its Sovereign Good, ceaselessly desires to achieve this end while it is still within the body. But the senses, by means of which the soul is able to have intelligence of its Sovereign Good, are dim and carnal because of the sins of our forefather Adam and consequently can reveal to the soul only those things which are visible and have some nearer approximation to perfection. The soul runs after these things, vainly thinking that in some external beauty, in some visible grace and in the moral virtues it will find the sovereign beauty, the sovereign grace and the sovereign virtue. But once the soul has searched out these things and tried and tested them, once it has failed to find in them Him whom it loves, it passes beyond. In the same way children, when they are small, like dolls and all manner of little things that are attractive to the eye and think that the pebbles they collect will make them rich; but then, as they grow up, the dolls they love are living people and the things they collect are the necessities of human life. Then, when they learn through experience that in earthly and transitory things there is neither perfection nor felicity, they desire to seek the source and maker of these things. Yet, if God does not open the eyes of faith, they will be in danger of leaving ignorance behind only to become infidel philosophers. For only faith can reveal and make the soul receive that Good which carnal and animal man cannot understand."

"Do you not see," said Longarine, "that uncultivated ground is desirable, although it bears nothing but useless trees and grasses, because it offers the hope that one day, when it is sown, it will bring forth good fruit? In the same way, if the heart of man feels no love for visible things, it will never attain the love of God when His word is sown therein. For the earth of his heart is sterile, cold and damned."

"So that's why most of your doctors of theology aren't spiritual doctors!" said Saffredent. "It's because all they'll ever like is good wine and ugly, sluttish chambermaids. They never try out what it's like to love ladies who are more refined!"

"If I could speak Latin properly," said Simontaut, "I'd quote St. John to you. He says 'he who loves not his brother whom he has seen, how can he love God whom he cannot see?'[11] For it is through things visible that one is drawn to the love of things invisible."

"But who is the man who is so perfect?" asked Ennasuite. *"Quis est ille, et laudabimus eum?"*[12]

To this Dagoucin replied: "There *are* men," he said, "who love so deeply and so perfectly that they would rather die than feel any desire that was contrary to the honor and conscience of their ladies, and yet they would not wish their ladies or anyone else to be aware of their feelings."

"Men like that," said Saffredent, "are chameleons—they live on nothing but air! The fact is that there's no such thing as a man who doesn't want to declare his love and know it's returned. What is more, if it *isn't* returned, I don't think there was ever a love fever that wasn't cured instantaneously. I've seen miracles enough to prove it!"

* * *

"But [said Parlamente] I don't think that these days there is a single man alive who is genuinely good with regard to ladies, and who can be trusted with a lady's honor and conscience. Women who believe it is otherwise, and accordingly act in complete confidence, end up by being deceived! They enter into such liaisons by way of God, and often get out of them by way of the Devil. I know many women who, under the guise of talking about God, embarked on a liaison which they later wanted to break but couldn't, because they were caught up in their own cloak of respectability. You see, vicious love disintegrates of its own accord, and is unable to survive in a heart that is pure. But 'virtuous' love has such subtle bonds that one gets caught before one notices them."

"From what you say," said Ennasuite, "no woman would ever want to be in love with a man. But your law is so harsh that it cannot endure."

"I know," said Parlamente, "but in spite of that, I still think it desirable that every woman should be content with her own husband, as I am with mine!"

Ennasuite felt that these words were aimed at her and colored: "I don't think you should assume the rest of us are any different at heart from yourself," she said, "unless you regard yourself as more perfect than we are."

"Well," said Parlamente, "so as not to get into an argument, let's see who Hircan will pick to speak next."

"I choose Ennasuite," he said, "to make up for what my wife has said."

"Well, since it's my turn," said Ennasuite, "I shall spare neither men nor women, in order to make everything equal. And seeing that you can't bring yourselves to admit that men can be good and virtuous, I'll take up the thread of the last story, and tell you one that is very similar."

[11] First Epistle of John 4:20.
[12] Latin: "Who is he, and we will praise him?"

STORY THIRTY-SIX

It is about a man who was president of the Parlement of Grenoble[1]—a man whose name I can't reveal, although I can tell you he wasn't a Frenchman. He was married to a very beautiful woman, and they lived a happy and harmonious life together. However, the President was getting on in years, and the wife began an affair with a young clerk who was called Nicolas. Every morning, when her husband went off to the Palais de Justice,[2] Nicolas would go to her bedroom to take his place. This was noticed by one of the President's servants, a man who had been in his household for thirty years, and who, being loyal to his master, could not do otherwise than tell him. The President was a prudent man, and was not prepared to believe the story without further evidence. He said that the servant was merely trying to sow discord between his wife and himself. If it was true, he said, then he ought to be able to show him the living proof. If he could not do so, then he would conclude that the man had been lying in order to destroy the love which he and his wife had for one another. The servant assured him that he should see with his own eyes what he had described.

One morning, as soon as the President had left for the courts and Nicolas had gone into the bedroom, the servant sent one of his fellow-servants to tell the master to come, while he stayed by the door to make sure Nicolas did not leave. When the President saw the servant give him the signal, he pretended he was feeling unwell, left the court, and hurried back home, where he found his other faithful old servant by the bedroom door assuring him that Nicolas was inside and that he had indeed only just gone in.

"Do not move from here," said the President. "As you know, there is no way in or out except through the small private room to which I alone have the key."

In went the President and found his wife and Nicolas in bed together. Nicolas, who had nothing on but his shirt, threw himself at the President's feet, begging forgiveness, while the wife started to weep.

"Your misdemeanor is a serious one, as you well know," said the President to his wife. "However, I do not wish to see my household dishonored or the daughters I have had by you disadvantaged. Therefore, I order you to cry no more and to listen to what I mean to do. And you, Nicolas, hide in my private room and make no noise."

Then he opened the door, called his old servant, and said:

"Did you not tell me that you would show me Nicolas and my wife in bed together? I came here on the strength of your word and might have killed my poor wife. I have found nothing to bear out what you have told me. I have looked all over the room and there is no one here, as I now desire to demonstrate to you."

[1] The Court of Justice of Grenoble, a city in southeastern France. The President, in this story, is modeled on a certain Geoffroy Carles, a northern Italian, who died in 1516. (His method of disposing of his wife was somewhat different, however, from what the story relates.) The theme of Stories 31–40, told on the fourth day, is the virtuous patience of wives in cementing their marriages and the prudence of men in preserving the honor of their houses.

[2] The law court building.

So saying, he made the servant look under the beds and everywhere else in the room. When he found nothing, the old man was amazed, and said to his master: "The Devil must have carried him off! I saw him come in, and he didn't come out through the door—yet I can see that he is not here!"

Then his master replied: "You are a miserable servant to try to sow discord between my wife and myself. Therefore I give you leave to depart. For the services that you have rendered I shall pay what I owe you and more. But leave quickly and take care not to be found in this town when twenty-four hours have passed!"

The President gave him five or six years' wages in advance, and knowing how loyal he was, said that he hoped to reward him further. So the servant went off in tears, and the President brought Nicolas out of his hiding-place. After telling his wife and her lover what he thought of their wicked behavior, he forbade them to give any hint of it to anyone. He then instructed his wife to dress more elegantly than usual and to take part in all the social gatherings, dances and festivities. He ordered Nicolas too to make merry more than before, but added that the moment he whispered in his ear the words "Leave this place!" he should take care to be out of town within three hours. So saying, he returned to the Palais de Justice without the slightest hint that anything had happened.

For the next fortnight he set about entertaining his friends and neighbors—something he had not at all been in the habit of doing. After the banquets which he gave, there were musicians with drums for the ladies to dance to. On one occasion he noticed that his wife wasn't dancing, and told Nicolas to be her partner. Nicolas, thinking the President had forgotten what had happened, danced with her quite gaily. But after the dance was over, the President, on the pretext of giving him some instructions about domestic duties, whispered into Nicolas's ear: "Leave this place and never return!"

Now Nicolas was sorry indeed to leave his lady, but none the less glad to escape with his life. The President impressed upon all his relatives, friends and neighbors how much he loved his wife. Then, one fine day in the month of May, he went into his garden and picked some herbs for a salad. After eating it, his wife did not live more than twenty-four hours, and the grief that the President showed was so great that nobody suspected that he was the agent of her death. And so he avenged himself on his enemy and saved the honor of his house.

* * *

"It is not my wish, Ladies, to praise the President's conscience, but rather to portray a woman's laxity, and the great patience and prudence of a man. And do not take offense, Ladies, I beg you, because the truth sometimes speaks just as much against you as against men. Both men and women have their share of vice as well as of virtue."

"If all those women who've had affairs with their domestics," said Parlamente, "were obliged to eat salads like that one, then I know a few who wouldn't be quite so fond of their gardens as they are, but would pull up all their herbs to avoid the ones that restore the honor of families by taking the lives of wanton mothers!"

Hircan, who guessed full well why she said this, replied angrily, "A woman of honor ought never to accuse another of doing things she herself would never do!"

"Knowing something is not the same as making foolish accusations," said Parlamente. "The fact remains that this poor woman paid a penalty which not a few deserve. And I think that the husband, considering that he was intent on revenge, conducted himself with remarkable prudence and good sense."

"And also with great malice," said Longarine, "as well as vindictiveness that was both protracted and cruel—which shows that he had neither God nor conscience in mind."

"And what would you have wanted him to do, then," asked Hircan, "to avenge himself for the worst outrage a woman can perpetrate against a man?"

"I would rather," she said, "that he had killed her out of anger, for the learned doctors say that such a sin is remissible,[3] because the first movements of the soul are not within man's powers. So if he had acted out of anger he might have received forgiveness."

"Yes," said Geburon, "but his daughters and his descendants would have borne the stigma for ever."

"He shouldn't have killed her," said Longarine, "for once rage had subsided, she could have lived with him as an honorable woman and the whole thing would have been forgotten."

"Do you really think," said Saffredent, "that he had really calmed down, just because he had managed to conceal his anger? I think that the day he made the salad he was just as angry as at first, because there are people whose first movements never subside till their passion is put into effect. And I'm glad to say the theologians regard this kind of sin as readily pardonable. I share their view on this."

"One needs to watch one's words with people as dangerous as you," said Parlamente, "but what I said was meant to apply to cases where the passion is so great that it suddenly overwhelms the senses, and does so to such an extent that reason cannot operate."

"Taking that point further," said Saffredent, "I would argue that a man who is deeply in love does not commit a sin, or only commits a venial sin, whatever he does. Because I'm certain that if he is in the grip of perfect love, he will not hear the voice of reason, either in his heart or in his understanding. And, if we're truthful about it, there's not one among us who's not experienced this wild passion, which, I believe, is readily pardonable. What is more, I believe that God is not even angered by sin of this kind, since it is one step in the ascend to perfect love of Him, to which one cannot ascend without passing up the ladder of worldly love. For St John says: 'How shall you love God, whom you see not, unless you love him whom you see?'"[4]

"There is not a single text in Holy Scripture, however beautiful," Oisille said, "that you would not turn to your own ends. But take care lest, like the

[3] Forgivable. The "doctors" are theologians.

[4] First Epistle of John 4:20. Compare the quotation of this text in the discussion following Story Nineteen.

spider, you turn wholesome meat into poison. Be you assured that it is indeed dangerous to draw on Scripture out of place and without necessity."

"Do you call telling the truth 'out of place' and 'without necessity'?" said Saffredent. "Do you mean to say, then, that when we're talking to you unbelieving ladies and call God to our aid, do you mean that we're taking His name in vain? But if there is any sin in *that,* it's you who should take the blame—because it's *your* unbelief that obliges us to look for all the oaths we can possibly think of. And even then we can't kindle the fire of charity in your icy hearts!"

"That just shows," said Longarine, "that you're all liars—for the truth is so mighty that we could do no other than believe you, were truth in the words you spoke. But the danger is that the daughters of Eve are too ready to believe this serpent."

"I can see, Parlamente, that women are invincible," replied Saffredent. "So I shall keep quiet, to see who Ennasuite will choose to speak next."

* * *

"You make me laugh when you mention conscience," said Simontaut. "Conscience is something I would rather a woman never troubled herself about."

"It would serve you right," said Nomerfide, "to have a wife like the one who, after her husband's death, turned out to be more concerned about his cash than his conscience."

"Then will you tell us the story," asked Saffredent, "if I invite you to be the next speaker?"

"I hadn't intended to tell such a short story," replied Nomerfide, "but since it is to the point, I will do so."

STORY FIFTY-FIVE

In the town of Saragossa[1] there was a rich merchant. Seeing that his death was near, and that he could not take his wealth with him—wealth which perhaps he had not acquired altogether honestly—he thought that he might make some amends for his sins by making some little donation or other to God. As if God grants his grace in return for money! Anyway, he made arrangements regarding his house, and gave instructions that a fine Spanish horse of his should be sold, and the proceeds distributed to the poor mendicants.[2] It was his wife whom he requested to carry out these instructions as soon as possible after his death. No sooner was the burial over and the first few tears shed, than the wife, who to say the least was no more stupid than Spanish women in general, approached her servant, who had also heard her husband's wishes.

[1]A city in northeastern Spain. Stories 51–60, told on the sixth day, concern deceptions motivated by greed, hatred, and vengeance.

[2]Beggars soliciting alms.

"I think I've lost enough," said she, "in losing my husband whom I loved so dearly, without losing his property as well. Not that I want to disobey his instructions. In fact, I want to carry out his wishes even better than he intended. You see, the poor man was so taken in by those greedy priests. He thought he would make a sacrifice to God after his death by giving away a sum of money, not a single écu[3] of which he would have given away during his lifetime, however great the need, as you know. So I've made up my mind that we shall do what he instructed us to do after his death—indeed we shall do better, and do what he *would* have done himself, had he lived a fortnight longer. Only not a soul must hear of it!"

The servant gave his word, and she went on: "You will go and sell his horse, and when they ask you how much you want, you will say one ducat.[4] But I also have an excellent cat that I want to sell, and you will sell it at the same time, for ninety-nine ducats. Together the horse and the cat will fetch a hundred ducats, which is what my husband wanted for the horse alone."

So the servant promptly went off to do as his mistress requested. As he was leading the horse across the square, carrying the cat in his arms, he was approached by a certain nobleman who had seen the horse before and was interested in acquiring it. Having asked the price, the nobleman received the answer: "One ducat!"

"I should be obliged if you would be serious," said the man.

"I assure you, Monsieur, that the price is one ducat. You have to buy the cat with it, of course. I can't let the cat go for less than ninety-nine ducats!"

The nobleman thought this was a fair enough bargain. On the spot he paid one ducat for the horse, and ninety-nine for the cat, as requested, and led his purchases away. The servant took the money back to his mistress, who was extremely pleased, and lost no time in giving away the proceeds from the sale of the horse to the poor mendicants. As for the rest, that went to provide for the wants of herself and her children.

* * *

"Well, what do you think of her? Wasn't she wiser than her husband, and wasn't she just as much concerned about his conscience as she was about doing well for her family?"

"I think she loved her husband," said Parlamente, "but realized that most men's minds wander when they're on their deathbeds, and knowing what his real intention was, she wanted to interpret his wishes for the benefit of their children, and I think it was very wise of her to do so."

"What!" exclaimed Geburon. "Do you not think it a grave error to fail to execute the last will and testament of deceased friends?"

"Indeed I do!" replied Parlamente. "Provided the testator is sound of mind and not deranged."

"Do you call it deranged," replied Geburon, "to give away one's goods to the Church and to the poor mendicants?"

"I do not call it deranged," she replied, "if a man distributes to the poor that which God has placed within his power. But to give away as alms what

[3]A coin worth three francs.
[4]A gold coin.

belongs to other people—I do not think that shows great wisdom. It's all too common to see the world's greatest usurers putting up ornate and impressive chapels, in the hope of appeasing God for hundreds of thousands of ducats' worth of sheer robbery by spending ten thousand ducats on a building! As if God didn't know how to count!"

"Indeed, I am frequently astonished," said Oisille, "that they presume to be able to appease God by means of the very things, which, when He came to earth, He condemned—things such as fine buildings, gilded ornaments, decorations and paintings. But, if they had rightly understood what God has said of human offerings in a certain passage—that 'the sacrifice of God is a troubled spirit: a broken and contrite heart, O God, shalt thou not despise'—and again, in another passage, what Saint Paul has said—that 'ye are the temple of the living God, in which He will dwell'—if they had rightly heard these words, I say, they would have taken pains to adorn their conscience while they were yet alive.[5] They would not have waited till a time when man can do neither good nor evil. Nor would they have done what is even worse and placed upon those who remain the burden of dispensing their alms to those upon whom, during their lifetime, they did not even deign to look. But He who reads men's hearts will not be deceived, and He will judge them not only according to their works, but according to the faith and charity that they have shown towards Him."

"Why is it, then," said Geburon, "that the Franciscans and Mendicants[6] talk of nothing else when a man's dying but of how we ought to make bequests to their monasteries, with the assurance that they will send us to Paradise whether we want or not?"

"What, Geburon!" broke in Hircan. "Have you forgotten your story about the Franciscans, that you're asking how men like that can possibly lie? I'll tell you, as far as I'm concerned, there's no one on this earth tells lies like they do. It may be that those who speak for the good of their community as a whole aren't to be criticized; but there are some who forget their vow of poverty in order to satisfy their own greed."

Michel de Montaigne

(1533–1592)

"I have no more made my book than my book has made me," Michel de Montaigne wrote, "'tis a book consubstantial with the author, of a peculiar design, a member of my life, and whose business is not designed for others, as that of all other books is." The book is his *Essays,* and perhaps no other work has ever coincided so precisely with the personality of its author, who was an extraordinarily complex, attractive, and in some ways baffling man.

Montaigne was born in 1533, the son of Pierre Eyquem, a wealthy merchant and mayor of Bordeaux. (Montaigne later discarded the name Eyquem and took instead the name of the family estate, the château de Montaigne

[5] The biblical quotations are from Psalms 51:17 and 2 Corinthians 6:16.
[6] Religious orders of begging friars.

in Périgord, in southwestern France.) Montaigne's father was deeply impressed with Renaissance ideas, and he attempted to give his son an experimental education that would fit him for the spirit of the new age. He sent his son to be nursed by a peasant woman in a village on his estate, so that the young Montaigne would develop a love and respect for common people. A Latin tutor came from Germany to oversee his first attempts at speech, to keep him from hearing French until he had mastered Latin, and thus to make Latin his native tongue.

When he was six, Montaigne was sent to school at the famous Collège de Guienne in Bordeaux, where he studied under a number of learned men destined to become key figures in Renaissance thought. After he had completed his course at Bordeaux, he went on to the study of law, probably at Toulouse, home of one of the famous law schools of France. When he was twenty-one, he became a member of a court and, three years later, a member of the Parlement of Bordeaux, where he was one of sixty magistrates whose duty it was to enforce the king's law. In his function as magistrate, Montaigne was an observer of, and sometimes a participant in, the religious conflicts between Catholics and Protestant Huguenots and in the brutal suppression of Huguenot "heretics." Here he seems to have developed the strong distaste for cruelty and brutal punishments that appears frequently in the *Essays*. The other notable influence upon Montaigne during these years was an intense friendship with another young member of the Parlement, Étienne de la Boétie, which lasted six years and ended only with the early death of La Boétie. La Boétie was a Humanist and a fine scholar who translated Xenophon and Plutarch and wrote poetry in both Latin and French.

In 1570, Montaigne resigned from the Parlement of Bordeaux and retired to his estate, "to the bosom of the learned Virgins" (the Muses), as he put it. For the rest of his life, his chief employment was the writing of his *Essays*, though there were many interruptions and temporary returns to active life: a year and a half of traveling in 1580–1581, two terms as mayor of Bordeaux (during which the plague killed almost a third of the population of that city), and a period of exile from his château during the height of the plague and the Wars of Religion. The first two volumes of his *Essays* were published in 1580; in 1586–1588, he thoroughly revised and expanded the earlier volumes and wrote a third one. Even after the publication of the edition of 1588, he continued to revise and expand the *Essays* through marginal annotations during the last four years of his life. He died of a severe inflammation of the throat on September 13, 1592.

Montaigne's *Essays* represent a new genre in Western literature. The nineteenth-century English critic Edmund Gosse wrote, "It is not often that we can date with any approach to accuracy the arrival of a new class of literature into the world. But it was in the month of March 1571 that the essay was invented." This exaggeration neglects the long process by which Montaigne developed his characteristic form, but it does suggest the originality of his achievement. Montaigne began his work as a modest set of quotations from his readings, annotated with his own comments; a reminder of these origins remains in the many Latin quotations that punctuate the *Essays* in their final form. As he continued to write, however, his own comments began to outweigh the quotations and develop their own loose, rambling, almost free-associational structure. Frequently, the title of an essay serves only as the jumping-off place for a series of meditations that have little or no connection with the presumed subject. The style is easy and informal, though it can rise when appropriate to great eloquence; Montaigne's literary voice is distinctively witty, self-deprecating, and charming. Often long passages consist merely of a series of amusing and ingenious anecdotes, illustrations, and quotations spiraling around the subject. The nineteenth-century French critic Sainte-Beuve described Montaigne's style as "a continual epigram or a metaphor always renewing itself."

Montaigne's ideas have been the subject of almost continuous controversy since the *Essays* were first published. Some readers, noting that he regards human reason as powerless and the world as essentially unknowable, have concluded that his work implies indifference and resignation to ignorance. Others have found the essential spirit of modern science in his skeptical, inquiring spirit and his unwillingness to take anything merely on authority. His religious views are also variously interpreted. Few of his contemporaries found anything unorthodox in the *Essays,* but the Church later found their skeptical spirit questionable and in 1676 placed them on the *Index.* Some close students of Montaigne have found him profoundly Christian, while Ralph Waldo Emerson called his essay on Montaigne "The Skeptic," and Sainte-Beuve believed that he worked deliberately to undermine the teachings of Christianity. Equally controversial, across the centuries, has been the meaning of Montaigne's preoccupation with himself. In the seventeenth century, the French scientist and philosopher Pascal spoke of Montaigne's work as "the foolish project of painting himself." Others have seen this self-preoccupation as inspired both by the classical injunction to "know thyself" and the Renaissance emphasis on the importance of the individual mind, while modern readers have found in Montaigne a vivid anticipation of twentieth-century literature's intense interest in the inner world of the individual self.

The disagreements regarding Montaigne's work probably arise from attempts to impose a unity and consistency upon them that they do not have. Critics now usually divide his thought into three stages of development. In the first stage, he was deeply influenced by the philosophy of Seneca and by the personal model of Cato of Utica. During this period he held "Stoic" ideas of indifference to death, suffering, and misfortune. A second, "Skeptical" stage is marked by his writing of the long and important "Apology for Raymond Sebond." Skepticism had such a hold on Montaigne that in about 1576 he had a medal struck that depicted an evenly balanced scale above the personal motto, "*Que sçay-je?*" or "What do I know?" The third and last stage is often called the "Epicurean" stage; Montaigne's emphasis now shifts to the achievement of happiness through the exercise of the human faculties, physical as well as intellectual.

This tripartite scheme seems accurate as far as it goes, but even it may imply more consistency and order in Montaigne's work than actually exists. The real core of Montaigne's work is not a consistent set of ideas, but the continual presence of the man himself. He is constantly shifting and changing but is always vividly present at center stage. It is through Montaigne's constant attention to the details of his own life that he captures not only the quality of his own personality but also the rich variety and delight of life itself. The twentieth-century novelist and critic Virginia Woolf summed up this vitality in her essay on Montaigne: "It is life that emerges more and more clearly as these essays reach not their end, but their suspension in full career. It is life that becomes more and more absorbing as death draws near, one's self, one's soul, every part of existence: that one wears silk stockings summer and winter; puts water in one's wine; has one's hair cut after dinner; must have glass to drink from; has never worn spectacles; has a loud voice; carries a switch in one's hands; bites one's tongue, fidgets with one's feet; is apt to scratch one's ears; likes meat to be high; rubs one's teeth with a napkin (thank God, they are good!); must have curtains to one's bed; and, what is rather curious, began by liking radishes, then disliked them, and now likes them again. No fact is too little to let it slip through one's fingers."

Montaigne's spirit, as well as some of his recurring ideas and his characteristic style, are well illustrated in the two essays reprinted here. Montaigne's love of simplicity and "naturalness" is expressed vividly in the quaint but pointed essay "Of Cannibals." Montaigne, like most of his European contemporaries, was fascinated by reports of the New World; he had seen natives of Brazil at the court celebrations in Rouen in 1560 (celebrating the coming of age of Charles IX) and, as he tells us, had some Brazilian artifacts in his home. He delights in the curious details of cannibal life but, characteristically, lets his mind spiral around the implications of a comparison between the lives of these "noble savages" and his own life. "So we may well call these people barbarians," he writes, "in respect to the rules of reason, but not in respect to ourselves, who surpass them in every kind of barbarity." (This essay has an extrinsic interest in that Shakespeare adapted a passage from it, in John Florio's Elizabethan translation, and incorporated it into *The Tempest.*)

The most important fact to be noted about "Apology for Raymond Sebond," perhaps, is that it is not an apology for Raymond Sebond. Sebond, a fifteenth-century professor of medicine, theology, and philosophy at Toulouse, in Spain, had written a Latin work called *Liber Creaturarum,* or *Natural Theology* (1484), which Montaigne had translated into French for his father. In this book, Sebond had argued that human beings could arrive at a comprehensive knowledge of God through study of nature, God's creation. Montaigne apparently wrote his very long essay (only about 20 percent is represented in this excerpt) at the request of Princess Margaret of Valois, who asked him to defend the book he had translated. Montaigne's "apology" is halfhearted at best, and in the course of the essay, he comes close to defending a view precisely opposite to Sebond's: that the human mind is unable to know anything with certainty. The spine of his argument is simple: Human beings are ill-equipped to know the world; knowledge can make us neither happy nor good, and anyway it is impossible to acquire; our senses are deceptive; the world is in such flux that knowledge is impossible; and so on. But in the course of developing his argument, Montaigne brings such curious and idiosyncratic detail to it that the essay is a delight to read.

Both "Of Cannibals" and the "Apology for Raymond Sebond" may be seen as expressions of the love of ordinary life that Woolf noted in Montaigne and his corresponding distrust of high-flying claims to power and knowledge. "The virtue of the soul," he wrote in "Of Repentance," "does not consist in flying high, but in walking orderly," and his ideal is not the grandeur of an Alexander but the modesty of a Socrates, who wanted not to conquer the world but to "carry on human life conformably with its natural condition."

FURTHER READING: The standard biography is Donald M. Frame's *Montaigne: A Biography,* 1965. Frame's *Montaigne's "Essais": A Study,* 1969, is a lucid and thoughtful critical overview, as are Peter Burke's *Montaigne,* 1981, a volume in the Past Masters series, and Dorothy Coleman's *Montaigne's "Essais,"* 1987, in the Unwin Critical Library series. Erich Auerbach's chapter on Montaigne, "L'humaine condition," in *Mimesis: The Representation of Reality in Western Literature,* trans. Willard R. Trask, 1953, remains valuable and provocative. Of the many specialized studies that could be recommended, Barbara C. Bowen's *The Age of Bluff: Paradox and Ambiguity in Rabelais and Montaigne,* 1972, is especially readable and useful. Harold Bloom has edited two collections of essays on Montaigne: *Michel de Montaigne,* 1987, in the Modern Critical Views series, and *Montaigne's "Essays,"* 1987, in the Modern Critical Interpretations series. Both offer a good selection of recent criticism and guides to further reading. The former contains a fine essay by Catherine Demure: "The Paradox and the Miracle: Structure and Meaning in 'The Apology for Raymond Sebond.'" Two especially good advanced studies are Jean Starobinski's *Montaigne in Motion,* trans. Arthur Goldhammer, 1985, and Richard L. Regosin's *The Matter of My Book: Montaigne's "Essais" as the Book of the Self,* 1977. David Lewis Schaefer, *The Political Philosophy of Montaigne,* 1991, is valuable on its subject. Montaigne is among the authors discussed by the French feminist Christine Faure in *Democracy Without Women,* 1991.

ESSAYS

Translated by Donald M. Frame

OF CANNIBALS

When King Pyrrhus passed over into Italy, after he had reconnoitered the formation of the army that the Romans were sending to meet him, he said: "I do not know what barbarians these are" (for so the Greeks called all foreign nations), "but the formation of this army that I see is not at all barbarous."[1] The Greeks said as much of the army that Flamininus brought into their country,[2] and so did Philip, seeing from a knoll the order and distribution of the Roman camp, in his kingdom, under Publius Sulpicius Galba.[3] Thus we should beware of clinging to vulgar opinions, and judge things by reason's way, not by popular say.

I had with me for a long time a man who had lived for ten or twelve years in that other world which has been discovered in our century, in the place where Villegaignon landed, and which he called Antarctic France.[4] This discovery of a boundless country seems worthy of consideration. I don't know if I can guarantee that some other such discovery will not be made in the future, so many personages greater than ourselves having been mistaken about

[1] Pyrrhus (318–272 B.C.) was king of Epirus. This story is told in Plutarch's *Life of Pyrrhus.*

[2] T. Quintius Flamininus (230–144 B.C.) was a Roman general. See Plutarch's *Life of Flamininus* for this story.

[3] The reference is to Philip V, king of Macedon (221–179 B.C.). This story is told by the Roman historian Livy.

[4] The French explorer Villegaignon explored Brazil (Antarctic France) in 1557.

this one. I am afraid we have eyes bigger than our stomachs, and more curiosity than capacity. We embrace everything, but we clasp only wind.

Plato brings in Solon, telling how he had learned from the priests of the city of Saïs in Egypt that in days of old, before the Flood, there was a great island named Atlantis, right at the mouth of the Strait of Gibraltar, which contained more land than Africa and Asia put together, and that the kings of that country, who not only possessed that island but had stretched out so far on the mainland that they held the breadth of Africa as far as Egypt, and the length of Europe as far as Tuscany, undertook to step over into Asia and subjugate all the nations that border on the Mediterranean, as far as the Black Sea; and for this purpose crossed the Spains, Gaul, Italy, as far as Greece, where the Athenians checked them; but that some time after, both the Athenians and themselves and their island were swallowed up by the Flood.[5]

It is quite likely that that extreme devastation of waters made amazing changes in the habitations of the earth, as people maintain that the sea cut off Sicily from Italy—

> 'Tis said an earthquake once asunder tore
> These lands with dreadful havoc, which before
> Formed but one land, one coast
>
> VIRGIL

—Cyprus from Syria, the island of Euboea from the mainland of Boeotia; and elsewhere joined lands that were divided, filling the channels between them with sand and mud:

> A sterile marsh, long fit for rowing, now
> Feeds neighbor towns, and feels the heavy plow.
>
> HORACE

But there is no great likelihood that that island was the new world which we have just discovered; for it almost touched Spain, and it would be an incredible result of a flood to have forced it away as far as it is, more than twelve hundred leagues; besides, the travels of the moderns have already almost revealed that it is not an island, but a mainland connected with the East Indies on one side, and elsewhere with the lands under the two poles; or, if it is separated from them, it is by so narrow a strait and interval that it does not deserve to be called an island on that account.

It seems that there are movements, some natural, others feverish, in these great bodies, just as in our own. When I consider the inroads that my river, the Dordogne, is making in my lifetime into the right bank in its descent, and that in twenty years it has gained so much ground and stolen away the foundations of several buildings, I clearly see that this is an extraordinary disturbance; for if it had always gone at this rate, or was to do so in the future, the face of the world would be turned topsy-turvy. But rivers are subject to changes: now they overflow in one direction, now in another, now they keep to their course. I am not speaking of the sudden inundations whose causes

[5] The story of Atlantis appears in Plato's *Timaeus*.

are manifest. In Médoc,[6] along the seashore, my brother, the sieur d'Arsac, can see an estate of his buried under the sands that the sea spews forth; the tops of some buildings are still visible; his farms and domains have changed into very thin pasturage. The inhabitants say that for some time the sea has been pushing toward them so hard that they have lost four leagues of land. These sands are its harbingers; and we see great dunes of moving sand that march half a league ahead of it and keep conquering land.

The other testimony of antiquity with which some would connect this discovery is in Aristotle, at least if that little book *Of Unheard-of Wonders* is by him. He there relates that certain Carthaginians, after setting out upon the Atlantic Ocean from the Strait of Gibraltar and sailing a long time, at last discovered a great fertile island, all clothed in woods and watered by great deep rivers, far remote from any mainland; and that they, and others since, attracted by the goodness and fertility of the soil, went there with their wives and children, and began to settle there. The lords of Carthage, seeing that their country was gradually becoming depopulated, expressly forbade anyone to go there any more, on pain of death, and drove out these new inhabitants, fearing, it is said, that in course of time they might come to multiply so greatly as to supplant their former masters and ruin their state. This story of Aristotle does not fit our new lands any better than the other.

This man I had was a simple, crude fellow[7]—a character fit to bear true witness; for clever people observe more things and more curiously, but they interpret them; and to lend weight and conviction to their interpretation they cannot help altering history a little. They never show you things as they are, but bend and disguise them according to the way they have seen them; and to give credence to their judgment and attract you to it, they are prone to add something to their matter, to stretch it out and amplify it. We need a man either very honest, or so simple that he has not the stuff to build up false inventions and give them plausibility; and wedded to no theory. Such was my man; and besides this, he at various times brought sailors and merchants, whom he had known on that trip, to see me. So I content myself with his information, without inquiring what the cosmographers say about it.

We ought to have topographers who would give us an exact account of the places where they have been. But because they have over us the advantage of having seen Palestine, they want to enjoy the privilege of telling us news about all the rest of the world. I would like everyone to write what he knows, and as much as he knows, not only in this, but in all other subjects; for a man may have some special knowledge and experience of the nature of a river or a fountain, who in other matters knows only what everybody knows. However, to circulate this little scrap of knowledge, he will undertake to write the whole of physics. From this vice spring many great abuses.

Now, to return to my subject, I think there is nothing barbarous and savage in that nation, from what I have been told, except that each man calls barbarism whatever is not his own practice; for indeed it seems we have no other test of truth and reason than the example and pattern of the opinions

[6] Home of Montaigne's brother, Médoc is a district in southwestern France, northwest of Bordeaux.

[7] That is, the traveler referred to at the beginning of the essay.

and customs of the country we live in. *There* is always the perfect religion, the perfect government, the perfect and accomplished manners in all things. Those people are wild, just as we call wild the fruits that Nature has produced by herself and in her normal course; whereas really it is those that we have changed artificially and led astray from the common order, that we should rather call wild. The former retain alive and vigorous their genuine, their most useful and natural, virtues and properties, which we have debased in the latter in adapting them to gratify our corrupted taste. And yet for all that, the savor and delicacy of some uncultivated fruits of those countries is quite as excellent, even to our taste, as that of our own. It is not reasonable that art should win the place of honor over our great and powerful mother Nature. We have so overloaded the beauty and richness of her works by our inventions that we have quite smothered her. Yet wherever her purity shines forth, she wonderfully puts to shame our vain and frivolous attempts:

> Ivy comes readier without our care;
> In lonely caves the arbutus grows more fair;
> No art with artless bird song can compare.
>
> PROPERTIUS

All our efforts cannot even succeed in reproducing the nest of the tiniest little bird, its contexture, its beauty and convenience; or even the web of the puny spider. All things, says Plato, are produced by nature, by fortune, or by art; the greatest and most beautiful by one or the other of the first two, the least and most imperfect by the last.[8]

These nations, then, seem to me barbarous in this sense, that they have been fashioned very little by the human mind, and are still very close to their original naturalness. The laws of nature still rule them, very little corrupted by ours; and they are in such a state of purity that I am sometimes vexed that they were unknown earlier, in the days when there were men able to judge them better than we. I am sorry that Lycurgus and Plato did not know of them;[9] for it seems to me that what we actually see in these nations surpasses not only all the pictures in which poets have idealized the golden age and all their inventions in imagining a happy state of man, but also the conceptions and the very desire of philosophy. They could not imagine a naturalness so pure and simple as we see by experience; nor could they believe that our society could be maintained with so little artifice and human solder. This is a nation, I should say to Plato, in which there is no sort of traffic, no knowledge of letters, no science of numbers, no name for a magistrate or for political superiority, no custom of servitude, no riches or poverty, no contracts, no successions, no partitions, no occupations but leisure ones, no care for any but common kinship, no clothes, no agriculture, no metal, no use of wine or wheat. The very words that signify lying, treachery, dissimulation, avarice,

[8]Montaigne is paraphrasing a passage in Plato's *Laws*.

[9]Lycurgus was a Spartan lawgiver. Like Plato, he wrote of ideal societies, and, Montaigne suggests, both would have profited from knowing the culture of the New World cannibals.

envy, belittling, pardon—unheard of.[10] How far from this perfection would he find the republic that he imagined: *Men fresh sprung from the gods* [Seneca].

> These manners nature first ordained.
> VIRGIL

For the rest, they live in a country with a very pleasant and temperate climate, so that according to my witnesses it is rare to see a sick man there; and they have assured me that they never saw one palsied, bleary-eyed, toothless, or bent with age. They are settled along the sea and shut in on the land side by great high mountains, with a stretch about a hundred leagues wide in between. They have a great abundance of fish and flesh which bear no resemblance to ours, and they eat them with no other artifice than cooking. The first man who rode a horse there, though he had had dealings with them on several other trips, so horrified them in this posture that they shot him dead with arrows before they could recognize him.

The buildings are very long, with a capacity of two or three hundred souls; they are covered with the bark of great trees, the strips reaching to the ground at one end and supporting and leaning on one another at the top, in the manner of some of our barns, whose covering hangs down to the ground and acts as a side. They have wood so hard that they cut with it and make of it their swords and grills to cook their food. Their beds are of a cotton weave, hung from the roof like those in our ships, each man having his own; for the wives sleep apart from their husbands.

They get up with the sun, and eat immediately upon rising, to last them through the day; for they take no other meal than that one. Like some other Eastern peoples, of whom Suidas[11] tells us, who drank apart from meals, they do not drink then; but they drink several times a day, and to capacity. Their drink is made of some root, and is of the color of our claret wines. They drink it only lukewarm. This beverage keeps only two or three days; it has a slightly sharp taste, is not at all heady, is good for the stomach, and has a laxative effect upon those who are not used to it; it is a very pleasant drink for anyone who is accustomed to it. In place of bread they use a certain white substance like preserved coriander. I have tried it; it tastes sweet and a little flat.

The whole day is spent in dancing. The younger men go to hunt animals with bows. Some of the women busy themselves meanwhile with warming their drink, which is their chief duty. Some one of the old men, in the morning before they begin to eat, preaches to the whole barnful in common, walking from one end to the other, and repeating one single sentence several times until he has completed the circuit (for the buildings are fully a hundred paces long). He recommends to them only two things: valor against the enemy and love for their wives. And they never fail to point out this obligation, as their refrain, that it is their wives who keep their drink warm and seasoned.

There may be seen in several places, including my own house, specimens of their beds, of their ropes, of their wooden swords and the bracelets with

[10] The two sentences preceding are the famous passage adapted by Shakespeare in *The Tempest,* II.i.147.

[11] A tenth-century A.D. Greek lexicographer.

which they cover their wrists in combats, and of the big canes, open at one end, by whose sound they keep time in their dances. They are close shaven all over, and shave themselves much more cleanly than we, with nothing but a wooden or stone razor. They believe that souls are immortal, and that those who have deserved well of the gods are lodged in that part of heaven where the sun rises, and the damned in the west.

They have some sort of priests and prophets, but they rarely appear before the people, having their home in the mountains. On their arrival there is a great feast and solemn assembly of several villages—each barn, as I have described it, makes up a village, and they are about one French league from each other. The prophet speaks to them in public, exhorting them to virtue and their duty; but their whole ethical science contains only these two articles: resoluteness in war and affection for their wives. He prophesies to them things to come and the results they are to expect from their undertakings, and urges them to war or holds them back from it; but this is on the condition that when he fails to prophesy correctly, and if things turn out otherwise than he has predicted, he is cut into a thousand pieces if they catch him, and condemned as a false prophet. For this reason, the prophet who has once been mistaken is never seen again.

Divination is a gift of God; that is why its abuse should be punished as imposture. Among the Scythians, when the soothsayers failed to hit the mark, they were laid, chained hand and foot, on carts full of heather and drawn by oxen, on which they were burned.[12] Those who handle matters subject to the control of human capacity are excusable if they do the best they can. But these others, who come and trick us with assurances of an extraordinary faculty that is beyond our ken, should they not be punished for not making good their promise, and for the temerity of their imposture?

They have their wars with the nations beyond the mountains, further inland, to which they go quite naked, with no other arms than bows or wooden swords ending in a sharp point, in the manner of the tongues of our boar spears. It is astonishing what firmness they show in their combats, which never end but in slaughter and bloodshed; for as to routs and terror, they know nothing of either.

Each man brings back as his trophy the head of the enemy he has killed, and sets it up at the entrance to his dwelling. After they have treated their prisoners well for a long time with all the hospitality they can think of, each man who has a prisoner calls a great assembly of his acquaintances. He ties a rope to one of the prisoner's arms, by the end of which he holds him, a few steps away, for fear of being hurt, and gives his dearest friend the other arm to hold in the same way; and these two, in the presence of the whole assembly, kill him with their swords. This done, they roast him and eat him in common and send some pieces to their absent friends. This is not, as people think, for nourishment, as of old the Scythians used to do; it is to betoken an extreme revenge. And the proof of this came when they saw the Portuguese, who had joined forces with their adversaries, inflict a different kind of death on them when they took them prisoner, which was to bury them up to the waist, shoot the rest of their body full of arrows, and

[12] The Scythians were the inhabitants of a region in southeastern Europe and Asia, legendary for their barbarity. This story appears in the work of the Greek historian Herodotus.

afterward hang them. They thought that these people from the other world, being men who had sown the knowledge of many vices among their neighbors and were much greater masters than themselves in every sort of wickedness, did not adopt this sort of vengeance without some reason, and that it must be more painful than their own; so they began to give up their old method and to follow this one.

I am not sorry that we notice the barbarous horror of such acts, but I am heartily sorry that, judging their faults rightly, we should be so blind to our own. I think there is more barbarity in eating a man alive than in eating him dead; and in tearing by tortures and the rack a body still full of feeling, in roasting a man bit by bit,[13] in having him bitten and mangled by dogs and swine (as we have not only read but seen within fresh memory, not among ancient enemies, but among neighbors and fellow citizens, and what is worse, on the pretext of piety and religion), than in roasting and eating him after he is dead.

Indeed, Chrysippus and Zeno,[14] heads of the Stoic sect, thought there was nothing wrong in using our carcasses for any purpose in case of need, and getting nourishment from them; just as our ancestors, when besieged by Caesar in the city of Alésia, resolved to relieve their famine by eating old men, women, and other people useless for fighting.[15]

> The Gascons once, 'tis said, their life renewed
> By eating of such food.
>
> JUVENAL

And physicians do not fear to use human flesh in all sorts of ways for our health, applying it either inwardly or outwardly. But there never was any opinion so disordered as to excuse treachery, disloyalty, tyranny, and cruelty, which are our ordinary vices.

So we may well call these people barbarians, in respect to the rules of reason, but not in respect to ourselves, who surpass them in every kind of barbarity.

Their warfare is wholly noble and generous, and as excusable and beautiful as this human disease can be; its only basis among them is their rivalry in valor. They are not fighting for the conquest of new lands, for they still enjoy that natural abundance that provides them without toil and trouble with all necessary things in such profusion that they have no wish to enlarge their boundaries. They are still in that happy state of desiring only as much as their natural needs demand; anything beyond that is superfluous to them.

They generally call those of the same age, brothers; those who are younger, children; and the old men are fathers to all the others. These leave to their heirs in common the full possession of their property, without division or any other title at all than just the one that Nature gives to her creatures in bringing them into the world.

If their neighbors cross the mountains to attack them and win a victory, the gain of the victor is glory, and the advantage of having proved the

[13] These were accepted modes of execution in Montaigne's day.

[14] Chrysippus (291–208 B.C.) and Zeno (d. 264 B.C.) were, as noted, Stoic philosophers.

[15] This story of cannibalism appears in Caesar's *Gallic Wars*.

master in valor and virtue; for apart from this they have no use for the goods of the vanquished, and they return to their own country, where they lack neither anything necessary nor that great thing, the knowledge of how to enjoy their condition happily and be content with it. These men of ours do the same in their turn. They demand of their prisoners no other ransom than that they confess and acknowledge their defeat. But there is not one in a whole century who does not choose to die rather than to relax a single bit, by word or look, from the grandeur of an invincible courage; not one who would not rather be killed and eaten than so much as ask not to be. They treat them very freely, so that life may be all the dearer to them, and usually entertain them with threats of their coming death, of the torments they will have to suffer, the preparations that are being made for that purpose, the cutting up of their limbs, and the feast that will be made at their expense. All this is done for the sole purpose of extorting from their lips some weak or base word, or making them want to flee, so as to gain the advantage of having terrified them and broken down their firmness. For indeed, if you take it the right way, it is in this point alone that true victory lies:

> It is no victory
> Unless the vanquished foe admits your mastery.
>
> CLAUDIAN

The Hungarians, very bellicose fighters, did not in olden times pursue their advantage beyond putting the enemy at their mercy. For having wrung a confession from him to this effect, they let him go unharmed and unransomed, except, at most, for exacting his promise never again to take up arms against them.

We win enough advantages over our enemies that are borrowed advantages, not really our own. It is the quality of a porter, not of valor, to have sturdier arms and legs; agility is a dead and corporeal quality; it is a stroke of luck to make our enemy stumble, or dazzle his eyes by the sunlight; it is a trick of art and technique, which may be found in a worthless coward, to be an able fencer. The worth and value of a man is in his heart and his will; there lies his real honor. Valor is the strength, not of legs and arms, but of heart and soul; it consists not in the worth of our horse or our weapons, but in our own. He who falls obstinate in his courage, *if he has fallen, he fights on his knees* [Seneca]. He who relaxes none of his assurance, no matter how great the danger of imminent death; who, giving up his soul, still looks firmly and scornfully at his enemy—he is beaten not by us, but by fortune; he is killed, not conquered.

The most valiant are sometimes the most unfortunate. Thus there are triumphant defeats that rival victories. Nor did those four sister victories the fairest that the sun ever set eyes on—Salamis, Plataea, Mycale, and Sicily—ever dare match all their combined glory against the glory of the annihilation of King Leonidas and his men at the pass of Thermopylae.[16]

[16] Salamis, Plataea, Mycale, and Sicily were the sites of notable victories of the Greeks over the Persians and Carthaginians in the fifth century B.C. At Thermopylae, a narrow mountain pass in eastern Greece, a small band of Spartans held off the Persian army in 480 B.C.

Who ever hastened with more glorious and ambitious desire to win a battle than Captain Ischolas to lose one?[17] Who ever secured his safety more ingeniously and painstakingly than he did his destruction? He was charged to defend a certain pass in the Peloponnesus against the Arcadians. Finding himself wholly incapable of doing this, in view of the nature of the place and the inequality of the forces, he made up his mind that all who confronted the enemy would necessarily have to remain on the field. On the other hand, deeming it unworthy both of his own virtue and magnanimity and of the Lacedaemonian name to fail in his charge, he took a middle course between these two extremes, in this way. The youngest and fittest of his band he preserved for the defense and service of their country, and sent them home; and with those whose loss was less important, he determined to hold this pass, and by their death to make the enemy buy their entry as dearly as he could. And so it turned out. For he was presently surrounded on all sides by the Arcadians, and after slaughtering a large number of them, he and his men were all put to the sword. Is there a trophy dedicated to victors that would not be more due to these vanquished? The role of true victory is in fighting, not in coming off safely; and the honor of valor consists in combating, not in beating.

To return to our story. These prisoners are so far from giving in, in spite of all that is done to them, that on the contrary, during the two or three months that they are kept, they wear a gay expression; they urge their captors to hurry and put them to the test; they defy them, insult them, reproach them with their cowardice and the number of battles they have lost to the prisoners' own people.

I have a song composed by a prisoner which contains this challenge, that they should all come boldly and gather to dine off him, for they will be eating at the same time their own fathers and grandfathers, who have served to feed and nourish his body. "These muscles," he says, "this flesh and these veins are your own, poor fools that you are. You do not recognize that the substance of your ancestors' limbs is still contained in them. Savor them well; you will find in them the taste of your own flesh." An idea that certainly does not smack of barbarity. Those that paint these people dying, and who show the execution, portray the prisoner spitting in the face of his slayers and scowling at them. Indeed, to the last gasp they never stop braving and defying their enemies by word and look. Truly here are real savages by our standards; for either they must be thoroughly so, or we must be; there is an amazing distance between their character and ours.

The men there have several wives, and the higher their reputation for valor the more wives they have. It is a remarkably beautiful thing about their marriages that the same jealousy our wives have to keep us from the affection and kindness of other women, theirs have to win this for them. Being more concerned for their husbands' honor than for anything else, they strive and scheme to have as many companions as they can, since that is a sign of their husbands' valor.

Our wives will cry "Miracle!" but it is no miracle. It is a properly matrimonial virtue, but one of the highest order. In the Bible, Leah, Rachel, Sarah, and Jacob's wives gave their beautiful handmaids to their husbands; and Livia

[17] This story is told by the Greek historian Diodorus Siculus (first century B.C.).

seconded the appetites of Augustus, to her own disadvantage; and Stratonice, the wife of King Deiotarus, not only lent her husband for his use a very beautiful young chambermaid in her service, but carefully brought up her children, and backed them up to succeed to their father's estates.[18]

And lest it be thought that all this is done through a simple and servile bondage to usage and through the pressure of the authority of their ancient customs, without reasoning or judgment, and because their minds are so stupid that they cannot take any other course, I must cite some examples of their capacity. Besides the warlike song I have just quoted, I have another, a love song, which begins in this vein: "Adder, stay; stay, adder, that from the pattern of your coloring my sister may draw the fashion and the workmanship of a rich girdle that I may give to my love; so may your beauty and your pattern be forever preferred to all other serpents." This first couplet is the refrain of the song. Now I am familiar enough with poetry to be a judge of this: not only is there nothing barbarous in this fancy, but it is altogether Anacreontic.[19] Their language, moreover, is a soft language, with an agreeable sound, somewhat like Greek in its endings.

Three of these men, ignorant of the price they will pay some day, in loss of repose and happiness, for gaining knowledge of the corruptions of this side of the ocean; ignorant also of the fact that of this intercourse will come their ruin (which I suppose is already well advanced: poor wretches, to let themselves be tricked by the desire for new things, and to have left the serenity of their own sky to come and see ours!)—three of these men were at Rouen, at the time the late King Charles IX[20] was there. The king talked to them for a long time; they were shown our ways, our splendor, the aspect of a fine city. After that, someone asked their opinion, and wanted to know what they had found most amazing. They mentioned three things, of which I have forgotten the third, and I am very sorry for it; but I still remember two of them. They said that in the first place they thought it very strange that so many grown men, bearded, strong, and armed, who were around the king (it is likely that they were talking about the Swiss of his guard) should submit to obey a child, and that one of them was not chosen to command instead. Second (they have a way in their language of speaking of men as halves of one another), they had noticed that there were among us men full and gorged with all sorts of good things, and that their other halves were beggars at their doors, emaciated with hunger and poverty; and they thought it strange that these needy halves could endure such an injustice, and did not take the others by the throat, or set fire to their houses.

I had a very long talk with one of them; but I had an interpreter who followed my meaning so badly, and who was so hindered by his stupidity in taking in my ideas, that I could get hardly any satisfaction from the man. When I asked him what profit he gained from his superior position among his people (for he was a captain, and our sailors called him king), he told me that it was to march foremost in war. How many men followed him? He

[18] The story of Sarah and her maid Hagar appears in Genesis, chapter 16; that of Leah and Rachel in Genesis, chapter 30. The story of Livia is in Suetonius' *Life of Augustus* and that of Stratonice in Plutarch's *Bravery of Women.*

[19] Like the poetry of Anacreon (c. 563–c. 478 B.C.), a Greek poet known for his love poems.

[20] King Charles IX of France died in 1574.

pointed to a piece of ground, to signify as many as such a space could hold; it might have been four or five thousand men. Did all his authority expire with the war? He said that this much remained, that when he visited the villages dependent on him, they made paths for him through the underbrush by which he might pass quite comfortably.

All this is not too bad—but what's the use? They don't wear breeches.

from APOLOGY FOR RAYMOND SEBOND

In truth, knowledge is a great and very useful quality; those who despise it give evidence enough of their stupidity. But yet I do not set its value at that extreme measure that some attribute to it, like Herillus the philosopher, who placed in it the sovereign good, and held that it was in its power to make us wise and content. That I do not believe, nor what others have said, that knowledge is the mother of all virtue, and that all vice is produced by ignorance. If that is true, it is subject to a long interpretation.

[RAYMOND SEBOND'S BOOK][1]

My house has long been open to men of learning, and is well known to them. For my father, who ruled it for fifty years and more, inflamed with that new ardor with which King Francis I embraced letters and brought them into credit, sought with great diligence and expense the acquaintance of learned men, receiving them at his house like holy persons having some particular inspiration of divine wisdom, collecting their sayings and discourses like oracles, and with all the more reverence and religion as he was less qualified to judge them; for he had no knowledge of letters, any more than his predecessors. Myself, I like them well enough, but I do not worship them.

Among others, Pierre Bunel, a man of great reputation for learning in his time, after staying a few days at Montaigne in the company of my father with other men of his sort, made him a present, on his departure, of a book entitled "Natural Theology, or Book of Creatures, by Master Raymond de Sabonde." And because the Italian and Spanish languages were familiar to my father, and this book was composed in a Spanish scrambled up with Latin endings, Bunel hoped that with a very little help he could make his profit of it, and recommended it to him as a very useful book and suited to the time in which he gave it to him; this was when the innovations of Luther were beginning to gain favor and to shake our old belief in many places.

In this he was very well advised, rightly foreseeing by rational inference that this incipient malady would easily degenerate into an execrable atheism. For the common herd, not having the faculty of judging things in themselves, let themselves be carried away by chance and by appearances, when once they have been given the temerity to despise and judge the opinions that they had held in extreme reverence, such as are those in which their salvation is concerned. And when some articles of their religion have been

[1] Bracketed subheadings are not in the original but have been supplied by the editors.

set in doubt and upon the balance, they will soon after cast easily into like uncertainty all the other parts of their belief, which had no more authority or foundation in them than those that have been shaken; and they shake off as a tyrannical yoke all the impressions they had once received from the authority of the laws or the reverence of ancient usage—

> For eagerly is trampled what once was too much feared
>
> LUCRETIUS

—determined from then on to accept nothing to which they have not applied their judgment and granted their personal consent.

Now some days before his death, my father, having by chance come across this book under a pile of other abandoned papers, commanded me to put it into French for him. It is nice to translate authors like this one, where there is hardly anything but the matter to reproduce; but those who have given much care to grace and elegance of language are dangerous to undertake, especially to render them into a weaker idiom.[2] It was a very strange and a new occupation for me; but being by chance at leisure at the time, and being unable to disobey any command of the best father there ever was, I got through it as best I could; at which he was singularly pleased, and ordered it to be printed; and this was done after his death.

I found the ideas of this author fine, the arrangement and sequence of his work good, and his plan full of piety. Because many people are busy reading it, and especially the ladies, to whom we owe additional help, I have often found myself in a position to help them by clearing their book of two principal objections that are made against it. His purpose is bold and courageous, for he undertakes by human and natural reasons to establish and prove against the atheists all the articles of the Christian religion; wherein, to tell the truth, I find him so firm and felicitous that I do not think it is possible to do better in that argument, and I think that no one has equaled him.

Since this work seemed to me too rich and splendid for an author whose name is so little known, and of whom all we know is that he was a Spaniard professing medicine at Toulouse about two hundred years ago, I once inquired of Adrianus Turnebus, who knew everything, what could be the truth about this book. He replied that he thought it was some quintessence extracted from Saint Thomas Aquinas; for in truth that mind, full of infinite erudition and admirable subtlety, was alone capable of such ideas. At all events, whoever is the author and inventor (and it is not reasonable, without greater occasion, to rob Sebond of that title), he was a very able man with many fine qualities.

[FIRST OBJECTION TO SEBOND AND DEFENSE]

The first criticism that they make of his work is that Christians do themselves harm in trying to support their belief by human reasons, since it is conceived only by faith and by a particular inspiration of divine grace. In this objection there seems to be a certain pious zeal, and for this reason we must try

[2] That is, French, which was considered "weaker" than Latin.

with all the more mildness and respect to satisfy those who advance it. This would be rather the task for a man versed in theology than for myself, who know nothing about it.

However, I think thus, that in a thing so divine and so lofty, and so far surpassing human intelligence, as is this truth with which it has pleased the goodness of God to enlighten us, it is very necessary that he still lend us his help, by extraordinary and privileged favor, so that we may conceive it and lodge it in us. And I do not think that purely human means are at all capable of this; if they were, so many rare and excellent souls, so abundantly furnished with natural powers, in ancient times, would not have failed to arrive at this knowledge through their reason. It is faith alone that embraces vividly and surely the high mysteries of our religion.

But this is not to say that it is not a very fine and very laudable enterprise to accommodate also to the service of our faith the natural and human tools that God has given us. There can be no doubt that this is the most honorable use that we could put them to, and that there is no occupation or design more worthy of a Christian man than to aim, by all his studies and thoughts, to embellish, extend, and amplify the truth of his belief. We do not content ourselves with serving God with mind and soul, we also owe and render him a bodily reverence; we apply even our limbs and movements and external things to honor him. We must do the same here, and accompany our faith with all the reason that is in us, but always with this reservation, not to think that it is on us that faith depends, or that our efforts and arguments can attain a knowledge so supernatural and divine. . . .

[SECOND OBJECTION TO SEBOND AND DEFENSE]

I have already, without thinking about it, half involved myself in the second objection which I had proposed to answer for Sebond.

Some say that his arguments are weak and unfit to prove what he proposes, and undertake to shatter them with ease. These must be shaken up a little more roughly, for they are more dangerous and malicious than the others. People are prone to apply the meaning of other men's writings to suit opinions that they have previously determined in their minds; and an atheist flatters himself by reducing all authors to atheism, infecting innocent matter with his own venom. These men have some prepossession in judgment that makes their taste jaded for Sebond's reasons. Furthermore, it seems to them that they are given an easy game when set at liberty to combat our religion by purely human weapons, which they would not dare attack in its authoritative and commanding majesty.

The means I take to beat down this frenzy, and which seems fittest to me, is to crush and trample underfoot human arrogance and pride; to make them feel the inanity, the vanity and nothingness, of man; to wrest from their hands the puny weapons of their reason; to make them bow their heads and bite the ground beneath the authority and reverence of divine majesty. It is to this alone that knowledge and wisdom belong; it alone that can have some self-esteem, and from which we steal what we account and prize ourselves for:

> For God allows great thoughts to no one else.
>
> HERODOTUS

Let us beat down this presumption, the first foundation of the tyranny of the evil spirit. *For God resisteth the proud, and giveth grace to the humble* [Saint Peter]. Intelligence is in all gods, says Plato, and in very few men.

Now it is nevertheless a great consolation to the Christian to see our frail mortal tools so properly suited to our holy and divine faith, that when they are used on subjects that are by their nature frail and mortal, they are no more completely and powerfully appropriate. Let us see then if man has within his power other reasons more powerful than those of Sebond, or indeed if it is in him to arrive at any certainty by argument and reason.

For Saint Augustine, arguing against these people, has good cause to reproach them for their injustice in that they hold those parts of our belief to be false which our reason fails to establish. And to show that there can be and can have been plenty of things whose nature and causes our reason cannot possibly establish, he puts before his adversaries certain known and indubitable experiences into which man confesses he has no insight; and this he does, like all other things, with careful and ingenious research. We must do more, and teach them that to convict our reason of weakness, there is no need to go sifting out rare examples, and that she is so lame and so blind that there is nothing so clear and easy as to be clear enough to her; that the easy and the hard are one to her; that all subjects alike, and nature in general, disavow her jurisdiction and mediation.

What does truth preach to us, when she exhorts us to flee worldly philosophy, when she so often inculcates in us that our wisdom is but folly before God; that of all vanities the vainest is man; that the man who is presumptuous of his knowledge does not yet know what knowledge is; and that man, who is nothing, if he thinks he is something, seduces and deceives himself? These statements of the Holy Spirit express so clearly and so vividly what I wish to maintain, that no other proof would be needed against men who would surrender with all submission and obedience to its authority. But these men insist on being whipped to their own cost and will not allow us to combat their reason except by itself.

Let us then consider for the moment man alone, without outside assistance, armed solely with his own weapons, and deprived of divine grace and knowledge, which is his whole honor, his strength, and the foundation of his being. Let us see how much presence he has in this fine array. Let him help me to understand, by the force of his reason, on what foundations he has built these great advantages that he thinks he has over other creatures. Who has persuaded him that that admirable motion of the celestial vault, the eternal light of those torches rolling so proudly above his head, the fearful movements of that infinite sea, were established and have lasted so many centuries for his convenience and his service? Is it possible to imagine anything so ridiculous as that this miserable and puny creature, who is not even master of himself, exposed to the attacks of all things, should call himself master and emperor of the universe, the least part of which it is not in his power to know, much less to command? And this privilege that he attributes to himself of being the only one in this great edifice who has the capacity to recognize its beauty and its parts, the only one who can give thanks for it to the architect and keep an account of the receipts and expenses of the world: who has sealed him this privilege? Let him show us his letters patent for this great and splendid charge.

Have they been granted in favor of the wise only? Then they do not touch many people. Are the fools and the wicked worthy of such extraordinary favor, and, being the worst part of the world, of being preferred to all the rest?

Shall we believe this man? *For whom then shall a man say that the world was made? Naturally, for those souls who have the use of reason. These are gods and men, to whom certainly nothing is superior* [Cicero, quoting Balbus]. We shall never have flouted enough the impudence of this coupling.

But, poor wight, what has he in himself worthy of such an advantage? When we consider the incorruptible life of the celestial bodies, their beauty, their greatness, their continual motion by so exact a rule;

> When the vaults of heaven meet our sight,
> Infinite worlds above, ether with stars alight;
> And when the course of sun and moon come to our mind;
>
> LUCRETIUS

when we consider the dominion and power that those bodies have, not only over our lives and the conditions of our fortune,

> For on the stars men's deeds and lives depend,
>
> MANILIUS

but over our very inclinations, our reasonings, our wills, which they govern, drive, and stir at the mercy of their influences, as our reason finds and teaches us;

> He learns that stars remotely seen
> Govern by silent laws, and intervene;
> To move the universe they alternate,
> And rule by certain signs the twists of fate;
>
> MANILIUS

when we see that not merely a man, nor a king, but kingdoms, empires, and all this world below move in step with the slightest movements of the heavens;

> How great a change the slightest motion brings:
> So great this kingdom is that governs kings;
>
> MANILIUS

if our virtue, our vices, our competence and knowledge, and this very dissertation that we are making about the power of the stars and this comparison of them to us, comes as our reason judges, by their medium and their favor;

> One, in love's delirium,
> Can cross the sea and conquer Ilium;
> Another man is destined laws to build;
> Fathers kill sons, fathers by sons are killed,
> And brother wounds armed brother in the fray.

> This war is not of ours; Fate makes men stray,
> Punish themselves, their members lacerate.
> . . . .
> This too is fated, that I write of fate;
>
> MANILIUS

if we hold by the dispensation of heaven this portion of reason that we have, how can our reason make us equal to heaven? How subject its essence and conditions to our knowledge? All that we see in those bodies astonishes us. *What preparations, what instruments, what levers, what machines, what workmen performed so great a work?* [Cicero.]

Why do we deny them soul, and life, and reason? Have we recognized in them some inert, insensible stupidity, we who have no dealings with them except obedience? Shall we say that we have seen in no other creature than man the exercise of a rational soul? Well, have we seen anything like the sun? Does it fail to exist, because we have seen nothing like it, and its movements to exist, because there are none like them? If what we have not seen does not exist, our knowledge is marvelously shrunk: *How narrow are the limits of our mind!* [Cicero.]

Are these not dreams of human vanity, to make the moon a celestial earth, to imagine mountains and valleys there, like Anaxagoras; to plant habitations and human dwellings there, and set up colonies for our convenience, as Plato and Plutarch do; and to make our earth a bright star lighting the moon? *Among other human infirmities is this one also, mental fog, and not so much the need to err as the love of errors* [Seneca]. *The corruptible body weighs down the soul, and the earthy tabernacle oppresses the much pondering mind* [The Book of Wisdom, quoted by Saint Augustine].

[HUMAN BEINGS' PLACE IN CREATION]

Presumption is our natural and original malady. The most vulnerable and frail of all creatures is man, and at the same time the most arrogant. He feels and sees himself lodged here, amid the mire and dung of the world, nailed and riveted to the worst, the deadest, and the most stagnant part of the universe, on the lowest story of the house and the farthest from the vault of heaven, with the animals of the worst condition of the three;[3] and in his imagination he goes planting himself above the circle of the moon, and bringing the sky down beneath his feet. It is by the vanity of this same imagination that he equals himself to God, attributes to himself divine characteristics, picks himself out and separates himself from the horde of other creatures, carves out their shares to his fellows and companions the animals, and distributes among them such portions and faculties and powers as he sees fit. How does he know, by the force of his intelligence, the secret internal stirrings of animals? By what comparison between them and us does he infer the stupidity that he attributes to them?

When I play with my cat, who knows if I am not a pastime to her more than she is to me? Plato, in his picture of the golden age under Saturn, counts

[3] Animals were conventionally divided into those that walk, those that fly, and those that swim.

among the principal advantages of the man of that time the communication he had with the beasts; inquiring of them and learning from them, he knew the true qualities and differences of each one of them; whereby he acquired a very perfect intelligence and prudence, and conducted his life far more happily than we could possibly do. Do we need a better proof to judge man's impudence with regard to the beasts? That great author opined that in most of the bodily form that Nature gave them, she considered solely the use of prognostications that were derived from them in his time.

This defect that hinders communication between them and us, why is it not just as much ours as theirs? It is a matter of guesswork whose fault it is that we do not understand one another; for we do not understand them any more than they do us. By this same reasoning they may consider us beasts, as we consider them. It is no great wonder if we do not understand them; neither do we understand the Basques and the Troglodytes.[4] However, some have boasted of understanding them, like Apollonius of Tyana, Melampus, Tiresias, Thales, and others. And since it is a fact, as the cosmographers say, that there are nations that accept a dog as their king, they must give a definite interpretation to his voice and motions. We must notice the parity there is between us. We have some mediocre understanding of their meaning; so do they of ours, in about the same degree. They flatter us, threaten us, and implore us, and we them.

Furthermore, we discover very evidently that there is full and complete communication between them and that they understand each other, not only those of the same species, but also those of different species.

> Even dumb cattle and the savage beasts
> Varied and different noises do employ
> When they feel fear or pain, or thrill with joy.
>
> LUCRETIUS

In a certain bark of the dog the horse knows there is anger; at a certain other sound of his he is not frightened. Even in the beasts that have no voice, from the mutual services we see between them we easily infer some other means of communication; their motions converse and discuss:

> Likewise in children, the tongue's speechlessness
> Leads them to gesture what they would express.
>
> LUCRETIUS

Why not; just as well as our mutes dispute, argue, and tell stories by signs? I have seen some so supple and versed in this, that in truth they lacked nothing of perfection in being able to make themselves understood. Lovers grow angry, are reconciled, entreat, thank, make assignations, and in fine say everything, with their eyes:

> And silence too records
> Our prayers and our words.
>
> TASSO

[4]Cave dwellers who lived on the western shore of the Red Sea.

What of the hands? We beg, we promise, call, dismiss, threaten, pray, entreat, deny, refuse, question, admire, count, confess, repent, fear, blush, doubt, instruct, command, incite, encourage, swear, testify, accuse, condemn, absolve, insult, despise, defy, vex, flatter, applaud, bless, humiliate, mock, reconcile, commend, exalt, entertain, rejoice, complain, grieve, mope, despair, wonder, exclaim, are silent, and what not, with a variation and multiplication that vie with the tongue. With the head: we invite, send away, avow, disavow, give the lie, welcome, honor, venerate, disdain, demand, show out, cheer, lament, caress, scold, submit, brave, exhort, menace, assure, inquire. What of the eyebrows? What of the shoulders? There is no movement that does not speak both a language intelligible without instruction, and a public language; which means, seeing the variety and particular use of other languages, that this one must rather be judged the one proper to human nature. I omit what necessity teaches privately and promptly to those who need it, and the finger alphabets, and the grammars in gestures, and the sciences which are practiced and expressed only by gestures, and the nations which Pliny says have no other language.

An ambassador of the city of Abdera, after speaking at length to King Agis of Sparta, asked him: "Well, Sire, what answer do you wish me to take back to our citizens?" "That I allowed you to say all you wanted, and as much as you wanted, without ever saying a word." Wasn't that an eloquent and thoroughly intelligible silence?

Moreover, what sort of faculty of ours do we not recognize in the actions of the animals? Is there a society regulated with more order, diversified into more charges and functions, and more consistently maintained, than that of the honeybees? Can we imagine so orderly an arrangement of actions and occupations as this to be conducted without reason and foresight?

> Some, by these signs and instances inclined,
> Have said that bees share in the divine mind
> And the ethereal spirit.
>
> VIRGIL

Do the swallows that we see on the return of spring ferreting in all the corners of our houses search without judgment, and choose without discrimination, out of a thousand places, the one which is most suitable for them to dwell in? And in that beautiful and admirable texture of their buildings, can birds use a square rather than a round figure, an obtuse rather than a right angle, without knowing their properties and their effects? Do they take now water, now clay, without judging that hardness is softened by moistening? Do they floor their palace with moss or with down, without foreseeing that the tender limbs of their little ones will lie softer and more comfortably on it? Do they shelter themselves from the rainy wind and face their dwelling toward the orient without knowing the different conditions of these winds and considering that one is more salutary to them than the other? Why does the spider thicken her web in one place and slacken it in another, use now this sort of knot, now that one, unless she has the power of reflection, and thought, and inference?

We recognize easily enough, in most of their works, how much superiority the animals have over us and how feeble is our skill to imitate them.

We see, however, in our cruder works, the faculties that we use, and that our soul applies itself with all its power; why do we not think the same thing of them? Why do we attribute to some sort of natural and servile inclination these works which surpass all that we can do by nature and by art? Wherein, without realizing it, we grant them a very great advantage over us, by making Nature, with maternal tenderness, accompany them and guide them as by the hand in all the actions and comforts of their life; while us she abandons to chance and to fortune, and to seek by art the things necessary for our preservation, and denies us at the same time the power to attain, by any education and mental straining, the natural resourcefulness of the animals: so that their brutish stupidity surpasses in all conveniences all that our divine intelligence can do.

Truly, by this reckoning, we should be quite right to call her a very unjust stepmother. But this is not so; our organization is not so deformed and disorderly. Nature has universally embraced all her creatures; and there is none that she has not very amply furnished with all powers necessary for the preservation of its being. For these vulgar complaints that I hear men make (as the license of their opinions now raises them above the clouds, and then sinks them to the antipodes) that we are the only animal abandoned naked on the naked earth, tied, bound, having nothing to arm and cover ourselves with except the spoils of others; whereas all other creatures Nature has clothed with shells, husks, bark, hair, wool, spikes, hide, down, feathers, scales, fleece, and silk, according to the need of their being; has armed them with claws, teeth, or horns for attack and defense; and has herself instructed them in what is fit for them—to swim, to run, to fly, to sing—whereas man can neither walk, nor speak, nor eat, nor do anything but cry, without apprenticeship—

> The infant, like a sailor tossed ashore
> By raging seas, lies naked on the earth,
> Speechless, helpless for life, when at his birth
> Nature from out the womb brings him to light.
> He fills the place with wailing, as is right
> For one who through so many woes must pass.
> Yet flocks, herds, savage beasts of every class
> Grow up without the need for any rattle,
> Or for a gentle nurse's soothing prattle;
> They seek no varied clothes against the sky;
> Lastly they need no arms, no ramparts high
> To guard their own—since earth itself and nature
> Amply bring forth all things for every creature
>
> LUCRETIUS

—those complaints are false, there is a greater equality and a more uniform relationship in the organization of the world. Our skin is provided as adequately as theirs with endurance against the assaults of the weather: witness so many nations who have not yet tried the use of any clothes. Our ancient Gauls wore hardly any clothes; nor do the Irish, our neighbors, under so cold a sky. But we may judge this better by ourselves; for all the parts of the body that we see fit to expose to the wind and air are found fit to endure it: face, feet, hands, legs, shoulders, head, according as custom invites us. For if there is a part of us that is tender and that seems as though it should fear the cold, it should be the stomach, where digestion takes place; our fathers left it uncovered, and our ladies, soft and delicate as they are, sometimes go half bare down to the navel. Nor are the bindings and swaddlings of infants necessary either; and the Lacedaemonian mothers raised their children in complete freedom to move their limbs, without wrapping or binding them. Our weeping is common to most of the other animals; and there are scarcely any who are not observed to complain and wail long after their birth, since it is a demeanor most appropriate to the helplessness that they feel. As for the habit of eating, it is, in us as in them, natural and needing no instruction:

> For each one feels his powers and his needs.
>
> LUCRETIUS

Who doubts that a child, having attained the strength to feed himself would be able to seek his food? And the earth produces and offers him enough of it for his need, with no other cultivation or artifice; and if not in all weather, neither does she for the beasts: witness the provisions we see the ants and others make for the sterile seasons of the year. These nations that we have just discovered to be so abundantly furnished with food and natural drink, without care or preparation, have now taught us that bread is not our only food, and that without plowing, our mother Nature had provided us in plenty with all we needed; indeed, as seems likely, more amply and richly than she does now that we have interpolated our artifice:

> At first and of her own accord the earth
> Brought forth sleek fruits and vintages of worth,
> Herself gave harvests sweet and pastures fair,
> Which now scarce grow, despite our toil and care,
> And we exhaust our oxen and our men;
>
> LUCRETIUS

the excess and unruliness of our appetite outstripping all the inventions with which we seek to satisfy it.

As for weapons, we have more that are natural than most other animals, and more varied movements of our limbs; and we get more service out of them, naturally and without lessons. Those who are trained to fight naked are seen to throw themselves into dangers like our own men. If some animals surpass us in this advantage, we surpass many others. And the skill to fortify and protect the body by acquired means, we possess by a natural instinct and precept. As proof that this is so, the elephant sharpens and whets the teeth which he uses in war (for he has special ones for this purpose, which he spares, and does not use at all for his other functions). When bulls go into combat, they spread and toss the dust around them; boars whet their tusks; and the ichneumon,[5] when he is to come to grips with the crocodile, arms his body, coats it, and crusts it all over with mud, well pressed and well

[5]A kind of African mongoose, said to be able to kill a crocodile.

kneaded, as with a cuirass. Why shall we not say that it is just as natural to arm ourselves with wood and iron?

As for speech, it is certain that if it is not natural, it is not necessary. Nevertheless, I believe that a child who had been brought up in complete solitude, remote from all association (which would be a hard experiment to make), would have some sort of speech to express his ideas. And it is not credible that Nature has denied us this resource that she has given to many other animals: for what is it but speech, this faculty we see in them of complaining, rejoicing, calling to each other for help, inviting each other to love, as they do by the use of their voice? How could they not speak to one another? They certainly speak to us, and we to them. In how many ways do we not speak to our dogs? And they answer us. We talk to them in another language, with other names, than to birds, hogs, oxen, horses; and we change the idiom according to the species:

> So ants amidst their sable-colored band
> Greet one another, and inquire perchance
> The road each follows, and the prize in hand.
>
> DANTE

It seems to me that Lactantius attributes to beasts not only speech but also laughter. And the difference of language that is seen between us, according to the difference of countries, is found also in animals of the same species. Aristotle cites in this connection the various calls of partridges according to the place they are situated in,

> And various birds . . .
> Utter at different times far different cries . . .
> And some change with the changing of the skies
> Their raucous songs.
>
> LUCRETIUS

But it is yet to be known what language this child would speak; and what is said about it by conjecture has not much appearance of truth. If they allege to me, against this opinion, that men naturally deaf do not speak at all, I reply that it is not only because they could not be taught speech by ear, but rather because the sense of hearing, of which they are deprived, is related to that of speech, and they hold together by a natural tie: so that what we speak we must speak first to ourselves, and make it ring on our own ears inwardly, before we send it to other ears.

I have said all this to maintain this resemblance that exists to human things, and to bring us back and join us to the majority. We are neither above nor below the rest: all that is under heaven, says the sage, incurs the same law and the same fortune,

> All things are bound by their own chains of fate.
>
> LUCRETIUS

There is some difference, there are orders and degrees; but it is under the aspect of one and the same nature:

And all things go their own way, nor forget
Distinctions by the law of nature set.

LUCRETIUS

Man must be constrained and forced into line inside the barriers of this order. The poor wretch is in no position really to step outside them; he is fettered and bound, he is subjected to the same obligation as the other creatures of his class, and in a very ordinary condition, without any real and essential prerogative or preeminence. That which he accords himself in his mind and in his fancy has neither body nor taste. And if it is true that he alone of all the animals has this freedom of imagination and this unruliness in thought that represents to him what is, what is not, what he wants, the false and the true, it is an advantage that is sold him very dear, and in which he has little cause to glory, for from it springs the principal source of the ills that oppress him: sin, disease, irresolution, confusion, despair. . . .

[KNOWLEDGE CANNOT MAKE US HAPPY]

But to return to my subject, we have as our share inconstancy, irresolution, uncertainty, grief, superstition, worry over things to come, even after our life, ambition, avarice, jealousy, envy, unruly, frantic, and untamable appetites, war, falsehood, disloyalty, detraction, and curiosity. Indeed we have strangely overpaid for this fine reason that we glory in, and this capacity to judge and know, if we have bought it at the price of this infinite number of passions to which we are incessantly a prey. Unless we like to make much, as indeed Socrates does, of this notable prerogative over the other animals, that whereas Nature has prescribed to them certain seasons and limits to the pleasures of Venus, she has given us free rein at all hours and occasions. *As with wine for sick men, since it is rarely good and often bad, it is better not to use it at all, than in the hope of a doubtful benefit to incur a manifest risk; so I hardly know whether it would not have been better for the human race if this swift movement of thought, this acumen, this cleverness, which we call reason, had not been given to man at all, since it is a plague to many and salutary only to a few, rather than given so abundantly and so lavishly* [Cicero].

What good can we suppose it did Varro and Aristotle to know so many things? Did it exempt them from human discomforts? Were they freed from the accidents that oppress a porter? Did they derive from logic some consolation for the gout? For knowing how this humor lodges in the joints, did they feel it less? Were they reconciled to death for knowing that some nations rejoice in it, and with cuckoldry for knowing that wives are held in common in some region? On the contrary, though they held the first rank in knowledge, one among the Romans, the other among the Greeks, and in the period when knowledge flourished most, we have not for all that heard that they had any particular excellence in their lives; in fact the Greek has a hard time to clear himself of some notable spots in his.

Have they found that sensual pleasure and health are more savory to him who knows astrology and grammar?

Does the illiterate's tool stand less erect?

HORACE

And are shame and poverty less troublesome?

> Disease and weakness you of course will miss,
> Escape both grief and pain, and possibly
> Win longer life, a better destiny.
>
> JUVENAL

I have seen in my time a hundred artisans, a hundred plowmen, wiser and happier than rectors of the university, and whom I would rather resemble. Learning, in my opinion, has a place among things necessary for life, like glory, nobility, dignity, or at best like beauty, riches, and such other qualities which are really useful for it, but remotely, and a little more in fancy than in nature.

We hardly need any more offices, rules, and laws of living, in our community than do the cranes and ants in theirs. And nevertheless we see that they conduct themselves in a very orderly manner without erudition. If man were wise, he would set the true price of each thing according as it was most useful and appropriate for his life.

If anyone will sum us up by our actions and conduct, a greater number of excellent men will be found among the ignorant than among the learned: I mean in every sort of virtue. The old Rome seems to me to have borne men of greater worth, both for peace and for war, than that learned Rome that ruined itself. Even if the rest were exactly equal, at least worth and innocence would remain on the side of the old, for they dwell singularly well with simplicity.

But I leave this subject, which would lead me farther than I would follow. I will add only this, that humility and submissiveness alone can make a good man. The knowledge of his duty should not be left to each man's judgment; it should be prescribed to him, not left to the choice of his reason. Otherwise, judging by the imbecility and infinite variety of our reasons and opinions, we would finally forge for ourselves duties that would set us to eating one another, as Epicurus says. . . .

[KNOWLEDGE CANNOT MAKE US GOOD]

As by simplicity life becomes pleasanter, so also does it become better and more innocent, as I was starting to say a while back. The simple and ignorant, says Saint Paul, raise themselves to heaven, and take possession of it; and we, with all our learning, plunge ourselves into the infernal abyss. I do not stop to consider either Valentinian, a declared enemy of knowledge and letters, or Licinius, Roman emperors both, who called them the poison and plague of any political state; or Mohammed, who, so I have heard, forbade learning to his followers. But the example of the great Lycurgus, and his authority, should certainly have great weight, and the reverence of that divine Lacedaemonian government, so great, so admirable, and so long flourishing in virtue and good fortune without any teaching or practice of letters. Those who return from that new world which was discovered in our fathers' time by the Spaniards can testify to us how much more lawfully and regulatedly these nations live, without magistrates and without law, than ours, where there are more officers and laws than there are other men and actions:

Their hands are full of motions and petitions,
Their pockets stuffed with reams of briefs and writs,
With powers of attorney, depositions,
Decisions, and opinions, and *op. cit.*'s,
Designed to rob, with maximum efficience,
The simple folk of their remaining wits;
Before, behind, no matter where they turn is
A host of lawyers, notaries, attorneys.

ARIOSTO

It is what a Roman senator of the late period said, that their predecessors had a breath stinking of garlic, and a stomach perfumed with a good conscience; and that on the contrary those of his time smelled outwardly of nothing but perfume, though stinking within of every kind of vice. That is to say, so I think, that they had great learning and ability, and a great lack of integrity. Uncouthness, ignorance, simplicity, and crudity are prone to go with innocence; curiosity, subtlety, and learning bring malice in their train; humility, fear, obedience, and amenability (which are the principal qualities for the preservation of human society) require a soul that is open, docile, and with little presumption. . . .

[HUMAN BEINGS HAVE NO KNOWLEDGE]

Yet must I see at last whether it is in the power of man to find what he seeks, and whether that quest that he has been making for so many centuries has enriched him with any new power and any solid truth.

I think he will confess to me, if he speaks in all conscience, that all the profit he has gained from so long a pursuit is to have learned to acknowledge his weakness. The ignorance that was naturally in us we have by long study confirmed and verified.

To really learned men has happened what happens to ears of wheat: they rise high and lofty, heads erect and proud, as long as they are empty; but when they are full and swollen with grain in their ripeness, they begin to grow humble and lower their horns. Similarly, men who have tried everything and sounded everything, having found in that pile of knowledge and store of so many various things nothing solid and firm, and nothing but vanity, have renounced their presumption and recognized their natural condition.

It is what Velleius reproaches Cotta and Cicero for, that they learned from Philo that they had learned nothing.

Pherecydes, one of the Seven Sages, writing to Thales as he was dying, said: "I have ordered my friends, after they have buried me, to bring you my writings. If they satisfy you and the other sages, publish them; if not, suppress them: they contain no certainty that satisfies myself. Nor do I profess to know the truth and to attain it. I uncover things more than I discover them."

The wisest man that ever was,[6] when they asked him what he knew, answered that he knew this much, that he knew nothing. He was verifying

[6] Socrates.

what they say, that the greatest part of what we know is the least of those parts that we do not know; that is to say that the very thing we think we know is a part, and a very small part, of our ignorance.

We know things in a dream, says Plato, and we are ignorant of them in reality.

Almost all the ancients have said that nothing can be understood, nothing perceived, nothing known; that our senses are narrow, our minds weak, the course of our life short [Cicero].

As for Cicero himself, who owed all his worth to learning, Valerius says that in his old age he began to lose his esteem for letters. And while he practiced them, it was without obligation to any party, following what seemed probable to him now in one sect, now in another, keeping himself always in Academic doubt. *I must speak, but in such a way as to affirm nothing; I shall search into all things, doubting most of them and mistrusting myself* [Cicero].

I should have too easy a time if I wanted to consider man in his ordinary condition and in the mass; and yet I could do so according to his own rule, which judges the truth not by the weight of votes but by the number. Let us leave the people aside,

> Who waking snore . . .
> Whose life is dead, although they live and see,
>
> LUCRETIUS

who are not conscious of themselves, who do not judge themselves, who leave most of their natural faculties idle.

I wish to take man in his highest estate. Let us consider him in that small number of excellent and select men who, having been endowed with fine and particular natural ability, have further strengthened and sharpened it by care, by study, and by art, and have raised it to the highest pitch of wisdom that it can attain. They have fashioned their soul to all directions and all angles, supported and propped it with all the outside assistance that was fit for it, and enriched and adorned it with all they could borrow, for its advantage, from the inside and the outside of the world; it is in them that the utmost height of human nature is found. They have regulated the world with governments and laws; they have instructed it with arts and sciences, and instructed it further by the example of their admirable conduct.

I shall take into account only these people, their testimony, and their experience. Let us see how far they have gone and where they have halted. The infirmities and defects that we shall find in this assembly the world may well boldly acknowledge as its own.

Whoever seeks anything comes to this point: he says either that he has found it, or that it cannot be found, or that he is still in quest of it. All philosophy is divided into these three types. Its purpose is to seek out truth, knowledge, and certainty.

The Peripatetics, Epicureans, Stoics, and others thought they had found it. These established the sciences that we have, and treated them as certain knowledge.

Clitomachus, Carneades, and the Academics despaired of their quest, and judged that truth could not be conceived by our powers. The conclusion of these men was man's weakness and ignorance. This school had the greatest following and the noblest adherents.

Pyrrho and other Skeptics or Epechists—whose doctrines, many of the ancients maintained, were derived from Homer, the Seven Sages, Archilochus, and Euripides, and were held by Zeno, Democritus, Xenophanes—say that they are still in search of the truth. These men judge that those who think they have found it are infinitely mistaken; and that there is also an overbold vanity in that second class that assures us that human powers are not capable of attaining it. For this matter of establishing the measure of our power, of knowing and judging the difficulty of things, is a great and supreme knowledge, of which they doubt that man is capable:

> Whoever thinks that we know nothing does not know
> Whether we know enough to say that this is so.
>
> LUCRETIUS

Ignorance that knows itself, that judges itself and condemns itself, is not complete ignorance: to be that, it must be ignorant of itself. So that the profession of the Pyrrhonians is to waver, doubt, and inquire, to be sure of nothing, to answer for nothing. Of the three functions of the soul, the imaginative, the appetitive, and the consenting, they accept the first two; the last they suspend and keep it ambiguous, without inclination or approbation, however slight, in one direction or the other. . . .

Our speech has its weaknesses and its defects, like all the rest. Most of the occasions for the troubles of the world are grammatical. Our lawsuits spring only from debate over the interpretation of the laws, and most of our wars from the inability to express clearly the conventions and treaties of agreement of princes. How many quarrels, and how important, have been produced in the world by doubt of the meaning of that syllable *Hoc!*[7]

Let us take the sentence that logic itself offers us as the clearest. If you say "It is fine weather," and if you are speaking the truth, then it is fine weather. Isn't that a sure way of speaking? Still it will deceive us. To show this let us continue the example. If you say "I lie," and if you are speaking the truth, then you lie. The art, the reason, the force, of the conclusion of this one are the same as in the other; yet there we are stuck in the mud.

I can see why the Pyrrhonian philosophers cannot express their general conception in any manner of speaking; for they would need a new language. Ours is wholly formed of affirmative propositions, which to them are utterly repugnant; so that when they say "I doubt," immediately you have them by the throat to make them admit that at least they know and are sure of this fact, that they doubt. Thus they have been constrained to take refuge in this comparison from medicine, without which their attitude would be inexplicable: when they declare "I do not know" or "I doubt," they say that this proposition carries itself away with the rest, no more nor less than rhubarb, which expels evil humors and carries itself off with them.

[7] Montaigne is referring to the controversy between Catholics and Protestants over transubstantiation, which centered on the meaning of Christ's words *Hoc est corpus meum* ("This is my body").

This idea is more firmly grasped in the form of interrogation: "What do I know?"[8]—the words I bear as a motto, inscribed over a pair of scales. . . .

[WE CANNOT RELY ON OUR SENSES]

This subject has brought me to the consideration of the senses, in which lies the greatest foundation and proof of our ignorance. All that is known, is doubtless known through the faculty of the knower; for since judgment comes from the operation of him who judges, it stands to reason that he performs this operation by his means and will, not by the constraint of others, as would happen if we knew things through the power and according to the law of their own essence.

Now all knowledge makes its way into us through the senses; they are our masters:

> No shorter pathway can persuasion find
> Into the human heart and human mind.
>
> LUCRETIUS

Knowledge begins through them and is resolved into them.

After all, we would know no more than a stone, if we did not know that there is sound, smell, light, taste, measure, weight, softness, hardness, roughness, color, smoothness, breadth, depth. There are the base and the principles of the whole edifice of our knowledge. And according to some, knowledge is nothing else but sensation. Whoever can force me to contradict the senses has me by the throat; he could not make me retreat any further. The senses are the beginning and the end of human knowledge:

> Our senses, you will find, did first provide
> The idea of truth; they cannot be denied.
> . . . .
> In what then should we place a greater trust
> Than in the senses?
>
> LUCRETIUS

Attribute to them as little as you can, still you must grant them this, that by way of them and by their mediation proceeds all our instruction. Cicero says that Chrysippus, having tried to disparage the power and strength of the senses, presented himself with arguments to the contrary, and such violent objections, that he could not satisfy them. Whereupon Carneades, who was upholding the opposite side, boasted that he would use the very weapons and words of Chrysippus to combat him, and therefore exclaimed against him: 'O wretched man, your strength has defeated you!"

We cannot conceive of an absurdity more extreme than to maintain that fire does not heat, that light does not illumine, that there is no weight or hardness in iron; these are items of knowledge brought to us by the senses;

[8]A reference to the medal Montaigne had struck, with the motto *Que sçay-je?* and an evenly balanced set of scales. See the Introduction to Montaigne.

and man has no belief or knowledge that can compare with this sort for certainty.

The first consideration that I offer on the subject of the senses is that I have my doubts whether man is provided with all the senses of nature. I see many animals that live a complete and perfect life, some without sight, others without hearing; who knows whether we too do not still lack one, two, three, or many other senses? For if any one is lacking, our reason cannot discover its absence. It is the privilege of the senses to be the extreme limit of our perception. There is nothing beyond them that can help us to discover them; no, nor can one sense discover the other:

> Can ears the errors of the eyes detect?
> Touch refute ears, or taste our touch correct?
> Nose confute touch, and eyes in turn prevail?
> LUCRETIUS

Together they all form the farthest limit of our faculties:

> Its function is defined
> To each apart, to each its power assigned.
> LUCRETIUS

It is impossible to make a man who was born blind conceive that he does not see; impossible to make him desire sight and regret its absence. Wherefore we should take no assurance from the fact that our soul is content and satisfied with those senses we have, seeing that it has no means of feeling its malady and imperfection therein, if any there be. It is impossible to say anything to this blind man, by reason, argument, or comparison, that will place in his imagination any apprehension of light, color, and sight. There is nothing further behind that can push that sense into evidence. When we see men blind from birth desire to see, it is not because they understand what they ask: they have learned from us that they lack something, that they have something to desire, which is in us; which they name perfectly well, and its effects and consequences; but nevertheless they do not know what it is, nor do they have a close or distant apprehension of it.

I have seen a gentleman of a good house, born blind, or at least blind from such an age that he does not know what sight is. He understands so little what he lacks, that he uses and employs as we do words appropriate to sight, and applies them in a manner all private and his own. He was presented with a boy, whose godfather he was; taking him in his arms, he said: "My, what a handsome boy! How good it is to see him! What a gay face he has!" He will say like one of us: "This room has a fine view; it is a clear day, the sun is shining bright." There is more; for because hunting, tennis, and shooting are our sports, and he has heard this, he is fond of them and keenly interested in them, and thinks he has the same share in them that we do; he finds excitement and pleasure in them, and yet he takes them in only through his ears. They call to him that there goes a hare when they are in a bit of fine open country where he can spur his horse; and then they tell him later that there is a hare caught; and he is as proud of his catch as he hears the others say they are. The tennis ball he takes in his left hand and strokes with his racket; with the harquebus[9] he shoots at random, and gets his fun by having his men tell him that he is either over or beside the mark.

What do we know about whether mankind is doing something equally foolish for lack of some sense, and whether by this lack the greater part of the face of things is hidden from us? What do we know about whether the difficulties we find in many works of nature come from that? And whether many actions of the animals that exceed our capacity are produced by the operation of some sense that we lack? And whether some of them have by this means a fuller and more complete life than ours?

We grasp an apple by almost all our senses; we find in it redness, smoothness, smell, and sweetness; besides these it may have other properties, like drying up or shrinking, to which we have no sense that corresponds. The properties that we call occult in many things, as that of the magnet to attract iron—is it not likely that there are sensory faculties in nature suitable to judge them and perceive them, and that the lack of such faculties causes our ignorance of the true essence of such things? Perhaps it is some particular sense that reveals to cocks the hours of morning and midnight, and moves them to crow; that teaches hens, before any practice and experience, to fear a sparrow hawk, and not a goose or a peacock, which are bigger creatures; which warns chickens of the quality in the cat that is hostile to them, and not to distrust the dog: to beware of mewing, a rather caressing sound, and not of barking, a harsh and quarrelsome sound; that teaches wasps, ants, and rats always to select the best cheese and the best pear, before having tasted them; and that guides the stag, the elephant, the snake, to the knowledge of a certain herb suitable for their cure.

There is no sense that does not have great dominion, and bring us by its means to know an infinite number of things. If we lacked the understanding of sounds, of harmony.and the voice, this lack would bring inconceivable confusion upon all the rest of our knowledge. For besides what is attached to the proper effect of each sense, how many arguments, consequences, and conclusions we draw in other things by the comparison of one sense with another! Let an intelligent man imagine human nature as produced originally without sight, and think how much ignorance and confusion such a lack would bring him, how much shadow and blindness in our soul: it will be seen from this how important to our knowledge of the truth is the privation of another such sense, or two, or three—if this privation is in us. We have formed a truth by the consultation and concurrence of our five senses, but perhaps we needed the agreement of eight or ten senses, and their contribution, to perceive it certainly and in its essence.

The schools that dispute man's knowledge dispute it principally because of the uncertainty and weakness of our senses; for since all knowledge comes to us by their means and mediation, if they err in the report they make to us, if they corrupt or alter what they carry to us from without, if the light that flows through them into our soul is obscured in passage, we have nothing left to go by. From this extreme difficulty have arisen all these fancies: that each object has in itself all that we find in it; that it has nothing of what

[9]A heavy musket, invented in the fifteenth century.

we think we find in it; and this of the Epicureans, that the sun is no bigger than it looks to us:

> Whate'er it is, it has no greater size
> Than what it seems to be, seen by our eyes;
>
> LUCRETIUS

that the appearances that show a body to be big to him who is near, and smaller to him who is far, are both true,

> Nor grant we therefore that our eyes are blind;
> . . . .
> Blame not on eyes the error of the mind;
>
> LUCRETIUS

and, boldly, that there is no deception in the senses, that we must submit to their mercy, and seek elsewhere reasons to excuse the difference and contradiction that we find in them, in fact invent any other falsehood or reverie (they go as far as that) rather than accuse the senses.

Timagoras swore that however much he pressed or turned his eyes, he had never seen the light of a candle doubled; and that that appearance came from a defect of the mind, not of the organ.

Of all absurdities the most absurd to the Epicureans is to disavow the power and effect of the senses.

> Hence what the senses see is always true.
> And if our reason cannot well expound
> Why what from near was square, from far is round,
> Although we lack the cause, 'tis better still
> Either appearance to interpret ill,
> Than from our hands to let the obvious go,
> To spurn our primal trust and overthrow
> The bases on which life and safety stay.
> For not alone would reason fail; straightway
> Our very life would fall, unless we dare
> To trust our senses, shun great heights, beware
> Of other similar dangers.
>
> LUCRETIUS

This desperate and most unphilosophical advice means nothing else than that human knowledge can maintain itself only by unreasonable, mad, and senseless reason; but that still it is better for man, in order to assert himself, to use it and any other remedy, however fantastic, than to admit his necessary stupidity: such a disadvantageous truth! He cannot escape the fact that the senses are the sovereign masters of his knowledge; but they are uncertain and deceivable in all circumstances. It is there that we must fight it out, and if just forces fail us, as they do, use stubbornness, heedlessness, impudence.

In case what the Epicureans say is true, to wit, that we have no knowledge if the appearances of the senses are false; and if what the Stoics say is also true, that the appearances of the senses are so false that they can produce no knowledge for us; we shall conclude, at the expense of these two great dogmatic sects, that there is no knowledge.

As for the error and uncertainty of the operation of the senses, each man can furnish himself with as many examples as he pleases, so ordinary are the mistakes and deceptions that they offer us. At the echo in a valley, the sound of a trumpet seems to come from in front of us, when it comes from a league behind:

> Two distant mountains like as one are seen,
> Though on the sea great distance lies between.
> . . . .
> Astern the hills and meadows seem to fly,
> Which our ship skirts near by . . .
> . . . .
> . . . When in midstream our steed stops short,
> Some power seems to bear his body athwart
> And force him up against the rushing stream.
>
> LUCRETIUS

When rolling a harquebus bullet under the forefinger, the middle finger being entwined over it, we have to force ourselves hard to admit that there is only one, so strongly does our sense represent two to us. For that the senses are many a time masters of reason, and constrain it to receive impressions that it knows and judges to be false, is seen at every turn. I leave aside the sense of touch, whose operations are closer, more vivid and substantial, which, so many times, by the effect of the pain it brings to the body, overthrows all those beautiful Stoical resolutions, and compels the man to cry out at his stomach who has established with all resoluteness this doctrine in his soul, that the colic, like every other malady and pain, is an indifferent thing, not having the power to reduce at all the supreme happiness and felicity in which the sage is lodged by his virtue.

There is no heart so faint that the sound of our drums and trumpets will not warm it, or so hard that the sweetness of music will not awaken it and caress it; no soul so crabbed as not to feel touched by some reverence on contemplating the somber vastness of our churches, the diversity of ornaments, and the order of our ceremonies, and on hearing the devotional sound of our organs and the harmony, so solemn and religious, of our voices. Even those who enter with disdain feel a certain shiver in their heart, and a certain awe, which makes them distrust their opinion.

As for me, I do not consider myself strong enough to listen sedately to verses of Horace or Catullus sung by an adequate voice from a young and beautiful mouth. And Zeno was right to say that the voice was the flower of beauty.

Someone tried to make me believe that a man whom all we Frenchmen know had overimpressed me by reciting to me some verses he had composed; that they were not the same on paper as in the air, and that my eyes would judge them contrary to my ears, so much influence utterance has in giving value and style to the works that come into its mercy. In which connection Philoxenus was not too choleric when, hearing someone giving a bad tone to some composition of his, he began to stamp on and break some tiles that belonged to the offender, saying: "I disrupt what is yours as you corrupt what is mine."

For what reason did even those who had themselves put to death by their own sure resolve turn away their face in order not to see the stroke that they were having dealt them? And why cannot those who for their health desire and order someone to cut into them and cauterize them endure the sight of the preparations, instruments, and operations of the surgeon, since sight is to have no participation in this pain? Are these not fit examples to prove the authority that the senses have over the reason?

No matter if we are aware that these tresses are borrowed from a page or a lackey, that this rosy complexion is a product of Spain, and that this whiteness and smoothness comes from the ocean sea; still sight must compel us to find the object more lovely and agreeable for it, against all reason. For in this there is nothing of the lady's own:

> Jewels and gold hide flaws; we are tricked by art;
> The girl is of herself the smallest part.
> Oft in all this you ask where your love lies:
> By this Gorgon shield rich love deceives the eyes.
>
> OVID

How much power the poets ascribe to the senses, who make Narcissus madly in love with his own reflection—

> All he admires for which he is admired;
> Unwitting, loves himself; yearned for, he yearns;
> Seeking, is sought; with flame self-kindled burns
>
> OVID

—and Pygmalion's understanding so troubled by the impression of the sight of his ivory statue, that he loves and serves it as though it were alive:

> Kisses he gives, and thinks they are returned;
> Pursues and holds, and thinks the flesh gives way
> Beneath his fingers, fears a mark will stay.
>
> OVID

Put a philosopher in a cage of thin iron wire in large meshes, and hang it from the top of the towers of Notre Dame of Paris: he will see by evident reason that it is impossible for him to fall, and yet (unless he is used to the trade of the steeplejacks) he cannot keep the sight of this extreme height from terrifying and paralyzing him. For we have trouble enough feeling secure in the galleries that are in our steeples, if they are wrought with openwork, even though they are of stone. There are some who cannot even bear the thought of them. Lay a beam between these two towers of such width as we need to walk on: there is no philosophical wisdom of such great firmness that it can give us courage to walk on it as we should if it were on the ground.

I have often experienced this in our mountains on this side of the border (and yet I am one of those who are only moderately frightened at such things): that I could not endure the sight of that infinite depth without a shiver and a trembling of the back of my legs and thighs, even though I was fully my own length away from the actual edge, and could not have fallen unless I had conveyed myself purposely into danger. I have also noticed there that whatever the height might be, provided that in the side some tree or jutting rock is present to support our sight a little and break it up, this relieves us and gives us assurance, as if it were a thing from which in case of a fall we could get help; but that sheer and unbroken precipices we cannot even look at without vertigo: *such that we cannot look down without dizziness both of eyes and of mind* [Livy]; which is an evident imposture of our sight.

That fine philosopher put out his eyes[10] to relieve his soul of the distractions that it received from them, and to be able to philosophize in greater freedom.

But on that score he should also have had his ears stopped up, which Theophrastus says are the most dangerous instrument we have for receiving violent impressions to disturb and alter us; and he should in short have deprived himself of all the other senses, that is to say of his life and his being. For they all have this power to command our reason and our soul. *Again it often happens that our mind is struck more vehemently by some sight, some depth of voice, some songs; often again by care and fear* [Cicero].

The doctors hold that there are certain temperaments that are stirred even to fury by some sounds and instruments. I have seen some who could not hear a bone gnawed under their table without losing patience; and there is hardly a man who is not disturbed by that harsh and piercing noise made by files scraping on iron; just as many, on hearing someone chewing nearby, or someone talking who has the passages of his nose or throat stopped up, are moved to the point of anger and hatred. That piping prompter of Gracchus, who softened, hardened, or directed his master's voice whenever he made a harangue at Rome, what use was he, if the movement and quality of the sound had not the power to move and alter the judgment of the audience? Truly there is good reason to make so much of the firmness of that fine faculty,[11] that lets itself be manipulated and altered by the accidental movements of so light a wind!

This same deception that the senses convey to our understanding they receive in their turn. Our soul at times takes a like revenge; they compete in lying and deceiving each other. What we see and hear when stirred with anger, we do not hear as it is:

> A double sun appears, and twin cities of Thebes.
>
> VIRGIL

The object that we love seems to us more beautiful than it is—

> Thus women oft we see, ugly and bent,
> Receive men's love, and honors eminent
>
> LUCRETIUS

[10] This story was told, probably falsely, of Democritus.
[11] The judgment.

—and uglier the one that we loathe. To a man vexed and afflicted the brightness of the day seems darkened and gloomy. Our senses are not only altered, but often completely stupefied by the passions of the soul. How many things we see which we do not notice if our mind is occupied elsewhere!

> Even in plain things you can plainly see,
> Unless you pay attention, they will be
> As though remote in time, or far away.
>
> LUCRETIUS

It seems as though the soul draws the powers of the senses inward and occupies them. Thus both the inside and the outside of man is full of weakness and falsehood.

Those who have compared our life to a dream were perhaps more right than they thought. When we dream, our soul lives, acts, exercises all her faculties, neither more nor less than when she is awake; but if more loosely and obscurely, still surely not so much so that the difference is as between night and bright daylight; rather as between night and shade. There she sleeps, here she slumbers: more and less. It is always darkness, and Cimmerian darkness.

Sleeping we are awake, and waking asleep. I do not see so clearly in sleep; but my wakefulness I never find pure and cloudless enough. Moreover sleep in its depth sometimes puts dreams to sleep. But our wakefulness is never so awake as to purge and properly dissipate reveries, which are the dreams of the waking, and worse than dreams.

Since our reason and our soul accept the fancies and opinions which arise in it while sleeping, and authorize the actions of our dreams with the same approbation as they do those of the day, why do we not consider the possibility that our thinking, our acting, may be another sort of dreaming, and our waking another kind of sleep?

If the senses are our first judges, it is not ours alone that must be consulted, for in this faculty the animals have as much right as we have, or more. It is certain that some have hearing keener than man's, others sight, others smell, others touch or taste. Democritus said that the gods and the animals had much more perfect sensitive faculties than man.

Now between the effects of their senses and ours, the difference is extreme. Our saliva cleans and dries up our wounds; it kills a snake:

> So great the distance and the difference here,
> That one man's food others as poison fear.
> By man's saliva touched, snakes oft decay,
> And bite themselves to death.
>
> LUCRETIUS

What property shall we attribute to saliva? According to us, or according to the snake? By which of the two points of view shall we prove its real essence, which we are seeking? Pliny says that there are in the Indies certain seahares which are poison to us and we to them, so that by a mere touch we kill them. Which is really poisonous, man or the fish? Which are we to believe, the fish about man, or man about the fish?

A certain quality of air infects man, which does not harm the ox; another infects the ox, which does not harm man. Which of the two, in truth and in nature, is the pestilential quality?

Those who have jaundice see all things as yellowish and paler than we do:

> Moreover, all that jaundiced people see
> Becomes pale yellow.
>
> LUCRETIUS

Those who have that malady that the doctors call hyposphagma, which is a suffusion of blood under the skin, see everything as red and bloody. These humors which thus change the operations of our sight, how do we know but that they predominate in animals and are the ordinary thing with them? For we see some that have yellow eyes like our sufferers from jaundice, others that have them red and bloodshot. It is probable that to them the color of objects appears different than to us. Which of the two is the true judgment? For it is not said that the essence of things is referred to man alone. Hardness, whiteness, depth, and bitterness concern the service and knowledge of the animals as well as ours; nature has given to them the use of these as well as to us.

When we press our eye, we perceive the bodies that we are looking at as longer and more extended. Many animals have an eye thus pressed. So this lengthiness is perhaps the real shape of this body, not that which our eyes assign to it in their ordinary position. If we squeeze the eye from below, things seem double to us:

> Double the lights of lamps, flowering with flame,
> Double the face of man, his body twain.
>
> LUCRETIUS

If our ears are stopped with anything, or our passages of hearing constricted, we receive the sound otherwise than we ordinarily do. The animals that have hairy ears, or that have only a very tiny hole in place of an ear consequently do not hear what we hear, and receive the sound differently.

We see at festivals and in theaters that when we hold up a pane tinted with some color against the light of the torches, everything in the place appears to us green, or yellow, or violet:

> In our great theaters this oft is done
> By veils of yellow, red, or rust, which run
> From poles and timbers, billowing but stretched tight.
> They dye the assembly with their tinted light,
> And on the stage, on statues row on row
> Of gods and parents, make their colors flow.
>
> LUCRETIUS

It is likely that the eyes of animals, which we see are of different colors, make bodies appear to them as matching their eyes.

To judge the action of the senses, then, we should first of all be in agreement with the animals, and second, among ourselves. Which we are not in the least; and we get into disputes at every turn because one man hears, sees, or tastes something differently from someone else; and we dispute about the diversity of the images that the senses bring us as much as about anything else. By the ordinary rule of nature, a child hears, sees, and tastes otherwise than a man of thirty, and he otherwise than a sexagenarian.

The senses are in some people more obscure and dim, in others more open and acute. We receive things in one way and another, according to what we are and what they seem to us. Now since our seeming is so uncertain and controversial, it is no longer a miracle if we are told that we can admit that snow appears white to us, but that we cannot be responsible for proving that it is so of its essence and in truth; and, with this starting point shaken, all the knowledge in the world necessarily goes by the board.

What of the fact that our senses interfere with each other? A painting seems to the eye to be in relief, to the touch it seems flat. Shall we say that musk is agreeable or not, which rejoices our sense of smell and offends our taste? There are herbs and unguents suitable for one part of the body which injure another. Honey is pleasant to the taste, unpleasant to the sight. As for those rings which are cut in the form of feathers and are called in heraldry feathers without ends, there is no eye that can discern their width and that can defend itself against this illusion, that on one side they grow wider, and narrower and tapering on the other, even when you roll them around your finger; however, to the touch they seem equal in width and everywhere alike.

Those persons who, to enhance their voluptuousness, in ancient times used mirrors made to enlarge and magnify the object they reflect, so that the members which they were to put to work should please them the more by this ocular growth: to which of the two senses did they give the victory, to the sight which showed them these members stout and long as they liked, or to the touch which showed them small and contemptible?

Is it our senses that lend the object these differing qualities, and do the objects nevertheless have only one? As we see in the bread we eat: it is only bread, but our use makes of it bones, blood, flesh, hair, and nails:

> As food, dispersed through all our members, dies,
> And other substance of itself supplies.
>
> LUCRETIUS

The moisture that the root of a tree sucks up becomes trunk, leaf, and fruit; and the air, being but one, by being applied to a trumpet is diversified into a thousand kinds of sounds. Is it our senses, I say, which likewise fashion these objects out of various qualities, or do they really have them so? And in the face of this doubt, what can we decide about their real essence?

Moreover, since the accidents of illnesses, madness, or sleep make things appear to us otherwise than they appear to healthy people, wise men, and waking people, is it not likely that our normal state and our natural disposition can also assign to things an essence corresponding to our condition, and accommodate them to us, as our disordered states do? And that our health is as capable of giving them its own appearance as sickness? Why should the temperate man not have some vision of things related to himself, like the intemperate man, and likewise imprint his own character on them?

The jaded man assigns the insipidity to the wine; the healthy man, the savor; the thirsty man, the relish.

Now, since our condition accommodates things to itself and transforms them according to itself, we no longer know what things are in truth; for nothing comes to us except falsified and altered by our senses. When the compass, the square, and the ruler are off, all the proportions drawn from them, all the buildings erected by their measure, are also necessarily imperfect and defective. The uncertainty of our senses makes everything they produce uncertain:

> As in a building, if the rule is false,
> If a bent square gives verticals untrue,
> And if the level is at all askew,
> Then all must be defective and at fault,
> Forward or backward leaning, lame and halt;
> Some part already seems about to fall;
> Then, from those first mistakes, down tumbles all.
> Thus any reasoning of yours on things
> Must needs be false, that from false senses springs.
>
> LUCRETIUS

Furthermore, who shall be fit to judge these differences? As we say in disputes about religion that we need a judge not attached to either party, free from preference and passion, which is impossible among Christians, so it is in this. For if he is old, he cannot judge the sense perception of old age, being himself a party in this dispute; if he is young, likewise; healthy, likewise; likewise sick, asleep, or awake. We would need someone exempt from all these qualities, so that with an unprejudiced judgment he might judge of these propositions as of things indifferent to him; and by that score we would need a judge that never was.

To judge the appearances that we receive of objects, we would need a judicatory instrument; to verify this instrument, we need a demonstration; to verify the demonstration, an instrument: there we are in a circle.

Since the senses cannot decide our dispute, being themselves full of uncertainty, it must be reason that does so. No reason can be established without another reason: there we go retreating back to infinity.

Our conception is not itself applied to foreign objects, but is conceived through the mediation of the senses; and the senses do not comprehend the foreign object, but only their own impressions. And thus the conception and semblance we form is not of the object, but only of the impression and effect made on the sense; which impression and the object are different things. Wherefore whoever judges by appearances judges by something other than the object.

And as for saying that the impressions of the senses convey to the soul the quality of the foreign objects by resemblance, how can the soul and understanding make sure of this resemblance, having of itself no communication with foreign objects? Just as a man who does not know Socrates, seeing his portrait, cannot say that it resembles him.

Now if anyone should want to judge by appearances anyway, to judge by all appearances is impossible, for they clash with one another by their contradictions and discrepancies, as we see by experience. Shall some selected appearances rule the others? We shall have to verify this selection by another selection, the second by a third; and thus it will never be finished.

[EVERYTHING, EXCEPT GOD, IS IN CONSTANT CHANGE]

Finally, there is no existence that is constant, either of our being or of that of objects. And we, and our judgment, and all mortal things go on flowing and rolling unceasingly. Thus nothing certain can be established about one thing by another, both the judging and the judged being in continual change and motion.

We have no communication with being, because every human nature is always midway between birth and death, offering only a dim semblance and shadow of itself, and an uncertain and feeble opinion. And if by chance you fix your thought on trying to grasp its essence, it will be neither more nor less than if someone tried to grasp water: for the more he squeezes and presses what by its nature flows all over, the more he will lose what he was trying to hold and grasp. Thus, all things being subject to pass from one change to another, reason, seeking a real stability in them, is baffled, being unable to apprehend anything stable and permanent; because everything is either coming into being and not yet fully existent, or beginning to die before it is born.

Plato said that bodies never had existence, but did have birth; thinking that Homer had made the Ocean father of the gods, and Thetis mother, to show us that all things are in perpetual flux, change, and variation—an opinion common to all the philosophers before his time, as he says, except Parmenides alone, who denied things movement, on whose power he sets great store. Pythagoras thought that all matter is flowing and sliding. The Stoics, that there is no present time, and that what we call present is only the juncture and meeting of the future and the past. Heraclitus, that never had a man entered the same river twice.

Epicharmus, that he who once borrowed money does not owe it now; and that he who last night was invited to come to dine this morning, today comes uninvited, seeing that he and his hosts are no longer themselves: they have become others. And that no mortal substance can be found twice in the same state; for by the suddenness and nimbleness of its change, it is now dissipated, now reassembled; it comes, and then goes. So that what is beginning to be born never arrives at the perfection of being; forasmuch as this birth is never completed, and never stops as being at an end, but from the seed onward goes on ever changing and shifting from one thing into another. As from human seed is made first in the mother's womb a formless fruit, then a fully formed infant; then, outside the womb, an infant at the breast; afterward it becomes a boy; then in turn a youth; then a grown man; then an older man; finally a decrepit old man. So that the subsequent age and generation is always undoing and destroying the preceding one:

> Time alters all the nature of the world;
> From one state to another all must change;
> Nothing remains itself, but all things range;
> Nature modifies all and changes all.
>
> LUCRETIUS

And then we stupidly fear one kind of death, when we have already passed and are still passing through so many others. For not only, as Heraclitus used to say, is the death of fire the generation of air, and the death of air the generation of water; but even more obviously we can see it in ourselves. Our prime dies and passes when old age comes along, and youth ends in the prime of the grown man, childhood in youth, and infancy in childhood. And yesterday dies in today, and today will die in tomorrow, and there is nothing that abides and is always the same.

For, to prove that this is so, if we always remain one and the same, how is it that we rejoice now in one thing, and now in another? How is it that we love opposite things or hate them, praise them or blame them? How do we have different affections, no longer retaining the same feeling within the same thought? For it is not plausible that we take up different passions without changing; and what suffers change does not remain one and the same, and if it is not one and the same, it also *is* not; but together with its *being the same,* it also changes its simple *being,* from one thing always becoming another. And consequently the senses of nature are mistaken and lie, taking what appears for what is, for want of really knowing what it is that *is.*

But then what really is? That which is eternal: that is to say, what never had birth, nor will ever have an end; to which time never brings any change. For time is a mobile thing, which appears as in a shadow, together with matter, which is ever running and flowing, without ever remaining stable or permanent. To which belong the words *before* and *after,* and *has been* or *will be,* which at the very first sight show very evidently that time is not a thing that *is;* for it would be a great stupidity and a perfectly apparent falsehood to say that that *is* which is not yet in being, or which already has ceased to be. And as for these words, *present, immediate, now,* on which it seems that we chiefly found and support our understanding of time, reason discovering this immediately destroys it; for she at once splits and divides it into future and past, as though wanting to see it necessarily divided in two.

The same thing happens to nature that is measured, as to time that measures it. For there is nothing in it either that abides or is stable; but all things in it are either born, or being born, or dying. For which reason it would be a sin to say of God, who is the only one that *is,* that he *was* or *will be.* For those terms represent declinings, transitions, or vicissitudes of what cannot endure or remain in being. Wherefore we must conclude that God alone *is*—not at all according to any measure of time, but according to an eternity immutable and immobile, not measured by time or subject to any decline; before whom there is nothing, nor will there be after, nor is there anything more new or more recent; but one who really is—who by one single *now* fills the *ever;* and there is nothing that really is but he alone—nor can we say "He has been," or "He will be"—without beginning and without end.

To this most religious conclusion of a pagan I want to add only this remark of a witness of the same condition,[12] for an ending to this long and boring discourse, which would give me material without end: "O what a vile and abject thing is man," he says, "if he does not raise himself above humanity!"

That is a good statement and a useful desire, but equally absurd. For to make the handful bigger than the hand, the armful bigger than the arm, and to hope to straddle more than the reach of our legs, is impossible and unnatural. Nor can man raise himself above himself and humanity; for he can see only with his own eyes, and seize only with his own grasp.

He will rise, if God by exception lends him a hand; he will rise by abandoning and renouncing his own means, and letting himself be raised and uplifted by purely celestial means.

It is for our Christian faith, not for his Stoical virtue, to aspire to that divine and miraculous metamorphosis.

Miguel de Cervantes Saavedra

(1547–1616)

Don Quixote is one of the greatest works of art in Western literature, but in a sense it is surprising that it should have been a work of art at all. It began its life as a humble parody of contemporary popular literature, written by an elderly failed playwright in a more or less desperate attempt to make money, possibly even as he lay in prison for shortages in his accounts as a petty government official. Cervantes may have conceived of the total work in all its complexity and grandeur from the very beginning, but it seems more likely that even he was surprised at the way the work developed, from an unpretentious extended joke to an almost mythic narrative. Growing from roots deep in the popular culture of his time, it reached the loftiest heights of speculation about human nature.

Miguel de Cervantes Saavedra was born in 1547, the fourth of seven children of an impoverished physician. During Miguel's childhood the family moved from one village to another to flee from creditors. By 1564, when he was sixteen, the family had settled in Seville, where Miguel was enrolled in a Jesuit school; he seems later to have studied for a time at the University of Salamanca. Any hopes he may have had for an academic career, however, were blasted when he got involved, at the age of twenty-one, in a duel within the precincts of the royal palace in Madrid. The royal court sentenced him to lose his right hand and be exiled for ten years; Cervantes fled to Italy to escape the execution of the sentence.

He was not to return to Spain for twelve years, and those years were filled with hardships and adventures more spectacular than any in the romances he was to parody in *Don Quixote.* After a brief period of service in Rome in the retinue of the cardinal-elect Giulio Acquaviva, he enlisted in the Spanish forces of the Holy League opposing Turkish control of the Mediterranean. His first engagement was the famous Battle of Lepanto. Cervantes was on

[12] The Stoic philosopher Seneca (4 B.C.–A.D. 65).

board a ship called the *Marquesa* when the battle began, sick with a fever and confined to his bunk. Despite his condition, he immediately asked to be placed in the most dangerous position and fought gallantly throughout the battle. In the action, he received two shots in the chest and his left hand was shattered; he was never to recover full use of it. Cervantes received an increase in pay for his bravery and a letter of commendation from his commander, Don John of Austria, brother of King Philip II. After his convalescence, he spent four more years in the army, campaigning in Sardinia, Naples, and southern Italy.

Finally, in 1575, Cervantes set sail for Spain again in the company of his brother Rodrigo, who had joined the colors at the same time as Cervantes. Off the coast of southern France, the ship was attacked by pirates and captured, and everyone on board was carried off to Algiers to be sold as slaves. Cervantes remained in slavery for five years, conducting himself with the utmost gallantry. Four times he attempted to organize a general rising among the 24,000 Christian slaves in Algiers. All these attempts failed, and each time Cervantes took full responsibility, in spite of the potential penalty of death by torture. The Dey of Algiers, Hassan Pacha, each time pardoned him, however, since he privately admired Cervantes' courage. Rodrigo was ransomed comparatively early by his family back in Spain, but Cervantes' ransom price was much higher because of the letter of commendation to the Spanish king his captors found in his possession. He was not ransomed until 1580, half of the money coming from his hardpressed family and the other half from sympathetic Spanish residents of Algiers.

Cervantes was thirty-three when he finally returned to Spain. He was crippled and without a job; his family was deeply in debt. Don John was by now dead, and since his memory was hated by the king, Cervantes could not use his commendation to get preferment. He spent the next twenty-five years trying desperately to earn a meager living. He wrote a number of plays, none notably successful. During his theatrical days he fell in love with an actress, Ana Franca de Rojas. They had a child, Isabel, whom Cervantes was left to rear when Ana deserted him. In 1584, at the age of thirty-seven, he married a nineteen-year-old girl, Catalina de Palacios y Salazar Vozmediano; he then had to support a household consisting of his wife, Isabel, his mother, his two sisters, and his widowed mother-in-law. He finally succeeded in getting a government post as a traveling agent charged with requisitioning supplies for the Invincible Armada, the massive fleet that Philip was preparing to launch against England in 1588. As a "commissary," he not only had to face angry mobs of villagers who resented the army's appropriation of their goods but had to deal also with a government bureaucracy that at one point was two years behind with his salary. Cervantes was twice imprisoned for shortages in his accounts, owing to a combination of his superiors' own chaotic records, an untimely bank failure, and doubtless his own inadequacies as a bookkeeper. There is a tradition, based on an ambiguous passage in the Prologue to Book I of *Don Quixote* (the story was "just what might be begotten in a prison, where every discomfort is lodged and every dismal noise has its dwelling"), that he began his great novel in the prison at Seville in 1597.

However this may be, soon after his release Cervantes was hard at work on *Don Quixote,* which was first published in 1605, the year in which his contemporary Shakespeare produced *King Lear.* Cervantes' book was an immediate best-seller; it went through a number of printings the first year and was very promptly translated into French, Italian, and other European languages. Its success brought Cervantes little except the satisfaction of fame; he received no royalties beyond the small initial sum paid him by the publisher.

From the time the first part was published, Cervantes had planned a continuation, but it did not appear for ten years. In 1614, he had written fifty-nine chapters of the sequel when he learned that a pirated continuation had been published by one Alonso Fernandez de Avellaneda. Furious he rushed through the ending of Part II, incorporating in the part he had already finished an attack upon the "false Quixote." Part II was also successful, but again it did little to relieve the author's chronic poverty. Aged and ill, he spent the last two years of his life finishing *Persiles and Sigismunda,* an episodic romance he had begun in 1609. (It was published posthumously.) In the dedication to this work, written on his deathbed to his patron the Conde de Lemos, he wrote the famous lines, adapted from an old ballad, "With one foot in the stirrup, and in the anguish of death, My Lord, I write to thee." He died on April 23, 1616; ten days later in England, Shakespeare died, also on April 23 (since the English calendar was still unreformed).

Don Quixote is a long novel, one of the longest ever written, but it is not a word too long. An abridgment can only suggest the cumulative effect of the book's movement from primitive burlesque to the mysteriously moving climax. At the heart of the novel are the mad knight himself, his commonsensical squire Sancho, and their gradually unfolding relationship. Quixote and Sancho are inseparable, bound together like spirit and flesh as are their fictional descendants Sherlock Holmes and Dr. Watson, Stephen Dedalus and Leopold Bloom in Joyce's *Ulysses,* and Didi and Gogo in Beckett's *Waiting for Godot.* The division is not absolute: Quixote has his earthy side, and it is Sancho who clings to a dream of being governor of an island. It is not Sancho, finally, who represents the claims of unimaginative reality, but the barber and the curate, guardians of flesh and spirit in the everyday world in their respective roles as bleeder and spiritual advisor. Similarly, it is not Don Quixote himself who represents dreams kicked loose from all contact with the earth, but the romances with which he has addled himself. Quixote and Sancho are not allegorical figures but real human beings, each torn between dream and reality. The novel traces their profound, moving, and richly comic negotiation with each other. This negotiation consists of the gradual "Sanchification" of Quixote and the "Quixotification" of Sancho; the Knight moves from a world of pure delusion to a vision of real life ennobled by idealism, while Sancho begins to see the substantial world through the eyes of his master, as touched by the dream. By the end of the novel, all hope of his island gone, Sancho still longs for the quest: "Up with you this instant, out of your bed! . . . Who knows but we may find Lady Dulcinea behind a hedge, disenchanted and as fresh as a daisy!"

As, for his protagonists, Cervantes draws upon the most fundamental of human relationships, so for his plot he turns to the most basic of narratives, the journey. The key to all the great quest stories is the goal of the quest. Odysseus, on his journey home, is in quest of Ithaca and Penelope, the world of ordinary life after the heroic but distorted world of military action. Dante, in his dream journey through the afterlife, seeks to leave the Dark Wood of worldly confusion and find the security of God's holy order. Quixote's quest remains in the Dark Wood on this earth: the dusty and sterile landscape of La Mancha, the emblem of a modern world from which it seems all glory has fled. His quest, literally for chivalric adventure, is more fundamentally for the spark of imagination that redeems ordinary life. And ultimately he finds this spark, not in absurd romances but within himself.

FURTHER READING: Melveena McKendrick s biography *Cervantes,* 1980, is a good introduction for the general reader. Manuel Duran's *Cervantes,* 1974, a somewhat more succinct biography, contains a good introductory chapter on Spanish culture in Cervantes' time and includes a long discussion of *Don Quixote.* An excellent evaluation of Cervantes as a critical theorist can be found in E. C. Riley's *Cervantes' Theory of the Novel,* 1962, which places Cervantes' ideas in the literary context of his time and discusses such topics as structural unity, verisimilitude, and the function of history. Riley's later, more comprehensive study, *Don Quixote,* 1986, is an excellent historical and critical analysis of the work. Cervantes' role in the development of the novel is addressed in Michael McKeon, *The Origins of the English Novel, 1600 to 1740,* 1987, and in Stephen Gilman, *The Novel According to Cervantes,* 1989. Diverse critical approaches are represented in *Cervantes: A Collection of Critical Essays,* ed. Lowry Nelson, Jr., 1969. This volume includes Erich Auerbach's "The Enchanted Dulcinea" and Thomas Mann's "Voyage with Don Quixote." The essays on *Don Quixote* gathered in the Norton Critical Edition, ed. Joseph R. Jones and Kenneth Douglas, 1981, are also well selected. Ruth El Saffar's *Distance and Control in "Don Quixote,"* 1975, explores a wide variety of narrative techniques employed by Cervantes, concentrating on the dynamics of role switching by the characters. John C. Weiger's *The Individuated Self,* 1979, distinguishes "individuation" from individualism in an examination of personal freedom in *Don Quixote* and is interesting on the emergence of self-knowledge in the novel. John J. Allen's *Don Quixote: Hero or Fool?: A Study in Narrative Techniques,* 1969, discusses stylistic devices, levels of fiction, and the relationship between author, reader, and character. The subject of chivalry is the starting point for a provocative study in Howard Mancing's *The Chivalric World of Don Quijote: Style, Structure, and Narrative Technique,* 1982.

DON QUIXOTE

Translated by Walter Starkie

from PART I

CHAPTER I

Which tells of the quality and manner of life of the famous gentleman Don Quixote of La Mancha

At a village of La Mancha, whose name I do not wish to remember,[1] there lived a little while ago one of those gentlemen who are wont to keep a lance in the rack, an old buckler, a lean horse, and a swift greyhound. His stew

[1] Cervantes was purposely vague in describing Don Quixote's birthplace. An old Spanish ballad begins "At a village in La Mancha." (Notes are adapted and expanded from those of the translator.)

had more beef than mutton in it and most nights he ate a hodgepodge, pickled and cold. Lentil soup on Fridays, "tripe and trouble" on Saturdays,[2] and an occasional pigeon as an extra delicacy on Sundays consumed three quarters of his income. The remainder was spent on a jerkin of fine puce, velvet breeches, and slippers of the same stuff for holidays, and a suit of good, honest homespun for weekdays. His family consisted of a housekeeper about forty, a niece not yet twenty, and a lad who served him both in the field and at home and could saddle the horse or use the pruning knife. Our gentleman was about fifty years of age, of a sturdy constitution, but wizened and gaunt-featured, an early riser and a devotee of the chase. They say that his surname was Quixada or Quesada (for on this point the authors who have written on this subject differ), but we may reasonably conjecture that his name was Quixana. This, however, has very little to do with our story; enough that in its telling we swerve not a jot from the truth. You must know that the above-mentioned gentleman in his leisure moments (which was most of the year) gave himself up with so much delight and gusto to reading books of chivalry that he almost entirely neglected the exercise of the chase and even the management of his domestic affairs. Indeed his craze for this kind of literature became so extravagant that he sold many acres of arable land to purchase books of knight-errantry, and he carried off to his house as many as he could possibly find. Above all, he preferred those written by the famous Feliciano de Silva[3] because of the clarity of his writing and his intricate style, which made him value those books more than pearls, especially when he read of those courtships and letters of challenge that knights sent to ladies, often containing expressions such as: "The reason for your unreasonable treatment of my reason so enfeebles my reason that I have reason to complain of your beauty." And again: "The high heavens, which with your divinity divinely fortify you with stars, make you the deserver of the desert that is deserved by your greatness." These and similar rhapsodies bewildered the poor gentleman's understanding, for he racked his brain day and night to unbowel their meaning, which not even Aristotle himself could have done if he had been raised from the dead for that very purpose. He was not quite convinced of the number of wounds that Don Belianís gave and received in battle, for he considered that however skillful the surgeons that cured him may have been, the worthy knight's face and body must have been bedizened with scars and scabs. Nevertheless he praised the author for concluding his book with the promise of endless adventure, and many times he felt inclined to take up his pen and finish it off himself, as it is there promised. He doubtless would have done so, and successfully too, had he not been diverted by other plans and purposes of greater moment. He often debated with the curate of the village—a man of learning, a graduate of Sigüenza—on the relative merits of Palmerin of England and Amadis of Gaul. But Master Nicholas, the village barber, affirmed that no one could be compared with the Knight of the Sun and that if, indeed, any could be matched with him, it was Don Galaor, the brother of Amadis of Gaul, for he had a nature adapted to every whim

[2] Spaniards ate meagerly on Saturdays, in commemoration of a victory over the Moors in 1212.

[3] A sixteenth-century writer of romances, famous for *Don Florisel de Niquea* (1532), from which the following quotation is taken.

of fortune; he was not so namby-pamby and whimpering a knight as his brother, and as for valor, he was in every respect his equal.

In short, he so immersed himself in those romances that he spent whole days and nights over his books; and thus with little sleeping and much reading, his brains dried up to such a degree that he lost the use of his reason. His imagination became filled with a host of fancies he had read in his books—enchantments, quarrels, battles, challenges, wounds, courtships, loves, tortures, and many other absurdities. So true did all this phantasmagoria from books appear to him that in his mind he accounted no history in the world more authentic. He would say that the Cid Ruiz Díaz was a very gallant knight, but not to be compared with the Knight of the Burning Sword, who with a single thwart blow cleft asunder a brace of hulking, blustering giants. He was better pleased with Bernardo del Carpio, because at Roncesvalles he had slain Roland the Enchanted by availing himself of the stratagem Hercules had employed on Antaeus, the son of the Earth, whom he squeezed to death in his arms. He praised the giant Morgante, for he alone was courteous and well bred among that monstrous brood puffed up with arrogance and insolence. Above all, he admired Rinaldo of Montalbán,[4] especially when he saw him sallying out of his castle to plunder everyone who came his way, and when beyond the seas he made off with the idol of Mohammed which, as history says, was of solid gold. But he would have parted with his housekeeper and his niece into the bargain for the pleasure of rib roasting the traitor Galalón.[5]

At last, having lost his wits completely, he stumbled upon the oddest fancy that ever entered a madman's brain. He believed that it was necessary, both for his own honor and for service of the state, that he should become a knight-errant, roaming through the world with his horse and armor in quest of adventures and practicing all that had been performed by the knights-errant of whom he had read. He would follow their life, redressing all manner of wrongs and exposing himself to continual dangers, and at last, after concluding his enterprises, he would win everlasting honor and renown. The poor gentleman fancied himself already crowned emperor of Trebizond for the valor of his arm. And thus excited by these agreeable delusions, he hastened to put his plans into operation.

The first thing he did was to refurbish some rusty armor that had belonged to his great grandfather and had lain moldering in a corner. He cleaned it and repaired it as best he could, but he found one great defect: instead of a complete helmet there was just the simple morion.[6] This want he ingeniously remedied by making a kind of visor out of pasteboard, and when it was fitted to the morion, it looked like an entire helmet. It is true that in order to test its strength and see if it was swordproof, he drew his sword and gave it two strokes, the first of which instantly destroyed the result of a week's labor. It troubled him to see with what ease he had broken the helmet in

[4] One of Charlemagne's knights and the hero of Boiardo's romance *Orlando Innamorato (Roland in Love)*. Palmerin of England, Amadis of Gaul, The Knight of the Sun, The Cid Ruiz Diaz, The Knight of the Burning Sword, Bernardo del Carpio, and Morgante are all characters in actual romances.

[5] Galalón, or Ganelon of Mayence, was another of Charlemagne's knights who betrayed him at Rouncevalles. See *The Song of Roland*.

[6] Headpiece of a helmet, without the visor.

pieces, so to protect it from such an accident, he remade it and fenced the inside with a few bars of iron in such a manner that he felt assured of its strength, and without caring to make a second trial, he held it to be a most excellent helmet. Then he went to see his steed, and although it had more cracks in its hoof than there are quarters in a Spanish real[7] and more faults than Gonella's jade, which was all skin and bone,[8] he thought that neither the Bucephalus of Alexander nor the Cid's Babieca could be compared with it.[9] He spent four days deliberating over what name he would give the horse, for (as he said to himself) it was not right that the horse of so famous a knight should remain without a name. So he endeavored to find one that would express what the animal had been before he had been the mount of a knight-errant, and what he now was. It was indeed reasonable that when the master changed his state, the horse should change his name too and assume one pompous and high-sounding, as suited the new order he was about to profess. So after having devised, erased, and blotted out many other names, he finally decided to call the horse Rozinante—a name, in his opinion, lofty, sonorous, and significant, for it explained that he had been only an ordinary hack before he had been raised to his present status of first of all the hacks in the world.[10]

Now that he had given his horse a name so much to his satisfaction, he resolved to choose one for himself, and after seriously considering the matter for eight whole days, he finally determined to call himself Don Quixote. For that reason the authors who have related this most true story have deduced that his name must undoubtedly have been Quixada and not Quesada, as others would have it. Then, remembering that the valiant Amadis had not been content to call himself simply Amadis, but added thereto the name of his kingdom and native country to render it more illustrious, calling himself Amadis of Gaul, so he, like a good knight, also added the name of his province and called himself Don Quixote of La Mancha. In this way he openly proclaimed his lineage and country, and at the same time he honored it by taking its name.

Now that his armor was scoured, his morion made into a helmet, his horse and himself newly named, he felt that nothing was wanting but a lady of whom to be enamored, for a knight-errant who was loveless was a tree without leaves and fruit, a body without soul. "If," said he, "for my sins or through my good fortune I encounter some giant—a usual occurrence to knights-errant—and bowling him over at the first onset or cleaving him in twain, I finally vanquish and force him to surrender, would not it be better to have some lady to whom I may send him as a trophy? Then, when he comes into her presence, he may kneel before her and humbly say: 'Madam, I am the giant Caraculiambro, Lord of the Island of Malindrania, whom the never-adequately-praised Don Quixote of La Mancha has overcome in single combat. He has commanded me to present myself before you so that your highness may dispose of me as you wish.' " How glad was our knight

[7] A *real* was a silver coin. There were eight *cuartos,* or "cracks," in a real.

[8] Pedro Gonella was the clown of the Duke of Ferrara in the fifteenth century; his horse, all skin and bones, was the theme of many of his jokes.

[9] Bucephalus was Alexander the Great's horse, Babieca that of Ruy Diaz, hero of the twelfth-century Spanish epic *The Cid.*

[10] *Rozin,* or *rocin,* means an ordinary horse; *ante,* before.

when he had made these discourses to himself, but chiefly when he had found one whom he might call his lady! It happened that in a neighboring village there lived a good-looking country lass with whom he had been in love, although it is understood that she never knew or was aware of it. She was called Aldonza Lorenzo, and it was to her that he thought fit to entrust the sovereignty of his heart. He sought a name for her that would not vary too much from her own and yet would approach that of a princess or a lady of quality. At last he resolved to call her Dulcinea of El Toboso (she was a native of that town), a name in his opinion musical, uncommon, and expressive, like the others he had devised.

CHAPTER II

Which deals with our imaginative hero's first sally from his home

Once these preparations were made he was anxious to put his designs into operation without delay, for he was spurred on by the conviction that the world needed his immediate presence; so many were the grievances he intended to rectify, the wrongs he resolved to set right, the harms he meant to redress, the abuses he would reform, and the debts he would discharge. And so, without acquainting a living soul with his intentions, and wholly unobserved, one morning before daybreak (it was one of the hottest in the month of July), he armed himself cap-a-pie, mounted Rozinante, placed his ill-constructed helmet on his head, braced on his buckler, grasped his lance, and through the door of his back yard sallied forth into the open country, mightily pleased to note the ease with which he had begun his worthy enterprise. But scarcely had he issued forth when he was suddenly struck by so terrible a thought that he almost gave up his whole undertaking, for he just then remembered that he had not yet been dubbed a knight, and therefore, in accordance with the laws of chivalry, he neither could nor ought to enter the lists against any knight. Moreover, even if he had been dubbed, he should, as a novice, have worn white armor without any device on his shield until he had won it by force of arms. These thoughts made him stagger in his purpose; but as his madness prevailed over every reason, he determined to have himself knighted by the first person he should meet, like many others of whom he had read in the books that distracted him. As to white armor, he intended at the first opportunity to scour his own so that it would be whiter than ermine. In this way he calmed himself and continued his journey, letting his horse choose the way, believing that in this consisted the true spirit of adventure.

As our brand-new adventurer proceeded, he kept conversing with himself in this manner: "Who doubts but that in future ages, when the true story of my famous deeds is brought to light, the wise man who writes it will describe my first sally in the morning as follows: 'Scarcely had the rubicund Apollo spread over the face of the vast and spacious earth the golden tresses of his beautiful hair, and scarcely had the little painted birds with their tuneful tongues saluted in sweet and melodious harmony the coming of rosy Aurora, who, leaving the soft couch of her jealous husband, revealed herself to mortals through the gates and balconies of the Manchegan horizon, when the famous knight Don Quixote of La Mancha, quitting his downy bed of ease, mounted his renowned steed, Rozinante, and began to ride over the ancient and memorable plain of Montiel.' "[11] (And indeed he was doing so.) Continuing his discourse, he added: "O happy era, O happy age, wherein my famous deeds shall be revealed to the world, deeds worthy to be engraved in bronze, sculptured in marble, and painted in pictures for future record! O thou wise enchanter, whosoever thou mayest be, whose duty it will be to chronicle this strange history, do not, I beseech thee, forget my good horse, Rozinante, the everlasting companion of my wanderings." Then, as if really enamored, he cried: "O Dulcinea, my princess! Sovereign of this captive heart! Grievous wrong hast thou done me by dismissing me and by cruelly forbidding me by decree to appear in thy beauteous presence. I pray thee, sweet lady, to remember this poor, enslaved heart, which for love of thee suffers so many pangs."

To such words he added a sequence of other foolish notions all in the manner of those that his books had taught him, imitating their language as nearly as he could. And all the while he rode slowly on while the sun rose with such intense heat that it would have been enough to dissolve his brains, if he had had any left. He traveled almost the whole of that day without meeting any adventure worthy of note, wherefore he was much troubled, for he was eager to encounter someone upon whom he could try the strength of his doughty arm. Some authors say his first adventure was that of the Pass of Lápice; others hold it was that of the windmills, but according to my investigations and according to what is written in the annals of La Mancha, he traveled all that day, and at dusk both he and his horse were tired and nearly dead with hunger. He looked around him on every side to see whether he could discover any castle or shepherd's hut where he might rest and find nourishment. He then saw, not far from the road, an inn, which was as welcome to him as a star leading him not to the portals but to the very palace itself of his redemption. So he hastened on and reached it before dark.

Now there chanced to be standing at the door two young wenches who belonged to the category of women of the town, as they say. They were on their way to Seville in the company of certain carriers who halted for the night in that inn. As all our adventurer saw, thought, or imagined seemed to happen in accordance with what he had read in his books of chivalry, no sooner did he see the inn than it assumed in his eyes the semblance of a castle with four turrets, the pinnacles of which were of glittering silver including drawbridge, deep moat, and all the appurtenances with which such castles are depicted. And so he drew near to the inn (which he thought was a castle), and at a short distance from it, he halted Rozinante, expecting that some dwarf would mount the battlements to announce by trumpet blast the arrival of a knight-errant at the castle. But when he saw that they tarried, and as Rozinante was pawing the ground impatiently in eagerness to reach the stable, he approached the inn door and there saw the two young doxies, who appeared to him to be two beautiful damsels or graceful ladies

[11] Memorable because it was the scene of a famous battle in 1369.

enjoying the fresh air at the castle gate. It happened also at this very moment that a swineherd, as he gathered his hogs (I ask no pardon,[12] for so they are called) from the stubblefield, blew a horn that assembled them, and instantly Don Quixote imagined it was what he expected, namely, that some dwarf was giving notice of his arrival. Therefore, with extraordinary satisfaction he went up to the inn and the ladies. But when they saw a man armed in that manner draw near with lance and buckler, they started to take to their heels, full of fear. Don Quixote, perceiving their alarm, raised his pasteboard visor, and displaying his withered and dusty countenance, accosted them gently and gravely: "I beseech your ladyships, do not flee, nor fear the least offense. The order of chivalry that I profess does not permit me to do injury to anyone, and least of all to such noble maidens as your presences denote you to be."

The wenches kept gazing earnestly, endeavoring to catch a glimpse of his face, which its ill-fashioned visor concealed; but when they heard themselves called maidens, a thing so out of the way of their profession, they could not restrain their laughter, which was so boisterous that Don Quixote exclaimed in anger: "Remember that modesty is becoming in beautiful ladies, whereas laughter without cause denotes much folly. However," added he, "I do not say this to offend you or to incur your displeasure, for my one desire is to do you honor and service." The strange language of the knight was not understood by the ladies, and this, added to his uncouth appearance, increased their laughter and his annoyance, and he would have proceeded further but for the timely appearance of the innkeeper, a man who by reason of his extreme corpulence was of very peaceable disposition. As soon as he saw that uncomely figure all armed, in accouterments so ill sorted as were the bridle, lance, buckler, and corselet, he felt inclined to join the damsels in their mirth. But out of fear of such a medley of warlike gear, he resolved to be civil, and so he said: "Sir knight, if you are seeking a lodging, you will find all in abundance here, with the exception of a bed for there are none in this inn." Don Quixote, observing the humility of the governor of the fortress (for such the landlord and the inn appeared to him), answered: "Anything, sir castellan, suffices me:

My ornaments are arms,
My pastime is in war."

The host thought he called him a castellan because he took him to be one of the Simple-Simon Castilians,[13] whereas he was an Andalusian, one of those from the Sanlúcar shore, no less a thief than Cacus[14] and not less mischievous than a truant scholar or court page. And so he made the following reply: "If so, your worship's beds must be hard rocks and your sleep an everlasting watching;[15] wherefore you may boldly dismount and I can assure you that you can hardly miss being kept awake all year long in this house,

[12] Spanish peasants still beg one's pardon when mentioning pigs, a custom picked up from the neighboring Muslims, who abhor pork.

[13] *Castellano* means both "castellan" (a governor of a castle) and "Castilian" (a native of Castile).

[14] Cacus, in Roman mythology, stole some of Hercules' cattle.

[15] The innkeeper quotes the same ballad Quixote quotes above.

much less one single night." Saying this, he went and held Don Quixote's stirrup, who forthwith dismounted, though with much difficulty, for he had not broken his fast all that day. He then told the host to take great care of his horse, saying that he was one of the finest pieces of horseflesh that ever ate bread. The innkeeper looked him over but thought him not so good by half as his master had said. After stabling him, he returned to receive his guest's orders and found the damsels (who had now become reconciled to him) disarming him, but though they were able to take off the back- and breast-plates, they did not know how to undo his gorget[16] or remove his counterfeit helmet, which he had tied on with green ribbons in such a way that they could not be untied. It was necessary to cut them because the knots were so intricate, but he would not allow this to be done, and so remained all that night with his helmet on, and was the strangest and pleasantest sight imaginable.

And while he was being disarmed by those lights-o'-love whom he imagined to be ladies of quality of that castle, he said to them with great charm:

"There never was on earth a knight
So waited on by ladies fair
As once was he, Don Quixote hight,
When first he left his village dear:
Damsels to serve him ran with speed
And princesses to dress his steed.[17]

"Rozinante, ladies, is the name of my horse, and Don Quixote of La Mancha my own. I never intended to discover myself until deeds performed in your service should have proclaimed me, but the need of adapting to my present purpose the old ballad of Sir Lancelot has made my right name known to you prematurely. But the day will come when your ladyships shall command and I obey, and the valor of my arm make plain my desire to serve you."

The girls, unaccustomed to such flourishes of rhetoric, made no reply but asked whether he would eat anything. "Fain would I break my fast," answered Don Quixote, "for I think that a little food would be of great service to me." That day happened to be a Friday and there was nothing in the inn but some pieces of fish, called in Castile pollack, in Andalusia codfish, in some parts ling, and in others troutlets, or Poor Jack. They asked him if he would eat some troutlets, for they had no other fish to offer him. "Provided there are many little trout," answered Don Quixote, "they will supply the place of one salmon trout, for it is the same to me whether I receive eight single reals or one piece of eight. Moreover, those troutlets may turn out to be like unto veal, which is better than beef, and kid, which is superior to goat. Be that as it may, let it come in quickly, for the toil and weight of arms cannot be sustained without the good government of the guts." As the air was cool, they placed the table at the door of the inn, and the landlord brought a portion of ill-soaked and worse-cooked codfish and a piece of bread as black and moldy as the knight's arms. It was a laughable sight to see him eat, for as he had his helmet and his visor up, he could not feed himself, and so

[16] Throatpiece.
[17] Quixote is quoting, and altering, a ballad about Sir Lancelot, as he acknowledges below.

one of the ladies performed that service for him. But it would have been impossible for him to drink had not the innkeeper bored a cane, and placing one end in his mouth, poured in the wine at the other end. All this he endured patiently rather than cut the ribbons of his helmet.

While he was at his meal, a hog-gelder happened to sound his reed flageolet four or five times as he came near the inn. This was a still more convincing proof to Don Quixote that he was in a famous castle where they were entertaining him with music, that the codfish was salmon trout, the bread of the purest white, the whores ladies, and the innkeeper the governor of the fortress. All this made him applaud his own resolution and his enterprising sally. There was only one thing that vexed him: he regretted that he was not dubbed a knight, for he thought that he could not lawfully undertake any adventure until he had received the order of knighthood.

CHAPTER III

Which relates the pleasant method by which Don Quixote had himself dubbed knight

As he was tormented by that thought, he made short work of his meager, pothouse supper. Then he called for his host, shut himself up with him in the stable, and fell upon his knees, saying: "I will never rise from this place, valorous knight, until your courtesy grants me the boon I seek, one that will redound to your glory and to the advantage of the human race." The innkeeper, seeing his guest at his feet and hearing such words, stared at him in bewilderment, without knowing what to do or say. He tried to make him get up, but in vain, for the latter would not consent to do so until the boon he demanded was granted. "I expected no less from your magnificence," answered Don Quixote, "and so I say unto you that the boon I have demanded and that you, out of your liberality, have granted unto me is that tomorrow morning you will dub me knight. This night I shall watch over my arms in the chapel of your castle,[18] and tomorrow, as I have said, you will fulfill my earnest desires so that I may sally forth through the four parts of the world in quest of adventures on behalf of the distressed, as is the duty of knighthood and knights-errant who, like myself, are devoted to such achievements."

The host, who was, as we said before, a bit of a wag and already had some doubts about his guest's sanity, now found all his suspicions confirmed, but he resolved to humor him so that he might have sport that night. He told the knight that his wishes were very reasonable, for such pursuits were natural to knights so illustrious as he seemed and his gallant bearing showed him to be. He added that he himself in the days of his youth had devoted himself to the same honorable profession and had wandered over various parts of the world in search of adventures; and, moreover, he had not failed to visit the curing grounds of Málaga, the Isles of Riarán, the Precinct of Seville, the Quicksilver Square of Segovia, the Olive field of Valencia, the Circle of Granada, the Strand of Sanlúcar, the Colt Fountain of Córdoba, the Taverns of Toledo, and divers other haunts where he had proved the

[18] In chivalric romances, the "vigil" (watching over one's arms overnight) was an important part of the ceremony of knighthood.

nimbleness of his feet and the lightness of his fingers, committing wrongs in plenty, accosting many widows, deflowering sundry maidens, tricking some minors, and finally making himself known and famous to all the tribunals and courts over the length and breadth of Spain.[19] At last he had retired to this castle, where he lived on his own and on other men's revenues, entertaining therein knights-errant of every quality, solely for the great affection he bore them, and that they might share their goods with him in return for his benevolence. He further told him that in his castle there was no chapel where he could watch over his arms, for he had knocked it down to build it anew. However, in case of necessity, he might watch over the arms wherever he pleased, and therefore, he might watch that night in the castle courtyard. Then, the following morning, with God's help, the required ceremonies would be carried out in such a way that he would be dubbed a knight so effectively that nowhere in the world could one more perfect be found. He asked if Don Quixote had brought any money. "Not a farthing," answered the knight, "for I have never read in the stories of knights-errant that they ever carried money with them."

"You are mistaken," answered the landlord, "for although the stories are silent on this matter, seeing that the authors did not think it necessary to specify such obvious requirements as money and clean shirts, yet there is no reason to believe that the knights had none. On the contrary, it was an established fact that all knights-errant (whose deeds fill many a volume) carried their purses well lined against accidents, and moreover, they carried, in addition to shirts, a small chest of ointments to heal their wounds, for in the plains and deserts where they fought and were wounded, there was no one to cure them unless they were lucky enough to have some wise enchanter for friend who straightaway would send through the air in a cloud some damsel or dwarf with a vial of water possessed of such power that upon tasting a single drop of it, they would instantly find their wounds as perfectly cured as if they had never received any. But when the knights had no such friend, they always insisted that their squires should be provided with money and such necessities as lint and ointments; and when they had no squires (which was very seldom), they themselves carried those things on the crupper of their horse in saddlebags so small that they were scarcely visible, for except in such a case, the custom of carrying saddlebags was not allowed among knights-errant. I must, therefore, advise you," he continued, "nay, I might even command you, seeing that you are shortly to become my godson in chivalry, never from this day forward to travel without money or without the aforesaid necessities, and you will see how serviceable you will find them when least you expect it."

Don Quixote promised to follow his injunctions carefully, and an order was given for him to watch over his armor in a large yard adjoining the inn. When the knight had collected all his arms together, he laid them on a stone trough that was close by the side of a wall. Then embracing his buckler and grasping his lance, he began with stately air to pace up and down in front of the trough, and as he began his parade, night began to close in.

[19] The places the innkeeper names were all associated with robbers and thieves.

The landlord, meanwhile, told all who were in the inn of the madness of his guest, the arms vigil, and the knighthood dubbing that was to come. They were astonished at such a strange kind of madness and flocked to observe him from a distance. They saw that sometimes he paced to and fro and at other times he leaned on his lance and gazed fixedly at his arms for a considerable time. It was now night, but the moon shone so clearly that she might have almost vied with the luminary that lent her splendor, and thus every action of our new knight could be seen by the spectators.

Just at this moment one of the carriers in the inn took it into his head to water his team of mules, to do which would necessitate removing Don Quixote's arms from the trough. But the knight, as he saw him approach, cried out in a loud voice: "O thou, whosoever thou art, rash knight that dost prepare to lay hands upon the arms of the most valiant knight-errant who ever girded sword, take heed and touch them not if thou wouldst not leave thy life in guerdon[20] for thy temerity." The carrier paid no heed to this warning (it would have been better for him if he had), but seizing hold of the armor by the straps, he threw it a good way from him. No sooner did Don Quixote perceive this than, raising his eyes to heaven and fixing his thoughts (as it seemed) upon his lady, Dulcinea, he said: "Assist me, O lady, in this first affront that is offered to thy vassal's heart. Let not thy favor and protection fail me in this first encounter." Uttering these and similar words, he let slip his buckler, and raising the lance in both hands, he gave the carrier such a hefty blow on the pate that he felled him to the ground in so grievous a plight that if he had followed it with a second, there would have been no need of a surgeon to cure him. This done, he put back his arms and began to pace to and fro as peacefully as before.

Soon after, another carrier, not knowing what had happened (for the first still lay unconscious), came out with the same intention of watering his mules and began to take away the arms that were encumbering the trough, when Don Quixote, not saying a word or imploring assistance from a soul, once more dropped his buckler, lifted up his lance, and without breaking it to pieces, opened the second muleteer's head in four places. All the people in the inn rushed out when they heard the noise, and the landlord among them. As soon as Don Quixote saw them, he braced on his buckler and laid his hands upon his sword, saying: "O lady of beauty, strength and vigor of my enfeebled heart! Now is the time for thee to turn the eyes of thy greatness upon this thy captive knight, who stands awaiting so great an adventure." These words, it seemed to him, filled him with such courage that if all the muleteers in the world had attacked him he would not have retreated one step. The wounded men's companions, seeing them in such an evil plight, began from afar to rain a shower of stones upon Don Quixote, who defended himself as best he could with his buckler, but he did not dare to leave the trough for fear of leaving his arms unprotected. The landlord shouted at them to let him alone, for he had told them the man was mad, and as such, he would be acquitted even if he killed every one of them. Don Quixote shouted still louder, called them caitiffs and traitors, and the lord of the castle a cowardly, baseborn knight for allowing knights-errant to be treated in such a manner. "I would make thee understand," cried he, "what a traitorous scoundrel thou

[20] Recompense.

art had I but been dubbed a knight. But as for you, ye vile and base rabble, I care not a fig for you; fire on, advance, draw near, and hurt me as much as you dare. Soon ye shall receive the reward for your folly and presumption." Such was the undaunted boldness with which he uttered these words that his attackers were struck with terror. And so, partly through fear and partly through the persuasive words of the landlord, they ceased to fling stones at him, and he allowed them to carry off their wounded, after which he returned to the guard of his arms with as much calm gravity as before.

The landlord did not relish the mad pranks of his guest, so he determined to make an end of them and give him his accursed order of chivalry before any further misfortune occurred. And so, going up to him, he excused himself for the insolent way those low fellows had treated him, without his knowledge or consent, adding that they had been well chastised for their rashness. He repeated what he had said before: that there was no chapel in that castle, nor was one necessary for what remained to be done; that the chief point of the knighting ceremony consisted in the accolade and the tap on the shoulders, according to the ceremonial of the order,[21] and that might be administered in the middle of a field; that he had performed the duty of watching over his armor, for he had watched more than four hours, whereas only two were required. All this Don Quixote believed and said that he was then ready to obey him, but yet begged him to conclude with all the brevity possible, for if he should be attacked again when he was armed a knight, he was determined not to leave one person alive in the castle, except those whom, out of respect for the governor of the fortress and at his request, he would spare. The governor, being warned and alarmed at possible consequences, brought out forthwith a book in which he kept his account of the straw and barley supplied to the carriers, and with a stump of candle, which a boy held lighted in his hands, and accompanied by the two above-mentioned damsels, he went over to Don Quixote and ordered him to kneel. He then read in his manual as if he had been repeating some pious oration. In the midst of the prayer he raised his hand and gave him a good blow on the neck, and after that gave a royal thwack on the shoulders, all the time mumbling between his teeth as if praying. After this he commanded one of the ladies to gird on his sword, which she did with much discretion and aplomb, plenty of which was needed to prevent them all from bursting with laughter at every stage of the ceremonies; but the prowess they had beheld in the new knight made them restrain their laughter. As she girded on his sword, the good lady said: "God make you fortunate, knight, and give you success in your contests." Don Quixote demanded then how she was called that he might henceforward know to whom he was beholden for the favor received, for he was resolved to give her a share of the honor that his valor should merit. And she answered with great humility that she was called La Tolosa and was a cobbler's daughter from Toledo, who lived near Sancho Bienaya Square, and that she would always serve him and consider him her lord wherever she happened to be. Don Quixote replied, requesting her for his sake to call herself henceforth Lady Tolosa, which she promised to do. Then the other lady buckled on his spur and he addressed her in very nearly the same terms as the lady of the sword. He asked her name,

[21] The "accolade" (a ceremonial embrace) and a ceremonial tap on the shoulders with a sword were part of the ceremony conferring knighthood.

and she said she was called La Molinera and was daughter of an honest miller of Antequera. He begged her to take a title and call herself Lady Molinera, at the same time making new offers of service.

Don Quixote could not rest until he found himself mounted on horseback and sallying forth in quest of adventures, and after saddling Rozinante, he mounted, but not before he had embraced his host and said so many extravagant words in thanking him for having dubbed him knight that it is impossible to tell them. The landlord, that he might speed the parting guest, answered him in no less rhetorical flourishes but in briefer words, and without asking him to pay for his lodging, he let him go with a godspeed.

CHAPTER IV

What happened to our knight when he sallied from the inn

It was about daybreak when Don Quixote sallied forth from the inn, so happy, so lively, and so excited at finding himself knighted that his very horse girths were ready to burst for joy. But calling to mind the advice of his host concerning the necessary accouterments for his travels, especially the money and the clean shirts, he resolved to return home to provide himself with them and with a squire. He had in view a certain laboring man of the neighborhood who was poor and had children but was otherwise very well fitted for the office of squire to a knight. With this thought in mind he turned Rozinante toward his village, and the horse, knowing full well the way to his stable, began to trot so briskly that his hoofs seemed hardly to strike the ground. The knight had not traveled far when he thought he heard the faint cries of someone in distress from a thicket on his right hand. No sooner had he heard them than he said: "I render thanks to heaven for such a favor. Already I have an opportunity of performing the duty of my profession and of reaping the harvest of my good ambition. Those cries must surely come from some distressed man or woman who needs my protection." Then turning his reins, he guided Rozinante toward the place from which he thought the cries came. A short distance within the wood he saw a mare tied to an oak and to another a youth of about fifteen years of age naked from the waist up. It was he who was crying out, and not without reason, for a lusty countryman was flogging him with a leather strap, and every blow he accompanied with a word of warning and advice, saying, "Keep your mouth shut and your eyes skinned." The boy answered: "I'll never do it again, master. By God's passion, I won't do it again and I promise in future to be more careful of your flock."

When Don Quixote saw what was happening, he said in an angry voice: "Discourteous knight, it is a caitiff's deed to attack one who cannot defend himself. Get up on your horse and take your lance" (for the farmer, too, had a lance leaning against the oak tree to which the mare was tied) "I will show you that you have been acting a coward's part." The countryman, at the sight of the strange apparition in armor brandishing a lance over him, gave himself up for lost and so replied submissively: "Sir knight, this youth I am chastising is a servant of mine, whom I employ to look after a flock of sheep in the neighborhood, but he is so careless that every day he loses one, and when I punish him for his negligence or rascality, he says I do it because I am a skinflint and will not pay him his wages. Upon my life and soul, he lies."

"Have you the impudence to lie in my presence, vile serf?" said Don Quixote. "By the sun that shines on us I will pierce you through and through with this lance of mine. Pay him instantly and none of your denials. If not, by almighty God who rules us all, I will annihilate you this very moment. Untie him at once."

The countryman lowered his head and without a word untied his servant. Don Quixote then asked the boy how much his master owed him. He replied nine months' wages at seven reals a month. Don Quixote, having calculated the sum, found that it came to sixty-three reals and told the farmer to pay up the money unless he wished to die. The farmer, who was shaking with fear, then answered that on the word of one in a tight corner and also upon his oath (yet he had sworn nothing), he did not owe so much, for they must deduct three pairs of shoes that he had given the boy and a real for two bloodlettings that he had when he was sick.

"That is all very well," answered Don Quixote, "but let the shoes and the bloodletting stand for the blows that you have given him for no fault of his own; if he wore out the leather of the shoes you gave him, you wore out his skin, and if the barber drew blood from him when he was sick,[22] you drew blood from him when he was in good health; so in this matter he owes you nothing."

"The trouble is, sir knight," said the countryman, "that I have no money on me. If Andrés comes home with me, I'll pay him ready money down."

"I go home with him?" said the boy. "Not on your life, sir! I would not think of doing such a thing; the moment he gets me alone he'll flay me like a Saint Bartholomew."[23]

"He will not do so," answered Don Quixote. "I have only to command and he will respect me and do my behest. So I shall let him go free and guarantee payment to you, provided he swears by the order of knighthood that he has received."

"Take heed, sir, of what you are saying," said the boy. "My master is no knight; he has not received any order of knighthood. He is Juan Haldudo the wealthy, a native of Quintanar."

"That matters little," answered Don Quixote, "there may be Haldudos who are knights, especially as every man is the son of his own works."

"That's true," said Andrés, "but what kind of works is my master the son of? Isn't he denying me the wages of my sweat and toil?"

"I'm not denying them, brother Andrés," answered the countryman. "Do, please, come with me and I swear by all the orders of knighthood there are in the world to pay you, as I said before, every real down and even perfumed into the bargain."

"I'll spare you the perfume," said Don Quixote. "Give them to him in good, honest reals and I shall be satisfied; but see to it that you carry out your oath. If not, I swear by the same oath to return and chastise you, and I am sure to find you, even if you hide away from me more successfully than a lizard. And if you want to know who it is who gives you this command, learn that I am the valiant Don Quixote of La Mancha, the undoer of wrongs

[22] Barbers also functioned as surgeons.

[23] Saint Bartholomew, one of the twelve apostles and martyrs, was said to have been flayed to death.

and injuries. So, God be with you, and do not forget what you have promised and sworn, on pain of the penalty I have stated." With these words he spurred Rozinante and in a moment he was far away.

The countryman gazed after him, and when he saw that he had gone through the wood and was out of sight, he turned to his servant, Andrés, saying: "Come here, my boy; I want to pay you what I owe you in accordance with the commands of that undoer of wrongs."

"So you will, I swear," said Andrés; "and you had better obey the orders of that good knight—may he live a thousand years. He is such a courageous man and such a fair judge that by Saint Roch, if you don't pay me, he'll be back and he'll do what he threatened."

"And I'll swear I will too," answered the countryman, "and to show you my goodwill, I'll double the debt so that I can double the pay." Catching the boy by the arm, he tied him again to the oak and gave him such a drubbing that he left him for dead. "Now, master Andrés," said he, "call out to that undoer of wrongs and you'll find that he won't undo this one. Indeed I don't think I'm finished with you yet, for I've a mind to flay you alive as you feared a moment ago." At last he untied him and gave him leave to go off and fetch his judge to carry out the threatened sentence. As for Andrés, he went off sorely fretful, swearing that he would seek out the valiant Don Quixote of La Mancha and tell him all that happened, and he would make his tormentor pay sevenfold. However, he departed in tears, while his master stayed behind laughing.

Such was the manner in which the valiant Don Quixote undid that wrong.

Meanwhile the knight was quite pleased with himself, for he believed that he had begun his feats of arms in a most successful and dignified manner, and he went on riding toward his village, saying to himself in a low voice: "Well mayest thou call thyself the happiest of all women on earth, O Dulcinea of El Toboso, peerless among beauties, for it was thy fortune to have subject to thy will so valiant and celebrated a knight as is and shall be Don Quixote of La Mancha, who, as all the world knows, received only yesterday the order of knighthood and today has undone the greatest wrong that ever ignorance designed or cruelty committed. Today from the hand of that pitiless foe he seized the lash with which he so unjustly scourged that tender child."

Just then he came to a road that branched into four directions, and forthwith he was reminded of the crossroads where knights-errant would halt to consider which road they should follow. To imitate their example he paused for a moment's meditation, and then he slackened the reins, leaving Rozinante to choose the way. The horse followed his original intention, which was to make straight in the direction of his stable.

When Don Quixote had ridden about two miles, he saw a big company of people who, as it appeared later, were traders of Toledo on their way to buy silk in Murcia. There were six of them and they carried sunshades. They were accompanied by four servants on horseback and three muleteers on foot. No sooner had Don Quixote perceived them than he fancied a new adventure was at hand. So, imitating as closely as possible the exploits he had read about in his books, he resolved now to perform one that was admirably molded to the present circumstances. So, with a lofty bearing he fixed himself firmly in his stirrups, grasped his lance, covered himself with his buckler, and stood in the middle of the road waiting for those knights-errant to approach (for such he supposed them to be). As soon as they came within earshot, Don Quixote, raising his voice, cried out in an arrogant tone: "Let all the world stand still if all the world does not confess that there is not in all the world a fairer damsel than the Empress of La Mancha, the peerless Dulcinea of El Toboso."

At the sound of those words the traders pulled up and gazed in amazement at the grotesque being who uttered them. Both the tone and the appearance of the horseman gave clear proof of his insanity, but they wished to consider in more leisurely fashion the meaning of this confession that he insisted upon. So one of them, who was a trifle waggish in humor and had plenty of wit, addressed him as follows: "Sir knight, we do not know this lady you speak of. Show her to us, and if she is as beautiful as you say, we shall willingly and universally acknowledge the truth of your claim."

"If I were to show her to you," answered Don Quixote, "what merit would there be in acknowledging a truth so manifest to all? The important point is that you should believe, confess, affirm, swear, and defend it without setting eyes on her. If you do not, I challenge you to try battle with me, ye presumptuous and overweening band. Come on now, one by one as the traditions of chivalry declare, or else all together according to the foul custom of your breed. Here I stand waiting for you, trusting in the justice of my cause."

"Sir knight," answered the trader, "I beseech you in the name of all the princes here present not to force us to burden our consciences by confessing something we have never seen or heard, especially when it is so prejudicial to the empresses and queens of Alcarria and Extremadura.[24] Please show us some picture of that lady, even if it is no bigger than a grain of wheat, for a thread will enable us to judge the whole skein and we shall be satisfied and you yourself happy and content. I believe that we already are so much on your side that even if your lady's picture shows that one eye squints and the other drips vermilion and sulphur, yet in spite of all, to gratify you, we shall say all that you please in her favor."

"Drip indeed, you infamous scoundrels!" cried Don Quixote in a towering rage. "Nothing of the kind drips from her eyes, but only ambergris and civet in cotton wool. She is not squint-eyed nor hunchbacked, but straighter than a Guadarrama spindle. But you shall pay the penalty for the great blasphemy you have uttered against so peerless a beauty as my lady." With those words he attacked the man who had spoken to him, so fiercely with couched lance that if good fortune had not caused Rozinante to stumble and fall midway, the merchant would have paid dearly for his rashness. Rozinante fell and his master rolled a good distance over the ground. Although he tried to rise, he could not, for he was so impeded by the lance, the buckler, the spurs, the helmet, and the weight of the ancient armor. However, as he was struggling to arise, he kept on crying: "Flee not, cowardly rabble! Wait, slavish herd! It is not my fault, but the fault of my horse, that I am stretched here."

One of the muleteers of the company, who indeed was not very good-natured, when he heard the poor fallen knight say such arrogant words, could not resist the temptation to give him the answer on his ribs. So he went up

[24] Both backward, primitive regions.

to him, took the lance, broke it into pieces, and with one of them he so belabored our poor Don Quixote that in spite of his armor he thrashed him like a measure of wheat. His masters shouted to him not to beat him so much and to leave off; but the fellow was angry and would not stop the game until he had spent what remained of his rage. Then, running to get the rest of the pieces of the lance, he splintered them all on the wretched knight, who, in the midst of all this tempest of blows that rained on him, did not for a moment close his mouth, but bellowed out threats to heaven and earth and those villainous cutthroats (for so they appeared to him). At last the muleteer became wearied and the traders pursued their journey, carrying with them plenty of matter for conversation at the expense of the poor drubbed knight. And when he was alone, he tried to see if he could get up, but if he could not do so when he was hale and hearty, how could he do it when he was bruised and battered? And yet he counted himself lucky, for he thought that his misfortune was peculiar to knights-errant and he attributed the whole accident to the fault of his horse. But so bruised was his whole body that it was impossible for him to get up.

CHAPTER V

In which is continued the account of our knight's mishap

Seeing that he couldn't stir, he resolved to have recourse to his usual remedy, which was to think of some incident from one of his books. His madness made him remember that of the Marquess of Mantua and Baldwin, whom Carloto left wounded on the mountainside[25]—a story familiar to children, not unknown to youths, celebrated and even believed by old men, yet for all that, no more authentic than the miracles of Mohammed. Now this story, so he thought, exactly fitted his present circumstances, so with great display of affliction he began to roll about on the ground and to repeat in a faint voice the words that the wounded knight in the wood was supposed to have said:

> "Where art thou, lady of my heart,
> That for my woe thou dost not grieve?
> Alas, thou do know'st not my distress,
> Or thou art false and pitiless."

In this manner he repeated the ballad until he came to those verses that say: "O noble Marquess of Mantua, my uncle and liege lord." By chance there happened to pass by at that very moment a peasant of his own village, a neighbor, who was returning from bringing a load of wheat to the mill. And he, seeing a man lying stretched out on the ground, came over and asked him who he was and what was the cause of his sorrowful lamentation. Don Quixote, firmly believing that the man was the Marquess of Mantua, his uncle, would not answer but continued reciting his ballad, which told of his misfortunes and of the loves of the Emperor's son with his wife, just as the book relates

[25] Carloto, son of Charlemagne, was the hero of a well-known ballad, which Quixote quotes below.

it. The peasant was amazed to hear those extravagant words. Then taking off his visor, which had been broken to pieces in the drubbing, he wiped the dust off his face. No sooner had he done so than he recognized him and said: "Master Quixana" (for that must have been how people called him when he had his wits and had not been transformed from a staid gentleman into a knight-errant) "who left you in such a state?" But he kept on reciting his ballad and made no answer to what he was asked. The good man then, as best as he could, took off his breast- and back-plate to see if he was wounded, but he saw no blood or scar upon him. He managed to lift him up from the ground and with the greatest difficulty hoisted him on to his ass, thinking that beast an easier mount. Then he gathered together all his arms, not omitting even the splinters of the lance, tied them into a bundle, and laid them upon Rozinante's back. Then taking the horse by the bridle and the ass by the halter, he set off toward his village, meditating all the while on the foolish words that Don Quixote kept saying. And Don Quixote on his part was no less pensive, for he was so beaten and bruised that he could hardly hold himself onto the ass, and from time to time he uttered such melancholy sighs that seemed to pierce the skies that the peasant felt again moved to ask him what was the cause of his sorrow. But it must have been the Devil himself who supplied him with stories so similiar to his circumstances, for at that instant, forgetting Baldwin, he remembered the Moor Abindarráez whom the governor of Antequera, Rodrigo de Narváez, took prisoner to his castle.[26] So when the peasant asked him again how he was, he answered word for word as the captive Abindarráez answered Rodrigo de Narváez, just as he had read in Montemayor's *Diana,* where the story is told. And he applied it so artfully to his own case that the peasant wished he were in Hell rather than to have to listen to such a hodgepodge of foolishness. This convinced him that his neighbor was mad, so he made haste to reach the village and thereby escape being further plagued by Don Quixote's long discourse. The latter ended by saying: "I would have you know, Master Rodrigo de Narváez, that the beauteous Jarifa I have mentioned is now the fair Dulcinea of El Toboso, for whom I have done, still do, and shall do the most famous deeds of chivalry that ever have been, are, or ever shall be seen in the world." To this the peasant answered: "Take heed, sir, that I am neither Don Rodrigo de Narváez nor the Marquess of Mantua, but Pedro Alonso, your neighbor, and you are neither Baldwin nor Abindarráez, but the honorable gentleman Master Quixana."

"I know who I am," answered Don Quixote, "and I know that I can be not only those I have mentioned but also the Twelve Peers of France and even the Nine Worthies, for my exploits will surpass all they have ever jointly or separately achieved."[27]

With this and sundry topics of conversation they reached the village at sunset, but the peasant waited until it was dark so that no one would see the belabored knight so sorrily mounted. When he thought the time had come,

[26] There were a number of romance tales about the love of the captive Moor Abindarráez for the beautiful Jarifa. One version of the story is in Jorge de Montemayor's romance *Diana* (1561), which Quixote mentions.

[27] The Twelve Peers were Charlemagne's chief knights, all equal in rank. The Nine Worthies, in medieval lore, were nine famous men, three Jewish, three pagan, and three Christian, subjects of a number of tales and chronicles.

he entered the village and went to Don Quixote's house, which he found in an uproar. The curate and the village barber, great friends of Don Quixote, happened to be there and the housekeeper was addressing them in a loud voice: "What do you think, Master Licentiate Pedro Pérez" (that was the curate's name) "of my master's misfortune? For the past six days neither he, nor his horse, nor his buckler, nor his lance, nor his armor has appeared. Woe is me! I'm now beginning to understand, and I'm as sure of it as I am of death that those accursed books of chivalry that he continually reads have turned his brain topsy-turvy. Now that I think of it I remember hearing him say to himself many a time that he wished to become a knight-errant and go through the world in search of adventures. The Devil and Barabbas[28] take such books, for they have ruined the finest mind in all La Mancha!" The niece said the same and a little more: "You must know, Master Nicholas" (this was the name of the barber) "that it was a frequent occurrence for my uncle to read these soulless books of misadventures for days and nights on end. At the end of that time he would cast the book from his hands, clutch his sword, and begin to slash the walls. Then, when he was grown very weary, he would say that he had killed four giants as big as towers and that the sweat that dripped off him after his great exertions, he would say, was blood from the wounds he had received in battle. Then he would drink a great jugful of water and become calm and peaceable, saying that the water was a most precious liquor that his friend the great enchanter Esquife had given him. I, however, blame myself for all, for not having warned you of my uncle's extravagant behavior. You might have cured him before things reached such a state, and you would have burned all those excommunicated books (he has many, mind you), for they all deserve to be burned as heretics."

"I agree with that," said the curate, "and I hold that tomorrow must not pass without a public inquiry being made into them. They should be condemned to the fire to prevent them from tempting those who read them to do what my poor master must have done."

All this Don Quixote and the peasant heard. The latter finally understood the infirmity of his neighbor and began to shout: "Open your doors, all of you, to Sir Baldwin and the Marquess of Mantua, who is grievously wounded, and to the Moor Abindarráez, who is led captive by the valiant Rodrigo de Narváez, governor of Antequera."

Hearing these cries, they all rushed out and straightaway recognized their friend. They ran to embrace him, but he had not yet dismounted from the ass, for he was not able to do so. He said: "Stand back, all of you. I have been sorely wounded through the fault of my horse; carry me to my bed and, if possible, call the wise Urganda to examine and cure my wounds."

"A thousand curses," said the housekeeper then. "My heart told me clearly on which foot my master limped. Come on upstairs, sir; we'll know how to look after you here without that Urganda woman. Curses, aye, a hundred curses on those books of chivalry that have driven you to this!"

They carried him to his bed and searched his body for wounds, but could find none. He said he was all bruised after a great fall he had with his horse, Rozinante, when he was fighting ten giants, the fiercest and most overweening in the world.

[28] The robber whom Pilate pardoned instead of Christ; see, for example, Matthew 27:15–26.

"Aha!" said the curate. "So there are giants too in the dance. By the sign of the Cross I swear I'll burn the lot of them before tomorrow night."

They questioned Don Quixote a thousand times, but he would give no answer. He only asked them to give him food and allow him to sleep, for rest was what he needed most. . . .

[*In a chapter omitted here, the curate and the barber examine the contents of Don Quixote's library and burn all the books on knight-errantry. They examine the title pages and comment critically on the absurd contents.*]

CHAPTER VII

Of the second sally of our good knight Don Quixote of La Mancha

. . . . That same night the housekeeper burned all the books she could find in the courtyard and in the house, and some that perished in the flames deserved to be preserved forever in the archives, but fate and the laziness of the inquisitor did not allow it, and thus in their case the saying was fulfilled that the saint sometimes pays for the sinner. One of the remedies that the curate and the barber then prescribed for their friend's infirmity was to wall up the room where the books had been stored so that when he rose he should not find them, for once the cause had been removed, the effect might cease. And they agreed to tell him that an enchanter had whisked books, room, and all away. The plan was carried out with great speed.

Two days later Don Quixote got up, and the first thing he did was to go and see his books, and as he could not find the room in which he had left them, he went up and down and all over the house looking for it. He came to the place where the door used to be and felt the wall with his hands, staring around him on all sides without saying a word. At last he asked the housekeeper where was the study in which he kept his books. The housekeeper, who knew exactly what she had to answer, said: "What manner of study is your worship looking for? There are no studies or books in this house now, for the Devil in person took all away."

"It was not the Devil," said the niece, "but an enchanter who arrived on a cloud one night after you went away from here. He got down off the serpent on which he was riding and went into the room. I don't know what he did in there, but soon after he went flying out through the roof, leaving the house full of smoke. When we looked to see what he had done, we could see no books or room, but we remember very well, myself and the housekeeper, that when the wicked old man was about to depart, he said in a loud voice that owing to the secret enmity he bore against the owner of those books and of the room, he had done damage that would soon be clear. He also said that he was called Muñatón the wizard."

"Frestón was the name he wished to say," answered Don Quixote.

"I don't know," said the housekeeper, "whether he was called Frestón or Fritón; I only know that his name ended in *-tón*."

"That is true," said Don Quixote. "He is a wise enchanter, a great enemy of mine, and looks upon me with a malicious eye, for he knows by his skill and wisdom that in the course of time I shall fight in single combat with a knight whom he favors, and I shall win, in spite of all his machinations; so, he tries to do me all the hurt he can. But I affirm that he will never prevail over what has been ordained by Heaven."

"Who has any doubts on that score?" said the niece. "But, dear uncle, what have you to do with such quarrels? Is it not better to stay peacefully at home instead of roaming the world in search of better bread than is made of wheat, not to mention that many who go for wool come home shorn?"

"My dear niece," answered Don Quixote, "how far you are off the mark! Before they ever shear me, I'll have plucked and lopped off the beards of all who think they can touch the tip of a single hair of mine."

The two would not make any further reply, for they saw that his anger was rising. As a matter of fact, he remained a fortnight peacefully at home without showing any signs of wanting to repeat his former vagaries. During those days he held many pleasant arguments with his two old friends the curate and the barber. He would maintain that what the world needed most of all was plenty of knights-errant and that he himself would revive knight-errantry. The curate sometimes contradicted him; at other times he would give in to him, for had he not adopted this procedure, he could never have dealt with him.

During this interval Don Quixote made overtures to a certain laboring man, a neighbor of his and an honest fellow (if such a term can be applied to one who is poor), but with very little wit in his pate. In effect, he said so much to him and made so many promises that the poor wight resolved to set out with him and serve him as squire. Among other things Don Quixote told him that he should be most willing to go with him because some time or another he might meet with an adventure that would earn for him, in the twinkling of an eye, some island, and he would find himself governor of it. With those and other promises, Sancho Panza (for that was the fellow's name) left his wife and children and engaged himself as squire to his neighbor. Don Quixote then set about raising money, and by selling one thing, pawning another, and throwing away the lot for a mere song, he gathered a respectable sum. He furnished himself likewise with a buckler borrowed from a friend, repaired his broken helmet as best he could, and informed his squire, Sancho, of the day and hour when he intended to sally forth so that the latter might supply himself with all that was needed. He charged him particularly to carry saddlebags. Sancho said he would do so and added that he was thinking of bringing an ass with him, for he had a good one and he was not used to travel on foot. At the mention of the ass Don Quixote hesitated a little, racking his brains to remember any case of a knight-errant who was attended by a squire mounted on ass-back, but he could not remember any such case. Nevertheless, he resolved to let him take his ass, for he intended to present him with a more dignified mount when he got the opportunity, by unhorsing the first discourteous knight he came across. He also provided himself with shirts and other necessities, thus following the advice the innkeeper had given him.

After all these preparations had been made, Don Quixote, without saying farewell to his housekeeper and niece, Panza to his wife and children, set out one night from the village without being seen. They traveled so far that night that at daybreak they were sure that no one would find them, even if they were pursued.

Sancho Panza rode along on his ass like a patriarch, with his saddlebags and wineskin, full of a huge longing to see himself governor of the island his master had promised to him. Don Quixote happened to take the same road as on his first journey, that is, across the Plain of Montiel, which he now traveled with less discomfort than the last time, for as it was early in the morning, the rays of the sun did not beat down directly upon them, but slantwise, and so did not trouble them. Presently Sancho Panza said to his master: "Mind, your worship, sir knight-errant, you don't let slip from your memory the island you've promised me; I'll be able to rule it well, no matter how big it is."

To which Don Quixote replied: "I would have you know, my friend Sancho, that knights-errant of long ago were accustomed to make their squires governors of the islands or kingdoms they won, and I have resolved not to neglect so praiseworthy a custom. Nay, I wish to surpass them in it, for they sometimes, perhaps even on the majority of occasions, waited till their squires were grown old, and then when they were cloyed with service after enduring bad days and worse nights, they conferred upon them some title, such as count or at least marquess, of some valley of more or less account. But if you live and I live, I may, before six days have passed, even conquer a kingdom with a string of dependencies, which would fall in exactly with my plan of crowning you king of one of them. Do not, however, think this strange, for knights-errant of my kind meet with such extraordinary and unexpected chances that I might easily give you still more than I am promising."

"And so," answered Sancho Panza, "by that token, if I became king by one of those miracles you mention, at least my chuck[29] Juana Gutiérrez would become queen and my children princes."

"Who doubts it?" answered Don Quixote.

"I doubt it," replied Sancho Panza, "for I truly believe that even if God were to rain kingdoms down upon earth, none would sit well on the head of Mari Gutiérrez.[30] Believe me, sir, she's not worth two farthings as queen; countess would suit her better, and even then, God help her."

"Leave all in God's hands, Sancho," answered Don Quixote. "He will do what is best for her, but do not humble yourself so far as to be satisfied with anything less than the title of lord-lieutenant."

"I'll not indeed, sir," replied Sancho, "for a famous master like yourself will know what is fit for me and what I can carry."

CHAPTER VIII

Of the valiant Don Quixote's success in the terrifying and never-before-imagined adventure of the windmills, with other events worthy of happy remembrance

Just then they came in sight of thirty or forty windmills that rise from that plain, and no sooner did Don Quixote see them than he said to his squire: "Fortune is guiding our affairs better than we ourselves could have wished. Do you see over yonder, friend Sancho, thirty or forty hulking giants? I intend

[29] A term of endearment. Juana is Sancho's wife.

[30] Gutiérrez is Juana's (or Mari's) maiden name; elsewhere she is called Juana Panza.

to do battle with them and slay them. With their spoils we shall begin to be rich, for this is a righteous war and the removal of so foul a brood from off the face of the earth is a service God will bless."

"What giants?" asked Sancho Panza.

"Those you see over there," replied his master, "with their long arms; some of them have them well-nigh two leagues in length."

"Take care, sir," cried Sancho. "Those over there are not giants but windmills, and those things that seem to be arms are their sails, which when they are whirled around by the wind turn the millstone."

"It is clear," replied Don Quixote, "that you are not experienced in adventures. Those are giants, and if you are afraid, turn aside and pray whilst I enter into fierce and unequal battle with them."

Uttering these words, he clapped spurs to Rozinante, his steed, without heeding the cries of his squire, Sancho, who warned him that he was not going to attack giants but windmills. But so convinced was he that they were giants that he neither heard his squire's shouts nor did he notice what they were, though he was very near them. Instead, he rushed on, shouting in a loud voice: "Fly not, cowards and vile caitiffs; one knight alone attacks you!" At that moment a slight breeze arose and the great sails began to move. When Don Quixote saw this, he shouted again: "Although you flourish more arms than the giant Briareus, you shall pay for it![31]

Saying this and commending himself most devoutly to his lady, Dulcinea, whom he begged to help him in this peril, he covered himself with his buckler, couched his lance, charged at Rozinante's full gallop, and rammed the first mill in his way. He ran his lance into the sail, but the wind twisted it with such violence that it shivered the lance in pieces and dragged both rider and horse after it, rolling them over and over on the ground, sorely damaged.

Sancho Panza rushed up to his assistance as fast as his ass could gallop, and when he reached the knight, he found that he was unable to move, such was the blow that Rozinante had given him in the fall.

"God help us!" cried Sancho. "Did I not tell you, sir, to mind what you were doing, for those were only windmills? Nobody could have mistaken them unless he had windmills in his brain."

"Hold your peace, good Sancho," replied Don Quixote. "The affairs of war are, above all others, subject to continual change. Moreover, I am convinced, and that is the truth, that the magician Frestón, the one who robbed me of my study and books, has changed those giants into windmills to deprive me of the glory of victory; such is the enmity he bears against me. But in the end his evil arts will be of little avail against my doughty sword."

"God settle it in His own way," cried Sancho as he helped his master to rise and remount Rozinante, who was well-nigh disjointed by his fall.

They conversed about the recent adventure as they followed the road toward the Pass of Lápice, for there, Don Quixote said, they could not fail to find many and various adventures, seeing that it was a much frequented spot. Nevertheless he was very downcast at the loss of his lance, and in mentioning it to his squire, he said: "I remember having read of a Spanish knight

[31] Briareus was a hundred-armed, fifty-headed giant in Greek mythology. He helped Zeus to overthrow the Titans.

called Diego Pérez de Vargas, who, when he broke his sword in a battle, tore off a huge branch from an oak and with it did such deeds of prowess that day and pounded so many Moors that he earned the surname of Machuca,[32] and so he and his descendants were called from that day onwards Vargas y Machuca. I mention this because I intend to tear from the first oak tree we meet such a branch, with which I am resolved to perform such deeds that you will consider yourself fortunate to witness, exploits that men will scarcely credit."

"God's will be done," said Sancho. "I'll believe all your worship says; but straighten yourself a bit in the saddle, for you seem to be leaning over on one side, which must be from the bruises you received in your fall."

"That is true," replied Don Quixote, "and if I do not complain, it is because knights-errant must never complain of any wound, even though their guts are protruding from them."

"If that be so, I've no more to say," answered Sancho, "but God knows I'd be glad to hear you complain when anything hurts you. As for myself, I'll never fail to complain at the smallest twinge, unless this business of not complaining applies also to squires."

Don Quixote could not help laughing at the simplicity of his squire and told him that he might complain whenever he pleased and to his heart's content, for he had never read anything to the contrary in the order of chivalry. Sancho then bade his master consider that it was now time to eat, but the latter told him to eat whenever he fancied. As for himself, he had no appetite at the moment. Sancho no sooner had obtained leave than he settled himself as comfortably as he could upon his ass, and taking out of his saddlebags some of the contents, he jogged behind his master, munching deliberately; and every now and then he would take a stiff pull at the wineskin with such gusto that the ruddiest tapster in Málaga would have envied him. While he rode on, swilling away in that manner, he did not remember any promise his master might have made to him, and so far from thinking it a labor, he thought it a life of ease to go roaming in quest of adventures, no matter how perilous they might be.

They spent that night under some trees, and from one of them Don Quixote tore a withered branch that might, at a pinch, serve him as a lance, and he fixed to it the iron head of the one he had broken. All that night he did not sleep, for he kept thinking of his lady, Dulcinea. In this way he imitated what he had read in his books, where knights spent many sleepless nights in forests and wastes, reveling in memories of their fair ladies. Not so Sancho Panza, whose belly was full of something more substantial than chicory water. He made one long sleep of it, and if his master had not roused him, not even the rays of the sun beating on his face nor the joyful warbling of the hosts of birds would have awakened him. When he got up he tested the wineskin once more and found it somewhat flabbier than the night before. This saddened him, for he thought that they were not in the way to remedy that loss as soon as would satisfy him. Don Quixote would not break his fast, for as we have said before, he was resolved to nurture himself on savory remembrances. . . .

[32] The verb *machucar* means "to pound." The story of Diego Pérez de Vargas, a sort of Spanish Hercules, is told in another old ballad.

[*In the following chapters, Don Quixote attacks two monks and some muleteers who he thinks are necromancers carrying off a princess; he encounters a beautiful maiden, Marcella, who is as independent and idealistic as Quixote himself; he is beaten by herdsmen who object to Rozinante's amorous attentions to their mares; and he becomes embroiled in a dispute in an inn when he mistakenly thinks a servant girl is a beautiful princess who has fallen in love with him. This incident ends with Sancho being tossed in a blanket.*]

CHAPTER XVIII

In which an account is given of the conversation that took place between Sancho Panza and his master, Don Quixote, with other adventures worth recording

. . . . Suddenly Don Quixote saw a large, dense cloud of dust rolling toward them. Turning to Sancho, he said: "This is the day, Sancho, on which shall be clearly seen the good that fate has in store for us; this is the day, I say, on which I shall show the might of my arm and on which I intend to do deeds that shall be written in the books of fame for succeeding ages. Do you see that dust cloud, Sancho? Know then that it is churned up by a mighty army composed of sundry and innumerable people who are marching this way."

"If so, there must be two armies," said Sancho, "for here on this side there is as great a cloud of dust."

Don Quixote turned around to look at it, and seeing it was so, he rejoiced, for he fancied that there were indeed two armies coming to fight each other in the midst of that spacious plain. For his imagination at all hours of the day and night was full of battles, enchantments, adventures, follies, loves, and challenges as are related in the books of chivalry, and all his words, thoughts, and actions were turned to such things. As for the clouds of dust he had seen, they were raised by two large flocks of ewes and rams that were being driven along the same road from opposite directions, which, because of the dust, could not be seen until they came near.

So earnest was Don Quixote in calling them armies that Sancho came to believe it and asked: "Well, what are we to do?"

"What?" said Don Quixote. "Why, favor and help the distressed and needy. You must know, Sancho, that the army marching toward us in front is led by the mighty emperor Alifanfarón, lord of the great island of Trapobana;[33] the other, which is marching at our back, is the army of his foe, the king of the Garamantans, Pentapolín of the Naked Arm, for he always goes into battle with his right arm bare."

"Why do these two gentlemen hate each other so much?" asked Sancho.

"They are enemies," replied Don Quixote, "because Alifanfarón is a furious pagan and is in love with the daughter of Pentapolín, a beautiful, graceful lady and a Christian. Her father refuses to give her to the pagan king unless he abandon first the false religion of Mohammed and turn Christian."

"By my beard," said Sancho, "Pentapolín does right, and I'll help as best I can."

[33] Most of the high-sounding names in this passage are imaginary. Trapobana, or Taprobana, is the ancient name given the island of Sri Lanka.

"Then you will do your duty," said Don Quixote, "for it is not necessary to be dubbed a knight to engage in battles such as these."

"I understand," replied Sancho, "but where shall we tie this ass that we may be sure of finding him after the scuffle is over? I think it was never customary to go into battle mounted on such a beast."

"That is true," said Don Quixote. "What you must do is to leave the ass to his own devices. Let him take his chance whether he get lost or not, for after winning this battle we shall have so many horses that even Rozinante runs the risk of being exchanged for another. Now listen to me carefully while I give you an account of the principal knights in the two approaching armies. Let us withdraw to that hillock over there to get a better view of the two armies."

They did so, and standing on the top of the hill, they could have discerned the two flocks that Don Quixote had converted into armies had their eyes not been blinded by the clouds of dust. But seeing in his imagination what did not exist, he began to say in a loud voice: "The knight you see yonder with the yellow armor, who bears on his shield a crowned lion couchant at a damsel's feet, is the valiant Laurcalco, lord of the Silver Bridge. The other with armor flowered with gold, who bears on his shield three crowns argent on an azure field, is the fearsome Micocolembo, grand duke of Quirotia. The other, with gigantic limbs, who marches on his right, is the undaunted Brandabarbarán of Boliche, lord of the Three Arabias. He is wearing a serpent's skin and bears a gate as a shield, which, fame says, was one of those belonging to the temple that Samson pulled down when by his death he took revenge on his enemies.[34] Now turn your eyes to this other side, and there you will see, in front of this other army, the victorious and never vanquished Timonel of Carcajona, prince of New Biscay, who comes clad in armor quartered azure, vert, argent, and or. He bears on his shield a cat or on a field gules with a scroll inscribed *Miau,* which is the beginning of his mistress' name—according to report—the peerless Miaulina, daughter of Alfeñiquén, duke of Algarbe. The other, who weighs down and oppresses the back of that powerful and spirited charger, with armor as white as snow and a white shield without a device, is a novice knight of the French nation called Pierre Papin, lord of the baronies of Utrique. The other pricking with iron heel the flanks of that nimble zebra and carrying for arms the azure cups is the doughty duke of Nerbia, Espartafilardo of the Wood, who bears on his shield the device of an asparagus plant, with a motto in Castilian which says: *My fortune trails.*"

So he went on, naming many imaginary knights in each squadron as his fancy dictated and giving extemporaneously to each his armor, colors, devices, and mottoes, for he was completely carried away by his strangely deluded imagination. He continued without a pause: "That squadron in the front is composed of men of various nations: Here are they who drink of the sweet waters of the famous Xanthus; mountaineers who tread the Massilian fields; those who sift the pure and fine gold of Arabia; dwellers on the celebrated cool shores of clear Thermodon; those who drain in various ways the golden Pactolus; the Numidians, unreliable in their promises; Persians, famous for

[34] See Judges 16.

their bows and arrows; Parthians; Medes, who fight as they flee; Arabs, with their movable houses; Scythians as cruel as they are fair; Ethiopians with pierced lips; and countless other nations, whose faces I recognize and behold, although their names I do not recollect. In that other squadron come drinkers of the crystal waters of the olive-bearing Betis; men who burnish and polish their faces with the liquor of the ever-rich and golden Tagus; men who enjoy the health-giving waters of the divine Genil; dwellers in the Tartessian plain with their abundant pastures; men who enjoy the Elysian fields of Jérez; men of La Mancha rich and crowned with golden corn; men clad in iron, survivors of the ancient Gothic race; bathers in the Pisuerga, famous for its mild current; men who graze their flock on the broad pastures of the winding Guadiana, famous for its hidden current;[35] men who shiver with the cold of the wooded Pyrenees and among the white snows of the lofty Apennines; as many as all Europe contains and encloses."

By God! How many provinces did he name! How many nations did he enumerate, giving to each, with wonderful speed, its peculiar attributes, so absorbed and wrapped up was he in all that he had read in his lying books! Sancho Panza hung on his words without uttering one. Now and then he turned his head to see whether he could perceive the knights and giants his master named. Seeing none, he said at last: "Master, I'll commend to the Devil any man, giant, or knight of all those you mentioned who is actually here. At least I do not see them. Perhaps all may be enchantment like last night's specters."

"Why do you say that?" said Don Quixote. "Do you not hear the neighing of the horses, the blaring of the trumpets, and the rattle of the drums?"

"I hear nothing," answered Sancho, "but the bleating of sheep and lambs." And so it was, for now the two flocks were close at hand.

"The fear you are in," said Don Quixote, "allows you neither to see nor to hear correctly, for one of the effects of fear is to disturb the senses and make things seem different from what they are. If you are so afraid, stand to one side and leave me alone, for I alone am sufficient to give the victory to the side that I shall assist." With these words he clapped spurs to Rozinante, and with lance couched, rode down the hillside like a thunderbolt.

Sancho shouted at him: "Come back, master, come back! I swear to God that those you are going to charge are only sheep and lambs. Come back! Woe to the father who begat me! What madness is this? Look! There is neither giant, nor knight, nor cats, nor arms, nor shield quartered or entire, nor azures true or bedeviled. Sinner that I am, what are you doing?"

Don Quixote, however, did not turn back, but charged on, shouting as he went: "Ho! You knights who fight under the banners of the valiant emperor Pentapolín of the Naked Arm! Follow me, all of you, and you will see how easily I will take vengeance for him on his enemy, Alifanfarón of Trapobana."

With these words he dashed into the midst of the flock of sheep and began to spear them with as much courage and fury as if he were fighting his mortal enemies. The shepherds and herdsmen who came with the flock shouted to him to stop, but seeing that words were of no avail, they unloosed their slings and began to salute his ears with stones as big as one's fist. Don Quixote

[35] The Guadiana River runs underground through part of La Mancha.

took no notice of their stones but galloped to and fro, crying out: "Where are you, proud Alifanfarón? Where are you? Come to me, for I am but one knight and wish to try my strength with you, man to man, and take away your life for the wrong you do to the valiant Pentapolín." At that instant a smooth pebble hit him in the side and buried two ribs in his entrails. Finding himself in such a bad way, he thought for certain that he was killed or sorely wounded, and remembering his balsam, he took out his cruse[36] and raised it to his mouth to drink. But before he could swallow what he wanted, another pebble struck him full on the hand, broke the cruse to pieces, carried away with it three or four teeth and grinders out of his mouth, and badly crushed two fingers of his hand. And such was the force of those two blows that the poor knight fell off his horse onto the ground. The shepherds ran up to him, and believing that they had killed him, they collected their flocks in great haste, carried away their dead sheep, which were more than seven, and departed without further inquiry.

All this time Sancho stood on the hillock watching his master's mad escapade and tearing his beard and cursing the unlucky hour and moment when he first met him. But seeing him lying on the ground and the shepherds out of sight, he came down the hill, went up to his master, and found him in a very bad way, although not quite unconscious. So he said to him: "Did I not tell you, sir, to come back, for those you went to attack were not armies, but flocks of sheep?"

"That rascal of an enchanter, my enemy, can counterfeit and make men vanish. Know, Sancho, that it is a very easy matter for such men to make us see what they please, and this malignant persecutor of mine, envious of the glory that I was to reap in this battle, has changed the squadrons of enemy into flocks of sheep. Now, for my sake, Sancho, do one thing to undeceive yourself and see the truth of what I am telling you. Get up on your ass and follow them softly, and you will see that when they have gone a little distance away, they will return to their original shapes, and ceasing to be sheep, will become grown-up, mature men as when I described them to you at first. But do not go now, for I need your assistance. Come and see how many of my teeth are missing, for I do not think I have a single one left in my mouth."

Sancho went so close that he almost thrust his eyes into his mouth, and it was precisely at the fatal moment when the balsam that had been fretting in Don Quixote's stomach came up to the surface; and with the same violence that a bullet is fired out of a gun, all that he had in his stomach discharged itself upon the beard of the compassionate squire.

"Holy Mary!" cried Sancho. "What has happened to me? The poor sinner must be at death's door, for he's puking blood at the mouth." But reflecting a little, he was soon convinced by the color, smell, and taste that it was not blood, but the balsam that he had seen him drink; and so great was the loathing he felt that his own stomach turned, and he emptied its full cargo upon his master, and both were in a precious pickle. Sancho rushed to his ass to take something out of his saddlebags to clean himself and his master, and when he did not find them, he was on the verge of losing his mind. He cursed himself again and vowed in his heart to leave his master and return

[36] An earthen pot. "Balsam" is any soothing medicine.

to his home, although he would lose his wages for service and his hopes of becoming governor of the promised island.

Don Quixote had now risen, and keeping his left hand to his mouth lest the rest of his teeth fall out, with the other he took hold of Rozinante's bridle (who had not stirred from his master's side, such was his well-bred loyalty) and went over to his squire, who stood leaning against his ass with his cheek upon his hand, looking like the picture of a man lost in thought.

The knight, seeing him in that mood and so full of melancholy, said to him: "Learn, Sancho, that one man is not more than another unless he achieves more than another. All those storms that fall upon us are signs that soon the weather will be fair and that things will go smoothly, for it is not possible for evil or good to last forever. Hence we may infer that as our misfortunes have lasted so long, good fortunes must be near. So, you must not vex yourself about my mischances, for you have no share in them."

"How not?" replied Sancho. "I suppose him they tossed in a blanket yesterday was not my father's son? And the saddlebags that are missing today with all my chattels is someone else's misfortune?"

"What, are the saddlebags missing, Sancho?" asked Don Quixote.

"Yes, they are missing," answered Sancho.

"In that case, we have nothing to eat today," said Don Quixote.

"Very true," said Sancho, "if these fields are barren of the herbs that your worship says he knows all about and with which unfortunate knights-errant like yourself generally supply their wants."

"Nevertheless," answered Don Quixote, "at the present moment I would rather have a quarter-loaf of bread or a cottage loaf and a couple of heads of salted pilchards than all the herbs that Dioscorides describes, though his book be illustrated by Doctor Laguna.[37] But, good Sancho, get up on your ass and follow me, for God, who provides for all, will not desert us, especially being engaged, as we are, in His service. He does not abandon the gnats of the air, nor the worms of the earth, nor the tadpoles of the water, and He is so merciful that He maketh His sun shine on the good and the evil and He causeth the rain to fall upon the just and the unjust."

"Your worship," said Sancho, "were fitter to be a preacher than a knight-errant."

"Knights-errant, Sancho," said Don Quixote, "knew, and ought to know, somewhat of all things, for there have been knights-errant in past ages who were as ready to make a sermon or a speech on the king's highway as though they had taken their degrees at the University of Paris; whence it may be inferred that the lance never blunted the pen, nor the pen the lance."

"Well, may it turn out as you say," answered Sancho. "But let us be gone and endeavor to get a lodging tonight; and I pray to God we may find a place where there are no blankets, blanketeers, specters, or enchanted Moors; and if there are, may the Devil keep the lot of them."

"Ask that of God, my son," said Don Quixote, "and lead me where you please, for on this occasion I will leave the choice of lodging to you. But give me your hand and feel with your finger how many teeth and grinders I have lost on this right side of my upper jaw, for there I feel the pain."

[37] Andrés de Laguna, a famous sixteenth-century physician, translated the work of Dioscorides, a first-century A.D. Greek physician and pharmacologist.

Sancho put in his finger, and feeling about, asked: "How many grinders did your worship have before on this side?"

"Four," answered Don Quixote, "besides the wisdom tooth, all of them whole and sound."

"Mind well, master, what you say," answered Sancho.

"I say four, if not five," said Don Quixote, "for in all my life I have never had a tooth or grinder pulled from my mouth, nor has any fallen out or been destroyed by decay."

"Well then, on this lower side," said Sancho, "you have only two grinders and a half, but on the upper, not even half a one, for it is as smooth as the palm of my hand."

"Woe is me," cried Don Quixote, hearing these sad tidings from his squire. "I would rather they lopped off an arm, provided it were not my sword arm; for you must know, Sancho, that a mouth without grinders is like a mill without grindstone, and a tooth is far more to be prized than a diamond. But all this must be suffered by those who profess the stern order of chivalry. Mount, friend, and lead the way, for I will follow you at what pace you please. . . ."

[*In the succeeding sections, Don Quixote attacks a funeral party, mistakes a cloth mill for a supernatural danger, and deprives a barber of his basin, which he takes to be the "golden helmet of Mambrino," referred to in Ariosto's* Orlando Furioso.]

CHAPTER XXII

Of the liberty Don Quixote gave to a number of unfortunates who were being borne, much against their will, where they had no wish to go

Cide Hamete Benengeli, the Arabian and Manchegan author,[38] relates in this most grave, high-sounding, precise, pleasant, and imaginative history that after the conversation between the famous Don Quixote of La Mancha and Sancho Panza, his squire, which is reported at the end of the twenty-first chapter, Don Quixote raised his eyes and saw coming, along the road he was taking, about a dozen men on foot strung together like beads on a great iron chain. The chain was fastened around their necks and they were handcuffed. With them were two men on horseback, and two others followed on foot. The horsemen had firelocks, and those on foot pikes and swords.

As soon as Sancho Panza saw them he said: "Here's a chain of galley slaves, men forced by the king, going to serve in the galleys."

"How! Men forced?" answered Don Quixote. "Is it possible that the king forces anybody?"

"I don't say that," answered Sancho, "but they are people condemned for their offenses to serve the king in the galleys."

"Then it is a fact," replied Don Quixote, "however you put it, that these men are being taken to their destination by force and not by their own free will."

[38] Cide Hamete Benengeli is the imaginary author Cervantes has earlier introduced as the writer of an old manuscript, in Arabic, containing the history of Don Quixote. This device allows the narrator to step in and out of the story, commenting on the presentation as well as on the content of the narrative.

"That is so," said Sancho.

"Then," said his master, "here is the opportunity for me to carry out my duty: to redress grievances and give help to the poor and the afflicted."

"I beg you, sir," said Sancho, "to consider that justice, which is the king himself, does no violence to these men, but only punishes those who have committed crime."

By this time the chain gang came up, and Don Quixote in very courteous words asked those in charge to be good enough to inform him why they conducted people away in that manner. One of the guardians on horseback replied that they were slaves condemned by His Majesty to the galleys and that there was no more to be said, nor ought Don Quixote to desire any further information.

"Nevertheless," answered Don Quixote, "I would like to hear from each one of them individually the cause of his disgrace." To this the guardian on horseback answered: "Though we have here the register of the crimes of all these unlucky fellows, this is no time to produce and read them. Draw near, sir, and ask it from themselves. No doubt they'll tell you their tales, for men of their sort take delight in boasting of their rascalities."

With this leave, which Don Quixote would have taken for himself if they had not given it, he went up to the gang and asked the first man for what crimes he found himself in such straits. The man answered that it was for being in love.

"For that and no more?" cried Don Quixote. "If men are sent to the galleys for being in love, I should have been pulling an oar there long ago."

"My love was not of the kind your worship imagines," replied the galley slave. "Mine was that I loved too much a basket of fine linen, which I embraced so lovingly that if the law had not taken it from me by violence, I should not of my own free will have forsaken it even to this present day. I was caught in the act, so there was no need for torture. The case was a short one. They gave my shoulders a hundred lashes and in addition three years' hard labor in the *gurapas,* and that's an end of it."

"What are *gurapas?*" said Don Quixote.

"*Gurapas* are galleys," answered the convict, who was a young man of about twenty-four, born, as he said, at Piedrahita.

Don Quixote put the same question to the second, who returned no answer, for he seemed too downcast and melancholy to speak. But the first one spoke for him and said: "Sir, this gentleman goes for being a canary bird—I mean a musician or singer."

"Is it possible," said Don Quixote, "that musicians and singers are sent to galleys?"

"I should say so, sir," replied the galley slave. "There's nothing worse than to sing under torture."

"Well," said Don Quixote, "I, on the contrary, have heard it said: 'Who sings in grief, procures relief.'"

"Down here it's the exact opposite," said the slave, "for he who sings once, weeps the rest of his life."

"I do not understand it," said Don Quixote. One of the guards then said to him: "You know, sir, among these unsanctified folk 'to sing under torture' means to confess on the rack. They put this poor sinner to the torture and he confessed his crime of being a rustler, which means that he was a cattle thief; and because he confessed, he was condemned to the galleys for six years, with the addition of two hundred lashes that he carries on his shoulders. He's always sad and pensive, for the other thieves bully, abuse, and despise him because he confessed and hadn't the courage to say a couple of *nos*. For as they say, 'A *nay* has as many letters as a *yea,*' and it is good luck for a criminal when there are no witnesses and proofs and his fate depends on his own tongue. In my opinion there's much truth in that."

"I think so also," said Don Quixote, and he passed on to where the third slave stood, and put to him the same question as to the others. The man replied quickly and coolly, saying: "I'm off to their ladyship the galleys because I wanted ten ducats."

"I will give you twenty with all my heart to free you from that misfortune," said Don Quixote.

"That," replied the slave, "would be like one who has money in the middle of the sea and yet is perishing of hunger because he has nowhere to buy what he needs. I say this because, if I'd had the twenty ducats your worship offers me at the right time, I would have greased the lawyer's palm with them and so sharpened my advocate's wit that I would now be strolling about in the marketplace at Toledo instead of being trailed along here like a greyhound. But God is great; patience is enough."

Don Quixote passed on to the fourth, who was a man of venerable appearance, with a white beard reaching below his chest. No sooner was he asked the reason for his being there than he began to weep and would not answer a word; but the fifth convict lent him a tongue and said: "This honest gentleman is off for four years to the galleys after having appeared in the usual procession dressed in full pomp and mounted."[39]

"That means, I suppose," said Sancho, "carried to shame in view of the whole people."

"You have said it," answered the galley slave, "and the offense for which they gave him this punishment was for having been an ear broker, and a body broker too. What I mean to say is that this gentleman goes for pimping and for fancying himself as a bit of a wizard."

"If it had been merely for pimping," said Don Quixote, "he certainly did not deserve to go rowing in the galleys, but rather to command them and be their captain. For the profession of pimp is no ordinary office, but one requiring wisdom and most necessary in any well-governed state. None but wellborn persons should practice it. In fact, it should have its overseers and inspectors, as there are of other offices, limited to a certain appointed number, like exchange brokers.[40] If this were done, many evils would be prevented, which now take place because this profession is practiced only by foolish and ignorant persons such as silly women, page boys, and mountebanks of few years' standing and less experience, who, in moments of difficulty, when the utmost skill is needed, allow the tidbit to freeze between their fingers and their mouth and scarcely know which is their right hand. I should like to

[39] Those condemned for witchcraft or wizardry were dealt with by the Holy Office. They were mounted on mules with face to the tail and led in procession through the streets accompanied by a noisy crowd. They wore a *coroza* or paper miter, carried a lighted candle, and were flogged through the streets.

[40] Don Quixote's ironic praise of pimps echoes a stock joke in sixteenth-century Spanish literature.

go on and give reasons why it is right to make special choice of those who have to fill such an important office in the state, but this is not the place to do it. Some day I will tell my views to those who may provide a remedy; at present I only wish to say that the sorrow I felt at seeing your gray hairs and venerable countenance in so much distress for pimping has entirely vanished when I learn that you are a wizard; though I know well that there are no sorceries in the world that can affect and force the will, as some simple people imagine. Our will is free and no herb nor charm can compel it. What such gullible wenches and lying rascals do is to mix some potion or poison that drives men crazy, claiming that it has the power to rouse love; whereas I maintain that it is impossible to force a man's will."

"That is true, sir," said the worthy old man; "and indeed I was not guilty of witchcraft; as for being a pimp, I couldn't deny it, but I never thought there was any harm in it, for all my intention was that the whole world should enjoy themselves and live together in peace and quiet without quarrels or troubles. But my good intentions could not save me from going to a place from which I have no hope of return, laden as I am with years and so worried with a bladder trouble that does not give me a moment's rest." He now began to weep as before, and Sancho felt so sorry for him that he drew from his purse a four-real piece and gave it to him as alms.

Don Quixote passed on and asked another what his offense was. He answered with much more pleasantness than the former: "I am here because I played a little too much of a game with two cousins of mine and with two other sisters who were not mine. In short, I carried the game so far with them all that the result of it was the increasing of my kindred so intricately that no devil could make it out. It was all proved against me, I hadn't a friend, and I hadn't a groat; my neck was in the utmost danger; they gave me six years in the galleys; I concurred: it's fair punishment for my guilt; I'm young; if only my life lasts, all will turn out for the best. If you, sir, have anything about you to relieve us poor devils, God will repay you in Heaven and we will have care on earth to ask God in our daily prayers to give you as long and prosperous a life and health as your kind presence deserves."

This convict was dressed in a student's habit, and one of the guards told Don Quixote that he was a great talker and a fine Latin scholar.

Behind all these came a man about thirty years of age, of very comely looks, except that he had a slight squint. He was differently tied from the rest, for he wore a chain to his leg so long that it wound around his whole body. He had, besides, around his neck two iron rings, one of which was fastened to the chain, and the other, called a keep friend or friend's foot, had two irons that came down from it to his waist, at the ends of which were fixed two manacles. These held his hands locked with a great padlock so that he could neither put his hands to his mouth nor bend down his head to his hands.

Don Quixote asked why this man was loaded with more fetters than the rest. The guard answered that it was because he had committed more crimes than all the rest put together and that he was such a desperate rascal that, though they carried him fettered in that way, they were not sure of him but feared that he might give them the slip.

"What crimes did he commit," said Don Quixote, "that have deserved no greater penalty than being sent to the galleys?"

"He is going for ten years," said the guard, "which is the same as civil death. I need only tell you that this man is the famous Ginés de Pasamonte, alias Ginesillo de Parapilla."

"Master commissary," said the galley slave, "don't go so fast and don't let us start defining names and surnames. Ginés is my name, not Ginesillo, and Pasamonte is my family name, not Parapilla as you say. Let every man first look to himself and he'll do a good deal."

"Keep a civil tongue, mister out-and-out robber," answered the commissary. "Otherwise we'll shut you up, whether you like it or not."

"I know," answered the galley slave, "that man goes as God pleases; but one day someone will know whether my name is Ginesillo de Parapilla or not."

"Don't they call you that, you lying trickster?"

"They do," answered Ginés, "but I'll make them stop calling me by that name or I'll shear them where I don't care to mention in company. And now, sir, if you have something to give us, hand it out and good-bye, for you tire us with your inquiries about other men's lives. If you want to know mine, I am Ginés de Pasamonte, whose life has been written by these very fingers of mine."

"He speaks the truth," said the commissary. "He himself has written his own history—as good a one as you could wish, and he pawned the book in jail for two hundred reals."

"Aye, and I intend to redeem it," said Ginés, "even if it stood at two hundred ducats."

"Is it good?" said Don Quixote.

"It is so good," answered Ginés, "that it means trouble for *Lazarillo de Tormes*[41] and for all that has been written or ever shall be written in that style. I assure you it deals with truths and truths so attractive and entertaining that no fiction could compare with them."

"What is the title of the book?" asked Don Quixote.

"*The Life of Ginés de Pasamonte,*" answered Gines himself.

"Is it finished yet?" asked Don Quixote.

"How can it be finished," answered Gines, "when my life isn't finished yet? What is written tells everything from my birth down to this last time I was packed off to the galleys."

"Then you have been there before?" said Don Quixote.

"To serve God and the king," answered Ginés; "on the last occasion I was there for four years, and I know already the taste of hard tack and the lash. I'm not too sorry to return there, for I'll have an opportunity to finish my book. I've still many things to say, and in the galleys of Spain there's more than enough leisure, though I don't need much for what I have to write because I know it by heart."

"You seem to be a clever fellow," said Don Quixote.

"Aye. And an unlucky one," replied Ginés, "for bad luck always pursues genius."

"It pursues knaves," interrupted the commissary.

"I've already told you, sir commissary," answered Pasamonte, "not to go so fast. The lords of the land didn't give you that rod to mistreat us but to

[41]An anonymous "rogue novel" published in 1554.

guide us and take us where His Majesty has ordered. If not, by Heaven—But enough! Perhaps one day the dirty work that was done in the inn may come out in the wash; in the meantime mum's the word, and let every man live well and speak better. Now let us move on, for we've had too much of this diversion."

The commissary raised his rod to strike Pasamonte in answer to his threats, but Don Quixote intervened, asking him not to ill-treat the convict since it was only fair that one who had his hands so tied should be somewhat free with his tongue. Then, turning toward the gang, he said: "I have gathered from all you have said, dearest brethren, that although they punish you for your faults, yet the pains you suffer do not please you, and that you go to them with ill will and against your inclination. I realize, moreover, that perhaps it was the lack of courage of one fellow on the rack, the want of money of another, the want of friends of a third, and finally the biased sentence of the judge that have been the cause of your not receiving the justice to which you were entitled. Now all this prompts and even compels me to perform on your behalf the task for which I was sent into the world, and for which I became a knight-errant, and to which end I vowed to succor the needy and help those who are oppressed by the powerful. But as it is prudent not to do by evil means what can be done by fair, I wish to entreat these gentlemen, your guardians and the commissary, to be kind enough to loose you and let you go in peace, for there will be plenty of men to serve the king on worthier occasions; it seems to me a harsh thing to make slaves of those whom God and nature made free. What is more, gentlemen of the guard," added Don Quixote, "these unfortunate creatures have done nothing against you yourselves. Let each man be answerable for his own sins; there is a God in Heaven who does not fail to punish the wicked nor to reward the good. It is not right that honest men should be executioners of others when they have nothing to do with the case. I ask this boon of you in a peaceable and quiet manner, and if you grant it, I shall give you my thanks. If, on the other hand, you will not grant it willingly, then shall this lance and sword of mine, wielded by my invincible arm, force you to do my bidding."

"This is a pleasant jest," answered the commissary. "You have ended your ranting with a fine joke. Do you want us to hand over to you those the king has imprisoned, as if we had the authority to let them go or you to order us to do it? Go your way, good sir, and a pleasant journey. Settle the basin straight on your pate, and don't go looking for a cat with three legs."[42]

"You are a cat, a rat, and a knave," answered Don Quixote. Without another word he ran at him so fiercely that, not giving him time to defend himself, he struck him to the ground badly wounded by his lance. It was lucky for the knight that this was the one who carried the firelock. The guards were astounded at this unexpected event. But they recovered themselves, and the horsemen drew their swords, the footmen clutched their pikes, and all of them threw themselves upon Don Quixote, who quietly waited for their attack. No doubt he would have been in great danger if the slaves, seeing a chance of liberty, had not broken the chain by which they were tied together. The confusion was such that the guards, first trying to prevent the galley slaves from getting loose, then defending themselves against Don Quixote, who

[42]A proverbial expression that means "Don't go looking for the impossible."

attacked them, did nothing to any purpose. Sancho, for his part, helped to release Ginés de Pasamonte, who was the first that leaped free and unfettered upon the plain. The latter then set upon the fallen commissary and relieved him of his sword and firelock, with which, aiming first at one and then at another, although he never fired it, he cleared the plain of guards, for they all fled no less from Pasamonte's firelock than from the showers of stones that the liberated slaves flung at them.

Sancho was much worried by all that had happened, for he had a shrewd suspicion that the guards who had fled would report the matter to the Holy Brotherhood,[43] who would raise the alarm and sally out in pursuit of the criminals, and he said so to his master, begging him to leave that place at once and hide themselves in the neighboring sierra.

"That is all very well," answered Don Quixote, "but I know what we should do now." Then he called all the galley slaves, who were now running hither and thither in a riotous mood and had stripped the commissary to the skin, and when they had gathered around him in a circle, he addressed them as follows: "It is the duty of well-bred people to be grateful for benefits received, and ingratitude is one of the most hateful sins in the eyes of God. I say this, sirs, because you know what favor you have received from me, and the only return I wish and demand is that you all go from here, laden with the chains from which I have just freed your necks, to the city of El Toboso. There you are to present yourselves before Lady Dulcinea of El Toboso and tell her that her Knight of the Rueful Figure sent you there to commend his service to her. You are to tell her, point by point, the details of this famous adventure, and when you have done this, you may then go whichever way you please and good luck be with you."

Ginés de Pasamonte answered for all the rest, saying: "That which you demand, sir, is impossible to perform, because we must not travel the roads together, but go alone and separate so that we may not be found by the men of the Holy Brotherhood, who will be sure to come out to search for us. What you can do, and ought to do, is to change this service and duty to the Lady Dulcinea of El Toboso into a certain number of Ave Marias and credos that we shall say for your worship's intention. And this we may do by night or by day, resting or on the run, at peace or at work; but if you think that we are now going to return to the fleshpots of Egypt—to our chains, I mean—and start off on the road to El Toboso, you might as well imagine that it's already nighttime, whereas it is not yet ten o'clock in the morning. To expect this from us is like expecting pears off an elm tree."

"I vow then," said Don Quixote in a rage, "sir whoreson, Don Ginesillo de Parapilla, or whatever you call yourself, that you will go alone, with your tail between your legs and the whole length of chain on your back."

Pasamonte, who was a truculent fellow (he now understood that Don Quixote was not very sane, seeing the foolish thing he had done by setting them free), would not stand being abused in this manner; so he winked at his companions, and they from a distance began to rain a shower of stones on Don Quixote, whose buckler gave him scant cover; and poor Rozinante paid no more attention to the spur than if his flanks were made of bronze. Sancho took cover behind his ass and thus sheltered himself against the squall

[43]A tribunal organized to punish highway robbers.

of stones that burst about them. Don Quixote was less able to shield himself against the countless stones that hit him with such force that at last they stretched him on the ground. Scarcely had he fallen when the student Ginés jumped upon him, and taking the basin from his head, gave him three or four blows with it on the shoulders and then struck it repeatedly on the ground, almost breaking it into pieces. They then stripped him of a tunic he wore over his armor, and they would have seized his hose too had they not been hindered by his greaves.[44] They took Sancho's cloak, leaving him in his underclothes, and after dividing among themselves the rest of the spoils, each went his own way, with more thought of escaping the Holy Brotherhood than of dragging their chains to Lady Dulcinea of El Toboso.

All that remained were the ass, Rozinante, Sancho, and Don Quixote. The ass pensively hanging his head, shaking his ears every now and then as if he thought the storm of stones was not yet over; Rozinante prostrate lying beside his master on the ground; Sancho in his underclothes, trembling at the thought of the Holy Brotherhood; and Don Quixote, in the dumps at finding himself so ill-treated by those for whom he had done so much.

[*Don Quixote decides to do penance in the wilderness of the Sierra Morena as other knights-errant do who have been absent too long from their mistresses. He sends Sancho to deliver a letter to Dulcinea. Quixote then meets a young man, Cardenio (whom Quixote calls the "Knight of the Wood"), who has lost his love to a false friend, Ferdinand. Meanwhile Sancho meets the curate and the barber, and they persuade him to join in a strategem to get Don Quixote to return to his village. They and Cardenio meet Dorothea, a woman deceived and abandoned by Cardenio's betrayer Ferdinand; she agrees to help them deceive the knight by playing the role of a princess, "Micomicona." They return to Quixote, and charmed by "Micomicona," he agrees to help her regain her "kingdom." The party stops at an inn on the way back to the village—the same inn where Sancho was tossed in a blanket. Here the curate reads them a manuscript called* A Tale of Ill-Advised Curiosity, *in which a husband comes to grief through testing his wife's fidelity. The story raises some of the same questions of reality and illusion explored in the novel itself. At the inn, Cardenio is reunited with his Lucinda, and Ferdinand claims Dorothea as his true wife. A returned captive of the Turks arrives at the inn and tells the party of his experiences and his escape (experiences reminiscent of Cervantes' own). Other guests arrive, including a judge with a beautiful young daughter who is pursued by a lovesick boy posing as a muleteer. After the ugly servant woman Maritornes plays a cruel trick on Quixote, the curate and the barber place him in a barred oxcart to take him back to his village. On the journey, Sancho manages to free his master from the cart. Quixote meets a goatherd and offers to rescue his lover from a nunnery; the goatherd, however, becomes angry and beats Quixote.*]

CHAPTER LII

Of the quarrel that Don Quixote had with the goatherd, with the rare adventure of the disciplinants, which he successfully achieved with the sweat of his brow

. . . . It so happened that year that the clouds had denied the earth their moisture; so, throughout the valleys of that region, processions, public prayers, and penances were ordered to beseech Heaven to open the flood

[44]Armor for the lower legs.

gates of its mercy and send them rain. It was for this purpose, therefore, that the people of a neighboring village were coming in procession to a holy shrine that stood on a hill at the edge of the valley. Don Quixote, as soon as he saw the strange attire of the disciplinants, did not pause to recall the many occasions on which he had seen a similar sight before but immediately imagined that it was some kind of adventure that was reserved for him alone as knight-errant. He was all the more confirmed in his opinion by mistaking an image that they carried all swathed in mourning for some noble lady whom those ruffians and unmannerly churls were carrying away against her will. No sooner did this thought flash through his mind than he rushed over to Rozinante, who was grazing nearby, and taking off the bridle and buckler that hung from the pommel of the saddle, he bridled him in an instant. Then, asking Sancho for his sword, he mounted Rozinante, and bracing his buckler, he cried in a loud voice to all those present: "Now, valiant company, ye shall see how necessary it is that there be in the world knights who profess the order of knight-errantry; now, I say, shall ye see, in the restoration of that captive lady to liberty, whether knights-errant ought to be valued!"

Saying this, he clapped his heels to Rozinante (for spurs he had none), and at a half gallop (for nowhere in all this truthful history can one read that Rozinante ever went at full speed) he advanced to encounter the disciplinants, though the curate and the barber tried to stop him. But all their efforts were in vain, nor could he be stopped by the screams of Sancho, who shouted: "Master, where are you going? What devils in your heart are driving you on to attack our Catholic faith? Mind, sir! Bad 'cess to it! That is a procession of disciplinants and the lady they're carrying on the bier is the most blessed image of the Immaculate Virgin. Take heed, sir, what you're doing; this time I can assure you that it's not what you think."

Sancho wasted his breath, for his master was so set upon encountering the sheeted ones and upon freeing the lady in black that he heard not a word, and even if he had, he would not have turned back though the king himself had commanded him. When he reached the procession, he stopped Rozinante, who already wanted to rest a little, and in a hoarse, angry voice he cried out: "You there, who cover up your faces probably because you are evil, halt and pay heed to my words!"

The first to halt were those who were carrying the image. Then, one of the four priests who chanted the litanies, noticing the strange appearance of Don Quixote, the leanness of Rozinante, and other ludicrous details, answered him, saying: "Brother, if you have anything to say, say it quickly, for these brethren are scourging their flesh, and we cannot, nor is it right that we should, stop to listen to anything that may not be said in two words."

"I will say it in one," replied Don Quixote. "You must instantly free that beauteous lady whose tears and sad appearance show clearly that you are bearing her away against her will and that you have done her some grievous wrong. But I, who came into the world to redress such injuries, will not allow you to move one single step forward till you have restored to her the liberty she desires and deserves."

From these words all who heard them concluded that Don Quixote must be some madman, and they began to laugh heartily. But their laughter only served to add gunpowder to the knight's fury, for without another word he drew his sword and attacked the litter. One of those who carried it, leaving the burden to his comrades, stepped forward to encounter Don Quixote, brandishing a forked pole on which they propped the litter while resting, and with it he parried the heavy stroke that the knight aimed at him. The force of the stroke snapped the pole in two, but with the remaining stump that was left in his hand he dealt the knight such a thwack on the shoulder of his sword-arm that his buckler was unable to shield him against the rustic onslaught, and down came poor Don Quixote to the ground in a bad way. Sancho, who came panting after him, seeing him fall, called out to his assailant not to strike him again, for he was a poor enchanted knight who had done nobody any harm all his life. The peasant stopped, not, however, on account of Sancho's appeal, but because he saw that Don Quixote stirred neither hand nor foot. And, believing that he had killed him, he hastily tucked up his habit to his girdle and set off, racing like a deer across the country.

By that time everyone in Don Quixote's company had reached where he lay, but when the men in the procession saw them running in their direction and with them troopers of the Holy Brotherhood with their crossbows, they feared some trouble. So, they clustered in a circle about the image: the penitents lifted their hoods and grasped their lashes; the priests brandished their tapers, and all waited for the attack with the firm resolve to defend themselves, and if they could, to take the offensive against their aggressors. But Fortune arranged matters better than they expected, for Sancho did nothing but cast himself upon the body of his master, making over him the most sorrowful and drollest lament in the world, for he truly believed that Don Quixote was dead. Our curate was recognized by one of the priests in the procession, and this calmed the apprehension of both sides. Our curate in a few words told the second curate of Don Quixote's condition; then, he and the whole crowd of disciplinants went to see whether or not the poor knight was dead, and heard Sancho Panza proclaim with tears in his eyes: "O flower of chivalry, one single blow of a cudgel has finished the course of your well-spent years! O glory of your race, honor and credit to all La Mancha, and even to the whole world, which, now that you are gone, will be overrun with evildoers, who will no longer fear punishment for their iniquities! O liberal above all the Alexanders, since for a mere eight months' service you have given me the best island that the sea surrounds! O humble to the haughty and arrogant to the humble! Resister of perils, sufferer of affronts, lover without cause, imitator of the good, scourge of the wicked, enemy of the base! In a word, knight-errant, which is the highest thing anyone could say!"

At the cries and groans of Sancho, Don Quixote revived, and the first words he said were: "He who lives absent from thee, sweet Dulcinea, endures far greater sufferings than these. Help me, friend Sancho, to lift myself into the enchanted cart, for I am no longer in a condition to press the saddle of Rozinante; this shoulder of mine is broken to pieces."

"That I'll do with all my heart, dear master," replied Sancho, "and let us go back to our village in the company of these gentlemen, and there we will make schemes for another sally that may be more profitable to us."

"You speak well, Sancho," answered the knight. "It is prudent for us to wait until the evil influence of the stars that now reigns passes away."

The canon, the curate, and the barber approved this resolution, and after they had enjoyed Sancho Panza's fooleries to the full, they placed Don Quixote on the cart as before. The procession resumed its former order and went on its way. The goatherd took his leave of them all, and as the troopers refused to go any further, the curate paid them what he owed them. The canon then begged the curate to let him know what might happen to Don Quixote (whether he recovered from his madness or remained in it), and with this he took his leave. Thus they all parted and went their several ways.

The party now consisted only of the curate, the barber, Don Quixote, Sancho, and good Rozinante, who bore all the ups and downs as patiently as his master. The wagoner yoked his oxen, and having laid Don Quixote on a bundle of hay, plodded his way at his usual calm, deliberate pace, following the directions of the curate; and at the end of six days they reached Don Quixote's village. They made their entrance at noon, and as it happened to be Sunday, all the people were in the marketplace when the wagon passed through. Everyone rushed to see who was in it, and when they recognized their townsman, they were amazed. A boy ran off at full speed to give the news to his housekeeper and his niece that their master and uncle was coming home lean and yellow, stretched out on a bundle of hay in an oxcart. It was a pathetic thing to hear the cries of the two ladies, the blows they gave themselves, the execrations they uttered afresh against the books of chivalry, all of which were repeated when they saw Don Quixote enter the door of his house.

As soon as she received news of Don Quixote's arrival, Sancho Panza's wife ran there, and as soon as she saw Sancho, her first inquiry was whether the ass had come home in good condition. Sancho replied that he was in better health than his master.

"Thanks be to God," said she, "for this great favor. Now tell me, husband, what good have you got from your squireship? What petticoat have you brought for me? What dainty shoes for your children?"

"I've brought you nothing of the kind, dear wife," said Sancho, "But I've other things of more consequence."

"I'm glad to hear so," answered the wife. "Show me those things of more consequence. I'm dying to see them to gladden my heart, for I've been mournful and down in the mouth all those ages you've been away."

"I'll show them to you at home, wife," said Sancho. "For the present, hold your soul in patience. Please God we may sally out another time in search of adventures and you'll soon see me count or governor of an island, and not one of those around here, but the finest that can be found."

"May the Lord be pleased to grant it, husband, for we're in sore need of it. Tell me now; what's all this about islands? I don't catch your meaning."

"Honey is not for an ass's mouth," answered Sancho. "You'll see in good time, wife, aye, and you'll be all agape at hearing yourself called ladyship by all your vassals."

"What are you prating about ladyships, islands, and vassals?" cried Juana Panza, for that was the name of Sancho's wife, not because they were relatives, but because in La Mancha it is customary for wives to take their husbands' last name.

"Don't fret yourself, Juana, and be in such a hurry to know everything at once; it's enough for you to know that I'm telling the truth, so mum's the word; but I can tell you one thing by the way, namely, that there's nothing in this world so pleasant as for an honest man to be squire to a knight-errant on the prowl for adventures. It's true that most of those we encountered were not as comfortable as a body would wish, for out of a hundred adventures, ninety-nine usually turned out cross and crooked. I know by experience, for from some I came off blanketed and from others bruised and battered, but when all's said and done, it's a fine thing to be gadding about spying for chances, crossing mountains, exploring woods, climbing rocks, visiting castles, lodging in inns at our own sweet will, with devil a maravedi to pay."

While this conversation was passing between Sancho Panza and Juana Panza, his wife, Don Quixote's housekeeper and niece received the knight, undressed him, and put him into his old bed. He looked at them with squinting eyes, for he could not make out where he was. The curate told the niece to take very good care of her uncle and to be very watchful lest he should make another sally, telling her the trouble it had cost to get him home. The two women began their lamentations once more, again execrating the books of chivalry and imploring Heaven to plunge the authors of so many lies and absurdities into the bottomless abyss. In fact, they were at their wits' end, for they were afraid they might lose their master and uncle the moment he felt a little better. And events turned out as they feared.

But though the author of this history has eagerly and diligently inquired after Don Quixote's exploits on his third sally, he has not been able to discover any account of them, at least from any authentic documents. Only tradition has preserved in the memory of La Mancha that the third time Don Quixote left his home he went to Saragossa, where he took part in some famous jousts in that city, and that he had adventures there worthy of his valor and of his sound intelligence. Nor would our author have been able to discover any details of his death, nor would he even have heard of it, if Fortune had not thrown in his path an aged physician who had in his possession a leaden box that he said he had discovered among the ruined foundations of an ancient hermitage that was being rebuilt. In this box he had found certain parchments written in the Gothic script, but in Castilian verse, which contained many of his exploits and emphasized the beauty of Dulcinea of El Toboso, the shape of Rozinante, the fidelity of Sancho Panza, and the burial of Don Quixote himself, with various epitaphs and eulogies on his life and character. Such as could be deciphered and interpreted the trustworthy author of this original and matchless history has set down here, and he asks no recompense from his readers for the immense pains it has cost him to ransack all the archives of La Mancha to drag it into light. All he asks is that they should give it as much credit as sensible men are wont to give to the books of chivalry, which are held in such high esteem in the world. With this he will reckon himself well paid and satisfied, and he will be encouraged to go in search of other histories, perhaps less truthful than this one, but at least as inventive and entertaining. . . .

William Shakespeare
(1564–1616)

Shakespeare's plays and poems, taken together, have a quality of impersonality, or suprapersonality, transcending the limitations and biases that one normally finds in a single author. If we try to understand Shakespeare through his works, he is everything and everyone. Each of his plays is its own place, with a distinctive mood, method, and thematic emphasis; collectively, they define a mind and a sensibility that seem nearly as inclusive as the world itself. It is appropriate, then, if also tantalizing, that we know so little about the inner workings of the mind of Shakespeare as an individual and artist. Nineteenth-century critical tradition tended to find autobiographical revelations in the plays and some of the poems (especially the *Sonnets*), and modern psychoanalytic criticism purports to find in them revelations of Shakespeare's unconscious mind, but all the hard facts we have about him are impersonal or external: records of law and vital statistics, annals of the Elizabethan and Jacobean stage, and references to him by contemporary authors and playgoers.

Shakespeare was born in the town of Stratford, in the geographic heart of England, in April 1564. His father was a tradesman and prominent member of the town government, his mother a descendant of a very old family. Although he did not go to a university, he got a good education at the Stratford grammar school, especially in the Latin classics. (Ovid seems to have been one of his favorite authors.) In 1582 he married Anne Hathaway, by whom he had two daughters and a son who died in boyhood. How and where Shakespeare spent his early twenties is obscure; by 1590 or so, however, he was active in the London theater. During the next decade he became highly popular as a playwright and poet (among his nondramatic works are *Venus and Adonis, The Rape of Lucrece,* and the famous *Sonnets*), apparently making a good living and also acquiring influential friends. In 1596, almost certainly through Shakespeare's efforts, his family was granted a coat of arms. By 1612 or so, when he stopped writing, he had composed more than three dozen plays. He died on April 23, 1616—very nearly on the same day Cervantes died.

Shakespeare wrote his plays for performance; he had little or no interest in having them printed and published. A reading audience for plays did exist, however, and many of Shakespeare's plays were in fact published during his lifetime—some in good versions, others in very poor ones. In 1623, seven years after Shakespeare died, the First Folio, a comprehensive collection of almost all his plays, was issued under the supervision of two members of Shakespeare's old company. The Folio contains a famous tribute by the eminent contemporary poet and playwright Ben Jonson. Not a man to bestow praise lightly, Jonson rated Shakespeare above all his contemporary dramatists. His true peers, according to Jonson, were Aeschylus, Sophocles, and Euripides; in comedy, Jonson asserted, Shakespeare was peerless. This tribute has proved to be an accurate prophecy of Shakespeare's reputation in later ages.

Beginning with the First Folio, it has been customary to divide Shakespeare's plays into three categories: tragedies, comedies, and histories.

But these labels are inadequate; Shakespeare's plays are typically blends of different tones and genres. Some of the histories (*Richard the Second,* for example) can accurately be called tragedies. The comedies are of several different kinds; the early *Comedy of Errors* and *Taming of the Shrew* are mainly farcical; *A Midsummer Night's Dream* combines farce with lyrical fantasy; the "romantic" comedies of Shakespeare's middle period (including *As You Like It* and *Twelfth Night*) are warmly exuberant works that place fairly realistic characters in never-never-land settings; the "dark" comedies, like *Measure for Measure,* include some disturbing, uncomic elements; the late *Winter's Tale* and *Tempest* treat serious themes but with a disregard for realism that has earned for them the name romances. Some of the tragedies mingle comic episodes with their prevalent high seriousness (as in *Romeo and Juliet* and *Macbeth*), and several are based on history, especially that of ancient Rome (*Julius Caesar, Antony and Cleopatra, Coriolanus*).

To enumerate briefly the qualities that make Shakespeare great is impossible, since the individual plays and poems are so different from one another. Every age, from Shakespeare's time to the present, has found something different in him to admire. All ages, however, have recognized his supreme skill in inventing sharply etched characters; it frequently happens that long after one has forgotten the exact story of a play one remembers its people with absolute vividness. It is true, paradoxically, that many of Shakespeare's characters represent universal types; Romeo's name has become a synonym for the fervent young lover, and the adjective *Falstaffian* has entered the common vocabulary of English as an epithet for robust, expansive heartiness. But none of Shakespeare's characters is merely a type. Scores of them are fully realized persons, absolutely individualized new creations even when they are adapted from earlier sources. (Few of Shakespeare's stories were wholly invented by him.) More than anything else, it is his power to create such characters that has prompted extravagant praise of Shakespeare's "godlike" genius. Some critics, in fact, have speculated about the characters, even those Shakespeare wholly invented, almost as though they had a real existence outside of the plays. Such excesses, odd as they may seem, are understandable, for the characters do seem to speak and act as of their own volition, with the combination of inevitability and unpredictability that one finds in living human beings.

The power to create characters and tell compelling stories underlies one traditional view of Shakespeare: that his plays are children of "nature" rather than of "art." That view of him no longer has much currency. Both in their total conception and in their craftsmanship, most Shakespearean plays are both powerful and skillfully controlled. He is expert in managing plot lines and is particularly fond of double plotting.

Perhaps the ultimate reason for Shakespeare's power is simply his mastery of language as an expressive and poetic medium. The many pages given to Shakespeare in dictionaries of quotations attest the beauty and memorability of his words. But such excerpting, which removes Shakespeare's lines from their dramatic context, also does him a disservice, suggesting as it does that he was a gnomic philosopher at large. The well known lines from *Hamlet* "To thine own self be true, / And it must follow, as the night the day, / Thou canst not then be false to any man" have been quoted countless times without an awareness that in the play they illustrate a pompous old man's self-importance.

The true measure of Shakespeare's language is its effectiveness in the play where it occurs; much of Shakespeare's artistry lies in his skill in giving different characters different poetic imaginations and voices. Moreover, the quality of a play's language—plain or ornate, ceremonial or colloquial, quiet or declamatory, direct or fraught with images and figures of speech—is intimately wedded to the governing themes and distinctive atmospheres. Whether the plays generated their linguistic texture or the other way around is a difficult question. Whatever the answer, it remains true that language—prose or verse—is the principal shaping force of Shakespearean drama.

The Tempest (1611) is the last of four romances that Shakespeare wrote at the end of his career, the others being *Pericles* (1608–1609), *Cymbeline* (1609–1610), and *The Winter's Tale* (1610–1611). The romances all have fairy-tale-like plots, full of magic and other wonders. They are also tragicomic, bringing tragic or potentially tragic stories to happy conclusions. Their recurring theme is reconciliation, often brought about by a daughter who succeeds in healing her wounded family. *The Tempest* is unusual among the romances, and among Shakespeare's plays as a whole, for its tight construction and observance of the unities of time, place, and action. While the other romances are rather loose, sprawling plays, *The Tempest*'s action is confined to the island and to a space of about three hours.

The story of *The Tempest* seems to be original to Shakespeare; no source has ever been discovered. Nevertheless, the play is resonant with echoes of classical works, especially Virgil's *Aeneid.* Prospero's island is in the Mediterranean, somewhere between Tunis and Naples, near the route of Aeneas's journey from Carthage to Rome. *The Tempest* begins, as the *Aeneid* does, with a violent storm, followed by wanderings that involve a banquet with harpies (*Aeneid,* Book III, II. 222–229). Sycorax recalls in some ways Circe, whose island is near the route of Aeneas. There are other reminiscences in the play of Ovid's *Metamorphoses,* Apuleius's *Golden Ass,* and even the Bible (the names of the spirits are of Hebrew origin; "Ariel" comes from Isaiah 29:1).

Despite the nominal placement of the island and the classical allusions, Shakespeare, in writing *The Tempest,* seems to have had America very much on his mind, as the two most important sources alluded to in the play suggest: Montaigne's essay "Of Cannibals" and a group of so-called Burmuda pamphlets. Gonzalo's speech about the ideal commonwealth in Act II is drawn from Montaigne's essay; more important, the essay raises one of the central issues in the play—the relation between the "civilized" and the "uncivilized" worlds. The Burmuda pamphlets were accounts of a shipwreck in the New World. In June 1609, a fleet of seven ships and two smaller vessels set out from Plymouth to Jamestown, Virginia. The flagship, the *Sea Adventure,* carried the new governor of Virginia, Sir Thomas Gates, among other notables. When the fleet reached Burmuda, it was scattered by a terrible storm. Eight vessels reached Jamestown, but the *Sea Adventure* was missing and presumed lost. About nine months later, however, the missing men arrived in Jamestown with a marvelous tale. The *Sea Adventure* had not sunk but had run aground without loss of life. The passengers and crew had lived on an island for nine months and had built two boats from the wreckage of the *Sea Adventure* and managed to complete their journey. The most important to Shakespeare of the various accounts of this episode was *A True Reportory of the Wreck and Redemption of Sir Thomas Gates, Knight* by William Strachey, a member of the marooned party. It was not published until after Shakespeare's death, but it is virtually certain that he read it in manuscript and drew upon it not only for details of the island but for its tone of wonder at the discovery of a "brave new world."

The sense that many readers and playgoers have that Shakespeare's plays are capacious and comprehensive may come from his practice of juxtaposing many levels of experience, from the largest scale to the smallest. Prospero, as a *magus* or practitioner of "white magic," deals with the cosmic forces of nature itself. He is also an earthly ruler, the former Duke of Milan and presently lord of the island on which he has been marooned. He is a father as well, trying to ensure the welfare of his daughter, Miranda, and her husband-to-be, Ferdinand. Finally, he is also an individual, responsible for ruling himself, as well as nature, the state, and his family, torn between the base impulse toward revenge and the loftier one toward forgiveness.

The question of "rule," in all these dimensions, runs throughout the play and is focused with special vividness in the character of Caliban. Caliban is the Natural Man, close kin to Montaigne's cannibals (his very name is an anagram of "cannibal"). But far from being an innocent child of nature, he is the most ignoble of savages, longing only to kill Prospero and rape his daughter. There is a certain amount of justice on his side—Prospero did usurp his island after deceiving him with gifts and a dissembled friendship—but Shakespeare finally characterizes Caliban as a natural slave and Prospero, the white civilized European, as his natural ruler.

Not surprisingly, *The Tempest*'s ideology of European rule has come to seem less "natural" in the four centuries of relentless European colonization that followed its first production, and a number of adaptations and replies have "written back" to *The Tempest.* Robert Browning's "Caliban upon Setebos" (1864) and W. H. Auden's "The Sea and the Mirror" (1945) both draw on the characters and the situations of *The Tempest.* Aimé Cesaire's *A Tempest* (1969) inverts the play, making Prospero a tyrannical white colonizer and Caliban a heroic revolutionary. The classic science-fiction film *Forbidden Planet* (1956) places Prospero and Miranda on the planet Altair-4 in the year 2200, while Peter Greenaway's *Prospero's Books* (1991) offers John Gielgud speaking Shakespeare's lines in lush, ornate settings.

NOTE ON SHAKESPEARE'S STAGE

The public theaters of Shakespeare's day were modeled architecturally on inn-yards, where, a generation or so earlier, plays had commonly been presented by itinerant troupes of actors. The theaters were large, three-story structures, round, square, or multisided in shape, surrounding an open-air arena. Three sides of the theater consisted of galleries, facing inward toward the arena. From the fourth side, a large platform stage, about 5 feet high, perhaps 40 feet deep and 25 feet wide, projected into the arena; around it stood those spectators ("groundlings") who paid the lowest price of admission. At the back of this stage were two doors and a curtained alcove used for "discovery" scenes. There was some sort of acting space on the second level, as well, perhaps another curtained alcove and perhaps a projecting balcony, supported by posts rising from the main stage. There may have been a third level as well, occasionally used by actors but intended primarily for musicians. To avoid harassment by the Puritanically minded London government, the theaters were built outside the city limits, especially on the south bank of the Thames. A theater could accommodate about 2,000 people, drawn from every social level from the laboring class through the titled aristocracy. As in ancient Greek drama, spectacle was important on Shakespeare's stage. Costumes were elaborate, and the style of acting was emphatic and declamatory. All the actors were male; the female roles were played by boys. There was little or no scenery, and action flowed continuously without scene or act divisions. Because the plays were performed in the afternoon, under the sky, settings such as storms or night scenes had to be evoked by the play's language; the imagination of the audience thus played a crucial part, as in modern radio drama.

Shakespeare's theater was literally what a modern director and critic has called "the empty space," to be filled by the playwright's, the actors', and the audience's imaginations. The Greek *skene* building and *orchestra* were well suited for plays that took place "before the palace" and dramatized the public lives of scapegoat-kings. The neutral, fluid space of the Elizabethan stage was ideally suited to drama, calling for the free movement of the imagination. The line between illusion and reality, nebulous in any kind of theater, was especially so in Shakespeare's, and his plays are full of scenes that question what is "real," as in *King Lear*, Act IV, scene vi, in which the blind Gloucester thinks he is on the top of a cliff. Edgar knows that Gloucester is "really" in a flat field, while we see that the field is as imaginary as the cliff and that the characters are really on a wooden stage.

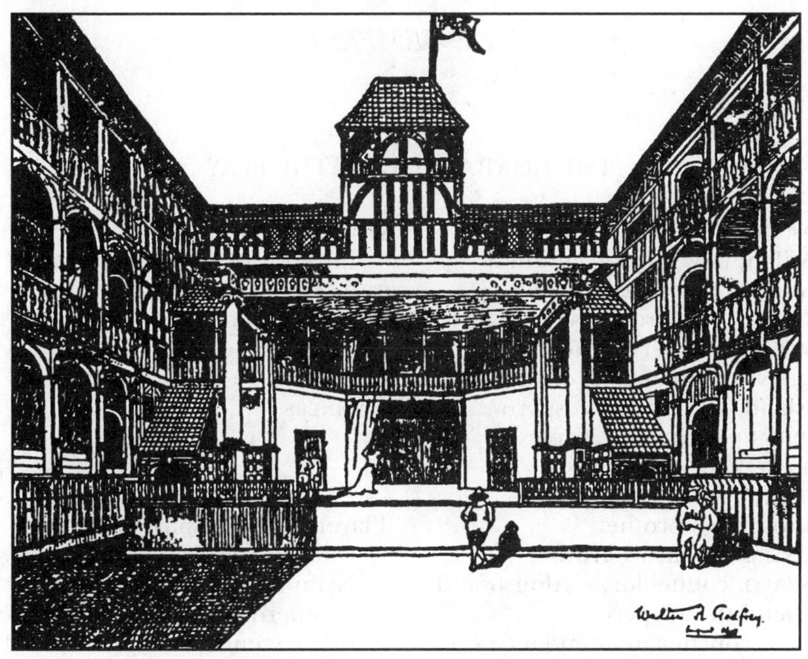

A reconstruction of the Fortune Theater by Walter H. Godfrey. (From Shakespeare's Theatre *by Ashley H. Thorndike.)*

FURTHER READING: S. Schoenbaum's *William Shakespeare: A Compact Documentary Life,* 1977, sums up what is known about Shakespeare's life and reprints the key documents upon which that knowledge is based. Germaine Greer's *Shakespeare,* 1986, in the *Past Masters* series, is a refreshing overview from the perspective of a nonspecialist. Stanley Wells's *Shakespeare: The Writer and His Work,* 1978, is a useful handbook that surveys, among other topics, criticism of Shakespeare. Gary Taylor's *Reinventing Shakespeare: A Cultural History from the Restoration to the Present,* 1989, is a lively history of the reception of Shakespeare. On Shakespeare's theater, see Andrew Gurr's *Playgoing in Shakespeare's London,* 1987. On Shakespeare's language, see Randal Robinson, *Unlocking Shakespeare's Language: Help for the Teacher and Student,* 1989. Among the many books on Shakespeare that include distinctive readings of *The Tempest* are C. L. Barber's *Shakespeare's Festive Comedy,* 1959; Northrop Frye's *A Natural Perspective,* 1965; and Howard Felperin's *Shakespearean Romance,* 1972. O. Mannoni's *Prospero and Caliban: The Psychology of Colonization,* tr. Pamela Powesland, 1956, is not so much a reading of the play as a study of the colonial relationships implicit in it. Alden T. Vaughan and Virginia Mason Vaughan's *Shakespeare's Caliban: A Cultural History,* 1991, explores not only the sources of Caliban but his subsequent treatment in various media. Key postcolonial readings of *The Tempest* include Paul Brown, "'This thing of darkness I acknowledge mine': *The Tempest* and the Discourse of Colonialism," in *Political Shakespeare: New Essays in Cultural Materialism,* ed. Jonathan Dollimore and Alan Sinfield, 1985; and Stephen J. Greenblatt, "Martial Law in the Land of Cockaigne," in *Shakespearean Negotiations,* 1988; and "Learning to Curse: Aspects of Linguistic Colonialism in the Sixteenth Century," in *Learning to Curse: Essays in Early Modern Culture,* 1990.

THE TEMPEST

THE CHARACTERS IN THE PLAY

PROSPERO, the former duke of Milan, now a magician on a Mediterranean island
MIRANDA, Prospero's daughter
ARIEL, a spirit, servant to Prospero
CALIBAN, an inhabitant of the island, servant to Prospero
FERDINAND, prince of Naples
ALONSO, king of Naples
ANTONIO, duke of Milan and Prospero's brother
SEBASTIAN, Alonso's brother
GONZALO, councillor to Alonso and friend to Prospero
ADRIAN, courtier in attendance on Alonso
FRANCISCO, courtier in attendance on Alonso
TRINCULO, servant to Alonso
STEPHANO, Alonso's butler
SHIPMASTER
BOATSWAIN
MARINERS

Players who, as spirits, take the roles of Iris, Ceres, Juno, Nymphs, and Reapers in Prospero's masque, and who, in other scenes, take the roles of "islanders" and of hunting dogs

ACT 1

SCENE 1

A tempestuous noise of thunder and lightning heard.[1]
Enter a Shipmaster and a Boatswain.

MASTER. Boatswain!
BOATSWAIN. Here, master. What cheer?
MASTER. Good,[2] speak to th' mariners. Fall to 't yarely[3] or we run ourselves aground. Bestir, bestir! *He exits.*

Enter Mariners.

BOATSWAIN. Heigh, my hearts! Cheerly, cheerly, my hearts! Yare, yare! Take in the topsail.[4] Tend[5] to th' Master's whistle.—Blow till thou burst thy wind, if room[6] enough!

Enter Alonso, Sebastian, Antonio, Ferdinand, Gonzalo, and others.

ALONSO. Good boatswain, have care. Where's the Master? Play the men.[7]
BOATSWAIN. I pray now, keep below.
ANTONIO. Where is the Master, boatswain? 10
BOATSWAIN. Do you not hear him? You mar our labor. Keep your cabins. You do assist the storm.
GONZALO. Nay, good, be patient.
BOATSWAIN. When the sea is. Hence! What care these roarers for the name of king? To cabin! Silence! Trouble us not.
GONZALO. Good, yet remember whom thou hast aboard.
BOATSWAIN. None that I more love than myself. You are a councillor; if you can command these elements to silence, and work the peace of the present,[8] we will not hand a rope more. Use your authority. If you cannot, give thanks you have lived so long, and 20 make yourself ready in your cabin for the mischance of the hour, if it so hap.—Cheerly, good hearts!—Out of our way, I say! *He exits.*
GONZALO. I have great comfort from this fellow. Me-thinks he hath no drowning mark upon him. His complexion is perfect gallows.[9] Stand fast, good Fate, to his hanging. Make the rope of his destiny our cable, for our own doth little advantage. If he be not born to be hanged, our case is miserable.
He exits with Alonso, Sebastian, and the other courtiers.

[1]The ship is in great danger. The wind is blowing hard from the sea; on the other side lies the rocky island, and between there is too little sea room for her to sail past without being driven ashore by the drift. (All annotations to *The Tempest* are by G. B. Harrison.)
[2]My good man. [3]Quickly, smartly. [4]I.e., to lessen the drift. [5]Attend.
[6]Sea room. [7]Act like men. [8]Bring us peace at once.
[9]Gonzalo remembers the proverb "He that is born to be hanged will never be drowned," and the boatswain looks like a gallows bird.

Enter Boatswain.

BOATSWAIN. Down with the topmast! Yare! Lower, lower! Bring her to try wi' th' main course.[10] (*A cry within.*) A plague upon this howling! They are louder than the weather or our office.[11] 30

Enter Sebastian, Antonio, and Gonzalo.

Yet again? What do you here? Shall we give o'er and drown? Have you a mind to sink?

SEBASTIAN. A pox o' your throat, you bawling, blasphemous, incharitable dog!

BOATSWAIN. Work you, then.

ANTONIO. Hang, cur, hang, you whoreson,[12] insolent noisemaker! We are less afraid to be drowned than thou art.

GONZALO. I'll warrant him for drowning,[13] though the ship were no stronger than a nutshell and as leaky as an unstanched wench.

BOATSWAIN. Lay her ahold, ahold![14] Set her two courses.[15] Off to sea again! Lay her off! 40

Enter more Mariners, wet.

MARINERS. All lost! To prayers, to prayers! All lost!

Mariners exit.

BOATSWAIN. What, must our mouths be cold?[16]

GONZALO. The King and Prince at prayers. Let's assist them, for our case is as theirs.

SEBASTIAN. I am out of patience.

ANTONIO. We are merely cheated of our lives by drunkards. This wide-chopped[17] rascal—would thou mightst lie drowning the washing of ten tides![18]

Boatswain exits.

GONZALO. He'll be hanged yet, though every drop of water swear against it and gape at wid'st to glut[19] him. 50

A confused noise within: "Mercy on us!"—"We split, we split!"—"Farewell, my wife and children!"—"Farewell, brother!"—"We split, we split, we split!"

ANTONIO. Let's all sink wi' th' King.

SEBASTIAN. Let's take leave of him.

He exits with Antonio.

GONZALO. Now would I give a thousand furlongs of sea for an acre of barren ground: long heath,[20] brown furze,[21] anything. The wills above be done, but I would fain die a dry death.

He exits.

[10]I.e., use only the mainsail to heave her to. [11]Business. [12]Bastard.
[13]Guarantee him against drowning. [14]Close to the wind.
[15]Two sails, i.e., set the foresail as well. The maneuver of heaving-to has failed; the boatswain now hopes to get the ship moving into the wind enough to pass the island.
[16]Here the boatswain abandons hope and falls to drinking.
[17]Large-cheeked, because full of liquor.
[18]Pirates were hanged on the seashore and left until three high tides had passed over them.
[19]Swallow. [20]Rough grass. [21]A prickly bushy shrub.

SCENE 2

Enter Prospero and Miranda.

MIRANDA.
If by your art, my dearest father, you have
Put the wild waters in this roar, allay[1] them.
The sky, it seems, would pour down stinking pitch,
But that the sea, mounting to th' welkin's[2] cheek,
Dashes the fire out. O, I have suffered
With those that I saw suffer! A brave vessel,
Who had, no doubt, some noble creature in her,
Dashed all to pieces. O, the cry did knock
Against my very heart! Poor souls, they perished.
Had I been any god of power, I would 10
Have sunk the sea within the earth or ere
It should the good ship so have swallowed, and
The fraughting[3] souls within her.

PROSPERO.
Be collected.[4]
No more amazement. Tell your piteous heart
There's no harm done.

MIRANDA.
O, woe the day!

PROSPERO.
No harm.
I have done nothing but in care of thee,
Of thee, my dear one, thee, my daughter, who
Art ignorant of what thou art, naught knowing
Of whence I am, nor that I am more better
Than Prospero, master of a full[5] poor cell, 20
And thy no greater father.

MIRANDA.
More to know
Did never meddle[6] with my thoughts.

PROSPERO.
'Tis time
I should inform thee farther. Lend thy hand
And pluck my magic garment from me.
Putting aside his cloak.
So,
Lie there, my art.—Wipe thou thine eyes. Have comfort.
The direful spectacle of the wrack, which touched
The very virtue of compassion in thee,
I have with such provision[7] in mine art
So safely ordered that there is no soul—
No, not so much perdition[8] as an hair, 30
Betid[9] to any creature in the vessel
Which thou heard'st cry, which thou saw'st sink. Sit down,
For thou must now know farther. *They sit.*

[1]Abate. [2]Sky's. [3]Literally, who were her freight. [4]Calm. [5]Exceedingly.
[6]Interfere, i.e., cause to be curious. [7]Foresight. [8]Loss. [9]Befallen.

MIRANDA. You have often
Begun to tell me what I am, but stopped
And left me to a bootless inquisition,[10]
Concluding "Stay. Not yet."
PROSPERO. The hour's now come.
The very minute bids thee ope thine ear.
Obey, and be attentive. Canst thou remember
A time before we came unto this cell?
I do not think thou canst, for then thou wast not 40
Out[11] three years old.
MIRANDA. Certainly, sir, I can.
PROSPERO.
By what? By any other house or person?
Of anything the image tell me that
Hath kept with thy remembrance.
MIRANDA. 'Tis far off
And rather like a dream than an assurance
That my remembrance warrants. Had I not
Four or five women once that tended me?
PROSPERO.
Thou hadst, and more, Miranda. But how is it
That this lives in thy mind? What seest thou else
In the dark backward and abysm of time?[12] 50
If thou remembʼrest aught ere thou camʼst here,
How thou camʼst here thou mayst.
MIRANDA. But that I do not.
PROSPERO.
Twelve year since, Miranda, twelve year since,
Thy father was the Duke of Milan and
A prince of power.
MIRANDA. Sir, are not you my father?
PROSPERO.
Thy mother was a piece of virtue, and
She said thou wast my daughter. And thy father
Was Duke of Milan, and his only heir
And princess no worse issued.
MIRANDA. O, the heavens!
What foul play had we that we came from thence? 60
Or blessèd was 't we did?
PROSPERO. Both, both, my girl.
By foul play, as thou sayst, were we heaved thence,
But blessedly holp[13] hither.
MIRANDA. O, my heart bleeds
To think o' th' teen[14] that I have turned you to,
Which is from my remembrance. Please you, farther.
PROSPERO.
My brother and thy uncle, called Antonio—
I pray thee, mark me—that a brother should

[10]Vain inquiry. [11]More than. [12]I.e., the past, which is like a dark abyss.
[13]Helped. [14]Sorrow.

Be so perfidious!—he whom next thyself
Of all the world I loved, and to him put
The manage[15] of my state, as at that time 70
Through all the signories[16] it was the first,
And Prospero the prime[17] duke, being so reputed
In dignity, and for the liberal arts[18]
Without a parallel. Those being all my study,
The government I cast upon my brother
And to my state grew stranger, being transported
And rapt in secret studies. Thy false uncle—
Dost thou attend me?

MIRANDA. Sir, most heedfully.

PROSPERO.
Being once perfected[19] how to grant suits,
How to deny them, who t' advance, and who 80
To trash for overtopping,[20] new created[21]
The creatures that were mine, I say, or changed 'em,
Or else new formed 'em, having both the key[22]
Of officer and office, set all hearts i' th' state
To what tune pleased his ear, that now he was
The ivy which had hid my princely trunk
And sucked my verdure out on 't. Thou attend'st not.[23]

MIRANDA.
O, good sir, I do.

PROSPERO. I pray thee, mark me.
I, thus neglecting worldly ends, all dedicated
To closeness[24] and the bettering of my mind 90
With that which, but by being so retired,[25]
O'erprized all popular rate,[26] in my false brother
Awaked an evil nature, and my trust,
Like a good parent, did beget of him
A falsehood in its contrary as great
As my trust was, which had indeed no limit,
A confidence sans[27] bound. He being thus lorded,
Not only with what my revenue yielded
But what my power might else exact, like one
Who, having into truth by telling of it, 100
Made such a sinner of his memory
To credit his own lie, he did believe
He was indeed the Duke,[28] out o' th' substitution

[15]Management. [16]Lordships. [17]Leading. [18]Academic learning.
[19]Become perfect by practice.
[20]Check for running ahead, a metaphor from training a pack of hounds.
[21]Made them new creatures—by altering their minds.
[22]Tool used for tuning a stringed instrument.
[23]You are not listening. [24]Privacy.
[25]Except that it kept me away from state affairs.
[26]Was worth more than it is commonly regarded. [27]Without.
[28]He, getting such greatness not only from my wealth but also by abusing my power, began to believe as he had hitherto pretended, that he was in truth the Duke.

And executing th' outward face of royalty
With all prerogative.[29] Hence, his ambition growing—
Dost thou hear?

MIRANDA.
Your tale, sir, would cure deafness.

PROSPERO.
To have no screen between this part he played
And him he played it for, he needs will be
Absolute Milan.[30] Me, poor man, my library 110
Was dukedom large enough. Of temporal royalties[31]
He thinks me now incapable; confederates,[32]
So dry[33] he was for sway, wi' th' King of Naples
To give him annual tribute, do him homage,
Subject his coronet to his crown,[34] and bend
The dukedom, yet unbowed—alas, poor Milan!—
To most ignoble stooping.

MIRANDA. O, the heavens!

PROSPERO.
Mark his condition and th' event.[35] Then tell me
If this might be a brother.

MIRANDA. I should sin
To think but nobly of my grandmother. 120
Good wombs have borne bad sons.

PROSPERO. Now the condition.
This King of Naples, being an enemy
To me inveterate, hearkens my brother's suit,
Which was that he, in lieu o' th' premises[36]
Of homage and I know not how much tribute,
Should presently[37] extirpate[38] me and mine
Out of the dukedom, and confer fair Milan,
With all the honors, on my brother; whereon,
A treacherous army levied, one midnight
Fated to th' purpose did Antonio open 130
The gates of Milan, and i' th' dead of darkness
The ministers for th' purpose hurried thence
Me and thy crying self.

MIRANDA. Alack, for pity!
I, not rememb'ring how I cried out then,
Will cry it o'er again. It is a hint[39]
That wrings mine eyes to 't.

PROSPERO. Hear a little further,
And then I'll bring thee to the present business
Which now 's upon 's, without the which this story
Were most impertinent.

[29]From being my substitute and acting outwardly as Duke with all the rights of a ruler.
[30]Duke of Milan, in fact. [31]Worldly power. [32]Conspires. [33]Thirsty.
[34]I.e., pay homage as to his overlord. The coronet was worn as a symbol by rulers of lower rank than that of king.
[35]Sequel. [36]In return for these conditions. [37]Immediately.
[38]Root out. [39]Occasion.

MIRANDA. Wherefore did they not
That hour destroy us?
PROSPERO. Well demanded, wench. 140
My tale provokes that question. Dear, they durst not,
So dear the love my people bore me, nor set
A mark so bloody on the business, but
With colors fairer painted their foul ends.
In few,[40] they hurried us aboard a bark,
Bore us some leagues to sea, where they prepared
A rotten carcass of a butt,[41] not rigged,
Nor tackle, sail, nor mast; the very rats
Instinctively have quit it. There they hoist us
To cry to th' sea that roared to us, to sigh 150
To th' winds, whose pity, sighing back again,
Did us but loving wrong.
MIRANDA. Alack, what trouble
Was I then to you!
PROSPERO. O, a cherubin
Thou wast that did preserve me. Thou didst smile,
Infusèd with a fortitude from heaven,
When I have decked the sea with drops full salt,
Under my burden groaned, which raised in me
An undergoing stomach[42] to bear up
Against what should ensue.
MIRANDA. How came we ashore? 160
PROSPERO. By providence divine.
Some food we had, and some fresh water, that
A noble Neapolitan, Gonzalo,
Out of his charity, who being then appointed
Master of this design, did give us, with
Rich garments, linens, stuffs, and necessaries,
Which since have steaded much.[43] So, of his gentleness,
Knowing I loved my books, he furnished me
From mine own library with volumes that
I prize above my dukedom.
MIRANDA. Would I might 170
But ever see that man.
PROSPERO, *standing.* Now I arise.
Sit still, and hear the last of our sea-sorrow.
Here in this island we arrived, and here
Have I, thy schoolmaster, made thee more profit
Than other princes can, that have more time
For vainer hours and tutors not so careful.
MIRANDA.
Heavens thank you for 't. And now I pray you, sir—
For still 'tis beating[44] in my mind—your reason
For raising this sea storm?

[40]In a few words. [41]Tub.
[42]Courage to endure, the stomach being regarded as the seat of valor.
[43]Have been of great benefit. [44]Throbbing.

PROSPERO. Know thus far forth:
By accident most strange, bountiful Fortune,[45] 180
Now my dear lady,[46] hath mine enemies
Brought to this shore; and by my prescience[47]
I find my zenith[48] doth depend upon
A most auspicious star, whose influence
If now I court not,[49] but omit, my fortunes
Will ever after droop. Here cease more questions.
Thou art inclined to sleep. 'Tis a good dullness,
And give it way. I know thou canst not choose.

Miranda falls asleep.
Prospero puts on his cloak.

Come away, servant, come. I am ready now.
Approach, my Ariel. Come. 190

Enter Ariel.

ARIEL.
All hail, great master! Grave sir, hail! I come
To answer thy best pleasure. Be 't to fly,
To swim, to dive into the fire, to ride
On the curled clouds, to thy strong bidding task[50]
Ariel and all his quality.[51]
PROSPERO. Hast thou, spirit,
Performed to point[52] the tempest that I bade thee?
ARIEL. To every article.
I boarded the King's ship; now on the beak,
Now in the waist,[53] the deck, in every cabin,
I flamed amazement.[54] Sometimes I'd divide 200
And burn in many places. On the topmast,
The yards, and bowsprit would I flame distinctly,
Then meet and join. Jove's lightning, the precursors[55]
O' th' dreadful thunderclaps, more momentary
And sight-outrunning were not. The fire and cracks
Of sulfurous roaring the most mighty Neptune
Seem to besiege and make his bold waves tremble,
Yea, his dread trident shake.
PROSPERO. My brave spirit!
Who was so firm, so constant, that this coil[56]
Would not infect his reason?
ARIEL. Not a soul 210
But felt a fever of the mad,[57] and played
Some tricks of desperation.[58] All but mariners

[45]I.e., I will now tell you more. [46]Fortune (once my foe) is now kind to me.
[47]Foreknowledge. [48]The highest point of my fortunes.
[49]Do not seek to win. [50]Impose a task on. [51]Ability.
[52]In all points, exactly. [53]That part of the ship that lies between forecastle and poop.
[54]Appeared in the form of fire, which caused amazement. This phenomenon, known as Saint Elmo's fire or a "corposant," is sometimes seen on ships during a storm.
[55]Forerunners. [56]Confusion. [57]Fever of madness. [58]Desperate tricks.

Plunged in the foaming brine and quit the vessel,
Then all afire with me. The King's son, Ferdinand,
With hair up-staring—then like reeds, not hair—
Was the first man that leaped; cried "Hell is empty,
And all the devils are here."

PROSPERO. Why, that's my spirit!
But was not this nigh shore?

ARIEL. Close by, my master.

PROSPERO.
But are they, Ariel, safe?

ARIEL. Not a hair perished.
On their sustaining[59] garments not a blemish, 220
But fresher than before; and, as thou bad'st me,
In troops I have dispersed them 'bout the isle.
The King's son have I landed by himself,
Whom I left cooling of the air with sighs
In an odd angle[60] of the isle, and sitting,
His arms in this sad knot.[61] *He folds his arms.*

PROSPERO. Of the King's ship,
The mariners say how thou hast disposed,
And all the rest o' th' fleet.

ARIEL. Safely in harbor
Is the King's ship. In the deep nook, where once
Thou called'st me up at midnight to fetch dew 230
From the still-vexed Bermoothes,[62] there she's hid;
The mariners all under hatches stowed,
Who, with a charm joined to their suffered labor,[63]
I have left asleep. And for the rest o' th' fleet,
Which I dispersed, they all have met again
And are upon the Mediterranean float,[64]
Bound sadly home for Naples,
Supposing that they saw the King's ship wracked
And his great person perish.

PROSPERO. Ariel, thy charge
Exactly is performed. But there's more work. 240
What is the time o' th' day?

ARIEL. Past the mid season.

PROSPERO.
At least two glasses.[65] The time 'twixt six and now
Must by us both be spent most preciously.

ARIEL.
Is there more toil? Since thou dost give me pains,[66]
Let me remember[67] thee what thou hast promised,
Which is not yet performed me.

PROSPERO. How now? Moody?
What is 't thou canst demand?

[59]Which bore them up. [60]Corner. [61]Sadly folded. Ariel imitates the posture.
[62]Ever stormy Burmudas. [63]As well as the labor they had endured.
[64]Sea. [65]I.e., hours, turns of the hourglass. [66]Toil. [67]Remind.

ARIEL. My liberty.

PROSPERO.
Before the time be out? No more.

ARIEL. I prithee,
Remember I have done thee worthy service,
Told thee no lies, made no mistakings, served 250
Without or grudge or grumblings. Thou did promise
To bate[68] me a full year.

PROSPERO. Dost thou forget
From what a torment I did free thee?

ARIEL. No.

PROSPERO.
Thou dost, and think'st it much to tread the ooze
Of the salt deep,
To run upon the sharp wind of the north,
To do me business in the veins o' th' earth
When it is baked with frost.

ARIEL. I do not, sir.

PROSPERO.
Thou liest, malignant thing. Hast thou forgot
The foul witch Sycorax, who with age and envy 260
Was grown into a hoop?[69] Has thou forgot her?

ARIEL. No, sir.

PROSPERO.
Thou hast. Where was she born? Speak. Tell me.

ARIEL.
Sir, in Argier.[70]

PROSPERO. O, was she so? I must
Once in a month recount what thou hast been,
Which thou forget'st. This damned witch Sycorax,
For mischiefs manifold, and sorceries terrible
To enter human hearing,[71] from Argier,
Thou know'st, was banished. For one thing she did[72]
They would not take her life. Is not this true? 270

ARIEL. Ay, sir.

PROSPERO.
This blue-eyed[73] hag was hither brought with child
And here was left by th' sailors. Thou, my slave,
As thou report'st thyself, was then her servant,
And for thou wast a spirit too delicate
To act her earthy and abhorred commands,
Refusing her grand hests,[74] she did confine thee,
by help of her more potent ministers
And in her most unmitigable[75] rage,

[68]Abate, lessen. [69]Bent double. [70]Algiers.
[71]For a human being to hear. [72]This good action is not recalled.
[73]With dark rings under the eyes. [74]Commands.
[75]Absolute.

Into a cloven pine, within which rift 280
Imprisoned thou didst painfully remain
A dozen years; within which space she died
And left thee there, where thou didst vent thy groans
As fast as mill wheel strike.[76] Then was this island
(Save for the son that she did litter here,
A freckled whelp, hag-born[77] not honored with
A human shape.

ARIEL. Yes, Caliban, her son.

PROSPERO.
Dull thing, I say so; he, that Caliban
Whom now I keep in service. Thou best know'st
What torment I did find thee in. Thy groans 290
Did make wolves howl, and penetrate the breasts
Of ever-angry bears. It was a torment
To lay upon the damned, which Sycorax
Could not again undo. It was mine art,
When I arrived and heard thee, that made gape
The pine and let thee out.

ARIEL. I thank thee, master.

PROSPERO.
If thou more murmur'st, I will rend an oak[78]
And peg thee in his knotty entrails till
Thou hast howled away twelve winters.

ARIEL. Pardon, master.
I will be correspondent[79] to command 300
And do my spiriting[80] gently.

PROSPERO. Do so, and after two days
I will discharge thee.

ARIEL. That's my noble master.
What shall I do? Say, what? What shall I do?

PROSPERO.
Go make thyself like a nymph o' th' sea. Be subject
To no sight but thine and mine, invisible
To every eyeball else. Go, take this shape,
And hither come in 't. Go, hence with diligence!

Ariel exits.

Awake, dear heart, awake. Thou hast slept well.
Awake. 310

MIRANDA. The strangeness of your story put
Heaviness in me.

PROSPERO. Shake it off. Come on,
We'll visit Caliban, my slave, who never
Yields us kind answer.

MIRANDA, *rising*. 'Tis a villain, sir,
I do not love to look on.

[76]I.e., the continuous clack of a water mill. [77]Child of a hag.
[78]I.e., a far worse torment than imprisonment in a pine. [79]Agreeable, submissive.
[80]My work as a spirit.

PROSPERO. But, as 'tis,
We cannot miss[81] him. He does make our fire,
Fetch in our wood, and serves in offices
That profit us.—What ho, slave, Caliban!
Thou earth,[82] thou, speak!
CALIBAN, *within.* There's wood enough within.
PROSPERO.
Come forth, I say. There's other business for thee. 320
Come, thou tortoise. When?

Enter Ariel like a water nymph.

Fine apparition! My quaint[83] Ariel,
Hark in thine ear. *He whispers to Ariel.*
ARIEL. My lord, it shall be done. *He exits.*
PROSPERO, *to Caliban.*
Thou poisonous slave, got[84] by the devil himself
Upon thy wicked dam,[85] come forth!

Enter Caliban.

CALIBAN.
As wicked dew as e'er my mother brushed
With raven's feather from unwholesome fen
Drop on you both. A southwest[86] blow on you
And blister you all o'er.
PROSPERO.
For this, be sure, tonight thou shalt have cramps, 330
Side-stitches that shall pen thy breath up. Urchins[87]
Shall forth at vast[88] of night that they may work
All exercise on thee. Thou shalt be pinched
As thick as honeycomb, each pinch more stinging
Than bees that made 'em.
CALIBAN. I must eat my dinner.
This island's mine by Sycorax, my mother,
Which thou tak'st from me. When thou cam'st first,
Thou strok'st me and made much of me, wouldst give me
Water with berries in 't,[89] and teach me how
To name the bigger light and how the less, 340
That burn by day and night. And then I loved thee,
And showed thee all the qualities[90] o' th' isle,
The fresh springs, brine pits, barren place and fertile.
Cursed be I that did so! All the charms
Of Sycorax, toads, beetles, bats, light on you,

[81]Do without. [82]Lump of dirt. [83]Elegant. [84]Begotten. [85]Mother.
[86]Regarded as an unhealthy wind. [87]Goblins or hedgehogs. [88]Desolate period.
[89]Shakespeare apparently took this from an account by William Strachey of being cast ashore on Bermuda. He records that the castaways made a pleasant drink from cedar berries.
[90]Good spots.

For I am all the subjects that you have,
Which first was mine own king; and here you sty[91] me
In this hard rock, whiles you do keep from me
The rest o' th' island.

PROSPERO. Thou most lying slave,
Whom stripes[92] may move, not kindness, I have used thee, 350
Filth as thou art, with humane care, and lodged thee
In mine own cell, till thou didst seek to violate
The honor of my child.

CALIBAN.
O ho, O ho! Would 't had been done!
Thou didst prevent me. I had peopled else
This isle with Calibans.

MIRANDA. Abhorrèd slave,
Which any print[93] of goodness wilt not take,
Being capable of all ill! I pitied thee,
Took pains to make thee speak, taught thee each hour
One thing or other. When thou didst not, savage, 360
Know thine own meaning, but wouldst gabble like
A thing most brutish, I endowed thy purposes
With words that made them known. But thy vile race,
Though thou didst learn, had that in 't which good natures
Could not abide to be with. Therefore wast thou
Deservedly confined into this rock,
Who hadst deserved more than a prison.

CALIBAN.
You taught me language, and my profit on 't
Is I know how to curse. The red plague[94] rid[95] you
For learning[96] me your language!

PROSPERO. Hagseed,[97] hence! 370
Fetch us in fuel; and be quick, thou 'rt best,
To answer other business. Shrugg'st thou, malice?
If thou neglect'st or dost unwillingly
What I command, I'll rack thee with old[98] cramps,
Fill all thy bones with aches,[99] make thee roar
That beasts shall tremble at thy din.

CALIBAN. No, pray thee.
Aside. I must obey. His art is of such power
It would control my dam's god, Setebos,
And make a vassal[100] of him.

PROSPERO. So, slave, hence.

Caliban exits.

[91]Pen. [92]Blows. [93]Impression. [94]Bubonic plague. [95]Destroy.
[96]Teaching. [97]Son of a hag. [98]Abundant.
[99]A two-syllable word, pronounced like "h's."
[100]Slave.

Enter Ferdinand; and Ariel, invisible, playing and singing.

Song.

ARIEL.

Come unto these yellow sands, 380
And then take hands.
Curtsied when you have, and kissed
The wild waves whist.[101]
Foot it featly[102] *here and there,*
And sweet sprites bear
The burden.[103] *Hark, hark!*
Burden dispersedly, within: *Bow-wow.*
The watchdogs bark.
Burden dispersedly, within: *Bow-wow.*
Hark, hark! I hear 390
The strain of strutting chanticleer
Cry cock-a-diddle-dow.

FERDINAND.

Where should this music be? I' th' air, or th' earth?
It sounds no more; and sure it waits upon
Some god o' th' island. Sitting on a bank,
Weeping again the King my father's wrack,
This music crept by me upon the waters,
Allaying both their fury and my passion[104]
With its sweet air. Thence I have followed it,
Or it hath drawn me rather. But 'tis gone. 400
No, it begins again.

Song.

ARIEL.

Full fathom five thy father lies.
Of his bones are coral made.
Those are pearls that were his eyes.
Nothing of him that doth fade
But doth suffer a sea change
Into something rich and strange.
Sea nymphs hourly ring his knell.
Burden, within: *Ding dong.*
Hark, now I hear them: ding dong bell. 410

FERDINAND.

The ditty does remember my drowned father.
This is no mortal business, nor no sound
That the earth owes.[105] I hear it now above me.

[101]Silent. [102]Smartly. [103]Refrain. [104]Emotion, sorrow.
[105]Owns, possesses.

PROSPERO, *to Miranda.*
The fringèd curtains of thine eye advance[106]
And say what thou seest yond.
MIRANDA. What is 't? A spirit?
Lord, how it looks about! Believe me, sir,
It carries a brave form.[107] But 'tis a spirit.
PROSPERO.
No, wench, it eats and sleeps and hath such senses
As we have, such. This gallant which thou seest
Was in the wrack; and, but he's something stained 420
With grief—that's beauty's canker[108]—thou might'st call him
A goodly person. He hath lost his fellows
And strays about to find 'em.
MIRANDA. I might call him
A thing divine, for nothing natural
I ever saw so noble.
PROSPERO, *aside.* It goes on,[109] I see,
As my soul prompts it. *To Ariel.* Spirit, fine spirit, I'll free thee
Within two days for this.
FERDINAND, *seeing Miranda.* Most sure, the goddess
On whom these airs attend![110]—Vouchsafe my prayer
May know if you remain upon this island,[111] 430
And that you will some good instruction give
How I may bear me[112] here. My prime request,
Which I do last pronounce, is—O you wonder!—
If you be maid or no.[113]
MIRANDA. No wonder, sir,
But certainly a maid.
FERDINAND. My language! Heavens!
I am the best of them[114] that speak this speech,
Were I but where 'tis spoken.
PROSPERO. How? The best?
What wert thou if the King of Naples heard thee?
FERDINAND.
A single[115] thing, as I am now, that wonders
To hear thee speak of Naples. He does hear me, 440
And that he does I weep. Myself am Naples,
Who with mine eyes, never since at ebb,[116] beheld
The King my father wracked.
MIRANDA. Alack, for mercy!

[106]Raise. [107]Fine shape. [108]Maggot.
[109]I.e., Prospero's plan that Miranda and Ferdinand shall fall in love.
[110]Wait on. [111]Grant my prayer, which is to know whether you inhabit this island.
[112]Behave myself. [113]I.e., a mortal or a goddess.
[114]I.e., I am now King of Naples since my father's death.
[115]Lonely. [116]I.e., have not ceased to flow.

FERDINAND.
Yes, faith, and all his lords, the Duke of Milan
And his brave son being twain.[117]
PROSPERO, *aside.* The Duke of Milan
And his more braver daughter could control thee,
If now 'twere fit to do 't. At the first sight
They have changed eyes.[118]—Delicate Ariel,
I'll set thee free for this. *To Ferdinand.* A word, good sir.
I fear you have done yourself some wrong. A word. 450
MIRANDA.
Why speaks my father so ungently? This
Is the third man that e'er I saw, the first
That e'er I sighed for. Pity move my father
To be inclined my way.
FERDINAND. O, if a virgin,
And your affection not gone forth,[119] I'll make you
The Queen of Naples.
PROSPERO. Soft, sir, one word more.
Aside. They are both in either's powers. But this swift business
I must uneasy make, lest too light winning
Make the prize light. *To Ferdinand.* One word more. I charge thee
That thou attend me. Thou dost here usurp 460
The name thou ow'st not, and hast put thyself
Upon this island as a spy, to win it
From me, the lord on 't.
FERDINAND. No, as I am a man!
MIRANDA.
There's nothing ill can dwell in such a temple.[120]
If the ill spirit have so fair a house,
Good things will strive to dwell with 't.
PROSPERO, *to Ferdinand.* Follow me.
To Miranda. Speak not you for him. He's a traitor.
To Ferdinand. Come,
I'll manacle thy neck and feet together.
Sea water shalt thou drink. Thy food shall be 470
The fresh-brook mussels, withered roots, and husks
Wherein the acorn cradled. Follow.
FERDINAND. No,
I will resist such entertainment till
Mine enemy has more power.
He draws, and is charmed from moving.
MIRANDA. O dear father,
Make not too rash a trial of him, for
He's gentle and not fearful.[121]

[117]I.e., two of those drowned.
[118]Fallen in love. [119]I.e., been bestowed on someone else.
[120]I.e., beautiful body. [121]To be feared.

PROSPERO. What, I say,
My foot my tutor?[122]—Put thy sword up, traitor,
Who mak'st a show, but dar'st not strike, thy conscience
Is so possessed with guilt. Come from thy ward,[123]
For I can here disarm thee with this stick 480
And make thy weapon drop.
MIRANDA. Beseech you, father—
PROSPERO.
Hence! Hang not on my garments.
MIRANDA. Sir, have pity.
I'll be his surety.
PROSPERO. Silence! One word more
Shall make me chide thee, if not hate thee. What,
An advocate for an imposter? Hush.
Thou think'st there is no more such shapes as he,
Having seen but him and Caliban. Foolish wench,
To th' most of men this is a Caliban,
And they to him are angels.
MIRANDA. My affections
Are then most humble. I have no ambition 490
To see a goodlier man.
PROSPERO, *to Ferdinand.* Come on, obey.
Thy nerves[124] are in their infancy again
And have no vigor in them.
FERDINAND. So they are.
My spirits, as in a dream, are all bound up.
My father's loss, the weakness which I feel,
The wrack of all my friends, nor this man's threats
To whom I am subdued, are but light to me,
Might I but through my prison once a day
Behold this maid. All corners else o' th' earth 500
Let liberty make use of. Space enough
Have I in such a prison.
PROSPERO, *aside.* It works.—Come on.—
Thou hast done well, fine Ariel.—Follow me.
To Ariel. Hark what thou else shalt do me.
MIRANDA, *to Ferdinand.* Be of comfort.
My father's of a better nature, sir,
Than he appears by speech. This is unwonted[125]
Which now came from him.
PROSPERO, *to Ariel.* Thou shalt be as free
As mountain winds; but then exactly do
All points of my command.
ARIEL. To th' syllable.
PROSPERO, *to Ferdinand.*
Come follow. *To Miranda.* Speak not for him. 510
They exit.

[122]The head is the tutor to the body, but Miranda (who is by nature subordinate and so the foot) is trying to tell her father what he should do.
[123]Position of defense. [124]Sinews. [125]Unusual.

ACT 2

SCENE 1

Enter Alonso, Sebastian, Antonio, Gonzalo, Adrian, Francisco, and others.

GONZALO, *to Alonso.*
Beseech you, sir, be merry. You have cause—
So have we all—of joy, for our escape
Is much beyond our loss.[1] Our hint of woe
Is common; every day some sailor's wife,
The masters of some merchant,[2] and the merchant[3]
Have just our theme of woe. But for the miracle—
I mean our preservation—few in millions
Can speak like us. Then wisely, good sir, weigh
Our sorrow with our comfort.

ALONSO. Prithee, peace.

SEBASTIAN, *aside to Antonio.* He receives comfort like cold porridge. 10

ANTONIO. The visitor[4] will not give him o'er so.

SEBASTIAN. Look, he's winding up the watch of his wit. By and by it will strike.

GONZALO, *to Alonso.* Sir—

SEBASTIAN. One. Tell.[5]

GONZALO. When every grief is entertained[6] that's offered, come to th' entertainer—

SEBASTIAN. A dollar.

GONZALO. Dolor comes to him indeed. You have spoken truer than you purposed. 20

SEBASTIAN. You have taken it wiselier than I meant you should.

GONZALO, *to Alonso.* Therefore, my lord—

ANTONIO. Fie, what a spendthrift is he of his tongue.

ALONSO, *to Gonzalo.* I prithee, spare.

GONZALO. Well, I have done. But yet—

SEBASTIAN, *aside to Antonio.* He will be talking.

ANTONIO, *aside to Sebastian.* Which, of he or Adrian, for a good wager, first begins to crow?

SEBASTIAN. The old cock.

ANTONIO. The cockerel. 30

SEBASTIAN. Done. The wager?

ANTONIO. A laughter.[7]

[1]Occasion. [2]Captains of merchant ships. [3]I.e., the owner.

[4]Visiting minister. Sebastian means that Gonzalo will insist on having his say whether Alonso wishes to hear him or not.

[5]Count. [6]Received.

[7]The winner is to have the laugh on the loser, on the principle of the proverb "He laughs that wins."

SEBASTIAN. A match!
ADRIAN. Though this island seem to be desert—
ANTONIO. Ha, ha, ha.
SEBASTIAN. So. You're paid.[8]
ADRIAN. Uninhabitable and almost inaccessible—
SEBASTIAN. Yet—
ADRIAN. Yet—
ANTONIO. He could not miss 't.[9] 40
ADRIAN. It must needs be of subtle, tender, and delicate temperance.
ANTONIO. Temperance was a delicate wench.
SEBASTIAN. Ay, and a subtle, as he most learnedly delivered.[10]
ADRIAN. The air breathes upon us here most sweetly.
SEBASTIAN. As if it had lungs, and rotten ones.
ANTONIO. Or as 'twere perfumed by a fen.
GONZALO. Here is everything advantageous to life.
ANTONIO. True, save means to live.
SEBASTIAN. Of that there's none, or little.
GONZALO. How lush and lusty the grass looks! How green! 50
ANTONIO. The ground indeed is tawny.
SEBASTIAN. With an eye[11] of green in 't.
ANTONIO. He misses not much.
SEBASTIAN. No, he doth but mistake the truth totally.
GONZALO. But the rarity[12] of it is, which is indeed almost beyond credit[13]—
SEBASTIAN. As many vouched[14] rarities are.
GONZALO. That our garments, being, as they were, drenched in the sea, hold notwithstanding their freshness and gloss, being rather new-dyed than stained with salt water. 60
ANTONIO. If but one of his pockets could speak,[15] would it not say he lies?
SEBASTIAN. Ay, or very falsely pocket up his report.
GONZALO. Methinks our garments are now as fresh as when we put them on first in Afric, at the marriage of the King's fair daughter Claribel to the King of Tunis.
SEBASTIAN. 'Twas a sweet marriage, and we prosper well in our return.
ADRIAN. Tunis was never graced[16] before with such a paragon to[17] their queen.
GONZALO. Not since widow Dido's time.[18] 70

[8]The words "So, you're paid" may belong to Antonio, who is telling Sebastian that he has had his laugh (as winner).

[9]I.e., if he begins the first clause with "though," he is sure to follow it up with a "yet."

[10]Declared. [11]Tinge. [12]Strange thing. [13]Belief. [14]Guaranteed.

[15]I.e., his pockets are still wet. [16]Honored. [17]For.

[18]Dido was the Queen of Carthage (near the modern Tunis) who entertained Aeneas on his way from Troy to Italy. She was a widow and had vowed eternal fidelity to the memory of her husband, but she fell in love with Aeneas. When he deserted her, she committed suicide.

ANTONIO. Widow? A pox[19] o' that! How came that "widow" in?[20]
Widow Dido!

SEBASTIAN. What if he had said "widower Aeneas" too? Good Lord, how you take it!

ADRIAN, *to Gonzalo.* "Widow Dido," said you? You make me study of that. She was of Carthage, not of Tunis.

GONZALO. This Tunis, sir, was Carthage.

ADRIAN. Carthage?

GONZALO. I assure you, Carthage.

ANTONIO. His word is more than the miraculous harp.[21] 80

SEBASTIAN. He hath raised the wall, and houses too.

ANTONIO. What impossible matter will he make easy next?

SEBASTIAN. I think he will carry this island home in his pocket and give it his son for an apple.

ANTONIO. And sowing the kernels of it in the sea, bring forth more islands.

GONZALO. Ay.

ANTONIO. Why, in good time.

GONZALO, *to Alonso.* Sir, we were talking that our garments seem now as fresh as when we were at Tunis at the marriage of your 90 daughter, who is now queen.

ANTONIO. And the rarest that e'er came there.

SEBASTIAN. Bate[22], I beseech you, widow Dido.

ANTONIO. O, widow Dido? Ay, widow Dido.

GONZALO, *to Alonso.* Is not, sir, my doublet as fresh as the first day I wore it? I mean, in a sort.[23]

ANTONIO. That "sort" was well fished for.[24]

GONZALO, *to Alonso.* When I wore it at your daughter's marriage.

ALONSO.
You cram these words into mine ears against
The stomach of my sense. Would I had never 100
Married my daughter there, for coming thence
My son is lost, and, in my rate,[25] she too,
Who is so far from Italy removed
I ne'er again shall see her.—O, thou mine heir
Of Naples and of Milan, what strange fish
Hath made his meal on thee?

FRANCISCO. Sir, he may live.
I saw him beat the surges[26] under him
And ride upon their backs. He trod the water,
Whose enmity he flung aside, and breasted

[19]Plague; venereal disease. [20]Why do you call her a widow?

[21]According to the legends told by Ovid, the walls of Thebes came together at the music of Amphion's harp. By a similar miracle, Gonzalo has erected a Carthage at Tunis.

[22]Except. [23]After a fashion. [24]I.e., he had to add "after a fashion."

[25]Estimation. [26]Waves.

The surge most swoll'n[27] that met him. His bold head 110
'Bove the contentious waves he kept, and oared
Himself with his good arms in lusty stroke
To th' shore, that o'er his wave-worn basis bowed,[28]
As stooping to relieve him. I not doubt
He came alive to land.

ALONSO. No, no, he's gone.

SEBASTIAN.
Sir, you may thank yourself for this great loss,
That would not bless our Europe with your daughter,
But rather lose her to an African,
Where she at least is banished from your eye,
Who hath cause to wet[29] the grief on 't.

ALONSO. Prithee, peace. 120

SEBASTIAN.
You were kneeled to and importuned otherwise
By all of us; and the fair soul herself
Weighed[30] between loathness[31] and obedience at
Which end o' th' beam[32] should bow. We have lost your son,
I fear, forever. Milan and Naples have
More widows in them of this business' making
Than we bring men to comfort them.
The fault's your own.

ALONSO. So is the dear'st[33] o' th' loss.

GONZALO. My lord Sebastian,
The truth you speak doth lack some gentleness 130
And time to speak it in. You rub the sore
When you should bring the plaster.

SEBASTIAN. Very well.

ANTONIO. And most chirurgeonly.[34]

GONZALO, *to Alonso*
It is foul weather in us all, good sir,
When you are cloudy.

SEBASTIAN. Foul weather?

ANTONIO. Very foul.

GONZALO.
Had I plantation[35] of this isle, my lord—

ANTONIO.
He'd sow 't with nettle seed.

SEBASTIAN. Or docks, or mallows.[36]

[27]Swollen. [28]Hung over its base, which had been worn away by the sea.
[29]Weep for. [30]Balanced. [31]Reluctance. [32]Which scale should sink.
[33]Most grievous. [34]Like a good surgeon.
[35]Colonization, but Antonio pretends to take it literally as "planting."
[36]Common English weeds.

GONZALO.
And were the King on 't, what would I do?
SEBASTIAN. Scape being drunk, for want of wine.
GONZALO.
I' th' commonwealth[37] I would by contraries[38] 140
Execute all things, for no kind of traffic[39]
Would I admit; no name of magistrate;
Letters[40] should not be known; riches, poverty,
And use of service,[41] none; contract;[42] succession,[43]
Bourn,[44] bound[45] of land, tilth,[46] vineyard, none;
No use of metal,[47] corn, or wine, or oil;
No occupation;[48] all men idle, all,
And women too, but innocent and pure;
No sovereignty—
SEBASTIAN. Yet he would be king on 't.
ANTONIO. The latter end of his commonwealth forgets the beginning. 150
GONZALO.
All things in common nature should produce
Without sweat or endeavor; treason, felony,
Sword, pike, knife, gun, or need of any engine[49]
Would I not have; but nature should bring forth
Of its own kind all foison,[50] all abundance,
To feed my innocent people.
SEBASTIAN. No marrying 'mong his subjects?
ANTONIO. None, man, all idle: whores and knaves.
GONZALO.
I would with such perfection govern, sir,
T' excel the Golden Age.[51]
SEBASTIAN. Save[52] his Majesty! 160
ANTONIO.
Long live Gonzalo!
GONZALO. And do you mark me, sir?
ALONSO.
Prithee, no more. Thou dost talk nothing to me.
GONZALO. I do well believe your Highness, and did it to minister occasion[53] to these gentlemen, who are of such sensible[54] and nimble lungs that they always use to laugh at nothing.
ANTONIO. 'Twas you we laughed at.
GONZALO. Who in this kind of merry fooling am nothing to you. So you may continue, and laugh at nothing still.

[37]This speech is based on Montaigne's essay "Of Cannibals."
[38]Contrary to the usual plan. [39]Trade. [40]Learning.
[41]No one should have servants. [42]Legal agreements. [43]Right of inheritance.
[44]Boundary. [45]Limit, i.e., private property rights. [46]Tillage.
[47]I.e., exchange of money. [48]Manual labor. [49]Instrument of warfare. [50]Plenty.
[51]The days of perfect innocence at the beginning of the world.
[52]God save. [53]Provide opportunity. [54]Sensitive.

ANTONIO. What a blow was there given!
SEBASTIAN. An[55] it had not fallen flatlong.[56] 170
GONZALO. You are gentlemen of brave mettle.[57] You would lift the moon out of her sphere[58] if she would continue in it five weeks without changing.

Enter Ariel invisible, playing solemn music.

SEBASTIAN. We would so, and then go a batfowling.[59]
ANTONIO, *to Gonzalo.* Nay, good my lord, be not angry.
GONZALO. No, I warrant you, I will not adventure my discretion so weakly.[60] Will you laugh me asleep? For I am very heavy.
ANTONIO. Go sleep, and hear us.

All sink down asleep except Alonso, Antonio, and Sebastian.

ALONSO.
What, all so soon asleep? I wish mine eyes
Would, with themselves, shut up my thoughts. I find 180
They are inclined to do so.
SEBASTIAN. Please you, sir,
Do not omit the heavy offer of it.[61]
It seldom visits sorrow; when it doth,
It is a comforter.
ANTONIO. We two, my lord,
Will guard your person while you take your rest,
And watch your safety.
ALONSO. Thank you. Wondrous heavy.

Alonso sleeps. Ariel exits.

SEBASTIAN.
What a strange drowsiness possesses them!
ANTONIO.
It is the quality[62] o' th' climate.
SEBASTIAN. Why
Doth it not then our eyelids sink? I find
Not myself disposed to sleep. 190
ANTONIO. Nor I. My spirits are nimble.
They fell together all, as by consent.
They dropped as by a thunderstroke. What might,
Worthy Sebastian, O, what might—? No more.
And yet methinks I see it in thy face
What thou shouldst be. Th' occasion speaks thee,[63] and
My strong imagination sees a crown
Dropping upon thy head.

[55]If. [56]On the flat side of the sword. [57]Material, stuff. [58]Course.
[59]Hunting for birds at night with the aid of torches and sticks or bats.
[60]Risk my reputation as a discreet man so easily, by showing anger at such as you.
[61]Do not lose this chance of sleeping. [62]Nature.
[63]Opportunity calls you.

SEBASTIAN. What, art thou waking[64]?

ANTONIO.
Do you not hear me speak?

SEBASTIAN. I do, and surely
It is a sleepy language, and thou speak'st 200
Out of thy sleep. What is it thou didst say?
This is a strange repose, to be asleep
With eyes wide open—standing, speaking, moving—
And yet so fast asleep.

ANTONIO. Noble Sebastian,
Thou let'st thy fortune sleep, die rather, wink'st
Whiles thou art waking.

SEBASTIAN. Thou dost snore distinctly.
There's meaning in thy snores.

ANTONIO.
I am more serious than my custom. You
Must be so too, if heed me;[65] which to do
Trebles thee o'er.[66]

SEBASTIAN. Well, I am standing water.[67] 210

ANTONIO.
I'll teach you how to flow.[68]

SEBASTIAN. Do so. To ebb
Hereditary sloth instructs me.

ANTONIO. O,
If you but knew how you the purpose cherish
Whiles thus you mock it, how in stripping it
You more invest it.[69] Ebbing men indeed
Most often do so near the bottom run
By their own fear or sloth.[70]

SEBASTIAN. Prithee, say on.
The setting[71] of thine eye and cheek proclaim
A matter[72] from thee, and a birth indeed
Which throes thee much to yield.[73]

ANTONIO. Thus, sir: 220
Although this lord of weak remembrance—this,[74]
Who shall be of as little memory
When he is earthed—hath here almost persuaded—
For he's a spirit of persuasion, only
Professes to persuade—the King his son's alive,

[64]Awake. [65]If you will listen to me. [66]Makes you three times the man you are.

[67]I.e., at the standing of the tide, which for a while neither ebbs nor flows.

[68]Advance (like the rising tide).

[69]If you would only realize how much you are moved by the prospect of becoming king, even while you mock it; how in stripping it of its glamour you make it more attractive.

[70]*Ebbing men* (i.e., the lazy and unambitious) often run aground through fear or sloth.

[71]Expression. [72]Something serious. [73]Is very painful to bring forth.

[74]I.e., Francisco.

'Tis as impossible that he's undrowned
As he that sleeps here swims.

SEBASTIAN. I have no hope
That he's undrowned.

ANTONIO. O, out of that no hope
What great hope have you! No hope that way is
Another way so high a hope that even 230
Ambition cannot pierce a wink beyond,
But doubt discovery there.[75] Will you grant with me
That Ferdinand is drowned?

SEBASTIAN. He's gone.

ANTONIO. Then tell me,
Who's the next heir of Naples?

SEBASTIAN. Claribel.

ANTONIO.
She that is Queen of Tunis; she that dwells
Ten leagues beyond man's life;[76] she that from Naples
Can have no note, unless the sun were post[77]—
The man i' th' moon's too slow—till newborn chins
Be rough and razorable;[78] she that from whom
We all were sea-swallowed, though some cast[79] again, 240
And by that destiny to perform an act
Whereof what's past is prologue, what to come
In yours and my discharge.[80]

SEBASTIAN. What stuff is this? How say you?
'Tis true my brother's daughter's Queen of Tunis,
So is she heir of Naples, 'twixt which regions
There is some space.

ANTONIO. A space whose ev'ry cubit
Seems to cry out "How shall that Claribel
Measure us[81] back to Naples? Keep[82] in Tunis
And let Sebastian wake." Say this were death 250
That now hath seized them, why, they were no worse
Than now they are. There be that can rule Naples
As well as he that sleeps, lords that can prate
As amply and unnecessarily
As this Gonzalo. I myself could make
A chough of as deep chat,[83] O, that you bore
The mind that I do, what a sleep were this
For your advancement! Do you understand me?

[75]I.e., your certainty that the true heir is drowned gives you a greater hope in another direction (i.e., of being king yourself), where even your ambition cannot look higher.
[76]Ten leagues farther than a man could travel in his lifetime. [77]Messenger.
[78]I.e., newborn children are grown men. [79]Vomited up. [80]Task to be performed.
[81]Retrace her journey after us. [82]Let her remain.
[83]I could make a jackdaw (*chough*, rhyming with rough) talk as profoundly as he does.

SEBASTIAN.
Methinks I do.
ANTONIO. And how does your content
Tender your own good fortune?
SEBASTIAN. I remember 260
You did supplant your brother Prospero.
ANTONIO. True,
And look how well my garments sit upon me,
Much feater[84] than before. My brother's servants
Were then my fellows;[85] now they are my men.[86]
SEBASTIAN. But, for your conscience?
ANTONIO.
Ay, sir, where lies that? If 'twere a kibe,
'Twould put me to my slipper,[87] but I feel not
This deity in my bosom. Twenty consciences
That stand 'twixt me and Milan, candied be they
And melt ere they molest![88] Here lies your brother, 270
No better than the earth he lies upon.
If he were that which now he's like—that's dead—
Whom I with this obedient steel, three inches of it,
Can lay to bed forever; whiles you, doing thus,
To the perpetual wink[89] for aye might put
This ancient morsel, this Sir Prudence, who
Should not upbraid our course. For all the rest,
They'll take suggestion as a cat laps milk.
They'll tell the clock to[90] any business that
We say befits the hour.
SEBASTIAN. Thy case, dear friend, 280
Shall be my precedent: as thou got'st Milan,
I'll come by Naples. Draw thy sword. One stroke
Shall free thee from the tribute which thou payest,
And I the King shall love thee.
ANTONIO. Draw together,
And when I rear my hand, do you the like
To fall[91] it on Gonzalo. *They draw their swords.*
SEBASTIAN. O, but one word.
They talk apart.

Enter Ariel, invisible, with music and song.

ARIEL, *to the sleeping Gonzalo.*
My master through his art foresees the danger

[84]More trimly. [85]Equals. [86]Servants.
[87]A chilblain, which would make me wear a slipper.
[88]I.e., if twenty consciences had stood between me and the dukedom of Milan, I should have let them melt like candy before they would have disturbed me.
[89]Everlasting sleep. [90]Say it is time for. [91]Let fall.

That you, his friend, are in, and sends me forth—
For else his project dies—to keep them living.
Sings in Gonzalo's ear.
While you here do snoring lie, 290
Open-eyed conspiracy
His time[92] *doth take.*
If of life you keep a care,
Shake off slumber and beware.
Awake, awake!

ANTONIO, *to Sebastian.* Then let us both be sudden.

GONZALO, *waking.* Now, good angels preserve the King! *He wakes Alonso.*

ALONSO, *to Sebastian.*
Why, how now, ho! Awake? Why are you drawn?
Wherefore this ghastly looking?

GONZALO, *to Sebastian.* What's the matter?

SEBASTIAN.
Whiles we stood here securing[93] your repose, 300
Even now, we heard a hollow burst of bellowing
Like bulls, or rather lions. Did 't not wake you?
It struck mine ear most terribly.

ALONSO. I heard nothing.

ANTONIO.
O, 'twas a din to fright a monster's ear,
To make an earthquake. Sure, it was the roar
Of a whole herd of lions.

ALONSO. Heard you this, Gonzalo?

GONZALO.
Upon mine honor, sir, I heard a humming,
And that a strange one too, which did awake me.
I shaked you, sir, and cried. As mine eyes opened, 310
I saw their weapons drawn. There was a noise,
That's verily.[94] 'Tis best we stand upon our guard,
Or that we quit this place. Let's draw our weapons.

ALONSO.
Lead off this ground, and let's make further search
For my poor son.

GONZALO. Heavens keep him from these beasts,
For he is, sure, i' th' island.

ALONSO. Lead away.

ARIEL, *aside*
Prospero my lord shall know what I have done.
So, king, go safely on to seek thy son.

They exit.

[92]Opportunity. [93]Keeping safe. [94]Truth.

SCENE 2

Enter Caliban with a burden of wood. A noise of thunder heard.

CALIBAN.
All the infections that the sun sucks up
From bogs, fens, flats, on Prosper fall and make him
By inchmeal[1] a disease! His spirits hear me,
And yet I needs must curse. But they'll nor pinch,
Fright me with urchin-shows[2], pitch me i' th' mire,
Nor lead me like a firebrand[3] in the dark
Out of my way, unless he bid 'em. But
For every trifle are they set upon me,
Sometimes like apes, that mow[4] and chatter at me
And after bite me; then like hedgehogs, which 10
Lie tumbling in my barefoot way and mount[5]
Their pricks at my footfall. Sometime am I
All wound with adders, who with cloven tongues
Do hiss me into madness. Lo, now, lo!
Here comes a spirit of his, and to torment me
For bringing wood in slowly. I'll fall flat.
Perchance he will not mind me.
He lies down and covers himself with a cloak.

Enter Trinculo.

TRINCULO. Here's neither bush nor shrub to bear off any weather at all. And another storm brewing; I hear it sing i' th' wind. Yond same black cloud, yond huge one, looks like a foul bombard[6] 20 that would shed his liquor. If it should thunder as it did before, I know not where to hide my head. Yond same cloud cannot choose but fall by pailfuls. *Noticing Caliban.* What have we here, a man or a fish? Dead or alive? A fish, he smells like a fish—a very ancient and fishlike smell, a kind of not-of-the-newest poor-John.[7] A strange fish. Were I in England now, as once I was, and had but this fish painted,[8] not a holiday fool there but would give a piece of silver. There would this monster make a man.[9] Any strange beast there makes a man. When they will not give a doit[10] to relieve a lame beggar, they will lay out ten to see a dead 30 Indian. Legged like a man, and his fins like arms! Warm, o' my troth! I do now let loose my opinion, hold it no longer: this is no fish, but an islander that hath lately suffered by a thunder-bolt. *Thunder.* Alas, the storm is come again. My best way is to

[1]By inches. [2]The appearance of goblins. [3]Will-o'-the-wisp. [4]Make faces.
[5]Raise. [6]Large black leathern jug. [7]Dried salt hake.
[8]Had a poster of this fish painted. [9]I.e., his fortune. [10]A small Dutch coin, a cent.

creep under his gaberdine.[11] There is no other shelter hereabout. Misery acquaints a man with strange bedfellows. I will here shroud[12] till the dregs of the storm be past. *He crawls under Caliban's cloak.*

Enter Stephano singing.

STEPHANO.

I shall no more to sea, to sea.
Here shall I die ashore—

This is a very scurvy[13] tune to sing at a man's funeral. 40
Well, here's my comfort. *Drinks.*

Sings.

The master, the swabber, the boatswain, and I,
The gunner and his mate,
Loved Mall, Meg, and Marian, and Margery,
But none of us cared for Kate.
For she had a tongue with a tang,[14]
Would cry to a sailor "Go hang!"
She loved not the savor[15] *of tar nor of pitch,*
Yet a tailor might scratch her where'er she did itch.
Then to sea, boys, and let her go hang! 50

This is a scurvy tune too. But here's my comfort. *Drinks.*

CALIBAN. Do not torment me! O!

STEPHANO. What's the matter? Have we devils here? Do you put tricks upon 's with savages and men of Ind?[16] Ha? I have not scaped drowning to be afeard now of your four legs, for it hath been said "As proper[17] a man as ever went on four legs cannot make him give ground," and it shall be said so again while Stephano breathes at's nostrils.

CALIBAN. The spirit torments me. O!

STEPHANO. This is some monster of the isle with four legs, who hath got, as I take it, an ague.[18] Where the devil should he learn our language? I will give him some relief, if it be but for that. If I can recover[19] him and keep him tame and get to Naples with him, he's a present for any emperor that ever trod on neat's leather.[20] 60

CALIBAN. Do not torment me, prithee. I'll bring my wood home faster.

STEPHANO. He's in his fit now, and does not talk after the wisest. He shall taste of my bottle. If he have never drunk wine afore, it will go near to remove his fit. If I can recover him and keep

[11]Cloak. [12]Cover myself. [13]"Lousy." [14]A sharp sound. [15]Taste. [16]Native of India. [17]Fine. [18]Fever, which makes him shiver. [19]Cure. [20]I.e., shoes.

him tame, I will not take too much for him.[21] He shall pay for him that hath him, and that soundly. 70

CALIBAN. Thou dost me yet but little hurt. Thou wilt anon; I know it by thy trembling.[22] Now Prosper works upon thee.

STEPHANO. Come on your ways. Open your mouth. Here is that which will give language to you, cat. Open your mouth. This will shake your shaking, I can tell you, and that soundly. *Caliban drinks.* You cannot tell who's your friend. Open your chaps[23] again.

TRINCULO. I should know that voice. It should be—but he is drowned, and these are devils. O, defend me! 80

STEPHANO. Four legs and two voices—a most delicate monster! His forward voice now is to speak well of his friend. His backward voice is to utter foul speeches and to detract. If all the wine in my bottle will recover him, I will help his ague. Come. *Caliban drinks.* Amen! I will pour some in thy other mouth.

TRINCULO. Stephano!

STEPHANO. Doth thy other mouth call me? Mercy, mercy, this is a devil, and no monster! I will leave him; I have no long spoon.[24]

TRINCULO. Stephano! If thou be'st Stephano, touch me and speak to me, for I am Trinculo—be not afeard—thy good friend Trinculo. 90

STEPHANO. If thou be'st Trinculo, come forth. I'll pull thee by the lesser legs. If any be Trinculo's legs, these are they. *He pulls him out from under Caliban's cloak.* Thou art very Trinculo indeed. How cam'st thou to be the siege[25] of this mooncalf[26]? Can he vent Trinculos?

TRINCULO. I took him to be killed with a thunderstroke. But art thou not drowned, Stephano? I hope now thou art not drowned. Is the storm overblown? I hid me under the dead mooncalf's gaberdine for fear of the storm. And art thou living, Stephano? O Stephano, two Neapolitans scaped! 100

STEPHANO. Prithee, do not turn me about. My stomach is not constant.[27]

CALIBAN, *aside.* These be fine things, an if they be not sprites. That's a brave god and bears celestial liquor. I will kneel to him. *He crawls out from under the cloak.*

[21]I'll not take even an excessive price.

[22]Trinculo is the trembler, for he believes that the voice of Stephano comes from a ghost. Trinculo is a natural coward.

[23]Chops, jaws.

[24]"He that sups with the Devil needs a long spoon"—a proverb from the time when men dipped into a common dish. A long spoon was needed, as the Devil's claws were long and sharp, and his table manners nasty.

[25]Excrement. [26]Misshapen monster, freak.

[27]Steady. Trinculo is pawing him all over and turning him round in his excitement.

STEPHANO, *to Trinculo.* How didst thou scape? How cam'st thou hither? Swear by this bottle how thou cam'st hither—I escaped upon a butt of sack,[28] which the sailors heaved o'er board—by this bottle, which I made of the bark of a tree with mine own hands, since I was cast ashore. 110

CALIBAN. I'll swear upon that bottle to be thy true subject, for the liquor is not earthly.

STEPHANO, *to Trinculo.* Here. Swear then how thou escapedst.

TRINCULO. Swum ashore, man, like a duck. I can swim like a duck, I'll be sworn.

STEPHANO. Here, kiss the book. *Trinculo drinks.* Though thou canst swim like a duck, thou art made like a goose.

TRINCULO. O Stephano, hast any more of this?

STEPHANO. The whole butt, man. My cellar is in a rock by th' seaside, where my wine is hid.—How now, mooncalf, how does thine ague? 120

CALIBAN. Hast thou not dropped from heaven?

STEPHANO. Out o' th' moon, I do assure thee. I was the man i' th' moon when time was.[29]

CALIBAN. I have seen thee in her, and I do adore thee. My mistress showed me thee, and thy dog, and thy bush.[30]

STEPHANO. Come, swear to that. Kiss the book. I will furnish is anon with new contents. Swear. *Caliban drinks.*

TRINCULO. By this good light, this is a very shallow monster. I afeard of him? A very weak monster. The man i' th' moon? A most poor, credulous monster!—Well drawn,[31] monster, in good sooth![32] 130

CALIBAN. I'll show thee every fertile inch o' th' island, and I will kiss thy foot. I prithee, be my god.

TRINCULO. By this light, a most perfidious and drunken monster. When 's god's asleep, he'll rob his bottle.

CALIBAN. I'll kiss thy foot. I'll swear myself thy subject.

STEPHANO. Come on, then. Down, and swear.

Caliban kneels.

TRINCULO. I shall laugh myself to death at this puppy-headed monster. A most scurvy monster. I could find in my heart to beat him— 140

STEPHANO. Come, kiss.

TRINCULO. But that the poor monster's in drink. An abominable monster.

[28]A dry wine from Spain. [29]Once upon a time.

[30]The man in the moon had his dog and bush of thorns, as Quince in *A Midsummer Night's Dream* knows.

[31]Sucked. [32]Truth.

CALIBAN.

I'll show thee the best springs. I'll pluck thee berries.
I'll fish for thee and get thee wood enough.
A plague upon the tyrant that I serve.
I'll bear him no more sticks, but follow thee,
Thou wondrous man.[33] 150

TRINCULO. A most ridiculous monster, to make a wonder of a poor drunkard.

CALIBAN, *standing.*

I prithee, let me bring thee where crabs[34] grow,
And I with my long nails will dig thee pignuts,[35]
Show thee a jay's nest, and instruct thee how
To snare the nimble marmoset.[36] I'll bring thee
To clustering filberts, and sometimes I'll get thee
Young scamels[37] from the rock. Wilt thou go with me?

STEPHANO. I prithee now, lead the way without any more talking.—Trinculo, the King and all our company else being drowned, 160 we will inherit here.—Here, bear my bottle.—Fellow Trinculo, we'll fill him by and by again.

CALIBAN *sings drunkenly.*

Farewell, master farewell, farewell.

TRINCULO. A howling monster, a drunken monster.

CALIBAN *sings.*

No more dams I'll make for fish,
Nor fetch in firing
At requiring,
Nor scrape trencher,[38] nor wash dish.
'Ban, 'ban, Ca-caliban
Has a new master. Get a new man. 170

Freedom, high-day! High-day, freedom! Freedom, high-day, freedom!

STEPHANO. O brave monster! Lead the way.

They exit.

[33]Caliban's line echoes Miranda's reaction to first seeing Ferdinand in the preceding scene.
[34]Crab apples.
[35]Called also earthnut, a plant producing edible tubers.
[36]Kind of small monkey.
[37]A much-discussed word that does not occur elsewhere and so has been variously interpreted or emended, the likeliest guess being *seamel*: sea gull.
[38]Wooden plate.

ACT 3

SCENE 1

Enter Ferdinand bearing a log.

FERDINAND.
There be some sports are painful, and their labor
Delight in them sets off;[1] some kinds of baseness
Are nobly undergone; and most poor matters
Point[2] to rich ends. This my mean task
Would be as heavy to me as odious, but
The mistress which I serve quickens[3] what's dead
And makes my labors pleasures. O, she is
Ten times more gentle than her father's crabbed,
And he's composed of harshness. I must remove
Some thousands of these logs and pile them up, 10
Upon a sore injunction.[4] My sweet mistress
Weeps when she sees me work, and says such baseness
Had never like executor.[5] I forget,
But these sweet thoughts do even refresh my labors,
Most busiest when I do it.[6]

Enter Miranda; and Prospero at a distance, unobserved.[7]

MIRANDA. Alas now, pray you,
Work not so hard. I would the lightning had
Burnt up those logs that you are enjoined to pile.
Pray, set it down and rest you. When this burns
'Twill weep[8] for having wearied you. My father
Is hard at study. Pray now, rest yourself. 20
He's safe for these three hours.
FERDINAND. O most dear mistress,
The sun will set before I shall discharge
What I must strive to do.
MIRANDA. If you'll sit down,
I'll bear your logs the while. Pray, give me that.
I'll carry it to the pile.

[1]The delight they bring outweighs the fatigue. [2]Lead. [3]Brings to life.
[4]A command enforced with penalties against disobedience.
[5]Performer.
[6]This line has been much discussed and may be corrupt. It means apparently "I am most busy when I am idle, for then I think so many sweet thoughts."
[7]Probably Miranda enters the main stage and Prospero enters the balcony above. The balcony was a most convenient place for eavesdroppers.
[8]Drip with sap when burning.

FERDINAND. No, precious creature,
I had rather crack my sinews, break my back,
Than you should such dishonor undergo
While I sit lazy by.

MIRANDA. It would become me
As well as it does you, and I should do it
With much more ease, for my good will is to it, 30
And yours it is against.

PROSPERO, *aside.* Poor worm, thou art infected.
This visitation[9] shows it.

MIRANDA. You look wearily.

FERDINAND.
No, noble mistress, 'tis fresh morning with me
When you are by at night. I do beseech you,
Chiefly that I might set it in my prayers,
What is your name?

MIRANDA. Miranda.—O my father,
I have broke your hest[10] to say so!

FERDINAND. Admired Miranda[11]!
Indeed the top[12] of admiration, worth
What's dearest to the world! Full many a lady 40
I have eyed with best regard, and many a time
Th' harmony of their tongues hath into bondage
Brought my too diligent ear. For several[13] virtues
Have I liked several women, never any
With so full soul but some defect in her
Did quarrel with the noblest grace she owed,
And put it to the foil[14] But you, O you,
So perfect and so peerless, are created
Of every creature's best.

MIRANDA. I do not know
One of my sex, no woman's face remember, 50
Save, from my glass, mine own. Nor have I seen
More that I may call men than you, good friend,
And my dear father. How features are abroad
I am skilless of,[15] but by my modesty,
The jewel in my dower, I would not wish
Any companion in the world but you,
Nor can imagination form a shape
Besides yourself to like of. But I prattle
Something too wildly, and my father's precepts
I therein do forget. 60

[9]Visit. [10]Command.
[11]A play on her name, for *miranda* in Latin means "she who ought to be wondered at." "Admired" at this time had a stronger meaning than today.
[12]Summit. [13]Separate, individual. [14]Bring it to disgrace.
[15]I have no experience of how people look elsewhere.

FERDINAND. I am in my condition
A prince, Miranda; I do think a king—
I would, not so!—and would no more endure
This wooden slavery[16] than to suffer
The flesh-fly blow[17] my mouth. Hear my soul speak:
The very instant that I saw you did
My heart fly to your service, there resides
To make me slave to it, and for your sake
Am I this patient log-man.
MIRANDA. Do you love me?
FERDINAND.
O heaven, O earth, bear witness to this sound, 70
And crown what I profess with kind event[18]
If I speak true; if hollowly, invert
What best is boded[19] me to mischief. I,
Beyond all limit of what else i' th' world,
Do love, prize, honor you.
MIRANDA. I am a fool
To weep at what I am glad of.
PROSPERO, *aside.* Fair encounter
Of two most rare affections. Heavens rain grace
On that which breeds between 'em!
FERDINAND. Wherefore weep you?
MIRANDA.
At mine unworthiness, that dare not offer
What I desire to give, and much less take 80
What I shall die to want.[20] But this is trifling,
And all the more it seeks to hide itself,
The bigger bulk it shows. Hence, bashful cunning,
And prompt me, plain and holy innocence.
I am your wife if you will marry me.
If not, I'll die your maid. To be your fellow[21]
You may deny me, but I'll be your servant
Whether you will or no.
FERDINAND.
My mistress, dearest, and I thus humble ever.
MIRANDA.
My husband, then?
FERDINAND. Ay, with a heart as willing[22] 90
As bondage e'er of freedom. Here's my hand.
MIRANDA, *clasping his hand*
And mine, with my heart in 't. And now farewell
Till half an hour hence.
FERDINAND. A thousand thousand.[23]

They exit.

[16]I.e., task of having to carry wood. [17]Lay its eggs on, foul. [18]Result.
[19]The best fate that is prophesied. [20]Be without. [21]Equal. [22]Eager.
[23]I.e., farewells.

PROSPERO.
So glad of this as they I cannot be,
Who[24] are surprised withal;[25] but my rejoicing
At nothing can be more: I'll to my book,
For yet ere suppertime must I perform
Much business appertaining.

He exits.

SCENE 2

Enter Caliban, Stephano, and Trinculo.

STEPHANO, *to Trinculo.* Tell not me. When the butt is out, we will drink water; not a drop before. Therefore bear up[1] and board 'em.—Servant monster, drink to me.

TRINCULO. Servant monster? The folly of this island![2] They say there's but five upon this isle; we are three of them. If th' other two be brained like us, the state totters.

STEPHANO. Drink, servant monster, when I bid thee. Thy eyes are almost set[3] in thy head.

Caliban drinks.

TRINCULO. Where should they be set else? He were a brave monster indeed if they were set in his tail. 10

STEPHANO. My man-monster hath drowned his tongue in sack. For my part, the sea cannot drown me. I swam, ere I could recover the shore, five-and-thirty leagues[4] off and on, by this light.—Thou shalt be my lieutenant, monster, or my standard.[5]

TRINCULO. Your lieutenant, if you list. He's no standard.

STEPHANO. We'll not run, Monsieur Monster.

TRINCULO. Nor go neither. But you'll lie like dogs, and yet say nothing neither.

STEPHANO. Mooncalf, speak once in thy life, if thou be'st a good mooncalf. 20

CALIBAN. How does thy Honor? Let me lick thy shoe. I'll not serve him; he is not valiant.

TRINCULO. Thou liest, most ignorant monster. I am in case[6] to justle a constable. Why, thou debauched fish, thou! Was there ever man a coward that hath drunk so much sack as I today? Wilt thou tell a monstrous lie, being but half a fish and half a monster?

CALIBAN. Lo, how he mocks me! Wilt thou let him, my lord?

[24]I.e., Ferdinand and Miranda. [25]Therewith.
[1]Crowd on more sail. [2]What a silly place this island is. [3]Closed, dazed with drink.
[4]Three miles.
[5]Standard-bearer (or ensign), the junior officer in the company, the others being the captain and the lieutenant. Caliban is now too unsteady to be a satisfactory *standard.*
[6]In a condition.

TRINCULO. "Lord," quoth he? That a monster should be such a natural![7]

CALIBAN. Lo, lo again! Bite him to death, I prithee. 30

STEPHANO. Trinculo, keep a good tongue in your head. If you prove a mutineer, the next tree. The poor monster's my subject, and he shall not suffer indignity.

CALIBAN. I thank my noble lord. Wilt thou be pleased to harken once again to the suit I made to thee?

STEPHANO. Marry,[8] will I. Kneel and repeat it. I will stand, and so shall Trinculo.

Enter Ariel, invisible.

CALIBAN, *kneeling.* As I told thee before, I am subject to a tyrant, a sorcerer, that by his cunning hath cheated me of the island.

ARIEL, *in Trinculo's voice.* Thou liest. 40

CALIBAN, *to Trinculo.* Thou liest,[9] thou jesting monkey, thou. *He stands.* I would my valiant master would destroy thee, I do not lie.

STEPHANO. Trinculo, if you trouble him any more in 's tale, by this hand, I will supplant[10] some of your teeth.

TRINCULO. Why, I said nothing.

STEPHANO. Mum then, and no more. *Trinculo stands aside.* Proceed.

CALIBAN.
I say by sorcery he got this isle;
From me he got it. If thy Greatness will,
Revenge it on him, for I know thou dar'st, 50
But this thing dare not.

STEPHANO. That's most certain.

CALIBAN.
Thou shalt be lord of it, and I'll serve thee.

STEPHANO. How now shall this be compassed?[11] Canst thou bring me to the party?

CALIBAN.
Yea, yea, my lord. I'll yield him thee asleep,
Where thou mayst knock a nail into his head.

ARIEL, *in Trinculo's voice.* Thou liest. Thou canst not.

CALIBAN.
What a pied ninny's[12] this!—Thou scurvy patch![13]—
I do beseech thy Greatness, give him blows 60
And take his bottle from him. When that's gone,
He shall drink naught but brine, for I'll not show him
Where the quick freshes[14] are.

STEPHANO. Trinculo, run into no further danger. Interrupt the

[7]Born fool. [8]Mary, by the Virgin. [9]Caliban supposes the voice to be Trinculo's.
[10]Displace. [11]Brought about.
[12]Patched fool, because Trinculo as a jester wears motley, the "patched" or particolored dress of his profession.
[13]Fool. [14]Running springs of fresh water.

monster one word further, and by this hand, I'll turn my mercy out o' doors and make a stockfish of thee.

TRINCULO. Why, what did I? I did nothing. I'll go farther off.

STEPHANO. Didst thou not say he lied?

ARIEL, *in Trinculo's voice.* Thou liest.

STEPHANO. Do I so? Take thou that. *He beats Trinculo.* As you like this, give me the lie[15] another time. 70

TRINCULO. I did not give the lie! Out o' your wits and hearing too? A pox o' your bottle! This can sack and drinking do. A murrain[16] on your monster, and the devil take your fingers!

CALIBAN. Ha, ha, ha!

STEPHANO. Now forward with your tale. *To Trinculo.* Prithee, stand further off.

CALIBAN.

Beat him enough. After a little time
I'll beat him too.

STEPHANO. Stand farther. *Trinculo moves farther away.* Come, proceed. 80

CALIBAN.

Why, as I told thee, 'tis a custom with him
I' th' afternoon to sleep. There thou mayst brain him,
Having first seized his books, or with a log
Batter his skull, or paunch him with a stake[17]
Or cut his weasand[18] with thy knife. Remember
First to possess his books, for without them
He's but a sot, as I am, nor hath not
One spirit to command. They all do hate him
As rootedly[19] as I. Burn but his books.
He has brave utensils[20]—for so he calls them— 90
Which, when he has a house, he'll deck withal.
And that most deeply to consider is
The beauty of his daughter. He himself
Calls her a nonpareil.[21] I never saw a woman
But only Sycorax my dam and she;
But she as far surpasseth Sycorax
As great'st does least.

STEPHANO. Is it so brave a lass?

CALIBAN.

Ay, lord, she will become thy bed, I warrant,
And bring thee forth brave brood.

STEPHANO. Monster, I will kill this man. His daughter and I will be king and queen—save our Graces!—and Trinculo and thyself shall be viceroys.—Dost thou like the plot, Trinculo? 100

TRINCULO. Excellent

STEPHANO. Give me thy hand. I am sorry I beat thee. But while thou liv'st, keep a good tongue in thy head.

CALIBAN.

Within this half hour will he be asleep.
Wilt thou destroy him then?

[15]Call me a liar. [16]Plague. [17]Stab him in the belly. [18]Windpipe.
[19]Fixedly. [20]Furnishings. [21]Without equal.

STEPHANO. Ay, on mine honor.
ARIEL, *aside.* This will I tell my master.
CALIBAN.
Thou mak'st me merry. I am full of pleasure.
Let us be jocund. Will you troll the catch[22] 110
You taught me but whilere?[23]
STEPHANO. At thy request, monster, I will do reason,[24] any reason.—
Come on, Trinculo, let us sing. *Sings.*
Flout[25] 'em and cout[26] 'em
And scout 'em and flout 'em!
Thought is free.
CALIBAN. That's not the tune.
Ariel plays the tune on a tabor[27] and pipe.
STEPHANO. What is this same?
TRINCULO. This is the tune of our catch played by the picture of Nobody.[28] 120
STEPHANO, *to the invisible musician.* It thou be'st a man, show thyself in thy likeness. If thou be'st a devil, take 't as thou list.
TRINCULO. O, forgive me my sins!
STEPHANO. He that dies pays all debts.—I defy thee!—Mercy upon us.
CALIBAN. Art thou afeard?
STEPHANO. No, monster, not I.
CALIBAN.
Be not afeard. The isle is full of noises,[29]
Sounds and sweet airs that give delight and hurt not.
Sometimes a thousand twangling instruments
Will hum about mine ears, and sometimes voices 130
That, if I then had waked after long sleep,
Will make me sleep again; and then, in dreaming,
The clouds methought would open, and show riches
Ready to drop upon me, that when I waked
I cried to dream again.
STEPHANO. This will prove a brave kingdom to me, where I shall have my music for nothing.
CALIBAN. When Prospero is destroyed.
STEPHANO. That shall be by and by.[30] I remember the story.
TRINCULO. The sound is going away. Let's follow it, and after do our work. 140
STEPHANO. Lead, monster. We'll follow.—I would I could see this taborer. He lays it on. Wilt come?
TRINCULO. I'll follow, Stephano.

They exit.

[22]Sing a rowdy song. In a "catch," each singer in turn catches up the song a few words after the others.
[23]Just now. [24]Anything within reason. [25]Mock. [26]Deride. [27]Small drum.
[28]I.e., by an invisible player. There is a picture of Nobody in a play called *Nobody and Somebody*, printed 1606. It is all head and no body, like Humpty Dumpty.
[29]Music. [30]In the near future.

SCENE 3

Enter Alonso, Sebastian, Antonio, Gonzalo, Adrian, Francisco, etc.

GONZALO.
By 'r lakin,[1] I can go no further, sir.
My old bones aches. Here's a maze trod indeed
Through forthrights and meanders.[2] By your patience,
I needs must rest me.
ALONSO. Old lord, I cannot blame thee,
Who am myself attached[3] with weariness
To th' dulling of my spirits. Sit down and rest.
Even here I will put off my hope and keep it
No longer for my flatterer. He is drowned
Whom thus we stray to find, and the sea mocks
Our frustrate[4] search on land. Well, let him go. 10
ANTONIO, *aside to Sebastian.*
I am right glad that he's so out of hope.
Do not, for one repulse, forgo the purpose
That you resolved t' effect.
SEBASTIAN, *aside to Antonio.* The next advantage
Will we take throughly.[5]
ANTONIO, *aside to Sebastian.* Let it be tonight;
For now they are oppressed with travel, they
Will not nor cannot use such vigilance
As when they are fresh.
SEBASTIAN, *aside to Antonio.* I say tonight. No more. 20

Solemn and strange music, and enter Prospero on the top invisible.

ALONSO.
What harmony is this? My good friends, hark.
GONZALO. Marvelous sweet music!

Enter several strange shapes, bringing in a banquet,[6]
and dance about it with gentle actions of salutations.

ALONSO.
Give us kind keepers, heavens! What were these?
SEBASTIAN.
A living drollery![7] Now[8] I will believe
That there are unicorns, that in Arabia

[1]By Our Lady.
[2]We have wandered as in a maze by straight paths (*forthrights*) and winding paths (*meanders*).
[3]Overcome by; literally, arrested. [4]Vain. [5]Thoroughly.
[6]Light refreshments, such as fruit and jellies.
[7]Puppet show. [8]I.e., after this we can believe any fantastic traveler's yarn.

There is one tree, the phoenix'[9] throne, one phoenix
At this hour reigning there.

ANTONIO. I'll believe both;
And what does else want credit,[10] come to me
And I'll be sworn 'tis true. Travelers ne'er did lie,
Though fools at home condemn 'em.

GONZALO. If in Naples 30
I should report this now, would they believe me?
If I should say I saw such islanders—
For, certes,[11] these are people of the island—
Who, though they are of monstrous shape, yet note
Their manners are more gentle, kind, than of
Our human generation[12] you shall find
Many, nay, almost any.

PROSPERO, *aside.* Honest lord,
Thou hast said well, for some of you there present
Are worse than devils.

ALONSO. I cannot too much muse[13]
Such shapes, such gesture, and such sound, expressing— 40
Although they want the use of tongue—a kind
Of excellent dumb discourse.

PROSPERO, *aside.* Praise in departing.[14]

Inviting the King, etc., to eat, the shapes depart.

FRANCISCO. They vanished strangely.

SEBASTIAN. No matter, since
They have left their viands behind, for we have stomachs.
Will 't please you taste of what is here?

ALONSO. Not I.

GONZALO.
Faith, sir, you need not fear. When we were boys,
Who would believe that there were mountaineers
Dewlapped[15] like bulls, whose throats had hanging at 'em
Wallets of flesh? Or that there were such men 50
Whose heads stood in their breasts?[16] Which now we find

[9]A mythical bird. According to the legend, only one phoenix was alive at a time. It lived for 500 years. Then it built itself a nest of spices, which were set alight by the rapid beating of its wings. From the ashes a new phoenix was born.

[10]Is not believed. [11]Certainly. [12]Breed. [13]Wonder at.

[14]A proverb meaning "Don't give thanks for your entertainment until you see how it will end."

[15]Having folds of loose skin hanging from the throat.

[16]Sir Walter Raleigh in his account of Guiana (1595) noted "a nation of people whose heads appear not above their shoulders; which though it may be thought a mere fable, yet for mine own part I am resolved it is true, because every child in the provinces of Arromaia and Canuri affirms the same. They are called Ewaipanoma. They are reported to have their eyes in their shoulders, and their mouths in the middle of their breasts, and that a long train of hair groweth backward between their shoulders."

Each putter-out of five for one[17] will bring us
Good warrant of.

ALONSO. I will stand to and feed.
Although my last, no matter, since I feel
The best is past. Brother, my lord the Duke,
Stand to, and do as we.

Alonso, Sebastian, and Antonio move toward the table.

Thunder and lightning. Enter Ariel, like a Harpy,[18] claps his wings upon the table, and with a quaint device[19] the banquet vanishes.

ARIEL *as Harpy.*
You are three men of sin, whom Destiny,
That hath to instrument this lower world
And what is in 't,[20] the never-surfeited[21] sea
Hath caused to belch up you, and on this island, 60
Where man doth not inhabit, you 'mongst men
Being most unfit to live. I have made you mad;
And even with such-like valor, men hang and drown
Their proper[22] selves.

Alonso, Sebastian, and Antonio draw their swords.

You fools, I and my fellows
Are ministers of Fate. The elements
Of whom your swords are tempered may as well
Wound the loud winds or with bemocked-at stabs
Kill the still-closing[23] waters as diminish
One dowl[24] that's in my plume.[25] My fellow ministers
Are like invulnerable. If you could hurt, 70
Your swords are now too massy[26] for your strengths
And will not be uplifted. But remember—
For that's my business to you—that you three
From Milan did supplant good Prospero,
Exposed unto the sea, which hath requit[27] it,
Him and his innocent child, for which foul deed,
The powers—delaying, not forgetting—have
Incensed the seas and throes, yea, all the creatures
Against your peace. Thee of thy son, Alonso,
They have bereft; and do pronounce by me 80
Ling'ring perdition,[28] worse than any death
Can be at once, shall step by step attend

[17]In Shakespeare's time voyages to distant and strange ports were so risky that the traveler sometimes left a sum of money with a merchant at home on condition that he should receive five times the amount if he returned; if he did not, the premium was forfeited.

[18]A foul creature, half bird of prey, half woman. This episode was suggested by an event in Virgil's *Aeneid* when the harpies seize and foul the food of Aeneas and his followers.

[19]Piece of ingenious stage machinery.

[20]Destiny (Providence), which uses this world below and its powers as its instrument.

[21]Never overfull. A surfeit is an excess of food. Even the sea, which can retain most things, cannot stomach Alonso and his fellow sinners.

[22]Own. [23]Always closing up, i.e., which cannot be wounded. [24]Downy feather.
[25]Wing. [26]Heavy. [27]Paid back. [28]Destruction.

You and your ways, whose wraths to guard you from—
Which here, in this most desolate isle, else falls
Upon your heads—is nothing but[29] heart's sorrow
And a clear[30] life ensuing. *He vanishes in thunder.*

Then, to soft music, enter the shapes again, and dance, with mocks[31] and mows,[32] and carrying out the table.

PROSPERO, *aside.*
Bravely the figure of this Harpy hast thou
Performed, my Ariel. A grace it had, devouring.[33]
Of my instruction has thou nothing bated[34]
In what thou hadst to say. So, with good life[35] 90
And observation[36] strange,[37] my meaner ministers[38]
Their several kinds[39] have done. My high charms work,
And these mine enemies are all knit up[40]
In their distractions.[41] They now are in my power;
And in these fits I leave them while I visit
Young Ferdinand, whom they suppose is drowned,
And his and mine loved darling. *He exits, above.*

GONZALO, *to Alonso.*
I' th' name of something holy, sir, why stand you
In this strange stare?

ALONSO. O, it is monstrous, monstrous!
Methought the billows spoke and told me of it; 100
The winds did sing it to me, and the thunder,
That deep and dreadful organ pipe, pronounced
The name of Prosper. It did bass my trespass.[42]
Therefor my son i' th' ooze is bedded, and
I'll seek him deeper than e'er plummet[43] sounded,
And with him there lie mudded. *He exits.*

SEBASTIAN. But one fiend at a time,
I'll fight their legions o'er.

ANTONIO. I'll be thy second.
They exit.

GONZALO.
All three of them are desperate. Their great guilt,
Like poison given to work a great time after, 110
Now 'gins to bite the spirits. I do beseech you
That are of suppler joints, follow them swiftly
And hinder them from what this ecstasy[44]
May now provoke them to.

ADRIAN. Follow, I pray you.
They all exit.

[29]I.e., only repentance will guard you from destruction. [30]Innocent.
[31]Mocking gestures. [32]Grimaces.
[33]The action of devouring was splendidly (*bravely*) performed.
[34]Abated, left out. [35]Realistically. [36]Obedience. [37]Unusual.
[38]Lesser servants. [39]Particular tasks. [40]Entangled. [41]Fits of madness.
[42]Proclaim my sin in a deep note.
[43]The lead weight at the end of a cord used by sailors to discover the depth of the water.
[44]Mad fit.

ACT 4

SCENE 1

Enter Prospero, Ferdinand, and Miranda.

PROSPERO, *to Ferdinand.*
If I have too austerely punished you,
Your compensation makes amends, for I
Have given you here a third[1] of mine own life,
Or that for which I live; who once again
I tender[2] to thy hand. All thy vexations
Were but my trials of thy love, and thou
Hast strangely[3] stood the test. Here afore heaven
I ratify this my rich gift. O Ferdinand,
Do not smile at me that I boast of her,
For thou shalt find she will outstrip all praise 10
And make it halt[4] behind her.
FERDINAND. I do believe it
Against an oracle.[5]
PROSPERO
Then, as my gift and thine own acquisition
Worthily purchased, take my daughter. But
If thou dost break her virgin-knot before
All sanctimonious[6] ceremonies may
With full and holy rite be ministered,
No sweet aspersion[7] shall the heavens let fall
To make this contract grow[8]; but barren hate,
Sour-eyed disdain, and discord shall bestrew 20
The union of your bed with weeds so loathly
That you shall hate it both. Therefore take heed,
As Hymen's[9] lamps shall light you.
FERDINAND. As I hope
For quiet days, fair issue,[10] and long life,
With such love as 'tis now, the murkiest den,
The most opportune place, the strong'st suggestion[11]
Our worser genius[12] can shall never melt
Mine honor into lust to take away
The edge of that day's celebration
When I shall think or Phoebus' steeds are foundered 30
Or night kept chained below.[13]

[1]I.e., a great part of. [2]Hand over. [3]Exceptionally.
[4]Come limping; i.e., she will excel all praise. [5]I.e., even if a god had said the contrary.
[6]Religious. [7]Blessing; literally, sprinkling. [8]Prosper. [9]The god of marriage.
[10]Children. [11]Temptation. [12]Evil angel.
[13]Either the horses of the Sun have fallen or Night has been imprisoned; i.e., my wedding day, when night seems never to come.

PROSPERO. Fairly spoke.
Sit then and talk with her. She is thine own.
Ferdinand and Miranda move aside.
What, Ariel, my industrious servant, Ariel!

Enter Ariel.

ARIEL.
What would my potent master? Here I am.
PROSPERO.
Thou and thy meaner fellows your last service
Did worthily perform, and I must use you
In such another trick. Go bring the rabble,
O'er whom I give thee power, here to this place.
Incite them to quick motion, for I must
Bestow upon the eyes of this young couple 40
Some vanity[14] of mine art. It is my promise,
And they expect it from me.
ARIEL. Presently?[15]
PROSPERO. Ay, with a twink.[16]
ARIEL.
Before you can say "Come" and "Go,"
And breathe twice, and cry "So, so,"
Each one, tripping on his toe,
Will be here with mop[17] and mow.
Do you love me, master? No?
PROSPERO.
Dearly, my delicate Ariel. Do not approach
Till thou dost hear me call.
ARIEL. Well; I conceive.[18] 50
He exits.
PROSPERO, *to Ferdinand.*
Look thou be true; do not give dalliance[19]
Too much the rein. The strongest oaths are straw
To th' fire i' th' blood. Be more abstemious,
Or else goodnight your vow.
FERDINAND. I warrant you, sir,
The white cold virgin snow upon my heart
Abates the ardor of my liver.[20]
PROSPERO. Well.—
Now come, my Ariel. Bring a corollary[21]
Rather than want[22] a spirit. Appear, and pertly.
Soft music.[23]
No tongue. All eyes. Be silent.

[14]Display. [15]At once. [16]The twinkling of an eye. [17]Grimace.
[18]Understand. [19]Fondling. [20]Passion. The liver was regarded as the seat of passion.
[21]Excess; i.e., too many rather than too few. [22]Be without.
[23]Prospero now produces a little wedding masque in honor not only of the lovers, Ferdinand and Miranda, but as a compliment to the Princess Elizabeth and her bridegroom.

Enter Iris.[24]

IRIS.
Ceres,[25] most bounteous lady, thy rich leas[26] 60
Of wheat, rye, barley, vetches, oats, and peas;
Thy turfy mountains, where live nibbling sheep,
And flat meads[27] thatched with stover,[28] them to keep;
Thy banks with pionèd and twillèd brims,[29]
Which spongy April at thy hest[30] betrims[31]
To make cold nymphs chaste crowns; and thy broom[32] groves,
Whose shadow the dismissèd[33] bachelor loves,
Being lass-lorn;[34] thy poll-clipped[35] vineyard,
And thy sea marge,[36] sterile and rocky hard,
Where thou thyself dost air—the Queen o' th' sky,[37] 70
Whose wat'ry arch[38] and messenger am I,
Bids thee leave these, and with her sovereign grace,
Here on this grass-plot, in this very place,
To come and sport. Her peacocks[39] fly amain.[40]
Approach, rich Ceres, her to entertain.

Enter Ceres.

CERES.
Hail, many-colored messenger, that ne'er
Dost disobey the wife of Jupiter;
Who with thy saffron[41] wings upon my flowers
Diffusest honey drops, refreshing showers;
And with each end of thy blue bow dost crown 80
My bosky[42] acres and my unshrubbed down,[43]
Rich scarf[44] to my proud earth. Why hath thy queen
Summoned me hither to this short-grassed green?

IRIS.
A contract of true love to celebrate,
And some donation[45] freely to estate[46]
On the blest lovers.

[24]The female messenger of the gods, also the personification of the rainbow.
[25]Goddess of corn and plenty. [26]Arable lands. [27]Meadows.
[28]Covered over with grass for fodder.
[29]A difficult phrase, much disputed and emended. The likeliest explanation is that *pioned* means dug, and *twilled,* heaped up; i.e., with high banks.
[30]Command.
[31]Trims with wild flowers, especially kingcups, a kind of buttercup that grows by streams.
[32]A shrub with yellow flowers. [33]Rejected. [34]Without his girl.
[35]Poles embraced by vines. [36]Seashore. [37]The goddess Juno, wife of Jupiter.
[38]I.e., the rainbow. [39]Birds sacred to Juno. [40]Swiftly. [41]Yellow.
[42]Wooded. [43]Rolling, open country, without shrubs. [44]Adornment.
[45]Present. [46]Donate.

CERES. Tell me, heavenly bow,
If Venus or her son, as thou dost know,
Do now attend the Queen? Since they did plot
The means that dusky Dis[47] my daughter got,
Her and her blind boy's[48] scandaled[49] company 90
I have forsworn.

IRIS. Of her society
Be not afraid. I meet her deity
Cutting the clouds towards Paphos,[50] and her son
Dove-drawn[51] with her. Here thought they to have done
Some wanton charm upon this man and maid,
Whose vows are that no bed-right shall be paid
Till Hymen's torch[52] be lighted—but in vain.
Mars's hot minion[53] is returned again;
Her waspish-headed[54] son has broke his arrows,
Swears he will shoot no more, but play with sparrows, 100
And be a boy right out.

Juno descends.

CERES. Highest queen of state,
Great Juno comes. I know her by her gait.

JUNO.
How does my bounteous sister? Go with me
To bless this twain, that they may prosperous be
And honored in their issue.

They sing.

JUNO.
Honor, riches, marriage-blessing,
Long continuance, and increasing,
Hourly joys be still[55] *upon you.*
Juno sings her blessings on you.

CERES.
Earth's increase, foison[56] *plenty,* 110
Barns and garners never empty,
Vines with clust'ring bunches growing,
Plants with goodly burden bowing;
Spring come to you at the farthest
In the very end of harvest.[57]
Scarcity and want shall shun you.
Ceres' blessing so is on you.

[47]Pluto, god of the underworld, and so dark. He seized Ceres' daughter Persephone and carried her down to his kingdom. [48]Cupid. [49]Scandalous.
[50]In Sicily, a town sacred to Venus. [51]In a chariot drawn by doves.
[52]The torches of the wedding god were lit to escort bride and bridegroom to bed.
[53]Mars' lusty darling; i.e., Venus. [54]Quick-tempered. [55]Always.
[56]Bounteous harvest.
[57]May spring follow autumn; i.e., may there be no bitterness of winter in your lives.

FERDINAND.
This is a most majestic vision, and
Harmonious charmingly. May I be bold
To think these spirits?

PROSPERO. Spirits, which by mine art 120
I have from their confines[58] called to enact
My present fancies.[59]

FERDINAND. Let me live here ever.
So rare a wondered[60] father and a wife
Makes this place paradise.

Juno and Ceres whisper, and send Iris on employment.

PROSPERO. Sweet now, silence.
Juno and Ceres whisper seriously.
There's something else to do. Hush, and be mute,
Or else our spell is marred.

IRIS.
You nymphs, called naiads[61] of the windring[62] brooks,
With your sedged[63] crowns and ever-harmless looks,
Leave your crisp[64] channels and on this green land 130
Answer your summons, Juno does command.
Come, temperate[65] nymphs, and help to celebrate
A contract of true love. Be not too late.

Enter certain Nymphs.

You sunburned sicklemen,[66] of August weary,
Come hither from the furrow and be merry.
Make holiday: your rye-straw hats put on,
And these fresh nymphs encounter every one
In country footing.[67]

Enter certain Reapers, properly habited. They join with the Nymphs in a graceful dance, towards the end whereof Prospero starts suddenly and speaks.

PROSPERO.
I had forgot that foul conspiracy
Of the beast Caliban and his confederates 140
Against my life. The minute of their plot
Is almost come.—Well done. Avoid.[68] No more.

To a strange, hollow, and confused noise, the spirits heavily[69] vanish.

FERDINAND, *to Miranda.*
This is strange. Your father's in some passion
That works him strongly.

[58]Places of confinement. [59]Devices of my imagination. [60]Wonderful.
[61]Water nymphs. [62]Wandering, winding. [63]Covered with sedge, a kind of water grass.
[64]Curled, rippling. [65]Chaste. [66]Reapers, who cut the wheat with sickles.
[67]Dancing. [68]Be gone. [69]Sorrowfully.

MIRANDA. Never till this day
Saw I him touched with anger, so distempered.[70]

PROSPERO, *to Ferdinand.*
You do look, my son, in a moved sort,[71]
As if you were dismayed. Be cheerful, sir.
Our revels now are ended. These our actors,
As I foretold you, were all spirits and
Are melted into air, into thin air; 150
And like the baseless fabric[72] of this vision,
The cloud-capped towers, the gorgeous palaces,
The solemn temples, the great globe itself,
Yea, all which it inherit, shall dissolve,
And, like this insubstantial pageant faded,
Leave not a rack[73] behind. We are such stuff
As dreams are made on, and our little life
Is rounded[74] with a sleep. Sir, I am vexed.
Bear with my weakness. My old brain is troubled.
Be not disturbed with my infirmity. 160
If you be pleased, retire into my cell
And there repose. A turn or two I'll walk
To still my beating[75] mind.

FERDINAND/MIRANDA. We wish your peace.

They exit.

Enter Ariel.

PROSPERO.
Come with a thought. I thank thee, Ariel. Come.

ARIEL.
Thy thoughts I cleave to. What's thy pleasure?

PROSPERO. Spirit,
We must prepare to meet with Caliban.

ARIEL.
Ay, my commander. When I presented[76] Ceres,
I thought to have told thee of it, but I feared
Lest I might anger thee.

PROSPERO.
Say again, where didst thou leave these varlets[77]? 170

ARIEL.
I told you, sir, they were red-hot with drinking,
So full of valor that they smote the air

[70]Disturbed. [71]As if you were distressed. [72]Unreal stuff. [73]Cloud.
[74]Completed; i.e., life is but a moment of consciousness in an everlasting sleep.
[75]Throbbing.
[76]Either introduced the masques or acted the part of Ceres. There is, however, very little time for a change of costume between Ariel's exit at l. 50 and Ceres' entrance at l. 75.
[77]Knaves.

For breathing in their faces, beat the ground
For kissing of their feet; yet always bending[78]
Towards their project. Then I beat my tabor,
At which, like unbacked[79] colts, they pricked their ears,
Advanced their eyelids, lifted up their noses
As[80] they smelt music. So I charmed their ears
That, calf-like, they my lowing followed through
Toothed briers, sharp furzes,[81] prickling gorse, and thorns, 180
Which entered their frail shins. At last I left them
I' th' filthy-mantled[82] pool beyond your cell,
There dancing up to th' chins, that the foul lake
O'erstunk their feet.

PROSPERO. This was well done, my bird.
Thy shape invisible retain thou still.
The trumpery[83] in my house, go bring it hither
For stale[84] to catch these thieves.

ARIEL. I go, I go. *He exits.*

PROSPERO.
A devil, a born devil, on whose nature
Nurture[85] can never stick; on whom my pains,
Humanely taken, all, all lost, quite lost; 190
And as with age his body uglier grows,
So his mind cankers.[86] I will plague them all
Even to roaring.

Enter Ariel, loaden with glistering[87] apparel, etc.

Come, hang them on this line.[88]

Enter Caliban, Stephano, and Trinculo, all wet, as Prospero and Ariel look on.

CALIBAN. Pray you, tread softly that the blind mole may not hear a footfall. We now are near his cell.

STEPHANO. Monster, your fairy, which you say is a harmless fairy, has done little better than played the jack[89] with us.

TRINCULO. Monster, I do smell all horse piss, at which my nose is in great indignation.

STEPHANO. So is mine.—Do you hear, monster. If I should take a dis- 200
pleasure against you, look you—

TRINCULO. Thou wert but a lost monster.

CALIBAN.
Good my lord, give me thy favor still.

[78]Inclining. [79]Never saddled. [80]As if. [81]Prickly, bushy shrubs. [82]Covered with scum. [83]Cheap finery. [84]Bait. [85]Education. [86]Grows malignant. [87]Glittering. [88]Lime tree. [89]Knave.

Be patient, for the prize I'll bring thee to
Shall hoodwink this mischance.[90] Therefore speak softly.
All's hushed as midnight yet.

TRINCULO. Ay, but to lose our bottles in the pool!

STEPHANO. There is not only disgrace and dishonor in that, monster, but an infinite loss.

TRINCULO. That's more to me than my wetting. Yet this is your harmless fairy, monster! 210

STEPHANO. I will fetch off[91] my bottle, though I be o'er ears[92] for my labor.

CALIBAN.
Prithee, my king, be quiet. Seest thou here,
This is the mouth o' th' cell. No noise, and enter.
Do that good mischief which may make this island
Thine own forever, and I, thy Caliban,
For aye thy foot-licker.

STEPHANO. Give me thy hand. I do begin to have bloody thoughts.

TRINCULO, *seeing the apparel.* O King Stephano,[93] O peer, O worthy Stephano, look what a wardrobe here is for thee! 220

CALIBAN.
Let it alone, thou fool. It is but trash.

TRINCULO. Oho, monster, we know what belongs to a frippery.[94] *He puts on one of the gowns.* O King Stephano.

STEPHANO. Put off that gown, Trinculo. By this hand, I'll have that gown.

TRINCULO. Thy Grace shall have it.

CALIBAN.
The dropsy drown this fool! What do you mean
To dote thus on such luggage?[95] Let 't alone,
And do the murder first. If he awake, 230
From toe to crown he'll fill our skins with pinches,
Make us strange stuff.

STEPHANO. Be you quiet, monster.—Mistress[96] Line, is not this my jerkin? *He takes a jacket from the tree.* Now is the jerkin under the line.—Now, jerkin, you are like to lose your hair and prove a bald jerkin.

[90]Blindfold this misfortune; i.e., make us forget it. [91]Rescue.

[92]Up to my ears in the pond.

[93]The sight of all the clothes reminds Trinculo of the old ballad "King Stephen was a worthy peer."

[94]Secondhand-clothing shop. [95]Baggage, which will hinder them.

[96]These lines have mystified editors, and indeed elaborate Elizabethan jokes, especially when made by a half-drunk butler, are not always easy to follow. Stephano begins by addressing the lime tree as "Mistress Line" as if he were talking to the dealer in an old-clothes shop. He appeals to her to decide whether the jerkin is his or Trinculo's. Having taken the jerkin for himself, he then puns on "under the line" (i.e., south of the Equator), where the various skin diseases common to long voyages in the tropics caused hair to fall out. Trinculo caps the remark by a further pun on "line and level"; i.e., "on the square," literally, by the bricklayer's instruments for ensuring perpendicular and horizontal exactness.

TRINCULO. Do, do. We steal by line and level, an 't like your Grace.

STEPHANO. I thank thee for that jest. Here's a garment for 't. Wit shall not go unrewarded while I am king of this country. "Steal by line and level" is an excellent pass of pate.[97] There's another garment for 't. 240

TRINCULO. Monster, come, put some lime[98] upon your fingers, and away with the rest.

CALIBAN.
I will have none on't. We shall lose our time
And all be turned to barnacles[99] or to apes
With foreheads villainous low.

STEPHANO. Monster, lay to your fingers. Help to bear this away where my hogshead of wine is, or I'll turn you out of my kingdom. Go to, carry this. 250

TRINCULO. And this.

STEPHANO. Ay, and this.

A noise of hunters heard.

Enter divers spirits in shape of dogs and hounds, hunting them about, Prospero and Ariel setting them on.

PROSPERO. Hey, Mountain, hey!

ARIEL. Silver! There it goes, Silver!

PROSPERO.
Fury, Fury! There, Tyrant,[100] there! Hark, hark!

Caliban, Stephano, and Trinculo are driven off.

Go, charge my goblins that they grind their joints
With dry convulsions, shorten up their sinews
With agèd cramps,[101] and more pinch-spotted make them
Than pard[102] or cat o' mountain.[103]

ARIEL. Hark, they roar.

PROSPERO.
Let them be hunted soundly. At this hour 260
Lies at my mercy all mine enemies.
Shortly shall all my labors end, and thou
Shalt have the air at freedom. For a little
Follow and do me service.

They exit.

[97]Sally of wit.

[98]Birdlime, to make them sticky, because Caliban disgustedly drops the garments.

[99]Tree geese. It was believed, even by serious botanists, that from the barnacles, which grow on rotten wood immersed in sea water, emerged creatures which grew into birds, like geese.

[100]Mountain, Silver, Fury, and Tyrant are the names of the hounds.

[101]The cramps that come with old age. [102]Leopard.

[103]Mountain cat.

ACT 5

SCENE 1

Enter Prospero in his magic robes, and Ariel.

PROSPERO.
Now does my project gather to a head.
My charms crack not,[1] my spirits obey, and time
Goes upright with his carriage.[2]—How's the day?

ARIEL.
On the sixth hour, at which time, my lord,
You said our work should cease.

PROSPERO. I did say so
When first I raised the tempest. Say, my spirit,
How fares the King and 's followers?

ARIEL. Confined together
In the same fashion as you gave in charge,
Just as you left them; all prisoners, sir,
In the line grove[3] which weather-fends[4] your cell. 10
They cannot budge till your release. The King,
His brother, and yours abide all three distracted,
And the remainder mourning over them,
Brimful of sorrow and dismay; but chiefly
Him that you termed, sir, the good old Lord Gonzalo.
His tears runs down his beard like winter's drops
From eaves of reeds.[5] Your charm so strongly works 'em
That if you now beheld them, your affections
Would become tender.

PROSPERO. Dost thou think so, spirit?

ARIEL.
Mine would, sir, were I human.

PROSPERO. And mine shall. 20
Hast thou, which art but air, a touch, a feeling
Of their afflictions, and shall not myself,
One of their kind, that relish[6] all as sharply
Passion[7] as they, be kindlier moved than thou art?
Though with their high wrongs I am struck to th' quick,
Yet with my nobler reason 'gainst my fury
Do I take part. The rarer action is
In virtue than in vengeance.[8] They being penitent,
The sole drift[9] of my purpose doth extend

[1]Do not break down.
[2]Time bears his burden without stopping, because it has now grown so light.
[3]Grove of lime trees. [4]Protects from the weather. [5]A thatched roof.
[6]Feel. [7]Suffer emotion.
[8]It is a finer action to be self-controlled than to take vengeance.
[9]Intention.

Not a frown further. Go, release them, Ariel. 30
My charms I'll break, their senses I'll restore,
And they shall be themselves.

ARIEL. I'll fetch them, sir.

He exits.

Prospero draws a large circle on the stage with his staff.

PROSPERO.

You elves of hills, brooks, standing lakes, and groves,
And you that on the sands with printless foot[10]
Do chase the ebbing Neptune,[11] and do fly him
When he comes back; you demi-puppets[12] that
By moonshine do the green sour[13] ringlets[14] make,
Whereof the ewe not bites; and you whose pastime
Is to make midnight mushrumps,[15] that rejoice
To hear the solemn curfew[16]; by whose aid, 40
Weak masters though you be, I have bedimmed
The noontide sun, called forth the mutinous winds,
And 'twixt the green sea and the azured vault[17]
Set roaring war; to the dread rattling thunder
Have I given fire, and rifted[18] Jove's stout oak
With his own bolt; the strong-based promontory
Have I made shake, and by the spurs[19] plucked up
The pine and cedar; graves at my command
Have waked their sleepers, oped, and let 'em forth
By my so potent art. But this rough magic 50
I here abjure, and when I have required
Some heavenly music, which even now I do,

Prospero gestures with his staff.

To work mine end upon their senses that
This airy charm is for, I'll break my staff,
Bury it certain fathoms in the earth,
And deeper than did ever plummet[20] sound
I'll drown my book.[21]

Solemn music.

Here enters Ariel before; then Alonso with a frantic gesture, attended by Gonzalo; Sebastian and Antonio in like manner attended by Adrian and Francisco. They all enter the circle which Prospero had made, and there stand charmed; which Prospero observing, speaks.

[10]Without leaving a footprint. [11]I.e., the outgoing tide.
[12]Tiny creatures, half the size of a puppet. [13]I.e., unacceptable to the cattle.
[14]Fairy rings, circles of grass on a darker green often seen in English meadows, supposed to be caused by the fairies dancing in a ring.
[15]As mushrooms grow in a single night, they were thought to be the work of fairies.
[16]Rung at 9 P.M. to warn people to go indoors. Thereafter the fairies can work without interruption.
[17]Blue sky. [18]Split. [19]Roots. [20]See III.3.101, note 43. [21]I.e., of magic spells.

A solemn air,[22] and the best comforter
To an unsettled fancy, cure thy brains,
Now useless, boiled,[23] within thy skull. There stand, 60
For you are spell-stopped.—
Holy Gonzalo, honorable man,
Mine eyes, e'en sociable[24] to the show of thine,
Fall[25] fellowly[26] drops.—The charm dissolves apace,[27]
And as the morning steals upon the night,
Melting the darkness, so their rising senses
Begin to chase the ignorant fumes[28] that mantle[29]
Their clearer reason.—O good Gonzalo,
My true preserver and a loyal sir
To him thou follow'st, I will pay thy graces 70
Home,[30] both in word and deed.—Most cruelly
Didst thou, Alonso, use me and my daughter.
Thy brother was a furtherer in the act.—
Thou art pinched for 't now, Sebastian.—Flesh and blood,
You, brother mine, that entertained ambition,
Expelled remorse[31] and nature, whom, with Sebastian,
Whose inward pinches therefore are most strong,
Would here have killed your king, I do forgive thee,
Unnatural though thou art.—Their understanding
Begins to swell, and the approaching tide 80
Will shortly fill the reasonable shore[32]
That now lies foul and muddy. Not one of them
That yet looks on me, or would know me.—Ariel,
Fetch me the hat and rapier in my cell.

Ariel exits and at once returns with Prospero's ducal robes.

I will discase[33] me and myself present
As I was sometime Milan.[34]—Quickly, spirit,
Thou shalt ere long be free.

ARIEL *sings, and helps to attire him.*

Where the bee sucks, there suck I.
In a cowslip's bell I lie.
There I couch[35] when owls do cry. 90
On the bat's back I do fly
After summer merrily.
Merrily, merrily shall I live now
Under the blossom that hangs on the bow.

[22]Musical air. [23]Boiling. [24]Of fellow feeling. [25]Let fall. [26]In sympathy. [27]Quickly. [28]Mists of ignorance. [29]Cloak. [30]Reward your kind deeds fully. [31]Pity. [32]Shore of reason, i.e., sanity is beginning to flow back like the incoming tide. [33]Remove my outer garment. Prospero is still in his magic robe and so not recognized by his former associates. [34]As I was when I was Duke of Milan. [35]Lie.

PROSPERO.
Why, that's my dainty Ariel. I shall miss
Thee, but yet thou shalt have freedom. So, so, so.[36]
To the King's ship, invisible as thou art.
There shalt thou find the mariners asleep
Under the hatches. The master and the boatswain
Being awake, enforce them to this place, 100
And presently, I prithee.

ARIEL.
I drink the air before me, and return
Or ere your pulse twice beat. *He exits.*

GONZALO.
All torment, trouble, wonder, and amazement
Inhabits here. Some heavenly power guide us
Out of this fearful country!

PROSPERO, *to Alonso.* Behold, sir king,
The wrongèd Duke of Milan, Prospero.
For more assurance that a living prince
Does now speak to thee, I embrace thy body.
He embraces Alonso.
And to thee and thy company I bid 110
A hearty welcome.

ALONSO. Whe'er thou be'st he or no,
Or some enchanted trifle[37] to abuse[38] me
(As late I have been) I not know. Thy pulse
Beats as of[39] flesh and blood; and since I saw thee,
Th' affliction of my mind amends, with which
I fear a madness held me. This must crave,
An if this be at all,[40] a most strange story.
Thy dukedom I resign, and do entreat
Thou pardon me my wrongs.[41] But how should Prospero
Be living and be here?

PROSPERO, *to Gonzalo.* First, noble friend, 120
Let me embrace thine age, whose honor cannot
Be measured or confined.

GONZALO. Whether this be
Or be not, I'll not swear.

PROSPERO. You do yet taste
Some subtleties[42] o' th' isle, that will not let you
Believe things certain. Welcome, my friends all.
Aside to Sebastian and Antonio. But you, my brace of lords, were
I so minded,
I here could pluck his Highness' frown upon you
And justify you traitors. At this time
I will tell no tales.

[36]"So," used thus, often indicates movement. [37]Hallucination caused by enchantment.
[38]Deceive. [39]As if composed of. [40]If all this is really true.
[41]The wrongs that I have committed. [42]You still have the taste of the magic nature.

SEBASTIAN, *aside.* The devil speaks in him.
PROSPERO, *aside to Sebastian.* No. 130
To Antonio. For you, most wicked sir, whom to call brother
Would even infect my mouth, I do forgive
Thy rankest fault, all of them, and require
My dukedom of thee, which perforce I know
Thou must restore.
ALONSO. If thou be'st Prospero,
Give us particulars of thy preservation,
How thou hast met us here, whom three hours since
Were wracked upon this shore, where I have lost—
How sharp the point of this remembrance is!—
My dear son Ferdinand.
PROSPERO. I am woe for 't,[43] sir. 140
ALONSO.
Irreparable is the loss, and patience
Says it is past her cure.
PROSPERO. I rather think
You have not sought her help, of whose soft grace,
For the like loss, I have her sovereign[44] aid
And rest myself content.
ALONSO. You the like loss?
PROSPERO.
As great to me as late, and supportable
To make the dear loss have I means much weaker
Than you may call to comfort you, for I
Have lost my daughter.
ALONSO. A daughter? 150
O heavens, that they were living both in Naples,
The King and Queen there! That they were, I wish
Myself were mudded in that oozy bed
Where my son lies!—When did you lose your daughter?
PROSPERO.
In this last tempest. I perceive these lords
At this encounter do so much admire[45]
That they devour their reason, and scarce think
Their eyes do offices of truth,[46] their words
Are natural breath.—But howsoe'er you have
Been justled from your senses, know for certain 160
That I am Prospero and that very duke
Which was thrust forth of Milan, who most strangely
Upon this shore, where you were wracked, was landed
To be the lord on 't. No more yet of this,
For 'tis a chronicle of day by day,
Not a relation for a breakfast, nor
Befitting this first meeting. *To Alonso.* Welcome, sir.

[43]Sorry for it. [44]All-powerful. [45]Wonder. [46]True service.

This cell's my court. Here have I few attendants,
And subjects none abroad. Pray you, look in.
My dukedom since you have given me again, 170
I will requite[47] you with as good a thing,
At least bring forth a wonder to content you
As much as me my dukedom.

Here Prospero discovers[48] Ferdinand and Miranda, playing at chess.

MIRANDA, *to Ferdinand.*
Sweet lord, you play me false.

FERDINAND. No, my dearest love,
I would not for the world.

MIRANDA.
Yes, for a score of kingdoms you should wrangle,
And I would call it fair play.

ALONSO. If this prove
A vision of the island, one dear son
Shall I twice lose.

SEBASTIAN. A most high miracle!

FERDINAND, *seeing Alonso and coming forward.*
Though the seas threaten, they are merciful. 180
I have cursed them without cause. *He kneels.*

ALONSO. Now, all the blessings
Of a glad father compass thee about!
Arise, and say how thou cam'st here.

Ferdinand stands.

MIRANDA, *rising and coming forward.* O wonder!
How many goodly creatures are there here!
How beauteous mankind is! O, brave new world
That has such people in 't!

PROSPERO. 'Tis new to thee.

ALONSO, *to Ferdinand.*
What is this maid with whom thou wast at play?
Your eld'st[49] acquaintance cannot be three hours.
Is she the goddess that hath severed us
And brought us thus together?

FERDINAND. Sir, she is mortal, 190
But by immortal providence she's mine.
I chose her when I could not ask my father
For his advice, nor thought I had one. She
Is daughter to this famous Duke of Milan,
Of whom so often I have heard renown,
But never saw before, of whom I have
Received a second life; and second father
This lady makes him to me.

ALONSO. I am hers.
But, O, how oddly will it sound that I
Must ask my child[50] forgiveness!

[47]Pay back. [48]Reveals by drawing back the curtain. [49]Longest.
[50]I.e., Miranda, who is about to become his daughter-in-law.

PROSPERO. There, sir, stop. 200
Let us not burden our remembrances with
A heaviness that's gone.

GONZALO. I have inly wept
Or should have spoke ere this. Look down, you gods,
And on this couple drop a blessèd crown,
For it is you that have chalked forth[51] the way
Which brought us hither.

ALONSO. I say "Amen," Gonzalo.

GONZALO.
Was Milan thrust from Milan, that his issue
Should become kings of Naples? O, rejoice
Beyond a common joy, and set it down
With gold on lasting pillars: in one voyage 210
Did Claribel her husband find at Tunis,
And Ferdinand, her brother, found a wife
Where he himself was lost; Prospero his dukedom
In a poor isle; and all of us ourselves
When no man was his own.

ALONSO, *to Ferdinand and Miranda.* Give me your hands.
Let grief and sorrow still embrace[52] his heart
That doth not wish you joy!

GONZALO. Be it so. Amen.

Enter Ariel, with the Master and Boatswain amazedly[53] following.

O, look, sir, look, sir, here is more of us.
I prophesied if a gallows were on land, 220
This fellow could not drown.[54] Now, blasphemy,[55]
That swear'st grace o'erboard,[56] not an oath on shore?
Hast thou no mouth by land? What is the news?

BOATSWAIN.
The best news is that we have safely found
Our king and company. The next: our ship,
Which, but three glasses since, we gave out split,
Is tight and yare and bravely rigged as when
We first put out to sea.

ARIEL, *aside to Prospero.* Sir, all this service
Have I done since I went.

PROSPERO, *aside to Ariel.* My tricksy[57] spirit!

ALONSO.
These are not natural events. They strengthen 230
From strange to stranger.—Say, how came you hither?

BOATSWAIN.
If I did think, sir, I were well awake,
I'd strive to tell you. We were dead of sleep

[51]Marked out (as with a chalk line). [52]Always cling to. [53]In amazement.
[54]See I.1.31–32. [55]You blasphemer.
[56]That by your swearing drives the grace of God away. [57]Clever.

And—how, we know not—all clapped[58] under hatches,
Where, but even now, with strange and several noises
Of roaring, shrieking, howling, jingling chains,
And more diversity of sounds, all horrible,
We were awaked, straightway at liberty,
Where we, in all her trim, freshly beheld
Our royal, good, and gallant ship, our master 240
Cap'ring[59] to eye her. On a trice, so please you,
Even in a dream were we divided from them
And were brought moping hither.

ARIEL, *aside to Prospero.* Was 't well done?

PROSPERO, *aside to Ariel.*
Bravely, my diligence. Thou shalt be free.

ALONSO.
This is as strange a maze as e'er men trod,
And there is in this business more than nature
Was ever conduct of. Some oracle
Must rectify[60] our knowledge.

PROSPERO. Sir, my liege,
Do not infest your mind with beating on
The strangeness of this business. At picked leisure, 250
Which shall be shortly, single[61] I'll resolve[62] you,
Which to you shall seem probable, of every
These happened accidents; till when, be cheerful
And think of each thing well. *Aside to Ariel.*
Come hither, spirit;
Set Caliban and his companions free.
Untie the spell. *Ariel exits.* How fares my gracious sir?
There are yet missing of your company
Some few odd lads that you remember not.

Enter Ariel, driving in Caliban, Stephano, and Trinculo in their stolen apparel.

STEPHANO. Every man shift for all the rest, and let no man take care for himself, for all is but fortune. Coraggio,[63] bull monster, coraggio. 260

TRINCULO. If these be true spies[64] which I wear in my head, here's a goodly sight.

CALIBAN. O Setebos, these be brave spirits indeed! How fine my master is! I am afraid he will chastise me.

SEBASTIAN. Ha, ha!
What things are these, my Lord Antonio?
Will money buy 'em?

ANTONIO. Very like. One of them
Is a plain fish and no doubt marketable.

[58]Shut in. [59]Dancing for joy. [60]Prove true. [61]Alone.
[62]Inform. [63]Courage. [64]Eyes.

PROSPERO.
Mark but the badges[65] of these men, my lords, 270
Then say if they be true. This misshapen knave,
His mother was a witch, and one so strong
That could control the moon, make flows and ebbs,
And deal in her command[66] without her power.[67]
These three have robbed me, and this demi-devil,
For he's a bastard one, had plotted with them
To take my life. Two of these fellows you
Must know and own. This thing of darkness I
Acknowledge mine.

CALIBAN. I shall be pinched to death.

ALONSO.
Is not this Stephano, my drunken butler? 280

SEBASTIAN. He is drunk now. Where had he wine?

ALONSO.
And Trinculo is reeling ripe. Where should they
Find this grand liquor that hath gilded 'em?[68]
To Trinculo. How cam'st thou in this pickle?

TRINCULO. I have been in such a pickle since I saw you last that I fear me will never out of my bones. I shall not fear flyblowing.[69]

SEBASTIAN. Why, how now, Stephano?

STEPHANO. O, touch me not! I am not Stephano, but a cramp.

PROSPERO. You'd be king o' the isle, sirrah?

STEPHANO. I should have been a sore one, then. 290

ALONSO, *indicating Caliban.*
This is as strange a thing as e'er I looked on.

PROSPERO.
He is as disproportioned in his manners[70]
As in his shape. *To Caliban.* Go, sirrah, to my cell.
Take with you your companions. As you look
To have my pardon, trim[71] it handsomely.

CALIBAN.
Ay, that I will, and I'll be wise hereafter
And seek for grace.[72] What a thrice-double ass
Was I to take this drunkard for a god,
And worship this dull fool!

PROSPERO. Go to, away!

ALONSO, *to Stephano and Trinculo.*
Hence, and bestow your luggage where you found it. 300

SEBASTIAN. Or stole it, rather.

Caliban, Stephano, and Trinculo exit.

PROSPERO.
Sir, I invite your Highness and your train
To my poor cell, where you shall take your rest

[65]A nobleman's servant wore a badge displaying his master's coat of arms.
[66]I.e., take over the moon's power of controlling the tides.
[67]Without the aid of the moon. [68]Made them glow.
[69]I.e., shall never go bad, for I have been so well pickled.
[70]Behavior. [71]Make tidy. [72]Favor.

For this one night, which part of it I'll waste
With such discourse as, I not doubt, shall make it
Go quick away: the story of my life
And the particular accidents[73] gone by
Since I came to this isle. And in the morn
I'll bring you to your ship, and so to Naples,
Where I have hope to see the nuptial 310
Of these our dear-belovèd solemnized,
And thence retire me to my Milan, where
Every third thought shall be my grave.

ALONSO. I long
To hear the story of your life, which must
Take the ear strangely.

PROSPERO. I'll deliver all,
And promise you calm seas, auspicious[74] gales,
And sail so expeditious that shall catch
Your royal fleet far off. *Aside to Ariel.* My Ariel, chick,
That is thy charge. Then to the elements
Be free, and fare thou well.—Please you, draw near. 320

They all exit.

EPILOGUE,[75]

spoken by Prospero.

Now my charms are all o'erthrown,
And what strength I have 's mine own,
Which is most faint. Now 'tis true
I must be here confined by you,
Or sent to Naples. Let me not,
Since I have my dukedom got
And pardoned the deceiver, dwell
In this bare island by your spell,
But release me from my bands[76]
With the help of your good hands.[77] 10
Gentle breath[78] of yours my sails
Must fill, or else my project fails,
Which was to please. Now I want[79]
Spirits to enforce, art to enchant,
And my ending is despair,
Unless I be relieved by prayer,
Which pierces so that it assaults
Mercy itself, and frees all faults.
As you from crimes would pardoned be,
Let your indulgence set me free. 20

He exits.

[73]Events. [74]Favorable.
[75]A concluding epilogue is fairly common in Elizabethan plays, especially those performed before a courtly audience. It is usually a conventional apology for the inadequacies of the performance and an appeal for applause.
[76]Bonds. [77]I.e., by clapping. [78]Kindly criticism. [79]Lack.

John Milton
(1608–1674)

John Milton was one of the world's greatest and most influential poets, the author of the definitive English epic, the last towering figure of the European Renaissance, and a prominent partisan, on the Puritan and Republican side, in the momentous English Civil War, fought in the seventeenth century over issues of church and civil government. The issues of his day in certain ways mark the beginning of the modern political era.

Milton was born in London in 1608; his father, disinherited for converting from Roman Catholicism to Protestantism, was a successful businessman (and a gifted musician) who found it proper, the family having risen in the world, to give his son John the best of humanist educations, through private tutors and at St. Paul's School. The precocious evidence John gave of intellectual and poetic ability made the church, rather than a more worldly profession, seem his natural calling, and, although Milton later in his life chose not to be ordained, he remained grateful that his education had not been narrow and merely pragmatic. In 1625 he entered Cambridge University; there, after problems with his first tutor, he achieved distinction, though he chafed at what he considered the university's intellectual conservatism. At Cambridge he earned the nickname "The Lady" because of his delicate good looks, his religious seriousness, and the ascetic tendencies that (as his later life would reveal) coexisted with a passionate and even sensuous side of his character. In 1629 he wrote his first great poem in English (he composed in Latin and Italian also), the *Ode on the Morning of Christ's Nativity,* which anticipates *Paradise Lost* by its references to the overcoming of the heathen gods at the coming of Christ. After taking his B.A. in 1629 and his M.A. in 1632, he retired to his father's estate, where he studied intensively, preparing himself, as he felt, for some great enterprise in literature or public life. Before the age of thirty, when this period of retirement ended, Milton had also written *L'Allegro* and *Il Penseroso* (twin poems praising, respectively, the cheerful and contemplative characters), the brief masque *Arcades,* the longer masque *Comus* (a platonic celebration of the triumph of virtue and chastity over evil and sensuality), and *Lycidas,* a pastoral elegy that some critics consider the greatest lyric poem in English. Written to commemorate the premature death of an acquaintance, *Lycidas* dramatizes Milton's concern over the mystery and injustice of death, the possible unfulfillment of his own hopes in life, and the assurance of spiritual victory through submission to divine Providence—all this in the context of an almost unbelievably rich pattern of classical allusion and creative imitation.

In 1638 Milton left England to spend fifteen months on the Continent, mainly in Florence, Rome, and Naples. During this "grand tour," he met a number of eminent men of learning and culture, including Hugo Grotius, the Dutch expositor of international law, and Galileo, who at the time was in trouble with the Church because of his speculations in astronomy. Milton was for the most part gratified by his reception, which gave him increased confidence in his powers. It is both characteristic and prophetic that, as Milton later put it, he "openly defended . . . the reformed religion in the very metropolis of popery" despite plots said to have been hatched against him by the Jesuits. He aborted a trip to Sicily and Greece when he learned of the outbreak of civil disturbances in England, and some months later he was back there. Around the time of his return, King Charles I was forced to convene a hostile Parliament; over the next two decades, during which many battles were fought between the Royalists/Episcopalians and their Republican/Puritan antagonists, the Presbyterian party first rose to power, being succeeded later by an even more radical party of Independents; Charles I was beheaded in 1649; a republic (the "Commonwealth") was declared; Oliver Cromwell was named Lord Protector (dictator, virtually) between 1653 and his death in 1658; his ineffectual son Richard succeeded him but abdicated; and finally, to Milton's dismay, the monarchy was restored in 1660 in the person of the heretofore exiled Charles II.

After returning from his Italian tour, Milton pondered an ambitious literary work, particularly a drama on an English or scriptural subject, and it is possible that he did begin a play on his favorite topic, the fall of humankind, which he later chose for his epic. But his sense of commitment to the cause of religious and civil freedom as he understood it made him put aside his ambitious literary plans for the greater part of two decades, during which he composed many treatises and pamphlets directed against his personal and political enemies and those of the revolutionary government. His first efforts dealt with the evils of the episcopal system (rule by bishops) in the Church of England, an issue that Milton conceived to be part of the larger issue of general human freedom. An ill-considered marriage, which for a time was broken off, prompted a series of tracts boldly arguing for the legality of divorce on grounds of incompatibility, a position that in its alleged libertinism alienated not only the Royalists but the Presbyterians as well. In 1644, in opposition to a parliamentary censorship law, he wrote *Areopagitica,* a classic rationale for freedom of the press and individual responsibility that, curiously, uses arguments against an artificially sheltered, untested virtue that seem at least to be similar to those Satan and Eve use in Book IX of *Paradise Lost* to justify eating the fruit of the Tree of Knowledge of Good and Evil. He also wrote on education, history, and theology. In 1649, the year Charles was beheaded, he wrote *The Tenure of Kings and Magistrates,* a tract that earned him the favor of the regicide regime by arguing that a king's tenure and very life were subject to the will of the people. Milton was made Latin Secretary in the government, a post that involved foreign correspondence and official defenses of the regime against its opponents at home and abroad. But his eyesight, which for some time had been failing, deteriorated until total blindness came in 1652, after which time he was gradually relieved of official duties and was able (especially after 1654) to turn his energies again to literature. Milton was sustained in part by his belief that loss of literal vision was compensated by a strengthened inner light and vision—a hope that was later expressed movingly in the hymn to light that opens Book III of *Paradise Lost.* In the latter 1650s he began his epic *Paradise Lost,* which he completed by 1665; it was published in 1667, in a ten-book version that he later altered to twelve. Meanwhile, the restoration of the Royalists brought Milton's life into peril, though for reasons not entirely clear he was released, after being arrested, with just a fine. Thereafter, despite reduced financial circumstances and some friction with his relatives, he lived a fairly regular and outwardly uneventful life, composing verse (the inspiration for which is said to have come mainly in the winter during the hours before dawn), singing and playing music, walking in his garden, meditating and being read to, receiving admiring visitors. In 1671 were published the "short epic" *Paradise Regained* (a sequel to *Paradise Lost* that centers on Christ's resistance to Satan's temptations in the wilderness as narrated, for example, in the fourth chapter of Matthew's gospel) and the drama *Samson Agonistes*. The latter, based on the story of Samson in Judges 13–16, has irresistible autobiographical relevance as the story of a blinded hero, living his last days in captivity, who undergoes a spiritual renewal and finally triumphs over his wicked captors. *Samson Agonistes* has been praised as the nearest English equivalent of ancient Greek drama and as a work on the same level of greatness as *Paradise Lost*. Thus Milton's stature as a poet is attested in all three traditional poetic modes: lyric (his sonnets must be mentioned along with works already named), epic, and drama. After a final pamphlet in 1673 warning against resurgent "popery" under Charles II, Milton died, in 1674, of gout.

In *Paradise Lost* Milton aimed at grandeur, comprehensiveness, and universal relevance. This is most clearly true in the choice of subject itself, for to Christians no theme could be more awesome than that of the fall of our first parents, which "Brought death into the world, and all our woe" (I.3) and the counterpoised Redemption that is outlined theologically in Book III and historically in Book XII. It was a theme, Milton tells us, that he was "long choosing and beginning late" (IX.26). The question to what extent the poem transcends the interests of Christian theology has been much debated. Milton's approach can be cited on both sides: On one hand, he is careful to integrate into his poem the whole fabric of pagan antiquity, thus achieving something like mythic universality; on the other hand, he takes pains to distinguish the distorted versions of truth expressed by the pagans from the literal and naked truth of biblical revelation on which his epic is based. The pagan gods, for example, are the true devils in disguise. Aiming at universality, Milton subordinates in *Paradise Lost* the notes of political and religious partisanship he sounds in his tracts. His political opposition to the restored monarchy appears chiefly by innuendo, and although there is in the poem some peculiarly Miltonic theology (his apparently unorthodox view of the Trinity, for example), and some direct sectarian invective, his treatment of the Son's redeeming self-sacrifice is essentially in the mainstream of Christian tradition.

Whatever limitations Milton's theology, idiosyncratic or more broadly Christian, may imply for the persuasiveness of his *answers*, it is hardly questionable that he defines compellingly the ultimate *issues* explored in all theodicies (attempts to "justify God's ways")—questions of cosmic justice, the origin of physical suffering and of moral evil, and the relationship of these to human free will. Indeed, the motif of liberty is at the heart of *Paradise Lost* and is perhaps the most vital link between the values of the poem and those Milton cherished in his personal and public life. Moreover, his treatment of liberty is complex. His belief that we stand or fall essentially on our own, without either the compulsion or the effective help of earthly authority, is part both of radical Protestantism and of modern libertarianism. Yet it is also true that the Son's obedient submission to the Father is for Milton the prototype of all true liberty. *Paradise Lost* thus raises some questions about the relationship between absolute human autonomy and acquiescence in the cosmic order that assert themselves in any age, under any system.

Milton's claim to have raised the subject matter of epic to a new level of grandeur and truth is itself part of the epic tradition. In this claim he is following the precedent of Virgil, who (to apply a phrase of Milton's) also tried to be "doctrinal and exemplary to a nation" by implicitly substituting for Homeric objectivity and concern with war a set of values that, while still communal, are more inward, ethical, philosophical. Like Virgil, Milton tells a story whose historical, and not merely mythical, dimension is important to him. The matter is of the greatest possible public import. Yet Milton, while insisting on the literal existence of hell, heaven, and the earthly paradise, gives them also an extended spiritual dimension. Hell is a state of mind, one that Satan creates for himself and carries with him everywhere he goes. Paradise is lost by Adam and Eve, but Book XII assures them that, through faith in and imitation of the redeeming Son of God, they can achieve "A Paradise within thee, happier far" (XII.587) than the one they forfeited. In a passage where he both acknowledges and repudiates his epic ancestry, Milton substitutes for "Wars, hitherto the only argument / Heroic deemed" the "better fortitude / Of patience and heroic martyrdom" (IX.28–32). It is enormously significant that in *Paradise Regained* he balances against the "disobedience" *(Paradise Lost,* I.1) of the fallen Adam not the climax of Jesus' public life in the Passion and Resurrection but the most private incident in his career, the obedience to his Father manifested in the Temptation in the Wilderness.

Much of the power of *Paradise Lost* comes from qualities that might seem alien to the opinionated Milton: a kind of evenhandedness or at least intellectual and imaginative empathy that he extends to ideas and characters opposed to what he is championing. Easily the best example is Satan, one of the supreme triumphs of literary characterization. Shelley and other interpreters in the Romantic tradition went so far as to consider him the real hero of the poem. That was surely not Milton's intent, yet it remains true that Satan is given dramatic autonomy. He is treated with grandeur, in, for example, Books I and II, and sometimes with touches of pathos as in the soliloquy that opens Book IV. (Ironically, as it has seemed to some readers, the Milton who in life defended rebellion against monarchy identifies the insubordinate Satan in the epic poem as the origin of evil.) Belial, whom Milton calls "lewd," "gross," and one who could "make the worse appear / The better reason" (I.490–491; II.113–114), is endowed with breathtaking imagination and made to utter a noble encomium on the human mind, "this intellectual being, / Those thoughts that wander through eternity" (II.147–148). And, as mentioned earlier, Satan and Eve sound somewhat like *Areopagitica.* Such anomalies can suggest a failure by Milton to control the tone of the poem or else, as William Blake's *Marriage of Heaven and Hell* charges, a lapse in self-knowledge by Milton. Against which it might be argued that in true epics heroes and heroism have worthy, however evil, adversaries. If the temptations and errors of Satan and humankind had no plausibility and seductive power, their fall would seem not tragic but fatuous.

Paradise Lost is a consummate work of art, in architecture and surface. The sublime hymn to light in Book III, for example, serves structurally to emphasize the emergence of Satan, and the poem, from the sulfurous horror of hell and darkness to the ambrosial brightness of heaven. These same transitional lines also mark the elaborate parallelism between the council scenes of Books II and III, including the antithetical offers by Satan and the Son of God, respectively, to destroy and to save humanity. Figures of speech are powerful; the modulation of the metaphysical praise of light into Milton's mourning for his personal blindness is capped by a sublime metaphor in which the outward-radiating natural sun that fertilizes the world and dispels darkness becomes the emblem of a fertilizing spiritual sun that shines toward a center:

> So much the rather thou celestial Light
> Shine inward, and the mind through all her powers
> Irradiate, there plant eyes, all mist from thence
> Purge and disperse, that I may see and tell
> Of things invisible to mortal sight. (III.51–55)

The grand style in *Paradise Lost,* the style generally called "Miltonic," is the high ceremonial one that Milton recognized as appropriate to epic. Vowel sounds are often sonorous ("To bellow through the vast and boundless deep"—I.177). Half-repetitions (the "Miltonic turn") have an effect that can be both epigrammatic and swelling ("Thus high uplifted beyond hope, aspires / Beyond thus high"—II.7–8). Exotic, evocative proper names are heaped on one another (IV.268–83). Long-extended similes are used as in Homer and Virgil (I.302–313, 768–792), often with even greater psychological suggestiveness. Sentences are prolonged through whole "verse paragraphs," the sense drawn out inexorably from one line to the next—sustaining elevation of tone or creating suspense or introducing bold imaginative surprises that one is not allowed to linger over as climaxes.

In fact, however, the poem has many voices. The speeches in the infernal council in Book II are not just magniloquent; they are specifically modeled on parliamentary oratory. Moreover, even this section is varied within itself, the headlong Moloch sounding not at all like the subtle, intellectually speculative Belial. Satan's soliloquy in Book IV is in itself a mixture of tones, from subdued remorse to anguish to desperate recklessness. Adam and Eve can address each other like royal consorts in their unfallen state but with colloquial acrimony at the end of Book IX after their fall. Milton abandoned the dramatic genre for the epic, but he retained the variety of speech one finds in the best dramas.

Although Shakespeare may have been rated as highly, Milton's influence on English literature in the 150 years following his death in 1674 was much greater, indeed incalculable. To imitate Shakespeare, who created in his plays and poems a score of different worlds, is nearly equivalent to imitating the whole variety of human experience. But Milton's work, despite its wide variety of genre and tone, has a kind of finished architectural coherence that, blending with the events of his life and his forcefully expressed ideas, has the effect of a single massive literary and personal presence. He dominated the eighteenth-century imagination as Newton dominated its science, partly because of his grandeur of manner, partly because of the fascination of his theological argument, partly because he synthesized while he transformed a vast body of ancient and Renaissance culture. The English Romantic poets, especially Blake, Wordsworth, Shelley, and Keats, all took Milton, in one way or another, as a touchstone for their most considered statements about human values and the place of humanity in the cosmic order.

FURTHER READING: William Riley Parker's *Milton: A Biography,* 2 vols., 1968, is a standard modern biography; as an introduction, Douglas Bush's *John Milton: A Sketch of His Life and Writings,* 1964, is recommended. Also very good, especially for new readers of Milton, is A. N. Wilson, *The Life of John Milton,* 1983. The subject identified in his book's title is treated topically in James Thorpe, *John Milton: The Inner Life,* 1983. An admirable introduction to *Paradise Lost,* discussing the poem as psychology, doctrine, drama, and from several other perspectives, is G. K. Hunter, *Paradise Lost,* 1980. Arnold Stein's *Answerable Style: Essays on "Paradise Lost,"* 1953, is an excellent study of the poem. C. S. Lewis's *A Preface to "Paradise Lost,"* 1942, rev. 1960, discusses the poem's ideas and style in a lively, rigorous fashion, in the contexts of classical and Christian tradition. An excellent introduction is David M. Miller's *John Milton: Poetry,* 1978, which includes a biographical introduction and discussions of *Paradise Lost, Paradise Regained,* and *Samson Agonistes,* in a manner suitable for general readers. Northrop Frye's *The Return of Eden,* 1965, contains excellent essays, including Frye's celebrated analysis of foreground and background action in *Paradise Lost.* Douglas Bush's *"Paradise Lost" in Our Time,* 1945, discusses the negative reaction to Milton's epic in the twentieth century, Milton's religion and ethics, methods of characterization, and other topics. Helen Gardner's *A Reading of "Paradise Lost,"* 1965, contains a helpful discussion of the modern meaning of *Paradise Lost;* an appendix contains Gardner's earlier (1948) and important essay on Satan and his appeal as a heroic figure. Joan Webber's *Milton and His Epic Tradition,* 1979, surveys early epics beginning with Homer and relates this tradition to *Paradise Lost* and *Paradise Regained. New Essays on "Paradise Lost,"* ed. Thomas Kranidas, 1971, contains good essays on the theme of Book III, innocence and experience in *Paradise Lost,* the Fall, and other topics. Don Cameron Allen's *The Harmonious Vision,* 1954, deals with nearly all of Milton's poetry in an attempt to define the overall unity of Milton's thought. Gender issues are addressed by Phillip Gallagher in *Milton, the Bible, and Misogyny,* 1990; and by John T. Shawcross in his biography *John Milton,* 1993. The classic attack on Milton as a sexist is Mary Wollstonecraft's in *A Vindication of the Rights of Woman,* 1792. Diane Kelsey McColley, *Milton's Eve,* 1983, asserts Eve's positive role in the scheme of *Paradise Lost,* taking issue with the idea that the portrayal of her is antifeminist. Catherine Belsey's *John Milton,* 1988, in the Rereading Literature series, reconsiders critical issues from a contemporary theoretical perspective. On Milton's status as humanist and his political background, see Joan S. Bennett, *Reviving Liberty,* 1989.

PARADISE LOST

Selected Notes by James Holly Hanford

THE VERSE: The measure is English heroic verse without rime, as that of Homer in Greek, and of Virgil in Latin; rime being no necessary adjunct or true ornament of poem or good verse, in longer works especially, but the invention of a barbarous age, to set off wretched matter and lame metre; graced indeed since by the use of some famous modern poets, carried away by custom, but much to their own vexation, hindrance, and constraint to express many things otherwise, and for the most part worse than else they would have expressed them. Not without cause, therefore, some both Italian and Spanish poets of prime note have rejected rime both in longer and shorter works, as have also, long since, our best English tragedies, as a thing of itself, to all judicious ears, trivial and of no true musical delight; which consists only in apt numbers, fit quantity of syllables, and the sense variously drawn out from one verse into another, not in the jingling sound of like endings, a fault avoided by the learned ancients both in poetry and all good oratory. This neglect then of rime so little is to be taken for a defect, though it may seem so perhaps to vulgar readers, that it rather is to be esteemed an example set, the first in English, of ancient liberty recovered to heroic poem from the troublesome and modern bondage of riming.

from BOOK I

THE ARGUMENT

This first book proposes first in brief the whole subject, Man's disobedience, and the loss thereupon of Paradise wherein he was placed: then touches the prime cause of his fall, the Serpent, or rather Satan in the Serpent; who revolting from God, and drawing to his side many legions of angels, was by the command of God driven out of Heaven with all his crew into the great Deep. Which action passed over, the poem hastes into the midst of things, presenting Satan with his angels now fallen into Hell, described here, not in the center (for Heaven and Earth may be supposed as yet not made, certainly not yet accursed) but in a place of utter darkness, fitliest called Chaos. Here Satan with his angels lying on the burning lake, thunderstruck and astonished, after a certain space recovers, as from confusion, calls up him who next in order and dignity lay by him; they confer of their miserable fall. Satan awakens all his legions, who lay till then in the same manner confounded; they rise: their numbers, array of battle, their chief leaders named, according to the idols known afterwards in Canaan and the countries adjoining. To these Satan directs his speech, comforts them with hope yet of regaining Heaven, but tells them lastly of a new world and new kind of creature to be created, according to an ancient prophecy or report in Heaven; for that angels were long before this visible creation, was the opinion of many ancient Fathers. To find out the truth of this prophecy, and what to determine thereon, he refers to a full council. What his associates thence attempt. Pandemonium the palace of Satan rises, suddenly built out of the Deep; the infernal peers there sit in council.

Of Man's first disobedience, and the fruit*
Of that forbidden tree, whose mortal taste
Brought death into the world, and all our woe,
With loss of Eden, till one greater Man
Restore us, and regain the blissful seat,

*All footnotes are by Hanford unless otherwise stated. Some notes are abridged. The Arguments are by Milton.

1 ff. Milton follows the conventional epic procedure in his opening. For the various elements or steps in this procedure, cf. *Iliad* i. 1 ff., *Aeneid* i. 1 ff.

2. mortal, deadly.

Sing Heavenly Muse, that on the secret top
Of Oreb, or of Sinai, didst inspire
That shepherd, who first taught the chosen seed,
In the beginning how the Heavens and Earth
Rose out of Chaos; or if Sion hill 10
Delight thee more, and Siloa's brook that flowed
Fast by the oracle of God, I thence
Invoke thy aid to my adventurous song,
That with no middle flight intends to soar
Above the Aonian mount, while it pursues
Things unattempted yet in prose or rhyme.
And chiefly thou O Spirit, that dost prefer
Before all temples the upright heart and pure,
Instruct me, for thou knowest; thou from the first
Wast present, and with mighty wings outspread 20
Dove-like sat'st brooding on the vast Abyss
And madest it pregnant: what in me is dark
Illumine, what is low raise and support;
That to the height of this great argument
I may assert Eternal Providence,
And justify the ways of God to men.
Say first, for Heaven hides nothing from thy view,
Nor the deep tract of Hell, say first what cause
Moved our grand parents in that happy state,
Favored of Heaven so highly, to fall off 30
From their Creator, and transgress his will
For one restraint, lords of the world besides?
Who first seduced them to that foul revolt?
The infernal Serpent; he it was, whose guile,
Stirred up with envy and revenge, deceived
The Mother of Mankind; what time his pride

6. Heavenly Muse. The Christian poets adopted the classical muse of Astronomy, whose name (Urania, the Heavenly) qualified her for the new office, as the patroness of their divine inspiration. Milton identifies her with the Holy Spirit of Scripture and so turns his invocation into a prayer.

7. of Oreb or of Sinai. Cf. Exod. 19:20 and Deut. 4:10. Milton carefully follows Scripture even in its apparent contradiction.

8. That shepherd, Moses.

10. Sion hill, Mount Zion, one of the hills on which the city of Jerusalem is built.

11. Siloa's brook, "the waters of Shiloah that go softly" (Isa. 8:6).

12. Fast by the oracle of God, i.e., close to the Temple of Jerusalem.

15. Above the Aonian mount. Milton means that his theme is loftier than any that the Pagan poets could sing. The **Aonian mount** is Helicon, sacred to the muses.

21. Gen. 1:1, 2. The Hebrew word translated in the Authorized Version "moved" can also be rendered "brooded." The Holy Spirit takes the form of a dove in Luke 3:22.

24. argument, subject.

25. assert, maintain the cause of.

26. justify, make apparent the justice of. The real issue in Milton's mind is whether an intelligent and righteous will rules man's destiny, or a blind or capricious or malicious one. The justification hinges on (1) the affirmation of man's freedom and responsibility, and (2) the scheme of salvation through Christ which is set forth in the poem as a whole.

29. our grand parents, i.e., our original ancestors, Adam and Eve.

32. for, because of.

Had cast him out from Heaven, with all his host
Of rebel angels, by whose aid aspiring
To set himself in glory above his peers,
He trusted to have equalled the Most High, 40
If he opposed; and with ambitious aim
Against the throne and monarchy of God,
Raised impious war in Heaven and battle proud
With vain attempt. Him the Almighty Power
Hurled headlong flaming from the ethereal sky
With hideous ruin and combustion down
To bottomless perdition, there to dwell
In adamantine chains and penal fire,
Who durst defy the Omnipotent to arms.
Nine times the space that measures day and night 50
To mortal men, he with his horrid crew
Lay vanquished, rolling in the fiery gulf
Confounded though immortal. But his doom
Reserved him to more wrath; for now the thought
Both of lost happiness and lasting pain
Torments him; round he throws his baleful eyes,
That witnessed huge affliction and dismay
Mixed with obdurate pride and steadfast hate.
At once as far as angel's ken he views
The dismal situation waste and wild: 60
A dungeon horrible, on all sides round
As one great furnace flamed, yet from those flames
No light, but rather darkness visible
Served only to discover sights of woe,
Regions of sorrow, doleful shades, where peace
And rest can never dwell, hope never comes
That comes to all; but torture without end
Still urges, and a fiery deluge, fed
With ever-burning sulphur unconsumed:
Such place Eternal Justice had prepared 70
For those rebellious, here their prison ordained
In utter darkness, and their portion set
As far removed from God and light of Heaven
As from the center thrice to the utmost pole.
Oh how unlike the place from whence they fell!

53. Confounded, defeated and ruined. **57. witnessed,** bore witness to, expressed.

59. angel's ken, an angel's range of vision.

63. darkness visible, darkness not quite absolute. The words perhaps express also the idea of the darkness having a positive quality.

64. discover, reveal.

66. Cf. Dante, *Inferno,* iii: "All hope abandon, ye who enter here."

68. urges, afflicts.

72. utter, outer—as in Scripture. But there is also a suggestion of the modern sense.

74. from the center thrice to the utmost pole. The center is the center of the earth; the **utmost pole** is the pole of the outermost sphere of the visible heavens. The distance from hell to the empyrean (the supreme heaven) is ordinarily felt by Milton to be much greater than this exact calculation makes it.

There the companions of his fall, o'erwhelmed
With floods and whirlwinds of tempestuous fire,
He soon discerns, and weltering by his side
One next himself in power, and next in crime,
Long after known in Palestine, and named 80
Beëlzebub. To whom the Arch-Enemy,
And thence in Heaven called Satan, with bold words
Breaking the horrid silence thus began.
"If thou beest he; but Oh how fallen! how changed
From him, who in the happy realms of light
Clothed with transcendent brightness didst outshine
Myriads, though bright: if he whom mutual league,
United thoughts and counsels, equal hope
And hazard in the glorious enterprise,
Joined with me once, now misery hath joined 90
In equal ruin: into what pit thou seest
From what height fallen, so much the stronger proved
He with his thunder, and till then who knew
The force of those dire arms? Yet not for those,
Nor what the potent victor in his rage
Can else inflict, do I repent or change,
Though changed in outward luster, that fixed mind
And high disdain, from sense of injured merit,
That with the Mightiest raised me to contend,
And to the fierce contention brought along 100
Innumerable force of spirits armed
That durst dislike his reign, and, me preferring,
His utmost power with adverse power opposed
In dubious battle on the plains of Heaven,
And shook his throne. What though the field be lost?
All is not lost; the unconquerable will,
And study of revenge, immortal hate,
And courage never to submit or yield:
And what is else not to be overcome?
That glory never shall his wrath or might 110
Extort from me. To bow and sue for grace
With suppliant knee, and deify his power
Who from the terror of this arm so late
Doubted his empire, that were low indeed,
That were an ignominy and shame beneath
This downfall; since by fate the strength of gods
And this empyreal substance cannot fail,
Since through experience of this great event,

81. Beëlzebub. Cf. Matt. 12:24. **Arch-Enemy.** Satan in Hebrew means "adversary."

84 ff. If thou beest he, etc. The sentence is not completed. The entire speech is made disjointed to indicate Satan's emotional stress.

110. That glory, i.e., the glory of subduing Satan's will.

114. Doubted, feared for.

116 ff. since by fate, etc. Satan denies that he was created by and is therefore subordinate to God. His egotism makes him a polytheist or more specifically a Manichee.

In arms not worse, in foresight much advanced,
We may with more successful hope resolve 120
To wage by force or guile eternal war,
Irreconcilable to our grand foe,
Who now triumphs, and in the excess of joy
Sole reigning holds the tyranny of Heaven."
So spake the apostate Angel, though in pain,
Vaunting aloud, but racked with deep despair;
And him thus answered soon his bold compeer.
"O Prince, O Chief of many thronëd Powers,
That led the embattled Seraphim to war
Under thy conduct, and in dreadful deeds 130
Fearless, endangered Heaven's perpetual King,
And put to proof his high supremacy,
Whether upheld by strength, or chance, or fate;
Too well I see and rue the dire event,
That with sad overthrow and foul defeat
Hath lost us Heaven, and all this mighty host
In horrible destruction laid thus low,
As far as gods and heavenly essences
Can perish: for the mind and spirit remains
Invincible, and vigor soon returns, 140
Though all our glory extinct, and happy state
Here swallowed up in endless misery.
But what if he our conqueror (whom I now
Of force believe almighty, since no less
Than such could have o'erpowered such force as ours)
Have left us this our spirit and strength entire,
Strongly to suffer and support our pains,
That we may so suffice his vengeful ire,
Or do him mightier service as his thralls
By right of war, whate'er his business be, 150
Here in the heart of Hell to work in fire,
Or do his errands in the gloomy deep;
What can it then avail, though yet we feel
Strength undiminished, or eternal being
To undergo eternal punishment?"
Whereto with speedy words the Arch-Fiend replied.
"Fallen Cherub, to be weak is miserable,
Doing or suffering: but of this be sure,
To do aught good never will be our task,
But ever to do ill our sole delight, 160
As being the contrary to his high will
Whom we resist. If then his providence
Out of our evil seek to bring forth good,

120. successful hope, hope of success.

128–29. throned Powers, Seraphim. The angelic orders in Dante and the Catholic theologians are, from lowest to highest, as follows: Angels, Archangels, Principalities, Powers, Virtues, Dominions, Thrones, Cherubim, Seraphim. Milton uses many of these names interchangeably.

148. suffice, satisfy.

Our labor must be to pervert that end,
And out of good still to find means of evil;
Which oft-times may succeed, so as perhaps
Shall grieve him, if I fail not, and disturb
His inmost counsels from their destined aim.
But see the angry victor hath recalled
His ministers of vengeance and pursuit 170
Back to the gates of Heaven; the sulphurous hail
Shot after us in storm, o'erblown hath laid
The fiery surge, that from the precipice
Of Heaven received us falling, and the thunder,
Winged with red lightning and impetuous rage,
Perhaps hath spent his shafts, and ceases now
To bellow through the vast and boundless deep.
Let us not slip the occasion, whether scorn,
Or satiate fury yield it from our foe.
Seest thou yon dreary plain, forlorn and wild, 180
The seat of desolation, void of light,
Save what the glimmering of these livid flames
Casts pale and dreadful? Thither let us tend
From off the tossing of these fiery waves,
There rest, if any rest can harbor there,
And re-assembling our afflicted powers,
Consult how we may henceforth most offend
Our enemy, our own loss how repair,
How overcome this dire calamity,
What reinforcement we may gain from hope; 190
If not, what resolution from despair."
Thus Satan talking to his nearest mate
With head uplift above the wave, and eyes
That sparkling blazed; his other parts besides,
Prone on the flood, extended long and large,
Lay floating many a rood, in bulk as huge
As whom the fables name of monstrous size,
Titanian or Earth-born, that warred on Jove,
Briareos or Typhon, whom the den
By ancient Tarsus held, or that sea-beast 200
Leviathan, which God of all his works
Created hugest that swim the ocean stream:
Him haply slumbering on the Norway foam,

167. if I fail not, unless I mistake. **178. Let us not slip,** Let us not let slip.
186. afflicted powers, routed forces. **197. as whom,** as those whom.
198. Titanian, or Earth-born. The Titans and Giants in classical mythology were sons of Heaven (Uranus) and Earth (Ge).
199. Briareos or Typhon. The former was a Titan, the latter a Giant.
201. Leviathan. Cf. Psalms 104:26, and Job 41. The monster was often associated with the whale or the crocodile. Milton does not specifically identify it with either, although he suggests characteristics of both.
203 ff. This is an old traveller's story, the most familiar version being in the *Arabian Nights.* **night-foundered,** i.e., lost in the darkness as completely as a sunken ship is lost in the ocean.

The pilot of some small night-foundered skiff,
Deeming some island, oft, as seamen tell,
With fixëd anchor in his scaly rind,
Moors by his side under the lee, while night
Invests the sea, and wishëd morn delays:
So stretched out huge in length the Arch-Fiend lay
Chained on the burning lake; nor ever thence 210
Had risen or heaved his head, but that the will
And high permission of all-ruling Heaven
Left him at large to his own dark designs,
That with reiterated crimes he might
Heap on himself damnation, while he sought
Evil to others, and enraged might see
How all his malice served but to bring forth
Infinite goodness, grace and mercy shown
On Man by him seduced, but on himself
Treble confusion, wrath and vengeance poured. 220
  Forthwith upright he rears from off the pool
His mighty stature; on each hand the flames
Driven backward slope their pointing spires, and rolled
In billows, leave in the midst a horrid vale.
Then with expanded wings he steers his flight
Aloft, incumbent on the dusky air
That felt unusual weight, till on dry land
He lights, if it were land that ever burned
With solid, as the lake with liquid fire,
And such appeared in hue; as when the force 230
Of subterranean wind transports a hill
Torn from Pelorus, or the shattered side
Of thundering Ætna, whose combustible
And fuellëd entrails thence conceiving fire,
Sublimed with mineral fury, aid the winds,
And leave a singëd bottom all involved
With stench and smoke: such resting found the sole
Of unblest feet. Him followed his next mate,
Both glorying to have scaped the Stygian flood
As gods, and by their own recovered strength, 240
Not by the sufferance of supernal power.
  "Is this the region, this the soil, the clime,"
Said then the lost Archangel, "this the seat
That we must change for Heaven, this mournful gloom

208. invests, covers as with a garment.

226. incumbent, leaning on.

232. Pelorus, Cape Faro in Sicily, near Mt. Aetna.

235. sublimed, sublimated, converted to gaseous form, but also with the original sense of lifted up; **the winds,** i.e., the winds or gases within the earth which were supposed to be the cause of earthquakes.

236. involved, wrapped in.

244. change for, take in exchange for.

For that celestial light? Be it so, since he
Who now is sovran can dispose and bid
What shall be right. Farthest from him is best,
Whom reason hath equalled, force hath made supreme
Above his equals. Farewell happy fields
Where joy for ever dwells: Hail horrors, hail 250
Infernal world, and thou profoundest Hell
Receive thy new possessor: one who brings
A mind not to be changed by place or time.
The mind is its own place, and in itself
Can make a Heaven of Hell, a Hell of Heaven.
What matter where, if I be still the same,
And what I should be, all but less than he
Whom thunder hath made greater? Here at least
We shall be free; the Almighty hath not built
Here for his envy, will not drive us hence: 260
Here we may reign secure, and in my choice
To reign is worth ambition, though in Hell:
Better to reign in Hell than serve in Heaven.
But wherefore let we then our faithful friends,
The associates and co-partners of our loss,
Lie thus astonished on the oblivious pool,
And call them not to share with us their part
In this unhappy mansion; or once more
With rallied arms to try what may be yet
Regained in Heaven, or what more lost in Hell?" 270
So Satan spake, and him Beëlzebub
Thus answered. "Leader of those armies bright,
Which but the Omnipotent none could have foiled,
If once they hear that voice, their liveliest pledge
Of hope in fears and dangers, heard so oft
In worst extremes, and on the perilous edge
Of battle when it raged, in all assaults
Their surest signal, they will soon resume
New courage and revive, though now they lie
Grovelling and prostrate on yon lake of fire, 280
As we erewhile, astounded and amazed;
No wonder, fallen such a pernicious height!"
He scarce had ceased when the superior Fiend
Was moving toward the shore; his ponderous shield,

246. sovran, sovereign, supreme in power.

254–255. The supremacy of the mind is one of Milton's favorite ideas. The corollary of this utterance of Satan's is to be found in IV, 20–23.

257–258. all but less than, etc. Usually interpreted as "all but equal to" or "less only than," but other or additional meanings are possible. "What I should be" is, in Satan's mind, God's equal. He would rather be anything but inferior and, since the mind is its own place, he *can* be equal in everything but power. The confusion of grammar is no greater than the confusion of frustrated human emotion.

266. oblivious, causing forgetfulness. Milton is thinking of the classical Lethe.

276. edge. Latin *acies,* edge, means also battle line.

Ethereal temper, massy, large, and round,
Behind him cast; the broad circumference
Hung on his shoulders like the moon, whose orb
Through optic glass the Tuscan artist views
At evening from the top of Fesolë,
Or in Valdarno, to descry new lands, 290
Rivers or mountains in her spotty globe.
His spear, to equal which the tallest pine
Hewn on Norwegian hills, to be the mast
Of some great ammiral, were but a wand,
He walked with, to support uneasy steps
Over the burning marle, not like those steps
On Heaven's azure; and the torrid clime
Smote on him sore besides, vaulted with fire.
Nathless he so endured, till on the beach
Of that inflamëd sea, he stood and called 300
His legions, angel forms, who lay entranced,
Thick as autumnal leaves that strew the brooks
In Vallombrosa, where the Etrurian shades
High over-arched embower; or scattered sedge
Afloat, when with fierce winds Orion armed
Hath vexed the Red-Sea coast, whose waves o'erthrew
Busiris and his Memphian chivalry
While with perfidious hatred they pursued
The sojourners of Goshen, who beheld
From the safe shore their floating carcasses 310
And broken chariot wheels; so thick bestrewn
Abject and lost lay these, covering the flood,
Under amazement of their hideous change.
He called so loud, that all the hollow deep
Of Hell resounded. "Princes, Potentates,
Warriors, the flower of Heaven, once yours, now lost,

288. the Tuscan artist, Galileo, whom Milton had visited during his stay in Italy.

289. Fesolë, Fiesole, a small town located on a hill just outside Florence.

290. Valdarno, the valley of the Arno, in which Florence is located. Galileo's last residence was at Arcetri, west of the main part of the city. He was blind or almost so when Milton visited him and lamented that he could no longer look at the universe which his discoveries had made more wonderful.

294. ammiral, admiral, flagship.

296. marle, soil.

299. Nathless, nevertheless.

302 ff. Note the series of brilliant Homeric similes used to emphasize the numbers of the fallen angels. They are compared (1) when lying on the lake, to fallen leaves and floating seaweed; (2) when flying, to a cloud of locusts; (3) when alighted, to a huge invading army.

303. Vallombrosa, a district about eighteen miles from Florence, containing a famous monastery which Milton is said to have visited. The name is Italian for "shady valley."

305. Orion, a constellation proverbially associated with storms.

307 ff. Cf. Exod. 14. **Busiris** was an ancient Egyptian king, whom Milton for some reason identifies with the Pharaoh whose hosts were drowned in the Red Sea. **Memphian** is here equivalent to Egyptian, Memphis being the ancient capital of Egypt. **The sojourners of Goshen** are, of course, the Israelites.

312. Abject, cast down (Latin *abjectus*).

If such astonishment as this can seize
Eternal spirits; or have ye chosen this place
After the toil of battle to repose
Your wearied virtue, for the ease you find 320
To slumber here, as in the vales of Heaven?
Or in this abject posture have ye sworn
To adore the conqueror, who now beholds
Cherub and Seraph rolling in the flood
With scattered arms and ensigns, till anon
His swift pursuers from Heaven gates discern
The advantage, and descending tread us down
Thus drooping, or with linkëd thunderbolts
Transfix us to the bottom of this gulf.
Awake, arise, or be for ever fallen!" 330
They heard and were abashed, and up they sprung
Upon the wing, as when men wont to watch
On duty, sleeping found by whom they dread,
Rouse and bestir themselves ere well awake.
Nor did they not perceive the evil plight
In which they were, or the fierce pains not feel;
Yet to their general's voice they soon obeyed
Innumerable. As when the potent rod
Of Amram's son in Egypt's evil day
Waved round the coast, up called a pitchy cloud 340
Of locusts, warping on the eastern wind,
That o'er the realm of impious Pharaoh hung
Like night, and darkened all the land of Nile:
So numberless were those bad angels seen
Hovering on wing under the cope of Hell
'Twixt upper, nether, and surrounding fires;
Till, as a signal given, the uplifted spear
Of their great Sultan waving to direct
Their course, in even balance down they light
On the firm brimstone, and fill all the plain; 350
A multitude, like which the populous North
Poured never from her frozen loins, to pass
Rhene or the Danaw, when her barbarous sons
Came like a deluge on the South, and spread

320. virtue, valor, strength (Latin *virtus*).
328. linkëd thunderbolts. The thunderbolts are compared to linked cannon balls.
335. Nor did they not, i.e., they did.
338 ff. As when the potent rod, etc. Cf. Exod. 10:12–15. Moses was Amram's son.
340. pitchy, dark as pitch.
341. warping, working slowly forward with a bending or swerving motion. The term is primarily nautical.
345. cope, vault or canopy.
351. A multitude, etc. Milton concentrates in a simile the history of the barbarian invasions of the Roman Empire. Successive inroads were made by the Goths, the Vandals, and the Huns.
353. Rhene, the Rhine (from Latin *Rhenus*). **Danaw,** the Danube (from German *Donau*).

Beneath Gibraltar to the Libyan sands.
Forthwith from every squadron and each band
The heads and leaders thither haste where stood
Their great commander; godlike shapes and forms
Excelling human, Princely Dignities,
And Powers that erst in Heaven sat on thrones; 360
Though of their names in heavenly records now
Be no memorial, blotted out and rased
By their rebellion from the Books of Life.
Nor had they yet among the sons of Eve
Got them new names, till wandering o'er the Earth,
Through God's high sufferance for the trial of Man,
By falsities and lies the greatest part
Of mankind they corrupted to forsake
God their Creator, and the invisible
Glory of him that made them to transform 370
Oft to the image of a brute, adorned
With gay religions full of pomp and gold,
And devils to adore for deities:
Then were they known to men by various names,
And various idols through the heathen world.

* * *

Meanwhile the wingëd heralds by command
Of sovran power, with awful ceremony
And trumpet's sound, throughout the host proclaim
A solemn council forthwith to be held
At Pandemonium, the high capitol
Of Satan and his peers; their summons called
From every band and squarëd regiment
By place or choice the worthiest; they anon
With hundreds and with thousands trooping came 760
Attended. All access was thronged, the gates
And porches wide, but chief the spacious hall
(Though like a covered field, where champions bold
Wont ride in armed, and at the Soldan's chair
Defied the best of Paynim chivalry
To mortal combat or career with lance)

355. Beneath Gibraltar, i.e., south of Gibraltar. The Vandals crossed from Spain into North Africa.

364 ff. Nor had they yet, etc. The idea that the fallen angels become the pagan divinities goes back to early Patristic sources. The identification furnishes Milton with abundant biblical and mythological data regarding the inhabitants of hell.

753. awful, awe-inspiring.

756. Pandemonium, the abode of all the demons. The name, which is a Miltonic coinage, may have been suggested by *Pantheon,* the abode of all the gods.

757 ff. their summons, etc. The council is in reality a sort of military Parliament.

763–766. The allusion is to the single combats between Pagans and Crusaders described in the Italian romances of chivalry. **Soldan** is a variant of Sultan.

Thick swarmed, both on the ground and in the air,
Brushed with the hiss of rustling wings. As bees
In spring time, when the sun with Taurus rides,
Pour forth their populous youth about the hive 770
In clusters; they among fresh dews and flowers
Fly to and fro, or on the smoothëd plank,
The suburb of their straw-built citadel,
New rubbed with balm, expatiate and confer
Their state affairs. So thick the airy crowd
Swarmed and were straitened; till the signal given,
Behold a wonder! they but now who seemed
In bigness to surpass Earth's giant sons,
Now less than smallest dwarfs, in narrow room
Throng numberless, like that Pygmean race 780
Beyond the Indian mount, or fairy elves,
Whose midnight revels, by a forest side
Or fountain, some belated peasant sees
Or dreams he sees, while overhead the Moon
Sits arbitress, and nearer to the Earth
Wheels her pale course; they on their mirth and dance
Intent, with jocund music charm his ear;
At once with joy and fear his heart rebounds.
Thus incorporeal spirits to smallest forms
Reduced their shapes immense, and were at large, 790
Though without number still, amidst the hall
Of that infernal court. But far within,
And in their own dimensions like themselves,
The great Seraphic Lords and Cherubim
In close recess and secret conclave sat,
A thousand demi-gods on golden seats,
Frequent and full. After short silence then
And summons read, the great consult began.

from BOOK II

THE ARGUMENT

The consultation begun, Satan debates whether another battle is to be hazarded for the recovery of Heaven: some advise it, others dissuade. A third proposal is

769. when the Sun with Taurus rides, i.e., when the sun is in the zodiacal sign of the Bull (between April 19 and May 20).

774. excpatiate and confer, walk abroad and discuss.

776. straitened, crowded.

780 ff. The **Indian mount** is probably Imaus in the Himalayas.

781 ff. Milton is here drawing on the traditions of English fairy poetry.

785. arbitress, spectator. **790. were at large,** had ample room.

793. like themselves, i.e., in their own shapes. **795. recess,** retirement.

797. frequent, crowded.

preferred, mentioned before by Satan, to search the truth of that prophecy or tradition in Heaven concerning another world, and another kind of creature, equal, or not much inferior, to themselves, about this time to be created. Their doubt who shall be sent on this difficult search; Satan, their chief, undertakes alone the voyage; is honoured and applauded. The council thus ended, the rest betake them several ways and to several employments, as their inclinations lead them, to entertain the time till Satan return. He passes on his journey to Hell's gates, finds them shut, and who sat there to guard them; by whom at length they are opened, and discover to him the great gulf between Hell and Heaven; with what difficulty he passes through, directed by Chaos, the Power of that place, to the sight of this new world which he sought.

High on a throne of royal state, which far
Outshone the wealth of Ormus and of Ind,
Or where the gorgeous East with richest hand
Showers on her kings barbaric pearl and gold,
Satan exalted sat, by merit raised
To that bad eminence; and from despair
Thus high uplifted beyond hope, aspires
Beyond thus high, insatiate to pursue
Vain war with Heaven, and by success untaught,
His proud imaginations thus displayed. 10
"Powers and Dominions, Deities of Heaven,
For since no deep within her gulf can hold
Immortal vigor, though oppressed and fallen,
I give not Heaven for lost. From this descent
Celestial Virtues rising, will appear
More glorious and more dread than from no fall,
And trust themselves to fear no second fate.
Me though just right, and the fixed laws of Heaven
Did first create your leader, next, free choice,
With what besides, in counsel or in fight, 20
Hath been achieved of merit, yet this loss
Thus far at least recovered, hath much more
Established in a safe unenvied throne
Yielded with full consent. The happier state
In Heaven, which follows dignity, might draw
Envy from each inferior; but who here
Will envy whom the highest place exposes
Foremost to stand against the Thunderer's aim
Your bulwark, and condemns to greatest share
Of endless pain? Where there is then no good 30
For which to strive, no strife can grow up there

2. Ormus, a city on the Persian Gulf, famous as a market for precious stones. It is often mentioned by Renaissance travelers. **Ind,** India.

4. barbaric pearl and gold. The sprinkling of powdered pearls and gold dust on a monarch at his coronation was an Oriental custom.

9. success, i.e., ill-success, the outcome of his former attempt.

17. trust themselves, etc., i.e., their experience has given them such confidence that they will not fear to fall again.

24 ff. Satan, like Belial (112 ff.), knows how to "make the worse appear the better reason."

From faction; for none sure will claim in Hell
Precedence, none whose portion is so small
Of present pain, that with ambitious mind
Will covet more. With this advantage then
To union, and firm faith, and firm accord,
More than can be in Heaven, we now return
To claim our just inheritance of old,
Surer to prosper than prosperity
Could have assured us; and by what best way, 40
Whether of open war or covert guile,
We now debate; who can advise, may speak."
  He ceased, and next him Moloch, sceptred king,
Stood up, the strongest and the fiercest spirit
That fought in Heaven; now fiercer by despair.
His trust was with the Eternal to be deemed
Equal in strength, and rather than be less
Cared not to be at all; with that care lost
Went all his fear: of God, or Hell, or worse
He recked not, and these words thereafter spake. 50
  "My sentence is for open war. Of wiles,
More unexpert, I boast not; them let those
Contrive who need, or when they need, not now.
For while they sit contriving, shall the rest,
Millions that stand in arms, and longing wait
The signal to ascend, sit lingering here
Heaven's fugitives, and for their dwelling-place
Accept this dark opprobrious den of shame,
The prison of his tyranny who reigns
By our delay? No, let us rather choose, 60
Armed with Hell flames and fury, all at once
O'er Heaven's high towers to force resistless way,
Turning our tortures into horrid arms
Against the Torturer; when to meet the noise
Of his almighty engine he shall hear
Infernal thunder, and for lightning see
Black fire and horror shot with equal rage
Among his angels, and his throne itself
Mixed with Tartarean sulphur and strange fire,
His own invented torments. But perhaps 70
The way seems difficult and steep to scale
With upright wing against a higher foe.

50. thereafter spake, spoke accordingly.

51. sentence, judgment, opinion (Latin *sententia*). Moloch is the type of blunt warrior who knows no other method of winning an object than to fight for it. Milton must have known such among the leaders of the Commonwealth.

63. tortures, i.e., the flames which torture.

65. engine, instrument—referring to the thunderbolt.

69. Tartarean, infernal (from Tartarus, a classical name for hell).

Let such bethink them, if the sleepy drench
Of that forgetful lake benumb not still,
That in our proper motion we ascend
Up to our native seat; descent and fall
To us is adverse. Who but felt of late
When the fierce foe hung on our broken rear
Insulting, and pursued us through the deep,
With what compulsion and laborious flight 80
We sunk thus low? The ascent is easy then;
The event is feared; should we again provoke
Our stronger, some worse way his wrath may find
To our destruction; if there be in Hell
Fear to be worse destroyed; what can be worse
Than to dwell here, driven out from bliss, condemned
In this abhorrëd deep to utter woe;
Where pain of unextinguishable fire
Must exercise us without hope of end
The vassals of his anger, when the scourge 90
Inexorably, and the torturing hour
Calls us to penance? More destroyed than thus
We should be quite abolished and expire.
What fear we then? what doubt we to incense
His utmost ire? which to the height enraged,
Will either quite consume us, and reduce
To nothing this essential, happier far
Than miserable to have eternal being;
Or if our substance be indeed divine,
And cannot cease to be, we are at worst 100
On this side nothing; and by proof we feel
Our power sufficient to disturb his Heaven,
And with perpetual inroads to alarm,
Though inaccessible, his fatal throne;
Which if not victory is yet revenge."
He ended frowning, and his look denounced
Desperate revenge, and battle dangerous

73. such, i.e., those who reason thus. **sleepy drench,** sleep-producing drink. The word **drench** suggests contempt.

74. forgetful, causing forgetfulness. Cf. I, 266 and note.

75–77. The natural (**proper**) motion of Spirits, as of fire, is upward. For them to fall is therefore unnatural (**adverse**).

79. Insulting. The original Latin meaning (*insultans,* leaping upon) is implied.

82. event, outcome.

89. exercise, torment.

94. what doubt we, i.e., why do we hesitate.

97. essential, essence, spiritual being.

104. fatal, upheld by fate. Admitting that the throne is so upheld, Moloch is forced to grant its inaccessibility.

106. denounced, proclaimed.

To less than gods. On the other side up rose
Belial, in act more graceful and humane;
A fairer person lost not Heaven; he seemed 110
For dignity composed and high exploit;
But all was false and hollow; though his tongue
Dropped manna, and could make the worse appear
The better reason, to perplex and dash
Maturest counsels: for his thoughts were low;
To vice industrious, but to nobler deeds
Timorous and slothful: yet he pleased the ear,
And with persuasive accent thus began.
"I should be much for open war, O Peers,
As not behind in hate, if what was urged 120
Main reason to persuade immediate war,
Did not dissuade me most, and seem to cast
Ominous conjecture on the whole success:
When he who most excels in fact of arms,
In what he counsels and in what excels
Mistrustful, grounds his courage on despair
And utter dissolution, as the scope
Of all his aim, after some dire revenge.
First, what revenge? The towers of Heaven are filled
With armëd watch, that render all access 130
Impregnable; oft on the bordering deep
Encamp their legions, or with óbscure wing
Scout far and wide into the realm of Night
Scorning surprise. Or could we break our way
By force, and at our heels all Hell should rise
With blackest insurrection, to confound
Heaven's purest light, yet our great enemy
All incorruptible would on his throne
Sit unpolluted, and the ethereal mould
Incapable of stain would soon expel 140
Her mischief, and purge off the baser fire,
Victorious. Thus repulsed, our final hope
Is flat despair; we must exasperate
The almighty victor to spend all his rage,
And that must end us, that must be our cure,
To be no more; sad cure; for who would lose,
Though full of pain, this intellectual being,
Those thoughts that wander through eternity,

109. act, bearing.

113. manna. Cf. Exod. 16:31: "the taste of it was like wafers made with honey."

119 ff. Cf. with the abrupt beginning of Moloch's speech the insinuating oratory of Belial. Like a skilled debater, he turns his opponent's own argument against him.

124. fact of arms, feat of arms (Latin *factum,* deed).

136. blackest insurrection. Cf. 65–70. Belial answers Moloch point by point.

139. mould, substance.

141. Her mischief, i.e., the damage or pollution caused by hell-fire.

To perish rather, swallowed up and lost
In the wide womb of uncreated Night, 150
Devoid of sense and motion? And who knows,
Let this be good, whether our angry foe
Can give it, or will ever? How he can
Is doubtful; that he never will is sure.
Will he, so wise, let loose at once his ire,
Belike through impotence, or unaware,
To give his enemies their wish, and end
Them in his anger, whom his anger saves
To punish endless? 'Wherefore cease we then?'
Say they who counsel war; 'we are decreed, 160
Reserved, and destined to eternal woe;
Whatever doing, what can we suffer more,
What can we suffer worse?' Is this then worst,
Thus sitting, thus consulting, thus in arms?
What when we fled amain, pursued and struck
With Heaven's afflicting thunder, and besought
The Deep to shelter us? this Hell then seemed
A refuge from those wounds. Or when we lay
Chained on the burning lake? that sure was worse.
What if the breath that kindled those grim fires 170
Awaked should blow them into sevenfold rage
And plunge us in the flames? or from above
Should intermitted vengeance arm again
His red right hand to plague us? What if all
Her stores were opened, and this firmament
Of Hell should spout her cataracts of fire,
Impendent horrors, threatening hideous fall
One day upon our heads; while we perhaps
Designing or exhorting glorious war,
Caught in a fiery tempest shall be hurled 180
Each on his rock transfixed, the sport and prey
Of racking whirlwinds, or for ever sunk
Under yon boiling ocean, wrapped in chains;
There to converse with everlasting groans,
Unrespited, unpitied, unreprieved,
Ages of hopeless end; this would be worse.
War therefore, open or concealed, alike
My voice dissuades; for what can force or guile
With him, or who deceive his mind, whose eye

152. Let this be good, i.e., granting that this (annihilation) is desirable.

156. Belike, no doubt. As frequently in Shakespeare, the word implies irony. **impotence,** lack of self-control.

165. What when, i.e., how was it when. **amain,** with all haste, precipitately.

177. Impendent, overhanging.

182. racking, twisting, torturing.

185. Note how the repetition of the prefix intensifies the effect of utter hopelessness.

186. of hopeless end, without hope of end.

Views all things at one view? He from Heaven's height 190
All these our motions vain, sees and derides;
Not more almighty to resist our might
Than wise to frustrate all our plots and wiles.
Shall we then live thus vile, the race of Heaven
Thus trampled, thus expelled to suffer here
Chains and these torments? Better these than worse,
By my advice; since fate inevitable
Subdues us, and omnipotent decree,
The victor's will. To suffer, as to do,
Our strength is equal, nor the law unjust 200
That so ordains: this was at first resolved,
If we were wise, against so great a foe
Contending, and so doubtful what might fall.
I laugh when those who at the spear are bold
And venturous, if that fail them, shrink and fear
What yet they know must follow, to endure
Exile, or ignominy, or bonds, or pain,
The sentence of their conqueror: this is now
Our doom; which if we can sustain and bear,
Our súpreme foe in time may much remit 210
His anger, and perhaps, thus far removed,
Not mind us not offending, satisfied
With what is punished; whence these raging fires
Will slacken, if his breath stir not their flames.
Our purer essence then will overcome
Their noxious vapor, or inured not feel,
Or changed at length, and to the place conformed
In temper and in nature, will receive
Familiar the fierce heat, and void of pain;
This horror will grow mild, this darkness light, 220
Besides what hope the never-ending flight
Of future days may bring, what chance, what change
Worth waiting, since our present lot appears
For happy though but ill, for ill not worst,
If we procure not to ourselves more woe."
Thus Belial with words clothed in reason's garb,
Counselled ignoble ease, and peaceful sloth,
Not peace; and after him thus Mammon spake.
"Either to disenthrone the King of Heaven
We war, if war be best, or to regain 230

191. motions, proposals, plots.

213. With what is punished, i.e., with the punishment already inflicted.

219. Familiar the fierce heat, etc., i.e., the fierce heat, by becoming familiar, will be no longer painful. The considerations which move Belial are in complete accordance with his character and philosophy.

224. For happy, etc., i.e., viewed as a happy situation the present one is bad, but it is not so bad as it might be.

Our own right lost. Him to unthrone we then
May hope, when everlasting Fate shall yield
To fickle Chance, and Chaos judge the strife:
The former, vain to hope, argues as vain
The latter; for what place can be for us
Within Heaven's bound, unless Heaven's Lord supreme
We overpower? Suppose he should relent
And publish grace to all, on promise made
Of new subjection; with what eyes could we
Stand in his presence humble, and receive 240
Strict laws imposed, to celebrate his throne
With warbled hymns, and to his Godhead sing
Forced halleluiahs; while he lordly sits
Our envied Sovran, and his altar breathes
Ambrosial odors and ambrosial flowers,
Our servile offerings. This must be our task
In Heaven, this our delight; how wearisome
Eternity so spent in worship paid
To whom we hate. Let us not then pursue,
By force impossible, by leave obtained 250
Unacceptable, though in Heaven, our state
Of splendid vassalage, but rather seek
Our own good from ourselves, and from our own
Live to ourselves, though in this vast recess,
Free, and to none accountable, preferring
Hard liberty before the easy yoke
Of servile pomp. Our greatness will appear
Then most conspicuous, when great things of small,
Useful of hurtful, prosperous of adverse
We can create, and in what place soe'er 260
Thrive under evil, and work ease out of pain
Through labor and endurance. This deep world
Of darkness do we dread? How oft amidst
Thick clouds and dark doth Heaven's all-ruling Sire
Choose to reside, his glory unobscured,
And with the majesty of darkness round
Covers his throne; from whence deep thunders roar,
Mustering their rage, and Heaven resembles Hell!
As he our darkness, cannot we his light
Imitate when we please? This desert soil 270
Wants not her hidden luster, gems and gold;
Nor want we skill or art, from whence to raise
Magnificence; and what can Heaven show more?

234. argues, proves.
249. pursue, seek to regain.
271. Wants not, is not without.

Our torments also may in length of time
Become our elements, these piercing fires
As soft as now severe, our temper changed
Into their temper; which must needs remove
The sensible of pain. All things invite
To peaceful counsels, and the settled state
Of order, how in safety best we may 280
Compose our present evils, with regard
Of what we are and where, dismissing quite
All thoughts of war: ye have what I advise."
He scarce had finished, when such murmur filled
The assembly, as when hollow rocks retain
The sound of blustering winds, which all night long
Had roused the sea, now with hoarse cadence lull
Seafaring men o'erwatched, whose bark by chance
Or pinnace anchors in a craggy bay
After the tempest: such applause was heard 290
As Mammon ended, and his sentence pleased,
Advising peace; for such another field
They dreaded worse than Hell: so much the fear
Of thunder and the sword of Michaël
Wrought still within them; and no less desire
To found this nether empire, which might rise
By policy and long process of time,
In emulation opposite to Heaven.
Which when Beëlzebub perceived, than whom,
Satan except, none higher sat, with grave 300
Aspéct he rose, and in his rising seemed
A pillar of state; deep on his front engraven
Deliberation sat and public care;
And princely counsel in his face yet shone,
Majestic though in ruin: sage he stood,
With Atlantean shoulders fit to bear
The weight of mightiest monarchies; his look
Drew audience and attention still as night
Or summer's noontide air, while thus he spake.

278. sensible, sense. The use of an adjective for a noun is a Latinism which Milton frequently adopts.

281. Compose, adjust.

290 ff. such applause, etc. Mammon's proposal is an improvement on Belial's in that it supplies an activity consistent with the abandonment of a futile renewal of the attempt on Heaven. But the desire for revenge expressed by Moloch and felt by all the demons remains to be satisfied.

299. Beëlzebub. Cf. I, 79–81 and note. In the Old Testament the name is applied to the sun-god of the Philistines.

302. front, forehead.

306. Atlantean shoulders, shoulders like those of Atlas, who in Greek mythology supported the heavens.

"Thrones and imperial Powers, Offspring of Heaven, 310
Ethereal Virtues; or these titles now
Must we renounce, and changing style, be called
Princes of Hell? for so the popular vote
Inclines, here to continue, and build up here
A growing empire; doubtless; while we dream,
And know not that the King of Heaven hath doomed
This place our dungeon, not our safe retreat
Beyond his potent arm, to live exempt
From Heaven's high jurisdiction, in new league
Banded against his throne, but to remain 320
In strictest bondage, though thus far removed,
Under the inevitable curb, reserved
His captive multitude. For he, be sure,
In height or depth, still first and last will reign
Sole king, and of his kingdom lose no part
By our revolt, but over Hell extend
His empire, and with iron scepter rule
Us here, as with his golden those in Heaven.
What sit we then projecting peace and war?
War hath determined us, and foiled with loss 330
Irreparable; terms of peace yet none
Vouchsafed or sought; for what peace will be given
To us enslaved, but custody severe,
And stripes, and arbitrary punishment
Inflicted? and what peace can we return,
But to our power hostility and hate,
Untamed reluctance, and revenge though slow,
Yet ever plotting how the conqueror least
May reap his conquest, and may least rejoice
In doing what we must in suffering feel? 340
Nor will occasion want, nor shall we need
With dangerous expedition to invade
Heaven, whose high walls fear no assault or siege
Or ambush from the Deep. What if we find
Some easier enterprise? There is a place
(If ancient and prophetic fame in Heaven
Err not), another world, the happy seat
Of some new race called Man, about this time
To be created like to us, though less
In power and excellence, but favored more 350
Of him who rules above; so was his will

313. the popular vote, i.e., the state of opinion indicated by the applause given Mammon.
315. doubtless. The word is used sarcastically.
330. determined us, ended us or perhaps determined our future.
336. to our power, up to the limits of our power.
337. Untamed reluctance, untamable resistance.
346. fame, rumor.

Pronounced among the gods, and by an oath,
That shook Heaven's whole circumference, confirmed.
Thither let us bend all our thoughts, to learn
What creatures there inhabit, of what mould
Or substance, how endued, and what their power,
And where their weakness, how attempted best,
By force or subtlety. Though Heaven be shut,
And Heaven's high Arbitrator sit secure
In his own strength, this place may lie exposed, 360
The utmost border of his kingdom, left
To their defence who hold it; here perhaps
Some advantageous act may be achieved
By sudden onset, either with Hell fire
To waste his whole creation, or possess
All as our own, and drive as we were driven,
The puny habitants; or if not drive,
Seduce them to our party, that their God
May prove their foe, and with repenting hand
Abolish his own works. This would surpass 370
Common revenge, and interrupt his joy
In our confusion, and our joy upraise
In his disturbance; when his darling sons
Hurled headlong to partake with us, shall curse
Their frail original, and faded bliss,
Faded so soon. Advise if this be worth
Attempting, or to sit in darkness here
Hatching vain empires." Thus Beëlzebub
Pleaded his devilish counsel, first devised
By Satan, and in part proposed; for whence, 380
But from the author of all ill, could spring
So deep a malice, to confound the race
Of Mankind in one root, and Earth with Hell
To mingle and involve, done all to spite
The great Creator? But their spite still serves
His glory to augment. The bold design
Pleased highly those infernal States, and joy
Sparkled in all their eyes; with full assent

354. Thither let us, etc. Beëlzebub's proposal does not exclude Mammon's, which had itself appropriated Belial's; but it goes beyond both in supplying a rational project of revenge. The whole movement of the discussion has been constructively forward toward the formation of a policy satisfactory to all, and Beëlzebub, who is Satan's mouthpiece, has been simply waiting the opportune moment to introduce Satan's own scheme. His intelligence is far more comprehensive than that of the preceding speakers. It is easy to believe that Milton had been present at deliberations of the Council of State, and that he had noted with care the play of mind in them.

356. endued, equipped.

375. original, originator, i.e., Adam.

380. in part proposed, i.e., in an earlier speech, I, 645 ff.

382. confound, destroy completely.

387. States, princes or representatives.

They vote: whereat his speech he thus renews.
"Well have ye judged, well ended long debate, 390
Synod of gods, and like to what ye are,
Great things resolved; which from the lowest deep
Will once more lift us up, in spite of Fate,
Nearer our ancient seat; perhaps in view
Of those bright confines, whence with neighboring arms
And opportune excursion we may chance
Re-enter Heaven; or else in some mild zone
Dwell not unvisited of Heaven's fair light
Secure, and at the brightening orient beam
Purge off this gloom; the soft delicious air, 400
To heal the scar of these corrosive fires
Shall breathe her balm. But first whom shall we send
In search of this new world? whom shall we find
Sufficient? who shall tempt with wandering feet
The dark unbottomed infinite Abyss
And through the palpable obscure find out
His uncouth way, or spread his airy flight
Upborne with indefatigable wings
Over the vast abrupt, ere he arrive
The happy isle; what strength, what art can then 410
Suffice, or what evasion bear him safe
Through the strict senteries and stations thick
Of angels watching round? Here he had need
All circumspection, and we now no less
Choice in our suffrage; for on whom we send,
The weight of all and our last hope relies."
This said, he sat; and expectation held
His look suspense, awaiting who appeared
To second, or oppose, or undertake
The perilous attempt; but all sat mute, 420
Pondering the danger with deep thoughts; and each
In other's countenance read his own dismay
Astonished; none among the choice and prime
Of those Heaven-warring champions could be found
So hardy as to proffer or accept
Alone the dreadful voyage; till at last
Satan, whom now transcendent glory raised
Above his fellows, with monarchal pride
Conscious of highest worth, unmoved thus spake.

404. tempt, attempt, try.
406. palpable obscure, tangible darkness.
407. uncouth, unknown, strange.
409. the vast abrupt, the region of Chaos, which is a gulf or breach (Lat. *abruptum*), an emptiness.
412. stations, outposts, guards.
415. Choice in our suffrage, care in our selection.
418. suspense, suspended.

"O Progeny of Heaven, empyreal Thrones, 430
With reason hath deep silence and demur
Seized us, though undismayed. Long is the way
And hard, that out of Hell leads up to light;
Our prison strong, this huge convex of fire,
Outrageous to devour, immures us round
Ninefold, and gates of burning adamant
Barred over us prohibit all egress.
These passed, if any pass, the void profound
Of unessential Night receives him next
Wide gaping, and with utter loss of being 440
Threatens him, plunged in that abortive gulf.
If thence he scape into whatever world,
Or unknown region, what remains him less
Than unknown dangers and as hard escape.
But I should ill become this throne, O Peers,
And this imperial sovranty, adorned
With splendor, armed with power, if aught proposed
And judged of public moment, in the shape
Of difficulty or danger, could deter
Me from attempting. Wherefore do I assume 450
These royalties, and not refuse to reign,
Refusing to accept as great a share
Of hazard as of honor, due alike
To him who reigns, and so much to him due
Of hazard more, as he above the rest
High honored sits? Go therefore mighty Powers,
Terror of Heaven, though fallen; intend at home,
While here shall be our home, what best may ease
The present misery, and render Hell
More tolerable; if there be cure or charm 460
To respite or deceive, or slack the pain
Of this ill mansion; intermit no watch
Against a wakeful foe, while I abroad
Through all the coasts of dark destruction seek
Deliverance for us all: this enterprise
None shall partake with me." Thus saying rose
The Monarch, and prevented all reply;
Prudent, lest from his resolution raised
Others among the chief might offer now

431. demur, hesitation.

439. unessential, having no real being. Night and Chaos are thought of by Milton as merely negative, not really created.

441. abortive, prematurely brought forth and therefore unformed.

445 ff. But I should ill, etc. Satan's offer is parallel to that of Christ in III, 217 ff.

450. Me. Note the emphasis given by the meter.

457. intend, plan, consider. **461. deceive,** beguile.

467. prevented, anticipated (a good example of the transition from the older, literal meaning of the word to the modern).

468. from his resolution raised, encouraged by his bravery.

(Certain to be refused) what erst they feared; 470
And so refused might in opinion stand
His rivals, winning cheap the high repute
Which he through hazard huge must earn. But they
Dreaded not more the adventure than his voice
Forbidding; and at once with him they rose;
Their rising all at once was as the sound
Of thunder heard remote. Towards him they bend
With awful reverence prone; and as a god
Extol him equal to the Highest in Heaven.
Nor failed they to express how much they praised, 480
That for the general safety he despised
His own: for neither do the spirits damned
Lose all their virtue; lest bad men should boast
Their specious deeds on Earth, which glory excites,
Or close ambition varnished o'er with zeal.
  Thus they their doubtful consultations dark
Ended rejoicing in their matchless chief:
As when from mountain tops the dusky clouds
Ascending, while the North wind sleeps, o'erspread
Heaven's cheerful face, the louring element 490
Scowls o'er the darkened landscape snow or shower;
If chance the radiant sun with farewell sweet
Extend his evening beam, the fields revive,
The birds their notes renew, and bleating herds
Attest their joy, that hill and valley rings.
O shame to men! Devil with devil damned
Firm concord holds, men only disagree
Of creatures rational, though under hope
Of heavenly grace; and God proclaiming peace,
Yet live in hatred, enmity, and strife 500
Among themselves, and levy cruel wars,
Wasting the Earth, each other to destroy:
As if (which might induce us to accord)
Man had not hellish foes enow besides,
That day and night for his destruction wait!

* * *

477–479. This deification of Satan is a precedent for the idolatries of men.

483. virtue, merit—but not moral goodness, for that, Milton would hold, is inconsistent with disobedience to God.

484. specious deeds, deeds which, though having all the appearance of being public-spirited and self-sacrificing, are really the fruit of personal ambition masquerading as zeal for the common good. Under Milton's theory the demons can furnish a precedent for all that is great and magnanimous in men except the one essential of a righteous will. He never forgets that Satan and the rest are angels fallen.

490. element, sky.

492. If chance, if it chances that.

from BOOK III

THE ARGUMENT

God, sitting on his throne, sees Satan flying towards this World, then newly created; shows him to the Son, who sat at his right hand; foretells the success of Satan in perverting mankind; clears his own justice and wisdom from all imputation, having created Man free and able enough to have withstood his tempter; yet declares his purpose of grace towards him, in regard he fell not of his own malice, as did Satan, but by him seduced. The Son of God renders praises to his Father for the manifestation of his gracious purpose towards Man; but God again declares that grace cannot be extended towards Man without the satisfaction of Divine Justice: Man hath offended the majesty of God by aspiring to Godhead, and therefore, with all his progeny, devoted to death, must die, unless some one can be found sufficient to answer for his offence, and undergo his punishment. The Son of God freely offers himself a ransom for Man: the Father accepts him, ordains his incarnation, pronounces his exaltation above all names in Heaven and Earth; commands all the angels to adore him: they obey, and hymning to their harps in full choir, celebrate the Father and the Son. Meanwhile Satan alights upon the bare convex of this World's outermost orb; where wandering he first finds a place since called the Limbo of Vanity; what persons and things fly up thither; thence comes to the gate of Heaven, described ascending by stairs, and the waters above the firmament that flow about it. His passage thence to the orb of the sun: he finds there Uriel, the regent of that orb, but first changes himself into the shape of a meaner angel, and pretending a zealous desire to behold the new creation, and Man whom God had placed here, inquires of him the place of his habitation, and is directed; alights first on Mount Niphates.

Hail holy Light, offspring of Heaven first-born,
Or of the Eternal coeternal beam
May I express thee unblamed? since God is light,
And never but in unapproachëd light,
Dwelt from eternity, dwelt then in thee,
Bright effluence of bright essence increate.
Or hear'st thou rather pure ethereal stream,
Whose fountain who shall tell? Before the sun,
Before the Heavens thou wert, and at the voice
Of God, as with a mantle didst invest 10
The rising world of waters dark and deep,
Won from the void and formless infinite.
Thee I revisit now with bolder wing,
Escaped the Stygian pool, though long detained
In that obscure sojourn, while in my flight
Through utter and through middle darkness borne

2–3. May I, without blame, call thee coeternal with God?
6. Light is God's essence and as such is uncreated; but it is also what flows from him (effluence) and was the first created thing.
7–8. Or hear'st. Milton now says that the relation of the effluence to the essence is a mystery.
16. utter, outer, i.e., Hell.

With other notes than to the Orphean lyre
I sung of Chaos and eternal Night,
Taught by the heavenly Muse to venture down
The dark descent, and up to re-ascend, 20
Though hard and rare: thee I revisit safe,
And feel thy sovran vital lamp; but thou
Revisit'st not these eyes, that roll in vain
To find thy piercing ray, and find no dawn;
So thick a drop serene hath quenched their orbs,
Or dim suffusion veiled. Yet not the more
Cease I to wander where the Muses haunt
Clear spring, or shady grove, or sunny hill,
Smit with the love of sacred song; but chief
Thee Sion, and the flowery brooks beneath 30
That wash thy hallowed feet, and warbling flow,
Nightly I visit; nor sometimes forget
Those other two equalled with me in fate,
So were I equalled with them in renown,
Blind Thamyris and blind Mæonides,
And Tiresias and Phineus prophets old:
Then feed on thoughts, that voluntary move
Harmonious numbers; as the wakeful bird
Sings darkling, and in shadiest covert hid
Tunes her nocturnal note. Thus with the year 40
Seasons return; but not to me returns
Day, or the sweet approach of even or morn,
Or sight of vernal bloom, or summer's rose,
Or flocks, or herds, or human face divine;
But cloud instead, and ever-during dark
Surrounds me, from the cheerful ways of men
Cut off, and for the book of knowledge fair
Presented with a universal blank
Of Nature's works to me expunged and razed,
And wisdom at one entrance quite shut out. 50
So much the rather thou celestial Light
Shine inward, and the mind through all her powers
Irradiate, there plant eyes, all mist from thence
Purge and disperse, that I may see and tell
Of things invisible to mortal sight.
  Now had the Almighty Father from above,
From the pure Empyrean where he sits

17. Orphean lyre. There was an Orphic hymn to night. Milton means that his poem is of higher inspiration, being based on Scripture.

25. drop serene, a translation of the medical term *gutta serena,* used of blindness in which the eye is not clouded. The "clear drop" is a humor which blocks the optic nerve.

26. dim suffusion, cataract.

29. sacred song, poetry, which is divine as coming from the muses.

30. To visit the brooks by Sion is to read Scripture.

35. Mæonides, Homer.

High throned above all height, bent down his eye,
His own works and their works at once to view.
About him all the sanctities of Heaven 60
Stood thick as stars, and from his sight received
Beatitude past utterance; on his right
The radiant image of his glory sat,
His only Son; on Earth he first beheld
Our two first parents, yet the only two
Of mankind, in the happy garden placed,
Reaping immortal fruits of joy and love,
Uninterrupted joy, unrivalled love
In blissful solitude. He then surveyed
Hell and the gulf between, and Satan there 70
Coasting the wall of Heaven on this side Night
In the dun air sublime, and ready now
To stoop with wearied wings and willing feet
On the bare outside of this World, that seemed
Firm land imbosomed without firmament,
Uncertain which, in ocean or in air.
Him God beholding from his prospect high,
Wherein past, present, future he beholds,
Thus to his only Son foreseeing spake.
"Only begotten Son, seest thou what rage 80
Transports our Adversary, whom no bounds
Prescribed, no bars of Hell, nor all the chains
Heaped on him there, nor yet the main Abyss
Wide interrupt can hold; so bent he seems
On desperate revenge, that shall redound
Upon his own rebellious head. And now
Through all restraint broke loose he wings his way
Not far off Heaven, in the precincts of light,
Directly towards the new-created World,
And Man there placed, with purpose to assay 90
If him by force he can destroy, or worse,
By some false guile pervert; and shall pervert;
For Man will hearken to his glozing lies,
And easily transgress the sole command,

72. sublime, elevated.

74–76. Satan is ready to light on the *primum mobile,* the outer shell of the created universe, not on the earth itself. The substance of this shell is indeterminate. The "firmament" is the visible sky, which separates the waters above from the waters beneath the earth. The shell is "without," i.e., outside of this firmament, or perhaps rather not composed of it, as the other spheres must be. The "waters above" constitute the crystalline sphere, inside the *primum mobile,* but also make a sea on top of it. Milton is not only adjusting the biblical account of creation to the Ptolemaic idea of the spheres but making the conception philosophic as well. The *primum mobile* is a link between God and his universe.

76. Uncertain which, it being uncertain whether the shell hung in water or in air. Milton suggests that the business about the firmament and the waters is obscure, as indeed it is.

Sole pledge of his obedience; so will fall
He and his faithless progeny. Whose fault?
Whose but his own? Ingrate, he had of me
All he could have; I made him just and right,
Sufficient to have stood, though free to fall.
Such I created all the Ethereal Powers 100
And spirits, both them who stood and them who failed;
Freely they stood who stood, and fell who fell.
Not free, what proof could they have given sincere
Of true allegiance, constant faith, or love,
Where only what they needs must do, appeared,
Not what they would? what praise could they receive?
What pleasure I from such obedience paid,
When will and reason (reason also is choice)
Useless and vain, of freedom both despoiled,
Made passive both, had served necessity, 110
Not me. They therefore as to right belonged,
So were created, nor can justly accuse
Their Maker, or their making, or their fate,
As if predestination overruled
Their will, disposed by absolute decree
Or high foreknowledge; they themselves decreed
Their own revolt, not I. If I foreknew,
Foreknowledge had no influence on their fault,
Which had no less proved certain unforeknown.
So without least impulse or shadow of fate, 120
Or aught by me immutably foreseen,
They trespass, authors to themselves in all,
Both what they judge and what they choose; for so
I formed them free, and free they must remain,
Till they enthrall themselves: I else must change
Their nature, and revoke the high decree
Unchangeable, eternal, which ordained
Their freedom; they themselves ordained their fall.
The first sort by their own suggestion fell,
Self-tempted, self-depraved; Man falls, deceived 130
By the other first; Man therefore shall find grace,
The other none. In mercy and justice both,
Through Heaven and Earth, so shall my glory excel,
But mercy first and last shall brightest shine."
  Thus while God spake, ambrosial fragrance filled
All Heaven, and in the blessed spirits elect
Sense of new joy ineffable diffused.
Beyond compare the Son of God was seen

114 ff. Predestination, in Milton's theology, was a conditional decree of God, not an absolute one, as in strict Calvinism. Milton is not the first or the last thinker to maintain the paradox that God foresees but not immutably.

Most glorious; in him all his Father shone
Substantially expressed; and in his face 140
Divine compassion visibly appeared,
Love without end, and without measure grace,
Which uttering thus he to his Father spake.
"O Father, gracious was that word which closed
Thy sovran sentence, that Man should find grace;
For which both Heaven and Earth shall high extol
Thy praises with the innumerable sound
Of hymns and sacred songs, wherewith thy throne
Encompassed shall resound thee ever blest.
For should Man finally be lost, should Man 150
Thy creature late so loved, thy youngest son
Fall circumvented thus by fraud, though joined
With his own folly? that be from thee far,
That far be from thee, Father, who art judge
Of all things made, and judgest only right.
Or shall the Adversary thus obtain
His end, and frustrate thine, shall he fulfil
His malice, and thy goodness bring to nought,
Or proud return though to his heavier doom,
Yet with revenge accomplished, and to Hell 160
Draw after him the whole race of mankind,
By him corrupted? or wilt thou thyself
Abolish thy creation, and unmake,
For him, what for thy glory thou hast made?
So should thy goodness and thy greatness both
Be questioned and blasphemed without defence."
To whom the great Creator thus replied.
"O Son, in whom my soul hath chief delight,
Son of my bosom, Son who art alone
My word, my wisdom, and effectual might, 170
All hast thou spoken as my thoughts are, all
As my eternal purpose hath decreed:
Man shall not quite be lost, but saved who will,
Yet not of will in him, but grace in me
Freely vouchsafed; once more I will renew
His lapsëd powers, though forfeit and enthralled
By sin to foul exorbitant desires;
Upheld by me, yet once more he shall stand
On even ground against his mortal foe,
By me upheld, that he may know how frail 180
His fallen condition is, and to me owe
All his deliverance, and to none but me.
Some I have chosen of peculiar grace

175–176. Man's free will, like Satan's, has lapsed with his disobedience. Because his sin came from an outside suggestion his power to choose good is renewed by an act of Grace, as Satan's is not.

Elect above the rest; so is my will.
The rest shall hear me call, and oft be warned
Their sinful state, and to appease betimes
The incensëd Deity, while offered grace
Invites; for I will clear their senses dark,
What may suffice, and soften stony hearts
To pray, repent, and bring obedience due. 190
To prayer, repentance, and obedience due,
Though but endeavored with sincere intent,
Mine ear shall not be slow, mine eye not shut.
And I will place within them as a guide
My umpire Conscience, whom if they will hear,
Light after light well used they shall attain,
And to the end persisting, safe arrive.
This my long sufferance and my day of grace
They who neglect and scorn shall never taste;
But hard be hardened, blind be blinded more, 200
That they may stumble on, and deeper fall;
And none but such from mercy I exclude.
But yet all is not done; Man disobeying,
Disloyal breaks his fealty, and sins
Against the high supremacy of Heaven,
Affecting Godhead, and so losing all,
To expiate his treason hath nought left,
But to destruction sacred and devote,
He with his whole posterity must die;
Die he or justice must; unless for him 210
Some other able, and as willing, pay
The rigid satisfaction, death for death.
Say Heavenly Powers, where shall we find such love?
Which of ye will be mortal to redeem
Man's mortal crime, and just the unjust to save?
Dwells in all Heaven charity so dear?"
He asked, but all the heavenly choir stood mute,
And silence was in Heaven; on Man's behalf
Patron or intercessor none appeared,
Much less that durst upon his own head draw 220
The deadly forfeiture, and ransom set.
And now without redemption all mankind
Must have been lost, adjudged to Death and Hell
By doom severe, had not the Son of God,
In whom the fulness dwells of love divine,
His dearest mediation thus renewed.

184. Elect. In Calvinistic thought the elect include all who are to be saved, in contrast to the "reprobate," who are predestined before their birth to be damned; with Milton, on the other hand, the elect are only a special group of saints to whom goodness and salvation come easily. The rest of mankind are prone to sin but capable of repentance.

203 ff. God's immutable decree cannot be evaded. If justice is to be satisfied there must be death for sin. The solution is the sacrifice of Christ, who, like Adam, is the representative of mankind.

"Father, thy word is passed, Man shall find grace;
And shall grace not find means, that finds her way,
The speediest of thy wingëd messengers,
To visit all thy creatures, and to all 230
Comes unprevented, unimplored, unsought?
Happy for Man, so coming; he her aid
Can never seek, once dead in sins and lost;
Atonement for himself or offering meet
Indebted and undone, hath none to bring.
Behold me then, me for him, life for life
I offer; on me let thine anger fall;
Account me Man; I for his sake will leave
Thy bosom, and this glory next to thee
Freely put off, and for him lastly die 240
Well pleased; on me let Death wreak all his rage;
Under his gloomy power I shall not long
Lie vanquished; thou hast given me to possess
Life in myself for ever; by thee I live;
Though now to Death I yield, and am his due
All that of me can die, yet that debt paid,
Thou wilt not leave me in the loathsome grave
His prey, nor suffer my unspotted soul
For ever with corruption there to dwell;
But I shall rise victorious, and subdue 250
My vanquisher, spoiled of his vaunted spoil;
Death his death's wound shall then receive, and stoop
Inglorious, of his mortal sting disarmed.
I through the ample air in triumph high
Shall lead Hell captive maugre Hell, and show
The powers of darkness bound. Thou at the sight
Pleased, out of Heaven shalt look down and smile,
While by thee raised I ruin all my foes,
Death last, and with his carcass glut the grave:
Then with the multitude of my redeemed, 260
Shall enter Heaven long absent, and return,
Father, to see thy face, wherein no cloud
Of anger shall remain, but peace assured
And reconcilement; wrath shall be no more
Thenceforth, but in thy presence joy entire."
His words here ended, but his meek aspéct
Silent yet spake, and breathed immortal love
To mortal men, above which only shone
Filial obedience. As a sacrifice
Glad to be offered, he attends the will 270
Of his great Father. Admiration seized
All Heaven, what this might mean, and whither tend
Wondering; but soon the Almighty thus replied.

236 ff. Christ's highly dramatic offer, with its reception, is in studied contrast to Satan's in Book II, 430 ff.

"O thou in Heaven and Earth the only peace
Found out for mankind under wrath, O thou
My sole complacence! well thou know'st how dear
To me are all my works, nor Man the least
Though last created, that for him I spare
Thee from my bosom and right hand, to save,
By losing thee a while, the whole race lost! 280
Thou therefore whom thou only canst redeem,
Their nature also to thy nature join;
And be thyself Man among men on Earth,
Made flesh, when time shall be, of virgin seed,
By wondrous birth; be thou in Adam's room
The head of all mankind, though Adam's son.
As in him perish all men, so in thee
As from a second root shall be restored,
As many as are restored; without thee, none.
His crime makes guilty all his sons; thy merit 290
Imputed shall absolve them who renounce
Their own both righteous and unrighteous deeds,
And live in thee transplanted, and from thee
Receive new life. So Man, as is most just,
Shall satisfy for Man, be judged and die,
And dying rise, and rising with him raise
His brethren, ransomed with his own dear life.
So heavenly love shall outdo hellish hate,
Giving to death, and dying to redeem,
So dearly to redeem what hellish hate 300
So easily destroyed, and still destroys
In those who, when they may, accept not grace. . . ."

* * *

from BOOK IV

THE ARGUMENT

Satan, now in prospect of Eden, and nigh the place where he must now attempt the bold enterprise which he undertook alone against God and Man, falls into many doubts with himself, and many passions, fear, envy, and despair; but at length confirms himself in evil, journeys on to Paradise, whose outward prospect and situation is described, overleaps the bounds, sits in the shape of a cormorant on the Tree of Life, as highest in the Garden, to look about him. The Garden described; Satan's first sight of Adam and Eve; his wonder at their excellent form and happy state, but with resolution to work their fall; overhears their discourse; thence gathers that the Tree of Knowledge was forbidden them to eat of under penalty of death, and thereon intends to found his temptation by seducing them to transgress; then leaves them a while, to know further of their state by some other means. Meanwhile Uriel, descending on a sunbeam, warns Gabriel, who had in charge the gate of Paradise, that some evil spirit had escaped the Deep, and passed at noon by his sphere, in the shape of a good angel, down to Paradise; discovered after by his furious gestures in the mount. Gabriel promises to find him ere morning. Night coming on, Adam and Eve discourse of going to their rest: their bower described; their evening worship. Gabriel, drawing forth his bands of night-watch to walk the round of Paradise, appoints two strong angels to Adam's bower, lest the evil spirit should be there doing some harm to Adam or Eve sleeping; there they find him at the ear of Eve, tempting her in a dream, and bring him, though unwilling, to Gabriel; by whom questioned, he scornfully answers, prepares resistance, but hindered by a sign from Heaven, flies out of Paradise.

O for that warning voice, which he who saw
The Apocalypse heard cry in Heaven aloud,
Then when the Dragon, put to second rout,
Came furious down to be revenged on men,
"Woe to the inhabitants on Earth!" that now,
While time was, our first parents had been warned
The coming of their secret foe, and scaped,
Haply so scaped, his mortal snare; for now
Satan, now first inflamed with rage, came down,
The tempter ere the accuser of mankind, 10
To wreak on innocent frail Man his loss
Of that first battle, and his flight to Hell.
Yet not rejoicing in his speed, though bold,
Far off and fearless, nor with cause to boast,
Begins his dire attempt, which nigh the birth
Now rolling, boils in his tumultuous breast,
And like a devilish engine back recoils
Upon himself; horror and doubt distract
His troubled thoughts, and from the bottom stir
The Hell within him, for within him Hell 20
He brings, and round about him, nor from Hell
One step no more than from himself can fly
By change of place. Now conscience wakes despair
That slumbered, wakes the bitter memory
Of what he was, what is, and what must be
Worse; of worse deeds worse sufferings must ensue.
Sometimes towards Eden which now in his view
Lay pleasant, his grievëd look he fixes sad,
Sometimes towards Heaven and the full-blazing sun,
Which now sat high in his meridian tower. 30
Then much revolving, thus in sighs began.
"O thou that with surpassing glory crowned,
Look'st from thy sole dominion like the god

1 ff. This opening passage is based on the vision of St. John recorded in Rev. 12.

10. The tempter ere the accuser. In St. John's vision, Satan, routed from heaven for the second time, comes down to earth as "the accuser of our brethren" (Rev. 12:10). But, as Milton points out, he first came to earth in the role of tempter. The word "devil" is a corruption of the Greek *diabolos,* meaning literally "slanderer" or "accuser."

11. wreak, avenge.

27. The literal meaning of **Eden** is "delight."

31. much revolving, pondering many things.

Of this new world; at whose sight all the stars
Hide their diminished heads; to thee I call,
But with no friendly voice, and add thy name
O Sun, to tell thee how I hate thy beams
That bring to my remembrance from what state
I fell, how glorious once above thy sphere;
Till pride and worse ambition threw me down 40
Warring in Heaven against Heaven's matchless King.
Ah wherefore! He deserved no such return
From me, whom he created what I was
In that bright eminence, and with his good
Upbraided none; nor was his service hard.
What could be less than to afford him praise,
The easiest recompense, and pay him thanks,
How due! Yet all his good proved ill in me,
And wrought but malice; lifted up so high
I 'sdeined subjection, and thought one step higher 50
Would set me highest, and in a moment quit
The debt immense of endless gratitude,
So burdensome still paying, still to owe;
Forgetful what from him I still received,
And understood not that a grateful mind
By owing owes not, but still pays, at once
Indebted and discharged; what burden then?
Oh had his powerful destiny ordained
Me some inferior angel, I had stood
Then happy; no unbounded hope had raised 60
Ambition. Yet why not? some other Power
As great might have aspired, and me though mean
Drawn to his part; but other Powers as great
Fell not, but stand unshaken, from within
Or from without, to all temptations armed.
Hadst thou the same free will and power to stand?
Thou hadst. Whom hast thou then or what to accuse,
But Heaven's free love dealt equally to all?
Be then his love accurst, since love or hate,
To me alike it deals eternal woe. 70
Nay cursed be thou; since against his thy will
Chose freely what it now so justly rues.
Me miserable! which way shall I fly
Infinite wrath and infinite despair?
Which way I fly is Hell; myself am Hell;
And in the lowest deep a lower deep
Still threatening to devour me opens wide,

41. Cf. I, 116, 117 and note. The uncompromising egotism of Satan's public utterances now gives way to a secret admission of God's supremacy.

50. 'sdeined, disdained.

51. quit, requite, pay.

52–57. Satan means that gratitude is in itself payment, whereas payment alone does not release from a debt of gratitude.

To which the Hell I suffer seems a Heaven.
O then at last relent: is there no place
Left for repentance, none for pardon left? 80
None left but by submission; and that word
Disdain forbids me, and my dread of shame
Among the spirits beneath, whom I seduced
With other promises and other vaunts
Than to submit, boasting I could subdue
The Omnipotent. Ay me, they little know
How dearly I abide that boast so vain,
Under what torments inwardly I groan;
While they adore me on the throne of Hell,
With diadem and scepter high advanced 90
The lower still I fall, only supreme
In misery; such joy ambition finds.
But say I could repent, and could obtain
By act of grace my former state; how soon
Would height recall high thoughts, how soon unsay
What feigned submission swore: ease would recant
Vows made in pain, as violent and void.
For never can true reconcilement grow
Where wounds of deadly hate have pierced so deep;
Which would but lead me to a worse relapse 100
And heavier fall: so should I purchase dear
Short intermission bought with double smart.
This knows my Punisher; therefore as far
From granting he, as I from begging peace.
All hope excluded thus, behold instead
Of us, outcast, exiled, his new delight,
Mankind created, and for him this World.
So farewell hope, and with hope farewell fear,
Farewell remorse! All good to me is lost;
Evil be thou my good; by thee at least 110
Divided empire with Heaven's King I hold
By thee, and more than half perhaps will reign;
As Man ere long, and this new World shall know."
  Thus while he spake, each passion dimmed his face
Thrice changed with pale, ire, envy, and despair,
Which marred his borrowed visage, and betrayed
Him counterfeit, if any eye beheld.
For heavenly minds from such distempers foul
Are ever clear. Whereof he soon aware,
Each perturbation smoothed with outward calm, 120
Artificer of fraud; and was the first

87. abide, suffer for.
90. advanced, elevated. **Me** (89) is the word modified.
115. Thrice changed with pale, i.e., each of the passions (**ire, envy, and despair**) dims the natural luster of his countenance. **Pale** is of course used as a noun.

That practised falsehood under saintly show,
Deep malice to conceal, couched with revenge.
Yet not enough had practised to deceive
Uriel once warned; whose eye pursued him down
The way he went, and on the Assyrian mount
Saw him disfigured, more than could befall
Spirit of happy sort. His gestures fierce
He marked and mad demeanor, then alone,
As he supposed, all unobserved, unseen. 130
So on he fares, and to the border comes
Of Eden, where delicious Paradise,
Now nearer, crowns with her enclosure green,
As with a rural mound the champaign head
Of a steep wilderness, whose hairy sides
With thicket overgrown, grotesque and wild,
Access denied; and overhead up grew
Insuperable height of loftiest shade,
Cedar, and pine, and fir, and branching palm,
A sylvan scene, and as the ranks ascend 140
Shade above shade, a woody theater
Of stateliest view. Yet higher than their tops
The verdurous wall of Paradise up sprung;
Which to our general sire gave prospect large
Into his nether empire neighboring round.
And higher than that wall a circling row
Of goodliest trees loaden with fairest fruit,
Blossoms and fruits at once of golden hue
Appeared, with gay enamelled colors mixed;
On which the sun more glad impressed his beams 150
Than in fair evening cloud, or humid bow,
When God hath showered the earth; so lovely seemed
That landscape. And of pure now purer air
Meets his approach, and to the heart inspires
Vernal delight and joy, able to drive
All sadness but despair; now gentle gales
Fanning their odoriferous wings dispense
Native perfumes, and whisper whence they stole
Those balmy spoils. As when to them who sail
Beyond the Cape of Hope, and now are past 160
Mozambic, off at sea north-east winds blow
Sabæan odors from the spicy shore
Of Araby the Blest, with such delay

123. couched with, lying hidden with.
126. the Assyrian mount, Niphates.
132 ff. Eden is apparently thought of as embracing the greater part of the Tigris and Euphrates region. Paradise is a garden in the east of Eden.
134. champaign head, level summit.
145. nether empire, i.e., the outlying territories of Eden.
149. enamelled, bright and variegated.

Well pleased they slack their course, and many a league
Cheered with the grateful smell old Ocean smiles.
So entertained those odorous sweets the Fiend
Who came their bane, though with them better pleased
Than Asmodëus with the fishy fume,
That drove him, though enamored, from the spouse
Of Tobit's son, and with a vengeance sent 170
From Media post to Egypt, there fast bound.
Now to the ascent of that steep savage hill
Satan had journeyed on, pensive and slow;
But further way found none, so thick entwined,
As one continued brake, the undergrowth
Of shrubs and tangling bushes had perplexed
All path of man or beast that passed that way.
One gate there only was, and that looked east
On the other side; which when the Arch-Felon saw,
Due entrance he disdained, and in contempt, 180
At one slight bound high overleaped all bound
Of hill or highest wall, and sheer within
Lights on his feet. As when a prowling wolf,
Whom hunger drives to seek new haunt for prey,
Watching where shepherds pen their flocks at eve
In hurdled cotes amid the field secure,
Leaps o'er the fence with ease into the fold;
Or as a thief bent to unhoard the cash
Of some rich burgher, whose substantial doors,
Cross-barred and bolted fast, fear no assault, 190
In at the window climbs, or o'er the tiles:
So clomb this first grand thief into God's fold;
So since into his Church lewd hirelings climb.
Thence up he flew, and on the Tree of Life,
The middle tree and highest there that grew,
Sat like a cormorant; yet not true life
Thereby regained, but sat devising death
To them who lived; nor on the virtue thought
Of that life-giving plant, but only used
For prospect, what well used had been the pledge 200
Of immortality. So little knows
Any, but God alone, to value right
The good before him, but perverts best things
To worst abuse, or to their meanest use.

167 ff. The allusion is to an episode related in the apocryphal Book of Tobit, 8. Tobit's son is married to a maiden of Media, who is beloved by the evil spirit Asmodeus; to get rid of this spirit he is instructed by the angel Raphael to burn the heart and liver of a fish. The odor drives Asmodeus into Egypt, where the angel binds him.

172. savage, woody.

176. perplexed, made difficult.

181. bound . . . bound. Note the play on words.

194. Tree of Life. Cf. Gen.

196. like a cormorant, i.e., in the shape of a ravenous bird of prey.

Beneath him with new wonder now he views
To all delight of human sense exposed
In narrow room Nature's whole wealth, yea more,
A Heaven on Earth, for blissful Paradise
Of God the garden was, by him in the east
Of Eden planted; Eden stretched her line 210
From Auran eastward to the royal towers
Of great Seleucia, built by Grecian kings,
Or where the sons of Eden long before
Dwelt in Telassar. In this pleasant soil
His far more pleasant garden God ordained;
Out of the fertile ground he caused to grow
All trees of noblest kind for sight, smell, taste;
And all amid them stood the Tree of Life,
High-eminent, blooming ambrosial fruit
Of vegetable gold; and next to life 220
Our death the Tree of Knowledge grew fast by,
Knowledge of good bought dear by knowing ill.
Southward through Eden went a river large,
Nor changed his course, but through the shaggy hill
Passed underneath ingulfed, for God had thrown
That mountain as his garden mould, high raised
Upon the rapid current, which through veins
Of porous earth with kindly thirst up drawn,
Rose a fresh fountain, and with many a rill
Watered the garden; thence united fell 230
Down the steep glade, and met the nether flood,
Which from his darksome passage now appears,
And now divided into four main streams,
Runs diverse, wandering many a famous realm
And country whereof here needs no account;
But rather to tell how, if art could tell,
How from that sapphire fount the crispëd brooks,
Rolling on orient pearl and sands of gold,
With mazy error under pendent shades
Ran nectar, visiting each plant, and fed 240
Flowers worthy of Paradise, which not nice art
In beds and curious knots, but Nature boon
Poured forth profuse on hill and dale and plain,

211. Auran, a district of Syria, about fifty miles south of Damascus.

212. Seleucia, a city on the Tigris, about twenty miles southeast of modern Bagdad.

214. Telassar, an ancient site in Mesopotamia.

219. blooming, bearing.

223 ff. Southward . . . no account. Cf. Gen. 2:10. In IX, 71–73 Milton identifies this river with the Tigris.

233. four main streams. Cf. Gen. 2:10–14.

238. orient, lustrous.

239. error, wandering (the literal meaning of Latin *error*).

241–242. The natural profusion of Paradise is contrasted with the artificial arrangement of an Italian garden. **nice,** fastidious. **boon,** bounteous. This passage played a part in supporting later preference for the so-called English garden and for the love of natural scenery generally.

Both where the morning sun first warmly smote
The open field, and where the unpierced shade
Imbrowned the noon-tide bowers. Thus was this place,
A happy rural seat of various view;
Groves whose rich trees wept odorous gums and balm,
Others whose fruit burnished with golden rind
Hung amiable, Hesperian fables true, 250
If true, here only, and of delicious taste.
Betwixt them lawns, or level downs, and flocks
Grazing the tender herb, were interposed,
Or palmy hillock, or the flowery lap
Of some irriguous valley spread her store,
Flowers of all hue, and without thorn the rose.
Another side, umbrageous grots and caves
Of cool recess, o'er which the mantling vine
Lays forth her purple grape, and gently creeps
Luxuriant; meanwhile murmuring waters fall 260
Down the slope hills, dispersed, or in a lake,
That to the fringëd bank with myrtle crowned
Her crystal mirror holds, unite their streams.
The birds their choir apply; airs, vernal airs,
Breathing the smell of field and grove, attune
The trembling leaves, while universal Pan,
Knit with the Graces and the Hours in dance,
Led on the eternal Spring. Not that fair field
Of Enna, where Proserpine gathering flowers
Herself a fairer flower by gloomy Dis 270
Was gathered, which cost Ceres all that pain
To seek her through the world; nor that sweet grove
Of Daphne by Orontes, and the inspired
Castalian spring, might with this Paradise
Of Eden strive; nor that Nyseian isle,
Girt with the river Triton, where old Cham
Whom Gentiles Ammon call and Lybian Jove,

247. various view, varied aspect.

250–251. Milton means that here, if anywhere, was to be found such fruit as classical myth attributed to the Garden of the Hesperides. **amiable,** lovely.

255. irriguous, well-watered.

266 ff. Classical writers often made "the dance of the Hours" symbolic of the orderly succession of the seasons.

269 ff. Enna, etc. Proserpine (Greek Persephone), the daughter of Ceres, goddess of agriculture (Greek Demeter), was abducted by Dis, god of the Underworld, from her garden in Enna (in Sicily). After a long search, Ceres found her daughter in the Underworld and arranged that she should spend part of her time there and part on the earth. The myth obviously describes the alternation of the seasons. (Editors' note.)

273. Daphne, a town situated on the river **Orontes,** about five miles from Antioch. It contained a grove and fountain sacred to Apollo, the fountain being named after the more famous **Castalian spring** at Delphi.

275. that Nyseian isle, the island of Nysa, situated in the midst of the river **Triton** in northern Africa. The identification of Jupiter Ammon with Noah's son Ham (**Cham**) is an interesting Miltonic touch.

Hid Amalthea and her florid son
Young Bacchus from his stepdame Rhea's eye;
Nor where Abassin kings their issue guard, 280
Mount Amara, though this by some supposed
True Paradise, under the Ethiop line
By Nilus' head, enclosed with shining rock,
A whole day's journey high, but wide remote
From this Assyrian garden, where the Fiend
Saw undelighted all delight, all kind
Of living creatures new to sight and strange.
Two of far nobler shape erect and tall,
God-like erect, with native honor clad
In naked majesty seemed lords of all, 290
And worthy seemed, for in their looks divine
The image of their glorious Maker shone,
Truth, wisdom, sanctitude severe and pure,
Severe but in true filial freedom placed;
Whence true authority in men; though both
Not equal, as their sex not equal seemed;
For contemplation he and valor formed,
For softness she and sweet attractive grace;
He for God only, she for God in him.
His fair large front and eye sublime declared 300
Absolute rule; and hyacinthine locks
Round from his parted forelock manly hung
Clustering, but not beneath his shoulders broad:
She as a veil down to the slender waist
Her unadornëd golden tresses wore
Dishevelled, but in wanton ringlets waved
As the vine curls her tendrils, which implied
Subjection, but required with gentle sway,
And by her yielded, by him best received,
Yielded with coy submission, modest pride, 310
And sweet reluctant amorous delay.
Nor those mysterious parts were then concealed;
Then was not guilty shame; dishonest shame
Of Nature's works, honor dishonorable,

281. Mount Amara, a high hill on the Abyssinian plateau, the place of seclusion where, according to tradition, the Abyssinian princes were sent to be educated.

282. Ethiop line, the equator.

289. God-like erect. Milton makes man's upright stature a symbol of his superiority to the brutes and of his instinctive aspiration.

295 ff. Throughout the poem Milton carefully distinguishes between the relative endowments and obligations of man and woman. The sexes are not equal, he insists, and authority quite properly belongs to the male. But the position which he accords woman, when considered in the light of theological tradition, is exceedingly high.

300. front, brow.

301. hyacinthine, i.e., dark in color.

306. wanton, loose, unbound.

313. dishonest, unchaste.

Sin-bred, how have ye troubled all mankind
With shows instead, mere shows of seeming pure,
And banished from man's life his happiest life,
Simplicity and spotless innocence.
So passed they naked on, nor shunned the sight
Of God or angel, for they thought no ill; 320
So hand in hand they passed, the loveliest pair
That ever since in love's embraces met:
Adam the goodliest man of men since born
His sons, the fairest of her daughters Eve.
Under a tuft of shade that on a green
Stood whispering soft, by a fresh fountain side
They sat them down; and after no more toil
Of their sweet gardening labor than sufficed
To recommend cool Zephyr, and made ease
More easy, wholesome thirst and appetite 330
More grateful, to their supper-fruits they fell,
Nectarine fruits which the compliant boughs
Yielded them, sidelong as they sat recline
On the soft downy bank damasked with flowers.
The savory pulp they chew, and in the rind
Still as they thirsted scoop the brimming stream;
Nor gentle purpose, nor endearing smiles
Wanted, nor youthful dalliance, as beseems
Fair couple linked in happy nuptial league,
Alone as they. About them frisking played 340
All beasts of the earth, since wild, and of all chase
In wood or wilderness, forest or den;
Sporting the lion ramped, and in his paw
Dandled the kid; bears, tigers, ounces, pards,
Gambolled before them; the unwieldy elephant
To make them mirth used all his might, and wreathed
His lithe proboscis; close the serpent sly
Insinuating, wove with Gordian twine
His braided train, and of his fatal guile
Gave proof unheeded; others on the grass 350
Couched, and now filled with pasture gazing sat,
Or bedward ruminating; for the sun
Declined was hasting now with prone career

323. the goodliest man of men since born, etc. The idiom is obviously illogical, but it has ample precedent in Elizabethan English as well as in Greek and Latin.

333. recline, i.e., reclining.

334. damasked, ornamented with a variegated pattern.

337. purpose, conversation.

343. ramped, reared on his hind legs.

348. Gordian twine, intricate tangle. The reference is to the famous Gordian knot, which no one could untie but which Alexander the Great finally cut with his sword.

352. ruminating, chewing the cud.

To the Ocean Isles, and in the ascending scale
Of Heaven the stars that usher evening rose:
When Satan still in gaze, as first he stood,
Scarce thus at length failed speech recovered sad.
"Oh Hell! what do mine eyes with grief behold!
Into our room of bliss thus high advanced
Creatures of other mould, earth-born perhaps, 360
Not spirits, yet to heavenly spirits bright
Little inferior; whom my thoughts pursue
With wonder, and could love, so lively shines
In them divine resemblance, and such grace
The hand that formed them on their shape hath poured.
Ah gentle pair, ye little think how nigh
Your change approaches, when all these delights
Will vanish and deliver ye to woe,
More woe, the more your taste is now of joy;
Happy, but for so happy ill secured 370
Long to continue, and this high seat your Heaven
Ill fenced for Heaven to keep out such a foe
As now is entered; yet no purposed foe
To you whom I could pity thus forlorn
Though I unpitied. League with you I seek,
And mutual amity so strait so close,
That I with you must dwell, or you with me
Henceforth; my dwelling haply may not please
Like this fair Paradise, your sense, yet such
Accept your Maker's work; he gave it me, 380
Which I as freely give; Hell shall unfold,
To entertain you two, her widest gates,
And send forth all her kings; there will be room,
Not like these narrow limits, to receive
Your numerous offspring; if no better place,
Thank him who puts me loath to this revenge
On you who wrong me not, for him who wronged.
And should I at your harmless innocence
Melt, as I do, yet public reason just,
Honor and empire with revenge enlarged, 390
By conquering this new World, compels me now
To do what else though damned I should abhor."
So spake the Fiend, and with necessity,
The tyrant's plea, excused his devilish deeds.
Then from his lofty stand on that high tree
Down he alights among the sportful herd
Of those four-footed kinds, himself now one,

354. the Ocean Isles, i.e., the extreme west. Milton may here have in mind the Azores, but the figure is used by classical writers without definite geographical reference.

389. By excusing his crime on the ground of political expediency, Satan once more demonstrates his proficiency in Machiavellian statecraft. That he can feel human pity is a survival of the divine endowment which he has perverted.

Now other, as their shape served best his end
Nearer to view his prey, and unespied
To mark what of their state he more might learn 400
By word or action marked. About them round
A lion now he stalks with fiery glare;
Then as a tiger, who by chance hath spied
In some purlieu two gentle fawns at play,
Straight couches close, then rising changes oft
His couchant watch, as one who chose his ground
Whence rushing he might surest seize them both
Griped in each paw; when Adam first of men
To first of women Eve thus moving speech,
Turned him all ear to hear new utterance flow. 410
"Sole partner and sole part of all these joys,
Dearer thyself than all, needs must the Power
That made us, and for us this ample World,
Be infinitely good, and of his good
As liberal and free as infinite,
That raised us from the dust and placed us here
In all this happiness, who at his hand
Have nothing merited, nor can perform
Aught whereof he hath need, he who requires
From us no other service than to keep 420
This one, this easy charge, of all the trees
In Paradise that bear delicious fruit
So various, not to taste that only Tree
Of Knowledge, planted by the Tree of Life,
So near grows death to life, whate'er death is,
Some dreadful thing no doubt; for well thou know'st
God hath pronounced it death to taste that Tree;
The only sign of our obedience left
Among so many signs of power and rule
Conferred upon us, and dominion given 430
Over all other creatures that possess
Earth, air, and sea. Then let us not think hard
One easy prohibition, who enjoy
Free leave so large to all things else, and choice
Unlimited of manifold delights;
But let us ever praise him, and extol
His bounty, following our delightful task
To prune these growing plants, and tend these flowers,
Which were it toilsome, yet with thee were sweet."
To whom thus Eve replied. "O thou for whom 440
And from whom I was formed flesh of thy flesh,
And without whom am to no end, my guide
And head, what thou hast said is just and right.

411. Note the double play on words: **partner . . . part; sole . . . sole.** The first *sole* is used in the ordinary sense of "only," the second in the sense of "unrivaled," or "chief."

For we to him indeed all praises owe,
And daily thanks, I chiefly who enjoy
So far the happier lot, enjoying thee
Pre-eminent by so much odds, while thou
Like consort to thyself canst nowhere find.
That day I oft remember, when from sleep
I first awaked, and found myself reposed 450
Under a shade on flowers, much wondering where
And what I was, whence thither brought, and how.
Not distant far from thence a murmuring sound
Of waters issued from a cave and spread
Into a liquid plain, then stood unmoved
Pure as the expanse of Heaven; I thither went
With unexperienced thought, and laid me down
On the green bank, to look into the clear
Smooth lake, that to me seemed another sky.
As I bent down to look, just opposite 460
A shape within the watery gleam appeared
Bending to look on me: I started back,
It started back, but pleased I soon returned,
Pleased it returned as soon with answering looks
Of sympathy and love; there I had fixed
Mine eyes till now, and pined with vain desire,
Had not a voice thus warned me. 'What thou seest,
What there thou seest, fair creature, is thyself,
With thee it came and goes; but follow me,
And I will bring thee where no shadow stays 470
Thy coming, and thy soft embraces, he
Whose image thou art, him thou shalt enjoy
Inseparably thine; to him shalt bear
Multitudes like thyself, and thence be called
Mother of human race.' What could I do
But follow straight, invisibly thus led?
Till I espied thee, fair indeed and tall,
Under a platane; yet methought less fair,
Less winning soft, less amiably mild,
Than that smooth watery image; back I turned, 480
Thou following cried'st aloud, 'Return fair Eve,
Whom fliest thou? whom thou fliest, of him thou art,
His flesh, his bone; to give thee being I lent
Out of my side to thee, nearest my heart,
Substantial life, to have thee by my side
Henceforth an individual solace dear.
Part of my soul I seek thee, and thee claim
My other half.' With that thy gentle hand

470. stays, awaits.
479. less amiably mild, i.e., less fitted to inspire love.
486. individual, inseparable.

Seized mine, I yielded, and from that time see
How beauty is excelled by manly grace 490
And wisdom, which alone is truly fair."
So spake our general mother, and with eyes
Of conjugal attraction unreproved,
And meek surrender, half embracing leaned
On our first father; half her swelling breast
Naked met his under the flowing gold
Of her loose tresses hid. He in delight
Both of her beauty and submissive charms
Smiled with superior love, as Jupiter
On Juno smiles, when he impregns the clouds 500
That shed May flowers; and pressed her matron lip
With kisses pure. Aside the Devil turned
For envy, yet with jealous leer malign
Eyed them askance, and to himself thus plained.
"Sight hateful, sight tormenting! thus these two
Imparadised in one another's arms,
The happier Eden, shall enjoy their fill
Of bliss on bliss, while I to Hell am thrust,
Where neither joy nor love, but fierce desire,
Among our other torments not the least, 510
Still unfulfilled with pain of longing pines;
Yet let me not forget what I have gained
From their own mouths. All is not theirs, it seems;
One fatal tree there stands, of Knowledge called,
Forbidden them to taste. Knowledge forbidden?
Suspicious, reasonless. Why should their Lord
Envy them that? can it be sin to know,
Can it be death? and do they only stand
By ignorance, is that their happy state,
The proof of their obedience and their faith? 520
O fair foundation laid whereon to build
Their ruin! Hence I will excite their minds
With more desire to know, and to reject
Envious commands, invented with design
To keep them low whom knowledge might exalt
Equal with gods. Aspiring to be such,
They taste and die; what likelier can ensue?
But first with narrow search I must walk round
This garden, and no corner leave unspied;

493. unreproved, unreprovable.

500. impregns, impregnates. Hera typifies the lower air or haze which surrounds the earth, Zeus the upper air (aether). The mingling of the two produces the spring with its flowers.

504. plained, complained, murmured.

521 ff. Satan's own experience has taught him the allurement of godlike power, and the outcome of any attempt to gain it. He therefore has little difficulty in determining the most effective temptation. Cf. IX, 705 ff.

A chance but chance may lead where I may meet 530
Some wandering spirit of Heaven, by fountain side,
Or in thick shade retired, from him to draw
What further would be learned. Live while ye may,
Yet happy pair; enjoy, till I return,
Short pleasures, for long woes are to succeed."
 So saying, his proud step he scornful turned,
But with sly circumspection, and began
Through wood, through waste, o'er hill, o'er dale, his roam.

* * *

 Now came still Evening on, and Twilight gray
Had in her sober livery all things clad;
Silence accompanied, for beast and bird, 600
They to their grassy couch, these to their nests
Were slunk, all but the wakeful nightingale;
She all night long her amorous descant sung;
Silence was pleased. Now glowed the firmament
With living sapphires; Hesperus that led
The starry host, rode brightest, till the Moon
Rising in clouded majesty, at length
Apparent queen unveiled her peerless light,
And o'er the dark her silver mantle threw.
When Adam thus to Eve. "Fair consort, the hour 610
Of night, and all things now retired to rest
Mind us of like repose, since God hath set
Labor and rest, as day and night to men
Successive, and the timely dew of sleep
Now falling with soft slumberous weight inclines
Our eye-lids; other creatures all day long
Rove idle, unemployed, and less need rest;
Man hath his daily work of body or mind
Appointed, which declares his dignity,
And the regard of Heaven on all his ways; 620
While other animals unactive range,
And of their doings God takes no account.
To-morrow ere fresh morning streak the east
With first approach of light, we must be risen,
And at our pleasant labor, to reform
Yon flowery arbors, yonder alleys green,
Our walks at noon, with branches overgrown,
That mock our scant manuring, and require
More hands than ours to lop their wanton growth.
Those blossoms also, and those dropping gums, 630
That lie bestrown unsightly and unsmooth,

530. A chance but, there is a chance that.
603. descant, a song, or rather a soprano part. **605. Hesperus,** the evening star.
608. Apparent, manifest. **628. manuring,** cultivating.

Ask riddance, if we mean to tread with ease;
Meanwhile, as Nature wills, night bids us rest."
  To whom thus Eve with perfect beauty adorned.
"My author and disposer, what thou bidd'st
Unargued I obey; so God ordains.
God is thy law, thou mine; to know no more
Is woman's happiest knowledge and her praise.
With thee conversing I forget all time,
All seasons and their change, all please alike. 640
Sweet is the breath of Morn, her rising sweet,
With charm of earliest birds; pleasant the Sun
When first on this delightful land he spreads
His orient beams, on herb, tree, fruit, and flower,
Glistering with dew; fragrant the fertile Earth
After soft showers; and sweet the coming on
Of grateful Evening mild, then silent Night
With this her solemn bird and this fair Moon,
And these the gems of Heaven, her starry train:
But neither breath of Morn when she ascends 650
With charm of earliest birds, nor rising Sun
On this delightful land, nor herb, fruit, flower,
Glistering with dew, nor fragrance after showers,
Nor grateful Evening mild, nor silent Night,
With this her solemn bird, nor walk by moon,
Or glittering star-light, without thee is sweet.
But wherefore all night long shine these? for whom
This glorious sight, when sleep hath shut all eyes?"
  To whom our general ancestor replied.
"Daughter of God and Man, accomplished Eve, 660
Those have their course to finish, round the Earth
By morrow evening, and from land to land
In order, though to nations yet unborn,
Ministering light prepared, they set and rise;
Lest total Darkness should by night regain
Her old possession, and extinguish life
In nature and all things; which these soft fires
Not only enlighten, but with kindly heat
Of various influence foment and warm,
Temper or nourish, or in part shed down 670
Their stellar virtue on all kinds that grow

640. All seasons, i.e., all times of the day. Spring is the only season of the year that Eve has yet experienced.

642. charm, song.

650 ff. Note how the imagery of the preceding nine lines is repeated with subtle variations in phrasing. Milton frequently makes effective use of repetition, but nowhere else does he work it into so elaborate a pattern. He is adorning or sophisticating a Homeric device, as he does in his use of similes, and in his structural adaptation of the epic throwback.

665. total Darkness, i.e., the darkness of Chaos.

667 ff. The doctrine of stellar influence, which formed the basis of astrology, was still widely current in the seventeenth century. Milton seems to take its validity for granted.

On Earth, made hereby apter to receive
Perfection from the sun's more potent ray.
These then, though unbeheld in deep of night,
Shine not in vain, nor think, though men were none,
That Heaven would want spectators, God want praise;
Millions of spiritual creatures walk the Earth
Unseen, both when we wake, and when we sleep.
All these with ceaseless praise his works behold
Both day and night. How often from the steep 680
Of echoing hill or thicket have we heard
Celestial voices to the midnight air,
Sole, or responsive each to other's note,
Singing their great Creator; oft in bands
While they keep watch, or nightly rounding walk,
With heavenly touch of instrumental sounds
In full harmonic number joined, their songs
Divide the night, and lift our thoughts to Heaven."
Thus talking, hand in hand alone they passed
On to their blissful bower; it was a place 690
Chosen by the sovran Planter, when he framed
All things to Man's delightful use; the roof
Of thickest covert was inwoven shade,
Laurel and myrtle, and what higher grew
Of firm and fragrant leaf; on either side
Acanthus, and each odorous bushy shrub
Fenced up the verdant wall; each beauteous flower,
Iris all hues, roses, and jessamine
Reared high their flourished heads between, and wrought
Mosaic; underfoot the violet, 700
Crocus, and hyacinth with rich inlay
Broidered the ground, more colored than with stone
Of costliest emblem. Other creature here,
Beast, bird, insect, or worm durst enter none;
Such was their awe of Man. In shadier bower
More sacred and sequestered, though but feigned,
Pan or Sylvanus never slept, nor Nymph
Nor Faunus haunted. Here in close recess
With flowers, garlands, and sweet-smelling herbs
Espousëd Eve decked first her nuptial bed, 710
And heavenly choirs the hymenæan sung,
What day the genial angel to our sire
Brought her in naked beauty more adorned,

688. Divide the night, i.e., into watches.

703. emblem, embossed or inlaid ornamentation.

707. Pan, Sylvanus, and Faunus were classical deities of the fields and woods. The qualifying **though but feigned** phrase, used with reference to their haunts, implies a judgment on much of the subject matter of pagan poetry. Milton frequently asserts the superior truth of his own materials. Cf. 250, 251, and note.

712. genial, nuptial, instrumental to marriage.

More lovely than Pandora, whom the gods
Endowed with all their gifts, and O too like
In sad event, when to the unwiser son
Of Japhet brought by Hermes, she ensnared
Mankind with her fair looks, to be avenged
On him who had stole Jove's authentic fire.
Thus at their shady lodge arrived, both stood, 720
Both turned, and under open sky adored
The God that made both sky, air, Earth, and Heaven,
Which they beheld, the moon's resplendent globe
And starry pole: "Thou also mad'st the night,
Maker Omnipotent, and thou the day,
Which we in our appointed work employed
Have finished happy in our mutual help
And mutual love, the crown of all our bliss
Ordained by thee, and this delicious place
For us too large, where thy abundance wants 730
Partakers, and uncropped falls to the ground.
But thou hast promised from us two a race
To fill the Earth, who shall with us extol
Thy goodness infinite, both when we wake,
And when we seek, as now, thy gift of sleep."
This said unanimous, and other rites
Observing none, but adoration pure
Which God likes best, into their inmost bower
Handed they went; and eased the putting off
These troublesome disguises which we wear, 740
Straight side by side were laid, nor turned, I ween,
Adam from his fair spouse, nor Eve the rites
Mysterious of connubial love refused;
Whatever hypocrites austerely talk
Of purity and place and innocence,
Defaming as impure what God declares
Pure, and commands to some, leaves free to all.
Our Maker bids increase; who bids abstain
But our destroyer, foe to God and Man?
Hail wedded Love, mysterious law, true source 750
Of human offspring, sole propriety
In Paradise of all things common else.

714 ff. The allusion is to a myth related by Hesiod. To be avenged on Prometheus, who had stolen fire from heaven for the use of mortals, Jove sent to earth **Pandora** ("the all-gifted"), on whom each of the gods had bestowed some fatal charm. Hermes conducted her to Epimetheus, the **unwiser son of Japhet,** who married her, despite the warning of his brother. Thereupon all the ills which she had brought from heaven were released to afflict humanity.

719. authentic, original.

739. Handed, hand in hand.

744 ff. Whatever hypocrites, etc. Throughout this passage, Milton is quite obviously taking issue with the advocates of monasticism and celibacy.

751. sole propriety, sole property. Their love for each other is the one thing in Paradise which Adam and Eve have as their exclusive possession.

By thee adulterous lust was driven from men
Among the bestial herds to range; by thee,
Founded in reason, loyal, just, and pure,
Relations dear, and all the charities
Of father, son, and brother first were known.
Far be it, that I should write thee sin or blame,
Or think thee unbefitting holiest place,
Perpetual fountain of domestic sweets, 760
Whose bed is undefiled and chaste pronounced,
Present or past, as saints and patriarchs used.
Here Love his golden shafts employs, here lights
His constant lamp, and waves his purple wings,
Reigns here and revels; not in the bought smile
Of harlots, loveless, joyless, unendeared,
Casual fruition; nor in court-amours,
Mixed dance, or wanton mask, or midnight ball,
Or serenate, which the starved lover sings
To his proud fair, best quitted with disdain. 770
These lulled by nightingales, embracing slept,
And on their naked limbs the flowery roof
Showered roses, which the morn repaired. Sleep on
Blest pair; and O yet happiest if ye seek
No happier state, and know to know no more.

* * *

BOOK V: THE ARGUMENT

Morning approached, Eve relates to Adam her troublesome dream; he likes it not, yet comforts her; they come forth to their day labors; their morning hymn at the door of their bower. God, to render Man inexcusable, sends Raphael to admonish him of his obedience, of his free estate, of his enemy near at hand—who he is, and why his enemy, and whatever else may avail Adam to know. Raphael comes down to Paradise; his appearance described; his coming discerned by Adam afar off, sitting at the door of his bower; he goes out to meet him, brings him to his lodge, entertains him with the choicest fruits of Paradise got together by Eve; their discourse at table. Raphael performs his message, minds Adam of his state and of his enemy; relates, at Adam's request, who that enemy is, and how he came to be so, beginning from his first revolt in Heaven, and the occasion thereof; how he drew his legions after him to the parts of the North, and there incited them to rebel with him, persuading all but only Abdiel, a Seraph, who in argument dissuades and opposes him, then forsakes him.

756. charities, affections.

767. nor in court-amours, etc. Milton may be thinking specifically of the court of Charles II; but he is also thinking of the general chivalric tradition, the artificial conventions of which he believes to be irreconcilable with the ideal domestic relationship.

769. serenate, serenade. **starved,** i.e., suffering from cold.

775. know to know no more, i.e., are wise enough not to seek further knowledge.

BOOK VI: THE ARGUMENT

Raphael continues to relate how Michael and Gabriel were sent forth to battle against Satan and his angels. The first fight described; Satan and his Powers retire under night. He calls a council; invents devilish engines, which, in the second day's fight, put Michael and his angels to some disorder; but they at length, pulling up mountains, overwhelmed both the force and machines of Satan. Yet, the tumult not so ending, God, on the third day, sends Messiah his Son, for whom he had reserved the glory of that victory. He, in the power of his Father, coming to the place, and causing all his legions to stand still on either side, with his chariot and thunder driving into the midst of his enemies, pursues them, unable to resist, towards the wall of Heaven; which opening, they leap down with horror and confusion into the place of punishment prepared for them in the deep. Messiah returns with triumph to his Father.

BOOK VII: THE ARGUMENT

Raphael, at the request of Adam, relates how and wherefore this World was first created: that God, after the expelling of Satan and his angels out of Heaven, declared his pleasure to create another World, and other creatures to dwell therein; sends his Son with glory, and attendance of angels, to perform the work of creation in six days: the angels celebrate with hymns the performance thereof, and his reascension into Heaven.

BOOK VIII: THE ARGUMENT

Adam inquires concerning celestial motions; is doubtfully answered, and exhorted to search rather things more worthy of knowledge. Adam assents, and still desirous to detain Raphael, relates to him what he remembered since his own creation: his placing in Paradise, his talk with God concerning solitude and fit society, his first meeting and nuptials with Eve. His discourse with the angel thereupon; who, after admonitions repeated, departs.

BOOK IX

THE ARGUMENT

Satan, having compassed the Earth, with meditated guile returns as a mist by night into Paradise; enters into the serpent sleeping. Adam and Eve in the morning go forth to their labors, which Eve proposes to divide in several places, each laboring apart: Adam consents not, alleging the danger, lest that enemy, of whom they were forewarned, should attempt her found alone. Eve, loth to be thought not circumspect or firm enough, urges her going apart, the rather desirous to make trial of her strength; Adam at last yields. The Serpent finds her alone: his subtle approach, first gazing, then speaking, with much flattery extolling Eve above all other creatures. Eve, wondering to hear the Serpent speak, asks how he attained to human speech and such understanding, not till now; the Serpent answers, that by tasting of a certain tree in the garden he attained both to speech and reason, till then void of both. Eve requires him to bring her to that tree, and finds it to be the Tree of Knowledge forbidden. The Serpent, now grown bolder, with many wiles and arguments induces her at length to eat; she, pleased with the taste, deliberates a while whether to impart thereof to Adam or not; at last brings him of the fruit; relates what persuaded her to eat thereof. Adam, at first amazed, but perceiving her lost, resolves through vehemence of love to perish with her, and, extenuating the trespass, eats also of the fruit. The effects thereof in them both; they seek to cover their nakedness; then fall to variance and accusation of one another.

No more of talk where God or angel guest
With Man, as with his friend, familiar used
To sit indulgent, and with him partake
Rural repast, permitting him the while
Venial discourse unblamed. I now must change
Those notes to tragic; foul distrust and breach
Disloyal on the part of man, revolt
And disobedience; on the part of Heaven
Now alienated, distance and distaste,
Anger and just rebuke, and judgment given, 10
That brought into this World a world of woe,
Sin and her shadow Death, and Misery
Death's harbinger. Sad task, yet argument
Not less but more heroic than the wrath
Of stern Achilles on his foe pursued
Thrice fugitive about Troy wall; or rage
Of Turnus for Lavinia disespoused;
Or Neptune's ire or Juno's, that so long
Perplexed the Greek and Cytherea's son;
If answerable style I can obtain 20
Of my celestial patroness, who deigns
Her nightly visitation unimplored,
And dictates to me slumbering, or inspires
Easy my unpremeditated verse;
Since first this subject for heroic song
Pleased me long choosing and beginning late;
Not sedulous by nature to indite

1 ff. The long conversation between Raphael and Adam, forming the substance of Books V–VIII, has introduced the antecedent action and illuminated more fully the existing situation. Now before entering upon the climax of his narrative, Milton pauses for a brief meditative interlude. The personal allusions in the opening lines of this book are of exceptional interest.

6–12. Cf. I, 3. The theme announced at the beginning of the poem is repeated in expanded form.

13 ff. Having restated his theme, Milton here asserts its superiority to the themes of the three great classical epics: (1) the *Iliad,* which deals with **the wrath of stern Achilles;** (2) the *Odyssey,* which relates the outcome of **Neptune's ire** against the Greek Odysseus; (3) the *Aeneid,* the first part of which is motivated by the hostility of **Juno** toward Aeneas (**Cytherea's son**), and the second part by the anger of **Turnus** at the loss of **Lavinia.**

20. answerable style, i.e., a style commensurate with the dignity of the theme.

21–23. Cf. III, 29–40. The implication is that with Milton composition was a spontaneous process, based on a passive reception of impressions and ideas.

25 ff. From the Cambridge MS. it is evident that the subject of *Paradise Lost* (together with various other subjects drawn from biblical and British history) was in Milton's mind by 1640 or soon after. The actual composition of the epic could not have been begun much before 1658.

Wars, hitherto the only argument
Heroic deemed, chief mastery to dissect
With long and tedious havoc fabled knights 30
In battles feigned; the better fortitude
Of patience and heroic martyrdom
Unsung; or to describe races and games,
Or tilting furniture, imblazoned shields,
Impresses quaint, caparisons and steeds,
Bases and tinsel trappings, gorgeous knights
At joust and tournament; then marshalled feast
Served up in hall with sewers and seneshals,
The skill of artifice or office mean,
Not that which justly gives heroic name 40
To person or to poem. Me of these
Nor skilled nor studious, higher argument
Remains, sufficient of itself to raise
That name, unless an age too late, or cold
Climate, or years damp my intended wing
Depressed, and much they may, if all be mine,
Not hers who brings it nightly to my ear.
The sun was sunk, and after him the star
Of Hesperus, whose office is to bring
Twilight upon the Earth, short arbiter 50
'Twixt day and night, and now from end to end
Night's hemisphere had veiled the horizon round;
When Satan who late fled before the threats
Of Gabriel out of Eden, now improved
In meditated fraud and malice, bent
On Man's destruction, maugre what might hap
Of heavier on himself, fearless returned.
By night he fled, and at midnight returned
From compassing the Earth, cautious of day,
Since Uriel, regent of the sun, descried 60
His entrance, and forewarned the Cherubim
That kept their watch; thence full of anguish driven,
The space of seven continued nights he rode
With darkness, thrice the equinoctial line
He circled, four times crossed the car of Night

33. races and games. Milton is thinking of the detailed accounts in *Iliad* xxiii, and *Aeneid* v.

34. tilting furniture, etc., i.e., the trappings of chivalry.

35. impresses, devices on shields.

36. bases, kilt-like garments worn by knights on horseback.

41–43. Me . . . remains. To me, who am, etc., there remains.

44–45. an age too late, i.e., too late a period in the world's history. The notion of universal retrogression was fairly common in the seventeenth century. Though Milton had argued against the theory, he here shows that he is not unaffected by fear that it may be true. **or cold Climate.** The idea that a northern climate is unfavorable to works of the mind goes back to Aristotle.

56. maugre, in spite of.

From pole to pole, traversing each colure;
On the eighth returned, and on the coast averse
From entrance or cherubic watch, by stealth
Found unsuspected way. There was a place,
Now not, though sin, not time, first wrought the change, 70
Where Tigris at the foot of Paradise
Into a gulf shot under ground, till part
Rose up a fountain by the Tree of Life;
In with the river sunk, and with it rose
Satan involved in rising mist, then sought
Where to lie hid; sea he had searched and land
From Eden over Pontus, and the pool
Mæotis, up beyond the river Ob;
Downward as far antarctic; and in length
West from Orontes to the ocean barred 80
At Darien, thence to the land where flows
Ganges and Indus. Thus the orb he roamed
With narrow search, and with inspection deep
Considered every creature, which of all
Most opportune might serve his wiles, and found
The serpent subtlest beast of all the field.
Him after long debate, irresolute
Of thoughts revolved, his final sentence chose
Fit vessel, fittest imp of fraud, in whom
To enter, and his dark suggestions hide 90
From sharpest sight; for in the wily snake,
Whatever sleights none would suspicious mark,
As from his wit and native subtlety
Proceeding, which in other beasts observed,
Doubt might beget of diabolic power
Active within beyond the sense of brute.
Thus he resolved, but first from inward grief
His bursting passion into plaints thus poured.
"O Earth, how like to Heaven, if not preferred
More justly, seat worthier of Gods, as built 100
With second thoughts, reforming what was old!
For what God after better worse would build?

66. traversing each colure. The colures are two great circles intersecting at the poles, one passing through the equinoxes, the other (at right angles to it) through the solstices. Satan follows each of these lines from south to north and back, keeping always within the earth's shadow.

69 ff. Cf. IV, 223–230. Satan makes his entrance from the north side. Satan's wanderings, first described astronomically, are here described geographically. Northward he had gone over the Black Sea (**Pontus**) and the Sea of Azof (**the pool Mæotis**), beyond the Siberian river **Ob** to the pole; thence southward to the Antarctic. Westward he had gone along the Syrian river **Orontes,** over the Mediterranean and Atlantic to the Isthmus of Panama (**Darien**), and from there across the Pacific to India (the land of **Ganges and Indus**).

82. orb, the world. **88. sentence,** decision. **89. imp,** offspring.

99 ff. "O Earth," etc. Cf. Satan's soliloquy on first gaining sight of Eden, IV, 32 ff. As then, he is torn by passion, but now there is less of remorse, more of bitterness and despair.

Terrestrial Heaven, danced round by other Heavens
That shine, yet bear their bright officious lamps,
Light above light, for thee alone, as seems,
In thee concentring all their precious beams
Of sacred influence. As God in Heaven
Is center, yet extends to all, so thou
Centring receivest from all those orbs; in thee,
Not in themselves, all their known virtue appears 110
Productive in herb, plant, and nobler birth
Of creatures animate with gradual life
Of growth, sense, reason, all summed up in Man.
With what delight could I have walked thee round,
If I could joy in aught, sweet interchange
Of hill and valley, rivers, woods, and plains,
Now land, now sea, and shores with forest crowned,
Rocks, dens, and caves; but I in none of these
Find place or refuge; and the more I see
Pleasures about me, so much more I feel 120
Torment within me, as from the hateful siege
Of contraries; all good to me becomes
Bane, and in Heaven much worse would be my state.
But neither here seek I, no nor in Heaven
To dwell, unless by mastering Heaven's Supreme;
Nor hope to be myself less miserable
By what I seek, but others to make such
As I, though thereby worse to me redound:
For only in destroying I find ease
To my relentless thoughts; and him destroyed, 130
Or won to what may work his utter loss,
For whom all this was made, all this will soon
Follow, as to him linked in weal or woe;
In woe then, that destruction wide may range.
To me shall be the glory sole among
The infernal Powers, in one day to have marred
What he Almighty styled, six nights and days
Continued making, and who knows how long
Before had been contriving, though perhaps
Not longer than since I in one night freed 140
From servitude inglorious well nigh half
The angelic name, and thinner left the throng
Of his adorers. He to be avenged,
And to repair his numbers thus impaired,
Whether such virtue spent of old now failed
More angels to create, if they at least
Are his created, or to spite us more,
Determined to advance into our room

103. danced round by other Heavens. Milton frequently compares the motion of the heavenly bodies to a dance.
142. name, race, stock.

A creature formed of earth, and him endow,
Exalted from so base original, 150
With heavenly spoils, our spoils. What he decreed
He effected; Man he made, and for him built
Magnificent this World, and Earth his seat,
Him lord pronounced, and, O indignity!
Subjected to his service angel wings,
And flaming ministers to watch and tend
Their earthy charge. Of these the vigilance
I dread, and to elude, thus wrapped in mist
Of midnight vapor glide obscure, and pry
In every bush and brake, where hap may find 160
The serpent sleeping, in whose mazy folds
To hide me, and the dark intent I bring.
O foul descent! that I who erst contended
With Gods to sit the highest, am now constrained
Into a beast, and, mixed with bestial slime,
This essence to incarnate and imbrute,
That to the height of deity aspired;
But what will not ambition and revenge
Descend to? Who aspires must down as low
As high he soared, obnoxious first or last 170
To basest things. Revenge, at first though sweet,
Bitter ere long back on itself recoils;
Let it; I reck not, so it light well aimed,
Since higher I fall short, on him who next
Provokes my envy, this new favorite
Of Heaven, this man of clay, son of despite,
Whom us the more to spite his Maker raised
From dust: spite then with spite is best repaid."
So saying, through each thicket dank or dry,
Like a black mist low creeping, he held on 180
His midnight search, where soonest he might find
The serpent. Him fast sleeping soon he found
In labyrinth of many a round self-rolled,
His head the midst, well stored with subtle wiles;
Not yet in horrid shade or dismal den,
Nor nocent yet, but on the grassy herb
Fearless unfeared he slept. In at his mouth
The Devil entered, and his brutal sense,
In heart or head, possessing soon inspired
With act intelligential, but his sleep 190
Disturbed not, waiting close the approach of morn.
Now whenas sacred light began to dawn
In Eden on the humid flowers, that breathed
Their morning incense, when all things that breathe,

163 ff. Satan's imbruting himself within the serpent is the final step in his progressive degeneration. His own words explain the symbolism.

170. obnoxious, liable, subject.

From the Earth's great altar send up silent praise
To the Creator, and his nostrils fill
With grateful smell, forth came the human pair
And joined their vocal worship to the choir
Of creatures wanting voice; that done, partake
The season, prime for sweetest scents and airs; 200
Then commune how that day they best may ply
Their growing work; for much their work outgrew
The hands' dispatch of two gardening so wide.
And Eve first to her husband thus began.
"Adam, well may we labor still to dress
This garden, still to tend plant, herb, and flower,
Our pleasant task enjoined, but till more hands
Aid us, the work under our labor grows,
Luxurious by restraint; what we by day
Lop overgrown, or prune, or prop, or bind, 210
One night or two with wanton growth derides
Tending to wild. Thou therefore now advise
Or hear what to my mind first thoughts present:
Let us divide our labors, thou where choice
Leads thee, or where most needs, whether to wind
The woodbine round this arbor, or direct
The clasping ivy where to climb, while I
In yonder spring of roses intermixed
With myrtle, find what to redress till noon.
For while so near each other thus all day 220
Our task we choose, what wonder if so near
Looks intervene and smiles, or object new
Casual discourse draw on, which intermits
Our day's work, brought to little, though begun
Early, and the hour of supper comes unearned."
To whom mild answer Adam thus returned.
"Sole Eve, associate sole, to me beyond
Compare above all living creatures dear,
Well hast thou motioned, well thy thoughts employed
How we might best fulfil the work which here 230
God hath assigned us, nor of me shalt pass
Unpraised; for nothing lovelier can be found
In woman, than to study household good,
And good works in her husband to promote.
Yet not so strictly hath our Lord imposed
Labor, as to debar us when we need
Refreshment, whether food, or talk between,
Food of the mind, or this sweet intercourse
Of looks and smiles, for smiles from reason flow,

199–200. partake The season, i.e., share the beauties of the morning. As in IV, 640, **season** refers to the time of day.
218. spring, clump, thicket.
229. motioned, proposed.

To brute denied, and are of love the food, 240
Love not the lowest end of human life.
For not to irksome toil, but to delight
He made us, and delight to reason joined.
These paths and bowers doubt not but our joint hands
Will keep from wilderness with ease, as wide
As we need walk, till younger hands ere long
Assist us. But if much converse perhaps
Thee satiate, to short absence I could yield;
For solitude sometimes is best society,
And short retirement urges sweet return. 250
But other doubt possesses me, lest harm
Befall thee severed from me; for thou know'st
What hath been warned us, what malicious foe
Envying our happiness, and of his own
Despairing, seeks to work us woe and shame
By sly assault; and somewhere nigh at hand
Watches, no doubt, with greedy hope to find
His wish and best advantage, us asunder,
Hopeless to circumvent us joined, where each
To other speedy aid might lend at need; 260
Whether his first design be to withdraw
Our feälty from God, or to disturb
Conjugal love, than which perhaps no bliss
Enjoyed by us excites his envy more;
Or this, or worse, leave not the faithful side
That gave thee being, still shades thee and protects.
The wife, where danger or dishonor lurks,
Safest and seemliest by her husband stays,
Who guards her, or with her the worst endures."
  To whom the virgin majesty of Eve, 270
As one who loves, and some unkindness meets,
With sweet austere composure thus replied.
  "Offspring of Heaven and Earth, and all Earth's lord,
That such an enemy we have, who seeks
Our ruin, both by thee informed I learn,
And from the parting angel overheard
As in a shady nook I stood behind,
Just then returned at shut of evening flowers.
But that thou shouldst my firmness therefore doubt
To God or thee, because we have a foe 280
May tempt it, I expected not to hear.
His violence thou fear'st not, being such,
As we, not capable of death or pain,
Can either not receive, or can repel.
His fraud is then thy fear, which plain infers

245. wilderness, wildness (i.e., too luxuriant growth of vegetation).
265. Or this, or worse, i.e., whether his design (261) be this or worse.
276. from the parting angel, i.e., from Raphael as he was parting from Adam.

Thy equal fear that my firm faith and love
Can by his fraud be shaken or seduced;
Thoughts, which how found they harbor in thy breast,
Adam, misthought of her to thee so dear?"
To whom with healing words Adam replied. 290
"Daughter of God and Man, immortal Eve,
For such thou art, from sin and blame entire;
Not diffident of thee do I dissuade
Thy absence from my sight, but to avoid
The attempt itself, intended by our foe.
For he who tempts, though in vain, at least asperses
The tempted with dishonor foul, supposed
Not incorruptible of faith, not proof
Against temptation. Thou thyself with scorn
And anger wouldst resent the offered wrong, 300
Though ineffectual found. Misdeem not then,
If such affront I labor to avert
From thee alone, which on us both at once
The enemy, though bold, will hardly dare,
Or daring, first on me the assault shall light.
Nor thou his malice and false guile contemn;
Subtle he needs must be, who could seduce
Angels, nor think superfluous others' aid.
I from the influence of thy looks receive
Access in every virtue, in thy sight 310
More wise, more watchful, stronger, if need were
Of outward strength; while shame, thou looking on,
Shame to be overcome or overreached,
Would utmost vigor raise, and raised unite.
Why shouldst not thou like sense within thee feel
When I am present, and thy trial choose
With me, best witness of thy virtue tried."
So spake domestic Adam in his care
And matrimonial love; but Eve, who thought
Less attributed to her faith sincere, 320
Thus her reply with accent sweet renewed.
"If this be our condition, thus to dwell
In narrow circuit straitened by a foe,
Subtle or violent, we not endued
Single with like defence, wherever met,
How are we happy, still in fear of harm?
But harm precedes not sin: only our foe
Tempting affronts us with his foul esteem
Of our integrity; his foul esteem
Sticks no dishonor on our front, but turns 330

292. entire, untouched. **310. access,** growth, increase.
318. domestic, devoted to home life and its duties.
320. less, too little.
328. affronts. The literal meaning "strikes on the forehead" is implied (Latin *ad* + *frons*). Note how the image is expanded in the two lines following.

Foul on himself; then wherefore shunned or feared
By us? who rather double honor gain
From his surmise proved false, find peace within,
Favor from Heaven, our witness, from the event.
And what is faith, love, virtue, unassayed
Alone, without exterior help sustained?
Let us not then suspect our happy state
Left so imperfect by the Maker wise,
As not secure to single or combined.
Frail is our happiness, if this be so, 340
And Eden were no Eden thus exposed."
  To whom thus Adam fervently replied.
"O Woman, best are all things as the will
Of God ordained them; his creating hand
Nothing imperfect or deficient left
Of all that he created, much less Man,
Or aught that might his happy state secure,
Secure from outward force: within himself
The danger lies, yet lies within his power;
Against his will he can receive no harm. 350
But God left free the will, for what obeys
Reason is free, and Reason he made right,
But bid her well be ware, and still erect,
Lest by some fair appearing good surprised
She dictate false, and misinform the will
To do what God expressly hath forbid.
Not then mistrust, but tender love enjoins,
That I should mind thee oft, and mind thou me.
Firm we subsist, yet possible to swerve,
Since Reason not impossibly may meet 360
Some specious object by the foe suborned,
And fall into deception unaware,
Not keeping strictest watch, as she was warned.
Seek not temptation then, which to avoid
Were better, and most likely if from me
Thou sever not; trial will come unsought.
Wouldst thou approve thy constancy, approve
First thy obedience; the other who can know,
Not seeing thee attempted, who attest?
But if thou think trial unsought may find 370

335. And what is faith, love, virtue, etc., i.e., what value have these qualities unless they have been tested and found able to stand by their own merits. Milton here puts in the mouth of Eve an argument which he himself used in *Areopagitica.* Cf. the famous passage: "I cannot praise a fugitive and cloistered virtue," etc.

339. to single or combined, i.e., to us singly or together.

341. no Eden, no place of delight. Cf. note on IV, 27, 28.

348 ff. within himself . . . no harm. The principle of human responsibility is fundamental to Milton's whole philosophy.

353. still erect, ever alert.

367. approve, give proof of, confirm.

Us both securer than thus warned thou seem'st,
Go; for thy stay, not free, absents thee more;
Go in thy native innocence, rely
On what thou hast of virtue, summon all,
For God towards thee hath done his part, do thine."
 So spake the patriarch of mankind, but Eve
Persisted; yet submiss, though last, replied.
 "With thy permission then, and thus forewarned,
Chiefly by what thy own last reasoning words
Touched only, that our trial, when least sought, 380
May find us both perhaps far less prepared,
The willinger I go, nor much expect
A foe so proud will first the weaker seek;
So bent, the more shall shame him his repulse."
 Thus saying, from her husband's hand her hand
Soft she withdrew, and like a wood-nymph light,
Oread or Dryad, or of Delia's train,
Betook her to the groves, but Delia's self
In gait surpassed and goddess-like deport,
Though not as she with bow and quiver armed, 390
But with such gardening tools as art yet rude,
Guiltless of fire had formed, or angels brought.
To Pales, or Pomona, thus adorned,
Likest she seemed, Pomona when she fled
Vertumnus, or to Ceres in her prime,
Yet virgin of Proserpina from Jove.
Her long with ardent look his eye pursued
Delighted, but desiring more her stay.
Oft he to her his charge of quick return
Repeated, she to him as oft engaged 400
To be returned by noon amid the bower,
And all things in best order to invite
Noontide repast, or afternoon's repose.
O much deceived, much failing, hapless Eve,
Of thy presumed return! event perverse!
Thou never from that hour in Paradise
Found'st either sweet repast or sound repose;
Such ambush, hid among sweet flowers and shades,
Waited with hellish rancor imminent
To intercept thy way, or send thee back 410
Despoiled of innocence, of faith, of bliss.

371. securer, i.e., "less prepared" (381).

387. Oread or Dryad, a nymph of the mountains or of the trees. **Delia,** the goddess Diana, born on the island of Delos.

392. Guiltless of fire. The uses of fire are not discovered until after the fall.

393 ff. Pales was a Roman goddess of flocks, **Pomona** of fruits, **Ceres** of agriculture; **Vertumnus** was god of the changing seasons.

396. Yet virgin of, not yet the mother of.

402. And all things in best order, i.e., to have all things in best order.

For now, and since first break of dawn the Fiend,
Mere serpent in appearance, forth was come,
And on his quest, where likeliest he might find
The only two of mankind, but in them
The whole included race, his purposed prey.
In bower and field he sought, where any tuft
Of grove or garden-plot more pleasant lay,
Their tendance or plantation for delight,
By fountain or by shady rivulet. 420
He sought them both, but wished his hap might find
Eve separate; he wished, but not with hope
Of what so seldom chanced; when to his wish,
Beyond his hope, Eve separate he spies,
Veiled in a cloud of fragrance, where she stood,
Half spied, so thick the roses bushing round
About her glowed, oft stooping to support
Each flower of slender stalk, whose head though gay
Carnation, purple, azure, or specked with gold,
Hung drooping unsustained; them she upstays 430
Gently with myrtle band, mindless the while
Herself, though fairest unsupported flower,
From her best prop so far, and storm so nigh.
Nearer he drew, and many a walk traversed
Of stateliest covert, cedar, pine, or palm,
Then voluble and bold, now hid, now seen
Among thick-woven arborets and flowers
Imbordered on each bank, the hand of Eve:
Spot more delicious than those gardens feigned
Or of revived Adonis, or renowned 440
Alcinous, host of old Laertes' son,
Or that, not mystic, where the sapient king
Held dalliance with his fair Egyptian spouse.
Much he the place admired, the person more.
As one who long in populous city pent,
Where houses thick and sewers annoy the air,
Forth issuing on a summer's morn to breathe
Among the pleasant villages and farms
Adjoined, from each thing met conceives delight,

432. Herself . . . flower. The metaphor is repeated from IV, 270.

436. voluble, rolling (Latin *volubilis*).

437. arborets, small trees, shrubs.

438. hand, handiwork.

439 ff. The gardens of Alcinous, the Phaeacian ruler who entertained Odysseus (**old Laertes' son**), are described in *Odyssey* vii. The garden of Solomon (**the sapient king**) is mentioned in Scripture; hence, from Milton's point of view, it is not **feigned** or **mystic** (i.e., mythical) like the others. Cf. Song of Sol. 7:2, and I Kings 3:1.

440, 442. Or . . . or, either . . . or.

445 ff. The attitude toward nature revealed in this simile anticipates Wordsworth's. Note especially the idea that natural objects, lovely in themselves, are enhanced in meaning by their human associations. Milton's treatment is ordinarily more impersonal.

446. annoy, pollute, render noisome.

The smell of grain, or tedded grass, or kine, 450
Or dairy, each rural sight, each rural sound;
If chance with nymph-like step fair virgin pass,
What pleasing seemed, for her now pleases more,
She most, and in her look sums all delight.
Such pleasure took the Serpent to behold
This flowery plat, the sweet recess of Eve
Thus early, thus alone; her heavenly form
Angelic, but more soft and feminine,
Her graceful innocence, her every air
Of gesture or least action overawed 460
His malice, and with rapine sweet bereaved
His fierceness of the fierce intent it brought.
That space the Evil One abstracted stood
From his own evil, and for the time remained
Stupidly good, of enmity disarmed,
Of guile, of hate, of envy, of revenge;
But the hot hell that always in him burns,
Though in mid Heaven, soon ended his delight,
And tortures him now more, the more he sees
Of pleasure not for him ordained; then soon 470
Fierce hate he recollects, and all his thoughts
Of mischief, gratulating, thus excites.
"Thoughts, whither have ye led me, with what sweet
Compulsion thus transported to forget
What hither brought us, hate, not love, nor hope
Of Paradise for Hell, hope here to taste
Of pleasure, but all pleasure to destroy,
Save what is in destroying; other joy
To me is lost. Then let me not let pass
Occasion which now smiles, behold alone 480
The woman, opportune to all attempts,
Her husband, for I view far round, not nigh,
Whose higher intellectual more I shun,
And strength, of courage haughty, and of limb
Heroic built, though of terrestrial mould,
Foe not informidable, exempt from wound,
I not; so much hath Hell debased, and pain
Enfeebled me, to what I was in Heaven.
She fair, divinely fair, fit love for Gods,
Not terrible, though terror be in love 490
And beauty, not approached by stronger hate,
Hate stronger, under shew of love well feigned,
The way which to her ruin now I tend."
So spake the Enemy of mankind, enclosed
In serpent, inmate bad, and toward Eve

450. tedded grass, grass just mown and spread out for drying.
465. Stupidly good, i.e., stupefied into goodness.
485. of terrestrial mould, of earthly substance.

Addressed his way, not with indented wave,
Prone on the ground as since, but on his rear,
Circular base of rising folds, that towered
Fold above fold a surging maze; his head
Crested aloft, and carbuncle his eyes; 500
With burnished neck of verdant gold, erect
Amidst his circling spires, that on the grass
Floated redundant. Pleasing was his shape,
And lovely, never since of serpent kind
Lovelier; not those that in Illyria changed
Hermione and Cadmus, or the god
In Epidaurus; nor to which transformed
Ammonian Jove, or Capitoline was seen,
He with Olympias, this with her who bore
Scipio the height of Rome. With tract oblique 510
At first, as one who sought access, but feared
To interrupt, sidelong he works his way.
As when a ship by skilful steersman wrought
Nigh river's mouth or foreland, where the wind
Veers oft, as oft so steers, and shifts her sail;
So varied he, and of his tortuous train
Curled many a wanton wreath in sight of Eve,
To lure her eye; she busied heard the sound
Of rustling leaves, but minded not, as used
To such disport before her through the field, 520
From every beast, more duteous at her call,
Than at Circean call the herd disguised.
He bolder now, uncalled before her stood,
But as in gaze admiring. Oft he bowed
His turret crest, and sleek enamelled neck,
Fawning, and licked the ground whereon she trod.
His gentle dumb expression turned at length
The eye of Eve to mark his play; he glad
Of her attention gained, with serpent tongue
Organic, or impulse of vocal air, 530
His fraudulent temptation thus began:

500. carbuncle, i.e., deep red, suggesting passion.

502. spires, coils. **505. changed,** took the place of.

506. Hermione and her husband **Cadmus,** king of Thebes, were changed into serpents at their own request, in order to escape the miseries of human life. The god of medicine, Aesculapius, took the form of a serpent when going from **Epidaurus** to Rome for the purpose of staying a pestilence.

507. nor to which transformed, etc., i.e., nor those serpents into which Jove was seen transformed. According to a myth told by Plutarch, Jupiter Ammon (**Ammonian Jove**) was the father of Alexander the Great, having been observed in the shape of a serpent with **Olympias,** Alexander's mother. A similar myth portrayed Jupiter Capitolinus as the father of Scipio Africanus.

517. wanton, playful.

522. Circean call. The allusion is to the well-known myth of Circe, an enchantress who changed men into beasts and kept them in complete subjection to her will.

529. with serpent tongue, etc. Satan either uses the serpent's vocal organs directly or causes his words seemingly to come from them.

"Wonder not, sovran mistress, if perhaps
Thou canst, who art sole wonder, much less arm
Thy looks, the heaven of mildness, with disdain,
Displeased that I approach thee thus, and gaze
Insatiate, I thus single, nor have feared
Thy awful brow, more awful thus retired.
Fairest resemblance of thy Maker fair,
Thee all things living gaze on, all things thine
By gift, and thy celestial beauty adore, 540
With ravishment beheld, there best beheld
Where universally admired; but here
In this enclosure wild, these beasts among,
Beholders rude, and shallow to discern
Half what in thee is fair, one man except,
Who sees thee? (and what is one?) who shouldst be seen
A Goddess among Gods, adored and served
By angels numberless, thy daily train."
So glozed the Tempter, and his proem tuned;
Into the heart of Eve his words made way, 550
Though at the voice much marvelling; at length
Not unamazed she thus in answer spake.
"What may this mean? Language of man pronounced
By tongue of brute, and human sense expressed?
The first at least of these I thought denied
To beasts, whom God on their creation-day
Created mute to all articulate sound;
The latter I demur, for in their looks
Much reason, and in their actions, oft appears.
Thee, Serpent, subtlest beast of all the field 560
I knew, but not with human voice endued;
Redouble then this miracle, and say,
How cam'st thou speakable of mute, and how
To me so friendly grown above the rest
Of brutal kind, that daily are in sight?
Say, for such wonder claims attention due."
To whom the guileful Tempter thus replied.
"Empress of this fair World, resplendent Eve,
Easy to me it is to tell thee all
What thou command'st, and right thou shouldst be obeyed. 570
I was at first as other beasts that graze
The trodden herb, of abject thoughts and low,
As was my food, nor aught but food discerned
Or sex, and apprehended nothing high:
Till on a day roving the field, I chanced
A goodly tree far distant to behold

544. shallow, i.e., too shallow.
549. glozed, smoothed over his real motive with flattery.
558. demur, remain in doubt about.
563. How cam'st thou speakable of mute, i.e., how did you, being mute, become capable of speech.

Loaden with fruit of fairest colors mixed,
Ruddy and gold. I nearer drew to gaze;
When from the boughs a savory odor blown,
Grateful to appetite, more pleased my sense 580
Than smell of sweetest fennel or the teats
Of ewe or goat dropping with milk at even,
Unsucked of lamb or kid, that tend their play.
To satisfy the sharp desire I had
Of tasting those fair apples, I resolved
Not to defer; hunger and thirst at once,
Powerful persuaders, quickened at the scent
Of that alluring fruit, urged me so keen.
About the mossy trunk I wound me soon,
For high from ground the branches would require 590
Thy utmost reach or Adam's: round the tree
All other beasts that saw, with like desire
Longing and envying stood, but could not reach.
Amid the tree now got, where plenty hung
Tempting so nigh, to pluck and eat my fill
I spared not, for such pleasure till that hour
At feed or fountain never had I found.
Sated at length, ere long I might perceive
Strange alteration in me, to degree
Of reason in my inward powers, and speech 600
Wanted not long, though to this shape retained.
Thenceforth to speculations high or deep
I turned my thoughts, and with capacious mind
Considered all things visible in Heaven,
Or Earth, or middle, all things fair and good;
But all that fair and good in thy divine
Semblance, and in thy beauty's heavenly ray
United I beheld; no fair to thine
Equivalent or second, which compelled
Me thus, though importune perhaps, to come 610
And gaze, and worship thee of right declared
Sovran of creatures, universal Dame."
So talked the spirited sly Snake; and Eve
Yet more amazed unwary thus replied.
"Serpent, thy overpraising leaves in doubt
The virtue of that fruit, in thee first proved.
But say, where grows the tree, from hence how far?
For many are the trees of God that grow
In Paradise, and various, yet unknown
To us; in such abundance lies our choice, 620
As leaves a greater store of fruit untouched,

581. According to popular belief, serpents were especially fond of fennel and were in the habit of sucking milk from sheep and goats.

605. middle, i.e., the air.

612. universal Dame, mistress of the universe.

613. spirited, i.e., inspired by Satan.

Still hanging incorruptible, till men
Grow up to their provision, and more hands
Help to disburden Nature of her birth."
  To whom the wily Adder, blithe and glad.
"Empress, the way is ready, and not long;
Beyond a row of myrtles, on a flat,
Fast by a fountain, one small thicket past
Of blowing myrrh and balm; if thou accept
My conduct, I can bring thee thither soon." 630
  "Lead then," said Eve. He leading swiftly rolled
In tangles, and made intricate seem straight,
To mischief swift. Hope elevates, and joy
Brightens his crest, as when a wandering fire,
Compact of unctuous vapor, which the night
Condenses, and the cold environs round,
Kindled through agitation to a flame,
Which oft, they say, some evil spirit attends,
Hovering and blazing with delusive light,
Misleads the amazed night-wanderer from his way 640
To bogs and mires, and oft through pond or pool,
There swallowed up and lost, from succor far.
So glistered the dire Snake, and into fraud
Led Eve our credulous mother, to the tree
Of prohibition, root of all our woe;
Which when she saw, thus to her guide she spake.
  "Serpent, we might have spared our coming hither,
Fruitless to me, though fruit be here to excess,
The credit of whose virtue rest with thee,
Wondrous indeed, if cause of such effects. 650
But of this tree we may not taste nor touch;
God so commanded, and left that command
Sole daughter of his voice; the rest, we live
Law to ourselves, our reason is our law."
  To whom the Tempter guilefully replied.
"Indeed? Hath God then said that of the fruit
Of all these garden trees ye shall not eat,
Yet lords declared of all in Earth or air?"
  To whom thus Eve yet sinless. "Of the fruit
Of each tree in the garden we may eat, 660
But of the fruit of this fair tree amidst
The garden, God hath said, 'Ye shall not eat
Thereof, nor shall ye touch it, lest ye die.'"

622. incorruptible, incapable of decay.
624. birth, i.e., the products to which she has given birth.
629. blowing, blossoming.
634 ff. This description of the ignis fatuus combines a semiscientific explanation with a popular superstition. Whether Milton actually believed the phenomenon the work of an evil spirit he does not say.
643. fraud, offense, harm. **653. the rest,** as for the rest.
661–663. Milton here follows very closely the phraseology of Gen. 3:1–3.

She scarce had said, though brief, when now more bold
The Tempter, but with show of zeal and love
To Man, and indignation at his wrong,
New part puts on, and as to passion moved,
Fluctuates disturbed, yet comely and in act
Raised, as of some great matter to begin.
As when of old some orator renowned 670
In Athens or free Rome, where eloquence
Flourished, since mute, to some great cause addressed,
Stood in himself collected, while each part,
Motion, each act won audience ere the tongue,
Sometimes in height began, as no delay
Of preface brooking through his zeal of right.
So standing, moving, or to height upgrown,
The Tempter all impassioned thus began.
"O sacred, wise, and wisdom-giving Plant,
Mother of science, now I feel thy power 680
Within me clear, not only to discern
Things in their causes, but to trace the ways
Of highest agents, deemed however wise.
Queen of this Universe, do not believe
Those rigid threats of death; ye shall not die:
How should ye? by the fruit? it gives you life
To knowledge; by the threatener? look on me,
Me who have touched and tasted, yet both live,
And life more perfect have attained than fate
Meant me, by venturing higher than my lot. 690
Shall that be shut to Man, which to the beast
Is open? or will God incense his ire
For such a petty trespass, and not praise
Rather your dauntless virtue, whom the pain
Of death denounced, whatever thing death be,
Deterred not from achieving what might lead
To happier life, knowledge of good and evil;
Of good, how just? of evil, if what is evil
Be real, why not known, since easier shunned?
God therefore cannot hurt ye, and be just; 700
Not just, not God; not feared then, nor obeyed:
Your fear itself of death removes the fear.
Why then was this forbid? Why but to awe,
Why but to keep ye low and ignorant,
His worshippers; he knows that in the day
Ye eat thereof, your eyes that seem so clear,

668. Fluctuates. The word is used literally. Milton means that the serpent moves his body to and fro, in order to give visible expression to his assumed emotion.

679 ff. "O sacred, wise . . ." The serpent's speech is a masterpiece of persuasion, uniting intense emotional fervor with closely packed and seemingly irrefutable arguments. Milton does not wish to make Eve too easy a victim.

680. science, knowledge (Latin *scientia*).

687. To, in addition to.

Yet are but dim, shall perfectly be then
Opened and cleared, and ye shall be as Gods,
Knowing both good and evil as they know.
That ye should be as Gods, since I as Man, 710
Internal Man, is but proportion meet,
I of brute human, ye of human Gods.
So ye shall die perhaps, by putting off
Human, to put on Gods, death to be wished,
Though threatened, which no worse than this can bring.
And what are Gods, that Man may not become
As they, participating godlike food?
The Gods are first, and that advantage use
On our belief, that all from them proceeds;
I question it, for this fair Earth I see, 720
Warmed by the sun, producing every kind,
Them nothing. If they all things, who enclosed
Knowledge of good and evil in this tree,
That whoso eats thereof, forthwith attains
Wisdom without their leave? and wherein lies
The offence, that Man should thus attain to know?
What can your knowledge hurt him, or this tree
Impart against his will, if all be his?
Or is it envy, and can envy dwell
In heavenly breasts? These, these and many more 730
Causes import your need of this fair fruit.
Goddess humane, reach then, and freely taste!"
He ended, and his words replete with guile
Into her heart too easy entrance won.
Fixed on the fruit she gazed, which to behold
Might tempt alone, and in her ears the sound
Yet rung of his persuasive words, impregned
With reason, to her seeming, and with truth;
Meanwhile the hour of noon drew on, and waked
An eager appetite, raised by the smell 740
So savory of that fruit, which with desire,
Inclinable now grown to touch or taste,
Solicited her longing eye; yet first
Pausing a while, thus to herself she mused.
"Great are thy virtues, doubtless, best of fruits,
Though kept from Man, and worthy to be admired,
Whose taste, too long forborne, at first assay
Gave elocution to the mute, and taught
The tongue not made for speech to speak thy praise.
Thy praise he also who forbids thy use 750
Conceals not from us, naming thee the Tree

732. humane, gracious, gentle in demeanor.
737. impregned, impregnated.
739–743. Physical appetite is an important factor in Eve's decision, but she does not admit it to herself.

Of Knowledge, knowledge both of good and evil;
Forbids us then to taste, but his forbidding
Commends thee more, while it infers the good
By thee communicated, and our want;
For good unknown sure is not had, or had
And yet unknown, is as not had at all.
In plain then, what forbids he but to know,
Forbids us good, forbids us to be wise?
Such prohibitions bind not. But if Death 760
Bind us with after-bands, what profits then
Our inward freedom? In the day we eat
Of this fair fruit, our doom is, we shall die.
How dies the Serpent? He hath eaten and lives,
And knows, and speaks, and reasons, and discerns,
Irrational till then. For us alone
Was death invented? or to us denied
This intellectual food, for beasts reserved?
For beasts it seems; yet that one beast which first
Hath tasted, envies not, but brings with joy 770
That good befallen him, author unsuspect,
Friendly to man, far from deceit or guile.
What fear I then, rather what know to fear
Under this ignorance of good and evil,
Of God or death, of law or penalty?
Here grows the cure of all, this fruit divine,
Fair to the eye, inviting to the taste,
Of virtue to make wise; what hinders then
To reach, and feed at once both body and mind?"
So saying, her rash hand in evil hour 780
Forth reaching to the fruit, she plucked, she eat.
Earth felt the wound, and Nature from her seat
Sighing through all her works gave signs of woe,
That all was lost. Back to the thicket slunk
The guilty Serpent, and well might, for Eve
Intent now only on her taste, nought else
Regarded; such delight till then, as seemed,
In fruit she never tasted, whether true
Or fancied so, through expectation high
Of knowledge, nor was Godhead from her thought. 790
Greedily she ingorged without restraint,

758. In plain, frankly (i.e., in plain terms).

771. author unsuspect, informant not to be suspected.

778. Of virtue, i.e., having the power.

781. eat. Milton regularly uses this form of the preterite. Since the pronunciation corresponds to the spelling, lines 781 and 782 form a rhymed couplet, giving effective emphasis to a crucial point in the action.

791. Greedily she ingorged without restraint. In terms of human ethics as opposed to theology, Milton interprets the sin of Adam and Eve as a sin of excess, a violation of temperance. Eve's initial greed is therefore a symbol of all the other forms of excess in which she and Adam afterwards indulge.

And knew not eating death. Satiate at length,
And heightened as with wine, jocund and boon,
Thus to herself she pleasingly began.
"O sovran, virtuous, precious of all trees
In Paradise, of operation blest
To sapience, hitherto obscured, infamed,
And thy fair fruit let hang, as to no end
Created; but henceforth my early care,
Not without song, each morning, and due praise, 800
Shall tend thee, and the fertile burden ease
Of thy full branches offered free to all;
Till dieted by thee I grow mature
In knowledge, as the Gods who all things know;
Though others envy what they cannot give;
For had the gift been theirs, it had not here
Thus grown. Experience, next to thee I owe,
Best guide; not following thee, I had remained
In ignorance, thou open'st Wisdom's way,
And givest access, though secret she retire. 810
And I perhaps am secret; Heaven is high,
High and remote to see from thence distinct
Each thing on Earth; and other care perhaps
May have diverted from continual watch
Our great Forbidder, safe with all his spies
About him. But to Adam in what sort
Shall I appear? Shall I to him make known
As yet my change, and give him to partake
Full happiness with me, or rather not,
But keep the odds of knowledge in my power 820
Without copartner? so to add what wants
In female sex, the more to draw his love,
And render me more equal, and perhaps,
A thing not undesirable, sometime
Superior; for inferior who is free?
This may be well. But what if God have seen
And death ensue? then I shall be no more,
And Adam wedded to another Eve,
Shall live with her enjoying, I extinct;
A death to think. Confirmed then I resolve 830
Adam shall share with me in bliss or woe.

792. knew not eating, i.e., knew not that she was eating.

793. boon, gay.

795. virtuous, precious of all trees, i.e., most virtuous, most precious, etc. The idiom is classical.

796-97. of operation blest To sapience, i.e., so blest as to have the power of conferring wisdom.

797. infamed, not known.

815. safe, not likely to do harm.

817 ff. Shall I to him, etc. The first fruits of Eve's sin are selfishness and jealousy—the negation of her original qualities.

So dear I love him, that with him all deaths
I could endure, without him live no life."
  So saying, from the tree her step she turned,
But first low reverence done, as to the power
That dwelt within, whose presence had infused
Into the plant sciential sap, derived
From nectar, drink of Gods. Adam the while
Waiting desirous her return, had wove
Of choicest flowers a garland to adorn 840
Her tresses, and her rural labors crown,
As reapers oft are wont their harvest queen.
Great joy he promised to his thoughts, and new
Solace in her return, so long delayed;
Yet oft his heart, divine of something ill,
Misgave him; he the faltering measure felt;
And forth to meet her went, the way she took
That morn when first they parted. By the Tree
Of Knowledge he must pass; there he her met,
Scarce from the tree returning; in her hand 850
A bough of fairest fruit that downy smiled,
New gathered, and ambrosial smell diffused.
To him she hasted; in her face excuse
Came prologue, and apology to prompt,
Which with bland words at will she thus addressed.
  "Hast thou not wondered, Adam, at my stay?
Thee I have missed, and thought it long, deprived
Thy presence, agony of love till now
Not felt, nor shall be twice, for never more
Mean I to try what rash untried I sought, 860
The pain of absence from thy sight. But strange
Hath been the cause, and wonderful to hear:
This tree is not as we are told, a tree
Of danger tasted, nor to evil unknown
Opening the way, but of divine effect
To open eyes, and make them Gods who taste;
And hath been tasted such. The Serpent wise,
Or not restrained as we, or not obeying,
Hath eaten of the fruit, and is become
Not dead as we are threatened, but thenceforth 870

835–836. Eve's perverted conception of God quickly manifests itself in idolatry.

837. sciential, capable of bestowing knowledge.

838–844. Adam the while . . . delayed. The situation closely parallels that in *Iliad* xxii, where Andromache is described making preparations for Hector's return, not knowing that he is already slain.

845. divine of, foreboding.

846. faltering measure, i.e., the uneven beating of his heart.

853–854. in her face . . . prompt. Milton means that the appearance of Eve's face served as a fitting introduction to her verbal apology. The stage imagery is perhaps intended to suggest her insincerity; she approaches Adam in an assumed character.

Endued with human voice and human sense,
Reasoning to admiration, and with me
Persuasively hath so prevailed, that I
Have also tasted, and have also found
The effects to correspond, opener mine eyes,
Dim erst, dilated spirits, ampler heart,
And growing up to Godhead; which for thee
Chiefly I sought, without thee can despise.
For bliss, as thou hast part, to me is bliss;
Tedious, unshared with thee, and odious soon. 880
Thou therefore also taste, that equal lot
May join us, equal joy, as equal love;
Lest thou not tasting, different degree
Disjoin us, and I then too late renounce
Deity for thee, when fate will not permit."
 Thus Eve with countenance blithe her story told;
But in her cheek distemper flushing glowed.
On the other side, Adam, soon as he heard
The fatal trespass done by Eve, amazed,
Astonied stood and blank, while horror chill 890
Ran through his veins, and all his joints relaxed;
From his slack hand the garland wreathed for Eve
Down dropped, and all the faded roses shed.
Speechless he stood and pale, till thus at length
First to himself he inward silence broke.
 "O fairest of creation, last and best
Of all God's works, creature in whom excelled
Whatever can to sight or thought be formed,
Holy, divine, good, amiable, or sweet!
How art thou lost, how on a sudden lost, 900
Defaced, deflowered, and now to death devote!
Rather how hast thou yielded to transgress
The strict forbiddance, how to violate
The sacred fruit forbidden! Some cursëd fraud
Of enemy hath beguiled thee, yet unknown,
And me with thee hath ruined, for with thee
Certain my resolution is to die;
How can I live without thee, how forgo
Thy sweet converse and love so dearly joined,
To live again in these wild woods forlorn? 910
Should God create another Eve, and I
Another rib afford, yet loss of thee
Would never from my heart; no, no! I feel
The link of nature draw me: flesh of flesh,
Bone of my bone thou art, and from thy state

872. to admiration, in a way to be admired.

877–878. which for . . . Chiefly I sought. Eve ends her plea with an open falsehood. Cf. 816–825.

901. devote, doomed, accursed.

914 ff. flesh of flesh, etc. Cf. Gen. 2:23.

Mine never shall be parted, bliss or woe."
  So having said, as one from sad dismay
Recomforted, and after thoughts disturbed
Submitting to what seemed remediless,
Thus in calm mood his words to Eve he turned. 920
  "Bold deed thou hast presumed, adventurous Eve,
And peril great provoked, who thus hast dared,
Had it been only coveting to eye
That sacred fruit, sacred to abstinence
Much more to taste it under ban to touch.
But past who can recall, or done undo?
Not God Omnipotent, nor Fate. Yet so
Perhaps thou shalt not die; perhaps the fact
Is not so heinous now, foretasted fruit,
Profaned first by the Serpent, by him first 930
Made common and unhallowed ere our taste,
Nor yet on him found deadly; he yet lives,
Lives, as thou saidst, and gains to live as Man
Higher degree of life, inducement strong
To us, as likely tasting to attain
Proportional ascent, which cannot be
But to be Gods, or angels, demi-gods.
Nor can I think that God, Creator wise,
Though threatening, will in earnest so destroy
Us his prime creatures, dignified so high, 940
Set over all his works, which in our fall,
For us created, needs with us must fail,
Dependent made; so God shall uncreate
Be frustrate, do, undo, and labor lose,
Not well conceived of God, who though his power
Creation could repeat, yet would be loth
Us to abolish, lest the Adversary
Triumph and say: 'Fickle their state whom God
Most favors, who can please him long? Me first
He ruined, now mankind; whom will he next?' 950
Matter of scorn not to be given the Foe;
However, I with thee have fixed my lot,
Certain to undergo like doom: if death
Consort with thee, death is to me as life;
So forcible within my heart I feel
The bond of nature draw me to my own,
My own in thee, for what thou art is mine;
Our state cannot be severed; we are one,
One flesh; to lose thee were to lose myself."

928. fact, deed (Latin *factum*).

932. he yet lives, etc. Having determined his course on nonrational grounds, Adam proceeds to rationalize just as Eve had done.

953. Certain, resolved.

So Adam, and thus Eve to him replied. 960
"O glorious trial of exceeding love,
Illustrious evidence, example high!
Engaging me to emulate, but short
Of thy perfection, how shall I attain,
Adam, from whose dear side I boast me sprung,
And gladly of our union hear thee speak,
One heart, one soul in both; whereof good proof
This day affords, declaring thee resolved,
Rather than death or aught than death more dread
Shall separate us, linked in love so dear, 970
To undergo with me one guilt, one crime,
If any be, of tasting this fair fruit,
Whose virtue (for of good still good proceeds,
Direct, or by occasion) hath presented
This happy trial of thy love, which else
So eminently never had been known.
Were it I thought death menaced would ensue
This my attempt, I would sustain alone
The worst, and not persuade thee, rather die
Deserted, than oblige thee with a fact 980
Pernicious to thy peace, chiefly assured
Remarkably so late of thy so true,
So faithful love unequalled; but I feel
Far otherwise the event, not death, but life
Augmented, opened eyes, new hopes, new joys,
Taste so divine, that what of sweet before
Hath touched my sense, flat seems to this and harsh.
On my experience, Adam, freely taste,
And fear of death deliver to the winds."
So saying, she embraced him, and for joy 990
Tenderly wept, much won that he his love
Had so ennobled, as of choice to incur
Divine displeasure for her sake, or death.
In recompense (for such compliance bad
Such recompense best merits) from the bough
She gave him of that fair enticing fruit
With liberal hand; he scrupled not to eat
Against his better knowledge, not deceived,
But fondly overcome with female charm.
Earth trembled from her entrails, as again 1000
In pangs, and Nature gave a second groan;
Sky loured, and muttering thunder, some sad drops

977–983. Were it I thought . . . unequalled. Cf. 826–33. **oblige,** render liable to punishment.

1000 ff. Earth trembled, etc. The idea that the fall was marked by convulsions of the earth and other signs of nature's grief is a literary and theological tradition. While it has no direct scriptural authority, it may have been suggested by the analogous portents accompanying the crucifixion of Christ (Matt. 27:51).

Wept at completing of the mortal sin
Original; while Adam took no thought,
Eating his fill, nor Eve to iterate
Her former trespass feared, the more to soothe
Him with her loved society, that now
As with new wine intoxicated both
They swim in mirth, and fancy that they feel
Divinity within them breeding wings 1010
Wherewith to scorn the Earth. But that false fruit
Far other operation first displayed,
Carnal desire inflaming: he on Eve
Began to cast lascivious eyes, she him
As wantonly repaid; in lust they burn,
Till Adam thus 'gan Eve to dalliance move.
"Eve, now I see thou art exact of taste
And elegant, of sapience no small part,
Since to each meaning savor we apply,
And palate call judicious; I the praise 1020
Yield thee, so well this day thou hast purveyed.
Much pleasure we have lost, while we abstained
From this delightful fruit, nor known till now
True relish, tasting; if such pleasure be
In things to us forbidden, it might be wished
For this one tree had been forbidden ten.
But come; so well refreshed, now let us play,
As meet is, after such delicious fare;
For never did thy beauty since the day
I saw thee first and wedded thee, adorned 1030
With all perfections, so inflame my sense
With ardor to enjoy thee, fairer now
Than ever, bounty of this virtuous tree."
So said he, and forbore not glance or toy
Of amorous intent, well understood
Of Eve, whose eye darted contagious fire.
Her hand he seized, and to a shady bank,
Thick overhead with verdant roof embowered,
He led her nothing loth; flowers were the couch,
Pansies, and violets, and asphodel, 1040
And hyacinth, Earth's freshest softest lap.
There they their fill of love and love's disport
Took largely, of their mutual guilt the seal,
The solace of their sin, till dewy sleep
Oppressed them, wearied with their amorous play.

1003–1004. the mortal sin Original. This is Milton's only use in the poem of the theological term "original sin."

1019. The word **savor** is derived from Latin *sapere,* which means both "to taste" and "to be wise." Milton represents Adam as playing on this double meaning in explaining why Eve's *taste* can properly be called **judicious.**

1034. toy, caress.

Soon as the force of that fallacious fruit,
That with exhilarating vapor bland
About their spirits had played, and inmost powers
Made err, was now exhaled, and grosser sleep,
Bred of unkindly fumes, with conscious dreams 1050
Encumbered, now had left them, up they rose
As from unrest, and each the other viewing,
Soon found their eyes how opened, and their minds
How darkened; innocence, that as a veil
Had shadowed them from knowing ill, was gone,
Just confidence, and native righteousness,
And honor from about them, naked left
To guilty Shame. He covered, but his robe
Uncovered more. So rose the Danite strong,
Herculean Samson, from the harlot-lap 1060
Of Philistean Delilah, and waked
Shorn of his strength, they destitute and bare
Of all their virtue. Silent, and in face
Confounded, long they sat, as strucken mute,
Till Adam, though not less than Eve abashed,
At length gave utterance to these words constrained.
"O Eve, in evil hour thou didst give ear
To that false worm, of whomsoever taught
To counterfeit Man's voice, true in our fall,
False in our promised rising; since our eyes 1070
Opened we find indeed, and find we know
Both good and evil, good lost and evil got,
Bad fruit of knowledge, if this be to know,
Which leaves us naked thus, of honor void,
Of innocence, of faith, of purity,
Our wonted ornaments now soiled and stained,
And in our faces evident the signs
Of foul concupiscence; whence evil store,
Even shame, the last of evils; of the first
Be sure then. How shall I behold the face 1080
Henceforth of God or angel, erst with joy
And rapture so oft beheld? those heavenly shapes
Will dazzle now this earthly, with their blaze
Insufferably bright. Oh might I here
In solitude live savage, in some glade
Obscured, where highest woods impenetrable
To star or sunlight, spread their umbrage broad
And brown as evening! Cover me ye pines,
Ye cedars, with innumerable boughs

1050. unkindly, contrary to nature.
1058. He covered, etc. i.e., shame covered them with his robe, but in so doing revealed to them their nakedness.
1059. So rose the Danite strong, etc. Cf. Judg. 16:4–20.
1068. worm, serpent.
1079. the last of evils, i.e., the greatest (Latin *extremus*). **the first,** i.e., the lesser.

Hide me, where I may never see them more. 1090
But let us now, as in bad plight, devise
What best may for the present serve to hide
The parts of each from other that seem most
To shame obnoxious, and unseemliest seen,
Some tree whose broad smooth leaves together sewed,
And girded on our loins, may cover round
Those middle parts, that this new comer, Shame,
There sit not, and reproach us as unclean."
So counselled he, and both together went
Into the thickest wood; there soon they chose 1100
The fig-tree, not that kind for fruit renowned,
But such as at this day to Indians known
In Malabar or Decan spreads her arms
Branching so broad and long, that in the ground
The bended twigs take root, and daughters grow
About the mother tree, a pillared shade
High overarched, and echoing walks between;
There oft the Indian herdsman shunning heat
Shelters in cool, and tends his pasturing herds
At loop-holes cut through thickest shade. Those leaves 1110
They gathered, broad as Amazonian targe,
And with what skill they had, together sewed,
To gird their waist, vain covering if to hide
Their guilt and dreaded shame; Oh how unlike
To that first naked glory. Such of late
Columbus found the American so girt
With feathered cincture, naked else and wild
Among the trees on isles and woody shores.
Thus fenced, and as they thought, their shame in part
Covered, but not at rest or ease of mind, 1120
They sat them down to weep, nor only tears
Rained at their eyes, but high winds worse within
Began to rise, high passions, anger, hate,
Mistrust, suspicion, discord, and shook sore
Their inward state of mind, calm region once
And full of peace, now tossed and turbulent;
For Understanding ruled not, and the Will
Heard not her lore, both in subjection now
To sensual Appetite, who from beneath
Usurping over sovran Reason claimed 1130
Superior sway. From thus distempered breast,
Adam, estranged in look and altered style,
Speech intermitted thus to Eve renewed.

1094. obnoxious. Cf. note on 170.

1103. Malabar refers to the western coast of Hindustan, especially the southern part. **Decan,** or **Deccan,** is a name applied to the entire peninsula.

1111. Amazonian targe, shield of the Amazons.

1127 ff. For Understanding . . . sway. The tripartite division of the soul, which underlies this passage, is Platonic. Cf. 351–356.

"Would thou hadst hearkened to my words, and stayed
With me, as I besought thee, when that strange
Desire of wandering this unhappy morn,
I know not whence possessed thee; we had then
Remained still happy, not as now, despoiled
Of all our good, shamed, naked, miserable.
Let none henceforth seek needless cause to approve 1140
The faith they owe; when earnestly they seek
Such proof, conclude, they then begin to fail."
To whom soon moved with touch of blame thus Eve.
"What words have passed thy lips, Adam severe!
Imputest thou that to my default, or will
Of wandering, as thou call'st it, which who knows
But might as ill have happened thou being by,
Or to thyself perhaps? Hadst thou been there,
Or here the attempt, thou couldst not have discerned
Fraud in the Serpent, speaking as he spake; 1150
No ground of enmity between us known,
Why he should mean me ill, or seek to harm.
Was I to have never parted from thy side?
As good have grown there still a lifeless rib.
Being as I am, why didst not thou the head
Command me absolutely not to go,
Going into such danger as thou saidst?
Too facile then, thou didst not much gainsay,
Nay didst permit, approve, and fair dismiss.
Hadst thou been firm and fixed in thy dissent, 1160
Neither had I transgressed, nor thou with me."
To whom then first incensed Adam replied.
"Is this the love, is this the recompense
Of mine to thee, ingrateful Eve, expressed
Immutable when thou wert lost, not I,
Who might have lived and joyed immortal bliss,
Yet willingly chose rather death with thee?
And am I now upbraided, as the cause
Of thy transgressing? not enough severe,
It seems, in thy restraint. What could I more? 1170
I warned thee, I admonished thee, foretold
The danger, and the lurking enemy

1141. owe, possess.

1163 ff. Adam's statement is a fascinating mixture of right and wrong judgment, self-knowledge, and self-deception. In Milton's theory he is the superior being, but his reasoning is flawed by passion: "Understanding ruled not." Lines 1166–1167 are certainly not a fair representation of the facts, being inconsistent with what he said in lines 908–910, above: "How can I live without thee?" On the other hand, he has come to the point of partly recognizing his own weakness: "And perhaps I also erred." How detached Milton himself is in all this it is really very difficult to say.

1164. expressed, demonstrated.

That lay in wait; beyond this had been force,
And force upon free will hath here no place.
But confidence then bore thee on, secure
Either to meet no danger or to find
Matter of glorious trial; and perhaps
I also erred in overmuch admiring
What seemed in thee so perfect, that I thought
No evil durst attempt thee, but I rue 1180
That error now, which is become my crime,
And thou the accuser. Thus it shall befall
Him who to worth in women overtrusting
Lets her will rule; restraint she will not brook,
And left to herself, if evil thence ensue,
She first his weak indulgence will accuse."
Thus they in mutual accusation spent
The fruitless hours, but neither self-condemning,
And of their vain contest appeared no end.

from BOOK X

THE ARGUMENT

Man's transgression known, the guardian angels forsake Paradise, and return up to Heaven to approve their vigilance, and are approved; God declaring that the entrance of Satan could not be by them prevented. He sends his Son to judge the transgressors; who descends, and gives sentence accordingly; then in pity clothes them both, and reascends. Sin and Death, sitting till then at the gates of Hell, by wondrous sympathy feeling the success of Satan in this new world, and the sin by Man there committed, resolve to sit no longer confined in Hell, but to follow Satan, their sire, up to the place of Man. To make the way easier from Hell to this world to and fro, they pave a broad highway or bridge over Chaos, according to the track that Satan first made; then, preparing for Earth, they meet him, proud of his success, returning to Hell; their mutual gratulation. Satan arrives at Pandemonium; in full assembly relates, with boasting, his success against Man; instead of applause is entertained with a general hiss by all his audience, transformed, with himself also, suddenly into serpents, according to his doom given in Paradise; then, deluded with a show of the Forbidden Tree springing up before them, they greedily reaching to take of the fruit chew dust and bitter ashes. The proceedings of Sin and Death; God foretells the final victory of his Son over them, and the renewing of all things; but for the present commands his angels to make several alterations in the heavens and elements. Adam, more and more perceiving his fallen condition, heavily bewails, rejects the condolement of Eve; she persists, and at length appeases him: then, to evade the curse likely to fall on their offspring, proposes to Adam violent ways, which he approves not, but, conceiving better hope, puts her in mind of the late promise made them, that her seed should be revenged on the Serpent, and exhorts her with him to seek peace of the offended Deity by repentance and supplication.

Thus began
Outrage from lifeless things; but Discord first,
Daughter of Sin, among the irrational,
Death introduced through fierce antipathy.
Beast now with beast 'gan war, and fowl with fowl, 710
And fish with fish; to graze the herb all leaving,
Devoured each other; nor stood much in awe
Of Man, but fled him, or with countenance grim
Glared on him passing. These were from without
The growing miseries, which Adam saw
Already in part, though hid in gloomiest shade,
To sorrow abandoned, but worse felt within,
And in a troubled sea of passion tossed,
Thus to disburden sought with sad complaint.
"O miserable of happy! is this the end 720
Of this new glorious World, and me so late
The glory of that glory, who now, become
Accurst of blessed, hide me from the face
Of God, whom to behold was then my height
Of happiness. Yet well, if here would end
The misery; I deserved it, and would bear
My own deservings; but this will not serve:
All that I eat or drink, or shall beget,
Is propagated curse. O voice once heard
Delightfully, 'Increase and multiply,' 730
Now death to hear! for what can I increase
Or multiply, but curses on my head?
Who of all ages to succeed, but feeling
The evil on him brought by me, will curse
My head: 'Ill fare our Ancestor impure,
For this we may thank Adam'; but his thanks
Shall be the execration; so besides
Mine own that bide upon me, all from me
Shall with a fierce reflux on me redound,
On me as on their natural center light 740
Heavy, though in their place. O fleeting joys
Of Paradise, dear bought with lasting woes!
Did I request thee, Maker, from my clay
To mould me Man, did I solicit thee
From darkness to promote me, or here place
In this delicious garden? As my will
Concurred not to my being, it were but right
And equal to reduce me to my dust,
Desirous to resign and render back
All I received, unable to perform 750
Thy terms too hard, by which I was to hold
The good I sought not. To the loss of that,
Sufficient penalty, why hast thou added
The sense of endless woes? inexplicable

Thy justice seems; yet to say truth, too late
I thus contest; then should have been refused
Those terms whatever, when they were proposed.
Thou didst accept them; wilt thou enjoy the good,
Then cavil the conditions? And though God
Made thee without thy leave, what if thy son 760
Prove disobedient, and reproved, retort,
'Wherefore didst thou beget me? I sought it not.'
Wouldst thou admit for his contempt of thee
That proud excuse? yet him not thy election,
But natural necessity begot.
God made thee of choice his own, and of his own
To serve him, thy reward was of his grace,
Thy punishment then justly is at his will.
Be it so, for I submit, his doom is fair,
That dust I am, and shall to dust return. 770
O welcome hour whenever! Why delays
His hand to execute what his decree
Fixed on this day? Why do I overlive,
Why am I mocked with death, and lengthened out
To deathless pain? How gladly would I meet
Mortality my sentence, and be earth
Insensible, how glad would lay me down
As in my mother's lap! There I should rest
And sleep secure; his dreadful voice no more
Would thunder in my ears, no fear of worse 780
To me and to my offspring would torment me
With cruel expectation. Yet one doubt
Pursues me still, lest all I cannot die,
Lest that pure breath of life, the spirit of Man
Which God inspired, cannot together perish
With this corporeal clod; then in the grave
Or in some other dismal place, who knows
But I shall die a living death? O thought
Horrid, if true! Yet why? It was but breath
Of life that sinned; what dies but what had life 790
And sin? the body properly hath neither.
All of me then shall die: let this appease
The doubt, since human reach no further knows.
For though the Lord of all be infinite,
Is his wrath also? Be it, Man is not so,
But mortal doomed. How can he exercise
Wrath without end on Man whom death must end?
Can he make deathless death? That were to make
Strange contradiction, which to God himself
Impossible is held, as argument 800
Of weakness, not of power. Will he draw out,
For anger's sake, finite to infinite
In punished Man, to satisfy his rigor

Satisfied never? That were to extend
His sentence beyond dust and Nature's law,
By which all causes else according still
To the reception of their matter act,
Not to the extent of their own sphere. But say
That death be not one stroke, as I supposed,
Bereaving sense, but endless misery 810
From this day onward, which I feel begun
Both in me and without me, and so last
To perpetuity: Ay me, that fear
Comes thundering back with dreadful revolution
On my defenceless head; both Death and I
Am found eternal, and incorporate both,
Nor I on my part single, in me all
Posterity stands cursed. Fair patrimony
That I must leave ye, sons; oh were I able
To waste it all myself, and leave ye none! 820
So disinherited how would ye bless
Me now your curse! Ah, why should all mankind
For one man's fault thus guiltless be condemned,
If guiltless? But from me what can proceed
But all corrupt, both mind and will depraved,
Not to do only, but to will the same
With me? How can they then acquitted stand
In sight of God? Him after all disputes
Forced I absolve; all my evasions vain
And reasonings, though through mazes, lead me still 830
But to my own conviction: first and last
On me, me only, as the source and spring
Of all corruption, all the blame lights due;
So might the wrath. Fond wish! couldst thou support
That burden heavier than the Earth to bear,
Than all the World much heavier, though divided
With that bad woman? Thus what thou desirest
And what thou fearst, alike destroys all hope
Of refuge, and concludes thee miserable
Beyond all past example and future, 840
To Satan only like, both crime and doom.
O Conscience, into what abyss of fears
And horrors hast thou driven me; out of which
I find no way, from deep to deeper plunged!"
Thus Adam to himself lamented loud
Through the still night, not now, as ere Man fell,
Wholesome and cool and mild, but with black air
Accompanied, with damps and dreadful gloom,
Which to his evil conscience represented

805–808. In all other matters where causes produce effects, the effect is in accordance with the nature and properties of the thing being acted on. (Editors' note.)

All things with double terror. On the ground 850
Outstretched he lay, on the cold ground, and oft
Cursed his creation, Death as oft accused
Of tardy execution, since denounced
The day of his offence. "Why comes not Death,"
Said he, "with one thrice-acceptable stroke
To end me? Shall Truth fail to keep her word,
Justice divine not hasten to be just?
But Death comes not at call, Justice divine
Mends not her slowest pace for prayers or cries.
O woods, O fountains, hillocks, dales, and bowers, 860
With other echo late I taught your shades
To answer, and resound far other song."
Whom thus afflicted when sad Eve beheld,
Desolate where she sat, approaching nigh,
Soft words to his fierce passion she assayed;
But her with stern regard he thus repelled.
"Out of my sight, thou serpent, that name best
Befits thee with him leagued, thyself as false
And hateful; nothing wants, but that thy shape,
Like his, and color serpentine, may show 870
Thy inward fraud, to warn all creatures from thee
Henceforth; lest that too heavenly form, pretended
To hellish falsehood, snare them. But for thee
I had persisted happy, had not thy pride
And wandering vanity, when least was safe,
Rejected my forewarning, and disdained
Not to be trusted, longing to be seen
Though by the Devil himself, him overweening
To overreach, but with the Serpent meeting
Fooled and beguiled, by him thou, I by thee, 880
To trust thee from my side, imagined wise,
Constant, mature, proof against all assaults,
And understood not all was but a show
Rather than solid virtue, all but a rib
Crooked by nature, bent, as now appears,
More to the part sinister from me drawn;
Well if thrown out, as supernumerary
To my just number found. Oh why did God,
Creator wise, that peopled highest Heaven
With spirits masculine, create at last 890
This novelty on Earth, this fair defect
Of Nature, and not fill the World at once
With men as angels without feminine,
Or find some other way to generate
Mankind? This mischief had not then befallen,
And more that shall befall, innumerable
Disturbances on Earth through female snares,
And strait conjunction with this sex. For either
He never shall find out fit mate, but such

As some misfortune brings him, or mistake, 900
Or whom he wishes most shall seldom gain,
Through her perverseness, but shall see her gained
By a far worse, or if she love, withheld
By parents, or his happiest choice too late
Shall meet, already linked and wedlock-bound
To a fell adversary, his hate or shame;
Which infinite calamity shall cause
To human life, and household peace confound."
He added not, and from her turned, but Eve
Not so repulsed, with tears that ceased not flowing, 910
And tresses all disordered, at his feet
Fell humble, and embracing them, besought
His peace, and thus proceeded in her plaint:
"Forsake me not thus, Adam, witness Heaven
What love sincere and reverence in my heart
I bear thee, and unweeting have offended,
Unhappily deceived; thy suppliant
I beg, and clasp thy knees; bereave me not,
Whereon I live, thy gentle looks, thy aid,
Thy counsel in this uttermost distress, 920
My only strength and stay. Forlorn of thee,
Whither shall I betake me, where subsist?
While yet we live, scarce one short hour perhaps,
Between us two let there be peace, both joining,
As joined in injuries, one enmity
Against a foe by doom express assigned us,
That cruel Serpent. On me exercise not
Thy hatred for this misery befallen,
On me already lost, me than thyself
More miserable. Both have sinned, but thou 930
Against God only, I against God and thee,
And to the place of judgment will return,
There with my cries importune Heaven, that all
The sentence from thy head removed may light
On me, sole cause to thee of all this woe,
Me, me only, just object of his ire."
She ended weeping, and her lowly plight,
Immovable till peace obtained from fault
Acknowledged and deplored, in Adam wrought
Commiseration; soon his heart relented 940
Towards her, his life so late and sole delight,
Now at his feet submissive in distress,
Creature so fair his reconcilement seeking,
His counsel whom she had displeased, his aid;
As one disarmed, his anger all he lost,
And thus with peaceful words upraised her soon:
"Unwary, and too desirous, as before,
So now, of what thou knowst not, who desirest
The punishment all on thyself; alas,

Bear thine own first, ill able to sustain 950
His full wrath whose thou feel'st as yet least part,
And my displeasure bear'st so ill. If prayers
Could alter high decrees, I to that place
Would speed before thee, and be louder heard,
That on my head all might be visited,
Thy frailty and infirmer sex forgiven,
To me committed and by me exposed.
But rise, let us no more contend, nor blame
Each other, blamed enough elsewhere, but strive
In offices of love, how we may lighten 960
Each other's burden in our share of woe;
Since this day's death denounced, if aught I see,
Will prove no sudden, but a slow-paced evil,
A long day's dying to augment our pain,
And to our seed (O hapless seed!) derived."
To whom thus Eve, recovering heart, replied.
"Adam, by sad experiment I know
How little weight my words with thee can find,
Found so erroneous, thence by just event
Found so unfortunate; nevertheless, 970
Restored by thee, vile as I am, to place
Of new acceptance, hopeful to regain
Thy love, the sole contentment of my heart
Living or dying, from thee I will not hide
What thoughts in my unquiet breast are risen,
Tending to some relief of our extremes,
Or end, though sharp and sad, yet tolerable,
As in our evils, and of easier choice.
If care of our descent perplex us most,
Which must be born to certain woe, devoured 980
By Death at last (and miserable it is
To be to others cause of misery,
Our own begotten, and of our loins to bring
Into this cursëd World a woeful race,
That after wretched life must be at last
Food for so foul a monster), in thy power
It lies, yet ere conception, to prevent
The race unblest, to being yet unbegot.
Childless thou art, childless remain; so Death
Shall be deceived his glut, and with us two 990
Be forced to satisfy his ravenous maw.
But if thou judge it hard and difficult,
Conversing, looking, loving, to abstain
From love's due rites, nuptial embraces sweet,
And with desire to languish without hope,
Before the present object languishing
With like desire, which would be misery
And torment less than none of what we dread,
Then both our selves and seed at once to free

From what we fear for both, let us make short, 1000
Let us seek Death, or he not found, supply
With our own hands his office on ourselves;
Why stand we longer shivering under fears
That show no end but death, and have the power,
Of many ways to die the shortest choosing,
Destruction with destruction to destroy."
She ended here, or vehement despair
Broke off the rest; so much of death her thoughts
Had entertained as dyed her cheeks with pale.
But Adam with such counsel nothing swayed, 1010
To better hopes his more attentive mind
Laboring had raised, and thus to Eve replied.
"Eve, thy contempt of life and pleasure seems
To argue in thee something more sublime
And excellent than what thy mind contemns;
But self-destruction therefore sought, refutes
That excellence thought in thee, and implies,
Not thy contempt, but anguish and regret
For loss of life and pleasure overloved.
Or if thou covet death, as utmost end 1020
Of misery, so thinking to evade
The penalty pronounced, doubt not but God
Hath wiselier armed his vengeful ire than so
To be forestalled; much more I fear lest death
So snatched will not exempt us from the pain
We are by doom to pay; rather such acts
Of contumacy will provoke the Highest
To make death in us live. Then let us seek
Some safer resolution, which methinks
I have in view, calling to mind with heed 1030
Part of our sentence, that thy seed shall bruise
The Serpent's head; piteous amends, unless
Be meant, whom I conjecture, our grand foe
Satan, who in the serpent hath contrived
Against us this deceit. To crush his head
Would be revenge indeed; which will be lost
By death brought on ourselves, or childless days
Resolved, as thou proposest; so our foe
Shall scape his punishment ordained, and we
Instead shall double ours upon our heads. 1040
No more be mentioned then of violence
Against ourselves, and wilful barrenness,
That cuts us off from hope, and savors only
Rancor and pride, impatience and despite,
Reluctance against God and his just yoke
Laid on our necks. Remember with what mild

1015. what thy mind contemns, the life and pleasure your mind shows contempt for. (Editors' note.)

And gracious temper he both heard and judged,
Without wrath or reviling; we expected
Immediate dissolution, which we thought
Was meant by death that day, when lo, to thee 1050
Pains only in child-bearing were foretold,
And bringing forth, soon recompensed with joy,
Fruit of thy womb; on me the curse aslope
Glanced on the ground: with labor I must earn
My bread; what harm? Idleness had been worse;
My labor will sustain me; and lest cold
Or heat should injure us, his timely care
Hath unbesought provided, and his hands
Clothed us unworthy, pitying while he judged;
How much more, if we pray him, will his ear 1060
Be open, and his heart to pity incline,
And teach us further by what means to shun
The inclement seasons, rain, ice, hail, and snow,
Which now the sky with various face begins
To show us in this mountain, while the winds
Blow moist and keen, shattering the graceful locks
Of these fair spreading trees; which bids us seek
Some better shroud, some better warmth to cherish
Our limbs benumbed, ere this diurnal star
Leave cold the night, how we his gathered beams 1070
Reflected, may with matter sere foment,
Or by collision of two bodies grind
The air attrite to fire, as late the clouds
Justling or pushed with winds rude in their shock
Tine the slant lightning, whose thwart flame driven down
Kindles the gummy bark of fir or pine,
And sends a comfortable heat from far,
Which might supply the sun. Such fire to use,
And what may else be remedy or cure
To evils which our own misdeeds have wrought, 1080
He will instruct us praying, and of grace
Beseeching him, so as we need not fear
To pass commodiously this life, sustained
By him with many comforts, till we end
In dust, our final rest and native home.
What better can we do, than to the place
Repairing where he judged us, prostrate fall
Before him reverent, and there confess
Humbly our faults, and pardon beg, with tears
Watering the ground, and with our sighs the air 1090

1070–1078. Various means of inventing or producing fire.
1071. matter sere, dry materials. **foment,** increase the heat of.
1073. attrite, rubbed together.
1075. Tine, kindle. **thwart,** slanting.
1078. supply the sun, replace the heat of the sun. (Notes to lines 1070–1078 are by the anthology editors.)

Frequenting, sent from hearts contrite, in sign
Of sorrow unfeigned, and humiliation meek.
Undoubtedly he will relent and turn
From his displeasure; in whose look serene,
When angry most he seemed and most severe,
What else but favor, grace, and mercy shone?"
  So spake our father penitent, nor Eve
Felt less remorse. They forthwith to the place
Repairing where he judged them, prostrate fell
Before him reverent, and both confessed 1100
Humbly their faults, and pardon begged, with tears
Watering the ground, and with their sighs the air
Frequenting, sent from hearts contrite, in sign
Of sorrow unfeigned, and humiliation meek.

BOOK XI: THE ARGUMENT

The Son of God presents to his Father the prayers of our first parents now repenting, and intercedes for them. God accepts them, but declares that they must no longer abide in Paradise; sends Michael with a band of Cherubim to dispossess them, but first to reveal to Adam future things; Michael's coming down. Adam shows to Eve certain ominous signs; he discerns Michael's approach; goes out to meet him; the Angel denounces their departure. Eve's lamentation. Adam pleads, but submits; the Angel leads him up to a high hill; sets before him in vision what shall happen till the Flood.

from BOOK XII

THE ARGUMENT

The Angel Michael continues from the Flood to relate what shall succeed; then, in the mention of Abraham, comes by degrees to explain, who that Seed of the Woman shall be which was promised Adam and Eve in the Fall; his incarnation, death, resurrection, and ascension; the state of the Church till his second coming. Adam greatly satisfied and recomforted by these relations and promises descends the hill with Michael; wakens Eve, who all this while had slept, but with gentle dreams composed to quietness of mind and submission. Michael in either hand leads them out of Paradise, the fiery sword waving behind them, and the Cherubim taking their stations to guard the place.

  Here Adam interposed. "O sent from Heaven, 270
Enlightener of my darkness, gracious things
Thou hast revealed, those chiefly which concern
Just Abraham and his seed. Now first I find
Mine eyes true opening, and my heart much eased,
Erewhile perplexed with thoughts what would become
Of me and all mankind; but now I see
His day, in whom all nations shall be blest,
Favor unmerited by me, who sought
Forbidden knowledge by forbidden means.

This yet I apprehend not, why to those 280
Among whom God will deign to dwell on Earth
So many and so various laws are given;
So many laws argue so many sins
Among them; how can God with such reside?"
To whom thus Michael. "Doubt not but that sin
Will reign among them, as of thee begot;
And therefore was law given them to evince
Their natural pravity, by stirring up
Sin against law to fight; that when they see
Law can discover sin, but not remove, 290
Save by those shadowy expiations weak,
The blood of bulls and goats, they may conclude
Some blood more precious must be paid for Man,
Just for unjust, that in such righteousness
To them by faith imputed, they may find
Justification towards God, and peace
Of conscience, which the law by ceremonies
Cannot appease, nor man the moral part
Perform, and not performing cannot live.
So law appears imperfect, and but given 300
With purpose to resign them in full time
Up to a better covenant, disciplined
From shadowy types to truth, from flesh to spirit,
From imposition of strict laws, to free
Acceptance of large grace, from servile fear
To filial, works of law to works of faith.
And therefore shall not Moses, though of God
Highly beloved, being but the minister
Of law, his people into Canaan lead;
But Joshua whom the Gentiles Jesus call, 310
His name and office bearing, who shall quell
The adversary Serpent, and bring back
Through the world's wilderness long-wandered Man
Safe to eternal Paradise of rest.
Meanwhile they in their earthly Canaan placed
Long time shall dwell and prosper, but when sins
National interrupt their public peace,
Provoking God to raise them enemies,
From whom as oft he saves them penitent
By judges first, then under kings; of whom 320
The second, both for piety renowned

287. evince, to demonstrate. In Milton's theology the Mosaic law was given "for the hardness of men's hearts." It was abrogated by the new testament of love in Christ, the "better covenant" of line 302.

303. shadowy types. Christian interpretation found allegorical illustrations of the truth everywhere in Old Testament history. Thus the burnt offerings are a symbol of the true sacrifice of a contrite heart; Moses is a mediator and foreshadows the office of the Redeemer; Joshua, leading his people into the promised land, is again Christ making possible salvation for the elect.

And puissant deeds, a promise shall receive
Irrevocable, that his regal throne
For ever shall endure; the like shall sing
All prophecy: that of the royal stock
Of David (so I name this king) shall rise
A Son, the Woman's Seed to thee foretold,
Foretold to Abraham, as in whom shall trust
All nations, and to kings foretold, of kings
The last, for of his reign shall be no end. 330
But first a long succession must ensue,
And his next son for wealth and wisdom famed,
The clouded ark of God till then in tents
Wandering, shall in a glorious temple enshrine.
Such follow him, as shall be registered
Part good, part bad, of bad the longer scroll,
Whose foul idolatries and other faults
Heaped to the popular sum, will so incense
God, as to leave them, and expose their land,
Their city, his temple, and his holy ark 340
With all his sacred things, a scorn and prey
To that proud city, whose high walls thou saw'st
Left in confusion, Babylon thence called.
There in captivity he lets them dwell
The space of seventy years, then brings them back,
Remembering mercy, and his covenant sworn
To David, stablished as the days of Heaven.
Returned from Babylon by leave of kings
Their lords, whom God disposed, the house of God
They first re-edify, and for a while 350
In mean estate live moderate, till grown
In wealth and multitude, factious they grow;
But first among the priests dissension springs,
Men who attend the altar, and should most
Endeavor peace; their strife pollution brings
Upon the temple itself; at last they seize
The scepter and regard not David's sons,
Then lose it to a stranger, that the true
Anointed King Messiah might be born
Barred of his right; yet at his birth a star 360
Unseen before in Heaven proclaims him come,
And guides the eastern sages, who inquire
His place, to offer incense, myrrh, and gold;
His place of birth a solemn angel tells
To simple shepherds, keeping watch by night;
They gladly thither haste, and by a choir
Of squadroned angels hear his carol sung.
A Virgin is his mother, but his Sire
The Power of the Most High; he shall ascend

332. his next son. Solomon. See I Kings 6–7 and II Chron. 3–4.

The throne hereditary, and bound his reign 370
With Earth's wide bounds, his glory with the Heavens."
  He ceased, discerning Adam with such joy
Surcharged, as had like grief been dewed in tears,
Without the vent of words, which these he breathed.
  "O prophet of glad tidings, finisher
Of utmost hope! now clear I understand
What oft my steadiest thoughts have searched in vain,
Why our great Expectation should be called
The Seed of Woman: Virgin Mother, hail,
High in the love of Heaven, yet from my loins 380
Thou shalt proceed, and from thy womb the Son
Of God Most High; so God with Man unites.
Needs must the Serpent now his capital bruise
Expect with mortal pain: say where and when
Their fight, what stroke shall bruise the Victor's heel."
  To whom thus Michael. "Dream not of their fight
As of a duel, or the local wounds
Of head or heel: not therefore joins the Son
Manhood to Godhead, with more strength to foil
Thy enemy; nor so is overcome 390
Satan, whose fall from Heaven, a deadlier bruise,
Disabled not to give thee thy death's wound;
Which he, who comes thy Savior, shall recure,
Not by destroying Satan, but his works
In thee and in thy seed. Nor can this be,
But by fulfilling that which thou didst want,
Obedience to the law of God, imposed
On penalty of death, and suffering death,
The penalty to thy transgression due,
And due to theirs which out of thine will grow: 400
So only can high justice rest appaid.
The law of God exact he shall fulfil
Both by obedience and by love, though love
Alone fulfil the law; thy punishment
He shall endure by coming in the flesh
To a reproachful life and cursëd death,
Proclaiming life to all who shall believe
In his redemption, and that his obedience
Imputed becomes theirs by faith, his merits
To save them, not their own, though legal works. 410
For this he shall live hated, be blasphemed,
Seized on by force, judged, and to death condemned
A shameful and accursed, nailed to the cross
By his own nation, slain for bringing life;
But to the cross he nails thy enemies,
The law that is against thee, and the sins
Of all mankind, with him there crucified,

373. had, would have. **383. capital,** of the head, but with the idea also of "chief."

Never to hurt them more who rightly trust
In this his satisfaction; so he dies,
But soon revives, Death over him no power 420
Shall long usurp; ere the third dawning light
Return, the stars of morn shall see him rise
Out of his grave, fresh as the dawning light,
Thy ransom paid, which Man from Death redeems,
His death for Man, as many as offered life
Neglect not, and the benefit embrace
By faith not void of works. This godlike act
Annuls thy doom, the death thou shouldst have died,
In sin for ever lost from life; this act
Shall bruise the head of Satan, crush his strength 430
Defeating Sin and Death, his two main arms,
And fix far deeper in his head their stings
Than temporal death shall bruise the Victor's heel,
Or theirs whom he redeems, a death like sleep,
A gentle wafting to immortal life.
Nor after resurrection shall he stay
Longer on Earth than certain times to appear
To his disciples, men who in his life
Still followed him; to them shall leave in charge
To teach all nations what of him they learned 440
And his salvation, them who shall believe
Baptizing in the profluent stream, the sign
Of washing them from guilt of sin to life
Pure, and in mind prepared, if so befall,
For death, like that which the Redeemer died.
All nations they shall teach; for from that day
Not only to the sons of Abraham's loins
Salvation shall be preached, but to the sons
Of Abraham's faith wherever through the world;
So in his seed all nations shall be blest. 450
Then to the Heaven of Heavens he shall ascend
With victory, triumphing through the air
Over his foes and thine; there shall surprise
The Serpent, Prince of air, and drag in chains
Through all his realm, and there confounded leave;
Then enter into glory, and resume
His seat at God's right hand, exalted high
Above all names in Heaven; and thence shall come,
When this world's dissolution shall be ripe,
With glory and power to judge both quick and dead, 460
To judge the unfaithful dead, but to reward
His faithful, and receive them into bliss,
Whether in Heaven or Earth, for then the Earth
Shall all be Paradise, far happier place
Than this of Eden, and far happier days."
So spake the Archangel Michael, then paused,
As at the world's great period; and our Sire

Replete with joy and wonder thus replied.
"O goodness infinite, goodness immense!
That all this good of evil shall produce, 470
And evil turn to good; more wonderful
Than that which by creation first brought forth
Light out of darkness! full of doubt I stand,
Whether I should repent me now of sin
By me done and occasioned, or rejoice
Much more, that much more good thereof shall spring,
To God more glory, more good will to men
From God, and over wrath grace shall abound.
But say, if our Deliverer up to Heaven
Must reascend, what will betide the few 480
His faithful, left among the unfaithful herd,
The enemies of truth; who then shall guide
His people, who defend? will they not deal
Worse with his followers than with him they dealt?"
"Be sure they will," said the Angel; "but from Heaven
He to his own a Comforter will send,
The promise of the Father, who shall dwell
His Spirit within them, and the law of faith
Working through love, upon their hearts shall write,
To guide them in all truth, and also arm 490
With spiritual armor, able to resist
Satan's assaults, and quench his fiery darts,
What man can do against them, not afraid,
Though to the death, against such cruelties
With inward consolations recompensed,
And oft supported so as shall amaze
Their proudest persecutors. For the Spirit
Poured first on his Apostles, whom he sends
To evangelize the nations, then on all
Baptized, shall them with wondrous gifts endue 500
To speak all tongues, and do all miracles,
As did their Lord before them. Thus they win
Great numbers of each nation to receive
With joy the tidings brought from Heaven: at length
Their ministry performed, and race well run,
Their doctrine and their story written left,
They die; but in their room, as they forewarn,
Wolves shall succeed for teachers, grievous wolves,

473 ff. The paradox which makes the Fall of Man at once the greatest of human calamities and the occasion of man's highest experience of good is a commonplace of Christian thinking.

508 ff. Wolves shall succeed for teachers. In this review of the perversion of the Church Milton touches on every essential point in the attack of Protestant against Catholic, of Puritan against Anglican. The clergy have substituted "man-made tradition" for the "plain truth of Scripture"; they have sought rank and title instead of imitating the simplicity of the early church; they have invoked secular power for the suppression of dissent; they have taught that authority and not inner conviction should rule the individual in matters of belief, and that salvation may be obtained by ritualistic observance rather than by repentance. Milton had been saying these things more or less all his life.

Who all the sacred mysteries of Heaven
To their own vile advantages shall turn 510
Of lucre and ambition, and the truth
With superstitions and traditions taint,
Left only in those written records pure,
Though not but by the Spirit understood.
Then shall they seek to avail themselves of names,
Places and titles, and with these to join
Secular power, though feigning still to act
By spiritual, to themselves appropriating
The Spirit of God, promised alike and given
To all believers; and from that pretence, 520
Spiritual laws by carnal power shall force
On every conscience; laws which none shall find
Left them enrolled, or what the Spirit within
Shall on the heart engrave. What will they then
But force the Spirit of Grace itself, and bind
His consort Liberty; what but unbuild
His living temples, built by faith to stand,
Their own faith, not another's: for on earth
Who against faith and conscience can be heard
Infallible? yet many will presume: 530
Whence heavy persecution shall arise
On all who in the worship persevere
Of Spirit and Truth; the rest, far greater part,
Will deem in outward rites and specious forms
Religion satisfied; Truth shall retire
Bestuck with slanderous darts, and works of faith
Rarely be found. So shall the world go on,
To good malignant, to bad men benign,
Under her own weight groaning till the day
Appear of respiration to the just, 540
And vengeance to the wicked, at return
Of Him so lately promised to thy aid,
The Woman's Seed, obscurely then foretold,
Now amplier known thy Savior and thy Lord,
Last in the clouds from Heaven to be revealed
In glory of the Father, to dissolve
Satan with his perverted world, then raise
From the conflagrant mass, purged and refined,
New Heavens, new Earth, ages of endless date
Founded in righteousness and peace and love, 550
To bring forth fruits joy and eternal bliss."
He ended; and thus Adam last replied.
"How soon hath thy prediction, Seer blest,
Measured this transient world, the race of time,
Till time stand fixed: beyond is all abyss,
Eternity, whose end no eye can reach.
Greatly instructed I shall hence depart,
Greatly in peace of thought, and have my fill

Of knowledge, what this vessel can contain;
Beyond which was my folly to aspire. 560
Henceforth I learn, that to obey is best,
And love with fear the only God, to walk
As in his presence, ever to observe
His providence, and on him sole depend,
Merciful over all his works, with good
Still overcoming evil, and by small
Accomplishing great things, by things deemed weak
Subverting worldly strong, and worldly wise
By simply meek; that suffering for truth's sake
Is fortitude to highest victory, 570
And to the faithful death the gate of life;
Taught this by his example whom I now
Acknowledge my Redeemer ever blest."
  To whom thus also the Angel last replied.
"This having learned, thou hast attained the sum
Of wisdom; hope no higher, though all the stars
Thou knew'st by name, and all the ethereal powers,
All secrets of the deep, all Nature's works,
Or works of God in heaven, air, earth, or sea,
And all the riches of this world enjoy'dst, 580
And all the rule, one empire; only add
Deeds to thy knowledge answerable, add faith,
Add virtue, patience, temperance, add love,
By name to come called charity, the soul
Of all the rest: then wilt thou not be loth
To leave this Paradise, but shalt possess
A Paradise within thee, happier far.
Let us descend now therefore from this top
Of speculation; for the hour precise
Exacts our parting hence; and see the guards, 590
By me encamped on yonder hill, expect
Their motion, at whose front a flaming sword,
In signal of remove, waves fiercely round;
We may no longer stay: go, waken Eve;
Her also I with gentle dreams have calmed
Portending good, and all her spirits composed
To meek submission: thou at season fit
Let her with thee partake what thou hast heard,
Chiefly what may concern her faith to know,
The great deliverance by her seed to come 600
(For by the Woman's Seed) on all mankind.
That ye may live, which will be many days,
Both in one faith unanimous though sad,
With cause for evils past, yet much more cheered
With meditation on the happy end."

591–592. expect Their motion, await the moment of moving.

He ended, and they both descend the hill;
Descended, Adam to the bower where Eve
Lay sleeping ran before, but found her waked;
And thus with words not sad she him received.
"Whence thou return'st, and whither went'st, I know; 610
For God is also in sleep, and dreams advise,
Which he hath sent propitious, some great good
Presaging, since with sorrow and heart's distress
Wearied I fell asleep. But now lead on;
In me is no delay; with thee to go,
Is to stay here; without thee here to stay,
Is to go hence unwilling; thou to me
Art all things under Heaven, all places thou,
Who for my wilful crime art banished hence.
This further consolation yet secure 620
I carry hence; though all by me is lost,
Such favor I unworthy am vouchsafed,
By me the Promised Seed shall all restore."
So spake our mother Eve, and Adam heard
Well pleased, but answered not; for now too nigh
The Archangel stood, and from the other hill
To their fixed station, all in bright array
The Cherubim descended; on the ground
Gliding meteorous, as evening mist
Risen from a river o'er the marish glides, 630
And gathers ground fast at the laborer's heel
Homeward returning. High in front advanced,
The brandished sword of God before them blazed
Fierce as a comet; which with torrid heat,
And vapor as the Libyan air adust,
Began to parch that temperate clime; whereat
In either hand the hastening angel caught
Our lingering parents, and to the eastern gate
Led them direct, and down the cliff as fast
To the subjected plain; then disappeared. 640
They looking back, all the eastern side beheld
Of Paradise, so late their happy seat,
Waved over by that flaming brand, the gate
With dreadful faces thronged and fiery arms.
Some natural tears they dropped, but wiped them soon;
The world was all before them, where to choose
Their place of rest, and Providence their guide.
They hand in hand with wandering steps and slow,
Through Eden took their solitary way.

614 ff. Eve's words suggest those of Ruth, "Whither thou goest I will go," but also Andromache's to Hector in the *Iliad*.

Renaissance Lyric Poetry
(c. 1500–c. 1660)

One traditional model in the study of literature suggests that we can assign to the epic the expression of national and broadly religious values, to drama the expression of social values, and to lyric poetry the expression of individual values and states of feeling. The Renaissance was an era of great achievement in all three of these literary modes. The lyric poetry of this era has a special significance; even if we regard skeptically the nineteenth-century exaggeration that the Renaissance was a sudden explosion of individualism, that view has a certain amount of truth. Just as painters of the period began to sign their names to their canvases, thus staking a claim to some kind of achievement or style different from those of other painters, so poets also cultivated voices that were uniquely their own. The following section of this anthology presents a concert, so to speak, of such voices, Seven of them are Spanish: Garcilaso de la Vega (c. 1501–1536), Santa Teresa de Jesús, or St. Teresa of Jesus (1515–1582), Fray Luis de León (c. 1527–1591), San Juan de la Cruz, or St. John of the Cross (1542–1591), Luis de Góngora (1561–1627), Bartolomé Leonardo de Argensola (1562–1631), and Lope de Vega (1562–1635). Two are French: Joachim Du Bellay (1522–1560) and Pierre de Ronsard (1524–1585). Seven are English: Edmund Spenser (1552–1599), Michael Drayton (1563–1631), William Shakespeare (1564–1616), Thomas Campion (1567–1620), John Donne (1572–1631), Robert Herrick (1591–1674), and John Milton (1608–1674). A number of facts are worth noting incidentally in connection with this roster—that some of the poets are even better known for their work in the larger genres; for example, Lope de Vega and Shakespeare in drama, Spenser and Milton in epic; that the Spanish poetry has an especially strong religious coloring (except for Garcilaso, all seven Spanish poets were priests or belonged to other religious orders, and two are canonized saints); and that, as the dates indicate, the distinctively Renaissance lyric impulse flourished later in England than on the continent.

If the poems included here had been recently discovered, without the poets' names, it would be no harder to determine who wrote them than it is for music enthusiasts today to identify established singers or composers; in both cases, distinctive rhythms, ways of handling melody and theme, and other stylistic traits would permit firm identification. (The two included poems by Campion, incidentally, are literally song lyrics, the music for which has survived.) It is also true, however, that artists of any given era tend to share certain habits of style, attitude, and preference in subject matter. In the Renaissance lyric these habits, most easily identifiable in the poetry of love and religion, are essentially a blending of classical with late-medieval Christian elements.

The main model for this blending was the lyric poetry of the fourteenth-century Italian humanist Francis Petrarch, whose presence loomed over almost all the significant lyric poets of the following two or three centuries. In his time Petrarch had been the foremost apostle of the revival of the ancient classical spirit, tone, and forms. He was involved, for example, in rediscovering the passionate but formally elegant love poetry of Catullus, perhaps the most powerful expression in ancient poetry of both the bliss and agony of love. But behind Petrarch lay several other, more recent European traditions: the courtly love tradition of the troubadours of southern France, which made a kind of religion of the worship of an unattainable beloved; the *Divine Comedy* and *Vita Nuova* ("New Life") of Dante, whose sensuously beautiful Beatrice was an emblem of God's revealed truth; and a number of other Christian influences including medieval "Mariolatry," a quasi-worship of the Virgin Mary often expressed in terms of sensuous art and lyrical language. All these strands, along with others, went into the poetic creation of Petrarch's beloved Laura, celebrated in the sonnet form that became a hallmark of the poet and in other lyric forms he developed from classical precedents. Laura was the occasion for the poet's highest happiness and sorest suffering, and in her very name femininity blended with the associations of the laurel wreath that, in classic antiquity, had symbolized the loftiest achievements in the sphere of poetry. Petrarch, far more even than Dante, set the example for the Renaissance thought-pattern by which religious experience could be described in terms of sexual love and love described in terms of religion.

The result, in Petrarch and his countless followers, was a poetry that fused with one another the supernal fervor of Christianity, the secular discipline of classical form, and overtones of ancient philosophy. Plato's works, with their combination of lyricism and otherworldliness, exerted an especially strong influence as they became better known in the centuries after Petrarch, reinforcing the blend of sensuousness and idealism in the "religion" of love. Significantly, this "religion" was developed almost exclusively from a male point of view. To the poets, most of them men, women were the desired but alien Other and were treated with profound ambivalence. On the one hand, they were regarded with something of the old distrust (the more primitive inheritance from the Middle Ages), so that misplaced devotion to them was a bar to salvation, but they could also be regarded as avenues to the highest reaches of spiritual experience, not to mention other varieties of ecstasy. Such a state of mind has an obvious seductive appeal, a form of having one's cake and eating it too. It is, just as obviously, a fragile construction singularly open to the jeers of the skeptical and irreverent. The Petrarchan tradition ultimately was to undergo this kind of undercutting and ironic subversion, most notably at the hands of John Donne.

In the Renaissance, every country of Western Europe had to come to terms with this Italian influence and the Italian cast given in the Renaissance to classical models. The result, commonly, was another immensely powerful cultural ambivalence. The Italian models had obvious attractions, not to mention the fact that Rome, a still-flourishing modern city, was a present reminder of classical glories. On the other hand, the Italian states and city-states were perennial pawns or enemies in the wars of expansion conducted by France and Spain, which were flexing their muscles as newly centralized modern nations. In the countries of northern Europe where the Protestant Reformation made headway, most obviously in England, Italian religion and culture were also suspect for other reasons. On top of that, the generally recognized cultural superiority of Italy engendered in other parts of Europe a kind of militant inferiority complex that imitated Italian achievements while sometimes chafing under the awareness of an allegiance or debt to Italy. Ronsard, Du Bellay, and the other five members of the sixteenth-century French group called the Pléiade wanted to create a new, consciously French literature that could compete with Italian excellence, but also bypass Italy for more direct use of ancient literary models. In some countries and in some authors, this ambivalence produced a powerful tension; for example, Edmund Spenser in England (with his medievally flavored epic *The Faerie Queene*) and Lope de Vega in Spain (with his old-Spanish type of ballads) were both in many ways modernists (which in the Renaissance meant being classicists) but were reluctant to join any modernist movement that would jeopardize the more popular medieval heritage, which was dear to them as a repository of their respective national traditions.

Thus, the Petrarchan and classicizing craze that became epidemic in Europe was accompanied by a self-consciousness that could be very intense. Even the simplest, most straightforward repetitions of ancient themes—for example, adaptations by Garcilaso de la Vega, Ronsard, and Herrick of the *carpe diem* ("seize the day") theme traceable to such ancient poems as Catullus' "Come, Lesbia, let us live and love"—could be construed as cultural gestures of international import. Edmund Spenser's "Epithalamion," perhaps the most heartfelt and beautiful wedding poem ever written, a personal statement if there ever was one, could also be seen, with its repeated appeals to mythology and its recollections of Catullus' wedding poems, as part of a general European classicizing program. To invoke the religious theme of the Good Shepherd familiar in the Old and New Testaments was a half-automatic temptation to imitate the pastoral genre of ancient pagan literature.

The more direct indebtedness to Petrarch was even more self-conscious, whether it was being followed meekly or subverted. Shakespeare's Sonnet 18, "Shall I compare thee to a summer's day?," works without restlessness within the Petrarchan gallery of images and similes, but his Sonnet 130, "My mistress's eyes are nothing like the sun," is a direct repudiation of Petrarchism. The self-loathing in Sonnet 129, "The expense of spirit in a waste of shame," is conveyed partly through the Petrarchan images, now reviled, of heaven and hunted game animals. The sonneteering cliché that lovers are sustained by sighs and tears is evoked by John Donne in "Love's Diet" with a literalism that amusingly calls the whole convention into question while also, in a wry way, affirming its validity: The speaker, tired of being in love, tries to cure the obesity of his (personified) love by calorie-counting, as it were, as he indulges in sighs and tears. Luis de Góngora, writing at the time when the Spanish Renaissance was beginning to yield to the Baroque era, does similarly jarring things with the Petrarchan and sonneteering conventions. His poem "A Rose" mourns not so much the flower's brevity of life and beauty as its being born at all. "The Spring" compares the mistress's beauty to the sun not as life-giving but as killing. "Allegory of the Brevity of Things Human" (if we take the speaker to be a human being) reverses the usual similitudes by asking flowers to take a lesson from the brevity of human life. More cheerfully, "The Rosemary Spray" has flowers turning not to ashes and dust but to honey.

To some modern readers, of course, the wonder is not that poets should eventually have come to look askance at such apparently artificial conventions, but rather that they should have survived in any form, heartfelt or ironic, for 300 years. One reason is their hallowed pedigree. Another is that they were not wholly conventional; for example, the medieval view (expressed by Dante and many others) that the celestial spheres of the sun and planets literally dispensed love and other heavenly favors was still significantly alive. In any case, to the extent that we recognize and accept those many Petrarchan clichés that have survived and been infinitely repeated in modern popular music (my sweetheart is an angel) and other equally shopworn clichés of emotion (I'm laughing, but I'm crying inside, etc.), we ought to be careful about casting stones. Or, if those examples seem too lightweight, we might ponder the recurrence in the more solemn black spirituals and folk songs of certain interchangeable phrases and images ("The river of Jordan [death and deliverance] is muddy and cold, / It chills the body but not the soul"). It would be rash indeed to regard these perennial formulas as emotional posing.

It might seem that by the time one has enumerated all the traditions governing the Renaissance lyric—survivals of medieval attitudes such as the *contemptus mundi* (disdain of the world), biblical and other Christian influences, classical models of form and of attitude, neoplatonism, and the rest—all traces of original expression will have been explained away. What such enumeration cannot explain is the peculiar energy of Renaissance poetry at its best—its freshness, fragrance, and intensity. To say that these qualities are the product of the spiritual challenge of a rapidly changing world, full of new perils and opportunities, political and cultural, may sound romantic, but it also may well be true. The greatest era of Spanish literature, for example, undoubtedly coincides closely with the era of Spain's greatest influence on the world's stage. Nor would it be at all accurate to regard Spain as an enclave sealed off from the energy and ferment of the Reformation. The Counter-Reformation launched in and from Spain was not merely an attempt to contain the Protestant movement; it was also a genuine deepening of spiritual experience, and it involved some risks. The three greatest religious poets of sixteenth-century Spain—St. Teresa of Jesus, Fray Luis de León, and St. John of the Cross—were all members of religious orders, but they were also innovators who, in their own day, were challenged by the Inquisition, imprisoned, or both. Teresa and John collaborated in vitally important conventual and monastic reform movements, and in John's poetry and other writings are expressed some of the most powerful mystical religious experiences of which we have a record.

One especially interesting thing about Spanish Renaissance poetry is the way in which it daringly unites different traditions, modes of poetry, and modes of feeling. Lope de Vega (another cleric, though an unlikely one in light of his amorous and other adventures), in his sonnet "The Good Shepherd," St. John of the Cross, in "A Shepherd, Young and Mournful, Grieves Alone," and Luis de León, in "The Life of the Blessed," all combine the settings of ancient pastoral with the biblical Good Shepherd motif. In his "Ode to Francisco Salinas," Fray Luis yokes together Christian otherworldliness, neoplatonism, Ptolemaic cosmology, and Pythagorean philosophy, while in certain other poems his impulse to withdraw from the fevered world owes something to the let's-get-away-from-the-city theme in the ancient Latin poems of Horace. But the most daring conjunctions are those of eroticism and mysticism, as achieved by St. John of the Cross in certain of his poems, where he sometimes also surprisingly inverts the sexual role of the speaker. In his pastoral poem noted earlier, he also inverts the role of the Savior and humankind, so that the Savior is the lovesick shepherd. This strategy of daring and surprise in religious poetry is by no means unique; it has its roots in the eroticism of the Song of Songs in the Old Testament, and it reappears later in the love songs sung by Christ and the soul in the church music of J. S. Bach (not to mention other centrist Protestant hymns, such as "The Church's One Foundation"). But St. John carries the strategy much farther than in most realizations of the "bride of Christ" tradition. In this respect, the closest analogues to St. John's poems are those of Donne, who has long been notorious for converting sex into religion and vice versa.

The most lasting formal legacy of Petrarch was the sonnet—a fourteen-line poem broken by rhyme scheme and strategy into an eight-line octave and a six-line sestet. (In England, the Shakespearean form, three quatrains and a couplet, was often used instead.) Considered simply as a verse form, the sonnet has its attractions and advantages, and poets have demonstrated its enormous versatility. (It has never gone out of style in English poetry except during the century or so after Milton.) That it should have become popular is not surprising, but that it became so nearly universal an obsession during the Renaissance is one of the mysteries of literary history. It is possible, though unlikely, that the sonnet form provides a basic, if unconscious, satisfaction, as the AABA song form apparently does. The sonnet's expressiveness was well demonstrated by Milton in "On the Late Massacre in Piedmont," where all the lines end with a howling, angry wail in o and a sounds and the poem's compression is important to its effect. It is not clear, however, why this effect would not be equally powerful in other short lyric forms.

We get a clue to the secret of the sonnet's fascination from Shakespeare's play *Romeo and Juliet,* where the protagonists fall in love at first sight, in the course of speaking a perfect sonnet in dialogue. In the first quatrain, Romeo flirts his way (to the accompanying Petrarchan obbligato of religious imagery) to kissing Juliet's hand:

> If I profane with my unworthiest hand
> This holy shrine, the gentle fine is this,
> My lips, two blushing pilgrims, ready stand
> To smooth that rough touch with a tender kiss.

She proffers some maidenly resistance, telling him that handshakes should be enough, and introducing a pun on *palm* and *palmer* (religious pilgrim):

> Good pilgrim, you do wrong your hand too much,
> Which mannerly devotion shows in this:
> For saints have hands that pilgrims' hands do touch,
> And palm to palm is holy palmer's kiss.

Seizing on this last hint, Romeo presses his advantages:

> ROM. Have not saints lips, and holy palmers too?
> JUL. Ay, pilgrim, lips that they must use in pray'r.
> ROM. O then, dear saint, let lips do what hands do,
> They pray—grant thou, lest faith turn to despair.
> JUL. Saints do not move, though grant for prayers' sake.
> ROM. Then move not while my prayer's effect I take.

He is now ready to kiss her, on the lips, and does so twice as they speak a few more lines. "You kiss by th' book," says the bemused Juliet, in one of Shakespeare's best lines. Both she and Romeo understand sonnet form, including the climactic effect of the end couplet.

Like the limerick, the sonnet is a way of saying things "by the book," of living within certain arbitrarily hard-and-fast rules, and if this is true, it perhaps explains why certain quite expressive variations on sonnet form, invented by Spenser, John Keats, and certain other poets, have not taken hold. Poets rely on formal expectations that are themselves part of the poem's effect. Drayton's sonnet "Since There's No Help," another poem about handshakes and kisses, is of the Shakespearean type, divided 4–4–4–2, and the movement of supposedly cooling love between the parting kiss that opens the first quatrain and the handshake that opens the second one is inseparable from the sonnet form itself. The ultimate specimen of the game aspect of the genre is Lope de Vega's "Sonnet All of a Sudden," which is totally devoid of substantive content, an example of poetic form concerned entirely with itself. Even when the sonnet is used to comment on serious events of great moment, as in Milton's massacre poem, formal expectations play a part, in this case (Petrarchan, 8–6) because the poet's rage pushes him past the paltry barrier that is supposed to neatly separate the octave and sestet. Even that effect, however, of disdain for mere calculated art, was presumably calculated, the poem's ferocious anger and high-mindedness notwithstanding. If so, we are reminded that our present-day distinction between sincerity and artifice is something the Renaissance poets probably would not have appreciated or perhaps even understood.

FURTHER READING: Extensive bilingual collections of Spanish-language poetry, for those who wish to sample it more extensively, include John A. Crow, ed., *An Anthology of Spanish Poetry from the Beginnings to the Present Day*, 1979; Angel Flores, ed., *An Anthology of Spanish Poetry from Garcilaso to García Lorca in English Translation*, 1961; and Eleanor L. Turnbull and Pedro Salinas, eds., *Ten Centuries of Spanish Poetry*, 1955. Stephen Minta's *Petrarch and Petrarchism: The English and French Traditions*, 1980, is a collection of poems by Petrarch and by French and English poets whom he influenced. *The Continental Renaissance: 1500–1600*, 1978, by W. A. Coupe, A. J. Krailsheimer, J. A. Scott, and R. W. Truman, is a helpful and well-written general survey of the period and includes discussions of individual French and Spanish poets (and of poets of other nationalities as well). An analogous survey of French Renaissance literature appears in I. D. McFarlane, *A Literary History of France: Renaissance France 1470–1589*, 1974. Surveys and other general treatments of English Renaissance lyrics include J. W. Lever, *The Elizabethan Love Sonnet*, 1956; Douglas Peterson, *The English Lyric from Wyatt to Donne: A History of the Plain and Eloquent Styles*, 1967; Hallett Smith, *Elizabethan Poetry: A Study in Convention, Meaning, and Expression*, 1952; and Rosemond Tuve, *Elizabethan and Metaphysical Imagery: Renaissance Poetic and Twentieth Century Critics*, 1947. On individual authors, see the following books, all either overviews or studies described by their titles: Helmut Hatzfeld, *Santa Teresa de Ávila*, 1969; A. W. Satterthwaite, *Spenser, Ronsard, and Du Bellay: A Renaissance Comparison*, 1960; K. R. W. Jones, *Pierre de Ronsard*, 1970; Manuel Durán, *Luis de León*, 1971; Gerald Brenan, *St. John of the Cross*, with translations by Lynda Nicholson, 1973; A. Kent Hieatt, *Short Time's Endless Monument The Symbolism of Numbers in Edmund Spenser's Epithalamion*, 1960; Francis C. Hayes, *Lope de Vega*, 1968; Angel Flores, *Lope de Vega: Monster of Nature*, 1969; John Carey, *John Donne: Life, Mind, and Art*, 1981; Arnold Stein, *John Donne's Lyrics: The Eloquence of Action*, 1962; and James Winny, *A Preface to Donne*, 1970. The introduction, notes, and apparatus in *The Complete English Poems of John Donne*, ed. C. A. Patrides, 1985, are very helpful and useful.

Garcilaso de la Vega

(c. 1501–1536)

YOUR FACE IS WRITTEN IN MY SOUL . . .[1]

Your face is written in my soul, and when
I want to write about you, you alone
Become the writer, I but read the line;
I watch you where you still watch me, within.

This state I am and always will be in. 5
For though my soul imprints a half-design
Of what I see in you, the good unknown
Is taken on a trusting regimen.

What was I born for if not to adore you?
My ills have shaped you to the bent they give. 10
I love you by a daily act of soul.

All that I have I must confess I owe you.
For you I came to life, for you I live,
For you I'd die, and do die, after all.

WHILE THERE IS STILL THE COLOR OF A ROSE . . .[1]

While there is still the color of a rose
And of a lily in your countenance,
And you with such an ardent candid glance
Can fire the heart, and check the flames it shows;

And while that golden hair of yours that flows 5
Into a knot can leap into a dance
As the wind blows with livelier dalliance
Upon the fairest proud white neck it knows:

Gather together from your happy spring
Fruits that are sweet, before time ravages 10
With angry snow the beauty of your head.

The rose will wither as the cold wind rages,
And age come gently to change everything,
Lest our desire should change old age instead.

[1]Spanish title: *Escrito está en mi alma vuestro gesto*; translated by Edwin Morgan.
[1]*En tanto que de rosa y azucena*; translated by Edwin Morgan.

Santa Teresa de Jesús

(1515–1582)

IF, LORD, THY LOVE FOR ME IS STRONG[1]

If, Lord, Thy love for me is strong
As this which binds me unto Thee,
What holds me from Thee, Lord, so long,
What holds Thee, Lord, so long from me?

O soul, what then desirest thou? 5
—Lord, I would see Thee, who thus choose Thee.
What fears can yet assail thee now?
—All that I fear is but to lose Thee.

Love's whole possession I entreat,
Lord, make my soul Thine own abode, 10
And I will build a nest so sweet
It may not be too poor for God.

O soul in God hidden from sin,
What more desires for thee remain,
Save but to love, and love again, 15
And, all on flame with love within,
Love on, and turn to love again?

LET NOTHING DISTURB THEE[1]

Let nothing disturb thee,
Nothing affright thee;
All things are passing;
God never changeth;
Patient endurance 5
Attaineth to all things;
Who God possesseth
In nothing is wanting;
Alone God sufficeth.

[1]Spanish title: *Si el amor que me tenéis*; translated by Arthur Symons.

[1]*Nada te turbe*; translated by Henry Wadsworth Longfellow. This poem is also known as "St. Teresa's Bookmark." It was found, after her death, inscribed on the bookmark she used in her breviary (the book of prescribed prayers and readings used by members of religious orders).

Joachim Du Bellay
(1522–1560)

REGRETS, XXXI[1]

How happy is the man who has traveled the ways
Of Jason or Ulysses,[2] and then returned
To his home again, wise, and having learned
To live among his own the rest of his days.

When will I see again the wisps which rise 5
From the chimneys of my town, what spring or fall
Will I see the little garden behind my wall—
Greater than any province in my eyes?

More pleasant is my family's humble home
Than any gaudy palace front in Rome, 10
More than their marble does that slate roof please.

I'd rather have my Loire and hilltop town
Than the Latin Tiber and Mount Palatine,
And rather than salty air, the sweet Anjou breeze.[3]

FROM A WINNOWER OF WHEAT TO THE WINDS[1]

To you, light airy flock,
Who, on the wing, pass
Over this world of ours
And softly sweep the grass,
And make the treetops shake, 5
With soft, rustling murmurs,

[1]French title: *Les Regrets, XXXI, Heureux, qui, comme Ulysse*; translated by David Sanders.
[2]Two great travelers and adventurers from Greek myth: Jason captained the Argonauts in their voyage to capture the Golden Fleece, Odysseus sailed all over the Mediterranean in his ten-years' voyage home from the Trojan war.
[3]The Loire is a river flowing through the old province of Anjou, in western France. The Tiber is the river of Rome, the Palatine one of the city's seven hills.
[1]*D'un Vanneur de blé aux vents*; translated by David Sanders.

I offer these violets,
These daisies, these lilies,
And some roses, too,
Scarlet roses, all these 10
Newly blossomed florets,
And carnations, for you.

So fan this tract of land
With your sweet breath,
Fan this farm, while I 15
Separate the chaff
From the wheat I fan
In the heat of the day.

Pierre de Ronsard
(1524–1585)

TO CASSANDRE[1]

I'm sending you this fresh bouquet of flowers
Which, if my fingers hadn't picked them tonight,
Would all be withered up and shriveled tight,
And have dropped their petals in a few short hours.

There is in this a lesson meant for you: 5
The delicate flower your beauty has become
Will also wither up and drop in time
And someday, like these flowers, perish too.

Time goes on, my dearest, time goes on.
Alas! not time, it's we who have to go, 10
And we who'll lie beneath the family stone.

And the love of which we've both been talking so
Will mean just nothing when our lives are through;
So love me, while your beauty is still new.

[1]French title: *Je vous envoie un bouquet, que ma main*; translated by David Sanders.

ON THE DEATH OF MARIE[1]

Just as the rose on the branch one sees in May,
In youthful beauty budding, in first flower,
Turns the sky jealous of its deep color
When the Dawn's tears bathe it at break of day

(Grace held in its leaf and Love that lies 5
Inside anoint the gardens and trees with scents),
But beaten by rain or by the sun's intense
Heat, leaf by open leaf, it dies;

So in your young and first unfolding bloom
While the earth and sky honored your beauty's powers, 10
The Fates killed you, and laid you in an ashen bed.

Accept these tears I offer at your tomb,
This vase of milk, this basket full of flowers,
And let your body be roses, alive and dead.

TO HÉLÈNE[1]

When you are old and sitting by the fire,
Spinning your threads of yarn by candlelight,
Singing my songs, you'll say to yourself one night,
"Ronsard praised me when I was his desire."

You'll have no maid who hears you tell this story 5
Though already half-asleep from working hard,
Who won't wake up at the sound of the name Ronsard,
Blessing your name with songs of lasting glory.

By then I'll be a ghost, long since dead,
Buried in the shade of the myrtle overhead, 10
And you'll be an old crone crouching at the fire

Regretting my lost love and your cold scorning.
Live now, if you believe me, don't wait till morning;
Come out and cut the roses from your brier.

[1] *Sonnet sur la mort de Marie*; translated by David Sanders.
[1] *Sonnets pour Hélène: Quand vous serez bien vieille*; translated by David Sanders.

SONNET TO AN UNNAMED PERSON[1]

I give these eggs to you. The egg is a sphere
Resembling heaven, which holds within its girth
The water of oceans, the fire, the air and earth,[2]
And contains without confining all that's here.

The egg's membrane is like the air; the raw 5
Egg white, the sea from which all things spring;
The yolk, a fire igniting everything;
The shell, the fertile earth which can bear them all.

Both heaven and eggs are covered with white. It's this,
My gift to you in a shell: the universe. 10
The present is perfection—if you care.

As perfect as it is, it cannot equal
The perfection of you, to which nothing can compare,
And of which the gods alone are entitled to tell.

Fray Luis de León

(c. 1527–1591)

ODE TO FRANCISCO SALINAS[1]

The air grows calm and clear
And clothes itself in beauty and strange light,
Salinas, when the extreme
Art of your music strikes
Out from that skilled and tempering hand I admire. 5

It is a heavenly sound
That makes my dull, all-too-forgetful soul
Find its senses and rouse
Its lost recollections of those
First days in its primordial glorious home. 10

[1] *Les Amours diverses, XLVIII: Je vous donne des oeufs*; translated by David Sanders.
[2] This line names the four elements of which all things were believed to be constituted.
[1] Spanish title: *Oda a Francisco Salinas*; translated by Edwin Morgan. Salinas (1530–1590), who was blind, was a distinguished musician and music theorist on the faculty of the University of Salamanca.

Yes, it goes back, it remembers;
In thoughts, and fate, it grows a better thing;
For gold, it loses fervor:
Let that brittle glint
Trap the adoring slavelike mob, not this 15

Soul that crosses space,
Climbs till it has reached the highest sphere,[2]
And hears a music there
That's made for other ears,
Unfading notes and the first notes to speak.[3] 20

It sees the master player
With that great cosmic cithern[4] in his arms
Pluck out sure and clear
The sacred chord that guards
This everlasting temple from all harm.[5] 25

And since it is itself
Composed of many chords, it quickly gives
Its answer in an echo,
And both together mix
Their vying sounds in sweetest harmony. 30

Now through a sea of sweetness
The soul goes voyaging on, until at last
It plunges drowned so deep there
That neither eye nor heart
Takes notice of what happens above or apart. 35

O blessed loss of sense!
O life-enhancing death! O sweet forgetting!
If I could enjoy your rest
Without regaining, ever,
This consciousness so earthbound and so wretched! 40

To this blessing I call you,
Glory of Apollo's holy choir,[6] friends
I love more dearly than all the
Things that are treasured well,
For what is all the rest but a lament? 45

[2]The Primum Mobile, or first mover, the outermost shell of the universe in the Ptolemaic system.

[3]The "music of the spheres" was produced, according to ancient Pythagorean philosophy, by the ordered movements of the heavens. This philosophy also posited the existence of numerical correspondences between the heavens and the soul.

[4]A guitar-like instrument of the sixteenth century.

[5]The harmony of chords is also based on numerical ratios.

[6]Fellow-poets (Apollo being the god of poets).

O play, still play, Salinas,
Still sound the sound of music in my ear;
Let this unblind the feelings
Till the divine good appears
And every other thing stays sunk in sleep. 50

THE LIFE OF THE BLESSED[1]

Region of life and light!
Land of the good whose earthly toils are o'er!
Nor frost nor heat may blight
Thy vernal beauty, fertile shore,
Yielding thy blessed fruits for evermore! 5

There, without crook or sling,
Walks the Good Shepherd; blossoms white and red
Round his meek temples cling;
And, to sweet pastures led,
His own loved flock beneath his eye is fed. 10

He guides, and near him they
Follow delighted; for he makes them go
Where dwells eternal May,
And heavenly roses blow,
Deathless, and gathered but again to grow. 15

He leads them to the height
Named of the infinite and long-sought Good,
And fountains of delight;
And where his feet have stood,
Springs up, along the way, their tender food. 20

And when, in the mid skies,
The climbing sun has reached his highest bound,
Reposing as he lies,
With all his flock around,
He witches the still air with numerous[2] sound. 25

From his sweet lute flow forth
Immortal harmonies, of power to still
All passions born of earth,
And draw the ardent will
Its destiny of goodness to fulfil. 30

[1] *Morada del cielo*; translated by William Cullen Bryant.
[2] Musical; metrical.

Might but a little part,
A wandering breath, of that high melody
Descend into my heart,
And change it till it be
Transformed and swallowed up, O love! in thee: 35

Ah! then my soul should know,
Beloved! where thou liest at noon of day;
And from this place of woe
Released, should take its way
To mingle with thy flock, and never stray. 40

AT THE ASCENSION[1]

Good Shepherd, have You skipped away, to leave
Your flock in this deep, hidden vale,
Their lonely legacy to grieve
Their stay, while You, beyond the blue sky's trail,
Attain assuring immortality. 5

They are now reft of joy who once were filled
From the fond kindness of Your breast;
Where can the leaderless, who willed
To follow, turn? the hungry, lest
They lose their way, seek out Your company? 10

What vision in this world can satisfy
Those who have gazed upon Your face?
Less beauty but disturbs the eye;
The music in this world is dull, lacks grace,
For those who heard Your words' sweet harmony. 15

Who is there now to calm the white-foamed lake?
Who now to still the roaring gales?
Now that a cloud has lowered to take
And cover You, how can we set our sails
For port? What north star pilots destiny? 20

Why do you run so fast, O cloud, as though
You envied us brief happiness?
Why hoard the sun, only to show
How rich you are?—miser without largesse,
Scorning our blindness and our poverty! 25

[1]*En la Ascensión*; translated by James Edward Tobin. According to Luke 24:53, after the Ascension of Jesus into heaven his disciples "returned to Jerusalem with great joy, and were continually in the temple, praising and blessing God."

THE ASSUMPTION OF THE VIRGIN[1]

Lady! thine upward flight
The opening heavens receive with joyous song;
Blest, who thy garments bright
May seize, amid the throng,
And to the sacred mount float peacefully along. 5

Bright angels are around thee,
They that have served thee from thy birth are here:
Their hands with stars have crowned thee;
Thou,—peerless Queen of air,
As sandals to thy feet the silver moon dost wear. 10

Celestial dove! so meek
And mild and fair! oh, let thy peaceful eye
This thorny valley seek,
Where such sweet blossoms lie,
But where the sons of Eve in pain and sorrow sigh. 15

For if the imprisoned soul
Could catch the brightness of that heavenly way,
'Twould own its sweet control
And gently pass away,
Drawn by the magnet power to an eternal day. 20

San Juan de la Cruz
(1542–1591)

ONE DISMAL NIGHT . . .[1]

One dismal night
With the ardors of love aflame
O venture bright!
Unobserved I slipped away
While my dwelling still unstirring lay. 5

[1]*A la Asunción de Nuestra Señora*; translated by Henry Wadsworth Longfellow. Roman Catholics believe that the Virgin Mary was bodily assumed into heaven at her death.

[1]Spanish title: *En una noche obscura*; translated by Kate Flores. The poem is probably, to some extent, literal description, of the author's escape from a Toledo prison, in which he had been confined by fellow-friars opposed to his attempts at monastic reform. Juan (St. John of the Cross) also wrote a prose commentary expanding on the mystical significance of the poem, as he did with certain others including "O Living Flame of Love."

In disguise of night
By the secret stair's security
O venture bright!
Into the dark and stealthily
While my dwelling still unstirring lay. 10

In the secrecy
Of the glorious night, unseen my face
Nor able any part to see
Having no light to guide my way
Save the one within my heart ablaze. 15

This more luminously
Led me than the radiance of noon
Thence to where in waiting for me
One to me well known
Kept a place where no one had been drawn. 20

O that night that guided me
O night lovelier than the dawn
O that night of ecstasy
When Beloved and Lover joined,
Into Lover the Beloved transformed! 25

On my flowering breast,
Kept for Him alone away,
Him I caressed
And He drowsed and stayed
And all my senses languished there. 30

The turreted breeze
In stroking His hair
With fingers serene
My throat touched near
And all my senses languished there. 35

Lingering and forgetting
Face in the Lover reposing fair
All lapsed and I surrendered
Surrendering my care
Amidst the lilies remembering no more. 40

O LIVING FLAME OF LOVE . . .[1]

O living flame of love,
How tender is your wound,
Your burning at the center of my soul!
You are no longer shy—

[1] *¡Oh llama de amor viva!*; translated by Stephen Stepanchev. See the note to "One Dismal Night."

Please finish, know me at the source; 5
Break the hymen of our sweet intercourse!

O easy cautery![2]
Oh wound that is really gift!
Oh gentle hand! Oh delicate touch of a knife
That brings eternal life 10
And pays all petty debts!
Killing, you turn my death into flaming life!

O lamps of living fire,
In whose renewing splendors
The deep and smoking caverns of the senses, 15
Which once were black and blind,
Provide amazing delights,
Give heat and light to their awaking lover!

How tender, mild, and blessed
Is your image in my breast, 20
Where, secretly, you live alone, a king;
And with your soft breathing,
The bliss and glory of the Dove,
How delicately you induce my love!

I ENTERED WHERE I DID NOT KNOW . . .[1]

I entered where I did not know,
And there remained unknowing,
All reason now transcended.

I did not know the door
But when I found the way, 5
Unknowing where I was,
I learned unheard of things,
But what I heard I cannot say,
For I remained unknowing,
All reason now transcended. 10

My knowledge was fulfilled
With piety and peace.
In deepest solitude
I found the narrow way:
A secret giving such release 15
That I was left there stammering,
All reason now transcended.

[2]Medical treatment with a hot iron or needle.
[1]*Entréme donde no supe*; translated by Willis Barnstone.

I was so fully drunk,
So dazed and far away,
My senses were released 20
From feelings of my own.
My mind had found a surer way:
A knowledge of unknowing,
All reason now transcended.

And he who does arrive, 25
Collapses as in sleep;
For all he knew before
Now seems of little worth,
And so his knowledge grows so deep
That he remains unknowing, 30
All reason now transcended.

The higher he ascends,
The darker is the wood;
It is the shadowy cloud
That clarified the night, 35
And so the one who understood
Remains at last unknowing,
All reason now transcended.

This knowledge by unknowing
Is such a soaring force 40
That scholars argue long
But never leave the ground.
Their reason always fails the source:
To understand unknowing,
All reason now transcended. 45

This knowledge is supreme
And meets a blazing height,
Though formal reason tries,
It crumbles in the dark.
For one who would control the night, 50
By knowledge of unknowing
He will have all transcended.

This is my final word,
The highest learning lead
To an ecstatic feeling 55
Of the most holy Being;
And from his mercy comes his deed:
To make one stay unknowing,
All reason now transcended.

A SHEPHERD, YOUNG AND MOURNFUL, GRIEVES ALONE . . .[1]

A shepherd, young and mournful, grieves alone,
Alien his pleasure, absent his content;
The shadow-memory of his shepherdess
Strikes at his heart as though love were a stone.

Physical pain does not evoke lament, 5
Such suffering is not what brings the hurt;
Although his heart is battered by the blow,
He weeps to realize neglect is meant.

In realizing thus that he is not
The center of his shepherdess's life 10
He sadly finds his heart is wounded more;
Alien to joy, he hears love taunt: Forgot.

The shepherd cries: Why does she stand apart?
Ah, woe to him who holds her distantly,
Keeps her in willing absence from my side, 15
Shutting her eyes to how love tears my heart.

He stretched his lovely, loving arms out wide,
Climbing a tree in time to hold them so;
His heart still deeply wounded by her love,
He clung there, waiting her, until he died. 20

I KNOW FULL WELL THE WATER'S FLOWING POWER . . .[1]

I know full well the water's flowing power,
Though it be dark.

A secret font, an everlasting force—
I know exactly where it has its source,
Though it be dark. 5

And yet I do not know; for therein lies
The origin from which origins rise,
Though it be dark.

[1] *Un pastorcico solo está penado*; translated by James Edward Tobin.

[1] *Que bien sé yo la fonte que mana y corre*; translated by James Edward Tobin. As with "One Dismal Night," this devotional and theological poem may have had a circumstantial origin, in the darkness of Juan's imprisonment in Toledo. The poem's images develop the idea of the divine Trinity.

I know that nothing can be quite so fair
And that earth drinks from it as well as air, 10
Though it be dark.

I know its depth cannot be sounded, know
That none can cross against the eddies' flow,
Though it be dark.

Nothing can dim its ever-brilliant gleam, 15
From which all other light and wisdom stream,
Though it be dark.

I know its many branches stretch and wind
To reach all heights and depths and all mankind,
Though it be dark. 20

I know how well this nourished current laves
Each bank, how very powerful its waves,
Though it be dark.

Both source and swirling stream are one, I sense—
Their unity permits no precedence— 25
Though it be dark.

Its deathless strength, its hidden riverhead,
Are in grace-giving eucharistic Bread,
Though it be dark.

And all mankind is called and asked to share 30
The nourishment of hidden mystery there,
Though it be dark.

Desiring and desired, this mystery
Within the Bread of life I clearly see,
Though it be dark. 35

Edmund Spenser

(1552–1599)

EPTHALAMION[1]

Ye learnèd sisters,[2] which have oftentimes
Been to me aiding, others to adorn,
Whom ye thought worthy of your graceful rhymes,

[1]*Epithalamion,* or *epithalamium,* is the generic name (derived from Greek) for a wedding song. Spenser was married on June 11, 1594, to Elizabeth Boyle.
[2]The Muses, the goddesses of inspiration.

That even the greatest did not greatly scorn
To hear their names sung in your simple lays,[3] 5
But joyèd in their praise;
And when ye list[4] your own mishaps to mourn,
Which death, or love, or fortune's wreck did raise,
Your string could soon to sadder tenor turn,
And teach the woods and waters to lament 10
Your doleful dreariment:
Now lay those sorrowful complaints aside;
And, having all your heads with garlands crowned,
Help me mine own love's praises to resound;
Nor let the same of any be envide: 15
So Orpheus did for his own bride![5]
So I unto myself alone will sing;
The woods shall to me answer, and my echo ring.

Early, before the world's light-giving lamp
His golden beam upon the hills doth spread, 20
Having dispersed the night's uncheerful damp,
Do ye awake; and, with fresh lusty-hed,[6]
Go to the bower of my belovèd love,
My truest turtle dove;
Bid her awake; for Hymen[7] is awake, 25
And long since ready forth his mask to move,[8]
With his bright Tead[9] that flames with many a flake,
And many a bachelor to wait on him,
In their fresh garments trim.
Bid her awake therefore, and soon her dight,[10] 30
For lo! the wishèd day is come at last,
That shall, for all the pains and sorrows past,
Pay to her usury of long delight:
And, whilst she doth her dight,
Do ye to her of joy and solace sing, 35
That all the woods may answer, and your echo ring.

Bring with you all the Nymphs that you can hear,
Both of the rivers and the forests green,
And of the sea that neighbors to her near,[11]
All with gay garlands goodly well beseen. 40
And let them also with them bring in hand
Another gay garland,

[3]Poems. Spenser's longest and greatest work, *The Faerie Queene*, was written to honor Queen Elizabeth I.
[4]It pleases you.
[5]Orpheus, the mythical poet and musician, loved his wife Eurydice so strongly that he undertook to rescue her from the realm of the dead.
[6]Zestful pleasure. [7]The god of weddings.
[8]To lead the festive wedding procession. [9]Torch. [10]Array; adorn.
[11]The bride's residence was near the ocean. The Nymphs were minor nature-goddesses: they included naiads (of rivers), dryads (of trees), nereids (of ocean).

For my fair love, of lilies and of roses,
Bound truelove wise with a blue silk riband;
And let them make great store of bridal posies, 45
And let them eke[12] bring store of other flowers,
To deck the bridal bowers.
And let the ground whereas her foot shall tread,
For fear the stones her tender foot should wrong,
Be strewed with fragrant flowers all along, 50
And diapered like the discolored mead;[13]
Which done, do at her chamber door await,
For she will waken straight;[14]
The whiles do ye this song unto her sing,
The woods shall to you answer, and your echo ring. 55

Ye Nymphs of Mulla,[15] which with careful heed
The silver scaly trouts do tend full well,
And greedy pikes which use therein to feed
(Those trouts and pikes all others do excel);
And ye likewise, which keep the rushy lake, 60
Where none do fishes take;
Bind up the locks the which hang scattered light,
And in his waters, which your mirror make,
Behold your faces as the crystal bright,
That when you come whereas my love doth lie, 65
No blemish she may spy.
And eke, ye lightfoot maids, which keep the deer,
That on the hoary mountain used to tower;[16]
And the wild wolves, which seek them to devour,
With your steel darts do chase from coming near; 70
Be also present here,
To help to deck her, and to help to sing,
That all the woods may answer, and your echo ring.

Wake, now, my love, awake! for it is time;
The rosy morn long since left Tithon's bed,[17] 75
All ready to her silver coach to climb;
And Phoebus[18] 'gins to show his glorious head.
Hark, how the cheerful birds do chant their lays[19]
And carol of love's praise.
The merry lark her matins[20] sings aloft; 80
The thrush replies; the mavis descant[21] plays;
The ouzel shrills; the ruddock warbles soft;
So goodly all agree, with sweet consent,
To this day's merriment.

[12]Also. [13]*diapered:* decorated. *discolored mead:* many-colored meadow.
[14]Straightway; immediately. [15]A river valley in Ireland, where the wedding is taking place.
[16]To dwell in a high place.
[17]Tithonus was the mate of Eos, or Aurora, goddess of the dawn.
[18]Apollo, god of the sun. [19]Songs. [20]Morning prayers. [21]Treble part.

Ah! my dear love, why do ye sleep thus long, 85
When meeter[22] were that ye should now awake,
To await the coming of your joyous mate,
And hearken to the birds' love-learnèd song,
The dewy leaves among!
For they of joy and pleasance to you sing, 90
That all the woods them answer, and their echo ring.

My love is now awake out of her dreams,
And her fair eyes, like stars that dimmèd were
With darksome cloud, now show their goodly beams
More bright than Hesperus[23] his head doth rear. 95
Come now, ye damsels, daughters of delight,
Help quickly her to dight:
But first come, ye fair hours, which were begot
In Jove's sweet paradise of Day and Night;[24]
Which do the seasons of the year allot, 100
And all that ever in this world is fair,
Do make and still repair:
And yet three handmaids of the Cyprian queen,[25]
The which do still adorn her beauty's pride,
Help to adorn my beautifulest bride; 105
And as ye her array, still throw between
Some graces to be seen,
And, as ye use to Venus, to her sing,
The whiles the woods shall answer, and your echo ring.

Now is my love all ready forth to come: 110
Let all the virgins therefore well await:
And yet fresh boys, that tend upon her groom,
Prepare yourselves; for he is coming straight;
Set all your things in seemly good array,
Fit for so joyful day: 115
The joyfulest day that ever sun did see.
Fair Sun! show forth thy favorable ray,
And let thy life-full heat not fervent be,
For fear of burning her sunshiny face,
Her beauty to disgrace. 120
O fairest Phoebus! father of the Muse![26]
If ever I did honor thee aright,
Or sing the thing that might thy mind delight,
Do not thy servant's simple boon[27] refuse;

[22]More fitting. [23]Venus as evening star.

[24]The Hours were goddesses of order and the seasons. In Renaissance poetry Jove, king of the gods, was a near-synonym for God.

[25]The three Graces were minor goddesses personifying charm, brilliance, and freshness. They were attendants on Aphrodite/Venus, the goddess of love, who was worshiped especially in Cyprus.

[26]Phoebus Apollo was god both of the sun and of poetry. [27]Requested favor.

But let this day, let this one day, be mine; 125
Let all the rest be thine.
Then I thy sovereign praises loud will sing,
That all the woods shall answer, and their echo ring.

Hark! how the Minstrels 'gin to shrill aloud
Their merry music that resounds from far. 130
The pipe, the tabor, and the trembling croud,
That well agree withouten breach or jar.[28]
But, most of all, the Damsels do delight
When they their timbrels[29] smite,
And thereunto do dance and carol sweet, 135
That all the senses they do ravish quite;
The whiles the boys run up and down the street,
Crying aloud with strong confusèd noise,
As if it were one voice,
Hymen, iö Hymen, Hymen, they do shout;[30] 140
That even to the heavens their shouting shrill
Doth reach, and all the firmament doth fill;
To which the people standing all about,
As in approvance, do thereto applaud,
And loud advance her laud;[31] 145
And evermore they Hymen, Hymen sing,
That all the woods them answer, and their echo ring.

Lo! where she comes along with portly pace,
Like Phoebe,[32] from her chamber of the East,
Arising forth to run her mighty race, 150
Clad all in white, that seems a virgin best.
So well it her beseems, that ye would ween
Some angel she had been.
Her long loose yellow locks like golden wire,
Sprinkled with pearl, and pearling flowers atween, 155
Do like a golden mantle her attire;
And, being crownèd with a garland green,
Seem like some maiden queen.
Her modest eyes, abashèd to behold
So many gazers as on her do stare, 160
Upon the lowly ground affixèd are;
Nor dare lift up her countenance too bold,
But blush to hear her praises sung so loud,
So far from being proud.
Nathless do ye still loud her praises sing, 165
That all the woods may answer, and your echo ring.

Tell me, ye merchants' daughters, did ye see
So fair a creature in your town before:

[28]*tabor:* drum. *croud:* fiddle. *jar:* dissonance. [29]Tambourines.
[30]The traditional exclamation of joy in classical wedding poetry, such as Catullus' Poem 62.
[31]Praise. [32]Goddess of the moon; sister of Phoebus Apollo.

So sweet, so lovely, and so mild as she,
Adorned with beauty's grace and virtue's store? 170
Her goodly eyes like sapphires shining bright,
Her forehead ivory white,
Her cheeks like apples which the sun hath ruddied,
Her lips like cherries charming men to bite,
Her breast like to a bowl of cream uncrudded,[33] 175
Her paps[34] like lilies budded,
Her snowy neck like to a marble tower;
And all her body like a palace fair,
Ascending up, with many a stately stair,
To honor's seat and chastity's sweet bower. 180
Why stand ye still, ye virgins, in amaze,
Upon her so to gaze,
Whiles ye forget your former lay to sing,
To which the woods did answer, and your echo ring?

But if ye saw that which no eyes can see, 185
The inward beauty of her lively spright,[35]
Garnished with heavenly gifts of high degree,
Much more then would ye wonder at that sight,
And stand astonished like to those which read
Medusa's mazeful head.[36] 190
There dwells sweet love, and constant chastity,
Unspotted faith, and comely womanhood,
Regard of honor, and mild modesty;
There virtue reigns as queen in royal throne,
And giveth laws alone, 195
The which the base affections[37] do obey,
And yield their services unto her will;
Nor thought of thing uncomely ever may
Thereto approach to tempt her mind to ill.
Had ye once seen these her celestial treasures, 200
And unrevealèd pleasures,
Then would ye wonder, and her praises sing,
That all the woods should answer, and your echo ring.

Open the temple gates unto my love,
Open them wide that she may enter in, 205
And all the posts adorn as doth behove,
And all the pillars deck with garlands trim,
For to receive this Saint with honor due,
That cometh in to you.
With trembling steps, and humble reverence, 210
She cometh in, before the Almighty's view;

[33]Uncurdled. [34]Nipples. [35]Spirit.
[36]*read:* saw. Medusa was a monster, with snakes for hair, who turned to stone anyone who gazed on her. [37]Lower passions and feelings.

Of her ye virgins learn obedience,
When so ye come into those holy places,
To humble your proud faces:
Bring her up to the high altar, that she may 215
The sacred ceremonies there partake,
The which do endless matrimony make;
And let the roaring organs loudly play
The praises of the Lord in lively notes;
The whiles, with hollow throats, 220
The choristers the joyous Anthem sing,
That all the woods may answer, and their echo ring.

Behold, whiles she before the altar stands,
Hearing the holy priest that to her speaks,
And blesseth her with his two happy hands, 225
How the red roses flush up in her cheeks,
And the pure snow, with goodly vermill stain
Like crimson dyed in grain:[38]
That even the Angels, which continually
About the sacred altar do remain, 230
Forget their service and about her fly,
Oft peeping in her face, that seems more fair,
The more they on it stare.
But her sad[39] eyes, still fastened on the ground,
Are governèd with goodly modesty, 235
That suffers not one look to glance awry,
Which may let in a little thought unsound.
Why blush ye, love, to give to me your hand,
The pledge of all our band?[40]
Sing, ye sweet Angels, Alleluja sing, 240
That all the woods may answer, and your echo ring.

Now all is done: bring home the bride again;
Bring home the triumph of our victory:
Bring home with you the glory of her gain;
With joyance bring her and with jollity. 245
Never had man more joyful day than this,
Whom heaven would heap with bliss.
Make fast therefore now all this live-long day;
This day for ever to me holy is.
Pour out the wine without restraint or stay, 250
Pour not by cups, but by the belly full,
Pour out to all that will,
And sprinkle all the posts and walls with wine,
That they may sweat, and drunken be withal.
Crown ye God Bacchus[41] with a coronal, 255
And Hymen also crown with wreaths of vine;

[38]*vermill:* vermilion. *grain:* fast dye. [39]Serious.
[40]Union. [41]God of wine.

And let the Graces dance unto the rest,
For they can do it best:
The whiles the maidens do their carol sing,
To which the woods shall answer, and their echo ring. 260

Ring ye the bells, ye young men of the town,
And leave your wonted[42] labors for this day:
This day is holy; do ye write it down,
That ye for ever it remember may.
This day the sun is in his chiefest height, 265
With Barnaby the bright,[43]
From whence declining daily by degrees,
He somewhat loseth of his heat and light,
When once the Crab[44] behind his back he sees.
But for this time it ill ordainèd was, 270
To choose the longest day in all the year,
And shortest night, when longest fitter were:
Yet never day so long, but late would pass.
Ring ye the bells, to make it wear away,
And bonfires make all day; 275
And dance about them, and about them sing,
That all the woods may answer, and your echo ring.

Ah! when will this long weary day have end,
And lend me leave to come unto my love?
How slowly do the hours their numbers spend? 280
How slowly does sad Time his feathers move?
Haste thee, O fairest Planet,[45] to thy home,
Within the Western foam:
Thy tirèd steeds long since have need of rest.
Long though it be, at last I see it gloom, 285
And the bright evening-star with golden crest
Appear out of the East.
Fair child of beauty! glorious lamp of love!
That all the host of heaven in ranks dost lead,
And guidest lovers through the night's sad dread, 290
How cheerfully thou lookest from above,
And seems to laugh atween thy twinkling light,
As joying in the sight
Of these glad many, which for joy do sing,
That all the woods them answer, and their echo ring! 295

Now, cease, ye damsels, your delights fore-past;[46]
Enough is it that all the day was yours:

[42]Usual.

[43]June 11, the feats of St. Barnabas, was the longest day of the year before the Gregorian calendar was adopted, which omitted the dates of ten consecutive days. Since then, June 21 has been the longest day.

[44]The constellation Cancer, which the sun enters at the summer solstice.

[45]The sun. [46]Gone by.

Now day is done, and night is nighing fast,
Now bring the bride into the bridal bowers.
The night is come, now soon her disarray, 300
And in her bed her lay;
Lay her in lilies and in violets,
And silken curtains over her display,
And odored sheets, and Arras[47] coverlets.
Behold how goodly my fair love does lie, 305
In proud humility!
Like unto Maia, when as Jove her took
In Tempe, lying on the flowery grass,
'Twixt sleep and wake, after she weary was,
With bathing in the Acidalian brook.[48] 310
Now it is night, ye damsels may be gone,
And leave my love alone,
And leave likewise your former lay to sing:
The woods no more shall answer, nor your echo ring.

Now welcome, night! thou night so long expected, 315
That long day's labor dost at last defray,
And all my cares, which cruel Love collected,
Hast summed in one, and cancellèd for aye:
Spread thy broad wing over my love and me,
That no man may us see; 320
And in thy sable mantle us enwrap,
From fear of peril and foul horror free.
Let no false treason seek us to entrap,
Nor any dread disquiet once annoy
The safety of our joy; 325
But let the night be calm, and quietsome,
Without tempestuous storms or sad affray:
Like as when Jove with fair Alcmena lay,
When he begot the great Tirynthian groom:[49]
Or like as when he with thyself[50] did lie 330
And begot Majesty.
And let the maids and young men cease to sing;
Nor let the woods them answer, nor their echo ring.

Let no lamenting cries, nor doleful tears,
Be heard all night within, nor yet without: 335
Nor let false whispers, breeding hidden fears,
Break gentle sleep with misconceivèd doubt.
Let no deluding dreams, nor dreadful sights,
Make sudden sad affrights;

[47]A city in France where tapestries were made.

[48]Maia was the mother of the god Hermes, or Mercury. Tempe was a valley near Mt. Olympus, the home of the gods in northern Greece. The Acidalian brook was sacred to Aphrodite.

[49]Hercules, son of Alcmena, born at Tiryns; the greatest of the Greek heroes.

[50]Night.

Nor let house-fires, nor lightning's helpless[51] harms, 340
Nor let the Puck,[52] nor other evil sprites,
Nor let mischievous witches with their charms,
Nor let hobgoblins, names whose sense we see not,
Fray[53] us with things that be not:
Let not the screech-owl nor the stork be heard, 345
Nor the night raven, that still deadly yells;
Nor damnèd ghosts, called up with mighty spells,
Nor grizzly vultures, make us once afraid:
Nor let the unpleasant choir of frogs still croaking
Make us to wish their choking. 350
Let none of these their dreary accents sing;
Nor let the woods them answer, nor their echo ring.

But let still Silence true night-watches keep,
That sacred Peace may in assurance reign,
And timely Sleep, when it is time to sleep, 355
May pour his limbs forth on your[54] pleasant plain;
The whiles an hundred little wingèd loves,
Like divers-feathered doves,
Shall fly and flutter round about your bed,
And in the secret dark, that none reproves, 360
Their pretty stealths shall work, and snares shall spread
To filch away sweet snatches of delight,
Concealed through covert night.
Ye sons of Venus,[55] play your sports at will!
For greedy pleasure, careless of your toys,[56] 365
Thinks more upon her paradise of joys,
Than what ye do, albeit good or ill.
All night therefore attend your merry play,
For it will soon be day:
Now none doth hinder you, that say or sing; 370
Nor will the woods now answer, nor your echo ring.

Who is the same, which at my window peeps?
Or whose is that fair face that shines so bright?
Is it not Cynthia,[57] she that never sleeps,
But walks about high heaven all the night? 375
O! fairest goddess, do thou not envy
My love with me to spy:
For thou likewise didst love, though now unthought,
And for a fleece of wool, which privily[58]
The Latmian shepherd once unto thee brought, 380
His pleasures with thee wrought.

[51]For which there is no help. [52]A mischievous fairy. [53]Frighten.
[54]Night's. [55]Cupids (the "loves" of line 357). [56]Trivial amusements.
[57]Another name for the goddess of the moon. Proverbially chaste, she nevertheless fell in love with Endymion, a shepherd of Mt. Latmos, to whom she came in his sleep.
[58]Secretly.

Therefore to us be favorable now;
And since of women's labors thou hast charge,
And generation goodly dost enlarge,
Incline thy will to effect our wishful vow, 385
And the chast womb inform with timely seed,
That may our comfort breed:
Till which we cease our hopeful hap[59] to sing;
Nor let the woods us answer, nor our echo ring.

And thou, great Juno![60] which with awful might 390
The laws of wedlock still dost patronize,
And the religion of the faith first plight[61]
With sacred rites hast taught to solemnize;
And eke for comfort often callèd art
Of women in their smart;[62] 395
Eternally bind thou this lovely band,
And all thy blessings unto us impart.
And thou, glad Genius![63] in whose gentle hand
The bridal bower and genial bed remain,
Without blemish or stain: 400
And the sweet pleasures of their love's delight
With secret aid dost succor and supply,
Till they bring forth the fruitful progeny;
Send us the timely fruit of this same night.
And thou, fair Hebe![64] and thou, Hymen free! 405
Grant that it may so be.
Till which we cease your further praise to sing;
Nor any woods shall answer, nor your echo ring.

And ye high heavens, the temple of the gods,
In which a thousand torches flaming bright 410
Do burn, that to us wretched earthly clods
In dreadful darkness lend desirèd light;
And all ye powers which in the same remain,
More than we men can feign,[65]
Pour out your blessing on us plenteously, 415
And happy influence upon us rain,
That we may raise a large posterity,
Which from the earth, which they may long possess
With lasting happiness,
Up to your haughty[66] palaces may mount; 420
And, for the guerdon[67] of their glorious merit,
May heavenly tabernacles there inherit,
Of blessèd Saints for to increase the count.

[59]Good fortune. [60]Queen of the gods; goddess of matrimony.
[61]*religion:* tie. *plight:* pledged. [62]Pains of childbirth.
[63]Spirit of fertility; compare *genial* in the following line. [64]Goddess of youth.
[65]Imagine. [66]Lofty. [67]Reward.

So let us rest, sweet love, in hope of this,
And cease till then our timely joys to sing: 425
The woods no more us answer, nor our echo ring!

Song! made in lieu of many ornaments,
With which my love should duly have been decked,
Which cutting off through hasty accidents,[68]
Ye would not stay your due time to expect, 430
But promised both to recompense;
But unto her a goodly ornament,
And for short time[69] *an endless monument.*

Luis de Góngora
(1561–1627)

A ROSE[1]

Blown[2] in the morning, thou shalt fade ere noon,
What boots[3] a life which in such haste forsakes thee?
Thou'rt wondrous frolic, being to die so soon,
And passing proud a little colour makes thee.
If thee thy brittle beauty so deceives, 5
Know then the thing that swells thee is thy bane;[4]
For the same beauty doth, in bloody leaves,
The sentence of thy early death contain.
Some clown's[5] coarse lungs will poison thy sweet flower,
If by the careless plough thou shalt be torn; 10
And many Herods lie in wait each hour
To murder thee as soon as thou art born[6]—
Nay, force thy bud to blow—their tyrant breath
Anticipating life, to hasten death!

[68]Accidents caused by hate. The wedding poem is a gift in lieu of "ornaments" (presents) which have not yet arrived.

[69]*for short time:* of this one brief (wedding) day.

[1]Spanish title: *Vana rosa*; translated by Sir Richard Fanshawe (1608–1666).

[2]Blossomed. [3]Profits. [4]Ruin. [5]Peasant's; boor's.

[6]King Herod ordered a wholesale massacre of infants with the intent of killing the new-born Jesus; Matthew 2:1–16.

A NIGHTINGALE[1]

With such variety and dainty skill
Yon nightingale divides[2] her mournful song,
As if ten thousand of them through one bill
Did sing in parts the story of their wrong.[3]
Nay, she accuses with such vehemence 5
Her ravisher, I think she would incline
The conscious grove thereof to have a sense
And print it on the leaves of that tall pine.
Yet happy she, who may her pain declare
In moving notes, and wandering through the woods 10
With uncut wings, but change divert her care!
But let Him melt away in silent floods,
Whom his Medusa turned into a stone,[4]
That he might neither change, nor make his moan.

THE SPRING[1]

Those whiter lilies which the early morn
Seems to have newly woven of sleaved[2] silk,
To which (on banks of wealthy Tagus[3] borne)
Gold was their cradle, liquid pearl their milk:
These blushing roses, with whose virgin leaves 5
The wanton wind to sport himself presumes,
Whilst from their rifled wardrobe he receives
For his wings purple, for his breath perfumes:
But those, and these,[4] my Celia's pretty foot
Trod up. But if she should her face display, 10
And fragrant breast, they'd dry down to the root,
(As with the blasting of the midday's ray)
And this soft wind which both perfumes and cools
Pass like the unregarded breath of Fools.

[1] *Con fiderencia tal, con gracia tanta;* translated by Sir Richard Fanshawe.
[2] A musical term, meaning to sing a rapid melody in harmony.
[3] In the Greek myth, Philomela was raped by her brother-in-law Tereus, who cut out her tongue to prevent her revealing the fact. She was later transformed into a nightingale.
[4] Medusa, one of the Gorgons, turned those who gazed on her to stone.
[1] *Los blancos lilios que de ciento en ciento*; translated by Sir Richard Fanshawe.
[2] Made from finely separated threads. [3] A river flowing through Spain and Portugal.
[4] Both the lilies and the roses.

SOAR HIGH, MY LOVE[1]

Soar high, my Love, check not thy gallant flight
With thought of that ill-fated youth, to whom
(Fallen like a star from his presumptuous height)
The grey sea was a diaphanous tomb.[2]
Thy downy wings stretch to the gentle wind, 5
Avoiding the dead sea of cold despair,
And raised above the clouds, a passage fine,
To the most flaming region of the air.
With active circles crown that golden sphere,
'Gainst which the Royal Bird[3] refines his sight, 10
Showing what kind he is by looking there,
And melt thy wings yet at the noblest light.
Since to the Ocean and her pearly shore,
My glorious ruin now adds one title more.

LIFE'S GREATEST MISERY. ADDRESSED TO A FRIEND ON HIS MARRIAGE[1]

To dine on meats high-spiced, and find your flask
Has leak'd, and not a drop your thirst to tame;
To reach your posting-house[2] dead-tired, and ask
For mules, and find one trotting brute dead-lame;
To try new boots, with luck not quite the same, 5
One with great pain you fit, and one you tear;
To play Primero,[3] and,—to win your game
Wanting the King,—to find the Knave is there;
To ply with gifts a thankless lady fair;
To owe to bankers punctual as the day; 10
To ride uncloak'd, unfenced, through spungy air;[4]
To feed bad grooms who steal your corn and hay:
Count all the griefs you've known since life began;
The worst remains—to be a married man.

[1]*No enfrene tu gallardo pensamiento*; translated by Sir Richard Fanshawe.
[2]Daedalus, the legendary master-craftsman, made wings for himself and his son Icarus, but Icarus flew too near the sun, which melted the wax fastenings. He then fell to his death in the sea.
[3]The eagle, proverbially keen-sighted and able to gaze at the sun.
[1]*Comer salchicas y hallar sin gota*; translated by Edward Churton.
[2]Station for changing mounts. [3]A sixteenth- and seventeenth-century card game.
[4]*unfenced:* unprotected. *spungy:* damp.

ALLEGORY OF THE BREVITY OF THINGS HUMAN[1]

Learn, flowers, from me, what parts we play
From dawn to dusk. Last noon the boast
And marvel of the fields, today
I am not even my own ghost.

The fresh aurora was my cot, 5
The night my coffin and my shroud;
I perished with no light, save what
The moon could lend me from a cloud.
And thus, all flowers must die—of whom
Not one of you can cheat the doom. 10

Learn, flowers, from me, what parts we play
From dawn to dusk. Last noon the boast
And marvel of the fields, today
I am not even my own ghost.

What most consoles me from my fleetness 15
Is the carnation fresh with dew,
Since that which gave me one day's sweetness
To her conceded scarcely two:
Ephemerids[2] in briefness view
My scarlet and her crimson die. 20

Learn, flowers, from me, what parts we play
From dawn to dusk. Last noon the boast
And marvel of the fields, today
I am not even my own ghost.

The jasmine, fairest of the flowers, 25
Is least in size as in longevity.
She forms a star, yet lives less hours
Than it has rays. Her soul is brevity.
If amber could a flower be grown
It would be she, and she alone! 30

Learn, flowers, from me, what parts we play
From dawn to dusk. Last noon the boast
And marvel of the fields, today
I am not even my own ghost.

[1]*Alegoría de la brevedad de las cosas humanas*; translated by Roy Campbell. The speaker can be thought of as the poet or as a flower, the morning glory.

[2]Short-lived creatures.

The gillyflower, though plain and coarse, 35
Enjoys on earth a longer stay.
And sees more suns complete their course
—As many as there shine in May.
Yet better far a marvel die
Than live a gillyflower, say I! 40

Learn, flowers, from me, what parts we play
From dawn to dusk. Last noon the boast
And marvel of the fields, today
I am not even my own ghost.

To no flower blooming in our sphere did 45
The daystar[3] grant a longer pardon
Than to the Sunflower, golden-bearded
Methusaleh[4] of every garden.
Eying him through as many days
As he shoots petals forth like rays. 50

Learn, flowers, from me, what parts we play
From dawn to dusk. Last noon the boast
And marvel of the fields, today
I am not even my own ghost.

THE ROSEMARY SPRAY[1]

The flowers upon the rosemary spray,
  Young Maid, may school thy sorrow;
The blue-eyed flower, that blooms to-day,
  To honey turns to-morrow.

A tumult stirs thy tender breast, 5
  With jealous pain true-hearted,
That he, whom thy first love hath bless'd
  From thee hath coldly parted.

Ungracious boy, who slights thy love,
  And overbold, disdaining 10
To ask forgiveness, and remove
  The cause of thy complaining.

Hope, come and drive those tears away!
  For lovers' jealous sorrow,
Like dewy blue-eyed flower on spray, 15
  To honey turns to-morrow.

[3]The sun. [4]A biblical figure who lived 969 years; Genesis 5:27.
[1]*Las flores del romero*; translated by Edward Churton.

By thine own joy thou wast undone:
  A bliss thou could'st not measure,
Like star at dawn too near the sun,
  Eclipsed thee by its pleasure. 20

Walk forth with eyes serene and fair;
  The pearls that deck the morning,
Are wasted in the day's fierce glare;
  With calmness tame his corning.

Disperse those clouds that but dismay; 25
  Distrust that jealous sorrow:
The blue-eyed flower, that blooms to-day,
  To honey turns to-morrow.

Bartolome Leonardo de Argensola

(1562–1631)

I MUST CONFESS, DON JUAN[1]

I must confess, Don Juan, on due inspection,
That dame Elvira's[2] charming red and white,
Though fair they seem, are only hers by right,
In that her money purchased their perfection;
But thou must grant as well, on calm reflection, 5
That her sweet lie hath such a luster bright,
As fairly puts to shame the paler light,
And honest beauty of a true complexion!
And yet no wonder I distracted go
With such deceit, when 'tis within our ken[3] 10
That nature blinds us with the self-same spell;
For that blue heaven above that charms us so,
Is neither heaven nor blue! Sad pity then
That so much beauty is not truth as well.

[1]Spanish title: *Yo os quiero confesar, Don Juan*; translated by James Young Gibson.
[2]Wife of the legendary lover and seducer Don Juan.
[3]Range of observation.

MARY MAGDALENE[1]

Blessed, yet sinful one, and broken-hearted!
The crowds are pointing at the thing forlorn,
In wonder and in scorn!
Thou weepest days of innocence departed;
Thou weepest, and thy tears have power to move 5
The Lord to pity and love.

The greatest of thy follies is forgiven,
Even for the least of all the tears that shine
On that pale cheek of thine.
Thou didst kneel down to Him who came from heaven, 10
Evil and ignorant, and thou shalt rise
Holy, and pure, and wise.

It is not much that to the fragrant blossom
The ragged brier should change; the bitter fir
Distill Arabian myrrh; 15
Nor that, upon the wintry desert's bosom,
The harvest should rise plenteous, and the swain
Bear home the abundant grain.

But come and see the bleak and barren mountains
Thick to their tops with roses; come and see 20
Leaves on the dry, dead tree:
The perished plant, set out by living fountains,
Grows fruitful, and its beauteous branches rise
For ever towards the skies.

Lope de Vega
(1562–1635)

THE GOOD SHEPHERD[1]

Shepherd! who with thine amorous, sylvan song
Hast broken the slumber that encompassed me,
Who mad'st Thy crook from the accursèd tree
On which Thy powerful arms were stretched so long!

[1]*A Santa María Magdalena*; translated by William Cullen Bryant. Mary Magdalene was traditionally identified with the repentant harlot (Luke 7:36–50) who washes Jesus' feet with her tears and wipes them with her hair. An onlooker is scandalized, but Jesus says of her, "Her sins, which are many, are forgiven, for she loved much."

[1]Spanish title: *Rimas sacras, Soneto XIV: Pastor, que con tus silbos amorosos*; translated by Henry Wadsworth Longfellow.

Lead me to mercy's ever-flowing fountains; 5
For Thou my shepherd, guard, and guide shalt be;
I will obey Thy voice, and wait to see
Thy feet all beautiful upon the mountains.
Hear, Shepherd, Thou who for Thy flock art dying,
Oh, wash away these scarlet sins, for Thou 10
Rejoicest at the contrite sinner's vow!
Oh, wait! to Thee my weary soul is crying,
Wait for me: Yet why ask it, when I see,
With feet nailed to the cross, Thou'rt waiting still for me!

TOMORROW[1]

Lord, what am I, that with unceasing care
Thou did'st seek after me, that Thou did'st wait
Wet with unhealthy dews before my gate,
And pass the gloomy nights of winter there?
Oh, strange delusion, that I did not greet 5
Thy blest approach, and oh, to heaven how lost
If my ingratitude's unkindly frost
Has chilled the bleeding wounds upon Thy feet.
How oft my guardian angel gently cried,
"Soul from thy casement look, and thou shalt see 10
How He persists to knock and wait for thee!"
And oh, how often to that Voice of sorrow,
"Tomorrow we will open," I replied,
And when the morrow came I answered still "Tomorrow."

AT DAWN THE VIRGIN IS BORN . . .[1]

At dawn the Virgin is born
And with her the sun,
Banishing the night
Of our griefs.
The bright dawn 5
Tramples down the night;
Heaven's smile
Tells of her peace
And time stands still
To gaze upon her 10
Banishing the night
Of our griefs.

[1] *Rimas sacras, Soneto XVIII: ¿Qué tengo yo, que mi amistad procuras?*; translated by Henry Wadsworth Longfellow.
[1] *Nace el Alba María;* translated by W. S. Merwin.

That she may be
Mistress of heaven, this holy
Child lifts up 15
Her light, which is the dawn;
And the light sings while she weeps
Divine pearls,
Banishing the night
Of our griefs. 20

That pure light
From the sun proceeds,
For all beauty which is
His to give he gives her:
The dawn, whose promise is 25
That he follows after,
Banishing the night
Of our griefs.

ICE AND FIRES CONTEND WITH MY CHILD . . .[1]

Ice and fires
Contend with my child;
Only love
Would suffer such torment.

The fire of love 5
And the cold of time
Rob my sweet love
Of his peace.
So that I say
When I find him smiling: 10
Only love
Would suffer such torment.

Whatever breast freeze
Or soul blaze
It will be seen that love 15
Alone could have wrought it.
Child contented
With ice and fire,
Only love
Would suffer such torment. 20

[1] *A mi niño combaten fuegos y hielos*; translated by W. S. Merwin.

WHERE ARE YOU GOING, MAIDEN . . . ?[1]

Where are you going, maiden,
Alone on the mountain?[2]
But who bears the sun
Does not fear the night.

Where are you going, Mary, 5
Divine bride,
Glorious mother
Of him who made us?
What would you do if the day
Should sink in the west 10
And night overtake you
On the mountain?
But who bears the sun
Does not fear the night.

The sight of the stars 15
Troubles me,
But your eyes
Are brighter than they.
Now with the stars
The dark night comes, 20
And the light of your beauty
Is hidden away,
But who bears the sun
Does not fear the night.

A LITTLE CAROL OF THE VIRGIN[1]

Angels walking under the palm trees,
holy angels,
let my child sleep,
hold back the branches.

Palms of Bethlehem, 5
tossing in angry wind,
rustling so loud:
for his sake quieten, sway gently—
let my child sleep,
hold back the branches. 10

[1] *¿Dónde vais, zagala?*; translated by W. S. Merwin.

[2] "And Mary arose in those days, and went into the hill country with haste" (Luke 1:39). The reference is to Mary's journey, after the Annunciation, to her cousin Elisabeth, herself then pregnant with John the Baptist.

[1] *Cantarcillo de la Virgen*; translated by Denise Levertov.

The holy child
is tired
of crying for his rest
on earth;
he craves a little respite 15
from his pathetic plaint.
Let my child sleep,
hold back the branches.

All about him
the bitter frost; 20
see, I have nothing
with which to shelter him.
Blessed angels,
flying past,
let my child sleep, 25
hold back the branches.

A SONNET ALL OF A SUDDEN[1]

Violante has commanded me to write
A sonnet. Oh! what trouble I am in!
Though here go three lines, eager to begin,
A sonnet's lines must number fourteen, quite!

I never thought that I should find a rhyme, 5
And look! the second quatrain[2] is begun:
But nothing in the quatrains would I shun
If I reach the first tercet[3] in good time.

I enter the first tercet in effect,
And I came in on the right foot, it seems, 10
Because the end of this verse is in sight.

Already in the second, I suspect
That I am finishing just thirteen lines:
Count them! If there are fourteen, it is right.

[1]*Soneto de repente,* from the play *La niña de plata*; translated by Doreen Bell.
[2]Unit of four lines. [3]Unit of three lines.

Michael Drayton
(1563–1631)

HOW MANY PALTRY, FOOLISH, PAINTED THINGS

How many paltry, foolish, painted things,
That now in coaches trouble ev'ry street,
Shall be forgotten, whom no poet sings,
Ere they be well wrapped in their winding sheet![1]
Where I to thee eternity shall give, 5
When nothing else remaineth of these days,
And queens hereafter shall be glad to live
Upon the alms of thy superfluous praise;
Virgins and matrons reading these my rhymes
Shall be so much delighted with thy story 10
That they shall grieve they lived not in these times,
To have seen thee, their sex's only[2] glory.
So shalt thou fly above the vulgar throng.
Still to survive in my immortal song.

SINCE THERE'S NO HELP

Since there's no help, come let us kiss and part;
Nay, I have done, you get no more of me,
And I am glad, yea glad with all my heart
That thus so cleanly I myself can free;
Shake hands forever, cancel all our vows, 5
And when we meet at any time again,
Be it not seen in either of our brows
That we one jot of former love retain.
Now at the last gasp of love's latest breath,
When, his pulse failing, passion speechless lies, 10
When faith is kneeling by his bed of death,
And innocence is closing up his eyes,
Now if thou wouldst, when all have given him over,
From death to life thou mightst him yet recover.

[1]Shroud.
[2]Preeminent (but perhaps with the modern meaning also).

William Shakespeare
(1564–1616)

SONNET 18

Shall I compare thee to a summer's day?
Thou art more lovely and more temperate.
Rough winds do shake the darling buds of May,
And summer's lease hath all too short a date.
Sometime too hot the eye of heaven shines, 5
And often is his gold complexion dimmed.
And every fair from fair[1] sometime declines,
By chance or nature's changing course untrimmed.[2]
But thy eternal summer shall not fade,
Nor lose possession of that fair thou owest,[3] 10
Nor shall Death brag thou wander'st in his shade
When in eternal lines to time thou grow'st.
So long as men can breathe, or eyes can see,
So long lives this, and this gives life to thee.

SONNET 30

When to the sessions of sweet silent thought
I summon up remembrance of things past,
I sigh the lack of many a thing I sought,
And with old woes new wail my dear time's waste.
Then can I drown an eye, unused to flow, 5
For precious friends hid in death's dateless[1] night,
And weep afresh love's long since canceled woe,
And moan the expense of many a vanished sight.
Then can I grieve at grievances foregone,
And heavily from woe to woe tell o'er[2] 10
The sad account of forebemoanèd moan,
Which I new-pay as if not paid before.
But if the while I think on thee, dear friend,
All losses are restored and sorrows end.

[1]*fair from fair:* beauty from beauty. [2]Deprived of adornment.
[3]Possess; own.
[1]Eternal. [2]Total up.

SONNET 64

When I have seen by Time's fell[1] hand defaced
The rich-proud cost of outworn buried age;
When sometime[2] lofty towers I see down-razed,
And brass eternal slave to mortal rage;
When I have seen the hungry ocean gain 5
Advantage on the kingdom of the shore,
And the firm soil win of the weary main,
Increasing store[3] with loss, and loss with store;
When I have seen such interchange of state,
Or state itself confounded to decay; 10
Ruin hath taught me thus to ruminate,
That Time will come and take my love away.
This thought is as a death, which cannot choose
But weep to have that which it fears to lose.

SONNET 73

That time of year thou mayst in me behold
When yellow leaves, or none, or few, do hang
Upon those boughs which shake against the cold,
Bare ruined choirs where late the sweet birds sang.
In me thou see'st the twilight of such day 5
As after sunset fadeth in the west,
Which by and by black night doth take away,
Death's second self, that seals up all in rest.
In me thou see'st the glowing of such fire,
That on the ashes of his youth doth lie 10
As the deathbed whereon it must expire,
Consumed with that which it was nourished by.
This thou perceivest, which makes thy love more strong,
To love that well which thou must leave ere long.

SONNET 116

Let me not to the marriage of true minds
Admit impediments. Love is not love
Which alters when it alteration finds,
Or bends with the remover to remove:

[1]Cruel; evil. [2]Formerly. [3]Plenty; supply.

O, no! it is an ever-fixed mark,
That looks on tempests and is never shaken;
It is the star to every wandering bark,[1]
Whose worth's unknown, although his height be taken.[2]
Love's not Time's fool, though rosy lips and cheeks
Within his bending sickle's compass come;
Love alters not with his brief hours and weeks,
But bears it out even to the edge of doom.
If this be error, and upon me proved,
I never writ, nor no man ever loved.

SONNET 129

The expense[1] of spirit in a waste of shame
Is lust in action; and till action, lust
Is perjured, murderous, bloody, full of blame,
Savage, extreme, rude, cruel, not to trust;
Enjoyed no sooner but despisèd straight;[2]
Past reason hunted, and no sooner had,
Past reason hated, as a swallowed bait,
On purpose laid to make the taker mad.
Mad in pursuit, and in possession so;
Had, having, and in quest to have, extreme;
A bliss in proof; and proved,[3] a very woe;
Before, a joy proposed; behind, a dream.
All this the world well knows, yet none knows well
To shun the Heaven that leads men to this Hell.

SONNET 130

My mistress' eyes are nothing like the sun;
Coral is far more red than her lips' red;
If snow be white, why then her breasts are dun;[1]
If hairs be wires, black wires grow on her head.
I have seen roses damasked, red and white,
But no such roses see I in her cheeks;
And in some perfumes is there more delight
Than in the breath that from my mistress reeks.
I love to hear her speak, yet well I know
That music hath a far more pleasing sound;
I grant I never saw a goddess go;[2]
My mistress, when she walks, treads on the ground:
And yet, by heaven, I think my love as rare
As any she belied with false compare.

[1]Sailing ship. [2]*his height be taken:* its celestial altitude be measurable.
[1]Spending. [2]Straightway; immediately.
[3]*in proof:* while being tried or experienced. *proved:* after being experienced.
[1]Lightless, dull brown. [2]Walk. Gait and carriage were distinctive marks of a goddess.

SONNET 138

When my love swears that she is made of truth,
I do believe her, though I know she lies,
That she might think me some untutor'd youth,
Unlearned in the world's false subtleties.
Thus vainly thinking that she thinks me young, 5
Although she knows my days are past the best,
Simply I credit her false-speaking tongue:
On both sides thus is simple truth supprest.
But wherefore says she not she is unjust?[1]
And wherefore say not I that I am old? 10
O, love's best habit is in seeming trust,
And age in love loves not to have years told:[2]
Therefore I lie with her, and she with me,
And in our faults by lies we flatter'd be.

Thomas Campion

(1567–1620)

I CARE NOT FOR THESE LADIES

I care not for these ladies
That must be wooed and prayed,
Give me kind Amaryllis,
The wanton country maid;
Nature art disdaineth, 5
Her beauty is her own;
Her when we court and kiss,
She cries forsooth let go,
But when we come where comfort is,
She never will say no. 10

If I love Amaryllis
She gives me fruit and flowers,
But if we love these ladies
We must give golden showers.[1]
Give them gold that sell love; 15
Give me the nut-brown lass
Who when we court and kiss
She cries forsooth let go,
But when we come where comfort is,
She never will say no. 20

[1]Unfaithful. [2]Counted.
[1]In Greek myth, Zeus made love to Danaë in the guise of a shower of gold.

These ladies must have pillows
And beds by strangers wrought;
Give me a bower of willows,
Of moss and leaves unbought,
And fresh Amaryllis 25
With milk and honey fed,
Who when we court and kiss
She cries forsooth let go,
But when we come where comfort is,
She never will say no. 30

FOLLOW YOUR SAINT

Follow your saint, follow with accents sweet;
Haste you, sad notes, fall at her flying feet.
There, wrapped in cloud of sorrow, pity move,
And tell the ravisher of my soul I perish for her love.
But if she scorns my never-ceasing pain, 5
Then burst with sighing in her sight and ne'er return again.

All that I sung still[1] to her praise did tend,
Still she was first, still she my songs did end.
Yet she my love and music both doth fly,
The music that her echo is and beauty's sympathy. 10
Then let my notes pursue her scornful flight:
It shall suffice that they were breathed and died for her delight.

John Donne
(1572–1631)

THE GOOD-MORROW

I wonder by my troth, what thou and I
Did, till we lov'd? were we not wean'd till then?
But suck'd on country pleasures,[1] childishly?
Or snorted we in the seven sleepers' den?[2]

[1]Always; constantly.

[1]Rural pleasures, but also a sexual pun.

[2]The seven sleepers were seven Christian youths of Ephesus who were said to have taken refuge in a cave during the persecution of the Emperor Decius and slept for two centuries.

'Twas so; but this,[3] all pleasures fancies be. 5
If ever any beauty I did see,
Which I desir'd, and got, 'twas but a dream of thee.

And now good-morrow to our waking souls,
Which watch not one another out of fear;
For love all love of other sights controls, 10
And makes one little room[4] an everywhere.
Let sea-discoverers to new worlds have gone,
Let maps to other, worlds on worlds have shown,
Let us possess one world, each hath one, and is one.[5]

My face in thine eye, thine in mine appears, 15
And true plain hearts do in the faces rest;
Where can we find two better hemispheres[6]
Without sharp North, without declining West?
What ever dies, was not mixt equally;[7]
If our two loves be one, or thou and I 20
Love so alike that none do slacken, none can die.

SONG

Go, and catch a falling star,
Get with child a mandrake root,[1]
Tell me, where all past years are,
Or who cleft the Devil's foot,[2]
Teach me to hear Mermaids singing, 5
Or to keep off envy's stinging,
And find
What wind
Serves to advance an honest mind.

If thou be'st born to strange sights, 10
Things invisible to see,
Ride ten thousand days and nights,
Till age snow white hairs on thee,
Thou, when thou return'st, wilt tell me
All strange wonders that befell thee, 15
And swear
No where
Lives a woman true, and fair.

[3]Compared to this love. [4]Their bedroom.
[5]That is, each has the world of the other, and each is a world to the other.
[6]Donne may have been thinking of "cordiform" maps which depicted each hemisphere as a heart.
[7]An axiom in alchemy. *Equally* here means "uniformly."
[1]The forked root of the mandrake looks like the lower half of a human body.
[2]The devil is said to be recognizable by his cloven hoof.

If thou find'st one, let me know,
  Such a Pilgrimage were sweet; 20
Yet do not, I would not go,
  Though at next door we might meet,
Though she were true, when you met her,
And last, till you write your letter,
      Yet she 25
      Will be
False, ere I come, to two, or three.

THE CANONIZATION

For God's sake hold your tongue, and let me love;
  Or chide my palsy, or my gout,
My five grey hairs, or ruin'd fortune flout;
  With wealth your state, your mind with arts improve,
    Take you a course,[1] get you a place,[2] 5
    Observe his Honour, or his Grace,[3]
Or the King's real, or his stamped face[4]
  Contemplate; what you will, approve,[5]
  So you will let me love.

Alas, alas, who's injur'd by my love? 10
  What merchant's ships have my sighs drown'd?
Who says my tears have overflow'd his ground?
  When did my colds a forward spring remove?
    When did the heats which my veins fill
    Add one more to the plaguy bill?[6] 15
Soldiers find wars, and lawyers find out still
  Litigious men, which quarrels move,[7]
  Though she and I do love.

Call us what you will, we are made such by love;
  Call her one, me another fly,[8] 20
We're tapers too, and at our own cost die,[9]
  And we in us find the Eagle and the Dove.[10]
    The Phoenix riddle[11] hath more wit
    By us; we two being one, are it.

[1]That is, a course of action leading to worldly success. [2]A job.
[3](1) A judge or a nobleman, (2) the qualities of honor and grace.
[4]Stamped on a coin. [5]Try out, test.
[6]The list of deaths from the plague. [7]Who start quarrels.
[8]The taper-fly, which was attracted to flame and burned itself in it, was said to be hermaphroditic and resurrectable.
[9]Sexual intercourse was thought to shorten life. Therefore lovers are like candles, which get shorter as they burn. *Die* is a slang term for having sexual intercourse.
[10]Symbols, in medieval literature, of righteousness and mercy.
[11]The Phoenix bird, which was resurrected from its own ashes, was also said to be hermaphroditic.

So to one neutral thing both sexes fit, 25
We die and rise the same,[12] and prove
Mysterious by this love.

We can die by it, if not live by love,
And if unfit for tombs and hearse[13]
Our legend be, it will be fit for verse; 30
And if no piece of Chronicle we prove,[14]
We'll build in sonnets pretty rooms;[15]
As well a well-wrought urn becomes
The greatest ashes, as half-acre tombs,
And by these hymns, all shall approve 35
Us canonized for Love:

And thus invoke us; You whom reverend love
Made one another's hermitage;
You, to whom love was peace, that now is rage;
Who did the whole world's soul contract, and drove 40
Into the glasses of your eyes[16]
(So made such mirrors, and such spies,
That they did all to you epitomize,)
Countries, Towns, Courts: beg from above
A pattern of your love![17] 45

THE FUNERAL

Whoever comes to shroud me, do not harm
Nor question much
That subtle wreath of hair, which crowns my arm;[1]
The mystery, the sign you must not touch,
For 'tis my outward Soul, 5
Viceroy to that, which then to heaven being gone,
Will leave this to control,
And keep these limbs, her Provinces, from dissolution.

For if the sinewy thread my brain lets fall
Through every part,[2] 10
Can tie those parts, and make me one of all;

[12]In sexual intercourse, we become sexless (*neutral*), because one sex cancels out the other. But after intercourse, we mysteriously are two different sexes again. *Die* and *rise* also have sexual meanings.

[13]Funereal poems were pinned to hearses.

[14]If we are not recorded in history, or if we do not beget children as described in I Chronicles 1–9.

[15]Mausoleum rooms and stanzas (in Italian).

[16]That is, drove the whole world into each other's eyes by gazing at each other.

[17]Ask the god of love for a pattern of your love.

[1]Such bracelets found on corpses are described by several medieval writers, including Giraldus Cambrensis.

[2]The nervous system which makes him one being.

These hairs which upward grew, and strength and art
Have from a better brain,
Can better do 't;[3] except[4] she meant that I
By this should know my pain, 15
As prisoners then are manacled, when they're condemn'd to die.

Whate'er she meant by it, bury it with me,
For since I am
Love's martyr, it might breed idolatry,
If into others' hands these Reliques came; 20
As 'twas humility
To afford to it all that a Soul can do,[5]
So, 'tis some bravery,
That since you would save none of me, I bury some of you.

THE FLEA

Mark but this flea, and mark in this,
How little that which thou deny'st me is;
It suck'd me first, and now sucks thee,
And in this flea, our two bloods mingled be;[1]
Thou know'st that this cannot be said 5
A sin, nor shame, nor loss of maidenhead,
Yet this enjoys before it woo,
And pamper'd swells with one blood made of two,
And this, alas, is more than we would do.

Oh stay, three lives in one flea spare, 10
Where we almost, yea more than married are.
This flea is you and I, and this
Our marriage bed, and marriage temple is;
Though parents grudge, and you, we're met,
And cloistered in these living walls of jet. 15
Though use make you apt to kill me,
Let not to that, self murder added be,
And sacrilege,[2] three sins in killing three.

Cruel and sudden, hast thou since
Purpled thy nail, in blood of innocence? 20
Wherein could this flea guilty be,
Except in that drop which it suck'd from thee?

[3]That is, tie the parts of the body together. [4]Unless.
[5]It was submission to give to it all that a soul can do.
[1]The three united in the flea—the flea himself, the lover, and the mistress—thus echo the Trinity, an idea that recurs throughout the poem.
[2]Sacrilege because the flea is a "marriage temple."

Yet thou triumph'st, and say'st that thou
Find'st not thyself, nor me the weaker now;
'Tis true, then learn how false, fears be; 25
Just so much honour, when thou yield'st to me,
Will waste, as this flea's death took life from thee.

A VALEDICTION: FORBIDDING MOURNING[1]

As virtuous men pass mildly away,
And whisper to their souls, to go,
Whilst some of their sad friends do say,
The breath goes now, and some say, no:

So let us melt, and make no noise, 5
No tear-floods, nor sigh-tempests move,
'Twere profanation of our joys
To tell the laity our love.

Moving of th' earth brings harms and fears,
Men reckon what it did and meant, 10
But trepidation of the spheres,[2]
Though greater far, is innocent.

Dull sublunary[3] lovers' love
(Whose soul is sense[4]) cannot admit
Absence, because it doth remove 15
Those things which elemented[5] it.

But we by a love, so much refin'd,
That ourselves know not what it is,
Inter-assurèd of the mind,
Care less eyes, lips, and hands to miss. 20

Our two souls therefore, which are one,
Though I must go, endure not yet[6]
A breach, but an expansion,
Like gold to aery thinness beat.

If they be two, they are two so 25
As stiff twin compasses[7] are two,
Thy soul the fixed foot, makes no show
To move, but doth, if th' other do.

[1]Donne wrote this poem to his wife when he went to the Continent with Sir Robert Drury in 1611.

[2]*Trepidation* was the term used for the trembling of the outermost sphere (the *primum mobile*) in the Ptolemaic universe; this gave movement to the other spheres. The word also means "fear" of heavenly disturbances.

[3]Beneath the moon; earthly. [4]Dependent upon sensual gratification.

[5]Created or composed. [6]Nevertheless do not allow.

[7]That is, the two legs of a compass.

And though it in the centre sit,
  Yet when the other far doth roam, 30
It leans, and hearkens after it,
  And grows erect, as that comes home.

Such wilt thou be to me, who must
  Like th' other foot, obliquely[8] run;
Thy firmness makes my circle just, 35
  And makes me end, where I begun.

LOVE'S DIET

To what a cumbersome unwieldiness
And burdenous corpulence my love had grown,
  But that I did, to make it less,
  And keep it in proportion,
Give it a diet, made it feed upon 5
That which love worst endures, *discretion.*

Above one sigh a day I allow'd him not,
Of which my fortune, and my faults had part;
  And if sometimes my stealth he got
  A she sigh from my mistress's heart, 10
And thought to feast on that, I let him see
'Twas neither very sound, nor meant to me.[1]

If he wrung from me a tear, I brined[2] it so
With scorn or shame, that him it nourish'd not;
  If he suck'd hers, I let him know 15
  'Twas not a tear, which he had got,
His drink was counterfeit, as was his meat;
For, eyes which roll towards all, weep not, but sweat.

Whatever he would dictate, I writ that,
But burnt my letters; when she writ to me, 20
  And that that favour made him fat,
  I said, if any title be
Convey'd by this, Ah, what doth it avail,
To be the fortieth name in an entail?[3]

[8]Not in a straight line. The lover travels in a circle, and then, when the compass is closed, returns to his starting place.

[1]This is a difficult line. It probably means either, "The *she sigh* was neither a true ("very") sound, nor meant *for* me," or "The *she sigh* was to me neither a true sound nor sincerely intended."

[2]Salted.

[3]An *entail* is a paper documenting a line of descent of ownership or inheritance. The lover doubts that he will win the mistress, since he is so far down on the list.

Thus I reclaim'd my buzzard[4] love, to fly 25
At what, and when, and how, and where I choose;
Now negligent of sport I lie,
And now as other falconers use,
I spring[5] a mistress, swear, write, sigh and weep:
And the game kill'd, or lost, go talk, and sleep. 30

ELEGY XIX
TO HIS MISTRESS GOING TO BED

Come, Madam, come, all rest my powers defy,
Until I labour, I in labour lie.[1]
The foe oft-times having the foe in sight,
Is tired with standing though he never fight[2]
Off with that girdle, like heaven's Zone glistering, 5
But a far fairer world encompassing.
Unpin that spangled breastplate which you wear,
That th' eyes of busy fools may be stopt there.
Unlace yourself, for that harmonious chime
Tells me from you, that now it is bed time. 10
Off with that happy busk,[3] which I envy,
That still can be, and still can stand so nigh.
Your gown going off, such beauteous state reveals,
As when from flowry meads th' hill's shadow steals.
Off with that wiry Coronet and show 15
The hairy Diadem which on you doth grow:
Now off with those shoes, and then safely tread
In this love's hallow'd temple, this soft bed.
In such white robes, heaven's Angels used to be
Receiv'd by men; thou Angel bring'st with thee 20
A heaven like Mahomet's Paradise;[4] and though
Ill spirits walk in white, we easily know,
By this these Angels from an evil sprite,
Those set our hairs, but these our flesh upright.
Licence my roving hands, and let them go, 25
Before, behind, between, above, below.
O my America! my new-found-land,
My kingdom, safeliest when with one man mann'd,
My Mine of precious stones, My Empery,
How blest am I in this discovering thee! 30
To enter in these bonds, is to be free;
Then where my hand is set, my seal[5] shall be.

[4]That is, rapacious but slow. [5]Rouse from hiding, as in hunting with falcons.
[1]Until I get to work at sexual intercourse, I lie in agony waiting.
[2]Note sexual double meanings. [3]Corset.
[4]The paradise of Islam was supposed to be full of fleshly pleasure.
[5]Both "impression" and "sign of ownership."

Full nakedness! All joys are due to thee,
As souls unbodied, bodies uncloth'd must be,
To taste whole joys. Gems which you women use 35
Are like Atlanta's balls,[6] cast in men's views,
That when a fool's eye lighteth on a Gem,
His earthly soul may covet theirs, not them.
Like pictures, or like books' gay coverings made
For lay-men, are all women thus array'd; 40
Themselves are mystic books, which only we
(Whom their imputed grace will dignify)
Must see reveal'd. Then since that I may know,[7]
As liberally,[8] as to a Midwife, show
Thyself: cast all, yea, this white linen hence, 45
There is no penance due to innocence.
To teach thee, I am naked first; why then
What needst thou have more covering than a man.

HOLY SONNETS

X

Death be not proud, though some have called thee
Mighty and dreadful, for, thou art not so,
For, those, whom thou think'st, thou dost overthrow,
Die not, poor death, nor yet canst thou kill me.
From rest and sleep, which but thy pictures be, 5
Much pleasure, then from thee, much more must flow,
And soonest our best men with thee do go,
Rest of their bones, and soul's delivery.
Thou art slave to Fate, Chance, kings, and desperate men,
And dost with poison, war, and sickness dwell, 10
And poppy, or charms can make us sleep as well,
And better than thy stroke; why swell'st thou then?
One short sleep past, we wake eternally,
And death shall be no more; death, thou shalt die.

XIV

Batter my heart, three-person'd God; for, you
As yet but knock, breathe, shine, and seek to mend;
That I may rise, and stand, o'erthrow me, and bend
Your force, to break, blow, burn and make me new.
I, like an usurp'd town, to another due, 5
Labour to admit you, but Oh, to no end,

[6]Atalanta (usually so spelled) lost a race to Hippomenes because she paused three times to pick up three golden apples that Venus had given him and that he threw in her path.
[7]Both "have knowledge" and "have intercourse." [8]Both "freely" and "lewdly."

Reason your viceroy in me, me should defend,
But is captiv'd, and proves weak or untrue.
Yet dearly I love you, and would be loved fain,
But am betroth'd unto your enemy: 10
Divorce me, untie, or break that knot again,
Take me to you, imprison me, for I
Except you enthrall me, never shall be free,
Nor ever chaste, except you ravish me.

A HYMN TO GOD THE FATHER

I

Wilt Thou forgive that sin where I begun,[1]
Which is my sin, though it were done before?[2]
Wilt Thou forgive that sin, through which I run,
And do run still: though still I do deplore?
When Thou hast done, Thou hast not done, 5
For I have more.

II

Wilt Thou forgive that sin by which I have worn
Others to sin? and, made my sin their door?
Wilt Thou forgive that sin which I did shun
A year, or two: but wallowed in, a score? 10
When Thou hast done, Thou hast not done,
For I have more.

III

I have a sin of fear, that when I have spun
My last thread, I shall perish on the shore;[3]
Swear by Thyself, that at my death Thy son 15
Shall shine as He shines now, and heretofore;
And, having done that, Thou hast done,
I fear no more.

[1]Original sin.
[2]Note the pun on Donne's name, here and following.
[3]As opposed to going to heaven.

Robert Herrick

(1591–1674)

TO THE VIRGINS, TO MAKE MUCH OF TIME

Gather ye rosebuds while ye may,
    Old time is still[1] a-flying,
And this same flower that smiles today
    Tomorrow will be dying.

The glorious lamp of heaven, the sun, 5
    The higher he's a-getting,
The sooner will his race be run,
    And nearer he's to setting.

That age is best which is the first,
    When youth and blood are warmer; 10
But being spent, the worse, and worst
    Times still succeed the former.

Then be not coy,[2] but use your time,
    And while ye may, go marry;
For having lost but once your prime, 15
    You may for ever tarry.

TO DAFFODILS

Fair daffodils, we weep to see
    You haste away so soon;
As yet the early-rising sun
    Has not attained his noon.
        Stay, stay, 5
    Until the hasting day
        Has run
    But to the even-song;[1]
And, having prayed together, we
    Will go with you along. 10

We have short time to stay as you,
    We have as short a spring,
As quick a growth to meet decay
    As you, or any thing.

[1]Always. [2]Unwilling; retiring.
[1]Evensong is the Church of England evening prayer service.

We die 15
As your hours do, and dry
Away,
Like to the summer's rain,
Or as the pearls of morning's dew,
Ne'er to be found again. 20

John Milton
(1608–1674)

ON THE LATE MASSACRE IN PIEDMONT[1]

Avenge, O Lord, thy slaughtered saints, whose bones
Lie scattered on the Alpine mountains cold;
Even them who kept thy truth so pure of old,
When all our fathers worshipped stocks and stones,
Forget not: in thy book record their groans 5
Who were thy sheep, and in their ancient fold
Slain by the bloody Piedmontese, that rolled
Mother with infant down the rocks. Their moans
The vales redoubled to the hills, and they
To heaven. Their martyred blood and ashes sow 10
O'er all the Italian fields, where still doth sway
The triple tyrant;[2] that from these may grow
A hundredfold, who, having learnt thy way,
Early may fly the Babylonian woe.[3]

WHEN I CONSIDER HOW MY LIGHT IS SPENT[1]

When I consider how my light is spent
Ere half my days, in this dark world and wide,
And that one talent which is death to hide,
Lodged with me useless, though my soul more bent

[1]In April 1655, the Waldenses, an early-Protestant sect dwelling in the Piedmont (Alpine foothills) of northern Italy, were victims of a religious massacre by soldiers under the Duke of Savoy.

[2]The Pope, with his three-crowned tiara.

[3]The biblical book of Revelation (chapters 17, 18) portrayed ancient Rome as the Whore of Babylon; militant Protestants often applied the figure to the contemporary Church of Rome.

[1]Milton, whose eyesight had deteriorated over several years, became totally blind in the early 1650s. *Spent* means gone or exhausted.

To serve therewith my Maker, and present 5
My true account, lest he returning chide,
"Doth God exact day-labour, light denied?"
I fondly ask;[2] but Patience, to prevent
That murmur, soon replies, "God doth not need
Either mans' work or his own gifts; who best 10
Bear his mild yoke, they serve him best. His state
Is kingly. Thousands at his bidding speed
And post o'er land and ocean without rest:
They also serve who only stand and wait."

Sor Juana Inés de la Cruz

(c. 1650–1695)

ON HER PORTRAIT[1]

What here you see in deceiving tints,
Vaunting its crafty artistry
In specious syllogisms of color,
Is a discreet delusion of the sense;

This which flattery would fain pretend 5
Could expiate the horrors of the years,
The cruelties of time obliterate,
And triumph over age and nothingness,

'Tis but of apprehensiveness a futile artifice,
'Tis but a brittle blossom in the wind, 10
'Tis against fate an unavailing wall,

'Tis merely a folly diligently mistaken,
'Tis merely a senile ardor, and truly seen
'Tis a corpse, dust, shadow, nothing at all.

[2]Lines 3–8 refer to the parable of the talents in Matthew 24:30, which compares God to a rich man who demands that his servants invest, at a profit, the talents (sums of money) he allots to them. The master punishes harshly the servant who failed to multiply his capital.

[1]Spanish title: *A su retrato*; translated by Kate Flores. Sister Juana of the Cross was a Mexican poet. An intellectual prodigy in her childhood and youth, she began writing poetry early, then suddenly entered the convent at the age of nineteen. As a nun, she got into trouble for a time because of her passion for secular art and learning and her feminist sentiments, but she also demonstrated exceptional religious devotion and self-sacrifice, dying of the plague after ministering to other nuns infected with it.

THIS EVENING WHEN I SPOKE TO YOU . . .[1]

This evening when I spoke to you, my dear,
When in your face and gesture I perceived
That I could not persuade you with my words,
Then I desired that you should see my heart.

And love, that came to help my purposes, 5
Accomplished that which seemed impossible,
For there among the tears that sorrow spilled
Was drop by drop my wasting heart distilled.

Enough of harshness now, my dear, enough;
Nor let cruel jealousy torment you more, 10
Nor base suspicion attack your virtue now
With foolish shadows, empty evidence,
Since here in watery medium you have seen
And felt within your hands my wasted heart.

ELUSIVE SHADOW OF MY SUBSTANCE, STAY . . .[1]

Elusive shadow of my substance, stay,
Bewitching image that I want too well,
Illusion fair for whom in joy I die,
Fiction sweet for whom in pain I dwell.

If to the magnet of your gracious charms 5
My breast obedient as steel is drawn,
Why do you entice my enamored arms
If you would but escape me then in scorn?

Yet you must not think in your tyranny
That you quite succeed in vanquishing me: 10
For although you mock the tenuous ties
That ever will your phantom form despise,
What matter if my arms and breast you flee
If I keep you prisoner in my fantasy?

VERSES AGAINST THE INCONSEQUENCE OF MEN'S TASTE AND STRICTURES[1]

You stupid men, who do accuse
Women without good reason,
You are the cause of what you blame,
Yet this inference you refuse.

[1]*Esta tarde, mi bien, cuando te hablaba*; translated by Muriel Kittel.
[1]*Deténte, sombra de mi bien esquivo*; translated by Kate Flores.
[1]*Arguye de inconsecuentes el gusto y la censura de los hombres*; translated by Muriel Kittel.

If you seek women's favor to win 5
With ardor beyond compare,
Why require them to be good,
When 'tis you who urge their sin?

You break down their resistance,
Then say quite seriously 10
That their lightness has achieved
What you won by your persistence.

You seek with stupid presumption
To find her whom you pursue
To be Thais when you woo her, 15
And Lucretia in your possession.[2]

No woman can your favor win
Since even the most discreet
Is ungrateful if she keeps you out
And loose if she lets you in. 20

So how could she be born
Who would gain your love,
If an ungrateful woman displeases
And a complaisant one you scorn?

Your amorous labors give 25
Wings to their indiscretions,
When you have made women wicked
You wish them virtuously to live.

In a passion that is guilty
Who bears the greater blame: 30
She who falls on being entreated
Or he who falls to make entreaty?

When each is guilty of sin,
Which is the most to blame:
She who sins for payment, 35
Or he who pays for the sin?

Why are you so surprised
At the fault that is your own?
Either prize women as you make them,
Or make them to be prized. 40

To them no longer urge your suit,
And then with much more reason
Can you blame their affection
When they are in pursuit.

To assert this I have every right; 45
Your pride has many weapons,
Your persistence and your promises
Devil, world, and flesh unite.

[2]Thais was a notorious seductive courtesan of ancient Athens, mistress of Alexander the Great; Lucretia was an ancient Roman matron known for her heroic chastity.

Cultural Texts of the Renaissance

Giovanni Pico della Mirandola

(1463–1494)

from *ORATION ON THE DIGNITY OF MAN*[1]

I have read in the records of the Arabians, reverend Fathers, that Abdala the Saracen, when questioned as to what on this stage of the world, as it were, could be seen most worthy of wonder, replied: "There is nothing to be seen more wonderful than man." In agreement with this opinion is the saying of Hermes Trismegistus: "A great miracle, Asclepius, is man."[2] But when I weighed the reason for these maxims, the many grounds for the excellence of human nature reported by many failed to satisfy me—that man is the intermediary between creatures, the intimate of the gods, the king of the lower beings, by the acuteness of his senses, by the discernment of his reason, and by the light of his intelligence the interpreter of nature, the interval between fixed eternity and fleeting time, and (as the Persians say) the bond, nay, rather, the marriage song of the world, on David's testimony but little lower than the angels.[3] Admittedly great though these reasons be, they are not the principal grounds, that is, those which may rightfully claim for themselves the privilege of the highest admiration. For why should we not admire more the angels themselves and the blessed choirs of heaven? At last it seems to me I have come to understand why man is the most fortunate of creatures and consequently worthy of all admiration and what precisely is that rank which is his lot in the universal chain of Being—a rank to be envied not only by brutes but even by the stars and by minds beyond this world. It is a matter past faith and a wondrous one. Why should it not be? For it is on this very account that man is rightly called and judged a great miracle and a wonderful creature indeed.

[1]Translated by Elizabeth Livermoore Forbes. Pico, one of the most brilliant of Renaissance philosophers, used his considerable skills in languages and newly recovered classical texts to formulate a philosophy that attempted to reconcile Plato and Aristotle and to show that both were consistent with Christianity. This oration, the best known of his works, was never delivered. It was prepared as an introduction to nine hundred theses he prepared for a public disputation. Thirteen of the theses were condemned as heretical, and Pico was forced to flee. Although Pope Alexander VI later absolved him of the charge of heresy, he spent the rest of his short life under the protection of Lorenzo de Medici in Florence. He died at the age of thirty-one. "Oration on the Dignity of Man" develops the familiar Renaissance view of the human being as a microcosm of the world. It also expresses Pico's faith that all faiths and all philosophies ultimately express a single truth.

[2]Hermes Trismegistus was a legendary figure to whom were attributed a number of "Hermetic" texts of Neo-Platonist, Judaic, and cabbalistic teachings. The equally legendary Asclepius is represented in Homer as a mortal; later he was regarded as the god of healing.

[3]Psalms 8:5.

But hear, Fathers, exactly what this rank is and, as friendly auditors, conformably to your kindness, do me this favor. God the Father, the supreme Architect, had already built this cosmic home we behold, the most sacred temple of His godhead, by the laws of His mysterious wisdom. The region above the heavens He had adorned with Intelligences, the heavenly spheres He had quickened with eternal souls, and the excrementary and filthy parts of the lower world He had filled with a multitude of animals of every kind. But, when the work was finished, the Craftsman kept wishing that there were someone to ponder the plan of so great a work, to love its beauty, and to wonder at its vastness. Therefore, when everything was done (as Moses and Timaeus[4] bear witness), He finally took thought concerning the creation of man. But there was not among His archetypes that from which He could fashion a new offspring, or was there in His treasure-houses anything which He might bestow on His new son as an inheritance, nor was there in the seats of all the world a place where the latter might sit to contemplate the universe. All was now complete; all things had been assigned to the highest, the middle, and the lowest orders. But in its final creation it was not the part of the Father's power to fail as though exhausted. It was not the part of His wisdom to waver in a needful matter through poverty of counsel. It was not the part of His kindly love that he who was to praise God's divine generosity in regard to others should be compelled to condemn it in regard to himself.

At last the best of artisans ordained that that creature to whom He had been able to give nothing proper to himself should have joint possession of whatever had been peculiar to each of the different kinds of being. He therefore took man as a creature of indeterminate nature and, assigning him a place in the middle of the world, addressed him thus: "Neither a fixed abode nor a form that is thine alone nor any function peculiar to thyself have we given thee, Adam, to the end that according to thy longing and according to thy longing and according to thy judgment thou mayest have and possess what abode, what form, and what functions thou thyself shalt desire. The nature of all other beings is limited and constrained within the bounds of laws prescribed by Us. Thou, constrained by no limits, in accordance with thine own free will, in whose hand We have placed thee, shalt ordain for thyself the limits of thy nature. We have set thee at the world's center that thou mayest from thence more easily observe whatever is in the world. We have made thee neither of heaven nor of earth, neither mortal nor immortal, so that with freedom of choice and with honor, as though the maker and molder of thyself, thou mayest fashion thyself in whatever shape thou shalt prefer. Thou shalt have the power to degenerate into the lower forms of life, which are brutish. Thou shalt have the power, out of thy soul's judgment, to be reborn into the higher forms, which are divine."

O supreme generosity of God the Father, O highest and most marvelous felicity of man! To him it is granted to have whatever he chooses, to be whatever he wills. Beasts as soon as they are born (so says Lucilius)[5] bring with them from their mother's womb all they will ever possess. Spiritual beings, either from the beginning or soon thereafter, become what they are to be

[4]See Plato's dialogue *Timaeus.*
[5]Latin satiric poet, second century B.C. The comment appears in his *Sixth Satire.*

for ever and ever. On man when he came into life the Father conferred the seeds of all kinds and the germs of every way of life. Whatever seeds each man cultivates will grow to maturity and bear in him their own fruit. If they be vegetative, he will be like a plant. If sensitive, he will become brutish. If rational, he will grow into a heavenly being. If intellectual, he will be an angel and the son of God. And if, happy in the lot of no created thing, he withdraws into the center of his own unity, his spirit, made one with God, in the solitary darkness of God, who is set above all things, shall surpass them all. Who would not admire this our chameleon? Or who could more greatly admire aught else whatever? It is man who Asclepius of Athens, arguing from his mutability of character and from his self-transforming nature, on just grounds says was symbolized by Proteus[6] in the mysteries.

* * *

I come now to the things I have elicited from the ancient mysteries of the Hebrews and have cited for the confirmation of the inviolable Catholic faith. Lest perchance they should be deemed fabrications, trifles, or the tales of jugglers by those to whom they are unfamiliar, I wish all to understand what they are and of what sort, whence they come, by what and by how illustrious authors supported, and how mysterious, how divine, and how necessary they are to the men of our faith for defending our religion against the grievous misrepresentations of the Hebrews. Not only the famous doctors of the Hebrews, but also from among men of our opinion Esdras, Hilary, and Origen[7] write that Moses on the mount received from God not only the Law, which he left to posterity written down in five books, but also a true and more occult explanation of the Law. It was, moreover, commanded him of God by all means to proclaim the Law to the people but not to commit the interpretation of the Law to writing or to make it a matter of common knowledge. He himself should reveal it only to Iesu Nave, who in his turn should unveil it to the other high priests to come after him, under a strict obligation of silence.[8] It was enough through guileless story to recognize now the power of God, now his wrath against the wicked, his mercy to the righteous, his justice to all; and through divine and beneficial precepts to be brought to a good and happy way of life and the worship of true religion. But to make public the occult mysteries, the secrets of the supreme Godhead hidden beneath the shell of the Law and under a clumsy show of words—what else were this than to give a holy thing to dogs and to cast pearls before swine?[9] Therefore to keep hidden from the people the things to be shared by the initiate, among whom alone, Paul says, he spoke wisdom,[10] was not the part of human deliberation but of divine command. This custom the ancient philosophers most reverently observed, for Pythagoras wrote nothing except a few trifles, which he intrusted on his deathbed to his daughter Dama. The Sphinxes carved on the temples of the Egyptians reminded them that mystic doctrines should

[6]The Greek seagod Proteus had the power to assume different shapes.

[7]Esdras (or Ezra) was a sixth-century B.C. Jewish priest and scribe. St. Hilary (fourth century A.D.) was Bishop of Poitiers. Origen (c. 185–254) was, along with St. Augustine, the most influential theologian of his time.

[8]See the Apocryphal book IV Esdras 14:45–47.

[9]Matthew 7:6.

[10]I Corinthians 2:6.

be kept inviolable from the common herd by means of the knots of riddles. Plato, writing certain things to Dion concerning the highest substances, said: "It must be stated in riddles, lest the letter should fall by chance into the hands of others and what I am writing to you should be apprehended by others."[11] Aristotle used to say that his books of *Metaphysics*, in which he treated of things divine, were both published and not published. What further? Origen asserts that Jesus Christ, the Teacher of life, made many revelations to his disciples, which they were unwilling to write down lest they should become commonplaces to the rabble. This is in the highest degree confirmed by Dionysius the Areopagite, who says that the occult mysteries were conveyed by the founders of our religion *εκ νου ειζ νουν δια μεσον λογου*, from mind to mind, without writing, through the medium of speech.

In exactly the same way, when the true interpretation of the Law according to the command of God, divinely handed down to Moses, was revealed, it was called the Cabala, a word which is the same among the Hebrews as "reception" among ourselves; for this reason, of course, that one man from another, by a sort of hereditary right, received that doctrine not through written records but through a regular succession of revelations. But after the Hebrews were restored by Cyrus from the Babylonian captivity, and after the temple had been established anew under Zorobabel, they brought their attention to the restoration of the Law. Esdras, then the head of the church, after the book of Moses had been amended, when he plainly recognized that, because of the exiles, the massacres, the flights, and the captivity of the children of Israel, the custom instituted by their forefathers of transmitting the doctrine from mouth to mouth could not be preserved, and that it would come to pass that the mysteries of the heavenly teachings divinely bestowed on them would be lost, since the memory of them could not long endure without the aid of written records, decided that those of the elders then surviving should be called together and that each one should impart to the gathering whatever he possessed by personal recollection concerning the mysteries of the Law and that scribes should be employed to collect them into seventy volumes (about the number of elders in the Sanhedrin). That you may not have to rely on me alone in this matter, Fathers, hear Esdras himself speak thus: "And it came to pass, when the forty days were fulfilled, that the Most High spake unto me, saying, The first that thou hast written publish openly, and let the worthy and the unworthy read it: but keep the seventy last books, that thou mayst deliver them to such as be wise among thy people: for in them is the spring of understanding, the fountain of wisdom, and the stream of knowledge. And I did so."[12] And these are the words of Esdras to the letter. These are the books of cabalistic lore. In these books principally resides, as Esdras with a clear voice justly declared, the spring of understanding, that is, the ineffable theology of the supersubstantial deity; the fountain of wisdom, that is, the exact metaphysic of the intellectual and angelic forms; and the stream of knowledge, that is, the most steadfast philosophy of natural things. Pope Sixtus the Fourth who last preceded the pope under whom we are now fortunate to be living, Innocent the Eighth, took the greatest pains and interest in seeing that

[11]Plato, *Epistle II*.
[12]IV Esdras 14:45–47.

these books should be translated into the Latin tongue for a public service to our faith, and, when he died, three of them had been done into Latin. Among the Hebrews of the present day these books are cherished with such devotion that it is permitted no man to touch them unless he be forty years of age.

When I had purchased these books at no small cost to myself, when I had read them through with the greatest diligence and with unwearying toil, I saw in them (as God is my witness) not so much the Mosaic as the Christian religion. There is the mystery of the Trinity, there the Incarnation of the Word, there the divinity of the Messiah; there I have read about original sin, its expiation through Christ, the heavenly Jerusalem, the fall of the devils, the orders of the angels, purgatory, and the punishments of hell, the same things we read daily in Paul and Dionysius, in Jerome and Augustine. But in those parts which concern philosophy you really seem to hear Pythagoras and Plato, whose principles are so closely related to the Christian faith that our Augustine gives immeasurable thanks to God that the books of the Platonists have come into his hands. Taken altogether, there is absolutely no controversy between ourselves and the Hebrews on any matter, with regard to which they cannot be refuted and gainsaid out of the cabalistic books, so that there will not be even a corner left in which they may hide themselves. I have as a most weighty witness of this fact that very learned man Antonius Chronicus who, when I was with him at a banquet, with his own ears heard Dactylus, a Hebrew trained in this lore, with all his heart agree entirely to the Christian idea of the Trinity.

Desiderius Erasmus

(c. 1466–1536)

from *IN PRAISE OF FOLLY*[1]

[A WORLD OF FOOLS]

Come now then as many of you as challenge the respect of being accounted wise, ingenuously confess how many insurrections of rebellious thoughts, and pangs of a laboring mind, ye are perpetually thrown and tortured with; reckon up all those inconveniences that you are unavoidably subject to, and then

[1]Translated by White Kennett. Erasmus, a Dutch humanist, was one of the great figures of the Renaissance. He edited Greek and Latin classics and translated the New Testament from Greek into Latin. He supported ecclesiastical reform but opposed the Protestant Reformation. He was also a witty satirist in his original works *In Praise of Folly* (1509) and *The Education of a Christian Prince* (1515). *In Praise of Folly* is written in the persona of the allegorical figure of Folly, a device that permits Erasmus to direct his satire at a wide range of social foibles as well as at the Church and popular religious practices.

tell me [Folly] whether fools, by being exempted from all these embroilments, are not infinitely more free and happy than yourselves? Add to this, that fools do not barely laugh, and sing, and play the good-fellow alone to themselves: but as it is the nature of good to be communicative, so they impart their mirth to others, by making sport for the whole company they are at any time engaged in, as if providence purposely designed them for an antidote to melancholy: whereby they make all persons so fond of their society, that they are welcomed to all places, hugged, caressed, and defended, a liberty given them of saying or doing anything; so well beloved, that none dares to offer them the least injury; nay, the most ravenous beasts of prey will pass them by untouched, as if by instinct they were warned that such innocence ought to receive no hurt. Farther, their converse is so acceptable in the court of princes, that few kings will banquet, walk, or take any other diversion, without their attendance;[2] nay, and had much rather have their company, than that of their gravest counsellors, whom they maintain more for fashion-sake than good-will; nor is it so strange that these fools should be preferred before graver politicians, since these last, by their harsh, sour advice, and ill-timing the truth, are fit only to put a prince out of the humor, while the others laugh, and talk, and joke, without any danger of disobliging.

It is one farther very commendable property of fools, that they always speak the truth, than which there is nothing more noble and heroical. For so, though Plato relate it as a sentence of Alcibiades, that in the sea of drunkenness truth swims uppermost, and so wine is the only teller of truth[3], yet this character may more justly be assumed by me, as I can make good from the authority of Euripides, who lays down this as an axiom μωρα μωροδ λφγφι, Children and fools always speak the truth.[4] Whatever the fool has in his heart he betrays it in his face; or what is more notifying, discovers it by his words: while the wise man, as Euripides observes, carries a double tongue[5]; the one to speak what may be said, the other what ought to be; the one what truth, the other what the time requires: whereby he can in a trice so alter his judgment, as to prove that to be now white, which he had just before swore to be black[6]; like the satyr at his porridge, blowing hot and cold at the same breath[7]; in his lips professing one thing, when in his heart he means another.

Furthermore, princes in their greatest splendor seem upon this account unhappy, in that they miss the advantage of being told the truth, and are shammed off by a parcel of insinuating courtiers, that acquit themselves as flatterers more than as friends. But some will perchance object, that princes do not love to hear the truth, and therefore wise men must be very cautious how they behave themselves before them, lest they should take too great a liberty in speaking what is true, rather than what is acceptable. This must be confessed, truth indeed is seldom palatable to the ears of kings; yet fools have so great a privilege as to have free leave, not only to speak bare truths,

[2]Renaissance kings often included jesters or "fools" among their retinues, witty entertainers who were allowed considerable license in their speech and behavior. The Fool in Shakespeare's *King Lear* is the best-known literary example.

[3]Erasmus is citing a mistranslation of a line from the *Symposium*.

[4]The statement appears in *The Bacchae*.

[5]The line is quoted from *Rhesus*, a play erroneously attributed to Euripides.

[6]The Roman satirist Juvenal mentions changing black into white: *Satires* III.30.

[7]The satyr that can blow hot and cold at the same time appears in Aesop's *Fables*.

but the most bitter ones too; so as the same reproof, which had it come from the mouth of a wise man would have cost him his head, being blurted out by a fool, is not only pardoned, but well taken, and rewarded. For truth has naturally a mixture of pleasure, if it carry with it nothing of offence to the person whom it is applied to; and the happy knack of ordering it so is bestowed only on fools. 'Tis for the same reason that this sort of men are more fondly beloved by women, who like their tumbling them about, and playing with them, though never so boisterously; pretending to take that only in jest, which they would have to be meant in earnest, as that sex is very ingenious in palliating, and dissembling the bent of their wanton inclinations.

But to return. An additional happiness of these fools appears farther in this, that when they have run merrily on to their last stage of life, they neither find any fear nor feel any pain to die, but march contentedly to the other world, where their company sure must be as acceptable as it was here upon earth.

Let us draw now a comparison between the condition of a fool and that of a wise man, and see how infinitely the one outweighs the other.

Give me any instance then of a man as wise as you can fancy him possible to be, that has spent all his younger years in poring upon books, and trudging after learning, in the pursuit whereof he squanders away the pleasantest time of his life in watching, sweat, and fasting; and in his latter days he never tastes one mouthful of delight, but is always stingy, poor, dejected, melancholy, burdensome to himself, and unwelcome to others, pale, lean, thin-jawed, sickly, contracting by his sedentariness such hurtful distempers as bring him to an untimely death, like roses plucked before they shatter. Thus have you the draught of a wise man's happiness, more the object of a commiserating pity than of an ambitioning envy.[8]

But now again come the croaking Stoics, and tell me, in mood and figure, that nothing is more miserable than the being mad: but the being a fool is the being mad, therefore there is nothing more miserable than the being a fool. Alas, this is but a fallacy, the discovery whereof solves the force of the whole syllogism. Well then, they argue subtly, 'tis true; but as Socrates in Plato makes two Venuses and two Cupids,[9] and shows how their actions and properties ought not to be confounded; so these disputants, if they had not been made themselves, should have distinguished between a double madness in others: and there is certainly a great difference in the nature as well as in the degrees of them, and they are not both equally scandalous: for Horace seems to take delight in one sort, when he says:

> Does welcome frenzy make me thus mistake?[10]

And Plato in his *Phædon* ranks the madness of poets, of prophets, and of lovers among those properties which conduce to a happy life. And Virgil, in the sixth *Æneid,* gives this epithet to his industrious *Æneas*:

> If you will proceed to these your mad attempts.[11]

[8]In his negative portrait of the wise man, Erasmus appears to be parodying himself.
[9]Plato's *Symposium* divides love into the physical and the spiritual.
[10]*Odes* III.4. [11]*Aeneid* VI:135.

And indeed there is a two-fold sort of madness; the one that which the furies bring from hell; those that are herewith possessed are hurried on to wars and contentions, by an inexhaustible thirst of power and riches, inflamed to some infamous and unlawful lust, enraged to act the parracide, seduced to become guilty of incest, sacrilege, or some other of those crimson-dyed crimes; or, finally, to be so pricked in conscience as to be lashed and stung with the whips and snakes of grief and remorse. But there is another sort of madness that proceeds from Folly, so far from being any way injurious or distasteful that it is thoroughly good and desirable; and this happens when by a harmless mistake in the judgment of things the mind is freed from those cares which would otherwise gratingly afflict it, and smoothed over with a content and satisfaction it could not under other circumstances so happily enjoy. And this is that comfortable apathy or insensibleness which Cicero, in an epistle to his friend Atticus,[12] wishes himself master of, that he might the less take to heart those insufferable outrages committed by the tyrannizing triumvirate, Lepidus, Antonius, and Augustus. That Grecian[13] likewise had a happy time of it, who was so frantic as to sit a whole day in the empty theatre laughing, shouting, and clapping his hands, as if he had really seen some pathetic tragedy acted to the life, when indeed all was no more than the strength of imagination, and the efforts of delusion, while in all other respects the same person behaved himself very discreetly, was

> Sweet to his friends, to his wife, obliging, kind,
> And so averse from a revengeful mind,
> That had his men unsealed his bottled wine,
> He would not fret, nor doggedly repine.

And when by a course of physic he was recovered from this frenzy, he looked upon his cure so far from a kindness, that he thus reasons the case with his friends:

> This remedy, my friends, is worse i' th' main
> Than the disease, the cure augments the pain;
> My only hope is a relapse again.

And certainly they were the more mad of the two who endeavored to bereave him of so pleasing a delirium, and recall all the aches of his head by dispelling the mists of his brain.

I have not yet determined whether it be proper to include all the defects of sense and understanding under the common genius of madness. For if any one be so short-sighted as to take a mule for an ass, or so shallow-pated as to admire a paltry ballad for an elegant poem, he is not thereupon immediately censured as mad. But if any one let not only his senses but his judgment be imposed upon in the most ordinary common concerns, he shall come under the scandal of being thought next door to a madman. As suppose any one should hear an ass bray, and should take it for ravishing music[14];

[12] *Letters to Atticus* III.13.
[13] The mad Greek appears in Horace's *Epistles* III.2.
[14] The Greek didactic poet Theognis (6th century B.C.) tells this story.

or if any one, born a beggar, should fancy himself as great as a prince, or the like. But this sort of madness, if (as is most usual) it be accompanied with pleasure, brings a great satisfaction both to those who are possessed with it themselves, and those who deride it in others, though they are not both equally frantic. And this species of madness is of larger extent than the world commonly imagines. Thus the whole tribe of madmen make sport among themselves, while one laughs at another; he that is more mad many times jeering him that is less so. But indeed the greater each man's madness is, the greater is his happiness, if it be but such a sort as proceeds from an excess of folly, which is so epidemical a distemper that it is hard to find any one man so uninfected as not to have sometimes a fit or two of some sort of frenzy. There is only this difference between the several patients; he that shall take a broom-stick for a straitbodied woman is without more ado sentenced for a madman, because this is so strange a blunder as very seldom happens; whereas he whose wife is a common jilt, that keeps a warehouse free for all customers, and yet swears she is as chaste as an untouched virgin, and hugs himself in his contented mistake, is scarce taken notice of, because he fares no worse than a great many more of his good-natured neighbors. Among these are to be ranked such as take an immoderate delight in hunting, and think no music comparable to the sounding of horns and the yelping of beagles; and were they to take physic, would no question think the most sovereign virtues to be in the *album Græcum*[15] of a dog's turd. When they have run down their game, what strange pleasure they take in cutting of it up! Cows and sheep may be slaughtered by common butchers, but what is killed in hunting must be broke up by none under a gentleman, who shall throw down his hat, fall devoutly on his knees, and drawing out a slashing hanger (for a common knife is not good enough), after several ceremonies shall dissect all the parts as artificially as the best skilled anatomist, while all that stand round shall look very intently, and seem to be mightily surprised with the novelty, though they have seen the same an hundred times before; and he that can but dip his finger, and taste of the blood, shall think his own bettered by it: and though the constant feeding on such diet does but assimilate them to the nature of those beasts they eat of, yet they will swear that venison is meat for princes, and that their living upon it makes them as great as emperors.

Near akin to these are such as take a great fancy for building: they raise up, pull down, begin anew, alter the model, and never rest till they run themselves out of their whole estate, taking up such a compass for buildings, till they leave themselves not one foot of land to live upon, nor one poor cottage to shelter themselves from cold and hunger: and yet all the while are mighty proud of their contrivances, and sing a sweet *requiem* to their own happiness.

To these are to be added those plodding virtuosos, that plunder the most inward recesses of nature for the pillage of a new invention, and rake over sea and land for the turning up some hitherto latent mystery; and are so continually tickled with the hopes of success, that they spare for no cost nor pains, but trudge on, and upon a defeat in one attempt, courageously tack

[15]"Greek white," the dung of dogs or hyenas, which turns white when it dries and was used to dress leather.

about to another, and fall upon new experiments, never giving over till they have calcined their whole estate to ashes, and have not money enough left unmelted to purchase one crucible or limbeck. And yet after all, they are not so much discouraged, but that they dream fine things still, and animate others what they can to the like undertakings; nay, when their hopes come to the last gasp, after all their disappointments, they have yet one *salvo* for their credit, that:

In great exploits our bare attempts suffice.[16]

And so inveigh against the shortness of their life, which allows them not time enough to bring their designs to maturity and perfection.

Whether dice-players may be so favorably dealt with as to be admitted among the rest is scarce yet resolved upon: but sure it is hugely vain and ridiculous, when we see some persons so devoutly addicted to this diversion that at the first rattle of the box their heart shakes within them, and keeps consort with the motion of the dice: they are egged on so long with the hopes of always winning, till at last, in a literal sense, they have thrown away their whole estate, and made shipwreck of all they have, scarce escaping to shore with their own clothes to their backs; thinking it in the meanwhile a great piece of religion to be just in the payment of their stakes, and will cheat any creditor sooner than him who trusts them in play: and that poring old men, that cannot tell their cast without the help of spectacles, should be sweating at the same sport; nay, that such decrepit blades, as by the gout have lost the use of their fingers, should look over, and hire others to throw for them. This indeed is prodigiously extravagant; but the consequence of it ends so oft in downright madness, that it seems rather to belong to the furies than to folly.

The next to be placed among the regiment of fools are such as make a trade of telling or inquiring after incredible stories of miracles and prodigies: never doubting that a lie will choke them, they will muster up a thousand several strange relations of spirits, ghosts, apparitions, raising of the devil, and such like bugbears of superstition, which the farther they are from being probably true, the more greedily they are swallowed, and the more devoutly believed. And these absurdities do not only bring an empty pleasure, and cheap divertisement, but they are a good trade, and procure a comfortable income to such priests and friars as by this craft get their gain. To these again are nearly related such others as attribute strange virtues to the shrines and images of saints and martyrs, and so would make their credulous proselytes believe that if they pay their devotion to St. Christopher[17] in the morning, they shall be guarded and secured the day following from all dangers and misfortunes: if soldiers, when they first take arms, shall come and mumble over such a set prayer before the picture of St. Barbara,[18] they shall return safe form all engagements: or if any pray to Erasmus[19] on such

[16]Propertius II.10.

[17]St. Christopher was represented in medieval statues and paintings as enormous in stature. It was believed that if one saw such an image in the morning, one would not die on that day.

[18]St. Barbara was executed by her own father, who was struck dead by lightning when he had killed her. The patron saint of gunners, she protected soldiers in battle.

[19]St. Erasmus, an early 4th-century martyr, was the patron saint of wealth.

particular holidays, with the ceremony of wax-candles, and other fopperies, he shall in a short time be rewarded with a plentiful increase of wealth and riches. The Christians have now their gigantic St. George,[20] as well as the pagans had their Hercules; they paint the saint on horseback, and drawing the horse in splendid trappings, very gloriously accoutred, they scarce refrain in a literal sense from worshipping the very beast.

What shall I say of such as cry up and maintain the cheat of pardons and indulgences? that by these compute the time of each soul's residence in purgatory, and assign them a longer or shorter continuance, according as they purchase more or fewer of these paltry pardons, and saleable exemptions? Or what can be said bad enough of others who pretend that by the force of such magical charms, or by the fumbling over the beads in the rehearsal of such and such petitions (which some religious imposters invented, either for diversion, or what is more likely for advantage), they shall procure riches, honor, pleasure, health, long life, a lusty old age, nay, after death a sitting at the right hand of our Saviour in His kingdom; though as to this last part of their happiness, they care not how long it be deferred, having scarce any appetite toward a-tasting the joys of heaven, till they are surfeited, glutted with, and can no longer relish their enjoyments on earth. By this easy way of purchasing pardons, any notorious highwayman, any plundering soldier, or any bribe-taking judge, shall disburse some part of their unjust gains, and so think all their grossest impieties sufficiently atoned for; so many perjuries, lusts, drunkenness, quarrels, blood-sheds, cheats, treacheries, and all sorts of debaucheries, shall all be, as it were, struck a bargain for, and such a contract made, as if they had paid off all arrears, and might now begin upon a new score.[21]

And what can be more ridiculous, than for some others to be confident of going to heaven by repeating daily those seven verses out of the Psalms, which the devil taught St. Bernard, thinking thereby to have put a trick upon him, but that he was overreached in his cunning.[22]

Several of these fooleries, which are so gross and absurd as I myself am even ashamed to own, are practiced and admired, not only by the vulgar, but by such proficients in religion as one might well expect should have more wit.

From the same principles of folly proceeds the custom of each country's challenging their particular guardian-saint; nay, each saint has his distinct office allotted to him, and is accordingly addressed to upon the respective occasions: as one for the toothache, a second to grant an easy delivery in child-birth, a third to help persons to lost goods, another to protect seamen in a long voyage, a fifth to guard the farmer's cows and sheep, and so on; for to rehearse all instances would be extremely tedious.

[20]St. George was usually depicted on horseback, slaying a dragon with his lance.

[21]The selling of indulgences, supposed to reduce the time one spent in Purgatory, was a notorious abuse of the medieval Church and was the focus of Luther's criticism. Erasmus is careful to criticize, through Folly, only the selling of false indulgences.

[22]According to legend, a devil told St. Bernard that there were seven verses from the Psalms that, if repeated daily, would ensure salvation. He would not tell Bernard what they were, but Bernard told him that since he recited all the Psalms every day, he must be saying the crucial seven.

There are some more Catholic saints petitioned to upon all occasions, as more especially the Virgin Mary, whose blind devotees think it manners not to place the mother before the Son.

And of all the prayers and intercessions that are made to these respective saints the substance of them is no more than downright Folly. Among all the trophies that for tokens of gratitude are hung upon the walls and ceilings of churches, you shall find no relics presented as a memorandum of any that were ever cured of Folly, or had been made one dram the wiser. One perhaps after shipwreck got safe to shore; another recovered when he had been run through by an enemy; one, when all his fellow-soldiers were killed upon the spot, as cunningly perhaps as cowardly, made his escape from the field; another, while he was a-hanging, the rope broke, and so he saved his neck, and renewed his licence for practising his old trade of thieving; another broke jail, and got loose; a patient, against his physician's will, recovered of a dangerous fever; another drank poison, which putting him into a violent looseness, did his body more good than hurt, to the great grief of his wife, who hoped upon this occasion to have become a joyful widow[23]; another had his wagon overturned, and yet none of his horses lamed; another had caught a grievous fall, and yet recovered from the bruise; another had been tampering with his neighbor's wife, and escaped very narrowly from being caught by the enraged cuckold in the very act. After all these acknowledgments of escapes from such singular dangers, there is none (as I have before intimated) that return thanks for being freed from Folly; Folly being so sweet and luscious, that it is rather sued for as a happiness, than deprecated as a punishment. But why should I launch out into so wide a sea of superstitions?

> Had I as many tongues as Argus eyes,
> Briareus hands, they all would not suffice
> Folly in all her shapes t' epitomize.[24]

Almost all Christians being wretchedly enslaved to blindness and ignorance, which the priests are so far from preventing or removing, that they blacken the darkness, and promote the delusion; wisely foreseeing that the people (like cows, which never give down their milk so well as when they are gently stroked), would part with less if they knew more, their bounty proceeding only from a mistake of charity. Now if any grave wise man should stand up, and unseasonably speak the truth, telling every one that a pious life is the only way of securing a happy death; that the best title to a pardon of our sins is purchased by a hearty abhorrence of our guilt, and sincere resolutions of amendment; that the best devotion which can be paid to any saints is to imitate them in their exemplary life: if he should proceed thus to inform them of their several mistakes, there would be quite another estimate put upon tears, watchings, masses, fastings, and other severities, which before were so much prized, as persons will now be vexed to lose that satisfaction they formerly found in them.

[23]The story of the woman who tried to kill her husband by giving him two poisons was told by the Latin poet Ausonius (4th century B.C.). He survived because each poison was the antidote of the other.

[24]The lines are adapted from the *Aeneid* VI.625–627.

In the same predicament of fools are to be ranked such, as while they are yet living, and in good health, take so great a care how they shall be buried when they die, that they solemnly appoint how many torches, how many escutcheons, how many gloves to be given, and how many mourners they will have at their funeral; as if they thought they themselves in their coffins could be sensible of what respect was paid to their corpse; or as if they doubted they should rest a whit the less quiet in the grave if they were with less state and pomp interred.[25]

Now though I am in so great haste, as I would not willingly be stopped or detained, yet I cannot pass by without bestowing some remarks upon another sort of fools; who, though their first descent was perhaps no better than from a tapster or tinker, yet highly value themselves upon their birth and parentage. One fetches his pedigree from Æneas, another from Brute, a third from king Arthur: they hang up their ancestors' wormeaten pictures as records of antiquity, and keep a long list of their predecessors, with an account of all their offices and titles, while they themselves are but transcripts of their forefathers' dumb statues, and degenerate even into those very beasts which they carry in their coat of arms as ensigns of their nobility: and yet by a strong presumption of their birth and quality, they live not only the most pleasant and unconcerned themselves, but there are not wanting others too who cry up these brutes almost equal to the gods. But why should I dwell upon one or two instances of Folly, when there are so many of like nature? Conceitedness and self-love making many by strength of Fancy believe themselves happy, when otherwise they are really wretched and despicable. Thus the most ape-faced, ugliest fellow in the whole town, shall think himself a mirror of beauty: another shall be so proud of his parts that if he can but mark out a triangle with a pair of compasses, he thinks he has mastered all the difficulties of geometry, and could outdo Euclid[26] himself. A third shall admire himself for a ravishing musician, though he have no more skill in the handling of any instrument than a pig playing on the organs: and another that rattles in the throat as hoarse as a cock crows, shall be proud of his voice, and think he sings like a nightingale.

There is another very pleasant sort of madness, whereby persons assume to themselves whatever of accomplishment they discern in others. Thus the happy rich churl in Seneca, who had so short a memory as he could not tell the least story without a servant standing by to prompt him, and was at the same time so weak that he could scarce go upright, yet he thought he might adventure to accept a challenge to a duel because he kept at home some lusty, sturdy fellows whose strength he relied upon instead of his own.[27]

It is almost needless to insist upon the several professors of arts and sciences who are all so egregiously conceited that they would sooner give up their title to an estate in lands than part with the reversion of their wits: among these, more especially stage-players, musicians, orators, and poets, each of which, the more of duncery they have, and the more of pride, the greater is their ambition: and how notoriously soever dull they be, they meet with

[25]Erasmus's satire on those who are overconcerned with their own funerals is based on Seneca's *Of the Brevity of Life*, chap. 20.

[26]Fourth-century Greek mathematician who presented the principles of geometry in his *Elements*.

[27]The story of the rich man with the bad memory is taken from Seneca's *Letters*.

their admirers; nay, the more silly they are the higher they are extolled; Folly (as we have before intimated) never failing of respect and esteem. If therefore every one, the more ignorant he is, the greater satisfaction he is to himself, and the more commended by others, to what purpose is it to sweat and toil in the pursuit of true learning, which shall cost so many gripes and pangs of the brain to acquire, and when obtained, shall only make the laborious student more uneasy to himself, and less acceptable to others?

As nature in her dispensation of conceitedness has dealt with private persons, so has she given a particular smatch of self-love to each country and nation. Upon this account it is that the English challenge the prerogative of having the most handsome women, of the being most accomplished in the skill of music, and of keeping the best tables: the Scotch brag of their gentility, and pretend the genius of their native soil inclines them to be good disputants: the French think themselves remarkable for complaisance and good breeding: the Sorbonists of Paris pretend before any others to have made the greatest proficiency in polemic divinity: the Italians value themselves for learning and eloquence; and, like the Grecians of old, account all the world barbarians in respect of themselves; to which piece of vanity the inhabitants of Rome are more especially addicted, pretending themselves to be owners of all those heroic virtues which their city so many ages since was deservedly famous for. The Venetians stand upon their birth and pedigree. The Grecians pride themselves in having been the first inventors of most arts, and in their country being famed for the product of so many eminent philosophers. The Turks, and all the other refuse of Mahometism, pretend they profess the only true religion, and laugh at all Christians for superstitious, narrow-souled fools. The Jews to this day expect their Messias as devoutly as they believe in their first prophet Moses. The Spaniards challenge the repute of being accounted good soldiers. And the Germans are noted for their tall, proper stature, and for their skill in magic. But not to mention any more, I suppose you are already convinced how great an improvement and addition to the happiness of human life is occasioned by self-love: next step to which is flattery; for as self-love is nothing but the coaxing up of ourselves, so the same currying and humoring of others is termed flattery.

Flattery, it is true, is now looked upon as a scandalous name, but it is by such only as mind words more than things. They are prejudiced against it upon this account, because they suppose it jostles out all truth and sincerity, whereas indeed its property is quite contrary, as appears from the examples of several brute creatures. What is more fawning than a spaniel? And yet what is more faithful to his master? What is more fond and loving than a tame squirrel? And yet what is more sporting and inoffensive? This little frisking creature is kept up in a cage to play withal, while lions, tigers, leopards, and such other savage emblems of rapine and cruelty are shown only for state and rarity, and otherwise yield no pleasure to their respective keepers.

There is indeed a pernicious destructive sort of flattery wherewith rookers and sharks work their several ends upon such as they can make a prey of, by decoying them into traps and snares beyond recovery: but that which is the effect of folly is of a much different nature; it proceeds from a softness of spirit, and a flexibleness of good humor, and comes far nearer to virtue than that other extreme of friendship, namely, a stiff, sour, dogged moroseness: it refreshes our minds when tired, enlivens them when melancholy, reinforces them when languishing, invigorates them when heavy, recovers them when sick, and pacifies them when rebellious: it puts us in a method how to procure friends, and how to keep them; it entices children to swallow the bitter rudiments of learning; it gives a new ferment to the almost stagnated souls of old men; it both reproves and instructs principles without offense under the mask of commendation: in short, it makes every man fond and indulgent of himself, which is indeed no small part of each man's happiness, and at the same time renders him obliging and complaisant in all company, where it is pleasant to see how the asses rub and scratch one another.[28]

This again is a great accomplishment to an orator, a greater to a physician, and the only one to a poet: in fine, it is the best sweetener to all afflictions, and gives a true relish to the otherwise insipid enjoyments to our whole life. Ay, but (say you) to flatter is to deceive; and to deceive is very harsh and hurtful; no, rather just contrary; nothing is more welcome and bewitching than the being deceived. They are much to be blamed for an undistinguishing head, that make a judgment of things according to what they are in themselves, when their whole nature consists barely in the opinions that are had of them. For all sublunary matters are enveloped in such a cloud of obscurity that the short-sightedness of human understanding, cannot pry through and arrive to any comprehensive knowledge of them; hence the sect of academic philosophers have modestly resolved that all things being no more than probable, nothing can be known as certain; or if there could, yet would it but interrupt and abate from the pleasure of a more happy ignorance. Finally, our souls are so fashioned and molded that they are sooner captivated by appearances than by real truths; of which, if any one would demand an example, he may find a very familiar one in churches, where, if what is delivered from the pulpit be a grave, solid, rational discourse, all the congregation grow weary, and fall asleep, till their patience be released; whereas if the preacher (pardon the impropriety of the word, the prater I would have said) be zealous, in his thumps of the cushion, antic gestures, and spend his glass in the telling of pleasant stories, his beloved shall then stand up, tuck their hair behind their ears, and be very devoutly attentive. So among the saints, those are most resorted to who are most romantic and fabulous: as for instance, a poetic St. George, a St. Christopher, or a St. Barbara, shall be oftener prayed to than St. Peter, St. Paul, nay, perhaps than Christ himself; but this, it is possible, may more properly be referred to another place.[29]

In the meanwhile observe what a cheap purchase of happiness is made by the strength of fancy. For whereas many things even of inconsiderable value would cost a great deal of pains and perhaps pelf to procure; opinion spares charges, and yet gives us them in as ample a manner by conceit as if we possessed them in reality. Thus he who feeds on such a stinking dish of fish as another must hold his nose at a yard's distance from, yet if he feed heartily, and relish them palatably, they are to him as good as if they were fresh caught: whereas, on the other hand, if any one be invited to never so

[28]The mules who engage in reciprocal scratching are proverbial. Erasmus includes them in his *Adages*.

[29]Erasmus calls Sts. George, Christopher, and Barbara "romantic and fabulous"; he stops short, though, of calling them false. They were removed from the calendar in the twentieth century.

dainty a jowl of sturgeon, if it go against his stomach to eat any, he may sit a-hungry, and bite his nails with greater appetite than his victuals. If a woman be never so ugly and nauseous, yet if her husband can but think her handsome, it is all one to him as if she really were so: if any man have never so ordinary and smutty a draught, yet if he admires the excellency of it, and can suppose it to have been drawn by some old Apelles, or modern Vandyke, he is as proud of it as if it had really been done by one of their hands. I knew a friend of mine that presented his bride with several false and counterfeit stones, making her believe that they were right jewels, and cost him so many hundred thousand crowns; under his mistake the poor woman was as choice of pebbles, and painted glass, as if they had been so many natural rubies and diamonds, while the subtle husband saved a great deal in his pocket, and yet made his wife as well pleased as if he had been at ten hundred times the cost. What difference is there between them that, in the darkest dungeon, can with a platonic brain survey the whole world in idea, and him that stands in the open air, and takes a less deluding prospect of the universe? If the beggar in Lucian, that dreamt he was a prince, had never waked, his imaginary kingdom had been as great as a real one.[30] Between him therefore that truly is happy, and him that thinks himself so, there is no perceivable distnction; or if any, the fool has the better of it: first, because his happiness costs him less, standing him only in the price of a single thought; and then, secondly, because he has more fellow-companions and partakers of his good fortune: for no enjoyment is comfortable where the benefit is not imparted to others; nor is any one station of life desirable, where we can have no converse with persons of the same condition with ourselves: and yet this is the hard fate of wise men, who are grown so scarce that like Phœnixes they appear but one in an age. The Grecians, it is true, reckoned up seven within the narrow precincts of their own country; yet I believe were they to cast up their accounts anew, they would not find a half, nay, not a third part, of one in far larger extent.

Farther, when among the several good properties of Bacchus this is looked upon as the chief, namely, that he drowns the cares and anxieties of the mind, though it be indeed but for a short while; for after a small nap, when our brains are a little settled, they all return to their former corrodings: how much greater is the more durable advantage which I bring? while by one uninterrupted fit of being drunk in conceit, I perpetually cajole the mind with riots, revels, and all the excess and energy of joy.

Add to this, that I am so communicative and bountiful, as to let no one particular person pass without some token of my favor; whereas other deities bestow their gifts sparingly to their elect only. Bacchus has not thought fit that every soil should bear the same juice-yielding grape: Venus has not given to all a like portion of beauty: Mercury endows but few with the knack of an accomplished eloquence: Hercules gives not to all the same measure of wealth and riches: Jupiter has ordained but a few to be born to a kingdom: Mars in battle gives a complete victory but to one party; nay, he often makes them both losers: Apollo does not answer the expectation of all that consult his oracles: Jove oft thunders: Phœbus sometimes shoots the plague, or some other infection, at the point of his darts: and Neptune swallows down

[30]The Latin satirist Lucian tells this story in *The Dream or the Cock.*

more than he bears up: not to mention their Jupiters, their Plutos, their Ate, goddess of loss, their evil geniuses, and such other monsters of divinity as had more of the hangman than the god in them, and were worshipped only to deprecate that hurt which used to be inflicted by them: I say, not to mention these, I am that high and mighty goddess whose liberality is of as large an extent as her omnipotence: I give to all that ask: I never appear sullen, nor out of humor, nor ever demand any atonement or satisfaction for the omission of any ceremonious punctilio in my worship: I do not storm or rage, if mortals in their addresses to the other gods pass me by unregarded, without the acknowledgement of any respect or application: whereas all the other gods are so scrupulous and exact, that it often proves less dangerous manfully to despise them than sneakingly to attempt the difficulty of pleasing them. Thus some men are of that captious, forward humor, that a man had better be wholly strangers to them than never so intimate friends.

Well, but there are none (say you) build any altars, or dedicate any temple to Folly. I admire (as I have before intimated) that the world should be so wretchedly ungrateful. But I am so good natured as to pass by and pardon this seeming afront, though indeed the charge thereof, as unnecessary, may well be saved; for to what purpose should I demand the sacrifice of frankincense, cakes, goats, and swine, since all persons everywhere pay me that more acceptable service which all divines agree to be more effectual and meritorious, namely, an imitation of my communicable attributes? I do not therefore any way envy Diana for having her altars bedewed with human blood: I think myself then most religiously adored, when my respective devotees (as is their usual custom) conform themselves to my practice, transcribe my pattern, and so live the copy of me their original. And truly this pious devotion is not so much in use among Christians as is much to be wished it were: for how many zealous votaries are there that pay so profound respect to the Virgin Mary, as to place lighted tapers even at noon day upon her altars? And yet how few of them copy after her untouched chastity, her modesty, and her other commendable virtues, in the imitation whereof consists the truest esteem of divine worship? Farther, why should I desire a temple, since the whole world is but one ample continued choir, entirely dedicated to my use and service? Nor do I want worshippers at any place where the earth wants not inhabitants. And as to the manner of my worship, I am not yet so irrecoverably foolish as to be prayed to by proxy, and to have my honor intermediately bestowed upon senseless images and pictures which quite subvert the true end of religion; while the unwary supplicants seldom distinguish betwixt the things themselves and the objectives they represent. The same respect in the meanwhile is paid to me in a more legitimate manner; for to me there are as many statutes erected as there are moving fabrics of mortality; every person, even against his own will, carrying the image of me, *i.e.*, the signal of Folly instamped on his countenance. I have not therefore the least tempting inducement to envy the more seeming state and splendor of the other gods, who are worshipped at set times and places; as Phœbus at Rhodes, Venus in her Cyprian isle, Juno in the city Argos, Minerva at Athens, Jupiter on the hill Olympus, Neptune at Tarentum, and Priapus in the town of Lampsacum; while my worship extending as far as my influence, the whole world is my one altar, whereupon the most valuable incense and sacrifice is perpetually offered up.

Niccolo Machiavelli

(1469–1527)

from *THE PRINCE*[1]

[RULES FOR PRINCES]

OF THE QUALITIES IN RESPECT OF WHICH MEN, AND MOST OF ALL PRINCES, ARE PRAISED OR BLAMED

It now remains for us to consider what ought to be the conduct and bearing of a Prince in relation to his subjects and friends. And since I know that many have written on this subject, I fear it may be thought presumptuous in me to write of it also; the more so, because in my treatment of it I depart from the views that others have taken.

But since it is my object to write what shall be useful to whosoever understands it, it seems to me better to follow the real truth of things than an imaginary view of them. For many Republics and Princedoms have been imagined that were never seen or known to exist in reality.[2] And the manner in which we live, and that in which we ought to live, are things so wide asunder, that he who quits the one to betake himself to the other is more likely to destroy than to save himself; since any one who would act up to a perfect standard of goodness in everything, must be ruined among so many who are not good. It is essential, therefore, for a Prince who desires to maintain his position, to have learned how to be other than good, and to use or not to use his goodness as necessity requires.

Laying aside, therefore, all fanciful notions concerning a Prince, and considering those only that are true, I say that all men when they are spoken of, and Princes more than others from their being set so high, are characterized by some one of those qualities which attach either praise or blame. Thus one is accounted liberal,[3] another miserly (which word I use, rather than *avaricious*, to denote the man who is too sparing of what is his own, *avarice* being the disposition to take wrongfully what is another's); one is generous, another greedy; one cruel, another tender-hearted; one is faithless, another true to his word; one effeminate and cowardly, another high-spirited and courageous; one is courteous, another haughty; one impure, another

[1]Translated by N. Hill Thomson. Machiavelli knew the world of power politics firsthand. As defense secretary of the Florentine republic, he travelled widely and meet many European princes, including Cesare Borgia. When the Medici family returned to power in Florence, he was dismissed from office, imprisoned, and tortured. Upon his release, he retired in his mid-forties to his country estates and spent the rest of his life writing works about politics, as well as poems and plays. His contemporaries professed to be shocked by "Machiavellianism," the ruthless, amoral policy described in *The Prince*; modern readers are more likely to see it as a realistic description of how politics works, behind idealistic rationalizations.

[2]For example, in Plato's *Republic.*

[3]Free-giving; generous.

chaste; one simple, another crafty; one firm, another facile; one grave, another frivolous; one devout, another unbelieving; and the like. Every one, I know, will admit that it would be most laudable for a Prince to be endowed with all of the above qualities that are reckoned good; but since it is impossible for him to possess or constantly practice them all, the conditions of human nature not allowing it, he must be discreet enough to know how to avoid the infamy of those vices that would deprive him of his government, and, if possible, be on his guard also against those which might not deprive him of it; though if he cannot wholly restrain himself, he may with less scruple indulge in the latter. He need never hesitate, however, to incur the reproach of those vices without which his authority can hardly be preserved; for if he well consider the whole matter, he will find that there may be a line of conduct having the appearance of virtue, to follow which would be his ruin, and that there may be another course having the appearance of vice, by following which his safety and well-being are secured.

OF LIBERALITY AND MISERLINESS

Beginning, then, with the first of the qualities above noticed, I say that it may be a good thing to be reputed liberal, but, nevertheless, that liberality without the reputation of it is hurtful; because, though it be worthily and rightly used, still if it be not known, you escape not the reproach of its opposite vice. Hence, to have credit for liberality with the world at large, you must neglect no circumstance of sumptuous display; the result being, that a Prince of a liberal disposition will consume his whole substance in things of this sort, and, after all, be obliged, if he would maintain his reputation for liberality, to burden his subjects with extraordinary taxes, and to resort to confiscations and all the other shifts whereby money is raised. But in this way he becomes hateful to his subjects, and growing impoverished is held in little esteem by any. So that in the end, having by his liberality offended many and obliged few, he is worse off than when he began, and is exposed to all his original dangers. Recognizing this, and endeavoring to retrace his steps, he at once incurs the infamy of miserliness.

A Prince, therefore, since he cannot without injury to himself practice the virtue of liberality so that it may be known, will not, if he be wise, greatly concern himself though he be called miserly. Because in time he will come to be regarded as more and more liberal, when it is seen that through his parsimony his revenues are sufficient; that he is able to defend himself against any who make war on him; that he can engage in enterprises against others without burdening his subjects; and thus exercise liberality towards all from whom he does not take, whose number is infinite, while he is miserly in respect of those only to whom he does not give, whose number is few.

In our own days we have seen no Princes accomplish great results save those who have been accounted miserly. All others have been ruined. Pope Julius II, after availing himself of his reputation for liberality to arrive at the Papacy, made no effort to preserve that reputation when making war on the King of France, but carried on all his numerous campaigns without levying from his subjects a single extraordinary tax, providing for the increased expenditure out of his long-continued savings. Had the present King of Spain been accounted liberal, he never could have engaged or succeeded in so many enterprises.

A Prince, therefore, if he is enabled thereby to forbear from plundering his subjects, to defend himself, to escape poverty and contempt, and the necessity of becoming rapacious, ought to care little though he incur the reproach of miserliness, for this is one of those vices which enable him to reign.

And should any object that Cæsar by his liberality rose to power, and that many others have been advanced to the highest dignities from their having been liberal and so reputed, I reply, "Either you are already a Prince or you seek to become one; in the former case liberality is hurtful, in the latter it is very necessary that you be thought liberal; Cæsar was one of those who sought the sovereignty of Rome; but if after obtaining it he had lived on without retrenching his expenditure, he must have ruined the Empire." And if it be further urged that many Princes reputed to have been most liberal have achieved great things with their armies, I answer that a Prince spends either what belongs to himself and his subjects, or what belongs to others; and that in the former case he ought to be sparing, but in the latter ought not to refrain from any kind of liberality. Because for a Prince who leads his armies in person and maintains them by plunder, pillage, and forced contributions, dealing as he does with the property of others this liberality is necessary, since otherwise he would not be followed by his soldiers. Of what does not belong to you or to your subjects you should, therefore, be a lavish giver, as were Cyrus, Cæsar, and Alexander; for to be liberal with the property of others does not take from your reputation, but adds to it. What injures you is to give away what is your own. And there is no quality so self-destructive as liberality; for while you practice it you lose the means whereby it can be practiced, and become poor and despised, or else, to avoid poverty, you become rapacious and hated. For liberality leads to one or other of these two results, against which, beyond all others, a Prince should guard.

Wherefore it is wiser to put up with the name of being miserly, which breeds ignominy, but without hate, than to be obliged, from the desire to be reckoned liberal to incur the reproach of rapacity, which breeds hate as well as ignominy.

OF CRUELTY AND CLEMENCY AND WHETHER IT IS BETTER TO BE LOVED OR FEARED

Passing to the other qualities above referred to, I say that every Prince should desire to be accounted merciful and not cruel. Nevertheless, he should be on his guard against the abuse of this quality of mercy. Cesare Borgia was reputed cruel, yet his cruelty restored Romagna, united it, and brought it to order and obedience; so that if we look at things in their true light, it will be seen that he was in reality far more merciful than the people of Florence, who, to avoid the imputation of cruelty, suffered Pistoja to be torn to pieces by factions.[4]

A Prince should therefore disregard the reproach of being thought cruel where it enables him to keep his subjects united and obedient. For he who

[4]Pitoja was a city near Florence, under its control. Florence failed to assert its power and allowed a bloody civil war to continue.

quells disorder by a very few signal examples will in the end be more merciful than he who from too great leniency permits things to take their course and so to result in rapine and bloodshed; for these hurt the whole State, whereas the severities of the Prince injure individuals only.

And for a new Prince, of all others, it is impossible to escape a name for cruelty, since new States are full of dangers. Wherefore Virgil, by the mouth of Dido, excuses the harshness of her reign on the plea that it was new, saying:

> A fate unkind, and newness in my reign
> Compel me thus to guard a wide domain.[5]

Nevertheless, the new Prince should not be too ready of belief, nor too easily set in motion; nor should he himself be the first to raise alarms; but should so temper prudence with kindliness that too great confidence in others shall not throw him off his guard, nor groundless distrust render him insupportable.

And here comes in the question whether it is better to be loved rather than feared, or feared rather than loved. It might perhaps be answered that we should wish to be both; but since love and fear can hardly exist together, if we must choose between them, it is far safer to be feared than loved. For of men it may generally be affirmed that they are thankless, fickle, false, studious to avoid danger, greedy of gain, devoted to you while you are able to confer benefits upon them, and ready, as I said before, while danger is distant, to shed their blood, and sacrifice their property, their lives, and their children for you; but in the hour of need they turn against you. The Prince, therefore, who without otherwise securing himself builds wholly on their professions in undone. For the friendships which we buy with a price, and do not gain by greatness and nobility of character, though they be fairly earned are not made good, but fail us when we have occasion to use them.

Moreover, men are less careful how they offend him who makes himself loved than him who makes himself feared. For love is held by the tie of obligation, which, because men are a sorry breed, is broken on every whisper of private interest; but fear is bound by the apprehension of punishment which never relaxes its grasp.

Nevertheless a Prince should inspire fear in such a fashion that if he do not win love he may escape hate. For a man may very well be feared and yet not hated, and this will be the case so long as he does not meddle with the property or with the women of his citizens and subjects. And if constrained to put any to death, he should do so only when there is manifest cause or reasonable justification. But, above all, he must abstain from the property of others. For men will sooner forget the death of their father than the loss of their patrimony. Moreover, pretexts for confiscation are never to seek, and he who has once begun to live by rapine always finds reasons for taking what is not his; whereas reasons for shedding blood are fewer, and sooner exhausted.

But when a Prince is with his army, and has many soldiers under his command, he must needs disregard the reproach of cruelty, for without such a

[5]Dido is explaining to the shipwrecked Trojans that, having only recently founded and settled Carthage, she and her people must take extreme security precautions.

reputation in its Captain, no army can be held together or kept under any kind of control. Among other things remarkable in Hannibal[6] this has been noted, that having a very great army, made up of men of many different nations and brought to fight in a foreign country, no dissension ever arose among the soldiers themselves, nor any mutiny against their leader, either in his good or in his evil fortunes. This we can only ascribe to the transcendent cruelty, which, joined with numberless great qualities, rendered him at once venerable and terrible in the eyes of his soldiers; for without this reputation for cruelty these other virtues would not have produced the like results.

Unreflecting writers, indeed, while they praise his achievements, have condemned the chief cause of them; but that his other merits would not by themselves have been so efficacious we may see from the case of Scipio, one of the greatest Captains, not of his own time only but of all times of which we have record, whose armies rose against him in Spain from no other cause than his too great leniency in allowing them a freedom inconsistent with military strictness. With which weakness Fabius Maximus[7] taxed him in the Senate House, calling him the corrupter of the Roman soldiery. Again, when the Locrians were shamefully outraged by one of his lieutenants,[8] he neither avenged them, nor punished the insolence of his officer; and this from the natural easiness of his disposition. So that it was said in the Senate by one who sought to excuse him, that there were many who knew better how to refrain from doing wrong themselves than how to correct the wrong-doing of others. This temper, however, must in time have marred the name and fame even of Scipio, had he continued in it, and retained his command. But living as he did under the control of the Senate, this hurtful quality was not merely disguised, but came to be regarded as a glory.

Returning to the question of being loved or feared, I sum up by saying, that since his being loved depends upon his subjects, while his being feared depends upon himself, a wise Prince should build on what is his own, and not on what rests with others. Only, as I have said, he must do his utmost to escape hatred.

HOW PRINCES SHOULD KEEP FAITH

Every one understands how praiseworthy it is in a Prince to keep faith, and to live uprightly and not craftily. Nevertheless, we see from what has taken place in our own days that Princes who have set little store by their word, but have known how to overreach men by their cunning, have accomplished great things, and in the end got the better of those who trusted to honest dealing.

Be it known, then, that there are two ways of contending, one in accordance with the laws, the other by force; the first of which is proper to men, the second to beasts. But since the first method is often ineffectual, it becomes necessary to resort to the second. A Prince should, therefore, understand

[6]Carthaginian general (247–182 B.C.), victorious against Rome for a time but finally defeated by Scipio. One of Hannibal's most spectacular feats was to lead his invading army across the Alps from Spain to Italy.

[7]Fabius Cunctator ("The Delayer"), noted for his tactic of harassing Hannibal's army without meeting it head-on. He became dictator of Rome in 217 B.C.

[8]Scipio took Locri, in southern Italy, in 205 B.C.

how to use well both the man and the beast. And this lesson has been covertly taught by the ancient writers, who relate how Achilles and many others of these old Princes were given over to be brought up and trained by Chiron the Centaur; since the only meaning of their having for instructor one who was half man and half beast[9] is, that it is necessary for a Prince to know how to use both natures, and that the one without the other has no stability.

But since a Prince should know how to use the beast's nature wisely, he ought of beasts to choose both the lion and the fox; for the lion cannot guard himself from the toils, nor the fox from wolves. He must therefore be a fox to discern toils, and a lion to drive off wolves.

To rely wholly on the lion is unwise; and for this reason a prudent Prince neither can nor ought to keep his word when to keep it is hurtful to him and the causes which led him to pledge it are removed. If all men were good, this would not be good advice, but since they are dishonest and do not keep faith with you, you, in return, need not keep faith with them; and no prince was ever at a loss for plausible reasons to cloak a breach of faith. Of this numberless recent instances could be given, and it might be shown how many solemn treaties and engagements have been rendered inoperative and idle through want of faith in Princes, and that he who was best known to play the fox has had the best success.

It is necessary, indeed, to put a good color on this nature, and to be skillful in simulating and dissembling. But men are so simple, and governed so absolutely by their present needs, that he who wishes to deceive will never fail in finding willing dupes. One recent example I will not omit. Pope Alexander VI had no care or thought but how to deceive, and always found material to work on. No man ever had a more effective manner of asseverating, or made promises with more solemn protestations, or observed them less. And yet, because he understood this side of human nature, his frauds always succeeded.

It is not essential, then, that a Prince should have all the good qualities which I have enumerated above, but it is most essential that he should seem to have them; I will even venture to affirm that if he has and invariably practices them all, they are hurtful, whereas the appearance of having them is useful. Thus, it is well to seem merciful, faithful, humane, religious, and upright, and also to be so; but the mind should remain so balanced that were it needful not to be so, you should be able and know how to change to the contrary.

And you are to understand that a Prince, and most of all a new Prince, cannot observe all those rules of conduct in respect whereof men are accounted good, being often forced, in order to preserve his Princedom, to act in opposition to good faith, charity, humanity, and religion. He must therefore keep his mind ready to shift as the winds and tides of Fortune turn, and, as I have already said, he ought not to quit good courses if he can help it, but should know how to follow evil courses if he must.

A Prince should therefore be very careful that nothing ever escapes his lips which is not replete with the five qualities above named, so that to see and hear him, one would think him the embodiment of mercy, good faith, integrity, humanity, and religion. And there is no virtue which it is more necessary for him to seem to possess that this last; because men in general judge

[9]Centaurs were half-man, half-horse.

rather by the eye than by the hand, for every one can see but few can touch. Every one sees what you seem, but few know what you are, and these few dare not oppose themselves to the opinion of the many who have the majesty of the State to back them up.

Moreover, in the actions of all men, and most of all of Princes, where there is no tribunal to which we can appeal, we look to results. Wherefore if a Prince succeeds in establishing and maintaining his authority, the means will always be judged honorable and be approved by every one. For the vulgar are always taken by appearances and by results, and the world is made up of the vulgar, the few only finding room when the many have no longer ground to stand on.

A certain Prince of our own days, whose name it is as well not to mention,[10] is always preaching peace and good faith, although the mortal enemy of both; and both, had he practiced them as he preaches them, would, oftener than once, have lost him his kingdom and authority.

Nicholas Copernicus

(1473–1543)

from *THE REVOLUTIONS OF THE CELESTIAL SPHERES*[1]

[THE EARTH AND THE SUN]

THAT THE UNIVERSE IS SPHERICAL

In the first place, we must allow that the universe is spherical; whether because the form itself, since it is a complete whole, needing no joining, is the most perfect of all; or because it is the most spacious form, which is especially suited to contain and retain all things; or also because each distinct part of the universe, I mean the sun, the moon, and the stars, are seen to be of such form; or because all things seek to be defined by this form, a fact which appears in drops of water and in other liquid bodies, so long as they wish to be complete within themselves. No one then will doubt that such form has been given to the heavenly bodies!

[10]King Ferdinand of Spain.

[1]Translated by Anna E. Gilbert. Niklas Koppernigk (Latin name: Nicholas Copernicus) was a Polish astronomer. A cleric, he held the post of canon of the cathedral in Frauenburg, Poland. His interests were chiefly scientific, however, and he spent his life disproving the Earth-centered view of the universe and proving instead that Earth revolved daily around its axis and yearly around the Sun. He did not allow his complete statement of his theory, *The Revolutions of the Celestial Spheres*, to be published until the very end of his life; tradition has it that he received the first copy on his death bed.

THAT THE EARTH IS LIKEWISE SPHERICAL

The earth also is spherical because it is supported on all sides from its center. Although the perfect sphere does not appear at once on account of the very great height of the mountains and the depths of the valleys, still these in no way alter the general sphericity of the earth. This is evident in the following manner: For to people traveling from any place to the North, the north pole of the daily revolution gradually rises, while the south pole falls an equal amount. Also, most of the stars around the Great Bear appear not to set, and in the South some stars appear no longer to rise. Thus Italy does not see Canopus, which is visible to the Egyptians. And Italy sees the farthermost star of the stream, which to us in a section of a colder region is not known. On the other hand, to those passing over to the South, those stars rise higher in the heavens, while these which are higher to us become lower. And the inclinations of the poles hold the same relation everywhere to a traversed space of the earth, a fact which obtains for no other form than that of a sphere. From this it is clear that the earth is enclosed between poles, and for this reason is spherical. Add to this, also, the fact that inhabitants of the East do not see the eclipses of the sun or the moon which occur in the evening, and those who live in the West do not see the eclipses which occur in the morning, while those who live midway between Eat and West see the former later, and the latter, in fact, earlier.

Furthermore, it is known by sailors that water has this same shape, because the land which is not seen from the ship is seen from the top of the mast. And, conversely, when a light is placed on the top of the mast, it appears to those on the shore gradually to drop as the ship recedes until finally the light disappears as if it were sinking into the water. It is clear, also, that water flowing in accordance with its own nature always seeks lower levels, the same as does the earth, and does not seek to rise to a higher level at the shore than its own convexity allows. For this reason it is clear that the land rises above the ocean by only so much as it happens to be higher than the ocean.

THAT THE MOTIONS OF THE HEAVENLY BODIES ARE UNIFORM, CIRCULAR, UNINTERRUPTED, OR ARE MADE UP OF COMBINED CIRCULAR MOTIONS

Now, we shall mention that the motion of heavenly bodies is circular. A sphere when it is in motion revolves, expressing by this very activity its own form as that of the simplest of bodies, in which there is found neither a beginning nor an end; nor is the one to be distinguished from the other, so long as the sphere moves through the intermediate points to its original position. But there are many motions belonging to a multitude of circles. The best known of all is the daily revolution which the Greeks called Nychthemeron, that is, the period of day and night. It is thought that the whole universe, with the exception of the earth, moves through this daily revolution from east to west. This measure is understood to be common to all motions, since even time itself is measured principally by the number of days. Then we see other revolutions just as if they were retrograde, that is, moving from west to east; namely, those of the sun, the moon and the five planets. By means of this revolution, the sun measures the year for us, and the moon the month, as the most common units of time. In this way each of the other five planets completes its own revolution. Still in many ways they are different: first, in that they do not revolve about those same poles around which that first motion takes place, but are moving rapidly in the oblique path of the Zodiac; second, in that they do not seem to move uniformly in their own orbits, for the sun and the moon are discovered moving now with a slower, now with a faster motion. Moreover, we see the other five planets at times going backward and, in the transition, becoming stationary. And although the sun moves always in its own direct path, the planets roam in various ways, wandering sometimes toward the South, sometimes toward the North, for which reason they are called planets.[2] Add to this the fact that they come nearer to the earth at times, where they are called at perigee; at other times, when they are more remote, they are said to be at apogee. It must be admitted, nevertheless, that the motions are circular, or are constructed from many circles, or are constructed from many circles; for thus such irregularities would occur according to a fixed law and fixed periods, which could not happen if they were not circles. For the circle alone can bring back the past, as the sun, for example, through its motion made up of circles brings back to us the irregularities of days and nights, and the four seasons of the year; in which many motions are recognized, since it cannot happen that a simple heavenly body moves irregularly in a single orbit. Were this to happen, it must be caused either by an instability in the nature of the moving force, whether the instability be of an outward or an inward nature, or it must be due to an irregularity of the revolving body. Since, in truth, reason is opposed to both, and it is unworthy to think such a thing concerning that which has been arranged in the best order, one must admit that the regular motions seem to us irregular, either because of the different poles of their circles, or because the earth is not in the center of the circles in which the planets move; and to us who observe the motions of the stars from the earth, the planets because of the varying distances appear larger when near us than when they are in more remote paths (as can be proved in optics). In this way the motions which take place in equal times in equal arcs seem to us unequal on account of the different distances. For this reason I think it necessary before all else that we investigate carefully the relation of the earth to the heavens, so that when we wish to study the most noble things in nature we may not leave out of consideration those things that are nearest to us and erroneously attribute to the heavenly bodies what belongs to the earth.

WHETHER THE EARTH HAS A CIRCULAR MOTION, AND CONCERNING THE POSITION OF THE EARTH

Now, since it has been shown that the earth, too, has the form of a sphere, I think that we must also decide whether motion results from its form, and what place the earth holds in the universe. Without this knowledge it is not possible to make a true calculation in regard to the phenomena in the heavens. Although among writers it is agreed, generally, that the earth is at rest in the center of the universe, so that they regard it unbelievable and indeed

[2]The word *planet* comes from the Greek *planes* ("to wander").

even ridiculous to think the contrary; nevertheless, if one considers the matter carefully, one will see that this question is not yet settled, and for that reason must by no means be disregarded. For every change which is seen according to position is due either to the motion of the object observed or to that of the observer, or to the motions of both, naturally in different directions; for no motion is perceived between objects when both are moving uniformly in the same direction, that is, the observed object and the observer. But the earth is the place from which the revolution of the heavens is observed and to which, in turn, it is brought to our sight. If, therefore any motion of the earth is to be considered, that very same motion will appear in everything in the universe which is outside of the earth, but will be in the opposite direction just as if everything were passing by the earth. Of this sort the daily revolution of the earth is foremost. For this motion seems to possess the whole universe, excepting the earth itself, and everything that is near the earth. However, if one should admit that the heavens possess none of this motion, but that the earth rotates from west to east, and if one should consider this seriously in respect to the apparent rising and setting of the sun, of the moon, and of the stars, one would find that it is true. Since the heavens, which contain and retain all things, are the common location of all things, it does not appear at once why a motion is not ascribed rather to the thing contained than to the containing, to the thing placed rather than to the placing. Of course, the Pythagoreans, Heracleides and Ekphantus, and the Syracusean Nicetas (according to Cicero) were of the opinion that the earth revolves in the center of the universe.

Indeed, they thought that the stars set because of the intervening of the earth and rose because of the receding of the earth.

From this assumption follows the other not less important doubt concerning the position of the earth, although now it is accepted and believed by almost every one that this earth occupies the center of the universe.

Still, if anyone should deny that the earth is in the middle or center of the universe, and yet should admit that the distance between the two is not so great as to be comparable to the sphere of the fixed stars, but marked and evident in the orbits of the sun and other planets; and if he should think that for this reason the motions of the planets appear irregular, just as if they were controlled from a center other than that of the earth, he might, perhaps, be able to give the true reason for their apparently irregular motion. Since, indeed, the planets are seen now nearer to, now more remote from, the earth, this necessarily proves that the center of the earth is not the center of those circular orbits. Still it is not known whether the earth withdraws (to a distance) from them or they from the earth.

Nor would it be strange if someone should ascribe to the earth another motion in addition to that of its daily revolution. For the belief that the earth rotates and even moves along irregularly with various motions, and that it is one of the planets, is said to have been held by Philolaus the Pythagorean, not an ordinary mathematician, inasmuch as Plato did not delay a visit to Italy for the pleasure of seeing him, as those who have written the life of Plato tell us. Many, in truth, have thought that it could be proved by mathematical calculation that the earth is situated in the center of the universe, and that compared to the immensity of the heavens it is like a point, that it occupies the central position and for this reason is immovable; because, if the universe moves, the center point of it must remain motionless, and those parts which are nearest to the center must move more slowly.

REFUTATION OF THE ARGUMENTS AND THEIR INSUFFICIENCY

Now from these and similar reasons it is claimed that the earth is at rest in the center of the universe, and that without doubt this is true. But yet, if anyone believes that the earth rotates, he will, at least, admit that this motion is, therefore, natural and not violent. In fact, whatever happens in accordance with nature produces effects opposite to those which happens through violence. For those things which violence or fury attacks must be destroyed and are unable to resist for any length of time. But things which occur in accordance with nature retain their position and are preserved according to their own best arrangement.

It is said, moreover, that outside of the heavens there is no body, no place, no empty space, in fact, absolutely nothing, and, therefore, nothing exists into which the heavens could expand; then it is very strange, if something can be contained in nothing. But if the heavens were infinite, and were bounded only by their own hollowness, perhaps the truth would be evident that there is nothing outside the heavens, since everything, whatever its size, is within them, but the heavens would remain motionless. For the most important argument on which depends the proof that the earth is finite, is motion. Therefore, whether the world is finite or infinite, we shall leave to the discussions of the natural philosophers, while we hold it to be true that the earth, enclosed within poles, is bounded by a spherical surface. Why, then, should we still hesitate to concede to it a motion natural and appropriate to its form, rather than to assume that the whole world, whose boundary is unknown, and cannot be known, moves, and why not confess that the appearance of its daily revolution belongs to the heavens, its reality belongs to the earth? Vírgil expresses a similar case in the Aeneid, when he says: "We sail out from the harbor, and land and cities recede." For when a ship is sailing in a calm sea, all things which are outside of it seem to those on shipboard to be moving with a motion corresponding to that of the ship, and the sailors, in turn, think that they, and all things with them, are at rest. So, without doubt, this can be applied to the motion of the earth, and it may seem as if the whole world were revolving.

WHETHER MORE MOTIONS CAN BE ATTRIBUTED TO THE EARTH, AND CONCERNING THE CENTER OF THE UNIVERSE

Since, therefore, nothing prevents the mobility of the earth, I think we must now investigate whether there are several motions possible to it, so that it may be considered one of the planets. The fact that it is not the center of all the revolutions is shown by the visible irregular motions of the planets and their varying distances from the earth, which cannot be explained as concentric circles with the earth at the center. Therefore, since there are many apparent centers, not without cause will anyone doubt whether the center of the universe, or some other central point, is the center of gravity of the earth. Indeed, I think that gravity is nothing else than a certain natural force implanted, by the Divine foresight of the Maker of the World, into its parts, so that coming together in the form of a sphere, they might form a unity and a whole. This natural force is believed to belong also to the sun, to the moon, and to the planets, and by its inherent power they remain in the spherical form in which they present themselves, while they nevertheless complete their revolutions in many ways. If, therefore, the earth too makes other revolutions besides that around its center, they must necessarily be those which appear similar in many and appropriate ways, among which we find the yearly revolution.

Since, if the yearly revolution should be transferred from the sun to the earth, then (granting the immobility of the sun) the rising and setting of the constellations and that of the fixed stars, means by which they become morning and evening stars, will appear in the same way as now; it will thus become apparent that the arrested motions and the retrogressions and progressions of the planets do not belong to them, but to the terrestrial motion which gives them the appearance of being planetary motions. Finally, we shall be convinced that the sun itself occupies the center of the universe.

All these things are taught us by a law of succession in which things succeed one another in regular order, also by the harmony of the entire universe, if we but look (as they say) with both eyes.

Baldassare Castiglione

(1478–1529)

from *THE BOOK OF THE COURTIER*[1]

[THE PERFECT COURTIER]

Within myself I have long doubted, dearest messer Alfonso, which of two things were the harder for me: to deny you what you have often begged of me so urgently, or to do it. For while it seemed to me very hard to deny

[1]Translated by Leonard Opdycke. *Il cortegiano* (*The Book of the Courtier*) was not only the bible of aristocratic manners throughout the fifteenth and sixteenth centuries throughout Europe, it was also a celebration of an ideal character and ethical system that was powerfully influential throughout the Renaissance. Castiglione always denied that it was a self-portrait, but certainly the life it describes and the life its author lived coincide closely. Born near Mantua, Italy, Castiglione received a good humanist education in Milan and then spent his life in the service of princes, first in the courts of Mantua and Urbino and later in the service of the Pope. *The Book of the Courtier* was written between 1513 and 1518 but was not published until 1528. Castiglione died the following year and thus did not live to see the enormous success of his book, which was almost immediately translated into a number of European languages and remained popular for two centuries. *The Book of the Courtier* is in the form of a dialogue among seven speakers, based on seven of Castiglione's friends. In the short selection included here, no attempt has been made to identify the separate speakers.

anything (and especially a thing in the highest degree laudable) to one whom I love most dearly and by whom I feel myself to be most dearly loved, yet to set about an enterprise that I am not sure of being able to finish, seemed to me ill befitting a man who esteems just censure as it ought to be esteemed. At last, after much thought, I am resolved to try in this matter how much aid my assiduity may gain from that affection and intense desire to please, which in other things are so wont to stimulate the industry of man.

You ask me then to write what is to my thinking the form of Courtiership most befitting a gentleman who lives at the court of princes, by which he may have the ability and knowledge perfectly to serve them in every reasonable thing, winning from them favor, and praise from other men; in short, what manner of man he ought to be who may deserve to be called a perfect Courtier without flaw. Wherefore, considering your request, I say that had it not seemed to me more blameworthy to be reputed somewhat unamiable by you than too conceited by everyone else, I should have avoided this task, for fear of being held over bold by all who know how hard it is, from among such a variety of customs as are in use at the courts of Christendom, to choose the perfect form and as it were the flower of Courtiership. For custom often makes the same thing pleasing and displeasing to us; whence it sometimes follows that customs, habits, ceremonies and fashions that once were prized, become vulgar, and contrariwise the vulgar become prized. Thus it is clearly seen that use rather than reason has power to introduce new things among us, and to do away with the old; and he will often err who seeks to determine which are perfect. Therefore being conscious of this and many other difficulties in the subject set before me to write of, I am constrained to offer some apology, and to testify that this error (if error it may indeed be called) is common to us both, to the end that if I be blamed for it, the blame may be shared by you also; for your offense in setting me a task beyond my powers should not be deemed less than mine in having accepted it.

So now let us make a beginning of our subject, and if possible let us form such a Courtier that any prince worthy to be served by him, although of but small estate, might still be called a very great lord.

* * *

"I wish, then, that this Courtier of ours should be nobly born and of gentle race; because it is far less unseemly for one of ignoble birth to fail in worthy deeds, than for one of noble birth, who, if he strays from the path of his predecessors, stains his family name, and not only fails to achieve but loses what has been achieved already; for noble birth is like a bright lamp that manifests and makes visible good and evil deeds, and kindles and stimulates to virtue both by fear of shame and by hope of praise. And since this splendor of nobility does not illumine the deeds of the humbly born, they lack that stimulus and fear of shame, nor do they feel any obligation to advance beyond what their predecessors have done; while to the nobly born it seems a reproach not to reach at least the goal set them by their ancestors. And thus it nearly always happens that both in the profession of arms and in other worthy pursuits the most famous men have been of noble birth, because nature has implanted in everything that hidden seed which gives a certain force and quality of its own essence to all things that are derived from it, and makes them like itself: as we see not only in the breeds of horses and of other animals, but also in trees, the shoots of which nearly always resemble the trunk; and if they sometimes degenerate, it arises from poor cultivation. And so it is with men, who if rightly trained are nearly always like those from whom they spring, and often better; but if there be no one to give them proper care, they become like savages and never reach perfection.

"It is true that, by favor of the stars or of nature, some men are endowed at birth with such graces that they seem not to have been born, but rather as if some god had formed them with his very hands and adorned them with every excellence of mind and body. So too there are many men so foolish and rude that one cannot but think that nature brought them into the world out of contempt or mockery. Just as these can usually accomplish little even with constant diligence and good training, so with slight pains those others reach the highest summit of excellence. And to give you an instance: you see my lord Don Ippolite d'Este, Cardinal of Ferrara, who has enjoyed such fortune from his birth, that his person, his aspect, his words and all his movements are so disposed and imbued with this grace, that—although he is young—he exhibits among the most aged prelates such weight of character that he seems fitter to teach than to be taught; likewise in conversation with men and woman of every rank, in games, in pleasantry and in banter, he has a certain sweetness and manners so gracious, that who so speaks with him or even sees him, must needs remain attached to him forever.

"But to return to our subject: I say that there is a middle state between perfect grace on the one hand and senseless folly on the other; and those who are not thus perfectly endowed by nature, with study and toil can in great part polish and amend their natural defects. Besides this noble birth, then, I would have the Courtier favored in this regard also, and endowed by nature not only with talent and beauty of person and feature, but with a certain grace and (as we say) air that shall make him at first sight pleasing and agreeable to all who see him; and I would have this an ornament that should dispose and unite all his actions, and in his outward aspect give promise of whatever is worthy the society and favor of every great lord."

* * *

"But to come to some details, I am of opinion that the principal and true profession of the Courtier ought to be that of arms; which I would have him follow actively above all else, and be known among others as bold and strong, and loyal to whomsoever he serves. And he will win a reputation for these good qualities by exercising them at all times and in all places, since one may never fail in this without severest censure. And just as among women, their fair fame once sullied never recovers its first lustre, so the reputation of a gentleman who bears arms, if once it be in the least tarnished with cowardice or other disgrace, remains forever infamous before the world and full of ignominy. Therefore the more our Courtier excels in this art, the more he will be worthy of praise; and yet I do not deem essential in him that perfect knowledge of things and those other qualities that befit a commander; since this would be too wide a sea, let us be content, as we have said, with perfect loyalty and unconquered courage, and that he be always seen to possess them. For the courageous are often recognized even more in small things than in great; and frequently in perils of importance and where there are many spectators, some men are to be found, who, although their hearts be dead within them, yet, moved by shame or by the presence of others, press forward almost with their eyes shut, and do their duty God knows how. While on occasions of little moment, when they think they can avoid putting themselves in danger without being detected, they are glad to keep safe. But those who, even when they do not expect to be observed or seen or recognized by anyone, show their ardor and neglect nothing, however paltry, that may be laid to their charge,—they have that strength of mind which we seek in our Courtier."

* * *

". . . And of such sort I would have our Courtier's aspect; not so soft and effeminate as is sought by many, who not only curl their hair and pluck their brows, but gloss their faces with all those arts employed by the most wanton and unchaste women in the world; and in their walk, posture and every act, they seem so limp and languid that their limbs are like to fall apart; and they pronounce their words so mournfully that they appear about to expire upon the spot: and the more they find themselves with men of rank, the more they affect such tricks. Since nature has not made them women, as they seem to wish to appear and be, they should be treated not as good women but as public harlots, and driven not merely from the courts of great lords but from the society of honest men.

"Then coming to the bodily frame, I say it is enough if this be neither extremely short nor tall, for both of these conditions excite a certain contemptuous surprise, and men of either sort are gazed upon in much the same way that we gaze on monsters. Yet if we must offend in one of the two extremes, it is preferable to fall a little short of the just measure of height than to exceed it, for besides often being dull of intellect, men thus huge of body are also unfit for every exercise of agility, which thing I should much wish in the Courtier. And so I would have him well built and shapely of limb, and would have him show strength and lightness and suppleness, and know all bodily exercises that befit a man of war; whereof I think the first should be to handle every sort of weapon well on foot and on horse, to understand the advantages of each, and especially to be familiar with those weapons that are ordinarily used among gentlemen; for besides the use of them in war, where such subtlety in contrivance is perhaps not needful, there frequently arise differences between one gentleman and another, which afterwards result in duels often fought with such weapons as happen at the moment to be within reach: thus knowledge of this kind is a very safe thing. Nor am I one of those who say that skill is forgotten in the hour of need; for he whose skill forsakes him at such a time, indeed gives token that he has already lost heart and head through fear.

"Moreover I deem it very important to know how to wrestle, for it is a great help in the use of all kinds of weapons on foot. Then, both for his own sake and for that of his friends, he must understand the quarrels and differences that may arise, and must be quick to seize an advantage, always showing courage and prudence in all things. Nor should he be too ready to fight except when honor demands it; for besides the great danger that the uncertainty of fate entails, he who rushes into such affairs recklessly and without urgent cause, merits the severest censure even though he be successful.

But when he finds himself so far engaged that he cannot withdraw without reproach, he ought to be most deliberate, both in the preliminaries to the duel and in the duel itself, and always show readiness and daring. Nor must he act like some, who fritter the affair away in disputes and controversies, and who, having the choice of weapons, select those that neither cut nor pierce, and arm themselves as if they were expecting a cannonade; and thinking it enough not to be defeated, stand ever on the defensive and retreat,—showing therein their utter cowardice. . . ."

* * *

"But as Count Ludovico has explained very minutely the chief profession of the Courtier, and has insisted it be that of arms, methinks it is also fitting to tell what in my judgment is that of the Court Lady: and when I have done this, I shall think myself quit of the greater part of my duty.

"Laying aside, then, those faculties of the mind that she ought to have in common with the Courtier (such as prudence, magnanimity, continence, and many others), and likewise those qualities that befit all women (such as kindness, discretion, ability to manage her husband's property and her house and children if she be married, and all those capacities that are requisite in a good housewife), I say that in a lady who lives at court methinks above all else a certain pleasant affability is befitting, whereby she may be able to entertain politely every sort of man with agreeable and seemly converse, suited to the time and place, and to the rank of the person with whom she may speak, uniting with calm and modest manners, and with that seemliness which should ever dispose all her actions, a quick vivacity of spirit whereby she may show herself alien to all indelicacy; but with such a kindly manner as shall make us think of her no less chaste, prudent and benign, than agreeable, witty and discreet: and so she must preserve a certain mean (difficult and composed almost of contraries), and must barely touch certain limits but not pass them.

"Thus, in her wish to be thought good and pure, the Lady ought not to be so coy and seem so to abhor company and talk that are a little free, as to take her leave as soon as she finds herself therein; for it might easily be thought that she was pretending to be thus austere in order to hide something about herself which she feared others might come to know; and such prudish manners are always odious. Nor ought she, on the other hand, for the sake of showing herself free and agreeable, to utter unseemly words or practice a certain wild and unbridled familiarity and ways likely to make that believed of her which perhaps is not true; but when she is present at such talk, she ought to listen with a little blush and shame.

"Likewise she ought to avoid an error into which I have seen many women fall, which is that of saying and of willingly listening to evil about other women. For those women who, on hearing the unseemly ways of other women described, grow angry thereat and seem to disbelieve it and to regard it almost monstrous that a woman should be immodest,—they, by accounting the offense so heinous, give reason to think that they do not commit it. But those who go about continually prying into other women's intrigues, and narrate them so minutely and with such zest, seem to be envious of them and to wish that everyone may know it, to the end that like matters may not be reckoned as a fault in their own case; and thus they fall into certain laughs and ways that show they then feel greatest pleasure. And hence it comes that men, while seeming to listen gladly, usually hold such women in small respect and have very little regard for them, and think these ways of theirs are an invitation to advance father, and thus often go such lengths with them as bring them deserved reproach, and finally esteem them so lightly as to despise their company and even find them tedious.

"And on the other hand, there is no man so shameless and insolent as not to have reverence for those women who are esteemed good and virtuous; because this gravity (tempered with wisdom and goodness) is as it were a shield against the insolence and coarseness of the presumptuous. Thus we see that a word or laugh or act of kindness (however small it be) from a virtuous woman is more prized by everyone, than all the endearments and caresses of those who show their lack of shame so openly; and if they are not immodest, by their unseemly laughter, their loquacity, insolence and like scurrile manners, they give sign of being so.

"And since words that carry no meaning of importance are vain and puerile, the Court Lady must have not only the good sense to discern the quality of him with whom she is speaking, but knowledge of many things, in order to entertain him graciously; and in her talk she should know how to choose those things that are adapted to the quality of him with whom she is speaking, and should be cautious lest occasionally, without intending it, she utter words that may offend him. Let her guard against wearying him by praising herself indiscreetly or by being too prolix. Let her not go about mingling serious matters with her playful or humorous discourse, or jests and jokes with her serious discourse. Let her not stupidly pretend to know that which she does not know, but modestly seek to do herself credit in that which she does know,—in all things avoiding affectation, as has been said. In this way she will be adorned with good manners, and will perform with perfect grace the bodily exercises proper to women; her discourse will be rich and full of prudence, virtue and pleasantness; and thus she will be not only loved but revered by everyone, and perhaps worthy to be placed side by side with this great Courtier as well in qualities of the mind as in those of the body."

* * *

". . . Hence I think that the perfect Courtier, such as Count Ludovico and messer Federico have described, may be a truly good thing and worthy of praise, not however simply, and in himself, but in respect to the end to which he may be directed. For indeed if by being nobly born, graceful, agreeable, and expert in so many exercises, the Courtier brought forth no other fruit than merely being what he is, I should not deem it right for a man to devote so much study and pains to acquiring this perfection of Courtiership, as anyone must who wishes to attain it. Nay, I should say that many of those accomplishments that have been ascribed to him (like dancing, merry-making, singing and playing) were follies and vanities, and in a man of rank worthy rather of censure than of praise: for these elegances, devices, mottoes, and other like things that pertain to discourse about women and love, although perhaps many other men think the contrary, often serve only to effeminate the mind, to corrupt youth, and to reduce it to great wantonness of living; whence then it comes to pass that the Italian name is brought into opprobrium, and but few are to be found who dare, I will not say to die, but even to run into danger.

"And surely there are countless other things, which, if industry and study were spent upon them, would be of much greater utility in both peace and war than this kind of Courtiership in itself merely; but if the Courtier's actions are directed to that good end to which they ought, and which I have in mind, methinks they are not only not harmful or vain, but very useful and deserving of infinite praise.

"I think then that the aim of the perfect Courtier, which has not been spoken of till now, is so to win for himself, by means of the accomplishments ascribed to him by these gentlemen, the favor and mind of the prince whom he serves, that he may be able to say, and always shall say, the truth about everything which it is fitting for the prince to know, without fear, or risk of giving offense thereby; and that when he sees his prince's mind inclined to do something wrong, he may be quick to oppose, and gently to make use of the favor acquired by his good accomplishments, so as to banish every bad intent and lead his prince into the path of virtue. And thus, possessing the goodness which these gentlemen have described, together with readiness of wit and pleasantness, and shrewdness and knowledge of letters and many other things,—the Courtier will in every case be able deftly to show the prince how much honor and profit accrue to him and his from justice, liberality, magnanimity, gentleness, and the other virtues that become a good prince; and on the other hand how much infamy and loss proceed from the vices opposed to them. Therefore I think that just as music, festivals, games, and the other pleasant accomplishments are as it were the flower, in like manner to lead or help one's prince towards right, and to frighten him from wrong, are the true fruit of Courtiership.

"And since the merit of well-doing lies chiefly in two things, one of which is the choice of an end for our intentions that shall be truly good, and the other ability to find means suitable and fitting to conduce to that good end marked out,—certain it is that man's mind tends to the best end, who purposes to see to it that his prince shall be deceived by no one, shall hearken not to flatterers or to slanderers and liars, and shall distinguish good and evil, and love the one and hate the other."

* * *

"Nor do I think that Aristotle and Plato would have scorned the name of perfect Courtier, for we clearly see that they performed the works of Courtiership and wrought to this end,—the one with Alexander the Great, the other with the kings of Sicily.[2] And since the office of a good Courtier is to know the prince's character and inclinations, and thus to enter tactfully into his favor according to need and opportunity, as we have said, by those ways that afford safe access, and then to lead him towards virtue,—Aristotle so well knew the character of Alexander, and tactfully fostered it so well, that he was loved and honored more than a father by Alexander. Thus, among many other tokens that Alexander gave him of good will, the

[2]Aristotle was tutor to the young Alexander the Great at the Macedonian court (342–339 B.C.). Plato was tutor to the young Dionysius the Younger (fl. 368–344 B.C.) at the court of Syracuse.

king ordered the rebuilding of his native city, Stagira, which had been destroyed; and besides directing Alexander to that most glorious aim,—which was the desire to make the world as one single universal country, and all men as a single people to live in amity and mutual concord under a single government and a single law, which should shine equally on all like the light of the sun,—Aristotle so instructed him in the natural sciences and in the virtues of the mind as to make him most wise, brave, continent, and a true moral philosopher, not only in words but in deeds; for a nobler philosophy cannot be imagined than to bring into civilized living such savage people as those who inhabited Bactria and Caucasia, India, Scythia; and to teach them marriage, agriculture, honor to their fathers, abstention from rapine, murder and other evil ways; to build so many very noble cities in distant lands;—so that countless men were by his laws reduced from savage life to civilization. And of these achievements of Alexander the author was Aristotle, using the means of a good Courtier: which Callisthenes knew not how to do, although Aristotle showed him; for in his wish to be a pure philosopher and austere minister of naked truth, without mingling Courtiership therewith, he lost his life and brought not help but rather infamy to Alexander.

"By these same means of Courtiership, Plato schooled Dio of Syracuse; and having afterwards found the tyrant Dionysius like a book all full of faults and errors and in need of complete erasure rather than of any change or correction (since it was not possible to remove from him that tinge of tyranny wherewith he had so long been stained), Plato was unwilling to practise the ways of Courtiership upon him, thinking that they all would surely be in vain. Which our Courtier also ought to do, if by chance he finds himself in the service of a prince of so evil a disposition as to be inveterate in vice, like consumptives in their malady; for in such case he ought to escape that bondage, in order not to receive blame for his lord's evil deeds, and in order not to feel that distress which all good men feel who serve the wicked."

Martin Luther
(1483–1546)

from *THE NINETY-FIVE THESES*[1]

The pope does excellently when he grants remission to the souls in purgatory on account of intercessions made on their behalf, and not by the power of the keys (which he cannot exercise for them).

[1]Translated by Bertram Lee Woolf. Martin Luther was a German priest who protested the corruption and spiritual laxity of the sixteenth-century Catholic Church. A particular target of his criticism was the sale of indulgences, pardons for temporal punishments due for sin. When John Tetzel, a cleric who defended the sale of indulgences, visited Saxony in 1517, Luther protested by nailing his ninety-five theses to the door of the castle church. The theses were widely debated and led to Luther's excommunication in 1521; they are usually regarded as the beginning of the Protestant Reformation.

There is no divine authority for preaching that the soul flies out of purgatory immediately the money clinks in the bottom of the chest.

It is certainly possible that when the money clinks in the bottom of the chest avarice and greed increase; but when the church offers intercession, all depends on the will of God.

Who knows whether all souls in purgatory wish to be redeemed in view of what is said of St. Severinus and St. Paschal.[2]

No one is sure of the reality of his own contrition, much less of receiving plenary forgiveness.[3]

One who *bona fide* buys indulgences is as rare as a *bona fide* penitent man, i.e., very rare indeed.

All those who believe themselves certain of their own salvation by means of letters of indulgence, will be eternally damned, together with their teachers.

We should be most carefully on our guard against those who say that the papal indulgences are an inestimable divine gift, and that a man is reconciled to God by them.

For the grace conveyed by these indulgences relates simply to the penalties of the sacramental "satisfactions" decreed merely by man.

It is not in accordance with Christian doctrine to preach and teach that those who buy off souls, or purchase confessional licenses, have no need to repent of their own sins.

Any Christian whatsoever, who is truly repentant, enjoys plenary remission from penalty and guilt, and this is given him without letters of indulgence.

Any true Christian whatsoever, living or dead, participates in all the benefits of Christ and the Church; and this participation is granted to him by God without letters of indulgence.

Yet the pope's remission and dispensation are in no way to be despised, for, as already said, they proclaim the divine remission.

It is very difficult, even for the most learned theologians, to extol to the people the great bounty contained in the indulgences, while, at the same time, praising contrition as a virtue.

A truly contrite sinner seeks out, and loves to pay, the penalties of his sins; whereas the very multitude of indulgences dulls men's consciences, and tends to make them hate the penalties.

Papal indulgences should only be preached with caution, lest people gain a wrong understanding, and think that they are preferable to other good works: those of love.

Christians should be taught that the pope does not at all intend that the purchase of indulgences should be understood as at all comparable with works of mercy.

Christians should be taught that one who gives to the poor, or lends to the needy, does a better action than if he purchases indulgences;

Because, by works of love, love grows and a man becomes a better man; whereas, by indulgences, he does not become a better man, but only escapes certain penalties.

[2]Both saints are said to have refused to have their periods of penance in Purgatory shortened.

[3]Complete forgiveness.

Christians should be taught that he who sees a needy person, but passes him by although he gives money for indulgences, gains no benefit from the pope's pardon, but only incurs the wrath of God.

Christians should be taught that, unless they have more than they need, they are bound to retain what is necessary for the upkeep of their home, and should in no way squander it on indulgences.

Christians should be taught that they purchase indulgences voluntarily, and are not under obligation to do so.

Christians should be taught that, in granting indulgences, the pope has more need, and more desire, for devout prayer on his own behalf than for ready money.

Christians should be taught that the pope's indulgences are useful only if one does not rely on them, but most harmful if one loses the fear of God through them.

Christians should be taught that, if the pope knew the exactions of the indulgence-preachers, he would rather the church of St. Peter were reduced to ashes than be built with the skin, flesh, and bones of his sheep.

Chronology

THE ANCIENT WORLD

Political and Social Events

B.C.

ca. 2750 Date of possibly historical Gilgamesh
ca. 2100–2000 Empire of Ur
ca. 1830 First dynasty of Babylonian kings begins
13th *c.* Hebrew Exodus from Egypt into Canaan
1193–1184 Trojan War
ca. 1100 Dorians migrate into Peloponnesus
953 Dedication of Temple at Jerusalem

931 Jews split into the Northern Kingdom of Israel and the Southern Kingdom of Judah
826 Founding of Carthage
776 First Olympic games in Greece
753 Traditional date of founding of Rome by Romulus and Remus
750–500 Era of Greek colonization

597 Babylonian captivity of the Jews
6th *c.* Ascendancy of the Persian Empire

538 The Persians under Cyrus capture Babylon and free the Jews

509 Traditional date of the founding of the Roman Republic
490 Athenians defeat Persians at the Battle of Marathon
480 The Greek fleet defeats the Persians at the Battle of Salamis
461–429 The Periclean Age in Athens

431-404 Peloponnesian War and the fall of Athens

336–323 Conquests of Alexander

264–146 Punic Wars
146 Roman conquest of Greece

Intellectual and Cultural Events

ca. 3000 Bricks first used by Egyptians and Assyrians. Invention of the wheel.
ca. 2700 Egyptian ruler Cheops builds Great Pyramid at Giza
ca. 2500 Early Minoan civilization in Crete
ca. 1860 Construction of Stonehenge begins in Britain
10th *c.* Oral traditions of Jews attain first written form (the J strand); oral epics in circulation among the Greeks

6th *c.* Rise of free statuary and Doric and Ionic temple architecture
586 The piper Sakadas wins the pipe contest at the Greek Pythian games with a piece representing Apollo's fight with a dragon
585 Thales makes the first prediction of a solar eclipse
534 Thespis' dramatic performances in Athens

432 The Parthenon completed
429 The Acropolis completed

399 The death of Socrates
334 Founding of the Library at Alexandria

ca. 150 Frieze from the Altar of Zeus at Pergamon

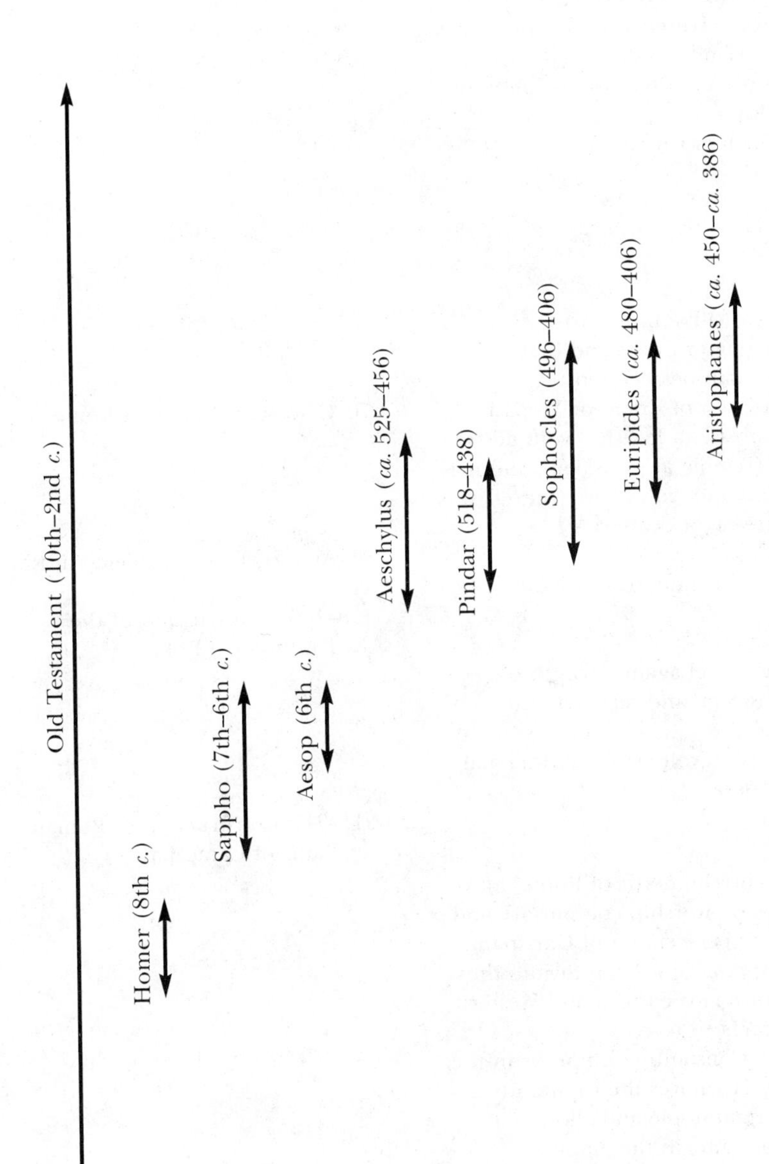

Gilgamesh (*ca.* 2000 B.C.)
Old Testament (10th–2nd *c.*)
Homer (8th *c.*)
Sappho (7th–6th *c.*)
Aesop (6th *c.*)
Aeschylus (*ca.* 525–456)
Pindar (518–438)
Sophocles (496–406)
Euripides (*ca.* 480–406)
Aristophanes (*ca.* 450–*ca.* 386)
Theocritus (3rd *c.*)

Political and Social Events	*Intellectual and Cultural Events*
60 First Triumvirate (Pompey, Julius Caesar, Crassus)	
58–50 Caesar's Gallic Wars	
44 Assassination of Caesar	
43 Second Triumvirate (Antony, Octavian, Lepidus)	
27–A.D.14 Augustus Caesar Emperor of Rome	
ca. 4 Birth of Christ	
A.D.	
ca. 29 Crucifixion of Christ	
64 Burning of Rome and first Christian persecutions	
70 Titus, son of Emperor Vespasian, suppresses a Jewish revolt, destroys the Temple at Jerusalem, and massacres and exiles Jews (the *Diaspora,* or Scattering)	70 Colosseum begun at Rome
	81 Arch of Titus completed at Rome
84 Roman conquest of Britain	
	118–126 Construction of the Pantheon at Rome
132 Jews rebel again, recapture Jerusalem, and set up a state of Israel	
135 Jewish revolt crushed; the Final Diaspora	
	211–217 Construction of Roman Baths of Caracalla
250 Decius, Emperor of Rome, makes emperor-worship compulsory and orders persecution of Christians	
286 Emperor Diocletian divides the Empire into Eastern and Western Empires	
323–337 Constantine Emperor in the East. He moves the capital to Constantinople and allows Christianity in the empire	
351 Emperor Julian attempts to reintroduce paganism in place of Christianity	
395 Emperor Theodosius makes Christianity the official religion of Rome	

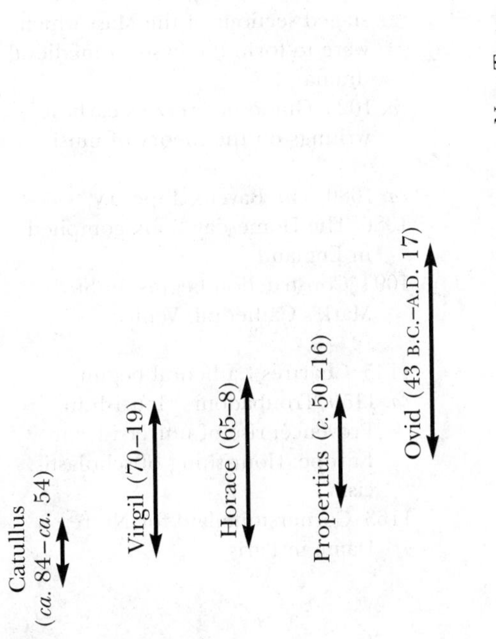
Catullus (*ca.* 84–*ca.* 54)
Virgil (70–19)
Horace (65–8)
Propertius (*c.* 50–16)
Ovid (43 B.C.–A.D. 17)
New Testament (1st and 2nd *c.*)

Political and Social Events	*Intellectual and Cultural Events*
401 Pope Innocent I claims universal jurisdiction over the Roman Church	413 St. Augustine, *The City of God*
	ca. 450 Establishment of the seven liberal arts as regular course of study
476 The end of the Roman Empire	

THE MIDDLE AGES

Political and Social Events	*Intellectual and Cultural Events*
	527–565 Construction of the Hagia Sophia, Constantinople
622–624 Beginning of Mohammedan Era and Holy War	622 Hegira of Mohammed
711 Conquest of Spain by Arabs	
	ca. 750 Arabic science brought to Europe
768–814 Charlemagne ruler of Franks and Holy Roman Emperor	
9th *c.* Feudal system develops among the Franks and spreads across Europe	9th *c.* Music cultivated in monasteries; development of "sequences" (elaborated passages) in liturgical music
856–875 Vikings overrun England	
	ca. 925 The *Quem Quaeritis* trope, earliest surviving example of the staged sections of the Mass which were to form the basis of medieval drama
	ca. 1025 Guido of Arezzo's earliest writings on the theory of music
1066 Norman conquest of England	
	ca. 1080 The Bayeux Tapestry
	1086 The Domesday Book compiled in England
	1094 Construction begins on St. Mark's Cathedral, Venice
1095–1291 Period of the Crusades	
	1145 Chartres Cathedral begun
	ca. 1150 Troubadours flourish in Provence; rise of universities in Europe; flourishing of scholasticism
	1163 Cornerstone laid for Notre Dame in Paris

Koran (7th *c.*)

Cattle Raid of Cooley (7th–8th *c.*)

Hrafnkel the Priest of Frey (12th–14th *c.*)

Marie de France (late 12th *c.*)

Renard the Fox (12th–13th *c.*)

Political and Social Events

1233 Inquisition established in Spain

1271 Beginning of Marco Polo's travels

1309–1378 The "Babylonian Captivity": papal see removed to Avignon, France

1337–1453 The Hundred Years' War between France and England

1348 Outbreak of Black Death in Europe

1431 Joan of Arc burned as a witch

1453 Fall of Constantinople to Ottoman Turks ends the Byzantine Empire and marks the end of the Middle Ages

Intellectual and Cultural Events

1167 Oxford University founded

1170 Beginning of the University of Paris

ca. 1200 Trouvères flourish in northern France, Minnesingers in Germany

1209 Cambridge University founded

1213–1380 Construction of the Alhambra

ca. 1240 The motet becomes the most important form of polyphonic composition

ca. 1250 Period of the *ars antiqua* polyphonic style in music

1270 St. Thomas Aquinas, *Summa Theologica*

1300–1370 Period of *ars nova* in France, the "new art" of musical composition

1305 Giotto, the Arena chapel frescoes

1308 Duccio begins painting the Siena panels

1327 Petrarch meets Laura

1360 Guillaume Machaut, Mass of Notre Dame

1376 Wycliffe's translation of the Bible

1426 Jan and Hubert Van Eyck begin the Ghent Altarpiece

1436 Guillaume Dufay, *Nuper rosarum flores*

ca. 1450 Ascendancy of humanism in Italy

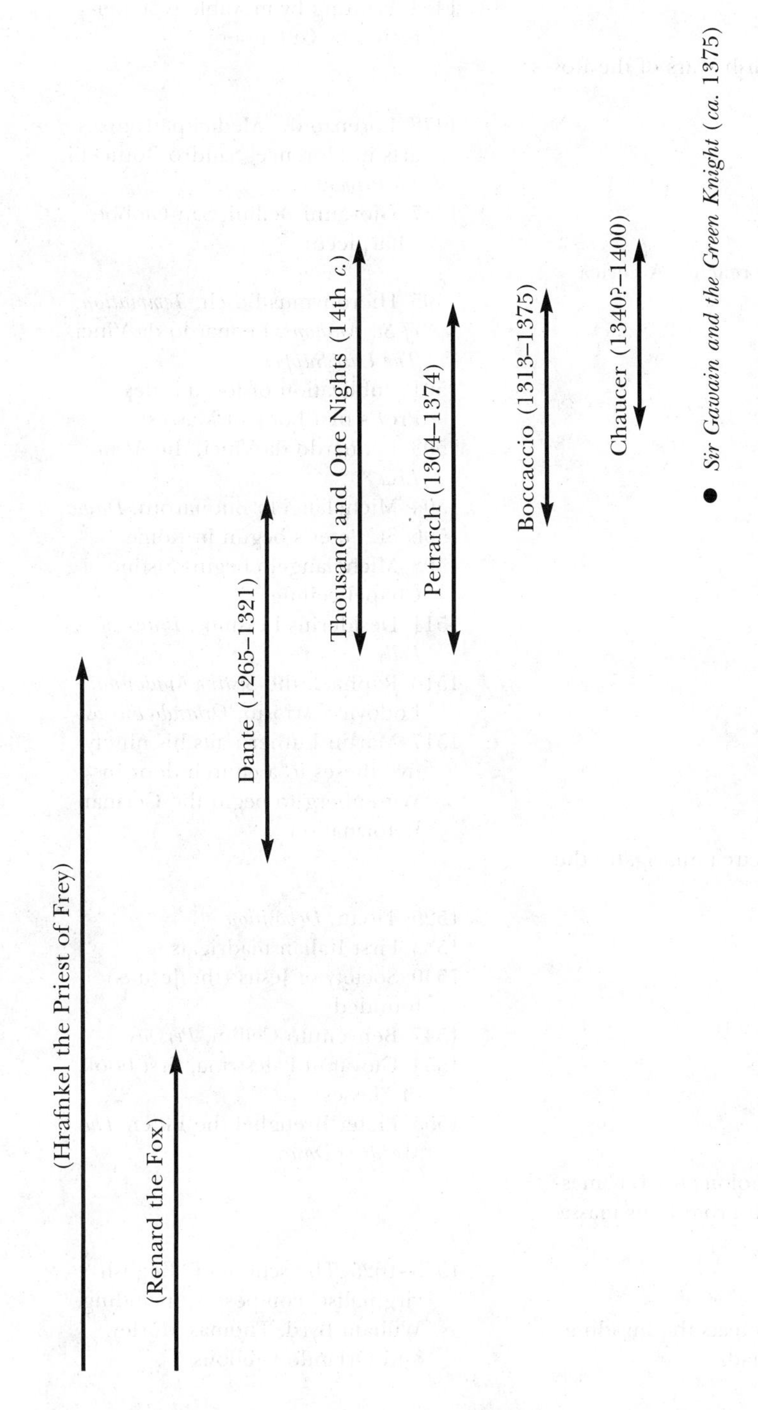
(Hrafnkel the Priest of Frey)
(Renard the Fox)
Dante (1265–1321)
Thousand and One Nights (14th c.)
Petrarch (1304–1374)
Boccaccio (1313–1375)
Chaucer (1340?–1400)
Sir Gawain and the Green Knight (*ca.* 1375)
Christine de Pizan (1364–*ca.* 1430)

THE RENAISSANCE

Political and Social Events

1455–1485 English Wars of the Roses

1492 Columbus reaches America

1522 Magellan circumnavigates the globe

1572 Saint Bartholomew's Day massacre: French Protestants massacred

1588 England defeats the invading Spanish Armada

Intellectual and Cultural Events

1454 Printing by movable type perfected by Gutenberg

1478 Lorenzo de' Medici patronizes arts in Florence; Sandro Botticelli, *La Primavera*

1487 Giovanni Bellini, San Giobbe Altarpiece

1495 Hieronymus Bosch, *Temptation of St. Anthony;* Leonardo da Vinci, *The Last Supper*

1501 Publication of Josquin des Prez's first book of Masses

1503 Leonardo da Vinci, the *Mona Lisa*

1504 Michelangelo Buonarotti, *David*

1506 St. Peter's begun in Rome

1508 Michelangelo begins Sistine Chapel ceiling

1511 Desiderius Erasmus, *Praise of Folly*

1516 Raphael, the *Sistine Madonna;* Lodovico Ariosto, *Orlando Furioso*

1517 Martin Luther nails his ninety-five theses to a church door in Wittenberg to begin the German Reformation

1525 Titian, *Deposition*

1533 First Italian madrigals

1540 Society of Jesus (the Jesuits) founded

1547 Benvenuto Cellini, *Perseus*

1554 Giovanni Palestrina, first book of Masses

1555 Pieter Breughel the Elder, *The Wedding Dance*

1575–1625 The school of "English virginalist" composers, including William Byrd, Thomas Morley, and Orlando Gibbons

Lives of Authors

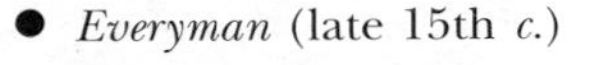

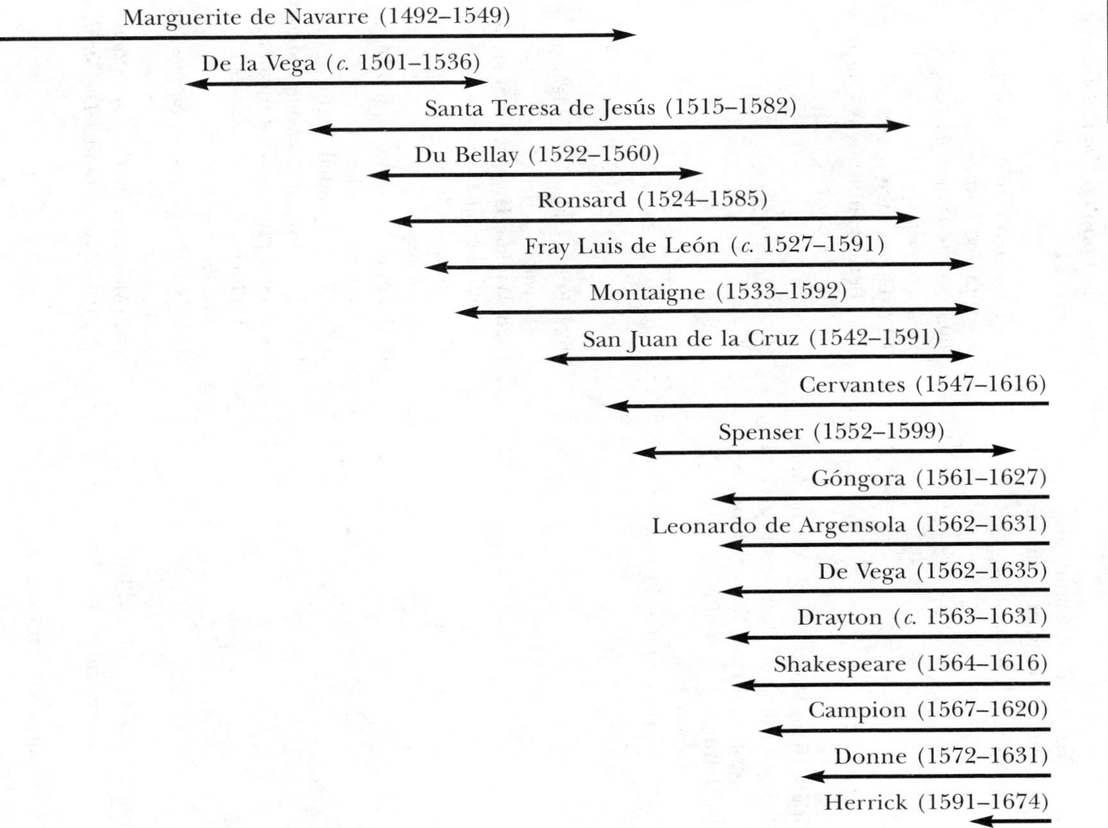

Political and Social Events

1598 The Edict of Nantes gives French Protestants equal political rights with Roman Catholics

1618–1648 Thirty Years' War between Catholics and Protestants over succession of Holy Roman Empire

1619 Introduction of Negro slavery into America

1620 Pilgrims land at Plymouth Rock

1642–1660 English Civil War, Commonwealth, and Protectorate

1643 Louis XIV crowned King of France

1649 Charles I of England executed

1665 Great Plague in London

1666 Great Fire in London

Intellectual and Cultural Events

1592 Tintoretto, *The Last Supper*

1597 Jacopo Peri, *Dafne* (the first opera)

1602 Galileo Galilei discovers the law of falling bodies

1605 Monteverdi, *Fifth Book of Madrigals*

1612 The Louvre begun

1614 Peter Paul Rubens, *The Descent from the Cross*

1624 Franz Hals, *The Laughing Cavalier*

1628 William Harvey, *Essay on the Motion of the Heart and Blood*

1629 Heinrich Schütz, *Sacred Symphony I*

1631 Rembrandt van Rijn, *The Anatomy Lesson*

1634 The Taj Mahal begun

1636 Founding of Harvard College

1637 First public opera theater (Venice); René Descartes, *Discourse on Method*

1639 Nicholas Poussin, *Shepherds in Arcadia*

1642 Monteverdi, *The Coronation of Poppea;* Rembrandt, *The Night Watch*

1650 Carissimi, *Jephta*

1651 Thomas Hobbes, *Leviathan*

1653 Jean-Baptiste Lully becomes court composer at Paris

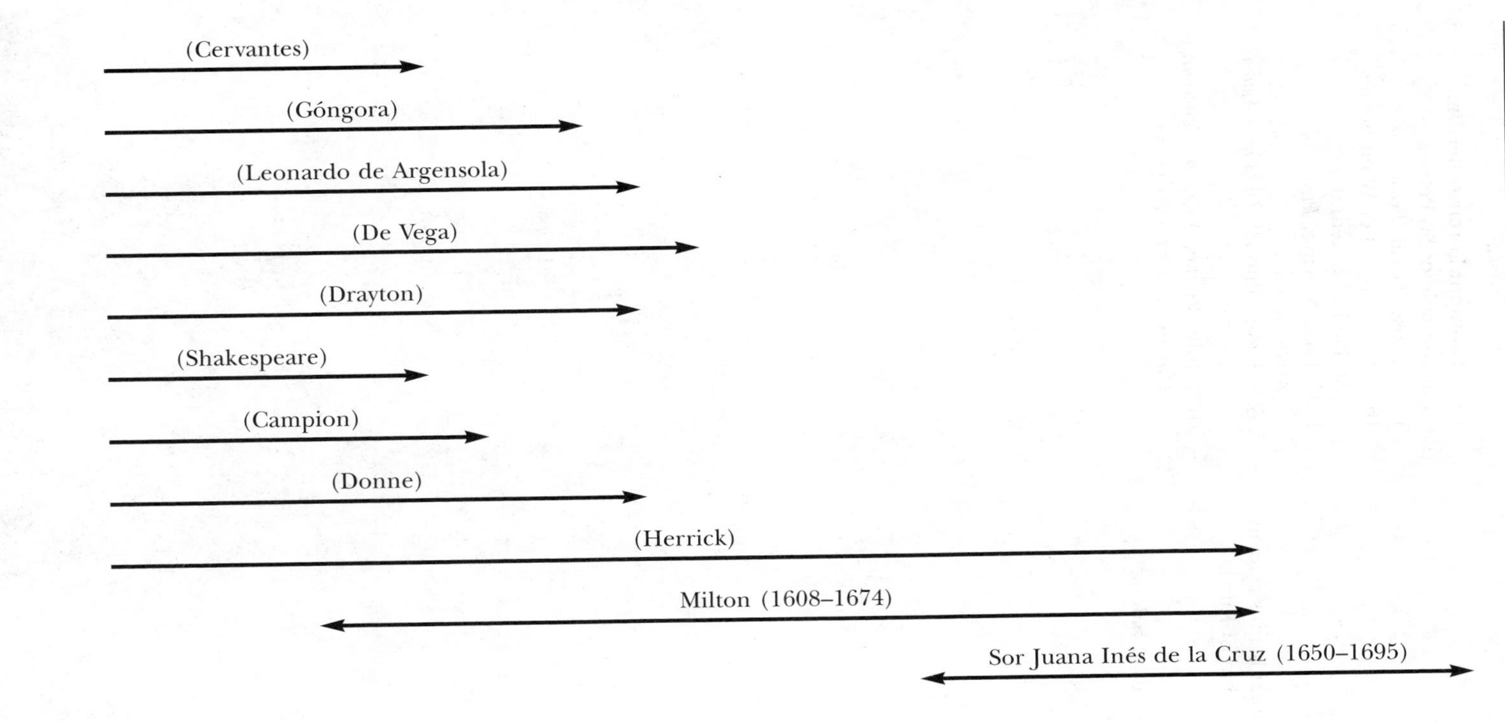
(Cervantes)
(Góngora)
(Leonardo de Argensola)
(De Vega)
(Drayton)
(Shakespeare)
(Campion)
(Donne)
(Herrick)
Milton (1608–1674)
Sor Juana Inés de la Cruz (1650–1695)

Political and Social Events

1689 Peter the Great begins reform and modernization of Russia

1692 Witchcraft trials at Salem, Massachusetts

Intellectual and Cultural Events

1667 Giovanni Lorenzo Bernini, colonnade of St. Peter's

1670 Blaise Pascal, *Pensées*

1675 Sir Christopher Wren begins St. Paul's Cathedral

1687 Isaac Newton, *Principia Mathematica*

1689 Henry Purcell, *Dido and Aeneas*

1690 John Locke, *An Essay Concerning Human Understanding*

Acknowledgments

AESCHYLUS, "Agamemnon," "The Libation Bearers," and "The Eumenides," from *The Oresteia*, translated by Robert Fagles. Copyright © 1966, 1967, 1975 by Robert Fagles. Reprinted with the permission of Viking Penguin, a division of Penguin Putnam Inc.

AESOP fables from *The Complete Fables*, translated by Olivia and Robert Temple. Copyright © 1998 by Olivia and Robert Temple. Reprinted with the permission of Summit House.

DANTE ALIGHERI, "Inferno," excerpts from "Purgatory," and excerpts from "Paradise," from *The Divine Comedy*, translated by H. R. Huse. Copyright 1954 by Howard R. Huse. Reprinted with the permission of Harcourt, Inc.

ANONYMOUS, "The Story of Sindbad the Sailor," from *The Arabian Nights II*, translated by Husain Haddaway. Copyright © 1995 by Husain Haddaway. Reprinted with the permission of W. W. Norton & Company, Inc.

ANONYMOUS, *The Epic of Gilgamesh*, Second Edition. Verse rendition by Danny P. Jackson, Introduction by Robert Riggs, Appreciation by James G. Keenan, Illustrations by Thom Kapheim. Copyright © 1997 by Bolchazy-Carducci Publishers, Inc. Reprinted by permission.

ANONYMOUS, "Exile of the Sons of Uisliu," from *The Tain*, translated by Thomas Kinsella (London, New York: Oxford University Press, 1970). Reprinted with the permission of the translator.

ANONYMOUS, "Hrafnkel the Priest of Frey," translated by Gwyn Jones, from *Eirik the Red and Other Icelandic Sagas*. Reprinted with the permission of Oxford University Press, Ltd.

ANONYMOUS, *Sir Gawain and the Green Knight*, translated by Theodore Howard Banks, Jr. (New York: Appleton, 1929). Used with the permission of Penguin Putnam Inc.

ARISTOPHANES, "Lysistrata," from *Aristophanes: Four Comedies*, translated by Dudley Fitts. Copyright 1954 by Harcourt Brace Jovanovich, Inc. and renewed © 1982 by Cornelia Fitts, Daniel H. Fitts, and Deborah Fitts. Reprinted with the permission of Harcourt Brace and Company. Caution: Professionals and amateurs are hereby warned that all titles included in this volume, being fully protected under the laws of the United States of America, the British Commonwealth, and all other countries which are signatories to the Universal Copyright Convention and the International Copyright Union, are subject to royalty. All rights, including professional, amateur, motion picture, recitation, lecturing, public reading, radio broadcasting, and television, and the rights of translation into foreign languages, are strictly reserved. Inquiries on professional rights should be addressed to Lucy Kroll Agency, 390 West End Avenue, New York, NY 10024. Inquiries on all other rights should be addressed to Harcourt, Inc., Permissions Department, Orlando, FL 32887-6777.

ARISTOTLE, excerpt from "Poetics," translated by Samuel Henry Butcher and Louise Ropes Loomis, from *On Man in the Universe*. Copyright 1943. Reprinted with permission.

Aristotle, "The Golden Mean," and Books II.6, II.7 and II.9, from "Nichomachean Ethics," translated by W. D. Ross. Reprinted with the permission of Oxford University Press, Ltd.

Francis Bacon, "Experimental Science," from *Opus Majus*, translated by Robert Belle Burke. Copyright 1928 by The University of Pennsylvania Press. Reprinted with permission.

Giovanni Boccaccio, excerpts from *The Decameron*, translated by Richard Aldington. Copyright 1930 by Richard Aldington. Reprinted with the permission of Rosica Colin Ltd.

Andreas Capellanus, excerpts from *The Art of Courtly Love*, translated by John Jay Perry. Copyright 1941 by Columbia University Press. Reprinted with the permission of the publishers.

Catullus, poems from *The Poems of Catullus*, translated by Horace Gregory. Copyright © 1956 by Horace Gregory. Reprinted with the permission of Alison M. Bond, Literary Agent.

Miguel de Cervantes Saavedra, excerpts from *Don Quixote*, translated by Walter Starkie. Copyright 1954 by Walter Starkie. Reprinted with the permission of Macmillan Press Ltd.

Geoffrey Chaucer, excerpts from *The Portable Chaucer*, translated and edited by Theodore Morrison. Copyright © 1997 by Arlie Russell Hochschild. Copyright 1949, © 1975 and renewed © 1977 by Theodore Morrison. Reprinted with the permission of Viking Penguin, a division of Penguin Putnam Inc.

San Juan de la Cruz, "One Dismal Night," translated by Kate Flores, "O Living Flame of Love," translated by Stephen Stepanchev, "I Entered Where I Did Not Know," translated by Willis Barnstone, "A Shepherd, Young and Mournful, Grieves Alone," and "I Know Full Well the Water's Flowing Power," translated by James Edward Tobin, from *An Anthology of Spanish Poetry from Garcilaso to García Lorca*, edited by Angel Flores (New York: Anchor Books, 1961). Copyright © 1961 by Angel Flores. All reprinted with the permission of the Estate of Angel Flores, c/o The Permissions Company.

Euripides, "Medea," from *Medea and Other Plays*, translated by Philip Vellacott. Copyright (c) 1963 by Philip Vellacott. Reprinted with the permission of Penguin Books Ltd.

Euripides, "Helen," from *The Bacchae and Other Plays*, translated by Philip Vellacott. Copyright © 1973 by Philip Vellacott. Reprinted with the permission of Penguin Books Ltd.

Marie de France, "Bisclavret (The Werewolf)" and "Yonec" from *The Lais of Marie de France*, translated by Robert Henning and Joan Ferrante. Copyright © 1982. Reprinted with the permission of The Labyrinth Press.

Marie de France, "The Mouse and the Frog," "The Frogs Who Asked for a King," "The Wolf King," "The Peasant and His Jackdaw," "The Vole Who Sought a Wife," and "Epilogue," from *Marie de France: Fables*, edited and translated by Harriet Spiegel. Copyright © 1987. Reprinted with the permission of University of Toronto Press.

Luis de Góngora, "Allegory of the Brevity of Things Human," translated by Roy Campbell, from *An Anthology of Spanish Poetry from Garcilaso to García Lorca*, edited by Angel Flores (New York: Anchor Books, 1961). Copyright © 1961 by Angel Flores. Reprinted with the permission of the Estate of Angel Flores, c/o The Permissions Company.

Goodman of Paris, excerpt from *The Goodman of Paris*, translated by Eileen Power. Copyright 1928. Reprinted with the permission of Routledge.

Homer, excerpts from *The Iliad*, translated by Robert Fitzgerald. Copyright © 1974 by Robert Fitzgerald. Reprinted with the permission of Doubleday, a division of Random House, Inc. *The Odyssey*, translated by Robert Fitzgerald. Copyright © 1961, 1963 by Robert Fitzgerald, renewed 1989, 1991 by Benedict R. C.

Fitzgerald. Reprinted with the permission of Farrar, Straus & Giroux, LLC. Book 1, Numbers 1, 2, 3, 4, 5, 6, 7, 8, and 9, from *The Complete Odes and Epodes of Horace,* translated by David West. Copyright © 1997. Reprinted with the permission of Oxford University Press, Ltd. Ode 1.1, translated by Anthony Hecht, as "An Old Malediction," from *Collected Earlier Poems.* Copyright © 1990 by Anthony E. Hecht. Reprinted with the permission of Alfred A. Knopf, a division of Random House, Inc.

John of Salisbury, excerpt from *The Statesman's Book of John of Salisbury,* translated by John Dickinson. Copyright 1927. Reprinted with permission.

The Koran, "The Opening," excerpt from "The Cow," "Light," "Ya Sin," and "Sincere Religion," from *The Koran Interpreted,* translated by Arthur J. Arberry. Copyright © 1955 by George Allen & Unwin Ltd. Reprinted with the permission of George Allen & Unwin Ltd., a division of HarperCollins Publishers Ltd.

Fray Luis de León, "Ode to Francisco Salinas . . .," translated by Edwin Morgan, and "At the Ascension," translated by James Edward Tobin, from *An Anthology of Spanish Poetry from Garcilaso to García Lorca,* edited by Angel Flores (New York: Anchor Books, 1961). Copyright © 1961 by Angel Flores. Reprinted with the permission of the Estate of Angel Flores, c/o The Permissions Company.

Robert Lowell, "The Ghost," from *Lord Weary's Castle.* Copyright © 1974 by Robert Lowell. Reprinted with the permission of Harcourt, Inc.

John Milton, excerpts from *Paradise Lost,* in James Holly Hanford (ed.), *The Poems of John Milton,* Second Edition. Copyright 1953 by Scott, Foresman and Company. Reprinted with the permission of the translator.

Michel de Montaigne, "Of Cannibals" and excerpt from "Apology for Raymond Sebond," from *The Complete Essays of Montaigne,* translated by Donald M. Frame. Copyright © 1958 by the Board of Trustees of the Leland Stanford Junior University. Reprinted with the permission of the publishers, Stanford University Press.

Marguerite de Navarre, stories from *The Heptameron,* translated by P.A. Chilton. Copyright © 1984 by P. A. Chilton. Reprinted with the permission of Penguin Books Ltd.

Ovid, excerpts from *Amores,* in *The Erotic Poems,* translated by Peter Green. Copyright © 1982 by Peter Green. Reprinted with the permission of Penguin Books, Ltd. "Paris to Helen (XVI)" and "Helen to Paris (XVII)," translated by Daryl Hine, from *Ovid's Heroides.* Copyright © 1991 by Yale University. Reprinted with the permission of Yale University Press. Excerpts from *Metamorphoses,* translated by Rolfe Humphries. Copyright © 1955 by Rolfe Humphries, renewed 1983 by Winifred Davies. Reprinted with the permission of Indiana University Press.

Francis Petrarch, rhymes from *Selected Poems,* translated by Anthony Mortimer. Copyright © 1977 by The University of Alabama Press. Reprinted with the permission of the publishers.

Pindar, "First Olympian Ode," from *Pindar's Victory Songs,* translated by Frank Nisetich, pp. 82–85. Copyright © 1980 by The Johns Hopkins University Press. Reprinted with the permission of the publishers.

Christine de Pizan, excerpts from *The Book of the City of Ladies,* translated by Earl Jeffrey Richards. Copyright © 1982, 1998 by Persea Books, Inc. Reprinted with the permission of Persea Books, Inc., New York.

Ezra Pound, "Midnight, and a letter comes to me," from "Homage to Sextus Propertius," from *Collected Poems.* Copyright 1926 by Ezra Pound. Reprinted with the permission of New Directions Publishing Corporation.

Propertius, Book 1, Number 6 and Book 2, Number 15, from *The Poems of Propertius,* translated by Constance Carrier. Reprinted with the permission of Indiana University Press.

Pierre de Saint-Cloud, "The Trial of Renard," from *Renard the Fox,* translated by Patricia Terry. Copyright © 1983 by Patricia Terry. Reprinted with the permission of the University of California Press.

SAPPHO, poems from *Sappho: A New Translation,* translated by Mary Barnard. Copyright © 1958 by The Regents of the University of California, renewed 1984 by Mary Barnard. Reprinted with the permission of the University of California Press.

SOPHOCLES, *Oedipus the King,* translated by Stephen Berg and Diskin Clay. Copyright © 1978 by Stephen Berg and Diskin Clay. Reprinted with the permission of Oxford University Press, Inc. *Antigone,* from *Three Theban Plays,* translated by Robert Fagles. Copyright © 1982 by Robert Fagles. Reprinted with the permission of Viking Penguin, a division of Penguin Putnam Inc.

THEOCRITUS, "Idyll 1: Song of Thyrsis," from *The Idylls of Theocritus: A Verse Translation,* translated by Thelma Sargent. Copyright © 1982 by Thelma Sargent. Reprinted with the permission of W. W. Norton & Company, Inc.

GARCILASO DE LA VEGA, "Your Face Is Written in My Soul..." and "While There Is Still the Color of a Rose...," translated by Edwin Morgan, from *An Anthology of Spanish Poetry from Garcilaso to García Lorca,* edited by Angel Flores (New York: Anchor Books, 1961). Copyright © 1961 by Angel Flores. Reprinted with the permission of the Estate of Angel Flores, c/o The Permissions Company.

LOPE DE VEGA, "At Dawn the Virgin Is Born . . . ," "Ice and Fires Contend with My Child...," and "Where Are You Going, Maiden...?," translated by W. S. Merwin, "A Little Carol of the Virgin," translated by Denise Levertov, and "A Sonnet All of a Sudden," translated by Doreen Bell, from *An Anthology of Spanish Poetry from Garcilaso to García Lorca,* edited by Angel Flores (New York: Anchor Books, 1961). Copyright © 1961 by Angel Flores. All reprinted with the permission of the Estate of Angel Flores, c/o The Permissions Company.

VIRGIL, "Book I: The Landing Near Carthage," "Book II: The Fall of Troy," "The Wanderings of Aeneas," "Book IV: Aeneas and Dido," excerpt from "Book V: The Funeral Games for Anchises," "Book VI: The Lower World," excerpt from "Book VIII: Aeneas at the Site of Rome," and excerpt from "Book XII: The Final Combat," from *The Aeneid,* translated by Rolfe Humphries. Copyright 1951 by Rolfe Humphries. Reprinted with the permission of Scribner, a division of Simon & Schuster, Inc.

Index

Note: First lines of short and middle-length poems are in roman type. Titles of long works are in italics. Titles of short works are in italics in the general alphabetical listing but in roman type when listed as sub-entries under their authors' names.